ook of Private Schools

S0-AJH-574

MAINE

VERMONT **New England**

NEW HAMPSHIRE

NNESOTA

MASSACHUSETTS

WISCONSIN

NEW YORK RHODE ISLAND
CONNECTICUT

MICHIGAN

Great Lakes PENNSYLVANIA NEW JERSEY

Middle Atlantic

IOWA OHIO DELAWARE

DISTRICT OF COLUMBIA
MARYLAND

ILLINOIS INDIANA WEST VIRGINIA

VIRGINIA

MISSOURI

KENTUCKY NORTH CAROLINA

TENNESSEE

ARKANSAS SOUTH CAROLINA

Southern

MISSISSIPPI ALABAMA GEORGIA

h Central

FLORIDA

LOUISIANA

s

The Porter Sargent Handbook Series

THE HANDBOOK OF
PRIVATE SCHOOLS

PUBLISHER'S STATEMENT

Esteemed educational and social critic Porter Sargent established *The Handbook of Private Schools* in 1914, with the aim "to present a comprehensive and composite view of the private school situation as it is today. No attempt has been made at completeness. The effort on the contrary has been to include only the best, drawing the line somewhat above the average."

Today, **The Porter Sargent Handbook Series** continues its founder's mission: to serve parents, educators and others concerned with the independent and critical evaluation of primary and secondary educational options, leading to a suitable choice for each student.

The Handbook of Private Schools, Guide to Summer Programs (1924) and *Guide to Private Special Education* (2011) provide the tools for objective comparison of programs in their respective fields.

THE HANDBOOK OF
PRIVATE SCHOOLS

AN ANNUAL DESCRIPTIVE SURVEY
OF INDEPENDENT EDUCATION

NINETY-THIRD EDITION

PORTER SARGENT HANDBOOKS
A Division of Carnegie Communications

2 LAN Drive, Suite 100
Westford, Massachusetts 01886
Tel: 978-842-2812   Fax: 978-692-2304
info@portersargent.com   www.portersargent.com

Copyright © 2012 by Carnegie Communications
Previous editions copyrighted 1915-2011

PRINTED IN THE UNITED STATES OF AMERICA

LIBRARY OF CONGRESS CATALOG CARD NUMBER 15-12869

ISBN 978-0-87558-176-7
ISSN 0072-9884

All information as reported to Porter Sargent Handbooks as of June 29, 2012.
Schools and organizations should be contacted for updated information.

All rights reserved. No part of this book may be reproduced or transmitted in
any form or by any means, electronic or mechanical, including photocopying,
recording, or by any information storage and retrieval system, without permission in writing from the publisher.

*Cost: US$99.00 plus shipping and handling. Additional copies are available from
booksellers, or from Porter Sargent Handbooks, 2 LAN Dr., Ste. 100, Westford,
MA 01886. Tel: 978-692-9708. Fax: 978-692-2304. info@portersargent.com.
www.portersargent.com.*

TABLE OF CONTENTS

A GUIDE TO THE *HANDBOOK*

FEATURED SCHOOLS

This section is provided as a supplement to the basic descriptions. Schools have paid for this space to portray—in their own words and images—their programs, objectives and ideals. Schools in other countries are included that are not elsewhere described in the Handbook.

SCHOOL FEATURE INDEXES

LEADING PRIVATE SCHOOLS

Schools in this section have been listed in the Handbook *for at least five consecutive years. In addition to responding to our annual update questionnaires, schools described here typically meet most of the following criteria: accreditation by educational associations; regional or national appeal; a strong graduate placement record; and a varied curriculum that includes advanced courses, multiple foreign languages, computer instruction and a strong arts program.*

CONCISE SCHOOL LISTINGS

These are, in many ways, schools similar to those found in the Leading Private Schools section. Schools that have been listed in the Handbook *for fewer than five consecutive years appear in this section, as do those institutions that have failed to respond regularly to annual update questionnaires. This section also includes schools that offer a more limited curriculum and those that enroll students from a strictly local area.*

TERM PROGRAMS

This section describes secondary-level academic term programs (usually operating on a semester system) that combine credit-bearing course work with experiential learning. Programs may have an environmental focus and typically employ the local environs as a significant teaching tool. Curricula are designed to promote academic continuity between the student's home school and the term program.

ASSOCIATIONS AND ORGANIZATIONS

CLASSIFIED DIRECTORIES OF
FIRMS AND AGENCIES

THE HANDBOOK OF PRIVATE SCHOOLS

Senior Editor   Daniel P. McKeever

Production Manager   Leslie A. Weston

PORTER SARGENT HANDBOOKS
A division of Carnegie Communications

President & CEO   Joseph F. Moore

Vice President, Publishing   Meghan Dalesandro

Publishers

1914-1950	Porter E. Sargent
1951-1975	F. Porter Sargent
1976-1999	J. Kathryn Sargent
2000-2007	Cornelia Sargent

PREFACE

The original guide to nonpublic elementary and secondary schools in the United States, *The Handbook of Private Schools* was first published by eminent social critic Porter Sargent in 1915. The annual *Handbook* soon became a trusted resource for parents, educational advisors and others concerned with private education and interested in placing children in suitable private school settings.

Now in its 93rd edition, the *Handbook* remains the one truly objective resource on nonpublic education in the United States. Unlike other available school guides, this book does not require listed schools to subscribe for space. Programs are selected on the basis of their merits, as evaluated by our editorial staff.

The aim of the *Handbook* is not to briefly list every operating nonpublic elementary and secondary program. Rather, we seek to provide in-depth information on schools that satisfy our criteria. We have established strict guidelines for acceptance into the *Handbook*. Prior to consideration, schools must complete at least five academic years of operation. Other criteria weighed by our editors during the evaluative process include accreditation earned by the school, appeal to readers beyond the immediate vicinity of the school, institutions attended by school graduates, and the overall depth and breadth of the curriculum.

Two components of the School Feature Indexes (which precede the editorial listings) particularly merit explanation here: 1) the evaluation of each school's affordability relative to other schools listed in this edition, and 2) the appraisal of the school's admission selectivity (along a scale ranging from nonselective to very selective). While these measures are necessarily somewhat subjective in nature, our editors weighed certain statistical figures in making their determinations. By examining tuition data presented by the schools, we found that we could classify both boarding and day schools into three affordability bands. (Please see the School Feature Indexes for details about tuition bands.) While we certainly ascribe to the belief that cost should not be the primary determinant in school selection, financial realities play an indisputable role in choosing an appropriate school. When assessing a school's affordability, parents and advisors should factor in the availability of financial aid at the school; listings include merit scholarship and need-based financial aid information whenever it has been furnished.

Appraisals of admission selectivity, while more fluid than those of affordability, also have a statistical basis. Schools accepting less than one-quarter of applicants generally have been designated as "very selective"; those accepting between 25 and about 85 percent of applicants (by far the largest group of schools) typically have been identified as "selective"; institutions accepting more than 85 percent of their applicants are described as "somewhat selective"; and schools accepting all (or virtually all) of their applicants have been designated as "nonselective." In the case of selectivity, we consider the school's self-appraisal in this regard prior to making a designation, as numbers alone do not always accurately reflect selectivity.

We invite our readers to refer to the *Handbook*'s companion website, www.privateschoolsearch.com. This destination features much of the same data presented on the pages of the *Handbook,* thereby making it an important online partner to the hardcover volume, and features articles—written by our staff—addressing numerous topics related to private education. In addition, schools formerly a part of our *Schools Abroad of Interest to Americans* (no longer being published) can be found in searches by country. Readers interested in residential summer programming may wish to visit www.summerprogramsearch.com, an online companion to our biennial *Guide to Summer Programs.*

In closing, please note that we often cannot list schools—however well they may fit our selection criteria—unless the schools complete our annual *Handbook* questionnaire. Consequently, some eligible programs do not appear in this volume; however, the roster of listed schools is both impressive and varied and will appeal to readers with a broad range of interests.

We wish to express our gratitude to the many school administrators who have devoted the requisite time and effort to updating their school listings for this edition.

EDITORIAL POLICY

We offer the following remarks to clarify the aim of the *Handbook* and the lines of editorial policy that necessarily follow. They are intended to assist readers in understanding our reporting methods and school administrators who feel that their requests for editorial change are overlooked. The following should be read in conjunction with the section How to Read the School Descriptions.

In the Leading Private Schools and Concise School Listings sections, we present—at no cost or obligation to the schools—the information parents and advisors want and ought to know. The statistics are printed as supplied by the schools, whose thorough response to our annual questionnaire enables yearly revisions to be computerized readily and smoothly. Inadequately completed questionnaires jeopardize comprehensive updating of statistics, or even retention in the Leading Private Schools or Concise School Listings sections.

A long-standing purpose of the paragraph descriptions has been to provide a historical summary of each school and, consequently, of independent education. Growth is organic, even among institutions, and the recounting of previous trends often helps to convey the tenor of a school. Consistent support has served to strengthen this intent. Our annual invitation to schools to supply new and interesting material has continued to elicit many useful suggestions—as well as a significant number of protestations. From an aggregate of information, we select those aspects that seem to most effectively characterize a school in the limited space available.

In revising the paragraphs, all suggestions are carefully reviewed, but our editorial staff reserves the right to determine which changes are pertinent and significant in keeping with our long tradition of impartial reporting of facts. Suggested revisions often cite a school's stimulating atmosphere, emphasis on basic skills, small classes and concern for the individual. While such statements may be undeniably valid, their reiteration for school after school is out of place in a compendium serving persons who seek reliable, specific information. Moreover, many of these generalizations are evidenced in a more focused way by the statistics reported above the paragraphs.

We often receive the broad remark that a particular item, or even whole entry, is obsolete, superseded or misleading, but without a specific reason or supporting evidence. Alternatively, a school may submit a totally new fact without indicating how it relates to a whole series of other facts long included in the write-up, thus resulting in more questions than answers. When error or new information is clearly identified and substantiated, we endeavor to respond quickly and appropriately.

The technique of vanity publishing—where length of listing is determined by purchase of advertising space—has never been part of the policy in publishing the *Handbook.* No school pays for a listing in the book, and space is allotted solely on the basis of our judgment of a school's interest to our audience. Nor does a school's purchase of space in the autonomous Featured Schools section affect the length or content of its free listing.

The 93rd edition of the *Handbook* comprises free listings of 1700 schools. In addition, many schools elect to reserve space in the Featured Schools section. Through this option, schools are able to stress features they consider most significant in describing their programs and aims. All those concerned with independent education welcome the opportunity to read these distinctive statements, and a sponsoring school thereby furthers not only recruitment, but also public relations in general.

The most complete and meaningful presentation of a school is achieved through the editor's independent report in conjunction with the school's own statement of purpose in the Featured Schools section. The one is objective reporting of facts, the other an individualized account of each school's philosophy, policy and spirit. These two views provide a perspective that cannot be achieved by either alone.

HOW TO READ THE
SCHOOL DESCRIPTIONS

The Leading Private Schools are arranged geographically by region, progressing from east to west across the country, then alphabetically by state and alphabetically by city or town within each state. Each city or town is briefly described prior to listings for that city. Refer also to the US map on the front end leaf. For information on additional schools, consult the Concise Listing of Schools section or refer to the Index of Schools.

1.   **PORTER SARGENT ACADEMY**

Bdg — Boys Gr 9-PG; Day — Coed PS (Age 3)-PG

2. **Westford, MA 01886. 2 LAN Dr, Ste 100. Tel: 978-692-9708. Fax: 978-692-2304.**
   www.portersargent.com   E-mail: info@portersargent.com

3. **Herbert Paul Brooks, Head (1980).** BA, Univ of Minnesota-Twin Cities, MEd, EdD, Cornell Univ. **Bryan Ferry, Adm.**

4. **Col Prep. IB Diploma. Elem math**—Kumon. **AP (exams req'd; 75 taken, 79% 3+)**—Eng Calc US_Hist. **Feat**—Fr Lat Span Stats Comp_Sci Ethics Art_Hist Music Journ. **Supp**—Dev_Read ESL Makeup Rem_Math Rem_Read Rev Tut. Outdoor ed. Sat classes. **Dual enr: MIT.**

5. **Sports (req'd)**—Basket X-country Soccer Tennis Track. B: Baseball Golf. G: F_Hockey Softball Volley. **Activities: 20.**

6. **Selective adm (Bdg Gr 9-11; Day Gr PS-10):** 100/yr. Usual entry: PS, K, 6 & 9. Bdg 30. Day 70. Appl fee: $100. Appl due: Feb. Applied: 307. Accepted: 64%. Yield: 51%. **Tests** IQ SSAT.

7. **Enr 480.** B 275. G 205. Bdg 95. Day 385. Elem 196. Sec 270. PG 14. Wh 88%. Latino 4%. Blk 3%. Native Am 1%. Asian 4%. Intl 12%. Avg class size: 18. Stud/fac: 10:1. Uniforms. **Fac 75.** M 25/F 50. FT 72/PT 3. Wh 90%. Latino 5%. Blk 5%. Adv deg: 31%. In dorms 27.

8. **Grad '11—90. Col—85.** (Boston U 4, Brown 3, Yale 3, Stanford 2, Trinity Col-CT 2, Marist 1). Athl schol 4. **Avg SAT:** CR 560. M 660. W 630. **Mid 50% SAT:** CR 610-720. M 590-700. W 600-710. Avg ACT: 26. **Col couns:** 5. Alum donors: 13%.

9. **Tui '12-'13: Bdg $42,900** (+$1250). **Day $19,250-25,470** (+$800-1100). **Intl Bdg $44,900** (+$1500-6000). **Aid:** Merit 23 ($86,000). Need 360 ($2,500,000). Work prgm 2 ($12,000).

10. **Summer (enr 120):** Acad Enrich. Tui Bdg $4000. Tui Day $1475/crse. 6 wks.

11. Endow $45,750,000. Plant val $75,000,000. Acres 12. Bldgs 20 (50% ADA). Dorms 2. Dorm rms 76. Class rms 32. 2 Libs 25,000 vols. Sci labs 4. Lang labs 1. Art studios 2. Music studios 3. Gyms 2. Fields 4. Courts 12. Pools 1. Comp labs 2. Comp/stud: 1:1 Laptop prgm Gr 6-8.

12. Est 1914. Nonprofit. Religious Society of Friends (5% practice). Tri (Sept-June). **Assoc** CLS NEASC.

13. Founded in Boston's Beacon Hill neighborhood by Robert Gordon Orr, long a leader in progressive education, PSA continues to maintain a reputation for sound college preparation. Originally a boys' boarding high school, it began accepting day boys and girls and opened an elementary division in 1960. The academy moved to its current campus, on a 12-acre site in Westford, in July 2010.

PSA's experiential lower school curriculum includes French from grade 2, and Latin and Spanish from grade 6. The upper school offers a broad curriculum with liberal arts electives, Advanced Placement courses and a strong foreign language department. Qualified seniors may participate in on- or off-campus independent study or may spend a trimester at an affiliated secondary school in Paris, France. Most graduates enter New England colleges, although an increasing number now attend schools in other parts of the country.

The weeklong interim program each February consists of enrichment courses and classes in nontraditional subjects. All boys and girls in grades 9-PG perform 30 hours of annual community service.

14.   **See Also Page 1500**

1.   SCHOOL NAME and TYPE. Sex and grade range of students are provided here. Age spans replace grade ranges for ungraded programs. Prekindergarten programs are indicated by "PS," with an age reference frequently included in parentheses to indicate entry age of the youngest pupils [e.g., "PS (Age 3)" for a school that enrolls three-year-olds in its preschool]. If the school conducts both boys' and girls' single-gender programs, the term "Coord" (Coordinate) appears prior to the grade range to distinguish the school from coeducational institutions. Consult the Glossary for more information about coordinate programs.

2.   CITY or TOWN, STATE, ZIP CODE, STREET ADDRESS, TELEPHONE and FAX NUMBERS, and WEB SITE and E-MAIL ADDRESSES. If a school has divisions at more than one location, additional location addresses will follow the school's fax number.

3.   ACADEMIC HEAD OF SCHOOL. An active president or superintendent may be listed for larger schools, followed in many cases by the head of school or the principal. When available, year of installation follows the head's title in parentheses. Whenever possible, degrees and granting institutions are also given. The director of admissions (or the administrator who fills this role) immediately follows, unless the academic head serves in this capacity.

4.   ACADEMIC ORIENTATION and CURRICULUM. The basic curriculum is described as college preparatory, pre-preparatory, general academic or, in some cases, vocational or business.

Availability of one or more of the curricula designed by the International Baccalaureate Organization is indicated next. The Primary Years Program (PYP) serves children ages 3-12, the Middle Years Program (MYP) runs from age 11 through age 16, and the Diploma Program is offered to pupils ages 16-19. Schools that prepare students for the French Baccalaureate are so designated. Consult the Glossary for further details about these international programs.

Bilingual programs are then noted. Additional information about bilingual instruction is provided in the school's paragraph description. Institutions following alternative curricula such as Montessori and Waldorf are identified thusly. Schools that primarily serve underachievers or students with learning disabilities are indicated as such, as are institutions with specialized programs for athletes or aspiring artists. Next, formal math and reading curricula utilized during the elementary years are indicated. For a full listing of specific course offerings, consult the school's catalogue.

"AP" indicates regularly offered Advanced Placement courses. In the model, AP course work is offered in English, calculus and US history. Available in the upper high school grades, courses listed here follow the curriculum formulated by the College Board and prepare students for standardized Advanced Placement examinations. If a school offering AP courses requires students to take the AP exam for each AP class completed, it is so noted parenthetically. The total number of AP exams administered by the school in the previous year follows, as does the percentage of test takers who scored a 3 (out of 5) or above.

"Feat" denotes courses of interest that the school does not offer at the Advanced Placement level. Disciplines commonly addressed in this section include foreign language, computer and the arts.

Supplemental areas of instruction appear after the notation "Supp" and comprise limited learning disabilities programs, tutoring, review, remedial and developmental reading, remedial math, makeup and English as a Second Language.

"Outdoor ed" designates the presence of outdoor education programming. Schools that regularly conduct classes on Saturdays carry the designation "Sat classes." "Dual enr" indicates that the secondary school allows qualified pupils to enroll in dual-credit courses available through the college(s) specified.

5.   SPORTS AND ACTIVITIES. A listing of varsity sports appears next. A parenthetical notation identifies schools that require competitive athletic participation in some or all sports seasons. Sports available to both genders (or, in some instances, ones for which gender information has not been furnished) are listed first; teams serving boys and girls only are then delineated. For secondary schools, the total number of interest clubs and other activities (excepting interscholastic athletics) often follows.

6.   ADMISSIONS. An appraisal of the school's admissions selectivity follows, with schools categorized as "very selective," "selective," "somewhat selective" and "nonselective" (consult the Glossary for details). A parenthetical grade range is present for schools that do not accept new pupils at all grade levels. The total number of new students enrolled during the previous year and the usual grade(s) of entry follow. When available, the number of new boarding and day pupils is listed.

The application fee, the annual application due month (or "Rolling" if applications are considered year-round), the total number of annual applications, the percentage of applicants accepted and the percentage of accepted students who enroll ("Yield") follow. Reported next are the abbreviations of tests used (though not necessarily required) for admission purposes by the school. Consult the Key to Admission Tests for details.

7.   ENROLLMENT and FACULTY. The total number of students enrolled during the current academic year is reported with the following breakdown: number of

boys; number of girls; number of boarders; number of day pupils; and an enumeration of students in elementary, secondary and postgraduate divisions. Information about the student body's racial makeup appears in many listings. Should the school choose to provide the percentage of minority pupils instead of the various ethnicities, the percentage of non-Caucasian students is listed. The percentage of international students is reported if it is at least five percent of the enrollment. Average class size and student-faculty ratio follow. "Uniforms" indicates that the school requires its students to wear uniforms; if the school instead maintains a formal or casual dress code, the appropriate designation is made.

Faculty figures are detailed as follows: total faculty; number of males/number of females; number of full-time teachers/number of part-time teachers. When provided by the school, racial composition of the teaching staff is indicated next. Should the school choose to provide the percentage of minority teaching faculty instead of the various ethnicities, the percentage of non-Caucasian faculty is detailed.

The percentage of teaching faculty members who have earned advanced degrees follows. At boarding schools, faculty members may reside on campus. "In dorms" reports the number of resident teaching faculty dwelling in dormitories. (This figure does not include instructors who live elsewhere on campus.) The student-teacher ratio can be deduced from a comparison of teaching faculty and enrollment figures.

8.   GRADUATE RECORD. These figures specify the total number of students in a recent academic year's graduating class and the number who matriculated at nonpublic preparatory schools or at two- or four-year colleges. As many as six schools entered by the largest number of class members are cited. Where applicable, the number of college athletic scholarships for the most recent high school graduating class follows. Secondary school listings may include average math, critical reading and writing Scholastic Aptitude Test (SAT) scores, in addition to ACT assessment results. In some cases, combined math/critical reading or math/ critical reading/writing scores (designated by "CR/M" or "CR/M/W") are relayed. Also, many listings include mid-50th percentile SAT and ACT scores instead of (or in addition to) straight averages. Some elementary schools report average scores for students taking the Secondary School Admission Test (SSAT). For high schools, the total number of college counselors on staff may appear. The percentage of alumni/-ae who have contributed to the school financially in the past year follows.

9.   TUITION and AID. When both boarding and day departments are maintained, both tuitions are given. If international boarding students pay a higher tuition rate, this rate is also provided. Grouped tuition figures (e.g., $19,250-25,470) typically show the fee span from the lowest to the highest grade. Tuition figures for young children who do not attend for five full school days per week are omitted. The school's estimate of extra expenses incurred by the average student follows in parentheses. Note: Reference school year for listed tuition figure(s) precedes this data.

The number of students receiving merit scholarships is reported with the school's total scholarship allotment. Financial aid figures follow, with total dollar amount provided again listed after number of recipients. Finally, the number of students participating in remunerative work programs, with corresponding dollar values, is cited where applicable. Children of faculty members are excluded from all aid categories.

10.   SUMMER SESSION. The total enrollment, type, orientation, fees and duration are specified for schools with summer programs.

11.   PLANT EVALUATION and ENDOWMENT. Following the dollar values of the

endowment and the physical plant is a brief listing of the school's facilities. When the school has supplied this data, listings parenthetically indicate the percentage of school buildings that meet the standards set in the wake of the Americans with Disabilities Act.

The number of computers per student, expressed as a ratio, often appears. Schools that require students to rent or purchase laptop computers for class work are denoted by "Laptop prgm," followed by the grade range involved. Costs associated with laptop program participation typically fall under estimated tuition extras.

12. ESTABLISHMENT and CALENDAR. The establishment date, the organizational nature (for those schools that are incorporated or incorporated nonprofit) and the religious or other affiliation are cited. When it has been provided, the percentage of students who practice the school's sponsoring religion is also indicated. Division of the academic year and months of operation follow.

Accreditation by the seven associations listed under "Accrediting Associations" in the Associations and Organizations section is recorded based upon lists provided by these associations. Advocacy, testing, school membership and professional organizations are also part of the Associations and Organizations compilation.

13. PARAGRAPH DESCRIPTION. These comments often begin with highlights of the school's founding and early development. Significant aspects of the academic and cocurricular programs are then summarized.

Descriptions are based upon annual questionnaires and supplementary literature submitted by school officials. Material is not presented when it does not serve to objectively define a school. The descriptions are intended to be impartial and factual and are not designed to be school-composed promotional pieces. Editors review all revisions suggested by the schools according to the publisher's Editorial Policy.

14. PAGE CROSS-REFERENCE TO FEATURED SCHOOLS SECTION. Many schools supply their own appraisals of ideals and objectives in the Featured Schools section. Page cross-references are appended to the paragraph descriptions of participating schools.

GLOSSARY

ACT assessment: Composed of a multiple-choice section that addresses English, math, reading and science, as well as an optional writing section that measures skill in planning and writing a short essay, this college entrance exam assesses high school students' general educational development and evaluates their ability to complete college-level work.

advanced degree: Regarding teaching faculty members, this figure designates the percentage of teachers who hold any degree more advanced than a bachelor's degree.

Advanced Placement: "AP" courses, which comprise advanced material and follow the syllabi set forth by the College Board (see Testing Organizations), are listed after the AP designation in the statistical portion of the editorial listing. Upon completing each AP course, students may sit for the standardized Advanced Placement examination. Favorable scores on these examinations may lead to advanced standing at the college level.

coordinate: Used to describe schools that share some key administrators and admit both boys and girls, yet operate separate boys' and girls' divisions. Classes at such schools are not typically coeducational, although there are exceptions. Some schools operate coeducationally at certain grade levels and coordinately at others.

country day school: This concept became popular in the 1930s, when day schools (with boarding school aspirations in terms of academic rigor) flourished in rustic settings and placed importance on physical education as a complement to academics. The term lives on in many school names, although it now has no concrete meaning.

developmental reading: Instruction that focuses upon fundamental reading skills.

elementary: In the statistical portion of the editorial listing, "Elem" refers to preschool through grade 8.

elementary math: In the statistical portion of the editorial listing, specifies formal math curricula used during the elementary years.

elementary reading: In the statistical portion of the editorial listing, specifies formal reading curricula used during the elementary years.

endowment: Funds or property donated to a school as a source of income.

enrichment: Supplemental instruction (such as a field trip) intended to amplify or extend classroom learning.

French-American Baccalaureate: Formulated jointly by the French Ministry of Education and the College Board and first offered in fall 2010, the FAB combines the French Baccalaureate curriculum with the College Board's Advanced Placement program. Students take three Advanced Placement courses in place of the corresponding French subjects, thereby achieving proficiency in both French and English in a bicultural environment.

French Baccalaureate: The completion of the French high school curriculum leads to this diploma. Taught entirely in French and found primarily in the US at French-American schools, it follows curricular guidelines established by the French Ministry of Education. Students must complete grade 12 and pass externally assessed examinations to earn the French Baccalaureate.

honors: Many high schools designate certain advanced courses with this label. Unlike Advanced Placement courses, however, honors courses meet no specific curricular requirements and thus gain the honors distinction at the discretion of the school.

independent school: An institution of this type does not rely upon local or federal government funding, instead operating on the basis of tuition fees, donations and, in many instances, the investment yield gained from the school's endowment.

interim program: Commonly referred to as "Winterim" (or "winterim") when it operates in the winter, this program enables students to explore topics of interest or participate in internships on an intensive, short-term basis. The program typically lasts a week or two and runs between two school terms.

International Baccalaureate: The International Baccalaureate Organization (IBO) is a nonprofit, international foundation that works with more than 3400 schools (in 143 countries) to oversee three distinct programs. The Primary Years Program (PYP), for students ages 3-12, is a comprehensive international curriculum that comprises learning guidelines, a teaching methodology and assessment strategies. The Middle Years Program (MYP) is a five-year program for students ages 11-16 that is flexible enough to encompass other subjects not determined by the IBO but required by local authorities. The Diploma Program, the most commonly utilized IB program in the United States, is a two-year, precollege course of study that leads to standardized examinations. It is designed for highly motivated students ages 16-19. While these programs form a continuous sequence, each may be offered independently.

laptop program: When used in the editorial listings, this refers strictly to one-to-one laptop programs in which students use owned or rented laptops at both home and school. Schools with mobile laptop cart programs—but not one-to-one programs—do not carry a laptop program designation.

learning disabilities: Comprising such conditions as dyslexia, dysgraphia and dyscalculia, learning disabilities are a group of neurological disorders that affect the brain's ability to receive, process, store and respond to information and stimuli.

makeup: An opportunity for the student to retake a course in which mastery was not previously displayed.

merit scholarship: Tuition assistance granted in recognition of noteworthy academic achievement or a special talent. It is often provided to students with accompanying financial need.

mid-50th percentile: Presented as a range, this sample of a school's Scholastic Aptitude Test or ACT scores progresses from the 25th percentile to the 75th percentile. Many schools prefer this method of reporting to a straight average, as they believe mid-50th percentile scores provide a more accurate representation of student achievement.

Montessori: Developed in the early 1900s by Maria Montessori, Italy's first female physician, the Montessori method of education incorporates manipulative materials with which children essentially teach themselves. Multi-age groupings are commonly found in Montessori settings, and the Montessori approach is usually employed during the early elementary years.

need-based aid: Tuition assistance granted to families in recognition of financial need.

nonprofit: Refers to schools that are legally categorized as Section 501(c)(3) organizations, and thus not designed to be profit-making businesses.

nonselective: Indicates that admission to the school is noncompetitive (virtually all applicants are accepted).

plant: The physical facilities and land owned by the school.

postgraduate: Typically a year in duration, "PG" offers course work to high school graduates who wish to bolster their academic credentials, improve their readiness for college, or both.

preschool: For reasons of standardization, "PS" in the statistical portion of the editorial listings refers to any schooling prior to five-year-old kindergarten (for example, nursery, transitional kindergarten or prekindergarten), regardless of how the school itself refers to such grade levels. An age parenthically appended to "PS" indicates entry age of the youngest students [e.g., "PS (Age 3)" for a school that enrolls three-year-olds in its preschool].

remedial: Intended to remedy a deficit, often in the areas of math or reading.

review: Reinforcement of previously covered material.

Saturday classes: Some schools, typically those with boarding divisions, hold classes on Saturday on a regular basis as a means of maximizing instructional time.

secondary: When used in the statistical portion of the editorial listing, "Sec" refers to grades 9-12.

selective: Indicates that admission to the school is competitive; such schools typically accept between 25 and 85 percent of annual applicants.

somewhat selective: Indicates that admission to the school is minimally competitive; such schools typically accept upwards of 85 percent of annual applicants.

Sudbury Valley: This alternative educational approach, which originated at the Sudbury Valley School in Framingham, MA, is now followed at more than 30 schools around the world. Students are free to do as they wish during the school day (as long as they follow school rules), and they need not attend class. The nontraditional classes involve no tests or grades, and students and teachers are treated equally. Sudbury Valley schools are governed democratically by a weekly school meeting that involves both pupils and staff.

tutoring: One-on-one or small-group instruction for students requiring extra assistance in a subject.

underachiever: Underachieving students, who are typically of average or above-average intelligence, have failed to learn to potential due to motivational, emotional, behavioral or learning problems.

very selective: Indicates that admission to the school is highly competitive; such schools typically accept fewer than one-quarter of annual applicants.

Waldorf: Developed by Austrian intellectual Rudolf Steiner in 1919, Waldorf education typically incorporates play and toys as important learning tools for children. Instructors follow a developmental approach that seeks to address the changing needs of the child as he or she grows and matures.

work program: Opportunities for students to perform chores or other duties that aid in the maintenance of the school. Only those programs that result in tuition reimbursement are referenced in the statistical portion of the editorial listing, although nonpaying work programs are frequently noted in the paragraph descriptions.

yield: The percentage of accepted students who matriculate at a school.

KEY TO ABBREVIATIONS

Commonly accepted abbreviations do not appear on this list. For further clarification, refer to How to Read the School Descriptions.

Achieve	Achievement
Actg	Acting
ADA	Americans with Disabilities Act Compliance
Adm	Admissions, Director of Admission(s)
Admin	Administration, Administrator
Anat	Anatomy
Anthro	Anthropology
AP	Advanced Placement (College Board)
Appl	Application(s)
Architect	Architectural, Architecture
ASL	American Sign Language
Athl	Athletic
Aud	Auditorium
B	Boys
Bac	Baccalaureate
Bdg	Boarding
Blk	Black
Bus	Business
CC	Community College
Chrm	Chairman
Co Day	Country Day
Comp	Comparative, Computer
Comp/stud	Computer-to-Student Ratio
Coord	Coordinate
Couns	Counselor(s)
CR	Critical Reading (SAT Score)
CR/M	Critical Reading/Math (Combined SAT Score)
CR/M/W	Critical Reading/Math/Writing (Combined SAT Score)
Crse	Course
Dev	Development, Developmental
Ec, Econ	Economics
Ed, Educ	Education
Elem	Elementary (Preschool–Grade 8)
Endow	Endowment
Enr	Enrollment
Enrich	Enrichment
Environ	Environmental
F	Females
F_Hockey	Field Hockey
Feat	Featured Courses

Fr	French
FT	Full-time
G	Girls
Gr	Grade(s)
Hand	Handball
Head	Head of School, Headmaster, Headmistress
IB	International Baccalaureate
Int	Interim
Japan	Japanese
JC	Junior College
Journ	Journalism
JROTC	Junior Reserve Officers Training Corps
M	Males, Math (SAT Score)
Mid 50%	Mid-50th Percentile
Milit	Military
MYP	Middle Years Program
PG	Postgraduate
Philos	Philosophy
Physiol	Physiology
Pol	Political, Politics
Prgm	Program
PS	Preschool
PT	Part-time
PYP	Primary Years Program
Rem	Remedial
Req'd	Required
Res	Residential
Schol	Scholarships
Sculpt	Sculpture
Sec	Secondary (Grades 9–12)
Sem	Semester
Ses	Session
Sociol	Sociology
Speak	Speaking
SSAT	Secondary School Admission Test
Stud	Student, Studies
Tech	Technical, Technology
Tri	Trimester
Trng	Training
Tui	Tuition
Tut	Tutorial, Tutoring
W	Writing (SAT Score)
W_Polo	Water Polo
X-country	Cross-country

KEY TO ADMISSION TESTS

Standardized tests of ability, aptitude and achievement are frequently requisites for admission to independent schools. These tests may be administered by the school, an agency or a testing service. Listed below are major tests utilized by schools in the Handbook.

CEEB COLLEGE ENTRANCE EXAMINATION BOARD tests include the PSAT/NMSQT (Preliminary SAT/National Merit Scholarship Qualifying Test), the SAT I and the SAT II. The PSAT prepares high school juniors for the SAT I, which is designed to measure a student's ability to perform in college. Both the PSAT and the SAT I comprise critical reading and mathematical sections, while the SAT II measures knowledge in specific subjects. Changes effected to the SAT in March 2005 were the addition of an essay writing section and modifications to the critical reading and mathematics sections.

CTP 4 COMPREHENSIVE TESTING PROGRAM measures achievement in grades 1-11, as well as verbal and quantitative ability in grades 3-11.

DAT DIFFERENTIAL APTITUDE TESTS measure aptitudes of adolescents in grades 7-12.

HSPT HIGH SCHOOL PLACEMENT TEST, developed by Scholastic Testing Service (STS) but administered by the schools themselves, is utilized for the evaluation of middle school students by many Roman Catholic high schools. The test consists of five multiple-choice sections: verbal, reading, qualitative, math and language.

IQ INTELLIGENCE QUOTIENT: Intelligence tests, designed to evaluate an individual's academic aptitude, are many, with varying purposes, scales and results. The most common are the Stanford-Binet, WISC and Otis-Lennon.

ISEE INDEPENDENT SCHOOL ENTRANCE EXAMINATION, for students in grades 4-12, comprises tests for verbal and quantitative ability, reading comprehension and mathematics achievement, in addition to an essay.

MAT METROPOLITAN ACHIEVEMENT TESTS, for grades K-12, measure student achievement in reading, mathematics, language, science and social studies.

MRT   METROPOLITAN READINESS TESTS assess literacy and mathematics development in prekindergarten to grade 1.

SSAT   SECONDARY SCHOOL ADMISSION TEST assesses scholastic ability of students applying for admission to independent secondary schools. The test's five sections include quantitative, verbal and reading categories.

Stanford   STANFORD ACHIEVEMENT TEST, for grades K-12, measures student achievement in reading, mathematics, language, spelling, study skills, science, social science and listening.

TACHS   TEST FOR ADMISSION INTO CATHOLIC HIGH SCHOOLS is a Roman Catholic high school entrance test, similar in structure to the HSPT, that is employed predominantly in the Archdiocese of New York.

TOEFL   TEST OF ENGLISH AS A FOREIGN LANGUAGE, which evaluates the English proficiency of individuals whose native language is not English, consists of three sections: listening comprehension, structure and written expression, and reading comprehension.

KEY TO
ACCREDITING ASSOCIATIONS

Association accreditation and membership data are supplied by the following associations and recorded in each school listing.

Listed below are the six regional accrediting associations serving the United States and its territories at the elementary, secondary and college levels.

MSA   Middle States Association of Colleges and Schools

NCA   North Central Association
Commission on Accreditation and School Improvement

NEASC   New England Association of Schools and Colleges

NWAC   Northwest Accreditation Commission

SACS   Southern Association of Colleges and Schools
Council on Accreditation and School Improvement

WASC   Western Association of Schools and Colleges

The association listed below accredits secondary schools from throughout the United States.

CLS   Cum Laude Society

For more information about the above associations—as well as other organizations that serve independent schools, parents and educational professionals—refer to the list of Associations and Organizations beginning on page 1233.

FEATURED SCHOOLS

Schools in this section have paid for space to supplement their basic descriptions in the editorial listing sections of the book.

INDEX TO
FEATURED SCHOOLS

Parenthetical information indicates the school type. The pages have been arranged based on the reservation of space date.

ST. ANDREW'S SCHOOL
63 Federal Rd.
BARRINGTON, RI 02806
Tel: 401-246-1230
Web: www.standrews-ri.org

St. Andrew's School is a coeducational, college preparatory boarding and day school for students in grades 3-12, with the boarding program starting in the ninth grade. The School is located on a 100-acre campus one mile from the center of Barrington (population 16,000), a suburban community 10 miles southeast of Providence on Narragansett Bay. Its proximity to Providence and Newport, as well as Boston, offers a wide variety of cultural opportunities for students.

St. Andrew's School was founded in 1893 by Rev. William Merrick Chapin as a school for homeless boys. From these simple beginnings through its years as a working farm school to its present role as a coeducational boarding and day college preparatory school, St. Andrew's steadfastly maintains the same sense of purpose and concern for the individual. St. Andrew's was named an exemplary School by the nationally recognized Schools Attuned program. Every teacher at St. Andrew's is trained to teach using a multisensory approach, to identify students individual learning styles, and to teach students how they learn best, thereby helping them to maximize their strengths. Academic expectations are high, but support is always available for those who need it. Small classes (7-12 students), an overall student to faculty ratio of 5:1, and a twice-daily advisor program ensure that no student is overlooked and he or she receives the attention they need. The homelike community, nurturing environment, and the hands-on approach to learning and teaching help maintain close student-teacher relationships. St. Andrew's students find that when they go to college, they are well prepared to handle the course work because they have a true understanding of how they learn and an awareness of the tools they need to achieve the best.

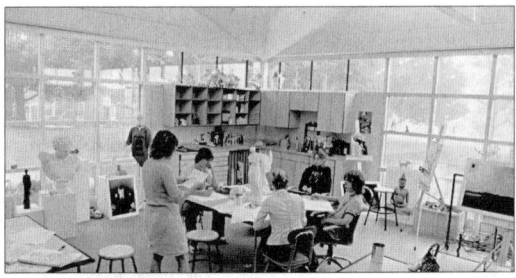

Over the years, St. Andrew's School has attracted boarding students from all corners of the United States and other countries, including China, Germany, India, Israel, Jamaica, Japan, South Korea, and Taiwan. The School is also committed to ensuring that our students who demonstrate need receive financial aid; the result is a student body that is economically and culturally diverse.

St. Andrew's seeks to motivate each student to strive for his or her personal best in the classroom, athletics or creative pursuits, and in life, while offering strong faculty support in all areas of endeavor. The St. Andrew's campus includes two gymnasiums, a state-of-the-art fitness center including a weight room, playing field, tennis courts, a Project Adventure ropes course, a recently renovated facility to house the new Lower School (3-5), and a new Arts Center provides facilities including a fully equipped, 287-seat theatre for a burgeoning fines arts program. The campus is also fully networked, providing access to a world of information via the internet.

The 48-member faculty of St. Andrew's has been led since 1996 by Head Master John D. Martin, a graduate of Northfield Mount Hermon School and Tufts University. Mr. Martin holds a M.Ed. from American International College and a M.Div. from Yale University. He has held faculty, admissions, and chaplain positions at Tabor Academy, The Peddie School, and Sewickley Academy.

St. Andrew's is accredited by the New England Association of Schools and Colleges (NEASC). It is a member of the National Association of Independent Schools (NAIS), the Association of Independent Schools of New England (AISNE), The Association of Boarding Schools (TABS), and the Independent School Association of Rhode Island (ISARI).

Parents seeking a private school education for their child have many excellent choices in New York City. But there is no school quite like ours.

Located in historic downtown Manhattan, Léman Manhattan is the school that offers the rigorous academics and will offer an International Baccalaureate Diploma by May 2015.

It's the school that teaches the critical thinking skills that are keys to preparing today's graduates to succeed at top choice colleges and throughout their lives.

It's the school that believes learning courage, resilience, empathy and open-mindedness is just as important as learning calculus, chemistry and history.

It's the school with state-of-the-art facilities including: a light-filled library, performing arts auditoriums, rock climbing wall, roof-top playground, regulation-size gymnasiums, personal training room and two competition-size pools.

It's the school that offers small classes and Personal Learning Plans designed to challenge and excite each student to reach his or her potential.

It's the only preparatory school in Manhattan with established sister schools in Europe, Asia, Latin America and throughout the US offering our students exciting opportunities to participate in international academic, athletic, music and art exchange programs.

Léman Manhattan offers a one-of-a-kind international boarding program where students from around the world can share culture and diverse perspectives to create a truly global community.

All of this contributes to a learning experience that is second to none.

where does your child go to school?

LÉMAN MANHATTAN
———— PREPARATORY SCHOOL ————

WORLD VIEWS FROM EVERY CLASSROOM

WWW.LEMANMANHATTAN.ORG   #MYLEMAN
JANET BARRETT, DIRECTOR OF ADMISSIONS
(212) 232-0266 EXT. 259   J.BARRETT@LEMANMANHATTAN.ORG

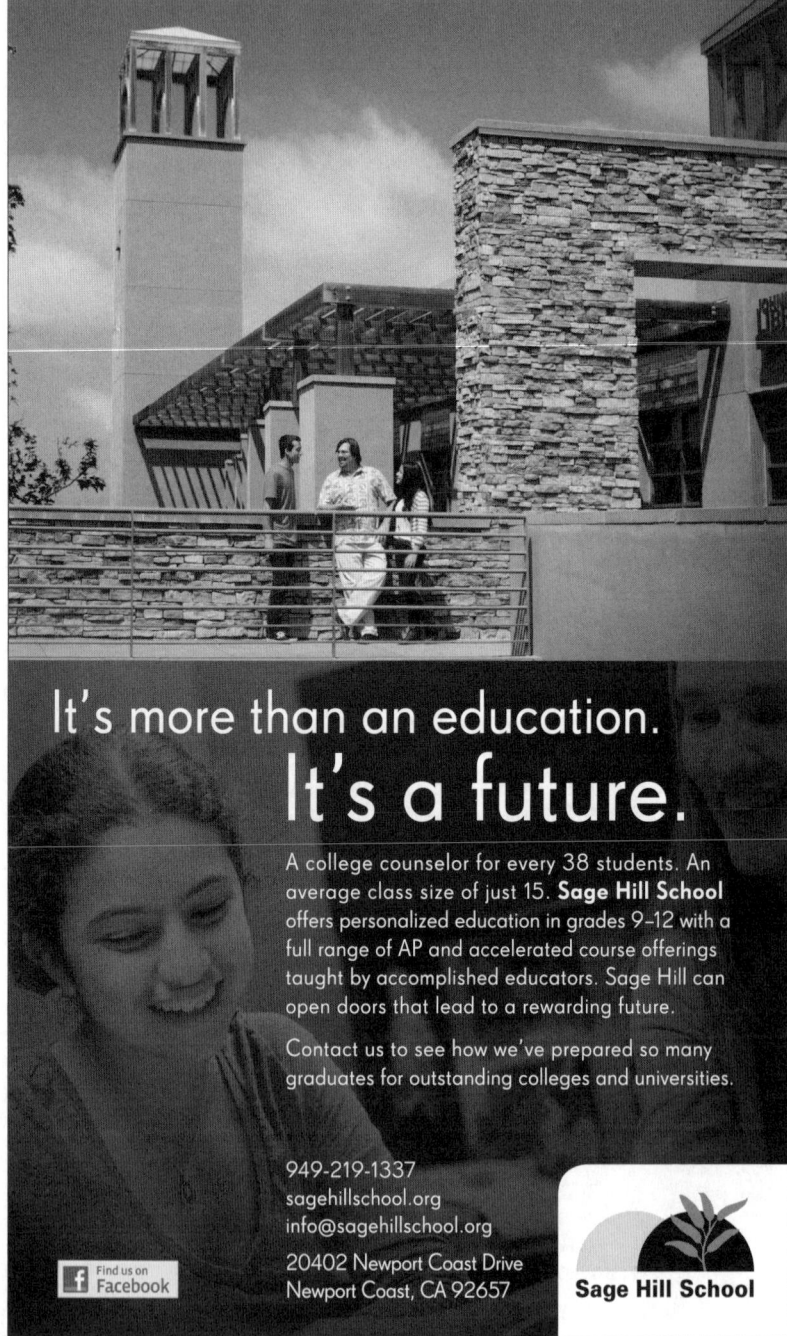

It's more than an education.
It's a future.

A college counselor for every 38 students. An average class size of just 15. **Sage Hill School** offers personalized education in grades 9–12 with a full range of AP and accelerated course offerings taught by accomplished educators. Sage Hill can open doors that lead to a rewarding future.

Contact us to see how we've prepared so many graduates for outstanding colleges and universities.

949-219-1337
sagehillschool.org
info@sagehillschool.org

20402 Newport Coast Drive
Newport Coast, CA 92657

Find us on Facebook

Sage Hill School

THE ROEPER SCHOOL

BIRMINGHAM AND BLOOMFIELD HILLS, MICHIGAN
41190 WOODWARD AVENUE, BLOOMFIELD HILLS, MI 48304
DAVID FELDMAN, HEAD OF SCHOOL

248.203.7300
WWW.ROEPER.ORG

Metro Detroit parents have many excellent options for schools, but for gifted children, none matches the education offered by The Roeper School. Founded in 1941, the school has an international reputation for its approach to educating gifted children.

The approach, pioneered by the Roepers, focuses on the whole child while uniquely accommodating the complexity of gifted children. Educationally, it offers the intellectual rigor gifted children crave and allows them to explore personal passions deeply and imaginatively. Emotionally, it embraces the complicated path gifted children travel to maturity as they juggle cognitive and emotional stages that are frequently out of sync. Developmentally, it teaches gifted children, who have a fierce desire to control their own learning, how to do so constructively and responsibly.

The Roeper School is an independent, coeducational day school for gifted students, pre-kindergarten through grade 12, with campuses in Bloomfield Hills (pre-K through 5th grade) and Birmingham (grades 6-12). Decision-making, problem-solving, social responsibility and leadership are interwoven throughout the school's curriculum. Roeper students receive local and national recognition on a regular basis. Roeper has a strong college preparatory program, with early access to many advanced placement courses, as well as highly regarded fine arts, drama, robotics and athletic departments.

ST. STEPHEN'S SCHOOL
ROME, ITALY

Lesley Jane Murphy, *Head of School*

Located in the historic center of Rome, St. Stephen's School is a non-denominational, co-educational college preparatory day and boarding school which has served the American and international communities in Rome and Italy since 1964. The boarding and day program offered spans grades 9 through 12, with a postgraduate year option. In addition to its regular 4 year program, St. Stephen's welcomes a limited number of students, usually in their junior year, from respected American preparatory schools who wish to take advantage of our curriculum, especially with regard to our Classical Studies, Art History, Latin and Italian classes for one or two semesters.

The curriculum adapts a traditional independent school model to its unique Roman setting and fosters rigorous learning in an atmosphere of international fellowship, harmony and trust. St. Stephen's School is accredited by the New England Association of Schools and Colleges and the Council of International Schools. Since 1975, it has offered the International Baccalaureate program, which is now a recognized entrance qualification for universities throughout the world. The School's early recognition of the potential importance of the IB attests to its pioneering spirit in the world of international education.

Enrollment is maintained at around 250 pupils because St. Stephen's believes that students are best served by keeping the student body small, thus allowing each student wider access to our first-rate faculty and campus resources. These resources include new chemistry and physics laboratories; a renovated library and the newly renovated performing arts/assembly hall and tennis, volleyball, and basketball courts; new art studios; and a photography lab, dance studio, and landscaped courtyard and terrace. In further pursuit of its educational mission, St. Stephen's maintains a selective admissions procedure. Students are chosen on the basis of personal promise and their potential to benefit from the School's curriculum. St. Stephen's welcomes students of all races, nationalities, religions and persuasions.

With students from approximately 30 nations, St. Stephen's is truly international in character. Students who have elected to follow the traditional American high school curriculum, many of whom have also participated in our AP program, have recently been accepted to North American universities such as NYU, Macalester College, Bard, and Chicago. Recent acceptances to universities in the UK include Oxford, Edinburgh, Cambridge, Kings College London, University College London, and Imperial College London.

The two and one half acre campus—just a ten minute walk from the Colosseum and the Roman Forum—offers students unique cultural, educational, and recreational advantages as well as frequent school-sponsored travel opportunities to other cities in Italy and the Mediterranean area. Life at St. Stephen's is intense and enjoyable with a happy blend of relaxation and rigor.

Contact: Admissions Office, St. Stephen's School, Via Aventina 3, 00153 Rome, Italy. Tel: (3906) 575.0605. Fax: (3906) 574.1941. E-mail: admissions@ststephens-rome.com. Website: www.sssrome.it.

HILLSDALE ACADEMY

One Academy Lane
Hillsdale, Michigan 49242
517.439.8644
www.hillsdale.edu/academy

Headmaster: Dr. Kenneth Calvert

Founded in 1990, the Academy serves as a model kindergarten-through-twelfth grade school. Under the auspices of Hillsdale College, the Academy bases its curriculum on fundamental academic skills, an exploration of the arts and sciences, and an understanding of the foundational tenets of our Judeo-Christian and Greco-Roman heritage. Originally K-8, the Upper School was incorporated in 1998.

Hillsdale Academy offers an academically enriched alternative to students in Hillsdale County and the surrounding area. Students are admitted to the Academy based on the combined strengths of their application and interview, inasmuch as these show evidence of personal motivation.

RILEY SCHOOL, Inc.

Physical address: Warrenton Rd, Glen Cove, ME 04846
Postal address: PO Box 587, Rockland, ME 04841
Tel: 207-596-6405
E-mail: info@rileyschool.org   Web: www.rileyschool.org

Since 1972, the Riley School has supported the needs of young children and adolescents during their critical years of cognitive, emotional, and social growth. Riley offers a unique and creative approach to learning in which children learn by doing, questioning, and discovering. Small, integrated classes provide opportunities for children to express themselves and to build their self-esteem, thus helping them to develop the skills and attitudes that will help them become life-long learners and creative, independent thinkers.

The comprehensive elementary academic program, which provides children with individual attention to their unique skills and behavior, reflects the school's educational philosophy of meaningful and child-centered education based upon continued study of the children and their ways of knowing.

The school champions the ability of all people to collaborate and to help others through cooperative work, fosters a sense of responsibility toward the natural environment, and strives to promote its goals within a setting that includes appropriate adult role models and a secure, loving atmosphere for learning.

At Riley, children learn how to learn, how to pursue their special interests, and how to realize their potential.

THE GRIER SCHOOL
TYRONE, PA

A supportive faculty and warm environment contribute to the success of the academic program at Grier. Students are encouraged to excel in their academic strengths and passions and have many choices through the Elite Scholars Program, which prepares students for the top American colleges and universities via honors and advanced courses. Students can choose from the 16 Advanced Placement (AP) courses offered at Grier. In addition to the academic rigor available at Grier, students may avail themselves of Grier School's LEAP! (LEArning Power) program, which seeks to empower students with the tools needed to close gaps and improve skills. Grier School's college counseling department supports students throughout high school and works with students and families to ensure a successful transition to university.

Other signature programs, such as the visual and performing arts, enhance the Grier experience. Students interested in the visual arts choose from studio classes in drawing, painting, printmaking, photography, graphic design, batik, weaving, costume design, stagecraft, metal arts, and ceramics, while students wishing to concentrate in the visual arts participate in many of the aforementioned classes in addition to AP studio art and AP art history. Grier's performing arts offerings include instrumental and vocal instruction and ensembles, straight and musical drama troupes, and dance. Grier's dance department offers classes in tap, jazz, ballet, modern, hip hop, and choreography at the beginning, intermediate, and advanced levels. All of the performing arts have options to perform and compete regularly throughout the year.

The sports program at Grier is diverse and attuned to the interests and needs of the students. Varsity programs include soccer, tennis, volleyball, basketball and fencing. Other offerings include recreational versions of soccer, tennis, volleyball, and basketball in addition to options such as karate, Zumba, yoga, body sculpting, and skiing/snowboarding.

Grier's renowned signature equestrian program offers instruction for all riders, from beginning through advanced, in both the English and Western styles. Varsity riders can log upwards of 15-20 hours per week and show regularly throughout the school year in both IEA team competitions and rated competitions in multiple organizations.

Faculty, staff, and facilities are designed to support students in all their endeavors at Grier. In addition to the teaching faculty, full-time resident advisors and guidance counselors add to the supportive and rich environment of the school. All existing structures on campus have been recently renovated and modernized, and many of our signature programs, including the visual arts, the performing arts, and the equestrian program, now reside in new state-of-the-art buildings.

Contact Andrew Wilson, Grier School, Tyrone PA 16686. Tel: 814-684-3000. Fax: 814-684-2177. Email: admissions@grier.org. Web: www.grier.org.

GRIER SUMMER CAMPS

Box 308
TYRONE, PA 16686
Tel: 814-684-3000 , ext 113
E-mail: bestcamp@grier.org
Web: www.bestcamp.org

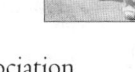

Accredited by the American Camp Association

Helen Zientek, *Director*

Located in the Allegheny Mountains of beautiful central Pennsylvania, Grier Summer Camps offers camp programs using the campus of the Grier School, a historic girls boarding school. Whether a camper chooses horseback riding, visual or performing arts or a combination of all three opportunities, each venue offers state of the art facilities.

Founded in 1975, Allegheny Riding Camp was the first Grier Summer program. Allegheny Riding Camp is our premier camp for girls ages 7 to 17 who love horses! In order to assure a personalized experience for every camper, Allegheny Riding Camp accommodates no more than 70 riding campers at a time. We maintain an excellent staff ratio to provide a caring atmosphere for everyone. We have a rich tradition of teaching girls self-confidence through English horsemanship, and this summer will add Western saddle to our Show Camper program. Our staff teaches girls to realize their potential through horsemanship, friendship, and respect for animals.

Allegheny Camp of the Arts is perfect for girls, ages 8-17, looking for a fun camp experience in a beautiful, serene location with top-notch arts facilities. Grier Summer offers a three-week program in creative and performing arts. Campers choose four different elective activities from a variety of creative and recreational options. Counselors, Grier School teachers, or professionals hired for summer activities, teach activities. Activities are offered only if there is a qualified or experienced instructor.

Grier Summer also offers three intensive art programs, Dance, Art Portfolio and Musical Theatre.

In a three-week session at Grier Summer, each camper follows her individual activity schedule for 13 days of the session, including Saturdays and Sundays. On Thursdays,

we have special events such as theme days with entertainers. On Mondays, campers attend field trips to local attractions. Campers range in age from 7 to 17 and come from of a variety of religious backgrounds and cultures from across the US and around the world.

In order to assure a personalized experience for every camper, Grier Summer maintains an excellent staff ratio. We take pride in giving every camper the special attention she deserves.

The Roxbury Latin School
Grades 7-12 independent boys' school founded in 1645

The Roxbury Latin School
101 St. Theresa Avenue
West Roxbury, Massachusetts 02132
617.325.4920
www.roxburylatin.org

No application fee.
Need-blind admission.
Ample financial aid.

Throughout its history,
Roxbury Latin has been
proud to celebrate the academic
laurels its students have
earned, but has never lost
sight of its primary concern:
the moral character of its boys.
At Roxbury Latin, the
fundamental promise made
to families is that their boy
will be known and loved.

NOBLE AND GREENOUGH SCHOOL

10 Campus Dr.
DEDHAM, MA 02026

Robert P. Henderson, Jr., A.B., A.M., Dartmouth College, *Head*

Noble and Greenough School is a coeducational independent day and five-day boarding school located on a 187-acre campus on the banks of the Charles River in Dedham. Founded in 1866 in Boston by George Washington Copp Noble, the school draws students in grades seven through 12 from 95 cities and towns. The unique five-day boarding program, which allows boarders to return to their families every weekend, is open to some 50 young men and women of Upper School (grades 9-12) age, a few of whom come from abroad, most from communities in Massachusetts beyond daily commuting range. The new student and faculty residential hall was recently completed and the new Arts facility, containing a two-storied theater, art gallery, recital hall and practice rooms, was completed in 2006.

Nobles, as it is familiarly called, moved to Dedham in 1922, locating on the Nickerson estate. The original home, known as the Castle and designed by the eminent architectural firm of H.H. Richardson, is still used for daily meals as well as special functions that celebrate the school. Besides the Castle, the Nobles campus includes two main classroom buildings (one for the Upper School and one for the Middle School), a science building, a library, a state-of-the-art athletic center, an arts center, a multi-purpose indoor ice hockey facility and boathouses.

Nobles' academic and afternoon (extra-curricular) programs offer a balance among intellectual, moral and physical disciplines intended to inculcate values of honesty, self-respect, curiosity, commitment to others, integrity and civility. The curriculum combines a core of academic courses requisite to an educated person; elective courses are designed to fit the special needs and interests of the many unique individuals in the community. Students taking part in the school's Advanced Placement program are given a choice of 20 selections. In the semester prior to graduation, students may create and execute independent studies projects within the Greater Boston community. The afternoon program electives offer opportunities in service learning, athletics (including fitness training), performing arts, visual arts and outdoor education. A wide range of clubs and activities is also available, including yearbook and newspaper, photography, drama, a cappella groups, cooking club, multicultural and foreign language societies. Nobles faculty annually guide upwards of 15 school-sanctioned trips both internationally and across the USA. Most trips focus on learning through service and cultural immersion.

Nobles students go on to the most select colleges across the country, with close to 90 percent typically entering their first- or second-choice schools.

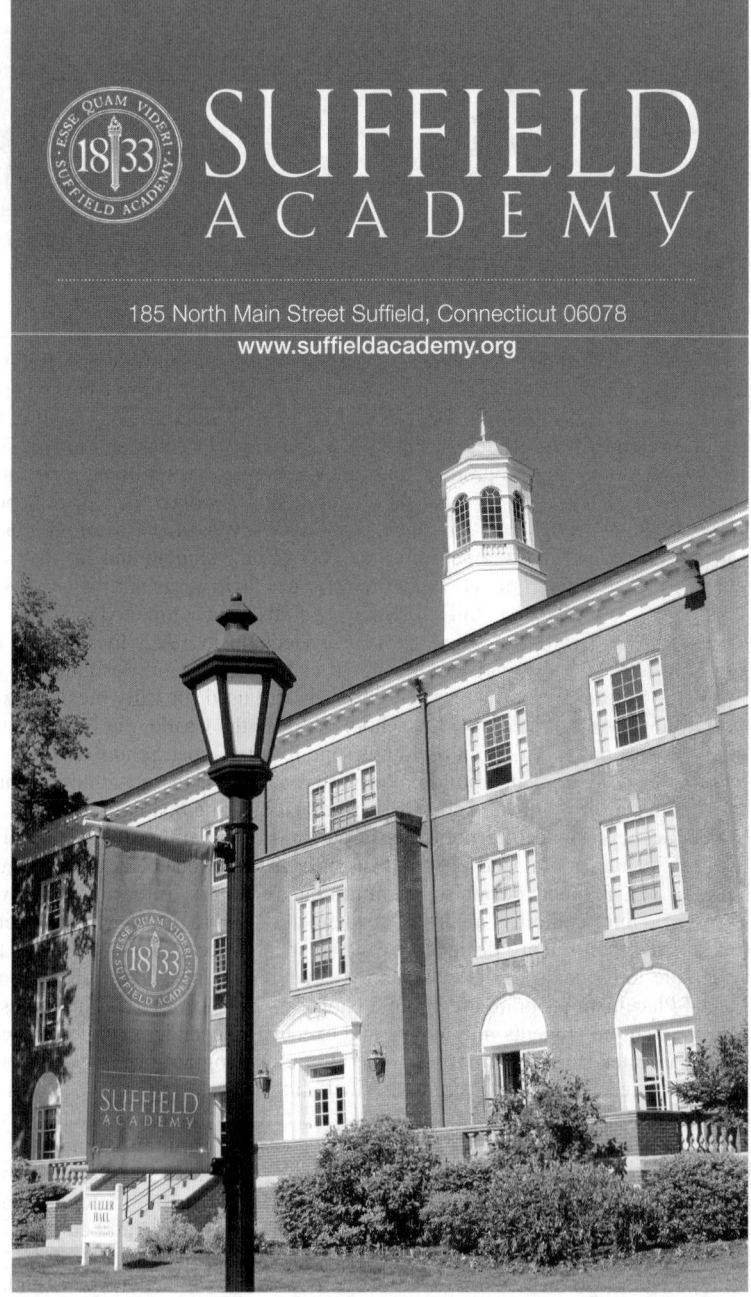

SUFFIELD ACADEMY

185 North Main Street Suffield, Connecticut 06078
www.suffieldacademy.org

- FOUNDED IN 1833 • GRADES 9-12 (PG) • 400 STUDENTS
- 5:1 STUDENT & FACULTY RATIO • CO-ED BOARDING & DAY

Suffield Academy is a school grounded in **rich tradition** with a healthy **respect for community** and an eye toward **innovation**. Come to Suffield and discover **endless opportunities** for you to create your Suffield experience.

Suffield Academy does not discriminate on the basis of sex, race, color, religion, creed, national or ethnic origin, citizenship, physical attributes, disability, age, or sexual orientation. We administer our admissions, financial aid, educational, athletic, extracurricular, and other policies so that each student is equally accorded all the rights, privileges, programs, and facilities made available by the school.

➜ Scan for the Suffield experience

LANDMARK SCHOOL

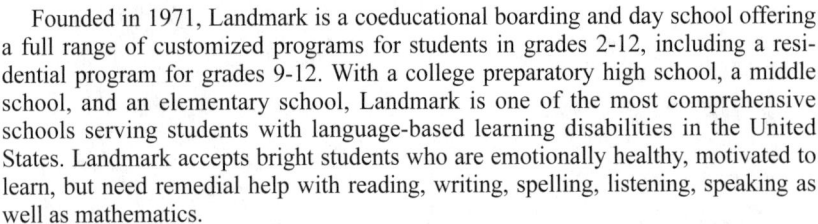

PRIDES CROSSING, MA
Tel: 978-236-3000
E-mail: admission@landmarkschool.org
Web: www.landmarkschool.org

Robert J. Broudo, MEd, *Head of School*

Founded in 1971, Landmark is a coeducational boarding and day school offering a full range of customized programs for students in grades 2-12, including a residential program for grades 9-12. With a college preparatory high school, a middle school, and an elementary school, Landmark is one of the most comprehensive schools serving students with language-based learning disabilities in the United States. Landmark accepts bright students who are emotionally healthy, motivated to learn, but need remedial help with reading, writing, spelling, listening, speaking as well as mathematics.

Landmark individualizes instruction for each student, emphasizing the development of language and learning skills within a uniquely supportive and structured living and learning environment.

With a 1:3 teacher-student ratio, the key to Landmark's successful model is the daily one-to-one tutorial. A customized tutorial curriculum is designed to remediate specific language needs, which may encompass decoding, fluency, phonological awareness, written composition, and organizational skills. In addition, Landmark provides small group classes in language arts, math, science, social studies, auditory/oral expression, literature, as well as study skills and electives. Students from both campuses may choose from electives such as art, auto mechanics, woodworking, and computers/programming. Performing Arts, photography, creative writing, television production, yearbook and newspaper are offered at the High School Campus. Computer technology is integrated across the entire curriculum. Extracurricular activities include drama, intramural sports and community service. Landmark's athletic program includes soccer, basketball, lacrosse, tennis, wrestling, track and field which provide opportunities for physical fitness and a greater sense of achievement and success.

The High School curriculum addresses the spectrum of needs for students; based on their unique abilities and skill levels, students are assigned to a schedule of courses. The curriculum is designed to teach the students to become independent learners. Individual assessments are made continually to determine the appropriate approach of remediation. When a student makes progress within one year of grade level, their case manager may consider a transition to more advanced levels of courses.

Situated on two beautiful campuses just 25 miles north of Boston, students take advantage of its North Shore location and many cultural opportunities.

The Glenholme School

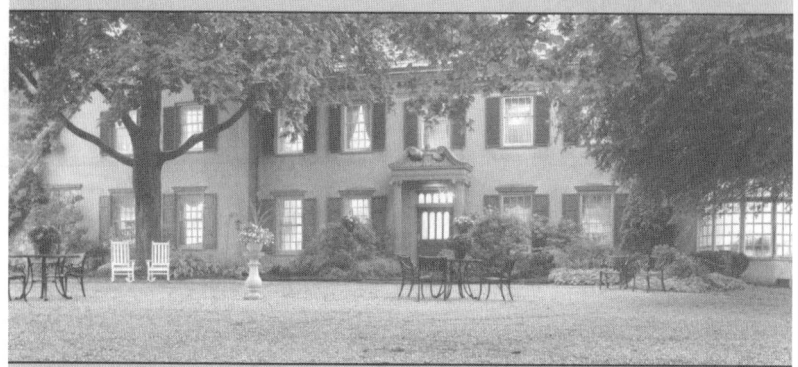

The Glenholme School is a therapeutic boarding school for young people diagnosed with Asperger's, ADHD, PDD, OCD, Tourette's, depression, anxiety, and various learning differences. The program provides a treatment milieu designed to build competence socially and academically. Our learning environment supports and enhances the success of special needs students.

Enrollment is open for Glenholme's middle school, high school, Summer Program and Glen Ridge post-secondary program.

81 Sabbaday Lane, Washington, CT 06793
Phone: (860) 868-7377 • Fax: (860) 868-7413
www.theglenholmeschool.org
Devereux CONNECTICUT

The Oxbow School
Semester Program

The Oxbow School is a unique, interdisciplinary semester program for high-school students. Our mission is to strengthen students' abilities in creative and critical inquiry by combining rigorous studio art practice with innovative academics. Our vision is for Oxbow students to develop a stronger sense of identity, self-worth, and the confidence to embrace the responsibility for their own learning and lives.

The Oxbow School curriculum is sequential, project-based, experiential, and interdisciplinary. Courses are team-taught across disciplines and media. Academic and art projects are based on reading, writing, research, and study skills that extend the student's ability to fully engage with the topics through experimentation, testing, and revision. With a heuristic emphasis on taking risks and assuming personal responsibility for decision-making, the sequence of the projects deepens basic foundation skills so that at the end of twelve weeks, each student is prepared to embark upon a comprehensive, month-long Final Project on a topic of their choice, supported by research in relevant domains.

Teaching for a future we cannot imagine. Essential to the Oxbow experience is the presence of compassionate adults—as artists, teachers, mentors, and advisors—in every aspect of the life of the students and the School. Oxbow faculty members are passionate about sharing the excitement of inquiry-based learning and personal growth with students. Their firm commitment to developmental concepts such as self-reliance, individual responsibility, resourcefulness, and self-reflection, leads students to the development of the skills and habits of mind that lead to life-long learning.

The Visiting Artist Program is integral to the overall concept and character of the school. Twice each semester, nationally (often internationally) known artists join the faculty in residence at Oxbow. In this setting, students, faculty, and artists explore the nature of creative thinking and the role of the artist in contemporary society and culture.

The Oxbow School
530 Third Street, Napa, CA 94559
P 707.255.6000; F 707.255.6006
mail@oxbowschool.org
www.oxbowschool.org

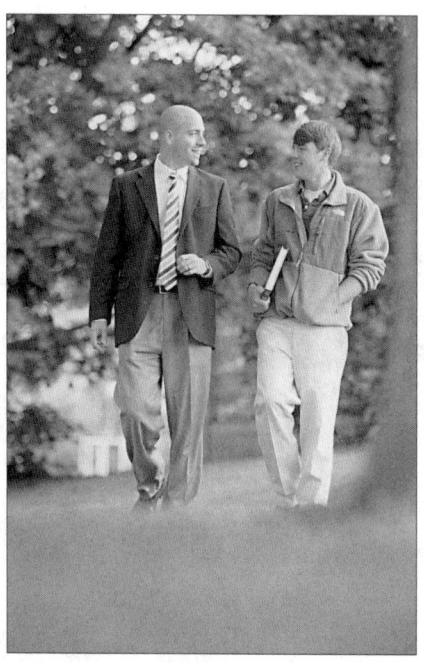

THE OXFORD ACADEMY
WESTBROOK, CT

Since 1906, Oxford Academy has specialized in educating young men between the ages of 14 and 20 of average to above average intelligence who wish to accelerate their course work, or who seek an alternative to the traditional academic approach. With a classroom ratio of one teacher to one pupil, each student is instructed at the level and pace most appropriate to his own ability and learning style. Students at Oxford benefit from carefully designed individual curricula, proctored study halls and close academic guidance in a caring community atmosphere. Specific programs include Advanced Placement and English-as-a-Second Language. Each student participates daily in intramural or varsity sports throughout the year.

In recent years, 99% of the students accepted for admission were referred to Oxford by educational consultants, parents of graduates or former students, other private school headmasters or school counselors. Instruction and guidance is provided by 22 faculty members, 11 of whom live on campus. Enrollment is limited to 48 boys with approximately one-third of the student body coming from outside the United States. The school is located along the Connecticut shoreline, midway between New York and Boston.

RYE COUNTRY DAY SCHOOL

Rye, New York 10580
Tel: 914.925.4513
www.RyeCountryDay.org

Rye Country Day School is a coeducational, college preparatory school in Rye, New York, dedicated to providing students from Pre-Kindergarten through Grade 12 with an excellent education using both traditional and innovative approaches. In a nurturing and supportive environment, we offer a challenging program that stimulates individuals to achieve their maximum potential through academic, athletic, creative, and social endeavors. We are actively committed to diversity. We expect and promote moral responsibility, and strive to develop strength of character within a respectful school community. Our goal is to foster a lifelong passion for learning, understanding, and service in an ever-changing world.

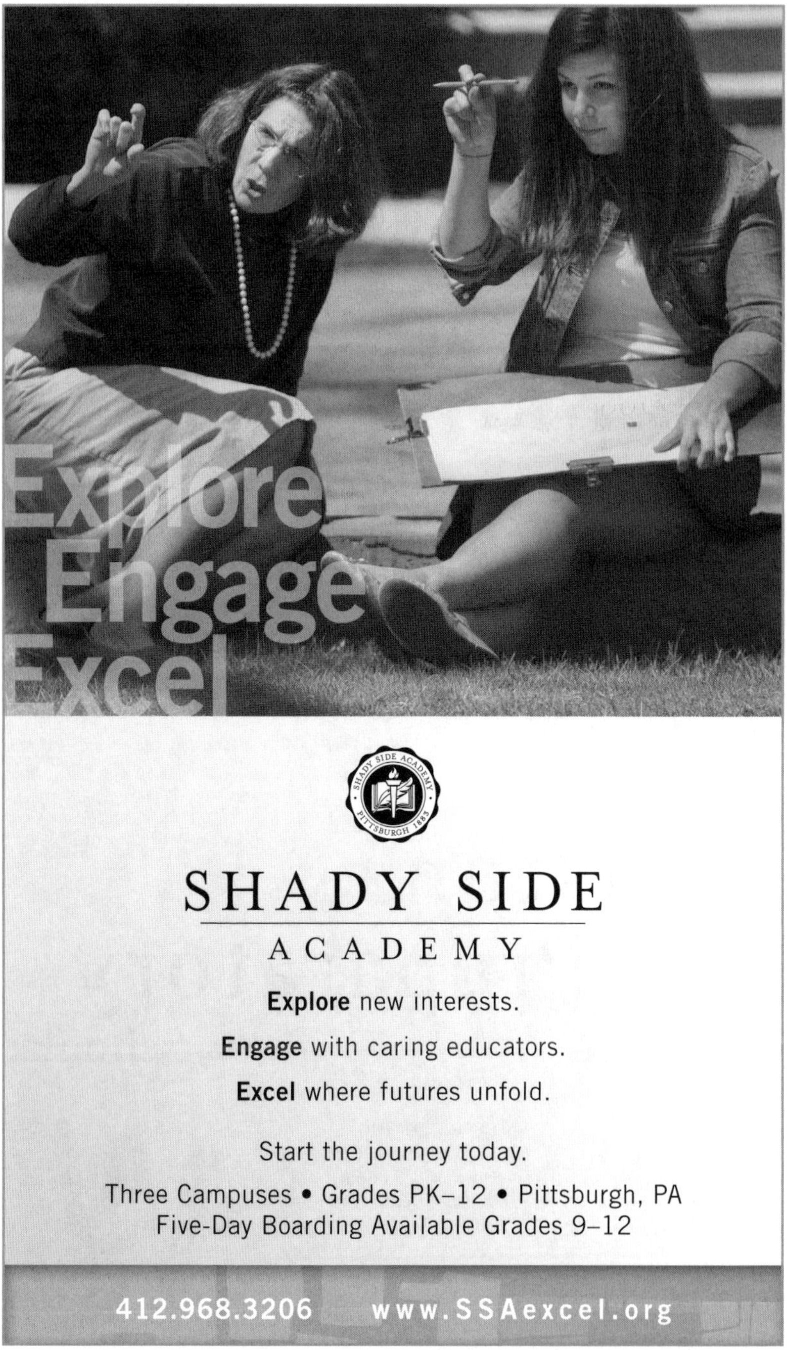

SHADY SIDE

ACADEMY

Explore new interests.

Engage with caring educators.

Excel where futures unfold.

Start the journey today.

Three Campuses • Grades PK–12 • Pittsburgh, PA
Five-Day Boarding Available Grades 9–12

412.968.3206   www.SSAexcel.org

If your child is struggling with school...

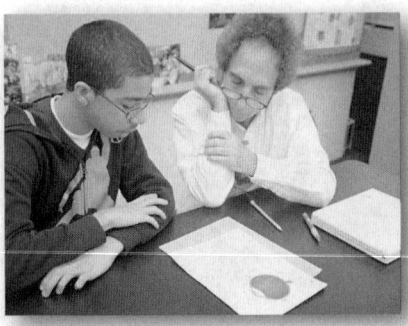

"Someone mentioned to me that if I had a creative and bright child, he would thrive at Winston Prep.

Winston changed his life."

Jenifer Levin, mother of Mak Levin
Winston Prep Class of 2008
Roger Williams University Class of 2012

...we can help.

The
Winston
Preparatory
Schools

NEW YORK
126 W. 17th St.
New York City, NY 10011
646.638.2705 x634

CONNECTICUT
57 West Rocks Road
Norwalk, CT 06851
203.229.0465 x535

www.winstonprep.edu

ORINDA ACADEMY
PARENTS, STUDENTS & TEACHERS WORKING TOGETHER

College Prep • Grades 6-12 • Small Classes

19 Altarinda Rd., Orinda, CA 94563
925.254.7553 • www.OrindaAcademy.org

Orinda Academy has a 30 year history of providing a superb college preparatory education for students, grades 6-12. The school's hallmarks are structure and support for engendering success for students with various learning styles. Small class size, student teacher ratio 9:1, inclusive and diverse student population, and a full compliment of co-curricular activities make Orinda Academy a special jewel in the redwood hills, accessible to all San Francisco East Bay communities. Our mission is to provide the support to help each student reach his full potential by engaging parents, students and teachers in working together.

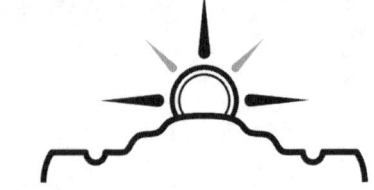

FOUNTAIN VALLEY SCHOOL
OF COLORADO

A classic boarding school education in
the Rocky Mountain West

"Academics, Athletics, Arts"

Fountain Valley School combines intellectual rigor with a spirit of adventure
and exploration. FVS offers a college
preparatory program for motivated
students who seek a diverse and challenging learning experience within a
close-knit and supportive community.

www.fvs.edu
6155 Fountain Valley School Road
Colorado Springs, CO 80911
admission@fvs.edu * 719.390.7035
Boarding/Day * Co-ed * Grades 9-12

Great Expectations
You have them. So do we.

Leaders in the classroom, on the playing field,
and in the community — since 1886.

Learn more. Call Admissions Director
Scott Wade at 763-381-8200.

www.breckschool.org

Breck School | 123 Ottawa Ave N | Minneapolis MN 55422-5189

CHARLOTTE COUNTRY DAY SCHOOL
1440 Carmel Road, Charlotte NC 28226
(704) 943-4530 • www.charlottecountryday.org

Founded in 1941, Charlotte Country Day School is the oldest and largest independent college preparatory day school in the Charlotte area. With superior, highly professional teachers, state-of-the-art facilities, and a commitment to "living our mission," we offer students in junior kindergarten through grade 12 hands-on experiences and individualized attention in a diverse and nurturing environment.

- **Our Mission:** CCDS is a mission-driven school committed to developing fully the potential of every student by fostering intellectual curiosity, principled character, ethical leadership, and a responsibility to serve.
- **Rigorous Curriculum:** Students are challenged academically at every grade level by innovative and caring teachers. We offer the International Baccalaureate diploma program and more than 20 Advanced Placement courses. Our graduates annually receive in excess of $4 million in scholarship offers.
- **Global Connections:** Foreign language and cultural instruction begins in junior kindergarten. Students are offered numerous opportunities for foreign travel and language immersion beginning in sixth grade. CCDS also offers international students the opportunity to learn the language skills necessary to succeed both academically and socially through the English as Second Language (ESL).
- **Two Campuses:** Our Middle School students thrive on a separate, close-knit campus dedicated specifically to nurturing the hearts and minds of adolescents.
- **Creative Expression:** Students at every grade level have opportunities for fine and performing arts instruction and extracurricular activities, including visual arts, vocal and instrumental music, drama, and dance.
- **Full-Participation Athletics:** The athletics program supports 66 teams, and 90 percent of our students participate in some form of organized athletics on the Middle School, junior varsity, or varsity levels.
- **Guidance:** A strong advisory program begins in Middle School, and three dedicated college guidance counselors assist Upper School students in their college selections.
- **Community Outreach:** Service to others is an integral part of the Charlotte Country Day School experience.

We invite you to visit our school and discover how our programs and teachers will bring out the very best in your child.

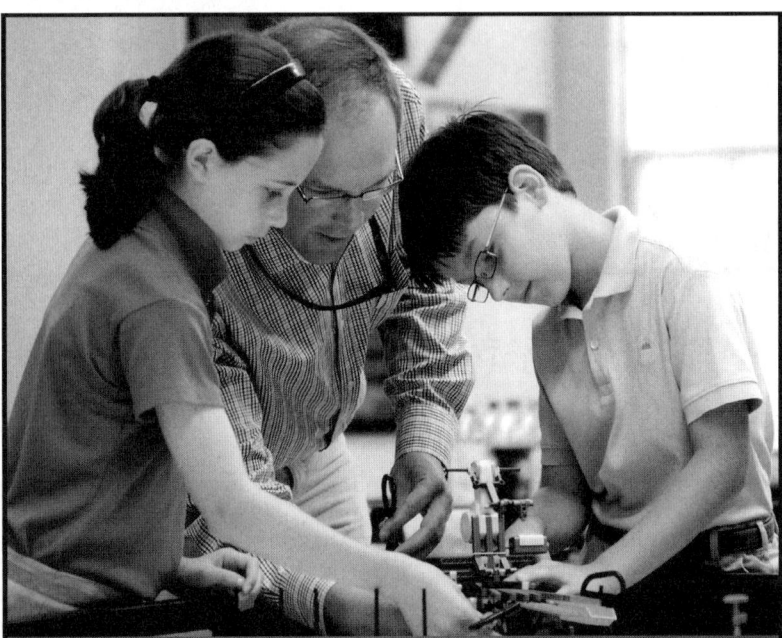

Collaboration and perseverance.
Important in physics. And in life.

We're proud of the ways we challenge students academically. It's rewarding to see them excel. But we're even prouder of the character lessons we teach. We help students learn to work well on teams and keep striving for the best solutions as they reach for their goals.

When they're adults, the problems our students will face will be more complex than designing self-propelled robots. That's why we actively teach collaboration, perseverance, flexibility, and other habits of mind and behavior that lead to personal and professional success.

Think private school is out of reach? Think again.

We offer financial support so students who are highly motivated to learn can take advantage of all LFCDS has to offer. *Contact the Office of Admission for details.*

LAKE FOREST COUNTRY DAY SCHOOL

145 South Green Bay Road | Lake Forest, IL 60045
(847) 615-6151 | admission@lfcds.org | www.lfcds.org

TRINITY-PAWLING SCHOOL
PAWLING, NY
Archibald A. Smith, III, BS, Trinity, MALS, Wesleyan, *Headmaster*

Trinity-Pawling, founded in 1907, is a college preparatory, Episcopal, boarding school for boys. The school is located in Pawling, New York, 67 miles north of New York City along the Connecticut border. The campus, set on 140 acres of rolling hills, is just over an hour's drive from New York's major airports.

It is Trinity-Pawling's belief that an appreciation of one's own worth can best be discovered by experiencing the worth of others, by understanding the value of one's relationship with others, and by acquiring a sense of self-confidence that comes through living and working competently at the level of one's own potential.

Trinity-Pawling respects and recognizes the differences in individuals and the different processes required to achieve their educational potential.

At the heart of Trinity-Pawling's philosophy is the effort system. This system rewards a boy based on his effort in various aspects of school life including academic, athletic, extracurricular, and dormitory. We acknowledge that boys have different strengths and weaknesses, and it is our belief that by rewarding students for hard work, each boy will be motivated to reach his own potential in all areas of school life.

Trinity-Pawling offers over 100 courses including 17 AP courses. A student teacher ratio of 7 to 1 and a residential faculty allow for an intimate academic setting where additional instruction is always available. The Language Program, a curriculum based program for bright students who have been diagnosed as having a mild language based learning disability is also offered on a limited basis.

Students benefit from an extensive physical plant. The Dann Building includes 6 new classrooms, 4 new science labs, 2 science lecture halls, 2 computer labs and an auditorium. There are is a 25,000+ volume library, chapel, Arts Center, Scully Hall, a new dining facility, and 8 dormitories.

Athletic facilities include McGraw Pavilion, with a multi-purpose wrestling room, a newly renovated hockey arena, the Carleton Gymnasium that includes 5 international-sized squash courts, a Nautilus and free weights room, a cardioroom, 11 tennis courts, 8 playing fields, a state-of-the-art track, stadium football field, and baseball diamond.

A wide variety of extracurricular activities is offered and there are athletic teams and intramural programs for students of all levels of ability.

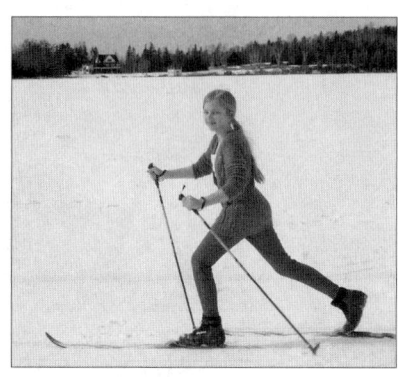

NORTH COUNTRY SCHOOL
4382 Cascade Rd.
LAKE PLACID, NY 12946

E-mail: admissions@northcountryschool.org
Web: www.northcountryschool.org

David Hochschartner, *Director*

North Country School offers a unique learning environment for children including a full working farm, a recreational setting in Olympic Lake Placid, and an optional seven week summer camp. The educational program is experientially based and designed to speak to a variety of intelligences. Gifted children thrive as do classroom resistant learners. The ratio of 3-1 provides guidance for individualized student learning initiatives as well as good caretaking. Children live in groups of 8-10 with houseparents.

The 200-acre campus include a lake, organic gardens, a sugar bush, meadows, and a ski hill. There are also skating ponds, tree houses and slides by every staircase. Studio and performing arts, horseback riding, skiing, mountaineering, camping and regular farm chores supplement the enriched academic program.

The school's goals are character development, intellectual competence, self-reliance, self-confidence and a natural and healthy childhood.

BUXTON SCHOOL
291 South St., Williamstown, MA 01267
Tel: 413-458-3919, Admissions ext. 108
Fax: 413-458-9428
Email: Admissions@BuxtonSchool.org

Buxton School is a coed college-preparatory boarding and day school for students who are looking for stimulating, participatory academics; a committed arts program; and a community experience that is supportive and intentional. For over 80 years, Buxton has been educating students in the progressive tradition—we believe that all people learn best by doing, and that experience is the most powerful teacher of all. Our goal is to find the appropriate balance between a challenging academic curriculum and a community life that is rich and fulfilling. Discussion-based classes are the norm; ESL instruction and learning support are available.

Central to the school experience is the value of students contributing their ideas, energy, and labor to the care and maintenance at the school; the commitment we make to traveling within and outside our country to better understand how communities and governments work; and the importance of artistic exploration and expression. Buxton is also committed to diversity of every kind, as it serves to enrich students' experiences at school as well as in the world beyond.

In addition to a varied curriculum that readies students for the rigors of college, Buxton offers extensive arts courses and activities that include studio art, music (composition, theory, and performance), theater, ceramics, photography, video production, creative writing, and drum and dance—Afro-Caribbean and Balinese.

Our campus—with new art and music studios and a renovated classroom/science complex—provides students with the best of both worlds: the charm and history of traditional buildings with the opportunities offered by state-of-the-art facilities. Nearby are the exceptional resources of Williams College, the Clark Art Institute, and MASS MoCA.

THE PEGASUS SCHOOL

19692 Lexington Lane
Huntington Beach, CA 92646
www.thepegasusschool.org
Tel: 714-964-1224 • Fax: 714-962-6047

The Pegasus School, where bright minds soar, is an independent co-educational school for pre-kindergarten through grade eight dedicated to academic excellence and the development of lifelong learners who are confident, caring, and courageous.

The Pegasus School is accredited by the California Association of Independent Schools (CAIS) and is a proud member of National Association of Independent Schools (NAIS).

WINDWARD SCHOOL
13 Windward Ave.
WHITE PLAINS, NY 10605
Tel: 914-949-6968
Fax: 914-949-8220
Web: www.windwardny.org

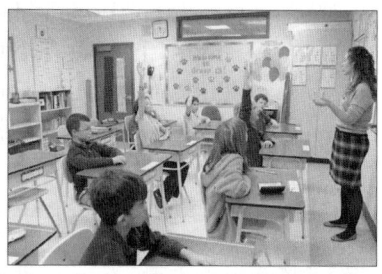

Windward is an independent, coeducational day school, grades 1-9, dedicated to providing an excellent instructional program for children with language-based learning disabilities. The multisensory curriculum is designed for students of average to superior intelligence who can benefit from the unique educational experience provided. Through direct instruction in small class settings, a trained staff assists students to improve their language skills. Academic success, combined with opportunities for social and emotional growth, enables students to understand their learning styles, build confidence, and develop self-advocacy skills. Windward is committed to helping students achieve their full potential in preparation for a successful return to the mainstream educational environment. To meet these goals, the school provides ongoing training to its faculty based on the most current research and also shares its expertise with the parent body, other educators, and the broader community.

**Getting
an education
shouldn't be
a desk job.**

St. Andrew's-Sewanee School offers:
- Innovative courses such as Chinese, Film making, and Environmental Studies
- An emphasis on creativity and problem solving
- A supportive, close-knit community that won't let you get lost in the crowd
- Study and organizational skills support
- Better than AP - Free college courses at an outstanding liberal arts college
- Personalized college counseling
- Family-style residences
- Outdoor adventure on 550 beautiful acres

ST.ANDREW'S
SEWANEE

www.sasweb.org   931.598.5651

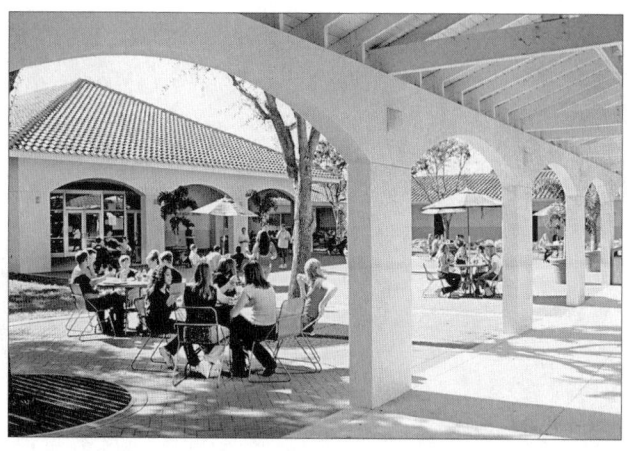

CANTERBURY SCHOOL
FORT MYERS, FL

John Anthony (Tony) Paulus, *Head of School*

Canterbury is the only independent, co-educational, PK-12, college preparatory day-school serving the rapidly growing Fort Myers and Lee County vicinities.

The school's 12 building, 32-acre campus is located adjacent to Edison College. Canterbury has a total enrollment of 600, with approximately 200 students in grades 9-12; 22% of students receive financial aid. An Honor Code administered by the Student Council was adopted in 1990.

An Upper School complex contains seventeen classrooms, four science labs, two art studios, a band room, a drama room, a computer lab, a language lab and a lecture hall. The campus includes a Performing Arts Center, two gymnasiums, a dining hall, and a marine science, touch-tank lab opened in 2006.

Canterbury provides a rigorous, traditional liberal arts course of study within a supportive atmosphere, emphasizing good citizenship and personal responsibility. Advanced Placement courses are offered in all disciplines, and beyond that, extraordinary opportunities are available in the sciences. Additional offerings include a strong advisor program, an extensive college guidance program, rapidly expanding foreign student exchanges, a vigorous athletic program, varied extra-curricular opportunities, and a required community service component. All graduates continue their education; many enroll in leading colleges and universities.

A member of the National Association of Independent Schools and the Cum Laude Society, Canterbury is fully accredited by the Florida Council of Independent Schools and the Southern Association of Colleges and Schools/Council on Accreditation and School Improvement (SACS/CASI). Other memberships include the National Association of College Admissions, the Southern Association of College Admissions, and the Florida Kindergarten Council.

PROVIDENCE HIGH SCHOOL
YOU BELONG HERE.

- Real-World Expertise in our Medical, Media and Technology Focus Programs
- Award-Winning Visual and Performing Arts
- Competitive Sports

Campus Ministry Programs 2011 CIF Champion for Character School
Catholic, College Preparatory School
Member of CAIS
Accredited by WASC & WCEA • Applications & Financial Assistance Available

PROVIDENCE
High School

511 S. Buena Vista St.
Burbank, CA 91505
(818) 846-8141
www.providencehigh.org

MAKE OF YOUR LIFE
A DREAM; AND OF THAT
DREAM, A REALITY.

FAIS DE TA VIE UN RÊVE,
ET D'UN RÊVE, UNE RÉALITÉ.

ANTOINE DE SAINT-EXUPÉRY

We teach the world.

English or French College Prep
Preschool–12th grade

www.LyceeLA.org
(310) 836-3464

OPENINGS AVAILABLE

Admissions Information:
(310) 836-3464, ext 315
admissions@LyceeLA.org

Accredited by both WASC and the
French Ministry of Education

1964
Cogito Ergo Sum

Le Lycee Francais de Los Angeles

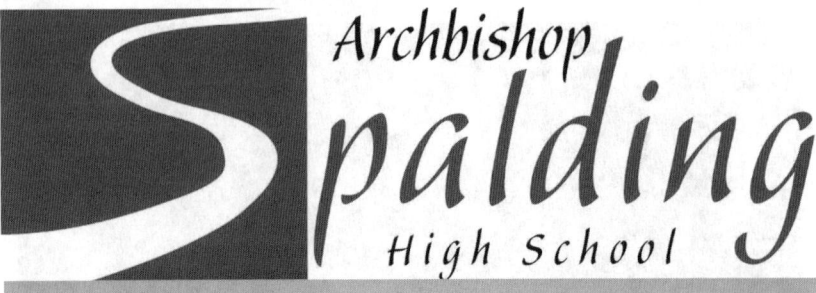

8080 New Cut Road Severn, MD 21144

Profile: Founded in 1966, Archbishop Spalding High School welcomes students from throughout the greater Annapolis, Baltimore and Washington, DC areas. Archbishop Spalding High School is situated on a 52-acre campus with state-of-the-art academic and athletic facilities. Archbishop Spalding annually welcomes students from more than 50 middle schools. Archbishop Spalding offers College Preparatory, Honors, *Pathways to Engineering,* and (19) Advanced Placement courses balanced with more than 60 athletic, artistic, and cocurricular activities, including one of the premiere Music and Arts programs in the state. Archbishop Spalding High School is committed to the development of every student academically, spiritually, physically, and socially.

Tuition Assistance: Decisions to invite an applicant to attend Archbishop Spalding High School are distinct from, and do not take into account, the financial situation of an applicant. Families requesting financial assistance (re)apply each year. Applications must be submitted to the school Scholarship Service of Princeton, NJ no later than January 7, 2013. Financial need is viewed as "the difference between a family's resources and the child's total educational expenses." A fee is charged by S.S.S. to process an application.

Scholarships: Archbishop Spalding awards scholarships for academics, leadership, and musical achievement.

Transportation: Limited bus service is available (additional cost).

Shadow Dates: Parents register online at www.archbishopspalding.org or contact the Admissions office at 410-969-9105, ext. 232 to schedule.

Tuition for 2012-2013: $12, 950 **Fees:** Application Fee: $100

Open House: October 28, 2012

Presentations and tours begin at 12:00pm, 12:30pm, 1:00pm, 1:30pm, and 2:00pm

Application Deadline (for applicants to the class of 2017): January 7, 2013

Year of Founding: 1966

Grade 9-12 Enrollment: 1230

Athletic Conferences: M.I.A.A. & Baltimore Catholic League (Boys); I.A.A.M. (Girls)

www.archbishopspalding.org

BELMONT DAY SCHOOL

55 Day School Ln.
BELMONT, MA 02478

Tel: 617-484-3078   Fax: 617-489-1942
Web: www.belmontday.org

Belmont Day School is an intimate school with an expansive vision. The school provides deep and thoughtful academic preparation for elementary and middle school students within a secure, purposeful, and highly personal community. It is a school where deep research leads to an independent project presented to the community, where students cultivate a garden to learn about sustainability, where an artist captains a varsity team, and where engineering problems are solved collaboratively in the woodshop. Honesty, caring, joy, responsibility, respect, and excellence are the values that guide every decision and interaction. Students leave Belmont Day School with a strong sense of self, an appreciation of the wide and complicated world around them, an understanding of the possibilities and privileges of an effective community, an enthusiasm for learning, and a commitment to balance their own perspectives with those of others. Belmont Day is a school where all voices speak big ideas, where children embrace compelling and uncommon challenges - and grow into independent learners.

After school, extended day, summer session and vacation session programs are offered. Financial aid is available to qualified applicants. Tuition: $20,470 to $32,340. Annette Raphel (Northeastern Univ, BS; Bridgewater State Univ, MEd; Harvard Univ, CAS) is Head of School; Deborah Brissenden is Director of Admissions.

THE LOVETT SCHOOL

4075 Paces Ferry Road, NW
Atlanta, GA 30327
(404) 262-3032
www.lovett.org

William S. Peebles IV, AB, MBA, *Headmaster*

The Lovett School, located on 100 acres bordering the Chattahoochee River in northwest Atlanta, is a college-preparatory school for approximately 1,585 boys and girls in kindergarten through grade 12. Founded in 1926 by Eva Edwards Lovett, the school retains her emphasis on the development of the whole child.

Lovett combines challenging academics with a strong sense of community. Distinctive features of the curriculum include experiential education and interdisciplinary studies, as well as honors and Advanced Placement courses. An Academic Resource Center provides individualized instruction and academic support.

The Fuqua Center houses Lovett's fine arts program, considered one of the best in the Southeast. Comprehensive programs in orchestra, band, voice, music, drama, and art are available at every level. A full athletic program provides each student an opportunity to experience the value of team effort and sportsmanship. The school fields more than 65 competitive teams in 15 sports, in addition to intramurals.

Students participate in a variety of community service activities, and nondenominational chapel services are held weekly in all school divisions. Extracurricular activities include various faculty-sponsored groups, ranging from cooking clubs to honor societies. Summer programs provide academic courses, outdoor experiences, travel opportunities, and athletic offerings.

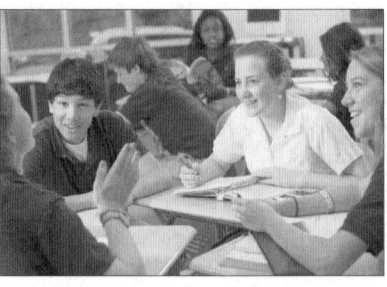

Lovett seeks students from all ethnic, cultural, racial, and religious backgrounds who can benefit from a challenging academic program. We encourage you to visit The Lovett School campus and tour our facilities, which include a Lower School, Upper School, Student Activities Center, and a LEED-Gold certified Middle School.

For more information, please contact the Admission Office.

HAMPSHIRE COUNTRY SCHOOL

Bernd Föcking, Headmaster

Hampshire Country School is for boys of very high ability who, despite difficulties elsewhere, would thrive in a small school with an abundance of adult attention and a focus on abilities rather than problems or deficits.

The education program features flexible classes for students in grades 3 through 6, and traditional English, math, science, history, and foreign language courses for students in grade 7 and above. Class size is 3 to 6 students.

All students are 7-day boarders, and all faculty live on campus, forming a small school community that shares an interest in education and a healthy lifestyle. The school property includes the main campus and hundreds of acres of fields, forests, streams, and lakes.

Activities are informal but structured. They include recreational sports, music lessons, art, drama, board and strategy games, hiking, fishing, camping, caring for farm animals, skiing, and lots of outdoor play.

Enrollment is limited to 25 students. Ideally, they enter when they are 8 to 12 years old and stay for about 3 to 5 years.

28 Patey Circle, Rindge, New Hampshire 03461
www.hampshirecountryschool.org

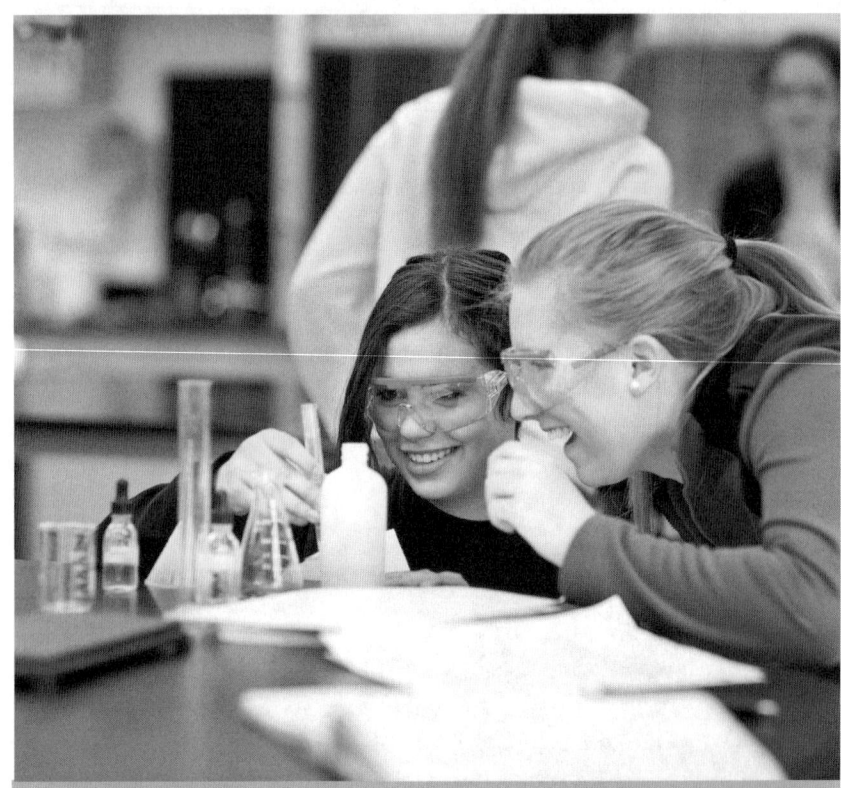

DANA HALL LOVES A GOOD CHALLENGE

Briefly: 475 blazingly intelligent girls from 16 countries. Middle School day program, grades 6-8; Upper School boarding and day programs, grades 9-12. Remarkably accomplished alumnae. Amazing resources for science, arts, athletics, service. Steps away from Wellesley Center (shops, cafes, village life), 12 miles from Boston (center of the world).

Much more: www.danahall.org or 781.235.3010.

Southfield School for girls
Dexter School for boys

 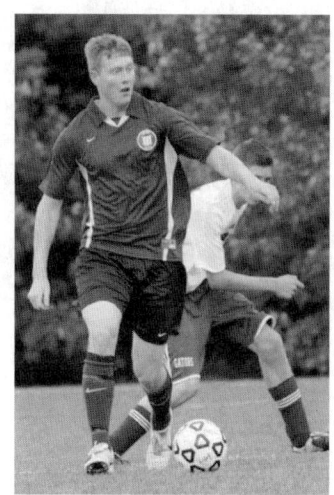

Two independent schools,
one campus community

Academics | Athletics | Arts | Community Service

Early childhood through Grade 12
Building character as well as skills

20 Newton Street, Brookline
(617) 454-2721
www.southfield.org
www.dexter.org

THE WHITE MOUNTAIN SCHOOL
371 West Farm Rd
BETHLEHEM, NH 03574
Tel: 603-444-2928
admissions@whitemountain.org
www.whitemountain.org

Allison Kimmerle, *Director of Admissions*

Set among the beautiful mountains of northern New Hampshire, The White Mountain School is a coeducational, college preparatory, boarding and day school for students in grades 9-12 (and PG). Since our founding in 1886, we have maintained a clear focus on educating each student as an individual. Within our small school community our talented faculty encourage, support, and challenge our students in their studies, provide extracurricular opportunities that nurture their individual interests, and help them begin to build meaningful lives. Our community includes students from 13 states and 9 foreign countries. Students do not "fall between the cracks" at WMS and we are fond of saying, "This is what high school should be!"

Through challenging coursework, discussion-based classes and innovative instruction, students learn to think critically and creatively. We encourage hands-on learning through creative projects, field trips, outdoor labs, and Saturday project blocks. Our Field Courses—one week long and twice per year—offer unique combinations of academic and experiential education in locations both within and outside of the US.

With a solid grounding in core academics and support from caring teachers, our students discover that learning for the sake of learning is rewarding. Additionally, we feel that a successful education is dependent on gaining an understanding of the surrounding world and environment. Our student-faculty ratio is 5:1 and our average class size is 10. We offer eight AP classes and a diverse selection of electives such as Buddhism, Climate & Energy, and Modern African History.

Our Learning Center provides academic support to students who need extra attention within a mainstream academic program. Our college counseling program, which begins junior year, provides individualized guidance from an experienced college counselor.

Performing and fine arts, sustainability studies, community service, and a variety of athletic and extracurricular offerings are integral parts of a WMS education. Team and outdoor sport opportunities include: hiking, kayaking, canoeing, rock climbing, mountain and road biking, soccer, basketball, lacrosse, cross country, ice climbing, Nordic and alpine skiing, snowboarding, and freestyle skiing. Student clubs and committees include: Citizens of the World, a capella, Social Committee, Student Counsel, Art Club, Sustainability Club, China Care, WMS Students Against Cancer, and Yearbook. Theater, dance, community service and participation in our Farm/Forest program are also extracurricular options.

In the classroom, in the dining hall and dormitories, and in the great outdoors, our students learn to be responsible global citizens who understand the complexity of natural systems and the links among ecological integrity, economic security, and social equity. They are empowered to put their education to use through social, environmental, and cultural action.

The 250-acre campus is easily accessible from I-93 and is a beautiful drive from Manchester, Boston, or Hartford airports. The school is governed by a 18-member Board of Trustees and welcomes students from diverse backgrounds and all religious traditions.

School accreditations: NEACS, TABS, ISANNE, SSATB, NHS, NAIS, SBSA. Our Outdoor Education Department is accredited by the Association for Experiential Education and our Climbing Program is accredited by the American Mountain Guides Association.

Wildwood School

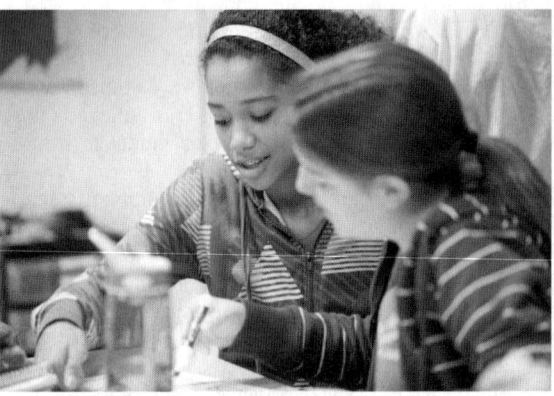

At Wildwood School, we believe success demands more than the mastery of content. Students must learn how to learn - to adapt, collaborate, and gain perspective in a global society that is increasingly interconnected. Wildwood students begin to develop these skills in kindergarten and continue through 12th grade.

A nationally-acclaimed independent day school, Wildwood emphasizes academic excellence and instills a genuine passion for learning. Armed with knowledge, creativity, curiosity, and passion, Wildwood students graduate with the power to make a difference in the world. To learn more about Wildwood, please visit our website, www.wildwood.org.

Elementary Campus   **Middle and Upper Campus**
12201 Washington Place   11811 Olympic Boulevard
Los Angeles, CA 90066   Los Angeles, CA 90064
(310) 397-3134   (310) 478-7189

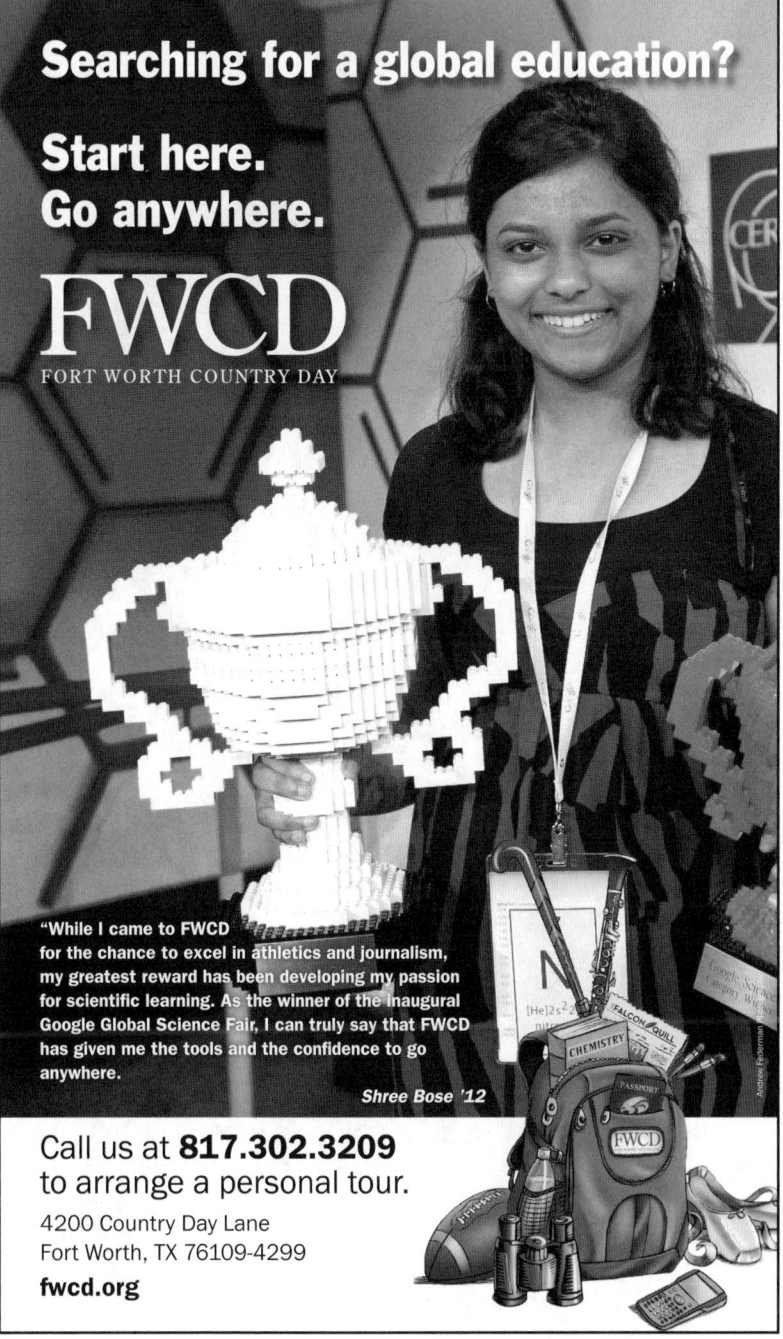

Searching for a global education?

Start here.
Go anywhere.

FWCD
FORT WORTH COUNTRY DAY

"While I came to FWCD for the chance to excel in athletics and journalism, my greatest reward has been developing my passion for scientific learning. As the winner of the inaugural Google Global Science Fair, I can truly say that FWCD has given me the tools and the confidence to go anywhere.

Shree Bose '12

Call us at **817.302.3209**
to arrange a personal tour.

4200 Country Day Lane
Fort Worth, TX 76109-4299

fwcd.org

A boy's education without
Christian Worldview and *Consistent Structure*
misses the goal.

Our personalized instruction provides the right equipment
C H A M B E R L A I N - H U N T . C O M
Tel 601.437.8855 | Fax 601.437.3212

ST. MARTIN'S EPISCOPAL SCHOOL
METAIRIE, LA

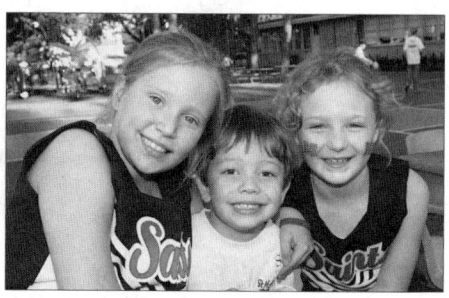

*We prepare students to thrive in college and in life through
faith, scholarship and service*

St. Martin's Episcopal School is a vibrant learning community with a rich history, engaging and bright students, topnotch faculty, nationally recognized academic, artistic, and athletic programs, as well as a state of the art campus second to none in the greater New Orleans area.

Founded in 1947, St. Martin's is an independent, co-educational school serving students ages two years through twelfth grade. The school is located on 18 tree-shaded acres convenient to any location in the Greater New Orleans area. Although affiliated with the Episcopal Diocese of Louisiana, St. Martin's enrolls students of many faiths and in the Episcopal tradition, welcomes and encourages learning about and respect for all religious faiths.

The strong academic curriculum provides honors and advanced placement courses as well as a wide range of extracurricular activities including athletics and fine and performing arts. Service and leadership are hallmarks of a St. Martin's education, and our students are involved in serving the community and developing their skills as leaders from the youngest grades.

The people of St. Martin's provide the foundation for what makes St. Martin's excel. Our students are intellectually curious, motivated, and have an authentic desire to serve others. Our faculty members are experienced and caring. They understand that all children learn differently and that it is their responsibility to create learning experiences that tap into each child's unique interests and innate curiosity.

To learn more, visit St. Martin's Episcopal School on the web at www.stmsaints.com or call the Admission Office at (504) 736-9917.

BROOKFIELD ACADEMY

3460 N. Brookfield Rd.
BROOKFIELD, WI 53045
Tel: 262-783-3200

Brookfield Academy is a college preparatory school for students in Pre-K through Grade 12. The Academy offers a solid and wide range of educational opportunities which are offered in an atmosphere of traditional American values. Students are encouraged to appreciate the institutions and histories of free societies and to practice the skills of responsible, constructive free people.

The academic programs in the Lower School are built upon a phonics approach to reading, emphasis on writing and vocabulary development, the Singapore approach to reasoning and computation in math, strong sequences in history and literature, and introductions to Spanish and French. Studies in the Middle School continue with languages, add more emphasis on science, and place continued emphasis on grammar and correct use of English. The Upper School offers high-level academic studies, leading to advanced placement courses in English, art, calculus, economics, biology, chemistry, physics, and languages. The particular course selections in the Upper School are tailored to the individual student with the aim to prepare all students for acceptance and success in a competitive college atmosphere.

In addition to their strong academic programs the students participate in a wide range of interscholastic athletic competition, including girls' field hockey and volleyball, boys' football and baseball, and girls' and boys' basketball, cross country, fencing, golf, skiing, soccer, swimming, tennis, and track. Physical education, art, and music are taught in the Lower and Middle Schools as extracurricular supplements to the academic studies. In the Upper School, extracurricular activities include Academic Decathlon, Ambassadors Club, Service Club, Chess Club, Drama Club, Entrepreneurs Club, Forensics Team, International Travel, Journalism Club, Art Club, Math Society, Mock Trial, Newspaper Staff, Science Club, Student Council, Yearbook Staff, and language clubs.

The school was founded in 1962 as the Academy of Basic Education by a group of families who were concerned that the education of their children should develop reason and a respect for factual knowledge, should revere religious inspiration and guidance, and should retain an understanding of the nature of a free society and a capitalistic economy. Those purposes, and the program in which they are embodied, have been embraced by hundreds of families who have brought their children to the Academy since its founding.

Educating Inquisitive Minds To Their Potential

Accelerated Programs

The award-winning Nysmith School nourishes minds with a caring environment and daily science, computers, foreign language and logic. Most importantly, subjects can be accelerated to reach the full potential of every child.

Private Tours Daily.
Call Today.
Limited Space.
(703) 552-2912
info-pa@nysmith.com
www.NysmithSchool.com

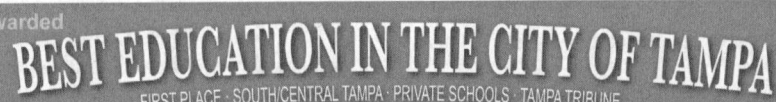

Awarded

BEST EDUCATION IN THE CITY OF TAMPA
FIRST PLACE · SOUTH/CENTRAL TAMPA · PRIVATE SCHOOLS · TAMPA TRIBUNE

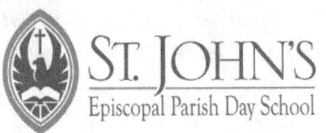

ST. JOHN'S
Episcopal Parish Day School

**A Superior Educational Experience
in a Nurturing Christian Environment**

Accelerated K(4) - 8th Grade

Cindy M. Fenlon
Director of Admissions

(813) 600-4348
www.stjohnseagles.org

906 South Orleans Ave
Tampa, Florida 33606

EAGLE HILL-SOUTHPORT
214 Main St., Southport, CT 06890
Tel: 203-254-2044   Fax: 203-255-4052
Web: www.eaglehillsouthport.org
E-mail: info@eaglehillsouthport.org

Eagle Hill-Southport is a non-profit school for children with learning disabilities. Serving boys and girls ages 6 to 14 in a supportive, structured, success-oriented program, the 3:1 student/staff ratio allows for individualized instruction to address the learning style and level of each child. The school is transitional and non-graded, designed to reinforce students' skills through tutorials and small group classes that prepare them for return to more traditional placements.

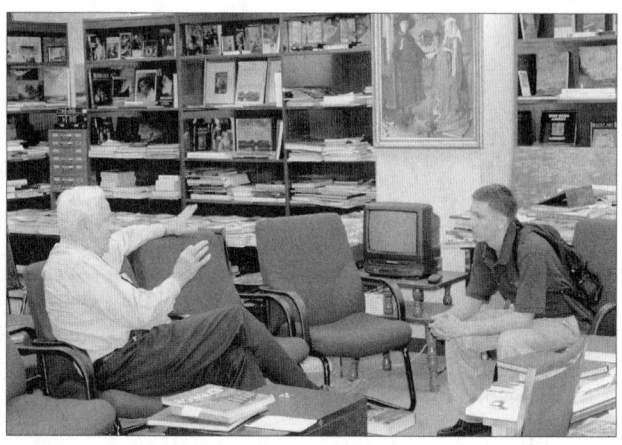

FORDHAM PREPARATORY SCHOOL
BRONX, NY 10458

Rev. Kenneth J. Boller, SJ, *President*
Mr. Robert J. Gomprecht '65, *Principal*

Fordham Prep is a Jesuit, college preparatory school for male day students founded in 1841. Located on the campus of Fordham University, it is an independent school with its own Board of Trustees. The school's two buildings contain classrooms, labs, two gyms, fitness center, library, computer center and the 1,000-seat Leonard Theatre. There are 950 students. The student to teacher ratio is 11:1.

Fordham prep offers an advanced program of individualized study for highly motivated young men. Its goals in both academic studies and personal growth are realized in the daily interaction between students and teachers. The ideal of Jesuit education is the well-rounded person who is intellectually competent, open to growth, religious, loving and committed to doing justice in generous service to other people. A program of retreats, days of renewal and a 4-year service program combine with curricular and co-curricular activities to provide a rich experience for our students in preparation for college and for life. Our graduates are accepted at the finest colleges and universities in the country.

Our location is ideally suited for its combination of students from all across the metropolitan area. The geographic, ethnic and religious diversity of the students is one of the special features of the Prep and a point of pride for both students and faculty. We strive to include qualified students of limited financial resources by providing substantial financial assistance.

Fordham Prep offers an education that emphasizes faith, scholarship and service, engaging the whole person: mind, heart, imagination and feelings. A Jesuit education is an experience that shapes a lifetime.

RIVER OAKS BAPTIST SCHOOL
2300 Willowick Rd.
HOUSTON, TX 77027
Tel: 713-623-6938   Web: www.robs.org

Founded in 1955, River Oaks Baptist School has grown into one of the premier independent schools in the Houston area. R.O.B.S. gives its students a firm foundation for life—academically, morally, spiritually, socially, and physically. Rigorous academics are balanced with a nurturing environment and multi-dimensional character and spiritual development. In 2004, R.O.B.S. was one of 10 schools to be recognized as a National School of Character by the Character Education Partnership.

The curriculum includes award-winning foreign language, fine arts, and athletics programs. In 2008, R.O.B.S. was the only school in the nation to receive the prestigious Melba Woodruff Award for Exemplary Elementary Foreign Language Program. The fine arts program includes musical and theatrical performances and visual arts classes at every grade level. In the athletic program, teamwork and respect are stressed so that sports become an opportunity to build community and character. The School's athletic teams bring home conference championships, too.

R.O.B.S. believes that education is enriched when students with different experiences, perspectives, and ideas learn together. The 850 students at R.O.B.S. are drawn from a wide geographic area, varied economic backgrounds, and more than 20 distinct Christian and non-Christian traditions. Students range from age 2 to eighth grade. Over 95% of R.O.B.S. graduates typically are accepted into their first or second high school of choice.

Through an R.O.B.S. education, students are prepared to meet life's challenges and lead tomorrow's world through a superior educational program undergirded by faith in Jesus Christ and Christian principles. Dedicated faculty and involved parents join together to create a stimulating and supportive school environment—one that produces children who are smart *and* good.

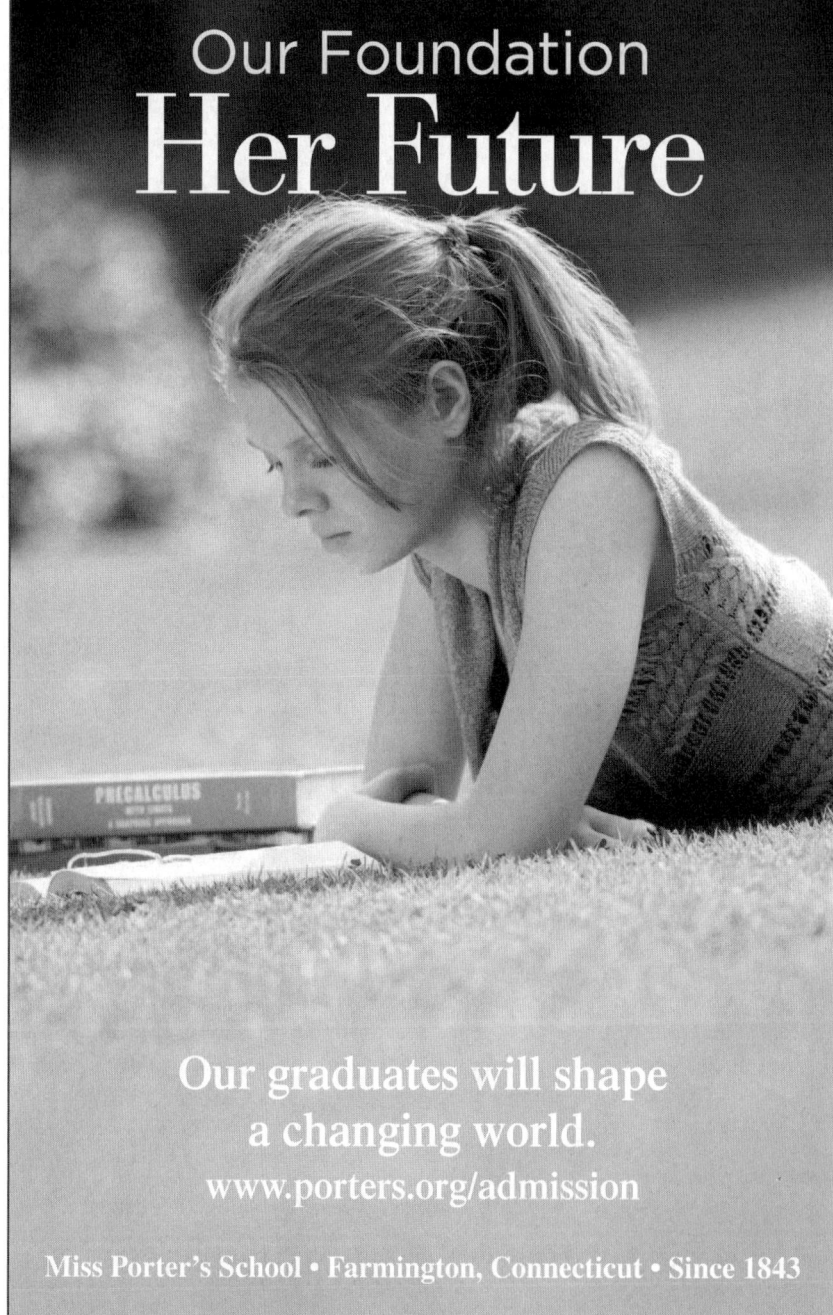

Our Foundation

Her Future

Our graduates will shape
a changing world.
www.porters.org/admission

Miss Porter's School • Farmington, Connecticut • Since 1843

"Her education means the world to me."

Explore all that Winsor means to academically promising girls in grades 5-12. Our reputation as a top day school has drawn Boston-area families for 125 years. They want the world for their daughters. So do *we*.

Winsor teachers expect the best from every girl. They know that girls learn best when they listen actively, think critically and voice their own ideas. To learn more about our urban day school, call 617 735-9503 or visit us online.

THE WINSOR SCHOOL   *Pilgrim Road, Boston, Massachusetts 02215*

www.winsor.edu/admission

A lifelong love of learning starts here!

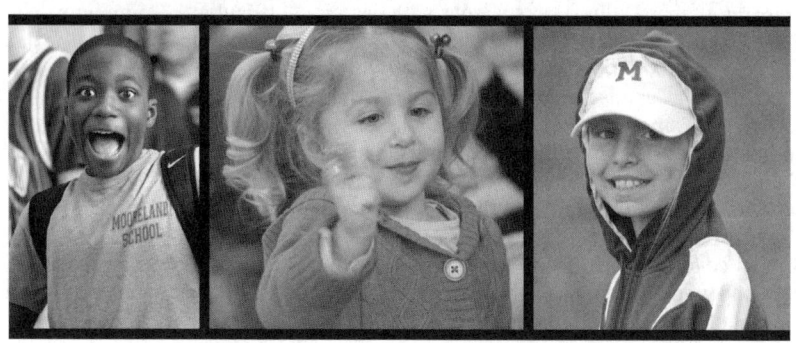

Mooreland Hill School is an independant, co-educational
day school serving central Connecticut students
in kindergarten though grade nine.

•

What interests and talents will we nurture in your child?

Please call to schedule a personal tour.

166 Lincoln Street, Kensington CT 06037
Easy proximity to I-84, RT 9, and I-91

860.223.6428 • mooreland.org

*Mooreland Hill admits
students of every race, color,
creed, ethnic & national origin*

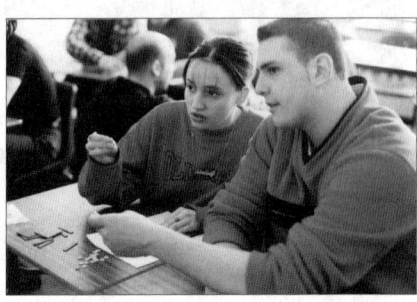

COMMUNITY HIGH SCHOOL
1135 Teaneck Rd.
TEANECK, NJ 07666

Toby Braunstein, *Director of Education*
Dennis Cohen, *Director of Program*

Community High School provides a full, rich four year college and career preparatory curriculum for students with learning difficulties. Community High School serves students from New York City, Northern New Jersey, and Rockland County. Transportation from New York City is provided.

Adolescent counseling groups, career counseling, college counseling, SAT preparation, small class groupings, individualized instruction, skilled remediation, additional tutorials in reading language and speech, and wide range of study skills classes are provided. Courses follow the traditional high school curriculum, are completely departmentalized, and include computer programming, photography, video production, computer graphics, graphics, keyboarding, music, drama, and drivers education. Extracurricular activities include theater and music productions, newspaper and yearbook production, a complete intramural athletic program and an interscholastic athletic program.

For admissions contact Toby Braunstein: 201-862-1796.

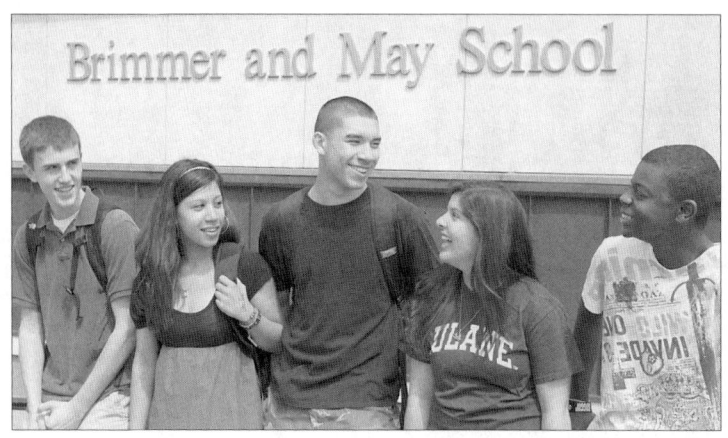

BRIMMER AND MAY SCHOOL
CHESTNUT HILL, MA
Web: www.brimmerandmay.org

Judy Guild, BS, ALM, *Head of School*

Brimmer and May, a coeducational, diverse, independent, nonsectarian, pre-kindergarten through grade twelve day school, in Chestnut Hill, has been cited as a 'Model School' by The National Association of Independent Schools. A total of five U.S. schools were so designated based on their ongoing efforts to successfully adopt eight "Essential Capacities for the 21st Century."

The Committee identified eight unifying themes that comprise 'Essential Capacities for the 21st Century' and which independent schools should work to adopt: Academically Demanding; Project-based Learning; Classrooms that Extend Beyond School Walls; Digital Technologies and a Global Perspective that Infuse the Program; Vibrant Arts Programs; Learning Communities; A Culture of Engagement and Support; and Transformational Leadership.

Brimmer and May launched a new Global Studies Diploma Program in 2010, and the new Honors Program offers students an intellectual extension to the required class work. The Creative Arts Diploma Program provides students with the opportunity to delve more deeply into a chosen art form.

Pre-kindergartners begin with the study French and students may study French, Spanish, or Mandarin in later grades.

Upper School students participate in Winterim, a study tour program. Students will travel to the Galapagos Islands, Italy, Spain, Ireland, Senegal and China in 2013.

EPISCOPAL HIGH SCHOOL

BELLAIRE, TX

Tel: 713-512-3400   Fax: 713-512-3603
Web: ehshouston.org

Founded in 1982, Episcopal High School of Houston is a four-year coeducational day school within the Episcopal Diocese of Texas. The school community is faith-centered and provides instruction to college-bound students with a wide range of abilities. The strong academic program is complemented by extensive offerings in the arts, religion, and athletics. EHS is located on a 35-acre campus in the suburban residential community of Bellaire, which is surrounded by Houston.

In August 1998, EHS made history and entered the 21st century as a Compaq laptop computer was put in the hands of each student and teacher. Anticipating the direction of many colleges and universities, EHS embraced the Anytime, Anywhere Learning program promoted by the Microsoft Corporation. By equipping all teachers with laptops and piloting a laptop classroom, EHS began to look ahead to the next great innovation. Currently, students peer-edit with e-mail, make presentations with PowerPoint, discover geometry with Sketchpad, conduct laboratory experiments with probes, and analyze data in Excel. Many teachers have built Web pages as homes for their course resources and Internet links. Students all over campus have expanded the walls of the classroom by communicating with teachers and classmates via a wireless network. As a result, they are more engaged with their studies, taking charge of their own learning, and collaborating more often with their peers. And the skills they once practiced mechanically in a computer lab are now mastered for real applications, as they need them. EHS manages this innovation as an educational program, not a technology diversion, and students with financial aid also receive assistance in purchasing their laptops.

To learn more, visit Episcopal High School on the Web at www.ehshouston.org.

SANTA CATALINA SCHOOL

Girls | Resident & Day | Grades 9-12
1500 Mark Thomas Drive, Monterey CA
831.655.9356 | santacatalina.org

Founded in 1950, Santa Catalina School is an independent, Catholic, college preparatory day and boarding school for young women located on 36-acres in beautiful Monterey, Califormia. Santa Catalina seeks girls with intellectual curiosity and an adventurous spirit. We select students who indicate they can succeed here, not only academically, but as contributing members of our community.

2011-12 School Facts
- 243 girls (130 day, 113 resident)
- Average class size is 12 students; student-faculty ratio is 7:1
- Classical liberal arts curriculum, with honors and 18 Advanced Placement courses offered
- Introductory and advanced level courses in art, photography, music, dance, and theatre
- Extensive advisory and college counseling programs
- Interscholastic sports: basketball, cross country, equestrian team, field hockey, golf, lacrosse, soccer, softball, swimming and diving, tennis, track and field, volleyball, and water polo

2011-12 Faculty
- 34 teaching faculty
- 28 with advanced degrees

Facilities
- Professional-level 500-seat performing arts center
- 150-seat recital hall and dance studio
- Science laboratories and classrooms
- Gymnasium, pool, tennis courts, track, and field

2012 College Acceptances
Acceptances included: Amherst, Georgetown, MIT, NYU, Notre Dame, UC Berkeley, UCLA, UPenn, and USC

If you were to open an album of OLDFIELDS lore, you would find 140 years worth of images steeped in history, memory and tradition. The first page would tell you about Anna Austen McCulloch, the School's founder, and her little yellow clapboard home that has since grown and become the heart of the OLDFIELDS campus. Early pictures would show the first graduating classes, young equestrians on their horses, and a teacher working one-on-one with a student at dinner. Pages later, you would see new buildings, signifying the growth of the School. In the pages and memories most recently created, you might find pictures of a girl scoring the winning goal in the **lacrosse** championships, visiting the **Eiffel Tower**, building a rocket in the Physics lab, and contemplating her art-work in preparation for the Annual Art  Show. Other pages might include images of another girl using her **L A P T O P** to update the web page she designed for her AP Spanish class, enjoying an Orioles baseball game at Camden Yards, or dancing with her *prom* date.

In every picture, each girl would look, feel, and be contented because at OLDFIELDS, we ensure each girl's success. Girls are challenged to find their gifts and talents and allow them to soar. At Oldfields, a girl can be a **scholar**, an **athlete**, and an artist. At OLDFIELDS, a girl can be an **individual**.

The School's admission officers ask that students simply come to
OLDFIELDS ready to make the
most of their academic and personal
potential, to **work hard** and play
hard, and to contribute to a community of courage, humility, and
largeness of heart, values stated

in the motto we live and breathe. The School's mission
reverberates: OLDFIELDS *is committed to the intellectual and moral development of young women. In a culture
of kindness and mutual respect, we encourage each student to
make the most of her academic and personal potential. We
seek to guide each student to grow in character, confidence, and
knowledge by encouraging her to embrace the values of personal honesty, intellectual curiosity, and social responsibility.*

Located 25 miles north of Baltimore, near Hunt
Valley, MD, OLDFIELDS is an all girls' boarding school
of 165 students in grades 8-PG.

If you are already picturing yourself at
OLDFIELDS, we want to get to know you better. For
more information, please contact the Admission Office at

410.472.4800, or 1500 Glencoe
Road, Glencoe, MD 21152.
E-mail us at
Admissions@OldfieldsSchool.org,
and visit our website at
www.OldfieldsSchool.org.

THE JOHN COOPER SCHOOL
THE WOODLANDS, TX
Tel: 281-367-0900   Fax: 281-298-5715
Web: www.johncooper.org

Michael F. Maher, *Head of School*

The John Cooper School is a PK-12 non-sectarian, co-educational, college preparatory day school, located on a wooded 43-acre campus in The Woodlands, Texas. The mission of The John Cooper School is to provide a challenging education in a caring environment to a diverse group of select students enabling them to become creative thinkers, responsible citizens and leaders, and lifetime learners. The school focuses on the development of each child—intellectually, artistically and athletically—within the context of a strong academic program taught by a nationally recognized faculty. Organized community service programs are offered at all levels of the school.

Since 1988, The John Cooper School has grown from 175 students to a current PK-12 enrollment of 998. Current facilities include: a Lower School building (PK-5) with adjacent playgrounds, covered basketball pavilion and outdoor learning centers—the Children's Garden, Arboretum and Environmental Science Center; and a Middle/ Upper School for grades 6-8 and 9-12. All Cooper students utilize two fully equipped gymnasiums, softball and soccer fields, a cross country course, a football and track and field facility, tennis courts, baseball field; and extensive visual arts facilities nicknamed "the Art Barn." Additional facilities include a Student Center and a 38,000-square-foot Performing Arts Center that houses a main stage theater, black box theater, choir, drama and dance classrooms.

The John Cooper School curriculum is traditional and conforms to standards recommended by the National Association of Independent Schools (NAIS). Admission is competitive and students are selected largely on the basis of aptitude and potential for success in a rigorous college preparatory program of study. Class size is limited to ensure individualized attention and to facilitate open and regular communication with teachers. The Class of 2012 has 78 members, of whom 5 have been named National Merit Finalists and 1 a semifinalist, 13 named Commended Scholars, and 3 named Scholars in the National Hispanic Recognition Program. Student athletes compete on 18 different athletic teams. Varsity athletes compete in the Southwest Preparatory Conference.

The John Cooper School is accredited by the Independent Schools Association of the Southwest and is a member of NAIS, the College Entrance Examination Board, Educational Records Bureau, National Association of College Admission Counselors and the Cum Laude Society. Confidential, need-based financial aid is available. Cooper welcomes students of any race, color, religion or national/ethnic background, and does not discriminate on the basis of physical handicap or gender.

INDEPENDENT
COEDUCATIONAL
GRADES 7-12

Striking a Balance

BURROUGHS
J O H N   B U R R O U G H S   S C H O O L

755 South Price Road • St. Louis, MO 63124
314/993-4040 • jburroughs.org

THE DERRYFIELD SCHOOL
2108 River Road, MANCHESTER, NH 03104-1396
Tel: 603-669-4524 Fax: 603-641-9521
Web: www.derryfield.org

Mission
The Derryfield School inspires bright, motivated young people to be their best and provides them with the skills and experiences needed to be valued, dynamic, confident, and purposeful members of any community.

Core Values
Aim High: Young people achieve their best in a culture of high expectations and encouragement.

Balance: We offer inspiring academic, artistic, and athletic opportunities, promoting the development of healthy habits of mind, body, and spirit, and the skill to balance creative tension.

Character: We actively cultivate respect, integrity, compassion, and perseverance in our community members.

Community: We seek a diverse community defined and sustained by close relationships, social interdependence, and service.

Families: We embrace the family's role in the life of our day school, celebrating collaboration between home and school.

Individuality: We encourage young people to grow as unique individuals through the discovery of new passions and a love for learning, self-knowledge, critical inquiry, and reflection.

CONVENT OF THE SACRED HEART

1177 King St.
GREENWICH, CT 06831
Tel: 203-531-6500
Web: cshgreenwich.org

Pamela Juan Hayes, *Head of School*
Catherine Cullinane, *Director of Admission*

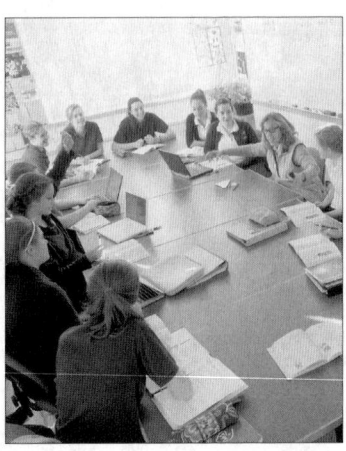

Convent of the Sacred Heart is an independent, college preparatory, Catholic day school for young women serving students from Preschool through Grade 12. Founded in 1848 in New York City, the school relocated to Greenwich in 1945. Convent of the Sacred Heart is part of a worldwide network of Sacred Heart schools in 35 countries that has been educating women for more than 200 years. The 22 Sacred Heart Schools in the United States share a common set of Goals and Criteria that guide the decisions made by our 22-member Board of Trustees. Committed to each girl's intellectual, spiritual, social and physical development, our dedicated faculty and staff provide a rigorous academic program, enrichment and honors study, a supportive advisory program and opportunities for creative exploration, entrepreneurship and independent study. Middle and Upper Schools students have an opportunity to participate in an international exchange program with other Sacred Heart schools. The school is dedicated to developing confident young women who have a strong sense of self, independence of judgment and social awareness so that they can become leaders with broad intellectual and spiritual horizons.

Technology enables Sacred Heart to develop new programs which promote creativity and exploration for the development of 21st century learners. The Lower, Middle and Upper Schools are equipped with the latest in technology. The Lower School students have computers in their classrooms, as well as in a dual-platform Computer Lab which each class visits regularly. iPads are used extensively in the Lower School, including Preschool and Prekindergarten, and are being introduced into the Middle School. Fifth graders will have net books and the lap top program will now include the sixth grade, as well as grades 7-12. A computer laptop program for grades 6-12 is incorporated into the curriculum across all disciplines. Using the latest in technology, the Broadcast Journalism and Science Research programs provide students with many opportunities to excel.

In preschool through grade 4, individual, small group and whole group instruction is used in the core disciplines of mathematics, science, language arts, social studies, theology and world languages. In addition to regular classroom instruction, academic teaching specialists meet with Lower School students and classroom teachers.

In grades 5 through 8, each student has an advisor who guides and encourages the students in all aspects of school life. The curriculum is departmentalized to include mathematics, science, computer, language arts, theology, social studies and world languages. Lower and Middle School students receive instruction in library skills, music, drama, dance, art, and physical education/health.

In the Upper School, the curriculum offers more than 70 courses in mathematics, science, English, social sciences, history, theology, world languages, fine arts, technology and physical education/health. Honors courses are taught in geometry, algebra II/trigonometry, precalculus, biology, chemistry, physics, history, English, Arabic, Chinese, French and Spanish. Advanced Placement courses are offered in calculus AB and BC; statistics;

computer science; biology; studio art; physics; chemistry; environmental science; psychology; microeconomics; English literature; American and European history; comparative government; art history; Chinese, French, Latin and Spanish languages; and Spanish literature. All academic disciplines employ the computer as a tool for writing, research, analysis and presentation.

College guidance begins informally in ninth grade when the importance of curriculum and extra curriculars is discussed with parents and students. In tenth grade, students take their first PSAT and the PLAN tests to begin preparing for standardized tests. A second PSAT is administered in junior year. Formal guidance classes begin in junior year and continue into senior year. Continuing a tradition of academic excellence, students in the Class of 2012 attend colleges and universities with strong national reputations. Over 95 percent of the class was accepted at colleges listed as "Most" or "Highly" competitive by Barron's Profiles of American Colleges. Among the 2012 graduates, Sacred Heart had one National Merit Scholarship winner, two National Merit Scholarship finalists and four National Merit Commended Students.

Convent of the Sacred Heart is accredited by the New England Association of Schools and Colleges and is approved by the Connecticut State Board of Education. It is a member of the National Association of Independent Schools, the Connecticut Association of Independent Schools, Coalition of Girls' Schools and the Network of Sacred Heart Schools, The College Board, and National Association of College Admission Counselors.

The campus occupies a 118-acre property with the main building housing the administrative offices, chapel, art gallery, art and music studios, college guidance, and classrooms. An academic wing contains a new performing arts center, Upper School Core Center, classrooms and academic offices. A 29,000 square foot science center has state-of-the-art laboratories for all three divisions, in addition to art and photo studios, dark room, and classrooms. Students have access to an outdoor observatory housing a 16-inch telescope in a moving, domed facility augmenting the ten eight-inch telescopes located on an outdoor pad.

Stuart Hall, a new four-level building, features the Middle School and the library/media center. The two-level library, which serves the School's students from preschool through grade 12, contains the School's collections of books, periodicals, DVDs and online databases. It features space for individual and group study, computer labs, a storytelling room and a broadcast journalism suite. The Middle School features beautiful, spacious classrooms equipped with state-of-the art technology.

Students in the Middle and Upper Schools may study participate in an exchange program at a Sacred Heart school domestically or internationally. The students live with host families and reciprocate, when their host student visits Sacred Heart on exchange. The program provides a unique opportunity for students to broaden their global awareness both academically and socially. Recently, our students have studied in New Orleans and San Francisco, in addition to Australia, Austria, England; Ireland; France, Scotland; Spain, and Taiwan.

Athletic facilities include playing fields for soccer, softball, field hockey and lacrosse, six tennis courts, gymnasium, fitness room, dance studio, indoor pool and three-mile cross country course. Interscholastic athletic competition (Fairchester Athletic Association and Western New England Prep School Association) includes crew, field hockey, soccer, lacrosse, softball, tennis, golf, basketball, cross-country, squash, diving and swimming, and volleyball.

Middle School students participate in: Student Council, Bell Choir, Chorus, theater, dance, instrumental music, Math Club, Martin Luther King, Jr. Club, Great Books Club, Literary Magazine and environmental education. Interscholastic athletic competition includes cross-country, softball, squash, field hockey, soccer, lacrosse, basketball, swimming, volleyball, tennis and golf. In the Lower School: physical education, swimming, dance (ballet, tap, jazz), and the arts.

Wilmington
Friends 1748 *School*

From our Early Learning Center to our signature international programs, global education at Friends prepares students for the opportunities and challenges of their future, even those that we cannot predict.

Our students learn how to engage complex questions intellectually and in action ~ in and outside of the classroom ~ with a sense of confidence and responsibility.

IB, School Year Abroad, Chinese, "1-to-1" laptop program, lower school STEM Lab ~ Please visit us to learn more.

www.wilmingtonfriends.org • 302.576.2930

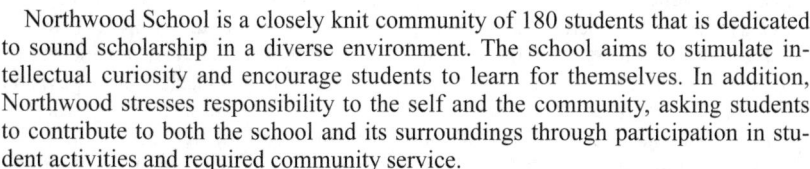

NORTHWOOD SCHOOL

P.O. Box 1070
LAKE PLACID, NY 12946
Tel: 518-523-3357   Fax: 518-523-3405
Web: www.northwoodschool.com

Edward M. Good, *Headmaster*

Northwood School is a closely knit community of 180 students that is dedicated to sound scholarship in a diverse environment. The school aims to stimulate intellectual curiosity and encourage students to learn for themselves. In addition, Northwood stresses responsibility to the self and the community, asking students to contribute to both the school and its surroundings through participation in student activities and required community service.

Classes at Northwood are small by design, permitting exacting supervision and close individual counseling. Students learn to participate in their academic experience developing strong communication skills and confidence. A core curriculum that stresses skill development and achievement through effort is supplemented by Advanced Placement and honors courses, as well as such electives as Art Exploration, Instrumental Ensemble, Steel Drums, Great Issues, and Irish and Adirondack history.

Northwood School has access to the Olympic facilities of Lake Placid. The 3 ice surfaces at the Olympic Arena and the challenging slopes of Whiteface Mountain Ski Area service our most competitive athletes. A recent $5 million renovation includes a fitness center with a squash court, rock climbing wall, cybex weight system, a student center with a walk-in book store, home theatre, post office, recreational area, dining room and kitchen facilities, science building with 4 science labs, classrooms and a greenhouse, and an enhanced art facility.

Class offerings in art, music, drama, journalism, and photography enhance the academic curriculum. Ice Hockey, Alpine Skiing, Lacrosse, Crew, Soccer, Tennis and Golf are established varsity sports. Our "Wilderness Skills" program includes rock climbing, canoeing and kayaking, camping and survival skills in all seasons of the year.

Recent graduates have enrolled at Boston College, Williams College, Brown University, Cornell University, the University of New Hampshire, Connecticut College, Boston University, Harvard, and Princeton.

BLAIR ACADEMY

T. Chandler Hardwick, Headmaster

Blairstown, NJ 07825

(908) 362-2024   (800) 462-5247   admissions@blair.edu

In its 164th year, Blair continues to offer a superior academic college-preparatory program while holding firmly to its tradition of being a community fully focused on the development of each individual student. In this environment, students learn to advocate for themselves, become service-minded, and develop the leadership skills necessary for success in college and beyond. The balance between high academic and personal expectations and a willingness to provide individual focus is, if not unique to Blair, perhaps its greatest strength. The classrooms at Blair serve as forums for open debate, participation, and experiential learning. Passionate about their subjects, a talented and diverse faculty brings enthusiasm and global perspective to lessons. Traditional sports, plus golf, skiing, squash, ice hockey, and crew are offered. In addition, Blair boasts a notable fine and performing arts program featuring six theatrical productions each year, instrumental and choral music ensembles, architecture, graphic design, video production, and numerous other arts offerings.

Points of Distinction

- Approximately 1/3 of graduates annually earn admission to Ivy League or comparably -tiered schools (i.e.–Stanford, Duke, M.I.T., Williams).
- Blair, with an enrollment of 445 students, is located in the foothills of the Pocono Mountains, with easy access to New York City and Philadelphia.
- Four students in recent years have been recipients of the following prestigious academic scholarships:
    - *Morehead Scholarship,* University of North Carolina at Chapel Hill (2)
    - *Jefferson Scholarship,* University of Virginia
    - *Belk Scholarship,* Davidson College
- 23 AP offerings with electives in Roman History, Asian Studies, Mandarin Chinese, Epidemiology, Ethical Philosophy, Video Production, Architecture, and more . . .
- College-level lecture series, *The Society of Skeptics,* enters its 33rd year.
- 7:1 student/faculty ratio; average class size: 11; 95% of faculty live on campus.
- 160 students sat for 269 AP exams in 2010.
- Blair Academy Singers have completed two European tours in 5 years and the String Orchestra completed a performance tour of Prague, Vienna, and Budapest.
- Enhanced and newly renovated athletic facilities that include 10 tennis courts, an all weather track, turf field with game lights, 7 squash courts, and 3 basketball courts.
- Foreign travel with students and faculty includes trips to Ecuador, China, Kenya, Cayman Islands, and multiple European destinations.

Le Jardin Academy

"A Challenged Mind . . . A Sound Character"

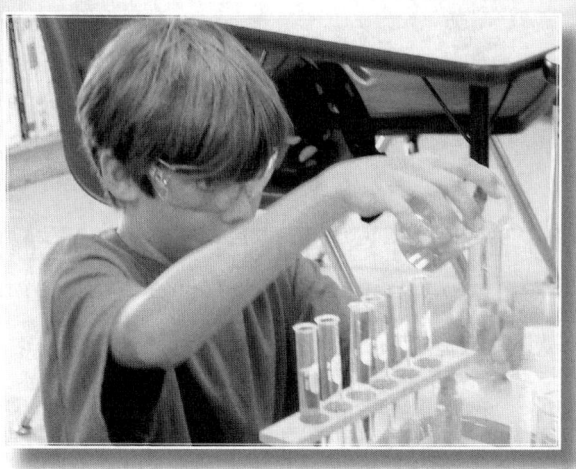

Coed Pre-School through High School
Rigorous Academics
Fine and Performing Arts
Brand-new Athletic Facilities
International Baccalaureate Programme

917 Kalanianaole Hwy. • Kailua, HI 96734
www.lejardinacademy.com
808-261-0707

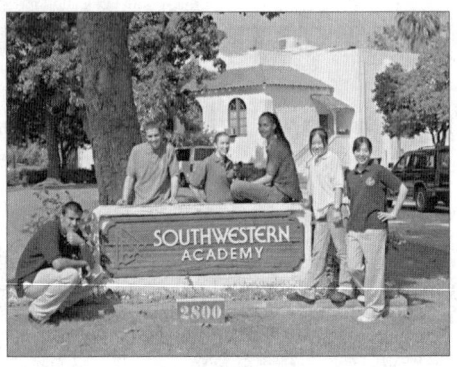

SOUTHWESTERN ACADEMY
One School, Two Campuses, Two Learning Environments

SAN MARINO, CA   RIMROCK, AZ

Southwestern Academy prepares students to be lifelong learners, critical thinkers, and self-motivated leaders who will positively impact the natural and global community in the 21st century. Techniques and methodology focus on application of knowledge and skills while incorporating the cultural differences and individual learning styles, abilities, and interests of each student.

Southwestern Academy was founded by Maurice Veronda in 1924 "for capable students who could do better" in small, supportive classes. While maintaining that commitment, Southwestern provides college preparatory and general academic coursework to U.S. and international students with strong academic abilities who are eager to learn and strengthen English language skills as well as pursue a college preparatory program. Departmentalized and supportively structured classes are limited to 9-12 students. Small classes allow for individualized attention in a non-competitive environment for regular school year and summer programs.

A mix of U.S. and international students from as many as 25 countries offers a unique blend of cultural, social, and educational opportunities for all. Every effort is made to enroll a well-balanced student body that represents the rich ethnic diversity of U.S. citizens and students from around the world. The student body consists of 175 students who prefer a small, personalized education; above average students who have the potential to become excellent academic achievers in the right learning environment; and average to under-achieving students who, with supportive structure, can achieve academic success. Southwestern is not a behavioral or therapeutic school and will not accept students with serious disciplinary, emotional, attitudinal problems, or significant learning differences.

High school graduation requirements are based on University of California requirements. The academic term is mid-September through mid-June. International students are offered three levels of classes in English as a second language

(ESL), including a transition class that prepares them to enter and succeed in other academic areas. Advanced placement classes are available in history, math, and science. Review and remedial classes are made available to students who need additional instruction.

Beginning in the ninth grade, students receive support and guidance in researching colleges and universities that complement their interests and academic achievement levels. A variety of college representatives are invited annually to visit each campus. Approximately 35 students graduate each year from Southwestern. 100% of graduating students enter a U.S. college or university of their choice.

Southwestern Academy offers students the opportunity to study at either of two distinctly different and beautiful campuses. If space permits, students may study at both in order to benefit from each learning environment.

The San Marino, California campus is located near Pasadena and Los Angeles and occupies eight acres in the residential suburb of San Marino ten miles from downtown Los Angeles and immediately south of Pasadena. The Arizona campus, known as Beaver Creek Ranch, is a 180-acre site located in north central Arizona 100 miles north of Phoenix, 18 miles from the resort community of Sedona, and 35 miles south of Flagstaff. A breathtaking, creek-watered, red rock oasis provides an ideal setting for general academic and college preparatory study.

A central theme of the academic program at Beaver Creek Campus is the development of an appreciation for the importance of environmental sustainability and the role individuals must play as socially responsible citizens.

Southwestern Academy offers summer programs at each campus. The program at San Marino offers an accelerated ESL program for international students to improve their knowledge and use of English. Students may also attend classes to earn credits toward high school graduation or for review and enhancement purposes. Students participate in special daily activities and a variety of field trips that support learning in the classroom and offer recreation and relaxation.

The summer curriculum at Beaver Creek is designed for students who wish to enhance their academic performance by combining high adventure activities and field trips with science-based learning and outdoor education that supports the overall theme and focus of the campus.

Call for a DVD or catalog.
Tel: 626-799-5010 x5
Fax: 626-799-0407
E-mail: Admissions@SouthwesternAcademy.edu
Web: www.SouthwesternAcademy.edu

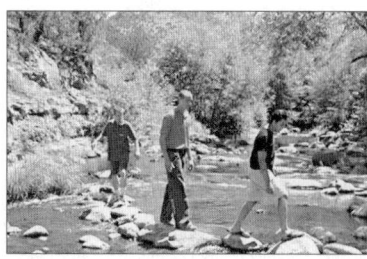

THAYER ACADEMY

745 Washington St.
BRAINTREE, MA 02184
Tel: 781-843-3580
E-mail: admissions@thayer.org
Web: www.thayer.org

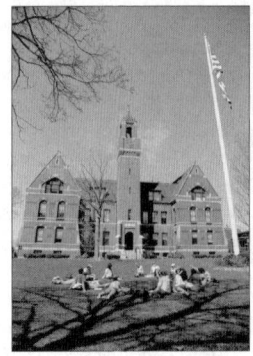

LOCATED IN HISTORIC BRAINTREE, THAYER ACADEMY is a co-educational day school for students in grades 6-12. The Academy's Mission is to inspire a diverse community of students to moral, intellectual, aesthetic, and physical excellence so that each may rise to honorable achievement and contribute to the common good.

FOUNDER, GENERAL SYLVANUS THAYER

Thayer Academy was founded in 1877, in accordance with the will of General Sylvanus Thayer, a native of Braintree, who led a distinguished life as a soldier, engineer, educator, and philanthropist. Thayer graduated from Dartmouth College as valedictorian of his class in 1807. The following year, he graduated from the U.S. Military Academy at West Point, again at the head of his class, with the rank of Second Lieutenant of Engineers. He maintained long-term relationships with both schools, and they continue to benefit from his achievements today.

At Dartmouth, he established the Thayer School of Engineering with an endowment of $70,000 and 2,000 volumes on military science, architecture, and civil engineering. His own achievements in engineering and architecture influenced colleges and universities nationwide as they tried to meet the demands of a new technological age set in motion by the Industrial Revolution. His work was exemplary to such a degree that he is now honored in the Hall of Fame for Great Americans as "Father of Technological Education in the United States."

At West Point, where he returned to serve as Superintendent, he elevated the quality of education by holding the cadets to high standards in scholarship, discipline, and performance evaluation. In this way, he earned the epithet "Father of the U.S. Military Academy."

Through a lifetime of service to the United States Military, Sylvanus Thayer reluctantly became a man of great wealth. He was opposed to the practice of granting certain commissions to army officers, but when he learned that large sums would become part of his estate whether he liked it or not, he decided to invest the money in the institution he valued most: Education.

QUALITIES OF A THAYER EDUCATION

General Thayer was devoted to the principle of excellence in education, and to this day, the objectives of Thayer Academy—inspiring excellence in the moral, intellectual, aesthetic, and physical pursuits of its students—keep the founder's ideals alive. Every member of the Thayer community – teachers, students, parents, alumni, trustees, administrators, staff, and friends of the Academy – are stewards of this mission and share in its rewards. Thayer draws to its faculty extraordinary teachers whose devotion to scholarship and careful attention to the individual development of each student embody the Academy's mission.

High standards of scholarship, along with courses and activities designed for self-expression in the arts, and opportunities to compete in interscholastic athletics motivate students to reach their full potential. Students are challenged in a supportive environment, and encouraged to reach beyond what they perceive to be the limits of their own capabilities – to achieve what they think they can't. Students learn to recognize the intangible but lasting merits of perseverance, taking calculated risks, and doing every job well. Thayer students are extremely well prepared for college and for future success.

FACTS & FIGURES

Thayer offers a challenging academic program that prepares students for college and adulthood with a 6:1 student-faculty ratio; 111 faculty members, 69% of whom have master's or doctoral degrees, and 18 of whom have taught at Thayer more than 25 years; 13 AP courses; 135 total courses, including 4 foreign languages (French, Spanish, Latin, and Chinese); 79 electives, 18

of which are courses in visual and performing arts; a Learning-Through-Travel Program with 4 international sister-school exchange programs and 6 study-abroad programs; library holdings of 21,000 volumes, 58 periodical subscriptions, and 50+ online database subscriptions for scholarly research; a 2:1 student-to-computer ratio, 13 computer labs, 345 computers for student use, and all classrooms with Internet access; 30 extra-curricular activities and 80+ sports teams; situated on a 34-acre campus comprising 8 buildings and 54 classrooms.

Thayer recently completed facilities improvements that include 6 state-of-the-art science labs; a 2-story strength and conditioning facility; 4 turf playing fields; a new Middle School Library; a completely refurbished Upper School Library; a new Center for the Arts with a 550-seat theater, 1 dance studio, 3 visual art classrooms, 7 instrumental or vocal practice rooms; 2 spacious rehearsal rooms – 1 for vocal groups and the other for instrumental ensembles; and a new campus student center.

Over 200 AP exams are taken each year, and 90% of students taking AP exams earn scores of 3 or better. Thayer graduates consistently earn admittance to the most challenging and selective universities around the country. Over 85% attend colleges listed in Princeton Review's top colleges. As of September 2012, tuition is $36,575 with 33% of students receiving financial aid from a $5.5 million financial aid budget. The campus is easily accessible from the major surrounding highways (routes 3, 93, 95) and from public transportation.

INTERNATIONAL STUDY

The Learning-Through-Travel Program, comprised of a rich set of sister-school cultural exchanges and study-abroad programs, sets Thayer apart from other independent schools. The programs not only allow for travel and study in new cultures, but they establish long-term relationships with schools and students around the world. Many students recall their international experience as a turning point in their lives. Thayer hosts exchanges with the Lycée Stanislas in Cannes, the Northampton School for Boys in England, the WeiYu High School in Shanghai, and the Chirec School near Hyderabad, India. An Artists-in-Residence program in Cortona, Italy allows student artists to take workshops with Italian instructors, to view original work by such masters as Michelangelo, DaVinci, or Brunelleschi, and to do field work out in the Cortona countryside. Latin and history students can explore classical Roman sites, and those interested in doing community service or academic study abroad will find opportunities directed by Thayer faculty members in Quebec, Peru, and Costa Rica.

A BALANCED EDUCATIONAL PROGRAM — ARTS, ACADEMICS, ATHLETICS

Thayer is proud to offer an overall program that respects the value of academics, arts, athletics, and community service in equal measures.

The arts are woven into the daily fabric of student life at Thayer, where arts, academics, athletics, and service work in concert to ensure a well-balanced education. The key to this balance is in careful scheduling:

- Eighteen different arts classes form an integral part of the overall curriculum, and as such, they meet during the regular school day.
- Rehearsals for the extra-curricular theater productions are scheduled to avoid conflict with athletic practices. Thayer students do not have to choose between their artistic and athletic interests. They are free to develop as artists and athletes at the same time.

Athletic competition at Thayer enjoys a tradition of excellence that complements a rigorous academic program. All students, from grades six through twelve can choose to play on inter-scholastic teams. Over 90% of our students play at least one sport, and many are two- or three-season athletes. Thayer athletic programs are designed to encourage students to reach their potential in physical fitness, skill development, and teamwork. At every level, coaches emphasize sportsmanship, discipline, and lealeadership discipline, and leadership.

GRIT & GRACE

Our motto - grit and grace - defines and distinguishes our school. It represents a tradition, a culture, an aspiration, a way of life for our students and faculty, a distinct advantage for our graduates.

Westminster School

Co-ed boarding and day, grades 9-12
200-acre campus in Simsbury, Conn.
www.gritgrace.org (860) 408-3060

Westminster School welcomes students of every race, religion, color, nationality and ethnic origin.

Far Hills Country Day School

Academic Excellence & Character Development

The Journey Starts in Primary School. Come See Our Classrooms in Action!

PreK-Grade 8

Kassandra Hayes
Admission Director

908.766.0622 x455

697 Mine Brook Road (Rte 202) • Far Hills, NJ 07931

www.fhcds.org

EAGLE HILL SCHOOL
GREENWICH
45 Glenville Rd.
GREENWICH, CT 06831
Tel: 203-622-9240   FAX: 203-622-8668

Marjorie Castro, PhD, *Head of School*

Founded in 1975, Eagle Hill–Greenwich offers specialized instruction to bright children who, because of a learning disability, are unable to realize their full potential in traditional educational environments. Using a language immersion approach in an ungraded, non-competitive setting, students are provided with individualized and small group instruction. All teachers receive continued professional development.

Eagle Hill's main objective is to provide intensive, remedial instruction and then to return the child to the educational mainstream. A transitional program is incorporated into the plan to develop the academic skills, study strategies, self-advocacy and risk taking necessary to function independently in a traditional school setting. Students are placed in a range of boarding schools, local independent schools and public programs across the country. In addition to the extensive academic programs, the campus includes a professional library, a 15,000-volume children's library, art and music rooms, while advanced educational technology enhances the academic program and provides students with state-of-the-art facilities in which to develop their study skills and writing proficiency.

Eagle Hill offers a wide variety of activities. Electives include art, music, photography, cooking, newspaper, and community service programs. Full interscholastic and intra-mural sports programs include competition in soccer, cross country, field hockey, lacrosse, basketball, ice hockey, baseball, softball and tennis. Regular physical education classes, karate, jazz dance, aerobics, biking, ultimate frisbee and flag football round out the physical activity options.

Eagle Hill–Greenwich is a coed day and five-day residential program for students ages six through 16. The residential population at Eagle Hill ranges in ages from 10-16. Most students live within a two hour commute of Greenwich, and go home on weekends. The living situation is a warm, family-like setting, with close faculty supervision, guidance and interaction.

Eagle Hill houses a Lower School, ages six-11, and an Upper School, ages 11½-16. An active Advisor system ensures communication among staff and between school and home, and provides an advocate for the child within the program throughout the child's matriculation. Eagle Hill also runs a separate five and a half week summer school for children ages six-12, and two week workshops for students entering grade six through 9. For information regarding Eagle Hill–Greenwich, please contact Tom Cone, Director of Admissions and Placement at t.cone@eaglehill.org.

Celebrating over 50 Years

A fine arts boarding high school, offering the highest quality artistic training combined with comprehensive college-preparatory academics. The Academy also offers post-graduate opportunities.

Interlochen Majors include:

Comparative Arts • Creative Writing • Dance
Motion Picture Arts • Music • Theatre • Visual Arts

academy.interlochen.org

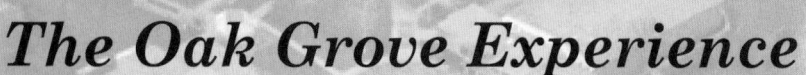

The Oak Grove Experience

Founded in 1906, Oak Grove Lutheran School serves students Pre-K through 12.

- Committed to providing an outstanding academic experience with a strong grounding in Christian faith
- Small class sizes; 12:1 student – teacher ratio
- Full range of co-curricular activities with many opportunities for student involvement
- Emphasis on service which fosters awareness and compassion for one another
- Nearly all Oak Grove graduates pursue degrees in higher education
- Safety and respect for one another
- Strong sense of community

The mission of Oak Grove is to express God's love by nurturing students for academic achievement, lifelong Christian commitment and loving service throughout the world.

OAK GROVE
LUTHERAN SCHOOL

6 – 12: 124 N Terrace, Fargo, ND 58102
Pre-K – 5: 2720 32nd Ave S, Fargo, ND 58103
Director of Admissions: (701) 373-7114   www.oakgrovelutheran.com/admissions/

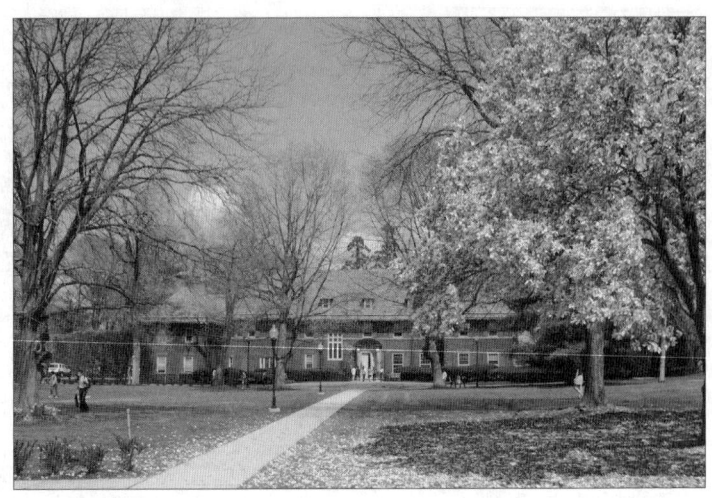

MORAVIAN ACADEMY
4313 Green Pond Rd.
BETHLEHEM, PA 18020

George N. King, Jr., *Headmaster*
Dr. Richard Krohn, *Director—Upper School*
Robert A. Bovee, *Director—Middle School*
Susan Paren, *Director—Lower School*

Founded in 1742, Moravian Academy is a coeducational day school for students in prekindergarten through grade twelve. The curriculum at the Upper School is college-preparatory with an emphasis on academics. We believe that the moral and physical development of students should complement their academic achievements. The student-teacher ratio is 9:1, giving teachers the opportunity to work closely with students in the classroom and after school, both in individual conferences and in numerous extracurricular activities. Academic excellence, challenge, respect and service—this is Moravian Academy. For more information about admissions, please call 610-691-1600.

Army and Navy Academy
College Preparatory Boarding School for Boys, Grades 7-12

Since 1910, Army and Navy Academy has sought to develop scholarship and honorable character in young men. To achieve these results, the Academy demands high curriculum standards in combination with essential life management, good citizenship and leadership skills.

Accreditation
The Army and Navy Academy is accredited by the Western Association of Schools and Colleges (WASC), in association with the California Association of Independent Schools (CAIS).

Academics
One of our core competencies is the academic achievement of our students. On a regular basis, students show significant improvement in their G.P.A., often within the first semester of attendance. Small class sizes, a highly committed staff and individualized support enable students to achieve better results and improve their chances for attending a college or university of their choice.

Students can benefit from a structured schedule, small classes and study skills training. Our challenging college-prep curriculum is based on the standards established by the University of California system requirements (a-g).

The Academic Department provides a variety of academic support services for cadets including daily tutorial, supervised study hall, academic counseling, and college planning services.

Campus Setting
The Academy has been established in its current oceanfront location in Carlsbad, CA since 1936. It is 35 miles north of San Diego and approximately 80 miles south of Los Angeles. The campus consists of 29 buildings on 16.5 acres, including a gymnasium, cafeteria, library media center, classroom buildings, recreation center, chapel, dormitories, and faculty houses. In addition, the campus contains administrative offices, a swimming pool, tennis courts, athletic field, and beach access.

Athletics
The Academy participates in interscholastic sports competitions. We are members of the Coastal Conference, which is part of the San Diego section of the California Interscholastic Federation (CIF), the governing body for all high school sports. For grades 9-12, we compete in Football, Cross-Country and Water Polo in the fall. Basketball, Wrestling and Soccer are offered in the winter and Baseball, Golf, Tennis, Swimming, Track and Field and Lacrosse are offered in the spring. For the 7th and 8th grades, we offer Flag Football, Basketball, Soccer and Baseball.

Residential Life
Safety and security are important at the Academy. Residential Life Officers oversee cadets and serve as a cadet's mentor/advisor for time spent outside of the classroom.

Leadership Opportunities
Leadership opportunities are one of the unique aspects of the Army and Navy Academy program.

Whether it's participating in one of the Academy's 20+ clubs or in the Leadership, Education and Training program (LET), opportunities to participate and lead are within reach for all cadets. Leadership training provides an underlying foundation that prepares high school students for leadership roles and cultivates independence, responsibility, accountability and self-discipline.

To arrange a campus visit or for more information, please contact us:
Email: admission@armyandnavyacademy.org
Phone: 888-762-2338
Address: 2605 Carlsbad Blvd., Carlsbad, CA. 92008
Visit our Website: www.armyandnavyacademy.org

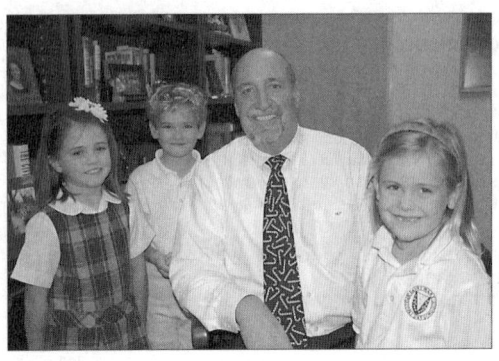

ST. MARY'S EPISCOPAL DAY SCHOOL

2101 S. Hubert Ave., TAMPA, FL 33629

Tel: 813-258-5508   Fax: 813-258-5603

E-mail: info@smeds.org   Web: www.smeds.org

St. Mary's Episcopal Day School is an independent, co-educational Pre-Kindergarten through eighth grade school, which inspires curiosity, kindness, and dignity in a caring Christian community. *At St. Mary's, children are taught to 'Learn ~ Love ~ Lead.'* St. Mary's provides a highly qualified faculty, rigorous academics, and well-balanced arts and sports programs, with the expectation that students can and will achieve their best. The accelerated curriculum includes Language Arts, Novel Study, Grammar, and Writing Workshops; advanced levels of Math; Social Studies, Geography, and History; Environmental Sciences, Life Sciences, Physical Science, and Global Awareness; Latin and Spanish; Religion; Physical Education; Performing Arts, Visual Arts, Music, Public Speaking, Community Service, and more. Technology is integrated into the curriculum at all levels, and each classroom is equipped with computers, an interactive Smartboard, and iPads. Educational and recreational field trips to local museums, theaters and attractions commence in Pre-Kindergarten, and students in upper grades enjoy overnight field trips including Sea Camp and a senior trip to Washington, DC. Specific character-development goals include integrity, self-discipline, self-motivation, good citizenship, friendliness, and a love of learning. Religious tradition follows that of the Episcopal Church, however children of many denominations attend. Parental involvement at school is highly encouraged.

THE WINDSOR SCHOOL
136-23 Sanford Ave.
FLUSHING, NY 11355
Tel: 718-359-8300   Fax: 718-359-1876
E-mail: admin@thewindsorschool.com
Web: windsorschool.com

- Accredited by the Middle States Association
  of Colleges and Secondary Schools
- Registered by the New York State Education Department
- Elected to membership in the College Entrance Examination Board and the College
  Scholarship Service

The Windsor School, grades 6-12 and Pre-University year, is dedicated to giving attention, identity, guidance and college preparation, not only to the gifted youngster, but also to the middle-range youngster, who is overlooked in larger schools. Small classes and involved teachers are the hallmark of the Windsor School.

All students have open, easy and informal access to all faculty members, guidance counselors and administrators—appointments are not necessary. College guidance is organized, thorough and successful.

The school is authorized under federal law to enroll non-immigrant alien students. If an international student is accepted, an I-20 form is issued. Recently we have had students from 21 foreign countries for

grades 7-12, or for the special Pre-University year: Hong Kong, Taiwan, Brazil, Korea, China, Russia, Israel, Egypt, Thailand, India, Angola, Singapore, Indonesia, Pakistan, Sudan, etc.

The modern school building is centrally located near public transportation—buses, subway and Long Island Railroad.

THE PINGRY SCHOOL

MARTINSVILLE, NJ
SHORT HILLS, NJ
www.pingry.org

Nathaniel E. Conard, *Headmaster*
BS, Yale University
MBA, Dartmouth College

Founded in 1861, The Pingry School is an independent co-educational college preparatory day school for students in K-12. Pingry has a national reputation for its long tradition of academic excellence and its commitment to an unparalleled education that emphasizes honor and character, respect, and service. Building on this 150-year-old foundation, Pingry today is a vibrant learning community dedicated to generating intellectual engagement and fostering honor and character in a diverse and inclusive environment. The Pingry experience is based on mutual respect and personal integrity. The foundation of this belief is Pingry's Honor Code, which, since 1926, has set the ethical standard that underlies every dimension of school life.

Pingry promotes excellence and honor at all levels of school life. Students participate in a demanding college preparatory program, complemented by extensive co-curricular opportunities. Our students are curious, creative, and involved—in the classroom, on the athletic fields, in the studios, on the stage, and in their communities. Our graduates go on to attend the nation's most selective colleges and universities such as Cornell, Dartmouth, Duke, Georgetown, Harvard, Middlebury, Princeton, Yale, and the University of Pennsylvania.

The Pingry School is also committed to sustaining a welcoming and supportive environment for all children and families in its community and those interested in joining the Pingry family. Pingry values and celebrates ethnic, racial, religious, and socioeconomic diversity. All members of our community, including trustees, administration, faculty, staff, students, parents, and alumni, contribute to the School in many different ways but share a unified and consistent commitment to Pingry's mission. The core of this commitment, and the link between Pingry's past and future, is John Pingry's founding motto: *"Greatest respect is due students."*

During the admission process, we are looking for academically focused and community oriented students who represent a variety of interests, talents, and experiences and who are eager to embrace the challenges and opportunities that Pingry offers. To arrange for a visit or to request further information, contact our Admission Office at 908-647-6419.

AN INDEPENDENT K-8 SCHOOL FOR CHILDREN OF ALL FAITHS

THE CATHEDRAL SCHOOL
of St. John the Divine

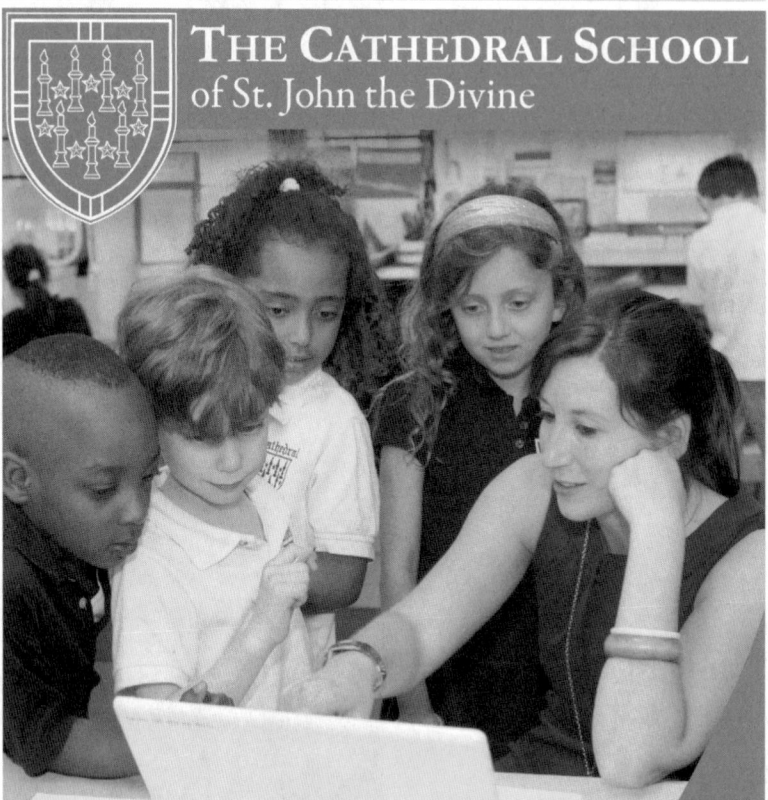

Visit our website at **cathedralnyc.org** to learn more about our:
- Rigorous academic program
- Diverse and welcoming community
- Commitment to character education
- Excellent track record of high school placement
- Spectacular campus on the 13-acre Close of The Cathedral of St. John the Divine

For more than 100 years, our school has helped young people mature into articulate, confident, and responsible citizens of the world.

1047 Amsterdam Ave
New York, NY 10025
Tel. 212-316-7500
cathedralnyc.org
Marsha K. Nelson,
Head of School
Lisa Smoots,
Director of Admission

MENLO SCHOOL

50 Valparaiso Avenue
ATHERTON, CA 94027
Tel: 650-330-2000
Fax: 650-330-2002
Web: www.menloschool.org

Menlo School (coed, grades 6-12) is dedicated to providing a challenging academic curriculum complemented by outstanding fine arts and athletic programs. The School helps students develop positive values and nurtures character development in a supportive environment that upholds the highest moral and ethical standards. Menlo's program encourages students to reach their fullest potential and develop the skills necessary to respond intelligently and humanely to the complexities of an increasingly diverse world.

ST. PETER'S SCHOOL

319 Lombard St.
PHILADELPHIA, PA 19147
Tel: 215-925-3963
Web: www.St-Peters-School.org

Shawn Kelly, *Head of School*

An independent, multi-denominational, co-ed day school, preschool through eighth grade. Founded in 1834, St. Peter's draws children of all socio-economic backgrounds, races, and religions. Music, art, poetry, and French enhance a traditional academic curriculum. Science, technology, and physical education are integral to the student's experience. Before, After and Summer School Programs are available.

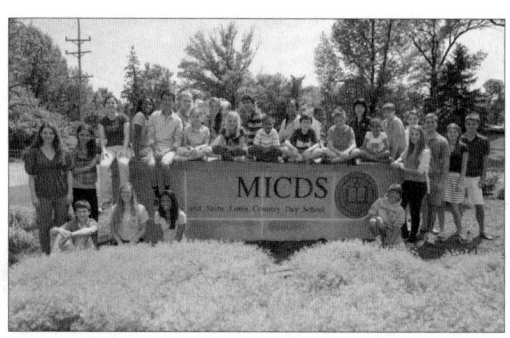

MARY INSTITUTE AND SAINT LOUIS COUNTRY DAY SCHOOL

IOI N. Warson Rd., ST. LOUIS, MO 63124

Tel: 314-993-5100   Fax: 314-995-7470

Web: www.micds.org

Founded in 1859, Mary Institute and Saint Louis Country Day School (MICDS) is today considered one of the nation's pre-eminent independent schools. MICDS is a coed, college-preparatory school serving 1,230 students. Grades Junior Kindergarten through four and grades nine through twelve are coed, while Middle School students in grades five through eight learn within a framework of single-gender and coed classes.

MICDS is committed to living its mission of preparing young people for higher learning and lives of purpose and service. The school's outstanding education balances strong academics, an innovative arts program, community service, a wide variety of extracurricular activities, and an athletics program that has claimed 23 state championships and 45 district championships over the past decade. In 2011, the School unveiled plans to add a state-of-the-art Science, Technology, Engineering and Mathematics (STEM) facility and Center for Community to its campus.Teachers and students benefit from a strong mission, a caring and diverse community and exceptional facilities for learning. MICDS welcomes students from all backgrounds, with 28% of our student body identifying themselves as students of color, and new students last year came from 109 different public/private/parochial/independent schools. The student-to-teacher ratio is 8:1, and class size ranges from 14-16 students. More than 75% of the faculty hold advanced degrees.

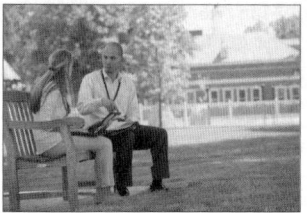

The 155 graduates of the Class of 2012 have enrolled at 89 different four-year colleges and universities. Approximately 24% of the student body receives some financial aid, which last school year totaled over $3.7 million. Tuition for the 2012-2013 school year ranges from $16,950 to $22,700.

THE HOTCHKISS SCHOOL
LAKEVILLE, CT

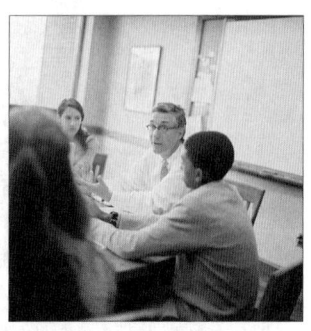

Malcolm H. McKenzie, *Head of School*

*The aspect of Hotchkiss which gives the school its usefulness and meaning
is challenge.*   — a student

Hotchkiss is a middle-sized, coeducational boarding school with a demanding academic curriculum and an extensive athletic and extracurricular program. The School strives to help students develop the confidence and clarity of thought necessary to express themselves, make decisions, assume responsibilities, and respond sensitively to the needs of others.

*I came to Hotchkiss in order to receive an excellent academic education.
I was successful in obtaining this objective, but I gained a lot more personally—more than I could have imagined three years ago.*— a student

Hotchkiss has long maintained its tradition of academic excellence. Classes range in size from 1 to 16 students. There are 123 full-time faculty members (and administrators) dedicated to the personal growth of each student. Most faculty members live on campus and all take an active role on campus by coaching, advising, leading activities, supervising in dormitories, and participating in the life of the School. Hotchkiss is small enough to retain an intimacy and sense of community which encourage close relationships between faculty members and students. It is also large enough—595 students in grade 9 through 12 & PG—to offer a variety of programs to meet the ever-expanding needs and interests of students.

*The holistic approach to education is what I like about teaching at a
boarding school. You're teaching the students, you're coaching the students,
you're eating meals with them.*   — a faculty member

Extracurricular activities are an important aspect of Hotchkiss life. Students can participate in any of the following clubs and groups: student newspapers, a literary review, radio station, a community service club, choral groups including a gospel choir, instrumental groups, major dramatic productions as well as numerous small-stage performances, scuba diving, computer club, and many other activities. There is ample opportunity to lead. Many senior students serve as proctors in dormitories, head tour guides, discipline committee members, or social committee members. All students participate in a school service program.

*The setting is lovely, the facilities are superb, the students are able, and
perhaps more important, the administration is committed to involvement in
the daily life of the School.*   — a faculty member

Hotchkiss is located on 815 acres of meadows and woodland in the foothills of the Berkshires. The academic facilities and life of the School are centered in the Main Building. Here there are 37 classrooms; 2 computer labs networked for Apple and PC platforms; 7 art studios; two auditoriums; a black box theater; a dance studio; a language laboratory with video server; and the outstanding Edsel Ford Memorial Library which boasts over 95,000 titles in print, and on video and DVD. Recently opened is a new music and performing arts wing which houses an auditorium for orchestral performance and new practice rooms. The school chapel and dining hall are attached to either end of the Main Building. The Griswold Science Building adjacent to the Main Building boasts 3 floors of laboratory space with independent project rooms, the latest scientific equipment including a scanning electron microscope, a weather station, plant "grow" rooms, a lecture hall equipped for video and computer projection, and state-of-the-art photography studios.

Boarding students at Hotchkiss live in twelve dormitories, where they are organized by class year, with about 15 to 25 students per corridor. Faculty members and senior proctors reside on each corridor, providing supervision and guidance. The dormitories are fully networked with voice and data access for every single student; day students enjoy this access as well as boarding students.

At Hotchkiss, I've learned to push myself and fully discover my capabilities in the classroom and on the field. — a student

Students participate in sports on many different levels; most interscholastic sports have not only a varsity team, but also a junior varsity and third team. Club sports are intramural. At all levels, students have full use of the school athletic facilities. Hotchkiss has 20 professional tennis courts in addition to a three-court indoor facility, 8 squash courts, 2 hockey rinks, a nine-hole golf course, and an indoor gymnasium complex with a wrestling room, 4 basketball courts, a ten-lane, 25-yard swimming pool, an indoor exercise complex, and a six-lane, all-weather surface track. Hotchkiss' facilities were expanded into a new 200,000-sq. ft. athletic and fitness center, which opened in the fall of 2002. The School borders on Lake Wononscopomuc, the deepest natural lake in Connecticut. Students use the lake for swimming, sailing, ice skating, and scientific research.

Four counselors guide students in the selection of colleges and in the application process. Over 100 college representatives visit the campus each year. The colleges most frequently attended by recent Hotchkiss graduates are Georgetown, Middlebury, Cornell, University of Pennsylvania, Bowdoin, Duke, Yale, Harvard, Brown and University of Virginia.

RANNEY SCHOOL

235 Hope Rd.
TINTON FALLS, NJ 07724
Tel: 732-542-4777

Lawrence S. Sykoff, Ed.D.
Head of School

Ranney School is a co-educational, independent, college preparatory, day school for grades Beginners (3 years old) through twelve. The traditional, structured academic program features an average class size of 15 students. Total enrollment averages 800 students.

Ranney School was founded in 1960 by Russell G. Ranney as an outgrowth of the Rumson Reading Institute. Emphasis on language arts skills remain the cornerstone of a Ranney education at all grade levels.

For the capable student, the school offers Algebra I in 7th grade. This allows the opportunity for 6 year advanced mathematics/science programs. A total of 17 Advanced Placement courses are offered in the Upper School, as well as standard and Honors courses in math, science, history, foreign language, and English.

French, Spanish, Mandarin Chinese, computer science, art, and music are introduced in Lower School. Latin, French, Spanish, and Chinese are available starting in 6th grade.

The Lower School is comprised of 3 buildings and has its own library, cafeteria, and computer and science labs. The new state-of-the-art Lower School Academic Complex opened its doors in the fall of 2008 and houses grades one through five. The Middle and Upper School building offers modern, high-tech classrooms and science laboratories, a foreign language laboratory, college guidance center, library, and a unique Distance Learning Center. Middle and Upper School has its own dining hall.

A full sports program makes use of the school's beautiful campus. Swimming in a 25-meter indoor pool is a weekly event for all grades. Two gyms provide space for indoor sports. In addition, these facilities include a fitness center with a certified athletic trainer on duty.

Other extracurricular activities include forensics, drama, chess, and various student publications. An optional after-school program allows students to participate in a large number of supervised activities, both academic and social.

AN EXCEPTIONAL EDUCATION
FOR AN EXCEPTIONAL COMMUNITY

Small class sizes, dynamic curriculum, creatively-inspired education for preschool through grade 9 in Park City, Utah.

INTEGRITY · RESPONSIBILITY · RESPECT

TEAMWORK · COMPASSION

AT PARK CITY DAY SCHOOL, WE SEE YOUR CHILD'S UNIQUE STRENGTHS,

and we work together as a community to nuture those strengths and advance new skills each and every day. It's how we give our students the fundamental grounding they need to realize their full potential in school - and in life.

P A R K   C I T Y

D A Y   S C H O O L

FOR MORE INFORMATION:
Park City Day School
3120 Pinebrook Road
Park City, UT 84098
www.parkcitydayschool.org

Tess Miner-Farra
Associate Head of School
435.649.2791 x14
info@parkcitydayschool.org

THE PENNINGTON SCHOOL
a coeducational day and boarding school for grades 6–12

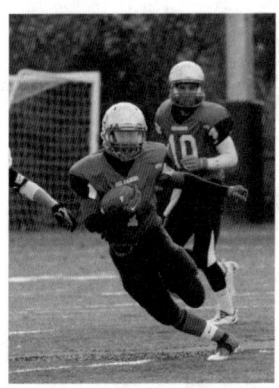

The Pennington School is an independent coeducational school for students in grades 6 through 12, in both day and boarding programs, with a current enrollment of approximately 475 students. The curriculum is college preparatory, with an emphasis on fostering the development of the whole student through academics, athletics, community service, and the creative and performing arts. Within the curriculum there are also small programs for international students and for students with learning differences. Founded in 1838, Pennington values both tradition and innovation, blending values gleaned from centuries of learning with the most up-to-date knowledge, and guides students in applying the result to a rapidly changing world. The School's faculty members focus not only on what they can teach the students but also on what the varied perspectives of the student body can impart to the overall educational experience.

AIGLON COLLEGE
1885 CHESIERES-VILLARS, SWITZERLAND
Tel: +41 24 496 6161   Fax: +41 24 496 6162
Email: info@aiglon.ch   Web: www.aiglon.ch

Aiglon College, founded in 1949 by John Corlette, offers a well-rounded education in a secure and friendly international community. It is an independent, non-profit, co-educational, international boarding school with an enrolment of over 60 nationalities. The school is a member of the Round Square, is accredited by ECIS and NEASC, and is registered as a charitable trust in Switzerland, the UK, USA, Netherlands and Canada. It is situated on a 25-acre alpine site 4,000 feet above the Rhone Valley. There are four houses for girls and four houses for boys (two of which form a separate Junior School), each with its own houseparents.

The school is divided into Junior (ages 9-13), Middle (13-15) and Upper (15-18) schools; courses are taught in English and the average of 8 students in each class permits the school to care for each student and provide learning support when necessary. The academic programme prepares students for British GCSE examinations and for the final two years of study we offer the International Baccalaureate (IB) Diploma. Facilities include a language centre, eight science laboratories, a library and outstanding art, drama and music departments. The school is also a centre for the College Board/SATs and IELTS exams at subsidiary levels. Aiglon's graduates are currently enrolled in leading universities and colleges in the USA, UK and Europe.

Academic study is complemented by a very high degree of pastoral care and a challenging programme of sports and outdoor activities. Sports include skiing, basketball, tennis, soccer, athletics, gymnastics, swimming and volleyball. Each weekend students can go on expedition and partake in a variety of outdoor activities including camping, hiking, climbing, canoeing, and skiing. Service and responsibility are fostered through social service projects amongst the local Swiss community and through the Round Square organisation worldwide.

Language schools combined with outdoor activities are offered during Easter and the Summer.

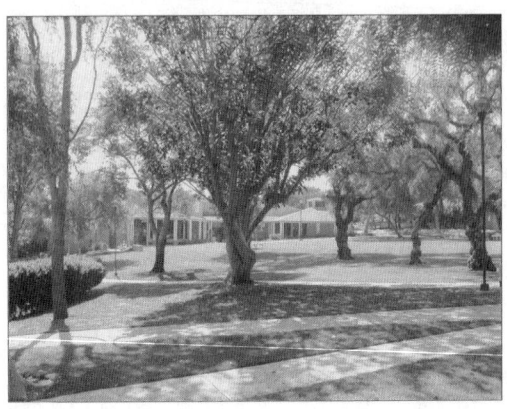

CHADWICK SCHOOL
26800 S. Academy Dr.
PALOS VERDES PENINSULA, CA 90274
Tel: 310-377-1543
Web: www.chadwickschool.org
Accredited by WASC

Chadwick School, founded in 1935, is a nonprofit, nondenominational, coeducational day school that serves a culturally and economically diverse student body in Grades K-12. Chadwick's mission encourages personal excellence, the development of exemplary character, the mastery of academic, athletic and artistic skills, and the growth of social and individual responsibility. Chadwick School is located on 45 acres atop the beautiful Palos Verdes Peninsula, where approximately one third of the faculty lives on campus. In the Village School (Grades K-6), class size is 18 to 20 students. The faculty is made up of classroom teachers and specialists in art, music, science, technology, global languages and physical education.

With an average class size of 17 students, the Middle and Upper Schools offer a rigorous college preparatory core curriculum with courses in English, history, science, mathematics, global languages, visual and performing arts and technology. A full range of honors and Advanced Placement courses is available in all disciplines, as well as an individualized college counseling program. Outdoor education is an integral part of the curriculum: this course of study culminates in a three-week senior trip just prior to graduation. A variety of choices is available for students in competitive athletics, community service programs, special interest clubs, student publications, and international study and service. Chadwick has a second campus in Songdo, near Incheon, South Korea.

For more information, please contact the Office of Admission, (310) 377-1543, ext. 4025, or admissions@chadwickschool.org.

PASADENA WALDORF SCHOOL
209 E. Mariposa St.
ALTADENA, CA 91001
Tel: 626-794-9564   Web: www.pasadenawaldorf.org
E-mail: admissions@pasadenawaldorf.org

Established in 1979, Pasadena Waldorf School currently serves 240 students, from preschool through eighth grade, on its beautiful and historic three-and-a-half-acre campus in Altadena. Our high school opens fall, 2012.

Pasadena Waldorf students pursue academic excellence in a balanced, nurturing, non-competitive environment, with a curriculum originally developed by Rudolf Steiner for the first Waldorf School, 1919. We teach both Japanese and Spanish beginning in first grade; in addition to our handwork program for all the grades, our fourth through eighth graders learn woodworking. Our music program includes string instruction for third and fourth grades, wind instruction for fifth grade, and instrumental ensemble for the middle school. Our middle school students participate in a weekly choir class and are encouraged to play in the after-school sports program. All students learn Eurythmy, a movement program and internationally-recognized performance art developed by Rudolf Steiner. PWS students explore their world on school trips all over California (and sometimes beyond). Festivals, plays, and assemblies throughout the year bring the students together to celebrate seasonal rhythms and traditions. The result: well-grounded, culturally literate, competent, creative students, curious about the world and eager to explore its wonders.

The Williston Northampton School enrolls 460 students in grades 9 through PG—280 boarding boys and girls and 180 day students. Forty-six percent of our students receive financial aid and eighteen percent are students of color. Located in the heart of Massachusetts' Pioneer Valley— 14 miles north of Springfield, MA, 150 miles north of New York City, and 90 miles west of Boston—Williston offers superior college preparation. Through the Williston⁺ program, students benefit from having the resources of the Five Colleges in our community—Amherst, Hampshire, Mount Holyoke, and Smith Colleges and the University of Massachusetts, Amherst—brought into the classroom. This unique learning environment provides students and faculty with opportunities to engage and explore like no other boarding school in the country.

Academic preparation for college lies at the heart of Williston's program, but the faculty also recognize their important role in helping young people develop the necessary skills to lead a successful life. Williston's varied, challenging, and broad-based curriculum—including 22 AP courses—offers students the opportunity to explore, to investigate, and to question. In addition to traditional college preparatory courses with numerous electives, we offer special programs such as School Year Abroad, the Writers' Workshop and our Photographers' Lecture Series, which bring to campus internationally acclaimed authors and photographers who present their work to the community and discuss it with students. Students can also participate in School Year Abroad while at Williston. The school helps students develop responsible independence by fostering cooperation, mutual respect, and the development of personal leadership skills. We actively seek a diverse student body to encourage students to take advantage of the cultural richness and diversity of our world.

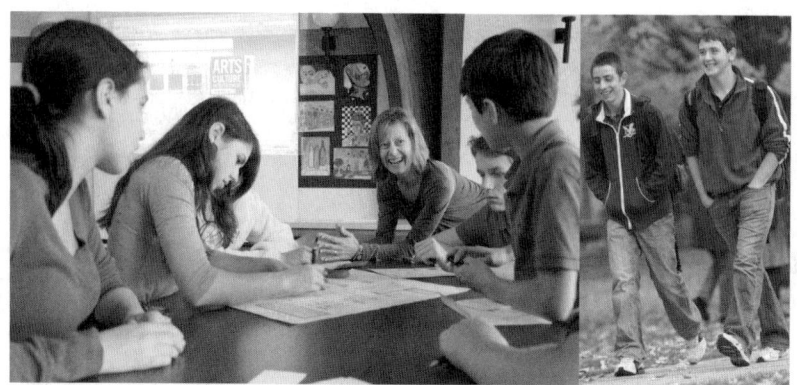

Williston's 125-acre suburban setting lies only a few miles from the base of Mt. Tom. The surrounding area offers excellent outdoor activities and a culturally rich environment of fine museums, libraries, and theater programs. The school's activities office arranges many fine events for students, including trips to New England Patriots, Boston Celtics, and Red Sox games, visits to Boston and New York City, weekend ski excursions to Stratton and Stowe in Vermont, and many films, plays, concerts, and dance performances at the area colleges, and in Hartford and Springfield. These off-campus events complement the busy weekends on campus that feature dances and coffee houses, talent shows, visiting lecturers, and film series, among many other events. The Williston Northampton School offers over 30 extracurricular opportunities. The Williston Theatre is one of the school's extracurricular highlights, and with several theater productions each year, students have the opportunity to develop their talents in acting or the technical aspects of theater.

Williston also offers a comprehensive athletic program that allows students to compete in more than 30 competitive sports. The athletic program features excellent facilities, including a state-of-the-art athletic center with two basketball courts, a six-lane pool, four squash courts, a fitness center, a multi-use aerobics and wrestling room, and a training room. Williston also has two synthetic turf playing fields (one with lights); an eight-lane all-weather track and field facility; a refurbished ice rink; a 12-court tennis complex; and a 3.1 mile cross country course. The ski team practices at Berkshire East, and the golf teams use three local courses.

The Williston Northampton School

Head of School Robert W. Hill III

19 Payson Avenue, Easthampton, MA 01027 | 413.529.3000 | www.williston.com

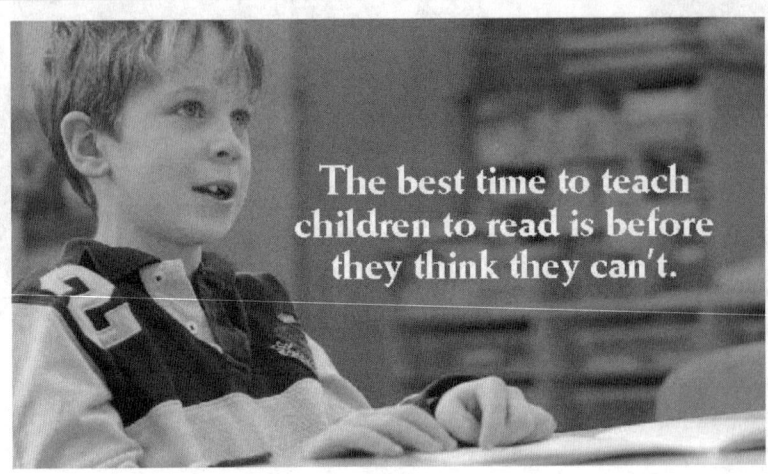

The best time to teach children to read is before they think they can't.

THE BEGINNING READERS PROGRAM
AT THE CARROLL SCHOOL

Proper intervention can help kids who have trouble reading overcome their problems at an early age. With over 40 years of experience teaching children with language-based learning disabilities, Carroll excels in this field. Our Beginning Readers Program provides first grade children the customized instruction, enriched curriculum, and personal attention they need to learn to read and enjoy academic success.

 Carroll School

Lincoln and Waltham, MA | 781-259-8342 | www.carrollschool.org

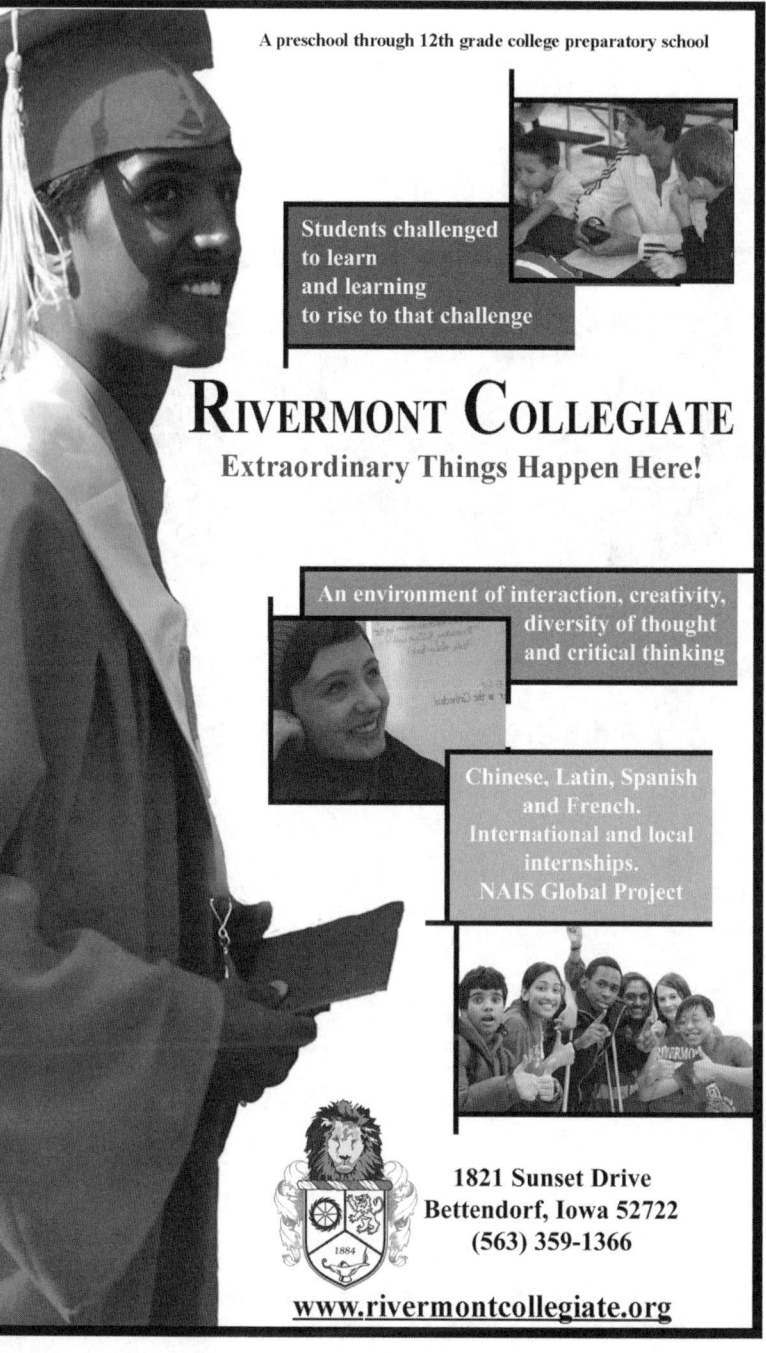

A preschool through 12th grade college preparatory school

Students challenged
to learn
and learning
to rise to that challenge

RIVERMONT COLLEGIATE
Extraordinary Things Happen Here!

An environment of interaction, creativity,
diversity of thought
and critical thinking

Chinese, Latin, Spanish
and French.
International and local
internships.
NAIS Global Project

**1821 Sunset Drive
Bettendorf, Iowa 52722
(563) 359-1366**

www.rivermontcollegiate.org

Rolling Hills Country Day School
Kindergarten through Grade 8

Small class sizes, specialized teachers in art, music, physical education, Spanish, science, and computer

Call Today to Learn More

(310) 377-4848 ✏ www.rhcds.com

26444 Crenshaw Blvd., Rolling Hills Estates, CA 90274

The Heiskell School

Excellence in Christian Education Since 1949

The Heiskell School's accelerated academic program and its focus on building Godly character have had a life-changing impact in the lives of children for more than 60 years.

www.heiskell.net

**Preschool · Elementary · Junior High
Two Years through 8th Grade**

Located in Buckhead in Northwest Atlanta
3260 Northside Drive, NW, Atlanta, Georgia 30305

404-262-2233

THE GREENWOOD SCHOOL

14 Greenwood Lane
Putney, VT 05346
Stewart Miller, *Headmaster*

Founded in 1978, Greenwood is a boarding and day school for young men in grades 6 through 12. Greenwood empowers bright and talented boys who face dyslexia, related language-based learning differences, ADHD, and executive function weakness with the skills necessary to bridge the gap between their outstanding promise and present abilities. Greenwood offers comprehensive, individualized teaching balanced with an emphasis on enrichment programs designed to awaken students' hidden talents. The result is a school that transforms lives by providing the best environment possible for students with learning differences to maximize their academic, social, and creative potentials.

- 2:1 student : teacher ratio
- All students receive a daily, hour-long individualized tutorial
- Integrated, support services:

    o   Speech and Language Therapy
    o   Occupational Therapy
    o   Social Pragmatics
    o   Life Skills

- Focus on multi-sensory instruction and experiential learning
- All teachers are trained learning specialists
- State of the art technology: laptop program, SMART Boards, assistive technology
- Enrichment opportunities including art, music, athletics, woodworking, robotics, community service and outdoor leadership
- 100+ acre campus on a rural Vermont hillside

Contact: Melanie Miller, Director of Admission
tel: 802-387-4545   fax: 802-387-5396
email: admissions@greenwood.org   web: www.greenwood.org

BURGUNDY

Where learning comes alive!

Pre-Kindergarten - 8th Grade

· Exciting, experiential curriculum

· Diverse, nurturing community

· Extended day and enrichment opportunities

· Bus transportation in MD, VA and DC

· 25-acre Alexandria campus

· 500-acre Center for Wildlife Studies

Join us for an
Open House!
Or call to schedule a tour:
703.329.6968

Burgundy Farm Country Day School
3700 Burgundy Road · Alexandria, VA · 22303
703.329.6968 · info@burgundyfarm.org
www.burgundyfarm.org

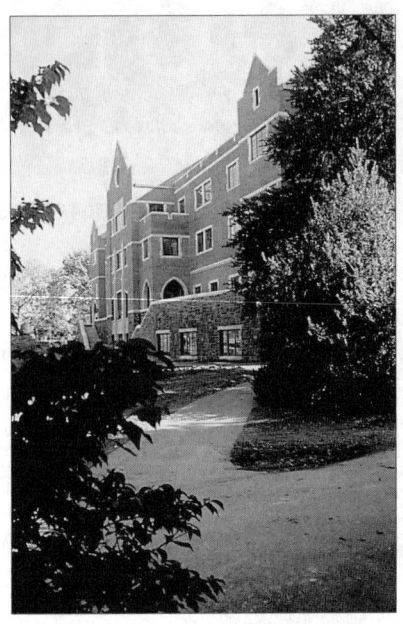

THE HILL SCHOOL
717 E. High St.
POTTSTOWN, PA 19464
Tel: 610-326-1000
www.thehill.org

The Hill School prepares students from across the United States and around the world for excellence in college, careers, and life. Dedicated to developing the minds, bodies, and character of all students, the School combines a challenging liberal arts curriculum with moral direction and leadership opportunities in a traditionally structured, supportive residential community. Hill's stimulating academic program is founded on classical and Judeo-Christian principles that value refinement of thought and inspire responsibility for the common good. Hill's outstanding teachers develop students' skills and core knowledge, lead students to a global perspective on the world, and encourage life-long learning.

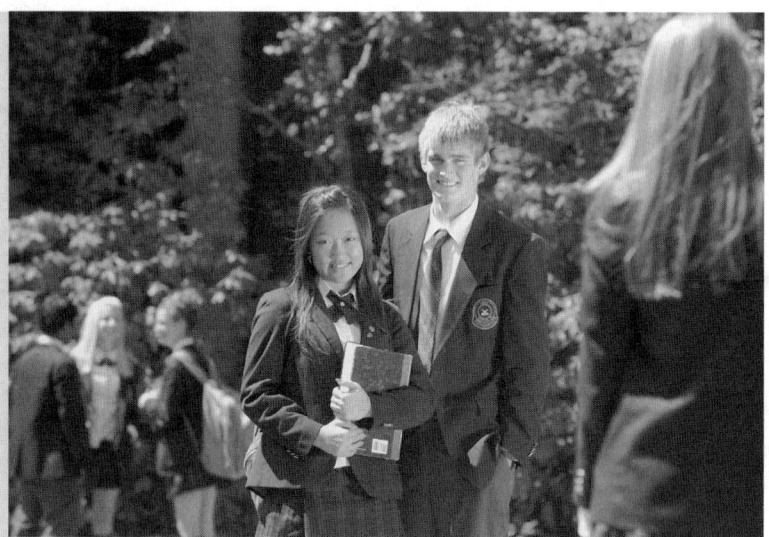

Never, Never, Never Quit.

F|ROM A FAMILY'S FIRST CAMPUS VISIT to Graduation Day, these words echo throughout the Linsly Experience. To persevere through adversity. To show grace in victory and defeat. To respect the opposition. These values serve students well while they are at Linsly and through their college and professional lives.

Call for information about 2012-2013 CAMPUS VISIT DAYS 304-233-1436

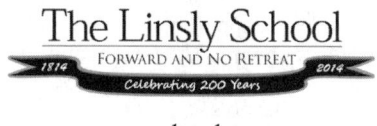

The Linsly School
FORWARD AND NO RETREAT
1814   2014
Celebrating 200 Years

www.linsly.org
admit@linsly.org

 FACEBOOK.COM/LINSLYSCHOOL    TWITTER.COM/LINSLY

THE LINSLY SCHOOL, 60 KNOX LANE, WHEELING, WV 26003
THE LINSLY SCHOOL IS AN EQUAL OPPORTUNITY SCHOOL

CRANBROOK SCHOOLS
BLOOMFIELD HILLS, MI

Arlyce Seibert, *Director of Schools*
Drew Miller, *Director of Admission*

Cranbrook Schools is a college-preparatory, coeducational day and boarding school committed to academic excellence. The school consists of Brookside Lower School (pre-kindergarten-5), Cranbrook Kingswood Middle School (6-8) with separate programs for boys and girls, and Cranbrook Kingswood Upper School (day and boarding, 9-12).

Cranbrook Kingswood Upper School offers students the advantages of both coeducational and single-sex learning environments, activities and traditions. Students have full access to two campuses characterized by unique architectural styles and outstanding facilities. At the same time, male and female boarders enjoy the privacy of dormitory living on separate campuses.

The school is a part of Cranbrook Educational Community, an internationally renowned educational and cultural center occupying 319 acres in Bloomfield Hills, 45 minutes north of Detroit. Founded by the late George G. Booth and his wife, Ellen Scripps Booth, Cranbrook is primarily active in the fields of science, education, and art. The Community includes the Cranbrook Academy of Art and Museum, Cranbrook Institute of Science with its planetarium and observatory, and Cranbrook Schools.

Underlying the creation of these institutions was the founders' conviction that beauty and culture are part of education. Accordingly, Eliel Saarinen was retained as architect and designed the complex. Today several of its buildings are acknowledged architectural masterpieces. In addition, Carl Milles was brought to Cranbrook as artist-in-residence and much of his sculpture, together with many other works of art, enhance the beautiful grounds of the Community.As a result of this broad educational approach, Cranbrook Schools has an unusual and refreshing atmosphere of warmth, cordiality and friendship, which is reflected among the boys and girls themselves. Between faculty and students, there is a strong feeling of working together in a common enterprise. The school offers a wide range of academic courses and, beyond that, extraordinary opportunities in the sciences and visual and performing arts. The multi-faceted Gordon Science Center is highlighted by seven wireless laboratories, solarium, computer center, aquatic center, animal room, library, and classrooms.

Virtually all graduates go on to college, with the majority of students attending Boston University, Brown, Cornell, Georgetown, Johns Hopkins, Kenyon, Miami University–Ohio, Michigan State, MIT, Northwestern, Princeton, Purdue, University of Chicago, University of Michigan, University of Pennsylvania, Williams, and Yale.

All students participate in a vigorous athletic program. The school's athletic facilities include five gymnasia, twelve large playing fields for football, baseball, soccer, field hockey, lacrosse, fifteen tennis courts, a year-round ice arena, a dance studio, a performing arts center and an eight lane indoor swimming pool. Intramural and interscholastic competition is held on all age levels.

The men and women teaching at Cranbrook Schools, some from foreign countries, are selected not only for their unusual academic expertise, but also for their interests in young students. Most Upper School faculty members and their families live on campus, and students share the warmth of family relationships. Cranbrook Schools challenges each individual to do his very best, emphasizes pride in real accomplishment and promotes self-confidence. An extensive financial aid program allows for a student body of wide geographical and economic backgrounds, and the school enrolls students without regard to race, religion, color, national origin, age, sex or handicap.

Out-of-Door At a Glance

Accredited by Florida Council of Independent Schools and Florida Kindergarten Council

Enrollment is over 600 students (PreK – 12th)

Faculty are caring, dedicated professionals with a student-teacher ratio of 10:1 and a talented support staff.

Academics are rigorous and comprehensive. Recent graduating classes have:
~ Average SATs over 1200
~ 100% matriculation to four-year colleges or universities
~ 70% matriculation outside Florida

Athletics stress physical skill development, self-confidence, teamwork, and sportsmanship with 38 varsity, junior varsity, and middle school teams. Member of the Florida High School Athletics Association.

Arts incorporate drama, music, and the visual arts. Meaningful experiences are created by linking projects to academic studies and performing for community and school functions.

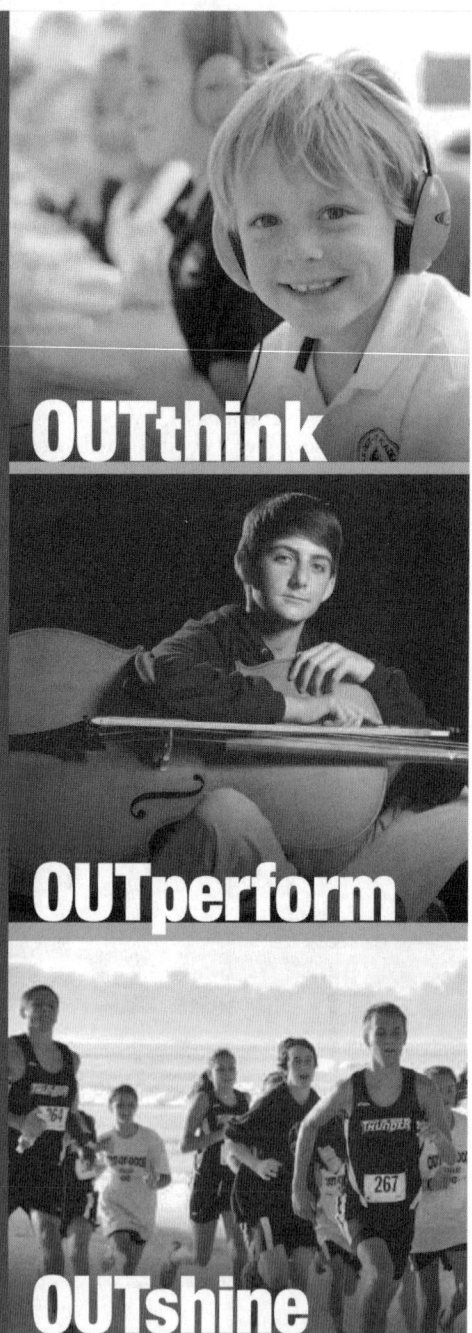

OUTthink

OUTperform

OUTshine

In 1924, our founders, Fanneal Harrison and Catherine Gavin, sought to establish a uniquely progressive school committed to high academic standards and to nourishing the minds, bodies, and spirits of children...

85 years later, we remain inspired by their vision.

From PreK through 12th grade, we are passionate about educating the whole child through a rigorous balance of academics, athletics, arts, and character development. We value a strong partnership with our parent community and, together, prepare our students to meet life's challenges with knowledge, integrity, courage, and poise so that they, in turn, can make a difference in the world.

As an independent, college preparatory school, our mission is to provide an environment in which students strive to achieve their highest academic goals and to build character through a balanced program of academics, athletics, and the arts. While words and pictures can provide an exciting glimpse of The Out-of-Door Academy experience, ultimately we are about relationships and community. We encourage you to visit our campuses, meet our students and teachers, and see our comprehensive program in action first-hand.

THE OUT-OF-DOOR ACADEMY est.1924

Admissions: 941.554.3400 ~ www.oda.edu
Siesta Key Campus, Grades PreK–6
Uihlein Campus at Lakewood Ranch, Grades 7–12

BOLLES
ALL THINGS POSSIBLE

Established in 1933 as a military school for boys in grades 7-12, Bolles dropped its military affiliation in 1962 and became coeducational in 1971. The school's balanced college preparatory program combines academics, offerings in the fine and performing arts, approximately three dozen athletic teams, leadership and service opportunities, and a nationally-known guidance program. The boarding program, in which boys and girls reside on different campuses, complements the coeducational learning environment. After-school activities on each campus include many coeducational pursuits.

7400 San Jose Blvd   Jacksonville FL 32217   (904) 256-5030   www.Bolles.org

The Bolles School is a drug-free workplace, admitting students regardless of gender, race, religion, color or national origin.

SAINT JOSEPH HIGH SCHOOL
A Brothers of the Sacred Heart School

145 Plainfield Avenue Metuchen, NJ 08840
732-549-7600   www.stjoes.org
Mr. John A. Anderson '70, Principal

Where excellence is a habit . . .

Accomplishments of the class of 2012

100% College Acceptance
84% of seniors received a College Scholarship
$24.5 Million in College Scholarships (to date)
1 attendee US Naval Academy Annapolis
1 attendee US Coast Guard Academy
7 Commended Students National Merit Scholarship Competition
1 Finalist National Hispanic Recognition Competition
1 National Merit Finalist
MSG Varsity The New Jersey Challenge Championship (College Bowl)
New Jersey Team History Championship and Invitation to the Nationals
(5th place finish at Nationals)
New Jersey History Bowl State Individual Championship
1st place Individual Varsity National History Championship
Individual World Championship, World History Bee, Grasse France
Robotics Invitation to Nationals
Falcon Newspaper National Honors
Evergreen Yearbook National Honors
Vignette Literary Magazine National Honors
Top 1% Finisher National American Association of German Teachers
Catholic Math League Regional Championship
New Jersey Math League Middlesex County Champions
5 Athletic Divisional Championships
5 Athletic County Championships
Non Public A Boys Basketball State Championship

. . . not a goal

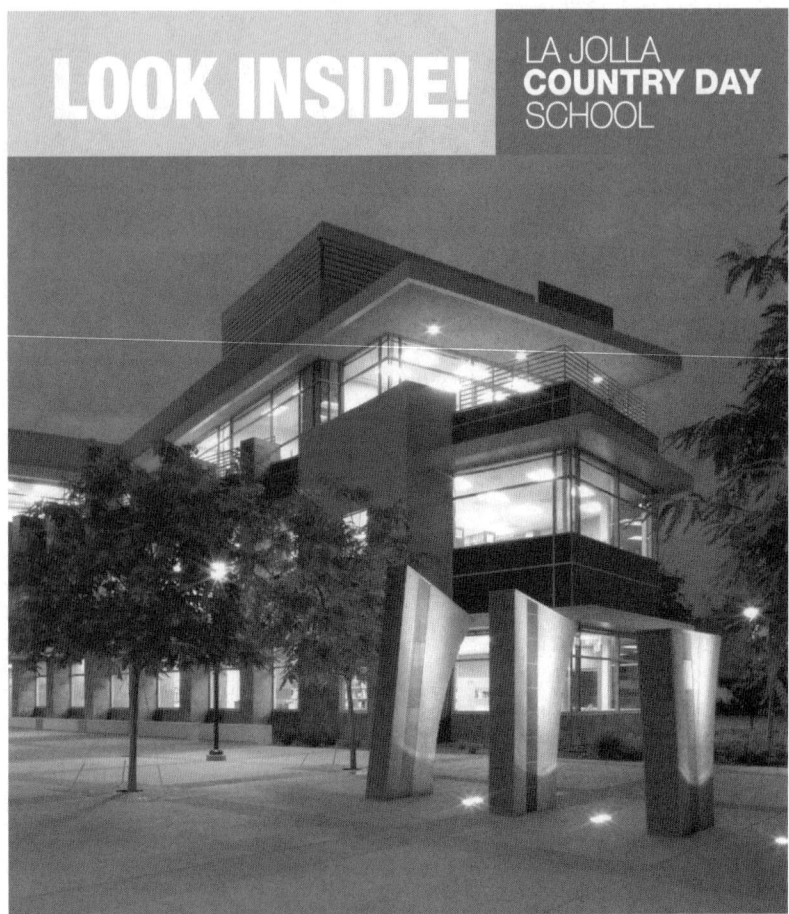

LOOK INSIDE! LA JOLLA **COUNTRY DAY** SCHOOL

AT LA JOLLA COUNTRY DAY SCHOOL YOU WILL SEE:

- Superior college preparation.
- Age 3 to Grade 12 students on one campus.
- $46-million campus redevelopment complete.
- Small classes enabling individualized attention.
- Experienced, world-class faculty.

LaJollaCountryDaySchool.org

THE HUDSON SCHOOL
Grades 5−12 • Founded 1978 • Coeducational Day School

Open House October 13, 2012, 2-4 p.m.

- Highest Academic and Ethical Standards
- Small Classes
- Dedicated and Professional Faculty
- International Student Body
- Computer and Technology Courses
- Challenging College Preparatory Curriculum
- AP Courses
- Art, Drama, Instrumental Music, Choral and Dance Instruction
- Modern and Classical Languages
- Community Service Required

For the intellectually curious student who loves to learn and doesn't mind a bit of hard work.

Accredited by the Middle States Association of Colleges and Schools

601 Park Avenue • Hoboken, NJ 07030
201-659-8335 • www.thehudsonschool.org

KEY TO SCHOOL FEATURE INDEXES

Selectivity column *(see Glossary for a definition of the below terms)*

O	Open (nonselective) admission
•	Somewhat selective admission
••	Selective admission
•••	Very selective admission

Tuition column

0	Tuition is free
$	Bdg tuition $39,499 or less; Day tuition $12,549 or less
$$	Bdg tuition $39,500-47,499; Day tuition $12,550-20,900
$$$	Bdg tuition $47,500 and up; Day tuition $20,901 and up

LD column

F	Designates an LD focus
P	Designates an LD program

Summer column

O	Indicates summer program is open to students not enrolled at the school
•	Summer program available to enrolled students only

Religion column

A	Anglican	LMS	Lutheran-Missouri Synod
B	Baptist	Mn	Mennonite
CS	Christian Science	Mth	Methodist
CG	Church of God (Seventh-Day)	Mr	Moravian
CB	Church of the Brethren	NC	Nondenom Christian
CLC	Church of the Lutheran Confession	OJ	Orthodox Jewish
Cg	Congregational	P	Presbyterian
Ec	Ecumenical	RSF	Religious Society of Friends
Ep	Episcopal	RC	Roman Catholic
Ev	Evangelical	Swk	Schwenkfelder
EvC	Evangelical Covenant	SA	Seventh-day Adventist
GB	Grace Brethren	SB	Southern Baptist
I	Islamic	UU	Unitarian Universalist
J	Jewish	UCC	United Church of Christ
L	Lutheran	UM	United Methodist
		W	Wesleyan

SCHOOL FEATURE INDEXES

SCHOOLS WITH A SPECIAL FOCUS

INDEXES OF SPECIAL INTEREST

School	Town	Girls' Grade Range Bdg	Girls' Grade Range Day	Boys' Grade Range Bdg	Boys' Grade Range Day	Enrollment	Selectivity	Tuition	AP Courses	Learning Disabilities	ESL	Varsity Sports	Summer	Religion	Page
ALABAMA															
DONOHO	Amniston		PS-12		PS-12	374	•	$	9			10	O		561
ADVENT EPISCOPAL	Birmingham		PS-8		PS-8	319	••	$				4		Ep	983
ALTAMONT	Birmingham		5-12		5-12	340	••	$$	14			10	O		561
HIGHLANDS-AL	Birmingham		PS-8		PS-8	280	••	$				3	O		983
LYMAN WARD	Camp Hill			6-12		122	••	$				4	O		983
BAYSIDE	Daphne		PS-12		PS-12	750	••	$	10	P		11	•		984
HOUSTON ACAD	Dothan		PS-12		PS-12	632	••	$	9			9			563
MARS HILL	Florence		PS-12		PS-12	598	•	$	4			9		NC	984
RANDOLPH SCH	Huntsville		K-12		K-12	997	••	$$	17			12	O		564
INDIAN SPRINGS	Indian Springs	9-12	8-12	9-12	8-12	269	••	$	17			9	O		562
SPRINGWOOD	Lanett		PS-12		PS-12	309	••	$	3			7			564
MADISON	Madison		PS-12		PS-12	899	•	$	4			10		NC	984
MCGILL-TOOLEN	Mobile		9-12		9-12	1130	••	$	13	P		12	•	RC	985
ST LUKE'S EPIS-AL	Mobile		PS-12		PS-12	696	•	$	8			12	O	Ep	985
ST PAUL'S EPIS-AL	Mobile		PS-12		PS-12	1262	••	$	12	P	•	12	O	Ep	565
AL CHRISTIAN	Montgomery		PS-12		PS-12	987	•	$	5			9		NC	986
MONTGOMERY ACAD	Montgomery		K-12		K-12	821	••	$	18		•	12	•		566
ST JAMES SCH-AL	Montgomery		PS-12		PS-12	1112	••	$	11			13			986
TUSCALOOSA ACAD	Tuscaloosa		PS-12		PS-12	400	•	$	12		•	11	O		986
ALASKA															
GRACE CHRISTIAN	Anchorage		K-12		K-12	577	•	$	8	P		7		NC	1171
PACIFIC NORTHERN	Anchorage		PS-8		PS-8	135	••	$$							1171
ARIZONA															
ORME	Mayer	8-12	6-12	8-12	6-12	124	••	$$	8		•	7	•		789

School	City	Grades	Grades	Enroll		$						Affil	Page
IMMACULATE HEART	Oro Valley	9-12	9-12	71	•	$			•	6		RC	795
PHOENIX CO DAY	Paradise Valley	PS-12	PS-12	722	••	$$$	13			10	O		791
ALL SAINTS' EPIS-AZ	Phoenix	PS-8	PS-8	519	••	$$	21			4	•	Ep	790
BROPHY	Phoenix	9-12	9-12	1270	•	$$				13	O	RC	790
PARADISE VALLEY PREP	Phoenix	PS-12	PS-12	335	•	$				6		NC	1160
PHOENIX CHRISTIAN	Phoenix	PS-12	PS-12	571	•	$	9		•	12		NC	1160
ST MARY'S CATHOLIC	Phoenix	9-12	9-12	503	•	$	7		•	11	•	RC	1160
SCOTTSDALE CHRISTIAN	Phoenix	PS-12	PS-12	850	••	$	3	P	•	12	•	NC	1161
SOUTHWESTERN-AZ	Rimrock	9-PG	9-PG	40	O	$	4		•	5	O		792
CAMELBACK DESERT	Scottsdale	PS-8	PS-8	176	O	$$				3	O		1161
VERDE VALLEY	Sedona	9-12	9-12	102	••	$$			•	3	O		792
FENSTER	Tucson	6-PG	6-PG	23	••	$		P	•	3	O		793
GREEN FIELDS	Tucson	K-12	K-12	181	••	$$	11			5			794
ST GREGORY COL PREP	Tucson	6-12	6-12	304	••	$$	16			10	O		1162
ST MICHAEL'S PARISH	Tucson	K-8	K-8	337	•	$				5	O	Ep	1162
SALPOINTE	Tucson	9-12	9-12	1117	•	$	17			13	O	RC	1162
OAK CREEK	West Sedona	7-12	7-12	90	•	$$		F	•	6	O		1163
ARKANSAS													
ANTHONY	Little Rock	PS-8	PS-8	415	•	$				10	O		1122
MT ST MARY-AR	Little Rock	9-12	9-12	500	O	$				11	•	RC	1122
PULASKI	Little Rock	PS-12	PS-12	1335	••	$	18			13			749
CENTRAL AR CHRISTIAN	North Little Rock	PS-12	PS-12	985	•	$	5			11		NC	1122
SUBIACO	Subiaco	7-12	7-12[5]	175	••	$	9		•	8	O	RC	750
CALIFORNIA													
RAMONA	Alhambra	7-12	7-12	392	••	$	13			8		RC	1171
PASADENA WALDORF	Altadena	PS-8	PS-8	220	••	$$				2	•		1172
CORNELIA CONNELLY	Anaheim	9-12	9-12	259	•	$$	10			10	O	RC	1172

School	Town	Girls' Grade Range Bdg	Girls' Grade Range Day	Boys' Grade Range Bdg	Boys' Grade Range Day	Enrollment	Selectivity	Tuition	AP Courses	Learning Disabilities	ESL	Varsity Sports	Summer	Religion	Page
CA															
FAIRMONT	Anaheim		PS-12		PS-12	2230	•	$$	17			8	•		1173
ST CATHERINE'S ACAD	Anaheim			4-8[5]	K-8	170	••	$$			•	4	O	RC	801
SERVITE	Anaheim				9-12	957	••	$$	17			13	O	RC	1173
MENLO	Atherton		6-12		6-12	795	••	$$$	19			14	O		801
NOTRE DAME-BELMONT	Belmont		9-12			450	••	$$	11	P		9	O	RC	1173
ECOLE BILINGUE-CA	Berkeley		PS-8		PS-8	546	••	$$$			•	2	•		1174
PROVIDENCE HS	Burbank		9-12		9-12	400	•	$$	13			8	O	RC	1174
VIEWPOINT	Calabasas		K-12		K-12	1215	••	$$$	22			13	O		821
ARMY & NAVY	Carlsbad			7-12	7-12	320	••	$	10		•	11	O		802
ALL SAINTS' EPIS-CA	Carmel		PS-8		PS-8	215	••	$$				5	O	Ep	1175
JESUIT HS-CA	Carmichael				9-12	1065	••	$	13			13	•	RC	1175
ST MICHAEL'S EPIS	Carmichael		PS-8		PS-8	231	••	$				4	O	Ep	1175
CATE	Carpinteria	9-12		9-12	9-12	265	••	$$	16			13			855
CHAMINADE PREP-CA	Chatsworth		6-12		6-12	1320	••	$$	21			16	O	RC	1176
CHATSWORTH HILLS	Chatsworth		PS-8		PS-8	250	••	$$				3	O		1176
SIERRA CANYON	Chatsworth		PS-12		PS-12	922	••	$$$	15			10	O		1177
FOOTHILL CO DAY	Claremont		PS-8		PS-8	228	••	$$				3	O		803
WEBB SCHS-CA	Claremont	9-12[C]	9-12[C]	9-12[C]	9-12[C]	400	••	$$$	15			14	•		804
HARBOR DAY	Corona del Mar		K-8		K-8	408	••	$$				4			805
MARIN CO DAY	Corte Madera		K-8		K-8	560	•••	$$$		P		5			805
TURNING POINT	Culver City		PS-8		PS-8	373	••	$$$				8	•		820
HILLDALE	Daly City		PS-8		PS-8	93	••	$$							1177
ATHENIAN	Danville	9-12	6-12	9-12	6-12	455	••	$$$	9		•	11			806
CHRISTIAN UNIFIED	El Cajon		K-12		K-12	820	•	$	11		•	13	•	B	1177
PROSPECT SIERRA	El Cerrito		K-8		K-8	479	••	$$$				5			1178

School Feature Indexes

Page 154

School	Town	Girls' Bdg	Girls' Day	Boys' Bdg	Boys' Day	Enrollment	Selectivity	Tuition	AP Courses	Learning Disabilities	ESL	Varsity Sports	Summer	Religion	Page
CA															
JOHN THOMAS DYE	Los Angeles		K-6		K-6	333	•••	$$$				6	O		815
LYCEE FRANCAIS-LA	Los Angeles		PS-12		PS-12	726	•••	$$$	11		•	6	O		816
LOYOLA HS-CA	Los Angeles				9-12	1256	••	$$	16			12	O	RC	1185
LYCEE INTL–LOS ANGEL	Los Angeles		PS-12		PS-12	900	•	$$				6	O		1186
MARLBOROUGH	Los Angeles		7-12			530	••	$$$	18			11	O		817
MARYMOUNT HS	Los Angeles		9-12			368	••	$$$	15			14	O	RC	817
MIRMAN	Los Angeles		1-9		1-9	330	••	$$$				5	O		818
NOTRE DAME ACAD-CA	Los Angeles		9-12			400	••	$	12			7	O	RC	1186
PAGE	Los Angeles		PS-8		PS-8	250	•	$$				2	O		1186
PILGRIM	Los Angeles	9-12	PS-12	9-12	PS-12	350	••	$$	8		•	6	O	Cg	820
SACRED HEART HS-CA	Los Angeles		9-12			370	•	$	6			6	O	RC	1187
WILDWOOD	Los Angeles		K-12		K-12	716	••	$$$				11	•		822
WINDWARD-CA	Los Angeles		7-12		7-12	525	•••	$$$	12			11	O		1187
HILLBROOK	Los Gatos		PS-8		PS-8	315	••	$$$				3	O		823
DUNN	Los Olivos	9-12	6-12	9-12	6-12	229	••	$$	11	P		8	•		823
MIDLAND	Los Olivos	9-12		9-12		88	••	$				5	•		824
PHILLIPS BROOKS	Menlo Park		PS-5		PS-5	276	••	$$$				5	O		1187
MARIN HORIZON	Mill Valley		PS-8		PS-8	287	••	$$$				5	O		1188
MT TAMALPAIS	Mill Valley		K-8		K-8	260	•••	$$$				4	O		1188
CENTRAL CATHOLIC-CA	Modesto		9-12		9-12	410	••	$	8			14		RC	1188
SANTA CATALINA	Monterey	9-12	9-12			243	••	$$	16			13	O	RC	825
YORK SCH	Monterey		8-12		8-12	229	••	$$$	15			11	O	Ep	826
SAKLAN	Moraga		PS-8		PS-8	110	•	$$$					O		1189
JUSTIN-SIENA	Napa		9-12		9-12	646	•	$$	8	P		14	O	RC	1189
OXBOW	Napa	11-PG	11-PG			96	•	$$							1230

School	Town	Girls' Grade Range Bdg	Girls' Grade Range Day	Boys' Grade Range Bdg	Boys' Grade Range Day	Enrollment	Selectivity	Tuition	AP Courses	Learning Disabilities	ESL	Varsity Sports	Summer	Religion	Page
CA															
MAYFIELD JR	Pasadena		K-8		K-8	508	••	$$				10	O	RC	1195
MAYFIELD SR	Pasadena		9-12			304	•	$$$	12			12	O	RC	1195
POLYTECH SCH	Pasadena		K-12		K-12	861	•••	$$$	13			15	•		835
WALDEN	Pasadena		PS-6		PS-6	215	••	$$					O		1196
WESTRIDGE	Pasadena		4-12			487	••	$$$	15			11	O		836
STEVENSON	Pebble Beach	9-12	PS-12	9-12	PS-12	730	••	$$$	16			15	O		837
WOODSIDE PRIORY	Portola Valley	9-12	6-12	9-12	6-12	371	••	$$$	21			11		RC	833
ST JOHN'S EPIS-CA	Rancho Santa Margarita		PS-8		PS-8	650	•	$$				5	O	Ep	1196
MERCY HS-RED BLUFF	Red Bluff		9-12		9-12	91	O	$	8			12	O	RC	1196
VALLEY PREP	Redlands		PS-8		PS-8	170	•	$				3	O		837
ALPHA BEACON	Redwood City		PS-12		PS-12	150	•	$	2		•	6	O	NC	1197
PENINSULA HERITAGE	Rolling Hills Estates		K-6		K-6	110	••	$$$					•		1197
ROLLING HILLS CO DAY	Rolling Hills Estates		K-8		K-8	375	••	$$				5	O		1197
BRANSON	Ross		9-12		9-12	319	••	$$$	10			13	O		838
BROOKFIELD SCH	Sacramento		K-8		K-8	150	••	$				7			1198
SACRAMENTO CO DAY	Sacramento		PS-12		PS-12	479	••	$$$	15			12	O		839
SAN DOMENICO	San Anselmo	9-12	PS-12		PS-8	580	••	$$$	15	P		7	O	RC	840
ACAD OUR LADY PEACE	San Diego		9-12			750	•	$$$	12		•	8	O	RC	1198
FRANCIS PARKER-CA	San Diego		PS-12		PS-12	1237	••	$$$	22			11	O		841
ST AUGUSTINE HS	San Diego				9-12	700	••	$$	18			13	•	RC	1198
WARREN-WALKER	San Diego		PS-8		PS-8	395	••	$$				8	O		1199
CATHEDRAL SCH BOYS	San Francisco				K-8	270	••	$$$				6	O	Ep	842
CHIN AMER INTL	San Francisco		PS-8		PS-8	468	•	$$$	6		•	5	O		1199
DREW	San Francisco		9-12		9-12	250	••	$$$		P	•	8	O		843
INTL HS	San Francisco		PS-12		PS-12	1008	••	$$$			•	9			843

School	City	Grades	Grades	Enroll.		Cost								Code	Page
HAMLIN	San Francisco	K-8		404	••	$$$					4		•			844
HILLWOOD	San Francisco	K-8	K-8	56	••	$					5		O			1200
IMMACULATE CONCEPT	San Francisco	9-12		250	••	$	3				5		O		RC	1200
JEWISH COMMUNITY HS	San Francisco	9-12	9-12	174	••	$$$	9	P			5		O		J	1200
KATHERINE D BURKE	San Francisco	K-8		400	••	$$$					4					845
LICK-WILMERDING	San Francisco	9-12	9-12	444	•••	$$$					11					846
LIVE OAK	San Francisco	K-8		272	••	$$$					3		O			1201
MERCY-SAN FRANCISCO	San Francisco	9-12		450	••	$$	9	P			9		O		RC	1201
PRESIDIO HILL	San Francisco	K-8		193	••	$$$					4					846
ST IGNATIUS-CA	San Francisco	9-12		1446	•••	$$	15	P			15		•		RC	1201
SAN FRANCISCO DAY	San Francisco	K-8		400	•••	$$$					4					847
SAN FRANCISCO SCH	San Francisco	PS-8		276	•••	$$$					4		•			847
SAN FRANCISCO U HS	San Francisco	9-12		396	••	$$$	15				14		O			848
SCHS-SACRED HEART	San Francisco	K-12^C	K-12^C	996	••	$$$	20				12		O		RC	849
TOWN SCH FOR BOYS	San Francisco	K-8		404	••	$$$					6		O			850
URBAN	San Francisco	9-12		377	••	$$					10					850
CLAIRBOURN	San Gabriel	PS-8		351	••	$$					10		O		CS	1202
BELLARMINE	San Jose	9-12		1600	••	$$	21				13		O		RC	1202
HARKER	San Jose	K-12		1790	•••	$$$	23				14		O			851
PRESENTATION	San Jose	9-12		750	••	$$	10				11		O		RC	1203
ST MARGARET'S EPIS	San Juan Capistrano	PS-12		1221	••	$$$	20				14		O		Ep	852
CHIN CHRISTIAN	San Leandro	K-12		695	•	$	14		•		6		O		NC	1203
SOUTHWESTERN-CA	San Marino	6-PG	6-PG	153	••	$	6		•		5		O			853
JUNIPERO SERRA	San Mateo	9-12		900	••	$$	11	P			14		O		RC	1204
ROLLING HILLS PREP	San Pedro	6-12		225	••	$$$	9		•		9					1204
MARIN ACAD	San Rafael	9-12		409	••	$$$	2				12		O			854
ST MARK'S SCH-CA	San Rafael	K-8		380	•	$$$					4		O			1204

	School	Town	Girls' Grade Range Bdg	Girls' Grade Range Day	Boys' Grade Range Bdg	Boys' Grade Range Day	Enrollment	Selectivity	Tuition	AP Courses	Learning Disabilities	ESL	Varsity Sports	Summer	Religion	Page
CA	MATER DEI HS	Santa Ana		9-12		9-12	2049	•	$	13			15	O	RC	1205
	CRANE	Santa Barbara		K-8		K-8	250	••	$$$		P		3	O		1205
	LAGUNA BLANCA	Santa Barbara		K-12		K-12	350	••	$$$	17			10	O		856
	MARYMOUNT SANTA BARB	Santa Barbara		PS-8		PS-8	216	•••	$$$					O		1206
	ST LAWRENCE ACAD	Santa Clara		9-12		9-12	260	••	$$	4	P		10		RC	1206
	CARLITHORP	Santa Monica		K-6		K-6	280	•••	$$$				3			1206
	CROSSROADS-CA	Santa Monica		K-12		K-12	1147	••	$$$				10	O		856
	PS 1	Santa Monica		K-6		K-6	215	••	$$$							1207
	SONOMA ACAD	Santa Rosa		9-12		9-12	237	••	$$$	8	P		7			1207
	SONOMA CO DAY	Santa Rosa		K-8		K-8	250	•	$$$				4	O		1207
	BAYMONTE	Scotts Valley		PS-8		PS-8	450	•	$				4	O	NC	1208
	BUCKLEY SCH-CA	Sherman Oaks		K-12		K-12	770	••	$$$	19			11	O		812
	NOTRE DAME-SHER OAKS	Sherman Oaks		9-12		9-12	1200	••	$	19			13	•	RC	1208
	ST MICHAEL'S PREP	Silverado			9-12[5]		65	••	5		F	4	•	RC		1209
	BRIDGES	Studio City		5-12		5-12	130	••	$$$				3	O		1209
	WOODCREST	Tarzana		K-5		K-5	161	••	$				3	O		1209
	LAURENCE	Valley Glen		K-6		K-6	315	••	$$$				4	•		1209
	MONTCLAIR COL PREP	Van Nuys		7-12		7-12	350	••	$$	9		•	10	O		1210
	DORRIS-EATON	Walnut Creek		PS-8		PS-8	425	••	$$				3	O		1210
	SEVEN HILLS-CA	Walnut Creek		PS-8		PS-8	375	••	$$$				6	O		1211
	MONTE VISTA	Watsonville	9-12	6-12	9-12	6-12	629	••	$	18		•	11	O	Ev	857
	PACIFIC HILLS	West Hollywood		6-12		6-12	180	••	$$$	10			8	O		1211
	HERITAGE OAK	Yorba Linda		PS-8		PS-8	515	••	$$				3	O		1211
	COLORADO															
	ASPEN CO DAY	Aspen		PS-8		PS-8	207	••	$$$							779

School	City	Grades	Grades	Enroll		Tuition							Page
REGIS JESUIT	Aurora	9-12^C	9-12^C	1599	••	$	15			16	•	RC	1152
FRIENDS' SCH-CO	Boulder	PS-5	PS-5	172	••	$$					O		1152
SHINING MTN	Boulder	PS-12	PS-12	295	••	$$				3	O		1153
HOLY FAMILY HS	Broomfield	9-12	9-12	580	••	$	8			11	•	RC	1153
CO ROCKY MTN	Carbondale	9-12	9-12	154	••	$$	4	•		2	O		783
CO SPRINGS SCH	Colorado Springs	PS-12	PS-12	305	••	$$	13			7	O		779
FOUNTAIN VALLEY	Colorado Springs	9-12	9-12	244	••	$$	17	P	•	11	•		780
ST MARY'S HS-CO	Colorado Springs	9-12	9-12	340	•	$	7			14	•	RC	1153
CO ACAD	Denver	PS-12	PS-12	909	•••	$$$	13			12	O		781
DENVER ACAD	Denver	1-12	1-12	387	•	$$$		F		7	O		1154
DENVER JEWISH DAY	Denver	K-12	K-12	361	••	$$	2		•	4		J	1154
DENVER MONTCLAIR	Denver	PS-7	PS-7	472	••	$$				2	O		1154
GRALAND	Denver	K-8	K-8	631	••	$$$				8			782
LOGAN	Denver	K-8	K-8	286	••	$$					O		1155
ST ANNE'S EPISCOPAL	Denver	PS-8	PS-8	423	••	$$				5			1155
CO TIMBERLINE	Durango	9-PG	9-PG	42	•	$			•	3			1155
KENT DENVER	Englewood	6-12	6-12	664	••	$$$	11			12	O		783
EVERGREEN CO DAY	Evergreen	PS-8	PS-8	215	•	$$				3	O		1156
BEACON	Greenwood Village	PS-8	PS-8	152	•	$$					O		1156
ALEXANDER DAWSON-CO	Lafayette	K-12	K-12	460	••	$$	13			8	O		784
HIGH MTN INST	Leadville	11-12	11-12	42	••	$$$	2						1229
CAMPION	Loveland	9-12	9-12	151	•	$	1			4		SA	1157
LOWELL WHITEMAN	Steamboat Springs	9-12	9-12	85	••	$	5			1			785
VAIL MTN	Vail	K-12	K-12	350	••	$$	10	P		5	O		786
CONNECTICUT													
AVON	Avon	9-PG	9-PG	404	••	$$	16			14	O		237
ACAD HOLY FAMILY	Baltic	9-12	9-12	58	•	$	3		•	3		RC	877

School	Town	Girls' Bdg	Girls' Day	Boys' Bdg	Boys' Day	Enrollment	Selectivity	Tuition	AP Courses	Learning Disabilities	ESL	Varsity Sports	Summer	Religion	Page
CT															
WOODHALL	Bethlehem			9-12	9-12	42	••	$$$	7	F	•	5			238
BESS & PAUL SIGEL	Bloomfield		PS-8		PS-8	95	○	$$			•	2	○	J	877
ST PAUL CATHOLIC	Bristol		9-12		9-12	331	•	$	10			12	○	RC	877
CHESHIRE	Cheshire	9-PG	8-PG	9-PG	8-PG	368	••	$$	15			17	○		239
IMMACULATE HS	Danbury		9-12		9-12	352	••	$	12		•	13	•	RC	878
WOOSTER	Danbury		PS-12		PS-12	335	••	$$$	16			8	○	Ep	240
ENFIELD MONTESSORI	Enfield		PS-6		PS-6	120	○	$						RC	878
FAIRFIELD COL PREP	Fairfield				9-12	900	••	$$	11			15	•	RC	241
FAIRFIELD CO DAY	Fairfield				PS-9	253	••	$$$				8	○		241
UNQUOWA	Fairfield		PS-8		PS-8	178	••	$$$				5	○		242
MISS PORTER'S	Farmington	9-12	9-12			333	••	$$	17			17	○		242
GREENS FARMS	Greens Farms		K-12		K-12	685	••	$$$	16			14	○		278
BRUNSWICK	Greenwich				PS-12	940	•••	$$$	18			14	○		244
CONVENT SAC HEART-CT	Greenwich		PS-12			769	••	$$$	20	F		12	•	RC	244
EAGLE HILL-GREENWICH	Greenwich	10-16[5] A	6-16	10-16[5] A	6-16	250	•	$$$				10	○		878
GREENWICH ACAD	Greenwich		PS-12			804	••	$$$	20			15	○		245
GREENWICH CO DAY	Greenwich		PS-9		PS-9	873	••	$$$				15	○		246
STANWICH	Greenwich		PS-11		PS-11	375	••	$$$				11	○		879
WHITBY	Greenwich		PS-8		PS-8	404	••	$$$				6	○		247
HAMDEN HALL	Hamden		PS-12		PS-12	563	••	$$$	14			14	○		258
SACRED HEART ACAD-CT	Hamden		9-12			490	••	$	13			13		RC	879
WATKINSON	Hartford		6-PG		6-PG	247	••	$$$		P		12	○		249
MOORELAND HILL	Kensington		K-9		K-9	45	••	$$$				6			238
KENT SCH-CT	Kent	9-PG	9-PG	9-PG	9-PG	565	••	$$$	20		•	15		Ep	249
MARVELWOOD	Kent	9-PG	9-PG	9-PG	9-PG	169	••	$$$	6	F	•	12	○		250

NAME	City					Enr	Bd	$					O	Rel	Pg
INDIAN MTN	Lakeville	6-9	PS-9	6-9	PS-9	246	••	$$			•	12	O		252
FORMAN	Litchfield	9-PG	9-PG	9-PG	9-PG	173	••	$$		F	•	14	•		253
COUNTRY SCH-CT	Madison		PS-8	PS-8	PS-8	220	••	$$$				8			880
GROVE SCH	Madison	7-PG	7-PG	7-PG	7-PG	126	••	$$$	3	F	•	3	O		880
WESTOVER	Middlebury	9-12	9-12		9-12	212	••	$$	18			11	O		254
INDEPENDENT DAY-CT	Middlefield		PS-8	PS-8	PS-8	187	••	$$$				4	O		255
MERCY HS-CT	Middletown	9-12	9-12			651	•	$	13			12		RC	880
XAVIER-CT	Middletown			9-12		866	••	$	13		•	16		RC	881
ACAD OUR LADY MERCY	Milford	9-12	9-12		9-12	460	••	$$	13			15		RC	881
NEW CANAAN COUNTRY	New Canaan		PS-9	PS-9	PS-9	650	••	$$$				10			255
ST LUKE'S SCH-CT	New Canaan	5-12	5-12		5-12	524	••	$$$	16			14	O		256
COLD SPRING	New Haven	PS-6	PS-6		PS-6	121	••	$$							257
FOOTE	New Haven	K-9	K-9		K-9	470	••	$$$				8	O		257
HOPKINS	New Haven	7-12	7-12		7-12	687	••	$$$	15			18	O		259
ST THOMAS'S DAY	New Haven	K-6	K-6		K-6	136	•	$$						Ep	260
WILLIAMS-CT	New London	7-12	7-12		7-12	259	•	$$$	10		•	11			260
CANTERBURY-CT	New Milford	9-PG	9-PG	9-PG	9-PG	358	••	$$$	16	P		18		RC	261
WASH MONTESSORI	New Preston	PS-8	PS-8		PS-8	241	••	$$				5	O		882
ST THOMAS MORE-CT	Oakdale		8-PG			200	••	$$		F	•	10	O	RC	262
S CT HEBREW	Orange	PS-8	PS-8		PS-8	173	O	$			•	1		J	882
POMFRET	Pomfret	9-PG	9-PG	9-PG	9-PG	350	••	$$$	18			15	O		263
RECTORY	Pomfret	5-9	K-9	5-9	K-9	249	••	$$		P	•	13	O	Ep	263
RIDGEFIELD	Ridgefield	PS-8	PS-8		PS-8	336	••	$$$				7	•		882
SALISBURY-CT	Salisbury		9-PG	9-PG		305	••	$$$	13			13	O	Ep	264
ETHEL WALKER	Simsbury	9-PG	6-PG		9-PG	239	••	$$$	17			12	O		265
WESTMINSTER SCH-CT	Simsbury	9-PG	9-PG	9-PG	9-PG	390	••	$$$	22			14			267

School	Town	Girls' Bdg	Girls' Day	Boys' Bdg	Boys' Day	Enrollment	Selectivity	Tuition	AP Courses	Learning Disabilities	ESL	Varsity Sports	Summer	Religion	Page
CT															
SOUTH KENT	South Kent			9-PG	9-PG	177	••	$$	7	P	•	10		Ep	268
EAGLE HILL-SOUTHPORT	Southport		6-14^A		6-14^A	112	•	$$$		F		5	O		883
BI-CULTURAL DAY	Stamford		K-8		K-8	395	•	$$		P		5		J	883
KING LOW HEY THOMAS	Stamford		PS-12		PS-12	685	••	$$$	15			14	O		268
LONG RIDGE	Stamford		PS-5		PS-5	110	••	$$$					O		269
MEAD SCH	Stamford		PS-8		PS-8	127	••	$$$				3	O		883
TRINITY CATHOLIC	Stamford		9-12		9-12	430	•	$	8			12	O	RC	884
PINE PT	Stonington		PS-9		PS-9	246	••	$$$				6	•		270
SUFFIELD	Suffield	9-PG	9-12	9-PG	9-12	410	••	$$	15	P		17	O		270
MARIANAPOLIS	Thompson	9-PG	9-PG	9-PG	9-PG	340	••	$	12		•	13	•	RC	271
CHRISTIAN HERITAGE	Trumbull		K-12		K-12	470	••	$$	10		•	7	O	NC	884
CHOATE	Wallingford	9-PG	9-PG	9-PG	9-PG	850	•••	$$$	22			20	O		272
GLENHOLME	Washington	5-PG	5-PG	5-PG	5-PG	89	•		F		5	0		884	
GUNNERY	Washington	9-PG	9-PG	9-PG	9-PG	285	••	$$$	15		•	13			273
RUMSEY	Washington Depot	5-9	K-9	5-9	K-9	319	••	$$	16		•	14	O		274
CHASE	Waterbury		PS-12		PS-12	460	••	$$$				12	O		275
TAFT	Watertown	9-PG	9-PG	9-PG	9-PG	577	•••	$$$	23			17	O		276
HARTFORD CHRISTIAN	West Hartford		K-12		K-12	70	•	$	5			3		B	885
HEBREW HS	West Hartford		9-12		9-12	79	•	$$	5			4		J	885
KINGSWOOD OXFORD	West Hartford		6-12		6-12	497	••	$$$	14			16	•		247
NORTHWEST CATHOLIC	West Hartford		9-12		9-12	625	••	$$	13			16	O	RC	885
RENBROOK	West Hartford		PS-9		PS-9	435	••	$$$		P		11	O		248
NOTRE DAME HS-CT	West Haven				9-12	650	••	$	5			12	•	RC	886
MASTER'S SCH-CT	West Simsbury		PS-12		PS-12	303	••	$$	4			8	O	NC	266
OXFORD ACAD	Westbrook	9-PG		9-PG		48	•	$$$	2	F	•	3	O		277

School	City	Bdg Grades	Day Grades	Enroll	Sel	Cost						Affil	Page
EZRA	Woodbridge	K-8	K-8	165	•	$$	8		•	4			886
HYDE SCH-WOODSTOCK	Woodstock	9-PG	9-PG	171	••	$$$			•	10	O		280
DELAWARE													
ARCHMERE	Claymont		9-12	476	••	$$$	15			15		RC	382
SANFORD	Hockessin		PS-12	575	•	$$$	16			12	O		382
ST ANDREW'S SCH-DE	Middletown	9-12	9-12	295	••	$$				13		Ep	381
INDEPENDENCE	Newark		PS-8	675	••	$$		F		11	•		909
PILOT	Wilmington		K-8	153	••	$$$					•		909
ST EDMOND'S	Wilmington		PS-8	286	••	$$				7	O	RC	909
ST MARK'S HS	Wilmington		9-12	1100	••	$	19	P		18		RC	910
SALESIANUM	Wilmington		9-12	980	••	$	20			13		RC	910
TATNALL SCH	Wilmington		PS-12	640	••	$$$	13			15	O		383
TOWER HILL	Wilmington		PS-12	753	••	$$$				14	O		384
URSULINE ACAD-DE	Wilmington		PS-3	650	••	$$	14			10	O	RC	911
WILMINGTON FRIENDS	Wilmington		PS-12	777	••	$$$	2			13		RSF	384
DISTRICT OF COLUMBIA													
BEAUVOIR	Washington		PS-3	393	••	$$$					O	Ep	386
BRITISH SCH OF WASH	Washington		PS-12	452	•	$$$				6			911
CAPITOL HILL DAY	Washington		PS-8	214	••	$$$				4	O		911
EMERSON	Washington		9-12	40	•	$$$	3		•		•		386
FIELD	Washington		6-12	320	••	$$$				12			912
GEORGETOWN DAY	Washington		PS-12	1075	•••	$$$	16			13	O		387
GEORGETOWN VISITAT	Washington		9-12	480	••	$$$	17			11	•	RC	387
GONZAGA COL HS	Washington		9-12	957	••	$$	20			16	O	RC	912
LAB SCH	Washington		1-12	340	••	$$$		F		9	O		913
LOWELL SCH	Washington		PS-8	300	••	$$$				7	O		913

School	Town	Girls' Grade Range Bdg	Girls' Grade Range Day	Boys' Grade Range Bdg	Boys' Grade Range Day	Enrollment	Selectivity	Tuition	AP Courses	Learning Disabilities	ESL	Varsity Sports	Summer	Religion	Page
DC															
MARET	Washington		K-12		K-12	633	•••	$$$	4			13	O		388
NATL CATHEDRAL	Washington		4-12			584	•••	$$$	15			12	O	Ep	389
NATL PRESBYTERIAN	Washington		PS-6		PS-6	276	••	$$$				4	O	P	913
PARKMONT	Washington		6-12		6-12	52	••	$$$		F					914
ST ALBANS	Washington			9-12	4-12	578	••	$$$	13			13	O	Ep	390
ST ANSELM'S	Washington				6-12	232	••	$$$	19		•	8	O	RC	391
ST JOHN'S COL HS	Washington		9-12		9-12	1046	••	$$	15	P		16	•	RC	914
ST PATRICK'S EPIS	Washington		PS-8		PS-8	500	•••	$$$				6	O	Ep	915
SHERIDAN	Washington		K-8		K-8	226	••	$$$				5	O		391
SIDWELL FRIENDS	Washington		PS-12		PS-12	1109	••	$$$				14	O	RSF	392
WASH INTL	Washington		PS-12		PS-12	923	••	$$$			•	9	O		393
FLORIDA															
BOCA RATON CHRISTIAN	Boca Raton		PS-12		PS-12	535	•	$	8			11	•	NC	987
DONNA KLEIN	Boca Raton		K-12		K-12	702	••	$$	8			5		J	987
GRANDVIEW	Boca Raton		PS-12		PS-12	250	•	$$	10			8			988
ST ANDREW'S SCH-FL	Boca Raton	9-12	PS-12	9-12	PS-12	1315	••	$$	20			16	•	Ep	568
BRADENTON CHRISTIAN	Bradenton		PS-12		PS-12	540	•	$	6			11		NC	988
ST STEPHEN'S EPIS-FL	Bradenton		PS-12		PS-12	664	••	$$	15			13	O	Ep	568
BRANDON ACAD	Brandon		PS-8		PS-8	264	•	$				7	•		989
ST PAUL'S SCH-FL	Clearwater		PS-8		PS-8	346	••	$$		F	•	7	O	Ep	989
NORTH BROWARD PREP	Coconut Creek	6-12	PS-12	6-12	PS-12	1381	•	$$	20			17	O		989
GULLIVER	Coral Gables		PS-12		PS-12	2200	••	$$$	23			15	O		577
ST PHILIP'S	Coral Gables		PS-5		PS-5	180	••	$$					O	Ep	990
ST THOMAS EPISCOPAL	Coral Gables		PS-5		PS-5	425	••	$$					O	Ep	990
... LUTHERAN	...		PS-12			506	•	$	5	P		12		L	990

School	Town	Girls' Grade Range Bdg	Girls' Grade Range Day	Boys' Grade Range Bdg	Boys' Grade Range Day	Enrollment	Selectivity	Tuition	AP Courses	Learning Disabilities	ESL	Varsity Sports	Summer	Religion	Page
FL															
HOLY TRINITY ACAD	Melbourne		PS-12		PS-12	854	••	$	19		•	13	O	Ep	997
ALEXANDER MONTESSORI	Miami		PS-5		PS-5	560	•	$$			•	9	O		998
ATLANTIS-MIAMI	Miami		K-12		K-12	180	••	$$		F	•	11	O		998
CARROLLTON SCH	Miami		PS-12				••	$$$	7			11	•	RC	998
CUSHMAN	Miami		PS-8		PS-8	487	••	$$$		P		7	O		999
DADE CHRISTIAN	Miami		PS-12		PS-12	924	••	$	11			10	•	B	999
IMMACULATA-LA SALLE	Miami		9-12		9-12	630	••	$	9			6	•	RC	999
MIAMI CO DAY	Miami		PS-12		PS-12	935	••	$$$	16			13	•		578
PALMER TRINITY	Miami		6-12		6-12	625	••	$$$	22			12	O	Ep	578
PINEWOOD ACRES	Miami		PS-8		PS-8	280	••	$				17	O		1000
RANSOM EVERGLADES	Miami		6-12		6-12	1079	•	$$$	23			10	O		579
MONTVERDE	Montverde	7-PG	PS-12	7-PG	PS-12	705	•	$$$	19		•	13	O	NC	1000
COMMUNITY SCH-FL	Naples		PS-12		PS-12	726	•	$$$	26			13	O		580
NAPLES CHRISTIAN	Naples		PS-8		PS-8	160	••	$				5		NC	1000
BENJAMIN	North Palm Beach		PS-12		PS-12	1144	•	$$$	14			15	O		1001
ST JOHNS CO DAY	Orange Park		PS-12		PS-12	650	•	$$	15			13	O		581
BISHOP MOORE	Orlando		9-12		9-12	1100	••	$$	22			17	•	RC	1001
LAKE HIGHLAND	Orlando		PS-12		PS-12	2030	••	$$	20			16	O		1002
NEW SCH PREP	Orlando		K-8		K-8	129	••	$				6	O		1002
PALM BEACH DAY	Palm Beach		PS-9		PS-9	519	•	$$$				6	O		581
WESTMINSTER-MIAMI	Palmetto Bay		PS-12		PS-12	1040	••	$$	15			13	O	NC	1002
PENSACOLA CATHOLIC	Pensacola		9-12		9-12	565	•	$	5			13	O	RC	1003
AM HERITAGE	Plantation		PS-12		PS-12	2541	•	$$$	20	P	•	14	O		1003
CARDINAL MOONEY-FL	Sarasota		9-12		9-12	477	O	$	11	P		14		RC	1005
JULIE ROHR	Sarasota		PS-8		PS-8	190	•	$		P			O		1005

School	City	Grades	Grades	Enroll		Tuition						Affil	Page
OUT-OF-DOOR	Sarasota	PS-12	PS-12	599	••	$$	18			13			585
ST JOSEPH ACAD-FL	St Augustine	6-12⁵	9-12	275	•	$	8			13	O	RC	1004
ADMIRAL FARRAGUT	St Petersburg	6-12⁵	PS-12	409	••	$	12	•		13	O		582
CANTERBURY SCH OF FL	St Petersburg		PS-12	390	••	$$	21			12		Ep	583
KESWICK	St Petersburg		PS-12	487	••	$	8			11		NC	1004
SHORECREST	St Petersburg		PS-12	946	••	$$	21			12	O		584
PINE SCH	Stuart		PS-12	465	•	$$	5			9	O		585
HOLY COMFORTER	Tallahassee		PS-8	595	O	$				11	O	Ep	1006
MACLAY	Tallahassee		PS-12	910	••	$	21			13	O		586
ACAD HOLY NAMES	Tampa		PS-12	855	•	$$	10			9	O	RC	1006
BAYSHORE	Tampa		PS-12	215	•	$	5			10	O	UM	1006
BERKELEY PREP	Tampa		PS-12	1250	••	$$	20			14	O	Ep	587
CAMBRIDGE CHRISTIAN	Tampa		PS-12	579	••	$$	10			11	•	NC	1007
CARROLLWOOD	Tampa		PS-12	799	••	$$				11	O		1007
JESUIT HS-FL	Tampa		9-12	733	••	$	10			12	•	RC	1008
ST JOHN GREEK ORTH	Tampa		PS-8	125	•	$				7	O	GO	1008
ST JOHNS EPIS PARISH	Tampa		PS-8	586	•	$				10	O	Ep	1008
ST MARY'S EPIS DAY	Tampa		PS-8	443	••	$				10	O	Ep	588
TAMPA PREP	Tampa		6-12	600	••	$$	19			15	O		588
UNIVERSAL ACAD OF FL	Tampa		PS-12	359	•	$	6			2		I	1009
FL COL ACAD	Temple Terrace		PS-9	150	•					7		NC	1009
ST EDWARD'S SCH	Vero Beach		PS-12	500	•	$$$	18	•		14		Ep	589
ARTHUR I MEYER	West Palm Beach	K-8	K-8	340	•	$$				6		J	1009
CARDINAL NEWMAN	West Palm Beach	9-12	9-12	572	••	$	8			15	•	RC	1010
WINDERMERE PREP	Windermere	9-12	PS-12	1068	•	$$	9			11	O		1010
TRINITY PREP	Winter Park		6-12	834	••	$$	21	•		14	O	Ep	590

GEORGIA

	School	Town	Girls' Grade Range Bdg	Girls' Grade Range Day	Boys' Grade Range Bdg	Boys' Grade Range Day	Enrollment	Selectivity	Tuition	AP Courses	Learning Disabilities	ESL	Varsity Sports	Summer	Religion	Page
GA	DEERFIELD-WINDSOR	Albany		PS-12		PS-12	832	•	$	8			11	O		1011
	ATHENS ACAD	Athens		PS-12		PS-12	957	••	$$	12			11	O		1011
	ATLANTA INTL	Atlanta		PS-12		PS-12	1020	•	$$				8	O		591
	BRANDON HALL	Atlanta	7-PG	6-PG	7-PG	6-PG	130	••	$$$	5	F	•	9	O		591
	GALLOWAY	Atlanta		PS-12		PS-12	725	••	$$$	17		•	9	O		1011
	HEISKELL	Atlanta		PS-8		PS-8	360	••	$$				5		NC	592
	HOLY INNOCENTS'	Atlanta		PS-12		PS-12	1300	••	$$	19			14	O	Ep	1012
	HOLY SPIRIT PREP	Atlanta		PS-12		PS-12	787	••	$$	18			11		RC	1012
	HORIZONS	Atlanta	8-12	K-12	8-12	K-12	122	••	$	3		•	3	O		1013
	LOVETT	Atlanta		K-12		K-12	1585	••	$$$	18			15	O		592
	MARIST	Atlanta		7-12		7-12	1076	••	$$	21			14	•	RC	593
	MT VERNON	Atlanta		PS-12		PS-12	740	••	$$	11			12	•	P	1013
	PACE ACAD	Atlanta		K-12		K-12	1075	••	$$$	20			15	O		594
	PAIDEIA	Atlanta		PS-12		PS-12	974	••	$$	9			10	O		595
	ST MARTIN'S-GA	Atlanta		PS-8		PS-8	575	••	$$				8		Ep	1014
	ST PIUS-GA	Atlanta		9-12		9-12	1100	••	$	17			14		RC	1014
	TRINITY SCH-GA	Atlanta		PS-6		PS-6	627	••	$$				15			1014
	WESTMINSTER SCHS-GA	Atlanta		K-12		K-12	1854	•••	$$$	16			17	O		595
	AQUINAS HS	Augusta		9-12		9-12	320	•	$	5	P		11		RC	1015
	EPISCOPAL DAY	Augusta		PS-8		PS-8	450	•	$				10	O	Ep	1015
	WESTMINSTER-AUGUSTA	Augusta		PS-12		PS-12	598	•	$	14			11	O	NC	1015
	OAK MTN	Carrollton		PS-12		PS-12	184	••	$	6			11	O	NC	1016
	WOODWARD	College Park		PS-12		PS-12	2735	••	$$$	17			15			596
	BROOKSTONE	Columbus		PS-12		PS-12	792	••	$$	16			12	O		598
	LANDMARK CHRISTIAN	Fairburn		PS-12		PS-12	807	••	$$	10			12		NC	1016

School	Town	Girls' Grade Range Bdg	Girls' Grade Range Day	Boys' Grade Range Bdg	Boys' Grade Range Day	Enrollment	Selectivity	Tuition	AP Courses	Learning Disabilities	ESL	Varsity Sports	Summer	Religion	Page
HI HANAHAUOLI	Honolulu		PS-6		PS-6	208	••	$$					O		859
HOLY NATIVITY	Honolulu		PS-6		PS-6	147	••	$$					O	Ep	1212
IOLANI	Honolulu		K-12		K-12	1870	•••	$$	21			16	O	Ep	859
LA PIETRA	Honolulu		6-12			233	••	$$	4			13	O		1212
MARYKNOLL	Honolulu		PS-12		PS-12	1400	••	$$	9			15	O	RC	1212
MID-PACIFIC	Honolulu		PS-12		PS-12	1550	••	$$	10		•	16	O		860
PUNAHOU	Honolulu		K-12		K-12	3743	•••	$$	16			16	O		861
SACRED HRTS ACAD-HI	Honolulu		PS-12			1150	••	$	4		•	12	O	RC	1213
ST ANDREW'S PRIORY	Honolulu		K-12			450	••	$$	11		•	12	O	Ep	862
ST FRANCIS SCH-HI	Honolulu		PS-12		PS-12	497	••	$	7		•	14	O	RC	1213
LE JARDIN	Kailua		PS-12		PS-12	800	••	$$	9			7	O		862
HI PREP	Kamuela	6-12[S]	K-12	6-12[S]	K-12	600	••	$$	17		•	13	O		863
ISLAND SCH	Lihue		PS-12		PS-12	365	•	$				8	•		1214
LANAKILA	Waipahu		K-12		K-12	250	•	$				7	•	B	1214
IDAHO															
BISHOP KELLY	Boise		9-12		9-12	675	O	$	9			16	O	RC	1157
GEM ST ADVENTIST	Caldwell	9-12[S]	9-12	9-12[S]	9-12	115	••	$	1			2		SA	1157
COMMUNITY SCH-ID	Sun Valley		PS-12		PS-PS	307	••	$$$		P		6	O		787
ILLINOIS															
ST VIATOR	Arlington Heights		9-12		9-12	1000	••	$	12			16	•	RC	1064
QUEEN OF PEACE	Burbank		9-12			400	•	$	10			8	O	RC	1064
BR RICE-IL	Chicago				9-12	887	••	$	11	P		17		RC	1065
CHICAGO ACAD ARTS	Chicago		9-12		9-12	144	••	$$$	5						675
CHICAGO WALDORF	Chicago		PS-12		PS-12	353	••	$$				4			1065
DE LA SALLE INST	Chicago		9-12[C]		9-12[C]	1122	••	$	7			16	•	RC	1065

	School	Town	Girls' Grade Range Bdg	Girls' Grade Range Day	Boys' Grade Range Bdg	Boys' Grade Range Day	Enrollment	Selectivity	Tuition	AP Courses	Learning Disabilities	ESL	Varsity Sports	Summer	Religion	Page
IL	KEITH	Rockford		PS-12		PS-12	290	•	$$	6			6	O		683
	WHEATON	West Chicago		9-12		9-12	639	••	$$	13	P		12	O	Ev	1072
	ST FRANCIS HS-IL	Wheaton		9-12		9-12	769	••	$	12			12	O	RC	1073
	LOYOLA ACAD	Wilmette		9-12		9-12	2000	••	$$	23	P		20	O	RC	1073
	N SHORE CO DAY	Winnetka		PS-12		PS-12	500	••	$$$	11			10	O		684
	INDIANA															
	U HS OF IN	Carmel		9-12		9-12	278	•	$$	13			9	O		1074
	CULVER	Culver	9-PG	9-PG	9-PG	9-PG	791	•	$	20		•	21	O		685
	EVANSVILLE DAY	Evansville		PS-12		PS-12	325	•	$$	8			4	O		686
	BISHOP DWENGER	Fort Wayne		9-12		9-12	1019	O	$	6			14	O	RC	1074
	BISHOP LUERS	Fort Wayne		9-12		9-12	567	•	$	8			14		RC	1075
	CANTERBURY-IN	Fort Wayne		PS-12		PS-12	982	••	$$	13			11	O		687
	CONCORDIA LUTH-IN	Fort Wayne		9-12		9-12	697	•	$	9	P		14	O	LMS	1075
	HOWE	Howe	7-12	7-12	7-12	7-12	141	•	$	4			8	O	Ep	688
	BREBEUF	Indianapolis		9-12		9-12	785	••	$$	21			17	O	RC	1075
	HERITAGE CHRISTIAN	Indianapolis		PS-12		PS-12	1371	•	$	7	P	•	13		NC	1076
	LUTHERAN HS-IN	Indianapolis		9-12		9-12	237	O	$	7			10		LMS	1076
	ORCHARD	Indianapolis		PS-8		PS-8	615	••	$$				9	O		689
	PARK TUDOR	Indianapolis		PS-12		PS-12	987	••	$$	15			16	O		689
	ST RICHARD'S	Indianapolis		PS-8		PS-8	300	••	$$				7	•	Ep	690
	SYCAMORE	Indianapolis		PS-8		PS-8	391	••	$$				10	O		691
	LA LUMIERE	La Porte		9-PG	9-PG	9-PG	210	••	$	6		•	10	O	RC	691
	FOREST RIDGE ACAD	Schererville		PS-8		PS-8	155	••	$$				2	O		1077
	STANLEY CLARK	South Bend		PS-8		PS-8	322	•	$$				7	O		692
	IOWA															

School	Town	Girls' Grade Range Bdg	Girls' Grade Range Day	Boys' Grade Range Bdg	Boys' Grade Range Day	Enrollment	Selectivity	Tuition	AP Courses	Learning Disabilities	ESL	Varsity Sports	Summer	Religion	Page
KY VILLA MADONNA	Villa Hills		K-12		K-12	510	•	$	14			12		RC	1027
LOUISIANA															
HOLY SAVIOR MENARD	Alexandria		7-12		7-12	481	•	$	4			11		RC	1123
CATHOLIC HS-LA	Baton Rouge				8-12	1028	•	$	6			11	O	RC	1123
DUNHAM	Baton Rouge		PS-12		PS-12	802	••	$	13	P		13	•	NC	1124
EPISCOPAL HS-LA	Baton Rouge		PS-12		PS-12	1034	••	$$	18			13	O	Ep	751
EPISCOPAL ACADIANA	Cade		PS-12		PS-12	530	••	$$	10			11	O	Ep	1124
SCHS SACRED HEART-LA	Grand Coteau	7-12C5	PS-12C		PS-9C	476	•	$	4		•	8		RC	1125
ARCHBISHOP SHAW	Marrero				8-12	491	••	$	5			9	O	RC	1125
CRESCENT CITY CHRIST	Metairie		PS-12		PS-12	325	•	$			•	5		NC	1125
METAIRIE PARK CO DAY	Metairie		PS-12		PS-12	721	••	$$	12			12	O		752
RIDGEWOOD PREP	Metairie		PS-12		PS-12	275	••	$				9			752
ST MARTIN'S-LA	Metairie		PS-12		PS-12	559	•	$$	11			11	O	Ep	753
ACAD SAC HRT-NEW ORL	New Orleans		PS-12			781	••	$$	11			11	O	RC	754
HOLY CROSS SCH-LA	New Orleans				5-12	747	••	$	5			12	•	RC	1126
ISIDORE NEWMAN	New Orleans		PS-12		PS-12	920	••	$$	17			14	O		755
JESUIT HS-LA	New Orleans				8-12	1358	•	$$	4			10	•	RC	1126
LOUISE S MCGEHEE	New Orleans		PS-12		PS-PS	525	••	$$	4			9		RC	755
MT CARMEL	New Orleans		8-12			1172	••	$	5			10	•	RC	1126
ST ANDREW'S EPIS-LA	New Orleans		PS-8		PS-8	177	••	$				4	•	Ep	1127
ST MARY'S DOMINICAN	New Orleans		8-12			919	••	$	8			9	•	RC	1127
STUART HALL-LA	New Orleans				PS-7	332	••	$				5	O	RC	1128
TRINITY EPIS-LA	New Orleans		PS-8		PS-8	331	••	$$	7			7	O	Ep	1128
URSULINE ACAD-LA	New Orleans		PS-12			754	••	$	4			9	•	RC	1128
WSTMNSTR CHRISTN-LA	Opelousas		PS-12		PS-12	1039	••	$	3	P		10	O	NC	1129

School	City	Grades	Grades	Enroll	•	$	5	P	•	10	O	Aff	Page
CEDAR CREEK	Ruston	PS-12	PS-12	682	•	$				10	O		1129
SOUTHFIELD-LA	Shreveport	PS-8	PS-8	458	•	$			•	6	O		756
MAINE													
JOHN BAPST	Bangor	9-12[5]	9-12	440	•	$	17		•	16	•		887
HYDE SCH-BATH	Bath	9-PG	9-PG	138	••	$$	4			10	O		281
GOULD	Bethel	9-PG	9-PG	248	••	$$$	9		•	11			282
GEO STEVENS	Blue Hill	9-12	9-12	300	••	$	8	P	•	13			887
OCEAN CLASSROOM	Boothbay Harbor	10-PG	10-PG	22	••	$		P			O		1227
FOXCROFT ACAD	Dover-Foxcroft	9-12	9-12	430	••	$	9		•	14	•		888
WASH ACAD	East Machias	9-12	9-12	430	•	$	11	P	•	13	•		888
DECK HOUSE	Edgecomb	9-12	9-12	12	•	$$$			•	9			889
FRYEBURG	Fryeburg	9-12[5]	9-12	638	•	$$	14	P	•	15	•		284
RILEY	Glen Cove	PS-9	PS-9	80	•	$					O		889
HEBRON	Hebron	9-PG	6-PG	256	••	$$$	9	P	•	13			285
KENTS HILL	Kents Hill	9-PG	9-PG	250	••	$$	10	P	•	13			286
BRIDGTON	North Bridgton	PG-PG	PG-PG	188	••	$$		P	•	9			283
ME CENTRAL	Pitsfield	9-PG	9-PG	450	••	$$	6	P	•	11	O		287
BREAKWATER	Portland	PS-8	PS-8	130	••	$$			•		O		889
CATHERINE MCAULEY	Portland		9-12	200	•	$$	6	P		11	O	RC	890
CHEVERUS	Portland	9-12	9-12	497	••	$$	13	P		17	O	RC	890
WAYNFLETE	Portland	PS-12	PS-12	556	••	$$$				13	O		287
BERWICK	South Berwick	PS-PG	PS-PG	566	••	$$$	12			12	O		282
CHEWONKI SEMESTER	Wiscasset	11-12	11-12	72	•	$$	5						1227
CHOP POINT	Woolwich	8-12[5]	K-12	95	•	$	2		•	2	O	NC	890
N YARMOUTH	Yarmouth	5-12	5-12	265	••	$$$	12			13	O		288
MARYLAND													
ALEPH BET	Annapolis	K-5	K-5	34	•	$						J	915

School	Town	Girls' Grade Range Bdg	Girls' Grade Range Day	Boys' Grade Range Bdg	Boys' Grade Range Day	Enrollment	Selectivity	Tuition	AP Courses	Learning Disabilities	ESL	Varsity Sports	Summer	Religion	Page
MD															
ANNAPOLIS CHRISTIAN	Annapolis		PS-12		PS-12	886	••	$$	11	P		12	O	NC	915
KEY	Annapolis		PS-12		PS-12	700	••	$$$				10	O		395
ST ANNE'S-ANNAPOLIS	Annapolis		PS-8		PS-8	200	••	$$				6	O	Ep	916
CHESAPEAKE-MD	Arnold		PS-5		PS-5	321	••	$$				12	O		916
BOYS' LATIN	Baltimore				K-12	600	••	$$$	12			15			396
BRYN MAWR	Baltimore		PS-12		PS-PS	811	••	$$$	19			18	O		396
CALVERT HALL	Baltimore				9-12	1225	•	$	25	P		10	O	RC	397
CALVERT SCH	Baltimore		PS-8		PS-8	612	••	$$$				13	O		398
CATHOLIC HS OF BALT	Baltimore		9-12			308	••	$	9			4	•	RC	916
CONSERVATORY BALT	Baltimore		K-12		K-12	30	••	$	8				O		917
DAY SCH-BALT HEBREW	Baltimore		PS-8		PS-8	80	••	$$				14		J	917
FRIENDS SCH-MD	Baltimore		PS-12		PS-12	972	••	$$$				16	O	RSF	399
GILMAN	Baltimore				K-12	1022	••	$$$	21			9	O		399
MERCY HS-MD	Baltimore		9-12			400	••	$	5	P		14		RC	918
MT ST JOSEPH HS	Baltimore				9-12	1085	•	$	19	P		10	•	RC	918
PARK SCH-MD	Baltimore		PS-12		PS-12	865	••	$$$	8			14	O		400
ROLAND PARK	Baltimore		K-12			700	••	$$$	20			12			401
SETON KEOUGH	Baltimore		9-12			400	•	$	9	P			O	RC	918
BARNESVILLE	Barnesville		PS-8		PS-8	182	••	$$				4	O		919
HARFORD DAY	Bel Air		PS-8		PS-8	325	•	$$				4	•		402
JOHN CARROLL	Bel Air		9-12		9-12	691	••	$$	15			17	•	RC	919
WORCESTER PREP	Berlin		PS-12		PS-12	540	••	$	7			6	O		920
FR INTL	Bethesda		PS-12		PS-12	1040	••	$$			•				920
HARBOR SCH-MD	Bethesda		PS-2		PS-2	109	••	$$				13	O		920
HOLTON-ARMS	Bethesda		3-12			645	••	$$$	17			13	O		403

School	City		Grades	Enroll		Cost							Page
LANDON	Bethesda		3-12	689	••	$$$	17			14	O		404
NORWOOD	Bethesda		K-8	480	••	$$$$				8	O		921
PRIMARY DAY	Bethesda		PS-2	146	••	$$$							921
STONE RIDGE	Bethesda		PS-12	660	••	$$$	21			10	O	RC	405
WASH EPISCOPAL	Bethesda		PS-8	280	••	$$				5	O	Ep	921
WOODS	Bethesda		PS-8	295	••	$$				5	O	RC	922
ELIZABETH SETON	Bladensburg		9-12	608	••	$	10	P		11	•	RC	922
MARYVALE	Brooklandville		6-12	365	••	$$	10			7	O	RC	923
ST PAUL'S SCH-MD	Brooklandville		K-4	800	••	$$$	1			14	O	Ep	405
ST PAUL'S SCH GIRLS	Brooklandville		5-12	414	••	$$$	17			12	O	Ep	406
GUNSTON	Centreville		9-12	136	•	$$$	12		•	9	O		407
KENT SCH-MD	Chestertown		PS-8	192	••	$$				4	O		923
MT AVIAT	Childs		PS-8	250	••	$				3			923
W NOTTINGHAM	Colora	9-12	9-12	120	••	$$	5	P	•	8		RC	408
COUNTRY SCH-MD	Easton		K-8	288	••	$$				4	O		409
GLENELG COUNTRY	Ellicott City		PS-12	777	••	$$$	16			10	O		409
TRINITY SCH-MD	Ellicott City		PS-8	382	••	$				3	O	RC	924
BANNER	Frederick		PS-8	167	••	$				4	O		924
ST JOHN'S CATHOLIC	Frederick		9-12	274	•	$$	16			11		RC	924
OLDFIELDS	Glencoe	8-PG[5]	6-PG	155	••	$$	1			9			410
HOLY TRINITY DAY	Glenn Dale		PS-8	520	••	$				3	O	Ep	925
CALVERTON	Huntingtown		PS-12	385	••	$$	11			8	O		925
DEMATHA	Hyattsville		9-12	900	••	$$	15			14	O	RC	925
GRACE EPISCOPAL	Kensington		PS-5	239	••	$$				3	O	Ep	926
ST VINCENT PALLOTTI	Laurel		9-12	510	••	$$	7	P		13	O	RC	926
LEONARD HALL	Leonardtown		6-12	50	•	$				2			927
ST JAMES ACAD	Monkton		K-8	349	••	$$				5		Ep	927

School	Town	Girls' Grade Range Bdg	Girls' Grade Range Day	Boys' Grade Range Bdg	Boys' Grade Range Day	Enrollment	Selectivity	Tuition	AP Courses	Learning Disabilities	ESL	Varsity Sports	Summer	Religion	Page
MD															
GEORGETOWN PREP	North Bethesda			9-12	9-12	480	••	$$$	19		•	14	O	RC	402
TOME	North East		K-12		K-12	495	••	$	1			7	•		927
ST JOHN'S EPIS-MD	Olney		PS-8		PS-8	235	•	$$				4		Ep	411
GARRISON FOREST	Owings Mills	8-12^5	PS-12		PS-K	675	••	$$	11		•	12	O		412
MCDONOGH	Owings Mills	9-12^5	K-12	9-12^5	K-12	1296	••	$$$	17			19	•		413
EAGLE COVE	Pasadena		PS-5		PS-5	70	••	$$							414
BULLIS	Potomac		3-12		3-12	618	••	$$$	16			14	•		414
CONNELLY HOLY CHILD	Potomac		6-12			295	••	$$$	9			11		RC	415
FOURTH PRESBYTERIAN	Potomac		PS-8		PS-8	105	•	$$				5	O	P	928
GERMAN SCH	Potomac		PS-12		PS-12	565	••	$$	8			5	O		928
HEIGHTS	Potomac				3-12	460	••	$$$	18			12	O	RC	928
MCLEAN	Potomac		K-12		K-12	411	••	$$$	8			8	O		415
ST ANDREW'S EPIS-MD	Potomac		PS-12		PS-12	542	••	$$$	12			13	O	Ep	416
CHARLES E SMITH	Rockville		K-12		K-12	1514	•	$$$				9	•	J	929
GREEN ACRES	Rockville		PS-8		PS-8	300	••	$$$	8			5	O		417
MELVIN J BERMAN	Rockville		PS-12		PS-12	700	••	$$	13	P		6	O	J	929
SALISBURY-MD	Salisbury		PS-12		PS-12	345	••	$$	15	P		6	O		929
SANDY SPRING FRIENDS	Sandy Spring	9-12^5	PS-12	9-12^5	PS-12	571	••	$$$	10	P	•	9	O	RSF	418
ARCHBISHOP SPALDING	Severn		9-12		9-12	1230	••	$$	19	P		17		RC	930
SEVERN	Severna Park		6-12		6-12	584	••	$$$	12			12	O		419
BARRIE	Silver Spring		PS-12		PS-12	301	••	$$$	6			6	O		420
CHELSEA	Silver Spring		5-12		5-12	74	••	$$$	2	F		4			930
NORA	Silver Spring		9-12		9-12	53	••	$$$		P		3			930
ST JAMES SCH-MD	St James	8-12	8-12	8-12	8-12	202	••	$	14	P	•	12		Ep	418
ST TIMOTHY'S	Stevenson	9-12	9-12			150	••	$$				12	O	Ep	421

School	City	Grades				Enr.	Rtg.	Cost						Affil.	Page
NOTRE DAME PREP-MD	Towson	6-12				773	••	$$	16			11		RC	931
MASSACHUSETTS														
PHILLIPS ACAD	Andover	9-PG	9-PG	9-PG	9-PG	1109	•••	$$	16			20	O		290
PIKE	Andover	PS-9		PS-9		441	••	$$$				10			292
CUSHING	Ashburnham	9-PG	9-PG		9-PG	445	••	$$$	7			14	O		292
TRINITY CHRISTIAN-MA	Barnstable	PS-12				135	•	$	1	•		2	O	NC	293
BELMONT DAY	Belmont	PS-8		PS-8		273	•••	$$$				7	O		294
BELMONT HILL	Belmont	7-12		9-12[5]		442	••	$$$	15			14	O		294
SHORE	Beverly	PS-9		PS-9		440	••	$$$				8	O		296
WARING	Beverly	6-12		6-12		151	••	$$$	3			4	O		891
GLEN URQUHART	Beverly Farms	K-8		K-8		232	••	$$$			•	4	•		891
BOSTON COL HS	Boston	7-12				1604	••	$$		•		16	O	RC	892
BOSTON U ACAD	Boston	9-12		9-12		159	••	$$$	20			8	O		297
COMMONWEALTH SCH	Boston	9-12		9-12		151	••	$$$				4			297
KINGSLEY	Boston	PS-6		PS-6		210	••	$$$					•		298
LEARNING PROJECT	Boston	K-6		K-6		118	••	$$					O		298
NEWMAN	Boston	9-PG		9-PG		230	••	$$			•	9	O		892
WINSOR	Boston	5-12				430	•••	$$$	8			13	O		300
THAYER	Braintree	6-12		6-12		694	••	$$$	13			16	O		301
DEXTER	Brookline	PS-12[C]		PS-12[C]		415	••	$$$	15			12	•		304
PARK SCH-MA	Brookline	PS-9		PS-9		562	•••	$$$				9	•		305
SOUTHFIELD-MA	Brookline	PS-12[C]		PS-12[C]		321	••	$$$	15			12	O		305
GOVERNOR'S ACAD	Byfield	9-12	9-12	9-12		401	••	$$$	17			15	O		306
BUCKINGHAM BROWNE	Cambridge	PS-12		PS-12		1012	•••	$$$	14			16	O		307
CAMBRIDGE FRIENDS	Cambridge	PS-8		PS-8		193	••	$$$				2	O	RSF	308
CAMBRIDGE MONTESSORI	Cambridge	PS-8		PS-8		220	••	$$$				4	O		893

School	Town	Girls' Grade Range Bdg	Girls' Grade Range Day	Boys' Grade Range Bdg	Boys' Grade Range Day	Enrollment	Selectivity	Tuition	AP Courses	Learning Disabilities	ESL	Varsity Sports	Summer	Religion	Page
MA															
FAYERWEATHER	Cambridge		PS-8		PS-8	205	••	$$$				3	O		309
SHADY HILL	Cambridge		PS-8		PS-8	518	••	$$$				10	O		309
BEAVER CO DAY	Chestnut Hill		6-12		6-12	452	••	$$$				13	•		302
BRIMMER & MAY	Chestnut Hill		PS-12		PS-12	393	••	$$$	12		•	9	O		302
CHESTNUT HILL SCH	Chestnut Hill		PS-6		PS-6	272	••	$$$				4	O		303
CONCORD ACAD	Concord	9-12	9-12	9-12	9-12	363	••	$$$				14			310
FENN	Concord		4-9		4-9	305	••	$$$				10	O		311
MIDDLESEX	Concord	9-12	9-12	9-12	9-12	372	•••	$$$	22			16	O		311
NASHOBA BROOKS	Concord		PS-8		PS-3	306	••	$$$				9			312
CLARK	Danvers		K-12		K-12	90	•	$$					O		893
ST JOHN'S PREP-MA	Danvers				9-12	1200	••	$$	20			20	O	RC	313
DEDHAM CO DAY	Dedham		PS-8		PS-8	252	••	$$$				10	O		314
NOBLE & GREENOUGH	Dedham	9-12[5]	7-12	9-12[5]	7-12	591	•••	$$$	14			15	O		315
URSULINE ACAD-MA	Dedham		7-12			396	••	$$	6		•	12	O	RC	893
BEMENT	Deerfield	3-9[5]	K-9	3-9[5]	K-9	246	••	$$	8			11	O		316
DEERFIELD ACAD	Deerfield	9-PG	9-PG	9-PG	9-PG	630	•••	$$$				19			317
EAGLEBROOK	Deerfield			6-9	6-9	255	••	$$$			•	15	O		317
EPIPHANY-MA	Dorchester		5-8		5-8	85	••	0		P		4	•	Ep	894
CHARLES RIVER	Dover		PS-8		PS-8	207	••	$$$				5	O		318
RIVERVIEW	East Sandwich	6-PG	6-PG	6-PG	6-PG	207	••	$$$		F		8	O		339
WILLISTON NORTHAMPT	Easthampton	9-PG	7-PG	9-PG	7-PG	545	••	$$$	18		•	19			319
POPE JOHN XXIII	Everett		9-12		9-12	280	•	$	8		•	11	O	RC	894
ANTIOCH	Fall River		PS-8		PS-8	87	•	$							894
FALMOUTH	Falmouth		7-12		7-12	190	•	$$$				3	O		320
APPI EWI D	Fitchburg		K-8		K-8	186	•	$$$				5	O		321

School	City	Grades	Grades	Grades	Grades	Enroll.	●●	$	#	F/P	●	#	○	Affil.	Page
SAGE	Foxboro		PS-8		PS-8	163	••	$$$				2	O		895
SUDBURY VALLEY	Framingham	4-19A	4-19A		4-19A	160	O	$				9	O		322
MACDUFFIE	Granby	6-12⁵	6-12	6-12⁵	6-12	200	••	$$$	10		•	8	O		343
STONELEIGH-BURNHAM	Greenfield	7-PG	7-PG		7-PG	132	••	$$$	4		•	8		Ep	322
GROTON	Groton	8-12	8-12	8-12	8-12	370	•••	$$$	10			12	O		323
LAWRENCE ACAD	Groton	9-12	9-12	9-12	9-12	399	•••	$$$	6		•	15	•		324
EAGLE HILL-MA	Hardwick	8-12	8-12	8-12	8-12	184	•••	$$$		F		8	O		325
DERBY	Hingham		PS-8		PS-8	333	••	$$$				8	O		326
SACRED HEART HS-MA	Kingston		7-12		7-12	412	••	$	6			15	•	RC	895
BERKSHIRE CO DAY	Lenox		PS-9		PS-9	188	••	$$$			•	4			326
LEXINGTON CHRISTIAN	Lexington	6-12	6-12	6-12	6-12	310	••	$$$	10	P		9	O	NC	327
CARROLL	Lincoln	1-9	1-9		1-9	370	••	$$$		F		3	O		328
OAK MEADOW MONTESSOR	Littleton		PS-8		PS-8	253	••	$$		P		2	•		895
MALDEN CATHOLIC	Malden			9-12	9-12	600	••	$$	10		•	13	•	RC	896
BROOKWOOD	Manchester		PS-8		PS-8	404	••	$$$				5	O		329
TOWER SCH	Marblehead		PS-8		PS-8	298	••	$$$				3	O		329
TABOR	Marion	9-12	9-12	9-12	9-12	517	••	$$$	16		•	16	O		330
HILLSIDE	Marlborough	5-9⁵		5-9⁵	5-9	145	••	$$$		F	•	10	O		331
MONTROSE	Medfield		6-12		6-12	172	••	$$	5			4		RC	896
DELPHI	Milton		PS-8		PS-8	150	•••	$					O		897
MILTON ACAD	Milton	9-12	K-12	9-12	K-12	980	••	$$$	11			18			332
NORTHFIELD MT HERMON	Mount Hermon	9-PG	9-PG	9-PG	9-PG	665	••	$$$	19		•	19	O		336
WALNUT HILL	Natick	9-PG	9-PG	9-PG	9-PG	300	••	$$$			•		O		333
ST SEBASTIAN'S	Needham				7-12	364	••	$$$	16			9		RC	333
NEWTON CO DAY	Newton	5-12			5-12	385	••	$$$	19			13	•	RC	335
SOLOMON SCHECHTER-MA	Newton	K-8	K-8		K-8	465	••	$$$				4		J	897
BROOKS	North Andover	9-12	9-12	9-12	9-12	370	••	$$$	12			13	O	Ep	290

School	Town	Girls' Grade Range Bdg	Girls' Grade Range Day	Boys' Grade Range Bdg	Boys' Grade Range Day	Enrollment	Selectivity	Tuition	AP Courses	Learning Disabilities	ESL	Varsity Sports	Summer	Religion	Page
MA															
BISHOP STANG	North Dartmouth		9-12		9-12	707	•	$	7			16		RC	897
FRIENDS ACAD-MA	North Dartmouth		PS-8		PS-8	267	•	$$$		P		5	O		314
SMITH COL CAMPUS SCH	Northampton		K-6		K-6	270	••	$					•		336
CAPE COD ACAD	Osterville		PS-12		PS-12	327	••	$$$	8			8			337
MISS HALL'S	Pittsfield	9-12	9-12			180	••	$$$	13		•	8			338
LANDMARK SCH	Prides Crossing	8-12	2-12	8-12	2-12	461	••	$$$		F		9	O		295
AUSTIN PREP	Reading		6-12		6-12	700	••	$$	16			16		RC	898
BERKSHIRE SCH	Sheffield	9-PG	9-PG	9-PG	9-PG	380	••	$$$	14			16			340
ST JOHN'S HS-MA	Shrewsbury		9-12			1036	••	$	21			15	•	RC	898
PINGREE	South Hamilton		9-12		9-12	341	••	$$$	10			15	O		340
FAY	Southborough	7-9	PS-9	7-9	PS-9	441	••	$$$				13	O		341
ST MARK'S SCH-MA	Southborough	9-12	9-12	9-12	9-12	349	••	$$$	18		•	14		Ep	342
PIONEER VALLEY	Springfield		PS-12		PS-12	263	•	$	2	P		7		Ev	899
CORWIN-RUSSELL	Sudbury	6-PG	6-PG	6-PG	6-PG	55	•••	$$$		F			•		899
WILLOW HILL	Sudbury		6-12		6-12	60	••	$$$		F		4			344
ACAD OF NOTRE DAME	Tyngsboro	PS-12	PS-12		PS-8	611	••	$	8			9		RC	899
CHAPEL HILL-CHAUNCY	Waltham	9-PG	9-PG	9-PG	9-PG	165	••	$$$	2	P	•	10	O		344
ATRIUM	Watertown		PS-6		PS-6	100	••	$$$							900
DANA HALL	Wellesley	9-12	6-12			475	••	$$$	17			14	O		345
TENACRE	Wellesley		PS-6		PS-6	192	••	$$$				5	O		346
FESSENDEN	West Newton			5-9[5]	PS-9	485	••	$$$			•	11	O		334
CATHOLIC MEMORIAL	West Roxbury				7-12	745	••	$$	15			12	•	RC	900
ROXBURY LATIN	West Roxbury				7-12	296	•••	$$$	11			10			299
CAMBRIDGE SCH-MA	Weston	9-PG	9-PG	9-PG	9-PG	325	••	$$$	2		•	7	O		347
MEADOWBROOK-MA	Weston		PS-8		PS-8	305	••	$$$				10	O		348

School	City					Enroll	Tuition					Coed	Rel	Page
RIVERS	Weston		6-12	6-12	••	458	$$$	14			12	O		348
XAVERIAN BROS	Westwood			9-12	••	978	$$	13			16	O	RC	900
WILBRAHAM & MONSON	Wilbraham	9-PG	6-PG	6-PG	••	394	$$$	18	P	•	17	O		349
BUXTON	Williamstown	9-12	9-12	9-12	••	90	$$$		P	•	2	O		350
PINE COBBLE	Williamstown		PS-9	PS-9	•	120	$$				3	•		351
WINCHENDON	Winchendon	9-PG	9-PG	9-PG	••	240	$$$	1	F	•	9	O		351
CHILDREN'S OWN	Winchester		PS-K	PS-K	•	80	$					•		901
BANCROFT	Worcester		K-12	K-12	•	522	$$$	16			14	O		352
HOLY NAME	Worcester		7-12	7-12	•	620	$	7			12	O	RC	901
NOTRE DAME-WORCESTER	Worcester		9-12	9-12	••	300	$	2		•	10	O	RC	353
WORCESTER ACAD	Worcester	9-PG[5]	6-12	6-12	••	642	$$$	16			17	O		353
MICHIGAN														
GREENHILLS-MI	Ann Arbor		6-12	6-12	••	545	$$	10			12	O		693
SUMMERS-KNOLL	Ann Arbor		K-8	K-8	••	58	$$					O		1077
DETROIT CO DAY	Beverly Hills		PS-12	PS-12	•	1624	$$$	20			18	•		696
OUR LADY QN MARTYRS	Beverly Hills		PS-8	PS-8	•	235	$				7	O	RC	1077
ACAD SACRED HEART-MI	Bloomfield Hills	PS-12[C]	PS-8[C]	PS-8[C]	•	475	$$$	3			9	O	RC	693
BR RICE-MI	Bloomfield Hills		9-12	9-12	••	685	$	9			13	•	RC	1078
CRANBROOK	Bloomfield Hills	9-12[C]	PS-12[C]	PS-12[C]	••	1656	$	13		•	16			694
ROEPER	Bloomfield Hills		PS-12	PS-12	••	549	$$$	13			7	O		695
DETROIT WALDORF	Detroit		PS-8	PS-8	•	127	$					O		1078
FRIENDS SCH-DETROIT	Detroit		PS-8	PS-8	••	110	$				2		RSF	1078
MERCY HS-MI	Farmington Hills		9-12	9-12	•	742	$	7			15		RC	1079
VALLEY SCH-MI	Flint		PS-12	PS-12	•	54	$				4			1079
LEELANAU	Glen Arbor	9-12[5]	9-12[5]	9-12	•	60	$$$	2	F	•	4	O		698
GRAND RAPIDS CHRIST	Grand Rapids		PS-12	PS-12	O	2100	$	9		•	18	O	NC	1079
GROSSE POINTE	Grosse Pointe Farms		PS-8	PS-8	••	280	$$				6	•		697

School	Town	Girls' Grade Range Bdg	Girls' Grade Range Day	Boys' Grade Range Bdg	Boys' Grade Range Day	Enrollment	Selectivity	Tuition	AP Courses	Learning Disabilities	ESL	Varsity Sports	Summer	Religion	Page
MI															
U LIGGETT	Grosse Pointe Woods		PS-12		PS-12	583	••	$$$	1			13			697
HILLSDALE	Hillsdale		K-12		K-12	183	•	$				6			1080
INTERLOCHEN	Interlochen	9-PG	9-PG	9-PG		474	••	$$$	3		•		O		699
MONSIGNOR HACKETT	Kalamazoo		9-12		9-12	321	•	$	6	P		12		RC	1080
LANSING CATHOLIC	Lansing		9-12		9-12	490	•	$	8			16		RC	1081
LADYWOOD	Livonia		9-12			322	•	$	10			16		RC	1081
ST MARY CATHOLIC	Monroe		9-12		9-12	430	O	$	4			15		RC	1081
ORCHARD ST MARY'S	Orchard Lake			9-12[5]	9-12	500	•	$	6		•	12		RC	1082
SPRING VALE	Owosso	9-12	9-12	9-12	9-12	48	O	$				3		CG	1082
KINGSBURY CO DAY	Oxford		PS-8		PS-8	93	••	$				4	•		700
NOTRE DAME PREP-MI	Pontiac		9-12		9-12	699	••	$	16	F		15	•	RC	1082
KALAMAZOO	Portage		PS-8		PS-8	180	••	$		P		2			1083
SHRINE	Royal Oak		9-12		9-12	280	••	$	7		•	13	O	RC	1083
MI LUTHERAN	Saginaw	9-12	9-12	9-12	9-12	234	••	$			•	8		L	1084
DE LA SALLE	Warren				9-12	778	•	$	13			13		RC	1084
MINNESOTA															
MARANATHA CHRISTIAN	Brooklyn Park		PS-12		PS-12	660	•	$	5			9		NC	1104
ST JOHN'S PREP-MN	Collegeville	9-PG[5]	6-PG	9-PG[5]	6-PG	313	•	$	3		•	11	O	RC	727
MARSHALL	Duluth		4-12		4-12	460	••	$$	10			12			1104
INTL. SCH OF MN	Eden Prairie		PS-12		PS-12	450	••	$$	16		•	4	O		728
BETHLEHEM	Faribault		7-12		7-12	281	••	$				10		RC	1104
SHATTUCK-ST MARY'S	Faribault	6-PG	6-PG	6-PG	6-PG	434	••	$$	15	P	•	9	O	Ep	728
HILLCREST	Fergus Falls	10-12	7-12	10-12	7-12	197	O	$	5		•	8	O	L	1105
BLAKE	Hopkins		PS-12		PS-12	1383	••	$$$	12			15	O		729
MAYER LUTHERAN	Mayer		9-12		9-12	252	•	$	2			12	O	LMS	1105

School	City			Enroll		Cost							Page
CONVENT VISITATION	Mendota Heights	PS-12	PS-6	548	•	$$	10			12	O	RC	731
ST THOMAS ACAD	Mendota Heights		7-12	675	•	$$$	11	P		13	•	RC	733
BRECK	Minneapolis	PS-12	PS-12	1131	••	$$$	11			15	O	Ep	730
DE LA SALLE HS-MN	Minneapolis	9-12	9-12	630	••	$	5			13	O	RC	1105
LAKE COUNTRY	Minneapolis	PS-9	PS-9	300	•••	$$					O		1106
MINNEHAHA	Minneapolis	PS-12	PS-12	965	•	$$	18	P		15	O	EvC	731
MARTIN LUTHER-MN	Northrop	9-12	9-12	71	O	$	2			11		LMS	1106
PROVIDENCE ACAD	Plymouth	PS-12	PS-12	910	•	$$				12	O	RC	1106
BENILDE-ST MARGARET	St Louis Park	7-12	7-12	1184	••	$	13			15	O	RC	1107
GROVES ACAD	St Louis Park	1-12	1-12	207	••	$$$		F			O		1107
FRIENDS SCH OF MN	St Paul	K-8	K-8	162	••	$$					O	RSF	1108
ST AGNES SCH	St Paul	K-12	K-12	516	•	$	7	P		11	O	RC	1108
ST PAUL ACAD-SUMMIT	St Paul	K-12	K-12	872	••	$$$				14	O		732
COTTER	Winona	9-12[5]	7-12	380	••	$	10	P	•	15	O	RC	1108
NEW LIFE ACAD	Woodbury	PS-12	PS-12	647	•	$	7	P		11	O	NC	1109
MISSISSIPPI													
ST STANISLAUS	Bay St Louis		7-PG	414	••	$	9	P	•	11	O	RC	1130
JACKSON ACAD	Jackson	PS-12	PS-12	1263	•	$	9	P		11	O		1130
JACKSON PREP	Jackson	6-12	6-12	805	•	$	14	P		9	O		1130
CATHEDRAL SCH-MS	Natchez	PS-12	PS-12	625	•	$	3	P		13	O	RC	1131
OXFORD U SCH	Oxford	PS-5	PS-5	140	•	$				1	O		1131
CHAMBERLAIN-HUNT	Port Gibson	7-12	7-12	120	••	$	1		•	7	O	NC	1131
ST ANDREW'S EPIS-MS	Ridgeland	PS-12	PS-12	1184	••	$$	20			15	O	Ep	758
MISSOURI													
CHESTERFIELD DAY	Chesterfield	PS-6	PS-6	190	•	$$					O		1109
WILSON SCH-MO	Clayton	PS-6	PS-6	190	••	$$				3	O		744
OAKHILL DAY	Gladstone	PS-8	PS-8	295	•	$				5	O		1110

School	Town	Girls' Grade Range Bdg	Girls' Grade Range Day	Boys' Grade Range Bdg	Boys' Grade Range Day	Enrollment	Selectivity	Tuition	AP Courses	Learning Disabilities	ESL	Varsity Sports	Summer	Religion	Page
MO															
ARCHBISHOP O'HARA	Kansas City		9-12		9-12	353	••	$	8			12	•	RC	1110
BARSTOW	Kansas City		PS-12		PS-12	646	•	$$	17			11	O		735
LUTHERAN HS-MO	Kansas City		9-12		9-12	108	O	$				9		LMS	1110
NOTRE DAME DE SION	Kansas City		PS-12		PS-8	754	••	$	9			10	•	RC	1111
PEMBROKE HILL	Kansas City		PS-12		PS-12	1168	••	$$	19			14	O		735
ROCKHURST	Kansas City				9-12	1089	•	$	16			11	O	RC	1111
ST PAUL'S EPIS DAY	Kansas City		PS-8		PS-8	475	••	$				5	O	Ep	1112
WENTWORTH	Lexington	9-PG	9-PG	9-PG	9-PG	215	••	$			•	9	O		736
JFK CATHOLIC-MO	Manchester		9-12		9-12	400	•	$	2			12	O	RC	1112
MO MILIT	Mexico			6-PG[5]	6-PG	240	•	$	11		•	10	O		737
BISHOP DUBOURG	St Louis		9-12		9-12	575	•	$		P		12	O	RC	1112
CHAMINADE PREP-MO	St Louis			6-12[5]	6-12	789	•	$	18		•	15	O	RC	738
CHRISTIAN BROS-MO	St Louis				9-12	940	•	$$	10			16		RC	1113
COMMUNITY SCH-MO	St Louis		PS-6		PS-6	350	••	$$					O		739
COR JESU	St Louis		9-12			575	••	$	16			12	O	RC	1113
CROSSROADS-MO	St Louis		7-12		7-12	233	•	$$	9			6	O		1114
DE SMET	St Louis				9-12	1103	•	$	10			13		RC	1114
FORSYTH SCH	St Louis		PS-6		PS-6	393	•	$$					O		740
INCARNATE WORD-MO	St Louis		9-12			450	•	$	4			10	O	RC	1114
JOHN BURROUGHS	St Louis		7-12		7-12	600	••	$$	8			16			740
LOGOS	St Louis		6-12		6-12	150	•	$$$	1			4			1115
LUTHERAN HS N	St Louis		9-12		9-12	314	•	$	3	F		11		L	1115
MARY INST ST LOUIS	St Louis		PS-12		PS-12	1233	•	$$$	17			18	O		741
NEW CITY	St Louis		PS-6		PS-6	350	••	$$					O		1116
NOTRE DAME HS-MO	St Louis		9-12			320	•	$	2			10		RC	1116

School	Town	Girls' Grade Range Bdg	Girls' Grade Range Day	Boys' Grade Range Bdg	Boys' Grade Range Day	Enrollment	Selectivity	Tuition	AP Courses	Learning Disabilities	ESL	Varsity Sports	Summer	Religion	Page
NEW HAMPSHIRE															
PROCTOR	Andover	9-PG	9-PG	9-PG	9-PG	345	••	$$$	9	P		12			355
WHITE MTN	Bethlehem	9-PG	9-PG	9-PG	9-PG	112	••	$$	7	P	•	5	O	Ep	356
CARDIGAN MTN	Canaan			6-9	6-9	201	••	$$			•	11	O		357
ST PAUL'S SCH-NH	Concord	9-12		9-12		539	•••	$$$	13		•	16	O	Ep	357
ST THOMAS AQUINAS-NH	Dover		9-12		9-12	640	••	$	9			17	•	RC	902
DUBLIN	Dublin	9-12	9-12	9-12	9-12	130	••	$$$	7	F	•	7			358
PHILLIPS EXETER	Exeter	9-PG	9-PG	9-PG	9-PG	1063	•••	$$	7			19	O		359
OLIVERIAN	Haverhill	9-PG		9-PG		50	•	$$$	1	F		1	O		902
DERRYFIELD	Manchester		6-12		6-12	370	••	$$$	12		•	13	O		361
KIMBALL UNION	Meriden	9-PG	9-PG	9-PG	9-PG	314	••	$$	18		•	12	O		361
NEW HAMPTON	New Hampton	9-PG	9-PG	9-PG	9-PG	305	••	$$$	4		•	12	O		362
HOLDERNESS	Plymouth	9-12	9-12	9-12	9-12	282	••	$$$	14	F		12		Ep	363
HAMPSHIRE COUNTRY	Rindge			3-12		23	•	$$$	14	F					364
TILTON	Tilton	9-PG	9-PG	9-PG	9-PG	260	••	$$$	14	P	•	13		Mth	365
WATERVILLE VALLEY	Waterville Valley	6-12	6-12	6-12	6-12	60	••	$	6			1			902
PINE HILL	Wilton		PS-8		PS-8	187	••	$$				1			903
BREWSTER	Wolfeboro	9-PG	9-PG	9-PG	9-PG	364	••	$$$	10	P	•	14	O		366
NEW JERSEY															
BLAIR	Blairstown	9-PG	9-PG	9-PG	9-PG	447	••	$$$	22			17		P	423
WOODLAND CO DAY	Bridgeton		PS-8		PS-8	147	•	$	5			5	O		424
DOANE ACAD	Burlington	PS-12	PS-12			210	•	$$	13			6	O	Ep	424
KING'S CHRISTIAN	Cherry Hill	PS-12	PS-12			321	•	$	5	P	•	7	•	NC	932
ACAD OF ST ELIZABETH	Convent Station	9-12	9-12			206	•	$$	10			11		RC	435
HOLY CROSS HS-NJ	Delran	9-12	9-12	9-12	9-12	601	••	$	8			15	O	RC	932

School	Town	Girls' Grade Range Bdg	Girls' Grade Range Day	Boys' Grade Range Bdg	Boys' Grade Range Day	Enrollment	Selectivity	Tuition	AP Courses	Learning Disabilities	ESL	Varsity Sports	Summer	Religion	Page
NJ															
VILLA WALSH	Morristown		7-12			257	••	$$	12			9		RC	937
WILSON SCH-NJ	Mountain Lakes		PS-8		PS-8	75	••	$$$				2	O	Ec	438
FRIENDS MULLICA HILL	Mullica Hill		PS-8		PS-8	200	•	$$				5	O	RSF	438
OUR LADY OF MERCY	Newfield		9-12			170	O	$				9		RC	938
BARNSTABLE	Oakland		5-12		5-12	103	••	$$$		F		5	O		942
YAVNEH	Paramus		PS-8		PS-8	695	••	$$		P				OJ	938
PENNINGTON	Pennington	8-12	6-12	8-12	6-12	485	••	$$	18	P		15		UM	439
TIMOTHY CHRISTIAN-NJ	Piscataway		K-12		K-12	491	•	$	5	P		8	O	Ev	938
PURNELL	Pottersville	9-12[5]	9-12			100	••	$$$		P		3			440
AM BOYCHOIR	Princeton			4-8	4-8	50	•	$			•				440
CHAPIN-NJ	Princeton		PS-8		PS-8	312	••	$$$				5			441
HUN	Princeton	9-PG	6-PG	9-PG	6-PG	610	••	$$$	14	P	•	15	O		442
PRINCETON ACAD	Princeton				PS-8	228	••	$$$				8	O	RC	939
PRINCETON DAY	Princeton		PS-12		PS-12	907	••	$$$	14			14	O		442
PRINCETON FRIENDS	Princeton		PS-8		PS-8	135	••	$$$					O	RSF	939
STUART CO DAY	Princeton		PS-12		PS-PS	471	••	$$$	15	P		10	O	RC	443
RUMSON	Rumson		PS-8		PS-8	440	•	$$$				7			444
SADDLE RIVER	Saddle River		K-12		K-12	315	••	$$$	12			9	O		445
FAR BROOK	Short Hills		PS-8		PS-8	229	••	$$$				4	•		446
RUTGERS PREP	Somerset		PS-12		PS-12	702	••	$$$	20			11	O		447
HILLTOP	Sparta		PS-8		PS-8	230	••	$$					O		939
KENT PLACE	Summit		PS-12		PS-PS	636	••	$$$	21			11	O		447
OAK KNOLL	Summit		K-12		K-6	540	••	$$$	14			13	O	RC	448
COMMUNITY SCH-NJ	Teaneck		9-12		9-12	185	•	$$$		F		8	O		940
RANNEY	Tinton Falls		PS-12		PS-12	821	••	$$$	14			13	O		449

School	Town	Girls' Bdg	Girls' Day	Boys' Bdg	Boys' Day	Enrollment	Selectivity	Tuition	AP Courses	Learning Disabilities	ESL	Varsity Sports	Summer	Religion	Page
NY															
RIVERDALE	Bronx		PS-12		PS-12	1130	••	$$$				18			455
BERKELEY CARROLL	Brooklyn		PS-12		PS-12	820	••	$$$	11			9	O		456
BISH KEARN-BROOKLYN	Brooklyn		9-12			674	•	$	8			9	O	RC	943
BISHOP LOUGHLIN	Brooklyn				9-12	880	•	$	2			10	•	RC	944
BROOKLYN FRIENDS	Brooklyn		PS-12		PS-12	750	••	$$$				7	O	RSF	457
BROOKLYN HTS MONT	Brooklyn		PS-8		PS-8	223	••	$$$		P		3	O		944
PACKER	Brooklyn		PS-12		PS-12	997	••	$$$	17			9	O		457
POLY PREP	Brooklyn		PS-12		PS-12	1012	•••	$$$	18			16	O		458
ST ANN'S-NY	Brooklyn		PS-12		PS-12	1090	••	$$$				10	O		459
LONG ISLAND LUTHERAN	Brookville		6-12		6-12	600	••	$	13			13	O	L	944
BUFFALO SEMINARY	Buffalo	9-12[5]	9-12			170	••	$	13			11	O		460
CANISIUS	Buffalo				9-12	826	••	$	19			17	•	RC	945
ELMWOOD FRANKLIN	Buffalo		PS-8		PS-8	334	••	$$				4	O		461
NARDIN	Buffalo		PS-12		PS-8	922	••	$$	12			14	O	RC	945
NICHOLS	Buffalo		5-12		5-12	580	••	$$	17			15	O		461
ST JOSEPH'S COLLEG	Buffalo				9-12	722	••	$	16			16	O	RC	946
GREEN MEADOW	Chestnut Ridge		PS-12		PS-12	382	••	$	4			6	O		946
ST AGNES HS	College Point		9-12			390	•	$	4		•	7		RC	946
ROCKLAND CO DAY	Congers	8-12	PS-12	8-12	PS-12	130	O	$$$	10			2			501
BROOKWOOD-NY	Cooperstown		PS-6		PS-6	111		$					O		947
NY MILIT	Cornwall-on-Hudson	7-12	7-12	7-12	7-12	146	••	$	4		•	15	O		463
STORM KING	Cornwall-on-Hudson	8-PG	8-PG	8-PG	8-PG	132	••	$$$	9	P	•	11			463
MANLIUS PEBBLE HILL	DeWitt		PS-PG		PS-PG	558	••	$$	18		•	12	O		514
CITYTERM	Dobbs Ferry	11-12	11-12	11-12		30	••	$$	4		•				1228
MASTERS SCH-NY	Dobbs Ferry	9-12[C5]	5-12[C]	9-12[C5]	5-12[C]	580	••	$$$	16			12			464

School	Town	Girls' Grade Range Bdg	Girls' Grade Range Day	Boys' Grade Range Bdg	Boys' Grade Range Day	Enrollment	Selectivity	Tuition	AP Courses	Learning Disabilities	ESL	Varsity Sports	Summer	Religion	Page
NY															
URSULINE SCH	New Rochelle		6-12			792	••	$$	15			12		RC	953
ABRAHAM JOSHUA HESCH	New York		PS-12		PS-12	793	•••	$$$			•	4		J	954
ALLEN-STEVENSON	New York				K-9	418	•••	$$$				7	O		472
BEEKMAN	New York		9-PG		9-PG	80	••	$$$			•	7	O		473
BIRCH WATHEN LENOX	New York		K-12		K-12	565	•••	$$$	10			10	•		473
BREARLEY	New York		K-12			701	•••	$$$	11			13	O		474
BROWNING	New York				K-12	388	••	$$$				9	•		475
BUCKLEY SCH-NY	New York				K-9	374	•••	$$$				9			476
CAEDMON	New York		PS-5		PS-5	275	••	$$$					O		954
CALHOUN	New York		PS-12		PS-12	734	•••	$$$				7	O		476
CATHEDRAL SCH-NY	New York				K-8	290	•••	$$$				7		Ep	477
CHAPIN-NY	New York		K-12			713	•••	$$$	14			15	•		478
CHILDREN'S STOREFRNT	New York				PS-8	174	••	0							954
CITY & COUNTRY	New York		PS-8		PS-8	360	•••	$$$				4			478
COLLEGIATE-NY	New York				K-12	648	•••	$$$	11			9			479
COLUMBIA GRAMMAR	New York		PS-12		PS-12	1220	•••	$$$	19	P	•	11			480
CONVENT SAC HEART-NY	New York		PS-12			691	•••	$$$	15			9	O	RC	481
CORLEARS	New York		PS-5		PS-5	165	••	$$$					•		955
DALTON	New York		K-12		K-12	1279	•••	$$$				13	O		481
DOMINICAN ACAD	New York		9-12			225	••	$	10			7		RC	955
DWIGHT SCH	New York		PS-12		PS-12	555	••	$$$			•	8			482
FRIENDS SEMINARY	New York		K-12		K-12	733	••	$$$	10			10	O	RSF	483
GRACE CHURCH	New York		PS-8		PS-8	410	•••	$$$				5		Ep	484
HEWITT	New York		K-12			525	••	$$$	6			9	•		484
LA SCUOLA D'ITALIA	New York		PS-12		PS-12	250	•	$$			•	4			485

School	Town	Girls' Grade Range Bdg	Girls' Grade Range Day	Boys' Grade Range Bdg	Boys' Grade Range Day	Enrollment	Selectivity	Tuition	AP Courses	Learning Disabilities	ESL	Varsity Sports	Summer	Religion	Page
NY															
UN INTL	New York		K-12		K-12	1541	••	$$$			•	7	O		499
WINSTON PREP	New York		6-12		6-12	198	••	$$$		F		5	O		958
XAVIER-NY	New York				9-12	1050	••	$$	11			13	•	RC	959
YORK PREP	New York		6-12		6-12	350	•••	$$$	5	P		9	•		500
WOODLAND HILL	North Greenbush		PS-8		PS-8	245	••	$				4	O		959
HOLY CHILD ACAD-NY	Old Westbury		PS-8		PS-8	245	••	$$				3	•	RC	959
E WOODS	Oyster Bay		PS-8		PS-8	233	••	$$$				7	O		502
TRINITY-PAWLING	Pawling			9-PG	7-PG	300	••	$$$	18	P		13	O	Ep	502
SETON CATHOLIC	Plattsburgh	7-12	7-12	7-12	7-12	157	••	$	6			10		RC	960
VINCENT SMITH	Port Washington		4-12		4-12	60	••	$$$		F		3	O		503
OAKWOOD FRIENDS	Poughkeepsie	9-12⁵	6-12	9-12⁵	6-12	171	••	$$	7	P	•	8	O	RSF	504
POUGHKEEPSIE DAY	Poughkeepsie		PS-12		PS-12	297	••	$$$				6	O		505
DOANE STUART	Rensselaer		PS-12		PS-12	289	••	$$				9		Ep	451
ALLENDALE COLUMBIA	Rochester		PS-12		PS-12	325	••	$$	16			11	O		507
AQUINAS INST	Rochester		PS-12		PS-12	1417	••	$	12			16		RC	960
BISH KEARN-ROCHESTER	Rochester		7-12		7-12	413	••	$	9			14	•	RC	961
HARLEY	Rochester		PS-12		PS-12	520	•	$$$	17			11	O		507
MCQUAID	Rochester				7-12	838	•	$	17			18	O	RC	961
BUCKLEY CO DAY	Roslyn		PS-8		PS-8	339	••	$$$				5	O		508
RYE CO DAY	Rye		PS-12		PS-12	887	••	$$$	18			16	O		509
SCH OF HOLY CHILD	Rye		5-12			345	••	$$$	10			13	O	RC	509
PARK SCH-NY	Snyder		PS-12		PS-12	253	•	$$	7		•	7	O		462
JFK CATHOLIC-NY	Somers		9-12		9-12	610	••	$	9			17		RC	961
ST ANTHONY'S	South Huntington		9-12		9-12	2250	••	$	14			19	•	RC	962
GOW	South Wales	7-12	7-12	7-12	7-12	130	•	$$$		F		9	O		512

School	Town	Girls' Bdg	Girls' Day	Boys' Bdg	Boys' Day	Enrollment	Selectivity	Tuition	AP Courses	Learning Disabilities	ESL	Varsity Sports	Summer	Religion	Page
NC															
CHARLOTTE CHRISTIAN	Charlotte		PS-12		PS-12	1002	••	$$	19			14	O	NC	1028
CHARLOTTE CO DAY	Charlotte		PS-12		PS-12	1617	••	$$$	22		•	16	O		612
CHARLOTTE LATIN	Charlotte		K-12		K-12	1388	••	$$	14			15	O		613
CHARLOTTE PREP	Charlotte		PS-8		PS-8	350	••	$$	8			8	O		1028
NORTHSIDE CHRISTIAN	Charlotte		PS-12		PS-12	540	•	$	4			10	O	B	1029
PROVIDENCE DAY	Charlotte		PS-12		PS-12	1545	••	$$$	21			15	O		614
CANNON	Concord		PS-12		PS-12	876	••	$$	15			13	O		615
CAMELOT	Durham		K-12		K-12	95	••	$	7		•	3	O	RSF	1029
CAROLINA FRIENDS	Durham		PS-12		PS-12	483	••	$$	5			8	O	RSF	615
DURHAM ACAD	Durham		PS-12		PS-12	1145	••	$$	19	P		12	O		616
FAYETTEVILLE	Fayetteville		PS-12		PS-12	393	••	$$	11			10	O		617
GASTON DAY	Gastonia		PS-12		PS-12	503	•	$$	11	P		11	O		1030
WAYNE	Goldsboro		PS-12		PS-12	252	••	$	7			8	•		1030
AM HEBREW	Greensboro	9-12	9-12	9-12	9-12	156	••	$	11		•	9	O	J	1030
CANTERBURY-NC	Greensboro		K-8		K-8	337	••	$$				6	O	Ep	1031
GREENSBORO DAY	Greensboro		PS-12		PS-12	875	••	$$	16		•	14	O		618
NEW GARDEN FRIENDS	Greensboro		PS-12		PS-12	275	•	$$				6	O	RSF	1031
HARRELLS CHRISTIAN	Harrells		K-12		K-12	396	••	$	5			9		NC	1032
KERR-VANCE	Henderson		PS-12		PS-12	430	••	$	6			12	•		1032
HICKORY	Hickory		PS-8		PS-8	68	•	$					O		1032
WESTCHESTER CO DAY	High Point		K-12		K-12	399	•	$$	14			10	O		619
HOBGOOD	Hobgood		K-12		K-12	220	•	$	7			7	•		1033
FORSYTH CO DAY	Lewisville		PS-12		PS-12	849	••	$$	11	P	•	13	O		620
OAK RIDGE	Oak Ridge	8-PG	8-PG	8-PG	8-PG	63	•	$			•	10	O		620
OUTDOOR ACAD	Pisgah Forest	10-11	10-11	10-11	10-11	30	••	$							1229

School	Town	Girls' Grade Range Bdg	Girls' Grade Range Day	Boys' Grade Range Bdg	Boys' Grade Range Day	Enrollment	Selectivity	Tuition	AP Courses	Learning Disabilities	ESL	Varsity Sports	Summer	Religion	Page
OH															
SCHILLING	Cincinnati		K-12		K-12	45	••	$$	2			1			1088
SEVEN HILLS-OH	Cincinnati		PS-12		PS-12	1000	••	$$$	12	P		13	O		704
SUMMIT CO DAY	Cincinnati		PS-12		PS-12	1082	••	$	18			16	O	RC	705
URSULINE ACAD-OH	Cincinnati		9-12			649	••	$	12			10		RC	1088
BENEDICTINE HS-OH	Cleveland				9-12	380	••	$	9			12	•	RC	1088
ST IGNATIUS-OH	Cleveland				9-12	1461	••	$$	16			15	O	RC	1089
BEAUMONT	Cleveland Heights		9-12			442	••	$	9			11	•	RC	1089
BISHOP WATTERSON	Columbus		9-12		9-12	1019	••	$	15			16	O	RC	1090
COLUMBUS SCH GIRLS	Columbus		PS-12			609	••	$$	19			10	O		708
MARBURN	Columbus		1-12		1-12	152	•••	$$		F		6	O		1090
WELLINGTON	Columbus		PS-12		PS-12	577	•	$$	13		•	8	O		708
CUYAHOGA VALLEY CHR	Cuyahoga Falls		7-12		7-12	850	••	$	9			15	•	NC	1091
WALSH	Cuyahoga Falls		9-12		9-12	936	••	$	13			16	•	RC	1091
MIAMI VALLEY	Dayton		PS-12		PS-12	449	•	$$	11	P		11	O		709
ST JOHN'S HS-OH	Delphos		9-12		9-12	259	•	$				9		RC	1092
COLUMBUS ACAD	Gahanna		PS-12		PS-12	1072	••	$$	11			13	O	RC	707
GILMOUR	Gates Mills	7-12	PS-12	7-12	PS-12	695	••	$	11			14	O	RC	710
HAWKEN	Gates Mills		PS-12		PS-12	971	••	$$$	17			13	O		711
STEPHEN T BADIN	Hamilton		9-12		9-12	450	•	$	6	P		14		RC	1092
WESTERN RESERVE	Hudson	9-PG	9-PG	9-PG	9-PG	390	••	$$	17			15	•		712
ST EDWARD	Lakewood				9-12	828	••	$	14			16	•	RC	1092
TUSCARAWAS CATHOLIC	New Philadelphia		7-12		7-12	184	O	$	3			10		RC	1093
LAKE RIDGE	North Ridgeville		K-12		K-12	359	••	$$$	14			8	O		713
PADUA	Parma		9-12		9-12	837	•	$	9	P		14	O	RC	1093
LILLIAN-BETTY RATNER	Pepper Pike		PS-8		PS-8	217	••	$$		P	•		O	J	1093

School	City	Boarding Grades	Grades	Enroll	Sel	Brd	Cost	#	P	#	O	L	Page
LUTHERAN HS W	Rocky River		9-12	450	••		$	8		11			1094
MAGNIFICAT	Rocky River		9-12	774	••		$	12		13	•	RC	1094
HATHAWAY BROWN	Shaker Heights		PS-12	861	••		$$$	15		12	•		714
LAUREL SCH	Shaker Heights		PS-12	673	••		$$$	15		11			714
MAUMEE VALLEY	Toledo		PS-12	475	•	•	$$	9		9	O		716
ST FRANCIS DE SALES	Toledo		9-12	606	•		$	18		14	O	RC	1095
ANDREWS OSBORNE	Willoughby	7-12[5]	PS-12	350	••	•	$	7		10	O		706
CARDINAL MOONEY-OH	Youngstown		9-12	590	•		$	5		15	O	RC	1095
OKLAHOMA													
CASADY	Oklahoma City		PS-12	859	••		$$	16		13	O	Ep	759
HERITAGE HALL	Oklahoma City		PS-12	930	•		$$$	13		13	O		759
ST JOHN'S EPIS-OK	Oklahoma City		PS-8	120	•		$			2	O	Ep	1132
WESTMINSTER SCH-OK	Oklahoma City		PS-8	537	•		$			5	O		1132
BISHOP KELLEY	Tulsa		9-12	807	••		$	16	P	13	•	RC	1133
CASCIA HALL	Tulsa		6-12	579	••		$	12	P	12	O	RC	1133
HOLLAND HALL	Tulsa		PS-12	958	•		$$	6		13	O	Ep	760
MONTE CASSINO	Tulsa		PS-8	904	••		$			8	O	RC	1134
U SCH-OK	Tulsa		PS-8	235	•		$				O		1134
OREGON													
VALLEY CATHOLIC	Beaverton		PS-12	716	••	•	$	11		11	O	RC	1214
MILO ADVENTIST	Days Creek	9-12	9-12	103	••	•	$	2		5		SA	1215
OAK HILL SCH-OR	Eugene		K-12	115	•	•	$$	18		5			1215
NESKOWIN VALLEY	Neskowin		PS-8	45	O		$			3	O		1215
CATLIN GABEL	Portland		PS-12	746	•••		$$$			9	O		865
CENTRAL CATHOLIC-OR	Portland		9-12	830	••		$	8		12	O	RC	1216
INTL SCH-OR	Portland		PS-5	465	O		$$				O		1216
JESUIT HS-OR	Portland		9-12	1260	••		$	12		13	O	RC	1216

School	Town	Girls' Grade Range Bdg	Girls' Grade Range Day	Boys' Grade Range Bdg	Boys' Grade Range Day	Enrollment	Selectivity	Tuition	AP Courses	Learning Disabilities	ESL	Varsity Sports	Summer	Religion	Page
OR															
NORTHWEST ACAD	Portland		6-12		6-12	121	••	$$							1217
OR EPISCOPAL	Portland	9-12	PS-12	9-12	PS-12	844	••	$$$	10		•	9	O	Ep	865
PORTLAND LUTHERAN	Portland		PS-12		PS-12	245	•	$	2		•	5		L	866
ST MARY'S ACAD	Portland		9-12			640	•	$	7			10	O	RC	1217
BLANCHET	Salem		6-12		6-12	372	•	$	2		•	11	O	RC	1218
W MENNONITE	Salem	9-12[5]	6-12	9-12[5]	6-12	250	•	$			•	6	O	Mn	1218
DELPHIAN	Sheridan	3-12	K-12	3-12	K-12	272	••	$	3		•	4	O		1218
PENNSYLVANIA															
ALLENTOWN CATHOLIC	Allentown		9-12		9-12	900	•	$	7			15		RC	966
SWAIN	Allentown		PS-8		PS-8	300	••	$$				5	O		519
BISHOP GUILFOYLE	Altoona		9-12		9-12	320	O	$	3			10		RC	966
QUIGLEY	Baden		9-12		9-12	178	O	$	4			7		RC	967
BEAVER COUNTY CHRIST	Beaver Falls		K-12		K-12	214	•	$	3			3			967
HOLY GHOST PREP	Bensalem				9-12	498	••	$$	17			12	O	RC	967
MORAVIAN	Bethlehem		PS-12		PS-12	777	•	$$$	12			14	O	Mr	519
BALDWIN	Bryn Mawr		PS-12			535	••	$$$				13	O		521
CO DAY SACRED HEART	Bryn Mawr		PS-12			310	••	$$	7			11	O	RC	522
ST ALOYSIUS	Bryn Mawr				K-8	228	•	$				6	O	RC	968
SHIPLEY	Bryn Mawr		PS-12		PS-12	835	••	$$$	1			13			523
MONTGOMERY SCH	Chester Springs		PS-8		PS-8	271	•	$$$				8	O		523
DEVON PREP	Devon				6-12	259	••	$$	14			8	O	RC	968
HOLY CHILD ACAD-PA	Drexel Hill		PS-8		PS-8	225	••	$$				5	O	RC	969
BISHOP CARROLL	Ebensburg	9-12	9-12	9-12	9-12	240	•	$	4			12		RC	969
ERIE DAY	Erie		PS-8		PS-8	154	••	$$			•	4	•	RC	969
CHURCH FARM	Exton			7-12	7-12	190	••	$	6			10		Ep	524

School	Town	Girls' Grade Range Bdg	Girls' Grade Range Day	Boys' Grade Range Bdg	Boys' Grade Range Day	Enrollment	Selectivity	Tuition	AP Courses	Learning Disabilities	ESL	Varsity Sports	Summer	Religion	Page
PA															
WALDRON MERCY	Merion Station		PS-8		PS-8	514	•	$				10	•	RC	974
CARSON LONG	New Bloomfield			6-12[5]	6-12	120	•	$			•	7			535
SOLEBURY	New Hope	9-PG	7-12	9-PG	7-12	235	••	$$	10	P	•	11		RSF	536
GEORGE SCH	Newtown	9-12	9-12	9-12	9-12	530	••	$$$	11		•	17	O	RSF	537
NEWTOWN FRIENDS	Newtown		PS-8		PS-8	253	••	$$				6		RSF	538
DE COUNTY CHRISTIAN	Newtown Square		PS-12		PS-12	795	••	$$	10	P	•	13	O	NC	975
EPISCOPAL ACAD	Newtown Square		PS-12		PS-12	1227	••	$$$	18			18	O	Ep	540
STRATFORD FRIENDS	Newtown Square		K-8		K-8	78	••	$$$		F			O	RSF	975
DE VALLEY FRIENDS	Paoli		6-12		6-12	176	••	$$$		F		7	O	RSF	975
PERKIOMEN	Pennsburg	7-PG	6-PG	7-PG	6-PG	303	••	$$	22	P	•	12	O		539
ARCHBISHOP RYAN	Philadelphia		9-12		9-12	1611	••	$	10	P		19		RC	976
CREFELD	Philadelphia		7-12		7-12	96	••	$$$		F		2	O		540
FR JUDGE	Philadelphia				9-12	1143	•	$	6			16	•	RC	976
FRIENDS SELECT	Philadelphia		PS-12		PS-12	552	••	$$$			•	10	•	RSF	541
GERMANTOWN FRIENDS	Philadelphia		K-12		K-12	855	••	$$$			•	12	O	RSF	543
GIRARD	Philadelphia	1-12[5]		1-12[5]		475	••	2			10	0			977
GREENE ST FRIENDS	Philadelphia		PS-8		PS-8	360	••	$$				3	•	RSF	544
JOHN W HALLAHAN	Philadelphia		9-12			650	••	$	5			9	O	RC	977
NAZARETH	Philadelphia		9-12			415	•	$	12			13	O	RC	977
PHILADELPHIA SCH	Philadelphia		PS-8		PS-8	387	••	$$$				5	O		978
ST PETER'S SCH	Philadelphia		PS-8		PS-8	214	••	$$$				2	O		545
NEUMANN-GORETTI	Philadelphia		9-12		9-12	1091	••	$	5		•	10		RC	978
SPRINGSIDE	Philadelphia		PS-12[C]		PS-12[C]	1129	••	$$$	11			17	O		545
W PHILADELPHIA CATH	Philadelphia		9-12		9-12	487	•	$	5			9	O	RC	979
WM PENN CHARTER	Philadelphia		PS-12		PS-12	955	••	$$$	12			16	•	RSF	546

School	City	Grades	Grades (B)	Enroll	Type	Tuition					O	Affil	Page
ELLIS	Pittsburgh	PS-12	PS-12	448	••	$$$	13			10	○		547
FALK	Pittsburgh	K-8	K-8	323	••	$				4			548
FOX CHAPEL	Pittsburgh	PS-5	PS-5	90	••	$$		P		5	○	Ep	979
ST EDMUND'S	Pittsburgh	PS-8	PS-8	298	••	$$	7			5	○		548
SHADY SIDE	Pittsburgh	PS-12	9-12[5]	928	••	$$$	7			16	○		549
WINCHESTER THURSTON	Pittsburgh	PS-12	PS-12	643	•	$$$	12		•	9	○		550
PLYMOUTH MEETING	Plymouth Meeting	PS-6	PS-6	145	••	$$				5	○	RSF	979
PORTERSVILLE CHRIST	Portersville	PS-12	PS-12	262	••	$	2					Ev	980
HILL SCH-PA	Pottstown	9-PG	9-PG	494	••	$$$	22			17	○		551
WYNDCROFT	Pottstown	PS-8	PS-8	238	•	$$				5	○		552
UNITED FRIENDS	Quakertown	PS-8	PS-8	118	•	$$	13			4	○	RSF	980
SCH IN ROSE VALLEY	Rose Valley	PS-6	PS-6	125	••	$$				13	○		534
AGNES IRWIN	Rosemont	PS-12	PS-12	687	••	$$$	13			5	○		520
HILL TOP PREP	Rosemont	5-12	5-12	71	••	$$$		F		5	○		980
ROSEMONT	Rosemont	PS-8	PS-8	323	•	$$	12			5	○	RC	981
KISKI	Saltsburg	9-PG	9-PG	195	••	$$			•	11	○		552
SEWICKLEY	Sewickley	PS-12	PS-12	708	••	$$$	15			12	○		553
WOODLLYNDE	Strafford	1-12	1-12	240	••	$$$	2			8	○		981
GRIER	Tyrone	7-PG	7-PG	262	••	$$	15	P	•	7	○		554
VALLEY FORGE	Wayne	7-PG	7-PG	280	••	$$	5		•	11		NC	555
WEST CHESTER FRIENDS	West Chester	PS-5	PS-5	110	••	$$					○	RSF	981
WESTTOWN	West Chester	PS-10	9-12	700	••	$$			•	14	○	RSF	555
HARRISBURG	Wormleysburg	PS-12	PS-12	396	••	$$	4			5	•		526
LA SALLE COL HS	Wyndmoor	9-12	9-12	1068	••	$$	20	P		16	○	RC	544
FRIENDS' CENTRAL	Wynnewood	PS-12	PS-12	890	••	$$$				16	○	RSF	557
CHRISTIAN SCH YORK	York	PS-12	PS-12	378	•	$	1	P	•	9	○	NC	982
YORK CO DAY	York	PS-12	PS-12	216	••	$$	13			5	○		558

School	Town	Girls' Grade Range Bdg	Girls' Grade Range Day	Boys' Grade Range Bdg	Boys' Grade Range Day	Enrollment	Selectivity	Tuition	AP Courses	Learning Disabilities	ESL	Varsity Sports	Summer	Religion	Page
RHODE ISLAND															
ST ANDREW'S SCH-RI	Barrington	9-12	3-12	9-12	3-12	213	••	$$	4	P	•	6	O		367
MERCYMOUNT	Cumberland		PS-8		PS-8	463	O	$		P		5	O	RC	903
ROCKY HILL	East Greenwich		PS-12		PS-12	325	••	$$$	12		•	8	O		368
GORDON SCH	East Providence		PS-8		PS-8	407	••	$$$				8	O		371
PROVIDENCE CO DAY	East Providence		6-12		6-12	215	••	$$$	8	P		14	O		373
ST GEORGE'S SCH-RI	Middletown	9-12	9-12	9-12	9-12	357	••	$$$	22			15	O	Ep	369
ST MICHAEL'S CO DAY	Newport		PS-8		PS-8	226	••	$$$				4	O		370
PENNFIELD	Portsmouth		PS-8		PS-8	184	•	$$				4	O		904
PORTSMOUTH	Portsmouth	9-12	9-12	9-12	9-12	350	••	$$	19			15	O	RC	368
COMMUNITY PREP	Providence		3-8		3-8	152	••	$$				5	O		904
FR-AMER SCH OF RI	Providence		PS-8		PS-8	170	••	$$					O		904
LA SALLE ACAD	Providence		7-12		7-12	1477	••	$$	16			16	•	RC	905
LINCOLN	Providence		PS-12		PS-PS	353	••	$$$	12			9	O	RSF	371
MOSES BROWN	Providence		PS-12		PS-12	765	••	$$$	11			17	•	RSF	372
WHEELER	Providence		PS-12		PS-12	801	••	$$$	8	P		14	O		373
PROUT	Wakefield		9-12		9-12	647	••	$	5			12	O	RC	905
MT ST CHARLES	Woonsocket		7-12		7-12	873	••	$	14			14	O	RC	905
SOUTH CAROLINA															
MEAD HALL	Aiken		PS-12		PS-12	356	•	$$	4			6		Ep	1035
BEAUFORT	Beaufort		PS-12		PS-12	275	••	$	7	P		10			626
CAMDEN MILIT	Camden			7-PG		302	••	$	4			10	•		626
ASHLEY HALL	Charleston		PS-12		PS-K	652	••	$$	12			10	O		627
CHARLESTON DAY	Charleston		1-8		1-8	206	••	$$				6	O		628
MASON	Charleston		1-8		1-8	330	••	$				4	O		1036

	City												Page
PORTER-GAUD	Charleston	1-12	1-12	902	••	$$	17			14	O	Ep	628
BEN LIPPEN	Columbia	6-12	PS-12	777	••	$	8		•	13	O	NC	1036
HAMMOND	Columbia	PS-12	PS-12	902	••	$$	16			14	O		1036
HEATHWOOD	Columbia	PS-12	PS-12	773	••	$$	13			15	O	Ep	629
BYRNES	Florence	PS-12	PS-12	200	•	$	7			9	O		1037
BOB JONES	Greenville	9-12	PS-12	1178	••	$				3	•	NC	1037
CHRIST CHURCH EPIS	Greenville	K-12	K-12	1025	••	$$	19			15	O	Ep	630
ST JOSEPH'S CATHOLIC	Greenville	6-12	6-12	611	•	$	15	P	•	12	O	RC	1038
SHANNON FOREST	Greenville	PS-12	PS-12	424	•	$	7	P		10	•	NC	1038
CAMBRIDGE ACAD	Greenwood	PS-8	PS-8	167	•	$				7			1038
HILTON HEAD PREP	Hilton Head Island	PS-12	PS-12	440	••	$$	12	P		8	O		1039
TRIDENT	Mount Pleasant	K-12	K-12	100	•	$$$		F		7	O		1039
LOWCOUNTRY	Pawleys Island	PS-12	PS-12	160	••	$	7			7	O		1039
SPARTANBURG DAY	Spartanburg	PS-12	PS-12	473	••	$$	16	P		11	O		631
PINEWOOD PREP	Summerville	PS-12	PS-12	800	••	$	13			13	O		1040
WILSON HALL	Sumter	PS-12	PS-12	838	••	$	16			13	O		1040
SOUTH DAKOTA													
FREEMAN	Freeman	9-12	5-12	67	••	$		P		7		Mn	1120
ST THOMAS MORE HS	Rapid City	9-12	9-12	234	•	$	8			10	O	RC	1121
SIOUX FALLS CHRISTN	Sioux Falls	PS-12	PS-12	875	•	$	5	F		7	O	NC	1121
TENNESSEE													
WEBB SCH-BELL BUCKLE	Bell Buckle	7-PG[5]	6-12	304	••	$$	13	P	•	10	O		632
BRENTWOOD ACAD	Brentwood	6-12	6-12	765	•	$$	13			14	O	NC	1041
CURREY INGRAM	Brentwood	K-12	K-12	340	••	$$$				7	O		1041
BAYLOR	Chattanooga	9-12	6-12	1053	••	$$	18		•	17	O		633
BOYD-BUCHANAN	Chattanooga	PS-12	PS-12	898	••	$	7			10	O	NC	1041
BRIGHT SCH	Chattanooga	PS-5	PS-5	327	••	$$				6	O		633

School	Town	Girls' Grade Range Bdg	Girls' Grade Range Day	Boys' Grade Range Bdg	Boys' Grade Range Day	Enrollment	Selectivity	Tuition	AP Courses	Learning Disabilities	ESL	Varsity Sports	Summer	Region	Page
TN															
CHATTANOOGA CHRIST	Chattanooga		K-12		K-12	1147	•	$	4	P		13	•	NC	1042
GIRLS PREP	Chattanooga		6-12			600	••	$$	17			13	O		634
MCCALLIE	Chattanooga			9-12	6-12	889	••	$$	19			13	O	NC	635
NOTRE DAME HS-TN	Chattanooga		9-12		9-12	471	••	$	6	P		14	•	RC	1042
COLUMBIA ACAD	Columbia				PS-12	706	•	$	2			12	O	NC	1043
EVANGELICAL CHRIST	Cordova		PS-12		PS-12	1068	•	$$	10			12	O	Ev	1043
BATTLE GROUND	Franklin		K-12		K-12	886	••	$$	11			14	O		1044
SUMNER	Gallatin		PS-8		PS-8	212	•	$				6			1044
ST GEORGE'S SCH-TN	Germantown		PS-12		PS-12	1203	••	$$	14			14	•		636
POPE JOHN PAUL II	Hendersonville		9-12		9-12	615	••	$	16			16	O	RC	1044
U SCH OF JACKSON	Jackson		PS-12		PS-12	1180	•	$	13		•	10	O		636
EPISCOPAL KNOXVILLE	Knoxville		K-8		K-8	321	••	$$				8	O	Ep	1045
WEBB SCH KNOXVILLE	Knoxville		K-12		K-12	1047	••	$$	20			17	O		637
FRIENDSHIP CHRISTIAN	Lebanon		PS-12		PS-12	600	•	$	1			14	O	NC	1045
GRACE-ST LUKE'S	Memphis		PS-8		PS-8	510	••	$$	6			10	O	Ep	638
HARDING-MEMPHIS	Memphis		PS-12		PS-12	1475	••	$	6			13	O	NC	1046
HUTCHISON	Memphis		PS-12			894	••	$$	18			10	•		639
LAUSANNE	Memphis		PS-12		PS-12	809	••	$$	14		•	12	O		639
MEMPHIS U SCH	Memphis				7-12	660	••	$$	17			13	O		640
PRESBYTERIAN DAY	Memphis				PS-6	644	••	$$				13	O	P	641
ST MARY'S EPIS SCH	Memphis		PS-12			845	••	$$	15			10	O	Ep	641
WOODLAND PRESBY	Memphis		PS-8		PS-8	362	•	$		P		9	O	P	1046
MIDDLE TN CHRISTIAN	Murfreesboro		PS-12		PS-12	696	••	$	5			12		NC	1046
DAVID LIPSCOMB	Nashville		PS-12		PS-12	1386	••	$	4			13		NC	1047
ENSWORTH	Nashville		K-12		K-12	1045	••	$$$	20			15	O		642

	City		Grades	Grades	Enrollment		$		P						Code	Page
FR RYAN	Nashville		9-12	9-12	940	•	$$	21				16	•		RC	643
FRANKLIN RD	Nashville		PS-12	PS-12	800	••	$$	16				15	O		NC	1047
HARDING-NASHVILLE	Nashville		K-8	K-8	482	••	$$$	11				13	•			1048
HARPETH HALL	Nashville		5-12		645	••	$$$					11	O			644
MONTGOMERY BELL	Nashville		7-12		713	••	$$	23				14	O			644
OAK HILL SCH-TN	Nashville		PS-6	PS-6	513	••	$$		P			6	O		NC	1048
OVERBROOK	Nashville		PS-8	PS-8	331	••	$					6			RC	1048
ST CECILIA	Nashville		9-12	9-12	259	••	$$	14				11	•		RC	1049
U SCH OF NASHVILLE	Nashville		K-12	K-12	1039	••	$$	13				14	O			645
ST ANDREW'S-SEWANEE	Sewanee	9-12	6-12	6-12	255	••	$$	8		•		12	O		Ep	646
KING'S ACAD	Seymour	6-12^5	PS-12	6-12^5	455	•	$			•		9	O		SB	1049
		TEXAS														
GREENHILL-TX	Addison		PS-12	PS-12	1270	••	$$$	11				14	O			764
OAKRIDGE	Arlington		PS-12	PS-12	877	••	$$	18				14	O			762
AUSTIN INTL	Austin		PS-5	PS-5	150	•	$			•			O			1134
HYDE PARK	Austin		K-12	K-12	524	••	$$	14		•		10			B	1135
KIRBY HALL	Austin		PS-12	PS-12	105	••	$	8					O		NC	1135
REGENTS	Austin		K-12	K-12	900	••	$	3				10			NC	1136
ST STEPHEN'S EPIS-TX	Austin	8-12	6-12	6-12	665	••	$$			•		14	O		Ep	762
ALL SAINTS-BEAUMONT	Beaumont		PS-8	PS-8	396	••	$			•		8			Ep	1136
EPISCOPAL HS-TX	Bellaire		9-12	9-12	672	•	$$$	18				15	O		Ep	1136
ALLEN	Bryan		PS-12	PS-12	310	••	$	12		•		10	•			763
CARROLLTON CHRISTIAN	Carrollton		PS-12	PS-12	325	•	$	1	P			11			NC	1137
INCARNATE WORD-TX	Corpus Christi		PS-12	PS-12	889	••	$	11				11			RC	1137
ST JAMES EPISCOPAL	Corpus Christi		PS-8	PS-8	214	•	$					7	O		Ep	1138
ANN & NATE LEVINE	Dallas		PS-8	PS-8	400	•	$$			•		3			J	1138
DALLAS INTL	Dallas		PS-12	PS-12	600	••	$$					4	O			1138

School	Town	Girls' Grade Range Bdg	Girls' Grade Range Day	Boys' Grade Range Bdg	Boys' Grade Range Day	Enrollment	Selectivity	Tuition	AP Courses	Learning Disabilities	ESL	Varsity Sports	Summer	Religion	Page
TX															
DALLAS LUTHERAN	Dallas		7-12		7-12	200	•	$$	3			10		LMS	1139
EPISCOPAL SCH DALLAS	Dallas		PS-12		PS-12	1170	••	$$$	18			14	O	Ep	1139
FIRST BAPTIST ACAD	Dallas		PS-12		PS-12	285	••	$$	8	P		11	•	Ev	1139
HOCKADAY	Dallas	8-12	PS-12			1087	•••	$$	19			13	O		765
JESUIT COL PREP	Dallas				9-12	1040	••	$$	16		•	17	O	RC	765
LAKEHILL	Dallas		K-12		K-12	400	••	$$	13			10	O		1140
LAMPLIGHTER	Dallas		PS-4		PS-4	440	••	$$$					O		766
PARISH EPISCOPAL	Dallas		PS-12		PS-12	1150	••	$$$	17			13	O	Ep	1140
ST MARK'S SCH OF TX	Dallas				1-12	854	••	$$$	19			15	O		767
ST THOMAS AQUINAS-TX	Dallas		PS-8		PS-8	875	O	$		P		9	O	RC	1141
SHELTON	Dallas		PS-12		PS-12	853	••	$$$		F		10	O		1141
URSULINE ACAD DALLAS	Dallas		9-12			800	••	$$	19			12	•	RC	1141
WINSTON SCH-TX	Dallas		1-12		1-12	200	••	$$$		F		10	O		1142
SELWYN	Denton		PS-12		PS-12	178	••	$$	8	P		6	O		768
CANTERBURY EPISCOPAL	DeSoto		K-12		K-12	265	•	$$	10			9	O	Ep	1142
MARY IMMACULATE	Farmers Branch		K-8		K-8	510	••	$				11	O	RC	1143
FT WORTH ACAD	Fort Worth		K-8		K-8	240	••	$$				7	O		1143
FT WORTH CO DAY	Fort Worth		K-12		K-12	1110	••	$$	20			14	O		768
HOLY FAMILY CATHOLIC	Fort Worth		PS-8		PS-8	232	••	$				6	O	RC	1143
NOLAN	Fort Worth		9-12		9-12	956	••	$$	17			12	•	RC	1144
ST IGNATIUS-TX	Fort Worth		9-12		9-12	38	••	$					O	RC	1144
ST RITA	Fort Worth		PS-8		PS-8	200	O	$				6		RC	1144
TRINITY VALLEY	Fort Worth		K-12		K-12	960	••	$$	16			12	O		769
TRINITY EPIS SCH-TX	Galveston		PS-8		PS-8	200	•	$				4	O	Ep	1145
MARINE MILIT	Harlingen				8-PG	222	••	$	9		•	10	O		770

School	Town	Girls' Grade Range Bdg	Girls' Grade Range Day	Boys' Grade Range Bdg	Boys' Grade Range Day	Enrollment	Selectivity	Tuition	AP Courses	Learning Disabilities	ESL	Varsity Sports	Summer	Religion	Page
UTAH															
WASATCH	Mount Pleasant	7-12[5]	7-12	7-12[5]	7-12	250	••	$$	10	P	•	11	O		1169
PARK CITY DAY	Park City		PS-9		PS-9	175	•	$$				4	O		1169
REID	Salt Lake City		PS-9		PS-9	212	••	$			•		O		1170
ROWLAND HALL	Salt Lake City		PS-12		PS-12	1005	••	$$	15			10	O	Ep	800
WATERFORD	Sandy		PS-12		PS-12	900	••	$$	14			8	•		1170
VERMONT															
ROCK PT	Burlington	9-PG	9-PG	9-PG	9-PG	40	••	$$$		F	•			Ep	375
LONG TRAIL	Dorset	6-12	6-12	6-12	6-12	166	•	$$	8	P		6	O		375
LYNDON	Lyndon Center	9-12[5]	9-12	9-12[5]	9-12	600	••	$$	10		•	13	O		906
BURR & BURTON	Manchester	9-12	9-12	9-12	9-12	682	••	$$	10	P	•	12	O		906
GRAMMAR	Putney		PS-8		PS-8	119	••	$$				3	O		376
GREENWOOD	Putney			6-11	6-11	47	••	$$$		F	•	3	O		377
PUTNEY	Putney	9-12	9-12	9-12	9-12	220	•	$$	8		•	7	O		377
MT ST JOSEPH ACAD-VT	Rutland	9-12	9-12	9-12	9-12	95	•	$	6	P	•	9		RC	907
VT ACAD	Saxtons River	9-PG	9-PG	9-PG	9-PG	225	••	$$	9	P	•	15	O		379
RICE	South Burlington		9-PG		9-PG	370	•	$	8		•	14		RC	907
ST JOHNSBURY	St Johnsbury	9-PG	9-12	9-PG	9-12	889	•	$$	20	F	•	18	O		378
STRATTON MTN	Stratton Mountain	7-PG	7-12	7-PG	7-12	140	••	$$			•	5	O		908
MTN SCH	Vershire	11-11	11-11	11-11	11-11	45	••	$$	6						1228
VIRGINIA															
ALEXANDRIA CO DAY	Alexandria		K-8		K-8	228	••	$$$				6	O		1050
BISHOP IRETON	Alexandria		9-12		9-12	828	••	$$	14			16	O	RC	1050
BROWNE ACAD	Alexandria		PS-8		PS-8	300	••	$$$				3	O		1050
BURGUNDY FARM	Alexandria		PS-8		PS-8	288	•	$$$				6	O		648

School	City													
STUART HALL-VA	Staunton	8-12[5]	PS-12	PS-12	333	••	$	9		•	7		Ep	667
NANSEMOND-SUFFOLK	Suffolk		PS-12	PS-12	930	••	$$	17			14	O		668
ST MARGARET'S SCH	Tappahannock	8-12	8-12		123	•	$$$	9		•	10	O	Ep	669
WAKEFIELD	The Plains		PS-12	PS-12	432	•	$$$	15			10	O		660
GREEN HEDGES	Vienna		PS-8	PS-8	190	••	$$$				4	O		1061
CAPE HENRY	Virginia Beach		PS-12	PS-12	853	••	$$	14		•	15	O		669
TIDEWATER	Wakefield		PS-12	PS-12	227	••	$	4			7	O		1061
HIGHLAND-VA	Warrenton		PS-12	PS-12	480	••	$$$	15	P		12	O		670
FISHBURNE	Waynesboro		7-PG	7-PG	200	•	$				11	O		671
WALSINGHAM	Williamsburg		PS-12	PS-12	755	••	$	14			13	O	RC	1062
WILLIAMSBURG CHRIST	Williamsburg		PS-12	PS-12	265	•	$	9	P		8		NC	1062
WOODBERRY FOREST	Woodberry Forest			9-12	406	••	$$	13			13	O		672
MASSANUTTEN	Woodstock	7-PG	7-PG	7-PG	175	••	$	6		•	14	O	NC	673
WASHINGTON														
COLUMBIA ADVENTIST	Battle Ground		9-12	9-12	108	O	$	2			3		SA	1219
LITTLE SCH	Bellevue		PS-6	PS-6	165	••	$$					O		1219
SPRING ST INTL	Friday Harbor		6-12	6-12	76	•	$	7						1219
ST THOMAS SCH	Medina		PS-7	PS-7	284	••	$$$					O		1220
BEAR CREEK	Redmond		PS-12	PS-12	756	••	$$	10		•	8	O	NC	1220
OVERLAKE	Redmond		5-12	5-12	535	••	$$$	13			8			868
BERTSCHI	Seattle		PS-5	PS-5	235	••	$$		P			O		1221
BUSH	Seattle		K-12	K-12	575	••	$$$			•	11	O		868
EPIPHANY-WA	Seattle		PS-5	PS-5	233	••	$$							1221
HOLY NAMES ACAD	Seattle		9-12	9-12	675	••	$	13	P		13	O	RC	1221
JFK MEMORIAL	Seattle		9-12	9-12	865	••	$	3		•	13	•	RC	1222
LAKESIDE SCH	Seattle		5-12	5-12	796	•••	$$$				14	O		869
NORTHWEST SCH	Seattle	9-12	6-12	6-12	474	••	$$			•	6	O		870

School	Town	Girls' Bdg	Girls' Day	Boys' Bdg	Boys' Day	Enrollment	Selectivity	Tuition	AP Courses	Learning Disabilities	ESL	Varsity Sports	Summer	Religion	Page
WA															
SEATTLE CO DAY	Seattle		K-8		K-8	334	••	$$$				6			1222
SEATTLE PREP	Seattle		9-12		9-12	702	••	$$	5			13	•	RC	1223
SEATTLE WALDORF	Seattle		PS-12		PS-12	360	••	$$		P		9			1223
U PREP	Seattle		6-12		6-12	510	••	$$$				9			871
EVERGREEN SCH	Shoreline		PS-8		PS-8	455	••	$$$				7	O		1223
GONZAGA	Spokane		9-12		9-12	902	••	$	11			13		RC	1224
ST GEORGE'S SCH-WA	Spokane		K-12		K-12	381	••	$$	14			8	O		872
ANNIE WRIGHT	Tacoma	9-12[5]	PS-12		PS-8	441	••	$$			•	7	O	Ep	872
CHARLES WRIGHT	Tacoma		PS-12		PS-12	676	••	$$$	14			9			873
WEST VIRGINIA															
NOTRE DAME HS-WV	Clarksburg		7-12		7-12	149	••	$	10			10	•	RC	1062
COUNTRY DAY	Kearneysville		PS-8		PS-8	110	•	$					•		1063
LINSLY	Wheeling	7-12	5-12	7-12	5-12	444	••	$	10			13	O		674
WISCONSIN															
WAYLAND	Beaver Dam		9-12	9-12	9-12	220	••	$$	12		•	14			718
BROOKFIELD ACAD	Brookfield		PS-12		PS-12	884	•	$$	16			13	O		719
CATHOLIC CENTRAL-WI	Burlington		9-12		9-12	148	•	$	2			14	O	RC	1095
ST JOHN'S NORTHWEST	Delafield			7-PG	7-12	341	••	$	7		•	11	O	Ep	719
IMMANUEL LUTHERAN	Eau Claire	9-12	9-12	9-12	9-12	121	•	$				6		CLC	1096
NOTRE DAME BAIE	Green Bay		9-12		9-12	740	•	$$				12	•	RC	1096
U LAKE	Hartland		PS-12		PS-12	280	•	$	7			9	O		720
ARMITAGE	Kenosha		K-8		K-8	71	•	$							1097
LAKESIDE LUTHERAN	Lake Mills		9-12		9-12	424	•	$	2			10		L	1097
EDGEWOOD	Madison		9-12		9-12	650	•	$	12	P		13	•	RC	1097
MARQUETTE U HS	Milwaukee				9-12	1064	••	$	14			13	•	RC	1098

						$	8	P		12	•	LMS	1098
MILWAUKEE LUTHERAN	Milwaukee	9-12	9-12	622	••	$	8			12	•	LMS	1098
PIUS	Milwaukee	9-12	9-12	992	•	$	12	•		15	O	RC	1098
U SCH OF MILWAUKEE	Milwaukee	PS-12	PS-12	1058	••	$$$	16			14	O		721
ST LAWRENCE SEMINARY	Mount Calvary		9-12	196	••	$				7	O	RC	1099
PRAIRIE HILL	Pewaukee	PS-8	PS-8	160	O	$				3	O		1099
PRAIRIE SCH	Racine	PS-12	PS-12	694	•	$$	11		•	8	O		722
DOMINICAN HS-WI	Whitefish Bay	9-12	9-12	278	••	$	7			12	O	RC	1100
WYOMING													
JOURNEYS	Jackson	PS-12	PS-12	176	••	$$				11	O		1159

SCHOOLS WITH A SPECIAL FOCUS

ALTERNATIVE EDUCATION

ALTERNATIVE EDUCATION *(CONT.)*

ARTS

Interlochen .... Interlochen, MI...........699
    (Perform_Arts Visual_Arts Creative_Writing)

Am Boychoir...Princeton, NJ...........440
    (Perform_Arts)

Professional Child.. New York, NY...........491
    (Perform_Arts Visual_Arts)

St Thomas Choir .... New York, NY...........495
    (Perform_Arts)

Northwest Acad... Portland, OR.........1217
    (Perform_Arts Visual_Arts)

BILINGUAL

Ecole Bilingue-CA *(Fr)*...Berkeley, CA.........1174
San Diego Fr-Amer *(Fr)*... La Jolla, CA.........1182
Lycee Francais-LA *(Fr)*...Los Angeles, CA...........816
Lycee Intl-Los Angel *(Fr)*..Los Angeles, CA.........1186
Intl Sch Peninsula *(Chin Fr)*...Palo Alto, CA...........832
Chin Amer Intl *(Chin)*... San Francisco, CA.........1199
Intl HS *(Fr)* .... San Francisco, CA...........843
Wash Intl *(Dutch Fr Span)* ....Washington, DC...........393
Atlanta Intl *(Fr Ger Span)*...Atlanta, GA...........591
Fr Intl *(Fr)*... Bethesda, MD...........920
German Sch *(Ger)*...Potomac, MD...........928
Waring *(Fr)* ....Beverly, MA...........891
Solomon Schechter-WC *(Hebrew)* .... Hartsdale, NY...........949
Fr-Amer Sch *(Fr)* .... Larchmont, NY...........951
La Scuola d'Italia *(Ital)* .... New York, NY...........485
Lycee Francais-NYC *(Fr)*... New York, NY...........487
Lyceum Kennedy *(Fr)* .... New York, NY...........488
Solomon Schecht-NYC *(Hebrew)* .... New York, NY...........957
Intl Sch-OR *(Chin Japan Span)* .... Portland, OR.........1216
Fr-Amer Sch of RI *(Fr)* .... Providence, RI...........904
Austin Intl *(Fr Span)* ....Austin, TX.........1134
Dallas Intl *(Fr Span)*...Dallas, TX.........1138
Awty *(Arabic Fr Ger Ital Span)* ....Houston, TX...........771

INTERNATIONAL (IB), FRENCH (FB) AND FRENCH-AMERICAN (Fr-Am) BACCALAUREATE

Verde Valley *(IB)* ....Sedona, AZ...........792
Mt St Mary-AR *(IB)* ....Little Rock, AR.........1122
Fairmont *(IB)* .... Anaheim, CA.........1173
Lycee Francais-LA *(FB & Fr-Am_Bac)* .... Los Angeles, CA...........816
Lycee Intl-Los Angel *(IB)*.......................................Los Angeles, CA.........1186
Intl HS *(IB & FB)* .... San Francisco, CA...........843
Cheshire *(IB)*..Cheshire, CT...........239
Wilmington Friends *(IB)*...Wilmington, DE...........384
British Sch of Wash *(IB)*..Washington, DC...........911
Wash Intl *(IB)*..Washington, DC...........393
St Andrew's Sch-FL *(IB)* .... Boca Raton, FL...........568
North Broward Prep *(IB)* ....Coconut Creek, FL...........989
Carrollton Sch *(IB)* .... Miami, FL...........998
Gulliver *(IB)*..Coral Gables, FL...........577
Carrollwood *(IB)*... Tampa, FL.........1007
Cardinal Newman *(IB)*.....................................West Palm Beach, FL.........1010
Windermere Prep *(IB)*... Windermere, FL.........1010
Atlanta Intl *(IB)*... Atlanta, GA...........591
St Andrew's Sch-GA *(IB)* .... Savannah, GA.........1022
Mid-Pacific *(IB)* .... Honolulu, HI...........860
Trinity HS-IL *(IB)* ....River Forest, IL.........1072
Fr Intl *(FB)* .... Bethesda, MD...........920
St Paul's Sch-MD *(IB)* ....Brooklandville, MD...........405
St Timothy's *(IB)* ....Stevenson, MD...........421
Newman *(IB)*...Boston, MA...........892
Detroit Co Day *(IB)* .... Beverly Hills, MI...........696
Notre Dame Prep-MI *(IB)*.....................................Pontiac, MI.........1082
St John's Prep-MN *(IB)* .... Collegeville, MN...........727
New Hampton *(IB)* .... New Hampton, NH...........362
Newark Acad *(IB)* ....Livingston, NJ...........431
Armand Hammer *(IB)*..Montezuma, NM...........798
Brooklyn Friends *(IB)*...Brooklyn, NY...........457
Fr-Amer Sch *(FB)* .... Larchmont, NY...........951
Dwight Sch *(IB)*... New York, NY...........482
Lycee Francais-NYC *(FB & Fr-Am_Bac)*............................. New York, NY...........487
Lyceum Kennedy *(FB)* .... New York, NY...........488
UN Intl *(IB)*... New York, NY...........499
Charlotte Co Day *(IB)*..Charlotte, NC...........612
St Edward *(IB)* ....Lakewood, OH.........1092

LEARNING DISABILITIES AND UNDERACHIEVEMENT

LEARNING DISABILITIES
AND UNDERACHIEVEMENT *(CONT.)*

SPORTS

INDEXES OF SPECIAL INTEREST

SCHOOLS WITH COORDINATE SINGLE-GENDER PROGRAMS

BOARDING PROGRAMS BEGINNING IN GRADE 6 OR EARLIER

SCHOOLS WITH 25% OR MORE INTERNATIONAL STUDENTS

SCHOOLS WITH 25% OR MORE
INTERNATIONAL STUDENTS *(CONT.)*

SCHOOLS WITH 25% OR MORE
NONWHITE FACULTY

SCHOOLS WITH 25% OR MORE
NONWHITE FACULTY *(CONT.)*

Corlears *(31%)*	New York, NY	955
Manhattan Country *(43%)*	New York, NY	489
Metropolitan Mont *(36%)*	New York, NY	956
Philosophy Day *(29%)*	New York, NY	956
Town Sch-NY *(32%)*	New York, NY	497
Trinity-Pawling *(25%)*	Pawling, NY	502
Oak Ridge *(41%)*	Oak Ridge, NC	620
Old Trail *(39%)*	Bath, OH	701
Community Prep *(53%)*	Providence, RI	904
Incarnate Word-TX *(50%)*	Corpus Christi, TX	1137
Duchesne *(31%)*	Houston, TX	1146
Strake Jesuit *(25%)*	Houston, TX	1148
Trinity Sch-TX *(28%)*	Midland, TX	1150
Alexander Sch-TX *(43%)*	Richardson, TX	1150
TX Milit *(29%)*	San Antonio, TX	776
U Prep *(25%)*	Seattle, WA	871

SCHOOLS WITH 50% OR MORE
NONWHITE STUDENTS

St Mary's Catholic *(87%)*	Phoenix, AZ	1160
Southwestern-AZ *(60%)*	Rimrock, AZ	792
Fenster *(52%)*	Tucson, AZ	793
Ramona *(96%)*	Alhambra, CA	1171
Cornelia Connelly *(66%)*	Anaheim, CA	1172
Providence HS *(83%)*	Burbank, CA	1174
Army & Navy *(55%)*	Carlsbad, CA	802
Foothill Co Day *(58%)*	Claremont, CA	803
Hilldale *(55%)*	Daly City, CA	1177
St Lucy's *(61%)*	Glendora, CA	1180
Moreau *(78%)*	Hayward, CA	1180
Idyllwild *(62%)*	Idyllwild, CA	809
Damien *(60%)*	La Verne, CA	1183
Lutheran HS-CA *(52%)*	La Verne, CA	1183
Bishop Conaty *(99%)*	Los Angeles, CA	1185
Loyola HS-CA *(51%)*	Los Angeles, CA	1185
Notre Dame Acad-CA *(67%)*	Los Angeles, CA	1186
Sacred Heart HS-CA *(97%)*	Los Angeles, CA	1187
Bishop O'Dowd *(57%)*	Oakland, CA	1191
Holy Names HS *(73%)*	Oakland, CA	1191

SCHOOLS WITH 50% OR MORE
NONWHITE STUDENTS *(CONT.)*

LEADING PRIVATE SCHOOLS

These schools are presented together in the belief that they are of first interest to the readers of the Handbook. *They may be included because of their international and historical renown, because they command general respect of parents and educators, and also because our information discloses unique or significant aspects of their programs that are deserving of the reader's attention.*

New England States

CONNECTICUT

AVON, CT. (8 mi. WNW of Hartford, CT; 98 mi. NE of New York, NY) Suburban. Pop: 15,832. Alt: 201 ft.

AVON OLD FARMS SCHOOL
Bdg and Day — Boys Gr 9-PG

Avon, CT 06001. 500 Old Farms Rd. Tel: 860-673-3244, 800-464-2866.
Fax: 860-675-6051.
www.avonoldfarms.com   E-mail: admissions@avonoldfarms.com
Kenneth H. LaRocque, Head (1998). AB, EdM, Harvard Univ. **Brendon Welker, Adm.**
Col Prep. AP (exams req'd; 125 taken, 72% 3+)—Eng Fr Span Calc Stats Comp_ Sci Bio Environ_Sci Physics US_Hist World_Hist Econ US_Govt & Pol Studio_Art. **Feat**—Lat Forensic_Sci Geol WWI & WWII Intl_Relations Law Asian_Stud Philos Architect Ceramics Drawing Photog Theater Chorus Music Jazz_Band Public_Speak Woodworking. **Supp**—Tut. Sat classes.
Sports (req'd)—B: Baseball Basket X-country Football Golf Ice_Hockey Lacrosse Ski Soccer Squash Swim Tennis Track Wrestling. **Activities:** 45.
Selective adm: 150/yr. Bdg 115. Day 35. Appl fee: $50. Appl due: Jan. Accepted: 44%. Yield: 56%. **Tests** CEEB IQ SSAT TOEFL.
Enr 404. Bdg 305. Day 99. Sec 384. PG 20. Intl 13%. Avg class size: 12. Stud/fac: 6:1. Uniform. **Fac 56.** M 39/F 17. FT 49/PT 7. Adv deg: 50%. In dorms 20.
Grad '11—121. Col—121. (Johns Hopkins, Wake Forest, Northwestern, U of CT, U of San Diego, Yale). **Avg SAT:** CR 551. M 584. W 556. **Col couns:** 3.
Tui '11-'12: Bdg $46,650 (+$2800). **Day $35,300** (+$2800). **Aid:** Need 133 ($3,700,000).
Summer: Gr K-8. Rec. 6 wks.
Endow $35,000,000. Plant val $100,000,000. Acres 850. Bldgs 41. Dorms 7. Dorm rms 196. Class rms 51. Lib 24,000 vols. Sci labs 6. Lang labs 2. Dark rms 1. Auds 1. Theaters 1. Art studios 1. Music studios 8. Wood shops 1. Gyms 1. Fields 12. Courts 9. Rinks 1. Weight rms 1. Comp labs 3. Laptop prgm Gr 9-PG.
Est 1927. Nonprofit. Quar (Sept-May). **Assoc** CLS NEASC.

Theodate Pope Riddle designed and founded this architecturally unique school. Its location within 850 acres of forested land provides for a number of outdoor activities, including fishing, hiking, camping, biking and cross-country skiing.

The curriculum focuses on the development of writing, reading and mathematical skills. The academic courses are college preparatory, with electives provided in music, drama and the arts. Advanced Placement courses are available in every discipline, including computer science. Computer technology is an important aspect of school life; students have the option of purchasing a laptop computer through the school.

An enrichment hour each weekday evening provides opportunities for extra help. The day student program is unusual in that boys are strongly encouraged to take part in many boarding activities, including evening functions. In addition, the school assigns each pupil a campus job.

Every student participates in a sport or an alternate activity of his choice each season.

BERLIN, CT. (10 mi. SSW of Hartford, CT; 91 mi. NE of New York, NY) Suburban. Pop: 18,215. Alt: 64 ft. Area also includes Kensington.

MOORELAND HILL SCHOOL
Day — Coed Gr K-9

Kensington, CT 06037. 166 Lincoln St. Tel: 860-223-6428. Fax: 860-223-3318.
www.mooreland.org   E-mail: info@mooreland.org
Michael D. Dooman, Head (2006). BA, Drew Univ, MA, Trinity College (CT). **Kathryn J. West, Adm.**
Pre-Prep. Feat—Humanities Fr Lat Span Studio_Art Drama Music.
Sports (req'd)—Basket Soccer Tennis. B: Baseball. G: F_Hockey Softball.
Selective adm: 15/yr. Usual entry: 4, 5 & 6. Appl fee: $40. Appl due: Feb. **Tests** CTP_4 ISEE.
Enr 45. B 24. G 21. Wh 81%. Latino 2%. Blk 13%. Asian 2%. Other 2%. Avg class size: 8. Stud/fac: 5:1. **Fac 10.** M 4/F 6. FT 8/PT 2. Wh 100%. Adv deg: 30%.
Grad '11—7. Prep—7. (Avon 2, Miss Porter's 2, Loomis Chaffee 1, Miss Hall's 1, Salisbury-CT 1).
Tui '12-'13: Day $11,500-22,150. Aid: Need 16 ($125,480).
Endow $150,000. Plant val $2,000,000. Bldgs 5. Class rms 10. Libs 1. Sci labs 1. Photog labs 1. Auds 1. Art studios 1. Gyms 1. Fields 2. Basketball courts 1. Comp labs 1.
Est 1930. Nonprofit. Tri (Aug-June).

Founded as the Shuttle Meadow School by New Britain industrialist families, the school became Mooreland Hill in 1937, in gratitude for property donated by E. Allen Moore. Today, the school enrolls students from more than two dozen central Connecticut towns. The school structure features multi-age groupings in kindergarten and grade 1, grades 2 and 3, and grades 4 and 5, then individual grades thereafter.

The curriculum is traditional, with emphasis placed on English, literature, history, math and science. Complementing the basics are offerings in French, Spanish, Latin, humanities, art, music, and human growth and development. Mooreland Hill maintains small average class sizes, and the curriculum includes advanced-level courses in all major disciplines.

In addition to interscholastic athletics, the school offers such noncompetitive options as photography, hiking and life sports. Each pupil completes daily chores. Children in all grades participate in off-campus learning experiences, such as history and science trips to nearby cities; visits to local art museums, concerts and plays; and out-of-state class trips.

See Also Page 89

BETHLEHEM, CT. (28 mi. WSW of Hartford, CT; 77 mi. NNE of New York, NY) Rural. Pop: 3422. Alt: 880 ft.

THE WOODHALL SCHOOL
Bdg and Day — Boys Gr 9-12

Bethlehem, CT 06751. 58 Harrison Ln, PO Box 550. Tel: 203-266-7788.
Fax: 203-266-5896.
www.woodhallschool.org   E-mail: woodhallschool@woodhallschool.org
Matthew C. Woodhall, Head. BA, Vassar College, MA, Columbia Univ.
Col Prep. LD. Underachiever. AP (exams req'd; 22 taken)—Eng Calc Bio Chem Eur_ Hist US_Hist. **Feat**—Fr Greek Lat Span. **Supp**—Dev_Read ESL Makeup Rem_Math Rev Tut. Outdoor ed. Sat classes.
Sports—B: Basket X-country Lacrosse Soccer Wrestling. **Activities:** 8.
Selective adm (Gr 9-11): 15/yr. Bdg 15. Day 0. Appl fee: $100. Appl due: Rolling.

Accepted: 50%. Yield: 60%.
Enr 42. Wh 88%. Latino 5%. Blk 7%. Intl 5%. Avg class size: 4. Stud/fac: 4:1. **Fac 16.** M 12/F 4. FT 16. Wh 86%. Latino 7%. Asian 7%. Adv deg: 75%. In dorms 13.
Grad '11—8. Col—8. (Guilford, Eckerd, Northeastern U, Hartwick, U of VT, Wash Col). **Avg SAT:** CR 600. M 540. W 550.
Tui '12-'13: Bdg $59,500. Day $45,810.
Endow $100,000. Plant val $7,500,000. Acres 38. Bldgs 8. Dorms 2. Dorm rms 22. Class rms 15. Lib 3000 vols. Sci labs 2. Auds 1. Art studios 1. Gyms 1. Fields 1. Courts 2.
Est 1983. Nonprofit. Tri (Sept-June). **Assoc** NEASC.

Located on a 38-acre campus, the school enrolls boys who have not succeeded in traditional school environments. Woodhall accepts students of average to superior intellectual ability who have no serious emotional or behavioral problems and no chemical dependencies. Applicants may display one or more of the following characteristics: lack of motivation and low achievement; a mild learning disability; difficulty with reading, writing or math; poor concentration and attention; lack of self-confidence or poor self-esteem; long school absences due to illness; or school changes due to family mobility.

The school provides small classes within a core college preparatory or general secondary-level curriculum in English, math, social studies, science and foreign languages; remedial programs in language arts, reading, writing and math; and English as a Second Language instruction. The intensive academic program is integrated with proctored study periods, small study groups and an evening study hall.

Communications groups help students develop skills of self-expression, and a daily athletic program promotes physical fitness, sportsmanship and teamwork and includes interscholastic options. Each boy completes a compulsory service project every trimester. Woodhall conducts social and recreational activities and clubs on campus and in cooperation with nearby prep schools. Theater, concerts, and educational field trips to New Haven, Hartford and New York City complete the program.

CHESHIRE, CT. (21 mi. SSW of Hartford, CT; 79 mi. NE of New York, NY) Suburban. Pop: 28,543. Alt: 161 ft.

CHESHIRE ACADEMY

Bdg — Coed Gr 9-PG; Day — Coed 8-PG

Cheshire, CT 06410. 10 Main St. Tel: 203-272-5396. Fax: 203-250-7209.
www.cheshireacademy.org   E-mail: admissions@cheshireacademy.org
Gerald Larson, Int Head (2012). John Ettore, Adm.
Col Prep. IB Diploma. AP (exams req'd; 238 taken, 62% 3+)—Eng Fr Span Calc Stats Comp_Sci Bio Chem Physics Eur_Hist US_Hist Psych US_Govt & Pol Music_Theory.
Feat—Playwriting Chin Anat & Physiol Ecol Environ_Sci Web_Design Amer_Stud Econ Ceramics Fine_Arts Photog Sculpt Studio_Art Acting Chorus Public_Speak.
Supp—ESL Rev Tut. Sat classes.
Sports—Arch Basket X-country Fencing Golf Lacrosse Soccer Swim Tennis Track Ultimate_Frisbee. B: Baseball Football Wrestling. G: F_Hockey Softball Volley. **Activities:** 30.
Selective adm: 109/yr. Bdg 70. Day 39. Appl due: Feb. Accepted: 65%. Yield: 50%. **Tests** ISEE SSAT TOEFL.
Enr 368. Elem 30. Sec 325. PG 13. Wh 46%. Latino 5%. Blk 7%. Native Am 1%. Asian 34%. Other 7%. Intl 30%. Avg class size: 12. **Fac 70.** M 27/F 43. FT 66/PT 4. Wh 89%. Latino 4%. Blk 3%. Asian 2%. Other 2%. Adv deg: 68%. In dorms 26.
Grad '11—90. Col—90. (Carnegie Mellon 3, Sch of the Art Inst of Chicago 3, U of WA 3, Furman 2, Gettysburg 2, Dickinson 2). Athl schol 8. **Avg SAT:** CR 513. M 622. W 543. Avg ACT: 20.6. **Col couns:** 4.
Tui '12-'13: Bdg $44,900-46,900 (+$1500). **Day $27,860-33,320** (+$800-1000). **Aid:**

Need 120 ($2,000,000).
Summer (enr 90): Acad Enrich. Tui Bdg $5295. Tui Day $3995. 4 wks.
Endow $7,405,000. Plant val $30,000,000. Acres 104. Bldgs 20. Dorms 6. Dorm rms 90. Class rms 43. Lib 17,000 vols. Comp ctrs 1. Auds 1. Theaters 1. Art studios 2. Music studios 1. Gyms 2. Fields 7. Tennis courts 10. Pools 1. Comp labs 2.
Est 1794. Nonprofit. Sem (Aug-June). **Assoc** NEASC.

Founded as a coeducational community school, Cheshire Academy was established as the Episcopal Academy of Connecticut. In the mid-1800s, it became a boys' boarding school and, during the Civil War, adopted a military program. In the early 1900s, it gave up its military program and religious affiliation; renamed the Roxbury School, it then served as a preparatory school for Yale and other comparable institutions. In 1937, the school assumed its present name. It returned to coeducation in 1969.

The school offers small classes and supervision of each student's progress, supplemented by one-on-one instruction where advisable. The traditional upper school curriculum includes Advanced Placement and honors courses, as well as programs in the fine arts, technology, study skills and SAT preparation. Since 2010, Cheshire has offered the two-year International Baccalaureate Diploma Program to upperclassmen. Independent study can be arranged by department heads in grades 9-PG, and semester-long study abroad opportunities are also available to qualified pupils. Upper schoolers perform 10 hours of required community service each year.

DANBURY, CT. (48 mi. WSW of Hartford, CT; 56 mi. NNE of New York, NY) Suburban. Pop: 74,848. Alt: 378 ft.

WOOSTER SCHOOL
Day — Coed Gr PS (Age 3)-12

Danbury, CT 06810. 91 Miry Brook Rd. Tel: 203-830-3900. Fax: 203-790-7147.
    www.woosterschool.org   E-mail: admissions@woosterschool.org
Timothy B. Golding, Head (2007). BA, Haverford College, MA, Villanova Univ. **Tad Jacks, Adm.**
    Col Prep. AP (exams req'd)—Eng Fr Span Calc Stats Comp_Sci Bio Chem Physics Eur_Hist US_Hist Econ Studio_Art Music_Theory. **Elem math**—Singapore Math. **Feat**—Lat Russ Marine_Bio/Sci Engineering Pol_Sci Psych Ethics World_Relig Ceramics Photog Sculpt Chorus Music Study_Skills. **Supp**—ESL Tut. Outdoor ed.
    Sports—Basket X-country Lacrosse Soccer Tennis. B: Baseball Softball. G: Volley.
    Selective adm: 75/yr. Appl fee: $50. Appl due: Feb. Accepted: 50%. Yield: 55%. **Tests** ISEE SSAT.
    Enr 335. B 170. G 165. Elem 210. Sec 125. Wh 81%. Latino 6%. Blk 4%. Asian 3%. Other 6%. Intl 5%. Avg class size: 15. Casual. **Fac 78.** M 29/F 49. FT 46/PT 32. Wh 86%. Latino 2%. Blk 2%. Asian 2%. Other 8%. Adv deg: 48%.
    Grad '11—45. Col—45. (Tufts 3, Bates 1, U of CT 1, NYU 1, Skidmore 1). **Avg SAT:** CR 618. M 601. Alum donors: 28%.
    Tui '12-'13: Day $17,850-31,200 (+$100-600). **Aid:** Need 105 ($1,900,000).
    Summer (enr 500): Gr PS-9. Acad Enrich Rec. Sports. Tui Day $500/2-wk ses. 6 wks.
    Endow $4,700,000. Plant val $24,000,000. Acres 100. Bldgs 15. Libs 2. Sci labs 3. Theaters 1. Art studios 5. Music studios 3. Drama studios 1. Gyms 3. Fields 5. Courts 2. Pools 1. Comp labs 2.
    Est 1926. Nonprofit. Episcopal. Sem (Sept-June). **Assoc** CLS NEASC.

Since its founding, Wooster has sought academic excellence and a diverse student body, while emphasizing community responsibility and spiritual growth. The college preparatory curriculum provides a grounding in the basics of liberal education, while offering enough flexibility for individual interests. Special programs include Advanced Placement, a year abroad in

France or Spain, independent study for seniors, individualized college guidance, and extensive fine arts and music offerings.

Students may participate in such extracurricular activities as team sports, music, art and publications. All pupils, under the direction of the senior class, are accountable for the daily maintenance of the campus. Boys and girls satisfy the following community service requirements: 15 hours in grade 6, 7 or 8, then 100 cumulative hours in grades 9-12.

FAIRFIELD, CT. (48 mi. NE of New York, NY; 53 mi. SW of Hartford, CT) Suburban. Pop: 57,340. Alt: 25 ft.

FAIRFIELD COLLEGE PREPARATORY SCHOOL
Day — Boys Gr 9-12

Fairfield, CT 06824. 1073 N Benson Rd. Tel: 203-254-4200. Fax: 203-254-4108.
www.fairfieldprep.org E-mail: gmarshall@fairfieldprep.org
Rev. John J. Hanwell, SJ, Pres (2006). BA, Boston College, MA, Middlebury College, MA, MDiv, Weston School of Theology. **Robert A. Perrotta, Prin.** JD, Univ of Connecticut, EdD, Fordham Univ. **Gregory H. Marshall, Adm.**
  Col Prep. AP—Eng Fr Lat Span Calc Bio Chem Physics US_Hist US_Govt & Pol. **Feat**—Shakespeare African-Amer_Lit Environ_Sci Computers Middle_Eastern_Hist Sociol Asian_Stud Theol Architect_Drawing Drawing Studio_Art Acting Drama Band Drafting. **Supp**—Tut. **Dual enr:** Fairfield.
  Sports—B: Baseball Basket Bowl X-country Football Golf Ice_Hockey Lacrosse Rugby Ski Soccer Swim Tennis Track Wrestling. **Activities:** 34.
  Selective adm (Gr 9-11): 250/yr. Usual entry: 9. Appl fee: $60. Applied: 500. Accepted: 50%. Yield: 70%. **Tests** HSPT.
  Enr 900. Wh 81%. Latino 6%. Blk 5%. Asian 3%. Other 5%. Avg class size: 21. Formal. **Fac 70.** M 46/F 24. FT 68/PT 2. Adv deg: 61%.
  Grad '11—195. Col—194. (Fairfield, U of CT, Fordham, Boston Col, Holy Cross, Providence). **Avg SAT:** CR 578. M 589. W 580. **Mid 50% SAT:** CR 510-630. M 530-640. W 510-640. Avg ACT: 24.9. Mid 50% ACT: 21-29. **Col couns:** 2.
  Tui '11-'12: Day $16,400 (+$500-875). **Aid:** Need 225 ($2,100,000).
  Summer: Acad Enrich Rev Rem. 4 wks.
  Endow $9,000,000. Acres 200. Bldgs 4 (100% ADA). Sci labs 4. Auds 1. Theaters 2. Art studios 2. Music studios 1. Gyms 1. Fields 5. Courts 7. Pools 1. Comp labs 4.
  Est 1942. Nonprofit. Roman Catholic (80% practice). Sem (Aug-June). **Assoc** NEASC.

Situated on a 200-acre campus, this Jesuit-directed school offers a college preparatory program. Freshmen must complete a computer literacy course, and all students take part in a four-year developmental service program, working within the church and the community. Community service requirements are as follows: 20 hours of service in grade 10, 30 hours in grade 11, and weekly service work in grade 12.

FAIRFIELD COUNTRY DAY SCHOOL
Day — Boys Gr PS (Age 4)-9

Fairfield, CT 06824. 2970 Bronson Rd. Tel: 203-259-2723. Fax: 203-259-3249.
www.fairfieldcountryday.org E-mail: admissions@fcdsmail.org
John R. Munro, Jr., Head (2010). BA, Hamilton College, MALS, Wesleyan Univ. **Richard Runkel, Adm.**
  Pre-Prep. Feat—Fr Lat Span Computers Studio_Art Chorus Music Study_Skills. **Supp**—Rem_Math Rem_Read Tut.
  Sports (req'd)—B: Baseball Basket X-country Football Ice_Hockey Lacrosse Soccer Squash.

Selective adm (Gr PS-8): 53/yr. Usual entry: PS, K, 1, 4 & 6. Appl fee: $50. Appl due: Rolling. Applied: 95. **Tests** ISEE SSAT.
Enr 253. Elem 241. Sec 12. Wh 90%. Latino 3%. Blk 3%. Asian 4%. Avg class size: 14. Stud/fac: 6:1. Formal. **Fac 43.** M 16/F 27. FT 41/PT 2. Adv deg: 58%.
Grad '11—20. Prep—16. (Fairfield Col Prep 4, Salisbury-CT 2, Hopkins 2, Taft 1, St Paul's Sch-NH 1, St George's Sch-RI 1).
Tui '12-'13: Day $30,500-32,700. Aid: Need 32 ($645,800).
Summer: Coed. Enrich Rec. Tui Day $410/wk. 8 wks.
Endow $6,372,000. Plant val $12,947,000. Bldgs 4. Class rms 20. Lib 10,200 vols. Sci labs 3. Lang labs 1. Gyms 1. Fields 5. Courts 2. Rinks 1. Laptop prgm Gr 6-9.
Est 1936. Nonprofit. Tri (Sept-June).

FCDS' academic program emphasizes the mastery of core subjects and the development of critical-thinking and problem-solving skills. Computer instruction is an integral part of the program. Extracurricular activities and a broad-based athletic program complement class work.

THE UNQUOWA SCHOOL
Day — Coed Gr PS (Age 3)-8

Fairfield, CT 06825. 981 Stratfield Rd. Tel: 203-336-3801. Fax: 203-336-3479.
www.unquowa.org   E-mail: suellen.hansen@unquowa.org
Sharon Lauer, Head (2004). BS, Millersville Univ of Pennsylvania. **Suellen Hansen, Adm.**
Pre-Prep. Gen Acad. Feat—Span Environ_Sci Computers Studio_Art Drama Music.
Sports—Basket Lacrosse Soccer Tennis. G: F_Hockey.
Selective adm: 50/yr. Appl fee: $60. Appl due: Rolling. Applied: 105. Accepted: 84%. Yield: 57%. **Tests** ISEE.
Enr 178. B 73. G 105. Wh 80%. Latino 2%. Blk 7%. Asian 7%. Other 4%. Avg class size: 12. Stud/fac: 5:1. Uniform. **Fac 34.** M 3/F 31. Wh 95%. Blk 3%. Asian 2%. Adv deg: 52%.
Grad '11—26. Prep—18. (Hopkins 6, Acad of Our Lady of Mercy 4, Fairfield Col Prep 2, King Low Heywood Thomas 1, St Luke's Sch-CT 1).
Tui '12-'13: Day $23,750-25,850. Aid: Need 42 ($552,000).
Summer: Acad Rec. Farm Camp. Art. Yoga. Tui Day $100-300. 1-4 wks.
Endow $325,000. Plant val $3,500,000. Acres 5. Bldgs 1. Class rms 20. Lib 10,000 vols. Sci labs 1. Comp ctrs 1. Art studios 1. Music studios 2. Gyms 1. Fields 1. Comp labs 3.
Est 1917. Nonprofit. Tri (Sept-June).

Situated on a five-acre tract bordering the London and Horse Tavern brooks, Unquowa conducts a traditional liberal arts curriculum that follows a progressive approach. Academic offerings center around a problem-solving approach within the major disciplines. Fine arts and foreign language classes begin in early childhood. The schoolwide ecology program features a regional, seasonal dining component. Boys and girls engage in daily physical education at all grade levels, and upper schoolers may participate in interscholastic sports. High school placement services begin toward the end of grade 7.

FARMINGTON, CT. (8 mi. WSW of Hartford, CT; 93 mi. NE of New York, NY) Suburban. Pop: 23,641. Alt: 245 ft.

MISS PORTER'S SCHOOL
Bdg and Day — Girls Gr 9-12

Farmington, CT 06032. 60 Main St. Tel: 860-409-3530. Fax: 860-409-3531.

www.porters.org   E-mail: admission@missporters.org
Katherine G. Windsor, Head (2008). BA, Univ of Rochester, MA, College of Notre Dame of Maryland, EdD, Univ of Pennsylvania. **Elizabeth Schmitt, Adm.**
Col Prep. AP (exams req'd; 296 taken, 92% 3+)—Chin Fr Lat Span Calc Stats Comp_ Sci Bio Chem Environ_Sci Physics Eur_Hist US_Hist Art_Hist Studio_Art Music_ Theory. **Feat**—Creative_Writing Anat & Physiol Forensic_Sci Marine_Bio/Sci Engineering Neuroanatomy Comp_Design African_Hist Lat-Amer_Hist Middle_Eastern_ Hist Modern_Chin_Hist Modern_Japan_Hist Amer_Stud Econ Intl_Relations Psych Ethics World_Relig Photog Printmaking Theater Music Dance Journ Public_Speak. **Supp**—Tut.
Sports—G: Badminton Basket Crew X-country Equestrian F_Hockey Golf Lacrosse Ski Soccer Softball Squash Swim Tennis Track Ultimate_Frisbee Volley. **Activities:** 45.
Selective adm (Bdg Gr 9-12; Day 9-11): 107/yr. Bdg 70. Day 37. Appl fee: $50. Appl due: Jan. Applied: 456. Accepted: 43%. Yield: 54%. **Tests** ISEE SSAT TOEFL.
Enr 333. Bdg 223. Day 110. Intl 13%. Avg class size: 11. Stud/fac: 8:1. Casual. **Fac 52.** M 20/F 32. FT 39/PT 13. Adv deg: 63%.
Grad '11—87. Col—87. (Hobart/Wm Smith 6, Northeastern U 4, Cornell 3, Gettysburg 3, Yale 3, U of PA 2). Athl schol 1. **Avg SAT:** CR 627. M 636. W 633. **Mid 50% SAT:** CR 570-680. M 580-700. W 580-680. **Avg ACT:** 27.4. Mid 50% ACT: 25-30. **Col couns:** 3. Alum donors: 42%.
Tui '11-'12: Bdg $46,650 (+$1925). **Day $36,850** (+$1415). **Aid:** Need 127 ($3,540,000).
Summer: Acad Rec. Leadership. 2 wks.
Endow $100,000,000. Plant val $55,000,000. Acres 50. Bldgs 56. Dorms 8. Dorm rms 106. Class rms 37. Lib 22,100 vols. Sci labs 5. Lang labs 1. Auds 1. Theaters 1. Art studios 5. Music studios 5. Dance studios 1. Gyms 2. Fields 4. Courts 15. Comp labs 6.
Est 1843. Nonprofit. Sem (Sept-May). **Assoc** CLS NEASC.

Sarah Porter, sister of onetime Yale president Noah Porter, founded this school that bears her name. The school's 19th-century curriculum emphasized traditional values and service to others, offering a curriculum that included Latin, French and German languages, plus reading, spelling, arithmetic, trigonometry, history and geography. Because Sarah Porter believed in women receiving educations equal to those available to men, the program also featured chemistry, physiology, botany, geology and astronomy, as well as arts and music instruction.

After Sarah Porter's death in 1900, management of the school remained in the hands of her nephew, Robert Porter Keep, and his wife. From 1917 to 1943, under the leadership of Robert Porter Keep, Jr., the school increasingly emphasized college preparation. Miss Porter's was incorporated as a nonprofit institution in 1943.

Today, the school conducts a rigorous liberal arts curriculum that emphasizes collaboration, connections among disciplines, and both critical and creative thinking. Honors and Advanced Placement courses are offered in all departments, and many electives are also available. Campus art studios provide girls with opportunities in photography, painting, sculpture, printmaking, jewelry making and graphic design. Athletics are an area of emphasis: Girls must play a sport each season and must also pass a swimming test prior to graduation.

Students at all levels can engage in independent study. Juniors may spend a school year abroad. All girls complete an experiential education requirement: an intensive, focused experience for at least 80 hours in successive weeks of summer, winter or spring break. Options include professional internships, community service projects and cultural and language immersion. Girls entering as freshmen or sophomores perform 20 hours of cumulative community service; those entering as juniors or seniors contribute 10 hours during their time at Porter's.

See Also Page 87

GREENWICH, CT. (30 mi. NNE of New York, NY) Urban. Pop: 61,010. Alt: 28 ft.

BRUNSWICK SCHOOL
Day — Boys Gr PS (Age 4)-12

Greenwich, CT 06830. 100 Maher Ave. Tel: 203-625-5843. Fax: 203-625-5863.
  www.brunswickschool.org   E-mail: gina_hurd@brunswickschool.org
Thomas W. Philip, Head (2001). BA, Bucknell Univ, MA, Wesleyan Univ. **Gina Hurd, Adm.**
  Col Prep. AP (exams req'd; 458 taken, 96% 3+)—Chin Fr Lat Span Calc Stats Comp_ Sci Bio Chem Environ_Sci Physics Eur_Hist US_Hist Econ Human_Geog Psych US_Govt & Pol Art_Hist Studio_Art. **Feat**—Creative_Writing Shakespeare African-Amer_Lit Ital Arabic Astron Oceanog Physiol Animal_Behavior Lat-Amer_Hist Milit_Hist Vietnam_War Law Ethics Philos Photog Drama Music. **Supp**—Dev_Read Rem_Math Rem_Read Rev.
  Sports (req'd)—B: Baseball Basket Crew X-country Fencing Football Golf Ice_Hockey Lacrosse Soccer Squash Tennis W_Polo Wrestling.
  Very selective adm: 124/yr. Usual entry: PS, K, 5, 6, 9 & 10. Appl fee: $75. Appl due: Dec. Applied: 527. Accepted: 23%. Yield: 91%. **Tests** CEEB CTP_4 IQ ISEE SSAT.
  Enr 940. Elem 584. Sec 356. Wh 81%. Latino 4%. Blk 5%. Asian 4%. Other 6%. Avg class size: 15. Stud/fac: 5:1. Formal. **Fac 166.** M 80/F 86. FT 166. Wh 90%. Latino 2%. Blk 3%. Asian 3%. Other 2%. Adv deg: 65%.
  Grad '11—78. Col—78. (Georgetown 7, Duke 6, U of VA 6, U of PA 4, Yale 3, Dartmouth 3). **Avg SAT:** CR 660. M 668. W 660.
  Tui '12-'13: Day $27,300-35,700 (+$750). **Aid:** Need 85 ($2,000,000).
  Summer: Acad Enrich Rev. Tui Day $2500. 4 wks.
  Endow $83,000,000. Plant val $76,000,000. Acres 118. Bldgs 10. Class rms 35. 3 Libs 19,000 vols. Sci labs 8. Lang labs 2. Auds 3. Art studios 3. Music studios 2. Shops 1. Gyms 4. Fields 4. Rinks 1. Comp labs 4. Laptop prgm Gr 9-12.
  Est 1902. Nonprofit. Sem (Sept-June). **Assoc** CLS NEASC.

Founded and directed for 30 years by George E. Carmichael, this school is divided into lower, middle and upper divisions. In the upper school, the majority of classes are conducted on a coordinate basis with Greenwich Academy, a neighboring girls' school. The rigorous college preparatory program provides honors and Advanced Placement courses in every subject and a comprehensive arts curriculum.

All students take part in the athletic program, through either intramural or interscholastic competition. Every boy in grades 9-12 also participates in a class community service project. Computer instruction is integrated into the curriculum at all grade levels, and upper school students lease wireless-equipped laptops for use in the classroom and at home.

CONVENT OF THE SACRED HEART
Day — Girls Gr PS (Age 3)-12

Greenwich, CT 06831. 1177 King St. Tel: 203-531-6500. Fax: 203-531-5206.
  www.cshgreenwich.org   E-mail: admission@cshgreenwich.org
Pamela Juan Hayes, Head (2009). BA, Briarcliffe College, MAT, Manhattanville College **Catherine Cullinane, Adm.**
  Col Prep. AP (exams req'd)—Eng Chin Fr Lat Span Calc Stats Comp_Sci Bio Chem Environ_Sci Physics Eur_Hist US_Hist Comp_Govt & Pol Econ Psych Art_Hist Studio_Art. **Feat**—Creative_Writing Shakespeare African-Amer_Lit Arabic Multivariable_Calc Astron Web_Design Ethics Theol Drawing Photog Sculpt Drama Chorus Music_Theory Orchestra Journ Speech. **Supp**—Rev Tut.
  Sports—G: Basket Crew X-country F_Hockey Golf Lacrosse Soccer Softball Squash Swim Tennis Volley. **Activities:** 50.
  Selective adm (Gr PS-10): Appl fee: $50. Appl due: Feb. **Tests** CTP_4 ISEE SSAT.

Enr 769. Elem 484. Sec 285. Avg class size: 13. Uniform. **Fac 113.** Adv deg: 80%.
Grad '11—79. Col—79. (Georgetown 6, Holy Cross 3, Bucknell 3, Duke 3, NYU 3, Villanova 3). **Col couns:** 2. Alum donors: 30%.
Tui '12-'13: Day $28,300-34,500 (+$300-1750). **Aid:** Need 138 ($2,500,000).
Summer: Enrich. 2-3 wks.
Endow $28,588,000. Plant val $22,900,000. Acres 118. Bldgs 10. Class rms 45. Chapels 1. Sci labs 7. Observatories 1. Theaters 1. Art studios 2. Music studios 3. Dance studios 1. Art galleries 1. Photog studios 1. Gyms 1. Fields 5. Courts 6. Pools 1. Student ctrs 2. Comp labs 3. Comp/stud: 1:1 Laptop prgm Gr 5-12.
Est 1848. Nonprofit. Roman Catholic (75% practice). Tri (Sept-June). **Assoc** CLS NEASC.

Founded in New York City, the school moved to its 118-acre Greenwich campus in 1945. Sacred Heart integrates a rigorous academic program, the foundation of a strong faith, and the development of social responsibility. The curriculum emphasizes advanced course work and independent study; honors and AP courses are offered. Religious education begins in the lower school and includes prayer services, liturgies, retreats and other campus ministry programs. Students are evaluated for their work with various community agencies.

An exchange program for girls in the middle and upper schools is conducted with other Sacred Heart schools in the United States and abroad. Various academic, community and social activities involving local boys' high schools, such as dances, sports and dramatic arts, complement the extracurricular program. All girls participate in at least one extracurricular activity each year. Community service begins informally in the earliest grades, and each upper school student performs 25 hours of compulsory service per year.

Sacred Heart conducts two distinct summer programs: one offering enrichment and recreational options to inner-city youth (for a nominal fee), the other providing enrichment for CSH pupils and their siblings. **See Also Pages 98-9**

GREENWICH ACADEMY

Day — Girls Gr PS (Age 4)-12

Greenwich, CT 06830. 200 N Maple Ave. Tel: 203-625-8900. Fax: 203-625-8912.
Other locations: 16 Ridgeview Ave, Greenwich 06830.
www.greenwichacademy.org E-mail: admission@greenwichacademy.org
Molly H. King, Head (2004). BA, Bowdoin College, EdM, Harvard Univ. **Abby S. Katz, Adm.**
Col Prep. AP (419 exams taken, 98% 3+)—Fr Lat Span Calc Stats Comp_Sci Bio Chem Environ_Sci Physics Eur_Hist US_Hist World_Hist Econ Human_Geog Psych US_Govt & Pol Art_Hist Studio_Art Music_Theory. **Elem math**—Singapore Math.
　　Feat—Creative_Writing Chin Ital Arabic Astron Geol Oceanog Physiol Comp_Graphics Film Theater Chorus Music Dance.
Sports—Basket Crew X-country F_Hockey Golf Ice_Hockey Lacrosse Sail Soccer Softball Squash Swim Tennis Track Volley.
Selective adm (Gr PS-11): 106/yr. Usual entry: PS, K, 5, 6, 9 & 10. Appl fee: $75. Appl due: Dec. Applied: 352. Accepted: 38%. Yield: 79%. **Tests** CTP_4 ISEE SSAT.
Enr 804. Elem 457. Sec 347. Avg class size: 13. Stud/fac: 7:1. Uniform. **Fac 121.** M 29/F 92. FT 111/PT 10. Wh 85%. Latino 6%. Blk 5%. Asian 2%. Other 2%. Adv deg: 75%.
Grad '11—80. Col—80. (Yale 7, Dartmouth 5, Duke 4, Georgetown 4, Princeton 4, Bucknell 4). Athl schol 1. **Avg SAT:** CR 679. M 669. W 698. **Mid 50% SAT:** CR 620-730. M 610-730. W 670-770. Avg ACT: 29. **Col couns:** 3. Alum donors: 33%.
Tui '12-'13: Day $30,700-36,050 (+$100-1800). **Aid:** Need 92 ($2,722,685).
Summer: Enrich. 3-10 wks.
Endow $75,000,000. Plant val $85,960,000. Acres 39. Bldgs 12. Class rms 84. 3 Libs 29,500 vols. Sci labs 9. Lang labs 1. Auds 2. Theaters 2. Art studios 6. Music studios 4. Dance studios 2. Perf arts ctrs 1. Art galleries 1. Gyms 2. Athletic ctrs 1. Fields 4. Tennis courts 6. Squash courts 5. Comp labs 2. Laptop prgm Gr 7-12.
Est 1827. Nonprofit. Quar (Sept-June). **Assoc** CLS NEASC.

Located on a 39-acre campus, Greenwich Academy is a traditional girls' school with a structured liberal arts curriculum. Clearly defined requirements in English, mathematics, history, language arts and science are supplemented by a wide range of electives offered both at GA and through coordination with neighboring Brunswick School for boys. Honors and Advanced Placement courses are available in most disciplines; in addition, the use of laptop computers leased from the school is required in grades 7-12. Classes and projects in the arts are central to the curriculum, with choices in the performing and visual arts.

Interscholastic athletic competition begins in grade 7 with a variety of individual and team sports. All students are encouraged to perform community service. GA's coordinated program with Brunswick provides not only coeducational classes, but also many joint music, drama, art and community service projects.

The Ridgeview Avenue campus accommodates preschool and kindergarten children.

GREENWICH COUNTRY DAY SCHOOL
Day — Coed Gr PS (Age 3)-9

Greenwich, CT 06836. 401 Old Church Rd, PO Box 623. Tel: 203-863-5600.
Fax: 203-622-6046.
www.gcds.net   E-mail: admission@gcds.net
Adam C. Rohdie, Head (2004). BA, Wesleyan Univ, MA, Stanford Univ. **Kirby Williams, Adm.**
Pre-Prep. Gen Acad. Feat—Chin Fr Lat Span Computers Visual_Arts Band Chorus. Supp—Dev_Read Rem_Read Tut.
Sports (req'd)—Basket Crew X-country Golf Ice_Hockey Lacrosse Soccer Squash Swim Tennis. B: Baseball Football Wrestling. G: F_Hockey Softball.
Selective adm (Gr PS-8): 115/yr. Usual entry: PS, K, 5 & 6. Appl fee: $75. Appl due: Dec. Applied: 503. Accepted: 26%. Yield: 88%. **Tests** CEEB CTP_4 ISEE.
Enr 873. Elem 820. Sec 53. Wh 89%. Latino 2%. Blk 5%. Asian 3%. Other 1%. Avg class size: 18. Stud/fac: 9:1. **Fac 127.** M 39/F 88. FT 127. Wh 88%. Latino 7%. Blk 3%. Asian 2%. Adv deg: 37%.
Grad '10—53. Prep—53. (Deerfield Acad, Greenwich Acad, Brunswick, Rye Co Day, Choate, Westminster Acad).
Tui '11-'12: Day $24,600-31,800. Aid: Need 71 ($1,584,250).
Summer (enr 300): Rec. Tui Day $1100-2700. 3-6 wks.
Endow $41,276,000. Plant val $102,981,000. Acres 84. Bldgs 29. Class rms 54. 3 Libs 20,000 vols. Sci labs 3. Auds 3. Art studios 2. Music studios 7. Gyms 4. Fields 8. Tennis courts 4. Pools 2. Rinks 1. Comp labs 3. Comp/stud: 1:3 (1:1 Laptop prgm Gr 7-9).
Est 1926. Nonprofit. Tri (Sept-June).

GCDS emphasizes academic preparation while maintaining a varied extracurricular and artistic program. English, math, science and social studies are required at all grade levels, with a conversational Spanish language program and computer education both beginning in kindergarten. Beginning in grade 6, students choose from Spanish, French, Latin, or Mandarin. Art and choral music are offered, and the school has two full bands, piano, drama, and print and wood shops. The regular program also includes two- to five-day trips for students in grades 5-9 to such places as Mystic; Washington, DC; and outdoor education centers in New Jersey and New York State.

Upper school students (grades 7-9) purchase required tablet computers through the school. Athletics are required, combining physical education with interscholastic competition in the upper school. Dance, ice hockey and physical fitness balance a standard competitive program. Community service is stressed, with students serving both on campus and in community agencies and institutions. Students complete five hours of required service in grade 7 and 10 hours in grade 8.

WHITBY SCHOOL
Day — Coed Gr PS (Age 2)-8

Greenwich, CT 06831. 969 Lake Ave. Tel: 203-869-8464. Fax: 203-869-2215.
www.whitbyschool.org   E-mail: info@whitbyschool.org
Barbara Brent, Int Co-Head (2011). BA, Rollins College, MS, College of New Rochelle.
Nelyda Miguel, Int Co-Head. MA, MEd, Columbia Univ, MA, Fairfield Univ. **Nadia Meier, Adm.**
Pre-Prep. Montessori. IB PYP. IB MYP. Feat—Chin Fr Span Computers Studio_Art Drama Band Music Dance. **Supp**—Dev_Read Rem_Math Rem_Read Rev Tut.
Sports—Basket X-country Soccer Tennis. B: Baseball. G: Softball.
Selective adm: 85/yr. Appl fee: $75. Appl due: Rolling. Accepted: 65%. Yield: 95%. **Tests** CTP_4 ISEE.
Enr 404. Intl 12%. Avg class size: 20. Stud/fac: 6:1. Uniform. **Fac 76.** M 12/F 64. FT 71/PT 5. Adv deg: 46%.
Grad '11—17. Prep—13. (Greens Farms, Greenwich Acad, Ethel Walker, Masters Sch-NY, Hackley, Stanwich).
Tui '12-'13: Day $29,750-31,000 (+$650-1650). **Aid:** Need 55 ($507,419).
Summer (enr 85): Acad Enrich Rev Rem Rec. Tui Day $270-1200. 1-3 wks.
Endow $630,000. Plant val $11,140,000. Acres 25. Bldgs 4. Class rms 20. Lib 4000 vols. Art studios 1. Music studios 1. Gyms 1. Fields 3. Tennis courts 2. Comp labs 1.
Est 1958. Nonprofit. Tri (Sept-June).

The oldest Montessori school in the country, Whitby continues to follow the fundamental principles of this educational method while also incorporating International Baccalaureate curricular elements. The school's multi-age approach allows students to stay with the same teacher for two to three years, thus enabling the instructor to follow each child's progress through an entire developmental cycle. The primary (ages 3-6) and lower school (grades 1-4) divisions follow the IB Primary Years Program, while the middle school curriculum (grades 5-8) utilizes the IB Middle Years Program. The transdisciplinary IB programs emphasize holistic learning, intercultural awareness and communicational skills.

The sharing of values and the development of a sense of community are integral parts of school life. The 25-acre campus, located in the backcountry of Greenwich, has its own pond, woods and playing fields. Students enroll from Fairfield and Westchester counties.

HARTFORD, CT. (65 mi. W of Providence, RI; 100 mi. NE of New York, NY) Urban. Pop: 121,578. Alt: 38 ft. Area also includes West Hartford.

KINGSWOOD OXFORD SCHOOL
Day — Coed Gr 6-12

West Hartford, CT 06119. 170 Kingswood Rd. Tel: 860-727-5000. Fax: 860-236-3651.
www.kingswoodoxford.org   E-mail: admission@k-o.org
Dennis Bisgaard, Head (2006). BA, MA, Univ of Southern Denmark, MEd, Columbia Univ.
James E. O'Donnell, Adm.
Col Prep. AP (exams req'd; 372 taken, 80% 3+)—Eng Fr Lat Span Calc Stats Comp_ Sci Bio Chem Physics US_Hist Econ US_Govt & Pol Art_Hist. **Feat**—Creative_Writing Shakespeare African-Amer_Lit Women's_Lit Chin Marine_Bio/Sci Robotics Chin & Japan_Hist Anthro Philos Relig Photog Studio_Art Theater_Arts Music Journ. **Supp**—Tut.
Sports (req'd)—Basket X-country Ice_Hockey Lacrosse Ski Soccer Squash Swim Tennis Track. B: Baseball Football Golf. G: F_Hockey Softball Volley. **Activities:** 50.
Selective adm (Gr 6-11): 114/yr. Usual entry: 6 & 9. Appl fee: $55. Appl due: Feb. Applied: 319. Accepted: 57%. Yield: 59%. **Tests** IQ SSAT.
Enr 497. B 247. G 250. Elem 150. Sec 347. Wh 86%. Latino 2%. Blk 6%. Asian 4%. Other 2%. Avg class size: 13. Stud/fac: 7:1. **Fac 69.** M 30/F 39. FT 66/PT 3. Wh 95%. Latino

4%. Asian 1%. Adv deg: 44%.
Grad '11—98. Col—98. (Union Col-NY 4, U of CT 4, Tufts 3, Skidmore 3, Boston U 3, Syracuse 3). **Avg SAT:** CR 616. M 601. W 622. Avg ACT: 25. **Col couns:** 2. Alum donors: 18%.
Tui '11-'12: Day $32,771 (+$775-1300). **Aid:** Merit 31 ($225,000). Need 172 ($2,700,000).
Endow $25,700,000. Plant val $16,598,000. Acres 30. Bldgs 9. Class rms 41. 2 Libs 35,000 vols. Sci labs 11. Comp ctrs 1. Auds 1. Theaters 1. Art studios 5. Music studios 5. Dance studios 1. Gyms 3. Athletic ctrs 1. Fields 8. Squash courts 4. Rinks 1. Comp labs 4.
Est 1909. Nonprofit. Sem (Sept-June). **Assoc** CLS NEASC.

KO is the result of the 1969 merger of Kingswood School for boys and Oxford School for girls. In fall 2003, the middle school (grades 6-8) moved from the former Oxford campus to the main, 30-acre former Kingswood campus, where the upper school (grades 9-12) has long been located. The student body represents a cross section of central Connecticut residents in their religious, social and economic backgrounds.

Offering a college preparatory program, the school maintains small classes and close contact between students and faculty. The well-rounded curriculum, which includes course work in English, history, math, science, foreign language, computer science, and the performing and visual arts, culminates in a wide selection of Advanced Placement classes. Independent study is encouraged.

All pupils in grades 9-12 satisfy a 30-hour community service requirement prior to graduation. Seniors compose a required thesis during the third quarter of the academic year, and they may also pursue an on- or off-campus project during the last quarter.

RENBROOK SCHOOL

Day — Coed Gr PS (Age 3)-9

West Hartford, CT 06117. 2865 Albany Ave. Tel: 860-236-1661. Fax: 860-231-8206.
   www.renbrook.org   E-mail: admission@renbrook.org
Armistead C. G. Webster, Head (2010). BA, Princeton Univ, MA, New York Univ, PhD, Univ of Colorado-Boulder. **Amy L. Clemons, Adm.**
Pre-Prep. Elem math—Everyday Math. **Feat**—Lib_Skills Fr Lat Span Computers Studio_Art Band Chorus Music Study_Skills.
Sports—Basket Ice_Hockey Lacrosse Ski Soccer Squash Tennis. B: Football. G: F_ Hockey Gymnastics Softball.
Selective adm: 82/yr. Appl fee: $50. Appl due: Feb. Applied: 156. Accepted: 78%. Yield: 67%.
Enr 435. B 223. G 212. Elem 404. Sec 31. Wh 72%. Blk 10%. Other 18%. Stud/fac: 6:1. **Fac 72.** M 19/F 53. FT 57/PT 15. Wh 97%. Blk 3%. Adv deg: 62%.
Grad '11—27. Prep—25. (Loomis Chaffee 5, Westminster Sch-CT 2, Miss Porter's 2, Hotchkiss 2, Northwest Catholic 2, Taft 1). Alum donors: 12%.
Tui '12-'13: Day $18,700-30,750 (+$75-600). **Aid:** Need 94 ($1,950,228).
Summer (enr 899): Enrich Rec. Tui Day $885-2575. 3-6 wks.
Endow $11,186,000. Plant val $24,801,000. Acres 75. Bldgs 11 (90% ADA). Class rms 65. Lib 33,000 vols. Sci labs 5. Math ctrs 1. Auds 2. Theaters 2. Art studios 4. Music studios 6. Gyms 2. Fields 4. Courts 3. Pools 3. Ropes crses 2. Playgrounds 4. Ponds 1. Comp labs 5.
Est 1935. Nonprofit. (Sept-June).

Located on the 75-acre Rentschler estate, Renbrook comprises three divisions: the beginning (beginners, junior kindergarten and kindergarten), lower (grades 1-5) and upper (grades 6-9) schools.

At all grade levels, children study science, math, library studies, music, art and physical education. The school's curriculum includes 10 years of French and Spanish, social studies, technology, learning strategies and lab science; Latin is part of the program in grades 6-9.

Honors courses, independent study options, service learning opportunities and leadership classes complete the curriculum.

The 12-year physical education program includes four years of interscholastic sports. Pupils in grades 4-9 participate in Project Adventure, an on-campus high and low ropes course. Renbrook also offers extended-day services, an after-school program, vacation care and a summer day camp.

WATKINSON SCHOOL

Day — Coed Gr 6-PG

Hartford, CT 06105. 180 Bloomfield Ave. Tel: 860-236-5618. Fax: 860-233-8295.
www.watkinson.org   E-mail: info@watkinson.org
John W. Bracker, Head (1999). BA, Haverford College, MEd, Harvard Univ. **John J. Crosson, Adm.**
> **Col Prep. Feat**—ASL Fr Span Anat & Physiol Zoology Global_Stud Ceramics Photog Sculpt Studio_Art Music Debate. **Supp**—Dev_Read LD Makeup Rev Tut. **Dual enr:** U of Hartford.
> **Sports**—Basket Crew X-country Golf Lacrosse Soccer Tennis Track Ultimate_Frisbee. B: Baseball. G: Softball Volley. **Activities:** 35.
> **Selective adm:** 71/yr. Appl fee: $50. Appl due: Feb. Applied: 147. Accepted: 43%. Yield: 66%. **Tests** ISEE SSAT.
> **Enr 247.** B 138. G 109. Elem 83. Sec 161. PG 3. Wh 64%. Latino 10%. Blk 8%. Native Am 1%. Asian 5%. Other 12%. Avg class size: 11. Stud/fac: 6:1. Casual. **Fac 45.** M 13/F 32. FT 43/PT 2. Wh 95%. Latino 1%. Blk 4%. Adv deg: 71%.
> **Grad '11—43. Col—41.** (High Pt 2, McDaniel 2, Mitchell 2, U of VT 2, Lynn 2). **Avg SAT:** CR 582. M 553. W 554. Avg ACT: 26. **Col couns:** 1. Alum donors: 4%.
> **Tui '12-'13: Day $34,125** (+$500). **Aid:** Need 75 ($1,343,150).
> **Summer (enr 28):** Acad Enrich Rev Rem. Tui Day $45-58/hr. 6 wks.
> Endow $3,539,000. Plant val $13,900,000. Acres 40. Bldgs 10 (25% ADA). Class rms 26. Lib 8000 vols. Sci labs 2. Auds 1. Theaters 1. Art studios 3. Music studios 1. Dance studios 1. Gyms 1. Fields 2. Courts 4. Comp labs 3. Comp/stud: 1:2.5.
> **Est 1881.** Nonprofit. Tri (Sept-June). **Assoc** NEASC.

The school, established through the liberal bequest of David Watkinson, occupies 40 rural Hartford acres, 10 minutes from downtown and the state capitol. The campus includes a performing arts and athletic center that houses an indoor amphitheater where daily school meetings are held. The core college preparatory curriculum is enhanced by programs in writing, learning skills, global studies, creative arts, computers and community service. The creative arts and global studies programs culminate in a special diploma for preprofessional students.

Closely affiliated with the neighboring University of Hartford, with which it shares many cooperative programs, Watkinson provides access to the resources of a large university, as well as the opportunity for seniors to graduate with college credits. The Academy at Watkinson (the school's postgraduate program) bridges secondary school and college.

KENT, CT. (41 mi. W of Hartford, CT; 77 mi. NNE of New York, NY) Suburban. Pop: 2858. Alt: 395 ft.

KENT SCHOOL

Bdg and Day — Coed Gr 9-PG

Kent, CT 06757. 1 Macedonia Rd, PO Box 2006. Tel: 860-927-6111, 800-538-5368. Fax: 860-927-6109.
www.kent-school.edu   E-mail: admissions@kent-school.edu

Rev. Richardson W. Schell, Head (1980). AB, Harvard Univ, MDiv, Yale Univ. **Kathryn F. Sullivan, Adm.**

Col Prep. AP (exams req'd; 477 taken)—Eng Fr Ger Lat Span Calc Stats Comp_Sci Bio Chem Environ_Sci Physics Eur_Hist US_Hist Econ Psych US_Govt & Pol Art_ Hist Studio_Art. **Feat**—Poetry Playwriting Chin Greek Astron Genetics Geol Sports_ Med Biotech Meteorology African-Amer_Hist Civil_War Philos World_Relig Architect Ceramics Photog Sculpt Acting Music_Theory. **Supp**—ESL. Sat classes.

Sports—Basket Crew X-country Equestrian Golf Ice_Hockey Lacrosse Soccer Squash Swim Tennis. B: Baseball Football. G: F_Hockey Softball. **Activities:** 36.

Selective adm: 165/yr. Bdg 155. Day 10. Appl fee: $65. Appl due: Jan. Accepted: 47%. Yield: 46%. **Tests** CEEB SSAT TOEFL.

Enr 565. B 311. G 254. Bdg 515. Day 50. Sec 550. PG 15. Nonwhite 13%. Intl 18%. Avg class size: 12. Stud/fac: 8:1. Formal. **Fac 66.** M 40/F 26. FT 66. Adv deg: 71%. In dorms 30.

Grad '09—164. Col—164. (Geo Wash 6, Boston U 5, St Lawrence 4, Trinity Col-CT 4, Col of Charleston 4, Boston Col 3). **Avg SAT:** CR/M 1240. **Col couns:** 4.

Tui '12-'13: Bdg $49,500 (+$3000). **Day** $39,000 (+$2700). **Aid:** Need 187 ($6,200,000).

Endow $78,300,000. Plant val $87,000,000. Acres 1200. Bldgs 16. Dorms 6. Dorm rms 241. Class rms 46. Lib 57,000 vols. Sci labs 12. Lang labs 7. Sci ctrs 1. Observatories 1. Auds 2. Art studios 3. Music studios 8. Dance studios 1. Gyms 2. Fields 18. Squash courts 3. Field houses 1. Pools 1. Rinks 1. Riding rings 6. Stables 1. Weight rms 1. Rowing ctrs 1. Comp labs 2. Comp/stud: 1:1 Laptop prgm Gr 9-PG.

Est 1906. Nonprofit. Episcopal. Tri (Sept-June). **Assoc** CLS NEASC.

Kent has been characterized since its founding by simplicity, self-reliance and directness of purpose. Rev. Frederick H. Sill, a man of extraordinary genius and vigor, started the school in a small farm building. He developed the Kent plan of self-help, still in practice today, whereby students participate in a daily work program.

Kent became coeducational in 1960, when it opened a campus for girls near its boys' campus. After operating for more than 30 years on two campuses, Kent consolidated its operations on one campus in 1992. The school facilities include St. Joseph's Chapel, a fine Norman chapel—complete with bell tower and cloister—at the center of the campus.

The school has a rigorous liberal arts program with Advanced Placement courses in every discipline—including computer science, environmental science and economics—and provides a course in study skills for all freshmen. The classics program includes Greek and Latin language study and an emphasis on classical literature and mythology.

THE MARVELWOOD SCHOOL

Bdg and Day — Coed Gr 9-PG

Kent, CT 06757. 476 Skiff Mountain Rd, PO Box 3001. Tel: 860-927-0047, 800-440-9107. Fax: 860-927-0021.

www.marvelwood.org   E-mail: admissions@marvelwood.org

Arthur F. Goodearl, Jr., Head (2011). AB, Harvard Univ, MALS, Wesleyan Univ. **Katherine Almquist, Adm.**

Col Prep. LD. Underachiever. AP (exams req'd)—Calc Stats Chem Eur_Hist US_Hist. **Feat**—Creative_Writing Shakespeare Fr Lat Span Anat & Physiol Ecol Environ_Sci Ethology Limnology Ornithology Comp_Sci Asian_Hist Psych Comp_Relig Art_Hist Ceramics Filmmaking Photog Studio_Art Drama Directing Music Public_Speak. **Supp**—ESL Rem_Math Rev Tut. Sat classes.

Sports (req'd)—Basket X-country Golf Ski Soccer Tennis Ultimate_Frisbee. B: Baseball Lacrosse Wrestling. G: Softball Volley.

Selective adm: 65/yr. Bdg 63. Day 2. Appl fee: $50. Appl due: Rolling. Accepted: 80%. **Tests** CEEB SSAT TOEFL.

Enr 169. B 112. G 57. Bdg 152. Day 17. Intl 19%. Avg class size: 11. Stud/fac: 4:1. Uniform. **Fac 52.** M 25/F 27. Adv deg: 48%. In dorms 16.

Grad '08—41. Col—40. (Purdue 3, Pace 2, Syracuse 1, SUNY-Binghamton 1, Boston U

1, U of IL-Urbana 1). **Col couns:** 2.
Tui '12-'13: Bdg $48,200 (+$1250). **Day $31,500** (+$1250). **Aid:** Need 42 ($540,000).
Summer: Acad Enrich Rem. Tui Bdg $5600 (+$600). Tui Day $2000 (+$300). 4 wks.
Endow $1,422,000. Plant val $10,000,000. Acres 83. Bldgs 17. Dorms 4. Dorm rms 92.
Class rms 25. Lib 8500 vols. Labs 3. Theaters 1. Art studios 2. Music studios 1. Wood
shops 1. Gyms 1. Fields 5. Courts 6. Comp/stud: 1:16.9.
Est 1956. Nonprofit. Tri (Sept-June). **Assoc** NEASC.

Marvelwood was founded by Robert A. Bodkin especially to help youngsters of average to above-average intelligence who have not lived up to academic potential in traditional school settings.

The college preparatory curriculum is sensitive to the individual who needs a structured program in order to fully realize his or her potential. One-quarter of the student body participates in a tutorial program designed to improve reading, writing, organizational and study skills. An extensive interscholastic sports program and many outdoor activities are offered. Graduates attend many different colleges.

In addition to a full range of competitive team sports, Marvelwood offers a year-round Wilderness Ways program that provides experiences in hiking, cross-country skiing, canoeing and mountain biking. All students participate in a weekly community service program.

LAKEVILLE, CT. (41 mi. WNW of Hartford, CT; 93 mi. NNE of New York, NY) Rural. Pop: 1800. Alt: 800 ft.

THE HOTCHKISS SCHOOL
Bdg and Day — Coed Gr 9-PG

Lakeville, CT 06039. 11 Interlaken Rd, PO Box 800. Tel: 860-435-3102.
Fax: 860-435-0042.
www.hotchkiss.org E-mail: admission@hotchkiss.org
Malcolm H. McKenzie, Head (2006). BA, Univ of Cape Town (South Africa), MA, Oxford
Univ (England), MA, Lancaster Univ (England). **Jane Reynolds, Adm.**
Col Prep. AP (630 exams taken)—Eng Chin Fr Ger Lat Span Calc Stats Comp_Sci Bio
Chem Environ_Sci Physics Eur_Hist US_Hist Comp_Govt & Pol Econ Human_Geog
Art_Hist Studio_Art Music_Theory. **Feat**—Creative_Writing Humanities Shakespeare
African-Amer_Lit Irish_Lit Native_Amer_Lit Victorian_Lit Greek Russ Linear_Algebra
Multivariable_Calc Number_Theory Astron Bioethics Ecol Forensic_Sci Limnology
Organic_Chem Neuroanatomy Robotics Web_Design Holocaust Middle_Eastern_
Hist Amer_Stud Comp_Relig Ethics Philos Architect Ceramics Photog Video_Pro-
duction Printmaking Acting Directing Jazz_Hist Ballet Dance Public_Speak. **Supp**—
Rev Tut. Sat classes.
Sports—Basket X-country Golf Ice_Hockey Lacrosse Sail Soccer Squash Swim Tennis
Track Ultimate_Frisbee. B: Baseball Football Wrestling. G: F_Hockey Softball Volley
W_Polo. **Activities:** 65.
Very selective adm: 193/yr. Bdg 183. Day 10. Appl fee: $50-65. Appl due: Jan. Applied:
1869. Accepted: 18%. Yield: 56%. **Tests** CEEB ISEE SSAT TOEFL.
Enr 597. B 300. G 297. Bdg 555. Day 42. Sec 580. PG 17. Wh 59%. Latino 4%. Blk 10%.
Asian 16%. Other 11%. Intl 13%. Avg class size: 12. Stud/fac: 5:1. Formal. **Fac 129.**
M 74/F 55. FT 117/PT 12. Wh 90%. Latino 1%. Blk 3%. Asian 5%. Other 1%. Adv deg:
75%. In dorms 39.
Grad '10—169. Col—169. (NYU 7, Dartmouth 6, U of PA 6, Columbia 5, Princeton 5,
Colgate 5). **Avg SAT:** CR 655. M 680. W 660. **Col couns:** 4.
Tui '12-'13: Bdg $47,950 (+$850). **Day $40,750** (+$850). **Aid:** Need 199 ($7,331,223).
Summer: Ages 12-15. Acad. Music. Environ Sci. Tui Bdg $4000. 3 wks.
Endow $358,000,000. Plant val $335,000,000. Acres 815. Bldgs 86. Dorms 12. Dorm
rms 521. Class rms 37. Lib 95,000 vols. Sci labs 13. Lang labs 1. Photog labs 1.
Dark rms 5. Comp ctrs 1. Auds 2. Theaters 2. Art studios 7. Music studios 25. Dance

studios 1. Arts ctrs 1. Art galleries 1. Fields 14. Tennis courts 19. Squash courts 8. Field houses 1. Pools 1. Rinks 2. Tracks 2. Fitness ctrs 1. Golf crses 1. Comp labs 2. Comp/stud: 1:1 Laptop prgm Gr 9-11.
Est 1891. Nonprofit. Sem (Sept-June). **Assoc** CLS NEASC.

At the urging of Yale University president Timothy Dwight, the school was founded by Maria Harrison Bissell Hotchkiss, who provided the land, the original buildings and the money for additional buildings. Originally intended to prepare young men for enrollment at Yale, in 1974 Hotchkiss became a coeducational school.

The curriculum includes both required and elective courses in English, mathematics, history, modern and classical languages, science and the arts, and additional elective courses in such fields as computer science, philosophy and religion. All departments offer electives, independent study and advanced courses at the AP level and beyond. Students may qualify for a classics diploma by completing extensive formal and independent work in Greek and Latin. Lectures, concerts and exhibits enrich the program. Affiliations with the English-Speaking Union, Round Square and the School Year Abroad program encourage foreign study experiences. A summer arts program in Italy offers intensive study in music and the visual arts.

A wide selection of interest clubs, student publications, community service organizations, and music and performance ensembles form the extracurricular program. Interscholastic, intramural and club sports are offered. Weekend activities include Saturday morning classes and afternoon athletic competitions, ski trips to nearby summits, visits to museums and performances in New York City and master classes conducted by visiting artists.

See Also Pages 122-3

INDIAN MOUNTAIN SCHOOL

Bdg — Coed Gr 6-9; Day — Coed PS (Age 4)-9

Lakeville, CT 06039. 211 Indian Mountain Rd. Tel: 860-435-0871. Fax: 860-435-1380.
Other locations: 204 Interlaken Rd, Lakeville 06039.
    www.indianmountain.org   E-mail: mimi_babcock@indianmountain.org
Mark A. Devey, Head (2006). BA, Univ of North Carolina-Chapel Hill, MEd, Columbia Univ.
Mimi Babcock, Adm.
Pre-Prep. Feat—Humanities Chin Lat Span Computers Film Photog Studio_Art Drama Music. **Supp**—Dev_Read ESL Tut.
Sports (req'd)—Basket X-country Lacrosse Ski Soccer Squash Tennis. B: Baseball Football Ice_Hockey. G: Softball Volley.
Selective adm: 65/yr. Bdg 37. Day 28. Appl due: Rolling. Accepted: 50%. Yield: 65%.
Tests IQ TOEFL.
Enr 246. B 135. G 111. Bdg 75. Day 171. Wh 73%. Latino 8%. Blk 5%. Asian 11%. Other 3%. Intl 17%. Avg class size: 10. Stud/fac: 4:1. Formal. **Fac 73.** M 30/F 43. FT 51/PT 22. Wh 98%. Blk 1%. Asian 1%. Adv deg: 41%. In dorms 9.
Grad '11—42. **Prep**—42. (Hotchkiss, Salisbury-CT, Millbrook, Berkshire Sch, Westminster Sch-CT, St George's Sch-RI).
Tui '11-'12: Bdg $46,250 (+$2500). **Day $15,650-24,400** (+$1500). **Aid:** Need 48 ($477,335).
Summer: Enrich. Art. Film. 2 wks.
Endow $5,000,000. Plant val $20,000,000. Acres 650. Bldgs 12. Dorms 4. Dorm rms 42. Class rms 33. Lib 10,000 vols. Sci labs 3. Sci/art ctrs 1. Comp ctrs 2. Auds 1. Theaters 1. Art studios 4. Music studios 5. Gyms 2. Fields 9. Tennis courts 3. Ropes crses 1. Skiing facilities. Comp labs 2.
Est 1922. Nonprofit. Tri (Sept-June).

Founded as a boarding school for boys by Francis Behn Riggs, a Groton graduate and friend of Dr. Endicott Peabody, Indian Mountain has maintained high academic standards over the years. Girls, long admitted as day students, were first accepted into the boarding program in 1991. In 2003, IMS effected a merger with the Town Hill School, a nearby elementary school that dates back to 1938, thereby expanding the day program from prekindergarten through grade 9. The program for children in grades pre-K-4 operates at the 10-acre Town Hill campus on Interlaken Road.

The curriculum is traditional, with strong emphasis placed on verbal and written skills and disciplined study habits. Curricular offerings include earth science and biology, a two-year American history course for seventh and eighth graders, and weekly computer instruction for pupils in grades 7-9. Special-help classes are held four times a week to reinforce classroom work. Students' effort and attitude are evaluated every two weeks and are discussed with their faculty advisors. IMS also operates a learning skills center that provides supportive, remedial and English as a Second Language tutoring.

The school's 600-acre main campus, which includes ponds, marshes and woodland, provides opportunities for exploration and outdoor education. The outdoor program features a ropes course.

LITCHFIELD, CT. (26 mi. W of Hartford, CT; 84 mi. NNE of New York, NY) Suburban. Pop: 8316. Alt: 956 ft.

FORMAN SCHOOL
Bdg and Day — Coed Gr 9-PG

Litchfield, CT 06759. 12 Norfolk Rd, PO Box 80. Tel: 860-567-8712. Fax: 860-567-8317.
www.formanschool.org   E-mail: admissions@formanschool.org
Adam K. Man, Head (2008). BA, Bard College at Simon's Rock, MA, Univ of New Hampshire. Sara Lynn Leavenworth, Adm.
Col Prep. LD. Feat—ASL Fr Span Graphic_Arts Photog Studio_Art Visual_Arts. Supp—Dev_Read ESL Rem_Math Rem_Read Tut. Sat classes.
Sports (req'd)—Basket X-country Ice_Hockey Lacrosse Ski Soccer Tennis Ultimate_Frisbee. B: Baseball Football Wrestling. G: Equestrian Golf Volley.
Selective adm: 56/yr. Appl fee: $50. Appl due: Rolling. Accepted: 40%. Yield: 71%. Tests IQ.
Enr 173. Bdg 151. Day 22. Wh 90%. Latino 1%. Blk 7%. Native Am 1%. Asian 1%. Intl 8%. Avg class size: 8. Stud/fac: 3:1. Casual. Fac 56.
Grad '08—41. Col—41. (Lynn, Curry, Hofstra, Colby-Sawyer, Roger Williams, New England Col). Avg SAT: CR/M 850. Col couns: 4. Alum donors: 5%.
Tui '12-'13: Bdg $61,700. Day $50,400. Aid: Need 42 ($1,000,000).
Endow $3,500,000. Plant val $20,200,000. Acres 104. Bldgs 26. Dorms 12. Class rms 25. Lib 6000 vols. Sci labs 2. Auds 1. Art studios 1. Music studios 1. Arts ctrs 1. Art galleries 1. Gyms 1. Fields 4. Courts 6. Comp labs 1.
Est 1930. Nonprofit. Tri (Sept-June). Assoc NEASC.

The school was founded by John N. Forman as a school for young boys who would benefit from close personal attention. An upper school was added in 1935, and a girls' school was incorporated in 1942 under the direction of Mrs. Forman.

Serving pupils with learning differences, the school offers a college preparatory curriculum with a wide variety of courses. Language and math training programs are specifically designed to help students with learning differences.

MIDDLEBURY, CT. (28 mi. SW of Hartford, CT; 73 mi. NE of New York, NY) Suburban. Pop: 6451.

WESTOVER SCHOOL
Bdg and Day — Girls Gr 9-12

Middlebury, CT 06762. 1237 Whittemore Rd, PO Box 847. Tel: 203-758-2423.
Fax: 203-577-4588.
www.westoverschool.org   E-mail: admission@westoverschool.org
Ann S. Pollina, Head (1997). BA, Fordham Univ, MA, New York Univ. Laura Volovski, Adm.

Col Prep. AP (exams req'd; 159 taken)—Eng Fr Lat Span Calc Stats Comp_Sci Bio Chem Environ_Sci Physics Eur_Hist US_Hist US_Govt & Pol Art_Hist Studio_Art Music_Theory. **Feat**—Poetry Shakespeare Etymology Chin Astron Genetics Geol Ornithology Robotics Boston_Hist WWII Psych Ceramics Drawing Photog Video_ Production Drama Dance Journ. **Supp**—ESL Tut. Outdoor ed.

Sports—G: Basket X-country F_Hockey Golf Lacrosse Soccer Softball Squash Swim Tennis Volley. **Activities:** 24.

Selective adm (Gr 9-11): 63/yr. Bdg 40. Day 23. Appl fee: $50. Appl due: Feb. Applied: 247. Accepted: 44%. Yield: 58%. **Tests** ISEE SSAT TOEFL.

Enr 212. Bdg 133. Day 79. Wh 74%. Latino 5%. Blk 6%. Asian 10%. Other 5%. Intl 18%. Avg class size: 12. Stud/fac: 8:1. **Fac 37.** M 14/F 23. FT 23/PT 14. Wh 95%. Asian 5%. Adv deg: 78%. In dorms 1.

Grad '10—50. Col—50. (Dickinson 3, Boston Col 2, Middlebury 2, NYU 2, Occidental 1, Yale 1). **Mid 50% SAT:** CR 540-630. M 540-650. W 550-710. Mid 50% ACT: 24-29. Alum donors: 45%.

Tui '11-'12: Bdg $45,500 (+$2000). **Day $32,500** (+$1500). **Aid:** Need 98 ($2,550,000).

Summer: Gr 7-9. Acad Enrich. Arts. Tui Bdg $800-1400. 1-2 wks.

Endow $38,100,000. Plant val $31,000,000. Acres 145. Bldgs 11. Dorms 1. Dorm rms 71. Class rms 30. Lib 18,000 vols. Sci labs 3. Lang labs 1. Auds 1. Theaters 1. Art studios 3. Music studios 5. Dance studios 3. Gyms 2. Fields 2. Courts 21. Comp labs 2.

Est 1909. Nonprofit. Tri (Sept-June). **Assoc** NEASC.

Established by Mary Robbins Hillard, formerly a principal at a local day school, with the assistance of her friend Theodate Pope Riddle, Connecticut's first female architect, Westover offers a college preparatory curriculum with a wide selection of electives and Advanced Placement courses. Visiting speakers complement the academic program. Girls perform at least four hours of community service annually.

A special cocurricular program, Women in Science and Engineering (WISE), is conducted in conjunction with Rensselaer Polytechnic Institute in Troy, NY. Girls who display an aptitude for and an interest in science and math may participate in this program. WISE combines the traditional Westover curriculum with additional math and science courses that meet primarily on Saturdays. Students design independent projects, often conducted with nearby corporations or universities.

Two separate programs allow girls of outstanding ability in music or dance to complete a traditional Westover program and, on Saturdays, to attend either the Manhattan School of Music Pre-College Division in New York City or the Brass City Ballet in Waterbury.

An outdoor program consists of overnight camping, mountain climbing and canoeing. Weekend social activities involve nearby boys' schools. Westover conducts exchanges with schools in Australia, England, France, Jordan, South Africa and Spain.

MIDDLEFIELD, CT. (17 mi. S of Hartford, CT; 87 mi. NE of New York, NY) Suburban. Pop: 4203. Alt: 236 ft.

THE INDEPENDENT DAY SCHOOL
Day — Coed Gr PS (Age 3)-8

Middlefield, CT 06455. 115 Laurel Brook Rd. Tel: 860-347-7235. Fax: 860-347-8852.
www.independentdayschool.org E-mail: ids@independentdayschool.org
John Barrengos, Head (2007). BA, Tufts Univ, MA, EdM, EdD, Columbia Univ. **Robin Nichols, Adm.**
Pre-Prep. Elem math—Everyday Math. **Feat**—Span Computers Fine_Arts Performing_Arts Music. **Supp**—Dev_Read Rem_Math Rem_Read Rev.
Sports—Basket X-country Lacrosse Soccer.
Selective adm (Gr PS-7): 26/yr. Appl fee: $55. Appl due: Rolling. Applied: 56. Accepted: 64%. Yield: 70%. **Tests** IQ.
Enr 187. B 94. G 93. Wh 77%. Latino 2%. Blk 3%. Asian 3%. Other 15%. Avg class size: 16. Stud/fac: 6:1. **Fac 33.** M 4/F 29. FT 30/PT 3. Wh 94%. Latino 3%. Other 3%. Adv deg: 57%.
Grad '11—14. Prep—13. (Mercy HS-CT 3, Choate 2, Kingswood Oxford 2, Miss Porter's 2, Loomis Chaffee 1, Suffield 1).
Tui '12-'13: Day $22,385-25,849 (+$300-425). **Aid:** Need 35 ($238,452).
Summer: Acad Enrich Rev Rec. Tui Day $245-395/wk. Drama. Tui Day $1500. 6 wks.
Endow $176,000. Plant val $3,500,000. Acres 35. Bldgs 3. Class rms 30. Lib 7000 vols. Sci labs 2. Lang labs 2. Theaters 1. Art studios 1. Music studios 2. Gyms 1. Fields 2. Basketball courts 1. Comp labs 2.
Est 1961. Nonprofit. Tri (Sept-June).

IDS provides preparation for college preparatory secondary schools. Classes for three-year-olds and older children through grade 5 are self-contained and reflect high standards of scholarship and citizenship. During these years, children develop a sound foundation in the essential subjects. In preparation for the departmentalization they will encounter in grades 6-8, fifth graders change teachers for reading, math and social studies instruction. The curriculum includes humanities, computers, Spanish, field trips, and a particular emphasis on reading, writing, organizational and study skills, as well as the fine and performing arts.

In addition to physical education three times each week, boys and girls in grades 6-8 may participate in interscholastic sports. Beginning at age 3, children in each grade take part in age-appropriate community service projects.

NEW CANAAN, CT. (40 mi. NE of New York, NY) Suburban. Pop: 19,395. Alt: 550 ft.

NEW CANAAN COUNTRY SCHOOL
Day — Coed Gr PS (Age 3)-9

New Canaan, CT 06840. 545 Ponus Ridge, PO Box 997. Tel: 203-972-0771.
Fax: 203-966-5924.
www.countryschool.net E-mail: nhayes@countryschool.net
Timothy R. Bazemore, Head (2000). BA, Middlebury College, MA, Univ of Pennsylvania. **Nancy R. Hayes, Adm.**
Pre-Prep. Feat—Chin Fr Lat Span Studio_Art Drama Music Dance Indus_Arts Woodworking. **Supp**—Rem_Read Tut.
Sports (req'd)—Basket X-country Ice_Hockey Lacrosse Soccer. B: Baseball Football. G: F_Hockey Softball Volley.
Selective adm (Gr PS-8): 106/yr. Appl fee: $75. Appl due: Jan. **Tests** ISEE.
Enr 650. B 326. G 324. Elem 600. Sec 50. Wh 86%. Latino 2%. Blk 6%. Asian 3%. Other

3%. Avg class size: 15. Stud/fac: 6:1. Casual. **Fac 124.** M 40/F 84. FT 106/PT 18. Wh 89%. Latino 2%. Blk 5%. Asian 2%. Other 2%. Adv deg: 45%.
Grad '11—60. Prep—45. (Greens Farms 7, Greenwich Acad 5, Choate 4, Hotchkiss 3, St Luke's Sch-CT 3, Westminster Sch-CT 3). Alum donors: 17%.
Tui '11-'12: Day $29,200-31,260 (+$35-3000). **Aid:** Need 78 ($1,903,500).
Endow $30,319,000. Plant val $100,000,000. Acres 75. Bldgs 8 (95% ADA). Class rms 67. 2 Libs 26,965 vols. Sci labs 5. Auds 1. Art studios 4. Music studios 3. Dance studios 1. Wood shops 1. Gyms 2. Fields 7. Rinks 1. Comp labs 2. Comp/stud: 1:1 Laptop prgm Gr 7-9.
Est 1916. Nonprofit. Sem (Sept-June).

NCCS was founded as The Community School by Edith Dudley and Effie Dunton, coprincipals from the founding date to 1933. Due to the growth of its student body, the school moved in 1936 to Grace Hill, where the institution assumed its present name. The campus has since undergone significant expansion and improvement.

The academic program features the basic disciplines of English, math, social studies, science and foreign language. Latin, Spanish, Mandarin and French constitute the foreign language program, and computer instruction begins in the lower school. All pupils are involved in a broad and varied creative arts program that makes music, art, wood shop, creative dance and drama an integral part of each student's education.

Field trips, guest speakers, films and community resources are used extensively to enrich the curriculum. Pupils in grades 6-9 embark on excursions of up to seven days to such destinations as Washington, DC; the Florida Keys; Nantucket, MA; Memphis, TN; Gettysburg, PA; and outdoor education centers in Connecticut and Massachusetts. Boys and girls perform community service projects on and off campus, and all upper schoolers take part in interscholastic athletics.

ST. LUKE'S SCHOOL

Day — Coed Gr 5-12

New Canaan, CT 06840. 377 N Wilton Rd. Tel: 203-966-5612. Fax: 203-972-3450.
www.stlukesct.org   E-mail: info@stlukesct.org
Mark C. Davis, Head (2002). MA, Yale Univ, MALS, Wesleyan Univ. **Ginny Bachman, Adm.**
Col Prep. AP (exams req'd; 146 taken, 79% 3+)—Eng Fr Lat Span Calc Comp_Sci Bio Chem Physics Eur_Hist US_Hist US_Govt & Pol Art_Hist Studio_Art Music_Theory. **Feat**—Creative_Writing Shakespeare Chin Forensic_Sci Geol Marine_Bio/Sci Robotics Anthro Psych Global_Stud Theater Theater_Arts Public_Speak. **Supp**—Rev Tut.
Sports—Basket Crew X-country Golf Lacrosse Ski Soccer Squash Tennis. B: Baseball Football. G: F_Hockey Softball Volley. **Activities:** 27.
Selective adm (Gr 5-11): 117/yr. Usual entry: 5,6 & 9. Appl fee: $75. Appl due: Jan. Applied: 357. Accepted: 48%. Yield: 62%. **Tests** ISEE SSAT.
Enr 524. B 275. G 249. Elem 232. Sec 292. Wh 83%. Latino 1%. Blk 8%. Asian 4%. Other 4%. Avg class size: 12. Stud/fac: 8:1. Uniform. **Fac 74.** M 41/F 33. FT 74. Wh 88%. Latino 2%. Blk 6%. Other 4%. Adv deg: 91%.
Grad '11—69. Col—69. (Bucknell 7, Colby 3, Villanova 3, NYU 3, Middlebury 2). Athl schol 2. **Avg SAT:** CR 610. M 620. W 610. Avg ACT: 27. **Col couns:** 2.
Tui '12-'13: Day $33,320-34,610 (+$2500). **Aid:** Need 70 ($1,700,000).
Summer: Squash. Tui Day $450/wk. 2 wks.
Endow $20,000,000. Plant val $45,000,000. Acres 46. Bldgs 5 (100% ADA). Class rms 55. Lib 16,000 vols. Sci labs 6. Lang labs 2. Art studios 4. Music studios 4. Photog studios 1. Gyms 2. Fields 6. Tennis courts 5. Squash courts 5. Comp labs 4. Comp/stud: 1:3.
Est 1928. Nonprofit. Sem (Sept-June). **Assoc** CLS NEASC.

St. Luke's developmentally tailored middle school program, which places emphasis on skill acquisition and seeks to instill in boys and girls an appreciation of learning, prepares students for rigorous secondary school course work. The upper school curriculum integrates science and technology and stresses critical thinking skills and the development of aesthetic sensibilities. Honors and Advanced Placement courses are available in every discipline. Each upper school student performs 20 hours of community service annually.

The school draws its enrollment primarily from New Canaan, Stamford, Darien, Norwalk, Ridgefield and Westchester County, NY.

NEW HAVEN, CT. (34 mi. SSW of Hartford, CT; 69 mi. NE of New York, NY) Urban. Pop: 123,626. Alt: 10 ft. Area also includes Hamden.

COLD SPRING SCHOOL
Day — Coed Gr PS (Age 3)-6

New Haven, CT 06513. 263 Chapel St. Tel: 203-787-1584. Fax: 203-787-9444.
www.coldspringschool.org E-mail: coldspring@coldspringschool.org
Merrill S. Hall, Int Dir (2011). BA, MA, Louisiana State Univ-Baton Rouge, MA, Johns Hopkins Univ. **Sara Armstrong, Adm.**
Pre-Prep. Gen Acad. Feat—Span Computers Studio_Art Music. **Supp**—Tut.
Selective adm: 26/yr. Usual entry: PS, K & 1. Appl fee: $30. Appl due: Feb. Applied: 75. Accepted: 73%. Yield: 48%.
Enr 121. B 61. G 60. Wh 63%. Latino 9%. Blk 5%. Native Am 1%. Asian 9%. Other 13%. Avg class size: 16. **Fac 20.** M 3/F 17. FT 16/PT 4. Wh 79%. Latino 11%. Blk 5%. Asian 5%. Adv deg: 35%.
Grad '11—16. Prep—11. (Hopkins 5, Foote 2, Hamden Hall 2, Cheshire 1, Winston Prep 1).
Tui '11-'12: Day $13,440-19,740. Aid: Need 41 ($334,500).
Endow $124,000. Plant val $4,100,000. Class rms 8. Lib 15,000 vols. Art studios 1. Music studios 1. Dance studios 1. Gyms 1. Fields 1. Playgrounds 2.
Est 1982. Nonprofit. Sem (Sept-June).

Founded by a small group of local parents, Cold Spring enrolls boys and girls from 16 towns in Greater New Haven. The school follows a thematic approach that integrates the study of the traditional disciplines and incorporates creative projects, field trips, experiments and collaboration as learning tools. Under the direction of both a master teacher and an associate teacher, classes consist of mixed-age groups with two grades per classroom. CSS places considerable emphasis on technology, with computer availability and use increasing as children progress. Spanish instruction begins in preschool and continues through grade 6.

Older children develop leadership skills through interaction with younger children in reading, fitness and classroom situations. Extended-day programming and seasonal after-school activities are daily options.

FOOTE SCHOOL
Day — Coed Gr K-9

New Haven, CT 06511. 50 Loomis Pl. Tel: 203-777-3464. Fax: 203-777-2809.
www.footeschool.org E-mail: laltshul@footeschool.org
Carol Maoz, Head (2009). BA, Univ of Massachusetts-Amherst, MEd, Harvard Univ. **Laura O. Altshul, Adm.**
Pre-Prep. Gen Acad. Feat—Humanities Fr Lat Span Computers Studio_Art Drama Music.
Sports—Basket Lacrosse Soccer Swim Tennis. B: Baseball. G: F_Hockey Softball.
Selective adm: 71/yr. Usual entry: K. Appl fee: $30. Appl due: Feb.
Enr 470. B 236. G 234. Wh 68%. Latino 2%. Blk 8%. Asian 8%. Other 14%. Avg class size: 17. Stud/fac: 6:1. **Fac 86.** M 15/F 71. FT 83/PT 3. Adv deg: 62%.

Grad '11—21. Prep—13. (Choate 7, Notre Dame HS-CT 2, Westover 1, Westminster Sch-CT 1, Berkshire Sch 1, Williams-CT 1).
Tui '12-'13: Day $20,560-24,040. Aid: Need 99 ($1,400,000).
Summer: Enrich Rec. Ages 4-18. Tui Day $300/wk. Theater. Gr 6-12. Tui Day $1400. 6 wks.
Endow $7,500,000. Plant val $18,000,000. Acres 18. Bldgs 10. Class rms 41. Lib 47,000 vols. Sci labs 2. Theaters 1. Art studios 2. Music studios 3. Gyms 1. Fields 3. Comp/stud: 1:2.
Est 1916. Nonprofit. (Sept-June).

Founded by Martha Babcock Foote, the school occupies a 18-acre, wooded site near Yale University. The strong academic program, which is complemented by art, music, drama and computers, includes a required six-subject course schedule in the upper grades. Lower school pupils take two years of both French and Spanish, then choose one language to study in grades 4-9; Latin is added to the curriculum in grades 7-9. Ninth graders participate in a compulsory Monday afternoon community service program.

The school maintains an association with a sister school in Changsha, China. A Chinese guest teacher comes to Foote each autumn semester, and students from Yali Middle School (the sister school) visit during the fall. Each year, Foote's ninth graders visit Yali and tour parts of China over spring break.

Foote's summer program provides various enrichment, recreational and theatrical options for boys and girls ages 4-18. An after-school program that includes enrichment mini-courses is available daily to children in grades K-6, and alternative programs operate during certain school vacations and holidays.

HAMDEN HALL COUNTRY DAY SCHOOL
Day — Coed Gr PS (Age 3)-12
Hamden, CT 06517. 1108 Whitney Ave. Tel: 203-752-2600. Fax: 203-752-2651.
www.hamdenhall.org   E-mail: admissions@hamdenhall.org
Robert J. Izzo, Head (2006). BA, Univ of Rhode Island, MBA, Bryant College. **Janet B. Izzo, Adm.**
  Col Prep. AP (exams req'd; 132 taken, 85% 3+)—Eng Fr Lat Span Calc Stats Bio Eur_ Hist US_Hist World_Hist Econ. **Feat**—Creative_Writing Multivariable_Calc Astron Geol Marine_Bio/Sci Comp_Sci Vietnam_War Studio_Art Music Outdoor_Ed.
  Sports (req'd)—Basket X-country Golf Lacrosse Soccer Swim. B: Baseball Football Ice_Hockey Tennis Wrestling. G: F_Hockey Softball Volley. **Activities:** 36.
  Selective adm (Gr PS-11): 110/yr. Appl fee: $50. Appl due: Feb. Applied: 352. Accepted: 65%. Yield: 48%. **Tests** ISEE SSAT.
  Enr 563. B 324. G 239. Elem 296. Sec 267. Wh 75%. Latino 2%. Blk 10%. Asian 5%. Other 8%. Avg class size: 13. Stud/fac: 7:1. **Fac 82.** M 30/F 52. FT 71/PT 11. Adv deg: 79%.
  Grad '10—65. Col—65. (Brandeis 3, Lafayette 3, Muhlenberg 3, Rensselaer Polytech 2, Trinity Col-CT 2, Union Col-NY 2). **Avg SAT:** CR/M 1200. **Col couns:** 3.
  Tui '11-'12: Day $14,000-29,990 (+$425). **Aid:** Need 214.
  Summer: Acad Enrich Rev Rem Rec. Tui Day $250-1800. 1-9 wks.
  Endow $7,275,000. Plant val $25,276,000. Acres 30. Bldgs 8. Class rms 46. 2 Libs 25,000 vols. Sci labs 6. Lang labs 3. Theaters 1. Art studios 3. Music studios 3. Gyms 1. Fields 2. Courts 6. Field houses 1. Comp labs 4. Comp/stud: 1:3.
  Est 1912. Nonprofit. Sem (Sept-June). **Assoc** CLS NEASC.

One of the earlier country day schools, Hamden Hall has developed from a boys' elementary school to the present completely coed preparatory program. In the upper grades, students take at least five major academic subjects and have a variety of required courses, electives and independent study opportunities to choose from. Advanced Placement and honors courses are offered in all academic disciplines, and the curriculum prepares graduates for a variety of selective colleges.

In addition to fielding interscholastic sports, the school offers various noncompetitive options, among them an outdoors program and a running club.

HOPKINS SCHOOL
Day — Coed Gr 7-12

New Haven, CT 06515. 986 Forest Rd. Tel: 203-397-1001. Fax: 203-389-2249.
www.hopkins.edu   E-mail: admissions@hopkins.edu
Barbara M. Riley, Head (2002). BA, MA, MPhil, Yale Univ. **Pamela R. McKenna, Adm.**
   Col Prep. AP (431 exams taken, 94% 3+)—Chin Fr Lat Span Calc Stats Comp_Sci Bio Chem Environ_Sci Physics Eur_Hist US_Hist Human_Geog Art_Hist Music_Theory. **Feat**—Creative_Writing Russ_Lit Greek Ital Anat & Physiol Ecol Forensic_Sci African-Amer_Hist Holocaust Psych Asian_Stud Urban_Stud Philos Architect Video_Production Acting Drama Orchestra Jazz-Rock_Ensemble Outdoor_Ed. **Supp**—Dev_Read Tut.
Sports—Basket Crew X-country Fencing Golf Lacrosse Soccer Squash Swim Tennis Track. B: Baseball Football Wrestling. G: F_Hockey Softball Volley W_Polo. **Activities:** 73.
Selective adm (Gr 7-10): 150/yr. Usual entry: 7 & 9. Appl fee: $75. Appl due: Jan. Applied: 454. Accepted: 50%. Yield: 68%. **Tests** ISEE SSAT.
   Enr 687. B 347. G 340. Elem 157. Sec 530. Wh 75%. Latino 1%. Blk 6%. Asian 10%. Other 8%. Intl 28%. Avg class size: 12. **Fac 123.** M 52/F 71. FT 117/PT 6. Wh 90%. Latino 3%. Blk 3%. Asian 3%. Other 1%. Adv deg: 73%.
Grad '10—131. Col—131. (Brown 6, Colgate 6, Yale 5, Johns Hopkins 5, Wesleyan U 4, Georgetown 4). Athl schol 1. **Avg SAT:** CR 673. M 662. W 681. Avg ACT: 30. **Col couns:** 3. Alum donors: 30%.
Tui '12-'13: Day $33,700 (+$350). **Aid:** Need 108 ($2,508,639).
Summer (enr 139): Ages 8-18. Acad Enrich Rev Rem Rec. Sports. 6 wks.
Endow $55,800,000. Plant val $68,000,000. Acres 108. Bldgs 10. Class rms 39. Lib 22,000 vols. Sci labs 10. Auds 1. Theaters 1. Art studios 9. Music studios 5. Gyms 2. Fields 8. Tennis courts 11. Squash courts 6. Pools 1. Comp labs 4.
   Est 1660. Nonprofit. Sem (Sept-June). **Assoc** CLS NEASC.

Edward Hopkins, seven-time governor of Connecticut Colony, bequeathed a portion of his estate to the American colonies to found schools dedicated to "the breeding up of hopeful youths . . . for the public service of the country in future times." With a portion of that bequest, Hopkins Grammar School was founded in the 17th century in a one-room building on the New Haven Green and settled in its present location on a hill overlooking the city in 1925. Two prominent girls' schools, the Day School (founded in 1907) and the Prospect Hill School (founded in 1930), consolidated in 1960 to form a strong center for the education of the area's young women. Cooperative ventures between Hopkins Grammar and Day Prospect Hill led to the 1972 merger that formed the present-day school.

Every student participates in athletics throughout the year, selecting either interscholastics or an informal sport in each of the three seasons, although seniors may opt to take off one season. An independent athletics program enables boys and girls to pursue activities not offered at Hopkins, among them ballet and horseback riding. Service to others—in school, community and country—as envisioned by founder Edward Hopkins, remains an important element of student life.

The school's proximity to Yale University and New Haven provides students access to museums; historical sites; theatrical, orchestral and dance performances; and professional sporting events.

ST. THOMAS'S DAY SCHOOL
Day — Coed Gr K-6

New Haven, CT 06511. 830 Whitney Ave. Tel: 203-776-2123. Fax: 203-776-3467.
www.stthomasday.org   E-mail: info@stthomasday.org
Fred Acquavita, Head (1981). BS, Kansas State College of Pittsburg, MS, Southern Connecticut State College, MS, Bank Street College of Education. **Roxanne Turekian, Adm.**
Pre-Prep. Elem math—Pearson. **Elem read**—Macmillan/McGraw-Hill. **Feat**—Span Computers Relig Studio_Art Music.
Selective adm: 22/yr. Usual entry: K. Appl fee: $40. Appl due: Feb. Applied: 52. Accepted: 54%. Yield: 79%.
Enr 136. B 68. G 68. Wh 65%. Latino 4%. Blk 11%. Asian 14%. Other 6%. Avg class size: 19. Uniform. **Fac 25.** M 6/F 19. FT 16/PT 9. Wh 88%. Blk 12%. Adv deg: 52%.
Grad '11—19. Prep—15. (Hopkins 12, Foote 2, Hamden Hall 1). Alum donors: 4%.
Tui '11-'12: Day $18,025 (+$150). **Aid:** Need 33 ($346,000).
Endow $914,000. Plant val $1,795,000. Bldgs 2 (50% ADA). Libs 1. Sci labs 1. Comp ctrs 1. Art studios 1. Gyms 1. Playgrounds 2. Comp/stud: 1:5.
Est 1956. Nonprofit. Episcopal (15% practice). Sem (Sept-June).

This Episcopal school serves children from diverse faiths and backgrounds. Small classes encourage students to work at an appropriate level. The reading program at St. Thomas's is based on a linguistic approach, and playwriting and drama are integral parts of the curriculum. Music programming emphasizes choral work and music appreciation at all levels. Religion, Spanish, science, art, music, library and physical education are also included in the academic program.

An extended-day program includes such activities as computer, drama, sports, cooking and art.

NEW LONDON, CT. (43 mi. SE of Hartford, CT; 89 mi. SW of Boston, MA) Urban. Pop: 25,671. Alt: 45 ft.

THE WILLIAMS SCHOOL
Day — Coed Gr 7-12

New London, CT 06320. 182 Mohegan Ave. Tel: 860-443-5333. Fax: 860-439-2796.
www.williamsschool.org   E-mail: 1891@williamsschool.org
Mark Fader, Head (2004). BA, Hampden-Sydney College, MA, College of William and Mary. **Cristan Harris, Adm.**
Col Prep. AP (exams req'd; 108 taken, 80% 3+)—Fr Lat Span Calc Bio Chem Physics US_Hist Music_Theory. **Feat**—Stats Environ_Sci Ger_Hist Econ Govt Film Studio_Art Acting Theater Music Dance Accounting Journ. **Supp**—Rev Tut. **Dual enr:** CT Col, U of CT.
Sports—Basket X-country Golf Lacrosse Sail Soccer Squash Swim Tennis. B: Baseball. G: F_Hockey. **Activities:** 25.
Somewhat selective adm: 56/yr. Usual entry: 7 & 9. Appl fee: $50. Appl due: Feb. Applied: 105. Accepted: 95%. Yield: 55%. **Tests** SSAT.
Enr 259. B 119. G 140. Elem 42. Sec 217. Wh 81%. Latino 2%. Blk 2%. Native Am 2%. Asian 6%. Other 7%. Avg class size: 13. Stud/fac: 8:1. Casual. **Fac 34.** M 15/F 19. FT 31/PT 3. Wh 95%. Latino 3%. Native Am 2%. Adv deg: 55%.

Grad '11—49. Col—47. (U of CT 4, CT Col 3, Trinity Col-CT 2, Tufts 2, Wheaton-MA 2).
Avg SAT: CR 609. M 591. W 600. Avg ACT: 26. **Col couns:** 2. Alum donors: 15%.
Tui '11-'12: Day $25,835 (+$500-2850). **Aid:** Need 95 ($1,135,500).
Summer (enr 85): Acad Rec. 1-6 wks.
Endow $5,000,000. Plant val $12,000,000. Acres 200. Bldgs 1 (100% ADA). Class rms
18. Lib 5000 vols. Sci labs 5. Auds 1. Art studios 2. Music studios 1. Dance studios 1.
Gyms 2. Fields 3. Student ctrs 1. Comp labs 2. Comp/stud: 1:5.
Est 1891. Nonprofit. Quar (Aug-June). **Assoc** CLS NEASC.

Williams' college preparatory program emphasizes critical-thinking and research skills, as well as student and teacher collaboration during the learning process. Pupils follow a seven-day rotating schedule—with major subjects meeting six of the seven days—that allows for variety, flexibility, and time for work on individual or group projects. The curriculum balances traditional humanities offerings with those in math and science.

A particularly strong arts program commences with theater, music and dance courses in grades 7 and 8, and juniors and seniors may enroll in a digital film course. Technology education begins during the middle school years. Honors and Advanced Placement courses and independent study opportunities provide additional challenge for qualified older students.

All students take part in an advisor program that enables boys and girls to receive assistance with their academic, social and personal needs.

NEW MILFORD, CT. (39 mi. WSW of Hartford, CT; 69 mi. NNE of New York, NY) Suburban. Pop: 25,343. Alt: 480 ft.

CANTERBURY SCHOOL
Bdg and Day — Coed Gr 9-PG

New Milford, CT 06776. 101 Aspetuck Ave. Tel: 860-210-3800. Fax: 860-210-4425.
www.cbury.org   E-mail: admissions@cbury.org
Thomas J. Sheehy III, Head (1990). BA, Bowdoin College, MA, Pennsylvania State Univ.
Keith R. Holton, Adm.
Col Prep. AP—Eng Fr Span Calc Stats Bio Chem Eur_Hist US_Hist World_Hist Econ
Studio_Art Music_Theory. **Feat**—Shakespeare Victorian_Lit Greek Lat Multivariable_Calc Anat & Physiol Ecol Geol Oceanog Biotech Programming Holocaust Anthro Psych Women's_Stud Theol World_Relig Art_Hist Ceramics Film Sculpt.
Supp—ESL LD Rev Tut. Sat classes.
Sports—Basket Crew X-country Ice_Hockey Lacrosse Soccer Squash Swim Tennis Track. B: Baseball Football Golf W_Polo Wrestling. G: F_Hockey Softball Volley.
Activities: 15.
Selective adm (Gr 9-11): 140/yr. Bdg 100. Day 40. Appl fee: $65. Appl due: Jan. Applied:
607. Accepted: 49%. Yield: 45%. **Tests** SSAT TOEFL.
Enr 358. B 200. G 158. Bdg 229. Day 129. Sec 341. PG 17. Intl 9%. Avg class size: 11.
Stud/fac: 6:1. **Fac 76.** M 44/F 32. FT 76. Adv deg: 91%. In dorms 40.
Grad '08—105. Col—104. (Salve Regina 6, Fairfield 5, Colgate 3, Endicott 3, Fordham
3, U of IL-Urbana 3). **Avg SAT:** CR/M 1100. **Col couns:** 2.
Tui '11-'12: Bdg $46,725 (+$2000). **Day $36,225** (+$1000).
Endow $16,000,000. Plant val $20,000,000. Acres 150. Bldgs 26. Dorms 8. Dorm rms
240. Class rms 40. Lib 18,000 vols. Sci labs 4. Auds 1. Theaters 1. Art studios 3.
Music studios 2. Gyms 2. Fields 10. Courts 6. Field houses 1. Pools 1. Rinks 1. Comp
labs 2.
Est 1915. Nonprofit. Roman Catholic (60% practice). Sem (Sept-June). **Assoc** NEASC.

Long holding a leadership position among Catholic boarding schools and appealing to families not only in New England but throughout the world, Canterbury is conducted by Catholic laity. The work accomplished by the first headmaster, Dr. Nelson Hume, was recognized by Pope Pius XI, who appointed him to the Order of the Knights of St. Gregory in 1938.

Canterbury offers a college preparatory curriculum, with graduates attending both Catholic and nonsectarian colleges around the country. A wide range of elective courses, with such offerings as ethics, political philosophy, oceanography, studio art and literature of women over the years, supplements required academics.

OAKDALE, CT. (34 mi. SE of Hartford, CT; 84 mi. SW of Boston, MA) Rural. Pop: 400.

ST. THOMAS MORE SCHOOL
Bdg — Boys Gr 8-PG

Oakdale, CT 06370. 45 Cottage Rd. Tel: 860-859-1900. Fax: 860-823-3863.
www.stmct.org   E-mail: triordan@stmct.org
James Fox Hanrahan, Jr., Head. BS, Fairfield Univ, MEd, Boston College. **Todd Holt, Adm.**

Col Prep. LD. Underachiever. Feat—British_Lit Mythology Span Calc Environ_Sci Physiol Programming Comp_Relig Theol Fine_Arts Studio_Art. **Supp**—ESL Rev Tut.

Sports—B: Baseball Basket X-country Football Golf Ice_Hockey Lacrosse Soccer Tennis Track.

Selective adm: 115/yr. Appl fee: $75. Appl due: Rolling. Accepted: 75%. **Tests** CEEB IQ SSAT TOEFL.

Enr 200. Intl 35%. Avg class size: 12. Stud/fac: 6:1. Uniform. **Fac 27.** M 22/F 5. FT 27. Adv deg: 48%. In dorms 10.

Grad '11—48. **Col**—48. (Fordham, Quinnipiac, U of CT, Syracuse, St Anselm, U of MA-Amherst). **Avg SAT:** CR/M 1010. **Col couns:** 2.

Tui '12-'13: **Bdg $43,900** (+$1000). **Intl Bdg $43,900** (+$5000).

Summer: Gr 7-12. Acad Enrich Rev Rem Rec. Tui Bdg $5495. Tui Day $3000. ESL. Tui Bdg $2998-5995. 2½-5 wks.

Endow $9,100,000. Plant val $10,500,000. Acres 110. Bldgs 14. Dorms 3. Dorm rms 121. Class rms 18. Lib 6500 vols. Chapels 1. Sci labs 2. Lang labs 1. Auds 1. Art studios 1. Gyms 1. Fields 5. Courts 6. Pools 1. Tracks 1. Comp labs 2.

Est 1962. Nonprofit. Roman Catholic. Quar (Sept-May). **Assoc** NEASC.

St. Thomas More prepares boys for college entrance by emphasizing study and organizational skills, which are incorporated into the regular curriculum. The school typically enrolls underachieving students of average to above-average intelligence who have no chronic social, emotional or behavioral problems. Classes are small and highly structured.

The school maintains a postgraduate program offering separate English and math courses to prepare students for college-level work. Special emphasis is given to preparation for the SAT exam. International pupils, who may enroll in a grade 7 program that is reserved for them, take part in an intensive English as a Second Language program that provides preparation for the TOEFL.

POMFRET, CT. (29 mi. W of Providence, RI; 57 mi. WSW of Boston, MA) Suburban. Pop: 3798. Alt: 389 ft.

POMFRET SCHOOL
Bdg and Day — Coed Gr 9-PG

Pomfret, CT 06258. 398 Pomfret St, PO Box 128. Tel: 860-963-6100.
Fax: 860-963-2042.
www.pomfretschool.org   E-mail: admission@pomfretschool.org
J. Timothy Richards, Head (2011). BA, Connecticut College, MA, Middlebury College.
Carson Roy, Adm.
Col Prep. AP (exams req'd; 218 taken, 88% 3+)—Eng Fr Lat Span Calc Bio Chem Environ_Sci Physics Eur_Hist US_Hist Econ US_Govt & Pol Studio_Art Music_Theory.
Feat—Creative_Writing Shakespeare E_Asian_Lit Mystery_Lit Playwriting Chin Stats Anat & Physiol Astron Ecol Forensic_Sci Microbio Oceanog Organic_Chem Programming Web_Design Civil_War Middle_Eastern_Hist Vietnam_War Anthro Law World_Relig Art_Hist Ceramics Sculpt Drama Dance Public_Speak. Supp—Tut. Outdoor ed. Sat classes.
Sports (req'd)—Basket Crew X-country Ice_Hockey Lacrosse Soccer Squash Tennis. B: Baseball Football Golf Wrestling. G: F_Hockey Softball Volley. Activities: 25.
Selective adm: 130/yr. Bdg 109. Day 21. Usual entry: 9. Appl fee: $60. Appl due: Jan. Applied: 773. Accepted: 51%. Yield: 33%. Tests CEEB SSAT TOEFL.
Enr 350. B 186. G 164. Bdg 263. Day 87. Sec 339. PG 11. Wh 88%. Latino 1%. Blk 3%. Native Am 1%. Asian 7%. Intl 16%. Avg class size: 12. Stud/fac: 6:1. Formal. Fac 58. M 34/F 24. FT 51/PT 7. Wh 80%. Latino 2%. Blk 5%. Native Am 1%. Asian 12%. Adv deg: 67%. In dorms 18.
Grad '11—106. Col—105. (St Lawrence 6, Gettysburg 5, Geo Wash 3, Boston U 3, Boston Col 2, Yale 2). Avg SAT: CR 586. M 605. W 581. Avg ACT: 23. Col couns: 4. Alum donors: 33%.
Tui '12-'13: Bdg $50,900 (+$850). Day $31,900 (+$550). Aid: Need 118 ($2,962,310). Endow $40,000,000. Plant val $100,000,000. Acres 500. Bldgs 23. Dorms 9. Dorm rms 150. Class rms 31. Lib 17,000 vols. Observatories 1. Auds 1. Theaters 1. Art studios 2. Music studios 6. Dance studios 1. Gyms 1. Athletic ctrs 1. Fields 10. Courts 8. Field houses 1. Rinks 1. Weight rms 1. Boathouses 1.
Est 1894. Nonprofit. Tri (Sept-May). Assoc CLS NEASC.

William E. Peck, the former principal of St. Mark's School, established Pomfret as a preparatory school for boys. The school instituted coeducation in 1968, however, and now enrolls a varied student body that represents roughly 30 states and a dozen foreign countries.

Pomfret offers a varied curriculum with a wide range of electives to supplement a mandatory core of traditional courses. The school's curriculum comprises both yearlong classes and term courses that last for one or two trimesters. Students typically take six courses per term. Honors and Advanced Placement sections are available in all academic disciplines. All boys and girls enroll in one class in Pomfret's digital arts department, which offers course work in graphics, design, film, animation and mechanical engineering.

A cocurricular structure allows students to devote part of the day to athletics and the arts. Each pupil enrolls in arts courses the equivalent of two trimesters per year; classes, which convene during the week and every other Saturday, combine theory and instruction with hands-on work in the studio. All students are also involved in the athletic program, with options for both interscholastic and intramural participation.

THE RECTORY SCHOOL
Bdg — Coed Gr 5-9; Day — Coed K-9

Pomfret, CT 06258. 528 Pomfret St, PO Box 68. Tel: 860-928-1328. Fax: 860-928-4961.
www.rectoryschool.org   E-mail: admissions@rectoryschool.org

Frederick W. Williams, Head (2009). BA, Boston Univ, MEd, Lesley Univ. **Vincent Ricci, Adm.**

Pre-Prep. **Feat**—Lib_Skills Fr Lat Span Computers Studio_Art Music. **Supp**—Dev_ Read ESL LD Makeup Rem_Math Rem_Read Rev Tut.

Sports—Basket X-country Fencing Golf Lacrosse Soccer Tennis Track. B: Baseball Football Ice_Hockey Wrestling. G: Softball.

Selective adm (Bdg Gr 5-9; Day K-8): 90/yr. Bdg 65. Day 25. Appl fee: $50. Appl due: Rolling. Accepted: 82%. Yield: 70%. **Tests** IQ SSAT Stanford.

Enr 249. Bdg 183. Day 66. Wh 66%. Latino 7%. Blk 5%. Native Am 2%. Asian 20%. Intl 30%. Avg class size: 10. Stud/fac: 4:1. **Fac 60.** M 22/F 38. FT 60. Wh 96%. Latino 2%. Blk 2%. Adv deg: 51%. In dorms 23.

Grad '08—44. Prep—37. (Avon 2, Pomfret 2, Proctor 2, Gunnery 2, Tilton 2, Salisbury-CT 1).

Tui '09-'10: Bdg $38,950 (+$9000). **Day $17,400-19,450** (+$6500).

Summer: Acad Enrich Rev Rem. Tui Bdg $5725. Tui Day $1295. 4 wks.

Endow $11,000,000. Plant val $29,000,000. Acres 138. Bldgs 24. Dorms 10. Dorm rms 120. Class rms 42. Lib 8000 vols. Sci labs 3. Auds 1. Art studios 3. Music studios 2. Perf arts ctrs 1. Gyms 1. Athletic ctrs 1. Fields 6. Tennis courts 6. Pools 1. Weight rms 1. Ropes crses 1. Ponds 1. Comp labs 3. Comp/stud: 1:2.

Est 1920. Nonprofit. Episcopal. Tri (Sept-June).

Rev. Frank H. Bigelow and his wife, Mabel, began this school as a small tutoring group in their home. Their pervasive kindness and untiring energy immediately attracted students.

Students receive a thorough grounding in the fundamentals as they prepare for many secondary boarding schools. All grades are divided homogeneously, and there are accelerated programs in various subject areas. Boys and girls enrolled in Rectory's individualized instruction program convene five days a week for one-to-one sessions tailored to pupils' learning needs, strengths and interests. In addition to languages, math, science, social studies and a coordinated computer program, the curriculum includes courses in the arts, crafts and music.

SALISBURY, CT. (41 mi. WNW of Hartford, CT; 95 mi. NNE of New York, NY) Suburban. Pop: 3977. Alt: 685 ft.

SALISBURY SCHOOL
Bdg and Day — Boys Gr 9-PG

Salisbury, CT 06068. 251 Canaan Rd. Tel: 860-435-5700. Fax: 860-435-5750.
www.salisburyschool.org   E-mail: admissions@salisburyschool.org

Chisholm S. Chandler, Head (2003). BA, Brown Univ, MEd, Harvard Univ. **Peter B. Gilbert, Adm.**

Col Prep. **AP (exams req'd)**—Eng Lat Span Calc Stats Comp_Sci Bio Chem Environ_Sci Physics US_Hist World_Hist Econ. **Feat**—Chin Fr Anat Ecol Geol Forestry Chin_Hist Civil_War Middle_Eastern_Hist Intl_Relations Bible Ethics Photog Studio_ Art Music Bus. **Supp**—Tut. Sat classes.

Sports—B: Baseball Basket Crew X-country Football Golf Ice_Hockey Lacrosse Ski Soccer Squash Tennis Wrestling. **Activities:** 35.

Selective adm: 100/yr. Bdg 100. Day 0. Appl fee: $50. Appl due: Feb. Applied: 560. Accepted: 39%. Yield: 60%. **Tests** CEEB ISEE SSAT TOEFL.

Enr 305. Bdg 285. Day 20. Sec 293. PG 12. Nonwhite 11%. Intl 22%. Avg class size: 11. Stud/fac: 5:1. Formal. **Fac 51.** M 44/F 7. FT 46/PT 5. Adv deg: 43%.

Grad '09—82. Col—78. (US Milit Acad 4, U of CT 4, Trinity Col-CT 3, Hobart/Wm Smith 3, U of PA 2, SMU 2). **Avg SAT:** CR 560. M 590. W 560. **Col couns:** 4. Alum donors: 25%.

Tui '12-'13: Bdg $49,750 (+$1100). **Day $39,750** (+$750). **Aid:** Need 97 ($3,500,000).

Summer (enr 100): Coed. Gr 8-12. Acad Enrich Rem Rec. ESL. Tui Bdg $7150 (+$250). Tui Day $5150 (+$250). 5 wks.

Endow $43,900,000. Plant val $44,000,000. Acres 700. Bldgs 25. Dorms 10. Dorm rms 163. Class rms 35. Lib 25,000 vols. Chapels 1. Sci labs 5. Lang labs 1. Dark rms 1. Theaters 1. Art studios 3. Music studios 3. Ceramics studios 1. Athletic ctrs 1. Fields 6. Basketball courts 2. Tennis courts 10. Volleyball courts 1. Squash courts 8. Rinks 1. Weight rms 2. Boathouses 1. Comp/stud: 1:1 Laptop prgm Gr 9-PG. **Est 1901.** Nonprofit. Episcopal. Tri (Sept-May). **Assoc** CLS NEASC.

Founded by Rev. Dr. George Emerson Quaile on a hilltop campus that now spans 700 acres, Salisbury School offers a traditional curriculum that successfully prepares students for competitive colleges. Electives and Advanced Placement courses are available to juniors and seniors. An interdisciplinary program in grades 9-11 combines English, history and art instruction. Salisbury issues a laptop computer to each pupil.

The school's entrepreneurial studies program enables boys to create and manage a student-run business. The Residential Life Program complements academics with dorm-based discussions, all-school meetings, speakers, seminars and events, all of which revolve around annual themes. A learning center offers support to students in need of additional help.

Salisbury encourages all boys to participate in community service projects, and seniors fulfill a 15-hour service requirement. An active student entertainment committee plans gatherings with nearby girls' schools throughout the year. Athletics are extensive: Interscholastic sports are available at various levels, and recreational options are also part of the program.

SIMSBURY, CT. (10 mi. NW of Hartford, CT; 97 mi. WSW of Boston, MA) Suburban. Pop: 23,234. Alt: 164 ft. Area also includes West Simsbury.

THE ETHEL WALKER SCHOOL
Bdg — Girls Gr 9-PG; Day — Girls 6-PG

Simsbury, CT 06070. 230 Bushy Hill Rd. Tel: 860-408-4200. Fax: 860-408-4201.
www.ethelwalker.org E-mail: admission@ethelwalker.org
Elizabeth Cromwell Speers, Head (2007). BA, Middlebury College, MLA, Johns Hopkins Univ. **Margy Foulk, Adm.**
  Col Prep. AP (exams req'd; 146 taken, 64% 3+)—Eng Chin Fr Lat Span Calc Stats Bio Chem Environ_Sci Physics Eur_Hist US_Hist Econ Psych Studio_Art. **Feat—** Women's_Lit Astron African_Stud Asian_Stud Lat-Amer_Stud Ethics World_Relig Art_Hist Ceramics Photog Drama Music Music_Theory Dance Debate. **Supp**—Rev Tut. Outdoor ed. **Dual enr:** U of Hartford.
  Sports—G: Basket Equestrian F_Hockey Golf Lacrosse Ski Soccer Softball Squash Swim Tennis Volley. **Activities:** 35.
  Selective adm (Bdg Gr 9-PG; Day 6-11): 80/yr. Bdg 58. Day 22. Appl fee: $60. Appl due: Feb. Applied: 280. Accepted: 54%. Yield: 53%. **Tests** SSAT TOEFL.
  Enr 239. Bdg 138. Day 101. Elem 31. Sec 207. PG 1. Wh 63%. Latino 6%. Blk 11%. Native Am 1%. Asian 15%. Other 4%. Intl 22%. Avg class size: 12. Casual. **Fac 42.** M 10/F 32. FT 42. Wh 91%. Latino 2%. Blk 5%. Asian 2%. Adv deg: 66%. In dorms 6.
  Grad '11—61. Col—61. (Amherst 1, Bates 1, Wellesley 1, Dartmouth 1, U of MI 1, Hamilton 1). Athl schol 1. **Avg SAT:** CR 570. M 570. W 610. Avg ACT: 25. **Col couns:** 2.
  Tui '12-'13: Bdg $49,925 (+$1180). **Day $31,850-36,350** (+$900-1550). **Intl Bdg $50,925** (+$1180). **Aid:** Need 107 ($3,200,000).
  Summer (enr 65): Acad Enrich Rev Rec. Arts. Riding. Tui Bdg $1500-4900. Tui Day $300-650. 1-3 wks.
  Endow $17,900,000. Plant val $72,000,000. Acres 300. Bldgs 30. Dorms 3. Dorm rms 90. Class rms 25. Lib 24,000 vols. Chapels 1. Sci labs 5. Lang labs 1. Auds 1. Theaters 1. Art studios 4. Music studios 9. Dance studios 1. Perf arts ctrs 1. Art galleries 1. Media ctrs 1. Gyms 1. Fields 6. Riding rings 4. Stables 1. Comp labs 5. Comp/stud: 1:2.
  Est 1911. Nonprofit. Sem (Sept-June). **Assoc** CLS NEASC.

Ethel Walker opened this school in Lakewood, NJ, moving it to its present site in 1917. The founder designed the program to give her students a sound college preparatory curriculum and instill a sense of responsibility and self-discipline. Ahead of its time, the school was distinguished by its purpose: to prepare young women for college. In 1990, Ethel Walker opened a middle school division that now serves pupils in grades 6-8.

The long-maintained standards of college preparation continue, and the curriculum provides a complete program in math, science, languages, literature, history and the arts, with Advanced Placement and honors courses offered in every discipline. Wellness and service are important elements of the program. Elective courses offered in all departments produce an extensive and varied preparatory curriculum, and independent study is encouraged. The classroom experience offers opportunities for hands-on, project-based learning, and a senior project allows students to participate in an on- or off-campus internship to explore an academic or career interest.

Athletic, social and leadership opportunities balance academics. Outdoor life is emphasized through equestrian instruction and competition and a faculty-led outdoor adventure program. Walker's special-events schedule includes musical and dance performances, lectures, career panels and weekend social activities.

THE MASTER'S SCHOOL

Day — Coed Gr PS (Age 3)-12

West Simsbury, CT 06092. 36 Westledge Rd. Tel: 860-651-9361. Fax: 860-651-9363.
www.masterschool.org   E-mail: jeldridge@masterschool.org
Jon F. Holley, Head (2008). BA, Wheaton College (IL), MA, Middlebury College. **Robin Egan, Adm.**

> **Col Prep. AP (exams req'd; 27 taken, 70% 3+)**—Eng Calc Bio US_Hist. **Feat**—British_Lit Creative_Writing Fr Span Stats Anat & Physiol Astron Pol_Sci Psych Bible Sculpt Studio_Art Video_Production Music.
> **Sports**—Basket Lacrosse Ski Soccer Tennis. B: Baseball. G: Softball Volley.
> **Selective adm:** Appl fee: $50. Appl due: Rolling. Accepted: 66%. **Tests** Stanford.
> **Enr 303.** B 158. G 145. Elem 196. Sec 107. Wh 83%. Latino 6%. Blk 10%. Asian 1%. Avg class size: 15. Casual. **Fac 39.** M 10/F 29. FT 27/PT 12. Wh 94%. Latino 4%. Blk 2%. Adv deg: 38%.
> **Grad '09—27. Col—27.** (Drew 2, Northwestern CT CC 2, Tunxis CC 2). **Avg SAT:** CR 521. M 549. W 530. Alum donors: 3%.
> **Tui '12-'13: Day $9250-16,800** (+$150-1050). **Aid:** Merit 5 ($4670). Need 51 ($238,885).
> **Summer:** Enrich Rec. 1 wk.
> Plant val $6,800,000. Acres 72. Bldgs 11. Class rms 28. Lib 8000 vols. Art studios 5. Music studios 2. Photog studios 1. Gyms 1. Fields 3. Courts 2. Comp labs 1.
> **Est 1970.** Nonprofit. Nondenom Christian. Sem (Sept-June). **Assoc** NEASC.

This nondenominational Christian school conducts four divisions: the early childhood center, the lower school, and the middle and upper schools. Reading and math are stressed in the lower school, with computers, French, music and art offered from grade 1. Strong emphasis is placed on academics in all programs.

Students in the middle and upper schools may follow an "aggressive" or a "standard" college preparatory program, depending on the level of math, science and language courses they elect. Curricular elements include Advanced Placement classes and a focus on Biblical principles. In addition, pupils take part in an interactive science and technology program. Seniors have two special program options: 1) a senior seminar, incorporating different academic disciplines, that provides an overview of Western thought and Christian worldviews, and 2) an independent study program that provides hands-on experience in a field of particular interest.

WESTMINSTER SCHOOL
Bdg and Day — Coed Gr 9-PG

Simsbury, CT 06070. 995 Hopmeadow St. Tel: 860-408-3060. Fax: 860-408-3001.
www.westminster-school.org E-mail: admit@westminster-school.org
William V. N. Philip, Head (2010). BA, Yale Univ, MALS, Wesleyan Univ. **Jon C. Deveaux, Adm.**

Col Prep. AP (exams req'd; 431 taken, 90% 3+)—Eng Fr Lat Span Calc Stats Comp_ Sci Bio Chem Environ_Sci Physics Eur_Hist US_Hist Comp_Govt & Pol Econ Psych Art_Hist Studio_Art Music_Theory. **Feat**—Creative_Writing Humanities Gothic_Lit Chin Anat & Physiol Astron Geol Engineering Philos Architect_Drawing Film Photog Theater_Arts Jazz_Ensemble Public_Speak. **Supp**—Tut. Sat classes.

Sports (req'd)—Basket X-country Golf Ice_Hockey Lacrosse Soccer Squash Swim Tennis Track. B: Baseball Football. G: F_Hockey Softball. **Activities:** 32.

Selective adm: 138/yr. Bdg 101. Day 37. Usual entry: 9 & 10. Appl fee: $75. Appl due: Jan. Applied: 1028. Accepted: 29%. Yield: 46%. **Tests** CEEB SSAT TOEFL.

Enr 390. B 215. G 175. Bdg 269. Day 121. Sec 380. PG 10. Wh 85%. Latino 3%. Blk 6%. Asian 2%. Other 4%. Intl 16%. Avg class size: 12. Stud/fac: 5:1. Formal. **Fac 56.** M 34/F 22. FT 50/PT 6. Wh 89%. Latino 5%. Blk 5%. Other 1%. Adv deg: 71%. In dorms 23.

Grad '11—110. Col—107. (Middlebury 7, U of Richmond 5, St Lawrence 5, Franklin & Marshall 5, Bucknell 4, Wesleyan Col 3). **Avg SAT:** CR 620. M 620. W 631. **Col couns:** 3. Alum donors: 40%.

Tui '12-'13: Bdg $49,500 (+$1600). **Day $36,800** (+$1100). **Aid:** Need 105 ($3,258,000).

Endow $70,000,000. Plant val $120,000,000. Acres 200. Bldgs 38. Dorms 6. Dorm rms 148. Class rms 41. Lib 26,000 vols. Chapels 1. Sci labs 7. Lang labs 1. Dark rms 3. Observatories 1. Planetariums 1. Auds 1. Theaters 1. Art studios 4. Music studios 6. Dance studios 14. Arts ctrs 1. Perf arts ctrs 1. Architect studios 1. Gyms 2. Fields 10. Tennis courts 14. Squash courts 12. Paddleball courts 2. Pools 1. Rinks 1. Greenhouses 1. Student ctrs 2. Comp labs 2. Comp/stud: 1:1

Est 1888. Nonprofit. Tri (Sept-June). **Assoc** NEASC.

The educational experience at Westminster is distinguished by complementary characteristics: breadth and depth of curriculum, yet small in class sizes and individual attention. Academic emphasis is on a liberal arts college preparatory program, balanced by athletic requirements, the arts, community service and afternoon commitment to work programs and student organizations. Art studios and a performing arts center house a comprehensive creative arts program in which most students take part. College preparatory work is of a high standard, and graduates enter a variety of competitive colleges.

The school motto "grit and grace" is infused in the entire Westminster experience, from the classroom, to the playing field, to the stage and beyond campus. High academic and character standards and expectations are grounded in the schools ever-present core values: community, character, balance and involvement.

Westminster opened a new 85,000 square foot academic center in 2009. It is a four-level facility that incorporates all disciplines other than the arts. The building is LEED Gold certified and is equipped with the latest in technology, including computer labs, language studio, planetarium and lecture hall. It's central atrium is a gathering place of twice-weekly all-school meetings. Construction began in spring 2012 for a new synthetic turf field and for two new dormitories to replace two existing ones. **See Also Page 108**

SOUTH KENT, CT. (41 mi. W of Hartford, CT; 74 mi. NNE of New York, NY) Rural. Pop: 108. Alt: 395 ft.

SOUTH KENT SCHOOL
Bdg and Day — Boys Gr 9-PG

South Kent, CT 06785. 40 Bulls Bridge Rd. Tel: 860-927-3539. Fax: 888-803-0040.
www.southkentschool.org   E-mail: southkent@southkentschool.org
Andrew J. Vadnais, Head. BA, Williams College, MA, Univ of Delaware. **Kenneth W. Brown, Adm.**

Col Prep. AP—Eng Calc Stats US_Hist Econ Psych US_Govt & Pol. **Feat**—Creative_ Writing Lat Span Ecol Environ_Sci Studio_Art Music_Theory. **Supp**—ESL LD Tut. Sat classes.

Sports—B: Baseball Basket Crew X-country Football Golf Ice_Hockey Lacrosse Soccer Tennis.

Selective adm: 68/yr. Appl fee: $50. Appl due: Feb. Accepted: 46%. **Tests** CEEB SSAT TOEFL.

Enr 177. Intl 20%. Avg class size: 8. Stud/fac: 5:1. Uniform. **Fac 35.** M 22/F 13. FT 30/PT 5. Adv deg: 57%. In dorms 11.

Grad '11—61. **Col**—61. (Endicott, Dickinson, Trinity Col-CT, Lafayette, U of MA-Amherst, Wash & Jefferson). **Avg SAT:** CR 500. M 600. W 500.

Tui '12-'13: Bdg $44,000 (+$3600). **Day $26,000** (+$3600). **Intl Bdg $44,000** (+$5350-10,350).

Endow $6,000,000. Plant val $29,000,000. Acres 460. Bldgs 32. Dorms 7. Dorm rms 120. Class rms 31. Lib 24,000 vols. Chapels 1. Sci labs 4. Lang labs 1. Auds 1. Theaters 1. Art studios 3. Music studios 1. Dance studios 1. Gyms 1. Fields 3. Courts 10. Pools 1. Rinks 1. Boating facilities. Student ctrs 1. Comp labs 3. Laptop prgm Gr 9-PG.

Est 1923. Nonprofit. Episcopal. Tri (Sept-May). **Assoc** CLS NEASC.

South Kent was founded by Samuel S. Bartlett and Richard M. Cuyler with the help of Rev. Frederick H. Sill, founder and headmaster of Kent School. Mr. Bartlett and Mr. Cuyler, graduates of Kent, adopted the Kent ideal of the self-help system.

The school's structured college preparatory curriculum places equal emphasis on essential academic skills and course content. Strong humanities, science and math programs are available, and Advanced Placement classes are open to qualified students. The school provides a full range of support services for those with different learning styles. The school organizes exchange programs with schools in France and the Czech Republic, and students may spend a winter term in the High Mountain Institute Semester program.

Founded as an Episcopal school, South Kent maintains an active chapel program that meets the needs of students of all faiths. An extensive activities schedule includes dances and other social events with various girls' and coed schools.

STAMFORD, CT. (36 mi. NE of New York, NY) Urban. Pop: 117,083. Alt: 34 ft.

KING LOW HEYWOOD THOMAS
Day — Coed Gr PS (Age 4)-12

Stamford, CT 06905. 1450 Newfield Ave. Tel: 203-322-3496. Fax: 203-504-6288.
www.klht.org   E-mail: admission@klht.org
Thomas B. Main, Head (2002). BA, Bates College, MA, Wesleyan Univ. **Carrie J. Salvatore, Adm.**

Col Prep. AP (exams req'd; 154 taken, 73% 3+)—Eng Fr Span Calc Stats Bio Chem Physics Eur_Hist US_Hist Econ. **Feat**—Creative_Writing Poetry Chin Forensic_Sci

Meteorology Comp_Sci Anthro Archaeol Philos Photog Studio_Art Acting Theater_ Arts Music_Theory. **Supp**—Dev_Read Rev Tut.

Sports (req'd)—Basket X-country Golf Ice_Hockey Lacrosse Soccer Squash Tennis Volley. B: Baseball Football. G: Cheer F_Hockey Softball.

Selective adm (Gr PS-11): 130/yr. Appl fee: $75. Appl due: Jan. Applied: 490. Accepted: 41%. Yield: 70%. **Tests** CTP_4 ISEE SSAT.

Enr 685. B 386. G 299. Elem 377. Sec 308. Wh 77%. Latino 2%. Blk 2%. Native Am 1%. Asian 13%. Other 5%. Avg class size: 15. Stud/fac: 7:1. Uniform. **Fac 99.** M 32/F 67. FT 94/PT 5. Wh 74%. Latino 6%. Blk 3%. Asian 1%. Other 16%. Adv deg: 76%.

Grad '10—66. Col—65. (Bucknell 4, U of Richmond 4, Northeastern U 4, Colgate 3, Boston U 3, Wake Forest 3). Athl schol 5. **Avg SAT:** CR 591. M 606. W 596. Avg ACT: 25. Alum donors: 11%.

Tui '11-'12: Day $29,820-33,800 (+$225-2010). **Aid:** Need 81 ($1,800,000).

Summer (enr 250): Acad Enrich Rec. Sports. Tui Day $475-1630/crse. 3-6 wks.

Endow $17,000,000. Plant val $40,500,000. Acres 36. Bldgs 9 (22% ADA). Class rms 50. 2 Libs 35,000 vols. Sci labs 7. Lang labs 2. Auds 1. Theaters 1. Art studios 3. Music studios 3. Perf arts ctrs 1. Gyms 2. Fields 4. Courts 2. Comp labs 3. Comp/stud: 1:1.5 (1:1 Laptop prgm Gr 9-12).

Est 1865. Nonprofit. (Sept-June). **Assoc** CLS NEASC.

In 1988, the Low-Heywood Thomas School for girls (founded in 1865) and the King School for boys (founded in 1875) consolidated. The two schools had been located on adjacent campuses, and the resulting coeducational school continues to occupy the combined 36-acre area in North Stamford.

The school's curriculum emphasizes the liberal arts and sciences, including English, foreign languages, mathematics, history, biology, chemistry, physics and computer science, with Advanced Placement courses in all major subjects. In addition, King conducts academic enrichment classes in the lower, middle and upper schools. Small classes and individual attention prepare graduates for entrance to competitive colleges. Students in grade 8 perform at least 12 hours of required community service.

THE LONG RIDGE SCHOOL

Day — Coed Gr PS (Age 2)-5

Stamford, CT 06903. 478 Erskine Rd. Tel: 203-322-7693. Fax: 203-322-0406.
www.longridgeschool.org E-mail: mail@longridgeschool.org

Crystal Klein Bria, Head (1988). BA, Carnegie Mellon Univ, MA, Columbia Univ, MEd, Bank Street College of Education. **Caroline Lesando, Adm.**

Pre-Prep. Feat—Lib_Skills Span Computers Studio_Art Drama Music Movement. **Supp**—Rem_Read Rev Tut.

Selective adm: 32/yr. Appl fee: $50. Appl due: Rolling.

Enr 110. Nonwhite 26%. Avg class size: 14. **Fac 20.** FT 14/PT 6. Adv deg: 75%.

Grad '10—10. Prep—10. (New Canaan Country 2, Harvey 2, St Luke's Sch-CT 2, King Low Heywood Thomas 1).

Tui '12-'13: Day $25,800 (+$550).

Summer: Rec. 8 wks.

Acres 14. Bldgs 3. Class rms 18. Lib 6000 vols. Sci labs 1. Lang labs 1. Auds 1. Theaters 1. Art studios 1. Music studios 1. Dance studios 1. Gyms 1. Fields 2. Courts 1. Pools 3. Gardens 1.

Est 1938. Nonprofit. Sem (Sept-June).

Founded as a nursery school in the home of educator Harriet Rowland, Long Ridge has gradually added elementary grades over the years. The school, which occupies 14 wooded acres in the Long Ridge section of the city, serves students from southern Connecticut and Westchester County, NY.

At all grade levels, Long Ridge follows a hands-on, multisensory approach. Academic groupings are small and are adjusted to the needs and capabilities of students. Classes are integrated around a core theme and involve projects to maintain high levels of interest and to develop critical-thinking skills. Instructors employ developmentally appropriate methods and materials to promote successful learning experiences for every child. Strong emphasis is placed on the arts, science, computers and the environment. Spanish instruction begins in kindergarten.

STONINGTON, CT. (42 mi. SW of Providence, RI; 83 mi. SW of Boston, MA) Suburban. Pop: 16,953. Alt: 7 ft.

PINE POINT SCHOOL
Day — Coed Gr PS (Age 3)-9

Stonington, CT 06378. 89 Barnes Rd. Tel: 860-535-0606. Fax: 860-535-8033.
   www.pinepoint.org   E-mail: ppoint@pinepoint.org
Stephen Bennhoff, Head (2011). BA, Northwestern Univ. MEd, Harvard Univ. **Julie W. Abbiati, Adm.**
   Pre-Prep. Feat—Humanities Fr Lat Span Computers Studio_Art Music Dance. **Supp**—Dev_Read ESL Makeup Rem_Math Rem_Read Rev Tut.
   Sports (req'd)—Basket X-country Lacrosse Soccer. G: F_Hockey Gymnastics.
   Selective adm: 55/yr. Appl fee: $50. Appl due: Rolling. Accepted: 74%. **Tests** IQ SSAT.
   Enr 246. Avg class size: 11. Stud/fac: 7:1. Casual. **Fac 38.** M 11/F 27. FT 32/PT 6. Adv deg: 71%.
   Grad '11—13. Prep—8. (Loomis Chaffee, Kent Sch-CT, Deerfield Acad, Choate, Hotchkiss, Pomfret).
   Tui '12-'13: Day $13,900-22,985 (+$150). **Aid:** Need 67 ($565,815).
   Summer: Enrich Rec. 8 wks.
   Endow $1,346,000. Plant val $3,932,000. Acres 26. Bldgs 3. Class rms 15. Lib 9000 vols. Labs 2. Auds 1. Art studios 2. Music studios 1. Dance studios 1. Gyms 1. Fields 3. Courts 1.
   Est 1948. Nonprofit. Sem (Sept-June).

   Pine Point offers a highly integrated, developmental program at the primary level that emphasizes problem solving and the basic skills. Creative writing/publishing, computer, art, music, dance and community service are available to all students. The middle school program (grades 6-9) features three foreign languages, advanced mathematics and English, an international studies program for ninth graders, environmental and oceanographic sciences, interscholastic athletics, and visits to such regional locations as Mystic Aquarium, Mystic Seaport, the Palmer House Museum and Martha's Vineyard, MA.

   Pine Point's Global Education Outreach program offers home stay residencies and ESL support to international students in grades 7-9.

SUFFIELD, CT. (15 mi. N of Hartford, CT; 87 mi. WSW of Boston, MA) Suburban. Pop: 13,552. Alt: 124 ft.

SUFFIELD ACADEMY
Bdg — Coed Gr 9-PG; Day — Coed 9-12

Suffield, CT 06078. 185 N Main St, PO Box 999. Tel: 860-668-7315. Fax: 860-668-2966.
   www.suffieldacademy.org   E-mail: saadmit@suffieldacademy.org
Charles Cahn III, Head (2003). BA, Univ of Michigan, MALS, Wesleyan Univ. **Terry Breault, Adm.**
   Col Prep. AP (exams req'd; 236 taken, 56% 3+)—Eng Fr Span Calc Stats Comp_Sci

Bio Chem Physics US_Hist Econ US_Govt & Pol. **Feat**—Playwriting Chin Ital Multivariable_Calc Anat & Physiol Astron Environ_Sci Forensic_Sci Engineering Civil_War Modern_Middle_Eastern_Hist Native_Amer_Stud Comp_Relig Architect Art_Hist Ceramics Photog Studio_Art Acting Theater_Arts Directing Music Music_Hist Bus Outdoor_Ed. **Supp**—ESL LD Rem_Math Tut. Outdoor ed. Sat classes.

Sports (req'd)—Basket X-country Golf Lacrosse Ski Soccer Squash Swim Tennis Track W_Polo. B: Baseball Football Wrestling. G: F_Hockey Softball Volley. **Activities:** 16.

Selective adm (Bdg Gr 9-PG; Day 9-11): 132/yr. Bdg 80. Day 52. Appl fee: $50. Appl due: Jan. Applied: 934. Accepted: 30%. Yield: 51%. **Tests** CEEB SSAT TOEFL.

Enr 410. B 219. G 191. Bdg 275. Day 135. Sec 400. PG 10. Intl 15%. Avg class size: 10. Stud/fac: 5:1. Formal. **Fac 81.** M 45/F 36. FT 75/PT 6. Wh 92%. Latino 1%. Blk 5%. Asian 2%. Adv deg: 69%.

Grad '11—131. Col—131. (Trinity Col-CT 8, Bentley 7, SMU 6, Gettysburg 4, St Lawrence 3, Boston Col 3). **Avg SAT:** CR 539. M 581. W 546. Avg ACT: 24.8. Mid 50% ACT: 19-26. **Col couns:** 4. Alum donors: 40%.

Tui '11-'12: Bdg $46,500 (+$2050-2200). **Day $32,900** (+$2050-2200). **Aid:** Merit 16 ($246,000). Need 108 ($2,089,025).

Summer (enr 130): Acad Enrich. ESL. Tui Bdg $6800 (+$500). Tui Day $3750 (+$100). 5 wks.

Endow $34,751,000. Plant val $129,000,000. Acres 350. Bldgs 50. Dorms 13. Dorm rms 250. Class rms 47. Lib 20,000 vols. Comp ctrs 1. Theaters 1. Art studios 3. Music studios 2. Perf arts ctrs 1. Gyms 1. Fields 14. Courts 9. Field houses 1. Pools 1. Tracks 1. Weight rms 1. Rifle ranges 1. Comp/stud: 1:1 Laptop prgm Gr 9-PG.

Est 1833. Nonprofit. Tri (Sept-May). **Assoc** CLS NEASC.

Known at first as the Connecticut Literary Institution, the school initially prepared young men for the ministry. In 1843, Suffield Academy became coeducational; after World War II, however, it emerged as an independent, all-male, nondenominational boarding and day school. Suffield returned to coeducation in 1974.

The traditional liberal arts curriculum of more than 100 courses, including Advanced Placement work and term electives, prepares graduates for leading colleges throughout the country. All students participate in a leadership program, and boys and girls in grades 9-12 perform 20 hours of required community service per year.

The 350-acre campus is located in a small New England town, and students take advantage of athletic and cultural events in the nearby cities of Hartford and Springfield, MA.

See Also Pages 48-9

THOMPSON, CT. (25 mi. WNW of Providence, RI; 51 mi. WSW of Boston, MA) Suburban. Pop: 8878. Alt: 540 ft.

MARIANAPOLIS PREPARATORY SCHOOL

Bdg and Day — Coed Gr 9-PG

Thompson, CT 06277. 26 Chase Rd, PO Box 304. Tel: 860-923-9245.
Fax: 860-923-3730.
www.marianapolis.org   E-mail: admissions@marianapolis.org

Joseph C. Hanrahan, Head (2011). BA, State University of New York, MA, Providence College, MBA, Univ of Connecticut. **Daniel M. Harrop, Adm.**

Col Prep. AP (exams req'd)—Eng Span Calc Stats Bio Chem Physics Eur_Hist US_Hist Econ Psych US_Govt & Pol. **Feat**—Japan_Lit Sci_Fiction Chin Fr Anat & Physiol Astron Bioethics Ecol Comp_Sci Web_Design Civil_Rights Civil_War Cold_War Vietnam_War Theol World_Relig Film Photog Studio_Art Music_Hist Music_Theory Debate Journ. **Supp**—ESL Rev Tut.

Sports—Basket X-country Golf Indoor_Track Lacrosse Soccer Tennis Track Ultimate_Frisbee. B: Baseball Wrestling. G: Softball Volley. **Activities:** 26.

Selective adm (Bdg Gr 9-PG; Day 9-11): 123/yr. Bdg 65. Day 58. Appl fee: $50-100.

Appl due: Rolling. Accepted: 65%. **Tests** CEEB SSAT TOEFL.
Enr 340. B 184. G 156. Wh 50%. Latino 15%. Blk 5%. Asian 20%. Other 10%. Intl 40%. Avg class size: 16. Stud/fac: 8:1. Formal. **Fac 40.** M 23/F 17. FT 35/PT 5. Wh 98%. Asian 2%. Adv deg: 42%. In dorms 15.
Grad '10—84. Col—83. (Purdue, U of CT, Suffolk, Drexel, Northeastern U, UCLA). **Avg SAT:** CR/M 1140. **Col couns:** 1.
Tui '12-'13: Bdg $39,170 (+$2000). **Day $11,950** (+$500). **Intl Bdg $44,920** (+$2000). **Aid:** Merit 2 ($16,012). Need ($600,000).
Summer: Acad Enrich Rev. ESL. Tui Bdg $6000. Tui Day $2000/crse. 6 wks.
Plant val $7,000,000. Acres 150. Bldgs 8. Dorms 5. Class rms 26. Lib 10,000 vols. Labs 4. Music studios 1. Gyms 1. Fields 6. Courts 4.
Est 1926. Nonprofit. Roman Catholic. Quar (Sept-June). **Assoc** NEASC.

Originally for boys, Marianapolis was established by the Congregation of Marians of the Immaculate Conception. It moved to its present, 150-acre site, on an arboretum in the heart of the 440-acre Thompson Hill Historic District, in 1931. The coeducational day program was instituted in 1974, and in 1989 girls were admitted to the boarding program.

The school offers a college preparatory program that includes honors as well as standard sections in most academic subjects. Advanced Placement classes are offered in several areas. In addition, there are four levels of English taught to students for whom it is a second language.

Marianapolis plans weekend trips to New York City, Boston, MA, and Providence, RI, as well as various seasonal activities. Residential students also have the opportunity to engage in many other weekend activities.

WALLINGFORD, CT. (23 mi. SSW of Hartford, CT; 80 mi. NE of New York, NY) Urban. Pop: 43,026. Alt: 100 ft.

CHOATE ROSEMARY HALL
Bdg and Day — Coed Gr 9-PG

Wallingford, CT 06492. 333 Christian St. Tel: 203-697-2000. Fax: 203-697-2629.
www.choate.edu   E-mail: admission@choate.edu
Alex D. Curtis, Head (2011). BA, Swarthmore College, PhD, Princeton Univ. **Ray Diffley III, Adm.**
Col Prep. AP (684 exams taken, 95% 3+)—Eng Chin Fr Lat Span Calc Stats Comp_Sci Bio Chem Environ_Sci Physics Eur_Hist US_Hist World_Hist Econ Psych US_Govt & Pol Art_Hist Music_Theory. **Feat**—Creative_Writing Irish_Lit Lat-Amer_Lit Greek Ital Arabic Linear_Algebra Multivariable_Calc Anat & Physiol Astron Ecol Marine_Bio/Sci Microbio Geosci Organic_Chem Robotics Middle_Eastern_Hist Modern_Chin_Hist Modern_Japan_Hist Middle_Eastern_Hist Amer_Stud Abnormal_Psych Logic Relig Architect_Drawing Photog Video_Production Acting Theater_Arts Band Chorus Orchestra Dance. Sat classes.
Sports—Arch Basket Crew X-country Golf Ice_Hockey Lacrosse Soccer Squash Swim Tennis Track Ultimate_Frisbee Volley W_Polo. B: Baseball Football Wrestling. G: F_ Hockey Softball. **Activities:** 97.
Very selective adm: 267/yr. Bdg 201. Day 66. Usual entry: 9 & 10. Appl fee: $60. Appl due: Jan. Applied: 1987. Accepted: 21%. Yield: 67%. **Tests** CEEB ISEE SSAT TOEFL.
Enr 850. B 422. G 428. Bdg 629. Day 221. Sec 830. PG 20. Wh 54%. Latino 7%. Blk 9%. Asian 22%. Other 8%. Intl 13%. Avg class size: 12. Stud/fac: 6:1. **Fac 122.** M 67/F 55. FT 109/PT 13. Wh 85%. Latino 5%. Blk 3%. Asian 6%. Other 1%. Adv deg: 68%. In dorms 47.
Grad '11—254. Col—251. (Boston U 8, Georgetown 8, Lehigh 8, Amherst 7, Columbia 7, Yale 7). Athl schol 4. **Mid 50% SAT:** CR 600-720. M 610-740. W 610-730. Mid 50% ACT: 26-31. **Col couns:** 6. Alum donors: 30%.

Tui '12-'13: Bdg $48,890 (+$890). **Day** $37,000 (+$840). **Aid:** Need 272 ($8,800,000). **Summer (enr 550):** Acad Enrich Rev. Tui Day $2270/crse. Study Abroad. Tui Bdg $6970. 5 wks.
Endow $286,500,000. Plant val $111,000,000. Acres 458. Bldgs 121 (50% ADA). Dorms 29. Dorm rms 409. Class rms 106. Lib 68,000 vols. Sci labs 15. Lang labs 1. Photog labs 1. Sci ctrs 1. Auds 2. Theaters 3. Art studios 5. Music studios 16. Dance studios 1. Arts ctrs 1. Art galleries 2. Gyms 2. Fields 13. Tennis courts 22. Squash courts 12. Pools 1. Rinks 1. Fitness ctrs 1. Boathouses 1. Climbing walls 1. Comp labs 4. Comp/stud: 1:3.
Est 1890. Nonprofit. Tri (Sept-June). **Assoc** CLS NEASC.

In 1890, Mary Atwater Choate, a descendent of one of Wallingford's first settlers, invited Caroline Ruutz-Rees, a young scholar from England, to establish a school for girls, Rosemary Hall. Six years after Rosemary Hall's founding, William Choate, Mary Atwater Choate's husband, established The Choate School for boys. Choate and Rosemary Hall announced the coordination of the two schools in 1968, and Rosemary Hall relocated from Greenwich to Wallingford in 1971. The schools officially merged and assumed the current name in 1974.

Located on 458 acres of open fields, rolling hills and woods, the school occupies a campus that reflects a melding of the old with the new. The older school buildings are mostly Georgian in style, and the campus also includes two modern I. M. Pei-designed buildings: an arts center and a science center. All academic buildings and dormitory commons are outfitted for wireless Internet access.

The sense of community at the school is strengthened by diverse residences where five to 66 students, who come from dozens of states and foreign countries, live closely with faculty and their families.

Choate's rigorous curriculum includes core requirements in six academic departments: English; math and computer science; science; history, philosophy, religion and social sciences; languages; and arts. In addition to traditional course offerings, students choose from a wide array of electives, may pursue honors and Advanced Placement course work, and may undertake directed studies. Boys and girls perform 30 hours of compulsory community service prior to graduation.

Signature academic programs at Choate are the Arts Concentration Program, which allows particularly talented students to design their own programs in music, theater or the visual arts and the Science Research Program, which enables 16 motivated science pupils to move beyond the traditional classroom while practicing independent laboratory science in a university setting.

The Arabic and Eastern Studies (AMES) program offers students a working knowledge of modern Arabic and features the study of the history, art, culture and architecture of the classical Arab world, as well as the history and the politics of the modern Middle East. Opened in 2012, the Kohler Environmental Center (KEC) is a teaching and research institution that serves as a working laboratory for Choate students and others. KEC features a yearlong interdisciplinary curriculum for juniors that focuses on the environment.

Term abroad programs operate in Spain, France, Italy and China. Other cross-cultural pursuits include summer studies opportunities at schools in China, France and Spain.

WASHINGTON, CT. (34 mi. WSW of Hartford, CT; 74 mi. NNE of New York, NY) Suburban. Pop: 3596. Alt: 740 ft. Area also includes Washington Depot.

THE GUNNERY

Bdg and Day — Coed Gr 9-PG

Washington, CT 06793. 99 Green Hill Rd. Tel: 860-868-7334. Fax: 860-868-1614.
www.gunnery.org   E-mail: admissions@gunnery.org
Peter W. E. Becker, Head (2012). BA, Univ of Virginia, MA, Yale Univ. **Shannon Baudo, Adm.**

Col Prep. AP (exams req'd; 170 taken)—Eng Fr Span Calc Comp_Sci Bio Chem Physics Eur_Hist US_Hist Econ Studio_Art. **Feat**—Creative_Writing Humanities Chin Stats Anat & Physiol Ecol Environ_Sci Marine_Bio/Sci Middle_Eastern_Hist Psych Sociol Sports_Psych Ethics Art_Hist Ceramics Photog Video_Production Acting Music Public_Speak. **Supp**—ESL Tut. Sat classes.

Sports (req'd)—Basket Crew X-country Golf Ice_Hockey Lacrosse Soccer Tennis. B: Baseball Football Wrestling. G: F_Hockey Softball.

Selective adm (Gr 9-12): 116/yr. Bdg 92. Day 24. Appl fee: $50. Appl due: Jan. Applied: 553. Accepted: 50%. Yield: 35%. **Tests** CEEB SSAT TOEFL.

Enr 285. B 165. G 120. Bdg 220. Day 65. Sec 272. PG 13. Wh 80%. Latino 1%. Blk 6%. Asian 13%. Intl 20%. Avg class size: 12. Formal. **Fac 59.** M 34/F 25. FT 59. Wh 98%. Blk 1%. Other 1%. Adv deg: 69%. In dorms 27.

Grad '11—76. Col—76. (Dickinson 2, Hamilton 2, NYU 2). **Avg SAT:** CR/M/W 1680. **Col couns:** 3.

Tui '12-'13: Bdg $49,200 (+$2000). **Day $37,000** (+$2000). **Aid:** Merit 24 ($327,000). Need 120 (2,800,000).

Acres 220. Bldgs 5. Dorms 10. Dorm rms 105. Class rms 22. Lib 15,000 vols. Sci labs 4. Auds 1. Theaters 1. Art studios 2. Music studios 2. Perf arts ctrs 1. Gyms 2. Fields 4. Courts 8. Rinks 1. Comp labs 2.

Est 1850. Nonprofit. Tri (Sept-June). **Assoc** CLS NEASC.

This historic school was established by abolitionist and teacher Frederick W. Gunn and his wife, Abigail Brinsmade. The school provides a rigorous, traditional education in readying its students for college. Students are graded on a nine-tier scale. An independent study program and seminars are available for seniors, and The Gunnery emphasizes the development of writing and speaking skills at all grade levels. Boys and girls may prepare for Advanced Placement tests in every major discipline.

Students participate in compulsory athletics each term, although juniors and seniors may devote one term to the ski program, the outdoor club, community service or independent study.

RUMSEY HALL SCHOOL

Bdg — Coed Gr 5-9; Day — Coed K-9

Washington Depot, CT 06794. 201 Romford Rd. Tel: 860-868-0535. Fax: 860-868-7907. www.rumseyhall.org E-mail: admiss@rumseyhall.org

Thomas W. Farmen, Head (1985). BA, New England College, MSA, Western Connecticut State Univ. **Matthew S. Hoeniger, Adm.**

Pre-Prep. Feat—Fr Lat Span Computers Studio_Art Music Health. **Supp**—Dev_Read ESL Rem_Read Tut.

Sports—Basket Crew X-country Ice_Hockey Ski Tennis. B: Baseball Football Lacrosse Soccer Wrestling. G: F_Hockey Softball Volley.

Selective adm (Bdg Gr 5-8; Day K-8): 106/yr. Bdg 60. Day 46. Appl fee: $50-100. Appl due: Rolling. Applied: 201. Accepted: 50%. Yield: 75%. **Tests** IQ.

Enr 319. B 179. G 140. Bdg 132. Day 187. Intl 51%. Avg class size: 12. Stud/fac: 8:1. Formal. **Fac 58.** M 28/F 30. FT 58. Adv deg: 43%. In dorms 45.

Grad '11—61. Prep—61. (Gunnery 9, Canterbury-CT 5, Suffield 4, Brewster 2, Lawrenceville 2, Mercersburg 2).

Tui '12-'13: Bdg $47,335 (+$2000). **Day $18,270-22,470** (+$1000). **Aid:** Need 49 ($1,000,000).

Summer (enr 65): Acad Enrich Rev Rem Rec. Tui Bdg $6300. Tui Day $2250. 5 wks.

Endow $6,200,000. Plant val $30,000,000. Acres 147. Bldgs 32. Dorms 8. Dorm rms 72. Class rms 25. Lib 5000 vols. Sci labs 4. Theaters 1. Art studios 1. Music studios 1. Gyms 2. Fields 9. Courts 6. Rinks 1. Comp labs 2. Comp/stud: 1:3.

Est 1900. Nonprofit. Tri (Sept-June).

Lillias Rumsey Sanford founded Rumsey Hall in Seneca Falls, NY, with the idea that children need a structured environment with an emphasis on effort. The school moved to larger quarters in Cornwall in 1907 and to the present campus, situated in the foothills of the Berkshires, in 1949. Effort continues to be a focus and earns students various privileges.

The traditional structure of the school provides a family atmosphere, and full sports and extracurricular programs complement the academic curriculum. All students take art and music classes and participate in afternoon athletics. An outdoor adventure program is available for those who wish a less competitive program.

In addition to an array of sports and traditional activities, students may also become involved in fishing, bicycling, swimming, hiking and backpacking, and overnight camping trips. Rumsey Hall schedules off-campus trips and various pursuits on weekends for boarders.

WATERBURY, CT. (23 mi. SW of Hartford, CT; 77 mi. NE of New York, NY) Urban. Pop: 107,271. Alt: 260 ft.

CHASE COLLEGIATE SCHOOL
Day — Coed Gr PS (Age 3)-12

Waterbury, CT 06708. 565 Chase Pky. Tel: 203-236-9500. Fax: 203-236-9503.
www.chasecollegiate.org   E-mail: admissions@chasemail.org
John Durling Fixx, Head (2003). BA, Wesleyan Univ, MBA, Univ of Connecticut. **Melissa Medeiros, Adm.**
   Col Prep. AP (exams req'd; 189 taken, 70% 3+)—Eng Fr Lat Span Calc Comp_Sci Bio Chem Environ_Sci Physics US_Hist World_Hist Econ Art_Hist. **Feat**—Poetry Shakespeare Playwriting Greek Stats Astron Ecol Forensic_Sci Geol Oceanog Web_Design Comp_Animation Modern_Japan_Hist Archaeol Intl_Relations Adolescent_Psych Ethics Drawing Film Filmmaking Painting Photog Sculpt Studio_Art Acting Theater Music_Theory Handbells Journ.
   Sports—Basket X-country Lacrosse Soccer Swim Tennis Ultimate_Frisbee. B: Baseball Golf Wrestling. G: Softball Volley. **Activities:** 36.
   Selective adm (Gr PS-11): 100/yr. Appl fee: $60. Appl due: Jan. Accepted: 81%. Yield: 68%. **Tests** SSAT.
   Enr 460. B 238. G 222. Elem 260. Sec 200. Wh 83%. Latino 2%. Blk 4%. Native Am 1%. Asian 5%. Other 5%. Avg class size: 12. Casual. **Fac 58.** FT 58. Adv deg: 81%.
   Grad '11—35. Col—35. (Worcester Polytech, Brown, Boston U, Clark U, CT Col, Geo Wash). **Avg SAT:** CR 603. M 585. W 603. **Col couns:** 2. Alum donors: 15%.
   Tui '12-'13: Day $16,810-32,425 (+$800). **Aid:** Need 230 ($3,440,000).
   Summer: Acad Enrich Rev Rec. Tui Day $115-275/wk. 6 wks.
   Endow $13,000,000. Plant val $15,620,000. Acres 47. Bldgs 10. Class rms 62. Lib 22,000 vols. Sci labs 7. Lang labs 1. Dark rms 1. Auds 1. Theaters 1. Art studios 3. Music studios 6. Arts ctrs 1. Wood shops 1. Gyms 2. Fields 9. Tennis courts 8. Field houses 1. Comp labs 6. Comp/stud: 1:1.5.
   Est 1865. Nonprofit. Sem (Sept-June). **Assoc** CLS NEASC.

Formerly called St. Margaret's-McTernan School, the school resulted from the 1972 merger of St. Margaret's School (founded in 1865), a girls' boarding school, and the McTernan School (established in 1912), a boys' day school. Chase Collegiate assumed its current name in July 2005. The school occupies a 47-acre, wooded campus on a hill overlooking the city. Separate buildings house the lower, middle and upper schools.

A rigorous traditional curriculum in English, history, mathematics, science and foreign languages is complemented by numerous electives in art, music, drama and computer technology. Many students take advantage of the array of honors and Advanced Placement courses. Field trips in each grade are planned throughout the academic year, with the focus on extending and enriching the classroom experience; the school sponsors European trips during March break. Drama internships are available through Waterbury's Seven Angels Theatre.

Frequent public affairs seminars bring students and guest professionals together to discuss various issues. Interscholastic sports begin in grade 6, and community service projects are an important part of Chase Collegiate's extracurricular program at all grade levels.

WATERTOWN, CT. (25 mi. WSW of Hartford, CT; 78 mi. NNE of New York, NY) Urban. Pop: 21,661. Alt: 484 ft.

TAFT SCHOOL
Bdg and Day — Coed Gr 9-PG

Watertown, CT 06795. 110 Woodbury Rd. Tel: 860-945-7777. Fax: 860-945-7808.
www.taftschool.org   E-mail: admissions@taftschool.org
William R. MacMullen, Head (2001). BA, Yale Univ, MA, Middlebury College. **Peter A. Frew, Adm.**

Col Prep. AP (exams req'd; 676 taken, 90% 3+)—Eng Chin Fr Lat Span Calc Stats Comp_Sci Bio Chem Environ_Sci Physics Eur_Hist US_Hist Comp_Govt & Pol Econ Psych US_Govt & Pol Art_Hist Studio_Art Music_Theory. **Feat**—Humanities Poetry Chin & Japan_Lit Russ_Lit Southern_Lit Multivariable_Calc Anat Astron Foren-sic_Sci Oceanog Zoology Engineering Robotics Civil_Rights WWII Middle_East-ern_Stud Comp_Relig Philos Buddhism Architect Ceramics Drawing Film Photog Sculpt Video_Production Acting Music Jazz Dance Finance Marketing. **Supp**—Rev Tut. Sat classes.

Sports—Basket Crew X-country Golf Ice_Hockey Lacrosse Ski Soccer Squash Tennis Track. B: Baseball Football Wrestling. G: F_Hockey Softball Volley. **Activities:** 70.

Very selective adm: 199/yr. Bdg 167. Day 32. Usual entry: 9 & 10. Appl fee: $50. Appl due: Jan. Applied: 1620. Accepted: 24%. Yield: 50%. **Tests** CEEB ISEE SSAT TOEFL.

Enr 577. B 298. G 279. Bdg 472. Day 105. Sec 555. PG 22. Wh 72%. Latino 4%. Blk 7%. Asian 11%. Other 6%. Intl 15%. Avg class size: 12. Stud/fac: 5:1. Casual. **Fac 98.** M 59/F 39. FT 88/PT 10. Wh 84%. Latino 5%. Blk 5%. Asian 4%. Other 2%. Adv deg: 91%. In dorms 42.

Grad '11—178. Col—171. (Boston Col 9, Geo Wash 9, Georgetown 7, Trinity Col-CT 7, Cornell 6, Bucknell 5). **Avg SAT:** CR 647. M 656. W 662. **Mid 50% SAT:** CR 600-690. M 600-710. W 610-710. Avg ACT: 28. Mid 50% ACT: 25-31. **Col couns:** 4. Alum donors: 38%.

Tui '12-'13: Bdg $48,360 (+$2000). **Day $35,775** (+$1800). **Aid:** Need 216 ($6,700,000).

Summer (enr 150): Acad Enrich Rev. ESL. SAT/SSAT Prep. Arts. Sports. Tui Bdg $6150. Tui Day $3500. 5 wks.

Endow $207,779,000. Plant val $199,500,000. Acres 225. Bldgs 23 (75% ADA). Dorms 8. Dorm rms 278. Class rms 40. Lib 60,500 vols. Sci labs 10. Lang labs 1. Dark rms 2. Math/sci ctrs 1. Learning ctrs 1. Auds 2. Theaters 2. Art studios 2. Music studios 3. Dance studios 1. Arts ctrs 1. Art galleries 1. Woodworking studios 2. Gyms 2. Fields 16. Basketball courts 4. Tennis courts 16. Volleyball courts 2. Squash courts 8. Rinks 2. Tracks 2. Weight rms 1. Climbing walls 1. Golf crses 1. Comp labs 3. Comp/stud: 1:1 Laptop prgm Gr 9-PG.

Est 1890. Nonprofit. Sem (Sept-June). **Assoc** CLS NEASC.

Horace Dutton Taft, brother of the 27th president, devoted 46 years to the creation and the development of this school. He began as a lawyer, but a love of teaching drew him first (in 1887) to Yale, where he tutored Latin, and then to establish his own school. In 1927, he placed the school under the control of a board of trustees, and in 1936 Mr. Taft ended his 46-year tenure as headmaster. The school became fully coeducational in 1971, with girls being admit-ted into all grades as boarding and day students. In the ensuing years, Taft made major campus improvements, greatly elevated its endowment, expanded the scholarship program and further diversified its student body.

Taft's curriculum begins with foundation courses, then broadens into a diverse and challenging selection of honors and Advanced Placement courses and equally challenging upper-level electives. An independent studies program enables selected upper school students to pursue individual creative work of a high caliber. The school also supports lecture and concert series, in addition to a program of art and historical exhibits.

Taft's Center for Teacher Education attracts public, private and parochial school teachers and administrators from all parts of the country. These summer workshops are devoted to developing specific curricula and teaching techniques for Advanced Placement, science and values courses.

Patronage is national and international, and the financial aid program assists many students who otherwise might not be able to attend Taft. Graduates enter leading colleges and universities.

Numerous athletic facilities occupy Taft's 225-acre campus, and the athletic program, which is both intramural and interscholastic, provides competition in most sports. Student-faculty policymaking committees and an active student government offer practical experience in organizational leadership.

WESTBROOK, CT. (36 mi. SSE of Hartford, CT; 89 mi. ENE of New York, NY) Suburban. Pop: 6292. Alt: 34 ft.

OXFORD ACADEMY

Bdg — Boys Gr 9-PG

Westbrook, CT 06498. 1393 Boston Post Rd. Tel: 860-399-6247. Fax: 860-399-6805.
www.oxfordacademy.net   E-mail: admissions@oxfordacademy.net
Philip B. Cocchiola, Head (2010). BS, Univ of Connecticut, MS, Univ of New Haven. **Patti Davis, Adm.**
Col Prep. Gen Acad. LD. Underachiever. AP (exams req'd)—Eng US_Hist. **Feat**—Fr Ger Lat Span Calc Stats Botany Ecol Environ_Sci Marine_Bio/Sci Microbio Civil_War Holocaust Econ Pol_Sci Psych Sociol Art_Hist Drawing Painting Photog Study_Skills. **Supp**—Dev_Read ESL Makeup Rem_Math Rem_Read Rev Tut.
Sports—B: Basket Soccer Tennis.
Somewhat selective adm: 17/yr. Appl fee: $65. Appl due: Rolling. Accepted: 75%. Yield: 90%. **Tests** IQ TOEFL.
Enr 48. Wh 86%. Latino 4%. Asian 6%. Other 4%. Intl 25%. Avg class size: 1. Stud/fac: 1:1. **Fac 21.** M 13/F 8. FT 17/PT 4. Wh 95%. Latino 5%. Adv deg: 42%. In dorms 6.
Grad '07—18. Col—18. (Cabrini, Columbia Col-IL, Hampshire, Manhattanville, Rochester Inst of Tech, Savannah Col of Art & Design). Athl schol 1. **Avg SAT:** CR 476. M 544. W 495. **Col couns:** 1.
Tui '12-'13: Bdg $54,900 (+$2000).
Summer: Rev. Tui Bdg $7298. 5 wks.
Endow $200,000. Plant val $3,700,000. Bldgs 10. Dorms 2. Dorm rms 26. Class rms 20. Lib 3100 vols. Sci labs 2. Lang labs 1. Art studios 1. Gyms 1. Fields 2. Courts 3. Comp labs 1.
Est 1906. Nonprofit. 5 terms (Sept-June). **Assoc** NEASC.

Founded in Pleasantville, NJ, by Joseph M. Weidberg, this school moved to Westbrook in 1973, after a fire had destroyed the main building. The academy, which draws its enrollment from throughout the country and the world, has successfully developed and pursued a program of totally individualized instruction that prepares all of its students for college or further secondary preparation.

The school serves young men who have experienced learning difficulties in a traditional school setting, as well as those who wish to accelerate. The Socratic method of teaching is used, and a full curriculum extends from basic courses through Advanced Placement. Each class consists of one student and one teacher. An English as a Second Language program helps students from other countries to improve their English and prepare for entrance to American colleges.

Extracurricular activities include trips to concerts, museums, movies, deep-sea fishing sites and nearby points of interest.   **See Also Page 53**

WESTPORT, CT. (44 mi. NE of New York, NY; 56 mi. SW of Hartford, CT) Suburban. Pop: 25,749. Alt: 26 ft. Area also includes Greens Farms.

GREENS FARMS ACADEMY
Day — Coed Gr K-12

Greens Farms, CT 06838. 35 Beachside Ave, PO Box 998. Tel: 203-256-0717. Fax: 203-256-7501.
www.gfacademy.org   E-mail: admission@gfacademy.org
Janet M. Hartwell, Head (2003). BA, University of Leeds (England), DipEd, Univ of Edinburgh (Scotland), MA, Columbia Univ. **Stephanie B. Whitney, Adm.**

   Col Prep. AP (exams req'd; 310 taken, 90% 3+)—Eng Chin Fr Lat Span Calc Stats Bio Chem Environ_Sci Physics Eur_Hist US_Hist Studio_Art Music_Theory. **Elem math**—Scott Foresman-Addison Wesley. **Feat**—Greek_Lit Nature_Writing Astron Bioethics Econ Intl_Relations Photog Video_Production Theater Jazz & Blues Journ.
   Sports (req'd)—Basket X-country Fencing Golf Lacrosse Sail Soccer Squash Tennis. B: Baseball Wrestling. G: F_Hockey Softball Volley. **Activities:** 25.
   Selective adm (Gr K-11): 134/yr. Usual entry: K, 6, 9 & 10. Appl fee: $75. Appl due: Jan. Applied: 512. Accepted: 38%. Yield: 68%. **Tests** ISEE SSAT.
   Enr 685. B 323. G 362. Elem 377. Sec 308. Wh 83%. Latino 3%. Blk 3%. Asian 4%. Other 7%. Avg class size: 13. Stud/fac: 7:1. **Fac 94.** M 33/F 61. FT 83/PT 11. Wh 87%. Latino 4%. Blk 1%. Asian 4%. Other 4%. Adv deg: 58%.
   Grad '11—71. Col—71. (Dartmouth 3, Brown 2, MIT 2, Johns Hopkins 2, McGill-Canada 2, Wesleyan U 2). **Avg SAT:** CR 659. M 649. W 675. Avg ACT: 28. **Col couns:** 2. Alum donors: 15%.
   Tui '11-'12: Day $31,150-34,870 (+$500). **Aid:** Need 72 ($1,837,590).
   Summer (enr 300): Acad Enrich Rev Rec. Tui Day $160-1950. 1-6 wks.
   Endow $32,500,000. Plant val $43,700,000. Acres 43. Bldgs 4. Class rms 81. Lib 24,408 vols. Sci labs 9. Lang labs 1. Art studios 5. Music studios 5. Gyms 3. Fields 5. Courts 8. Comp/stud: 1:1 Laptop prgm Gr 6-12.
   Est 1925. Nonprofit. Sem (Sept-June). **Assoc** CLS NEASC.

The traditional college preparatory curriculum emphasizes study skills, the basics of the major disciplines, ample opportunities in the arts and, for upper school students, a wide array of Advanced Placement offerings. Students may choose to broaden their program further through independent study, study abroad or off-campus projects.

All students participate in the community service program. Beginning in grade 6, all pupils must supply a laptop computer for classroom use.

WINDSOR, CT. (6 mi. NNE of Hartford, CT; 90 mi. WSW of Boston, MA) Suburban.
Pop: 28,237. Alt: 61 ft.

THE LOOMIS CHAFFEE SCHOOL

Bdg and Day — Coed Gr 9-PG

Windsor, CT 06095. 4 Batchelder Rd. Tel: 860-687-6000. Fax: 860-298-8756.
www.loomischaffee.org   E-mail: erby_mitchell@loomis.org
Sheila Culbert, Head (2008). BEd, Univ of Nottingham (England), MA, PhD, Indiana Univ.
Erby Mitchell, Adm.
Col Prep. AP (504 exams taken, 84% 3+)—Eng Chin Fr Lat Span Calc Stats Comp_
Sci Chem Environ_Sci Physics US_Hist Econ Studio_Art Music_Theory. **Feat**—Cre-
ative_Writing Shakespeare Satire Women's_Lit Arabic Linear_Algebra Multivari-
able_Calc Anat & Physiol Astron Genetics Geol Molecular_Bio Comp_Animation
Civil_War Middle_Eastern_Hist Modern_African_Hist Psych Philos Relig Video_Pro-
duction Animation Drama Music. Sat classes.
Sports—Basket X-country Golf Ice_Hockey Lacrosse Ski Soccer Squash Swim Tennis
Track W_Polo. B: Baseball Football Wrestling. G: F_Hockey Softball Volley. **Activi-
ties:** 50.
Selective adm: 231/yr. Bdg 134. Day 97. Appl fee: $75. Appl due: Jan. Applied: 1680.
Accepted: 28%. Yield: 46%. **Tests** CEEB ISEE SSAT TOEFL.
Enr 680. B 357. G 323. Bdg 409. Day 271. Sec 658. PG 22. Nonwhite 23%. Intl 17%. Avg
class size: 12. Stud/fac: 5:1. Casual. **Fac 160.** M 75/F 85. Adv deg: 68%. In dorms
42.
Grad '11—185. Col—185. (Trinity Col-CT 7, Syracuse 7, Colgate 5, Geo Wash 5,
Georgetown 5, Hamilton 5). **Mid 50% SAT:** CR 590-700. M 610-720. W 590-700. **Col
couns:** 5. Alum donors: 34%.
Tui '12-'13: Bdg $49,220 (+$1075-1705). **Day** $37,570 (+$875). **Aid:** Need 231
($7,700,000).
Endow $200,000,000. Plant val $260,000,000. Acres 300. Bldgs 66. Dorms 10. Dorm
rms 271. Class rms 57. Lib 60,000 vols. Sci labs 9. Lang labs 1. Comp ctrs 1. Plan-
etariums 1. Theaters 1. Art studios 12. Music studios 10. Dance studios 1. Arts ctrs 1.
Gyms 3. Fields 17. Tennis courts 11. Squash courts 8. Pools 1. Rinks 1. TV stations
1. Radio stations 1.
Est 1914. Nonprofit. Tri (Sept-June). **Assoc** CLS NEASC.

In 1874, five members of the Loomis family, bereft of heirs, dedicated their resources and
drew up a charter for a school on what had been (since 1639) the Loomis homestead, "for the
free and gratuitous education of all persons of the age of 12 years and upwards to 20 years in
all the departments of learning which are now taught or hereafter may be taught in the various
grades of schools in this country . . . so far as the funds of the institute will permit." While
members of the Loomis family and residents of Windsor were given preference under the charter, the school rapidly developed a wide geographical distribution of patronage.

Originally conceived as a coeducational institution, the Loomis Institute was divided in
its early years into Loomis, a boys' boarding school, and Chaffee, a girls' day school. This
separation came to an end in 1970 when Chaffee, returning from the far side of the Farmington
River, moved into a spacious new building on the Loomis campus. In the spring of 1972, the
operating name of The Loomis Institute became The Loomis Chaffee School.

The curriculum, constantly reviewed, offers an extensive selection of courses. Pupils choose
from traditional subjects, as well as technological and globally inclusive ones. Course work
and school life incorporate current world issues and social concerns. Electives are available
in all departments, as are independent study programs. Loomis Chaffee's fully equipped art
center supports a strong visual arts program. Each year, several guest speakers visit the campus
to discuss topical issues with students.

The School Year Abroad program offers opportunities to study in France, Spain, India, Italy
and Beijing, China. Athletics are both interscholastic and intramural. Other activities include
cycling, aerobics, cross-country skiing, jogging and Outward Bound activities.

All students and faculty participate in a work program that involves the daily maintenance of buildings, the efficient functioning of the dining facility, and assistance in many areas of school life. Student points of view are presented to the faculty by the elected student council. Among extracurricular activities are several publications, numerous clubs, dramatics, music, hobbies and two volunteer service organizations.

WOODSTOCK, CT. (30 mi. WNW of Providence, RI; 56 mi. WSW of Boston, MA) Rural. Pop: 7221. Alt: 592 ft.

HYDE SCHOOL AT WOODSTOCK
Bdg — Coed Gr 9-PG

Woodstock, CT 06281. 150 Rte 169, PO Box 237. Tel: 860-963-9096, 888-234-4933. Fax: 860-928-0612.
www.hyde.edu   E-mail: woodstock.admissions@hyde.edu
Laura Gauld, Head (2006). BS, Univ of Southern Maine. **Jason Warnick, Adm.**
  Col Prep. AP (exams req'd; 46 taken, 30% 3+)—Eng Calc Environ_Sci Physics Eur_ Hist US_Hist Human_Geog. **Feat**—Fr Span Multivariable_Calc Anat & Physiol 20th-Century_Hist Econ Chin_Stud Lat-Amer_Stud Ethics Philos World_Relig Art_Hist Ceramics Painting Photog Visual_Arts Theater_Arts Directing Music_Theory Song-writing. **Supp**—ESL Rem_Math Rev Tut. Sat classes.
  Sports (req'd)—Basket X-country Equestrian Lacrosse Soccer Tennis Track. B: Football Wrestling. G: F_Hockey.
  Selective adm: 40/yr. Appl fee: $100. Appl due: Rolling. Accepted: 60%. Yield: 71%.
  Enr 171. Wh 74%. Latino 3%. Blk 10%. Asian 13%. Intl 13%. Avg class size: 12. Stud/fac: 5:1. Formal. Fac 31. M 16/F 15. FT 30/PT 1. Wh 91%. Blk 3%. Asian 6%. Adv deg: 25%. In dorms 22.
  Grad '10—56. Col—54. (Endicott 3, Champlain 2, U of CO-Boulder 2, E CT St 2, Eckerd 1, Goucher 1). Athl schol 1. Avg SAT: CR 525. M 499. W 494. Mid 50% SAT: CR 460-580. M 430-570. W 440-540. Avg ACT: 19.9. Mid 50% ACT: 17-22. Alum donors: 8%.
  Tui '12-'13: Bdg $48,500 (+$2500). Intl Bdg $48,500 (+$4195). Aid: Need 60 ($1,150,000).
  Summer: Acad Enrich Rec. Leadership. Tui Bdg $1200/wk. 4 wks.
  Endow $2,158,000. Plant val $44,000,000. Acres 119. Bldgs 11 (83% ADA). Dorms 3. Dorm rms 10. Sci labs 2. Lang labs 2. Theaters 1. Art studios 1. Music studios 1. Dance studios 1. Gyms 1. Fields 3. Courts 1. Comp labs 1. Comp/stud: 1:3.5.
  Est 1996. Nonprofit. Tri (Sept-May). Assoc NEASC.

An outgrowth of Hyde School at Bath (see separate listing), this school was founded in response to a growing demand for Hyde's character-based curriculum. The rural campus occupies a 123-acre site that once served as the location of a Catholic women's college.

Hyde's program focuses upon three elements: character development, college preparation and family involvement. All students fulfill requirements in athletics, the performing arts and community service. In addition to traditional grading, faculty and peer evaluations are stressed. An unusual amount of responsibility is given to each student in the overall decision-making and operation of the school. Parents must participate in the Family Education Program, which consists of a three-day, on-campus seminar; regional monthly meetings; twice-annual family weekends; and yearly regional retreats.

Acceptance to Hyde is based on a family interview conducted on campus, in conjunction with papers composed after the interview by both the prospective student and his or her parents. Admission to the school is year-round.

MAINE

BATH, ME. (26 mi. NE of Portland, ME; 126 mi. NNE of Boston, MA) Suburban. Pop: 9266. Alt: 79 ft.

HYDE SCHOOL AT BATH
Bdg and Day — Coed Gr 9-PG

Bath, ME 04530. 616 High St. Tel: 207-443-5584. Fax: 207-443-1450.
www.hyde.edu   E-mail: bath.admissions@hyde.edu
Malcolm W. Gauld, Pres (1998). BA, Bowdoin College, MA, Harvard Univ. **Donald W. Mac-Millan, Head.** AB, Bowdoin College, MEd, Harvard Univ, MA, Antioch New England Graduate School. **Ross Sanner, Adm.**
Col Prep. AP (exams req'd)—Eng Calc Physics US_Hist. **Feat**—Chin Span Comp_Sci Theater_Arts Music. **Supp**—Tut.
Sports—Basket X-country Indoor_Track Lacrosse Soccer Swim Tennis Track. B: Football Wrestling.
Selective adm (Gr 9-11): 44/yr. Bdg 44. Day 0. Appl fee: $100. Appl due: Rolling. Accepted: 65%. Yield: 85%.
Enr 138. Wh 83%. Latino 2%. Blk 11%. Asian 3%. Other 1%. Intl 8%. Avg class size: 12. Stud/fac: 5:1. Formal. **Fac 36.** Wh 99%. Blk 1%.
Grad '08—53. **Col**—52. (Dean 2, U of CO-Boulder 2, U of Denver 2, U of ME-Orono 2, CO Col 1, U of San Diego 1). **Avg SAT:** CR/M 1039. Alum donors: 15%.
Tui '11-'12: Bdg $46,200 (+$3250). **Day $24,500** (+$1450). **Aid:** Need 46 ($820,000).
Summer: Acad Enrich. Leadership. Tui Bdg $1200/wk. 4 wks.
Plant val $24,000,000. Acres 145. Bldgs 32. Dorms 6. Dorm rms 92. Class rms 21. Lib 6000 vols. Sci labs 2. Lang labs 1. Auds 1. Theaters 1. Art studios 1. Music studios 1. Gyms 1. Fields 3. Pools 1. Tracks 1. Comp labs 1.
Est 1966. Nonprofit. Tri (Sept-May). **Assoc** NEASC.

After several years of planning and with the handsome estate of shipbuilder John S. Hyde for a campus, this school was opened by Joseph Gauld in 1966. The school became coeducational in 1971.

Hyde's college preparatory program is character based and promotes an interdisciplinary curriculum encompassing traditional secondary academics, athletics, the performing arts and community service. In addition to traditional grading, faculty and peer evaluations are stressed. An unusual amount of responsibility is given to each student in the overall decision-making and operation of the school. The Family Education Center, founded in 1977, assists parents in understanding Hyde's program and helps with a network of regional parent groups. Acceptance to Hyde is based on a family interview conducted on campus, in conjunction with papers composed after the interview by both the prospective student and his or her parents. Admission to the school is year-round.

Since July 1996, Hyde has operated a second campus in Woodstock, CT (see separate listing).

BERWICK, ME. (43 mi. SW of Portland, ME; 65 mi. N of Boston, MA) Suburban. Pop: 6353. Alt: 102 ft. Area also includes South Berwick.

BERWICK ACADEMY
Day — Coed Gr PS (Age 4)-PG

South Berwick, ME 03908. 31 Academy St. Tel: 207-384-2164. Fax: 207-384-3332.
www.berwickacademy.org E-mail: kcampbell@berwickacademy.org
Gregory Schneider, Head (2007). BA, Amherst College, EdM, Harvard Univ. **Andrew Kasprzak, Adm.**

Col Prep. AP (exams req'd; 131 taken, 80% 3+)—Eng Fr Lat Span Calc Comp_Sci Bio Chem Physics US_Hist Studio_Art. **Elem math**—TERC Investigations. **Feat**—Creative_Writing Poetry Stats Anat & Physiol Astron Environ_Sci Geol Holocaust Middle_Eastern_Hist Russ_Hist Amer_Stud Irish_Stud Women's_Stud Ceramics Photog Sculpt Chorus Music Music_Theory Orchestra Dance Journ Metal_Shop. **Supp**—Tut.

Sports (req'd)—Basket X-country Golf Ice_Hockey Lacrosse Ski Soccer Swim Tennis. B: Baseball. G: F_Hockey Softball. **Activities:** 23.

Selective adm: 119/yr. Usual entry: PS, K, 6 & 9. Appl fee: $50. Appl due: Dec. Applied: 298. Accepted: 66%. Yield: 62%. **Tests** CTP_4 ISEE SSAT.

Enr 566. B 271. G 295. Elem 292. Sec 274. Wh 99%. Asian 1%. Avg class size: 14. Stud/fac: 8:1. Casual. **Fac 82.** M 29/F 53. FT 64/PT 18. Wh 100%. Adv deg: 57%.

Grad '10—63. Col—61. (U of VT 3, Geo Wash 2, Dartmouth 1, Cornell 1, Northwestern 1, Johns Hopkins 1). **Mid 50% SAT:** CR 560-660. M 560-650. W 600-680. **Col couns:** 3.

Tui '11-'12: Day $13,550-26,400 (+$2000). **Aid:** Need 200 ($2,259,200).

Summer: Acad Enrich. Study Skills. Tui Day $400. 2 wks. Sports. Tui Day $100-200. 1 wk.

Endow $20,000,000. Plant val $3,500,000. Acres 72. Bldgs 14. Class rms 31. Lib 11,000 vols. Sci ctrs 1. Art studios 4. Music studios 4. Gyms 1. Athletic ctrs 1. Fields 4. Courts 6. Laptop prgm Gr 7-12.

Est 1791. Nonprofit. Tri (Sept-June). **Assoc** CLS NEASC.

The oldest school in Maine, BA holds a charter as an institution of higher learning, signed by Gov. John Hancock when Maine was a possession of Massachusetts. Albert L. Kerr, who assumed direction in 1957, established a college preparatory program that now offers a competitively rigorous curriculum, with training in fundamental academic skills, as well as honors and Advanced Placement courses. After 17 years as a combined boarding and day school, the academy reverted to country day status in 1976 and now predominantly enrolls students from southern Maine and New Hampshire.

Berwick encourages boys and girls to participate in its daily program of sports and activities. A common period on Tuesdays enables upper schoolers to work with advisors, take part in wellness pursuits, organize class activities or attend performances. All students in grades 7-12 purchase laptop or tablet computers for use in class and to connect to the campus wireless network.

BETHEL, ME. (59 mi. NNW of Portland, ME; 143 mi. N of Boston, MA) Suburban. Pop: 2411. Alt: 643 ft.

GOULD ACADEMY
Bdg and Day — Coed Gr 9-PG

Bethel, ME 04217. 39 Church St, PO Box 860. Tel: 207-824-7700. Fax: 207-824-7711.

www.gouldacademy.org E-mail: admissions@gouldacademy.org
Matthew Ruby, Head (2012). BA, Carleton College, MA, Univ of Minnesota-Twin Cities.
Todd Ormiston, Adm.
   Col Prep. AP (exams req'd; 134 taken, 56% 3+)—Eng Calc Stats Bio Chem Physics US_Hist US_Govt & Pol. **Feat**—British_Lit Creative_Writing Chin Fr Span Astron Environ_Sci Comp_Sci Robotics Econ Psych Drawing Filmmaking Painting Photog Sculpt Studio_Art Theater Chorus Music_Hist Music_Theory Design Study_Skills. **Supp**—ESL.
   Sports (req'd)—Basket X-country Equestrian Golf Lacrosse Ski Soccer Tennis. B: Baseball. G: F_Hockey Softball.
   Selective adm: 91/yr. Bdg 70. Day 21. Appl fee: $30. Appl due: Feb. Accepted: 77%. Yield: 55%. **Tests** CEEB IQ SSAT TOEFL.
   Enr 248. B 150. G 98. Bdg 179. Day 69. Sec 243. PG 5. Intl 26%. Avg class size: 11. Stud/fac: 7:1. Casual. **Fac 49.** M 23/F 26. FT 32/PT 17. Wh 100%. Adv deg: 57%. In dorms 15.
   Grad '11—81. Col—80. (U of VT 2, U of ME-Orono 1, UNH 1, Syracuse 1, NYU 1, Wheaton-MA 1). **Mid 50% SAT:** CR 470-600. M 480-640. W 450-600. Mid 50% ACT: 19-26. **Col couns:** 3.
   Tui '11-'12: Bdg $47,730 (+$1000). **Day $28,170** (+$1000). **Aid:** Need 94 ($1,355,000).
   Endow $9,500,000. Plant val $17,000,000. Acres 500. Bldgs 30. Dorms 5. Class rms 35. Lib 15,000 vols. Sci labs 5. Gyms 2. Fields 4. Courts 8. Comp labs 3. Comp/stud: 1:1 Laptop prgm Gr 9-PG.
   Est 1836. Nonprofit. Tri (Sept-June). **Assoc** NEASC.

Coeducational from its founding, Gould is situated adjacent to the White Mountain National Forest. Students enroll from many states and foreign countries.

The college preparatory program combines traditional curricular elements with forward-looking electives. Honors and Advanced Placement courses in most disciplines are available for talented students, and qualified pupils may pursue independent studies in fields of interest to them. Ninety-minute class blocks facilitate in-depth inquiry in humanities, social science and laboratory science courses.

Special offerings include experiential education programs; exchange programs with schools in Germany, France, Spain and Hungary; a university-level computer network; and noteworthy programs in the visual arts, science and technology. The school's location allows for an extensive outdoor program and a strong winter sports program.

BRIDGTON, ME. (38 mi. NW of Portland, ME; 120 mi. N of Boston, MA) Suburban. Pop: 4883. Alt: 405 ft. Area also includes North Bridgton.

BRIDGTON ACADEMY
Bdg and Day — Boys PG Year

North Bridgton, ME 04057. Rte 37, PO Box 292. Tel: 207-647-3322. Fax: 207-647-8513.
   www.bridgtonacademy.org E-mail: cwebb@bridgtonacademy.org
Graydon E. Vigneau, Jr., Head (2008). BS, Univ of New Hampshire, MBA, Columbia Univ.
Chris Webb, Adm.
   Col Prep. Feat—Creative_Writing Calc Stats Anat & Physiol Ecol Environ_Sci Oceanog Comp_Sci Civil_War WWII Econ Law Pol_Sci Psych Sociol Logic Philos Relig Graphic_Arts Communications Journ SAT_Prep. **Supp**—LD. **Dual enr:** U of S ME, U of New England, Plymouth St.
   Sports—B: Baseball Basket Football Golf Ice_Hockey Lacrosse Ski Soccer Tennis.
   Selective adm: 188/yr. Bdg 185. Day 3. Appl fee: $50. Appl due: Rolling. Accepted: 83%. Yield: 66%. **Tests** CEEB.
   Enr 188. Bdg 185. Day 3. Nonwhite 15%. Avg class size: 13. Stud/fac: 9:1. **Fac 24.** In dorms 8.

Grad '08—188. Col—181. (Quinnipiac, Sacred Heart, S NH, Assumption, US Naval Acad, St Anselm). **Avg SAT:** CR 500. M 480. **Col couns:** 3.
Tui '11-'12: Bdg $42,000 (+$1500). **Day $23,500** (+$1500). **Aid:** Need 94.
Endow $4,700,000. Plant val $8,484,000. Acres 55. Bldgs 24. Dorms 8. Dorm rms 84. Class rms 11. Lib 7000 vols. Chapels 1. Sci labs 4. Writing labs 1. Auds 1. Art studios 1. Music studios 1. Museums 1. Gyms 1. Fields 5. Courts 2. Rinks 1. Weight rms 1. Comp labs 1. Comp/stud: 1:2.8.
Est 1808. Nonprofit. Sem (Sept-May). **Assoc** NEASC.

Bridgton was established by the Massachusetts legislature at a time when Maine was part of Massachusetts. The impetus for founding came from 37 local residents who furnished financial support to provide secondary schooling for boys and girls. In 1964, the academy adopted a new academic plan that resulted in the discontinuance of coeducation and the elimination of the lower grades: Bridgton became a one-year college preparatory school offering specific programs for older boys in grade 12 and for postgraduates. The present-day school serves postgraduate students who attend for one year only.

All aspects of school life address the needs of the boy capable of college-level work who stands to benefit from an additional year of study and growth prior to college entrance. The curriculum emphasizes writing, computation and critical reading, in addition to electives. Qualified students may take college courses for transferable college credit through partnerships with the University of Southern Maine, the University of New England and Plymouth State College. A separate program provides academic support for pupils who have been diagnosed with mild learning disabilities.

Students are encouraged to participate in interscholastic sports or in skiing, intramurals or the outing club. Most teams compete against college junior varsity squads, as well as against traditional prep school rivals. Bridgton schedules various guest lectures and performances.

FRYEBURG, ME. (45 mi. WNW of Portland, ME; 116 mi. N of Boston, MA) Rural. Pop: 1549. Alt: 420 ft.

FRYEBURG ACADEMY
Bdg and Day — Coed Gr 9-12

Fryeburg, ME 04037. 745 Main St. Tel: 207-935-2001. Fax: 207-935-4475.
 www.fryeburgacademy.org E-mail: admissions@fryeburgacademy.org
Daniel G. Lee, Jr., Head (1993). BA, Yale Univ, MA, Wesleyan Univ. **Christopher Hibbard, Adm.**
 Col Prep. Gen Acad. AP (exams req'd)—Eng Fr Span Calc Stats Comp_Sci Bio Chem Physics Eur_Hist US_Hist Music_Theory. **Feat**—Creative_Writing Gothic_Lit Holocaust_Lit Chin Lat Anat & Physiol Ecol Organic_Chem Econ Psych Sociol Ethics Architect Filmmaking Photog Studio_Art Theater Public_Speak Indus_Arts Woodworking Health. **Supp**—Dev_Read ESL LD Rem_Math Rem_Read Tut.
 Sports—Basket Cheer X-country Golf Lacrosse Ski Soccer Tennis Track. B: Baseball Football Ice_Hockey Wrestling. G: F_Hockey Softball. **Activities:** 41.
 Somewhat selective adm: 200/yr. Bdg 65. Day 135. Appl fee: $50. Appl due: Rolling. Accepted: 88%. Yield: 60%.
 Enr 638. Bdg 154. Day 484. Intl 13%. Avg class size: 17. Casual. **Fac 64.** FT 56/PT 8. In dorms 10.
 Grad '10—186. Col—143. (S ME CC 16, U of S ME 8, U of ME-Orono 7, Plymouth St 6, Central ME CC 5, White Mtns CC 5). **Avg SAT:** CR 510. M 540. **Col couns:** 3.
 Tui '12-'13: Bdg $42,300 (+$1200). **5-Day Bdg $33,800** (+$1200). **Day $20,200** (+$700). **Intl Bdg $42,300** (+$3700).
 Endow $5,000,000. Plant val $24,000,000. Acres 34. Bldgs 14. Dorms 4. Dorm rms 120. Class rms 60. Lib 13,000 vols. Sci labs 6. Lang labs 1. Art studios 1. Music studios 1. Gyms 1. Fields 6. Courts 3. Comp labs 2.

Est 1792. Nonprofit. Sem (Sept-June). **Assoc** NEASC.

Started and since maintained as a coeducational school, FA enjoyed as its first headmaster Paul Langdon, the Bernard Langdon of Oliver Wendell Holmes' novel *Elsie Venner.* His most eminent successor was Daniel Webster, who here made his first and only attempt at teaching school.

Serving the community through its day program, the academy also offers boarding enrollment to its students, who pursue either a college preparatory or a general course of study. AP courses, tutorials and learning-disability services complement the academic program, and English as a Second Language courses are available for an additional fee. FA maintains particularly strong drama and music programs.

HEBRON, ME. (38 mi. NNW of Portland, ME; 132 mi. NNE of Boston, MA) Rural. Pop: 1053. Alt: 600 ft.

HEBRON ACADEMY

Bdg — Coed Gr 9-PG; Day — Coed 6-PG

Hebron, ME 04238. 339 Paris Rd, PO Box 309. Tel: 207-966-2100, 888-432-7664. **Fax:** 207-966-2304.
www.hebronacademy.org   **E-mail: admissions@hebronacademy.org**
John J. King, Head (2001). BA, Williams College. **Joseph M. Hemmings, Adm.**
   Col Prep. AP (exams req'd)—Eng Calc Bio Chem Physics US_Hist Studio_Art. **Feat**— Humanities Fr Lat Span Anat & Physiol Astron Environ_Sci Genetics Geol Comp_Sci Web_Design Psych Philos World_Relig Architect Drawing Painting Photog Sculpt Music Music_Theory. **Supp**—ESL LD Tut. Outdoor ed.
   Sports—Basket X-country Golf Lacrosse Ski Soccer Tennis Track. B: Baseball Football Ice_Hockey. G: F_Hockey Softball.
   Selective adm: 103/yr. Bdg 80. Day 23. Appl fee: $50. Appl due: Feb. Applied: 350. Accepted: 63%. Yield: 48%. **Tests** CEEB CTP_4 IQ SSAT Stanford TOEFL.
   Enr 256. B 162. G 94. Bdg 163. Day 93. Elem 23. Sec 222. PG 11. Wh 82%. Latino 1%. Blk 6%. Native Am 1%. Asian 10%. Intl 30%. Avg class size: 12. Stud/fac: 7:1. Casual.
   Fac 45. Wh 100%. In dorms 31.
   Grad '11—70. Col—70. (Cornell, Columbia, US Milit Acad, US Naval Acad, Boston Col, Bowdoin). **Avg SAT:** CR/M/W 1540. **Col couns:** 2.
   Tui '12-'13: Bdg $49,900 (+$1500). **Day** $22,400-27,400 (+$400). **Aid:** Need 127 ($1,500,000).
   Endow $16,000,000. Plant val $30,000,000. Acres 1500. Bldgs 9. Dorms 3. Dorm rms 107. Class rms 19. Lib 20,000 vols. Comp ctrs 1. Theaters 2. Art studios 2. Gyms 1. Courts 8. Rinks 1.
   Est 1804. Nonprofit. Tri (Sept-June). **Assoc** CLS NEASC.

The school was founded by Revolutionary War veterans as a coeducational academy. Affiliated with Colby College until 1956, it became a boys' boarding school in the early 20th century before once again admitting girls and day students in 1972. In 1991, Hebron's trustees adopted a middle school program for students in grades 6-8. The academy occupies a 1500-acre campus in the foothills of western Maine, distinguished by the work of architect John Calvin Stevens at the turn of the century.

The curriculum prepares students for higher education and includes a full range of Advanced Placement and honors courses. Hebron conducts a well-regarded program for students with minor learning differences, and English as a Second Language is part of the repertoire of course instruction. The interdisciplinary nature studies program consists of academic study and outdoor skills instruction. Classroom course work involves specialized, trimester-long English, math, science and history classes. In addition, students choose from extensive course offerings in art and music and a full complement of activities and interscholastic sports.

A variety of environmental and outdoor education experiences, including kayaking, canoeing, rock climbing, hiking, camping, skiing and snowboarding, is offered. The cultural resources of nearby Lewiston, Auburn and Portland provide theater, sporting and concert opportunities for students and faculty.

KENTS HILL, ME. (52 mi. NNE of Portland, ME; 152 mi. NNE of Boston, MA) Rural. Pop: 90.

KENTS HILL SCHOOL

Bdg and Day — Coed Gr 9-PG

Kents Hill, ME 04349. 1614 Main St, PO Box 257. Tel: 207-685-4914.
　Fax: 207-685-9529.
　www.kentshill.org　E-mail: info@kentshill.org
Jeremy LaCasse, Head (2011). AB, Bowdoin College, MA, Columbia Univ. **Amy Smucker, Adm.**
　Col Prep. AP (exams req'd; 129 taken)—Eng Calc Stats Bio Chem Environ_Sci Physics Eur_Hist US_Hist Studio_Art. **Feat**—Shakespeare Holocaust_Lit Playwriting Chin Fr Span Anat & Physiol Astron Ecol Forensic_Sci Web_Design African_Hist Econ Psych Comp_Relig Ethics Philos Art_Hist Ceramics Filmmaking Photog Sculpt Theater Music_Theory Dance Journ Woodworking. **Supp**—ESL LD Rev Tut. Sat classes.
　Sports—Basket X-country Fencing Golf Ice_Hockey Lacrosse Ski Soccer Tennis. B: Baseball Football. G: F_Hockey Softball.
　Selective adm: 90/yr. Bdg 75. Day 15. Appl fee: $50. Appl due: Feb. Applied: 350. Accepted: 70%. Yield: 45%. **Tests** SSAT TOEFL.
　Enr 250. B 150. G 100. Bdg 190. Day 60. Sec 240. PG 10. Wh 75%. Latino 3%. Blk 6%. Native Am 1%. Asian 15%. Intl 25%. Avg class size: 11. Stud/fac: 6:1. Formal. **Fac 44.** M 26/F 18. FT 44. Wh 96%. Blk 2%. Native Am 2%. Adv deg: 54%. In dorms 20.
　Grad '11—75. Col—72. (U of ME-Orono 4, Bryant 3, UNH 2, Colby 2, Gettysburg 2, High Pt 2). Athl schol 4. **Mid 50% SAT:** CR 420-580. M 490-640. W 450-560. Mid 50% ACT: 19-25. **Col couns:** 3.
　Tui '11-'12: Bdg $46,400 (+$500). **Day $25,300** (+$500). **Aid:** Need 103 ($2,254,100). Endow $4,500,000. Plant val $45,000,000. Acres 400. Bldgs 22 (35% ADA). Dorms 5. Dorm rms 102. Class rms 32. Lib 10,000 vols. Photog labs 1. Comp ctrs 2. Theaters 1. Art studios 4. Music studios 1. Perf arts ctrs 1. Gyms 1. Athletic ctrs 1. Fields 7. Basketball courts 1. Rinks 1. Riding rings 1. Stables 1. Weight rms 1. Fitness ctrs 1. Equestrian ctrs 1.
　Est 1824. Nonprofit. Tri (Sept-June). **Assoc** CLS NEASC.

One of the oldest coeducational boarding schools in the country, Kents Hill was established by Luther D. Sampson to offer "an educational program calculated to inspire intellectual growth and develop character."

The curriculum includes a wide variety of courses, ranging from the traditional to the progressive. Numerous electives supplement required courses. The school's learning center provides students with one-on-one instruction, and SAT preparation is available on a weekly basis. Sophomores and juniors may participate in exchange programs with schools in the US and Europe. All boys and girls take part in two community service days annually.

Kents Hill owns and operates its own on-campus ski and snowboard slope and complex of cross-country trails, providing for a strong emphasis on winter sports. Nearby Lovejoy Pond is available for environmental research, as well as for canoeing, fishing and swimming. The school also plans hiking, rock climbing and biking trips in the area. Kents Hill's proximity to Portland and to Colby, Bates and Bowdoin colleges enables students to attend lectures, concerts, dances, athletic contests and other events.

PITTSFIELD, ME. (87 mi. NNE of Portland, ME; 187 mi. NNE of Boston, MA) Rural. Pop: 4214. Alt: 223 ft.

MAINE CENTRAL INSTITUTE

Bdg and Day — Coed Gr 9-PG

Pittsfield, ME 04967. 295 Main St. Tel: 207-487-3355. Fax: 207-487-3512.
www.mci-school.org   E-mail: cwilliams@mci-school.org
Christopher J. Hopkins, Head (2008). BA, MA, Middlebury College. **Clint Williams, Adm.**

> **Col Prep. Gen Acad. AP (exams req'd)**—Eng Calc Bio Chem Physics Studio_Art. **Feat**—Humanities Fr Lat Span Anat & Physiol Astron Botany Environ_Sci Meteorology Comp_Sci Sociol Asian_Stud Architect_Drawing Video_Production Music_Hist Ballet Debate Mech_Drawing. **Supp**—ESL LD. **Dual enr:** Colby, U of ME-Augusta, U of ME-Orono.
>
> **Sports**—Basket Soccer Track. B: Baseball Football Golf Wrestling. G: Cheer F_Hockey Ski Softball.
>
> **Selective adm:** 177/yr. Bdg 71. Day 106. Appl fee: $75. Appl due: Rolling. Accepted: 70%. Yield: 53%. **Tests** CEEB SSAT TOEFL.
>
> **Enr 450.** Bdg 140. Day 310. Sec 437. PG 13. Intl 28%. Avg class size: 15. Casual. **Fac 53.** M 23/F 30. FT 43/PT 10. Adv deg: 24%. In dorms 11.
>
> **Grad '08—120. Col—90.** (U of ME-Orono, Syracuse, U of New England, IN U, Albany Col of Pharmacy, Champlain). **Avg SAT:** CR 425. M 474. W 420. Avg ACT: 23. Alum donors: 5%.
>
> **Tui '12-'13: Bdg $40,850** (+$2500). **Day $10,000.**
>
> **Summer:** Acad Enrich Rec. ESL. 4 wks.
>
> Endow $4,200,000. Plant val $14,200,000. Acres 23. Bldgs 16. Dorms 4. Dorm rms 56. Class rms 43. Lib 17,000 vols. Sci labs 3. Lang labs 3. Art studios 1. Music studios 1. Dance studios 2. Gyms 2. Fields 6. Courts 8. Comp labs 4.
>
> **Est 1866.** Nonprofit. Sem (Aug-June). **Assoc** NEASC.

Established by Rev. Oren Cheney, who had founded Bates College six years prior, MCI conducts a rigorous educational program for students of varying ability levels and interests. The school requires four years of math and science study, and its humanities curriculum integrates history, literature, art and music. Pupils may take Advanced Placement courses in grades 11 and 12, and honors classes are also part of the curriculum.

The senior project, a graduation requirement, encourages students to explore areas of interest in detail prior to delivering formal presentations. MCI's English as a Second Language program serves the university-bound international student, while the Personalized Learning Program offers content tutoring and yearlong instructional support for those requiring extra help in the classroom.

The Bossov Ballet, headed by dancer Andrei Bossov, formerly of Russia's Kirov Ballet, is in residence at the school. Boys and girls may also take part in highly regarded vocal and instrumental jazz ensembles; approximately one-third of MCI's students participate in music, while many others are involved in drama and the visual arts. MCI's annual, three-day winter carnival is an enduring tradition.

PORTLAND, ME. (101 mi. NNE of Boston, MA) Urban. Pop: 64,249. Alt: 26 ft.

WAYNFLETE SCHOOL

Day — Coed Gr PS (Age 3)-12

Portland, ME 04102. 360 Spring St. Tel: 207-774-5721. Fax: 207-772-4782.

www.waynflete.org   E-mail: admissionoffice@waynflete.org
Mark W. Segar, Head (1994). AB, Harvard Univ, EdD, Univ of Massachusetts-Amherst.
Lynne Breen, Adm.
Col Prep. Feat—British_Lit African_Lit Chin Fr Lat Span Calc Stats Astron Bioethics
   Environ_Sci Marine_Bio/Sci Russ_Hist Psych Philos Ceramics Printmaking Acting
   Music_Theory. **Supp**—Tut.
Sports (req'd)—Basket Crew X-country Golf Lacrosse Ski Soccer Swim Tennis. B:
   Baseball. G: F_Hockey Ice_Hockey Softball. **Activities:** 28.
Selective adm (Gr PS-11): 102/yr. Usual entry: PS, K, 4, 6 & 9. Appl fee: $40. Appl due:
   Feb. Applied: 234. Accepted: 54%. Yield: 78%.
Enr 556. B 258. G 298. Elem 304. Sec 252. Wh 76%. Blk 6%. Asian 7%. Other 11%. Avg
   class size: 13. Stud/fac: 9:1. **Fac 134.** M 84/F 50. FT 69/PT 65. Wh 94%. Latino 1%.
   Blk 3%. Asian 1%. Other 1%. Adv deg: 30%.
Grad '11—61. Col—61. (Northeastern U 4, CT Col 3, Brown 2, Bowdoin 2, Wheaton-
   MA 2, Bates 2). **Avg SAT:** CR 620. M 600. W 610. **Col couns:** 4. Alum donors: 23%.
Tui '12-'13: Day $20,355-25,375. Aid: Need 128 ($2,086,860).
Summer (enr 500): Acad Enrich Rec. Arts. Theater. Sports. Tui Day $125-425. 1-3 wks.
   Marine Sci. Tui Bdg $4000. 4 wks.
Endow $17,900,000. Plant val $39,000,000. Acres 37. Bldgs 11 (93% ADA). Class rms
   44. Lib 18,558 vols. Sci labs 6. Auds 1. Art studios 3. Music studios 2. Dance studios
   1. Art galleries 2. Gyms 2. Fields 4. Courts 6. Comp labs 1. Comp/stud: 1:3.
Est 1898. Nonprofit. Sem (Sept-June). **Assoc** CLS NEASC.

Founders Agnes Lowell and Caroline Crisfield, who came to Portland from the Ogontz School in Philadelphia, PA, and served Waynflete until 1924, named the school after 15th-century British statesman and educator William Waynflete. Rapid early growth prompted Lowell and Crisfield to relocate the campus to the former Horace Dudley estate, situated in the city's residential West End. In addition to its urban campus, Waynflete maintains a 35-acre site along the Fore River for athletics and outdoor education. Students enroll from approximately 50 Greater Portland communities.

The lower school comprises four multi-age groups: early childhood (ages 3 and 4), kindergarten and grade 1, grades 2 and 3, and grades 4 and 5. As the program progresses, children assume additional responsibility and gain more independence. During the middle school years (grades 6-8), students build upon the skills they began developing in the lower school. Special programs provide enrichment, and competitive athletics and cocurricular activities supplement academics.

In the upper school, the rigorous college preparatory curriculum combines instruction in the traditional subject areas with electives, survey courses, interdisciplinary courses and seminar. Visual and performing arts offerings are noteworthy, and an applied arts program incorporates the musical resources of Greater Portland. All boys and girls engage in one athletic program per season, in either a competitive sport or an alternative area such as yoga or weight training.

Community service, in the form of service days and projects, is an integral part of the program at all grade levels; in addition, juniors and seniors perform 25 hours of compulsory volunteer work in the community annually. Upper schoolers participate in a fall outdoor program in wilderness areas of northern New England, and juniors may pursue off-campus study opportunities through the Chewonki Semester School or the CITYterm program.

YARMOUTH, ME. (9 mi. N of Portland, ME; 109 mi. NNE of Boston, MA) Suburban. Pop: 8360. Alt: 87 ft.

NORTH YARMOUTH ACADEMY
Day — Coed Gr 5-12
Yarmouth, ME 04096. 148 Main St. Tel: 207-846-9051. Fax: 207-846-8829.

www.nya.org   E-mail: lhyndman@nya.org
Brad Choyt, Head (2011). AB, Brown Univ, MFA, Univ of Pennsylvania. **Laurie Hyndman, Adm.**
Col Prep. AP (146 exams taken, 82% 3+)—Eng Fr Lat Span Calc Bio Environ_Sci Eur_Hist US_Hist Art_Hist Studio_Art Music_Theory. **Feat**—Stats Genetics Comp_ Graphics Cold_War Lat-Amer_Hist Middle_Eastern_Hist Criminal_Justice Photog Drama Music Jazz_Band Dance Yoga. **Supp**—Tut. Outdoor ed.
Sports—Basket X-country Golf Ice_Hockey Indoor_Track Lacrosse Ski Soccer Tennis Track. G: F_Hockey Softball Volley.
Selective adm: 70/yr. Appl fee: $45. Appl due: Feb. Accepted: 69%. Yield: 76%. **Tests** ISEE SSAT.
Enr 265. Avg class size: 14. Stud/fac: 8:1. **Fac 36.** M 17/F 19. FT 31/PT 5. Wh 100%. Adv deg: 50%.
Grad '11—52. Col—51. (Bowdoin, Williams, Hamilton, U of ME-Orono, Georgetown, CT Col). **Mid 50% SAT:** CR 510-670. M 520-650. W 500-660. Mid 50% ACT: 21-28. **Col couns:** 1.
Tui '11-'12: Day $20,800-24,500 (+$500).
Summer: Sports. Writing. 8 wks.
Endow $3,000,000. Plant val $7,793,000. Acres 25. Bldgs 11. Class rms 20. Lib 9000 vols. Sci labs 3. Dark rms 1. Auds 1. Theaters 1. Art studios 2. Music studios 2. Dance studios 1. Perf arts ctrs 1. Pottery studios 1. Gyms 1. Fields 3. Tennis courts 3. Rinks 1. Greenhouses 1. Comp/stud: 1:4.
Est 1814. Nonprofit. Tri (Sept-June). **Assoc** CLS NEASC.

Located on a 25-acre campus in the center of the village of Yarmouth, the academy serves approximately 35 communities. NYA offers students a structured academic program with strong faculty and parental support for academic, social and athletic development. An advisor system, small classes, opportunities for extra help and tutoring, and Advanced Placement course work in several major disciplines are integral to the academy's liberal arts curriculum. Pupils also choose from a variety of fine arts courses.

All students participate in either the afternoon arts program or athletics. In addition, boys and girls may engage in wilderness trips, publications, school government and various activities. Social service is also emphasized at NYA, with group activities organized at all levels and each senior completing a two- to three-week service project prior to graduation.

MASSACHUSETTS

ANDOVER, MA. (23 mi. NNW of Boston, MA) Suburban. Pop: 29,063. Alt: 85 ft. Area also includes North Andover.

BROOKS SCHOOL
Bdg and Day — Coed Gr 9-12

North Andover, MA 01845. 1160 Great Pond Rd. Tel: 978-725-6272.
Fax: 978-725-6298.
www.brooksschool.org   E-mail: admission@brooksschool.org
John R. Packard, Head (2008). BA, Franklin and Marshall College, MALS, Wesleyan Univ.
Andrew C. Hirt, Adm.
Col Prep. AP (320 exams taken, 76% 3+)—Eng Chin Fr Lat Span Calc Bio Chem Environ_Sci Physics US_Govt & Pol Art_Hist. **Feat**—African-Amer_Lit Lat-Amer_Lit Playwriting Southern_Lit Greek Multivariable_Calc Anat Forensic_Sci Engineering Robotics African_Hist Chin_Hist Middle_Eastern_Hist Econ Psych Philos Theol Ceramics Film Photog Studio_Art Theater Music Music_Theory Jazz_Hist. **Supp**— Rev Tut. Sat classes.
Sports (req'd)—Basket Crew X-country Ice_Hockey Lacrosse Soccer Squash Tennis. B: Baseball Football Wrestling. G: F_Hockey Softball.
Selective adm (Bdg Gr 9-11; Day 9-10): 113/yr. Bdg 82. Day 31. Usual entry: 9 & 10. Appl fee: $50. Appl due: Feb. Applied: 1026. Accepted: 26%. Yield: 42%. **Tests** CEEB ISEE SSAT TOEFL.
Enr 370. B 196. G 174. Bdg 254. Day 116. Wh 78%. Latino 5%. Blk 3%. Native Am 1%. Asian 13%. Intl 14%. Avg class size: 12. Stud/fac: 5:1. Formal. **Fac 77.** M 42/F 35. FT 77. Nonwhite 7%. Adv deg: 81%. In dorms 29.
Grad '11—102. Col—102. (Boston U 5, Middlebury 4, U of VT 4, U of Denver 4, Tufts 3, Colby 3). **Mid 50% SAT:** CR 570-670. M 590-690. W 560-660. Avg ACT: 27.1. **Col couns:** 3. Alum donors: 33%.
Tui '12-'13: Bdg $49,365 (+$500). **Day $37,180** (+$500). **Aid:** Need 77 ($2,640,000).
Summer: Acad Enrich Rev. Tui Day $385-2900. 1-8 wks.
Endow $58,700,000. Acres 251. Bldgs 49. Dorms 10. Class rms 33. Lib 36,000 vols. Sci labs 8. Lang labs 1. Auds 3. Theaters 2. Art studios 3. Music studios 5. Gyms 1. Fields 9. Courts 3. Rinks 1. Student ctrs 1. Comp labs 2. Comp/stud: 1:2.
Est 1926. Nonprofit. Episcopal. Sem (Sept-June). **Assoc** CLS NEASC.

Brooks was founded by Rev. Endicott Peabody, founder and onetime headmaster of Groton School. Named in honor of Phillips Brooks, former bishop of Massachusetts and native of North Andover, the school was given its land and original buildings by the Russell family. Girls were first admitted in 1979.

Students follow a flexible liberal arts curriculum and readily enter leading colleges. The school offers Advanced Placement courses in the major disciplines. Each student may choose his or her own faculty advisor; faculty and students share in many aspects of school governance and committee work. The Students on the Forefront of Science program places talented fifth form students in summer research internships at universities and laboratories.

Brooks conducts exchange programs with schools in Kenya, Scotland, South Africa and Hungary.

PHILLIPS ACADEMY
Bdg and Day — Coed Gr 9-PG
Andover, MA 01810. 180 Main St. Tel: 978-749-4000. Fax: 978-749-4123.

www.andover.edu E-mail: admissions@andover.edu
John Palfrey, Head (2012). AB, JD, Harvard Univ, MPhil, Univ of Cambridge (England).
Jim Ventre, Int Adm.
> **Col Prep. AP (842 exams taken, 97% 3+)**—Chin Fr Ger Japan Span Calc Stats Comp_Sci Bio Chem Physics Econ Art_Hist Studio_Art Music_Theory. **Feat**—Creative_Writing Shakespeare African-Amer_Lit Caribbean_Lit James_Joyce Greek Lat Russ Arabic Linear_Algebra Anat & Physiol Astron Bioethics Ecol Forensic_Sci Genetics Geol Microbio Cosmology Fluid_Mechanics Meteorology Comp_Animation E_Asian_Hist Middle_Eastern_Hist Intl_Relations Psych Lat-Amer_Stud Race_Relations Urban_Stud Architect Ceramics Filmmaking Photog Sculpt Theater Music Music_Hist Dance Study_Skills. **Supp**—Tut.
Sports—Basket Crew X-country Golf Ice_Hockey Lacrosse Ski Soccer Squash Swim Tennis Track Ultimate_Frisbee Volley W_Polo. B: Baseball Football Wrestling. G: F_Hockey Softball. **Activities:** 100.
Very selective adm: 350/yr. Appl fee: $40. Appl due: Feb. Applied: 2910. Accepted: 14%. Yield: 84%. **Tests** CEEB ISEE SSAT TOEFL.
Enr 1109. B 553. G 556. Bdg 818. Day 291. Sec 1085. PG 24. Nonwhite 40%. Intl 8%. Avg class size: 13. Stud/fac: 5:1. **Fac 220.** M 115/F 105. FT 220. Wh 78%. Latino 7%. Blk 7%. Asian 7%. Other 1%. Adv deg: 72%. In dorms 79.
Grad '11—329. Col—323. (Harvard 15, Stanford 15, Columbia 14, Yale 14, Cornell 11, USC 10). **Avg SAT:** CR 683. M 694. W 677. Avg ACT: 29.9. **Col couns:** 6. Alum donors: 38%.
Tui '12-'13: Bdg $44,500 (+$2500). **Day $34,500** (+$2500). **Aid:** Need 506 ($17,100,000).
Summer (enr 550): Acad Enrich. Tui Bdg $7850. Tui Day $4800. 5 wks.
Endow $770,000,000. Plant val $534,395,000. Acres 500. Bldgs 151. Dorms 43. Dorm rms 589. Class rms 95. 2 Libs 120,000 vols. Chapels 1. Sci labs 10. Lang labs 1. Observatories 1. Sci ctrs 1. Auds 2. Theaters 2. Art studios 5. Music studios 15. Dance studios 2. Music ctrs 1. Gyms 3. Fields 18. Basketball courts 2. Tennis courts 18. Squash courts 8. Pools 2. Rinks 2. Museums 2. Radio stations 1. Comp labs 3.
Est 1778. Nonprofit. Tri (Sept-June). **Assoc** CLS NEASC.

Often referred to as Andover, the academy was founded by Samuel Phillips, Jr., during the American Revolution. Paul Revere designed the school's seal, and John Hancock signed its Act of Incorporation. Andover seeks students from diverse ethnic, racial, socioeconomic and geographic backgrounds, drawing students from nearly every state and roughly 30 foreign countries and providing financial aid for both needy and middle-class families.

With some 300 course offerings in 18 academic departments, the curriculum comprises a required core of studies fundamental to a liberal education and includes elective courses designed to address individual interests. Courses at the Advanced Placement level and beyond are offered in virtually every department. Among several complementary programs are an exchange with a school in China, as well as School Year Abroad, which offers juniors and seniors a full academic year of study in China, France, Spain or Italy. The Abbott Independent Scholars Program provides opportunities for independent work with faculty members.

The athletic department features sport, dance and exercise options at every level of instruction. Recreational athletes have various intramural and instructional options, while interscholastic athletes prepare for competition with other prep schools and with Boston-area colleges. Outdoor adventure opportunities, including rock climbing, winter camping, and white-water canoeing and kayaking, are also available.

Pupils choose from many interest clubs and organizations, and more than half of the student body fulfill the mandate of the school's motto, *Non Sibi* ("Not for Self"), by volunteering in an extensive community service program. In addition, each student takes part in a schoolwide work-duty program by engaging in such tasks as dorm cleaning, school office assistance and dining hall duties.

PIKE SCHOOL
Day — Coed Gr PS (Age 4)-9

Andover, MA 01810. 34 Sunset Rock Rd. Tel: 978-475-1197. Fax: 978-475-3014.
www.pikeschool.org E-mail: information@pikeschool.org
John M. Waters, Head (1994). BA, Middlebury College, MA, Trinity College (CT). **Angela Brown, Adm.**

Pre-Prep. Elem math—TERC Investigations. **Feat**—Humanities Fr Lat Span Studio_Art Drama Music. **Supp**—Dev_Read Tut. Outdoor ed.

Sports—Basket X-country Ice_Hockey Lacrosse Soccer Tennis Track. B: Baseball. G: F_Hockey Softball.

Selective adm: 75/yr. Usual entry: PS, K & 6. Appl fee: $45. Appl due: Jan. Applied: 216. Accepted: 35%. Yield: 80%. **Tests** SSAT.

Enr 441. B 206. G 235. Elem 431. Sec 10. Wh 67%. Latino 6%. Blk 3%. Asian 17%. Other 7%. Avg class size: 14. Stud/fac: 8:1. **Fac 58.** M 11/F 47. FT 55/PT 3. Wh 97%. Asian 3%. Adv deg: 86%.

Grad '11—61. Prep—54. (Phillips Acad 12, Brooks 11, Governor's Acad 5, Central Catholic-MA 4, Middlesex 3, St John's Prep-MA 3).

Tui '12-'13: Day $20,990-26,650 (+$635-2390). **Aid:** Need 57 ($935,000).

Endow $5,767,000. Plant val $31,000,000. Acres 35. Bldgs 5. Class rms 47. Lib 20,000 vols. Sci labs 6. Media/tech ctrs 1. Art studios 5. Music studios 2. Gyms 1. Fields 4. Courts 1. Comp/stud: 1:1.8.

Est 1926. Nonprofit. Tri (Sept-June).

Founded by Mrs. Walter E. Pike, this school serves Andover and the communities of the Merrimack Valley. The school's five major buildings and athletic fields are located on a 36-acre tract of former farmland. The lower school (grades PS-2), the middle school (grades 3-5) and the upper school (grades 6-9) offer a coordinated academic program that emphasizes fundamental skills in the basic disciplines. Technology resources include mobile laptop computer labs, classrooms outfitted with interactive whiteboards and campuswide wireless connectivity.

Outdoor education, which stresses environmental issues, begins in grade 5, while foreign language instruction commences in grade 6. Physical education and visual and performing arts offerings are integral to the program at all grade levels.

ASHBURNHAM, MA. (50 mi. WNW of Boston, MA) Suburban. Pop: 5546. Alt: 1100 ft.

CUSHING ACADEMY
Bdg and Day — Coed Gr 9-PG

Ashburnham, MA 01430. 39 School St, PO Box 8000. Tel: 978-827-7000.
Fax: 978-827-7500.
www.cushing.org E-mail: admissions@cushing.org
James Tracy, Head (2006). BA, Univ of Massachusetts-Boston, MBA, Boston Univ, PhD, Stanford Univ. **Deborah A. Gustafson & Adam J. Payne, Adms.**

Col Prep. AP (exams req'd; 157 taken, 84% 3+)—Calc Bio Physics US_Hist Econ US_Govt & Pol. **Feat**—Playwriting Chin Fr Lat Span Stats Ecol Programming Web_Design Cold_War Holocaust Vietnam_War Psych Sociol Comp_Relig Ethics Architect_Drawing Art_Hist Fine_Arts Painting Photog Stained_Glass Acting Drama Music Dance Silversmithing. **Supp**—Dev_Read ESL Rem_Math Rem_Read Rev Tut.

Sports—Basket X-country Golf Ice_Hockey Lacrosse Ski Soccer Tennis Track. B: Baseball Football. G: F_Hockey Softball Volley. **Activities:** 23.

Selective adm: 191/yr. Bdg 170. Day 21. Appl fee: $50. Appl due: Feb. Accepted: 65%. Yield: 44%. **Tests** CEEB SSAT TOEFL.

Enr 445. B 267. G 178. Bdg 372. Day 73. Sec 421. PG 24. Wh 60%. Latino 2%. Blk 5%.

Native Am 1%. Asian 18%. Other 14%. Intl 25%. Avg class size: 12. Stud/fac: 8:1. Casual. **Fac 66.** M 39/F 27. FT 55/PT 11. Wh 97%. Latino 1%. Blk 1%. Asian 1%. Adv deg: 60%. In dorms 32.
Grad '10—124. Col—124. (Roger Williams 4, Boston U 3, Emory 3, U of MA-Amherst 3, Wheaton-MA 3, Dartmouth 2). **Col couns:** 3. Alum donors: 12%.
Tui '12-'13: Bdg $51,575 (+$3000). **Day $37,500** (+$1300). **Aid:** Merit 12 ($60,000). Need 78 ($1,600,000).
Summer: Acad Enrich. Studio Art. Tui Bdg $6200. Tui Day $3000. ESL. Tui Bdg $6200. 5 wks.
Endow $22,600,000. Plant val $33,000,000. Acres 162. Bldgs 19. Dorms 11. Dorm rms 167. Class rms 23. Lib 10,000 vols. Sci labs 9. Lang labs 1. Auds 1. Art studios 5. Music studios 7. Gyms 1. Fields 8. Courts 6. Rinks 1. Comp labs 2. Laptop prgm Gr 9-PG.
Est 1865. Nonprofit. Tri (Sept-June). **Assoc** CLS NEASC.

Founded by a benefaction from Thomas Parkman Cushing, a native of Ashburnham, and enriched by several bequests, this academy owes its early growth chiefly to Dr. Hervey S. Cowell, beloved by his students and in office for nearly 40 years. Over the years, the school has seen an improvement of facilities and physical plant, with steady increases in enrollment and faculty, as well as heightened academic standards.

Cushing's college preparatory program features Advanced Placement courses, well-developed fine arts and computer curricula, opportunities for independent study, language development courses, ESL classes and trimester-length seminars. All students must purchase laptop computers, and a wireless Internet network covers all academic buildings.

An important facet of the academic program, The Cushing Institute for 21st Century Leadership, brings current issues into the classroom, facilitates global travel experiences and hosts various guest speakers. The institute also provides leadership and entrepreneurial opportunities on campus and coordinates both internships and the Cushing Scholars, an enrichment program for a chosen group of high-potential students. In 2009, the academy changed its library into a primarily digital learning center that houses a collection of electronic readers and online data sources.

Many faculty members reside on campus, and each pupil has a faculty advisor. The school draws its enrollment from many states and foreign countries.

BARNSTABLE, MA. (57 mi. SE of Boston, MA; 58 mi. E of Providence, RI) Suburban. Pop: 47,821. Alt: 37 ft.

TRINITY CHRISTIAN ACADEMY
Day — Coed Gr PS (Age 4)-12

Barnstable, MA 02630. 979 Mary Dunn Rd. Tel: 508-790-0114. Fax: 508-790-1293.
www.trinitychristiancapecod.org   E-mail: tcafrontdesk@comcast.ne
Ben Haskell, Head (2009). BA, Univ of Massachusetts-Amherst, MA, Grace Theological Seminary. **Denise Wiegand, Adm.**
Col Prep. Gen Acad. AP—Calc. **Feat**—Fr Lat Span Anat & Physiol Comp_Sci Bible Studio_Art Music Music_Theory. **Supp**—Tut. **Dual enr:** Cape Cod CC.
Sports—Basket Soccer. **Activities:** 5.
Somewhat selective adm: 24/yr. Appl fee: $60. Appl due: Rolling. Applied: 28. Accepted: 90%. Yield: 90%.
Enr 135. B 69. G 66. Elem 117. Sec 18. Wh 75%. Latino 3%. Blk 5%. Native Am 1%. Asian 3%. Other 13%. Avg class size: 10. Uniform. **Fac 27.** M 6/F 21. FT 20/PT 7. Wh 100%. Adv deg: 7%.
Grad '11—5. Col—5. (Cape Cod CC 3, Framingham St 1, MA Maritime 1). **Avg SAT:** CR 593. M 520. **Col couns:** 1. Alum donors: 10%.
Tui '12-'13: Day $6707-8298 (+$200). **Aid:** Merit 5. Need 46.

Summer: Acad Enrich Rec. Tui Day $160/wk. 8 wks.
Plant val $2,000,000. Acres 7. Bldgs 1 (100% ADA). Class rms 17. Lib 2000 vols. Sc
 labs 1. Fields 1. Comp labs 1. Comp/stud: 1:10.
Est 1967. Nonprofit. Nondenom Christian. (Sept-June).

Characterized by a favorable student-faculty ratio, this Cape Cod school stresses reading instruction (with emphasis placed on the developmental approach) while offering strong programs in math and science. Staff also direct attention to the spiritual life of each child within a traditional Christian framework. Pupils attend Bible classes each day and a chapel service each week. Boys and girls perform 100 hours of required community service prior to graduation.

Trinity schedules experiential trips to local museums and theaters, as well as annual excursions to the Cape Cod National Seashore NEEDS Program and to Washington, DC.

BELMONT, MA. (9 mi. WNW of Boston, MA) Suburban. Pop: 24,194. Alt: 39 ft.

BELMONT DAY SCHOOL
Day — Coed Gr PS (Age 4)-8
Belmont, MA 02478. 55 Day School Ln. Tel: 617-484-3078. Fax: 617-489-1942.
www.belmontday.org   E-mail: info@belmontday.org
Annette Raphel, Head (2011). BS, Northeastern Univ, MEd, Bridgewater State College
Deborah Brissenden, Adm.
 Pre-Prep. Feat—Fr Span Computers Studio_Art Drama Music Orchestra Woodworking
  Supp—Dev_Read Rem_Read Tut.
 Sports—Basket X-country Lacrosse Soccer Tennis Track. G: F_Hockey.
 Very selective adm (Gr PS-7): 46/yr. Usual entry: PS & 5. Appl fee: $45. Appl due: Jan
  Applied: 191. Accepted: 24%. Yield: 82%. **Tests** ISEE SSAT.
 Enr 273. B 132. G 141. Wh 75%. Latino 2%. Blk 3%. Asian 7%. Other 13%. Avg class
  size: 13. Stud/fac: 8:1. **Fac 40.** M 9/F 31. FT 31/PT 9. Wh 97%. Latino 1%. Blk 1%
  Asian 1%. Adv deg: 80%.
 Grad '11—31. Prep—25. (Concord Acad 6, Dana Hall 2, Gann Acad 2, Milton Acad 2)
  Alum donors: 6%.
 Tui '12-'13: Day $20,470-32,340. Aid: Need 45 ($893,145).
 Summer (enr 300): Acad Enrich Rec. Tui Day $1150/2-wk ses. 8 wks.
 Endow $14,813,000. Plant val $14,292,000. Acres 11. Bldgs 1 (100% ADA). Class rms
  23. Lib 13,000 vols. Sci labs 1. Lang labs 1. Auds 1. Theaters 1. Art studios 2. Music
  studios 1. Gyms 1. Fields 3. Courts 1. Pools 2. Comp labs 2. Comp/stud: 1:2 (1:1
  Laptop prgm Gr 7-8).
 Est 1927. Nonprofit. Sem (Sept-June).

Founded by parents, this elementary and middle school prepares students for independent secondary schools in and around Boston. Children are taught in small learning groups that allow for individual attention. The developmentally structured program combines academics with social competency skills instruction.

Belmont Day's core curriculum of language arts, math, social studies and science is enhanced by course work in studio art, music, orchestra, drama, technology, French, Spanish, physical education and athletics. Extended-day, after-school enrichment, and vacation and summer programs complement the regular academic sessions.   See Also Page 7

BELMONT HILL SCHOOL
5-Day Bdg — Boys Gr 9-12; Day — Boys 7-12
Belmont, MA 02478. 350 Prospect St. Tel: 617-993-5220. Fax: 617-484-4688.
www.belmonthill.org   E-mail: mkinnealey@belmonthill.org

Richard I. Melvoin, Head (1993). AB, Harvard Univ, MA, PhD, Univ of Michigan. **Stephen W. Carr, Jr., Adm.**

Col Prep. AP (280 exams taken, 96% 3+)—Eng Fr Lat Span Calc Stats Bio Chem Environ_Sci Physics Eur_Hist US_Hist US_Govt & Pol. **Feat**—British_Lit Creative_Writing Shakespeare African-Amer_Lit Southern_Lit Chin Greek Astron Geol Comp_Sci Vietnam_War Econ Intl_Relations Psych Art_Hist Photog Sculpt Studio_Art Acting Music. **Supp**—Tut.

Sports—B: Baseball Basket Crew X-country Football Ice_Hockey Lacrosse Sail Ski Soccer Squash Tennis Track Wrestling. **Activities:** 54.

Selective adm (Bdg Gr 9-11; Day 7-11): 90/yr. Usual entry: 7, 8 & 9. Appl fee: $40. Appl due: Feb. Applied: 419. Accepted: 28%. Yield: 71%. **Tests** ISEE SSAT.

Enr 442. Bdg 25. Day 417. Elem 110. Sec 332. Wh 80%. Latino 5%. Blk 7%. Asian 5%. Other 3%. Avg class size: 12. Stud/fac: 6:1. Formal. **Fac 68.** M 53/F 15. FT 63/PT 5. Adv deg: 72%. In dorms 4.

Grad '11—80. Col—80. (Harvard 6, U of PA 5, Holy Cross 4, Georgetown 3, Tufts 3, Boston Col 3). **Avg SAT:** CR 671. M 699. W 686. **Col couns:** 3. Alum donors: 51%.

Tui '11-'12: 5-Day Bdg $42,700 (+$835). **Day $35,950** (+$835). **Aid:** Need 124 ($3,250,000).

Summer (enr 500): Acad Enrich Rev Rec. 6 wks.

Endow $60,000,000. Acres 34. Bldgs 16. Dorms 2. Dorm rms 22. Class rms 32. Lib 18,000 vols. Chapels 1. Labs 4. Art studios 2. Music studios 1. Gyms 2. Fields 6. Courts 11. Rinks 1. Comp/stud: 1:2.

Est 1923. Nonprofit. Sem (Sept-May). **Assoc** CLS NEASC.

Belmont Hill provides a strong college preparatory program that combines a traditional curriculum with many elective opportunities. Expansion of opportunities in both curricular and extracurricular activities has been made possible by loyal alumni and parental support. The sectioning of classes allows for Advanced Placement in languages, mathematics, science, computer science and history. Qualified students may engage in independent study.

Exchange study programs to France, Spain and China are conducted during junior year. Belmont Hill often coordinates extracurricular activities with the Winsor School for girls in Boston.

BEVERLY, MA. (18 mi. NNE of Boston, MA) Urban. Pop: 39,862. Alt: 26 ft. Area also includes Prides Crossing.

LANDMARK SCHOOL

Bdg — Coed Gr 8-12; Day — Coed 2-12

Prides Crossing, MA 01965. 429 Hale St, PO Box 227. Tel: 978-236-3000. Fax: 978-927-7268.

Other locations: 167 Bridge St, PO Box 1489, Manchester-by-the-Sea 01944.

www.landmarkschool.org   E-mail: admission@landmarkschool.org

Robert J. Broudo, Head (1990). BA, Bates College, MEd, Boston Univ. **Carolyn Orsini Nelson, Adm.**

Col Prep. LD. Feat—Anat & Physiol Environ_Sci Marine_Bio/Sci Anthro Psych Sociol Studio_Art Acting Drama Chorus Dance Woodworking Study_Skills. **Supp**—Dev_ Read Rem_Math Rem_Read Rev Tut. Sat classes.

Sports—Basket X-country Golf Lacrosse Soccer Tennis. B: Baseball Wrestling. G: Volley.

Selective adm: 128/yr. Bdg 39. Day 89. Appl due: Rolling. Applied: 335. Accepted: 52%. Yield: 73%. **Tests** IQ.

Enr 461. B 301. G 160. Bdg 159. Day 302. Elem 150. Sec 311. Wh 78%. Latino 3%. Blk 2%. Native Am 1%. Asian 2%. Other 14%. Avg class size: 7. Casual. **Fac 222.** M 90/F 132. FT 222. Adv deg: 63%. In dorms 22.

Grad '11—72. Col—69. (Curry, U of AZ, UNH, Colby-Sawyer, Westfield St, Dean). **Avg**

SAT: CR 447. M 425. W 445.
Tui '12-'13: Bdg $64,200 (+$1600). **Day $48,200** (+$200).
Summer (enr 135): Acad Rem Rec. Tui Bdg $7775. 6 wks. Tui Day $4625-6450. 4-5
wks.
Endow $10,000,000. Plant val $40,000,000. Bldgs 27. Dorms 6. Dorm rms 89. Class
rms 81. Libs 2. Sci labs 3. Art studios 2. Music studios 1. Dance studios 1. Gyms 2.
Fields 4. Comp labs 5.
Est 1971. Nonprofit. Quar (Sept-June). **Assoc** NEASC.

Landmark is designed to help those intellectually capable and emotionally healthy students
who are not able to achieve in school because of language-based learning disabilities. The
school is not capable of addressing the needs of boys and girls with more pervasive learning
disabilities such as nonverbal learning disabilities, Asperger's syndrome, pervasive developmental disorder, bipolar disorder and developmental delay.

An intensive program of diagnostic prescriptive teaching based on one-on-one tutorials is
provided. The school offers remedial, expressive language and college preparatory programs
on two campuses along Boston's North Shore: the high school campus in Prides Crossing and
the elementary and middle schools in Manchester-by-the-Sea.   **See Also Page 50**

SHORE COUNTRY DAY SCHOOL

Day — Coed Gr PS (Age 4)-9

Beverly, MA 01915. 545 Cabot St. Tel: 978-927-1700. Fax: 978-927-1822.
www.shoreschool.org   E-mail: lcarey@shoreschool.org
Lawrence A. Griffin, Head (1987). BA, Florida Atlantic Univ, MALS, Dartmouth College.
Lilia N. Carey, Adm.
Pre-Prep. Feat—Lat Span Studio_Art Theater Music Outdoor_Ed. **Supp**—Dev_Read.
Sports—Basket Lacrosse Soccer Squash. B: Baseball Ice_Hockey. G: F_Hockey Soft-
ball.
Selective adm: 70/yr. Usual entry: PS, K, 1 & 5. Appl fee: $35. Appl due: Feb. Applied
200. Accepted: 50%. Yield: 70%.
Enr 440. B 225. G 215. Elem 420. Sec 20. Wh 85%. Latino 2%. Blk 2%. Asian 5%. Other
6%. Avg class size: 16. Stud/fac: 8:1. Casual. **Fac 60.** M 17/F 43. FT 57/PT 3. Wh
89%. Latino 3%. Blk 5%. Asian 3%. Adv deg: 58%.
Grad '10—25. Prep—24. (St Paul's Sch-NH 6, Phillips Acad 5, Pingree 4, Middlesex 3
Buckingham Browne & Nichols 3, Governor's Acad 3). Avg SSAT: 75%. Alum donors
20%.
Tui '11-'12: Day $21,910-29,750 (+$500). **Aid:** Need 55 ($1,000,000).
Summer: Rec. Sports. Tui Day $300/wk. 6 wks.
Endow $10,000,000. Plant val $19,500,000. Acres 17. Bldgs 4. Class rms 47. Lib 18,000
vols. Sci labs 5. Theaters 1. Art studios 2. Music studios 2. Gyms 2. Fields 6. Climbing
walls 1. Comp labs 2. Comp/stud: 1:2.
Est 1936. Nonprofit. Tri (Sept-June).

With its roots in the Shore School and the North Shore Country Day School, the present
school was incorporated in 1936. Courses in computer, science, world language, art, music,
health and physical education enhance the traditional curriculum at all grade levels. Drama
instruction is introduced in grade 4, and sports replace physical education in grades 6-9. The
school's program was expanded in 1982 to include a readiness year for children of school age
who are bright but not developmentally ready for kindergarten. The academic program culminates in a grade 9 curriculum that includes language, history, geometry, biology and major
course electives in Latin, advanced studio art and advanced theater arts.

Leadership and service opportunities, independent studies, a community code, camping and
interdisciplinary trips are noteworthy aspects of Shore's program. Ninth graders perform 15
hours of required community service, while younger students participate in grade-specific service projects. Graduates enter leading preparatory boarding and day school programs at both
ninth- and 10th-grade levels.

BOSTON, MA. Urban. Pop: 589,141. Alt: to 169 ft. Area also includes West Roxbury.

BOSTON UNIVERSITY ACADEMY
Day — Coed Gr 9-12

Boston, MA 02215. 1 University Rd. Tel: 617-353-9000. Fax: 617-353-8999.
  www.buacademy.org   E-mail: academy@buacademy.org
James Berkman, Head (2006). BA, JD, Harvard Univ, MPhil, Oxford Univ (England). **Paige Brewster, Adm.**
  Col Prep. **Feat**—Chin Fr Ger Greek Hebrew Ital Japan Lat Portuguese Russ Span African_Lang Hindi Korean Comp_Sci Philos Art_Hist Drawing Graphic_Arts Painting Sculpt Drama Chorus Music. **Dual enr:** Boston U.
  Sports—Basket Crew X-country Fencing Sail Soccer Tennis Ultimate_Frisbee. **Activities:** 25.
  Selective adm (Gr 9-11): 46/yr. Usual entry: 9. Appl fee: $45. Appl due: Jan. Applied: 189. Accepted: 51%. Yield: 48%. **Tests** SSAT.
  Enr 159. B 87. G 72. Wh 72%. Latino 5%. Blk 1%. Asian 14%. Other 8%. Avg class size: 12. Stud/fac: 8:1. **Fac 21.** M 13/F 8. FT 14/PT 7. Adv deg: 85%.
  Grad '11—34. Col—33. (Boston U 3, Brandeis 2, Harvey Mudd 2). **Avg SAT:** CR 718. M 724. W 722. **Col couns:** 2. Alum donors: 14%.
  Tui '11-'12: Day $32,950 (+$1100). **Aid:** Need 57 ($1,089,800).
  Summer (enr 50): Acad Enrich. Tui Day $0. 5 wks.
  Acres 6. Bldgs 1. Class rms 19. Lib 3,000,000 vols. Sci labs 5. Lang labs 1. Auds 3. Theaters 1. Art studios 3. Music studios 1. Dance studios 1. Gyms 3. Fields 3. Courts 3. Pools 1. Rinks 1. Comp labs 2.
  Est 1993. Nonprofit. Sem (Sept-June). **Assoc** NEASC.

Utilizing the resources of Boston University, BUA provides students with an integrated program that seeks to explore the ethical and historical dimensions of knowledge, in addition to requiring basic skill mastery and the learning of facts.

The classically based core curriculum begins with a broad liberal arts introduction in grades 9 and 10, including two years of either Latin or ancient Greek. The program's accelerated pace enables pupils to enroll in undergraduate courses with BU faculty and students during junior year: up to two classes per semester in grade 11, up to four per semester in grade 12. All 12th graders enroll in a yearlong senior thesis research project. Students graduate with as many as 40 transferable college credits.

All pupils perform 20 required hours of community service per year.

COMMONWEALTH SCHOOL
Day — Coed Gr 9-12

Boston, MA 02116. 151 Commonwealth Ave. Tel: 617-266-7525. Fax: 617-266-5769.
  www.commschool.org   E-mail: admissions@commschool.org
William D. Wharton, Head (2000). AB, MA, Brown Univ. **Helene T. Carter, Adm.**
  Col Prep. **AP exams taken: 165 (99% 3+).** **Feat**—Creative_Writing Poetry African_Lit Fr Lat Span Calc Stats Multivariable_Calc Astron Environ_Sci Comp_Sci Japan_Hist Lat-Amer_Hist Econ Psych Constitutional_Law Ethics Art_Hist Ceramics Film Painting Photog Studio_Art Acting Music Music_Theory Dance. **Supp**—Tut.
  Sports—Basket Fencing Soccer Ultimate_Frisbee.
  Selective adm: 35/yr. Appl fee: $40-50. Appl due: Feb. Applied: 174. Accepted: 48%. Yield: 48%. **Tests** ISEE SSAT.
  Enr 151. B 72. G 79. Wh 69%. Latino 6%. Blk 10%. Asian 15%. Avg class size: 12. Stud/fac: 5:1. **Fac 33.** M 14/F 19. FT 28/PT 5. Wh 81%. Latino 10%. Blk 3%. Asian 3%. Other 3%. Adv deg: 90%.
  Grad '09—41. Col—41. (U of Chicago 5, Bard-NY 3, Amherst 2, Brown 2, Mt Holyoke 2,

Reed 2). **Avg SAT:** CR 750. M 710. W 720. **Col couns:** 4. Alum donors: 23%.
Tui '11-'12: Day $33,080 (+$1306). **Aid:** Need 53 ($1,026,926).
Endow $12,000,000. Plant val $4,300,000. Bldgs 1 (0% ADA). Class rms 12. Lib 7000 vols. Sci labs 2. Lang labs 1. Dark rms 1. Art studios 3. Comp labs 1.
Est 1957. Nonprofit. Sem (Sept-May). **Assoc** NEASC.

Charles Merrill founded Commonwealth, which currently occupies two renovated Back Bay townhouses, with an eye toward taking advantage of its location in the heart of the city. The rigorous curriculum emphasizes effective writing; history, especially readings and research from primary sources; math; the sciences; the visual and performing arts; and close literary analysis of major works in both English and other languages. The school utilizes locations and resources across the city to support academic, artistic and athletic programming. Students complete 70 hours of required community service prior to the start of grade 11.

Twice a year, the school community spends extended weekends at a lakeside camp in southern Maine, where pupils and teachers jointly plan meals and recreational activities. During the spring semester, boys and girls devote a week (or, in the case of seniors, a month) to an intensive project in an area of interest, such as politics, scientific research, the arts or community service. Approximately two dozen students use this time for exchange trips to France or Spain.

KINGSLEY MONTESSORI SCHOOL

Day — Coed Gr PS (Age 2)-6

Boston, MA 02116. 30 Fairfield St. Tel: 617-226-4900. Fax: 617-536-7507.
Other locations: 26 Exeter St, Boston 02116.
   www.kingsley.org   E-mail: kate_k@kingsley.org
Renee DuChainey-Farkes, Head (1998). BS, MEd. **Kate Kimball, Adm.**
   Pre-Prep. Montessori. Feat—Span Computers Visual_Arts Drama Music. **Supp—**Dev_Read Rem_Read Tut.
   Selective adm: 36/yr. Appl due: Jan. Accepted: 40%.
   Enr 210. Intl 5%. Avg class size: 18. **Fac 39.** M 4/F 35. FT 36/PT 3. Adv deg: 46%.
   Tui '12-'13: Day $22,650-24,100 (+$150-300).
   Summer: Enrich Rec. 6 wks.
   Plant val $1,500,000. Bldgs 2. Class rms 10. 2 Libs 2000 vols. Sci labs 2. Lang labs 1. Art studios 2. Music studios 1.
   Est 1938. Nonprofit. Tri (Sept-June).

Located in Boston's Back Bay in the historic Saltonstall homestead, this school began as a Montessori preschool and later added an elementary curriculum that extends through grade 6. The school offers a Montessori program featuring multi-age groupings, with children placed into three-year age groups.

Preschool classrooms are staffed by a head teacher and an assistant teacher, and two co-teachers lead each elementary classroom. The program makes use of Boston-area museums and cultural institutions, and the science curriculum incorporates study of the nearby Charles River. Kingsley's outdoor program features overnight trips to the White Mountains and other sites. After-school and summer programs serve children ages 3-12. The elementary campus is located one block away on Exeter Street.

THE LEARNING PROJECT ELEMENTARY SCHOOL

Day — Coed Gr K-6

Boston, MA 02116. 107 Marlborough St. Tel: 617-266-8427. Fax: 617-266-3543.
   www.learningproject.org   E-mail: tlp@learningproject.org
Michael McCord, Head (1973). BA, Wesleyan Univ. **Andrew Gallagher, Adm.**
   Pre-Prep. Gen Acad. Elem math—Saxon. **Elem read—**Open Court. **Feat—**Span Studio_Art Music. **Supp—**Dev_Read Rem_Math Rem_Read Rev Tut.

Selective adm: 21/yr. Usual entry: K. Appl due: Jan. Applied: 95. Yield: 90%.
Enr 118. B 60. G 58. Wh 66%. Latino 5%. Blk 15%. Asian 14%. Avg class size: 17.
Stud/fac: 6:1. Casual. **Fac 19.** M 2/F 17. FT 19. Wh 85%. Blk 10%. Asian 5%. Adv
deg: 42%.
Grad '11—17. Prep—5. (Park Sch-MA 1, Boston Col HS 1, Buckingham Browne &
Nichols 1, Noble & Greenough 1, Winsor 1). Alum donors: 18%.
Tui '12-'13: Day $18,300-18,900. Aid: Need 29 ($352,200).
Summer (enr 85): Acad Rec. Tui Day $0-700. 2 wks.
Endow $1,900,000. Plant val $2,265,000. Bldgs 1. Class rms 9. Sci labs 1. Art studios
1. Laptop prgm Gr 4-6.
Est 1973. Nonprofit. Tri (Sept-June).

Located in an original schoolhouse in the Back Bay, the school maintains a small enrollment and a favorable average class size to permit children of different ages to teach and learn
from each other. Program emphasis is on the study of basic skills, and the school takes an
integrated approach to its curriculum. Social studies, science, language arts, Spanish, computers, physical education, art, problem solving, music and math form the core of each child's
weekly schedule.

Children in grades 3-6 undertake a major independent study project in the spring, and field
trips include a week in Washington, DC, for sixth graders. Students also stage three major
musical performances annually. Three extended-day programs, serving children in grades 1-3
and 4-6, are available for an additional fee.

ROXBURY LATIN SCHOOL

Day — Boys Gr 7-12

West Roxbury, MA 02132. 101 St Theresa Ave. Tel: 617-325-4920. Fax: 617-325-3585.
www.roxburylatin.org   E-mail: admission@roxburylatin.org
Kerry P. Brennan, Head (2004). BA, Amherst College, MA, Columbia Univ. **Thomas R.**
Guden, Adm.
Col Prep. AP (248 exams taken, 92% 3+)—Fr Lat Span Calc Stats Comp_Sci Econ
US_Govt & Pol Music_Theory. **Feat**—Greek Photog Studio_Art Drama Music.
Sports—B: Baseball Basket X-country Football Ice_Hockey Lacrosse Soccer Tennis
Track Wrestling. **Activities:** 14.
Very selective adm (Gr 7-10): 57/yr. Usual entry: 7 & 9. Appl fee: $0. Appl due: Jan.
Accepted: 14%. Yield: 88%. **Tests** ISEE SSAT.
Enr 296. Elem 86. Sec 210. Wh 68%. Latino 4%. Blk 12%. Asian 11%. Other 5%. Avg
class size: 13. Stud/fac: 8:1. Casual. **Fac 39.** M 34/F 5. FT 38/PT 1. Adv deg: 76%.
Grad '11—51. Col—50. (Dartmouth 5, Harvard 4, Columbia 4, Princeton 3, Vanderbilt 3,
Bowdoin 2). **Avg SAT:** CR 724. M 738. W 731. **Col couns:** 1. Alum donors: 50%.
Tui '12-'13: Day $24,300 (+$400). **Aid:** Need 118 ($1,918,650).
Endow $116,000,000. Plant val $63,000,000. Acres 117. Bldgs 10. Class rms 27. Lib
13,000 vols. Tech ctrs 2. Sci ctrs 1. Arts ctrs 1. Gyms 2. Fields 8. Courts 7. Comp/stud:
1:2.
Est 1645. Nonprofit. Quar (Aug-June). **Assoc** CLS NEASC.

Founded during the reign of King Charles I by Rev. John Eliot, a church teacher who later
gained renown as an apostle to the Indians and translator of the Bible into the Algonquin
language, Roxbury Latin is the oldest school in continuous existence in North America. The
school occupied a wood-frame building on Kearsarge Avenue in Roxbury from 1860 until
1927. At that time, it assumed its present campus on an estate in West Roxbury that has grown
over the years from 50 to 117 acres.

Although the school has no formal religious affiliation and enrolls students from diverse
faiths and backgrounds, it is committed to the essential values of its Judeo-Christian heritage.
A substantial endowment and a supportive school community enable Roxbury Latin to admit a
diverse Greater Boston student body without regard to families' ability to pay.

Modeled on the English grammar school, RL maintains a connection to its classical heritage by requiring three years of both Latin and a modern Romance language, in addition to

offering three years of Homeric Greek as an elective. The academic program for younger boys emphasizes the development of basic skills in the arts, English, history, classical and modern languages, computer science, math and science. As they mature, students gain increasing flexibility in scheduling through elective options and independent study opportunities. In addition, they engage in Roxbury Latin's extensive athletic and activity programs. All boys participate in on- and off-campus service projects.   **See Also Page 46**

WINSOR SCHOOL

Day — Girls Gr 5-12

Boston, MA 02215. Pilgrim Rd. Tel: 617-735-9500. Fax: 617-739-5519.
   www.winsor.edu   E-mail: admissions@winsor.edu
Rachel Friis Stettler, Dir (2004). AB, Princeton Univ, MA, New School for Social Research.
Pamela Parks McLaurin, Adm.
   Col Prep. AP (exams req'd; 202 taken, 82% 3+)—Fr Lat Span Bio Chem Environ_Sci Physics. **Feat**—British_Lit Creative_Writing Poetry Shakespeare African_Lit Chin_Lit Indian_Lit Islamic_Lit Chin Astron Marine_Bio/Sci Engineering Comp_Sci African_ Hist Lat-Amer_Hist Russ_Hist Psych Architect Art_Hist Photog Studio_Art Drama Music Dance. **Supp**—Dev_Read.
   Sports—Sail. G: Basket Crew X-country F_Hockey Ice_Hockey Lacrosse Soccer Softball Squash Swim Tennis Track. **Activities:** 33.
   Very selective adm (Gr 5-11): 74/yr. Usual entry: 5 & 6. Appl fee: $45. Appl due: Jan. Applied: 388. Accepted: 20%. Yield: 70%. **Tests** ISEE SSAT.
   Enr 430. Wh 71%. Latino 4%. Blk 10%. Asian 15%. Avg class size: 13. Stud/fac: 7:1. Casual. **Fac 70.** M 12/F 58. FT 55/PT 15. Wh 86%. Latino 4%. Blk 4%. Asian 6%. Adv deg: 88%.
   Grad '09—62. Col—62. (Harvard 6, Boston Col 4, U of PA 4, Vanderbilt 4, Brown 3, Wesleyan U 3). **Mid 50% SAT:** CR 650-740. M 660-740. W 700-790. **Col couns:** 2. Alum donors: 36%.
   Tui '11-'12: Day $35,500 (+$600). **Aid:** Need 108 ($3,000,000).
   Endow $50,500,000. Plant val $14,000,000. Acres 7. Bldgs 2. Class rms 37. Lib 27,000 vols. Sci labs 7. Lang labs 1. Photog labs 1. Sci ctrs 1. Comp ctrs 1. Auds 1. Art studios 3. Music studios 5. Gyms 1. Fields 2. Tennis courts 6. Comp labs 3. Comp/stud: 1:2.8.
   Est 1886. Nonprofit. Sem (Sept-June). **Assoc** NEASC.

The curriculum at Winsor reflects a sound balance between courses that stress fundamentals and those that allow students to pursue their own interests. Studies in math and science are extensive: Most students elect to study four years of science in the upper school. Offerings in the arts and a program of physical education complement academics.

Coordinate activities with Belmont Hill School and Roxbury Latin School include drama programs and the joint publication of a school newspaper. Winsor is also a member of the Mountain School Program of Milton Academy, which gives juniors an opportunity to participate for a semester in a coeducational residential experience in Vershire, VT. Another study option for juniors is CITYterm, a semester-long program that combines classroom study at The Masters School in Dobbs Ferry, NY, with fieldwork in New York City. The school's urban location makes it accessible by public transportation.   **See Also Page 88**

BRAINTREE, MA. (9 mi. S of Boston, MA) Urban. Pop: 33,828. Alt: 94 ft.

THAYER ACADEMY
Day — Coed Gr 6-12

Braintree, MA 02184. 745 Washington St. Tel: 781-664-2221. Fax: 781-843-2916.
www.thayer.org   E-mail: admissions@thayer.org
W. Theodore Koskores, Head (2003). BA, Boston Univ, MALS, Columbia Univ. **Jonathan R. White, Adm.**

Col Prep. AP (exams req'd; 216 taken, 83% 3+)—Eng Fr Lat Span Calc Comp_Sci Bio Chem Environ_Sci Physics US_Hist. **Feat**—Poetry Sports_Lit Chin Anat & Physiol Astron Marine_Bio/Sci African_Hist Holocaust Irish_Hist Vietnam_War Archaeol Econ Psych Australian_Stud Foreign_Policy Graphic_Arts Painting Photog Studio_Art Video_Production Architect_Design Acting Drama Directing Chorus Music Dance. **Supp**—Rev Tut.

Sports—Basket Crew X-country Golf Ice_Hockey Lacrosse Ski Soccer Swim Tennis Track Wrestling. B: Baseball Football. G: F_Hockey Softball. **Activities:** 28.

Selective adm (Gr 6-11): 148/yr. Usual entry: 6, 7 & 9. Appl fee: $50. Appl due: Feb. Applied: 521. Accepted: 44%. Yield: 60%. **Tests** ISEE SSAT.

Enr 694. B 340. G 354. Elem 210. Sec 484. Wh 87%. Latino 1%. Blk 6%. Asian 6%. Avg class size: 15. Stud/fac: 6:1. **Fac 111.** M 57/F 54. FT 100/PT 11. Wh 95%. Latino 1%. Blk 2%. Native Am 1%. Asian 1%. Adv deg: 68%.

Grad '11—115. Col—115. (Northeastern U 6, Trinity Col-CT 5, Syracuse 4, Providence 4, MA Col of Pharmacy 4, Boston Col 3). **Mid 50% SAT:** CR 530-560. M 560-660. W 570-670. Mid 50% ACT: 23-28. **Col couns:** 4. Alum donors: 20%.

Tui '12-'13: Day $36,575 (+$500). **Aid:** Need 220 ($5,000,000).

Summer: Enrich Rec. Tui Day $450-2850. 1-8 wks.

Endow $38,000,000. Plant val $60,000,000. Acres 34. Bldgs 8 (90% ADA). Class rms 54. Lib 22,000 vols. Observatories 1. Auds 2. Theaters 2. Art studios 2. Music studios 2. Dance studios 1. Gyms 3. Athletic ctrs 1. Fields 11. Courts 6. Pools 2. Comp labs 11. Comp/stud: 1:2.

Est 1877. Nonprofit. Tri (Sept-June). **Assoc** CLS NEASC.

Thayer Academy was founded in 1877 by the will of Gen. Sylvanus Thayer, native of Braintree, "Father of West Point," and now honored in the Hall of Fame for Great Americans as the "Father of Technological Education in the United States."

The curricula of the middle and upper schools form one continuous program of college preparation. Middle school teachers emphasize the development of sound study and organizational skills, which provide a foundation for achievement at the upper school level. Public speaking is integral to the middle school program, with each student first memorizing a piece of published literature, then making a presentation in English class.

The upper school course of studies features honors and Advanced Placement options in every subject area. Boys and girls take classes in the five major disciplines each term and choose from an array of electives. Most pupils take an arts elective; more than two dozen electives are available in studio art, music and theater. At all grade levels, Thayer offers classes at two levels: accelerated/Advanced Placement and college preparatory. Technology is an important learning tool, and the school maintains several hundred computers for student use.

Although Thayer does not have a community service graduation requirement, most students take part in the school's service program. Participating boys and girls volunteer weekly at local nursing homes, hospitals and shelters. **See Also Pages 106-7**

BROOKLINE, MA. (6 mi. W of Boston, MA) Suburban. Pop: 57,107. Alt: 43 ft. Area also includes Chestnut Hill.

BEAVER COUNTRY DAY SCHOOL
Day — Coed Gr 6-12

Chestnut Hill, MA 02467. 791 Hammond St. Tel: 617-738-2700. Fax: 617-738-2701.
www.bcdschool.org   E-mail: admission@bcdschool.org
Peter R. Hutton, Head (1992). BA, St Lawrence Univ, MA, Wesleyan Univ. **Shamikhah Baker, Adm.**

    Col Prep. Feat—Poetry Shakespeare Fiction_Writing Fr Span Calc Stats Anat & Physiol Astron Bioethics Ecol Forensic_Sci Geol Biotech Organic_Chem Programming Genocide Middle_Eastern_Hist Psych World_Relig Ceramics Painting Photog Sculpt Studio_Art Acting Theater Chorus Jazz_Theory Study_Skills. **Supp**—Tut.

    Sports—Basket X-country Fencing Golf Lacrosse Soccer Tennis Ultimate_Frisbee. B: Baseball Wrestling. G: F_Hockey Softball Volley. **Activities:** 35.

    Selective adm (Gr 6-11): 121/yr. Appl fee: $45. Appl due: Jan. Accepted: 45%. Yield: 50%. **Tests** ISEE SSAT.

    Enr 452. B 235. G 217. Elem 123. Sec 329. Wh 73%. Latino 5%. Blk 15%. Asian 7%. Avg class size: 15. Casual. **Fac 60.** M 35/F 25. FT 54/PT 6. Wh 78%. Latino 7%. Blk 12%. Asian 3%. Adv deg: 70%.

    Grad '11—70. Col—70. (Smith 4, Syracuse 4, Boston Col 4, U of VT 3, Middlebury 2, Skidmore 2). **Col couns:** 3.

    Tui '11-'12: Day $36,930 (+$400). **Aid:** Need 105 ($2,049,896).

    Summer: Ages 3-15. Rec. Sports. Tui Day $490-1390. 1-2 wks.

    Endow $4,000,000. Plant val $12,000,000. Acres 17. Bldgs 3. Class rms 38. Lib 16,500 vols. Sci labs 5. Auds 1. Theaters 2. Art studios 7. Music studios 6. Dance studios 1. Gyms 2. Fields 4. Courts 4. Pools 3. Comp labs 2. Laptop prgm Gr 6-12.

    Est 1920. Nonprofit. Tri (Sept-June). **Assoc** CLS NEASC.

Shortly after World War I, a group of liberal-minded parents, desirous of bringing to the city more progressive educational methods than were then available, asked Eugene Randolph Smith, who had successfully developed the Park School of Baltimore, MD, to organize a similar school in Boston. He was extraordinarily successful in his 22 years as headmaster, adding constantly to the activities and the plant of the school, which became nationally noted as a leader in progressive education.

Beaver's rigorous academic program is unusually rich in the sciences, the humanities, and the performing and visual arts. Upper school students select from a variety of honors and advanced courses, and independent study is also available. All boys and girls purchase a laptop computer for school use.

All students take part in the school's afternoon program of activities, community service and athletics. Pupils in grades 9-12 accumulate 40 hours of required community service, 20 of which must be performed at one location.

BRIMMER AND MAY SCHOOL
Day — Coed Gr PS (Age 4)-12

Chestnut Hill, MA 02467. 69 Middlesex Rd. Tel: 617-738-8695. Fax: 617-734-5147.
www.brimmerandmay.org   E-mail: admissions@brimmer.org
Judith Guild, Head (2012). BS, State Univ of New York-Oswego, ALM, Harvard Univ. **Brian Beale, Upper & Middle Sch Adm; Ellen Foley, Lower Sch Adm.**

    Col Prep. AP (exams req'd)—Eng Fr Span Calc Bio Environ_Sci Physics Econ Studio_Art Music_Theory. **Feat**—Creative_Writing Screenwriting Chin Stats Anat & Physiol Oceanog Web_Design Comp_Graphics Anthro Intl_Relations Law Psych Middle_Eastern_Stud Ceramics Drawing Photog Video_Production Theater_Arts Music Public_Speak. **Supp**—ESL Tut. Outdoor ed.

Sports (req'd)—Basket X-country Golf Lacrosse Soccer Tennis. B: Baseball. G: F_ Hockey Softball. **Activities:** 20.
Selective adm (Gr 9-11): 88/yr. Usual entry: PS, K, 6, 7 & 9. Appl fee: $50. Appl due: Jan. **Tests** ISEE SSAT TOEFL.
Enr 393. B 181. G 212. Elem 265. Sec 128. Wh 64%. Latino 9%. Blk 7%. Asian 11%. Other 9%. Intl 13%. Avg class size: 12. Stud/fac: 6:1. **Fac 68.** M 22/F 46. FT 62/PT 6. Adv deg: 67%.
Grad '11—32. Col—32. (CT Col 2, Syracuse 2, Fordham 2, Brown 1, Wellesley 1, Boston U 1). Athl schol 3. **Col couns:** 2. Alum donors: 25%.
Tui '12-'13: Day $23,200-38,600 (+$1000). **Aid:** Need 106 ($2,149,000).
Summer: Acad Rec. 1-10 wks.
Endow $8,000,000. Plant val $14,500,000. Bldgs 7. Class rms 45. Lib 19,000 vols. Sci labs 4. Writing ctrs 1. Theaters 1. Art studios 4. Music studios 2. Art/sci ctrs 2. Gyms 1. Fields 2. Pools 1. Comp/stud: 1:3.
Est 1880. Nonprofit. Sem (Sept-June). **Assoc** NEASC.

Brimmer and May School grew out of two schools originally founded on Boston's Beacon Hill: Miss Folsom's in 1880 and Miss Brown's Classical in 1887. Miss Folsom's School came to be known as the May School in 1902, while under the leadership of Mary May. The Classical School for Girls became the Brimmer School in 1914, offering a coeducational lower school and college preparatory girls' middle and upper schools. In 1939, the two schools merged and, in 1954, moved to Chestnut Hill. Brimmer and May became fully coeducational in 1994.

In the lower school, basic skills and programs in the creative arts and physical education are emphasized. Middle and upper school students take a program of academic subjects that is enriched by experiential learning programs, as well as community service, creative arts and athletic offerings. Brimmer and May's curriculum emphasizes problem solving, critical thinking, and analytical reading and writing. Juniors perform 40 hours of required community service, while also engaging in three group projects.

Located three miles west of Boston, the school utilizes the cultural and educational resources of the city to further enrich the classroom experience. **See Also Page 91**

THE CHESTNUT HILL SCHOOL

Day — Coed Gr PS (Age 3)-6

Chestnut Hill, MA 02467. 428 Hammond St. Tel: 617-566-4394. Fax: 617-738-6602.
www.tchs.org   E-mail: admissions@tchs.org
Steven B. Tobolsky, Head (2007). AB, Princeton Univ. MA, PhD, Columbia Univ. **Wendy W. Borosavage, Adm.**
Pre-Prep. Elem math—Everyday Math. **Feat**—Lib_Skills Lat Span Computers Studio_ Art Music Violin Woodworking. **Supp**—Dev_Read Tut.
Sports (req'd)—Basket Soccer. B: Baseball. G: Softball.
Selective adm (Gr PS-5): 49/yr. Usual entry: PS & K. Appl fee: $55. Appl due: Jan. Applied: 144. Accepted: 47%. Yield: 72%.
Enr 272. B 121. G 151. Wh 61%. Latino 2%. Blk 10%. Asian 11%. Other 16%. Avg class size: 16. Stud/fac: 8:1. **Fac 54.** M 12/F 42. FT 40/PT 14. Wh 70%. Latino 2%. Blk 20%. Asian 2%. Other 6%. Adv deg: 57%.
Grad '11—20. Prep—16. (Dana Hall 4, Noble & Greenough 4, Belmont Hill 2, Roxbury Latin 2, Dexter 2, Beaver Co Day 1). Alum donors: 9%.
Tui '11-'12: Day $21,500-30,300. Aid: Need 45 ($819,600).
Summer (enr 400): Rec. Creative Arts. Sports. Tui Day $1086/2-wk ses. 9 wks.
Endow $5,044,000. Plant val $12,104,000. Acres 5. Bldgs 1. Class rms 24. Lib 7000 vols. Sci labs 1. Lang labs 2. Amphitheaters 1. Auds 1. Theaters 1. Art studios 2. Music studios 2. Wood shops 1. Gyms 1. Fields 1. Pools 2. Playgrounds 2. Comp labs 1. Comp/stud: 1:2.
Est 1860. Nonprofit. Sem (Sept-June).

One of the rooms in CHS' original building, modeled on the design of the Old Ship Church in Hingham, was the first church in Chestnut Hill and now serves as a library. The school is situated on a five-acre campus in a residential section of Newton.

CHS' developmentally appropriate program, which emphasizes the development of critical-thinking and problem-solving skills, includes two sections at each grade level. The early childhood program, which accommodates children beginning at age 3, features one-on-one interactions with teachers designed to provide support and to instill good work habits. Field trips provide enrichment at all grade levels. Beginning in grade 4, boys and girls assume leadership roles while assisting younger students. An advisor program offers one-on-one mentoring and support to sixth graders. Optional before- and after-school programs are available.

DEXTER SCHOOL
Day — Boys Gr PS (Age 4)-12

Brookline, MA 02445. 20 Newton St. Tel: 617-522-5544. Fax: 617-522-8166.
www.dexter.org   E-mail: administration@dexter.org
Todd A. **Vincent, Head (2011).** BA, Allegheny College, EdM, Boston Univ. **William H. Southwick, Adm.**

Col Prep. AP (exams req'd; 37 taken, 78% 3+)—Eng Fr Lat Span Calc Stats Bio Chem Physics Eur_Hist US_Hist Music_Theory. **Elem math**—Sadlier-Oxford. **Feat**—British_Lit Greek Multivariable_Calc Anat & Physiol Astron Environ_Sci Marine_Bio/Sci Astrophysics Cold_War Modern_Chin_Hist Modern_Russ_Hist Pol_Sci Constitutional_Law Art_Hist Drawing Photog Sculpt Studio_Art Acting Theater Music Woodworking. **Supp**—Tut.

Sports—B: Baseball Basket Crew X-country Football Golf Ice_Hockey Lacrosse Soccer Squash Swim Tennis. **Activities: 23.**

Selective adm: 49/yr. Usual entry: K, 6, 7 & 9. Appl fee: $0. Appl due: Feb. Applied: 231. **Tests** CEEB HSPT ISEE MRT SSAT TOEFL.

Enr 415. Elem 266. Sec 149. Wh 95%. Blk 2%. Asian 2%. Other 1%. Avg class size: 14. Formal. **Fac 101.** M 52/F 49. FT 100/PT 1. Adv deg: 55%.

Grad '10—19. Col—19. (Bentley 2, Harvard 1, USC 1, Vanderbilt 1, RI Sch of Design 1, St Lawrence 1). **Col couns:** 2.

Tui '10-'11: Day $20,595-36,795 (+$500-1000). **Aid:** Need 141 ($4,206,465).

Summer: Acad Enrich Rec. Tui Day $625/wk. 8 wks. Hockey. Tui Day $1195/2-wk ses. 8 wks. Sci & Tech. Tui Day $625/wk. 8 wks. Marine Sci. Tui Bdg $895/wk. 8 wks. Sailing. Tui Bdg $895/wk. 8 wks.

Endow $26,436,000. Plant val $61,280,000. Acres 36. Bldgs 11 (90% ADA). Class rms 69. Lib 18,900 vols. Sci labs 4. Observatories 1. Auds 2. Art studios 3. Music studios 2. Arts ctrs 1. Shops 1. Gyms 1. Fields 5. Courts 4. Pools 1. Rinks 2. Comp labs 2. Comp/stud: 1:2 (1:1 Laptop prgm Gr 9-12).

Est 1926. Nonprofit. Sem (Sept-June).

Located on a 36-acre hilltop estate opposite Larz-Anderson Park, Dexter was founded as a successor to the lower school of Noble and Greenough. After decades as an elementary institution, the school added a high school division in fall 2003.

Classes in the lower school combine work in the fundamental academic areas with such subjects as geography, history and science. Boys study Latin beginning in grade 7 and may choose either French or Spanish in grade 8. Upper school students master content and skills while also developing critical-thinking abilities. Honors, Advanced Placement and independent study courses are part of the upper school program. Among Dexter's many facilities are a science and technology center, a boathouse on the Charles River and the Briarwood Marine Science Center on Cape Cod. Comprehensive intramural and interscholastic athletic programs balance academics.

Students attend a chapel assembly each week, and boys in grades 10-12 perform compulsory community service: 20 hours in grade 10, then 40 hours per year in grades 11 and 12. All boys participate in a public speaking program that commences in kindergarten and continues through grade 12. Over the summer, the school operates enrichment, recreational, ice hockey, science and technology, marine science and sailing camps. Dexter founded its sister school, Southfield (separately listed), in 1992 on the same campus.   **See Also Page 75**

PARK SCHOOL

Day — Coed Gr PS (Age 4)-9

Brookline, MA 02445. 171 Goddard Ave. Tel: 617-277-2456. Fax: 617-232-1261.
www.parkschool.org   E-mail: admission@parkschool.org
Jerrold I. Katz, Head (1993). AB, Univ of Michigan, MEd, Boston Univ, EdD, Harvard Univ. **Merle Jacobs, Adm.**

Pre-Prep. Elem math—TERC Investigations. **Feat**—Fr Lat Span Computers Studio_Art Drama Music. **Supp**—Tut.

Sports—Basket X-country Lacrosse Soccer Track. B: Ice_Hockey Wrestling. G: F_ Hockey Softball.

Very selective adm (Gr PS-8): 80/yr. Usual entry: PS, K, 1, 6 & 7. Appl fee: $60. Appl due: Jan. Applied: 326. Accepted: 24%. Yield: 73%. **Tests** ISEE SSAT.

Enr 562. B 269. G 293. Elem 539. Sec 23. Wh 65%. Latino 3%. Blk 9%. Asian 10%. Other 13%. Avg class size: 14. **Fac 99.** FT 81/PT 18. Wh 85%. Latino 2%. Blk 10%. Asian 2%. Other 1%. Adv deg: 70%.

Grad '11—31. Prep—27. (Beaver Co Day 4, Buckingham Browne & Nichols 3, Concord Acad 3, Deerfield Acad 2, Boston U Acad 2, Brooks 2).

Tui '12-'13: Day $24,650-35,385. Aid: Need 107 ($2,041,210).

Summer: Ages 4-8. Enrich Rec. Ages 8-15. Creative Arts. Ages 4-15. Sports. 1-8 wks.

Endow $35,757,000. Plant val $63,875,000. Acres 25. Bldgs 2. Class rms 36. Lib 30,000 vols. Sci labs 5. Theaters 1. Art studios 3. Music studios 3. Gyms 2. Fields 6. Tennis courts 1. Pools 1. Playgrounds 3. Greenhouses 1. Comp labs 3.

Est 1888. Nonprofit. Tri (Sept-June).

Founded by Caroline A. Pierce as a small neighborhood school, Park now provides a diverse student body from the Greater Boston area with a strong coeducational program. In 1970, the school moved to a 25-acre site across from Larz Anderson Park, where the long tradition of small classes, rigorous academics and close contact with parents continues to be fostered.

The curriculum is designed to build basic skills and instill self-confidence. Music, art, drama and athletics are regular parts of the program. Two-week work-study opportunities and language-study trips to France, Spain and Italy are integral to the grade 9 curriculum.

An after-school program offers both structured activities and free play time for the younger children in a relaxed atmosphere. During the summer, Park also conducts several day camp and special activity programs for children ages 4-15, the largest of which is a creative arts program.

SOUTHFIELD SCHOOL

Day — Girls Gr PS (Age 4)-12

Brookline, MA 02445. 10 Newton St. Tel: 617-522-6980. Fax: 617-522-8166.
www.southfield.org   E-mail: admissions@southfield.org
Todd A. Vincent, Head (2011). BA, Allegheny College, EdM, Boston Univ. **William H. Southwick, Adm.**

Col Prep. AP (exams req'd; 39 taken, 79% 3+)—Eng Fr Lat Span Calc Stats Bio Chem Physics Eur_Hist US_Hist Music_Theory. **Elem math**—Sadlier-Oxford. **Feat**—Women's_Lit Greek Multivariable_Calc Anat & Physiol Astron Marine_Bio/Sci Comp_Sci Cold_War Modern_Chin_Hist Modern_Russ_Hist Women's_Hist Pol_Sci Constitutional_Law Ethics Art_Hist Photog Sculpt Studio_Art Printmaking Theater Music Jazz_Ensemble Woodworking. **Supp**—Tut.

Sports—G: Basket Crew X-country F_Hockey Golf Ice_Hockey Lacrosse Soccer Softball Squash Swim Tennis. **Activities:** 23.

Selective adm: 30/yr. Usual entry: K, 6, 7 & 9. Appl fee: $0. Appl due: Feb. **Tests** CEEB

HSPT ISEE MRT SSAT TOEFL.
Enr 321. Avg class size: 14. Casual. **Fac 96.** M 40/F 56. FT 94/PT 2. Adv deg: 58%.
Grad '10—16. Col—16. (Boston Col 3, Bentley 2, Harvard 1, Dartmouth 1, Tufts 1, Hamilton 1). **Col couns:** 3.
Tui '12-'13: Day $22,245-39,995 (+$500-1500). **Aid:** Need 95 ($2,909,885).
Summer: Enrich. Tui Day $625/wk. Rec. Tui Day $595/wk. Sci & Tech. Tui Day $650/wk. Marine Sci. Tui Bdg $895/wk. Hockey. Tui Day $1195/2-wk ses. Sailing. Tui Bdg $895/wk. 8 wks.
Endow $4,593,000. Plant val $61,280,000. Acres 36. Bldgs 11 (90% ADA). Class rms 69. Lib 18,900 vols. Sci labs 3. Observatories 1. Auds 2. Art studios 2. Music studios 1. Shops 1. Gyms 1. Fields 5. Courts 3. Pools 1. Rinks 2. Comp labs 4. Comp/stud: 1:4 (1:1 Laptop prgm Gr 9-12).
Est 1992. Nonprofit. Sem (Sept-June).

Established as a sister school to Dexter School for boys, Southfield is located on a 36-acre estate opposite Larz-Anderson Park, a campus that the school shares with Dexter. After more than a decade as an elementary institution, the school added a high school division in September 2004.

The lower school curriculum emphasizes the fundamental academic areas, as well as such subjects as history, social studies, geography and science. Girls study Latin beginning in grade 7 and may choose either French or Spanish in grade 8. Additional courses include offerings in art, woodworking, music and health. In addition to mastery of content and basic skills, the upper school emphasizes the development of critical-thinking abilities. Honors, Advanced Placement and independent study options are available to qualified pupils.

Among Southfield's many facilities are a science and technology center, a boathouse on the Charles River and the Briarwood Marine Science Center on Cape Cod. A chapel assembly is held weekly, and girls in grades 10-12 satisfy a community service requirement: 20 hours in grade 10 and 40 hours per year in grades 11 and 12. **See Also Page 75**

BYFIELD, MA. (29 mi. N of Boston, MA) Rural. Pop: 1200. Alt: 66 ft.

THE GOVERNOR'S ACADEMY
Bdg and Day — Coed Gr 9-12

Byfield, MA 01922. 1 Elm St. Tel: 978-465-1763. Fax: 978-462-1278.
www.thegovernorsacademy.org   E-mail: admissions@govsacademy.org
Peter H. Quimby, Head (2011). BA, Bowdoin College, MA, PhD, Univ of Wisconsin-Madison. Michael J. Kinnealey, Adm.

Col Prep. AP (exams req'd)—Eng Fr Lat Span Calc Stats Comp_Sci Bio Chem Physics US_Hist World_Hist Econ Psych Studio_Art. **Feat**—Creative_Writing Children's_Lit Chin Ger Anat & Physiol Environ_Sci African_Hist Chin_Hist Middle_Eastern_Hist Russ_Hist Amer_Stud Pol_Sci Women's_Stud Comp_Relig Architect Ceramics Film Photog Drama Theater_Arts Chorus Music_Hist Music_Theory Jazz_Band. **Supp**—ESL.
Sports—Basket X-country Golf Ice_Hockey Indoor_Track Lacrosse Soccer Tennis Track. B: Baseball Football Wrestling. G: F_Hockey Softball Volley. **Activities:** 60.
Selective adm (Gr 9-11): 108/yr. Appl fee: $50. Appl due: Jan. Applied: 867. Accepted: 32%. Yield: 53%. **Tests** ISEE SSAT TOEFL.
Enr 401. B 215. G 186. Bdg 257. Day 144. Nonwhite 17%. Intl 12%. Avg class size: 12. Stud/fac: 5:1. Casual. **Fac 83.** FT 83. Wh 93%. Latino 3%. Blk 3%. Other 1%. Adv deg: 65%. In dorms 21.
Grad '11—100. Col—100. (Boston U, NYU, Bates, Colby, Harvard, Occidental). **Mid 50% SAT:** CR 540-650. M 570-680. W 550-660. **Col couns:** 3.
Tui '12-'13: Bdg $48,550 (+$2000). **Day $38,415** (+$1500). **Aid:** Need 120 ($3,200,000).
Summer: Enrich Rec. Dance. 8 wks.

Endow $68,000,000. Plant val $61,000,000. Acres 450. Bldgs 48. Dorms 10. Dorm rms 227. Class rms 40. Lib 35,000 vols. Sci labs 8. Lang labs 1. Sci ctrs 1. Auds 1. Theaters 2. Art studios 4. Music studios 8. Dance studios 1. Perf arts ctrs 1. Gyms 1. Athletic ctrs 1. Fields 10. Courts 10. Field houses 1. Rinks 1. Tracks 1. Golf crses 1. Comp labs 2. Comp/stud: 1:3.
Est 1763. Nonprofit. Sem (Sept-May). **Assoc** CLS NEASC.

The oldest boarding school in continuous operation in the country, the academy was founded as Governor Dummer Academy by Lt. Gov. William Dummer of the Massachusetts Bay Colony, who bequeathed his beautiful Byfield home and 600-acre farm for that purpose. Under the celebrated Samuel Moody, who made it a grammar school of the earlier type, so many boys were prepared for "the College" that, between 1768 and 1790, one-fourth of Harvard's graduates were from the academy. Originally a boys' school, the school first accepted girls as day students in 1971, then as boarders in 1973. The academy assumed its present name in July 2006.

The school's curriculum stresses in-depth exploration of critical academic skills and abilities. Longer class sessions (lasting 60 or 90 minutes), an emphasis on discussion and debate, and the use of a variety of methods and materials are characteristics of the curriculum. Hands-on lab and field experiments, oral presentations, group research, exhibits and technology-assisted presentations supplement traditional assessments (exams and papers). In addition, the academy maintains such structures as extra-help sessions, an advisory system and a supervised evening study program to assist boys and girls with time-management and study skills.

An afternoon program provides opportunities in athletics, drama and community service. Boys and girls complete 50 hours of community service prior to graduation. Student exchanges are arranged with two boarding schools in Kenya. The academy offers a full visual and performing arts program, in addition to numerous clubs and activities. Students are encouraged to develop self-discipline, individual responsibility, and respect for and an ability to work with others.

CAMBRIDGE, MA. (6 mi. WNW of Boston, MA) Urban. Pop: 101,355. Alt: 40 ft.

BUCKINGHAM BROWNE & NICHOLS SCHOOL
Day — Coed Gr PS (Age 4)-12

Cambridge, MA 02138. 80 Gerry's Landing Rd. Tel: 617-800-2131. Fax: 617-576-1139.
Other locations: 80 Sparks St, Cambridge 02138; 10 Buckingham St, Cambridge 02138.
www.bbns.org E-mail: gmitchell@bbns.org
Rebecca T. Upham, Head (2001). BA, Middlebury College, MA, Columbia Univ. **Geordie Mitchell, Adm.**
Col Prep. AP (280 exams taken, 88% 3+)—Chin Fr Lat Span Calc Stats Comp_Sci Bio Physics Eur_Hist Econ US_Govt & Pol Art_Hist. **Feat**—Russ Arabic Multivariable_Calc Environ_Sci Physiol Chin_Hist Anthro Govt Pol_Sci Philos World_Relig Architect Ceramics Drawing Film Photog Sculpt Studio_Art Drama Chorus Music Orchestra Jazz_Ensemble Dance Woodworking. **Supp**—Tut.
Sports (req'd)—Basket Crew X-country Fencing Golf Ice_Hockey Lacrosse Sail Soccer Tennis. B: Baseball Football Wrestling. G: F_Hockey Softball Volley. **Activities:** 25.
Very selective adm (Gr PS-11): 150/yr. Appl fee: $50. Appl due: Feb. Applied: 900. Accepted: 17%. Yield: 60%. **Tests** ISEE SSAT.
Enr 1012. B 505. G 507. Elem 499. Sec 513. Nonwhite 26%. Avg class size: 14. **Fac 132.** M 53/F 79. FT 106/PT 26. Adv deg: 89%.
Grad '07—114. Col—113. (Harvard, Cornell, NYU, Columbia, Georgetown, Yale). **Avg SAT:** CR 652. M 680. W 668. Avg ACT: 29.3. **Col couns:** 4. Alum donors: 25%.
Tui '12-'13: Day $27,360-38,030 (+$700). **Aid:** Need 232 ($6,418,370).
Summer: Rec. Sports. 8 wks.
Endow $60,700,000. Plant val $28,273,000. Bldgs 25. Class rms 64. 4 Libs 20,000 vols.

Theaters 2. Studios 5. Wood shops 1. Gyms 2. Fields 6. Courts 4. Rinks 1. Boathouses 1.
Est 1883. Nonprofit. Sem (Sept-June). **Assoc** CLS NEASC.

BB&N resulted from the January 1974 merger of two distinguished Cambridge independent schools, the Buckingham School and the Browne & Nichols School, both of which date from the 19th century. Offering a coordinated program, the school maintains three geographically separate campuses: lower (Buckingham Street), middle (Sparks Street) and upper (Gerry's Landing Road).

Students are drawn from many parts of Greater Boston by the broad and challenging curriculum, which is enriched by many extracurricular activities. The school provides a program that meets the individual student's needs. Simple schedules within the lower school emphasize basic instruction in a relaxed atmosphere, while the middle school incorporates participatory activities into student instruction. The upper school program balances core subjects with a wide array of elective courses, including six foreign language options. Opportunities for international study and exchanges are available. Participation in team sports is required in grades 7-9, and pupils total 40 hours of required community service in grades 9-12.

BB&N conducts extensive programs in instrumental and vocal music, as well as in the visual arts.

CAMBRIDGE FRIENDS SCHOOL
Day — Coed Gr PS (Age 4)-8

Cambridge, MA 02140. 5 Cadbury Rd. Tel: 617-354-3880. Fax: 617-876-1815.
www.cfsmass.org   E-mail: cfsadmission@cfsmass.org
Peter Sommer, Head (2008). AB, Hamilton College, MA, Princeton Univ. **Sarah Turner, Adm.**
   Pre-Prep. Elem math—TERC Investigations. **Elem read**—Wilson Fundations. **Feat**—Lib_Skills Span Studio_Art Drama Music. **Supp**—Dev_Read Tut.
   Sports—Basket Soccer.
   Selective adm: 47/yr. Usual entry: PS, K, 1, 6 & 7. Appl fee: $50. Appl due: Jan. Applied: 131. Accepted: 66%. Yield: 54%. **Tests** ISEE.
   Enr 193. B 101. G 92. Wh 61%. Latino 12%. Blk 6%. Asian 9%. Other 12%. Avg class size: 12. Stud/fac: 6:1. **Fac 33.** M 6/F 27. FT 23/PT 10. Wh 85%. Latino 3%. Blk 9%. Asian 3%. Adv deg: 63%.
   Grad '11—23. Prep—9. (Cambridge Sch-MA 5, Concord Acad 1, Beaver Co Day 1, Gifford 1, Matignon 1).
   Tui '12-'13: Day $21,800-27,950 (+$215-5355). **Aid:** Need 62 ($921,646).
   Endow $4,571,000. Plant val $10,442,000. Bldgs 1 (100% ADA). Class rms 19. Lib 14,000 vols. Labs 2. Theaters 1. Art studios 2. Music studios 1. Dance studios 1. Gyms 1. Fields 1. Comp/stud: 1:3 (1:1 Laptop prgm Gr 4-8).
   Est 1961. Nonprofit. Religious Society of Friends (8% practice). Sem (Sept-June).

Guided by Quaker principles, CFS conducts an integrated curriculum that emphasizes problem solving, critical thinking and comprehensive literacy. Course work in language arts and social studies is particularly strong. Classroom teachers and specialists work together to integrate these subjects with course work in science, mathematics and the arts.

Beginning in kindergarten, children utilize computers as a tool for developing their research, writing and math skills, and CFS introduces Spanish instruction in grade 5. Physical education classes, which are taught at all grade levels, focus upon both individual fitness and cooperative play. Learning specialists and a counselor work with students, parents and teachers to address pupils' needs.

FAYERWEATHER STREET SCHOOL
Day — Coed Gr PS (Age 4)-8

Cambridge, MA 02138. 765 Concord Ave. Tel: 617-876-4746. Fax: 617-520-6700.
www.fayerweather.org   E-mail: admit@fayerweather.org
Edward Kuh, Head (2005). BA, Michigan State Univ, MEd, Univ of Washington. **Cynthia Bohrer, Adm.**
Pre-Prep. Gen Acad. Elem math—TERC Investigations. **Feat**—Lib_Skills Span Studio_Art Music Woodworking. **Supp**—Dev_Read Rem_Read Rev Tut.
Sports—Basket Soccer Ultimate_Frisbee.
Selective adm (Gr PS-7): 40/yr. Usual entry: PS, K, 6 & 7. Appl fee: $60. Appl due: Jan.
Enr 205. Wh 71%. Latino 1%. Blk 4%. Asian 4%. Other 20%. Avg class size: 21. Stud/fac: 11:1. **Fac 39.** M 5/F 34. FT 31/PT 8. Wh 76%. Latino 9%. Blk 9%. Native Am 3%. Asian 3%. Adv deg: 69%.
Grad '11—24. Prep—12. (Cambridge Sch-MA, Concord Acad, Boston U Acad, Commonwealth Sch, Chapel Hill-Chauncy Hall, Buckingham Browne & Nichols).
Tui '12-'13: Day $21,960-27,365. Aid: Need 53 ($600,000).
Summer: Enrich Rec. Engineering. Arts. Tui Day $290-390/wk. 3 wks.
Plant val $3,000,000. Bldgs 1. Class rms 11. Lib 15,000 vols. Sci labs 1. Lang labs 1. Art studios 2. Music studios 1. Wood shops 1. Gyms 1. Fields 1. Courts 1.
Est 1967. Nonprofit. Sem (Sept-June).

Started by a group of Cambridge parents and educators, this school stresses competence in literacy, communication and computation; problem defining, research and problem solving; physical coordination; and interpersonal relations. Beginning in prekindergarten, children are presented with choices and learn to assess their results.

After kindergarten, in grades 1-8, learning occurs in mixed-age groups. Individualized folder work supplements choice times, literature and math groups, art, science and social studies activities, and daily times for writing and reading. Children work with specialist teachers in Spanish, wood shop, music, library and sports. Eighth graders perform in-school community service as part of their program.

An after-school program that includes a variety of focused activities is available at all grade levels. The school's location allows for field trips that utilize the rich educational and cultural resources of the Boston/Cambridge community.

SHADY HILL SCHOOL
Day — Coed Gr PS (Age 4)-8

Cambridge, MA 02138. 178 Coolidge Hill. Tel: 617-520-5260. Fax: 617-520-9387.
www.shs.org   E-mail: admissions@shs.org
Mark J. Stanek, Head (2010). BA, Hamilton College, MEd, Columbia Univ. **Cassie Firenze, Adm.**
Pre-Prep. Feat—Chin Fr Span Computers Studio_Art Chorus Orchestra Jazz_Band Woodworking. **Supp**—Dev_Read Tut.
Sports—Basket X-country F_Hockey Ice_Hockey Lacrosse Soccer Tennis Track Ultimate_Frisbee Volley.
Selective adm: 73/yr. Usual entry: PS, K, 3 & 6. Appl fee: $50. Applied: 373. Accepted: 24%. Yield: 82%. **Tests** ISEE SSAT.
Enr 518. B 249. G 269. Wh 66%. Latino 2%. Blk 7%. Native Am 1%. Asian 7%. Other 17%. Avg class size: 16. Stud/fac: 8:1. Casual. **Fac 93.** M 21/F 72. FT 75/PT 18. Wh 81%. Latino 1%. Blk 9%. Asian 3%. Other 6%. Adv deg: 86%.
Grad '11—63. Prep—46. (Milton Acad 10, Concord Acad 4, Cambridge Sch-MA 4, Commonwealth Sch 3, Phillips Acad 3, Middlesex 2). Alum donors: 24%.
Tui '12-'13: Day $22,310-31,560. Aid: Need 60 ($1,605,000).
Summer (enr 100): Enrich Rec. Tui Day $890/2-wk ses. 8 wks.
Endow $42,727,000. Plant val $40,139,000. Acres 11. Bldgs 18. Class rms 37. Lib 25,000 vols. Sci labs 5. Art studios 6. Music studios 3. Arts ctrs 1. Gyms 3. Fields 2.

Tennis courts 1. Playgrounds 4. Comp labs 3. Comp/stud: 1:2.
Est 1915. Nonprofit. Tri (Sept-June).

Bearing the name of the estate of Charles Eliot Norton, Shady Hill was founded by Professor and Mrs. William Ernest Hocking on the porch of their Cambridge home. The school grew out of the desire of a group of local parents to build on the ideas of Frances Parker, John Dewey and Alfred Whitehead, and its program continues to strike a balance between innovation and continuity.

From kindergarten through grade 8, the curriculum is built around Central Subject, the yearlong study of a people via their history, literature, geography, and arts and sciences. This approach to learning stresses the interrelationships of many disciplines and the use of original sources rather than textbooks. Foreign language study begins in grade 7, and all students participate in the visual and performing arts, as well as in shop. The sports program stresses movement education in the lower grades and the acquisition of team sports skills later on.

CONCORD, MA. (19 mi. WNW of Boston, MA) Suburban. Pop: 16,993. Alt: 121 ft.

CONCORD ACADEMY

Bdg and Day — Coed Gr 9-12

Concord, MA 01742. 166 Main St. Tel: 978-402-2250. Fax: 978-402-2345.
www.concordacademy.org   E-mail: admissions@concordacademy.org
Richard G. Hardy, Head (2009). BA, Univ of New Hampshire, MA, Brown Univ. **Marie D. Myers, Adm.**
   Col Prep. AP exams taken: **186 (94% 3+). Feat**—Creative_Writing Irish_Lit Native_ Amer_Lit Screenwriting Chin Fr Ger Lat Span Calc Stats Astron Geol Oceanog Comp_Sci Web_Design African_Hist Korean_Hist Middle_Eastern_Hist Comp_Relig Architect Art_Hist Film Photog Theater Music_Hist Music_Theory Dance Journ. **Supp**—Rev Tut.
   Sports—Basket X-country Golf Lacrosse Sail Ski Soccer Squash Tennis. B: Baseball Wrestling. G: F_Hockey Softball Volley. **Activities:** 54.
   Selective adm (Bdg Gr 9-11; Day 9-10): 100/yr. Bdg 48. Day 52. Appl fee: $50. Appl due: Jan. Applied: 760. Accepted: 33%. Yield: 43%. **Tests** ISEE SSAT TOEFL.
   Enr 363. B 171. G 192. Bdg 151. Day 212. Nonwhite 25%. Intl 10%. Avg class size: 12. Stud/fac: 6:1. Casual. **Fac 63.** M 28/F 35. FT 29/PT 34. Nonwhite 18%. Adv deg: 87%. In dorms 12.
   Grad '11—97. Col—97. (Brown 5, Tufts 4, Yale 3, Barnard 3, Columbia 3, Skidmore 3). **Avg SAT:** CR 690. M 691. W 750. **Mid 50% SAT:** CR 650-740. M 640-750. W 640-750. **Col couns:** 4. Alum donors: 30%.
   Tui '12-'13: Bdg $50,075 (+$500-700). **Day $40,500** (+$500-700). **Aid:** Need 88 ($3,340,000).
   Endow $55,000,000. Acres 39. Bldgs 29. Dorms 6. Dorm rms 83. Class rms 75. Lib 20,000 vols. Sci labs 6. Lang labs 1. Auds 1. Theaters 1. Art studios 4. Music studios 8. Dance studios 1. Arts ctrs 1. Film/TV studios 3. Gyms 1. Fields 4. Tennis courts 6. Squash courts 4. Pools 1. Student ctrs 1. Comp labs 3.
   Est 1922. Nonprofit. Sem (Sept-May). **Assoc** NEASC.

CA was incorporated as a result of the combined efforts of a group of local parents. The campus lies along the Sudbury River, a block and a half from the center of Concord. Residential campus buildings consist of 11 historic homes that once housed such luminaries as Ralph Waldo Emerson, Henry David Thoreau, Ulysses S. Grant, Sarah Orne Jewett and Daniel Chester French.

The traditional academic curriculum combines electives in every discipline with required courses. Visual arts electives include drawing, painting, ceramics, photography, filmmaking, fiber, sculpture, bookmaking, printmaking and art history. The performing arts department offers musical electives such as music theory, music history, improvisation, vocal and instrumental instruction, chorus, orchestra, and jazz and percussion ensembles. In addition, dance (both ballet and modern) is taught at five levels. Qualified upperclassmen may engage in independent study in many disciplines.

In addition to a full interscholastic athletic program, the academy also conducts wide-ranging courses in skills and in fitness. CA's student center offers a program of events and activities designed to enrich the weekend life of boarders and day students by combining athletics and fitness, the performing arts and student life.

Students may attend school abroad for one year through one or several programs, or they may participate in a biennial summer exchange with a school in Kassel, Germany. In addition, juniors may take part in the Mountain School, a semester-long academic and environmental program in Vermont; CITYterm, a one-semester academic and urban studies program in New York City; or High Mountain Institute Semester, which emphasizes experiential education.

FENN SCHOOL
Day — Boys Gr 4-9

Concord, MA 01742. 516 Monument St. Tel: 978-369-5800. Fax: 978-371-7520.
www.fenn.org   E-mail: info@fenn.org
Gerard J. G. Ward, Head. BA, Boston Univ, MEd, Harvard Univ. **Amy Louise Jolly, Adm.**
 Pre-Prep. Gen Acad. Feat—Lat Span Computers Ceramics Painting Photog Studio_Art Video_Production Drama Theater_Arts Music Debate Woodworking. **Supp**—Dev_ Read Rem_Math Rem_Read Rev Tut.
 Sports—B: Baseball Basket X-country Football Ice_Hockey Lacrosse Soccer Tennis Track Wrestling.
 Selective adm (Gr 4-8): 72/yr. Appl fee: $50. Appl due: Jan. Accepted: 50%. Yield: 85%. **Tests** IQ ISEE SSAT.
 Enr 305. Elem 279. Sec 26. Wh 85%. Latino 6%. Blk 2%. Asian 6%. Other 1%. Avg class size: 14. Casual. **Fac 56.** M 27/F 29. FT 41/PT 15. Adv deg: 73%.
 Grad '08—70. **Prep**—43. (Middlesex, Concord Acad, Lawrence Acad, Phillips Acad, Buckingham Browne & Nichols, St Mark's Sch-MA). Alum donors: 22%.
 Tui '12-'13: Day $29,480-35,200 (+$500).
 Summer: Enrich Rec. Arts. 3 wks.
 Endow $13,000,000. Plant val $19,000,000. Acres 21. Bldgs 13. Class rms 34. Lib 14,000 vols. Sci labs 4. Dark rms 1. Auds 1. Theaters 1. Art studios 5. Music studios 2. Shops 1. Gyms 2. Fields 4. Pools 1. Climbing walls 1. Comp labs 1. Comp/stud: 1:1.5.
 Est 1929. Nonprofit. Tri (Sept-June).

Founded and headed until 1960 by Roger C. Fenn, this school sends its graduates largely to New England college preparatory schools. The academic curriculum emphasizes study habits and fundamentals. The use of flexible sectioning and a departmentalized faculty allows the school to respond to the student's individual needs. Woodworking, art, drama and music are integral parts of each boy's program. In addition to computer labs and wireless laptop carts, all classrooms contain networked computers. Photography and video production classes utilize digital imaging software.

All Fenn students participate in athletics, with interscholastic competition beginning in grade 8. Fenn's marching band is a well-known attraction in the Concord area, and its chorus has performed abroad.

MIDDLESEX SCHOOL
Bdg and Day — Coed Gr 9-12

Concord, MA 01742. 1400 Lowell Rd, PO Box 9122. Tel: 978-371-6524.
 Fax: 978-402-1400.
 www.mxschool.edu   E-mail: admissions@mxschool.edu
Kathleen C. Giles, Head (2003). AB, JD, MEd, Harvard Univ. **Douglas C. Price, Adm.**

Col Prep. AP (528 exams taken, 94% 3+)—Eng Chin Fr Lat Span Calc Stats Comp_ Sci Bio Chem Environ_Sci Physics Eur_Hist US_Hist Econ US_Govt & Pol Art_Hist Studio_Art Music_Theory. **Feat**—Creative_Writing Medieval_Lit Greek Astron Bio-ethics Marine_Bio/Sci Holocaust Vietnam_War Psych Asian_Stud Relig Photog Sculpt Video_Production Drama Music. **Supp**—Tut. Sat classes.

Sports (req'd)—Basket Crew X-country Golf Ice_Hockey Lacrosse Ski Soccer Squash Tennis Track. B: Baseball Football Wrestling. G: F_Hockey Softball. **Activities:** 61.

Very selective adm (Gr 9-11): 95/yr. Bdg 75. Day 20. Usual entry: 9 & 10. Appl fee: $50. Appl due: Jan. Applied: 1020. Accepted: 19%. Yield: 50%. **Tests** ISEE SSAT TOEFL.

Enr 372. B 183. G 189. Bdg 260. Day 112. Wh 71%. Latino 4%. Blk 8%. Asian 15%. Other 2%. Intl 9%. Avg class size: 12. Stud/fac: 5:1. Casual. **Fac 61.** M 31/F 30. FT 60/PT 1. Wh 81%. Latino 5%. Blk 11%. Asian 3%. Adv deg: 73%. In dorms 19.

Grad '11—86. **Col**—86. (Middlebury 4, Cornell 3, Dartmouth 3, Harvard 3, MIT 3). **Avg SAT:** CR 680. M 680. W 690. **Col couns:** 1. Alum donors: 48%.

Tui '11-'12: Bdg $48,390 (+$1200). **Day $38,710** (+$1200). **Aid:** Need 112 ($4,100,000).

Summer: Enrich. Arts. Tui Day $1100-2625. 2-5 wks.

Endow $160,000,000. Plant val $130,000,000. Acres 350. Bldgs 35. Dorms 9. Dorm rms 237. Class rms 37. Lib 41,000 vols. Sci labs 7. Lang labs 1. Sci ctrs 1. Auds 1. Theaters 2. Art studios 3. Music studios 5. Dance studios 1. Gyms 1. Fields 8. Squash courts 8. Rinks 1. Boathouses 1. Ponds 1. Comp labs 2.

Est 1901. Nonprofit. Sem (Sept-June). **Assoc** NEASC.

Frederick Winsor, with the aid of his brother and a group of Harvard colleagues, established Middlesex, where he combined elements of the house system with some of the features of the church schools in England. In the mid-1930s, to aid in recruiting pupils from a distance, he introduced his plan of competitive prize scholarships for boys from all parts of the country. In 1974, the school became coeducational.

From the start, the school has maintained a college preparatory curriculum that emphasizes critical-thinking, analytical and communicational skills. Each academic department is organized into the humanities, arts, social sciences or natural sciences division, with distributive requirements established by each division.

In the junior and senior years, students may choose from the unusually rich elective offerings, which include Advanced Placement courses in some two dozen subject areas; all juniors take AP English. Advanced electives and an independent study program enable pupils to study beyond the AP level in any discipline. The school conducts small classes and maintains a low student-teacher ratio.

Located on 350 acres, the well-equipped campus allows for a wide variety of team and individual sports. Facilities are provided for drama, figure drawing, oil painting, watercolor, ceramics, woodworking, printmaking and photography.

Students produce three major theater productions annually, and Middlesex schedules various on-campus social and cultural activities throughout the year. The school's proximity to Boston and Cambridge offers further opportunities for enrichment.

NASHOBA BROOKS SCHOOL

Day — Boys Gr PS (Age 3)-3, Girls PS (Age 3)-8

Concord, MA 01742. 200 Strawberry Hill Rd. Tel: 978-369-4591. Fax: 978-287-6038. www.nashobabrooks.org   E-mail: admission@nashobabrooks.org

Danielle Boyd Heard, Head (2012). BA, Williams College, MEd, Harvard Univ. **Susanne C. Carpenter, Adm.**

Pre-Prep. Feat—Lat Span Computers Visual_Arts Drama Music Health. **Supp**—Dev_ Read.

Sports—G: Basket X-country F_Hockey Lacrosse Soccer Softball Squash Tennis Track.

Selective adm: 62/yr. Usual entry: PS, K & 4. Appl fee: $50. Appl due: Jan. Applied: 120. Accepted: 61%. Yield: 88%. **Tests** ISEE.

Enr 306. B 66. G 240. Wh 81%. Latino 2%. Blk 1%. Asian 8%. Other 8%. Avg class size: 16. Casual. **Fac 52.** M 3/F 49. FT 40/PT 12. Adv deg: 78%.
Grad '10—30. Prep—20. (Cambridge Sch-MA, Concord Acad, Rivers, Middlesex, St George's Sch-RI, Milton Acad). Alum donors: 10%.
Tui '12-'13: Day $22,900-32,690 (+$100-500). **Aid:** Need 31 ($331,945).
Endow $6,600,000. Plant val $11,000,000. Acres 30. Bldgs 3 (100% ADA). Class rms 32. Lib 14,000 vols. Sci labs 3. Sci ctrs 2. Auds 1. Theaters 1. Art studios 2. Music studios 2. Gyms 2. Fields 2. Comp labs 3. Comp/stud: 1:1
Est 1980. Nonprofit. Tri (Sept-June).

Situated on a 30-acre campus, Nashoba Brooks is the result of a merger between the Brooks School of Concord (founded in 1928) and Nashoba Country Day School (founded in 1958). Coeducational classes in the early years (age 3 through grade 3) lead into girls-only classes in grades 4-8. The educational program stresses a thorough grounding in fundamental skills and study habits and includes art, music, foreign languages and athletics. Computer specialists, who assist students of all ages, work with faculty to facilitate the integration of technology into the curriculum.

All children and faculty become involved in age-appropriate community service projects. Service consists of both direct assistance and indirect help (such as fundraising).

DANVERS, MA. (17 mi. NNE of Boston, MA) Suburban. Pop: 25,212. Alt: 50 ft.

ST. JOHN'S PREPARATORY SCHOOL
Day — Boys Gr 9-12

Danvers, MA 01923. 72 Spring St. Tel: 978-774-1050. Fax: 978-774-5069.
www.stjohnsprep.org E-mail: pmcmanus@stjohnsprep.org
Edward P. Hardiman, Head (2011). BA, Fairfield Univ, MA, PhD, Boston College. **Keith A. Crowley, Prin.** BS, MS, Springfield College, PhD, Boston College. **Philip McManus, Adm.**
Col Prep. AP (522 exams taken)—Eng Chin Fr Ger Lat Span Calc Stats Comp_Sci Bio Chem Physics Eur_Hist US_Hist Econ US_Govt & Pol. **Feat—**Playwriting Anat & Physiol Environ_Sci Zoology Neurosci Robotics Web_Design Holocaust African-Amer_Stud Constitutional_Law Ethics Philos World_Relig Ceramics Drawing Painting Sculpt Studio_Art Acting Drama Music Music_Theory Jazz_Ensemble. **Supp—**Tut.
Sports—B: Baseball Basket X-country Fencing Football Golf Ice_Hockey Indoor_Track Lacrosse Rugby Sail Ski Soccer Swim Tennis Track Ultimate_Frisbee Volley W_Polo Wrestling. **Activities:** 60.
Selective adm (Gr 9-11): 300/yr. Appl fee: $0. Appl due: Dec. **Tests** HSPT SSAT.
Enr 1200. Avg class size: 19. Stud/fac: 11:1. Casual. **Fac 107.** M 67/F 40. FT 107. Adv deg: 80%.
Grad '11—333. Col—326. (Northeastern U 18, Boston Col 17, U of VT 17, Holy Cross 14, U of MA-Amherst 13, Fairfield 9). **Avg SAT:** CR 591. M 613. W 597. **Col couns:** 8.
Tui '11-'12: Day $18,695. Aid: Need ($2,800,000).
Summer: Coed. Gr 7-12. Enrich Rem Rec. Tui Day $550/2-wk ses. 8 wks.
Endow $9,000,000. Plant val $35,784,000. Acres 175. Bldgs 9. Class rms 64. Lib 21,500 vols. Chapels 1. Labs 6. Arts ctrs 1. Fields 5. Courts 5. Comp/stud: 1:2.2.
Est 1907. Nonprofit. Roman Catholic (70% practice). Quar (Sept-June). **Assoc** NEASC.

Sponsored by the Xaverian Brothers, St. John's occupies a 175-acre campus two miles from the center of town. Classes are offered at four ability levels in a curriculum that features many Advanced Placement and elective classes. Boys take compulsory religious studies classes during all four years, and students are expected to enroll in at least one fine arts course before graduation. International exchange programs with schools in Taiwan and Spain are available.

Boys are encouraged to take part in St. John's wide range of extracurricular activities. Inter-scholastic and intramural offerings constitute the athletic program. An active campus ministry program provides retreats at all grade levels, student-centered liturgies, and ample opportuni-ties for service locally, in other parts of the country and internationally.

DARTMOUTH, MA. (26 mi. ESE of Providence, RI; 48 mi. S of Boston, MA) Sub-urban. Pop: 30,666. Alt: 153 ft. Area also includes North Dartmouth.

FRIENDS ACADEMY
Day — Coed Gr PS (Age 3)-8

North Dartmouth, MA 02747. 1088 Tucker Rd. Tel: 508-999-1356. Fax: 508-997-0117.
www.friendsacademy1810.org   E-mail: cdeane@friendsacademy1810.org
Stephen K. Barker, Head (2011). MEd, Harvard Univ. **Cheryl Deane, Adm.**
Pre-Prep. Elem read—Orton-Gillingham. **Feat**—Lib_Skills Lat Span Studio_Art Drama Music Outdoor_Ed. **Supp**—LD Tut. Outdoor ed.
Sports—Basket X-country Lacrosse Soccer. G: F_Hockey.
Somewhat selective adm: 46/yr. Usual entry: PS, K, 6 & 7. Appl fee: $50. Appl due: Jan. Applied: 68. Accepted: 90%. Yield: 75%. **Tests** IQ ISEE.
Enr 267. B 133. G 134. Wh 84%. Latino 3%. Blk 1%. Asian 4%. Other 8%. Avg class size: 12. Stud/fac: 7:1. **Fac 43.** M 13/F 30. FT 41/PT 2. Wh 96%. Blk 4%.
Grad '11—31. Prep—19. (Tabor 3, Bishop Stang 3, Moses Brown 2, Phillips Acad 1, Milton Acad 1, Wilbraham & Monson 1).
Tui '12-'13: Day $15,500-23,300. Aid: Need 81 ($1,063,990).
Summer: Gr K-8. Acad Enrich Rec. Tui Day $110-1800. 1-6 wks.
Endow $1,400,000. Plant val $10,000,000. Acres 65. Bldgs 3. Class rms 23. Lib 13,000 vols. Labs 3. Auds 1. Art studios 2. Music studios 2. Perf arts ctrs 1. Gyms 1. Fields 4. Comp/stud: 1:2 (1:1 Laptop prgm Gr 6-8).
Est 1810. Nonprofit. Tri (Sept-June).

Founded by a group of New Bedford Quakers, the academy became nondenominational in 1855. In 1949, it moved from New Bedford to its present, 65-acre campus in North Dart-mouth.

The curriculum emphasizes the fundamentals and is enriched by offerings in world lan-guages, technology, art, music, drama, library and physical education. The Sally Borden School at Friends Academy, established in 2007, provides special programming for an addi-tional fee for boys and girls of average to superior cognitive ability who have language-based learning differences. These differences may include difficulty in mastering reading, spelling, written expression, math, organizational or study skills due to dyslexia or a specific learning disability.

The academy's diverse student body enrolls from various Massachusetts and Rhode Island communities.

DEDHAM, MA. (10 mi. SW of Boston, MA) Suburban. Pop: 23,464. Alt: 119 ft.

DEDHAM COUNTRY DAY SCHOOL
Day — Coed Gr PS (Age 4)-8

Dedham, MA 02026. 90 Sandy Valley Rd. Tel: 781-329-0850. Fax: 781-329-0551.
www.dedhamcountryday.org   E-mail: etretter@dcds.net
Nicholas S. Thacher, Head (2004). AB, Yale University, MPhil, Oxford Univ (England).

Ellen Tretter, Adm.
Pre-Prep. Feat—Lat Span Computers Studio_Art Drama Music Public_Speak Woodworking. **Supp**—Rem_Read Tut.
Sports (req'd)—Basket X-country Ice_Hockey Lacrosse Soccer Squash Tennis. B: Baseball. G: F_Hockey Softball.
Selective adm (Gr PS-7): 39/yr. Usual entry: PS, K, 1, 4 & 6. Appl fee: $50. Appl due: Jan. Applied: 148. Yield: 70%. **Tests** ISEE SSAT.
Enr 252. B 121. G 131. Wh 79%. Latino 1%. Blk 5%. Asian 3%. Other 12%. Avg class size: 12. Stud/fac: 6:1. **Fac 49.** M 12/F 37. FT 38/PT 11. Wh 89%. Latino 2%. Blk 9%. Adv deg: 61%.
Grad '11—26. Prep—24. (Thayer 4, Xaverian Bros 3, Milton Acad 2, Noble & Greenough 2, Beaver Co Day 2, Rivers 1). Alum donors: 15%.
Tui '12-'13: Day $21,220-33,650. Aid: Need 56 ($1,181,090).
Summer: Rec. Sports. Tui Day $435/wk. 8 wks.
Endow $3,900,000. Plant val $8,221,000. Acres 17. Bldgs 5. Class rms 20. Lib 13,600 vols. Sci labs 2. Auds 1. Theaters 1. Art studios 2. Music studios 4. Dance studios 1. Shops 1. Gyms 2. Fields 4. Pools 2. Comp labs 2. Comp/stud: 1:1.75 (1:1 Laptop prgm Gr 6-8).
Est 1903. Nonprofit. Tri (Sept-June).

A developmentally based school that balances traditional and progressive educational approaches, DCD attracts students from 30 communities in and around Boston. Academic programming emphasizes preparation in the basic disciplines, with Spanish offered in grades 4-8 and Latin in grades 6-8. Art, vocal and instrumental music, drama and wood shop are integral parts of the curriculum, as are athletics and physical education.

In addition to frequent one-day field trips, Dedham Country Day schedules an excursion of several days' duration in grades 5-8. Students at all grade levels participate in class service projects.

NOBLE AND GREENOUGH SCHOOL

5-Day Bdg — Coed Gr 9-12; Day — Coed 7-12

Dedham, MA 02026. 10 Campus Dr. Tel: 781-326-3700. Fax: 781-320-1329.
www.nobles.edu E-mail: admissions@nobles.edu
Robert P. Henderson, Jr., Head (2000). AB, AM, Dartmouth College. **Jennifer Hines, Adm.**
Col Prep. AP (318 exams taken, 87% 3+)—Fr Japan Lat Span Calc Stats Comp_Sci Bio Chem Physics Eur_Hist Art_Hist Studio_Art. **Feat**—Creative_Writing Poetry Shakespeare Lat-Amer_Lit Southern_Lit Chin Greek Environ_Sci Marine_Bio/Sci Organic_Chem Boston_Hist Middle_Eastern_Hist Vietnam_War Econ Gender_Stud Ethics Ceramics Painting Photog Drama Theater Chorus Music Music_Theory Dance Journ Public_Speak. **Supp**—Rev Tut.
Sports (req'd)—Basket Crew X-country Golf Ice_Hockey Lacrosse Ski Soccer Squash Tennis. B: Baseball Football Wrestling. G: F_Hockey Softball. **Activities:** 53.
Very selective adm (Bdg Gr 9-11; Day 7-11): 141/yr. Bdg 13. Day 128. Usual entry: 7 & 9. Appl fee: $50. Appl due: Jan. Applied: 774. Accepted: 26%. Yield: 69%. **Tests** CEEB ISEE SSAT TOEFL.
Enr 591. B 290. G 301. Bdg 47. Day 544. Elem 122. Sec 469. Wh 75%. Latino 4%. Blk 8%. Native Am 1%. Asian 7%. Other 5%. Avg class size: 12. Stud/fac: 5:1. Casual. **Fac 127.** M 65/F 62. FT 115/PT 12. Wh 77%. Latino 5%. Blk 6%. Native Am 1%. Asian 6%. Other 5%. Adv deg: 63%. In dorms 6.
Grad '11—117. Col—117. (Dartmouth 8, Colgate 5, Boston Col 4, Brown 4, Davidson 4, Duke 4). Athl schol 2. **Avg SAT:** CR 670. M 674. W 673. **Mid 50% SAT:** CR 630-730. M 600-740. W 610-730. **Col couns:** 5. Alum donors: 50%.
Tui '11-'12: 5-Day Bdg $42,500 (+$1000). **Day $37,300** (+$1000). **Aid:** Need 117 ($3,311,150).
Summer (enr 1578): Rec. Tui Day $450-535/wk. 8 wks.
Endow $101,000,000. Plant val $63,103,000. Acres 188. Bldgs 28 (95% ADA). Dorms 1.

Dorm rms 24. Class rms 62. Lib 35,000 vols. Labs 7. Auds 2. Theaters 1. Art studios 7. Music studios 4. Recital halls 1. Gyms 4. Athletic ctrs 1. Fields 11. Tennis courts 12. Squash courts 6. Pools 3. Rinks 1. Rowing facilities. Comp/stud: 1:1.4.
Est 1866. Nonprofit. Sem (Sept-June). **Assoc** CLS NEASC.

Established on Beacon Hill by George W. C. Noble, who was joined after a quarter of a century by James J. Greenough, this school originally tutored students for entrance to Harvard. Although some continue to enter Harvard, others attend such institutions as Dartmouth, Princeton, Middlebury and Williams. In 1892, the school changed its name to Noble and Greenough. After absorbing the Volkmann School in 1917, the school relocated to Dedham in 1922.

Nobles' college preparatory academic program offers a broad range of courses, including interdisciplinary history electives and options for independent study. The required afternoon program comprises athletics, community service, the arts, outdoor education and independent projects. Students may participate in study-abroad and service-learning programs in Spain, France, South Africa, China and Japan, or in the Chewonki Semester School program or School Year Abroad.   **See Also Page 47**

DEERFIELD, MA. (54 mi. N of Hartford, CT; 82 mi. W of Boston, MA) Suburban. Pop: 4750. Alt: 152 ft.

BEMENT SCHOOL

Bdg — Coed Gr 3-9; Day — Coed K-9

Deerfield, MA 01342. 94 Old Main St, PO Box 8. Tel: 413-774-7061. Fax: 413-774-7863.
  www.bement.org   E-mail: admit@bement.org
Shelley Borror Jackson, Head (1999). BA, Wheaton College (MA), MA, Ohio State Univ.
  Kimberly C. Loughlin, Adm.
  Pre-Prep. Feat—Chin Fr Lat Span Computers Studio_Art Drama Music. **Supp**—ESL Rev Tut.
  Sports (req'd)—Basket X-country Lacrosse Ski Soccer Squash Swim Track. B: Baseball. G: F_Hockey Softball.
  Selective adm: 48/yr. Bdg 12. Day 36. Usual entry: K, 6 & 7. Appl fee: $50. Appl due: Feb. Applied: 127. Accepted: 65%. Yield: 67%. **Tests** IQ SSAT.
  Enr 246. B 129. G 117. Bdg 38. Day 208. Elem 222. Sec 24. Wh 81%. Latino 4%. Blk 2%. Asian 12%. Other 1%. Intl 13%. Avg class size: 12. Stud/fac: 6:1. **Fac 38.** M 14/F 24. FT 38. Wh 95%. Blk 2%. Asian 2%. Other 1%. Adv deg: 50%. In dorms 7.
  Grad '11—23. Prep—23. (Deerfield Acad 4, Northfield Mt Hermon 3, Hotchkiss 2, Williston Northampton 2, Proctor 2, Suffield 2).
  Tui '12-'13: Bdg $46,225 (+$3500). **5-Day Bdg $38,270** (+$2000). **Day $14,360-20,980** (+$1000). **Aid:** Need 84 ($653,340).
  Summer: Ages 2-15. Rec. Tui Day $400-450. 2 wks. ESL. Tui Bdg $4350. 3 wks.
  Endow $5,500,000. Plant val $6,700,000. Bldgs 12. Dorms 4. Dorm rms 18. Class rms 28. Libs 1. Sci labs 2. Art studios 3. Music studios 2. Dance studios 1. Fields 3. Comp labs 3.
  Est 1925. Nonprofit. Tri (Sept-June).

Developed from an informal group that Grace Bement taught in her own home, this school for younger children has grown into a thriving boarding and day establishment housed in restored colonial buildings.

Art, music, drama and athletics are a daily part of the pre-preparatory curriculum. Between Thanksgiving and Christmas, Bement schedules a three-week mini-term that combines special courses, electives and speakers as a thematic focus for the entire school. Students engage in compulsory community service projects that vary by grade. Bement's advisory program matches each students with a faculty member for weekly meetings and activities.

DEERFIELD ACADEMY

Bdg and Day — Coed Gr 9-PG

Deerfield, MA 01342. 7 Boyden Ln, PO Box 87. Tel: 413-774-1400. Fax: 413-772-1100.
www.deerfield.edu   E-mail: admission@deerfield.edu
Margarita O'Byrne Curtis, Head (2006). BA, Tulane Univ, BS, Mankato State Univ, PhD, Harvard Univ. **Patricia L. Gimbel, Adm.**
Col Prep. AP (exams req'd; 823 taken, 90% 3+)—Calc Stats Comp_Sci Bio Chem Physics Art_Hist Studio_Art. **Feat**—Creative_Writing Humanities Shakespeare 1950s_Lit Lat-Amer_Lit NYC_Lit Chin Fr Greek Lat Span Arabic Anat & Physiol Astron Geol Asian_Hist Amer_Stud Econ Ethics Philos Relig World_Relig Islamic_Stud Architect Ceramics Photog Video_Production Acting Band Chorus Music Music_Theory Dance Health.
Sports—Basket Crew X-country Golf Ice_Hockey Lacrosse Ski Soccer Squash Swim Tennis Track W_Polo. B: Baseball Football Wrestling. G: F_Hockey Softball Volley. **Activities: 23.**
Very selective adm: 203/yr. Bdg 177. Day 26. Usual entry: 9. Appl fee: $60. Appl due: Jan. Applied: 2361. Accepted: 13%. Yield: 65%. **Tests** CEEB ISEE SSAT TOEFL.
Enr 630. B 319. G 311. Bdg 553. Day 77. Sec 610. PG 20. Wh 74%. Latino 4%. Blk 5%. Asian 12%. Other 5%. Intl 14%. Avg class size: 12. Stud/fac: 6:1. Formal. **Fac 119.** M 62/F 57. FT 115/PT 4. Wh 87%. Latino 3%. Blk 3%. Asian 5%. Other 2%. Adv deg: 74%. In dorms 48.
Grad '11—189. Col—189. (Middlebury 12, Georgetown 10, Bowdoin 7, U of VA 7, Yale 6, Princeton 6). Athl schol 4. **Avg SAT:** CR 660. M 670. W 670. **Col couns:** 4. Alum donors: 48%.
Tui '12-'13: Bdg $47,500 (+$2125). **Day $34,050** (+$1870). **Aid:** Need 223 ($7,003,000).
Endow $368,000,000. Plant val $132,000,000. Acres 280. Bldgs 81 (90% ADA). Dorms 17. Dorm rms 491. Class rms 60. Lib 75,000 vols. Sci labs 15. Lang labs 1. Planetariums 1. Auds 2. Theaters 2. Art studios 7. Music studios 2. Dance studios 2. Gyms 3. Fields 20. Tennis courts 21. Squash courts 13. Pools 1. Rinks 1. Tracks 1. Boathouses 1. Comp labs 3. Comp/stud: 1:1 Laptop prgm Gr 9-PG.
Est 1797. Nonprofit. Tri (Sept-June). **Assoc** CLS NEASC.

On March 1, 1797, Gov. Samuel Adams signed a bill granting a charter for the founding of this academy in Deerfield, which now occupies a 280-acre campus in the historic village. After operating as a boys' school for nearly two centuries, the school became coeducational in the fall of 1989.

The Deerfield curriculum offers accelerated course sequences in all academic departments. A spring-term elective program and independent study opportunities give teachers and students a chance to work in areas of special interest or expertise. Faculty teach a number of interdisciplinary subjects as well. Seniors are encouraged to participate in the alternate study program, which may include a congressional internship, volunteer work in a hospital or a unique program designed by the student. Deerfield participates in off-campus and exchange programs located in Europe, Africa, Asia, Australia, and rural and coastal New England. All students are provided with laptop computers, the cost of which is included in tuition. Academic buildings and public spaces are outfitted for wireless Internet access.

Participation in athletics, theater, or some significant activity or program each term is required of all students. Among the academy's musical opportunities are chamber music, jazz ensembles and various singing groups. In addition, a range of student organizations, social activities and cultural programs, as well as the opportunity to take part in community service projects, is available.

EAGLEBROOK SCHOOL

Bdg and Day — Boys Gr 6-9

Deerfield, MA 01342. 271 Pine Nook Rd, PO Box 7. Tel: 413-774-9111.
Fax: 413-774-9119.

www.eaglebrook.org   E-mail: admissions@eaglebrook.org
Andrew C. Chase, Head (2002). BA, Williams College. **Theodore J. Low, Adm.**
   Pre-Prep. Feat—Creative_Writing Chin Fr Lat Span Anat Comp_Design Civil_War Middle_Eastern_Hist Amer_Stud Anthro Govt Ethics Architect_Drawing Ceramics Photog Sculpt Studio_Art Drama Band Chorus Music Public_Speak Woodworking. **Supp**—ESL Rev Tut.
   Sports (req'd)—B: Baseball Basket X-country Football Golf Ice_Hockey Lacrosse Ski Soccer Squash Swim Tennis Track W_Polo Wrestling.
   Selective adm (Gr 6-8): 102/yr. Bdg 87. Day 15. Appl fee: $50. Appl due: Rolling. **Tests** IQ SSAT.
   Enr 255. Bdg 200. Day 55. Wh 78%. Latino 9%. Blk 3%. Asian 10%. Intl 25%. Avg class size: 10. Stud/fac: 5:1. **Fac 70.** Adv deg: 44%. In dorms 33.
   Grad '10—86. Prep—84. (Deerfield Acad, Phillips Exeter, Choate, Northfield Mt Hermon, Westminster Sch-CT, Hotchkiss).
   Tui '12-'13: Bdg $49,700 (+$3000). **Day $31,800** (+$600). **Intl Bdg $49,700** (+$4000). **Aid:** Need ($1,600,000).
   Summer (enr 60): Coed. Acad Enrich Rec. Tui Bdg $5700. 4 wks.
   Endow $65,000,000. Plant val $70,000,000. Acres 750. Bldgs 15. Dorms 5. Dorm rms 120. Class rms 38. Lib 13,000 vols. Sci labs 3. Auds 1. Theaters 1. Art studios 7. Music studios 6. Photog studios 1. Shops 1. Gyms 1. Fields 7. Courts 10. Field houses 1. Pools 1. Rinks 1. Tracks 1. Rifle ranges 1. Skiing facilities. Comp labs 2.
   Est 1922. Nonprofit. Tri (Sept-May).

Under the direction of Dr. C. Thurston Chase, associate of the founder, Howard B. Gibbs, and headmaster from 1928 to 1966, Eaglebrook became one of the leading boarding schools for younger boys. Parents and alumni help endow and expand the plant, which now covers more than 750 acres. The former classroom building, now used primarily for the arts, includes facilities for woodworking, stained glass, architectural design, computer-aided design, ceramics and photography, as well as acting and music rehearsal rooms.

Eaglebrook boys go on to secondary school having already had wide opportunities for responsibility and leadership in student government and in committees that direct many aspects of school life. Accelerated sections, as well as remedial classes, and the flexible program offer boys challenges at all levels. The curriculum is enriched by many electives, with particular emphasis placed on music and the arts. Programs of cultural value are held bimonthly.

Each student participates every season in one of the many interscholastic and individual sports, and school service activities take place on Saturday mornings. Although community service is not a graduation requirement, Eaglebrook encourages boys to partake of local outreach opportunities.

The fall Country Fair, the Winter Carnival and Grandparents' Day are special occasions that bring parents and alumni to the school. In addition, International Day and Cultural and Racial Awareness Day promote social and cultural maturity.

DOVER, MA. (15 mi. WSW of Boston, MA) Suburban. Pop: 5558. Alt: 156 ft.

CHARLES RIVER SCHOOL
Day — Coed Gr PS (Age 4)-8

Dover, MA 02030. 6 Old Meadow Rd, PO Box 339. Tel: 508-785-0068.
   Fax: 508-785-8290.
   www.charlesriverschool.org   E-mail: info@charlesriverschool.org
Catherine H. Gately, Head (1992). BA, MEd, Boston Univ. **Susan A. Mantilla-Goin, Adm.**
   Pre-Prep. Feat—Lib_Skills Fr Span Computers Studio_Art Drama Music. **Supp**—Tut.
   Sports—Basket Lacrosse Soccer Tennis. G: F_Hockey.
   Selective adm (Gr PS-7): 29/yr. Usual entry: PS, K, 4 & 5. Appl fee: $50. Appl due: Jan.

Applied: 92. Accepted: 45%. Yield: 65%. **Tests** ISEE.
Enr 207. B 91. G 116. Wh 77%. Latino 1%. Blk 13%. Asian 9%. Avg class size: 22. Stud/
fac: 11:1. Casual. **Fac 37.** M 9/F 28. FT 31/PT 6. Wh 91%. Latino 2%. Blk 2%. Asian
5%. Adv deg: 67%.
Grad '11—22. Prep—20. (Milton Acad 2, Concord Acad 2, St Mark's Sch-MA 2, Thayer
2, Buckingham Browne & Nichols 2, Dana Hall 2). Alum donors: 16%.
Tui '12-'13: Day $21,450-32,950 (+$300). **Aid:** Need 29 ($550,165).
Summer (enr 543): Enrich Rec. Creative Arts. Tui Day $2250/4-wk ses. 8 wks.
Endow $7,000,000. Plant val $10,000,000. Acres 16. Bldgs 5 (80% ADA). Class rms 22.
Lib 8000 vols. Sci labs 2. Lang labs 1. Dark rms 1. Amphitheaters 1. Auds 1. Theaters
1. Art studios 2. Music studios 2. Gyms 2. Fields 2. Courts 2. Pools 1. Climbing walls
1. Comp labs 1. Comp/stud: 1:1.5.
Est 1911. Nonprofit. Sem (Sept-June).

Founded by area parents on the banks of the Charles River in Needham, CRS moved to
Dover in 1917. The school offers a varied, rigorous elementary program to children from
roughly 30 towns in suburban Boston. Parents and faculty play an active role in the direction
of the school.

The interdisciplinary, thematic curriculum emphasizes critical-thinking, reading, writing
and math skills, as well as science, social studies, computer, and health and wellness. The arts
are integral to the program. Instructional groups are limited to 10 or 11 pupils per teacher. In
all grades, consideration is given to each student's developmental level and learning style.
The school offers three years of both French and Spanish. Global awareness and community
service are important aspects of school life: Boys and girls in grades 7 and 8 perform 10 compulsory hours of service at school and five hours in the wider community.

EASTHAMPTON, MA. (35 mi. N of Hartford, CT; 85 mi. W of Boston, MA) Suburban. Pop: 15,994. Alt: 169 ft.

THE WILLISTON NORTHAMPTON SCHOOL
Bdg — Coed Gr 9-PG; Day — Coed 7-PG

Easthampton, MA 01027. 19 Payson Ave. Tel: 413-529-3000. Fax: 413-527-9494.
www.williston.com   E-mail: admission@williston.com
Robert W. Hill III, Head (2010). BA, MA, Middlebury College. **Christopher J. Dietrich,
Adm.**
Col Prep. AP (exams req'd; 264 taken)—Eng Fr Lat Span Calc Stats Comp_Sci Bio
Chem Physics Eur_Hist US_Hist Comp_Govt & Pol Econ Psych. **Feat**—Poetry
Shakespeare Lat-Amer_Lit Playwriting Chin Discrete_Math Astron Ecol Forensic_Sci
Genetics Marine_Bio/Sci Animal_Behavior Organic_Chem African_Hist Japan_Hist
Intl_Relations Ethics Philos Relig World_Relig Ceramics Fine_Arts Photog Sculpt
Theater Music Dance. **Supp**—ESL Tut. Sat classes.
Sports (req'd)—Basket Crew X-country Golf Ice_Hockey Lacrosse Ski Soccer Squash
Swim Tennis Track W_Polo. B: Baseball Football Wrestling. G: F_Hockey Softball
Volley.
Selective adm: 160/yr. Bdg 100. Day 60. Usual entry: 7, 9 & 10. Appl fee: $50. Appl due:
Feb. Applied: 852. Accepted: 34%. Yield: 47%. **Tests** CEEB ISEE SSAT TOEFL.
Enr 545. Elem 80. Sec 450. PG 15. Wh 84%. Latino 2%. Blk 5%. Asian 7%. Other 2%.
Intl 17%. Avg class size: 13. Stud/fac: 7:1. Casual. **Fac 69.** M 35/F 34. FT 65/PT 4.
Adv deg: 62%. In dorms 27.
Grad '11—122. Col—117. (Hobart/Wm Smith 4, U of MA-Amherst 4, Colby 3, NYU 3,
Union Col-NY 3, Northeastern U 3). Athl schol 4. **Avg SAT:** CR 576. M 616. W 587.
Avg ACT: 26. **Col couns:** 4. Alum donors: 21%.
Tui '12-'13: Bdg $49,400 (+$1400). **Day $27,600-33,800** (+$1000). **Aid:** Merit 7
($79,000). Need 229 ($4,995,206).
Endow $42,000,000. Plant val $50,000,000. Acres 125. Bldgs 56. Dorms 11. Dorm rms

188. Class rms 60. Lib 45,000 vols. Sci labs 7. Comp ctrs 1. Theaters 1. Art studios 6. Music studios 5. Dance studios 1. Gyms 1. Athletic ctrs 1. Fields 10. Squash courts 5. Pools 1. Rinks 1. Tracks 1. Comp labs 7. Comp/stud: 1:7 (1:1 Laptop prgm Gr 7-8). **Est 1841.** Nonprofit. Sem (Sept-June). **Assoc** CLS NEASC.

Founded by local manufacturer Samuel Williston to provide the education of which he was deprived, Williston Seminary offered English, science and mathematics on an equal plane with the classics, a radical but realistic policy for that time. In the fall of 1971, Williston Academy merged with the Northampton School for Girls, founded in 1924 by Sarah B. Whitaker and Dorothy Bement. Today, the school maintains a traditional college preparatory curriculum and places its graduates in selective colleges throughout the country.

The core academic program is supplemented by a broad selection of elective options. Course work places particular emphasis on the development of critical-thinking and writing skills. The school's proximity to the Five Colleges (Amherst, Hampshire, Mount Holyoke, Smith and the University of Massachusetts) allows for further academic and cultural explorations. Juniors and seniors may participate in the School Year Abroad program in China, France, Spain or Italy, while seniors in good academic standing may undertake an internship or pursue independent study on or off campus. The writer's workshop series meets twice weekly and welcomes established writers and poets for public readings and hands-on instruction.

See Also Pages 130-1

FALMOUTH, MA. (46 mi. ESE of Providence, RI; 58 mi. SSE of Boston, MA) Suburban. Pop: 29,030. Alt: 45 ft.

FALMOUTH ACADEMY
Day — Coed Gr 7-12

Falmouth, MA 02540. 7 Highfield Dr. Tel: 508-457-9696. Fax: 508-457-4112.
   www.falmouthacademy.org   E-mail: mearley@falmouthacademy.org
David C. Faus, Head (2005). BA, Kenyon College, MSEd, Univ of Pennsylvania. **Michael J. Earley, Adm.**
   Col Prep. AP exams taken: 14 (93% 3+). Feat—Fr Ger Stats Comp_Sci Photog Studio_Art Music Woodworking. **Supp**—Tut.
   Sports—Basket Lacrosse Soccer. **Activities:** 40.
   Somewhat selective adm: 53/yr. Usual entry: 7 & 9. Appl fee: $50. Appl due: Mar. Applied: 90. Accepted: 85%. Yield: 90%. **Tests** SSAT.
   Enr 190. B 91. G 99. Elem 75. Sec 115. Wh 91%. Latino 3%. Native Am 1%. Asian 3%. Other 2%. Avg class size: 12. Casual. **Fac 44.** M 18/F 26. FT 32/PT 12. Wh 99%. Latino 1%. Adv deg: 93%.
   Grad '11—35. Col—35. (CT Col 2, Sarah Lawrence 2, Wake Forest 2, Simmons 2). **Avg SAT:** CR 642. M 615. W 660. **Col couns:** 1. Alum donors: 13%.
   Tui '12-'13: Day $24,860 (+$350). **Aid:** Merit 4 ($8000). Need 90 ($1,050,000).
   Summer (enr 120): Acad Rec. Arts. Sports. 7 wks.
   Endow $6,000,000. Plant val $6,000,000. Acres 34. Bldgs 3 (100% ADA). Class rms 16. Lib 8000 vols. Sci labs 5. Dark rms 1. Auds 1. Theaters 1. Art studios 1. Music studios 1. Gyms 1. Fields 2. Field houses 1. Comp labs 1. Comp/stud: 1:9.
   Est 1977. Nonprofit. Tri (Sept-June). **Assoc** NEASC.

On a 34-acre campus located next to Beebe Woods conservation area and overlooking Martha's Vineyard, FA draws students from Cape Cod, the Vineyard and southeastern Massachusetts. Within the traditional college preparatory curriculum, students are required each year to study English, math, foreign languages, science and history, with an emphasis placed on writing. More than three dozen electives are offered in the fine and performing arts, publications, and other curricular areas.

The academy conducts exchanges with Holderlin Gymnasium in Heidelberg, Germany, and the Lycee Honore Estienne d'Orves in Nice, France. The math and science programs take advantage of the academy's proximity to the Woods Hole scientific community, and field trips are common. Each class completes an annual community service project. Students attend an all-school daily meeting.

FITCHBURG, MA. (44 mi. WNW of Boston, MA) Urban. Pop: 39,102. Alt: 438 ft.

APPLEWILD SCHOOL
Day — Coed Gr K-8

Fitchburg, MA 01420. 120 Prospect St. Tel: 978-342-6053. Fax: 978-345-5059.
www.applewild.org   E-mail: ebracchita@applewild.org
Christopher B. Williamson, Head (2004). BA, Williams College, MEd, Univ of New Hampshire. **Emily Walker Bracchitta, Adm.**
Pre-Prep. Gen Acad. Feat—Lib_Skills Fr Lat Span Computers Studio_Art Visual_Arts Drama Music Indus_Arts. **Supp**—Tut.
Sports (req'd)—Basket X-country Lacrosse Soccer. G: F_Hockey.
Somewhat selective adm: 38/yr. Usual entry: K, 1 & 6. Appl fee: $50. Appl due: Feb. Applied: 72. Accepted: 91%. Yield: 58%. **Tests** ISEE MRT.
Enr 186. B 108. G 78. Wh 83%. Latino 2%. Blk 2%. Asian 6%. Other 7%. Avg class size: 15. Stud/fac: 6:1. Casual. **Fac 30.** M 9/F 21. FT 25/PT 5. Wh 100%. Adv deg: 50%.
Grad '11—38. Prep—8. (Cushing, Worcester Acad, Bancroft, Concord Acad, Lawrence Acad, St Mark's Sch-MA). Alum donors: 8%.
Tui '12-'13: Day $16,972-23,914. Aid: Merit 16 ($36,305). Need 80 ($951,835).
Summer: Acad Rec. Tui Day $450/2-wk ses. 6 wks.
Endow $8,400,000. Plant val $5,286,000. Acres 26. Bldgs 7 (50% ADA). Class rms 30. 2 Libs 17,000 vols. Sci labs 4. Theaters 2. Art studios 2. Music studios 2. Ceramics studios 1. Gyms 2. Fields 3. Pools 1. Comp labs 2. Comp/stud: 1:2.
Est 1957. Inc. Sem (Sept-June).

Located on the former estate of Mr. and Mrs. Charles T. Crocker, Applewild serves students from 37 communities in north-central Massachusetts and southern New Hampshire. The 26-acre campus is situated on a hill overlooking Fitchburg that abuts hundreds of acres of conservation land.

Applewild's traditional academic program stresses the application of basic skills and ideas, and the school groups students according to achievement and ability in certain disciplines at appropriate age levels. Departmentalization begins in grade 6. The school's visual arts program consists of drawing, printmaking, sculpture, 3-D construction, photography and collage, while the industrial arts program allows participants to progress from simple woodworking in the lower school to advanced furniture making in the upper school. All children take chorus starting in kindergarten; instrumental music instruction begins in grade 4.

Athletics are a mandatory part of the curriculum, and Applewild sponsors interscholastic sports teams for pupils in grades 6-8. Upper school students may participate in the theater program or in art or furniture-making mentor programs in lieu of a season of athletics. The community service program allows pupils to volunteer at area agencies, such as the Head Start Program and a care facility for the elderly.

FRAMINGHAM, MA. (22 mi. W of Boston, MA) Urban. Pop: 66,910. Alt: 189 ft.

SUDBURY VALLEY SCHOOL
Day — Coed Ages 4-19

Framingham, MA 01701. 2 Winch St. Tel: 508-877-3030. Fax: 508-788-0674.
www.sudval.org   E-mail: office@sudval.org
Penelope Jungreis, Pres. Hanna Greenberg, Adm.
  Col Prep. Gen Acad. Sudbury Valley.
  Nonselective adm: 30/yr. Appl fee: $30. Appl due: Rolling. Accepted: 99%.
  Enr 160. B 95. G 65. **Fac 9.** M 4/F 5. FT 9.
  Grad '11—16.
  Tui '12-'13: Day $7400.
  Plant val $2,000,000. Acres 10. Bldgs 2. Lib 15,000 vols. Art studios 1. Music studios 1.
    Fields 1. Comp labs 1.
  Est 1968. Nonprofit. (Sept-June).

Sudbury Valley offers alternative education stressing self-motivation and self-direction. The ungraded program encourages students to learn at their own rates in an informal and personal atmosphere. While addressing individual needs, the school's major emphasis is on promoting a sense of responsibility.

The school's location on the 10-acre former estate of Nathaniel Bowditch, adjoining parkland and conservation land, allows for a variety of outdoor activities. Opportunities for ice skating and fishing at the nearby millpond are accompanied by seasonal field trips. Informal athletic activities include skiing and hiking.

GREENFIELD, MA. (57 mi. N of Hartford, CT; 83 mi. WNW of Boston, MA) Suburban. Pop: 13,716. Alt: 240 ft.

STONELEIGH-BURNHAM SCHOOL
Bdg and Day — Girls Gr 7-PG

Greenfield, MA 01301. 574 Bernardston Rd. Tel: 413-774-2711. Fax: 413-772-2602.
www.sbschool.org   E-mail: admissions@sbschool.org
Sally L. Mixsell, Head (2008). BA, Wells College, MA, Columbia Univ. **Eric Swartzentruber, Adm.**
  Col Prep. AP—Calc Bio US_Hist. **Feat**—Chin Fr Span Anat & Physiol Environ_Sci Econ
    Psych Ceramics Drawing Painting Weaving Acting Chorus Music Music_Theory
    Dance. **Supp**—ESL Tut.
  Sports (req'd)—G: Basket X-country Equestrian Lacrosse Soccer Softball Tennis
    Volley.
  Selective adm: 52/yr. Appl fee: $50. Appl due: Feb. Applied: 210. Accepted: 49%. Yield:
    76%. **Tests** SSAT TOEFL.
  Enr 132. Bdg 99. Day 33. Elem 32. Sec 99. PG 1. Intl 38%. Avg class size: 10. Stud/fac:
    6:1. Casual. **Fac 33.** M 9/F 24. FT 24/PT 9. Wh 95%. Asian 2%. Other 3%. Adv deg:
    54%. In dorms 11.
  Grad '11—26. Col—24. (Smith, Boston U, Mt Holyoke, St Lawrence, NYU, Wheaton-
    MA). **Col couns:** 1.
  Tui '12-'13: Bdg $48,443 (+$2375). **Day $28,890** (+$2045). **Aid:** Merit 4 ($20,000).
    Need 65 ($900,000).
  Summer: Rec. Debate. Dance. Riding. Sports. Tui Bdg $450-2500. 1-2 wks.
  Endow $2,000,000. Plant val $16,500,000. Acres 100. Bldgs 11. Dorms 2. Dorm rms
    100. Class rms 20. Lib 10,000 vols. Sci labs 5. Photog labs 1. Theaters 1. Art studios
    4. Music studios 7. Dance studios 1. Gyms 1. Fields 4. Pools 1. Riding rings 4. Stables

2. Comp labs 5.
Est 1869. Nonprofit. Tri (Sept-June). **Assoc** NEASC.

SBS traces its origins to five New England girls' schools, beginning with the Prospect Hill School in Greenfield, which was founded in 1869. The Mary A. Burnham School, which was located in Northampton for over 90 years, and Stoneleigh-Prospect Hill School, which occupied the present 100-acre, wooded campus in residential Greenfield, merged in 1968 to form Stoneleigh-Burnham School. After operating for many years solely as a high school, SBS opened a middle school division in the fall of 2004. The school began offering the two-year International Baccalaureate Diploma Program in fall 2011.

The college preparatory curriculum stresses language, mathematics, science and history. Broad course offerings include electives, a strong skills program, English as a Second Language and the opportunity to pursue the IB Diploma. These curricular features are enhanced by opportunities in the visual, performing and communicative arts.

The school maintains its own equestrian facilities. Competition includes jumping, equitation and dressage. Girls interested in competing have frequent opportunities to show.

GROTON, MA. (34 mi. WNW of Boston, MA) Suburban. Pop: 8083. Alt: 300 ft.

GROTON SCHOOL

Bdg and Day — Coed Gr 8-12

Groton, MA 01450. 282 Farmers Row, PO Box 991. Tel: 978-448-7510.
Fax: 978-448-9623.
www.groton.org   E-mail: admission_office@groton.org
Richard B. Commons, Head (2004). BA, Univ of Virginia, MA, Stanford Univ, MA, Middlebury College. Ian Gracey, Adm.
Col Prep. AP (exams req'd; 425 taken, 89% 3+)—Fr Lat Span Stats Comp_Sci Bio Chem Environ_Sci Physics Music_Theory. **Feat**—Poetry Shakespeare Playwriting Chin Greek Arabic Calc Anat & Physiol Astron Bioethics Ecol Middle_Eastern_Hist Modern_Chin_Hist Modern_Indian_Hist S_African_Hist Archaeol Econ Intl_Relations Ethics Relig Art_Hist Ceramics Photog Video_Production Visual_Arts Acting Music Music_Hist Dance Woodworking. **Supp**—Tut. Sat classes.
Sports—Basket Crew X-country Ice_Hockey Lacrosse Soccer Squash Tennis Track. B: Baseball Football. G: F_Hockey. **Activities: 20.**
Very selective adm (Gr 8-11): 92/yr. Bdg 78. Day 14. Appl fee: $50. Appl due: Jan. Applied: 1120. Accepted: 14%. Yield: 56%. **Tests** ISEE SSAT TOEFL.
Enr 370. B 190. G 180. Bdg 317. Day 53. Elem 26. Sec 344. Wh 69%. Latino 4%. Blk 8%. Asian 11%. Other 8%. Intl 10%. Avg class size: 13. Stud/fac: 5:1. Casual. **Fac 63.** M 36/F 27. FT 52/PT 11. Wh 93%. Latino 2%. Blk 2%. Asian 3%. Adv deg: 82%. In dorms 18.
Grad '11—91. Col—90. (Princeton 4, Trinity Col-CT 4, Colby 4, Harvard 3, Georgetown 3, Middlebury 3). **Avg SAT:** CR 702. M 688. W 702. **Col couns:** 3.
Tui '12-'13: Bdg $51,800 (+$1000). **Day $40,150** (+$600). **Aid:** Need 127 ($4,689,450).
Endow $309,285,000. Plant val $300,000,000. Acres 400. Bldgs 16 (90% ADA). Dorm rms 184. Class rms 39. Lib 60,000 vols. Chapels 1. Sci labs 4. Auds 1. Art studios 4. Music studios 7. Dance studios 1. Arts ctrs 1. Perf arts ctrs 2. Athletic ctrs 1. Fields 10. Basketball courts 3. Squash courts 12. Pools 2. Rinks 2. Tracks 1. Boathouses 1. Fitness ctrs 1. Comp labs 4. Comp/stud: 1:1 Laptop prgm Gr 8-12.
Est 1884. Nonprofit. Episcopal. Tri (Sept-June). **Assoc** NEASC.

Rev. Endicott Peabody founded Groton in order to provide a thorough education not only for college but also for the "active work of life." Established with close links to the Episcopal Church, the school draws its present student body and faculty from many different religious backgrounds. It was Mr. Peabody's hope that many of the graduates would engage in public service, and a significant number have entered the professions of government, education, medicine and religion. Originally a six-year boarding school, Groton now offers grades 8-12 (forms II-VI) to boarding and day boys and girls. Nearly all the main school buildings on the 385-acre campus are grouped around a central green.

Open-minded in introducing innovations in advance of his peers, Mr. Peabody expanded the curriculum to include printing, woodworking, academic science in all its forms, music and studio art. His plan to have faculty and students live together to foster the students' maturity and participation in social and academic affairs continues today, with a faculty resident living in each dormitory. Additionally, every student has a faculty advisor, and sports are coached almost entirely by the teachers, thus further encouraging faculty-student relationships.

In all forms, the rigorous academic program is conducted in small classes, with emphasis on student participation and group discussion. In the upper forms, students choose from a variety of electives; seniors may pursue independent study projects and tutorials. Advanced Placement courses are part of the curriculum in most subject areas. Students must purchase laptops for classroom use.

LAWRENCE ACADEMY

Bdg and Day — Coed Gr 9-12

Groton, MA 01450. 26 Powderhouse Rd, PO Box 992. Tel: 978-448-6535.
Fax: 978-448-9208.
www.lacademy.edu   E-mail: admiss@lacademy.edu
Dan Scheibe, Head (2012). BA, Yale Univ, MDiv, Princeton Univ, MALS, Wesleyan Univ.
Tony Hawgood, Adm.
  Col Prep. AP (exams req'd; 124 taken)—Eng Calc Comp_Sci Environ_Sci US_Govt & Pol Music_Theory. Feat—Creative_Writing Poetry Fr Lat Span Stats Anat & Physiol Astron Botany Forensic_Sci Marine_Bio/Sci Entomology Ornithology Boston_Hist Middle_Eastern_Hist Vietnam_War WWII Psych Ceramics Film Filmmaking Photog Sculpt Printmaking Dance. Supp—ESL Rev Tut.
  Sports—Basket X-country Golf Ice_Hockey Lacrosse Ski Soccer Tennis Track. B: Baseball Football Wrestling. G: F_Hockey Softball Volley. Activities: 30.
  Selective adm (Gr 9-11): 113/yr. Appl fee: $50. Appl due: Feb. Accepted: 42%. Yield: 50%. Tests SSAT TOEFL.
  Enr 399. B 208. G 191. Bdg 199. Day 200. Wh 75%. Latino 1%. Blk 4%. Asian 5%. Other 15%. Intl 13%. Avg class size: 14. Stud/fac: 5:1. Casual. Fac 57. M 30/F 27. FT 57. Adv deg: 57%. In dorms 17.
  Grad '11—96. Col—93. (Northeastern U 6, Boston Col 5, Boston U 4, Union Col-NY 3, Providence 3, Bentley 3). Athl schol 12. Col couns: 4. Alum donors: 50%.
  Tui '12-'13: Bdg $52,640 (+$400-1200). Day $40,510 (+$400-1200). Aid: Need 100 ($3,100,000).
  Summer: Acad Enrich Rec. Arts. Sports. Tui Day $200-600. 1-2 wks.
  Endow $20,000,000. Plant val $71,000,000. Acres 120. Bldgs 19. Dorms 10. Dorm rms 100. Class rms 30. Lib 20,000 vols. Sci labs 6. Lang labs 1. Theaters 1. Art studios 7. Music studios 4. Dance studios 1. Arts ctrs 1. Art galleries 1. Gyms 1. Athletic ctrs 1. Fields 8. Courts 14. Rinks 1. Student ctrs 1. Radio stations 1. Comp/stud: 1:2.
  Est 1793. Nonprofit. Tri (Sept-June). Assoc CLS NEASC.

Founded as the coeducational Groton Academy and renamed in 1846 in honor of Amos and William Lawrence, who endowed it, this college preparatory school enrolled only boys from 1898 to 1971, when it again became coeducational. Although one of the older schools in the country, its charter having been signed by Gov. John Hancock, Lawrence is modern in method and facilities.

The school's academic program allows students to select from a wide variety of courses, including honors and Advanced Placement classes and interdisciplinary offerings. The arts, namely dance, drama, music and the visual arts, are an integral part of the learning experience. Other program features include independent study options; the Independent Immersion Program (IIP), which allows select students to build a course of study around an area of strong interest, such as music composition, journalism, astronomy or genetics; and the two-week Winterim program, which offers each student the opportunity to learn from a hands-on experience that may involve travel, on-campus activities or community service.

Every pupil meets daily with his or her faculty advisor.

HARDWICK, MA. (61 mi. W of Boston, MA) Rural. Pop: 2622. Alt: 880 ft.

EAGLE HILL SCHOOL
Bdg and Day — Coed Gr 8-12

Hardwick, MA 01037. 242 Old Petersham Rd, PO Box 116. Tel: 413-477-6000.
Fax: 413-477-6837.
www.ehs1.org   E-mail: admission@ehs1.org
Peter John McDonald, Head (1998). BS, Purdue Univ, MEd, Cambridge College, EdD, Univ of Massachusetts-Amherst. Dana M. Harbert, Adm.

Col Prep. LD. Feat—British_Lit Creative_Writing Sci_Fiction Fr Lat Russ Span Calc Anat & Physiol Botany Environ_Sci Forensic_Sci Oceanog Zoology Meteorology Microbio Web_Design Civil_War Holocaust Middle_Eastern_Hist Vietnam_War WWI WWII Psych Child_Dev Gender_Stud World_Relig Film Filmmaking Painting Studio_Art Directing Music_Theory Journ Woodworking Health. Supp—Dev_Read Rem_Math Rem_Read Rev Tut.

Sports—Basket X-country Soccer Tennis Ultimate_Frisbee. B: Golf Wrestling. G: Softball. Activities: 15.

Very selective adm (Gr 8-11): 56/yr. Bdg 48. Day 8. Appl fee: $100. Appl due: Rolling. Applied: 257. Accepted: 23%. Yield: 96%. Tests IQ.

Enr 184. B 108. G 76. Bdg 166. Day 18. Wh 87%. Latino 3%. Blk 4%. Native Am 1%. Asian 3%. Other 2%. Intl 8%. Avg class size: 5. Stud/fac: 4:1. Casual. Fac 45. M 19/F 26. Wh 95%. Latino 1%. Blk 1%. Native Am 1%. Asian 1%. Other 1%. Adv deg: 66%. In dorms 8.

Grad '11—37. Col—37. (Brandeis, Norwich, Curry, U of MA-Amherst, Hofstra, Purdue). Avg ACT: 22.

Tui '11-'12: Bdg $59,839 (+$4500). Day $42,351 (+$1000). Aid: Need 4 ($230,000).

Summer (enr 90): Ages 10-18. Acad Enrich Rev Rem Rec. Tui Bdg $7800. Tui Day $6800. 5 wks.

Endow $6,000,000. Plant val $31,000,000. Acres 210. Bldgs 16 (94% ADA). Dorms 4. Dorm rms 145. Class rms 48. Lib 5000 vols. Sci labs 6. Dark rms 1. Art studios 3. Wood shops 1. Gyms 1. Athletic ctrs 1. Fields 1. Tennis courts 3. Pools 1. Ropes crses 1. Comp labs 5. Comp/stud: 1:1

Est 1967. Nonprofit. (Sept-June). Assoc NEASC.

One of the few independent schools designed for the adolescent who has been diagnosed with a specific learning disability, attention deficit disorder or both, Eagle Hill accepts only students of average or above-average intelligence who are free of primary emotional and behavioral difficulties. The college preparatory program allows faculty to take advantage of the pupil's strengths while also providing remediation of learning deficits. An important aspect of the curriculum is the Pragmatics Program, which assists students with their verbal and non-verbal communicational skills. Eagle Hill also conducts a student leadership program.

Specialized training in perceptual speech and language development is available. In addition, the residential program facilitates the development of organizational, time management and social skills.

Students in grades 9-12 satisfy a 10-hour annual community service requirement.

HINGHAM, MA. (10 mi. SE of Boston, MA) Suburban. Pop: 19,882. Alt: 21 ft.

DERBY ACADEMY
Day — Coed Gr PS (Age 4)-8

Hingham, MA 02043. 56 Burditt Ave. Tel: 781-749-0746. Fax: 781-740-2542.
  www.derbyacademy.org   E-mail: admissions@derbyacademy.org
Andrea Archer, Head (2007). MA, DipEd, Oxford Univ (England), MSc, Univ of Warwick (England). **Scot Chandler, Adm.**
  Pre-Prep. Elem math—Everyday Math. **Elem read**—Open Court/Orton-Gillingham. **Feat**—Fr Lat Span Computers Ceramics Studio_Art Drama Music Public_Speak Indus_Arts Sewing. **Supp**—Tut.
  Sports (req'd)—Basket X-country Lacrosse Soccer. B: Baseball Ice_Hockey. G: F_ Hockey Softball.
  Selective adm: 67/yr. Appl fee: $75. **Tests** ISEE.
  Enr 333. B 169. G 164. Wh 88%. Latino 1%. Blk 2%. Other 9%. Avg class size: 14. Stud/fac: 6:1. **Fac 65.** M 16/F 49. FT 53/PT 12. Wh 93%. Latino 2%. Blk 5%. Adv deg: 49%.
  Grad '10—40. Prep—32. (Thayer 10, Tabor 7, Milton Acad 5, Noble & Greenough 3, Phillips Acad 2). Alum donors: 6%.
  Tui '12-'13: Day $17,750-28,370. Aid: Need 42 ($960,000).
  Summer (enr 300): Enrich Rec. Arts. Sports. Tui Day $200-2350. 1-5 wks.
  Endow $6,874,000. Plant val $10,942,000. Acres 27. Bldgs 14. Class rms 33. 2 Libs 16,000 vols. Sci labs 2. Auds 1. Theaters 1. Art studios 2. Music studios 2. Arts ctrs 2. Gyms 2. Fields 4. Basketball courts 3. Comp labs 3. Comp/stud: 1:3 (1:1 Laptop prgm Gr 8).
  Est 1784. Nonprofit. Quar (Sept-June).

Founded by Madame Sarah Derby and in continuous operation since 1791, Derby Academy is the oldest independent, coeducational day school in New England. The school, situated on a 27-acre campus, moved from its original site in 1965, when the trustees deeded the old academy building to the Hingham Historical Society.

The nondenominational program emphasizes a well-balanced education with challenging academics, enriching arts, physical education and competitive team sports. In addition to traditional courses, the curriculum includes studio art, pottery, woodworking, music, sewing, dramatics and computer instruction. Derby's three divisions—lower school (grades pre-K-3), middle school (grades 4-6) and upper school (grades 7 and 8)—provide age-appropriate settings for its student body.

Summer Arts at Derby utilizes the campus in July and August, enrolling students interested in exploring fine arts and recreational offerings taught by area professionals. Most of the school's graduates continue their secondary education at independent schools, both boarding and day, in New England.

LENOX, MA. (34 mi. SE of Albany, NY; 116 mi. W of Boston, MA) Suburban. Pop: 5077. Alt: 1210 ft.

BERKSHIRE COUNTRY DAY SCHOOL
Day — Coed Gr PS (Age 2)-9

Lenox, MA 01240. PO Box 867. Tel: 413-637-0755. Fax: 413-637-8927.
  www.berkshirecountryday.org   E-mail: info@berkshirecountryday.org
L. Paul Lindenmaier, Head (2008). BA, Goddard College, MEd, Arcadia Univ. **Alicia Rossie, Adm.**

Pre-Prep. Feat—Classics Shakespeare Fr Lat Span Computers Film Graphic_Arts Studio_Art Theater Theater_Arts Band Chorus Music Indus_Arts. **Supp**—Dev_Read ESL Rem_Math Rem_Read Rev Tut.
Sports—Basket Lacrosse Ski Soccer.
Selective adm: 26/yr. Appl fee: $0. Appl due: Rolling. Applied: 54. Accepted: 40%. Yield: 80%. **Tests** CTP_4 IQ ISEE SSAT TOEFL.
Enr 188. B 109. G 79. Elem 178. Sec 10. Wh 95%. Latino 1%. Blk 3%. Asian 1%. Avg class size: 6. Casual. **Fac 33.** FT 32/PT 1. Nonwhite 1%. Adv deg: 84%.
Grad '11—14. Prep—9. (Berkshire Sch 2, Darrow 1, Concord Acad 1, Cambridge Sch-MA 1, Putney 1).
Tui '12-'13: Day $11,800-24,240 (+$1200-4200). **Aid:** Need 49 ($613,610).
Endow $1,073,000. Plant val $4,075,000. Acres 27. Bldgs 8. Class rms 37. Lib 5800 vols. Sci labs 2. Lang labs 3. Theaters 1. Art studios 2. Music studios 2. Wood shops 1. Gyms 1. Fields 7. Comp labs 2.
Est 1946. Nonprofit. Tri (Sept-June). **Assoc** NEASC.

Located on 27 acres neighboring Tanglewood, BCD is housed in the attractive remodeled farm buildings of the former Anson Phelps Stokes estate. In the early grades (grades PS-3), classes are staffed by homeroom teachers and specialists in science, French, art, music, chorus, library and physical education. Beginning in grade 4, students have two homeroom teachers and subject teachers.

Travel opportunities include domestic options (Florida's Everglades; Washington, DC; Vermont; and Rhode Island) and overseas trips to Spain and France. All students complete at least one annual community service project.

LEXINGTON, MA. (13 mi. NW of Boston, MA) Suburban. Pop: 30,355. Alt: 200 ft.

LEXINGTON CHRISTIAN ACADEMY
Bdg and Day — Coed Gr 6-12

Lexington, MA 02420. 48 Bartlett Ave. Tel: 781-862-7850. Fax: 781-863-8503.
www.lca.edu   E-mail: admissions@lca.edu
Mark R. Davis, Head of School (2006). BA, Northwestern College, MEd, Univ of South Florida. **Brook Berry, Adm.**
Col Prep. AP—Eng Calc Stats Comp_Sci Bio Physics Eur_Hist US_Hist. **Feat**—British_Lit Japan_Lit Fr Lat Span Anat & Physiol Pol_Sci Psych Bible Architect Ceramics Painting Photog Sculpt Studio_Art Stained_Glass Acting Theater_Arts Music Music_Theory Journ. **Supp**—LD Tut.
Sports—Basket X-country Golf Lacrosse Soccer. B: Baseball Wrestling. G: F_Hockey Softball. **Activities:** 20.
Selective adm: 84/yr. Usual entry: 6 & 9. Appl fee: $50. Appl due: Feb. Accepted: 70%. Yield: 68%. **Tests** ISEE SSAT TOEFL.
Enr 310. Wh 63%. Latino 6%. Blk 10%. Asian 20%. Other 1%. Intl 6%. Avg class size: 16. Stud/fac: 10:1. **Fac 37.** M 17/F 20. FT 33/PT 4. Wh 92%. Latino 2%. Blk 4%. Asian 2%. Adv deg: 81%.
Grad '10—61. Col—61. (Boston U, U of PA, MIT, Northeastern U, Georgetown, Wheaton-IL). **Avg SAT:** CR 623. M 633. W 613.
Tui '11-'12: Bdg $49,500. Day $20,200-22,500. Intl Bdg $53,000. Aid: Merit 70 ($150,000). Need 116 ($556,000).
Summer: Acad Enrich Rec. 8 wks.
Endow $3,000,000. Plant val $25,000,000. Acres 30. Bldgs 1. Class rms 23. Lib 10,000 vols. Art studios 2. Music studios 2. Gyms 1. Fields 3. Courts 2. Pools 1. Comp labs 2.
Est 1946. Nonprofit. Nondenom Christian. Sem (Sept-June). **Assoc** NEASC.

Originally located in Boston and known as Boston Christian High School, the school moved to Cambridge in 1949 as the Christian High School. Since 1965, it has been located on a 30-acre campus in historic Lexington and, in 1970, the school changed its name to Lexington Christian Academy. After decades of operation as a day school, LCA opened a boarding division for regional and international students in fall 2011.

The integration of faith and learning is central to LCA's college preparatory curriculum, which also features the visual arts, music and theater. Honors and Advanced Placement courses are available at the upper school level (grades 9-12), and various electives during these years address student interests and talents. Community service is part of the freshman year Bible curriculum; boys and girls then fulfill 15- and 20-hour service requirements in grades 10 and 11, respectively. The school provides academic support services for highly motivated students who have documented learning differences.

LCA holds an annual fine arts festival each spring.

LINCOLN, MA. (16 mi. WNW of Boston, MA) Suburban. Pop: 8056. Alt: 258 ft.

CARROLL SCHOOL
Day — Coed Gr 1-9

Lincoln, MA 01773. 25 Baker Bridge Rd. Tel: 781-259-8342. Fax: 781-259-8852.
Other locations: 1841 Trapelo Rd, Waltham 02451.
www.carrollschool.org   E-mail: admissions@carrollschool.org
Stephen M. Wilkins, Head (2005). BA, Colgate Univ, MEd, Harvard Univ, PhD, Johns Hopkins Univ. **Lesley Fowler Nesbitt, Adm.**

> **Pre-Prep. LD. Elem read**—Orton-Gillingham. **Feat**—Computers Studio_Art Drama Music Woodworking Outdoor_Ed. **Supp**—Rem_Math Rem_Read Tut.
>
> **Sports**—Basket Soccer Track.
>
> **Selective adm:** 106/yr. Appl fee: $75. Appl due: Rolling. Applied: 221. Accepted: 75%. Yield: 64%. **Tests** IQ.
>
> **Enr 370.** B 236. G 134. Wh 91%. Latino 2%. Blk 2%. Native Am 1%. Asian 3%. Other 1%. Avg class size: 7. Stud/fac: 3:1. **Fac 142.** M 27/F 115. Adv deg: 61%.
>
> **Grad '11—61. Prep—50.**
>
> **Tui '12-'13: Day $39,838. Aid:** Need 42 ($780,000).
>
> **Summer (enr 175):** Acad Enrich Rem Rec. Tui Day $4275-5100. 5 wks.
>
> Endow $4,900,000. Plant val $13,500,000. Acres 23. Bldgs 5. Auds 2. Art studios 2. Gyms 2. Fields 3. Comp labs 5. Laptop prgm Gr 6-9.
>
> **Est 1967.** Nonprofit. Quar (Sept-June). **Assoc** NEASC.

Carroll specializes in the education and the remediation of children of average to superior intelligence who have been diagnosed with dyslexia or a language-based learning disability. The program helps the language-disabled child grow to the point where he or she can successfully return to a regular public or private school setting. Children are grouped according to language competency and grade. In all subjects, teachers use a multisensory approach to learning and place emphasis on improving reading, writing and organizational skills.

A full academic program includes language, math, science, social studies, performing arts, drama, art, woodworking and an Outward Bound-type program. Sports and physical education are offered at all levels, with interscholastic competition available in soccer, basketball and track. After-school electives are numerous and entail additional fees. Computers are employed in all classes.

The day camp complements the academic summer school. The academic summer program includes one-on-one tutoring and small-group instruction in language and math; in addition to a choice of electives, it offers a full range of activities aimed at building self-confidence.

In the fall of 2010, Carroll opened a new lower school campus (grades 1-5) in Waltham. The same year, the middle school program in Lincoln grew with the addition of grade 9.

See Also Page 132

MANCHESTER, MA. (21 mi. NE of Boston, MA) Suburban. Pop: 5228. Alt: 30 ft.

BROOKWOOD SCHOOL
Day — Coed Gr PS (Age 4)-8

Manchester, MA 01944. 1 Brookwood Rd. Tel: 978-526-4500. Fax: 978-526-9303.
  www.brookwood.edu   E-mail: info@brookwood.edu
John C. Peterman, Head (1992). BA, Wittenberg Univ, MEd, Loyola Univ of Chicago. **Lindsay Murphy, Adm.**
  Pre-Prep. Elem math—Holt McDougal/Pearson-Prentice Hall/TERC Investigations.
    Feat—Chin Fr Span Computers Visual_Arts Drama Music Woodworking. **Supp**—Dev_Read Rem_Read Tut.
  Sports—Basket Ice_Hockey Lacrosse Soccer. G: F_Hockey.
  Selective adm: 63/yr. Usual entry: PS, K, 5 & 6. Appl fee: $40. Appl due: Feb. Yield: 72%.
    Tests IQ ISEE.
  Enr 404. B 195. G 209. Wh 90%. Latino 2%. Blk 1%. Asian 3%. Other 4%. Avg class size: 17. Stud/fac: 8:1. **Fac 60.** M 19/F 41. FT 46/PT 14. Wh 93%. Latino 3%. Blk 2%. Asian 2%. Adv deg: 75%.
  Grad '11—53. Prep—45. (Pingree 9, Phillips Acad 8, Governor's Acad 7, Middlesex 3, St John's Prep-MA 3, Westover 2).
  Tui '12-'13: Day $20,100-28,440. Aid: Need 59 ($965,225).
  Summer: Enrich Rec. Sports. Tui Day $140-480. 1-2 wks.
  Endow $9,728,000. Plant val $23,000,000. Acres 28. Bldgs 3 (100% ADA). Class rms 40. Lib 15,000 vols. Sci labs 4. Lang labs 1. Art studios 3. Music studios 2. Gyms 2. Fields 2. Comp labs 2. Comp/stud: 1:1.4.
  Est 1956. Nonprofit. Tri (Sept-June).

Founded by Philip Cutler, formerly at St. George's School in Newport, RI, Brookwood occupies a 30-acre tract on Boston's North Shore. The school's campus features a writing center, a recording studio, extensive computer technology (including interactive whiteboards in many classrooms), and various athletic facilities.

The broad academic curriculum emphasizes critical thinking, problem solving and creativity. Brookwood also conducts a particularly strong creative arts program. Interscholastic sports in grades 7 and 8, service learning, field trips and a cultural enrichment assembly program supplement academics. Before-school care and various after-school opportunities are also available.

MARBLEHEAD, MA. (14 mi. NE of Boston, MA) Suburban. Pop: 20,377. Alt: 65 ft.

TOWER SCHOOL
Day — Coed Gr PS (Age 4)-8

Marblehead, MA 01945. 75 W Shore Dr. Tel: 781-631-5800. Fax: 781-631-2292.
  www.towerschool.org   E-mail: contact@towerschool.org
Peter S. Philip, Head (2000). BA, Yale Univ, MALS, Wesleyan Univ. **Elizabeth D. Parker, Adm.**
  Pre-Prep. Feat—Lib_Skills Lat Span Environ_Sci Computers Studio_Art Woodworking.
    Supp—Dev_Read Rem_Math Tut.
  Sports (req'd)—Basket Lacrosse Soccer.
  Selective adm: 43/yr. Usual entry: PS, K & 4. Appl fee: $45. Appl due: Jan. **Tests** IQ.
  Enr 298. B 154. G 144. Wh 88%. Latino 2%. Blk 2%. Asian 3%. Other 5%. Avg class size: 17. Stud/fac: 8:1. **Fac 69.** M 17/F 52. FT 67/PT 2. Wh 97%. Latino 2%. Asian 1%. Adv deg: 52%.
  Grad '10—32. Prep—21. (St John's Prep-MA 7, St Paul's Sch-NH 2, Governor's Acad 2,

Phillips Acad 2, St George's Sch-RI 1, Middlesex 1). Alum donors: 5%.
Tui '11-'12: Day $18,000-24,800. Aid: Need 83 ($1,029,300).
Summer: Enrich Rec. Tui Day $575-1375. 2-3 wks.
Endow $5,000,000. Plant val $10,200,000. Acres 5. Bldgs 1 (100% ADA). Class rms 25.
Lib 10,000 vols. Sci labs 3. Lang labs 2. Theaters 1. Art studios 2. Music studios 2.
Wood shops 1. Gyms 1. Fields 1. Pools 1. Comp labs 2. Comp/stud: 1:4 (1:1 Laptop
prgm Gr 3-8).
Est 1912. Nonprofit. Quar (Sept-June).

Established by Adeline Lane Tower in Salem and moved to Marblehead in 1941, the school emphasizes a strong program with offerings in reading, math, science, history, geography, global studies, Spanish, Latin, art, woodworking, music and physical education. The school encourages all students to participate in service projects. Pupils enroll from a wide area of the North Shore, and the majority go on to New England preparatory schools.

MARION, MA. (35 mi. ESE of Providence, RI; 46 mi. SSE of Boston, MA) Suburban.
Pop: 5123. Alt: 38 ft.

TABOR ACADEMY
Bdg and Day — Coed Gr 9-12

Marion, MA 02738. 66 Spring St. Tel: 508-748-2000. Fax: 508-291-6666.
www.taboracademy.org   E-mail: admissions@taboracademy.org
John H. Quirk, Jr., Head (2012). Andrew L. McCain, Adm.
Col Prep. AP (exams req'd; 349 taken, 78% 3+)—Eng Chin Fr Lat Span Stats Bio Chem Environ_Sci Physics Eur_Hist US_Hist World_Hist Econ. **Feat**—Creative_ Writing Greek Calc Anat & Physiol Astron Marine_Bio/Sci Oceanog Asian_Hist Civil_ War Vietnam_War Govt Psych Philos Art_Hist Ceramics Drawing Painting Photog Sculpt Studio_Art Acting Chorus Music_Hist Jazz_Hist Nautical_Sci. **Supp**—ESL. Sat classes.
Sports (req'd)—Basket Crew X-country Ice_Hockey Lacrosse Sail Soccer Squash Tennis Track. B: Baseball Football Golf Wrestling. G: F_Hockey Softball. **Activities:** 30.
Selective adm: 163/yr. Bdg 122. Day 41. Appl fee: $50. Appl due: Jan. Accepted: 51%.
Tests CEEB SSAT TOEFL.
Enr 517. B 289. G 228. Bdg 359. Day 158. Nonwhite 6%. Intl 18%. Avg class size: 12. Stud/fac: 6:1. Formal. **Fac 93.**
Grad '11—133. Col—133. (Boston U, Bates, Hobart/Wm Smith, Harvard, NYU, Rollins).
Avg SAT: CR 600. M 620. W 592. **Col couns:** 5.
Tui '12-'13: Bdg $49,400 (+$400-900). **Day $35,400** (+$400-750). **Aid:** Need ($3,726,325).
Summer: Enrich Rev Rec. Tui Bdg $1700-8000. 1-6 wks. Tui Day $495-2575. 1-6 wks.
Endow $36,535,000. Plant val $65,000,000. Acres 85. Bldgs 42. Dorms 19. Class rms 72. Libs 1. Auds 4. Theaters 3. Art studios 2. Music studios 10. Dance studios 1. Gyms 1. Athletic ctrs 1. Fields 9. Tennis courts 11. Squash courts 9. Field houses 1. Rinks 1. Tracks 1. Comp labs 3.
Est 1876. Nonprofit. Sem (Sept-June). **Assoc** CLS NEASC.

Endowed and named by a wealthy whaling family, Tabor occupies a waterfront location near Cape Cod on Buzzards Bay. The school's curriculum, size and facilities have been increased over the years. Girls were readmitted as day students in 1979, and a boarding section was added in 1982.

The curriculum includes Advanced Placement courses and honors sections in all major disciplines. In addition to the basic subjects, pupils may study oceanology, creative writing, ceramics, ethics, government, acting and music. Opportunities for celestial navigation, piloting and seamanship are available aboard the school's 92-foot schooner, *Tabor Boy,* which cruises the waters of southern New England during the fall and the spring. In addition to taking part in an annual community service day, all boys and girls satisfy a five-hour service requirement each year. Tabor is a nationally recognized Naval Honor School, allowing the school to nominate students to the US service academies.

MARLBOROUGH, MA. (27 mi. W of Boston, MA) Suburban. Pop: 36,255. Alt: 700 ft.

HILLSIDE SCHOOL

Bdg and Day — Boys Gr 5-9

Marlborough, MA 01752. 404 Robin Hill Rd. Tel: 508-485-2824. Fax: 508-485-4420.
www.hillsideschool.net   E-mail: admissions@hillsideschool.net
David Z. Beecher, Head. BA, Lake Forest College. Kristen J. Naspo, Adm.
  Pre-Prep. Gen Acad. LD. Underachiever. Feat—Fr Lat Span Studio_Art Music Study_
    Skills. Supp—Dev_Read ESL Rem_Math Rem_Read Rev Tut.
  Sports (req'd)—B: Baseball Basket X-country Golf Ice_Hockey Lacrosse Soccer Tennis
    Track Wrestling.
  Selective adm (Bdg Gr 5-9; Day 5-8): 55/yr. Bdg 40. Day 15. Appl fee: $50. Appl due:
    Rolling. Accepted: 72%. Yield: 90%. Tests IQ SSAT TOEFL.
  Enr 145. Bdg 94. Day 51. Wh 69%. Latino 5%. Blk 12%. Asian 10%. Other 4%. Intl 15%.
    Avg class size: 10. Stud/fac: 7:1. Formal. Fac 35. M 23/F 12. FT 35. Wh 90%. Latino
    2%. Blk 8%. Adv deg: 31%. In dorms 14.
  Grad '09—30. Prep—26. (Kent Sch-CT, Millbrook, Lawrence Acad, Brewster, Cushing,
    Choate). Alum donors: 5%.
  Tui '11-'12: Bdg $49,500 (+$1000). 5-Day Bdg $44,145 (+$1000). Day $29,500
    (+$500). Aid: Need 29 ($1,000,000).
  Summer: Coed. Ages 9-16. Enrich Rec. ESL. Farm. Leadership. Tui Bdg $2300/2-wk
    ses. Tui Day $1250/2-wk ses. 4 wks.
  Endow $3,300,000. Plant val $20,000,000. Acres 200. Bldgs 15. Dorms 6. Dorm rms 30.
    Class rms 14. Lib 7000 vols. Sci labs 2. Auds 1. Art studios 1. Music studios 1. Gyms
    1. Fields 2. Courts 2. Pools 1. Farms 1. Comp labs 1.
  Est 1901. Nonprofit. Tri (Sept-June).

Hillside School was founded as a farm school by Miss Charlotte Drinkwater and her sister, Mrs. Mary Drinkwater Warren, on a farm near the western boundary of Greenwich. When the original site was flooded in 1927 to create the Quabbin Reservoir, the school relocated to its current location on 200 acres of fields, ponds and forestland.

Hillside provides a structured and supportive environment for traditional learners and boys of average to above-average intelligence who have learning differences, attentional disorders or both. In grades 7-9, the academic program includes English, history, science, math, studio art, wood shop, and foreign language; children in grades 5 and 6 receive instruction in math, language arts, social studies, reading, art, music and science. The curriculum is supplemented with organizational, socialization and subject-specific tutorials for those students in need of additional support. Regular evaluations of each pupil's social and academic behavior is another important element of school life.

All students must participate in a sport or an athletic activity each trimester. Selected boys who are interested in assisting with the farm program may live on the farm and are responsible for getting up early each morning to feed and provide water for the animals.

MILTON, MA. (7 mi. SSW of Boston, MA) Suburban. Pop: 26,062. Alt: 24 ft.

MILTON ACADEMY
Bdg — Coed Gr 9-12; Day — Coed K-12

Milton, MA 02186. 170 Centre St. Tel: 617-898-1798. Fax: 617-898-1701.
  www.milton.edu   E-mail: admissions@milton.edu
Todd Bland, Head (2009). BA, Bowdoin College, MEd, Harvard Univ. **Paul S. Rebuck,
  Adm.**
  Col Prep. AP—Fr Lat Span Calc Stats Comp_Sci Comp_Govt & Pol Econ Psych US_
    Govt & Pol Art_Hist. **Feat**—Creative_Writing Poetry Shakespeare Chin Greek Anat
    & Physiol Astron Ecol Environ_Sci Genetics Geol Marine_Bio/Sci Asian_Hist Afri-
    can-Amer_Hist Middle_Eastern_Hist Anthro Philos Architect Ceramics Film Photog
    Studio_Art Drama Music_Hist Music_Theory Dance. **Supp**—Rev Tut. Outdoor ed.
  Sports—Basket X-country Golf Ice_Hockey Lacrosse Sail Ski Soccer Squash Swim
    Tennis Track. B: Baseball Football Wrestling. G: F_Hockey Softball Volley. **Activities:**
    46.
  Very selective adm (Bdg Gr Gr 9-11; Day K-10): 200/yr. Bdg 100. Day 100. Usual
    entry: K, 4, 6, 9, 10 & 11. Appl fee: $50. Appl due: Jan. Applied: 1312. Accepted: 25%.
    Yield: 60%. **Tests** CEEB ISEE SSAT TOEFL.
  Enr 980. B 490. G 490. Bdg 335. Day 645. Elem 305. Sec 675. Wh 58%. Latino 4%. Blk
    10%. Asian 19%. Other 9%. Intl 10%. Avg class size: 14. Stud/fac: 5:1. **Fac 130.** Adv
    deg: 85%.
  Grad '11—181. Col—181. (Harvard 13, Cornell 7, Boston Col 6, Geo Wash 6, Tufts 6).
    Avg SAT: CR 673. M 678. W 684. **Col couns:** 4.
  Tui '12-'13: Bdg $47,520 (+$1250). **Day $21,830-39,000** (+$900).
  Endow $193,000,000. Plant val $53,000,000. Acres 125. Bldgs 62. Dorms 8. Lib 46,000
    vols. Lang labs 1. Photog labs 1. Art studios 6. Music studios 5. Perf arts ctrs 1. Art
    galleries 1. Gyms 4. Athletic ctrs 1. Fields 12. Tennis courts 13. Squash courts 7.
    Rinks 1.
  Est 1798. Nonprofit. Sem (Sept-June). **Assoc** CLS NEASC.

In 1798, Milton was chartered to provide education for the families then living in the small
colonial village and on farms scattered through the forested Blue Hills area. Though Milton
was originally coeducational, the academy was divided into separate schools in 1901, reacting
to a marked increase in the interest in separate education for young women. For many years,
the Milton Academy boys' school and girls' school maintained separate faculties, facilities and
student bodies; in 1973, however, the academy returned to coeducation.

Boarders enroll from numerous states and foreign countries, and day students, who commute from many communities of Metropolitan Boston, are invited to participate in the full
schedule of on-campus weekend activities. Although the school is bordered to the south by
6000 acres of preservation land, it is located 10 miles south of Boston, which is accessible
by subway. The upper school (grades 9-12) and the K-8 school share the academy's 125-acre
campus.

The academic program combines demanding training with innovative approaches. Upper
school students are placed at course levels and in sections according to interest and ability,
rather than grade or age. The curriculum is varied, with many electives offered in all areas
of study. The required one-year arts program offers creative writing, dance, drama, speech,
improvisational music, studio art and photography. Students may apply for an independent
study project under faculty guidance. Seniors may design five-week spring term projects with
faculty approval and supervision.

Activities and organizations are fully coeducational. The chamber singers have traveled to
Romania, Kenya, Germany, the Czech Republic and Hawaii, and student publications, orchestra, speech team, the visual and graphic arts, and drama are prominent in school life. Milton
has its own six-week exchange program for foreign study in France, Spain or China, and the
academy is also an affiliate of School Year Abroad. In 1983, Milton purchased the Mountain

School in Vershire Center, VT, to create a semester-long program for juniors from Milton and other member schools (see separate listing).

NATICK, MA. (17 mi. WSW of Boston, MA) Suburban. Pop: 32,170. Alt: 158 ft.

WALNUT HILL SCHOOL
Bdg and Day — Coed Gr 9-PG
Natick, MA 01760. 12 Highland St. Tel: 508-650-5020. Fax: 508-655-3726.
www.walnuthillarts.org E-mail: admissions@walnuthillarts.org
Antonio Viva, Head (2010). BA, MA, Union College (NY). **Lorie Komlyn, Adm.**
Col Prep. Perform_Arts Visual_Arts Creative_Writing. Feat—Creative_Writing Fr Span Stats Comp_Sci Art_Hist Studio_Art Visual_Arts Theater Music_Hist Music_ Theory Ballet Dance. **Supp**—ESL Tut.
Activities: 20.
Selective adm (Gr 9-12): 115/yr. Bdg 88. Day 27. Appl fee: $65. Appl due: Feb. Accepted: 46%. **Tests** SSAT TOEFL.
Enr 300. Sec 299. PG 1. Intl 25%. Avg class size: 14. **Fac 41.** M 20/F 21. FT 36/PT 5. Adv deg: 70%. In dorms 10.
Grad '09—100. Col—99. (New England Conservatory of Music 8, Juilliard 5, RI Sch of Design 5, Boston U 4, Boston Conservatory 3, Parsons Sch of Design 3). **Col couns:** 2.
Tui '12-'13: Bdg $48,500 (+$1650-4000). **Day $36,500** (+$1650-4000). **Aid:** Need 140 ($2,300,000).
Summer: Perform Arts. Visual Arts. Creative Writing. 2-5 wks.
Endow $6,135,000. Plant val $20,000,000. Dorm rms 185. Class rms 25. Lib 7500 vols. Lang labs 1. Writing ctrs 1. Theaters 2. Art studios 6. Music studios 6. Dance studios 5. Arts ctrs 1. Practice rms 20. Fields 1. Courts 4. Pools 1.
Est 1893. Nonprofit. Sem (Sept-June). **Assoc** CLS NEASC.

Walnut Hill was founded as a college preparatory school for Wellesley College. In 1971, the trustees voted to form a coeducational cocurricular program, fully integrating the academic program with training in the fine and performing arts.

The curriculum provides a broad range of both college preparatory and performing and visual arts courses, with requirements in English, mathematics, science, foreign language and social science. Each student must also be accepted into one of the arts departments and must major in music, ballet, theater, visual arts or creative writing. The school program is enhanced by an affiliation with the New England Conservatory of Music. This combination of arts study and academics provides students with the preparation necessary for entrance into universities, conservatories, art colleges and professional dance companies.

NEEDHAM, MA. (12 mi. WSW of Boston, MA) Suburban. Pop: 28,911. Alt: 169 ft.

ST. SEBASTIAN'S SCHOOL
Day — Boys Gr 7-12
Needham, MA 02492. 1191 Greendale Ave. Tel: 781-449-5200. Fax: 781-449-5630.
www.saintsebastiansschool.org E-mail: admissions@stsebs.org
William L. Burke III, Head (1990). BA, Middlebury College, MA, Boston College. **Gregory W. Wishart, Adm.**
Col Prep. AP (exams req'd; 260 taken)—Eng Lat Span Calc Stats Comp_Sci Bio Chem

Physics US_Hist US_Govt & Pol Art_Hist Studio_Art Music_Theory. **Feat**—Writing
Greek Anat & Physiol Govt Ethics Ceramics. **Supp**—Rev Tut.
Sports—B: Baseball Basket X-country Football Golf Ice_Hockey Lacrosse Soccer
Tennis.
Selective adm (Gr 7-10): 68/yr. Usual entry: 7, 8 & 9. Appl fee: $40. Appl due: Jan.
Applied: 275. Accepted: 41%. Yield: 60%. **Tests** ISEE SSAT.
Enr 364. Elem 102. Sec 262. Wh 88%. Latino 3%. Blk 5%. Asian 4%. Avg class size: 11.
Stud/fac: 7:1. **Fac 63.** M 50/F 13. FT 63. Wh 94%. Blk 4%. Asian 2%. Adv deg: 49%.
Grad '10—60. Col—60. (Villanova 5, Boston Col 4, Holy Cross 3, Dartmouth 3, Princeton
2, Middlebury 2). **Avg SAT:** CR 640. M 640. **Col couns:** 2. Alum donors: 31%.
Tui '11-'12: Day $34,750 (+$250). **Aid:** Need 88 ($2,040,885).
Endow $9,562,000. Plant val $29,532,000. Acres 25. Bldgs 5 (100% ADA). Class rms 32.
Lib 10,000 vols. Sci labs 5. Auds 1. Theaters 1. Art studios 2. Music studios 1. Gyms
2. Fields 5. Tennis courts 3. Rinks 1. Comp labs 2. Comp/stud: 1:4.
Est 1941. Inc. Roman Catholic. Quar (Sept-June). **Assoc** CLS NEASC.

Established by Cardinal O'Connell, this college preparatory school combines the traditions
of the New England independent school with Catholic education. The college preparatory
curriculum is highly structured, with required courses in English, foreign language, social
science, mathematics and laboratory science. Opportunities exist for honors and Advanced
Placement work. All seniors participate in an intensive, five-week community service immersion program.

NEWTON, MA. (10 mi. W of Boston, MA) Suburban. Pop: 83,829. Alt: 33 ft. Area
also includes West Newton.

FESSENDEN SCHOOL

Bdg — Boys Gr 5-9; Day — Boys PS (Age 4)-9

West Newton, MA 02465. 250 Waltham St. Tel: 617-630-2300. Fax: 617-630-2303.
www.fessenden.org   E-mail: admissions@fessenden.org
David B. Stettler, Head (2011). AB, Princeton Univ, MA, Columbia Univ. **Caleb W. Thomson, Adm.**
Pre-Prep. Feat—Lat Span Computers Ceramics Photog Studio_Art Video_Production
Drama Music. **Supp**—ESL Tut.
Sports (req'd)—B: Baseball Basket X-country Football Ice_Hockey Lacrosse Soccer
Squash Tennis Track Wrestling.
Selective adm (Bdg Gr 5-9; Day K-7): 124/yr. Bdg 34. Day 90. Appl fee: $50. Applied:
255. Accepted: 61%. Yield: 79%. **Tests** IQ ISEE SSAT.
Enr 485. Bdg 100. Day 385. Elem 436. Sec 49. Wh 91%. Blk 6%. Asian 3%. Intl 8%. Avg
class size: 11. **Fac 94.** M 38/F 56. FT 64/PT 30. Adv deg: 60%. In dorms 43.
Grad '11—49. Prep—49. (Brooks, Loomis Chaffee, St George's Sch-RI, Deerfield Acad,
Milton Acad, Phillips Acad).
Tui '11-'12: Bdg $48,750-49,600 (+$1000). **5-Day Bdg $42,750-43,600** (+$1000).
Day $23,775-33,750 (+$300). **Intl Bdg $53,475-54,325** (+$1000). **Aid:** Need 38
($1,000,000).
Summer: Coed. Ages 10-16. Acad. ESL. Tui Bdg $5225. 5 wks.
Endow $24,900,000. Plant val $40,000,000. Acres 43. Bldgs 25. Dorms 7. Dorm rms
105. Class rms 39. Lib 17,000 vols. Sci labs 4. Art studios 5. Music studios 3. Arts
ctrs 1. Gyms 3. Athletic ctrs 1. Fields 7. Courts 13. Pools 2. Rinks 1. Comp labs 4.
Comp/stud: 1:2.
Est 1903. Nonprofit. Tri (Sept-June).

Founded by Frederick J. Fessenden, the school balances a traditional curriculum with
instruction in the visual and performing arts and training in athletics. Honors, regular and
moderately paced sections accommodate individual needs in many subject areas. The lower

school program emphasizes the basic skills of reading, oral and written language, and mathematics, enriched by courses in social studies, science and geography. In addition, Fessenden begins instruction in Spanish at the kindergarten level.

Team sports begin in grade 5, and boys choose one athletic offering every season from a varied list of competitive team, intramural and recreational sports. Ninth-grade students are required to complete 10 hours of community service. The school's nonacademic programs (NAP) provide trips and activities for recreation and relaxation every weekend. Among the numerous options, which take advantage of the resources of Boston and New England, are seasonal outdoor activities, cultural and sporting events, school dances, sightseeing trips and movie nights.

NEWTON COUNTRY DAY SCHOOL OF THE SACRED HEART
Day — Girls Gr 5-12

Newton, MA 02458. 785 Centre St. Tel: 617-244-4246. Fax: 617-965-5313.
www.newtoncountryday.org   E-mail: mdelaney@newtoncountryday.org
Sr. Barbara Rogers, RSCJ, Head (1989). BA, Manhattanville College, MBA, Yale Univ.
Mary E. Delaney, Adm.
Col Prep. AP (exams req'd; 194 taken, 80% 3+)—Eng Fr Lat Span Calc Stats Bio Chem Environ_Sci Physics Eur_Hist US_Hist Comp_Govt & Pol US_Govt & Pol Art_Hist Studio_Art. **Feat**—British_Lit Creative_Writing Chin Anat & Physiol Astron Comp_Sci Econ Psych World_Relig Photog Visual_Arts Drama Chorus Music Music_Theory Dance. **Supp**—Rev. **Dual enr:** Boston Col.
Sports—G: Basket Crew X-country F_Hockey Golf Ice_Hockey Lacrosse Sail Soccer Softball Squash Tennis Volley. **Activities:** 35.
Selective adm (Gr 5-9): 68/yr. Appl fee: $50. Appl due: Feb. Accepted: 35%. Yield: 62%. **Tests** ISEE SSAT.
Enr 385. Avg class size: 15. Stud/fac: 7:1. **Fac 58.** M 19/F 39. FT 52/PT 6. Adv deg: 74%.
Grad '10—52. Col—51. (Holy Cross, Boston Col, Colby, Trinity Col-CT, Princeton, Harvard). **Avg SAT:** CR/M 1280. Alum donors: 16%.
Tui '11-'12: Day $36,700 (+$750).
Summer: Rec. Sports. 3 wks.
Endow $20,181,000. Plant val $23,811,000. Acres 18. Bldgs 6. Class rms 40. Libs 1. Sci labs 6. Theaters 2. Art studios 3. Music studios 2. Dance studios 1. Gyms 1. Fields 2. Courts 4. Rinks 1. Comp labs 1. Laptop prgm Gr 9-12.
Est 1880. Nonprofit. Roman Catholic. Quar (Sept-June). **Assoc** NEASC.

A member of the international Network of Sacred Heart Schools, NCDS provides a college preparatory curriculum for highly motivated girls from more than 65 communities in the Greater Boston area. At all grade levels, the program is designed to be developmentally appropriate. The middle school curriculum (grades 5-8) emphasizes the development of writing, reading and math skills, while the upper school program (grades 9-12) culminates in Advanced Placement classes in the major disciplines during the junior and senior years. Qualified pupils may earn college credit for courses taken at nearby Boston College.

The religious studies program instructs students in the Hebrew and Christian scriptures. Outside of the classroom, students engage in peer and Eucharistic ministry, retreats and weekly chapel services. In addition, all girls perform community service: 40 hours during junior year, required class projects in the other grades.

NORTHAMPTON, MA. (39 mi. N of Hartford, CT; 85 mi. W of Boston, MA) Suburban. Pop: 28,978. Alt: 124 ft.

SMITH COLLEGE CAMPUS SCHOOL

Day — Coed Gr K-6

Northampton, MA 01063. Gill Hall, 33 Prospect St. Tel: 413-585-3270.
Fax: 413-585-3285.
www.smith.edu/sccs   E-mail: campusschool@smith.edu
Cathy Hofer Reid, Dir. BA, Hamline Univ, MS, Utah State Univ, PhD, Univ of Connecticut.
Tim Lightman, Prin. BA, New York Univ, MS, MEd, Bank Street College of Education, EdD, Columbia Univ. **Maureen Litwin, Adm.**
  Pre-Prep. Gen Acad. **Feat**—Lib_Skills Span Computers Visual_Arts Music. **Supp**—Dev_Read.
  Selective adm: 50/yr. Appl fee: $40. Appl due: Mar. Accepted: 44%.
  Enr 270. B 117. G 153. Wh 81%. Latino 5%. Blk 4%. Native Am 1%. Asian 5%. Other 4%. Avg class size: 20. Stud/fac: 10:1. **Fac 23.** M 7/F 16. FT 17/PT 6. Wh 96%. Blk 4%. Adv deg: 91%.
  Grad '08—39. Prep—18. (Williston Northampton, Eaglebrook, Wilbraham & Monson, MacDuffie).
  Tui '12-'13: Day $9930 (+$145-440).
  Summer: Rec. 3 wks.
  Bldgs 2. Class rms 20. Lib 14,000 vols. Labs 1. Art studios 1. Music studios 1. Gyms 1. Fields 2.
  Est 1926. Nonprofit. Sem (Sept-May).

As a laboratory school for the Department of Education and Child Study at Smith College, the Campus School enrolls children of Northampton and surrounding towns in the Connecticut River Valley. Classroom teachers work closely with student teachers, and college faculty members visit classes often and act as a resource for teachers as they develop curriculum and activities. Among the Smith facilities open to the Campus School are a science center, a plant house, a theater, a chapel, a student center, a computer center and an arboretum.

The academic program emphasizes concept mastery and skill development in the core subjects. Special programs in art, vocal and instrumental music, Spanish, computers and physical education are integrated with major subjects whenever possible. Spanish instruction begins in grade 3 and progresses from oral language practice to written and grammatical study in grades 5 and 6.

NORTHFIELD, MA. (66 mi. N of Hartford, CT; 77 mi. WNW of Boston, MA) Suburban. Pop: 1141. Alt: 300 ft. Area also includes Mount Hermon.

NORTHFIELD MOUNT HERMON SCHOOL

Bdg and Day — Coed Gr 9-PG

Mount Hermon, MA 01354. 1 Lamplighter Way. Tel: 413-498-3227. Fax: 413-498-3152.
www.nmhschool.org   E-mail: admission@nmhschool.org
Peter B. Fayroian, Head (2012). BA, Univ of Vermont, MA, Middlebury College. **Claude Anderson, Adm.**
  Col Prep. AP (exams req'd; 249 taken, 92% 3+)—Eng Fr Lat Span Calc Comp_Sci Bio Chem Environ_Sci Physics Eur_Hist US_Hist Econ Psych Studio_Art Music_Theory. **Feat**—Creative_Writing Shakespeare Satire Chin Russ Arabic Multivariable_Calc Astron Bioethics Botany Ecol Geol Civil_Rights Anthro Bible Ethics Philos Relig Theater Dance Outdoor_Ed. **Supp**—ESL Rev Tut. Outdoor ed.

Sports—Basket Crew X-country Golf Ice_Hockey Lacrosse Ski Soccer Swim Tennis Track Ultimate_Frisbee Volley W_Polo. B: Baseball Football Wrestling. G: F_Hockey Softball. **Activities:** 63.

Selective adm (Bdg Gr 9-PG; Day 9-11): 239/yr. Bdg 198. Day 41. Appl fee: $50. Appl due: Feb. **Tests** CEEB ISEE SSAT TOEFL.

Enr 665. B 346. G 319. Bdg 545. Day 120. Intl 25%. Avg class size: 12. Stud/fac: 7:1. Casual. **Fac 95.** Adv deg: 66%.

Grad '11—203. Col—191. (CT Col, Boston U, Brown, Trinity Col-CT, Dickinson, U of PA). **Avg SAT:** CR/M/W 1854. Avg ACT: 24. **Col couns:** 4. Alum donors: 28%.

Tui '12-'13: Bdg $49,700 (+$1850). **Day $34,200** (+$1880). **Intl Bdg $49,700** (+$2630). **Aid:** Need 226 ($6,850,000).

Summer: Acad Enrich. Tui Bdg $6400. Tui Day $1600. ESL. Tui Bdg $6700. Tui Day $1900. Travel Abroad. Tui Bdg $6500-6700. 5 wks.

Endow $123,000,000. Plant val $199,240,000. Acres 1565. Bldgs 73. Dorm rms 515. Class rms 92. Lib 65,000 vols. Chapels 1. Sci labs 15. Lang labs 2. Auds 1. Gyms 2. Fields 11. Tennis courts 15. Pools 1. Rinks 1. Comp labs 2.

Est 1879. Nonprofit. Sem (Sept-June). **Assoc** CLS NEASC.

In 1879, Dwight L. Moody founded the Northfield Seminary for young ladies. Two years later, he founded Mount Hermon School for boys. Located on opposite banks of the Connecticut River, the schools were associated from the beginning in a variety of social, artistic and religious endeavors. In 1971, the schools joined to form a single coeducational institution on two campuses. Then, in the fall of 2005, NMH consolidated school operations onto the Mount Hermon campus on what is now known as Lamplighter Way.

Students take three major courses per semester that meet for extended class periods, resulting in a total of six rigorous college preparatory courses a year. Cocurricular enrichment classes and a ninth-grade foundation program complement these major courses. Spiritual opportunities at the school include religious studies courses and faculty-supported spiritual life groups. The Moody system of advising matches teachers with small groups of seven pupils. Small classes and a strong college counseling department are other notable aspects of NMH's program.

All students participate in the work program, contributing four hours each week to the operation of the school community through a variety of jobs. The outreach volunteer program, offered on an extracurricular basis, allows students to work at elementary schools, nursing homes, soup kitchens, animal shelters and other area service organizations.

The school participates in an international studies program that permits juniors and seniors to live in New Zealand, Egypt, South Africa, Costa Rica, Australia, Italy, Ireland, Greece, France, the Dominican Republic or China; summer study options include an intensive language program in Spain. Students who develop appropriate apprenticeship placement also earn credit.

OSTERVILLE, MA. (55 mi. ESE of Providence, RI; 59 mi. SSE of Boston, MA) Suburban. Pop: 2911. Alt: 70 ft.

CAPE COD ACADEMY

Day — Coed Gr PS (Age 4)-12

Osterville, MA 02655. 50 Osterville-W Barnstable Rd. Tel: 508-428-5400. Fax: 508-428-0701.
www.capecodacademy.org   E-mail: admissions@capecodacademy.org
Phillip P. Petru, Head (2011). BA, Wake Forest Univ, MS, Univ of Pennsylvania. **Laurie A. Wyndham, Adm.**

Col Prep. AP—Eng Calc Stats Bio US_Hist Studio_Art. **Feat**—British_Lit Creative_Writing Mythology Fr Ger Lat Span Environ_Sci Programming Philos Ceramics Drawing Photog Sculpt Theater_Arts Chorus Music Music_Theory. **Supp**—Tut.

Sports—Basket X-country Lacrosse Soccer Tennis. B: Baseball Golf Ice_Hockey. **Activ-**

ities: 19.

Selective adm: 89/yr. Appl fee: $95. Appl due: Feb. Accepted: 40%. **Tests** ISEE SSAT.
Enr 327. B 154. G 173. Elem 161. Sec 166. Wh 96%. Latino 2%. Blk 1%. Asian 1%. Avg class size: 16. Stud/fac: 8:1. **Fac 60.** Adv deg: 83%.
Grad '11—43. Col—43. (Wheaton-MA 3, Assumption 2, Emmanuel 2, Rensselaer Polytech 2, UNH 2, Harvard 1). **Avg SAT:** CR 595. M 624. W 600. **Col couns:** 2.
Tui '11-'12: Day $19,400-23,380 (+$150). **Aid:** Need 91 ($470,945).
Endow $2,500,000. Plant val $12,500,000. Acres 46. Bldgs 1. Class rms 32. 2 Libs 8000 vols. Sci labs 7. Sci ctrs 1. Art studios 3. Gyms 2. Fields 3. Basketball courts 2. Comp labs 2. Comp/stud: 1:2.
Est 1976. Nonprofit. Tri (Sept-June). **Assoc** CLS NEASC.

Situated on a 46-acre campus and drawing students from throughout southeastern Massachusetts, the school has experienced rapid growth since its establishment. Boys and girls engage in a rigorous scholastic program while enrolling in five or six academic courses per year in grades 7-12. All pupils take Latin in grades 7 and 8, and those in grades 9-12 take at least three years of Spanish or French. Older students choose among Advanced Placement courses in most disciplines.

Students in grades 7-12 must participate in one season of interscholastic athletics each year. Boys and girls have community service opportunities at all grade levels. Seniors devote at least 80 hours to a self-designed service project with a local nonprofit organization during the final month of the school year.

PITTSFIELD, MA. (31 mi. ESE of Albany, NY; 115 mi. W of Boston, MA) Urban. Pop: 45,793. Alt: 1013 ft.

MISS HALL'S SCHOOL

Bdg and Day — Girls Gr 9-12

Pittsfield, MA 01202. 492 Holmes Rd, PO Box 1166. Tel: 413-443-6401, 800-233-5614. Fax: 413-448-2994.
www.misshalls.org   E-mail: info@misshalls.org
Margaret A. Jablonski, Head (2012). BA, MEd, Univ of Massachusetts-Amherst, EdD, Boston Univ. **Julie Bradley, Adm.**
Col Prep. AP (exams req'd; 1022 taken, 9% 3+)—Eng Fr Lat Span Calc Stats Bio Chem Eur_Hist US_Hist Human_Geog Studio_Art. **Feat**—British_Lit Chin Anat & Physiol Forensic_Sci Web_Design Chin_Hist Civil_War Japan_Hist Law Philos Relig Art_Hist Ceramics Drawing Photog Drama Chorus Music Music_Hist Modern_Dance Debate. **Supp**—ESL Rev Tut.
Sports (req'd)—G: Basket X-country Lacrosse Ski Soccer Softball Tennis Volley. **Activities:** 33.
Selective adm: 68/yr. Bdg 55. Day 13. Appl fee: $50. Appl due: Feb. Applied: 250. Accepted: 43%. Yield: 67%. **Tests** SSAT TOEFL.
Enr 180. Bdg 136. Day 44. Intl 30%. Avg class size: 10. Stud/fac: 5:1. Casual. **Fac 35.** M 6/F 29. FT 34/PT 1. Adv deg: 80%. In dorms 9.
Grad '11—44. Col—44. (NYU, U of IL-Urbana, PA St, Wm & Mary, Brown, Trinity Col-CT). **Col couns:** 3. Alum donors: 35%.
Tui '12-'13: Bdg $48,400 (+$900). **Day $30,000** (+$900). **Intl Bdg $48,400** (+$3550). **Aid:** Need 100 ($2,329,020).
Endow $16,000,000. Plant val $22,000,000. Acres 85. Bldgs 17. Dorms 2. Dorm rms 84. Class rms 25. Lib 15,000 vols. Sci labs 3. Photog labs 1. Auds 2. Theaters 1. Art studios 1. Music studios 4. Dance studios 1. Arts ctrs 1. Gyms 1. Athletic ctrs 1. Fields 4. Courts 8. Ski chalets 1. Student ctrs 1. Comp labs 2.
Est 1898. Nonprofit. Sem (Sept-June). **Assoc** CLS NEASC.

The school was established by Mira Hinsdale Hall as a successor institution to the first girls' boarding school founded in Massachusetts in 1800. Upon her aunt's death in 1937, Margaret Hall assumed direction of the school, continuing the family tradition, conservative tone and standards of scholarship.

Miss Hall's offers both an honors tier and Advanced Placement courses, in addition to various electives. An established expressive arts program features photography, studio art, modern dance, theater and music. Internships with area businesses and science and cultural organizations add breadth to the traditional college preparatory program. Girls take part in community service each Thursday morning.

The athletic program comprises interscholastic and recreational sports, as well as a wilderness program. All students participate in an athletic activity each term, including at least one team sport each year. Emphasis is placed on attracting a geographically diverse student body and maintaining a family-style atmosphere.

SANDWICH, MA. (48 mi. SE of Boston, MA; 48 mi. E of Providence, RI) Suburban. Pop: 17,119. Alt: 20 ft. Area also includes East Sandwich.

RIVERVIEW SCHOOL
Bdg and Day — Coed Gr 6-PG

East Sandwich, MA 02537. 551 Rte 6A. Tel: 508-888-0489. Fax: 508-833-7001.
www.riverviewschool.org   E-mail: admissions@riverviewschool.org
Maureen B. Brenner, Head (2001). BA, University College Dublin (Ireland), MEd, Bridgewater State College. **Jeanne M. Pacheco, Adm.**

Col Prep. LD. Feat—Computers Photog Studio_Art Drama Indus_Arts. **Supp**—Dev_ Read Rem_Math Rem_Read.

Sports—Basket X-country Soccer Swim Tennis Track. B: Baseball. G: Softball. **Activities: 28.**

Selective adm: 52/yr. Bdg 49. Day 3. Usual entry: 9. Appl fee: $75. Appl due: Rolling. Applied: 203. Accepted: 50%. Yield: 50%. **Tests** IQ.

Enr 207. B 117. G 90. Bdg 187. Day 20. Elem 9. Sec 86. PG 112. Wh 89%. Latino 5%. Blk 2%. Asian 2%. Other 2%. Avg class size: 8. Stud/fac: 8:1. Casual. **Fac 48.** M 15/F 33. FT 45/PT 3. Wh 89%. Blk 11%. Adv deg: 54%.

Grad '11—35. Col—32. (Cape Cod CC 28, Lesley 2, Col of Charleston 1, Clemson 1).

Tui '11-'12: Bdg $69,750. Day $41,674. Aid: Need 24 ($330,000).

Summer (enr 152): Ages 12-22. Acad Enrich Rev Rem Rec. Computers. Sports. Tui Bdg $6984. Tui Day $4260. 5 wks.

Endow $4,500,000. Plant val $30,000,000. Acres 16. Bldgs 20 (75% ADA). Dorms 10. Dorm rms 62. Class rms 29. Libs 1. Sci labs 1. Dark rms 1. Auds 1. Art studios 1. Music studios 1. Gyms 1. Athletic ctrs 1. Fields 1. Courts 1. Greenhouses 1. Comp labs 3. Comp/stud: 1:1

Est 1957. Nonprofit. Quar (Sept-June). **Assoc** NEASC.

Riverview serves adolescents without significant behavioral or emotional problems who have complex language, learning and cognitive disabilities. Students, who have an IQ between 70 and 100, typically have experienced lifelong difficulties in academics and in making friends. The thematic, integrated program features academic, remedial and computer course work, while also addressing independent living skills and social skills development.

The program includes small, individualized academic classes, as well as reading, speech and language therapies. Speech/language pathologists and reading specialists provide assistance as needed. Structured evening and weekend programs offer support and are an important element of Riverview's predictable learning environment.

All juniors take part in a weekly community service program.

SHEFFIELD, MA. (42 mi. NW of Hartford, CT; 104 mi. NNE of New York, NY) Suburban. Pop: 3335. Alt: 679 ft.

BERKSHIRE SCHOOL

Bdg and Day — Coed Gr 9-PG

Sheffield, MA 01257. 245 N Undermountain Rd. Tel: 413-229-1003. Fax: 413-229-1016. www.berkshireschool.org E-mail: admission@berkshireschool.org

Michael J. Maher, Head (2004). BA, Univ of Vermont, MA, Wesleyan Univ. **Andrew L. Bogardus, Adm.**

Col Prep. AP (exams req'd; 249 taken, 75% 3+)—Eng Fr Span Calc Bio Chem Environ_Sci Physics Eur_Hist US_Hist US_Govt & Pol Studio_Art. **Feat**—Creative_Writing Chin Lat Stats Linear_Algebra Multivariable_Calc Astron Ecol Psych Constitutional_Law Ethics Ceramics Filmmaking Photog Acting Chorus Music Music_Theory Journ. **Supp**—ESL Tut. Outdoor ed. Sat classes.

Sports—Basket Crew X-country Golf Ice_Hockey Lacrosse Ski Soccer Squash Tennis Track. B: Baseball Football. G: F_Hockey Softball Volley. **Activities:** 27.

Selective adm: 147/yr. Bdg 128. Day 19. Appl fee: $75. Appl due: Jan. Applied: 975. Accepted: 35%. Yield: 47%. Tests CEEB SSAT TOEFL.

Enr 380. B 218. G 162. Bdg 333. Day 47. Sec 364. PG 16. Intl 19%. Avg class size: 12. Stud/fac: 5:1. Formal. **Fac 61.** M 40/F 21. FT 58/PT 3. Wh 92%. Blk 5%. Asian 3%. Adv deg: 63%. In dorms 35.

Grad '11—113. Col—108. (Union Col-NY 6, Boston Col 3, Emory 3, Tufts 3, Colby 2). Athl schol 5. **Col couns:** 5.

Tui '12-'13: Bdg $49,900 (+$1000). **Day $39,900** (+$800). **Aid:** Need ($4,100,000).

Endow $94,000,000. Plant val $190,000,000. Acres 550. Bldgs 33. Dorms 10. Dorm rms 185. Class rms 45. Lib 40,500 vols. Comp ctrs 2. Observatories 1. Theaters 1. Art studios 5. Music studios 4. Dance studios 1. Art galleries 1. Gyms 1. Athletic ctrs 1. Fields 9. Courts 13. Rinks 2. Student ctrs 1. Radio stations 1.

Est 1907. Nonprofit. Sem (Sept-May). **Assoc** CLS NEASC.

In the fall of 1907, Mr. and Mrs. Seaver B. Buck rented the buildings of the Glenny farm at the foot of Mt. Everett and founded Berkshire School. For 35 years, the Bucks devoted themselves to educating young men about the values of academic pursuit and high personal standards. In 1969, this dedication to excellence was extended to girls, as the school became coeducational.

Berkshire provides a traditional curriculum, with honors and accelerated classes leading to a variety of Advanced Placement courses. Emphasis is placed on the acquisition of sound research skills, the integration of knowledge and an awareness of global issues. The school allows qualified students to explore specialized interests through independent study. Boys and girls are encouraged to develop their leadership skills and to take an active role in the governance of the school.

Located on 550 acres in the hills of western Massachusetts, the school provides competition in many interscholastic sports, with recreational offerings available in skiing and mountain climbing. Berkshire schedules frequent lectures, concerts and art exhibits.

SOUTH HAMILTON, MA. (20 mi. NNE of Boston, MA) Suburban. Pop: 2720. Alt: 55 ft.

PINGREE SCHOOL

Day — Coed Gr 9-12

South Hamilton, MA 01982. 537 Highland St. Tel: 978-468-4415. Fax: 978-468-3758.

www.pingree.org   E-mail: estacey@pingree.org
Timothy M. Johnson, Head (2009). BA, Bowdoin College, MFA, Maryland Institute College of Art, EdD, Univ of Pennsylvania. **Eric Stacey, Adm.**
Col Prep. AP (exams req'd; 158 taken, 81% 3+)—Fr Span Calc Stats Bio Environ_Sci Physics US_Hist Art_Hist Music_Theory. **Feat**—Creative_Writing Chin Lat Anat & Physiol Ecol Oceanog Programming Comp_Animation Philos Ceramics Drawing Photog Sculpt Studio_Art Theater_Arts Dance. **Supp**—Tut.
Sports (req'd)—Basket X-country Golf Ice_Hockey Lacrosse Sail Ski Soccer Swim Tennis Ultimate_Frisbee. B: Baseball Football. G: Softball Volley. **Activities:** 40.
Selective adm (Gr 9-11): 99/yr. Usual entry: 9. Appl fee: $50. Appl due: Jan. Accepted: 48%. Yield: 54%. **Tests** ISEE SSAT.
Enr 341. B 154. G 187. Wh 94%. Latino 3%. Blk 1%. Asian 2%. Avg class size: 15. Stud/fac: 8:1. Casual. **Fac 50.** M 18/F 32. FT 47/PT 3. Wh 86%. Latino 6%. Blk 4%. Other 4%. Adv deg: 64%.
Grad '11—85. Col—79. (Bentley 5, Boston Col 5, St Lawrence 4, Boston U 3, Lafayette 3, Amherst 2). **Avg SAT:** CR 590. M 615. W 590. **Mid 50% SAT:** CR 540-650. M 530-660. W 530-660. Avg ACT: 27. **Col couns:** 3. Alum donors: 22%.
Tui '12-'13: Day $36,100 (+$750). **Aid:** Merit 8 ($110,725). Need 83 ($2,071,931).
Summer: Enrich Rec. Sports. Tui Day $375-2640. 1-8 wks.
Endow $9,800,000. Plant val $21,000,000. Acres 105. Bldgs 7 (100% ADA). Class rms 28. Lib 16,000 vols. Sci labs 5. Lang labs 1. Writing ctrs 1. Auds 1. Theaters 1. Art studios 1. Music studios 1. Gyms 1. Fields 8. Rinks 1. Comp labs 4. Comp/stud: 1:4.
Est 1961. Nonprofit. Sem (Sept-June). **Assoc** CLS NEASC.

In 1961, Mr. and Mrs. Sumner Pingree gave their home and 50 acres of land as the site of this school. Pingree opened with 50 girls and became coeducational in 1971.

Serving the North Shore, the school offers a curriculum that consists of a balanced sequence of requirements, providing a solid foundation in the liberal arts and sciences. The arts are a basic component of the educational program. Students are required to take two semesters of art and may choose from such courses as drawing and painting, photography, theater arts, chamber music and modern dance. Students interested in advanced work may elect Advanced Placement and honors courses, which are available in every department.

All students participate in an afternoon program all three seasons; seniors must fulfill the requirement for two seasons. Those who are not interested in competitive sports may take part in the outdoor education program or earn credit for community service work, drama, dance or an independent project. Prior to graduation, each student must complete 50 hours of service to the community, either during one athletic season, on weekends or vacations, or by playing an essential role in the organization and operation of a major community service project.

SOUTHBOROUGH, MA. (26 mi. W of Boston, MA) Suburban. Pop: 8781. Alt: 314 ft.

FAY SCHOOL

Bdg — Coed Gr 7-9; Day — Coed PS (Age 4)-9

Southborough, MA 01772. 48 Main St, PO Box 9106. Tel: 508-485-0100.
Fax: 508-481-7872.
www.fayschool.org   E-mail: fayadmit@fayschool.org
Robert J. Gustavson, Jr., Head (2008). BA, MEd, Univ of Virginia. **Beth Whitney, Adm.**
Pre-Prep. Feat—Chin Fr Lat Span Computers Econ Govt Law Studio_Art Music. **Supp**—ESL Tut.
Sports (req'd)—Basket X-country Ice_Hockey Lacrosse Soccer Tennis Track. B: Baseball Football Wrestling. G: F_Hockey Softball Volley.
Selective adm: 144/yr. Bdg 52. Day 92. Usual entry: PS & 5. Appl fee: $50. Appl due: Rolling. Applied: 410. Accepted: 51%. Yield: 69%. **Tests** IQ ISEE SSAT TOEFL.

Enr 441. Elem 412. Sec 29. Wh 65%. Latino 3%. Blk 4%. Asian 20%. Other 8%. Intl 15%. Avg class size: 13. Stud/fac: 6:1. **Fac 80.** M 23/F 57. FT 70/PT 10. Wh 94%. Latino 1%. Blk 1%. Asian 1%. Other 3%. Adv deg: 68%. In dorms 18.

Grad '11—46. Prep—45. (St Mark's Sch-MA 9, Brooks 3, Cushing 2, Northfield Mt Hermon 2, Phillips Acad 2, Phillips Exeter 2). Avg SSAT: 90%.

Tui '11-'12: Bdg $46,900-47,800 (+$2070). **Day $18,500-28,750** (+$525-725). **Intl Bdg $49,375-55,800** (+$2070). **Aid:** Need 51 ($1,377,060).

Summer (enr 200): Acad Enrich Rec. ESL. Tui Bdg $9600. 6 wks. Rec. Tui Day $475/wk. 8 wks.

Endow $32,795,000. Plant val $58,486,000. Acres 62. Bldgs 32. Dorms 6. Lib 13,000 vols. Sci labs 5. Dark rms 1. Theaters 1. Art studios 2. Music studios 3. Dance studios 1. Arts ctrs 1. Gyms 2. Fields 9. Basketball courts 6. Tennis courts 8. Pools 1. Comp labs 3. Comp/stud: 1:3.

Est 1866. Nonprofit. Tri (Sept-June).

The oldest junior boarding school in America, Fay School was founded by Harriet Burnett and Eliza Burnett Fay. Waldo B. Fay was headmaster from 1896 to 1918; his son, Edward Winchester Fay, served from 1918 to 1942. The school became coeducational in 1972, with the acceptance of girls. Boarding students in grades 7-9 enroll from various states and foreign countries, creating a diverse student body.

The traditional primary curriculum in the lower school is enriched by arts, French, Spanish, music instruction and age-appropriate physical education. In the upper school, which prepares students for leading secondary schools, the curriculum encompasses course work for the academically advanced and for students who require academic support. French and Spanish are introduced in prekindergarten, Latin and Mandarin in grade 6. English courses within the upper school emphasize writing, novels, poetry, grammar and public speaking. A strong laboratory-oriented science curriculum includes biology and conceptual physics. Technology is an integral aspect of the curriculum. Fay conducts academic field trips and weekend enrichment excursions in Boston and throughout the surrounding area.

SAINT MARK'S SCHOOL

Bdg and Day — Coed Gr 9-12

Southborough, MA 01772. 25 Marlborough Rd, PO Box 9105. Tel: 508-786-6000. Fax: 508-786-6120.

www.stmarksschool.org   E-mail: admission@stmarksschool.org

John Warren, Head (2007). BA, MA, Stanford Univ, MEd, EdD, Harvard Univ. **Anne E. Behnke, Adm.**

Col Prep. AP (exams req'd; 342 taken, 90% 3+)—Eng Fr Lat Span Calc Stats Bio Chem Physics Eur_Hist US_Hist Human_Geog Psych Art_Hist Studio_Art Music_Theory. **Feat**—Ger Greek Astron Forensic_Sci Comp_Sci Robotics Civil_War Russ_Hist Anthro Ethics Relig Ceramics Film Photog Sculpt Theater Music_Hist. **Supp**—Tut. Sat classes.

Sports (req'd)—Basket Crew X-country Ice_Hockey Lacrosse Soccer Squash Tennis. B: Baseball Football Golf Wrestling. G: F_Hockey Softball. **Activities:** 63.

Selective adm (Gr 9-11): 121/yr. Bdg 93. Day 28. Usual entry: 9. Appl fee: $50. Appl due: Jan. Applied: 722. Accepted: 36%. Yield: 46%. **Tests** SSAT TOEFL.

Enr 349. B 178. G 171. Bdg 269. Day 80. Wh 80%. Latino 3%. Blk 5%. Native Am 1%. Asian 5%. Other 6%. Intl 20%. Avg class size: 12. Stud/fac: 5:1. Casual. **Fac 76.** M 42/F 34. FT 75/PT 1. Wh 84%. Latino 5%. Blk 7%. Native Am 1%. Asian 1%. Other 2%. Adv deg: 73%. In dorms 24.

Grad '11—95. Col—95. (Geo Wash 5, Lehigh 5, Trinity Col-CT 4, Tufts 3, Boston Col 3, Villanova 3). Athl schol 3. **Avg SAT:** CR 630. M 670. W 640. Avg ACT: 27. **Col couns:** 2. Alum donors: 30%.

Tui '12-'13: Bdg $49,130 (+$1800). **Day $39,225** (+$1700). **Aid:** Need 87 ($3,500,000).

Endow $130,000,000. Plant val $125,000,000. Acres 250. Bldgs 24. Dorms 13. Dorm rms 180. Class rms 37. Lib 30,000 vols. Sci labs 8. Lang labs 1. Auds 2. Theaters 3.

Art studios 5. Music studios 12. Dance studios 1. Mech drawing studios 1. Gyms 2. Fields 9. Basketball courts 2. Tennis courts 10. Squash courts 7. Pools 1. Rinks 1. Weight rms 1. Comp labs 3.
Est 1865. Nonprofit. Episcopal (30% practice). Sem (Sept-June). **Assoc** CLS NEASC.

Founded by Joseph Burnett as an Episcopal school, Saint Mark's remains grounded in its Judeo-Christian heritage. The school meets as a group five times per week in either the chapel or the student center. The 250-acre campus is centered around the main building, a large Tudor structure built in 1890.

The liberal arts curriculum includes requirements in English, mathematics, foreign language, history, science, religion and the arts. All departments except religion offer Advanced Placement courses, and students with demonstrated interest in a particular subject may pursue independent study under the guidance of a faculty advisor. Opportunities for study abroad and student exchanges complement Saint Mark's varied foreign language program. Wired and wireless Internet access is available throughout the campus, including dorm rooms.

Each student takes part in the school's athletic program. Third- and fourth-form students participate on interscholastic teams each season; fifth and sixth formers may instead pursue recreational athletics or, with faculty approval, independent study in the arts for one season each year. The school's proximity to Boston allows students to attend numerous cultural and sporting events.

SPRINGFIELD, MA. (25 mi. NNE of Hartford, CT; 80 mi. W of Boston, MA) Urban. Pop: 152,082. Alt: 119 ft. Area also includes Granby.

THE MacDUFFIE SCHOOL
Bdg and Day — Coed Gr 6-12

Granby, MA 01033. 66 School St. Tel: 413-467-1601. Fax: 413-467-1607.
www.macduffie.com   E-mail: admissions@macduffie.org
Steven Griffin, Head (2011). BS, Univ of Waterloo (Canada), BEd, Univ of Western Ontario (Canada), MA, Univ of Toronto (Canada). **Linda Keating, Adm.**
Col Prep. AP (exams req'd; 80 taken, 92% 3+)—Eng Fr Lat Calc Stats Chem Eur_ Hist World_Hist. **Feat**—British_Lit Creative_Writing Chin Span Environ_Sci Biotech Meteorology Econ Psych Peace_Stud Philos World_Relig Architect Art_Hist Drawing Film Painting Sculpt Studio_Art Visual_Arts Acting Drama Music_Hist Music_Theory Dance Journ. **Supp**—ESL Tut.
Sports—Basket X-country Soccer Tennis Ultimate_Frisbee. B: Baseball. G: Lacrosse Softball Volley.
Selective adm: 74/yr. Bdg 22. Day 52. Appl fee: $50-100. Appl due: Rolling. Accepted: 58%. Yield: 68%. **Tests** SSAT TOEFL.
Enr 200. B 94. G 106. Bdg 103. Day 97. Elem 41. Sec 159. Nonwhite 55%. Intl 18%. Avg class size: 12. Stud/fac: 6:1. Casual. **Fac 28.** Adv deg: 71%.
Grad '09—44. Col—44. (NYU 3, Mt Holyoke 3, Clark U 3, Rensselaer Polytech 2, MA Col of Pharmacy 2, Harvard 1). **Avg SAT:** CR 577. M 610. W 588. **Col couns:** 1.
Tui '12-'13: Bdg $47,250-52,500 (+$1500-2000). **5-Day Bdg $45,000** (+$1500-2000). **Day $19,500-24,500** (+$500-800).
Plant val $10,800,000.
Est 1890. Sem (Sept-May). **Assoc** CLS NEASC.

The school was founded as a college preparatory school for girls by Dr. John MacDuffie, a Harvard alumnus, and his wife, Abby, a member of Radcliffe's first graduating class. The MacDuffie family directed the school until 1941.

The course of studies at MacDuffie features an integrated curriculum at all levels. Teams of teachers work together in both the middle school and the upper school to create an interrelated program that includes the arts and the core subjects of English, mathematics, history, foreign languages and science. Advanced Placement and honors courses are offered in all subject areas. The school also conducts after-school extra-help sessions on a regular basis.

Students take advantage of Springfield's cultural opportunities by attending events at the civic center, theaters, museums and the many local colleges of the western Massachusetts area.

SUDBURY, MA. (21 mi. W of Boston, MA) Suburban. Pop: 16,841. Alt: 201 ft.

WILLOW HILL SCHOOL
Day — Coed Gr 6-12

Sudbury, MA 01776. 98 Haynes Rd. Tel: 978-443-2581. Fax: 978-443-7560.
www.willowhillschool.org   E-mail: mfoley@willowhillschool.org
Rhonda Taft-Farrell, Head (2011). EdD. Melissa Foley-Procko, Adm.
  Col Prep. LD. Feat—Computers Filmmaking Photog Studio_Art Drama Music Outdoor_ Ed. Supp—Dev_Read Makeup Rem_Math Rem_Read Rev Tut. Outdoor ed. Dual enr: Middlesex CC.
  Sports—Basket Soccer Track Ultimate_Frisbee. Activities: 7.
  Selective adm (Gr 6-11): 16/yr. Appl fee: $0. Appl due: Rolling. Applied: 99. Accepted: 46%. Yield: 50%. Tests IQ.
  Enr 60. B 43. G 17. Elem 20. Sec 40. Wh 100%. Avg class size: 8. Stud/fac: 4:1. Casual. Fac 17. M 8/F 9. FT 16/PT 1. Wh 100%. Adv deg: 88%.
  Grad '11—11. Col—11. (Landmark 2, Middlesex CC 2, Anna Maria 1, Plymouth St 1, Castleton St 1, Westfield St 1). Col couns: 2.
  Tui '11-'12: Day $48,574.
  Plant val $4,928,000. Acres 26. Bldgs 4. Class rms 17. Lib 5300 vols. Sci labs 2. Art studios 1. Arts ctrs 1. Gyms 1. Comp labs 2. Comp/stud: 1:1 Laptop prgm Gr 6-12.
  Est 1970. Nonprofit. Quar (Sept-June). Assoc NEASC.

The school offers comprehensive educational services for students of average to high intelligence who have been diagnosed with learning disabilities, nonverbal learning disabilities or Asperger's syndrome. The college preparatory curriculum includes course work in art, drama and technology. Willow Hill also provides highly individualized one-on-one and small-group tutorials, sports, a wilderness exploration program and extracurricular activities.

WALTHAM, MA. (12 mi. WNW of Boston, MA) Urban. Pop: 59,226. Alt: 51 ft.

CHAPEL HILL-CHAUNCY HALL SCHOOL
Bdg and Day — Coed Gr 9-PG

Waltham, MA 02452. 785 Beaver St. Tel: 781-314-0800. Fax: 781-894-5205.
www.chch.org   E-mail: lpelrine@chch.org
Siri Akal Khalsa, Pres (2009). BA, MS, City Univ of New York, MFA, Brandeis Univ, MA, EdD, Columbia Univ. Lance Conrad, Head. BA, Bowdoin College, MAT, Marlboro College, MEd, Harvard Univ. Lisa Pelrine, Adm.
  Col Prep. AP (exams req'd)—Eng Studio_Art. Feat—Humanities Chin Fr Span Calc Stats Anat & Physiol Econ Pol_Sci Adolescent_Psych Ethics Art_Hist Graphic_Arts Photog Visual_Arts Theater_Arts Chorus Music_Theory Public_Speak. Supp—ESL LD Tut. Outdoor ed.
  Sports—Basket X-country Golf Lacrosse Soccer Ultimate_Frisbee. B: Baseball Wrestling. G: Softball Volley.
  Selective adm: 50/yr. Bdg 22. Day 28. Appl fee: $50. Appl due: Feb. Tests IQ SSAT

TOEFL.
Enr 165. B 83. G 82. Bdg 74. Day 91. Intl 25%. Avg class size: 12. Stud/fac: 5:1. **Fac 35.** Adv deg: 65%. In dorms 11.
Grad '10—48. Col—48. (Roger Williams 3, Clark U 2, Curry 2, Drew 2, U of IL-Urbana 2, Wheaton-MA 2). **Avg SAT:** CR 518. M 578. W 538. **Mid 50% SAT:** CR 460-590. M 450-690. W 470-580. Avg ACT: 22.4. Mid 50% ACT: 17-25.
Tui '12-'13: Bdg $47,800 (+$950). **Day $25,000-34,900** (+$650). **Intl Bdg $46,000** (+$2145). **Aid:** Need 25 ($513,189).
Summer: Enrich Rev Rem Rec. Tui Day $380-480/wk. 8 wks.
Endow $1,800,000. Plant val $11,800,000. Acres 37. Bldgs 16. Dorms 3. Dorm rms 52. Class rms 25. Lib 13,000 vols. Sci labs 3. Auds 1. Theaters 1. Art studios 1. Music studios 1. Dance studios 1. Wood shops 1. Gyms 1. Fields 2. Pools 1. Greenhouses 1. Comp labs 6. Comp/stud: 1:2.
Est 1828. Nonprofit. Tri (Sept-June). **Assoc** NEASC.

Chapel Hill School for girls, a boarding school founded by New Church members in 1860, merged with the Chauncy Hall School for boys (established in 1828), a day school, on the Chapel Hill campus in 1971.

Enrolling students from throughout the country and the world, CH-CH stresses personal growth and independence while providing a structured, supportive environment that is flexible enough to address the varied needs and talents of its diverse student body. Within the traditional college preparatory curriculum, the school offers a learning center and a ninth-grade program specifically designed to support first-year students. Pupils partake of many cultural events in and around Boston.

WELLESLEY, MA. (14 mi. W of Boston, MA) Suburban. Pop: 26,613. Alt: 140 ft.

DANA HALL SCHOOL
Bdg — Girls Gr 9-12; Day — Girls 6-12
Wellesley, MA 02482. 45 Dana Rd, PO Box 9010. Tel: 781-235-3010.
Fax: 781-239-1383.
www.danahall.org   E-mail: admission@danahall.org
Caroline Kent Erisman, Head (2008). BA, Wellesley College, JD, New York Univ, MA, Columbia Univ. **Wendy Sibert Secor, Adm.**
Col Prep. AP (exams req'd; 195 taken, 91% 3+)—Eng Chin Fr Lat Span Calc Stats Comp_Sci Bio Chem Physics Eur_Hist US_Hist Studio_Art. **Feat**—Creative_Writing Greek Astron Econ Pol_Sci African_Stud E_Asian_Stud Lat-Amer_Stud Russ_Stud Architect Art_Hist Ceramics Drawing Photog Acting Theater_Arts Chorus Music Jazz_Ensemble Dance Journ. **Supp**—Tut. Outdoor ed.
Sports—G: Basket X-country Equestrian Fencing F_Hockey Golf Ice_Hockey Lacrosse Soccer Softball Squash Swim Tennis Volley. **Activities:** 30.
Selective adm (Bdg Gr 9-12; Day 6-11): 132/yr. Bdg 54. Day 78. Usual entry: 6 & 9. Appl fee: $50. Appl due: Feb. Applied: 537. Accepted: 51%. Yield: 48%. **Tests** CEEB ISEE SSAT TOEFL.
Enr 475. Bdg 138. Day 337. Elem 120. Sec 355. Wh 82%. Latino 4%. Blk 7%. Asian 4%. Other 3%. Intl 17%. Avg class size: 13. Stud/fac: 9:1. Casual. **Fac 61.** M 21/F 40. FT 55/PT 6. Wh 87%. Latino 4%. Blk 7%. Asian 2%. Adv deg: 67%.
Grad '11—103. Col—103. (Johns Hopkins 4, Brandeis 4, CT Col 3, NYU 3, Trinity Col-CT 3, U of PA 2). **Avg SAT:** CR 600. M 632. W 632. **Mid 50% SAT:** CR 540-660. M 570-690. W 570-690. Avg ACT: 28. **Col couns:** 2. Alum donors: 22%.
Tui '12-'13: Bdg $52,131 (+$500-1500). **Day $39,266** (+$500-1500). **Intl Bdg $52,867** (+$500-1500). **Aid:** Need 90 ($3,163,219).
Summer (enr 80): Ages 7-14. Rec. Sports. Tui Day $1095/2-wk ses. 6 wks. Gr 9. Leadership. Tui Bdg $850. 1 wk.
Endow $18,368,000. Plant val $61,225,000. Acres 55. Bldgs 34 (25% ADA). Dorms 6.

Dorm rms 81. Class rms 51. Lib 32,000 vols. Sci labs 6. Lang labs 1. Photog labs 1. Writing labs 1. Math labs 1. Auds 2. Theaters 1. Art studios 3. Music studios 10. Dance studios 1. Fields 4. Squash courts 4. Pools 1. Riding rings 3. Stables 1. Weight rms 1. Climbing walls 1. Comp labs 3.
Est 1881. Nonprofit. Tri (Sept-June). **Assoc** CLS NEASC.

In 1881, Wellesley College president Henry F. Durant encouraged the sisters Sarah and Julia Eastman to leave their teaching positions at Wellesley to establish a new college preparatory school a short distance from the college campus, on land donated by Charles B. Dana.

From the beginning, Dana Hall stressed that overall personal development was as important as "strict mental training." Under the leadership of Helen Temple Cooke from 1899 to 1951, the school achieved national prominence.

Numerous states and foreign countries are represented in the student body. All girls prepare for college and choose from many cocurricular activities. The curriculum includes Advanced Placement courses in all major disciplines. In addition, Dana Hall maintains a writing center and math and language labs to assist pupils with the review of material, essays, papers and college applications. Sophomores satisfy a 20-hour community service requirement.

Students make good use of the cultural advantages of Boston: Dana Hall schedules off-campus activities in Boston and Cambridge and at nearby universities. The school provides foreign study and travel opportunities in such locations as Italy and Australia, and pupils may also take part in the Rocky Mountain Institute in Colorado.

Dana Hall's middle school occupies its own on-campus building, although middle schoolers utilize upper school science, library and dining facilities. The middle school enrolls day students from the surrounding area.   **See Also Page 74**

TENACRE COUNTRY DAY SCHOOL
Day — Coed Gr PS (Age 4)-6
Wellesley, MA 02482. 78 Benvenue St. Tel: 781-235-2282. Fax: 781-237-7057.
   www.tenacrecds.org   E-mail: sam_reece@tenacrecds.org
Christian B. Elliot, Head (1996). AB, Princeton Univ. **Sam Reece, Adm.**
   Pre-Prep. Elem math—Singapore Math. **Feat**—Span Computers Studio_Art Music.
      Supp—Dev_Read Rem_Math Rem_Read.
   Sports—Basket Soccer. B: Baseball. G: F_Hockey Softball.
   Selective adm: 26/yr. Usual entry: PS, K, 1 & 3. Appl fee: $50. Appl due: Jan. Applied: 148. Accepted: 29%. Yield: 74%.
   Enr 192. B 93. G 99. Wh 71%. Latino 11%. Blk 5%. Asian 9%. Other 4%. Avg class size: 24. Stud/fac: 11:1. Casual. **Fac 36.** M 7/F 29. FT 30/PT 6. Wh 89%. Blk 8%. Asian 3%. Adv deg: 69%.
   Grad '11—24. Prep—23. (Dana Hall 6, Noble & Greenough 5, Belmont Hill 3, Rivers 3, Buckingham Browne & Nichols 2, Roxbury Latin 2).
   Tui '12-'13: Day $21,405-29,990. Aid: Need 5.
   Summer: Ages 3-12. Rec. Tui Day $810-3970. 2-8 wks.
   Endow $16,205,000. Plant val $5,416,000. Acres 13. Bldgs 4. Class rms 20. Lib 10,000 vols. Sci labs 1. Auds 1. Theaters 1. Art studios 1. Music studios 1. Gyms 1. Fields 2. Courts 2. Comp labs 1. Comp/stud: 1:1.3.
   Est 1910. Nonprofit. Sem (Sept-June).

Originally the elementary division of Dana Hall School, Tenacre formed its own corporation and board of trustees in 1972. The school has been coeducational since 1942, and it was reorganized on its present campus as an elementary day school in 1952. Today, students enroll from more than two dozen nearby communities.

In addition to an emphasis on fundamental learning skills in language arts and mathematics, the comprehensive program devotes a large amount of instructional time to social studies, science, art, music, computer, Spanish and physical education. The school maintains small classes and employs team teaching, assigning two teachers to each homeroom. Parental involvement is encouraged.

WESTON, MA. (15 mi. W of Boston, MA) Suburban. Pop: 11,469. Alt: 161 ft.

THE CAMBRIDGE SCHOOL OF WESTON
Bdg and Day — Coed Gr 9-PG

Weston, MA 02493. 45 Georgian Rd. Tel: 781-642-8650. Fax: 781-398-8344.
www.csw.org   E-mail: admissions@csw.org
Jane Moulding, Head (2002). BA, Univ of Warwick (England), ALM, Harvard Univ. **Trish Saunders, Adm.**

Col Prep. AP (29 exams taken, 83% 3+)—Calc. **Feat**—Creative_Writing ASL Chin Fr Lat Span Stats Botany Ecol Environ_Sci Geol Marine_Bio/Sci Physiol Zoology Web_Design Cold_War Child_Dev Native_Amer_Stud Art_Hist Film Photog Drama Theater Music Dance Journ. **Supp**—ESL.

Sports—Basket X-country Soccer Tennis Ultimate_Frisbee. B: Baseball. G: F_Hockey. **Activities:** 21.

Selective adm: 105/yr. Bdg 32. Day 73. Appl fee: $50. Appl due: Feb. Applied: 384. Accepted: 55%. Yield: 58%. **Tests** ISEE SSAT TOEFL.

Enr 325. Bdg 81. Day 244. Nonwhite 15%. Intl 12%. Avg class size: 13. Stud/fac: 6:1. **Fac 50.** Adv deg: 70%.

Grad '11—93. **Col**—93. (Oberlin, Haverford, Smith, Beloit, Goucher, Cornell). **Mid 50% SAT:** CR 570-690. M 580-680. W 590-700. **Col couns:** 4. Alum donors: 16%.

Tui '12-'13: Bdg $49,800 (+$1000-1500). **Day $38,300** (+$1000-1500). **Intl Bdg $49,800** (+$1000-3600). **Aid:** Need 81.

Endow $4,200,000. Plant val $21,000,000. Acres 65. Bldgs 24. Dorms 4. Dorm rms 50. Class rms 30. Lib 19,343 vols. Sci labs 6. Lang labs 1. Auds 1. Theaters 2. Art studios 6. Music studios 10. Dance studios 2. Gyms 1. Fields 3. Pools 2. Comp labs 2.

Est 1886. Nonprofit. 7 terms (Sept-June). **Assoc** NEASC.

The school was founded by Arthur Gilman to prepare young women for Radcliffe College, which he had established in 1879. In 1931, the school moved from Cambridge to its present wooded, 65-acre campus in suburban Weston; at that time, it became coeducational and instituted boarding.

In 1973, CSW devised the Module Plan, in which the academic year is divided into seven five-week terms, or "modules." The school day consists of three academic blocks, each 90 minutes long, allowing intensive learning in two or three subjects at a time; a fourth block is set aside at the end of the day for interscholastic and recreational sports and other activities. More than 300 courses—ranging from molecular biology to documentary filmmaking—are available, including requirements in English, mathematics, history, science and foreign language; integrated studies (team-taught, interdisciplinary courses); and, to address personal interests, electives. The visual and performing arts are an integral part of the curriculum, and by graduation students must complete a variety of arts courses, including art history.

In addition, CSW provides two distinct programs for postgraduates: liberal arts, for students who wish to add an extra year of study to their high school record, and visual arts, designed for students who need an extra year to prepare portfolios for art school applications, as well as for those wishing to explore their artistic potential.

Each year, students must earn athletic credits through participation in competitive interscholastics or in a combination of recreational sports, major theatrical productions, wilderness experiences and dance courses. The wilderness program offers day and weekend trips for hiking, rock climbing, bicycling, rafting, cross-country skiing, canoeing, mountain biking and survival camping. One block each year, boys and girls perform school service as daycare interns, office workers or admissions guides, and in other positions at such places as the dining hall and the campus store. CSW students also perform 15 hours of off-campus community service annually.

Students and faculty serve together on many committees, and students participate in the school's decision-making process, from all-school town meetings (where students and faculty meet regularly to discuss campus issues and make recommendations to the head of school) to the board of trustees.

MEADOWBROOK SCHOOL

Day — Coed Gr PS (Age 4)-8

Weston, MA 02493. 10 Farm Rd. Tel: 781-894-1193. Fax: 781-894-0557.
www.meadowbrook-ma.org   E-mail: admissions@meadowbrook-ma.org
Stephen T. Hinds, Head (1986). BSEd, Miami Univ (OH), MEd, Boston Univ. **Barbara T. Vincent, Adm.**

Pre-Prep. Feat—Fr Lat Span Performing_Arts Studio_Art Video_Production Music. **Supp**—Dev_Read.

Sports—Basket X-country Lacrosse Ski Soccer Squash Tennis Track. B: Baseball. G: Softball.

Selective adm (Gr PS-7): 45/yr. Usual entry: PS, 4 & 6. Appl fee: $60. Appl due: Feb. Applied: 159. Accepted: 37%. Yield: 78%. **Tests** CTP_4 IQ ISEE SSAT TOEFL.

Enr 305. B 146. G 159. Wh 74%. Latino 2%. Blk 4%. Asian 9%. Other 11%. Intl 5%. Avg class size: 24. Stud/fac: 7:1. **Fac 53.** M 17/F 36. FT 48/PT 5. Adv deg: 81%.

Grad '11—33. Prep—29. (Noble & Greenough 4, St Mark's Sch-MA 4, Milton Acad 2, Buckingham Browne & Nichols 2, Belmont Hill 2, Cushing 2). Avg SSAT: 90%. Alum donors: 13%.

Tui '12-'13: Day $22,025-30,110 (+$200-2200). **Aid:** Need 23 ($537,650).

Summer (enr 612): Gr K-6. Rec. Tui Day $2262-4700. 4-8 wks.

Endow $11,263,000. Plant val $26,212,000. Acres 26. Bldgs 8 (100% ADA). Class rms 27. Lib 15,800 vols. Sci labs 2. Lang labs 3. Theaters 1. Art studios 3. Music studios 3. Wood shops 1. Gyms 2. Fields 4. Tennis courts 4. Pools 2. Comp labs 2. Comp/stud: 1:2 (1:1 Laptop prgm Gr 4-8).

Est 1923. Nonprofit. Sem (Sept-June).

Situated on a 26-acre campus, Meadowbrook maintains a low student-teacher ratio as it offers the opportunity for individual attention in a strong academic setting. Boys and girls learn from two teachers in each homeroom in junior kindergarten through grade 3, and three teachers in grades 4 and 5. Art, music, ceramics and computer studies are offered at all levels. Spanish is available from junior kindergarten, along with French, Mandarin and Latin in grades 5-8. The eighth grade global studies program includes a 10-day cultural exchange trip to Costa Rica. A modified Outward Bound program, field trips, class projects and a competitive athletic program are among the activities.

The school also conducts an after-school program and two recreational summer camps. Graduates matriculate at leading New England secondary schools.

THE RIVERS SCHOOL

Day — Coed Gr 6-12

Weston, MA 02493. 333 Winter St. Tel: 781-235-9300. Fax: 781-239-3614.
www.rivers.org   E-mail: info@rivers.org
Thomas P. Olverson, Head (1997). AB, Duke Univ, MAEd, College of William and Mary. **Gillian M. Lloyd, Adm.**

Col Prep. AP (exams req'd; 206 taken, 99% 3+)—Eng Fr Lat Span Calc Stats Bio Chem Environ_Sci Physics Eur_Hist US_Hist Econ. **Feat**—Poetry Shakespeare Crime_Fiction Playwriting Southern_Lit Chin Anat & Physiol Astron Sports_Med Robotics Civil_Rights Holocaust Pol_Sci Ethics Ceramics Drawing Film Filmmaking Painting Photog Sculpt Chorus Jazz_Band Jazz_Choir. **Supp**—Tut.

Sports—Basket X-country Ice_Hockey Lacrosse Ski Soccer Tennis Track. B: Baseball Football. G: F_Hockey Softball. **Activities:** 22.

Selective adm (Gr 6-11): 93/yr. Usual entry: 6 & 9. Appl fee: $40. Appl due: Feb. Applied: 535. Accepted: 44%. Yield: 45%. **Tests** ISEE SSAT.

Enr 458. B 240. G 218. Elem 114. Sec 344. Wh 85%. Latino 4%. Blk 4%. Asian 5%. Other 2%. Avg class size: 12. Stud/fac: 6:1. Casual. **Fac 74.** M 40/F 34. FT 71/PT 3. Wh 92%. Latino 2%. Blk 3%. Other 3%. Adv deg: 63%.

Grad '10—79. Col—79. (Hamilton 3, Tufts 3, Wesleyan U 2, Carnegie Mellon 2, Johns Hopkins 2, Middlebury 2). Athl schol 4. **Avg SAT:** CR 665. M 690. W 680. Avg ACT:

29. **Col couns:** 2.
Tui '11-'12: Day $36,950 (+$600). **Aid:** Need 120 ($3,093,000).
Summer: Ages 4-14. Rec. Tui Day $565-4370. 1-8 wks.
Endow $17,500,000. Plant val $66,000,000. Acres 60. Bldgs 13 (90% ADA). Class rms 38. Lib 18,000 vols. Sci labs 6. Lang labs 1. Theater/auds 2. Art studios 6. Music studios 24. Gyms 2. Fields 6. Courts 6. Field houses 1. Rinks 1. Comp labs 2. Comp/stud: 1:2.
Est 1915. Nonprofit. Tri (Sept-June). **Assoc** CLS NEASC.

At the suggestion of a group of prominent Boston physicians, Robert W. Rivers created an open-air school for boys in Brookline; it was widely believed that the open-air concept, popular in England, promoted good health in an environment conducive to scholarship and learning. Twenty-six years and one new campus later, the Country Day School for Boys of Boston merged with Rivers. The school moved its location twice more before settling on the Loker Farm acreage, surrounded by conservation wetlands and a pond, in 1960. Rivers became coeducational in 1989.

Rivers provides a traditional liberal arts curriculum supplemented by electives and cocurricular activities. The broad scope of the arts department is enhanced by The Rivers School Conservatory, a community music school located on campus. Athletics at Rivers include interscholastic and intramural competition, individualized activities and fitness programs for the recreational athlete. Students are required to take part in athletics each year; those not participating during a given term must undertake other afternoon activities. In addition, boys and girls accumulate 30 hours of compulsory service in grades 9-12. Also offered are various outdoor programs and organized trips abroad.

WILBRAHAM, MA. (29 mi. NNE of Hartford, CT; 74 mi. W of Boston, MA) Suburban. Pop: 3554. Alt: 119 ft.

WILBRAHAM & MONSON ACADEMY
Bdg — Coed Gr 9-PG; Day — Coed 6-PG

Wilbraham, MA 01095. 423 Main St. Tel: 413-596-6811, 800-616-3659.
  Fax: 413-596-2448.
  www.wmacademy.org E-mail: admission@wma.us
Rodney J. LaBrecque, Head (2002). BA, MA, Clark Univ. Chris Sparks, Adm.
  Col Prep. AP—Eng Fr Lat Span Calc Stats Bio Chem Environ_Sci Physics Eur_Hist US_Hist Econ Studio_Art Music_Theory. **Feat**—Poetry Asian_Lit Hemingway Playwriting Chin Multivariable_Calc Anat & Physiol Genetics Marine_Bio/Sci Web_Design Vietnam_War Sociol World_Relig Ceramics Drawing Painting Photog Sculpt Acting Marketing SAT_Prep. **Supp**—ESL LD Tut.
  Sports—Basket X-country Golf Lacrosse Ski Soccer Swim Tennis Track W_Polo. B: Baseball Football Rugby Wrestling. G: F_Hockey Softball Volley.
  Selective adm: 159/yr. Bdg 76. Day 83. Appl fee: $75. Appl due: Feb. **Tests** IQ SSAT TOEFL.
  Enr 394. B 206. G 188. Bdg 180. Day 214. Elem 67. Sec 313. PG 14. Avg class size: 14. Stud/fac: 7:1. Formal. **Fac 65.** M 34/F 31. FT 52/PT 13. Adv deg: 47%.
  Grad '11—79. Col—79. (Boston U 3, Merrimack 3, Babson 2, Dickinson 2, Geo Wash 2, Northeastern U 2). **Avg SAT:** CR 533. M 617. W 562. **Col couns:** 2.
  Tui '11-'12: Bdg $48,500 (+$1275-2175). **Day** $14,000-30,905 (+$850-1850). **Intl Bdg** $48,500 (+$5200-6795).
  Summer: Ages 5-12. Rec. Tui Day $410/2-wk ses. 6 wks.
  Acres 350. Bldgs 23. Dorms 3. Dorm rms 130. Class rms 31. Lib 12,000 vols. Labs 8. Auds 1. Theaters 1. Art studios 7. Gyms 1. Fields 11. Courts 9. Pools 1.
  Est 1804. Nonprofit. Tri (Sept-June). **Assoc** CLS NEASC.

The school resulted from the 1971 merger of Monson Academy, founded in 1804, and Wilbraham Academy, established in 1817. Located in the center of town, Wilbraham & Monson continues to occupy its fully renovated, historic buildings, and the academy has a listing in the National Register of Historic Places.

The college preparatory curriculum features honors courses in all departments and a variety of Advanced Placement classes. As an alternative to a study hall arrangement, Wilbraham & Monson encourages boys and girls to seek day and evening help from their teachers and peer tutors. The English as a Second Language program serves the academy's substantial international population, and the school also maintains an academic services program for students with diagnosed learning differences.

WILLIAMSTOWN, MA. (31 mi. E of Albany, NY; 114 mi. WNW of Boston, MA) Suburban. Pop: 4754. Alt: 604 ft.

BUXTON SCHOOL
Bdg and Day — Coed Gr 9-12

Williamstown, MA 01267. 291 South St. Tel: 413-458-3919. Fax: 413-458-9428.
www.buxtonschool.org　E-mail: admissions@buxtonschool.org
C. **William Bennett, Co-Dir** (1983). BA, Williams College. **Peter Smith, Co-Dir.** BA, Clark Univ. **Franny Shuker-Haines, Adm.**

　Col Prep. Feat—Poetry 20th-Century_Lit Chin Fr Span Bahasa_Indonesia Calc Astron Environ_Sci Marine_Bio/Sci Oceanog Anthro Econ Psych Gender_Stud Architect Ceramics Film Photog Sculpt Studio_Art Video_Production Drama Music Music_Theory. **Supp**—ESL LD Tut.

　Sports—Basket Soccer.

　Selective adm (Gr 9-11): 35/yr. Bdg 31. Day 4. Usual entry: 9 & 10. Appl fee: $50. Appl due: Feb. **Tests** IQ SSAT TOEFL.

　Enr 90. B 44. G 46. Bdg 80. Day 10. Wh 47%. Latino 6%. Blk 26%. Asian 20%. Other 1%. Intl 25%. Avg class size: 9. Stud/fac: 5:1. Casual. **Fac 22.** M 12/F 10. FT 17/PT 5. Wh 77%. Latino 9%. Asian 9%. Other 5%. Adv deg: 22%. In dorms 10.

　Grad '11—30. Col—26. (Bennington 3, Bard-NY 3, Guilford 2, Barnard 1, Oberlin 1, Williams 1).

　Tui '12-'13: Bdg $47,500 (+$2000-2500). **Day $29,000** (+$2000-2500). **Intl Bdg $47,500** (+$2000-6300). **Aid:** Need 44 ($1,300,000).

　Summer: Day. Ages 7-13. Arts. 2 wks.

　Endow $1,900,000. Plant val $7,200,000. Acres 120. Bldgs 18 (50% ADA). Dorms 3. Dorm rms 33. Class rms 15. Lib 7000 vols. Sci labs 3. Photog labs 1. Theaters 1. Art studios 1. Music studios 1. Dance studios 1. Ceramics studios 1. Fields 2. Basketball courts 1. Weight rms 1. Fitness rms 1. Skiing facilities. Greenhouses 1. Ponds 3. Comp labs 3. Comp/stud: 1:3.

　Est 1928. Nonprofit. Sem (Sept-June). **Assoc** NEASC.

Buxton School, established in Williamstown in 1947, grew out of the Buxton Country Day School, which was founded as a progressive school in New Jersey in 1928 by Ellen Geer Sangster. She retired in 1963.

The traditional college preparatory curriculum also includes courses and activities in art, ceramics, photography, video production, music, drama, creative writing, dance and drumming. Courses of study are tailored to individual needs, with ample opportunities for advanced study. An essential element of the school is the ongoing attention given to community life. A work program and the annual all-school trip to investigate aspects of a major city are of central importance; trip destinations have included Atlanta, GA; Chicago, IL; El Paso, TX; Philadelphia, PA; Washington, DC; Toronto, Canada; Havana, Cuba; San Juan, Puerto Rico; Mexico City, Mexico; and three cities in Nicaragua.　　　　**See Also Page 64**

PINE COBBLE SCHOOL
Day — Coed Gr PS (Age 2)-9

Williamstown, MA 01267. 163 Gale Rd. Tel: 413-458-4680. Fax: 413-458-8174.
www.pinecobble.org   E-mail: l.cushman@pinecobble.org
Susannah H. Wells, Head (2010). BA, Williams College. **Lisa Cushman, Adm.**
    Pre-Prep. Gen Acad. Feat—Fr Lat Computers Photog Studio_Art Drama Music.
      Supp—Dev_Read Makeup Rem_Math Rem_Read Rev Tut.
    Sports—Lacrosse. B: Soccer. G: F_Hockey.
    Selective adm: 22/yr. Appl fee: $45. Appl due: Rolling. **Tests** IQ Stanford.
    Enr 120. Wh 90%. Latino 1%. Blk 4%. Asian 5%. Avg class size: 10. Stud/fac: 5:1. **Fac
    28.** M 6/F 22. FT 25/PT 3. Wh 100%. Adv deg: 53%.
    Grad '10—16. Prep—1. (Williston Northampton 1).
    Tui '11-'12: Day $12,700-17,700 (+$400). **Aid:** Need 48 ($250,000).
    Summer: Acad Enrich Rec. Tui Day $120-400. 1-2 wks.
    Endow $1,000,000. Plant val $3,600,000. Acres 20. Bldgs 5 (40% ADA). Class rms 15.
    Lib 5000 vols. Sci labs 2. Dark rms 1. Comp ctrs 1. Art studios 1. Music studios 2.
    Dance studios 1. Shops 1. Fields 2. Basketball courts 1. Tennis courts 2. Pools 1.
    Comp labs 2.
    Est 1937. Nonprofit. Sem (Sept-June).

Founded by Dr. and Mrs. Edgar W. Flinton, with the cooperation of a group of parents, Pine Cobble serves northern Berkshire County and adjacent communities in eastern New York State and southern Vermont. Within a traditional country day school environment, the program develops basic academic skills and offers a broad cocurricular program that features art, music, drama and athletics. French begins in kindergarten, while Latin and Spanish are available from grade 7. Cross-grade grouping in the upper school (grades 6-9) allows the program to address individual needs and provide opportunities for accelerated study.

In 1993, the school purchased a second campus in the hills just south of Williamstown. The main building, formerly the estate of George Alfred Cluett, and four classroom buildings occupy 20 acres. Field trips and outdoor experiences are numerous, and the entire school participates in an annual mountain climb and hike. A winter athletic program offers instruction in both cross-country and downhill skiing to children in grade 1 and above.

WINCHENDON, MA. (58 mi. WNW of Boston, MA) Suburban. Pop: 4246. Alt: 1180 ft.

THE WINCHENDON SCHOOL
Bdg and Day — Coed Gr 9-PG

Winchendon, MA 01475. 172 Ash St. Tel: 978-297-1223, 800-622-1119.
    Fax: 978-297-0911.
    www.winchendon.org   E-mail: admissions@winchendon.org
John A. Kerney, Head (2008). BA, Middlebury College. **Ellyn Baldini, Adm.**
    Col Prep. LD. Underachiever. AP—Calc. **Feat**—British_Lit Fr Span Stats Forensic_Sci
      Comp_Sci Psych Ceramics Drawing Painting Drama Public_Speak. **Supp**—Dev_
      Read ESL Makeup Rem_Math Rem_Read Rev Tut.
    Sports—Basket X-country Ice_Hockey Lacrosse Soccer Tennis. B: Baseball Golf. G:
      Volley.
    Somewhat selective adm: 110/yr. Bdg 100. Day 10. Appl fee: $50. Appl due: Rolling.
      Accepted: 90%. Yield: 90%. **Tests** IQ.
    Enr 240. B 188. G 52. Bdg 218. Day 22. Sec 196. PG 44. Wh 38%. Latino 3%. Blk 8%.
      Asian 50%. Other 1%. Intl 65%. Avg class size: 7. Formal. **Fac 36.** M 25/F 11. FT
      35/PT 1. Wh 100%. Adv deg: 25%. In dorms 12.
    Grad '07—83. Col—81. (Boston U, U of MA-Amherst, UNH, Bentley, Curry, Northeast-
      ern U). **Avg SAT:** CR 550. M 600. W 500. **Col couns:** 1. Alum donors: 30%.

Tui '12-'13: Bdg $48,600. Day $27,600. Intl Bdg $48,600 (+$2600-4600). **Aid:** Need ($2,000,000).
Summer: Acad Rev Rem. ESL. Tui Bdg $6500 (+$330). 6 wks.
Endow $21,000,000. Plant val $29,000,000. Acres 350. Bldgs 35. Dorms 5. Dorm rms 162. Class rms 27. Lib 15,000 vols. Sci labs 4. Art studios 2. Music studios 1. Dance studios 1. Gyms 1. Athletic ctrs 1. Fields 4. Courts 2. Pools 1. Rinks 1. Golf crses 1. Comp labs 1.
Est 1926. Nonprofit. Quar (Sept-June). **Assoc** NEASC.

Formerly the Hatch School of Newport, RI, this school adopted its present name in 1961 upon moving to Winchendon, where it occupies 350 wooded acres. Through personal attention to the academic capabilities of each student, the school has been able to aid those who have not previously developed sound study habits.

The curriculum is college preparatory, with an emphasis on small, student-centered classes. In 1973, a remedial program for students with minor learning disabilities was added, and in 1974 the first female boarders were enrolled. Daily tutoring periods are available.

WORCESTER, MA. (41 mi. W of Boston, MA) Urban. Pop: 172,648. Alt: 482 ft. Area also includes Shrewsbury.

BANCROFT SCHOOL

Day — Coed Gr K-12

Worcester, MA 01605. 110 Shore Dr. Tel: 508-853-2640. Fax: 508-853-7824.
www.bancroftschool.org　　E-mail: admission@bancroftschool.org
Scott R. Reisinger, Head (1999). BA, MA, Univ of Rochester, MPhil, Columbia Univ. **Susan Cranford, Adm.**
　Col Prep. AP (exams req'd; 196 taken, 93% 3+)—Eng Fr Lat Span Calc Comp_Sci Bio Chem Physics Eur_Hist US_Hist US_Govt & Pol Studio_Art. **Elem math**—Everyday Math. **Elem read**—McGraw-Hill/Reader's Workshop. **Feat**—Creative_Writing Chin Stats Anat & Physiol Marine_Bio/Sci Biotech Comp_Graphics Women's_Hist Anthro Econ Psych Philos Relig Ceramics Photog Drama Music Music_Theory. **Supp**—Rev Tut. **Dual enr:** Holy Cross.
　Sports—Basket Crew X-country Golf Lacrosse Ski Soccer Tennis Track. B: Baseball Wrestling. G: F_Hockey Softball Volley. **Activities:** 29.
　Somewhat selective adm (Gr K-11): 83/yr. Usual entry: K, 6 & 9. Appl fee: $50. Appl due: Feb. Applied: 144. Accepted: 88%. Yield: 65%. **Tests** CEEB CTP_4 IQ ISEE SSAT.
　Enr 522. B 225. G 297. Elem 290. Sec 232. Wh 77%. Latino 4%. Asian 12%. Other 7%. Avg class size: 13. Casual. **Fac 82.** M 26/F 56. FT 80/PT 2. Wh 94%. Latino 2%. Blk 2%. Asian 2%. Adv deg: 63%.
　Grad '11—54. Col—54. (Boston Col 5, Tufts 4, Brown 3, U of Chicago 2, Trinity Col-CT 2, Holy Cross 2). **Mid 50% SAT:** CR 570-720. M 590-710. W 560-700. Avg ACT: 28. **Col couns:** 1. Alum donors: 12%.
　Tui '11-'12: Day $20,950-25,900 (+$750). **Aid:** Need 145 ($1,663,800).
　Summer (enr 300): Acad Enrich Rev Rec. Sports. Tui Day $110-600. 1-6 wks.
　Endow $11,069,000. Plant val $10,201,000. Acres 36. Bldgs 8 (87% ADA). Class rms 44. 2 Libs 22,571 vols. Sci labs 9. Lang labs 1. Sci ctrs 1. Theaters 1. Art studios 4. Music studios 4. Arts ctrs 1. Gyms 3. Fields 5. Courts 8. Comp labs 2. Comp/stud: 1:3.
　Est 1900. Nonprofit. Quar (Sept-June). **Assoc** CLS NEASC.

The oldest coeducational independent day school in central Massachusetts, the school was named for George Bancroft, a diplomat, secretary of the Navy and historian who was born in Worcester in 1800. After outgrowing the original school buildings on Elm Street, Bancroft moved to more spacious quarters on Sever Street in 1922; in 1958, the school first occupied its current, 36-acre campus.

Bancroft's college preparatory curriculum features Advanced Placement courses in the major disciplines, including all three available foreign languages. Academics are enhanced by sports, clubs and activities, drama, art and music. Middle school children perform nine hours of community service annually, while older students complete 30 hours of community service in grades 9-12.

NOTRE DAME ACADEMY

Day — Girls Gr 9-12

Worcester, MA 01609. 425 Salisbury St. Tel: 508-757-6200. Fax: 508-757-1888.
www.nda-worc.org   E-mail: mriordan@nda-worc.org
Sr. Ann E. Morrison, SND, Prin. BA, Emmanuel College, MA, St Louis Univ. **Mary F. Riordan, Adm.**
Col Prep. AP—Calc Art_Hist Music_Theory. **Feat**—Women's_Lit Fr Lat Span Anat & Physiol Comp_Sci Econ Psych Sociol Relig World_Relig Visual_Arts Drama Music.
Sports—G: Basket X-country F_Hockey Golf Indoor_Track Ski Softball Swim Tennis Track. **Activities:** 26.
Selective adm (Gr 6-11): 72/yr. Appl fee: $25. Appl due: Dec.
Enr 300. Wh 93%. Latino 1%. Blk 1%. Asian 3%. Other 2%. Avg class size: 17. Stud/fac: 9:1. **Fac 34.** Nonwhite 1%.
Grad '08—70. Col—70. (Boston Col, Assumption, Providence, Holy Cross, Boston U, Simmons). **Avg SAT:** CR 531. M 508. W 542. **Col couns:** 2.
Tui '12-'13: Day $11,700 (+$400).
Plant val $1,678,000. Acres 13. Bldgs 3. Class rms 25. Lib 16,000 vols. Sci labs 2. Theaters 1. Art studios 2. Music studios 2. Gyms 1. Fields 1. Student ctrs 1. Comp labs 1.
Est 1951. Nonprofit. Roman Catholic. Quar (Sept-June). **Assoc** NEASC.

Founded by the Sisters of Notre Dame de Namur, this school occupies a 13-acre campus in a residential area. Religious studies are integrated into NDA's college preparatory program, which also emphasizes community involvement; for instance, girls in grades 11 and 12 volunteer two hours per week in various service capacities. Qualified students may enroll in advanced courses in a number of subjects. Music, theater and arts classes; sports; and cocurricular activities enrich the program.

WORCESTER ACADEMY

Bdg — Coed Gr 9-PG; Day — Coed 6-12

Worcester, MA 01604. 81 Providence St. Tel: 508-754-5302. Fax: 508-752-2382.
www.worcesteracademy.org   E-mail: admission@worcesteracademy.org
Ronald M. Cino, Head (2012). BA, Trinity College (CT). **Gregory Cappello, Adm.**
Col Prep. AP (353 exams taken, 81% 3+)—Eng Fr Span Calc Comp_Sci Bio Chem Physics Eur_Hist US_Hist World_Hist US_Govt & Pol Studio_Art Music_Theory. **Feat**—Shakespeare African-Amer_Lit Chin Lat Anat & Physiol Geol Marine_Bio/Sci Web_Design Holocaust WWII Drama Theater_Arts Directing Music. **Supp**—ESL Tut.
Sports—Basket Crew X-country Lacrosse Ski Soccer Swim Tennis Track. B: Baseball Football Golf Ice_Hockey Wrestling. G: F_Hockey Softball Volley. **Activities:** 90.
Selective adm (Bdg Gr 9-PG; Day 6-11): 180/yr. Bdg 68. Day 112. Usual entry: 6, 7 & 9. Appl fee: $60. Appl due: Jan. Applied: 548. Accepted: 64%. Yield: 51%. **Tests** CEEB ISEE SSAT TOEFL.
Enr 642. Bdg 168. Day 474. Elem 140. Sec 479. PG 23. Wh 67%. Latino 2%. Blk 5%. Asian 22%. Other 4%. Intl 15%. Avg class size: 14. Stud/fac: 7:1. Formal. **Fac 86.** M 39/F 47. FT 78/PT 8. Wh 91%. Latino 2%. Blk 5%. Asian 2%. Adv deg: 76%. In dorms 12.
Grad '11—146. Col—146. (Boston U, U of VT, Geo Wash, U of MI, Johns Hopkins, Boston Col). Athl schol 11. **Avg SAT:** CR 587. M 633. W 600. Avg ACT: 26. **Col**

couns: 3. Alum donors: 21%.
Tui '12-'13: Bdg $51,400 (+$1250). **5-Day Bdg $42,490** (+$1250). **Day $26,980-29,190** (+$1250). **Intl Bdg $51,400** (+$4820). **Aid:** Need 244 ($4,600,000).
Summer: Enrich Rec. Arts. Tui Day $525-950. 2-6 wks. Sports. Tui Day $225-800. 1-6 wks. ESL. TOEFL/SAT Prep. Tui Bdg $4500. 3 wks.
Endow $34,200,000. Plant val $117,900,000. Acres 71. Bldgs 14 (40% ADA). Dorms 4. Dorm rms 75. Class rms 43. Lib 14,000 vols. Sci labs 6. Lang labs 1. Theaters 2. Art studios 2. Music studios 2. Gyms 2. Fields 8. Courts 4. Pools 1. Tracks 3. Comp labs 3. Comp/stud: 1:1 Laptop prgm Gr 6-12.
Est 1834. Nonprofit. Tri (Sept-June). **Assoc** CLS NEASC.

First organized as the Worcester County Manual Labor High School by a group of the leading men of Worcester, the school was renamed in 1844. Later reorganized as a boys' school, the academy again admitted girls into the student body in 1974. The campus includes six buildings listed in the National Register of Historic Places.

The academy's successful preparatory program combines academics, athletics and the arts. The curriculum includes clear requirements in the major disciplines and, through a full array of Advanced Placement courses, enables students to enroll in course sections appropriate to their abilities. Instruction in studio art, various aspects of drama, chorus and instrumental ensemble are part of the regular curriculum, and there is a strong emphasis on performance. Seniors may earn credit for internships with local theaters. Boys and girls perform a total of 60 compulsory hours of community service in grades 9-12. WA fields interscholastic teams at both the varsity and the junior varsity levels, as well as at the middle school level. All academic buildings and dorms are networked for wireless Internet access, and each student receives a laptop computer.

The academy's urban location enables its students to take full advantage of the collegiate, university and cultural facilities of Worcester.

NEW HAMPSHIRE

ANDOVER, NH. (86 mi. NNW of Boston, MA) Rural. Pop: 2109. Alt: 620 ft.

PROCTOR ACADEMY
Bdg and Day — Coed Gr 9-PG

Andover, NH 03216. 204 Main St, PO Box 500. Tel: 603-735-6000. Fax: 603-735-5129.
www.proctoracademy.org   E-mail: admissions@proctornet.com
Michael Henriques, Head (2005). BA, MA, Middlebury College, MFA, Warren Wilson College. **Christopher Bartlett, Adm.**

Col Prep. AP—Eng Fr Span Calc Bio Environ_Sci Physics US_Hist Art_Hist. **Feat**—British_Lit Poetry Playwriting Stats Anat & Physiol Astron Ecol Forensic_Sci Zoology Organic_Chem Comp_Sci Holocaust Middle_Eastern_Hist Vietnam_War Econ Psych Constitutional_Law Relig Architect_Drawing Ceramics Photog Studio_Art Drama Music_Hist Music_Theory Dance Journ Indus_Arts Mech_Drawing Woodworking. **Supp**—LD.

Sports—Basket X-country Golf Ice_Hockey Lacrosse Ski Soccer Tennis. B: Baseball Football. G: F_Hockey Softball.

Selective adm: 116/yr. Appl fee: $50. Appl due: Feb. Accepted: 48%. **Tests** CEEB ISEE SSAT TOEFL.

Enr 345. B 190. G 155. Bdg 270. Day 75. Sec 341. PG 4. Intl 8%. Avg class size: 12. Stud/fac: 5:1. Casual. **Fac 86.** M 39/F 47. FT 82/PT 4. Adv deg: 60%. In dorms 27.

Grad '10—101. Col—93. (U of VT 5, U of CO-Boulder 4, Hobart/Wm Smith 4, Rochester Inst of Tech 3, Savannah Col of Art & Design 3, UNH 3). **Avg SAT:** CR 550. M 533. W 530. **Mid 50% SAT:** CR 480-620. M 460-590. W 480-600. Avg ACT: 22.6. Mid 50% ACT: 18-25. **Col couns:** 3.

Tui '12-'13: Bdg $48,950 (+$1400). **Day $29,400** (+$1000).

Endow $24,000,000. Plant val $40,000,000. Acres 3000. Bldgs 39. Dorms 21. Dorm rms 125. Class rms 32. Lib 23,000 vols. Sci labs 6. Auds 2. Theaters 1. Art studios 2. Music studios 2. Dance studios 1. Shops 4. Gyms 1. Fields 8. Courts 10. Field houses 1. Rinks 1. Riding rings 1. Stables 1. Comp labs 4. Laptop prgm Gr 9-PG.

Est 1848. Nonprofit. Tri (Sept-June). **Assoc** NEASC.

This school, originally the coeducational Andover Academy, was renamed in 1879 in honor of a local benefactor and has long been affiliated with the Unitarian Church, although it has remained nondenominational in practice. In 1971, girls were admitted as boarding students and a coeducational day program was established. Over the years, the academy's campus has grown to encompass 3000 acres and now includes the central village of Andover and extensive woodland in Ragged Mountain.

Proctor's college preparatory program serves a cross section of college-bound students. Qualified pupils choose from a selection of honors and Advanced Placement courses, and the school also maintains a support system featuring structured extra-help and tutorial sessions. Laptop computers are issued to all students, and wireless Internet is available in classrooms and dormitories.

The curriculum is enhanced by an extensive arts program and an Outward Bound-inspired mountain classroom elective in the desert Southwest. Pupils studying Spanish or French may participate in a ten-week program at a Proctor campus in Segovia, Spain; Aix-en-Provence, France; or Tangier, Morocco. A sailing adventure option, offered each fall term, allows students to earn full academic credit while sailing from New England to the Caribbean.

BETHLEHEM, NH. (85 mi. WNW of Portland, ME; 138 mi. NNW of Boston, MA) Rural. Pop: 2199. Alt: 978 ft.

THE WHITE MOUNTAIN SCHOOL
Bdg and Day — Coed Gr 9-PG

Bethlehem, NH 03574. 371 W Farm Rd. Tel: 603-444-2928, 800-545-7813.
Fax: 603-444-5568.
www.whitemountain.org   E-mail: admissions@whitemountain.org
Timothy Breen, Head (2010). BA, Bucknell Univ, MS, PhD, Univ of Michigan. **Allison Kim-merle, Adm.**

> **Col Prep. AP (exams req'd)**—Eng Fr Span Calc Environ_Sci Human_Geog. **Feat**—Creative_Writing Contemporary_Lit Utopia/Dystopia Anat & Physiol Climate & Energy Comp_Sci Amer_Stud Lat-Amer_Stud Ethics Relig Buddhism Ceramics Photog Studio_Art Theater Music_Hist Music_Theory Journ. **Supp**—ESL LD Tut. Sat classes.
>
> **Sports**—X-country Lacrosse Ski Soccer. B: Basket. **Activities:** 23.
>
> **Selective adm:** 48/yr. Bdg 41. Day 7. Appl fee: $50. Appl due: Feb. Accepted: 60%. Yield: 75%. **Tests** IQ SSAT TOEFL.
>
> **Enr 112.** Wh 72%. Latino 1%. Blk 7%. Asian 20%. Intl 30%. Avg class size: 9. Stud/fac: 4:1. Casual. **Fac 26.** M 15/F 11. FT 19/PT 7. Wh 96%. Native Am 3%. Asian 1%. Adv deg: 53%. In dorms 10.
>
> **Grad '10—28. Col—26.** (St Lawrence, Earlham, U of CO-Boulder, MT St-Bozeman, Bard, U of VT). **Avg SAT:** CR 569. M 527. W 549.
>
> **Tui '12-'13: Bdg $46,000** (+$1500). **Day $22,600** (+$1500). **Aid:** Merit 8 ($75,000). Need 56 ($562,554).
>
> **Summer:** Rec. Outdoor Ed. Tui Bdg $1195-3195. 1-3 wks.
>
> Endow $1,500,000. Plant val $19,000,000. Acres 250. Bldgs 12 (30% ADA). Dorms 4. Dorm rms 70. Class rms 23. Lib 13,000 vols. Sci labs 4. Lang labs 1. Sci ctrs 1. Theaters 1. Art studios 4. Music studios 2. Gyms 1. Fields 2. Climbing walls 1. Gardens 1. Comp labs 3. Comp/stud: 1:4.
>
> **Est 1886.** Nonprofit. Episcopal. Sem (Sept-June). **Assoc** NEASC.

Founded as St. Mary's School for girls in Concord by the Episcopal Diocese of New Hampshire, the school moved to its current location in 1936, became coeducational in 1969 and assumed its present name in 1972.

Utilizing interdisciplinary learning and hands-on experiences, WMS encourages active learning through writing, independent study, small-group work, research and extended field trips. Although the school employs the traditional letter grading system, grades assess mastery of six areas: content knowledge, complex thinking, information processing, collaboration, communication and self-direction. Extensive studio arts courses and a residential curriculum round out the program. An optional learning assistance program serves students in need of additional help, and English as a Second Language is available to international pupils.

Throughout the year, WMS teaches wilderness skills classes after school and on weekends, and all students and faculty participate twice a year in five-day experiential learning expeditions. A service learning program comprises local weekly projects and optional Community Odysseys, with destinations as far afield as Haiti, Honduras and Nicaragua. All boys and girls participate in the upkeep of the school's grounds and facilities.   **See Also Pages 76-7**

CANAAN, NH. (104 mi. NNW of Boston, MA) Rural. Pop: 3319. Alt: 942 ft.

CARDIGAN MOUNTAIN SCHOOL
Bdg and Day — Boys Gr 6-9

Canaan, NH 03741. 62 Alumni Dr. Tel: 603-523-3548. Fax: 603-523-3565.
www.cardigan.org   E-mail: admissions@cardigan.org
David J. McCusker, Jr., Head (2007). BA, Dartmouth College. Chip Audett, Adm.
  Pre-Prep. Feat—Fr Lat Span Relig Studio_Art Music Woodworking. Supp—Dev_Read
    ESL Rem_Math Rem_Read Rev Tut. Sat classes.
  Sports (req'd)—B: Baseball Basket X-country Football Ice_Hockey Lacrosse Sail Ski
    Soccer Tennis Wrestling.
  Selective adm: 96/yr. Bdg 81. Day 15. Appl fee: $50. Appl due: Rolling. Accepted: 62%.
    Yield: 65%. Tests IQ ISEE SSAT.
  Enr 201. Elem 134. Sec 67. Wh 57%. Latino 15%. Blk 3%. Asian 23%. Other 2%. Intl
    45%. Avg class size: 12. Stud/fac: 4:1. Formal. Fac 44. M 34/F 10. FT 44. Wh 91%.
    Latino 2%. Asian 5%. Other 2%. Adv deg: 52%. In dorms 30.
  Grad '11—52. Prep—52. (Holderness, Brooks, St Mark's Sch-MA, Avon, Berkshire Sch,
    Kimball Union). Alum donors: 14%.
  Tui '11-'12: Bdg $45,865 (+$1370). Day $26,625. Aid: Need 48 ($1,031,000).
  Summer: Coed. Gr 3-9. Acad Enrich Rev Rem Rec. ESL. Tui Bdg $5304-8840. Tui Day
    $2808-4680. 3-6 wks.
  Endow $15,100,000. Plant val $37,700,000. Acres 525. Bldgs 30. Dorms 13. Dorm rms
    104. Class rms 37. Lib 12,000 vols. Lang labs 1. Auds 1. Theaters 1. Art studios 3.
    Music studios 3. Wood shops 1. Gyms 1. Fields 6. Courts 18. Rinks 1. Boathouses 1.
    Rifle/trap ranges 1.
  Est 1945. Nonprofit. Tri (Sept-May). Assoc NEASC.
  Located in the foothills of the White Mountains and on the shores of Canaan Street Lake,
Cardigan Mountain was established with the support of a group of industrialists and educators,
including Ernest Hopkins, former president of nearby Dartmouth College.
  The school's academic program incorporates a multitrack approach that caters to a broad
spectrum of students. Parallel scheduling allows boys to work to potential in each discipline.
A schoolwide learning support and self-advocacy program, PEAKS, meets four days per week
and revolves around study skills, technology and health topics.
  Cardigan Mountain's extensive athletic facilities allow boys to engage in an array of sports,
as well as such outdoor pursuits as downhill and cross-country skiing. A diversified club program supplements various interscholastic and intramural activities. The school's graduates
enter a wide range of secondary schools, predominantly ones in the Northeast.

CONCORD, NH. (68 mi. NNW of Boston, MA) Urban. Pop: 40,687. Alt: 244 ft.

ST. PAUL'S SCHOOL
Bdg — Coed Gr 9-12

Concord, NH 03301. 325 Pleasant St. Tel: 603-229-4600, 888-644-9611.
  Fax: 603-229-4771.
  www.sps.edu   E-mail: admissions@sps.edu
Michael Gifford Hirschfeld, Rector (2011). AB, Princeton Univ, MA, Dartmouth College.
  Scott Patrick Bohan, Adm.
  Col Prep. AP (185 exams taken)—Eng Chin Fr Ger Lat Span Calc Stats Bio Chem
    Physics Studio_Art. Feat—Creative_Writing Humanities Environ_Lit Hemingway
    Middle_Eastern_Lit Latino_Lit Southern_Lit Greek Japan Linear_Algebra Astron
    Bioethics Ecol Marine_Bio/Sci Engineering Comp_Design Programming Robot-

ics Cold_War Modern_Chin_Hist Amer_Stud Gender_Stud Philos Relig Architec
Art_Hist Ceramics Film Fine_Arts Photog Printmaking Music Music_Theory Balle
Dance. **Supp**—ESL Tut. Sat classes.

Sports—Basket Crew X-country Ice_Hockey Lacrosse Ski Soccer Squash Tennis Track
B: Baseball Football Softball Wrestling. G: F_Hockey Volley. **Activities:** 75.

Very selective adm (Gr 9-11): 152/yr. Appl fee: $50. Appl due: Jan. Applied: 1402
Accepted: 16%. Yield: 68%. **Tests** SSAT.

Enr 539. B 279. G 260. Wh 62%. Latino 5%. Blk 8%. Native Am 1%. Asian 18%. Othe
6%. Intl 18%. Avg class size: 11. Stud/fac: 5:1. Formal. **Fac 105.** FT 97/PT 8. Wh 82%
Latino 5%. Blk 8%. Asian 5%. Adv deg: 70%. In dorms 50.

Grad '11—135. Col—135. (Dartmouth 6, Georgetown 6, U of CA-Berkeley 6, Harvard 5
NYU 5, Columbia 4). **Avg SAT:** CR 667. M 678. W 670. **Col couns:** 4. Alum donors
50%.

Tui '12-'13: Bdg $48,250 (+$3595). **Aid:** Need 193 ($8,000,000).

Summer (enr 268): Acad. Tui Day $3500. 5 wks.

Endow $442,000,000. Plant val $85,000,000. Acres 2000. Bldgs 112. Dorms 18. Dorm
rms 250. Class rms 47. Lib 70,000 vols. Chapels 2. Sci labs 8. Lang labs 1. Observa
tories 3. Auds 1. Theaters 2. Art studios 6. Music studios 1. Dance studios 1. Art gal
leries 1. Drama studios 1. Gyms 2. Fields 11. Courts 15. Pools 1. Rinks 2. Tracks 1.

Est 1856. Nonprofit. Episcopal. Tri (Sept-June). **Assoc** CLS NEASC.

Founded the previous year by Dr. George Cheyne Shattuck of Boston, who gave his country
home in Concord for the school's use, St. Paul's opened on April 3, 1856, with an enrollmen
of three boys. St. Paul's has had a long-time association with the Episcopal Church. Faculty
and students continue to gather in the chapel four mornings each week.

Students attend classes six days per week. The curriculum offers a solid foundation in the
liberal arts and a wide range of elective options. Each student must complete courses in the
humanities, math, science, the arts and languages, and pupils also satisfy a 10-hour annua
community service graduation requirement. The arts offer students opportunities in music
dance, drama and the visual arts at a preprofessional level or as enriching cocurricular activi
ties, while studies in the humanities integrate the disciplines of literature, history, philosophy
and religious studies. Advanced Studies courses offer highly motivated sixth formers an addi
tional educational opportunity in a particular discipline once all courses in the division, includ
ing electives, have been fully exhausted.

St. Paul's cosponsors School Year Abroad programs in France, China, Italy, Spain and Viet
nam for students in the fifth and sixth forms. The school also has an association with Seike
School in Tokyo, Japan, in addition to conducting exchange programs with schools in England
France, Sweden, Germany, Chile, Ghana and Greece. An independent study program offer
sixth form students the opportunity to learn from study and experience outside the classroom
student projects may be academic, vocational, social service oriented or experiential.

DUBLIN, NH. (66 mi. NW of Boston, MA) Rural. Pop: 1476. Alt: 1493 ft.

DUBLIN SCHOOL

Bdg and Day — Coed Gr 9-12

Dublin, NH 03444. 18 Lehmann Way, PO Box 522. Tel: 603-563-8584.
Fax: 603-563-7121.
www.dublinschool.org   E-mail: admission@dublinschool.org
Bradford D. Bates, Head (2008). BA, MA, Dartmouth College. **Jill Hutchins, Adm.**

Col Prep. LD. AP (exams req'd)—Eng Calc Bio Physics US_Hist Studio_Art. **Feat**—F
Lat Span Stats Astron Environ_Sci Marine_Bio/Sci Programming Web_Design E
African_Hist Modern_Chin_Hist Econ Psych Ceramics Drawing Film Painting Photo
Sculpt Printmaking Acting Music Music_Theory Journ. **Supp**—ESL Rem_Read Re
Tut.

Sports—Basket Crew X-country Lacrosse Ski Soccer Tennis.
Selective adm (Bdg Gr 9-12; Day 9-10): 51/yr. Bdg 40. Day 11. Appl fee: $50. Appl due: Jan. **Tests** CEEB IQ SSAT TOEFL.
Enr 130. B 72. G 58. Bdg 97. Day 33. Intl 25%. Avg class size: 10. Stud/fac: 4:1. Formal.
Fac 25. M 13/F 12. FT 25. Wh 100%. Adv deg: 52%. In dorms 13.
Grad '08—30. Col—30. (Goucher, UNH, Johns Hopkins, Agnes Scott, Johnson & Wales, NYU). **Avg SAT:** CR 554. M 574. W 541. Avg ACT: 20.8. **Col couns:** 1.
Tui '12-'13: Bdg $48,200 (+$1000). **Day $28,000** (+$1000). **Intl Bdg $48,200** (+$1000-6300). **Aid:** Need 39.
Endow $2,300,000. Plant val $12,100,000. Acres 350. Bldgs 21. Dorms 7. Dorm rms 51. Class rms 17. Lib 12,000 vols. Sci labs 3. Lang labs 1. Sci ctrs 1. Auds 1. Theaters 1. Art studios 1. Music studios 2. Dance studios 1. Arts ctrs 1. Wood shops 1. Recording studios 1. Gyms 1. Fields 2. Tennis courts 6. Rinks 1. Weight rms 1. Skiing facilities. Boating facilities. Student ctrs 1. Lakes 1. Comp labs 3.
Est 1935. Nonprofit. Tri (Sept-June). **Assoc** NEASC.

Paul Lehmann founded this successful school with his wife, Nancy. Girls were admitted on a day basis in 1969, and the girls' boarding division (opened in 1970) has firmly established coeducation for the school. The traditional college preparatory curriculum seeks to develop academic skills, artistic talents and athletic abilities. Faculty and students work together in small classes that facilitate individualized instruction.

The curriculum comprises a distributed core of required courses, as well as electives in the disciplines of English, foreign language, math, science, art and history. Advanced courses and independent study options enrich the program, and qualified pupils may pursue an honors-level diploma. Seniors may arrange independent internships or design a yearlong interdisciplinary course on a topic of personal interest.

Dublin also conducts individualized learning skills and evening study programs for students who are intellectually capable but whose academic achievement has not yet matched their ability level. These programs may include boys and girls with diagnosed learning differences or those in need of organizational assistance. Each program represents a structured support system for the mainstream Dublin curriculum, not an alternative curriculum.

All students participate in the athletic program, which includes both interscholastic and recreational sports. Boys and girls must perform 10 hours of community service annually, and participation a campuswide jobs program is also compulsory. The school schedules frequent on- and off-campus weekend events.

EXETER, NH. (44 mi. N of Boston, MA) Suburban. Pop: 9759. Alt: 58 ft.

PHILLIPS EXETER ACADEMY
Bdg and Day — Coed Gr 9-PG

Exeter, NH 03833. 20 Main St. Tel: 603-777-3437. Fax: 603-777-4399.
www.exeter.edu   E-mail: admit@exeter.edu
Thomas Edward Hassan, Prin (2009). AB, Brown Univ, MEd, EdD, Harvard Univ. **Michael Gary, Adm.**
Col Prep. AP exams taken: 490 (98% 3+). Feat—British_Lit Creative_Writing Humanities Shakespeare African_Lit Irish_Lit Hemingway Nabokov Chin Fr Ger Greek Ital Japan Lat Russ Span Arabic Linear_Algebra Multivariable_Calc Astron Ecol Genetics Marine_Bio/Sci Physiol Biochem Ornithology Comp_Sci Robotics Web_Design Modern_Chin_Hist Modern_Japan Middle_Eastern_Hist Anthro Econ Law Psych Lat-Amer_Stud Relig Architect Ceramics Filmmaking Photog Sculpt Drama Dance. **Supp**—Tut. Sat classes.
Sports—Basket Crew X-country Golf Ice_Hockey Indoor_Track Lacrosse Soccer Squash Swim Tennis Track W_Polo. B: Baseball Football Wrestling. G: F_Hockey Softball Volley. **Activities:** 60.

Very selective adm: 333/yr. Appl fee: $50. Appl due: Jan. Applied: 3053. Accepted: 17%. Yield: 71%. **Tests** CEEB ISEE SSAT TOEFL.

Enr 1063. B 521. G 542. Bdg 859. Day 203. Sec 1030. PG 33. Wh 48%. Latino 7%. Blk 10%. Native Am 1%. Asian 27%. Other 7%. Intl 13%. Avg class size: 12. Stud/fac: 5:1. Formal. **Fac 209.** M 103/F 106. FT 189/PT 20. Wh 89%. Latino 4%. Blk 2%. Asian 4%. Other 1%. Adv deg: 81%. In dorms 69.

Grad '10—310. Col—310. (Harvard, Princeton, Yale, Georgetown, Dartmouth, Cornell). **Avg SAT:** CR 700. M 711. W 694. Avg ACT: 29. **Col couns:** 6. Alum donors: 51%.

Tui '12-'13: Bdg $44,470 (+$845). **Day $34,540** (+$350). **Aid:** Need 499 ($15,852,834).

Summer (enr 700): Acad Enrich. Tui Bdg $7350. Tui Day $1150/crse. 5 wks.

Endow $969,000,000. Acres 670. Bldgs 130. Dorms 29. Dorm rms 675. Class rms 119. Lib 169,853 vols. Sci labs 22. Lang labs 1. Sci ctrs 1. Theaters 1. Art studios 4. Music studios 8. Dance studios 1. Art galleries 1. Observatories 1. Gyms 2. Fields 15. Tennis courts 23. Squash courts 14. Pools 2. Rinks 2. Stadiums 1. Comp labs 3. Comp/stud: 1:1

Est 1781. Nonprofit. Tri (Sept-June). **Assoc** CLS NEASC.

Established by John Phillips, whose nephew Samuel Phillips, Jr., had founded Phillips Academy at Andover, MA, three years earlier, Exeter is known for its outstanding faculty, diverse student body, and excellent academic and athletic facilities. The academy has been coeducational since 1970, when girls were first admitted as day students. The boarding program became coed the following fall. The present-day school enrolls a diverse student body from nearly every state, as well as various foreign countries.

Exeter's curriculum exhibits noteworthy breadth in diploma requirements. Broadly distributed requirements in science, history and the humanities form the main thrust of a curriculum that stresses knowledge acquisition in a liberal arts framework. In lieu of an Advanced Placement curriculum, Exeter offers college-level courses in most subjects, including some that go beyond the AP level.

At the center of an Exeter education is the Harkness Plan, made possible in the early 1930s by gifts from Edward S. Harkness, benefactor to many schools and colleges. A teacher and 12 students sit around a table forming and expressing ideas—a classroom in the seminar mode, where maximum participation is encouraged.

Students are assigned at the outset, especially in mathematics and foreign languages, to courses and sections according to demonstrated ability. Help in cultivating effective learning, speaking and thinking habits establishes a sound foundation. Through close daily association of students with the faculty in all areas of school life, Exeter seeks also to blend goodness of character with the growth in intellectual skills fostered by the Harkness Plan.

Exeter's comprehensive music program provides opportunities for study and performance. An orchestra and a chorus are the largest activities, while a number of other musical groups are available. Both varsity athletes and nonathletic students are involved in a daily physical education program. A dance program is also available at elementary through advanced levels. Modern language, English and theater courses utilize classrooms incorporating tablet computers and multimedia equipment, and wireless Internet access is available in the library and the student center.

Off-campus programs include a term spent in Washington, DC, as a congressional intern and a half year at the Milton Mountain School in Vershire, VT. Through School Year Abroad, students may study in France, Italy or Spain, or may spend the fall term or full year in Beijing, China. Exchanges are also arranged with secondary schools in Germany, Mexico and Russia, and one-term programs are offered in England, France, Ireland and the Bahamas.

MANCHESTER, NH. (50 mi. NNW of Boston, MA) Urban. Pop: 107,006. Alt: 225 ft.

THE DERRYFIELD SCHOOL
Day — Coed Gr 6-12

Manchester, NH 03104. 2108 River Rd. Tel: 603-669-4524. Fax: 603-641-9521.
www.derryfield.org   E-mail: admission@derryfield.org
Mary Halpin Carter, Int Head (2012). AB, Dartmouth College, MEd, Harvard Univ, PhD, Univ of New Hampshire. **Allison M. Price, Adm.**
   Col Prep. AP (exams req'd; 135 taken, 89% 3+)—Eng Fr Lat Span Calc Stats Chem Physics US_Hist. **Feat**—Creative_Writing Shakespeare Mythology Urban_Lit Chin Greek Anat & Physiol Engineering Comp_Sci Robotics Web_Design Holocaust Philos Ceramics Film Photog Studio_Art Drama Band Chorus Music_Theory Study_Skills.
   Sports (req'd)—Basket Crew X-country Equestrian Golf Lacrosse Ski Soccer Swim Tennis. B: Baseball. G: F_Hockey Softball. **Activities:** 35.
   Selective adm: 80/yr. Usual entry: 6, 7 & 9. Appl fee: $50. Appl due: Feb. **Tests** SSAT.
   Enr 370. B 168. G 202. Elem 121. Sec 249. Wh 91%. Latino 1%. Blk 2%. Asian 5%. Other 1%. Avg class size: 15. Stud/fac: 8:1. Casual. **Fac 47.** M 25/F 22. FT 45/PT 2. Wh 95%. Latino 2%. Blk 1%. Asian 1%. Other 1%. Adv deg: 51%.
   Grad '11—64. Col—64. (UNH 6, Syracuse 4, Northeastern U 4, Wm & Mary 3, Middlebury 3, St Lawrence 3). **Mid 50% SAT:** CR 550-680. M 530-640. W 530-660. Mid 50% ACT: 23-30. **Col couns:** 3. Alum donors: 14%.
   Tui '12-'13: Day $27,730 (+$500-1000). **Aid:** Merit 25 ($20,600). Need 86 ($1,435,675).
   Summer: Ages 8-16. Rec. Theater. Tui Day $450. 2 wks.
   Endow $4,700,000. Plant val $10,700,000. Acres 84. Bldgs 5 (20% ADA). Class rms 32. Lib 16,477 vols. Sci labs 5. Auds 1. Theaters 1. Art studios 2. Music studios 1. Perf arts ctrs 1. Gyms 1. Fields 4. Courts 6. Comp labs 1.
   Est 1964. Nonprofit. Tri (Sept-June). **Assoc** NEASC.

Serving more than 40 southern New Hampshire communities, Derryfield provides a traditional preparatory curriculum in combination with extensive sports, fine arts, extracurricular and community service programs.

Middle school course work progresses from the concrete to the abstract and seeks increasing sophistication and autonomy. Upper school students choose from a variety of Advanced Placement subjects, interdisciplinary courses and term electives. Seniors may design a six-week independent study program in the spring, with past projects including service learning, internships, study abroad and the arts. Students in grades 7-12 are required to participate in two seasons of interscholastic or noncompetitive athletics.

Derryfield also conducts Breakthrough Manchester, a tuition-free program for academically talented public school students. High school and college pupils interested in teaching serve as instructors for this eight-week summer program.

Each year, the school arranges host family living accommodations for a limited number of international students.   **See Also Page 97**

MERIDEN, NH. (104 mi. NW of Boston, MA) Rural. Pop: 500. Alt: 1000 ft.

KIMBALL UNION ACADEMY
Bdg and Day — Coed Gr 9-PG

Meriden, NH 03770. 7 Campus Center Dr, PO Box 188. Tel: 603-469-2100.
   Fax: 603-469-2041.
   www.kua.org   E-mail: admissions@kua.org

Michael J. Schafer, Head (2003). BA, Colby College, MEd, Harvard Univ. **Richard Ryerson, Adm.**

Col Prep. AP (exams req'd; 208 taken, 70% 3+)—Eng Fr Lat Span Calc Stats Comp_ Sci Bio Chem Environ_Sci Physics Eur_Hist US_Hist World_Hist Human_Geog Art_Hist Studio_Art. **Feat**—Creative_Writing Humanities Playwriting Chin Multivariable_Calc Anat & Physiol Geol Wildlife_Bio Chin_Hist Amer_Stud Anthro Econ Intl_ Relations Law Psych Photog Sculpt Jewelry Drama Music Music_Production Dance Public_Speak Woodworking Study_Skills. **Supp**—Tut. Sat classes.

Sports—Basket X-country Ice_Hockey Lacrosse Ski Soccer Swim Tennis. B: Baseball Rugby. G: F_Hockey Softball.

Selective adm: 130/yr. Bdg 87. Day 43. Appl fee: $50. Appl due: Feb. Applied: 371. Accepted: 60%. Yield: 53%. **Tests** CEEB ISEE SSAT TOEFL.

Enr 314, B 184. G 130. Bdg 207. Day 107. Sec 307. PG 7. Wh 83%. Latino 2%. Blk 4%. Native Am 1%. Asian 10%. Intl 25%. Avg class size: 11. Stud/fac: 6:1. **Fac 45.** M 28/F 17. FT 39/PT 6. Wh 97%. Asian 2%. Other 1%. Adv deg: 66%. In dorms 20.

Grad '11—99. Col—94. (UNH 9, Trinity Col-CT 4, St Lawrence 4, Lake Forest 3, Boston U 2, Skidmore 2). Athl schol 2. **Col couns:** 4.

Tui '11-'12: Bdg $45,990 (+$1200). **Day $28,850** (+$750). **Intl Bdg $48,990** (+$4200). **Aid:** Merit 4 ($40,000). Need 150 ($3,407,420).

Summer: Acad Enrich Rec. ESL. Tui Bdg $2800-5940. 2-4 wks. Tui Day $1490. 2 wks. Travel Abroad. Tui Bdg $3990. 3 wks.

Endow $14,600,000. Plant val $45,000,000. Acres 1300. Bldgs 35 (100% ADA). Dorms 9. Dorm rms 145. Class rms 26. Lib 20,000 vols. Sci labs 6. Lang labs 1. Theaters 1. Art studios 3. Music studios 2. Dance studios 2. Arts ctrs 1. Gyms 2. Fields 9. Courts 8. Pools 1. Rinks 1. Fitness ctrs 1. Comp labs 2. Laptop prgm Gr 9-PG.

Est 1813. Nonprofit. Tri (Sept-May). **Assoc** CLS NEASC.

Founded as a coeducational school, Kimball Union followed educational trends in 1935 and became a boys' school, which it remained until coeducation was reintroduced in 1974. The present-day institution, located 13 miles south of Dartmouth College, attracts a diverse student body from throughout the world.

The challenging liberal arts curriculum features small classes, as well as honors and Advanced Placement courses in every discipline. Graduation requirements include three years of foreign language and arts courses. An extensive environmental studies program makes use of Snow Mountain, the school's 750-acre wilderness area. Kimball Union issues laptop computers to all students.

All students participate in two seasons of a team activity each year and can spend the third in an activity such as recreational skiing, or in an arts program such as visual arts or photography. Arts programs involving larger groups—such as chorus, jazz and rock bands, dance and theater—have an exclusively allotted period around the dinner hour.

KUA offers many leadership opportunities. Students and staff gather for an all-school meeting twice weekly.

NEW HAMPTON, NH. (93 mi. NNW of Boston, MA) Rural. Pop: 1950. Alt: 574 ft.

NEW HAMPTON SCHOOL

Bdg and Day — Coed Gr 9-PG

New Hampton, NH 03256. 70 Main St. Tel: 603-677-3400. Fax: 603-677-3481.
www.newhampton.org   E-mail: admissions@newhampton.org

Andrew V. Menke, Head (2005). BS, Towson State Univ, MA, Dartmouth College. **Suzanne Buck, Adm.**

Col Prep. IB Diploma. AP (101 exams taken, 90% 3+)—Eng Stats US_Hist Studio_ Art. **Feat**—Chin Fr Span Anat & Physiol Sports_Med Engineering Web_Design Econ Psych Film Photog Drama Music Dance. **Supp**—ESL Tut. Sat classes.

Sports (req'd)—Basket X-country Golf Ice_Hockey Lacrosse Ski Soccer Tennis. B: Baseball Football. G: F_Hockey Softball.
Selective adm: 150/yr. Bdg 120. Day 30. Appl fee: $50. Appl due: Feb. Accepted: 60%.
Tests CEEB SSAT.
Enr 305. B 175. G 130. Bdg 245. Day 60. Sec 280. PG 25. Wh 75%. Latino 3%. Blk 6%. Asian 12%. Other 4%. Intl 17%. Avg class size: 12. Stud/fac: 5:1. Casual. **Fac 61.** M 35/F 26. FT 61.
Grad '11—103. Col—100. (St Lawrence, UNH, Plymouth St, St Anselm, Boston Col, High Pt). **Mid 50% SAT:** CR 420-550. M 420-560. W 410-540. Mid 50% ACT: 17-21. **Col couns:** 3. Alum donors: 13%.
Tui '12-'13: Bdg $49,500. Day $29,800. Intl Bdg $50,500. Aid: Need 109 ($2,150,000).
Summer: Acad Enrich Rec. ESL. Arts. Sports. 1-2 wks.
Endow $10,164,000. Plant val $22,044,000. Acres 300. Bldgs 47. Dorms 13. Dorm rms 150. Class rms 50. Lib 15,000 vols. Sci labs 5. Lang labs 1. Photog labs 1. Auds 1. Theaters 1. Art studios 1. Music studios 1. Dance studios 1. Gyms 2. Fields 5. Tennis courts 9. Rinks 1. Comp labs 3. Comp/stud: 1:1 Laptop prgm Gr 9-10.
Est 1821. Nonprofit. Sem (Sept-May). **Assoc** CLS NEASC.

New Hampton offers a well-regarded program that adheres to a national model for experience-based education. Recognizing that students learn in different ways and come from varying academic backgrounds, the school designs its classes to provide different learning experiences and to accommodate boys and girls with a range of academic skills. Honors, Advanced Placement and standard college preparatory offerings are available in each discipline, as are fine and performing arts courses, academic support services and English as a Second Language instruction. Juniors and seniors may pursue the International Baccalaureate Diploma.

Participation in an after-school program is compulsory during each of the three terms. Several Saturday mornings throughout the fall and spring terms are devoted to schoolwide community service efforts. Another program, Alongside Saturdays, enables students to conduct workshops for their peers and teachers. Various other service opportunities are available during the winter term. In total, boys and girls perform at least 24 hours of required service each year.

PLYMOUTH, NH. (103 mi. NNW of Boston, MA) Rural. Pop: 5892. Alt: 514 ft.

HOLDERNESS SCHOOL
Bdg and Day — Coed Gr 9-12

Plymouth, NH 03264. 33 Chapel Ln, PO Box 1879. Tel: 603-536-1257.
Fax: 603-536-1267.
www.holderness.org   E-mail: info@holderness.org
R. Phillip Peck, Head. BA, Dartmouth College, MA, MEd, Columbia Univ. **Tyler Lewis, Adm.**
Col Prep. AP (128 exams taken, 80% 3+)—Eng Fr Lat Span Calc Stats Bio Environ_ Sci Eur_Hist US_Hist Music_Theory. **Feat**—Anat & Physiol Comp_Sci Cold_War Middle_Eastern_Hist Women's_Hist Econ Theol Art_Hist Ceramics Photog Sculpt Studio_Art Acting Theater Music. **Supp**—Tut. Outdoor ed. Sat classes.
Sports—Basket X-country Golf Ice_Hockey Lacrosse Ski Soccer Tennis. B: Baseball Football. G: F_Hockey Softball.
Selective adm: 103/yr. Bdg 85. Day 18. Appl fee: $50. Appl due: Feb. Accepted: 50%.
Tests IQ SSAT TOEFL.
Enr 282. Bdg 240. Day 42. Intl 12%. Avg class size: 11. Stud/fac: 6:1. Formal. **Fac 49.** Adv deg: 67%.
Grad '08—80. Col—80. (UNH, U of CO-Boulder, St Lawrence, Bates, CO Col, U of VT). **Avg SAT:** CR 548. M 561. W 554. **Col couns:** 3.
Tui '11-'12: Bdg $47,500 (+$1000). **Day $28,500** (+$150). **Aid:** Need 113

($2,500,000).
Endow $44,000,000. Plant val $19,741,000. Acres 682. Bldgs 23. Dorms 16. Dorm rms 110. Class rms 30. Lib 16,000 vols. Sci labs 6. Auds 1. Theaters 1. Art studios 4. Music studios 2. Gyms 1. Fields 3. Courts 6. Rinks 1. Comp labs 3.
Est 1879. Nonprofit. Episcopal. Sem (Sept-May). **Assoc** CLS NEASC.

The Holderness curriculum emphasizes the acquisition of those skills that prepare students for college entrance; in particular, course work addresses reading comprehension and clarity in writing. Focus in math and the physical science classes (as well as in the social sciences and languages) remains on critical thinking and application of the principals of logic. Art, music and drama, in addition to a daily job program, complement standard course offerings.

Classes are held six days each week, with half-days on Wednesdays and Saturdays allowing for afternoon athletics. During the month of March, pupils engage in grade-specific special programs. Freshmen and returning sophomores participate in Artward Bound, a creative collaboration with artists-in-residence that ends with an art exhibition, while returning sophomores take part in Habitat for Humanity community service projects. Juniors partake of an outdoor education experience in the White Mountains that calls upon both individual and team survival techniques. Seniors choose from either an intensive, college-style course taught by school faculty and visiting professors on a topic in the humanities, or an independent project that begins with two to three weeks of research and culminates in the composition of a 10-page paper and the delivery of an oral presentation to other students.

Holderness offers a wide selection of competitive athletics. The school's proximity to mountains also enables boys and girls to join Alpine ski teams or engage in recreational skiing or snowboarding.

RINDGE, NH. (58 mi. WNW of Boston, MA) Suburban. Pop: 5451. Alt: 1400 ft.

HAMPSHIRE COUNTRY SCHOOL

Bdg — Boys Gr 3-12

Rindge, NH 03461. 28 Patey Cir. Tel: 603-899-3325. Fax: 603-899-6521.
www.hampshirecountryschool.org
E-mail: admissions@hampshirecountryschool.net
Bernd Foecking, Head (2009). BA, Ruhr Univ Bochum (Germany), MEd, Plymouth State Univ. **William Dickerman, Adm.**
    Col Prep. Gen Acad. LD. Underachiever. Feat—Fr Anat & Physiol Environ_Sci 20th-Century_Hist. **Supp**—Rev Tut. Outdoor ed.
    Somewhat selective adm (Gr 3-7): 6/yr. Usual entry: 3 & 7. Appl fee: $0. Appl due: Rolling. **Tests** IQ.
    Enr 23. Elem 16. Sec 7. Wh 83%. Latino 4%. Native Am 9%. Other 4%. Avg class size: 4. Stud/fac: 2:1. Casual. **Fac 9.** M 4/F 5. FT 8/PT 1. Wh 100%. Adv deg: 33%. In dorms 5.
    Grad '10—3. Col—3. (La Salle 1, Morningside 1, Paul Smith's 1).
    Tui '12-'13: Bdg $49,000 (+$1000).
    Plant val $2,000,000. Acres 1700. Bldgs 7. Dorms 4. Dorm rms 20. Class rms 7. Lib 3000 vols. Sci labs 1. Theaters 1. Music studios 1. Fields 1. Tennis courts 1. Comp labs 1. Comp/stud: 1:5.
    Est 1948. Nonprofit. Tri (Sept-June). **Assoc** NEASC.

Within the framework of a traditional educational program, HCS educates students of above-average ability who have been unable to succeed in other settings. Pupils typically enroll at middle school age and remain at the school for three or four years before transferring to competitive New England preparatory schools, although some complete their high school studies at HCS. The school can accommodate such special needs as hyperactivity, difficulty in dealing with peers or adults, unusually timid or fearful behavior, school phobia, nonverbal learning disability and Asperger's syndrome. A favorable student-teacher ratio meets the needs of students who require extra structure and attention.

Located on 1700 acres of farm and woodland, the school offers an activities program that includes skating, sledding, soccer, canoeing, swimming, tennis, hiking and skiing.

See Also Page 73

TILTON, NH. (82 mi. NNW of Boston, MA) Suburban. Pop: 3477. Alt: 453 ft.

TILTON SCHOOL

Bdg and Day — Coed Gr 9-PG

Tilton, NH 03276. 30 School St. Tel: 603-286-1733. Fax: 603-286-1705.
www.tiltonschool.org E-mail: admissions@tiltonschool.org
Peter Saliba, Head (2012). BA, Middlebury College, MLA, Dartmouth College. **Beth A. Skoglund, Adm.**
Col Prep. AP—Eng Fr Span Calc Stats Bio Chem Physics Eur_Hist Econ Psych. **Feat**—World_Lit Chin Japan Anat & Physiol Ecol Forensic_Sci Geol Marine_Bio/Sci Animal_Sci Asian_Hist Pol_Sci Sociol Global_Stud World_Relig Ceramics Drawing Graphic_Arts Painting Photog Studio_Art Band Chorus Music_Theory. **Supp**—ESL LD Rev Tut. Sat classes.
Sports—Basket X-country Golf Ice_Hockey Lacrosse Ski Soccer Tennis. B: Baseball Football Wrestling. G: F_Hockey Softball. **Activities:** 30.
Selective adm: Usual entry: 9. Appl fee: $50. Appl due: Feb. Applied: 488. Accepted: 83%. Yield: 32%. **Tests** CEEB IQ ISEE SSAT TOEFL.
Enr 260. B 169. G 91. Bdg 196. Day 64. Sec 240. PG 20. Wh 71%. Latino 3%. Blk 5%. Asian 20%. Other 1%. Intl 28%. Avg class size: 11. Stud/fac: 6:1. Casual. **Fac 40.** M 27/F 13. FT 34/PT 6. Wh 95%. Asian 2%. Other 3%. Adv deg: 30%. In dorms 21.
Grad '11—85. Col—79. (Bates, Bentley, Gettysburg, Quinnipiac, U of IL-Urbana). Athl schol 6. **Avg SAT:** CR 524. M 567. W 534. **Mid 50% SAT:** CR 460-580. M 490-660. W 480-580. Avg ACT: 20. **Col couns:** 3. Alum donors: 14%.
Tui '12-'13: Bdg $47,600 (+$750). **Day $27,400** (+$750). **Intl Bdg $48,350** (+$1500). **Aid:** Merit 19 ($125,500). Need 108 ($2,360,145).
Endow $14,600,000. Plant val $48,000,000. Acres 153. Bldgs 29. Dorms 5. Dorm rms 122. Class rms 22. Lib 17,500 vols. Chapels 1. Sci labs 4. Auds 1. Theaters 1. Art studios 1. Music studios 1. Dance studios 1. Gyms 1. Athletic ctrs 1. Fields 8. Tennis courts 3. Squash courts 2. Pools 1. Rinks 1. Comp labs 2. Comp/stud: 1:1
Est 1845. Nonprofit. Methodist. Sem (Sept-May). **Assoc** CLS NEASC.

Founded as a secondary school for boarding and day boys and girls, the school was founded in Northfield, across the Winnipesaukee River from the present campus. A fire in the 1860s led the school to move to its current location. Over the years, Tilton has fulfilled different functions, according to community need: It has been a coeducational boarding school, a boys' boarding school, a public school, a female college, a junior college, and a secondary school with both college and general courses. In 1939, the school stopped serving as the local high school and became a strictly independent boys' boarding and day school. General diploma courses were dropped in 1958, as the school focused solely on college preparation. Tilton reinstituted its girls' division in 1970.

The college preparatory curriculum, which qualifies graduates for many competitive colleges, includes Advanced Placement and honors courses. A learning center provides academic support, and the school schedules weekly extra-help periods and small-group advisor meetings. The +5 program requires participation beyond the school day in arts and culture, team athletics, outdoor experiences, community service and leadership activities.

Located on a 153-acre tract in New Hampshire's White Mountains and Lakes Region, the school's campus includes fields, trails, woodland, streams and ponds. Several ski areas are a short distance away.

WOLFEBORO, NH. (51 mi. W of Portland, ME; 87 mi. N of Boston, MA) Suburban. Pop: 2979. Alt: 508 ft.

BREWSTER ACADEMY
Bdg and Day — Coed Gr 9-PG

Wolfeboro, NH 03894. 80 Academy Dr. Tel: 603-569-7200. Fax: 603-569-7272.
www.brewsteracademy.org   E-mail: admissions@brewsteracademy.org
Michael E. Cooper, Head (2003). BA, State Univ of New York-Albany, MEd, St Lawrence Univ, PhD, Syracuse Univ. **Lynne M. Palmer, Adm.**

>**Col Prep. AP (exams req'd; 123 taken, 63% 3+)**—Eng Calc Stats Bio Physics Eur_Hist US_Hist Econ. **Feat**—Fr Span Astron Ecol Environ_Sci Comp_Design Comp_Sci Web_Design Ceramics Filmmaking Photog Animation Theater Theater_Arts Jazz_ Band Dance Journ Yoga. **Supp**—ESL LD Tut. Outdoor ed. Sat classes.
>**Sports (req'd)**—Basket Crew X-country Equestrian Golf Ice_Hockey Lacrosse Sail Ski Soccer Tennis. B: Baseball. G: F_Hockey Softball. **Activities:** 25.
>**Selective adm:** 135/yr. Bdg 118. Day 17. Usual entry: 9 & 10. Appl fee: $50. Appl due: Feb. Applied: 502. Accepted: 56%. Yield: 49%. **Tests** IQ SSAT TOEFL.
>**Enr 364.** B 213. G 151. Bdg 294. Day 70. Sec 351. PG 13. Wh 74%. Latino 3%. Blk 5%. Native Am 1%. Asian 14%. Other 3%. Intl 18%. Avg class size: 11. Stud/fac: 6:1. Formal. **Fac 64.** M 34/F 30. FT 62/PT 2. In dorms 33.
>**Grad '11—117. Col—114.** (Hobart/Wm Smith 5, Boston U 4, Susquehanna 4, North-eastern U 3, St Michael's 3, NYU 2). Athl schol 13. **Avg SAT:** CR 500. M 526. W 498. Avg ACT: 22. **Col couns:** 2. Alum donors: 9%.
>**Tui '12-'13: Bdg $47,980** (+$2000). **Day $29,550** (+$600). **Aid:** Need 105 ($2,600,000).
>**Summer (enr 50):** Acad Enrich Rev Rec. Outdoor Ed. Tui Bdg $7380-7850. Tui Day $4200. 6 wks.
>Endow $9,800,000. Plant val $43,000,000. Acres 91. Bldgs 43. Dorms 20. Dorm rms 278. Class rms 40. Lib 45,000 vols. Sci labs 3. Theaters 3. Art studios 4. Music studios 5. Gyms 1. Athletic ctrs 1. Fields 6. Tennis courts 9. Tracks 1. Boathouses 1. Climbing walls 1. Student ctrs 1. Comp labs 2. Comp/stud: 1:1 Laptop prgm Gr 9-12.
>**Est 1820.** Nonprofit. Tri (Sept-June). **Assoc** NEASC.

This small college preparatory school's concern for personal growth and development attracts students from dozens of states and foreign countries. The traditional college preparatory curriculum stresses an individualized approach to learning, facilitated by a low student-teacher ratio. In addition to its core classes, Brewster offers a variety of electives, among them visual and performing arts, computer graphics, performance poetry and freshwater ecology. Qualified pupils may also pursue honors and Advanced Placement courses.

An academic support department includes a writing center and an English as a Second Language program. Integrated technology enhances the curriculum: All students use laptop computers and connect to the Brewster network and Internet at classroom workstations, in dormitories and in all campus buildings. Saturday classes convene biweekly.

Located in a resort village, the 91-acre campus on the shores of Lake Winnipesaukee provides the setting for a year-round sports program.

RHODE ISLAND

BARRINGTON, RI. (8 mi. SE of Providence, RI; 44 mi. SSW of Boston, MA) Suburban. Pop: 16,819. Alt: 24 ft.

ST. ANDREW'S SCHOOL

Bdg — Coed Gr 9-12; Day — Coed 3-12

Barrington, RI 02806. 63 Federal Rd. Tel: 401-246-1230. Fax: 401-246-0510.
www.standrews-ri.org   E-mail: inquiry@standrews-ri.org
John D. Martin, Head (1996). BA, Tufts Univ, MEd, American International College, MDiv, Yale Univ. **R. Scott Telford, Adm.**

Col Prep. AP (exams req'd; 15 taken, 80% 3+)—Calc Stats Physics Music_Theory. **Elem read**—Open Court. **Feat**—Fr Span Anat & Physiol Astron Environ_Sci Oceanog Comp_Sci Global_Issues Ethics Ceramics Drawing Fine_Arts Graphic_Arts Photog Drama Theater_Arts Chorus Music Music_Hist. **Supp**—Dev_Read ESL LD Rem_Read Tut.

Sports (req'd)—Basket X-country Lacrosse Soccer Tennis. B: Golf.

Selective adm: 73/yr. Bdg 18. Day 55. Usual entry: 9. Appl fee: $50. Appl due: Jan. Applied: 243. Accepted: 57%. Yield: 48%. **Tests** IQ ISEE TOEFL.

Enr 213. Bdg 60. Day 153. Elem 51. Sec 162. Wh 65%. Latino 1%. Blk 12%. Asian 17%. Other 5%. Intl 17%. Avg class size: 10. Stud/fac: 5:1. Casual. **Fac 47.** M 21/F 26. FT 47. Wh 96%. Blk 4%. Adv deg: 61%. In dorms 24.

Grad '11—39. Col—37. (Emory, Mitchell, Mt Ida, Rollins, Worcester St, Dean). **Avg SAT:** CR 480. M 508. W 477. **Col couns:** 2.

Tui '11-'12: Bdg $44,700 (+$2000). **Day $28,650-29,800** (+$400). **Intl Bdg $45,175** (+$2000-8100). **Aid:** Need 100 ($2,073,450).

Summer: Gr 1-12. Acad Enrich Rem Rec. Computers. Art. Sports. Tui Bdg $425/wk. Tui Day $195-350/wk. 7 wks.

Endow $16,000,000. Plant val $37,500,000. Acres 100. Bldgs 33 (33% ADA). Dorms 4. Dorm rms 60. Lib 11,000 vols. Sci labs 4. Lang labs 2. Auds 1. Theaters 1. Art studios 2. Music studios 1. Ceramics studios 1. Gyms 2. Fields 4. Tennis courts 4. Ropes crses 1. Comp labs 3. Comp/stud: 1:3.

Est 1893. Nonprofit. Quar (Sept-June). **Assoc** NEASC.

Founded by Rev. William M. Chapin, this nondenominational school has an Episcopal heritage. St. Andrew's provides a traditional college preparatory curriculum within a structured environment. After offering middle and upper school programming from its founding, the school added a lower school (grades 3-5) to its day division in the fall of 2008.

The curriculum is designed to help students develop sound academic skills and study habits, to provide college preparation, and to expose students to a variety of cocurricular activities. Small classes and a daily advisory system ensure individualized attention. The Resource and Focus programs, both of which are available for an additional fee, offer extra support to pupils with mild language-based learning disabilities or attentional concerns.

Beginning in grade 9, students fulfill a community service requirement: 10 hours annually for freshman, 20 hours for sophomores, 30 hours for juniors and 40 hours for seniors. The school, which occupies a 100-acre site, offers a full range of athletic and extracurricular offerings as a complement to academics. **See Also Pages 36-7**

EAST GREENWICH, RI. (11 mi. S of Providence, RI; 52 mi. SSW of Boston, MA) Suburban. Pop: 12,948. Alt: 31 ft.

ROCKY HILL SCHOOL
Day — Coed Gr PS (Age 3)-12

East Greenwich, RI 02818. 530 Ives Rd. Tel: 401-884-9070. Fax: 401-885-4985.
www.rockyhill.org   E-mail: cwashburn@rockyhill.org
Jonathan M. Schoenwald, Head (2011). PhD, Stanford Univ. Catherine T. Washburn, Adm.

   Col Prep. AP (exams req'd)—Eng Fr Lat Span Calc Stats Bio Chem Environ_Sci Physics US_Hist. Feat—Creative_Writing Shakespeare Chin Marine_Bio/Sci Physiol Comp_Sci Holocaust Psych Global_Stud Ceramics Drawing Photog Studio_Art Drama Music Journ SAT_Prep. Supp—ESL Rev Tut. Outdoor ed.
   Sports (req'd)—Basket X-country Golf Lacrosse Soccer Tennis. B: Ice_Hockey. G: F_ Hockey. Activities: 18.
   Selective adm: 65/yr. Appl fee: $50. Appl due: Feb. Accepted: 80%. Yield: 60%. Tests ISEE SSAT TOEFL.
   Enr 325. B 162. G 163. Wh 82%. Latino 5%. Blk 5%. Native Am 1%. Asian 5%. Other 2%. Intl 5%. Avg class size: 14. Stud/fac: 6:1. Casual. Fac 64. M 24/F 40. FT 59/PT 5. Wh 96%. Latino 1%. Blk 1%. Asian 2%. Adv deg: 57%.
   Grad '11—39. Col—39. (Geo Wash 6, URI 3, Wheaton-MA 3, U of VT 2, Barnard 1, Tufts 1). Avg SAT: CR 587. M 589. W 616.
   Tui '12-'13: Day $26,100-29,200 (+$300-2600). Aid: Merit 8 ($34,750). Need 66 ($962,500).
   Summer: Enrich Rec. Arts. Sports. Tui $75-240/wk. 6 wks.
   Endow $1,800,000. Plant val $8,000,000. Acres 88. Bldgs 13. Class rms 52. 2 Libs 13,000 vols. Sci labs 8. Auds 1. Art studios 3. Music studios 3. Wood shops 1. Gyms 1. Fields 5. Courts 4. Sailing facilities. Comp labs 2. Laptop prgm Gr 9-12.
   Est 1934. Nonprofit. Sem (Sept-June). Assoc NEASC.

   Located on a historic, 88-acre estate that borders Narragansett Bay, Rocky Hill makes use of its waterfront facilities for various activities and conducts marine and environmental programs at all grade levels. Students in grades 5-12 utilize Harkness tables, and boys and girls in grades 9-12 must have a laptop computer. Elective courses, Advanced Placement classes, an SAT preparation course and a senior project program are available in the upper school, with both AP biology and AP environmental science enriched by the school's natural setting.

   Arts are emphasized, with specialized offerings provided in instrumental music, band, chorus, drama, drawing, painting, ceramics and sculpture.

NEWPORT, RI. (25 mi. SSE of Providence, RI; 61 mi. SSW of Boston, MA) Suburban. Pop: 26,475. Alt: 6 ft. Area also includes Middletown and Portsmouth.

PORTSMOUTH ABBEY SCHOOL
Bdg and Day — Coed Gr 9-12

Portsmouth, RI 02871. 285 Cory's Ln. Tel: 401-643-1248. Fax: 401-643-1355.
www.portsmouthabbey.org   E-mail: admissions@portsmouthabbey.org
James M. De Vecchi, Head (2000). BA, St Francis College, MS, PhD, Univ of New Hampshire. Meghan M. Fonts, Adm.

   Col Prep. AP (exams req'd; 248 taken, 66% 3+)—Eng Fr Lat Span Calc Stats Comp_ Sci Bio Chem Physics Eur_Hist US_Hist World_Hist Econ Art_Hist Music_Theory. Feat—Creative_Writing Humanities Chin Greek Environ_Sci Physiol Irish_Hist Intl_Relations Pol_Sci Constitutional_Law Relig Ceramics Photog Studio_Art Drama

Music. **Supp**—Tut. Sat classes.
Sports (req'd)—Basket X-country Golf Ice_Hockey Lacrosse Sail Soccer Squash Swim Tennis Track. B: Baseball Football. G: F_Hockey Softball. **Activities:** 25.
Selective adm (Bdg Gr 9-11; Day 9): 113/yr. Bdg 81. Day 32. Usual entry: 9. Appl fee: $50. Appl due: Jan. Applied: 467. Accepted: 55%. Yield: 46%. **Tests** CEEB SSAT.
Enr 350. B 173. G 177. Bdg 250. Day 100. Wh 89%. Latino 2%. Blk 3%. Asian 6%. Intl 11%. Avg class size: 13. Stud/fac: 7:1. Formal. **Fac 51.** M 31/F 20. FT 47/PT 4. Wh 98%. Blk 1%. Asian 1%. Adv deg: 72%. In dorms 25.
Grad '10—107. Col—100. (Catholic U 5, Boston Col 4, Col of Charleston 3, NYU 3, Salve Regina 3, Trinity Col-CT 3). **Mid 50% SAT:** CR 530-670. M 540-690. W 540-650. **Col couns:** 3.
Tui '11-'12: Bdg $46,650 (+$1000). **Day $31,750** (+$750). **Intl Bdg $46,650** (+$1825). **Aid:** Merit 16 ($300,000). Need 115 ($2,900,000).
Summer: Gr 7-10. Acad Enrich Rec. Tui Bdg $5850. Tui Day $3350. 4 wks.
Endow $38,000,000. Plant val $37,500,000. Acres 550. Bldgs 25. Dorms 8. Dorm rms 155. Class rms 25. 2 Libs 55,076 vols. Labs 3. Auds 1. Art studios 1. Music studios 10. Gyms 2. Athletic ctrs 1. Fields 10. Tennis courts 6. Squash courts 8. Rinks 1. Riding rings 1. Stables 1. Tracks 1. Boating facilities. Golf crses 1. Radio stations 1.
Est 1926. Nonprofit. Roman Catholic (70% practice). Tri (Sept-May). **Assoc** CLS NEASC.

Founded by Rev. Dom John Hugh Diman and known as the Portsmouth Priory School until 1969, when the monastery of the English Benedictine Congregation that conducts the school was raised to the status of an abbey, Portsmouth Abbey occupies a 550-acre site on Narragansett Bay. The school continues its goal of instilling in students "a genuine appreciation of scholarship, excellence in academic work and a belief in a broad and liberal education." The faculty comprises both monastic and lay members.

Portsmouth Abbey's traditional college preparatory curriculum features Advanced Placement courses, and a wide range of electives are available to juniors and seniors. All pupils study Latin in grade 9, while a signature humanities program begins in grade 10. Graduation requirements include four years of Christian doctrine and a senior independent study project. Open conference periods built into each academic day allow students to consult with teachers and attend extra-help sessions.

The school requires students to participate in interscholastic sports every season, although drama or community service may be substituted for athletics in one term of grades 9-11 and two terms of grade 12. Sophomores complete a 10-hour service requirement. Portsmouth Abbey schedules cultural expeditions to Boston, MA, and Providence.

ST. GEORGE'S SCHOOL

Bdg and Day — Coed Gr 9-12

Middletown, RI 02842. 372 Purgatory Rd. Tel: 401-842-6600. Fax: 401-842-6696.
www.stgeorges.edu   E-mail: admissions_office@stgeorges.edu
Eric F. Peterson, Head (2004). AB, Dartmouth College, JD, Northwestern Univ. **James A. Hamilton, Adm.**
Col Prep. AP (exams req'd; 399 taken, 71% 3+)—Eng Chin Fr Lat Span Calc Stats Comp_Sci Bio Chem Environ_Sci Physics Eur_Hist US_Hist World_Hist Econ US_ Govt & Pol Studio_Art Music_Theory. **Feat**—Creative_Writing Gothic_Lit Marine_Bio/ Sci Preveterinary_Sci Civil_War Global_Stud World_Relig Art_Hist Photog Acting Journ. **Supp**—Tut. Sat classes.
Sports (req'd)—Basket X-country Golf Ice_Hockey Lacrosse Sail Soccer Squash Swim Tennis Track. B: Baseball Football. G: F_Hockey Softball.
Selective adm (Gr 9-11): 107/yr. Bdg 96. Day 11. Usual entry: 9 & 10. Appl fee: $50. Appl due: Feb. Applied: 700. **Tests** ISEE SSAT TOEFL.
Enr 357. B 176. G 181. Bdg 292. Day 65. Intl 11%. Avg class size: 12. Stud/fac: 10:1. **Fac 66.** M 37/F 29. FT 65/PT 1. Adv deg: 78%. In dorms 37.
Grad '11—93. Col—93. (Georgetown 5, Boston Col 5, Brown 4, Dartmouth 3, Stanford 2, Middlebury 2). **Avg SAT:** CR 623. M 632. W 638. **Col couns:** 3. Alum donors:

37%.
Tui '12-'13: Bdg $49,750 (+$1000). **Day** $34,150 (+$700). **Aid:** Need 100 ($3,400,000).
Endow $112,215,000. Acres 200. Bldgs 46. Dorms 21. Dorm rms 195. Class rms 48. Lib 22,000 vols. Sci labs 5. Photog labs 1. Auds 1. Theaters 1. Art studios 10. Music studios 5. Dance studios 1. Gyms 4. Fields 12. Tennis courts 12. Squash courts 1. Field houses 1. Pools 1. Rinks 2. Comp labs 5. Comp/stud: 1:1 Laptop prgm Gr 9-12.
Est 1896. Nonprofit. Episcopal. Sem (Sept-May). **Assoc** CLS NEASC.

St. George's was founded by Rev. John B. Diman, who later established Portsmouth Abbey, and in 1901 moved to its present, 200-acre campus overlooking the Atlantic Ocean and the city of Newport.

St. George's offers a traditional college preparatory curriculum with opportunities for numerous electives and advanced work. Art offerings—drawing, painting, printmaking, architecture, photography and art history—religious studies, and computer applications and programming are important curricular features. The music program offers diploma credit for private instruction in voice and instrumental music. Students attend from many states and foreign countries, and graduates enter leading colleges.

St. George's conducts work and study internships, as well as year-round research cruises for full academic credit that allow students to live and study for six weeks aboard the school research vessel, *Geronimo*. Marine biology and field research concentrate on the study of sea turtles, while oceanography (including meteorology and navigation) and English are taught by the on-board staff; pupils take other courses by correspondence with their teachers at the school. All incoming freshmen purchase tablet computers, and most campus buildings feature wireless Internet access.

ST. MICHAEL'S COUNTRY DAY SCHOOL

Day — Coed Gr PS (Age 3)-8

Newport, RI 02840. 180 Rhode Island Ave. Tel: 401-849-5970. Fax: 401-849-7890.
www.smcds.org   E-mail: scasey@smcds.org
Whitney C. Slade, Head. BA, Tufts Univ, MEd, Harvard Univ. **Sally Casey, Adm.**
  Pre-Prep. Feat—Fr Span Computers Studio_Art Drama Music. **Supp**—Tut.
  Sports (req'd)—Basket Lacrosse Soccer Tennis.
  Selective adm: 47/yr. Appl fee: $50. Appl due: Mar. Accepted: 83%. Yield: 85%. **Tests** SSAT.
  Enr 226. Wh 93%. Latino 2%. Blk 2%. Asian 3%. **Fac 55.** Adv deg: 50%.
  Grad '08—21. Prep—19. (Portsmouth 4, Rocky Hill 4, St George's Sch-RI 3, Prout 2, Gould 2, Groton 1).
  Tui '12-'13: Day $19,480-22,015 (+$390).
  Summer: Ages 3-18. Enrich Rec. Sports. 7 wks. Theater. 3 wks.
  Endow $158,000. Plant val $2,163,000. Acres 7. Bldgs 4. Class rms 28. 2 Libs 8500 vols. Sci labs 2. Art studios 2. Music studios 2. Arts ctrs 1. Gyms 1. Fields 3. Playgrounds 3. Comp labs 1.
  Est 1938. Nonprofit. Sem (Sept-June).

Founded by Rt. Rev. James DeWolf Perry, onetime bishop of Rhode Island, St. Michael's moved to its current location in 1943 and served as the parish day school of Trinity Church for many years. In 1976, the school was reincorporated as a nondenominational independent school with a self-perpetuating board of trustees.

Situated on a seven-acre tract in a historic residential section of Newport, St. Michael's provides an interdisciplinary curriculum at all grade levels. French, computer, library, art, music, drama and physical education classes enrich the program throughout. Field trips and special activities complement class work. The school also sponsors the Publishing House, a volunteer-run program in which children in grades K-4 write, illustrate and bind their own books. All eighth graders perform at least 20 hours of required community service.

St. Michael's offers an extended-day option that includes outdoor and enrichment activities. All students in grades 6-8 participate in interscholastic athletics.

PROVIDENCE, RI. (41 mi. SSW of Boston, MA) Urban. Pop: 173,618. Alt: 12 ft. Area also includes East Providence.

GORDON SCHOOL
Day — Coed Gr PS (Age 3)-8

East Providence, RI 02914. 45 Maxfield Ave. Tel: 401-434-3833. Fax: 401-431-0320.
www.gordonschool.org E-mail: admission@gordonschool.org
Ralph L. Wales, Head (1994). AB, MEd, Harvard Univ. Emily C. Anderson, Adm.
  Pre-Prep. Elem math—Col Prep Math. **Feat**—Fr Span Computers Photog Studio_Art Music Jazz_Band. **Supp**—Dev_Read Tut.
  Sports—Baseball Basket X-country Lacrosse Soccer Tennis Track. G: F_Hockey.
  Selective adm: 67/yr. Usual entry: PS & K. Appl fee: $50. Appl due: Feb. Applied: 206. Accepted: 76%. Yield: 42%. **Tests** CTP_4 ISEE SSAT.
  Enr 407. B 195. G 212. Wh 73%. Latino 2%. Blk 3%. Asian 8%. Other 14%. Avg class size: 14. Stud/fac: 7:1. **Fac 56.** M 14/F 42. FT 51/PT 5. Wh 79%. Latino 3%. Blk 9%. Native Am 2%. Asian 7%. Adv deg: 75%.
  Grad '11—36. Prep—33. (Wheeler 11, Moses Brown 9, Providence Co Day 6, Rocky Hill 2, Lincoln 1). Alum donors: 55%.
  Tui '12-'13: Day $22,260-26,745 (+$495). **Aid:** Need 124 ($1,429,000).
  Summer (enr 90): Rec. Tui Day $270/wk. 2 wks.
  Endow $6,800,000. Plant val $9,000,000. Acres 12. Bldgs 5. Class rms 29. Lib 20,000 vols. Sci labs 3. Art studios 2. Music studios 1. Gyms 1. Fields 2. Playgrounds 2. Ponds 1. Gardens 2. Comp labs 2.
  Est 1910. Nonprofit. Sem (Sept-June).

Dr. Helen West Cooke, a female pediatrician, founded this school for her son Gordon. The oldest independent, coeducational elementary school in the state, the school conducts a child-centered program for a diverse student population.

A rigorous, integrated and multicultural curriculum forms the basis for Gordon's academic program. The middle school (grades 5-8) provides an integrated math/science and humanities curriculum, as well as an individualized advisory program, leadership opportunities and community service. Spanish begins in kindergarten and is part of a more extensive middle school language program that also includes French.

Team sports commence in grade 5, and extended-day programs are available to all children. Each year, students in grade 8 travel to Georgia and Alabama as part of the civil rights curriculum. Then, in May, eighth graders devote three weeks to a service learning project.

LINCOLN SCHOOL
Day — Boys Gr PS (Age 3)-PS (Age 4), Girls PS (Age 3)-12

Providence, RI 02906. 301 Butler Ave. Tel: 401-331-9696. Fax: 401-751-6670.
Other locations: 160 Danforth St, Rehoboth, MA 02769.
  www.lincolnschool.org E-mail: info@lincolnschool.org
Julia Russell Eells, Head (2005). BA, William Smith College, MH, Wesleyan Univ. Jennifer Devine, Adm.
  Col Prep. AP (exams req'd; 120 taken, 73% 3+)—Eng Fr Lat Span Calc Stats Bio Chem Physics Eur_Hist US_Hist Art_Hist. **Feat**—Arabic Robotics Ethics Studio_Art Theater Chorus Music. **Supp**—Tut.
  Sports—G: Basket Crew X-country F_Hockey Lacrosse Soccer Squash Swim Tennis. **Activities:** 20.
  Selective adm: 82/yr. Appl fee: $50. Appl due: Feb. **Tests** ISEE SSAT.
  Enr 353. Elem 186. Sec 167. Nonwhite 19%. Avg class size: 13. Uniform. **Fac 70.** Adv deg: 67%.
  Grad '11—28. Col—28. (Geo Wash 3, Brown 2, Stonehill 2, Salve Regina 2, Johns Hopkins 1, Harvard 1). **Mid 50% SAT:** CR 540-680. M 520-650. W 560-710. **Col couns:**

1. Alum donors: 26%.
Tui '11-'12: Day $21,315-28,105 (+$500-1000). **Aid:** Need ($2,000,000).
Summer: Rec. Tui Day $175-300/wk. 10 wks.
Endow $7,000,000. Plant val $18,001,000. Bldgs 6. Class rms 36. 2 Libs 12,000 vols.
Labs 8. Art studios 3. Music studios 2. Gyms 2. Fields 3. Tennis courts 4.
Est 1884. Nonprofit. Religious Society of Friends. Sem (Sept-June). **Assoc** CLS NEASC.

The school, enrolling students from Rhode Island, Connecticut and Massachusetts, has long been noted for its strong academic program and commitment to Quaker values. Emphasis is on basic academics in preparation for college, with Advanced Placement courses available in most disciplines.

Lincoln has a 33-acre farm in Rehoboth, MA, with full athletic facilities and opportunities for indoor and outdoor learning projects. Expanded facilities, a computer arts studio, and a middle school guided-study program complement the basic curriculum. Athletic, science, public speaking, music, health, theater, world language, computer and art programs commence in the earliest grades, encouraging students with special interests in these fields.

MOSES BROWN SCHOOL
Day — Coed Gr PS (Age 3)-12

Providence, RI 02906. 250 Lloyd Ave. Tel: 401-831-7350. Fax: 401-455-0084.
www.mosesbrown.org   E-mail: administration@mosesbrown.org
Matt Glendinning, Head (2009). BA, Dartmouth College, MEd, Arcadia Univ, PhD, Univ of North Carolina-Chapel Hill. **Hugh Madden, Adm.**
Col Prep. AP—Eng Fr Lat Span Calc Stats Bio Chem Physics Comp_Govt & Pol. **Feat**—Chin Ital Russ Anat & Physiol Astron Environ_Sci Marine_Bio/Sci Engineering Meteorology Programming Robotics Women's_Hist Econ World_Relig Art_Hist Ceramics Painting Photog Studio_Art Acting Chorus Music_Theory. **Supp**—Tut.
Sports—Basket X-country Golf Indoor_Track Lacrosse Sail Soccer Squash Swim Tennis Track. B: Baseball Football Ice_Hockey Wrestling. G: F_Hockey Softball. **Activities:** 21.
Selective adm (Gr PS-11): 130/yr. Appl fee: $55. Appl due: Feb. Accepted: 38%. Yield: 75%. **Tests** ISEE SSAT.
Enr 765. Wh 84%. Latino 4%. Blk 3%. Native Am 1%. Asian 5%. Other 3%. Avg class size: 15. Stud/fac: 8:1. Casual. **Fac 97.** M 33/F 64. FT 82/PT 15. Wh 77%. Latino 5%. Blk 3%. Asian 3%. Other 12%. Adv deg: 73%.
Grad '11—91. Col—89. (Boston U, Brown, Georgetown, U of PA, Wash U, Vanderbilt). **Avg SAT:** CR 641. M 648. W 652. Avg ACT: 27. **Col couns:** 2.
Tui '11-'12: Day $24,920-28,385 (+$1002-1853). **Aid:** Need 230.
Summer: Enrich Rec. Sports. 1-9 wks.
Endow $16,000,000. Plant val $25,000,000. Acres 33. Bldgs 16. Class rms 90. 2 Libs 30,000 vols. Sci labs 8. Lang labs 2. Art studios 5. Music studios 4. Dance studios 1. Perf arts ctrs 1. Wood shops 1. Fields 8. Field houses 1. Comp/stud: 1:2.8.
Est 1784. Nonprofit. Religious Society of Friends. Sem (Sept-June). **Assoc** CLS NEASC.

Opened as Friends School in Portsmouth, this institution was reestablished in Providence in 1819 through the energy and generosity of Moses Brown, an influential Quaker whose family established Brown University. It was further endowed by his son, Obadiah, and the present name was adopted in 1904. The school remained coeducational until 1926, when the girls' department ceased operation. In 1976, girls were readmitted and the school reinstated coeducation.

The school has upper, middle and lower divisions. All students must meet basic requirements, but there are many electives and extracurricular activities available as well. Offerings include Advanced Placement courses in English, world languages, science and mathematics. A feature of the school's Quaker heritage is the requirement that every student complete a 40-hour community service project during the upper school years (grades 9-12). When appropriate, students in the upper school may also pursue independent study, and the senior projects program allows students to focus on independent inquiry and personal growth outside the classroom.

PROVIDENCE COUNTRY DAY SCHOOL
Day — Coed Gr 6-12

East Providence, RI 02914. 660 Waterman Ave. Tel: 401-438-5170. Fax: 401-435-4514.
www.providencecountryday.org
E-mail: admissions@providencecountryday.org
Vince Watchorn, Head (2011). Ashley Randlett, Adm.

Col Prep. AP (exams req'd; 122 taken)—Eng Lat Span Calc Bio US_Hist US_Govt & Pol Art_Hist. **Feat**—Creative_Writing Mythology Fr Astron Bioethics Forensic_Sci Comp_Design Comp_Sci Intl_Relations Photog Sculpt Printmaking Chorus Music Jazz_Ensemble Public_Speak. **Supp**—Dev_Read LD Rev Tut.

Sports (req'd)—Basket X-country Golf Indoor_Track Lacrosse Sail Soccer Swim Tennis Track. B: Baseball Football Ice_Hockey Wrestling.

Selective adm (Gr 6-11): 44/yr. Usual entry: 6 & 9. Appl fee: $55. Appl due: Feb. Applied: 142. Accepted: 82%. Yield: 44%. **Tests** CEEB ISEE SSAT.

Enr 215. Wh 85%. Latino 5%. Blk 4%. Asian 2%. Other 4%. Avg class size: 12. Stud/fac: 7:1. **Fac 41.** M 17/F 24. FT 38/PT 3. Adv deg: 63%.

Grad '10—47. Col—46. (CT Col 3, URI 3, Worcester Polytech 3, Colby 2, Gettysburg 2, Skidmore 2). **Col couns:** 1.

Tui '12-'13: Day $29,400-29,900 (+$800-1200). **Aid:** Need 102 ($1,489,000).

Endow $1,500,000. Plant val $10,000,000. Acres 18. Bldgs 6. Class rms 27. Lib 15,000 vols. Sci labs 4. Auds 1. Art studios 2. Music studios 1. Gyms 1. Fields 4. Field houses 1. Comp labs 2.

Est 1923. Nonprofit. Tri (Sept-June). **Assoc** CLS NEASC.

The school was founded by a group of business leaders, educators and parents who were interested in establishing a college preparatory school in a rural setting. Originally a boys' school, PCD first enrolled girls in the fall of 1991. In 1997, an extensive consolidation and building project culminated in the movement and subsequent renovation of two historic buildings (both erected in 1927) to the east side of campus. Several other plant improvements accompanied this building project.

Structured yet individualized in approach, both the middle school and the upper school follow a rigorous college preparatory program. An extensive selection of Advanced Placement and elective courses is available. In addition, PCD's curriculum features a broad selection of visual and performing arts classes, including instrumental ensemble offerings at the nearby Rhode Island Philharmonic School of Music. All students participate in athletics and the arts. Upper school boys and girls accumulate 45 hours of required community service prior to the start of senior year. All 12th graders take part in independent senior projects for four weeks in the spring.

Middle school pupils take a variety of off-campus trips, ranging in duration from two to five days, that emphasize experiential learning. While the school designs some experiences each year to complement course material or respond to student interest, PCD schedules others annually to provide benchmarks for learning and development.

WHEELER SCHOOL
Day — Coed Gr PS (Age 3)-12

Providence, RI 02906. 216 Hope St. Tel: 401-421-8100. Fax: 401-751-7674.
Other locations: 357 Walker St, Seekonk, MA 02771.
www.wheelerschool.org   E-mail: annadistefano@wheelerschool.org
Dan B. Miller, Head (2003). BA, Amherst College, MA, PhD, Harvard Univ. **Jeanette**

Epstein, Adm.
Col Prep. AP (exams req'd; 217 taken, 89% 3+)—Fr Span Calc Comp_Sci Bio Chem Environ_Sci US_Hist. **Feat**—Chin Anat & Physiol Engineering Psych Performing_ Arts Drama Music Handbells. **Supp**—Dev_Read LD Tut.
Sports—Basket X-country Indoor_Track Lacrosse Soccer Squash Tennis Track. B: Baseball Football Golf Ice_Hockey. G: F_Hockey Softball. **Activities:** 51.
Selective adm: 131/yr. Usual entry: K, 6 & 9. Appl fee: $60. Appl due: Jan. Applied: 320. Accepted: 72%. Yield: 58%. **Tests** ISEE SSAT.
Enr 801. B 433. G 368. Elem 484. Sec 317. Wh 79%. Latino 2%. Blk 3%. Asian 7%. Other 9%. Avg class size: 15. Stud/fac: 6:1. **Fac 130.** M 41/F 89. FT 127/PT 3. Wh 93%. Latino 2%. Asian 3%. Other 2%. Adv deg: 63%.
Grad '11—96. Col—95. (Boston Col 6, Brown 5, Vassar 3, Boston U 3, Columbia 2, Princeton 2). **Avg SAT:** CR 630. M 650. W 650. **Col couns:** 1. Alum donors: 18%.
Tui '12-'13: Day $26,640-28,960 (+$100-400). **Aid:** Need 172 ($2,586,213).
Summer (enr 441): Acad Enrich Rec. Tui Day $255/wk. 8 wks.
Endow $20,600,000. Plant val $43,051,000. Acres 135. Bldgs 12 (95% ADA). Class rms 85. 2 Libs 33,557 vols. Sci labs 8. Auds 1. Art studios 9. Music studios 6. Gyms 2. Fields 10. Courts 8. Pools 1. Comp labs 4. Comp/stud: 1:4.
Est 1889. Nonprofit. Quar (Sept-June). **Assoc** CLS NEASC.

The school bears the name of its founder, Mary Colman Wheeler, a leader in art and education in the early 1900s. The college preparatory program, which includes Advanced Placement courses in most academic areas, is further enriched by classes in music, art and theater and prepares graduates for success in college. The school strives to develop the individual talents of each student in a supportive educational atmosphere.

The traditional curriculum is supplemented at all levels by a variety of elective courses, special-interest activities and enrichment experiences. The school's computer center promotes the acquisition of computer skills at all levels of the instructional program. A substantial enrichment program features specially designed activities, games and studies several times per week. Qualified juniors may spend a semester studying overseas or in New York, Vermont or Colorado.

The Hamilton School at Wheeler, established in 1988, serves high-potential language-disabled students in grades 1-8. The curriculum is based on a structured, multisensory approach applied to reading, spelling, grammar and writing skills.

Wheeler owns a 120-acre farm a few miles east in Seekonk, MA. The farm houses athletic fields and facilities and serves as a summer camp location.

VERMONT

BURLINGTON, VT. (186 mi. NW of Boston, MA) Urban. Pop: 38,889. Alt: 113 ft.

ROCK POINT SCHOOL
Bdg and Day — Coed Gr 9-PG

Burlington, VT 05408. 1 Rock Point Rd. Tel: 802-863-1104. Fax: 802-863-6628.
www.rockpoint.org   E-mail: ledson@rockpoint.org
Camillo J. Spirito, Head (2011). BA, MEd, St Michael's College. **Hillary Kramer, Adm.**
    Col Prep. Gen Acad. LD. Underachiever. Feat—20th-Century_Lit Photog Studio_Art Animation Stained_Glass Theater. **Supp**—Dev_Read Makeup Rem_Math Rem_ Read Rev Tut. Outdoor ed.
    Activities: 10.
    Selective adm (Gr 9-12): 16/yr. Bdg 13. Day 3. Appl fee: $50. Appl due: Rolling. Accepted: 70%. Yield: 90%. **Tests** IQ.
    Enr 40. B 17. G 23. Wh 91%. Latino 3%. Asian 6%. Avg class size: 10. Casual. **Fac 8.** M 2/F 6. FT 5/PT 3. Wh 100%. Adv deg: 37%.
    Grad '10—11. Col—10. (Champlain 2, Burlington Col 1, Hartwick 1, Knox 1, McDaniel 1, U of CA-Santa Cruz 1). **Avg SAT:** CR 560. M 500. W 500. Alum donors: 10%.
    Tui '11-'12: Bdg $51,000 (+$500). **Day $26,000. Aid:** Need 9 ($140,000).
    Endow $1,600,000. Plant val $5,300,000. Acres 150. Bldgs 2. Dorms 2. Dorm rms 29. Class rms 6. Lib 3000 vols. Sci labs 1. Art studios 2. Fields 1. Courts 1. Comp labs 1. Comp/stud: 1:2.5.
    Est 1928. Nonprofit. Episcopal. Quar (Sept-June). **Assoc** NEASC.

Rock Point conducts a high school program for students of average to above-average intelligence who stand to benefit from the structure and personal contact available in a small-school environment. The school places particular emphasis on the arts and community service. A senior seminar assists boys and girls with college placement and applications.

The 150-acre campus is situated on a peninsula in Lake Champlain, about one mile from the center of the city. Rock Point stresses accountability and work within the school community: Students attend frequently scheduled school meetings and meet with an advisor for 40 minutes once a week. Prominent evening and weekend offerings include trips to Montreal, Canada, and Boston, MA, as well as an off-campus outdoor program that features hiking, camping, cross-country skiing, snowboarding, and local music and sporting event attendance.

DORSET, VT. (54 mi. NE of Albany, NY; 123 mi. WNW of Boston, MA) Rural. Pop: 2036. Alt: 899 ft.

LONG TRAIL SCHOOL
Day — Coed Gr 6-12

Dorset, VT 05251. 1045 Kirby Hollow Rd. Tel: 802-867-5717. Fax: 802-867-0147.
www.longtrailschool.org   E-mail: lts@longtrailschool.org
John H. Suitor III, Head (2008). BA, Univ of Vermont, MA, Georgetown Univ. **Courtney M. Callo, Adm.**
    Col Prep. IB Diploma. AP (exams req'd)—Eng Span Calc Stats Environ_Sci US_Hist Psych Studio_Art. **Feat**—Creative_Writing Mythology Fr Programming Web_Design Econ Law Pol_Sci Architect Art_Hist Ceramics Drawing Painting Photog Sculpt Acting Theater_Arts Music Music_Theory. **Supp**—Dev_Read ESL LD Makeup Rem_Math

Rem_Read Rev Tut.
Sports—Golf Ski Soccer Tennis. B: Baseball. G: Softball. **Activities:** 19.
Somewhat selective adm: 48/yr. Appl fee: $75. Appl due: Rolling. Accepted: 91%.
Enr 166. Elem 77. Sec 89. Wh 93%. Latino 3%. Blk 1%. Asian 3%. Avg class size: 10.
     Stud/fac: 6:1. Casual. **Fac 32.** M 13/F 19. FT 20/PT 12. Adv deg: 50%.
Grad '11—15. Col—15. (Clarkson, Colgate, Davidson, Middlebury, Rochester Inst of
     Tech, Williams). **Mid 50% SAT:** CR 550-640. M 480-630. W 510-600. Mid 50% ACT:
     23-28. **Col couns:** 1.
Tui '12-'13: Day $16,500 (+$500-1100).
Summer: Gr PS-9. Acad Rec. Arts. Drama. 2 wks.
Endow $5,000,000. Plant val $10,000,000. Acres 14. Bldgs 1. Class rms 21. Lib 8000
     vols. Sci labs 3. Theaters 1. Art studios 3. Music studios 2. Dance studios 1. Gyms 1.
     Fields 2. Comp labs 2.
Est 1975. Nonprofit. Sem (Sept-June). **Assoc** NEASC.

LTS features small-group instruction and maintains a family-like environment. Each student completes a common core of subjects in the disciplines of English, math, science, social studies and world languages during each year of attendance. Requirements also include participation in Arts Core, a two-year overview of the dramatic, musical and visual arts, and Connections, a multidisciplinary course that focuses on critical thinking and knowledge acquisition. A wide selection of Advanced Placement classes provides additional challenge, as does the two-year International Baccalaureate Diploma Program. All boys and girls perform at least eight hours of community service each year.

The LTS community convenes for a morning meeting four days a week, and for three or four days each fall the entire student body and faculty participate in a team-building experience off campus that emphasizes cooperation, teamwork, trust and self-confidence. A limited number of students with learning disabilities enroll each year. International students in grades 9-12 may board with local host families.

PUTNEY, VT. (68 mi. ENE of Albany, NY; 88 mi. WNW of Boston, MA) Rural. Pop: 2634. Alt: 251 ft.

THE GRAMMAR SCHOOL

Day — Coed Gr PS (Age 3)-8

Putney, VT 05346. 69 Hickory Ridge Rd S. Tel: 802-387-5364. Fax: 802-387-4744.
     www.thegrammarschool.org   E-mail: tgs@thegrammarschool.org
Steve Lorenz, Head (2006). BA, Univ of Dayton, MS, Long Island Univ. **Philip Blood,**
     Adm.
     Pre-Prep. Feat—Lib_Skills Fr Span Computers Studio_Art Drama Music Study_Skills.
        Supp—Tut.
     Sports—X-country Ski Soccer.
     Selective adm: 26/yr. Appl fee: $30. Appl due: Mar. Applied: 48. Accepted: 79%. Yield:
        80%.
     Enr 119. B 53. G 66. Wh 91%. Latino 2%. Blk 3%. Asian 3%. Other 1%. Avg class size:
        12. Stud/fac: 8:1. **Fac 26.** M 7/F 19. FT 14/PT 12. Wh 100%. Adv deg: 50%.
     Grad '11—15. Prep—11. (VT Acad 7, Northfield Mt Hermon 3, Putney 3).
     Tui '12-'13: Day $12,450-16,250 (+$40-575). **Aid:** Need 49 ($189,000).
     Summer (enr 45): Enrich Rec. Arts. Tui Day $185-280/wk. 4 wks.
     Endow $200,000. Plant val $1,003,000. Acres 60. Bldgs 3. Class rms 9. Lib 9000 vols.
        Art studios 1. Music studios 1. Fields 2. Comp labs 1. Laptop prgm Gr 5-8.
     Est 1960. Nonprofit. Tri (Sept-June). **Assoc** NEASC.

The curriculum prepares students for secondary school by emphasizing language arts; history; geography; the physical, environmental and life sciences; and mathematics. The visual and performing arts, computer literacy and physical skills development are also incorporated. In addition, French is taught in grades K-8 and Spanish in grades 6-8.

TGS utilizes the rural and recreational assets of southern Vermont extensively.

THE GREENWOOD SCHOOL

Bdg and Day — Boys Gr 6-11

Putney, VT 05346. 14 Greenwood Ln. Tel: 802-387-4545. Fax: 802-387-5396.
www.greenwood.org   E-mail: admissions@greenwood.org
Stewart Miller, Head (2004). Melanie Miller, Adm.
   Gen Acad. LD. Feat—Computers Studio_Art Music Speech Metal_Shop Woodworking.
      Supp—Dev_Read ESL Rem_Math Rem_Read Tut. Outdoor ed.
   Sports—Basket Soccer. B: Baseball.
   Selective adm: 12/yr. Bdg 12. Day 0. Appl fee: $75. Appl due: Rolling. Applied: 65.
      Accepted: 60%. Yield: 85%. **Tests** IQ.
   Enr 47. Bdg 42. Day 5. Wh 92%. Latino 2%. Asian 4%. Other 2%. Intl 5%. Avg class size:
      4. Stud/fac: 2:1. Casual. **Fac 29.** FT 22/PT 7. Adv deg: 82%. In dorms 7.
   Grad '11—11. Prep—8. (Eagle Hill-MA 4, Brewster 2, Dublin 1, Brehm Prep 1).
   Tui '11-'12: Bdg $65,870 (+$2000). **Day $50,400** (+$300). **Aid:** Need 5 ($249,290).
      Endow $840,000. Plant val $3,226,000. Acres 100. Bldgs 17 (100% ADA). Dorms 1.
      Dorm rms 18. Class rms 19. Lib 5500 vols. Art studios 1. Music studios 1. Gyms 1.
      Fields 1. Comp/stud: 1:1. Laptop prgm Gr 6-11.
   Est 1978. Nonprofit. Tri (Sept-June). **Assoc** NEASC.

Greenwood's program is designed to help boys of average to above-average intelligence overcome such learning differences as dyslexia, attentional disorders and executive functioning deficits. Instruction combines individualized remedial programming with enrichment. The school presents course work in the traditional subject areas in a manner that enables students to practice literary skills and organizational strategies across the curriculum; the residential life skills program further reinforces these strategies outside the classroom. Support services include occupational therapy, social pragmatics and speech therapy.

Greenwood's 100-acre, forested campus provides boys with athletic and recreational opportunities in soccer, baseball, downhill and cross-country skiing, rock climbing, ice skating, fishing, canoeing, mountain biking and skateboarding, among others.   **See Also Page 136**

THE PUTNEY SCHOOL

Bdg and Day — Coed Gr 9-12

Putney, VT 05346. Elm Lea Farm, 418 Houghton Brook Rd. Tel: 802-387-6219.
   Fax: 802-387-6278.
   www.putneyschool.org   E-mail: info@putneyschool.org
Emily H. Jones, Dir (2007). AB, Harvard Univ, MA, Yale Univ. **Richard H. Cowan, Adm.**
   Col Prep. Feat—Creative_Writing Poetry Shakespeare Fr Span Stats Anat & Physiol
      Astron Ecol Environ_Sci Forensic_Sci Genetics Comp_Sci African_Hist Middle_East-
      ern_Hist Lat-Amer_Hist Econ Comp_Relig Philos Ceramics Drawing Painting Photog
      Sculpt Printmaking Drama Music Dance. **Supp**—ESL Rev Tut. Sat classes.
   Sports—Basket Crew X-country Lacrosse Ski Soccer Ultimate_Frisbee.
   Somewhat selective adm (Bdg Gr 9-12; Day 9-11): 77/yr. Bdg 62. Day 15. Usual entry:
      9. Appl fee: $50. Appl due: Jan. Applied: 126. Accepted: 85%. Yield: 65%. **Tests** SSAT
      TOEFL.
   Enr 220. B 97. G 123. Bdg 169. Day 51. Wh 86%. Latino 5%. Blk 5%. Native Am 1%.
      Asian 3%. Intl 21%. Stud/fac: 6:1. **Fac 42.** M 20/F 22. FT 29/PT 13. Adv deg: 69%.
      In dorms 19.
   Grad '11—39. Col—37. (Goucher 3, U of VT 3, New Sch U 2, Hampshire 2, Sarah Law-
      rence 2, Savannah Col of Art & Design 2). **Avg SAT:** CR 637. M 559. Avg ACT: 25.
   Col couns: 2. Alum donors: 29%.

Tui '12-'13: Bdg $46,900 (+$1500-2000). **Day $29,900** (+$1500). **Aid:** Need 88 ($2,200,000).
Summer: Arts. ESL. Farm. Writing. Tui Bdg $3900-7200. Tui Day $1375-2350. 3-6 wks.
Endow $14,000,000. Plant val $18,000,000. Acres 500. Bldgs 37. Dorms 9. Dorm rms 95. Class rms 32. Lib 26,000 vols. Sci labs 3. Auds 1. Theaters 1. Art studios 7. Music studios 14. Dance studios 1. Arts ctrs 1. Fields 3. Field houses 1. Riding rings 2. Stables 1. Weight rms 1. Greenhouses 2. Sugarhouses 1. Barns 2. Comp labs 1.
Est 1935. Nonprofit. Sem (Sept-June). **Assoc** NEASC.

"To make school life a more real, less sheltered, less self-centered venture; to educate the individual in the light of what he can later do toward solving the problems of society" was Carmelita Hinton's vision in opening this preparatory school. Vigorous, dynamic, broad-visioned, unsparing of her energy, Mrs. Hinton selected her faculty, including many specialists in the arts, from outstanding progressive and conservative schools and colleges in this country and in Europe.

Through small, seminar-style classes, Putney offers students opportunities for acceleration and for independence in academic pursuits. The curriculum is complemented by a Vermont farm experience, an outdoor program with competitive and noncompetitive sports, and opportunities in the arts. The wide range of student activities includes an evening activity period two times a week during which students learn about such subjects as jewelry making, blacksmithing, jazz, chamber music, African drumming, photography, pottery, weaving and woodworking.

Every student participates in the work program, rotating through jobs in the kitchen, the barns, the dairy, the forest, the gardens and other sites on campus. The school community is, in many ways, self-sustaining, producing much of its own food, firewood and lumber.

ST. JOHNSBURY, VT. (153 mi. NNW of Boston, MA) Rural. Pop: 6319. Alt: 711 ft.

ST. JOHNSBURY ACADEMY

Bdg — Coed Gr 9-PG; Day — Coed 9-12

St Johnsbury, VT 05819. 1000 Main St, PO Box 906. Tel: 802-751-2130.
Fax: 802-748-5463.
www.stjohnsburyacademy.org   E-mail: hilltoppers@stjacademy.org
Thomas W. Lovett, Head. BA, Providence College, AM, Brown Univ. Mary Ann Gessner, Adm.
  Col Prep. Voc. Bus. LD. Underachiever. AP (exams req'd; 281 taken, 82% 3+)—Eng Fr Japan Span Calc Stats Comp_Sci Bio Chem Environ_Sci Physics Eur_Hist US_ Hist Psych US_Govt & Pol Studio_Art Music_Theory. **Feat**—Creative_Writing Chin Lat Multivariable_Calc Anat & Physiol Astron Forensic_Sci Genetics Engineering Robotics Web_Design Philos Photog Acting Theater Dance Accounting Journ Drafting Culinary_Arts Nutrition. **Supp**—Dev_Read ESL Rem_Math Tut.
  Sports—Basket X-country Golf Indoor_Track Lacrosse Ski Soccer Tennis Track Ultimate_Frisbee. B: Baseball Football Ice_Hockey Wrestling. G: Cheer F_Hockey Gymnastics Softball. **Activities:** 63.
  Somewhat selective adm: 331/yr. Bdg 122. Day 209. Appl fee: $20. Appl due: Rolling. Accepted: 89%. Yield: 85%. **Tests** SSAT TOEFL.
  Enr 889. Bdg 248. Day 641. Sec 888. PG 1. Wh 75%. Latino 5%. Blk 2%. Native Am 1%. Asian 12%. Other 5%. Intl 18%. Avg class size: 12. Stud/fac: 10:1. Formal. **Fac 115.** M 65/F 50. FT 115. Wh 94%. Latino 2%. Blk 1%. Asian 3%. Adv deg: 66%. In dorms 26.
  Grad '10—260. **Col**—223. (U of VT 20, Lyndon St 19, U of WI-Madison 5, UNH 5, Purdue 5, Rochester Inst of Tech 3). **Avg SAT:** CR 516. M 550. **Col couns:** 5.
  Tui '12-'13: Bdg $44,700. Day $14,570. Aid: Need 39 ($782,900).
  Summer: Acad. ESL. Tui Bdg $5900. 6 wks.

Endow $14,000,000. Plant val $60,000,000. Acres 142. Bldgs 28. Dorms 9. Dorm rms 91. Class rms 85. Lib 20,000 vols. Sci labs 7. Lang labs 2. Auds 1. Theaters 2. Music studios 2. Dance studios 1. Gyms 2. Fields 6. Courts 4. Field houses 1. Pools 1. Comp labs 5. Comp/stud: 1:3.
Est 1842. Nonprofit. Sem (Aug-June). **Assoc** NEASC.

This old New England academy was founded by Erastus, Joseph and Thaddeus (inventor of the platform scale) Fairbanks to provide intellectual, moral and religious training for their own children and those of the community. Since then, the academy has provided a secondary education to youth of the northeastern Vermont area through its day school and to students from all over the world through its boarding program. It presently occupies a campus of 142 acres.

A comprehensive high school, the academy offers courses for students of all levels of ability, including remedial education and Advanced Placement work. In all academic courses, students are grouped according to ability. Graduates go on to attend colleges throughout the US and Canada.

The academy also maintains a technical education department that offers courses in electricity/electronics, construction trades, drafting, forestry and culinary arts, each in a two-year sequence. All of these programs incorporate hands-on experiences in real-world projects; the construction trades class annually builds a house.

SAXTONS RIVER, VT. (73 mi. ENE of Albany, NY; 94 mi. NW of Boston, MA) Rural. Pop: 519. Alt: 528 ft.

VERMONT ACADEMY
Bdg and Day — Coed Gr 9-PG

Saxtons River, VT 05154. 10 Long Walk, PO Box 500. Tel: 802-869-6229.
  Fax: 802-869-6242.
  www.vermontacademy.org   E-mail: admissions@vermontacademy.org
Sean P. Brennan, Head (2009). BA, MA, Middlebury College. **David Hodgson, Adm.**
  Col Prep. AP—Eng Fr Span Calc Stats Bio Chem Environ_Sci. **Feat**—British_Lit Poetry Women's_Lit Lat Russ Astron Bioethics Kinesiology Organic_Chem Comp_Design Programming Holocaust Econ Psych Women's_Stud Architect Art_Hist Filmmaking Graphic_Arts Photog Studio_Art Music_Theory Jazz_Ensemble Ballet Dance Jazz_Dance Public_Speak Study_Skills. **Supp**—ESL LD Rev Tut. Outdoor ed. Sat classes.
  Sports (req'd)—Basket Crew X-country Equestrian Golf Ice_Hockey Lacrosse Ski Soccer Tennis Track. B: Baseball Football. G: F_Hockey Softball.
  Selective adm: 94/yr. Appl fee: $50. Appl due: Feb. Applied: 369. Accepted: 65%. Yield: 40%. **Tests** CEEB CTP_4 IQ ISEE MAT MRT SSAT Stanford TOEFL.
  Enr 225. B 135. G 90. Bdg 180. Day 45. Sec 215. PG 10. Wh 90%. Latino 5%. Blk 5%. Intl 21%. Avg class size: 11. Stud/fac: 7:1. Casual. **Fac 46.** M 25/F 21. FT 41/PT 5. Wh 92%. Latino 2%. Native Am 2%. Other 4%. Adv deg: 41%. In dorms 22.
  Grad '10—66. Col—65. (U of VT 3, St Lawrence 3, Suffolk 3, U of IL-Urbana 2, UNH 2, New England Col 2). **Avg SAT:** CR 500. M 542. W 488. Avg ACT: 22. **Col couns:** 2. Alum donors: 15%.
  Tui '12-'13: Bdg $45,600 (+$2500). **Day $25,800** (+$1000). **Intl Bdg $47,100** (+$2500).
  Aid: Need 75 ($1,200,000).
  Endow $7,300,000. Plant val $44,000,000. Acres 515. Bldgs 25 (25% ADA). Dorms 10. Dorm rms 155. Class rms 32. Lib 14,000 vols. Sci labs 3. Observatories 1. Auds 1. Art studios 4. Music studios 6. Perf arts ctrs 1. Gyms 1. Fields 7. Courts 6. Rinks 1. Ropes crses 1. Skiing facilities. Comp labs 1.
  Est 1876. Nonprofit. Sem (Sept-May). **Assoc** CLS NEASC.

Located on a 515-acre campus, this nationally known college preparatory institution serves primarily as a boarding school. High-achieving pupils may enroll in VA's honors courses, while students who need extra help may, for an additional fee, take part in a learning skills program that emphasizes study skills. The academy maintains small classes and a low student-teacher ratio. Senior seminars allow students to pursue independent projects while working with faculty and adults outside of VA. Laptop computers are available for lease and a wireless Internet network connects all campus buildings.

A full complement of activities and athletics serves pupils at all levels of ability. All boys and girls take part in competitive athletics at least two seasons per year; for the third, students may instead participate in an activity such as photography, drama, community service, rock climbing, mountain biking, silversmithing or outdoor challenge.

Middle Atlantic States

DELAWARE

MIDDLETOWN, DE. (22 mi. SSW of Wilmington, DE; 49 mi. SW of Philadelphia, PA) Suburban. Pop: 6161. Alt: 67 ft.

ST. ANDREW'S SCHOOL
Bdg — Coed Gr 9-12

Middletown, DE 19709. 350 Noxontown Rd. Tel: 302-285-4231. Fax: 302-285-4275.
www.standrews-de.org   E-mail: dfagan@standrews-de.org
Daniel T. Roach, Jr., Head (1997). BA, Williams College, MA, Middlebury College. **Louisa H. Zendt, Adm.**

Col Prep. Feat—Creative_Writing Chin Fr Greek Lat Span Calc Stats Multivariable_ Calc Environ_Sci Comp_Sci E_Asian_Hist Middle_Eastern_Hist Amer_Stud Global_ Stud Philos World_Relig Art_Hist Ceramics Film Photog Studio_Art Drama Music Music_Theory. Sat classes.

Sports—Basket Crew X-country Lacrosse Soccer Squash Swim Tennis. B: Baseball Football Wrestling. G: F_Hockey Volley. **Activities:** 25.

Selective adm (Gr 9-11): 81/yr. Appl fee: $50. Appl due: Jan. Applied: 464. Accepted: 28%. Yield: 62%. **Tests** SSAT TOEFL.

Enr 295. B 156. G 139. Wh 69%. Latino 3%. Blk 13%. Asian 15%. Intl 13%. Avg class size: 11. Stud/fac: 5:1. **Fac 78.** M 46/F 32. FT 78. Wh 90%. Latino 1%. Blk 5%. Asian 2%. Other 2%. Adv deg: 64%. In dorms 24.

Grad '11—68. Col—68. (Davidson, Haverford, Williams, Boston Col, U of DE, Franklin & Marshall). **Avg SAT:** CR 629. M 647. W 625. **Mid 50% SAT:** CR 580-680. M 600-700. W 570-680. **Col couns:** 5. Alum donors: 39%.

Tui '11-'12: Bdg $47,000 (+$1500). **Aid:** Need 129 ($4,504,050).

Endow $170,000,000. Plant val $63,000,000. Acres 2200. Bldgs 12. Dorms 6. Dorm rms 144. Class rms 28. Lib 35,000 vols. Chapels 1. Sci labs 3. Lang labs 1. Theaters 1. Music studios 6. Arts ctrs 1. Gyms 2. Fields 11. Tennis courts 17. Squash courts 5. Pools 1. Weight rms 1. Boathouses 1. Gardens 1. Comp labs 4. Comp/stud: 1:3.

Est 1930. Nonprofit. Episcopal. Sem (Sept-May). **Assoc** MSA.

Founded and endowed by Alexis Felix Du Pont, this Episcopal school is situated on 2200 acres of wetlands, farmland and forestland. Rev. Walden Pell, a St. Mark's graduate, headmaster from the founding, developed sound scholarship and a loyal following during his administration.

St. Andrew's offers its students a rigorous and varied college preparatory program that sends graduates to leading colleges. The traditional curriculum includes theater, studio art, music and advanced electives in the sciences, history, computer science and mathematics. Although courses are not labeled as Advanced Placement, advanced study options in most subjects prepare students for AP exams. Advanced topics tutorials are individualized and often student-directed courses allowing further advanced study in particular disciplines. Reading- and writing-intensive spring tutorials, designed by faculty for three or fewer sixth form students, more closely approximate the collegiate academic experience.

WILMINGTON, DE. (28 mi. SW of Philadelphia, PA) Urban. Pop: 72,664. Alt: 134 ft. Area also includes Claymont and Hockessin.

ARCHMERE ACADEMY
Day — Coed Gr 9-12

Claymont, DE 19703. 3600 Philadelphia Pike. Tel: 302-798-6632. Fax: 302-798-7290.
www.archmereacademy.com   E-mail: jjordan@archmereacademy.org
Michael A. Marinelli, Head (2010). EdD, Wilmington College (DE). **William J. Doyle, Prin.** BS, West Chester Univ, MEd, Univ of Delaware, EdD, Widener Univ. **John J. Jordan, Adm.**

Col Prep. AP (exams req'd; 361 taken, 88% 3+)—Eng Fr Ger Span Calc Stats Bio Chem Environ_Sci Physics Eur_Hist US_Hist World_Hist Studio_Art. **Feat**—British_Lit Creative_Writing Women's_Lit Anat & Physiol Astron Botany Ecol Forensic_Sci Marine_Bio/Sci Biotech Electronics Engineering Programming Robotics Cold_War Econ Law Psych Global_Stud World_Relig Architect Ceramics Drawing Painting Photog Sculpt Watercolor Chorus Music_Theory Finance Speech Driver_Ed. **Supp**—Tut.

Sports—Basket X-country Golf Ice_Hockey Lacrosse Soccer Swim Tennis Track. B: Baseball Football Wrestling. G: F_Hockey Softball Volley. **Activities:** 46.

Selective adm (Gr 9-11): 118/yr. Appl fee: $35. Appl due: Dec. Yield: 70%.

Enr 476. Wh 90%. Latino 2%. Blk 2%. Asian 6%. Avg class size: 15. Stud/fac: 10:1. Uniform. **Fac 60.** M 33/F 27. FT 60. Adv deg: 80%.

Grad '11—115. Col—115. (U of DE 19, PA St 6, St Joseph's U 6, U of Pittsburgh 6, NYU 5, Drexel 5). **Avg SAT:** CR 614. M 600. W 632. **Mid 50% SAT:** CR 560-670. M 540-660. W 580-680. **Col couns:** 2. Alum donors: 14%.

Tui '11-'12: Day $21,825 (+$1100-1600). **Aid:** Need 175 ($990,000).

Endow $9,500,000. Plant val $32,700,000. Acres 35. Bldgs 5. Class rms 34. Lib 12,000 vols. Sci labs 6. Lang labs 1. Auds 1. Art studios 4. Music studios 2. Perf arts ctrs 1. Gyms 2. Fields 6. Courts 6. Weight rms 1. Comp labs 3. Comp/stud: 1:5.

Est 1932. Nonprofit. Roman Catholic. Sem (Sept-June). **Assoc** MSA.

Founded by the Norbertine Fathers, Archmere is situated on a 35-acre campus. Pupils fulfill graduation requirements in foreign language, religion, speech and electives, and Advanced Placement courses are available. The science department occupies a separate facility containing six laboratory classrooms, a two-story physics lab with frictionless tables, a greenhouse and more than 60 computers with wireless Internet access. Archmere has organized field study trips to such locations as Costa Rica, Kenya and Fiji.

SANFORD SCHOOL
Day — Coed Gr PS (Age 4)-12

Hockessin, DE 19707. 6900 Lancaster Pike, PO Box 888. Tel: 302-239-5263. Fax: 302-239-5389.
www.sanfordschool.org   E-mail: admission@sanfordschool.org
Mark J. Anderson, Head (2011). BS, Univ of Missouri-Columbia, MA, Maryville Univ. **Andrew R. N. Walpole, Adm.**

Col Prep. AP (exams req'd; 110 taken, 85% 3+)—Eng Fr Lat Span Calc Stats Comp_Sci Bio Chem Environ_Sci Physics US_Hist World_Hist Studio_Art. **Feat**—Creative_Writing Anat & Physiol Ecol Web_Design Civil_War Anthro Econ Law Psych Photog Music Public_Speak.

Sports—Basket X-country Indoor_Track Lacrosse Soccer Swim Tennis. B: Baseball Golf Wrestling. G: F_Hockey Volley. **Activities:** 25.

Somewhat selective adm: 77/yr. Usual entry: PS, K & 9. Appl fee: $40. Appl due: Rolling. Applied: 160. Accepted: 85%. Yield: 56%. **Tests** CTP_4 ISEE SSAT.

Enr 575. B 271. G 304. Elem 351. Sec 224. Wh 75%. Latino 2%. Blk 10%. Asian 4%. Other 9%. Intl 5%. Avg class size: 15. Stud/fac: 12:1. **Fac 71.** Wh 94%. Latino 4%.

Blk 2%.
Grad '10—54. Col—54. (U of DE 13, Lynchburg 3, Cornell 2, Elizabethtown 2, Gettysburg 2, Randolph Col 2). Athl schol 1. **Mid 50% SAT:** CR 520-650. M 530-640. W 500-650. **Col couns:** 2. Alum donors: 15%.
Tui '11-'12: Day $14,000-22,000 (+$300-600). **Aid:** Need 160 ($1,400,000).
Summer: Acad Enrich Rev Rec. Tui Day $225-375/crse. 2-6 wks.
Endow $7,600,000. Plant val $25,000,000. Acres 93. Bldgs 15. Class rms 58. 3 Libs 32,000 vols. Sci labs 6. Art studios 7. Music studios 3. Gyms 2. Fields 6. Courts 9. Pools 1. Comp labs 7.
Est 1930. Nonprofit. Tri (Sept-June). **Assoc** CLS MSA.

Founded as a boarding school by Ellen Q. Sawin, Sanford made the transition to a day school in the late 1970s. A capital campaign established in 2000 enabled the school to complete significant renovation and new construction on the 93-acre campus in the ensuing years.

The liberal arts college preparatory curriculum features a world languages program that commences in junior kindergarten, humanities, studio and performing arts, an individualized reading program in the lower school, history, mathematics, sciences, computer science and Advanced Placement courses. An extensive athletic program and various other extracurricular options complement academics.

TATNALL SCHOOL

Day — Coed Gr PS (Age 3)-12

Wilmington, DE 19807. 1501 Barley Mill Rd. Tel: 302-892-4285. **Fax:** 302-892-4387.
www.tatnall.org   E-mail: admissions@tatnall.org
Eric G. Ruoss, Head (1996). BA, Ursinus College, MDiv, Union Theological Seminary, MSEd, Iona College, PhD, Univ of Virginia. **Eric S. Peters, Adm.**
Col Prep. AP (136 exams taken, 93% 3+)—Eng Fr Lat Span Calc Stats Bio Environ_Sci Physics Eur_Hist US_Hist Psych. **Feat**—Humanities Shakespeare Multivariable_Calc Astron Botany Microbio Electronics Comp_Sci Vietnam_War Govt Native_Amer_Stud Ceramics Drawing Sculpt Drama Theater_Arts Chorus Music. **Supp**—Rev Tut.
Sports—Basket X-country Indoor_Track Lacrosse Soccer Swim Tennis Track. B: Baseball Football Golf Ice_Hockey Wrestling. G: F_Hockey Volley.
Selective adm (Gr PS-11): 78/yr. Appl fee: $40. Appl due: Jan. Applied: 239. Accepted: 67%. Yield: 50%. **Tests** CTP_4 ISEE SSAT.
Enr 640. B 322. G 318. Elem 386. Sec 254. Wh 85%. Latino 1%. Blk 8%. Asian 2%. Other 4%. Intl 5%. Avg class size: 11. Stud/fac: 11:1. **Fac 88.** M 25/F 63. FT 81/PT 7. Wh 93%. Blk 5%. Asian 1%. Other 1%.
Grad '09—70. Col—70. (U of DE 19, U of CO-Boulder 2, Loyola Col 2, Yale 2, Villanova 2, Lynn 2). Athl schol 3. **Avg SAT:** CR 580. M 593. W 594. **Col couns:** 2.
Tui '12-'13: Day $17,400-24,400 (+$200-400). **Aid:** Need 136 ($1,644,168).
Summer: Enrich Rec. 2-6 wks.
Endow $17,000,000. Plant val $31,000,000. Acres 110. Bldgs 4 (100% ADA). Class rms 60. 3 Libs 38,000 vols. Sci labs 8. Theaters 2. Art studios 5. Music studios 4. Gyms 3. Fields 12. Courts 8. Pools 4. Comp labs 5.
Est 1930. Nonprofit. Tri (Sept-June). **Assoc** CLS MSA.

The school, founded by Frances D. S. Tatnall in her home, moved in 1952 to its present 110-acre, wooded campus. The broad liberal arts curriculum is college preparatory and is enriched by public speaking, computer science, foreign languages, community service and athletics. Honors and Advanced Placement courses are available in many subjects. Tatnall places particular emphasis on the arts, with students of all ages taking part in a program that combines exposure, instruction and participation. Upper schoolers take a service learning course, then complete a compulsory, 40-hour community service project prior to graduation. Junior and senior students may complete a professional internship in the field of their choice as an elective.

Boys and girls of all ability levels choose from a wide selection of interscholastic sports, and various other activities are also available. In addition, the school operates a year-round extended-day program.

TOWER HILL SCHOOL
Day — Coed Gr PS (Age 3)-12

Wilmington, DE 19806. 2813 W 17th St. Tel: 302-575-0550. Fax: 302-657-8366.
www.towerhill.org   E-mail: thinfo@towerhill.org
Christopher D. Wheeler, Head (2005). BA, Univ of the Arts, MA, PhD, State Univ of New York-Stony Brook. **Kelly M. Deshane, Adm.**
Col Prep. AP exams taken: 57 (93% 3+). Feat—British_Lit Creative_Writing Shakespeare Russ_Lit Fr Lat Span Calc Anat Environ_Sci Engineering Web_Design Vietnam_War Psych Art_Hist Drawing Filmmaking Painting Photog Sculpt Studio_Art Acting Chorus Music_Theory Woodworking.
Sports (req'd)—Basket X-country Golf Indoor_Track Lacrosse Soccer Swim Tennis Track. B: Baseball Football Wrestling. G: F_Hockey Volley. **Activities:** 32.
Selective adm (Gr PS-11): 93/yr. Usual entry: PS, K, 5 & 9. Appl fee: $40. Appl due: Jan. Applied: 223. Accepted: 64%. Yield: 64%. **Tests** CTP_4 IQ SSAT.
Enr 753. B 373. G 380. Elem 517. Sec 236. Wh 80%. Latino 1%. Blk 7%. Asian 9%. Other 3%. Avg class size: 16. Stud/fac: 7:1. Casual. **Fac 97.** M 39/F 58. FT 94/PT 3. Wh 96%. Latino 2%. Blk 2%. Adv deg: 52%.
Grad '11—55. Col—55. (U of DE 9, Am U 4, Lehigh 3, Stanford 2, Columbia 2, Boston Col 2). **Avg SAT:** CR 627. M 651. W 639. Avg ACT: 28.4. **Col couns:** 1. Alum donors: 24%.
Tui '12-'13: Day $13,425-25,675 (+$870-1280). **Aid:** Merit 8 ($30,000). Need 136 ($1,742,042).
Summer (enr 220): Acad Enrich Rev. Sports. Tui Day $175/wk. 9 wks.
Endow $30,275,000. Plant val $33,495,000. Acres 45. Bldgs 5 (50% ADA). Class rms 30. 2 Libs 24,000 vols. Sci labs 7. Lang labs 1. Auds 1. Theaters 1. Art studios 6. Music studios 3. Dance studios 1. Arts ctrs 1. Gyms 2. Fields 6. Courts 8. Field houses 1. Tracks 2. Comp labs 4. Comp/stud: 1:2.
Est 1919. Nonprofit. Quar (Sept-June). **Assoc** CLS MSA.

Tower Hill's strong college preparatory program includes accelerated courses, various electives and a technology component. In addition to academic work, all upper schoolers complete a community service project. Tower Hill's well-developed arts program culminates in the spring with an all-school evening of exhibits and performances. Student publications and musical activities supplement the school's varied dramatic and visual arts offerings.

In the upper school, all students participate in the athletic program, although juniors and seniors may elect not to take part in one season each year.

WILMINGTON FRIENDS SCHOOL
Day — Coed Gr PS (Age 2)-12

Wilmington, DE 19803. 101 School Rd. Tel: 302-576-2900. Fax: 302-576-2939.
www.wilmingtonfriends.org   E-mail: admissions@wilmingtonfriends.org
Bryan K. Garman, Head (2006). BA, Bucknell Univ, PhD, Emory Univ. **Kathleen Hopkins, Adm.**
Col Prep. IB Diploma. AP (61 exams taken, 69% 3+)—Calc Stats. **Elem math**—Everyday Math. **Elem read**—Wilson Fundations. **Feat**—Chin Fr Span Environ_Sci Comp_Sci Peace_Stud World_Relig Theater Jazz Journ.
Sports (req'd)—Basket X-country Indoor_Track Lacrosse Soccer Swim Tennis Track. B: Baseball Football Wrestling. G: F_Hockey Volley. **Activities:** 41.
Selective adm: 106/yr. Usual entry: PS, K, 6 & 9. Appl fee: $50. Appl due: Rolling. Applied: 291. Accepted: 56%. Yield: 65%. **Tests** CEEB CTP_4 ISEE SSAT.

Enr 777. B 377. G 400. Elem 511. Sec 266. Wh 77%. Blk 11%. Asian 3%. Other 9%. Avg class size: 14. Stud/fac: 9:1. Casual. **Fac 88.** M 30/F 58. FT 76/PT 12. Wh 75%. Latino 6%. Blk 9%. Asian 3%. Other 7%. Adv deg: 56%.
Grad '11—68. Col—66. (U of DE 14, Gettysburg 4, Bryn Mawr 2, Emory 2, Geo Wash 2, Princeton 2). **Avg SAT:** CR 608. M 611. W 625. Avg ACT: 27.3. **Col couns:** 2. Alum donors: 26%.
Tui '11-'12: Day $15,650-22,475 (+$300). **Aid:** Need 186 ($2,077,995).
Endow $19,800,000. Plant val $23,019,000. Acres 57. Bldgs 4 (90% ADA). Class rms 48. 2 Libs 30,000 vols. Sci labs 9. Auds 1. Art studios 5. Music studios 3. Gyms 5. Athletic ctrs 1. Fields 6. Courts 6. Comp labs 4. Comp/stud: 1:2.4 (1:1 Laptop prgm Gr 5-12).
Est 1748. Nonprofit. Religious Society of Friends (5% practice). Sem (Sept-June). **Assoc** MSA.

Founded by area Quakers to educate children of diverse backgrounds, Wilmington Friends is one of the oldest independent preparatory schools in the country and the oldest in Delaware. Although enrollment is interdenominational, the school emphasizes the principles of the Society of Friends at all grade levels.

Wilmington Friends' global curriculum includes Mandarin language instruction, summer and school-year options through School Year Abroad, and the two-year International Baccalaureate Diploma Program. In addition, juniors and seniors may take individual IB courses. Independent and advanced study options are also available. Service learning is a programmatic component from preschool on, and each upper schooler completes at least 50 hours of community service with one agency or organization prior to graduation.   **See Also Page 100**

DISTRICT OF COLUMBIA

WASHINGTON, DC. Urban. Pop: 572,059. Alt: 50 ft.

BEAUVOIR
THE NATIONAL CATHEDRAL ELEMENTARY SCHOOL
Day — Coed Gr PS (Age 4)-3

Washington, DC 20016. 3500 Woodley Rd NW. Tel: 202-537-6485. Fax: 202-537-5778.
www.beauvoirschool.org   E-mail: beauvoiradmissions@cathedral.org
Paula J. Carreiro, Head. BS, Northeastern State Univ. **Margaret Hartigan, Adm.**
  Pre-Prep. Feat—Lib_Skills Span Studio_Art Music. **Supp**—Dev_Read.
  Selective adm: 84/yr. Usual entry: PS & K. Appl fee: $65. Appl due: Jan. Yield: 85%.
    Tests IQ.
  Enr 393. B 197. G 196. Avg class size: 22. Stud/fac: 7:1. **Fac 60.** M 12/F 48. FT 60.
  Grad '07—71. Prep—69. (Natl Cathedral 28, St Albans 27, Georgetown Day 3, Landon
    2, Maret 2). Alum donors: 7%.
  Tui '11-'12: Day $30,120 (+$700). **Aid:** Need 58 ($1,000,000).
  Summer: Acad Enrich Rec. 7 wks.
  Endow $8,500,000. Plant val $11,000,000. Acres 60. Bldgs 1. Class rms 20. Lib 17,000
    vols. Sci labs 1. Lang labs 1. Auds 1. Art studios 1. Music studios 1. Gyms 1. Fields
    1. Pools 1. Playgrounds 2.
  Est 1933. Nonprofit. Episcopal. (Sept-June). **Assoc** MSA.

Founded as a coeducational primary school for students that would move onto one of the
Cathedral Schools (St. Alban's or the National Cathedral School), in 1939 Beauvoir was established as a separate and independent school in the Cathedral system. The school provides a
broadly based, integrated academic curriculum that is supplemented by resources in science,
technology, music, library, media, the visual arts, Spanish and physical education. Computers
are available in all classrooms.

Beauvoir's Global Studies Program, conducted from January to March each year, engages
students in integrated explorations of countries from one of five geographical regions. The
school also offers an extended-day program and after-school enrichment courses.

Chapel is held in the National Cathedral, and teachers frequently utilize the 60-acre Cathedral Close, as well as other resources in the Washington area. Beauvoir organizes age-appropriate projects in the community at all grade levels.

EMERSON PREPARATORY SCHOOL
Day — Coed Gr 9-12

Washington, DC 20036. 1324 18th St NW. Tel: 202-785-2877. Fax: 202-785-2228.
www.emersonprep.net   E-mail: info@emersonprep.net
John Morris Glick, Head (2009). BA, Univ of California-Berkeley, MEd, Loyola College
  (MD).
  Col Prep. Gen Acad. Underachiever. AP—Eng Calc US_Hist. **Feat**—Humanities
    Japan Arabic Astron Environ_Sci Anthro Econ. **Supp**—Dev_Read ESL Tut.
  Somewhat selective adm: 45/yr. Appl fee: $50. Appl due: Rolling. Accepted: 90%. Yield:
    86%. **Tests** IQ.
  Enr 40. B 19. G 21. Wh 70%. Latino 3%. Blk 19%. Asian 8%. Intl 10%. Avg class size: 7.
    Stud/fac: 7:1. **Fac 15.** Adv deg: 80%.
  Grad '09—17. Col—14. (Drew, Goucher, U of MD-Col Park, U of VT, Wash Col, Geo
    Wash). **Avg SAT:** CR 659. M 534. W 614.
  Tui '11-'12: Day $22,000-25,000 (+$500-700).

Summer: Acad. Tui Day $1000/crse. 4 wks.
Plant val $4,000,000. Bldgs 2. Class rms 11. Libs 1. Sci labs 1. Courtyards 1. Comp
labs 1.
Est 1852. Nonprofit. Sem (Sept-June).

The intensive program at this school, which evolved from the Emerson Institute, allows for the completion of a full year of high school academic work in each subject in one four-and-a-half-month term. An SAT preparation course provides instruction in verbal and math skills. Summer session offerings include math, science, history, government, English composition and literature, as well as an English workshop for foreign students.

GEORGETOWN DAY SCHOOL
Day — Coed Gr PS (Age 4)-12

Washington, DC 20016. 4200 Davenport St NW. Tel: 202-274-3210. Fax: 202-274-3211.
Other locations: 4530 MacArthur Blvd NW, Washington 20007.
www.gds.org   **E-mail: hsadmissions@gds.org**
Russell Shaw, Head (2010). BA, Yale Univ, MEd, Columbia Univ. **Vincent Rowe, Adm.**
   Col Prep. AP (exams req'd; 458 taken, 89% 3+)—Fr Lat Span Calc Stats Comp_Sci
Bio Chem Environ_Sci Physics US_Hist Comp_Govt & Pol Psych US_Govt & Pol
Studio_Art Music_Theory. **Feat**—Creative_Writing Chin Astron Physiol Lat-Amer_
Hist Amer_Stud Anthro Econ Art_Hist Film Photog Sculpt Theater Chorus Music.
   Sports—Basket Crew X-country Golf Indoor_Track Lacrosse Soccer Tennis Track. B:
Baseball Wrestling. G: Softball Volley.
   Very selective adm: 162/yr. Usual entry: PS, K, 1, 3, 4, 6, 7 & 9. Appl fee: $65. Appl due:
Jan. Accepted: 18%. Yield: 85%. **Tests** IQ ISEE SSAT.
   Enr 1075. B 537. G 538. Elem 575. Sec 500. Intl 5%. Avg class size: 14. Stud/fac: 7:1.
   Fac 160. M 51/F 109. FT 147/PT 13. Adv deg: 55%.
   Grad '08—118. Col—118. (Harvard, Princeton, Yale, Oberlin, Cornell, U of PA). **Avg
SAT:** CR/M 1343. **Col couns:** 2.
   Tui '11-'12: Day $29,170-33,615 (+$500-1225). **Aid:** Need 157 ($1,900,000).
   Summer: Enrich Rec. 2-4 wks.
Endow $6,240,000. Plant val $22,000,000. Acres 10. Bldgs 2. Class rms 80. Lib 22,000
vols. Sci labs 10. Theaters 2. Art studios 6. Music studios 4. Gyms 2. Comp/stud:
1:2.
   Est 1945. Nonprofit. Sem (Sept-June). **Assoc** MSA.

The first racially integrated school in the city, this parent-owned school now enrolls a student body with one-third pupils of color. The curriculum combines college preparation with an emphasis on the humanities and the arts and sciences. Features of the lower school program (grades pre-K-5) are the commencement of regular science study in prekindergarten and foreign language instruction beginning in grade 3. During the middle school years (grades 6-8), academic demands increase and pupils take part in such projects as the consumer science fair, on-site studies of Chesapeake Bay, and a two-month study of constitutional issues that includes personal interviews with national experts. GDS' varied high school curriculum (grades 9-12) incorporates block scheduling, as well as honors and Advanced Placement classes in most disciplines, and students have increased flexibility in course selection.

High school students fulfill a 60-hour community service requirement prior to senior year through involvement with local, national and international service organizations. The lower and middle schools—which are conducted on MacArthur Boulevard Northwest—require boys and girls to engage in class service projects.

GEORGETOWN VISITATION PREPARATORY SCHOOL
Day — Girls Gr 9-12

Washington, DC 20007. 1524 35th St NW. Tel: 202-337-3350. Fax: 202-342-5733.

www.visi.org   E-mail: info@visi.org
Daniel M. Kerns, Jr., Head. BA, St Bonaventure Univ, JD, George Mason Univ. **Janet Keller, Adm.**
  Col Prep. AP (exams req'd)—Eng Fr Span Calc Comp_Sci Bio Chem Environ_Sci Physics Eur_Hist US_Hist Comp_Govt & Pol Psych Art_Hist Studio_Art. **Feat**—Humanities Lat Relig Fine_Arts Theater_Arts Chorus Dance. **Supp**—Tut. **Dual enr:** Georgetown.
  Sports—G: Basket Crew X-country F_Hockey Lacrosse Soccer Softball Swim Tennis Track Volley. **Activities:** 40.
  Selective adm: 125/yr. Usual entry: 9. Appl fee: $50. Appl due: Dec. Accepted: 35%. Yield: 77%.
  Enr 480. Wh 79%. Latino 3%. Blk 8%. Asian 3%. Other 7%. Avg class size: 15. Stud/fac: 13:1. Uniform. **Fac 48.** M 9/F 39. FT 37/PT 11. Wh 90%. Blk 6%. Other 4%. Adv deg: 64%.
  Grad '08—121. Col—121. (U of VA, Georgetown, U of SC, U of MD-Col Park, Miami U-OH, James Madison). **Avg SAT:** CR 638. M 616. W 660. **Col couns:** 3.
  Tui '11-'12: Day $23,500 (+$450). **Aid:** Merit 24 ($60,000). Need 119 ($1,600,000).
  Summer: Acad Enrich. Tui Day $425-800/crse. 6 wks.
  Endow $14,600,000. Acres 20. Bldgs 8. Class rms 40. Lib 15,000 vols. Art studios 1. Music studios 3. Perf arts ctrs 1. Gyms 1. Athletic ctrs 1. Fields 2. Tennis courts 4. Comp labs 4.
  Est 1799. Nonprofit. Roman Catholic. Sem (Sept-May). **Assoc** CLS MSA.

Georgetown Visitation traces its origins to the end of the 18th century, when Archbishop Leonard Neale, president of Georgetown College, asked "three pious ladies" to found a school for young women. The main academic building, Founders Hall, was completely reconstructed after it was destroyed by a fire in 1993. While the school has a Roman Catholic religious tradition, students enroll from all backgrounds and religions. The present-day campus occupies 20 acres in the city's Georgetown section.

Visitation's curriculum emphasizes literature and the arts, and the technology program is particularly strong. Girls choose from a series of electives in science, English, math and social studies, and both honors and Advanced Placement courses are available. Qualified students may take courses at neighboring Georgetown University. The school's campus ministry conducts school liturgies and retreats throughout the year.

All students engage in community service work, with 80 cumulative hours required for graduation.

MARET SCHOOL

Day — Coed Gr K-12

Washington, DC 20008. 3000 Cathedral Ave NW. Tel: 202-939-8800.
  Fax: 202-939-8884.
  www.maret.org   E-mail: admission@maret.org
Marjo Talbott, Head (1994). BA, Williams College, MEd, Harvard Univ. **Annie Farquhar, Adm.**
  Col Prep. AP (245 exams taken, 92% 3+)—Lat Calc US_Hist. **Elem math**—Everyday Math. **Feat**—British_Lit Classics Creative_Writing Humanities Shakespeare African-Amer_Lit Women's_Lit World_Lit Chin Fr Span Stats Anat & Physiol Ecol Environ_Sci Geol Comp_Sci 20th-Century_Africa 20th-Century_Europe Econ Lat-Amer_Stud Comp_Relig Art_Hist Ceramics Film Photog Sculpt Studio_Art Drama Music Woodworking. **Supp**—Tut.
  Sports—Basket X-country Golf Lacrosse Soccer Swim Tennis. B: Baseball Football Wrestling. G: Softball Track Volley. **Activities:** 53.
  Very selective adm: 90/yr. Usual entry: K, 1, 4, 6 & 9. Appl fee: $65. Appl due: Jan. Accepted: 10%. **Tests** CEEB IQ ISEE SSAT.
  Enr 633. B 326. G 307. Elem 327. Sec 306. Wh 61%. Latino 3%. Blk 17%. Asian 8%. Other 11%. Intl 5%. Avg class size: 18. Stud/fac: 7:1. Casual. **Fac 94.** M 34/F 60. FT 76/PT 18. Wh 81%. Latino 3%. Blk 11%. Other 5%. Adv deg: 85%.

Grad '10—72. Col—72. (U of MI 5, U of PA 5, Wash U 5, Duke 4, Yale 3). **Avg SAT:** CR 685. M 691. W 687. **Col couns:** 3.
Tui '11-'12: Day $27,515-31,670 (+$250-800). **Aid:** Need 108 ($2,110,653).
Summer: Acad Enrich Rev. Tui Day $450-1175. Travel Abroad. Tui Bdg $4300-5000. 3-6 wks. Ecol. 6 wks.
Endow $12,700,000. Plant val $24,000,000. Acres 8. Bldgs 6. Class rms 62. 2 Libs 12,000 vols. Sci labs 6. Auds 1. Art studios 4. Music studios 3. Dance studios 1. Gyms 2. Fields 1. Comp labs 3.
Est 1911. Nonprofit. Sem (Sept-June). **Assoc** CLS MSA.

Since its founding by Louise Maret, a teacher born in Switzerland and educated in the US, the school has undergone several evolutions. Originally a girls' boarding school for French nationals preparing for the Baccalaureate exams, it expanded to include boys in 1937, added a traditional American college preparatory program in the 1940s, and finally abandoned the Baccalaureate program in 1969. In 1952, the school moved to its present location on the former Woodley Oaks Estate, a site that was considered for the Capitol by George Washington and, in the 19th century, became the summer residence of two presidents.

Maret's cross-disciplinary approach begins in kindergarten, when the humanities department integrates English and social studies curricula. In addition to satisfying course requirements in math and humanities, each student takes foreign language, science, computers, art and music from kindergarten through the high school years. Middle school pupils study Latin and a second foreign language of their choice. Dozens of electives are open to juniors and seniors.

Summer study in Honduras and a summer subtropical ecology program in Sanibel Island, FL, are conducted under the direction of the Maret faculty.

NATIONAL CATHEDRAL SCHOOL
Day — Girls Gr 4-12

Washington, DC 20016. Mt St Alban. Tel: 202-537-6374. Fax: 202-537-2382.
www.ncs.cathedral.org   E-mail: ncs_admissions@cathedral.org
Kathleen O'Neill Jamieson, Head (2003). BA, Univ of Maryland-College Park, MA, Columbia Univ. **Maureen Miller, Int Adm.**
Col Prep. AP (exams req'd; 320 taken)—Fr Japan Lat Span Calc Stats Comp_Sci Bio Chem Physics US_Hist Human_Geog US_Govt & Pol. **Feat**—British_Lit Creative_Writing Poetry Shakespeare African-Amer_Lit Comp_Lit Travel_Lit Chin Greek Anat & Physiol Environ_Sci Zoology Engineering Modern_African_Hist Econ Pol_Sci Social_Psych Bible Ethics Relig Islam Ceramics Drawing Filmmaking Painting Photog Sculpt Studio_Art Acting Theater_Arts Directing Chorus Music Music_Theory Dance Public_Speak. **Supp**—Rev Tut. Outdoor ed.
Sports—G: Basket Crew X-country F_Hockey Ice_Hockey Lacrosse Soccer Softball Swim Tennis Track Volley. **Activities:** 32.
Very selective adm (Gr 4-11): 97/yr. Usual entry: 4, 6, 7 & 9. Appl fee: $75. Appl due: Jan. Applied: 297. Accepted: 47%. Yield: 67%. **Tests** CTP_4 IQ ISEE SSAT.
Enr 584. Elem 271. Sec 313. Wh 65%. Latino 4%. Blk 11%. Asian 9%. Other 11%. Intl 7%. Avg class size: 14. Stud/fac: 7:1. **Fac 100.** M 26/F 74. Adv deg: 72%.
Grad '11—76. Col—76. (Stanford, Trinity Col-CT, Yale, U of Chicago, Harvard, U of VA). **Avg SAT:** CR 701. M 676. W 711. Avg ACT: 31. Mid 50% ACT: 28-33. **Col couns:** 3. Alum donors: 35%.
Tui '12-'13: Day $35,120 (+$2800-3000). **Aid:** Need 108 ($2,439,840).
Endow $23,000,000. Plant val $35,000,000. Acres 57. Bldgs 7. Class rms 44. 2 Libs 60,000 vols. Sci labs 7. Lang labs 1. Auds 3. Theaters 2. Art studios 4. Music studios 3. Dance studios 2. Gyms 3. Fields 2. Courts 3. Comp labs 4.
Est 1899. Nonprofit. Episcopal. Quar (Sept-May). **Assoc** CLS MSA.

After seven years of planning by Henry Yates Satterlee, the first Episcopal bishop of Washington, and local philanthropist and educator Phoebe Apperson Hearst, this girls' school opened with an enrollment of 16 day students and 32 boarders. The school's early years were closely linked with the beginning of the Diocese of Washington and the 1907 construction of the Cathedral of St. Peter and St. Paul. Today, NCS shares the 57-acre Cathedral Close with two related schools: Beauvoir, a coeducational primary school, and St. Albans, a boys' school consisting of grades 4-12. Since the 1970s, National Cathedral has conducted a program of coordinate classes and activities with St. Albans.

NCS is essentially a college preparatory school. A structured, interdisciplinary course of studies in the lower school (grades 4-6) prepares children for an increasing degree of latitude in course selection during the middle school years (grades 7 and 8). The middle school program emphasizes complex thinking, in preparation for the upper school (grades 9-12). The upper school curriculum features a full complement of Advanced Placement courses and electives. Girls at this level design their own course schedules around a core of college preparatory classes. Seniors may pursue special interests in greater depth through credit-bearing independent study.

International programs include fellowships for travel and study abroad; community service in Haiti; and exchange programs with schools in London, England, Paris, France, and Cape Coast, Ghana. Opportunities in publications, art, music, drama and sports are numerous. Girls perform 60 hours of compulsory community service prior to the start of senior year.

ST. ALBANS SCHOOL

Bdg — Boys Gr 9-12; Day — Boys 4-12

Washington, DC 20016. Mount St Alban. Tel: 202-537-6435. Fax: 202-537-6434.
www.stalbansschool.org   E-mail: sta_admission@cathedral.org
Vance Wilson, Head (1999). BA, Yale Univ, MA, Univ of Virginia. **Hart Roper, Adm.**

> **Col Prep. AP (exams req'd)**—Fr Japan Lat Span Calc Comp_Sci Bio Chem Physics Eur_Hist Human_Geog US_Govt & Pol Art_Hist. **Feat**—British_Lit Creative_Writing Poetry Shakespeare African-Amer_Lit Southern_Lit Women's_Lit Chin Greek Russ Stats Anat & Physiol Environ_Sci Forensic_Sci Geol Zoology Web_Design Civil_Rights Econ Govt Ethics Relig Ceramics Drawing Photog Studio_Art Drama Theater_Arts Music. **Supp**—Rev Tut.
>
> **Sports (req'd)**—B: Baseball Basket Crew X-country Football Golf Ice_Hockey Lacrosse Soccer Swim Tennis Track Wrestling. **Activities:** 35.
>
> **Selective adm (Bdg Gr 9-11; Day 4-11):** 93/yr. Bdg 6. Day 87. Usual entry: 4, 6, 7 & 9. Appl fee: $80. Appl due: Jan. Accepted: 30%. Yield: 76%. **Tests** IQ ISEE SSAT TOEFL.
>
> **Enr 578.** Bdg 29. Day 549. Elem 266. Sec 312. Wh 67%. Latino 4%. Blk 12%. Asian 8% Other 9%. Avg class size: 13. Stud/fac: 7:1. Formal. **Fac 77.** M 54/F 23. FT 77. Adv deg: 71%. In dorms 6.
>
> **Grad '11—82. Col—82.** (Yale 4, U of MI 4, Bowdoin 3, Colby 3, Cornell 3, Lafayette 3) **Col couns:** 3.
>
> **Tui '12-'13: Bdg $52,301** (+$1000). **Day $36,973** (+$500-2350). **Aid:** Need 143 ($3,400,000).
>
> **Summer:** Acad Enrich Rev Rem Rec. Tui Day $400-1000. 6 wks.
>
> Endow $45,000,000. Plant val $14,879,000. Acres 57. Bldgs 7. Dorms 1. Class rms 30 Lib 17,000 vols. Labs 6. Theaters 1. Art studios 3. Music studios 3. Gyms 2. Fields 2 Courts 14. Pools 1.
>
> **Est 1909.** Nonprofit. Episcopal. Sem (Sept-May). **Assoc** CLS.

Founded as the National Cathedral School for Boys by the bequest of Harriet Lane Johnston, St. Albans has use of the 57-acre Close of Washington Cathedral. Well-equipped for both academic and extracurricular programs, with unusual opportunities for music at the cathedral the school provides honors courses in history, math, science and languages. Reflecting the worldwide importance of Washington, the school enrolls students from many countries, with graduates entering leading colleges.

St. Albans provides many of the advantages of coeducation while retaining the strengths of separate education, for its sister school, the National Cathedral School, is also located in the Cathedral Close. Approximately 30 coordinate courses are open to students. The two school come together for such extracurricular activities as glee club, dramatics and social events. St. Albans offers a vigorous sports program and provides opportunities for students to engage in social service activities in the Greater Washington area. Boys fulfill a 60-hour community service requirement prior to the start of senior year.

ST. ANSELM'S ABBEY SCHOOL
Day — Boys Gr 6-12

Washington, DC 20017. 4501 S Dakota Ave NE. Tel: 202-269-2350. Fax: 202-269-2373.
www.saintanselms.org   E-mail: schooloffice@saintanselms.org
Rev. Peter Weigand, OSB, Pres (2008). BA, St Mary's College (MN), MTS, Catholic Univ of America. **Louis Silvano, Head.** BMus, Univ of London (England), MA, Marymount College (NY). **Kirk Otterson, Adm.**
Col Prep. AP (exams req'd; 112 taken, 87% 3+)—Eng Fr Lat Span Calc Stats Comp_ Sci Bio Chem Environ_Sci Physics US_Hist Comp_Govt & Pol Econ US_Govt & Pol Art_Hist Music_Theory. **Feat**—Humanities Greek Arabic Multivariable_Calc Engineering Lat-Amer_Hist Anthro Native_Amer_Stud Ethics World_Relig Studio_Art Acting Theater_Arts Speech. **Supp**—ESL Rev Tut.
Sports—B: Baseball Basket X-country Fencing Soccer Tennis Track Wrestling. **Activities:** 31.
Selective adm (Gr 6-11): 53/yr. Appl fee: $50. Appl due: Rolling. Applied: 100. Accepted: 46%.
Enr 232. Wh 77%. Latino 6%. Blk 9%. Asian 8%. Avg class size: 12. Stud/fac: 6:1. Uniform. **Fac 44.** Adv deg: 84%.
Grad '11—35. Col—35. (U of MD-Col Park 4, U of PA 2, U of Chicago 2, VA Polytech 2, Notre Dame 2, James Madison 2). **Avg SAT:** CR 684. M 667. W 667. Avg ACT: 29. **Col couns:** 2. Alum donors: 18%.
Tui '12-'13: Day $22,600-23,600 (+$650-1000). **Aid:** Need 85 ($850,000).
Summer: Acad Enrich Rev Rem Rec. Sports. 3-6 wks.
Acres 43. Bldgs 3 (100% ADA). Class rms 20. Lib 12,000 vols. Sci labs 4. Auds 1. Theaters 1. Art studios 1. Music studios 4. Perf arts ctrs 1. Gyms 1. Athletic ctrs 1. Fields 1. Courts 6. Comp labs 1. Comp/stud: 1:5.
Est 1942. Nonprofit. Roman Catholic (60% practice). (Aug-May). **Assoc** MSA.

Founded by a group of Benedictine monks from Fort Augustus in Scotland, St. Anselm's Abbey is one of 10 monasteries that form the English Benedictine Congregation. The school's curriculum is based on a balanced and thorough exposure to the major disciplines: religion, language and literature, mathematics, the natural and physical sciences, and history. Boys follow a set curriculum in grades 6-10, with elective options first available during junior year.

Retreats are an integral part of school life: Students in grades 6-10 participate in daylong or overnight retreats, while juniors and seniors go on extended, three-day trips. Juniors and seniors take part in a Tuesday morning community service program.

SHERIDAN SCHOOL
Day — Coed Gr K-8

Washington, DC 20008. 4400 36th St NW. Tel: 202-362-7900. Fax: 202-244-9696.
www.sheridanschool.org   E-mail: admission@sheridanschool.org
C. Randall Plummer, Head (1997). BS, Univ of Missouri-Columbia, MEd, Boston Univ. **Margie Gottfried, Adm.**
Pre-Prep. Feat—Fr Span Computers Studio_Art Music. **Supp**—Rev Tut.
Sports—Basket X-country Soccer Softball Track.
Very selective adm: 36/yr. Appl fee: $60. Appl due: Jan. Accepted: 22%. Yield: 84%. **Tests** IQ ISEE SSAT.
Enr 226. Avg class size: 26. Stud/fac: 6:1. **Fac 35.** M 7/F 28. FT 35. Adv deg: 60%.
Grad '11—26. Prep—26. (Georgetown Day 8, Field 4, Maret 3, Edmund Burke 3, St

Andrew's Sch-DE 3, Sidwell Friends 2). Alum donors: 20%.
Tui '12-'13: Day $27,740-30,440. Aid: Need 45 ($760,000).
Summer: Enrich. Arts. Tui Day $305-910. 1-3 wks.
Endow $3,700,000. Plant val $6,500,000. Bldgs 1. Class rms 10. Lib 8689 vols. Sci labs 2. Lang labs 2. Auds 1. Theaters 1. Art studios 1. Music studios 1. Gyms 1. Comp labs 1.
Est 1927. Nonprofit. Tri (Sept-June). **Assoc** MSA.

In 1927, Mrs. Frank Cummings Cook took over Miss Tomlin's School, a small, coed primary school, and renamed it Mrs. Cook's School. When she retired in 1952, the school was renamed "Sheridan" because of its location at Sheridan Circle on Massachusetts Avenue, NW. In 1962, it was incorporated by a group of parents as a nonprofit organization and expanded through grade 8. The school moved to its present location in 1964.

Through immersion in an inquiry- and concept-based curriculum, this small family school offers a strong academic program that provides a solid grounding in the basic skills. Sheridan's writing program, which is consistent throughout the school, commences with five- to 15-minute lessons that focus on specific skills or writing techniques, then progresses to journal-writing time and a chance to receive individualized instruction from the teacher. French and Spanish instruction begins in kindergarten, and music and art are integral parts of the program. The school schedules trips to local cultural and historical points of interest.

A 130-acre campus in the Shenandoah Valley offers outdoor educational experiences for children at all grade levels, including trips during the school year, optional weekend backpacking excursions, and longer winter and summer educational sojourns. Boys and girls engage in both in-class and schoolwide community service projects. An after-school program, vacation camps and summer programs are open to all students.

SIDWELL FRIENDS SCHOOL
Day — Coed Gr PS (Age 4)-12

Washington, DC 20016. 3825 Wisconsin Ave NW. Tel: 202-537-8100.
Fax: 202-537-8138.
Other locations: 5100 Edgemoor Ln, Bethesda, MD 20814.
   www.sidwell.edu   E-mail: admissions@sidwell.edu
Thomas B. Farquhar, Head (2010). BA, Earlham College, MEd, Univ of Pennsylvania.
Joshua Wolman, Adm.
   Col Prep. Feat—Classics Shakespeare Chin Fr Lat Span Calc Stats Linear_Algebra Environ_Sci Marine_Bio/Sci Neurosci Comp_Sci African_Hist African-Amer_Hist Chin_Hist E_Asian_Hist Lat-Amer_Hist Amer_Stud Econ Comp_Relig Philos Art_Hist Photog Studio_Art Acting Drama Theater_Arts Music Music_Theory Jazz_Ensemble Dance. **Supp—**Tut.
   Sports—Basket X-country Lacrosse Soccer Swim Tennis Track. B: Baseball Football Golf Wrestling. G: F_Hockey Softball Volley. **Activities:** 50.
   Selective adm (Gr PS-11): 118/yr. Usual entry: PS, K, 3, 6, 7 & 9. Appl fee: $60. Appl due: Jan. **Tests** IQ ISEE SSAT.
   Enr 1109. B 564. G 545. Elem 644. Sec 465. Wh 60%. Latino 3%. Blk 13%. Asian 8%. Other 16%. Avg class size: 16. Casual. **Fac 150.**
   Grad '10—111. Col—111. Avg SAT: CR/M 1400. **Col couns:** 3.
   Tui '11-'12: Day $31,960-32,960 (+$300-600). **Aid:** Need 254 ($5,400,000).
   Summer: Gr PS-12. Acad Enrich Rev Rem Rec. 11 wks.
   Acres 20. Bldgs 11. Class rms 217. 3 Libs 39,242 vols. Sci labs 7. Lang labs 2. Meeting-houses 2. Auds 2. Art studios 6. Music studios 3. Dance studios 1. Arts ctrs 1. Gyms 2. Fields 6. Courts 5. Tracks 1. Playgrounds 2. Comp labs 4. Laptop prgm Gr 6-8.
   Est 1883. Nonprofit. Religious Society of Friends (5% practice). Sem (Sept-June). **Assoc** MSA.

Thomas W. Sidwell established and then conducted this school for 53 years according to Quaker concepts of education, emphasizing simplicity, friendliness, democratic group processes, and personal and community responsibility. The school began with 11 students in a

Friends meetinghouse in downtown Washington, moving to its present, 15-acre location in 1922. Under five successive headmasters, the school developed this site and added a five-acre Bethesda, MD, campus in 1963 to house the lower school (grades PS-4).

The competitive academic program has strong departments of English, sciences, mathematics, languages, social studies and the arts being supplemented by extensive athletics. Boys and girls complete a 60-hour annual community service project over a 12-month period in grades 9-11; they also participate in a compulsory work program in grades 9-12. A weekly Meeting for Worship is central to the life of the school. Students of diverse racial, economic and cultural backgrounds enter leading colleges throughout the country.

Taking advantage of its location in the nation's capital, the school offers many learning environments and teaching approaches. Sidwell's Chinese Studies program comprises major units in all divisions' social studies curricula, six years of language study, elective courses at the upper level, summer group trips and student/teacher exchanges with sister schools in Beijing, Shanghai and Hangzhou. Upper school students have further opportunities for specialized study through the School Year Abroad program in France, Spain, China, Italy and Vietnam.

WASHINGTON INTERNATIONAL SCHOOL
Day — Coed Gr PS (Age 4)-12

Washington, DC 20008. 3100 Macomb St NW. Tel: 202-243-1815. Fax: 202-243-1807. Other locations: 1690 36th St NW, Washington 20007.
www.wis.edu   E-mail: admissions@wis.edu
Clayton Lewis, Head (2007). BA, Rhodes College, MS, Vanderbilt Univ. **Kathleen Visconti, Adm.**
- **Col Prep. IB Diploma. IB PYP. Bilingual (Dutch Fr Span). AP exams taken: 41 (98% 3+). Feat**—Chin Dutch Environ_Sci Comp_Sci Econ Film Studio_Art Drama Music Journ Design. **Supp**—ESL Tut.
- **Sports**—Basket X-country Golf Soccer Tennis Track. B: Baseball. G: Softball Volley. **Activities:** 20.
- **Selective adm (Gr PS-11):** 148/yr. Usual entry: PS, 6 & 9. Appl fee: $50. Appl due: Jan. Applied: 572. Accepted: 36%. Yield: 71%.
- **Enr 923.** B 443. G 480. Elem 662. Sec 261. Wh 56%. Latino 11%. Blk 7%. Asian 4%. Other 22%. Intl 40%. Avg class size: 13. Stud/fac: 8:1. **Fac 104.** M 29/F 75. FT 96/PT 8. Wh 59%. Latino 18%. Blk 3%. Asian 11%. Other 9%. Adv deg: 57%.
- **Grad '11—55. Col—55.** (McGill-Canada 5, U of MI 4, U of St Andrews-Scotland 4, U of VA 3, Tufts 2, U of Toronto-Canada 2). **Avg SAT:** CR 652. M 629. W 669. **Mid 50% SAT:** CR 620-710. M 580-690. W 610-730. Avg ACT: 30.1. Mid 50% ACT: 30-31. **Col couns:** 2.
- **Tui '12-'13: Day $28,930-32,250** (+$400). **Aid:** Need 113 ($3,100,000).
- **Summer:** Acad Enrich Rec. 1-3 wks.
- Endow $3,000,000. Plant val $55,000,000. Acres 9. Bldgs 9. Class rms 56. Libs 2. Auds 1. Theaters 1. Art studios 4. Music studios 4. Gyms 2. Fields 3. Comp labs 2.
- **Est 1966.** Nonprofit. Sem (Sept-June). **Assoc** MSA.

WIS provides an international education for both American and international students, offering the cultural richness of an international staff and a curriculum that draws upon different educational traditions.

The primary school program includes language immersion classes in the prekindergarten and kindergarten, and children in grades 1-5 follow a bilingual curriculum with half the instruction in English and the remainder in French, Spanish or, for native speakers, Dutch. Intensive courses in Spanish and English are available for new pupils in grade 2 and above. History and geography are taught in French and Spanish through grade 8, although English-language sections are also available for newly enrolled students.

WIS offers the International Baccalaureate Primary Years Program in grades pre-K-5. In their last two years of the upper school, all students follow the IB Diploma Program, a rigorous, comprehensive course of studies recognized by many colleges around the world.

The school maintains two locations: Grades pre-K-5 are located on the primary school campus at Reservoir Road and 36th Street NW, while middle and upper school classes and activities take place at Tregaron, a 20-acre former residential estate in the northwestern part of the city.

MARYLAND

ANNAPOLIS, MD. (23 mi. SSE of Baltimore, MD; 28 mi. E of Washington, DC) Suburban. Pop: 35,838. Alt: 40 ft.

KEY SCHOOL
Day — Coed Gr PS (Age 3)-12

Annapolis, MD 21403. 534 Hillsmere Dr. Tel: 410-263-9231. Fax: 410-280-5516.
www.keyschool.org E-mail: inquiry@keyschool.org
Marcella Yedid, Head (1999). BS, Indiana Univ, MA, Brown Univ. **Jessie D. Dunleavy, Adm.**
Col Prep. AP exams taken: 149 (58% 3+). Feat—Playwriting Women's_Lit Fr Lat Span Calc Stats Astron Ecol Comp_Sci Anthro Russ_Stud Philos Art_Hist Photog Studio_Art Video_Production Music Music_Theory Dance Outdoor_Ed. **Supp**—Tut. Outdoor ed.
Sports—Basket X-country Golf Lacrosse Sail Soccer Tennis Track. G: Equestrian F_ Hockey. **Activities:** 100.
Selective adm: 118/yr. Appl fee: $45. Appl due: Rolling. Applied: 314. Accepted: 49%. Yield: 77%. **Tests** ISEE.
Enr 700. B 307. G 393. Elem 490. Sec 210. Wh 68%. Latino 4%. Blk 16%. Native Am 1%. Asian 3%. Other 8%. Avg class size: 17. Stud/fac: 8:1. **Fac 112.** M 28/F 84. Wh 90%. Latino 4%. Blk 2%. Native Am 1%. Asian 3%. Adv deg: 58%.
Grad '11—34. Col—34. (U of MD-Col Park 5, U of VT 4, Lynchburg 3, Brown 2, High Pt 2, Barnard 1). **Mid 50% SAT:** CR 560-670. M 560-650. W 510-650. **Col couns:** 2.
Tui '11-'12: Day $16,145-23,950 (+$380-965). **Aid:** Need 174 ($1,694,515).
Summer (enr 500): Acad Enrich Rec. 1-8 wks.
Endow $6,483,000. Plant val $20,000,000. Acres 15. Bldgs 16. Class rms 60. Libs 3. Sci labs 6. Lang labs 1. Auds 1. Theaters 1. Art studios 3. Music studios 3. Gyms 2. Fields 3. Comp labs 3.
Est 1958. Nonprofit. (Sept-June).

Founded by several tutors from nearby St. John's College who were determined to bring strong teachers and able students together, the school soon established a program combining experiential learning with a rigorous, essentially classical curriculum. Originally serving 18 pupils in grades 1-3, Key added one grade in each ensuing year until the 1970s, when the program ran from prekindergarten through grade 12 and enrollment had grown to 360 students. Ongoing plant renovations and new construction in the 1980s and 1990s enabled the school to meet the needs of a larger student body and an expanding educational program.

Boys and girls in the middle school (grades 5-8) take part in various multidisciplinary experiences and hands-on activities. Key's Orff Schulwerk music program, which begins in preschool and continues through middle school, is nationally recognized. All boys and girls in the program engage in the daily study of speech, rhythm, instruments, singing, creative movement and dance, drama and improvisation. Students also learn to read music while gaining an understanding of basic theoretical concepts.

The college preparatory upper school curriculum (grades 9-12) features extensive modern and classical language and fine and performing arts programs. Instructors place emphasis on writing, critical reading and analytical thinking, and the curriculum incorporates experiential education and interdisciplinary learning techniques wherever possible (such as in the three-year core humanities sequence that commences in grade 9). Although Key does not explicitly follow the Advanced Placement curriculum, advanced courses in most disciplines prepare students for AP exams.

Extensive field trips (such as outdoor education camping excursions) are integral to school life.

BALTIMORE, MD. Urban. Pop: 651,154. Alt: to 445 ft.

BOYS' LATIN SCHOOL

Day — Boys Gr K-12

Baltimore, MD 21210. 822 W Lake Ave. Tel: 410-377-5192. Fax: 410-377-4312.
www.boyslatinmd.com   E-mail: cbradfield@boyslatinmd.com
Christopher J. Post, Head (2008). BA, Johns Hopkins Univ, MA, Boston Univ. **James W.
Currie, Jr., Upper & Middle Sch Adm; Kathleen M. Berger, Lower Sch Adm.**

> **Col Prep. AP (exams req'd; 136 taken, 71% 3+)**—Eng Calc Stats Bio Chem Environ_Sci Physics Eur_Hist US_Hist. **Elem read**—Wilson Fundations. **Feat**—African-Amer_Lit Fr Lat Span Multivariable_Calc Forensic_Sci African-Amer_Hist Milit_Hist Govt Psych Studio_Art Acting Music Music_Theory Journ. **Supp**—Tut.
> **Sports**—B: Baseball Basket X-country Football Golf Ice_Hockey Lacrosse Soccer Squash Tennis Volley Wrestling. **Activities: 43.**
> **Selective adm:** 76/yr. Usual entry: K, 1, 6 & 9. Appl fee: $50. Appl due: Rolling. Applied: 216. Accepted: 63%. Yield: 55%. **Tests** CTP_4 IQ ISEE MRT Stanford.
> **Enr 600.** Elem 310. Sec 290. Wh 84%. Latino 1%. Blk 13%. Asian 2%. Avg class size: 14. Stud/fac: 8:1. **Fac 88.** M 42/F 46. FT 85/PT 3. Wh 92%. Latino 1%. Blk 6%. Native Am 1%. Adv deg: 56%.
> **Grad '10—80. Col—78.** (U of MD-Col Park 8, Wash Col 5, VA Polytech 3, U of DE 3, UNC-Chapel Hill 2, Villanova 2). **Avg SAT:** CR 531. M 571. W 530. Avg ACT: 23. **Col couns:** 3. Alum donors: 39%.
> **Tui '11-'12: Day $19,500-22,520. Aid:** Need 170 ($1,540,000).
> Endow $31,000,000. Plant val $75,000,000. Acres 41. Bldgs 8. Class rms 64. 2 Libs 15,000 vols. Sci labs 6. Lang labs 1. Photog labs 1. Auds 1. Theaters 1. Art studios 2. Music studios 2. Gyms 2. Fields 5. Courts 6. Comp labs 3. Comp/stud: 1:2.
> **Est 1844.** Nonprofit. Quar (Sept-June). **Assoc** MSA.

Founded by Evert M. Topping, a Princeton professor, Boys' Latin serves the needs of young men in the Baltimore area. Originally located downtown, the school moved in 1960 to its present location, a 41-acre campus in Roland Park.

The oldest independent, nonsectarian school for boys in the state, Boys' Latin combines college preparatory academics, arts, athletics and cocurricular activities with a character development program. The lower school emphasizes language arts and mathematics, while the middle school stresses the five traditional subjects. In the upper school, qualified juniors and seniors may choose from a variety of electives and Advanced Placement courses beyond the traditional disciplines. Students in grades 9-12 perform 10 hours of required community service per year.

THE BRYN MAWR SCHOOL

Day — Boys Gr PS (Age 2)-PS (Age 4), Girls PS (Age 2)-12

Baltimore, MD 21210. 109 W Melrose Ave. Tel: 410-323-8800. Fax: 410-477-8963.
www.brynmawrschool.org   E-mail: admissions@brynmawrschool.org
Maureen E. Walsh, Head (2002). BA, Wesleyan Univ, MEd, Columbia Univ. **Talia Busby
Titus, Adm.**

> **Col Prep. AP (exams req'd; 246 taken, 80% 3+)**—Eng Chin Fr Lat Span Calc Stats Comp_Sci Bio Chem Environ_Sci Physics World_Hist Comp_Govt & Pol Econ Psych US_Govt & Pol Art_Hist. **Elem math**—GO Math!. **Feat**—Creative_Writing Poetry Shakespeare African-Amer_Lit Irish_Lit Mythology Russ_Lit Ger Greek Russ Arabic Multivariable_Calc Anat & Physiol Astron Forensic_Sci Genetics Engineering Web_Design Holocaust Modern_Chin_Hist Intl_Relations Law Native_Amer_Stud Ethics Architect_Drawing Film Fine_Arts Photog Studio_Art Drama Music Music_Theory Dance Finance Journ.
> **Sports**—G: Badminton Basket Crew X-country F_Hockey Golf Ice_Hockey Lacrosse

Soccer Softball Squash Swim Tennis Track Volley. **Activities:** 64.
Selective adm: 98/yr. Usual entry: K, 1, 6 & 9. Appl fee: $60. Appl due: Jan. Accepted: 60%. **Tests** ISEE.
Enr 811. B 40. G 771. Elem 516. Sec 295. Wh 65%. Latino 1%. Blk 15%. Asian 10%. Other 9%. Avg class size: 14. Stud/fac: 7:1. Uniform. **Fac 147.** M 22/F 125. FT 119/PT 28. Wh 86%. Latino 1%. Blk 9%. Asian 3%. Other 1%. Adv deg: 43%.
Grad '11—77. Col—76. (U of MD-Col Park 4, Wake Forest 4, Wash U 4, U of PA 3, Brown 2, Dartmouth 2). Athl schol 3. **Avg SAT:** CR 661. M 641. W 675. Avg ACT: 27.9. **Col couns:** 4. Alum donors: 39%.
Tui '12-'13: Day $24,000-25,490 (+$230-2030). **Aid:** Need 205 ($2,880,200).
Summer: Acad Enrich Rec. Tui Day $175-990. 1-3 wks. Sports. Tui Day $260-295/wk. 9 wks.
Endow $27,024,000. Plant val $32,000,000. Acres 26. Bldgs 23 (65% ADA). Class rms 50. 2 Libs 27,000 vols. Sci ctrs 1. Auds 1. Theaters 1. Art studios 3. Music studios 4. Dance studios 1. Gyms 2. Fields 4. Tennis courts 6. Comp labs 3. Comp/stud: 1:2.5 (1:1 Laptop prgm Gr 6-12).
Est 1885. Nonprofit. Sem (Sept-June). **Assoc** CLS MSA.

Bryn Mawr School, one of the nation's first college preparatory schools for girls, is located on a 26-acre, wooded campus within the city limits. The school was originally established to prepare graduates for Bryn Mawr College. Among the five young Baltimore women who founded Bryn Mawr was M. Carey Thomas, the first dean and second president of Bryn Mawr College and a pioneer in women's education, and Mary Garrett, a Baltimore philanthropist who later made possible the founding of Johns Hopkins Medical School by donating a sum of money contingent upon the admission of women. Edith Hamilton, author of *The Greek Way,* was the first headmistress.

The rigorous college preparatory curriculum includes drama, art, physical education, music, values education and computer studies. These areas are complemented in the upper school by requirements in public speaking and community service. Bryn Mawr's coordinate program with neighboring Gilman School for boys and Roland Park Country School for girls allows for expanded Advanced Placement and elective course offerings. French instruction begins in kindergarten and is joined by Latin and Spanish in the middle school and by German, Greek, Russian, Chinese and Arabic in the upper school. Foreign exchange programs are also available. All girls accumulate 50 hours of required community service in grades 9-12.

Bryn Mawr's coeducational preschool program enrolls two- to five-year-olds. The division also includes an infant/toddler daycare center for children ages 2 months-2½.

CALVERT HALL COLLEGE HIGH SCHOOL
Day — Boys Gr 9-12

Baltimore, MD 21286. 8102 La Salle Rd. Tel: 410-825-4266. Fax: 410-825-6826.
www.calverthall.com   E-mail: chc@calverthall.com
Br. Thomas Zoppo, FSC, Pres (2009). BS, Villanova Univ, MS, Manhattan College. **Louis E. Heidrick, Prin.** BS, MBA, Loyola College. **Chris Bengel, Adm.**
Col Prep. AP (exams req'd; 407 taken, 79% 3+)—Eng Fr Ger Lat Span Calc Stats Comp_Sci Bio Chem Environ_Sci Physics Eur_Hist US_Hist World_Hist Comp_Govt & Pol Econ Psych US_Govt & Pol Studio_Art Music_Theory. **Feat**—Humanities Ital Russ Anat & Physiol Engineering Web_Design World_Relig Fine_Arts Accounting Bus. **Supp**—LD Rev Tut.
Sports—B: Baseball Basket Crew X-country Football Golf Ice_Hockey Indoor_Track Lacrosse Rugby Soccer Squash Swim Tennis Track Volley W_Polo Wrestling. **Activities:** 50.
Somewhat selective adm: 335/yr. Usual entry: 9. Appl fee: $25. Appl due: Dec. Applied: 685. Accepted: 88%. Yield: 57%. **Tests** HSPT.
Enr 1225. Wh 87%. Latino 2%. Blk 8%. Asian 3%. Avg class size: 21. Stud/fac: 13:1. Formal. **Fac 100.** M 72/F 28. FT 100. Wh 92%. Latino 1%. Blk 3%. Asian 3%. Other 1%. Adv deg: 65%.
Grad '11—301. Col—295. (Towson 53, U of MD-Col Park 35, WV U 17, U of MD-Balti-

more County 8, Salisbury 8, VA Polytech 7). Athl schol 12. **Avg SAT:** CR 537. M 553. W 520. **Col couns:** 2. Alum donors: 21%.

Tui '12-'13: Day $12,500 (+$250). **Aid:** Merit 100 ($350,000). Need 400 ($1,000,000).

Summer (enr 300): Acad Enrich Rev Rem. Tui Day $335-365/wk. 5 wks.

Endow $4,000,000. Plant val $25,000,000. Acres 32. Bldgs 5. Class rms 50. Lib 23,000 vols. Sci labs 3. Lang labs 1. Auds 1. Theaters 1. Art studios 1. Music studios 1. Perf arts ctrs 1. Gyms 2. Fields 3. Pools 1. Stadiums 2. Comp/stud: 1:4.

Est 1845. Nonprofit. Roman Catholic (71% practice). Sem (Sept-June). **Assoc** MSA.

Founded by the Brothers of the Christian Schools, Calvert Hall has occupied its present, 32-acre campus since 1960. The curriculum is college preparatory, offering a variety of programs.

A four-year scholars program includes courses designed for intellectually gifted students, incorporating accelerated content, in-depth study, small-group discussions, interdisciplinary approaches and experiential learning. The writing program includes a staffed writing center. Juniors complete 24 hours of required community service.

The school conducts a program for students with identified language-learning difficulties. Students in this program are fully integrated into the academic environment and receive additional instruction from a language specialist.

CALVERT SCHOOL

Day — Coed Gr PS (Age 4)-8

Baltimore, MD 21210. 105 Tuscany Rd. Tel: 410-243-6054. Fax: 410-243-0384.

    www.calvertschoolmd.org   E-mail: info@calvertschoolmd.org

Andrew D. Martire, Head (2004). AB, Princeton Univ, MLA, Johns Hopkins Univ, EdD, Univ of Pennsylvania. **Nicole H. Webster, Adm.**

Pre-Prep. Feat—Mythology Fr Lat Span Art_Hist Studio_Art Music.

Sports—Basket X-country Lacrosse Soccer Squash Track. B: Baseball Football. G: F_Hockey Softball.

Selective adm (Gr PS-7): 80/yr. Usual entry: PS & K. Appl fee: $75. Appl due: Jan. Applied: 199. Accepted: 59%. Yield: 78%. **Tests** IQ.

Enr 612. B 295. G 317. Wh 81%. Blk 7%. Asian 4%. Other 8%. Avg class size: 16. Stud/fac: 9:1. Uniform. **Fac 72.** M 18/F 54. FT 70/PT 2. Wh 91%. Latino 2%. Blk 5%. Native Am 2%. Adv deg: 54%.

Grad '11—34. Prep—34. (Roland Park 6, Gilman 5, Bryn Mawr 4, St Paul's Sch-MD 4, Friends Sch-MD 3, Garrison Forest 3). Alum donors: 31%.

Tui '12-'13: Day $20,700-22,000. Aid: Need 126 ($1,349,000).

Summer (enr 275): Acad Rec. Sports. Tui Day $150-300/wk. 5 wks.

Endow $38,000,000. Plant val $40,000,000. Acres 13. Bldgs 2. Class rms 52. 2 Libs 15,000 vols. Sci labs 3. Planetariums 1. Auds 1. Theaters 1. Art studios 2. Music studios 2. Dance studios 1. Gyms 3. Fields 3. Comp labs 3. Laptop prgm Gr 5-8.

Est 1897. Nonprofit. Sem (Sept-June). **Assoc** MSA.

Calvert, located in the Tuscany-Canterbury neighborhood, features a curriculum of science, geography, composition, foreign language, art history, music, art and grammar, in addition to the core subjects. The library, science and computer labs and a planetarium provide a solid resource base for students, and the athletic program fosters physical development and sportsmanship. Boys and girls begin to study French or Spanish in grade 2, and all eighth graders study Latin alongside French or Spanish. Each middle schooler purchases a laptop computer from Calvert for school use. Community service is a middle school requirement.

A home instruction program (grades K-8), developed and tested in the day school, helps parents to teach supplementary or enrichment courses at home. It is specially designed for parents without previous teaching experience or training.

FRIENDS SCHOOL

Day — Coed Gr PS (Age 4)-12

Baltimore, MD 21210. 5114 N Charles St. Tel: 410-649-3200. Fax: 410-649-3302.
www.friendsbalt.org E-mail: admissions@friendsbalt.org
Matthew W. **Micciche, Head (2005).** BA, Amherst College, MAT, Tufts Univ, MA, Middlebury College. **Karen Dates Dunmore, Adm.**
Col Prep. AP exams taken: 50 (96% 3+). Elem math—Singapore Math. **Elem read**—Wilson Fundations. **Feat**—British_Lit Poetry Shakespeare African_Lit Russ_Lit Fr Lat Russ Span Calc Stats Ecol Environ_Sci Geol Comp_Sci Cold_War Middle_Eastern_Hist Anthro Econ Govt Peace_Stud Photog Studio_Art Animation Theater Music Dance Finance Journ. **Supp**—Rem_Math Rem_Read Tut. Outdoor ed. **Dual enr:** Johns Hopkins.
Sports (req'd)—Basket X-country Golf Lacrosse Soccer Squash Tennis. B: Baseball Football Wrestling. G: Badminton F_Hockey Softball Volley. **Activities:** 45.
Selective adm: 146/yr. Usual entry: PS, 1, 6 & 9. Appl fee: $50. Appl due: Dec. Applied: 486. Accepted: 73%. Yield: 41%. **Tests** ISEE.
Enr 972. B 523. G 449. Elem 560. Sec 412. Wh 75%. Latino 2%. Blk 13%. Asian 3%. Other 7%. Avg class size: 16. Stud/fac: 9:1. Casual. **Fac 104.** M 36/F 68. FT 92/PT 12. Wh 90%. Blk 7%. Asian 1%. Other 2%. Adv deg: 71%.
Grad '10—95. Col—95. (U of MD-Col Park 6, U of PA 3, St Mary's Col of MD 3, Vanderbilt 2, Reed 2, U of VT 2). **Mid 50% SAT:** CR 600-680. M 600-690. W 610-690. Mid 50% ACT: 25-30. **Col couns:** 3.
Tui '11-'12: Day $19,610-22,735 (+$175-700). **Aid:** Need 249 ($3,000,000).
Summer: Acad Enrich Rec. Tui Day $135-2020. 1-8 wks.
Endow $17,700,000. Plant val $45,459,000. Acres 31. Bldgs 13. Class rms 75. 3 Libs 43,735 vols. Sci labs 10. Auds 1. Art studios 1. Dance studios 1. Gyms 2. Fields 6. Courts 4. Pools 1. Comp labs 7.
Est 1784. Nonprofit. Religious Society of Friends (5% practice). Sem (Sept-June). **Assoc** CLS MSA.

Providing a program from preprimary through high school, Friends carries forward the Quaker tradition from the school's 18th-century founding. Occupying a 31-acre site in northern Baltimore, the school's plant includes eight major educational buildings.

Quaker ideals serve as the cornerstone of the school's extensive social service program. Students in grades 9-12 must perform 60 hours of community service in a 12-month period. The school offers a country day program providing a broad liberal education that prepares its graduates for competitive colleges.

GILMAN SCHOOL

Day — Boys Gr K-12

Baltimore, MD 21210. 5407 Roland Ave. Tel: 410-323-3800. Fax: 410-864-2825.
www.gilman.edu E-mail: admissions@gilman.edu
John E. **Schmick, Head (2007).** BA, Univ of Pennsylvania, MEd, Towson Univ. **William H. Gamper, Adm.**
Col Prep. AP (exams req'd; 348 taken, 76% 3+)—Eng Chin Fr Lat Span Calc Stats Comp_Sci Bio Chem Environ_Sci Physics US_Hist Comp_Govt & Pol Econ Psych US_Govt & Pol Art_Hist Music_Theory. **Elem math**—Macmillan/McGraw-Hill. **Feat**—Creative_Writing Sci_Fiction Ger Greek Russ Arabic Anat & Physiol Genetics Web_Design African-Amer_Hist Holocaust Islamic_Stud Architect_Drawing Acting Drama Music_Hist Finance Speech Indus_Arts Study_Skills. **Supp**—Rev Tut.
Sports (req'd)—B: Baseball Basket X-country Football Golf Ice_Hockey Indoor_Track Lacrosse Soccer Squash Swim Tennis Track Volley W_Polo Wrestling. **Activities:** 30.
Selective adm (Gr K-11): 145/yr. Usual entry: K, 1, 6 & 9. Appl fee: $50. Appl due: Jan. Applied: 425. Accepted: 43%. Yield: 70%. **Tests** ISEE.
Enr 1022. Elem 557. Sec 465. Wh 73%. Latino 2%. Blk 13%. Asian 11%. Other 1%. Avg

class size: 16. Stud/fac: 8:1. **Fac 144.** M 89/F 55. FT 140/PT 4. Wh 85%. Latino 3%. Blk 8%. Asian 3%. Other 1%. Adv deg: 71%.
Grad '11—106. Col—106. (U of MD-Col Park 11, Clemson 5, U of VA 4, Dickinson 4, Princeton 3, U of MD-Baltimore County 3). **Avg SAT:** CR 652. M 667. W 649. **Col couns:** 4. Alum donors: 35%.
Tui '12-'13: Day $19,900-25,200 (+$50-650). **Aid:** Need 252 ($3,497,400).
Summer (enr 350): Acad Enrich Rev Rem Rec. Tui Day $250-800. 1-6 wks.
Endow $97,771,000. Plant val $54,299,000. Acres 68. Bldgs 15 (100% ADA). 3 Libs 48,000 vols. Sci labs 16. Auds 1. Theaters 1. Art studios 3. Music studios 4. Gyms 2. Fields 10. Courts 9. Pools 1. Comp labs 3. Comp/stud: 1:2.3.
Est 1897. Nonprofit. Sem (Sept-June). **Assoc** CLS.

Founded as The Country School for Boys of Baltimore City by Anne Galbraith Carey, a mother seeking a strong school for her sons, Gilman was established as the nation's first country day school. In addition to enrolling students from all parts of the city, the school accepts boys of varying religious, cultural and socioeconomic backgrounds.

Gilman provides a solid preparatory curriculum supplemented by many electives. During the lower school years (grades K-5), the program combines a focus on the fundamental skills of reading, writing and math with projects in such areas as science, music, art and woodworking. The middle school (grades 6-8) supplements content learning with instruction in study skills and organization, note taking, problem solving and communication. Boys in the upper school (grades 9-12) have increased scheduling flexibility to pursue interests and determine academic strengths.

The school extends its reach to the broader Baltimore community through community service programs and coordinate classes with two nearby girls' schools, Bryn Mawr School and Roland Park Country School. Lower school children engage in mandatory community service projects, while middle schoolers complete 20 hours of service and upper school students devote at least 50 hours of successive involvement to one project. Athletic participation is compulsory at the upper school level.

PARK SCHOOL

Day — Coed Gr PS-12

Baltimore, MD 21208. 2425 Old Court Rd. Tel: 410-339-4130. Fax: 410-339-4127.
www.parkschool.net   E-mail: admission@parkschool.net
Daniel J. Paradis, Head (2008). AB, Princeton Univ, MAT, Brown Univ. **Megan Ford, Adm.**
Col Prep. AP (113 exams taken, 87% 3+)—Fr Span Calc Stats Comp_Sci Environ_Sci US_Hist Music_Theory. **Feat**—Shakespeare Anat & Physiol Astron Robotics Criminology Art_Hist Film Photog Acting Drama Theater_Arts Outdoor_Ed. **Supp**—Tut.
Sports—Basket X-country Lacrosse Soccer Squash Tennis. B: Baseball. G: F_Hockey Softball Track.
Selective adm: 109/yr. Usual entry: PS, K, 1, 6 & 9. Appl fee: $50. Appl due: Jan. Accepted: 56%. Yield: 51%. **Tests** IQ ISEE Stanford.
Enr 865. B 443. G 422. Elem 540. Sec 325. Avg class size: 16. Stud/fac: 7:1. **Fac 120.** M 45/F 75. FT 105/PT 15. Adv deg: 60%.
Grad '08—75. Col—75. (Columbia, Wash U, Geo Wash, Yale, Wesleyan U, Oberlin). **Avg SAT:** CR 660. M 640. **Col couns:** 2.
Tui '12-'13: Day $23,120-25,420 (+$400-1000). **Aid:** Need 164 ($2,700,000).
Summer: Enrich Rec. Sci. Arts. Challenge Prgm. 2-6 wks.
Endow $21,447,000. Plant val $25,651,000. Acres 100. Bldgs 4. Class rms 60. 2 Libs 45,000 vols. Sci labs 7. Sci/math/tech ctrs 1. Auds 1. Theaters 1. Art studios 4. Music studios 2. Dance studios 1. Gyms 3. Fields 9. Courts 5. Pools 1. Riding rings 1. Stables 1. Tracks 1. Comp labs 3.
Est 1912. Nonprofit. Sem (Sept-June).

One of the nation's first progressive institutions, Park was the laboratory school at which Eugene Randolph Smith developed his nationally known methods. Since 1959, the school has occupied a 100-acre, wooded campus.

Within a broad liberal arts curriculum, the program emphasizes inquiry, analysis, problem solving, independent thinking and fundamental skills. In the early years, Park's integrated curriculum is characterized by an experiential approach that provides room for individualization. At upper grade levels, a broad range of electives complements required course work. Advanced classes are available in all disciplines, and the school's senior term features a required six-week, off-campus project. Park conducts student exchanges with schools in Central America and France.

ROLAND PARK COUNTRY SCHOOL
Day — Girls Gr K-12

Baltimore, MD 21210. 5204 Roland Ave. Tel: 410-323-5500. Fax: 410-323-2164.
www.rpcs.org   E-mail: info@rpcs.org

Jean Waller Brune, Head (1992). BA, Middlebury College, MLA, Johns Hopkins Univ. Peggy K. Wolf, Adm.

Col Prep. AP (exams req'd; 358 taken, 84% 3+)—Eng Chin Fr Span Calc Stats Comp_ Sci Bio Chem Environ_Sci Physics Eur_Hist US_Hist Econ Psych US_Govt & Pol Studio_Art Music_Theory. Feat—Ger Greek Lat Russ Arabic Art_Hist Photog Drama Music_Hist Dance. Outdoor ed.

Sports—G: Badminton Basket Crew X-country F_Hockey Golf Lacrosse Soccer Softball Squash Swim Tennis Track Volley.

Selective adm: 100/yr. Usual entry: K, 1, 6 & 9. Appl fee: $50. Appl due: Jan. Tests CTP_4 ISEE.

Enr 700. Elem 410. Sec 290. Wh 79%. Latino 3%. Blk 12%. Asian 6%. Avg class size: 15. Stud/fac: 6:1. Uniform. Fac 98. Adv deg: 76%.

Grad '10—76. Col—76. (U of MD-Col Park 5, U of VA 3, Georgetown 2, U of PA 2, NYU 2, Syracuse 2). Athl schol 3. Avg SAT: CR 563. M 567. W 589. Mid 50% SAT: CR 510-620. M 500-640. W 530-650. Avg ACT: 26. Mid 50% ACT: 23-27. Col couns: 2. Alum donors: 35%.

Tui '11-'12: Day $23,335 (+$300-2000). Aid: Need 196 ($2,000,000).

Endow $50,000,000. Plant val $32,600,000. Acres 21. Bldgs 1. Class rms 75. Lib 20,382 vols. Sci labs 7. Theaters 1. Music studios 5. Arts ctrs 1. Gyms 3. Athletic ctrs 1. Fields 2. Courts 6. Comp labs 2. Laptop prgm Gr 7-12.

Est 1901. Nonprofit. Sem (Sept-June). Assoc CLS.

Located on a 21-acre estate originally owned by Jerome Bonaparte, RPCS combines modern facilities with the original 19th-century mansion. The school offers a strong academic program that is complemented by more than 50 electives, extracurricular activities, community service opportunities, and interscholastic and intramural sports. Academic standards are high, and there are opportunities for students to take Advanced Placement courses in all disciplines, as well as for foreign travel and study in France, Spain, England, Russia and Germany.

Students perform a total of 60 hours of community service in grades 9-12, including 40 hours at one location. There is the opportunity for career exploration through a senior internship, and a coordinate program with the neighboring Gilman School for boys provides possibilities for additional electives in a coed setting. After-school care is available for lower school girls. Computer instruction begins in kindergarten, and students in grades 7-12 must purchase their own tablet computers. The campus wireless Internet network enhances classroom instruction, laboratory work and library research.

BEL AIR, MD. (21 mi. NE of Baltimore, MD) Suburban. Pop: 10,080. Alt: 380 ft.

HARFORD DAY SCHOOL
Day — Coed Gr PS (Age 4)-8

Bel Air, MD 21014. 715 Moores Mill Rd. Tel: 410-838-4848. Fax: 410-836-5918.
  www.harfordday.org E-mail: info@harfordday.org
Susan G. Harris, Head (1993). BS, Bucknell Univ. **Ellen Kelly, Adm.**
  Pre-Prep. **Feat**—Fr Lat Span Computers Studio_Art Drama Music. **Supp**—Dev_Read
    Rem_Math Rem_Read Tut.
  Sports—Basket Lacrosse Soccer. G: F_Hockey.
  Somewhat selective adm: 44/yr. Usual entry: PS & K. Appl fee: $55. Appl due: Feb.
    Accepted: 85%. Yield: 85%. **Tests** SSAT.
  Enr 325. B 164. G 161. Wh 83%. Latino 2%. Blk 3%. Asian 11%. Other 1%. Avg class
    size: 18. Stud/fac: 9:1. **Fac 42.** M 10/F 32. FT 40/PT 2. Wh 94%. Blk 2%. Asian 4%.
    Adv deg: 42%.
  Grad '10—36. Prep—28. (John Carroll 15, Notre Dame Prep-MD 4, Bryn Mawr 4, St
    Paul's Sch-MD 3, Oldfields 2). Alum donors: 12%.
  Tui '11-'12: Day $14,000 (+$150-200). **Aid:** Need 75 ($397,290).
  Summer: Enrich Rec. 1-4 wks.
  Endow $1,950,000. Plant val $7,612,000. Acres 12. Bldgs 3. Class rms 37. Lib 10,880
    vols. Sci labs 2. Art studios 1. Music studios 1. Gyms 2. Fields 3. Field houses 1.
    Comp labs 2. Comp/stud: 1:3.
  Est 1957. Nonprofit. Quar (Sept-June).

Located 20 miles northeast of Baltimore, this school offers a comprehensive curriculum that includes Spanish, which is taught from prekindergarten. French instruction begins in grade 4, and Latin is taught in grade 8. Reading, writing, language arts and math skills, as well as reasoning and independent thinking, are emphasized. Each grade receives computer instruction, and students participate in art, music and dramatics. Frequent field trips to Baltimore, Washington, DC, and Philadelphia, PA, enrich classroom learning, and small classes permit faculty members to address individual student needs.

Beginning in grade 6, when they serve 10 hours during the year, boys and girls perform compulsory community service. Seventh graders complete a minimum of 20 hours of service per year, eighth graders at least 30 hours. The school offers an optional extended-day program.

BETHESDA, MD. (8 mi. NW of Washington, DC) Urban. Pop: 55,277. Alt: 340 ft.
Area also includes North Bethesda.

GEORGETOWN PREPARATORY SCHOOL
Bdg and Day — Boys Gr 9-12

North Bethesda, MD 20852. 10900 Rockville Pike. Tel: 301-493-5000.
  Fax: 301-493-5905.
  www.gprep.org E-mail: admissions@gprep.org
Rev. Michael J. Marco, SJ, Pres (2010). BA, Creighton Univ, MDiv, Weston Jesuit School
  of Theology, MEd, Boston College. **Jeffrey Jones, Head.** BA, Chaminade Univ of Hono-
  lulu. **Brian J. Gilbert, Adm.**
  Col Prep. AP (exams req'd)—Eng Fr Ger Lat Span Calc Stats Comp_Sci Bio Chem
    Physics Eur_Hist US_Hist World_Hist Econ US_Govt & Pol Art_Hist Studio_Art.
    Feat—Greek Multivariable_Calc Anat & Physiol Relig Photog Stained_Glass Band
    Chorus Orchestra Jazz_Band Driver_Ed. **Supp**—ESL Rev Tut.
  Sports—B: Baseball Basket X-country Fencing Football Golf Ice_Hockey Lacrosse

Rugby Soccer Swim Tennis Track Wrestling. **Activities:** 25.
Selective adm (Gr 9-11): 135/yr. Usual entry: 9 & 11. Appl fee: $50. Appl due: Jan. Applied: 371. Accepted: 27%. Yield: 80%. **Tests** SSAT.
Enr 480. Bdg 110. Day 370. Wh 65%. Latino 10%. Blk 12%. Asian 12%. Other 1%. Intl 15%. Avg class size: 16. Stud/fac: 8:1. Uniform. **Fac 53.** M 35/F 18. FT 49/PT 4. Wh 99%. Latino 1%. Adv deg: 88%. In dorms 7.
Grad '11—117. Col—117. (Georgetown 8, Miami U-OH 4, U of MD-Col Park 4, Notre Dame 4, Clemson 3, Holy Cross 3). **Avg SAT:** CR 620. M 643. W 627. Avg ACT: 27.
Tui '12-'13: Bdg $50,465 (+$500). **Day $29,625** (+$500). **Intl Bdg $50,465** (+$500-6620). **Aid:** Need 100 ($1,900,000).
Summer: Ages 14-17. ESL. Tui Bdg $6800. Tui Day $4150. 6 wks. Ages 5-18. Sports. 1 wk.
Endow $20,000,000. Plant val $70,000,000. Acres 90. Bldgs 8. Dorms 2. Dorm rms 65. Class rms 26. Lib 20,000 vols. Sci labs 3. Lang labs 1. Auds 1. Theaters 1. Art studios 2. Music studios 2. Dance studios 1. Gyms 2. Fields 7. Tennis courts 6. Pools 1. Tracks 2. Golf crses 1. Comp labs 4.
Est 1789. Nonprofit. Roman Catholic (70% practice). Sem (Sept-June). **Assoc** MSA.

Archbishop John Carroll (America's first Catholic bishop) founded this institution, the oldest Catholic secondary school and the only Jesuit boarding school in the country, as a part of Georgetown University. It has been independent since 1919, when it moved to its present, 90-acre campus across the Maryland line.

The school maintains a traditional liberal arts curriculum that prepares graduates for competitive colleges throughout the country. Graduation requirements include four years of English, math and religion; three and a half years of social studies; two years of science, Latin and a modern language; and a year of fine arts course work. In addition to Advanced Placement courses, Georgetown Prep offers accelerated math classes and an honors track in the sciences. Community service requirements are as follows: class project in grade 9, eight hours in grade 10, 12 hours in grade 11 and 50 hours during the summer prior to grade 12.

The school's proximity to Washington, DC, permits visits to cultural and historic destinations, including the US Capitol, the National Gallery of Art and the Smithsonian Institute.

HOLTON-ARMS SCHOOL

Day — Girls Gr 3-12

Bethesda, MD 20817. 7303 River Rd. Tel: 301-365-5300. Fax: 301-365-6071.
www.holton-arms.edu   E-mail: contactus@holton-arms.edu
Susanna A. Jones, Head (2007). AB, Princeton Univ, MA, MPhil, Columbia Univ. **Sharron K. Rodgers, Adm.**
Col Prep. AP (exams req'd; 395 taken, 79% 3+)—Chin Fr Lat Span Calc Stats Bio Environ_Sci Physics Eur_Hist US_Hist Econ Psych US_Govt & Pol Art_Hist. **Feat**—Forensic_Sci Engineering Comp_Sci Philos Existentialism Ceramics Drawing Painting Photog Acting Music Dance.
Sports—G: Basket Crew X-country F_Hockey Ice_Hockey Indoor_Track Lacrosse Soccer Softball Swim Tennis Track Volley. **Activities:** 49.
Selective adm: 108/yr. Appl fee: $60. Appl due: Jan. **Tests** IQ ISEE SSAT.
Enr 645. Elem 313. Sec 332. Avg class size: 15. Stud/fac: 7:1. Uniform. **Fac 92.** Adv deg: 80%.
Grad '11—74. Col—74. (Dartmouth, Davidson, Geo Wash, Georgetown, U of MD-Col Park, Miami U-OH). **Avg SAT:** CR 675. M 668. W 705. **Mid 50% SAT:** CR 660-740. M 610-720. W 630-760. Avg ACT: 29.4. **Col couns:** 2.
Tui '12-'13: Day $31,886-33,441 (+$500). **Aid:** Need 161.
Summer: Enrich Rec. Fine Arts. 6 wks.
Endow $51,030,000. Plant val $43,069,000. Acres 57. Bldgs 8. Class rms 52. 2 Libs 50,000 vols. Sci labs 9. Lang labs 1. Photog labs 1. Theaters 2. Art studios 3. Music studios 4. Dance studios 3. Perf arts ctrs 1. Gyms 2. Athletic ctrs 1. Fields 3. Tennis courts 7. Pools 1. Tracks 1. Weight rms 1. Comp labs 4. Laptop prgm Gr 7-12.
Est 1901. Nonprofit. Sem (Sept-June). **Assoc** CLS MSA.

Founded in Washington, DC, as a small girls' school by Jessie Moon Holton and Carolyn Hough Arms, this school has been at its present, suburban campus since 1963. Faculty utilize a variety of teaching methods while emphasizing the processes of inquiry, critical thinking and reading, and problem solving.

The sequential college preparatory curriculum features strong arts and athletic programs, honors and Advanced Placement courses, and a number of electives, particularly in the pure and applied sciences and the social sciences. Juniors and seniors may complete an independent study course and may register for consortium classes at any of four nearby schools. Girls perform 50 hours of community service prior to senior year. In May, all seniors take part in either a senior project or a structured seminar. Students in grades 7-12 must purchase laptop computers for classroom use.

LANDON SCHOOL

Day — Boys Gr 3-12

Bethesda, MD 20817. 6101 Wilson Ln. Tel: 301-320-3200. Fax: 301-320-2787. www.landon.net   E-mail: landon@landon.net
David M. Armstrong, Head (2004). BA, Princeton Univ, JD, Univ of Denver. **George C. Mulligan, Adm.**

Col Prep. AP (exams req'd; 311 taken, 83% 3+)—Fr Lat Span Calc Stats Comp_Sci Bio Chem Environ_Sci Physics Eur_Hist US_Hist Econ US_Govt & Pol Art_Hist Studio_Art Music_Theory. **Feat**—Humanities Chin Forensic_Sci Oceanog Meteorology Middle_Eastern_Hist Intl_Relations Constitutional_Law Architect Music Public_Speak. **Supp**—Rev Tut.

Sports—B: Baseball Basket X-country Football Golf Ice_Hockey Lacrosse Rugby Soccer Swim Tennis Track W_Polo Wrestling. **Activities:** 30.

Selective adm (Gr 3-9): 126/yr. Usual entry: 3, 4, 7 & 9. Appl fee: $75. Appl due: Jan. Applied: 350. Accepted: 52%. Yield: 64%. **Tests** ISEE SSAT.

Enr 689. Elem 353. Sec 336. Wh 73%. Latino 4%. Blk 13%. Native Am 1%. Asian 7%. Other 2%. Avg class size: 16. Stud/fac: 6:1. Formal. **Fac 107.** M 83/F 24. FT 100/PT 7. Adv deg: 60%.

Grad '11—82. Col—82. (U of MD-Col Park 6, Davidson 6, Tulane 4, Dartmouth 4). Athl schol 5. **Avg SAT:** CR 624. M 641. W 633. Avg ACT: 27.5. **Col couns:** 4. Alum donors: 33%.

Tui '12-'13: Day $31,000-32,000 (+$1000). **Aid:** Need 143 ($2,588,975).

Summer (enr 700): Acad Enrich Rem Rec. Arts. Music. Sports. Travel. 1-3 wks.

Endow $14,000,000. Plant val $39,000,000. Acres 75. Bldgs 13 (15% ADA). Class rms 44. 3 Libs 25,000 vols. Labs 9. Auds 1. Theaters 1. Art studios 7. Music studios 15. Media ctrs 3. Gyms 3. Fields 9. Courts 12. Pools 1. Rifle ranges 1. Comp/stud: 1:3.

Est 1929. Nonprofit. Quar (Sept-June). **Assoc** CLS MSA.

Paul Landon Banfield, a graduate of St. John's College who had taught and coached at Emerson Institute and Dewitt Preparatory School, founded this school for boys with his wife, Mary Lee. The school relocated in 1934 from its original location on Massachusetts Avenue in Washington, DC, to a campus on Bradley and Wilson lanes in Bethesda. Two years later, the school moved to its present, 75-acre location.

Landon's structured college preparatory program emphasizes a solid grounding in fundamental academic skills while seeking to promote intellectual curiosity, artistic impression and social awareness. Leadership and character development are a top priority at all levels. In grades 3 and 4, the school provides a self-contained, traditional classroom setting. Departmentalization begins in grade 5. During the middle school years (grades 6-8), the rigorous academic program focuses on the development of critical-thinking skills.

Upon reaching the upper school (grades 9-12), boys encounter a less structured program that allows for independent study and a greater degree of personal responsibility. Required courses—including a junior year humanities class—and activities are replaced by increased elective choices, and pupils select from a broad range of advanced classes. Community service, which is built into the lower and middle school curricula, is a popular optional activity for upper school students.

STONE RIDGE SCHOOL OF THE SACRED HEART
Day — Boys PS (Age 4)-K, Girls Gr PS (Age 4)-12

Bethesda, MD 20814. 9101 Rockville Pike. Tel: 301-657-4322. Fax: 301-657-4393.
www.stoneridgeschool.org E-mail: mtobias@stoneridgeschool.org
Catherine Ronan Karrels, Head (2008). BA, Boston College, MA, San Francisco State Univ. **Mary Tobias, Adm.**
Col Prep. AP (exams req'd; 234 taken, 71% 3+)—Eng Fr Lat Span Calc Stats Comp_ Sci Bio Chem Physics Eur_Hist US_Hist Comp_Govt & Pol Econ Psych US_Govt & Pol Art_Hist Studio_Art. **Feat**—British_Lit Creative_Writing Multivariable_Calc Anat & Physiol Astron Environ_Sci Forensic_Sci Engineering Molecular_Bio Sociol Theol Ceramics Filmmaking Fine_Arts Graphic_Arts Photog Drama Handbells Journ.
Sports—G: Basket X-country F_Hockey Lacrosse Soccer Softball Swim Tennis Track Volley. **Activities:** 44.
Selective adm (Gr PS-11): 138/yr. Appl fee: $50. Applied: 325. **Tests** CTP_4 SSAT.
Enr 660. B 7. G 653. Elem 338. Sec 322. Wh 62%. Latino 7%. Blk 14%. Asian 8%. Other 9%. Avg class size: 16. Uniform. **Fac 85.** M 17/F 68. FT 68/PT 17. Wh 83%. Latino 9%. Blk 4%. Asian 4%. Adv deg: 62%.
Grad '11—66. Col—66. (Bucknell 2, Georgetown 2, NYU 2, U of PA 2, U of MD-Col Park 2, Villanova 2). Athl social 2. **Col couns:** 2. Alum donors: 25%.
Tui '11-'12: Day $20,250-25,200 (+$250-750). **Aid:** Merit 38. Need 118 ($1,438,000).
Summer (enr 700): Acad Enrich. Tui Day $600-1300. 3-6 wks.
Endow $30,000,000. Plant val $19,100,000. Acres 35. Bldgs 12. Class rms 38. Libs 3. Sci labs 6. Art studios 5. Music studios 3. Gyms 3. Fields 3. Tennis courts 4. Pools 1. Comp labs 3. Laptop prgm Gr 9-12.
Est 1923. Nonprofit. Roman Catholic. Sem (Aug-June). **Assoc** CLS MSA.

Founded by the Society of the Sacred Heart and a member of the Network of Sacred Heart Schools, Stone Ridge occupies a 35-acre campus and draws its student body from a 50-mile radius. The school conducts a college preparatory program for girls in grades 1-12, as well as coeducational prekindergarten and kindergarten programs. The upper school (grades 9-12) offers accelerated and advanced courses, in addition to independent study and expanded course options through the Bethesda Independent Schools' Consortium. Through Stone Ridge's exchange program, students may spend one semester at a Sacred Heart school in the United States or abroad.

Community service is integrated into the upper school curriculum. Beginning with a year-long orientation in grade 9, girls devote six hours every other Wednesday (from October through April) to service work. All seniors take part in a five-day, 40-hour internship in the Washington, DC, metropolitan area that enables each student to experience a job setting and meet professionals in a particular career field.

BROOKLANDVILLE, MD. (9 mi. NNW of Baltimore, MD) Suburban. Pop: 800. Alt: 300 ft.

ST. PAUL'S SCHOOL
Day — Boys Gr K-12, Girls K-4

Brooklandville, MD 21022. 11152 Falls Rd, PO Box 8100. Tel: 410-825-4400.
Fax: 410-427-0390.
www.stpaulsschool.org E-mail: admissions@stpaulsschool.org

Thomas J. Reid, Head (2002). BA, Univ of Pennsylvania, MA, Univ of Connecticut. **Peter Hawley, Adm.**

> **Col Prep. IB Diploma. AP**—Studio_Art. **Feat**—Fr Ger Japan Span Stats Anat & Physiol Environ_Sci Forensic_Sci Cold_War Econ Geog Psych Ethics World_Relig Graphic_ Arts Photog Drama Theater_Arts Music Jazz_Band Dance. **Supp**—Dev_Read Rem_ Math Rem_Read Rev Tut.
>
> **Sports (req'd)**—B: Baseball Basket Crew X-country Football Golf Ice_Hockey Lacrosse Soccer Squash Swim Tennis Volley Wrestling.
>
> **Selective adm:** 146/yr. Usual entry: K, 5, 6 & 9. Appl fee: $50. Appl due: Jan. Applied: 456. Accepted: 69%. Yield: 47%. **Tests** ISEE Stanford.
>
> **Enr 800.** Wh 79%. Latino 1%. Blk 15%. Asian 2%. Other 3%. Avg class size: 16. Stud/fac: 9:1. Formal. **Fac 110.** Wh 93%. Blk 3%. Asian 3%. Other 1%.
>
> **Grad '11—77. Col—77.** (U of MD-Col Park, U of CO-Boulder, Tulane, Elon, UNC-Wilmington). **Mid 50% SAT:** CR 560-650. M 560-670. W 560-650. **Col couns:** 5.
>
> **Tui '11-'12: Day $19,450-23,850** (+$400). **Aid:** Need 200 ($2,400,000).
>
> **Summer:** Enrich Rec. Sports. Tui Day $180-405/wk. 6 wks.
>
> Endow $30,300,000. Plant val $28,600,000. Acres 95. Bldgs 27. 3 Libs 30,600 vols. Sci labs 6. Lang labs 1. Theaters 1. Art studios 4. Music studios 8. Gyms 4. Fields 8. Tennis courts 14. Ropes crses 1. Comp labs 3. Laptop prgm Gr 9-12.
>
> **Est 1849.** Nonprofit. Episcopal. Sem (Sept-June). **Assoc** CLS.

Affiliated with the Episcopal Church, St. Paul's was founded in a Sunday school room of St. Paul's Parish in downtown Baltimore. In 1952, the school moved to its current, 95-acre campus, which includes Brooklandwood, a mansion built in 1793 by Charles Carroll, a signer of the Declaration of Independence. St. Paul's is coordinated with the adjacent St. Paul's School for Girls, and a common center for the arts joins the two campuses. St. Paul's lower school is coeducational through grade 4, and most of the girls proceed to St. Paul's School for Girls. During the middle and upper school years, boys and girls of the two schools share many activities, projects and classes, including all electives and most language courses.

The school places an emphasis on the arts, beginning in the lower school, when children take such courses as visual arts, music and dance, and movement. Middle school pupils gain exposure to various artistic media, while upper schoolers may pursue the arts through group classes, private lessons, and performances and shows. Upper school students may pursue the International Baccalaureate Diploma. Among the graduation requirements are electives, study of world religions, one year of art and 60 cumulative hours of community service.

A three-week program at the end of May enables seniors to gain career insights through internships with community businesses and organizations, and the Mountain School program of Milton Academy provides juniors and seniors the opportunity to study for a semester in a rural setting in Vermont. St. Paul's also encourages foreign exchange and travel programs and is involved in study programs in Spain, Germany and France. Middle school students take part in an outdoor education program, and upper school students must participate in 10 of 12 athletic seasons.

ST. PAUL'S SCHOOL FOR GIRLS

Day — Girls Gr 5-12

Brooklandville, MD 21022. 11232 Falls Rd. Tel: 410-823-6323. **Fax:** 410-828-7238. www.spsfg.org   **E-mail:** bsmith@spsfg.org

Lila B. Lohr, Int Head (2012). BA, Vassar College, MEd, Goucher College. **Susan A. Hasler, Adm.**

> **Col Prep. AP (exams req'd; 187 taken, 88% 3+)**—Eng Fr Span Calc Stats Bio Chem Environ_Sci Physics Eur_Hist US_Hist World_Hist Econ Psych Studio_Art. **Feat**— Poetry Shakespeare 20th-Century_Lit Chin Ger Japan Cold_War Amer_Stud Women's_Stud Ethics World_Relig Art_Hist Fine_Arts Performing_Arts Photog Theater Music Jazz_Band Dance Journ. **Supp**—Dev_Read Rem_Math Rev Tut.
>
> **Sports**—G: Badminton Basket Crew X-country F_Hockey Golf Lacrosse Soccer Softball Swim Tennis Volley. **Activities:** 24.

Selective adm (Gr 5-11): 73/yr. Appl fee: $50. Appl due: Jan. Accepted: 50%. **Tests** ISEE.
Enr 414. Elem 158. Sec 256. Wh 76%. Latino 2%. Blk 13%. Asian 3%. Other 6%. Avg class size: 17. Stud/fac: 6:1. Uniform. **Fac 74.** M 11/F 63. Wh 89%. Latino 2%. Blk 8%. Asian 1%. Adv deg: 72%.
Grad '11—76. Col—76. (Cornell, Duke, Wake Forest, U of MD-Col Park, Wash U, U of VA). Athl schol 3. **Mid 50% SAT:** CR 540-700. M 540-650. W 580-700. **Col couns:** 2.
Tui '12-'13: Day $22,455-23,570 (+$1000). **Aid:** Need 124.
Summer (enr 100): Coed. Arts. Dance. Sports. Tui Day $200/wk. 4 wks.
Endow $7,000,000. Plant val $17,209,000. Acres 38. Bldgs 3. Class rms 34. Lib 10,191 vols. Chapels 1. Sci labs 8. Theaters 1. Art studios 3. Music studios 2. Dance studios 1. Arts ctrs 1. Gyms 2. Fields 1. Tennis courts 4. Weight rms 1. Fitness ctrs 1. Comp labs 2. Comp/stud: 1:3 (1:1 Laptop prgm Gr 5-12).
Est 1959. Nonprofit. Episcopal. (Sept-June). **Assoc** CLS.

Affiliated with the nearby St. Paul's School, St. Paul's School for Girls has separate facilities and administration. Children in the middle school follow a developmentally appropriate, interdisciplinary curriculum, while students in the upper school pursue a college preparatory program of traditional liberal arts subjects. Advanced Placement courses are offered in many subject areas.

Girls in grades 9-12 satisfy a 60-hour community service requirement. Faculty and students alternately conduct daily assemblies and weekly chapel services, with the assistance of outside speakers.

CENTREVILLE, MD. (34 mi. ESE of Baltimore, MD) Rural. Pop: 1970. Alt: 61 ft.

THE GUNSTON SCHOOL
Day — Coed Gr 9-12

Centreville, MD 21617. 911 Gunston Rd, PO Box 200. Tel: 410-758-0620.
Fax: 410-758-0628.
www.gunston.org   E-mail: dhenry@gunston.org
John A. Lewis IV, Head (2010). BA, Georgetown Univ, EdM, Harvard Univ, MA, Columbia Univ. **David G. Henry, Adm.**
Col Prep. AP (exams req'd; 44 taken, 59% 3+)—Eng Lat Span Calc Bio Chem Environ_Sci Physics Eur_Hist US_Hist World_Hist Studio_Art. **Feat**—Ecol Comp_Sci Robotics Psych Ethics Photog Drama Music SAT_Prep. **Supp**—ESL Tut. **Dual enr:** Chesapeake, Wash Col, Anne Arundel CC.
Sports—Basket Crew Golf Lacrosse Sail Soccer Swim Tennis. G: F_Hockey.
Somewhat selective adm: 50/yr. Appl fee: $50. Appl due: Feb. Applied: 63. Accepted: 95%. Yield: 67%. **Tests** ISEE SSAT.
Enr 136. B 67. G 69. Wh 80%. Blk 1%. Asian 19%. Intl 19%. Avg class size: 8. Stud/fac: 6:1. Casual. **Fac 27.** M 16/F 11. FT 27. Wh 98%. Asian 1%. Other 1%. Adv deg: 59%.
Grad '11—42. Col—42. (St Mary's Col of MD 4, High Pt 3, Rochester Inst of Tech 2, Guilford 2, Wash Col 2, Tufts 1). Athl schol 1. **Avg SAT:** CR 575. M 528. W 546. **Mid 50% SAT:** CR 500-640. M 480-590. W 470-630. **Col couns:** 1. Alum donors: 30%.
Tui '12-'13: Day $21,950 (+$600). **Aid:** Merit 2 ($20,000). Need 62 ($750,400).
Summer (enr 200): Acad Enrich Rec. Tui Day $170-300/wk. 9 wks.
Endow $1,000,000. Plant val $3,000,000. Acres 35. Bldgs 3. Class rms 18. Lib 5000 vols. Sci labs 3. Dark rms 1. Comp ctrs 1. Auds 1. Art studios 2. Music studios 1. Dance studios 1. Gyms 1. Fields 3. Tennis courts 4. Field houses 1. Boathouses 1. Comp/stud: 1:3.
Est 1911. Nonprofit. Sem (Sept-June). **Assoc** MSA.

Samuel and Mary Middleton opened this school on their Corsica River farm to educate their own children and those of their friends and neighbors. For many years, Gunston continued to provide a family environment for girls on Maryland's Eastern Shore. In 1996, the school first admitted boys as day students and also discontinued its boarding division. Students enroll from throughout the Upper Bay region.

Gunston offers a strong core of traditional academics and features Advanced Placement and honors classes, as well as electives in music, drama, dance and the studio arts. A compulsory, interdisciplinary bay studies program allows students to learn about the Chesapeake Bay as an ecological, historical and cultural resource.

Trips to museums, art galleries and the theater complement the curriculum. Students accumulate 45 hours of required community service in grades 9-12.

COLORA, MD. (37 mi. NE of Baltimore, MD) Rural. Pop: 160. Alt: 450 ft.

WEST NOTTINGHAM ACADEMY
Bdg and Day — Coed Gr 9-12

Colora, MD 21917. 1079 Firetower Rd. Tel: 410-658-9279. Fax: 410-658-9264.
www.wna.org   E-mail: admissions@wna.org
Stephen J. Brotschul, Head (2012). BS, Univ of Massachusetts-Amherst, MA, California State Univ-San Bernardino. Joseph Izokaitis, Adm.
  Col Prep. AP (7 exams taken, 43% 3+)—Eng Calc Physics Eur_Hist US_Hist. Feat—Creative_Writing Fr Span Anat & Physiol Computers Aesthetics Ethics Relig Studio_ Art Acting Music. Supp—ESL LD Rem_Math Rem_Read Tut.
  Sports—Basket X-country Lacrosse Soccer. B: Baseball Golf. G: Softball Volley. Activities: 12.
  Selective adm: 53/yr. Appl fee: $50. Appl due: Rolling. Accepted: 52%. Yield: 84%. Tests SSAT TOEFL.
  Enr 120. B 64. G 56. Bdg 78. Day 42. Wh 62%. Latino 3%. Blk 15%. Asian 20%. Intl 37%. Avg class size: 10. Stud/fac: 7:1. Casual. Fac 32. M 19/F 13. FT 32. Wh 95%. Latino 5%. Adv deg: 71%. In dorms 13.
  Grad '10—36. Col—36. (NYU 3, Syracuse 3, James Madison 2, U of MD-Col Park 2, U of MD-Baltimore County 2, Dickinson 2). Athl schol 2. Avg SAT: CR 556. M 549. W 534. Col couns: 1.
  Tui '11-'12: Bdg $42,380 (+$1100). Day $16,150 (+$600). Intl Bdg $44,564 (+$1100-8100). Aid: Need 42.
  Endow $3,000,000. Plant val $14,000,000. Acres 120. Bldgs 16. Dorms 4. Dorm rms 65. Class rms 25. Lib 8500 vols. Sci labs 3. Comp ctrs 1. Auds 1. Art studios 1. Music studios 1. Dance studios 1. Gyms 1. Fields 6. Courts 3. Field houses 1. Pools 1. Comp labs 1.
  Est 1744. Nonprofit. Tri (Aug-June). Assoc MSA.

Noted graduates of this school, founded by Rev. Samuel Finley, include colonial leaders Benjamin Rush and Richard Stockton, both signers of the Declaration of Independence. The campus is located on 120 acres of northeastern Maryland countryside.

West Nottingham offers a college preparatory curriculum and supports students through its advisor program and individual academic support. A strong sense of community exists in campus life. As a complement to the academic program, the academy offers a well-developed athletic program and makes use of the recreational and cultural resources of the Baltimore/ Philadelphia, PA, area. All boys and girls complete 15 hours of required community service prior to graduation.

In addition to its traditional program, WNA offers the Chesapeake Learning Center curriculum (available for an additional fee), a regular high school course of studies adapted for students with learning differences who are of average to above-average intelligence. The multisensory CLC Program features smaller classes, a structured study hall and ongoing tutorial assistance.

As a third program option, West Nottingham provides a well-developed English as a Second Language curriculum that prepares international students for US colleges. The program, available at beginning, intermediate and advanced levels, also includes instruction in mathematics, science, history and the arts. Participants incur an additional fee.

EASTON, MD. (47 mi. SE of Baltimore, MD) Urban. Pop: 11,708. Alt: 38 ft.

COUNTRY SCHOOL
Day — Coed Gr K-8

Easton, MD 21601. 716 Goldsborough St. Tel: 410-822-1935. Fax: 410-822-1971.
www.countryschool.org E-mail: kbalderson@countryschool.org
Neil Mufson, Head (1990). AB, Brown Univ, MEd, Tufts Univ. **Kimerly C. Balderson, Adm.**
  Pre-Prep. Gen Acad. Feat—Lat Span Ecol Computers Band Music Outdoor_Ed. **Supp**—Tut.
  Sports—Basket Lacrosse Soccer. G: F_Hockey.
  Selective adm: 48/yr. Appl fee: $50. Appl due: Rolling. **Tests** CTP_4.
  Enr 288. B 137. G 151. Nonwhite 20%. Avg class size: 17. Stud/fac: 10:1. Uniform. **Fac 38.** Adv deg: 31%.
  Grad '10—31. Prep—15. (Gunston Day, Mercersburg, George Sch, Madeira, St Andrew's Sch-DE). Alum donors: 15%.
  Tui '11-'12: Day $13,250. Aid: Need 101.
  Summer: Acad Enrich Rec Rev Rec. Art. Tui Day $100-150/wk. 2 wks.
  Endow $7,741,000. Plant val $6,613,000. Acres 9. Bldgs 1. Class rms 28. Lib 17,620 vols. Sci labs 2. Auds 1. Gyms 1. Fields 2. Comp labs 2.
  Est 1934. Nonprofit. Tri (Sept-June).

The school provides a traditional and structured yet child-centered curriculum that features small classes and individual attention in a family setting. Varied nonacademic activities, including the fine and performing arts, outdoor education, instrumental music, community service, physical education and life skills, are offered. The interscholastic sports program commences in grade 6.

ELLICOTT CITY, MD. (12 mi. W of Baltimore, MD) Suburban. Pop: 56,397. Alt: 580 ft.

GLENELG COUNTRY SCHOOL
Day — Coed Gr PS (Age 4)-12

Ellicott City, MD 21042. 12793 Folly Quarter Rd. Tel: 410-531-7347.
Fax: 410-531-7363.
www.glenelg.org E-mail: admission@glenelg.org
Gregory J. Ventre, Head (2007). BA, St John's Univ (NY), MA, New York Univ. **Karen K. Wootton, Adm.**
  Col Prep. AP (exams req'd; 195 taken, 59% 3+)—Eng Fr Lat Span Calc Stats Comp_ Sci Bio Chem Environ_Sci Physics Eur_Hist Econ Art_Hist Studio_Art Music_Theory. **Feat**—British_Lit Creative_Writing Humanities Chin Anat & Physiol Astron Anthro Psych Asian_Stud Islamic_Stud Philos Photog Sculpt Drama Theater_Arts Chorus.

Supp—Rev Tut.
Sports—Basket X-country Lacrosse Soccer Tennis. B: Baseball Golf Ice_Hockey. G: F_Hockey Volley.
Selective adm (Gr PS-11): 126/yr. Appl fee: $75. Appl due: Feb. Accepted: 75%. Yield: 67%. **Tests** CTP_4 ISEE SSAT Stanford.
Enr 777. Elem 488. Sec 289. Wh 60%. Latino 3%. Blk 15%. Asian 10%. Other 12%. Avg class size: 15. Stud/fac: 6:1. Uniform. **Fac 118.** Adv deg: 43%.
Grad '11—70. Col—70. (VA Polytech, Randolph-Macon, James Madison, Dickinson, Vanderbilt, U of MD-Baltimore County). **Mid 50% SAT:** CR 540-670. M 520-690. **Col couns:** 2. Alum donors: 25%.
Tui '12-'13: Day $20,350-24,170 (+$675-775). **Aid:** Need 303 ($2,500,000).
Summer: Acad Enrich Rev Rec. Drama. Adventure. Sports. 1-6 wks.
Plant val $60,000,000. Acres 87. Bldgs 6. Class rms 55. 4 Libs 18,000 vols. Sci labs 6. Auds 1. Theaters 1. Art studios 4. Music studios 3. Dance studios 1. Gyms 2. Fields 4. Courts 1. Pools 1. Comp labs 4. Comp/stud: 1:2.2.
Est 1954. Nonprofit. Quar (Sept-June). **Assoc** CLS MSA.

Located in historic Glenelg Manor (dating from 1740) on 87 acres of fields and woodland, GCS was established for students in Howard County and the surrounding area. Emphasis is placed on academics, with creative arts, athletics and mandatory community service included.

French and Spanish are offered from prekindergarten, Latin from grade 6 and Chinese from grade 9. Each year of high school features a compulsory interdisciplinary course: Freshmen take a humanities class that combines the origins of human society, history, anthropology and sociology with English literature; sophomores take a course combining Western literature with arts and ideas; juniors study American literature and expository writing in conjunction with a US history course; and seniors take part in an integrative seminar that reflects upon the "product and process of learning" across the curriculum. Advanced Placement courses, internships and independent study opportunities broaden the academic program.

Upper school boys and girls perform 25 hours of community service annually. Also part of the curriculum are field trips to Baltimore and Washington, DC, that enable students to take advantage of cultural amenities such as art galleries, museums, the theater and historical sites.

GLENCOE, MD. (17 mi. N of Baltimore, MD) Rural. Pop: 215. Alt: 600 ft.

OLDFIELDS SCHOOL

Bdg — Girls Gr 8-PG; Day — Girls 6-PG

Glencoe, MD 21152. 1500 Glencoe Rd. Tel: 410-472-4800. Fax: 410-472-6839.
www.oldfieldsschool.org E-mail: admission@oldfieldsschool.org
Taylor Smith, Head (2008). BA, Wesleyan Univ, MEd, Loyola College. **Parnell P. Hagerman, Adm.**
Col Prep. AP (58 exams taken)—Chem. **Feat**—Creative_Writing Chin Fr Span Calc Stats Anat & Physiol Environ_Sci Forensic_Sci Marine_Bio/Sci Equine_Sci Comp_Sci Pol_Sci Ceramics Photog Drama Dance. **Supp**—Rev Tut.
Sports (req'd)—G: Badminton Basket X-country F_Hockey Lacrosse Soccer Softball Tennis Volley. **Activities:** 25.
Selective adm (Bdg Gr 8-12; Day 6-12): 65/yr. Bdg 45. Day 20. Usual entry: 9 & 10. Appl fee: $50. Appl due: Feb. Applied: 350. Accepted: 55%. Yield: 45%. **Tests** CEEB CTP_4 HSPT IQ ISEE MAT SSAT TOEFL.
Enr 155. Bdg 97. Day 58. Elem 20. Sec 135. Wh 60%. Latino 5%. Blk 17%. Asian 6%. Other 12%. Intl 19%. Avg class size: 10. Stud/fac: 5:1. Casual. **Fac 45.** Wh 94%. Latino 2%. Blk 2%. Other 2%. Adv deg: 42%. In dorms 25.
Grad '10—43. Col—42. (Brown, Wm & Mary, Randolph-Macon, Dickinson, U of PA,

Gettysburg). **Mid 50% SAT:** CR 450-570. M 420-570. W 450-540. Mid 50% ACT: 19-22. **Col couns:** 1. Alum donors: 45%.
Tui '12-'13: Bdg $46,500. 5-Day Bdg $44,700. Day $28,500. Intl Bdg $46,500 (+$1500). **Aid:** Need 32 ($1,000,000).
Endow $12,000,000. Plant val $14,300,000. Acres 230. Bldgs 22. Dorms 7. Dorm rms 76. Class rms 23. Lib 10,000 vols. Sci labs 5. Theaters 1. Art studios 4. Music studios 2. Dance studios 1. Gyms 1. Fields 4. Courts 5. Pools 1. Riding rings 3. Stables 1. Barns 1. Comp labs 2. Laptop prgm Gr 8-PG.
Est 1867. Nonprofit. Tri (Aug-June). **Assoc** MSA.

Mrs. John Sears McCulloch founded Oldfields to provide instruction to her own and neighboring girls. Mrs. McCulloch fostered high standards among her girls and at the same time always retained the family-like atmosphere of the school. Under the leadership of Mrs. McCulloch and succeeding members of her family, Oldfields was among the first schools to offer girls complete programs in chemistry, athletics, the fine and performing arts, riding and student government. The McCulloch family directed the school through 1960, when the last McCulloch retired. Oldfields is operated as a nonsectarian school under a board of trustees composed of parents, past parents and alumnae.

School life is informal, but structured. From its beginnings, the school has helped each girl select a course of study appropriate to her needs, and, since early this century, Oldfields has offered a personalized curriculum. Flexible scheduling enables college preparatory course work to accommodate both the motivated student of average ability and the gifted pupil. Each spring, Oldfields conducts the May Program, which comprises two-week, self-contained programs in a variety of academic and social disciplines for all students. Options include faculty-supervised language and cultural immersion experiences in France, Spain, Peru and Belize, as well as on-campus programs and internship opportunities for seniors. During her tenure at Oldfields, each girl must select at least one May Program trip that focuses upon community service.

Extensive extracurricular opportunities, field trips, outings and weekend activities enrich the academic experience and routinely take students to places of interest in the four-state area. The school offers a particularly strong equestrian program. Among the riding facilities are an indoor riding arena, two outdoor show rings, an extensive cross-country course and trails along the Gunpowder River. **See Also Pages 94-5**

OLNEY, MD. (17 mi. NNW of Washington, DC) Suburban. Pop: 31,438. Alt: 544 ft.

ST. JOHN'S EPISCOPAL SCHOOL
Day — Coed Gr PS (Age 3)-8

Olney, MD 20832. 3427 Olney-Laytonsville Rd. Tel: 301-774-6804. Fax: 301-774-2375. www.stjes.com E-mail: mark.woodson@stjes.com
Thomas R. Stevens, Head (2011). BA, Yale Univ, MA, Columbia Univ. **Mark Woodson, Adm.**
Pre-Prep. Feat—Fr Lat Span Environ_Sci Relig Studio_Art Music. **Supp**—Tut.
Sports—Basket X-country Lacrosse Soccer.
Selective adm: 38/yr. Usual entry: PS & K. Appl fee: $50. Appl due: Feb. Accepted: 70%. **Tests** IQ.
Enr 235. Wh 91%. Latino 4%. Blk 2%. Asian 3%. Avg class size: 16. Uniform. **Fac 33.** M 4/F 29. FT 29/PT 4. Adv deg: 48%.
Grad '11—35. Prep—31. (Our Lady of Good Counsel, Holton-Arms, Stone Ridge, Connelly Sch of the Holy Child).
Tui '12-'13: Day $11,925-18,820.
Endow $285,000. Plant val $4,800,000. Bldgs 2. Lib 10,000 vols. Sci labs 2. Music studios 2. Gyms 1. Fields 1. Comp labs 2.
Est 1961. Nonprofit. Episcopal. Tri (Sept-June).

Serving Montgomery County, this Episcopal school offers a well-balanced curriculum and small classes, giving students a solid grounding in the fundamentals. The school strives to develop students' study, organizational and test-taking skills through its standard pre-preparatory curriculum.

Emphasis on reading and writing begins with an introduction to phonics in kindergarten and culminates with the preparation of research papers in the upper grades. Math classes are tracked beginning in grade 6, allowing qualified students to take algebra in grade 8. Field trips to local historical sites and science and nature facilities supplement social studies and science instruction. Spanish study begins in kindergarten, while Latin starts in grade 7.

Community service is part of the curriculum at all grade levels: Children in grades PS-4 participate in an annual class project, while boys and girls in 5-8 engage in individual service work. Weekly chapel, social outreach participation and family involvement are integral aspects of school life.

OWINGS MILLS, MD. (12 mi. NW of Baltimore, MD) Rural. Pop: 9474. Alt: 496 ft.

GARRISON FOREST SCHOOL

Bdg — Girls Gr 8-12; Day — Boys PS (Age 2)-K, Girls PS (Age 2)-12

Owings Mills, MD 21117. 300 Garrison Forest Rd. Tel: 410-363-1500.
  Fax: 410-363-8441.
  www.gfs.org   E-mail: admission@gfs.org
G. Peter O'Neill, Jr., Head (1995). BA, St Michael's College, MA, Trinity College (CT).
  Leslie D. Tinati, Adm.
  Col Prep. AP—Eng Fr Lat Span Calc Bio Chem Environ_Sci US_Hist Art_Hist Studio_ Art. **Feat**—Creative_Writing Chin Stats Multivariable_Calc Anat & Physiol Ecol Animal_Behavior Comp_Sci Econ Child_Dev Middle_Eastern_Stud Peace_Stud Ethics World_Relig Drawing Photog Drama Theater_Arts Music Dance. **Supp**— ESL.
  Sports—G: Basket X-country Equestrian F_Hockey Golf Lacrosse Soccer Softball Squash Tennis Track W_Polo. **Activities:** 20.
  Selective adm (Bdg Gr 8-11; Day PS-11): 116/yr. Bdg 27. Day 89. Usual entry: K, 1, 6 & 9. Appl fee: $50. Appl due: Jan. Applied: 273. Accepted: 58%. Yield: 63%. **Tests** ISEE SSAT TOEFL.
  Enr 675. B 19. G 656. Bdg 70. Day 605. Elem 385. Sec 290. Wh 72%. Latino 3%. Blk 17%. Asian 5%. Other 3%. Intl 14%. Avg class size: 14. Stud/fac: 7:1. Uniform. **Fac 99.** M 10/F 89. FT 99. Wh 88%. Latino 3%. Blk 4%. Asian 5%. Adv deg: 69%. In dorms 6.
  Grad '10—67. Col—67. (U of VA 6, U of MD-Col Park 6, U of VT 3, Clemson 3, Wash & Lee 2, Rensselaer Polytech 2). Athl schol 14. **Avg SAT:** CR 619. M 611. W 605. Avg ACT: 27. **Col couns:** 2.
  Tui '11-'12: Bdg $34,600-43,860 (+$2500). **5-Day Bdg $34,600** (+$2500). **Day $21,700- 23,990** (+$200-1075). **Aid:** Merit 2 ($21,220). Need 168 ($2,265,280).
  Summer: Rec. 6 wks.
  Endow $39,000,000. Plant val $31,000,000. Acres 115. Bldgs 18. Dorms 3. Dorm rms 50. Class rms 50. Lib 16,000 vols. Chapels 1. Comp ctrs 3. Theaters 1. Art studios 5. Music studios 6. Dance studios 1. Arts ctrs 1. Gyms 2. Athletic ctrs 1. Fields 4. Tennis courts 7. Riding rings 4. Stables 2. Weight rms 1. Student ctrs 1. Laptop prgm Gr 5-12.
  Est 1910. Nonprofit. Quar (Sept-June). **Assoc** CLS MSA.

Established by Mary M. Livingston, Garrison Forest has always been characterized by high academic standards and a close association between faculty and students. The curriculum, with an emphasis on academic fundamentals, prepares students for leading colleges. In addition to the core courses of English, history, math, science, modern languages and Latin, girls choose among electives in the humanities, science and the arts. Seniors may explore academic or career interests in May through a three-week independent project or a professional internship. GFS assigns tablet computers to all students in grade 4; girls in grades 5-12 then purchase their own tablets. Beginning in first grade, all classrooms are equipped with wireless data projectors and mounted speakers.

The Women in Science and Engineering (WISE) program, a partnership between the school and Johns Hopkins University, recruits junior and senior girls from within the school and around the country to spend a semester in residence at GFS. In addition to following a customized curriculum, participants spend two afternoons a week on the Johns Hopkins campus engaging in hands-on research, science immersion experiences and mentoring activities with university faculty.

Boys may enroll in the preschool and kindergarten programs only.

McDONOGH SCHOOL

5-Day Bdg — Coed Gr 9-12; Day — Coed K-12

Owings Mills, MD 21117. 8600 McDonogh Rd. Tel: 410-363-0600. Fax: 410-581-4777.
www.mcdonogh.org   E-mail: tfish@mcdonogh.org
Charles W. Britton, Head (2007). BA, Lake Forest College, MA, Middlebury College. **Tim Fish, Int Adm.**

Col Prep. AP—Eng Fr Ger Span Calc Comp_Sci Bio Chem Physics Eur_Hist US_Hist World_Hist Econ US_Govt & Pol Studio_Art Music_Theory. **Elem math**—Everyday Math. **Elem read**—Balanced Literacy. **Feat**—Poetry Shakespeare African-Amer_Lit Jewish-Amer_Lit Sci_Fiction Chin Lat Anat Astron Ecol Genetics Marine_Bio/Sci Engineering African_Hist Civil_War Middle_Eastern_Hist Russ_Hist Intl_Relations Psych Philos Ceramics Photog Sculpt Music Dance. **Supp**—Dev_Read Rem_Read.

Sports—Basket X-country Equestrian Golf Indoor_Track Lacrosse Soccer Squash Swim Track Ultimate_Frisbee W_Polo. B: Baseball Football Wrestling. G: Cheer F_ Hockey Softball Tennis. **Activities: 57.**

Selective adm: 178/yr. Bdg 6. Day 172. Usual entry: K, 6 & 9. Appl fee: $45-50. Appl due: Dec. Applied: 762. Accepted: 35%. Yield: 66%. **Tests** IQ ISEE Stanford.

Enr 1296. B 689. G 607. Elem 708. Sec 588. Avg class size: 18. Stud/fac: 9:1. Uniform. **Fac 157.** M 56/F 101. Adv deg: 83%. In dorms 4.

Grad '11—141. Col—139. (U of MD-Col Park 12, Bucknell 5, Franklin & Marshall 4, Col of Charleston 4, Cornell 3, Wash U 3). **Mid 50% SAT:** CR 560-670. M 590-700. W 580-670. Mid 50% ACT: 25-30. **Col couns:** 3.

Tui '11-'12: 5-Day Bdg $33,830 (+$220-320). **Day $22,620-25,160** (+$220-320). **Aid:** Need 236 ($3,700,000).

Summer: Acad Rec. 2 wks.

Endow $83,050,000. Plant val $95,000,000. Acres 800. Bldgs 44. Dorms 2. Class rms 58. Lib 30,000 vols. Theaters 2. Art studios 6. Music studios 12. Dance studios 1. Perf arts ctrs 1. Art galleries 1. Gyms 2. Athletic ctrs 1. Fields 19. Tennis courts 20. Pools 1. Riding rings 4. Stables 1. Tracks 1. Stadiums 1. Comp labs 5.

Est 1873. Nonprofit. Tri (Sept-June). **Assoc** CLS.

Established by the endowment of John McDonogh as a school for scholarship students, this institution began accepting paying students in 1922. In 1975, coeducation was instituted in the day department. The boarding department became coeducational in 1983.

All upper schoolers complete 40 hours of community service prior to graduation. Athletic participation is not required, but those who do not take part in a sport must take physical education classes. The riding program features 80 horses and extensive professional facilities on the school's 800-acre campus.

International programs include upper school trips to France, Germany, Japan, Spain and the Ukraine, as well as a yearlong exchange program with Seijo and Gauken Senior High School in Tokyo, Japan. Out-of-state and international students boarding at McDonough may reside with host families.

PASADENA, MD. (13 mi. SSE of Baltimore, MD) Urban. Pop: 12,093. Alt: 80 ft.

EAGLE COVE SCHOOL
Day — Coed Gr PS (Age 4)-5

Pasadena, MD 21122. 5191 Mountain Rd. Tel: 410-255-5370. Fax: 410-255-0416.
  www.eaglecoveschool.org E-mail: schoolsecretary@eaglecoveschool.org
Laura Kang, Head (2008). BS, Univ of Kansas, MS, Loyola College (MD). **Jane C. Pehlke,
  Adm.**
  Pre-Prep. Elem math—Scott Foresman-Addison Wesley. **Elem read**—Reading Street.
    Feat—Lib_Skills Span Environ_Sci Computers Studio_Art Music. **Supp**—Rev Tut.
  Selective adm: 20/yr. Appl fee: $60. Appl due: Mar. Accepted: 80%.
  Enr 70. B 40. G 30. Wh 87%. Latino 2%. Blk 7%. Asian 4%. Avg class size: 7. Uniform.
    Fac 16. M 2/F 14. FT 13/PT 3. Wh 94%. Blk 6%. Adv deg: 12%.
  Grad '11—7. Prep—6. (Severn 3, Indian Creek 3).
  Tui '12-'13: Day $10,915-12,760 (+$300).
  Endow $1,500,000. Plant val $2,000,000. Acres 6. Bldgs 3. Class rms 13. Lib 4000 vols.
    Sci labs 1. Lang labs 1. Auds 1. Art studios 1. Music studios 1. Gyms 1. Fields 1.
    Comp labs 1. Comp/stud: 1:3 (1:1 Laptop prgm Gr 5).
  Est 1947. Nonprofit. Tri (Sept-June).

Founded as Gibson Island Country School to serve the expanding needs of the area, this primary school has grown from its initial enrollment of 43 and now serves 13 communities in Anne Arundel County. ECS assumed its current name in 2010, in large part as a reflection of its location and environmental emphasis.

Classes are small, allowing teachers to work individually with students. Instructors emphasize a strong academic foundation, and the program integrates Spanish, music, art, library, computer, physical education and waterfront studies. Field trips and leadership opportunities complement academics. Boys and girls engage in classwide community service projects.

POTOMAC, MD. (13 mi. NW of Washington, DC) Suburban. Pop: 44,822. Alt: 360 ft.

THE BULLIS SCHOOL
Day — Coed Gr 3-12

Potomac, MD 20854. 10601 Falls Rd. Tel: 301-299-8500. Fax: 301-299-9050.
  www.bullis.org E-mail: admission@bullis.org
Gerald L. Boarman, Head (2010). BA, MA, Univ of Maryland-College Park, EdD, Nova
  Southeastern Univ. **Timothy Simpson, Adm.**
  Col Prep. AP (237 exams taken, 79% 3+)—Eng Fr Lat Span Calc Stats Comp_Sci Bio
    Chem Physics US_Hist World_Hist Psych Art_Hist Studio_Art Music_Theory. **Feat**—
    British_Lit Econ Asian_Stud Ceramics Fine_Arts Photog. Outdoor ed.
  Sports—Basket X-country Lacrosse Soccer Swim Tennis Track. B: Baseball Football
    Golf Ice_Hockey Wrestling. G: F_Hockey Softball. **Activities:** 30.
  Selective adm: 144/yr. Usual entry: 3,6, 7 & 9. Appl due: Feb. **Tests** CTP_4 IQ ISEE
    SSAT.
  Enr 618. B 340. G 278. Elem 239. Sec 379. Intl 5%. Avg class size: 15. Uniform. **Fac 98.**
    M 43/F 55. FT 87/PT 11. Adv deg: 66%.
  Grad '10—100. Col—99. (U of MD-Col Park, Syracuse, Geo Wash, Boston U, Gettys-
    burg, Georgetown). **Mid 50% SAT:** CR 510-640. M 540-660. Mid 50% ACT: 22-30.
    Col couns: 2.
  Tui '11-'12: Day $28,775-31,925 (+$380-1005). **Aid:** Need 87 ($1,326,600).
  Summer: Enrich Rec. Sports. 1-3 wks.
  Acres 80. Bldgs 12. Class rms 70. Libs 1. Sci labs 6. Photog labs 1. Theater/auds 1. Art

studios 6. Dance studios 1. Gyms 2. Fields 6. Courts 11. Comp labs 5.
Est 1930. Nonprofit. Tri (Sept-June). **Assoc** MSA.

Founded in Washington, DC, as a one-year preparatory school for the US service academies, the school moved to Silver Spring four years later. At that time, Bullis began to offer a four-year program. In 1963, the school's present, 80-acre tract in Potomac was purchased. The program subsequently grew to encompass grades 3-12.

In the lower and middle schools, students develop research and study skills in preparation for future academic work. The upper school's curriculum enables pupils to choose from various Advanced Placement courses, as well as a number of social studies, visual and performing arts, computer science and foreign language electives.

CONNELLY SCHOOL OF THE HOLY CHILD

Day — Girls Gr 6-12

Potomac, MD 20854. 9029 Bradley Blvd. Tel: 301-365-0955. Fax: 301-365-0981.
  www.holychild.org   E-mail: admissions@holychild.org
Maureen K. Appel, Head. BA, Rosemont College, MA, Long Island Univ. **Pat Harden, Adm.**
  Col Prep. AP (exams req'd; 95 taken)—Eng Fr Span Calc Stats Bio Chem US_Hist.
    Feat—British_Lit Creative_Writing Humanities Anat & Physiol Environ_Sci
    Forensic_Sci Genetics Oceanog Middle_Eastern_Hist Econ Psych Relig World_Relig
    Art_Hist Photog Studio_Art Drama Theater_Arts Music Music_Theory.
  Sports—G: Basket X-country Equestrian F_Hockey Lacrosse Soccer Softball Swim
    Tennis Track Volley. **Activities:** 27.
  Selective adm: 64/yr. Appl fee: $50. Appl due: Dec. Accepted: 80%. Yield: 51%. **Tests**
    CEEB ISEE SSAT.
  Enr 295. Avg class size: 15. Uniform. **Fac 60.** M 10/F 50. FT 44/PT 16. Adv deg: 66%.
  Grad '10—78. Col—78. (U of MD-Col Park 6, U of SC 4, Catholic U 3, James Madison
    3, Villanova 3, VA Polytech 3). **Col couns:** 1.
  Tui '12-'13: Day $23,535-25,675 (+$675-925). **Aid:** Need 68 ($562,380).
  Acres 9. Bldgs 4. Class rms 26. Lib 13,000 vols. Sci labs 4. Art studios 2. Music studios
    2. Dance studios 1. Gyms 1. Fields 2. Comp labs 2.
  Est 1961. Nonprofit. Roman Catholic (75% practice). (Sept-June). **Assoc** MSA.

Founded by the Society of the Holy Child Jesus, the school offers a college preparatory curriculum in a supportive Christian environment. Drawing its enrollment from the Greater Washington, DC, area, the school takes advantage of the resources of the nation's capital. Campus ministry and service programs reinforce Christian values.

Courses in religion, English, math, science, social studies, foreign languages and fine arts, as well as physical education, are required of all students. Honors and Advanced Placement courses are available in most disciplines, and seminars in various subjects are offered jointly with area independent schools. Holy Child conducts tours abroad each spring.

McLEAN SCHOOL OF MARYLAND

Day — Coed Gr K-12

Potomac, MD 20854. 8224 Lochinver Ln. Tel: 301-299-8277. Fax: 301-299-1639.
  www.mcleanschool.org   E-mail: admission@mcleanschool.org
Darlene B. Pierro, Head. AB, Sweet Briar College, MEd, Univ of Maryland-College Park.
  Judy Jankowski, Adm.
  Col Prep. AP (exams req'd; 39 taken, 67% 3+)—Eng Span Calc Bio Chem US_Hist
    US_Govt & Pol Studio_Art. **Feat**—Creative_Writing ASL Lat Anat & Physiol Environ_Sci Anthro Relig Ceramics Graphic_Arts Photog Chorus Jazz_Band Debate.
    Supp—Tut.
  Sports—Basket X-country Lacrosse Track. B: Soccer Wrestling. G: Softball Volley.

Selective adm (Gr K-11): 77/yr. Usual entry: K, 1, 3, 5, 7 & 9. Appl fee: $100. Appl due: Feb. Applied: 200. Accepted: 60%. Yield: 65%. **Tests** CTP_4 IQ SSAT.

Enr 411. B 273. G 138. Elem 332. Sec 79. Wh 78%. Latino 2%. Blk 7%. Asian 4%. Other 9%. Avg class size: 10. Stud/fac: 6:1. **Fac 73.** M 17/F 56. FT 64/PT 9. Wh 77%. Latino 5%. Blk 7%. Asian 7%. Other 4%. Adv deg: 61%.

Grad '10—40. Col—36. (Guilford 2, McDaniel 2, Muhlenberg 2). **Avg SAT:** CR 609. M 551. W 605. Avg ACT: 23. Alum donors: 1%.

Tui '12-'13: Day $28,095-33,950 (+$885-1585). **Aid:** Need 54 ($892,658).

Summer: Acad Enrich Rev Rec. Sports. Tui Day $250-375/wk. 10 wks.

Endow $2,400,000. Plant val $10,300,000. Acres 9. Bldgs 1 (100% ADA). Class rms 67. Lib 26,000 vols. Sci labs 7. Lang labs 3. Art studios 3. Music studios 3. Gyms 2. Fields 2. Courts 2. Comp labs 3. Comp/stud: 1:1.5.

Est 1954. Nonprofit. Quar (Sept-June).

Founded by local businesspersons and parents Delbert and Lenore Foster, McLean conducts a flexible academic program that addresses the needs of a broad range of learners. After many years of serving children in grades K-9, the school extended its program through the high school years by adding grade 10 in 2000, grade 11 in 2001 and grade 12 in 2002.

The lower school (grades K-4) and the middle school (grades 5-8) curricula emphasize language arts and math and include art, music, computer and daily physical education classes. Upper school classes are departmentalized, with both English and literature studies provided. Art, music and computer are among the requirements.

ST. ANDREW'S EPISCOPAL SCHOOL
Day — Coed Gr PS (Age 2)-12

Potomac, MD 20854. 8804 Postoak Rd. Tel: 301-983-5200. Fax: 301-983-4620.
Other locations: 10033 River Rd, Potomac 20854.
　　www.saes.org　E-mail: admission@saes.org
Robert F. Kosasky, Head (2002). BA, Yale Univ, MA, Columbia Univ. **Julie Jameson, Gr 4-12 Adm; Spring C. Swinehart, Gr PS-3 Adm.**

　Col Prep. AP (184 exams taken, 85% 3+)—Eng Fr Lat Span Calc Bio US_Hist Econ Psych Art_Hist Studio_Art. **Feat**—British_Lit Creative_Writing Stats Multivariable_ Calc Forensic_Sci Robotics Lat-Amer_Stud Middle_Eastern_Stud Bible Ethics Theol World_Relig Ceramics Photog Acting Theater Chorus Orchestra Jazz_Band Dance Journ Public_Speak.

　Sports—Basket X-country Equestrian Indoor_Track Lacrosse Soccer Tennis Track. B: Baseball Golf Wrestling. G: Softball Volley.

Selective adm: 145/yr. Appl fee: $50. Appl due: Feb. **Tests** ISEE SSAT.

Enr 542. B 252. G 290. Elem 273. Sec 269. Wh 54%. Latino 5%. Blk 13%. Asian 7%. Other 21%. Avg class size: 12. Stud/fac: 6:1. Casual. **Fac 66.** Wh 93%. Latino 4%. Blk 1%. Native Am 1%. Other 1%. Adv deg: 66%.

Grad '11—68. Col—68. (Wake Forest 4, U of DE 4, U of MD-Col Park 3, Am U 3, Duke 3, Bryn Mawr 2). Athl schol 2. **Col couns:** 2.

Tui '12-'13: Day $19,990-34,835 (+$400-1700). **Aid:** Need 112 ($2,240,544).

Summer: Acad Enrich Rec. 8 wks.

Endow $5,469,000. Plant val $14,268,000. Bldgs 8 (75% ADA). Class rms 67. Lib 14,000 vols. Sci labs 6. Lang labs 9. Theater/auds 5. Art studios 6. Music studios 6. Dance studios 2. Gyms 2. Fields 5. Courts 6. Comp labs 10.

Est 1978. Nonprofit. Episcopal (21% practice). Tri (Sept-June). **Assoc** CLS MSA.

St. Andrew's emphasizes thorough college preparation in a program that combines academics, the arts, athletics and spiritual life. After serving students in grades 6-12 for 30 years, the school merged with St. Francis Episcopal Day School, a coeducational day school for children in grades PS-3, in July 2008. The former St. Francis campus on River Road serves as the lower school location for St. Andrew's. An intermediate school, which opened with the addition of grade 4 in the fall of 2009 and extends through grade 6, operates at the main campus on Postak Road.

In the lower school (grades PS-3), children gain an introduction to the major disciplines, as well as computers, Spanish, library skills and music. The experiential middle school program, which addresses the developmental needs of early adolescents, emphasizes problem solving and study skills in a structured setting.

Building on the middle school program, the upper school (grades 9-12) incorporates sequential skill instruction in a college preparatory setting. Upper schoolers satisfy requirements in such areas as religion and the arts, complete an independent research paper, and fulfill a 120-hour community service requirement prior to graduation (including 60 hours during senior year). Expanded Advanced Placement and elective offerings are available to seniors as part of a consortium with four other local independent schools. Students and faculty convene once a week for all-school chapel.

ROCKVILLE, MD. (14 mi. NNW of Washington, DC) Urban. Pop: 47,388. Alt: 451 ft.

GREEN ACRES SCHOOL
Day — Coed Gr PS (Age 4)-8

Rockville, MD 20852. 11701 Danville Dr. Tel: 301-881-4100, 888-410-4152.
   Fax: 301-881-3319.
   www.greenacres.org   E-mail: gasinfo@greenacres.org
Neal M. Brown, Head (2008). BA, MAT, Brown Univ, EdM, EdD, Harvard Univ. Susan Friend, Gr 2-8 Adm; Nina Chibber, Gr PS-1 Adm.
   Pre-Prep. Feat—Humanities Span Computers Ethics Ceramics Photog Studio_Art Drama Chorus Music Handbells Movement Outdoor_Ed. Supp—Tut.
   Sports—Basket X-country Lacrosse Soccer. G: Softball.
   Selective adm (Gr PS-6): 41/yr. Appl fee: $75. Appl due: Jan. Applied: 117. Accepted: 69%. Yield: 51%.
   Enr 300. Wh 70%. Latino 6%. Blk 4%. Asian 5%. Other 15%. Avg class size: 12. Stud/fac: 6:1. Fac 47. M 8/F 39. FT 39/PT 8. Wh 77%. Latino 6%. Blk 6%. Other 11%. Adv deg: 65%.
   Grad '11—27. Prep—21. (Georgetown Day 10, St Andrew's Episcopal-MD 6, Field 2, Sandy Spring Friends 2, Our Lady of Good Counsel 1). Alum donors: 10%.
   Tui '12-'13: Day $30,215 (+$240-1025). Aid: Need 58 ($1,118,991).
   Summer (enr 320): Rec. Tui Day $2230. 6 wks.
   Endow $4,000,000. Plant val $18,000,000. Acres 15. Bldgs 6 (100% ADA). Class rms 40. Lib 22,000 vols. Sci labs 3. Photog labs 1. Amphitheaters 1. Auds 2. Theaters 1. Art studios 2. Music studios 2. Dance studios 1. Perf arts ctrs 1. Gyms 1. Fields 2. Courts 2. Pools 1. Playgrounds 3. Comp labs 2. Laptop prgm Gr 5-6.
   Est 1934. Nonprofit. Sem (Sept-June).

Green Acres has its roots in the traditions of progressive education. The school's board of trustees is composed of parents, teachers and community members. An active parents' association provides parents with many opportunities for involvement in the school community.

Green Acres' integrated, multicultural programs and curricula are developmentally oriented and consider the needs and interests of the students. Small classes allow teachers to work with children individually and in small groups, and Green Acres also encourages cooperation among students. Emphasis is placed on pupils involving themselves in their own learning through exploration, experimentation, reading, discussion, research and practice. Spanish instruction begins in grade 5.

The school's 15-acre campus in suburban Washington, DC, provides opportunities for pupils to study animal and plant life in woods and streams. Environmental concerns are integral to the curriculum.

ST. JAMES, MD. (60 mi. NW of Washington, DC) Rural. Pop: 100. Alt: 464 ft.

SAINT JAMES SCHOOL
Bdg and Day — Coed Gr 8-12

St James, MD 21740. 17641 College Rd. Tel: 301-733-9330. Fax: 301-739-1310.
www.stjames.edu   E-mail: admissions@stjames.edu
Rev. D. Stuart Dunnan, Head (1992). AB, AM, Harvard Univ, MA, DPhil, Oxford Univ (England). Ben Douglass, Adm.

Col Prep. AP (exams req'd; 149 taken, 77% 3+)—Eng Fr Lat Span Calc Bio Chem Physics Eur_Hist US_Hist World_Hist Studio_Art Music_Theory. Feat—Stats Anat & Physiol Environ_Sci Econ Pol_Sci Ethics Theol Chorus Music Orchestra. Supp—Tut.

Sports (req'd)—Basket Lacrosse Soccer Tennis. B: Baseball X-country Football Golf Wrestling. G: F_Hockey Softball Volley. Activities: 12.

Selective adm: 63/yr. Bdg 42. Day 21. Usual entry: 8 & 9. Appl fee: $65. Appl due: Jan. Applied: 227. Accepted: 66%. Yield: 54%. Tests CEEB SSAT TOEFL.

Enr 202. B 128. G 74. Bdg 144. Day 58. Elem 23. Sec 179. Wh 64%. Latino 1%. Blk 8%. Asian 24%. Other 3%. Intl 18%. Avg class size: 11. Stud/fac: 7:1. Formal. Fac 32. M 20/F 12. FT 30/PT 2. Wh 94%. Latino 3%. Blk 3%. Adv deg: 50%. In dorms 16.

Grad '10—53. Col—53. (Boston U 2, Carnegie Mellon 2, Elon 2, Eckerd 2, U of MD-Col Park 2, Princeton 1). Mid 50% SAT: CR 530-680. M 560-690. W 540-700. Mid 50% ACT: 23-27. Col couns: 1. Alum donors: 49%.

Tui '12-'13: Bdg $39,000 (+$1500). Day $26,000 (+$900). Intl Bdg $39,000 (+$3000). Aid: Need 72 ($1,277,950).

Endow $11,100,000. Plant val $37,641,000. Acres 900. Bldgs 31. Dorms 5. Dorm rms 101. Class rms 25. Lib 25,000 vols. Chapels 1. Sci labs 5. Auds 1. Theaters 1. Art studios 1. Music studios 1. Dance studios 2. Gyms 1. Fields 12. Courts 12. Field houses 1. Comp labs 8. Comp/stud: 1:3.

Est 1842. Nonprofit. Episcopal. Tri (Aug-June). Assoc CLS MSA.

Saint James is the oldest Episcopal boarding school in America modeled on the English "public school" plan. Originally a boys' preparatory school and college, Saint James dropped the college division when it reopened after the Civil War. Girls were admitted as day students during the 1970s, and the school became fully coeducational with the addition of female boarders in 1991.

The school's traditional core curriculum is designed to provide pupils with a firm foundation in the major disciplines while preparing them for college attendance. Advanced and Advanced Placement courses are available for able students who wish to pursue subjects in greater depth. In addition, upper school electives provide enrichment and allow students to explore areas of individual interest. Beginning in grade 9, boys and girls satisfy a 15-hour annual community service requirement. Chapel attendance is mandatory of all students.

SANDY SPRING, MD. (25 mi. WSW of Baltimore, MD) Rural. Pop: 1200. Alt: 484 ft.

SANDY SPRING FRIENDS SCHOOL
Bdg — Coed Gr 9-12; Day — Coed PS (Age 4)-12

Sandy Spring, MD 20860. 16923 Norwood Rd. Tel: 301-774-7455. Fax: 301-924-1115.
www.ssfs.org   E-mail: admissions@ssfs.org
Thomas R. Gibian, Head (2010). BA, College of Wooster, MBA, Univ of Pennsylvania. Yasmin McGinnis, Adm.

Col Prep. AP (exams req'd; 171 taken, 65% 3+)—Eng Fr Span Calc Stats Chem Environ_Sci US_Hist Music_Theory. Feat—British_Lit Russ_Lit Chin Bioethics African-

Amer_Hist Modern_Chin_Hist Native_Amer_Hist Russ_Hist Quakerism Ceramics Drawing Photog Studio_Art Video_Production Weaving Drama Music Handbells Dance Woodworking Yoga. **Supp**—ESL.

Sports—Basket X-country Lacrosse Soccer Tennis Track. B: Baseball. G: Softball Volley. **Activities:** 30.

Selective adm (Bdg Gr 9-11; Day PS-11): 106/yr. Appl fee: $75. Appl due: Jan. Applied: 322. Accepted: 62%. Yield: 52%. **Tests** IQ SSAT TOEFL.

Enr 571. B 274. G 297. Bdg 60. Day 511. Elem 320. Sec 251. Wh 60%. Latino 2%. Blk 13%. Asian 17%. Other 8%. Intl 7%. Avg class size: 15. Stud/fac: 8:1. **Fac 69.** M 22/F 47. FT 65/PT 4. Wh 85%. Latino 5%. Blk 7%. Asian 3%. Adv deg: 56%. In dorms 5.

Grad '11—74. Col—72. (U of MD-Col Park, St Mary's Col of MD, Dickinson, Parsons Sch of Design, Col of Wooster, GA Inst of Tech). Athl schol 1. **Avg SAT:** CR 620. M 610. W 620. **Mid 50% SAT:** CR 570-640. M 560-620. W 530-640. Avg ACT: 27. Mid 50% ACT: 25-29. **Col couns:** 2.

Tui '12-'13: Bdg $52,200 (+$2000). **5-Day Bdg $41,700** (+$1700). **Day $20,475-28,300** (+$500). **Intl Bdg $52,200** (+$3050). **Aid:** Need 151 ($2,262,828).

Summer: Enrich Rec. ESL. Service. 10 wks.

Endow $1,046,000. Plant val $48,410,000. Acres 140. Bldgs 13. Dorms 1. Dorm rms 28. Class rms 33. Lib 25,000 vols. Sci labs 5. Theaters 1. Art studios 4. Music studios 3. Perf arts ctrs 1. Wood shops 1. Print shops 1. Gyms 3. Fields 4. Courts 4. Comp labs 4.

Est 1961. Nonprofit. Religious Society of Friends (9% practice). Sem (Sept-June).

Established as a result of community effort by the Sandy Spring Monthly Meeting, this school provides a college preparatory program within the framework of the Quaker philosophy. The school operated as a boarding and day high school until 1982, when it added a middle school division (grades 6-8). The lower school was added in 1993, when Sandy Spring Friends effected a merger with Friends Elementary School.

Curricular features include a foreign language program that enables students to take Spanish from age 5 through graduation, a sequential math program that allows acceleration beginning in the middle school, and integrated English and history offerings. The ninth-grade curriculum emphasizes both academic and organizational skills development and an awareness of social and community issues. An extensive selection of courses, including Advanced Placement offerings in the core subjects, is available in the upper school.

The school's spring intersession allows pupils to engage in a one- to two-week project pertaining to community service, intensive arts study, a rigorous physical activity or travel. Upper schoolers accumulate 100 hours of required community service during their four years.

Excursions to Washington, DC, and Baltimore; dances; camping trips; and service-oriented projects are among the extracurricular and weekend activities.

SEVERNA PARK, MD. (15 mi. S of Baltimore, MD) Suburban. Pop: 28,507. Alt: 50 ft.

SEVERN SCHOOL

Day — Coed Gr 6-12

Severna Park, MD 21146. 201 Water St. Tel: 410-647-7700. Fax: 410-544-9451.

www.severnschool.com   E-mail: info@severnschool.com

Douglas H. Lagarde, Head (2006). AB, College of William and Mary, MEd, Harvard Univ. Andrew Greeley, Upper Sch Adm; Ellen Murray, Middle Sch Adm.

Col Prep. AP (exams req'd; 339 taken, 89% 3+)—Eng Fr Lat Span Calc Stats Comp_ Sci Bio Physics Eur_Hist US_Hist. **Feat**—British_Lit Creative_Writing Shakespeare Anat & Physiol Astron Environ_Sci Forensic_Sci Marine_Bio/Sci Engineering Robotics Cold_War Middle_Eastern_Hist Econ Psych Global_Stud Art_Hist Ceramics Drawing Painting Photog Sculpt Studio_Art Acting Theater Chorus Dance Journ

Public_Speak.
Sports (req'd)—Basket X-country Lacrosse Sail Soccer Swim Tennis Track. B: Baseball Football Golf. G: F_Hockey. **Activities:** 33.
Selective adm: 117/yr. Appl fee: $55. Appl due: Jan. **Tests** ISEE.
Enr 584. Avg class size: 14. Stud/fac: 10:1. Uniform. **Fac 79.** M 34/F 45. FT 79. Adv deg 74%.
Grad '11—99. Col—99. (U of MD-Col Park 9, U of AL-Tuscaloosa 4, Boston U 3, Col of Charleston 3, Elon 3, Johns Hopkins 3). **Mid 50% SAT:** CR 540-650. M 550-680. W 560-680. **Col couns:** 2.
Tui '11-'12: Day $22,150 (+$800). **Aid:** Need ($1,500,000).
Summer: Enrich Rec. Sports. Tui Day $125-375. 1-2 wks.
Acres 19. Bldgs 3. Class rms 39. Lib 20,000 vols. Sci labs 3. Lang labs 1. Auds 1. Art studios 4. Music studios 1. Dance studios 1. Gyms 1. Athletic ctrs 1. Fields 4. Comp labs 8.
Est 1914. Nonprofit. Sem (Aug-June). **Assoc** CLS MSA.

Founded by Rolland M. Teel as a boarding school designed to prepare boys for the US Naval Academy, Severn has since 1958 sent graduates to colleges throughout the country. The school became coeducational in the day department in 1971 and dropped its boarding division in 1973. Located on a 19-acre campus between Annapolis and Baltimore, the school is roughly 40 miles from Washington, DC.

Notable elements of the curriculum include foreign language study in three languages beginning in grade 6, independent study possibilities in the fine arts and an emphasis on computer technology. At the upper school level (grades 9-12), boys and girls enroll in a minimum of six courses per semester. Students participate in at least one sport each year and also must attain CPR certification by graduation. Middle schoolers (grades 6-8) take part in community service days, while upper school pupils perform a minimum of 10 hours of annual service.

SILVER SPRING, MD. (8 mi. N of Washington, DC) Suburban. Pop: 76,540. Alt: 340 ft.

THE BARRIE SCHOOL
Day — Coed Gr PS (Age 2)-12

Silver Spring, MD 20906. 13500 Layhill Rd. Tel: 301-576-2800. Fax: 301-576-2803.
www.barrie.org   E-mail: admissions@barrie.org
Charlie Abelmann, Head (2010). AB, Duke Univ, EdM, EdD, Harvard Univ. **Alyssa Jahn,** Adm.
Col Prep. Montessori. AP (exams req'd)—Fr Span Calc Stats Environ_Sci. Feat—Multivariable_Calc Programming Robotics Ceramics Drawing Film Studio_Art Drama Music_Theory. **Supp**—Tut. Outdoor ed.
Sports—Basket Equestrian Soccer Tennis Track. G: Volley. **Activities:** 14.
Selective adm: 82/yr. Appl fee: $50. Appl due: Jan. Applied: 161. Accepted: 50%. Yield 71%. **Tests** IQ ISEE SSAT TOEFL.
Enr 301. B 155. G 146. Elem 238. Sec 63. Wh 64%. Latino 2%. Blk 18%. Asian 8%. Other 8%. Avg class size: 13. Stud/fac: 12:1. **Fac 36.** FT 31/PT 5. Wh 70%. Latino 10%. Blk 5%. Native Am 5%. Asian 5%. Other 5%. Adv deg: 80%.
Grad '11—22. Col—21. (U of MD-Col Park 2, Bucknell 1, Brandeis 1, U of VA 1, Am U 1, Northeastern U 1). **Avg SAT:** CR 625. M 626. W 628. **Mid 50% SAT:** CR 550-670. M 540-660. Avg ACT: 25. **Col couns:** 1.
Tui '12-'13: Day $19,000-26,100 (+$1200). **Aid:** Need 165.
Summer (enr 893): Rec. Tui Day $870/2-wk ses. 8 wks.
Endow $1,111,000. Acres 45. Bldgs 25. Class rms 50. 3 Libs 20,000 vols. Sci labs 2. Theaters 1. Art studios 1. Music studios 2. Gyms 2. Fields 3. Pools 1. Riding rings 1. Stables 1. Comp labs 4.
Est 1932. Nonprofit. Quar (Aug-June). **Assoc** MSA.

The school is located on a wooded, 45-acre campus just north of Washington, DC. At all grade levels, the experiential program provides opportunities to explore individual interests. Barrie's lower school (grades pre-K-5) employs a Montessori approach that emphasizes the development of fundamental academic skills and problem-solving strategies.

In addition to course requirements in humanities, math, science, foreign language, art and physical education, the middle and upper school programs (grades 6-12) include community service (96 cumulative hours prior to graduation), special on- and off-campus study opportunities, and athletics. Barrie also conducts Extended Study Week, an intensive, experiential program that enables students to explore material beyond the standard curriculum through local, national or international study.

STEVENSON, MD. (9 mi. NW of Baltimore, MD) Rural. Pop: 600. Alt: 320 ft.

ST. TIMOTHY'S SCHOOL

Bdg and Day — Girls Gr 9-12

Stevenson, MD 21153. 8400 Greenspring Ave. Tel: 410-486-7401. Fax: 410-486-1167.
www.stt.org   E-mail: admis@stt.org
Randy S. Stevens, Head (2003). BA, Univ of South Carolina, MPA, Cornell Univ. **Deborah Haskins, Adm.**
Col Prep. IB Diploma. Feat—Chin Fr Lat Span Econ Ethics Relig World_Relig Art_Hist Photog Studio_Art Visual_Arts Drama Music. **Supp**—ESL LD Tut.
Sports (req'd)—G: Badminton Basket Equestrian F_Hockey Golf Ice_Hockey Lacrosse Soccer Softball Squash Tennis Volley. **Activities:** 30.
Selective adm (Bdg Gr 9-11; Day 9-12): 51/yr. Bdg 43. Day 8. Appl fee: $50. Appl due: Feb. Applied: 190. Accepted: 45%. Yield: 57%. **Tests** CEEB ISEE SSAT TOEFL.
Enr 150. Bdg 120. Day 30. Intl 30%. Avg class size: 9. Stud/fac: 6:1. Uniform. **Fac 33.** M 9/F 24. FT 33. Wh 87%. Latino 5%. Blk 5%. Asian 3%. Adv deg: 63%. In dorms 6.
Grad '11—35. Col—35. (Geo Wash 4, USC 3, U of MD-Col Park 2, Brown 1, U of VA 1, Wake Forest 1). **Avg SAT:** CR 500. M 550. W 530. **Mid 50% SAT:** CR 440-540. M 460-640. W 470-590. Avg ACT: 23. Mid 50% ACT: 20-25. Alum donors: 25%.
Tui '12-'13: Bdg $46,800 (+$2000). **Day $27,200** (+$1500). **Intl Bdg $46,800** (+$2000-5500). **Aid:** Merit 6 ($76,000). Need 74 ($2,000,000).
Summer: Gr 8-12. Acad Rec. ESL. Tui Bdg $5800. Col Prep. Tui Bdg $4800. Col Prep & Riding. Tui Day $6000. 4 wks.
Endow $9,000,000. Plant val $9,700,000. Acres 145. Bldgs 23. Dorms 2. Dorm rms 45. Class rms 18. Lib 22,000 vols. Sci labs 3. Auds 1. Theaters 1. Art studios 2. Music studios 7. Dance studios 1. Perf arts ctrs 1. Gyms 2. Fields 2. Platform tennis courts 2. Pools 1. Riding rings 2. Stables 1. Student ctrs 1. Comp labs 3. Comp/stud: 1:2 (1:1 Laptop prgm Gr 9-12).
Est 1882. Nonprofit. Episcopal. Tri (Sept-June). **Assoc** CLS MSA.

The school, founded in Catonsville by the Misses Sally and Polly Carter, moved to its present, rural site in the Green Spring Valley in 1951. In 1974, St. Tim's merged with the Hannah More Academy, which, founded in 1832, was the oldest Episcopal girls' school in the country. Named after the Englishwoman who had pioneered for girls' education, Hannah More Academy had served as the diocesan school since 1873. Effective with the merger was the transfer of all school activities to the St. Tim's campus.

St. Timothy's academic program prepares students to pursue the International Baccalaureate Diploma, which includes a 150-hour community service requirement. The two-week Winterim enables girls to break from the regular curriculum and choose from leadership, government, political and international experiences. The school schedules an international trip each summer.

All girls participate in sports. Among the athletic options is an equestrian program that accommodates both competitive and noncompetitive riders. Students take part in various school organizations, including a social services club that provides opportunities for volunteerism. Extensive cultural and social options, among them concerts, mixers and outdoor activities, round out the program.

NEW JERSEY

BLAIRSTOWN, NJ. (68 mi. N of Philadelphia, PA) Suburban. Pop: 5747. Alt: 351 ft.

BLAIR ACADEMY

Bdg and Day — Coed Gr 9-PG

Blairstown, NJ 07825. 2 Park St, PO Box 600. Tel: 908-362-2024, 800-462-5247.
Fax: 908-362-7975.
www.blair.edu   E-mail: admissions@blair.edu
T. Chandler Hardwick III, Head (1989). BA, Univ of North Carolina-Chapel Hill, MA, Middlebury College. **Peter Curran, Adm.**

Col Prep. AP (exams req'd; 302 taken, 80% 3+)—Eng Chin Fr Lat Span Calc Stats Comp_Sci Bio Chem Environ_Sci Physics Eur_Hist US_Hist World_Hist Comp_Govt & Pol Econ US_Govt & Pol Art_Hist Studio_Art Music_Theory. **Feat**—Marine_Bio/ Sci Biotech Roman_Hist Asian_Stud Architect Ceramics Filmmaking Graphic_Arts Painting Photog Video_Production Theater Music. **Supp**—Tut. Sat classes.

Sports—Basket Crew X-country Golf Lacrosse Ski Soccer Squash Swim Tennis Track. B: Baseball Football Ice_Hockey Wrestling. G: F_Hockey Softball. **Activities:** 13.

Selective adm (Bdg Gr 9-PG; Day 9-11): 145/yr. Bdg 119. Day 26. Usual entry: 9 & 10. Appl fee: $50. Appl due: Feb. Applied: 773. Accepted: 32%. Yield: 59%. **Tests** ISEE SSAT TOEFL.

Enr 447. B 249. G 198. Bdg 344. Day 103. Wh 70%. Latino 2%. Blk 7%. Asian 14%. Other 7%. Intl 17%. Avg class size: 11. Stud/fac: 6:1. Casual. **Fac 64.** M 40/F 24. FT 64. Wh 90%. Latino 1%. Blk 5%. Asian 4%. Adv deg: 70%. In dorms 30.

Grad '11—134. Col—134. (Cornell, Wash & Lee, Bucknell, Lehigh, U of PA, Swarthmore). **Avg SAT:** CR 608. M 611. W 614. **Col couns:** 3. Alum donors: 32%.

Tui '12-'13: Bdg $49,500. Day $35,100. Aid: Need 148 ($3,978,200).

Endow $66,500,000. Plant val $110,500,000. Acres 423. Bldgs 61. Dorms 10. Dorm rms 215. Class rms 39. Lib 22,000 vols. Sci labs 5. Lang labs 1. Auds 2. Theaters 3. Art studios 5. Music studios 7. Dance studios 2. Arts ctrs 1. Gyms 3. Fields 8. Tennis courts 10. Squash courts 7. Pools 1. Golf crses 1. Comp labs 7.

Est 1848. Nonprofit. Presbyterian. Sem (Sept-May). **Assoc** CLS MSA.

Opening with a coeducational enrollment, then, in 1915, serving boys only, the school once again became completely coeducational in 1970, and it now draws students from roughly two dozen states and a similar number of foreign countries. Though Presbyterian-affiliated, the school selects a multidenominational enrollment.

With a program grounded in the academic fundamentals, Blair has sent graduates to more than 200 different colleges over the years. Advanced Placement courses and electives are available, and seniors also participate in independent study projects. The fine and performing arts departments are particularly strong, as evidenced by such offerings as architecture, video production, orchestra and jazz ensemble. The Society of Skeptics, a weekly lecture series sponsored by the history department and in continuous operation since 1977, features speakers from the fields of business, government, science, academia and the arts.

Students may take advantage of outdoor opportunities provided by Blair's proximity to the Delaware Water Gap and the Pocono Mountains. Weekend school-sponsored trips to New York City and Philadelphia, PA, enable boys and girls to partake of urban culture (such as shows and museums).

See Also Page 102

BRIDGETON, NJ. (40 mi. S of Philadelphia, PA) Urban. Pop: 22,771. Alt: 30 ft.

WOODLAND COUNTRY DAY SCHOOL
Day — Coed Gr PS (Age 4)-8

Bridgeton, NJ 08302. 1216 Roadstown Rd. Tel: 856-453-8499. Fax: 856-453-1648.
www.wcdsnj.org E-mail: school@wcdsnj.org
Cosmo F. Terrigno, Head (2004). BA, Rowan Univ, MA, Villanova Univ. **Jennifer Bifulco, Adm.**
  Pre-Prep. Gen Acad. Feat—Lat Span Computers Studio_Art Music Study_Skills. **Supp**—Rem_Math Rem_Read.
  Sports—Basket. B: Lacrosse Soccer. G: F_Hockey Softball.
  Somewhat selective adm (Gr PS-7): 17/yr. Appl fee: $75. Appl due: Rolling. Accepted: 90%. Yield: 78%. **Tests** ISEE.
  Enr 147. Avg class size: 13. **Fac 26.** M 5/F 21. FT 18/PT 8. Adv deg: 19%.
  Grad '11—15. Prep—11. (St Augustine Col Prep, Archmere, Salesianum, Bishop Eustace, Paul VI HS).
  Tui '12-'13: Day $6990-11,390 (+$400). **Aid:** Need ($100,000).
  Summer: Acad Enrich Rev Rec. Tui Day $180/wk. 10 wks.
  Endow $900,000. Plant val $1,200,000. Acres 12. Bldgs 7. Class rms 24. Lib 10,000 vols. Sci labs 1. Art studios 1. Music studios 1. Gyms 1. Fields 3. Playgrounds 3. Comp labs 2.
  Est 1959. Nonprofit. Sem (Sept-June). **Assoc** MSA.

Founded as St. John's Day School by a group of families from Salem and Cumberland counties, Woodland serves students within a 30-mile radius. The school moved from its quarters in the parish hall of St. John's Episcopal Church in Salem to the historic Wood Mansion in Jericho. Computer, science lab, music and art supplement the traditional curriculum. Woodland offers Spanish from prekindergarten, Latin in grades 7 and 8.

BURLINGTON, NJ. (16 mi. ENE of Philadelphia, PA) Urban. Pop: 9736. Alt: 14 ft.

DOANE ACADEMY
Day — Coed Gr PS (Age 4)-12

Burlington, NJ 08016. 350 Riverbank. Tel: 609-386-3500. Fax: 609-386-5878.
www.doaneacademy.org E-mail: info@doaneacademy.org
John F. McGee, Head (2000). BA, MA, Univ of Notre Dame. **Jane Affleck, Adm.**
  Col Prep. AP (38 exams taken, 26% 3+)—Eng Lat Span Calc Comp_Sci Bio Chem Eur_Hist US_Hist Psych US_Govt & Pol Studio_Art. **Feat**—Poetry Shakespeare Stats Environ_Sci Forensic_Sci Genetics Engineering Organic_Chem Robotics Civil_War Econ Law Sociol Ethics World_Relig Fine_Arts Photog Band Chorus Music_Hist Journ Public_Speak. **Supp**—Tut. Outdoor ed. **Dual enr:** Burlington County.
  Sports (req'd)—Basket Crew X-country Soccer. B: Baseball. G: Softball. **Activities:** 12.
  Somewhat selective adm (Gr PS-11): 40/yr. Usual entry: PS, K & 9. Appl fee: $35. Appl due: Feb. Accepted: 90%. Yield: 69%. **Tests** CEEB CTP_4 ISEE MAT SSAT.
  Enr 210. Wh 65%. Latino 1%. Blk 30%. Asian 4%. Avg class size: 12. Stud/fac: 8:1. Uniform. **Fac 33.** M 12/F 21. FT 28/PT 5. Wh 91%. Latino 6%. Blk 3%. Adv deg: 36%.
  Grad '11—25. Col—25. (Alvernia 2, Ursinus 2, Am U 1, Worcester Polytech 1, Col of NJ 1, Drexel 1). **Avg SAT:** CR 555. M 520. W 535. **Col couns:** 1. Alum donors: 13%.
  Tui '11-'12: Day $10,500-16,100 (+$1000). **Aid:** Merit 20 ($54,100). Need 63 ($222,270).
  Summer: Acad Enrich Rec. Engineering. 2-6 wks.

Endow $1,243,000. Plant val $3,520,000. Acres 10. Bldgs 5. Class rms 32. Sci labs 4. Art studios 2. Music studios 2. Gyms 1. Fields 3. Comp labs 3. Comp/stud: 1:4. **Est 1837.** Nonprofit. Episcopal. Tri (Sept-June). **Assoc** CLS MSA.

Founded as a girls' boarding school by Rt. Rev. George Washington Doane, second Episcopal bishop of New Jersey, St. Mary's Hall became a day school in 1953, accepting boys in the elementary grades. Classes became coed in 1974, when the school merged with Doane Academy, founded in 1965 as a coordinate boys' school for students in grades 6-12. Long known as St. Mary's Hall/Doane Academy, the school assumed its current name in 2008. It is now fully coeducational.

The academy's college preparatory curriculum prepares graduates for many leading colleges. Reading instruction, which takes a phonics- and literature-based approach, enables children to read age-appropriate novels beginning in grade 2; writing skills are also a focus of the early grades. Math and science instruction is tailored to the student's ability level throughout the school.

EDISON, NJ. (24 mi. WSW of New York, NY) Suburban. Pop: 97,687.

THE WARDLAW-HARTRIDGE SCHOOL
Day — Coed Gr PS (Age 3)-12

Edison, NJ 08820. 1295 Inman Ave. Tel: 908-754-1882. Fax: 908-754-9678.
  www.whschool.org   E-mail: admission@whschool.org
Andrew Webster, Head (2005). AB, Brown Univ, MA, Univ of Virginia. **Linda Coleman, Adm.**

  Col Prep. AP (exams req'd; 103 taken, 81% 3+)—Eng Fr Lat Span Calc Stats Comp_ Sci Bio Chem Physics Eur_Hist US_Hist Comp_Govt & Pol Econ Psych US_Govt & Pol Art_Hist Studio_Art Music_Theory. **Feat**—Creative_Writing Chin Ital Environ_Sci Forensic_Sci Marine_Bio/Sci Law Sculpt Bus Journ Driver_Ed. **Supp**—ESL Tut.

  Sports—Basket Golf Soccer Swim Tennis Track. B: Baseball. G: Cheer Softball Volley. **Activities:** 26.

  Selective adm (Gr PS-10): 99/yr. Appl fee: $65-75. Appl due: Feb. Applied: 207. Accepted: 72%. Yield: 70%. **Tests** ISEE TOEFL.

  Enr 450. B 225. G 225. Elem 263. Sec 187. Wh 31%. Latino 10%. Blk 14%. Asian 36%. Other 9%. Avg class size: 16. Stud/fac: 7:1. Uniform. **Fac 59.** M 16/F 43. FT 55/PT 4. Wh 83%. Latino 8%. Blk 3%. Asian 5%. Other 1%. Adv deg: 55%.

  Grad '11—36. Col—36. (Rutgers 5, Geo Wash 2, Seton Hall 2, Harvard 1, Cornell 1, U of CA-Berkeley 1). **Avg SAT:** CR 586. M 614. W 605. **Mid 50% SAT:** CR 510-640. M 540-650. W 520-680. Avg ACT: 25.5. Mid 50% ACT: 21-29. **Col couns:** 1.

  Tui '12-'13: Day $14,560-31,150 (+$450-2000). **Aid:** Merit 29 ($190,416). Need 207 ($3,77,607).

  Summer (enr 202): Acad Enrich Rev Rem Rec. ESL. Tui Day $950-1400. 6 wks.

  Endow $2,202,000. Plant val $18,100,000. Acres 36. Bldgs 1 (95% ADA). Class rms 54. Lib 28,000 vols. Sci labs 6. Lang labs 1. Sci/tech ctrs 1. Art studios 3. Music studios 3. Gyms 2. Fields 6. Courts 9. Pools 1. Weight rms 1. Comp labs 4. Comp/stud: 1:1.3 (1:1 Laptop prgm Gr 9-12).

  Est 1882. Nonprofit. Sem (Sept-June). **Assoc** CLS.

The school was reconfigured in 1976 when the Wardlaw Country Day School, founded in 1882, merged with the Hartridge School, founded in 1884. Situated on a 36-acre tract, the school now occupies a single campus. All high school students utilize laptop computers in a variety of required and elective subjects. Honors and Advanced Placement courses are available, and pupils are encouraged to select enrichment courses in the areas of art, music and computers. Twelfth graders deliver a compulsory senior speech and present a senior public policy thesis on an issue of contemporary concern.

A weeklong trip is integrated into the curriculum in each middle school year (grades 6-8). In grades 5-8, all boys and girls participate in interscholastic competition; those in grades 9-12 may elect to play on athletic teams.

ENGLEWOOD, NJ. (15 mi. N of New York, NY) Suburban. Pop: 26,203. Alt: 24 ft.

DWIGHT-ENGLEWOOD SCHOOL
Day — Coed Gr PS (Age 3)-12

Englewood, NJ 07631. 315 E Palisade Ave. Tel: 201-569-9500. Fax: 201-568-9451.
www.d-e.org E-mail: browns@d-e.org
Rodney V. De Jarnett, Head. BS, Kutztown Univ, MS, Rensselaer Polytechnic Institute, EdD, Univ of Pennsylvania. **Sherronda L. Brown, Adm.**
Col Prep. AP—Eng Lat Span Calc Stats Comp_Sci Chem Environ_Sci US_Hist Art_ Hist. **Feat**—Creative_Writing Shakespeare Fr Greek Multivariable_Calc Bioethics Forensic_Sci NYC_Hist Econ Philos Architect_Drawing Painting Sculpt Studio_Art Acting Theater_Arts Music Journ. **Supp**—Dev_Read Makeup Rem_Math Rem_ Read Rev Tut.
Sports—Basket X-country Golf Lacrosse Soccer Tennis Track. B: Baseball Fencing Football. G: Cheer F_Hockey Softball Volley. **Activities:** 40.
Selective adm: 182/yr. Appl fee: $65. **Tests** ISEE.
Enr 932. Elem 478. Sec 454. Avg class size: 15. Stud/fac: 9:1. **Fac 130.** Adv deg: 63%.
Grad '11—107. Col—107. (NYU 9, Geo Wash 6, U of MI 4, USC 4, U of MD-Col Park 3, Emory 3). **Avg SAT:** CR 609. M 630. W 636. Mid 50% ACT: 24-30. **Col couns:** 3.
Tui '12-'13: Day $24,000-32,750 (+$75-2975).
Summer: Acad Enrich Rec. Sports. 6 wks.
Endow $4,550,000. Plant val $26,000,000. Acres 23. Bldgs 10. Class rms 78. 2 Libs 20,000 vols. Sci labs 10. Lang labs 1. Auds 1. Theaters 1. Art studios 2. Music studios 2. Arts ctrs 1. Gyms 3. Fields 4. Courts 5. Comp labs 4. Laptop prgm Gr 6-12.
Est 1889. Nonprofit. Sem (Sept-June). **Assoc** CLS MSA.

Dwight-Englewood School resulted from the merger of Dwight School, a girls' school founded in 1889, and Englewood School for Boys, founded in 1928. After a decade of increasingly coordinated campuses and classes, the two schools were completely merged in 1974. In 1992, Dwight-Englewood expanded its upper and middle school curriculum to include the lower grades when it incorporated Bede School, an elementary school that opened in 1963.

Enrolling students from northern New Jersey, Rockland County and the New York City metropolitan area, the school offers a preschool and kindergarten program. In the lower and middle grades, emphasis is on building a strong foundation in the core disciplines and in problem-solving skills. The upper school program, which includes honors and Advanced Placement courses and a fully integrated math/science/technology program, prepares graduates for admission to selective colleges. Students in grades 6-12 utilize tablet computers in class. Boys and girls perform 40 cumulative hours of required community service in grades 9-12.

THE ELISABETH MORROW SCHOOL
Day — Coed Gr PS (Age 3)-8

Englewood, NJ 07631. 435 Lydecker St. Tel: 201-568-5566. Fax: 201-568-1209.
www.elisabethmorrow.org E-mail: admissions@elisabethmorrow.org
David M. Lowry, Head (2000). BA, Haverford College, MS, PhD, Columbia Univ. **Blair Talcott Orloff, Adm.**
Pre-Prep. Feat—Lib_Skills Fr Lat Span Computers Ceramics Studio_Art Theater Music Orchestra Dance. **Supp**—Dev_Read ESL Tut.
Sports—Basket X-country Lacrosse Soccer. B: Baseball Ice_Hockey. G: Softball Volley.

Selective adm (Gr PS-7): 83/yr. Appl fee: $60. Appl due: Rolling. **Tests** ISEE.
Enr 445. B 195. G 250. Avg class size: 18. Stud/fac: 7:1. Casual. **Fac 70.** M 5/F 65. FT 70. Adv deg: 70%.
Grad '09—32. Prep—32. (Dwight-Englewood 7, Acad of the Holy Angels 4, Blair 2, Dwight Sch 2, Horace Mann 2).
Tui '11-'12: Day $17,300-27,900 (+$130-1530).
Summer: Acad Enrich Rec. 6 wks.
Endow $4,900,000. Plant val $15,800,000. Acres 14. Bldgs 4. Class rms 43. 3 Libs 23,000 vols. Sci labs 3. Lang labs 2. Theaters 1. Art studios 2. Music studios 2. Dance studios 1. Gyms 2. Fields 1. Playgrounds 3. Comp labs 2.
Est 1930. Nonprofit. Sem (Sept-June).

Originally the Little School, the school was renamed in 1948 for its cofounder, a daughter of Dwight Morrow. Located on a 14-acre, wooded campus in a residential area 10 miles from New York City, the school draws students from more than 50 surrounding communities.

The curriculum stresses a thematic approach to learning developmentally appropriate skills. Literature-based reading and writing and problem solving in mathematics form the core of the program. After-school, summer and childcare programs are available.

FAR HILLS, NJ. (36 mi. W of New York, NY) Rural. Pop: 859. Alt: 200 ft.

FAR HILLS COUNTRY DAY SCHOOL

Day — Coed Gr PS (Age 3)-8

Far Hills, NJ 07931. 697 Old Mine Brook Rd, PO Box 8. Tel: 908-766-0622.
Fax: 908-766-6705.
www.fhcds.org   E-mail: khayes@fhcds.org
Jayne Geiger, Head (1993). BA, MEd, Rutgers Univ, MS, Bank Street College of Education. **Kassandra Hayes, Adm.**
Pre-Prep. Elem math—Everyday Math/McDougal Littell. **Feat—**Chin Fr Lat Span Computers Studio_Art Drama Music Health.
Sports (req'd)—Basket X-country Fencing Ice_Hockey Lacrosse Soccer Tennis Track Volley. G: F_Hockey.
Selective adm: 59/yr. Usual entry: PS & K. Appl fee: $100. Appl due: Feb. Applied: 115. Accepted: 61%. Yield: 74%. **Tests** CTP_4 ISEE SSAT.
Enr 440. B 217. G 223. Wh 92%. Latino 1%. Blk 2%. Asian 3%. Other 2%. Avg class size: 15. Stud/fac: 8:1. Uniform. **Fac 60.** M 4/F 56. FT 47/PT 13. Wh 95%. Latino 1%. Asian 4%. Adv deg: 85%.
Grad '11—36. Prep—35. (Morristown-Beard, Hotchkiss, Delbarton, Kent Place, Pingry, Lawrenceville). Alum donors: 8%.
Tui '12-'13: Day $18,500-30,820. Aid: Merit 2 ($15,000). Need 57 ($700,000).
Summer: Acad Enrich. Tui Day $365-640. 1 wk. Musical Theater. Tui Day $650. 2 wks.
Endow $9,000,000. Plant val $30,000,000. Acres 54. Bldgs 5 (0% ADA). Class rms 42. Lib 12,000 vols. Sci labs 3. Comp ctrs 1. Theaters 1. Art studios 3. Music studios 8. Gyms 1. Athletic ctrs 2. Fields 4. Courts 3. Ropes crses 1. Comp/stud: 1:3.
Est 1929. Nonprofit. Tri (Sept-June). **Assoc** MSA.

Founded in Morristown as the Mount Kemble School, FHCDS moved to its present site and assumed its current name in 1944. The rural, 54-acre campus in Somerset County is accessible to both New York City and Princeton.

In the primary and intermediate schools (grades pre-K-5), children take part in self-contained classes in most academic areas, while specialists provide instruction in art, music, library, computer, science, Mandarin, Spanish and physical education. Public speaking is an important component of the program at all levels. The fully departmentalized upper school (grades 6-8) features such supplemental offerings as forensics, concert choir, bell choir, band and drama. In addition, all pupils take Latin in grades 7 and 8. Community service is integrated into the curriculum throughout, and boys and girls must complete 12 hours of service prior to the end of grade 8.

The school's adventure program, which commences in grade 5, consists of experiential learning and adventure pursuits.   **See Also Page 109**

GLADSTONE, NJ. (38 mi. W of New York, NY) Rural. Pop: 2111. Alt: 300 ft.

GILL ST. BERNARD'S SCHOOL

Day — Coed Gr PS (Age 3)-12

Gladstone, NJ 07934. St Bernard's Rd, PO Box 604. Tel: 908-234-1611.
   Fax: 908-234-1712.
   www.gsbschool.org   E-mail: admission@gsbschool.org
Sidney A. Rowell, Head (2001). BA, MA, Trinity College (CT). **Karen A. Loder, Adm.**
   Col Prep. AP (exams req'd; 158 taken, 80% 3+)—Eng Fr Span Calc Comp_Sci Bio Chem Environ_Sci Physics Eur_Hist US_Hist Psych US_Govt & Pol. **Elem math**—Singapore Math. **Feat**—Creative_Writing Poetry Lat Stats Astron Forensic_Sci Oceanog Web_Design Holocaust Philos Art_Hist Film Photog Studio_Art Acting Woodworking. **Supp**—Tut.
   Sports—Basket X-country Fencing Golf Soccer Swim Tennis Track. B: Baseball. G: Softball. **Activities:** 18.
   Selective adm (Gr PS-11): 123/yr. Usual entry: PS, K & 9. Appl fee: $75. Appl due: Feb. Applied: 225. Accepted: 66%. Yield: 77%. **Tests** CTP_4 ISEE SSAT.
   Enr 710. B 328. G 382. Elem 400. Sec 310. Wh 81%. Latino 2%. Blk 3%. Asian 6%. Other 8%. Avg class size: 15. Stud/fac: 9:1. Casual. **Fac 103.** M 35/F 68. FT 103. Adv deg: 52%.
   Grad '10—47. Col—47. (Villanova 4, Georgetown 2, U of DE 2, Fairfield 2, Williams 1, McGill-Canada 1). Athl schol 1. **Mid 50% SAT:** CR 550-680. M 550-680. W 550-690. **Col couns:** 3. Alum donors: 34%.
   Tui '12-'13: Day $20,800-30,900 (+$200-600). **Aid:** Merit 11 ($55,000). Need 85 ($1,350,000).
   Summer: Acad Enrich Rev Rec. 6 wks.
   Endow $6,500,000. Plant val $25,000,000. Acres 72. Bldgs 18. Class rms 53. 3 Libs 20,000 vols. Sci labs 4. Theaters 2. Art studios 3. Music studios 1. Dance studios 1. Art galleries 1. Gyms 2. Fields 7. Courts 5. Pools 1. Tracks 1. Comp labs 3.
   Est 1900. Nonprofit. Sem (Sept-June). **Assoc** CLS MSA.

The school resulted from the 1972 merger of the Gill School in Bernardsville, which was founded by Elizabeth Gill in 1934, and St. Bernard's School in Gladstone, founded by Rev. Thomas Conover as an Episcopal boarding school in 1900. GSB now occupies a 72-acre campus on the border of Morris and Somerset counties.

The lower school offers a curriculum that includes language arts, computers, world languages, Singapore Math, social studies, science, art and music at all levels. The Spring Unit is an important element of the upper school curriculum. For two weeks at the end of the academic year, upper school students engage in learning outside of the classroom context.

HIGHTSTOWN, NJ. (37 mi. ENE of Philadelphia, PA) Suburban. Pop: 5216. Alt: 97 ft.

PEDDIE SCHOOL

Bdg and Day — Coed Gr 9-PG

Hightstown, NJ 08520. 201 S Main St. Tel: 609-490-7500. Fax: 609-944-7901.
www.peddie.org   E-mail: admission@peddie.org
John F. Green, Head (2001). BA, Wesleyan Univ, MEd, Harvard Univ. **Raymond H. Cabot, Adm.**
Col Prep. AP (exams req'd; 411 taken, 98% 3+)—Chin Fr Lat Span Calc Stats Bio Chem Eur_Hist US_Hist Psych Art_Hist Music_Theory. **Feat**—Poetry Shakespeare Playwriting Astron Environ_Sci Forensic_Sci Genetics Programming Robotics Modern_E_Asian_Hist Modern_Indian_Hist Amer_Stud Econ Film Acting Drama Music Opera. **Supp**—Dev_Read ESL Tut. Sat classes.
Sports (req'd)—Basket Crew X-country Golf Lacrosse Soccer Swim Tennis Track. B: Baseball Football Wrestling. G: F_Hockey Softball. **Activities:** 35.
Very selective adm: 167/yr. Bdg 110. Day 57. Appl fee: $50. Appl due: Jan. Applied: 1561. Accepted: 20%. Yield: 55%. **Tests** CEEB SSAT TOEFL.
Enr 572. Sec 557. PG 15. Wh 59%. Latino 7%. Blk 8%. Asian 13%. Other 13%. Intl 12%. Avg class size: 12. Stud/fac: 6:1. Casual. **Fac 84.** M 48/F 36. FT 84. Adv deg: 69%. In dorms 28.
Grad '11—140. Col—140. (Johns Hopkins 8, Cornell 7, NYU 5, U of PA 4, Carnegie Mellon 4, Geo Wash 4). Athl schol 8. **Avg SAT:** CR 620. M 663. W 635. Avg ACT: 28.3. **Col couns:** 3.
Tui '12-'13: Bdg $47,500 (+$700). **Day $39,000** (+$350). **Aid:** Need 229 ($5,300,000).
Summer: Acad Enrich Rev Rec. Tui Day $525/crse. 6 wks.
Endow $228,000,000. Plant val $116,000,000. Acres 280. Bldgs 57. Dorms 14. Dorm rms 322. Class rms 47. Lib 33,000 vols. Chapels 1. Sci labs 11. Theaters 1. Art studios 4. Music studios 2. Gyms 1. Athletic ctrs 1. Fields 9. Courts 14. Pools 2. Golf crses 1. Student ctrs 1. Comp labs 2. Comp/stud: 1:1 Laptop prgm Gr 9-PG.
Est 1864. Nonprofit. Tri (Sept-May). **Assoc** CLS MSA.

Located on a 280-acre campus, Peddie offers a demanding academic program that attracts intelligent students from roughly 20 states and 30 countries. The broad college preparatory curriculum includes core courses and a wide variety of electives (available in one-, two- and three-term sequences) in the performing and visual arts, music, science, math, computer and information technology, and history. Honors and Advanced Placement sections are available in the major disciplines. Technology is an important aspect of Peddie's program, as each pupil receives a laptop computer upon enrollment. The school's library maintains a direct link with Princeton University, and all academic buildings and dormitories feature wireless Internet access.

All students take part in a physical education program that includes both interscholastic and intramural sports. Boys and girls fulfill a 20-hour community service requirement (or five hours for postgraduates and one-year seniors). Study abroad opportunities are also available.

JERSEY CITY, NJ. (7 mi. WNW of New York, NY) Urban. Pop: 240,055. Alt: 83 ft.

ST. PETER'S PREPARATORY SCHOOL

Day — Boys Gr 9-12

Jersey City, NJ 07302. 144 Grand St. Tel: 201-547-6400. Fax: 201-547-2341.
www.spprep.org   E-mail: irvinej@spprep.org

Rev. Robert E. Reiser, SJ, Pres (2006). BS, Canisius College, MA, Fordham Univ, MDiv, Weston Jesuit School of Theology, ThM, Harvard Univ, MEd, Univ of Rochester. **James C. DeAngelo, Prin.** BA, Boston College, MA, St Peter's College. **John Irvine, Adm.**

   Col Prep. AP (exams req'd; 257 taken)—Eng Lat Span Calc Stats Comp_Sci Bio Chem US_Hist. **Feat**—Creative_Writing Shakespeare Fr Ger Greek Ital Environ_Sci Middle_Eastern_Hist Law Ethics Relig Sculpt Studio_Art Chorus Music. **Supp**—Rev Tut.

   Sports—B: Baseball Basket Bowl Crew X-country Fencing Football Golf Ice_Hockey Lacrosse Rugby Soccer Swim Tennis Track Volley W_Polo Wrestling. **Activities:** 37.

   Selective adm: 300/yr. Usual entry: 9. Appl fee: $0. Appl due: Nov. Applied: 904. Accepted: 45%. Yield: 65%. **Tests** SSAT TACHS.

   Enr 938. Wh 63%. Latino 13%. Blk 10%. Asian 10%. Other 4%. Avg class size: 22. Stud/fac: 12:1. Formal. **Fac 72.** M 49/F 23. FT 67/PT 5. Wh 93%. Latino 4%. Blk 2%. Asian 1%. Adv deg: 66%.

   Grad '11—184. Col—182. (Rutgers 22, Boston Col 8, St Peter's 8, St Joseph's U 7, Kean 5, Col of NJ 5). Athl schol 8. **Avg SAT:** CR 623. M 639. W 633. Avg ACT: 24.3. **Col couns:** 4. Alum donors: 27%.

   Tui '11-'12: Day $11,500 (+$750-1050). **Aid:** Merit 150 ($450,000). Need 301 ($950,000).

   Summer (enr 100): Acad Enrich. Tui Day $300. 5 wks.

   Endow $18,000,000. Plant val $30,000,000. Bldgs 6 (80% ADA). Libs 1. Sci labs 10. Art studios 2. Gyms 1. Fields 1. Comp labs 2. Comp/stud: 1:8.

   Est 1872. Nonprofit. Roman Catholic (80% practice). Quar (Sept-June). **Assoc** MSA.

Located in the historic Paulus Hook section of the city, this Jesuit school offers a college preparatory curriculum enriched by Advanced Placement, honors and religion courses. All boys fulfill a two-year Latin requirement, and Prep maintains a strong fine arts department featuring courses that combine theory and practice. Technology forms an integral component of academic life at the school: Computers are employed extensively in science classes, and workstations in the computer center are available to students at lunchtime and after school (as well as in computer science courses).

As part of the foreign language program, St. Peter's plans noncredit exchanges for students of German, French, Spanish and Italian. In addition to its formal exchange programs, Prep regularly conducts summer tours to such countries as France, Spain and Mexico.

Boys perform 20 hours of annual community service during their freshman and sophomore years, then accumulate another 60 hours in grade 11.

LAWRENCEVILLE, NJ. (30 mi. NE of Philadelphia, PA) Suburban. Pop: 4081. Alt: 123 ft.

LAWRENCEVILLE SCHOOL
Bdg and Day — Coed Gr 9-PG

Lawrenceville, NJ 08648. 2500 Main St, PO Box 6008. Tel: 609-896-0400, 800-735-2030. Fax: 609-895-2217.

   www.lawrenceville.org   E-mail: admissions@lawrenceville.org

Elizabeth A. Duffy, Head (2003). AB, Princeton Univ, MBA, AM, Stanford Univ. **Gregg W. M. Maloberti, Adm.**

   Col Prep. AP exams taken: 801 (92% 3+). Feat—Humanities Poetry African-Amer_Lit Asian-Amer_Lit Irish_Lit Russ_Lit Southern_Lit Chin Fr Greek Japan Lat Span Stats Multivariable_Calc Astron Bioethics Ecol Environ_Sci Physiol Programming Robotics Chin_Hist Japan_Hist Middle_Eastern_Hist Russ_Hist Amer_Stud Econ Ethics Philos Relig Hinduism Architect Art_Hist Ceramics Studio_Art Visual_Arts Theater Music Music_Theory Dance Journ. Outdoor ed. Sat classes.

   Sports—Basket Crew X-country Fencing Golf Ice_Hockey Indoor_Track Lacrosse Soccer Squash Swim Tennis Track W_Polo. B: Baseball Football Wrestling. G: F_

Hockey Softball Volley. **Activities:** 90.
Very selective adm: 240/yr. Appl fee: $50. Appl due: Jan. Applied: 1940. Accepted: 22%. Yield: 64%. **Tests** CEEB ISEE SSAT TOEFL.
Enr 810. B 425. G 385. Bdg 548. Day 262. Intl 9%. Avg class size: 12. Stud/fac: 8:1. **Fac 141.** FT 139/PT 2. Adv deg: 75%. In dorms 37.
Grad '10—228. Col—226. (Georgetown 14, NYU 12, U of PA 11, Princeton 10, Columbia 9, Yale 8). **Avg SAT:** CR 676. M 694. W 698. **Col couns:** 5. Alum donors: 42%.
Tui '12-'13: Bdg $51,025 (+$1170). **Day $42,185** (+$750). **Aid:** Need ($10,160,000).
Endow $270,000,000. Plant val $300,000,000. Acres 700. Bldgs 35. Dorms 18. Dorm rms 430. Class rms 105. Lib 63,000 vols. Chapels 1. Sci labs 14. Lang labs 1. Sci ctrs 1. Theaters 1. Art studios 4. Music studios 6. Dance studios 1. Arts ctrs 1. Music ctrs 1. Gyms 1. Fields 17. Squash courts 10. Field houses 1. Pools 1. Rinks 1. Tracks 1. Weight rms 2. Golf crses 1. Ropes crses 1. Boathouses 1. Greenhouses 1. Comp labs 2.
Est 1810. Nonprofit. Tri (Sept-June). **Assoc** CLS MSA.

The school was founded when Isaac Van Arsdale Brown, a Presbyterian minister, began to teach lessons to nine local boys in his front parlor. Initially known as the Academy of Maidenhead, for the town's original name, and run under such names as Lawrenceville High School and the Lawrenceville Classical and Commercial High School for some 70 years thereafter, it was not until 1883 that it became the Lawrenceville School. The center of the 700-acre campus is the Circle, which was landscaped and designed by Frederick Law Olmsted and has been designated a national historic landmark.

Two noteworthy features are the house system and the conference plan. The first is a dormitory system that follows the example of such English public schools as Rugby and Eton. House identity is maintained through separate dining rooms in the dining center and athletic teams that compete intramurally. Each house has its own student government and traditions and, as students move through different levels, they assume increased responsibility for management of themselves and their house. The conference style of teaching allows for approximately a dozen students, along with the instructor, to sit around an oval Harkness table, thus challenging students to be well prepared and to participate in the discussion.

Based on a traditional approach to education, Lawrenceville's program exposes its students to courses in many disciplines through electives and departmental requirements. The comprehensive curriculum prepares students to take AP examinations and is complemented by an array of opportunities in the visual and performing arts. Other options include off-campus projects, independent study and Island School, a semester-long, intensive marine science program open to sophomores and juniors that utilizes the resources of the marine environment in Eleuthera, Bahamas. In addition, pupils who have completed their second year of Spanish or French may spend a term at an affiliated institution in either Alicante, Spain or Angouleme, France.

Students must participate in an approved athletic activity at least four times a week until the senior year, when they are required to take part three times a week. Among the choices are interscholastics, a comprehensive intramural program and instruction in any of a number of lifetime sports (such as aerobics, cricket, golf, karate, kayaking, riding and tennis). All students who spend more than one year at Lawrenceville perform at least 40 hours of cumulative community service; those attending for only one year satisfy a 20-hour commitment.

LIVINGSTON, NJ. (22 mi. WNW of New York, NY) Suburban. Pop: 27,391. Alt: 307 ft.

NEWARK ACADEMY

Day — Coed Gr 6-12

Livingston, NJ 07039. 91 S Orange Ave. Tel: 973-992-7000. Fax: 973-992-8962.
www.newarka.edu   E-mail: info@newarka.edu

Donald M. Austin, Head (2007). AB, Georgetown Univ, MA, MPhil, New York Univ. **Willard Taylor, Adm.**
  Col Prep. IB Diploma. AP (exams req'd; 281 taken, 81% 3+)—Eng Fr Lat Span Calc Stats Comp_Sci Bio Environ_Sci Physics Eur_Hist US_Hist Econ Art_Hist. **Feat**—Creative_Writing Humanities Chin Anat & Physiol Ecol Geol Zoology Biotech Robotics Holocaust Ethics Philos World_Relig Ceramics Film Visual_Arts Acting Drama Theater_Arts Music Music_Composition Dance Finance. **Supp**—Rev Tut.
  Sports—Basket X-country Fencing Golf Lacrosse Soccer Swim Tennis Track. B: Baseball Football Wrestling. G: F_Hockey Softball Volley. **Activities:** 40.
  Selective adm (Gr 6-11): 125/yr. Usual entry: 6 & 9. Appl fee: $65. Appl due: Dec. Applied: 490. Accepted: 26%. Yield: 73%. **Tests** ISEE SSAT.
  Enr 565. Elem 169. Sec 396. Nonwhite 25%. Avg class size: 13. Casual. **Fac 68.** Wh 82%. Latino 6%. Blk 6%. Asian 6%. Adv deg: 79%.
  Grad '11—98. Col—96. (Cornell 6, NYU 6, Wash U 5, U of PA 4, Harvard 4, Emory 4). **Avg SAT:** CR 657. M 678. W 681. Avg ACT: 29. **Col couns:** 3. Alum donors: 14%.
  Tui '12-'13: Day $31,725 (+$1870-1880). **Aid:** Need ($2,000,000).
  Summer: Acad Enrich. Tui Day $200-1140. 1-6 wks.
  Endow $18,300,000. Plant val $50,000,000. Acres 68. Bldgs 1. Class rms 44. Lib 22,000 vols. Sci labs 7. Lang labs 1. Auds 1. Theaters 1. Art studios 3. Music studios 2. Dance studios 1. Gyms 3. Fields 8. Courts 8. Field houses 1. Pools 1. Tracks 2. Weight rms 1. Comp labs 2.
  Est 1774. Nonprofit. Tri (Sept-June). **Assoc** CLS MSA.

Founded in Newark by Alexander Macwhorter, a leading New Jersey cleric and advisor to George Washington, Newark Academy closed during the Revolution and reopened in newly built quarters in 1792. The school opened a separate division for girls in 1802, but the program was discontinued in 1859. In 1964, the academy moved from Newark to Livingston, and it became fully coeducational in 1971.

Qualified students at the academy may elect to work towards the IB Diploma or choose a sampling of individual IB courses. Each department offers Advanced Placement courses, and all seniors choose and work on independent projects during the month of May. From middle school through upper school, all pupils take classes in the arts. In addition, participation in community service is a graduation requirement: Students in grades 9-12 perform a minimum of 10 hours of service annually, and the academy encourages boys and girls to donate additional hours.

MARTINSVILLE, NJ. (33 mi. W of New York, NY) Rural. Pop: 900. Alt: 306 ft.

THE PINGRY SCHOOL
Day — Coed Gr K-12

Martinsville, NJ 08836. Martinsville Rd, PO Box 366. Tel: 908-647-6419. Fax: 908-647-3703.
Other locations: 50 Country Day Dr, Short Hills 07078.
  www.pingry.org   **E-mail: info@pingry.org**
Nathaniel E. Conard, Head (2005). BS, Yale Univ, MBA, Dartmouth College. **Allison C. Brunhouse, Adm.**
  Col Prep. AP (exams req'd; 741 taken, 87% 3+)—Fr Ger Lat Span Calc Stats Comp_Sci Bio Chem Physics Eur_Hist US_Hist Econ Psych US_Govt & Pol Art_Hist Studio_Art Music_Theory. **Feat**—British_Lit Creative_Writing Shakespeare Anat & Physiol Civil_War Philos World_Relig Filmmaking Photog Sculpt Acting Drama Dance.
  Sports—Basket X-country Fencing Golf Ice_Hockey Lacrosse Ski Soccer Squash Swim Tennis Track W_Polo. B: Baseball Football Wrestling. G: F_Hockey Softball.
  Selective adm (Gr K-11): 162/yr. Usual entry: K, 3, 5, 6 & 9. Appl fee: $75-100. Appl due: Jan. Accepted: 30%. Yield: 82%. **Tests** CTP_4 ISEE SSAT.
  Enr 1065. B 539. G 526. Elem 527. Sec 538. Wh 54%. Latino 3%. Blk 8%. Asian 21%.

Other 14%. Avg class size: 15. Stud/fac: 9:1. **Fac 160.** Nonwhite 14%. Adv deg: 65%.
Grad '11—132. Col—127. (Cornell 7, Columbia 7, Lehigh 5, Princeton 5, Wm & Mary 5, Colgate 4). **Mid 50% SAT:** CR 620-740. M 640-740. W 650-750. **Col couns:** 4. Alum donors: 24%.
Tui '11-'12: Day $27,050-31,615 (+$500-3000). **Aid:** Need 161 ($3,600,000).
Summer: Acad Enrich Rev. Tui Day $890-5250. 2-6 wks. Sports. Tui Day $150-695. 1-2 wks.
Endow $68,000,000. Plant val $46,282,000. Bldgs 2. Class rms 70. Lib 37,500 vols. Labs 9. Theaters 3. Art studios 6. Music studios 8. Arts ctrs 1. Gyms 3. Fields 8. Courts 12. Pools 1. Tracks 1.
Est 1861. Nonprofit. Sem (Sept-June). **Assoc** CLS MSA.

Dr. John F. Pingry founded the school in Elizabeth to provide boys with moral education and scholastic training in the classical tradition. The school remained at its original site until 1953, at which time it moved a short distance to Hillside. In the early 1970s, Pingry first enrolled girls and also effected a merger with Short Hills Country Day School, thereby expanding the program to kindergarten through grade 12 and increasing the size of the student body. In 1983, the school moved from Hillside to Martinsville; this campus now serves pupils in grades 6-12. The Short Hills campus on Country Day Drive, located about 25 minutes away, accommodates children in grades K-5.

The school draws its students from 100 central and northern New Jersey communities. The curriculum features small classes and a varied selection of Advanced Placement and honors courses in the upper school. Spanish is taught daily from first grade, and in grades 7 and 8 pupils study Latin and either French, Spanish or Chinese. The honor code, one of Pingry's traditions, dates from 1926 and remains an important component of school life. Students in grades 6-12 complete 10 hours of compulsory community service per year and participate in interscholastic athletics, physical education or dance each term.   **See Also Page 118**

MONTCLAIR, NJ. (18 mi. NW of New York, NY) Suburban. Pop: 38,977. Alt: 41 ft.

MONTCLAIR KIMBERLEY ACADEMY
Day — Coed Gr PS (Age 4)-12

Montclair, NJ 07042. 201 Valley Rd. Tel: 973-746-9800. Fax: 973-509-4526.
Other locations: 224 Orange Rd, Montclair 07042; 6 Lloyd Rd, Montclair 07042.
    www.mka.org   E-mail: admissions@mka.org
Thomas W. Nammack, Head (2005). AB, Brown Univ, MEd, Univ of Pennsylvania. **Sarah Rowland, Adm.**
  Col Prep. AP (exams req'd; 198 taken, 93% 3+)—Eng Fr Lat Span Calc Stats Comp_ Sci Chem Physics Studio_Art. **Elem math**—Everyday Math. **Feat**—British_Lit Poetry Shakespeare Satire Women's_Lit World_Lit Chin Astron Oceanog Web_Design Chin_Hist Japan_Hist Econ Pol_Sci Irish_Stud Lat-Amer_Stud Ethics Visual_Arts Drama Theater_Arts Music Music_Theory Dance. **Supp**—Tut. Outdoor ed.
  Sports—Basket X-country Fencing Golf Lacrosse Soccer Swim Tennis Track. B: Baseball Football Ice_Hockey Wrestling. G: F_Hockey Softball Volley. **Activities:** 50.
  Selective adm (Gr PS-11): 200/yr. Usual entry: PS, 6 & 9. Appl fee: $50. Appl due: Jan. **Tests** ISEE SSAT.
  Enr 1040. B 560. G 480. Elem 610. Sec 430. Wh 74%. Latino 3%. Blk 11%. Asian 6%. Other 6%. Avg class size: 14. Stud/fac: 6:1. **Fac 157.** M 58/F 99. FT 157. Adv deg: 77%.
  Grad '11—105. Col—105. (NYU 4, Geo Wash 4, Princeton 3, Georgetown 3, Yale 2, U of PA 2). **Avg SAT:** CR 630. M 647. W 650. **Mid 50% SAT:** CR 570-680. M 590-770. W 590-710. **Col couns:** 5.
  Tui '12-'13: Day $24,200-32,000 (+$1000). **Aid:** Need 81 ($1,447,800).

Summer: Enrich Rec. Tui Day $550/wk. 6 wks.
Endow $12,000,000. Plant val $23,000,000. Acres 27. Bldgs 11. Class rms 90. 3 Libs 32,000 vols. Sci labs 11. Auds 3. Theaters 1. Art studios 5. Music studios 2. Dance studios 1. Drama studios 2. Gyms 4. Fields 4. Courts 6. Pools 2. Comp labs 5. Laptop prgm Gr 4-12.
Est 1887. Nonprofit. Sem (Sept-June). **Assoc** CLS MSA.

In 1974, Montclair Academy for boys (founded in 1887) merged with The Kimberley School for girls (founded in 1906). The academy's three campuses, located in residential northern New Jersey on Orange Road (grades PS-3), Valley Road (4-8) and Lloyd Road (9-12), enroll a diverse student population from Montclair and more than 70 neighboring communities.

The college preparatory upper school curriculum features various elective, honors and Advanced Placement courses. Classes meet in 75-minute blocks. MKA's Core Works program enables pupils at all grade levels to undertake in-depth study of notable works of literature and art from both Western and non-Western traditions. Writing is taught as a cumulative, continuous process across classrooms and campuses; teachers formally evaluate student portfolios in grades 3, 7 and 11. The academy integrates technology into the curriculum at all grade levels, and a one-to-one laptop program serves boys and girls in grades 4-12. The foreign studies program combines classroom learning with educational travel and exchange programs.

Outdoor education, field trips at all grade levels, and community and school service activities afford students opportunities to learn outside the classroom. The fine and performing arts are integrated into the school's curriculum, and pupils on all three campuses participate in musical and dramatic productions. Students in grades 11 and 12 satisfy a 10-hour community service requirement each year.

MOORESTOWN, NJ. (11 mi. ESE of Philadelphia, PA) Suburban. Pop: 19,017. Alt: 71 ft.

MOORESTOWN FRIENDS SCHOOL

Day — Coed Gr PS (Age 3)-12

Moorestown, NJ 08057. 110 E Main St. Tel: 856-235-2900. Fax: 856-235-6684.
www.mfriends.org E-mail: admiss@mfriends.org
Laurence R. Van Meter, Head (2001). BA, Hamilton College, MBA, Dartmouth College.
Karin B. Miller, Adm.
Col Prep. AP (exams req'd; 156 taken, 58% 3+)—Eng Fr Span Calc Stats Comp_Sci Bio Chem Environ_Sci Physics US_Hist Comp_Govt & Pol Psych Studio_Art Music_Theory. Feat—Creative_Writing Short_Fiction Chin Anat & Physiol Geol Molecular_Bio Robotics African_Hist Cold_War Middle_Eastern_Hist Archaeol Relig Ceramics Painting Photog Sculpt Printmaking Finance. Supp—Rem_Read Rev Tut.
Sports—Basket Crew X-country Fencing Golf Lacrosse Soccer Swim Tennis. B: Baseball. G: F_Hockey. Activities: 38.
Selective adm: 108/yr. Usual entry: PS, 6 & 9. Appl fee: $45. Appl due: Rolling. Applied: 254. Accepted: 58%. Yield: 77%. Tests CTP_4 Stanford.
Enr 711. B 342. G 369. Elem 422. Sec 289. Wh 66%. Latino 4%. Blk 11%. Asian 12%. Other 7%. Avg class size: 18. Stud/fac: 9:1. Fac 92. M 27/F 65. FT 80/PT 12. Wh 86%. Latino 7%. Blk 3%. Asian 4%. Adv deg: 61%.
Grad '11—75. Col—75. (Rutgers 5, Cornell 4, PA St 3, Johns Hopkins 2, Swarthmore 2, Bucknell 2). Avg SAT: CR 628. M 641. W 644. Alum donors: 25%.
Tui '12-'13: Day $15,400-24,600 (+$400). Aid: Need 175 ($2,281,425).
Endow $7,880,000. Plant val $23,206,000. Acres 48. Bldgs 21. Class rms 50. Lib 66,000 vols. Sci labs 6. Auds 1. Art studios 2. Music studios 2. Gyms 4. Fields 7. Courts 5. Pools 1. Comp labs 4. Comp/stud: 1:2.
Est 1785. Nonprofit. Religious Society of Friends. Quar (Sept-June). Assoc CLS MSA.

Moorestown Friends, operated under the care of the Moorestown Monthly Meeting, originated when the Quakers opened a school on the present, 48-acre site. All students, faculty and staff attend weekly meetings for worship. The school draws students of all backgrounds from South Jersey communities.

The college preparatory program in the middle and upper schools is varied, with attention given to the arts and learning experiences that provide off-campus opportunities each year. Weeklong intensive learning workshops each March allow for experiential, in-depth study of specific topics. Seniors engage in pre-professional or service projects in May, and upper school students fulfill a 50-hour community service requirement prior to graduation.

In the lower school, children are grouped in traditional grade levels. The developmental curriculum incorporates thematic and experiential learning. Three- and four-year-old students learn in a separate house on campus; the program emphasizes socialization and developmentally appropriate early childhood experiences.

MORRISTOWN, NJ. (29 mi. WNW of New York, NY) Suburban. Pop: 18,544. Alt: 350 ft. Area also includes Convent Station.

ACADEMY OF SAINT ELIZABETH
Day — Girls Gr 9-12

Convent Station, NJ 07961. PO Box 297. Tel: 973-290-5200. Fax: 973-290-5232.
www.aosenj.org   E-mail: admin@aosenj.org
Sr. Patricia Costello, OP, Prin (2003). BA, Caldwell College, MA, Seton Hall Univ. **Kathleen Thomas, Adm.**

Col Prep. AP (46 exams taken, 83% 3+)—Eng Fr Lat Span Calc Bio Chem Eur_Hist US_Hist. **Feat**—British_Lit Bioethics Ecol Environ_Sci Physiol Comp_Sci Psych Sociol Relig World_Relig Art_Hist Photog Studio_Art Theater Chorus Dance Journ Driver_Ed. **Supp**—Tut. **Dual enr:** Col of St Elizabeth.

Sports—G: Basket X-country F_Hockey Golf Lacrosse Soccer Softball Swim Tennis Track Volley. **Activities:** 30.

Somewhat selective adm: 71/yr. Appl fee: $100. Appl due: Nov. Accepted: 85%.

Enr 206. Avg class size: 15. Uniform. **Fac 27.** M 6/F 21. FT 25/PT 2. Adv deg: 37%.

Grad '11—56. Col—56. (Loyola U MD 3, U of Scranton 3, Seton Hall 2, Fairfield 2, Rutgers 2, Fordham 2). **Avg SAT:** CR 572. M 558. W 599. **Col couns:** 2.

Tui '12-'13: Day $16,000 (+$1550).

Acres 200. Bldgs 2. Class rms 20. Libs 1. Chapels 1. Sci labs 3. Auds 1. Theaters 1. Art studios 1. Music studios 1. Dance studios 1. Gyms 1. Fields 4. Courts 1. Pools 1. Comp labs 1.

Est 1860. Nonprofit. Roman Catholic. Quar (Sept-June). **Assoc** MSA.

In 1859, Mother Mary Xavier, a young Sister of Charity from New York, was commissioned by Bishop James Roosevelt Bayley to establish this school for young women; it is the oldest girls' high school in the state. The academy offers Advanced Placement programs in calculus, chemistry, English, US history and foreign languages, and honors classes in each major academic discipline. The academy offers a career-oriented program to seniors during the last two weeks before graduation in which each student chooses an area of interest and selects a mentor in that field. Internship participants follow up with reports submitted to the entire student body at an assembly.

The academy fields a full complement of varsity teams, and intramural programs are offered in riding and skiing. Students also plan and participate in liturgical celebrations, lead the school in daily prayer and volunteer for service projects. Annual retreats are conducted off campus for each class. The school's foreign travel program sponsors a two-week trip each year.

DELBARTON SCHOOL

Day — Boys Gr 7-12

Morristown, NJ 07960. 230 Mendham Rd. Tel: 973-538-3231. Fax: 973-538-8836.
www.delbarton.org   E-mail: admissions@delbarton.org
Br. Paul Diveny, OSB, Head (2007). BA, Catholic Univ of America, MA, Middlebury College. **David Donovan, Adm.**

Col Prep. AP (570 exams taken, 85% 3+)—Eng Fr Ger Lat Span Calc Stats Comp_Sci Bio Chem Physics Eur_Hist US_Hist Econ Psych Art_Hist Studio_Art Music_Theory. **Feat**—Creative_Writing Ital Russ Environ_Sci Intl_Relations Philos Film. **Supp**—Tut.

Sports—B: Baseball Basket Bowl X-country Football Golf Lacrosse Ski Soccer Squash Swim Tennis Track Wrestling. **Activities:** 69.

Selective adm (Gr 7-11): 122/yr. Usual entry: 7 & 9. Appl fee: $65. Appl due: Nov. Applied: 436. Accepted: 29%. Yield: 91%. **Tests** IQ Stanford.

Enr 550. Elem 66. Sec 484. Wh 83%. Latino 5%. Blk 3%. Asian 8%. Other 1%. Avg class size: 15. Stud/fac: 7:1. **Fac 83.** M 66/F 17. FT 58/PT 25. Wh 92%. Latino 7%. Asian 1%. Adv deg: 61%.

Grad '11—112. Col—112. (Villanova 14, Notre Dame 9, Georgetown 7, Princeton 5, Johns Hopkins 4, Boston Col 4). **Avg SAT:** CR/M 1330. **Col couns:** 3. Alum donors: 48%.

Tui '12-'13: Day $30,200 (+$1900). **Aid:** Need 85 ($1,295,000).

Summer (enr 400): Acad Enrich. Tui Day $1150. Tui Day $525. 5 wks.

Endow $20,900,000. Plant val $16,600,000. Acres 400. Bldgs 5. Class rms 40. Lib 20,000 vols. Sci labs 6. Lang labs 1. Art studios 2. Music studios 3. Gyms 2. Fields 8. Tennis courts 6. Pools 1. Greenhouses 1. Comp labs 5.

Est 1939. Nonprofit. Roman Catholic (80% practice). Tri (Sept-June). **Assoc** MSA.

Founded on the Delbarton estate of Luther Kountze by Benedictine monks, this preparatory school offers a strict academic curriculum integrated with religious study in the Benedictine tradition. The campus, which includes spacious playing fields, ponds and woodland, is adjacent to Jockey Hollow National Park.

In addition to traditional liberal arts classes, the curriculum offers Advanced Placement courses in all disciplines and such electives as economics and film study. Delbarton provides one-on-one music lessons in many instruments.

MORRISTOWN-BEARD SCHOOL

Day — Coed Gr 6-12

Morristown, NJ 07960. 70 Whippany Rd. Tel: 973-539-3032. Fax: 973-539-1590.
www.mobeard.org   E-mail: admission@mobeard.org
Peter J. Caldwell, Head (2011). BA, Bowdoin College, MEd, Harvard Univ. **Hillary Nastro, Adm.**

Col Prep. AP (exams req'd)—Eng Fr Lat Span Calc Bio Chem Physics Eur_Hist US_Hist Studio_Art. **Feat**—Creative_Writing Stats Forensic_Sci Sports_Med Comp_Sci Irish_Hist Middle_Eastern_Hist Vietnam_War Women's_Hist Econ Constitutional_Law Architect Ceramics Photog Sculpt Acting Theater Band Chorus Music_Theory Dance Journ.

Sports—Basket X-country Ice_Hockey Lacrosse Ski Soccer Swim Tennis Track. **B:** Baseball Football Golf. **G:** F_Hockey Softball Volley.

Selective adm (Gr 6-11): 131/yr. Usual entry: 6, 7 & 9. Appl fee: $55. Appl due: Feb. Accepted: 60%. Yield: 60%. **Tests** ISEE SSAT.

Enr 544. B 288. G 256. Elem 150. Sec 394. Avg class size: 12. Stud/fac: 7:1. **Fac 93.** Adv deg: 58%.

Grad '11—92. Col—91. (Am U, U of CT, Rollins, Muhlenberg, Rutgers, Fordham). **Avg SAT:** CR 571. M 607. W 592. **Mid 50% SAT:** CR 520-630. M 570-650. W 540-650. Avg ACT: 26. Mid 50% ACT: 23-27. **Col couns:** 2.

Tui '11-'12: Day $30,650-31,850 (+$2905). **Aid:** Need ($1,700,000).

Summer: Acad Enrich Rec. Arts. 6 wks.
Endow $10,000,000. Plant val $50,000,000. Acres 22. Bldgs 10. Class rms 51. Lib
14,500 vols. Sci labs 8. Theaters 1. Art studios 3. Music studios 2. Gyms 2. Fields 4.
Courts 4. Pools 1. Comp labs 5.
Est 1891. Nonprofit. Sem (Sept-June). **Assoc** CLS MSA.

Morristown-Beard was formed in 1971 by a merger of the Morristown School for boys and
the Beard School for girls. Morristown, which was founded in 1891 by three Harvard graduates—Thomas Q. Browne, Arthur P. Butler and Francis C. Woodman—was long considered
a preparatory school for Harvard. Beard was established the same year in Orange by Lucie C.
Beard.

The school is located on a 22-acre campus that is bordered on two sides by a county park
arboretum. The college preparatory curriculum features a full complement of Advanced Placement, honors, independent study and elective courses. The math center allows students access
to a system of microcomputers. Students in grades 9-12 satisfy a 16-hour community service
requirement, and boys and girls must also complete a senior project. Advanced seminars allow
talented and motivated juniors and seniors to explore an intellectual area in depth, under the
guidance of selected faculty members.

THE PECK SCHOOL

Day — Coed Gr K-8

Morristown, NJ 07960. 247 South St. Tel: 973-539-8660. Fax: 973-539-6894.
www.peckschool.org E-mail: eceder@peckschool.org
John J. Kowalik, Head (2003). BA, Williams College, MA, Columbia Univ. **Erin K. Ceder,**
Adm.
  Pre-Prep. Elem math—Scott Foresman-Addison Wesley. **Elem read**—Guided Read.
    Feat—Lib_Skills Fr Lat Span Computers Studio_Art Music Woodworking. **Supp**—
    Dev_Read.
  Sports (req'd)—Basket X-country Ice_Hockey Lacrosse Volley. B: Baseball Soccer. G:
    F_Hockey Softball.
  Selective adm: 53/yr. Usual entry: K & 5. Appl fee: $100. Appl due: Jan. Accepted: 45%.
    Yield: 76%. **Tests** CTP_4.
  Enr 336. B 182. G 154. Wh 81%. Blk 3%. Asian 10%. Other 6%. Intl 6%. Avg class size:
    15. Stud/fac: 6:1. Uniform. **Fac 51.** M 15/F 36. FT 39/PT 12. Wh 90%. Latino 2%. Blk
    2%. Asian 6%. Adv deg: 60%.
  Grad '11—37. Prep—36. (Pingry 6, Delbarton 5, Hotchkiss 5, Kent Place 2, Oak Knoll
    2, Lawrenceville 2). Avg SSAT: 95%. Alum donors: 15%.
  Tui '12-'13: Day $27,250-31,350 (+$1500). **Aid:** Need 21 ($458,832).
  Summer (enr 246): Acad Enrich Rev Rec. Sports. Tui Day $300-550/wk. 3 wks.
  Endow $10,000,000. Plant val $23,500,000. Acres 14. Bldgs 7 (86% ADA). Class rms
    38. Lib 12,000 vols. Sci labs 4. Auds 1. Art studios 2. Music studios 2. Wood shops 1.
    Gyms 2. Fields 3. Comp labs 1. Comp/stud: 1:1.3 (1:1 Laptop prgm Gr 5-8).
  Est 1893. Nonprofit. Tri (Sept-June). **Assoc** MSA.

Founded and for many years conducted by Lorraine T. Peck, the school, upon his retirement in 1944, was incorporated by a group of parents, and the activities and the curriculum
broadened.

Located on a wooded, 14-acre campus, Peck emphasizes a traditional academic program.
The acquisition of skills is stressed in English and mathematics, with enrichment in social studies, foreign language, science, and the fine and performing arts. French and Spanish instruction
begins in kindergarten and is joined by Latin in grades 6-8. Math and languages are grouped
into standard and honors sections in grades 7 and 8. Technology is fully integrated into the
curriculum; students in grades 5 and 6 participate in a school-based laptop program, while
those in grades 7 and 8 engage in a take-home laptop program. Upper school pupils belong to
an advisory group of eight to nine students that meets twice a week.

Physical education begins in kindergarten, and boys and girls choose from intramural
(beginning in grade 3) and interscholastic (in grades 5-8) athletic programs.

MOUNTAIN LAKES, NJ. (30 mi. WNW of New York, NY) Suburban. Pop: 4256. Alt: 513 ft.

THE WILSON SCHOOL
Day — Coed Gr PS (Age 4)-8

Mountain Lakes, NJ 07046. 271 Boulevard. Tel: 973-334-0181. Fax: 973-334-1852.
   www.thewilsonschool.com   E-mail: info@thewilsonschool.com
Carolyn K. Borlo, Head (1998). BA, Lake Erie College, MAT, Colgate Univ, MAEd, New
   York Univ. **Chris Vakulchik, Adm.**
   Pre-Prep. Feat—Writing Fr Span Computers Studio_Art Drama Music. **Supp**—Tut.
   Sports—Swim Volley.
   Selective adm (Gr PS-7): 25/yr. Appl fee: $75. Appl due: Rolling. Accepted: 75%. Yield:
   60%. **Tests** CTP_4 IQ ISEE.
   Enr 75. B 40. G 35. Wh 60%. Latino 10%. Blk 20%. Asian 10%. Avg class size: 9. Uni-
   form. **Fac 22.** M 2/F 20. FT 18/PT 4. Wh 85%. Blk 5%. Asian 10%. Adv deg: 27%.
   Grad '09—6. Prep—4. (Morristown-Beard 1, Oak Knoll 1, Newark Acad 1).
   Tui '11-'12: Day $17,700-22,800 (+$750). **Aid:** Merit 3 ($3000). Need 20 ($100,000).
   Summer: Acad Enrich Rec. 4 wks.
   Endow $225,000. Plant val $4,000,000. Acres 2. Bldgs 3. Class rms 15. Lib 10,000 vols.
   Sci labs 1. Auds 1. Theaters 1. Art studios 1. Music studios 1. Gyms 1. Pools 1. Comp
   labs 1. Comp/stud: 1:2.
   Est 1909. Nonprofit. Ecumenical. Tri (Sept-June). **Assoc** MSA.

Formerly St. John's School and continuing to be nonsectarian in practice, this school was renamed in 1965 after its founder, Rev. Henry B. Wilson. Consisting of a lower school (grades pre-K-4) and a middle school (grades 5-8), Wilson seeks to meet the specific needs of its students. Teacher teams assigned to each grade meet regularly to review children's progress and determine future class themes. Community service is integrated into the curriculum.

An extended-day program is available.

MULLICA HILL, NJ. (19 mi. SSW of Philadelphia, PA) Rural. Pop: 1658. Alt: 97 ft.

FRIENDS SCHOOL MULLICA HILL
Day — Coed Gr PS (Age 4)-8

Mullica Hill, NJ 08062. 15 High St. Tel: 856-478-2908. Fax: 856-478-0263.
   www.friendsmh.org   E-mail: info@friendsmh.org
Bruce S. Haines, Head (2010). BA, Earlham College, JD, Rutgers Univ. **Patti Sanderson,**
   Prin. Beth Reaves, Adm.
   Pre-Prep. Gen Acad. Elem math—Everyday Math. **Feat**—Lib_Skills Span Computers
   Art_Hist Studio_Art Drama Music. **Supp**—Rem_Math Rem_Read.
   Sports—Basket Soccer Softball Track. G: F_Hockey.
   Somewhat selective adm: 41/yr. Appl fee: $30. Appl due: Rolling. Accepted: 85%.
   Tests ISEE.
   Enr 200. Wh 73%. Latino 1%. Blk 21%. Asian 5%. Avg class size: 14. **Fac 30.** M 9/F 21.
   FT 30. Adv deg: 26%.
   Grad '11—14. Prep—9. (Westtown, Wilmington Friends, Moorestown Friends, Friends
   Select, DE Valley Friends, Tatnall Sch).
   Tui '12-'13: Day $13,950-16,950. Aid: Need 50 ($19,000).
   Summer: Acad Rec. Tui Day $400-2800. 1-8 wks.
   Endow $130,000. Plant val $1,320,000. Acres 13. Bldgs 6. Class rms 23. Lib 5000 vols.
   Sci labs 2. Art studios 1. Music studios 1. Gyms 1. Comp labs 1.
   Est 1969. Nonprofit. Religious Society of Friends. Tri (Sept-June). **Assoc** MSA.

FSMH provides an academic program based on the traditional concepts of a Quaker education. The curriculum in the lower school is rounded out by classes in art, music, physical education and Spanish. Spanish courses continue in the middle school, and all students receive computer instruction. After-school sports begin in grade 6; all teams abide by a no-cut policy. Students are active in community service.

PENNINGTON, NJ. (29 mi. NE of Philadelphia, PA) Suburban. Pop: 2699. Alt: 189 ft.

THE PENNINGTON SCHOOL
Bdg — Coed Gr 8-12; Day — Coed 6-12

Pennington, NJ 08534. 112 W Delaware Ave. Tel: 609-737-6128. Fax: 609-730-1405.
www.pennington.org E-mail: admiss@pennington.org
Stephanie G. Townsend, Head (2006). BA, Univ of Connecticut, MA, Middlebury College.
Stephen D. Milich, Adm.
Col Prep. AP (exams req'd; 229 taken, 55% 3+)—Eng Fr Ger Lat Span Calc Stats Bio Chem Physics Eur_Hist US_Hist Econ US_Govt & Pol Studio_Art Music_Theory. Feat—Chin Ecol Forensic_Sci Oceanog Organic_Chem Comp_Sci Robotics Psych Relig Ceramics Photog Drama Chorus Music. Supp—ESL LD.
Sports (req'd)—Basket X-country Golf Indoor_Track Lacrosse Soccer Swim Tennis Track W_Polo. B: Baseball Football Ice_Hockey. G: F_Hockey Softball. Activities: 35.
Selective adm (Bdg Gr 8-11; Day 6-11): 111/yr. Bdg 26. Day 85. Usual entry: 6 & 9. Appl fee: $50. Appl due: Feb. Applied: 600. Accepted: 38%. Tests SSAT TOEFL.
Enr 485. B 273. G 212. Bdg 115. Day 370. Elem 85. Sec 400. Intl 11%. Avg class size: 13. Stud/fac: 8:1. Formal. Fac 87. M 38/F 49. Wh 94%. Latino 2%. Blk 3%. Asian 1%. Adv deg: 73%. In dorms 25.
Grad '11—95. Col—95. (Hobart/Wm Smith 5, NYU 4, Fairfield 3, High Pt 3, U of Richmond 3, Syracuse 3). Athl schol 12. Avg SAT: CR 526. M 548. W 537. Avg ACT: 24.4. Col couns: 3.
Tui '12-'13: Bdg $46,100 (+$665). Day $30,950 (+$405). Intl Bdg $46,100 (+$6815). Aid: Need 120 ($3,000,000).
Endow $26,000,000. Plant val $20,500,000. Acres 54. Bldgs 18. Dorms 3. Dorm rms 130. Class rms 65. Lib 17,000 vols. Sci labs 4. Theaters 2. Art studios 4. Music studios 4. Gyms 2. Tennis courts 5. Pools 1. Tracks 1. Comp labs 3. Comp/stud: 1:1.5.
Est 1838. Nonprofit. United Methodist. Quar (Sept-June). Assoc MSA.

Founded as a school for boys by the New Jersey Conference of the Methodist Church, Pennington served a coeducational student body from 1854 to 1910, at which time single-gender male education returned. More than six decades later, in 1972, the school once again began to admit girls.

Pennington offers a college preparatory curriculum that features honors and Advanced Placement courses in all major disciplines. Boys and girls choose from a variety of athletic, community service, and creative and performing arts options. The school maintains small programs for international pupils and students with learning differences.   **See Also Page 126**

POTTERSVILLE, NJ. (41 mi. W of New York, NY) Rural. Pop: 400. Alt: 228 ft.

PURNELL SCHOOL

Bdg and Day — Girls Gr 9-12

Pottersville, NJ 07979. 51 Pottersville Rd, PO Box 500. Tel: 908-439-2154.
Fax: 908-439-2090.
www.purnell.org   E-mail: info@purnell.org
Ayanna Hill-Gill, Head (2007). BS, Dickinson College, MA, Columbia Univ. **Nicole Moon, Adm.**

    Col Prep. Feat—Creative_Writing Shakespeare Fr Span Anat & Physiol Marine_Bio/Sci Russ_Hist Law Psych World_Relig Photog Studio_Art Drama Music Dance. **Supp**— ESL LD Rev Tut.

    Sports—G: Basket Soccer Softball. **Activities:** 14.

    Selective adm (Gr 9-11): 53/yr. Appl fee: $50. Appl due: Rolling. Applied: 85. Accepted: 75%. Yield: 50%. **Tests** IQ SSAT TOEFL.

    Enr 100. Intl 24%. Avg class size: 9. Stud/fac: 4:1. Uniform. **Fac 24.** M 4/F 20. FT 24. Wh 91%. Blk 9%. Adv deg: 75%. In dorms 6.

    Grad '11—24. Col—24. (Mitchell, Boston Col, PA St, Alfred, Arcadia, High Pt). **Col couns:** 2. Alum donors: 16%.

    Tui '12-'13: Bdg $52,550 (+$1500). **5-Day Bdg $50,550** (+$1500). **Day $44,350** (+$1500). **Intl Bdg $54,050** (+$2500). **Aid:** Need 26 ($550,000).

    Endow $10,000,000. Plant val $8,200,000. Acres 83. Bldgs 23. Dorms 3. Dorm rms 59. Class rms 17. Lib 7000 vols. Labs 1. Theaters 1. Art studios 3. Music studios 4. Dance studios 1. Athletic ctrs 1. Fields 3. Courts 5. Comp/stud: 1:1

    Est 1963. Nonprofit. Sem (Sept-June). **Assoc** MSA.

Situated on an 83-acre former farm/estate, Purnell conducts a noncompetitive academic program that incorporates cooperative learning opportunities and places a particular emphasis on the studio and performing arts. The curriculum is interdisciplinary and highly structured in grades 9 and 10; older students choose electives from among the subjects of English, history/ social studies, foreign language, math, science, performing arts and studio arts. The school accepts girls with mild learning disabilities, in addition to those who excel academically. A learning center provides support for all students.

In midwinter, students participate in Project Exploration, a hands-on, project-oriented mini-term during which they work intensely on a project in a field of interest; time is built in for field trips as well. All students perform 10 hours of required community service per year. Juniors and seniors have the opportunity to travel for two weeks in a French- or Spanish-speaking country, at which time they take French or Spanish language courses and engage in cultural immersion.

Each senior takes part in a compulsory internship, as well as in a public speaking course that culminates in a speech delivered to the student body about her high school experience. Every girl meets with her faculty advisor weekly; advisors then confer weekly to assess student progress.

PRINCETON, NJ. (35 mi. NE of Philadelphia, PA) Suburban. Pop: 14,203. Alt: 290 ft.

AMERICAN BOYCHOIR SCHOOL

Bdg and Day — Boys Gr 4-8

Princeton, NJ 08540. 19 Lambert Dr. Tel: 609-924-5858, 888-269-2464.
Fax: 609-924-5812.
www.americanboychoir.org   E-mail: admissions@americanboychoir.org

Lisa Eckstrom, Head (2011). BA, St John's College (MD), MA, Princeton Univ.
  Pre-Prep. Perform_Arts. Feat—Span Chorus Music_Theory Piano. **Supp**—Dev_Read Rev Tut.
  Somewhat selective adm (Gr 4-7): 14/yr. Bdg 9. Day 5. Usual entry: 4, 5 & 6. Appl fee: $0. Appl due: Rolling. Applied: 25. Accepted: 88%. Yield: 56%.
  Enr 50. Bdg 31. Day 19. Wh 70%. Latino 1%. Blk 10%. Asian 12%. Other 7%. Avg class size: 12. Stud/fac: 8:1. Uniform. **Fac 13.** M 6/F 7. FT 10/PT 3. Wh 98%. Latino 1%. Blk 1%. Adv deg: 53%.
  Grad '11—13. Prep—6. (Lawrenceville 2, Pennington 1, St Paul's Sch-NH 1, Hotchkiss 1, Webb Sch of Knoxville 1). Alum donors: 25%.
  Tui '11-'12: Bdg $25,350-29,550 (+$1500). **Day** $21,100-23,300 (+$1500). **Aid:** Need 35 ($453,905).
  Summer (enr 80): Enrich Rec. Vocal & Instrumental Music. Tui Bdg $1420/2-wk ses. Tui Day $1115/2-wk ses. 4 wks.
  Endow $6,700,000. Plant val $6,500,000. Acres 17. Bldgs 5. Dorms 2. Dorm rms 21. Class rms 7. Lib 1800 vols. Sci labs 1. Music studios 6. Fields 2. Courts 2. Pools 1. Comp labs 1.
  Est 1937. Nonprofit. Sem (Sept-June). **Assoc** MSA.

Founded by Herbert Huffman as Columbus Boychoir School in Columbus, OH, this school moved to Princeton in 1950 and became the American Boychoir School in 1980. The school's program includes professional concert tours with renowned orchestras, conducted domestically and abroad, as well as classroom instruction, physical education and music study. International tours have included trips to Japan, Latvia, Sweden and Denmark.

Boys are admitted on the basis of musical potential, as demonstrated by an audition, and scholastic aptitude. Instruction covers all areas of academics, vocal performance and music theory. Class size is small and academic study is closely supervised, with required evening study and extra help. A special curriculum is designed for those occasions when the choir is on tour, an opportunity that affords many educational and cultural opportunities.

CHAPIN SCHOOL
Day — Coed Gr PS (Age 4)-8

Princeton, NJ 08540. 4101 Princeton Pike. Tel: 609-924-2449. Fax: 609-924-2364.
  www.chapinschool.org   E-mail: inquiries@chapinschool.org
Richard D. Johnson, Head (1999). AB, Princeton Univ, MEd, Univ of Virginia. **Barbara P. Pasteris, Adm.**
  Pre-Prep. Feat—Fr Span Computers Studio_Art Drama Music Study_Skills.
  Sports—Basket X-country Lacrosse Soccer Softball.
  Selective adm: 69/yr. Usual entry: PS & K. Appl fee: $40. Appl due: Feb. **Tests** SSAT.
  Enr 312. Fac 46. FT 40/PT 6.
  Grad '11—30. Prep—26. (Princeton Day 5, Hun 5, Peddie 5, Lawrenceville 4, George Sch 3, Middlesex 1).
  Tui '12-'13: Day $21,900-26,500 (+$350).
  Endow $8,200,000. Acres 15. Bldgs 3. Class rms 31. Lib 14,000 vols. Sci labs 2. Auds 1. Art studios 1. Music studios 1. Art galleries 1. Gyms 1. Fields 3. Comp labs 3. Comp/stud: 1:6.
  Est 1931. Nonprofit. (Sept-June). **Assoc** MSA.

Founded by Frances Chapin, this school served students in grades K-12 until 1949. After moving several times in its early years, the school moved to its current Lawrence Township location in 1957.

Chapin's curriculum emphasizes the acquisition of fundamental reading, writing, computing and critical thinking skills, while also exposing boys and girls to art, music, drama and foreign languages. Small classes provide opportunities for hands-on learning and allow pupils to gain proficiency in communicational and study skills. An on-campus art gallery hosts six professional shows annually.

Community service projects are part of the curriculum at all grade levels, and eighth graders enroll in a trimester-long course on service learning.

THE HUN SCHOOL OF PRINCETON
Bdg — Coed Gr 9-PG; Day — Coed 6-PG

Princeton, NJ 08540. 176 Edgerstoune Rd. Tel: 609-921-7600. Fax: 609-279-9398.
www.hunschool.org   E-mail: admiss@hunschool.org
Jonathan G. Brougham, Head (2009). BA, Williams College, JD, MA, Columbia Univ.
Steven C. Bristol, Adm.
   Col Prep. AP (242 exams taken)—Eng Fr Span Calc Stats Comp_Sci Bio Chem Physics Eur_Hist US_Hist Art_Hist Studio_Art Music_Theory. **Feat**—Creative_Writing Lat Multivariable_Calc Anat & Physiol Environ_Sci Forensic_Sci Marine_Bio/Sci Astrophysics E_Asian_Hist Amer_Stud Econ Govt Ethics Architect Photog Video_Production Music Public_Speak Woodworking. **Supp**—ESL LD Tut.
   Sports—Basket Crew X-country Fencing Golf Lacrosse Soccer Swim Tennis Track. B: Baseball Football Ice_Hockey. G: F_Hockey Softball. **Activities:** 54.
   Selective adm (Bdg Gr 9-PG; Day 6-12): 183/yr. Bdg 57. Day 126. Appl fee: $50. Appl due: Jan. **Tests** SSAT TOEFL.
   Enr 610. Bdg 150. Day 460. Elem 87. Sec 514. PG 9. Avg class size: 15. Stud/fac: 7:1. **Fac 83.** M 43/F 40. FT 81/PT 2. Adv deg: 57%. In dorms 16.
   Grad '11—131. Col—130. (PA St 6, Princeton 5, Lehigh 4, U of Miami 4, NYU 3, Lafayette 3). **Mid 50% SAT:** CR 530-630. M 550-640. W 540-650. Avg ACT: 28. **Col couns:** 3.
   Tui '12-'13: Bdg $48,550 (+$500-1500). **Day $33,400** (+$500-1500). **Intl Bdg $48,550** (+$500-11,135). **Aid:** Merit 1 ($32,000). Need 148 ($3,468,000).
   Summer: Acad Enrich Rev. Tui Bdg $5575. Tui Day $1298-2165. ESL. Tui Bdg $6800. Tui Day $3250. 5 wks.
   Endow $14,300,000. Plant val $35,000,000. Acres 45. Bldgs 14. Dorms 3. Dorm rms 96. Class rms 32. Lib 35,000 vols. Sci labs 6. Photog labs 2. Aquariums 1. Theaters 1. Art studios 2. Music studios 1. Ceramics/sculpture studios 1. Wood shops 1. Gyms 2. Athletic ctrs 1. Fields 6. Tennis courts 8. Tracks 1. Boathouses 1. Ponds 1. Comp labs 3.
   Est 1914. Nonprofit. Sem (Sept-June). **Assoc** CLS MSA.

The school was established as the Princeton Math School by John Gale Hun, an assistant professor of mathematics at Princeton University, and it originally met in a few small rooms near the university campus. The program's founding goal was to tutor Princeton University undergraduates. By 1925, when the school assumed its present name, it had evolved into a college preparatory institution with boarding facilities. Hun moved to its present location, a 45-acre campus just west of the university, in 1942. Girls were first enrolled as day students in 1971 and as boarders in 1975. The middle school was established in 1973, and grade 6 was added in 1977.

The traditional curriculum includes foreign language and fine arts requirements, electives and interdisciplinary courses. Advanced Placement and honors courses are provided in all disciplines. The fine and performing arts are an integral part of a Hun education; in addition to completing course work in the arts, all students attend arts assemblies during the year. Boys and girls satisfy the following community service requirements: 10 hours per year in grades 9 and 10, 15 hours in grade 11, and 20 hours in both grade 12 and postgraduate year.

A program for students of above-average ability having specific, diagnosed learning differences is also available (for an additional fee).

PRINCETON DAY SCHOOL
Day — Coed Gr PS (Age 4)-12

Princeton, NJ 08542. 650 Great Rd, PO Box 75. Tel: 609-924-6700. Fax: 609-924-8944.

www.pds.org   E-mail: krosko@pds.org
Paul J. Stellato, Head (2008). BA, Hamilton Colllege, MFA, Columbia Univ. **Kelly Dun, Adm.**
  Col Prep. AP (exams req'd; 356 taken, 85% 3+)—Fr Lat Span Calc Stats Bio Chem Physics Eur_Hist US_Hist Comp_Govt & Pol US_Govt & Pol Art_Hist Music_Theory. **Feat**—Creative_Writing Poetry Shakespeare Utopian_Lit Chin Astron Environ_Sci Forensic_Sci Physiol Programming Middle_Eastern_Hist Asian_Stud Lat-Amer_ Stud Comp_Relig Philos Architect Ceramics Photog Studio_Art Drama Music Jazz_ Ensemble Woodworking. **Supp**—Tut.
  Sports—Basket X-country Fencing Golf Ice_Hockey Lacrosse Soccer Squash Tennis. B: Baseball Football. G: F_Hockey Softball Volley. **Activities:** 45.
  Selective adm (Gr PS-11): 119/yr. Usual entry: PS, K, 6 & 9. Appl fee: $55. Appl due: Jan. Applied: 428. Accepted: 40%. Yield: 70%. **Tests** SSAT.
  Enr 907. B 457. G 450. Elem 515. Sec 392. Wh 80%. Latino 3%. Blk 7%. Asian 10%. Avg class size: 15. **Fac 130.** M 45/F 85. FT 113/PT 17. Wh 88%. Latino 5%. Blk 5%. Asian 2%. Adv deg: 60%.
  Grad '11—97. Col—97. (Middlebury 4, Princeton 4, Dickinson 4, Dartmouth 3, Colby 3, Tufts 3). **Avg SAT:** CR 648. M 653. W 662. Avg ACT: 29. **Col couns:** 2. Alum donors: 25%.
  Tui '12-'13: Day $24,070-29,490 (+$230-900). **Aid:** Need 140 ($3,200,000).
  Summer: Acad Enrich Rec. Tui Day $220-1045. 1-4 wks.
  Endow $43,000,000. Plant val $75,000,000. Acres 105. 3 Libs 45,000 vols. Sci labs 8. Lang labs 1. Photog labs 1. Sci ctrs 1. Planetariums 1. Auds 2. Theaters 1. Art studios 3. Music studios 4. Art galleries 1. Gyms 3. Fields 11. Tennis courts 8. Rinks 1. Greenhouses 1. Comp labs 3. Comp/stud: 1:1.3.
  Est 1899. Nonprofit. Tri (Sept-June). **Assoc** CLS MSA.

PDS traces its origins to the late 1800s, when May Margaret Fine founded a school in Princeton to prepare girls for college. Miss Fine's School was very unusual for its time, as women were not then expected to attend college, and only a small percentage of girls even went to elementary and secondary school. In 1927, a small group of area parents established an elementary school for boys, locating it next to Miss Fine's School. Although this school, which was named Princeton Country Day School, and Miss Fine's School fared quite well over the years, the two institutions decided in 1965 to merge and form a coeducational school.

The college preparatory program at PDS, which places particular emphasis on verbal and quantitative reasoning and creative self-expression, includes a variety of courses in literature, languages, history, math, computer and the sciences. Instructors encourage boys and girls to apply their learning skills to problem solving in the traditional subject areas. Notable curricular features are fine arts, music, drama, architecture and religion classes. Each senior arranges for an independent project to be completed in the last six weeks of the third trimester; projects have included internships, performing arts, community service and research projects through the school or local universities.

PDS' peer leadership training program selects 18 group leaders to conduct weekly discussions helping freshmen with the transition to upper school. International and domestic exchange programs and educational travel opportunities are also available.

STUART COUNTRY DAY SCHOOL OF THE SACRED HEART
Day — Boys Gr PS (Age 3)-PS (Age 4), Girls PS (Age 3)-12

Princeton, NJ 08540. 1200 Stuart Rd. Tel: 609-921-2330. Fax: 609-497-0784.
  www.stuartschool.org   E-mail: admissions@stuartschool.org
Patricia L. Fagin, Head (2010). BA, Fontbonne College, MA, Webster Univ, PhD, Univ of North Carolina-Greensboro. **Kyle Morse, Adm.**
  Col Prep. AP (exams req'd; 419 taken, 89% 3+)—Eng Fr Lat Span Calc Stats Comp_ Sci Chem Environ_Sci Physics Eur_Hist US_Hist Comp_Govt & Pol Studio_Art. **Feat**—Creative_Writing World_Lit Astron Marine_Bio/Sci Oceanog Web_Design Comp_Animation Econ Intl_Relations Ethics Relig World_Relig Film Photog Sculpt Visual_Arts Drama Music Music_Hist Debate. **Supp**—Tut. **Dual enr:** Princeton.

Sports—G: Basket X-country F_Hockey Golf Lacrosse Soccer Squash Tennis Track Volley. **Activities:** 24.

Selective adm (Gr PS-11): 78/yr. Usual entry: PS, K, 6 & 9. Appl fee: $75. Appl due: Jan. Applied: 186. Accepted: 72%. Yield: 60%. **Tests** SSAT.

Enr 471. B 4. G 467. Elem 333. Sec 138. Wh 65%. Latino 6%. Blk 11%. Asian 10%. Other 8%. Intl 5%. Avg class size: 15. Stud/fac: 6:1. **Fac 73.** M 5/F 68. FT 59/PT 14. Wh 81%. Latino 3%. Blk 4%. Asian 3%. Other 9%. Adv deg: 47%.

Grad '11—31. Col—31. (Cornell 2, Vassar 1, Notr 1, Princeton 1, U of MI 1). **Avg SAT:** CR/M 1273. Avg ACT: 27. Mid 50% ACT: 25-29.

Tui '12-'13: Day $21,300-31,800 (+$100-600). **Aid:** Need 94.

Summer: Acad Enrich Rec. Arts. 9 wks.

Endow $11,200,000. Plant val $40,000,000. Acres 55. Bldgs 2. Class rms 50. 2 Libs 24,800 vols. Chapels 1. Sci labs 6. Auds 1. Theaters 1. Art studios 5. Music studios 2. Gyms 2. Fields 2. Tennis courts 5. Comp labs 2. Laptop prgm Gr 6-12.

Est 1963. Nonprofit. Roman Catholic (50% practice). Tri (Sept-June). **Assoc** MSA.

Founded as an independent girls' school, Stuart is part of the Network of Sacred Heart schools. The school seeks to integrate a strong academic foundation with an awareness and an appreciation of the religious dimensions of life. Students represent many different faiths.

In the lower school (grades PS-5), emphasis is placed on the acquisition of basic skills. Foreign language study begins in with an introduction to Spanish in junior kindergarten. French is introduced in kindergarten, and students choose to study either language in grade 1. The upper school (grades 9-12) includes an increased choice of electives and Advanced Placement courses, and qualified seniors may enroll in certain courses at Princeton University.

An international exchange program links students with girls studying in French- and Spanish-speaking Sacred Heart schools in Europe or South America, and individual exchanges are also available with Sacred Heart schools in the US and abroad. Senior peer leaders receive training from faculty and lead discussions with small groups of freshmen. Upper school students perform 50 hours of community service each year.

Physical education is offered at every level, and middle and upper school teams compete interscholastically.

RUMSON, NJ. (21 mi. S of New York, NY) Suburban. Pop: 7137. Alt: 15 ft.

RUMSON COUNTRY DAY SCHOOL

Day — Coed Gr PS (Age 3)-8

Rumson, NJ 07760. 35 Bellevue Ave. Tel: 732-842-0527. Fax: 732-758-6528.
Other locations: 101 Ridge Rd, Rumson 07760.
  www.rcds.org   E-mail: spost@rcds.org
Chad Browning Small, Head (1989). BA, Ohio Wesleyan Univ, MEd, Univ of Virginia, EdD, Seton Hall Univ. **Suzanne R. Post, Adm.**

Pre-Prep. Gen Acad. Feat—Fr Lat Span Computers Filmmaking Studio_Art Music Woodworking. **Supp**—LD Tut.

Sports—Basket Lacrosse Soccer. B: Baseball Football. G: F_Hockey Softball.

Somewhat selective adm: 79/yr. Usual entry: PS & 8. Appl fee: $50-75. Appl due: Rolling. Applied: 124. Accepted: 94%. Yield: 64%. **Tests** CTP_4.

Enr 440. Wh 90%. Latino 3%. Blk 3%. Asian 4%. Avg class size: 13. Stud/fac: 7:1. Uniform. **Fac 65.** M 15/F 50. FT 61/PT 4. Wh 92%. Latino 2%. Blk 3%. Asian 2%. Other 1%. Adv deg: 36%.

Grad '10—42. Prep—23. (Blair 4, Christian Bros-NJ 3, Lawrenceville 2, Peddie 2, Phillips Acad 2, Hotchkiss 1). Alum donors: 13%.

Tui '11-'12: Day $15,350-20,985 (+$250-1000). **Aid:** Need 45 ($380,000).

Endow $7,800,000. Plant val $20,600,000. Acres 14. Bldgs 3. Class rms 48. 3 Libs 15,000 vols. Sci labs 3. Observatories 1. Auds 1. Art studios 2. Music studios 2. Shops

1. Gyms 2. Fields 4. Comp labs 1. Comp/stud: 1:2.
Est 1926. Nonprofit. Tri (Sept-June). **Assoc** MSA.

Rumson enrolls students from more than 30 communities in the semirural shore area. The school is divided into two administrative departments: the lower school (grades PS-4) is organized by heterogeneous homerooms; the upper school (grades 5-8) is departmentalized, with honors courses available beginning in grade 6. In addition to offering a traditional academic program, Rumson provides instruction in computer literacy, music, drama, art, crafts, woodworking and technology. French language instruction begins in kindergarten, with a choice of French or Spanish in grades 5-8, and a required Latin course in grades 7 and 8.

The school also offers nonacademic minicourses that meet weekly, an interscholastic athletic program for children in grades 5-8, a strong community service program and after-school care for all students. Rumson's School Within a School program provides individualized instruction for children with language-based learning differences.

The preschool occupies separate quarters on Ridge Road.

SADDLE RIVER, NJ. (26 mi. NNW of New York, NY) Suburban. Pop: 3201. Alt: 175 ft.

SADDLE RIVER DAY SCHOOL
Day — Coed Gr K-12

Saddle River, NJ 07458. 147 Chestnut Ridge Rd. Tel: 201-327-4050.
Fax: 201-327-6161.
www.saddleriverday.org   E-mail: glee@saddleriverday.org
Eileen Lambert, Head (2009). BA, Bowdoin Univ, MA, Univ of Cincinnati. **Gretchen Lee, Adm.**

Col Prep. AP (exams req'd)—Eng Fr Span Calc Bio Chem Physics Eur_Hist US_Hist US_Govt & Pol. **Feat**—Lat Stats Anat & Physiol Astron Marine_Bio/Sci Comp_Sci Econ Psych Graphic_Arts Studio_Art Drama Theater_Arts Chorus Music Music_Theory. **Supp**—Dev_Read Rev Tut.
Sports—Basket X-country Soccer Tennis Track. B: Baseball Golf. G: Softball Volley.
Selective adm (Gr K-11): 60/yr. Appl fee: $50. Appl due: Feb. Applied: 153. Accepted: 59%. Yield: 67%. **Tests** ISEE.
Enr 315. Wh 80%. Latino 5%. Blk 7%. Asian 7%. Other 1%. Intl 7%. Avg class size: 12. Stud/fac: 7:1. **Fac 50.**
Grad '09—31. Col—30. (Franklin & Marshall 3, Geo Wash 3, Fordham 2, Boston U 2, Col of NJ 2, Skidmore 1). Athl schol 2. **Avg SAT:** CR 561. M 610. W 586. Avg ACT: 29.
Tui '12-'13: Day $19,240-29,870 (+$1475). **Aid:** Need 63 ($858,375).
Summer (enr 80): Acad Enrich Rec. Theater. 2 wks.
Endow $5,150,000. Plant val $12,000,000. Acres 26. Bldgs 3. Class rms 32. 2 Libs 30,000 vols. Sci labs 6. Lang labs 1. Amphitheaters 1. Comp ctrs 2. Theaters 1. Art studios 2. Music studios 1. Arts ctrs 1. Gyms 2. Athletic ctrs 1. Fields 2. Tennis courts 1. Comp/stud: 1:1.
Est 1957. Nonprofit. Sem (Sept-June). **Assoc** CLS MSA.

Serving able, college-bound students from roughly 60 communities in New Jersey and New York State, this coeducational day school offers concentrated work in five major academic areas. Foreign language instruction consists of French and Spanish in grades K-12, and Latin in grades 8-12. Music and performing and visual arts offerings complement course work in the standard subjects. Honors and Advanced Placement courses are offered, and eligible seniors may participate in an independent project in the final term of the year. Small class size and a low student-teacher ratio are maintained.

The extracurricular program includes field trips in the Metropolitan New York City area. In addition, there are publications and recreational and interest clubs. The school is actively involved in the North Jersey Cultural Council programs, the Academic Decathlon, the New Jersey Math League and the Cum Laude Society. The foreign language department sponsors a cultural trip abroad in the spring and conducts exchange programs with French and Spanish schools.

SHORT HILLS, NJ. (21 mi. WNW of New York, NY) Suburban. Pop: 19,500. Alt: 600 ft.

FAR BROOK SCHOOL
Day — Coed Gr PS (Age 4)-8

Short Hills, NJ 07078. 52 Great Hills Rd. Tel: 973-379-3442. Fax: 973-379-9237.
www.farbrook.org   E-mail: farbrook@farbrook.org
Amy M. Ziebarth, Head (2010). Mikki Murphy, Adm.
  Pre-Prep. Gen Acad. Feat—Fr Computers Studio_Art Drama Chorus Music Music_ Theory Dance Woodworking. **Supp**—Rem_Math Rem_Read Tut.
  Sports (req'd)—B: Baseball Soccer. G: F_Hockey Softball.
  Selective adm (Gr PS-7): 36/yr. Appl fee: $100. Appl due: Jan. Accepted: 29%. **Tests** CTP_4 SSAT.
  Enr 229. B 127. G 102. Nonwhite 36%. Intl 7%. Avg class size: 18. Stud/fac: 6:1. **Fac 45.** FT 38/PT 7. Wh 97%. Blk 3%. Adv deg: 48%.
  Grad '11—19. Prep—13. (Newark Acad, Kent Place, Newark Acad, Pingry, Montclair Kimberley, Shattuck-St Mary's).
  Tui '12-'13: Day $23,250-29,900 (+$250-1600). **Aid:** Need 35 ($550,000).
  Summer: Rec. 7 wks.
  Endow $4,806,000. Plant val $7,000,000. Acres 9. Bldgs 11. Class rms 19. Lib 19,000 vols. Sci labs 2. Lang labs 1. Auds 1. Art studios 1. Music studios 4. Wood shops 1. Gyms 1. Fields 1. Comp labs 2. Comp/stud: 1:4.
  Est 1948. Nonprofit. (Sept-June). **Assoc** MSA.

A group of parents, led by former director Winifred Moore, subsidized its own independent school in 1948. The curriculum at Far Brook is based on the discipline of great subject matter, humanized and sustained by the arts, with an emphasis placed on choral music and drama.

The lower school program stresses the development of sound basic skills and problem-solving processes. The middle school and junior high programs focus on the history of man, with courses on Ancient Egypt, Greece, Rome, the Middle Ages, the Renaissance and American history. Each grade studies a civilization or historical period extensively, learning about its architecture, music, art, literature, science, agriculture, clothing and everyday life. Science offers a strong foundation of basic concepts and techniques through observation and active participation in experiments. Students also conduct studies utilizing the seven acres of woodland, meadow and swamp on which the school is located.

Every fall, the junior high takes a five-day wilderness trip with faculty to northern New York State. Each June, a Shakespearean play is performed by graduating students. Traditional events at Far Brook include daily morning meetings, Pergolesi's *Stabat Mater*, the Thanksgiving Processional and the Medieval Masque. All boys and girls participate in interscholastic athletics beginning in grade 5.

SOMERSET, NJ. (31 mi. WSW of New York, NY) Suburban. Pop: 24,938. Alt: 92 ft.

RUTGERS PREPARATORY SCHOOL
Day — Coed Gr PS (Age 3)-12

Somerset, NJ 08873. 1345 Easton Ave. Tel: 732-545-5600. Fax: 732-214-1819.
www.rutgersprep.org   E-mail: glace@rutgersprep.org
Steven A. Loy, Head (1992). AB, Princeton Univ, MA, Stanford Univ, EdD, Univ of California-Los Angeles. **Tara Klipstein, Gr 7-12 Adm; Diane Glace, Gr PS-6 Adm.**
Col Prep. AP (376 exams taken, 79% 3+)—Eng Fr Lat Span Calc Stats Comp_Sci Bio Chem Environ_Sci Physics Eur_Hist US_Hist World_Hist Econ Psych US_Govt & Pol. **Feat**—Creative_Writing Shakespeare African-Amer_Lit Irish_Lit Mythology Japan Arabic Multivariable_Calc Web_Design Holocaust Architect Ceramics Drawing Painting Photog Acting Chorus Music_Hist Orchestra Journ. **Supp**—Tut.
Sports—Basket X-country Lacrosse Soccer Swim Tennis. B: Baseball Golf Wrestling. G: Softball Volley.
Selective adm: 117/yr. Appl fee: $75. Appl due: Rolling. **Tests** SSAT.
Enr 702. Elem 369. Sec 333. Stud/fac: 7:1. **Fac 105.**
Grad '11—94. Col—93. (NYU 4, Rutgers 4, Case Western Reserve 3, Dickinson 3, URI 3, U of Rochester 2). **Mid 50% SAT:** CR 530-660. M 540-690. W 540-670. **Col couns:** 2.
Tui '12-'13: Day $29,650 (+$500). **Aid:** Need ($2,000,000).
Summer: Acad Enrich Rec. Sports. 6 wks.
Acres 35. Lib 32,000 vols. Sci labs 6. Photog labs 1. Gyms 2. Fields 2. Climbing walls 2. Comp labs 4. Comp/stud: 1:2.1.
Est 1766. Nonprofit. (Sept-June). **Assoc** CLS MSA.

Rutgers Prep was founded under the colonial charter of Queen's College (now Rutgers University). The oldest independent school in New Jersey, RPS became fully independent from the university in 1957. The present-day institution enrolls students from approximately 80 communities in central New Jersey.

RPS provides an integrated liberal arts curriculum designed for college preparation. The program at all grade levels is enhanced by computer science, as well as by fine and performing arts offerings. In the upper school (grades 9-12), boys and girls perform at least 10 hours of required community service per year. Enrichment activities include international study trips, local field trips and outdoor education.

The Senior Exploration program, conducted in the time between senior exams and commencement, enables grade 12 students to choose a project from a menu of options suggested by RPS faculty. Explorations vary in terms of time commitment, location and cost to suit the needs and ambitions of the pupils involved. Past projects have dealt with improvisation in art; math and poetry in New York City; and the culinary arts.

SUMMIT, NJ. (22 mi. W of New York, NY) Suburban. Pop: 21,131. Alt: 540 ft.

KENT PLACE SCHOOL
Day — Boys Gr PS (Age 3)-PS (Age 4), Girls PS (Age 3)-12

Summit, NJ 07902. 42 Norwood Ave. Tel: 908-273-0900. Fax: 908-273-9390.
www.kentplace.org   E-mail: admission@kentplace.org
Susan C. Bosland, Head (1999). BA, Denison Univ, MA, Columbia Univ. **Julia Wall, Adm.**
Col Prep. AP (exams req'd)—Eng Fr Lat Span Calc Stats Comp_Sci Bio Chem Environ_Sci Physics Eur_Hist US_Hist Econ US_Govt & Pol Art_Hist Studio_Art

Music_Theory. **Feat**—British_Lit Creative_Writing Russ_Lit Chin Anat & Physiol Web_Design Women's_Stud Drama Music_Hist Dance.

Sports—G: Basket X-country F_Hockey Golf Lacrosse Soccer Softball Swim Tennis Track Volley.

Selective adm (Gr PS-11): 96/yr. Usual entry: PS, K, 6 & 9. Appl fee: $70. Appl due: Jan. **Tests** CTP_4 ISEE SSAT.

Enr 636. B 9. G 627. Elem 359. Sec 277. Wh 75%. Latino 4%. Blk 10%. Asian 11%. Avg class size: 17. Stud/fac: 7:1. **Fac 90.** M 17/F 73. FT 87/PT 3. Wh 91%. Latino 6%. Blk 2%. Other 1%. Adv deg: 85%.

Grad '11—63. Col—63. (Boston Col, U of PA, Cornell, Colgate, Princeton, Lehigh). **Avg SAT:** CR/M 1283. **Col couns:** 2.

Tui '12-'13: Day $26,450-34,493 (+$500-2000).

Summer: Coed. Ages 4-14. Enrich. Arts. Tui Day $350-2680. 1-6 wks.

Endow $15,000,000. Plant val $14,000,000. Acres 26. Bldgs 6. Class rms 48. Lib 17,000 vols. Labs 9. Auds 1. Theaters 1. Art studios 3. Music studios 11. Dance studios 1. Fields 2. Courts 5. Field houses 1. Laptop prgm Gr 6-12.

Est 1894. Nonprofit. Tri (Sept-June). **Assoc** CLS MSA.

This college preparatory school is located on a suburban, 26-acre campus, embracing both half-timbered Old English and modern buildings. Boys enroll in the nursery and prekindergarten programs only. Students select from a broad range of academic offerings, with opportunities in more than a dozen areas affording qualified girls Advanced Placement credit. Activities emphasize publications, art, drama, music, language clubs, service work and a student-faculty senate.

The school's location enables pupils to take advantage of the museums, theaters and other cultural facilities of nearby New York City.

OAK KNOLL SCHOOL OF THE HOLY CHILD

Day — Boys Gr K-6, Girls K-12

Summit, NJ 07901. 44 Blackburn Rd. Tel: 908-522-8100. Fax: 908-277-1838.
www.oakknoll.org   E-mail: admissions@oakknoll.org
Timothy J. Saburn, Head (2005). BA, St Lawrence Univ, EdM, Harvard Univ. **Suzanne Kimm Lewis, Adm.**

Col Prep. AP (exams req'd; 110 taken, 77% 3+)—Eng Fr Span Calc Comp_Sci Bio Chem Physics Eur_Hist US_Hist World_Hist Studio_Art. **Feat**—Irish_Lit Southern_ Lit Women's_Lit Writing Ital Genetics Marine_Bio/Sci Engineering Web_Design Law Psych African-Amer_Stud Lat-Amer_Stud Native_Amer_Stud Theol Photog Drama Music Dance.

Sports—G: Basket X-country Fencing F_Hockey Golf Indoor_Track Lacrosse Soccer Softball Swim Tennis Track Volley. **Activities:** 36.

Selective adm (Gr K-10): Appl fee: $50-100. **Tests** CTP_4 ISEE SSAT.

Enr 540. Avg class size: 16. Stud/fac: 7:1. Uniform. **Fac 73.** Adv deg: 97%.

Grad '11—63. Col—63. (Providence 5, Villanova 5, Boston Col 4, Boston U 3, NYU 3, U of PA 2). **Avg SAT:** CR 621. M 625. W 656. **Col couns:** 2.

Tui '12-'13: Day $23,600-32,900 (+$350-1300). **Aid:** Need ($1,400,000).

Summer: Acad Enrich Rev. 2-6 wks. Ages 3-16. Rec. 1-7 wks.

Acres 11. Bldgs 4. Laptop prgm Gr 9-12.

Est 1924. Nonprofit. Roman Catholic. Tri (Sept-June). **Assoc** CLS MSA.

Oak Knoll is part of a network of schools operated by the Sisters of the Holy Child Jesus, an order founded by Cornelia Connelly in 1846. The lower school (grades K-6) is coeducational, while the upper school (grades 7-12) enrolls girls only.

The lower school features an innovative teaching program based on small groups and learning centers, with an enrichment program that includes computers, music, art, drama, dance and after-school activities. The upper school's curriculum, which focuses on the liberal arts in a value-centered environment, provides a rigorous college preparatory program. Students in grades 9-12 lease laptop computers from the school for use in class. Oak Knoll's campus ministry conducts a volunteer service program.

TINTON FALLS, NJ. (28 mi. SSW of New York, NY) Suburban. Pop: 15,053. Alt: 45 ft.

RANNEY SCHOOL
Day — Coed Gr PS (Age 3)-12

Tinton Falls, NJ 07724. 235 Hope Rd. Tel: 732-542-4777. Fax: 732-460-1078.
www.ranneyschool.org   E-mail: admission@ranneyschool.org
Lawrence S. Sykoff, Head (1995). BBA, City Univ of New York, MEd, EdD, Univ of San Diego. **Joseph M. Tweed, Adm.**
   Col Prep. AP (exams req'd; 321 taken, 77% 3+)—Eng Fr Span Calc Comp_Sci Bio Chem Physics Eur_Hist Econ Art_Hist Studio_Art Music_Theory. **Feat**—Shakespeare African-Amer_Lit Chin Stats Anat & Physiol Environ_Sci Web_Design British_Hist Lat-Amer_Hist Govt Psych Ceramics Music.
   Sports—Basket X-country Fencing Golf Indoor_Track Lacrosse Soccer Swim Tennis Track. B: Baseball. G: F_Hockey Softball. **Activities:** 30.
   Selective adm (Gr PS-10): 123/yr. Appl fee: $75. Appl due: Rolling. **Tests** CTP_4.
   Enr 821. B 406. G 415. Avg class size: 15. Stud/fac: 9:1. Formal. **Fac 95.** Adv deg: 53%.
   Grad '11—56. Col—56. (NYU 5, Cornell 4, Geo Wash 4, Loyola U MD 2, Georgetown 2, Johns Hopkins 2). Athl schol 4. **Avg SAT:** CR 600. M 606. W 620. **Mid 50% SAT:** CR 560-680. M 550-690. W 580-700. **Col couns:** 3.
   Tui '12-'13: Day $16,350-25,750 (+$150-900). **Aid:** Need 56 ($375,000).
   Summer: Acad Enrich Rec. 4-8 wks.
   Plant val $18,000,000. Acres 60. Bldgs 11. Class rms 96. 2 Libs 21,500 vols. Sci labs 5. Lang labs 1. Theaters 1. Art studios 3. Music studios 2. Gyms 2. Fields 6. Tennis courts 5. Pools 1. Weight rms 1. Playgrounds 1. Comp labs 3. Laptop prgm Gr 6-12.
   Est 1960. Nonprofit. Sem (Sept-June). **Assoc** CLS MSA.

With a strong preparatory course, Ranney places particular emphasis upon the development of reading, composition and effective study skills. The 60-acre campus, situated on a former country estate, has ample facilities for a full sports program. Regular preparatory work, starting as early as grade 7, has produced notable test results on College Board examinations and the National Merit Scholarship Test. Seniors may choose to complete a Capstone Project, a yearlong independent research study on a topic of their own design

An optional after-school program of athletic and cultural activities is available to students beginning in grade 2.   **See Also Page 124**

NEW YORK

ALBANY, NY. (84 mi. NW of Hartford, CT; 138 mi. N of New York, NY) Urban. Pop: 95,658. Alt: to 30 ft. Area also includes Rensselaer.

THE ALBANY ACADEMIES
Day — Coed Gr PS (Age 3)-12
(Coord — Day PS (Age 3)-10)

Albany, NY 12208. 135 Academy Rd. Tel: 518-429-2300. Fax: 518-427-7016.
Other locations: 140 Academy Rd, Albany 12208.
www.albanyacademies.org   E-mail: buranb@albanyacademies.org
Douglas M. North, Head (2009). BA, Yale Univ, MA, Syracuse Univ, PhD, Univ of Virginia.
Bramble Buran, Adm.
Col Prep. AP (296 exams taken, 71% 3+)—Eng Fr Lat Span Calc Stats Bio Chem Physics Eur_Hist US_Hist Comp_Govt & Pol Econ US_Govt & Pol Studio_Art. **Elem math**—Singapore Math. **Feat**—Chin Anat & Physiol Astron Computers Civil_War Psych Philos Ceramics Drawing Photog Theater Music Music_Theory Dance. **Supp**—Rem_Math Rem_Read Tut.
Sports (req'd)—Basket X-country Ice_Hockey Lacrosse Ski Soccer Swim Tennis Track. B: Baseball Football Golf Wrestling. G: F_Hockey Softball Volley.
Selective adm (Gr PS (Age 3)-9): 160/yr. Usual entry: PS, 6 & 9. Appl fee: $50. Appl due: Rolling. Applied: 294. Accepted: 75%. Yield: 73%. **Tests** CEEB CTP_4 ISEE SSAT.
Enr 725. B 372. G 353. Elem 361. Sec 364. Wh 82%. Latino 1%. Blk 6%. Asian 4%. Other 7%. Avg class size: 14. Stud/fac: 6:1. Uniform. **Fac 95.** Adv deg: 67%.
Grad '10—102. Col—99. (Union Col-NY 4, Boston U 3, Holy Cross 3, Syracuse 3, Cornell 2, NYU 2). **Avg SAT:** CR 576. M 599. W 574. **Mid 50% SAT:** CR 500-630. M 530-660. W 520-630. Avg ACT: 26. Mid 50% ACT: 23-29. **Col couns:** 2.
Tui '12-'13: Day $13,250-18,750 (+$1000). **Aid:** Merit 34 ($146,375). Need 274 ($2,056,217).
Summer: Rec. 12 wks.
Endow $10,500,000. Plant val $14,500,000. Acres 50. Bldgs 4. Class rms 66. 3 Libs 31,000 vols. Sci labs 8. Lang labs 1. Auds 1. Theaters 1. Art studios 4. Music studios 3. Dance studios 3. Media ctrs 1. Gyms 4. Fields 8. Squash courts 2. Pools 1. Rinks 1. Tracks 1. Weight rms 1. Comp labs 5. Laptop prgm Gr 7-8.
Est 1813. Nonprofit. Tri (Sept-June). **Assoc** CLS.

After operating as separate boys' and girls' institutions for nearly two centuries, The Albany Academy and Albany Academy for Girls effected a merger in the summer of 2007. AAG's campus is at 140 Academy Rd., across the street from AA.

The two schools retained their names under the combined institution, and the single-gender tradition continues with the school's coordinate program in grades PS-10. Boys and girls complete their high school years with coeducational classes in grades 11 and 12; in earlier grades, only honors courses are coed. Single-gender classes account for differences in learning styles between boys and girls. The joint curriculum provides a full complement of Advanced Placement courses and electives. All upper school students participate in a leadership program, while also performing eight cumulative hours of required community service in grades 9 and 10 and 12 total hours in grades 11 and 12.

Although the school does not offer a residential program, some international pupils live with area host families.

DOANE STUART SCHOOL

Day — Coed Gr PS (Age 3)-12

Rensselaer, NY 12144. 199 Washington Ave. Tel: 518-465-5222. Fax: 518-465-5230.
www.doanestuart.org   E-mail: admissions@doanestuart.org
Richard D. Enemark, Head (1998). BA, Colgate Univ, MA, Univ of Vermont, MPhil, PhD, Columbia Univ. Michael P. Green, Adm.

Col Prep. AP exams taken: 8 (88% 3+). Feat—Shakespeare African-Amer_Lit Austen Dickens Ger_Lit Tolstoy Wilde Fr Span Stats Econ Psych Sociol Ethics Philos Relig Buddhism Existentialism Art_Hist Fine_Arts Photog Sculpt Studio_Art Music_Hist Jazz_Ensemble SAT_Prep. Supp—Rev Tut. Dual enr: SUNY-Albany, Albany Col of Pharmacy.

Sports—Basket Crew X-country Soccer Tennis Track. B: Baseball. G: Softball Volley.
Selective adm: 75/yr. Appl fee: $75. Appl due: Rolling. Applied: 207. Accepted: 52%. Yield: 69%. Tests CTP_4 ISEE SSAT.
Enr 289. B 144. G 145. Elem 162. Sec 127. Wh 67%. Latino 1%. Blk 12%. Asian 3%. Other 17%. Avg class size: 14. Stud/fac: 7:1. Uniform. Fac 39. M 19/F 20. FT 37/PT 2. Wh 99%. Native Am 1%. Adv deg: 64%.
Grad '11—29. Col—29. (Vassar, Tufts, Rensselaer Polytech, Northeastern U, Hampshire, Williams).
Tui '12-'13: Day $14,370-22,225 (+$350). Aid: Need 158 ($1,624,495).
Endow $1,000,000. Plant val 20,000,000. Acres 27. Bldgs 3 (100% ADA). Class rms 25. 2 Libs 23,000 vols. Chapels 1. Sci labs 5. Photog labs 2. Auds 1. Theaters 1. Art studios 2. Music studios 2. Gyms 1. Fields 3. Courts 4. Playgrounds 2. Comp labs 1.
Est 1852. Nonprofit. Episcopal. Sem (Sept-June). Assoc CLS.

Doane Stuart was established upon the 1975 merger of Kenwood Academy, founded in 1852 by the Religious of the Sacred Heart, and Saint Agnes School, founded in 1870 by the Episcopal Diocese of Albany. The resulting institution represents the only successful merger between Catholic and Protestant private schools. Today, the school enrolls pupils of all faiths and backgrounds on a 27-acre campus that overlooks the Hudson River.

The curriculum is college preparatory, with a broad range of electives. There are opportunities in grades 11 and 12 for participation in classes at the University at Albany (State University of New York), Albany College of Pharmacy, the Irish/American Exchange and the Albany Institute of Art. Students may also pursue independent study and internship or research options. Group community service projects are conducted in the lower and middle school; boys and girls in grades 9-12 perform 25 hours of compulsory individual service per year.

AMENIA, NY. (45 mi. W of Hartford, CT; 84 mi. NNE of New York, NY) Suburban. Pop: 5195. Alt: 573 ft.

THE KILDONAN SCHOOL

Bdg — Coed Gr 6-12; Day — Coed 2-12

Amenia, NY 12501. 425 Morse Hill Rd. Tel: 845-373-8111. Fax: 845-373-9793.
www.kildonan.org   E-mail: info@kildonan.org
Kevin Pendergast, Head. BA, State Univ of New York-Albany, MA, Fordham Univ, JD, Case Western Univ. Beth Rainey, Adm.

Col Prep. LD. Elem read—Orton-Gillingham. Feat—Computers Robotics Studio_Art. Supp—Tut.
Sports—Basket Lacrosse Soccer Tennis.
Somewhat selective adm: 26/yr. Appl fee: $50. Appl due: Rolling.
Enr 95. Elem 40. Sec 55. Wh 96%. Latino 2%. Blk 2%. Avg class size: 7. Stud/fac: 2:1. Fac 63. M 30/F 33. FT 62/PT 1. Wh 95%. Blk 3%. Asian 2%. Adv deg: 19%. In dorms 26.
Grad '08—18. Col—17. (Mitchell, Lynn, Curry, New England Col).

Tui '12-'13: Bdg $63,800 (+$1500). **5-Day Bdg $66,800** (+$1500). **Day $46,900** (+$500). **Aid:** Need 41 ($485,000).
Summer: Ages 8-16. Acad Rec. Tui Bdg $10,000. Tui Day $5000-7500. 6 wks.
Endow $636,000. Plant val $1,500,000. Acres 325. Bldgs 18. Dorms 3. Dorm rms 93.
Class rms 21. Lib 14,975 vols. Sci labs 1. Art studios 2. Athletic ctrs 1. Fields 4. Courts
3. Riding rings 1. Stables 1. Comp labs 1.
Est 1969. Nonprofit. Tri (Sept-June).

Located on a 325-acre campus, the school serves boys and girls of average to above-average intelligence with dyslexia and language-based learning differences. Each student receives daily, one-to-one Orton-Gillingham tutoring. Other notable aspects of the program include college preparatory classes, opportunities in the arts and interscholastic athletics.

Dunnabeck at Kildonan, the country's oldest camp for children with dyslexia, operates on campus. Established to address the needs of intelligent boys and girls who are underachieving or failing in their academic work due to dyslexia, this summer program's educational programming also centers around one-to-one Orton-Gillingham tutoring. Recreational activities at Dunnabeck include horseback riding, arts and crafts, and water-skiing.

BEDFORD, NY. (40 mi. NNE of New York, NY) Suburban. Pop: 16,906. Alt: 200 ft.

RIPPOWAM CISQUA SCHOOL

Day — Coed Gr PS (Age 3)-9

Bedford, NY 10506. 439 Cantitoe St, PO Box 488. Tel: 914-244-1250.
Fax: 914-244-1245.
Other locations: 325 W Patent Rd, Mount Kisco 10549.
www.rcsny.org   E-mail: betsy_carter@rcsny.org
Matthew Nespole, Head (2009). BA, Bates College, MA, Columbia Univ. **Elizabeth W. Carter & Ashley Harrington, Adms.**
Pre-Prep. Feat—Fr Lat Span Computers Studio_Art Drama Music. **Supp**—Dev_Read Makeup Rem_Math Rem_Read Rev Tut.
Sports (req'd)—Basket Ice_Hockey Lacrosse Soccer Track. B: Baseball Football. G: F_Hockey Softball.
Selective adm: 83/yr. Appl due: Jan. **Tests** ISEE.
Enr 522. B 264. G 258. Elem 504. Sec 18. Wh 89%. Latino 2%. Blk 3%. Asian 3%. Other 3%. Avg class size: 16. Stud/fac: 6:1. Uniform. **Fac 93.** M 21/F 72. FT 93. Adv deg: 54%.
Grad '11—45. Prep—42. (Greenwich Acad 3, Hackley 2, Choate 2, Rye Co Day 2, St Luke's Sch-CT 2, Taft 2).
Tui '12-'13: Day $26,450-32,750. Aid: Need 74 ($1,400,000).
Endow $20,000,000. Plant val $12,800,000. Acres 50. Bldgs 4. Class rms 39. 2 Libs 25,200 vols. Sci labs 5. Theaters 2. Art studios 4. Music studios 4. Gyms 3. Fields 8. Comp labs 3.
Est 1917. Nonprofit. Tri (Sept-June).

Resulting from a 1973 merger of the Bedford-Rippowam School and the Cisqua School, this country day school prepares graduates for secondary boarding, day and public schools.

The curriculum incorporates both traditional and hands-on educational programs. RCS offers allied arts and computer science programs in grades K-9, a Spanish curriculum that begins in kindergarten, a cross-cultural approach to humanities, social studies and foreign language beginning in the middle school years, and a portfolio and thesis project in grade 9. Optional in the lower grades, community service becomes compulsory in grade 9. Parental involvement is an important aspect of the program.

The Cisqua campus in Mount Kisco accommodates children in grades PS-4. Grades 5-9 convene on the Rippowam campus in Bedford.

BRONX, NY. Urban. Pop: 1,332,650. Alt: 70 ft.

ETHICAL CULTURE FIELDSTON SCHOOL
Day — Coed Gr PS (Age 4)-12

Bronx, NY 10471. 3901 Fieldston Rd. Tel: 718-329-7300. Fax: 718-329-7305.
Other locations: 33 Central Park W, New York 10023.
    www.ecfs.org   E-mail: admissions@ecfs.org
Damian J. Fernandez, Head (2011). BA, Princeton Univ, MA, Univ of Florida, PhD, Univ of Miami. **Taisha M. Thompson, Adm.**
    Col Prep. Feat—British_Lit Creative_Writing Poetry Shakespeare African-Amer_Lit Comedy & Satire Chin Fr Greek Lat Span Calc Stats Geol Marine_Bio/Sci Meteorology Programming African-Amer_Hist Holocaust Middle_Eastern_Hist NYC_Hist Psych Lat-Amer_Stud Comp_Relig Ethics Architect Art_Hist Ceramics Film Photog Studio_Art Drama Music Dance Journ. **Supp**—Dev_Read LD Makeup Rem_Math Rem_Read Rev Tut.
    Sports—Basket X-country Golf Indoor_Track Lacrosse Soccer Swim Tennis Track Ultimate_Frisbee. B: Baseball Football Ice_Hockey. G: F_Hockey Softball Volley. **Activities:** 50.
    Very selective adm: 193/yr. Usual entry: PS, K, 6 & 9. Appl fee: $60. Appl due: Nov. Applied: 1892. Accepted: 14%. Yield: 71%. **Tests** ISEE SSAT.
    Enr 1704. B 855. G 849. Elem 1109. Sec 595. Avg class size: 18. Stud/fac: 6:1. **Fac 273.** M 88/F 185. FT 230/PT 43. Wh 75%. Latino 6%. Blk 12%. Asian 5%. Other 2%. Adv deg: 71%.
    Grad '11—149. Col—149. (Oberlin 9, Northwestern 8, Brown 7, Wesleyan U 6, Col of Wooster 5, Yale 5). **Avg SAT:** CR 678. M 668. W 674. **Col couns:** 5. Alum donors: 19%.
    Tui '12-'13: Day $39,925 (+$600). **Aid:** Need 368 ($9,800,000).
    Summer (enr 850): Ages 5-12. Sports. Tui Day $500-950. 1-2 wks. Outdoor Ed. Tui Day $4000. 6 wks.
    Endow $59,000,000. Lib 60,000 vols. Photog labs 1. Theaters 2. Art studios 5. Music studios 5. Dance studios 1. Recording studios 1. Gyms 5. Fields 3. Pools 1. Comp/stud: 1:2.5.
    Est 1878. Nonprofit. Sem (Sept-June).

Since its establishment by Felix Adler, this school has provided an ethnically diverse student body with an enriched curriculum that integrates academics, the arts and sciences, and ethical values.

Both elementary facilities, Fieldston Lower, which shares the 18-acre, wooded grounds in Riverdale, and Ethical Culture, located at on Central Park West in midtown Manhattan, offer students in grades pre-K-5 a program that focuses on building basic skills within a modified core curriculum. Specialists augment the program with laboratory science, computer, ethics, art, music, library, social studies workshop, wood shop and drama.

Fieldston (grades 6-8) and Fieldston Upper (grades 9-12), located in the Riverdale section of the Bronx, offer many courses in the visual and performing arts to supplement academic college preparation. Semester-long English electives rotate on a two-year cycle, and history offerings alternate each year. Interdisciplinary options allow juniors and seniors to integrate related electives across academic departments, and senior projects explore areas outside of the curriculum. Upper school students perform 60 hours of community service prior to graduation.

FORDHAM PREPARATORY SCHOOL
Day — Boys Gr 9-12

Bronx, NY 10458. 441 E Fordham Rd. Tel: 718-367-7500. Fax: 718-367-7598.
    www.fordhamprep.org   E-mail: admissions@fordhamprep.org

Rev. Kenneth J. Boller, SJ, Pres (2004). BA, Fordham Univ, MA, New York Univ, MDiv, Woodstock College. **Robert J. Gomprecht, Prin.** BA, MA, Fordham Univ. **Christopher D. Lauber, Adm.**

Col Prep. AP (exams req'd; 336 taken, 70% 3+)—Eng Lat Span Calc Stats Comp_ Sci Bio Chem Physics Eur_Hist US_Hist World_Hist Econ US_Govt & Pol Art_Hist Studio_Art. **Feat**—Creative_Writing Chin Fr Ger Greek Ital Forensic_Sci Biochem Engineering Relig Architect_Drawing. **Dual enr:** Fordham.

Sports—B: Baseball Basket Bowl Crew Football Golf Ice_Hockey Lacrosse Rugby Soccer Swim Tennis Track Volley Wrestling. **Activities:** 61.

Selective adm (Gr 9-10): 253/yr. Usual entry: 9. Appl fee: $0. Appl due: Dec. Applied: 1141. Accepted: 49%. Yield: 46%. **Tests** HSPT ISEE SSAT TACHS.

Enr 950. Wh 74%. Latino 16%. Blk 7%. Asian 3%. Avg class size: 24. Stud/fac: 11:1. Formal. **Fac 87.** M 63/F 24. FT 81/PT 6. Wh 81%. Latino 17%. Blk 1%. Asian 1%. Adv deg: 90%.

Grad '11—221. Col—216. (Fordham, U of Scranton, Boston Col, Holy Cross, Manhattan Col, NYU). **Avg SAT:** CR 585. M 590. W 584. **Col couns:** 4. Alum donors: 20%.

Tui '12-'13: Day $16,720 (+$300). **Aid:** Merit 100 ($400,000). Need 349 ($2,200,000). Endow $18,000,000. Plant val $19,000,000. Acres 5. Bldgs 2. Class rms 51. Lib 10,000 vols. Sci labs 9. Comp ctrs 1. Theater/auds 1. Fields 3. Courts 9. Pools 1. Comp/stud: 1:5.

Est 1841. Nonprofit. Roman Catholic (80% practice). Quar (Sept-May). **Assoc** MSA.

This Jesuit preparatory school, located on a five-acre portion of the Fordham University campus, uses some of the university's facilities.

The academic program consists of a flexible system of scheduling that allows boys to work at different rates. Beginning in grade 9, Fordham Prep conducts honors and Advanced Placement courses, and all freshmen take biology and Latin or ancient Greek. A well-equipped computer center supports the technology program. Freshmen and sophomores engage in Christian service activities as part of the curriculum, while juniors perform 15 hours of service outside of school hours and seniors complete 70 hours. See Also Page 85

HORACE MANN SCHOOL
Day — Coed Gr PS (Age 3)-12

Bronx, NY 10471. 231 W 246th St. Tel: 718-432-4100. Fax: 718-432-3610.
Other locations: 55 E 90th St, New York 10128; 4440 Tibbett Ave, Bronx 10471.
www.horacemann.org   E-mail: admissions@horacemann.org
Thomas M. Kelly, Head (2005). BA, Fairfield Univ, MEd, MA, MPhil, PhD, Columbia Univ. **Jason H. Caldwell, Adm.**

Col Prep. AP (exams req'd; 676 taken)—Eng Fr Ger Japan Lat Span Calc Comp_Sci Bio Chem Environ_Sci Physics Eur_Hist US_Hist World_Hist Econ Psych Art_Hist Studio_Art Music_Theory. **Feat**—Chin Greek Ital Astron Biotech Robotics Web_ Design E_Asian_Hist Govt Ceramics Filmmaking Photog Video_Production Drama Theater_Arts Music_Hist Dance Finance. Outdoor ed.

Sports—Basket Crew X-country Fencing Indoor_Track Lacrosse Ski Soccer Swim Tennis Track Ultimate_Frisbee W_Polo. B: Baseball Football Golf Squash Wrestling G: F_Hockey Gymnastics Softball Volley. **Activities:** 60.

Selective adm (Gr PS-11): 234/yr. Appl fee: $25-50. Appl due: Dec. **Tests** ISEE SSAT.

Enr 1781. Elem 1058. Sec 723. Wh 71%. Latino 3%. Blk 6%. Asian 11%. Other 9%. Avg class size: 19. **Fac 220.** Adv deg: 95%.

Grad '10—178. Col—176. (U of PA, Columbia, Cornell, Harvard, Georgetown, Yale) **Col couns:** 3. Alum donors: 21%.

Tui '11-'12: Day $37,275 (+$70-570). **Aid:** Need 300 ($8,300,000).

Summer: Acad Enrich Rev Rem Rec. Tui Day $1900-3800. 6 wks.

Endow $93,000,000. Plant val $102,000,000. Acres 115. Bldgs 23. Class rms 95. Lib 50,000 vols. Sci labs 7. Lang labs 1. Auds 1. Theaters 2. Art studios 8. Music studios 4. Dance studios 1. Art galleries 1. Gyms 3. Fields 4. Courts 8. Pools 1. Comp labs 4.

Est 1887. Nonprofit. Tri (Sept-May). **Assoc** CLS MSA.

Horace Mann School was established by Nicholas Murray Butler as an experimental and demonstration unit of Teachers College, Columbia University. The coeducational school included all grades from kindergarten through high school until 1914, at which time Horace Mann School for Boys was established in its present location in the Riverdale section of the Bronx; it was among the first country day schools in the United States. The kindergarten, elementary and girls' school continued at Teachers College until 1946 and, in that same year, the boys' school received its own charter from the state board of regents and became an independent institution. In 1969, Horace Mann again became a coeducational school beginning with the youngest level. The 18-acre middle (grades 6-8) and upper (grades 9-12) division campus overlooks Van Cortlandt Park. Across the street on Tibbett Avenue, the lower school houses grades K-5, and the nursery school (nursery, prekindergarten and kindergarten) occupies a historic building on East 90th Street in Manhattan.

Horace Mann's program is strongly rooted in the liberal arts tradition, with AP courses, a wide variety of electives, interdisciplinary offerings, and options such as independent study and study abroad. Foreign language instruction begins in grade 1 with French and Spanish, and upper division students choose from eight languages, among them Chinese, Japanese and Russian. Middle and upper division course requirements include classes in the visual and performing arts, computer science and community service; children in the nursery and lower division also participate in activities in these areas. As they progress, pupils have an increasing degree of choice in their course options, including the chance to undertake an independent research seminar. Students design these research projects, which address subjects not included in the curriculum or provide further study of a topic covered in a previous course.

Frequent outings and field trips are arranged for the youngest students, while interest clubs and other extracurricular options are available to older boys and girls. Interscholastic athletic competition commences in grade 7. Beginning in grade 2, students partake of a variety of conservation, science and outdoor living experiences at the 265-acre John Dorr Nature Laboratory in Washington, CT.

RIVERDALE COUNTRY SCHOOL
Day — Coed Gr PS (Age 4)-12

Bronx, NY 10471. 5250 Fieldston Rd. Tel: 718-549-8810. Fax: 718-519-2795.
www.riverdale.edu   E-mail: info@riverdale.edu
Dominic A. A. Randolph, Head (2007). AB, EdM, Harvard Univ. Jenna R. King, Upper & Middle Sch Adm; Sarah Lafferty, Lower Sch Adm.
Col Prep. Feat—Shakespeare African-Amer_Lit Chin Fr Japan Lat Span Calc Stats Anat & Physiol Astron Marine_Bio/Sci Comp_Sci 20th-Century_Indian_Hist Econ Law Psych Middle_Eastern_Stud Philos World_Relig Art_Hist Ceramics Film Photog Sculpt Video_Production Theater Music_Theory.
Sports—Basket X-country Fencing Golf Lacrosse Soccer Squash Swim Tennis Track Ultimate_Frisbee. B: Baseball Football Wrestling. G: F_Hockey Gymnastics Softball Volley.
Selective adm (Gr PS-11): 157/yr. Usual entry: PS, K, 6 & 9. Appl fee: $60. Appl due: Dec. Tests ISEE SSAT.
Enr 1130. B 570. G 560. Elem 620. Sec 510. Avg class size: 16. Stud/fac: 8:1. Fac 163. M 48/F 115. FT 133/PT 30. Adv deg: 82%.
Grad '11—117. Col—117. (Cornell 10, Duke 7, Dartmouth 6, Harvard 5, Yale 4, Stanford 3). Col couns: 3. Alum donors: 20%.
Tui '12-'13: Day $40,750-42,000 (+$2000). Aid: Need ($5,261,725).
Endow $57,971,000. Plant val $87,000,000. Acres 27. Bldgs 13. Class rms 76. 2 Libs 35,000 vols. Sci labs 8. Lang labs 1. Observatories 1. Auds 2. Theaters 2. Art studios 8. Music studios 9. Arts ctrs 1. Gyms 2. Fields 4. Courts 8. Pools 1. Comp labs 6. Comp/stud: 1:2.4.
Est 1907. Nonprofit. Sem (Sept-June). Assoc CLS.

Established by Dr. Frank S. Hackett, this was among the earliest country day schools to be located near a metropolitan center. Through his vision and drive, the school quickly gained an enviable reputation. In 1972, the school became coeducational when the boys' and girls' divisions merged. In 1985, the school was significantly reorganized with the consolidation of the lower, middle and upper schools into two divisions—lower (grades pre-K-6) and upper (grades 7-12)—on separate campuses. The school was restructured in fall 2005 into three divisions, with the lower school (grades pre-K-5) on one campus and the middle school (grades 6-8) and upper school (grades 9-12) on another.

Riverdale's traditional college preparatory curriculum is characterized by unusual breadth in elective courses, languages, the arts and interdisciplinary studies. Middle and upper school pupils take part in compulsory group service projects throughout the year. Juniors may participate in semester- or yearlong off-campus and study abroad programs.

BROOKLYN, NY. Urban. Pop: 2,465,326. Alt: to 109 ft.

BERKELEY CARROLL SCHOOL
Day — Coed Gr PS (Age 3)-12

Brooklyn, NY 11217. 181 Lincoln Pl. Tel: 718-789-6060. Fax: 718-398-3640.
Other locations: 701 Carroll St, Brooklyn 11215; 515 6th St, Brooklyn 11215.
  www.berkeleycarroll.org   E-mail: bcs@berkeleycarroll.org
Robert D. Vitalo, Head (2006). BS, New York Univ, MA, Columbia Univ. **Vanessa C. Prescott, Upper & Middle Sch Adm; Amanda Pike, Lower Sch Adm.**
  Col Prep. AP (exams req'd)—Fr Lat Span Calc Stats Bio Chem Physics US_Hist Econ.
    Feat—Lib_Skills Poetry Lat-Amer_Lit Satire Environ_Sci Oceanog Comp_Sci African_Hist Anglo-Irish_Hist Holocaust Modern_Chin_Hist Modern_Japan_Hist Vietnam_War Gender_Stud Art_Hist Ceramics Film Sculpt Studio_Art Drama Music Dance Journ.
  Sports—Basket X-country Soccer Swim Tennis Track Volley. B: Baseball. G: Softball.
  Selective adm: 110/yr. Appl fee: $100. Appl due: Dec. **Tests** ISEE.
  Enr 820. Wh 77%. Latino 5%. Blk 13%. Asian 5%. Avg class size: 16. Stud/fac: 7:1. **Fac 110.** M 40/F 70. FT 104/PT 6. Adv deg: 82%.
  Grad '11—55. Col—55. (Reed 4, U of Chicago 3, Cornell 2, Haverford 2, Georgetown 2, U of CO-Boulder 2). **Col couns:** 2.
  Tui '12-'13: Day $29,920-34,500 (+$100-890).
  Summer: Ages 3-8. Enrich Rec. Tui Day $465-2035. 1-5 wks. Ages 8-14. Creative Arts. Tui Day $2200. 4 wks.
  Endow $2,000,000. Plant val $9,000,000. Bldgs 5. Class rms 45. 3 Libs 35,000 vols. Sci labs 3. Auds 1. Theaters 1. Art studios 3. Music studios 3. Dance studios 2. Gyms 3. Courts 1. Pools 1. Comp labs 3.
  Est 1982. Nonprofit. Sem (Sept-June). **Assoc** CLS.

The school resulted from a merger between the Carroll Street School (founded in 1966) and the Berkeley Institute (founded in 1886). Located in Brooklyn's historic Park Slope section, Berkeley Carroll's campus consists of two building complexes housing its lower school (grades PS-4) on Carroll Street, and its middle and upper schools (grades 5-12) on Lincoln Place. The school also operates a childcare center on 6th Street.

The comprehensive curriculum includes a full program of Advanced Placement courses, independent study and internships, as well as electives in creative writing, studio art and computer science. BCS arranges direct cultural and academic exchanges with secondary schools in France and Spain. Computer proficiency and a senior internship are required for graduation.

A visiting artists program brings professional artists to campus to work with middle and upper school students on skills and techniques they might not ordinarily learn in a classroom setting.

BROOKLYN FRIENDS SCHOOL

Day — Coed Gr PS (Age 3)-12

Brooklyn, NY 11201. 375 Pearl St. Tel: 718-852-1029. Fax: 718-643-4868.
Other locations: 55 Willoughby St, Brooklyn 11201.
www.brooklynfriends.org   E-mail: info@brooklynfriends.org
Larry Weiss, Head (2010). BA, MA, PhD, Columbia Univ. **Crystal Backus, Gr 6-12 Adm; Karine Blemur-Chapman, Gr PS-5 Adm.**

> **Col Prep. IB Diploma. Elem math**—TERC Investigations. **Feat**—Creative_Writing Shakespeare Women's_Lit Chin Fr Ital Lat Span Calc Stats Astron Environ_Sci Oceanog Programming Robotics African_Hist Lat-Amer_Hist Psych Media_Stud Ethics Relig Art_Hist Painting Photog Visual_Arts Drama Chorus Jazz_Ensemble Dance. **Supp**—Dev_Read Rev.
>
> **Sports**—Basket X-country Soccer Track Volley. B: Baseball. G: Softball. **Activities:** 50.
>
> **Selective adm (Gr PS-11):** 140/yr. Usual entry: K, 1, 5 & 9. Appl fee: $80-110. Appl due: Rolling. Applied: 500. Accepted: 50%. **Tests** IQ ISEE SSAT.
>
> **Enr 750.** B 360. G 390. Wh 60%. Latino 4%. Blk 17%. Asian 4%. Other 15%. Avg class size: 18. Stud/fac: 7:1. **Fac 130.** M 40/F 90. FT 125/PT 5. Wh 67%. Latino 10%. Blk 15%. Asian 8%. Adv deg: 84%.
>
> **Grad '11—49. Col—49.** (Bard-NY 3, Amherst 2, Swarthmore 1, U of PA 1, Wesleyan U 1, Northwestern 1). **Col couns:** 2. Alum donors: 15%.
>
> **Tui '12-'13: Day $21,100-33,100. Aid:** Merit 3 ($30,000). Need 150 ($2,250,000).
>
> **Summer (enr 100):** Enrich Rec. Fine Arts. 6 wks.
>
> Endow $1,000,000. Plant val $20,000,000. Bldgs 2. Class rms 59. 2 Libs 20,000 vols. Sci labs 5. Lang labs 1. Dark rms 1. Theaters 1. Art studios 5. Music studios 3. Dance studios 2. Wood shops 1. Gyms 2. Playgrounds 1. Comp labs 4. Laptop prgm Gr 5-12.
>
> **Est 1867.** Nonprofit. Religious Society of Friends (3% practice). Quar (Sept-June).

Founded by the Brooklyn Meeting of the Society of Friends, BFS continues to adhere to Friends' traditions and ideals. In keeping with Quaker custom, the school conducts weekly meetings to provide time for silence and reflection. After more than 100 years at 112 Schermerhorn St., the school moved in 1973 to its current location in downtown Brooklyn. The upper school building is two blocks away on Willoughby Street.

The school as a whole is divided into four sections: preschool (ages 3 and 4), lower (grades K-4), middle (grades 5-8) and upper (grades 9-12). The college preparatory upper school program features a faculty advisory system, electives, independent study options and travel abroad. In addition, juniors and seniors may enroll in the rigorous two-year IB Diploma Program. Brooklyn Friends issues laptop computers to students in grades 5, 6, 11 and 12.

Community service is built into the curriculum, and older students also satisfy the following service requirements: 50 cumulative hours in grades 9 and 10, and another 150 total hours in grades 11 and 12. An arts-based summer program and outdoor education are among BFS' other offerings.

PACKER COLLEGIATE INSTITUTE

Day — Coed Gr PS (Age 3)-12

Brooklyn, NY 11201. 170 Joralemon St. Tel: 718-250-0200. Fax: 718-875-1363.
www.packer.edu   E-mail: bknauer@packer.edu
Bruce L. Dennis, Head (2004). BA, MA, City Univ of New York, EdD, Columbia Univ. **Sheila Bogan, Gr 5-12 Adm; Denise De Bono, Gr PS-4 Adm.**

> **Col Prep. AP (exams req'd)**—Eng Chin Fr Lat Span Calc Stats Comp_Sci Bio Chem Physics Eur_Hist US_Hist US_Govt & Pol Art_Hist Studio_Art. **Elem math**—Everyday Math. **Feat**—Dostoevsky Irish_Lit Lat-Amer_Lit NYC_Lit Multivariable_Calc Anat & Physiol Astron Forensic_Sci Organic_Chem Robotics Modern_Chin_Hist Modern_ E_Asia Anthro Photog Sculpt Drama Band Chorus Music Orchestra Dance Journ.
>
> **Sports**—Basket X-country Soccer Squash Tennis Track Volley. B: Baseball. G: Softball.
>
> **Selective adm (Gr PS-11):** 159/yr. Usual entry: PS, K, 5 & 9. Appl fee: $50-60. Accepted: 27%. **Tests** CTP_4 ISEE SSAT.

Enr 997. B 481. G 516. Wh 72%. Latino 6%. Blk 10%. Asian 9%. Other 3%. Avg class size: 15. Stud/fac: 9:1. **Fac 109.**
Grad '10—82. Col—82. (Wesleyan U, Oberlin, Geo Wash, Skidmore, Yale, Middlebury).
   Avg SAT: CR 668. M 649. W 686. **Col couns:** 3. Alum donors: 23%.
Tui '11-'12: Day $30,135-31,555 (+$600-1300). **Aid:** Need 200 ($4,000,000).
Summer: Enrich Rec. Tui Day $850/2-wk ses. 6 wks.
Bldgs 8 (100% ADA). Class rms 77. 2 Libs 18,000 vols. Sci labs 10. Lang labs 4. Dark rms 1. Auds 1. Theaters 1. Art studios 1. Music studios 6. Dance studios 1. Gyms 2. Weight rms 1. Gardens 1. Comp labs 2. Laptop prgm Gr 5-12.
Est 1845. Nonprofit. Quar (Sept-June). **Assoc** CLS.

Founded as the Brooklyn Female Academy, the school took its current name in honor of William S. Packer, whose widow donated money to rebuild the original structure, which had burned in 1853. Coeducational since 1972, Packer Collegiate is located in the Brooklyn Heights historical district.

Packer comprises a preschool and lower school (grades pre-K-4), a middle school (grades 5-8) and an upper school (grades 9-12). In the upper school, freshmen, sophomores and juniors have a fairly structured curriculum, while seniors have more scheduling flexibility. Students fulfill course and elective requirements in English, a foreign language, mathematics, humanities and American history, science and the arts. Advanced Placement classes and upper-level electives are available across the academic departments. Computer instruction begins in grade 1 and students in grades 5-12 purchase required laptop computers.

Independent study is encouraged in grades 10-12, and a senior program allows interested students to pursue a self-designed course of study throughout the second semester. A science department program also provides opportunities for independent research. Travel abroad opportunities are offered and, each semester, a few juniors may enroll in Chewonki Semester School or the Rocky Mountain Institute.

Beginning in the middle school, students are encouraged to participate in an array of extracurriculars. Student activities include clubs and organizations, artistic programs and athletics. Students in grades 9-11 are required to complete 15 hours of annual service to the school community or to the community at large, and all pupils in grades 5-12 attend a nonsectarian chapel assembly at least once a week.

POLY PREP COUNTRY DAY SCHOOL

Day — Coed Gr PS (Age 3)-12

Brooklyn, NY 11228. 9216 7th Ave. Tel: 718-836-9800. Fax: 718-921-5112.
Other locations: 50 Prospect Park W, Brooklyn 11215.
   www.polyprep.org   E-mail: polyadmissions@polyprep.org
David B. Harman, Head (2001). AB, MEd, Harvard Univ, MAT, Reed College. **Lori W. Redell, Adm.**
   Col Prep. AP (exams req'd; 244 taken, 84% 3+)—Eng Fr Lat Span Calc Stats Comp_ Sci Bio Chem Physics Eur_Hist US_Hist World_Hist Art_Hist Music_Theory. **Feat**— British_Lit Poetry Shakespeare Brooklyn_Lit Lat-Amer_Lit Chin Environ_Sci Forensic_Sci Geol Web_Design Cuban_Hist Modern_Chin_Hist Econ Intl_Relations Law Psych Sociol World_Relig Comp_Philos Film Painting Sculpt Acting Theater_Arts Music_Hist Journ. **Supp**—Rev Tut. **Dual enr:** Polytechnic Inst of NYU.
   Sports—Basket X-country Indoor_Track Lacrosse Soccer Squash Swim Tennis Track. B: Baseball Football Golf Ice_Hockey Wrestling. G: Softball Volley. **Activities:** 30.
   Very selective adm (Gr PS-11): 175/yr. Appl fee: $50. Appl due: Dec. **Tests** CTP_4 ISEE SSAT.
   Enr 1012. B 551. G 461. Elem 525. Sec 487. Wh 70%. Latino 4%. Blk 12%. Asian 5%. Other 9%. Avg class size: 16. Stud/fac: 12:1. Casual. **Fac 144.** M 65/F 79. FT 142/PT 2. Wh 87%. Latino 2%. Blk 8%. Asian 1%. Other 2%. Adv deg: 93%.
   Grad '11—105. Col—105. (Hamilton 6, Cornell 5, CT Col 4, U of PA 3, Trinity Col-CT 3, Franklin & Marshall 3). **Mid 50% SAT:** CR 580-680. M 600-710. W 610-700. **Col couns:** 5. Alum donors: 18%.

Tui '12-'13: Day $26,500-34,650 (+$1000). **Aid:** Need ($5,250,000).
Summer (enr 1500): Acad Enrich Rev Rem Rec. Sports. Test Prep. Theater. Tui Day $180-2650. 1-6 wks.
Endow $22,000,000. Plant val $68,000,000. Acres 27. Bldgs 10. Class rms 44. 2 Libs 34,000 vols. Sci labs 9. Lang labs 3. Theaters 2. Art studios 6. Music studios 4. Dance studios 2. Gyms 3. Athletic ctrs 1. Fields 6. Tennis courts 9. Squash courts 4. Field houses 1. Pools 2. Playgrounds 1. Greenhouses 1. Comp labs 9. Comp/stud: 1:4 (1:1 Laptop prgm Gr 6).
Est 1854. Nonprofit. (Sept-June). **Assoc** CLS MSA.

Founded as Brooklyn Collegiate and Polytechnic Institute, this school conducted a largely college preparatory program for boys until 1871, when the institution began to award bachelor's degrees. To reflect this change in focus, the school shortened its name to Brooklyn Polytechnic Institute in 1887. Four years later, the college prep division separated from the collegiate division and became a stand-alone school. In 1917, the preparatory division moved to its present, 25-acre campus in the Dyker Heights section of Brooklyn and received a new charter as Polytechnic Preparatory Country Day School. Under the leadership of Joseph Dana Allen, an ardent follower of the country day movement, Poly Prep gained renown as a top school of its kind. The school became coeducational in 1977 and established a lower school serving children in nursery through grade 4 upon acquiring a second campus in Park Slope, on Prospect Park West, in 1995. The school eventually elected to shorten its name to Poly Prep Country Day School.

Employing ideas attributed to John Dewey, the lower school program emphasizes exploration, creativity and discovery. The lower school focuses on intellectual and social development, as well as on skill building. Middle and upper schoolers follow a college preparatory curriculum that is conducted in the classical tradition, and Poly Prep implements progressive pedagogical techniques and interdisciplinary learning approaches where appropriate. In the middle school (grades 5-8), a dual language program combines modern language study with Latin instruction. Accelerated math and science offerings commence in grade 7, and the Dyker Heights campus serves as an outdoor classroom for science classes.

The upper school curriculum (grades 9-12) includes Advanced Placement courses for qualified students, in addition to various electives, particularly in the English and history disciplines. Pupils may also propose topics for independent study. Ninth graders perform 15 hours of in-school community service, while all boys and girls complete 40 hours of compulsory service at a school-approved agency prior to graduation.

The arts are an area of emphasis in all three school divisions. Arts faculty, many of whom are practicing professionals in their fields, provide instruction in dance, music, theater and the visual arts. All students have access to the latest instructional technology; learn to use computers; and may pursue course work in graphic and digital design, photo and video creation, and Internet and database research. Extensive libraries housing books, various reference materials and databases support learning on both campuses.

SAINT ANN'S SCHOOL

Day — Coed Gr PS (Age 3)-12

Brooklyn, NY 11201. 129 Pierrepont St. Tel: 718-522-1660. Fax: 718-522-2599.
Other locations: 153 Pierrepont St, Brooklyn 11201; 124 Henry St, Brooklyn 11201; 26 Willow Pl, Brooklyn 11201.
   www.saintannsny.org   E-mail: admissions@saintannsny.org
Vincent Tompkins, Head (2010). Diana Lomask, Adm.
   Col Prep. AP exams taken: 206. Feat—Russ_Lit Chin Fr Greek Japan Lat Span Calc Astron Genetics Marine_Bio/Sci Programming Robotics Web_Design Econ Constitutional_Law Ethics Logic Architect Drawing Film Painting Photog Sculpt Animation Acting Theater Music_Theory Dance.
   Sports—Basket X-country Fencing Soccer Squash Track. B: Baseball. G: Gymnastics Softball Volley.
   Selective adm (Gr PS-10): 161/yr. Appl fee: $35-150. Appl due: Dec. **Tests** IQ ISEE.

Enr 1090. Fac 220.
Grad '11—81. Col—79. (Brown 6, Oberlin 5, Yale 4, U of Chicago 4, Reed 4, Dartmouth 3). **Avg SAT:** CR 705. M 670. W 710. **Mid 50% SAT:** CR 655-740. M 620-710. W 660-760. **Col couns:** 3.
Tui '12-'13: Day $27,000-33,100.
Summer: Rec. 3 wks.
Endow $5,000,000. Bldgs 7. Class rms 48. Libs 2. Sci labs 3. Theaters 1. Art studios 6. Music studios 4. Dance studios 1. Gyms 3. Comp labs 2.
Est 1965. Nonprofit. Sem (Sept-June).

Saint Ann's was founded "with the express purpose of affording bright children an education specifically tailored to their needs." No letter or numerical grades are given, and from grade 4 on students advance in different subjects from level to level according to ability and achievement rather than age. All teachers are specialists in their fields; music, art and theater are taught by professionals. The wide-ranging curriculum includes such offerings as organic chemistry, Chinese, Spanish and Russian literature.

The school has both a horizontal structure (division into lower, middle and high schools) and a vertical structure (each academic department extends from grades 4-12 with no break in curriculum or staff), thus allowing for two channels of information about each student.

BUFFALO, NY. (174 mi. NE of Cleveland, OH) Urban. Pop: 292,648. Alt: 600 ft. Area also includes Snyder.

BUFFALO SEMINARY

Bdg and Day — Girls Gr 9-12

Buffalo, NY 14222. 205 Bidwell Pky. Tel: 716-885-6780. Fax: 716-885-6785.
www.buffaloseminary.org   E-mail: admissions@buffaloseminary.org
Jody Douglass, Head (2007). BA, Bates College, MA, Middlebury College. **Carrie Auwarter, Adm.**
    Col Prep. AP (exams req'd; 116 taken, 69% 3+)—Eng Fr Span Calc Stats Bio Physics Eur_Hist US_Hist US_Govt & Pol Art_Hist. **Feat**—Gothic_Lit Astron Environ_Sci Computers Chin_Hist Econ Urban_Stud Graphic_Arts Performing_Arts Photog Studio_Art Music. **Supp**—Rev Tut.
    Sports—G: Basket Crew Fencing F_Hockey Golf Lacrosse Soccer Softball Squash Swim Tennis.
    Selective adm (Bdg Gr 9-12; Day 9-11): 40/yr. Appl fee: $25. Appl due: Nov. Accepted: 80%. Yield: 60%. **Tests** DAT IQ SSAT.
    Enr 170. Bdg 20. Day 150. Wh 75%. Latino 2%. Blk 10%. Asian 8%. Other 5%. Intl 12%. Avg class size: 11. Stud/fac: 10:1. Casual. **Fac 29.** M 4/F 25. FT 20/PT 9. Wh 100%. Adv deg: 89%. In dorms 3.
    Grad '10—42. Col—42. (Allegheny 2, Hobart/Wm Smith 2, SUNY-Buffalo 2, Trinity Col-CT 2, Col of Wooster 2, U of PA 1). **Avg SAT:** CR 560. M 533. W 565. **Mid 50% SAT:** CR 480-640. M 480-590. W 480-660. Alum donors: 40%.
    Tui '11-'12: Bdg $37,950 (+$1200). **5-Day Bdg $34,950** (+$1200). **Day $16,950** (+$1200). **Aid:** Merit 3 ($8000). Need 75 ($490,000).
    Summer: Acad Rec. Arts. Tui Day $275/wk. 6 wks.
    Endow $3,200,000. Plant val $7,100,000. Bldgs 2. Class rms 17. Lib 9850 vols. Sci labs 3. Auds 1. Theaters 1. Art studios 1. Music studios 1. Dance studios 1. Gyms 1. Fields 1. Comp labs 1. Comp/stud: 1:1 Laptop prgm Gr 9-12.
    Est 1851. Nonprofit. Sem (Sept-June). **Assoc** CLS MSA.

Established as one of the earlier nondenominational girls' academies, the school has a curriculum that includes instruction in mathematics, the sciences, English, history and cultures, languages, computers, and the visual and performing arts. Students must complete a two-week internship in May of senior year. The school does not prepare students for the New York State

Regents examinations, instead emphasizing Advanced Placement courses and Scholastic Aptitude Test preparation.

Buffalo Seminary began offering boarding on a limited basis in fall 2009.

ELMWOOD FRANKLIN SCHOOL
Day — Coed Gr PS (Age 4)-8

Buffalo, NY 14216. 104 New Amsterdam Ave. Tel: 716-877-5035. Fax: 716-877-9680.
www.elmwoodfranklin.org   E-mail: eacker@elmwoodfranklin.org
Margaret Keller-Cogan, Head (2012). BA, Univ of Windsor (Canada), MEd, Nazareth College, EdD, Univ of Rochester. **Elaine Zehr Acker, Adm.**
  Pre-Prep. Feat—ASL Fr Span Computers Studio_Art Drama Music Outdoor_Ed. **Supp**—Dev_Read Rem_Math Rem_Read Rev Tut.
  Sports—Basket Lacrosse Soccer. G: F_Hockey.
  Selective adm (Gr PS-7): 60/yr. Appl fee: $50. Appl due: Mar. Accepted: 52%. Yield: 75%. **Tests** IQ MAT.
  Enr 334. Nonwhite 25%. Avg class size: 18. Stud/fac: 8:1. Casual. **Fac 47.** M 6/F 41. FT 39/PT 8. Nonwhite 12%. Adv deg: 61%.
  Grad '08—34. Prep—30. (Nichols, Canisius, Buffalo Seminary, Park Sch-NY). Alum donors: 20%.
  Tui '12-'13: Day $14,602-17,518. Aid: Need 120 ($553,912).
  Summer: Acad Enrich Rec. 6 wks.
  Endow $6,350,000. Plant val $7,448,000. Acres 5. Bldgs 1. Class rms 40. Lib 15,610 vols. Sci labs 2. Lang labs 2. Auds 1. Theaters 1. Art studios 1. Music studios 2. Perf arts ctrs 1. Gyms 1. Fields 2. Comp labs 2. Comp/stud: 1:1.7.
  Est 1895. Nonprofit. Quar (Sept-June).

The oldest preschool through grade 8 independent school in western New York State, EFS conducts a varied program that emphasizes basic learning skills and traditional subject matter. During the early years, four-, five- and six-year-olds take part in a well-developed reading program that incorporates storytelling, art, discussion, writing and dramatization throughout the school day. The lower school curriculum augments the standard subjects with music, art, foreign language, drama and daily physical education classes. Small skill-based groupings allow for individualization, and reading and math labs complement classroom instruction.

Departmentalization begins in the upper school. Interdisciplinary themes integrate music, art, literature, history, science, math and foreign language. Elmwood Franklin's outdoor education program combines group problem solving with environmental and science studies. Special classes enable pupils to explore arts, computers, sports, science and nature, while extended winter options include skiing, tennis and extensive computer study.

From prekindergarten through grade 8, each class completes one community service project annually.

NICHOLS SCHOOL
Day — Coed Gr 5-12

Buffalo, NY 14216. 1250 Amherst St. Tel: 716-332-6300. Fax: 716-875-2169.
www.nicholsschool.org   E-mail: admissions@nicholsschool.org
Richard C. Bryan, Jr., Head (1994). BA, Trinity College (CT), MA, Univ of North Carolina-Charlotte. **Heather Newton, Adm.**
  Col Prep. AP (326 exams taken, 76% 3+)—Eng Fr Lat Span Calc Stats Bio Chem Physics Eur_Hist Comp_Govt & Pol Econ US_Govt & Pol Art_Hist Studio_Art. **Elem math**—Singapore Math. **Feat**—British_Lit Creative_Writing Poetry Chin Anat & Physiol Environ_Sci Engineering Comp_Sci Chin & Japan_Hist Psych Urban_Stud Philos Relig Photog Video_Production Theater Band Chorus Music Ballet Dance. **Supp**—Dev_Read Rem_Read Tut.
  Sports—Basket Crew X-country Golf Ice_Hockey Lacrosse Soccer Squash Tennis. B:

Baseball Football Wrestling. G: F_Hockey Softball Volley. **Activities:** 26.
Selective adm (Gr 5-11): 134/yr. Appl fee: $35. Appl due: Jan. Accepted: 80%. Yield: 55%. **Tests** CTP_4 IQ Stanford TOEFL.
Enr 580. B 296. G 284. Elem 191. Sec 389. Wh 85%. Latino 2%. Blk 5%. Native Am 2%. Asian 6%. Avg class size: 14. Stud/fac: 8:1. Formal. **Fac 84.** Wh 96%. Blk 1%. Asian 2%. Other 1%. Adv deg: 94%.
Grad '11—103. Col—103. (Hobart/Wm Smith 6, SUNY-Buffalo 5, Canisius 5, Boston Col 4, Niagara 3, U of VT 3). **Avg SAT:** CR 560. M 578. W 566. **Mid 50% SAT:** CR 490-650. M 510-640. W 510-640. **Col couns:** 2. Alum donors: 33%.
Tui '11-'12: Day $18,550-20,000 (+$610-910). **Aid:** Need 172 ($1,557,886).
Summer: Acad Enrich Rev Rem Rec. Sports. Tui Day $100-435. 1-6 wks.
Endow $26,000,000. Plant val $22,000,000. Acres 30. Bldgs 8. Class rms 38. 2 Libs 20,000 vols. Sci labs 7. Auds 1. Theaters 1. Art studios 4. Music studios 2. Dance studios 1. Perf arts ctrs 1. Gyms 2. Fields 5. Squash courts 2. Rinks 2. Comp labs 5.
Est 1892. Nonprofit. Quar (Sept-May). **Assoc** CLS.

Established by William Nichols of Boston, then under the vigorous leadership of Dr. Joseph Dana Allen beginning in 1909, Nichols has always been characterized by efficient college preparation. In January 1972, the school became coeducational, with girls being admitted into all grades.

In addition to the traditional courses offered as part of a college preparatory program, an extensive arts program (including photography, dance, painting, computer graphics, chorus and orchestra) is available. Nichols encourages all upper schoolers to perform community service.

For years, the middle school (grades 5-8) was located on the Nottingham campus, one mile from the upper school (grades 9-12). In August 2001, however, Nichols consolidated campuses by adding a middle school building at its Amherst Street location.

THE PARK SCHOOL
Day — Coed Gr PS (Age 4)-12

Snyder, NY 14226. 4625 Harlem Rd. Tel: 716-839-1242. Fax: 716-839-2014.
www.theparkschool.org   E-mail: admissions@theparkschool.org
Christopher J. Lauricella, Head. BS, State University of New York-Oneonta, MEd, Columbia Univ. **Jennifer A. Brady, Adm.**
Col Prep. AP—Eng Fr Span Calc Comp_Sci US_Hist US_Govt & Pol. **Feat**—Botany Microbio Studio_Art Drama Music Outdoor_Ed. **Supp**—ESL Rev Tut.
Sports—Basket Bowl Soccer Tennis. B: Golf Lacrosse. G: Softball.
Somewhat selective adm: 58/yr. Appl fee: $50. Appl due: Rolling. Accepted: 93%. Yield: 53%. **Tests** CTP_4 IQ ISEE.
Enr 253. B 121. G 132. Elem 156. Sec 97. Nonwhite 31%. Avg class size: 15. Stud/fac: 8:1. Casual. **Fac 40.** M 13/F 27. FT 31/PT 9. Adv deg: 47%.
Grad '07—26. Col—25. (Am U, Denison, Purdue, Rochester Inst of Tech, Sarah Lawrence, SUNY-Buffalo). **Avg SAT:** CR 587. M 581. W 594. Avg ACT: 25. **Col couns:** 1.
Tui '07-'08: Day $10,300-16,750 (+$300). **Aid:** Need 109.
Summer: Rec. 1-6 wks.
Endow $1,500,000. Plant val $3,500,000. Acres 34. Bldgs 14. Class rms 32. 2 Libs 18,500 vols. Sci labs 4. Photog labs 1. Theaters 1. Art studios 5. Music studios 2. Arts ctrs Wood shops 1. Gyms 2. Fields 3. Courts 4. Pools 1. Greenhouses 1. Comp labs 2.
Est 1912. Nonprofit. Sem (Sept-June).

First of the Park Schools headed by Mary H. Lewis, this one, founded by a group of parents, has remained markedly holistic and child centered throughout its history.

The college preparatory curriculum incorporates art, music and drama, and it features a sequence in outdoor education at all grade levels. Qualified students may take advanced courses at area colleges and have opportunities to undertake independent projects. Upper school pupils perform 20 hours of required community service annually. The 34-acre school plant permits firsthand investigation of many natural phenomena.

CORNWALL-ON-HUDSON, NY. (53 mi. N of New York, NY) Suburban. Pop: 3058. Alt: 282 ft.

NEW YORK MILITARY ACADEMY
Bdg and Day — Coed Gr 7-12

Cornwall-on-Hudson, NY 12520. 78 Academy Ave. Tel: 845-534-3710, 888-275-6962. **Fax:** 845-534-7699.
www.nyma.org   E-mail: admissions@nyma.org
Maj. Jeffrey E. Coverdale, USAR (Ret), Supt (2010). BBA, Oklahoma City Univ. **Alisa Southwell, Adm.**
  Col Prep. Milit. AP—Eng Eur_Hist US_Hist Human_Geog. **Feat**—Creative_Writing Fr Lat Span Environ_Sci Forensic_Sci Engineering Computers Govt/Econ Fine_Arts Studio_Art Band Music Finance Journ JROTC Aviation. **Supp**—ESL Tut.
  Sports—Basket X-country Equestrian Fencing Golf Soccer Swim Tennis Ultimate_Frisbee. B: Baseball Football Lacrosse Wrestling. G: Softball Volley. **Activities:** 10.
  Selective adm (Gr 7-11): 128/yr. Appl fee: $100. Appl due: Rolling. Accepted: 68%. **Tests** CEEB IQ SSAT Stanford TOEFL.
  Enr 146. B 110. G 36. Bdg 124. Day 22. Elem 46. Sec 100. Wh 56%. Latino 8%. Blk 24%. Asian 12%. Intl 12%. Stud/fac: 15:1. Uniform. **Fac 19.** M 12/F 7. FT 19. Wh 79%. Latino 7%. Blk 7%. Native Am 7%. Adv deg: 68%.
  Grad '11—25. Col—25. (US Naval Acad 1, US Milit Acad 1, Franklin & Marshall 1, U of MD-Col Park 1, Rochester Inst of Tech 1, Drew 1). Athl schol 7. **Col couns:** 1. Alum donors: 10%.
  Tui '11-'12: Bdg $35,210 (+$750-1500). **Day $21,190** (+$750-1500). **Intl Bdg $38,660** (+$750-1500). **Aid:** Need ($150,000).
  Summer: Acad Enrich Rem Rec. Band. Equestrian. 1-6 wks.
  Endow $2,500,000. Plant val $20,000,000. Acres 120. Bldgs 13. Dorms 4. Dorm rms 170. Class rms 47. Lib 16,000 vols. Sci labs 3. Auds 1. Art studios 1. Music studios 1. Gyms 1. Fields 6. Courts 10. Pools 3. Riding rings 1. Stables 1. Weight rms 1. Rifle ranges 1. Comp labs 2.
  Est 1889. Nonprofit. Sem (Sept-June). **Assoc** MSA.

Drawing its enrollment from many states and foreign countries, this well-known academy was founded by Col. Charles J. Wright. The school became coeducational in 1976, and today girls play an important role in all school activities.

The academic program is college preparatory, with special emphasis placed on science, mathematics, modern languages and composition. Science and the humanities are supplemented by numerous electives. Part of NYMA's technology program, a campuswide network enables all boarding cadets to have computer connections in their dorm rooms. A compulsory athletic program includes interscholastic sports and fitness training. In addition, students perform 50 hours of required community service in grades 9-12.

The guidance department counsels early on college choices and career development. Graduates matriculate at traditional colleges and universities as well as the nation's five service academies.

THE STORM KING SCHOOL
Bdg and Day — Coed Gr 8-PG

Cornwall-on-Hudson, NY 12520. 314 Mountain Rd. Tel: 845-534-9860, 800-225-9144. **Fax:** 845-534-4128.

www.sks.org E-mail: admissions@sks.org

Paul C. Domingue, Head (2012). BA, Providence College, MFA, Univ of Massachusetts-Dartmouth. **Joanna Evans, Adm.**

Col Prep. AP (exams req'd; 23 taken, 61% 3+)—Eng Calc Stats Comp_Sci Physics US_Hist Econ Psych Art_Hist Studio_Art. **Feat**—ASL Chin Span Environ_Sci Govt Philos Photog Video_Production Acting Theater_Arts Scriptwriting Music Songwriting Dance Outdoor_Ed. **Supp**—Dev_Read ESL LD Makeup Rem_Math Rem_Read Rev Tut. Outdoor ed.

Sports (req'd)—Basket Crew X-country Golf Soccer Tennis Ultimate_Frisbee. B: Lacrosse Wrestling. G: Softball Volley. **Activities:** 14.

Selective adm: 53/yr. Bdg 46. Day 7. Usual entry: 8, 9 & 10. Appl fee: $85. Appl due: Rolling. Applied: 273. Accepted: 56%. Yield: 42%. **Tests** CEEB IQ ISEE SSAT Stanford TOEFL.

Enr 132. B 79. G 53. Bdg 106. Day 26. Elem 7. Sec 124. PG 1. Wh 35%. Latino 3%. Blk 6%. Asian 42%. Other 14%. Intl 45%. Avg class size: 12. Stud/fac: 6:1. Uniform. **Fac 36.** M 21/F 15. FT 26/PT 10. Wh 88%. Latino 3%. Blk 6%. Asian 3%. Adv deg: 55%. In dorms 9.

Grad '11—31. Col—31. (Boston U 2, UCLA 2, Valparaiso U 2, Centenary-NJ 2, NYU 1, Cornell 1). **Avg SAT:** CR 436. M 602. W 464. Avg ACT: 24. **Col couns:** 1. Alum donors: 10%.

Tui '12-'13: Bdg $32,900-49,950 (+$1375). **Day $13,100-30,200** (+$1175). **Intl Bdg $32,900-49,950** (+$9525). **Aid:** Merit 12 ($110,000). Need 25 ($291,000).

Endow $1,000,000. Plant val $25,000,000. Acres 55. Bldgs 22 (92% ADA). Dorms 4. Dorm rms 73. Class rms 22. Libs 1. Sci labs 2. Lang labs 1. Observatories 1. Auds 1. Theaters 1. Art studios 4. Music studios 3. Dance studios 1. Gyms 1. Fields 3. Courts 5. Comp labs 1.

Est 1867. Nonprofit. Tri (Sept-June). **Assoc** CLS MSA.

Storm King conducts a flexible and individualized academic curriculum that features an array of Advanced Placement classes and electives. Performing and visual arts programs include studio art, sculpture, photography and printmaking, as well as theatrical productions and a variety of music and dance options.

The Mountain Center Program offers support and differentiated instruction in core classes to college-bound students with specific educational needs or mild learning differences. In addition, a learning center assists boys and girls with study and organizational skills.

All students must participate in a daily afternoon activity—either athletic or extracurricular—each season; boys and girls take part in one compulsory interscholastic sport per year and another required athletic offering. Pupils also engage in at least two compulsory community service experiences each year.

DOBBS FERRY, NY. (24 mi. N of New York, NY) Suburban. Pop: 10,662. Alt: 12 ft.

THE MASTERS SCHOOL

Bdg — Coed Gr 9-12; Day — Coed 5-12
(Coord — Day 6-8)

Dobbs Ferry, NY 10522. 49 Clinton Ave. Tel: 914-479-6420. Fax: 914-693-7295.
www.mastersny.org E-mail: admission@mastersny.org

Maureen Fonseca, Head (2000). BA, Vassar College, MA, PhD, Fordham Univ. **Mary A. Schellhorn, Adm.**

Col Prep. AP (exams req'd; 188 taken)—Eng Fr Lat Span Calc Stats Bio Chem Physics Eur_Hist US_Hist Studio_Art Music_Theory. **Feat**—Women's_Lit Chin Greek Bioethics Environ_Sci Programming Web_Design Amer_Stud Econ Pol_Sci Psych Ethics World_Relig Art_Hist Ceramics Film Graphic_Arts Photog Video_Production Drama Music_Hist Dance Journ. **Supp**—ESL.

Sports—Basket X-country Fencing Golf Lacrosse Soccer Tennis Track. B: Baseball. G:

F_Hockey Softball Volley.
Selective adm (Bdg Gr 9-11; Day 5-11): 158/yr. Bdg 58. Day 100. Appl fee: $50. Appl due: Jan. Accepted: 47%. Yield: 60%. **Tests** ISEE SSAT TOEFL.
Enr 580. Bdg 160. Day 420. Elem 160. Sec 420. Intl 14%. Avg class size: 14. Stud/fac: 6:1. **Fac 90.** M 41/F 49. FT 90. Wh 88%. Latino 4%. Blk 5%. Asian 3%. Adv deg: 91%. In dorms 47.
Grad '10—99. Col—96. (Cornell 5, NYU 5, Barnard 4, Skidmore 4, Geo Wash 4, U of Richmond 3). **Avg SAT:** CR/M 1235. **Col couns:** 3. Alum donors: 23%.
Tui '11-'12: Bdg $47,780 (+$1500). **5-Day Bdg $43,780** (+$1500). **Day $32,710-33,830** (+$1500). **Aid:** Need 145 ($3,800,000).
Endow $20,500,000. Plant val $20,280,000. Acres 96. Bldgs 12. Dorms 6. Dorm rms 120. Class rms 55. Lib 28,000 vols. Sci labs 4. Lang labs 1. Photog labs 2. Auds 1. Theaters 1. Art studios 2. Music studios 6. Dance studios 1. Gyms 1. Athletic ctrs 1. Fields 5. Tennis courts 9.
Est 1877. Nonprofit. Sem (Sept-June). **Assoc** CLS MSA.

Established as a school for girls by Eliza B. Masters and her sister, Sarah, the Masters School became coeducational in 1995, offering parallel middle schools (grades 5-8): one for girls and one for boys. The upper school (grades 9-12) presents a coeducational framework, following the Harkness method of teaching, which features an oval table in each classroom around which students and teacher actively engage in learning.

Masters offers a college preparatory curriculum that includes more than a dozen Advanced Placement courses. The visual and performing arts program has extensive facilities and is an integral part of the school. Teachers use the cultural resources of Westchester County and New York City to augment their courses. The school provides ESL instruction at intermediate and advanced levels. Seniors may complete a Masters Thesis, a rigorous, guided course of interdisciplinary study requiring two long papers and a creative project.

Some students are selected to participate in CITYterm, a semester-long, interdisciplinary urban studies program that draws upon the resources of New York City for its academic and experiential curriculum (see separate listing).

HOOSICK, NY. (28 mi. ENE of Albany, NY; 155 mi. NNE of New York, NY) Suburban. Pop: 6759. Alt: 458 ft.

HOOSAC SCHOOL

Bdg and Day — Coed Gr 8-PG

Hoosick, NY 12089. Pine Valley Rd, PO Box 9. Tel: 518-686-7331, 800-822-0159.
  Fax: 518-686-3370.
  www.hoosac.com   E-mail: info@hoosac.com
Dean S. Foster, Head (2011). BA, State Univ of New York-Albany, MA, George Washington Univ. **Michael Foster, Adm.**
Col Prep. AP—Eng Calc US_Hist Studio_Art. **Feat**—British_Lit Fr Astron Computers Holocaust Psych Ethics Theol Art_Hist Film Photog Sculpt Drama Music Dance Journ Marketing. **Supp**—ESL LD Rev Tut. Sat classes.
Sports—Basket Lacrosse Soccer. B: Baseball X-country Ice_Hockey Tennis.
Nonselective adm (Gr 8-10): 40/yr. Bdg 37. Day 3. Appl fee: $30. Appl due: Rolling. Applied: 140. Accepted: 100%.
Enr 120. B 83. G 37. Bdg 110. Day 10. Elem 7. Sec 110. PG 3. Wh 77%. Blk 8%. Asian 15%. Intl 25%. Avg class size: 8. **Fac 16.** M 10/F 6. FT 16. Wh 100%. Adv deg: 37%. In dorms 11.
Grad '10—37. Col—37. (Bowdoin, Boston Col, Purdue, Rensselaer Polytech, Cornell, Hobart/Wm Smith). **Avg SAT:** CR 600. M 600. W 600. Alum donors: 50%.
Tui '11-'12: Bdg $41,230 (+$1320). **Day $16,320** (+$200). **Intl Bdg $41,230** (+$1320-5320). **Aid:** Need 28 ($525,000).

Endow $1,093,000. Plant val $11,500,000. Bldgs 16. Dorms 9. Dorm rms 65. Class rms 15. Lib 10,000 vols. Sci labs 2. Dark rms 1. Observatories 1. Auds 1. Art studios 1. Arts ctrs 1. Wood shops 1. Gyms 1. Athletic ctrs 1. Fields 7. Courts 3. Pools 1. Skiing facilities. Ponds 1. Comp labs 2.
Est 1889. Nonprofit. Episcopal. Tri (Sept-June). **Assoc** MSA.

Founded by Dr. Edward D. Tibbits, Hoosac was perhaps the first American boarding school to develop a work program where students play a role in maintaining their environment.

The curriculum encompasses a wide range of academic skills and includes advanced work, independent projects and tutorials, in addition to formal and remedial classes. Classes are held six days each week with five-day breaks in the middle of each trimester and three-week vacations in winter and spring. Hoosac utilizes a mastery education approach whereby the student may retake an exam until he or she exhibits sufficient mastery of the subject matter. An advisor system and a low student-teacher ratio are important aspects of the school's program.

All students perform at least 10 hours of community service prior to graduation. In addition to a varied selection of varsity sports, Hoosac offers a skiing and snowboarding program.

KATONAH, NY. (43 mi. NNE of New York, NY) Rural. Pop: 2340. Alt: 320 ft.

THE HARVEY SCHOOL
5-Day Bdg — Coed Gr 9-12; Day — Coed 6-12

Katonah, NY 10536. 260 Jay St. Tel: 914-232-3161. Fax: 914-232-6034.
www.harveyschool.org   E-mail: admissions@harveyschool.org
Barry W. Fenstermacher, Head (1986). BA, Drew Univ. **William P. Porter III, Adm.**
Col Prep. AP (exams req'd; 72 taken)—Eng Lat Span Calc Comp_Sci Bio Chem Physics Eur_Hist US_Hist. **Feat**—Playwriting Fr Greek Japan Bioethics Ecol Forensic_Sci Genetics Sports_Med Women's_Hist Psych Art_Hist Ceramics Studio_Art Video_Production Theater Music Dance. **Supp**—Makeup Rev Tut.
Sports—Basket Soccer Tennis. B: Baseball Football Ice_Hockey Lacrosse Rugby. G: Softball Volley.
Selective adm: 95/yr. Bdg 8. Day 87. Appl fee: $50. Appl due: Rolling. Accepted: 45%. Yield: 80%.
Enr 345. Avg class size: 12. **Fac 64.** M 35/F 29. FT 55/PT 9. Adv deg: 42%. In dorms 8.
Grad '11—63. Col—63. (Boston U, Holy Cross, Drew, IN U, Occidental, Trinity Col-CT).
Col couns: 4. Alum donors: 3%.
Tui '11-'12: 5-Day Bdg $38,950 (+$600-800). **Day $31,000-31,950** (+$600-800).
Summer: Acad Enrich. 6 wks.
Endow $3,000,000. Plant val $6,000,000. Acres 100. Bldgs 12. Dorms 2. Dorm rms 30. Class rms 20. Lib 20,000 vols. Labs 4. Art studios 3. Music studios 1. Gyms 1. Fields 6. Rinks 1.
Est 1916. Nonprofit. Tri (Sept-June).

The school was founded by Dr. Herbert Carter, a physician from New York City. Originally located at Dr. Carter's farm in Hawthorne, Harvey provided the traditional education of an English prep school for boys in grades 4-8. In 1959, construction on the Taconic Parkway forced the school to relocate to the 100-acre Sylvan Weil estate, where it started to draw a population of day students. Harvey began the transition to its current structure with a middle and an upper school in 1969 and subsequently, in 1971, enrolled the first female day students. In 1987, the boarding program was converted to a five-day option and girls were given the option to board.

Harvey offers a traditional college preparatory curriculum, with classes ranging from basic levels to Advanced Placement and honors courses. Pupils attend small classes while fulfilling requirements in English, math, science, history and the arts. The Krasne Project provides for the integration of computer technology into most subjects and allows students to work at two

Internet-accessible computer labs. Strong art, music, drama and creative writing programs enrich the curriculum.

Extracurriculars are mandatory for all except junior and senior day students. Most compete in Harvey's interscholastic athletic program, and a range of clubs and other activities is also available. Pupils may specially arrange off-campus participation in such pursuits as gymnastics, martial arts, skiing and swimming.

LAKE PLACID, NY. (112 mi. N of Albany, NY) Rural. Pop: 2638. Alt: 1742 ft.

NORTH COUNTRY SCHOOL
Bdg and Day — Coed Gr 4-9

Lake Placid, NY 12946. 4382 Cascade Rd. Tel: 518-523-9329. Fax: 518-523-4858.
www.northcountryschool.org   E-mail: admissions@northcountryschool.org
David Hochschartner, Dir (1999). BA, Union College, MEd, Columbia Univ. Christine LeFevre, Adm.

Pre-Prep. Gen Acad. Feat—Span Computers Studio_Art Music Dance Mountaineering. **Supp**—Dev_Read ESL LD Rem_Math Rem_Read Tut.
Selective adm: 33/yr. Bdg 28. Day 5. Appl due: Rolling. Accepted: 75%.
Enr 89. B 40. G 49. Bdg 78. Day 11. Elem 63. Sec 26. Wh 88%. Blk 12%. Intl 22%. Avg class size: 13. Stud/fac: 3:1. **Fac 32.** M 15/F 17. FT 26/PT 6. Wh 94%. Latino 3%. Blk 3%. Adv deg: 18%. In dorms 16.
Grad '11—23. Prep—7. (Gould 4, Northfield Mt Hermon 1, Phillips Exeter 1, Dublin 1).
Tui '12-'13: Bdg $54,100 (+$200). **5-Day Bdg $44,100** (+$200). **Day $23,200** (+$200).
Intl Bdg $58,100 (+$200-4200). **Aid:** Need 25 ($543,538).
Summer: Enrich Rec. Tui Bdg $8300. 7 wks.
Endow $8,000,000. Plant val $3,000,000. Acres 200. Bldgs 11. Dorms 6. Dorm rms 40. Class rms 15. Lib 8000 vols. Sci labs 2. Lang labs 1. Auds 1. Art studios 4. Music studios 3. Dance studios 1. Gyms 1. Fields 2. Basketball courts 2. Riding rings 1. Skiing facilities. Barns 1. Comp labs 1. Comp/stud: 1:3.
Est 1938. Nonprofit. Tri (Sept-June).

NCS is located on a 200-acre working farm in the Adirondack Forest Preserve, a wilderness area of mountains, lakes and forests. Children, who live in house groups of eight to 10 under the supervision of a teaching-staff couple, participate in all phases of housework and farm work. The school grows many of its own vegetables organically. Along with formal school work, each child has some daily responsibility.

A solid curriculum in the basic subjects prepares graduates for leading preparatory schools and is reinforced through field trips to points of environmental, cultural and social significance. Facilities for music study in orchestral instruments, piano and voice are offered. The arts program offers creative work in painting, drawing, sculpture, weaving, ceramics, woodwork, batik and photography. Practical shop work is gained through routine repairs and construction around the premises.

Physical exercise balances useful, productive work with recreation and sport. Skating, skiing on the school's rope-tow-equipped hill, cross-country skiing and snowshoeing are winter pursuits. Mountaineering and hiking opportunities exist year-round, and Lake Placid's 1980 Winter Olympics facilities are only seven miles away.   **See Also Page 63**

NORTHWOOD SCHOOL
Bdg and Day — Coed Gr 9-PG

Lake Placid, NY 12946. 92 Northwood Rd, PO Box 1070. Tel: 518-523-3357.
Fax: 518-523-3405.

www.northwoodschool.com   E-mail: admissions@northwoodschool.com
Edward M. Good, Head (1997). AB, Bowdoin College, MAT, Brown Univ. **Timothy Weaver, Adm.**
 Col Prep. AP (exams req'd; 60 taken, 75% 3+)—Eng Calc Bio US_Hist. **Feat**—Fr Span Stats Environ_Sci Geol Irish_Hist Anthro Law Psych Sociol Ceramics Drawing Photog Sculpt Studio_Art Music Study_Skills. **Supp**—ESL Tut. Outdoor ed.
 Sports—Crew Ice_Hockey Lacrosse Ski Soccer Tennis.
 Selective adm: 82/yr. Bdg 68. Day 14. Appl fee: $50. Appl due: Rolling. Applied: 203. Accepted: 65%. Yield: 60%. **Tests** ISEE SSAT TOEFL.
 Enr 180. B 118. G 62. Bdg 144. Day 36. Sec 168. PG 12. Wh 87%. Latino 3%. Asian 10%. Intl 35%. Avg class size: 8. Stud/fac: 6:1. Casual. **Fac 30.** M 21/F 9. FT 25/PT 5. Adv deg: 53%. In dorms 16.
 Grad '10—57. **Col**—57. (Utica 4, Hobart/Wm Smith 3, Plymouth St 3, Skidmore 2, U of Pittsburgh 2, St Mary's U of MN 2). Athl schol 4. **Mid 50% SAT:** CR 480-590. M 500-630. W 490-600. Avg ACT: 23. **Col couns:** 2.
 Tui '12-'13: Bdg $46,425 (+$1125). **Day $26,725** (+$1125). **Intl Bdg $45,425** (+$2125-4125). **Aid:** Need 89 ($1,190,420).
 Endow $8,000,000. Plant val $6,000,000. Acres 85. Bldgs 9. Dorms 4. Dorm rms 105. Class rms 18. Lib 20,000 vols. Sci labs 4. Lang labs 1. Auds 1. Art studios 4. Music studios 1. Gyms 1. Fields 4. Courts 7. Comp labs 1.
 Est 1905. Nonprofit. Sem (Sept-June). **Assoc** CLS.

Northwood's rigorous academic program emphasizes college preparation in a structured, small-class setting. Advanced Placement and honors courses, as well as a varied choice of electives, supplement the standard curricular offerings. The school also maintains a particularly strong arts program.

Students gain opportunities for initiative and responsibility through a broadly based student government program. The school enables pupils to engage in many different kinds of community service projects. A strong board of trustees has aided the growth of the school, which attracts able students from a wide area.

Supplementing the full athletic program are local woodland and mountain areas and the nearby Olympic Arena, all of which provide opportunities for alpine and freestyle skiing, snowboarding and other winter sports. **See Also Page 101**

LOCUST VALLEY, NY. (24 mi. NE of New York, NY) Suburban. Pop: 3521. Alt: 121 ft.

FRIENDS ACADEMY

Day — Coed Gr PS (Age 3)-12

Locust Valley, NY 11560. 270 Duck Pond Rd. Tel: 516-676-0393. Fax: 516-393-4276.
www.fa.org   E-mail: admissions@fa.org
William G. Morris, Jr., Head. BA, Bucknell Univ, MA, Univ of Connecticut, MA, Columbia Univ. **Nina Waechter, Adm.**
 Col Prep. AP (exams req'd)—Eng Fr Lat Span Calc Stats Bio Chem Environ_Sci Physics Eur_Hist US_Hist US_Govt & Pol Studio_Art Music_Theory. **Feat**—Creative_Writing Poetry Shakespeare Sci_Fiction Chin Greek Anat & Physiol Genetics Marine_Bio/Sci Computers Web_Design Amer_Stud Econ Psych Relig Photog Video_Production Theater_Arts Music Journ. Outdoor ed.
 Sports—Basket Crew X-country Golf Indoor_Track Lacrosse Soccer Tennis Track. B: Baseball Football. G: Cheer F_Hockey Softball. **Activities:** 50.
 Selective adm: 137/yr. Appl fee: $55-75. Appl due: Jan. Applied: 394. Accepted: 44%. Yield: 79%. **Tests** CEEB SSAT.
 Enr 777. Elem 398. Sec 379. Wh 77%. Latino 2%. Blk 7%. Asian 6%. Other 8%. Avg class size: 13. Stud/fac: 7:1. **Fac 78.** M 43/F 35. FT 78. Wh 83%. Latino 1%. Blk 12%. Asian 4%. Adv deg: 80%.

Grad '11—87. Col—87. (Dartmouth 5, Bucknell 5, Barnard 4, Duke 3, Colgate 3, Cornell 3). Athl schol 12. **Avg SAT:** CR/M 1240. **Col couns:** 3.
Tui '11-'12: Day $23,500-27,600 (+$400-600). **Aid:** Need 88 ($1,528,200).
Summer (enr 250): Enrich Rec. Arts. Tui Day $3895-5995. 4-8 wks.
Endow $30,000,000. Plant val $79,800,000. Acres 65. Bldgs 10 (100% ADA). Class rms 50. 2 Libs 35,000 vols. Sci labs 5. Lang labs 2. Photog labs 1. Comp ctrs 1. Auds 1. Theaters 1. Art studios 5. Music studios 5. Dance studios 3. Gyms 2. Fields 6. Courts 7. Field houses 1. Pools 2. Comp labs 5. Comp/stud: 1:2 (1:1 Laptop prgm Gr 5-6).
Est 1876. Nonprofit. Religious Society of Friends. Sem (Sept-June). **Assoc** CLS.

Founded by local businessman Gideon Frost for "the children of Friends and those similarly sentimented," the academy continues to reflect Quaker educational principles. The college preparatory curriculum features Advanced Placement courses and an array of electives. Technology is an important aspect of the program. For three weeks each spring, seniors pursue off-campus independent service projects that are related to their special interests.

Students assist in decision making through the student-faculty board.

PORTLEDGE SCHOOL

Day — Coed Gr PS (Age 2)-12

Locust Valley, NY 11560. 355 Duck Pond Rd. Tel: 516-750-3100. Fax: 516-671-2039.
www.portledge.org E-mail: mcoope@portledge.org
Steven L. Hahn, Head (2006). AB, Princeton Univ, MA, EdM, Harvard Univ. **Michael Coope, Adm.**
Col Prep. AP (exams req'd)—Eng Fr Span Calc Chem Environ_Sci Physics US_Hist Music_Theory. **Feat**—Creative_Writing Shakespeare Stats Anat & Physiol Astron Comp_Sci Cold_War Russ_Hist Psych World_Relig Architect Ceramics Photog Sculpt Theater_Arts Music Journ Public_Speak.
Sports—Basket X-country Fencing Ice_Hockey Lacrosse Soccer Squash Tennis. B: Baseball Golf. G: Softball. **Activities:** 20.
Selective adm (Gr PS-11): 73/yr. Appl fee: $75. Appl due: Feb. Accepted: 58%. Yield: 65%. **Tests** SSAT.
Enr 381. Elem 208. Sec 173. Avg class size: 12. Stud/fac: 8:1. **Fac 70.** M 20/F 50. FT 66/PT 4. Adv deg: 54%.
Grad '11—55. Col—52. (Tulane 3, Fordham 2, Hofstra 2, Villanova 2, U of VT 2, NY Inst of Tech 2). **Avg SAT:** CR 662. M 620. W 598. Alum donors: 17%.
Tui '09-'10: Day $13,500-28,000 (+$300).
Summer: Acad Enrich Rec. Environ Sci. Music. Drama. Sports. 6 wks.
Endow $1,600,000. Plant val $9,000,000. Acres 62. Bldgs 5. Class rms 56. 2 Libs 17,000 vols. Sci labs 6. Dark rms 1. Auds 1. Art studios 2. Music studios 4. Wood shops 1. Gyms 2. Fields 4. Courts 5. Comp labs 2.
Est 1933. Nonprofit. Sem (Sept-June). **Assoc** CLS.

Serving Nassau and Suffolk counties, Portledge is located in the North Shore community of Locust Valley. The outgrowth of Miss Stoddart's elementary school, Portledge moved to its 62-acre campus in 1965 and began adding a grade each year. The school graduated its first senior class in 1976.

Portledge provides a traditional college preparatory program. French and computer instruction begin in kindergarten, lab science in grade 3, and ability grouping for academically advanced students in grade 5. Advanced Placement courses are available in all major disciplines, and the school also conducts strong art and music programs. Student government shares the responsibility for the implementation of rules and for participation in the community service program; boys and girls in grades 9-12 perform 10 hours of compulsory service per year.

The school's campus is adjacent to a 75-acre sanctuary.

MILLBROOK, NY. (52 mi. W of Hartford, CT; 78 mi. N of New York, NY) Rural. Pop: 1429. Alt: 567 ft.

DUTCHESS DAY SCHOOL
Day — Coed Gr PS (Age 3)-8

Millbrook, NY 12545. 415 Rte 343. Tel: 845-677-5014. Fax: 845-677-6722.
www.dutchessday.org E-mail: admissions@dutchessday.org
Nancy N. Hathaway, Head (2010). BA, Smith College, MA, Western Connecticut State Univ. **Christine Whiting, Adm.**
Pre-Prep. Feat—Fr Lat Span Computers Studio_Art Music Health Study_Skills. **Supp**—Tut.
Sports—Basket X-country Golf Lacrosse Soccer Squash Tennis Volley. G: F_Hockey.
Selective adm: 26/yr. Usual entry: PS, K & 5. Appl fee: $50. Appl due: Rolling. Accepted: 80%. Yield: 80%.
Enr 133. Wh 87%. Latino 4%. Blk 1%. Asian 8%. Avg class size: 17. Stud/fac: 6:1. **Fac 25.** M 3/F 22. FT 22/PT 3. Adv deg: 76%.
Grad '11—14. Prep—9. (Millbrook 2, Kent Sch-CT 2, Taft 1, Hotchkiss 1, Emma Willard 1, Berkshire Sch 1).
Tui '12-'13: Day $19,000-21,980 (+$300).
Summer: Acad Enrich Rec. 1 wk.
Endow $2,900,000. Acres 30. Bldgs 3. Class rms 17. Lib 6300 vols. Labs 2. Art studios 1. Music studios 1. Gyms 2. Fields 3. Ponds 1.
Est 1955. Nonprofit. Quar (Sept-June).

Founded by a group of local parents, DDS offers a traditional curriculum designed to prepare students for secondary school. The academic program emphasizes the development of fundamental skills, and small classes allow students to pursue individual projects and interests. Offerings in computer, foreign language and the arts enrich the curriculum. Students in grades 5-8 may take part in the interscholastic athletic program.

MILLBROOK SCHOOL
Bdg and Day — Coed Gr 9-PG

Millbrook, NY 12545. 131 Millbrook School Rd. Tel: 845-677-8261. Fax: 845-677-8598.
www.millbrook.org E-mail: admissions@millbrook.org
Drew J. Casertano, Head (1990). BA, Amherst College, EdM, Harvard Univ. **Jonathan Downs, Adm.**
Col Prep. AP (exams req'd)—Eng Fr Span Calc. **Feat**—Creative_Writing Playwriting Chin Lat Stats Discrete_Math Astron Environ_Sci Animal_Behavior Middle_Eastern_Hist Anthro Econ Psych Constitutional_Law Philos Ceramics Drawing Photog Video_Production Acting Music_Theory Public_Speak. **Supp**—ESL Tut. Sat classes.
Sports (req'd)—Basket X-country Golf Ice_Hockey Lacrosse Soccer Squash Tennis. B: Baseball. G: F_Hockey Softball. **Activities:** 48.
Selective adm (Gr 9-12): 86/yr. Bdg 71. Day 15. Appl fee: $50. Appl due: Jan. Applied: 420. Accepted: 47%. Yield: 42%. **Tests** CEEB ISEE SSAT TOEFL.
Enr 260. Bdg 208. Day 52. Sec 257. PG 3. Wh 88%. Latino 6%. Blk 3%. Asian 3%. Intl 12%. Avg class size: 14. Stud/fac: 5:1. Casual. **Fac 72.** M 34/F 38. FT 60/PT 12. Wh 98%. Latino 1%. Blk 1%. Adv deg: 48%. In dorms 24.
Grad '11—64. Col—64. (Geo Wash, Bucknell, Franklin & Marshall, Hobart/Wm Smith, Denison, Middlebury). **Avg SAT:** CR 569. M 567. W 561. **Mid 50% SAT:** CR 500-620. M 500-630. W 510-620. Avg ACT: 22. **Col couns:** 4. Alum donors: 34%.
Tui '12-'13: Bdg $49,400 (+$1450-1850). **Day $36,600** (+$1450-1850). **Intl Bdg $49,400** (+$1950-2350). **Aid:** Need 70 ($2,148,000).
Endow $23,000,000. Plant val $50,200,000. Acres 800. Bldgs 69. Dorms 7. Dorm rms 113. Class rms 31. Lib 18,000 vols. Sci labs 4. Dark rms 1. Comp ctrs 1. Observatories

1. Art studios 4. Music studios 5. Dance studios 1. Arts ctrs 1. Gyms 1. Athletic ctrs 1. Fields 9. Basketball courts 1. Tennis courts 7. Squash courts 4. Rinks 1. Stables 4. **Est 1931.** Nonprofit. Sem (Sept-June). **Assoc** CLS.

Founded by Edward Pulling, this small school combines college preparation with particularly strong science, arts and school service programs. Originally a boys' boarding school, Millbrook first admitted girls as day students in 1971, and as boarding students in 1975. The academic program offers a rigorous, traditional curriculum featuring a variety of AP courses, independent studies and electives, as well as field trips in the arts and sciences, forums with guest speakers, and student news and literary publications. In addition, the school conducts a weeklong intersession in which student explore interests outside the classroom or off campus.

The 800-acre campus includes a wetlands sanctuary and boardwalk, nature trails, a forest canopy walkway, the six-acre, nationally accredited Trevor Zoo, an observatory and a weather station. Science classes utilize these resources and the school's natural surroundings. Boys and girls interested in the sciences may engage in a special program at Trevor Zoo, a living laboratory that serves as a center for student research and service, for the captive breeding of endangered species and for the recovery of sick or injured native animals. Environmental science, astronomy and zoo research are among the many science electives.

A 34,000-square-foot arts center is the setting for Millbrook's well-developed arts program. Roughly three-quarters of the student body enroll in an arts course each term. Offerings include dance, choreography, ceramics, photography, acting, and musical performance and history. Pupils participating in the arts have frequent opportunities for performance and exhibition.

Each student plays an active role in the functioning of the school and is required to choose one activity in the community service program. Students may, for example, manage the school store, run the community outreach program, recycle and compost campus materials, work at the school bank or care for animals at the zoo. Boys and girls also have various leadership opportunities, and Millbrook maintains a peer counseling program in which students provide support for fellow pupils.

Students must play team sports during at least two of the three athletic seasons. Alternative selections include horseback riding, zoo squad, dance, an improvisational theater group and recreational sports.

NEW LEBANON, NY. (25 mi. SE of Albany, NY; 127 mi. NNE of New York, NY) Rural. Pop: 2454. Alt: 699 ft.

DARROW SCHOOL

Bdg and Day — Coed Gr 9-PG

New Lebanon, NY 12125. 110 Darrow Rd. Tel: 518-794-6000, 877-432-7769.
  Fax: 518-794-7065.
  www.darrowschool.org   E-mail: hicksj@darrowschool.org
Nancy Maslack Wolf, Head (2000). BA, Ithaca College, MEd, Loyola College. **Jamie Hicks-Furgang, Adm.**
  Col Prep. Feat—Fr Span Anat & Physiol Astron Ecol Environ_Sci Ornithology Comp_Sci Civil_Rights Econ Psych Ethics Ceramics Drawing Graphic_Arts Painting Studio_Art Woodworking. **Supp**—ESL Rev Tut. Outdoor ed. Sat classes.
  Sports (req'd)—Basket X-country Soccer Tennis Ultimate_Frisbee. B: Baseball Lacrosse. G: Softball.
  Selective adm (Gr 9-12): 44/yr. Bdg 34. Day 10. Appl fee: $50. Appl due: Rolling. Applied: 162. Accepted: 57%. Yield: 47%. **Tests** CEEB CTP_4 ISEE SSAT Stanford TOEFL.
  Enr 116. B 60. G 56. Bdg 90. Day 26. Intl 28%. Avg class size: 9. Stud/fac: 4:1. Casual.
  Fac 28. M 17/F 11. FT 28. Adv deg: 60%. In dorms 13.
  Grad '07—29. Col—28. (NYU, Northeastern U, Mt Holyoke, Hobart/Wm Smith). **Avg SAT:** CR/M 1025. **Col couns:** 1.

Tui '12-'13: Bdg $49,600 (+$3900-7800). **Day** $28,300 (+$3900-11,700). **Intl Bdg** $49,600 (+$3900-11,700). **Aid:** Need 36 ($1,001,850).
Summer (enr 8): ESL. Tui Bdg $3900. 3 wks.
Endow $2,500,000. Plant val $4,500,000. Acres 360. Bldgs 24. Dorms 6. Dorm rms 50. Class rms 15. Lib 15,000 vols. Sci labs 4. Theaters 1. Art studios 1. Arts ctrs 1. Gyms 1. Athletic ctrs 1. Fields 4. Courts 2. Skiing facilities. Comp labs 3. Comp/stud: 1:2.
Est 1932. Nonprofit. Sem (Sept-June). **Assoc** MSA.

Darrow occupies the 360-acre site and buildings of the first and largest organized Shaker village in America, established in 1787. Originally the Lebanon School for Boys, which opened its doors under the direction of Charles H. Jones, the school was later renamed after George Darrow, the farmer who had originally donated the land to the Shakers, and became coeducational in 1970.

The school offers a college preparatory curriculum within a structured, supportive environment. Small classes, individual advisors, supervised study and a strong tutorial program provide individual attention for each student.

Darrow recognizes different learning styles and serves students with a variety of abilities. The comprehensive curriculum offers a range of courses in English, history, languages, mathematics and science, as well as art, music and drama. A number of electives are also available. A weeklong program of intensive experiential learning courses is conducted each spring. An important aspect of the academic program is its environmental focus: An environmental center features a working wastewater treatment process situated in an 1800-square-foot greenhouse. Hands-on assistance with the center's operation familiarizes pupils with new technologies, and students develop public-speaking skills by conducting tours of the facility.

As an outgrowth of the Shaker motto "Hands to Work, Hearts to God," the school sets aside Wednesday mornings to foster the dignity of labor and cooperative effort. All members of the community—administrators, teachers and students—participate in such projects and tasks as chopping wood, making apple cider and maple syrup, landscaping, woodworking and Habitat for Humanity.

NEW YORK, NY. Urban. Pop: 7,428,162. Alt: 54 ft.

ALLEN-STEVENSON SCHOOL
Day — Boys Gr K-9

New York, NY 10075. 132 E 78th St. Tel: 212-288-6710. Fax: 212-288-6802.
www.allen-stevenson.org   E-mail: info@allen-stevenson.org
David R. Trower, Head (1990). AB, Brown Univ, MDiv, Union Theological Seminary. **Ronnie R. Jankoff, Adm.**
Pre-Prep. Feat—Fr Span Computers Music. **Supp**—Dev_Read Rem_Read Rev Tut.
Sports—B: Basket Football Ice_Hockey Lacrosse Soccer Track Wrestling.
Very selective adm: 65/yr. Usual entry: K & 6. Appl fee: $60. Appl due: Oct. Applied: 425. Accepted: 17%. Yield: 75%. **Tests** ISEE.
Enr 418. Elem 409. Sec 9. Wh 75%. Latino 3%. Blk 7%. Asian 5%. Other 10%. Avg class size: 20. Stud/fac: 7:1. Uniform. **Fac 122.** M 60/F 62. FT 68/PT 54. Wh 64%. Latino 12%. Blk 7%. Asian 9%. Other 8%. Adv deg: 47%.
Grad '11—35. Prep—32. (Riverdale 4, Phillips Exeter 3, Fieldston 3, Poly Prep 2, Trinity Sch-NY 2). Alum donors: 18%.
Tui '12-'13: Day $38,000. **Aid:** Need 59 ($1,570,370).
Summer (enr 70): Rec. Tui Day $840-1025. 2 wks.
Endow $20,000,000. Plant val $37,000,000. Bldgs 1. Class rms 26. Lib 13,234 vols. Sci labs 3. Auds 1. Theaters 1. Art studios 2. Music studios 2. Shops 1. Gyms 1. Comp labs 2. Comp/stud: 1:2.
Est 1883. Nonprofit. Sem (Sept-June).

Founded by Francis B. Allen, the school merged in 1904 with the one started by Robert A. Stevenson. Allen-Stevenson's traditional curriculum prepares students for entrance to secondary schools. In addition to the basic subjects, the curriculum includes foreign language, computers, shop, music, art and physical education.

Allen-Stevenson's after-school program, Alligator Soup, features interscholastic and intramural sports, academic enrichment opportunities, homework assistance, supplementary foreign language instruction, cooking and outdoor education.

BEEKMAN SCHOOL
Day — Coed Gr 9-PG

New York, NY 10022. 220 E 50th St. Tel: 212-755-6666. Fax: 212-888-6085.
www.beekmanschool.org   E-mail: georgeh@beekmanschool.org
George Higgins, Head (1990). BA, Salisbury Univ, MA, New York Univ.
    Col Prep. Gen Acad. AP exams taken: 15 (60% 3+). Feat—Creative_Writing Poetry Sci_Fiction Span Astron Ecol Computers Web_Design Comp_Animation Anthro Econ Govt Intl_Relations Pol_Sci Psych Philos Film Photog Studio_Art Finance. Supp—Dev_Read ESL Makeup Rem_Math Rem_Read Rev Tut.
    Activities: 4.
    Selective adm (Gr 9-12): 25/yr. Usual entry: 9. Appl fee: $0. Appl due: Rolling.
    Enr 80. B 42. G 38. Sec 79. PG 1. Wh 71%. Latino 5%. Blk 9%. Asian 15%. Avg class size: 8. Stud/fac: 7:1. Fac 13. M 6/F 7. FT 9/PT 4. Wh 65%. Latino 20%. Asian 15%. Adv deg: 76%.
    Grad '11—25. Col—24. (Sarah Lawrence, Boston U, NYU, AZ St, Fordham, Marymount Manhattan). Avg SAT: CR 556. M 519. W 543. Col couns: 1.
    Tui '12-'13: Day $33,000 (+$0-500).
    Summer (enr 38): Acad Enrich Rev Rem. Tui Day $2200. 6 wks.
    Plant val $2,500,000. Bldgs 1. Class rms 8. Libs 1. Sci labs 1. Art studios 1. Gyms 1. Pools 1. Gardens 1. Comp labs 1.
    Est 1925. Inc. Quar (Sept-June).

Founded by George Matthew as the Tutoring School of New York, this small preparatory school is located in an East Side Manhattan townhouse. In the highly individualized program, the school does not place boys and girls in grades according to age, but rather by ability level. Beekman maintains a maximum class size of 10 students, and schedules are arranged according to the pupil's needs and abilities. Students requiring extra help in a given subject receive daily small-group instruction as a supplement to regular course work. A full complement of electives is available.

BIRCH WATHEN LENOX SCHOOL
Day — Coed Gr K-12

New York, NY 10075. 210 E 77th St. Tel: 212-861-0404. Fax: 212-879-3388.
www.bwl.org   E-mail: admissions@bwl.org
Frank J. Carnabuci III, Head (1992). BA, Drew Univ, MA, Columbia Univ, EdM, Harvard Univ. Julianne Kaplan, Adm.
    Col Prep. AP (exams req'd; 85 taken, 94% 3+)—Eng Fr Span Calc Bio Physics Eur_Hist US_Hist Studio_Art. Feat—Creative_Writing Shakespeare Japan Stats Anat & Physiol Astron Ecol Genetics Oceanog Meteorology Comp_Sci Web_Design Civil_Rights Anthro Philos Art_Hist Ceramics Drawing Film Photog Sculpt Acting Music Journ. Dual enr: Marymount Manhattan.
    Sports—Basket X-country Golf Swim Tennis. B: Baseball Ice_Hockey Soccer. G: Softball Volley. Activities: 41.
    Very selective adm: 41/yr. Usual entry: K, 6 & 9. Appl fee: $50. Appl due: Nov. Applied: 572. Accepted: 11%. Yield: 65%. Tests CEEB ISEE SSAT.
    Enr 565. Wh 82%. Latino 6%. Blk 6%. Asian 6%. Intl 20%. Avg class size: 17. Stud/fac:

6:1. Uniform. **Fac 125.** M 35/F 90. FT 115/PT 10. Wh 95%. Blk 1%. Other 4%. Adv deg: 65%.
Grad '11—51. Col—51. (Wesleyan U 2, Columbia 1, Princeton 1, Cornell 1, Dartmouth 1, Harvard 1). **Avg SAT:** CR 650. M 650. W 700. **Col couns:** 3. Alum donors: 37%.
Tui '12-'13: Day $37,923-38,950 (+$1900). **Aid:** Need 74 ($2,000,000).
Summer: Rec. Tui Day $550/wk. 2 wks.
Endow $5,400,000. Plant val $51,000,000. Bldgs 1. Class rms 51. Lib 22,000 vols. Labs 6. Auds 3. Art studios 5. Music studios 3. Gyms 1.
Est 1916. Nonprofit. (Sept-June). **Assoc** CLS.

Formed by the 1991 consolidation of the Birch Wathen School (founded in 1921) and the Lenox School (founded in 1916), Birch Wathen Lenox provides a challenging academic curriculum with a commitment to maintaining a balance among traditional education, innovation, student achievement and social development. This is achieved through small classes, individual attention and a favorable student-teacher ratio.

The curriculum includes a program in English, composition, math, science, history, foreign languages beginning in grade 4, computer science at all grade levels, art, instrumental and vocal music, word processing and woodworking. Advanced courses are available in all major curricular areas. In addition, students in grades 8-12 may take part in an overseas program that enables them to study the humanities and the social sciences under the supervision and the guidance of BWL faculty. Qualified seniors may pursue a career- or service-oriented internship project or earn college credit through courses Marymount Manhattan College.

Boys and girls in grades 6-8 perform 10 hours of on- or off-campus community service annually. In fulfilling their 30-hour service requirement over two years, freshmen and sophomores typically tutor children in the lower grades, assist in the science lab or catalog resources in the library. Juniors and seniors, who also have a 30-hour cumulative requirement, work with an outside agency or, with approval, perform duties in the lower or middle school.

BREARLEY SCHOOL

Day — Girls Gr K-12

New York, NY 10028. 610 E 83rd St. Tel: 212-744-8582. Fax: 212-472-8020.
www.brearley.org E-mail: admission@brearley.org
Jane Foley Fried, Head (2012). BA, Bowdoin College, MEd, Tufts Univ. **Joan Kaplan, Upper & Middle Sch Adm; Winifred M. Mabley, Lower Sch Adm.**
Col Prep. Feat—Chin Fr Greek Lat Span Calc Linear_Algebra Astron Comp_Sci Web_Design Chin & Japan_Hist Middle_Eastern_Hist Econ Philos Art_Hist Ceramics Photog Studio_Art Printmaking Acting Drama Music Music_Theory. **Supp**—Dev_ Read Rem_Math Rem_Read Rev Tut.
Sports—G: Badminton Basket X-country F_Hockey Gymnastics Lacrosse Soccer Softball Squash Swim Tennis Track Volley. **Activities:** 30.
Very selective adm (Gr K-10): 86/yr. Usual entry: K, 5, 6, 7 & 9. Appl fee: $65. Appl due: Dec. Accepted: 20%. Yield: 65%. **Tests** ISEE.
Enr 701. Elem 482. Sec 219. Wh 58%. Latino 4%. Blk 5%. Asian 12%. Other 21%. Avg class size: 12. Stud/fac: 6:1. **Fac 152.** M 34/F 118. FT 122/PT 30. Wh 81%. Latino 3%. Blk 3%. Asian 9%. Other 4%. Adv deg: 67%.
Grad '11—50. Col—50. (Yale 8, U of PA 5, Princeton 4, Columbia 2, Harvard 2, Williams 2). **Avg SAT:** CR/M 1432.
Tui '12-'13: Day $38,200. Aid: Need 143 ($4,000,000).
Summer: Rec. Tui Day $550-950. 1-2 wks.
Endow $115,700,000. Plant val $42,500,000. Bldgs 2. Class rms 60. Lib 26,000 vols. Sci labs 6. Auds 1. Art studios 5. Music studios 5. Dance studios 1. Gyms 3. Fields 1. Field houses 1. Comp labs 2.
Est 1884. Nonprofit. Sem (Sept-June).

Established by Samuel Brearley to provide a more substantial college preparatory program than most girls' schools of the time offered, Brearley has continuously maintained scholastic standards in the forefront among preparatory schools.

With a substantial scholarship program, the school seeks racial, religious and economic diversity in its student body. Since 1929 in a building overlooking the East River, the school offers a curriculum integrating many of the academic subjects and affording strong work in music and the arts. Mandarin language is first introduced in grade 1, and an integrated language program in the middle school (grades 5-8) adds French, Latin and Spanish options. Although Brearley offers no honors or Advanced Placement courses, the school's standard curriculum prepares girls for AP exams in all major disciplines. Classrooms, which are structured around seminar circles of desks or tables, typically feature electronic whiteboards, laptop computers and other technology.

Qualified sophomores, juniors and seniors may enroll in advanced science classes at Columbia University on Saturday mornings. Other off-campus learning opportunities in New York City include Saturday science seminars at Barnard College and US history courses at the Gilder Lehrman Institute of American History. Brearley conducts annual student exchanges with the Godolphin and Latymer School or the Francis Holland School in London, England, in grade 9 and, in grades 10-12, independent schools in Tokyo, Japan; Melbourne, Australia; and Kansas City, MO. Scholarships are available for summer travel and study abroad.

The school participates in a coordinated interscholastic academic and afternoon program with seven other New York City schools. Club sports commence in grade 5, while interscholastic competition begins in grade 7. Integrated community service projects progress from group endeavors to individual projects in grades 10-12.

THE BROWNING SCHOOL

Day — Boys Gr K-12

New York, NY 10065. 52 E 62nd St. Tel: 212-838-6280. Fax: 212-355-5602.
www.browning.edu   E-mail: csmith@browning.edu
Stephen M. Clement III, Head (1988). BA, Yale Univ, MDiv, Union Theological Seminary, EdM, EdD, Harvard Univ. **Liane Pei, Adm.**

> **Col Prep. AP (45 exams taken)**—Eng Fr Lat Span Calc Stats Chem Physics Eur_Hist US_Hist Studio_Art. **Elem math**—Scott Foresman-Addison Wesley. **Feat**—Greek Anat & Physiol Geol Comp_Sci Pol_Sci Psych Philos Art_Hist Ceramics Drawing Painting Visual_Arts Drama Chorus Music.
>
> **Sports**—B: Baseball Basket Crew X-country Fencing Golf Soccer Tennis Track. **Activities:** 17.
>
> **Selective adm (Gr K-10):** 59/yr. Usual entry: K & 9. Appl fee: $50. Appl due: Rolling. **Tests** ISEE SSAT.
>
> **Enr 388.** Elem 276. Sec 112. Wh 80%. Latino 5%. Blk 4%. Asian 7%. Other 4%. Avg class size: 15. Formal. **Fac 60.** Wh 93%. Latino 3%. Blk 2%. Asian 2%. Adv deg: 83%.
>
> **Grad '09**—25. **Col**—25. (Lehigh 2, Brown 1, Duke 1, Geo Wash 1, NYU 1, Skidmore 1). **Col couns:** 1.
>
> **Tui '11-'12: Day $37,900-38,280. Aid:** Need 54 ($1,524,042).
>
> **Summer:** Rec. 2 wks.
>
> Endow $16,756,000. Plant val $9,343,000. Bldgs 3. Class rms 21. Lib 12,353 vols. Sci labs 4. Art studios 2. Music studios 1. Gyms 2. Fields 2.
>
> **Est 1888.** Nonprofit. Tri (Sept-May).

Since its founding by John A. Browning, the school has offered a solid college preparatory program to students of varied interests and strong academic backgrounds. The curriculum offers elective courses in every department, and a wide variety of advanced courses and extracurricular activities is available.

Browning participates in a cooperative program with seven other New York City schools that offers opportunities for academic sharing and extracurricular participation throughout the year. Older students may also take coordinate courses at such local girls' schools as Marymount School and Hewitt School.

THE BUCKLEY SCHOOL
Day — Boys Gr K-9

New York, NY 10021. 113 E 73rd St. Tel: 212-535-8787. Fax: 212-535-4622.
Other locations: 209 E 73rd St, New York 10021; 210 E 74th St, New York 10021.
www.buckleyschool.org E-mail: admission@buckleyschool.org
Gregory J. O'Melia, Head (2001). AB, EdM, Harvard Univ. **Jo Ann E. Lynch, Adm.**
Pre-Prep. Feat—Fr Lat Span Computers Studio_Art Music Woodworking. **Supp**—Tut.
Sports (req'd)—B: Baseball Basket X-country Football Gymnastics Lacrosse Soccer Track Wrestling.
Very selective adm (Gr K-7): 46/yr. Appl fee: $55. Appl due: Rolling. Applied: 300. **Tests** IQ ISEE.
Enr 374. Elem 364. Sec 10. Wh 80%. Latino 1%. Blk 3%. Asian 3%. Other 13%. Avg class size: 20. Stud/fac: 6:1. Formal. **Fac 65.** M 28/F 37. FT 62/PT 3. Wh 80%. Latino 9%. Blk 8%. Asian 2%. Other 1%. Adv deg: 49%.
Grad '11—37. Prep—36. (Trinity Sch-NY 4, Phillips Acad 3, Dalton 3, Poly Prep 3, Riverdale 3, Deerfield Acad 2). Alum donors: 38%.
Tui '11-'12: Day $35,900. Aid: Need 33 ($907,000).
Endow $52,332,000. Plant val $75,000,000. Bldgs 3 (100% ADA). Class rms 42. 2 Libs 11,000 vols. Sci labs 3. Math labs 1. Auds 1. Theaters 1. Art studios 2. Music studios 1. Wood shops 1. Gyms 4. Fields 4. Courts 1. Comp labs 3. Comp/stud: 1:2.3.
Est 1913. Nonprofit. Sem (Sept-June).

The school was founded by B. Lord Buckley, a professional educator and innovator. Originally located above a milliner's shop on Madison Avenue, the school moved to larger quarters on 74th Street in 1917. After experiencing significant plant and educational improvements in response to changing times and a growing enrollment in the 1930s and 1940s, Buckley was fully remodeled in 1963. It then expanded and connected to an addition on 73rd Street. This expansion resulted in a broadening of the teaching program and the eventual addition of grade 9. Other plant improvements have followed, particularly after the 1996 acquisition of adjacent property on 73rd Street.

The balanced curriculum emphasizes mastery of academic fundamentals. During the lower school years (grades K-3), boys develop basic skills in the areas of reading, writing and math. Understanding of concepts and successful application of new skills take precedence over the rate of knowledge acquisition. Lower schoolers do not receive letter grades; instead, faculty submit to parents twice-yearly written comments concerning each area of the student's progress. In the transitional middle school years (grades 4-6), boys gain an increased level of independence while improving their academic skills and study habits.

The upper school program (grades 7-9) continues to stress the fundamentals, and boys may undertake more independent research projects, assume greater responsibility for class participation and develop their abstract thinking skills. The arts are integral to the program, beginning in the early years. A skills and remediation specialist provides small-group instruction at all grade levels.

All boys participate in the athletic program. After playing sports intramurally in the lower and middle school, all students engage in interscholastic competition at the junior varsity or varsity level.

CALHOUN SCHOOL
Day — Coed Gr PS (Age 3)-12

New York, NY 10024. 433 W End Ave. Tel: 212-497-6500. Fax: 212-497-6530.
Other locations: 160 W 74th St, New York 10023.
www.calhoun.org E-mail: angela.fischer@calhoun.org
Steven J. Nelson, Head (1998). BA, Case Western Reserve Univ. **Andrew Hume, Adm.**
Col Prep. Feat—Creative_Writing Shakespeare Playwriting Chin Fr Span Calc Stats Astron Bioethics Botany Programming Middle_Eastern_Hist Anthro Econ Pol_Sci Psych Relig Drawing Painting Photog Sculpt Video_Production Acting Theater_Arts

Chorus Music Journ.
Sports—Basket X-country Golf Soccer Track. B: Baseball. G: Volley.
Very selective adm: 91/yr. Appl fee: $65. Appl due: Jan. Accepted: 28%. Yield: 56%.
Tests CTP_4 ISEE.
Enr 734. B 374. G 360. Elem 549. Sec 185. Avg class size: 14. Stud/fac: 7:1. **Fac 118.** M
48/F 70. FT 112/PT 6. Wh 69%. Latino 13%. Blk 12%. Asian 6%. Adv deg: 65%.
Grad '11—41. Col—41. (Oberlin 3, Dickinson 3, Skidmore 3, Drew 2, Syracuse 2, Cor-
nell 1). **Avg SAT:** CR 615. M 572. W 604. **Col couns:** 2.
Tui '12-'13: Day $36,500-39,900 (+$200-500). **Aid:** Need 147.
Summer: Ages 10-16. Theater. 6 wks.
Endow $2,480,000. Plant val $43,080,000. Bldgs 2. Class rms 69. 2 Libs 20,000 vols. Sci
labs 5. Lang labs 4. Auds 1. Theaters 2. Art studios 3. Music studios 4. Dance studios
1. Gyms 2. Comp labs 3.
Est 1896. Nonprofit. Sem (Sept-June).

Founded by Laura Jacobi as the Jacobi School for Girls, the school assumed its present
name in 1924, while under the leadership of Mary E. Calhoun. The school became coeducational in 1971. From its beginnings, it has been a college preparatory institution located on
Manhattan's Upper West Side. A second West Side campus on 74th Street hosts three-year-old
through first grade programs.

The curriculum reflects a progressive, interdisciplinary approach and allows for individualization through independent study projects and enrichment activities. A strong advisory
system supports students in all areas of school life. Other distinctive features include active
studio art and theater programs; computer literacy requirements; a student exchange program;
a 60-hour community service graduation requirement; leadership and peer tutoring programs;
and an extensive extracurricular program.

THE CATHEDRAL SCHOOL OF ST. JOHN THE DIVINE
Day — Coed Gr K-8

New York, NY 10025. 1047 Amsterdam Ave. Tel: 212-316-7500. Fax: 212-316-7558.
www.cathedralnyc.org   E-mail: admission@cathedralnyc.org
Marsha K. Nelson, Head (2004). BS, Univ of Texas-Austin, BME, Baylor Univ, MA, Colum-
bia Univ. **Lisa Smoots, Adm.**
Pre-Prep. Feat—Chin Fr Lat Span Computers Studio_Art Chorus Music. **Supp**—Dev_
Read.
Sports—Basket X-country Soccer Track. B: Baseball. G: Softball Volley.
Very selective adm (Gr K-7): 48/yr. Appl fee: $60. Appl due: Nov. Applied: 400. Accepted:
16%. **Tests** CTP_4 ISEE.
Enr 290. Avg class size: 17. Stud/fac: 7:1. Uniform. **Fac 45.** M 10/F 35. FT 37/PT 8. Wh
75%. Latino 4%. Blk 6%. Asian 6%. Other 9%. Adv deg: 80%.
Grad '11—24. Prep—24. (Riverdale, Dalton, Poly Prep, Miss Hall's, St Andrew's Sch-
DE, Trinity Sch-NY).
Tui '12-'13: Day $36,250 (+$800-1050). **Aid:** Need 97 ($1,934,870).
Endow $5,400,000. Acres 13. Bldgs 1 (0% ADA). Class rms 21. Lib 7000 vols. Chapels
1. Sci labs 2. Art studios 2. Music studios 1. Gyms 2. Playgrounds 2. Comp labs 1.
Comp/stud: 1:2.
Est 1901. Nonprofit. Episcopal. Tri (Sept-June).

The school was founded by Rt. Rev. Henry Codman Potter, the Episcopal bishop of New
York City, as a boys' boarding school to provide the choir for the Cathedral of St. John the
Divine. In 1964, Cathedral began enrolling male day students of all faiths. Girls were first
admitted in 1974.

Located in a building on the 13-acre Cathedral Close, the school offers a solid foundation
in the basic elementary school subjects that integrates the arts, athletics and leadership opportunities. French, Spanish and Mandarin instruction begins in kindergarten. Older pupils take
French or Spanish in grades 4-8, while also enrolling in Latin courses in grades 7 and 8. Every

student attends two chapel services weekly, and compulsory community service is part of the school day.

On the basis of auditions, 25 to 28 boys and girls in grades 4-8 have the option of serving as choristers of the affiliated Cathedral of St. John the Divine. In exchange, they receive a tuition stipend.   **See Also Page 119**

THE CHAPIN SCHOOL
Day — Girls Gr K-12

New York, NY 10028. 100 E End Ave. Tel: 212-744-2335. Fax: 212-628-2126.
www.chapin.edu   E-mail: admissions@chapin.edu
Patricia T. Hayot, Head (2003). BA, MA, Marquette Univ, PhD, Univ of Michigan. **Andrea Kassar, Upper & Middle Sch Adm; Therese Cruite, Lower Sch Adm.**

Col Prep. AP (exams req'd; 219 taken, 84% 3+)—Eng Fr Lat Span Calc Stats Comp_ Sci Bio Chem Physics US_Hist Art_Hist Studio_Art. **Feat**—Chin Greek Astron Forensic_Sci Engineering Neurosci Pharmacology Robotics Ceramics Photog Acting Drama Music Dance Woodworking. **Supp**—Rev Tut.

Sports—G: Badminton Basket X-country Fencing F_Hockey Golf Gymnastics Lacrosse Soccer Softball Squash Swim Tennis Track Volley. **Activities:** 36.

Very selective adm (Gr K-10): 88/yr. Usual entry: K, 6 & 9. Appl fee: $50. Appl due: Dec. Applied: 691. Accepted: 19%. **Tests** IQ ISEE.

Enr **713.** Wh 67%. Latino 3%. Blk 7%. Asian 10%. Other 13%. Avg class size: 16. Stud/fac: 7:1. Uniform. **Fac 117.** M 25/F 92. FT 109/PT 8. Adv deg: 70%.

Grad '10—**42.** Col—**42.** (Princeton 3, Yale 3, Trinity Col-CT 3, Harvard 2, Duke 2, Dartmouth 2). **Mid 50% SAT:** CR 640-730. M 670-730. W 700-780. Avg ACT: 31. **Col couns:** 2. Alum donors: 40%.

Tui '11-'12: Day $35,100 (+$1300-4800). **Aid:** Need 133 ($3,785,605).

Summer: Gr K-7. Acad Enrich Rec. Tui Day $1250. 2 wks.

Endow $85,281,000. Plant val $85,281,000. Bldgs 1. Class rms 62. Lib 32,000 vols. Sci labs 6. Lang labs 1. Theaters 1. Art studios 4. Music studios 2. Dance studios 2. Gyms 4. Greenhouses 1. Comp labs 2. Comp/stud: 1:1.7 (1:1 Laptop prgm Gr 6-12).

Est 1901. Nonprofit. (Sept-June).

Founded as a primary school by Maria Bowen Chapin under the name of Miss Chapin's School for Girls, this school was incorporated as an elementary and secondary school in 1925. In 1928, it moved from two brownstone houses on East 57th Street to its own building on East End Avenue at 84th Street. The school assumed its current name in 1934.

The course of study emphasizes the liberal arts, the sciences and technology. Pupils study Spanish in grades 1-4 before committing to a course of study in Spanish, French or Chinese in grade 5, with Latin added in grade 7 and Greek in grade 9. A laptop immersion program in grade 6 provides computers to all students, and courses incorporate laptops in activities and discussions. Elective courses and Advanced Placement options provide opportunities for study at an advanced level. A varied dance program begins in kindergarten, while drama joins the curriculum in grade 2.

Other noteworthy offerings include a senior individual study program, special off-campus term programs, volunteer community service, and an academic and extracurricular exchange through the eight-school New York City consortium.

CITY AND COUNTRY SCHOOL
Day — Coed Gr PS (Age 2)-8

New York, NY 10011. 146 W 13th St. Tel: 212-242-7802. Fax: 212-242-7996.
www.cityandcountry.org   E-mail: elisec@cityandcountry.org
Kate Turley, Prin (1999). BA, State Univ of New York-Oswego, MA, New York Univ. **Elise Clark, Adm.**

Pre-Prep. **Feat**—Lib_Skills Span Computers Filmmaking Studio_Art Drama Music

Orchestra Carpentry.
Sports—Basket Soccer Softball Volley.
Selective adm (Gr PS-6): 45/yr. Usual entry: PS & K. Appl fee: $50. Appl due: Dec.
Tests CTP_4 ISEE.
Enr 360. B 180. G 180. Wh 83%. Latino 5%. Blk 7%. Asian 5%. Avg class size: 16. **Fac
54.** M 12/F 42. FT 49/PT 5. Wh 81%. Latino 3%. Blk 7%. Asian 9%.
Grad '10—15. Prep—13. (Trevor, Packer, Dalton, Loyola Sch, Calhoun, Fieldston).
Tui '11-'12: Day $27,620-32,900. Aid: Need 49 ($950,000).
Plant val $26,000,000. Bldgs 7. Class rms 49. Lib 8000 vols. Sci labs 8. Dark rms 1.
Auds 1. Art studios 4. Music studios 2. Dance studios 1. Ceramics studios 1. Gyms 4.
Greenhouses 1. Comp labs 2.
Est 1914. Nonprofit. Sem (Sept-June).

Founded by Caroline Pratt, City and Country conducts a program designed to help students explore firsthand experiences, play and responsible work, and to develop social and academic skills in an atmosphere of trust. The lower school program begins at age 2. For children ages 8-13, a strong history and social studies curriculum is built around a job program in which each class runs a school service (supplies, mail service, print shop and so on). The program includes opportunities for individualized work and research at each age, as well as a natural daily impetus for perfecting reading, writing, mathematical and creative skills.

Art, woodworking, science, music, computer and rhythms are integral to the program. The library, specially developed over the years as a source for the social studies program, is notable for its collection of primary source material.

COLLEGIATE SCHOOL

Day — Boys Gr K-12

New York, NY 10024. 260 W 78th St. Tel: 212-812-8500. Fax: 212-812-8547.
www.collegiateschool.org   E-mail: admissions@collegiateschool.org
Lee M. Levison, Head (2006). BA, Amherst College, EdM, EdD, Harvard Univ. **Joanne P.
Heyman, Adm.**
Col Prep. AP (exams req'd; 272 taken, 94% 3+)—Fr Lat Span Calc Bio Chem Envi-
ron_Sci Physics Eur_Hist US_Hist Art_Hist. **Elem math**—TERC Investigations.
Feat—Creative_Writing Shakespeare 19th-Century_Lit Chin Greek Biotech Comp_
Sci African_Hist Middle_Eastern_Hist Econ Aesthetics Ethics Logic Relig Architect
Ceramics Film Studio_Art Drama Dance.
Sports—B: Baseball Basket X-country Indoor_Track Lacrosse Soccer Tennis Track
Wrestling. **Activities:** 40.
Very selective adm (Gr K-9): 67/yr. Usual entry: K, 5, 6, 7 & 9. Appl fee: $50. Appl due:
Dec. Applied: 853. Accepted: 9%. Yield: 83%. **Tests** ISEE SSAT.
Enr 648. Elem 419. Sec 229. Wh 58%. Latino 4%. Blk 6%. Asian 15%. Other 17%. Avg
class size: 16. Stud/fac: 6:1. **Fac 90.** M 44/F 46. FT 85/PT 5. Adv deg: 75%.
Grad '11—55. Col—54. (Williams 5, Yale 5, Brown 5, U of PA 5, Northwestern 3, Dart-
mouth 3). **Mid 50% SAT:** CR 660-740. M 660-770. W 670-770. Alum donors: 35%.
Tui '11-'12: Day $37,500 (+$100). **Aid:** Need 112 ($3,207,275).
Endow $70,900,000. Plant val $100,000,000. Acres 1. Bldgs 1 (50% ADA). Class rms
64. Lib 45,746 vols. Sci labs 8. Lang labs 4. Auds 1. Theaters 1. Art studios 6. Music
studios 8. Gyms 3. Courts 2. Comp labs 4. Comp/stud: 1:2.
Est 1628. Nonprofit. Sem (Sept-June). **Assoc** CLS.

The oldest school in the country, Collegiate traces its history back to the early settlement of Manhattan by the Dutch; it operated as a parish day school for two and a half centuries, interrupted only when the city was occupied by British troops during the Revolution. In 1887, it became a grammar school, in 1891 preparatory, and after 1894 for boys only. Incorporated in 1940 as a nonprofit institution, the school is governed by a board, one-fifth of which represents the consistory of the Collegiate Dutch Reformed Church. In 1978, Collegiate purchased the 12-story West End Plaza Hotel, which is adjacent to the school campus on 78th Street. Six floors of the building have been converted to school use. In the late 1990s, the school erected a new building and completed renovations to existing space, thereby increasing the physical plant by one-fourth.

The lower school (grades K-4) follows a structured yet flexible program, featuring the Investigations curriculum in mathematics and integrated computer instruction at all levels. Foreign language study begins in middle school with French, Spanish and Chinese introduced in grade 5 and Latin in grade 8.

The rigorous upper school academic program (grades 9-12) affords thorough grounding for leading colleges. There are many electives, especially in English and history. Both Advanced Placement courses and independent study opportunities are also part of the curriculum. Travel opportunities for upper school students have included community service in the Dominican Republic, school-sponsored study abroad trips and exchange programs with schools in Europe and South America. All boys perform compulsory community service during the upper school years.

COLUMBIA GRAMMAR AND PREPARATORY SCHOOL
Day — Coed Gr PS (Age 4)-12

New York, NY 10025. 5 W 93rd St. Tel: 212-749-6200. Fax: 212-865-4278.
  www.cgps.org   E-mail: info@cgps.org
Richard J. Soghoian, Head (1981). BA, Univ of Virginia, PhD, Columbia Univ. Elaine Perlman, Adm.
  Col Prep. AP (exams req'd; 222 taken, 69% 3+)—Eng Fr Japan Lat Span Calc Stats Bio Chem Environ_Sci Physics Eur_Hist US_Hist World_Hist Psych US_Govt & Pol Music_Theory. Elem math—TERC Investigations. Feat—Creative_Writing Shakespeare Mythology NY_Lit Satire Chin Anat & Physiol Ecol Genetics Geol Microbio Comp_Sci Econ Pol_Sci Lat-Amer_Stud Philos World_Relig Ceramics Film Photog Drama Band Chorus Orchestra Debate. Supp—Dev_Read ESL LD Makeup Rem_Math Rem_Read Rev Tut.
  Sports (req'd)—Basket X-country Soccer Tennis Track. B: Baseball Golf Ice_Hockey. G: Softball Swim Volley.
  Very selective adm (Gr PS-11): 244/yr. Usual entry: K & 9. Appl fee: $60. Appl due: Dec. Applied: 1072. Accepted: 18%. Yield: 80%. Tests ISEE.
  Enr 1220. B 629. G 591. Elem 782. Sec 438. Wh 84%. Latino 6%. Blk 4%. Asian 5%. Other 1%. Avg class size: 13. Stud/fac: 6:1. Fac 234. M 66/F 168. FT 208/PT 26. Wh 85%. Latino 4%. Blk 3%. Asian 4%. Other 4%. Adv deg: 64%.
  Grad '10—112. Col—112. (Yale 6, Wash U 5, NYU 5, Cornell 4, Johns Hopkins 4, Emory 4). Athl schol 1. Avg SAT: CR 631. M 630. W 653. Col couns: 2. Alum donors: 9%.
  Tui '11-'12: Day $36,390-38,340. Aid: Need 245 ($5,000,000).
  Endow $22,000,000. Plant val $150,000,000. Bldgs 11 (60% ADA). Class rms 80. Lib 27,500 vols. Sci labs 11. Dark rms 1. Theaters 2. Art studios 6. Music studios 7. Gyms 3. Pools 1. Comp labs 5. Comp/stud: 1:3.
  Est 1764. Nonprofit. Sem (Sept-June).

Founded as a preparatory school for Columbia College and under the direction of the university for 100 years, this school rose to high prominence in the mid-19th century under Dr. Charles Anthon, America's earliest classical scholar. Today, the school is an independent institution with a board of trustees.

The curriculum prepares graduates for leading colleges throughout the country. Elective courses are available in English, social sciences, science, math, art, film, drama and music. Although CGPS offers them in most disciplines, Advanced Placement courses are not necessarily the school's most demanding classes. A three-year science research program allows students to explore scientific and mathematical topics in depth, and selected seniors participate in a college-level seminar on global issues. Students perform at least 60 hours of community service in grades 9-12.

CONVENT OF THE SACRED HEART
Day — Girls Gr PS (Age 3)-12

New York, NY 10128. 1 E 91st St. Tel: 212-722-4745. Fax: 212-996-1784.
www.cshnyc.org   E-mail: admissions@cshnyc.org
Joseph J. Ciancaglini, Head (2007). AB, MA, Georgetown Univ, MEd, Boston Univ, EdD, Columbia Univ. **Elizabeth R. Santini, Adm.**
Col Prep. AP (exams req'd)—Eng Fr Lat Span Calc Stats Comp_Sci Bio Chem Eur_ Hist US_Hist US_Govt & Pol Studio_Art Music_Theory. **Feat**—British_Lit Chin Environ_Sci Lat-Amer_Hist World_Relig Film Photog Drama Chorus Dance Debate.
Sports—G: Basket X-country Lacrosse Soccer Softball Swim Tennis Track Volley.
Very selective adm (Gr PS-11): 89/yr. Usual entry: K & 9. Appl fee: $65. Appl due: Dec. Accepted: 17%. Yield: 80%. **Tests** ISEE.
Enr 691. Elem 491. Sec 200. Wh 72%. Latino 12%. Blk 5%. Asian 9%. Other 2%. Avg class size: 15. Uniform. **Fac 100.** M 16/F 84. FT 100. Adv deg: 80%.
Grad '10—48. Col—48. (Georgetown 6, Geo Wash 4, U of PA 3, Fordham 3, Dartmouth 2, Johns Hopkins 2). Alum donors: 30%.
Tui '11-'12: Day $37,395. Aid: Need 129 ($2,900,000).
Summer: Ages 6-15. Rec. Creative Arts. Tui Day $2500. 4 wks.
Endow $34,100,000. Plant val $64,500,000. Bldgs 2. Class rms 36. 3 Libs 35,000 vols. Chapels 1. Sci labs 3. Theaters 1. Art studios 3. Music studios 3. Gyms 2. Comp labs 3.
Est 1881. Nonprofit. Roman Catholic. Sem (Sept-June).

The oldest private girls' school in Manhattan, Sacred Heart offers a solid college preparatory program with an emphasis on small-class instruction, a diversity of backgrounds among faculty and students, and community service in the urban environment. Features of the curriculum include independent study, Advanced Placement courses, and a broad selection of electives that includes creative writing, studio art, pottery, photography, computer graphics and the theater arts. Girls in grades 8-12 satisfy an annual community service requirement.

Opportunities for exchange study are available within the worldwide Network of Sacred Heart Schools. Over the years, students have attended Sacred Heart schools in France, Spain and Belgium for a semester, as well as some of the schools in the US. Religion courses are required of all students.

Located on Fifth Avenue opposite Central Park, the school's two buildings have been designated as city landmarks for their architectural styles. The principal structure is the former Otto Kahn residence, a copy of an Italian Renaissance palace; the adjoining rococo-style mansion formerly belonged to James Burden.

DALTON SCHOOL
Day — Coed Gr K-12

New York, NY 10128. 108 E 89th St. Tel: 212-423-5200. Fax: 212-423-5259.
Other locations: 53 E 91st St, New York 10128; 200 E 87th St, New York 10128.
www.dalton.org   E-mail: admissions@dalton.org
Ellen Cohen Stein, Head (2001). BA, Univ of Pennsylvania, MBA, Columbia Univ. **Elisabeth Krents, Gr K-12 Adm; Shamilla Beasmoney, PS Adm.**
Col Prep. AP exams taken: 284. Feat—Creative_Writing Poetry Shakespeare African-Amer_Lit James_Joyce Russ_Lit Chin Fr Greek Lat Span Calc Stats Multivariable_Calc Environ_Sci Forensic_Sci Comp_Sci Robotics African-Amer_Hist Lat-Amer_Hist Govt Psych Ethics Philos Art_Hist Photog Sculpt Acting Drama Music Music_Hist Music_Theory Jazz_Ensemble Dance Journ. **Supp**—Rem_Math Rem_Read Tut.
Sports—Basket X-country Lacrosse Soccer Swim Tennis Track Volley. B: Baseball Football Golf Wrestling. G: Softball.
Very selective adm: 161/yr. Usual entry: K, 6 & 9. Appl fee: $60. Appl due: Nov. Accepted: 13%. Yield: 80%. **Tests** ISEE SSAT.
Enr 1279. B 625. G 654. Elem 834. Sec 445. Avg class size: 15. Stud/fac: 7:1. **Fac 203.**

M 59/F 144. FT 168/PT 35. Adv deg: 74%.
Grad '09—100. Col—100. (Brown 9, U of PA 6, Yale 5, Harvard 4, Geo Wash 4, Amherst
3). **Avg SAT:** CR 685. M 683. W 695. **Mid 50% SAT:** CR 640-750. M 635-740. W 640-
740. **Col couns:** 2. Alum donors: 19%.
Tui '11-'12: Day $36,970. Aid: Need 256 ($7,400,000).
Summer: Ages 3-10. Enrich Rec. 6 wks.
Endow $45,000,000. Plant val $33,000,000. Bldgs 5. Class rms 96. Lib 65,000 vols. Labs
4. Theaters 2. Art studios 4. Music studios 4. Gyms 4. Laptop prgm Gr 6-8.
Est 1919. Nonprofit. Sem (Sept-June).

Founded by Helen Parkhurst, the school applies the theories of her widely known Dalton
Plan. The plan utilizes "the House, the Assignment and the Laboratory" to assist each student
in accepting increasing responsibility for his or her education.

The present building opened in the autumn of 1929. Eleanor Roosevelt, who admired Miss
Parkhurst's work, played an important role in expanding the school by promoting a merger
between the Todhunter School and Dalton in 1939. Today, Miss Parkhurst's basic techniques
have been broadened and modernized from the First Program (grades K-3) through high
school. The East 89th Street facility houses the middle and upper grades, while the First Program occupies a separate building on East 91st Street. Sports and physical education facilities
are located on East 87th Street.

Dalton's progressive educational model is enhanced by the introduction of computer technology in kindergarten, an interdisciplinary archaeological unit in grade 3 and foreign languages from grade 5. Approximately 140 full-time and semester courses constitute the high
school curriculum. Students choose their own classes and plan laboratory time with the help of
an advisor. Dalton issues laptops to boys and girls in grades 6-8 for school and home use, and
computer science is a graduation requirement.

During the high school years, boys and girls complete four community service projects.
Seniors are able to pursue independent projects during second semester, and qualified pupils
may enroll in interschool courses at seven other New York City independent schools. Dalton
also offers internships and study projects in hospitals and business firms and funds a lecture-
ship at the Metropolitan Museum of Art and the American Museum of Natural History.

THE DWIGHT SCHOOL
Day — Coed Gr PS (Age 2)-12

New York, NY 10024. 291 Central Park W. Tel: 212-724-7524. Fax: 212-724-2539.
www.dwight.edu   E-mail: admissions@dwight.edu
Stephen H. Spahn, Chancellor (1969). AB, Dartmouth College, MA, Oxford Univ (Eng-
land). **Marina Bernstein, Gr 9-12 Adm; Alyson Waldman, Gr 1-8 Adm; Alicia Janiak,
PS Adm.**
  Col Prep. IB Diploma. IB PYP. IB MYP. Feat—Chin Fr Ger Ital Japan Lat Russ Span
    Environ_Sci Philos Art_Hist Film Theater_Arts Music Bus. **Supp**—ESL Makeup Rev
    Tut.
  Sports—Basket X-country Tennis Track. B: Baseball Golf Soccer. G: Volley. **Activities:**
    38.
  Selective adm (Gr PS-11): 120/yr. Appl fee: $50-75. Appl due: Dec. **Tests** CTP_4 ISEE
    SSAT.
  Enr 555. Elem 305. Sec 250. Wh 70%. Latino 5%. Blk 5%. Asian 10%. Other 10%. Intl
    30%. Avg class size: 15. Stud/fac: 6:1. **Fac 150.** M 55/F 95. FT 138/PT 12. Adv deg:
    46%.
  Grad '11—70. Col—70. (NYU, Columbia, McGill-Canada, Stanford, Wash U, Franklin &
    Marshall). **Avg SAT:** CR 600. M 600. **Col couns:** 3.
  Tui '12-'13: Day $29,300-38,000 (+$1500). **Aid:** Need ($1,400,000).
  Summer: Acad Enrich Rev. SAT Prep. 2 wks.
  Endow $5,000,000. Plant val $20,000,000. Bldgs 3. Class rms 34. 2 Libs 15,000 vols. Sci
    labs 5. Lang labs 1. Comp ctrs 1. Auds 1. Theaters 2. Art studios 2. Music studios 1.
    Dance studios 1. Gyms 3. Comp labs 1. Comp/stud: 1:2.5.

Est 1872. Inc. Tri (Sept-June). **Assoc** MSA.

The school was founded as an academy of classical studies. Most of its students at that time went on to Yale University. In 1888, Timothy Dwight, president of Yale, became active in school affairs, and the school was renamed in his honor. Dwight became the first independent day school in the US to establish a permanent international campus when it founded the Woodside Park School (now called the Dwight North London International School), in London, England, in 1972. In 1993, Dwight effected a merger with the Anglo-American International School.

The school comprises a preschool and four houses: Timothy House (grades K-4), Bentley House (grades 5-8), Franklin House (grades 9 and 10) and Anglo House (grades 11 and 12). Students follow the International Baccalaureate curriculum at all grade levels. The IB Primary Years Program addresses the child's social, physical, emotional and cultural needs, in addition to his or her academic welfare. The IB Middle Years Program provides a comprehensive, developmentally appropriate framework of academics and life skills instruction. The curriculum concludes with the IB Diploma Program, a rigorous pre-university course of studies that leads to examinations suitable for motivated high schoolers. Graduates attend competitive US colleges, as well as such foreign universities as McGill, Oxford and the University of Edinburgh.

Dwight's extensive foreign language curriculum commences with Spanish and Chinese classes in prekindergarten. Additional options for older students are French, Latin, German, Hebrew, Italian and Japanese.

Extracurricular activities include various athletic, music, visual arts and drama programs, student government and neighborhood outreach programs. All high school students must participate in some form of community service. The school arranges learning opportunities and trips each year to such countries as Canada, France, England, Turkey, Kenya, India, Morocco, China and the Dominican Republic. The QUEST program provides individualized instruction for pupils with mild learning differences.

FRIENDS SEMINARY

Day — Coed Gr K-12

New York, NY 10003. 222 E 16th St. Tel: 212-979-5030. Fax: 212-979-5034.
www.friendsseminary.org   E-mail: admissions@friendsseminary.org
Robert N. Lauder, Prin (2002). BA, Auburn Univ, MA, Univ of North Carolina-Chapel Hill.
Harriet Burnett, Adm.
   Col Prep. AP (exams req'd; 143 taken)—Fr Lat Span Calc Stats Physics US_Hist World_Hist US_Govt & Pol. **Feat**—Creative_Writing Playwriting Arabic Environ_Sci Middle_Eastern_Hist Modern_African_Hist Law Architect Photog Sculpt Drama Music Dance Wilderness_Ed. **Supp**—Rev. Outdoor ed. **Dual enr:** NYU.
   Sports—Basket X-country Soccer Squash Swim Tennis Track. B: Baseball. G: Softball Volley. **Activities:** 20.
   Selective adm (Gr K-11): 130/yr. Usual entry: K, 6 & 9. Appl fee: $75. Appl due: Jan. Accepted: 29%. Yield: 41%. **Tests** CTP_4 ISEE SSAT.
   Enr 733. B 372. G 361. Elem 468. Sec 265. Wh 70%. Latino 2%. Blk 6%. Asian 7%. Other 15%. Avg class size: 17. **Fac 96.** M 38/F 58. FT 96. Wh 81%. Latino 4%. Blk 7%. Asian 5%. Other 3%. Adv deg: 78%.
   Grad '11—70. Col—70. (Brown 3, NYU 3, Pitzer 3, Bowdoin 2, Haverford 2, Tufts 2).
   Avg SAT: CR 678. M 658. W 699. **Col couns:** 2. Alum donors: 18%.
   Tui '11-'12: Day $34,600 (+$1555-2555). **Aid:** Need 172 ($3,485,274).
   Summer: Acad Enrich Rec. SAT Prep. 8 wks.
   Endow $25,400,000. Plant val $8,085,000. Bldgs 8. Class rms 40. Lib 15,000 vols. Sci labs 5. Lang labs 1. Meetinghouses 1. Theaters 1. Art studios 5. Music studios 2. Dance studios 1. Gyms 2. Athletic ctrs 1. Comp labs 4. Comp/stud: 1:4 (1:1 Laptop prgm Gr K, 5 & 9).
   Est 1786. Nonprofit. Religious Society of Friends (2% practice). Sem (Sept-June).

Having long occupied gracious quarters on Rutherford Place, this Quaker school has undergone significant physical expansion over the years.

The lower school program (grades K-4) places particular emphasis on problem solving and creative thinking. The departmentalized middle school (grades 5-8) offers ample opportunities for boys and girls to participate in activities such as community service and team sports. Qualified seniors may enroll in courses at New York University at no additional charge. Traditional college preparatory course work in the upper school (grades 9-12) is complemented by foreign and classical languages, technology, Advanced Placement classes, visual and performing arts offerings (including the opportunity to perform in professional theater space at the nearby Vineyard Theater), and an extensive electives and athletics program.

Experiential education at Friends encompasses urban internships, senior projects and a wilderness and outdoor program. Pupils may take part in study-abroad programs in Spain, France and Italy, as well as in exchanges with schools in the Continental US. Friends requires community service of its students. The school provides iPads to students in kindergarten, grade 5 and grade 9.

GRACE CHURCH SCHOOL

Day — Coed Gr PS (Age 4)-8

New York, NY 10003. 86 4th Ave. Tel: 212-475-5609. Fax: 212-475-5015.
www.gcschool.org   E-mail: admissions@gcschool.org
George P. Davison, Head (1994). BA, Yale Univ, MA, Columbia Univ. **Margery H. Stone, Adm.**

Pre-Prep. Feat—Fr Lat Span Computers Ethics Relig Studio_Art Drama Music. **Supp**—Rem_Math Rem_Read Tut.

Sports—Basket Soccer. B: Baseball. G: Softball Volley.

Very selective adm: 60/yr. Usual entry: PS & K. Appl fee: $75. Appl due: Nov. Applied: 500. **Tests** IQ ISEE SSAT.

Enr 410. Avg class size: 22. Stud/fac: 7:1. Uniform. **Fac 69.** M 28/F 41. FT 69.

Grad '09—42. Prep—39. (Packer, Dalton, Fieldston, Friends Seminary, Columbia Grammar & Prep, Berkeley Carroll).

Tui '11-'12: Day $34,800 (+$50-440). **Aid:** Need 90 ($2,200,000).

Endow $20,000,000. Plant val $30,000,000. Bldgs 5 (100% ADA). Class rms 22. Lib 10,000 vols. Sci labs 3. Art studios 3. Music studios 1. Dance studios 1. Shops 1. Gyms 2. Greenhouses 1. Comp labs 3.

Est 1894. Nonprofit. Episcopal. Sem (Sept-June).

Established as a choir school for boys and still an integral part of Grace Church, GCS has evolved into a coeducational pre-preparatory school. Ethical and scholastic development and Judeo-Christian beliefs are emphasized, and upper school students perform regular community service. Preparing students for leading secondary schools, the curriculum features enrichment opportunities in computer, music, art and drama, as well as various electives in the upper grades.

All children in the racially and religiously diverse student body attend chapel and take courses in the Bible, world religions and ethics. The after-school program serves as an extension of the academic day and also includes the arts and sports. Students in grades 7 and 8 have the opportunity to participate in exchange programs with families in India, Japan, France, Spain and China.

HEWITT SCHOOL

Day — Girls Gr K-12

New York, NY 10021. 45 E 75th St. Tel: 212-288-1919. Fax: 212-472-7531.
Other locations: 3 E 76th St, New York 10021.
www.hewittschool.org   E-mail: lchu@hewittschool.org

Joan Z. Lonergan, Head (2010). BS, Univ of New Hampshire, EdM, Harvard Univ. **Jessica Acee, Upper & Middle Sch Adm; Kelly Pierre, Lower Sch Adm.**
    Col Prep. AP (exams req'd)—Eng Fr Lat Span Calc Bio Art_Hist. **Feat**—British_Lit Shakespeare Lat-Amer_Lit Stats Anat & Physiol Astron Environ_Sci Forensic_Sci Programming Robotics Russ_Hist Econ Psych World_Relig Ceramics Film Photog Studio_Art Drama Chorus Music Handbells Dance Journ Public_Speak.
    Sports—G: Badminton Basket Crew X-country Soccer Swim Tennis Track Volley. **Activities:** 17.
    Selective adm: 87/yr. Usual entry: K, 3, 6 & 9. Appl fee: $60. Appl due: Dec. Accepted: 46%. Yield: 41%. **Tests** ISEE.
    Enr 525. Avg class size: 11. Stud/fac: 7:1. Uniform. **Fac 74.** M 18/F 56. FT 73/PT 1. Adv deg: 75%.
    Grad '07—24. Col—24. (Muhlenberg 3, Fordham 2, CT Col 1, Denison 1, U of Chicago 1, Alfred U 1). **Avg SAT:** CR/M 1210. Alum donors: 8%.
    Tui '12-'13: Day $39,400. Aid: Need 89.
    Summer: Acad Enrich Rec. 1-2 wks.
    Endow $11,300,000. Plant val $25,376,000. Bldgs 3. Class rms 40. 2 Libs 12,000 vols. Sci labs 3. Dark rms 2. Auds 2. Theaters 1. Art studios 3. Music studios 3. Dance studios 1. Gyms 1. Comp labs 2. Laptop prgm Gr 9-12.
    Est 1920. Nonprofit. Sem (Sept-June). **Assoc** CLS.

The college preparatory curriculum at this small school provides students with a firm grounding in the liberal arts, with emphasis placed upon the humanities, the sciences and the arts. In the lower school (grades K-3, at the 76th Street campus), children develop basic academic skills through an interdisciplinary program that enables them to engage in problem solving and creative thinking. Foreign language study and the integrated use of technology both begin in kindergarten.

During the middle school years (grades 4-8), girls continue to build their analytical thinking and study skills through a content-rich curriculum that also prepares them for advanced work in the traditional disciplines. Upper schoolers (grades 9-12), who choose from a range of Advanced Placement and elective offerings, take four or five academic courses per year, as well as one or two arts classes. Hewitt issues laptop computers to upper school students for classroom use. A weeklong interim program in January features approximately a dozen academic and cultural electives for middle and upper school students.

Hewitt's Upper East Side location permits students and faculty to make extensive use of the city's museums, parks, galleries and theaters. Girls satisfy the following community service requirements: 10 hours annually in grades 4-8, 20 hours per year in grades 9-12.

LA SCUOLA D'ITALIA

Day — Coed Gr PS (Age 3)-12

New York, NY 10128. 12 E 96th St. Tel: 212-369-3290. Fax: 212-369-1164.
Other locations: 406 E 67th St, New York 10065.
    www.lascuoladitalia.org   E-mail: secretary@lascuoladitalia.org
Anna Fiore, Head (2008). MPhil, MA. **Pia Pedicini, Adm.**
    Col Prep. Bilingual (Ital). Feat—Fr Ital Lat Philos Art_Hist Drama Music. **Supp**—ESL Makeup Rem_Math Rem_Read Tut.
    Sports—Basket Fencing Soccer Volley. **Activities:** 10.
    Selective adm: 60/yr. Usual entry: PS. Appl fee: $100. Appl due: Rolling. Accepted: 80%. Yield: 80%. **Tests** CTP_4.
    Enr 250. B 136. G 114. Wh 92%. Latino 6%. Blk 1%. Asian 1%. Intl 70%. Avg class size: 15. Uniform. **Fac 48.** M 9/F 39. FT 36/PT 12. Wh 99%. Latino 1%. Adv deg: 43%.
    Grad '11—9. Col—9. (Fordham, Manhattanville, Lancaster U-England, Syracuse, CUNY, Bocconi-Italy). **Avg SAT:** CR/M 1200. **Col couns:** 1. Alum donors: 5%.
    Tui '12-'13: Day $20,600 (+$1600).
    Plant val $20,000,000. Bldgs 2. Class rms 15. Lib 3000 vols. Sci labs 2. Auds 1. Gyms 1. Comp labs 2. Comp/stud: 1:3.
    Est 1977. Nonprofit. Sem (Sept-June).

La Scuola d'Italia Guglielmo Marconi integrates educational features of Italian and American schools. It is legally recognized by the Italian Ministry of Education. Students become bilingual and bicultural through the use of English and Italian as languages of instruction from preschool through 12th grade. The main curriculum spans a wide range of studies in mathematics, the natural and physical sciences, the humanities, the social sciences and the arts. French is mandatory in grades 7 and 8, and, in the upper school, students follow a compulsory program of studies that includes a four-year Latin requirement. Boys and girls perform 40 hours of required community service prior to graduation.

Upon adding a second location on East 67th Street in September 2000, La Scuola launched a curriculum at the middle school level (grades 6-8) that employs English and Italian as the languages of instruction. This program combines a firm grounding in math, science and the liberal arts with rigorous language instruction that provides a strong foundation for advanced study at the high school and college levels. Participating students also develop a deeper appreciation of the Italian and European cultures.

La Scuola maintains cultural collaborations with various Italian institutions in the city, among them the Italian Cultural Institute and the Italian Consulate General. At the high school level, the school offers supplementary cultural project opportunities in New York City and abroad, including exchange programs with Italian schools and meetings with ambassadors and other dignitaries, as well as notable Italian artists and interpreters.

Italian fluency is not required for school entrance in grades pre-K-9. Those applying to higher grades must speak the language at an intermediate level or above.

LITTLE RED SCHOOL HOUSE AND ELISABETH IRWIN HIGH SCHOOL
Day — Coed Gr PS (Age 4)-12

New York, NY 10014. 272 6th Ave. Tel: 212-477-5316. Fax: 212-677-9159.
Other locations: 40 Charlton St, New York 10014.
www.lrei.org   E-mail: admissions@lrei.org
Philip Kassen, Dir (2004). Julia Heaton, Adm.
   Col Prep. Elem math—TERC Investigations. **Feat**—Creative_Writing Shakespeare Latino_Lit Toni_Morrison Chin Fr Span Calc Environ_Sci Comp_Design Robotics NYC_Hist Econ Law Asian_Stud Film Filmmaking Photog Studio_Art Video_Production Acting Drama Music Dance Indus_Arts. **Dual enr:** NYU.
   Sports—Basket X-country Soccer Tennis Track. B: Baseball Golf. G: Softball Volley.
   Selective adm (Gr PS-11): 104/yr. Usual entry: PS, K, 6 & 9. Appl fee: $75. Appl due Dec. Applied: 676. **Tests** ISEE.
   Enr 608. Elem 419. Sec 189. Avg class size: 15. **Fac 100.** Adv deg: 74%.
   Grad '11—44. **Col**—44. (Bard-NY 4, Hampshire 4, Skidmore 3, Wesleyan U 2, Smith 2, Hobart/Wm Smith 2). **Col couns:** 1.
   Tui '11-'12: Day $32,690-34,493.
   Summer: Acad Enrich Rec. Musical Theater. Tui Day $610-980/2-wk ses. 6 wks.
   Plant val $5,000,000. Bldgs 3. Class rms 34. 2 Libs 15,000 vols. Sci labs 3. Dark rms 1. Auds 1. Theaters 1. Art studios 3. Music studios 2. Wood shops 1. Gyms 3. Comp labs 2.
   Est 1921. Nonprofit. (Sept-June).

The student body at LREI comes from all parts of New York City, reflecting the city's economic, ethnic and cultural diversity. The school began as an experiment in the New York City public schools, but it has been independent since 1932.

The curriculum throughout the school revolves around core themes, integrating language arts/English and social studies/history, as well as a required arts program. Writing is emphasized in all curricular areas. In the lower school (grades pre-K-4), understanding and skills in reading, mathematics and science are stressed. The middle school (grades 5-8) was established as a formal entity in 1986. Its program, which is based on a strong humanities curriculum, stresses theme studies and skills development. The high school (grades 9-12), established in

1941 and located on Charlton Street, offers a college preparatory course of study with a wide range of electives.

Boys and girls perform 25 hours of community service in grades 9-12, and seniors complete a six-week independent project.

LOYOLA SCHOOL

Day — Coed Gr 9-12

New York, NY 10028. 980 Park Ave. Tel: 212-288-3522. Fax: 212-861-1021.
www.loyola-nyc.org   E-mail: admissions@loyola-nyc.org
Antal Oroszlany, Pres (2011). BA, Georgetown Univ, MBA, Fordham Univ. **James F. X. Lyness, Jr., Head.** BA, MST, Boston College, MSEd, Manhattan College. **Lillian Diaz-Imbelli, Adm.**

Col Prep. AP (exams req'd)—Eng Fr Lat Span Calc Stats Bio Chem Physics Eur_Hist US_Hist Music_Theory. **Feat**—Creative_Writing Comp_Sci Econ Pol_Sci Psych Theol World_Relig Graphic_Arts Photog Chorus Music Orchestra.

Sports—Basket X-country Golf Track. B: Baseball Soccer. G: Softball Volley. **Activities:** 25.

Selective adm (Gr 9-11): 60/yr. Appl fee: $80. Appl due: Dec. **Tests** HSPT ISEE SSAT.

Enr 205. B 103. G 102. Avg class size: 15. Stud/fac: 12:1. Uniform. **Fac 31.** M 16/F 15. FT 31. Adv deg: 93%.

Grad '10—54. Col—54. (Villanova, Boston Col, Fordham, Vassar, Geo Wash, Boston U). **Avg SAT:** CR 620. M 630. W 640.

Tui '11-'12: Day $29,400 (+$650).

Endow $7,000,000. Bldgs 2. Class rms 13. Lib 10,500 vols. Sci labs 2. Theaters 1. Art studios 1. Music studios 1. Gyms 1. Comp labs 1.

Est 1900. Nonprofit. Roman Catholic. Quar (Sept-May). **Assoc** MSA.

Advantageously located in close proximity to many of Manhattan's museums, libraries and theaters, this well-known Jesuit school offers a solid college preparatory program. The flexible curriculum includes Advanced Placement courses and electives. All students fulfill a theology requirement.

The performing and visual arts, instrumental and choral groups, community service programs and interest clubs complement academics. Students may compete in interscholastic or intramural athletics.

LYCEE FRANCAIS DE NEW YORK

Day — Coed Gr PS (Age 4)-12

New York, NY 10021. 505 E 75th St. Tel: 212-369-1400. Fax: 212-439-4200.
www.lfny.org   E-mail: admissions@lfny.org
Sean Lynch, Head. Martine Lala, Adm.

Col Prep. Bilingual (Fr). AP (exams req'd)—Eng Fr Ger Span. **Feat**—Chin Greek Ital Lat Comp_Sci Philos. **Supp**—ESL Rem_Read Rev Tut.

Sports—Basket X-country Golf Soccer Softball Tennis Track Volley.

Selective adm: 296/yr. Appl fee: $200. Accepted: 37%. Yield: 80%. **Tests** ISEE.

Enr 1350. B 634. G 716. Intl 42%. Avg class size: 20. Formal. **Fac 143.** M 40/F 103. FT 139/PT 4. Adv deg: 77%.

Grad '11—95. Col—95. (McGill-Canada 13, U of St Andrews-Scotland 5, NYU 4, U of Edinburgh-Scotland 3, U of PA 3, Cornell 3). **Col couns:** 3.

Tui '12-'13: Day $26,100 (+$50-4480). **Aid:** Need 297.

Summer: Rec. 5 wks.

Endow $11,000,000. Bldgs 1. Class rms 62. 2 Libs 18,000 vols. Sci labs 6. Theaters 1. Art studios 2. Music studios 3. Dance studios 1. Gyms 2. Comp labs 2.

Est 1935. Nonprofit. Tri (Sept-June).

The Lycee's academic program combines the traditional French program, a strong English program and a selection of courses that, while not required by the French Ministry of National Education, adhere to the educational approach of that institution. Among the school's curricular requirements are French and English language and literature classes, an additional classical or modern language, and course work in the traditional disciplines.

Knowledge of French is not required for admission until grade 1; students entering from that level onward must pass a language proficiency exam. LFNY conducts language support classes in both French and English at all grade levels, and pupils in grades 2-4 may enroll in an intensive language integration program. Non-Francophone boys and girls learn French in a small-group setting, then join regular classes the following year.

The school's Upper East Side location enables students to embark on frequent field trips to museums, art galleries, and educational and business organizations. Interschool athletic, artistic, musical and literary competitions are commonplace.

LYCEUM KENNEDY
FRENCH AMERICAN SCHOOL
Day — Coed Gr PS (Age 3)-12

New York, NY 10017. 225 E 43rd St. Tel: 212-681-1877. Fax: 212-681-1922.
Other locations: 1 Cross Rd, Ardsley 10502.
  www.lyceumkennedy.org   E-mail: lkmanhattan@lyceumkennedy.org
  Laurent Bonardi, Head (2011). PhD, Univ of Provence (France). **Isabelle Walsh, Adm.**
  Col Prep. Gen Acad. Fr Bac. Bilingual (Fr). AP (exams req'd)—Eng Fr Span US_Hist.
    Feat—Lat Govt Intl_Relations Studio_Art Music. **Supp**—Dev_Read ESL Rem_Math Rem_Read Tut.
  Activities: 17.
  Selective adm (Gr PS-11): 48/yr. Appl fee: $200. Appl due: Feb. Applied: 293. Accepted: 30%. Yield: 70%. **Tests** ISEE SSAT.
  Enr 280. B 130. G 150. Wh 31%. Latino 5%. Blk 64%. Intl 70%. Uniform. **Fac 26.** M 7/F 19. FT 26. Wh 94%. Latino 2%. Blk 2%. Asian 2%. Adv deg: 3%.
  Grad '11—5. Col—5. (SUNY-Stony Brook).
  Tui '12-'13: Day $20,090-26,500 (+$670-1010).
  Bldgs 1. Class rms 14. Lib 7000 vols. Sci labs 1. Auds 1. Art studios 1. Music studios 1. Dance studios 1. Gyms 1. Comp labs 1.
  Est 1964. Inc. Tri (Sept-June).

This French international bilingual school was founded for the education of French-speaking and American children and formerly used the same methods of teaching as the French school system. A new administration in 1986 resulted in a more international student body, and today the school provides a multilingual education that emphasizes a cross-cultural exchange of ideas. Lyceum Kennedy is accredited by both the French Government and the State of New York.

Subjects are taught in English and French, thereby enabling students to achieve fluency in both languages; even the youngest children are immersed in the French language and tradition. Two-thirds of the curriculum is conducted in French, while the remaining third is in English. Some basics of Latin are taught in grade 7, and pupils are introduced to Latin and Spanish literature beginning in grade 8. SAT preparation, as well as American history and government, is required in the senior high school, and older students work toward Advanced Placement tests. Graduates earn a high school diploma, and students may prepare for the French Baccalaureate.

Lyceum Kennedy also operates a Westchester County campus in Ardsley (914-479-0722).

MANHATTAN COUNTRY SCHOOL

Day — Coed Gr PS (Age 4)-8

New York, NY 10128. 7 E 96th St. Tel: 212-348-0952. Fax: 212-348-1621.
Other locations: 3536 New Kingston Rd, Roxbury 12474.
www.manhattancountryschool.org
E-mail: admissions@manhattancountryschool.org
Michele Sola, Dir (1997). BA, Cornell Univ, MAT, Indiana Univ, EdD, Boston Univ. **Lois Gelernt, Adm.**
Pre-Prep. Feat—Lib_Skills Span Computers Studio_Art Chorus Music Dance Indus_ Arts Woodworking. **Supp**—Dev_Read Tut.
Sports—Basket Soccer Track. G: Softball.
Very selective adm: 42/yr. Usual entry: PS, K & 6. Appl fee: $70. Applied: 246. Accepted: 20%. Yield: 43%. **Tests** ISEE.
Enr 199. B 98. G 101. Wh 43%. Latino 17%. Blk 31%. Asian 9%. Intl 5%. Avg class size: 20. Stud/fac: 9:1. **Fac 40.** M 12/F 28. FT 26/PT 14. Wh 57%. Latino 18%. Blk 18%. Asian 7%. Adv deg: 37%.
Grad '11—19. Prep—13. (Little Red & Elisabeth Irwin 2, Dwight-Englewood 1, Brooklyn Friends 1, Fieldston 1, Friends Seminary 1, St Ann's-NY 1).
Tui '12-'13: Day $33,500-36,500 (+$100). **Aid:** Need 152 ($2,617,750).
Summer: Rec. Farm Prgm. Tui Bdg $3000. 3 wks.
Endow $6,212,000. Plant val $2,783,000. Acres 185. Bldgs 2. Class rms 10. Lib 6500 vols. Sci labs 1. Art studios 2. Music studios 1. Shops 1. Farms 1. Comp labs 1. Comp/stud: 1:2.
Est 1966. Nonprofit. Sem (Sept-June).

Founded to carry out the ideas of Martin Luther King, Jr., by teaching and practicing democracy in the classroom, MCS enrolls a racially, culturally and economically diverse student body. Combining the progressive principles of John Dewey with a multicultural approach to its curriculum, the school's program includes both individualized instruction and group learning experiences within a defined structure.

The hands-on, experiential curriculum, which incorporates the resources of New York City, emphasizes analytical and critical-thinking skills. Spanish is available at all grade levels, and pupils also take art, music, shop, library and physical education. Electives are part of the curriculum in the upper grades.

The school owns a 185-acre farm in the Catskill Mountains to which all students above age 7 make regular, extended trips. Its program emphasizes sustainability through farm work, food production, cooking and nutrition, construction of textiles from the farm's wool, nature studies and the responsibilities of an interdependent community.

MARYMOUNT SCHOOL

Day — Boys Gr PS (Age 3)-PS (Age 4), Girls PS (Age 3)-12

New York, NY 10028. 1026 5th Ave. Tel: 212-744-4486. Fax: 212-744-0163.
Other locations: 2 E 82nd St, New York 10028; 116 E 97th St, New York 10029.
www.marymountnyc.org   E-mail: admissions@marymountnyc.org
Concepcion R. Alvar, Head (2004). BA, Maryknoll College (Philippines), MA, Columbia Univ. **Lillian Issa, Adm.**
Col Prep. AP (exams req'd; 121 taken, 92% 3+)—Eng Fr Lat Span Calc Stats Bio Chem Physics US_Hist Art_Hist Studio_Art. **Feat**—Greek Atmospheric_Sci Comp_ Sci Modern_Chin_Hist Econ African_Stud Middle_Eastern_Stud Ethics Relig Drama Music Speech.
Sports—G: Badminton Basket X-country Fencing F_Hockey Lacrosse Soccer Softball Swim Tennis Track Volley. **Activities:** 28.
Very selective adm (Gr PS-11): 88/yr. Usual entry: PS, K & 1. Appl fee: $70. Appl due: Nov. Applied: 592. Accepted: 15%. **Tests** ISEE.
Enr 612. B 7. G 605. Elem 407. Sec 205. Wh 71%. Latino 4%. Blk 4%. Asian 7%. Other 14%. Avg class size: 15. Stud/fac: 6:1. Uniform. **Fac 105.** M 18/F 87. FT 99/PT 6. Wh

87%. Latino 4%. Blk 3%. Asian 6%. Adv deg: 80%.
Grad '10—49. Col—49. (Boston Col 2, Brown 2, Columbia 2, Fairfield 2, Geo Wash 2, Tulane 2). **Avg SAT:** CR 670. M 620. W 670. Avg ACT: 28. Alum donors: 21%.
Tui '12-'13: Day $37,275-37,975. Aid: Need 135 ($2,730,598).
Summer (enr 200): Acad Enrich Rec. Sci & Tech. Theater. World Cultures. Tui Day $2000-3500. 2-5 wks.
Endow $8,063,000. Plant val $43,782,000. Bldgs 5 (50% ADA). Class rms 55. 3 Libs 16,504 vols. Chapels 1. Sci labs 10. Lang labs 1. Math labs 3. Auds 2. Art studios 6. Music studios 2. Gyms 2. Comp labs 3. Comp/stud: 1:1 Laptop prgm Gr 4-7.
Est 1926. Nonprofit. Roman Catholic (66% practice). Sem (Sept-June).

Mother Joseph Butler of the Religious of the Sacred Heart of Mary founded this school. Located directly opposite the Metropolitan Museum of Art and Central Park, Marymount occupies four turn-of-the-20th-century Beaux Arts mansions that are designated landmarks of the Metropolitan Museum Historic District. In 2010, the school added a fifth building, a former parochial school edifice, on East 97th Street.

At all grade levels, Marymount's interdisciplinary curriculum makes extensive use of the international network of Marymount schools, mobile computing technology and the nearby Metropolitan Museum of Art. The school places particular emphasis on science, technology, engineering and math; financial literacy; social justice; leadership; and philanthropy. The lower school (nursery through grade 3) aims to develop the child's language, reading, mathematical and science skills within a structured environment. Only boys with a sibling currently or formerly enrolled at the school may gain admittance to the coeducational preschool program. Marymount schedules weekly visits to science laboratories beginning at the nursery level, and children attend lab three times per week by grade 3. Art, music, dance and physical education form an integral part of the curriculum.

The middle school (grades 4-7), which occupies separate quarters on East 82nd Street, utilizes modified and gradually increasing departmentalization in the major subject areas. The foreign language program commences with Spanish in grade 3 and the addition of French and Latin in grade 4. Within the program, girls have various opportunities to achieve and to display independence and leadership.

The upper school curriculum (grades 8-12) features honors classes in all disciplines, a full Advanced Placement program, and various electives. Emphasizing the classic disciplines and scientific inquiry, the curriculum prepares students for competitive colleges. A strong extracurricular and athletic program; a five-week, off-campus internship for seniors; and community service at all levels complement academics. Girls may take part in international exchange programs, including a semester abroad at one of the overseas Marymount schools.

NIGHTINGALE-BAMFORD SCHOOL
Day — Girls Gr K-12

New York, NY 10128. 20 E 92nd St. Tel: 212-289-5020. Fax: 212-876-1045.
www.nightingale.org   E-mail: admissions@nightingale.org
Paul A. Burke, Head (2012). BA, Williams College, MEd, Columbia Univ.
Col Prep. AP (129 exams taken, 93% 3+)—Fr Lat Span Calc Stats Bio Chem Physics US_Hist Art_Hist. **Feat—**Shakespeare Russ_Lit Southern_Lit Chin Astron Environ_Sci Comp_Sci Amer_Stud Psych World_Relig Ceramics Drawing Film Painting Photog Sculpt Studio_Art Acting Theater_Arts Chorus Guitar Journ Public_Speak.
Sports—G: Badminton Basket X-country Indoor_Track Lacrosse Soccer Softball Swim Tennis Track Volley. **Activities:** 26.
Very selective adm (Gr K-11): 80/yr. Usual entry: K, 6 & 9. Appl fee: $65. Appl due: Dec. **Tests** IQ ISEE SSAT.
Enr 567. Elem 409. Sec 158. Nonwhite 30%. Avg class size: 12. Stud/fac: 7:1. Uniform. **Fac 93.** M 20/F 73. Wh 78%. Latino 5%. Blk 4%. Asian 11%. Other 2%. Adv deg: 82%.
Grad '11—43. Col—43. (Bates 3, Lafayette 3, U of PA 2, Northwestern 2, Colby 2, Kenyon 2). **Mid 50% SAT:** CR 630-740. M 610-680. W 630-760. **Col couns:** 1.

Tui '11-'12: Day $37,150 (+$1080). **Aid:** Need 179 ($3,700,000).
Summer: Gr K-4. Rec. Tui Day $795/wk. 3 wks.
Endow $66,000,000. Plant val $50,000,000. Bldgs 1 (100% ADA). Lib 65,000 vols. Sci labs 4. Lang labs 1. Auds 1. Theaters 1. Art studios 4. Music studios 2. Dance studios 1. Gyms 1. Comp labs 3.
Est 1920. Nonprofit. Sem (Sept-June). **Assoc** CLS.

Founded by Frances N. Nightingale and Maya Stevens Bamford, the school offers a classical college preparatory program to girls of varied backgrounds and interests. In a small-class setting, the school combines academics with the arts, athletics, leadership opportunities, clubs and activities, and community service.

The arts curriculum includes photography, drama, dance, music and studio art. An interdisciplinary visual education curriculum and the program in dramatic literature make use of New York's museum resources and theatrical productions. Students gain an introduction to Spanish, French and Mandarin in grade 3, then commence Latin study in grade 6. Math and science offerings include a science seminar, a summer biotechnology session and an eighth grade research trip to Costa Rica. Social service programming is part of the curriculum in all three school divisions, and upper school students must commit to a yearlong service project within the community.

Among Nightingale's enrichment opportunities are off-campus events, individual student projects, and academic exchanges through the city's inter-school consortium of eight schools. Children in grades K-4 may participate in a coed after-school program.

PROFESSIONAL CHILDREN'S SCHOOL

Day — Coed Gr 6-12

New York, NY 10023. 132 W 60th St. Tel: 212-582-3116. Fax: 212-307-6542.
www.pcs-nyc.org E-mail: pcs@pcs-nyc.org
James Dawson, Head (1995). BS, PhD, State Univ of New York-Albany. **Sherrie A. Hinkle, Adm.**

Col Prep. Gen Acad. Perform_Arts Visual_Arts. Sports (General). Feat—Fr Span African-Amer_Hist Govt Constitutional_Law Studio_Art Drama Music Music_Theory. **Supp**—Dev_Read ESL Rem_Math Tut.
Selective adm: 64/yr. Appl fee: $75. Appl due: Rolling. Applied: 124. Accepted: 71%. Yield: 72%. **Tests** CTP_4 ISEE SSAT.
Enr 196. B 64. G 132. Elem 31. Sec 165. Wh 64%. Latino 4%. Blk 3%. Asian 20%. Other 9%. Intl 15%. Avg class size: 15. **Fac 29.** FT 27/PT 2. Wh 87%. Latino 3%. Blk 7%. Asian 3%. Adv deg: 86%.
Grad '11—38. Col—33. (Fordham, New Sch U, NYU, Manhattan Sch of Music, Princeton, Pace). **Col couns:** 1. Alum donors: 22%.
Tui '11-'12: Day $32,250-35,300 (+$600-2500). **Aid:** Need 63 ($903,000).
Endow $3,219,000. Plant val $11,000,000. Bldgs 1 (100% ADA). Class rms 19. Lib 15,000 vols. Sci labs 2. Theaters 1. Art studios 1. Music studios 1. Gyms 1. Comp labs 1.
Est 1914. Nonprofit. Sem (Sept-June).

Located opposite Lincoln Center for the Performing Arts, this unique school offers a college preparatory education to professional, preprofessional and nonprofessional students. PCS conducts its program in an atmosphere that is respectful of the arts. Scheduling and guided-study assignments are arranged so that students may meet both their academic and their professional commitments without conflict.

Among PCS' alumni are doctors, lawyers and teachers, as well as well-known performing artists and competitive athletes.

REGIS HIGH SCHOOL

Day — Boys Gr 9-12

New York, NY 10028. 55 E 84th St. Tel: 212-288-1100. Fax: 212-794-1221.
www.regis-nyc.org E-mail: edimiche@regis-nyc.org
Rev. J. Philip G. Judge, SJ, Pres (2005). BA, MA, Fordham Univ, MA, Univ of California-Berkeley, MDiv, STM, Jesuit School of Theology at Berkeley. **Gary Tocchet, Prin.** BS, US Military Academy, MA, Naval War College, MA, PhD, Stanford Univ. **Eric P. DiMichele, Adm.**

Col Prep. AP exams taken: 363 (86% 3+). Feat—Creative_Writing Shakespeare Russ_Lit Chin Fr Ger Lat Span Calc Stats Organic_Chem Programming Web_Design Cold_War WWII Psych Theol Architect Art_Hist Film Filmmaking Graphic_Arts Studio_Art Theater Band Music Music_Hist Accounting Speech.

Sports—B: Baseball Basket X-country Soccer Track Volley.

Very selective adm (Gr 9): 135/yr. Usual entry: 9. Appl fee: $50. Appl due: Oct. Applied: 800. Accepted: 17%. Yield: 96%. **Tests** HSPT.

Enr 544. Wh 72%. Latino 15%. Blk 4%. Asian 9%. Avg class size: 12. Stud/fac: 10:1. Casual. **Fac 61.** Adv deg: 85%.

Grad '09—134. Col—134. (Georgetown, Boston Col, Yale, Fordham, Columbia, Holy Cross). **Avg SAT:** CR/M 1423. Alum donors: 60%.

Tui '12-'13: Day $0 (+$385).

Endow $60,000,000. Sci labs 5. Art studios 1. Gyms 2. Comp/stud: 1:6.

Est 1914. Nonprofit. Roman Catholic (100% practice). Tri (Sept-June). **Assoc** MSA.

Named for St. John Francis Regis, a French Jesuit who performed missionary work among southern France's poor in the early 17th century, the school began when a wealthy Catholic widow's looking to anonymously donate her fortune to charity met up with a parish pastor on Manhattan's Upper East Side. The widow agreed to help the pastor realize his dream of founding a tuition-free school for the education of Catholic boys. Virtually from Regis's inception, competition for admission has been extremely intense; to best select worthy new students, the school formulated an admissions process that initially involved a rigorous entrance examination and later incorporated interviews. The present-day school, which continues to charge no tuition, serves a socioeconomically diverse group of students who commute an average of one hour each way. As transfer pupils are not accepted, only eighth-grade boys may apply.

In accordance with the educational tradition of the Society of Jesus, the curriculum originally placed particular emphasis on the classical languages and the liberal arts. Over the years, developments in both education in general and the Jesuit educational tradition in particular have led to an increased curricular prominence of science, math, foreign languages and the fine arts. Course work, which is largely standard for all students during the first three years, is intensive and accelerated, with unusual latitude built into the schedule in the areas of independent study, individualized instruction and unscheduled time. Seniors fulfill requirements in English, physics (if not taken in grade 11) and theology, then select their remaining classes from electives in any discipline.

Each senior devotes Tuesday mornings to Christian service. During his final trimester, the student may either work full-time on his service project or undertake a full-time career internship with an area business.

ROBERT LOUIS STEVENSON SCHOOL

Day — Coed Gr 8-12

New York, NY 10023. 24 W 74th St. Tel: 212-787-6400. Fax: 212-873-1872.
www.stevenson-school.org E-mail: dherron@stevenson-school.org
Douglas Herron, Head (2011). MA.

Col Prep. LD. Underachiever. Feat—Poetry Ecol Comp_Sci Robotics Econ Psych Sociol Philos Film Studio_Art Theater. **Supp**—Rem_Math Rem_Read.

Selective adm: 34/yr. Appl due: Rolling. Applied: 81. Accepted: 50%. Yield: 80%. **Tests** IQ.

Enr 75. B 51. G 24. Elem 9. Sec 66. Wh 63%. Latino 16%. Blk 12%. Asian 9%. Avg class size: 8. Stud/fac: 4:1. **Fac 14.** M 7/F 7. FT 14. Adv deg: 50%.
Grad '09—21. Col—19. (Pace, SUNY-Purchase, CUNY, Northeastern U).
Tui '10-'11: Day $47,000.
Summer (enr 25): Acad Enrich Rev Rem. 4 wks.
Plant val $12,000,000. Bldgs 1. Class rms 11. Comp/stud: 1:1
Est 1908. Nonprofit. Quar (Sept-June).

Derived from the merger of the Scoville School (established in 1882) and the Robert Louis Stevenson School (established in 1908), this school has been located at its present site since 1960.

The Stevenson School accepts only bright underachievers, preparing them for high school graduation and college entrance and seeking to develop their organizational and study skills. The educational environment is designed to strengthen self-motivation, encouraging the fulfillment of each student's academic potential. Parental involvement is modified, and students are expected to complete homework assignments under school supervision and on their own initiative.

The school takes advantage of the cultural opportunities of New York City through both curricular and extracurricular activities.

RUDOLF STEINER SCHOOL

Day — Coed Gr PS (Age 2)-12

New York, NY 10075. 15 E 78th St. Tel: 212-879-1101. Fax: 212-794-1554.
Other locations: 15 E 79th St, New York 10075.
  www.steiner.edu   E-mail: malter@steiner.edu
Julia Hays, Upper Sch Adm; Irene Mantel, Lower Sch Adm.
  Col Prep. Waldorf. Feat—British_Lit Creative_Writing Poetry Shakespeare Russ_Lit Fr Ger Span Calc Botany Ecol Environ_Sci Physiol Zoology Programming Philos Architect Film Graphic_Arts Studio_Art Music Jazz_Band Eurythmy.
  Sports—Basket Soccer Softball Track. G: Volley.
  Selective adm (Gr PS-11): Appl fee: $55. Appl due: Jan. Accepted: 25%. **Tests** ISEE.
  Enr 320. Nonwhite 29%. Avg class size: 21. Stud/fac: 9:1. **Fac 52.** M 14/F 38. FT 40/PT 12.
  Grad '08—17. Col—17. (Sch of the Art Inst of Chicago 2, Bard-NY 1, Middlebury 1, Sarah Lawrence 1, Trinity Col-CT 1, U of Chicago 1). **Col couns:** 1.
  Tui '12-'13: Day $33,500-35,900 (+$0-1525). **Aid:** Need 96 ($1,870,000).
  Endow $1,500,000. Plant val $25,000,000. Bldgs 2. Class rms 21. Libs 2. Sci labs 1. Auds 1. Theaters 2. Art studios 4. Music studios 2. Wood shops 1. Comp labs 1.
  Est 1928. Nonprofit. Sem (Sept-June).

Instruction at this school is based on the educational principles of Rudolf Steiner, who founded the first Waldorf school in 1919 in Stuttgart, Germany. Literature, history, modern languages, the sciences and mathematics form the core academic curriculum. Intensive academic seminars, skills courses that run throughout the year, and workshops for studio art, drama and practical arts enhance different learning tasks.

Student exchanges may be arranged with Waldorf schools in Austria, France, Switzerland, Germany and Spain. Students in grades 9-11 perform 20 hours of community service annually, and seniors participate in a three-week vocational internship program before graduation.

The lower school is located nearby on 79th Street.

ST. BERNARD'S SCHOOL

Day — Boys Gr K-9

New York, NY 10029. 4 E 98th St. Tel: 212-289-2878. Fax: 212-410-6628.
  www.stbernards.org   E-mail: d_kripal@stbernards.org

Stuart H. Johnson III, Head. BA, Yale Univ. **Anne S. Nordeman & Heidi R. Gore, Adms.**
Pre-Prep. Feat—Fr Lat Span Computers Asian_Hist Geog Studio_Art Music. **Supp**—
Rev Tut.
Sports—B: Baseball Basket X-country Lacrosse Soccer Track.
Very selective adm: 53/yr. Appl fee: $0. Appl due: Dec. **Tests** ISEE.
Enr 385. Elem 377. Sec 8. Avg class size: 18. **Fac 64.** M 37/F 27. FT 62/PT 2. Adv deg:
70%.
Grad '11—34. Prep—31. (Riverdale 5, Trinity Sch-NY 3, Phillips Acad 3, St Paul's Sch-
NH 3, Phillips Exeter 1). Alum donors: 28%.
Tui '12-'13: Day $37,610.
Endow $75,000,000. Plant val $60,000,000. Bldgs 1. Class rms 38. Lib 15,000 vols.
Theaters 1. Art studios 1. Music studios 1. Gyms 3. Comp labs 1.
Est 1904. Nonprofit. Tri (Sept-June).

St. Bernard's prepares boys for their secondary years by providing a strong, traditional academic program. Kindergarten offers readiness activities in reading, mathematics, writing, and social studies. Creative writing, including poetry, is emphasized from the earliest levels. The junior school (grades K-3) arts program includes crafts and carpentry, in addition to music and studio art. Foreign language study begins in middle school (grades 4-6) with French and Latin; upper school (grades 7-9) students continue Latin study and choose either French or Spanish. Technology is integrated into the curriculum in all subjects.

Public speaking is an important part of school life: students recite poetry and speak at morning assembly, and the upper school holds an annual competition. Other activities outside the classroom include community service projects, academic competitions and student government. All boys take part in the athletic program; intramural competition begins in grade 3, and the middle and upper schools field interscholastic teams.

SAINT DAVID'S SCHOOL

Day — Boys Gr PS (Age 4)-8

New York, NY 10128. 12 E 89th St. Tel: 212-369-0058. Fax: 212-369-5788.
www.saintdavids.org   E-mail: admissions@saintdavids.org
P. David O'Halloran, Head (2004). BA, Brisbane College of Theology (Australia), MA, Bank
Street College of Education, PhD, Fordham Univ. **Allison Vella, Adm.**
Pre-Prep. Feat—Fr Lat Span Anat & Physiol Computers Art_Hist Studio_Art Drama
Music Woodworking. **Supp**—Dev_Read Tut.
Sports—B: Baseball Basket Ice_Hockey Lacrosse Soccer Track.
Very selective adm (Gr PS-7): 62/yr. Usual entry: PS & K. Appl fee: $60. Appl due: Dec.
Applied: 399. Accepted: 15%. Yield: 89%. **Tests** CTP_4 IQ ISEE.
Enr 407. Wh 80%. Latino 3%. Blk 3%. Asian 2%. Other 12%. Intl 15%. Avg class size:
18. Formal. **Fac 76.** M 30/F 46. FT 60/PT 16. Wh 85%. Latino 5%. Blk 4%. Asian 5%.
Other 1%. Adv deg: 67%.
Grad '11—38. Prep—36. (Trinity Sch-NY 4, Poly Prep 4, Loyola Sch 4, Horace Mann 3,
Regis HS 2, Hotchkiss 2). Alum donors: 23%.
Tui '12-'13: Day $25,425-38,125. Aid: Need 32 ($843,832).
Summer: Rec. Math. Tui Day $250/wk. 2 wks.
Endow $44,257,000. Plant val $35,373,000. Bldgs 5 (25% ADA). Class rms 26. 2 Libs
17,000 vols. Sci labs 3. Art studios 4. Music studios 2. Gyms 5. Comp labs 1. Comp/
stud: 1:2.
Est 1951. Nonprofit. Roman Catholic (50% practice). Tri (Sept-June).

Founded as an independent school by nine Catholic families, Saint David's enrolls boys of all religious and ethnic backgrounds. During the pre-primary years (prekindergarten and kindergarten), children learn to work and play together as they begin to pursue their own interests. Developmentally appropriate language arts and math programs, which begin in grade 1, promote mastery of carefully sequenced concepts and skills. Small-group reading instruction emphasizes phonics and comprehension, and writing is integral to the language arts program.

Weekly science, social studies, art, pottery and woodworking classes augment the core curriculum, and formal computer instruction commences in prekindergarten.

In grades 4-8 (the upper school), students further develop their reading, writing and reasoning abilities. Faculty stress study and note taking skills and the use of reference materials, and the curriculum synthesizes the study of literature, history and science. Ability grouping is utilized in the math department, allowing more able boys to progress rapidly to new material. Latin study is compulsory in grades 5 and 6, after which time it is available as an elective. Boys fulfill their foreign language requirement in grades 6-8 with either French or Spanish. A well-developed computer program allows students to progress from basic keyboarding skills to word processing, spreadsheets and databases. As in the lower school, parental involvement is an important element of the program.

Community service opportunities, which further enrich the curriculum, begin in the lower school. After-school activities are available (for an additional fee) to boys in grades K-8.

ST. LUKE'S SCHOOL

Day — Coed Gr PS (Age 4)-8

New York, NY 10014. 487 Hudson St. Tel: 212-924-5960. Fax: 212-924-1352.
 www.stlukeschool.org   E-mail: scosentino@stlukeschool.org
Bart Baldwin, Head (2007). BA, Univ of Georgia, MEd, College of William and Mary. **Susan Harriot, Adm.**
 Pre-Prep. Feat—Lib_Skills Fr Span Computers Comp_Relig World_Relig Studio_Art Drama Music Outdoor_Ed. **Supp**—Rem_Read.
 Sports—Basket Soccer Softball Volley.
 Selective adm (Gr PS-7): 41/yr. Usual entry: PS & K. Appl fee: $70. Appl due: Dec. Applied: 265. Accepted: 31%. Yield: 53%. **Tests** CTP_4 DAT.
 Enr 215. Wh 75%. Latino 2%. Blk 9%. Asian 7%. Other 7%. Avg class size: 23. Stud/fac: 6:1. Casual. **Fac 30.** M 10/F 20. FT 29/PT 1. Wh 85%. Latino 3%. Blk 6%. Asian 6%. Adv deg: 56%.
 Grad '11—22. Prep—18. (Friends Seminary, Berkeley Carroll, Marymount Sch, Brearley, Dalton, Trinity Sch-NY). Alum donors: 6%.
 Tui '12-'13: Day $33,125-34,425 (+$510-785). **Aid:** Need 43 ($586,870).
 Endow $1,600,000. Plant val $5,000,000. Acres 2. Bldgs 3. Class rms 15. Lib 18,000 vols. Chapels 1. Sci labs 1. Auds 1. Theaters 1. Art studios 1. Music studios 1. Gyms 1. Playgrounds 3. Comp labs 1.
 Est 1945. Nonprofit. Episcopal. Tri (Sept-June).

Established by the Church of Saint Luke in the Fields, the school prepares boys and girls of all faiths for independent secondary schools and specialized public high schools. Located in a historic residential neighborhood in the West Village, the school sits on a two-acre enclosed block with tree-shaded gardens and playgrounds.

The program at St. Luke's emphasizes the development of critical-thinking and academic skills using a variety of educational approaches and techniques. In addition to academics, students participate in a range of extracurricular activities. Chapel, comparative religion classes and service learning are important aspects of school life, as is outdoor education. Boys and girls in grades 7 and 8 perform 16 hours of required community service per year. After-school programming is available.

ST. THOMAS CHOIR SCHOOL

Boarding — Boys Grades 4-8; 5-Day Boarding — Boys 3

New York, NY 10019. 202 W 58th St. Tel: 212-247-3311. Fax: 212-247-3393.
 www.choirschool.org   E-mail: info@choirschool.org
Rev. Charles F. Wallace, Head (2004). BA, Univ of King's College (Canada), MDiv, Univ of Toronto (Canada). **Ruth S. Cobb, Adm.**

Pre-Prep. Perform_Arts. Elem math—Everyday Math. **Feat**—Fr Lat Computers Theol Studio_Art Music Music_Theory. **Supp**—Dev_Read Rem_Math Rem_Read Rev Tut.
Sports (req'd)—B: Basket Soccer Softball.
Selective adm (Gr 3-5): 12/yr. Appl fee: $0. Appl due: Rolling. Accepted: 30%. Yield: 93%. **Tests** Stanford.
Enr 36. Wh 70%. Latino 3%. Blk 11%. Asian 11%. Other 5%. Avg class size: 6. Stud/fac: 4:1. Uniform. **Fac 9.** M 7/F 2. FT 9. Wh 95%. Blk 5%. Adv deg: 88%.
Grad '10—7. Prep—5. (Hill Sch-PA 2, St Mark's Sch-MA 1, St George's Sch-RI 1, St Andrew's Sch-DE 1, Shattuck-St Mary's 1). Avg SSAT: 75%. Alum donors: 9%.
Tui '11-'12: Bdg $13,500 (+$300). **Aid:** Need 28 ($163,000).
Endow $18,000,000. Plant val $20,000,000. Bldgs 1. Dorms 1. Dorm rms 17. Class rms 7. Lib 7300 vols. Labs 1. Gyms 1.
Est 1919. Nonprofit. Episcopal. Quar (Sept-June).

The only church-affiliated choir school in the US that enrolls boarding students, St. Thomas combines the English choir tradition with an American independent school academic and sports program.

The Choir School's academic program features English, mathematics, history, science, art, computer technology, foreign languages, theology, music theory and instrumental study. Graduates of the school enter leading secondary schools or return to their local schools.

The choir rehearses daily and prepares sacred music each year for five weekly services at St. Thomas Church on Fifth Avenue. In addition, the choir presents a concert series, tours domestically and abroad, and makes recordings. Candidates for admission must demonstrate musical aptitude, but need not have prior musical training.

All students participate in interscholastic sports, some of which are played on fields in nearby Central Park. Field trips to museums and exhibitions in Manhattan round out the school's program. A five-day boarding program serves third-grade students, who do not sing in the choir but receive preparation that allows them to become full members earlier. Third graders also remain at the school for four to five weekends between Christmas and the end of the school year, including graduation weekend.

THE SPENCE SCHOOL

Day — Girls Gr K-12

New York, NY 10128. 22 E 91st St. Tel: 212-289-5940. Fax: 212-996-5689.
Other locations: 56 E 93rd St, New York 10128.
www.spenceschool.org   E-mail: sparker@spenceschool.org
Ellanor N. Brizendine, Head (2007). BS, Towson Univ, MLA, Johns Hopkins Univ. **Susan Parker, Adm.**
Col Prep. AP—Studio_Art. **Feat**—Creative_Writing Poetry Shakespeare Asian_Lit Lat-Amer_Lit Chin Fr Lat Span Calc Stats Environ_Sci Physiol Chin_Hist Lat-Amer_Hist Middle_Eastern_Hist Econ Psych World_Relig Art_Hist Ceramics Film Painting Photog Sculpt Acting Drama Chorus Orchestra Dance Speech.
Sports—G: Badminton Basket X-country F_Hockey Soccer Softball Swim Tennis Track Volley. **Activities:** 40.
Very selective adm (Gr K-11): 66/yr. Appl fee: $65. **Tests** ISEE.
Enr 704. Nonwhite 33%. Avg class size: 17. Stud/fac: 7:1. Uniform. **Fac 124.** M 29/F 95. Adv deg: 74%.
Grad '11—53. Col—53. (Harvard 5, Brown 3, U of PA 2, Yale 2, Cornell 2, Dartmouth 2). **Avg SAT:** CR 680. M 680. W 710. **Col couns:** 1.
Tui '11-'12: Day $37,500 (+$135-160). **Aid:** Need 134.
Summer: Enrich Rec. 2 wks.
Endow $69,500,000. Bldgs 1. Class rms 40. 2 Libs 25,013 vols. Sci labs 6. Dark rms 1. Auds 1. Art studios 6. Music studios 2. Dance studios 2. Gyms 2. Comp labs 1.
Est 1892. Nonprofit. Tri (Sept-June).

Founded by Clara B. Spence, this school for girls was originally located in midtown Manhattan, where it enrolled both boarding and day students. Spence's early growth necessitated two relocations to larger quarters, the second of which established the school on East 91st Street in 1929. Boarding was discontinued in 1952.

Drawing its enrollment from Manhattan, Brooklyn, Queens and the Bronx, as well as from nearby suburbs, Spence serves a student body that reflects the multiracial and international character of the city. The school's varied curriculum emphasizes skill development while encouraging creative thinking and clear expression.

In the lower school (grades K-5), the developmental approach to reading and writing emphasizes the connection between the two. Computer classes in the computer lab are part of the curriculum, and girls are introduced to French, Spanish and Chinese languages in grade 3. During the middle school years (grades 6-8), students gain more independence while also receiving the necessary support and structure. Departmentalization begins in grade 6, when girls begin to follow a more complex daily schedule. Middle school faculty also typically teach upper school courses, thus enabling instructors to prepare middle schoolers for the upper grades.

The upper school curriculum (grades 9-12) balances requirements and electives, giving pupils the chance to explore areas of interest. Students take at least one term of world literature and one term of non-Western history. In lieu of Advanced Placement classes, a wide range of elective options for juniors and seniors includes many college-level courses.

Spence capitalizes on its East Side location by scheduling cultural field trips to museums, theaters and other local points of interest. Study abroad and student exchange programs are available, as is an after-school program for lower schoolers.

In autumn 2003, Spence established a second campus on 93rd Street for children in grades K-4. The original East 91st Street location serves girls in grades 5-12.

THE TOWN SCHOOL
Day — Coed Gr PS (Age 3)-8

New York, NY 10021. 540 E 76th St. Tel: 212-288-4383. Fax: 212-988-5846.
www.thetownschool.org E-mail: admissions@townschool.org
Anthony G. Featherston IV, Head (2012). BA, Boston College, MA, Brown Univ. **Linda B. Shuffman, Adm.**
Pre-Prep. Feat—Fr Lat Span Computers Studio_Art Drama Music Dance.
Sports—Basket Soccer Track. B: Baseball. G: Softball.
Very selective adm: 59/yr. Usual entry: K. Appl fee: $65. Appl due: Nov. **Tests** ISEE.
Enr 402. B 200. G 202. Avg class size: 20. Stud/fac: 6:1. **Fac 68.** M 14/F 54. FT 68. Wh 68%. Latino 7%. Blk 7%. Asian 9%. Other 9%. Adv deg: 88%.
Grad '11—36. Prep—32. (Spence 5, Columbia Grammar & Prep 4, Trinity Sch-NY 3, Friends Seminary 2, Fieldston 2, Horace Mann 2).
Tui '12-'13: Day $33,800-37,000. **Aid:** Need 63 ($1,600,000).
Summer: Ages 3-7. Enrich Rec. Tui Day $1300-1400. 2 wks.
Endow $30,800,000. Plant val $9,000,000. Bldgs 3. Class rms 37. Lib 13,000 vols. Sci labs 2. Lang labs 2. Theaters 1. Art studios 2. Music studios 2. Dance studios 1. Gyms 1. Comp labs 1. Laptop prgm Gr 4.
Est 1913. Nonprofit. Tri (Sept-June).

Founded by Hazel Hyde as a small nursery school, the Town School expanded to a full elementary program and assumed its present location near the East River in 1961. Town prepares its graduates for independent day and boarding schools, as well as for the competitive city high schools.

The Town academic program balances traditional and innovative approaches. Core subjects are introduced in kindergarten, and the lower school (grades 1-4) program integrates technology and subject matter across the curriculum, including specialist-taught science and arts lessons. Language arts emphasizes the writing process and literary analysis at all levels as students discuss and respond to classroom texts and independent selections. Native speakers conduct immersion-based French and Spanish classes in grades 1-5, leading to comprehensive three-year programs in both languages and required Latin study in grades 7 and 8.

Community service projects begin in preschool, and interscholastic athletics are available in grades 5-8.

TREVOR DAY SCHOOL
Day — Coed Gr PS (Age 3)-12

New York, NY 10024. 1 W 88th St. Tel: 212-426-3360. Fax: 212-873-8520.
Other locations: 11 E 89th St, New York 10128; 4 E 90th St, New York 10128.
www.trevor.org
Pamela J. Clarke, Head (2005). BA, Vassar College, MA, Yale Univ, EdM, Harvard Univ. **Kristin Harman, Upper Sch Adm; Kathleen Cook, Lower Sch Adm.**
  Col Prep. AP (exams req'd; 58 taken, 79% 3+)—Fr Span Calc Stats US_Hist. **Feat**— Asian_Lit Lat-Amer_Lit Ital Lat Environ_Sci Genetics Programming Web_Design Chin_Hist Ceramics Film Photog Stained_Glass Theater Chorus Music Dance. **Supp**—Tut.
  Sports—Basket X-country Soccer Tennis Track. B: Baseball Wrestling. G: Softball Volley.
  Selective adm: 150/yr. Usual entry: PS, K, 6 & 9. Appl fee: $50. Appl due: Dec. **Tests** ISEE SSAT.
  Enr 835. B 440. G 395. Elem 593. Sec 242. Wh 73%. Latino 4%. Blk 5%. Asian 5%. Other 13%. Avg class size: 15. Stud/fac: 6:1. **Fac 135.** M 34/F 101. FT 135. Adv deg: 62%.
  Grad '11—52. Col—52. (Boston U 4, Bard-NY 4, Franklin & Marshall 4, U of MI 3, Barnard 2, Cornell 2). **Avg SAT:** CR 648. M 628. W 642. Avg ACT: 27. **Col couns:** 2.
  Tui '12-'13: Day $31,500-37,750 (+$2000). **Aid:** Need ($2,881,934).
  Summer: Ages 3-6. Rec. Sports. Tui Day $900-4010. 2-5 wks.
  Endow $12,000,000. Plant val $87,000,000. Bldgs 3 (67% ADA). Class rms 48. 3 Libs 32,000 vols. Sci labs 6. Dark rms 1. Auds 1. Theaters 1. Art studios 7. Music studios 4. Dance studios 1. Gyms 3. Comp/stud: 1.7:1 (1:1 Laptop prgm Gr 5-12).
  Est 1930. Nonprofit. Tri (Sept-June).

Founded as a nursery school called The Day School, the institution expanded its program through grade 8 in the 1960s, and a high school division was added in 1991. The school assumed its present name in 1997.

Trevor maintains a low student-teacher ratio, allowing for activity-based, experiential learning. The program emphasizes critical thinking, time management and collaborative work skills. Ample opportunities in the arts and other areas include dance, drama, choral music, instrumental music and ensembles, filmmaking, photography, student government, publications and a full sports program. A spring mini-term in grades 4-8 offers enrichment courses in subjects outside of the standard curriculum.

Service learning activities begin in grade 1. Boys and girls in grades 6-12 perform at least 20 hours of service each year, and seniors may elect to undertake an independent project. An after-school program for younger children is available, and an outdoor education program serves pupils in grades 2-12. All students in grades 5-12 purchase laptop computers through the school.

Joined facilities on East 89th and East 90th streets house nursery through grade 5.

TRINITY SCHOOL
Day — Coed Gr K-12

New York, NY 10024. 139 W 91st St. Tel: 212-873-1650. Fax: 212-932-6812.
  www.trinityschoolnyc.org
John C. Allman, Head (2009). BA, Yale Univ, MA, Univ of Virginia. **Jan S. Burton, Gr 5-12 Adm; Jennifer Levine, Gr K-4 Adm.**
  Col Prep. AP (475 exams taken, 84% 3+)—Fr Lat Span Calc Stats Art_Hist. **Feat**— Chin Greek Comp_Sci Relig Ceramics Photog Studio_Art Theater Music Speech.
  Sports—Basket X-country Indoor_Track Lacrosse Soccer Swim Tennis Track W_Polo.

B: Baseball Golf Wrestling. G: Softball Volley. **Activities:** 55.
Very selective adm (Gr K-11): 120/yr. Appl fee: $60. Appl due: Jan. Accepted: 13%.
Tests ISEE SSAT.
Enr 980. Elem 540. Sec 440. Wh 74%. Latino 6%. Blk 8%. Asian 12%. Avg class size: 15.
Fac 153. M 72/F 81. FT 121/PT 32. Adv deg: 70%.
Grad '07—116. Col—116. (Harvard, Columbia, Yale, Cornell, U of PA, Johns Hopkins).
Mid 50% SAT: CR 650-750. M 670-760. W 680-770. **Col couns:** 2.
Tui '11-'12: Day $36,500-37,500 (+$1135-1785).
Endow $50,000,000. Plant val $16,000,000. Bldgs 3. Class rms 75. 2 Libs 36,000 vols.
Chapels 2. Sci labs 8. Auds 1. Theaters 2. Art studios 4. Music studios 7. Gyms 3.
Fields 1. Courts 2. Pools 2. Comp labs 2.
Est 1709. Nonprofit. Episcopal. Sem (Sept-June). **Assoc** CLS.

Founded by royal charter, this school was housed at Trinity Church for its first 100 years and was formally affiliated with the parish until 1970. Although Trinity is no longer an Episcopal school, religion remains an important part of school life. An Episcopal chaplain leads weekly chapel services, students in grades 5 and 6 take introductory religion courses, and upper school students fulfill a religion requirement.

In the middle school, the fifth- and sixth-grade curriculum includes English, French or Spanish, mathematics, history, science, religion, music, art, computer and physical education. Latin begins in grade 6. Seventh- and eighth-grade studies in the traditional disciplines are complemented by an elective program in the arts. In the upper school, advanced classes, AP courses or both are available in every discipline, and the arts department offers instruction in studio art, drama, photography, music and art history. All ninth graders spend a night before the start of school at Frost Valley in the Catskills with 12th graders and faculty; seniors act as group advisors and bunk counselors.

The athletic program begins swimming instruction in kindergarten and tennis in grade 3, while interscholastic sports commence in grade 7. A student volunteer service organization oversees the work of several groups, and boys and girls in the middle school (grades 5-8) complete a compulsory community service project each year.

The student body comes primarily from Manhattan, but three other New York City boroughs—in addition to New Jersey—are represented.

UNITED NATIONS INTERNATIONAL SCHOOL
Day — Coed Gr K-12

New York, NY 10010. 24-50 FDR Dr. Tel: 212-584-3071. Fax: 212-685-5023.
Other locations: 173-53 Croydon Rd, Jamaica Estates 11432.
www.unis.org   E-mail: admissions@unis.org
David Shapiro, Actg Exec Dir (2012). BA, State Univ of New York-Oneonta, MEd, Univ of Hawaii. **Amelia Rattew, Adm.**
Col Prep. IB Diploma. Feat—Chin Fr Ger Ital Japan Russ Span Arabic Comp_Sci Anthro Econ Intl_Relations Psych Philos Film Photog Studio_Art Video_Production Drama Theater_Arts Chorus Journ. **Supp**—ESL Rev.
Sports—Basket X-country Soccer Track Volley. B: Baseball. G: Softball.
Selective adm: 258/yr. Appl fee: $75. Appl due: Nov. Accepted: 48%. Yield: 77%. **Tests** CTP_4 ISEE SSAT.
Enr 1541. B 763. G 778. Elem 1078. Sec 463. Intl 84%. Avg class size: 21. **Fac 215.** M 71/F 144. FT 183/PT 32. Adv deg: 75%.
Grad '11—111. Col—111. (McGill-Canada, Geo Wash, Cornell, Smith, Duke, NYU).
Avg SAT: CR 580. M 600. W 590. Alum donors: 3%.
Tui '12-'13: Day $27,430-30,535 (+$1950-2950). **Aid:** Need 127 ($838,651).
Summer: Ages 4-14. Enrich Rec. ESL. Tui Day $650-3900. 1-6 wks.
Endow $11,598,000. Plant val $20,502,000. Acres 3. Bldgs 2. Class rms 97. 3 Libs 63,000 vols. Sci labs 10. Lang labs 2. Theaters 1. Art studios 6. Music studios 15. Dance studios 1. Gyms 5. Courts 2. Comp labs 4. Comp/stud: 1:2.
Est 1947. Nonprofit. Sem (Sept-June).

Although it gives admission preference to United Nations families, UNIS also serves members of the local and international communities who are interested in a global education. The school prepares its students through the International Baccalaureate and US examinations for entrance to universities here and, to a lesser degree, abroad. Over the years, IB students have been granted advanced standing of up to one year at many US colleges. In addition to following a rigorous program of study in the liberal arts and sciences, students may specialize in music or art.

The school has approximately 120 nationalities represented in its enrollment, and more than 65 nationalities among its faculty and staff. English is the principal language of instruction, but students may enter without previous knowledge of the language. The curriculum includes eight foreign language options, as well as after-school mother tongue language programs for native speakers who need to work on reading and writing skills. In addition to the Manhattan campus, which overlooks the East River, the school maintains a second campus for children in grades K-8 in Jamaica Estates, a residential section of Queens.

An outdoor education program heightens awareness of environmental concerns through trips to the Delaware River and the Catskill Mountains. Students organize an annual UNIS/UN Conference, held at the UN General Assembly, on a topic of current global importance. Boys and girls perform 30 hours of required community service annually in grades 9 and 10, then accumulate 50 total hours of service during their junior and senior years.

YORK PREPARATORY SCHOOL

Day — Coed Gr 6-12

New York, NY 10023. 40 W 68th St. Tel: 212-362-0400. Fax: 212-362-7424.
www.yorkprep.org   E-mail: admissions@yorkprep.org

Ronald P. Stewart, Head (1969). BA, BCL, MA, Oxford Univ (England). **Robert Reese, Prin.** BS, Rensselaer Polytechnic Institute, MS, Cornell Univ, PsyD, Yeshiva Univ (NY). **Elizabeth Norton & Cathy Minaudo, Adms.**

Col Prep. AP—Eng Fr Span Calc US_Hist. **Feat**—ASL Chin Anat & Physiol Environ_ Sci Geol Marine_Bio/Sci Zoology Comp_Sci NYC_Hist Law Pol_Sci Psych Ethics World_Relig Film Graphic_Arts Studio_Art Animation. **Supp**—LD Tut.

Sports—Basket X-country Golf Indoor_Track Soccer Track Volley. B: Baseball. G: Softball. **Activities:** 63.

Very selective adm: 100/yr. Appl fee: $50. Appl due: Jan. Accepted: 25%. **Tests** CEEB ISEE.

Enr 350. B 197. G 153. Elem 105. Sec 245. Intl 5%. Avg class size: 15. Uniform. **Fac 62.** M 20/F 42. FT 62. Adv deg: 67%.

Grad '11—63. Col—63. (Am U 5, Syracuse 4, NYU 2, U of PA 2, Johns Hopkins 1, Brandeis 1). **Col couns:** 2.

Tui '12-'13: Day $38,350-38,950 (+$2350). **Aid:** Need 75 ($950,000).

Summer: Acad Enrich. 4-8 wks.

Plant val $10,000,000. Bldgs 1. Class rms 25. Lib 10,000 vols. Sci labs 2. Auds 1. Art studios 1. Music studios 1. Gyms 1. Comp labs 2.

Est 1969. Inc. Quar (Sept-June). **Assoc** MSA.

The school was originally chartered in 1896 as a branch of the New York Preparatory, but was not established until 1969, where it opened at 116 E. 85th St.; it relocated to its present site in 1997. Mr. Stewart, an Oxford-educated Englishman, has been the school's only headmaster.

Enrolling pupils from throughout the Metropolitan New York City area, York Prep offers a traditional academic program that emphasizes college preparation. The school's tracking system places every student in one of several ability groups maintained in each discipline, thus enabling pupils to learn with others of similar ability and ability levels.

The curriculum features electives in most fields, as well as several Advanced Placement courses. The Scholars Program, a three-year sequence that leads to an honors diploma, invites selected students to attend twice-weekly seminars on topics not covered in the standard curriculum. The school also allows qualified pupils to participate in independent study. Faculty utilize York's Upper West Side location by incorporating available cultural and recreational opportunities into their curricula.

Boys and girls in grades 9-12 satisfy a 25-hour community service requirement each year.

NYACK, NY. (29 mi. N of New York, NY) Suburban. Pop: 6737. Alt: 68 ft. Area also includes Congers.

ROCKLAND COUNTRY DAY SCHOOL
Bdg — Coed Gr 8-12; Day — Coed PS (Age 3)-12

Congers, NY 10920. 34 Kings Hwy. Tel: 845-268-6802. Fax: 845-268-4644.
www.rocklandcds.org   E-mail: tmayer@rocklandcds.org
Kimberly Morcate, Head (2011). BA, Oberlin College, EdM, Columbia Univ. **Tricia Mayer, Adm.**

Col Prep. AP (exams req'd; 67 taken, 81% 3+)—Eng Fr Span Calc Stats Bio Physics Eur_Hist US_Hist Music_Theory. **Elem math**—Everyday Math/Singapore Math. **Feat**—Multivariable_Calc Ecol Psych Sociol Philos Ceramics Photog Studio_Art Theater Music Dance Gardening. **Supp**—Rem_Math Rem_Read Rev Tut. Outdoor ed.

Sports—Basket Soccer. **Activities:** 7.

Selective adm (Bdg Gr 8-11; Day PS-11): 37/yr. Bdg 9. Day 28. Usual entry: PS, K, 6 & 9. Appl fee: $100. Appl due: Rolling. Applied: 84. Accepted: 79%. Yield: 56%. **Tests** ISEE TOEFL.

Enr 130. B 61. G 69. Bdg 16. Day 114. Elem 52. Sec 78. Wh 45%. Latino 4%. Blk 12%. Asian 27%. Other 12%. Intl 27%. Avg class size: 11. Stud/fac: 7:1. Casual. **Fac 27.** M 10/F 17. FT 15/PT 12. Wh 88%. Latino 6%. Blk 3%. Asian 3%. Adv deg: 62%.

Grad '11—18. Col—18. (Harvard 1, NYU 1, Fordham 1, Carnegie Mellon 1, Northeastern U 1, Brandeis 1). **Avg SAT:** CR 600. M 650. W 620. **Col couns:** 1.

Tui '12-'13: Bdg $49,975 (+$700-1000). **Day $15,900-29,975** (+$90-700). **Aid:** Need 50 ($778,000).

Plant val $2,000,000. Acres 20. Bldgs 5. Dorms 1. Class rms 21. Lib 16,256 vols. Sci labs 4. Art studios 1. Music studios 2. Gyms 1. Fields 3. Comp labs 2. Comp/stud: 1:2.

Est 1959. Nonprofit. Tri (Sept-June).

Founded in Nyack by a group of community leaders, RCDS moved to its present, 20-acre campus in 1962. The curriculum provides preparation for college and beyond, with an emphasis placed on critical-reading, problem-solving and writing skills.

French and Spanish begin in kindergarten and remain part of the program through grade 12. Performing and visual arts courses are elements of the core curriculum. Upper schoolers choose from various honors and Advanced Placement courses. Fitness for Life, the school's health and wellness program, is a course requirement at all grade levels. Outdoor programs, including work in RCDS' organic garden, seek to develop self-reliance and class cohesiveness. All students satisfy a community service requirement.

In fall 2012, after years of providing older international students with host family living accommodations, RCDS opened an on-campus boarding division for both international and domestic students from grade 8 onward.

OYSTER BAY, NY. (26 mi. ENE of New York, NY) Suburban. Pop: 6687. Alt: 8 ft.

EAST WOODS SCHOOL
Day — Coed Gr PS (Age 2)-8

Oyster Bay, NY 11771. 31 Yellow Cote Rd. Tel: 516-922-4400. Fax: 516-922-2589.
www.eastwoods.org   E-mail: crogers@eastwoods.org
Nathaniel W. Peirce, Head. BS, Northeastern Univ, EdM, Harvard Univ, EdD, Columbia Univ. **Carol Rogers, Adm.**
　Pre-Prep. Feat—Fr Lat Span Studio_Art Drama Music Woodworking. **Supp**—Rem_ Math Rem_Read Rev Tut.
　Sports—Basket X-country Ice_Hockey Lacrosse Soccer. B: Baseball. G: Softball.
　Selective adm (Gr PS-8): 46/yr. Appl due: Rolling. **Tests** CTP_4.
　Enr 233. B 127. G 106. Wh 89%. Latino 3%. Blk 4%. Native Am 1%. Asian 3%. Avg class size: 20. Stud/fac: 6:1. Uniform. **Fac 55.** M 8/F 47. FT 54/PT 1. Wh 99%. Latino 1%. Adv deg: 20%.
　Grad '11—24. Prep—18. (Friends Acad-NY 4, Portledge 4, St Paul's Sch-NH 1, Phillips Acad 1, Tabor 1, Eaglebrook 1).
　Tui '11-'12: Day $18,300-23,600 (+$2100). **Aid:** Need 48 ($656,200).
　Summer: Enrich Rec. Tui Day $1600-2200. 3-6 wks.
　Endow $5,400,000. Plant val $16,000,000. Acres 46. Bldgs 6. Class rms 30. Lib 19,000 vols. Sci labs 2. Art studios 2. Music studios 2. Shops 1. Gyms 2. Fields 4. Pools 2. Comp labs 2. Comp/stud: 1:4.
　Est 1946. Nonprofit. Tri (Sept-June).

Founded by a group of interested parents in Cold Spring Harbor, this school moved to its present, 46-acre campus in 1948. The school draws students from 22 school districts in Nassau and Suffolk counties.

The child-centered curriculum is characterized by academic rigor in all subject areas. Foreign language instruction, which commences in kindergarten with Spanish, includes French in grades 5-9 and compulsory Latin in grades 7 and 8. Advanced programs in science, math and technology complement standard course offerings, and writing and research projects are integral to the program. Boys and girls in grades 5-8 complete required community service projects each year.

A strong performing and creative arts program includes woodworking, drama and music. The physical education program includes movement education for preschool and elementary children and interscholastic athletics for older pupils.

PAWLING, NY. (49 mi. WSW of Hartford, CT; 64 mi. NNE of New York, NY) Rural. Pop: 7521. Alt: 465 ft.

TRINITY-PAWLING SCHOOL
Bdg — Boys Gr 9-PG; Day — Boys 7-PG

Pawling, NY 12564. 700 Rte 22. Tel: 845-855-3100. Fax: 845-855-4827.
www.trinitypawling.org   E-mail: kdefonce@trinitypawling.org
Archibald A. Smith III, Head (1975). BS, Trinity College (CT), MALS, Wesleyan Univ. **MacGregor Robinson, Adm.**
　Col Prep. AP (exams req'd)—Eng Chin Fr Lat Span Calc Stats Comp_Sci Bio Chem Environ_Sci Physics Eur_Hist US_Hist Econ Art_Hist. **Feat**—Astron Oceanog Meteorology Vietnam_War Law Pol_Sci Psych Bible Comp_Relig Philos Photog Studio_Art Drama Theater_Arts Music Public_Speak Mech_Drawing. **Supp**—Dev_Read ESL LD Rem_Read. Sat classes.

Sports—B: Baseball Basket X-country Football Golf Ice_Hockey Lacrosse Ski Soccer Squash Track Weightlifting Wrestling. **Activities:** 34.
Selective adm (Bdg Gr 9-PG; Day 7-12): 100/yr. Bdg 85. Day 15. Usual entry: 9. Appl fee: $50. Appl due: Feb. Applied: 352. Accepted: 76%. Yield: 41%. **Tests** CEEB IQ SSAT TOEFL.
Enr 300. Bdg 235. Day 65. Elem 18. Sec 270. PG 12. Wh 75%. Latino 2%. Blk 6%. Asian 14%. Other 3%. Intl 20%. Avg class size: 12. Stud/fac: 8:1. Formal. **Fac 60.** M 44/F 16. FT 60. Wh 75%. Latino 2%. Blk 6%. Asian 14%. Other 3%. Adv deg: 55%. In dorms 30.
Grad '11—85. Col—85. (Hobart/Wm Smith 3, Boston U 3, High Pt 3, Syracuse 3, Johns Hopkins 2, St Lawrence 2). **Avg SAT:** CR 580. M 560. W 550. **Col couns:** 2. Alum donors: 22%.
Tui '12-'13: Bdg $49,250 (+$2000). **Day $24,000-35,000** (+$750). **Intl Bdg $49,250** (+$9600). **Aid:** Need 115 ($3,200,000).
Endow $32,000,000. Plant val $75,000,000. Acres 140. Bldgs 20. Dorms 8. Dorm rms 135. Class rms 37. Lib 25,000 vols. Chapels 1. Labs 5. Theaters 1. Art studios 5. Music studios 5. Arts ctrs 1. Shops 1. Gyms 1. Fields 13. Tennis courts 11. Squash courts 5. Rinks 1. Weight rms 1. Laptop prgm Gr 7-PG.
Est 1907. Nonprofit. Episcopal. Tri (Sept-May). **Assoc** CLS.

Established and conducted by Frederick L. Gamage, this school merged with Trinity of New York City when the latter took over the property in 1946, and a year later the school transferred its small boarding department there. In 1978, a board of trustees for Trinity-Pawling School was established, an absolute charter was granted by the board of regents of New York State, and Trinity-Pawling became separate from and independent of Trinity School.

The school offers more than 100 courses, including Advanced Placement classes. Mandarin Chinese instruction, which begins in the middle school, progresses from the production of characters and written text to advanced study of Chinese literature and culture. A two-year language program for bright students who have been diagnosed with a mild language-based learning disability utilizes a modified Orton-Gillingham approach to reinforce reading and writing skills, as well as active learning and study strategies. **See Also Page 62**

PORT WASHINGTON, NY. (18 mi. NE of New York, NY) Suburban. Pop: 15,215.

VINCENT SMITH SCHOOL
Day — Coed Gr 4-12

Port Washington, NY 11050. 322 Port Washington Blvd. Tel: 516-365-4900.
Fax: 516-627-5648.
www.vincentsmithschool.org   E-mail: awishnew@vincentsmithschool.org
Arlene Wishnew, Head. BA, MS, Long Island Univ. **Christine V. Cralidis, Prin.** BA, Pace Univ, MS, Fordham Univ.
Col Prep. Gen Acad. LD. Underachiever. Elem read—Wilson Fundations. **Feat**—Span Computers Studio_Art Band Chorus. **Supp**—Dev_Read Rem_Math Rem_Read Rev Tut.
Sports—Basket Soccer Volley.
Selective adm: 15/yr. Appl fee: $100. Appl due: Rolling. Accepted: 70%. **Tests** IQ MAT.
Enr 60. B 37. G 23. Elem 24. Sec 36. Wh 80%. Latino 5%. Blk 10%. Other 5%. Avg class size: 10. Uniform. **Fac 17.** M 4/F 13. FT 15/PT 2. Wh 99%. Latino 1%. Adv deg: 35%.
Grad '11—11. Col—9. (Nassau CC 2, Molloy 2, Dowling 1, Berklee Col of Music 1, Lincoln Tech 1). **Avg SAT:** CR 500. M 440. W 450. Alum donors: 10%.
Tui '11-'12: Day $25,000-29,000 (+$750). **Aid:** Need 15 ($200,000).
Summer: Acad Enrich Rem. 2-6 wks.
Plant val $8,000,000. Acres 4. Bldgs 3. Class rms 20. Lib 5000 vols. Sci labs 1. Auds 1. Art studios 1. Music studios 1. Gyms 1. Fields 1. Comp labs 1. Comp/stud: 1:7.

Est 1924. Nonprofit. Quar (Sept-June).

Vincent Smith's highly structured program, known for its individualized approach to teaching reluctant learners and students with learning disabilities, emphasizes the development of reading, organizational and study skills. Suitable pupils may have attentional disorders, Asperger's syndrome, or expressive and receptive language issues. The school maintains a low student-teacher ratio, and tutoring, remedial reading services and writing skills classes are important aspects of the curriculum. In addition to traditional courses, boys and girls take compulsory classes in computers, art, music, health and physical education.

Boys and girls accumulate 30 hours of required community service prior to graduation.

POUGHKEEPSIE, NY. (64 mi. W of Hartford, CT; 71 mi. N of New York, NY) Urban. Pop: 29,871. Alt: 156 ft.

OAKWOOD FRIENDS SCHOOL

Bdg — Coed Gr 9-12; Day — Coed 6-12

Poughkeepsie, NY 12603. 22 Spackenkill Rd. Tel: 845-462-4200, 800-843-3341.
Fax: 845-462-4251.
www.oakwoodfriends.org   E-mail: admissions@oakwoodfriends.org
Peter F. Baily, Head (2000). BA, Earlham College, ME, Nasson College, MA, Bryn Mawr. Barbara Lonczak, Adm.

Col Prep. AP (exams req'd; 86 taken, 43% 3+)—Eng Fr Span Calc Bio Chem. **Feat**—Playwriting Ecol Robotics Anthro Pol_Sci Ethics Relig Existentialism Art_Hist Film Music_Theory Jazz_Hist. **Supp**—ESL LD.

Sports—Basket X-country Soccer Tennis Ultimate_Frisbee. B: Baseball. G: Softball Volley. **Activities:** 21.

Selective adm (Bdg Gr 9-11; Day 6-11): 47/yr. Bdg 24. Day 23. Appl fee: $40. Appl due: Rolling. Accepted: 62%. Yield: 68%. **Tests** TOEFL.

Enr 171. B 81. G 90. Bdg 76. Day 95. Elem 18. Sec 153. Wh 55%. Latino 7%. Blk 9%. Asian 24%. Other 5%. Intl 23%. Avg class size: 15. Stud/fac: 5:1. Casual. **Fac 32.** M 16/F 16. FT 28/PT 4. Wh 84%. Latino 6%. Blk 6%. Asian 3%. Other 1%. Adv deg: 78%. In dorms 8.

Grad '10—43. Col—43. (Goucher 2, NYU 2, Rensselaer Polytech 2, Art Inst of Chicago 1, Skidmore 1, Boston U 1). **Avg SAT:** CR 516. M 567. W 538. **Col couns:** 1. Alum donors: 21%.

Tui '11-'12: Bdg $40,365 (+$800). **5-Day Bdg $35,190** (+$800). **Day $19,665-23,288** (+$800). **Intl Bdg $42,953** (+$800). **Aid:** Need 67 ($800,000).

Summer: Ages 5-12. Rec. Tui Day $360-400. 2 wks.

Endow $3,000,000. Plant val $15,700,000. Acres 63. Bldgs 21. Dorms 2. Dorm rms 76. Class rms 20. Lib 11,000 vols. Sci labs 3. Photog labs 1. Dark rms 1. Auds 1. Art studios 1. Music studios 1. Dance studios 1. Media ctrs 1. Gyms 1. Fields 5. Tennis courts 6. Comp labs 3.

Est 1796. Nonprofit. Religious Society of Friends (5% practice). Tri (Sept-June).

A Quaker school, Oakwood enrolls a diverse student body that comes from overseas and from all sections of the US. In a simple, friendly atmosphere that promotes close relations between students and faculty, Oakwood maintains high academic standards.

In addition to providing a strong base in traditional subjects, Oakwood has developed a unified senior program that includes intensive interdisciplinary and Advanced Placement courses, as well as various off-campus community service opportunities. Boys and girls in all grades take part in group service projects, and seniors satisfy a 20-hour community service requirement.

Student leadership opportunities include clubs, committees and student government. A substantial drama program, with both on-stage and technical theater instruction, complements art and music offerings. All upper school pupils participate in interscholastic or noncompetitive athletics.

POUGHKEEPSIE DAY SCHOOL
Day — Coed Gr PS (Age 3)-12

Poughkeepsie, NY 12603. 260 Boardman Rd. Tel: 845-462-7600. Fax: 845-462-7602.
www.poughkeepsieday.org   E-mail: admissions@poughkeepsieday.org
Josie Holford, Head (2006). BA, Univ of Wales. **Carol Bahruth, Adm.**
 Col Prep. AP exams taken: 40 (65% 3+). Elem math—TERC Investigations. **Feat**—British_Lit Creative_Writing Playwriting Fr Span Calc Stats Anat & Physiol Astron Bioethics Ecol Environ_Sci Geol Animal_Behavior Comp_Sci Civil_Rights Holocaust WWI Econ Law Gender_Stud Islamic_Stud Art_Hist Film Studio_Art Drama Music Music_Theory. **Supp**—Dev_Read Rem_Math Rem_Read Tut. Outdoor ed.
 Sports—Basket X-country Soccer Ultimate_Frisbee. B: Baseball. G: Softball. **Activities:** 30.
 Selective adm (Gr PS-11): 66/yr. Usual entry: PS, K, 5, 6, 9 & 10. Appl fee: $50. Appl due: Jan. Applied: 133. Accepted: 70%. Yield: 72%.
 Enr 297. B 141. G 156. Elem 200. Sec 97. Wh 75%. Latino 5%. Blk 7%. Asian 9%. Other 4%. Avg class size: 12. Stud/fac: 7:1. **Fac 42.** M 11/F 31. FT 26/PT 16. Wh 88%. Latino 6%. Blk 2%. Asian 4%. Adv deg: 59%.
 Grad '11—26. Col—26. (Hobart/Wm Smith 3, Bennington 2, Hampshire 2, NYU 2, SUNY-Purchase 2, Princeton 1). **Avg SAT:** CR 660. M 600. W 640. Alum donors: 6%.
 Tui '12-'13: Day $18,300-22,500 (+$150). **Aid:** Need 74 ($453,055).
 Summer (enr 50): Ages 3-15. Enrich Rec. Tui Day $285/wk. 3 wks.
 Endow $4,100,000. Plant val $13,000,000. Acres 35. Bldgs 2 (100% ADA). Class rms 40. 2 Libs 18,000 vols. Sci labs 4. Auds 1. Theaters 1. Art studios 2. Music studios 2. Drama studios 1. Gyms 1. Fields 2. Basketball courts 1. Playgrounds 1. Comp labs 2. Comp/stud: 1:2 (1:1 Laptop prgm Gr 7-12).
 Est 1934. Nonprofit. Sem (Sept-June).

PDS was founded by Vassar College faculty and local families with the purpose of "advancing the cause of liberal and progressive education." The school's 35-acre campus overlooking the Catskill Mountains includes historic Kenyon House, a Mediterranean-style mansion. Influenced by the theories of John Dewey and Jean Piaget, the student-centered program utilizes an interdisciplinary, problem-solving approach to academic and creative study.

The school utilizes mixed-age groupings throughout. PDS requires community service participation, either on campus or in the larger Poughkeepsie area, of all middle and upper school students. In addition, all diploma candidates must complete a month-long, off-campus senior internship.

QUEENS, NY. Urban. Pop: 2,229,379. Alt: 75 ft. Area also includes Flushing and Forest Hills.

THE KEW-FOREST SCHOOL
Day — Coed Gr PS (Age 4)-12

Forest Hills, NY 11375. 119-17 Union Tpke. Tel: 718-268-4667. Fax: 718-268-9121.
www.kewforest.org   E-mail: info@kewforest.org
Mark Fish, Head (2009). MEd, Harvard Univ. **Henry Horne, Adm.**
 Col Prep. AP (exams req'd)—Eng Bio Chem Physics US_Hist. **Feat**—Fr Lat Span Calc Stats Anat & Physiol Geol Ethics Philos Art_Hist Studio_Art Chorus Music.
 Sports—Basket Soccer Tennis. B: Baseball. G: Softball Volley.

Somewhat selective adm: 82/yr. Appl fee: $75. Appl due: Jan. Accepted: 85%. Yield: 90%. **Tests** ISEE.
Enr 385. B 195. G 190. Elem 210. Sec 175. Intl 5%. Avg class size: 18. Uniform. **Fac 45.** M 23/F 22. FT 37/PT 8. Adv deg: 46%.
Grad '04—40. Col—40. (NYU, Cornell, Barnard, Columbia, Wesleyan U, Lafayette). **Avg SAT:** CR/M 1129. **Col couns:** 1.
Tui '12-'13: Day $22,575-30,500.
Summer: Gr 7-12. Acad Enrich. Gr K-6. Rec. 8 wks.
Endow $1,500,000. Plant val $12,000,000. Class rms 25. 2 Libs 6000 vols. Sci labs 2. Auds 1. Art studios 2. Music studios 2. Gyms 1.
Est 1918. Nonprofit. Tri (Sept-June). **Assoc** MSA.

Kew-Forest was founded by Louis D. Marriott and Guy H. Catlin. In 1941, upon the retirement of Mr. Marriott, the school was incorporated by the parents.

Attracting students from throughout Queens County and Long Island, the school stresses college preparation and sends graduates to leading colleges. Activities include performance groups, media and academic teams as well as a competitive athletic program for boys and girls in the middle and upper schools. An outdoor education program is incorporated into the middle school, and an active field trip program serves students in the lower and upper schools. Kew-Forest takes juniors and seniors on college visits.

WINDSOR SCHOOL
Day — Coed Gr 6-PG

Flushing, NY 11355. 136-23 Sanford Ave. Tel: 718-359-8300. Fax: 718-359-1876.
www.thewindsorschool.com   E-mail: admin@thewindsorschool.com
James L. Seery, Prin (1988). BA, St John's Univ (NY), MA, Fordham Univ. **Philip A. Stewart, Dir.** PhD.
Col Prep. AP (11 exams taken, 82% 3+)—Calc Stats Chem Physics Studio_Art. **Feat**—Span Environ_Sci Marine_Bio/Sci Programming Econ Govt Law Psych Sociol Fashion_Design Music Bus Marketing. **Supp**—Dev_Read ESL Makeup Rev Tut.
Sports—Basket Bowl Soccer Tennis Track.
Somewhat selective adm (Gr 6-12): 80/yr. Appl due: Rolling. Accepted: 92%.
Enr 180. Wh 30%. Latino 8%. Blk 12%. Asian 50%. Intl 30%. Avg class size: 12. Casual. **Fac 14.** M 7/F 7. FT 13/PT 1. Adv deg: 100%.
Grad '10—34. Col—32. (CUNY, SUNY, Adelphi, CO Sch of Mines, St John's U-NY, Cornell).
Tui '12-'13: Day $17,900-21,900 (+$825).
Summer (enr 500): Acad Enrich Rev Rem. Tui Day $550/crse. 6½ wks.
Plant val $3,250,000. Bldgs 3. Class rms 18. Libs 1. Sci labs 2. Art studios 2. Gyms 1. Fields 1. Comp labs 1.
Est 1968. Inc. Tri (Sept-June). **Assoc** MSA.

Windsor prepares its graduates for leading colleges throughout the country while emphasizing individual development and progress by means of a strong guidance program. A tutorial/extracurricular period is part of the regular school day. Those who already have a high school diploma may enroll in the postgraduate program.

Windsor enrolls international pupils and does not require prior fluency in English, as intensive ESL instruction is available. Students who have completed high school abroad and wish to attend college in the US may attend Windsor's five-month English Language Institute or its yearlong pre-university program.   **See Also Page 117**

ROCHESTER, NY. (66 mi. ENE of Buffalo, NY) Urban. Pop: 219,773. Alt: 513 ft.

ALLENDALE COLUMBIA SCHOOL
Day — Coed Gr PS (Age 3)-12

Rochester, NY 14618. 519 Allens Creek Rd. Tel: 585-381-4560. Fax: 585-383-1191.
 www.allendalecolumbia.org   E-mail: sscharr@allendalecolumbia.org
Michael D. J. Gee, Head (2010). BA, Loughborough Univ (England), MEd, Columbia Univ.
Sara Scharr, Adm.
 Col Prep. AP (exams req'd; 172 taken, 89% 3+)—Eng Fr Lat Span Calc Stats Comp_
  Sci Bio Chem Physics Eur_Hist US_Hist Studio_Art. **Elem math**—Scott Foresman-
  Addison Wesley. **Elem read**—McGraw-Hill/Open Court. **Feat**—Creative_Writing Anat
  Astron Anthro Econ Ceramics Drawing Photog Music.
 Sports (req'd)—Basket Bowl X-country Golf Soccer Swim Tennis Track. B: Baseball. G:
  Softball Volley.
 Selective adm: 65/yr. Usual entry: PS & K. Appl fee: $50. Appl due: Rolling. Applied:
  147. Accepted: 61%. Yield: 71%. **Tests** CTP_4.
 Enr 325. B 152. G 173. Elem 201. Sec 124. Wh 69%. Latino 3%. Blk 15%. Native Am 1%.
  Asian 12%. Intl 8%. Avg class size: 7. Casual. **Fac 56.** M 17/F 39. Wh 90%. Latino 4%.
  Asian 6%. Adv deg: 69%.
 Grad '11—34. Col—34. (U of Rochester 3, Rochester Inst of Tech 2, U of CA-Berkeley
  2, Ithaca 2, Harvard 1, Yale 1). **Avg SAT:** CR 612. M 646. W 618. **Col couns:** 1. Alum
  donors: 18%.
 Tui '12-'13: Day $17,750-20,250. Aid: Need 168 ($1,908,635).
 Summer: Rec. 1-7 wks.
 Endow $14,500,000. Plant val $19,000,000. Acres 30. Bldgs 5. Class rms 42. Lib 16,000
  vols. Lang labs 1. Theaters 1. Art studios 4. Music studios 3. Gyms 2. Fields 6. Courts
  4. Comp/stud: 1:3.
 Est 1890. Nonprofit. Sem (Sept-June). **Assoc** CLS.

The Columbia School for girls, established in 1890, and the Allendale School for boys,
established in 1926, merged in 1971 to form the current coeducational school. Students enroll
from the urban, suburban and rural areas of Rochester. The school has four main divisions:
preprimary (nursery through kindergarten), lower school (grades 1-5), middle school (grades
6-8) and upper school (grades 9-12).

Conducted in a small-class setting, Allendale Columbia's liberal arts curriculum emphasizes
college preparation. Beginning in the lower school, students receive instruction from specialists in foreign language and science. In addition to the traditional subjects, the school offers
art, music, library and computer classes. A majority of seniors take at least one Advanced
Placement course (AP classes are available in every major discipline), and qualified seniors
design, pursue and receive credit for community- or career-oriented off-campus internships in
the last month of school.

Interscholastic sports are offered in coordination with the Harley School. All students in
grades 9 and 10 elect at least one competitive sport per year.

HARLEY SCHOOL
Day — Coed Gr PS (Age 3)-12

Rochester, NY 14618. 1981 Clover St. Tel: 585-442-1770. Fax: 585-442-5758.
 www.harleyschool.org   E-mail: admissions@harleyschool.org
Valerie A. Myntti, Int Head (2012). BS, MS, Univ of Utah, JD, Rutgers Univ.
 Col Prep. AP (exams req'd; 144 taken, 68% 3+)—Eng Fr Lat Span Calc Stats Comp_
  Sci Bio Chem Physics Eur_Hist US_Hist Econ Psych US_Govt & Pol Studio_Art.
  Feat—Creative_Writing Ceramics Film Filmmaking Photog Sculpt Glassmaking The-
  ater Directing Speech. **Supp**—Tut.
 Sports (req'd)—Basket Bowl X-country Soccer Swim. B: Baseball Golf Track. G: Softball

Tennis Volley. **Activities:** 18.
Somewhat selective adm (Gr PS-11): 111/yr. Appl fee: $50. Appl due: Rolling. Applied: 147. Accepted: 91%. Yield: 83%.
Enr 520. B 230. G 290. Elem 357. Sec 163. Wh 75%. Latino 3%. Blk 5%. Asian 5%. Other 12%. Avg class size: 12. Stud/fac: 7:1. Casual. **Fac 77.** M 23/F 54. FT 68/PT 9. Wh 95%. Latino 2%. Blk 1%. Asian 1%. Other 1%. Adv deg: 71%.
Grad '11—46. Col—46. (Carleton 1, Cornell 1, Duke 1, U of Richmond 1, Skidmore 1, St Lawrence 1). **Avg SAT:** CR 615. M 618. W 601. **Col couns:** 2. Alum donors: 17%.
Tui '12-'13: Day $13,000-21,470. Aid: Need 170 ($2,100,000).
Summer (enr 100): Acad Enrich Rev Rem Rec. Arts. Tui Day $105-295/wk. 8 wks.
Endow $9,176,000. Plant val $21,375,000. Acres 25. Bldgs 1. Class rms 58. 2 Libs 67,000 vols. Sci labs 5. Theaters 1. Art studios 5. Music studios 3. Dance studios 1. Gyms 2. Fields 2. Courts 7. Pools 1. Comp labs 3. Comp/stud: 1:4.
Est 1917. Nonprofit. Tri (Sept-June).

The college preparatory program at Harley emphasizes individualized instruction, with a low student-teacher ratio maintained. Students satisfy broad distribution requirements for graduation, and academic flexibility is achieved through electives and opportunities for independent and off-campus study. Music and art are offered at all levels, and Advanced Placement courses are available.

Students engage in one required community service project per year. The summer program provides recreation and reinforces academic skills.

ROSLYN, NY. (18 mi. ENE of New York, NY) Rural. Pop: 2570. Alt: 37 ft.

BUCKLEY COUNTRY DAY SCHOOL
Day — Coed Gr PS (Age 2)-8

Roslyn, NY 11576. 2 I U Willets Rd. Tel: 516-627-1910. Fax: 516-627-8627.
    www.buckleycountryday.com   E-mail: aduffy@buckleycountryday.com
Jean-Marc Juhel, Head (2002). BA, Univ of Paris (France), MA, Columbia Univ, PhD, Michel de Montaigne Univ (France). **Ann V. Duffy, Adm.**
    Pre-Prep. Feat—Lib_Skills Fr Lat Span Computers Studio_Art Drama Band Music Dance Indus_Arts.
    Sports—Basket Lacrosse Soccer. B: Baseball. G: Softball.
    Selective adm (Gr PS-7): 86/yr. Appl fee: $0-40. Appl due: Rolling. Applied: 139. Accepted: 55%. Yield: 75%.
    Enr 339. B 155. G 184. Wh 56%. Latino 4%. Blk 5%. Asian 16%. Other 19%. Avg class size: 14. Stud/fac: 7:1. Uniform. **Fac 50.** M 6/F 44. FT 38/PT 12. Adv deg: 82%.
    Grad '11—27. Prep—24. (Friends Acad-NY 6, Chaminade HS 4, Sacred Heart Acad-CT 4, Collegiate-NY 2, Portledge 2, Waldorf Sch-Garden City 2). Avg SSAT: 94%.
    Tui '12-'13: Day $21,000-29,500. Aid: Need 53 ($684,600).
    Summer: Enrich Rec. Tui Day $2375-7245. 2-8 wks.
    Endow $2,858,000. Plant val $27,078,000. Acres 25. Bldgs 1 (50% ADA). Class rms 30. Lib 19,299 vols. Sci labs 2. Lang labs 3. Art studios 1. Music studios 1. Shops 1. Gyms 3. Fields 4. Courts 4. Pools 4. Comp labs 1. Comp/stud: 1:1.5 (1:1 Laptop prgm Gr 7-8).
    Est 1923. Nonprofit. Quar (Sept-June).

The school, one of the suburban schools founded by B. Lord Buckley and known until 1938 as Great Neck Preparatory, moved in 1955 from Great Neck to its present location with double the former acreage, as well as a new plant and facilities.

Pupils develop basic skills in reading, mathematics and writing through a variety of teaching techniques and technologies. French and Spanish are introduced in prekindergarten, Latin in grade 7. Buckley schedules regular periods for art, music, physical education, library and computers. Laptop computers are issued to pupils in grades 7 and 8. Students in grades 5-8 participate in on- and off-campus community service projects.

Physical education classes meet four times per week in prekindergarten through grade 8. Fall and spring interscholastic athletic competition begins in grades 5 and 6, with winter sports added in grades 7 and 8.

RYE, NY. (24 mi. NE of New York, NY) Suburban. Pop: 14,955. Alt: 49 ft.

RYE COUNTRY DAY SCHOOL
Day — Coed Gr PS (Age 4)-12

Rye, NY 10580. Cedar St. Tel: 914-967-1417. Fax: 914-967-1418.
www.ryecountryday.org   E-mail: rcds_admin@ryecountryday.org
Scott Alan Nelson, Head (1993). AB, Brown Univ, MS, Fordham Univ. **Matthew Suzuki, Adm.**

Col Prep. AP (exams req'd; 453 taken, 92% 3+)—Eng Chin Fr Lat Span Calc Stats Comp_Sci Bio Chem Environ_Sci Physics Eur_Hist US_Hist Psych US_Govt & Pol Art_Hist Studio_Art Music_Theory. **Elem math**—TERC Investigations. **Feat**—Creative_Writing African-Amer_Lit Astron Forensic_Sci Geol Physiol Comp_Design Econ Asian_Stud Film Photog Drama Music Public_Speak. Outdoor ed.
Sports—Basket X-country Fencing Golf Ice_Hockey Lacrosse Sail Soccer Squash Tennis Track. B: Baseball Football Wrestling. G: F_Hockey Softball. **Activities:** 40.
Selective adm (Gr PS-11): 143/yr. Usual entry: PS, K, 4, 6, 9 & 10. Appl fee: $75. Appl due: Dec. Applied: 688. Accepted: 26%. Yield: 80%. **Tests** ISEE SSAT.
Enr 887. B 449. G 438. Elem 493. Sec 394. Wh 73%. Latino 6%. Blk 5%. Asian 7%. Other 9%. Avg class size: 13. Stud/fac: 8:1. Casual. **Fac 121.** M 46/F 75. FT 117/PT 4. Wh 87%. Latino 4%. Blk 4%. Asian 5%. Adv deg: 86%.
Grad '11—97. Col—97. (U of PA 4, U of MI 4, Syracuse 4, Yale 3, Princeton 3, Columbia 3). Athl schol 2. **Avg SAT:** CR 663. M 665. W 685. Avg ACT: 30. **Col couns:** 2. Alum donors: 26%.
Tui '11-'12: Day $20,100-32,800 (+$590-2500). **Aid:** Need 109 ($3,183,190).
Summer (enr 100): Acad Enrich Rev. Driver Ed. Tui Day $950-3400/crse. 6 wks.
Endow $28,000,000. Plant val $61,000,000. Acres 25. Bldgs 6 (100% ADA). Class rms 40. 2 Libs 30,000 vols. Sci labs 9. Photog labs 2. Theaters 1. Art studios 3. Music studios 8. Dance studios 1. Perf arts ctrs 1. Gyms 2. Athletic ctrs 1. Fields 5. Tennis courts 4. Squash courts 4. Field houses 1. Rinks 1. Comp labs 4. Laptop prgm Gr 7-12.
Est 1869. Nonprofit. Sem (Sept-June). **Assoc** MSA.

This college preparatory school offers a comprehensive program and enrolls primarily students from Westchester and Fairfield counties and the Bronx. A required laptop computer program in grades 7-12, independent study and the creative arts are features of the school's curriculum. Juniors and seniors choose from elective courses in English, science, languages, the arts and history. Ancient Greek is available as an independent study offering. Seniors perform community service each June. A full physical education program offers interscholastic sports in grades 7-12.

Apart from the regular schedule, the school provides an academic summer session for motivated students of color, in addition to its regular summer school.   **See Also Page 54**

SCHOOL OF THE HOLY CHILD
Day — Girls Gr 5-12

Rye, NY 10580. 2225 Westchester Ave. Tel: 914-967-5622. Fax: 914-967-6476.
www.holychildrye.org   E-mail: admissions@holychildrye.org

Ann F. Sullivan, Head (1999). BA, Good Counsel College, MA, New York Univ. **Joli Moniz, Adm.**

Col Prep. AP—Eng Fr Span Calc Bio Physics US_Hist World_Hist. **Feat**—Chin Lat Stats Anat Anthro Econ Psych Theol World_Relig Film Photog Studio_Art Drama Chorus Music. **Supp**—Rev Tut.

Sports—G: Basket X-country F_Hockey Golf Indoor_Track Lacrosse Soccer Softball Squash Swim Tennis Track Volley. **Activities:** 31.

Selective adm (Gr 5-11): 78/yr. Appl fee: $50. **Tests** ISEE SSAT TACHS.

Enr 345. Elem 95. Sec 250. Nonwhite 25%. Avg class size: 14. Stud/fac: 7:1. Uniform. **Fac 44.** M 7/F 37. FT 32/PT 12. Wh 93%. Latino 4%. Asian 3%. Adv deg: 81%.

Grad '11—63. Col—63. (Holy Cross, Boston Col, Trinity Col-CT, Notre Dame, Dartmouth, Vanderbilt). **Avg SAT:** CR/M 1197. Alum donors: 24%.

Tui '11-'12: Day $27,000-29,000 (+$875). **Aid:** Need 76.

Summer: Enrich. Arts. Ital Culture. Sports. 3 wks.

Endow $3,000,000. Acres 18. Bldgs 2. Lib 9000 vols. Sci labs 3. Art studios 2. Music studios 3. Gyms 1. Fields 2. Laptop prgm Gr 7-12.

Est 1904. Nonprofit. Roman Catholic. Tri (Sept-June).

Holy Child offers girls college preparation while stressing Christian values in a small-class environment. Advanced Placement courses are available in all major disciplines, and theology is required at all grade levels. Pupils in grades 7-12 take part in the school's laptop program, and students may pursue independent study in selected advanced courses. High school students perform 25 hours of required community service each year.

Among the extracurricular activities are cultural field trips to New York City and spiritual retreats. Arts workshops and study abroad trips are offered during the summer and throughout the school year.

ST. JAMES, NY. (44 mi. ENE of New York, NY) Rural. Pop: 13,268. Alt: 163 ft.

HARBOR COUNTRY DAY SCHOOL
Day — Coed Gr PS (Age 3)-8

St James, NY 11780. 17 Three Sisters Rd. Tel: 631-584-5555. Fax: 631-862-7664.
www.hcdsny.org   E-mail: info@hcdsny.org

James J. Young III, Head (2011). BS, Univ of Rhode Island, EdM, Harvard Univ. **Sally Dessart, Adm.**

Pre-Prep. Feat—Fr Span Computers Studio_Art Music.

Sports—Basket Lacrosse Soccer.

Somewhat selective adm: 31/yr. Appl fee: $75. Appl due: Rolling. Applied: 48. Accepted: 89%. Yield: 72%.

Enr 111. B 51. G 60. Wh 74%. Latino 6%. Blk 3%. Asian 11%. Other 6%. Avg class size: 10. Stud/fac: 5:1. Uniform. **Fac 22.** M 5/F 17. FT 19/PT 3. Wh 91%. Asian 9%. Adv deg: 63%.

Grad '11—13. Prep—11. (St Anthony's 4, Deerfield Acad 1, Portledge 1, Montclair Kimberley 1, Cardigan Mtn 1, Our Lady of Mercy 1).

Tui '11-'12: Day $14,600 (+$245-510). **Aid:** Merit 4 ($46,720). Need 29 ($220,575).

Summer: Acad Enrich Rev Rem Rec. Art. Tui Day $103-577/wk. 7 wks.

Plant val $2,750,000. Acres 11. Bldgs 1. Class rms 17. Lib 10,000 vols. Sci labs 1. Art studios 1. Music studios 1. Gyms 1. Fields 3. Pools 1. Comp labs 1. Comp/stud: 1:2.

Est 1958. Nonprofit. Quar (Sept-June).

This traditional school, founded by a group of local parents, serves western Suffolk County. Beginning in prekindergarten, all boys and girls study a foreign language. Pupils learn to use technology in the context of their daily lessons through work in the computer lab and the availability of laptop computers for classroom use in the upper grades. Writing is an important element of Harbor's curriculum, which emphasizes development of the writing process across disciplines.

The school's practice of differentiation, a classroom teaching technique that utilizes continual assessment to address students' varying learning needs, enables children to acquire knowledge and develop skills according to their readiness, interests and learning styles.

Boys and girls in grades 5-8 participate in various optional community service projects during the course of the year.

THE KNOX SCHOOL
Bdg — Coed Gr 7-12; Day — Coed 6-12

St James, NY 11780. 541 Long Beach Rd. **Tel:** 631-686-1600. **Fax:** 631-686-1650.
www.knoxschool.org   **E-mail:** admissions@knoxschool.org
George K. Allison, Head (2008). AB, Union College, MA, Trinity College (CT). **Duncan L. Marshall, Adm.**
Col Prep. AP (27 exams taken, 78% 3+)—Eng Fr Span Calc Bio Chem Physics US_ Hist. **Feat**—British_Lit Creative_Writing Poetry Shakespeare Astron Ecol Environ_Sci Geol Econ Govt Art_Hist Photog Studio_Art Music_Hist Dance. **Supp**—Dev_Read ESL Tut.
Sports—Basket Crew X-country Equestrian Golf Tennis. B: Baseball Soccer. G: Softball Volley. **Activities:** 9.
Selective adm: 64/yr. Bdg 58. Day 6. Usual entry: 7 & 9. Appl fee: $75. Appl due: Rolling. Applied: 333. Accepted: 64%. Yield: 45%. **Tests** ISEE SSAT Stanford TOEFL.
Enr 143. Bdg 123. Day 20. Elem 8. Sec 135. Intl 72%. Avg class size: 12. Stud/fac: 6:1. Uniform. **Fac 25.** M 11/F 14. FT 23/PT 2. Wh 92%. Latino 2%. Blk 6%. Adv deg: 64%. In dorms 14.
Grad '11—20. Col—20. (Geo Wash, NYU, Lynn, Sarah Lawrence, U of MI, Chapman). **Avg SAT:** CR 484. M 640. W 542. Avg ACT: 24. **Col couns:** 4.
Tui '12-'13: Bdg $45,000 (+$1000). **5-Day Bdg $42,700** (+$1000). **Day $21,965-23,870** (+$1000). **Intl Bdg $45,000** (+$1000-10,000). **Aid:** Merit 2 ($42,528). Need 34 ($619,046).
Summer: Rec. Tui Day $465-3560. 1-7 wks.
Endow $2,500,000. Plant val $6,500,000. Acres 48. Bldgs 12. Dorms 5. Dorm rms 54. Class rms 24. Lib 25,000 vols. Sci labs 2. Photog labs 1. Art studios 1. Music studios 3. Dance studios 1. Gyms 1. Fields 6. Courts 4. Riding rings 2. Stables 1. Comp labs 2.
Est 1904. Nonprofit. Tri (Sept-May). **Assoc** MSA.

Established as a girls' school in Briarcliff Manor by Mary Alice Knox, the school occupied quarters in Tarrytown and Cooperstown before settling at its present campus, a 48-acre estate on Long Island's North Shore, in 1954. Knox first enrolled boys in 1973.

The school's structured college preparatory program, which is rooted in the liberal arts, features small classes, flexible scheduling and a varied curriculum. Course work in the visual and performing arts is integral to the program. Knox offers a full range of opportunities in athletics, including an extensive equestrian program. Boys and girls accumulate 25 hours of required community service prior to graduation. Its proximity to New York City enables the school to schedule frequent weekend activities there.

SOUTH WALES, NY. (19 mi. SE of Buffalo, NY; 181 mi. ENE of Cleveland, OH) Rural. Pop: 450. Alt: 900 ft.

THE GOW SCHOOL
Bdg — Boys Gr 7-12; Day — Coed 7-12

South Wales, NY 14139. 2491 Emery Rd, PO Box 85. Tel: 716-652-3450.
Fax: 716-652-3457.
www.gow.org   E-mail: admissions@gow.org
M. Bradley Rogers, Jr., Head (2004). BA, Univ of Dayton, MA, Johns Hopkins Univ. **Robert Garcia, Adm.**

> **Col Prep. LD. Feat**—Comp_Sci Robotics Econ Fine_Arts Drama Music Bus Journ. **Supp**—Dev_Read Makeup Rem_Math Rem_Read Rev Tut. Sat classes.
> **Sports**—B: Basket Crew X-country Lacrosse Soccer Squash Tennis Volley Wrestling.
> **Somewhat selective adm:** 50/yr. Appl fee: $100. Appl due: Rolling. Accepted: 90%. Yield: 68%. **Tests** IQ Stanford.
> **Enr 130.** Intl 18%. Stud/fac: 4:1. Uniform. **Fac 38.** M 30/F 8. FT 33/PT 5. Adv deg: 60%. In dorms 19.
> **Grad '07—22. Col—22.** (Rochester Inst of Tech, Notre Dame, Drexel, Lynn, Marshall, Curry). **Avg SAT:** CR 450. M 460. W 400. **Col couns:** 2.
> **Tui '12-'13: Bdg $54,500** (+$2500). **Day $35,000** (+$2500). **Aid:** Need ($800,000).
> **Summer:** Coed. Ages 8-16. Acad Rem Rec. Tui Bdg $6800. Tui Day $3200-4300. 5 wks.
> Endow $7,100,000. Plant val $15,142,000. Acres 100. Bldgs 21. Dorms 6. Dorm rms 75. Class rms 32. Lib 10,000 vols. Comp ctrs 5. Auds 1. Theaters 1. Art studios 2. Music studios 1. Gyms 1. Fields 5. Tennis courts 7. Squash courts 3. Weight rms 1. Comp labs 1. Laptop prgm Gr 7-PG.
> **Est 1926.** Nonprofit. Quar (Sept-May).

The school was established by Peter Gow as a college preparatory institution for those with dyslexia or similar language learning differences. Although primarily a boys' boarding school, Gow maintains a small day division for pupils of both genders. All programs are individually planned, and nearly all graduates enter college.

The school serves students of average to above-average intelligence who have specific language difficulties. Classes are small, averaging three to seven pupils each. The core of the program at Gow is "reconstructive language" and multisensory mathematics, both of which are designed to improve and extend the student's academic ability within a college preparatory setting.

Boys and girls attend classes six days each week. An Outward Bound-type outdoors program is one of Gow's activities.

STATEN ISLAND, NY. Urban. Pop: 443,728. Alt: 9 ft.

STATEN ISLAND ACADEMY
Day — Coed Gr PS (Age 4)-12

Staten Island, NY 10304. 715 Todt Hill Rd. Tel: 718-987-8100. Fax: 718-979-7641.
www.statenislandacademy.org   E-mail: hello-sia@statenislandacademy.org
Albert R. Cauz, Head (2012). BA, Boston College, MA, Middlebury College. **Ruth Teague, Adm.**

> **Col Prep. AP (exams req'd; 96 taken, 74% 3+)**—Eng Fr Lat Span Calc Stats Comp_ Sci Bio Chem Eur_Hist US_Hist Psych US_Govt & Pol Studio_Art Music_Theory. **Feat**—Anat & Physiol Astron Oceanog Web_Design Econ Intl_Relations Criminal_ Justice Gender_Stud Art_Hist Film Painting Photog Sculpt Music Music_Hist Dance

Public_Speak. **Supp**—Dev_Read ESL Rev Tut.
Sports—Basket X-country Golf Soccer Tennis. B: Baseball. G: Lacrosse Softball Volley. **Activities:** 23.
Selective adm (Gr PS-11): 50/yr. Usual entry: K, 6 & 9. Appl fee: $50. Appl due: Jan. **Tests** ISEE.
Enr 350. B 175. G 175. Elem 214. Sec 136. Wh 65%. Latino 4%. Blk 6%. Native Am 1%. Asian 7%. Other 17%. Intl 6%. Avg class size: 14. Stud/fac: 8:1. Uniform. **Fac 42.** M 11/F 31. FT 40/PT 2. Wh 84%. Latino 4%. Blk 4%. Asian 1%. Other 7%. Adv deg: 88%.
Grad '11—30. Col—30. (Boston Col 2, Lafayette 2, Marist 2, Princeton 1, U of Chicago 1, Dartmouth 1). **Avg SAT:** CR 570. M 612. W 587. **Col couns:** 2.
Tui '11-'12: Day $21,900-29,050 (+$850). **Aid:** Need 116 ($1,700,000).
Summer (enr 400): Enrich Rec Sports. Tui Day $582-613/wk. 8 wks.
Endow $4,000,000. Plant val $5,300,000. Acres 12. Bldgs 7. Lib 19,000 vols. Sci labs 3. Lang labs 1. Comp ctrs 2. Auds 1. Theaters 1. Art studios 2. Music studios 2. Gyms 1. Athletic ctrs 1. Fields 4. Courts 3. Pools 2. Comp/stud: 1:2.
Est 1884. Nonprofit. Sem (Sept-June). **Assoc** MSA.

The academy, which traces its origins back to the 19th century, is the only independent school on Staten Island. Expansion began in earnest in the 1930s, when the school combined with several other private schools before eventually merging with the Dongan Hall-Arden School. By 1963, SIA had moved all operations from its original location to a 12-acre site in Todt Hill that formerly served as the Dongan Hall-Arden campus.

Academic standards are rigorous and the curriculum is comprehensive in all three divisions. The lower school curriculum (grades pre-K-4) includes accelerated programs in English and math, as well as an enrichment program in science. Middle school pupils (grades 5-8) follow a developmentally appropriate program of studies. The upper school course of studies (grades 9-12) offers Advanced Placement courses in every discipline, an independent study program, electives, an advanced science track and an accelerated math curriculum. Boys and girls perform 40 hours of required community service prior to graduation.

STONY BROOK, NY. (46 mi. ENE of New York, NY) Suburban. Pop: 13,726. Alt: 108 ft.

THE STONY BROOK SCHOOL
Bdg and Day — Coed Gr 7-12

Stony Brook, NY 11790. 1 Chapman Pky. Tel: 631-751-1800. Fax: 631-751-4211.
www.stonybrookschool.org   E-mail: admissions@stonybrookschool.org
Robert E. Gustafson, Jr., Head (1997). BA, Univ of Virginia, MA, Gordon-Conwell Theological Seminary, MA, Columbia Univ. **Joseph R. Austin, Adm.**
Col Prep. AP (exams req'd; 214 taken, 84% 3+)—Eng Fr Lat Span Calc Stats Bio Chem Environ_Sci Physics Eur_Hist US_Hist Psych US_Govt & Pol Studio_Art. **Feat**—Marine_Bio/Sci Comp_Sci Ceramics Drawing Painting Photog Chorus Jazz_ Band. **Supp**—ESL Tut. **Dual enr:** SUNY-Stony Brook.
Sports (req'd)—Basket X-country Golf Sail Soccer Tennis Track. B: Baseball Football Wrestling. G: Softball Volley. **Activities:** 26.
Selective adm (Bdg Gr 7-12; Day 7-9): 102/yr. Bdg 55. Day 47. Usual entry: 7, 8, 9 & 10. Appl fee: $50. Appl due: Rolling. Applied: 375. Accepted: 39%. Yield: 69%. **Tests** SSAT.
Enr 314. B 175. G 139. Bdg 174. Day 140. Elem 62. Sec 252. Wh 47%. Latino 2%. Blk 11%. Asian 13%. Other 27%. Intl 29%. Avg class size: 13. Stud/fac: 8:1. Formal. **Fac 44.** M 25/F 19. FT 33/PT 11. Adv deg: 54%. In dorms 11.
Grad '11—69. Col—69. (NYU 3, Babson 3, Wheaton-IL 3, Rensselaer Polytech 2, USC 2, Boston Col 2). **Avg SAT:** CR 596. M 614. W 593. **Col couns:** 1. Alum donors: 13%.

Tui '12-'13: Bdg $41,500 (+$375). **5-Day Bdg $35,000** (+$375). **Day $20,700-24,500** (+$375). **Aid:** Need 94.
Summer (enr 600): Acad Enrich Rev Rec. Sci. Sail. Sports. Tui Bdg $2500-2995/2-wk ses. Tui Day $395-825/2-wk ses. 6 wks.
Endow $13,316,000. Plant val $60,000,000. Acres 55. Bldgs 37. Dorms 7. Class rms 25. Lib 22,196 vols. Chapels 1. Labs 5. Auds 1. Art studios 2. Gyms 1. Fields 6. Tennis courts 6. Field houses 1. Tracks 1. Stadiums 1. Comp/stud: 1:3.9.
Est 1922. Nonprofit. Nondenom Christian. Sem (Aug-May). **Assoc** CLS MSA.

Stony Brook's founding headmaster, Frank E. Gaebelein, was determined to establish a school where an educational program of rigorous college preparation would be conducted within the context of the Christian faith and basic values, at a time when many were moving toward secular approaches to education. The school preserves the classic tradition, which Dr. Gaebelein articulated, of integrating faith and learning.

Academics stress the development of abstract thinking, intensive reading and careful research from within a traditional liberal arts curriculum. The humanities are emphasized, with Advanced Placement courses offered in many subjects, and an independent learning program is available. The school hosts the Staley Lecture Series, held annually to foster intellectual curiosity and critical thinking.

Upper-class honor students participate in a program of tutoring, while seniors satisfy a 40-hour community service requirement. Student exchange opportunities include a year of postgraduate study in England and spring break trips abroad.

SYRACUSE, NY. (122 mi. WNW of Albany, NY) Urban. Pop: 147,306. Alt: 400 ft. Area also includes DeWitt.

MANLIUS PEBBLE HILL SCHOOL

Day — Coed Gr PS (Age 4)-PG

DeWitt, NY 13214. 5300 Jamesville Rd. Tel: 315-446-2452. Fax: 315-446-2620.
www.mph.net   E-mail: mphinfo@mph.net
D. **Scott Wiggins, Head** (2012). BA, Boston Univ, JD, Arizona State Univ. **Nicole Cicoria, Adm.**
Col Prep. AP (exams req'd; 161 taken, 92% 3+)—Eng Fr Lat Span Calc Stats Comp_ Sci Bio Chem Environ_Sci Physics Eur_Hist US_Hist Econ Studio_Art. **Elem math—** Everyday Math. **Feat—**Creative_Writing Chin Greek Astron Geol Physiol Web_Design Asian_Stud Constitutional_Law Criminal_Justice Ethics Philos Art_Hist Photog Sculpt Acting Theater Chorus Music Music_Theory Jazz_Band Dance Accounting Marketing. **Supp—**ESL Tut. **Dual enr:** Cazenovia, Onondaga CC, Le Moyne.
Sports—X-country Equestrian Golf Lacrosse Ski Soccer Tennis Track. B: Basket. G: Softball Swim Volley. **Activities:** 50.
Selective adm (Gr PS-12): 99/yr. Usual entry: K, 7 & 9. Appl fee: $50. Appl due: Rolling. Applied: 188. Accepted: 78%. Yield: 67%. **Tests** CTP_4.
Enr 558. B 258. G 300. Elem 308. Sec 250. Wh 70%. Latino 2%. Blk 6%. Native Am 6%. Asian 4%. Other 12%. Avg class size: 13. Stud/fac: 8:1. **Fac 81.** M 29/F 52. FT 63/PT 18. Wh 90%. Latino 2%. Blk 5%. Asian 2%. Other 1%. Adv deg: 65%.
Grad '11—77. Col—76. (Alfred 3, Boston U 3, Syracuse 3, U of Pittsburgh 3, Cornell 2, NYU 2). **Avg SAT:** CR 611. M 602. W 608. Avg ACT: 26.5. **Col couns:** 2.
Tui '12-'13: Day $13,889-18,779 (+$490-1640). **Aid:** Merit 87 ($812,581). Need 162 ($1,053,870).
Summer (enr 225): Enrich Rec. Tui Day $214/wk. 6 wks.
Endow $2,000,000. Plant val $6,000,000. Acres 26. Bldgs 10. Class rms 46. Lib 12,500 vols. Sci labs 4. Lang labs 4. Theaters 1. Art studios 4. Music studios 3. Dance studios 1. Gyms 1. Fields 4. Courts 4. Comp labs 3.
Est 1869. Nonprofit. Quar (Sept-June). **Assoc** MSA.

MPH was formed in 1970 by a merger of the Manlius School (a boys' military boarding school founded in 1869) and Pebble Hill School (a coeducational day school begun in 1927). With the merger, the military program was dropped and the school assumed its present status.

The lower school offers individualized instruction with an emphasis on skills in reading and mathematics, as well as full curricula in science and social studies. Foreign language conversation and culture are also introduced. All-day prekindergarten and kindergarten programs are available. Middle and upper school classes follow a college preparatory curriculum. MPH offers Advanced Placement courses in all disciplines, and the school also provides opportunities for independent study, community service and travel abroad. Fine and performing arts programs and physical education serve pupils at all grade levels.

A limited boarding program enables students in grades 9-PG to live with host families chosen from parents, faculty members and administrators.

TARRYTOWN, NY. (28 mi. N of New York, NY) Suburban. Pop: 11,090. Alt: 300 ft.

HACKLEY SCHOOL
5-Day Bdg — Coed Gr 9-12; Day — Coed K-12

Tarrytown, NY 10591. 293 Benedict Ave. Tel: 914-366-2642. Fax: 914-366-2636.
www.hackleyschool.org E-mail: admissions@hackleyschool.org
Walter C. Johnson, Head (1995). BA, Amherst College, MA, Univ of Pennsylvania, MA, Columbia Univ. Christopher T. McColl, Gr 7-12 Adm; Julie S. Core, Gr K-6 Adm.
Col Prep. AP (exams req'd; 380 taken, 95% 3+)—Fr Lat Span Calc Stats Comp_Sci Bio Chem Environ_Sci Physics Studio_Art Music_Theory. Feat—Creative_Writing Women's_Lit Chin Greek Ecol Genetics Marine_Bio/Sci Zoology Comp_Animation Anthro Econ Architect Art_Hist Photog Acting Drama Music. Supp—Rev Tut.
Sports—Basket X-country Fencing Golf Indoor_Track Lacrosse Soccer Squash Swim Tennis Track. B: Baseball Football Wrestling. G: F_Hockey Softball.
Selective adm (Bdg Gr 9-11; Day K-11): 118/yr. Bdg 7. Day 111. Appl fee: $55. Appl due: Dec. Applied: 528. Accepted: 29%. Yield: 69%. Tests CTP_4 ISEE SSAT.
Enr 836. B 415. G 421. Bdg 25. Day 811. Elem 453. Sec 383. Wh 70%. Latino 8%. Blk 8%. Asian 12%. Other 2%. Avg class size: 16. Fac 132. M 52/F 80. FT 132. Wh 84%. Latino 5%. Blk 5%. Asian 5%. Other 1%. Adv deg: 81%. In dorms 6.
Grad '10—96. Col—96. (Columbia, Cornell, Harvard, NYU, Princeton, Yale). Mid 50% SAT: CR 630-730. M 650-730. Col couns: 3. Alum donors: 28%.
Tui '11-'12: 5-Day Bdg $45,000 (+$1000). Day $30,900-35,700 (+$1000). Aid: Need 123 ($3,107,606).
Endow $29,100,000. Plant val $50,000,000. Acres 285. Bldgs 20. Dorms 2. Dorm rms 46. Class rms 70. Lib 33,000 vols. Labs 7. Auds 2. Theaters 2. Art studios 3. Music studios 3. Perf arts ctrs 1. Gyms 1. Athletic ctrs 1. Fields 6. Tennis courts 6. Squash courts 4. Pools 1. Comp/stud: 1:2.
Est 1899. Nonprofit. Sem (Sept-June). Assoc CLS.

Established as a liberal arts boarding school for boys, Hackley now offers a rigorous academic program for both boys and girls. The lower school stresses both art and music, in addition to the traditional disciplines. Projects, field trips and hands-on activities supplement daily instruction, and interdisciplinary projects are common. Community service, environmental awareness, international studies and geography are integral aspects of the curriculum at this level. The study of foreign languages begins in the lower school, and field trips, assemblies, extracurricular activities, sports and social events complement the middle school schedule.

Students in the upper school choose from a wider array of courses, sports and activities. In many disciplines, the program offers AP classes, as well as tutorials and seminars that provide extensive choice to the students through a wide range of electives. Graduation requirements include foreign language, laboratory sciences, and performing or visual arts course work.

The athletic program for grades 7 and 8 stresses team sports at the interscholastic level; in the upper school, those who do not participate in interscholastic sports must choose a noncompetitive activity each season for after-school recreation. Such fitness electives include dance, squash and golf. Hackley's performing arts program includes concerts, recitals, serious drama and musicals.

TROY, NY. (8 mi. NE of Albany, NY; 143 mi. N of New York, NY) Urban. Pop: 49,170. Alt: 35 ft.

EMMA WILLARD SCHOOL
Bdg and Day — Girls Gr 9-PG

Troy, NY 12180. 285 Pawling Ave. Tel: 518-833-1320. Fax: 518-833-1805.
www.emmawillard.org   E-mail: admissions@emmawillard.org
Trudy E. Hall, Head (2000). BS, St Lawrence Univ, EdM, Harvard Univ, MALS, Duke Univ.
Jeffrey E. Pilgrim, Adm.

Col Prep. AP (exams req'd; 219 taken, 90% 3+)—Eng Chin Fr Lat Span Calc Stats Comp_Sci Bio Chem Physics Eur_Hist US_Hist US_Govt & Pol Art_Hist Studio_Art. **Feat**—Poetry Shakespeare Playwriting Bioethics Animal_Behavior Neurosci African_Hist E_Asian_Hist Lat-Amer_Hist Econ Philos Ceramics Drawing Film Photog Theater Chorus Music Music_Theory Orchestra Ballet Dance Jazz_Dance. **Supp**— ESL Tut.

Sports—G: Basket Crew X-country F_Hockey Lacrosse Soccer Softball Swim Tennis Track Volley. **Activities:** 40.

Selective adm (Bdg Gr 9-PG; Day 9-11): 102/yr. Bdg 68. Day 34. Usual entry: 9. Appl fee: $50. Appl due: Feb. Applied: 450. Accepted: 36%. Yield: 62%. **Tests** CEEB ISEE SSAT TOEFL.

Enr 322. Bdg 203. Day 119. Sec 320. PG 2. Wh 83%. Latino 4%. Blk 9%. Asian 3%. Other 1%. Intl 27%. Avg class size: 12. Stud/fac: 6:1. Casual. **Fac 56.** M 13/F 43. FT 46/PT 10. Wh 94%. Latino 3%. Asian 3%. Adv deg: 73%. In dorms 4.

Grad '11—84. Col—84. (Rensselaer Polytech 4, Cornell 3, St Lawrence 3, Union Col-NY 3, U of PA 2, Williams 2). **Avg SAT:** CR 635. M 620. W 642. Avg ACT: 26. **Col couns:** 3. Alum donors: 33%.

Tui '11-'12: Bdg $43,650 (+$1350). **Day $27,700** (+$1000). **Aid:** Merit 10 ($105,000). Need 166 ($3,868,300).

Summer (enr 24): ESL. Tui Bdg $6100. 4 wks.

Endow $86,000,000. Plant val $180,000,000. Acres 137. Bldgs 43. Dorms 3. Dorm rms 144. Class rms 28. Lib 32,000 vols. Lang labs 1. Auds 2. Theaters 1. Art studios 5. Music studios 11. Gyms 1. Fields 3. Courts 9. Pools 1. Tracks 1. Comp/stud: 1:3 (1:1 Laptop prgm Gr 9-PG).

Est 1814. Nonprofit. Sem (Sept-June). **Assoc** CLS.

Emma Willard School maintains a tradition of scholastic excellence, enrolling girls from families of varying backgrounds from throughout the nation and the world. Founded in Middlebury, VT, by Emma Willard, pioneer in the education of women, in 1821 it came upon invitation to Troy as Troy Female Seminary, and was reorganized under its present name in 1892. Among educationally influential alumnae was Mrs. Russell Sage, who provided the site that the school has occupied since 1910.

All students have a core of required courses and are expected to develop a strong foundation of academic skills. The program encourages flexibility within the structure so that students take courses in all major areas. The program consists of divisions in the following areas: the arts, computer science, English, history, languages, math, physical education and health, and science. The foreign language curriculum includes tutorial Italian classes, while dance, drama, music and visual arts classes are among the arts division offerings. Tablet computers are issued to incoming students.

The well-supervised independent study program may include part-time projects in the Troy/Albany/Schenectady area. Projects have included internships with a veterinary clinic, the New York State Supreme Court and the New York State Assembly. Emma Willard also operates a speaker series that brings prominent individuals to the school for 24-hour residencies.

TUXEDO PARK, NY. (39 mi. NNW of New York, NY) Rural. Pop: 731. Alt: 620 ft.

TUXEDO PARK SCHOOL
Day — Coed Gr PS (Age 3)-9

Tuxedo Park, NY 10987. Mountain Farm Rd. Tel: 845-351-4737. Fax: 845-351-4219.
www.tuxedoparkschool.org   E-mail: kheard@tuxedoparkschool.org
Kathleen McNamara, Head (2011). BA, Rutgers Univ, MA, New York Univ. **Kristen Heard, Adm.**
  Pre-Prep. Feat—Fr Lat Span Computers Studio_Art Drama Music Dance. **Supp**—Dev_ Read Rem_Read Rev Tut.
  Sports (req'd)—Basket Lacrosse Tennis Track. B: Soccer. G: F_Hockey.
  Selective adm: 35/yr. Appl fee: $75. Appl due: Feb. **Tests** CTP_4.
  Enr 238. Nonwhite 40%. Avg class size: 17. Stud/fac: 7:1. Uniform. **Fac 35.** M 8/F 27. FT 35. Adv deg: 68%.
  Grad '10—21. Prep—16. (Lawrenceville 2, Masters Sch-NY 2, Salisbury-CT 2, Berkshire Sch 1, Peddie 1, Westover 1).
  Tui '11-'12: Day $24,150-30,900. Aid: Need 88.
  Endow $10,000,000. Plant val $13,000,000. Bldgs 3. Class rms 20. Lib 12,000 vols. Sci labs 3. Theaters 2. Art studios 2. Music studios 2. Gyms 2. Fields 2.
  Est 1900. Nonprofit. Tri (Sept-June).

Located just north of the New Jersey border, Tuxedo Park serves students from New York State and New Jersey who live within a 35-mile radius. A traditional academic approach—with particular emphasis placed on reading, writing and mathematics—is combined with innovative programs in science, computer, and the fine and performing arts. TPS features interdisciplinary learning projects at all grade levels.

Students in grades 7-9 choose from a variety of electives that includes photography, yearbook, literary magazine, choral performances, drama and set design. French study begins in kindergarten, and all pupils also take Latin in grades 7-9. Interscholastic athletic competition begins in grade 7.

WHITE PLAINS, NY. (26 mi. NNE of New York, NY) Suburban. Pop: 53,077. Alt: 201 ft.

WINDWARD SCHOOL
Day — Coed Gr 1-9

White Plains, NY 10605. 13 Windward Ave. Tel: 914-949-6968. Fax: 914-949-8220.
Other locations: 40 W Red Oak Ln, White Plains 10604.
  www.windwardny.org   E-mail: admissionsinquiry@windwardny.org
John J. Russell, Head (2007). EdD. Maureen A. Sweeney, Adm.
  LD. Elem read—Orton-Gillingham. **Feat**—Lib_Skills Studio_Art Music. **Supp**—Dev_ Read Rem_Math Rem_Read.
  Sports—Basket X-country Soccer. B: Lacrosse. G: Cheer Softball.
  Selective adm: Appl due: Rolling. Applied: 329. Accepted: 30%. Yield: 25%. **Tests** IQ.

Enr 546. B 336. G 210. Wh 89%. Latino 2%. Blk 3%. Asian 3%. Other 3%. Avg class size: 10. Stud/fac: 4:1. **Fac 139.** M 20/F 119. FT 139.
Grad '11—16. Prep—16.
Tui '11-'12: Day $44,700 (+$100). **Aid:** Need ($1,650,000).
Summer (enr 141): Acad Enrich Rem. Tui Day $2500. 4 wks.
Endow $4,300,000. Plant val $25,000,000. Acres 17. Bldgs 5. Class rms 40. Lib 14,000 vols. Labs 4. Art studios 4. Gyms 2. Fields 3.
Est 1926. Nonprofit. (Sept-June).

Windward's language-based curriculum serves students of average to superior intelligence who have learning disabilities. Small-group basic skills remediation is supplemented by physical education, art, computer and library skills. Boys and girls attend daily math, science and social studies classes. The goal is to academically prepare the student for a return to the independent or public school of his or her choice.

The middle school occupies a separate campus on West Red Oak Lane.

See Also Page 65

WOODMERE, NY. (12 mi. E of New York, NY) Suburban. Pop: 16,447. Alt: 30 ft.

LAWRENCE WOODMERE ACADEMY
Day — Coed Gr PS (Age 3)-12

Woodmere, NY 11598. 336 Woodmere Blvd. Tel: 516-374-9000. Fax: 516-374-4707.
www.lawrencewoodmere.org   E-mail: info@lawrencewoodmere.org
Alan Bernstein, Head (2004). BMus, Boston University, MS, City Univ of New York. **Elizabeth Glazer, Adm.**
Col Prep. AP (exams req'd)—Eng Fr Span Calc Comp_Sci Bio Chem Physics US_Hist World_Hist Studio_Art. **Feat**—Chin Anat & Physiol Astron Environ_Sci Genetics Ethics Drama Band Chorus Music Bus Journ. **Supp**—ESL Tut. Outdoor ed.
Sports—Basket X-country Soccer Tennis. B: Baseball Golf. G: Softball Volley. **Activities:** 17.
Selective adm (Gr PS-11): Appl fee: $50. Appl due: Rolling. **Tests** ISEE SSAT TOEFL.
Enr 275. Elem 145. Sec 130. Wh 50%. Blk 30%. Asian 20%. Intl 20%. Avg class size: 15. Stud/fac: 6:1. **Fac 50.** Adv deg: 72%.
Grad '11—31. Col—31. (Syracuse 2, U of New Haven 2, Wellesley 1, Wash U 1, Haverford 1, Harvey Mudd 1). **Avg SAT:** CR 550. M 580. W 550. **Col couns:** 1.
Tui '12-'13: Day $19,500-29,700 (+$500). **Aid:** Need 116 ($1,816,150).
Summer: Rec. Sports. Tui Day $2800-4950. 4-8 wks.
Plant val $4,000,000. Acres 7. Bldgs 1. Class rms 22. Lib 32,000 vols. Comp ctrs 3. Theaters 1. Art studios 1. Music studios 2. Gyms 1. Fields 3. Courts 3. Pools 2.
Est 1912. Inc. Sem (Sept-June). **Assoc** CLS.

The school was formed by the 1990 consolidation of Lawrence Country Day School (founded in 1891) and Woodmere Academy (founded in 1912). Writing skills are emphasized in all course work, while the traditional curriculum is enriched by honors and Advanced Placement courses in a variety of disciplines. Instruction follows an individualized approach at all grade levels.

PENNSYLVANIA

ALLENTOWN, PA. (45 mi. NNW of Philadelphia, PA) Urban. Pop: 106,632. Alt: 304 ft.

SWAIN SCHOOL
Day — Coed Gr PS (Age 3)-8

Allentown, PA 18103. 1100 S 24th St. Tel: 610-433-4542. Fax: 610-433-3844.
www.swain.org   E-mail: info@swain.org
Todd P. Stansbery, Head (2006). BA, College of Wooster, MS, Johns Hopkins Univ. **Leah Papp, Adm.**
Pre-Prep. Feat—Lib_Skills Lat Span Computers Studio_Art Drama Music. **Supp**—Dev_Read Rem_Read Tut.
Sports—Basket X-country Lacrosse. B: Soccer. G: F_Hockey.
Selective adm: 63/yr. Usual entry: PS, K, 1, 5 & 6. Appl fee: $65. Appl due: Rolling. Accepted: 83%. Yield: 81%. **Tests** ISEE.
Enr 300. B 145. G 155. Intl 5%. Avg class size: 12. Stud/fac: 9:1. Uniform. **Fac 55.** M 3/F 52. FT 45/PT 10. Adv deg: 30%.
Grad '11—20. Prep—16. (Moravian 6, Hill Sch-PA 3, Phillips Exeter 1, Blair 1, St Andrew's Sch-DE 1).
Tui '12-'13: Day $14,995-18,900 (+$210-1340).
Summer (enr 100): Enrich Rec. Sports. 9 wks.
Endow $1,800,000. Plant val $6,000,000. Acres 20. Bldgs 2. Lib 9800 vols. Sci labs 2. Comp ctrs 1. Theaters 1. Art studios 1. Music studios 2. Gyms 1. Fields 3. Comp labs 2. Laptop prgm Gr 5.
Est 1929. Nonprofit. Tri (Sept-June). **Assoc** MSA.

Located on a 20-acre campus five minutes from downtown Allentown, Swain has grown considerably since being established by Dr. D. Esther Swain as a single kindergarten class.

At all grade levels, classroom faculty work closely with specialists in science, art, music, drama, technology and library science. Conversational Spanish is introduced in kindergarten, while Latin instruction begins in grade 6.

The middle school stresses the basic disciplines, and emphasis is also placed on study, library and research skills. Swain offers such extracurricular activities as after-school enrichment courses, athletics and drama. Before- and after-school care is also available.

BETHLEHEM, PA. (45 mi. NNW of Philadelphia, PA) Urban. Pop: 71,329. Alt: 235 ft.

MORAVIAN ACADEMY
Day — Coed Gr PS (Age 4)-12

Bethlehem, PA 18020. 4313 Green Pond Rd. Tel: 610-691-1600. Fax: 610-691-3354.
Other locations: 11 W Market St, Bethlehem 18018; 422 Heckewelder Pl, Bethlehem 18018; 7 E Market St, Bethlehem 18018.
www.moravianacademy.org   E-mail: csnook@moravianacademy.org
George N. King, Jr., Head (2007). BA, Murray State Univ, MS, New England Conservatory of Music. **Daniel J. Axford, Gr 9-12 Adm; Christine L. Murphy, Gr 6-8 Adm; Ingrid Gerber, Gr PS-5 Adm.**
Col Prep. AP (exams req'd; 240 taken, 84% 3+)—Eng Fr Span Calc Stats Bio Chem Environ_Sci Eur_Hist US_Hist. **Feat**—Chin Lat Linear_Algebra Botany Ecol Zool-

ogy 20th_Century_China Econ Ethics World_Relig Art_Hist Film Photog Studio_Art Acting Drama Music Handbells Woodworking Health. **Supp**—Rev. Outdoor ed.

Sports—Basket X-country Golf Lacrosse Soccer Swim Tennis Track. B: Baseball Football Wrestling. G: F_Hockey Softball Volley. **Activities:** 50.

Somewhat selective adm (Gr PS-11): 141/yr. Usual entry: PS, K, 6 & 9. Appl fee: $65. Appl due: Rolling. Applied: 227. Accepted: 86%. Yield: 72%. **Tests** CTP_4 IQ.

Enr 777. B 372. G 405. Elem 493. Sec 284. Wh 72%. Latino 2%. Blk 5%. Asian 12%. Other 9%. Avg class size: 15. Stud/fac: 8:1. **Fac 99.** M 27/F 72. FT 90/PT 9. Wh 95%. Blk 1%. Asian 4%. Adv deg: 67%.

Grad '11—70. Col—70. (Lehigh 4, Bucknell 3, Villanova 3, Bryn Mawr 2, Cornell 2, U of DE 2). **Avg SAT:** CR 656. M 658. W 655. **Col couns:** 2. Alum donors: 12%.

Tui '12-'13: Day $13,950-23,550 (+$755-1220). **Aid:** Need 118 ($1,299,663).

Summer: Acad Enrich. 1 wk. Gr PS-9. Rec. 8 wks.

Endow $15,275,000. Plant val $27,500,000. Acres 120. Bldgs 15. Class rms 69. Lib 23,000 vols. Sci labs 5. Auds 3. Art studios 4. Music studios 4. Gyms 3. Fields 8. Courts 6. Pools 1. Comp/stud: 1:1.3 (1:1 Laptop prgm Gr 9).

Est 1742. Nonprofit. Moravian. (Aug-June). **Assoc** CLS MSA.

The school resulted from a 1971 merger between Moravian Seminary for Girls, the oldest American girls' boarding school, and Moravian Preparatory School, both founded in 1742. The lower and middle schools (on Heckewelder Place and West Market Street, respectively) occupy the old Preparatory campus in the midst of the historic colonial section of Bethlehem.

The seminary was founded by Countess Benigna, daughter of Count Zinzendorf of Saxony. Eleanor Lee, grandniece of Washington, was among its pupils, as were Chancellor Livingston's daughter, Cornelia, wife of Robert Fulton; two daughters of Nathaniel Greene; and others representing the old colonial families of Dutch, German, Quaker, French and English heritage. Some of the original buildings of the academy are now part of Moravian College. The upper school occupies a 120-acre country estate with modern buildings, the land being an alumna gift of one of the last pieces of property held by the heirs of William Penn in direct grant from the English crown.

In addition to classes in the standard disciplines, Moravian's college preparatory curriculum includes religion, fine arts and global language course work. MA's High School Scholars Program allows a limited number of qualified seniors to take college-level classes at nearby colleges. Upper school boys and girls perform 40 hours of community service by the end of junior year. Independent study programs may be arranged, and some pupils participate in a study abroad program. **See Also Page 114**

BRYN MAWR, PA. (10 mi. W of Philadelphia, PA) Suburban. Pop: 4382. Alt: 413 ft. Area also includes Rosemont.

AGNES IRWIN SCHOOL
Day — Girls Gr PS (Age 4)-12

Rosemont, PA 19010. Ithan Ave & Conestoga Rd. Tel: 610-525-8400.
Fax: 610-525-8908.
www.agnesirwin.org   E-mail: admission@agnesirwin.org

Mary F. Seppala, Head (2009). BSEd, MEd, Massachusetts College of Liberal Arts, EdD, Univ of Massachusetts-Amherst. **Sally Keidel, Adm.**

Col Prep. AP (exams req'd; 266 taken, 82% 3+)—Eng Fr Span Calc Bio Chem Environ_Sci Physics Eur_Hist US_Hist Studio_Art. **Elem math**—Math Expressions. **Feat**—War_Lit ASL Greek Lat Stats Bioethics Comp_Sci Robotics Japan_Hist Middle_Eastern_Hist Econ Intl_Relations Art_Hist Ceramics Photog Theater Band Chorus Music_Theory Choreography Media_Arts. **Supp**—Rev Tut.

Sports (req'd)—G: Basket Crew X-country F_Hockey Golf Lacrosse Soccer Softball Squash Swim Tennis Track Volley. **Activities:** 20.

Selective adm (Gr PS-11): 102/yr. Usual entry: PS, K, 1, 5, 6 & 9. Appl fee: $50. Appl due: Dec. Applied: 267. Accepted: 58%. Yield: 65%. **Tests** IQ ISEE SSAT.
Enr 687. Elem 413. Sec 274. Wh 79%. Latino 1%. Blk 9%. Asian 5%. Other 6%. Avg class size: 15. Stud/fac: 7:1. Uniform. **Fac 102.** M 21/F 81. FT 89/PT 13. Wh 92%. Latino 3%. Blk 2%. Asian 2%. Other 1%. Adv deg: 73%.
Grad '11—64. Col—64. (U of PA 5, Lehigh 4, Bucknell 4, U of DE 4, Boston Col 3, Syracuse 3). Athl schol 1. **Mid 50% SAT:** CR 580-690. M 610-700. W 630-740. Mid 50% ACT: 24-29. **Col couns:** 2. Alum donors: 28%.
Tui '12-'13: Day $20,400-29,300 (+$275-800). **Aid:** Need 158 ($2,439,530).
Summer (enr 754): Acad Enrich Rev Rec. Arts. Sports. 7 wks.
Endow $18,000,000. Plant val $8,192,000. Acres 18. Bldgs 5. Class rms 64. Lib 25,000 vols. Labs 7. Art studios 4. Music studios 4. Gyms 2. Fields 3. Tennis courts 5. Playgrounds 3. Comp/stud: 1:2.
Est 1869. Nonprofit. Tri (Sept-June). **Assoc** CLS MSA.

The school was founded by Agnes Irwin, who in 1894 was appointed first dean of Radcliffe College. Formerly in Wynnewood, the school in 1961 consolidated on an 18-acre campus in Rosemont, a half mile from Villanova University. Agnes Irwin's curriculum incorporates computer education at every grade level, and mobile laptop carts are employed in place of computer labs in the lower, middle and upper schools. In the upper school years, girls choose from honors and Advanced Placement offerings in all major disciplines. The visual, musical and dramatic arts are a important part of the curriculum. Girls satisfy a 40-hour cumulative community service requirement prior to graduation.

Physical education begins in the lower school, followed by the introduction of team sports and fitness instruction in the middle and upper schools. In the school's Special Studies Program, sophomores and juniors spend two weeks pursuing school-sponsored or self-designed academic study, internships, language immersion or service learning programs outside of class.

THE BALDWIN SCHOOL
Day — Girls Gr PS (Age 4)-12

Bryn Mawr, PA 19010. 701 W Montgomery Ave. Tel: 610-525-2700. Fax: 610-581-7231.
www.baldwinschool.org   E-mail: admissions@baldwinschool.org
Sally M. Powell, Head (2006). BA, MA, Cambridge Univ (England). **Sarah J. Goebel, Adm.**
Col Prep. AP exams taken: 69 (81% 3+). Elem math—Everyday Math. **Elem read**—Wilson Fundations. **Feat**—Creative_Writing Shakespeare Chin Fr Greek Lat Span Calc Stats Anat & Physiol Astron Environ_Sci Comp_Sci Econ Existentialism Art_Hist Ceramics Photog Sculpt Studio_Art Architect_Design Jewelry Drama Music Music_Theory Speech. **Supp**—Rem_Math Rem_Read.
Sports—G: Basket Crew X-country F_Hockey Golf Indoor_Track Lacrosse Soccer Softball Squash Swim Tennis Volley. **Activities:** 35.
Selective adm: 73/yr. Appl fee: $50. Appl due: Feb. Accepted: 64%. Yield: 57%. **Tests** IQ ISEE SSAT.
Enr 535. Elem 333. Sec 202. Wh 60%. Latino 3%. Blk 14%. Asian 14%. Other 9%. Avg class size: 15. Stud/fac: 7:1. Uniform. **Fac 92.** Wh 89%. Latino 2%. Blk 3%. Asian 3%. Other 3%. Adv deg: 69%.
Grad '11—58. Col—58. (U of PA 7, U of VA 4, Drexel 4, Cornell 3, Geo Wash 3, Harvard 1). **Avg SAT:** CR 660. M 660. W 682. **Mid 50% SAT:** CR 600-720. M 630-720. W 630-730. **Col couns:** 2. Alum donors: 30%.
Tui '12-'13: Day $19,000-30,495. Aid: Need 136 ($2,195,600).
Summer: Rec. Sports. Tui Day $225/wk. 6 wks.
Endow $10,000,000. Plant val $31,000,000. Acres 25. Bldgs 8. Class rms 71. 3 Libs 28,000 vols. Sci labs 5. Lang labs 1. Art studios 8. Music studios 4. Gyms 3. Fields 4. Courts 9. Pools 3. Comp labs 3. Comp/stud: 1:3.
Est 1888. Nonprofit. Tri (Sept-June). **Assoc** MSA.

Miss Florence Baldwin founded this school, which initially enrolled 13 girls, to prepare students for Bryn Mawr College. Located in Miss Baldwin's mother's house at the corner of Montgomery and Morris avenues, the school was met with disapproval upon its establishment, as education for young women in the late 1800s was widely considered unnecessary, and some felt it was potentially dangerous as well.

Baldwin's college preparatory curriculum prepares students for competitive colleges across the country. The school features strong art, music and drama programs, as well as a full athletic schedule. The Service League stresses personal contributions to the school and the community. The school's location enables girls to partake of Philadelphia's cultural and educational institutions, and to take advantage of programs at Bryn Mawr and Haverford. Academic and social activities are conducted regularly with nearby boys' and coed schools.

COUNTRY DAY SCHOOL OF THE SACRED HEART
Day — Girls Gr PS (Age 4)-12

Bryn Mawr, PA 19010. 480 S Bryn Mawr Ave. Tel: 610-527-3915. Fax: 610-527-0942. www.cdssh.org   E-mail: lnowlan@cdssh.org
Sr. Matthew Anita MacDonald, SSJ, Head (1992). AB, Chestnut Hill College, MA, PhD, Univ of Pennsylvania. **Laurie Nowlan, Adm.**

Col Prep. AP (exams req'd)—Eng Fr Lat Chem Eur_Hist US_Hist Studio_Art. **Feat**—Humanities World_Lit Span Environ_Sci Comp_Sci Amer_Stud Econ Psych Relig Art_Hist Film Music Music_Theory. **Dual enr:** Villanova, St Joseph's U, Cabrini.

Sports—G: Basket Crew X-country F_Hockey Golf Lacrosse Softball Squash Tennis Track Volley. **Activities:** 28.

Selective adm (Gr PS-11): 70/yr. Usual entry: PS, K, 5, 6 & 9. Appl fee: $35. Appl due: Rolling. Applied: 150. Accepted: 50%. Yield: 70%. **Tests** CTP_4 HSPT IQ ISEE Stanford.

Enr 310. Elem 130. Sec 180. Wh 87%. Latino 3%. Blk 9%. Asian 1%. Avg class size: 14. Stud/fac: 7:1. Uniform. **Fac 44.** Adv deg: 47%.

Grad '11—44. Col—44. (U of Pittsburgh 2, Catholic U 2, St Joseph's U 2, W Chester 2, Harvard 1, Notre Dame 1). **Avg SAT:** CR 610. M 600. W 620. **Col couns:** 1. Alum donors: 14%.

Tui '12-'13: Day $10,350-16,400 (+$250). **Aid:** Merit 68 ($283,500). Need 43 ($182,000).

Summer: Enrich. Fine Arts. 1-4 wks.

Endow $1,528,000. Plant val $3,288,000. Acres 16. Bldgs 3. Class rms 28. Lib 10,000 vols. Sci labs 2. Art studios 1. Music studios 1. Gyms 1. Athletic ctrs 1. Fields 2. Comp labs 3. Comp/stud: 1:3 (1:1 Laptop prgm Gr 10).

Est 1865. Nonprofit. Roman Catholic (70% practice). Quar (Sept-June). **Assoc** MSA.

Originally established in Philadelphia by the Religious of the Sacred Heart, the school was located in suburban Overbrook for many years before relocating to Bryn Mawr in 1978.

The college preparatory curriculum includes college-level courses in French, Latin, English, history, biology, chemistry and math. Students fulfill course requirements in religion and art history, and CDSSH integrates a particularly strong humanities program into its curriculum. The school's technology curriculum features an iPad cart program in the lower and middle schools, as well as a one-to-one iPad program during sophomore year. Frequent field trips throughout the Philadelphia area enrich classroom instruction.

Athletics, music, clubs and community service projects augment the traditional academics. The school offers exchange opportunities with 20 other Sacred Heart institutions throughout the US. International exchanges are also available, most notably with the network school in Sydney, Australia.

THE SHIPLEY SCHOOL
Day — Coed Gr PS (Age 4)-12

Bryn Mawr, PA 19010. 814 Yarrow St. Tel: 610-525-4300. Fax: 610-525-5082.
Other locations: 1030 Wyndon Ave, Bryn Mawr 19010.
www.shipleyschool.org E-mail: shipley@shipleyschool.org
Steven S. Piltch, Head (1992). BA, Williams College, MEd, EdD, Harvard Univ. **Dorothy Maddock, Adm.**
> **Col Prep. AP**—Studio_Art. **Feat**—Humanities Shakespeare Fr Lat Span Calc Stats Comp_Sci Amer_Stud Econ Global_Stud Art_Hist Theater_Arts Music_Theory. **Supp**—Tut.
> **Sports**—Basket Crew X-country Golf Lacrosse Soccer Squash Swim Tennis. B: Baseball. G: F_Hockey Softball Volley.
> **Selective adm (Gr PS-11):** 136/yr. Appl fee: $60. Appl due: Jan. Applied: 305. Accepted: 80%. Yield: 56%. **Tests** IQ ISEE SSAT.
> **Enr 835.** Elem 505. Sec 330. Avg class size: 15. Stud/fac: 7:1. **Fac 84.** M 23/F 61. FT 77/PT 7. Wh 91%. Latino 1%. Blk 4%. Asian 4%. Adv deg: 59%.
> **Grad '10—85. Col—85.** (USC 4, U of PA 4, NYU 4, Boston U 4, Syracuse 3, Geo Wash 3). **Avg SAT:** CR 633. M 647. W 645. **Mid 50% SAT:** CR 580-680. M 580-710. W 590-690. **Col couns:** 2. Alum donors: 27%.
> **Tui '12-'13: Day $22,400-31,375** (+$1300). **Aid:** Need 220 ($3,500,000).
> Endow $16,200,000. Plant val $32,265,000. Acres 36. Bldgs 15. Class rms 65. 2 Libs 25,000 vols. Sci labs 8. Dark rms 1. Auds 1. Theaters 1. Art studios 5. Music studios 4. Pottery rms 1. Gyms 3. Fields 7. Tennis courts 6. Squash courts 3. Comp labs 3. Comp/stud: 1:1.6.
> **Est 1894.** Nonprofit. Quar (Sept-June). **Assoc** MSA.

This nonsectarian school was founded by three Quaker sisters, the Misses Hannah, Elizabeth and Katherine Shipley. While established to prepare girls for Bryn Mawr College, Shipley became coeducational in 1972, and the school now enrolls roughly the same number of boys and girls.

The sound college preparatory program—which includes electives and a full complement of honors courses—and the friendly atmosphere have long appealed both to families in Philadelphia's Main Line suburbs and to families in the city. Use is made of the cultural advantages of Philadelphia and of nearby Bryn Mawr College, and to a lesser extent those of New York City and Washington, DC. Tutoring and community service opportunities help to broaden the basic curriculum, and students participate in conferences on national and international affairs. In addition, upper school boys and girls satisfy a 10-hour annual community service requirement. Sophomores, juniors and seniors may take academic trips during spring vacation or over the summer. Graduates attend an array of competitive colleges in the US and abroad.

The lower school (grades pre-K-5) occupies separate quarters on Wyndon Avenue.

CHESTER SPRINGS, PA. (25 mi. WNW of Wilmington, DE; 26 mi. WNW of Philadelphia, PA) Suburban. Pop: 4413. Alt: 260 ft.

MONTGOMERY SCHOOL
Day — Coed Gr PS (Age 4)-8

Chester Springs, PA 19425. 1141 Kimberton Rd. Tel: 610-827-7222.
Fax: 610-827-7639.
www.montgomeryschool.org E-mail: admissions@montgomeryschool.org
Kevin R. Conklin, Head (2000). BA, Lake Forest College, MA, Columbia Univ. **Tearson W. Morrison, Adm.**
> **Pre-Prep. Gen Acad. Feat**—Fr Span Environ_Sci Computers Studio_Art Drama Music Public_Speak. **Supp**—Rev Tut.

Sports (req'd)—Basket X-country Equestrian F_Hockey Lacrosse Soccer. B: Baseball. G: Softball.
Somewhat selective adm: 31/yr. Usual entry: PS, 1, 5 & 6. Appl fee: $50. Appl due: Feb. Applied: 44. Yield: 75%. **Tests** IQ ISEE.
Enr 271. B 135. G 136. Wh 85%. Blk 4%. Asian 4%. Other 7%. Avg class size: 15. Stud/fac: 7:1. Uniform. **Fac 38.** Wh 97%. Blk 1%. Asian 1%. Other 1%. Adv deg: 55%.
Grad '10—27. Prep—13. (Episcopal Acad, Hill Sch-PA, Malvern Prep, Haverford, Baldwin, Shipley). Alum donors: 7%.
Tui '10-'11: Day $14,835-22,765 (+$400). **Aid:** Need 55 ($677,149).
Summer: Rec. Tui Day $400/wk. 9 wks.
Plant val $10,000,000. Acres 60. Bldgs 10. Class rms 29. Lib 10,000 vols. Sci labs 3. Amphitheaters 1. Art studios 2. Music studios 2. Gyms 1. Fields 5. Pools 1. Gardens 1. Comp labs 2. Comp/stud: 1:2.
Est 1915. Nonprofit. (Sept-June).

Founded as a boys' preparatory school in Wynnewood by Rev. Gibson Bell, this school graduated its last senior class in 1938. In 1943, the school was reorganized as a coeducational elementary and middle school. A decline in middle-school-aged children in the 1980s resulted in Montgomery's relocation to Chester Springs in the summer of 1988.

The school's varied curriculum prepares students for competitive area independent and public high schools. A full-day prekindergarten program provides problem-solving, communicational and life skills training beginning at age 4. Later in the lower school grades, Montgomery supplements course work in the traditional elementary subjects with computer education and an introduction to foreign languages. The lower school music curriculum includes enriching field trips, special assembly programs and study, and children learn more about the visual arts through excursions to local museums and art shows.

In the middle school (grades 6-8), instruction in all subject areas becomes more in-depth to help students prepare for advanced high school courses. The arts programs at this level emphasize appreciation and participation in music, art and drama. Interscholastic sports begin in the middle school.

EXTON, PA. (21 mi. NNW of Wilmington, DE; 26 mi. W of Philadelphia, PA) Suburban. Pop: 4761. Alt: 320 ft.

CFS
THE SCHOOL AT CHURCH FARM
Bdg and Day — Boys Gr 7-12

Exton, PA 19341. 1001 E Lincoln Hwy. Tel: 610-363-5347. Fax: 610-280-6746.
www.gocfs.net   E-mail: admissions@gocfs.net
Rev. Edmund K. Sherrill II, Head (2009). BA, Macalester College, MDiv, Yale Univ. **Bart Bronk, Adm.**

Col Prep. AP (exams req'd; 43 taken, 72% 3+)—Eng Calc Bio Chem Physics US_Hist. **Feat**—Fr Span Anat & Physiol Engineering Comp_Sci Robotics Middle_Eastern_Hist Ceramics Fine_Arts Photog Music. **Supp**—Rev Tut. **Dual enr:** Immaculata.
Sports (req'd)—B: Baseball Basket X-country Fencing Golf Indoor_Track Soccer Tennis Track Wrestling. **Activities:** 25.
Selective adm (Gr 7-11): 62/yr. Bdg 52. Day 10. Usual entry: 7, 8 & 9. Appl fee: $25. Appl due: Feb. Applied: 247. Accepted: 36%. Yield: 67%. **Tests** ISEE SSAT TOEFL.
Enr 190. Bdg 175. Day 15. Elem 36. Sec 154. Wh 30%. Latino 12%. Blk 30%. Asian 17%. Other 11%. Intl 15%. Avg class size: 10. Stud/fac: 6:1. Formal. **Fac 32.** M 22/F 10. FT 25/PT 7. Wh 78%. Latino 3%. Blk 13%. Asian 6%. Adv deg: 53%. In dorms 2.
Grad '11—34. Col—34. (Cornell 2, PA St 2, MIT 1, Emory 1, Northwestern 1, Haverford 1). Athl schol 1. **Avg SAT:** CR 550. M 593. W 555. **Col couns:** 3. Alum donors: 20%.
Tui '12-'13: Bdg $30,000. Day $17,172. Aid: Need 167 ($3,479,895).

Endow $126,000,000. Plant val $40,000,000. Bldgs 19. Dorms 10. Dorm rms 120. Class rms 26. Lib 28,000 vols. Chapels 1. Sci labs 4. Auds 1. Art studios 1. Music studios 1. Gyms 2. Fields 4. Courts 6. Field houses 1. Pools 1. Weight rms 1. Comp labs 1. Comp/stud: 1:1 Laptop prgm Gr 7-12.
Est 1918. Nonprofit. Episcopal (10% practice). Sem (Sept-June). **Assoc** MSA.

Founded by Rev. Dr. Charles W. Shreiner, Sr., CFS has traditionally offered an affordable college preparatory program in a Christian environment for academically talented boys for whom the cost of a private education might otherwise be prohibitive. Originally operating exclusively as a boarding school, CFS established what has become an increasingly prominent day division in 1995. A robust endowment enables the school to provide financial aid for the vast majority of its student body.

The curriculum includes required and elective course work in the major content areas, as well as foreign language, religion, the fine arts, technology education, health and computer studies. Students may pursue Advanced Placement or honors courses in all major academic departments. Mandatory work and community service programs provide valuable nonclassroom experiences both on and off campus. CFS issues a MacBook computer to each student at no additional tuition cost.

As sports are an important component of school life, all boys participate in some sort of interscholastic or intramural athletic activity.

FAIRLESS HILLS, PA. (19 mi. NE of Philadelphia, PA) Urban. Pop: 8365. Alt: 100 ft.

THE PEN RYN SCHOOL
Day — Coed Gr PS (Age 3)-8

Fairless Hills, PA 19030. 235 S Olds Blvd. Tel: 215-547-1800. Fax: 215-946-2877.
www.penryn.org   E-mail: kfried@penryn.org
Liz Morton, Head (2007). Karen Fried, Adm.
  Pre-Prep. Feat—Lib_Skills Span Computers Studio_Art Music. **Supp**—Rem_Math Rem_Read Tut.
  Sports—Basket Bowl X-country Soccer Softball Tennis. G: Cheer.
  Selective adm: Appl fee: $50. Appl due: Rolling. **Tests** IQ.
  Enr 250. Wh 88%. Blk 3%. Asian 2%. Other 7%. Avg class size: 16. Stud/fac: 10:1. **Fac 26.** M 3/F 23. FT 26. Nonwhite 1%. Adv deg: 15%.
  Grad '11—35. Prep—27. (Villa Joseph Marie 6, Notre Dame HS-PA 5, Holy Ghost Prep 3, Pennington 2, Doane Acad 2, La Salle Col HS 2).
  Tui '12-'13: Day $8200-10,750 (+$250-350). **Aid:** Need 24 ($43,000).
  Endow $250,000. Plant val $5,000,000. Acres 15. Bldgs 1. Class rms 21. Lib 5000 vols. Sci labs 2. Auds 1. Art studios 1. Music studios 1. Gyms 1. Fields 2. Courts 1. Comp labs 2.
  Est 1946. Nonprofit. Quar (Sept-June). **Assoc** MSA.

Located on a 15-acre campus, Pen Ryn emphasizes fundamental skills in a small-class environment that allows for personalized attention. The curriculum provides a continuous foundation in the core subjects, and course work emphasizes reading, writing, math and study skills. Computer technology, art, music, library and Spanish complement the traditional subjects.

The extracurricular program offers enrichment classes and student leadership opportunities for boys and girls in all grades, and athletics begin in grade 5. Students enroll from northeast Philadelphia, Bucks County and New Jersey.

FREELAND, PA. (81 mi. NNW of Philadelphia, PA) Suburban. Pop: 3643. Alt: 1836 ft.

MMI PREPARATORY SCHOOL
Day — Coed Gr 6-12

Freeland, PA 18224. 154 Centre St. Tel: 570-636-1108. Fax: 570-636-0742.
　www.mmiprep.org　E-mail: mmi@mmiprep.org
Thomas G. Hood, Pres (2008). BS, US Military Academy, MS, Rensselaer Polytechnic Univ. **Aprilaurie Whitley, Adm.**
　Col Prep. AP (exams req'd; 151 taken, 50% 3+)—Eng Calc Comp_Sci Bio Chem Physics Eur_Hist US_Hist Studio_Art. **Feat**—Chin Ger Greek Lat Span Environ_Sci Geol Physiol Biotech Meteorology Organic_Chem Robotics Anthro Econ Pol_Sci Psych Ethics Music_Theory Journ. **Supp**—Tut. **Dual enr:** Wilkes, Lehigh Carbon CC.
　Sports—Basket X-country Golf Soccer Tennis. B: Baseball. G: Cheer Softball Volley. **Activities:** 15.
　Selective adm (Gr 6-11): 61/yr. Usual entry: 6, 7 & 9. Appl fee: $25. Appl due: June. Applied: 87. Accepted: 80%. Yield: 53%. **Tests** IQ.
　Enr 247. B 133. G 114. Elem 85. Sec 162. Wh 87%. Latino 2%. Blk 1%. Asian 10%. Avg class size: 16. Stud/fac: 10:1. Formal. **Fac 27.** M 14/F 13. FT 25/PT 2. Wh 97%. Asian 3%. Adv deg: 81%.
　Grad '11—39. Col—37. (U of Scranton, Moravian, Wilkes, Bucknell, PA St, NYU). Athl schol 2. **Avg SAT:** CR 573. M 577. W 574. Avg ACT: 26. **Col couns:** 1. Alum donors: 45%.
　Tui '12-'13: Day $10,100-13,100 (+$250). **Aid:** Merit 63 ($47,250). Need 150 ($863,250). Work prgm 20 ($30,000).
　Summer (enr 100): Acad Enrich Rev. Tui Day $150/wk. 6 wks.
　Endow $20,000,000. Plant val $6,000,000. Acres 3. Bldgs 1 (100% ADA). Class rms 18. Lib 9000 vols. Sci labs 3. Auds 1. Art studios 1. Music studios 1. Gyms 1. Fields 2. Comp labs 2.
　Est 1879. Nonprofit. Sem (Aug-May). **Assoc** MSA.

Founded by Eckley B. Coxe as the Mining and Mechanical Institute, an evening school for miners, the school became a college preparatory day school in 1902. In 1970, the school became coeducational and the present name was adopted. In 1977, a middle school was added as the result of an expressed community need, and the school first offered grade 6 in 1999.

Today, MMI offers students a traditional college preparatory education. Utilizing a developmental approach, the school provides a sequence of classes that proceeds from a general review of topics to highly specialized offerings during the junior and senior years. Electives designed to enrich the college preparatory program complement major academic classes.

HARRISBURG, PA. (81 mi. WNW of Wilmington, DE; 94 mi. WNW of Philadelphia, PA) Urban. Pop: 48,950. Alt: 374 ft. Area also includes Wormleysburg.

HARRISBURG ACADEMY
Day — Coed Gr PS (Age 3)-12

Wormleysburg, PA 17043. 10 Erford Rd. Tel: 717-763-7811. Fax: 717-975-0894.
　www.harrisburgacademy.org　E-mail: warren.j@harrisburgacademy.org
James Newman, Head (2003). BA, Bowdoin College, MS, Univ of Wisconsin-Madison, MA, PhD, Univ of Rochester. **Jessica A. Warren, Adm.**
　Col Prep. IB Diploma. AP—Calc Comp_Sci Chem Psych. **Feat**—Creative_Writing Fr Lat Span Stats Econ Architect Studio_Art Video_Production Band Chorus Music_Theory Orchestra Health. **Supp**—Tut.
　Sports—Basket Soccer Tennis. B: Lacrosse. G: F_Hockey.

Selective adm: 73/yr. Appl fee: $75. Appl due: Rolling.
Enr 396. B 198. G 198. Elem 296. Sec 100. Nonwhite 34%. Avg class size: 14. Stud/fac: 8:1. Casual. **Fac 56.** M 10/F 46. FT 48/PT 8. Wh 92%. Blk 4%. Asian 4%. Adv deg: 44%.
Grad '11—32. Col—32. (PA St, Ithaca, Bloomsburg, Drexel, U of MI, Harding). **Mid 50% SAT:** CR 570-680. M 520-640. W 560-680. Mid 50% ACT: 25-30.
Tui '09-'10: Day $9000-15,350. Aid: Need 112 ($785,850).
Summer (enr 100): Ages 3-11. Acad Enrich Rec. Tui Day $200/wk. 10 wks.
Endow $3,130,000. Plant val $4,500,000. Acres 24. Bldgs 1. Class rms 41. 2 Libs 15,000 vols. Sci labs 4. Auds 1. Art studios 2. Music studios 2. Gyms 1. Fields 2. Courts 4. Comp labs 2. Laptop prgm Gr 8-12.
Est 1784. Nonprofit. Quar (Aug-June). **Assoc** MSA.

The academy was a boarding and day school for boys until merging with Seiler School and becoming coeducational in 1947. The school is located in East Pennsboro, across the Susquehanna River from Harrisburg.

The academy's program features foreign language and drama in all grades. Varied electives in the upper school broaden the traditional curriculum. Weekly guidance periods and a Great Books program in the middle school, process writing in all divisions, and senior internships enrich the program. Students in grades 11 and 12 may pursue the International Baccalaureate diploma, or enroll in IB courses while pursuing a traditional diploma. The community service program in grades 9-12 is modeled on the IB Creativity, Action and Service requirement.

The summer session, in operation since 1969, consists of special-interest and sports camps, as well as study skills and enrichment courses for older students.

HAVERFORD, PA. (9 mi. W of Philadelphia, PA) Suburban. Pop: 48,498. Alt: 383 ft.

FRIENDS SCHOOL HAVERFORD
Day — Coed Gr PS (Age 3)-6

Haverford, PA 19041. 851 Buck Ln. Tel: 610-642-2334. Fax: 610-642-0870.
www.friendshaverford.org   E-mail: fsh@friendshaverford.org
Michael Zimmerman, Head (2010). AB, George Washington Univ, MS, Univ of Pennsylvania. **Andrea Dominic, Adm.**
Pre-Prep. Elem math—Connected Math/Math Trailblazers. **Feat**—Lib_Skills Span Computers Studio_Art Music. **Supp**—Dev_Read Rev.
Selective adm: 21/yr. Appl fee: $60. Appl due: Rolling. Applied: 50. Accepted: 66%. Yield: 62%. **Tests** IQ.
Enr 125. B 62. G 63. Wh 66%. Latino 3%. Blk 14%. Native Am 1%. Asian 10%. Other 6%. Avg class size: 14. Stud/fac: 7:1. **Fac 28.** M 2/F 26. FT 21/PT 7. Wh 98%. Latino 1%. Blk 1%. Adv deg: 46%.
Grad '10—16. Prep—12. (Friends' Central 5, Haverford 3, Shipley 2, Agnes Irwin 1, Rosemont 1). Alum donors: 14%.
Tui '11-'12: Day $12,000-20,150. Aid: Merit 1 ($5000). Need 48 ($550,500).
Summer: Enrich Rec. 1-8 wks.
Endow $1,900,000. Plant val $2,500,000. Bldgs 3 (100% ADA). Class rms 17. Lib 9000 vols. Sci labs 1. Auds 1. Art studios 1. Music studios 1. Gyms 1. Fields 3. Comp labs 1. Comp/stud: 1:2.
Est 1885. Nonprofit. Religious Society of Friends (5% practice). Sem (Sept-June).

Governed by its school committee under the care of the Haverford Monthly Meeting, FSH offers an academic curriculum in an environment based on Quaker values. The school's course of studies emphasizes core concepts, logical thinking and communicational skills. Art, music, technology, science, health, library, Spanish and physical education enrich the program.

Central to the life of the school is the weekly Meeting for Worship, at which children and adults gather for a brief time of quiet reflection. The school schedules regular field trips to cultural and historical sites in the Philadelphia area.

HAVERFORD SCHOOL
Day — Boys Gr PS (Age 4)-12

Haverford, PA 19041. 450 Lancaster Ave. Tel: 610-642-3020. Fax: 610-642-8724.
www.haverford.org   E-mail: stassoni@haverford.org
Joseph T. Cox, Head (1998). BA, Lafayette College, MA, PhD, Univ of North Carolina-Chapel Hill. **Henry D. Fairfax, Adm.**

Col Prep. Elem math—Everyday Math. **Feat**—Chin Lat Span Calc Stats Astron Physiol Electronics Engineering Molecular_Bio Middle_Eastern_Hist Vietnam_War Econ Ceramics Film Studio_Art Theater Music Music_Theory Woodworking. **Supp**—Dev_ Read Rem_Math Rem_Read.

Sports—B: Baseball Basket Crew X-country Football Golf Ice_Hockey Indoor_Track Lacrosse Soccer Squash Swim Tennis Track W_Polo Wrestling. **Activities:** 28.

Selective adm (Gr PS-11): 142/yr. Usual entry: PS, K, 5, 6 & 9. Appl fee: $50. Appl due: Rolling. Applied: 400. Accepted: 46%. Yield: 73%. **Tests** IQ ISEE SSAT.

Enr 992. Elem 573. Sec 419. Wh 77%. Latino 1%. Blk 12%. Asian 5%. Other 5%. Avg class size: 15. Stud/fac: 8:1. Uniform. **Fac 117.** M 63/F 54. FT 116/PT 1. Wh 86%. Latino 3%. Blk 8%. Asian 2%. Other 1%. Adv deg: 63%.

Grad '11—96. Col—96. (U of PA 9, Harvard 4, Dartmouth 4, Wake Forest 4, PA St 4, Vanderbilt 3). Athl schol 3. **Mid 50% SAT:** CR 580-700. M 600-710. W 590-710. Mid 50% ACT: 25-31. **Col couns:** 3. Alum donors: 43%.

Tui '12-'13: Day $20,500-33,500 (+$300-800). **Aid:** Merit 8 ($50,000). Need 275 ($5,067,000).

Endow $42,443,000. Plant val $78,369,000. Acres 30. Bldgs 10 (50% ADA). Class rms 80. 2 Libs 40,000 vols. Sci labs 11. Auds 2. Theaters 2. Art studios 6. Music studios 9. Gyms 3. Fields 4. Tennis courts 4. Squash courts 4. Pools 1. Tracks 1. Comp labs 5. Comp/stud: 1:1.5 (1:1 Laptop prgm Gr 6-7).

Est 1884. Nonprofit. Sem (Sept-June). **Assoc** CLS MSA.

Haverford has served boys since its founding. Established at the request of railroad executive Alexander Cassatt and his wife, Lois, under the guidance of Haverford College, the school began as the Haverford College Grammar School. It became independent of the college when it moved to its current location in 1903 and adopted its present name and nonsectarian orientation.

The curriculum, with close individual guidance, prepares boys for a variety of leading colleges. Distinctive offerings include schoolwide programs in computer education, music and the visual arts. Although upper school courses do not follow the Advanced Placement curriculum, Haverford's rigorous program prepares students for AP exams in many subjects. In addition to choosing from a variety of semester electives, English literature seminars and advanced laboratory research options, seniors may also pursue an independent study project.

JENKINTOWN, PA. (6 mi. N of Philadelphia, PA) Suburban. Pop: 4263. Alt: 211 ft.

ABINGTON FRIENDS SCHOOL
Day — Coed Gr PS (Age 2)-12

Jenkintown, PA 19046. 575 Washington Ln. Tel: 215-886-4350. Fax: 215-886-9143.
www.abingtonfriends.net   E-mail: wnewman@abingtonfriends.net
Richard F. Nourie, Head. BS, Brown Univ, EdM, Harvard Univ. **William Newman, Adm.**

Col Prep. AP (96 exams taken, 81% 3+)—Fr Lat Span Calc Stats Physics US_Hist.

Feat—Poetry Russ_Lit Astron Forensic_Sci Genetics Comp_Sci African_Hist Civil_ War E_Asian_Hist Lat-Amer_Hist Govt Ethics Quakerism Ceramics Drawing Painting Photog Sculpt Studio_Art Acting Theater_Arts Music Music_Theory Orchestra Health Study_Skills.
Sports—Basket X-country Golf Soccer Swim Tennis Track Ultimate_Frisbee. B: Baseball Wrestling. G: Lacrosse Softball.
Selective adm: 153/yr. Appl fee: $50. Accepted: 54%. Yield: 71%. **Tests** IQ ISEE SSAT.
Enr 666. Elem 404. Sec 262. Nonwhite 35%. Stud/fac: 13:1. Casual. **Fac 88.**
Grad '11—83. Col—83. (PA St, Muhlenberg, Tulane, U of PA, Am U, Geo Wash). **Avg SAT:** CR 622. M 623. **Col couns:** 2. Alum donors: 14%.
Tui '12-'13: Day $16,500-28,400 (+$50-400).
Summer: Enrich Rec. 8 wks.
Acres 50. Bldgs 8. Class rms 42. Lib 20,000 vols. Sci labs 5. Dark rms 1. Auds 1. Theaters 1. Art studios 3. Music studios 3. Dance studios 1. Gyms 3. Fields 4. Courts 6. Pools 2. Comp labs 4.
Est 1697. Nonprofit. Religious Society of Friends (8% practice). Sem (Sept-June).
Assoc CLS MSA.

Abington Friends is the third-oldest Quaker school in the country. Founded by the Religious Society of Friends, it is the only 17th-century school still occupying its original site, a 50-acre tract. The academic program, which emphasizes college preparation, includes Advanced Placement courses in most subjects, as well as an independent study option for qualified students. Emphasis is placed on character development and physical fitness.

Foreign travel and frequent excursions to the cultural and historical sites of Philadelphia are offered. Each student attends Meeting for Worship, a central dimension of the school's program, once a week. Community service is also an integral part of school life: Service is part of the curriculum in the elementary grades, while students in grades 9-12 fulfill a 10-hour service requirement each year.

KENNETT SQUARE, PA. (12 mi. NW of Wilmington, DE; 30 mi. WSW of Philadelphia, PA) Suburban. Pop: 5274. Alt: 310 ft.

UPLAND COUNTRY DAY SCHOOL
Day — Coed Gr PS (Age 4)-9

Kennett Square, PA 19348. 420 W Street Rd. Tel: 610-444-3035. Fax: 610-444-2961.
www.uplandcds.org   E-mail: info@uplandcds.org
David M. Suter, Head (2007). BA, College of the Holy Cross, MA, Wesleyan Univ, MEd, Columbia Univ. **Joseph Sailer, Adm.**
Pre-Prep. Feat—Lat Span Computers Studio_Art Visual_Arts Drama Music.
Sports (req'd)—Ice_Hockey Lacrosse Soccer. B: X-country. G: F_Hockey Volley.
Selective adm: 22/yr. Appl fee: $45. Appl due: Rolling. Accepted: 69%. **Tests** CTP_4 SSAT Stanford.
Enr 183. B 96. G 87. Elem 161. Sec 22. Wh 95%. Latino 1%. Blk 1%. Native Am 1%. Asian 1%. Other 1%. Avg class size: 14. Stud/fac: 5:1. Casual. **Fac 32.** M 6/F 26. FT 29/PT 3. Wh 93%. Latino 3%. Blk 3%. Native Am 1%. Adv deg: 46%.
Grad '09—23. Prep—18. (Tatnall Sch, Madeira, St Andrew's Sch-DE, Westminster Sch-CT, Westtown, Wilmington Friends). Avg SSAT: 53%.
Tui '12-'13: Day $14,500-21,400 (+$500). **Aid:** Need 44 ($550,000).
Endow $4,300,000. Plant val $7,000,000. Acres 23. Bldgs 7. Class rms 15. Lib 7000 vols. Sci labs 3. Lang labs 1. Art studios 2. Music studios 1. Gyms 1. Fields 4. Rinks 1. Comp labs 1.
Est 1948. Nonprofit. Tri (Sept-June).

Upland provides individualized attention within a traditional environment. The pre-preparatory curriculum, which meets the needs of both the average and the above-average student, emphasizes the acquisition of basic skills. Spanish instruction commences in kindergarten, Latin in grade 6. A full laboratory science program serves pupils in grades K-9. The curriculum also includes a well-developed computer science program and strong music, art, drama and athletic programs.

Classes on the 23-acre campus are supplemented by field trips to sites of historical, scientific, artistic and social interest. Boys and girls complete community service projects at all grade levels. All pupils in grades 8 and 9 have the opportunity to travel to Finland as part of Upland's overseas program.

LAHASKA, PA. (24 mi. NNE of Philadelphia, PA) Rural. Pop: 200. Alt: 290 ft.

BUCKINGHAM FRIENDS SCHOOL
Day — Coed Gr K-8

Lahaska, PA 18931. 5684 York Rd, PO Box 159. Tel: 215-794-7491. Fax: 215-794-7955. www.bfs.org
Lucretia M. Wells, Head (2011). BA, Boston Univ, MS, Portland State Univ. **Kathy Fluehr, Adm.**
Pre-Prep. Feat—Lib_Skills Fr Span Relig Studio_Art Music Woodworking.
Sports (req'd)—Basket. B: Soccer. G: F_Hockey Lacrosse.
Selective adm: Appl fee: $55. Appl due: Feb.
Enr 176. Avg class size: 20. Stud/fac: 9:1. **Fac 21.** M 6/F 15. Adv deg: 52%.
Grad '08—20. Prep—16. (George Sch, Solebury, Germantown Acad, Lawrenceville, Hill Sch-PA, Princeton Day).
Tui '10-'11: Day $16,500.
Summer: Rec. Arts. 4 wks.
Endow $2,800,000. Plant val $4,000,000. Acres 44. Bldgs 4. Class rms 12. Lib 10,000 vols. Labs 1. Auds 1. Theaters 1. Gyms 1. Fields 2. Laptop prgm Gr 6-8.
Est 1794. Nonprofit. Religious Society of Friends. Sem (Sept-June).

Founded by Buckingham Friends Meeting, BFS conducts a traditional curriculum and emphasizes the development of fundamental skills. Buckingham offers French, wood shop, art and music at all grade levels. Some remedial reading and math are provided for students who need extra help. Boys and girls in grades 6-8 each receive a laptop computer from the school.

BFS encourages students to engage in outreach projects and community service.

LANCASTER, PA. (46 mi. WNW of Wilmington, DE; 62 mi. W of Philadelphia, PA) Urban. Pop: 56,348. Alt: 357 ft.

LANCASTER COUNTRY DAY SCHOOL
Day — Coed Gr PS (Age 3)-PG

Lancaster, PA 17603. 725 Hamilton Rd. Tel: 717-392-2916. Fax: 717-392-0425. www.lancastercountryday.org   E-mail: townsendb@lancastercountryday.org
Steven D. Lisk, Head (2008). BA, Univ of North Carolina-Chapel Hill, MA, North Carolina State Univ. **Peter C. Anderson, Adm.**
Col Prep. AP (136 exams taken, 75% 3+)—Eng Fr Span Calc Stats Bio Chem Physics US_Hist. **Elem math**—Everyday Math. **Feat**—Creative_Writing Humanities Chin Lat Anat & Physiol Environ_Sci Marine_Bio/Sci Zoology Comp_Sci Econ Govt Psych Art_Hist Ceramics Drawing Painting Photog Sculpt Studio_Art Acting Chorus Music_ Theory Orchestra Dance. **Supp**—Tut. **Dual enr:** Franklin & Marshall, Millersville.

Sports—Basket X-country Golf Lacrosse Soccer Swim Tennis Track. B: Baseball Football Wrestling. G: F_Hockey Softball.
Selective adm: 103/yr. Appl fee: $50-75. Appl due: Rolling. Accepted: 84%. Yield: 81%. **Tests** CTP_4.
Enr 964. Nonwhite 17%. Avg class size: 15. Stud/fac: 8:1. **Fac 87.** FT 63/PT 24. Adv deg: 51%.
Grad '08—53. Col—53. (U of VT 3, Bucknell 2, Carnegie Mellon 2, Dickinson 2, U of PA 2, Millersville 2). **Avg SAT:** CR 620. M 615. W 600. Avg ACT: 27.5. **Col couns:** 1. Alum donors: 20%.
Tui '09-'10: Day $11,400-18,825 (+$600). **Aid:** Need 289 ($1,900,000).
Summer: Acad Enrich Rec. 6 wks.
Endow $10,000,000. Plant val $27,000,000. Acres 26. Bldgs 1 (80% ADA). Class rms 60. Lib 27,000 vols. Sci labs 5. Comp ctrs 4. Theaters 1. Art studios 5. Music studios 2. Gyms 2. Fields 5. Tennis courts 6. Gardens 1. Comp labs 4. Comp/stud: 1:4.
Est 1908. Nonprofit. Tri (Aug-June).

The Shippen School for Girls (founded in 1908) and the Franklin and Marshall Academy for boys (established in 1787) came together in 1943 to form LCDS. In 1949, the doors opened at the current 26-acre, suburban campus.

Country Day provides a college preparatory curriculum based in the liberal arts tradition, with AP subjects, opportunities for independent study, and arts requirements. Competitive athletics begin in the middle school (grades 6-8). Independent, off-campus senior projects include participation in the International Model UN in The Hague, The Netherlands.

Annual outdoor expeditions, athletics, clubs, student government, theater, music and field trips supplement the curriculum. LCDS constructed a Habitat for Humanity house as part of its service program.

LIGONIER, PA. (41 mi. ESE of Pittsburgh, PA) Rural. Pop: 6973. Alt: 1290 ft.

VALLEY SCHOOL OF LIGONIER
Day — Coed Gr K-9

Ligonier, PA 15658. PO Box 616. Tel: 724-238-6652. Fax: 724-238-6838.
www.valleyschoolofligonier.org   E-mail: jderose@valleyschoolofligonier.org
Clair Ward, Head (2008). BA, Hamilton College, MEd, Boston College. **Johnette DeRose, Adm.**
Pre-Prep. Gen Acad. Feat—Lat Span Computers Studio_Art Drama Music Design.
Supp—Dev_Read.
Sports (req'd)—Basket Soccer. B: Lacrosse. G: F_Hockey.
Somewhat selective adm (Gr K-8): 22/yr. Usual entry: K. Appl fee: $25. Appl due: Rolling. Applied: 28. Accepted: 86%. Yield: 79%. **Tests** CTP_4.
Enr 192. B 90. G 102. Elem 177. Sec 15. Wh 93%. Latino 2%. Blk 2%. Asian 3%. Avg class size: 13. Uniform. **Fac 24.** M 6/F 18. FT 23/PT 1. Wh 100%. Adv deg: 54%.
Grad '11—15. Prep—8. (Linsly 2, Winchester Thurston 1, Phillips Exeter 1, Avon 1, Mercersburg 1, Ethel Walker 1).
Tui '12-'13: Day $12,550 (+$0-300). **Aid:** Merit 11 ($17,500). Need 56 ($383,146).
Summer: Rec. Tui Day $190/wk. 5 wks.
Endow $27,154,000. Plant val $22,401,000. Acres 400. Bldgs 3. Class rms 16. Lib 13,000 vols. Sci labs 3. Lang labs 3. Comp ctrs 1. Auds 2. Art studios 1. Music studios 3. Gyms 2. Fields 4. Comp labs 2. Comp/stud: 1:3 (1:1 Laptop prgm Gr 9).
Est 1946. Nonprofit. Tri (Sept-June).

Established by Constance Prosser Mellon Gen. Richard King Mellon, Valley provided a country day elementary program for a first-year student body that consisted of 43 children. Mrs. Mellon sought to maintain a small-class learning environment and a moderate tuition level.

Originally housed in the former residence of William C. Carnegie, the school has renovated and expanded its facilities over the years to better serve its student body. The curriculum is traditional, with an emphasis on the development of basic skills. Art, music, computers, language, physical education and science are included in the curriculum at all grade levels, and computers are located in all classrooms. Spanish instruction begins in kindergarten, and Latin is added in grade 6.

Interscholastic athletic competition begins in grade 5. Outdoor education and recreation periods make use of the 400-acre campus of woods and streams.

LITITZ, PA. (50 mi. NW of Wilmington, DE; 63 mi. W of Philadelphia, PA) Suburban. Pop: 9029. Alt: 360 ft.

LINDEN HALL

Bdg and Day — Girls Gr 5-12

Lititz, PA 17543. 212 E Main St. Tel: 717-626-8512, 800-258-5778. Fax: 717-627-1384.
www.lindenhall.org   E-mail: admissions@lindenhall.org
Vincent M. Stumpo, Head (2006). BS, St Joseph's Univ, MA, PhD, Univ of Delaware.
Katherine R. Rill, Adm.

Col Prep. AP (exams req'd)—Eng Fr Span Calc Stats Bio Chem Environ_Sci Physics Eur_Hist US_Hist US_Govt & Pol Art_Hist Studio_Art. **Feat**—Creative_Writing Chin Lat Anat & Physiol Web_Design Ethics World_Relig Ceramics Film Photog Theater Music Dance SAT_Prep Study_Skills Equestrian_Stud. **Supp**—ESL Rev Tut.

Sports—G: Basket X-country Equestrian F_Hockey Lacrosse Soccer Softball Swim Tennis Track Volley.

Selective adm: 55/yr. Bdg 46. Day 9. Appl fee: $45. Appl due: Rolling. **Tests** SSAT TOEFL.

Enr 230. Bdg 160. Day 70. Avg class size: 12. Stud/fac: 8:1. Uniform. **Fac 22.** M 4/F 18. FT 18/PT 4. Wh 100%. Adv deg: 72%.

Grad '11—38. Col—38. (MIT, U of Chicago, U of VA, Emory, Cornell, Haverford). **Avg SAT:** CR/M/W 2095. **Col couns:** 1. Alum donors: 30%.

Tui '11-'12: Bdg $41,950 (+$2000). **5-Day Bdg $39,400** (+$2000). **Day $17,650** (+$1000). **Aid:** Need 75.

Summer: Ages 6-12. Acad Enrich Rec. 9 wks. ESL. Tui Bdg $3975. 4 wks.

Acres 47. Bldgs 12. Dorms 5. Dorm rms 60. Class rms 20. Lib 12,500 vols. Sci labs 2. Dark rms 1. Theaters 1. Art studios 4. Music studios 2. Dance studios 1. Arts ctrs 1. Perf arts ctrs 1. Art galleries 1. Gyms 1. Athletic ctrs 1. Fields 3. Courts 6. Pools 1. Riding rings 2. Stables 1. Comp labs 2. Laptop prgm Gr 5-12.

Est 1746. Nonprofit. Sem (Sept-May). **Assoc** MSA.

Linden Hall is the oldest continuously operating girls' boarding school in the country. The school's program prepares students for college, with special emphasis placed on the development of academic skills and sound study habits. The school specializes in helping each student achieve her optimal level of scholarship by providing an honors program and Advanced Placement courses for qualified pupils, as well as allotting time daily for extra help. Academics are enhanced by opportunities in the fine and performing arts, and Linden Hall maintains affiliations with the Pennsylvania Academy of Music and local colleges. A strong equestrian program and interscholastic competition are also part of the regular program.

The school's 47-acre campus, which combines both modern and traditional structures, contains the full range of facilities. Girls enroll from foreign countries and locations throughout the US, and English as a Second Language is available during the academic year for international students desiring to improve their command of written and spoken English. Linden Hall provides notebook computers for all girls.

MEADOWBROOK, PA. (8 mi. NNE of Philadelphia, PA) Rural. Pop: 150. Alt: 411 ft.

THE MEADOWBROOK SCHOOL
Day — Coed Gr PS (Age 3)-6

Meadowbrook, PA 19046. 1641 Hampton Rd. Tel: 215-884-3238. Fax: 215-884-9143.
www.themeadowbrookschool.org
E-mail: kmosteller@themeadowbrookschool.org
David B. Stephens, Head (2008). BS, Hobart College, MS, Syracuse Univ. **Kelly A. Mosteller, Adm.**
Pre-Prep. Feat—Lib_Skills Fr Span Computers Studio_Art Music. **Supp**—Tut.
Sports—Soccer Softball. B: Baseball. G: F_Hockey.
Selective adm: 34/yr. Appl fee: $50. Appl due: Rolling. Applied: 258. Accepted: 70%. Yield: 85%. **Tests** IQ SSAT.
Enr 133. B 71. G 62. Wh 69%. Blk 24%. Asian 7%. Avg class size: 12. Uniform. **Fac 32.** M 3/F 29. FT 24/PT 8. Wh 99%. Blk 1%. Adv deg: 21%.
Grad '11—14. Prep—9. (Springside 2, Wm Penn Charter 2, Germantown Friends 2, Germantown Acad 1, Chestnut Hill Acad 1). Alum donors: 4%.
Tui '12-'13: Day $11,440-18,200 (+$520-2995). **Aid:** Need 71 ($510,000).
Summer (enr 40): Acad Enrich. Tui Day $300/wk. 7 wks.
Endow $40,000. Plant val $1,508,000. Acres 14. Bldgs 6. Class rms 16. Lib 12,000 vols. Sci labs 1. Lang labs 1. Sci ctrs 1. Auds 1. Art studios 1. Music studios 1. Gyms 1. Fields 2. Tennis courts 3. Comp labs 1. Comp/stud: 1:4.
Est 1919. Nonprofit. Tri (Sept-June).

Located on a 14-acre, wooded campus, this school features a family atmosphere and small classes. A structured curriculum emphasizes the development of strong basic skills, and a number of special enrichment programs supplement the traditional academics. French, science, music, art, physical education, computer and library specialists complement the work of the regular classroom teachers.

Additional activities—such as choir, recorder, gymnastics, ice skating, interscholastic sports, clubs, yearbook, and a dining hall waiter program in which fifth and sixth graders serve hot lunches to younger children—complete the student's experiences.

MEDIA, PA. (15 mi. WSW of Philadelphia, PA; 15 mi. NNE of Wilmington, DE) Suburban. Pop: 5533. Alt: 330 ft. Area also includes Rose Valley.

MEDIA-PROVIDENCE FRIENDS SCHOOL
Day — Coed Gr PS (Age 3)-8

Media, PA 19063. 125 W 3rd St. Tel: 610-565-1960. Fax: 610-565-9866.
www.mpfs.org   E-mail: fstrathmann@fox.mpfs.org
Earl Sissell, Head (2009). Francy Strathmann, Adm.
Pre-Prep. Gen Acad. Feat—Span Environ_Sci Computers Fine_Arts.
Sports—Basket Soccer Tennis.
Selective adm (Gr PS-7): 37/yr. Usual entry: PS, K & 6. Appl fee: $50. Appl due: Rolling.
Enr 157. B 79. G 78. Wh 74%. Latino 2%. Blk 13%. Asian 3%. Other 8%. Avg class size: 13. Stud/fac: 8:1. Casual. **Fac 29.** M 6/F 23. FT 24/PT 5. Wh 81%. Latino 6%. Blk 10%. Asian 3%. Adv deg: 37%.
Grad '11—17. Prep—9.
Tui '11-'12: Day $14,000-17,760 (+$25-235). **Aid:** Need 54 ($375,000).
Summer: Enrich Rec. Tui Day $350/wk. 9 wks.
Bldgs 4. Libs 1. Sci labs 2. Lang labs 2. Art studios 1. Music studios 1. Gyms 1. Fields 1.

Comp labs 1. Comp/stud: 1:3.
Est 1876. Nonprofit. Religious Society of Friends. Tri (Sept-June).

Quaker principles and processes are an integral part of the program at this Delaware County elementary school, which serves a diverse student body that reflects the surrounding area. In 1908, the school enrolled children from several Doukhobor families that came to the US to escape religious persecution in Russia. Decades later, MPFS became the first independent school in the area to integrate upon its acceptance of an African-American pupil in 1937.

In a small-class setting, MPFS provides a strong foundation in reading, writing and math that also prepares boys and girls for course work in science, social studies, Spanish and the arts. The school integrates subjects whenever possible, thereby teaching children that knowledge is interconnected. Within the context of the program, instructors accommodate differences in learning rates and styles as students advance from the mastery of basic skills to higher-order thinking.

Eighth graders take a culminating trip to New Mexico that integrates art, science, social studies and Spanish in the culture of another locale.

THE SCHOOL IN ROSE VALLEY
Day — Coed Gr PS (Age 2)-6

Rose Valley, PA 19063. 20 School Ln. Tel: 610-566-1088. Fax: 610-566-4640.
www.theschoolinrosevalley.org E-mail: office@theschoolinrosevalley.org
Todd R. Nelson, Head (2010). BA, Bates College, MA, Tufts Univ. **Kim Schmucki, Adm.**
Pre-Prep. Gen Acad. Elem math—Everyday Math. **Feat**—Lib_Skills Span Environ_Sci Computers Studio_Art Music Woodworking. **Supp**—Rev Tut.
Selective adm: 30/yr. Appl fee: $50. Appl due: Mar. Accepted: 60%. Yield: 90%.
Enr 125. B 62. G 63. Wh 78%. Latino 1%. Blk 4%. Asian 6%. Other 11%. Avg class size: 13. Stud/fac: 8:1. **Fac 23.** M 1/F 22. FT 12/PT 11. Wh 87%. Blk 1%. Asian 12%. Adv deg: 39%.
Grad '11—9. Prep—2. (Shipley 1, Friends' Central 1).
Tui '12-'13: Day $14,850-17,093 (+$240). **Aid:** Need 29 ($130,000).
Summer (enr 160): Rec. Tui Day $390-2450. 1-7 wks.
Endow $1,000,000. Plant val $2,000,000. Acres 9. Bldgs 6 (100% ADA). Class rms 11. Lib 11,000 vols. Sci labs 1. Auds 2. Theaters 2. Art studios 1. Music studios 1. Wood shops 1. Gyms 1. Fields 1. Pools 2. Comp labs 3. Comp/stud: 1:3 (1:1 Laptop prgm Gr 3-6).
Est 1929. Nonprofit. Sem (Sept-June).

A group of parents organized this progressive school in cooperation with the department of education at Swarthmore College. Parents helped construct the buildings and continue to maintain a strong partnership with the staff and administration, helping to shape school philosophy and support the school's management. The developmentally appropriate curriculum, based on concrete experiences whenever possible, emphasizes shop, art, music, environmental science, computers and noncompetitive sports, in addition to language arts, math and social studies.

MERCERSBURG, PA. (118 mi. ESE of Pittsburgh, PA) Rural. Pop: 1540. Alt: 595 ft.

MERCERSBURG ACADEMY
Bdg and Day — Coed Gr 9-PG

Mercersburg, PA 17236. 300 E Seminary St. Tel: 717-328-6173. Fax: 717-328-6319.
www.mercersburg.edu E-mail: admission@mercersburg.edu
Douglas Hale, Head (1997). BA, Univ of Tennessee-Chattanooga, MA, Middlebury Col-

lege. **Thomas W. Adams, Adm.**
Col Prep. AP (408 exams taken, 88% 3+)—Eng Chin Fr Ger Span Calc Stats Comp_ Sci Bio Chem Environ_Sci Physics Eur_Hist US_Hist World_Hist Comp_Govt & Pol Econ US_Govt & Pol Art_Hist. **Feat**—Greek Lat Multivariable_Calc Anat & Physiol Astron Botany Genetics Robotics Amer_Stud World_Relig Buddhism Ceramics Drawing Painting Sculpt Studio_Art Acting Chorus Music_Hist Music_Theory Dance Journ. **Supp**—Tut.
Sports—Basket X-country Indoor_Track Lacrosse Ski Soccer Squash Swim Tennis Track. B: Baseball Football Golf Wrestling. G: F_Hockey Softball Volley. **Activities:** 45.
Selective adm (Bdg Gr 9-12; Day 9-11): 159/yr. Bdg 130. Day 29. Appl fee: $50. Appl due: Jan. Accepted: 38%. Yield: 59%. **Tests** CEEB SSAT TOEFL.
Enr 432. Bdg 354. Day 78. Intl 13%. Avg class size: 12. Stud/fac: 5:1. **Fac 96.** M 61/F 35. FT 93/PT 3. Wh 96%. Latino 2%. Blk 1%. Other 1%. Adv deg: 69%. In dorms 32.
Grad '11—126. Col—126. (US Naval Acad 7, Lehigh 5, Bucknell 4, US Milit Acad 4, USC 4, U of VA 3). **Mid 50% SAT:** CR 530-660. M 560-680. W 523-660. **Col couns:** 3. Alum donors: 21%.
Tui '12-'13: Bdg $48,825 (+$1000-1425). **Day $35,950** (+$1000-1425). **Aid:** Need 212 ($5,100,000).
Summer: Enrich Rec. ESL. Sports. 5 wks.
Endow $193,000,000. Plant val $150,000,000. Acres 300. Bldgs 23. Dorms 7. Dorm rms 182. Class rms 40. Lib 50,000 vols. Chapels 1. Sci labs 7. Lang labs 1. Comp ctrs 3. Auds 1. Theaters 2. Art studios 5. Music studios 5. Dance studios 2. Arts ctrs 1. Gyms 3. Fields 10. Tennis courts 14. Volleyball courts 1. Squash courts 10. Pools 1. Comp labs 3.
Est 1893. Nonprofit. Tri (Sept-June). **Assoc** CLS MSA.

The history of Mercersburg goes back to 1836, when Marshall College was founded here. In 1853, Marshall College moved to Lancaster, where it joined with Franklin College to become Franklin and Marshall College, but the preparatory department of the college continued on its original site under private direction until 1865, when it was chartered as Mercersburg College. In 1893, the board of regents of the college elected William Mann Irvine to lead the institution. Within months, Dr. Irvine changed the college's name to Mercersburg Academy and began his work as the founder and first headmaster of the present-day school. He opened the school that same year with an enrollment of 40 boys. The academy became coeducational in 1969.

The curriculum provides a rigorous college preparatory course of study. Admitting students of above-average ability who have been achieving well, the school maintains small classes. The major disciplines are English, foreign language, mathematics, science and history, with requirements in religion and the fine arts. Advanced Placement work is available in all academic areas. Foreign study opportunities are provided for a limited number of students through Mercerburg's affiliation with the School Year Abroad program and the English-Speaking Union.

Mercersburg maintains an extensive fine and performing arts department that features instrumental and voice opportunities; theater productions; ballet, modern dance and hip-hop; and musical theater.

NEW BLOOMFIELD, PA. (100 mi. WNW of Wilmington, DE; 112 mi. WNW of Philadelphia, PA) Rural. Pop: 1092. Alt: 800 ft.

CARSON LONG MILITARY ACADEMY
Bdg and Day — Boys Gr 6-12

New Bloomfield, PA 17068. 200 N Carlisle St. Tel: 717-582-2121. Fax: 717-582-8763.
www.carsonlong.org   E-mail: clcontact@carsonlong.org
Col. Matthew J. Brown, USA (Ret), Pres (2007). BS, US Military Academy, MS, Bucknell

Univ, MSS, US Army War College. **Capt. Craig A. Martel, Adm.**
Col Prep. Gen Acad. Milit. Feat—Fr Span Environ_Sci Comp_Sci Civil_War WWII Anthro Econ Philos Studio_Art Music Speech JROTC. **Supp**—ESL Makeup Rem_ Math Rem_Read Tut.
Sports—B: Baseball Basket X-country Football Soccer Tennis Track. **Activities:** 25.
Somewhat selective adm: 54/yr. Bdg 54. Day 0. Usual entry: 9 & 10. Appl fee: $65. Appl due: Rolling. Applied: 104. Accepted: 67%. Yield: 70%. **Tests** DAT.
Enr 120. Elem 13. Sec 107. Wh 50%. Latino 10%. Blk 25%. Asian 10%. Other 5%. Intl 25%. Avg class size: 8. Stud/fac: 5:1. Uniform. **Fac 23.** M 20/F 3. FT 22/PT 1. Wh 100%. Adv deg: 56%. In dorms 12.
Grad '10—29. Col—22. (Norwich 2, St Vincent 2, VA Polytech 2). **Avg SAT:** CR 447. M 423. W 375. Avg ACT: 19.5. **Col couns:** 1. Alum donors: 8%.
Tui '11-'12: Bdg $24,000 (+$2130). **5-Day Bdg $21,080** (+$2130). **Day $13,180** (+$2130). **Intl Bdg $24,000** (+$2130-3230). **Aid:** Merit 17 ($38,250). Need 32 ($76,000).
Endow $1,700,000. Plant val $6,500,000. Acres 56. Bldgs 11. Dorms 6. Dorm rms 77. Class rms 18. Lib 6758 vols. Chapels 1. Sci labs 3. Lang labs 2. Auds 1. Art studios 1. Music studios 1. Gyms 1. Fields 3. Tennis courts 5. Weight rms 1. Comp labs 4. Comp/stud: 1:3.
Est 1837. Nonprofit. Sem (Sept-June). **Assoc** MSA.

The school was founded by Theodore K. Long in the plant of the local academy. The basic curriculum combines college preparation with honors courses, English as a Second Language, Junior ROTC and vocational guidance. The structured and controlled environment offers small classes and supervised study. Significant emphasis is placed on public speaking for all students.

NEW HOPE, PA. (26 mi. NNE of Philadelphia, PA) Rural. Pop: 2252. Alt: 86 ft.

SOLEBURY SCHOOL

Bdg — Coed Gr 9-PG; Day — Coed 7-12

New Hope, PA 18938. 6832 Phillips Mill Rd. Tel: 215-862-5261. Fax: 215-862-3366.
www.solebury.org E-mail: admissions@solebury.org
Thomas G. Wilschutz, Head (2008). BA, Univ of Iowa, MA, Michigan State Univ. **Scott Eckstein, Adm.**
Col Prep. AP (exams req'd; 70 taken, 70% 3+)—Eng Fr Span Calc Stats Environ_Sci US_Hist US_Govt & Pol Studio_Art. **Feat**—Creative_Writing Poetry Shakespeare Short_Fiction Chin Anat & Physiol Ecol Forensic_Sci Comp_Design Programming Chin_Hist Vietnam_War Amer_Stud Archaeol Civics Psych Criminal_Justice Gender_Stud Ethics Philos World_Relig Art_Hist Ceramics Photog Sculpt Theater Chorus Public_Speak. **Supp**—ESL LD Rem_Math Tut.
Sports—Basket X-country Soccer Tennis Track. B: Baseball Golf Wrestling. G: F_Hockey Lacrosse Softball. **Activities:** 25.
Selective adm (Bdg Gr 9-12; Day 7-12): 70/yr. Bdg 20. Day 50. Usual entry: 7 & 9. Appl fee: $50. Appl due: Jan. Applied: 250. Accepted: 75%. Yield: 55%. **Tests** ISEE SSAT TOEFL.
Enr 235. B 120. G 115. Bdg 79. Day 156. Elem 30. Sec 205. Wh 66%. Latino 1%. Blk 13%. Asian 16%. Other 4%. Intl 15%. Avg class size: 11. Stud/fac: 6:1. **Fac 53.** M 27/F 26. FT 34/PT 19. Wh 90%. Blk 6%. Asian 4%. Adv deg: 41%. In dorms 7.
Grad '10—42. Col—41. (PA St 2, U of VT 2, Boston U 1, Brandeis 1, Geo Wash 1, Oberlin 1). **Mid 50% SAT:** CR 475-635. M 480-650. W 480-650. Alum donors: 28%.
Tui '11-'12: Bdg $45,850 (+$600). **Day $27,700-30,900** (+$600). **Aid:** Merit 15 ($105,000). Need 96 ($1,465,890).
Endow $3,600,000. Plant val $20,000,000. Acres 90. Bldgs 22. Dorms 3. Dorm rms 72. Class rms 37. Lib 13,000 vols. Sci labs 4. Sci ctrs 1. Theaters 1. Art studios 3. Music

Middle Atlantic States—PA

studios 1. Gyms 1. Fields 4. Courts 4. Pools 1. Comp labs 3. Comp/stud: 1:2. **Est 1925.** Nonprofit. Tri (Sept-June). **Assoc** MSA.

Situated on a 90-acre campus midway between Philadelphia and New York City, this school conducts a rigorous college preparatory program. Solebury's curriculum includes AP classes, honors courses in all disciplines, and opportunities for independent study. A number of electives and course work in computers and the arts are among the school's graduation requirements. Advanced middle school students may take some high school courses for credit. In mid-May, another element of the curriculum allows seniors in good standing to leave campus for three weeks to work as an apprentice or a volunteer, to conduct independent research, or to pursue a creative project.

Each year, an academic theme promoting interdisciplinary learning is highlighted for which both faculty and students participate in summer reading, workshops, special films and assemblies, department presentations, weekend activities, play productions and art shows. In addition, Solebury offers a learning skills program for bright pupils with learning differences and, for international students, spring, summer and full-year programs in English as a Second Language.

Students perform five hours of community service annually in middle school, then 10 hours per year in high school, totaling a minimum of 40 hours prior to graduation. In addition to a full interscholastic sports program, the school offers recreational rock climbing, horseback riding, golf and biking. Solebury schedules trips to such locations as France, Tanzania and Belize.

NEWTOWN, PA. (19 mi. NE of Philadelphia, PA) Suburban. Pop: 2523. Alt: 180 ft.

GEORGE SCHOOL

Bdg and Day — Coed Gr 9-12

Newtown, PA 18940. 1690 Newtown Langhorne Rd. Tel: 215-579-6500.
Fax: 215-579-6549.
www.georgeschool.org E-mail: admission@georgeschool.org
Nancy O. Starmer, Head (2000). BA, College of Wooster, MEd, Boston Univ. **Christian Donovan, Adm.**
Col Prep. IB Diploma. AP **(208 exams taken, 76% 3+)**—Fr Lat Span Calc Stats Bio Chem Physics US_Hist Human_Geog Studio_Art. **Feat**—Chin Environ_Sci Forensic_Sci Marine_Bio/Sci Neurology Programming African-Amer_Hist Women's_Hist Amer_Stud Econ Quakerism Ceramics Painting Video_Production Theater_Arts Chorus Music Orchestra Dance Design Woodworking Horticulture. **Supp**—ESL.
Sports—Basket Cheer X-country Equestrian Golf Indoor_Track Lacrosse Soccer Swim Tennis Track. B: Baseball Football Wrestling. G: F_Hockey Softball Volley. **Activities:** 31.
Selective adm: 182/yr. Bdg 105. Day 77. Usual entry: 9. Appl fee: $50. Applied: 506. Accepted: 57%. Yield: 62%. **Tests** SSAT.
Enr 530. B 254. G 276. Bdg 297. Day 233. Nonwhite 20%. Intl 15%. Avg class size: 14. Stud/fac: 7:1. **Fac 87.** M 35/F 52. FT 75/PT 12. Wh 81%. Latino 3%. Blk 6%. Asian 6%. Other 4%. Adv deg: 68%. In dorms 30.
Grad '11—135. Col—133. (Geo Wash, Syracuse, U of Rochester, Boston U, Carnegie Mellon, Drexel). Mid 50% SAT: CR 550-690. M 550-690. W 550-680. Mid 50% ACT: 22-28. **Col couns:** 3.
Tui '12-'13: Bdg **$48,910** (+$1000). Day **$32,860** (+$1000). **Aid:** Need 249 ($6,500,000).
Summer (enr 275): Coord. Rec. Tui Day $1215-3305. 3-7 wks.
Endow $77,200,000. Plant val $71,800,000. Acres 240. Bldgs 14. Dorms 8. Dorm rms 160. Class rms 40. Lib 20,000 vols. Sci labs 6. Lang labs 1. Meetinghouses 1. Art studios 7. Music studios 6. Gyms 2. Fields 10. Tennis courts 10. Pools 1. Riding rings

2. Stables 1. Greenhouses 1.
Est 1893. Nonprofit. Religious Society of Friends (15% practice). Tri (Sept-June). **Assoc** MSA.

This Friends' school owes its name to its founder, John M. George, whose will provided for the education of the children of Friends and others. The campus is located on 240 acres of wooded countryside in Bucks County, within easy access of the cultural centers of Philadelphia, Princeton, NJ, and New York City. The spirit of the school is in the Friends tradition, and students of every religious, racial and economic background attend from many states and foreign countries.

George School's curriculum includes traditional college preparatory courses and a variety of special term electives. Accommodating students with differing learning styles and abilities, the curriculum's four-level system enables students to study with appropriate degrees of intensity in each discipline. GS is one of the only boarding schools in the country that offers the two-year International Baccalaureate curriculum, a rigorous course of study (taken in grades 11 and 12) that often results in a full year of credit earned for US colleges or opportunities for university study abroad. Advanced Placement classes are also available to qualified pupils. An English as a Second Language program serves international students.

Complementing its academic offerings, the school provides a wide selection of extracurricular activities in the following areas: athletics, the performing and visual arts, and community service. Each year, students must participate in team or intramural sports, take a yearlong arts course and contribute to the school's cooperative work program. Service projects to coastal Georgia and Arizona's Navajo Nation, as well as international work camps conducted in Cuba, France, South Korea, Israel/Palestine, Vietnam, Nicaragua and South Africa, are part of GS' prominent community service program.

NEWTOWN FRIENDS SCHOOL
Day — Coed Gr PS (Age 4)-8

Newtown, PA 18940. 1450 Newtown-Langhorne Rd. Tel: 215-968-2225.
  Fax: 215-968-9346.
  www.newtownfriends.org   E-mail: info@newtownfriends.org
Dana Harrison, Head (2010). BS, Haverford College, MS, Arizona State Univ, MA, Columbia Univ. **Rebecca A. Niszczak, Adm.**
  Pre-Prep. Elem math—Singapore Math. **Feat**—Lib_Skills Lat Span Computers Studio_ Art Music. **Supp**—Dev_Read Rev.
  Sports—Basket X-country Lacrosse Soccer Softball. G: F_Hockey.
  Selective adm (Gr PS-7): 55/yr. Usual entry: PS, K, 1, 6 & 7. Appl fee: $45. Appl due: Rolling. Applied: 89. Accepted: 79%. Yield: 74%. **Tests** SSAT.
  Enr 253. B 132. G 121. Wh 81%. Latino 2%. Blk 4%. Asian 7%. Other 6%. Avg class size: 16. Stud/fac: 11:1. Casual. **Fac 29.** M 3/F 26. FT 22/PT 7. Wh 87%. Latino 7%. Blk 3%. Asian 3%. Adv deg: 44%.
  Grad '11—37. Prep—26. (George Sch 14, Solebury 3, Peddie 2, Lawrenceville 1, Phillips Exeter 1, Mercersburg 1).
  Tui '12-'13: Day $12,500-17,900. Aid: Merit 5 ($13,500). Need 60 ($496,500).
  Endow $2,200,000. Plant val $11,400,000. Acres 7. Bldgs 1. Class rms 21. Lib 10,000 vols. Sci labs 2. Auds 1. Art studios 1. Music studios 1. Gyms 1. Fields 2. Comp labs 3. Comp/stud: 1:6.
  Est 1948. Nonprofit. Religious Society of Friends (11% practice). Tri (Sept-June).

Occupying a seven-acre site in Bucks County, Newtown Friends was founded by area Quakers and parents. The curriculum comprises course work in language arts, math, science, foreign language (Spanish and Latin), social studies, music and drama, art, computer and physical education. In grades K-8, the school divides each grade into two sections of roughly 16 to 18 pupils; in the prekindergarten, there is one class of approximately 16 children. Instruction at all levels combines hands-on experiences, group and individual projects, interdisciplinary approaches and traditional methods.

An important aspect of school life is an intergenerational program that provides students with opportunities for interaction with individuals at Pennswood Village, a Friends' continuing care retirement community that occupies quarters next to Newtown Friends. In addition, the school's curriculum includes mandatory community service in grades 6-8.

PENNSBURG, PA. (33 mi. NW of Philadelphia, PA) Rural. Pop: 2732. Alt: 425 ft.

PERKIOMEN SCHOOL
Bdg — Coed Gr 7-PG; Day — Coed 6-PG

Pennsburg, PA 18073. 200 Seminary St. Tel: 215-679-9511. Fax: 215-679-1146.
www.perkiomen.org   E-mail: admissions@perkiomen.org
Christopher R. Tompkins, Head (2008). BA, Colby College, MS, Syracuse Univ. **Christian Brena, Adm.**
Col Prep. AP (exams req'd; 250 taken, 70% 3+)—Eng Ger Lat Span Calc Stats Comp_ Sci Bio Chem Environ_Sci Physics Eur_Hist US_Hist World_Hist Econ US_Govt & Pol Art_Hist Studio_Art Music_Theory. **Feat**—Chin Physiol Robotics Anthro Archaeol Pol_Sci Relig Photog Drama Music Music_Hist. **Supp**—ESL LD Rev Tut.
Sports—Basket Lacrosse Soccer Swim Tennis. B: Baseball X-country Football Golf Weightlifting. G: F_Hockey Softball. **Activities:** 12.
Selective adm (Bdg Gr 7-10; Day 6-9): 85/yr. Bdg 56. Day 29. Usual entry: 6 & 9. Appl fee: $50. Appl due: Feb. Accepted: 54%. Yield: 78%. **Tests** SSAT.
Enr 303. Wh 68%. Latino 3%. Blk 9%. Asian 20%. Intl 35%. Avg class size: 14. Stud/fac: 7:1. **Fac 51.** M 29/F 22. FT 48/PT 3. Wh 97%. Latino 1%. Blk 1%. Asian 1%. Adv deg: 56%. In dorms 22.
Grad '11—79. Col—78. (U of CA-Berkeley 3, Wm & Mary 3, Franklin & Marshall 2, Northwestern 1, U of PA 1, US Air Force Acad 1). **Mid 50% SAT:** CR 430-570. M 540-740. W 460-620. **Col couns:** 3. Alum donors: 23%.
Tui '12-'13: Bdg $45,525 (+$3750-3900). **Day $24,975-26,250** (+$650-1000). **Aid:** Merit 25 ($66,000). Need 77 ($1,219,000).
Summer (enr 300): Enrich Rec. ESL. 1-5 wks.
Endow $6,200,000. Plant val $52,000,000. Acres 165. Bldgs 19. Dorms 5. Dorm rms 160. Class rms 57. Lib 17,000 vols. Sci labs 5. Auds 1. Theaters 1. Art studios 4. Music studios 5. Dance studios 2. Gyms 1. Fields 8. Courts 6. Pools 1. Comp labs 3.
Est 1875. Nonprofit. Tri (Sept-May). **Assoc** CLS MSA.

In response to the limited educational opportunities then available in the area, Rev. Charles S. Wieand founded the school in the latter stages of the 19th century to provide a traditional college preparatory program for students from the Upper Perkiomen Valley and beyond. Perkiomen's upper school curriculum includes traditional course requirements and electives, such as language, history, science, math and the arts, in each grade. All departments offer Advanced Placement and honors classes. Two special programs supplement the traditional academic courses: A highly individualized developmental language program aids above-average students with mild learning disabilities or gaps in learning skills, while an extensive ESL program provides individual support for international students until they are proficient in speaking and writing. Religious studies consist of course offerings in the upper school and a chapel program that convenes regularly and addresses such topics as ethics, religion and life experiences.

The fine arts program includes both curricular and extracurricular options. During the academic day, course offerings encompass instrumental and voice instruction, studio art, theater and private lessons. Students in the middle school take fine art classes five times a week, while those in grades 9-12 participate in a variety of electives, among them art history, studio art, photography, drawing, digital art, ceramics, stage makeup and playwriting. After class, individualized programs in studio art, dance, voice and instrumental music are available to advanced students.

Students accumulate 24 hours of required community service in grades 9-12.

PHILADELPHIA, PA. Urban. Pop: 1,517,550. Alt: to 440 ft. Area also includes Fort Washington, Newtown Square and Wyndmoor.

CREFELD SCHOOL
Day — Coed Gr 7-12

Philadelphia, PA 19118. 8836 Crefeld St. Tel: 215-242-5545. Fax: 215-242-8869.
www.crefeld.org   E-mail: info@crefeld.org
George Zeleznik, Head (2011). BS, Indiana Univ of Pennsylvania, MA, Gratz College.
Stacey Cunitz, Adm.
Col Prep. LD. Underachiever. Feat—Span Environ_Sci Forensic_Sci Computers Psych Drawing Sculpt Bookbinding Glass_Blowing Acting Music Dance Debate. Supp—Tut. Outdoor ed.
Sports—Basket Soccer. Activities: 15.
Selective adm (Gr 7-11): 19/yr. Usual entry: 7, 8 & 9. Appl fee: $75. Appl due: Rolling. Applied: 45. Accepted: 65%.
Enr 96. B 60. G 36. Elem 16. Sec 80. Wh 74%. Latino 3%. Blk 20%. Asian 3%. Avg class size: 10. Stud/fac: 5:1. Casual. Fac 20. M 11/F 9. FT 16/PT 4. Wh 90%. Latino 5%. Blk 5%. Adv deg: 70%.
Grad '11—16. Col—16. (Arcadia 2, Clark U 1, Bennington 1, Drexel 1, Susquehanna 1, Temple 1). Mid 50% SAT: CR 520-630. M 450-550. W 500-600. Col couns: 1. Alum donors: 20%.
Tui '12-'13: Day $24,000-27,050 (+$300). Aid: Need 43 ($400,000).
Summer (enr 15): Enrich. Arts. Tui Day $800/4-wk ses. 8 wks.
Plant val $2,500,000. Acres 4. Bldgs 2. Class rms 21. Libs 1. Sci labs 1. Lang labs 1. Auds 1. Theaters 1. Art studios 3. Music studios 1. Dance studios 1. Gyms 1. Fields 1. Basketball courts 1. Comp labs 2. Comp/stud: 1:3.
Est 1970. Nonprofit. Sem (Sept-June). Assoc MSA.

Guided by the principles of the Coalition of Essential Schools and research on multiple intelligences and learning styles, this progressive school follows a flexible and collaborative approach to learning. Crefeld serves able students, some of whom have learning differences, and it accommodates differences in learning style through differentiated instruction. When necessary, the school works closely with both the student's parents and outside professionals to coordinate efforts and formulate strategic plans.

Various electives, with an emphasis on the arts, complement the academic program. All students satisfy a two-hour weekly community service requirement during the school day.

THE EPISCOPAL ACADEMY
Day — Coed Gr PS (Age 4)-12

Newtown Square, PA 19073. 1785 Bishop White Dr. Tel: 484-424-1444.
Fax: 484-424-1604.
www.episcopalacademy.org   E-mail: admission@episcopalacademy.org
L. Hamilton Clark, Jr., Head (2002). BA, Trinity College (CT), MEd, Harvard Univ. Rachel Tilney, Adm.
Col Prep. AP (exams req'd; 408 taken, 88% 3+)—Eng Fr Lat Span Calc Stats Comp_ Sci Bio Chem Physics Eur_Hist US_Hist World_Hist Econ US_Govt & Pol Art_Hist Studio_Art Music_Theory. Elem math—Singapore Math. Feat—British_Lit Creative_Writing Shakespeare Middle_Eastern_Lit Satire Urban_Lit Victorian_Lit Chin Greek Astron Ecol Russ_Hist Urban_Hist Psych Ethics Philos World_Relig Architect_Drawing Ceramics Film Photog Acting Theater_Arts Music. Supp—Dev_Read Tut. Outdoor ed.
Sports (req'd)—Basket Crew X-country Golf Indoor_Track Lacrosse Soccer Squash Swim Tennis Track W_Polo. B: Baseball Football Ice_Hockey Wrestling. G: F_Hockey Softball. Activities: 38.

Selective adm: 193/yr. Usual entry: PS, K, 1, 6 & 9. Appl fee: $50. Appl due: Jan. Applied: 595. Accepted: 46%. Yield: 70%. **Tests** IQ ISEE SSAT.
Enr 1227. B 648. G 579. Elem 716. Sec 511. Wh 78%. Latino 1%. Blk 7%. Asian 7%. Other 7%. Avg class size: 16. Stud/fac: 7:1. Formal. **Fac 155.** M 69/F 86. FT 147/PT 8. Wh 85%. Latino 2%. Blk 3%. Asian 6%. Other 4%. Adv deg: 55%.
Grad '11—125. Col—125. (U of PA 8, Boston Col 7, Cornell 5, Princeton 4, Georgetown 4, Amherst 4). Athl schol 10. **Avg SAT:** CR 636. M 653. W 659. Avg ACT: 27.6. **Col couns:** 5. Alum donors: 29%.
Tui '12-'13: Day $20,600-28,970 (+$200-750). **Aid:** Need 172 ($3,232,530).
Summer (enr 638): Acad Enrich Rev Rem Rec. Tui Day $100-1200/crse. 1-7 wks.
Endow $35,134,000. Plant val $193,000,000. Acres 123. Bldgs 11 (100% ADA). Class rms 69. 2 Libs 70,000 vols. Chapels 1. Sci labs 14. Lang labs 2. Auds 1. Theaters 2. Art studios 3. Music studios 3. Dance studios 1. Gyms 3. Fields 9. Courts 24. Pools 1. Comp labs 3. Comp/stud: 1:1.5.
Est 1785. Nonprofit. Episcopal. Sem (Sept-June). **Assoc** CLS MSA.

One of the country's largest Episcopal day schools, Episcopal Academy was founded in Philadelphia by the Right Reverend William White, the first Episcopal bishop of Pennsylvania and a signee of the Declaration of Independence. Originally established to teach boys Anglican doctrine and to train clergy, the academy soon opened free schools to educate a broader population. EA moved to Merion in 1921, opened a second campus for the lower school (grades PS-5) in 1973 in the western suburbs of Devon, and adopted coeducation in 1974. Recognizing the need for a larger, unified campus, the school moved in fall 2008 to its current, 123-acre campus in Newtown Square. Students enroll from a 30-mile radius.

The academy's student body represents diverse religious, racial and ethnic backgrounds. The college preparatory curriculum, with individualized student scheduling, features strong technology and fine and performing arts programs. The science department arranges intensive internships with scientists and institutions in a range of fields, usually in the summer. Competitive athletics and an inclusive chapel program are other important aspects of school life. EA provides boys and girls with various opportunities for foreign travel and study. Students voluntarily engage in community service both on and off campus.

FRIENDS SELECT SCHOOL
Day — Coed Gr PS (Age 4)-12

Philadelphia, PA 19103. 17th St & Benjamin Franklin Pky. Tel: 215-561-5900.
Fax: 215-864-2979.
www.friends-select.org E-mail: anita@friends-select.org
Rose Hagan, Head (1995). BA, Temple Univ, MA, Southern Illinois Univ. **Roger Dillow, Adm.**
Col Prep. Feat—Shakespeare Irish_Lit Chin Fr Ital Lat Span Calc Discrete_Math Astron Environ_Sci Comp_Sci Robotics Chin_Hist Quakerism Drawing Film Photog Sculpt Drama Chorus Music Metal_Shop. **Supp**—Dev_Read ESL.
Sports (req'd)—Basket Crew X-country Soccer Swim Tennis. B: Baseball Wrestling. G: F_Hockey Softball.
Selective adm: 93/yr. Appl fee: $40-70. Appl due: Jan. Accepted: 66%. **Tests** ISEE SSAT.
Enr 552. Wh 66%. Latino 4%. Blk 16%. Native Am 1%. Asian 7%. Other 6%. Intl 5%. Avg class size: 16. Stud/fac: 10:1. **Fac 88.** Adv deg: 63%.
Grad '08—49. Col—45. (U of PA, Temple, U of Pittsburgh, Geo Wash, Mt Holyoke, Columbia).
Tui '12-'13: Day $17,710-28,580 (+$125). **Aid:** Need 155.
Summer: Gr 4-12. Acad Enrich Rev. 6 wks.
Endow $9,500,000. Plant val $8,500,000. Bldgs 1. Class rms 30. 2 Libs 17,000 vols. Sci labs 3. Dark rms 2. Auds 1. Theaters 1. Art studios 4. Music studios 2. Dance studios 1. Gyms 2. Fields 2. Tennis courts 8. Pools 1. Weight rms 1. Playgrounds 1. Comp labs 2.
Est 1689. Nonprofit. Religious Society of Friends (5% practice). Sem (Sept-June).

Assoc CLS.

Located in the cultural, corporate and business center of Philadelphia, Friends Select traces its Quaker beginnings to 1689. Coeducational since 1886, the school is still under the direct management of Friends, and religious course work is provided.

The school's college preparatory curriculum, rooted in Quaker values, encourages the development of conceptual understanding and creative thought while emphasizing the ability to serve the community. Small classes and individual attention are program characteristics at all grade levels. Internships with local businesses can be arranged during spring of junior year or the following summer, and all seniors complete an independent project or internship. Essential research and presentation skills are taught beginning in prekindergarten. Upper school students meet once a week with a faculty advisor. Each spring, fine arts students spend two weeks at the Umberto Boccioni School in Milan, Italy, studying Renaissance art and culture.

Interscholastic sports begin in grade 6. The school also offers after-school and vacation care, as well as summer programs for young children.

GERMANTOWN ACADEMY
Day — Coed Gr PS (Age 4)-12

Fort Washington, PA 19034. 340 Morris Rd, PO Box 287. Tel: 215-646-3300. Fax: 215-646-1216.
www.germantownacademy.net   E-mail: admission@germantownacademy.org
James W. Connor, Head (1989). BA, Eckerd College, MA, Univ of Pennsylvania. **Laura B. Martin, Adm.**

> **Col Prep. AP (exams req'd; 345 taken, 90% 3+)**—Eng Fr Span Calc Stats Bio Chem Environ_Sci Physics Eur_Hist US_Hist World_Hist Music_Theory. **Feat**—Lat Russ Marine_Bio/Sci Biotech Civil_War Econ Film Acting Theater_Arts Orchestra. **Supp**—Dev_Read. Outdoor ed.
>
> **Sports**—Basket Crew X-country Golf Lacrosse Soccer Swim Tennis Track W_Polo. B: Baseball Football Ice_Hockey Wrestling. G: F_Hockey Softball Volley. **Activities:** 46.
>
> **Selective adm (Gr PS-11):** 163/yr. Usual entry: PS, K, 5, 6, 7 & 9. Appl fee: $40. Appl due: Dec. **Tests** IQ ISEE SSAT.
>
> **Enr 1089.** B 588. G 501. Elem 587. Sec 502. Wh 77%. Latino 1%. Blk 7%. Asian 10%. Other 5%. Avg class size: 15. Stud/fac: 8:1. Uniform. **Fac 122.** M 55/F 67. FT 119/PT 3. Wh 90%. Latino 2%. Blk 3%. Asian 3%. Other 2%. Adv deg: 61%.
>
> **Grad '11—121. Col—121.** (U of PA 8, U of Pittsburgh 5, Franklin & Marshall 5, U of DE 4, Bucknell 4). **Mid 50% SAT:** CR 560-690. M 570-700. W 570-690. Mid 50% ACT: 25-29. **Col couns:** 7. Alum donors: 16%.
>
> **Tui '12-'13: Day $20,315-29,165** (+$300). **Aid:** Need 254 ($3,500,000).
>
> **Summer (enr 1000):** Acad Enrich Rec. Sports. Tui Day $275-400/wk. 6 wks.
>
> Endow $32,000,000. Plant val $25,000,000. Acres 126. Bldgs 8 (50% ADA). Class rms 106. Lib 18,000 vols. Sci labs 6. Lang labs 12. Sci ctrs 1. Auds 1. Theaters 1. Art studios 2. Music studios 2. Arts ctrs 1. Photog studios 1. Design studios 1. Gyms 2. Field houses 1. Pools 1. Comp labs 2. Comp/stud: 1:4.
>
> **Est 1759.** Nonprofit. Sem (Sept-June). **Assoc** CLS MSA.

The oldest nonsectarian independent day school in the country, GA was founded as Germantown Union School. The academy served both boys and girls on its original campus in the Germantown section of Philadelphia until 1836, when, by virtue of demand for space, the enrollment was limited to boys. A generous land gift in 1959 facilitated the school's move to its present, 126-acre campus in Fort Washington in 1961; the same year, GA reinstated coeducation.

The curriculum includes course requirements in English, history, mathematics, science, foreign language, the visual and performing arts, and physical education. Qualified students may complete Advanced Placement work in computer science and the major disciplines. Technology is an important aspect of the program: in addition to classroom computers, the academy maintains computer labs and provides extensive Internet access. All middle and upper school pupils have E-mail addresses.

Among other opportunities are an independent, off-campus study project at the end of senior year; elective summer internship programs; the Academy Scholars program for sophomores and juniors; and foreign exchange programs in France, Spain and Latin America.

GA provides numerous opportunities for pupils to satisfy middle and upper school extracurricular requirements. An extensive interscholastic sports program begins at the middle school level, and many on-campus clubs and activities are also available. Choral and orchestral groups travel and perform abroad and throughout the US on an annual basis.

GERMANTOWN FRIENDS SCHOOL
Day — Coed Gr K-12

Philadelphia, PA 19144. 31 W Coulter St. Tel: 215-951-2300. Fax: 215-951-2312.
www.germantownfriends.org   E-mail: admissions@gfsnet.org
Richard L. Wade, Head (1993). BA, College of William and Mary, MA, Northwestern Univ.
Laura Sharpless Myran, Adm.
Col Prep. AP exams taken: 27 (63% 3+). Elem math—TERC Investigations. **Feat**— Creative_Writing Fr Greek Lat Span Calc Stats Programming Robotics Philos World_ Relig Art_Hist Photog Drama Theater_Arts Chorus Music_Theory. **Supp**—ESL Tut.
Sports (req'd)—Basket X-country Indoor_Track Soccer Squash Tennis Track. B: Baseball Wrestling. G: F_Hockey Lacrosse Softball. **Activities:** 43.
Selective adm: 128/yr. Usual entry: K, 7 & 9. Appl fee: $40-60. Appl due: Dec. Applied: 341. Accepted: 68%. Yield: 55%. **Tests** IQ ISEE SSAT.
Enr 855. B 430. G 425. Elem 507. Sec 348. Wh 68%. Latino 2%. Blk 15%. Asian 9%. Other 6%. Avg class size: 18. Stud/fac: 7:1. **Fac 135.** M 43/F 92. FT 87/PT 48. Wh 83%. Latino 1%. Blk 12%. Asian 4%. Adv deg: 64%.
Grad '11—90. Col—90. (U of PA 12, Brown 5, U of Pittsburgh 5, Stanford 3, Vanderbilt 3, Wesleyan U 3). **Avg SAT:** CR 680. M 640. W 680. **Col couns:** 7. Alum donors: 20%.
Tui '12-'13: Day $19,150-28,450 (+$550-750). **Aid:** Need 273 ($2,720,000).
Summer (enr 400): Acad Rec. Tui Day $250/wk. 10 wks.
Endow $24,000,000. Plant val $38,000,000. Acres 21. Bldgs 24 (38% ADA). Class rms 84. Lib 60,000 vols. Sci labs 11. Lang labs 5. Theaters 3. Art studios 7. Music studios 7. Gyms 5. Fields 7. Courts 13. Comp labs 3. Comp/stud: 1:3.
Est 1845. Nonprofit. Religious Society of Friends (7% practice). Sem (Sept-June). **Assoc** MSA.

The importance and the influence of this Friends school developed during the time of Stanley R. Yarnall, with the school from 1898, and principal from 1906 until his retirement in 1941. The present-day school serves a multicultural student body and combines Quaker principles with a strong academic program.

GFS' thematic lower school curriculum progresses to a team-taught middle school and a college preparatory upper school program. Students may pursue advanced courses in science, mathematics, English, history, and classical and modern languages. Strong programs in art, music and theater are integrated with academics. Also noteworthy is a double-credit Latin history course that combines intermediate Latin language instruction with study of the origins of civilization in the Near East and its development in the Bronze Age and classical Greece. With faculty approval, students in grades 10-12 may engage in directed independent study for credit at a standard or accelerated level. GFS organizes community service projects at all grade levels; in addition, juniors spend January performing compulsory independent service.

Pupils take part in numerous extracurricular activities, as well as local service projects. Students in grades 9 and 10 are required to play an interscholastic sport. International travel and exchange programs are available, particularly through the modern language department's exchanges with schools in France and Mexico, advanced language, choir and athletic trips, and Germantown Friends' membership in the National Network of Complementary Schools.

GREENE STREET FRIENDS SCHOOL
Day — Coed Gr PS (Age 4)-8

Philadelphia, PA 19144. 5511 Greene St. Tel: 215-438-7000. Fax: 215-438-1121.
www.greenestreetfriends.org E-mail: lclancy@greenestreetfriends.org
Edward Marshall, Head (1995). BA, Temple Univ, PhD, Univ of Pennsylvania. **Leanne G. Clancy, Adm.**
   Pre-Prep. Gen Acad. Feat—Span Computers Econ Studio_Art Drama Music. **Supp**—Rem_Read Tut.
   Sports (req'd)—Basket Soccer Softball.
   Selective adm: 74/yr. Appl fee: $50. Appl due: Jan. Accepted: 30%. **Tests** CTP_4 ISEE.
   Enr 360. Avg class size: 18. **Fac 31.** M 7/F 24. FT 31.
   Grad '08—20. Prep—8. (Germantown Friends, Abington Friends, La Salle Col HS, Bishop McDevitt, Friends Select, Haverford).
   Tui '12-'13: Day $12,250-13,150 (+$200). **Aid:** Need 140.
   Summer: Rec. 2-6 wks.
   Plant val $10,000,000. Bldgs 5. Class rms 20. Lib 5000 vols. Sci labs 1. Auds 1. Theaters 1. Art studios 1. Music studios 1. Gyms 1. Comp labs 1.
   Est 1855. Nonprofit. Religious Society of Friends. Tri (Sept-June).

This Friends school was founded for children of the Green Street Monthly Meeting and others in the Germantown community. The program includes music, art, computer instruction, foreign language and physical education, as well as training in the basic academic skills. In the middle school, students choose from such electives as sign language, nature study, and the practical and fine arts. After-school sports and an extended-day program are available. Each spring, seventh graders visit Costa Rica for a 10-day cultural and language immersion experience.

LA SALLE COLLEGE HIGH SCHOOL
Day — Boys Gr 9-12

Wyndmoor, PA 19038. 8605 Cheltenham Ave. Tel: 215-233-2911. Fax: 215-233-1418.
www.lschs.org E-mail: doughertyk@lschs.org
Br. James L. Butler, FSC, Pres (2012). Joseph Marchese, Prin. BA, MA, Univ of Rochester. **Kevin B. Dougherty, Adm.**
   Col Prep. AP (560 exams taken, 84% 3+)—Eng Fr Lat Span Calc Stats Comp_Sci Bio Chem Environ_Sci Physics Eur_Hist US_Hist World_Hist Econ Psych US_Govt & Pol. **Feat**—British_Lit Creative_Writing Shakespeare Chin Ger Greek Ital Anat & Physiol Astron Civil_War Vietnam_War Pol_Sci Relig World_Relig Ceramics Drawing Painting Sculpt Studio_Art Chorus Music Public_Speak Health. **Supp**—LD Rev Tut.
   Sports—B: Baseball Basket Bowl Crew X-country Football Golf Ice_Hockey Indoor_Track Lacrosse Soccer Swim Tennis Track W_Polo Wrestling. **Activities:** 27.
   Selective adm (Gr 9-11): 260/yr. Usual entry: 9. Appl fee: $50. Appl due: Dec. **Tests** HSPT.
   Enr 1068. Avg class size: 19. Stud/fac: 11:1. Casual. **Fac 94.** M 73/F 21. FT 88/PT 6. Adv deg: 98%.
   Grad '10—248. Col—248. (PA St, St Joseph's U, Drexel, La Salle, Temple, Villanova). **Avg SAT:** CR 578. M 593. W 573. **Col couns:** 3.
   Tui '12-'13: Day $18,700 (+$300-2380).
   Summer: Acad Enrich Rev. 5 wks.
   Endow $10,400,000. Plant val $29,000,000. Acres 83. Bldgs 10. Class rms 40. Lib 13,000 vols. Sci labs 6. Lang labs 1. Auds 2. Art studios 2. Music studios 3. Gyms 2. Athletic ctrs 1. Fields 5. Tennis courts 5. Pools 2. Comp labs 7. Comp/stud: 1:4.
   Est 1858. Nonprofit. Roman Catholic. Sem (Sept-June). **Assoc** MSA.

Founded in Philadelphia and relocated to its present, 83-acre campus in 1960, this school is conducted by the De La Salle Christian Brothers. Advanced Placement classes are available; electives in psychology, economics, computer programming and networking, music, studio art and other subjects are also provided. The curriculum includes a full four-year program of religious studies, an extensive community service program and a campus ministry program that organizes yearly retreats.

Jazz band, string and choral programs, and a competing band are notable components of the music program. Educational technology at La Salle includes interactive whiteboards and a sophisticated computer network.

ST. PETER'S SCHOOL
Day — Coed Gr PS (Age 3)-8

Philadelphia, PA 19147. 319 Lombard St. Tel: 215-925-3963. Fax: 215-925-3351.
www.st-peters-school.org E-mail: bmunsterteiger@st-peters-school.org
Shawn Kelly, Head (2012). BA, Univ of Rhode Island, EdM, Harvard Univ. **Brit Munsterteiger, Adm.**
Pre-Prep. Feat—Poetry Fr Computers Studio_Art Music. **Supp**—Tut.
Sports (req'd)—Basket Soccer.
Selective adm: 39/yr. Usual entry: PS & K. Appl fee: $50. Appl due: Jan. Applied: 110. Accepted: 35%. Yield: 80%. **Tests** IQ.
Enr 214. B 94. G 120. Wh 66%. Latino 1%. Blk 7%. Asian 6%. Other 20%. Avg class size: 10. Stud/fac: 9:1. Uniform. **Fac 40.** M 8/F 32. FT 37/PT 3. Wh 93%. Blk 5%. Asian 2%.
Grad '10—14. **Prep**—9. (Friends Select). Alum donors: 9%.
Tui '11-'12: Day $16,265-21,620. Aid: Need 49 ($650,000).
Summer (enr 150): Acad Enrich Rec. Tui Day $200-300/wk. 6 wks.
Endow $1,100,000. Plant val $1,300,000. Bldgs 3 (0% ADA). Class rms 22. Lib 4000 vols. Sci labs 1. Lang labs 1. Auds 1. Theaters 1. Art studios 3. Music studios 2. Gyms 1. Fields 1. Courts 1. Comp labs 1. Comp/stud: 1:12.
Est 1834. Nonprofit. Tri (Sept-June).

The school was established as a parish school for the girls of St. Peter's Church by Bishop William White, bishop to the Continental Congress during the Revolutionary War. In the following years it became coeducational, and from 1904 to 1964 it was a renowned boys' choir school for St. Peter's Episcopal Church. St. Peter's incorporated independently of the church in 1969 and grew from a student body of 89 to its present size.

Students of all economic backgrounds, races and religions enroll from the Metropolitan Philadelphia area. The traditional academic program emphasizes literature, mathematics, history and science, and St. Peter's requires students to take part in music, art, physical education and technology courses. The school takes full advantage of surrounding cultural and historic institutions, while offering field trips to the New Jersey Shore and the Pennsylvania mountains.

See Also Page 120

SPRINGSIDE CHESTNUT HILL ACADEMY
Day — Coed Gr PS (Age 4)-12
(Coord — Day PS (Age 4)-8)

Philadelphia, PA 19118. 500 W Willow Grove Ave. Tel: 215-247-4700.
Fax: 215-247-7308.
Other locations: 8000 Cherokee St, Philadelphia 19118.
www.sch.org E-mail: admissions@sch.org
Priscilla G. Sands, Pres (2011). BFA, Univ of Rhode Island, MA, Villanova Univ, PhD, Univ of Pennsylvania. **Francis P. Steel, Head.** BA, Yale Univ, MA, Univ of Pennsylvania. **Michael Reardon, Adm.**
Col Prep. AP (200 exams taken, 80% 3+)—Eng Fr Span Calc Stats Bio Physics Eur_Hist World_Hist US_Govt & Pol. **Elem math**—Everyday Math. **Feat**—Creative_Writing Mythology Chin Lat Environ_Sci Forensic_Sci Oceanog Physiol Pharmacology Robotics E_Asian_Hist Intl_Relations African_Stud Ceramics Drawing Film Painting

Photog Video_Production Theater_Arts Chorus Orchestra Handbells Jazz_Ensemble Dance Journ Woodworking. **Supp**—Rev Tut. Outdoor ed.
Sports—Basket Crew X-country Golf Indoor_Track Lacrosse Soccer Squash Swim Tennis Track. B: Football Ice_Hockey Wrestling. G: F_Hockey Softball Volley. **Activities:** 39.
Selective adm: 153/yr. Usual entry: PS, K, 5 & 9. Appl fee: $50. Appl due: Jan. Applied: 456. Accepted: 55%. Yield: 66%. **Tests** IQ ISEE SSAT.
Enr 1129. B 491. G 638. Wh 75%. Latino 2%. Blk 17%. Asian 3%. Other 3%. Avg class size: 16. Stud/fac: 8:1. **Fac 152.** M 43/F 109. FT 135/PT 17. Wh 90%. Latino 5%. Blk 4%. Asian 1%. Adv deg: 51%.
Grad '11—106. Col—105. (U of PA 7, Gettysburg 5, W Chester 4, Syracuse 3, Lafayette 2, Trinity Col-CT 2). Athl schol 2. **Avg SAT:** CR 612. M 611. W 652. **Mid 50% SAT:** CR 530-640. M 550-630. Avg ACT: 25. **Col couns:** 3.
Tui '12-'13: Day $17,250-29,250. Aid: Need 371 ($5,070,260).
Summer (enr 665): Acad Enrich Rec. Sports. Tui Day $200-400/wk. 11 wks.
Endow $40,000,000. Plant val $30,000,000. Acres 62. Class rms 45. Libs 4. Sci labs 9. Lang labs 3. Auds 2. Art studios 7. Music studios 4. Dance studios 2. Art galleries 1. Gyms 6. Athletic ctrs 1. Fields 5. Tennis courts 4. Squash courts 10. Tracks 1. Weight rms 1. Comp labs 6. Comp/stud: 1:2 (1:1 Laptop prgm Gr 7-12).
Est 1879. Nonprofit. Quar (Sept-June). **Assoc** CLS.

SCH resulted from the 2011 merger of Springside School for girls (founded in 1879) and Chestnut Hill Academy for boys (established in 1861). The academy comprises single-gender lower schools (serving grades pre-K-5), single-gender middle schools (grades 6-8) and a coeducational upper school (grades 9-12). SCH continues to utilize both the Cherokee Street campus (which formerly served as the Springside location) and the West Willow Grove Avenue campus (which had operated as the Chestnut Hill location).

Qualified juniors and seniors may select options of independent study or courses at area colleges. Students in grades 9-12 are provided with laptop computers for use in class. More than half of the school's graduates enter college with Advanced Placement credits.

WILLIAM PENN CHARTER SCHOOL

Day — Coed Gr PS (Age 4)-12

Philadelphia, PA 19144. 3000 W School House Ln. Tel: 215-844-3460.
Fax: 215-844-5537.
www.penncharter.com E-mail: sbonnie@penncharter.com
Darryl J. Ford, Head (2007). BA, BS, Villanova Univ, MA, PhD, Univ of Chicago. **Stephen A. Bonnie, Adm.**
Col Prep. AP—Lat Span Calc Stats Bio Chem Environ_Sci Physics US_Hist World_Hist US_Govt & Pol Art_Hist. **Feat**—Creative_Writing Shakespeare Irish_Lit Fr Botany Genetics Oceanog Biochem Organic_Chem Comp_Sci Middle_Eastern_Hist Econ Bible Comp_Relig Relig Architect_Drawing Ceramics Film Filmmaking Photog Sculpt Glassmaking Theater Music.
Sports (req'd)—Basket Crew X-country Lacrosse Soccer Squash Swim Tennis Track W_Polo. B: Baseball Football Golf Wrestling. G: F_Hockey Softball. **Activities:** 31.
Selective adm: 156/yr. Usual entry: PS, K, 6, 7 & 9. Appl fee: $30-45. Appl due: Dec. Accepted: 43%. Yield: 57%. **Tests** ISEE SSAT.
Enr 955. Elem 515. Sec 440. Avg class size: 16. Stud/fac: 9:1. **Fac 138.** Adv deg: 68%.
Grad '10—110. Col—108. (U of PA 8, Temple 8, Drexel 7, Johns Hopkins 6, Boston Col 3, Northwestern 3). **Mid 50% SAT:** CR 590-700. M 610-700. W 610-710. Mid 50% ACT: 26-31. **Col couns:** 4.
Tui '12-'13: Day $19,600-28,950 (+$1000-2500). **Aid:** Need 325 ($6,500,000).
Summer: Rec. 3 wks.
Endow $53,000,000. Plant val $50,200,000. Acres 44. Bldgs 9. Class rms 62. 2 Libs 26,563 vols. Sci labs 7. Auds 3. Theaters 1. Art studios 3. Music studios 3. Dance studios 1. Art galleries 1. Gyms 5. Fields 9. Courts 7. Field houses 1. Pools 1. Comp labs 3.

Est 1689. Nonprofit. Religious Society of Friends. Tri (Sept-June). **Assoc** CLS MSA.

In 1701, a dozen years after the school's founding, William Penn granted the first of three charters that were to define the school's operation. The oldest Quaker school in the world is still conducted under his final charter of 1711. Richard Mott Jones, who served as headmaster from 1874 to 1916, brought the school a national reputation, largely due to his further development of the arts and athletic programs. Increasing enrollment resulted in Penn Charter's 1925 move from 8 S. 12th St. to its present Germantown location. In 1980, the overseers voted to admit girls into all grades for the first time.

The cosmopolitan student body emphasizes self-government and community participation. The prekindergarten program emphasizes project-based learning and integrated arts instruction. Each lower school student (grades K-5) attends weekly Meeting for Worship, and a quarter-long course in grade 7 integrating Quakerism, art and service learning. Spanish instruction in the lower school is followed by a trimester each of French, Latin and Spanish in grade 6, the first in a four-year required sequence.

Penn Charter's upper school curriculum, with its rotating schedule, trimester system and wide scope of elective courses, permits not only sound preparation for college, but also admission with advanced standing and opportunities for major units in art. Math and writing centers provide additional assistance with student assignments, and a comprehensive senior project is required of all graduates.

PITTSBURGH, PA. Urban. Pop: 334,563. Alt: 715-1240 ft.

ELLIS SCHOOL
Day — Girls Gr PS (Age 3)-12

Pittsburgh, PA 15206. 6425 5th Ave. Tel: 412-661-5992. Fax: 412-661-2287.
www.theellisschool.org   E-mail: admissions@theellisschool.org
A. Randol Benedict, Head (2009). BA, Denison Univ, MSEd, Johns Hopkins Univ. **Sara Imbriglia Leone, Adm.**
  Col Prep. AP (exams req'd; 141 taken, 87% 3+)—Eng Fr Lat Span Calc Bio Chem Physics Eur_Hist US_Hist US_Govt & Pol Art_Hist Studio_Art. **Feat**—British_Lit Poetry Stats Multivariable_Calc Anat & Physiol Environ_Sci Programming Anthro Pol_Sci Gender_Stud. **Supp**—Rev Tut.
  Sports—G: Basket Crew X-country F_Hockey Lacrosse Soccer Softball Swim Tennis Track. **Activities:** 38.
  Selective adm: 59/yr. Appl fee: $50. Appl due: Rolling. Applied: 167. Accepted: 73%. Yield: 48%. **Tests** ISEE SSAT.
  Enr 448. Elem 271. Sec 177. Wh 67%. Latino 1%. Blk 13%. Asian 13%. Other 6%. Avg class size: 12. Stud/fac: 6:1. Uniform. **Fac 78.** M 14/F 64. FT 62/PT 16. Wh 96%. Blk 2%. Asian 1%. Other 1%. Adv deg: 66%.
  Grad '11—34. Col—34. (Northwestern 2, Davidson 2, IN U of PA 2, Duke 1, Harvard 1, MIT 1). **Avg SAT:** CR 637. M 632. W 635. **Mid 50% SAT:** CR 560-700. M 500-700. W 570-680. Avg ACT: 27.8. Mid 50% ACT: 25-32. **Col couns:** 1. Alum donors: 21%.
  Tui '12-'13: Day $14,950-25,680 (+$25-500). **Aid:** Need 127 ($1,483,065).
  Summer: Rec. Tui Day $240/wk. 2 wks.
  Endow $21,539,000. Plant val $10,879,000. Acres 8. Bldgs 9 (33% ADA). Class rms 44. 2 Libs 48,000 vols. Sci labs 7. Photog labs 1. AV rms 1. Auds 1. Art studios 4. Music studios 4. Gyms 4. Fields 1. Comp labs 5. Comp/stud: 1:2 (1:1 Laptop prgm Gr 8-12).
  Est 1916. Nonprofit. Sem (Sept-June). **Assoc** CLS.

Founded by Sara Frazer Ellis, Ellis has grown from its initial enrollment of 40 and faculty of six to meet the increasing demands of the community. The school has occupied its present, eight-acre campus since 1959, and it has expanded facilities on several occasions over the years.

The rigorous traditional curriculum is sufficiently flexible to meet the needs of individual students. In addition to a two-week minicourse program each spring, a full range of electives featuring art, drama and music is available. An athletic program encourages broad participation. The resources of the city are utilized in field trips, senior projects, independent study and volunteer work. Ellis provides students in grades 8-12 with laptop computers and access to the campus' wireless network.

FALK SCHOOL
Day — Coed Gr K-8

Pittsburgh, PA 15261. 4060 Allequippa St. Tel: 412-624-8020. Fax: 412-624-1303. www.falk-school.org   E-mail: wmcconn@pitt.edu
Wendell McConnaha, Dir (2004). BA, Wayne State College, MA, MS, EdS, Univ of Nebraska-Omaha, PhD, Purdue Univ. **Jill Sarada, Adm.**
    Gen Acad. Elem math—Bridges in Math. **Feat**—Lib_Skills Span Studio_Art Music.
      Supp—Dev_Read Rem_Math Rem_Read Tut.
    Sports—Basket X-country Soccer Tennis.
    Selective adm: 36/yr. Usual entry: K & 6. Appl fee: $40. Appl due: Rolling. Accepted: 30%.
    Enr 323. Wh 64%. Latino 5%. Blk 5%. Asian 14%. Other 12%. Avg class size: 20. Stud/fac: 10:1. **Fac 34.** M 5/F 29. FT 34. Wh 85%. Latino 6%. Blk 6%. Asian 3%. Adv deg: 100%.
    Grad '03—36.
    Tui '11-'12: Day $11,881 (+$750). **Aid:** Need 67 ($243,000).
    Plant val $20,300,000. Bldgs 2 (100% ADA). Class rms 18. Lib 12,000 vols. Labs 1. Art studios 1. Music studios 1. Gyms 1. Fields 1.
    Est 1931. Nonprofit. Quar (Sept-June).

Now a laboratory school on the campus of the University of Pittsburgh, Falk grew out of the Community School, established in 1922, and was presented to the university by Leon Falk, Jr. in 1931. Originally designated as a progressive, experimental school for demonstration purposes, Falk's current mission includes educational research, the development of innovative teaching practices and in-service education of experienced teachers.

The nongraded curriculum provides advanced work for those who exhibit the ability. Inquiry-based language arts instruction includes a three-year focus on research, analysis of media and media texts and self-designed reading studies. An environmental education strand runs throughout the middle school and culminates in an annual four-day trip to an environmental awareness center.

ST. EDMUND'S ACADEMY
Day — Coed Gr PS (Age 3)-8

Pittsburgh, PA 15217. 5705 Darlington Rd. Tel: 412-521-1907. Fax: 412-521-2988. www.stedmunds.net   E-mail: info@stedmunds.net
William L. Kindler, Head (2007). BS, George Williams College, MA, New York Univ, PhD, Northern Illinois Univ. **Lucy King, Adm.**
    Pre-Prep. Feat—Fr Lat Span Computers Comp_Relig Studio_Art Music Study_Skills.
      Supp—Dev_Read Rem_Math Rem_Read Rev Tut.
    Sports—Basket X-country Lacrosse Soccer. G: F_Hockey.
    Selective adm: 64/yr. Usual entry: PS, K, 1, 4 & 5. Appl fee: $50. Appl due: Rolling. Applied: 166. Accepted: 55%. Yield: 70%. **Tests** CTP_4.
    Enr 298. B 174. G 124. Wh 71%. Latino 2%. Blk 20%. Asian 5%. Other 2%. Avg class size: 15. Stud/fac: 7:1. Uniform. **Fac 40.** M 8/F 32. FT 32/PT 8. Wh 97%. Latino 3%. Adv deg: 45%.
    Grad '10—26. Prep—19. (Ellis 5, Shady Side 4, Western Reserve 3, Winchester Thurston 2, Mercersburg 1, St Paul's Sch-NH 1). Alum donors: 30%.

Tui '11-'12: Day $10,600-16,900. **Aid:** Merit 5 ($25,000). Need 101 ($737,072).
Summer: Gr PS-6. Enrich Rec. Tui Day $250/wk. 6 wks.
Endow $3,000,000. Plant val $5,075,000. Bldgs 5. Class rms 29. Lib 10,000 vols. Sci labs 2. Auds 1. Art studios 2. Music studios 2. Gyms 1. Fields 2. Comp labs 4. Comp/stud: 1:3.
Est 1947. Nonprofit. Sem (Sept-June). **Assoc** MSA.

Founded as Ascension Academy, a boys' school, St. Edmund's became coeducational in 1983. The school's present name was adopted in 1952 and, after moving several times in its early years, St. Edmund's assumed its current location in the city's Squirrel Hill section in 1955.

The school's traditional high school preparatory curriculum stresses academic and social development. The course of studies in grades 1-4 focuses on language arts for half of each school day. French and Spanish begin in grade 5, while compulsory Latin courses start in grade 7. Computer instruction commences in prekindergarten, and St. Edmund's maintains mobile laptop computer labs in grades 5-8. Each grade designs and carries out an annual community service project. The school conducts a nonsectarian chapel service each week.

SHADY SIDE ACADEMY

5-Day Bdg — Coed Gr 9-12; Day — Coed PS (Age 4)-12

Pittsburgh, PA 15238. 423 Fox Chapel Rd. Tel: 412-968-3000. Fax: 412-968-3213.
Other locations: 400 Braddock Ave, Pittsburgh 15221; 500 Squaw Run Rd E, Pittsburgh 15238.
www.shadysideacademy.org   E-mail: kmihm@shadysideacademy.org
Thomas M. Cangiano, Pres (2010). BA, Middlebury College, MAT, Tufts Univ, MA, MPhil, Columbia Univ. **Katherine H. Mihm, Adm.**
Col Prep. AP (exams req'd; 124 taken, 66% 3+)—Fr Ger Lat Span Calc Comp_Sci.
Feat—Poetry Shakespeare Austen & Dickens Native_Amer_Lit Chin Stats Multivariable_Calc Environ_Sci Organic_Chem Robotics Web_Design Pittsburgh_Hist Econ Ethics Philos World_Relig Architect Ceramics Photog Glass_Art Printmaking Theater Band Chorus Orchestra Jazz_Ensemble Dance. **Supp**—Dev_Read Rev Tut. **Dual enr:** U of Pittsburgh.
Sports—Basket X-country Golf Ice_Hockey Lacrosse Soccer Squash Swim Tennis Track. B: Baseball Football Wrestling. G: Cheer F_Hockey Softball. **Activities:** 40.
Selective adm (Bdg Gr 9-11; Day PS-11): 152/yr. Bdg 20. Day 132. Usual entry: PS, K, 6 & 9. Appl fee: $50. Appl due: Feb. Applied: 310. Accepted: 75%. Yield: 66%. **Tests** ISEE SSAT TOEFL.
Enr 928. B 441. G 487. Bdg 57. Day 871. Elem 441. Sec 487. Wh 78%. Latino 1%. Blk 7%. Asian 8%. Other 6%. Avg class size: 13. Stud/fac: 8:1. Casual. **Fac 119.** M 47/F 72. FT 107/PT 12. Wh 95%. Blk 4%. Asian 1%. Adv deg: 53%. In dorms 7.
Grad '11—116. Col—115. (Carnegie Mellon 9, U of Pittsburgh 7, PA St 5, Cornell 3, U of PA 3, Geo Wash 3). Athl schol 3. **Mid 50% SAT:** CR 560-690. M 600-700. W 590-700. Mid 50% ACT: 24-30. **Col couns:** 2. Alum donors: 20%.
Tui '12-'13: 5-Day Bdg $37,900 (+$300-800). **Day** $14,850-27,000 (+$300-800). **Aid:** Merit 9 ($95,000). Need 154 ($2,600,000).
Summer (enr 181): Acad Enrich Rev Rem Rec. Tui Day $375-1740. 1-8 wks.
Endow $50,000,000. Plant val $56,200,000. Acres 192. Bldgs 26. Dorms 2. Dorm rms 45. Class rms 80. 3 Libs 50,000 vols. Sci labs 4. Lang labs 1. Auds 3. Art studios 3. Music studios 4. Arts ctrs 1. Gyms 4. Fields 9. Tennis courts 10. Squash courts 3. Pools 1. Rinks 1. Tracks 1. Playgrounds 3. Comp labs 4.
Est 1883. Nonprofit. Tri (Sept-June). **Assoc** CLS MSA.

Founded in Pittsburgh's East End by W. R. Crabbe as a college preparatory school for boys, Shady Side Academy now occupies three campuses and enrolls both boys and girls in grades PS-12. The senior school moved from the Shadyside area of Pittsburgh to suburban Fox Chapel in 1922. At that time, a gift of land from the estate of trustee Wallace H. Rowe enabled Shady Side to establish a combination country day and boarding school on a 125-acre campus;

five-day boarding still remains an option during the senior school years. The middle school (on Squaw Run Road East) was established in 1958 with the acquisition of a 60-acre campus, in the same Fox Chapel area as the senior school. The junior school's seven-acre campus, on Braddock Avenue in the East End, once served as the site of the Arnold School, which merged with the academy in 1940. A prekindergarten program formed in 2007 occupies its own building on the junior school campus.

Enrolling students from western Pennsylvania, the school conducts a rigorous college preparatory curriculum that is rooted in the liberal arts tradition. The structured, integrated junior school curriculum (grades pre-K-5) addresses broad themes designed to help boys and girls make connections between subjects as they acquire basic skills and learn new concepts. At the middle school level (grades 6-8), the curriculum becomes more diverse and faculty prepare students for high school academics.

Critical and creative thinking are points of emphasis in the senior school program (grades 9-12), through which pupils gain a deeper understanding of the humanities, math and science, and the arts. Global education options include exchange programs in France, Spain, China and Germany; service learning in Peru; and fellowship grants for summer study and service around the world.   **See Also Page 55**

WINCHESTER THURSTON SCHOOL
Day — Coed Gr PS (Age 4)-12

Pittsburgh, PA 15213. 555 Morewood Ave. Tel: 412-578-7500. Fax: 412-578-7504. Other locations: 4225 Middle Rd, Allison Park 15101.
www.winchesterthurston.org   E-mail: admission@winchesterthurston.org
Gary J. Niels, Head (2002). BA, Univ of Maryland, MTh, Regent College (Canada), MEd, Columbia Univ. **Karyn Vella, Adm.**

    Col Prep. AP (exams req'd; 281 taken, 74% 3+)—Eng Fr Lat Span Calc Stats Comp_Sci Bio Chem Physics Eur_Hist US_Hist Art_Hist. **Elem math**—Houghton Mifflin. **Elem read**—Open Court. **Feat**—Creative_Writing Chin Anat Animal_Behavior Robotics Web_Design African-Amer_Hist Asian_Hist Native-Amer_Hist Women's_Hist Psych Constitutional_Law Architect Film Fine_Arts Visual_Arts Music Dance Journ Public_ Speak. **Supp**—ESL Tut. **Dual enr:** U of Pittsburgh, Carnegie Mellon.

    Sports—Basket Crew X-country Fencing Lacrosse Tennis. B: Golf Soccer. G: F_ Hockey.

    Somewhat selective adm (Gr PS-11): 111/yr. Usual entry: PS, K, 6 & 9. Appl fee: $50. Appl due: Jan. Applied: 240. Accepted: 85%. Yield: 56%. **Tests** ISEE SSAT.

    Enr 643. Wh 77%. Latino 2%. Blk 12%. Asian 9%. Avg class size: 15. Stud/fac: 7:1. **Fac 95.** Wh 91%. Latino 3%. Blk 6%. Adv deg: 51%.

    Grad '10—41. Col—41. (Carnegie Mellon, U of PA, Lehigh, U of Pittsburgh, Boston U, Boston Col). **Avg SAT:** CR 633. M 611. W 640. **Mid 50% SAT:** CR 530-670. M 550-660. W 540-700. **Col couns:** 2. Alum donors: 50%.

    Tui '11-'12: Day $14,200-25,450. **Aid:** Merit 5 ($23,000). Need 182 ($2,124,525).

    Summer (enr 200): Gr PS-8. Rec. 1-6 wks.

    Endow $7,500,000. Plant val $16,900,000. Acres 12. Bldgs 5 (100% ADA). Class rms 51. 4 Libs 25,000 vols. Sci labs 7. Auds 2. Art studios 4. Music studios 4. Dance studios 1. Drama studios 1. Gyms 2. Fields 2. Comp labs 5. Comp/stud: 1:5.

    Est 1887. Nonprofit. Tri (Aug-June). **Assoc** CLS.

WT derives from schools begun by Alice Thurston and Elizabeth and Mary Mitchell. The college preparatory curriculum emphasizes experiential learning and includes process writing, a hands-on science program, a literature-based reading and English program, applied and conceptual mathematics, and global awareness. Advanced Placement courses are offered, as is a bridge and tutoring program that provides one-on-one tutoring for students with learning differences. An array of visual and performing arts classes complement the academic program.

Located in the Oakland section of Pittsburgh, the school's main campus, serving students in grades pre-K-12, utilizes the many cultural, technological and educational resources of the area. In 1988, the school established the North Hills campus for children in grades pre-K-5 in

Allison Park. Both campuses utilize the same curriculum and faculty, and students have access to the opportunities and resources of each location. An extended-day program is available each day before and after school.

POTTSTOWN, PA. (32 mi. WNW of Philadelphia, PA; 36 mi. N of Wilmington, DE) Urban. Pop: 21,859. Alt: 250 ft.

THE HILL SCHOOL
Bdg and Day — Coed Gr 9-PG

Pottstown, PA 19464. 717 E High St. Tel: 610-326-1000. Fax: 610-705-1753.
www.thehill.org   E-mail: admission@thehill.org
Zachary Lehman, Head (2012). AB, Dartmouth College, JD, Harvard Univ. **Thomas Eccleston IV, Adm.**

Col Prep. AP (exams req'd; 368 taken, 80% 3+)—Eng Chin Fr Ger Lat Span Calc Stats Comp_Sci Bio Chem Environ_Sci Physics Eur_Hist US_Hist Econ Psych Art_Hist Studio_Art. **Feat**—Humanities Mythology Greek Astron Physiol Amer_Stud Archaeol World_Relig Photog Video_Production Acting Music Journ Drafting. **Supp**—Rev Tut. Sat classes.

Sports (req'd)—Basket X-country Golf Ice_Hockey Indoor_Track Lacrosse Soccer Squash Swim Track W_Polo. B: Baseball Football Wrestling. G: F_Hockey Softball Tennis.

Selective adm (Bdg Gr 9-PG; Day 9-11): 173/yr. Bdg 123. Day 50. Appl fee: $50. Appl due: Jan. Accepted: 39%. Yield: 56%. **Tests** ISEE SSAT.

Enr 494. B 277. G 217. Bdg 368. Day 126. Sec 471. PG 23. Wh 77%. Latino 3%. Blk 7%. Native Am 1%. Asian 10%. Other 2%. Intl 12%. Avg class size: 15. Stud/fac: 7:1. Formal. **Fac 72.** M 45/F 27. FT 54/PT 18. Wh 91%. Latino 3%. Blk 5%. Asian 1%. Adv deg: 83%. In dorms 33.

Grad '10—139. Col—135. (Boston U 7, Boston Col 4, U of PA 4, NYU 4, Cornell 3, US Naval Acad 3). **Mid 50% SAT:** CR 560-680. M 570-690. W 570-670. Avg ACT: 26.2. **Col couns:** 4. Alum donors: 29%.

Tui '11-'12: Bdg $47,500 (+$2000). **Day $32,800** (+$2000). **Aid:** Need 40 ($3,500,000).

Endow $124,535,000. Plant val $135,000,000. Acres 200. Bldgs 60. Dorms 12. Dorm rms 190. Class rms 66. Libs 1. Sci labs 9. Lang labs 1. Auds 1. Theaters 2. Art studios 1. Music studios 8. Gyms 3. Fields 13. Courts 23. Pools 1. Rinks 1. Golf crses 1. Trap/ skeet ranges 1. Greenhouses 1. Comp labs 1. Laptop prgm Gr 9-PG.

Est 1851. Nonprofit. Tri (Sept-May). **Assoc** CLS MSA.

Rev. Matthew Meigs, a Presbyterian minister, founded The Hill as The Family Boarding School. In 1920, ownership of the school was transferred from the Meigs family to Hill alumni. After more than a century of educating only boys, the school became coeducational in the fall of 1998.

The varied curriculum consists of required and elective courses in English, mathematics, history, modern and classical languages, science, the arts, humanities and theology. Honors and Advanced Placement courses are available in every discipline, and qualified seniors may pursue independent study under the guidance of a faculty member. The school integrates technology instruction into the curriculum for all students, who are required to purchase laptop computers. Students satisfy a 10-hour community service requirement between the start of grade 9 and the conclusion of grade 10. Some form of athletic participation is required.

See Also Page 139

THE WYNDCROFT SCHOOL
Day — Coed Gr PS (Age 3)-8

Pottstown, PA 19464. 1395 Wilson St. Tel: 610-326-0544. Fax: 610-326-9931.
www.wyndcroft.org   **E-mail: mschmidt@wyndcroft.org**
Gail L. Wolter, Head (2011). Maureen K. Schmidt, Adm.

   Pre-Prep. Feat—Fr Lat Computers Fine_Arts Music.
   Sports (req'd)—Basket X-country Lacrosse. B: Soccer. G: F_Hockey.
   Somewhat selective adm: 33/yr. Usual entry: PS, K & 5. Appl fee: $50. Appl due: Rolling. Accepted: 85%. **Tests** IQ.
   Enr 238. B 122. G 116. Wh 95%. Latino 1%. Blk 2%. Asian 2%. Avg class size: 12. Stud/fac: 8:1. **Fac 31.** M 4/F 27. FT 31. Wh 100%. Adv deg: 29%.
   Grad '11—29. Prep—28. (Hill Sch-PA 17, Perkiomen 4, Agnes Irwin 3, Baldwin 1, Germantown Friends 1, Villa Maria Acad 1).
   Tui '12-'13: Day $16,015-18,575 (+$150). **Aid:** Need 25 ($135,725).
   Plant val $3,200,000. Bldgs 1. Libs 1. Sci labs 2. Gyms 1. Comp labs 1.
   Est 1918. Nonprofit. Quar (Sept-June).

The school was founded on the Hill School campus by the wives of Hill School faculty who wanted to provide a sound elementary education for their young children. Although Wyndcroft has been independent since 1920, it continues to maintain a close relationship with Hill. The academic program provides a sound foundation in English, math, science, social studies and the arts. French instruction begins in the preschool program and continues through grade 8, while Latin is introduced in grade 5. Each grade works on a specific community service project during the year.

Music, art groups and field trips are among the extracurricular activities. All boys and girls in grades 6-8 take part in either a team sport or a coeducational athletic option each season.

SALTSBURG, PA. (28 mi. E of Pittsburgh, PA) Rural. Pop: 955. Alt: 852 ft.

KISKI SCHOOL
Bdg and Day — Boys Gr 9-PG

Saltsburg, PA 15681. 1888 Brett Ln. Tel: 724-639-3586, 877-547-5448.
Fax: 724-639-8596.
www.kiski.org   **E-mail: admissions@kiski.org**
Christopher A. Brueningsen, Head (2002). BS, Muhlenberg College, MEd, Indiana Univ of Pennsylvania. **William Ellis, Adm.**

   Col Prep. AP—Eng Chin Fr Span Calc Stats Bio Physics Eur_Hist US_Hist. **Feat**—Creative_Writing Anat & Physiol Environ_Sci Comp_Sci Econ Sociol Global_Stud Philos Architect Art_Hist Drawing Sculpt Studio_Art Jewelry Theater Chorus Music_Theory Speech Indus_Arts. **Supp**—ESL Rev.
   Sports (req'd)—B: Baseball Basket X-country Football Golf Ice_Hockey Lacrosse Soccer Swim Tennis Track. **Activities:** 19.
   Selective adm (Bdg Gr 9-PG; Day 9-11): 110/yr. Bdg 95. Day 15. Appl fee: $50. Appl due: Jan. Accepted: 71%. Yield: 80%. **Tests** CEEB SSAT TOEFL.
   Enr 195. Sec 185. PG 10. Intl 34%. Avg class size: 11. Stud/fac: 7:1. Uniform. **Fac 38.** Adv deg: 63%. In dorms 20.
   Grad '11—64. Col—62. (Mercyhurst 3, IN U 3, US Naval Acad 2, UNC-Chapel Hill 2, NYU 2, Col of Wooster 2). **Avg SAT:** CR 516. M 586. W 531. Avg ACT: 21. **Col couns:** 2.
   Tui '12-'13: Bdg $43,500 (+$750). **Day $25,500** (+$500). **Intl Bdg $47,250** (+$750). **Aid:** Need 78 ($1,600,000).
   Summer: Gr 5-8. Enrich Rec. 4 wks.
   Endow $10,000,000. Plant val $50,000,000. Acres 350. Bldgs 44. Dorms 9. Dorm rms 138. Class rms 28. Lib 23,000 vols. Labs 3. Music studios 1. Gyms 3. Fields 9. Courts

7. Pools 2. Stadiums 2. Golf crses 1. Skiing facilities. Radio stations 1. Laptop prgm Gr 9-PG.
Est 1888. Nonprofit. Tri (Sept-May). **Assoc** CLS MSA.

Founded by Dr. Andrew W. Wilson, director until 1933, Kiski prepares its students for college with a rigorous academic program. The curriculum consists of five main subject areas—English, history, math, science and foreign languages—and is supplemented by requirements in art and music and a senior research paper. Supervised study periods for underclassmen are held in dorm rooms each evening. Students have the opportunity to receive individual instruction during evening hours with resident faculty members. Honors and Advanced Placement courses are offered in the main subject areas. Technology is an important aspect of the curriculum: Each boy receives a tablet computer.

Kiski's diversified athletic program includes various individual and team-based interscholastic sports. Each student must participate in three sports during the year. An extensive extracurricular activities program features participation in a national forensic competition, a political and literary forum, and off-campus cultural events.

SEWICKLEY, PA. (13 mi. WNW of Pittsburgh, PA) Suburban. Pop: 3902. Alt: 732 ft.

SEWICKLEY ACADEMY
Day — Coed Gr PS (Age 4)-12

Sewickley, PA 15143. 315 Academy Ave. Tel: 412-741-2230. Fax: 412-741-1411.
www.sewickley.org   E-mail: admission@sewickley.org
Kolia J. O'Connor, Head. BA, Boston Univ, MA, Columbia Univ, MA, Univ of Avignon (France). **Brendan J. Schneider, Adm.**
Col Prep. AP (exams req'd; 254 taken, 89% 3+)—Fr Ger Span Calc Stats Comp_Sci Bio Chem Physics Eur_Hist US_Hist Studio_Art. **Feat**—Creative_Writing Poetry Humor & Satire Sci_Fiction Chin Ital Anat & Physiol Astron Environ_Sci Web_Design Civil_War Middle_Eastern_Hist Modern_Asia Psych African_Stud Art_Hist Ceramics Photog Drama Music Music_Theory. **Supp**—Dev_Read Tut.
Sports—Basket X-country Golf Lacrosse Soccer Swim Tennis Track. B: Baseball Ice_ Hockey. G: F_Hockey Softball. **Activities:** 55.
Selective adm (Gr PS-11): 94/yr. Appl fee: $50. Appl due: Feb. Applied: 214. Accepted: 71%. Yield: 75%. **Tests** CTP_4 ISEE SSAT.
Enr 708. B 375. G 333. Wh 81%. Latino 1%. Blk 6%. Asian 6%. Other 6%. Avg class size: 15. Stud/fac: 7:1. Casual. **Fac 116.** M 47/F 69. FT 111/PT 5. Wh 93%. Blk 3%. Asian 2%. Other 2%. Adv deg: 63%.
Grad '11—72. Col—72. (Allegheny 6, Boston U 4, Col of Wooster 4, Bucknell 3, Geo Wash 3, Princeton 2). **Avg SAT:** CR 638. M 658. W 649. **Mid 50% SAT:** CR 580-700. M 600-720. W 590-700. **Col couns:** 2.
Tui '12-'13: Day $18,615-23,125 (+$500-700). **Aid:** Need 99 ($991,491).
Summer: Acad Enrich Rec. Sports. Tui Day $100-350. 1-4 wks.
Endow $18,800,000. Plant val $30,000,000. Acres 30. Bldgs 11. Class rms 84. 2 Libs 29,400 vols. Sci labs 7. Lang labs 1. Auds 1. Theaters 1. Art studios 4. Music studios 3. Dance studios 1. Gyms 2. Fields 4. Courts 6. Comp labs 4. Comp/stud: 1:1.6.
Est 1838. Nonprofit. Sem (Sept-June). **Assoc** CLS.

The academy began as a classical elementary school for boys, then became coeducational 30 years later. It has occupied the present plant since 1929. Enrollment steadily increased in the years that followed, and a secondary school was added in 1963. The campus has since undergone further building and renovation, resulting in extensive physical improvements to each school division.

The comprehensive curriculum offers a full college preparatory program and an extensive use of technology across the disciplines. Exchange programs are conducted with schools in Australia, Spain, France, Switzerland, Germany and China. All students participate in community service projects, with upper school students contributing individual hours. Seniors who have met all academic and service requirements may arrange a 50-hour internship.

TYRONE, PA. (93 mi. E of Pittsburgh, PA) Suburban. Pop: 5528. Alt: 868 ft.

GRIER SCHOOL
Bdg and Day — Girls Gr 7-PG
Tyrone, PA 16686. PO Box 308. Tel: 814-684-3000. Fax: 814-684-2177.
www.grier.org   E-mail: admissions@grier.org
Andrew M. Wilson, Head (2007). BA, Middlebury College. **Gina Borst, Head.** BS, MEd, Pennsylvania State Univ.
   Col Prep. AP (exams req'd; 149 taken, 64% 3+)—Eng Fr Span Calc Stats Bio Chem Environ_Sci Physics US_Hist World_Hist Econ Art_Hist Studio_Art. **Feat**—Chin Women's_Stud Philos Ceramics Drawing Fine_Arts Graphic_Arts Painting Photog Video_Production Costume_Design Jewelry Printmaking Music Dance Choreography. **Supp**—Dev_Read ESL LD Makeup Rem_Math Rem_Read Rev Tut.
   Sports—G: Basket Cheer Equestrian Fencing Soccer Tennis Volley. **Activities:** 19.
   Selective adm (Bdg Gr 7-PG; Day 7-11): 130/yr. Appl fee: $50. Appl due: Rolling. Applied: 300. Accepted: 60%. Yield: 73%. **Tests** IQ SSAT TOEFL.
   Enr 262. Bdg 237. Day 25. Elem 39. Sec 223. Wh 40%. Latino 16%. Blk 9%. Asian 35%. Intl 50%. Avg class size: 9. Stud/fac: 6:1. Casual. **Fac 59.** M 14/F 45. FT 49/PT 10. Wh 95%. Asian 5%. Adv deg: 54%.
   Grad '11—54. Col—53. (U of WA 4, Savannah Col of Art & Design 3, Boston Col 2, U of CA-San Diego 2, Lehigh 2, PA St 2). **Avg SAT:** CR/M 1290. Avg ACT: 25. **Col couns:** 4. Alum donors: 25%.
   Tui '12-'13: Bdg $46,800 (+$3000). **Day $22,500** (+$1000). **Intl Bdg $46,800** (+$3000-7000). **Aid:** Merit 24 ($540,000). Need 67 ($1,400,000).
   Summer: Acad Enrich Rec. Tui Bdg $450-4900. ½-3 wks.
   Endow $11,000,000. Plant val $9,500,000. Acres 325. Bldgs 16 (27% ADA). Dorms 10. Dorm rms 124. Class rms 34. Lib 16,000 vols. Comp ctrs 3. Art studios 4. Music studios 2. Dance studios 2. Arts ctrs 1. Gyms 1. Fields 1. Tennis courts 5. Pools 1. Riding rings 3. Stables 3. Comp/stud: 1:1 Laptop prgm Gr 7-PG.
   Est 1853. Nonprofit. Sem (Sept-June). **Assoc** MSA.

Incorporated in 1853 by a group of local citizens, and in 1857 purchased by Dr. Lemuel G. Grier, the school has since been under the guidance of four generations of the Grier family. Alvin R. Grier succeeded his father in 1887. In 1932, the school came into the capable hands of his son, Thomas C. Grier, who served for 33 years. Mrs. Grier, cohead with her husband for 26 years, carried on his administration until 1969, when their son Douglas became headmaster (and later director).

The school conducts a two-track academic curriculum. The upper track offers honors courses. The second track, which is also college preparatory, is designed for students who require extra structure and intensive learning skills development. Crossover is permitted between the tracks, according to ability. Grier also provides a comprehensive English as a Second Language program for international students.

The creative arts program, which includes modern dance, jazz and ballet, complements the academic curriculum. While retaining a mellow charm, all older buildings have been modernized over the years. **See Also Pages 44-5**

WAYNE, PA. (14 mi. W of Philadelphia, PA) Suburban. Pop: 39,944. Alt: 404 ft.

VALLEY FORGE MILITARY ACADEMY
Bdg — Boys Gr 7-PG; Day — Boys 7-12
Wayne, PA 19087. 1001 Eagle Rd. Tel: 610-989-1490, 866-923-8362.
Fax: 610-340-2194.
http://academy.vfmac.edu   E-mail: admissions@vfmac.edu
Col. John Ford, Head (2008). BS, US Military Academy, MEd, Widener Univ. **La Toro Yates, Adm.**
Col Prep. Milit. AP (exams req'd; 47 taken, 38% 3+)—Eng Calc Stats Eur_Hist US_ Hist. **Feat**—Lib_Skills Chin Fr Lat Russ Span. **Supp**—Dev_Read ESL Rem_Math Rem_Read Tut. **Dual enr:** Valley Forge Milit.
Sports (req'd)—B: Baseball Basket X-country Football Golf Lacrosse Softball Swim Tennis Track Wrestling. **Activities:** 30.
Selective adm: 166/yr. Bdg 164. Day 2. Appl fee: $100. Appl due: Rolling. Applied: 508. Accepted: 53%. Yield: 54%. **Tests** CEEB IQ SSAT TOEFL.
Enr 280. Bdg 277. Day 3. Elem 32. Sec 233. PG 15. Wh 58%. Latino 7%. Blk 15%. Asian 20%. Intl 19%. Avg class size: 13. Stud/fac: 9:1. Uniform. **Fac 26.** M 18/F 8. FT 25/PT 1. Wh 88%. Blk 4%. Asian 8%. Adv deg: 88%.
Grad '11—62. Col—60. (Valley Forge Milit, US Milit Acad, VA Polytech, NY Inst of Tech, PA St). Athl schol 5. **Avg SAT:** CR 432. M 498. W 433. **Col couns:** 1.
Tui '12-'13: Bdg $38,495-39,925 (+$2155). **Day $24,500** (+$2155). **Intl Bdg $38,495-39,925** (+$4095). **Aid:** Merit ($385,000). Need 87 ($2,081,833).
Endow $12,000,000. Plant val $50,000,000. Acres 119. Bldgs 84. Dorms 6. Dorm rms 404. Class rms 65. Lib 100,000 vols. Labs 8. Music studios 1. Gyms 2. Fields 9. Courts 5. Pools 2. Riding rings 1. Stables 1. Rifle ranges 1. Comp/stud: 1:1 Laptop prgm Gr 9-12.
Est 1928. Nonprofit. Nondenom Christian. Sem (Aug-June). **Assoc** MSA.

Founded by Lt. Gen. Milton G. Baker, this well-known academy has an enrollment recruited from many states and foreign countries. The academy grew from a modest beginning to a campus that spans more than 119 acres. After enrolling only boarding boys for decades, VFMA added a day division in the fall of 2007. A five-day boarding program allows students to return home on weekends, although the tuition rate is the same.

A strong emphasis on leadership and character development is evident at all grade levels. Many activities and special programs complement academic work. Options include the Boy Scouts, raider challenge teams, ski club and other outdoor activity clubs, marksmanship, community service, flight training, instrumental and vocal music, and equitation.

WEST CHESTER, PA. (25 mi. W of Philadelphia, PA) Suburban. Pop: 18,461. Alt: 420 ft.

WESTTOWN SCHOOL
Bdg — Coed Gr 9-12; Day — Coed PS (Age 4)-10
West Chester, PA 19382. 975 Westtown Rd. Tel: 610-399-0123. Fax: 610-399-3760.
www.westtown.edu   E-mail: admissions@westtown.edu
John W. Baird, Head (2002). AB, Princeton Univ, MA, Providence College. **Nathan Bohn, Adm.**
Col Prep. Elem math—Singapore Math. **Feat**—Southern_Lit Chin Fr Ger Lat Span Calc Stats Ecol Environ_Sci Astrophysics Vietnam_War Lat-Amer_Hist Holocaust Relig World_Relig Quakerism Art_Hist Photog Sculpt Acting Theater Directing Band Music_Hist Music_Theory Orchestra Woodworking. **Supp**—ESL Tut. Outdoor ed.

Sports (req'd)—Basket X-country Golf Indoor_Track Lacrosse Soccer Swim Tennis Track. B: Baseball Wrestling. G: F_Hockey Softball Volley. **Activities:** 43.
Selective adm: 163/yr. Bdg 72. Day 91. Usual entry: PS, K, 6 & 9. Appl fee: $50-100. Appl due: Jan. Applied: 432. Accepted: 60%. Yield: 56%. **Tests** ISEE SSAT TOEFL.
Enr 700. Bdg 290. Day 410. Elem 312. Sec 388. Wh 82%. Latino 4%. Blk 6%. Asian 3%. Other 5%. Intl 10%. Avg class size: 17. **Fac 104.** Wh 91%. Latino 2%. Blk 6%. Asian 1%. Adv deg: 57%. In dorms 27.
Grad '10—113. Col—113. (Franklin & Marshall 7, Boston U 4, Temple 4, Geo Wash 3, Drexel 3, Northeastern U 3). **Avg SAT:** CR 610. M 640. W 620. **Mid 50% SAT:** CR 560-690. M 580-680. W 580-670. Alum donors: 34%.
Tui '12-'13: Bdg $46,400. Day $19,960-29,100 (+$1125). **Intl Bdg $46,400** (+$500). **Aid:** Need 237 ($5,314,192).
Summer: Acad Rec. Tui Day $150-550/wk. 6 wks.
Endow $72,000,000. Plant val $60,000,000. Acres 640. Bldgs 12. Dorms 4. Dorm rms 159. Class rms 61. 2 Libs 45,000 vols. Sci labs 6. Dark rms 1. Observatories 1. Theaters 1. Art studios 4. Music studios 9. Dance studios 1. Art galleries 1. Gyms 4. Fields 10. Tennis courts 14. Field houses 1. Pools 1. Weight rms 1. Greenhouses 1. Lakes 1. Comp labs 5.
Est 1799. Nonprofit. Religious Society of Friends (16% practice). Tri (Sept-June). **Assoc** MSA.

Philadelphia Quakers established Westtown as a coeducational boarding school emphasizing high academic standards and such Quaker values as peace, integrity, equality, personal responsibility and service. A diverse student body comprises pupils from many states and foreign countries.

Westtown's college preparatory curriculum combines strong academics with the flexibility to address individual talents and interests. Course work during grades 9 and 10 revolves around a core curriculum that provides a firm liberal arts foundation for future study. The program in grades 11 and 12 allows students to choose electives and pursue areas of interest in greater depth, and more than a dozen advanced courses are available. All seniors complete an independent project during the first two weeks of March. Boarding is an important aspect of school life: Roughly half of all freshmen and sophomores and all juniors and seniors live on campus.

The school's 640-acre campus, which includes woods, meadows, a lake, an arboretum and a working farm, provides many opportunities for the study of nature and the environment. Drama classes frequently attend theatrical productions, while art classes visit museums and galleries on a regular basis. In addition, Westtown schedules field trips to Philadelphia; Wilmington, DE; Washington, DC; and New York City as a means of enriching various subjects.

All upper school students must participate in interscholastic sports each term. Noncompetitive activities include dance, aerobics, weight training, swimming, jogging, indoor soccer and yoga.

WILKES-BARRE, PA. (94 mi. NNW of Philadelphia, PA) Urban. Pop: 43,123. Alt: 642 ft. Area also includes Kingston.

WYOMING SEMINARY

Bdg — Coed Gr 9-PG; Day — Coed PS (Age 3)-12

Kingston, PA 18704. 201 N Sprague Ave. Tel: 570-270-2160. Fax: 570-270-2191.
Other locations: 1560 Wyoming Ave, Forty Fort 18704.
    www.wyomingseminary.org   E-mail: admission@wyomingseminary.org
Kip P. Nygren, Pres (2007). BS, US Military Academy, MS, Stanford Univ, PhD, Georgia Institute of Technology. **David Damico, Adm.**
    Col Prep. AP (exams req'd; 297 taken, 79% 3+)—Eng Fr Lat Span Calc Stats Comp_ Sci Bio Chem Environ_Sci Physics Eur_Hist US_Hist Econ Psych US_Govt & Pol

Art_Hist Studio_Art Music_Theory. **Elem math**—Everyday Math. **Feat**—Poetry Shakespeare Women's_Lit Russ Multivariable_Calc Ecol Forensic_Sci Marine_Bio/ Sci Neurosci Comp_Design African-Amer_Hist Sociol Ceramics Fine_Arts Photog Drama Chorus Music_Hist Dance Speech. **Supp**—ESL Rev Tut.

Sports—Basket X-country Ice_Hockey Lacrosse Soccer Swim Tennis. B: Baseball Football Golf Wrestling. G: F_Hockey Softball. **Activities:** 30.

Selective adm: 178/yr. Bdg 75. Day 103. Usual entry: K, 5 & 9. Appl fee: $75. Appl due: Rolling. Applied: 485. Accepted: 56%. Yield: 65%. **Tests** CEEB ISEE SSAT TOEFL.

Enr 780. Bdg 185. Day 595. Wh 86%. Latino 2%. Blk 4%. Native Am 1%. Asian 5%. Other 2%. Intl 17%. Avg class size: 13. Stud/fac: 8:1. **Fac 116.** M 46/F 70. FT 116. Wh 96%. Latino 1%. Blk 1%. Asian 2%. Adv deg: 56%. In dorms 22.

Grad '10—141. Col—141. (Boston U 6, Wilkes 6, Drexel 5, NYU 4, Boston Col 3, Bucknell 3). Athl schol 5. **Mid 50% SAT:** CR 500-640. M 540-640. W 490-630. Avg ACT: 25. **Col couns:** 5. Alum donors: 22%.

Tui '11-'12: Bdg $41,950 (+$450). **Day $12,175-21,200** (+$1550). **Aid:** Merit 40 ($90,000). Need 390 ($4,630,600).

Summer: Acad Enrich. Tui Bdg $2500. Tui Day $625/crse. 4 wks. ESL. Tui Bdg $2200-4000. 1-4 wks. Performing Arts. Tui Bdg $2625-4975. Tui Day $975-1950. 3-6 wks.

Endow $43,300,000. Plant val $15,500,000. Bldgs 11. Dorms 4. Dorm rms 125. Class rms 56. 2 Libs 32,500 vols. Sci labs 5. Music labs 2. Auds 2. Art studios 4. Music studios 4. Dance studios 1. Gyms 3. Fields 5. Courts 6. Pools 1. Comp labs 2.

Est 1844. Nonprofit. Methodist (5% practice). Tri (Aug-May). **Assoc** CLS MSA.

Wyoming Seminary's Upper School offers a varied program that readies graduates for competitive colleges. There is a large choice of electives (including Advanced Placement courses) in history, the fine arts, mathematics, computer, science and English. College planning workshops, enrichment opportunities, ESL programs and an elite performing arts institute are among the summer offerings.

Boys and girls participate in a compulsory extracurricular program that comprises service to the community and campus activities, arts or interscholastic athletics. An active service program progresses from group projects in the middle school to more demanding individual commitments in the upper school, where students satisfy a 40-hour service requirement prior to graduation.

The Wyoming Seminary Lower School is separately located three miles away in Forty Fort. Academics include accelerated courses, and computer science, art, music, health and physical education are integral parts of the program. Instruction in French and Spanish begins in kindergarten, while Latin commences in grade 7.

WYNNEWOOD, PA. (7 mi. W of Philadelphia, PA) Suburban. Pop: 7700. Alt: 316 ft.

FRIENDS' CENTRAL SCHOOL
Day — Coed Gr PS (Age 3)-12

Wynnewood, PA 19096. 1101 City Ave. Tel: 610-649-7440. Fax: 610-649-5669.
Other locations: 228 Old Gulph Rd, Wynnewood 19096.
  www.friendscentral.org   E-mail: admission@friendscentral.org
Craig Normile Sellers, Head (2012). AB, Franklin and Marshall College, JD, New York Law School, MA, Columbia Univ. **Cynthia Harris, Int Adm.**

  Col Prep. AP exams taken: 6 (50% 3+). Elem math—Everyday Math/Miquon Math Series/Pearson Scott Foresman. **Elem read**—Explode the Code. **Feat**—Fr Lat Span Calc Stats Botany African_Hist Women's_Hist Intl_Relations Psych Peace_Stud Comp_Relig Philos Architect Ceramics Photog Studio_Art Drama Music Music_Hist Music_Theory Woodworking. **Supp**—Dev_Read Rem_Math Tut. **Dual enr:** U of PA, Villanova, Haverford.

  Sports (req'd)—Basket X-country Golf Indoor_Track Lacrosse Soccer Squash Swim Tennis Track W_Polo. B: Baseball Wrestling. G: Cheer F_Hockey Softball. **Activities:**

46.
Selective adm (Gr PS-11): 96/yr. Usual entry: PS, K, 6 & 9. Appl fee: $50. Appl due: Jan. Applied: 402. Accepted: 55%. Yield: 43%. **Tests** IQ ISEE SSAT.
Enr 890. B 449. G 441. Elem 500. Sec 390. Wh 76%. Latino 2%. Blk 14%. Asian 5%. Other 3%. Avg class size: 16. Stud/fac: 9:1. **Fac 128.** M 50/F 78. FT 115/PT 13. Wh 87%. Latino 5%. Blk 7%. Asian 1%. Adv deg: 60%.
Grad '11—88. Col—87. (U of PA 6, Drexel 4, Geo Wash 3, IN U 3, Ithaca 3, Muhlenberg 3). **Avg SAT:** CR 630. M 624. W 628. **Mid 50% SAT:** CR 600-730. M 530-670. W 590-740. **Col couns:** 2. Alum donors: 31%.
Tui '11-'12: Day $17,300-27,400 (+$400). **Aid:** Need 234 ($3,831,148).
Summer (enr 30): Gr 7-12. Acad Enrich Rev Rem. Tui Day $600-850. 3-6 wks.
Endow $21,000,000. Plant val $100,000,000. Acres 41. Bldgs 16 (60% ADA). Class rms 86. 2 Libs 30,000 vols. Sci labs 11. Lang labs 2. Auds 1. Theaters 1. Art studios 8. Music studios 4. Dance studios 1. Gyms 4. Fields 9. Courts 7. Pools 2. Comp labs 6. Comp/stud: 1:4.
Est 1845. Nonprofit. Religious Society of Friends (4% practice). Tri (Sept-June). **Assoc** CLS.

Friends' Central has conducted a comprehensive day program since 1925, when this Quaker school moved to its present middle and upper school site of 23 acres on the edge of the city. The lower school (nursery through grade 4) operates at an 18-acre second campus on Old Gulph Road.

Over the years, Friends' Central has enjoyed the direction of a number of notable educators. The integrated course of study begins with an individualized curriculum in the lower school that precedes an increasingly rigorous college preparatory program as students progress through the upper school (grades 9-12). Course work includes many opportunities in the arts and a number of departmental electives. During the final five weeks of the school year, seniors undertake a project of their own design (with the assistance of an advisor) in which they learn about a field of interest and also complete at least one week of service.

Upper school student government and faculty conduct a guest speakers program that features authors, musicians, artists, politicians and athletes. Weekly Meeting for Worship is an important aspect of school life. Each upper school student performs at least 40 hours of service annually.

YORK, PA. (66 mi. WNW of Wilmington, DE; 85 mi. W of Philadelphia, PA) Urban. Pop: 40,862. Alt: 370 ft.

YORK COUNTRY DAY SCHOOL
Day — Coed Gr PS (Age 2)-12

York, PA 17403. 1071 Regents Glen Blvd. Tel: 717-843-9805. Fax: 717-815-6769.
www.ycds.org   E-mail: agreer@ycds.org
Nathaniel W. Coffman, Head. BA, Claremont McKenna College, MSA, Univ of Notre Dame.
Alison C. Greer, Adm.
Col Prep. AP (exams req'd)—Eng Chin Fr Span Calc Stats Bio Chem US_Hist World_ Hist Studio_Art Music_Theory. **Elem math**—Everyday Math. **Elem read**—Junior Great Books. **Feat**—Lat Comp_Sci Acting Chorus Music. **Supp**—Dev_Read Rev Tut. **Dual enr:** York Col of PA.
Sports—Basket Soccer Tennis. G: F_Hockey Volley. **Activities:** 9.
Selective adm: 48/yr. Usual entry: PS, K, 6 & 9. Appl fee: $35. Appl due: Rolling. **Tests** IQ ISEE Stanford.
Enr 216. Wh 75%. Latino 4%. Blk 12%. Asian 8%. Other 1%. Avg class size: 12. Stud/fac: 6:1. Formal. **Fac 39.** M 12/F 27. FT 34/PT 5. Adv deg: 58%.
Grad '11—16. Col—16. (Ursinus 2, Millersville 2, PA St 1, Gettysburg 1, Boston U 1, Wash Col 1). **Mid 50% SAT:** CR 520-650. M 500-640.

Tui '12-'13: Day $3180-16,850 (+$350-1150). **Aid:** Need 45 ($523,030).
Summer: Acad Enrich Rec. Tui Day $150/wk. 8 wks.
Endow $900,000. Plant val $2,750,000. Acres 17. Bldgs 1. Class rms 25. 3 Libs 5000
vols. Sci labs 4. Art studios 2. Music studios 1. Gyms 1. Fields 3. Courts 1. Comp labs
1. Comp/stud: 1:3.
Est 1953. Inc. Spons: York College of Pennsylvania. Sem (Sept-June). **Assoc** MSA.

Founded by a group of parents seeking a demanding academic program for the children
of York County, the school prospered and grew under the leadership of its first headmaster,
J. Kenneth Snyder, and his wife, Elizabeth. Beginning in a converted home in York City, Mr.
Snyder built a new school in 1956 on a 17-acre plot in the suburbs southwest of York. In 1975,
the school became affiliated with York College of Pennsylvania; as a result, seniors and select
underclassmen may enroll in up to three semester courses per year at the college.

The liberal arts curriculum balances a combination of requirements and electives. Proficiency in the use of a computer is required, as are two semesters in the arts. Students in grade
9 are required to take a semester-long course in public speaking. Elective courses are available
in each department. Boys and girls perform 20 hours of required community service in grades
9-11, in addition to 30 hours in grade 12.

Scheduled activity periods each week allow students to pursue extracurricular interests.

Southern States

ALABAMA

ANNISTON, AL. (58 mi. E of Birmingham, AL; 80 mi. W of Atlanta, GA) Suburban. Pop: 24,276. Alt: 710 ft.

THE DONOHO SCHOOL
Day — Coed Gr PS (Age 3)-12

Anniston, AL 36207. 2501 Henry Rd. Tel: 256-237-5477. Fax: 256-237-6474.
www.donohoschool.com   E-mail: lphillips@donohoschool.com
Janice D. Hurd, Pres (2004). BS, Univ of Alabama-Tuscaloosa, MS, EdS, Jacksonville State Univ. **Sue Canter, Adm.**

Col Prep. AP (exams req'd; 17 taken, 76% 3+)—Eng Fr Span Calc Bio US_Hist Econ US_Govt & Pol. **Elem math**—Everyday Math/Saxon. **Elem read**—Elements of Literature/Open Court. **Feat**—Lat Govt Psych Fine_Arts Studio_Art Drama Band Music Journ Speech. **Supp**—Tut. **Dual enr:** Jacksonville St.

Sports—Basket X-country Golf Soccer Tennis Track. B: Baseball Football. G: Cheer Volley. **Activities:** 15.

Somewhat selective adm (Gr PS-11): 48/yr. Usual entry: PS. Appl fee: $50. Appl due: Rolling. Applied: 53. Accepted: 92%. Yield: 94%. **Tests** IQ.

Enr 374. B 177. G 197. Elem 273. Sec 101. Wh 87%. Latino 1%. Blk 3%. Asian 7%. Other 2%. Avg class size: 13. Stud/fac: 12:1. Casual. **Fac 34.** M 6/F 28. FT 28/PT 6. Wh 99%. Blk 1%. Adv deg: 88%.

Grad '11—20. Col—20. (Birmingham-Southern 5, Auburn 5, U of AL-Tuscaloosa 2, U of AL-Birmingham 2, Johns Hopkins 1, OH St 1). **Avg SAT:** CR 593. M 576. W 659. Avg ACT: 27.5. **Col couns:** 1. Alum donors: 3%.

Tui '12-'13: Day $6238-8841 (+$400). **Aid:** Need 60 ($139,000).
Summer (enr 100): Acad Enrich Rec. Tui Day $85-155/wk. 6 wks.
Endow $2,439,000. Plant val $8,068,000. Bldgs 5. Class rms 40. 2 Libs 12,770 vols. Sci labs 4. Art studios 1. Arts ctrs 1. Gyms 2. Fields 2. Courts 2. Comp labs 2. Comp/stud: 1:30.

Est 1963. Nonprofit. Sem (Aug-June). **Assoc** SACS.

Established to satisfy the need for a sound college preparatory program in the Anniston area, the school, since its inception, has maintained its original purpose, with all of its graduates accepted by colleges. The comprehensive academic program is complemented by interest clubs, publications and athletics. An intersession program provides students with the opportunity to work in various fields of career interest and to pursue independent study projects.

BIRMINGHAM, AL. (138 mi. W of Atlanta, GA) Urban. Pop: 242,820. Alt: 620 ft. Area also includes Indian Springs.

ALTAMONT SCHOOL
Day — Coed Gr 5-12

Birmingham, AL 35222. 4801 Altamont Rd S. Tel: 205-879-2006. Fax: 205-871-5666.
www.altamontschool.org   E-mail: tgoldsmith@altamontschool.org

Sarah W. Whiteside, Head (2007). BA, Randolph-Macon Woman's College, MA, Univ of North Carolina-Chapel Hill. **Thomas Goldsmith, Adm.**

Col Prep. AP (115 exams taken, 98% 3+)—Eng Fr Calc Bio Chem Environ_Sci Physics US_Hist Comp_Govt & Pol Psych Studio_Art Music_Theory. **Feat**—British_Lit Creative_Writing Shakespeare Southern_Lit Chin Greek Lat Span Stats Anat & Physiol Ecol Programming Web_Design Vietnam_War Econ World_Relig Art_Hist Photog Acting Theater_Arts Music_Hist Debate Journ. **Supp**—Rev Tut.

Sports—Basket X-country Golf Soccer Swim Tennis Track. B: Baseball. G: Softball Volley.

Selective adm: 74/yr. Usual entry: 5, 7 & 9. Appl fee: $50. Appl due: Jan. Accepted: 70%. Yield: 86%. **Tests** ISEE.

Enr 340. Elem 125. Sec 215. Wh 88%. Blk 7%. Asian 5%. Avg class size: 15. Stud/fac: 12:1. **Fac 49.** M 17/F 32. FT 48/PT 1. Wh 92%. Latino 2%. Blk 4%. Asian 2%. Adv deg: 57%.

Grad '11—35. Col—35. (U of AL-Tuscaloosa, Birmingham-Southern, U of the South, Auburn, Bowdoin, Vanderbilt). **Mid 50% SAT:** CR 580-670. M 570-690. W 590-670. Mid 50% ACT: 27-31. Alum donors: 20%.

Tui '11-'12: Day $13,104-17,508 (+$500). **Aid:** Need 78 ($590,307).

Summer: Gr 3-12. Acad Enrich Rev Rem Rec. Fine Arts. Sports. Tui Day $100-1000. 1-6 wks.

Endow $5,000,000. Plant val $14,200,000. Acres 28. Bldgs 2 (100% ADA). Class rms 47. Lib 20,000 vols. Sci labs 4. Lang labs 1. Robotics labs 1. Auds 1. Theaters 1. Art studios 1. Music studios 2. Arts ctrs 1. Art galleries 1. Gyms 3. Fields 4. Basketball courts 2. Tennis courts 6. Volleyball courts 3. Tracks 1. Weight rms 1. Comp labs 2.

Est 1922. Nonprofit. Sem (Sept-June). **Assoc** SACS.

Altamont was formed through the 1975 merger of the Birmingham University School, a well-established day school founded in 1922, and the Brooke Hill School for girls, founded in 1940.

Located at the crest of Red Mountain on the former Brooke Hill campus, the school conducts a traditional liberal arts curriculum that prepares students for colleges throughout the country. The October Project Week provides experiential learning opportunities through travel, service and outdoor activities; one of the options is a college trip that visits 12 to 15 institutions. Advanced pupils may enroll in semester-long senior seminars in English and history that offer college-level instruction. Other noteworthy aspects of school life are abundant opportunities in the arts, academic competitions, speech and debate participation, and a strong student advisory program. Each grade completes an annual community service project.

INDIAN SPRINGS SCHOOL

Bdg — Coed Gr 9-12; Day — Coed 8-12

Indian Springs, AL 35124. 190 Woodward Dr. Tel: 205-988-3350, 888-843-9477. Fax: 205-988-3797.

www.indiansprings.org   E-mail: admission@indiansprings.org

Gareth Vaughan, Dir (2008). BA, Univ of York (England), MA, George Washington Univ, MEd, Columbia Univ. **Jack Sweeney, Adm.**

Col Prep. AP (287 exams taken, 70% 3+)—Eng Fr Lat Span Calc Stats Bio Chem Environ_Sci Physics Eur_Hist US_Hist Econ US_Govt & Pol Studio_Art Music_Theory. **Feat**—Creative_Writing Poetry Irish_Lit Middle_Eastern_Lit Women's_Lit Chin Anat & Physiol Programming Web_Design Civil_War Milit_Hist Vietnam_War Psych Philos World_Relig Ceramics Film Photog Video_Production Acting Theater_Arts Music_Hist Jazz_Hist Debate Woodworking Culinary_Arts. **Supp**—Tut.

Sports—Basket X-country Golf Soccer Tennis. B: Baseball Ultimate_Frisbee. G: Softball Volley. **Activities:** 25.

Selective adm: 84/yr. Bdg 27. Day 57. Appl fee: $65-70. Appl due: Rolling. Accepted: 55%. Yield: 79%. **Tests** CEEB SSAT TOEFL.

Enr 269. B 138. G 131. Bdg 68. Day 201. Intl 9%. Avg class size: 12. Stud/fac: 8:1. **Fac 40.** M 22/F 18. FT 34/PT 6. Adv deg: 62%. In dorms 2.

Grad '11—72. Col—72. (Birmingham-Southern, U of AL-Tuscaloosa, Emory, Bard-NY, GA Inst of Tech, Northwestern). **Avg SAT:** CR 658. M 643. W 669. Alum donors: 26%.
Tui '12-'13: Bdg $34,000-38,750 (+$1000). **Day $18,450** (+$1000). **Intl Bdg $41,000** (+$2500). **Aid:** Need ($1,049,276).
Summer: Acad Enrich. ESL. 6 wks.
Endow $22,500,000. Plant val $16,000,000. Acres 350. Bldgs 17. Dorms 2. Dorm rms 68. Class rms 19. Lib 19,623 vols. Sci labs 3. Auds 1. Theaters 1. Art studios 3. Music studios 4. Dance studios 1. Gyms 2. Fields 4. Courts 4. Lakes 1. Comp labs 2.
Est 1952. Nonprofit. Sem (Aug-May). **Assoc** SACS.

Established through the bequest of Birmingham industrialist Harvey G. Woodward, ISS was conceived as a boys' school. Dr. Louis E. Armstrong, former chairman of the curriculum department of George Peabody College, served as the first director. Today, the school is coeducational, with a socially and culturally diverse student body.

Open only to students of above-average intelligence, the school offers a heavily academic curriculum and prepares its graduates for leading colleges. A favorable student-teacher ratio facilitates learning. Students govern themselves by "town meeting" and elected officials.

The spacious, landscaped campus is part of a 350-acre, school-owned tract, partly forested and cultivated, abutting Oak Mountain State Park.

DOTHAN, AL. (93 mi. SE of Montgomery, AL; 183 mi. SSW of Atlanta, GA) Urban. Pop: 57,737. Alt: 326 ft.

HOUSTON ACADEMY
Day — Coed Gr PS (Age 3)-12

Dothan, AL 36303. 901 Buena Vista Dr. Tel: 334-794-4106. Fax: 334-793-4053.
www.houstonacademy.com
John P. O'Connell, Jr., Head. BA, MA, Loyola Univ of Chicago.
  Col Prep. AP—Eng Fr Lat Span Calc Comp_Sci Eur_Hist US_Hist Studio_Art. **Feat—**Anat & Physiol 20th_Century_Hist Econ Psych Art_Hist Drama Band Chorus Journ. **Supp—**Tut.
  Sports—Basket Soccer Tennis. B: Baseball Football Golf. G: Cheer Softball Volley. **Activities:** 17.
  Selective adm: 84/yr. Appl fee: $75. Accepted: 80%. **Tests** IQ Stanford.
  Enr 632. B 344. G 288. Elem 348. Sec 284. Avg class size: 20. Stud/fac: 13:1. **Fac 54.** M 7/F 47. FT 54. Adv deg: 48%.
  Grad '08—48. Col—48. (Auburn, U of AL-Tuscaloosa, Birmingham-Southern, Furman, Notre Dame, Wash & Lee). **Mid 50% SAT:** CR 520-668. M 518-666. Mid 50% ACT: 23-29.
  Tui '11-'12: Day $5570-9630 (+$300). **Aid:** Need 90 ($345,290).
  Plant val $2,047,000. Acres 19. Bldgs 5. Class rms 44. Lib 10,500 vols. Labs 3. Art studios 1. Music studios 1. Gyms 2. Fields 2.
  Est 1970. Nonprofit. Sem (Aug-May). **Assoc** SACS.

Founded by local civic and business leaders, the school offers a full college preparatory program. The preschool curriculum incorporates a multisensory approach to learning, and social studies and science units are taught. In the intermediate school, children have the opportunity to move above their assigned grade levels in language arts and mathematics. The curricula for the middle and upper schools provide honors and college placement courses in English, foreign language, history, mathematics and science. Students may also choose from a variety of electives, including art, computer, chorus and journalism.

HUNTSVILLE, AL. (142 mi. WNW of Atlanta, GA) Urban. Pop: 158,216. Alt: 635 ft.

RANDOLPH SCHOOL

Day — Coed Gr K-12

Huntsville, AL 35802. 1005 Drake Ave SE. Tel: 256-799-6100. Fax: 256-881-1784.
Other locations: 4915 Garth Rd, Huntsville 35802.
www.randolphschool.net   E-mail: admissions@randolphschool.net
Byron C. Hulsey, Head (2006). BA, Univ of Virginia, MA, PhD, Univ of Texas-Austin. **Glynn Below, Adm.**

- **Col Prep. AP (exams req'd; 251 taken, 88% 3+)**—Eng Fr Lat Span Calc Bio Chem Physics Eur_Hist US_Hist Comp_Govt & Pol US_Govt & Pol Studio_Art Music_ Theory. **Elem math**—Everyday Math. **Elem read**—Junior Great Books/Macmillan/ McGraw-Hill. **Feat**—Stats Anat & Physiol Environ_Sci Marine_Bio/Sci Microbio Law Ceramics Film Graphic_Arts Photog Drama Band Music Journ. **Supp**—Rev Tut.
- **Sports**—Basket X-country Golf Soccer Swim Tennis Track. B: Baseball Football. G: Cheer Softball Volley. **Activities:** 35.
- **Selective adm (Gr K-11):** 137/yr. Usual entry: K, 6 & 9. Appl fee: $75. Appl due: Mar. Applied: 206. Accepted: 82%. Yield: 82%. **Tests** ISEE Stanford TOEFL.
- **Enr 997.** B 459. G 538. Elem 646. Sec 351. Wh 81%. Latino 2%. Blk 4%. Asian 11%. Other 2%. Avg class size: 16. Stud/fac: 14:1. **Fac 103.** M 31/F 72. FT 92/PT 11. Wh 85%. Latino 5%. Blk 4%. Asian 2%. Other 4%. Adv deg: 52%.
- **Grad '11—64. Col—62.** (Auburn 20, U of AL-Tuscaloosa 9, Vanderbilt 3, U of the South 2, Rice 2, SMU 2). **Avg SAT:** CR 652. M 664. W 634. **Mid 50% SAT:** CR 570-700. M 610-730. W 570-710. Avg ACT: 28.9. Mid 50% ACT: 26-33. **Col couns:** 2. Alum donors: 10%.
- **Tui '11-'12: Day $12,150-15,785** (+$500-625). **Aid:** Merit 7 ($4483). Need 65 ($464,360).
- **Summer:** Acad Rec. 4 wks.
- Endow $8,900,000. Plant val $50,000,000. Acres 74. Bldgs 11 (100% ADA). Class rms 84. 3 Libs 29,000 vols. Sci labs 9. Auds 2. Theaters 2. Art studios 5. Music studios 5. Gyms 2. Fields 4. Courts 6. Comp labs 4. Laptop prgm Gr 8-12.
- **Est 1959.** Nonprofit. Sem (Aug-May). **Assoc** CLS SACS.

Founded by a group of Huntsville parents, Randolph provides a balanced program for college-bound students in the northern part of the state. The curriculum is based on individual guidance, with students grouped according to ability, not chronological age. Art, music, drama and various electives are integrated with the traditional disciplines.

Laptop computers, required for students in grades 9-12, and a wireless Internet network enhance the curriculum. A weeklong interim enables middle and upper school students to pursue learning experiences outside of the regular program. Qualified juniors and seniors choose from a wide array of Advanced Placement courses.

The main location on Drake Avenue serves children in grades K-8, while the Garth Road campus accommodates students in grades 9-12.

LANETT, AL. (72 mi. WSW of Montgomery, AL; 77 mi. NE of Atlanta, GA) Rural. Pop: 7897. Alt: 640 ft.

SPRINGWOOD SCHOOL

Day — Coed Gr PS (Age 4)-12

Lanett, AL 36863. 1814 Cherry Dr, PO Box 1030. Tel: 334-644-2191. Fax: 334-644-2194.
www.springwoodschool.com   E-mail: ahixon@springwoodschool.com

Rick Johnson, Head (2012). Ann M. Hixon, Adm.
Col Prep. AP—Eng US_Hist Studio_Art. **Feat**—Fr Span Comp_Sci Psych Sociol Drama Band Chorus. **Supp**—Tut.
Sports—Basket X-country Tennis. B: Baseball Football. G: Cheer Softball.
Selective adm: Appl fee: $100. Appl due: Feb.
Enr 309. B 155. G 154. Nonwhite 12%. Avg class size: 17. Stud/fac: 14:1. Casual. **Fac 36.** M 11/F 25. FT 34/PT 2. Adv deg: 58%.
Grad '11—28. Col—27. (S Union St JC, Auburn, U of AL-Tuscaloosa, Troy St, Birmingham-Southern, U of Richmond). Avg ACT: 22.1. Alum donors: 20%.
Tui '12-'13: Day $5366-7336 (+$225-1525).
Endow $12,000,000. Plant val $9,145,000. Acres 45. Bldgs 7. Libs 1. Sci labs 2. Art studios 1. Music studios 1. Arts ctrs 1. Gyms 1. Fields 3. Courts 1. Weight rms 1. Stadiums 1. Playgrounds 1. Comp labs 3. Laptop prgm Gr 9-12.
Est 1970. Nonprofit. Sem (Aug-May). **Assoc** SACS.

Located on a 45-acre campus near the Chattahoochee River, Springwood was established through the cooperative efforts of 13 founding members. The college preparatory curriculum includes specialized instruction in Spanish, art, music, computer and physical education, in addition to honors and Advanced Placement courses in all major disciplines.

Students in grades 9-12 participate in an interim week each March that varies by grade level. Freshmen choose from an annually rotating selection of minicourses, while sophomores take day trips to museums, the theater, universities and other places of interest. Juniors complete community service throughout the area, and seniors observe professionals in areas of career interest.

Springwood's community service curriculum commences in grades 7 and 8, when the school encourages boys and girls to perform five hours of annual service. Compulsory service begins in grade 9, during which pupils complete 10 service hours. The annual commitment grows to 20 hours in grade 10, 50 hours in grade 11 (including interim week) and 60 hours in grade 12 (including in-class hours).

MOBILE, AL. (118 mi. ENE of New Orleans, LA) Urban. Pop: 198,915. Alt: 7 ft.

ST. PAUL'S EPISCOPAL SCHOOL
Day — Coed Gr PS (Age 4)-12

Mobile, AL 36608. 161 Dogwood Ln. Tel: 251-342-6700. Fax: 251-342-1844.
www.stpaulsmobile.net   E-mail: jtaylor@stpaulsmobile.net
F. Martin Lester, Jr., Head. BA, Millsaps College, JD, Cumberland School of Law, MEd, Univ of South Alabama. **Julie L. Taylor, Adm.**
Col Prep. AP (exams req'd; 207 taken)—Eng Calc Bio Chem Environ_Sci Physics Eur_Hist US_Hist Econ US_Govt & Pol Studio_Art. **Elem math**—Everyday Math. **Elem read**—Foundations & Frameworks. **Feat**—Fr Lat Span Anat & Physiol Marine_Bio/Sci Comp_Design Comp_Sci 20th-Century_Hist Photog Drama Journ Speech. **Supp**—Dev_Read ESL LD Rev Tut.
Sports—Basket X-country Golf Soccer Swim Tennis Track. B: Baseball Football. G: Cheer Softball Volley. **Activities:** 38.
Selective adm: 111/yr. Usual entry: PS, K, 6 & 9. Appl fee: $0. Appl due: Rolling. Applied: 210. Accepted: 82%. Yield: 53%. **Tests** CTP_4 IQ.
Enr 1262. B 618. G 644. Wh 96%. Blk 3%. Asian 1%. Avg class size: 21. Uniform. **Fac 160.** M 38/F 122. FT 144/PT 16. Wh 99%. Blk 1%. Adv deg: 73%.
Grad '11—130. Col—130. (U of AL-Tuscaloosa 36, Auburn 32, U of S AL 15, U of MS 8, Birmingham-Southern 3, Vanderbilt 2). Athl schol 15. **Mid 50% SAT:** CR 530-700. M 580-700. W 520-670. Mid 50% ACT: 23-29. **Col couns:** 2. Alum donors: 19%.
Tui '12-'13: Day $6036-10,176 (+$300). **Aid:** Need 72 ($353,000).
Summer: Acad Enrich Rem Rec. Sports. Travel. 7 wks.
Endow $1,600,000. Plant val $10,000,000. Acres 32. Bldgs 14. Class rms 85. 3 Libs

13,000 vols. Sci labs 4. Photog labs 1. Auds 1. Art studios 4. Music studios 5. Perf arts ctrs 1. Art galleries 1. Gyms 2. Fields 5. Field houses 3. Tracks 1. Weight rms 2. Comp labs 3. Comp/stud: 1:2 (1:1 Laptop prgm Gr 7-12). **Est 1947.** Nonprofit. Episcopal. Quar (Aug-May). **Assoc** SACS.

St. Paul's Episcopal School was founded as a nursery school and became an independent school with a board of trustees in 1969. In 1974, the first high school class graduated.

Teachers are available for tutoring after school, and extensive individual tutoring may be scheduled. Offering a college preparatory curriculum within a Christian environment, high school courses include journalism, computer science, chemistry and physics, as well as various honors and Advanced Placement offerings. All students in grades 7-12 purchase laptop computers and connect to the Internet via wireless access points throughout the school. Laptop sections in every discipline utilize innovative teaching techniques and make extensive use of online resources.

Boys and girls in grades 9-12 satisfy a 60-hour cumulative community service requirement by April of senior year.

MONTGOMERY, AL. (145 mi. SW of Atlanta, GA) Urban. Pop: 201,568. Alt: 190 ft.

THE MONTGOMERY ACADEMY
Day — Coed Gr K-12

Montgomery, AL 36106. 3240 Vaughn Rd. Tel: 334-272-8210, 888-345-8210.
Fax: 334-277-3240.
Other locations: 1550 Perry Hill Rd, Montgomery 36106.
www.montgomeryacademy.org
E-mail: susannah_cleveland@montgomeryacademy.org
David J. Farace, Head (2010). BA, Washington and Lee Univ, MA, Johns Hopkins Univ.
Susannah J. Cleveland, Adm.
  Col Prep. AP (exams req'd; 214 taken, 85% 3+)—Eng Fr Lat Span Calc Bio Chem Environ_Sci Physics Eur_Hist US_Hist Comp_Govt & Pol Econ Art_Hist Studio_Art Music_Theory. **Elem math**—Everyday Math. **Elem read**—SRA. **Feat**—Anat Comp_ Sci Cold_War Philos Film Photog Drama Chorus Debate. **Supp**—ESL.
  Sports—Basket X-country Golf Soccer Swim Tennis Track. B: Baseball Football. G: Cheer Softball Volley.
  Selective adm: 129/yr. Appl fee: $25-115. Appl due: Rolling. **Tests** CTP_4 IQ ISEE Stanford.
  Enr 821. Elem 592. Sec 229. Wh 88%. Blk 7%. Asian 2%. Other 3%. Avg class size: 16. Uniform. **Fac 95.** Adv deg: 75%.
  Grad '09—74. Col—74. (U of AL-Tuscaloosa 27, Auburn 19, U of the South 3, SMU 2, Wash & Lee 2, Vanderbilt). **Mid 50% SAT:** CR 540-650. M 520-630. W 570-640. Mid 50% ACT: 24-28. **Col couns:** 2.
  Tui '12-'13: Day $6925-12,408 (+$60-595). **Aid:** Need 64 ($311,145).
  Endow $2,800,000. Plant val $24,598,000. Acres 52. Bldgs 8. Class rms 70. 2 Libs 35,000 vols. Sci labs 4. Lang labs 1. Theaters 1. Art studios 7. Music studios 2. Gyms 3. Fields 5. Courts 5. Comp labs 5. Comp/stud: 1:2 (1:1 Laptop prgm Gr 5-12).
  Est 1959. Nonprofit. Sem (Aug-May). **Assoc** CLS SACS.

The academy offers a comprehensive college preparatory curriculum with a wide choice of elective courses. During the lower school years (grades K-4), course work highlights basic concepts and seeks to develop children's problem-solving abilities through the practical application of acquired skills. Specialists supplement core courses with instruction in art, music, computer, science lab, Spanish and physical education.

The transitional middle school (grades 5-8) prepares boys and girls for high school by shifting from the elementary model followed in grades 5 and 6 to the upper school model utilized in grades 7 and 8. Pupils in grades 5 and 6 follow a set schedule and change classes during the day, while those in the two next grades adhere to the same rotating schedule as the upper school. Honors and Advanced Placement courses provide opportunities for acceleration in the upper school (grades 9-12), which also maintains a strong advisory program. Students select from a variety of visual and performing arts offerings. Students in grades 5-12 use iPads in class.

The lower school occupies separate quarters on Perry Hill Road.

FLORIDA

BOCA RATON, FL. (42 mi. N of Miami, FL) Urban. Pop: 74,764. Alt: 16 ft.

SAINT ANDREW'S SCHOOL
Bdg — Coed Gr 9-12; Day — Coed PS (Age 4)-12

Boca Raton, FL 33434. 3900 Jog Rd. Tel: 561-210-2000. Fax: 561-210-2007.
www.saintandrews.net E-mail: admission@saintandrews.net
Ann Marie Krejcarek, Head (1997). EdD. Kilian J. Forgus, Adm.
  Col Prep. IB Diploma. AP (exams req'd; 574 taken, 87% 3+)—Eng Chin Fr Lat Span
  Calc Stats Comp_Sci Bio Chem Physics Eur_Hist US_Hist Human_Geog US_Govt
  & Pol Art_Hist Music_Theory. Feat—Creative_Writing Shakespeare Ital Anat &
  Physiol Astron Environ_Sci Econ Bible Ethics World_Relig Photog Sculpt Video_Pro-
  duction Drama Theater_Arts Band Chorus Jazz_Band Dance Journ Public_Speak.
  Supp—Tut.
  Sports—Basket Bowl X-country Golf Lacrosse Soccer Swim Tennis Track W_Polo. B:
  Baseball Football Wrestling. G: Cheer Softball Volley.
  Selective adm: 372/yr. Bdg 45. Day 327. Appl fee: $75-100. Appl due: Feb. Tests SSAT
  TOEFL.
  Enr 1315. Bdg 100. Day 1215. Nonwhite 10%. Intl 18%. Avg class size: 15. Stud/fac: 9:1.
  Fac 140. M 55/F 85. FT 140. Adv deg: 63%. In dorms 10.
  Grad '11—138. Col—138. (U of Miami 9, NYU 5, Geo Wash 5, U of FL 5, USC 4, Tulane
  4). Avg SAT: CR 596. M 634. W 610. Mid 50% ACT: 24-30. Col couns: 3.
  Tui '12-'13: Bdg $44,700 (+$2000). Day $18,540-25,170 (+$1000). Aid: Need 194
  ($2,580,000).
  Summer: Acad. Tui Day $420-1700. 2-3 wks.
  Endow $11,000,000. Plant val $37,500,000. Acres 81. Bldgs 38. Dorms 2. Dorm rms 63.
  Class rms 78. Lib 18,000 vols. Sci labs 9. Lang labs 1. Sci ctrs 1. Auds 1. Theaters
  1. Art studios 7. Music studios 2. Perf arts ctrs 1. Gyms 2. Fields 6. Courts 10. Pools
  1. Comp labs 7.
  Est 1961. Nonprofit. Episcopal. Sem (Aug-June). Assoc CLS SACS.

Originally a boys' boarding school, Saint Andrew's became coeducational in 1971. Situated on an 81-acre site, the school admits day students at all grade levels and boarding students in the high school grades.

The broad curriculum, which includes Advanced Placement and honors courses, affords rigorous preparation for colleges throughout the nation. Saint Andrew's began offering the two-year International Baccalaureate Diploma as an additional curricular option in fall 2010. Requirements in English, foreign language, math, science and history form the core of the academic program. Other graduation requirements include courses in the arts, theology and computer. Students also perform 40 cumulative hours of community service in grades 9-12.

BRADENTON, FL. (33 mi. S of Tampa, FL) Urban. Pop: 49,504. Alt: 25 ft.

SAINT STEPHEN'S EPISCOPAL SCHOOL
Day — Coed Gr PS (Age 3)-12

Bradenton, FL 34209. 315 41st St W. Tel: 941-746-2121. Fax: 941-746-5699.
www.saintstephens.org E-mail: saintstephen@saintstephens.org
Janet S. Pullen, Head (2003). BS, Florida State Univ, MEd, National-Louis Univ. Linda G.

Lutz, Adm.
Col Prep. AP (exams req'd; 212 taken, 82% 3+)—Eng Fr Lat Span Calc Comp_Sci Bio Chem Environ_Sci Physics Eur_Hist US_Hist World_Hist Art_Hist Studio_Art. **Feat**—Humanities Gothic_Lit Southern_Lit Chin Marine_Bio/Sci Organic_Chem Web_Design Holocaust Econ Govt Intl_Relations Psych Comp_Relig Ceramics Film Photog Drama Band Music Journ. **Supp**—Tut.
Sports—Basket X-country Golf Soccer Swim Tennis Track. B: Baseball Football Wrestling. G: Cheer Softball Volley. **Activities:** 41.
Selective adm: 114/yr. Appl fee: $200. Appl due: Rolling. Accepted: 67%. Yield: 91%. **Tests** CEEB CTP_4 IQ ISEE SSAT.
Enr 664. Elem 414. Sec 250. Wh 82%. Latino 5%. Blk 2%. Asian 5%. Other 6%. Avg class size: 16. Stud/fac: 11:1. **Fac 87.** M 30/F 57. FT 80/PT 7. Wh 89%. Latino 8%. Blk 1%. Asian 2%. Adv deg: 48%.
Grad '09—69. Col—68. (U of FL 5, Rollins 3, U of Miami 3, U of Central FL 3, Johns Hopkins 2, UNC-Chapel Hill 2). **Mid 50% SAT:** CR 530-670. M 540-650. W 550-660. Avg ACT: 25. Mid 50% ACT: 23-28. **Col couns:** 2. Alum donors: 3%.
Tui '11-'12: Day $10,500-15,900 (+$1020-3220). **Aid:** Need 67 ($395,000).
Summer: Acad Enrich Rev Rec. Sports. Tui Day $120-180/wk. 9 wks.
Endow $958,000. Plant val $22,000,000. Acres 35. Bldgs 11. Class rms 35. 2 Libs 12,000 vols. Sci labs 7. Lang labs 1. Art studios 3. Music studios 1. Drama studios 1. Gyms 1. Fields 3. Tennis courts 10. Comp labs 3.
Est 1970. Nonprofit. Episcopal (14% practice). Sem (Aug-June). **Assoc** CLS SACS.

Founded by a group of community leaders from Sarasota and Manatee counties, Saint Stephen's provides traditional college preparation. In the upper school, Advanced Placement classes are available in all departments. The fine arts department features courses in the visual arts, music and drama. A religious studies program, from which a compulsory component of community service is derived, is also available. Boys and girls accumulate 75 hours of community service in grades 9-12.

The school's Interim Quest program allows upper school students to participate in specialized studies on campus, internships in the business community, or domestic or foreign travel programs. Interscholastic sports competition begins in grade 7. Some out-of-town students reside at the IMG Sports Academies in Bradenton while pursuing their academic work at the school.

FORT LAUDERDALE, FL. (26 mi. N of Miami, FL) Urban. Pop: 152,397. Alt: 10 ft.

PINE CREST SCHOOL
Day — Coed Gr PS (Age 4)-12

Fort Lauderdale, FL 33334. 1501 NE 62nd St. Tel: 954-492-4100. Fax: 954-492-4188.
Other locations: 2700 St Andrews Blvd, Boca Raton 33434.
www.pinecrest.edu   E-mail: pcadmit@pinecrest.edu
Henry M. Battle, Jr., Pres (2011). BA, Univ of North Carolina-Greensboro, MA, Union Theological Seminary. **Elena Del Alamo, Adm.**
Col Prep. AP (exams req'd; 1509 taken, 77% 3+)—Eng Fr Ger Span Calc Stats Comp_Sci Bio Chem Environ_Sci Physics Eur_Hist US_Hist Comp_Govt & Pol Econ Human_Geog Psych Art_Hist Studio_Art Music_Theory. **Feat**—Chin Multivariable_ Calc Marine_Bio/Sci Sociol Comp_Relig Ethics Film Graphic_Arts Photog Drama Band Orchestra Dance Debate. **Supp**—Dev_Read Tut.
Sports—Basket Crew X-country Golf Lacrosse Soccer Swim Tennis Track Volley Weightlifting. B: Baseball Football. G: Cheer Softball. **Activities:** 40.
Selective adm: 204/yr. Appl fee: $100. Appl due: Rolling. **Tests** SSAT.
Enr 1680. Avg class size: 17. Stud/fac: 9:1. Uniform. **Fac 130.** M 36/F 94. FT 125/PT 5.
Grad '10—196. Col—196. (U of FL, FL St, U of PA, Harvard, Vanderbilt, U of Miami). **Avg SAT:** CR 640. M 659. W 661. Avg ACT: 29.

Tui '11-'12: Day $19,270-23,560 (+$1500-3325). **Aid:** Need 300 ($3,200,000).
Summer: Acad Enrich Rev Rec. 6 wks.
Endow $25,000,000. Plant val $30,000,000. Acres 49. Bldgs 27. Class rms 93. 2 Libs
60,000 vols. Sci labs 6. Lang labs 1. Auds 4. Theaters 2. Art studios 4. Music studios
15. Dance studios 2. Gyms 2. Fields 6. Courts 8. Pools 3. Comp labs 3. Laptop prgm
Gr 6-12.
Est 1934. Nonprofit. Tri (Aug-June). **Assoc** CLS SACS.

Founded by Mae McMillan, Pine Crest has grown from a tutoring school for winter visitors
to a large college preparatory program on a 49-acre campus. In 1987, Pine Crest merged with
Boca Raton Academy, forming a second campus in Boca Raton that serves students through
grade 8. Its graduates are invited to complete their preparatory school education on the Fort
Lauderdale campus.

Honors sections and Advanced Placement courses offer able students opportunities for more
intensive studies. Community service is part of the curriculum at all grade levels, and upper
schoolers satisfy hourly service requirements each year. The school also conducts a variety of
summer programs on both campuses.

UNIVERSITY SCHOOL OF NOVA SOUTHEASTERN UNIVERSITY
Day — Coed Gr PS (Age 4)-12

Fort Lauderdale, FL 33314. 3375 SW 75th Ave. Tel: 954-262-4400, 800-541-6682.
Fax: 954-262-3971.
www.uschool.nova.edu   E-mail: uschool@nsu.nova.edu
Jerome S. Chermak, Head (1999). BA, MAT, State Univ of New York-Binghamton, EdD,
Boston Univ. **Lynne Fazzio, Adm.**
    Col Prep. AP (exams req'd; 655 taken, 71% 3+)—Eng Fr Lat Span Calc Stats Comp_
    Sci Bio Chem Environ_Sci Physics US_Hist World_Hist Econ Human_Geog Psych
    US_Govt & Pol Art_Hist Studio_Art Music_Theory. **Feat**—Creative_Writing Chin
    Anat & Physiol Marine_Bio/Sci Film Video_Production Theater_Arts Orchestra.
    Supp—Rem_Read. **Dual enr:** Nova Southeastern.
    Sports—Basket X-country Golf Lacrosse Soccer Swim Tennis Track. B: Baseball Crew
    Football Ice_Hockey Wrestling. G: Cheer Softball Volley. **Activities:** 50.
    Selective adm: 313/yr. Appl fee: $100-125. Appl due: Rolling. Applied: 593. Accepted:
    78%. Yield: 80%. **Tests** SSAT.
    Enr 1902. B 981. G 921. Elem 1222. Sec 680. Wh 66%. Latino 12%. Blk 5%. Native Am
    1%. Asian 4%. Other 12%. Avg class size: 20. Uniform. **Fac 181.** M 57/F 124. FT 181.
    Wh 83%. Latino 8%. Blk 7%. Asian 1%. Other 1%. Adv deg: 54%.
    Grad '11—166. Col—166. (FL St 21, U of FL 20, U of Central FL 7, U of Miami 6, U of
    MI 5, Brandeis 4). **Avg SAT:** CR 599. M 601. W 613.
    Tui '12-'13: Day $15,900-20,500 (+$1650-1850). **Aid:** Need 249 ($1,781,719).
    Summer: Acad Rec. Tui Day $500-700/4-wk ses. 10 wks.
    Endow $750,000. Plant val $80,000,000. Acres 28. Bldgs 5. 3 Libs 34,067 vols. Sci labs
    14. Auds 1. Theaters 1. Art studios 4. Music studios 3. Dance studios 1. Gyms 2.
    Fields 3. Courts 7. Pools 1. Comp labs 6.
    Est 1971. Nonprofit. Sem (Aug-June). **Assoc** CLS SACS.

Offering group instruction and individualized learning activities, this school occupies 28
acres of the central Nova Southeastern University campus.

Programming for both average and academically advanced children begins in prekindergarten; other special programs include cultural arts offerings, internships and independent study.
Qualified upper school students may enroll in Advanced Placement and college courses held
at the school.

Students in grades 9-12 accumulate 75 hours of community service. Boys and girls serve
children with special needs and underprivileged young adults; work at local soup kitchens and
animal rescues; assist with environmental preservation; and provide support at events that benefit the March of Dimes, pediatric AIDS victims, local hospitals and disaster relief.

FORT MYERS, FL. (99 mi. SSE of Tampa, FL) Urban. Pop: 48,028. Alt: 10 ft.

CANTERBURY SCHOOL
Day — Coed Gr PS (Age 3)-12

Fort Myers, FL 33919. 8141 College Pky. Tel: 239-481-4323. Fax: 239-481-8339.
www.canterburyfortmyers.org   E-mail: jpeters@canterburyfortmyers.org
John Anthony Paulus, Head (2008). BA, Stanford Univ, MEd, Boston Univ. **Julie A. Peters, Adm.**

Col Prep. AP (exams req'd; 128 taken, 80% 3+)—Eng Fr Span Calc Stats Comp_Sci Bio Chem Environ_Sci Physics Eur_Hist Comp_Govt & Pol Econ Psych US_Govt & Pol. **Feat**—British_Lit Creative_Writing Lat Linear_Algebra Multivariable_Calc Anat & Physiol Marine_Bio/Sci Sociol World_Relig Art_Hist Ceramics Drawing Photog Sculpt Theater_Arts Bus Speech Aquaculture. **Supp**—Rev. **Dual enr:** FL Gulf Coast, Edison St.

Sports—Basket X-country Golf Lacrosse Soccer Swim Tennis Track. B: Baseball Football. G: Cheer Softball Volley. **Activities:** 22.

Selective adm (Gr PS-11): 93/yr. Usual entry: PS, K, 6 & 9. Appl fee: $75. Appl due: Rolling. Applied: 185. Accepted: 77%. Yield: 65%. **Tests** CTP_4 SSAT.

Enr 580. B 292. G 288. Elem 381. Sec 199. Wh 76%. Latino 8%. Blk 4%. Asian 5%. Other 7%. Avg class size: 20. Stud/fac: 10:1. Casual. **Fac 82.** M 27/F 55. FT 78/PT 4. Wh 98%. Latino 2%. Adv deg: 52%.

Grad '11—47. Col—47. (Stetson 5, U of Miami 3, Boston Col 2, Yale 2, Duke 2, FL St 2). Athl schol 4. **Avg SAT:** CR 632. M 627. W 622. Avg ACT: 28. **Col couns:** 2. Alum donors: 17%.

Tui '12-'13: Day $13,995-18,550 (+$1000). **Aid:** Merit 30 ($240,000). Need 144 ($1,398,374).

Summer (enr 128): Acad Enrich Rev Rec. 5 wks.

Endow $7,600,000. Plant val $23,750,000. Acres 32. Bldgs 15 (100% ADA). Class rms 45. 2 Libs 8800 vols. Sci labs 6. Lang labs 2. Auds 1. Theaters 1. Art studios 2. Music studios 2. Perf arts ctrs 1. Gyms 2. Fields 3. Courts 6. Comp labs 3. Comp/stud: 1:1.5.

Est 1964. Nonprofit. Sem (Sept-June). **Assoc** CLS SACS.

Canterbury's college preparatory curriculum is marked by high academic standards and rigorous academic requirements. Offerings commence with a prekindergarten program for three-year-olds. The full-day kindergarten programs, for four- and five-year-olds, prepare pupils in reading and math skills while stimulating social, physical and creative development. In the lower and intermediate schools, academic development is augmented by work in the areas of scientific techniques and technology and research skills. Language arts classes foster the development of critical thinking. Opportunities for curriculum-related field trips and culture study are available.

The middle and upper schools emphasize traditional academic subjects while providing opportunities for independent research. Qualified students may enroll in Advanced Placement courses, and additional electives are available in the arts, computer science and speech. Boys and girls accumulate at least 50 total hours of required community service in grades 9-12.

See Also Page 67

GULF STREAM, FL. (50 mi. N of Miami, FL) Rural. Pop: 716. Alt: 7 ft.

GULF STREAM SCHOOL
Day — Coed Gr PS (Age 3)-8

Gulf Stream, FL 33483. 3600 Gulf Stream Rd. Tel: 561-276-5225. Fax: 561-276-7115.
www.gulfstreamschool.org   E-mail: admissions@gulfstreamschool.org
Joseph J. Zaluski, Head (2006). BS, MS, Univ of Dayton. Helen C. Burns, Adm.
  Pre-Prep. Feat—Lat Span Computers Studio_Art Music. Supp—Dev_Read Tut.
  Sports—Basket Lacrosse Soccer. G: Volley.
  Selective adm: 41/yr. Appl fee: $100. Appl due: Feb. Accepted: 66%. Yield: 71%. Tests
    IQ.
  Enr 250. B 131. G 119. Wh 95%. Latino 1%. Blk 3%. Asian 1%. Avg class size: 18. Uni-
    form. Fac 40. M 10/F 30. FT 36/PT 4. Wh 99%. Blk 1%. Adv deg: 55%.
  Grad '11—29. Prep—23. (St Andrew's Sch-FL 15, Pope John Paul II-FL 1, Hotchkiss 1,
    Gunnery 1, N Broward Prep 1, Pine Sch 1). Avg SSAT: 71%. Alum donors: 20%.
  Tui '12-'13: Day $12,075-18,950 (+$800-1500).
  Summer: Ages 3-5. Enrich Rem Rec. Tui Day $220/wk. 4 wks.
  Endow $5,000,000. Plant val $4,000,000. Acres 5. Bldgs 9. Class rms 28. Lib 13,500
    vols. Chapels 1. Sci labs 2. Comp ctrs 2. Auds 1. Music studios 1. Arts ctrs 2. Fields
    1. Field houses 1. Laptop prgm Gr 6-8.
  Est 1938. Nonprofit. Tri (Sept-June).

  In addition to the school's regular primary curriculum, Gulf Stream also conducts a seasonal
tutorial program between January and March for pupils spending the winter with their families
in south Florida. Generally traditional in approach and tone, the school features innovative fine
arts, early childhood language study and computer programs; tablet computers are integrated
into classroom instruction in grades 6-8. Gulf Stream maintains a close faculty-student relationship and small classes.

JACKSONVILLE, FL. (127 mi. N of Orlando, FL) Urban. Pop: 695,877. Alt: 43 ft.

THE BOLLES SCHOOL
Bdg — Coed Gr 7-PG; Day — Coed PS (Age 4)-12

Jacksonville, FL 32217. 7400 San Jose Blvd. Tel: 904-256-5030. Fax: 904-733-0606.
Other locations: 2264 Bartram Rd, Jacksonville 32207; 200 ATP Tour Blvd, Ponte Vedra
    Beach 32082.
  www.bolles.org   E-mail: admissions@bolles.org
Brian E. M. Johnson, Pres (2012). AB, Stanford Univ, EdM, Harvard Univ. Bradford L.
    Reed, Adm.
  Col Prep. AP (408 exams taken, 96% 3+)—Eng Chin Fr Lat Span Calc Stats Comp_
    Sci Bio Chem Physics Eur_Hist US_Hist Comp_Govt & Pol US_Govt & Pol Art_Hist
    Studio_Art. Elem math—Primary Math. Elem read—Open Court. Feat—Humani-
    ties Mythology Japan Anat & Physiol Environ_Sci Marine_Bio/Sci Neurobio Robotics
    Middle_Eastern_Hist Econ Ceramics Photog Acting Theater_Arts Music Music_Hist
    Dance. Supp—ESL Tut. Dual enr: FL St, U of N FL.
  Sports—Basket Crew X-country Golf Soccer Swim Tennis Track. B: Baseball Football
    Lacrosse Wrestling. G: Cheer Softball Volley. Activities: 84.
  Selective adm: 285/yr. Bdg 36. Day 249. Usual entry: PS, K, 7 & 9. Appl fee: $45. Appl
    due: Jan. Applied: 679. Accepted: 62%. Yield: 68%. Tests CEEB ISEE SSAT.
  Enr 1644. B 853. G 791. Bdg 87. Day 1557. Elem 864. Sec 779. PG 1. Wh 79%. Latino
    4%. Blk 4%. Native Am 1%. Asian 5%. Other 7%. Intl 5%. Avg class size: 12. Stud/fac:
    10:1. Fac 161. M 46/F 115. FT 154/PT 7. Wh 94%. Latino 4%. Blk 1%. Asian 1%. Adv

deg: 56%. In dorms 5.
Grad '11—192. Col—190. (FL St 21, U of FL 15, U of AL-Tuscaloosa 13, U of GA 7, U of Central FL 6, SMU 5). Athl schol 27. **Mid 50% SAT:** CR 510-670. M 540-680. W 520-650. **Col couns:** 4. Alum donors: 13%.
Tui '12-'13: Bdg $41,450 (+$2500). **Day $12,350-20,280** (+$500-750). **Aid:** Need 241 ($2,838,244).
Summer (enr 90): Acad Enrich Rev Rem Rec. Driver Ed. Tui Day $310-500. 3-6 wks.
Endow $12,098,000. Plant val $34,330,000. Bldgs 18. Dorms 4. Dorm rms 40. Class rms 57. 2 Libs 16,500 vols. Sci labs 6. Lang labs 1. Auds 2. Art studios 4. Music studios 1. Dance studios 1. Perf arts ctrs 2. Art galleries 2. Gyms 2. Fields 6. Basketball courts 2. Volleyball courts 1. Pools 2. Weight rms 1. Boathouses 1. Student ctrs 1. Comp labs 4. Comp/stud: 1:3.
Est 1933. Nonprofit. Quar (Aug-May). **Assoc** SACS.

Established as a military school for boys in grades 7-12, Bolles dropped its military affiliation in 1962 and became coeducational in 1971. The school's balanced college preparatory program combines academics, offerings in the fine and performing arts, approximately three dozen athletic teams, leadership and service opportunities, and a nationally known guidance program. The boarding program, in which boys and girls reside on different campuses, complements the coeducational learning environment. After-school activities on each campus include many coeducational pursuits.

An ongoing development program has enabled the school to make substantial improvements to its physical plant over the years. In 1991, the school acquired the Bartram Road campus, which allowed for the addition of a separate middle school facility and a girls' boarding section. In addition, Bolles opened a campus in Ponte Vedra Beach in 1999 to serve students from the Beaches area in grades pre-K-5.

Continuing to stress efficient college preparation, with extensive work in languages, science and mathematics, Bolles sends graduates to many competitive colleges. Morning tutorials are provided for students requiring additional academic assistance. **See Also Page 144**

EPISCOPAL SCHOOL OF JACKSONVILLE

Day — Coed Gr 6-12

Jacksonville, FL 32207. 4455 Atlantic Blvd. Tel: 904-396-5751. Fax: 904-396-7209.
www.esj.org   E-mail: foxp@esj.org
Dale D. Regan, Head (2007). BA, Florida State Univ, MEd, Univ of North Florida. **Peggy P. Fox, Adm.**
Col Prep. AP (exams req'd; 411 taken, 78% 3+)—Eng Fr Ger Lat Span Calc Stats Bio Chem Environ_Sci Physics Eur_Hist US_Hist US_Govt & Pol Art_Hist Studio_Art Music_Theory. **Feat**—Marine_Bio/Sci Comp_Sci Econ Relig Ceramics Photog Theater Journ Public_Speak. **Supp**—Tut. **Dual enr:** FL CC-Jacksonville.
Sports—Basket Crew X-country Golf Lacrosse Soccer Swim Tennis Track. B: Baseball Football Weightlifting Wrestling. G: Cheer Softball Volley. **Activities:** 35.
Selective adm: 192/yr. Appl fee: $50. Appl due: Jan. Accepted: 76%. Yield: 69%. **Tests** CTP_4 ISEE.
Enr 871. B 438. G 433. Elem 307. Sec 564. Wh 88%. Latino 3%. Blk 6%. Asian 1%. Other 2%. Avg class size: 17. Stud/fac: 10:1. Uniform. **Fac 90.** M 34/F 56. FT 90. Nonwhite 4%. Adv deg: 67%.
Grad '10—143. Col—143. (U of FL, FL St, U of N FL, U of Central FL, U of the South, U of AL-Tuscaloosa). Athl schol 12. **Avg SAT:** CR 593. M 597. W 576. Avg ACT: 26. **Col couns:** 4. Alum donors: 13%.
Tui '11-'12: Day $17,550-18,400 (+$750). **Aid:** Need 150 ($1,369,000).
Summer (enr 500): Acad Enrich. Sports. 12 wks.
Endow $6,800,000. Plant val $38,100,000. Acres 88. Bldgs 26 (100% ADA). Class rms 40. Lib 19,122 vols. Sci labs 8. Lang labs 1. Theaters 2. Studios 6. Gyms 2. Fields 4. Courts 6. Pools 1.
Est 1966. Nonprofit. Episcopal (30% practice). Sem (Aug-May). **Assoc** CLS SACS.

Founded on a 88-acre campus on the south bank of the St. Johns River, Episcopal is located five miles from downtown Jacksonville. The establishment of the school was made possible by a broadly based community effort, augmented by Mrs. Alfred I. DuPont.

Religion, the arts and classical languages are distinctive features of the solid college preparatory curriculum, which is offered in a Christian environment. Students satisfy the following community service requirements: compulsory project work in grades 6-8, 100 cumulative hours of individual service in grades 9-12. While the majority of graduates attend Southern colleges, the school is well represented at competitive universities throughout the country.

JACKSONVILLE COUNTRY DAY SCHOOL

Day — Coed Gr PS (Age 3)-6

Jacksonville, FL 32256. 10063 Baymeadows Rd. Tel: 904-641-6644.
Fax: 904-646-4058.
www.jcds.com   E-mail: admiss@jcds.com
S. Terry Bartow, Head (2004). BS, Univ of Massachusetts-Amherst, MS, Cornell Univ. **Pat Walker, Adm.**
    Pre-Prep. Elem math—Singapore Math. **Elem read**—Harcourt. **Feat**—Lib_Skills Span Computers Studio_Art Music. **Supp**—Rev Tut.
    Selective adm: 103/yr. Appl fee: $100. Appl due: Rolling. **Tests** CTP_4 IQ Stanford.
    Enr 489. B 232. G 257. Wh 65%. Latino 4%. Blk 7%. Asian 14%. Other 10%. Avg class size: 22. Uniform. **Fac 56.** FT 49/PT 7. Wh 93%. Latino 1%. Blk 5%. Asian 1%. Adv deg: 37%.
    Grad '10—51. Prep—44. (Episcopal HS of Jacksonville, Bolles, St Johns Co Day).
    Tui '12-'13: Day $10,105-12,305 (+$655-975).
    Summer (enr 600): Acad Enrich Rec. Tui Day $320/2-wk ses. 8 wks.
    Plant val $6,400,000. Acres 17. Bldgs 7. Class rms 27. Lib 10,000 vols. Sci labs 1. Amphitheaters 1. Auds 1. Art studios 1. Music studios 1. Arts ctrs 1. Gyms 1. Fields 4. Courts 3. Pools 2. Comp labs 1. Laptop prgm Gr 6.
    Est 1960. Nonprofit. Tri (Aug-May). **Assoc** SACS.

Founded as Southside Country Day School, JCDS assumed its current name in 1975. The program is designed primarily for those who are planning to attend a college preparatory secondary school. The school moved in 1964 to its present spacious and modern campus, located on a 17-acre site in the center of Jacksonville.

Cocurricular offerings include art, music, Spanish, library skills and laboratory science. The school incorporates the use of technology and computers into every aspect of its curriculum and emphasizes parental participation at all grade levels. In addition to the comprehensive physical education program, JCDS conducts an after-school intramural sports program. Morning and afternoon extended care is available.

RIVERSIDE PRESBYTERIAN DAY SCHOOL

Day — Coed Gr PS (Age 3)-6

Jacksonville, FL 32204. 830 Oak St. Tel: 904-353-5511. Fax: 904-634-1739.
www.rpds.com   E-mail: sfrancis@rpds.com
H. Palmer Bell, Head (2008). BS, Denison Univ, MEd, Rutgers Univ. **Shirley Francis, Adm.**
    Pre-Prep. Gen Acad. Elem math—Singapore Math. **Feat**—Creative_Writing Span Computers Bible Studio_Art Music. **Supp**—Dev_Read Rem_Math Rem_Read Tut.
    Somewhat selective adm: 110/yr. Usual entry: PS. Appl fee: $50-100. Appl due: Rolling. Accepted: 94%. Yield: 92%. **Tests** CTP_4 IQ ISEE Stanford.
    Enr 520. B 268. G 252. Wh 88%. Latino 2%. Blk 4%. Asian 4%. Other 2%. Avg class size: 18. Stud/fac: 12:1. **Fac 44.** M 3/F 41. FT 43/PT 1. Wh 99%. Latino 1%. Adv deg: 38%.
    Grad '11—46. Prep—33. (Episcopal HS of Jacksonville 22, Bolles 8, St Johns Co Day

3). Alum donors: 15%.
Tui '12-'13: Day $7200-10,950 (+$100). **Aid:** Need 75 ($263,810).
Summer: Acad Enrich Rec. Tui Day $85-150. 1-2 wks.
Endow $3,400,000. Plant val $11,000,000. Acres 9. Bldgs 4. Class rms 29. Libs 1. Sci labs 1. Lang labs 1. Auds 1. Theaters 1. Art studios 2. Music studios 1. Fields 1. Courts 1. Comp labs 1. Comp/stud: 1:4.
Est 1948. Nonprofit. Presbyterian. Tri (Aug-June). **Assoc** SACS.

RPDS comprises three divisions: a developmental prekindergarten and kindergarten that follows a half-day schedule; primary grades 1-3; and upper elementary grades 4-6 (with departmentalization beginning in grade 5). At all grade levels, the reading program is enriched by various materials and resources, while the language arts curriculum places increasing emphasis on writing skills as children progress. Math instruction incorporates manipulatives to facilitate mastery of computation and a firm grasp of concepts. In addition to the basic subjects, children study art, music, Bible, computer, Spanish and library skills.

Other noteworthy elements of the curriculum include creative writing, chorus, dance, drama, study trips and outdoor educational experiences.

LAKE WALES, FL. (44 mi. SSW of Orlando, FL; 55 mi. E of Tampa, FL) Suburban. Pop: 10,194. Alt: 147 ft.

THE VANGUARD SCHOOL
Bdg and Day — Coed Gr 5-PG

Lake Wales, FL 33859. 22000 Hwy 27. Tel: 863-676-6091. Fax: 863-676-8297.
www.vanguardschool.org E-mail: vanadmin@vanguardschool.org
Cathy Wooley-Brown, Pres. BA, MA, EdS, PhD, Univ of South Florida. **Stephen White, Prin. Candi Medeiros, Adm.**
Col Prep. Gen Acad. LD. Underachiever. AP—Calc Physics. **Feat**—Creative_Writing ASL Span Comp_Sci Econ Govt Filmmaking Studio_Art Accounting Journ Speech Woodworking Culinary_Arts. **Supp**—Dev_Read Makeup Rem_Math Rem_Read Tut. Outdoor ed. Sat classes. **Dual enr:** Polk CC, U of S FL.
Sports—Basket X-country Golf Soccer Tennis Track. B: Football Weightlifting. G: Cheer Volley. **Activities:** 13.
Somewhat selective adm: 39/yr. Bdg 33. Day 6. Appl fee: $100. Appl due: Rolling. Applied: 39. Accepted: 100%. **Tests** IQ.
Enr 100. B 75. G 25. Bdg 82. Day 18. Elem 17. Sec 82. PG 1. Wh 59%. Latino 5%. Blk 5%. Native Am 2%. Asian 1%. Other 28%. Intl 34%. Avg class size: 6. Stud/fac: 4:1. Casual. **Fac 21.** M 8/F 13. FT 17/PT 4. Wh 57%. Latino 9%. Blk 9%. Asian 19%. Other 6%. Adv deg: 28%.
Grad '11—26. Col—23. (Johnson & Wales, Barry, Savannah Col of Art & Design, U of N TX, Mary Baldwin, Vincennes).
Tui '12-'13: Bdg $44,000 (+$650). **5-Day Bdg $38,000** (+$650). **Day $22,500** (+$650). **Intl Bdg $44,000** (+$1250). **Aid:** Need 70 ($560,000).
Summer (enr 20): Acad Rev Rem. Tui Bdg $3995/4-wk ses. Tui Day $995/4-wk ses. 8 wks.
Endow $3,000,000. Plant val $8,000,000. Acres 75. Bldgs 13. Dorms 3. Dorm rms 72. Class rms 20. Lib 6300 vols. Sci labs 1. Lang labs 3. Dark rms 1. Gyms 1. Athletic ctrs 1. Fields 3. Courts 2. Pools 1. Comp labs 2.
Est 1966. Nonprofit. Sem (Sept-June). **Assoc** SACS.

Vanguard provides an individualized program for students with dyslexia, attention deficit disorder and other learning disabilities through a combination of classroom instruction and individual tutorial sessions. Structured classes emphasize organizational skills, study habits and the acquisition of fundamental academic skills. The core subjects of reading, language arts and mathematics, complemented by science and social studies, form the basic curriculum. Spanish language study and electives in the creative and industrial arts complete the program.

Two diploma programs are available in the upper school: one geared toward college-oriented academics, the other focusing on career-oriented practical studies.

MELBOURNE, FL. (52 mi. ESE of Orlando, FL) Urban. Pop: 69,779. Alt: 21 ft.

FLORIDA AIR ACADEMY
Bdg and Day — Coed Gr 7-12

Melbourne, FL 32901. 1950 S Academy Dr. Tel: 321-723-3211, 877-422-2338.
Fax: 321-676-0422.
www.flair.com   E-mail: admissions@flair.com

Col. James Dwight, Pres. BA, Middlebury College, MA, Columbia Univ, MS, Florida Institude of Technology. **Antiny White, Prin.** BS, Univ of West Georgia, MS, Nova Southeastern Univ. **Bryan Bergeron, Adm.**

   Col Prep. Milit. AP (exams req'd)—Eng Span Calc Physics US_Hist. **Feat**—Astron Environ_Sci Geol Oceanog Aerospace_Sci Comp_Sci Web_Design Aviation_Hist Econ Govt Psych Sociol Film Photog Music Public_Speak JROTC. **Supp**—Dev_ Read ESL Makeup Rem_Math Rev Tut. **Dual enr:** FL Inst of Tech, Brevard CC.

   Sports—Basket Golf Soccer Swim Tennis Track Volley. B: Baseball Football Weightlifting Wrestling. G: Softball.

   Somewhat selective adm: 166/yr. Appl fee: $100. Appl due: Rolling. Accepted: 85%. **Tests** SSAT TOEFL.

   Enr 350. Bdg 200. Day 150. Intl 22%. Avg class size: 15. Stud/fac: 10:1. Uniform. **Fac 35.** M 14/F 21. FT 31/PT 4. Adv deg: 48%.

   Grad '08—65. Col—64. (Embry-Riddle, U of S FL, FL Intl, U of FL, St Leo, FL Inst of Tech). **Avg SAT:** CR/M/W 1550.

   Tui '11-'12: Bdg $35,000-36,500 (+$5000). **Day $13,000-13,500** (+$3000). **Intl Bdg $40,000-41,500** (+$8000). **Aid:** Need 64 ($450,000).

   Summer: Acad Enrich Rev Rec. Flight Trng. SAT Prep. ESL. Tui Bdg $6000 (+$1200). Tui Day $2600 (+$600). 6 wks.

   Plant val $5,000,000. Acres 32. Bldgs 12. Dorms 1. Dorm rms 72. Class rms 33. Lib 4500 vols. Sci labs 1. Lang labs 1. Art studios 1. Music studios 1. Gyms 1. Fields 1. Courts 2. Pools 1. Comp labs 3.

   Est 1961. Inc. Sem (Aug-May). **Assoc** SACS.

Founded by Col. Jonathan Dwight, Florida Air provides a combined program of academic study and leadership training. After enrolling only boys for more than 40 years, the school opened both its boarding and its day divisions to girls in the fall of 2005. The college preparatory curriculum, which is grounded in the core subjects, includes honors and Advanced Placement courses in the major disciplines. Structured classroom instruction and compulsory study periods are characteristics of the program. An intensive English as a Second Language program serves international students.

Operating as an official US Air Force Junior ROTC Unit, the school offers aerospace science and military instruction. Flight training for academic credit, including simulator instruction and aircraft experience, provides the groundwork needed to qualify for a private pilot certificate.

MIAMI, FL. Urban. Pop: 362,470. Alt: 10 ft. Area also includes Coral Gables.

GULLIVER SCHOOLS
Day — Coed Gr PS (Age 3)-12

Coral Gables, FL 33146. 1500 San Remo Ave, Ste 400. Tel: 305-666-6333. Fax: 305-666-6344.
Other locations: 12595 Red Rd, Coral Gables 33156; 7500 SW 120th St, Pinecrest 33156; 6575 N Kendall Dr, Pinecrest 33156; 8000 SW 56th St, Miami 33155.
www.gulliverschools.org   E-mail: sancj@gulliverschools.org
John Krutulis, Head (2008). BA, Embry-Riddle Aeronautical Univ. **Carol A. Bowen, Gr 9-12 Adm; Thelma Wassmann, Gr PS-8 Adm.**
Col Prep. IB Diploma. IB MYP. AP (exams req'd; 565 taken, 84% 3+)—Eng Fr Lat Span Calc Stats Comp_Sci Bio Chem Physics Eur_Hist US_Hist World_Hist Comp_Govt & Pol Econ Human_Geog Psych US_Govt & Pol Art_Hist Studio_Art. **Feat**—ASL Chin Japan Engineering Anthro Govt Law Ethics Video_Production Architect_Design Drama Music Music_Theory Dance Debate TV_Production. **Supp**—Dev_Read Rem_Math Rem_Read Tut. **Dual enr:** U of Miami, FL Intl, Miami Dade.
Sports—Basket Bowl X-country Golf Soccer Swim Tennis Track Volley W_Polo. B: Baseball Football Lacrosse. G: Cheer Softball. **Activities:** 100.
Selective adm: 431/yr. Appl fee: $100. Appl due: Mar. Applied: 1069. **Tests** CEEB IQ SSAT.
Enr 2200. Wh 57%. Latino 31%. Blk 2%. Asian 2%. Other 8%. Intl 18%. Avg class size: 14. Stud/fac: 8:1. Uniform. **Fac 285.** M 73/F 212. FT 278/PT 7. Wh 57%. Latino 36%. Blk 4%. Asian 2%. Other 1%. Adv deg: 46%.
Grad '11—206. Col—206. (U of Miami 25, FL Intl 15, FL St 10, U of FL 10, NYU 8). Athl schol 20. **Mid 50% SAT:** CR 500-640. M 510-660. W 550-670. Avg ACT: 26. Mid 50% ACT: 23-29. **Col couns:** 9.
Tui '12-'13: Day $13,510-26,900 (+$700-1100). **Aid:** Need 217 ($3,466,000).
Summer: Acad Enrich. 3-6 wks.
Endow $5,733,000. Plant val $47,000,000. Bldgs 37. Class rms 229. Lib 39,000 vols. Sci labs 17. Auds 1. Theaters 2. Art studios 6. Music studios 4. Dance studios 2. Gyms 1. Fields 7. Courts 6. Pools 2. Comp labs 8.
Est 1926. Nonprofit. Sem (Aug-June). **Assoc** CLS SACS.

Gulliver Schools, with campuses in Coral Gables and the Village of Pinecrest, traces it roots to Gulliver Academy, which was founded in Miami by Mr. and Mrs. Arthur Gulliver. Marian Krutulis purchased the school in 1952 and moved it 15 years later to the Coral Gables site. The first high school class graduated in 1977, a year before the high school was established on a separate campus. Today, the school occupies four locations within a two-mile radius: Gulliver Academy (grades pre-K-8) is situated in a residential area of Coral Gables five miles south of Miami; the Montgomery Road campus serves children in grades 5-8 on Southwest 120th Street; Gulliver Preparatory School (grades 9-12) is situated on North Kendall Drive; and the Miller Road campus (grades 9-12) is located on Southwest 56th Street.

The primary school encompasses prekindergarten through senior kindergarten. Conversational Spanish is offered in the lower school (grades 1-4), while an independent study program is available in grades 3-8. In the middle school (grades 5-8), French, Spanish and Latin are electives in grades 7 and 8, and the study of Latin is particularly encouraged as a basis for the study of other languages. The middle school follows the International Baccalaureate Middle Years Program, which emphasizes communication, international mindedness and critical thinking; all students must take all eight core MYP courses. Band, chorus and drama are electives during these years.

Gulliver Preparatory School offers the International Baccalaureate Diploma, in addition to signature programs in architecture, biomedical sciences, engineering, and law and litigation. Gulliver Prep also conducts college-credit programs with the University of Miami, Florida International University and Miami Dade College.

Students satisfy the following community service requirements: 10 hours each year in grades 5 and 6, 15 hours annually in grades 7 and 8, and 20 hours per year in grades 9-12.

MIAMI COUNTRY DAY SCHOOL
Day — Coed Gr PS (Age 3)-12

Miami, FL 33161. 601 NE 107th St. Tel: 305-759-2843. Fax: 305-759-4871.
www.miamicountryday.org   E-mail: admissions@miamicountryday.org
John P. Davies, Head. BS, Merrimack College, MA, Texas A&M Univ, EdD, Florida International Univ. **Jasmine Lake, Adm.**

Col Prep. AP (exams req'd; 248 taken)—Eng Fr Span Calc Stats Bio Chem Environ_Sci Physics US_Hist World_Hist US_Govt & Pol Music_Theory. **Feat**—Multivariable_Calc Robotics Web_Design Econ Psych Ethics Philos World_Relig Ceramics Drawing Film Painting Photog Sculpt Drama Directing Orchestra Dance Journ Outdoor_Ed.

Sports—Basket X-country Soccer Swim Tennis Track. B: Baseball Football Golf Lacrosse. G: Cheer Softball Volley.

Selective adm (Gr PS-11): 174/yr. Appl fee: $85-115. Appl due: Feb. Accepted: 61%. Yield: 70%. **Tests** ISEE.

Enr 935. Elem 580. Sec 355. Intl 20%. Avg class size: 20. Uniform. **Fac 114.** Adv deg: 53%.

Grad '10—81. Col—81. (FL St 10, FL Intl 6, U of PA 3, USC 3, NYU 3, Babson 3). **Avg SAT:** CR/M 1240. **Col couns:** 2.

Tui '10-'11: Day $17,832-23,625 (+$750-1250).

Summer: Acad Enrich Rev Rec. Tui Day $400-1900. 3-6 wks.

Endow $4,000,000. Plant val $20,000,000. Acres 16. Bldgs 12. Class rms 77. 2 Libs 47,000 vols. Sci labs 7. Auds 1. Art studios 3. Music studios 2. Gyms 1. Fields 2. Courts 3. Pools 1. Comp labs 3.

Est 1938. Nonprofit. Quar (Aug-June). **Assoc** SACS.

MCDS' college preparatory curriculum features small classes and emphasizes the mastery of academic fundamentals. The lower, middle and upper divisions of the school stress both scholastic achievement and student involvement in a full range of activities. International pupils, who enroll from approximately 30 countries, benefit from an academically rigorous support program.

Beginning in the middle school, students perform mandatory community service. Boys and girls perform between five and 15 hours of annual service in grades 6-8, then another 25 hours per year in grades 9-12.

PALMER TRINITY SCHOOL
Day — Coed Gr 6-12

Miami, FL 33157. 7900 SW 176th St. Tel: 305-251-2230. Fax: 305-251-2917.
www.palmertrinity.org   E-mail: scalleja@palmertrinity.org
Sean Murphy, Head. BA, Dartmouth College, MA, St John's College. **Danny E. Reynolds, Adm.**

Col Prep. AP (exams req'd; 218 taken, 73% 3+)—Eng Chin Fr Span Calc Stats Bio Chem Environ_Sci Physics Eur_Hist US_Hist World_Hist Econ Psych US_Govt & Pol Studio_Art Music_Theory. **Feat**—Creative_Writing Anat & Physiol Ecol Forensic_Sci Marine_Bio/Sci Oceanog Meteorology Programming Amer_Stud Lat-Amer_Stud Buddhism Islam Architect Art_Hist Ceramics Drawing Film Filmmaking Painting Acting Theater_Arts Band Chorus Orchestra Guitar Dance Debate Journ Public_Speak. **Supp**—ESL.

Sports—Basket X-country Golf Lacrosse Soccer Tennis Track. B: Baseball Football. G: Cheer Softball Volley. **Activities:** 38.

Selective adm: 125/yr. Appl due: Feb. Accepted: 40%. Yield: 88%. **Tests** CEEB ISEE

SSAT.
Enr 625. Intl 26%. Avg class size: 16. Uniform. **Fac 60.** M 27/F 33. FT 60. Adv deg: 75%.
Grad '08—92. Col—92. (U of FL, Boston U, U of PA, Duke, SMU, Santa Clara). **Mid 50% SAT:** CR 520-650. M 540-640. W 520-630. Mid 50% ACT: 23-29. **Col couns:** 2. Alum donors: 30%.
Tui '12-'13: Day $25,000 (+$2400-3200). **Aid:** Need ($1,900,000).
Summer: Acad Enrich Rev Rem Rec. 4 wks.
Endow $4,000,000. Plant val $15,000,000. Acres 22. Bldgs 7. Class rms 60. Lib 17,000 vols. Labs 9. Auds 1. Theaters 1. Art studios 3. Music ctrs 1. Gyms 1. Fields 4. Courts 4. Laptop prgm Gr 6-12.
Est 1973. Nonprofit. Episcopal. Sem (Aug-May). **Assoc** SACS.

The result of a 1991 merger between Palmer School (founded in 1973) and Trinity Episcopal School (established in 1983), Palmer Trinity is situated on a 22-acre campus near Biscayne Bay in the southeastern section of the city.

Students build a firm foundation in the basic subjects of English, math, science, history and foreign languages. Honors and Advanced Placement courses are offered in all major subjects, an intensive English as a Second Language instruction is available, and pupils in all grades participate in a wireless laptop program. Boys and girls perform 20 hours of compulsory community service prior to graduation.

RANSOM EVERGLADES SCHOOL
Day — Coed Gr 6-12

Miami, FL 33133. 3575 Main Hwy. Tel: 305-460-8800. Fax: 305-854-1846.
Other locations: 2045 S Bayshore Dr, Miami 33133.
  www.ransomeverglades.org   E-mail: asayfie@ransomeverglades.org
Ellen Y. Moceri, Head (2001). BA, MA, Washington Univ. **Amy Sayfie, Adm.**
  Col Prep. AP (exams req'd; 713 taken, 97% 3+)—Eng Fr Span Calc Stats Comp_Sci Bio Chem Environ_Sci Physics Eur_Hist US_Hist World_Hist Comp_Govt & Pol Econ Psych US_Govt & Pol Art_Hist Music_Theory. **Feat**—Shakespeare Chin Ecol Marine_Bio/Sci Lat-Amer_Stud Ethics Judaic_Stud Fine_Arts Outdoor_Ed. Outdoor ed.
  Sports—Basket Crew X-country Golf Sail Soccer Swim Tennis Track Volley W_Polo. B: Baseball Football Lacrosse Wrestling. G: Cheer Softball. **Activities:** 85.
  Selective adm: 173/yr. Usual entry: 6. Appl fee: $100. Appl due: Dec. Applied: 483. Accepted: 41%. Yield: 86%. **Tests** SSAT.
  Enr 1079. B 559. G 520. Elem 472. Sec 607. Wh 45%. Latino 43%. Blk 5%. Asian 5%. Other 2%. Avg class size: 14. Stud/fac: 11:1. **Fac 96.** M 43/F 53. Wh 77%. Latino 16%. Blk 1%. Asian 4%. Other 2%. Adv deg: 78%.
  Grad '11—141. Col—141. (Vanderbilt 10, U of Miami 9, Georgetown 8, U of MI 8, Tufts 7, NYU 5). **Mid 50% SAT:** CR 600-700. M 650-740. W 640-720. Mid 50% ACT: 28-32. **Col couns:** 3. Alum donors: 21%.
  Tui '11-'12: Day $26,560 (+$1760). **Aid:** Need 147 ($2,985,290).
  Summer (enr 1200): Acad Enrich Rev Rem Rec. Tui Day $700/2-wk ses. 6 wks.
  Endow $23,952,000. Plant val $48,357,000. Bldgs 23. Class rms 59. 2 Libs 33,000 vols. Sci labs 11. Auds 2. Theaters 2. Art studios 6. Music studios 3. Gyms 2. Fields 2. Courts 6. Pools 1. Comp labs 4. Comp/stud: 1:4.
  Est 1903. Nonprofit. Quar (Aug-May). **Assoc** CLS SACS.

Ransom Everglades was founded in 1974 upon the merger of two established secondary schools in the Coconut Grove area of Miami: the Ransom School for Boys, opened under the direction of Paul C. Ransom in 1903 and originally known as the Adirondack Florida School, and the Everglades School for Girls, established in 1955. Now completely coeducational in all operations, the school occupies two campuses, with the middle school located on South Bayshore Drive.

Ransom Everglades provides college preparation in a small-class setting. Academic offerings in the upper school include numerous Advanced Placement courses. A variety of computer-based programs, such as a writing workshop that utilizes the computer in the development of student writing skills, enriches the upper school curriculum. In addition to the basic academic program, a number of experiences in the visual and performing arts are also offered.

NAPLES, FL. (102 mi. WNW of Miami, FL) Urban. Pop: 20,976. Alt: 9 ft.

THE COMMUNITY SCHOOL OF NAPLES
Day — Coed Gr PS (Age 4)-12

Naples, FL 34109. 13275 Livingston Rd. Tel: 239-597-7575. Fax: 239-598-2973.
www.communityschoolnaples.org
E-mail: svasey@communityschoolnaples.org
John E. Zeller, Jr., Head (2001). BA, Miami Univ (OH). Scott Vasey, Adm.

Col Prep. AP (exams req'd; 468 taken, 76% 3+)—Eng Fr Lat Span Calc Stats Comp_ Sci Bio Chem Environ_Sci Physics Eur_Hist US_Hist World_Hist Comp_Govt & Pol Econ Human_Geog Psych US_Govt & Pol Art_Hist Studio_Art Music_Theory. Elem math—Saxon. Elem read—Rigby Literacy by Design. Feat—Creative_Writing Humanities Chin Anat & Physiol Forensic_Sci Marine_Bio/Sci Oceanog Robotics Web_Design Law Ethics Film Photog Jewelry Theater. Supp—Rem_Math Rem_ Read Rev Tut. Dual enr: FL Gulf Coast.

Sports—Basket X-country Golf Lacrosse Soccer Swim Tennis Track. B: Baseball Football. G: Cheer Softball Volley. Activities: 40.

Somewhat selective adm (Gr PS-11): 128/yr. Usual entry: PS, K, 6 & 9. Appl fee: $100. Appl due: Feb. Applied: 197. Accepted: 85%. Yield: 76%. Tests CEEB CTP_4 ISEE SSAT TOEFL.

Enr 726. B 356. G 370. Elem 444. Sec 282. Wh 85%. Latino 3%. Blk 1%. Native Am 2%. Asian 4%. Other 5%. Avg class size: 16. Fac 93. M 31/F 62. FT 80/PT 13. Wh 90%. Latino 3%. Blk 2%. Asian 4%. Other 1%. Adv deg: 65%.

Grad '11—75. Col—75. (FL St 8, U of FL 4, FL Gulf Coast 4, Rensselaer Polytech 3, Eckerd 3, Notre Dame 3). Athl schol 5. Avg SAT: CR 591. M 635. W 710. Mid 50% SAT: CR 520-670. M 570-710. W 530-670. Avg ACT: 27. Col couns: 2. Alum donors: 1%.

Tui '12-'13: Day $16,975-23,020 (+$200-1500). Aid: Merit 6 ($50,000). Need 146 ($1,590,385).

Summer (enr 150): Enrich Rec. 1-5 wks.

Endow $9,350,000. Plant val $38,693,000. Acres 110. Bldgs 17 (60% ADA). Class rms 88. Lib 26,000 vols. Sci labs 11. Lang labs 3. Theaters 1. Art studios 5. Music studios 3. Dance studios 1. Gyms 2. Fields 4. Tennis courts 6. Pools 1. Comp labs 8. Comp/ stud: 1:2.5.

Est 1982. Nonprofit. Quar (Aug-June).

Founded by a group of area parents seeking to address a community need, CSN began as a school serving fewer than 50 children in grades K-8. An increasing enrollment and an expanding campus over the years led the school to add a high school division in 1993; the first senior class graduated in 1996.

Community School provides a comprehensive curriculum that places emphasis on the development of basic skills and an appreciation of music and the arts. Maintaining a low student-teacher ratio, the school provides instruction at every level—beginning in prekindergarten—in Spanish, computers, library skills, photography, drama, music and physical education.

College preparation is an integral aspect of the program, with most middle and upper school classes taught at the honors level, and Advanced Placement courses available at various grade levels in all major disciplines. Graduates matriculate at competitive colleges throughout the country.

Community service is a graduation requirement: All students perform 80 hours of service during the high school years.

ORANGE PARK, FL. (12 mi. SSW of Jacksonville, FL; 116 mi. N of Orlando, FL) Suburban. Pop: 9081. Alt: 24 ft.

ST. JOHNS COUNTRY DAY SCHOOL

Day — Coed Gr PS (Age 3)-12

Orange Park, FL 32073. 3100 Doctors Lake Dr. Tel: 904-264-9572. Fax: 904-264-0375.
www.sjcds.net   E-mail: admissionsinfo@sjcds.net
Edward M. Ellison, Head (2011). BA, Tufts Univ, MBA, Harvard Univ. **Brian Pargman, Adm.**

Col Prep. AP (exams req'd; 108 taken, 82% 3+)—Eng Fr Lat Span Calc Stats Comp_ Sci Bio Physics US_Hist Psych Art_Hist Studio_Art Music_Theory. **Feat**—Astron Sports_Med Econ Govt Journ. **Supp**—Rem_Math Tut.

Sports—Basket Crew X-country Golf Soccer Swim Tennis Track. B: Baseball Football. G: Cheer Softball Volley. **Activities:** 37.

Somewhat selective adm: 120/yr. Appl fee: $35-50. Appl due: Rolling. Accepted: 90%. **Tests** IQ ISEE.

Enr 650. Avg class size: 18. Stud/fac: 10:1. **Fac 77.** Adv deg: 54%.

Grad '11—58. Col—58. (U of FL 8, FL St 8, Flagler 7, U of N FL 4, U of AL-Tuscaloosa 4, U of Central FL 3). Athl schol 5. **Avg SAT:** CR 604. M 580. W 590. Avg ACT: 25. **Col couns:** 1. Alum donors: 5%.

Tui '12-'13: Day $6650-14,600 (+$400). **Aid:** Need 133 ($773,900).

Summer: Acad Enrich Rev Rem. 6 wks.

Endow $4,118,000. Plant val $10,408,000. Acres 26. Bldgs 14. Class rms 50. Lib 15,000 vols. Sci labs 6. Lang labs 1. Theaters 1. Art studios 3. Music studios 1. Perf arts ctrs 1. Gyms 2. Fields 4. Tennis courts 4. Pools 1. Tracks 1. Playgrounds 2. Comp labs 2.

Est 1953. Nonprofit. Sem (Aug-June). **Assoc** CLS SACS.

Located just south of Jacksonville, this country day school offers a strong college preparatory program for able students at all grade levels. A diverse curriculum with honors and Advanced Placement courses, laboratory sciences, foreign language instruction beginning in kindergarten, and a fine arts program prepares students for selective colleges throughout the country.

Cultural exchange visits are ongoing with schools in England, France, Germany and Costa Rica. An academic program and a day camp with adventure components provide summertime opportunities on the St. Johns campus.

PALM BEACH, FL. (64 mi. N of Miami, FL) Suburban. Pop: 9646. Alt: 15 ft.

PALM BEACH DAY ACADEMY

Day — Coed Gr PS (Age 2)-9

Palm Beach, FL 33480. 241 Seaview Ave. Tel: 561-655-1188. Fax: 561-655-5794.
Other locations: 1901 S Flagler Dr, West Palm Beach 33401.
www.palmbeachdayacademy.org   E-mail: malbanese@pbday.org
Rebecca Van der Bogert, Head (2007). BA, MA, Syracuse Univ, EdD, Harvard Univ. **Meghan Albanese, Adm.**

Pre-Prep. Montessori. Feat—Fr Span Computers Art_Hist Studio_Art Drama Music. **Supp**—Dev_Read Rem_Math Rem_Read Rev Tut.

Sports—Basket Lacrosse Soccer. B: Football. G: F_Hockey Volley.
Somewhat selective adm: 89/yr. Appl fee: $100. Appl due: Rolling. Applied: 122. Accepted: 88%. Yield: 73%. **Tests** CTP_4 SSAT Stanford.
Enr 519. B 267. G 252. Elem 500. Sec 19. Wh 92%. Latino 3%. Blk 1%. Asian 2%. Other 2%. Avg class size: 12. Uniform. **Fac 79.** M 16/F 63. FT 71/PT 8. Wh 90%. Latino 5%. Blk 1%. Asian 2%. Other 2%. Adv deg: 32%.
Grad '10—38. Prep—28. (Benjamin 8, St Andrew's Sch-FL 7, Cardinal Newman 4, Palmer Trinity 3, Phillips Acad 1, Suffield 1). Avg SSAT: 70%. Alum donors: 5%.
Tui '11-'12: Day $16,600-24,000 (+$1500). **Aid:** Merit 2 ($43,970). Need 105 ($1,299,821).
Endow $7,730,000. Plant val $19,366,000. Acres 3. Bldgs 6. Class rms 51. 3 Libs 15,000 vols. Sci labs 1. Lang labs 1. Auds 2. Theaters 1. Art studios 4. Music studios 2. Gyms 1. Fields 2. Comp labs 3. Comp/stud: 1:4.
Est 1921. Nonprofit. Quar (Sept-June).

The result of a July 2006 merger between Palm Beach Day School and the Academy of the Palm Beaches, PBDA provides a traditional curriculum with an emphasis on basic skills, enhanced by extensive extracurricular programs. Learning styles programs in the lower, middle and upper schools address special student needs. Early study of Spanish and computer in the lower grades, combined with departmentalized instruction in all subjects from grade 6, provide for entrance at the secondary level. The school conducts a two-tier community service program: Student council members perform 20 hours of service annually in grades 5-8 and 30 hours in grade 9, while other boys and girls devote eight hours to service each year in grades 7-9.

The Flagler campus in West Palm Beach, which formerly housed the Academy of the Palm Beaches, serves children in grades PS-3, while the Seaview Avenue campus accommodates students in grades 4-9.

ST. PETERSBURG, FL. (17 mi. SW of Tampa, FL) Urban. Pop: 248,232. Alt: 44 ft.

ADMIRAL FARRAGUT ACADEMY
Bdg — Coed Gr 6-12; Day — Coed PS (Age 3)-12

St Petersburg, FL 33710. 501 Park St N. Tel: 727-384-5500, 877-394-1742.
Fax: 727-347-5160.
www.farragut.org   E-mail: admissions@farragut.org
Capt. Robert J. Fine, Jr., Head (1998). BA, Carroll College, MEd, National-Louis Univ.
Gretchen Herbst, Adm.
Col Prep. Milit. AP (exams req'd; 115 taken, 35% 3+)—Eng Fr Span Calc Stats Comp_Sci Bio Chem US_Hist US_Govt & Pol. **Elem math**—Everyday Math. **Elem read**—Macmillan/McGraw-Hill. **Feat**—Creative_Writing ASL Chin Anat & Physiol Environ_Sci Marine_Bio/Sci Meteorology Law Psych Ethics Drama Music_Hist Journ JROTC SAT_Prep Aviation. **Supp**—ESL Tut. Outdoor ed. **Dual enr:** St Petersburg Col.
Sports—Basket X-country Golf Soccer Swim Tennis Track. B: Baseball Football Lacrosse Wrestling. G: Softball Volley. **Activities:** 17.
Selective adm (Bdg Gr 6-11; Day PS-11): 106/yr. Bdg 61. Day 45. Appl fee: $100. Appl due: Rolling. Accepted: 80%. Yield: 75%. **Tests** CEEB CTP_4 IQ SSAT Stanford TOEFL.
Enr 409. B 283. G 126. Bdg 165. Day 244. Elem 146. Sec 263. Wh 79%. Latino 6%. Blk 4%. Native Am 1%. Asian 10%. Intl 24%. Avg class size: 16. Stud/fac: 10:1. Uniform. **Fac 71.** M 32/F 39. FT 70/PT 1. Wh 87%. Latino 8%. Blk 3%. Asian 2%. Adv deg: 40%. In dorms 16.
Grad '11—68. Col—68. (U of FL 5, FL St 5, U of Central FL 4, Embry-Riddle 3, FL Gulf Coast 3, Northeastern U 2). Athl schol 3. **Mid 50% SAT:** CR 450-580. M 450-570. W 420-550. Mid 50% ACT: 18-24. **Col couns:** 3.

Tui '12-'13: Bdg $37,600-38,400 (+$2500-3100). **5-Day Bdg $31,600-32,100** (+$2500-3100). **Day $11,600-18,400** (+$0-600). **Intl Bdg $39,600-40,600** (+$4500-5100). **Aid:** Need 83 ($711,000).
Summer: Rec. Leadership. 1-2 wks.
Endow $1,500,000. Plant val $9,500,000. Acres 35. Bldgs 11. Dorms 1. Dorm rms 80. Class rms 26. Lib 12,000 vols. Sci labs 3. Lang labs 1. Art studios 1. Music studios 1. Video studios 1. Gyms 2. Fields 4. Courts 5. Pools 1. Comp labs 2. Laptop prgm Gr 9-12.
Est 1933. Nonprofit. Sem (Aug-May). **Assoc** SACS.

Admiral Farragut Academy was founded as a boys' school at Pine Beach, NJ, under the leadership of Adm. S. S. Robison, USN (Ret), a former superintendent of the US Naval Academy, and Brig. Gen. Cyrus S. Radford, USMC (Ret). In 1945, when the school reached maximum enrollment, the Florida campus was established. (The New Jersey campus closed in 1994.) AFA became coeducational in January of 1990. The lower division (grades pre-K-5), which began accepting students in 1999, provides a nonmilitary program.

This naval preparatory school offers college preparatory work on a 35-acre campus on the state's Gulf Coast that permits outdoor activities throughout the school year. The highly structured academic program stresses math and science, while strong English and history departments emphasize reading and writing skills. Individual college advisement and SAT preparation, as well as a full English for Speakers of Other Languages program, give all possible assurance of each student's success.

All students in grades 9-12 fulfill an 80-hour community service requirement prior to graduation. High schoolers also enroll in the Naval JROTC program, which includes drill team, color guard, rifle team and summer cruises aboard naval vessels. In addition, boys and girls must earn a sailing certification prior to graduation.

CANTERBURY SCHOOL OF FLORIDA

Day — Coed Gr PS (Age 4)-12

St Petersburg, FL 33702. 990 62nd Ave NE. Tel: 727-525-1419. Fax: 727-525-2545.
Other locations: 1200 Snell Isle Blvd NE, St Petersburg 33704.
www.canterbury-fl.org   E-mail: info@canterbury-fl.org
Mac H. Hall, Head (2005). BS, MEd, Valdosta State Univ, EdS, Univ of Central Florida.
Michelle Robinson, Adm.
Col Prep. AP (exams req'd; 135 taken, 64% 3+)—Eng Fr Lat Span Calc Stats Bio Chem Environ_Sci Physics US_Hist Comp_Govt & Pol Econ Human_Geog Psych US_Govt & Pol Art_Hist Studio_Art. **Feat**—British_Lit Shakespeare Astron Marine_Bio/Sci Oceanog Comp_Sci Relig Ceramics Drawing Film Painting Drama Theater_Arts Music Music_Hist Speech. **Supp**—Tut. **Dual enr:** St Petersburg Col, U of FL, U of S FL.
Sports—Basket X-country Golf Soccer Swim Tennis Track. B: Baseball Football. G: Cheer Softball Volley. **Activities:** 48.
Selective adm (Gr PS-11): 75/yr. Appl fee: $75. Appl due: Rolling. Accepted: 80%. Yield: 90%. **Tests** CEEB CTP_4 IQ ISEE SSAT Stanford TOEFL.
Enr 390. Elem 235. Sec 155. Wh 84%. Latino 6%. Blk 5%. Native Am 1%. Asian 4%. Avg class size: 13. Stud/fac: 7:1. **Fac 62.** M 16/F 46. FT 57/PT 5. Wh 98%. Latino 1%. Native Am 1%. Adv deg: 40%.
Grad '11—33. Col—33. (FL St 3, U of Central FL 3, U of FL 2, Ringling Sch of Art & Design 2, U of S MS 2). Athl schol 2. **Mid 50% SAT:** CR 520-670. M 500-660. W 530-660. Mid 50% ACT: 23-27. **Col couns:** 1.
Tui '12-'13: Day $9800-16,500 (+$690-1050).
Summer: Acad Enrich Rec. Sports. Tui Day $75-450/wk. 10 wks.
Endow $123,000. Plant val $8,500,000. Acres 20. Bldgs 7. Class rms 27. 2 Libs 16,415 vols. Sci labs 7. Lang labs 1. Auds 1. Theaters 1. Art studios 3. Music studios 3. Art galleries 1. Gyms 1. Fields 4. Courts 1. Comp labs 2. Comp/stud: 1:4.
Est 1968. Nonprofit. Episcopal. Sem (Aug-June). **Assoc** SACS.

Although affiliated with the Episcopal Church, Canterbury enrolls students of all faiths. The curriculum provides honors and Advanced Placement courses, marine studies and an international program, in addition to an array of extracurricular activities that ranges from interscholastic athletics to offerings in the fine and performing arts.

An annual miniterm session gives all upper school students a chance to gain extensive exposure to subjects or activities beyond the scope of the regular curriculum. Offerings have included career shadowing, broadcasting, trips abroad, ecology trips to the Florida Keys, SAT review, technical theater and community service, among others. Juniors and seniors may use miniterm as a chance to embark on college visits.

Activities include study skills, leadership opportunities, and trips organized by grade level in the middle and upper schools. Prior to graduation, boys and girls must perform at least 80 hours of community service. In addition, all seniors enroll in a research and writing course.

Canterbury operates two campuses. The lower school (grades pre-K-4) conducts classes at the Hough campus on Snell Isle Boulevard Northeast, while the middle school (grades 5-8) and the upper school (grades 9-12) occupy the Knowlton campus on 62nd Avenue Northeast.

SHORECREST PREPARATORY SCHOOL

Day — Coed Gr PS (Age 3)-12

St Petersburg, FL 33703. 5101 1st St NE. Tel: 727-522-2111. Fax: 727-527-4191.
www.shorecrest.org   E-mail: admissions@shorecrest.org
Michael A. Murphy, Head (2005). BS, Univ of Dayton, MS, Miami Univ (OH). **Jean Carnes, Adm.**

Col Prep. AP (exams req'd; 269 taken, 88% 3+)—Eng Fr Lat Span Calc Comp_Sci Bio Chem Physics Eur_Hist US_Hist World_Hist Econ Human_Geog Psych Art_Hist Studio_Art Music_Theory. **Feat**—Humanities Playwriting Anat & Physiol Astron Marine_Bio/Sci Web_Design Pol_Sci World_Relig Fine_Arts Photog Video_Production Drama Journ. **Supp**—Tut.

Sports—Basket X-country Soccer Swim Tennis Track. B: Baseball Football Golf. G: Cheer Softball Volley.

Selective adm: 112/yr. Appl fee: $75. Appl due: Rolling. Applied: 194. Accepted: 78%. Yield: 74%. **Tests** CEEB CTP_4 ISEE SSAT.

Enr 946. B 476. G 470. Elem 663. Sec 283. Wh 86%. Latino 4%. Blk 3%. Asian 3%. Other 4%. Avg class size: 15. Stud/fac: 12:1. **Fac 97.** M 35/F 62. FT 83/PT 14. Wh 87%. Latino 8%. Blk 2%. Asian 1%. Other 2%. Adv deg: 54%.

Grad '09—55. Col—55. (FL St 5, Davidson 3, U of CO-Boulder 3, Harvard 2, SMU 2, U of Miami 2). **Avg SAT:** CR 610. M 604. W 596. Avg ACT: 29. **Col couns:** 3. Alum donors: 8%.

Tui '11-'12: Day $12,150-18,120 (+$500). **Aid:** Need 49 ($596,493).

Summer: Enrich Rec. Theater. Tui Day $300-3000. 2-6 wks.

Endow $1,492,000. Plant val $32,878,000. Acres 28. Bldgs 40. Class rms 73. Lib 24,500 vols. Sci labs 4. Lang labs 3. Theaters 2. Art studios 4. Music studios 3. Dance studios 1. Gyms 1. Fields 4. Courts 3. Comp labs 8.

Est 1923. Nonprofit. Sem (Aug-May). **Assoc** CLS SACS.

The oldest independent school in the Tampa Bay area, the school occupies a 28-acre campus in northeast St. Petersburg. Shorecrest conducts a college preparatory program with a broad range of honors and Advanced Placement courses.

A strong athletic program offers a full complement of sports for boys and girls. Fine arts enrichment at the school introduces students to various musical forms and theatrical performances. Boys and girls in the upper division (grades 9-12) satisfy a 20-hour community service requirement each year, and all pupils also take part in an annual service week.

SARASOTA, FL. (43 mi. S of Tampa, FL) Urban. Pop: 52,715. Alt: 27 ft.

OUT-OF-DOOR ACADEMY
Day — Coed Gr PS (Age 4)-12

Sarasota, FL 34240. 5950 Deer Dr. Tel: 941-349-3223. Fax: 941-907-1251.
Other locations: 444 Reid St, Sarasota 34242.
  www.oda.edu   E-mail: lmurphy@oda.edu
David V. Mahler, Head (2004). BA, Wesleyan Univ, MEd, Univ of Virginia. **Laura Murphy, Adm.**
  Col Prep. AP (122 exams taken, 79% 3+)—Eng Fr Lat Span Calc Stats Comp_Sci Bio
    Chem Physics Eur_Hist US_Hist US_Govt & Pol Studio_Art Music_Theory. **Feat**—
    Marine_Bio/Sci Econ Govt Drama Music. **Supp**—Dev_Read Rem_Math Rem_Read
    Rev Tut.
  Sports—Basket X-country Golf Sail Soccer Swim Tennis Track. B: Baseball Football. G:
    Cheer Softball Volley.
  Selective adm: 120/yr. Appl fee: $100. Appl due: Feb. Accepted: 80%. **Tests** CTP_4
    SSAT.
  Enr 599. B 308. G 291. Elem 408. Sec 191. Wh 95%. Latino 2%. Blk 1%. Asian 2%. Avg
    class size: 16. Stud/fac: 11:1. **Fac 64.** Wh 98%. Latino 1%. Blk 1%. Adv deg: 45%.
  Grad '10—54. Col—54. (U of Miami, Boston Col, Vanderbilt, SMU, Skidmore, Rollins).
    Avg SAT: CR/M/W 1789. Avg ACT: 26. **Col couns:** 2.
  Tui '11-'12: Day $13,000-18,500 (+$180-500). **Aid:** Need 69 ($452,000).
  Endow $4,400,000. Plant val $25,000,000. Bldgs 16. Class rms 61. 2 Libs 20,000 vols.
    Auds 1. Theaters 1. Art studios 4. Music studios 2. Gyms 1. Fields 2. Comp labs 5.
  Est 1924. Nonprofit. (Aug-June). **Assoc** CLS.

Founded as an elementary school on Siesta Key by Fanneal Harrison, ODA was purchased by a parent group and was incorporated as a not-for-profit corporation in 1977. The school opened a high school division in 1996 and now offers a full pre-K-12 program to students in Manatee, Sarasota and Charlotte counties.

The academy provides college preparatory instruction in the traditional disciplines, as well as a broad selection of enrichment classes. Small class size throughout the school results in individual attention. The lower school curriculum (grades pre-K-6) emphasizes the fundamentals of reading, language arts, mathematics, science and social studies. Children also receive instruction in marine science, computers, library skills, art, music and physical education.

While continuing to stress the traditional subject areas, the upper school program (grades 7-12) also includes honors and Advanced Placement course work. The use of technology is an important part of the curriculum at all grade levels. Both lower and upper school students may participate in after-school athletics. Boys and girls perform 20 hours of required community service each year.

The lower school occupies the original campus on Siesta Key, while the upper school is situated on the mainland at Lakewood Ranch on Deer Drive.   **See Also Pages 142-3**

STUART, FL. (98 mi. N of Miami, FL) Suburban. Pop: 14,633. Alt: 14 ft.

THE PINE SCHOOL
Day — Coed Gr PS (Age 3)-12

Stuart, FL 34996. 1300 E 10th St. Tel: 772-283-1222. Fax: 772-220-9149.
Other locations: 12350 SE Federal Hwy, Hobe Sound 33455.
  www.thepineschool.org   E-mail: blettengarver@thepineschool.org
Phyllis B. Parker, Int Head. Beth Lettengarver, Adm.

Col Prep. AP—Eng Bio Environ_Sci US_Hist World_Hist. **Feat**—Chin Span Comp_Sci Robotics Asian_Stud Studio_Art Music Dance. **Supp**—Tut.
Sports—Basket X-country Golf Lacrosse Soccer Swim Tennis. G: Softball Volley. **Activities:** 25.
Somewhat selective adm: 69/yr. Appl fee: $75. Appl due: Rolling. Accepted: 95%. **Tests** CTP_4 SSAT.
Enr 465. Wh 94%. Latino 1%. Blk 2%. Asian 3%. Avg class size: 12. Stud/fac: 9:1. Uniform. **Fac 71.** M 17/F 54. FT 71. Wh 88%. Latino 4%. Blk 4%. Asian 4%. Adv deg: 64%.
Grad '10—21. Col—21. Alum donors: 30%.
Tui '11-'12: Day $10,500-18,800 (+$2775-3835). **Aid:** Merit 1 ($20,000). Need 89 ($1,200,000).
Summer: Acad Enrich Rec. Tui $180/wk. 5 wks.
Endow $850,000. Plant val $33,000,000. Acres 154. Bldgs 9. Class rms 38. Lib 24,000 vols. Sci labs 4. Lang labs 2. Auds 1. Art studios 3. Music studios 3. Gyms 2. Fields 5. Courts 4. Comp labs 2. Laptop prgm Gr 9-12.
Est 1969. Nonprofit. Tri (Aug-May). **Assoc** SACS.

Founded as the Pine School, this institution changed its name to Saint Michael's Independent School in 1994, when the school ended its affiliation with the Episcopal Church. It again assumed the Pine School name in July 2006. With its lower school campus located on an 11-acre tract in the heart of Stuart, the school serves Martin, Palm Beach and St. Lucie counties.

The college preparatory curriculum is reinforced by individualized instruction and small classes. Early learning through grade 5 classes are self-contained, while grade 6 and up are departmentalized. Specialists in Spanish, Chinese, art, music, computers and physical education meet with students several times a week. Boys and girls choose from an array of Advanced Placement courses in the upper grades. Students perform 120 hours of required community service in grades 9-12.

The middle and upper schools (grades 7-12) are located at a separate, 143-acre campus in Hobe Sound.

TALLAHASSEE, FL. (157 mi. W of Jacksonville, FL) Urban. Pop: 150,624. Alt: 190 ft.

MACLAY SCHOOL
Day — Coed Gr PS (Age 3)-12

Tallahassee, FL 32312. 3737 N Meridian Rd. Tel: 850-893-2138. Fax: 850-893-7434.
www.maclay.org   E-mail: chgallagh@maclay.org
William W. Jablon, Pres (1976). BA, Boston College, MS, Florida State Univ. **Michael Obrecht, Adm.**

Col Prep. AP (exams req'd; 354 taken, 86% 3+)—Eng Fr Lat Span Calc Stats Comp_Sci Bio Chem Environ_Sci Physics Eur_Hist US_Hist World_Hist Econ Psych US_Govt & Pol Studio_Art. **Feat**—Humanities Marine_Bio/Sci Journ Driver_Ed. **Supp**—Makeup Rem_Math Rem_Read.
Sports—Basket Crew X-country Golf Soccer Tennis Track Weightlifting. B: Baseball Football Lacrosse. G: Softball Volley. **Activities:** 36.
Selective adm: 159/yr. Appl fee: $50. Appl due: Rolling. Applied: 198. Accepted: 80%.
Enr 910. B 471. G 439. Elem 555. Sec 355. Wh 82%. Latino 3%. Blk 7%. Asian 3%. Other 5%. Avg class size: 17. **Fac 102.** M 30/F 72. FT 92/PT 10. Wh 95%. Latino 2%. Blk 3%. Adv deg: 50%.
Grad '11—88. Col—87. (FL St 15, U of FL 11, Tallahassee CC 6, U of N FL 6, Auburn 4, U of WA 3). Athl schol 1. **Avg SAT:** CR 587. M 592. W 593. Avg ACT: 26. **Col couns:** 2. Alum donors: 3%.
Tui '12-'13: Day $9125-10,250 (+$250). **Aid:** Need 76 ($430,080).
Summer (enr 136): Acad Enrich. 3-6 wks.

Endow $2,800,000. Plant val $14,472,000. Acres 100. Bldgs 13 (100% ADA). Class rms 80. Lib 26,500 vols. Sci labs 7. Theaters 1. Art studios 3. Music studios 2. Gyms 2. Fields 5. Courts 12. Pools 1. Tracks 1. Comp labs 3. Comp/stud: 1:3. **Est 1968.** Nonprofit. Sem (Aug-May). **Assoc** CLS SACS.

Maclay offers a college preparatory curriculum on a 100-acre, wooded campus that includes independent facilities for prekindergarten, lower, middle and upper school divisions.

The lower school program emphasizes the development of the learning skills that will be necessary for future academic success. Age-appropriate field trips, environmental responsibility education and foreign language instruction begin in prekindergarten. Formal college counseling commences in grade 8, and Maclay's focus on college preparation is reflected by an array of Advanced Placement course options for older students. Technology plays an important role at all grade levels. Academic and civic clubs, extensive athletic offerings, after-school and summer programming, and study abroad opportunities are also available.

TAMPA, FL. Urban. Pop: 303,447. Alt: 57 ft.

BERKELEY PREPARATORY SCHOOL
Day — Coed Gr PS (Age 4)-12

Tampa, FL 33615. 4811 Kelly Rd. Tel: 813-885-1673. Fax: 813-886-6933.
www.berkeleyprep.org   E-mail: info@berkeleyprep.org
Joseph W. Seivold, Head (2011). BA, Univ of North Carolina-Chapel Hill, EdS, St Mary's Univ of Minnesota. **Janie McIlvaine, Adm.**

Col Prep. AP (exams req'd; 704 taken, 80% 3+)—Eng Chin Fr Lat Span Calc Stats Comp_Sci Bio Chem Environ_Sci Physics Eur_Hist US_Hist Comp_Govt & Pol Econ Psych US_Govt & Pol. **Elem math**—Everyday Math. **Feat**—Creative_Writing Mythology Anat & Physiol Astron Genetics Geol Microbio Meteorology Organic_ Chem Robotics Comp_Animation African_Hist 20th-Century_Asia World_Relig Film Studio_Art Video_Production Drama Band Chorus Music_Theory Orchestra Dance Speech. **Supp**—Tut.

Sports—Basket Crew X-country Golf Lacrosse Soccer Swim Tennis Track Volley. B: Baseball Football Wrestling. G: Softball. **Activities:** 70.

Selective adm: 198/yr. Appl fee: $50. Appl due: Jan. **Tests** IQ SSAT.

Enr 1250. Elem 700. Sec 550. Avg class size: 18. Stud/fac: 8:1. **Fac 176.** Adv deg: 47%.

Grad '11—144. Col—144. (U of FL 19, FL St 7, Duke 5, Wake Forest 5, Boston Col 5, U of MI 4). **Avg SAT:** CR 629. M 642. W 642. Avg ACT: 28.3. **Col couns:** 3.

Tui '11-'12: Day $16,320-19,420.

Summer (enr 2000): Acad Enrich Rev Rec. Arts. Sports. 10 wks.

Acres 80. Bldgs 12. Class rms 62. 2 Libs 19,000 vols. Sci labs 8. Lang labs 1. Auds 1. Theaters 1. Art studios 2. Music studios 2. Dance studios 1. Arts ctrs 1. Gyms 2. Fields 3. Tennis courts 7. Pools 1. Tracks 1. Weight rms 1. Student ctrs 1. Laptop prgm Gr 4-12.

Est 1960. Nonprofit. Episcopal. Quar (Aug-June). **Assoc** CLS SACS.

Located on an 80-acre, suburban site that includes separate lower, middle and upper division administrative and teaching facilities, Berkeley serves the Tampa Bay area. The school immerses all students in the core subjects of math, English, science, history and foreign language. Pupils begin taking Spanish, athletics, drama, music and visual arts in prekindergarten, while sixth graders participate in double sessions of English.

The flexible program in the upper division (grades 9-12) allows qualified students to begin Advanced Placement course work as early as sophomore year, and Berkeley also offers a selection of honors courses and advanced topics. Students in grades 4-12 purchase laptop computers for use in class and at home. Upper division pupils perform compulsory community service: 22 hours per year in grades 9-11, 10 hours in grade 12.

Berkeley's international studies office sponsors educational trips abroad and arranges student exchanges with private schools in Europe and Australia during spring and summer breaks. A full-year study abroad program in Barcelona, Spain, is an option for sophomores and juniors.

ST. MARY'S EPISCOPAL DAY SCHOOL
Day — Coed Gr PS (Age 4)-8

Tampa, FL 33629. 2101 S Hubert Ave. Tel: 813-258-5508. Fax: 813-258-5603.
www.smeds.org   E-mail: info@smeds.org
Scott D. Laird, Head (1996). BS, West Chester Univ of Pennsylvania, MEd, MA, Florida Atlantic Univ. **Kathleen Lopez, Adm.**
  Pre-Prep. Gen Acad. Feat—Lat Span Computers Relig Fine_Arts Video_Production Drama Public_Speak Study_Skills. **Supp**—Dev_Read Rev Tut.
  Sports—Basket X-country Lacrosse Soccer Tennis Track. B: Baseball. G: Cheer Softball Volley.
  Selective adm (Gr PS-7): 62/yr. Appl fee: $50. Appl due: Rolling. Applied: 118. Accepted: 62%. Yield: 85%.
  Enr 443. B 224. G 219. Wh 90%. Latino 4%. Blk 3%. Asian 1%. Other 2%. Avg class size: 22. Stud/fac: 9:1. Uniform. **Fac 51.** M 7/F 44. FT 46/PT 5. Wh 96%. Latino 4%. Adv deg: 50%.
  Grad '11—44. Prep—23. (Jesuit HS-FL 13, Acad of the Holy Names 5, Berkeley Prep 3, Tampa Prep 2). Alum donors: 2%.
  Tui '12-'13: Day $11,450 (+$1000). **Aid:** Need 54 ($302,800).
  Summer: Enrich Rev Rec. Tui Day $150/wk. 4 wks.
  Endow $969,000. Plant val $5,000,000. Acres 8. Bldgs 3 (100% ADA). Class rms 30. Lib 16,000 vols. Sci labs 2. Auds 1. Theaters 1. Art studios 1. Music studios 1. Gyms 1. Fields 1. Courts 2. Comp labs 2. Comp/stud: 1:2.
  Est 1953. Nonprofit. Episcopal. (Aug-May).

Located on an eight-acre campus, St. Mary's was founded by a group of parents who recognized the need for a church-affiliated school with a strong academic environment in the South Tampa area. Children are assigned to homerooms with consideration to the mix of personalities, but are placed in academic sections for mathematics and foreign language according to ability and achievement. Parents may choose a half- or full-day prekindergarten program. All students study Spanish through grade 5, Latin in grade 6, and either language in grades 7 and 8. Technology projects are integrated into the curriculum at all levels, and each classroom is equipped with at least four computers and an interactive whiteboard. Middle school students produce a morning news show in the video production studio.

Schoolwide chapel services are held twice weekly, and boys and girls attend religion courses once a week. Each grade engages in community service outreach with a specific group throughout the year. Educational and recreational field trips to local museums, theaters and attractions commence in preschool, and students in grade 8 travel to Washington, DC.

See Also Page 116

TAMPA PREPARATORY SCHOOL
Day — Coed Gr 6-12

Tampa, FL 33606. 727 W Cass St. Tel: 813-251-8481. Fax: 813-254-2106.
www.tampaprep.org   E-mail: admissions@tampaprep.org
Kevin M. Plummer, Head (2007). BA, Colby College, MA, Columbia Univ. **W. Dennis Facciolo, Adm.**
  Col Prep. AP (311 exams taken, 82% 3+)—Eng Fr Lat Span Calc Stats Comp_Sci Bio Chem Environ_Sci Physics Eur_Hist US_Hist World_Hist Econ US_Govt & Pol Art_Hist Studio_Art Music_Theory. **Feat**—Creative_Writing Anat Astron Bioethics Genetics Marine_Bio/Sci Sports_Med Comp_Design African-Amer_Hist Anthro

Psych Gender_Stud World_Relig Ceramics Fine_Arts Photog Video_Production
Drama Theater_Arts Dance. **Supp**—Rev Tut.
Sports—Basket Bowl Crew X-country Golf Sail Soccer Swim Tennis Track. B: Baseball
Lacrosse Wrestling. G: Softball Volley. **Activities:** 28.
Selective adm: 160/yr. Appl fee: $75. Appl due: Feb. **Tests** CEEB CTP_4 ISEE SSAT.
Enr 600. Elem 180. Sec 420. Wh 73%. Latino 9%. Blk 10%. Asian 8%. Avg class size:
18. **Fac 54.** M 23/F 31. FT 45/PT 9. Wh 92%. Latino 2%. Blk 4%. Native Am 2%. Adv
deg: 46%.
Grad '09—130. Col—130. (U of Central FL 11, FL St 10, U of FL 7, U of S FL 5, Emory
4, Vanderbilt 3). Athl schol 2. **Avg SAT:** CR 570. M 570. W 560. Avg ACT: 26. **Col
couns:** 2.
Tui '12-'13: Day $17,845-18,500 (+$2000). **Aid:** Merit 6 ($100,545). Need 79
($879,010).
Summer: Acad Enrich Rev Rec. Sports. Tui Day $975-1900. 3-6 wks.
Endow $1,925,000. Plant val $21,000,000. Acres 12. Bldgs 4. Lib 9000 vols. Sci labs 6.
Lang labs 1. Photog labs 1. Theaters 1. Art studios 4. Music studios 2. Dance studios
1. Gyms 1. Fields 2. Courts 4. Field houses 1. Pools 1. Comp labs 4. Comp/stud:
1:2.
Est 1974. Nonprofit. Sem (Aug-June). **Assoc** CLS SACS.

Located in downtown Tampa, the school conducts a rigorous college preparatory curriculum
in which most upper school courses are taught at three levels: honors, advanced honors and
Advanced Placement. Middle schoolers develop an academic foundation through such classes
as writing, computer literacy, Latin, life sciences, world geography and algebra, while also
developing their learning and study skills. Upper school pupils fulfill requirements in English,
math, history, science and foreign language; course work in computers, the fine arts and physical education rounds out the curriculum.

VERO BEACH, FL. (84 mi. SE of Orlando, FL) Suburban. Pop: 17,705. Alt: 20 ft.

SAINT EDWARD'S SCHOOL
Day — Coed Gr PS (Age 4)-12

Vero Beach, FL 32963. 1895 Saint Edward's Dr. Tel: 772-231-4136. Fax: 772-231-2427.
www.steds.org   E-mail: panderson@steds.org
Michael J. Mersky, Head (2009). BS, Lock Haven Univ, MS, St Joseph's Univ. **Peggy
Anderson, Adm.**
Col Prep. AP (exams req'd; 233 taken, 76% 3+)—Eng Chin Span Calc Stats Comp_
Sci Bio Chem Physics Eur_Hist US_Hist World_Hist Econ Human_Geog US_Govt &
Pol Music_Theory. **Elem math**—Singapore Math. **Feat**—Anat & Physiol Marine_Bio/
Sci Psych Sociol Ethics Graphic_Arts Studio_Art Theater_Arts Chorus Music Journ.
Supp—ESL Tut. **Dual enr:** Indian River St.
Sports—Basket Crew X-country Golf Lacrosse Soccer Swim Tennis Track Weightlifting.
B: Baseball Football. G: Cheer Volley.
Somewhat selective adm: 61/yr. Appl fee: $50. Appl due: Feb. Applied: 124. Accepted:
87%. Yield: 56%. **Tests** SSAT.
Enr 500. Elem 276. Sec 224. Wh 92%. Latino 2%. Blk 2%. Asian 4%. Avg class size:
13. Stud/fac: 8:1. Formal. **Fac 59.** Wh 90%. Latino 2%. Blk 1%. Asian 3%. Other 4%.
Adv deg: 54%.
Grad '11—62. Col—62. (U of Miami 6, U of FL 5, FL St 4, NYU 3, Elon 2, Geo Wash
2). **Mid 50% SAT:** CR 540-660. M 560-660. W 540-650. Mid 50% ACT: 24-29. **Col
couns:** 2. Alum donors: 5%.
Tui '12-'13: Day $18,200-24,900 (+$100-3000). **Aid:** Need 122 ($1,500,000).
Endow $3,965,000. Plant val $35,400,000. Acres 28. Bldgs 16 (100% ADA). Class rms
65. 2 Libs 26,000 vols. Sci labs 7. Theaters 1. Art studios 3. Music studios 3. Gyms 2.
Fields 5. Courts 2. Pools 1. Comp labs 1. Comp/stud: 1:1 Laptop prgm Gr 6-12.

Est 1965. Nonprofit. Episcopal (15% practice). Quar (Aug-June). **Assoc** CLS.

This traditional school was founded to fill a community need for sound college preparation. The curriculum emphasizes core subjects, and considerable interest is shown in athletics, dramatics, art, music and student government. Accelerated students may gain entrance into a rigorous two-year program that combines honors and Advanced Placement course work with special seminars and independent research.

Boys and girls complete 80 hours of required community service prior to graduation. A limited number of international pupils board with host families.

WINTER PARK, FL. (7 mi. NNE of Orlando, FL) Suburban. Pop: 24,090. Alt: 94 ft.

TRINITY PREPARATORY SCHOOL
Day — Coed Gr 6-12

Winter Park, FL 32792. 5700 Trinity Prep Ln. Tel: 407-671-4140. Fax: 407-671-6935.
www.trinityprep.org   E-mail: inquire@trinityprep.org

Craig S. Maughan, Head (1993). BA, Washington Univ, MSPH, Univ of North Carolina-Chapel Hill, MBA, Univ of Kansas. **Sherryn Hay, Adm.**

   Col Prep. AP (exams req'd; 547 taken, 88% 3+)—Eng Fr Lat Span Calc Stats Comp_ Sci Bio Chem Environ_Sci Physics US_Hist World_Hist Econ Psych US_Govt & Pol Studio_Art Music_Theory. **Feat**—Creative_Writing Humanities Playwriting Anat & Physiol Bible Comp_Relig Ethics Photog Sculpt Music Finance Journ Speech. **Supp**—Tut. Outdoor ed. **Dual enr:** U of Central FL.

   Sports—Basket Bowl X-country Golf Lacrosse Soccer Swim Tennis Track Weightlifting. B: Baseball Football. G: Softball Volley. **Activities:** 40.

   Selective adm (Gr 6-11): 168/yr. Usual entry: 6, 7 & 9. Appl fee: $50. Appl due: Jan. Applied: 300. Accepted: 65%. Yield: 82%. **Tests** CTP_4 ISEE SSAT TOEFL.

   Enr 834. B 442. G 392. Elem 392. Sec 442. Wh 79%. Latino 5%. Blk 4%. Asian 11%. Other 1%. Avg class size: 17. Stud/fac: 12:1. Casual. **Fac 78.** M 30/F 48. FT 74/PT 4. Wh 89%. Latino 9%. Blk 1%. Asian 1%. Adv deg: 66%.

   Grad '11—117. Col—117. (FL St, U of FL, U of Central FL, Auburn, Yale, Stanford). Athl schol 13. **Mid 50% SAT:** CR 570-700. M 590-690. W 590-680. Mid 50% ACT: 26-30. **Col couns:** 3. Alum donors: 8%.

   Tui '11-'12: Day $16,800 (+$1435-1860). **Aid:** Need 157 ($1,650,000).

   Summer: Acad Enrich Rev Rem Rec. 7 wks.

   Endow $7,300,000. Plant val $27,000,000. Acres 100. Bldgs 12. Class rms 54. Lib 10,000 vols. Sci labs 7. Lang labs 1. Auds 1. Theaters 1. Art studios 3. Music studios 2. Gyms 2. Fields 5. Tennis courts 7. Pools 1. Comp labs 3. Comp/stud: 1:2.5.

   Est 1966. Nonprofit. Episcopal (11% practice). Sem (Aug-June). **Assoc** CLS.

This independent Episcopal school was founded by a group of central Florida community leaders. The traditional liberal arts curriculum includes Advanced Placement and honors courses. Special-help sessions four days per week after school allow teachers to aid those students who need extra guidance or explanation in a particular discipline.

Additional opportunities for enrichment are offered through participation in academic, service and recreational activities. The school occupies a 100-acre campus bordered by lakes and woods.

GEORGIA

ATLANTA, GA. Urban. Pop: 416,474. Alt: 1032 ft. Area also includes College Park.

ATLANTA INTERNATIONAL SCHOOL
Day — Coed Gr PS (Age 4)-12
Atlanta, GA 30305. 2890 N Fulton Dr. Tel: 404-841-3840. Fax: 404-841-3873.
www.aischool.org   E-mail: info@aischool.org
Kevin Glass, Head (2009). BSc, Univ of Manchester (England), MA, Framingham State College. **Reid Mizell, Adm.**
- **Col Prep. IB Diploma. IB PYP. IB MYP. Bilingual (Fr Ger Span). Feat**—Chin Fr Ger Lat Span Comp_Sci Visual_Arts Theater_Arts Music. **Supp**—ESL Tut.
- **Sports**—Basket X-country Soccer Swim Tennis Ultimate_Frisbee. B: Golf. G: Volley. **Activities:** 8.
- **Selective adm:** 198/yr. Appl fee: $100. **Tests** SSAT.
- **Enr 1020.** B 455. G 565. Elem 723. Sec 297. Intl 50%. Avg class size: 16. **Fac 145.** M 35/F 110. Adv deg: 53%.
- **Grad '11—73. Col—72.** (GA Inst of Tech, Northeastern U, Wake Forest, Loyola U-LA, Cornell, MIT). **Avg SAT:** CR 650. M 627. **Mid 50% SAT:** CR 590-730. M 580-680. **Col couns:** 3.
- **Tui '11-'12: Day $18,092-20,640** (+$3000).
- **Summer:** Acad Enrich Rec. Tui Day $300-1150. 1-4 wks.
- Endow $5,004,000. Plant val $6,454,000. Acres 14. Bldgs 4 (100% ADA). Class rms 78. Lib 20,000 vols. Sci labs 6. Lang labs 1. Auds 1. Theaters 1. Art studios 3. Music studios 7. Dance studios 1. Gyms 2. Fields 1. Comp labs 3. Comp/stud: 1:3.6 (1:1 Laptop prgm Gr 6-7).
- **Est 1985.** Nonprofit. Sem (Aug-June). **Assoc** SACS.

Founded by a group of parents, international educators and members of the local business community, AIS is an International Baccalaureate World School that offers all three components of the IB curriculum and serves both American and international pupils. Students enroll from approximately 50 countries, while faculty and staff represent more than 30 nations.

Primary-age children (grades pre-K-5) begin the IB Program by studying core subjects in two languages: English and either French, German or Spanish. Secondary school pupils may study a third or fourth language beginning in grade 6. Students complete the secondary curriculum by selecting six core subjects and engaging in three learning opportunities: Theory of Knowledge; an extended essay; and Creativity, Action and Service. Graduates receive both the IB Diploma and the AIS diploma.

BRANDON HALL SCHOOL
Bdg — Coed Gr 7-PG; Day — Coed 6-PG
Atlanta, GA 30350. 1701 Brandon Hall Dr. Tel: 770-394-8177. Fax: 770-804-8821.
www.brandonhall.org   E-mail: admissions@brandonhall.org
John L. Singleton, Pres (2010). BS, MA, Gardner-Webb College, EdD, Univ of Phoenix. **Jeff Holloway, Adm.**
- **Col Prep. Gen Acad. LD. Underachiever. AP**—Eng Span Calc Chem Physics. **Feat**—Comp_Sci Fine_Arts Studio_Art Drama Music SAT_Prep. **Supp**—Dev_Read ESL Makeup Rem_Math Rem_Read Rev Tut. Sat classes.
- **Sports (req'd)**—Basket X-country Golf Soccer Tennis Track. B: Baseball Wrestling. G: Volley.
- **Somewhat selective adm:** 27/yr. Bdg 13. Day 14. Appl fee: $75. Appl due: Rolling.

Accepted: 85%. Yield: 90%.
Enr 130. Wh 73%. Latino 1%. Blk 12%. Asian 14%. Intl 20%. Stud/fac: 3:1. Uniform.
Fac 31. M 20/F 11. FT 31. Wh 85%. Latino 2%. Blk 5%. Other 8%. Adv deg: 35%. In dorms 1.
Grad '09—26. Col—26. (GA Southern, GA Inst of Tech, Limestone, N GA Col & State U, Seton Hall, Embry-Riddle).
Tui '12-'13: Bdg $49,995. Day $26,095. Intl Bdg $54,995 (+$4825). **Aid:** Need 9 ($155,800).
Summer (enr 35): Acad Enrich Rev Rem. Tui Bdg $2500-7500. Tui Day $1250-3750. 2-6 wks.
Endow $250,000. Plant val $9,500,000. Acres 26. Bldgs 10. Dorms 1. Dorm rms 36. Class rms 20. Lib 5000 vols. Sci labs 3. Lang labs 1. Auds 1. Theaters 1. Gyms 1. Fields 1. Courts 2. Comp labs 2. Comp/stud: 1:1 Laptop prgm Gr 6-12.
Est 1959. Nonprofit. Sem (Aug-May). **Assoc** SACS.

Brandon Hall stresses college preparatory skills, independent study habits and personal self-discipline for the underachiever and for other bright students with different learning styles. Learning disabilities supported include dyslexia, ADHD, dyscalculia, dysgraphia and expressive language disorders. Reconstruction of basic skills and accelerated course work are elements of the program. All seniors receive SAT preparation. Class size varies from one-on-one instruction (offered in all courses) to small groups of four to eight. All instructors provide comprehensive E-mail updates each week.

THE HEISKELL SCHOOL
Day — Coed Gr PS (Age 2)-8

Atlanta, GA 30305. 3260 Northside Dr. Tel: 404-262-2233. Fax: 404-262-2575.
www.heiskell.net E-mail: writeus@heiskell.net
Cyndie Heiskell, Dir (2001). BA, College of William and Mary, MA, Georgia State Univ.
Virginia G. Peebles, Adm.
Pre-Prep. Feat—Lat Span Computers Bible Studio_Art Music Ballet.
Sports—Basket X-country Track. G: Cheer Volley.
Selective adm: 100/yr. Appl fee: $75. Appl due: Rolling. **Tests** IQ SSAT.
Enr 360. Wh 80%. Blk 18%. Other 2%. Intl 5%. Avg class size: 15. Uniform. **Fac 30.**
Grad '09—10. Prep—10.
Tui '12-'13: Day $7825-13,200 (+$125-700). **Aid:** Need 40 ($150,000).
Plant val $1,750,000. Bldgs 2. Class rms 34. Lib 12,000 vols. Sci labs 1. Media labs 1. Art studios 1. Gyms 1. Fields 1. Tennis courts 1. Tracks 1. Playgrounds 2. Comp labs 1.
Est 1949. Inc. Nondenom Christian. Quar (Aug-June). **Assoc** SACS.

Founded as a nursery school and kindergarten by Mrs. James M. Heiskell, this nondenominational Christian school added an elementary division in 1970. Heiskell, located in the Buckhead section of northwest Atlanta, stresses the development of reading, mathematical and motor skills. A strong emphasis is placed on phonetics in the preschool.

Heiskell comprises three sections: preschool (age 2 through kindergarten), elementary (grades 1-5) and junior high (grades 6-8). Students take courses in art, music, computer and Bible, in addition to the basic disciplines.

Pupils join in worship services each week and participate in community service programs throughout the year. Heiskell schedules frequent field trips to local places of interest.

See Also Page 135

THE LOVETT SCHOOL
Day — Coed Gr K-12

Atlanta, GA 30327. 4075 Paces Ferry Rd NW. Tel: 404-262-3032. Fax: 404-261-1967.
www.lovett.org E-mail: admissions@lovett.org

William S. Peebles IV, Head (2003). AB, Princeton Univ, MBA, Univ of Virginia. **Debbie Lange, Adm.**
  Col Prep. AP (exams req'd; 416 taken, 91% 3+)—Eng Chin Fr Lat Span Calc Stats Comp_Sci Bio Chem Environ_Sci Physics Eur_Hist US_Hist US_Govt & Pol Art_Hist Music_Theory. **Elem math**—Everyday Math. **Feat**—Screenwriting Linear_Algebra Multivariable_Calc Anat Botany Genetics Marine_Bio/Sci Zoology Organic_Chem Comp_Design Robotics Amer_Stud African_Stud Asian_Stud Lat-Amer_Stud Philos Relig Film Photog Studio_Art Video_Production Architect_Design Drama Theater_ Arts Music Debate Journ.
  Sports—Basket X-country Golf Lacrosse Soccer Swim Tennis Track. B: Baseball Football Wrestling. G: Cheer Gymnastics Softball Volley. **Activities:** 31.
  Selective adm (Gr K-11): 215/yr. Usual entry: K, 5, 6 & 9. Appl fee: $75. Appl due: Feb. Applied: 751. Accepted: 29%. Yield: 61%. **Tests** SSAT.
  Enr 1585. B 765. G 820. Elem 987. Sec 598. Wh 82%. Latino 1%. Blk 9%. Asian 5%. Other 3%. Avg class size: 15. Stud/fac: 9:1. Uniform. **Fac 155.** M 54/F 101. FT 146/PT 9. Adv deg: 63%.
  Grad '11—139. Col—139. (U of GA 25, GA Inst of Tech 7, U of AL-Tuscaloosa 6, Auburn 4, Samford 4, TX Christian 4). **Mid 50% SAT:** CR 570-690. M 570-700. W 580-680. Mid 50% ACT: 25-30. **Col couns:** 3. Alum donors: 20%.
  Tui '12-'13: Day $19,210-22,740 (+$230-1030). **Aid:** Need ($2,600,000).
  Summer (enr 900): Acad Enrich Rev Rem Rec. 1-3 wks.
  Endow $57,300,000. Plant val $103,000,000. Acres 100. Bldgs 18. Class rms 91. 2 Libs 56,000 vols. Sci labs 9. Auds 1. Theaters 2. Art studios 9. Music studios 3. Drama studios 1. Gyms 3. Fields 7. Courts 10. Pools 1. Comp labs 8. Comp/stud: 1:2 (1:1 Laptop prgm Gr 4-9).
  Est 1926. Nonprofit. Sem (Aug-May). **Assoc** CLS SACS.

Mrs. Eva Edwards Lovett founded this school and remained head until 1954. During the next eight years, the school expanded to include a kindergarten and 12 grades. Since 1963, Lovett has been an independent school governed by a board of trustees.

Bordered by the Chattahoochee River, this college preparatory school is located on 100 wooded acres in northwest Atlanta. In addition to a selection of honors and Advanced Placement courses, Lovett's curriculum includes a varied fine arts program. Students in need of additional help receive one-on-one or small-group instruction through the academic resource center. The school concerns itself with the development of all aspects of the child.

Lovett schedules field trips and provides travel opportunities during spring and summer breaks to such locations as China, South Africa, France and Italy. Siempre Verde, the school's research station in Ecuador, specializes in the study of cloud forest ecology; groups of students visit Siempre Verde during the school year and over the summer. **See Also Page 72**

MARIST SCHOOL
Day — Coed Gr 7-12
Atlanta, GA 30319. 3790 Ashford-Dunwoody Rd NE. Tel: 770-457-7201.
  Fax: 770-457-8402.
  www.marist.com E-mail: admissions@marist.com
Rev. John H. Harhager, SM, Pres (2008). BA, American Univ, MA, Catholic Univ of America. **Rev. Joel M. Konzen, SM, Prin.** BA, St Meinrad College, MDiv, Notre Dame Seminary, MA, MAEd, Catholic Univ of America. **James G. Byrne, Adm.**
  Col Prep. AP (exams req'd; 804 taken, 95% 3+)—Eng Fr Ger Lat Span Calc Stats Comp_Sci Bio Chem Physics Eur_Hist US_Hist World_Hist Econ US_Govt & Pol Art_Hist Studio_Art Music_Theory. **Feat**—Creative_Writing Fantasy_Lit Southern_ Lit Chin Anat & Physiol Astron Forensic_Sci Geol Entomology Ornithology Holocaust Middle_Eastern_Hist Relig World_Relig Ceramics Fine_Arts Photog Drama Band Chorus Accounting Journ. **Supp**—Tut. Outdoor ed.
  Sports—Basket X-country Golf Lacrosse Soccer Swim Tennis Track. B: Baseball Football Wrestling. G: Cheer Softball Volley. **Activities:** 58.
  Selective adm: 204/yr. Usual entry: 7 & 9. Appl fee: $75. Appl due: Feb. Applied: 538.

Accepted: 46%. Yield: 82%. **Tests** SSAT.
Enr 1076. B 544. G 532. Wh 83%. Latino 5%. Blk 5%. Asian 3%. Other 4%. Avg class size: 18. Stud/fac: 11:1. Uniform. **Fac 95.** M 51/F 44. FT 92/PT 3. Wh 89%. Latino 1%. Blk 6%. Asian 3%. Other 1%. Adv deg: 74%.
Grad '11—182. Col—181. (U of GA 29, GA Inst of Tech 21, Auburn 10, Notre Dame 6, U of AL-Tuscaloosa 6, GA Southern 5). Athl schol 26. **Mid 50% SAT:** CR 570-680. M 580-680. W 580-670. Mid 50% ACT: 26-30. **Col couns:** 3. Alum donors: 22%.
Tui '12-'13: Day $16,300 (+$1000). **Aid:** Need 175 ($1,650,000).
Summer (enr 170): Acad Enrich. Tui Day $50/wk. 2 wks.
Endow $5,500,000. Plant val $38,000,000. Acres 77. Bldgs 18 (11% ADA). Class rms 50. Lib 22,000 vols. Chapels 1. Sci labs 8. Auds 1. Theaters 1. Art studios 2. Music studios 2. Dance studios 1. Gyms 3. Fields 7. Tennis courts 4. Pools 1. Tracks 1. Stadiums 1. Comp labs 3. Comp/stud: 1:3.
Est 1901. Nonprofit. Roman Catholic (75% practice). Tri (Aug-June). **Assoc** SACS.

Marist School was founded by Rev. John E. Gunn, a member of the Society of Mary (the Marists). Known as Marist College until 1962, the school moved from downtown Atlanta to its present, 77-acre campus in northeast Atlanta to accommodate a growing enrollment.

The college preparatory curriculum offers yearlong courses in most major disciplines and a large variety of term courses, including drama, creative writing, statistics, geology, political science, accounting and driver education. A wide selection of Advanced Placement courses is also available. Graduates requirements include an introductory technology course, four years of religion and 50 cumulative hours of community service.

PACE ACADEMY
Day — Coed Gr K-12

Atlanta, GA 30327. 966 W Paces Ferry Rd NW. Tel: 404-262-1345. Fax: 404-240-9124.
www.paceacademy.org   E-mail: cstrowd@paceacademy.org
Frederick G. Assaf, Head (2005). BA, Johns Hopkins Univ, MEd, Univ of Virginia. **Claire Strowd, Upper & Middle Sch Adm; Jennifer McGurn, Lower Sch Adm.**
Col Prep. AP (exams req'd; 397 taken, 86% 3+)—Eng Fr Lat Span Calc Stats Comp_ Sci Bio Chem Environ_Sci Physics Eur_Hist US_Hist World_Hist Comp_Govt & Pol US_Govt & Pol Art_Hist Studio_Art Music_Theory. **Elem math**—Everyday Math. **Elem read**—Open Court. **Feat**—Creative_Writing Multivariable_Calc Ecol Molecular_Bio Vietnam_War Psych Comp_Relig Ethics Architect_Drawing Ceramics Drawing Photog Sculpt Theater_Arts Music Music_Hist Debate Public_Speak. **Supp**—Tut.
Sports—Basket X-country Golf Lacrosse Soccer Swim Tennis. B: Baseball Football Wrestling. G: Cheer Gymnastics Softball Track Volley. **Activities:** 20.
Selective adm (Gr K-11): 151/yr. Usual entry: K, 6 & 9. Appl fee: $75. Appl due: Feb. Applied: 731. Accepted: 29%. Yield: 72%. **Tests** SSAT.
Enr 1075. Wh 86%. Latino 1%. Blk 6%. Asian 3%. Other 4%. Avg class size: 15. Stud/fac: 9:1. **Fac 149.** M 53/F 96. FT 149. Wh 89%. Latino 3%. Blk 7%. Asian 1%. Adv deg: 61%.
Grad '11—86. Col—86. (U of GA 11, GA Inst of Tech 5, Tulane 5, Elon 4, Vanderbilt 4, U of PA 3). Athl schol 2. **Avg SAT:** CR 641. M 654. W 650. **Col couns:** 3. Alum donors: 22%.
Tui '12-'13: Day $19,600-22,570 (+$1000). **Aid:** Need 68 ($818,875).
Summer: Acad Enrich Rev Rec. Theater. Debate. 8 wks.
Endow $32,000,000. Plant val $41,000,000. Acres 27. Bldgs 8. Class rms 60. 2 Libs 20,000 vols. Sci labs 11. Lang labs 7. Auds 1. Theaters 1. Art studios 6. Music studios 3. Gyms 2. Fields 5. Courts 4. Pools 1. Comp labs 7. Comp/stud: 1:1.7.
Est 1958. Nonprofit. Sem (Aug-May). **Assoc** CLS SACS.

Located on a 31-acre tract in a residential section of northern Atlanta, Pace offers a curriculum with the flexibility to address students' varying needs, abilities and learning styles. In addition, the school maintains 23- and eight-acre off-site athletic properties.

Balancing challenge and support, the program features single-gender math groups in grade 3, accelerated classes in grade 4, in-depth writing workshops in grade 5, honors courses in grade 8, and both honors and Advanced Placement classes for upper schoolers. Computer use commences in the early grades and becomes increasingly prominent as the pupil progresses. After-school extra-help sessions provide daily opportunities for individual assistance.

The creative and performing arts play an important role in school life. Among Pace's course options in this area are painting, sculpture, drawing, photography, ceramics and printmaking, and students also choose from three singing groups and three instrumental music groups. In addition, the academy conducts a well-regarded drama program.

Community service requirements are as follows: five hours annually in grades 6-8 and 10 hours per year in grades 9-12. A range of sports and athletic opportunities that includes intramural games and interscholastic teams accommodates boys and girls of varying skill levels.

THE PAIDEIA SCHOOL

Day — Coed Gr PS (Age 3)-12

Atlanta, GA 30307. 1509 Ponce de Leon Ave. Tel: 404-377-3491. Fax: 404-377-0032.
www.paideiaschool.org E-mail: desimone.liz@paideiaschool.org
Paul F. Bianchi, Head (1971). AB, MAT, Harvard Univ. **Caroline Quillian Stubbs, Adm.**

Col Prep. AP (180 exams taken)—Calc Stats Bio Chem Environ_Sci Physics US_Hist Psych. **Elem math**—Everyday Math. **Feat**—Fr Span Anat & Physiol Forensic_Sci Comp_Sci Anthro Relig Ceramics Photog Studio_Art Drama Chorus Music Orchestra Journ. **Supp**—Tut.

Sports—Basket X-country Soccer Swim Tennis Track Ultimate_Frisbee. B: Baseball. G: Softball Volley. **Activities:** 50.

Selective adm (Gr PS-11): 124/yr. Appl fee: $75. Appl due: Feb.

Enr 974. Wh 71%. Latino 7%. Blk 13%. Asian 8%. Other 1%. Avg class size: 14. Stud/fac: 9:1. **Fac 139.** M 60/F 79. FT 117/PT 22. Wh 81%. Latino 4%. Blk 12%. Asian 1%. Other 2%. Adv deg: 76%.

Grad '11—93. Col—92. (U of GA 15, Emory 8, Eckerd 4, Elon 3, GA Southern 3, Harvard 2). **Col couns:** 2. Alum donors: 16%.

Tui '12-'13: Day $18,132-20,448 (+$100-300). **Aid:** Need 132 ($1,849,178).

Summer (enr 725): Enrich Rec. Tui Day $450-570. 2-3 wks.

Endow $10,899,000. Plant val $47,763,000. Acres 22. Bldgs 16 (69% ADA). Class rms 79. 2 Libs 23,400 vols. Sci labs 6. Auds 1. Theaters 2. Art studios 5. Music studios 4. Gyms 2. Fields 3. Comp labs 4. Comp/stud: 1:1.5.

Est 1971. Nonprofit. Sem (Aug-June). **Assoc** SACS.

Paideia encompasses a half-day program (morning and afternoon sessions) for three- to five-year-olds and a full-day program for those in grades K-12. The academic curriculum is characterized by individualized instruction and achievement at a pace in keeping with the student's development. The college preparatory high school program includes classes, seminars, independent study and community service. High schoolers accumulate 60 hours of compulsory service prior to graduation.

The school year comprises two long terms of approximately 15 weeks each and two short terms—one in January and one in May—of about four weeks. Short terms enable pupils to work intensively in an academic or nonacademic area of interest.

THE WESTMINSTER SCHOOLS

Day — Coed Gr K-12

Atlanta, GA 30327. 1424 W Paces Ferry Rd NW. Tel: 404-355-8673. Fax: 404-355-6606.
www.westminster.net E-mail: mainoffice@westminster.net
William Clarkson IV, Pres (1991). BA, Duke Univ, MDiv, General Theological Seminary, DMin, Southern Methodist Univ. **Marjorie Mitchell, Adm.**

Col Prep. AP (exams req'd; 1124 taken, 92% 3+)—Eng Fr Lat Span Calc Stats Comp_Sci Bio Chem Environ_Sci Physics Eur_Hist US_Hist Econ Art_Hist Studio_ Art Music_Theory. **Elem math**—Everyday Math. **Feat**—Chin Geol Marine_Bio/Sci Amer_Stud Psych Bible World_Relig. **Supp**—Dev_Read Rev Tut.

Sports—Basket Crew X-country Golf Lacrosse Soccer Squash Swim Tennis Track. B: Baseball Football Wrestling. G: Cheer Gymnastics Softball Volley.

Very selective adm: 274/yr. Usual entry: K & 6. Appl fee: $75. Appl due: Feb. Accepted: 25%. Yield: 84%. **Tests** CEEB IQ SSAT.

Enr 1854. B 936. G 918. Elem 1041. Sec 813. Wh 76%. Latino 3%. Blk 8%. Asian 8%. Other 5%. Avg class size: 16. **Fac 272.** M 98/F 174. FT 251/PT 21. Wh 88%. Latino 4%. Blk 7%. Asian 1%. Adv deg: 78%.

Grad '11—197. **Col**—197. (U of GA 24, GA Inst of Tech 9, UNC-Chapel Hill 9, Vanderbilt 9, U of VA 9, Georgetown 8). **Mid 50% SAT:** CR 610-730. M 650-750. W 630-740. **Col couns:** 4. Alum donors: 30%.

Tui '12-'13: Day $19,025-22,270 (+$500). **Aid:** Need 313 ($4,095,918).

Summer (enr 375): Acad Enrich Rev. Tui Day $1460-2025. 3-6 wks.

Endow $194,600,000. Plant val $132,000,000. Acres 180. Bldgs 13. Class rms 166. 3 Libs 98,000 vols. Chapels 3. Sci labs 23. Lang labs 2. Photog labs 1. Auds 3. Theaters 3. Art studios 8. Music studios 6. Dance studios 1. Gyms 4. Fields 9. Squash courts 4. Pools 2. Greenhouses 1. Comp labs 12. Comp/stud: 1:4.

Est 1951. Nonprofit. Sem (Aug-May). **Assoc** CLS SACS.

Originally the North Avenue Presbyterian School (established in 1909), the institution assumed its present name and became nondenominational in 1951. Shortly thereafter, the school relocated to the northwest section of the city. Westminster later merged with Washington Seminary, founded in 1878.

Located on 180 acres, Westminster maintains a strong academic program. Pupils study either Spanish or French throughout elementary school, in classes taught entirely in the target language. Eighth graders enroll in semester-long workshops in writing and economics. The high school program features a wide range of Advanced Placement courses and extensive offerings in art, debate, drama and music, as well as options for credit through off-campus and summer programs. Technology is integrated across the curriculum, and students use the Internet on classroom computers and mobile wireless carts to conduct research and online projects at all levels.

In addition to daily devotionals and classroom discussions in the early grades, Bible instruction includes a required semester course in grade 7 and electives in high school. The school emphasizes service learning at all grade levels, featuring programs in urban studies in grade 5 and philanthropy in grade 12.

WOODWARD ACADEMY

Day — Coed Gr PS (Age 4)-12

College Park, GA 30337. 1662 Rugby Ave. Tel: 404-765-4000. Fax: 404-765-4009. Other locations: 2001 Walker Ave, College Park 30337; 6565 Boles Rd, Johns Creek 30097.

www.woodward.edu   E-mail: admissions@woodward.edu

F. Stuart Gulley, Pres (2010). BA, Vanderbilt Univ, MDiv, Emory Univ, PhD, Georgia State Univ. **D. Ron McCollum, Head.** BA, Millsaps College, MDiv, Emory Univ, MEd, EdS, Univ of Georgia. **Russell L. Slider, Adm.**

Col Prep. AP (470 exams taken, 94% 3+)—Eng Fr Span Calc Stats Comp_Sci Bio Chem Environ_Sci Physics Eur_Hist US_Hist Econ US_Govt & Pol Music_Theory. **Feat**—Creative_Writing Chin Japan Lat Anat & Physiol Astron Botany Oceanog Meteorology Robotics Web_Design E_Asian_Hist Middle_Eastern_Hist Comp_Relig Ceramics Photog Sculpt Studio_Art Video_Production Acting Chorus Music Dance Journ. **Supp**—Tut.

Sports—Basket Golf Lacrosse Soccer Swim Tennis Track Ultimate_Frisbee Weightlifting. B: Baseball Football Wrestling. G: Cheer Softball Volley. **Activities:** 21.

Selective adm: 400/yr. Appl fee: $75. Appl due: Jan. Accepted: 35%. **Tests** SSAT.

Enr 2735. Elem 1690. Sec 1045. Avg class size: 17. Stud/fac: 10:1. Uniform. **Fac 300.** Adv deg: 80%.
Grad '11—266. Col—266. (U of GA, U of VA, UNC-Chapel Hill, Vanderbilt, Furman, Davidson). **Mid 50% SAT:** CR 530-650. M 550-680. W 550-670. **Col couns:** 4.
Tui '12-'13: Day $14,600-21,950 (+$250-500). **Aid:** Need 328.
Endow $60,000,000. Plant val $70,000,000. Acres 110. Bldgs 55. Class rms 155. 5 Libs 40,000 vols. Sci labs 10. Lang labs 1. Art studios 12. Music studios 6. TV studios 1. Gyms 6. Fields 6. Courts 8.
Est 1900. Nonprofit. Sem (Aug-May). **Assoc** SACS.

Known from its founding date until 1966 as Georgia Military Academy, the largest independent school in the Continental US offers a strenuous program for college preparation. The transition program for bright students diagnosed with learning disabilities moves from a modified self-contained classroom in grades 3-6 to full inclusion in the mainstream in grades 9 through 12. Computer literacy and advanced programming courses are offered at each grade level. Woodward conducts a European travel program for juniors and seniors.

Woodward's 75-acre campus on Rugby Avenue in College Park includes a separate primary school building on Walker Avenue, adjacent to the main campus. The 35-acre Woodward North campus in Johns Creek accommodates students in grades PS-6.

AUGUSTA, GA. (75 mi. WSW of Columbia, SC; 142 mi. E of Atlanta, GA) Urban. Pop: 195,182. Alt: 143 ft. Area also includes Martinez.

AUGUSTA PREPARATORY DAY SCHOOL
Day — Coed Gr PS (Age 3)-12

Martinez, GA 30907. 285 Flowing Wells Rd. Tel: 706-863-1906. Fax: 706-863-6198.
www.augustaprep.org   E-mail: admission@augustaprep.org
Rebecca Gilmore, Head (2011). BA, Duke Univ, MEd, Univ of Virginia. **Rosie Herrmann, Adm.**
Col Prep. AP (exams req'd; 186 taken, 78% 3+)—Eng Fr Lat Span Calc Stats Bio Chem Physics Eur_Hist US_Hist Human_Geog Studio_Art. **Feat**—Creative_Writing Women's_Lit Discrete_Math Anat & Physiol Bioethics Ecol Environ_Sci Civil_Rights Geog Psych World_Relig Theater. **Supp**—Tut.
Sports—Basket X-country Golf Soccer Swim Tennis Track. B: Baseball. G: Cheer Volley.
Somewhat selective adm: 101/yr. Appl fee: $75. Appl due: Rolling. Accepted: 90%. **Tests** CTP_4 MRT.
Enr 525. Avg class size: 14. Stud/fac: 10:1. **Fac 63.** M 16/F 47. FT 60/PT 3. Wh 95%. Latino 1%. Blk 3%. Asian 1%. Adv deg: 34%.
Grad '10—54. Col—54. (U of GA, U of SC, Augusta St, Furman, U of PA, Auburn). **Mid 50% SAT:** CR 550-670. W 540-650. Mid 50% ACT: 23-30.
Tui '11-'12: Day $8610-13,350 (+$500). **Aid:** Need 71 ($250,000).
Endow $4,000,000. Plant val $6,000,000. Acres 50. Bldgs 5. Class rms 43. 2 Libs 20,000 vols. Sci labs 4. Sci ctrs 1. Gyms 1. Fields 3. Courts 4. Comp labs 3.
Est 1960. Nonprofit. Sem (Aug-June). **Assoc** CLS SACS.

Located on a 50-acre campus, this school resulted from a 1988 merger between Augusta Preparatory School (established in 1960) and Augusta Country Day School (founded in 1972). A traditional college preparatory program, with an integrated curriculum in the lower, middle and upper schools, is complemented by honors and Advanced Placement courses in the upper school. The program is characterized by an emphasis on fine arts, athletics and character development. All seniors complete a 10-day off-campus project.

COLUMBUS, GA. (83 mi. E of Montgomery, AL; 90 mi. SSW of Atlanta, GA) Urban. Pop: 185,781. Alt: 265 ft.

BROOKSTONE SCHOOL
Day — Coed Gr PS (Age 4)-12

Columbus, GA 31904. 440 Bradley Park Dr. Tel: 706-324-1392. Fax: 706-571-0178.
  www.brookstoneschool.org   E-mail: msnyder@brookstoneschool.org
Brian D. Kennerly, Head (2010). BS, PhD, Vanderbilt Univ, MA, Columbia Univ. **Mary S. Snyder, Adm.**
  Col Prep. AP (exams req'd; 240 taken, 73% 3+)—Eng Fr Lat Span Calc Stats Bio Chem Physics Eur_Hist US_Hist Econ Human_Geog US_Govt & Pol Studio_Art. **Elem math**—McGraw-Hill. **Elem read**—McGraw-Hill. **Feat**—Humanities Anat & Physiol Astron Ecol Marine_Bio/Sci Zoology Neuroanatomy Ornithology Web_Design Civil_War Law Psych Comp_Relig Art_Hist Ceramics Photog Piano SAT_Prep. **Supp**—Dev_Read Rev Tut.
  Sports—Basket X-country Golf Soccer Tennis Track. B: Baseball Football Wrestling. G: Cheer Softball Volley. **Activities:** 50.
  Selective adm (Gr PS-11): 109/yr. Usual entry: PS & 9. Appl fee: $50. Appl due: Rolling. Applied: 186. Accepted: 83%. Yield: 72%. **Tests** CEEB CTP_4 SSAT.
  Enr 792. Elem 516. Sec 276. Wh 87%. Latino 1%. Blk 5%. Asian 5%. Other 2%. Avg class size: 14. Stud/fac: 11:1. **Fac 82.** M 19/F 63. FT 75/PT 7. Wh 97%. Latino 3%. Adv deg: 62%.
  Grad '11—72. Col—72. (U of GA 16, U of AL-Tuscaloosa 7, Columbus St 6, Furman 4, Auburn 4, Col of Charleston 3). **Avg SAT:** CR 570. M 594. W 582. **Col couns:** 2. Alum donors: 15%.
  Tui '12-'13: Day $12,440-14,545 (+$80-800). **Aid:** Merit 56 ($380,455). Need 77 ($488,280).
  Summer: Enrich Rec. 6 wks.
  Endow $20,443,000. Plant val $26,874,000. Acres 112. Bldgs 14. Class rms 57. 2 Libs 20,120 vols. Sci labs 3. Lang labs 1. Auds 1. Art studios 2. Music studios 5. Arts ctrs 1. Gyms 2. Fields 3. Tennis courts 6. Stadiums 1. Fitness ctrs 1. Student ctrs 1. Comp labs 3. Comp/stud: 1.3:1 (1:1 Laptop prgm Gr 9-12).
  Est 1951. Nonprofit. Sem (Aug-May). **Assoc** CLS SACS.

Founded as Trinity School, Brookstone has occupied its present, 112-acre campus since 1969. The curriculum, designed for the college-bound student, offers Advanced Placement courses and a variety of electives. The school's learning center offers small-group courses and provides academic support that focuses on study skills and learning strategies. Pupils may take part in such activities as debate, one-act plays and literary events. Freshmen receive tablet computers, with families and school sharing the cost.

GAINESVILLE, GA. (50 mi. NE of Atlanta, GA) Suburban. Pop: 25,578. Alt: 1200 ft.

BRENAU UNIVERSITY EARLY COLLEGE PROGRAM
Bdg and Day — Girls Gr 11-12

Gainesville, GA 30501. 500 Washington St SE. Tel: 770-534-6286. Fax: 770-534-6298.
  www.brenau.edu   E-mail: kbroccolo@brenau.edu
Katie Broccolo, Adm.
  Col Prep. Feat—Chin Fr Ital Span Performing_Arts Visual_Arts Theater Music. **Supp**—Rev Tut. **Dual enr:** Brenau.
  Selective adm: Appl fee: $35. Appl due: Rolling. **Tests** CEEB TOEFL.
  Enr 10. Bdg 7. Day 3. Wh 60%. Blk 10%. Asian 30%. Intl 22%.

Grad '11—9. Col—8. (U of WA, Brenau, Berry, Johnson & Wales). **Avg SAT:** CR 510. M 540. W 520.
Tui '11-'12: Bdg $28,262 (+$600-700). **Day $13,070** (+$600-700).
Endow $35,000,000. Plant val $28,000,000. Acres 53. Bldgs 64. Dorms 3. Class rms 12. Lib 150,000 vols. Sci labs 1. Lang labs 1. Auds 2. Theaters 3. Art studios 1. Music studios 2. Dance studios 1. Arts ctrs 1. Gyms 1. Fields 1. Courts 9. Pools 1. Comp labs 2.
Est 1928. Nonprofit. Sem (Aug-May). **Assoc** SACS.

Founded as Brenau Academy by Dr. H. S. Pearce on the campus of Brenau University Women's College, Brenau's Early College Program enables academically advanced juniors and seniors to engage in a curriculum that satisfies traditional high school requirements while also providing girls with access to the full range of Women's College courses. Upon completing this program and graduating from Early College, the student will earn transferable college credits that could result in a two-year associate of arts degree from the university. The program's association with the university also enables pupils to attend lectures and concerts, and also to make use of the shared campus facilities. Academic and residential living support, academic advising and tutorial services are also available.

In addition to extracurricular clubs and activities, students may engage in cultural field trips, community pursuits, supervised weekend outings, and domestic and international travel opportunities. All girls fulfill a 30-hour annual service requirement.

LAKEVIEW ACADEMY
Day — Coed Gr PS (Age 4)-12

Gainesville, GA 30501. 796 Lakeview Dr NE. Tel: 770-532-4383. Fax: 770-536-6142.
www.lakeviewacademy.com E-mail: jaimie.harrison@lakeviewacademy.com
John P. Kennedy, Head (2010). BA, MA, Univ of Dayton, EdD, Univ of Minnesota-Twin Cities. **Jaimie Harrison, Adm.**
  Col Prep. AP (exams req'd; 88 taken, 62% 3+)—Eng Span Calc Bio Chem US_Hist World_Hist Studio_Art. **Feat**—Poetry ASL Fr Lat Comp_Sci Web_Design Ceramics Painting Theater Chorus Debate Journ Speech TV_Production. **Supp**—Dev_Read LD Rem_Read Rev Tut.
  Sports—Basket X-country Golf Soccer Tennis. B: Baseball Football. G: Cheer Volley. **Activities:** 14.
  Selective adm: 111/yr. Appl fee: $75. Appl due: Feb. Accepted: 90%. Yield: 92%. **Tests** CTP_4.
  Enr 526. Elem 334. Sec 192. Avg class size: 15. Stud/fac: 11:1. Uniform. **Fac 62.** M 15/F 47. FT 49/PT 13. Adv deg: 46%.
  Grad '11—34. Col—34. (Clemson, Furman, GA Col & State U, GA Inst of Tech, Samford, U of GA). **Mid 50% SAT:** CR 520-610. M 540-630. W 500-590. Mid 50% ACT: 20-26. **Col couns:** 1. Alum donors: 6%.
  Tui '12-'13: Day $9900-15,345 (+$500-3000).
  Summer: Acad Enrich Rev Rem Rec. 3 wks.
  Endow $1,000,000. Plant val $9,243,000. Acres 88. Bldgs 4. Libs 2. Sci labs 4. Auds 1. Theaters 1. Studios 2. Gyms 2. Fields 3. Courts 6. Comp labs 2. Laptop prgm Gr 9-12.
  Est 1970. Nonprofit. Sem (Aug-May). **Assoc** SACS.

Founded by a group of parents and community officials seeking to establish a college preparatory program for boys and girls in the region, Lakeview now draws students from throughout northeast Georgia to its 88-acre campus.

The hands-on lower school program (grades pre-K-5) utilizes the community as an extension of the classroom through field trips and guest speakers. Music, art, drama, Spanish, physical education and technology are elements of the curriculum. These same classes complement the core course work in the middle school (grades 6-8), which provides a transition between the lower and upper schools. Students in the upper school (grades 9-12) engage in a rigorous liberal arts curriculum that features varied athletic, artistic and extracurricular offerings.

Technology is integral to the curriculum at all grade levels. Lower schoolers begin acquiring basic skills in prekindergarten, while middle school pupils study elements of robotics, video editing, desktop publishing, keyboarding and Web design. A compulsory laptop program is part of the upper school curriculum, which includes an AP course and classes in different aspects of technology. Lakeview also emphasizes the arts, with students fulfilling a visual arts course requirement.

A community service graduation requirement has upper schoolers complete 60 hours of service work during their four years. Boys and girls interested in studying abroad choose from several cultural exchange programs.

RIVERSIDE MILITARY ACADEMY

Bdg and Day — Boys Gr 7-12

Gainesville, GA 30501. 2001 Riverside Dr. Tel: 770-532-6251, 800-462-2338. Fax: 678-291-3364.
www.riversidemilitary.com E-mail: apply@riversidemilitary.com
Col. James H. Benson, USMC (Ret), Pres (2009). BA, Bridgewater College, MS, Univ of Tennessee-Knoxville, MPA, Pennsylvania State Univ, EdD, George Washington Univ.
Lynne Henderson, Adm.
Col Prep. Milit. AP—Eng Calc Stats Bio Chem Physics US_Hist World_Hist. **Feat**—British_Lit Ger Lat Span Comp_Sci Govt/Econ Ethics Art_Hist Photog Studio_Art Music Journ Speech JROTC. **Supp**—ESL Tut. **Dual enr:** Athens Area Tech.
Sports—B: Baseball Basket Crew X-country Fencing Football Golf Lacrosse Soccer Swim Tennis Track Wrestling.
Somewhat selective adm: 130/yr. Appl fee: $100. Appl due: Rolling. Accepted: 90%. **Tests** IQ TOEFL.
Enr 370. Bdg 329. Day 41. Wh 45%. Latino 15%. Blk 15%. Asian 20%. Other 5%. Intl 38%. Avg class size: 14. Stud/fac: 14:1. Uniform. **Fac 40.** M 30/F 10. FT 40. Wh 80%. Latino 10%. Blk 10%. Adv deg: 87%.
Grad '11—54. Col—52. (N GA Col & State U, Citadel, FL St, W Carolina, US Milit Acad, VA Milit). **Col couns:** 2.
Tui '12-'13: Bdg $28,600 (+$2598). **Day $17,150** (+$2598). **Intl Bdg $32,250** (+$2598).
Summer (enr 125): Acad Enrich Rev Rem Rec. Tui Bdg $4450. Tui Day $2075. 4 wks.
Endow $53,000,000. Plant val $100,000,000. Acres 206. Bldgs 9 (100% ADA). Dorms 1. Dorm rms 500. Libs 1. Sci labs 3. Lang labs 3. Theaters 1. Art studios 3. Music studios 3. Arts ctrs 1. Gyms 1. Fields 5. Courts 6. Pools 1. Weight rms 1. Comp labs 3.
Est 1907. Nonprofit. Sem (Aug-May). **Assoc** SACS.

RMA offers a structured program for college-bound young men that emphasizes problem-solving and critical-thinking skills and features Advanced Placement and honors courses. Small classes, evening tutorial opportunities and weekly grade reports are programmatic elements designed to increase the student's likelihood for success. Instructors teach organizational and time-management skills, and cadets also learn how to take notes and study in a manner that accounts for their styles of processing information. All boys in grades 9-12 take part in Riverside's Junior ROTC program, which focuses upon citizenship, leadership and responsibility.

Athletics are an integral aspect of school life. Each cadet spends two hours per day engaging in a sport at the varsity, junior varsity or intramural level; certain options are also available as seventh and eighth grade prep sports.

NEWNAN, GA. (34 mi. SW of Atlanta, GA) Urban. Pop: 16,242. Alt: 1001 ft.

THE HERITAGE SCHOOL
Day — Coed Gr PS (Age 3)-12

Newnan, GA 30263. 2093 Hwy 29 N. Tel: 770-253-9898. Fax: 770-253-4850.
www.heritagehawks.org   E-mail: ariley@heritagehawks.org
Judith Griffith, Head (2003). BA, MEd, State Univ of West Georgia. **Amy Riley, Adm.**
  Col Prep. AP (exams req'd; 137 taken, 44% 3+)—Eng Fr Span Calc Chem Environ_Sci
    Physics Eur_Hist US_Hist Psych US_Govt & Pol Studio_Art. **Feat**—Lat Comp_Sci
    Graphic_Arts Video_Production Drama Chorus Music Public_Speak. **Supp**—Dev_
    Read Rev Tut.
  Sports—Basket X-country Golf Soccer Swim Tennis Track. B: Baseball Football. G:
    Cheer Softball. **Activities:** 25.
  Selective adm: 67/yr. Appl fee: $50. Appl due: Rolling. Accepted: 81%. Yield: 92%.
  Enr 425. Elem 280. Sec 145. Avg class size: 16. Stud/fac: 8:1. **Fac 49.**
  Grad '10—37. Col—37. (U of GA, GA Inst of Tech, Auburn, U of W GA, Mercer U, Geo
    Wash). **Mid 50% SAT:** CR 490-620. M 470-630. W 470-580. Mid 50% ACT: 20-28.
    Alum donors: 10%.
  Tui '10-'11: Day $9760-12,980 (+$300). **Aid:** Need 65 ($498,310).
  Endow $1,228,000. Plant val $5,880,000. Acres 62. Bldgs 13 (70% ADA). Class rms
    42. Lib 12,699 vols. Sci labs 2. Lang labs 4. Auds 1. Theaters 1. Art studios 2. Music
    studios 2. Gyms 1. Fields 3. Courts 4. Comp labs 2. Comp/stud: 1:8.
  Est 1970. Nonprofit. Sem (Aug-May). **Assoc** SACS.

Situated on a 62-acre campus in the midst of a pecan grove, the school serves students from
Coweta, Fayette and surrounding counties. The integrated lower school curriculum immerses
children in a historical period, thereby integrating the cultural perspective of the time with
the study of geography and the applied arts. The middle school, which serves as a transition
between the lower and upper schools, combines work in the traditional subjects with a strong
outdoor education curriculum that incorporates a climbing tower and off-campus adventure
trips. The upper school stresses the liberal arts and character education while preparing students for college entrance. Computer, language, music and art classes begin in kindergarten
and continue through grade 12. The foreign language sequence, which also begins in kindergarten, requires students to study three languages: French, Spanish and Latin.

Middle and upper schoolers engage in Heritage's weeklong interim program each fall.
Middle school students embark on field experiences related to the outdoor education curriculum. Freshmen take part in a curriculum-based trip, sophomores perform community service,
juniors tour nearby college campuses and seniors go on a retreat to St. Mary's/Cumberland
Island.

NORCROSS, GA. (17 mi. NE of Atlanta, GA) Suburban. Pop: 8410. Alt: 1057 ft.

WESLEYAN SCHOOL
Day — Coed Gr K-12

Norcross, GA 30092. 5405 Spalding Dr. Tel: 678-223-2267. Fax: 770-448-3699.
  www.wesleyanschool.org   E-mail: mbking@wesleyanschool.org
Zach Young, Head (1996). BA, Univ of Virginia, MEd, Harvard Univ. **Mari Beth King,
  Adm.**
  Col Prep. AP (exams req'd; 188 taken, 91% 3+)—Eng Fr Span Calc Stats Comp_Sci
    Bio Chem Physics Eur_Hist US_Hist Studio_Art Music_Theory. **Feat**—British_Lit
    Lat Anat & Physiol Environ_Sci Comp_Design Web_Design Econ Bible World_Relig

Filmmaking Photog Theater Chorus Music Public_Speak.
Sports—Basket X-country Golf Lacrosse Soccer Swim Tennis Track. B: Baseball Football Wrestling. G: Cheer Softball Volley. **Activities:** 19.
Selective adm: 155/yr. Appl fee: $85. Appl due: Feb. Accepted: 40%. Yield: 84%. **Tests** CEEB IQ SSAT.
Enr 1135. Elem 679. Sec 456. Nonwhite 11%. Avg class size: 17. Stud/fac: 8:1. Uniform. **Fac 135.** M 45/F 90. FT 126/PT 9. Adv deg: 65%.
Grad '10—105. Col—105. (U of GA, Auburn, U of AL-Tuscaloosa, GA Inst of Tech, Samford, U of MS). Athl schol 7. **Mid 50% SAT:** CR 550-650. M 550-670. W 550-660. **Col couns:** 3. Alum donors: 23%.
Tui '11-'12: Day $14,900-19,965 (+$500).
Summer: Acad Enrich Rev Rec. Sports. Tui Day $82-175/wk. 6 wks.
Endow $8,100,000. Acres 75. Bldgs 12. Class rms 94. 2 Libs 13,000 vols. Chapels 2. Sci labs 6. Lang labs 1. Theaters 2. Art studios 3. Music studios 6. Dance studios 1. Drama studios 1. Gyms 4. Fields 7. Basketball courts 5. Tennis courts 7. Pools 1. Tracks 1. Weight rms 2. Stadiums 3. Comp labs 7. Comp/stud: 1:3 (1:1 Laptop prgm Gr 5-12).
Est 1963. Nonprofit. Nondenom Christian. Sem (Aug-May). **Assoc** SACS.

This Christian school was established as a preschool by Sandy Springs United Methodist Church. Soon thereafter, Wesleyan expanded to include elementary and middle school divisions. Following the school's divestiture from the founding church and the addition of a high school program, Wesleyan relocated in summer 1996 to its current, 75-acre site.

The school conducts a varied curriculum at all grade levels. In the lower school (grades K-4), children develop a foundation in the fundamentals as they follow a core curriculum that includes Bible, foreign language, computer science, music and art classes. Wesleyan's middle school program (grades 5-8) serves as a bridge between the lower and high schools and helps students form sound study habits, assume a higher degree of responsibility for their learning and learn to budget time effectively. During the high school years (grades 9-12), the college preparatory curriculum provides opportunities for acceleration while also encouraging pupils to take part in a variety of activities within the arts, athletics and fellowship groups.

A strict honor code, uniform requirements and regular chapel programs are integral aspects of school life.

RABUN GAP, GA. (102 mi. NE of Atlanta, GA) Rural. Pop: 200. Alt: 2000 ft.

RABUN GAP-NACOOCHEE SCHOOL
Bdg — Coed Gr 7-12; Day — Coed 6-12

Rabun Gap, GA 30568. 339 Nacoochee Dr. Tel: 706-746-7467, 800-543-7467.
Fax: 706-746-2594.
www.rabungap.org   E-mail: admissions@rabungap.org
Anthony Sgro, Head (2011). BA, MPA, Virginia Polytechnic Institute, EdD, Univ of Pennsylvania. DaRel Christiansen, Adm.
Col Prep. AP (exams req'd; 125 taken, 75% 3+)—Eng Fr Lat Span Calc Bio Chem Environ_Sci Eur_Hist US_Hist Psych US_Govt & Pol Art_Hist Studio_Art Music_Theory. **Feat**—British_Lit World_Lit Stats Botany Comp_Sci Econ Architect_Drawing Music Journ Mech_Drawing Outdoor_Ed. **Supp**—ESL Rev Tut.
Sports—Basket X-country Golf Soccer Swim Tennis Track. B: Baseball. G: Softball Volley. **Activities:** 24.
Selective adm: 120/yr. Bdg 61. Day 59. Appl fee: $50-85. Appl due: Mar. Accepted: 69%. Yield: 69%. **Tests** ISEE SSAT TOEFL.
Enr 341. B 178. G 163. Bdg 187. Day 154. Elem 79. Sec 262. Intl 24%. Avg class size: 16. Stud/fac: 8:1. Uniform. **Fac 51.** M 29/F 22. FT 38/PT 13. Adv deg: 60%.
Grad '11—77. Col—77. (Presbyterian, UNC-Chapel Hill, U of GA, Emory, Purdue, Syracuse). **Mid 50% SAT:** CR 470-620. M 510-670. Mid 50% ACT: 21-28. **Col couns:** 2.

Alum donors: 7%.
Tui '12-'13: Bdg $38,300 (+$2500). **Day $16,650** (+$1500). **Intl Bdg $43,600** (+$2500-5500). **Aid:** Need ($3,500,000).
Endow $50,000,000. Plant val $75,000,000. Acres 1400. Bldgs 22. Dorms 7. Dorm rms 126. Class rms 32. Lib 13,000 vols. Sci labs 5. Lang labs 1. Observatories 1. Auds 1. Theaters 2. Art studios 2. Music studios 2. Dance studios 1. Arts ctrs 1. Museums 1. Art galleries 3. Gyms 2. Fields 4. Courts 4. Pools 1. Tracks 3. Weight rms 1. Lakes 2. Comp labs 10.
Est 1903. Nonprofit. Presbyterian (11% practice). Sem (Aug-June). **Assoc** SACS.

Formed by the 1927 merger of Rabun Gap School and Nacoochee Institute, this school was established by Harvard graduate Andrew J. Ritchie to provide educational opportunities for children from the surrounding mountains. Rabun Gap now enrolls students from approximately 15 states and a dozen foreign countries.

The academic program includes honors courses at all grade levels, as well as Advanced Placement courses in all major disciplines. All students work on campus, usually after school each afternoon. Among Rabun Gap's extracurricular activities are a comprehensive outdoor program and a farm program. Skiing is available at Georgia's only ski resort, located six miles from campus.

ROME, GA. (56 mi. NW of Atlanta, GA) Urban. Pop: 34,980. Alt: 610 ft.

DARLINGTON SCHOOL
Bdg — Coed Gr 9-PG; Day — Coed PS (Age 4)-PG
Rome, GA 30161. 1014 Cave Spring Rd. Tel: 706-235-6051, 800-368-4437. Fax: 706-232-3600.
www.darlingtonschool.org E-mail: admission@darlingtonschool.org
Thomas C. Whitworth III, Head (2005). AB, Univ of North Carolina-Chapel Hill, MEd, The Citadel. **James Milford, Adm.**
Col Prep. AP (exams req'd; 311 taken, 79% 3+)—Eng Fr Span Calc Stats Bio Chem Environ_Sci Physics US_Hist World_Hist Econ Psych Art_Hist Studio_Art Music_Theory. **Elem math**—Everyday Math. **Elem read**—Open Court. **Feat**—Creative_Writing Organic_Chem Robotics Web_Design World_Relig Graphic_Arts Video_Production Drama Chorus Music Orchestra. **Supp**—ESL LD Tut.
Sports—Basket Crew X-country Golf Lacrosse Soccer Swim Tennis Track. B: Baseball Football Wrestling. G: Cheer Softball Volley.
Selective adm (Bdg Gr 9-11; Day PS-11): 190/yr. Bdg 71. Day 119. Usual entry: 9. Appl fee: $50. Appl due: Feb. Applied: 324. Accepted: 48%. Yield: 62%. **Tests** CEEB IQ SSAT TOEFL.
Enr 880. B 479. G 401. Bdg 189. Day 691. Elem 399. Sec 481. Wh 65%. Latino 1%. Blk 9%. Asian 11%. Other 14%. Intl 11%. Avg class size: 14. Stud/fac: 12:1. Uniform. **Fac 84.** M 36/F 48. FT 83/PT 1. Wh 98%. Latino 1%. Blk 1%. Adv deg: 70%. In dorms 8.
Grad '11—119. Col—119. (U of GA 13, GA Inst of Tech 9, Auburn 8, GA Southern 4, Presbyterian 3, Stetson 3). Athl schol 12. **Mid 50% SAT:** CR 480-610. M 520-670. W 460-580. **Col couns:** 11. Alum donors: 20%.
Tui '12-'13: Bdg $42,300 (+$2000). **Day $13,700-18,200** (+$1000). **Intl Bdg $47,300** (+$2000). **Aid:** Merit 82 ($633,950). Need 233 ($2,680,175).
Summer: Acad Enrich. 3 wks. Rec. Sports. Tui Day $95-365/wk. 9 wks.
Endow $34,700,000. Plant val $34,461,000. Acres 500. Bldgs 17 (75% ADA). Dorms 6. Dorm rms 104. Class rms 47. Lib 19,224 vols. Chapels 1. Sci labs 5. Theaters 1. Art studios 3. Music studios 4. Dance studios 1. Gyms 4. Athletic ctrs 1. Fields 9. Courts 9. Pools 1. Comp labs 6.
Est 1905. Nonprofit. Sem (Aug-May). **Assoc** CLS SACS.

The school was founded as an independent day school by John Paul and Alice Allgood Cooper and was named for Joseph James Darlington, who had been Mr. Cooper's teacher at a private school in Rome. The boarding department opened in 1923, as did a lower school in 1973. That same year, Darlington established coeducation through a merger with the Thornwood School for girls, founded in 1958.

Students follow a required core curriculum including foreign language and the fine arts, and they may pursue special interests through a wide range of electives. Honors courses are available in most subject areas, and Advanced Placement courses are also offered in many disciplines. Students in grades 9-12 satisfy a 15-hour annual community service requirement.

Both boys and girls may participate in varsity athletics, and intramural offerings include traditional sports and such activities as aerobics and lacrosse. On-campus weekend activities are scheduled, as are frequent excursions to Atlanta and Chattanooga, TN.

A faculty advisor assists each resident student with academic and extracurricular matters. In addition, the school matches boarders with local families—usually headed by parents of a current day student—in an effort to provide further support.

SAVANNAH, GA. (85 mi. SW of Charleston, SC) Urban. Pop: 131,510. Alt: 42 ft.

SAVANNAH COUNTRY DAY SCHOOL
Day — Coed Gr PS (Age 4)-12

Savannah, GA 31419. 824 Stillwood Dr. Tel: 912-925-8800. Fax: 912-920-7800.
  www.savcds.org   E-mail: admissions@savcds.org
Marcia M. Hull, Head (2009). Terri S. Barfield, Adm.

  Col Prep. AP (exams req'd; 342 taken, 74% 3+)—Eng Fr Span Calc Stats Bio Chem Environ_Sci Physics Eur_Hist US_Hist Econ US_Govt & Pol Studio_Art Music_Theory. **Feat**—British_Lit Shakespeare Lat Anat & Physiol Marine_Bio/Sci Neurobio Comp_Sci Russ_Hist Psych World_Relig Art_Hist Ceramics Drawing Photog Sculpt Video_Production Drama Chorus Music Dance Journ Public_Speak Study_Skills. **Supp**—Dev_Read Rem_Math Rem_Read Tut. Outdoor ed.

  Sports—Basket Crew X-country Soccer Tennis Track. B: Baseball Football Golf Wrestling. G: Cheer Softball Volley. **Activities:** 39.

  Selective adm (Gr PS-11): 129/yr. Usual entry: PS. Appl fee: $175. Appl due: Jan. Applied: 187. Accepted: 81%. Yield: 85%. **Tests** CTP_4 IQ Stanford.

  Enr 890. B 468. G 422. Elem 644. Sec 246. Wh 82%. Latino 2%. Blk 4%. Asian 6%. Other 6%. Avg class size: 16. Stud/fac: 10:1. Uniform. **Fac 98.** M 31/F 67. Wh 96%. Latino 1%. Blk 1%. Other 2%. Adv deg: 70%.

  Grad '10—68. Col—68. (U of GA 16, GA Inst of Tech 5, Auburn 4, U of SC 3, Harvard 2, Emory 2). **Mid 50% SAT:** CR 600-680. M 600-690. W 590-690. **Col couns:** 2. Alum donors: 17%.

  Tui '11-'12: Day $11,420-17,135 (+$500). **Aid:** Need 146 ($1,021,300).

  Summer: Acad Enrich Rev Rec. 10 wks.

  Endow $4,010,000. Plant val $43,243,000. Acres 65. Bldgs 25. Class rms 109. 2 Libs 48,211 vols. Sci labs 7. Lang labs 3. Auds 1. Theaters 1. Art studios 5. Music studios 4. Gyms 3. Fields 6. Courts 6. Tracks 1. Weight rms 1. Stadiums 1. Comp labs 6. Comp/stud: 1:2 (1:1 Laptop prgm Gr 6-8).

  Est 1955. Nonprofit. Quar (Aug-May). **Assoc** CLS SACS.

Founded by a group of men and women interested in establishing a college preparatory private school in the area, Savannah Country Day now provides a full elementary and secondary program for a diverse student body. The upper school offers Advanced Placement courses, in addition to honors work in every subject. A varied arts program features jazz ensemble, strings instruction, photography and modern dance, among others. Boys and girls may volunteer in the school's well-developed community service program.

KENTUCKY

LEXINGTON, KY. (71 mi. ESE of Louisville, KY) Urban. Pop: 260,512. Alt: 946 ft.

THE LEXINGTON SCHOOL
Day — Coed Gr PS (Age 2)-8

Lexington, KY 40504. 1050 Lane Allen Rd. Tel: 859-278-0501. Fax: 859-278-8604.
www.thelexingtonschool.org   E-mail: admission@thelexingtonschool.org
Charles D. Baldecchi, Head (2004). BA, Denison Univ, MA, St John's College (MD). **Beth Pride, Adm.**
  Pre-Prep. Gen Acad. Montessori. Elem math—Everyday Math. Elem read—Open Court. Feat—Fr Span Geol Computers Govt Studio_Art Music. Supp—Dev_Read LD Tut.
  Sports—Basket Lacrosse Soccer Tennis Track. G: Cheer.
  Selective adm: 80/yr. Appl fee: $75. Appl due: Jan. Tests CTP_4 IQ.
  Enr 545. B 273. G 272. Wh 93%. Latino 2%. Blk 2%. Asian 3%. Avg class size: 15. Stud/fac: 8:1. Fac 60. M 14/F 46. FT 60. Adv deg: 55%.
  Grad '11—49. Prep—34. (Sayre, Episcopal HS-VA, Ethel Walker, Deerfield Acad, Phillips Acad, Phillips Exeter).
  Tui '12-'13: Day $16,690-18,820.
  Summer: Acad Rec. Tui Day $150-250/wk. 6 wks.
  Endow $7,000,000. Plant val $3,800,000. Acres 25. Bldgs 1. Class rms 52. Lib 15,000 vols. Theaters 1. Art studios 3. Music studios 3. Gyms 2. Fields 4. Comp labs 3.
  Est 1959. Nonprofit. Tri (Aug-June). Assoc SACS.

Located on a 25-acre campus four miles from the heart of the business district, this school opened with the primary grades and later added grades 7 and 8. A Montessori preschool class and a full-day kindergarten program are available. Basic skills form the core of the curriculum in grades 1-3.

Foreign language study is introduced in the preschool and departmentalized instruction commences in grade 4. The academic program is enriched by the visual and performing arts, as well as by instrumental and choral music.

SAYRE SCHOOL
Day — Coed Gr PS (Age 3)-12

Lexington, KY 40507. 194 N Limestone St. Tel: 859-254-1361. Fax: 859-231-0508.
www.sayreschool.org   E-mail: info@sayreschool.org
Stephen M. Manella, Head (2012). BA, Kenyon College, MA, New York Univ. **Jeff Oldham, Adm.**
  Col Prep. Montessori. AP (exams req'd; 207 taken, 75% 3+)—Eng Fr Span Calc Stats Comp_Sci Bio Chem Environ_Sci Physics Eur_Hist US_Hist US_Govt & Pol Studio_Art Music_Theory. Elem math—Everyday Math. Elem read—Open Court. Feat—Creative_Writing Shakespeare Anat & Physiol Vietnam_War Ceramics Photog Acting Public_Speak. Supp—Dev_Read Tut.
  Sports—Basket Golf Soccer Swim Tennis Track. B: Baseball Lacrosse. G: Cheer Softball. Activities: 23.
  Selective adm: 83/yr. Usual entry: PS, 6 & 9. Appl fee: $75. Appl due: Rolling. Yield: 87%. Tests Stanford TOEFL.
  Enr 530. B 245. G 285. Elem 310. Sec 220. Avg class size: 14. Stud/fac: 8:1. Fac 74. M 20/F 54. FT 70/PT 4. Adv deg: 63%.
  Grad '11—62. Col—62. (U of KY, Centre, U of SC, U of GA, U of the South, TX Chris-

tian). **Avg SAT:** CR 575. M 545. W 583. Avg ACT: 25.6. **Col couns:** 2. Alum donors: 35%.
Tui '12-'13: Day $13,000-19,970 (+$300-550). **Aid:** Merit 8 ($4000). Need 114 ($1,196,140).
Summer (enr 200): Acad Enrich Rec. 6 wks.
Endow $5,900,000. Plant val $35,000,000. Acres 67. Bldgs 11 (55% ADA). Class rms 80. Lib 20,000 vols. Sci labs 7. Lang labs 4. Auds 1. Art studios 4. Music studios 3. Gyms 1. Athletic ctrs 1. Fields 5. Courts 10. Comp labs 4. Comp/stud: 1:3 (1:1 Laptop prgm Gr 9-12).
Est 1854. Nonprofit. Sem (Aug-May). **Assoc** SACS.

Established as the Sayre Female Institute by David A. Sayre, this school was the first in the region to offer college-level work for women. At the turn of the 20th century, boys were admitted to the primary department. In the 1960s, when it was revitalized as Sayre School, the school became coeducational and now serves pupils from age 3 through high school.

The liberal arts curriculum includes a strong language arts program with an emphasis on writing skills. Modern language instruction begins in the lower grades, while fine arts classes are available at all grade levels. Advanced Placement courses are available in all major disciplines. All upper school students (grades 9-12) purchase laptop computers. Seniors are required to plan, design, and implement an internship experience in social service, career exploration or the arts.

Community service is an important part of the curriculum beginning in grade 1, and all upper school students complete three independent projects each year. Both Montessori and traditional curricula are provided for children ages 3-5, and an extended-day program is available for students in grades pre-K-5.

LOUISVILLE, KY. (92 mi. SW of Cincinnati, OH) Urban. Pop: 256,231. Alt: 462 ft.

KENTUCKY COUNTRY DAY SCHOOL
Day — Coed Gr PS (Age 4)-12

Louisville, KY 40241. 4100 Springdale Rd. Tel: 502-423-0440. Fax: 502-423-0445.
  www.kcd.org   E-mail: admissions@kcd.org
  Bradley E. Lyman, Head (2003). BA, Hanover College, MA, Armstrong Atlantic State Univ.
  Jeff Holbrook, Adm.
  Col Prep. AP (exams req'd; 323 taken, 72% 3+)—Eng Fr Lat Span Calc Stats Comp_ Sci Bio Chem Physics Eur_Hist US_Hist Psych US_Govt & Pol Studio_Art Music_ Theory. **Elem math**—Everyday Math. **Feat**—African_Lit Asian_Lit Nonfiction Women's_Lit Electronics Ornithology African-Amer_Hist Civil_War Holocaust Middle_ Eastern_Hist Vietnam_War WWI Ceramics Film Photog Drama Music. **Supp**—Tut.
  Sports—Basket X-country Golf Lacrosse Soccer Swim Tennis Track. B: Baseball Football. G: F_Hockey Softball Volley. **Activities:** 40.
  Selective adm: 120/yr. Appl fee: $75. Appl due: Jan. Accepted: 57%. Yield: 82%. **Tests** CTP_4 Stanford.
  Enr 948. Wh 75%. Latino 1%. Blk 3%. Asian 17%. Other 4%. Avg class size: 16. Stud/fac: 8:1. Casual. **Fac 111.** M 34/F 77. FT 95/PT 16. Wh 94%. Latino 1%. Blk 5%. Adv deg: 72%.
  Grad '11—81. Col—81. (Centre 5, IN U 5, U of Louisville 4, Miami U-OH 3, Northwestern 3, Furman 2). Athl schol 2. **Avg SAT:** CR 600. M 610. W 600. Avg ACT: 27. **Col couns:** 2. Alum donors: 6%.
  Tui '11-'12: Day $12,990-17,300 (+$85-3000). **Aid:** Need 113 ($1,733,216).
  Summer: Acad Enrich Rec. 7 wks.
  Endow $10,876,000. Plant val $19,200,000. Acres 85. Bldgs 3. Class rms 89. Lib 30,000 vols. Sci labs 6. Lang labs 2. Art studios 3. Music studios 3. Gyms 2. Fields 10. Courts 8. Tracks 1. Comp labs 3. Comp/stud: 1:2 (1:1 Laptop prgm Gr 9-12).
  Est 1972. Nonprofit. Tri (Aug-June). **Assoc** CLS SACS.

In 1972, the Kentucky Home for Girls (founded in 1863) merged with the Louisville Country Day School (founded in 1948), which had previously consolidated with Aquinas Preparatory School and Kentucky Military Institute, to become Kentucky Country Day School. KCD moved to its present, 85-acre campus in 1978.

The school offers Advanced Placement courses, in addition to a selection of electives. Sophomores may apply to KCD's honors program, a two-year interdisciplinary program exploring philanthropy and the humanities. An international internship program offers sophomores and juniors the opportunity to pursue summer internships in the US and abroad. All upper school students must purchase a laptop computer for in-class use. Seniors complete a compulsory, 30-hour community service project.

LOUISVILLE COLLEGIATE SCHOOL
Day — Coed Gr PS (Age 4)-12

Louisville, KY 40204. 2427 Glenmary Ave, PO Box 4369. Tel: 502-479-0340.
Fax: 502-454-8549.
www.loucol.com   E-mail: info@loucol.com
Junius Scott Prince, Head (2007). AB, Davidson College, MS, Univ of Pennsylvania.
Robin Seiler, Adm.
Col Prep. AP exams taken: 176 (94% 3+). Feat—Chin Fr Ger Span Calc Stats Anat & Physiol Environ_Sci Marine_Bio/Sci Civil_Rights Econ Psych Art_Hist Photog Studio_Art Video_Production Drama Music.
Sports—Basket X-country Golf Lacrosse Soccer Swim Tennis Track. G: Crew F_Hockey.
Activities: 21.
Selective adm: 115/yr. Appl fee: $50. Appl due: Dec. Accepted: 71%. Yield: 74%. **Tests** CTP_4 Stanford.
Enr 690. Wh 82%. Latino 3%. Blk 6%. Asian 3%. Other 6%. Avg class size: 13. Uniform.
Fac 80. Adv deg: 73%.
Grad '10—51. Col—50. (IN U, Centre, DePaul, MD Inst-Col of Art, U of Louisville). **Avg SAT:** CR 623. M 619. W 627. Avg ACT: 27. Alum donors: 35%.
Tui '12-'13: Day $14,300-20,600. Aid: Need ($2,000,000).
Endow $5,000,000. Plant val $23,310,000. Acres 37. Bldgs 8. Class rms 61. Lib 21,000 vols. Labs 5. Art studios 3. Music studios 2. Gyms 2. Fields 2. Comp/stud: 1:2.3.
Est 1915. Nonprofit. Sem (Aug-May). **Assoc** CLS SACS.

Louisville Collegiate emphasizes a liberal arts curriculum at all levels, with specialized instruction in areas such as art, music and laboratory science. A strong advisory program complements academic and extracurricular life at the school. All subjects are departmentalized from grade 5. World languages commence in junior kindergarten and continue through grade 12. A sequentially structured program emphasizing reading, writing, speaking and listening is used to develop communicational skills. Other aspects of the curriculum are an emphasis on sophisticated technology and a weeklong interim program that enables middle and upper schoolers to explore the outdoors, experience different cultures and engage in project work.

To prepare students for independent study projects in the upper school, the middle school emphasizes methods of inquiry: gathering information, analyzing concepts and organizing ideas. Upper school students may choose electives according to their talents and interests. Although Louisville Collegiate does not offer Advanced Placement courses, students may prepare for the AP exam through advanced courses in most disciplines. A progressively demanding community service program begins in the middle school. Boys and girls choose from various international travel and exchange opportunities.

ST. FRANCIS SCHOOL
Day — Coed Gr PS (Age 2)-12

Louisville, KY 40202. 233 W Broadway. Tel: 502-736-1000. Fax: 502-736-1049.

Other locations: 11000 US Hwy 42, Goshen 40026; 6710 Wolf Pen Branch, Harrods Creek 40027.

www.stfrancishighschool.com   E-mail: murphy@stfrancishighschool.com

Alexandra Schreiber Thurstone, Head (2003). AB, Harvard Univ, MBA, Univ of Chicago. **Annie Murphy, Adm.**

Col Prep. AP (74 exams taken, 82% 3+)—Eng Fr Span Calc Stats Bio Chem Environ_ Sci Physics Eur_Hist US_Hist. **Feat**—Creative_Writing Chin Forensic_Sci Anthro Ethics Philos Relig Photog Drama Journ. **Supp**—Rev Tut.

Sports—Basket Soccer Tennis Track. B: Lacrosse. G: F_Hockey. **Activities:** 22.

Somewhat selective adm: 45/yr. Appl fee: $50. Appl due: Jan. Accepted: 90%. Yield: 72%.

Enr 496. B 243. G 253. Elem 366. Sec 130. Intl 7%. Avg class size: 11. Stud/fac: 8:1. **Fac 71.**

Grad '10—36. Col—36. (Vanderbilt, Bowdoin, Kenyon, Mt Holyoke, MD Inst-Col of Art, Savannah Col of Art & Design).

Tui '12-'13: Day $18,950 (+$650).

Summer: Acad Enrich Rec. Tui Day $140-240. 1-2 wks.

Bldgs 1. Class rms 13. Libs 1. Sci labs 3. Lang labs 4. Dark rms 1. Theater/auds 1. Studios 1. Comp labs 1.

Est 1976. Nonprofit. Quar (Aug-May). **Assoc** SACS.

The school was formed by the summer 2012 merger of St. Francis High School (grades 9-12; established in 1976) and St. Francis School (grades PS-8; founded in 1965), with the resulting institution assuming the latter's name. St. Francis retained all three campuses: the preschool in Harrods Creek, the elementary division in Goshen and the high school division in Louisville.

The developmentally designed elementary curriculum provides individualized programs in basic skills, life skills and foreign language instruction in grades K-8, and an outdoor environmental science lab. In addition to the standard subjects, St. Francis emphasizes drama, music, the fine arts and physical education. Enrichment is provided through many field trips, as well as visits by artists, musicians and craftsmen.

During the high school years, St. Francis offers a progressive college preparatory program that utilizes the diverse resources of downtown Louisville. Advanced Placement and college-level courses, drama, photography and studio art courses are among the academic offerings. All students complete three community service group projects and also participate in six schoolwide service days. Seniors complete a compulsory interdisciplinary project.

NORTH CAROLINA

ARDEN, NC. (88 mi. ESE of Knoxville, TN; 97 mi. WNW of Charlotte, NC) Rural. Pop: 800. Alt: 2228 ft.

CHRIST SCHOOL

Bdg and Day — Boys Gr 8-12

Arden, NC 28704. 500 Christ School Rd. Tel: 828-684-6232, 800-422-3212. Fax: 828-209-0003.
www.christschool.org   E-mail: admission@christschool.org

Paul M. Krieger, Head (2003). BA, Gettysburg College, MA, Immaculata Univ. **Garrison Conner, Adm.**

Col Prep. AP (exams req'd; 110 taken, 63% 3+)—Eng Fr Lat Span Calc Comp_Sci Bio Chem Environ_Sci Physics Eur_Hist US_Hist US_Govt & Pol Art_Hist Studio_Art Music_Theory. **Feat**—Arabic Astron Geol Marine_Bio/Sci Electronics Web_Design E_Asian_Hist Middle_Eastern_Hist WWI Econ Govt Law Asian_Stud Relig Film Photog Drama Music Journ. **Supp**—ESL Tut. Sat classes.

Sports—B: Baseball Basket X-country Football Golf Lacrosse Soccer Swim Tennis Track Wrestling. **Activities:** 14.

Somewhat selective adm (Gr 8-11): 95/yr. Bdg 72. Day 23. Usual entry: 8, 9 & 10. Appl fee: $50. Appl due: Feb. Applied: 161. Accepted: 85%. Yield: 60%. **Tests** ISEE SSAT TOEFL.

Enr 240. Bdg 165. Day 75. Elem 22. Sec 218. Wh 84%. Latino 1%. Blk 8%. Asian 7%. Intl 12%. Avg class size: 11. Stud/fac: 5:1. Casual. **Fac 42.** M 31/F 11. FT 35/PT 7. Wh 92%. Latino 2%. Blk 2%. Native Am 2%. Other 2%. Adv deg: 73%. In dorms 12.

Grad '11—56. Col—56. (UNC-Chapel Hill 7, U of MS 2, Col of Charleston 2, TX Christian 2, VA Polytech 2, Appalachian St 2). Athl schol 6. **Avg SAT:** CR/M 1133. **Col couns:** 2. Alum donors: 20%.

Tui '12-'13: Bdg $41,660 (+$1000). **Day $21,735** (+$700). **Intl Bdg $41,660** (+$1000-4500). **Aid:** Merit 37 ($409,230). Need 76 ($1,398,970).

Endow $10,500,000. Plant val $22,995,000. Acres 500. Bldgs 16. Dorms 5. Dorm rms 97. Class rms 29. Lib 16,000 vols. Sci labs 3. Auds 1. Art studios 1. Music studios 1. Gyms 1. Fields 5. Courts 8. Student ctrs 1. Comp labs 1.

Est 1900. Nonprofit. Episcopal. Sem (Aug-May). **Assoc** SACS.

Established by Rev. and Mrs. Thomas Wetmore, this college preparatory school is situated on a wooded, 500-acre campus in the mountains of western North Carolina. Founded as a coeducational day school, the school has enrolled only boys since the late 1920s.

Christ School emphasizes preparation for leading colleges throughout the country. Although affiliated with the Episcopal Church, the school enrolls students of many religious faiths. A work program instituted at the school's founding includes each boy in the supervision and the maintenance of the campus.

All students fulfill a 10-hour annual community service requirement, and other service learning opportunities are also available. In addition to an array of interscholastic sports and extracurricular activities, the school conducts a particularly active outdoor program that enables boys to engage in various pursuits in the surrounding Blue Ridge and Smoky Mountain areas.

ASHEVILLE, NC. (83 mi. ESE of Knoxville, TN; 100 mi. WNW of Charlotte, NC) Suburban. Pop: 68,889. Alt: 2200 ft.

ASHEVILLE SCHOOL
Bdg and Day — Coed Gr 9-12

Asheville, NC 28806. 360 Asheville School Rd. Tel: 828-254-6345. Fax: 828-210-6109.
www.ashevilleschool.org   E-mail: maddenc@ashevilleschool.org
Archibald R. Montgomery IV, Head (2002). BA, Univ of Pennsylvania, JD, Univ of Texas-Austin. **Morgan B. Scoville, Adm.**

  Col Prep. AP (exams req'd; 226 taken, 83% 3+)—Eng Fr Lat Span Calc Stats Bio Chem Physics Eur_Hist US_Hist World_Hist Music_Theory. **Feat**—Humanities Chin Anat & Physiol Environ_Sci Studio_Art Music. **Supp**—ESL Makeup Rev Tut.

  Sports—Basket X-country Soccer Swim Tennis Track. B: Baseball Football Lacrosse Wrestling. G: F_Hockey Volley. **Activities:** 30.

  Selective adm: 108/yr. Appl fee: $50. Appl due: Feb. Accepted: 49%. **Tests** CEEB IQ ISEE SSAT TOEFL.

  Enr 270. B 133. G 137. Bdg 202. Day 68. Intl 14%. Avg class size: 13. Stud/fac: 4:1. Formal. **Fac 36.** Adv deg: 72%. In dorms 17.

  Grad '11—77. Col—77. (U of the South 5, Cornell 3, U of PA 3, UNC-Chapel Hill 3, Wake Forest 3, Geo Wash 3). **Mid 50% SAT:** CR 550-690. M 580-720. W 560-690. **Col couns:** 2. Alum donors: 22%.

  Tui '11-'12: Bdg $42,110 (+$600). **Day $24,385** (+$600). **Intl Bdg $42,110** (+$1100). **Aid:** Need 57 ($1,700,000).

  Summer: Gr 7-11. Acad Enrich Rec. 3 wks.

  Endow $30,000,000. Plant val $22,600,000. Acres 300. Bldgs 15. Dorms 3. Dorm rms 185. Class rms 31. Lib 15,000 vols. Chapels 1. Theaters 1. Art studios 2. Music studios 2. Arts ctrs 1. Gyms 1. Fields 7. Courts 10. Pools 1. Stables 1. Comp labs 3.

  Est 1900. Nonprofit. Sem (Aug-May). **Assoc** CLS SACS.

Located on a 300-acre tract in the Blue Ridge Mountains, the school was founded by Newton M. Anderson and Charles A. Mitchell, who earlier had combined their efforts to found University School in Cleveland, OH. Originally a boys' school, Asheville first enrolled girls in 1971.

Asheville's rigorous course of study emphasizes a traditional core curriculum of humanities, math, science, foreign language and the arts. Faculty pay particular attention to the fundamentals of effective writing, critical-thinking skills and clear communication. The humanities curriculum integrates the study of literature, history, religion, art, music, architecture, film and dance in a four-year sequence: ancient studies, world studies, European studies and American studies. English and history instructors jointly teach these classes, along with the school's music teacher and guest lecturers.

Seniors engage in a semester-long program of self-directed learning in which they select a topic for in-depth study. After engaging in reading, research and study on the topic, the student composes two lengthy analytical essays and makes a verbal defense of his or her thesis before a panel of teachers.

Participation in the school's mountaineering program exposes students to backpacking, rock climbing, white-water kayaking, cross-country skiing, and caving in the Blue Ridge and Great Smoky mountains. Between the start of sophomore year and graduation, boys and girls accumulate 40 hours of required community service.

CAROLINA DAY SCHOOL
Day — Coed Gr PS (Age 4)-12
(Coord — Day 6-7)

Asheville, NC 28803. 1345 Hendersonville Rd. Tel: 828-274-0757. Fax: 828-274-0756.
www.carolinaday.org   E-mail: admissions@carolinaday.org

Thomas F. H. Trigg, Head (2010). BA, Univ of Kansas, MEd, Harvard Univ, MA, Yale Univ. **Ryn Fleischer, Adm.**
Col Prep. AP (169 exams taken, 73% 3+)—Eng Fr Span Calc Stats Bio Chem Environ_Sci Physics Eur_Hist US_Hist Psych US_Govt & Pol Art_Hist Music_Theory. **Elem math**—Singapore Math. **Elem read**—Orton-Gillingham. **Feat**—Creative_Writing Shakespeare Chin Ecol Forensic_Sci Genetics Comp_Sci Photog Studio_Art Debate Speech. **Supp**—LD Tut. Outdoor ed.
Sports—Basket X-country Golf Soccer Swim Tennis Track. B: Baseball. G: F_Hockey Volley. **Activities:** 20.
Selective adm: 127/yr. Usual entry: PS, 6 & 9. Appl fee: $100. Appl due: Rolling. Applied: 156. Accepted: 70%. Yield: 93%. **Tests** CEEB CTP_4 IQ ISEE SSAT.
Enr 669. B 335. G 334. Elem 483. Sec 186. Wh 91%. Latino 2%. Blk 2%. Asian 2%. Other 3%. Avg class size: 18. Stud/fac: 9:1. **Fac 103.** M 33/F 70. FT 76/PT 27. Wh 95%. Latino 3%. Asian 2%. Adv deg: 46%.
Grad '11—34. Col—34. (UNC-Chapel Hill 3, Wofford 2, High Pt 2, UNC-Charlotte 2, Mt Holyoke 1, Northwestern 1). Athl schol 1. **Avg SAT:** CR 625. M 615. W 615. **Col couns:** 1. Alum donors: 9%.
Tui '12-'13: Day $12,000-20,700 (+$750). **Aid:** Merit 42 ($140,059). Need 113 ($1,312,550).
Summer (enr 338): Acad Enrich Rec. Tui Day $150-365/wk. 8 wks.
Endow $3,545,000. Plant val $18,253,000. Acres 60. Bldgs 10 (56% ADA). Class rms 63. 2 Libs 8521 vols. Sci labs 4. Auds 1. Art studios 4. Music studios 3. Gyms 2. Fields 5. Comp labs 4. Comp/stud: 1:5 (1:1 Laptop prgm Gr 6-8).
Est 1987. Nonprofit. (Aug-May). **Assoc** SACS.

Founded upon the merger of Asheville Country Day School (established in 1936) and St. Genevieve/Gibbons Hall School (established in 1908), Carolina Day School enrolls students from seven counties of western North Carolina into its college preparatory program.

Computer science, the fine arts, Advanced Placement courses, outdoor education, sports and community service projects are integrated into the curriculum. Children in grades 1-8 with language-based learning differences may enroll in a special program that features language tutorial courses, a 3:1 student-teacher ratio and an emphasis on skill development. In the lower school (grades PS-5), reading instruction progresses from the phonetic Orton-Gillingham approach to a literature-based curriculum. Students in grades 6 and 7 attend single-gender core classes.

The school's Summer Quest program offers enrichment in the arts, the sciences and athletics.

BURNSVILLE, NC. (93 mi. E of Knoxville, TN; 96 mi. WNW of Charlotte, NC) Rural. Pop: 1623. Alt: 2814 ft.

ARTHUR MORGAN SCHOOL
Bdg and Day — Coed Gr 7-9

Burnsville, NC 28714. 60 AMS Cir. Tel: 828-675-4262. Fax: 828-675-0003.
www.arthurmorganschool.org   E-mail: info@arthurmorganschool.org
Michelle Rehfield, Clerk (2010). Meghan Lundy-Jones, Adm.
Gen Acad. Elem math—Connected Math/Core-Plus Math Project. **Feat**—Ceramics Drawing Studio_Art Jewelry_Making Drama Music Dance Metal_Shop Woodworking Printmaking Blacksmithing Culinary_Arts Wilderness_Ed Organic_Gardening. **Supp**—Tut.
Sports—Soccer.
Somewhat selective adm (Gr 7-8): 12/yr. Bdg 6. Day 6. Usual entry: 7. Appl fee: $50. Appl due: Rolling. Applied: 15. Accepted: 92%. Yield: 68%.
Enr 27. B 15. G 12. Bdg 18. Day 9. Elem 19. Sec 8. Wh 84%. Blk 5%. Asian 8%. Other 3%. Avg class size: 7. Stud/fac: 2:1. **Fac 8.** M 5/F 3. FT 6/PT 2. Wh 100%. In dorms

4.
Grad '10—6. Alum donors: 13%.
Tui '11-'12: Bdg $22,945 (+$250). **Day $11,945** (+$100). **Aid:** Need 17 ($105,183). Work prgm 3 ($2187).
Summer (enr 12): Rec. Tui Bdg $1200. 2 wks.
Endow $1,000,000. Plant val $700,000. Acres 100. Bldgs 9 (11% ADA). Dorms 4. Dorm rms 10. Class rms 5. Lib 10,000 vols. Sci labs 1. Art studios 3. Music studios 1. Dance studios 1. Wood shops 1. Fields 3. Courts 1. Ponds 1. Comp/stud: 1:4.
Est 1962. Nonprofit. Sem (Sept-May).

Elizabeth Morgan founded this school in accordance with the principles of Montessori, Pestalozzi, Grundtvig, Gandhi and Arthur Morgan, as well as her own Quaker values. The program continues to address the needs and interests of early adolescents. The school occupies a 100-acre campus in the Black Mountains.

The program integrates academic and practical skills, relating them to community life. Students participate in a daily work program and an outdoor hiking program. Academics feature small classes held four times each week, and electives address an array of interests. Community service plays an important role in the educational experience, with multiple opportunities provided during the year. In addition, the school divides itself into three distinct field trip groups in the early spring; each field trip has a service orientation and adheres to an educational theme that has been selected by students and staff.

CHARLOTTE, NC. (80 mi. N of Columbia, SC) Urban. Pop: 540,828. Alt: 721 ft.

CHARLOTTE COUNTRY DAY SCHOOL
Day — Coed Gr PS (Age 4)-12

Charlotte, NC 28226. 1440 Carmel Rd. Tel: 704-943-4500. Fax: 704-943-4536.
Other locations: 5936 Green Rea Rd, Charlotte 28226.
 www.charlottecountryday.org   E-mail: robin.riggins@charlottecountryday.org
Mark E. Reed, Head (2009). BA, Univ of Houston, MAT, Columbia Univ. **Nancy R. Ehringhaus, Adm.**
 Col Prep. IB Diploma. AP (337 exams taken, 82% 3+)—Eng Fr Ger Lat Span Calc Stats Comp_Sci Bio Chem Environ_Sci Physics Eur_Hist US_Hist World_Hist Psych US_Govt & Pol Art_Hist Studio_Art Music_Theory. **Feat**—Creative_Writing Shakespeare Chin Anat & Physiol Bioethics Marine_Bio/Sci Biotech Web_Design Econ Photog Drama Chorus Dance. **Supp**—ESL Tut.
 Sports—Basket X-country Golf Indoor_Track Lacrosse Soccer Swim Tennis Track. B: Baseball Football Wrestling. G: Cheer F_Hockey Softball Volley. **Activities:** 37.
 Selective adm: 221/yr. Usual entry: PS & K. Appl fee: $90. Appl due: Jan. Applied: 483. Accepted: 74%. Yield: 66%. **Tests** CEEB CTP_4 IQ ISEE.
 Enr 1617. Elem 1128. Sec 489. Wh 88%. Blk 7%. Asian 3%. Other 2%. Intl 8%. Avg class size: 15. Stud/fac: 12:1. Casual. **Fac 213.** M 50/F 163. FT 204/PT 9. Wh 91%. Latino 2%. Blk 6%. Asian 1%. Adv deg: 55%.
 Grad '11—123. Col—123. (UNC-Chapel Hill 23, Col of Charleston 8, Clemson 6, U of SC 6, U of GA 5, Vanderbilt 3). Athl schol 7. **Avg SAT:** CR 626. M 649. W 624. **Mid 50% SAT:** CR 560-680. M 600-700. W 550-670. Avg ACT: 27. **Col couns:** 3. Alum donors: 27%.
 Tui '12-'13: Day $14,930-21,260 (+$500). **Aid:** Need 118 ($1,374,675).
 Summer (enr 200): Acad Enrich Rec. Tui Day $100-610. 1-6 wks.
 Endow $18,615,000. Plant val $60,000,000. Acres 118. Bldgs 25. Class rms 105. 3 Libs 43,000 vols. Sci labs 6. Lang labs 1. Theaters 1. Art studios 3. Music studios 7. Dance studios 2. Gyms 1. Fields 5. Courts 8. Comp labs 6. Comp/stud: 1:3 (1:1 Laptop prgm Gr 9-12).
 Est 1941. Nonprofit. Sem (Aug-June). **Assoc** CLS SACS.

Founded by Dr. Thomas Burton, Country Day is the oldest and largest independent school in the Charlotte area. The school moved to its permanent campus in the southeastern part of the city in 1960, and a 1979 merger with Carmel Academy gave CCDS two campuses. The upper and lower schools share the 60-acre Cannon campus on Carmel Road, while the middle school is situated four miles south on the 40-acre Bissell campus on Green Rea Road.

College preparation is the focus of the rigorous curriculum. The lower school (junior kindergarten through grade 4), which emphasizes early foreign language work, science, computer instruction and the arts, follows the International Baccalaureate Primary Years Program. The middle school (grades 5-8) enhances its academic program with a range of activities designed specifically for emerging adolescents. The upper school, which leads to the International Baccalaureate Diploma, features Advanced Placement courses and a varied foreign language curriculum. Well-established guidance and advisory programs aid pupils in all three divisions.

The academic program is enriched by strong visual and performing arts programs, computer technology and library facilities. In addition to boys' and girls' extracurricular sports teams and opportunities, the athletic program includes trainer-supervised weight and wellness conditioning.

The student population includes international students from many countries, and English as a Second Language is offered. The school cooperates with Andover in School Year Abroad programs to France, China and Spain, the Maine Coast Experience, teacher and student exchanges with King Edward VI School in Britain, other trips and exchanges in every division, and various summer travel opportunities. **See Also Page 60**

CHARLOTTE LATIN SCHOOL

Day — Coed Gr K-12

Charlotte, NC 28277. 9502 Providence Rd. Tel: 704-846-1100. Fax: 704-846-6990. www.charlottelatin.org   E-mail: admissions@charlottelatin.org
Arch N. McIntosh, Jr., Head (2001). BA, Marshall Univ, MEd, Univ of South Alabama. Peter Egan, Adm.
  Col Prep. AP (exams req'd; 374 taken, 95% 3+)—Eng Fr Lat Span Calc Stats Comp_ Sci Bio Chem Physics Eur_Hist US_Hist US_Govt & Pol Music_Theory. Elem math— Real Math. Elem read—Houghton Mifflin/Open Court. Feat—Greek Anat & Physiol Environ_Sci Sports_Med Engineering Web_Design Econ Psych Intl_Stud Fine_Arts Visual_Arts Theater_Arts Band Chorus Orchestra Debate. Supp—Dev_Read Rev Tut.
  Sports—Basket X-country Golf Soccer Swim Tennis Track Ultimate_Frisbee. B: Baseball Football Lacrosse Wrestling. G: F_Hockey Softball Volley. Activities: 23.
  Selective adm: 177/yr. Appl fee: $90. Appl due: Jan. Applied: 546. Accepted: 42%. Yield: 78%. Tests CEEB CTP_4 IQ ISEE SSAT.
  Enr 1388. B 683. G 705. Elem 896. Sec 492. Wh 87%. Latino 1%. Blk 3%. Asian 3%. Other 6%. Avg class size: 15. Stud/fac: 10:1. Fac 143. M 57/F 86. FT 122/PT 21. Wh 95%. Latino 2%. Blk 3%. Adv deg: 59%.
  Grad '11—118. Col—118. (UNC-Chapel Hill 19, U of AL-Tuscaloosa 5, Wake Forest 4, Elon 3, NC St 3, U of GA 3). Athl schol 9. Mid 50% SAT: CR 570-680. M 600-710. W 590-700. Mid 50% ACT: 25-31. Col couns: 3. Alum donors: 13%.
  Tui '12-'13: Day $15,650-19,650. Aid: Merit 15 ($197,690). Need 164 ($1,644,700).
  Summer (enr 850): Acad Enrich Rec. Sports. Tui Day $110-750. 1-6 wks.
  Endow $22,880,000. Plant val $45,000,000. Acres 122. Bldgs 15 (100% ADA). Class rms 99. Lib 47,000 vols. Sci labs 10. Auds 1. Theaters 1. Art studios 5. Music studios 5. Dance studios 1. Gyms 3. Fields 7. Courts 6. Pools 1. Comp labs 12. Comp/stud: 1:2.
  Est 1970. Nonprofit. Sem (Aug-June). Assoc CLS SACS.

Occupying a 122-acre campus, Latin offers a complete elementary and secondary program. Language arts, phonics and mathematics are emphasized in the lower school, and all students attend weekly computer and twice-weekly Spanish lessons. A transitional kindergarten program serves children who may need an additional year of social, emotional and cognitive growth.

The middle and upper schools (grades 6-12) operate on a semester system. Advanced middle school students may be placed above their grade level in math and foreign language. The upper school curriculum, featuring Advanced Placement and honors courses, is enhanced by programs in the arts and international studies. Latin organizes study abroad trips and hosts exchange students from sister schools in Argentina, China, France, Germany, Italy, South Africa and Spain. Students are expected to acquire independent study habits and to make use of both the school media center and outside sources of reference.

PROVIDENCE DAY SCHOOL

Day — Coed Gr PS (Age 4)-12

Charlotte, NC 28270. 5800 Sardis Rd. Tel: 704-887-6000. Fax: 704-887-7042.
www.providenceday.org   E-mail: pds.communications@providenceday.org
Glyn Cowlishaw, Head (2011). BEd, Univ of Reading (England), MEd, Univ of Leeds (England), EdS, The Citadel, EdD, South Carolina State Univ. **Cecil Stodghill, Adm.**

    Col Prep. AP (exams req'd; 577 taken, 91% 3+)—Eng Chin Fr Ger Lat Span Calc Stats Comp_Sci Bio Chem Environ_Sci Physics Eur_Hist US_Hist World_Hist Psych US_ Govt & Pol Art_Hist Studio_Art Music_Theory. **Elem math**—Houghton Mifflin. **Elem read**—Fountas & Pinnell/McGraw-Hill. **Feat**—Anat & Physiol Astron Bioethics Meteorology Robotics Civil_War Econ Global_Stud Relig Photog Theater. **Supp**—Tut.

    Sports—Basket X-country Golf Lacrosse Swim Tennis Track. B: Baseball Football Wrestling. G: Cheer F_Hockey Soccer Softball Volley. **Activities:** 61.

    Selective adm: 226/yr. Appl fee: $90. Appl due: Jan. Applied: 547. Accepted: 69%. Yield: 60%. **Tests** CEEB CTP_4 IQ ISEE SSAT.

    Enr 1545. B 796. G 749. Elem 995. Sec 550. Wh 79%. Latino 3%. Blk 8%. Native Am 1%. Asian 5%. Other 4%. Stud/fac: 9:1. **Fac 146.** M 62/F 84. FT 142/PT 4. Wh 87%. Latino 3%. Blk 6%. Asian 3%. Other 1%. Adv deg: 56%.

    Grad '11—135. Col—135. (UNC-Chapel Hill 19, U of SC 7, Appalachian St 6, Vanderbilt 4, NC St 4, U of AL-Tuscaloosa 3). Athl schol 10. **Avg SAT:** CR 632. M 648. W 628. **Mid 50% SAT:** CR 570-690. M 590-700. W 580-680. Avg ACT: 27.2. **Col couns:** 3. Alum donors: 6%.

    Tui '12-'13: Day $15,484-21,456. Aid: Need 206 ($2,734,830).

    Summer: Acad Enrich Rec. 9 wks.

    Endow $5,497,000. Plant val $40,000,000. Acres 45. Bldgs 14 (96% ADA). Class rms 84. Lib 53,000 vols. Sci labs 7. Lang labs 1. Sci/tech ctrs 1. Theaters 2. Art studios 3. Music studios 4. Gyms 2. Fields 5. Courts 10. Field houses 1. Playgrounds 1. Comp labs 6. Comp/stud: 1:3.

    Est 1970. Nonprofit. Sem (Aug-June). **Assoc** CLS SACS.

Since opening with an enrollment of 150, Providence Day has experienced noteworthy growth and expansion in curriculum, enrollment and plant. The 45-acre campus includes ample athletic facilities and areas for physical education instruction.

Language arts is emphasized in the lower-middle school, as are math, science, computers, health, social studies, art, music, theater and physical education. The upper school curriculum includes college preparatory material, as well as enrichment electives. Advanced Placement courses are offered in every major discipline. Upper school pupils may enroll in a global studies diploma program. Each senior engages in a two-week community project that provides the opportunity to sample various professions and in a senior venture program that stresses group dependency and leadership skills.

CONCORD, NC. (20 mi. NE of Charlotte, NC) Suburban. Pop: 55,977. Alt: 704 ft.

CANNON SCHOOL
Day — Coed Gr PS (Age 4)-12

Concord, NC 28027. 5801 Poplar Tent Rd. Tel: 704-786-8171. Fax: 704-788-7779.
www.cannonschool.org   E-mail: info@cannonschool.org
Matthew E. Gossage, Head (2006). BA, MAT, Vanderbilt Univ, MEd, Harvard Univ. **William Diskin, Adm.**

Col Prep. AP (exams req'd; 389 taken, 80% 3+)—Eng Fr Span Calc Bio Chem Environ_Sci Physics Eur_Hist US_Hist Psych US_Govt & Pol Studio_Art. **Elem math**—Everyday Math. **Elem read**—Open Court. **Feat**—Creative_Writing Poetry Chin Marine_Bio/Sci Comp_Sci Drawing Film Graphic_Arts Painting Photog Theater Chorus Music Orchestra Jazz_Band Dance. **Supp**—Tut.

Sports—Basket X-country Golf Soccer Swim Tennis Track. B: Baseball Football Lacrosse. G: Cheer Softball Volley.

Selective adm: 120/yr. Appl fee: $90. Appl due: Rolling. Accepted: 65%. Yield: 77%. **Tests** CTP_4 IQ ISEE MRT SSAT Stanford.

Enr 876. Elem 564. Sec 312. Nonwhite 20%. Avg class size: 18. Stud/fac: 9:1. **Fac 86.** Adv deg: 41%.

Grad '11—71. Col—70. (UNC-Chapel Hill, NC St, Clemson, Elon, U of SC, Stanford). **Mid 50% SAT:** CR 540-660. M 560-680. W 550-670. Mid 50% ACT: 24-30. **Col couns:** 2.

Tui '12-'13: Day $10,985-18,170 (+$1000). **Aid:** Need 166.
Summer: Acad Enrich Rec. Tui Day $90-320/wk. 6 wks.
Endow $2,958,000. Plant val $20,000,000. Acres 65. Bldgs 6. Class rms 63. 2 Libs 16,700 vols. Sci labs 6. Auds 1. Art studios 3. Music studios 4. Dance studios 1. Gyms 2. Fields 6. Courts 6. Tracks 1. Comp labs 4. Laptop prgm Gr 9-12.
Est 1969. Nonprofit. Quar (Aug-June). **Assoc** CLS SACS.

Established as Cabarrus Academy at the Concord residence of textile entrepreneur J. W. Cannon, this college preparatory school assumed its current name in 1998. Lower and middle school instruction emphasizes basic skills and study habits through the study of foreign languages, lab science, physical education, art and music. Beginning in kindergarten, technology is integrated into the curriculum to promote information literacy, creativity and critical-thinking abilities. Instruction progresses from basic graphics and word processing applications to Internet research and multimedia presentations, and students in grades 9-12 receive laptop computers for school use.

The upper school curriculum features Advanced Placement and honors options, and seniors complete an independent study project during the spring semester. A partnership with Tianli International School in Luzhou, China, provides for annual student and faculty exchange programs and supplements the Chinese language course offered in grades 5-12. Community service projects are included in the middle school curriculum (grades 5-8), while students in grades 9-12 perform 10 hours of independent service annually.

DURHAM, NC. (18 mi. NW of Raleigh, NC) Urban. Pop: 179,212. Alt: 406 ft.

CAROLINA FRIENDS SCHOOL
Day — Coed Gr PS (Age 3)-12

Durham, NC 27705. 4809 Friends School Rd. Tel: 919-383-6602. Fax: 919-383-6009.
Other locations: 404 Alexander Ave, Durham 27705; 531 Raleigh Rd, Chapel Hill 27514.
www.cfsnc.org   E-mail: admissions@cfsnc.org

Mike Hanas, Prin (2003). BA, College of the Holy Cross, MEd, Harvard Univ. **Kathleen Davidson, Adm.**

Col Prep. AP (13 exams taken, 100% 3+)—Fr Span Calc Stats Bio. **Feat**—Creative_ Writing African_Lit Playwriting Anat & Physiol Ecol Environ_Sci Genetics Engineering Comp_Sci Robotics Web_Design African-Amer_Hist Holocaust Philos Photog Studio_Art Acting Drama Dance Gardening.

Sports—Basket X-country Soccer Swim Tennis Ultimate_Frisbee. B: Baseball. G: Volley.

Selective adm: 95/yr. Usual entry: PS, K, 1, 6 & 9. Appl fee: $50. Appl due: Jan. Applied: 254. Accepted: 51%. Yield: 73%.

Enr 483. B 240. G 243. Elem 332. Sec 151. Wh 77%. Latino 5%. Blk 5%. Asian 3%. Other 10%. Avg class size: 13. Stud/fac: 9:1. Casual. **Fac 70.** M 25/F 45. FT 63/PT 7. Wh 90%. Latino 6%. Blk 4%. Adv deg: 50%.

Grad '11—39. Col—38. (UNC-Chapel Hill 8, Am U 2, Goucher 2, Oberlin 1, Mt Holyoke 1, NYU 1). **Avg SAT:** CR 602. M 550. W 608. **Mid 50% SAT:** CR 550-680. M 480-610. W 550-660. Avg ACT: 25. **Col couns:** 1.

Tui '12-'13: Day $14,220-16,580 (+$50-400). **Aid:** Need 123 ($839,000).

Summer: Rec. Tui Day $190-225/wk. 10 wks.

Endow $6,700,000. Plant val $5,916,000. Acres 121. Bldgs 17. Libs 2. Sci labs 2. Art studios 2. Music studios 3. Dance studios 1. Gyms 1. Fields 6. Comp labs 4. Comp/ stud: 1:4.

Est 1962. Nonprofit. Religious Society of Friends (6% practice). Tri (Aug-June).

Founded by local Quakers and still affiliated with the Society of Friends, this nonsectarian school encourages students to progress at their own rates in a challenging and cooperative environment. The wooded, 121-acre main campus is accessible to Hillsborough, Durham and Chapel Hill. CFS maintains three early schools for children ages 3-6: one on the main campus, a second in Durham near Duke University and a third in Chapel Hill near the University of North Carolina.

The early curriculum emphasizes the development of basic skills through an integrated program involving thematic studies, field trips and cooperative learning in small, mixed-age groups. In addition to required course work, middle and upper school pupils engage in electives in language arts, math, science, social studies, the visual and dramatic arts, music, dance, woodworking, physical education and community service. Mini-sessions between terms and at year's end encourage community involvement, experiential learning and self-reliance.

DURHAM ACADEMY

Day — Coed Gr PS (Age 4)-12

Durham, NC 27705. 3501 Ridge Rd. Tel: 919-493-5787. Fax: 919-489-4893.

Other locations: 3601 Ridge Rd, Durham, NC 27705; 3616 Academy Rd, Durham, NC 27707.

www.da.org   E-mail: admissions@da.org

Edward R. Costello, Head (1999). BA, Syracuse Univ, MA, Wesleyan Univ. **S. Victoria Muradi, Adm.**

Col Prep. AP (258 exams taken, 88% 3+)—Eng Fr Lat Span Calc Stats Comp_Sci Bio Chem Environ_Sci Physics Eur_Hist US_Hist Psych US_Govt & Pol Studio_Art Music_Theory. **Feat**—Creative_Writing Poetry Gothic_Lit Chin Multivariable_Calc Bioethics Forensic_Sci Geol Middle_Eastern_Hist Econ Relig Film Photog Video_ Production Animation Drama Dance. **Supp**—LD.

Sports—Basket X-country Golf Lacrosse Soccer Swim Tennis Track. B: Baseball. G: F_Hockey Softball Volley. **Activities:** 48.

Selective adm (Gr PS-11): 171/yr. Usual entry: PS, K, 1, 5, 6 & 9. Appl fee: $55-85. Appl due: Jan. Applied: 377. Accepted: 61%. Yield: 45%. **Tests** ISEE SSAT Stanford.

Enr 1145. B 553. G 592. Elem 748. Sec 397. Wh 71%. Latino 2%. Blk 8%. Native Am 1%. Asian 7%. Other 11%. Avg class size: 18. Stud/fac: 10:1. Casual. **Fac 144.** M 42/F 102. FT 120/PT 24. Wh 91%. Latino 4%. Blk 3%. Asian 1%. Other 1%. Adv deg: 40%.

Grad '10—88. Col—88. (UNC-Chapel Hill, Duke, Harvard, UNC-Wilmington, Cornell, Stanford). Athl schol 4. **Avg SAT:** CR 650. M 650. W 655. Avg ACT: 27. **Col couns:** 2.
Tui '12-'13: Day $12,940-20,780 (+$2275-2675). **Aid:** Need 117 ($1,730,000).
Summer: Acad Enrich Rec. 7 wks.
Endow $8,863,000. Plant val $24,447,000. Acres 84. Bldgs 19. Class rms 89. 3 Libs 58,000 vols. Sci labs 15. Auds 3. Art studios 6. Music studios 2. Dance studios 2. Arts ctrs 2. Gyms 3. Fields 9. Courts 6. Comp labs 7. Comp/stud: 1:3.
Est 1933. Nonprofit. Sem (Aug-June). **Assoc** CLS SACS.

Founded and known as the Calvert Method School for its first 25 years, DA occupies two campuses in the southwestern section of Durham, near Duke University and the University of North Carolina at Chapel Hill. In 1959, the academy assumed its current name and began expanding beyond the elementary school years, culminating in the establishment of the upper school (grades 9-12) in 1972. DA dedicated a new campus, on Academy Road, to the middle school in August 2002; on Ridge Road, one location hosts the preschool, lower school and admissions office, while a second is home to the upper school.

The college preparatory curriculum includes AP courses in all major subjects, as well as term- and yearlong electives and opportunities for advanced study. Students fulfill requirements in English, a foreign language, math, lab science, the fine arts, computer and physical education. Students in grades 9-11 engage in group community service projects, while seniors satisfy a 15-hour individual service requirement. Seniors may explore career options through a two-week internship in the community. Field trips incorporate outdoor education in grades 8-10, civil rights in grade 11 and wilderness adventure in grade 12.

The Hill Center, an affiliate of the academy, serves students with specific learning disabilities who do not have primary emotional or behavioral problems.

FAYETTEVILLE, NC. (53 mi. NNE of Raleigh, NC) Suburban. Pop: 121,015. Alt: 240 ft.

THE FAYETTEVILLE ACADEMY
Day — Coed Gr PS (Age 4)-12

Fayetteville, NC 28303. 3200 Cliffdale Rd. Tel: 910-868-5131. Fax: 910-868-7351.
www.fayettevilleacademy.com   E-mail: email@fayettevilleacademy.com
Richard D. Cameron, Head (2005). BS, Northeastern Univ, MEd, The Citadel. **Barbara E. Lambert, Adm.**
Col Prep. AP (exams req'd; 106 taken, 49% 3+)—Eng Span Calc Stats Bio Chem Eur_Hist US_Hist World_Hist Studio_Art. **Elem math**—Everyday Math. **Elem read**—Open Court. **Feat**—Lat Anat & Physiol Environ_Sci Sports_Med Comp_Sci Web_Design Psych Sociol Ceramics Film Video_Production Music Music_Theory.
Sports—Basket X-country Golf Soccer Swim Tennis Track. B: Baseball. G: Softball Volley. **Activities:** 22.
Selective adm: 84/yr. Usual entry: PS, K, 6 & 9. Appl fee: $50-100. Appl due: Rolling. Applied: 134. Accepted: 78%. Yield: 80%. **Tests** CTP_4 SSAT.
Enr 393. B 184. G 209. Elem 239. Sec 154. Wh 67%. Latino 5%. Blk 8%. Asian 11%. Other 9%. Avg class size: 13. Stud/fac: 13:1. Casual. **Fac 50.** M 9/F 41. FT 47/PT 3. Wh 93%. Latino 5%. Blk 2%. Adv deg: 52%.
Grad '11—32. Col—32. (NC St 5, UNC-Chapel Hill 4, E Carolina 3, UNC-Greensboro 2, Elon 2, UNC-Wilmington 1). Athl schol 1. **Avg SAT:** CR 560. M 570. W 545. Avg ACT: 24. **Col couns:** 1. Alum donors: 5%.
Tui '11-'12: Day $8320-12,999 (+$1200). **Aid:** Merit 4 ($25,736). Need 111 ($510,644).
Summer: Acad Enrich. Tui Day $150/wk. 7 wks.
Endow $340,000. Plant val $15,696,000. Acres 30. Bldgs 10. Class rms 45. Libs 2. Sci labs 5. Lang labs 1. Writing ctrs 1. Art studios 2. Music studios 2. Gyms 2. Athletic ctrs

1. Fields 4. Courts 4. Comp labs 2. Comp/stud: 1:4.
Est 1969. Nonprofit. Sem (Aug-June). **Assoc** SACS.

Established by local citizens interested in addressing the community's need for an independent elementary and secondary school, this college preparatory school serves boys and girls from Fayetteville, Cumberland County and surrounding areas.

At the lower school level (prekindergarten through grade 5), children develop basic skills in the core academic subjects while studying in self-contained classrooms. Specialists teach weekly computer, science, Spanish, art, music, physical education and media center classes. Field trips, extracurricular clubs and organizations, and special programs enrich the program.

The middle school (grades 6-8) provides a transition between the lower and upper schools. Students continue to work on their basic skills, and the curriculum includes enrichment courses in word processing, computer applications, art, music, band and physical education. First available at this level, interscholastic sports are quite popular, and student government and other extracurricular opportunities are also part of the middle school program.

The academy encourages upper schoolers (grades 9-12) to further develop specific interests and abilities in a small-class setting, and academics stress clear expression and creative thinking. Juniors and seniors commonly enroll in Advanced Placement courses.

GREENSBORO, NC. (68 mi. WNW of Raleigh, NC) Urban. Pop: 223,891. Alt: 843 ft.

GREENSBORO DAY SCHOOL
Day — Coed Gr PS (Age 4)-12

Greensboro, NC 27455. 5401 Lawndale Dr. Tel: 336-288-8590. Fax: 336-282-2905.
www.greensboroday.org   E-mail: admissions@greensboroday.org
Mark C. Hale, Head (2007). BA, BS, MEd, Univ of Washington. Robin Schenck, Adm.
Col Prep. AP (exams req'd; 337 taken, 74% 3+)—Eng Fr Lat Span Calc Stats Comp_Sci Bio Chem Physics Eur_Hist US_Hist Studio_Art. Feat—Creative_Writing Marine_Bio/Sci Sports_Med Psych Ceramics Photog Video_Production Drama Chorus Journ. Supp—ESL Rev Tut.
Sports—Basket Cheer X-country Golf Lacrosse Soccer Swim Tennis Track. B: Baseball Wrestling. G: F_Hockey Softball Volley. Activities: 39.
Selective adm: 134/yr. Appl fee: $50-75. Appl due: Rolling. Applied: 258. Accepted: 73%. Yield: 71%. Tests CEEB CTP_4 SSAT TOEFL.
Enr 875. B 415. G 460. Elem 511. Sec 364. Wh 86%. Latino 2%. Blk 6%. Asian 5%. Other 1%. Avg class size: 18. Stud/fac: 8:1. Fac 106. M 34/F 72. FT 94/PT 12. Wh 92%. Latino 2%. Blk 5%. Other 1%. Adv deg: 61%.
Grad '11—87. Col—87. (UNC-Chapel Hill 18, Elon 7, NC St 6, Wash & Lee 3, Appalachian St 3, Citadel 2). Athl schol 5. Avg SAT: CR 610. M 650. Col couns: 3. Alum donors: 22%.
Tui '12-'13: Day $12,500-19,690 (+$1000-2200). Aid: Need 182 ($1,987,286).
Summer: Acad Enrich Rev Rec. 8 wks.
Endow $6,654,000. Plant val $11,156,000. Acres 65. Bldgs 9. Class rms 61. 2 Libs 34,000 vols. Sci labs 9. Lang labs 1. Theaters 2. Art studios 5. Music studios 5. Dance studios 1. Gyms 3. Fields 7. Tennis courts 10. Tracks 1. Playgrounds 2. Comp labs 2. Laptop prgm Gr 6-12.
Est 1970. Nonprofit. Sem (Aug-June). Assoc CLS SACS.

Situated on a 65-acre campus a few miles north of Greensboro, this college preparatory school emphasizes the basic disciplines. Course offerings in art, music, physical education and experiential/outdoor education are also fundamental to the program.

The lower school stresses the child's development of specific abilities, attitudes and work habits. Art, music, foreign language, laboratory science, computers and physical education, as well as language and mathematical skills, are the curriculum's foundation. All boys and girls participate in a laptop computer program beginning in grade 6. An environmental awareness and outdoor education program is an integral part of the curriculum at all grade levels. Seniors pursue independent projects or internships for credit, and honors and Advanced Placement courses are available in all major subjects.

Interscholastic sports competition begins at the middle school level.

HIGH POINT, NC. (72 mi. NE of Charlotte, NC; 76 mi. W of Raleigh, NC) Urban. Pop: 85,839. Alt: 939 ft.

WESTCHESTER COUNTRY DAY SCHOOL
Day — Coed Gr K-12

High Point, NC 27265. 2045 N Old Greensboro Rd. Tel: 336-869-2128.
Fax: 336-869-6685.
www.westchestercds.org   E-mail: admissions@westchestercds.org
Cobb Atkinson, Head (2010). BA, Emory Univ, MA, Harvard Univ, MA, Columbia Univ, MA, Middlebury College. **Kerie Beth Scott, Adm.**
   Col Prep. AP (exams req'd; 98 taken, 67% 3+)—Eng Fr Span Calc Stats Comp_Sci Bio Chem Physics Eur_Hist US_Hist Art_Hist Studio_Art Music_Theory. **Feat**—Humanities Chin Anat & Physiol Kinesiology Film Music. **Supp**—Dev_Read Rem_Math Rem_Read Rev Tut.
   Sports—Basket X-country Golf Soccer Swim Tennis Track. B: Baseball. G: Cheer Volley. **Activities:** 15.
   Somewhat selective adm: 57/yr. Appl fee: $75. Appl due: Rolling. Applied: 75. Accepted: 93%. Yield: 96%. **Tests** CTP_4 IQ.
   Enr 399. B 221. G 178. Elem 245. Sec 154. Wh 83%. Blk 10%. Asian 5%. Other 2%. Avg class size: 16. Casual. **Fac 54.** M 13/F 41. FT 50/PT 4. Wh 98%. Blk 2%. Adv deg: 40%.
   Grad '11—40. Col—40. (UNC-Chapel Hill, NC St, U of SC, Hampden-Sydney, E Carolina, Baylor). **Avg SAT:** CR 580. M 570. W 586. **Col couns:** 1.
   Tui '12-'13: Day $6000-14,760 (+$600). **Aid:** Need 102 ($560,000).
   Summer: Acad Enrich Rem Rev Rec. Tui Day $100/wk. 8 wks.
   Endow $2,986,000. Plant val $5,261,000. Acres 53. Bldgs 7 (86% ADA). Class rms 35. Lib 12,000 vols. Sci labs 4. Auds 1. Art studios 2. Gyms 2. Fields 3. Comp labs 2. Comp/stud: 1:4.8.
   Est 1967. Nonprofit. Sem (Aug-June). **Assoc** SACS.

Westchester serves High Point, Greensboro, Winston-Salem (the Triad) and neighboring communities. Located in a country setting, the school's 53-acre campus in Davidson County is accessible to the varied educational opportunities and facilities of the Triad.

The program at Westchester follows the classical liberal arts tradition of academics, athletics and the arts. The lower school curriculum (grades K-5) combines work in the core disciplines with foreign language, art, music, library science, computers and physical education. Middle school boys and girls (grades 6-8) move from the self-contained classrooms of the lower school to a departmentalized setting that emphasizes self-discovery and mastery of either French or Spanish. The broad liberal arts program in the upper school (grades 9-12) provides opportunities for specialization and enrichment. Both honors and Advanced Placement courses are available to qualified upper school pupils.

Community service begins as early as grade 5 and continues through middle school, at which level each student chooses a month-long project. To fulfill a graduation requirement, all seniors plan, complete and report upon a weeklong project.

LEWISVILLE, NC. (66 mi. NNE of Charlotte, NC) Urban. Pop: 8826. Alt: 973 ft.

FORSYTH COUNTRY DAY SCHOOL
Day — Coed Gr PS (Age 3)-12

Lewisville, NC 27023. 5501 Shallowford Rd, PO Box 549. Tel: 336-945-3151.
Fax: 336-945-2907.
www.fcds.org   E-mail: cindykluttz@fcds.org
Nan Wodarz, Head (2011). BA, Univ of Illinois-Urbana, MS, National Lewis Univ, EdD, Northern Arizona Univ. **Cindy C. Kluttz, Adm.**
  Col Prep. AP (exams req'd; 407 taken, 72% 3+)—Eng Fr Span Calc Stats Comp_Sci Bio Chem Eur_Hist US_Hist US_Govt & Pol. **Feat**—Chin Lat Engineering Robotics Studio_Art Drama Music Music_Theory. **Supp**—ESL LD Tut.
  Sports—Basket X-country Soccer Swim Tennis Track. B: Baseball Football Golf Lacrosse Wrestling. G: F_Hockey Softball. **Activities:** 45.
  Selective adm: 120/yr. Appl fee: $100. Appl due: Rolling. Applied: 187. Accepted: 82%. Yield: 75%. **Tests** CTP_4.
  Enr 849. B 487. G 362. Elem 501. Sec 348. Wh 97%. Blk 2%. Asian 1%. Avg class size: 18. Stud/fac: 7:1. **Fac 137.** M 31/F 106. FT 137.
  Grad '11—110. Col—110. (UNC-Chapel Hill, NC St, UNC-Charlotte, VA Polytech, U of SC, High Pt). Athl schol 6. **Mid 50% SAT:** CR 530-670. M 550-680. Mid 50% ACT: 23-30.
  Tui '12-'13: Day $9300-19,910 (+$100).
  Summer: Enrich Rec. Sports. Tui Day $160-250. Basketball. Tui Day $90-130. 1 wk.
  Endow $13,000,000. Plant val $6,000,000. Acres 80. Bldgs 9. Class rms 60. 2 Libs 50,000 vols. Comp ctrs 1. Auds 1. Art studios 3. Music studios 2. Dance studios 1. Gyms 2. Fields 4. Courts 6. Comp labs 3. Comp/stud: 1:3.
  Est 1970. Nonprofit. Quar (Aug-June). **Assoc** CLS SACS.

Located on an 80-acre campus slightly west of Winston-Salem, Forsyth offers a traditional college preparatory education through its lower (grades PS-4), middle (grades 5-8) and upper (grades 9-12) schools. The upper school's academic offerings include courses in economics, microcomputers and psychology. Advanced Placement classes are available in all major disciplines.

Students who enroll at the school by grade 10 perform at least 30 hours of community service; at least 10 of these hours must take place off campus.

OAK RIDGE, NC. (73 mi. S of Roanoke, VA; 78 mi. WNW of Raleigh, NC) Rural. Pop: 950. Alt: 1040 ft.

OAK RIDGE MILITARY ACADEMY
Bdg and Day — Coed Gr 8-PG

Oak Ridge, NC 27310. 2317 Oak Ridge Rd, PO Box 498. Tel: 336-643-4131.
Fax: 336-643-1797.
www.oakridgemilitary.com   E-mail: blipke@ormila.com
Robert R. Rossi, Pres (2012). Bob Lipke, Adm.
  Col Prep. Milit. Feat—British_Lit Fr Span Anat Environ_Sci Comp_Sci Robotics African-Amer_Hist World_Relig Studio_Art JROTC SAT_Prep Aviation. **Supp**—ESL Makeup Rev Tut. **Dual enr:** UNC-Greensboro.
  Sports—Basket X-country Swim Track. B: Baseball Golf Soccer Tennis Wrestling. G: Equestrian. **Activities:** 11.
  Somewhat selective adm: Appl fee: $200. Appl due: Rolling. Accepted: 85%. Yield: 75%.

Enr 63. Elem 13. Sec 50. Wh 81%. Latino 5%. Blk 8%. Asian 6%. Intl 14%. Avg class size: 8. Stud/fac: 8:1. Uniform. **Fac 17.** M 8/F 9. FT 12/PT 5. Wh 59%. Latino 12%. Blk 24%. Asian 5%. Adv deg: 70%. In dorms 2.
Grad '11—23. Col—21. (Appalachian St, UNC-Charlotte, Citadel, E Carolina, UNC-Chapel Hill). **Avg SAT:** CR/M 1100. **Col couns:** 1.
Tui '12-'13: Bdg $27,000 (+$2380). **Day $14,000** (+$2380). **Intl Bdg $27,000** (+$4380). **Aid:** Merit 32 ($38,400).
Summer: Acad Enrich Rem Rec. Leadership Trng. Tui Bdg $1950-4475. Tui Day $1100-1950. 2½-5 wks.
Plant val $8,000,000. Acres 101. Bldgs 18. Dorms 4. Class rms 25. Lib 20,000 vols. Sci labs 3. Lang labs 1. Music studios 1. Gyms 2. Fields 4. Courts 6. Pools 1. Rifle ranges 2. Comp labs 1.
Est 1852. Nonprofit. Sem (Aug-May). **Assoc** SACS.

Oak Ridge was a private institution from its founding date until 1965, when it became the property of Oak Ridge Foundation, a nonprofit body dedicated to the preservation of the school's tradition. The country's first coeducational military academy, ORMA maintains a favorable student-teacher ratio, as well as faculty-supervised study halls and extra-help classes. Seniors satisfy a 20-hour community service requirement.

RALEIGH, NC. (130 mi. ENE of Charlotte, NC) Urban. Pop: 276,093. Alt: 316 ft.

RAVENSCROFT SCHOOL
Day — Coed Gr PS (Age 4)-12
Raleigh, NC 27615. 7409 Falls of the Neuse Rd. Tel: 919-847-0900. Fax: 919-846-2371. www.ravenscroft.org E-mail: admissions@ravenscroft.org
Doreen C. Kelly, Head (2003). BA, MS, Univ of Pennsylvania. **Pamela J. Jamison, Adm.**
Col Prep. AP (exams req'd; 485 taken, 91% 3+)—Eng Fr Lat Span Calc Stats Comp_ Sci Bio Chem Environ_Sci Physics Eur_Hist US_Hist Comp_Govt & Pol Econ Psych US_Govt & Pol Art_Hist Studio_Art. **Feat**—Creative_Writing African-Amer_Lit Chin Greek Multivariable_Calc Anat & Physiol Astron Sports_Med Biotech Engineering Web_Design Vietnam_War Civil_War Intl_Relations Photog Drama Music Music_ Theory Dance. **Supp**—Rev Tut.
Sports—Basket X-country Golf Lacrosse Soccer Swim Tennis Track. B: Baseball Football Wrestling. G: Cheer F_Hockey Softball Volley.
Selective adm: 166/yr. Usual entry: PS, K, 6 & 9. Appl fee: $70-125. Appl due: Dec. **Tests** CTP_4 SSAT.
Enr 1234. Elem 790. Sec 444. Avg class size: 17. Stud/fac: 7:1. **Fac 163.** M 52/F 111. FT 163. Wh 97%. Blk 3%. Adv deg: 56%.
Grad '11—104. Col—104. (Clemson, E Carolina, NC St, UNC-Chapel Hill, Wake Forest, U of SC). **Mid 50% SAT:** CR 570-680. M 600-700. W 590-700. **Col couns:** 2.
Tui '12-'13: Day $13,450-19,550 (+$3000).
Summer: Acad Enrich Rev Rec. Sports. 2-8 wks.
Endow $12,000,000. Plant val $30,000,000. Acres 125. Bldgs 13. Class rms 135. 3 Libs 32,004 vols. Labs 20. Theaters 2. Art studios 4. Music studios 8. Gyms 5. Fields 7. Courts 6. Pools 1. Tracks 1. Comp/stud: 1:2.
Est 1862. Nonprofit. Sem (Aug-June). **Assoc** CLS SACS.

Ravenscroft was operated by Christ Episcopal Church from its founding until 1968, when it was turned over to an independent board of trustees. The school is named for Rt. Rev. John Stark Ravenscroft, the first Episcopal bishop of North Carolina. In 1970, the school moved from its original location on Tucker Street to its present, 125-acre campus on the northern edge of Raleigh and expanded to include an upper school. Ravenscroft draws its students primarily from Raleigh and the surrounding communities.

In addition to including Advanced Placement courses in every discipline, the college preparatory program incorporates an array of summer programs and off-campus learning experiences. Boys and girls fulfill course requirements in English, math, science, social studies, foreign language and physical education. Pupils also perform at least 20 hours per year of mandatory community service in the upper school grades.

SAINT MARY'S SCHOOL
Bdg and Day — Girls Gr 9-12

Raleigh, NC 27603. 900 Hillsborough St. Tel: 919-424-4100, 800-948-2557.
Fax: 919-424-4122.
www.sms.edu   E-mail: admission@sms.edu
Monica M. Gillespie, Head (2012). BA, MEd, PhD, Univ of Virginia. **Kim McDowell, Adm.**
  Col Prep. AP (exams req'd; 308 taken, 60% 3+)—Eng Fr Lat Span Calc Stats Comp_ Sci Bio Chem Environ_Sci Physics US_Hist Psych US_Govt & Pol Studio_Art. **Feat**—Creative_Writing Astron Ecol Geol Women's_Stud Philos World_Relig Acting Drama Music Dance. **Supp**—Rev Tut.
  Sports—G: Basket X-country F_Hockey Golf Lacrosse Soccer Softball Swim Tennis Track Volley. **Activities:** 30.
  Selective adm (Gr 9-11): 83/yr. Bdg 44. Day 39. Appl fee: $100. Appl due: Jan. Applied: 171. Accepted: 83%. Yield: 58%. **Tests** SSAT TOEFL.
  Enr 274. Bdg 122. Day 152. Wh 80%. Latino 1%. Blk 7%. Asian 8%. Other 4%. Intl 7%. Avg class size: 10. Stud/fac: 8:1. **Fac 39.** M 11/F 28. FT 27/PT 12. Wh 98%. Latino 1%. Blk 1%. Adv deg: 74%. In dorms 8.
  Grad '11—87. Col—87. (UNC-Chapel Hill 10, NC St 8, Appalachian St 7, U of SC 5, Elon 4, U of GA 4). **Mid 50% SAT:** CR 520-630. M 500-630. W 520-640. **Col couns:** 1. Alum donors: 23%.
  Tui '12-'13: Bdg $40,800 (+$2950). **Day $19,100** (+$2950). **Aid:** Merit 58 ($120,150). Need 66 ($663,402).
  Summer: Enrich Rec. Arts. Sports. 1-2 wks.
  Endow $17,800,000. Plant val $38,600,000. Acres 23. Bldgs 27. Dorms 3. Class rms 34. Lib 40,000 vols. Lang labs 1. Auds 1. Art studios 3. Music studios 4. Dance studios 3. Gyms 1. Fields 2. Courts 6. Pools 1. Comp/stud: 1:1 Laptop prgm Gr 9-12.
  Est 1842. Nonprofit. Episcopal. Sem (Aug-May). **Assoc** SACS.

Situated on a 23-acre, wooded campus that is listed on the National Register of Historic Places, this Episcopal school became affiliated with the Church in the two Carolinas in 1897. Founder and, for 36 years, director was Rev. Dr. Aldert Smedes.

Saint Mary's provides a liberal arts curriculum that includes a selection of honors and Advanced Placement classes and is supplemented by a chapel program. A particularly strong arts program include a wide selection of courses and instrumental music lessons. All students fulfill a community service requirement of 10 hours per semester and 20 hours per year.

WILMINGTON, NC. (119 mi. SSE of Raleigh, NC) Urban. Pop: 75,838. Alt: 35 ft.

CAPE FEAR ACADEMY
Day — Coed Gr PS (Age 4)-12

Wilmington, NC 28412. 3900 S College Rd. Tel: 910-791-0287. Fax: 910-791-0290.
www.capefearacademy.org   E-mail: info@capefearacademy.org
Donald S. Berger, Head (2012). BA, Haverford College, MEd, Harvard Univ. **Susan Mixon Harrell, Adm.**
  Col Prep. AP (exams req'd; 240 taken, 83% 3+)—Eng Calc Stats Bio Environ_Sci Physics Eur_Hist US_Hist Comp_Govt & Pol US_Govt & Pol Music_Theory. **Elem**

math—Sadlier-Oxford. **Feat**—Lat Span Anat & Physiol Geol Marine_Bio/Sci Zoology Earth & Space_Sci Ceramics Film Photog Studio_Art Video_Production Drama Music Journ. **Supp**—Rev Tut. **Dual enr:** UNC-Wilmington, Cape Fear CC.
Sports—Basket X-country Lacrosse Soccer Swim. B: Golf Tennis. G: Cheer F_Hockey Softball Volley. **Activities:** 25.
Selective adm: 112/yr. Usual entry: PS, K, 6 & 9. Appl fee: $75. Appl due: Rolling. Applied: 182. Accepted: 69%. Yield: 88%. **Tests** CEEB CTP_4 ISEE SSAT.
Enr 627. B 307. G 320. Elem 395. Sec 232. Wh 92%. Latino 2%. Blk 2%. Asian 4%. Avg class size: 18. Uniform. **Fac 74.** M 20/F 54. FT 59/PT 15. Wh 100%. Adv deg: 45%.
Grad '11—56. Col—56. (UNC-Wilmington 7, UNC-Chapel Hill 6, E Carolina 5, NC St 4, Wake Forest 3, U of VA 2). **Avg SAT:** CR 596. M 575. W 555. Avg ACT: 26. **Col couns:** 1. Alum donors: 5%.
Tui '12-'13: Day $9800-14,720 (+$250-750). **Aid:** Merit 5 ($13,500). Need 96 ($794,774).
Summer: Acad Enrich Rev Rec. 1-8 wks.
Endow $565,000. Plant val $10,000,000. Acres 27. Bldgs 5 (100% ADA). Class rms 55. 2 Libs 6500 vols. Sci labs 5. Art studios 2. Music studios 3. Perf arts ctrs 1. Gyms 2. Fields 3. Tennis courts 4. Playgrounds 1. Comp labs 2. Comp/stud: 1:2 (1:1 Laptop prgm Gr 9-12).
Est 1967. Nonprofit. Sem (Aug-May). **Assoc** SACS.

The school originated along the Lower Cape Fear River in 1867, operating for 50 years as a school for boys. In 1967, a group of Wilmington citizens established the current coeducational school on a 27-acre, suburban site.

CFA's college preparatory curriculum emphasizes the development of study skills and higher-level thinking skills. Teaching strategies are varied, and students demonstrate additional evidence of their learning through verbal presentations, technology and written communication. Collaborative work among pupils is an important aspect of the program. Extensive fine arts offerings are available throughout, including instrumental ensembles in grades 6-12 and separate choral ensembles in the lower, middle and upper schools. Ceramics, sculpture and a strong drama program are among the academy's arts offerings.

During the lower school years (grades pre-K-5), specialists in art, music, science, computers, physical education, foreign language and library science supplement the basic curriculum. A technology program in the lower school supports math and technology course work.

The middle school (grades 6-8) encourages appropriate social development and critical-thinking skills through collaborative and creative projects. Students in the upper school (grades 9-12) prepare for college entrance with a selection of honors and Advanced Placement courses and electives supplementing the required curriculum. All incoming freshmen receive a netbook computer at no additional charge for school use. Upper school pupils satisfy a 72-hour community service requirement prior to graduation.

WINSTON-SALEM, NC. (70 mi. NNE of Charlotte, NC) Urban. Pop: 168,086. Alt: 1000 ft.

SALEM ACADEMY
Bdg and Day — Girls Gr 9-12

Winston-Salem, NC 27101. 500 E Salem Ave. Tel: 336-721-2643, 877-407-2536.
Fax: 336-917-5340.
www.salemacademy.com E-mail: academy@salem.edu
Karl J. Sjolund, Head (2007). BA, Virginia Military Institute, MA, Columbia Univ. **Lucia Uldrick, Adm.**
Col Prep. AP (127 exams taken, 86% 3+)—Eng Fr Lat Span Calc Stats Bio Chem Physics US_Hist World_Hist. **Feat**—African-Amer_Lit Environ_Sci Computers Anthro Econ Pol_Sci Psych Relig Studio_Art Drama Music Journ. **Supp**—ESL Tut.

Dual enr: Salem Col.

Sports—G: Basket X-country Fencing F_Hockey Golf Soccer Softball Swim Tennis Track Volley.

Selective adm (Gr 9-11): 71/yr. Bdg 41. Day 30. Appl fee: $50. Appl due: Rolling. Accepted: 70%. Yield: 63%. **Tests** SSAT TOEFL.

Enr 160. Bdg 108. Day 52. Wh 55%. Latino 3%. Blk 8%. Asian 33%. Other 1%. Intl 35%. Avg class size: 13. Stud/fac: 7:1. Casual. **Fac 23.** M 2/F 21. FT 22/PT 1. Wh 91%. Latino 4%. Blk 4%. Other 1%. Adv deg: 60%. In dorms 1.

Grad '10—43. Col—43. (UNC-Chapel Hill, Appalachian St, Elon, Guilford, NYU, NC St). **Avg SAT:** CR/M/W 1893. Alum donors: 17%.

Tui '11-'12: Bdg $39,030 (+$500). **Day $18,990** (+$500). **Aid:** Merit 15 ($50,000). Need 78 ($1,098,000).

Endow $6,500,000. Plant val $15,000,000. Acres 64. Dorms 4. Dorm rms 76. Class rms 164. Lib 8000 vols. Sci labs 3. Auds 3. Theaters 1. Art studios 1. Music studios 2. Dance studios 1. Gyms 2. Fields 5. Courts 12. Pools 1. Student ctrs 1. Comp labs 2.

Est 1772. Nonprofit. Moravian. Sem (Aug-May). **Assoc** SACS.

Located near the restored 18th-century Moravian village of Old Salem, the school provides girls with sound preparation for competitive colleges throughout the country. The curriculum is complemented by Salem College's lectures, concerts, facilities and classes, and advanced pupils may take courses at Salem College.

January Term, Salem's interim program, enables 10th and 11th graders to take on-campus enrichment classes, and also to engage in various evening programs. Juniors and seniors instead participate in an internship. In addition, all girls have the option to embark on an international trip. Destinations have included Germany, Austria, Switzerland, Australia, Greece and Italy, among others.

Music and theater are popular extracurricular pursuits, and the glee club performs locally, nationally and internationally. In addition to participation in activities, the academy encourages students to seek leadership positions.

SUMMIT SCHOOL

Day — Coed Gr PS (Age 4)-9

Winston-Salem, NC 27106. 2100 Reynolda Rd. Tel: 336-722-2777. Fax: 336-724-0099. www.summitschool.com   E-mail: kmemory@summitmail.org

Michael J. Ebeling, Head (2008). BA, Lake Forest College, MA, PhD, Univ of Virginia. **Nancy Tuohy, Adm.**

Pre-Prep. Gen Acad. Elem math—Everyday Math. **Feat**—Chin Fr Lat Span Computers Robotics Ceramics Photog Video_Production Animation. **Supp**—Dev_Read LD Rem_Read Tut.

Sports—Basket Golf Soccer Tennis Track. B: Baseball Football Lacrosse. G: F_Hockey Gymnastics Softball Volley.

Selective adm: 69/yr. Appl fee: $75. Appl due: Rolling. Applied: 128. Accepted: 50%. Yield: 77%.

Enr 520. Wh 82%. Latino 2%. Blk 11%. Asian 3%. Other 2%. Stud/fac: 5:1. **Fac 98.** Adv deg: 51%.

Grad '10—32. Prep—13. (Forsyth Co Day, Salem, Episcopal HS-VA, St Paul's Sch-NH).

Tui '12-'13: Day $11,150-21,600 (+$830-1050). **Aid:** Need 83 ($878,000).

Summer: Acad Enrich Rec. Tui Day $150/wk. 6 wks.

Endow $14,000,000. Plant val $46,000,000. Acres 28. Bldgs 10 (100% ADA). Class rms 53. 2 Libs 45,000 vols. Sci labs 5. Photog labs 1. Comp ctrs 7. Theaters 2. Art studios 2. Music studios 3. Pottery studios 1. Gyms 3. Athletic ctrs 1. Fields 4. Basketball courts 3. Tracks 1. Comp/stud: 1:1.2.

Est 1933. Nonprofit. Tri (Aug-June). **Assoc** SACS.

Summit combines recent methods of teaching with sound academic standards, while also making special provisions for acceleration. The 28-acre campus features a modern arts and technology building and athletic center. French and Spanish instruction begins in junior kindergarten, and Latin and Chinese language classes add to the curriculum in grades 4-9. The arts are integral to the curriculum at all grade levels.

Summit requires community service participation. Schoolwide service learning projects often emphasize environmental issues and global responsibility. In addition, older pupils satisfy the following service requirements: six hours in grade 6, eight hours in grade 7, 10 hours in grade 8 and 15 hours in grade 9.

SOUTH CAROLINA

BEAUFORT, SC. (48 mi. WSW of Charleston, SC) Suburban. Pop: 12,950. Alt: 15 ft.

BEAUFORT ACADEMY
Day — Coed Gr PS (Age 2)-12

Beaufort, SC 29907. 240 Sams Point Rd. Tel: 843-524-3393. Fax: 843-524-1171.
www.beaufortacademy.org E-mail: contact@beaufortacademy.org
Julie Stewart Corner, Int Head (2011). BA, MEd, Univ of Pittsburgh. **M. J. Simmons, Adm.**

Col Prep. AP (exams req'd; 66 taken, 74% 3+)—Eng Calc Bio Eur_Hist US_Hist Psych. **Feat**—British_Lit Creative_Writing Chin Lat Span Stats Anat & Physiol Marine_Bio/Sci Sports_Med Govt/Econ Photog Journ Public_Speak. **Supp**—LD Tut.

Sports—Basket Golf Soccer Swim Tennis. B: Baseball Football. G: Cheer Softball Volley.

Selective adm: Appl fee: $75. Appl due: Rolling. **Tests** CTP_4 IQ.

Enr 275. Elem 180. Sec 95. Wh 90%. Latino 3%. Blk 3%. Asian 2%. Other 2%. Avg class size: 16. **Fac 40.** Adv deg: 50%.

Grad '10—19. Col—19. (Furman 2, Clemson 2, Davidson 1, US Milit Acad 1, Carnegie Mellon 1, GA Inst of Tech 1). **Avg SAT:** CR 599. M 589. W 582. Avg ACT: 24.

Tui '12-'13: Day $8350-11,325 (+$350).

Endow $500,000. Plant val $4,000,000. Acres 37. Bldgs 8. Class rms 32. Lib 16,500 vols. Sci labs 2. Art studios 1. Music studios 1. Gyms 1. Fields 3. Courts 4. Tracks 1. Comp labs 2.

Est 1965. Nonprofit. Tri (Aug-May). **Assoc** SACS.

BA's lower, middle and upper schools occupy a 37-acre campus on Lady's Island in the Carolina low country. Students follow a core curriculum in all grades and have the opportunity for intensive and advanced study during the final two years. Foreign language study begins in kindergarten, and Latin is offered in the middle school. The academy maintains strong programs in the humanities, the fine arts and the sciences.

Mandatory in all school divisions, the three-week interim program enables boys and girls to travel, to receive academic support and enrichment, to undertake a challenging pursuit, to engage in community service or to complete an internship.

CAMDEN, SC. (22 mi. NE of Columbia, SC) Suburban. Pop: 6682. Alt: 222 ft.

CAMDEN MILITARY ACADEMY
Bdg — Boys Gr 7-PG

Camden, SC 29020. 520 Hwy 1 N. Tel: 803-432-6001, 800-948-6291.
Fax: 803-425-1020.
www.camdenmilitary.com E-mail: admissions@camdenmilitary.com
Col. Eric Boland, Head (2003). BA, MEd, Univ of South Carolina. **R. Casey Robinson, Adm.**

Col Prep. Milit. AP—Eng Calc Bio Chem. **Feat**—Fr Lat Span Comp_Sci Econ Psych Sociol Bible Music Finance Journ JROTC. **Supp**—Dev_Read Rem_Math Tut.

Sports—B: Baseball Basket X-country Football Golf Lacrosse Soccer Tennis Track Wrestling.

Selective adm: 151/yr. Appl fee: $100. Appl due: Rolling. Accepted: 80%.

Enr 302. Elem 100. Sec 200. PG 2. Wh 86%. Latino 2%. Blk 11%. Asian 1%. Intl 5%. Avg class size: 15. Stud/fac: 8:1. Uniform. **Fac 33.** M 31/F 2. FT 24/PT 9. Wh 79%. Latino 15%. Asian 6%. Adv deg: 51%.
Grad '08—67. Col—59. (Auburn, Appalachian St, Col of Charleston, Clemson, U of SC, Citadel). **Avg SAT:** CR/M 1050.
Tui '12-'13: Bdg $18,595 (+$1995). **Intl Bdg $20,895** (+$14,090).
Summer: Acad Rec. Tui Bdg $2295-4495. 6 wks.
Endow $1,000,000. Plant val $6,500,000. Bldgs 11. Dorms 4. Dorm rms 146. Class rms 17. Lib 9000 vols. Labs 4. Gyms 1. Fields 3. Tennis courts 3. Pools 1. Rifle ranges 1.
Est 1950. Nonprofit. Sem (Aug-May). **Assoc** SACS.

Originally founded as Camden Academy by a group of citizens, the academy began operating under the present administration in 1958, at which time the school assumed its present name.

In addition to the preparatory curriculum, the discipline of drill ceremonies and two classes in military educational training per week are required. Students may participate in a full program of athletics, band, debate and publications, among other extracurricular activities.

CHARLESTON, SC. (101 mi. SSE of Columbia, SC) Urban. Pop: 95,650. Alt: 10 ft.

ASHLEY HALL
Day — Boys PS (Age 2)-K, Girls Gr PS (Age 2)-12

Charleston, SC 29403. 172 Rutledge Ave. Tel: 843-722-4088. Fax: 843-720-2868.
www.ashleyhall.org   E-mail: admission@ashleyhall.org
Jill Swisher Muti, Head (2004). BMus, DePauw Univ, MA, Duke Univ. Amy Jenkins, Adm.

Col Prep. AP—Eng Fr Lat Span Calc Stats Bio Environ_Sci US_Hist Econ US_Govt & Pol Art_Hist Studio_Art. **Elem math**—Everyday Math. **Elem read**—Open Court.
Feat—Classics Creative_Writing Humanities Greek Ital Marine_Bio/Sci Oceanog Comp_Sci Milit_Hist Psych Women's_Stud Drama Music. **Supp**—Tut. **Dual enr:** Col of Charleston.
Sports—G: Basket X-country Equestrian Sail Soccer Softball Swim Tennis Track Volley. **Activities:** 35.
Selective adm: 105/yr. Usual entry: K, 5 & 9. Appl fee: $75. Appl due: Jan. Applied: 150. Accepted: 80%. Yield: 75%. **Tests** CTP_4 IQ ISEE SSAT.
Enr 652. B 38. G 614. Elem 477. Sec 175. Wh 92%. Latino 1%. Blk 4%. Asian 3%. Avg class size: 15. Stud/fac: 10:1. Uniform. **Fac 75.** M 5/F 70. FT 73/PT 2. Wh 97%. Latino 1%. Blk 1%. Asian 1%. Adv deg: 69%.
Grad '11—29. Col—29. (U of SC 4, Col of Charleston 3, Wash & Lee 2, Wofford 2, Harvard 1, Parsons Sch of Design 1). Athl schol 2. **Avg SAT:** CR 614. M 630. W 642. Avg ACT: 26.3. **Col couns:** 1. Alum donors: 40%.
Tui '12-'13: Day $13,170-20,130 (+$350-1780). **Aid:** Merit 30 ($50,000). Need 90 ($1,200,000). Work prgm 14 ($8000).
Summer (enr 100): Acad Rec. Tui Day $135-300/wk. 4 wks.
Endow $3,000,000. Plant val $10,000,000. Acres 5. Bldgs 9. Class rms 50. 2 Libs 20,000 vols. Sci labs 4. Photog labs 1. Auds 2. Art studios 2. Music studios 4. Dance studios 1. Recital halls 1. Gyms 1. Fields 1. Pools 1. Comp labs 3.
Est 1909. Nonprofit. Sem (Aug-May). **Assoc** SACS.

Founded by Mary Vardrine McBee, a graduate of Smith College, the school gained prominence through the breadth of educational ideals that she brought to bear and maintained for 40 years. Upon her retirement, the school was continued under the Ashley Hall Foundation.

The school's coeducational early education center, created in 1990, enrolls boys and girls in preschool (ages 2-4) and pre-first (age 5). Foreign language courses begin in the primary years and continue throughout. The upper school program includes Advanced Placement offerings, as well as various electives. Art, music and drama are part of the curriculum, and all students take physical education. Girls in grades 9-12 perform 40 hours of required community service each year.

CHARLESTON DAY SCHOOL

Day — Coed Gr 1-8

Charleston, SC 29401. 15 Archdale St. Tel: 843-377-0315. Fax: 843-720-2143.
www.charlestondayschool.org
E-mail: caroline.moore@charlestondayschool.org
Brendan J. O'Shea, Head (2004). BS, MEd, Univ of Virginia. **Caroline H. Moore, Adm.**
  Pre-Prep. Feat—Fr Span Computers Geog Ethics Studio_Art Music.
  Sports—Basket Soccer Tennis. B: Football Golf. G: Volley.
  Selective adm: 27/yr. Appl fee: $75. Appl due: Feb. Accepted: 52%. Yield: 45%. **Tests** CTP_4.
  Enr 206. Avg class size: 18. Stud/fac: 7:1. **Fac 26.** M 5/F 21. FT 20/PT 6. Adv deg: 69%.
  Grad '08—22. Prep—16. (Episcopal HS-VA 5, Ashley Hall 3, Porter-Gaud 1, Phillips Acad 1, Woodberry Forest 1). Alum donors: 12%.
  Tui '12-'13: Day $15,900.
  Endow $2,000,000. Plant val $3,000,000. Bldgs 5. Class rms 14. Lib 10,000 vols. Sci labs 1. Amphitheaters 1. Art studios 1. Music studios 1. Arts ctrs 1. Gyms 1. Comp labs 1. Laptop prgm Gr 1-8.
  Est 1937. Nonprofit. Sem (Aug-May). **Assoc** SACS.

Founded by Emily E. Tenney and Mary Stuart, who directed the school until 1971, CDS provides a varied elementary program for children in Greater Charleston. The school has relocated three times to accommodate growth and now occupies quarters in the city's historic district.

While Charleston Day places particular emphasis on its core curriculum (math, reading, language arts and science), pupils at all grade levels also take French, computer, art, music and physical education courses. Students in grades 5-8 may take Spanish and advanced math classes (including honors algebra). Special academic programs, team sports and fine arts productions provide enrichment. In addition, each class participates in an annual community outreach project.

PORTER-GAUD SCHOOL

Day — Coed Gr 1-12

Charleston, SC 29407. 300 Albemarle Rd. Tel: 843-556-3620. Fax: 843-556-7404.
www.portergaud.edu   E-mail: eleanor.hurtes@portergaud.edu
D. DuBose Egleston, Jr., Head (2009). BS, Furman Univ, MBA, The Citadel. **Eleanor W. Hurtes, Adm.**
  Col Prep. AP (exams req'd; 269 taken)—Eng Fr Span Calc Stats Comp_Sci Bio Chem Physics Eur_Hist US_Hist World_Hist Econ US_Govt & Pol Studio_Art. **Elem math**—Sadlier-Oxford. **Elem read**—Open Court. **Feat**—Mythology Chin Lat Environ_Sci Forensic_Sci Marine_Bio/Sci Ethics Relig Film Music Music_Theory Jazz_Ensemble Finance Journ.
  Sports—Basket X-country Sail Soccer Squash Swim Tennis Track. B: Baseball Football Golf. G: Cheer Softball Volley.
  Selective adm (Gr 1-11): 154/yr. Usual entry: 1, 6 & 9. Appl fee: $75. Appl due: Rolling. Applied: 250. Accepted: 80%. Yield: 75%. **Tests** CEEB CTP_4 IQ ISEE SSAT.
  Enr 902. B 542. G 360. Elem 560. Sec 342. Wh 89%. Latino 1%. Blk 5%. Asian 2%. Other 3%. Avg class size: 15. Uniform. **Fac 88.** Wh 99%. Blk 1%. Adv deg: 67%.
  Grad '11—94. Col—94. (Clemson, U of SC, Col of Charleston, UNC-Chapel Hill, U of VA, Citadel). Athl schol 6. **Avg SAT:** CR 626. M 612. W 635. Avg ACT: 27. **Col couns:**

2. Alum donors: 12%.
Tui '12-'13: Day $16,520-19,400 (+$1000). **Aid:** Need 180 ($1,800,000).
Summer: Enrich Rev Rem Rec. 1-10 wks.
Endow $10,000,000. Plant val $22,611,000. Acres 80. Bldgs 19. Class rms 72. 2 Libs 25,000 vols. Sci labs 11. Sci/tech ctrs 1. Auds 1. Art studios 3. Music studios 4. Gyms 2. Athletic ctrs 1. Fields 5. Courts 6. Comp labs 3.
Est 1867. Nonprofit. Episcopal (35% practice). Sem (Aug-May). **Assoc** CLS SACS.

In 1964, Gaud School for Boys (founded in 1908) merged with Porter-Military Academy (founded in 1867) to form the larger Porter-Gaud School, now located on an 80-acre campus overlooking the Ashley River. The school discontinued its military program at that time, and girls were first admitted in 1972.

Porter-Gaud conducts a traditional college preparatory program in a city that includes six colleges and universities. Music and art offerings are among the electives, and the school maintains hand bell choirs and both jazz and concert bands. A winterim program in middle school (grades 6-8) features community service, educational travel and nontraditional courses. Upper school students may participate in such community outreach programs as Habitat for Humanity, tutoring at an inner-city schools, working on food or toy drives, helping to feed the homeless, engaging in beach cleanups or providing peer counseling.

COLUMBIA, SC. (80 mi. S of Charlotte, NC) Urban. Pop: 116,278. Alt: 332 ft.

HEATHWOOD HALL EPISCOPAL SCHOOL
Day — Coed Gr PS (Age 3)-12

Columbia, SC 29201. 3000 S Beltline Blvd. Tel: 803-765-2309. Fax: 803-748-4755.
www.heathwood.org   E-mail: admissions@heathwood.org
Michael N. Eanes, Int Head (2011). BA, Ohio Wesleyan Univ, MA, Trinity College (CT).
Blair Mason, Gr 5-12 Adm; Pence Scurry, Gr PS-4 Adm.
Col Prep. AP (exams req'd; 144 taken, 89% 3+)—Eng Fr Lat Span Calc Stats Bio Environ_Sci Physics Eur_Hist US_Hist Studio_Art. **Elem math**—enVisionMATH. **Elem read**—Houghton Mifflin. **Feat**—Mythology Chin Anat & Physiol Astron Programming Web_Design Anthro Econ Psych World_Relig Ceramics Graphic_Arts Acting Theater_Arts Chorus Music_Theory Journ. **Supp**—Dev_Read Rem_Math Rem_Read Rev Tut. Outdoor ed.
Sports—Basket Bowl X-country Golf Soccer Swim Track. B: Baseball Football Lacrosse Wrestling. G: Cheer Softball Tennis Volley.
Selective adm: 124/yr. Appl fee: $80. Appl due: Rolling. Applied: 197. Accepted: 77%. Yield: 82%. **Tests** CTP_4.
Enr 773. B 371. G 402. Elem 533. Sec 240. Wh 82%. Latino 1%. Blk 14%. Asian 3%. Avg class size: 16. Stud/fac: 8:1. Casual. **Fac 98.** M 30/F 68. FT 82/PT 16. Adv deg: 70%.
Grad '11—52. Col—52. (U of SC, Clemson, Furman, Col of Charleston, Wofford, Vanderbilt). **Avg SAT:** CR 587. M 567. W 595. **Col couns:** 2.
Tui '11-'12: Day $12,565-15,490 (+$400-600). **Aid:** Merit 1 ($15,490). Need 173 ($1,277,266).
Summer: Acad Enrich Rev Rem Rec. SAT Prep. Sports. Tui Day $90-450/wk. 6 wks.
Endow $4,038,000. Plant val $20,000,000. Acres 122. Bldgs 24. Class rms 91. Lib 26,000 vols. Labs 7. Art studios 3. Music studios 3. Gyms 2. Fields 6. Tracks 1. Ropes crses 1. Comp/stud: 1:2.2.
Est 1951. Nonprofit. Episcopal. Sem (Aug-May). **Assoc** CLS SACS.

Heathwood Hall, founded by a group of parents in cooperation with the Episcopal Diocese of upper South Carolina, is the oldest independent school in Columbia. The school moved in 1974 to its present, 122-acre campus near the downtown area. The high school division, which opened in 1973, graduated its first class in 1977.

The curriculum is college preparatory, and admission is by examination. Instruction is highly personalized, with a low student-teacher ratio, special tutoring programs and customized curricular packages to meet pupils' needs. The interdenominational student body pursues intensive and rigorous academic and athletic programming.

Heathwood Hall's weeklong winterim for students in grades 9-12 focuses on five main areas: academic and cultural enrichment, leadership, service, wilderness education and internships. During their four years, boys and girls must participate in at least one winterim internship. Another compulsory program, Senior Exhibition, is a yearlong project for twelfth graders that requires sustained and substantive independent research in an academic area of the pupil's choosing. The Exhibition, which takes the form of an academic paper or an original product and contextualization, culminates in a public presentation.

Boys and girls accumulate 80 hours of required community service in grades 9-12. An after-school child development program operates throughout the school year for children through grade 8.

GREENVILLE, SC. (91 mi. WSW of Charlotte, NC; 139 mi. ENE of Atlanta, GA) Urban. Pop: 56,002. Alt: 1040 ft.

CHRIST CHURCH EPISCOPAL SCHOOL
Day — Coed Gr K-12

Greenville, SC 29607. 245 Cavalier Dr. Tel: 864-299-1522. Fax: 864-299-8861.
www.cces.org　E-mail: admission@cces.org
Leonard R. Kupersmith, Head (2010). BA, City Univ of New York, PhD, Kansas State Univ.
Kathy Vaughan Jones, Adm.
Col Prep. IB Diploma. IB PYP. AP (exams req'd; 218 taken, 82% 3+)—Eng Fr Lat Span Calc Stats Comp_Sci Bio Chem Environ_Sci Physics Eur_Hist US_Hist Comp_ Govt & Pol US_Govt & Pol Studio_Art Music_Theory. Feat—Chin Ger Greek Comp_ Design Chin & Japan_Hist Hist_of_the_South Anthro Econ Psych Theater_Arts. Supp—ESL Tut.
Sports—Basket X-country Golf Lacrosse Soccer Swim Tennis Track. B: Baseball Football Wrestling. G: Cheer F_Hockey Softball Volley.
Selective adm: 141/yr. Appl fee: $150. Appl due: Rolling. Applied: 267. Accepted: 64%. Yield: 82%. Tests CEEB CTP_4.
Enr 1025. B 527. G 498. Elem 683. Sec 342. Wh 83%. Latino 1%. Blk 4%. Asian 2%. Other 10%. Intl 8%. Avg class size: 18. Stud/fac: 9:1. Uniform. Fac 107. M 24/F 83. FT 98/PT 9. Adv deg: 66%.
Grad '11—74. Col—74. (Clemson 13, Col of Charleston 7, Wofford 6, U of SC 6, Wash & Lee 5, Furman 3). Avg SAT: CR 602. M 603. W 592. Avg ACT: 27. Col couns: 2. Alum donors: 14%.
Tui '12-'13: Day $12,700-16,920. Aid: Merit 18 ($114,203). Need 201 ($1,440,358).
Summer (enr 680): Acad Enrich Rec. Tui Day $120-750/wk. 6 wks.
Endow $10,700,000. Plant val $36,500,000. Acres 72. Bldgs 5. Class rms 85. 3 Libs 21,000 vols. Sci labs 6. Lang labs 2. Auds 1. Theaters 1. Art studios 5. Music studios 5. Gyms 1. Fields 5. Courts 5. Tracks 1. Comp labs 5. Comp/stud: 1:3.
Est 1959. Nonprofit. Episcopal. Sem (Aug-June). Assoc CLS SACS.

Established as an elementary school offering grades K-6, Christ Church expanded to grade 9 upon completion of the Parish House of Christ Church. In 1969, the vestry decided to add grades 9-12 and acquired the 72-acre campus that now houses all three school divisions.

CCES offers a broad college preparatory curriculum that features the International Baccalaureate Diploma, a full complement of Advanced Placement courses, and a strong fine and performing arts department. Christian education in the lower and middle schools and religious studies in formal classes are required for graduation, and all students attend chapel (although the school serves pupils of all faiths). Upper school students perform 15 hours of required community service each year.

The student body displays a significant international presence, with pupils enrolling from more than 20 countries.

SPARTANBURG, SC. (64 mi. WSW of Charlotte, NC; 164 mi. ENE of Atlanta, GA) Urban. Pop: 39,673. Alt: 680-875 ft.

SPARTANBURG DAY SCHOOL

Day — Coed Gr PS (Age 4)-12

Spartanburg, SC 29307. 1701 Skylyn Dr. Tel: 864-582-8380. Fax: 864-582-7530.
www.spartanburgdayschool.org   E-mail: susan.jeffords@sdsgriffin.org
Rachel Deems, Head (2012). BA, Judson College, MA, Univ of Alabama-Tuscaloosa.
Susan Jeffords, Adm.
Col Prep. Gen Acad. IB PYP. IB MYP. AP (exams req'd; 154 taken, 83% 3+)—Eng
    Fr Lat Span Calc Stats Bio Chem Environ_Sci Physics Eur_Hist US_Hist Art_Hist
    Studio_Art Music_Theory. **Elem math**—Singapore Math. **Elem read**—Open Court.
    Feat—Chin Astrophysics Comp_Sci Econ Native_Amer_Stud Philos Band Speech.
    Supp—Dev_Read LD Rem_Math Rem_Read Rev Tut.
Sports—Basket X-country Soccer Swim Tennis Track. B: Baseball Golf Lacrosse. G:
    F_Hockey Volley. **Activities:** 18.
Selective adm: 73/yr. Usual entry: PS, 7 & 9. Appl fee: $50. Appl due: Rolling. Applied:
    109. Accepted: 70%. Yield: 90%. **Tests** IQ Stanford.
Enr 473. B 229. G 244. Elem 347. Sec 126. Wh 90%. Latino 1%. Blk 2%. Asian 4%.
    Other 3%. Avg class size: 12. Stud/fac: 9:1. **Fac 64.** M 15/F 49. FT 54/PT 10. Wh 98%.
    Latino 2%. Adv deg: 67%.
Grad '10—41. Col—41. (Col of Charleston 6, Limestone 3, Presbyterian 2, Rhodes 2, U
    of VA 1, Wake Forest 1). **Avg SAT:** CR/M 1216. **Col couns:** 3. Alum donors: 10%.
Tui '10-'11: Day $6419-14,228 (+$300-500). **Aid:** Need 31 ($265,000).
Summer (enr 300): Acad Enrich Rev Rec. Tui Day $150/wk. 8 wks.
Endow $2,000,000. Plant val $9,137,000. Acres 50. Bldgs 9. Class rms 52. 3 Libs 18,631
    vols. Sci labs 4. Aud/gyms 1. Art studios 4. Music studios 3. Arts ctrs 1. Gyms 1. Fields
    4. Courts 9. Comp labs 3. Comp/stud: 1:2.8.
Est 1957. Nonprofit. Sem (Aug-May). **Assoc** CLS SACS.

With an emphasis on small classes, this school offers a classical college preparatory curriculum that stresses English and mathematical skills. Mathematics, English, art, music, history and science are departmentalized in grades 5-12. In the elementary grades, SDS offers the International Baccalaureate Primary Years and Middle Years programs. The foreign language program allows pupils to begin Chinese study in prekindergarten, Spanish in grade 5, Latin in grade 7 and French in grade 8.

A learning laboratory for boys and girls with learning differences is a noteworthy curricular feature. Art is required through grade 8 and available through grade 12. SDS' winter interim program, Special Studies Week, enables students in grades 9-12 to engage in off-campus enrichment, outdoor experiences, travel or community service.

TENNESSEE

BELL BUCKLE, TN. (46 mi. SSE of Nashville, TN) Rural. Pop: 391. Alt: 846 ft.

THE WEBB SCHOOL
Bdg — Coed Gr 7-PG; Day — Coed 6-12

Bell Buckle, TN 37020. 319 Webb Rd E, PO Box 488. Tel: 931-389-6003, 888-733-9322. Fax: 931-389-6657.
www.thewebbschool.com   E-mail: admissions@webbschool.com
Raymond S. Broadhead, Head (2010). BS, Univ of Pennsylvania, ScM, Brown Univ. **Julie Harris, Adm.**

   Col Prep. AP (exams req'd; 116 taken, 73% 3+)—Eng Lat Calc Stats Chem Physics Eur_Hist US_Hist Econ Studio_Art. **Feat**—Fr Span Anat & Physiol Comp_Sci Psych Ethics World_Relig Art_Hist Theater Music_Theory Speech Wilderness_Ed. **Supp**—ESL LD Tut. Outdoor ed.

   Sports—Basket X-country Golf Lacrosse Soccer Tennis. B: Baseball Football. G: Softball Volley. **Activities:** 26.

   Selective adm (Bdg Gr 7-11; Day 6-11): 71/yr. Bdg 35. Day 36. Usual entry: 6, 7 & 9. Appl fee: $50. Appl due: Feb. Applied: 127. Accepted: 71%. Yield: 69%. **Tests** CEEB ISEE SSAT Stanford TOEFL.

   Enr 304. B 151. G 153. Bdg 98. Day 206. Intl 15%. Avg class size: 12. Stud/fac: 7:1. Uniform. **Fac 44.** M 23/F 21. FT 44. Wh 96%. Latino 2%. Blk 2%. Adv deg: 61%. In dorms 10.

   Grad '11—49. Col—48. (Berry 7, U of the South 3, U of TN-Chattanooga 3, U of TN-Knoxville 3, Belmont U 2, Clemson 2). **Avg SAT:** CR 626. M 623. W 600. Avg ACT: 26. Mid 50% ACT: 23-27. **Col couns:** 1. Alum donors: 21%.

   Tui '12-'13: Bdg $39,600 (+$1700). **5-Day Bdg $31,150** (+$1200). **Day $15,900-17,000** (+$800). **Intl Bdg $39,600** (+$4400-13,400). **Aid:** Merit 4 ($154,000). Need 103 ($906,343).

   Endow $24,000,000. Plant val $30,000,000. Acres 150. Bldgs 24 (25% ADA). Dorms 4. Dorm rms 60. Class rms 25. Lib 22,000 vols. Sci labs 7. Lang labs 5. Dark rms 1. Auds 1. Theaters 1. Art studios 1. Music studios 2. Dance studios 1. Black-box theaters 1. Gyms 2. Fields 5. Courts 4. Comp labs 2. Comp/stud: 1:2.

   Est 1870. Nonprofit. Sem (Aug-May). **Assoc** CLS SACS.

The school was founded in Culleoka by William R. Webb, active in educational, religious, political, social and community affairs and affectionately known as "Old Sawney." His brother, John M. Webb, joined the school in 1874 and served as coprincipal from that time until his death in 1916. Through the united efforts of the two brothers, the school soon attracted boys from all over the South and became a center of influence in the region. In 1886, the school was moved from Culleoka to its present location at Bell Buckle. William R. Webb, Jr., son of Old Sawney, joined the faculty in 1897, became a principal along with his father and his uncle in 1908, and took over as sole principal in 1926, upon the death of his father. During the years of his service, the school began to develop its present dormitory system. Webb is situated on 150 acres in a rural setting, and school facilities have been improved and enlarged over the years.

Academically, the college preparatory program is structured. In a small-class setting, Webb conducts a two-track system that enables boys and girls to take accelerated classes (including Advanced Placement courses) in areas of particular academic strength. An extensive college counseling program begins early in each student's career at Webb. Among the school's activities is an outdoor education program that provides opportunities for leadership.

CHATTANOOGA, TN. (83 mi. ENE of Huntsville, AL) Urban. Pop: 155,554. Alt: 674 ft.

BAYLOR SCHOOL
Bdg — Coed Gr 9-12; Day — Coed 6-12

Chattanooga, TN 37405. 171 Baylor School Rd. Tel: 423-267-8505. Fax: 423-757-2525.
www.baylorschool.org   E-mail: admission@baylorschool.org
Scott A. Wilson, Pres (2009). BA, Univ of Georgia, MEd, Univ of South Carolina. **Jim Kennedy, Adm.**
 Col Prep. AP (exams req'd; 454 taken, 80% 3+)—Eng Fr Ger Lat Span Calc Stats Bio Chem Environ_Sci Physics Eur_Hist US_Hist Human_Geog Art_Hist Studio_Art. **Feat**—Creative_Writing Eur_Lit Mythology S_Amer_Lit Chin Astron Forensic_Sci Geol Comp_Sci Robotics Civil_War WWII Archaeol Econ Law Psych Ethics Drawing Painting Photog Acting Band Chorus Orchestra Mech_Drawing SAT_Prep. **Supp**—ESL Tut.
 Sports—Basket Bowl Crew X-country Fencing Golf Lacrosse Swim Tennis Track. B: Baseball Football Wrestling. G: Cheer Soccer Softball Volley. **Activities:** 60.
 Selective adm: 195/yr. Bdg 80. Day 115. Appl fee: $75. Appl due: Jan. **Tests** ISEE SSAT.
 Enr 1053. B 549. G 504. Bdg 200. Day 853. Intl 10%. Avg class size: 15. Stud/fac: 7:1. Uniform. **Fac 144.** M 77/F 67. FT 144. Adv deg: 63%. In dorms 39.
 Grad '08—191. Col—190. (U of TN-Knoxville 25, Auburn 13, U of AL-Tuscaloosa 11, U of TN-Chattanooga 7, TN Tech 6, Middle TN St 5). **Mid 50% SAT:** CR 500-640. M 520-660. W 510-640. Mid 50% ACT: 23-28. **Col couns:** 3.
 Tui '12-'13: Bdg $41,926 (+$1000). **Day $20,585** (+$500). **Intl Bdg $43,000-45,000** (+$1000). **Aid:** Need 284 ($2,000,000).
 Summer: Enrich Rec. Sports. Tui Bdg $175-975. 1 wk. Tui Day $85-500. 1-2 wks.
 Endow $65,000,000. Plant val $50,000,000. Acres 670. Bldgs 15. Dorms 5. Dorm rms 94. Class rms 70. Lib 50,000 vols. Sci labs 5. Lang labs 2. Art studios 4. Music studios 2. Arts ctrs 1. Gyms 4. Fields 12. Courts 17. Pools 1. Climbing walls 1. Comp labs 4. Comp/stud: 1:1.6.
 Est 1893. Nonprofit. (Aug-May). **Assoc** CLS SACS.

John Roy Baylor, selected for the task by a group of Chattanooga businessmen, established this college preparatory school to address a community need. Originally a boys' school, Baylor became coeducational in 1985.

The school, which occupies a 670-acre tract on the banks of the Tennessee River, offers a program featuring honors and Advanced Placement courses in most disciplines, in addition to an array of electives. A noteworthy aspect of the curriculum is the foreign language program, which comprises five languages (including Chinese). Beginning in grade 6 and continuing through senior year, Baylor assigns each student with an advisor who is also a faculty member.

Experiential learning is a point of emphasis at Baylor. The community service program includes a grant-writing course that enables pupils to secure funding for community programs. Travel opportunities are designed to broaden student perspective. Finally, a highly regarded wilderness program and freshman and senior annual trips also take an experiential approach.

THE BRIGHT SCHOOL
Day — Coed Gr PS (Age 3)-5

Chattanooga, TN 37405. 1950 Hixson Pike. Tel: 423-267-8546. Fax: 423-265-0025.
www.brightschool.com   E-mail: bmoore@brightschool.com
O. J. Morgan, Head (2004). BA, Colby College, MAT, Northwestern Univ, MTh, Harvard Univ. **Brooke Moore, Adm.**
 Pre-Prep. Elem math—Everyday Math. **Feat**—Writing Span Computers Studio_Art

Music Indus_Arts. **Supp**—Rem_Math Rem_Read Tut.
Sports—Basket X-country Soccer Track. B: Football Lacrosse.
Selective adm: 55/yr. Usual entry: PS. Appl due: Rolling. **Tests** CTP_4 Stanford.
Enr 327. B 154. G 173. Wh 81%. Latino 5%. Blk 4%. Asian 8%. Other 2%. Avg class size: 18. Stud/fac: 10:1. Uniform. **Fac 62.** Wh 100%. Adv deg: 40%.
Grad '08—50. **Prep**—47. (Girls Prep, Baylor, McCallie).
Tui '12-'13: Day $9750-12,975 (+$50). **Aid:** Need 76 ($400,860).
Summer: Enrich Rec. Tui Day $125/wk. 10 wks.
Endow $4,103,000. Plant val $6,561,000. Acres 22. Bldgs 1. Class rms 23. Lib 17,500 vols. Sci labs 1. Auds 1. Art studios 1. Music studios 1. Man arts studios 1. Gyms 1. Fields 2. Comp labs 1.
Est 1913. Nonprofit. Sem (Aug-May). **Assoc** SACS.

Founded by Mary Gardner Bright and under her direction for 48 years, this is the oldest independent elementary school in the state. The curriculum prepares students for local independent secondary schools. Specialized areas include music, art, manual arts, computer, Spanish and physical education.

Beyond the academic offerings, an extended-care program offers intramural athletics, music and art lessons, ballet and computer instruction. The school occupies a well-equipped, 22-acre campus.

GIRLS PREPARATORY SCHOOL

Day — Girls Gr 6-12

Chattanooga, TN 37405. 205 Island Ave, PO Box 4736. Tel: 423-634-7600.
Fax: 423-634-7675.
www.gps.edu   E-mail: dyoung@gps.edu
Stanley R. Tucker, Jr., Head (1987). BA, Jacksonville Univ, MEd, Univ of North Florida.
Debbie Young, Adm.
    Col Prep. AP (exams req'd; 235 taken, 80% 3+)—Eng Fr Lat Span Calc Comp_Sci Bio Chem Physics Eur_Hist US_Hist Comp_Govt & Pol US_Govt & Pol Art_Hist Studio_ Art. **Feat**—Chin Stats Astron Environ_Sci Forensic_Sci Marine_Bio/Sci Web_Design Comp_Animation Civil_Rights Govt World_Relig Graphic_Arts Visual_Arts Media_ Arts Drama Music Dance. **Supp**—Rev Tut. **Dual enr:** Chattanooga St CC.
    Sports—G: Basket Bowl Cheer Crew X-country Golf Lacrosse Soccer Softball Swim Tennis Track Volley. **Activities:** 50.
    Selective adm: 105/yr. Usual entry: 6. Appl fee: $50. Appl due: Rolling. Applied: 203. Accepted: 76%. Yield: 67%.
    Enr 600. Elem 244. Sec 356. Wh 82%. Blk 6%. Asian 8%. Other 4%. Avg class size: 14. Stud/fac: 9:1. Uniform. **Fac 75.** M 16/F 59. FT 69/PT 6. Wh 96%. Latino 2%. Blk 1%. Asian 1%. Adv deg: 62%.
    Grad '11—83. **Col**—83. (U of TN-Knoxville 12, U of TN-Chattanooga 9, Auburn 7, U of the South 4, Wash U 2, Furman 2). Athl schol 3. **Mid 50% SAT:** CR 540-650. M 540-650. W 550-670. Mid 50% ACT: 24-30. **Col couns:** 2. Alum donors: 21%.
    Tui '11-'12: Day $20,020 (+$750). **Aid:** Merit 2 ($40,040). Need 233 ($2,198,859).
    Summer (enr 400): Acad Enrich Rec. Sports. Tui Day $145-750. 1-2 wks.
    Endow $27,700,000. Plant val $49,498,000. Acres 57. Bldgs 11. Class rms 90. Lib 35,000 vols. Sci labs 9. Lang labs 1. Auds 1. Theaters 2. Art studios 5. Music studios 2. Dance studios 3. Gyms 2. Fields 4. Courts 17. Pools 1. Tracks 1. Weight rms 1. Comp labs 1. Comp/stud: 1:1 Laptop prgm Gr 8-12.
    Est 1906. Nonprofit. Sem (Aug-June). **Assoc** CLS SACS.

Founded by Grace McCallie, Tommie Duffy and Eula Jarnagin, Girls Preparatory School offers a college preparatory curriculum with honors and Advanced Placement courses in all disciplines. A coordinate program with the McCallie School combines GPS' single-gender school with coeducational extracurricular and social activities in such areas as the performing arts. Students participate in community service projects throughout the year. Beginning in grade 8 students purchase laptop computers for use in the classroom and to connect to the campuswide wireless network.

GPS schedules two optional trips over winter break for eighth graders and seniors.

McCALLIE SCHOOL

Bdg — Boys Gr 9-12; Day — Boys 6-12

Chattanooga, TN 37404. 500 Dodds Ave. Tel: 423-624-8300, 800-234-2163.
Fax: 423-493-5426.
www.mccallie.org   E-mail: admission@mccallie.org
Robert Kirk Walker, Jr., Head (1999). BA, Univ of North Carolina-Chapel Hill, MS, PhD, Vanderbilt Univ. **Troy Kemp, Adm.**

Col Prep. AP (exams req'd; 512 taken, 90% 3+)—Eng Fr Lat Span Calc Stats Comp_ Sci Bio Chem Physics Eur_Hist US_Hist World_Hist Econ Studio_Art. **Feat**—Poetry Shakespeare Southern_Lit Chin Ger Greek Japan Bioethics Anthro Psych Bible Film Photog Sculpt Music_Theory Speech. **Supp**—Tut. **Dual enr:** Chattanooga St Tech CC.

Sports—B: Baseball Basket Bowl Crew X-country Football Golf Lacrosse Soccer Swim Tennis Track Wrestling. **Activities: 25.**

Selective adm (Bdg Gr 9-11; Day 6-11): 203/yr. Bdg 87. Day 116. Appl fee: $50. Appl due: Feb. Applied: 458. Accepted: 78%. Yield: 55%. **Tests** ISEE SSAT TOEFL.

Enr 889. Bdg 244. Day 645. Elem 246. Sec 643. Avg class size: 13. Stud/fac: 8:1. Formal. **Fac 95.** M 75/F 20. FT 88/PT 7. Wh 96%. Latino 1%. Blk 3%. Adv deg: 56%. In dorms 32.

Grad '11—146. Col—146. (U of AL-Tuscaloosa 8, U of TN-Chattanooga 8, U of TN-Knoxville 8, U of MS 6, Vanderbilt 6, Wake Forest 6). Athl schol 6. **Mid 50% SAT:** CR 530-650. M 560-680. W 510-630. Mid 50% ACT: 24-30. **Col couns:** 2. Alum donors: 32%.

Tui '12-'13: Bdg $40,860 (+$300-800). **Day $21,690** (+$300-800). **Intl Bdg $41,860** (+$3000). **Aid:** Merit 62 ($747,014). Need 250 ($4,098,675).

Summer: Acad Rec. Sports. Tui Bdg $1950/2-wk ses. 6 wks.

Endow $65,000,000. Plant val $60,000,000. Acres 100. Bldgs 32. Dorms 5. Dorm rms 124. Class rms 41. Lib 32,000 vols. Art studios 4. Music studios 2. Black-box theaters 1. Gyms 6. Fields 7. Courts 14. Pools 2.

Est 1905. Nonprofit. Nondenom Christian. Sem (Aug-May). **Assoc** CLS SACS.

The McCallie brothers, Prof. Spencer J. McCallie and Dr. J. Park McCallie, conducted the school they founded from 1905 to 1949. With a consistently demanding faculty, they developed superior academic standards and athletic facilities comparable to those of Northern schools. Graduates go on to competitive colleges in the South and around the country. Through a year of Bible study, activities such as Young Life, FCA and Big Brothers, and the honor system, emphasis is put on the development of Christian character. A coordinate program with Girls Preparatory School provides a limited number of coed courses and joint theater productions, a cheerleading squad, activities and social events.

A weekend activities program and an extensive academic counseling program provide additional stimuli. Faculty members conduct one-on-one tutorials four times per week for those students requiring extra help. In addition to interscholastic sports, McCallie maintains a comprehensive physical fitness program in which all participate.

GERMANTOWN, TN. (12 mi. E of Memphis, TN) Urban. Pop: 37,348. Alt: 379 ft.

ST. GEORGE'S INDEPENDENT SCHOOL
Day — Coed Gr PS (Age 4)-12

Germantown, TN 38138. 8250 Poplar Ave. Tel: 901-261-2300. Fax: 901-261-2371.
Other locations: 3749 Kimball Ave, Memphis 38111; 1880 Wolf River Blvd, Collierville 38017.
www.sgis.org E-mail: jtaylor@sgis.org
William W. Taylor, Pres (2007). BA, Kenyon College, MAR, Yale Univ. Jennifer Taylor, Adm.

Col Prep. AP (exams req'd; 281 taken, 73% 3+)—Eng Fr Lat Span Calc Stats Bio Chem Physics Eur_Hist US_Hist World_Hist. Elem math—Everyday Math. Elem read—Open Court. Feat—Anat & Physiol Astron Environ_Sci Engineering Comp_Sci Econ Psych Relig Film Music Journ. Supp—Dev_Read Makeup Rem_Math Rem_Read Rev Tut. Dual enr: Christian Bros.

Sports—Basket X-country Golf Lacrosse Soccer Swim Tennis Track. B: Baseball Football Wrestling. G: Cheer Softball Volley. Activities: 37.

Selective adm: Usual entry: PS & 6. Appl fee: $25-50. Appl due: Rolling. Yield: 71%. Tests ISEE.

Enr 1203. B 606. G 597. Elem 816. Sec 387. Wh 75%. Latino 1%. Blk 18%. Asian 2%. Other 4%. Avg class size: 20. Stud/fac: 8:1. Fac 98. M 25/F 73. FT 90/PT 8. Wh 91%. Latino 2%. Blk 5%. Asian 1%. Other 1%. Adv deg: 70%.

Grad '11—89. Col—87. (MS St, U of AL-Tuscaloosa, SMU, U of MS, U of TN-Knoxville, U of AR-Fayetteville). Avg SAT: CR 621. M 615. W 616. Mid 50% SAT: CR 550-680. M 560-690. W 540-670. Avg ACT: 26.8. Mid 50% ACT: 23-30. Col couns: 2.

Tui '12-'13: Day $11,890-16,590 (+$200-1000).
Summer: Acad Enrich Rev Rec. Tui Day $200/wk. 5 wks.
Endow $2,200,000. Acres 250. Bldgs 16. Class rms 70. Lib 14,000 vols. Sci labs 2. Auds 2. Theaters 2. Art studios 2. Music studios 3. Gyms 4. Fields 8. Pools 1. Comp labs 2. Laptop prgm Gr 6-12.
Est 1959. Nonprofit. Tri (Aug-May). Assoc CLS SACS.

St. George's conducts elementary and secondary curricula that place strong emphasis on language arts, mathematics and science. Beginning in the middle school grades, classes are conducted by separate math, reading, science and social studies departments, while instruction in the lower grades is in self-contained homerooms with the involvement of specialty teachers.

The development of Judeo-Christian values is a recognized part of the educational process. Pupils study art, religion, foreign language, music, computers, physical education and library skills at all levels.

As part of a multi-phase expansion of the program, St. George's opened a second elementary campus in August 2001 in Memphis, then started a high school division (grades 6-12) in fall 2002 in Collierville.

JACKSON, TN. (76 mi. ENE of Memphis, TN) Urban. Pop: 59,643. Alt: 450 ft.

UNIVERSITY SCHOOL OF JACKSON
Day — Coed Gr PS (Age 2)-12

Jackson, TN 38305. 232 McClellan Rd. Tel: 731-664-0812. Fax: 731-664-5046.
www.usjbruins.org E-mail: kshearin@usjbruins.org
Clay Lilienstern, Head (2007). BA, Univ of Alabama-Tuscaloosa, JD, MBA, Univ of Houston, LLM, George Washington Univ, MTS, Southern Methodist Univ. Kay Shearin,

Adm.
Col Prep. AP (exams req'd; 153 taken, 88% 3+)—Eng Span Calc Bio Chem Environ_
Sci Physics Eur_Hist US_Hist Studio_Art Music_Theory. **Feat**—Fr Anat & Physiol
Ecol Comp_Sci Psych Govt/Econ World_Relig Music Accounting Journ Speech
Tech_Writing. **Supp**—ESL Tut.
Sports—Basket X-country Golf Soccer Tennis Track. B: Baseball Football. G: Softball
Volley.
Somewhat selective adm: 141/yr. Appl fee: $50. Appl due: Rolling. Applied: 180.
Accepted: 85%. Yield: 94%. **Tests** IQ.
Enr 1180. B 608. G 572. Wh 91%. Latino 1%. Blk 3%. Asian 4%. Other 1%. Avg class
size: 20. Stud/fac: 14:1. Uniform. **Fac 91.** M 17/F 74. FT 90/PT 1. Wh 95%. Blk 5%.
Adv deg: 57%.
Grad '11—83. Col—83. (U of MS, MS St, Union U, Middle TN St, TN Tech, U of TN-
Knoxville). Athl schol 2. **Avg SAT:** CR 542. M 553. W 543. **Mid 50% SAT:** CR 480-590.
M 490-610. W 480-600. Avg ACT: 25.9. Mid 50% ACT: 23-28. Alum donors: 20%.
Tui '12-'13: Day $6140-8125 (+$50-265). **Aid:** Need 44 ($100,000).
Summer: Acad Enrich Rev Rec. 12 wks.
Acres 140. Bldgs 3. Class rms 50. 3 Libs 17,000 vols. Sci labs 5. Theaters 2. Art studios
4. Music studios 4. Gyms 4. Fields 5. Courts 6. Field houses 2. Comp labs 5.
Est 1970. Nonprofit. Quar (Aug-May). **Assoc** SACS.

Situated on a 140-acre campus, this school offers a college preparatory curriculum for average and above-average students. Advanced Placement and honors classes are available in the
major disciplines. Spanish classes begin in prekindergarten, and French and Spanish are available in grades 3-12. Computer instruction begins in grade 1. The fine arts department includes
chorus, music, band, show choir, plays, musicals and speech. Students in grades 9-12 perform
50 cumulative hours of required community service.

Pupils may also participate in a comprehensive sports program. USJ organizes both regional
and international student trips.

KNOXVILLE, TN. (97 mi. NE of Chattanooga, TN) Urban. Pop: 173,890. Alt: 889 ft.

WEBB SCHOOL OF KNOXVILLE
Day — Coed Gr K-12

Knoxville, TN 37923. 9800 Webb School Dr. Tel: 865-693-0011. Fax: 865-691-8057.
www.webbschool.org   E-mail: susan_smith@webbschool.org
Scott L. Hutchinson, Pres (1999). BA, Duke Univ, MEd, College of William and Mary.
Susan M. Smith, Upper & Middle Sch Adm; Angie Crabtree, Lower Sch Adm.
Col Prep. AP (422 exams taken, 86% 3+)—Eng Fr Lat Span Calc Stats Comp_Sci Bio
Chem Environ_Sci Physics Eur_Hist US_Hist World_Hist Econ Psych US_Govt &
Pol Art_Hist Studio_Art Music_Theory. **Elem math**—Everyday Math. **Elem read**—
Reading Street. **Feat**—Poetry ASL Chin Engineering Robotics Civil_War Ethics Relig
World_Relig Film Photog Acting Theater Band Chorus Orchestra Handbells Journ.
Supp—Rem_Math Rem_Read Tut.
Sports—Basket Bowl X-country Golf Sail Soccer Swim Tennis Track. B: Baseball Foot-
ball Lacrosse Wrestling. G: Cheer F_Hockey Softball Volley. **Activities:** 33.
Selective adm: 156/yr. Usual entry: K, 6 & 9. Appl fee: $75. Appl due: Jan. Applied: 237.
Accepted: 66%. Yield: 90%. **Tests** ISEE.
Enr 1047. B 521. G 526. Elem 571. Sec 476. Wh 87%. Blk 2%. Asian 5%. Other 6%. Avg
class size: 17. Stud/fac: 10:1. Uniform. **Fac 102.** M 31/F 71. FT 95/PT 7. Wh 94%.
Latino 2%. Asian 3%. Other 1%. Adv deg: 69%.
Grad '11—117. Col—117. (U of TN-Knoxville 25, Auburn 9, U of AL-Tuscaloosa 7, U of
MS 5, GA Inst of Tech 3, Belmont U 3). Athl schol 3. **Avg SAT:** CR 606. M 587. W 604.
Avg ACT: 27. **Col couns:** 2. Alum donors: 10%.
Tui '12-'13: Day $14,950-16,640 (+$225-480). **Aid:** Need 99 ($969,790).

Summer (enr 3185): Ages 12-17. Acad Enrich Rev Rem. Tui Day $200-625/crse. Ages 5-12. Rec. Tui Day $220-235/wk. Ages 15-17. Driver Ed. Tui Day $400. 8 wks.
Endow $6,170,000. Plant val $52,200,000. Acres 108. Bldgs 10 (100% ADA). Class rms 88. 2 Libs 46,962 vols. Sci labs 8. Lang labs 3. Writing ctrs 1. Auds 1. Art studios 5. Music studios 4. Gyms 3. Fields 7. Courts 8. Pools 1. Comp labs 4. Comp/stud: 1:2 (1:1 Laptop prgm Gr 4-12).
Est 1955. Nonprofit. (Aug-May). **Assoc** CLS SACS.

Webb School of Knoxville was established in 1955 by Robert Webb, grandson of William R. Webb, founder of the first Webb School in Bell Buckle, TN. Originally enrolling four boys in a leased Presbyterian church, Webb moved to its present campus in 1959 and became coeducational in 1968. Kindergarten and grades 1-4 were added with the opening of the lower school in 1998, when fifth-grade classes were relocated from the middle school.

Webb offers a traditional college preparatory curriculum that includes Advanced Placement courses in all major disciplines. Character and leadership development are cornerstones of Webb's program. High school students satisfy an annual 25-hour annual community service requirement; service opportunities are available through Habitat for Humanity and the Boys and Girls Club, among other organizations.

MEMPHIS, TN. (136 mi. ENE of Little Rock, AR) Urban. Pop: 650,100. Alt: 273 ft.

GRACE-ST. LUKE'S EPISCOPAL SCHOOL

Day — Coed Gr PS (Age 3)-8

Memphis, TN 38104. 246 S Belvedere Blvd. Tel: 901-278-0200. Fax: 901-272-7119.
  www.gslschool.org   E-mail: enroll@gslschool.org
Thor A. **Kvande, Head (2011).** BA, Muhlenberg College, MEd, Univ of Delaware. **Shelly McGuire, Adm.**
  Pre-Prep. Elem math—Everyday Math. **Elem read**—Macmillan/McGraw-Hill/SRA.
  Feat—Lat Span Computers Relig Studio_Art Drama Music.
  Sports—Basket X-country Tennis Track. B: Baseball Football Golf. G: Cheer Softball Volley.
  Selective adm: 90/yr. Usual entry: PS & K. Appl fee: $60. Appl due: Rolling. Applied: 110. Accepted: 80%. Yield: 90%. **Tests** ISEE.
  Enr 510. Wh 90%. Latino 1%. Blk 4%. Asian 3%. Other 2%. Avg class size: 16. Stud/fac: 9:1. Uniform. **Fac 70.** M 6/F 64. FT 70. Wh 93%. Latino 1%. Blk 5%. Other 1%. Adv deg: 50%.
  Grad '11—39. Prep—31. (Memphis U Sch 12, Hutchison 7, Christian Bros-TN 6, St Agnes-St Dominic 2). Alum donors: 25%.
  Tui '12-'13: Day $7150-12,995 (+$1000). **Aid:** Need ($500,000).
  Summer: Acad Enrich Rev Rec. Tui Day $300/wk. 9 wks.
  Endow $1,000,000. Plant val $5,000,000. Bldgs 6 (75% ADA). Class rms 40. Lib 15,000 vols. Sci labs 3. Theaters 1. Art studios 2. Music studios 1. Gyms 2. Fields 1. Pools 1. Greenhouses 1. Comp labs 2. Comp/stud: 1:6.
  Est 1947. Nonprofit. Episcopal (40% practice). Tri (Aug-May). **Assoc** SACS.

Begun as a kindergarten, the school now draws students from eastern Arkansas and northern Mississippi, in addition to those from its home state. The college preparatory curriculum is academically advanced and provides a complete fine arts program. Supplementary after-school activities include a program for children through grade 5; a middle school study hall; enrichment in gymnastics, dance, music, drama and sports; and church-sponsored sports, choirs and scouting.

Seventh graders perform eight hours of required community service as part of the world religions curriculum. Students attend and participate in chapel services regularly.

HUTCHISON SCHOOL
Day — Girls Gr PS (Age 3)-12

Memphis, TN 38119. 1740 Ridgeway Rd. Tel: 901-761-2220, 877-396-4319. Fax: 901-683-3510.
www.hutchisonschool.org E-mail: info@hutchisonschool.org
Annette C. Smith, Head (2000). BA, MA, Louisiana State Univ-Baton Rouge, EdS, Univ of Louisiana, EdD, Univ of Mississippi. **Candy Covington, Adm.**
Col Prep. AP (132 exams taken, 89% 3+)—Eng Fr Lat Span Calc Bio Chem Physics US_Hist World_Hist Comp_Govt & Pol US_Govt & Pol Art_Hist Studio_Art Music_ Theory. **Feat**—British_Lit Creative_Writing Chin Multivariable_Calc Anat Environ_ Sci Genetics Comp_Sci Econ Govt Psych Women's_Stud Relig Film Graphic_Arts Photog Drama Theater Music Dance. **Supp**—Rev.
Sports—G: Basket Bowl X-country Golf Lacrosse Soccer Swim Tennis Track Volley. **Activities:** 18.
Selective adm: 98/yr. Appl fee: $50. Appl due: Rolling. Accepted: 55%. **Tests** CTP_4 IQ ISEE MRT.
Enr 894. Avg class size: 17. Stud/fac: 8:1. Uniform. **Fac 114.** M 13/F 101. FT 102/PT 12. Adv deg: 62%.
Grad '08—48. Col—48. (U of MS, U of TN-Knoxville, Vanderbilt, Auburn, Boston U, U of AL-Tuscaloosa). **Mid 50% SAT:** CR 530-680. M 540-660. W 570-700. Mid 50% ACT: 23-28. **Col couns:** 4.
Tui '12-'13: Day $11,260-17,760 (+$50-825). **Aid:** Need 73 ($625,000).
Summer: Acad Enrich Rec. 10 wks.
Endow $14,000,000. Plant val $29,250,000. Acres 52. Bldgs 6. Class rms 56. 2 Libs 21,100 vols. Sci labs 5. Auds 1. Theaters 1. Art studios 3. Music studios 2. Dance studios 1. Gyms 2. Fields 3. Tennis courts 12. Pools 1. Tracks 1. Weight rms 1. Comp labs 4. Laptop prgm Gr 5-12.
Est 1902. Nonprofit. Quar (Aug-May). **Assoc** CLS SACS.

The school, founded by Mary Grimes Hutchison, is located on a 50-acre campus in residential east Memphis. The upper school curriculum utilizes block scheduling and instructs each student in the traditional liberal arts disciplines, emphasizing the study of literature, languages, mathematics, history, science and the arts. Both honors and AP courses are available. In the upper school, a coordinate program with the adjacent Memphis University School for boys allows students and faculty to jointly participate in academic seminars, civic service projects and theater and music programs. The schools also share athletic facilities, including a tennis center built through joint fundraising activities.

Students aspiring to a career in dance, music, theater or visual arts may pursue a special certificate through Hutchison's Arts Academy. Technology resources include laptop computers (issued to students in grades 5-12), a digital media lab and schoolwide wireless Internet access. Girls in grades 9-12 perform 15 hours of required community service each year.

LAUSANNE COLLEGIATE SCHOOL
Day — Coed Gr PS (Age 3)-12

Memphis, TN 38120. 1381 W Massey Rd. Tel: 901-474-1030. Fax: 901-474-1010.
www.lausanneschool.com E-mail: admission@lausanneschool.com
Stuart McCathie, Head (2005). BEd, Lancaster Univ (England), MEd, Univ of North Carolina-Wilmington. **Molly B. Cook, Adm.**
Col Prep. IB Diploma. AP (exams req'd)—Eng Fr Span Calc Stats Bio Chem Physics US_Hist Comp_Govt & Pol Econ US_Govt & Pol. **Feat**—Creative_Writing Women's_ Lit Chin Lat Astron Ecol Environ_Sci Biotech Organic_Chem Psych Photog Studio_ Art Acting Theater_Arts Directing Chorus Journ. **Supp**—Dev_Read ESL Rev Tut.
Sports (req'd)—Basket Bowl Cheer X-country Golf Lacrosse Soccer Swim Tennis Track. B: Football. G: Volley.
Selective adm: 117/yr. Appl fee: $75. Appl due: Jan. Applied: 229. Accepted: 66%. Yield: 90%. **Tests** CEEB CTP_4 ISEE SSAT.

Enr 809. B 404. G 405. Elem 490. Sec 319. Wh 53%. Latino 4%. Blk 18%. Asian 10%. Other 15%. Intl 29%. Avg class size: 18. Stud/fac: 8:1. Casual. **Fac 80.** M 22/F 58. FT 80. Wh 88%. Latino 5%. Blk 5%. Asian 1%. Other 1%. Adv deg: 48%.
Grad '11—79. Col—79. (U of Memphis, GA Inst of Tech, Millsaps, Christian Bros, Northwestern, U of the South). **Avg SAT:** CR 660. M 670. W 700. Avg ACT: 26. **Col couns:** 2.
Tui '12-'13: Day $12,250-17,300 (+$1000-3000).
Summer: Acad Enrich Rec. 8 wks.
Endow $872,000. Plant val $7,700,000. Acres 28. Bldgs 6. Class rms 50. Lib 21,000 vols. Sci labs 4. Lang labs 4. Theaters 1. Art studios 4. Music studios 3. Dance studios 1. Perf arts ctrs 1. Gyms 2. Fields 2. Tennis courts 6. Tracks 1. Comp/stud: 1:2 (1:1 Laptop prgm Gr 5-12).
Est 1926. Nonprofit. Sem (Aug-May). **Assoc** CLS SACS.

One of the oldest continuously operating schools in the region, Lausanne was founded by Emma DeSaussure Jett and Bessie Satler as a girls-only institution on a rustic, 28-acre campus that is bordered by woodlands and Blue Heron Lake. After operating for more than 50 years as a single-gender program, the school became coeducational in 1977.

In the early years, three- to five-year-olds engage in a play-based curriculum that introduces them to pre-reading, music, art, math, social studies, science and Spanish. The lower school (junior kindergarten through grade 4) emphasizes mastery of the fundamental academic skills in a developmentally appropriate setting that incorporates cocurricular offerings in the fine arts, computer technology, Spanish and physical education. The transitional middle school (grades 5-8) demands increasing levels of student responsibility and provides opportunities for advancement in math, literature composition, foreign language, history and science. Art, music and drama classes are also available during these years, and each grade level embarks on an annual class trip.

College preparation is the primary focus of the rigorous upper school program (grades 9-12). The curriculum progresses from skill building in foundation subjects and exposure to various disciplines in grades 9 and 10 to the International Baccalaureate Diploma Program and a choice of Advanced Placement courses in grades 11 and 12. The arts are integral to the upper school course of studies, and a strong athletic program includes both individual and team sports.

MEMPHIS UNIVERSITY SCHOOL

Day — Boys Gr 7-12

Memphis, TN 38119. 6191 Park Ave. Tel: 901-260-1300. Fax: 901-260-1301.
www.musowls.org E-mail: ginny.cochran@musowls.org
Ellis L. Haguewood, Head (1995). BA, Harding College, MA, Memphis State Univ. **Peggy Williamson, Adm.**
Col Prep. AP (287 exams taken, 96% 3+)—Eng Fr Lat Span Calc Stats Bio Chem Physics Eur_Hist US_Hist Comp_Govt & Pol US_Govt & Pol Art_Hist Music_Theory. **Feat**—British_Lit Creative_Writing Humanities Poetry Shakespeare Southern_Lit Astron Environ_Sci Genetics Geol Molecular_Bio Comp_Sci Econ Psych Photog Sculpt Digital_Arts Theater Theater_Arts Music_Production. **Supp**—Rev Tut.
Sports—B: Baseball Basket Bowl X-country Fencing Football Golf Lacrosse Soccer Swim Tennis Track Wrestling. **Activities:** 44.
Selective adm (Gr 7-11): 133/yr. Usual entry: 7 & 9. Appl fee: $50. Appl due: Dec. Applied: 225. Accepted: 775%. Yield: 83%. **Tests** ISEE.
Enr 660. Elem 204. Sec 456. Wh 81%. Latino 1%. Blk 9%. Native Am 1%. Asian 8%. Avg class size: 17. Stud/fac: 10:1. **Fac 73.** M 53/F 20. FT 66/PT 7. Wh 97%. Latino 1%. Blk 2%. Adv deg: 73%.
Grad '11—91. Col—91. (U of MS 15, U of TN-Knoxville 5, Rhodes 4, U of AL-Tuscaloosa 4, U of Memphis 4, Vanderbilt 3). Athl schol 3. **Avg SAT:** CR 619. M 645. W 630. **Mid 50% SAT:** CR 560-700. M 590-700. W 570-690. Avg ACT: 29. **Col couns:** 2. Alum donors: 34%.

Tui '11-'12: Day $17,500 (+$1470). **Aid:** Need 220 ($2,100,000).
Summer: Acad Enrich Rev Rec. 1-4 wks.
Endow $23,000,000. Plant val $50,000,000. Acres 94. Bldgs 13 (60% ADA). Class rms 50. Lib 38,000 vols. Sci labs 7. Lang labs 3. Auds 2. Art studios 2. Music studios 1. Music rms 2. Gyms 2. Fields 6. Courts 12. Comp labs 3. Comp/stud: 1:5.
Est 1893. Nonprofit. Sem (Aug-May). **Assoc** CLS SACS.

Founded as the Werts and Rhea School, the school is the result of a 1954 reorganization and incorporation. Conducted on a 94-acre campus, the strong academic program emphasizes college preparation and features Advanced Placement courses in the major disciplines. Study skills instruction in grade 7 emphasizes organization, note taking, reading for content, idea mapping and outlining, and exam preparation. MUS maintains a coordinate program with the Hutchison School, a girls' school whose adjacent campus allows for joint academic and leadership programs.

An honor code plays a major role in school life. Students coordinate community service efforts to benefit local nonprofit organizations, churches and synagogues.

PRESBYTERIAN DAY SCHOOL
Day — Boys Gr PS (Age 3)-6

Memphis, TN 38111. 4025 Poplar Ave. Tel: 901-842-4600. Fax: 901-327-7564.
www.pdsmemphis.org E-mail: info@pdsmemphis.org
A. Lee Burns III, Head (2000). AB, Dartmouth College, MEd, Harvard Univ. **Jan Conder, Adm.**
   Pre-Prep. Feat—Chin Span Computers Bible Studio_Art Band Music. **Supp**—Tut.
   Selective adm: 109/yr. Usual entry: PS. Appl fee: $75. Appl due: Jan. Applied: 184. Accepted: 70%. Yield: 85%. **Tests** CTP_4 IQ ISEE.
   Enr 644. Wh 87%. Latino 1%. Blk 7%. Asian 3%. Other 2%. Avg class size: 18. Stud/fac: 9:1. Casual. **Fac 76.** M 11/F 65. FT 74/PT 2. Wh 98%. Blk 1%. Asian 1%. Adv deg: 52%.
   Grad '11—66. Prep—66. (Memphis U Sch 56, Evangelical Christian 4, Woodland Presbyterian 2, St Agnes-St Dominic 2, Grace-St Luke's 1).
   Tui '12-'13: Day $12,720-16,310 (+$900-1650).
   Summer: Acad Enrich Rev Rem Rec. Musical Theater. Sports. Tui Day $100-250/wk. 8 wks.
   Endow $6,000,000. Plant val $2,400,000. Bldgs 2 (100% ADA). Class rms 34. Lib 17,000 vols. Sci labs 1. Art studios 1. Music studios 2. Gyms 2. Fields 1. Comp labs 1. Comp/stud: 1:1 Laptop prgm Gr 5-6.
   Est 1949. Nonprofit. Presbyterian (25% practice). Tri (Aug-May). **Assoc** SACS.

Developed from a kindergarten when the Pentecost-Garrison School for Boys was closed, PDS now offers prekindergarten through grade 6. Although the school is affiliated with the Second Presbyterian Church of Memphis, boys of many other faiths enroll.

Academic standards are high, and extracurricular options include athletics, publications, computer, art, music and clubs. Many graduates enter Memphis University School, which was reactivated in 1955 as a direct outgrowth of PDS.

ST. MARY'S EPISCOPAL SCHOOL
Day — Girls Gr PS (Age 3)-12

Memphis, TN 38117. 60 Perkins Ext. Tel: 901-537-1405. Fax: 901-685-1098.
Other locations: 41 N Perkins Rd, Memphis 38117; 71 N Perkins Rd, Memphis 38117.
   www.stmarysschool.org E-mail: admission@stmarysschool.org
Albert L. Throckmorton, Head (2012). BA, MA, Rice Univ. **Nicole Hernandez, Adm.**
   Col Prep. AP (exams req'd; 305 taken, 85% 3+)—Eng Fr Lat Span Calc Bio Chem Physics US_Hist World_Hist Human_Geog Art_Hist Studio_Art Music_Theory. **Elem**

math—Everyday Math. **Elem read**—Open Court. **Feat**—Creative_Writing Humanities Chin Anat & Physiol Microbio Robotics Econ Govt Psych Global_Issues Comp_ Relig Drama Music_Hist. **Supp**—Tut.
Sports—G: Basket Bowl X-country Golf Lacrosse Soccer Swim Tennis Track Volley. **Activities:** 31.
Selective adm: 107/yr. Usual entry: PS. Appl fee: $75. Appl due: Rolling. Applied: 200. Accepted: 82%. Yield: 65%. **Tests** CTP_4 ISEE.
Enr 845. Elem 611. Sec 234. Wh 78%. Latino 2%. Blk 9%. Asian 8%. Other 3%. Avg class size: 18. Stud/fac: 9:1. Casual. **Fac 97.** M 10/F 87. FT 84/PT 13. Wh 96%. Latino 1%. Asian 3%. Adv deg: 51%.
Grad '11—59. Col—59. (U of TN-Knoxville 4, U of MS 4, Samford 3, Wash & Lee 3, U of VA 2, Vanderbilt 2). Athl schol 3. **Avg SAT:** CR 650. M 632. W 675. Avg ACT: 29. **Col couns:** 3. Alum donors: 36%.
Tui '12-'13: Day $12,500-17,500 (+$300-1050). **Aid:** Need 143 ($902,300).
Summer (enr 466): Enrich Rev Rec. Tui Day $175-400. 1-2 wks.
Endow $17,545,000. Plant val $31,281,000. Acres 25. Bldgs 11 (100% ADA). Class rms 81. 3 Libs 36,114 vols. Sci labs 4. Lang labs 12. Theaters 1. Art studios 5. Music studios 3. Dance studios 2. Gyms 2. Fields 2. Comp labs 12. Comp/stud: 1:1.3.
Est 1847. Nonprofit. Episcopal (15% practice). Sem (Aug-May). **Assoc** CLS SACS.

The school's program places significant emphasis on college preparation, with honors and Advanced Placement courses available in many disciplines. Chapel services, held weekly in the lower school and daily in grades 5-12, provide a focal point for community life. The school's Pursuits program offers after-school enrichment activities, overnight camps and coeducational summer classes.

The early childhood and lower school programs occupy a separate campus at 41 N. Perkins Rd., while after-school and summer enrichment programs take place at 71 N. Perkins Rd.

NASHVILLE, TN. (101 mi. N of Huntsville, AL) Urban. Pop: 545,524. Alt: 450 ft.

ENSWORTH SCHOOL
Day — Coed Gr K-12

Nashville, TN 37205. 211 Ensworth Ave. Tel: 615-383-0661. Fax: 615-269-4840.
Other locations: 7401 Hwy 100, Nashville 37221.
www.ensworth.com
David J. Braemer, Head (2012). BA, Amherst College, MEd, Boston College. **Allie Bohannon & Ann West, Gr 9-12 Adms; Rebekah Capps, Gr K-8 Adm.**
Col Prep. AP—Eng Fr Lat Span Calc Stats Bio Chem Environ_Sci Physics Eur_Hist US_Hist Comp_Govt & Pol Econ US_Govt & Pol Art_Hist Music_Theory. **Feat**—British_Lit Shakespeare African-Amer_ Lit Russ_Lit Women's_Lit ASL Chin Astron Ecol Forensic_Sci Computers Amer_Stud Psych Constitutional_Law Comp_Relig Architect Ceramics Drawing Painting Photog Studio_Art Acting Theater Chorus Music Dance Public_Speak.
Sports—Basket Bowl X-country Golf Lacrosse Soccer Swim Tennis Track. B: Baseball Football Ice_Hockey Wrestling. G: Softball Volley. **Activities:** 30.
Selective adm: Appl fee: $35-100. Appl due: Jan. **Tests** ISEE.
Enr 1045. Elem 622. Sec 423. Avg class size: 15. Stud/fac: 8:1. **Fac 138.** M 48/F 90. FT 138. Adv deg: 68%.
Grad '08—83. Col—83. Mid 50% SAT: CR 520-630. M 520-670. W 520-630. Mid 50% ACT: 24-29. **Col couns:** 3.
Tui '12-'13: Day $17,735-21,665 (+$1210-2535). **Aid:** Need 127 ($1,900,000).
Summer: Acad Enrich Rec. Travel. 1-2 wks.
Endow $58,000,000. Acres 142. Bldgs 3. Class rms 45. 2 Libs 22,000 vols. Sci labs 4. Auds 1. Theaters 1. Art studios 3. Music studios 3. Dance studios 1. Gyms 1. Fields 3. Courts 2. Comp labs 3.

Est 1958. Nonprofit. Quar (Aug-May). **Assoc** SACS.

Founded and operating for nearly half a century as an elementary school, Ensworth opened a high school division on a separate campus on Highway 100 in August 2004.

The lower school (grades K-5) provides sound training in the basic academic skills and subjects; in many ways, however, it is a progressive school operating within a traditional framework. The transitional middle school (grades 6-8) emphasizes organizational and study skills, as well as responsibility for one's work. High school programming (grades 9-12) centers around the following skills: collaboration, communication, observation, speculation and hypothesizing. Boys and girls in grades 9-12 participate in one community service day per quarter.

The Capstone Program enables qualified juniors and seniors to extensively explore an academic interest that lies beyond the normal Ensworth curriculum. Interested students investigate, propose and gain approval for a specific Capstone project in grade 11, then pursue that project as soon as spring break of junior year. Portions of the project may include extensions of courses taken at Ensworth or at other learning institutions. Independent research or participation in internship programs, workshops or seminars related to the topic of interest may also be part of the project.

FATHER RYAN HIGH SCHOOL
Day — Coed Gr 9-12

Nashville, TN 37204. 700 Norwood Dr. Tel: 615-383-4200. Fax: 615-383-9056.
www.fatherryan.org E-mail: goetzingerk@fatherryan.org
James A. McIntyre, Pres. BA, Univ of North Texas, MEd, Texas A&M Univ-Commerce.
Paul Davis, Prin. Kate Goetzinger, Adm.
Col Prep. AP (286 exams taken, 83% 3+)—Eng Fr Lat Span Calc Stats Comp_Sci Bio Chem Environ_Sci Physics Eur_Hist US_Hist Econ Psych US_Govt & Pol Studio_Art Music_Theory. **Feat**—Shakespeare Women's_Lit Chin Asian_Stud Lat-Amer_Stud Native_Amer_Stud Comp_Relig Theol Art_Hist Film Theater Chorus Music. **Supp**—Tut.
Sports—Basket Bowl X-country Golf Lacrosse Soccer Swim Tennis Track. B: Baseball Football Ice_Hockey Wrestling. G: Cheer Softball Volley. **Activities:** 35.
Somewhat selective adm: 280/yr. Appl fee: $85. Appl due: Jan. Accepted: 98%. Yield: 84%. **Tests** HSPT TOEFL.
Enr 940. Avg class size: 16. Stud/fac: 13:1. Uniform. **Fac 76.** M 40/F 36. FT 76. Wh 95%. Latino 3%. Blk 2%. Adv deg: 57%.
Grad '09—205. Col—203. (U of TN-Knoxville, Middle TN St, TN Tech, U of TN-Martin, St Louis U, W KY). Mid 50% ACT: 25-27. **Col couns:** 2.
Tui '12-'13: Day $15,885 (+$410). Catholic $11,440-12,740 (+$410).
Summer: Acad Enrich Rev. 4 wks.
Endow $5,000,000. Plant val $20,000,000. Acres 40. Bldgs 5. Class rms 57. Lib 22,000 vols. Sci labs 7. Theaters 1. Art studios 2. Music studios 1. Dance studios 1. Gyms 1. Fields 4. Comp labs 3.
Est 1925. Nonprofit. Roman Catholic. Sem (Aug-May). **Assoc** CLS SACS.

Father Ryan was founded as Nashville Catholic High School for Boys by Bishop Alphonse Smith. Upon moving to Elliston Place (near Vanderbilt University) in 1928, the school assumed its current name in honor of 19th-century Southern priest and poet Rev. Abram J. Ryan. Girls were first enrolled in 1970, and Father Ryan relocated to its present, 40-acre campus in Oak Hill in 1991.

The curriculum includes honors and advanced courses at all grade levels and in every major subject. In addition, AP courses are available to juniors and seniors. Daily prayer and opportunities for community service round out the program. Students complete 50 hours of required independent service by the end of junior year.

HARPETH HALL SCHOOL

Day — Girls Gr 5-12

Nashville, TN 37215. 3801 Hobbs Rd. Tel: 615-297-9543. Fax: 615-297-0480.
www.harpethhall.org   E-mail: binkley@harpethhall.org
Ann M. Teaff, Head (1998). BA, Fontbonne College, MAT, Vanderbilt Univ, MA, Columbia Univ. **Dianne B. Wild, Adm.**

Col Prep. AP (exams req'd)—Eng Fr Lat Span Calc Bio Chem Physics Eur_Hist US_Hist Art_Hist Studio_Art. **Feat**—Creative_Writing Ecol Environ_Sci Psych World_Relig Photog Theater Journ Nutrition. **Supp**—Rev Tut.

Sports—G: Basket Bowl X-country Golf Lacrosse Soccer Softball Swim Tennis Track Volley. **Activities:** 34.

Selective adm (Gr 5-11): 115/yr. Appl fee: $50. Appl due: Jan. Accepted: 80%. Yield: 75%. **Tests** ISEE.

Enr 645. Elem 269. Sec 376. Avg class size: 16. Stud/fac: 9:1. Uniform. **Fac 75.** M 18/F 57. FT 75. Adv deg: 90%.

Grad '11—80. Col—80. (Vanderbilt, SMU, U of TN-Knoxville, U of VA, Wake Forest, Auburn). **Col couns:** 2. Alum donors: 29%.

Tui '11-'12: Day $21,090-21,915 (+$2000). **Aid:** Need 110.

Summer: Acad Enrich Rec. 3 wks.

Endow $31,300,000. Plant val $37,000,000. Acres 39. Bldgs 7. Libs 1. Sci labs 9. Theaters 1. Art studios 3. Music studios 1. Dance studios 2. Gyms 2. Fields 3. Courts 8. Tracks 1. Comp labs 3. Comp/stud: 1:1 Laptop prgm Gr 8-12.

Est 1951. Nonprofit. Sem (Aug-May). **Assoc** CLS SACS.

Founded as a successor to The Ward-Belmont School, Harpeth Hall conducts a rigorous liberal arts curriculum complemented by more than a dozen AP courses, independent study, academic travel, work-study and community service. The school employs an interdisciplinary team-teaching approach in which teams are organized horizontally by grade and vertically by subject. All pupils in grades 8-12 own and use laptop computers.

A winterim program for three weeks each January provides opportunities for students to learn and achieve outside the classroom and in nontraditional areas: girls in grades 9 and 10 engage in focused seminars, while upperclassmen choose from off-campus work/study internships, independent study options and academic travel abroad opportunities.

The fine arts program features visual and performing arts pursuits ranging from photography and art to dance and theater. Harpeth Hall encourages girls to participate in both extracurricular activities and community service. A collaborative program with Montgomery Bell Academy augments the available curricular and extracurricular offerings and resources.

MONTGOMERY BELL ACADEMY

Day — Boys Gr 7-12

Nashville, TN 37205. 4001 Harding Rd. Tel: 615-298-5514. Fax: 615-297-0271.
www.montgomerybell.edu   E-mail: admission@montgomerybell.edu
Bradford Gioia, Head (1994). BA, Univ of the South, MA, Middlebury College. **Greg Ferrell, Adm.**

Col Prep. AP (exams req'd; 465 taken, 88% 3+)—Eng Chin Fr Ger Lat Span Calc Stats Comp_Sci Bio Chem Environ_Sci Physics Eur_Hist US_Hist World_Hist Comp_Govt & Pol US_Govt & Pol Art_Hist Studio_Art Music_Theory. **Feat**—Greek Anat & Physiol Astron Vietnam_War Econ Theater_Arts Music_Hist Speech. **Supp**—Rev Tut.

Sports (req'd)—B: Baseball Basket Bowl Crew X-country Football Golf Ice_Hockey Lacrosse Soccer Swim Tennis Track Wrestling. **Activities:** 30.

Selective adm: 147/yr. Usual entry: 7 & 9. Appl fee: $50. Appl due: Feb. Applied: 280. Accepted: 50%. Yield: 88%. **Tests** ISEE.

Enr 713. Wh 90%. Latino 1%. Blk 5%. Native Am 1%. Asian 2%. Other 1%. Avg class size: 14. Stud/fac: 8:1. **Fac 98.** M 80/F 18. FT 84/PT 14. Wh 95%. Latino 2%. Blk 1%. Asian 2%. Adv deg: 69%.

Grad '10—100. Col—100. (U of TN-Knoxville 14, Vanderbilt 5, U of VA 5, Rhodes 4, U

of the South 4, SMU 4). Athl schol 2. **Mid 50% SAT:** CR 570-730. M 610-710. W 590-720. Avg ACT: 28. Mid 50% ACT: 25-31. **Col couns:** 3. Alum donors: 49%.
Tui '11-'12: Day $20,425 (+$1000-1800). **Aid:** Need 148 ($1,570,000).
Summer (enr 368): Acad Enrich Rev Rem. 3-10 wks.
Endow $50,949,000. Plant val $61,999,000. Acres 45. Bldgs 8 (100% ADA). Libs 1. Auds 1. Theaters 1. Art studios 1. Music studios 1. Gyms 2. Fields 6. Courts 4. Comp/stud: 1:3.
Est 1867. Nonprofit. Sem (Aug-May). **Assoc** CLS SACS.

Located on 45 acres in West Nashville, MBA began as a two-room school serving 26 grammar school and high school boys. (During its early years, MBA also included a two-year junior college program.) The school was named for Pennsylvanian Montgomery Bell, who came to Dickson County around 1800 and achieved financial success as owner of an iron company. A monetary gift that Mr. Bell left to the University of Tennessee upon his death in 1855 was later used by John Berrien Lindsley to open the academy. The school now draws students from approximately 40 elementary schools in central Tennessee.

The academic program includes honors sections at all grade levels, in addition to an unusually broad selection of Advanced Placement courses. The school strongly encourages boys to take part in the community service program, and each high school student is required to participate in the after-school athletic program in two of the three seasons. MBA conducts student exchanges with schools in Australia, Great Britain, New Zealand, South Africa, China and Greece.

UNIVERSITY SCHOOL OF NASHVILLE

Day — Coed Gr K-12

Nashville, TN 37212. 2000 Edgehill Ave. Tel: 615-327-8000. Fax: 615-321-0889.
www.usn.org E-mail: info@usn.org
Vincent W. Durnan, Jr., Dir (2000). BA, Williams College, MEd, Harvard Univ. **Juliet C. Douglas, Adm.**
Col Prep. AP (355 exams taken, 89% 3+)—Eng Fr Span Calc Stats Bio Chem Environ_Sci Physics Eur_Hist US_Hist US_Govt & Pol Art_Hist. **Feat**—British_Lit Creative_Writing Playwriting Lat Anat & Physiol Astron Forensic_Sci Geol Engineering Programming Web_Design Econ Psych Comp_Relig Ethics Ceramics Drawing Filmmaking Painting Photog Sculpt Theater Music_Theory Dance Debate Journ. **Dual enr:** Vanderbilt.
Sports—Baseball Basket Bowl Cheer X-country Golf Lacrosse Soccer Softball Swim Tennis Track Ultimate_Frisbee Volley.
Selective adm: Appl fee: $50. Appl due: Dec. **Tests** ISEE.
Enr 1039. Elem 668. Sec 371. Intl 19%. Avg class size: 14. **Fac 97.** Adv deg: 67%.
Grad '11—91. Col—91. (Vanderbilt, Wash U, Northwestern, NYU, Belmont U, U of AL-Tuscaloosa). **Mid 50% SAT:** CR 600-730. M 600-730. W 580-720. Avg ACT: 28.5. Mid 50% ACT: 26-31. **Col couns:** 2.
Tui '11-'12: Day $16,450-18,340 (+$400-600). **Aid:** Need 181 ($1,700,000).
Summer: Enrich. Lang. Sports. 1-5 wks.
Acres 80. Bldgs 4. Class rms 84. Lib 23,600 vols. Sci labs 2. Lang labs 1. Auds 1. Art studios 4. Music studios 4. Dance studios 1. Gyms 2. Fields 6. Weight rms 1. Comp labs 3.
Est 1915. Nonprofit. (Aug-May). **Assoc** CLS SACS.

The University School of Nashville was founded by the George Peabody College for Teachers, now the school of education at Vanderbilt University, as a demonstration school. In 1975, USN became an independent college preparatory school emphasizing the mastery of basic skills amid a broad liberal arts curriculum.

The lower school (grades K-4) is in self-contained classrooms, providing a program that utilizes a balanced whole-language/phonics approach to reading and writing and a hands-on, manipulation-oriented method for math and science. Music, art, and cultural and language enrichment opportunities complement the lower school curriculum.

In the middle school (grades 5-8), faculty members meet regularly to coordinate the curriculum and offer academic and social support for students. Middle school pupils benefit from a range of curricular activities, including library research, science lab, written and oral presentations, and current issues analysis.

The high school (grades 9-12) features a range of academic electives, independent projects, community service opportunities and cocurricular activities. In addition, qualified students may take courses (generally on topics not covered in the regular curriculum) at Vanderbilt University. USN conducts student and faculty exchanges and visits with a school in Japan and one in Paris, France.

ST. ANDREWS, TN. (37 mi. WNW of Chattanooga, TN) Rural. Pop: 240. Alt: 1960 ft. Area also includes Sewanee.

ST. ANDREW'S-SEWANEE SCHOOL
Bdg — Coed Gr 9-12; Day — Coed 6-12

Sewanee, TN 37375. 290 Quintard Rd. Tel: 931-598-5651. Fax: 931-914-1224.
www.sasweb.org   E-mail: admissions@sasweb.org

Rev. John T. Thomas, Head (2008). BA, Univ of the South, MDiv, Virginia Theological Seminary. **Anne Chenoweth, Adm.**

Col Prep. AP exams taken: 18 (44% 3+). Feat—British_Lit Creative_Writing Poetry Mythology Southern_Lit Chin Fr Lat Span Calc Stats Environ_Sci Geol Relig Drawing Filmmaking Photog Studio_Art Acting Theater_Arts Chorus Orchestra. **Supp**—ESL. Outdoor ed. **Dual enr:** U of the South.

Sports—Basket X-country Golf Soccer Swim Tennis Track. B: Baseball Football Wrestling. G: Softball Volley. **Activities: 25.**

Selective adm: 75/yr. Bdg 35. Day 40. Usual entry: 6 & 9. Appl fee: $50. Appl due: Mar. Applied: 132. Accepted: 83%. Yield: 57%. **Tests** CEEB ISEE SSAT Stanford TOEFL.

Enr 255. B 120. G 135. Bdg 84. Day 171. Elem 68. Sec 187. Wh 82%. Latino 1%. Blk 5%. Asian 12%. Intl 16%. Avg class size: 13. Stud/fac: 7:1. Casual. **Fac 44.** M 18/F 26. FT 29/PT 15. Wh 94%. Latino 2%. Blk 2%. Asian 2%. Adv deg: 72%. In dorms 21.

Grad '11—42. Col—37. (U of the South 4, TN Tech 4, Eckerd 2, Emory 2, Boston U 2). Athl schol 1. **Mid 50% SAT:** CR 450-620. M 500-650. W 480-600. Mid 50% ACT: 21-27. **Col couns:** 1. Alum donors: 10%.

Tui '12-'13: Bdg $40,000 (+$1880-2080). **Day $16,000-16,500** (+$450-750). **Intl Bdg $39,475** (+$2300-2500). **Aid:** Merit 11 ($202,983). Need 118 ($1,499,125).

Summer (enr 140): Enrich Rec. Tui Day $80-225/wk. 5 wks.

Endow $10,800,000. Acres 550. Bldgs 16 (45% ADA). Dorms 8. Class rms 25. Lib 27,000 vols. Chapels 1. Sci labs 5. Auds 1. Theaters 1. Art studios 2. Music studios 1. Dance studios 1. Art galleries 1. Gyms 1. Fields 4. Basketball courts 1. Tennis courts 8. Volleyball courts 1. Tracks 1. Climbing walls 1. Student ctrs 1. Comp labs 2. Comp/stud: 1:3.

Est 1868. Episcopal (30% practice). Sem (Sept-May). **Assoc** CLS SACS.

SAS resulted from a 1981 merger between the Sewanee Academy of the University of the South (established in 1868) and St. Andrew's School (established in 1905). The curriculum provides progressive liberal arts preparation for college.

An extensive arts program features course work in music, theater, clay, studio art and film. SAS' Winterim program enables all pupils to take two short, weeklong classes in such areas as stop-motion photography. Qualified juniors and seniors may enroll in tuition-free courses for college credit at the University of the South, and all pupils engage in a year's study of art, drama or music, and religion. Students fulfill a 60-hour community service requirement prior to graduation; they also contribute an hour per week to campus labor.

Various athletic and outdoor activities are available. The LEADS (Leadership, Environment, Adventure, Discovery and Service) program fosters leadership skill development through such outdoor activities as mountain biking, rock climbing and kayaking.

SAS schedules field trips to sites of interest in Nashville and Chattanooga.

See Also Page 66

VIRGINIA

ALEXANDRIA, VA. (7 mi. SSW of Washington, DC) Urban. Pop: 128,283. Alt: 32 ft.

BURGUNDY FARM COUNTRY DAY SCHOOL
Day — Coed Gr PS (Age 4)-8

Alexandria, VA 22303. 3700 Burgundy Rd. Tel: 703-960-3431. Fax: 703-960-5056.
Other locations: HC 83, Box 38DD, Capon Bridge, WV 26711.
    www.burgundyfarm.org   E-mail: info@burgundyfarm.org
Jeff Sindler, Head (2006). BA, Duke Univ, MA, Middlebury College. **Lori Adams, Adm.**
    Pre-Prep. Feat—Fr Span Computers Studio_Art Drama Music. **Supp**—Dev_Read Tut.
    Sports—Basket X-country Soccer Softball Volley. B: Lacrosse.
    Selective adm: 45/yr. Usual entry: PS & K. Appl fee: $75. Appl due: Feb. Applied: 219.
    Accepted: 59%. Yield: 37%. **Tests** IQ.
    Enr 288. B 138. G 150. Wh 69%. Latino 4%. Blk 18%. Asian 3%. Other 6%. Avg class
    size: 15. Stud/fac: 8:1. **Fac 44.** M 7/F 37. FT 35/PT 9. Wh 76%. Latino 7%. Blk 11%.
    Asian 2%. Other 4%. Adv deg: 54%.
    Grad '11—31. Prep—16. (Episcopal HS-VA 2, Field 2, Flint Hill 2, Thomas Jefferson-VA
    2). Alum donors: 3%.
    Tui '12-'13: Day $23,592-26,000 (+$1000). **Aid:** Need 57 ($817,665).
    Summer: Rec. Tui Day $330/wk. 8 wks.
    Endow $1,092,000. Plant val $9,500,000. Acres 525. Bldgs 13. Class rms 23. Lib 21,000
    vols. Sci labs 2. Photog labs 1. Theaters 1. Art studios 2. Music studios 1. Gyms 1.
    Fields 1. Pools 1. Barns 1. Comp labs 1. Comp/stud: 1:2.5.
    Est 1946. Nonprofit. Quar (Sept-June).

The first racially integrated school in the state, Burgundy conducts a rigorous elementary curriculum that emphasizes critical thinking and integrates science, technology, multicultural studies and the fine arts. Burgundy follows a developmental approach, and parent involvement is an important aspect of school life. Students extend their classroom learning with hands-on experiences at the 500-acre Burgundy Center for Wildlife Studies in West Virginia.

Transportation and an extended-day enrichment and recreational program are available.

See Also Page 137

EPISCOPAL HIGH SCHOOL
Bdg — Coed Gr 9-12

Alexandria, VA 22302. 1200 N Quaker Ln. Tel: 703-933-4062, 877-933-4347.
    Fax: 703-933-3016.
    www.episcopalhighschool.org   E-mail: admissions@episcopalhighschool.org
F. Robertson Hershey, Head (1998). BA, Williams College, MEd, Univ of Virginia. **Scott
Conklin, Adm.**
    Col Prep. AP (exams req'd)—Eng Fr Ger Lat Span Calc Stats Comp_Sci Bio Chem
    Environ_Sci Physics Eur_Hist US_Hist Econ Human_Geog Studio_Art Music_
    Theory. **Feat**—Creative_Writing Shakespeare African-Amer_Lit Southern_Lit Chin
    Greek Anat & Physiol Astron Ecol Genetics Geol Biotech Cold_War Modern_Chin_
    Hist Psych Sociol Comp_Relig Ethics Theol Ceramics Photog Theater Orchestra
    Jazz_Band Dance. **Supp**—Rev Tut.
    Sports—Basket X-country Lacrosse Soccer Squash Tennis Track. B: Baseball Football
    Golf Wrestling. G: Crew F_Hockey Softball Volley.
    Selective adm (Gr 9-11): 139/yr. Appl fee: $50. Appl due: Jan. Applied: 581. Accepted:
    43%. Yield: 56%. **Tests** CEEB ISEE SSAT TOEFL.

Enr 435. B 235. G 200. Wh 76%. Latino 2%. Blk 9%. Asian 8%. Other 5%. Intl 9%. Avg class size: 12. Formal. **Fac 71.** M 39/F 32. FT 64/PT 7. Adv deg: 85%.
Grad '11—104. Col—104. (U of VA, UNC-Chapel Hill, Wash & Lee, U of the South, Wake Forest, U of SC). **Mid 50% SAT:** CR 580-680. M 590-680. W 580-700. **Col couns:** 2. Alum donors: 43%.
Tui '12-'13: Bdg $46,600 (+$0-2000). **Aid:** Need 139 ($4,200,000).
Summer: Gr 7-9. Acad Enrich Rec. 5 wks.
Endow $162,000,000. Plant val $230,000,000. Acres 135. Bldgs 63. Dorms 9. Dorm rms 230. Class rms 44. Libs 2. Chapels 1. Auds 3. Theaters 3. Art studios 1. Music studios 2. Dance studios 2. Gyms 2. Fields 9. Tennis courts 12. Squash courts 9. Field houses 1. Pools 1. Comp labs 2. Laptop prgm Gr 9-12.
Est 1839. Nonprofit. Episcopal. Sem (Sept-June). **Assoc** CLS SACS.

This renowned boarding school enrolls students from roughly 30 states and 20 foreign countries. Located 10 minutes from Washington, DC, the suburban campus occupies 135 acres.

EHS' college preparatory curriculum, which is based on a liberal arts approach, emphasizes analytical, reasoning and independent thinking skills. More than 40 Advanced Placement and honors courses are available, and the school maintains strong programs in the arts and community service. Integrated technology enhances classroom study—all students have laptop computers and classrooms are fully wired for individual network access—and the school's Washington Program (tours conducted each Wednesday) enables pupils to engage in discussions with professionals in fields that relate to course work. Seniors may pursue a month-long internship in which they work on Capitol Hill or with a local organization of personal interest.

Summer trips to France, Spain and Italy enhance the foreign language program. EHS also conducts an exchange with a school in Austria, and students may take advantage of additional overseas study opportunities through School Year Abroad.

Extensive arts opportunities, extracurriculars and activities supplement academics. Among the varied arts options are offerings in music, drama, the visual arts and dance. The school's athletic program combines interscholastic sports with noncompetitive options such as aerobics, an outdoor program and weight training. Weekends include social events, dorm activities, and excursions to museums and cultural events in Washington, DC. The honor code remains a central part of Episcopal life.

ST. STEPHEN'S & ST. AGNES SCHOOL
Day — Coed Gr PS (Age 4)-12

Alexandria, VA 22304. 1000 St Stephen's Rd. Tel: 703-212-2705. Fax: 703-838-0032.
Other locations: 400 Fontaine St, Alexandria 22302; 4401 W Braddock Rd, Alexandria 22304.
www.sssas.org   E-mail: admission@sssas.org
Joan G. Ogilvy Holden, Head (1984). BA, Tufts Univ, EdM, Harvard Univ. **Diane Dunning, Adm.**
Col Prep. AP (exams req'd; 442 taken, 74% 3+)—Eng Fr Lat Span Calc Stats Bio Chem Environ_Sci Physics Eur_Hist US_Hist Comp_Govt & Pol Econ Psych US_Govt & Pol Art_Hist Studio_Art Music_Theory. **Elem math**—Everyday Math. **Feat**—Creative_Writing Gothic_Lit Playwriting Chin Bioethics Forensic_Sci Sports_Med Programming Robotics Ethics Relig Sculpt Directing Music Jazz_Ensemble Video_Journ. **Supp**—Tut.
Sports—Basket X-country Golf Indoor_Track Lacrosse Soccer Swim Tennis Track. B: Baseball Football Ice_Hockey Wrestling. G: F_Hockey Softball Volley. **Activities:** 37.
Selective adm (Gr PS-11): 177/yr. Usual entry: K, 6 & 9. Appl fee: $70. Appl due: Jan. **Tests** IQ ISEE SSAT Stanford.
Enr 1140. B 558. G 582. Elem 695. Sec 445. Wh 73%. Latino 3%. Blk 14%. Asian 4%. Other 6%. Avg class size: 15. Stud/fac: 8:1. **Fac 133.** M 40/F 93. FT 126/PT 7. Wh 89%. Latino 2%. Blk 5%. Asian 4%. Adv deg: 61%.
Grad '11—105. Col—105. (Wm & Mary, U of VA, Duke, Wake Forest, Cornell, George-

town). Athl schol 8. **Avg SAT:** CR 627. M 632. W 629. **Col couns:** 2.
Tui '11-'12: Day $22,455-29,582 (+$1500-3500). **Aid:** Need 240 ($3,911,737).
Summer (enr 1700): Acad Enrich Rec. 10 wks.
Endow $19,458,000. Plant val $86,606,000. Acres 58. Bldgs 13. Class rms 107. 3 Libs 43,500 vols. Chapels 1. Sci labs 11. Lang labs 1. Theaters 1. Art studios 6. Music studios 6. Perf arts ctrs 1. Gyms 3. Fields 5. Courts 8. Tracks 1. Weight rms 1. Comp labs 3.
Est 1924. Nonprofit. Episcopal (23% practice). Quar (Sept-June). **Assoc** CLS.

St. Stephen's & St. Agnes School, a church school in the Episcopal diocese of Virginia, was created by the 1991 merger of St. Stephen's School (founded in 1944) and St. Agnes School (founded in 1924). The strong academic program includes single-gender science and math classes in grades 6-8, an interdisciplinary history program in grades 9-12, and many honors and Advanced Placement courses. In addition, SSSAS conducts comprehensive visual and performing arts programs and a varied athletic program.

Seminars and field trips to historical, cultural and political points of interest in Washington, DC, augment the academic program. Cocurricular programs offer opportunities to study and travel abroad. The lower school (junior kindergarten through grade 5) is located on Fontaine Street, the middle school (grades 6-8) operates on West Braddock Road and the upper school (grades 9-12) holds classes on St. Stephen's Road.

Students participate in a service learning program at all grade levels (including junior kindergarten) through such avenues as food drives, the Special Olympics and Habitat for Humanity. In addition, upper schoolers fulfill a 40-hour service requirement. An extended-day program serves children through grade 8, and transportation to and from campus is available.

CHARLOTTESVILLE, VA. (65 mi. WNW of Richmond, VA; 100 mi. SW of Washington, DC) Urban. Pop: 45,049. Alt: 480 ft.

ST. ANNE'S-BELFIELD SCHOOL
Bdg — Coed Gr 9-12; Day — Coed PS (Age 2)-12

Charlottesville, VA 22903. 2132 Ivy Rd. Tel: 434-296-5106. Fax: 434-979-1486.
www.stab.org   E-mail: admission@stab.org
David S. Lourie, Head (2006). BA, Yale Univ, MA, Columbia Univ. **Bo Perriello, Gr 5-12 Adm; Gib Staunton, Gr PS-4 Adm.**
Col Prep. AP (exams req'd; 242 taken, 79% 3+)—Eng Fr Lat Span Calc Stats Bio Chem Environ_Sci Physics Eur_Hist US_Hist Comp_Govt & Pol Econ Studio_Art Music_Theory. **Feat**—Humanities Poetry Shakespeare African-Amer_Lit Satire Chin Civil_War Intl_Relations Art_Hist Ceramics Photog Sculpt Drama Music. **Supp**—Dev_Read ESL Rem_Math Rev Tut. **Dual enr:** U of VA.
Sports—Basket X-country Golf Lacrosse Soccer Squash Swim Tennis Track. B: Baseball Football. G: F_Hockey Softball Volley. **Activities:** 41.
Selective adm: 156/yr. Bdg 20. Day 136. Usual entry: K, 5, 6 & 9. Appl fee: $30-50. Appl due: Feb. Applied: 369. Accepted: 50%. Yield: 82%. **Tests** CEEB SSAT TOEFL.
Enr 892. B 442. G 450. Bdg 60. Day 832. Elem 543. Sec 349. Wh 79%. Latino 2%. Blk 6%. Asian 4%. Other 9%. Intl 6%. Avg class size: 13. Stud/fac: 8:1. Uniform. **Fac 114.** Wh 93%. Latino 1%. Blk 2%. Asian 2%. Other 2%. Adv deg: 71%. In dorms 3.
Grad '11—88. Col—88. (U of VA 14, VA Polytech 4, High Pt 4, Wm & Mary 3, Yale 2, Georgetown 2). Athl schol 12. **Avg SAT:** CR 621. M 639. W 630. **Col couns:** 3.
Tui '12-'13: Bdg $46,000. 5-Day Bdg $36,200. Day $7700-22,000 (+$300). **Aid:** Need 262 ($3,148,439).
Summer: Acad Enrich Rev Rem Rec. 3-9 wks.
Endow $16,800,000. Plant val $60,000,000. Acres 49. Bldgs 10 (50% ADA). Dorms 1. Dorm rms 27. Class rms 84. 3 Libs 23,000 vols. Sci labs 7. Theaters 1. Art studios 3. Music studios 2. Gyms 3. Fields 7. Courts 6. Field houses 1. Comp labs 3. Comp/stud:

1:2.
Est 1910. Nonprofit. Tri (Aug-May). **Assoc** CLS.

St. Anne's-Belfield was formed in 1970 by the merger of Belfield Elementary School (founded in 1955) and Saint Anne's School, a girls' residential secondary school (established in 1910). The school occupies two campuses totaling approximately 50 acres.

The academic program, which includes a variety of Advanced Placement courses, provides a solid background in the major disciplines, and all students are required to supplement their program of studies with courses in art, music, drama and computer study. The independent study program encourages students to pursue original investigation and present their findings to the school community. A senior thesis option allows grade 12 students to design and pursue an academic question, passion or interest over the course of the entire year. Boys and girls in grades 9-12 perform 15 hours of compulsory community service annually.

CHATHAM, VA. (44 mi. SE of Roanoke, VA; 194 mi. SW of Washington, DC) Rural. Pop: 1338. Alt: 828 ft.

CHATHAM HALL

Bdg and Day — Girls Gr 9-12

Chatham, VA 24531. 800 Chatham Hall Cir. Tel: 434-432-2941. Fax: 434-432-1002.
www.chathamhall.org   E-mail: admission@chathamhall.org
Gary J. Fountain, Rector (2003). AB, Brown Univ, MAR, Yale Univ, PhD, Boston Univ. **Vicki Wright, Adm.**
   Col Prep. AP (exams req'd; 93 taken)—Eng Fr Lat Span Calc Bio Chem Physics Eur_ Hist US_Hist Human_Geog Studio_Art Music_Theory. **Feat**—Creative_Writing Chin Veterinary_Sci Comp_Sci Robotics Econ Psych Ethics Relig World_Relig Islamic_ Film Drama Theater_Arts Music Ballet Dance. **Supp**—ESL Rev Tut.
   Sports—G: Basket X-country Equestrian F_Hockey Soccer Swim Tennis. **Activities:** 27.
   Selective adm: 53/yr. Bdg 46. Day 7. Appl fee: $50. Appl due: Feb. Accepted: 65%. Yield: 50%. **Tests** CEEB CTP_4 ISEE SSAT TOEFL.
   Enr 129. Bdg 108. Day 21. Wh 85%. Latino 4%. Blk 5%. Asian 6%. Intl 27%. Avg class size: 8. Stud/fac: 7:1. Casual. **Fac 31.** M 14/F 17. FT 31. Nonwhite 1%. Adv deg: 61%. In dorms 5.
   Grad '10—37. Col—36. (Rhodes 2, Sweet Briar 2, James Madison 2, U of Richmond 1, VA Polytech 1, Johns Hopkins 1). **Mid 50% SAT:** CR 500-630. M 500-650. W 490-630. Avg ACT: 25. **Col couns:** 1. Alum donors: 43%.
   Tui '10-'11: Bdg $39,000 (+$500). **5-Day Bdg $34,000** (+$500). **Day $16,500** (+$500). **Intl Bdg $39,000** (+$500-4500). **Aid:** Need 52 ($1,434,250).
   Summer: Sci. Tui Bdg $1250/2-wk ses. Riding. Tui Bdg $1000/wk. 4 wks.
   Endow $53,217,000. Plant val $30,458,000. Acres 362. Bldgs 10. Dorms 3. Dorm rms 87. Class rms 20. Lib 30,000 vols. Sci labs 3. Lang labs 1. Theaters 1. Art studios 1. Music studios 5. Dance studios 1. Gyms 1. Fields 3. Courts 8. Riding rings 3. Stables 2.
   Est 1894. Nonprofit. Episcopal. Tri (Sept-June). **Assoc** CLS.

Founded by Rev. C. Orlando Pruden, this school was called Chatham Episcopal Institute until 1924. The college preparatory program emphasizes spoken and written expression, in addition to analytical and computational skills. Math and science courses make extensive use of computer technology. Many students take honors and Advanced Placement classes, and the school conducts well-developed dance and arts programs.

An honor code governs all aspects of school life. Chatham Hall offers school-based study abroad programs and also participates in the English-Speaking Union. Internships, extensive weekend activities and an endowed speaker series provide enrichment opportunities. Veterinary science courses are enhanced by the school's riding program, featuring more than 50 horses, three training rings and a permanent trial course.

Students attend required chapel services on Tuesdays, Fridays and Sundays, and participate in a variety of social activities with independent schools across Virginia, North Carolina and Maryland.

HARGRAVE MILITARY ACADEMY
Bdg and Day — Boys Gr 7-PG

Chatham, VA 24531. 200 Military Dr. Tel: 434-432-2481, 800-432-2480.
Fax: 434-432-3129.
www.hargrave.edu   E-mail: admissions@hargrave.edu
Brig. Gen. Don Broome, Jr., USA (Ret), Pres (2011). Amy Walker, Adm.

Col Prep. Gen Acad. Milit. AP—Span Bio. **Feat**—Fr Lat Astron Environ_Sci Comp_Sci Econ Govt Psych Sociol Bible Ethics Art_Hist Fine_Arts Video_Production Debate Journ TV_Production Study_Skills. **Supp**—Dev_Read ESL Rem_Math Rem_Read Rev Tut.

Sports—B: Baseball Basket X-country Football Golf Lacrosse Soccer Swim Tennis Wrestling.

Somewhat selective adm: 200/yr. Bdg 190. Day 10. Appl fee: $75. Appl due: Aug. Accepted: 90%. Yield: 90%.

Enr 350. Bdg 325. Day 25. Wh 78%. Latino 3%. Blk 13%. Asian 4%. Other 2%. Intl 7%. Avg class size: 14. Stud/fac: 11:1. Uniform. **Fac 28.** M 18/F 10. FT 28. Wh 96%. Latino 2%. Blk 2%. Adv deg: 50%.

Grad '10—77. Col—77. (E TN St 3, US Naval Acad 3, US Milit Acad 2, VA Milit 2, NC St 2, Liberty 2). **Avg SAT:** CR/M/W 1515.

Tui '11-'12: Bdg $28,600 (+$2200). **Day $12,750** (+$1500). **Intl Bdg $30,600** (+$2200). **Aid:** Merit 38 ($38,000). Need 60 ($248,000).

Summer (enr 150): Acad Enrich Rev Rem Rec. Tui Bdg $4000-4500. Tui Day $875. 4 wks.

Endow $4,000,000. Plant val $8,700,000. Acres 214. Bldgs 10 (20% ADA). Dorms 10. Dorm rms 240. Class rms 49. Lib 16,000 vols. Sci labs 4. Lang labs 1. Photog labs 1. Auds 1. Theaters 1. Art studios 1. Music studios 1. Gyms 2. Fields 4. Courts 6. Pools 1. Weight rms 1. Rifle ranges 1. Comp/stud: 1:1 Laptop prgm Gr 7-PG.

Est 1909. Nonprofit. Baptist. Sem (Sept-May). **Assoc** SACS.

When a Baptist minister with six sons convinced a local entrepreneur of the need for boys in the area to obtain a Christian education, the two men combined resources to establish a school. Rev. T. Ryland Sanford served as Chatham Training School's first president, and his benefactor, J. Hunt Hargrave, served as chairman of the board of trustees. In 1925, the school's name was changed to honor the man who had given form to Rev. Sanford's vision.

Hargrave offers a sound college preparatory curriculum, with the majority of graduates matriculating at competitive colleges. The cadet corps organization, based on an infantry battalion, provides opportunities for leadership development and the assumption of responsibility.

CHRISTCHURCH, VA. (52 mi. E of Richmond, VA; 93 mi. SSE of Washington, DC) Rural. Pop: 100. Alt: 89 ft.

CHRISTCHURCH SCHOOL
Bdg and Day — Coed Gr 9-12

Christchurch, VA 23031. 49 Seahorse Ln. Tel: 804-758-2306. Fax: 804-758-0721.
www.christchurchschool.org   E-mail: admission@christchurchschool.org

John E. Byers, Head (2000). BA, Washington and Lee Univ, MA, Virginia Commonwealth Univ. **Lawrence J. Jensen, Adm.**
Col Prep. Feat—Chin Span Calc Environ_Sci Marine_Bio/Sci Civil_War Econ Studio_ Art. **Supp**—ESL LD Tut. Outdoor ed.
Sports (req'd)—Basket Crew Golf Sail Soccer Swim Tennis. B: Baseball Football Lacrosse. G: F_Hockey Volley. **Activities:** 5.
Selective adm (Gr 9-11): 85/yr. Bdg 55. Day 30. Usual entry: 9. Appl fee: $50. Appl due: Feb. Applied: 159. Accepted: 75%. Yield: 67%. **Tests** CEEB IQ SSAT TOEFL.
Enr 226. B 177. G 49. Bdg 123. Day 103. Wh 69%. Latino 2%. Blk 7%. Other 22%. Intl 18%. Avg class size: 12. Stud/fac: 6:1. Casual. **Fac 39.** M 25/F 14. FT 39. Wh 97%. Blk 2%. Asian 1%. Adv deg: 82%. In dorms 10.
Grad '11—42. Col—42. (Radford 4, Christopher Newport 2, James Madison 2, U of Mary Wash 2, VA Polytech 2, Loyola U MD 2). Athl schol 9. **Avg SAT:** CR 521. M 554. W 516. **Col couns:** 1. Alum donors: 21%.
Tui '12-'13: Bdg $43,900 (+$2000). **Day $18,700** (+$1000). **Intl Bdg $43,900** (+$2000-9500). **Aid:** Need 87 ($1,493,200).
Summer: Enrich Rec. Tui Bdg $850/wk. Tui Day $550/wk. 4 wks.
Endow $2,000,000. Plant val $15,000,000. Acres 125. Bldgs 14. Dorms 3. Dorm rms 100. Class rms 24. Lib 9500 vols. Labs 4. Theaters 1. Art studios 1. Gyms 2. Fields 6. Tennis courts 6. Comp/stud: 1:1 Laptop prgm Gr 9-12.
Est 1921. Nonprofit. Episcopal (17% practice). Sem (Sept-May).

Christchurch provides a challenging environment for students of varying abilities. The traditional, structured college preparatory curriculum features honors courses in all content areas. Student support at Christchurch includes learning skills instruction, life skills programming, daily extra-help opportunities, a supervised evening study period and differentiated classroom instruction.

All boys and girls participate in cocurricular activities (including athletics) each season. Prior to graduation, each pupil performs 60 hours of required community service, at least 30 of which must related to a school-sponsored service activity.

DYKE, VA. (77 mi. NW of Richmond, VA; 94 mi. WSW of Washington, DC) Rural. Pop: 25. Area also includes St. George.

THE BLUE RIDGE SCHOOL
Bdg — Boys Gr 9-12

St George, VA 22935. 273 Mayo Dr. Tel: 434-985-2811. Fax: 434-985-7215.
www.blueridgeschool.com   E-mail: admissions@blueridgeschool.com
William A. Darrin III, Actg Head (2012). BA, George Washington Univ, MBA, Univ of Virginia. **Don Smith, Adm.**
Col Prep. Feat—Fr Lat Span Anat Astron Ecol Environ_Sci Comp_Sci African-Amer_ Hist Studio_Art Drama Chorus Outdoor_Ed SAT_Prep. **Supp**—ESL Tut. Outdoor ed. Sat classes.
Sports—B: Baseball Basket X-country Football Golf Lacrosse Soccer Tennis Track Volley Wrestling. **Activities:** 10.
Selective adm: 83/yr. Appl fee: $100. Appl due: Rolling. Accepted: 65%. Yield: 63%. **Tests** TOEFL.
Enr 189. Intl 20%. Avg class size: 9. Stud/fac: 6:1. Formal. **Fac 30.** M 24/F 6. FT 27/PT 3. Wh 94%. Latino 5%. Blk 1%. Adv deg: 43%. In dorms 10.
Grad '10—46. Col—45. (Emory, Citadel, Hampden-Sydney, Lynchburg, VA Milit). **Avg SAT:** CR/M 1120. **Col couns:** 1. Alum donors: 11%.
Tui '12-'13: Bdg $40,500 (+$2000). **Intl Bdg $40,500** (+$2000-9200). **Aid:** Need 57 ($1,195,505).
Endow $12,000,000. Plant val $17,445,000. Acres 751. Bldgs 11. Dorms 2. Dorm rms 103. Class rms 21. Lib 11,000 vols. Sci labs 1. Auds 1. Theaters 1. Art studios 1.

Music studios 1. Gyms 2. Fields 8. Courts 4. Pools 1. Driving ranges 1. Ropes crses 1. Climbing towers 1. Comp labs 2.
Est 1909. Nonprofit. Tri (Sept-May). **Assoc** SACS.

Founded as an Episcopal mission school, Blue Ridge reorganized as an independent boarding school and adopted its current focus in 1962. The school provides a college preparatory education for capable boys who are suited to a program that incorporates small classes, a faculty advisor program, and a predictable daily schedule designed to help students develop sound study habits and time-management skills. Sufficient flexibility is built into the program to allow instructors to work with the student's strengths and needs. A learning center provides additional academic support as needed.

Occupying 751 acres on the eastern slope of the Blue Ridge Mountains, the school's campus is accessible to Charlottesville, Richmond and Washington, DC. Blue Ridge's outdoor program provides opportunities for hiking, camping, mountain biking, canoeing, fishing and ropes work. The athletic program, in which participation is mandatory, accommodates all ability levels. Each student attends chapel services two mornings a week and on Sundays.

FORK UNION, VA. (46 mi. WNW of Richmond, VA; 104 mi. SW of Washington, DC) Suburban. Pop: 2500. Alt: 900 ft.

FORK UNION MILITARY ACADEMY
Bdg and Day — Boys Gr 6-PG

Fork Union, VA 23055. 4744 James Madison Hwy. Tel: 434-842-3212, 800-462-3862.
Fax: 434-842-4300.
www.forkunion.com   E-mail: admissions@fuma.org
Rear Adm. J. Scott Burhoe, Pres (2011). BA, Virginia Polytechnic Institute, MPA, American Univ. **Lt. Col. Steve Macek, Adm.**
   Col Prep. Milit. AP (20 exams taken)—Eng Calc Bio US_Hist Psych US_Govt & Pol.
      Feat—Creative_Writing Humanities African_Lit Fr Ger Lat Span Stats Astron Comp_ Sci Econ Intl_Relations Pol_Sci Sociol Relig Studio_Art Drama Band Chorus Journ.
      Supp—ESL Rev Tut. **Dual enr:** Piedmont VA CC.
   Sports—B: Baseball Basket X-country Football Golf Indoor_Track Lacrosse Soccer Swim Tennis Track Wrestling.
   Selective adm: 275/yr. Bdg 272. Day 3. Appl fee: $100. Appl due: Rolling. Accepted: 55%. Yield: 87%. **Tests** CEEB Stanford.
   Enr 525. Elem 90. Sec 375. PG 60. Avg class size: 15. Stud/fac: 10:1. Uniform. **Fac 50.** M 40/F 10. FT 50. Adv deg: 60%. In dorms 4.
   Grad '11—93. Col—91. (Geo Mason 5, Longwood 5, James Madison 4, Old Dominion 3, Radford 3). **Avg SAT:** CR/M/W 1525. Avg ACT: 22. **Col couns:** 2.
   Tui '12-'13: Bdg $28,700 (+$3300). **Day $19,650** (+$3300). **Intl Bdg $37,600** (+$3300).
      Aid: Merit 75 ($75,000). Need 90 ($500,000).
   Summer: Gr 8-12. Acad. Tui Bdg $3700. 4 wks.
   Endow $15,600,000. Plant val $34,000,000. Acres 1000. Bldgs 11. Dorms 4. Dorm rms 303. Class rms 58. Lib 19,500 vols. Sci labs 5. Lang labs 2. Auds 1. Music studios 1. Gyms 3. Fields 6. Courts 14. Pools 1. Tracks 2. Comp labs 5.
   Est 1898. Nonprofit. Baptist. Quar (Sept-May).

This military school has received wide acclaim, particularly for its One-Subject Plan, which has been in use since 1950 in the upper school. Students focus intensively on single subjects for seven-week periods throughout the school year. Honors, Advanced Placement and college-credit courses provide opportunities for acceleration. The middle school (grades 6-8), which operates in separate facilities, features a small-class learning environment.

Students represent a variety of denominations and enroll from many states and several foreign countries.

FRONT ROYAL, VA. (70 mi. W of Washington, DC) Suburban. Pop: 13,589. Alt: 492 ft.

RANDOLPH-MACON ACADEMY
Bdg and Day — Coed Gr 6-PG

Front Royal, VA 22630. 200 Academy Dr. Tel: 540-636-5200, 800-272-1172.
Fax: 540-636-5419.
www.rma.edu   E-mail: admissions@rma.edu
Maj. Gen. Henry M. Hobgood, USAF (Ret), Pres (1997). BA, North Carolina State Univ, MS, Troy State Univ. **Amy M. Harriman, Adm.**
Col Prep. Milit. AP (exams req'd)—Eng Ger Span Calc Stats Bio Chem Physics Eur_ Hist US_Hist US_Govt & Pol. **Feat**—Shakespeare Anat & Physiol Aerospace_Sci Comp_Sci Asian_Hist Psych Bible Comp_Relig Studio_Art Drama Band Chorus Music_Theory Handbells Journ. **Supp**—ESL Makeup Tut. **Dual enr:** Shenandoah.
Sports—Basket X-country Soccer Swim Tennis Track. B: Baseball Football Golf Lacrosse Wrestling. G: Cheer Softball Volley. **Activities:** 35.
Somewhat selective adm (Bdg Gr 6-PG; Day 6-12): 134/yr. Bdg 122. Day 12. Usual entry: 6 & 9. Appl fee: $75. Appl due: Feb. Applied: 191. Yield: 74%. **Tests** CEEB CTP_4 DAT HSPT IQ ISEE MAT SSAT Stanford TACHS TOEFL.
Enr 370. B 254. G 116. Bdg 290. Day 80. Elem 73. Sec 294. PG 3. Wh 56%. Latino 4%. Blk 21%. Native Am 1%. Asian 8%. Other 10%. Intl 25%. Avg class size: 14. Stud/fac: 10:1. Uniform. **Fac 40.** M 25/F 15. FT 38/PT 2. Wh 96%. Latino 2%. Blk 2%. Adv deg: 52%. In dorms 3.
Grad '11—73. Col—72. (James Madison 7, Norwich 4, VA Commonwealth 4, US Air Force Acad 2, Geo Mason 2, U of Pittsburgh 2). **Avg SAT:** CR 499. M 537. W 493. **Col couns:** 1.
Tui '12-'13: Bdg $30,371-32,286 (+$4160-4195). Day $14,096-16,166 (+$2250). **Intl Bdg $38,217** (+$5510). **Aid:** Merit 64 ($163,810). Need 74 ($511,044).
Summer (enr 160): Acad Enrich Rev Rem. ESL. Tui Bdg $3800. Tui Day $1500. 4 wks.
Endow $4,389,000. Plant val $49,971,000. Acres 135. Bldgs 11. Dorms 3. Dorm rms 225. Class rms 53. 2 Libs 9000 vols. Sci labs 9. Theaters 1. Gyms 1. Fields 8. Courts 5. Pools 1. Comp labs 3. Comp/stud: 1:1.2.
Est 1892. Nonprofit. Methodist (10% practice). Quar (Sept-June). **Assoc** SACS.

This United Methodist-affiliated preparatory academy became coeducational in 1974. Students enroll from many states and foreign countries. Graduates enter a wide variety of the nation's colleges, including the service academies. Air Force Junior ROTC is an integral part of the upper school curriculum, as is optional flight training in academy-owned aircraft. A military academy prep track is also available.

A cooperative program with Shenandoah University provides 29 hours of college credit in English, science, math and social science for qualified seniors and postgraduate students. R-MA encourages boys and girls to participate in weekly ecumenical chapel services, regardless of the student's religious affiliation.

Randolph-Macon's 135-acre campus is situated 70 miles west of Washington, DC.

LYNCHBURG, VA. (43 mi. ENE of Roanoke, VA) Urban. Pop: 65,269. Alt: 517 ft.

VIRGINIA EPISCOPAL SCHOOL
Bdg and Day — Coed Gr 9-12

Lynchburg, VA 24503. 400 Virginia Episcopal School Rd. Tel: 434-385-3607.
Fax: 434-385-3603.
www.ves.org   E-mail: mjones@ves.org

G. Thomas Battle, Jr., Head (2010). BA, Univ of Virginia, MBA, College of William and Mary. **Garth Ainslie, Adm.**

Col Prep. AP (exams req'd)—Eng Fr Lat Span Calc Stats Comp_Sci Bio Chem Eur_Hist US_Hist Studio_Art Music_Theory. **Feat**—Environ_Sci Sports_Med Econ World_Relig Art_Hist Fine_Arts Graphic_Arts Video_Production Drama Music_Hist Public_Speak. **Supp**—Tut.

Sports—Basket X-country Indoor_Track Lacrosse Soccer Swim Tennis Track. B: Baseball Football Golf Wrestling. G: F_Hockey Volley. **Activities:** 20.

Selective adm: 116/yr. Bdg 79. Day 37. Appl fee: $50. Appl due: Feb. Accepted: 65%. Yield: 69%. **Tests** CEEB SSAT.

Enr 180. Bdg 99. Day 81. Intl 20%. Avg class size: 13. Stud/fac: 5:1. Uniform. **Fac 36.**

Grad '10—56. Col—56. (U of SC, NC St, U of VA, U of Mary Wash, UNC-Chapel Hill, U of MS). **Col couns:** 1.

Tui '10-'11: Bdg $42,000 (+$1400). **5-Day Bdg $31,000** (+$1400). **Day $20,000** (+$900). **Intl Bdg $43,500** (+$1400). **Aid:** Need 81 ($1,000,000).

Endow $16,000,000. Plant val $15,740,000. Acres 160. Bldgs 10. Dorms 6. Dorm rms 89. Class rms 25. Lib 16,000 vols. Sci labs 4. Art studios 1. Gyms 4. Fields 7. Courts 8. Pools 1. Riding rings 1. Comp labs 1.

Est 1916. Nonprofit. Episcopal. Tri (Sept-May). **Assoc** CLS.

This church-related school was founded by the first bishop of the Diocese of Southwestern Virginia, Rev. Dr. Robert Carter Jett. The college preparatory curriculum is presented in an environment that emphasizes the student's academic, social and athletic development. At all grade levels, boys and girls satisfy a 30-hour annual community service requirement.

Lynchburg offers many cultural opportunities for supplementing the school program. Graduates of the traditional, thorough curriculum enter many colleges, predominantly institutions in the South.

McLEAN, VA. (9 mi. WNW of Washington, DC) Suburban. Pop: 38,929. Alt: 300 ft.

THE LANGLEY SCHOOL
Day — Coed Gr PS (Age 3)-8

McLean, VA 22101. 1411 Balls Hill Rd. Tel: 703-356-1920. Fax: 703-790-9712.
www.langleyschool.org   E-mail: admission@langleyschool.org

Doris E. Cottam, Head (2000). BS, MS, Brigham Young Univ. **Christina Tait, Adm.**

Pre-Prep. Feat—Chin Span Computers Studio_Art Video_Production Drama Music. **Supp**—Dev_Read.

Sports—Basket X-country Lacrosse Soccer. B: Baseball. G: Softball.

Selective adm: 72/yr. Appl fee: $75. Appl due: Jan. Applied: 192. Accepted: 67%. Yield: 56%. **Tests** IQ ISEE SSAT.

Enr 508. B 259. G 249. Wh 72%. Latino 3%. Blk 5%. Native Am 1%. Asian 6%. Other 13%. Avg class size: 18. Stud/fac: 7:1. **Fac 71.** M 12/F 59. FT 70/PT 1. Wh 83%. Latino 2%. Blk 4%. Asian 4%. Other 7%. Adv deg: 54%.

Grad '10—34. Prep—29. (Flint Hill 5, Madeira 4, Bullis 2, Georgetown Day 2, Natl Cathedral 2).

Tui '11-'12: Day $27,140-28,350 (+$200). **Aid:** Need 45 ($871,655).

Summer (enr 380): Acad Enrich Rev Rec. Tui Day $145/wk. 5 wks.

Endow $3,005,000. Plant val $18,291,000. Acres 9. Bldgs 9. Class rms 27. Lib 20,000 vols. Sci labs 3. Lang labs 2. Auds 1. Art studios 2. Music studios 2. Arts ctrs 1. Media studios 1. Gyms 2. Fields 1. Comp labs 3. Comp/stud: 1:2.

Est 1942. Nonprofit. Tri (Sept-June).

Langley's varied curriculum prepares students for leading area preparatory schools. World language instruction begins in kindergarten, and fine arts courses are integral to the program at all grade levels. Science classes utilize a hands-on approach and feature labs and field trips, while technology is integrated across the curriculum. Beginning in the primary school, boys and girls take part in age-appropriate service learning projects.

MADEIRA SCHOOL

Bdg and Day — Girls Gr 9-12

McLean, VA 22102. 8328 Georgetown Pike. Tel: 703-556-8200. Fax: 703-893-3289.
www.madeira.org   E-mail: admissions@madeira.org
Pilar Cabeza de Vaca, Head (2010). BA, Bryn Mawr College, MA, Univ of Alabama-Tuscaloosa. **Ann Miller, Adm.**

Col Prep. AP (223 exams taken, 92% 3+)—Chin Fr Lat Span Calc Stats Bio Chem Physics Eur_Hist US_Hist Comp_Govt & Pol Human_Geog US_Govt & Pol Art_Hist Studio_Art. **Feat**—British_Lit Ital Multivariable_Calc Bioethics Environ_Sci Forensic_ Sci Programming Women's_Hist Econ Comp_Relig Ethics Ceramics Photog Acting Theater_Arts Music Dance Public_Speak. **Supp**—ESL Rev Tut.

Sports—G: Basket X-country Equestrian F_Hockey Lacrosse Soccer Softball Squash Swim Tennis Track Volley. **Activities: 36.**

Selective adm: 88/yr. Bdg 49. Day 39. Appl fee: $70. Appl due: Jan. Accepted: 65%. **Tests** CEEB SSAT TOEFL.

Enr 321. Bdg 173. Day 148. Wh 73%. Latino 3%. Blk 8%. Native Am 1%. Asian 12%. Other 3%. Intl 13%. Avg class size: 12. Stud/fac: 6:1. **Fac 44.** Adv deg: 86%.

Grad '11—54. Col—54. (U of VA 6, Wm & Mary 4, PA St 3, Santa Clara 2, Wellesley 2, Bucknell 2). **Avg SAT:** CR 627. M 627. W 642. **Col couns:** 2.

Tui '12-'13: Bdg $50,437 (+$800). **Day $38,297** (+$800). **Intl Bdg $50,437** (+$800-4905). **Aid:** Need 68 ($2,400,000).

Summer: Rec. Tui Day $450-875. 1-2 wks. Riding. Tui Bdg 2495/2-wk ses. Tui Day $550-1695. 1-2 wks.

Endow $55,000,000. Plant val $20,000,000. Acres 376. Bldgs 34. Dorms 6. Dorm rms 116. Class rms 35. Lib 20,000 vols. Chapels 1. Photog labs 1. Dark rms 1. Auds 1. Theaters 1. Art studios 1. Music studios 1. Dance studios 1. Perf arts ctrs 1. Gyms 1. Fields 3. Courts 8. Pools 1. Riding rings 1. Stables 1. Comp/stud: 1:3.

Est 1906. Nonprofit. Tri (Sept-June).

Lucy Madeira established her school in Washington, DC, after teaching at Sidwell Friends School and serving as headmistress of Potomac School. The school moved 12 miles west of Washington, DC, to a 376-acre campus overlooking the Potomac River, in 1931.

The scholastic standards of the school have always been high. Students come from many states and foreign countries, and graduates go on to competitive colleges. The curriculum includes more than 100 courses, and Advanced Placement courses are offered in all academic departments. Courses as diverse as calculus, Irish literature and American studies are offered, and facilities are available for the studio and performing arts and athletics. Madeira also provides English as a Second Language instruction.

A Wednesday cocurricular program is an integral part of the academic program. Freshmen attend on-campus seminars that focus on leadership and skill development, and participate in Outdoor Adventure. Sophomores volunteer for off-campus community service organizations, while juniors spend Wednesdays as congressional interns. Seniors explore various career interests.

All girls belong to the student government association, through which they participate in forming and enforcing school rules, as well as developing programs. All students also play on junior varsity or varsity athletic teams or engage in such individual pursuits as dance, riding and fitness. The school plans events with nearby schools and takes advantage of the cultural and recreational activities of Washington, DC.

THE POTOMAC SCHOOL
Day — Coed Gr K-12

McLean, VA 22101. 1301 Potomac School Rd. Tel: 703-356-4100. Fax: 703-883-9031.
www.potomacschool.org   E-mail: potomac@potomacschool.org
Geoffrey A. Jones, Head (2000). BS, MS, Indiana State Univ. **Charlotte Nelsen, Adm.**
    Col Prep. AP (exams req'd)—Fr Lat Span Calc Stats Comp_Sci Bio Chem Physics US_Hist Music_Theory. **Elem math**—Everyday Math. **Feat**—Creative_Writing Non-fiction_Writing Chin Bioethics Environ_Sci Genetics Robotics African-Amer_Hist Lat-Amer_Hist Govt Intl_Relations Comp_Relig Ethics Architect Photog Visual_Arts Theater Music.
    Sports—Basket X-country Golf Lacrosse Soccer Squash Swim Tennis Track. B: Baseball Football Wrestling. G: F_Hockey Softball. **Activities:** 35.
    Selective adm (Gr K-11): 160/yr. Appl fee: $65. Appl due: Jan. Applied: 801. **Tests** IQ ISEE SSAT.
    Enr 1007. B 508. G 499. Elem 597. Sec 410. Wh 68%. Latino 2%. Blk 9%. Asian 7%. Other 14%. Avg class size: 16. **Fac 150.** M 43/F 107. FT 125/PT 25. Adv deg: 69%.
    Grad '11—98. Col—96. (U of VA 5, Georgetown 4, SMU 4, Villanova 4, Columbia 3, Cornell 3). **Avg SAT:** CR/M 1377. **Col couns:** 3.
    Tui '11-'12: Day $27,950-32,080. Aid: Need 126 ($2,600,000).
    Summer: Enrich Rec. Tui Day $660-1470/3-wk ses. 8 wks.
    Endow $28,000,000. Plant val $76,600,000. Acres 90. Class rms 90. Libs 3. Sci labs 12. Theaters 3. Art studios 5. Music studios 8. Gyms 2. Fields 5. Basketball courts 2. Tennis courts 6. Squash courts 4. Pools 1. Weight rms 1. Ponds 2. Comp labs 6. Laptop prgm Gr 6-8.
    Est 1904. Nonprofit. Sem (Sept-June).

Potomac was established as a girls' school in Washington, DC, by parents, with Lucy Madeira Wing as its first principal. The school completed its transition to a coeducational student body in 1964. In 1951, Potomac moved to its present location, where the cultural and educational resources of the city remain within easy reach of a quiet and spacious campus. Over the years, additions to the property enlarged it to 90 acres of hills, playing fields and nature trails.

The academic program is college preparatory in design. It provides a foundation in the liberal arts through its core curriculum and offers a variety of electives and Advanced Placement courses. Science, art and music begin in kindergarten, and foreign languages are introduced in grade 4. Academic technology at Potomac includes three computers in each lower school classroom, a one-to-one tablet PC program in grades 7 and 8, mobile laptop labs, and classrooms outfitted with electronic whiteboards and LCD projectors. Interscholastic teams compete in grades 7-12. The school conducts is a schoolwide community service program. Students enroll from the Washington, DC, metropolitan area.

MIDDLEBURG, VA. (39 mi. W of Washington, DC) Rural. Pop: 637. Alt: 492 ft. Area also includes The Plains.

FOXCROFT SCHOOL
Bdg and Day — Girls Gr 9-12

Middleburg, VA 20118. 22407 Foxhound Ln, PO Box 5555. Tel: 540-687-4340, 800-858-2364. Fax: 540-687-3627.
    www.foxcroft.org   E-mail: admissions@foxcroft.org
Mary Louise L. Leipheimer, Head (1989). BS, Indiana Univ of Pennsylvania. **Gina B. Finn, Adm.**
    Col Prep. AP (exams req'd; 175 taken, 59% 3+)—Eng Fr Span Calc Bio Chem Physics US_Hist Econ Human_Geog US_Govt & Pol. **Feat**—Creative_Writing Poetry Shake-

speare Chin Lat Stats Anat & Physiol Astron Environ_Sci Microbio Middle_Eastern_ Hist Intl_Relations World_Relig Art_Hist Ceramics Drawing Graphic_Arts Painting Photog Studio_Art Acting Theater_Arts Music_Theory. **Supp**—Rev Tut.

Sports (req'd)—G: Basket X-country Equestrian F_Hockey Lacrosse Soccer Softball Swim Tennis Volley. **Activities:** 33.

Somewhat selective adm (Bdg Gr 9-12; Day 9-10): 54/yr. Bdg 44. Day 10. Usual entry: 9. Appl fee: $50. Appl due: Feb. Applied: 160. Accepted: 86%. Yield: 39%. **Tests** CEEB IQ SSAT TOEFL.

Enr 154. Bdg 103. Day 51. Intl 18%. Avg class size: 12. Stud/fac: 6:1. Casual. **Fac 22.** M 5/F 17. FT 18/PT 4. Wh 90%. Blk 5%. Native Am 5%. Adv deg: 68%. In dorms 4.

Grad '11—46. Col—45. (Wm & Mary 3, U of Mary Wash 3, U of the South 2, Geo Wash 2, U of PA 1). **Col couns:** 1. Alum donors: 16%.

Tui '12-'13: Bdg $47,500 (+$2000). **Day $38,500** (+$2000). **Intl Bdg $44,900** (+$2000). **Aid:** Merit 6 ($31,320). Need 38 ($1,174,020).

Endow $22,800,000. Plant val $48,997,000. Acres 500. Bldgs 32 (100% ADA). Dorms 5. Dorm rms 55. Class rms 14. Lib 50,000 vols. Sci labs 3. Lang labs 1. Observatories 1. Auds 1. Theaters 1. Art studios 2. Music studios 2. Dance studios 1. Gyms 2. Fields 4. Courts 8. Pools 1. Riding rings 4. Stables 1. Weight rms 1. Fitness ctrs 1. Comp labs 3. Comp/stud: 1:1

Est 1914. Nonprofit. Sem (Sept-June). **Assoc** CLS.

Foxcroft, founded by Charlotte H. Noland, was given to the alumnae and reorganized as a nonprofit institution in 1937. The school is situated on 500 acres between the Blue Ridge and Bull Run mountains, one hour west of Washington, DC.

The school's structured college preparatory curriculum features a variety of electives, as well as Advanced Placement courses in all disciplines. Other features include a March interim program that focuses on global awareness and other current topics; career internships; independent study opportunities; a fellowship program that brings renowned figures to campus for classes and discussions; an annual, two-day poetry festival; and trips abroad.

Washington, DC, is used extensively for field trips to historical and cultural sites. Foxcroft's enrollment comprises students from a wide range of states and foreign countries.

HILL SCHOOL
Day — Coed Gr K-8

Middleburg, VA 20118. 130 S Madison St, PO Box 65. Tel: 540-687-5897.
Fax: 540-687-3132.
www.thehillschool.org   E-mail: tlord@thehillschool.org
Treavor Lord, Head (2010). BA, St Lawrence Univ, MEd, Univ of Virginia.

Pre-Prep. Feat—Lat Span Computers Studio_Art Drama Music. **Supp**—Dev_Read Makeup Rem_Read Tut.

Sports—Basket Lacrosse Soccer Track. G: F_Hockey Gymnastics.

Selective adm: 35/yr.

Enr 230. Fac 46. M 13/F 33. Adv deg: 43%.

Grad '11—31. Prep—26. (Middleburg 9, Foxcroft Sch 6, Highland-VA 6, Christchurch Sch 2, Georgetown Prep 1, Episcopal HS-VA 1).

Tui '12-'13: Day $15,900-20,900 (+$250). **Aid:** Need 61 ($1,400,000).

Summer: Enrich Rec. Sports. Theater. 6 wks.

Acres 137. Class rms 25. Lib 8000 vols. Labs 1. Art studios 1. Music studios 1. Perf arts ctrs 1. Athletic ctrs 1. Fields 4.

Est 1926. Nonprofit. Tri (Sept-June).

The program at this elementary school stresses the teaching of basic skills, with art, music and drama balanced in the curriculum. Computers are utilized in all classes. Language instruction commences with Spanish in grade 1, with Latin joining the curriculum in grade 6.

The Hill Theater provides opportunities for theater education and performances. Field trips to Washington, DC, 40 miles away, take place on a regular basis.

WAKEFIELD SCHOOL

Day — Coed Gr PS (Age 3)-12

The Plains, VA 20198. 4439 Old Tavern Rd, PO Box 107. Tel: 540-253-7500.
Fax: 540-253-5492.
www.wakefieldschool.org   E-mail: admissions@wakefieldschool.org
Peter A. Quinn, Head (1996). BA, Washington and Lee Univ, MA, Univ of Virginia. **Sarah K. McDonough, Adm.**

Col Prep. AP (exams req'd; 174 taken, 29% 3+)—Eng Fr Lat Span Calc Stats Bio Chem Physics Eur_Hist US_Hist US_Govt & Pol Studio_Art Music_Theory. **Elem math**—Everyday Math. **Elem read**—Saxon Phonics. **Feat**—Creative_Writing Ecol Zoology Programming Psych Asian_Stud Ethics Art_Hist Photog Acting Theater Chorus Journ. **Supp**—Rev Tut.

Sports—Basket X-country Golf Lacrosse Soccer Squash Swim Tennis. G: F_Hockey Volley.

Somewhat selective adm: 81/yr. Appl fee: $60. Appl due: Jan. Applied: 105. Accepted: 97%. Yield: 79%. **Tests** SSAT Stanford.

Enr 432. B 213. G 219. Elem 289. Sec 143. Wh 84%. Latino 3%. Blk 6%. Asian 3%. Other 4%. Avg class size: 12. Stud/fac: 10:1. Uniform. **Fac 50.** M 16/F 34. FT 48/PT 2. Adv deg: 64%.

Grad '11—31. Col—31. (U of VA 6, U of TN-Knoxville 2, Baylor 2, Hobart/Wm Smith 2, U of Richmond 1, Am U 1). **Avg SAT:** CR 590. M 560. W 590. **Mid 50% SAT:** CR 520-670. M 510-660. W 540-670. Avg ACT: 25.

Tui '12-'13: Day $10,200-22,700 (+$700-1000). **Aid:** Need 90 ($780,300).

Summer: Acad Enrich Rec. 1-2 wks.

Plant val $6,000,000. Acres 64. Bldgs 5 (100% ADA). Class rms 48. Lib 7000 vols. Sci labs 6. Art studios 3. Music studios 1. Gyms 2. Fields 3. Comp labs 3.

Est 1972. Nonprofit. Tri (Sept-June).

Located on the 64-acre site of Archwood Farm, Wakefield helps boys and girls in all three school divisions master content, develop sound study habits and learn to think independently. Notable aspects of the curriculum include inquiry-based science classes, an English curriculum in grades 1-12 that focuses on the acquisition and development of writing and communicational skills, and a program emphasis on interdisciplinary connections. Upper school students choose from a wide array of Advanced Placement courses and electives.

Middle school children (grades 6-8) take part in an annual week of experiential learning opportunities. The student chooses his or her offering from a selection that includes adventure, knowledge acquisition, culture and service options.

Beginning either in the summer preceding senior year (for the honors version) or at the start of grade 12, Wakefield's yearlong Senior Thesis Project requires pupils to explore a topic of deep personal interest and report on it comprehensively. In completing the project, boys and girls employ the tools of interdisciplinary research, original composition, and multimedia and written presentation. The resulting thesis is the equivalent of a 15- or 30-page college paper (for the standard and honors versions, respectively). At the conclusion of the school year, students present their work to various audiences within the academic community.

MOUTH OF WILSON, VA. (90 mi. WSW of Roanoke, VA) Rural. Pop: 100. Alt: 2500 ft.

OAK HILL ACADEMY

Bdg — Coed Gr 8-12

Mouth of Wilson, VA 24363. 2635 Oak Hill Rd. Tel: 276-579-2619. Fax: 276-579-4722.
www.oak-hill.net   E-mail: information@oak-hill.net
Michael D. Groves, Pres. BA, Marshall Univ, MDiv, PhD, Southern Baptist Theological

Seminary. **Mike Rodgers, Adm.**
Col Prep. Gen Acad. Underachiever. Feat—Creative_Writing Span Calc Anat Psych World_Relig Studio_Art Chorus Accounting Study_Skills. **Supp**—Dev_Read ESL Rem_Math Rem_Read Tut. Sat classes. **Dual enr:** Wytheville CC.
Sports—Basket Soccer Tennis. B: Baseball. G: Cheer Volley.
Somewhat selective adm: 74/yr. Day 0. Appl fee: $50. Appl due: Rolling. Accepted: 97%. Yield: 94%. **Tests** TOEFL.
Enr 148. B 98. G 50. Elem 5. Sec 143. Intl 33%. Avg class size: 9. Uniform. **Fac 18.** M 11/F 7. FT 16/PT 2. Wh 94%. Blk 6%. Adv deg: 61%.
Grad '09—39. Col—35. (Meredith, U of AZ, UNC-Charlotte, E Carolina, Radford, Geo Mason). Athl schol 8. **Avg SAT:** CR/M 970. Alum donors: 6%.
Tui '12-'13: Bdg $25,527 (+$1603). **Intl Bdg $33,960** (+$8350).
Summer: Acad Rec. Tui Bdg $3900. 5 wks.
Endow $1,900,000. Plant val $10,000,000. Acres 400. Bldgs 22. Dorms 5. Dorm rms 104. Class rms 21. Lib 5500 vols. Sci labs 2. Lang labs 1. Auds 1. Art studios 1. Music studios 2. Gyms 1. Fields 2. Courts 5. Riding rings 1. Stables 1. Parks 1. Lakes 1. Comp labs 2.
Est 1878. Nonprofit. Baptist (22% practice). Sem (Sept-May).

Designed to provide a suitable environment for boys and girls who have experienced difficulties at previous schools, Oak Hill conducts a structured, nonmilitary program that can meet the needs of underachievers and unmotivated pupils. The school offers general academic and college preparatory curricula in a Christian setting. Students may participate in the advanced studies honors program, and those who need extra assistance may seek help in the school's learning labs.

Students attend compulsory weekly services at the local church. The nearby New River and Grayson Highlands State Park provide opportunities for hiking, canoeing and picnicking.

NEWPORT NEWS, VA. (18 mi. NW of Norfolk, VA) Urban. Pop: 180,150. Alt: 20 ft.

HAMPTON ROADS ACADEMY
Day — Coed Gr PS (Age 4)-12

Newport News, VA 23602. 739 Academy Ln. Tel: 757-884-9148. Fax: 757-884-9137.
www.hra.org   E-mail: admissions@hra.org
Peter W. Mertz, Head (2011). BA, Williams College, MBA, Barry Univ. **Rebecca Bresee, Adm.**
Col Prep. AP (exams req'd; 278 taken, 69% 3+)—Eng Fr Ger Lat Span Calc Stats Bio Chem Environ_Sci Physics US_Hist World_Hist Psych US_Govt & Pol Art_Hist Studio_Art. **Feat**—Creative_Writing Shakespeare Anat & Physiol Bioethics Forensic_Sci Marine_Bio/Sci Programming Amer_Stud Comp_Relig Ceramics Photog Acting Drama Theater_Arts Band Orchestra Jazz_Improv Journ Public_Speak. **Supp**—Rev Tut.
Sports—Basket Cheer X-country Football Golf Sail Soccer Swim Tennis Track. B: Baseball Lacrosse. G: F_Hockey Softball Volley. **Activities:** 30.
Selective adm: 120/yr. Appl fee: $100. Appl due: Rolling. Applied: 571. Accepted: 30%. Yield: 69%. **Tests** CTP_4.
Enr 600. Elem 327. Sec 273. Wh 72%. Latino 1%. Blk 9%. Asian 6%. Other 12%. Avg class size: 16. Stud/fac: 10:1. **Fac 60.** M 26/F 34. FT 59/PT 1. Adv deg: 61%.
Grad '10—67. Col—67. (U of VA, Wm & Mary, James Madison, VA Polytech, VA Commonwealth, Hampden-Sydney). **Avg SAT:** CR 607. M 605. W 602. **Col couns:** 3.
Tui '12-'13: Day $8900-15,520 (+$335-1185). **Aid:** Need 60.
Summer: Enrich Rec. Sports. Tui Day $100-498/wk. 8 wks.
Plant val $10,000,000. Acres 50. Bldgs 3. Class rms 50. Lib 14,500 vols. Comp ctrs 2. Auds 1. Art studios 2. Drama studios 1. Gyms 3. Fields 6. Courts 6. Weight rms 1. Comp/stud: 1:2.2.

Est 1959. Nonprofit. Sem (Aug-June). **Assoc** CLS.

This college preparatory school occupies a 50-acre campus. Middle and upper school divisions prepare students for college entrance. Advanced Placement courses are available in many subjects, and the school maintains strong visual arts, music and drama programs. In 2008, the school added grades PS-5 through the incorporation of Hampton Roads Country Day School.

Boys and girls accumulate at least 40 hours of required community service in grades 9-12.

NORFOLK, VA. (80 mi. ESE of Richmond, VA) Urban. Pop: 234,403. Alt: 12 ft.

NORFOLK ACADEMY

Day — Coed Gr 1-12

Norfolk, VA 23502. 1585 Wesleyan Dr. Tel: 757-461-6236. Fax: 757-455-3181. www.norfolkacademy.org   E-mail: naadmissions@norfolkacademy.org
Dennis G. Manning, Head (2001). BA, MA, Wake Forest Univ. **Jay Lasley, Adm.**
   Col Prep. AP exams taken: 256 (84% 3+). Elem math—Everyday Math. **Feat**—Creative_Writing Shakespeare Fr Ger Ital Lat Span Calc Stats Ecol Lat-Amer_Hist Econ Govt Intl_Relations Art_Hist Film Studio_Art Drama Theater_Arts Music_Hist Music_ Theory Orchestra Jazz_Band Dance Public_Speak.
   Sports—Basket Crew X-country Lacrosse Sail Soccer Swim Tennis Track. B: Baseball Football Golf Wrestling. G: F_Hockey Softball Volley. **Activities: 15.**
   Selective adm (Gr 1-11): 142/yr. Usual entry: 1, 6 & 9. Appl fee: $35-85. Appl due: Jan. Accepted: 56%. Yield: 83%. **Tests** CEEB ISEE SSAT Stanford.
   Enr 1229. B 630. G 599. Elem 733. Sec 496. Wh 78%. Latino 1%. Blk 8%. Asian 5%. Other 8%. Avg class size: 20. Stud/fac: 9:1. Formal. **Fac 110.** Wh 92%. Blk 6%. Asian 2%.
   Grad '11—117. Col—117. (U of VA 28, Wm & Mary 7, VA Polytech 6, James Madison 5, Hampden-Sydney 3, U of Mary Wash 3). **Avg SAT:** CR 620. M 635. W 620. **Mid 50% SAT:** CR 570-660. M 590-673. W 570-680. Avg ACT: 28. **Col couns:** 2.
   Tui '12-'13: Day $17,500-20,500 (+$300). **Aid:** Need 213 ($2,200,000).
   Summer: Acad Enrich Rec. Tui Day $250/wk. 6 wks.
   Endow $31,700,000. Plant val $66,000,000. Acres 63. Bldgs 14. Class rms 54. 2 Libs 50,000 vols. Sci labs 10. Auds 1. Theaters 2. Art studios 4. Music studios 7. Dance studios 2. Arts ctrs 1. Gyms 2. Fields 11. Tennis courts 8. Pools 1. Tracks 1. Stadiums 2. Comp labs 6.
   Est 1728. Nonprofit. Sem (Aug-June). **Assoc** CLS SACS.

Located on a 63-acre campus between Norfolk and Virginia Beach, the academy has been in operation since before the American Revolution. The solid college preparatory curriculum, enriched by study of contemporary affairs and public speaking, as well as athletic, fine arts and community service programs, prepares students for competitive institutions throughout the country.

Although Norfolk does not participate in the Advanced Placement program, students prepare independently for AP tests in a range of subjects. Twice a year, faculty suspend classes to devote the school day to small-group seminar discussions about a selected piece of literature. Exchange programs with schools in France, Germany, Spain and South Africa are available.

ORANGE, VA. (60 mi. NW of Richmond, VA; 75 mi. SW of Washington, DC) Suburban. Pop: 4123. Alt: 521 ft.

GRYMES MEMORIAL SCHOOL
Day — Coed Gr PS (Age 4)-8

Orange, VA 22960. 13775 Spicer's Mill Rd, PO Box 1160. Tel: 540-672-1010.
Fax: 540-672-9167.
www.grymesschool.org   E-mail: info@grymesschool.org
Penny Work, Head (2005). MA, Univ of Pennsylvania, PhD, Princeton Univ. **Lee D. Berry, Adm.**

Pre-Prep. Elem math—TERC Investigations. **Feat**—Span Computers Studio_Art Drama Music. **Supp**—Rev Tut.

Sports—Basket Soccer. B: Lacrosse. G: F_Hockey.

Selective adm: 39/yr. Appl fee: $30. Appl due: Rolling. Accepted: 71%. Yield: 95%.

Enr 170. Wh 87%. Blk 13%. Avg class size: 16. Stud/fac: 7:1. **Fac 24.** M 3/F 21. FT 22/PT 2. Wh 100%. Adv deg: 37%.

Grad '10—9. Prep—6. (Woodberry Forest 3, Episcopal HS-VA 1, St Margaret's Sch 1).

Tui '11-'12: Day $9260-12,075 (+$200).

Endow $2,100,000. Acres 40. Bldgs 2. Lib 10,000 vols. Sci labs 1. Lang labs 1. Art studios 1. Music studios 1. Gyms 1. Fields 4. Comp labs 1. Comp/stud: 1:3.

Est 1947. Nonprofit. Sem (Sept-June).

Tracing its origins back to a program Emily Grymes began in her home, this school experienced rapid early growth before moving to its current site near the Blue Ridge Mountains in the 1950s. Grymes now provides a balanced elementary curriculum for pupils from Fredericksburg and the counties of Orange, Madison, Spotsylvania, Louisa, Culpeper and Greene.

Students receive a thorough background in the fundamentals as the majority prepare for entrance to independent high schools. Spanish instruction begins in prekindergarten and runs through grade 8. The arts constitute an integral part of the program, with art, music and drama carefully woven into the curriculum. Athletic competition and various leadership opportunities round out the program.

RICHMOND, VA. (98 mi. SSW of Washington, DC) Urban. Pop: 197,790. Alt: 20 ft.

COLLEGIATE SCHOOL
Day — Coed Gr K-12
(Coord — Day 5-8)

Richmond, VA 23229. 103 N Mooreland Rd. Tel: 804-740-7077. Fax: 804-741-9797.
www.collegiate-va.org   E-mail: admission@collegiate-va.org
Keith A. Evans, Head (1999). BA, Davidson College, EdM, Harvard Univ, MS, Univ of Tennessee-Knoxville. **Amanda L. Surgner, Adm.**

Col Prep. AP (exams req'd; 516 taken, 87% 3+)—Eng Fr Lat Span Calc Stats Bio Chem Physics US_Hist Econ. **Elem math**—Everyday Math. **Feat**—Poetry Russ_Lit Chin Comp_Sci WWII Asian_Stud Relig Photog Studio_Art Chorus Journ. **Supp**—Rev Tut. **Dual enr:** U of Richmond.

Sports (req'd)—Basket X-country Lacrosse Soccer Swim Tennis Track. B: Baseball Football Golf Wrestling. G: F_Hockey Softball Volley. **Activities:** 47.

Selective adm: 181/yr. Usual entry: K, 5 & 9. Appl fee: $50. Appl due: Rolling. Applied: 508. Accepted: 53%. Yield: 66%. **Tests** CEEB CTP_4 DAT IQ SSAT TOEFL.

Enr 1597. B 809. G 788. Elem 1081. Sec 516. Wh 87%. Blk 5%. Asian 4%. Other 4%. Avg class size: 15. **Fac 198.** M 58/F 140. FT 155/PT 43. Adv deg: 73%.

Grad '11—119. Col—119. (U of VA 12, VA Polytech 8, Elon 7, James Madison 7, High

Pt 4, Wm & Mary 3). **Mid 50% SAT:** CR 540-670. M 560-680. W 560-660. Mid 50% ACT: 23-30. **Col couns:** 3. Alum donors: 28%.
Tui '11-'12: Day $17,630-20,690 (+$500-800). **Aid:** Need 186 ($2,017,195).
Summer: Acad Enrich Rev Rem Rec. Sports. 8 wks.
Endow $40,000,000. Plant val $43,688,000. Acres 211. Bldgs 31 (100% ADA). Class rms 120. 2 Libs 39,000 vols. Sci labs 12. Lang labs 2. Auds 3. Theaters 2. Art studios 5. Music studios 4. Dance studios 1. Gyms 3. Athletic ctrs 2. Fields 18. Tennis courts 13. Comp labs 7. Comp/stud: 1:2.
Est 1915. Nonprofit. Sem (Aug-May). **Assoc** CLS SACS.

Collegiate was founded downtown as a girls' school. The coeducational Collegiate Country Day School was established in 1953 as a separate division on a campus 10 miles from the original Collegiate Town School. In 1960, the schools consolidated and now occupy a 55-acre campus. At one time divided into girls' and boys' schools, Collegiate reorganized in 1986 to form a coeducational lower school (grades K-4) and coordinate upper levels (grades 5-12), with boys' and girls' divisions operating on the same campus. A 1986 restructuring resulted in full coeducation. Classes in the lower and upper schools are coed, while boys and girls in the middle school (grades 5-8) attend same-sex academic classes.

Math, science, foreign languages, art, music, physical education, computer literacy and economics are required elements of the curriculum. Collegiate offers a global economics course in conjunction with the University of Richmond; in addition, a summer economics institute involving work at companies in the community is available.

A strong sports program serves boys and girls in grades 7-12. Collegiate maintains a 156-acre athletic expanse five miles west of its main campus.

ST. CATHERINE'S SCHOOL
Day — Girls Gr PS (Age 4)-12

Richmond, VA 23226. 6001 Grove Ave. Tel: 804-288-2804. Fax: 804-285-8169.
www.st.catherines.org   E-mail: admissions@st.catherines.org
Terrie H. Scheckelhoff, Head (2012). BS, Miami Univ (OH), MA, MBA, Ohio State Univ, PhD, Univ of Nebraska-Lincoln. **Jennifer Cullinan, Adm.**
Col Prep. AP (241 exams taken, 83% 3+)—Eng Fr Lat Span Calc Stats Comp_Sci Bio Chem Environ_Sci Physics Eur_Hist US_Hist World_Hist Comp_Govt & Pol Econ US_Govt & Pol Art_Hist Music_Theory. **Feat**—Creative_Writing African-Amer_Lit Chin Genetics Mech_Engineering Middle_Eastern_Hist Vietnam_War Women's_Hist Constitutional_Law Relig Ceramics Photog Studio_Art Hist_of_Architect Theater Dance Journ. **Supp**—Dev_Read Rev Tut.
Sports—G: Basket X-country F_Hockey Golf Indoor_Track Lacrosse Sail Soccer Softball Squash Swim Tennis Track Volley.
Selective adm: 121/yr. Usual entry: K, 5 & 9. Appl fee: $50. Appl due: Rolling. **Tests** SSAT TOEFL.
Enr 930. Elem 637. Sec 293. Wh 84%. Latino 2%. Blk 7%. Asian 3%. Other 4%. Casual. **Fac 117.** M 24/F 93. FT 98/PT 19. Adv deg: 62%.
Grad '11—58. Col—58. (U of VA, Wm & Mary, Wash & Lee, James Madison, Elon, Christopher Newport). **Mid 50% SAT:** CR 570-650. M 560-660. W 570-680. **Col couns:** 2.
Tui '12-'13: Day $15,950-22,500 (+$235-2255). **Aid:** Need ($3,000,000).
Summer: Enrich. Creative Arts. 3-6 wks.
Endow $45,700,000. Acres 16. Bldgs 28. Class rms 50. Lib 20,000 vols. Sci labs 6. Lang labs 1. Theaters 1. Art studios 3. Music studios 9. Dance studios 1. Gyms 3. Athletic ctrs 1. Fields 6. Courts 4. Pools 1. Comp labs 4. Laptop prgm Gr 7-12.
Est 1890. Nonprofit. Episcopal. Sem (Sept-June). **Assoc** CLS.

St. Catherine's, which was founded by Virginia Randolph Ellett to prepare girls for colleges requiring entrance exams, was acquired by the Episcopal Church in the Diocese of Virginia in 1920. The school discontinued its long-standing boarding division in 2006.

In addition to traditional course selections, St. Catherine's offers special opportunities in art, drama and modern dance; day or evening electives in creative writing, critical thinking and ceramics; and X-Term, a yearlong experiential learning opportunity for upper school girls that offers courses focusing on academic enrichment, cultural experiences overseas and in the US, career exploration and individual community service projects. Mandarin Chinese is a four-year language offering.

All graduates perform 25 hours of community service each year in grades 11 and 12. Through coordination with the nearby St. Christopher's School for boys, a substantial number of upper school classes and extracurriculars are coeducational.

ST. CHRISTOPHER'S SCHOOL
Day — Boys Gr PS (Age 4)-12

Richmond, VA 23226. 711 St Christopher's Rd. Tel: 804-282-3185. Fax: 804-673-6632. www.stchristophers.com   E-mail: admissions@stcva.org
Charles M. Stillwell, Head (1999). AB, Princeton Univ, MA, Brown Univ. **Cary C. Mauck, Adm.**

Col Prep. AP (exams req'd; 303 taken, 87% 3+)—Eng Fr Lat Span Calc Stats Comp_Sci Bio Chem Environ_Sci Physics US_Hist Econ US_Govt & Pol Art_Hist Music_Theory. **Feat**—Humanities African-Amer_Lit Russ_Lit Southern_Lit Genetics Geol Marine_Bio/Sci Web_Design Chin_Hist Middle_Eastern_Hist Vietnam_War Law Comp_Relig Ethics Photog Studio_Art Theater Music Music_Hist Ballet Dance Journ. **Supp**—Dev_Read Rem_Math Rem_Read Rev Tut.

Sports—B: Baseball Basket X-country Football Golf Indoor_Track Lacrosse Sail Soccer Squash Swim Tennis Track Wrestling.

Selective adm: 116/yr. Appl fee: $50. Appl due: Rolling. Applied: 312. Accepted: 62%. Yield: 60%. **Tests** CTP_4 IQ SSAT.

Enr 952. Elem 671. Sec 281. Wh 92%. Latino 1%. Blk 6%. Asian 1%. Avg class size: 16. **Fac 145.** M 60/F 85. FT 130/PT 15. Wh 95%. Latino 2%. Blk 2%. Asian 1%. Adv deg: 61%.

Grad '10—80. Col—80. (U of VA 12, VA Polytech 7, Hampden-Sydney 5, Wash & Lee 4, Wm & Mary 3). **Mid 50% SAT:** CR 570-680. M 580-680. W 590-700. Alum donors: 47%.

Tui '11-'12: Day $16,355-21,835 (+$670-1350). **Aid:** Merit 2 ($3000). Need 140 ($1,749,800).

Summer: Acad Enrich Rec. Sports. Tui Day $155-1070. 1-6 wks.

Endow $61,000,000. Plant val $32,000,000. Acres 46. Bldgs 23. Class rms 100. Lib 16,400 vols. Sci labs 8. Lang labs 1. Auds 2. Theaters 1. Art studios 3. Music studios 6. Dance studios 1. Gyms 5. Fields 6. Courts 9. Field houses 1. Pools 1. Weight rms 1. Comp labs 5.

Est 1911. Nonprofit. Episcopal (40% practice). Sem (Sept-June).

St. Christopher's offers a complete college preparatory program and provides a liberal arts education with an emphasis on Judeo-Christian ideals. At the lower school level (junior kindergarten through grade 5), teachers take into account boys' varying developmental needs and learning styles, while also emphasizing the development of independent and critical-thinking and problem-solving skills. The middle school (grades 6-8) continues to address differing intellectual needs as it emphasizes skill development in preparation for higher learning. Instruction moves from predominantly concrete intellectual exercises in grade 6 to more abstract forms of reasoning by grade 8.

In the upper school (grades 9-12), pupils follow a rigorous academic program that includes honors or Advanced Placement courses in all subject areas. A coordinate program with nearby St. Catherine's School during these years permits a broader curriculum and a wider choice of electives and AP courses in a coeducational context. Seniors have a two-week period of independent study in the spring. The coeducational Halsey Waterman Program involves upperclassmen in canoeing and rock climbing; ninth graders may enroll if space permits.

Upper school pupils accumulate at least 50 hours of community service over four years.

Leading Private Schools

THE STEWARD SCHOOL
Day — Coed Gr PS (Age 4)-12

Richmond, VA 23238. 11600 Gayton Rd. Tel: 804-740-3394. Fax: 804-740-1464.
www.stewardschool.org   E-mail: debbie.robson@stewardschool.org
Kenneth H. Seward, Head (2004). BA, Middlebury College, MA, Case Western Reserve Univ. **Debbie Robson, Adm.**
Col Prep. AP (65 exams taken, 78% 3+)—Eng Lat Span Calc Stats Bio Chem US_Hist US_Govt & Pol Studio_Art. **Feat**—Creative_Writing Anat & Physiol Environ_Sci Programming Econ Psych Sociol Comp_Relig Graphic_Arts Photog Acting Theater_Arts Chorus Music Journ Public_Speak Woodworking. **Supp**—ESL Tut.
Sports—Basket X-country Golf Lacrosse Soccer Tennis. B: Baseball. G: Cheer F_ Hockey Volley.
Selective adm: 138/yr. Appl fee: $50. Appl due: Rolling. Applied: 210. Accepted: 66%. **Tests** IQ ISEE.
Enr 609. B 324. G 285. Elem 406. Sec 203. Wh 92%. Latino 2%. Blk 4%. Asian 2%. Avg class size: 15. Stud/fac: 15:1. **Fac 75.** M 24/F 51. FT 70/PT 5. Wh 86%. Latino 2%. Blk 2%. Native Am 1%. Other 9%. Adv deg: 58%.
Grad '10—43. Col—42. (James Madison 4, Christopher Newport 4, U of GA 2, VA Polytech 2, Col of Charleston 2, U of MS 2). **Avg SAT:** CR 555. M 556. W 589. **Mid 50% SAT:** CR 500-620. M 490-610. W 540-630. Avg ACT: 24. Alum donors: 13%.
Tui '12-'13: Day $18,400-20,545 (+$900). **Aid:** Need 109 ($1,021,390).
Summer: Acad Enrich Rev Rem Rec. 2-6 wks.
Endow $8,400,000. Plant val $36,000,000. Acres 37. Bldgs 8 (100% ADA). Class rms 77. Lib 20,000 vols. Sci labs 5. Auds 1. Theaters 2. Art studios 4. Music studios 2. Gyms 2. Fields 4. Courts 9. Comp labs 5. Comp/stud: 1:6.
Est 1972. Nonprofit. Sem (Aug-June).

Steward's college preparatory program provides opportunities for pupils to receive one-on-one tutoring. Environmental studies is an integral part of the lower and upper school programs, and the fine arts are promoted throughout the curriculum. Students fulfill graduation requirements in public speaking, economics and computers.

In the early grades, boys and girls take part in community service class projects; during the upper school years, students accumulate 50 hours of service.

ROANOKE, VA. (138 mi. W of Richmond, VA) Urban. Pop: 94,911. Alt: 904 ft.

NORTH CROSS SCHOOL
Day — Coed Gr PS (Age 3)-12

Roanoke, VA 24018. 4254 Colonial Ave. Tel: 540-989-6641, 866-294-5284.
Fax: 540-989-7299.
www.northcross.org   E-mail: djessee@northcross.org
Christian Proctor, Head (2011). BA, Colgate Univ, MS, Duke Univ, PhD, Univ of North Carolina. **Deborah C. Jessee, Adm.**
Col Prep. AP (exams req'd; 130 taken)—Eng Fr Lat Span Calc Comp_Sci Chem Physics US_Hist Psych US_Govt & Pol Studio_Art. **Feat**—Stats Ecol Environ_Sci Forensic_Sci Sports_Med Web_Design Civil_War Women's_Hist Vietnam_War WWII Anthro Ethics Philos World_Relig Art_Hist Drawing Filmmaking Graphic_Arts Painting Photog Drama Chorus Music_Theory. **Supp**—Tut.
Sports—Basket X-country Golf Soccer Swim. B: Baseball Football Lacrosse Tennis Wrestling. G: F_Hockey Softball Volley.
Somewhat selective adm: 95/yr. Appl fee: $35. Accepted: 85%.
Enr 549. B 277. G 272. Elem 381. Sec 168. Wh 78%. Latino 2%. Blk 8%. Asian 12%. Avg class size: 13. Stud/fac: 8:1. **Fac 64.** Wh 90%. Blk 1%. Asian 4%. Other 5%. Adv deg: 45%.

Grad '09—30. Col—30. (U of VA, VA Polytech, U of Mary Wash, Davidson, Radford, U of the South). Mid 50% ACT: 21-27. **Col couns:** 1.
Tui '12-'13: Day $9480-14,320. Aid: Need 154 ($500,000).
Summer: Enrich Rec. Soccer. 4-8 wks.
Endow $8,000,000. Plant val $24,000,000. Acres 77. Bldgs 9. Class rms 45. Lib 12,000 vols. Sci labs 5. Theaters 1. Art studios 5. Music studios 2. Dance studios 1. Gyms 1. Fields 5. Courts 12. Pools 1. Comp labs 3.
Est 1960. Nonprofit. Tri (Sept-June). **Assoc** CLS.

Located on a 77-acre campus, North Cross was founded to provide college preparation for its students through a comprehensive program. A traditional core curriculum is the academic focus throughout the school and is supported by enrichment classes, electives, and a wide selection of cocurricular activities and athletic programs.

The phonics-based lower school program (junior kindergarten through grade 5) includes an introduction to foreign languages in junior kindergarten, in addition to course work in music, art, computer and library skills. The middle school (grades 6-8) continues to provide boys and girls with a grounding in the fundamentals and features choral and instrumental music. The upper school curriculum includes electives in every discipline and a full complement of Advanced Placement courses. Seniors complete an extended research project and deliver a subsequent presentation to faculty and students.

As part of its service program, the school devotes two school days per year to community work that involves much of the student body, faculty advisors, select staff members and parents.

STAUNTON, VA. (78 mi. NE of Roanoke, VA) Suburban. Pop: 23,853. Alt: 1379 ft.

STUART HALL SCHOOL
Bdg — Girls Gr 8-12; Day — Coed PS (Age 4)-12

Staunton, VA 24402. 235 W Frederick St, PO Box 210. Tel: 540-885-0356, 888-306-8926. Fax: 540-886-2275.
Other locations: 74 Quicks Mill Rd, Verona 24482.
www.stuarthallschool.org E-mail: sday@stuart-hall.org
Mark Hampton Eastham, Head (2004). BA, Washington and Lee Univ, MEd, Univ of Virginia. **Sally Day, Adm.**
Col Prep. AP (exams req'd; 79 taken, 67% 3+)—Eng Fr Calc Bio Environ_Sci US_Hist World_Hist US_Govt & Pol Music_Theory. **Feat**—British_Lit Span Philos Relig Studio_Art Visual_Arts Theater Chorus Music Journ. **Supp**—ESL Tut. **Dual enr:** Mary Baldwin.
Sports—Basket X-country Golf Lacrosse Soccer. G: Cheer Volley.
Selective adm: 91/yr. Bdg 15. Day 76. Appl fee: $45. Appl due: Rolling. Accepted: 83%. Yield: 76%. **Tests** SSAT Stanford TOEFL.
Enr 333. B 114. G 219. Bdg 43. Day 290. Wh 87%. Latino 1%. Blk 5%. Asian 6%. Other 1%. Intl 9%. Avg class size: 15. Uniform. **Fac 39.** M 12/F 27. FT 27/PT 12. Wh 100%. Adv deg: 35%. In dorms 4.
Grad '10—33. Col—33. (U of VA 3, PA St 1, Princeton 1, VA Milit 1, VA Polytech 1, U of TN-Knoxville 1). **Avg SAT:** CR 608. M 591. W 586. Alum donors: 17%.
Tui '11-'12: Bdg $39,000 (+$1600). **5-Day Bdg $32,000** (+$1600). **Day $7200-12,800** (+$1600). **Intl Bdg $39,000** (+$1600-5100). **Aid:** Need 125 ($1,040,000).
Endow $907,000. Plant val $8,972,000. Acres 28. Bldgs 3. Dorms 8. Dorm rms 68. Class rms 33. 2 Libs 17,000 vols. Sci labs 4. Auds 1. Theaters 1. Art studios 2. Music studios 1. Gyms 2. Fields 3. Courts 3. Comp labs 3. Comp/stud: 1:5.
Est 1844. Nonprofit. Episcopal. Sem (Sept-May).

The oldest girls' boarding school in Virginia, Stuart Hall was founded as Virginia Female Institute and was renamed in honor of Mrs. J.E.B. Stuart, who was principal for 19 years. Since its founding, the school has been affiliated with the Episcopal Diocese of Virginia. Boys first enrolled as day students in grades 6-8 in 1992, and in grades 9-12 in 1999. Stuart Hall effected a merger with Hunter McGuire School in the summer of 2007, resulting in the addition of a coeducational lower school (grades PS-5). The lower school occupies the former Hunter McGuire location in Verona.

Within a Christian setting, the school offers a curriculum that includes an honors program beginning in grade 9 and a selection of AP courses. The school's well-developed fine arts program awards specialized diplomas to students who pursue concentrations in visual arts, theater or music. Pupils requiring academic support or assistance with their organizational or study skills may meet with Stuart Hall's learning resource specialists.

SUFFOLK, VA. (27 mi. SW of Norfolk, VA) Urban. Pop: 81,332. Alt: 32 ft.

NANSEMOND-SUFFOLK ACADEMY
Day — Coed Gr PS (Age 3)-12

Suffolk, VA 23434. 3373 Pruden Blvd. Tel: 757-539-8789. Fax: 757-934-8363.
www.nsacademy.org   E-mail: drussell@nsacademy.org
Colley W. Bell III, Head (2008). BA, Univ of Kentucky, MA, Columbia Univ. **Deborah Russell, Adm.**

> **Col Prep. AP (exams req'd; 315 taken, 64% 3+)**—Eng Fr Lat Span Calc Stats Bio Chem Environ_Sci Physics Eur_Hist US_Hist US_Govt & Pol Studio_Art Music_Theory. **Feat**—Creative_Writing Mythology Programming Holocaust Econ Psych Film Photog Theater_Arts Chorus Debate Journ. **Supp**—Tut.
> **Sports**—Basket X-country Golf Lacrosse Soccer Swim Tennis Track Volley. B: Baseball Football. G: Cheer F_Hockey Softball. **Activities:** 25.
> **Selective adm:** 151/yr. Appl fee: $25-50. Appl due: Feb.
> **Enr 930.** Avg class size: 17. Stud/fac: 11:1. **Fac 90.** Adv deg: 51%.
> **Grad '09—78. Col—78.** (VA Polytech 9, Old Dominion 8, James Madison 4, U of SC 4, U of VA 4, VA Commonwealth 4). Athl schol 1. **Mid 50% SAT:** CR 480-610. M 500-630. W 500-620. **Col couns:** 2. Alum donors: 17%.
> **Tui '12-'13: Day $11,850-14,140** (+$3200-3360). **Aid:** Need ($747,000).
> **Summer:** Enrich Rec. Sports. Adventure. Tui Day $125-310. 1-2 wks.
> Acres 100. Bldgs 5. Class rms 70. Libs 2. Sci labs 8. Amphitheaters 1. Auds 1. Art studios 4. Fields 5. Tennis courts 6. Weight rms 1. Comp labs 3.
> **Est 1966.** Nonprofit. Tri (Aug-June). **Assoc** SACS.

Originally serving students in grades 1-7, the academy moved to its present, 100-acre campus and added an upper school in 1970, graduating its first senior class in 1972.

The strong college preparatory program, which is rooted in the liberal arts tradition, features the humanities, foreign languages, mathematics and the natural sciences. Honors and Advanced Placement classes provide for college-level study in the major disciplines, and gifted students may engage in independent study. The academy teaches five levels of French, Spanish and Latin, as well as computer programming courses.

An on-campus cultural enrichment committee schedules guest artists in the performing arts.

TAPPAHANNOCK, VA. (43 mi. NE of Richmond, VA) Rural. Pop: 2068. Alt: 22 ft.

ST. MARGARET'S SCHOOL
Bdg and Day — Girls Gr 8-12

Tappahannock, VA 22560. 444 Water Ln, PO Box 158. Tel: 804-443-3357.
Fax: 804-443-6781.
www.sms.org E-mail: admit@sms.org
Margaret R. Broad, Head (1989). BA, Denison Univ, MA, Univ of Virginia.
  Col Prep. AP (26 exams taken, 81% 3+)—Eng Fr Lat Span Calc Bio Eur_Hist US_Hist.
    Feat—Humanities Anat & Physiol Ecol Environ_Sci Econ Relig Art_Hist Ceramics
    Photog Studio_Art Fashion_Design Mosaics Music Music_Hist Piano Journ Driver_
    Ed Health. Supp—ESL. Dual enr: Rappahannock CC.
  Sports—G: Basket Crew X-country F_Hockey Golf Soccer Softball Swim Tennis Volley.
  Somewhat selective adm: 46/yr. Bdg 40. Day 6. Appl fee: $40. Appl due: Rolling.
    Applied: 86. Accepted: 87%. Yield: 61%. Tests CEEB SSAT TOEFL.
  Enr 123. Bdg 100. Day 23. Intl 27%. Avg class size: 8. Stud/fac: 6:1. Uniform. Fac 35. M
    6/F 29. FT 35. Adv deg: 80%. In dorms 9.
  Grad '10—33. Col—33. (MI St 2, Randolph Col 2, VA Commonwealth 2, James Madison
    1, Geo Wash 1, RI Sch of Design 1). Athl schol 2. Avg SAT: CR 533. M 573. W 563.
    Mid 50% SAT: CR 460-590. M 480-660. W 570-620. Avg ACT: 21.8. Col couns: 1.
  Tui '11-'12: Bdg $43,200 (+$2000). Day $16,800 (+$800). Intl Bdg $43,200 (+$2500-
    6000). Aid: Need 45 ($820,000).
  Endow $6,000,000. Plant val $17,500,000. Acres 49. Bldgs 18. Dorms 3. Dorm rms
    58. Class rms 24. Lib 10,000 vols. Sci labs 2. Tech ctrs 1. Theaters 1. Art studios 2.
    Music studios 1. Dance studios 1. Gyms 1. Fields 5. Courts 3. Pools 1. Comp labs 2.
    Comp/stud: 1:2.
  Est 1921. Nonprofit. Episcopal. Tri (Sept-June). Assoc SACS.

One of the church schools in the Episcopal Diocese of Virginia, St. Margaret's takes advantage of its small-town setting in the historic Virginia Tidewater. Girls learn in a Christian, homelike atmosphere in which they are held to high academic standards. The curriculum, emphasizing individual attention and college preparation, encompasses a variety of courses, ranging from world civilizations and physics to piano and studio art.

At all grade levels, girls perform 12 hours of compulsory community service annually. All seniors complete a two-week career exploration internship in the spring. The River Program spans the curriculum, co-curriculum and residential life and exposes girls to hands-on science, water sports and volunteer service. St. Margaret's participates in an exchange program with schools in Australia and New Zealand that are also members of the Queen Margaret of Scotland Girls' Schools Association.

VIRGINIA BEACH, VA. (17 mi. SE of Norfolk, VA) Suburban. Pop: 425,257. Alt: 18 ft.

CAPE HENRY COLLEGIATE SCHOOL
Day — Coed Gr PS (Age 3)-12

Virginia Beach, VA 23454. 1320 Mill Dam Rd. Tel: 757-481-2446. Fax: 757-481-9194.
www.capehenrycollegiate.org E-mail: comments@capehenry.org
John P. Lewis, Head (2002). BS, MA, Saint Peter's College, EdD, Seton Hall Univ. Richard
  Plank, Adm.
  Col Prep. AP (exams req'd; 91 taken)—Eng Fr Lat Span Calc Comp_Sci Bio Chem
    Environ_Sci Physics Eur_Hist US_Hist US_Govt & Pol Studio_Art. Feat—Creative_
    Writing Poetry Stats Anat & Physiol Ecol Forensic_Sci Marine_Bio/Sci Paleontol-

ogy Web_Design Asian_Hist Econ Sociol Ethics Photog Drama Music Music_Hist Music_Theory Ballet Dance Journ. **Supp**—ESL Tut.

Sports—Basket Crew X-country Golf Lacrosse Soccer Swim Tennis Track Volley. B: Baseball Wrestling. G: Cheer F_Hockey Softball.

Selective adm: 115/yr. Appl fee: $50. Appl due: Feb. Accepted: 55%. Yield: 65%. **Tests** CTP_4 ISEE.

Enr 853. Elem 477. Sec 376. Intl 7%. Avg class size: 16. Stud/fac: 10:1. Casual. **Fac 135.** M 42/F 93. FT 95/PT 40. Adv deg: 61%.

Grad '11—76. Col—76. (U of VA 7, James Madison 5, Radford 5, Wm & Mary 4, E Carolina 4, U of VA 3). **Mid 50% SAT:** CR 500-650. M 520-640. W 500-640. Mid 50% ACT: 21-28. **Col couns:** 2.

Tui '12-'13: Day $10,900-17,995 (+$220-1925). **Aid:** Merit 8 ($140,760). Need 171 ($1,300,000).

Summer: Acad Enrich Rev Rec. 10 wks.

Endow $7,000,000. Plant val $20,500,000. Acres 30. Bldgs 8. Class rms 89. Libs 2. Sci labs 14. Lang labs 1. Photog labs 1. Auds 1. Theaters 1. Art studios 4. Music studios 4. Dance studios 1. Gyms 1. Fields 5. Courts 8. Comp labs 5. Comp/stud: 1:4.

Est 1924. Nonprofit. Sem (Aug-June).

Formerly the Everett School, Cape Henry Collegiate is Virginia Beach's oldest independent school. Students are encouraged to balance academics, athletics, the arts and community involvement. Pupils enroll from Virginia Beach, Norfolk, Portsmouth and Chesapeake, as well as several foreign countries.

The curriculum is college preparatory, emphasizing English, math, foreign languages, social studies, science and global affairs. The developmental lower school program offers an extended-day program for children in grades pre-K-5. The middle school (grades 6-8) provides an interdisciplinary curriculum and an enrichment program that includes electives in literary magazine, newspaper, music, drama and art. Emphasis upon computer literacy in core subjects begins in the lower school and continues through the upper school. The upper school curriculum emphasizes writing, critical-thinking and research skills. Advanced Placement and honors courses in all disciplines, as well as a variety of activities and public speaking requirements, are featured.

Boys and girls in grades 6-8 perform six hours of compulsory community service per year, while those in grades 9-12 accumulate at least 10 hours annually.

WARRENTON, VA. (44 mi. WSW of Washington, DC) Suburban. Pop: 6670. Alt: 700 ft.

HIGHLAND SCHOOL

Day — Coed Gr PS (Age 3)-12

Warrenton, VA 20186. 597 Broadview Ave. Tel: 540-878-2700. Fax: 540-878-2731. www.highlandschool.org   E-mail: admission@highlandschool.org

Henry D. Berg, Head (2005). BA, Wake Forest Univ, MS, Texas Tech Univ. **Donna Tomlinson, Adm.**

Col Prep. AP (exams req'd; 166 taken, 86% 3+)—Eng Fr Span Calc Stats Bio Chem Physics Eur_Hist US_Hist World_Hist Studio_Art Music_Theory. **Feat**—Shakespeare Mythology Lat Environ_Sci Marine_Bio/Sci Comp_Design Comp_Sci African-Amer_ Hist Econ Law Psych Comp_Relig Architect Ceramics Filmmaking Photog Sculpt Drama Theater_Arts Band Chorus Music Debate Journ SAT_Prep. **Supp**—LD. **Dual enr:** Geo Mason.

Sports—Basket X-country Golf Lacrosse Soccer Swim Tennis. B: Baseball. G: Cheer F_Hockey Softball Volley. **Activities:** 9.

Selective adm: 121/yr. Appl fee: $75. Appl due: Jan. Accepted: 60%. Yield: 98%. **Tests** CEEB SSAT.

Enr 480. Elem 282. Sec 198. Nonwhite 11%. Avg class size: 11. **Fac 99.** M 31/F 68. FT 99. Adv deg: 51%.
Grad '08—54. Col—54. (Wm & Mary, Hampden-Sydney, James Madison, Cornell, IN U, Randolph-Macon). **Avg SAT:** CR 595. M 570. W 592. **Col couns:** 2.
Tui '12-'13: Day $8300-21,900 (+$100). **Aid:** Merit 24 ($125,000). Need 173 ($1,400,000).
Summer: Acad Enrich Rec. 6 wks.
Endow $3,600,000. Plant val $15,400,000. Acres 42. Bldgs 3. Class rms 45. 2 Libs 8000 vols. Sci labs 6. Photog labs 1. Theaters 2. Art studios 5. Music studios 3. Arts ctrs 1. Art galleries 1. Gyms 2. Fields 6. Tennis courts 4. Weight rms 1. Comp labs 2.
Est 1928. Nonprofit. Sem (Sept-June).

Founded as the Warrenton branch of the Calvert School of Baltimore, MD, this school initially utilized the Calvert curriculum. Founders Lavinia Hamilton and Dorothy Montgomery moved the school on a couple of occasions to accommodate growth; the institution assumed its present location in 1957. That same year, an independent program replaced the Calvert system, and the name was changed to Highland School. A group of community leaders acquired the school in 1961.

Developmental in nature, the prekindergarten through fifth grade program emphasizes skill development in language arts, mathematics, social studies, science, computer science, foreign language, music, art and physical education. Specialist teachers conduct science, computer, foreign language, music, art and physical education classes during these years. Children in grades 6-8 take six courses per semester in the standard disciplines, including Latin, as well as an elective from among art, drama, band, community service, forensics and chorus. Pupils in grades 4-8 participate in interscholastic athletics.

Highland's comprehensive college preparatory curriculum in grades 9-12 includes honors and Advanced Placement courses and selections in science, the humanities, and the fine and performing arts. The upper school provides both honors and standard college preparatory levels; pupils need not take classes at exclusively one level or the other, however. All Highland upper schoolers take a music course and an art class. Students in grades 9-11 perform 20 hours of required community service annually, while 12th graders complete a senior service project. Field trips provide enrichment in the arts and sciences.

WAYNESBORO, VA. (80 mi. NE of Roanoke, VA; 87 mi. WNW of Richmond, VA) Urban. Pop: 19,520. Alt: 1407 ft.

FISHBURNE MILITARY SCHOOL
Bdg and Day — Boys Gr 7-PG
Waynesboro, VA 22980. 225 S Wayne Ave, PO Box 988. Tel: 540-946-7706, 800-946-6773. Fax: 540-946-7738.
www.fishburne.org   E-mail: admissions@fishburne.org
Col. Roy F. Zinser, USA (Ret), Supt. Col. William W. Sedr, Jr., Head. BA, Virginia Military Institute, MA, Virginia Polytechnic Institute. **Brock Selkow, Adm.**
Col Prep. Milit. Feat—Fr Span Anat & Physiol Comp_Sci Econ Law Sociol Studio_Art Band Music Public_Speak JROTC SAT_Prep. **Supp**—Makeup Rev Tut.
Sports (req'd)—B: Baseball Basket X-country Football Golf Lacrosse Soccer Swim Tennis Track Wrestling.
Somewhat selective adm: 65/yr. Bdg 62. Day 3. Appl fee: $50. Appl due: Rolling. Accepted: 90%. Yield: 36%.
Enr 200. Bdg 178. Day 22. Elem 17. Sec 183. Intl 5%. Avg class size: 10. Stud/fac: 8:1. Uniform. **Fac 30.** M 27/F 3. FT 30. Adv deg: 36%.
Grad '09—42. Col—42. (TX A&M, Old Dominion, VA Commonwealth, VA Milit, Citadel, US Milit Acad). **Avg SAT:** CR 470. M 530. W 540. **Col couns:** 1.
Tui '11-'12: Bdg $26,400 (+$1500). **Day $15,240** (+$1500). **Aid:** Need 80 ($75,000).

Summer: Acad. JROTC. Tui Bdg $3660-3890. 5 wks.
Endow $6,500,000. Plant val $8,000,000. Acres 9. Bldgs 4. Dorms 1. Dorm rms 88. Class rms 21. Lib 10,000 vols. Sci labs 3. Lang labs 2. Comp ctrs 1. Auds 1. Art studios 1. Music studios 1. Gyms 1. Fields 1. Basketball courts 2. Tennis courts 5. Pools 1. Weight rms 1. Rifle ranges 1. Comp labs 2.
Est 1879. Nonprofit. Quar (Aug-May). **Assoc** SACS.

James Fishburne, a student and close friend of Robert E. Lee's, established this school at age 29 with the aim of preparing boys "for the duties and responsibilities of life."

The oldest and smallest of Virginia's military school's, Fishburne offers a college preparatory curriculum that is complemented by a full athletic program and such military organizations as rifle and drill teams. Supervised study halls and extra-help sessions are integral to the program, and the school also emphasizes test-taking, critical thinking, writing, reading, note-taking, memory enhancement and time-management skills. Most graduates matriculate at Eastern colleges.

WOODBERRY FOREST, VA. (64 mi. NW of Richmond, VA; 76 mi. SW of Washington, DC) Rural. Pop: 450.

WOODBERRY FOREST SCHOOL

Bdg — Boys Gr 9-12

Woodberry Forest, VA 22989. 898 Woodberry Forest Rd. Tel: 540-672-3900.
Fax: 540-672-6471.
www.woodberry.org   E-mail: info@woodberry.org
Dennis M. Campbell, Head (1997). AB, PhD, Duke Univ, BD, Yale Univ. **J. Harrison Stuart, Adm.**
   Col Prep. AP (exams req'd; 315 taken, 70% 3+)—Lat Calc Stats Bio Chem Environ_Sci Physics Econ Psych US_Govt & Pol Art_Hist Studio_Art Music_Theory. **Feat**—Creative_Writing Chin Fr Japan Span Geol Comp_Sci Law Bible Photog Sculpt Drama Chorus Mech_Drawing. **Supp**—Rev. Outdoor ed. Sat classes.
   Sports—B: Baseball Basket X-country Football Golf Indoor_Track Lacrosse Soccer Squash Swim Tennis Track Wrestling. **Activities:** 30.
   Selective adm (Gr 9-11): 128/yr. Appl fee: $50. Appl due: Feb. Accepted: 66%. Yield: 65%. **Tests** SSAT TOEFL.
   Enr 406. Wh 90%. Latino 1%. Blk 7%. Asian 2%. Intl 10%. Avg class size: 9. Stud/fac: 6:1. **Fac 58.** M 51/F 7. FT 57/PT 1. Adv deg: 62%. In dorms 14.
   Grad '10—86. Col—86. (U of SC, Wofford, Wm & Mary, NC St, U of the South, Wash & Lee). **Avg SAT:** CR 599. M 598. W 599. **Col couns:** 3. Alum donors: 51%.
   Tui '11-'12: Bdg $44,800 (+$500-700). **Aid:** Need 157 ($4,300,000).
   Summer: Ages 10-16. Basketball. Lacrosse. 1 wk. Sports. 3 wks.
   Endow $217,000,000. Plant val $100,000,000. Acres 1200. Bldgs 77. Dorms 9. Dorm rms 205. Lib 55,000 vols. Sci labs 4. Lang labs 1. Theaters 1. Art studios 5. Music studios 10. Gyms 2. Fields 11. Courts 17. Pools 2. Tracks 1. Golf crses 1. Comp labs 4.
   Est 1889. Nonprofit. Tri (Sept-May). **Assoc** CLS SACS.

Woodberry Forest was established by Capt. Robert S. Walker and was carried on under family ownership and control until 1926 by three of his six sons.

The school's college preparatory curriculum features honors and Advanced Placement courses in many disciplines. Students choose among electives in math, English, the humanities, computer science and general subjects.

Participation in athletics is required, and the school offers a range of interscholastic and intramural sports. Also available are summer study programs in France, Spain, Japan, England, Australia, Scotland and Israel. Graduates matriculate at competitive colleges.

WOODSTOCK, VA. (81 mi. W of Washington, DC) Suburban. Pop: 3952. Alt: 820 ft.

MASSANUTTEN MILITARY ACADEMY

Bdg and Day — Coed Gr 7-PG

Woodstock, VA 22664. 614 S Main St. Tel: 540-459-2167, 877-466-6222.
Fax: 540-459-5421.
www.militaryschool.com   E-mail: admissions@militaryschool.com
R. **Craig Jones, Head (2009).** BA, Virginia Military Institute, JD, Univ of Virginia. **Tom Huckabee, Adm.**
Col Prep. Milit. AP—Eng Calc Bio Chem US_Hist US_Govt & Pol. **Feat**—Fr Lat Russ Span Econ Ethics Philos Ceramics Painting Photog Band Orchestra Journ JROTC SAT_Prep. **Supp**—ESL Makeup Rev Tut. Sat classes. **Dual enr:** Shenandoah.
Sports—Basket Cheer X-country Golf Soccer Swim Tennis Track. B: Baseball Football Lacrosse Wrestling. G: Softball Volley.
Selective adm: 92/yr. Bdg 87. Day 5. Appl fee: $50. Appl due: Rolling. Applied: 240. Accepted: 75%. Yield: 55%.
Enr 175. B 135. G 40. Bdg 160. Day 15. Elem 15. Sec 148. PG 12. Wh 74%. Latino 3%. Blk 15%. Asian 5%. Other 3%. Avg class size: 10. Uniform. **Fac 24.** M 10/F 14. FT 21/PT 3. Wh 94%. Latino 2%. Blk 4%. Adv deg: 37%.
Grad '10—43. **Col**—43. (U of MS, Geo Mason, James Madison, VA Milit, U of S AL, U of AK-Anchorage). Athl schol 3. **Avg SAT:** CR/M 914. Avg ACT: 20. **Col couns:** 2.
Tui '11-'12: Bdg $29,100 (+$3500-4000). **Day $12,000** (+$3500). **Intl Bdg $29,100** (+$5500-7000). **Aid:** Merit 20 ($38,724). Need 64 ($234,523).
Summer (enr 160): Acad Enrich. JROTC. Tui Bdg $3625. Tui Day $1945. 5 wks.
Endow $11,000,000. Plant val $12,000,000. Acres 40. Bldgs 19. Dorms 4. Dorm rms 116. Class rms 23. Lib 6000 vols. Sci labs 3. Auds 2. Art studios 1. Music studios 1. Gyms 1. Fields 2. Tennis courts 1. Pools 1. Comp labs 3.
Est 1899. Nonprofit. Nondenom Christian. Quar (Aug-June). **Assoc** SACS.

The school was founded by the Virginia Classis of the Reformed Church to prepare the children of the Shenandoah Valley for college. For 50 years, with the assistance of a board of trustees representing several religious denominations, Howard J. Benchoff devoted his energies to its development. In 1917, the academy adopted a military program whose structured environment remains an integral part of school life. Robert J. Benchoff succeeded his father in 1955 and continued to expand the enrollment and the plant facilities until his death in 1968.

Within a small-class environment, MMA emphasizes its core curriculum of English, math, science, social studies and foreign language. Noteworthy aspects of the program include reading comprehension courses, dual-enrollment college-credit courses in math and American history, and various fine and performing arts offerings. A daily academic assistance period, an evening study period, a homework assistance program and an academic advisor program provide academic support.

The academy's rural location on 40 acres in the middle of the Shenandoah Valley allows for a variety of activities. Scheduled trips are made to cultural and athletic events in Washington, DC, and Baltimore, MD. Other pursuits include hiking and skiing in the nearby Massanutten Range of the Blue Ridge Mountains and in the George Washington National Forest.

WEST VIRGINIA

WHEELING, WV. (46 mi. WSW of Pittsburgh, PA) Urban. Pop: 31,419. Alt: 642 ft.

LINSLY SCHOOL
Bdg — Coed Gr 7-12; Day — Coed 5-12

Wheeling, WV 26003. 60 Knox Ln. Tel: 304-233-1436. Fax: 304-234-4614.
www.linsly.org E-mail: admit@linsly.org

Chad Barnett, Head (2009). BA, Bethany College, MA, West Virginia Univ. Craig Tredenick, Adm.

Col Prep. AP (226 exams taken, 64% 3+)—Eng Calc Bio Chem Physics US_Hist Human_Geog Psych. **Feat**—Creative_Writing Humanities Shakespeare Fr Ger Lat Span Environ_Sci Programming Web_Design Econ Ceramics Graphic_Arts Studio_Art Theater_Arts Chorus Music Journ. **Supp**—Tut.

Sports—Basket X-country Golf Ice_Hockey Soccer Swim Tennis Track. B: Baseball Football Lacrosse. G: Softball Volley.

Selective adm (Bdg Gr 7-11; Day 5-11): 96/yr. Bdg 40. Day 56. Appl due: Rolling. Accepted: 66%. Yield: 80%. **Tests** IQ TOEFL.

Enr 444. B 243. G 201. Bdg 108. Day 336. Elem 160. Sec 284. Wh 82%. Blk 4%. Asian 2%. Other 12%. Intl 6%. Avg class size: 15. Uniform. **Fac 48.** M 31/F 17. FT 48. Adv deg: 60%. In dorms 10.

Grad '11—75. Col—75. (U of PA, US Air Force Acad, OH St, WV U, NYU, Elon). **Avg SAT:** CR 560. M 580. W 570.

Tui '12-'13: Bdg $30,710 (+$1000). **Day $15,790** (+$1000).

Summer: Acad Enrich. 5 wks.

Acres 65. Bldgs 20. Dorms 4. Dorm rms 75. Class rms 37. Lib 7000 vols. Sci labs 5. Lang labs 1. Art studios 4. Music studios 1. Gyms 3. Fields 3. Courts 3. Pools 1. Comp labs 2.

Est 1814. Nonprofit. Sem (Aug-May). **Assoc** NCA.

Founded by Noah Linsly as the Wheeling Lancastrian Academy, Linsly, renamed for its benefactor, is the oldest independent preparatory school west of the Allegheny Mountains. The traditional college preparatory curriculum includes Advanced Placement classes in all the major disciplines, as well as a contemporary approach to the utilization of technology in the classroom. The program also features compulsory art and music appreciation courses.

Interscholastic athletic competition is offered from grade 5 through the varsity level. All students spend time each year at the Linsly Outdoor Center, an experiential and environmental training facility located on 300 acres of parkland. Boys and girls in grades 9-12 must join one of the school's community service organizations. **See Also Page 139**

Great Lakes States

ILLINOIS

CHICAGO, IL. Urban. Pop: 2,896,016. Alt: 593 ft.

CHICAGO ACADEMY FOR THE ARTS
Day — Coed Gr 9-12

Chicago, IL 60642. 1010 W Chicago Ave. Tel: 312-421-0202. Fax: 312-421-3816.
www.chicagoartsacademy.org   E-mail: generalinfo@chicagoartsacademy.org
Pamela Jordan, Head (2002). **Melissa Brookes, Adm.**
   Col Prep. Perform_Arts Visual_Arts. AP (exams req'd; 30 taken, 67% 3+)—Eng Fr
   Span Calc Eur_Hist Art_Hist. **Feat**—Chicago_Lit Anat Bus_Law Philos Visual_Arts
   Urban_Design Media_Arts Acting Theater Music Dance. **Supp**—Tut.
   Selective adm (Gr 9-11): 60/yr. Usual entry: 9. Appl fee: $65. Appl due: Dec. Applied:
   142. Accepted: 62%. Yield: 75%. **Tests** ISEE.
   Enr 144. B 54. G 90. Wh 62%. Latino 11%. Blk 13%. Asian 5%. Other 9%. Avg class
   size: 12. Stud/fac: 12:1. **Fac 45.** M 25/F 20. FT 20/PT 25. Wh 98%. Latino 1%. Blk
   1%. Adv deg: 42%.
   Grad '11—44. Col—43. (Juilliard, NYU, SUNY-Purchase, U of MI, Parsons Sch of
   Design, Loyola Marymount). **Avg SAT:** CR 574. M 519. W 568. Avg ACT: 23.3. **Col
   couns:** 1.
   Tui '12-'13: Day $22,105 (+$525-1475). **Aid:** Need 89 ($753,025).
   Endow $918,000. Bldgs 1. Libs 1. Sci labs 2. Theaters 1. Art studios 4. Music studios 4.
   Dance studios 3. Drama studios 1. Comp labs 1. Comp/stud: 1:6.
   Est 1981. Nonprofit. Quar (Sept-May). **Assoc** NCA.

The academy focuses on the integration of arts and academics. Every day, students spend five hours in college preparatory academic classes, followed by three hours of instruction in each student's major: visual arts, music, theater, dance, musical theater or media arts (film and creative writing). The academy offers more than 50 arts courses, among them ballet, jazz and modern dance, vocal and instrumental lessons, acting, directing, stagecraft, drawing, painting, sculpting, design, printmaking, film studies, video production, speech, poetry and prose fiction, and publishing.

The majority of graduates matriculate at colleges or conservatories, while others immediately begin professional arts careers.

FRANCIS W. PARKER SCHOOL
Day — Coed Gr PS (Age 4)-12

Chicago, IL 60614. 330 W Webster Ave. Tel: 773-353-3000. Fax: 773-549-4669.
www.fwparker.org   E-mail: admission@fwparker.org
Daniel B. Frank, Prin. BA, Amherst College, MA, PhD, Univ of Chicago. **Karen Fisher,
Adm.**
   Col Prep. **Feat**—British_Lit Creative_Writing Poetry Shakespeare Sci_Fiction Chin Fr
   Lat Span Calc Stats Astron Environ_Sci Engineering Paleontology Programming
   Web_Design African-Amer_Hist Econ Intl_Relations Psych Architect_Drawing Art_
   Hist Ceramics Drawing Photog Sculpt Video_Production Drama Chorus Orchestra
   Jazz_Band Dance Journ Woodworking. **Supp**—Dev_Read Rem_Math Rem_Read
   Rev Tut.

Sports—Basket X-country Golf Indoor_Track Soccer Tennis Track. B: Baseball. G: F_ Hockey Softball Volley.
Very selective adm: 116/yr. Appl fee: $70-80. Appl due: Dec. Accepted: 20%. **Tests** ISEE.
Enr 930. Avg class size: 18. Stud/fac: 8:1. **Fac 102.** M 38/F 64. FT 92/PT 10.
Grad '10—75. Col—75. (U of MI 5, U of VT 5, U of IL-Urbana 4, U of PA 4, CA Inst of the Arts 3, Wesleyan U 3). **Col couns:** 3.
Tui '12-'13: Day **$24,050-31,290** (+$180-2260). **Aid:** Need 158 ($3,000,000).
Summer: Acad Enrich Rec. ACT/SAT Prep. Writing. 2-6 wks.
Endow $10,900,000. Plant val $45,000,000. Acres 5. Bldgs 2. Class rms 56. Lib 46,000 vols. Sci labs 8. Lang labs 1. Auds 1. Art studios 7. Music studios 2. Dance studios 1. Gyms 3. Fields 1. Comp labs 5. Comp/stud: 1:1.9.
Est 1901. Nonprofit. Sem (Sept-June). **Assoc** NCA.

Flora J. Cooke founded this school to carry out the progressive educational concepts envisioned by John Dewey and Col. Francis Wayland Parker. She served as principal for 33 years.

The interdisciplinary approach to curriculum fosters a broad academic and social understanding of the world. Although the curriculum is a rigorous one, every effort is made to adapt academics to each child's needs. A wide range of work is provided in music, art, dramatics and shop. Emphasis is placed on the development of student responsibility and its attendant activities. In junior kindergarten through grade 5, a central topic provides an organized, yearlong approach to the curriculum. In the upper school (grades 9-12), Dewey Seminars offer semester-long explorations of various elective topics.

A formal community service program begins in the middle school, as small groups of mixed-grade students spend eight mornings each year working with different agencies throughout the Chicago community.

LATIN SCHOOL OF CHICAGO
Day — Coed Gr PS (Age 4)-12

Chicago, IL 60610. 59 W North Blvd. Tel: 312-582-6000. Fax: 312-582-6011.
Other locations: 45 W North Blvd, Chicago 60610; 1531 N Dearborn Pky, Chicago 60610.
www.latinschool.org   E-mail: info@latinschool.org
Randall C. Dunn, Head (2011). AB, Brown Univ, MEd, Harvard Univ. **Frankie Brown, Adm.**
    Col Prep. AP (295 exams taken, 85% 3+)—Chin Fr Lat Span Calc Stats Comp_Sci Bio Chem Environ_Sci Physics Eur_Hist US_Hist Psych US_Govt & Pol Art_Hist Studio_Art Music_Theory. **Elem math**—Everyday Math. **Feat**—Creative_Writing Shakespeare African_Lit Lat-Amer_Lit Multivariable_Calc Anat & Physiol Astron African_Hist Middle_Eastern_Hist Russian_Hist Anthro Econ Law World_Relig Photog Acting Dance.
    Sports—Basket X-country Ice_Hockey Soccer Swim Tennis Track Volley W_Polo. B: Baseball Golf. G: F_Hockey Softball. **Activities:** 42.
    Selective adm: 155/yr. Usual entry: PS, 5 & 9. Appl fee: $80. Appl due: Rolling. Applied: 725. Accepted: 33%. Yield: 69%. **Tests** ISEE.
    Enr 1105. B 524. G 581. Elem 678. Sec 427. Wh 67%. Latino 4%. Blk 6%. Asian 9%. Other 14%. Avg class size: 20. Stud/fac: 8:1. Casual. **Fac 140.** M 58/F 82. FT 136/PT 4. Adv deg: 71%.
    Grad '11—111. Col—106. (U of MI 6, Colgate 5, Northwestern 5, Vanderbilt 5, U of WI-Madison 4, Vassar 3). Athl schol 1. **Mid 50% SAT:** CR 600-700. M 580-730. W 620-710. Mid 50% ACT: 27-32. **Col couns:** 2. Alum donors: 17%.
    Tui '12-'13: Day **$24,825-28,985** (+$1000-1500). **Aid:** Need 134 ($2,800,000).
    Summer (enr 721): Acad Enrich Rev Rec. Sports. Travel. Tui Day $125-5000. 1-8 wks.
    Plant val $82,000,000. Bldgs 3 (100% ADA). Class rms 67. 2 Libs 41,200 vols. Dark rms 1. Comp ctrs 3. Theaters 1. Art studios 4. Music studios 2. Gyms 4. Fields 3. Pools 1. Comp/stud: 1:3.
    Est 1888. Nonprofit. Quar (Aug-June). **Assoc** CLS NCA.

Latin offers a traditional college preparatory curriculum supplemented by the performing and applied arts, clubs, athletics and student-run publications. The middle school curriculum includes interdisciplinary and project-based learning opportunities; a writing lab; and an arts cycle that consists of art, drama and music. A featured course for ninth graders is an interdisciplinary global studies class that that explores cultural centers around the world.

The upper school curriculum features four foreign languages; an extensive selection of electives in history, English and science; and AP courses in many subjects. An annual project week provides nontraditional learning opportunities for those in grades 6-12 in an on- or off-campus setting. Students perform two independent community service activities in grade 9 and four projects in grade 10.

Latin conducts an extensive interscholastic sports program; the vast majority of middle and upper school students participate in at least one sport annually.

MORGAN PARK ACADEMY
Day — Coed Gr PS (Age 3)-12

Chicago, IL 60643. 2153 W 111th St. Tel: 773-881-6700. Fax: 773-881-8409.
www.morganparkacademy.org   E-mail: info@morganparkacademy.org
Catherine Raaflaub, Head (2009). BS, Curtin Univ of Technology (Australia), MS, Niagara Univ, PhD, Univ of Waterloo (Canada). **Adriana Mourgelas, Adm.**
Col Prep. AP (117 exams taken, 84% 3+)—Eng Fr Span Calc Stats Bio Chem US_Hist Comp_Govt & Pol Human_Geog Studio_Art. **Feat**—Creative_Writing Astron Genetics Comp_Sci Pol_Sci World_Relig Filmmaking Acting Drama Music Journ.
Sports—Basket Soccer Tennis. B: Baseball Golf. G: Softball Volley. **Activities:** 35.
Selective adm: 104/yr. Appl fee: $50. Appl due: Jan. Accepted: 33%. **Tests** ISEE.
Enr 500. Avg class size: 14. **Fac 62.** M 16/F 46. FT 62. Adv deg: 54%.
Grad '10—38. Col—38. (U of IL-Urbana, U of Chicago, Northwestern, DePaul, Stanford, Butler). **Avg SAT:** CR 605. M 606. W 595. Avg ACT: 26.
Tui '11-'12: Day $13,600-20,100 (+$800).
Summer: Acad Enrich Rem Rec. Tui Day $1500/2-wk ses. 6 wks.
Endow $1,200,000. Plant val $16,500,000. Acres 20. Bldgs 6. Class rms 43. Lib 26,000 vols. Labs 5. Music studios 2. Arts ctrs 1. Gyms 1. Fields 2. Tennis courts 4.
Est 1873. Nonprofit. Sem (Sept-June). **Assoc** CLS NCA.

The academy is located 15 miles southwest of downtown Chicago in a residential community. Morgan Park served as the preparatory department of the University of Chicago from 1892 to 1907, then existed as a military academy until 1958. The program places special emphasis on English, foreign languages, history, science and mathematics.

Continuing emphasis is placed on small classes and the development of a competitive and selective academic school of exacting standards. Foreign language instruction begins in preschool, and throughout the school emphasis is placed on the development of reading and writing skills. Honors and Advanced Placement courses are available in all major disciplines in the upper school. Course offerings in the areas of art, computer science, drama, music and physical education are provided at all levels.

Two service learning days are held during the school year in which students and faculty participate in a variety of community service events. All boys and girls participate in eight community service days prior to graduation.

SACRED HEART SCHOOLS
Day — Coed Gr K-8
(Coord — Day 1-8)

Chicago, IL 60660. 6250 N Sheridan Rd. Tel: 773-262-4446. Fax: 773-262-6178.
www.shschicago.org   E-mail: admissions@shschicago.org
Nat Wilburn, Heads (2009). BA, Univ of Tennessee-Knoxville, MEd, Loyola Univ of Chi-

cago, MDiv, Catholic Univ of America. **Jan Farnsworth, Adm.**
Pre-Prep. Feat—Fr Span Computers Relig Studio_Art Music Health. **Supp**—LD Tut.
Sports (req'd)—Basket X-country Soccer Track Volley. B: Baseball. G: Softball.
Selective adm (Gr K-7): 96/yr. Usual entry: K. Appl fee: $60-75. Appl due: Dec. Applied:
298. Accepted: 39%. Yield: 82%.
Enr 700. B 349. G 351. Wh 76%. Latino 3%. Blk 3%. Asian 4%. Other 14%. Avg class
size: 19. Stud/fac: 9:1. Uniform. **Fac 87.** M 12/F 75. FT 86/PT 1. Wh 96%. Latino 1%.
Blk 2%. Native Am 1%. Adv deg: 63%.
Grad '11—66. Prep—48. (St Ignatius-IL 32, Loyola Acad 9, Latin 3, Woodlands Acad 1,
Culver 1). Alum donors: 6%.
Tui '12-'13: Day $16,065 (+$450). **Aid:** Need 140 ($1,332,407).
Summer (enr 225): Acad Enrich Rec. Tui Day $200-350/wk. 6 wks.
Endow $18,070,000. Plant val $19,603,000. Acres 2. Bldgs 5 (80% ADA). Class rms 48.
Lib 12,000 vols. Sci labs 4. Auds 1. Art studios 3. Music studios 2. Gyms 1. Courts 2.
Playgrounds 3. Comp labs 2. Comp/stud: 1:1
Est 1876. Nonprofit. Roman Catholic (60% practice). Sem (Sept-June). **Assoc** NCA.

Part of the Network of Sacred Heart Schools in the US, this school consists of a coeducational kindergarten and two distinct elementary programs for children in grades 1-8: the Academy of the Sacred Heart for girls and Hardey Preparatory School for boys. The academy, which was founded on Dearborn Street in 1876 as one of Chicago's first independent schools, moved to its current location overlooking Lake Michigan on Sheridan Road in 1928. Hardey Prep was added to the school complex in 1935.

Developmental readiness is at the core of the kindergarten program. In addition to language arts, math, social studies and science, children gain an exposure to music, art, French, physical education and religion. Beginning in first grade, boys and girls learn in single-gender classrooms in the core subjects. Students follow similar curricula and thematic study units while also sharing many school activities. Departmentalization begins in the middle school (grades 6-8). Among special subjects at this level are foreign language, music, art, computer, health and religion.

Beginning in kindergarten, all boys and girls engage in community service projects that revolve around an age-appropriate theme. Sacred Heart schedules frequent field trips at all grade levels.

THE UNIVERSITY OF CHICAGO LABORATORY SCHOOLS
Day — Coed Gr PS (Age 4)-12

Chicago, IL 60637. 1362 E 59th St. Tel: 773-702-9450. Fax: 773-702-7455.
www.ucls.uchicago.edu   E-mail: lab@ucls.uchicago.edu
David Magill, Dir (2003). BS, Ohio State Univ, EdM, EdD, Temple Univ. **Irene Reed, Adm.**
Col Prep. AP—Fr Ger Span Calc Stats Comp_Sci Music_Theory. **Elem math**—Everyday Math. **Feat**—Creative_Writing Chin Lat Bioethics Organic_Chem Web_Design African-Amer_Hist Holocaust Art_Hist Photog Sculpt Studio_Art Drama Music Journ.
Supp—Dev_Read Rem_Read. **Dual enr:** U of Chicago.
Sports—Basket X-country Fencing Golf Soccer Swim Tennis Track. B: Baseball. G: Volley. **Activities:** 40.
Selective adm (Gr PS-11): 204/yr. Usual entry: PS & 9. Appl fee: $80. Appl due: Jan. Applied: 615. Accepted: 41%. Yield: 81%. **Tests** ISEE.
Enr 1783. Wh 52%. Latino 2%. Blk 9%. Other 37%. Avg class size: 23. Stud/fac: 11:1.
Fac 223. M 55/F 168. FT 207/PT 16. Wh 81%. Latino 4%. Blk 8%. Asian 6%. Other 1%. Adv deg: 79%.
Grad '11—117. Col—116. (Northwestern 8, U of Chicago 7, Yale 6, U of MI 5, U of IL-Urbana 4, Tufts 4). **Avg SAT:** CR 681. M 675. W 668. Avg ACT: 29.4. **Col couns:** 2. Alum donors: 10%.
Tui '12-'13: Day $23,526-26,520 (+$50-1300). **Aid:** Need 220 ($1,574,194).
Summer: Acad Enrich Rec. Tui Day $360-3190. 2-6 wks.
Plant val $10,000,000. Bldgs 4. 2 Libs 80,000 vols. Lang labs 1. Auds 1. Theaters 2. Art studios 7. Music studios 8. Dance studios 1. Gyms 4. Fields 3. Courts 5. Pools 1.

Playgrounds 5. Comp labs 4. Comp/stud: 1:2.7.
Est 1896. Nonprofit. Quar (Sept-June). **Assoc** NCA.

The Laboratory Schools, established by John Dewey as a laboratory for curricular development and teacher training, are part of the University of Chicago. Approximately half of the pupils are children of university faculty and staff members, while the rest of the student body come from all parts of the Chicago metropolitan area. Graduates continue study at the college level, but beyond academic preparation for college, the program encourages autonomy in intellectual development and endeavors to provide an environment for healthy personal and social growth.

Students in the lower school (grades 1-4) move gradually away from a homeroom-centered day as foreign languages are introduced in grade 3 and musical instruments in grade 4. The high school curriculum includes Advanced Placement courses and a variety of quarter-long electives in the English department, and students may enroll in up to six University of Chicago undergraduate courses at no additional cost. Freshmen and sophomores meet with academic advisors twice weekly, and most seniors spend the month of May completing an independent project outside the classroom. Wireless Internet access is available throughout the campus.

Boys and girls perform two compulsory quarters of service, usually in grade 10. During these quarters, students devote at least an hour a week to service activities.

CHICAGO HEIGHTS, IL. (23 mi. S of Chicago, IL) Urban. Pop: 32,776. Alt: 689 ft.

MARIAN CATHOLIC HIGH SCHOOL
Day — Coed Gr 9-12

**Chicago Heights, IL 60411. 700 Ashland Ave. Tel: 708-755-7565. Fax: 708-755-0042.
www.marianchs.com E-mail: mchsinfo@marianchs.com**
Sr. Judine Hilbing, OP, Pres (2008). BA, St Ambrose Univ, MA, Univ of Illinois-Urbana. **Sr. Kathleen Anne Tait, OP, Prin.** BA, St Ambrose Univ, MA, Univ of St Thomas (MN). **Sr. Dorothy Marie Solak, OP, Adm.**
Col Prep. AP (exams req'd; 684 taken, 76% 3+)—Eng Lat Span Calc Stats Comp_Sci Bio Chem Physics Eur_Hist US_Hist World_Hist Econ Psych. **Feat**—Creative_Writing World_Lit Fr Anat & Physiol Astron Ecol Forensic_Sci Amer_Stud Govt Sociol Relig Photog Studio_Art Video_Production Drama Band Chorus Music Bus Journ. **Supp**—Makeup Rev Tut. **Dual enr:** Prairie St.
Sports—Basket X-country Fencing Golf Lacrosse Soccer Tennis Track Volley. B: Baseball Football Wrestling. G: Cheer Softball Swim W_Polo. **Activities:** 31.
Somewhat selective adm (Gr 9-11): 326/yr. Appl fee: $0. Appl due: Mar. Applied: 529. Accepted: 85%. Yield: 71%. **Tests** HSPT IQ.
Enr 1444. B 684. G 760. Wh 44%. Latino 9%. Blk 38%. Asian 1%. Other 8%. Avg class size: 23. Stud/fac: 15:1. Uniform. **Fac 79.** M 35/F 44. FT 73/PT 6. Wh 92%. Latino 1%. Blk 6%. Native Am 1%. Adv deg: 64%.
Grad '11—343. Col—340. (IL St 19, U of IL-Urbana 16, Loyola U of Chicago 15, N IL 14, U of MO-Columbia 12, S IL-Carbondale 12). Athl schol 13. **Mid 50% SAT:** CR 480-600. M 420-620. Avg ACT: 19. Mid 50% ACT: 21-27. **Col couns:** 8. Alum donors: 20%.
Tui '11-'12: Day $8650 (+$300). **Aid:** Merit 246 ($541,750). Need 267 ($349,250).
Summer: Acad Enrich Rem. Tui Day $400/3-wk ses. 6 wks.
Endow $6,500,000. Plant val $16,000,000. Acres 72. Bldgs 1 (100% ADA). Class rms 56. Lib 25,000 vols. Sci labs 8. Theaters 1. Art studios 1. Music studios 4. Gyms 2. Fields 6. Courts 8. Comp labs 3. Comp/stud: 1:2.
Est 1958. Nonprofit. Roman Catholic. Sem (Aug-June). **Assoc** NCA.

Owned and operated by the Dominican Sisters of Springfield, Marian Catholic is one of the largest coeducational Catholic college preparatory schools in Illinois. Students enroll from more than 50 nearby communities, covering a radius of over 400 miles. Located on a 72-acre campus, the plant has undergone five expansion projects since the school's establishment.

The curriculum concentrates on traditional college preparatory courses, and Marian Catholic requires daily religious instruction of all students. In addition, honors and Advanced Placement classes are provided in all of the major fields. Electives include speech, music, art, drama, business and computer courses.

DOWNERS GROVE, IL. (17 mi. W of Chicago, IL) Suburban. Pop: 48,724. Alt: 718 ft.

AVERY COONLEY SCHOOL
Day — Coed Gr PS (Age 3)-8

Downers Grove, IL 60515. 1400 Maple Ave. Tel: 630-969-0800. Fax: 630-969-0131.
   www.averycoonley.org   E-mail: agilla@averycoonley.org
Paul A. Barton, Head. BA, Loras College, MA, St John's College, MEd, DePaul Univ. **Andrew Gilla, Adm.**
   Pre-Prep. Gen Acad. Feat—Fr Computers Studio_Art Drama Music.
   Sports—Basket Soccer Track. G: Volley.
   Selective adm: 52/yr. Appl fee: $75. **Tests** IQ.
   Enr 378. Avg class size: 16. Stud/fac: 11:1. **Fac 33.** Wh 100%. Adv deg: 60%.
   Grad '08—31. Prep—13. (Benet 1, U of Chicago Lab Schs 1, Latin 1, Lake Forest Acad 1, Deerfield Acad 1, Hotchkiss 1).
   Tui '12-'13: Day $18,565-19,565 (+$75-1300). **Aid:** Need 15 ($90,250).
   Summer: Acad Enrich Rec. 2-6 wks.
   Endow $2,400,000. Plant val $8,000,000. Acres 11. Bldgs 2. Class rms 28. Lib 18,000 vols. Sci labs 2. Auds 1. Art studios 1. Music studios 1. Gyms 1. Fields 1. Pools 1. Comp labs 2. Laptop prgm Gr 6-8.
   Est 1906. Nonprofit. Tri (Aug-June).

Founded in Riverside by Mrs. Queene Ferry Coonley and Lucia Burton Morse and moved to its present location in 1929, ACS has gained more than local prominence over the years. Drawing students from roughly 40 suburban communities, Avery Coonley conducts a rigorous elementary program that emphasizes critical and independent thought.

Various accelerated and enriched programs serve a student body that consists of bright and academically gifted children. Courses in art, computer science, French, music and physical education begin in kindergarten and continue through grade 8. ACS issues tablet computers to boys and girls in grades 6-8. Academic and enrichment classes are available in the summer program.

ELGIN, IL. (34 mi. WNW of Chicago, IL) Urban. Pop: 94,487. Alt: 715 ft.

ELGIN ACADEMY
Day — Coed Gr PS (Age 3)-12

Elgin, IL 60120. 350 Park St. Tel: 847-695-0300. Fax: 847-695-5017.
   www.elginacademy.org   E-mail: admissions@elginacademy.org
John W. Cooper, Head (2000). BA, MA, Florida State Univ, PhD, Syracuse Univ. **Shannon Howell, Adm.**
   Col Prep. AP (exams req'd; 112 taken, 87% 3+)—Eng Fr Lat Span Calc Bio Chem Physics Eur_Hist US_Hist Psych. **Elem math**—Everyday Math. **Feat**—Environ_Sci

Pol_Sci Fine_Arts Performing_Arts Photog. **Supp**—ESL Tut. Sat classes.
Sports (req'd)—Basket X-country Soccer Tennis Track. B: Golf. G: F_Hockey Volley.
Activities: 17.
Selective adm: 113/yr. Appl fee: $50. Appl due: Rolling. Applied: 187. Accepted: 77%.
Yield: 78%. **Tests** CTP_4 ISEE TOEFL.
Enr 462. Elem 329. Sec 133. Wh 70%. Latino 4%. Blk 9%. Asian 13%. Other 4%. Avg
class size: 13. Stud/fac: 7:1. **Fac 58.** M 16/F 42. FT 46/PT 12. Wh 89%. Latino 2%. Blk
7%. Other 2%. Adv deg: 70%.
Grad '11—30. Col—30. (Kettering 2, U of Chicago 1, Wash U 1, Boston U 1, Vassar 1,
Geo Wash 1). **Avg SAT:** CR 637. M 618. W 656. Avg ACT: 26.4.
Tui '12-'13: Day $11,750-21,735 (+$700-3275). **Aid:** Merit 52 ($52,000). Need 198
($1,698,160).
Summer: Acad Enrich Rev Rec. 6 wks.
Endow $10,000,000. Plant val $12,729,000. Acres 18. Bldgs 6 (16% ADA). Class rms 30.
Lib 18,000 vols. Sci labs 4. Theaters 2. Art studios 2. Music studios 2. Gyms 1. Fields
2. Courts 4. Comp labs 2. Comp/stud: 1:2.
Est 1839. Nonprofit. Sem (Aug-June). **Assoc** CLS NCA.

The oldest independent preparatory school west of the Allegheny Mountains, the academy
was founded by James Gifford, who four years earlier had founded the city of Elgin. On an
18-acre campus, the plant has been expanded and remodeled over the years.

The liberal arts curriculum emphasizes college preparation. The fine arts, athletics and
extracurricular activities are integral to the program. Special features include a comprehensive lower and middle school world language program, as well as a month-long immersion
program that allows lower school pupils to learn about another country. Community service
opportunities are available at all levels. Upper school students participate in at least six seasons
of interscholastic athletics by the end of grade 11.

EVANSTON, IL. (14 mi. N of Chicago, IL) Suburban. Pop: 74,239. Alt: 603 ft.

ROYCEMORE SCHOOL

Day — Coed Gr PS (Age 3)-12

Evanston, IL 60201. 640 Lincoln St. Tel: 847-866-6055. Fax: 847-866-6545.
www.roycemoreschool.org   E-mail: info@roycemoreschool.org
Joseph A. Becker, Head (1976). BA, Northwestern Univ. **Amanda Avery, Adm.**
Col Prep. AP (50 exams taken, 66% 3+)—Eng Fr Span Calc Bio Physics Eur_Hist
US_Hist US_Govt & Pol Studio_Art. **Feat**—African-Amer_Lit Mythology Environ_Sci
Econ Intl_Relations Law Pol_Sci Sociol World_Relig Drawing Sculpt Music_Theory.
Dual enr: Northwestern.
Sports—Basket Soccer. G: Volley.
Selective adm: 69/yr. Appl fee: $75. Appl due: Rolling. Accepted: 67%.
Enr 252. B 144. G 108. Elem 176. Sec 76. Wh 70%. Latino 2%. Blk 12%. Asian 8%. Other
8%. Avg class size: 18. Stud/fac: 8:1. **Fac 37.** M 8/F 29. FT 33/PT 4. Wh 89%. Latino
3%. Blk 5%. Asian 3%. Adv deg: 54%.
Grad '09—23. Col—23. (DePaul 1, MIT 1, Sch of the Art Inst of Chicago 1, U of IL-
Urbana 1, Valparaiso U 1). **Avg SAT:** CR 578. M 543. W 569. Avg ACT: 23.
Tui '12-'13: Day $14,100-24,425 (+$1890-2250). **Aid:** Merit 7. Need 113 ($1,000,000).
Summer: Enrich. Gr PS-9. Tui Day $555/3-wk ses. 6 wks. Rec. Gr PS-7. Tui Day $149-
328/wk. 9 wks.
Endow $1,000,000. Plant val $3,000,000. Acres 1. Bldgs 1. Class rms 25. 2 Libs 8500
vols. Sci labs 2. Art studios 2. Music studios 1. Gyms 1. Fields 1. Comp labs 1.
Est 1915. Nonprofit. Sem (Aug-June).

This independent, nondenominational school, influential in Chicago, Evanston and the
North Shore, prepares students for competitive colleges throughout the country. Art, music,

dramatics, computer literacy and physical education complement traditional academic subjects. Foreign language study begins in kindergarten. The upper school's two-week January Short Term provides opportunities for independent or group projects or travel abroad.

Advanced students may take courses at Northwestern University for credit at no additional charge. Roycemore also conducts a summer program for gifted pupils.

LAKE FOREST, IL. (29 mi. NNW of Chicago, IL) Suburban. Pop: 20,059. Alt: 704 ft.

LAKE FOREST ACADEMY
Bdg and Day — Coed Gr 9-12

Lake Forest, IL 60045. 1500 W Kennedy Rd. Tel: 847-234-3210. Fax: 847-615-3299. www.lfanet.org   E-mail: lstrudwick@lfanet.org
John Strudwick, Head (2001). BSc, London School of Economics (England), MA, Queens Univ (Canada), PhD, Univ of Toronto (Canada). **Loring Strudwick, Adm.**

  Col Prep. AP (exams req'd)—Eng Chin Fr Lat Span Calc Stats Comp_Sci Bio Chem Environ_Sci Physics US_Hist World_Hist Econ Art_Hist Music_Theory. **Feat**—Shakespeare Mythology Playwriting Anat Electronics Holocaust Vietnam_War Amer_Stud Psych E_Asian_Stud Philos Ceramics Filmmaking Photog Drama Musical_Theater Orchestra Communications Journ Speech. **Supp**—ESL Rev Tut.
  Sports (req'd)—Basket X-country Ice_Hockey Soccer Squash Swim Tennis Track Volley. B: Baseball Football Golf Wrestling. G: Cheer F_Hockey Softball. **Activities:** 57.
  Selective adm: 123/yr. Bdg 52. Day 71. Appl fee: $50. Appl due: Jan. Accepted: 40%. **Tests** CEEB SSAT TOEFL.
  Enr 410. Bdg 200. Day 210. Intl 24%. Avg class size: 12. Stud/fac: 7:1. **Fac 43.** M 25/F 18. FT 41/PT 2. Wh 93%. Blk 7%. Adv deg: 67%. In dorms 16.
  Grad '10—101. Col—101. (Northwestern, U of IL-Urbana, U of MI, Carnegie Mellon, CO Col). **Avg SAT:** CR 576. M 659. W 589. Avg ACT: 27. **Col couns:** 5.
  Tui '10-'11: Bdg $44,300 (+$500). **Day $32,700** (+$500). **Intl Bdg $44,300** (+$2300). **Aid:** Need 103 ($3,000,000).
  Summer: Ages 13-19. ESL. Tui Bdg $6168. 5 wks.
  Endow $21,000,000. Plant val $26,500,000. Acres 162. Bldgs 9. Dorms 4. Dorm rms 100. Class rms 25. Lib 27,000 vols. Sci labs 3. Lang labs 1. Photog labs 1. Comp ctrs 1. Auds 1. Theaters 1. Art studios 3. Music studios 1. Dance studios 1. Perf arts ctrs 1. Gyms 1. Athletic ctrs 1. Fields 6. Courts 3. Pools 1. Rinks 1. Tracks 1. Comp labs 1.
  Est 1857. Nonprofit. Sem (Aug-May). **Assoc** CLS.

LFA resulted from the 1974 merger of two institutions known for their college preparatory programs: Lake Forest Academy for boys (established in 1857) and Ferry Hall School for girls (founded in 1869). Before the consolidation, the two schools had operated for four years as coordinated academic programs. The academy has occupied its present, 162-acre campus in this suburb on Chicago's North Shore since 1948.

The college preparatory curriculum is a rigorous, sequential program comprising a core of studies and a broad range of Advanced Placement and elective options. The seminar program provides guides each pupil in the development of insights about community, participation, leadership, wellness and self. Extracurricular programs are designed to take advantage of Chicago's cultural offerings. All students participate in service learning activities and interscholastic sports.

LAKE FOREST COUNTRY DAY SCHOOL
Day — Coed Gr PS (Age 2)-8

Lake Forest, IL 60045. 145 S Green Bay Rd. Tel: 847-234-2350. Fax: 847-234-2352.

www.lfcds.org E-mail: admission@lfcds.org
Michael E. Robinson, Head (2005). BS, Univ of Massachusetts-Amherst, MDiv, Virginia Theological Seminary. **Elizabeth Black, Adm.**
Pre-Prep. Gen Acad. Feat—Chin Fr Span Computers Studio_Art Drama Music Outdoor_Ed. **Supp**—LD Tut.
Sports (req'd)—Basket Soccer Track Volley. B: Baseball Football. G: F_Hockey Lacrosse.
Selective adm: 68/yr. Usual entry: PS, K & 5. Appl fee: $100. Appl due: Rolling. Applied: 167. Accepted: 75%. **Tests** CTP_4.
Enr 443. B 226. G 217. Intl 11%. Avg class size: 12. Stud/fac: 9:1. Casual. **Fac 60.** M 11/F 49. FT 51/PT 9. Wh 99%. Latino 1%. Adv deg: 68%.
Grad '09—43. Prep—26. (Lake Forest Acad 1, Loyola Acad 1). Avg SSAT: 94%. Alum donors: 13%.
Tui '12-'13: Day $15,500-21,940 (+$600-2500). **Aid:** Need 60 ($772,604).
Endow $20,857,000. Plant val $28,000,000. Acres 35. Bldgs 1. Class rms 51. Lib 22,000 vols. Sci labs 3. Auds 1. Art studios 2. Music studios 2. Perf arts ctrs 1. Gyms 2. Fields 3. Comp labs 1. Comp/stud: 1:2.4.
Est 1888. Nonprofit. Sem (Sept-June).

LFCDS was established in 1958 as the result of a merger of the Bell School, founded in 1888, and the Lake Forest Day School, founded in 1927.

The school's early childhood program (ages 2-6) seeks to develop decision-making and critical-thinking skills through an experiential learning approach. In the elementary and middle schools, strong emphasis is placed upon the acquisition of organizational skills and sound study habits. The curriculum features a literature-based language arts program, a skills-oriented math sequence, and a hands-on method in science classes. French and Spanish foreign language classes begin in senior kindergarten and continue through grade 8. The traditional core curriculum in grades 5-8 utilizes an interdisciplinary approach.

Field trips and use of the computer center and the library are integral parts of the curriculum. Athletics are required, and interscholastic competition is available in grades 6-8.

See Also Page 61

ROCKFORD, IL. (77 mi. WNW of Chicago, IL; 78 mi. SW of Milwaukee, WI) Urban. Pop: 150,115. Alt: 730 ft.

KEITH COUNTRY DAY SCHOOL
Day — Coed Gr PS (Age 3)-12

Rockford, IL 61107. 1 Jacoby Pl. Tel: 815-399-8823. Fax: 815-399-2470.
www.keithschool.com E-mail: marcia.aramovich@keithschool.net
Deb Dimke, Head (2012). Marcia Aramovich, Adm.
Col Prep. AP (exams req'd)—Eng Bio Chem Eur_Hist US_Hist Music_Theory. **Feat**—Fr Greek Lat Span Stats Environ_Sci Comp_Sci Govt World_Relig Ceramics Photog Studio_Art Drama Music Music_Hist Speech. **Supp**—Dev_Read Tut.
Sports—Basket X-country Soccer Tennis. B: Golf. G: Volley. **Activities:** 25.
Somewhat selective adm (Gr PS-11): 46/yr. Appl fee: $50. Appl due: Rolling. Applied: 115. Accepted: 85%. **Tests** CTP_4.
Enr 290. B 147. G 143. Elem 203. Sec 87. Wh 62%. Latino 3%. Blk 5%. Asian 16%. Other 14%. Avg class size: 16. Stud/fac: 12:1. Casual. **Fac 56.** M 11/F 45. FT 50/PT 6. Wh 96%. Latino 2%. Blk 1%. Asian 1%. Adv deg: 58%.
Grad '11—32. Col—32. (U of IL-Urbana 3, Knox 2, St Louis U 2, Augustana 2, Purdue 2, Yale 1). Athl schol 1. **Avg SAT:** CR 621. M 634. W 589. Avg ACT: 25.8. **Col couns:** 1.
Tui '12-'13: Day $8200-14,200 (+$200-600). **Aid:** Merit 29 ($107,900). Need 147 ($899,098).
Summer (enr 60): Acad Enrich Rec. Music. Tui Day $150/wk. 8 wks.

Endow $450,000. Plant val $1,750,000. Acres 15. Bldgs 3 (33% ADA). Class rms 38. Libs 1. Labs 3. Art studios 2. Music studios 2. Gyms 2. Fields 2. Comp/stud: 1:3 (1:1 Laptop prgm Gr 6-12).
Est 1916. Nonprofit. Sem (Aug-June).

Founded by artist Belle Emerson Keith, this school occupies a 15-acre campus overlooking the Rock River. Serving students from northern Illinois and southern Wisconsin, Keith introduces both Spanish and French in preschool and teaches the languages to all students through grade 5; Latin is added in grade 6. In the upper school, requirements include fine arts, computers, foreign language, speech, and research and reference, and Advanced Placement courses are offered. In addition, all pupils and faculty in grades 6-12 utilize laptop computers. A senior project is compulsory.

A student volunteer program requires each student to perform 90 hours of community service during the four high school years, and all are encouraged to participate in team sports, the fine arts and other after-school activities.

WINNETKA, IL. (19 mi. N of Chicago, IL) Suburban. Pop: 12,419. Alt: 655 ft.

NORTH SHORE COUNTRY DAY SCHOOL
Day — Coed Gr PS (Age 4)-12
Winnetka, IL 60093. 310 Green Bay Rd. Tel: 847-446-0674. Fax: 847-446-0675. www.nscds.org E-mail: communications@nscds.org
W. Thomas Doar III, Head. BA, Univ of Minnesota-Twin Cities, MA, Univ of St Thomas (MN), EdM, Columbia Univ. **Dale L. Wentz, Adm.**
   Col Prep. AP (exams req'd; 112 taken, 79% 3+)—Eng Fr Span Calc Stats Comp_Sci Bio Chem Physics US_Hist Studio_Art. **Feat**—Chin Ecol Marine_Bio/Sci Engineering Holocaust Vietnam_War Intl_Relations Psych Photog Acting Theater Music Music_ Theory. **Supp**—Dev_Read Tut.
   Sports (req'd)—Basket X-country Soccer Tennis Track. B: Baseball Football Golf. G: F_Hockey Volley. **Activities:** 25.
   Selective adm (Gr PS-11): 94/yr. Appl fee: $50-100. **Tests** CTP_4 ISEE SSAT.
   Enr 500. B 242. G 258. Elem 300. Sec 200. Wh 83%. Latino 2%. Blk 4%. Asian 4%. Other 7%. Avg class size: 14. Stud/fac: 8:1. Casual. **Fac 68.** M 18/F 50. FT 65/PT 3. Adv deg: 55%.
   Grad '11—47. Col—47. (U of IL-Urbana 3, Vanderbilt 2, Rice 2, Northwestern 2, Lawrence U 2, Bradley U 2). **Mid 50% SAT:** CR 680-770. M 640-770. W 700-760. Mid 50% ACT: 27-32. **Col couns:** 2. Alum donors: 24%.
   Tui '11-'12: Day $15,340-24,905 (+$1500). **Aid:** Need 72 ($1,000,000).
   Summer (enr 650): Acad Enrich Rec. Tui Day $1050-3900. 2-8 wks.
   Endow $20,000,000. Plant val $17,300,000. Acres 16. Bldgs 9. Class rms 36. 2 Libs 26,000 vols. Sci labs 7. Photog labs 1. Auds 1. Theaters 1. Art studios 3. Music studios 2. Arts ctrs 1. Art galleries 1. Shops 1. Gyms 1. Fields 2. Tennis courts 3. Pools 1. Playgrounds 1. Greenhouses 1. Comp labs 4. Comp/stud: 1:2.
   Est 1919. Nonprofit. Sem (Sept-June).

North Shore offers a strong academic program that includes electives in many areas, including drama, computer science and Asian studies. Technology is an integral part of the program at all grade levels. Language instruction includes Spanish from junior kindergarten, French beginning in grade 6 and Mandarin Chinese commencing in grade 9. Advanced Placement courses are offered in the major disciplines for qualified students.

Independent study is emphasized in all subjects at the junior and senior levels. An interim week for pupils in grades 9-12 provides in-depth experiences off campus and frequently includes travel abroad. Upper school students participate in at least two theater productions and eight seasons of athletics. Community service, which is integrated into the curriculum at all grade levels, culminates in a compulsory, two-week senior service project.

INDIANA

CULVER, IN. (33 mi. SSW of South Bend, IN; 78 mi. ESE of Chicago, IL) Rural. Pop: 1539. Alt: 743 ft.

CULVER ACADEMIES
Bdg and Day — Coed Gr 9-PG

Culver, IN 46511. 1300 Academy Rd, Box 157. Tel: 574-842-7100, 800-528-5837.
Fax: 574-842-8066.
www.culver.org   E-mail: admissions@culver.org
John Buxton, Head (1999). AB, Brown Univ. **J. Michael Turnbull, Adm.**

> **Col Prep. Milit. AP (516 exams taken)**—Eng Fr Ger Lat Span Calc Stats Comp_Sci Bio Environ_Sci Physics Eur_Hist US_Hist Comp_Govt & Pol Econ US_Govt & Pol Music_Theory. **Feat**—Creative_Writing Humanities Chin Anat & Physiol Astron Psych Global_Stud Comp_Relig Art_Hist Film Photog Studio_Art Drama Music Dance Horsemanship. **Supp**—ESL Tut.
>
> **Sports**—Basket Crew X-country Equestrian Fencing Golf Ice_Hockey Lacrosse Polo Sail Soccer Swim Tennis Track. B: Baseball Football Rugby Wrestling. G: Cheer Softball Volley. **Activities:** 39.
>
> **Somewhat selective adm (Gr 9-12):** 266/yr. Bdg 246. Day 20. Usual entry: 9. Appl fee: $40. Appl due: May. Accepted: 93%. Yield: 54%. **Tests** CEEB ISEE SSAT TOEFL.
>
> **Enr 791.** B 461. G 330. Bdg 750. Day 41. Sec 790. PG 1. Wh 68%. Latino 9%. Blk 4%. Asian 15%. Other 4%. Intl 20%. Avg class size: 13. Stud/fac: 9:1. Uniform. **Fac 97.** Wh 94%. Latino 3%. Blk 2%. Asian 1%. Adv deg: 100%. In dorms 4.
>
> **Grad '11—211. Col—206.** (IN U 11, Miami U-OH 7, Purdue 5, Boston U 4, Carnegie Mellon 4, Hobart/Wm Smith 4). Athl schol 5. **Col couns:** 4.
>
> **Tui '12-'13: Bdg $39,000** (+$3000-4500). **Day $29,000** (+$1000-1850). **Aid:** Merit 92 ($2,326,500). Need 267 ($6,649,000).
>
> **Summer (enr 1350):** Ages 9-17. Acad Enrich Rec. Naval. Woodcraft. Horsemanship. Tui Bdg $4800. 6 wks.
>
> Endow $280,000,000. Acres 1800. Bldgs 39 (100% ADA). Dorms 7. Dorm rms 366. Class rms 59. Lib 50,000 vols. Sci labs 9. Lang labs 2. Auds 1. Theaters 1. Art studios 4. Music studios 12. Dance studios 1. Gyms 2. Fields 17. Courts 15. Pools 1. Rinks 2. Riding rings 1. Stables 1. Golf crses 1. Student ctrs 1. Comp labs 6. Comp/stud: 1:1 Laptop prgm Gr 9-PG.
>
> **Est 1894.** Nonprofit. Quar (Aug-June). **Assoc** CLS.

Culver Military Academy was founded by Henry Harrison Culver of St. Louis, MO, as a selective military academy for boys. His stated purpose at that time was that of "thoroughly preparing young men for the best colleges, scientific schools, and businesses of America," and he believed that a system of military discipline would best accomplish his objective.

In 1896, a fire at Missouri Military Academy resulted in its consolidation with Culver. Col. Alexander F. Fleet, Missouri Military's headmaster at that time, assumed command of the newly formed school and led a period of significant progress at Culver. By 1939, under the leadership of Gen. Leigh Gignilliat, the school had achieved national and international prominence. Girls first enrolled at the school in 1971, when Culver Girls Academy was founded on the same campus. Unlike the boys' division, the girls' leadership program is based on the classical British prefect system. Classes at the school are coeducational.

Graduates in recent years have attended more than 200 colleges throughout the country. The extensive curriculum provides Advanced Placement courses, as well as independent study options and a variety of elective courses. In addition to academic preparation for college, the academies stress self-discipline and leadership skills for all pupils. All seniors satisfy a 30-hour community service requirement.

Culver's 1800-acre campus provides many athletic and extracurricular opportunities. Both boys and girls choose from various varsity sports, and intramural athletics are offered for those not involved in interscholastic competition. Religious, athletic, hobby and student groups are also available.

During the summer, Culver conducts programs in sailing, horsemanship, aquatics and athletics for girls and boys ages 9-17.

EVANSVILLE, IN. (100 mi. W of Louisville, KY; 154 mi. ESE of St. Louis, MO) Urban. Pop: 121,582. Alt: 394 ft.

EVANSVILLE DAY SCHOOL
Day — Coed Gr PS (Age 3)-12

Evansville, IN 47715. 3400 N Green River Rd. Tel: 812-476-3039. Fax: 812-476-4061.
www.evansvilledayschool.org   E-mail: kbayles@evansvilledayschool.org
Kendell Berry, Head (2007). BS, Lynchburg College, MS, Univ of Virginia. **Karen Bayles, Adm.**

> **Col Prep. AP (31 exams taken, 87% 3+)**—Eng Fr Span Calc Bio Chem US_Hist US_ Govt & Pol. **Feat**—Creative_Writing Zoology Comp_Sci Econ Psych Sociol Asian_ Stud World_Relig Art_Hist Music Journ. **Supp**—Rev Tut. **Dual enr:** U of Evansville, U of S IN.
> **Sports**—Basket Soccer Tennis. B: Golf.
> **Somewhat selective adm:** 65/yr. Appl fee: $30. Appl due: Rolling. Accepted: 95%. Yield: 95%. **Tests** CTP_4.
> **Enr 325.** Elem 256. Sec 69. Wh 84%. Latino 1%. Blk 6%. Asian 1%. Other 8%. Avg class size: 22. **Fac 42.** M 12/F 30. FT 36/PT 6. Wh 98%. Latino 1%. Asian 1%. Adv deg: 42%.
> **Grad '08—14. Col—14.** (Purdue, Emory, IN U, Smith, Wabash, Franklin Col). **Avg SAT:** CR 612. M 608. W 612. Avg ACT: 25. Alum donors: 3%.
> **Tui '12-'13: Day $8915-14,875** (+$100-2000). **Aid:** Merit 12 ($111,675). Need 42 ($260,000).
> **Summer:** Acad Enrich. Tui Day $200/wk. 2 wks.
> Endow $700,000. Plant val $3,000,000. Acres 57. Bldgs 1. Class rms 40. Lib 8000 vols. Sci labs 4. Auds 1. Art studios 1. Music studios 1. Gyms 1. Fields 3. Comp labs 3. Comp/stud: 1:3.
> **Est 1946.** Nonprofit. Quar (Aug-May).

Established as an outgrowth of the Evansville Pre-School, under the direction of J. B. Davis, the Evansville Day School expanded rapidly. New facilities in 1961 permitted the addition of secondary grades, and the school has since offered a full college preparatory program. In 1968, the school moved to its current, 57-acre campus.

The program in grades 8-12 features 90-minute classes, and the curriculum is supplemented by specialized short-term courses in photography, ecology and ceramics, French films and theater appreciation. Intersession opportunities and senior projects provide students with off-campus curricular options.

FORT WAYNE, IN. (72 mi. SE of South Bend, IN; 142 mi. ESE of Chicago, IL) Urban. Pop: 205,727. Alt: 790 ft.

CANTERBURY SCHOOL
Day — Coed Gr PS (Age 2)-12

Fort Wayne, IN 46804. 3210 Smith Rd. Tel: 260-407-3553. Fax: 260-407-3551.
Other locations: 5601 Covington Rd, Fort Wayne 46804.
www.canterburyschool.org   E-mail: admissions@canterburyschool.org
Jonathan M. Hancock, Head (1982). BA, MA, Oxford Univ (England), EdM, Harvard Univ.
Susan Johnson, Gr 9-12 Adm; Krista Lohmar, Gr K-8 Adm; Paula Pritchard, PS Adm.
Col Prep. AP (exams req'd; 291 taken, 90% 3+)—Eng Fr Lat Span Calc Stats Comp_ Sci Bio Chem Physics Eur_Hist US_Hist. **Elem math**—Everyday Math. **Feat**—British_Lit Creative_Writing Shakespeare Japan Astron Geol Marine_Bio/Sci Physiol Meteorology Japan_Hist Middle_Eastern_Hist Psych Ethics World_Relig Photog Studio_Art Theater Music. Outdoor ed. **Dual enr:** IN U-Purdue Ft Wayne.
Sports—Basket X-country Golf Soccer Swim Tennis Track. B: Baseball. G: Cheer Softball Volley. **Activities:** 22.
Selective adm: 170/yr. Usual entry: K, 5 & 9. Appl fee: $35-75. Appl due: Rolling. Accepted: 49%. Yield: 74%. **Tests** ISEE.
Enr 982. B 506. G 476. Elem 644. Sec 338. Wh 76%. Latino 2%. Blk 3%. Asian 11%. Other 8%. Avg class size: 17. Stud/fac: 9:1. **Fac 102.** M 28/F 74. FT 82/PT 20. Wh 92%. Latino 1%. Blk 1%. Native Am 1%. Asian 5%. Adv deg: 56%.
Grad '11—71. Col—71. (IN U 11, Purdue 5, High Pt 2, Northwestern 2, Cedarville 2, St Mary's Col-IN 2). **Avg SAT:** CR 614. M 619. W 611. Avg ACT: 27.8. **Col couns:** 2. Alum donors: 16%.
Tui '12-'13: Day $11,950-14,450 (+$1000). **Aid:** Merit 53 ($53,000). Need 295 ($1,829,231).
Summer: Acad Enrich. Arts. Sports. 2-3 wks.
Endow $9,700,000. Plant val $14,830,000. Acres 55. Bldgs 2 (100% ADA). 3 Libs 18,000 vols. Sci labs 4. Dark rms 1. Auds 2. Art studios 4. Gyms 2. Fields 3. Tennis courts 10. Tracks 1. Greenhouses 1. Comp labs 4. Comp/stud: 1:2.
Est 1977. Nonprofit. (Aug-June). **Assoc** CLS NCA.

First opened in the educational wing of Trinity Episcopal Church to students in grades K-6, this school now enrolls students in an early childhood through high school program. Canterbury occupies two campuses: lower and middle school classes (early childhood through grade 8) are held at the Covington Road campus, while the high school program (grades 9-12) is conducted at the Smith Road address. The curriculum, which emphasizes academic achievement, features a required fine arts course of study and a competitive athletics program.

Instruction in French, Spanish, computers and the fine arts begins in the primary grades, where small classes provide for individual attention and development. An accelerated middle school program in all major disciplines includes a four-year science program and mathematics through advanced algebra II. Pupils choose either Spanish or French for four years of study in grades 5-8, and they may add Latin or Japanese as an additional language in grades 7 and 8. High school course work focuses upon accelerated college preparation. An Advanced Placement program offers college-level studies in many disciplines.

Canterbury conducts May Term, a three-week interim program, in grades 9-11. Students engage in minicourses during this session, while seniors instead take part in an internship program. To fulfill another high school requirement, boys and girls complete 20 hours of community service in grade 10 and 40 hours in grade 11.

HOWE, IN. (44 mi. E of South Bend, IN; 117 mi. E of Chicago, IL) Rural. Pop: 550.
Alt: 882 ft.

THE HOWE SCHOOL
Bdg and Day — Coed Gr 7-12

Howe, IN 46746. PO Box 240. Tel: 260-562-2131. Fax: 260-562-3678.
  www.thehoweschool.org   E-mail: admissions@thehoweschool.org
David Watson, Head (2010). MEd, Western Michigan Univ. **Al Heminger, Adm.**
  Col Prep. Milit. AP—Eng Calc Bio Chem. **Feat**—Creative_Writing Fr Ger Span Anat &
    Physiol Environ_Sci Organic_Chem Computers. Comp_Graphics Econ Geog Govt
    Sociol Ethics World_Relig Music Bus Journ Indus_Arts Furniture_Making JROTC.
    Supp—Makeup Rem_Math Rev Tut. **Dual enr:** Trine, IN U-Purdue Ft Wayne.
  Sports—Basket Golf Soccer Tennis Track. B: Baseball Wrestling. G: Volley. **Activities:**
    25.
  Somewhat selective adm: 74/yr. Bdg 72. Day 2. Appl fee: $100. Accepted: 90%. Yield:
    64%. **Tests** IQ.
  Enr 141. B 116. G 25. Bdg 138. Day 3. Elem 29. Sec 112. Wh 67%. Latino 3%. Blk 9%.
    Asian 16%. Other 5%. Intl 18%. Avg class size: 10. Stud/fac: 8:1. Uniform. **Fac 22.** M
    14/F 8. FT 21/PT 1. Wh 95%. Blk 5%.
  Grad '10—28. Col—27. (Purdue 2, Norwich 2, IN U-Purdue Indianapolis 2, Syracuse 1,
    St Mary's Col-IN 1, U of IL-Urbana 1). Alum donors: 15%.
  Tui '11-'12: Bdg $30,000. Day $16,947. Intl Bdg $32,000.
  Summer (enr 70): Acad Rev Rec. Milit Trng. Tui Bdg $1400-3500. 2-6 wks.
  Acres 100. Bldgs 19. Dorms 5. Class rms 26. Lib 15,000 vols. Labs 4. Auds 1. Music
    studios 2. Gyms 2. Fields 4. Courts 5. Pools 1. Rifle ranges 1.
  Est 1884. Nonprofit. Episcopal (1% practice). Sem (Aug-June). **Assoc** CLS NCA.

The school was made possible by a bequest of John Badlam Howe, who provided in his
will for the foundation of a school to train young men for the Episcopal priesthood. The military program was instituted in 1895 and, since 1920, Howe has had a high school ROTC unit
sponsored by the Department of the Army. Female students were admitted beginning in the
fall of 1988.

Howe emphasizes spiritual, intellectual and physical education in a structured environment.
The campus houses two separate schools: a junior high school (grades 7 and 8) and a senior
high school (grades 9-12). The junior high provides a standard curriculum consisting of English, reading, mathematics, science and social studies; eighth graders may enroll in an elective
class for high school credit. The college preparatory high school course of study includes
units from the fields of English, mathematics, science, social studies, foreign language, physical education, health and computer education, supplemented by electives in the fine arts, the
industrial arts and business.

The mandatory JROTC program provides classroom instruction, physical training, and
practice in conducting parades and ceremonies. The military department also sponsors a drill
team, a rifle team and an adventure group. Cadets must participate in sports, either organized
or intramural, and attendance and participation at worship is a required part of the school
program.

INDIANAPOLIS, IN. (109 mi. NNW of Louisville, KY) Urban. Pop: 781,870. Alt: 708 ft.

THE ORCHARD SCHOOL
Day — Coed Gr PS (Age 3)-8

Indianapolis, IN 46260. 615 W 64th St. Tel: 317-251-9253. Fax: 317-253-9707.
www.orchard.org   E-mail: khein@orchard.org
Joseph P. Marshall, Head. BA, Franklin and Marshall College, MEd, Hofstra Univ. **Kristen J. Hein, Adm.**
   Pre-Prep. Feat—Span Computers Studio_Art Drama Band Chorus Orchestra Dance Outdoor_Ed. **Supp**—Dev_Read Rem_Math Rem_Read Tut.
   Sports—Basket X-country Soccer Tennis Track. B: Baseball Football. G: Softball Volley.
   Selective adm: 113/yr. Appl fee: $75. Appl due: Feb. Accepted: 56%. Yield: 81%. **Tests** ISEE.
   Enr 615. Wh 77%. Latino 1%. Blk 8%. Asian 5%. Other 9%. Avg class size: 18. Stud/fac: 7:1. **Fac 80.** Adv deg: 52%.
   Grad '08—57. Prep—50. (Brebeuf 20, Park Tudor 16, U HS of IN 6). Alum donors: 8%.
   Tui '12-'13: Day $15,471-16,975. Aid: Need 185 ($1,600,000).
   Summer: Acad Enrich Rev Rec. Travel. 8 wks.
   Endow $30,000,000. Plant val $16,747,000. Acres 43. Bldgs 2. Class rms 51. Lib 19,200 vols. Sci labs 3. Dark rms 1. Aquariums 2. Weather stations 1. Theaters 1. Art studios 2. Music studios 3. Dance studios 1. Gyms 2. Fields 4. Tracks 1. Ropes crses 1. Ponds 1. Comp labs 3. Comp/stud: 1:2 (1:1 Laptop prgm Gr 5-8).
   Est 1922. Nonprofit. Quar (Aug-May).

Nine local women established Orchard as a progressive school for 20 children in a frame house located at 5050 N. Meridian St. The present-day school occupies a 43-acre wooded campus and serves a student body some 30 times larger.

The comprehensive curriculum integrates language arts, literature, social studies, math, music, art, drama, science, Spanish and physical education, as well as technology and outdoor education. Classroom instruction incorporates multiple perspectives and approaches while emphasizing problem solving and critical thinking. Student government, multicultural education and field trips are features of the program, and service learning is built into the curriculum as well. Outdoor education experiences are structured to support, reinforce and enrich the classroom curriculum. Learning support, speech-language therapy, assessment and evaluation, and school counseling are available.

Orchard conducts an intramural sports program in grades 1-4, in addition to an interscholastic program in the later grades. The school offers extended-day activities both before and after school.

PARK TUDOR SCHOOL
Day — Coed Gr PS (Age 3)-12

Indianapolis, IN 46240. 7200 N College Ave. Tel: 317-415-2700. Fax: 317-254-2714.
www.parktudor.org   E-mail: info@parktudor.org
Matthew D. Miller, Head (2011). BA, Dickinson College, BA, MA, Oxford Univ (England), MA, Univ of California-Berkeley, EdD, Univ of Pennsylvania. **David A. Amstutz, Adm.**
   Col Prep. AP (540 exams taken, 81% 3+)—Eng Fr Lat Span Calc Stats Comp_Sci Bio Chem Physics US_Hist World_Hist Art_Hist Music_Theory. **Feat**—Creative_Writing Chin Greek Anat & Physiol Environ_Sci Web_Design Milit_Hist Econ Psych Sociol Ethics Studio_Art Drama Music_Hist Journ Speech. **Supp**—Dev_Read Tut.
   Sports—Basket Crew X-country Golf Lacrosse Soccer Swim Tennis Track. B: Baseball Football Ice_Hockey Wrestling. G: Cheer Softball Volley. **Activities:** 32.
   Selective adm: 157/yr. Appl fee: $50. Accepted: 51%. Yield: 77%. **Tests** CTP_4 ISEE.
   Enr 987. B 504. G 483. Elem 568. Sec 419. Avg class size: 14. Stud/fac: 9:1. **Fac 152.** M

58/F 94. FT 126/PT 26. Adv deg: 58%.

Grad '11—104. Col—104. (IN U, DePauw, Case Western Reserve, Miami U-OH, Wittenberg, SMU). **Avg SAT:** CR 629. M 627. W 628. Avg ACT: 27.5. **Col couns:** 3. Alum donors: 14%.

Tui '12-'13: Day $14,810-18,190 (+$1000). **Aid:** Need 316 ($2,800,000).

Summer: Acad Enrich Rec. 1-3 wks.

Endow $89,600,000. Plant val $36,600,000. Acres 52. Bldgs 9. Class rms 57. 4 Libs 38,000 vols. Sci labs 7. Sci ctrs 1. Auds 1. Theaters 1. Art studios 2. Music studios 6. Dance studios 1. Gyms 3. Fields 6. Courts 12. Comp labs 9.

Est 1970. Nonprofit. Quar (Aug-May). **Assoc** CLS NCA.

Park Tudor was established in 1970 from the merger of two long-standing private schools: Tudor Hall School for Girls, founded in 1902, and Park School for Boys, founded in 1914. The present-day school continues the tradition established by its predecessors by offering a liberal arts curriculum, small class size, a support staff of counselors and learning specialists, and fully equipped facilities.

Located on a 52-acre campus, Park Tudor offers a sequential curriculum that provides children with age-appropriate learning experiences grounded in the basics and aimed at college preparation. Advanced Placement and elective courses in English, history, math, foreign languages and the sciences make use of the school's resources, as well as the cultural opportunities of Indianapolis. The Global Scholars Program for highly motivated juniors and seniors comprises advanced course work, independent research and presentation, self-assessment and service learning.

The fine arts program offers curricular and extracurricular experiences in drama, vocal and instrumental music, the visual arts and dance.

ST. RICHARD'S SCHOOL

Day — Coed Gr PS (Age 3)-8

Indianapolis, IN 46205. 33 E 33rd St. Tel: 317-926-0425. Fax: 317-921-3367.
www.strichardsschool.org   E-mail: mfisher@strichardsschool.org
Patricia Swenson, Head (2008). Melinda Fisher, Adm.

Pre-Prep. Feat—Fr Lat Span Computers Relig Studio_Art Music. **Supp**—Tut.

Sports—Basket X-country Soccer Tennis Track. G: Cheer Volley.

Selective adm: 83/yr. Appl fee: $75. Appl due: Jan. Accepted: 60%. **Tests** IQ.

Enr 300. Intl 10%. Avg class size: 16. Stud/fac: 10:1. **Fac 41.** M 5/F 36. FT 40/PT 1. Wh 90%. Blk 5%. Other 5%. Adv deg: 39%.

Grad '10—42. Prep—25. (Park Tudor 8, Brebeuf 6, U HS of IN 3, Culver 2).

Tui '11-'12: Day $13,810-14,430 (+$400). **Aid:** Need ($400,000).

Summer: Enrich Rec. 1-9 wks.

Endow $2,021,000. Plant val $11,300,000. Bldgs 3. Class rms 20. Lib 3500 vols. Sci labs 1. Auds 1. Art studios 1. Music studios 2. Gyms 1. Fields 1. Comp labs 1.

Est 1960. Nonprofit. Episcopal (14% practice). Tri (Sept-June).

Affiliated with Trinity Episcopal Church and founded by Rev. G. Ernest Lynch in honor of St. Richard of Chichester, an English saint and scholar, this school patterned itself after Great Britain's parish day schools. St. Richard's first teachers, who were brought to the US from Britain specifically to teach at the school, imparted a British flavor that remains manifest today.

Technology is an important element of the curriculum: all pupils have access to computers and to one on-site computer lab. French is required from transitional kindergarten through grade 5, while Spanish and Latin are added as foreign language options in the later grades. Chapel services are conducted daily. Interscholastic sports (with a no-cut policy) are available to students in grade 5 and above; intramural programs begin in grade 1. Students in grades 6 and 7 attend overnight retreats, and the eighth grade takes an annual graduation trip to Washington, DC, Monticello (VA) and Williamsburg, VA.

SYCAMORE SCHOOL
Day — Coed Gr PS (Age 2)-8

Indianapolis, IN 46260. 1750 W 64th St. Tel: 317-202-2500. Fax: 317-202-2501.
www.sycamoreschool.org   E-mail: skarpicke@sycamoreschool.org
Diane Borgmann, Head (2009). BA, DePauw Univ, MS, Butler Univ. **Susan Karpicke, Adm.**

Pre-Prep. Gen Acad. Feat—Humanities Span Computers Studio_Art Music.
Sports—Basket X-country Soccer Tennis Track. B: Baseball Football Wrestling. G: Softball Volley.
Selective adm: 59/yr. Appl fee: $50-100. Appl due: Feb. Applied: 124. Accepted: 59%. Yield: 81%. **Tests** IQ.
Enr 391. B 193. G 198. Wh 66%. Latino 1%. Blk 5%. Asian 16%. Other 12%. Avg class size: 20. **Fac 59.** M 8/F 51. FT 34/PT 25. Nonwhite 2%. Adv deg: 32%.
Grad '10—39. Prep—16. (U HS of IN 6, Brebeuf 4, Lutheran HS-IN 3, Park Tudor 2, Culver 1). Alum donors: 14%.
Tui '11-'12: Day $14,500 (+$115-1050). **Aid:** Need 46 ($328,411).
Summer: Acad Enrich Rec. Tui Day $90-120/wk. 8 wks.
Endow $1,500,000. Plant val $7,309,000. Acres 16. Bldgs 3. Class rms 24. Lib 17,654 vols. Sci labs 3. Theaters 1. Art studios 2. Music studios 2. Gyms 1. Fields 2. Tracks 1. Comp labs 2.
Est 1984. Nonprofit. Tri (Aug-May). **Assoc** NCA.

Founded by area parents and educators to address a community need, Sycamore provides acceleration and enrichment for academically gifted students. The curriculum exhibits greater complexity and depth and maintains a faster learning pace than do programs found in traditional elementary schools. In addition to the core academic subjects, students receive instruction from specialists in art, music, computer science, Spanish and physical education. Children learn through various means, and Sycamore enriches its program with guest speakers and field trips.

Lower school children may take part in intramural team sports, while upper school pupils may play on interscholastic teams.

LA PORTE, IN. (24 mi. W of South Bend, IN; 53 mi. ESE of Chicago, IL) Urban. Pop: 21,621. Alt: 812 ft.

LA LUMIERE SCHOOL
Bdg and Day — Coed Gr 9-PG

La Porte, IN 46350. 6801 N Wilhelm Rd. Tel: 219-326-7450. Fax: 219-325-3185.
www.lalumiere.org   E-mail: momalley@lalumiere.org
Michael H. Kennedy, Head. BA, Boston College, MS, Univ of Notre Dame. **Mary O'Malley, Adm.**

Col Prep. AP—Eng Calc Physics US_Hist. **Feat**—Creative_Writing Shakespeare Fr Lat Span Stats Anat & Physiol Programming Econ Govt Intl_Relations Psych Ethics Philos World_Relig Studio_Art Drama. **Supp**—ESL Rev Tut.
Sports (req'd)—X-country Golf Lacrosse Soccer Tennis Track. B: Baseball Basket Football. G: Volley. **Activities:** 30.
Selective adm: 57/yr. Bdg 32. Day 25. Appl fee: $50. Appl due: Rolling. Accepted: 65%. Yield: 69%. **Tests** CEEB SSAT TOEFL.
Enr 210. Bdg 75. Day 135. Intl 11%. Avg class size: 12. Stud/fac: 8:1. Uniform. **Fac 27.** M 14/F 13. FT 26/PT 1. Adv deg: 51%.
Grad '08—42. Col—42. (Purdue, IN U, Loyola U of Chicago, U of WI-Madison, DePaul, Ball St). **Avg SAT:** CR/M 1135. **Avg ACT:** 24. Alum donors: 12%.
Tui '11-'12: Bdg $33,370 (+$500). **Day $10,260** (+$500). **Intl Bdg $39,990** (+$500). **Aid:** Need 55.

Endow $1,000,000. Plant val $5,000,000. Acres 144. Bldgs 12. Dorms 5. Class rms 16.
Lib 9000 vols. Sci labs 2. Lang labs 2. Theaters 1. Art studios 1. Music studios 1.
Gyms 2. Fields 4. Courts 2. Tracks 1. Ropes crses 1. Lakes 1. Comp labs 1.
Est 1963. Nonprofit. Roman Catholic. Sem (Aug-May). **Assoc** NCA.

Founded by Catholic families, La Lumiere provides a rigorous college preparatory education for students from a rich diversity of backgrounds who enroll from various states and foreign countries. The wooded, 144-acre campus lies 60 miles southeast of Chicago, IL, thus enabling pupils to make use of that city's scholastic and cultural facilities.

Course work emphasizes critical thinking and the mastery of verbal and writing skills. The cross-curricular writing program requires students to compose and revise weekly papers in preparation for college writing. Foreign language, art, ethics, computer science and theology classes, as well as a range of electives, supplement the core curriculum. Qualified students may pursue independent study projects, and Advanced Placement courses are available. All students participate in three athletic seasons. All students satisfy a 45-hour community service requirement prior to graduation.

SOUTH BEND, IN. (74 mi. E of Chicago, IL) Urban. Pop: 107,789. Alt: 726 ft.

THE STANLEY CLARK SCHOOL
Day — Coed Gr PS (Age 3)-8

South Bend, IN 46614. 3123 Miami St. Tel: 574-291-4200. Fax: 574-299-4170.
www.stanleyclark.org　　E-mail: apriemer@stanleyclark.org
Melissa L. Grubb, Head (2010). BA, MA, Austin College. **Alexandra Sobieski Priemer, Adm.**

Pre-Prep. Gen Acad. Feat—Fr Lat Span Computers Studio_Art Drama Music. **Supp**—Dev_Read Rem_Math Rem_Read Rev Tut.

Sports—Basket X-country Golf Ice_Hockey Soccer Tennis Volley.

Somewhat selective adm: 45/yr. Appl fee: $100. Appl due: Rolling. Applied: 54. Accepted: 92%. Yield: 90%. **Tests** IQ.

Enr 322. Wh 78%. Latino 4%. Blk 10%. Asian 8%. Avg class size: 20. Stud/fac: 10:1. **Fac 40.** M 11/F 29. FT 31/PT 9. Wh 91%. Latino 3%. Blk 3%. Asian 3%. Adv deg: 60%.

Grad '10—31. Prep—21. (Marian Catholic 11, Culver 3, La Lumiere 1). Alum donors: 12%.

Tui '11-'12: Day $10,950-14,550 (+$100-470). **Aid:** Need 79 ($612,185).

Summer: Acad Enrich Rec. Tui Day $130-250. 6 wks.

Endow $4,284,000. Plant val $5,836,000. Acres 35. Bldgs 3 (50% ADA). Class rms 35.
Lib 10,000 vols. Sci labs 2. Art studios 2. Music studios 2. Dance studios 1. Gyms 3.
Fields 2. Comp labs 4. Comp/stud: 1:2.
Est 1958. Nonprofit. Tri (Aug-June). **Assoc** NCA.

This school for boys and girls of above-average to superior intelligence strives to provide each student with the solid foundation necessary for educational achievement. A program in computer science is available, and foreign languages are offered beginning in kindergarten. The fine arts, physical education and an enrichment center supplement academic offerings.

MICHIGAN

ANN ARBOR, MI. (36 mi. WSW of Detroit, MI) Urban. Pop: 114,024. Alt: 840 ft.

GREENHILLS SCHOOL
Day — Coed Gr 6-12

Ann Arbor, MI 48105. 850 Greenhills Dr. Tel: 734-769-4010. Fax: 734-205-4056.
www.greenhillsschool.org   E-mail: admission@greenhillsschool.org
Carl Pelofsky, Head (2012). BA, Harvard Univ, MA, EdS, Univ of Missouri-Columbia. **Betsy Ellsworth, Adm.**

Col Prep. AP (exams req'd; 216 taken, 80% 3+)—Eng Fr Lat Span Calc Stats Eur_Hist US_Hist Econ US_Govt & Pol. **Feat**—Creative_Writing Shakespeare Crime_Fiction Southern_Lit Chin Astron Comp_Sci African-Amer_Hist Chin_Stud Middle_Eastern_ Stud Russ_Stud Ceramics Fine_Arts Photog Studio_Art Theater Chorus Orchestra Jazz_Band. **Supp**—Rev Tut.

Sports—Basket Equestrian Golf Soccer Swim Tennis Track. B: Baseball Lacrosse. G: F_Hockey Softball Volley.

Selective adm (Gr 6-11): 119/yr. Usual entry: 6 & 9. Appl fee: $50. Appl due: Jan. Applied: 214. Accepted: 50%. Yield: 94%. **Tests** CEEB SSAT TOEFL.

Enr 545. B 250. G 295. Wh 65%. Latino 2%. Blk 7%. Asian 14%. Other 12%. Avg class size: 15. Stud/fac: 7:1. **Fac 72.** Wh 96%. Latino 1%. Blk 2%. Asian 1%. Adv deg: 83%.

Grad '11—90. Col—90. (U of MI, MI St, Col of Wooster, Cornell, Yale, Wash U). **Avg SAT:** CR 659. M 672. W 660. Avg ACT: 29. **Col couns:** 2.

Tui '11-'12: Day $18,565-18,940 (+$900). **Aid:** Need 103 ($1,000,000).

Summer: Acad Rec. 6 wks.

Endow $7,100,000. Plant val $22,000,000. Acres 30. Bldgs 1 (100% ADA). Class rms 51. Lib 15,901 vols. Sci labs 4. Theaters 1. Art studios 1. Music studios 2. Dance studios 1. Gyms 2. Fields 4. Courts 8. Tracks 1. Weight rms 1. Climbing walls 1. Comp labs 2.

Est 1968. Nonprofit. Sem (Sept-June). **Assoc** CLS.

Located on a wooded, 30-acre campus, Greenhills offers a traditional liberal arts program designed to prepare students for college. Emphasis is on the development of critical-thinking and communicational skills, as well as creative expression. The program accommodates a broad range of students and includes advanced courses and off-campus field trips.

Cocurricular programs and social, cultural and athletic activities are also available. Boys and girls in grades 6-12 perform at least 10 hours of community service annually.

BLOOMFIELD HILLS, MI. (15 mi. NNW of Detroit, MI) Suburban. Pop: 3940. Alt: 850 ft.

ACADEMY OF THE SACRED HEART
Day — Boys Gr PS (Age 2)-8, Girls PS (Age 2)-12
(Coord — Day 5-8)

Bloomfield Hills, MI 48304. 1250 Kensington Rd. Tel: 248-646-8900.
Fax: 248-646-4143.
www.ashmi.org   E-mail: admissions@ashmi.org
Sr. Bridget Bearss, RSCJ, Head (2000). BA, Maryville College, MA, Washington Univ.

Barbara Lopiccolo, Adm.
Col Prep. AP (exams req'd; 48 taken, 38% 3+)—Eng Calc US_Hist. **Elem math**— TERC Investigations. **Elem read**—Fountas & Pinnell. **Feat**—Fr Lat Span Environ_Sci Genetics Comp_Sci Web_Design Econ Psych Sociol Theol Art_Hist Photog Drama Music Debate TV_Production. **Supp**—Tut.
Sports—G: Basket Equestrian F_Hockey Golf Lacrosse Ski Softball Tennis Volley. **Activities:** 12.
Somewhat selective adm (Girls Gr PS-11): 68/yr. Usual entry: PS, K & 9. Appl fee: $50-100. Appl due: Rolling. Applied: 113. Accepted: 88%. Yield: 73%. **Tests** HSPT Stanford.
Enr 475. Wh 83%. Latino 2%. Blk 8%. Asian 3%. Other 4%. Avg class size: 12. Stud/fac: 7:1. Uniform. **Fac 79.** M 17/F 62. FT 66/PT 13. Wh 91%. Latino 6%. Blk 1%. Asian 1%. Other 1%. Adv deg: 48%.
Grad '10—34. Col—34. (U of MI 11, MI St 3, Oakland U 3, Notre Dame 1, Brown 1, Denison 1). **Avg SAT:** CR 550. M 531. W 540. Avg ACT: 24. **Col couns:** 2. Alum donors: 20%.
Tui '12-'13: Day $11,720-21,520 (+$400-500). **Aid:** Need 119 ($1,560,945).
Summer (enr 195): Acad Enrich Rec. Tui Day $195-200/wk. 6 wks.
Endow $3,367,000. Plant val $21,633,000. Acres 44. Bldgs 1 (100% ADA). Class rms 64. 2 Libs 16,200 vols. Sci labs 4. Lang labs 1. Photog labs 1. Auds 1. Theaters 1. Art studios 5. Music studios 1. Dance studios 2. Gyms 3. Fields 3. Courts 8. Comp labs 3. Comp/stud: 1:2 (1:1 Laptop prgm Gr 9-12).
Est 1851. Nonprofit. Roman Catholic (70% practice). Quar (Sept-June). **Assoc** NCA.

The school moved to its present, 44-acre campus in 1958, over a century after the founding date. In 2006, the academy effected a merger with Kensington Academy, a coeducational elementary school that began on the ASH campus in 1969.

The curriculum, which is highly individualized in the coeducational early grades (from an infant and toddler program through grade 4), emphasizes college preparation throughout. Boys and girls learn in single-gender settings during the middle school years (grades 5-8). Girls in the upper school (grades 9-12) choose from independent study and Advanced Placement options in a variety of subjects. Upper school requirements include two hours of community service each week (beginning in grade 10) and 20 hours of online course work each year. All upper schoolers must purchase tablet computers for in-class use.

Middle schoolers spend several days to a week off campus while engaged in enrichment programs that range from day trips into Detroit to participation in outdoor camps. High school girls take part in the compulsory Project Term, which enables them to study a focused unit of study through community service experiences, personal challenges or career exploration in a local, national or international setting.

As part of an international network of schools, Sacred Heart provides students with the opportunity to participate in exchanges abroad or within the United States.

CRANBROOK SCHOOLS

Bdg — Coed Gr 9-12; Day — Coed PS (Age 3)-12
(Coord — Day 6-8)

Bloomfield Hills, MI 48303. PO Box 801. Tel: 248-645-3610. Fax: 248-645-3025.
www.schools.cranbrook.edu E-mail: admission@cranbrook.edu
Arlyce M. Seibert, Dir (1996). AB, Univ of Detroit, MAT, Oakland Univ. **Drew Miller, Adm.**
Col Prep. AP (exams req'd; 551 taken, 88% 3+)—Fr Lat Span Calc Stats Comp_Sci Bio Chem Physics Eur_Hist US_Hist World_Hist. **Feat**—Humanities Poetry Shakespeare Detroit_Lit Chin Ger Astron Botany Genetics Engineering Comp_Design Middle_Eastern_Hist Econ Geog Psych Philos Relig Ceramics Photog Studio_Art Weaving Drama Theater_Arts Music Dance Public_Speak Metal_Shop Wilderness_ Ed. **Supp**—ESL Tut.
Sports—Basket Crew X-country Golf Ice_Hockey Lacrosse Ski Soccer Swim Tennis Track. B: Baseball Football. G: F_Hockey Softball Volley. **Activities:** 42.
Selective adm: 308/yr. Bdg 107. Day 201. Appl fee: $50. Appl due: Jan. Accepted: 34%.

Yield: 68%. **Tests** CEEB ISEE SSAT TOEFL.

Enr 1656. Bdg 258. Day 1398. Elem 857. Sec 799. Intl 12%. Avg class size: 16. **Fac 220.** M 109/F 111. FT 220. Adv deg: 80%. In dorms 15.

Grad '08—203. Col—203. (U of MI 43, MI St 15, Cornell 4, Boston U 4, Johns Hopkins 4, Brown 3). **Avg SAT:** CR 631. M 638. W 622. Avg ACT: 28. **Col couns:** 4.

Tui '12-'13: Bdg $38,900 (+$1500). **Day $18,900-28,300** (+$800). **Aid:** Need 551 ($7,000,000).

Endow $150,000,000. Plant val $150,000,000. Acres 315. Bldgs 21. Dorms 5. Dorm rms 214. Class rms 120. 7 Libs 100,000 vols. Sci labs 12. Lang labs 2. Theaters 2. Art studios 8. Music studios 13. Gyms 4. Fields 17. Courts 15. Pools 1. Rinks 1. Lakes 1.

Est 1922. Nonprofit. Sem (Sept-June). **Assoc** CLS NCA.

Founded by Mr. and Mrs. George G. Booth as part of the Cranbrook Educational Community, the Cranbrook and Kingswood campuses were designed by the Finnish architect Eliel Saarinen. Within walking distance of one another, the campuses are a part of a 315-acre estate of woods, lakes and rolling hills.

Cranbrook School for boys and Kingswood School for girls were united to form one school in 1984, although coordinated classes had been conducted since 1971. The school consists of one coeducational upper school (grades 9-12), a middle school with separate programs for boys and girls (grades 6-8) and Brookside School, the coeducational elementary division (grades pre-K-5).

From its opening, Cranbrook Schools has enrolled students from throughout the US and from other countries. Affiliation with Cranbrook Institute of Science and Cranbrook Academy of Art and Museum enriches the academic and cultural life of the school. Other distinctive features are the Tennessee Wilderness Expedition for sophomores, Senior May during the spring term, and Advanced Placement preparation in 16 test areas. In addition, juniors may study in England for a semester. Elective courses are available in all departments.

Brookside enrolls students in grades pre-K-5. The traditional academic curriculum is augmented by a strong emphasis on the arts and physical education, as well as by enrichment programs not generally offered in other schools. Included are the science, library, visual studies and drama programs; reading enrichment; and Orff-Schulwerk, instrumental and strings music programs. Computer studies are integrated into the classroom curriculum. Authors, illustrators and performing groups visit the school throughout the year.

Small class size, a nurturing environment and a talented, dedicated faculty are the cornerstones of the school. Most students progress to the Cranbrook Kingswood Middle School, where the gender-specific academic program continues the traditional academic curriculum with special emphasis on the basics of writing and mathematics.   **See Also Pages 140-1**

THE ROEPER SCHOOL

Day — Coed Gr PS (Age 3)-12

Bloomfield Hills, MI 48304. 41190 Woodward Ave. Tel: 248-203-7300.
Fax: 248-203-7310.

Other locations: 1051 Oakland Ave, Birmingham 48009.
www.roeper.org   E-mail: info@roeper.org

David H. Feldman, Head (2012). BS, Univ of Wisconsin-Madison, JD, John Marshall Law School. **Lori Zinser, Adm.**

Col Prep. AP (142 exams taken, 99% 3+)—Eng Fr Lat Span Calc Stats Bio Chem Physics Eur_Hist US_Hist Comp_Govt & Pol Art_Hist Music_Theory. **Elem math**—Singapore Math. **Feat**—Shakespeare African-Amer_Lit Russ_Lit Satire Sci_Fiction Women's_Lit Chin Bioethics Forensic_Sci Organic_Chem Comp_Sci Web_Design Civil_War Native_Amer_Hist Econ Law Comp_Relig Philos Drawing Film Photog Studio_Art Theater Jazz_Band Dance Finance Journ. **Supp**—Tut. Outdoor ed. Sat classes. **Dual enr:** Oakland U.

Sports—Basket X-country Golf Soccer Track. B: Baseball. G: Volley. **Activities:** 38.

Selective adm: 100/yr. Appl fee: $75. Appl due: Rolling. Applied: 227. Accepted: 74%. Yield: 60%. **Tests** IQ.

Enr 549. B 308. G 241. Elem 358. Sec 191. Wh 69%. Latino 1%. Blk 14%. Asian 5%. Other 11%. Avg class size: 14. Stud/fac: 9:1. **Fac 82.** M 17/F 65. FT 66/PT 16. Wh 83%. Latino 1%. Blk 6%. Asian 2%. Other 8%. Adv deg: 59%.
Grad '11—43. Col—42. (U of MI 20, W MI 3, Northwestern 2, U of Chicago 2). **Col couns:** 1. Alum donors: 8%.
Tui '12-'13: Day $16,500-23,350 (+$500). **Aid:** Need 200 ($1,795,925).
Summer (enr 1110): Enrich. Tui Day $145-250. 1 wk. Rec. Tui Day $555. 2 wks. Theater. Tui Day $470-730. 2-3 wks.
Endow $6,000,000. Plant val $21,500,000. Acres 15. Bldgs 11. Class rms 43. Lib 10,000 vols. Sci labs 6. Art studios 2. Music studios 3. Fields 2. Pools 2. Comp labs 3.
Est 1941. Nonprofit. Sem (Sept-June). **Assoc** NCA.

The school was founded by Annemarie and George Roeper, noted German educators who immigrated to the US during World War II, and in 1956 it became a pioneer by structuring its programs for gifted children. The open classroom approach is utilized in the lower school, and stress is placed on individualized, child-centered education at all grade levels. The expansion to a complete high school program was completed in 1969. George A. Roeper retired as headmaster of the upper school in 1979, and Annemarie Roeper retired as head of the lower school the following year.

Roeper admits students with outstanding ability and seeks enrollment from a wide variety of geographical, social and economic backgrounds. An extensive selection of course offerings and electives meets the diverse needs of gifted students. Admission is based on tests, interviews and teacher evaluations. Students in the middle school (grades 6-8) and the upper school (grades 9-12) attend classes at Roeper's campus in Birmingham.   **See Also Page 41**

DETROIT, MI. Urban. Pop: 951,270. Alt: 579 ft. Area also includes Beverly Hills, Grosse Pointe Farms and Grosse Pointe Woods.

DETROIT COUNTRY DAY SCHOOL

Day — Coed Gr PS (Age 3)-12

Beverly Hills, MI 48025. 22305 W 13 Mile Rd. Tel: 248-646-7717. Fax: 248-646-2458.
Other locations: 3003 W Maple Rd, Bloomfield Hills 48301; 3600 Bradway Blvd, Bloomfield Hills 48301; 22400 Hillview Ln, Beverly Hills 48025.
    www.dcds.edu   E-mail: mreimer@dcds.edu
Glen P. Shilling, Head (2007). BA, Albion College, MDiv, Harvard Univ, JD, Univ of Detroit.
    Jorge Dante Hernandez Prosperi, Gr 6-12 Adm; Joseph D'Angelo, Gr 3-5 Adm; Ruth Rebold, Gr PS-2 Adm.
    Col Prep. IB Diploma. AP (400 exams taken, 90% 3+)—Eng Fr Ger Lat Span Calc Stats Comp_Sci Bio Chem Environ_Sci Physics Eur_Hist US_Hist Econ Psych US_Govt & Pol Art_Hist Studio_Art Music_Theory. **Feat**—Humanities Japan Anat & Physiol Astron Ecol Genetics Oceanog Civil_War African-Amer_Stud Photog Sculpt Printmaking Theater Music Orchestra Dance. **Supp**—Tut.
    Sports (req'd)—Basket Bowl X-country Golf Ice_Hockey Lacrosse Ski Swim Track Ultimate_Frisbee. B: Baseball Football Soccer Tennis. G: Cheer F_Hockey Softball Volley. **Activities:** 40.
    Selective adm: 265/yr. Appl fee: $50. Appl due: Rolling. Accepted: 65%. Yield: 60%. **Tests** IQ ISEE Stanford.
    Enr 1624. B 870. G 754. Avg class size: 15. Stud/fac: 8:1. Uniform. **Fac 181.** M 53/F 128. FT 181. Adv deg: 61%.
    Grad '08—175. Col—175. (U of MI, MI St, Princeton, Johns Hopkins, Columbia, Harvard). **Avg SAT:** CR 655. M 661. W 632. Avg ACT: 27. **Col couns:** 3.
    Tui '12-'13: Day $17,300-26,600 (+$750-2350). **Aid:** Need 123 ($2,600,000).
    Summer: Acad Enrich Rev Rem Rec. 1-5 wks.
    Endow $9,000,000. Plant val $30,377,000. Acres 66. Bldgs 9. Class rms 115. 4 Libs 25,000 vols. Sci labs 14. Lang labs 2. Art studios 8. Music studios 6. Perf arts ctrs 1.

Gyms 4. Fields 8. Courts 10. Comp labs 5. Laptop prgm Gr 6-12.
Est 1914. Nonprofit. Tri (Sept-June). **Assoc** CLS.

Since its establishment, DCDS has emphasized sound scholarship, a natural, caring atmosphere, and a program comfortably filled with activities. The school maintains four campuses: the lower school (grades pre-K-2), the junior school (grades 3-5), the middle school (grades 6-8), and the upper school (grades 9-12). Country Day's computer-based learning program requires all middle and upper school pupils to employ laptops for class exercises, homework, tests and research.

Qualified students may enter the two-year International Baccalaureate Diploma Program beginning in grade 11. A cultural enrichment program is also available.

GROSSE POINTE ACADEMY
Day — Coed Gr PS (Age 2)-8

Grosse Pointe Farms, MI 48236. 171 Lake Shore Rd. Tel: 313-886-1221.
Fax: 313-886-2904.
www.gpacademy.org E-mail: mmcdermott@gpacademy.org
Lars Kuelling, Head (2012). BA, Univ of Virginia, MA, Univ of New Mexico. **Molly McDermott, Adm.**
Pre-Prep. Montessori. Feat—Chin Fr Span Environ_Sci Relig Studio_Art Music.
Sports (req'd)—Basket X-country Soccer Tennis. B: Lacrosse. G: Volley.
Selective adm: 52/yr. Appl fee: $50. Appl due: Rolling. **Tests** CTP_4.
Enr 280. Wh 92%. Blk 8%. Avg class size: 15. Uniform. **Fac 44.** M 7/F 37. FT 44. Adv deg: 25%.
Grad '10—25. Prep—25. (U Liggett, Cranbrook).
Tui '12-'13: Day $11,150-17,900. Aid: Need 56 ($550,000).
Summer: Enrich. Sports. 8 wks.
Endow $10,000,000. Plant val $10,000,000. Acres 20. Bldgs 7. Class rms 33. Lib 7200 vols. Sci labs 2. Auds 1. Art studios 2. Music studios 1. Gyms 1. Fields 3. Courts 4. Field houses 1. Comp labs 1.
Est 1885. Nonprofit. Sem (Sept-June).

Founded as the Academy of the Sacred Heart and originally operated by the Society of the Sacred Heart, GPA assumed its present name and nondenominational status in 1969. A Montessori early school program, the oldest of its kind in Michigan, serves children ages 2½-5. The school's pre-preparatory curriculum stresses basic skills development and features French, Spanish, Chinese, art, environmental science, music and religion courses. Various electives are also available.

Located on a 20-acre campus overlooking Lake St. Clair, the academy supplements in-class instruction with museum visits, a daylong on-site biology class, and a multi-day trip to Washington, DC. Girls and boys in grades 7 and 8 fulfill a 20-hour annual service requirement, with 10 hours to be completed outside of school time. Eighth graders complete a research project in art, literature, journalism or science.

UNIVERSITY LIGGETT SCHOOL
Day — Coed Gr PS (Age 3)-12

Grosse Pointe Woods, MI 48236. 1045 Cook Rd. Tel: 313-884-4444.
Fax: 313-884-1775.
Other locations: 850 Briarcliff Dr, Grosse Pointe Woods 48236.
www.uls.org E-mail: kbreen@uls.org
Joseph P. Healey, Head (2007). AB, Pontificia Universita Gregoriana (Italy), PhD, Harvard Univ. **Kevin Breen, Adm.**
Col Prep. AP (203 exams taken, 52% 3+)—US_Govt & Pol. **Feat**—British_Lit Chin Fr Lat Span Calc Anat & Physiol Environ_Sci Comp_Animation Vietnam_War Psych

Philos Ceramics Drawing Photog Drama Band Chorus Music_Theory Jazz_Hist Journ. **Supp**—Tut.
Sports—Basket X-country Ice_Hockey Lacrosse Soccer Swim Tennis Track. B: Baseball Football. G: F_Hockey Softball Volley. **Activities:** 27.
Selective adm: Usual entry: PS, 6 & 9. Appl fee: $50. Appl due: Rolling. Yield: 76%. **Tests** CEEB CTP_4 SSAT.
Enr 583. Elem 300. Sec 283. Avg class size: 16. Stud/fac: 8:1. **Fac 74.** M 23/F 51. FT 73/PT 1. Wh 96%. Latino 1%. Asian 3%. Adv deg: 68%.
Grad '11—55. Col—55. (U of MI 13, Kalamazoo Col 4, Denison 3, MI St 2, U of Chicago 2, Wayne St 2). **Avg SAT:** CR 607. M 589. W 576. Avg ACT: 26.5.
Tui '12-'13: Day $14,010-21,420 (+$625). **Aid:** Need 326 ($3,244,705).
Endow $30,799,000. Plant val $48,200,000. Acres 50. Bldgs 5. Class rms 87. 3 Libs 24,000 vols. Sci labs 9. Auds 3. Art studios 4. Music studios 4. Dance studios 1. Gyms 3. Fields 9. Tennis courts 12. Pools 2. Rinks 1. Comp labs 4.
Est 1878. Nonprofit. Sem (Sept-June). **Assoc** CLS.

ULS came into being when the Liggett School and Grosse Pointe University School merged in 1969. The Liggett School, founded by Rev. James D. Liggett in 1878, was the oldest coeducational independent school in Michigan. The Grosse Pointe University School was the result of a 1954 consolidation of the Detroit University School and the Grosse Pointe Country Day School.

The present school occupies two campuses: The lower (grades pre-K-5) and upper (grades 9-12) schools are situated on a 40-acre site on Cook Road, while the middle school (grades 6-8) is located on a 10-acre campus on Briarcliff Drive. While most pupils are from the Grosse Pointes, a significant number come from Detroit, elsewhere in southeastern Michigan or Canada.

The curriculum provides honors courses in all fields and also meets the needs of the average student. Boys and girls must participate in athletics and the creative and performing arts, and all seniors complete a month-long independent project or internship in the spring.

GLEN ARBOR, MI. (135 mi. N of Grand Rapids, MI; 161 mi. NE of Milwaukee, WI) Rural. Pop: 788. Alt: 591 ft.

LEELANAU SCHOOL

Bdg and Day — Coed Gr 9-12

Glen Arbor, MI 49636. 1 Old Homestead Rd. Tel: 231-334-5800, 800-533-5262.
Fax: 231-334-5898.
www.leelanau.org   E-mail: info@leelanau.org
Matt Ralston, Pres (2009). BS, MA, Ohio State Univ. **Brian Chatterley, Adm.**
Col Prep. LD. Underachiever. AP (exams req'd)—Calc Stats. Feat—Classics Creative_Writing Humanities Fr Span Anat & Physiol Astron Ecol Environ_Sci Psych World_Relig Drawing Studio_Art Drama Music Bus. **Supp**—Dev_Read ESL Tut.
Sports—Basket Soccer Tennis Volley.
Somewhat selective adm: 20/yr. Bdg 19. Day 1. Appl fee: $50. Appl due: Rolling. **Tests** SSAT TOEFL.
Enr 60. Intl 10%. Avg class size: 6. Stud/fac: 6:1. **Fac 18.** M 11/F 7. FT 16/PT 2. Adv deg: 38%. In dorms 4.
Grad '08—18. Col—18. (N MI, MI St, Albion, MI Tech, Allegheny, DePaul).
Tui '12-'13: Bdg $54,500 (+$1500). **5-Day Bdg $46,500** (+$1500). **Day $27,250** (+$500). **Intl Bdg $54,500** (+$1500-3000). **Aid:** Need 21 ($289,679).
Summer: ESL. Tui Bdg $7950. 6 wks.
Endow $400,000. Plant val $5,000,000. Acres 42. Bldgs 13. Dorms 5. Dorm rms 48. Class rms 13. Lib 10,000 vols. Observatories 1. Auds 1. Art studios 3. Music studios 1. Gyms 1. Fields 3. Courts 4. Weight rms 1. Greenhouses 1.
Est 1929. Nonprofit. Sem (Aug-May).

The school is located on the Crystal River, within the 72,000-acre Sleeping Bear Dunes National Park on the western shore of Lake Michigan. Leelanau is an experientially based college preparatory school that serves students with learning differences. Parents may track their children's progress through updates that are available every 72 hours.

Leelanau's multisensory approach utilizes an integrated curriculum. Within the humanities department, for example, instructors place emphasis on the historical timelines and events that correlate with the literature of the time; in a similar fashion, math and science course work enables boys and girls to study the relationship between mathematical models and scientific principles. During a compulsory senior seminar course, pupils produce a 10- to 12-page research paper and make a formal presentation of their findings.

Recreational and competitive sports, opportunities in the arts and community service options complement the curriculum.

INTERLOCHEN, MI. (116 mi. N of Grand Rapids, MI; 155 mi. NE of Milwaukee, WI) Rural. Pop: 150. Alt: 849 ft.

INTERLOCHEN ARTS ACADEMY
Bdg and Day — Coed Gr 9-PG

Interlochen, MI 49643. 4000 Hwy M-137, PO Box 199. Tel: 231-276-7472, 800-681-5912. Fax: 231-276-7464.
www.interlochen.org   E-mail: admission@interlochen.org
Jeffrey S. Kimpton, Pres (2003). BA, MA, Univ of Illinois-Urbana. **James R. Bekkering, Adm.**

> Col Prep. Gen Acad. Perform_Arts Visual_Arts Creative_Writing. AP (38 exams taken, 82% 3+)—Calc Stats Physics. **Feat**—Poetry Shakespeare Playwriting Screenwriting Fr Ger Span Anat Ecol Geol Comp_Sci Pol_Sci Film Filmmaking Visual_Arts Drama Theater_Arts Music_Theory Orchestra Ballet Dance Pointe. **Supp**—Dev_ Read ESL Makeup Rem_Math Rev Tut. Sat classes.
> **Selective adm:** 251/yr. Appl fee: $60. Appl due: Feb. Accepted: 58%.
> **Enr 474.** Sec 459. PG 15. Wh 76%. Latino 1%. Blk 6%. Asian 17%. Intl 19%. Avg class size: 13. Uniform. **Fac 77.** M 47/F 30. FT 77. Adv deg: 77%.
> **Grad '07—209. Col—184.** (U of MI, U of Rochester, Oberlin, Juilliard, Manhattan Sch of Music, Johns Hopkins). **Avg SAT:** CR 591. M 553. W 555. Avg ACT: 24. **Col couns:** 3.
> **Tui '11-'12: Bdg $48,250-51,725** (+$2320). **Day $30,850-32,750** (+$2320). **Aid:** Need 356 ($8,000,000).
> **Summer:** Ages 8-18. Rec. Arts. Tui Bdg $900-7000. 1-6 wks.
> Endow $22,000,000. Plant val $26,200,000. Acres 1200. Bldgs 25. Dorms 5. Dorm rms 246. Class rms 55. 2 Libs 21,000 vols. Labs 12. Theaters 4. Art studios 5. Music studios 29. Fields 1. Courts 2.
> **Est 1961.** Nonprofit. Sem (Sept-May). **Assoc** NCA.

Interlochen was founded by Dr. Joseph E. Maddy as an outgrowth of the National Music Camp, now known as Interlochen Arts Camp. The 1200-acre, wooded campus hugs the shores of two northern Michigan glacial lakes, and encompasses both rivers and fields. The academy combines preprofessional training in the fine arts with comprehensive college preparatory academics. Both high school and postgraduate year opportunities are available.

Students major in creative writing, dance, motion picture arts, music, theater arts, visual arts or comparative arts. A variety of offerings in English and literature, English as a Second Language, world languages, history and political science, science, mathematics, and physical and health education is available. Students are regularly exposed to a wide range of talent in their fields, as visiting artist-instructors hold master classes at the academy. Off-campus performance tours in the different arts divisions are an integral part of the curriculum.

Movies, theatrical performances, coffeehouses, dances, art exhibits, orchestra, band and small-ensemble concerts, readings, recitals and jam sessions are some of the regularly scheduled on-campus activities. In addition, each weekday evening, the academy provides organized physical recreation. Boarding students perform at least two hours of weekly community service on campus; work responsibilities may include food service, residence hall desk duty, tech crew, recycling crew, mail delivery or academic tutoring.

While many graduates continue studying in their arts specialty, others pursue varied careers unrelated to the arts.   **See Also Page 112**

OXFORD, MI. (31 mi. NNW of Detroit, MI) Suburban. Pop: 3540. Alt: 1062 ft.

KINGSBURY COUNTRY DAY SCHOOL
Day — Coed Gr PS (Age 4)-8

Oxford, MI 48370. 5000 Hosner Rd. Tel: 248-628-2571. Fax: 248-628-3612.
  www.kingsburyschool.org   E-mail: adibble@kingsburyschool.org
Tom Mecsey, Head. Audrey Smith-Dibble, Adm.
  Pre-Prep. Feat—Span Environ_Sci Computers Studio_Art Drama Music.
  Sports—Basket Soccer. B: Baseball. G: Volley.
  Selective adm: 35/yr. Appl fee: $100. Appl due: Mar.
  Enr 93. Avg class size: 14. Stud/fac: 6:1. **Fac 18.** M 3/F 15. FT 18. Adv deg: 16%.
  Grad '08—15. Prep—15. (Cranbrook, Notre Dame Prep-MI, Detroit Co Day, Acad of the Sacred Heart-MI, Roeper, Greenhills-MI).
  Tui '12-'13: Day $8075-9500.
  Summer: Enrich Rec. 3 wks.
  Endow $1,200,000. Plant val $5,000,000. Acres 125. Bldgs 3. Class rms 16. Lib 8061 vols. Sci labs 1. Lang labs 1. Art studios 1. Music studios 1. Gyms 1. Fields 2. Climbing walls 1. Comp labs 1.
  Est 1953. Nonprofit. Quar (Sept-June).

In the early grades, Kingsbury's developmentally oriented curriculum emphasizes basic academic skills. The middle school program (grades 6-8) provides broader curricular choices in the form of electives, offered in about 20 areas of study each term. At all grade levels, pupils utilize computers in the classroom and the computer lab. The athletic program features an all-school skiing program, as well as interscholastic and intramural sports for older students.

The school's 125-acre, rural campus serves as a natural setting of woods, fields, ponds, wetlands and trails for the environmental studies program.

OHIO

AKRON, OH. (29 mi. SSE of Cleveland, OH) Urban. Pop: 217,074. Alt: 873 ft. Area also includes Bath.

OLD TRAIL SCHOOL
Day — Coed Gr PS (Age 2)-8

Bath, OH 44210. 2315 Ira Rd, PO Box 827. Tel: 330-666-1118. Fax: 330-666-2187.
  www.oldtrail.org   E-mail: sholding@oldtrail.org
John S. Farber, Head (2000). BA, Trinity Univ, MA, Antioch Univ. **Susan Holding, Adm.**
  Pre-Prep. Feat—Creative_Writing Poetry Fr Lat Span Computers Photog Studio_Art Video_Production Theater_Arts Chorus Music Orchestra Metal_Shop. **Supp**—Dev_ Read Rem_Math Rem_Read Rev Tut.
  Sports—Basket X-country Lacrosse Soccer Swim Tennis Track. G: F_Hockey.
  Selective adm: 95/yr. Appl due: Rolling. Accepted: 72%. Yield: 75%. **Tests** ISEE.
  Enr 578. B 301. G 277. Wh 75%. Blk 5%. Asian 6%. Other 14%. Avg class size: 18. Stud/fac: 10:1. Casual. **Fac 59.** Wh 61%. Latino 1%. Blk 18%. Native Am 1%. Asian 19%. Adv deg: 54%.
  Grad '11—60. Prep—60. (Western Reserve, Walsh, Archbishop Hoban, U Sch-OH).
  Tui '11-'12: Day $12,300-16,550. Aid: Need 116 ($450,000).
  Summer: Acad Enrich Rem. Tui Day $110/wk. 9 wks.
  Endow $5,257,000. Plant val $35,000,000. Acres 62. Bldgs 6. Class rms 42. Lib 14,000 vols. Sci labs 2. Auds 1. Art studios 4. Music studios 2. Gyms 2. Fields 3. Courts 3. Pools 1. Greenhouses 1. Comp labs 2. Comp/stud: 1:2.
  Est 1920. Nonprofit. Quar (Aug-June). **Assoc** NCA.

Old Trail offers a liberal arts elementary education on a 62-acre campus within the Cuyahoga Valley National Park. Drawing students from a five-county region that includes the Akron and Cleveland suburbs, the school offers art, music, performing arts, technology and world languages from preschool on. Service learning is an important element of the curriculum at all grade levels.

Class trips commence in grade 5. Past destinations include outdoor experiences in northern Michigan, Yosemite National Park and the Smoky Mountains, as well as urban excursions to major American cities. Old Trail's location within a national park provides the school with an array of curricular and service opportunities.

CANTON, OH. (49 mi. SSE of Cleveland, OH) Urban. Pop: 80,806. Alt: 1052 ft.

CANTON COUNTRY DAY SCHOOL
Day — Coed Gr PS (Age 3)-8

Canton, OH 44718. 3000 Demington Ave NW. Tel: 330-453-8279. Fax: 330-453-6038.
  www.cantoncountryday.org   E-mail: pmonks@cantoncountryday.org
Pamela Shaw, Head (2002). BA, Providence College, MEd, Boston Univ. **R. Paul Monks, Adm.**
  Gen Acad. Elem math—Everyday Math. **Feat**—Fr Span Computers Robotics Govt Studio_Art Music Dance. **Supp**—Dev_Read Tut.
  Sports—Basket Soccer Track.
  Selective adm: 34/yr. Usual entry: PS, K, 1 & 6. Appl fee: $45. Appl due: Rolling. Applied: 58. Accepted: 81%. Yield: 72%. **Tests** CTP_4 IQ.

Enr 175. B 94. G 81. Wh 76%. Latino 2%. Blk 10%. Native Am 1%. Asian 9%. Other 2%. Avg class size: 12. Stud/fac: 9:1. Casual. **Fac 22.** M 6/F 16. FT 16/PT 6. Nonwhite 10%. Adv deg: 40%.
Grad '11—22. Prep—2. (Western Reserve 1, Archbishop Hoban 1). Alum donors: 46%.
Tui '11-'12: Day $11,724-15,059 (+$300). **Aid:** Need 59 ($670,000).
Summer (enr 45): Enrich Rec. 5 wks.
Endow $4,100,000. Plant val $7,500,000. Acres 40. Bldgs 2 (100% ADA). Class rms 27. Libs 1. Sci labs 1. Music studios 2. Gyms 1. Fields 2. Comp labs 3. Comp/stud: 1:1.5 (1:1 Laptop prgm Gr 4-8).
Est 1964. Nonprofit. Tri (Aug-June).

As part of the school's elementary curriculum, CCDS students develop a solid foundation in language arts, science, foreign language and the fine arts. In addition to a variety of local and regional field trips, the program features educational trips in the middle school (grades 5-8) that include visits to Williamsburg, VA, and Washington, DC, and an outdoor experience at Nature's Classroom.

CINCINNATI, OH. (92 mi. NE of Louisville, KY; 98 mi. ESE of Indianapolis, IN) Urban. Pop: 331,285. Alt: 490 ft.

BETHANY SCHOOL
Day — Coed Gr K-8

Cincinnati, OH 45246. 555 Albion Ave. Tel: 513-771-7462. Fax: 513-771-2292.
www.bethanyschool.org   E-mail: pez@bethanyschool.org
Cheryl L. Pez, Head (1999). BS, MEd, Miami Univ (OH). Teri Mauntel, Adm.
   Pre-Prep. Feat—Span Computers Relig Music Debate Public_Speak. **Supp**—Dev_ Read Rem_Math Rem_Read Tut.
   Sports—Basket Golf Track. B: Football. G: Volley.
   Selective adm: 54/yr. Usual entry: K & 1. Appl fee: $50. Appl due: Rolling. **Tests** IQ Stanford.
   Enr 244. B 118. G 126. Wh 42%. Latino 1%. Blk 44%. Asian 10%. Other 3%. Avg class size: 15. Stud/fac: 15:1. Uniform. **Fac 32.** M 3/F 29. FT 27/PT 5. Wh 85%. Latino 6%. Blk 9%. Adv deg: 43%.
   Grad '11—24. Prep—23. (Ursuline Acad-OH 5, Summit Co Day 4, La Salle HS-OH 2, Archbishop Moeller 2, Mt Notre Dame 2, St Xavier-OH 2).
   Tui '12-'13: Day $8950 (+$385-525). **Aid:** Need 25 ($160,000).
   Acres 23. Bldgs 8. Class rms 23. Libs 1. Sci labs 1. Art studios 1. Music studios 1. Gyms 1. Fields 1. Comp labs 1.
   Est 1898. Nonprofit. Episcopal (17% practice). Quar (Aug-June).

Located on 23 wooded acres in the suburban village of Glendale, Bethany provides a challenging academic program for boys and girls from Cincinnati who plan to attend college. The school was established by the Episcopal Society of the Transfiguration; however, the diverse student body represents various religious backgrounds.

Bethany's curriculum places strong emphasis on the development of sound reading and math skills. In grades 1-8, wireless laptops are employed in each classroom. Computer education is an important part of the overall program for all boys and girls, and problem-solving labs provide further enrichment. Field trips, excursions and overnights are other integral instructional tools.

As part of extracurricular programming, students may participate in interscholastic academic competitions in such areas as math, writing and social studies.

CINCINNATI COUNTRY DAY SCHOOL

Day — Coed Gr PS (Age 2)-12

Cincinnati, OH 45243. 6905 Given Rd. Tel: 513-979-0220. Fax: 513-527-7614.
www.countryday.net   E-mail: admission@countryday.net
Robert P. Macrae, Head (2004). BA, Wesleyan Univ, MA, Stanford Univ, MA, EdD, Columbia Univ. Aaron B. Kellenberger, Adm.
Col Prep. Montessori. AP (exams req'd; 200 taken, 86% 3+)—Eng Fr Span Calc Stats Comp_Sci Bio Chem US_Hist Studio_Art. Feat—Humanities Southern_Lit Lat Film Fine_Arts Performing_Arts Photog Drama Music. Supp—Rev Tut.
Sports—Basket Crew X-country Golf Lacrosse Soccer Swim Tennis Track. B: Baseball Football Wrestling. G: Gymnastics Softball Volley. Activities: 46.
Selective adm: 160/yr. Appl fee: $50. Appl due: Mar. Accepted: 70%. Yield: 67%. Tests CEEB CTP_4 IQ ISEE SSAT Stanford TOEFL.
Enr 820. Elem 545. Sec 275. Nonwhite 24%. Avg class size: 15. Stud/fac: 8:1. Fac 98.
Grad '09—62. Col—62. (Dartmouth 5, U of Cincinnati 3, Miami U-OH 3, Vanderbilt 3, Northwestern 2, Wake Forest 2). Avg SAT: CR 629. M 634. W 640. Avg ACT: 27. Col couns: 3. Alum donors: 22%.
Tui '12-'13: Day $17,700-18,700 (+$700). Aid: Merit 8 ($26,500). Need 136 ($1,382,800).
Summer: Acad Enrich Rev Rec. Sports. 1-10 wks.
Endow $22,000,000. Acres 62. Bldgs 6. Class rms 78. 2 Libs 15,000 vols. Comp ctrs 1. Observatories 1. Auds 3. Theaters 1. Art studios 3. Music studios 3. Gyms 2. Fields 8. Tennis courts 7. Pools 1. Tracks 1. Greenhouses 1. Laptop prgm Gr 5-12.
Est 1926. Nonprofit. Sem (Aug-June). Assoc CLS.

Located on a 62-acre campus in suburban Cincinnati, CCDS provides thorough college preparation for students that extends from early childhood through high school. The school conducts both Montessori and traditional programming for children ages 3-6. Technology is incorporated into every aspect of the curriculum, with all pupils having Internet and E-mail access, and each student in grades 5-12 being equipped with a tablet computer. Children gain exposure to physical education and the arts beginning in the early childhood program, and foreign language instruction commences in kindergarten.

The lower school (age 18 months through grade 2) provides developmentally appropriate instruction designed to stimulate an interest in learning. Increased levels of independence and collaboration, as well as more advanced reasoning skills, are in evidence during the elementary school years (grades 3-5). Middle school programming (grades 6-8) particularly addresses the varying learning and social needs of young adolescents. The upper school curriculum (grades 9-12) readies students for college through an emphasis on critical thinking, problem solving and the application of knowledge to new situations. Boys and girls perform 90 hours of community service prior to graduation.

ST. URSULA ACADEMY

Day — Girls Gr 9-12

Cincinnati, OH 45206. 1339 E McMillan St. Tel: 513-961-3410. Fax: 513-961-3856.
www.saintursula.org   E-mail: admissions@saintursula.org
Lelia K. Kramer, Pres (2011). Craig Maliborski, Prin. Sarah Catlin, Adm.
Col Prep. AP (exams req'd; 237 taken, 75% 3+)—Eng Fr Lat Span Calc Comp_Sci Bio Chem Environ_Sci Physics Eur_Hist US_Hist Psych US_Govt & Pol Art_Hist Studio_Art. Feat—British_Lit Creative_Writing Shakespeare Stats Anat & Physiol Econ Relig World_Relig Drawing Photog Sculpt Acting Theater_Arts Music_Hist Music_Theory Orchestra Design. Supp—LD.
Sports—G: Basket Bowl X-country F_Hockey Golf Lacrosse Soccer Softball Swim Tennis Track Volley. Activities: 40.
Somewhat selective adm (Gr 6-11): 167/yr. Usual entry: 9. Appl fee: $0. Appl due: Nov. Applied: 370. Accepted: 85%. Tests HSPT.
Enr 661. Wh 93%. Latino 1%. Blk 5%. Asian 1%. Avg class size: 20. Stud/fac: 15:1. Uni-

form. **Fac 58.** M 17/F 41. FT 48/PT 10. Wh 99%. Blk 1%. Adv deg: 79%.
Grad '10—165. Col—163. (U of Cincinnati 23, Miami U-OH 16, U of Dayton 13, OH St 9, Xavier-OH 7, U of SC 6). **Avg SAT:** CR 573. M 555. W 579. Avg ACT: 27. **Col couns:** 3. Alum donors: 23%.
Tui '11-'12: Day $11,320 (+$550). **Aid:** Merit 49 ($144,663). Need 121 ($420,780). Work prgm 28 ($15,600).
Acres 7. Bldgs 6. Class rms 48. Lib 15,003 vols. Sci labs 8. Lang labs 1. Theaters 1. Art studios 4. Music studios 7. Gyms 1. Fields 1. Student ctrs 1. Comp labs 3. Laptop prgm Gr 9-12.
Est 1910. Nonprofit. Roman Catholic (87% practice). Quar (Aug-June). **Assoc** NCA.

Sponsored by the Ursulines of Cincinnati, this Walnut Hills secondary school draws students from approximately 20 school districts in the Greater Cincinnati area. The academy conducts a rigorous college preparatory program in the fields of English, math, science, social studies, foreign language and religion. With the permission of the academic dean, qualified girls may pursue Advanced Placement course work during the junior or senior year. Incoming freshmen purchase tablet personal computers from the school to connect to the campus wireless network, complete classroom assignments and access course materials from home.

St. Ursula maintains a program for college-bound girls of above-average ability who have either dyslexia or another learning disability. Students enrolled in this program are completely mainstreamed within the regular curriculum, but certain modifications and services are in place to address their special learning needs. Program participants incur some additional costs.

THE SEVEN HILLS SCHOOL
Day — Coed Gr PS (Age 3)-12

Cincinnati, OH 45227. 5400 Red Bank Rd. Tel: 513-728-2400. Fax: 513-728-2408.
Other locations: 2726 Johnstone Pl, Cincinnati 45206.
   www.7hills.org   E-mail: janet.hill@7hills.org
Christopher P. Garten, Head (2009). BA, Princeton Univ, MA, Columbia Univ. **Janet Hill, Adm.**
Col Prep. AP (exams req'd; 228 taken, 96% 3+)—Eng Fr Lat Span Calc Comp_Sci Bio Chem Physics Eur_Hist US_Hist Art_Hist. **Feat**—Creative_Writing Chin Multivariable_Calc Anat & Physiol Environ_Sci Web_Design Econ Psych Drawing Graphic_Arts Painting Acting Drama Music Music_Hist Music_Theory Journ Speech. **Supp**—Dev_Read LD Rem_Math Rem_Read Tut.
Sports—Basket X-country Lacrosse Soccer Swim Tennis Track. B: Baseball Golf. G: Cheer Gymnastics Softball Volley. **Activities:** 56.
Selective adm: 131/yr. Appl fee: $50. **Tests** ISEE Stanford.
Enr 1000. Elem 720. Sec 280. Wh 77%. Latino 2%. Blk 6%. Asian 10%. Other 5%. Avg class size: 15. Stud/fac: 9:1. Casual. **Fac 105.** M 20/F 85. FT 96/PT 9. Wh 92%. Latino 2%. Blk 4%. Asian 2%. Adv deg: 54%.
Grad '11—70. Col—70. (U of Dayton 4, Princeton 3, Carleton 3, Kenyon 3, OH St 3, Tufts 2). **Avg SAT:** CR 661. M 663. W 666. **Mid 50% SAT:** CR 590-750. M 570-760. W 590-750. Avg ACT: 29. Mid 50% ACT: 27-32. **Col couns:** 3. Alum donors: 16%.
Tui '12-'13: Day $16,938-20,998 (+$400). **Aid:** Merit 24 ($100,000). Need 143 ($1,400,000).
Summer: Acad Enrich Rec. Tui Day $150-300/wk. 9 wks.
Endow $20,000,000. Plant val $55,000,000. Acres 44. Bldgs 21. Class rms 108. Libs 3. Art studios 5. Music studios 3. Gyms 4. Comp labs 4. Comp/stud: 1:1.3 (1:1 Laptop prgm Gr 6-12).
Est 1974. Nonprofit. Sem (Aug-June). **Assoc** CLS NCA.

Seven Hills traces its roots in the community back to 1906, when the College Preparatory School was founded in East Walnut Hills by Mary Harlan Doherty; to 1916, when Helen G. Lotspeich began the Clifton Open-Air School in her home; and to 1927, when community leaders founded Hillsdale School to provide an area alternative in private education. Today, the school is housed on two campuses located six miles apart: Doherty School for grades pre-

K-5 occupies the Doherty campus on Johnston Place in East Walnut Hills, while Lotspeich School, also pre-K-5, shares the 25-acre Hillsdale campus near Madisonville with the middle and upper schools.

In the lower school, every child works with specialists in art, music, Spanish, drama, library and physical education starting in kindergarten. Reading and math specialists offer learning support as needed. As part of the science curriculum, children work with teachers to care for rabbits, gerbils and rats in science laboratories. Lower schoolers may engage in service learning projects and organized sports begin in grade 1.

The middle school curriculum addresses the particular academic and interpersonal needs of young adolescents. Study skills are emphasized during these years. Foreign language offerings (French, Spanish and Latin), accelerated math groupings, art, music, drama, interest clubs, extracurricular activities and athletics accommodate individual abilities and interests.

In the upper school, every student must complete a traditional college preparatory program, pass writing and computer competency examinations, and complete both a 40-hour personal challenge project and a 30-hour community service project with a needy population. The fine and performing arts are integral to the curriculum, and honors and Advanced Placement courses are offered in all major disciplines. Students choose from a wide selection of electives and take advantage of a highly developed curriculum.

After-school enrichment (grades 1-5), extended-day and holiday care (grades pre-K-5), and summer programs (age 3 through grade 12) are also available.

SUMMIT COUNTRY DAY SCHOOL
Day — Coed Gr PS (Age 2)-12

Cincinnati, OH 45208. 2161 Grandin Rd. Tel: 513-871-4700. Fax: 513-533-5373.
   www.summitcds.org   E-mail: schiess_k@summitcds.org
Richard Wilson, Head (2010). BA, Davidson College, MBA, Univ of Chicago. **Kelley K. Schiess, Adm.**
   Col Prep. Montessori. AP (253 exams taken, 96% 3+)—Fr Lat Span Calc Stats Comp_Sci Bio Chem Environ_Sci Physics Eur_Hist US_Hist Human_Geog Psych US_Govt & Pol Music_Theory. **Elem read**—Common Core. **Feat**—Chin Anat & Physiol Robotics Web_Design Holocaust Philos World_Relig Ceramics Photog Drama Band Chorus Speech.
   Sports—Basket Bowl X-country Golf Lacrosse Soccer Swim Tennis Track. B: Baseball Football Wrestling. G: Cheer F_Hockey Softball Volley. **Activities:** 43.
   Selective adm: 181/yr. Usual entry: PS & 9. Appl fee: $50. Appl due: Rolling. Applied: 292. **Tests** CTP_4 HSPT ISEE Stanford.
   Enr 1082. Elem 687. Sec 395. Wh 83%. Latino 3%. Blk 7%. Asian 3%. Other 4%. Avg class size: 15. Stud/fac: 9:1. Uniform. **Fac 122.** M 26/F 96. FT 94/PT 28. Wh 95%. Latino 3%. Asian 2%. Adv deg: 36%.
   Grad '11—98. Col—98. (IN U, Carleton, Notre Dame, Denison, Wellesley, Geo Wash). **Avg SAT:** CR 612. M 605. W 593. Avg ACT: 26.3. **Col couns:** 2.
   Tui '12-'13: Day $15,300-19,100 (+$625).
   Summer: Acad Enrich Rev Rec. 13 wks.
   Endow $22,000,000. Plant val $45,000,000. Acres 24. Bldgs 10. Class rms 90. 4 Libs 15,000 vols. Sci labs 11. Lang labs 1. Auds 2. Theaters 1. Art studios 4. Music studios 13. Gyms 4. Athletic ctrs 2. Fields 5. Courts 4. Comp labs 7. Comp/stud: 1:2.
   Est 1890. Nonprofit. Roman Catholic (60% practice). Sem (Aug-June). **Assoc** NCA.

Founded by the Sisters of Notre Dame de Namur and now independently owned and governed by a board of trustees, Summit occupies a 24-acre site in Hyde Park. Three contiguous school divisions share the campus: a lower school comprising a Montessori toddler program and kindergarten, traditional grades 1-4, a middle school (grades 5-8) and an upper school (grades 9-12). Developmentally appropriate instruction characterizes each division.

Throughout, the curriculum places emphasis on technology: Keyboarding classes begin in grade 1, and middle and upper school pupils benefit from wireless mobile laptop labs and hardware and software resources through classroom computers, as well as Internet-based resources for home access. Programs in art, foreign language and religion are important aspects of the curriculum, and students also receive instruction in drama, music, health and library skills.

During the primary school years, students have a homeroom teacher who is responsible for instruction in the core subjects; specialists teach French, Spanish, technology, library, art, music and physical education classes. The middle school employs a team-teaching approach, with specialized teachers in each subject area and accelerated curricular offerings, including upper-school-level French, Spanish and Latin classes, as well as algebra I for qualified seventh graders. Study skills and leadership development are integral to the middle school program.

In the upper school, Advanced Placement and other advanced courses in many areas complement an array of electives. The college preparatory program stresses writing and incorporates the fine arts. Prior to graduation, pupils complete a senior project and fulfill a 48-hour community service requirement.

CLEVELAND, OH. Urban. Pop: 478,403. Alt: 690 ft. Area also includes Willoughby.

ANDREWS OSBORNE ACADEMY
Bdg — Coed Gr 7-12; Day — Coed PS (Age 3)-12

Willoughby, OH 44094. 38588 Mentor Ave. Tel: 440-942-3600, 800-753-4683. Fax: 440-954-3660.
Other locations: 150 Gillette St, Painesville 44077.
www.andrewsosborne.org　E-mail: admissions@andrewsosborne.org
Charles J. Roman, Head. Rachelle Sundberg, Adm.
　　Col Prep. AP (exams req'd)—Eng Fr Span Calc Bio Chem US_Hist. **Feat**—Russ_Lit Short_Fiction Stats Astron Environ_Sci Programming Web_Design Econ Govt Psych Ethics Ceramics Film Graphic_Arts Studio_Art Printmaking Theater_Arts Band Chorus Music_Theory Speech. **Supp**—ESL Rev Tut.
　　Sports—Basket X-country Golf Soccer Swim Tennis Volley. B: Baseball. G: Lacrosse Softball. **Activities:** 19.
　　Selective adm (Bdg Gr 7-11; Day PS-11): 92/yr. Bdg 35. Day 57. Appl fee: $40. Appl due: Rolling. Accepted: 80%. Yield: 75%. **Tests** ISEE SSAT TOEFL.
　　Enr 350. Intl 25%. Stud/fac: 8:1. Uniform. **Fac 62.** M 14/F 48. FT 62. Adv deg: 41%.
　　Grad '08—23. Col—23. (DePaul 2, Marietta 2, Geo Wash 1, Syracuse 1, U of VA 1, OH St 1). **Avg SAT:** CR/M 1120. Alum donors: 6%.
　　Tui '12-'13: Bdg $35,250 (+$750-1000). **5-Day Bdg $30,250** (+$750-1000). **Day $10,000-18,500** (+$200-1000). **Intl Bdg $40,250** (+$750-1000).
　　Summer: Rec. Equestrian. Girls. Ages 9-15. Coed. Ages 8-14. 8 wks.
　　Acres 300. Bldgs 19. Dorms 5. Class rms 30. Lib 13,100 vols. Sci labs 5. Lang labs 5. Auds 1. Theaters 1. Art studios 2. Music studios 1. Gyms 2. Fields 4. Courts 4. Field houses 1. Riding rings 7. Stables 80. Comp labs 7.
　　Est 1910. Nonprofit. Sem (Aug-June).

This nonsectarian school was established as the Andrews School in accordance with the will of area businessman Wallace Corydon Andrews and his wife, Margaret St. John Andrews. After more than 90 years as a girls' secondary school, the school became known as Andrews Osborne Academy upon effecting a merger with The Phillips-Osborne School in the summer of 2007. This merger resulted in the acquisition of a second campus in Painesville that houses a day division for students in grades PS-8. AOA is now fully coeducational.

In a small-class setting, the academic program encourages individual growth and prepares students for college. AOA's middle school curriculum (grades 6-8) integrates various projects and group activities, as well as enrichment field trips. Outdoor education is an important aspect of middle school life, as pupils develop riding skills in the equestrian center and also engage in such activities as rock climbing, canoeing, backpacking and work on the school's ropes course.

The liberal arts program during the upper school years (grades 9-12) features honors, Advanced Placement and independent study courses, as well as a senior research project. A wide selection of electives accommodates varying student interests. Also available is an English as a Second Language program for international students.

Community service requirements are as follows: 10 hours per year in grades 6-8 and 16 hours annually in grades 9-12.

COLUMBUS, OH. (100 mi. NE of Cincinnati, OH; 124 mi. SW of Cleveland, OH) Urban. Pop: 711,470. Alt: 744 ft. Area also includes Gahanna.

THE COLUMBUS ACADEMY
Day — Coed Gr PS (Age 4)-12

Gahanna, OH 43230. 4300 Cherry Bottom Rd. Tel: 614-475-2311. Fax: 614-475-0396.
www.columbusacademy.org   E-mail: wuorinen@columbusacademy.org
John M. Mackenzie, Head (1997). AB, Bowdoin College, MA, Columbia Univ. **John Wuorinen, Adm.**

Col Prep. AP exams taken: 356 (95% 3+). Feat—British_Lit Chin Fr Lat Span Calc Stats Environ_Sci Comp_Sci Chin & Japan_Hist Milit_Hist Russ_Hist S_African_Hist Econ Govt Psych Ethics Art_Hist Ceramics Drawing Photog Sculpt Studio_Art Band Chorus Music_Theory Jazz_Band Public_Speak. **Supp**—Dev_Read Rev Tut. **Dual enr:** OH St.

Sports—Basket X-country Soccer Swim Tennis Track. B: Baseball Football Golf Wrestling. G: F_Hockey Lacrosse Volley. **Activities:** 36.

Selective adm: 155/yr. Usual entry: PS, K, 5 & 9. Appl fee: $50-75. Appl due: Feb. Applied: 365. Accepted: 55%. Yield: 78%. **Tests** ISEE SSAT.

Enr 1072. B 548. G 524. Elem 720. Sec 352. Wh 77%. Latino 1%. Blk 7%. Asian 14%. Other 1%. Avg class size: 15. Stud/fac: 8:1. **Fac 135.** M 42/F 93. FT 118/PT 17. Wh 93%. Latino 3%. Blk 1%. Asian 3%. Adv deg: 67%.

Grad '10—93. Col—93. (OH St, Miami U-OH, Northwestern, Case Western Reserve, Denison, DePauw). **Avg SAT:** CR 643. M 660. W 658. **Mid 50% SAT:** CR 600-690. M 590-740. W 590-730. Avg ACT: 28. Mid 50% ACT: 24-31. **Col couns:** 2. Alum donors: 23%.

Tui '12-'13: Day $16,000-20,900 (+$300-700). **Aid:** Need 172 ($1,706,000).

Summer: Acad Enrich Rev Rem Rec. Arts. Tui Day $240/wk. 10 wks.

Endow $24,500,000. Plant val $44,000,000. Acres 231. Bldgs 10. Class rms 90. 3 Libs 35,543 vols. Sci labs 10. Lang labs 3. Comp ctrs 2. Theaters 1. Art studios 5. Music studios 3. Gyms 2. Fields 5. Courts 8. Pools 1. Comp labs 6.

Est 1911. Nonprofit. Sem (Aug-June). **Assoc** CLS.

Founded by Frank P. R. Van Syckel and conducted by him for 30 years, this was one of the earliest country day schools in the United States. Graduates of the traditional, thorough curriculum enter leading colleges in Ohio and throughout the country. In September 1968, the school moved to a new 230-acre, suburban campus. Originally enrolling boys only, the academy instituted coeducation in 1990.

The academy offers a broad educational program that incorporates a variety of electives in the upper grades, including course work in both the performing and the visual arts. Although courses are not designated as Advanced Placement, honors and advanced options prepare students for AP exams in most subjects. The school's East Asia Institute comprises six years of Chinese language study, courses in literature and history, visiting speakers and exchange programs for students and faculty. Juniors meet a public speaking requirement, and seniors complete an independent project, usually off-campus. Upper schoolers perform 50 hours of community service prior to graduation.

COLUMBUS SCHOOL FOR GIRLS
Day — Girls Gr PS (Age 3)-12

Columbus, OH 43209. 56 S Columbia Ave. Tel: 614-252-0781. Fax: 614-252-0571.
www.columbusschoolforgirls.org
E-mail: admissions2@columbusschoolforgirls.org
Elizabeth Lee, Head (2009). BA, Mount Holyoke College, MA, Columbia Univ. **Jenni Reeb Biehn, Adm.**

   Col Prep. AP (exams req'd; 233 taken, 75% 3+)—Eng Fr Ger Lat Span Calc Comp_Sci Bio Chem Physics Eur_Hist Comp_Govt & Pol Psych US_Govt & Pol Studio_Art Music_Theory. **Elem math**—Everyday Math/Singapore Math. **Feat**—British_Lit Chin Astron Environ_Sci Asian_Hist Civics Intl_Relations Philos World_Relig Art_Hist Ceramics Photog Sculpt Acting Theater Music Public_Speak. **Supp**—Dev_Read. **Dual enr:** OH St.

   Sports—G: Basket X-country F_Hockey Golf Lacrosse Soccer Swim Tennis Track Volley. **Activities:** 20.

   Selective adm: 86/yr. Appl fee: $50. Appl due: Feb. Applied: 160. Accepted: 79%. Yield: 68%. **Tests** CTP_4 ISEE TOEFL.

   Enr 609. Elem 400. Sec 209. Wh 75%. Latino 1%. Blk 7%. Asian 7%. Other 10%. Stud/fac: 9:1. Uniform. **Fac 77.** M 14/F 63. FT 73/PT 4. Wh 91%. Latino 3%. Blk 1%. Asian 5%. Adv deg: 74%.

   Grad '11—63. Col—63. (OH St 12, Miami U-OH 5, Col of Wooster 3, U of KY 3, NYU 2, U of Richmond 2). **Avg SAT:** CR 618. M 618. W 630. **Mid 50% SAT:** CR 560-670. M 560-680. W 570-690. Avg ACT: 27. Mid 50% ACT: 24-30. **Col couns:** 2.

   Tui '12-'13: Day $17,850-20,500. Aid: Need 122 ($1,111,500).

   Summer (enr 475): Acad Enrich Rev Rec. Tui Day $825/3-wk ses. 6 wks.

   Endow $22,496,000. Plant val $21,000,000. Acres 80. Bldgs 8 (80% ADA). Class rms 64. 2 Libs 39,700 vols. Sci labs 4. Theaters 1. Art studios 3. Music studios 3. Gyms 2. Athletic ctrs 1. Fields 5. Tennis courts 8. Pools 1. Comp labs 5. Comp/stud: 1:1.2 (1:1 Laptop prgm Gr 9-12).

   Est 1898. Nonprofit. Sem (Sept-June). **Assoc** CLS NCA.

Founded to offer girls a college preparatory education, CSG sends its graduates to leading colleges throughout the country. A strong academic program is complemented by an active school life that includes student government, team sports, journalism, fine arts, theater, music and compulsory community service.

The college preparatory curriculum features Advanced Placement courses, a modern and classical language program, and a one-to-one tablet computer program in grades 9-12. A month-long off-campus experience for seniors takes place each May. Upper school students perform 60 cumulative hours of community service prior to graduation.

WELLINGTON SCHOOL
Day — Coed Gr PS (Age 4)-12

Columbus, OH 43220. 3650 Reed Rd. Tel: 614-457-7883, 877-517-7883.
Fax: 614-442-3286.
www.wellington.org   E-mail: admissions@wellington.org
Robert D. Brisk, Head (2007). AB, Princeton Univ, MEd, Harvard Univ. **Maryline Kulewicz, Adm.**

   Col Prep. AP (exams req'd)—Eng Fr Lat Span Calc Bio Chem Eur_Hist US_Hist Studio_Art Music_Theory. **Feat**—Creative_Writing Shakespeare Lat-Amer_Lit Mythology Stats Astron Forensic_Sci Comp_Sci Econ Govt Comp_Relig Ethics Ceramics Drawing Film Photog Theater Journ Speech. **Supp**—ESL.

   Sports—Basket Golf Lacrosse Soccer Swim Tennis. B: Baseball. G: Softball.

   Selective adm: 97/yr. Appl fee: $50. Appl due: Rolling. **Tests** CTP_4.

   Enr 577. B 312. G 265. Elem 385. Sec 192. Wh 73%. Latino 3%. Blk 13%. Asian 11%. Stud/fac: 8:1. Uniform. **Fac 89.** M 25/F 64. FT 72/PT 17. Adv deg: 44%.

   Grad '11—49. Col—49. (OH St, Elon, Miami U-OH, Regis U, OH Wesleyan, George-

town). Athl schol 8. **Mid 50% SAT:** CR 540-690. M 530-650. W 510-670. Alum donors: 10%.
Tui '12-'13: Day $14,800-20,100 (+$650-925). **Aid:** Need 134.
Summer (enr 558): Acad Enrich Rev Rec. Tui Day $130-235/wk. 10 wks.
Plant val $12,000,000. Acres 21. Bldgs 2. Class rms 51. Lib 23,000 vols. Sci labs 4.
Lang labs 1. Dark rms 1. Theaters 1. Art studios 3. Music studios 4. Gyms 2. Fields 1.
Tennis courts 5. Weight rms 1. Greenhouses 1. Comp labs 3. Laptop prgm Gr 7-12.
Est 1982. Nonprofit. Tri (Aug-June). **Assoc** CLS NCA.

Originally serving grades K-6, Wellington began expanding in 1984 with the construction of an upper school building and the inclusion of an additional grade each year. The school graduated its first senior class in 1989.

The lower school program (pre-K-5) focuses on the core disciplines of math, social studies and language arts. Specialist teachers provide foreign language, music, physical education, science, art and technology instruction from the youngest age. During the middle school years (grades 6-8), boys and girls pursue content knowledge through individual and small-group work, creative projects, off-campus experiences and short lectures. Many students choose to participate in athletics, arts activities and service learning.

In a small-class setting, upper schoolers (grades 9-12) follow a college preparatory curriculum that typically includes interdisciplinary, honors and Advanced Placement course work. Faculty members continually assess student work through tests, computer-generated presentations, group projects, performances and written work.

Wellington maintains a varied arts curriculum. Children first gain an exposure to the fine arts, music and theater in prekindergarten. A formal art gallery provides a forum for artwork by pupils of all ages. The theater program ranges in scope from original pieces to large-scale musicals.

DAYTON, OH. (47 mi. NNE of Cincinnati, OH; 177 mi. SW of Cleveland, OH) Urban. Pop: 166,179. Alt: 740 ft.

MIAMI VALLEY SCHOOL
Day — Coed Gr PS (Age 3)-12

Dayton, OH 45429. 5151 Denise Dr. Tel: 937-434-4444. Fax: 937-434-1033.
www.mvschool.com   E-mail: admission@mvschool.com
Peter B. Benedict II, Head (2006). BA, Colorado State Univ, MA, Vanderbilt Univ. **C. S. Adams III, Adm.**

Col Prep. AP (132 exams taken, 78% 3+)—Calc Stats Comp_Sci Bio Chem Environ_ Sci Eur_Hist US_Hist Econ US_Govt & Pol. **Feat**—Native_Amer_Lit Southern_Lit Chin Fr Lat Span Astron Ecol Forensic_Sci Physiol Engineering Middle_Eastern_Hist Anthro Psych Ethics World_Relig Art_Hist Ceramics Drawing Film Sculpt Chorus Music_Theory Bus Communications Journ Speech Nutrition. **Supp**—LD. **Dual enr:** U of Dayton, Wright St, Sinclair CC.
Sports—Basket X-country Lacrosse Soccer Swim Tennis Track. B: Golf. G: Cheer Softball Volley. **Activities:** 40.
Selective adm: 77/yr. Appl fee: $70. Appl due: Rolling. Accepted: 66%. Yield: 76%. **Tests** IQ SSAT Stanford TOEFL.
Enr 449. Elem 260. Sec 189. Intl 5%. Avg class size: 16. Stud/fac: 9:1. **Fac 54.** M 12/F 42. FT 49/PT 5. Adv deg: 68%.
Grad '11—49. Col—49. (OH St, U of Richmond, Case Western Reserve, Denison, Miami U-OH, U of Dayton). **Mid 50% SAT:** CR 500-600. M 520-640. W 490-580. Mid 50% ACT: 22-28. **Col couns:** 3. Alum donors: 18%.
Tui '11-'12: Day $10,050-17,900 (+$150-5000). **Aid:** Need 162 ($1,500,000).
Summer: Enrich Rev Rec. 1-6 wks.
Endow $1,500,000. Plant val $10,000,000. Acres 22. Bldgs 4. Class rms 45. 2 Libs

12,000 vols. Labs 6. Art studios 2. Music studios 4. Black-box theaters 1. Gyms 2. Fields 4. Tennis courts 6. Comp/stud: 1:2.3.
Est 1956. Nonprofit. Tri (Aug-June).

Dayton's only independent college preparatory school, Miami Valley strikes a careful balance among academic fundamentals, creative activities and extracurricular opportunities. The elementary program emphasizes the measurement of educational needs through individualized and group instruction in self-contained classrooms. Specific contacts in the community enable older pupils to enroll in college-level courses or take part in internships relating to business, government, industry or the arts.

Independent study is available to eligible juniors and seniors, and March is reserved for in-depth seminars on selected subjects for those in grades 10-12. During the same time period, freshmen participate in a month of special academic and nonacademic pursuits. Boys and girls accumulate 75 hours of required community service in grades 9-12. Opportunities in sports, publications and the arts round out the upper school program.

Local companies, foundations and parents support the school's scholarship program. Miami Valley has occupied a 22-acre site in Washington Township since 1966.

GATES MILLS, OH. (14 mi. ENE of Cleveland, OH) Suburban. Pop: 2299. Alt: 750 ft.

GILMOUR ACADEMY
Bdg — Coed Gr 7-12; Day — Coed PS (Age 3)-12

Gates Mills, OH 44040. 34001 Cedar Rd. Tel: 440-442-1104. Fax: 440-473-8010.
www.gilmour.org E-mail: admissions@gilmour.org
Br. Robert E. Lavelle, CSC, Head. BS, St Edward's Univ, MEd, Kent State Univ. **Steve Scheidt, Upper & Middle Sch Adm; Megan Schlickmann, Lower Sch Adm.**
  Col Prep. Montessori. AP (exams req'd; 239 taken, 60% 3+)—Eng Fr Span Calc Stats Bio Chem Eur_Hist US_Hist. **Feat**—Creative_Writing Chin Lat Arabic Anat & Physiol Environ_Sci Forensic_Sci Oceanog Milit_Hist Econ Govt Constitutional_Law World_Relig Photog Studio_Art Acting Theater_Arts Music Music_Composition Journ Speech Design. **Supp**—Rev Tut. **Dual enr:** Kenyon.
  Sports—Basket X-country Lacrosse Soccer Swim Tennis Track. B: Baseball Football Golf Ice_Hockey. G: Cheer Softball Volley. **Activities:** 30.
  Selective adm: 158/yr. Bdg 28. Day 130. Usual entry: PS, 7 & 9. Appl fee: $35. Appl due: Jan. Applied: 350. Accepted: 80%. Yield: 50%. **Tests** CEEB ISEE SSAT TOEFL.
  Enr 695. Bdg 60. Day 635. Elem 271. Sec 422. PG 2. Intl 5%. Avg class size: 15. Stud/fac: 10:1. Uniform. **Fac 74.** Adv deg: 79%. In dorms 2.
  Grad '11—116. Col—112. (Notre Dame, Vanderbilt, Case Western Reserve, U of Dayton, Denison, Brown). Athl schol 5. **Avg SAT:** CR 566. M 574. W 564. Avg ACT: 26. **Col couns:** 2.
  Tui '12-'13: Bdg $38,895. Day $19,975-26,600.
  Summer: Rec. Gr PS-6. Tui Day $250-350/wk. Sports. Tui $350/wk. 6 wks.
  Endow $33,000,000. Plant val $25,000,000. Acres 144. Bldgs 22. Dorms 2. Dorm rms 55. Class rms 65. 2 Libs 25,000 vols. Chapels 1. Sci labs 7. Auds 1. Theaters 1. Art studios 3. Music studios 4. Gyms 2. Fields 7. Courts 6. Field houses 1. Pools 1. Rinks 1. Tracks 1. Weight rms 1. Stadiums 1. Driving ranges 1. Comp labs 5. Comp/stud: 1:1.5.
  Est 1946. Nonprofit. Roman Catholic (75% practice). Sem (Aug-June). **Assoc** CLS NCA.

Founded and still conducted by the Brothers of Holy Cross, this school began as a small boarding secondary school for boys. Significant growth occurred in the ensuing decades, and a 1982 merger with the Glen Oak School for girls opened Gilmour's enrollment to female students. A Montessori preschool commenced operations in 1985, and a coeducational program for children in preschool through grade 6 was in place by 1988. The academy now occupies a well-equipped, 144-acre campus.

Gilmour's curriculum, which has adapted over the years to reflect changes in business and technology, emphasizes critical-thinking, problem-solving and communicational skills. Students take seven courses per semester, each of which meets for 90 minutes every other class day. Advanced Placement offerings in the major disciplines challenge qualified pupils, and independent study allows boys and girls to pursue in-depth study in an area of particular interest.

Students accumulate at least 60 hours of required community service in grades 9-12. Another graduation requirement is successful completion of the senior project. Taking place during the final month of the school year, this project allows boys and girls to identify an area of interest, design an internship around it, and prepare and deliver a final presentation.

HAWKEN SCHOOL

Day — Coed Gr PS (Age 3)-12

Gates Mills, OH 44040. 12465 County Line Rd, PO Box 8002. Tel: 440-423-4446. Fax: 440-423-2960.
Other locations: 5000 Clubside Rd, Lyndhurst 44124; 10924 Magnolia Dr, Cleveland 44106.
www.hawken.edu   E-mail: admissions@hawken.edu
D. Scott Looney, Head (2006). BA, DePauw Univ, MA, Northwestern Univ. **Heather Willis Daly, Adm.**
   Col Prep. AP (exams req'd; 369 taken, 62% 3+)—Eng Fr Lat Span Calc Stats Bio Chem Environ_Sci Physics US_Hist Psych Studio_Art. **Feat**—Humanities Chin Ecol Physiol Engineering Archaeol African-Amer_Stud Graphic_Arts Acting Theater_Arts Music Music_Theory Accounting Bus. **Supp**—Tut. Outdoor ed.
   Sports—Basket X-country Golf Lacrosse Soccer Swim Tennis Track. B: Baseball Football. G: F_Hockey Softball Volley. **Activities: 31.**
   Selective adm: 175/yr. Appl fee: $25. Appl due: Dec. Applied: 362. Accepted: 79%. Yield: 62%. **Tests** ISEE.
   Enr 971. B 520. G 451. Elem 553. Sec 418. Wh 80%. Latino 1%. Blk 9%. Asian 6%. Other 4%. Avg class size: 15. Stud/fac: 14:1. Casual. **Fac 118.** M 44/F 74. FT 99/PT 19. Wh 94%. Latino 2%. Blk 2%. Asian 2%. Adv deg: 72%.
   Grad '11—94. Col—94. (Case Western Reserve 4, OH St 4, Miami U-OH 4, Wash U 4, U of Chicago 3, MIT 2). **Avg SAT:** CR 634. M 650. W 642. Avg ACT: 28. **Col couns:** 2. Alum donors: 25%.
   Tui '12-'13: Day $17,056-28,276. Aid: Merit ($162,000). Need ($5,000,000).
   Summer: Acad Enrich Rev Rec. Tui Day $353-1311. 3-6 wks.
   Endow $46,030,000. Plant val $50,685,000. Acres 346. Bldgs 25 (80% ADA). Class rms 101. 2 Libs 21,000 vols. Sci labs 8. Auds 2. Theaters 1. Art studios 4. Music studios 6. Dance studios 1. Gyms 5. Athletic ctrs 1. Fields 19. Courts 11. Pools 2. Comp labs 4. Comp/stud: 1:3 (1:1 Laptop prgm Gr 6-8).
   Est 1915. Nonprofit. Sem (Aug-June). **Assoc** CLS.

Established by James A. Hawken and a group of local parents, this school was founded as a boys' program serving children from Greater Cleveland in grades K-8. The school operated in Lyndhurst as an elementary school until 1961, when it added a second campus in Gates Mills to house an upper school. The school instituted coeducation in 1973 and opened its preschool in 1993. In 2009, Hawken opened a satellite campus in Cleveland's University Circle neighborhood.

The college preparatory program includes honors and Advanced Placement courses, and the school features a variety of electives, sports and extracurricular activities. Hawken offers upper school students more than 125 courses and considerable opportunities in the fine and performing arts, and computer literacy is emphasized at all grade levels. Pupils in grades 9-12 complete required community service projects. The athletic program features extensive interscholastic competition, as well as an intramural component that begins in the lower school.

Hawken's outdoor leadership program teaches wilderness survival skills to upper schoolers while utilizing the substantial woodland on its 325-acre Gates Mills campus. Students may participate in the School Year Abroad program; recent participants have studied in Spain, France and Israel. The Pathways Program enables upper schoolers to take part in internships with area professionals.

The school maintains a well-funded financial aid program that permits enrollment of academically qualified students from various backgrounds.

HUDSON, OH. (20 mi. SE of Cleveland, OH) Suburban. Pop: 22,439. Alt: 1055 ft.

WESTERN RESERVE ACADEMY
Bdg and Day — Coed Gr 9-PG

Hudson, OH 44236. 115 College St. Tel: 330-650-9717. Fax: 330-650-5858.
www.wra.net   E-mail: admission@wra.net
Christopher Burner, Head (2008). BA, Franklin and Marshall College, MALS, Dartmouth College, MEd, Harvard Univ. **Anne Sheppard, Adm.**

Col Prep. AP (exams req'd; 286 taken, 89% 3+)—Eng Fr Ger Lat Span Calc Stats Comp_Sci Bio Chem Physics Eur_Hist US_Hist Econ Art_Hist Music_Theory. **Feat**—Creative_Writing Chin Multivariable_Calc Astron Botany Environ_Sci Zoology Biotech Constitutional_Law Architect Photog Studio_Art Drama Music Music_Hist Dance Woodworking. **Supp**—Tut. Sat classes.

Sports—Basket X-country Lacrosse Soccer Swim Tennis Track. B: Baseball Football Golf Ice_Hockey Wrestling. G: F_Hockey Softball Volley. **Activities:** 53.

Selective adm: 93/yr. Bdg 50. Day 43. Appl fee: $50. Appl due: Rolling. Accepted: 55%. **Tests** CEEB ISEE SSAT TOEFL.

Enr 390. B 202. G 188. Bdg 249. Day 141. Intl 15%. Avg class size: 12. Stud/fac: 6:1. Uniform. **Fac 59.** Adv deg: 81%.

Grad '11—87. Col—87. (Denison 5, Wake Forest 5, NYU 3, Case Western Reserve 3, Boston Col 3, High Pt 3). **Col couns:** 3.

Tui '11-'12: Bdg $43,000 (+$500). **Day $30,500** (+$500). **Aid:** Need 133 ($3,600,000). Endow $97,700,000. Plant val $30,000,000. Acres 190. Bldgs 49. Dorms 9. Dorm rms 128. Class rms 49. Lib 45,000 vols. Sci labs 11. Lang labs 1. Observatories 1. Auds 1. Theaters 1. Art studios 2. Music studios 5. Dance studios 2. Gyms 3. Athletic ctrs 1. Fields 12. Basketball courts 2. Tennis courts 13. Field houses 1. Pools 1. Tracks 2. Stadiums 1. Comp labs 5. Comp/stud: 1:1.2.

Est 1826. Nonprofit. Quar (Sept-May). **Assoc** CLS NCA.

Established as the preparatory school of Western Reserve College, the academy took over the plant when the college moved to Cleveland in 1882. The affiliation between the two institutions continued until 1903, when the academy closed for lack of funds. Endowed in 1910 by James W. Ellsworth and reopened in 1916, the school came to more vigorous life in 1926 when it was reorganized on the Ellsworth Foundation with a trust fund of four million dollars.

Reserve has traditionally placed its major emphasis on college preparation. The academy offers a number of Advanced Placement courses, and its drama and music programs send some students on to advanced professional study. Courses for college credit at Kenyon College, independent study options and a variety of exchange programs are also available.

NORTH RIDGEVILLE, OH. (19 mi. WSW of Cleveland, OH) Suburban. Pop: 22,338. Alt: 700 ft.

LAKE RIDGE ACADEMY
Day — Coed Gr K-12

North Ridgeville, OH 44039. 37501 Center Ridge Rd. Tel: 440-327-1175. Fax: 440-327-3641.

www.lakeridgeacademy.org   E-mail: admission@lakeridgeacademy.org

Carol L. Klimas, Pres (2007). BA, Alvernia College. Sarah Moore, Gr 7-12 Adm; Edie Sweeterman, Gr K-6 Adm.

Col Prep. AP (exams req'd; 101 taken, 81% 3+)—Eng Fr Span Calc Stats Bio Chem Physics Eur_Hist US_Hist World_Hist Studio_Art. **Feat**—Creative_Writing Shakespeare World_Lit Ital Lat Astron Environ_Sci Forensic_Sci Comp_Sci Photog Video_Production Theater Musical_Theater Music. **Supp**—ESL Tut. **Dual enr:** Oberlin.

Sports—Basket Soccer Tennis Track. B: Baseball Golf. G: Softball Volley. **Activities:** 17.

Selective adm (Gr K-11): 86/yr. Usual entry: K, 6 & 9. Appl due: Rolling. Applied: 172. Accepted: 72%. Yield: 69%. **Tests** IQ ISEE Stanford TOEFL.

Enr 359. B 161. G 198. Elem 207. Sec 152. Wh 61%. Latino 5%. Blk 7%. Asian 12%. Other 15%. Intl 7%. Avg class size: 15. Stud/fac: 8:1. **Fac 50.** M 18/F 32. FT 43/PT 7. Wh 90%. Latino 4%. Blk 2%. Other 4%. Adv deg: 54%.

Grad '11—39. Col—39. (Purdue 3, DePaul 3, Rochester Inst of Tech 2, Northwestern 2, Yale 1, Brown 1). Athl schol 1. **Avg SAT:** CR 600. M 630. W 580. Avg ACT: 26. **Col couns:** 1. Alum donors: 10%.

Tui '11-'12: Day $15,750-24,250 (+$1500-2250). **Aid:** Merit 54 ($560,845). Need 148 ($1,799,934).

Summer (enr 150): Acad Enrich Rev Rec. Arts. Tui Day $150-560. 1-2 wks. Sports. Tui Day $100-300. 1-2 wks.

Endow $1,177,000. Plant val $17,270,000. Acres 88. Bldgs 12 (100% ADA). Class rms 55. 2 Libs 35,000 vols. Sci labs 7. Lang labs 6. Auds 1. Theaters 2. Art studios 4. Music studios 3. Gyms 1. Athletic ctrs 1. Fields 6. Courts 7. Barns 1. Comp labs 3. Comp/stud: 1:2.5.

Est 1963. Nonprofit. Sem (Aug-June).

LRA occupies an 88-acre campus on the eastern edge of Lorain County. The school draws students from about 45 communities in the Cleveland area, as well as international students from a number of foreign countries.

Lake Ridge's social and academic curricula emphasize college preparation. Art, music, foreign language, technology, and physical and outdoor education are incorporated into the lower school curriculum. Major emphasis is placed on literacy and math skills in the lower grades, and French and Spanish classes begin in kindergarten. The middle school's inquiry-based curriculum allows students to accelerate according to their individual needs.

The upper school curriculum consists of course work in the five basic disciplines, as well as technology. Students may enhance their studies with college-level courses (offered in cooperation with Oberlin College), Advanced Placement and independent study options. A two-year honors entrepreneurship program accommodates up to 40 upper school students each year and offers an extensive exploration of the principles of entrepreneurship.

Upper school students participate in various programs that allow them to pursue interests beyond the classroom through internships, community service, student exchanges, and two-week travel and study trips.

SHAKER HEIGHTS, OH. (7 mi. E of Cleveland, OH) Suburban. Pop: 29,405. Alt: 978 ft. Area also includes Chagrin Falls.

HATHAWAY BROWN SCHOOL
Day — Boys Gr PS (Age 2)-PS (Age 4), Girls PS (Age 2)-12

Shaker Heights, OH 44122. 19600 N Park Blvd. Tel: 216-932-4214. Fax: 216-371-1501. www.hb.edu   E-mail: admissions@hb.edu

H. William Christ, Head (1987). BA, Washington and Lee Univ, MA, Univ of Pennsylvania. Sarah Johnston, Adm.

Col Prep. AP—Eng Fr Lat Span Calc Stats Comp_Sci Bio Chem Physics US_Hist World_Hist Studio_Art. Feat—Chin Anat & Physiol Vietnam_War Amer_Stud Intl_ Relations Pol_Sci Relig Art_Hist Ceramics Graphic_Arts Photog Acting Theater Musical_Theater Chorus Music_Theory Orchestra Dance Journ. Supp—Tut.

Sports—G: Basket X-country F_Hockey Golf Indoor_Track Lacrosse Soccer Softball Swim Tennis Track Volley. Activities: 24.

Selective adm: 138/yr. Appl fee: $35-50. Accepted: 59%. Tests ISEE.

Enr 861. B 35. G 826. Avg class size: 15. Stud/fac: 8:1. Fac 114. M 15/F 99. FT 104/PT 10. Adv deg: 62%.

Grad '08—77. Col—77. (Syracuse 4, U of CO-Boulder 3, Brown 2, Georgetown 2, Williams 2, Boston Col 2). Avg SAT: CR 633. M 631. W 653. Col couns: 3.

Tui '12-'13: Day $17,310-24,270 (+$1700). Aid: Need 241 ($3,200,000).

Summer: Acad Enrich Rev Rec. 5 wks.

Endow $29,000,000. Plant val $46,000,000. Acres 16. Bldgs 3. Class rms 60. 3 Libs 14,000 vols. Sci labs 10. Lang labs 1. Theaters 2. Art studios 3. Music studios 2. Dance studios 2. Gyms 2. Fields 3. Tennis courts 6. Pools 1.

Est 1876. Nonprofit. Sem (Sept-June). Assoc CLS NCA.

Hathaway Brown traces its origins to the establishment of an afternoon program for girls at Brook School, a church school for boys. In 1886, Anne Hathaway Brown purchased the school and changed its name from Home and Day School to Miss Anne H. Hathaway Brown's School for Girls. HB has occupied its current, 16-acre campus in Shaker Heights since 1927.

Hathaway Brown's coeducational preschool consists of an early childhood program serving children ages 2½-5; grades K-12 admit girls only. Qualified students may participate in individual projects beyond the basic curriculum. The adventure learning program, which features a ropes course, is a required element of the middle school curriculum. The traditional college preparatory upper school program is supplemented by honors and Advanced Placement classes in most disciplines, as well as by fellowships in creativity. Special offerings include art, drama, music, photography, computer studies and Broad Horizons summer enrichment for academically and creatively gifted girls.

Students enrolled in the school's Science Research and Engineering Program conduct advanced research projects under the supervision of professionals from local universities, hospitals, museums and research centers.

LAUREL SCHOOL
Day — Boys Gr PS (Age 3)-PS (Age 4), Girls PS (Age 3)-12

Shaker Heights, OH 44122. 1 Lyman Cir. Tel: 216-464-1441. Fax: 216-464-8996. Other locations: 7420 Fairmount Rd, Russell 44072.
www.laurelschool.org   E-mail: admission@laurelschool.org

Ann V. Klotz, Head (2004). BA, Yale Univ, MA, New York Univ. Mary Lisa Geppert, Adm.

Col Prep. AP (142 exams taken, 65% 3+)—Eng Chin Fr Lat Span Calc Bio Chem Physics US_Hist US_Govt & Pol Art_Hist Studio_Art Music_Theory. Feat—Creative_Writing Stats Anat & Physiol Astron Environ_Sci Biotech Engineering Comp_Sci Philos Photog Acting Chorus Orchestra Dance Speech. Supp—Dev_Read Rem_Math Rem_Read Rev Tut. Dual enr: Kenyon.

Sports—G: Basket X-country F_Hockey Golf Lacrosse Soccer Softball Swim Tennis Track Volley.

Selective adm: 132/yr. Appl fee: $25. Appl due: Mar. Accepted: 70%. **Tests** ISEE.

Enr 673. B 33. G 640. Elem 405. Sec 268. Avg class size: 14. Stud/fac: 8:1. Uniform. **Fac 106.** Adv deg: 56%.

Grad '08—54. Col—54. (OH St, Dartmouth, NYU, Northwestern, Brown, Harvard). **Avg SAT:** CR 653. M 632. W 672. Avg ACT: 27. **Col couns:** 2. Alum donors: 45%.

Tui '09-'10: Day $8000-22,500 (+$1568-1983). **Aid:** Need 202 ($1,900,000).

Endow $39,000,000. Plant val $41,000,000. Acres 152. Bldgs 2. Class rms 57. 2 Libs 15,000 vols. Sci labs 6. Lang labs 1. Theaters 1. Art studios 2. Music studios 2. Dance studios 1. Gyms 2. Fields 9. Courts 12. Comp labs 3.

Est 1896. Nonprofit. Sem (Aug-June). **Assoc** CLS NCA.

This long-established school was founded in Cleveland when Jennie Prentiss opened a private school for girls in her own home. Laurel moved in 1928 to its present location in suburban Shaker Heights, where it has undergone subsequent expansion, including the 140-acre outdoor education and athletic facility in Russell, 20 minutes east of the main campus.

Laurel accepts both boys and girls into its early childhood center, which utilizes a hands-on, experiential approach. The theme-based primary school emphasizes fundamental academic skills, while the middle school offers an integrated approach to the sciences and the humanities and commences formal foreign language instruction. The upper school curriculum (grades 9-12) allows qualified girls to take Advanced Placement classes or to enroll in college-level courses through a program coordinated with Kenyon College. The school also maintains a program with the Cleveland Institute of Music.

During the upper school years, each student performs at least 50 hours of community service. Service is part of the curriculum in the lower and middle schools as well.

UNIVERSITY SCHOOL

Day — Boys Gr K-12

Chagrin Falls, OH 44022. 2785 SOM Center Rd. Tel: 216-831-2200. Fax: 216-292-7810. Other locations: 20701 Brantley Rd, Shaker Heights 44122.

www.us.edu   E-mail: admissions@us.edu

Stephen S. Murray, Head (2005). BA, Williams College, AM, MEd, Harvard Univ. **Sean Grosz, Gr 9-12 Adm; Christopher S. Barton, Gr 5-8 Adm; Marla Taub, Gr K-4 Adm.**

Col Prep. AP (401 exams taken, 75% 3+)—Eng Calc Stats Eur_Hist US_Hist Econ Psych US_Govt & Pol. **Feat**—Shakespeare Satire Chin Fr Greek Lat Span Astron Ecol Engineering Comp_Sci Chin_Hist Japan_Hist Lat-Amer_Hist Middle_Eastern_ Hist Art_Hist Film Photog Video_Production Drama Music Music_Theory Woodworking. **Supp**—Dev_Read. **Dual enr:** Kenyon.

Sports—B: Baseball Basket X-country Football Golf Ice_Hockey Lacrosse Soccer Squash Swim Tennis Track Wrestling.

Selective adm: 134/yr. Appl fee: $0. Appl due: Rolling. Accepted: 63%. Yield: 81%. **Tests** ISEE.

Enr 863. Elem 450. Sec 413. Avg class size: 14. Stud/fac: 8:1. Uniform. **Fac 140.** Adv deg: 80%.

Grad '09—104. Col—104. (Miami U-OH, Case Western Reserve, OH St, Boston Col, Yale, OH U). **Avg SAT:** CR 622. M 636. W 609. Avg ACT: 27.6. **Col couns:** 4.

Tui '12-'13: Day $16,500-25,500 (+$680-1290). **Aid:** Need ($3,500,000).

Summer: Acad Enrich Rev Rec. 4-6 wks.

Endow $52,000,000. Plant val $53,726,000. Acres 253. Bldgs 6. Class rms 69. Lib 20,000 vols. Labs 14. Auds 1. Theaters 2. Gyms 3. Fields 11. Courts 22. Pools 2.

Est 1890. Nonprofit. Tri (Aug-June). **Assoc** CLS NCA.

From its inception, this school has conducted a country day school program that features a strong college preparatory curriculum. The Shaker Heights campus on Brantley Road has been occupied since 1926 and now enrolls children in grades K-8. US added the Hunting Valley upper school campus (grades 9-12) in 1970.

The elementary school curriculum, which evolved out of an intensive study of the developmental patterns of very young boys, develops and coordinates skills in individual and group research projects. The college preparatory upper school features Advanced Placement courses in most disciplines and a wide range of electives. Liberal arts studies offer breadth of subject and approach, and there is frequent consideration of big ideas. Advanced physics and chemistry courses are offered through Kenyon College. Fellowship programs allow talented students to pursue independent study, research and creative writing projects.

US organizes school year and summer trips to Costa Rica, France, Honduras, Italy and Spain, and conducts regular student and teacher exchanges with schools in China. The Entrepreneur Institute arranges apprenticeships and hosts guest speakers. Students of all ages regularly use the 221-acre campus for projects, field studies in science, and other outdoor activities. Upper schoolers accumulate 40 hours of required community service during their four years.

TOLEDO, OH. (55 mi. SSW of Detroit, MI) Urban. Pop: 313,619. Alt: 587 ft.

MAUMEE VALLEY COUNTRY DAY SCHOOL
Day — Coed Gr PS (Age 3)-12

Toledo, OH 43614. 1715 S Reynolds Rd. Tel: 419-381-1313. Fax: 419-381-1314.
www.mvcds.org   E-mail: vkoelsch@mvcds.net
Gary Boehm, Head (2006). BA, Univ of Colorado-Boulder, MA, Wesleyan Univ. **Vicki Koelsch, Adm.**
    Col Prep. AP (exams req'd; 103 taken, 93% 3+)—Eng Calc Stats Bio Environ_Sci US_ Hist Studio_Art Music_Theory. **Feat**—Chin Fr Span Zoology Comp_Sci E_Asian_ Hist Human_Growth & Dev Intl_Stud Film Painting Sculpt Animation Drama Music. **Supp**—Dev_Read ESL Tut. Outdoor ed. **Dual enr:** U of Toledo.
    Sports—Basket Golf Indoor_Track Tennis Track. B: Baseball Soccer. G: F_Hockey Lacrosse. **Activities:** 21.
    Selective adm: 88/yr. Usual entry: PS, 1, 7 & 9. Appl fee: $50. Appl due: Rolling. Applied: 176. Accepted: 80%. Yield: 58%. **Tests** CEEB CTP_4 IQ ISEE SSAT TOEFL.
    Enr 475. B 250. G 225. Elem 299. Sec 176. Wh 62%. Latino 5%. Blk 11%. Asian 15%. Other 7%. Intl 15%. Avg class size: 15. Stud/fac: 10:1. Casual. **Fac 62.** M 23/F 39. FT 60/PT 2. Wh 79%. Latino 3%. Blk 7%. Asian 11%. Adv deg: 70%.
    Grad '11—39. Col—39. (Case Western Reserve 3, U of MI 3, OH St 3, Miami U-OH 2, NYU 2, Johns Hopkins 2). **Avg SAT:** CR 625. M 644. W 619. Avg ACT: 29. **Col couns:** 1. Alum donors: 22%.
    Tui '12-'13: Day $13,300-17,300 (+$150). **Aid:** Need 214 ($2,000,000).
    Summer (enr 125): Acad Enrich Rec. Tui Day $100-380. 1-2 wks.
    Endow $9,000,000. Plant val $18,000,000. Acres 72. Bldgs 6 (100% ADA). Class rms 46. 2 Libs 27,000 vols. Sci labs 3. Comp ctrs 1. Auds 1. Theaters 1. Art studios 3. Music studios 2. Dance studios 1. Arts ctrs 1. Art galleries 1. Gyms 3. Fields 3. Courts 4. Riding rings 1. Tracks 1. Comp labs 2. Comp/stud: 1:1
    Est 1884. Nonprofit. Sem (Aug-June). **Assoc** CLS.

As the only nonsectarian independent day school in Toledo, Maumee Valley has deep roots in the community that it serves. Originally the Smead School for Girls, the school moved in 1934 to its present, 72-acre campus, 10 miles from downtown Toledo.

Maumee Valley's college preparatory curriculum includes a wide variety of electives and places a strong emphasis on the fine arts, foreign languages and international experiences. Qualified students are able to earn college credit for work done in English, French, history and art. Boys and girls accumulate 45 hours of required community service in grades 9-12.

Each year, students engage in three weeks of intensive study during the school's winterim program. Options include electives, internships, independent study opportunities, language and cultural travel, work in the research laboratories of the Medical University of Ohio, and school exchanges.

There are separate units for the preschool, the lower school, the middle school and the upper school, with all sharing common dining facilities. International pupils may reside with host families.

WISCONSIN

BEAVER DAM, WI. (52 mi. WNW of Milwaukee, WI) Urban. Pop: 15,169. Alt: 872 ft.

WAYLAND ACADEMY
Bdg and Day — Coed Gr 9-12

Beaver Dam, WI 53916. 101 N University Ave. Tel: 920-885-3373, 800-860-7725.
Fax: 920-887-3373.
www.wayland.org   E-mail: admissions@wayland.org
Brian L. Cheek, Pres (2011). BA, Wesleyan Univ, MBA, Oregon State Univ. Paul D. Keller III, Adm.

    Col Prep. AP (exams req'd; 127 taken, 61% 3+)—Eng Ger Lat Span Calc Stats Bio Chem Physics Eur_Hist US_Hist Econ. **Feat**—Greek Ecol Govt Visual_Arts Drama Music. **Supp**—ESL Tut.

    Sports (req'd)—Basket X-country Golf Ski Soccer Swim Tennis Track. B: Baseball Football. G: F_Hockey Ice_Hockey Softball Volley.

    Selective adm: 84/yr. Bdg 67. Day 17. Usual entry: 9 & 10. Appl fee: $50. Appl due: Rolling. Applied: 229. Accepted: 72%. Yield: 66%. **Tests** CEEB CTP_4 SSAT Stanford.

    Enr 220. B 117. G 103. Bdg 151. Day 69. Wh 67%. Latino 5%. Blk 12%. Asian 14%. Other 2%. Intl 18%. Avg class size: 13. Formal. **Fac 31.** M 19/F 12. FT 30/PT 1. Wh 100%. Adv deg: 64%. In dorms 11.

    Grad '10—66. Col—66. (U of WI-Madison 4, Lawrence U 3, Marquette 2, U of MN-Twin Cities 2, Northwestern 1, Wellesley 1). **Avg SAT:** CR 533. M 593. W 523. Avg ACT: 24.6. Alum donors: 22%.

    Tui '11-'12: Bdg $39,993 (+$600). **Day $17,388** (+$600). **Intl Bdg $47,355** (+$600). **Aid:** Merit 98 ($356,600). Need 115 ($1,682,110).

    Endow $8,000,000. Plant val $35,000,000. Acres 55. Bldgs 25 (64% ADA). Dorms 4. Dorm rms 210. Class rms 25. Lib 21,500 vols. Sci labs 5. Lang labs 1. Dark rms 2. Observatories 1. Auds 1. Theaters 1. Art studios 1. Music studios 12. Dance studios 1. Gyms 2. Fields 5. Courts 11. Pools 1. Comp labs 1.

    Est 1855. Nonprofit. Sem (Aug-May). **Assoc** CLS NCA.

Initially called Wayland University, this school was named in honor of Dr. Francis Wayland, an educational reformer and onetime president of Brown University. The academy is the oldest continuously coeducational secondary boarding school in the country.

The curriculum offers college preparatory, honors and Advanced Placement levels of course work, with requirements in English, the fine arts, foreign language, mathematics, science, and social studies and history, in addition to compulsory academic electives, health education and athletics. An educational support program provides instruction in reading and study skills, as well as a coordinated tutorial program that enrolls a limited number of students in grades 9-11 who have identified special learning needs.

Students compete in a wide range of interscholastics and, as an alternative to organized athletics, sophomores, juniors and seniors may choose to participate in a variety of extracurricular activities through the Alternate Activities Program. AAP combines nonathletic and creative pursuits, such as yearbook, art, community service and photography, with lifetime sports, including cycling, aerobics and weight training.

All students take part in an annual service day, and boys and girls are encouraged to perform additional community service; Wayland recognizes those who donate noteworthy hours of service. The school schedules weekly chapel services, and at least four weekends are set aside each school year for trips that feature enrichment activities throughout the Midwest.

BROOKFIELD, WI. (8 mi. W of Milwaukee, WI) Suburban. Pop: 38,587. Alt: 835 ft.

BROOKFIELD ACADEMY
Day — Coed Gr PS (Age 4)-12

Brookfield, WI 53045. 3460 N Brookfield Rd. Tel: 262-783-3200. Fax: 262-783-3213.
www.brookfieldacademy.org   E-mail: admissions@brookfieldacademy.org
Robert E. Solsrud, Head (1993). BS, Univ of Wisconsin-Eau Claire, MEd, EdD, Marquette
Univ. **Sharon Koenings, Adm.**
  Col Prep. **AP (266 exams taken, 90% 3+)**—Eng Fr Ger Lat Span Calc Stats Comp_Sci
    Bio Chem Physics Eur_Hist US_Hist Econ Studio_Art. **Elem math**—Singapore Math.
    Feat—Creative_Writing Asian_Hist Middle_Eastern_Hist Milit_Hist Govt Art_Hist
    Fine_Arts Drama Music Journ Public_Speak. **Supp**—Tut.
  Sports—Basket X-country Fencing Golf Ski Soccer Swim Tennis Track. B: Baseball
    Football. G: F_Hockey Volley. **Activities: 27.**
  Somewhat selective adm: 148/yr. Appl fee: $25. Appl due: Rolling. Applied: 271. **Tests**
    ISEE.
  Enr 884. B 438. G 446. Elem 590. Sec 294. Stud/fac: 9:1. Casual. **Fac 109.** M 29/F 80.
    FT 93/PT 16. Wh 97%. Latino 1%. Asian 1%. Other 1%. Adv deg: 38%.
  Grad '11—63. Col—63. (U of WI-Madison 12, U of WI-Milwaukee 4, Notre Dame 3,
    Marquette 3, Loyola U of Chicago 2, Harvard 2). Athl schol 1. **Avg SAT:** CR 599. M
    608. W 596. **Mid 50% SAT:** CR 540-650. M 550-660. W 530-640. Avg ACT: 27.4. Mid
    50% ACT: 24-31. **Col couns:** 2. Alum donors: 16%.
  Tui '12-'13: Day $14,840-15,660 (+$75-500). **Aid:** Merit 45 ($168,250). Need 80
    ($677,083).
  Summer (enr 450): Acad Enrich Rev Rec. ACT/SAT Prep. Community Service. Driver
    Ed. Tui Day $600. 1-2 wks.
  Endow $3,000,000. Plant val $48,559,000. Acres 116. Bldgs 6 (67% ADA). Class rms
    46. Libs 4. Sci labs 10. Theaters 1. Art studios 6. Music studios 4. Gyms 3. Fields 11.
    Courts 8. Comp labs 5. Comp/stud: 1:2.
  Est 1962. Nonprofit. Sem (Sept-June). **Assoc** CLS.

BA was founded in 1962 as the Academy of Basic Education. Located on 116 acres, the school combines a rigorous college preparatory curriculum with traditional values.

The lower school (grades pre-K-5) focuses on establishing and strengthening the basic skills of reading, writing and mathematics. Reading is taught through a phonics approach. Students are also exposed to music, art, languages, physical education, history, geography, computers, science and English grammar.

The middle school curriculum (grades 6-8) emphasizes reading, composition, classics, Latin, math, science, history and geography. French and Spanish are offered in grades 7 and 8. Students also have classes in music, art, information skills, speech and drama.

The upper school prepares students for a wide variety of competitive colleges. Students are required to take four years of English, four of math, three of science, three of history (including one year of economics) and four of a foreign language. Advanced Placement courses are available in the major disciplines. **See Also Page 82**

DELAFIELD, WI. (22 mi. W of Milwaukee, WI) Rural. Pop: 6472. Alt: 1242 ft.

ST. JOHN'S NORTHWESTERN MILITARY ACADEMY
Bdg — Boys Gr 7-PG; Day — Boys 7-12

Delafield, WI 53018. 1101 Genesee St. Tel: 262-646-7199, 800-752-2338.
  Fax: 262-646-7128.

www.sjnma.org　E-mail: admissions@sjnma.org
Jack H. Albert, Jr., Pres (2004). BA, Glenville State College, MEd, James Madison Univ.
Duane Rutherford, Adm.
　Col Prep. Milit. AP—Eng Calc Stats Bio Chem Physics US_Hist. **Feat**—Chin Ger Span
　　Environ_Sci Programming Web_Design Geog Psych Sociol Comp_Relig Studio_Art
　　Drama Band Chorus Journ JROTC SAT_Prep Aviation_Sci. **Supp**—ESL Tut.
　Sports—B: Baseball Basket X-country Football Golf Rugby Soccer Swim Tennis Track
　　Wrestling.
　Selective adm: 128/yr. Bdg 123. Day 5. Appl fee: $100. Appl due: Rolling. Accepted:
　　55%. **Tests** SSAT TOEFL.
　Enr 341. Bdg 330. Day 11. Elem 40. Sec 301. Wh 68%. Latino 18%. Blk 5%. Native Am
　　2%. Asian 2%. Other 5%. Intl 16%. Avg class size: 11. Stud/fac: 12:1. Uniform. **Fac
　　38.** M 30/F 8. FT 35/PT 3. Wh 94%. Latino 2%. Blk 2%. Native Am 2%. Adv deg: 50%.
　　In dorms 2.
　Grad '07—58. Col—58. (DePaul, Embry-Riddle, Marquette, Purdue, U of IL-Urbana, U
　　of WI-Madison). Avg ACT: 22. **Col couns:** 1.
　Tui '11-'12: Bdg $25,000-33,500 (+$4000). **Day $12,500** (+$2000). **Intl Bdg $26,000-
　　34,500** (+$4000). **Aid:** Merit 62 ($120,000). Need 61 ($520,711).
　Summer: Acad Rec. Adventure. ESL. Tui Bdg $1500-3875. Tui Day $950-2175. 2-5
　　wks.
　Endow $4,000,000. Plant val $23,000,000. Acres 150. Bldgs 20. Dorms 3. Dorm rms
　　197. Class rms 42. Lib 14,000 vols. Sci labs 6. Art studios 1. Music studios 1. Gyms 1.
　　Fields 7. Courts 9. Pools 1. Golf crses 1. Rifle ranges 2. Comp labs 2.
　Est 1884. Nonprofit. Episcopal. Sem (Sept-June). **Assoc** NCA.

SJNMA was formed by the 1995 merger of St. John's Military Academy, which was established in 1884, and Northwestern Military and Naval Academy, founded in 1888. A number of required courses are supplemented by electives in each discipline. The supervised two-hour study period each evening is an integral part of the academic day, and daily tutorials are available for individual help. The military program, which promotes a structured cadet lifestyle, requires JROTC leadership training each year for all high school students.

A course in aviation science is available; in addition, those students who earn a private pilot's license during junior year may take an advanced course leading to an instrument rating. Cadets attend nondenominational chapel services twice a week.

St. John's Northwestern conducts three separate postgraduate programs: the first for students interested in attending one of the country's five service academies, a second for those seeking admission to a particular university, and a third for athletes wishing to play Division I or Division II college basketball.

HARTLAND, WI. (19 mi. W of Milwaukee, WI) Suburban. Pop: 7905. Alt: 930 ft.

UNIVERSITY LAKE SCHOOL

Day — Coed Gr PS (Age 3)-12

Hartland, WI 53029. 4024 Nagawicka Rd. Tel: 262-367-6011. Fax: 262-367-3146.
　www.universitylake.org　E-mail: deb.smith@universitylake.org
Paul B. Atkinson, Head (2010). MSW, MAT, EdD. **Debra H. Smith, Adm.**
　Col Prep. AP—Eng Span Calc Chem US_Hist World_Hist Studio_Art. **Feat**—Comp_Sci
　　Drama Music. **Supp**—Dev_Read Rem_Math Rem_Read Rev Tut.
　Sports (req'd)—Basket X-country Golf Ski Tennis Track. B: Soccer. G: F_Hockey
　　Volley.
　Somewhat selective adm: 65/yr. Appl fee: $25. Appl due: Rolling. Accepted: 99%. Yield:
　　98%.
　Enr 280. B 140. G 140. Wh 93%. Latino 1%. Blk 1%. Asian 1%. Other 4%. Avg class size:
　　12. Stud/fac: 9:1. Casual. **Fac 39.** M 10/F 29. FT 39. Wh 100%. Adv deg: 64%.
　Grad '11—24. Col—24. (U of WI-Madison 2, Coe 2, U of Denver 2, U of WI-Milwaukee

1, Vanderbilt 1, DePauw 1). **Avg SAT:** CR 566. M 541. Avg ACT: 27. **Col couns:** 1.
Tui '12-'13: Day $14,275-16,875 (+$1000). **Aid:** Merit 19 ($36,000). Need 41 ($229,963).
Summer: Acad Enrich Rev Rem Rec. 1-6 wks.
Endow $12,060,000. Plant val $9,080,000. Acres 180. Bldgs 5. Class rms 30. 3 Libs 14,000 vols. Labs 3. Auds 1. Theaters 1. Art studios 2. Music studios 2. Gyms 3. Fields 5. Courts 3. Laptop prgm Gr 7-12.
Est 1956. Nonprofit. Sem (Sept-June). **Assoc** CLS.

ULS maintains a strong college preparatory program. The 180-acre, wooded campus, located in the lake country of northwestern Waukesha County, provides a rural setting.

The lower school emphasizes academics (reading, math, writing, history, science and Spanish) the arts—with offerings provided in music and movement—and athletics. This program continues in the middle school with the addition of dramatics, team sports and student government. Computer science is available in all grades, and the upper school curriculum includes Advanced Placement or honors courses in most subject areas. Boys and girls in grades 6-12 lease laptop computers for school use, the cost of which is incorporated into tuition.

MILWAUKEE, WI. Urban. Pop: 596,974. Alt: 750 ft.

UNIVERSITY SCHOOL OF MILWAUKEE

Day — Coed Gr PS (Age 3)-12

Milwaukee, WI 53217. 2100 W Fairy Chasm Rd. Tel: 414-352-6000. Fax: 414-352-8076.
www.usmk12.org   E-mail: admissions@usmk12.org
Laura J. Fuller, Head (2011). BS, MS, Univ of Wisconsin-Madison. **Kathleen Friedman, Adm.**

Col Prep. AP (326 exams taken, 93% 3+)—Eng Fr Span Calc Stats Comp_Sci Bio Chem Environ_Sci Physics Eur_Hist US_Hist Studio_Art. **Elem math**—Everyday Math. **Feat**—Creative_Writing Lat-Amer_Lit Chin Lat Multivariable_Calc Anat & Physiol Oceanog Robotics Econ Pol_Sci Psych World_Relig Art_Hist Drawing Film Painting Photog Sculpt Acting Theater_Arts Music Public_Speak. **Supp**—Tut.

Sports—Basket X-country Ice_Hockey Ski Soccer Swim Tennis Track. B: Baseball Football Golf Lacrosse. G: F_Hockey Volley. **Activities:** 50.

Selective adm: 171/yr. Appl fee: $50. Appl due: Rolling. Applied: 260. Accepted: 83%. Yield: 79%. **Tests** CTP_4 Stanford.

Enr 1058. B 535. G 523. Elem 701. Sec 357. Wh 79%. Latino 2%. Blk 7%. Asian 2%. Other 10%. Avg class size: 15. Stud/fac: 9:1. Formal. **Fac 102.** M 36/F 66. FT 90/PT 12. Wh 97%. Blk 2%. Asian 1%. Adv deg: 69%.

Grad '10—89. Col—89. (U of WI-Madison 9, Miami U-OH 5, SMU 4, Wash U 3, Wake Forest 3, U of Richmond 3). **Avg SAT:** CR 700. M 700. W 730. Avg ACT: 29. **Col couns:** 2. Alum donors: 17%.

Tui '12-'13: Day $15,342-21,999 (+$100-1000). **Aid:** Need 221 ($1,902,020).

Summer (enr 1300): Acad Enrich Rev Rec. Art. Sports. 1-10 wks.

Endow $42,000,000. Plant val $52,000,000. Acres 131. Bldgs 3 (100% ADA). Class rms 79. 3 Libs 45,814 vols. Sci labs 11. Theaters 1. Art studios 5. Music studios 5. Dance studios 1. Gyms 4. Fields 7. Courts 8. Rinks 1. Comp labs 5. Comp/stud: 1:2.

Est 1851. Nonprofit. Sem (Aug-June). **Assoc** CLS.

USM resulted from a 1964 merger of Milwaukee Country Day School, Milwaukee Downer Seminary and Milwaukee University School. The school occupies a 131-acre campus in suburban River Hills.

The lower school program (grades pre-K-4) integrates the core subjects—language arts, mathematics, social studies, science and world language—with the visual arts, music, dance, technology and daily physical education. Writing across the curriculum, the development of study skills, and the continuation of language and technology offerings are features of the middle school curriculum (grades 5-8). Academics in the upper school (grades 9-12) focus upon college preparation, and students at this level may enroll in Advanced Placement courses in all major disciplines.

Travel abroad programs are available both during the school year and over the summer.

RACINE, WI. (25 mi. SSE of Milwaukee, WI) Urban. Pop: 81,855. Alt: 626 ft.

THE PRAIRIE SCHOOL
Day — Coed Gr PS (Age 3)-12

Racine, WI 53402. 4050 Lighthouse Dr. Tel: 262-260-3845. Fax: 262-260-3790.
www.prairieschool.com   E-mail: msweetman@prairieschool.com
William Mark H. Murphy, Pres (1993). BA, Norwich Univ, MA, State Univ of New York-Buffalo. **Molly Lofquist Johnson, Adm.**

Col Prep. AP (97 exams taken, 90% 3+)—Eng Fr Span Calc Stats Bio Chem Environ_ Sci Eur_Hist US_Hist Music_Theory. **Feat**—Chin Anat & Physiol Astron Intl_Relations Comp_Relig Graphic_Arts Studio_Art Glass_Blowing Public_Speak. **Supp**— Dev_Read ESL Makeup Rem_Math Rem_Read Rev Tut.

Sports—Basket X-country Golf Soccer Tennis Track. B: Baseball. G: Volley.

Somewhat selective adm: 93/yr. Usual entry: K, 6 & 9. Appl fee: $50. Appl due: Rolling. Applied: 162. Accepted: 85%. Yield: 73%.

Enr 694. B 352. G 342. Elem 428. Sec 266. Wh 77%. Latino 3%. Blk 2%. Asian 7%. Other 11%. Intl 7%. Avg class size: 20. Stud/fac: 17:1. Formal. **Fac 76.** M 26/F 50. FT 68/PT 8. Wh 92%. Latino 3%. Blk 3%. Asian 1%. Other 1%. Adv deg: 60%.

Grad '11—72. Col—72. (U of WI-Madison 7, Marquette 5, U of Tampa 4, U of MN-Twin Cities 3, U of WI-Milwaukee 3). **Avg SAT:** CR 591. M 598. W 594. Avg ACT: 27.1. Mid 50% ACT: 24-30. **Col couns:** 2. Alum donors: 8%.

Tui '12-'13: Day $12,515-14,515 (+$300-1000). **Aid:** Merit 15 ($105,000). Need 280 ($1,500,000).

Summer: Acad Enrich Rev Rec. Sports. 11 wks.

Endow $35,000,000. Plant val $45,000,000. Acres 33. Bldgs 2. Class rms 35. Lib 25,000 vols. Sci labs 5. Photog labs 1. Theaters 1. Art studios 3. Dance studios 1. Perf arts ctrs 1. Gyms 3. Athletic ctrs 1. Courts 8. Field houses 1. Comp labs 2. Comp/stud: 1:1.4.

Est 1965. Nonprofit. Tri (Aug-June). **Assoc** CLS.

Prairie was established by area mothers Imogene Johnson and Willie Hilpert to fill a need for an independent college preparatory school in southeastern Wisconsin. Its name derives from the style of its buildings, which were designed by associates of Frank Lloyd Wright.

In the primary and middle schools, academics and the fine arts are blended with opportunities for individually guided work. Leadership and team-building programs are part of the curriculum beginning in the primary grades. The upper school curriculum is accented by Advanced Placement courses and opportunities in the fine, creative and performing arts. During Prairie's two-week interim program, juniors and seniors may embark on a school-sponsored trip abroad or to the Grand Canyon (or another national park), or they may engage in a career internship with a local organization.

Upper school pupils fulfill a 25-hour community service requirement each year.

Plains States

IOWA

DAVENPORT, IA. (62 mi. ESE of Cedar Rapids, IA) Urban. Pop: 98,359. Alt: 559 ft. Area also includes Bettendorf.

RIVERMONT COLLEGIATE
Day — Coed Gr PS (Age 3)-12

Bettendorf, IA 52722. 1821 Sunset Dr. Tel: 563-359-1366. Fax: 563-359-7576.
www.rvmt.org   E-mail: admission@rvmt.org
Rachel Chamberlain, Adm.
  Col Prep. AP (26 exams taken, 81% 3+)—Eng Fr Span Calc Stats Bio Econ Psych.
  Elem math—Everyday Math. **Elem read**—Open Court. **Feat**—Humanities Chin Lat
  Computers Comp_Design Middle_Eastern_Hist Studio_Art Drama Band Chorus.
  Supp—Tut. **Dual enr:** Augustana, St Ambrose, Scott CC.
  Sports—Basket X-country Track. G: Cheer Volley. **Activities:** 15.
  Somewhat selective adm (Gr PS-11): 50/yr. Usual entry: PS, 6 & 9. Appl fee: $50. Appl
    due: Rolling. Applied: 65. Accepted: 85%. Yield: 85%.
  Enr 200. B 92. G 108. Elem 164. Sec 36. Wh 64%. Latino 3%. Blk 5%. Asian 24%. Other
    4%. Avg class size: 13. Stud/fac: 9:1. Casual. **Fac 31.** M 4/F 27. FT 24/PT 7. Wh 91%.
    Latino 3%. Asian 3%. Other 3%. Adv deg: 29%.
  Grad '11—11. Col—11. (Case Western Reserve 1, U of Miami 1, Pratt 1, Philadelphia
    U 1, U of IA 1, U of IL-Urbana 1). **Avg SAT:** CR 639. M 637. W 630. Avg ACT: 29. **Col
    couns:** 1. Alum donors: 6%.
  Tui '12-'13: Day $10,890-11,840 (+$500-800).
  Summer (enr 58): Acad Enrich Rev. Tui Day $110/wk. 4 wks.
  Bldgs 5 (20% ADA). Class rms 23. Libs 1. Art studios 1. Gyms 1. Fields 1. Courts 1.
    Comp labs 2. Comp/stud: 1:3.
  Est 1884. Nonprofit. Quar (Aug-June). **Assoc** NCA.

Founded as St. Katharine's School, an Episcopal boarding and day program for girls, the school dropped its boarding program, instituted coeducation and added St Mark's to its name in 1968. Five years later, SKSM moved to its present location on a bluff overlooking the Mississippi River, formerly the home of businessman Joseph Bettendorf. In 1980, the school discontinued its affiliation with the Episcopal Church, and Rivermont Collegiate assumed its current name in 2001. Students enroll from eastern Iowa and western Illinois.

The college preparatory curriculum features independent study, interdisciplinary electives and Advanced Placement courses for qualified students. Rivermont's program stresses critical-thinking skills at all grade levels. Foreign language instruction commences in kindergarten.

See Also Page 133

WEST BRANCH, IA. (27 mi. SE of Cedar Rapids, IA) Rural. Pop: 2270. Alt: 750 ft.

SCATTERGOOD FRIENDS SCHOOL
Bdg and Day — Coed Gr 9-12
West Branch, IA 52358. 1951 Delta Ave. Tel: 319-643-7600, 888-737-4636.
Fax: 319-643-7485.
www.scattergood.org   E-mail: admissions@scattergood.org
Christine Ashley, Head (2010). BA, Vassar College. **Margaret Ozemet, Adm.**
   Col Prep. Feat—Humanities Span Govt Ethics Quakerism Ceramics Drawing Painting
   Photog Studio_Art Drama Music Dance Woodworking. **Supp**—ESL.
   Sports—Basket Soccer.
   Selective adm (Gr 9-11): 22/yr. Bdg 22. Day 0. Appl fee: $65. Appl due: Apr. Applied: 32.
   Accepted: 80%. Yield: 85%. **Tests** TOEFL.
   Enr 55. Wh 65%. Latino 3%. Blk 15%. Native Am 2%. Asian 15%. Intl 32%. Avg class
   size: 12. Stud/fac: 3:1. **Fac 25.** Adv deg: 56%. In dorms 3.
   Grad '11—11. Col—9. (Earlham, OH St, U of IA, Reed, Green Mtn, IA St). **Avg SAT:** CR
   570. M 578. W 540. **Col couns:** 1.
   Tui '11-'12: Bdg $26,536 (+$300). **5-Day Bdg $24,963** (+$300). **Day $16,317** (+$300).
   Intl Bdg $28,336 (+$300). **Aid:** Need 48.
   Endow $3,500,000. Acres 140. Bldgs 15. Dorms 2. Dorm rms 26. Class rms 11. Lib
   10,000 vols. Sci labs 2. Dark rms 1. Auds 1. Theaters 1. Art studios 3. Music studios
   1. Dance studios 1. Gyms 1. Fields 2. Stables 1. Farms 1. Laptop prgm Gr 9-12.
   Est 1890. Nonprofit. Religious Society of Friends. Quar (Sept-May).

Scattergood provides a sound college preparatory curriculum with an emphasis on community living and the arts. Academics follow a block system wherein courses last for one to eight four-week blocks; each class meets for either 50 or 100 minutes. Students are evaluated on a pass-fail basis, but they may complete additional work to receive honors credit. Course work emphasizes critical-reasoning skills and effective communication in the form of reading, writing and speaking. As a graduation requirement, all students must gain acceptance to an accredited four-year college.

Scattergood's February Intersession is a weeklong program devoted to classes not found in the regular curriculum. Some of these hands-on classes are taught by staff members, others by students or their parents. Pupils may also engage in community service projects during this time.

Under the guidance of the Iowa Yearly Meeting of Friends, the school's daily activities include Quaker meeting, work crews and physical education. A diversified farm and an organic garden contribute to the comprehensive educational experience in this diverse learning community. Boys and girls in all grades fulfill a 30-hour annual service commitment.

KANSAS

SALINA, KS. (105 mi. W of Topeka, KS) Urban. Pop: 45,679. Alt: 1200 ft.

ST. JOHN'S MILITARY SCHOOL
Bdg — Boys Gr 6-12

Salina, KS 67402. PO Box 5020. Tel: 785-823-7231, 866-704-5294. Fax: 785-309-5489.
www.sjms.org   E-mail: inquiry@sjms.org
E. Andrew England, Pres (2010). D. Dale Browning, Head. Maj. Robert Forde, Adm.
  Col Prep. Gen Acad. Milit. **Feat**—Span Comp_Sci Econ Relig Architect_Drawing
    Photog Studio_Art Video_Production Drama Band Music Speech Woodworking
    JROTC Study_Skills. **Supp**—Dev_Read ESL Tut.
  Sports (req'd)—B: Baseball Basket X-country Football Golf Soccer Tennis Track Wres-
    tling.
  Somewhat selective adm: 121/yr. Appl fee: $100. Appl due: Rolling. Accepted: 97%.
  Enr 231. Wh 76%. Blk 8%. Native Am 7%. Asian 9%. Intl 10%. Avg class size: 13. Stud/
    fac: 10:1. Uniform. **Fac 27.** M 17/F 10. FT 27. Wh 90%. Latino 10%. Adv deg: 59%.
    In dorms 2.
  Grad '11—34. **Col**—27. (U of VT, PA St, TX St-San Marcos, U of CT, OK St, CO St). **Avg
    SAT:** CR/M 950. Avg ACT: 22.
  Tui '12-'13: Bdg $32,650. Intl Bdg $38,200. Aid: Need ($150,000).
  Summer (enr 75): Enrich Rec. Tui Bdg $4400. 4 wks.
  Endow $9,000,000. Plant val $10,000,000. Acres 30. Bldgs 18. Dorms 3. Dorm rms 110.
    Class rms 22. Lib 8000 vols. Art studios 1. Music studios 1. Gyms 1. Fields 3. Courts
    2. Fitness ctrs 1. Rifle ranges 1. Comp labs 1.
  Est 1887. Nonprofit. Episcopal. Sem (Sept-May). **Assoc** NCA.

St. John's was founded by Rt. Rev. Elisha Smith Thomas and a group of concerned Salina
businessmen. Students must complete either the standard or the college preparatory curriculum, in addition to JROTC and religion. Both require units in language arts, math, science,
social science, computer science, physical education and health, plus electives; the latter
includes a mandatory foreign language. Elective courses are offered in such subjects as art,
band, philosophy and industrial careers, among others.

St. John's students participate in varsity athletics in high school, and a more limited range
of sports is available for boys in grades 6-8. Cadets who do not compete in varsity athletics
engage in a physical training program. Boys in all grades work on required community service
projects. Each student attends religious services three times per week.

WICHITA, KS. (129 mi. SW of Topeka, KS) Urban. Pop: 344,284. Alt: 1325 ft.

WICHITA COLLEGIATE SCHOOL
Day — Coed Gr PS (Age 2)-12

Wichita, KS 67206. 9115 E 13th St. Tel: 316-634-0433. Fax: 316-634-0273.
www.wcsks.com   E-mail: ssteed@wcsks.com
Tom Davis, Head. BS, Rice Univ, MBA, Wichita State Univ. Susie Steed, Adm.
  Col Prep. Montessori. **AP (126 exams taken, 79% 3+)**—Eng Fr Lat Span Calc Stats
    Comp_Sci Bio Chem Physics US_Hist Econ US_Govt & Pol. **Feat**—Humanities Envi-
    ron_Sci Photog Studio_Art Music. **Supp**—LD Rev Tut.
  Sports—Basket Bowl X-country Golf Swim Tennis Track. B: Baseball Football. G: Cheer

Softball Volley. **Activities:** 11.

Somewhat selective adm: 166/yr. Appl fee: $25-35. Appl due: Rolling. Accepted: 91%. Yield: 73%. **Tests** IQ Stanford.

Enr 1041. Avg class size: 15. **Fac 97.** M 24/F 73. FT 84/PT 13. Adv deg: 32%.

Grad '10—61. Col—61. (U of KS, U of PA, SMU, U of Tulsa, Wichita St, Georgetown). **Avg SAT:** CR/M 1206. Avg ACT: 25. **Col couns:** 2.

Tui '05-'06: Day $7195-10,995 (+$100-600). **Aid:** Need 142 ($631,294).

Summer: Acad Enrich Rec. 11 wks.

Endow $1,495,000. Plant val $21,000,000. Acres 42. Bldgs 7. Class rms 80. Lib 16,000 vols. Sci labs 5. Amphitheaters 1. Art studios 1. Music studios 2. Dance studios 1. Gyms 3. Fields 2. Tennis courts 6. Tracks 1. Playgrounds 2. Comp labs 2.

Est 1963. Nonprofit. Sem (Aug-May). **Assoc** CLS.

Founded by parents seeking an alternative to public education and commencing as an elementary program, this school gradually expanded to provide complete college preparation, adding grade 12 in 1966. Students follow a common prescribed curriculum that emphasizes traditional discipline. Pupils must take part in the AP program, and all have opportunities in the arts and interscholastic athletics. Boys and girls may participate in community service and mentor programs.

MINNESOTA

COLLEGEVILLE, MN. (69 mi. NW of Minneapolis, MN) Rural. Pop: 100. Alt: 1094 ft.

SAINT JOHN'S PREPARATORY SCHOOL

Bdg — Coed Gr 9-PG; Day — Coed 6-PG

Collegeville, MN 56321. 2280 Watertower Rd, PO Box 4000. Tel: 320-363-3321, 800-525-7737. Fax: 320-363-3322.
www.sjprep.net   E-mail: admitprep@csbsju.edu

Rev. Timothy Backous, Head (2006). BA, Saint John's Univ (MN), MA, PhD, Accademia Alphonsianum (Italy). **Matthew Reichert, Prin.** BA, Saint John's Univ (MN), MEd, MA, Univ of Notre Dame. **Jennine Klosterman, Adm.**

Col Prep. IB Diploma. AP (exams req'd; 67 taken, 66% 3+)—Eng Ger Span. **Feat**—British_Lit Creative_Writing World_Lit Chin Stats Astron Environ_Sci Comp_Sci Econ Law Theol World_Relig Ceramics Drawing Painting Photog Sculpt Studio_Art Acting Theater Music. **Supp**—ESL Tut. **Dual enr:** St John's U-MN, Col of St Benedict.

Sports (req'd)—Basket X-country Ice_Hockey Ski Soccer Tennis Track. B: Baseball Football. G: Softball Swim. **Activities:** 40.

Somewhat selective adm: 82/yr. Appl fee: $25. Appl due: Rolling. Applied: 153. Accepted: 87%. Yield: 84%. **Tests** SSAT TOEFL.

Enr 313. B 166. G 147. Elem 82. Sec 231. Wh 73%. Latino 5%. Blk 4%. Asian 16%. Other 2%. Intl 25%. Avg class size: 15. Stud/fac: 10:1. Casual. **Fac 39.** M 19/F 20. FT 34/PT 5. Wh 93%. Latino 3%. Blk 1%. Asian 3%. Adv deg: 74%.

Grad '11—61. Col—59. (U of WA 5, Col of St Benedict 4, St John's U-MN 4, U of MN-Twin Cities 4, Gustavus Adolphus 3, U of IL-Urbana 2). Athl schol 1. **Avg SAT:** CR 481. M 669. W 497. Avg ACT: 27.1. **Col couns:** 3. Alum donors: 12%.

Tui '11-'12: Bdg $32,248 (+$500). **5-Day Bdg $28,861** (+$500). **Day $4562-13,999** (+$100). **Intl Bdg $37,999** (+$500). **Aid:** Merit 332 ($31,350). Need 80 ($597,313). Work prgm 66 ($35,650).

Summer: Enrich Rec. Ger. Tui Bdg $200-380. ½-1 wk. Tui Day $225/wk. 6 wks.

Endow $9,600,000. Plant val $4,125,000. Acres 2700. Bldgs 12. Dorms 2. Dorm rms 117. Class rms 18. Lib 6000 vols. Sci labs 4. Auds 1. Theaters 1. Art studios 3. Music studios 2. Arts ctrs 1. Fields 6. Courts 9. Pools 2. Comp labs 2.

Est 1857. Nonprofit. Roman Catholic (50% practice). Sem (Aug-May). **Assoc** NCA.

Saint John's Preparatory School shares its 2700-acre campus with Saint John's University, a liberal arts college for men.

The school supplements its traditional college preparatory course of study with offerings in the fine arts, social studies and theology. Each department provides the opportunity for qualified students to participate in an independent study program. Advanced courses are available, including the two-year International Baccalaureate Diploma Program. In addition, pupils may take college courses at Saint John's University. A number of university facilities are open to Prep students, and the school's computer system is linked directly to the university's. Prep students also have access to the programs and facilities of the College of Saint Benedict, a nearby liberal arts college for women that operates in conjunction with the university. The residential program for girls, started in 1992, is conducted in cooperation with the college, located four miles away in St. Joseph. Girls live in a building on the college campus that is staffed by Prep professionals; the school provides free transportation between the two campuses.

The Melk Program, first offered in 1966, is a nine-month course of study and travel at the Benedictine Abbey School of Melk, Austria, that is open to members of the junior and senior classes. A weeklong interim program held each winter comprises nontraditional classes and experiences, among them travel and service options.

EDEN PRAIRIE, MN. (12 mi. SW of Minneapolis, MN) Urban. Pop: 54,901. Alt: 875 ft.

THE INTERNATIONAL SCHOOL OF MINNESOTA
Day — Coed Gr PS (Age 3)-12

Eden Prairie, MN 55344. 6385 Beach Rd. Tel: 952-918-1840. Fax: 952-918-1801.
www.internationalschoolmn.com   E-mail: admissions@ism-sabis.net
Christi Seiple-Cole, Dir (2011). Christine Brinkman, Adm.
  Col Prep. AP (126 exams taken, 86% 3+)—Eng Fr Span Calc Stats Comp_Sci Bio Chem Physics Eur_Hist Econ US_Govt & Pol Art_Hist Music_Theory. **Feat**—British_Lit Chin Govt Psych Philos Studio_Art. **Supp**—ESL Rev Tut. Outdoor ed.
  Sports—Basket Soccer Track. G: Volley. **Activities:** 30.
  Selective adm: Appl fee: $75. Appl due: Rolling. **Tests** CTP_4 IQ TOEFL.
  Enr 450. B 225. G 225. Elem 300. Sec 150. Wh 55%. Latino 8%. Blk 3%. Native Am 5%. Asian 21%. Other 8%. Intl 30%. Avg class size: 22. Uniform. **Fac 56.** M 12/F 44. FT 55/PT 1. Wh 87%. Latino 11%. Asian 2%. Adv deg: 46%.
  Grad '11—30. Col—30. (U of MN-Twin Cities, McGill-Canada, DePaul, Northwestern, USC). **Avg SAT:** CR/M 1284. Avg ACT: 29.
  Tui '12-'13: Day $15,650-17,100 (+$600). **Aid:** Need ($160,000).
  Summer (enr 150): Acad Enrich Rec. Tui Day $250/wk. 2-8 wks.
  Acres 55. Lib 18,000 vols. Sci labs 1. Auds 1. Art studios 1. Music studios 3. Gyms 1. Fields 2. Courts 8. Pools 1. Comp labs 2.
  Est 1985. Inc. Spons: SABIS. Tri (Aug-June).

ISM is part of the worldwide SABIS network, which was established in Lebanon in 1886. Offered in a multicultural setting, the curriculum features various Advanced Placement courses and places an emphasis on English, world languages, math, science and the humanities. In accordance with ISM's global approach, pupils begin participating in the daily world language program at the preschool level. The school's fine arts program is particularly strong.

Boys and girls at all grade levels complete an annual community service project. Students at the school, which occupies a 55-acre campus, enroll from more than 40 nations.

FARIBAULT, MN. (46 mi. S of Minneapolis, MN) Urban. Pop: 19,214. Alt: 981 ft.

SHATTUCK-ST. MARY'S SCHOOL
Bdg and Day — Coed Gr 6-PG

Faribault, MN 55021. 1000 Shumway Ave, PO Box 218. Tel: 507-333-1618, 800-421-2724. Fax: 507-333-1661.
www.s-sm.org   E-mail: admissions@s-sm.org
Nicholas J. B. Stoneman, Head (2003). BA, Bowdoin College, MEd, Columbia Univ. **Jesse W. Fortney, Adm.**
  Col Prep. Sports (Figure_Skating Ice_Hockey & Soccer). AP (exams req'd; 119 taken)—Eng Fr Lat Span Calc Stats Chem Environ_Sci Physics Eur_Hist US_Hist Psych Studio_Art. **Feat**—British_Lit Creative_Writing S_African_Lit Women's_Lit ASL Chin Anat & Physiol Astron Ecol Genetics Microbio Econ Govt Ethics World_ Relig Drawing Film Photog Sculpt Drama Theater_Arts Chorus Music_Theory Dance Public_Speak Nutrition. **Supp**—Dev_Read ESL LD Rev Tut.
  Sports—Basket Fencing Golf Ice_Hockey Lacrosse Soccer Tennis. B: Baseball. G: Volley.
  Selective adm (Gr 6-12): 108/yr. Bdg 81. Day 27. Appl fee: $50. Appl due: Rolling. Accepted: 57%. Yield: 64%. **Tests** SSAT TOEFL.
  Enr 434. B 263. G 171. Bdg 314. Day 120. Elem 53. Sec 380. PG 1. Intl 32%. Avg class

size: 15. Stud/fac: 7:1. **Fac 95.** M 54/F 41. FT 78/PT 17. Adv deg: 28%.
Grad '08—76. Col—59. (Princeton, Cornell, Harvard, U of MN-Twin Cities). **Mid 50%**
SAT: CR 460-750. M 520-710. W 470-590. Mid 50% ACT: 21-26. **Col couns:** 2.
Tui '12-'13: Bdg $40,450 (+$1500). **Day $26,950-28,950** (+$1500). **Intl Bdg $42,450**
(+$3000). **Aid:** Need 191 ($3,700,000).
Summer: Rec. Sports. 4 wks.
Endow $15,000,000. Plant val $35,000,000. Acres 250. Bldgs 12. Dorms 5. Dorm rms
110. Class rms 30. Lib 25,000 vols. Sci labs 4. Comp ctrs 1. Auds 1. Theaters 2. Art
studios 2. Music studios 3. Dance studios 1. Gyms 2. Fields 7. Courts 8. Rinks 2.
Tracks 1. Golf crses 1. Comp labs 3.
Est 1858. Nonprofit. Episcopal. Tri (Aug-May). **Assoc** CLS.

One of the oldest boarding schools in the Midwest, Shattuck-St. Mary's was founded by
Rev. James L. Breck as an Episcopal mission. Separate schools were established for boys and
girls in the 1860s and merged in 1972. Today, the school is located on 250 acres on a wooded
hilltop, 45 miles south of Minneapolis.

The curriculum is college preparatory, with honors, accelerated and Advanced Placement
courses offered in all major disciplines. The fine and performing arts curriculum is noteworthy
for its scope, and courses in religion, ethics and values are available. Cultural, social and recreational opportunities include a full athletic program in interscholastic and intramural sports
(featuring particularly strong ice hockey, soccer and figure skating programs), in addition to a
diverse selection of on-campus organizations and activities.

The middle school has separate faculty, facilities and programs.

MINNEAPOLIS, MN. Urban. Pop: 382,618. Alt: 812 ft. Area also includes Hopkins.

THE BLAKE SCHOOL
Day — Coed Gr PS (Age 4)-12

Hopkins, MN 55343. 110 Blake Rd S. Tel: 952-988-3420. Fax: 952-988-3455.
Other locations: 301 Peavey Ln, Wayzata 55391; 511 Kenwood Pky, Minneapolis 55403.
www.blakeschool.org E-mail: communications@blakeschool.org
Anne E. Stavney, Head (2012). BA, MA, PhD, Univ of Washington. **G. Bryan Fleming,**
Adm.
Col Prep. AP (559 exams taken, 87% 3+)—Eng Fr Lat Span Calc Stats Bio Chem
Physics Eur_Hist Studio_Art. **Feat**—Chin Comp_Sci Pol_Sci Drama Theater_Arts
Music Public_Speak. **Supp**—Rev. **Dual enr:** U of MN-Twin Cities.
Sports (req'd)—Basket X-country Fencing Golf Ice_Hockey Lacrosse Ski Soccer Swim
Tennis Track. B: Baseball Football. G: Softball Volley.
Selective adm: 171/yr. Usual entry: PS, K, 6 & 9. Appl fee: $75-100. Appl due: Jan.
Applied: 411. Accepted: 62%. Yield: 67%. **Tests** CEEB CTP_4 IQ.
Enr 1383. B 729. G 654. Elem 857. Sec 526. Wh 77%. Latino 2%. Blk 5%. Native Am 1%.
Asian 8%. Other 7%. Avg class size: 16. Stud/fac: 9:1. **Fac 138.** M 57/F 81. FT 130/PT
8. Wh 89%. Latino 1%. Blk 5%. Asian 3%. Other 2%. Adv deg: 57%.
Grad '11—133. Col—133. (Northwestern 5, Dartmouth 4, Wellesley 4, Boston Col 4,
Colby 4, Carleton 3). **Avg SAT:** CR 680. M 630. W 640. **Mid 50% SAT:** CR 580-700.
M 570-690. W 580-720. Avg ACT: 29. **Col couns:** 3. Alum donors: 22%.
Tui '12-'13: Day $19,825-23,525 (+$1250-2210). **Aid:** Need 181 ($3,307,000).
Summer: Acad Enrich Rev Rem Rec. Art. Sports. Driver Ed. 8 wks.
Endow $43,500,000. Plant val $64,000,000. Acres 55. Bldgs 5. Class rms 150. Libs 4.
Chapels 1. Sci labs 9. Lang labs 1. Auds 2. Art studios 7. Music studios 7. Drama
studios 3. Gyms 4. Fields 6. Courts 10. Pools 1. Rinks 1. Comp labs 5. Laptop prgm
Gr 9-12.
Est 1900. Nonprofit. Sem (Sept-June). **Assoc** CLS.

One of the largest independent day schools in Greater Minneapolis/St. Paul, this coeducational school resulted from the 1972 merger of Blake School for boys, Northrop Collegiate School for girls and the Highcroft Country Day School. The school is located on three campuses, with the upper school (grades 9-12) on the Northrop campus in Minneapolis and the middle school (grades 6-8) and administrative offices on the Blake campus in Hopkins. The lower school operates at two locations: the Blake campus (grades pre-K-5) and the Highcroft campus (grades K-5) in Wayzata.

Blake's rigorous college preparatory course of studies features an integrated program of academic, artistic and athletic activities, and the school also offers a wide range of electives, Advanced Placement courses and independent study options for seniors. Students gain exposure to foreign languages in each division. Computer technology is integrated into the curriculum at all grade levels: Students work with online resources, software and multimedia processes to access information and develop presentations. The arts program is particularly strong, with such courses as ceramics, printmaking, photography, drama, chorus and instrumental music.

BRECK SCHOOL
Day — Coed Gr PS (Age 4)-12

Minneapolis, MN 55422. 123 Ottawa Ave N. Tel: 763-381-8100. Fax: 763-381-8288.
www.breckschool.org　E-mail: info@breckschool.org
Edward Kim, Head (2007). AB, Dartmouth College, MA, Columbia Univ. **Scott D. Wade, Adm.**

Col Prep. AP (exams req'd; 328 taken, 82% 3+)—Eng Fr Span Calc Bio Chem Physics Eur_Hist US_Hist Art_Hist Studio_Art. **Elem math**—Math Expressions. **Feat**—British_Lit Creative_Writing Shakespeare Chin Astron Middle_Eastern_Hist Russ_Hist Econ Ethics Relig Ceramics Acting Theater Music Dance. **Supp**—Rem_Math Rem_ Read Tut.

Sports—Basket X-country Golf Ice_Hockey Lacrosse Ski Soccer Swim Tennis Track. B: Baseball Football. G: Gymnastics Softball Volley.

Selective adm: 121/yr. Appl fee: $75. Appl due: Feb. Accepted: 40%. **Tests** CTP_4.

Enr 1131. B 530. G 601. Elem 731. Sec 400. Wh 71%. Latino 3%. Blk 12%. Native Am 1%. Asian 10%. Other 3%. Avg class size: 18. **Fac 114.** Adv deg: 50%.

Grad '10—94. Col—94. (St Olaf 7, Amherst 3, Boston Col 3, Bowdoin 3, CO Col 3, Pitzer 3). **Avg SAT:** CR 620. M 618. W 638. Avg ACT: 28. **Col couns:** 3.

Tui '12-'13: Day $21,870-25,215. Aid: Need 259 ($4,666,553).

Summer (enr 350): Acad Rec. Sports. Tui Day $175-600/2-wk ses. 6 wks.

Endow $43,194,000. Plant val $104,255,000. Acres 53. Bldgs 1. Class rms 73. 3 Libs 51,700 vols. Sci labs 8. Art studios 4. Music studios 5. Dance studios 1. Drama studios 2. Gyms 3. Fields 5. Basketball courts 4. Field houses 1. Pools 1. Rinks 1. Tracks 2. Weight rms 1. Comp labs 6. Comp/stud: 1:1 Laptop prgm Gr 4-12.

Est 1886. Nonprofit. Episcopal. Sem (Aug-June). **Assoc** CLS NCA.

Breck was established as an Episcopal school in Wilder by the same Bishop Whipple who founded the Faribault Schools. Named in honor of Rev. James Lloyd Breck, it relocated first (in 1917) to St. Paul and then, in 1956, to West River Parkway. In 1981, it moved to its present, 50-acre campus minutes west of downtown Minneapolis.

The curriculum features Spanish and Chinese instruction in grades K-12. All upper school students perform weekly community service and participate in the May Program, the two-week, in-depth study of an approved topic. Frequent field trips are made to Minneapolis and St. Paul theaters, museums, orchestra halls and zoological gardens, and annual trips are taken to China, France and other countries. Students in grades 4-12 receive laptop computers, and wireless Internet access is available throughout the school. Interested upper school students may participate in advanced research programs in history or science.

Breck conducts two chapel services per week for each division, as well as a monthly all-school service. Students in the upper school complete 20 hours of required community service over four years. **See Also Page 59**

MINNEHAHA ACADEMY
Day — Coed Gr PS (Age 3)-12

Minneapolis, MN 55406. 3100 W River Pky. Tel: 612-729-8321. Fax: 612-728-7757.
Other locations: 4200 W River Pky, Minneapolis 55406.
 www.minnehahaacademy.net   E-mail: admission@minnehahaacademy.net
Donna M. Harris, Pres (2009). BA, MA, San Jose State Univ, EdD, Univ of San Francisco.
 Heidi Shannon, Int Adm.
 Col Prep. AP (exams req'd; 545 taken, 70% 3+)—Eng Lat Span Calc Stats Comp_Sci
 Bio Chem Physics Eur_Hist US_Hist World_Hist Econ US_Govt & Pol Studio_Art.
 Elem math—McGraw-Hill. **Elem read**—Houghton Mifflin Harcourt/McGraw-Hill/
 Open Court. **Feat**—Shakespeare Chin Fr Anat & Physiol Environ_Sci Oceanog
 Sports_Med Psych Bible Ethics Philos Ceramics Drawing Filmmaking Painting
 Sculpt Acting Chorus Orchestra Debate Journ Speech Woodworking Study_Skills.
 Supp—Dev_Read LD Rem_Math Rem_Read Rev Tut.
 Sports—Basket X-country Golf Ice_Hockey Ski Soccer Tennis Track. B: Baseball Foot-
 ball Wrestling. G: Lacrosse Softball Swim Volley. **Activities:** 21.
 Somewhat selective adm: 137/yr. Usual entry: PS, K, 6 & 9. Appl fee: $100. Appl due:
 Mar. Applied: 246. Accepted: 92%. Yield: 61%.
 Enr 965. B 467. G 498. Elem 520. Sec 445. Wh 78%. Latino 3%. Blk 7%. Asian 4%. Other
 8%. Stud/fac: 10:1. Casual. **Fac 95.** M 42/F 53. FT 72/PT 23. Wh 93%. Blk 4%. Asian
 3%. Adv deg: 71%.
 Grad '11—134. Col—129. (Bethel U, U of MN-Twin Cities, U of WI-Madison, St Olaf, N
 Park, U of St Thomas-MN). Athl schol 1. **Avg SAT:** CR 612. M 612. W 597. Avg ACT:
 25.8. **Col couns:** 2. Alum donors: 7%.
 Tui '12-'13: Day $12,370-15,770 (+$435-730). **Aid:** Need 205 ($1,600,000).
 Summer (enr 400): Acad Enrich Rec. Tui Day $110-570. 1-2 wks.
 Endow $5,005,000. Plant val $42,000,000. Acres 25. Bldgs 3. Class rms 46. Lib 22,000
 vols. Lang labs 1. Auds 1. Theaters 1. Art studios 3. Music studios 6. Gyms 3. Basket-
 ball courts 1. Tennis courts 7. Rinks 1. Comp/stud: 1:2.
 Est 1913. Nonprofit. Evangelical Covenant (10% practice). (Aug-June).

This Christian school, large and well equipped, draws most of its enrollment from the
region. In addition to basic academics, Bible is taught at all grade levels. A full complement
of honors and Advanced Placement courses provides additional challenge for qualified pupils.
Extracurricular activities include musical groups, athletics and dramatics. Most classrooms are
outfitted with interactive whiteboards, and mobile laptop carts allow students to connect to the
campuswide wireless Internet network.

The lower and middle school campus (grades pre-K-8) occupies a separate site on West
River Parkway.

ST. PAUL, MN. (8 mi. E of Minneapolis, MN) Urban. Pop: 287,151. Alt: 703 ft. Area
also includes Mendota Heights.

CONVENT OF THE VISITATION SCHOOL
Day — Boys Gr PS (Age 2)-6, Girls PS (Age 2)-12

Mendota Heights, MN 55120. 2455 Visitation Dr. Tel: 651-683-1700.
 Fax: 651-454-7144.
 www.visitation.net   E-mail: info@vischool.org
Dawn Nichols, Head (2000). BA, Ursuline College, MA, Western Illinois Univ, EdD, Nova
 Southeastern Univ. **Patty Healy Janssen, Adm.**
 Col Prep. Montessori. AP (280 exams taken, 77% 3+)—Eng Fr Span Calc Stats Bio
 Eur_Hist US_Hist US_Govt & Pol. **Feat**—British_Lit Creative_Writing Chin Lat Anat
 Astron Environ_Sci Genetics Engineering Comp_Sci Psych Sociol World_Relig
 Drawing Graphic_Arts Sculpt Theater Ballet. **Supp**—Rem_Math Rem_Read Tut.

Sports—G: Basket X-country Golf Ice_Hockey Lacrosse Ski Soccer Softball Swim Tennis Track Volley. **Activities:** 25.
Somewhat selective adm: 105/yr. Appl fee: $25. Appl due: Rolling. Applied: 161. Accepted: 93%. Yield: 71%. **Tests** CTP_4 IQ Stanford.
Enr 548. B 62. G 486. Elem 244. Sec 304. Wh 87%. Latino 5%. Blk 3%. Asian 3%. Other 2%. Avg class size: 18. Stud/fac: 11:1. Uniform. **Fac 59.** M 7/F 52. FT 35/PT 24. Wh 88%. Latino 7%. Blk 2%. Asian 3%. Adv deg: 74%.
Grad '10—77. Col—77. (U of WI-Madison 8, Creighton 6, U of MN-Twin Cities 5, Fordham 4, Dartmouth 3, Marquette 3). Athl schol 1. **Avg SAT:** CR 619. M 586. W 607. Avg ACT: 27.5. **Col couns:** 2. Alum donors: 26%.
Tui '11-'12: Day $14,205-18,635 (+$1000). **Aid:** Need 165 ($1,385,500).
Summer: Gr K-6. Acad Enrich Rev Rem Rec. Tui Day $100-600/wk. 10 wks.
Endow $10,000,000. Plant val $23,000,000. Acres 35. Bldgs 7 (100% ADA). Class rms 42. 2 Libs 16,000 vols. Sci labs 4. Auds 1. Theaters 1. Art studios 2. Music studios 2. Dance studios 1. Gyms 2. Fields 3. Basketball courts 4. Tennis courts 8. Volleyball courts 4. Comp labs 2. Comp/stud: 1:3.
Est 1873. Nonprofit. Roman Catholic (85% practice). Quar (Aug-June). **Assoc** NCA.

This Catholic school was founded when six nuns from the Order of the Visitation, at the request of Bishop Thomas Grace, boarded a steamboat in St. Louis, MO, and traveled north to establish a school for young women in the St. Paul area. Over the years, the school has occupied four different campuses.

Today, Visitation comprises an early learning center, a Montessori preschool, a coeducational lower school, a middle school for boys and girls through grade 6—as well as for girls in grades 7 and 8—and an upper school for girls only. Visitation's upper school serves as the only all-girls secondary program in the state. Throughout, emphasis is placed on the fine arts, and a family-like atmosphere and a low student-teacher ratio provide individual attention. An extended-day program serves children in grades K-6.

The school's athletic program allows pupils to take part in team sports beginning in grade 5. Community service is an important aspect of school life, and seniors complete a 48-hour project each spring.

ST. PAUL ACADEMY AND SUMMIT SCHOOL

Day — Coed Gr K-12

St Paul, MN 55105. 1712 Randolph Ave. Tel: 651-698-2451. Fax: 651-698-6787.
Other locations: 1150 Goodrich Ave, St Paul 55105.
www.spa.edu   E-mail: hploen@spa.edu
Bryn S. Roberts, Head (2006). BA, Mount Allison Univ (Canada), MA, Univ of Western Ontario (Canada). **Heather Cameron Ploen, Adm.**
   Col Prep. AP exams taken: 73 (90% 3+). **Feat**—British_Lit Eastern_Lit Chin Fr Ger Span Calc Stats Marine_Bio/Sci Econ Law Psych Philos Ceramics Drawing Photog Drama Debate Journ Speech.
   Sports—Basket X-country Fencing Golf Ice_Hockey Ski Soccer Swim Track. B: Baseball Football. G: Softball Tennis Volley. **Activities:** 21.
Selective adm: 133/yr. Appl fee: $75. Appl due: Feb. Accepted: 70%. Yield: 76%. **Tests** CTP_4.
Enr 872. B 438. G 434. Elem 509. Sec 363. Wh 72%. Latino 5%. Blk 6%. Native Am 1%. Asian 16%. Avg class size: 14. Stud/fac: 7:1. **Fac 101.** M 44/F 57. FT 101. Wh 87%. Latino 3%. Blk 2%. Asian 4%. Other 4%. Adv deg: 67%.
Grad '11—87. Col—87. (U of WI-Madison 6, Wash U 5, Lewis & Clark 4, Carleton 3, U of Chicago 3, Boston U 3). **Avg SAT:** CR 624. M 645. W 631. **Mid 50% SAT:** CR 560-690. M 610-690. W 560-690. Avg ACT: 30. **Col couns:** 2. Alum donors: 16%.
Tui '12-'13: Day $23,310-25,560 (+$200). **Aid:** Need 196 ($2,983,750).
Endow $30,000,000. Plant val $41,000,000. Acres 34. Bldgs 3. Class rms 110. Lib 22,000 vols. Sci labs 9. Auds 1. Theaters 1. Art studios 5. Music studios 3. Gyms 3. Fields 9. Courts 12. Rinks 1. Playgrounds 2. Gardens 1. Comp labs 3. Laptop prgm Gr 7-10.
Est 1969. Nonprofit. Sem (Aug-June). **Assoc** CLS NCA.

SPA was formed in 1969 from the merger of St. Paul Academy for boys, founded in 1900, and Summit School for girls, founded in 1917. The upper school, for students in grades 9-12, shares the Randolph Avenue campus in Highland Park with the middle school (grades 6-8); the lower school (grades K-5) is located on Goodrich Avenue in St. Paul's Crocus Hill neighborhood.

Graduation requirements include foreign language study and a course in word processing. Electives are available beginning in grade 9, and work that prepares students to take AP examinations is offered in all academic disciplines. There is a strong emphasis on the fine arts: Most students pursue drama, visual arts and music beyond the requirements. Musical instrument training is offered on both campuses.

A senior speech before the student body is mandatory, and an optional senior project during the month of May incorporates self-designed study, community service and career exploration, culminating in an oral presentation to the review committee. Independent study provides students in grades 9-12 with an opportunity to study something that is not offered in the regular program or to learn it in a different way. Projects involve a variety of experiences, such as research, fieldwork, creative writing, courses at other institutions, training in music or art, correspondence study and community involvement.

Other learning opportunities include a course for students in grades 10-12 in which participants receive three weeks of training in preparation for a nine-day wilderness expedition and the option to study off campus for a full year, a semester or a quarter through a number of organizations. Students are encouraged to participate in community service.

SAINT THOMAS ACADEMY

Day — Boys Gr 7-12

Mendota Heights, MN 55120. 949 Mendota Heights Rd. Tel: 651-454-4570.
   Fax: 651-454-4574.
   www.cadets.com   E-mail: sta@cadets.com
Thomas B. Mich, Head (2004). MA, PhD, Univ of Minnesota-Twin Cities. **John Kenney, Adm.**

   Col Prep. Milit. AP (308 exams taken, 77% 3+)—Eng Fr Span Calc Stats Comp_Sci Bio US_Hist Econ US_Govt & Pol. **Feat**—Chin Lat Environ_Sci Amer_Stud Relig JROTC. **Supp**—LD Rev Tut. **Dual enr:** U of MN-Twin Cities, St Mary's U of MN.
   Sports—B: Baseball Basket X-country Football Golf Ice_Hockey Lacrosse Ski Soccer Swim Tennis Track Wrestling. **Activities:** 32.
   Somewhat selective adm: 164/yr. Usual entry: 7 & 9. Appl fee: $0. Appl due: Jan. Applied: 238. Accepted: 90%. Yield: 76%.
   Enr 675. Elem 116. Sec 559. Wh 90%. Latino 4%. Blk 4%. Asian 2%. Avg class size: 18. Stud/fac: 10:1. Uniform. **Fac 56.** M 34/F 22. FT 55/PT 1. Wh 95%. Latino 2%. Blk 3%. Adv deg: 78%.
   Grad '11—132. Col—126. (U of St Thomas-MN 20, U of MN-Twin Cities 8, U of ND 8, U of WI-Madison 8, St John's U-MN 7, IA St 4). Athl schol 4. **Avg SAT:** CR 611. M 626. W 585. Avg ACT: 26.3. **Col couns:** 1. Alum donors: 30%.
   Tui '12-'13: Day $17,950. Aid: Merit 35 ($69,000). Need 270 ($2,291,105).
   Summer: Acad Enrich Rev. Study Skills. Tui Day $125/½-wk ses. 4 wks.
   Endow $14,150,000. Plant val $39,924,000. Acres 75. Bldgs 3. Class rms 35. Lib 12,000 vols. Sci labs 5. Lang labs 4. Auds 1. Theaters 1. Art studios 2. Music studios 1. Gyms 2. Fields 7. Courts 6. Pools 1. Rinks 1. Stadiums 1. Rifle ranges 1. Comp labs 3. Comp/stud: 1:10.
   Est 1885. Nonprofit. Roman Catholic (75% practice). Sem (Aug-June). **Assoc** NCA.

Founded by Archbishop John Ireland, STA has offered a college preparatory, Catholic military program for boys since its establishment. It serves as the only secondary all-male school in the state. Academic instruction focuses on college preparation, with an emphasis on the development of strong study skills and on the core courses of English, history, foreign languages, math, the physical sciences and theology. Participation in a compulsory JROTC program hones pupils' leadership and life skills.

Prior to graduation, all seniors perform 140 hours of community service and also deliver a speech to the student body at Formation.

MISSOURI

KANSAS CITY, MO. Urban. Pop: 441,545. Alt: 750 ft.

THE BARSTOW SCHOOL
Day — Coed Gr PS (Age 3)-12

Kansas City, MO 64114. 11511 State Line Rd. Tel: 816-942-3255. Fax: 816-942-3227.
www.barstowschool.org   E-mail: admission@barstowschool.org
Shane A. Foster, Head (2008). BEd, Univ of Tasmania (Australia), MEd, Univ of Wisconsin-Madison, MS, Concordia Univ Wisconsin. **Kellye Crockett, Adm.**

Col Prep. AP (exams req'd; 108 taken, 76% 3+)—Eng Chin Fr Japan Span Calc Stats Comp_Sci Bio Chem Physics Eur_Hist US_Hist Econ US_Govt & Pol. **Feat**—Creative_Writing Astron Environ_Sci Engineering Web_Design Asian_Hist Ethics Art_Hist Ceramics Drawing Film Photog Studio_Art Acting Music Music_Theory Debate. **Supp**—Tut.

Sports—Basket X-country Golf Soccer Swim Tennis Track. B: Baseball. G: Cheer Softball Volley.

Somewhat selective adm (Gr PS-11): 105/yr. Appl fee: $45. Appl due: Feb. Accepted: 90%. Yield: 80%. **Tests** CTP_4 IQ.

Enr 646. Elem 433. Sec 213. Avg class size: 16. Stud/fac: 10:1. **Fac 63.**

Grad '11—45. Col—45. (U of KS 8, U of MO-Columbia 4, U of MO-Kansas City 2, Princeton 2, Rockhurst 2, SMU 2). **Avg SAT:** CR 668. M 630. W 622. Avg ACT: 27. **Col couns:** 2. Alum donors: 16%.

Tui '12-'13: Day $12,014-17,480 (+$1250-1335). **Aid:** Merit 21 ($162,594). Need 106 ($926,656).

Summer: Acad Enrich Rev Rec. 10 wks.

Endow $8,000,000. Plant val $20,400,000. Acres 40. Bldgs 5 (50% ADA). Class rms 64. 2 Libs 16,200 vols. Sci labs 4. Auds 1. Art studios 3. Music studios 2. Gyms 2. Fields 3. Courts 4. Comp labs 3. Laptop prgm Gr 6-12.

Est 1884. Nonprofit. Sem (Aug-May). **Assoc** CLS NCA.

Founded by Wellesley graduates Mary L. C. Barstow and Ada Brann at the request of several prominent Kansas City families, the school currently offers a holistic liberal arts program that emphasizes college preparation. Barstow draws its diverse student body from Greater Kansas City and Johnson County, KS.

A strong core of required courses is supplemented by electives in such areas as foreign languages, forensics, the social sciences and the arts. Pupils also benefit from a well-developed technology program. Beginning in grade 6 all students lease tablet computers, which are replaced before grade 10 with new models used until graduation. Boys and girls accumulate at least 40 hours of required community service prior to graduation. After-school enrichment activities, a comprehensive summer program and year-round extended care are available.

PEMBROKE HILL SCHOOL
Day — Coed Gr PS (Age 2)-12

Kansas City, MO 64112. 400 W 51st St. Tel: 816-936-1200. Fax: 816-936-1238.
Other locations: 5121 State Line Rd, Kansas City 64112.
www.pembrokehill.org   E-mail: phs@pembrokehill.org
Steven J. Bellis, Head (2007). BA, Kansas State Univ, MBA, Univ of Texas-Austin, EdD, Univ of Kansas. **Carolyn Sullivan, Adm.**

Col Prep. AP (exams req'd; 560 taken, 78% 3+)—Eng Fr Lat Span Calc Stats Comp_Sci Bio Chem Environ_Sci Physics US_Hist Econ Psych US_Govt & Pol Art_Hist

Studio_Art. **Feat**—Chin Botany Microbio Physiol Zoology Chin_Hist Middle_Eastern_Hist WWI Ceramics Filmmaking Photog Sculpt Drama Music Debate Silversmithing. **Supp**—Dev_Read Rem_Math Rem_Read.

Sports—Basket Cheer X-country Golf Soccer Swim Tennis Track. B: Baseball Football Lacrosse Wrestling. G: F_Hockey Volley.

Selective adm: 154/yr. Usual entry: PS, K, 6 & 9. Appl fee: $40. Appl due: Feb. Applied: 294. Accepted: 67%. Yield: 78%. **Tests** IQ.

Enr 1168. B 568. G 600. Elem 761. Sec 407. Wh 77%. Latino 1%. Blk 4%. Asian 8%. Other 10%. Avg class size: 15. Stud/fac: 11:1. Casual. **Fac 109.** M 35/F 74. FT 95/PT 14. Wh 84%. Latino 2%. Blk 8%. Asian 2%. Other 4%. Adv deg: 63%.

Grad '11—101. Col—101. (U of KS 10, SMU 8, U of Miami 6, U of MO-Columbia 5, Notre Dame 2, Vanderbilt 2). **Mid 50% SAT:** CR 590-700. M 590-690. W 590-700. Mid 50% ACT: 25-32. **Col couns:** 4. Alum donors: 20%.

Tui '12-'13: Day $15,855-18,515 (+$1200-1765). **Aid:** Need 230 ($2,000,000).

Summer: Acad Enrich Rev Rem Rec. Tui Day $165-495. 1-3 wks.

Endow $25,000,000. Plant val $100,000,000. Acres 36. Bldgs 17. Class rms 87. 3 Libs 45,000 vols. Sci labs 8. Lang labs 9. Auds 2. Theaters 2. Art studios 7. Music studios 4. Gyms 3. Fields 6. Field houses 2. Tracks 1. Comp labs 4.

Est 1910. Nonprofit. Sem (Aug-May). **Assoc** CLS.

Pembroke Hill was created in 1984 as the result of a merger of the Sunset Hill School for girls and the Pembroke-Country Day School for boys. Both predecessor schools were founded by Vassie Ward Hill and a group of progressive-minded parents.

The school maintains a low student-teacher ratio and provides a variety of course options in all disciplines, including languages, science, math, computer, history, English, and the visual and performing arts. Independent study projects and Advanced Placement courses are also offered. An extended-day program is available.

The school is located on two campuses less than a mile apart: the Wornall campus on West 51st Street for children in grades PS-5, and the Ward Parkway campus on State Line Road for students in grades 6-12.

LEXINGTON, MO. (37 mi. E of Kansas City, MO) Suburban. Pop: 4453. Alt: 806 ft.

WENTWORTH MILITARY ACADEMY
Bdg and Day — Coed Gr 9-PG

Lexington, MO 64067. 1880 Washington Ave. Tel: 660-259-2221, 800-962-7682. Fax: 660-259-2677.

www.wma.edu　E-mail: admissions@wma.edu

Col. William W. Sellers, Pres (2009). BS, Harvard Univ, JD, Univ of Missouri-Columbia. **Lt. Col. Robert Harmon, Adm.**

Col Prep. Gen Acad. Bus. Milit. Feat—Creative_Writing Mythology Fr Span Anat & Physiol Comp_Sci WWII Econ Govt Psych Sociol Drawing Studio_Art Chorus Journ Public_Speak JROTC. **Supp**—ESL Rem_Math Rev Tut. **Dual enr:** Wentworth Milit JC.

Sports—Basket X-country Golf Tennis Track. B: Baseball Football Wrestling. G: Volley. **Activities:** 14.

Selective adm: 110/yr. Bdg 108. Day 2. Appl fee: $25. Appl due: Rolling. Accepted: 65%. Yield: 85%. **Tests** Stanford.

Enr 215. B 165. G 50. Bdg 205. Day 10. Sec 87. PG 128. Wh 70%. Latino 17%. Blk 8%. Asian 5%. Intl 15%. Avg class size: 12. Stud/fac: 10:1. Uniform. **Fac 16.** M 13/F 3. FT 13/PT 3. Adv deg: 56%.

Grad '09—29. Col—29. (U of Central MO, U of MO-Columbia, U of KS, Central Methodist, MO U of Sci & Tech, Wentworth Milit JC). **Avg SAT:** CR/M/W 1650. Avg ACT: 24.

Tui '11-'12: Bdg $29,700. Intl Bdg $31,950. Aid: Merit 42 ($240,000). Need 27 ($160,000).

Summer (enr 100): Acad Enrich Rev Rec. Tui Bdg $3995/3-wk ses. 6 wks. Endow $1,200,000. Plant val $2,880,000. Acres 80. Bldgs 9. Dorms 4. Dorm rms 260. Class rms 30. Lib 20,000 vols. Labs 5. Music studios 1. Fields 4. Courts 10. Field houses 1. Pools 1. Golf crses 1. Rifle ranges 1. **Est 1880.** Nonprofit. Sem (Aug-May). **Assoc** NCA.

WMA shares its 80-acre campus with the affiliated Wentworth Military Junior College. Small classes, a strong English program supplemented by separately scheduled writing periods, a computer science program, and student participation in such extracurricular activities as marching band, chorus, drill team, flying, journalism, scouting, ranger platoon and clubs highlight the program. Boys and girls satisfy the following community service requirements: 14 hours in grade 9, 16 hours in grade 10, 18 hours in grade 11 and 20 hours in grade 12. Wentworth faculty supervise a mandatory evening study program, and tutorial services are available to those requiring extra help.

In 1993, Wentworth began accepting females into its affiliated junior college division; shortly thereafter, the academy started admitting girls into grades 10-12. Due to the school's relationship with its junior college, students may earn dual-enrollment credits. Each graduate of Wentworth Military Junior College enrolled in the Military Contract Program qualifies for commission as a second lieutenant in the Army, the Army Reserve or the Army National Guard.

MEXICO, MO. (95 mi. WNW of St. Louis, MO) Suburban. Pop: 11,320. Alt: 806 ft.

MISSOURI MILITARY ACADEMY

Bdg and Day — Boys Gr 6-PG

Mexico, MO 65265. 204 N Grand St. Tel: 573-581-1776, 888-564-6662.
Fax: 573-581-0081.
www.missourimilitaryacademy.org   E-mail: info@missourimilitaryacademy.org
Maj. Gen. Robert M. Flanagan, USMC (Ret), Pres (2007). AB, Univ of Michigan. **Lt. Col. Roger Hill,** Adm.
   Col Prep. Gen Acad. Milit. AP (exams req'd)—Eng Span Calc Stats Chem Physics US_Hist Econ Psych. **Feat**—Creative_Writing Humanities Chin Comp_Sci Robotics Govt Drawing Photog Studio_Art Drama Chorus Accounting Bus Journ Speech JROTC. **Supp**—Dev_Read ESL Rem_Math Tut. **Dual enr:** Moberly Area CC.
   Sports—B: Baseball Basket X-country Football Golf Soccer Swim Tennis Track Wrestling.
   Somewhat selective adm (Bdg Gr 6-12; Day 6-11): 96/yr. Bdg 95. Day 1. Appl fee: $100. Appl due: Rolling. Applied: 185. Accepted: 98%.
   Enr 240. Elem 50. Sec 190. Wh 61%. Latino 32%. Blk 1%. Asian 6%. Intl 35%. Avg class size: 10. Uniform. **Fac 37.** M 30/F 7. FT 36/PT 1. Wh 85%. Latino 5%. Blk 3%. Asian 7%. Adv deg: 56%. In dorms 6.
   Grad '11—42. Col—42. (Instituto Tecnologico de Monterrey-Mexico, IL St, U of MO-Kansas City, KS St, U of TX-Austin, U of CO-Boulder). Athl schol 3. **Avg SAT:** CR/M/ W 1511. Avg ACT: 23. **Col couns:** 2.
   Tui '12-'13: Bdg $29,900 (+$2200). **5-Day Bdg $25,000** (+$2200). **Day $8250-8750** (+$895). **Intl Bdg $29,900** (+$4100).
   Summer: Gr 7-12. Acad Enrich. Tui Bdg $3750. Tui Day $2500. 4 wks.
   Endow $43,000,000. Plant val $20,000,000. Acres 288. Bldgs 19. Dorms 4. Dorm rms 172. Class rms 28. Lib 8000 vols. Sci labs 4. Lang labs 1. Auds 1. Art studios 1. Music studios 10. Gyms 1. Fields 6. Courts 8. Field houses 1. Pools 1. Stables 1. Tracks 1. Rifle ranges 1. Comp labs 3. Laptop prgm Gr 6-PG.
   Est 1889. Nonprofit. Tri (Sept-May).

This military school was founded by Col. A. F. Fleet; Gov. Charles H. Hardin of Missouri served as MMA's first superintendent. After its original campus was destroyed by fire in 1896, the academy was reestablished in 1900 at its present location on the eastern outskirts of the city. The 70-acre main campus lies adjacent to a 218-acre wilderness area that features a lake, a lodge, a stream, and woodlands with riding and hiking trails.

MMA comprises a high school (grades 9-PG) and a separate middle school (grades 6-8). Learning resource centers operate at both schools. Instructors at these centers track and assist students in need of additional assistance with their academic work. Required extra-help sessions and supervised evening study are important elements of the program. Qualified students may take dual-enrollment courses, conducted in cooperation with a local college, that meet high school graduation requirements and lead to college credit.

The academy has been rated as an Honor School with Distinction by the Army JROTC for more than four decades. The student body is organized as a battalion, and student government is vested in a cadet council.

Among MMA's extracurricular activities are private instrumental and voice lessons, marching and stage bands, a drum and bugle corps, aviation, drill team and equitation.

ST. LOUIS, MO. Urban. Pop: 348,189. Alt: 455 ft. Area also includes Clayton and Webster Groves.

CHAMINADE COLLEGE PREPARATORY SCHOOL
Bdg and Day — Boys Gr 6-12

St Louis, MO 63131. 425 S Lindbergh Blvd. Tel: 314-993-4400, 877-378-6847.
Fax: 314-993-4403.
www.chaminade-stl.org   E-mail: admissions@chaminade-stl.com
Rev. Ralph A. Siefert, SM, Pres (1987). BA, St Mary's Univ of San Antonio, MA, North-western Univ, MA, St Louis Univ, DMin, Andover Newton Theological School. **Louis Peters, Prin.** BA, MA, EdD. **Matthew J. Saxer, Adm.**

Col Prep. AP (exams req'd; 211 taken, 76% 3+)—Eng Fr Lat Span Calc Stats Bio Chem Physics Eur_Hist US_Hist World_Hist Comp_Govt & Pol Econ Psych US_ Govt & Pol Studio_Art Music_Theory. **Feat**—Chin Greek Comp_Sci Theol Architect Film Drama Music Accounting Journ Speech. **Supp**—ESL Tut. **Dual enr:** St Louis U, U of MO-St Louis.

Sports—B: Baseball Basket Bowl X-country Football Golf Ice_Hockey Lacrosse Soccer Swim Tennis Track Volley W_Polo Wrestling. **Activities:** 25.

Somewhat selective adm (Gr 6-11): 191/yr. Bdg 28. Day 163. Usual entry: 6 & 9. Appl fee: $50. Appl due: Jan. Applied: 303. Accepted: 85%. Yield: 82%. **Tests** SSAT.

Enr 789. Bdg 43. Day 746. Elem 294. Sec 495. Wh 84%. Latino 1%. Blk 6%. Native Am 1%. Asian 7%. Other 1%. Intl 6%. Avg class size: 18. Stud/fac: 10:1. Casual. **Fac 82.** M 63/F 19. FT 80/PT 2. Wh 91%. Latino 3%. Blk 4%. Native Am 1%. Asian 1%. Adv deg: 79%. In dorms 5.

Grad '11—124. Col—123. (U of MO-Columbia, St Louis U, U of KS, U of Dayton, Purdue, U of IL-Urbana). Athl schol 17. Avg ACT: 26. Mid 50% ACT: 23-28. **Col couns:** 2. Alum donors: 27%.

Tui '12-'13: Bdg $33,081 (+$3000). **5-Day Bdg $31,931** (+$3000). **Day $15,765** (+$1500). **Intl Bdg $33,380** (+$2000). **Aid:** Merit 60 ($77,000). Need 230 ($1,500,000).

Summer (enr 400): Acad Enrich Rev Rec. Sports. 1-6 wks.

Endow $11,000,000. Plant val $64,800,000. Acres 55. Bldgs 12 (83% ADA). Dorms 1. Dorm rms 54. Class rms 56. Lib 20,000 vols. Sci labs 7. Theaters 1. Art studios 5. Music studios 3. Gyms 2. Fields 5. Tennis courts 8. Pools 1. Comp labs 3. Comp/stud: 1:1 Laptop prgm Gr 6-12.

Est 1910. Nonprofit. Roman Catholic (82% practice). Sem (Aug-May). **Assoc** NCA.

Sponsored by the Society of Mary, Chaminade offers honors and AP courses, as well as electives, and places a strong emphasis on the arts. Additional classes, taught by school faculty in affiliation with St. Louis University, allow students to receive college credit through the university. Chaminade also coordinates international exchange programs with schools in France, Spain and Mexico. All students are required to lease laptop computers from the school for use in class and to access electronic textbooks from home.

Retreats, a campus ministry and liturgical celebrations are among CCPS' religious activities. Depending upon grade level, all boys perform 10 to 50 hours of community service annually.

THE COLLEGE SCHOOL
Day — Coed Gr PS (Age 3)-8

Webster Groves, MO 63119. 7825 Big Bend Blvd. Tel: 314-962-9355.
   Fax: 314-962-5078.
   www.thecollegeschool.org   E-mail: admissions@thecollegeschool.org
Sheila Gurley, Head (2004). BSE, Arkansas State Univ, MA, Univ of Arkansas-Fayetteville.
   Adrienne Rusbarsky, Adm.
   Pre-Prep. Feat—Span Studio_Art Drama Music.
   Sports—Basket Soccer.
   Selective adm: 60/yr. Usual entry: PS, K & 6. Appl fee: $75. Appl due: Feb.
   Enr 260. B 130. G 130. Nonwhite 25%. Avg class size: 24. Stud/fac: 12:1. **Fac 31.** M 11/F
      20. FT 29/PT 2. Adv deg: 61%.
   Grad '11—27. Prep—20. (St Louis U HS, Nerinx Hall, Whitfield, St Joseph's Acad-MO,
      Westminster Christian-MO, John Burroughs).
   Tui '12-'13: Day $12,400-14,800 (+$240-1400).
   Summer (enr 300): Ages 4-15. Enrich Rec. Tui $450. 1-2 wks.
   Acres 28. Bldgs 1. Class rms 24. Lib 17,000 vols. Auds 1. Art studios 2. Music studios 1.
      Gyms 1. Fields 1. Tracks 1. Greenhouses 1. Comp labs 1.
   Est 1963. Nonprofit. Tri (Aug-May).

Founded as the Webster College Laboratory School, The College School became independent in 1978. A pioneer in the St. Louis area of the concept of thematic, experiential learning, the school teaches basic skills through hands-on experiences, both inside and outside the classroom. In addition to basic academic skills instruction, the curriculum includes the visual and performing arts, greenhouse science, outdoor adventure, physical education and foreign language. The early childhood program utilizes the Reggio Emilia Approach.

COMMUNITY SCHOOL
Day — Coed Gr PS (Age 3)-6

St Louis, MO 63124. 900 Lay Rd. Tel: 314-991-0005. Fax: 314-991-1512.
   www.communityschool.com   E-mail: mail@communityschool.com
Matthew A. Gould, Head (2004). BA, Earlham College, PhD, Univ of Chicago. **Dana Scott**
   Saulsberry, Adm.
   Pre-Prep. Elem math—Singapore Math. **Feat**—Fr Studio_Art Drama Band Music
      Woodworking. **Supp**—Dev_Read Tut.
   Selective adm: 57/yr. Usual entry: PS. Appl fee: $90. Appl due: Jan. **Tests** CTP_4.
   Enr 350. B 182. G 168. Wh 79%. Latino 1%. Blk 7%. Asian 6%. Other 7%. Avg class size:
      20. Stud/fac: 7:1. **Fac 50.** M 10/F 40. FT 44/PT 6. Wh 86%. Blk 7%. Asian 5%. Other
      2%. Adv deg: 50%.
   Grad '11—39. Prep—39. (John Burroughs, Mary Inst & St Louis Co Day, Whitfield,
      Chaminade Col Prep-MO, Westminster Christian-MO, Thomas Jefferson). Alum
      donors: 11%.
   Tui '12-'13: Day $16,120-16,925.
   Summer: Rec. Tui Day $150/wk. 6 wks.
   Endow $10,082,000. Acres 16. Bldgs 3. Class rms 17. Lib 25,000 vols. Sci labs 1. Lang
      labs 1. Art studios 1. Music studios 1. Man arts studios 1. Gyms 1. Fields 3. Comp
      labs 1. Comp/stud: 1:3.
   Est 1914. Nonprofit. Sem (Sept-June). **Assoc** NCA.

Founded in 1914 by a group of concerned parents, Community School, located on a 16-acre, wooded campus in Ladue, continues to encourage parental involvement in the life of the school. Community provides a full-day program for children from age 3 through grade 6. The integrated curriculum emphasizes reading at all grade levels. Nursery and kindergarten programs utilize a developmental approach, while the curriculum in grades 1-4 emphasizes secure computational and problem-solving skills and features creative writing, science, social studies and language arts. French instruction begins at age 3. Grades 5 and 6 are semidepartmentalized.

Students have physical education every day, and art, music and shop each week. Nature and outdoor activities form an integral part of the program.

FORSYTH SCHOOL

Day — Coed Gr PS (Age 3)-6

St Louis, MO 63105. 6235 Wydown Blvd. Tel: 314-726-4542. Fax: 314-726-0112.
www.forsythonline.com   E-mail: admissions@forsythonline.com
Michael J. Vachow, Head (2007). AB, Univ of Michigan, MA, Middlebury College. **Erica K. Axelbaum, Adm.**

> **Pre-Prep. Elem math**—Everyday Math. **Feat**—Lib_Skills Fr Lat Span Computers Performing_Arts Studio_Art Drama Band Music Movement Outdoor_Ed. **Supp**—Tut. Outdoor ed.
> **Selective adm:** 68/yr. Usual entry: PS & K. Appl fee: $85. Appl due: Feb. Applied: 146. Accepted: 55%. Yield: 81%. **Tests** CTP_4.
> **Enr 393.** B 188. G 205. Wh 73%. Latino 3%. Blk 6%. Asian 6%. Other 12%. Avg class size: 24. Stud/fac: 8:1. **Fac 48.** M 12/F 36. FT 48. Wh 92%. Latino 4%. Blk 4%. Adv deg: 50%.
> **Grad '11—42. Prep—41.** (John Burroughs 23, Mary Inst & St Louis Co Day 12, Villa Duchesne 2, Crossroads-MO 1, St Louis Priory 1, Westminster Christian-MO 1). Alum donors: 5%.
> **Tui '12-'13: Day $16,812. Aid:** Need 48 ($292,465).
> **Summer (enr 230):** Rec. Arts. Sports. Tui Day $250/wk. 8 wks.
> Endow $3,734,000. Plant val $6,745,000. Acres 3. Bldgs 8. Class rms 20. 2 Libs 14,000 vols. Sci labs 3. Art studios 1. Music studios 1. Perf arts ctrs 1. Gyms 1. Fields 1. Basketball courts 1. Tracks 1. Climbing walls 1. Ropes crses 1. Playgrounds 3. Comp labs 1. Comp/stud: 1:5 (1:1 Laptop prgm Gr 4-6).
> **Est 1961.** Nonprofit. Sem (Aug-June). **Assoc** NCA.

Forsyth, located across the street from Washington University, stresses individual attention by maintaining a low student-faculty ratio and team teaching in each classroom. Classes meet in five historic homes, all of which are equipped with modern classrooms. The challenging curriculum is enriched by full-time specialist teachers, a director of studies and a learning specialist.

Forsyth's extended-day program features after-school classes and year-round intramural sports.

JOHN BURROUGHS SCHOOL

Day — Coed Gr 7-12

St Louis, MO 63124. 755 S Price Rd. Tel: 314-993-4040, 800-264-4045.
Fax: 314-993-6458.
www.jburroughs.org   E-mail: admiss@jburroughs.org
Andrew H. Abbott, Head (2009). BA, Kenyon College, MA, Middlebury College. **Caroline G. LaVigne, Adm.**

> **Col Prep. AP (exams req'd; 340 taken, 93% 3+)**—Fr Ger Span Calc Comp_Sci Bio Chem Environ_Sci. **Feat**—Chin Greek Lat Russ Bioethics Engineering Neurosci Robotics Web_Design African-Amer_Stud Lat-Amer_Stud Architect_Drawing Art_

Hist Photog Video_Production Orchestra Jazz_Band Design Outdoor_Ed. **Supp—** Dev_Read Makeup Rem_Math Rem_Read Rev Tut. Outdoor ed.
Sports—Basket X-country Golf Lacrosse Racquet Soccer Swim Tennis Track. B: Baseball Football Ice_Hockey W_Polo Wrestling. G: F_Hockey Volley. **Activities:** 48.
Selective adm (Gr 7-9): 114/yr. Usual entry: 7. Appl fee: $40. Appl due: Jan. Applied: 271. Accepted: 46%. Yield: 91%. **Tests** SSAT.
Enr 600. B 295. G 305. Elem 198. Sec 402. Wh 72%. Latino 2%. Blk 10%. Asian 12%. Other 4%. Avg class size: 13. Stud/fac: 7:1. Casual. **Fac 107.** M 48/F 59. FT 73/PT 34. Wh 84%. Latino 5%. Blk 9%. Asian 2%. Adv deg: 71%.
Grad '11—103. Col—103. (Wash U 8, IN U 7, U of Miami 4, U of MO-Columbia 4, Vanderbilt 4, Dartmouth 3). **Avg SAT:** CR 670. M 700. W 690. **Mid 50% SAT:** CR 620-730. M 630-740. W 610-740. Avg ACT: 31. Mid 50% ACT: 29-33. **Col couns:** 6. Alum donors: 33%.
Tui '12-'13: Day $22,900 (+$1000). **Aid:** Need 101 ($1,429,200).
Endow $40,500,000. Plant val $62,059,000. Acres 48. Bldgs 7 (100% ADA). Class rms 50. Lib 30,000 vols. Sci labs 5. Lang labs 1. Auds 1. Art studios 2. Music studios 5. Dance studios 1. Art galleries 2. Gyms 3. Fields 9. Courts 10. Pools 2. Comp labs 5. Comp/stud: 1:3.4.
Est 1923. Nonprofit. Tri (Sept-May).

Located on a 47½-acre campus in the residential community of Ladue, Burroughs provides an educational experience that strikes a balance among academics, the arts, athletics and activities. The college preparatory curriculum provides a firm foundation in the five basic disciplines: English, science, math, social studies/history and languages. Although Burroughs does not emphasize the Advanced Placement program, several courses follow the AP curriculum and many others prepare students for AP exams. An outdoor, year-round laboratory in the Ozarks enhances the school's outdoor education projects and special programs that stress individual development.

The vast majority of students take part in Burroughs' voluntary community service program. Opportunities include schoolwide service projects on campus, a summer camp for underprivileged children, an academic enrichment program for at-risk children and a student group that organizes off-campus service activities. Each class contributes between 9000 and 13,000 cumulative hours of service while at the school. **See Also Page 97**

MARY INSTITUTE AND SAINT LOUIS COUNTRY DAY SCHOOL
Day — Coed Gr PS (Age 4)-12

St Louis, MO 63124. 101 N Warson Rd. Tel: 314-993-5100. Fax: 314-995-7470.
www.micds.org E-mail: admissions@micds.org
Lisa Lyle, Head (2007). BA, Univ of Texas-Austin, MA, Univ of Pennsylvania, MA, Columbia Univ. **Peggy B. Laramie, Adm.**
Col Prep. AP (exams req'd)—Fr Ger Lat Span Calc Stats Bio Chem Environ_Sci Physics Eur_Hist US_Hist Econ US_Govt & Pol Art_Hist Studio_Art Music_Theory. **Elem math**—Singapore Math. **Feat**—Creative_Writing Shakespeare Chin Ital Linear_Algebra Anat & Physiol Astron Forensic_Sci Animal_Behavior Engineering Comp_Sci Robotics Web_Design Civil_Rights Cold_War Holocaust Psych Architect Photog Sculpt Acting Drama Directing Music Speech. **Supp**—Tut.
Sports—Basket Crew X-country Golf Lacrosse Soccer Squash Swim Tennis Track. B: Baseball Football Ice_Hockey W_Polo Wrestling. G: Cheer F_Hockey Volley. **Activities:** 52.
Selective adm (Gr PS-11): 202/yr. Usual entry: PS, K, 1, 5, 6, 7 & 9. Appl fee: $40. Appl due: Jan. Applied: 442. Accepted: 66%. Yield: 65%. **Tests** ISEE SSAT TOEFL.
Enr 1233. Elem 613. Sec 620. Wh 72%. Latino 1%. Blk 9%. Asian 10%. Other 8%. Avg class size: 16. Stud/fac: 8:1. Casual. **Fac 148.** M 61/F 87. FT 142/PT 6. Wh 90%. Latino 5%. Blk 2%. Asian 1%. Other 2%. Adv deg: 72%.
Grad '11—135. Col—135. (U of MO-Columbia 10, TX Christian 6, Wash U 5, SMU 5, U of CO-Boulder 5, Vanderbilt 4). **Avg SAT:** CR/M/W 1910. Avg ACT: 29. **Col couns:** 5. Alum donors: 28%.

Tui '12-'13: Day $16,950-22,700 (+$300-500). **Aid:** Merit 13 ($65,000). Need 282 ($3,700,000).
Summer (enr 110): Acad Enrich. Tui Day $360-1500. 3-6 wks.
Endow $79,441,000. Plant val $78,292,000. Acres 103. Bldgs 9. Class rms 103. 3 Libs 55,000 vols. Sci labs 14. Lang labs 2. Photog labs 1. Auds 3. Theaters 3. Art studios 7. Music studios 4. Dance studios 1. AV rms 1. Gyms 3. Fields 12. Courts 15. Pools 1. Playgrounds 1. Comp/stud: 1:1.1 (1:1 Laptop prgm Gr 5-12).
Est 1859. Nonprofit. Tri (Aug-June). **Assoc** CLS.

Located on a 103-acre campus, MICDS comprises a lower school for children in grades pre-K-4, a middle school for those in grades 5-8, and an upper school serving grades 9-12. The entire school is coed, with single-gender academic classes in the core subjects conducted in the middle school.

Founded in the mid-19th century, Mary Institute and Smith Academy were departments of Washington University. In 1917, Saint Louis Country Day School became the successor to Smith Academy. Both schools were independent of the university by 1949. In 1992, the two schools joined together and began to function as one.

The lower school (junior kindergarten through grade 4) offers a literature-based reading program and an integrated core curriculum with specialists in science, Spanish, computer, art, music, drama and physical education. Middle schoolers take part in a departmentalized curriculum that features interdisciplinary units. Students in grades 5-8 attend single-gender advisories and classes in math, language arts, science history and physical education, as well as coeducational arts and foreign language classes, assemblies, lunch periods, activities and recess. Eighth graders satisfy a 20-hour community service requirement.

The upper school's college preparatory curriculum includes English, history, mathematics, science, foreign language, the arts and physical education. Advanced Placement exams are available in most disciplines, and most students take at least one AP class before graduating. Upper school students select from a variety of activities, including athletics. Boys and girls in grades 7-12 lease tablet personal computers, while each pupil in grades 5 and 6 has access to a netbook for in-school use.   **See Also Page 121**

SAINT LOUIS PRIORY SCHOOL
Day — Boys Gr 7-12

St Louis, MO 63141. 500 S Mason Rd. Tel: 314-434-3690. Fax: 314-576-7088.
www.stlprioryschool.org   E-mail: tmulvihill@priory.org
Rev. Linus Dolce, OSB, Head. PhD. **Tom Mulvihill, Adm.**
    Col Prep. AP—Lat Span Calc Stats Comp_Sci Bio Chem Physics Eur_Hist US_Hist US_Govt & Pol Studio_Art Music_Theory. **Feat**—Creative_Writing Shakespeare Fr Greek Astron Environ_Sci Comp_Relig Theol Art_Hist Filmmaking Photog Stained_Glass Acting Theater Theater_Arts.
    Sports (req'd)—B: Baseball Basket X-country Football Golf Ice_Hockey Rugby Soccer Tennis Track Wrestling.
    Selective adm: 75/yr. Appl fee: $50. Appl due: Jan. Accepted: 46%. **Tests** SSAT.
    Enr 390. Elem 138. Sec 252. Avg class size: 17. Stud/fac: 9:1. Formal. **Fac 51.** Adv deg: 74%.
    Grad '07—60. Col—60. (U of MO-Columbia, U of Miami, UNC-Chapel Hill, Notre Dame, Stanford, Georgetown). **Avg SAT:** CR 676. M 657. Avg ACT: 29. **Col couns:** 2.
    Tui '11-'12: Day $18,500 (+$1000). **Aid:** Need ($1,200,000).
    Summer: Acad Enrich Rev Rec. 6 wks.
    Endow $17,000,000. Plant val $18,500,000. Acres 150. Bldgs 18. Lib 65,000 vols. Gyms 2. Courts 9. Weight rms 1.
    Est 1956. Nonprofit. Roman Catholic (85% practice). Tri (Aug-May).

This college preparatory day school for boys is operated by Saint Louis Abbey, a Benedictine monastery founded by Ampleforth Abbey in England. Saint Louis Abbey and its school became independent of the founding Abbey in 1973. The 150-acre, wooded campus is situated on rolling hills in west St. Louis County.

The course of studies imparts a solid, traditional liberal arts education through the disciplines of religion, English, classical and modern foreign languages, mathematics, the natural sciences, history and computer science. Priory offers AP courses in most subjects, and independent study is an option for exceptional students in their junior and senior years. A special feature of the senior year is a thesis or exhibition; each student must submit a research thesis, a work of creative writing, or a project in the visual or performing arts. Service to the community is also required for graduation; juniors and seniors render service to the sick, the elderly, the young and many others in need. Once each week, the school community comes together to pray and to celebrate the liturgy.

Participation in athletics is required, and both interscholastic competition and noncompetitive physical activities are offered. Students in the high school are expected to take part in an interscholastic sport at least two trimesters each year.

THOMAS JEFFERSON SCHOOL
Bdg and Day — Coed Gr 7-12

St Louis, MO 63127. 4100 S Lindbergh Blvd. Tel: 314-843-4151. Fax: 314-843-3527.
www.tjs.org   E-mail: admissions@tjs.org
William C. Rowe, Head. BA, Wesleyan Univ, MA, Washington Univ. **Jane Roth & Ken Colston, Adms.**

Col Prep. AP (exams req'd)—Eng Fr Calc Bio Chem Physics Eur_Hist US_Hist Comp_Govt & Pol US_Govt & Pol. **Feat**—Greek Ital Lat Studio_Art Drama Music. **Supp**—ESL.
Sports—Basket Soccer Volley. **Activities:** 10.
Selective adm: 25/yr. Bdg 10. Day 15. Appl fee: $40. Appl due: Feb. Accepted: 63%. Yield: 100%. **Tests** SSAT TOEFL.
Enr 88. Intl 26%. Avg class size: 14. Stud/fac: 6:1. **Fac 13.** M 6/F 7. FT 13. Adv deg: 53%.
Grad '10—13. Col—13. (Emory 1, Case Western Reserve 1, Boston U 1, Johns Hopkins 1, U of PA 1, Bard-NY 1). **Avg SAT:** CR/M/W 2050.
Tui '12-'13: Bdg $39,500 (+$1800). **5-Day Bdg $37,750** (+$1800). **Day $22,750** (+$1800). **Intl Bdg $40,500** (+$3000). **Aid:** Need 35 ($394,450).
Summer: Enrich. European Travel. 3 wks.
Endow $800,000. Plant val $1,400,000. Acres 20. Bldgs 9. Dorms 7. Dorm rms 25. Class rms 9. Lib 3000 vols. Sci labs 2. Lang labs 2. Art studios 1. Gyms 1. Fields 1. Courts 5.
Est 1946. Nonprofit. Sem (Sept-May). **Assoc** NCA.

Thomas Jefferson was established as a boys' school by Robin McCoy, Charles Merrill, Jr., and Graham Spring, three Harvard alumni. Mr. McCoy was headmaster for 34 years, until his retirement in 1980, while Mr. Merrill taught for 10 years and eventually moved to Boston, MA, and started the Commonwealth School. The 20-acre campus is located on a former private estate in the residential neighborhood of Sunset Hills; its main building occupies the estate's original home. The school became coeducational in 1971.

English and mathematics form the foundation of the curriculum, along with science, social studies, and both classical and modern foreign languages. By the senior year, a typical student's program is entirely at the Advanced Placement level. All classes are held in the morning; part of the afternoon is spent engaged in study—the youngest pupils begin with a supervised study hall and advance to independent study at faculty discretion—while the rest is structured with labs, athletics and extracurricular meetings. A mandatory fine arts class meets two afternoons a week; typical options include choir, appreciation courses in art and music, and studio courses in drawing and painting, ceramics and photography.

Participation in athletics is required several days a week; students choose one sport or activity per season from among both interscholastic and intramural options. Student involvement in off-campus activities is encouraged, and all pupils fulfill a community service requirement of 75 total hours in grades 9-12. In addition, TJS schedules optional weekend activities such as concerts and sporting events.

The entire student body attends productions at the St. Louis Repertory Theater, and individual classes take field trips to the symphony, the art museum, and other exhibits and events. In addition, the headmaster leads a trip to Europe approximately every other summer. These trips, which focus on Florence, Italy, and London, England, with side excursions made to other cities, pay particular attention to art, architecture, theater and historical sites.

THE WILSON SCHOOL
Day — Coed Gr PS (Age 3)-6

Clayton, MO 63105. 400 DeMun Ave. Tel: 314-725-4999. Fax: 314-725-5242.
  www.wilsonschool.com   E-mail: info@wilsonschool.com
Thad M. Falkner, Head (2006). BS, MA, Univ of Missouri-St Louis. **Laura C. Hartung, Adm.**
  Pre-Prep. Feat—Lib_Skills Fr Lat Computers Studio_Art Music.
  Sports—Basket Soccer. B: Baseball.
  Selective adm: 32/yr. Usual entry: PS. Appl fee: $75. Appl due: Jan. **Tests** CTP_4 ISEE.
  Enr 190. B 95. G 95. Wh 77%. Latino 3%. Blk 13%. Native Am 1%. Asian 5%. Other 1%. Intl 18%. Avg class size: 20. Stud/fac: 8:1. **Fac 26.** M 4/F 22. FT 26. Wh 88%. Latino 3%. Blk 3%. Native Am 3%. Asian 3%. Adv deg: 38%.
  Grad '09—21. Prep—18. (John Burroughs, Mary Inst & St Louis Co Day, Villa Duchesne, Visitation, Whitfield, St Louis Priory).
  Tui '11-'12: Day $15,588 (+$140-2000). **Aid:** Need 33 ($161,520).
  Summer: Enrich Rec. Tui Day $220/wk. 9 wks.
  Plant val $1,600,000. Bldgs 1. Class rms 16. Lib 30,000 vols. Sci labs 1. Lang labs 1. Auds 1. Art studios 1. Music studios 1. Gyms 1. Fields 2. Comp labs 1.
  Est 1913. Nonprofit. Sem (Aug-June). **Assoc** NCA.

Named for its original director, Mabel Wilson, this school was founded as St. Louis' first independent preschool by a group of Central West End parents. Language arts, math, science, social studies, foreign language, art, music, physical education, library skills and technology form the core of the integrated curriculum at all grade levels. At all grade levels, the program emphasizes time management, writing and study skills.

The hands-on preschool program (pre-K and K), which enrolls children beginning at age 3, gears work and play toward developing a foundation in the basic skills; an emphasis on reading and an early exposure to computer technology are characteristics of the preschool. During the lower school years (grades 1-3), students further develop their reading and math skills, with classes becoming more challenging and daily homework beginning. Study of the environment, ecology and life science is part of the lower school science curriculum.

In the upper school (grades 4-6), course work in all departments allows for more depth. A substantial library book collection enriches the literature-based reading program. Technology is a strong component of the curriculum: Classrooms include computer workstations, and Internet access is available through the technology lab. Specialists teach classes in French, Latin, art, music, science, technology, library resource and physical education.

As a complement to traditional course work, all boys and girls participate in community service and character education programs. Wilson's proximity to Washington University, Forest Park, museums and concert halls provides opportunities for cultural enrichment.

NEBRASKA

ELKHORN, NE. (12 mi. W of Omaha, NE) Rural. Pop: 6062. Alt: 1200 ft.

MOUNT MICHAEL BENEDICTINE SCHOOL
Bdg and Day — Boys Gr 9-12

Elkhorn, NE 68022. 22520 Mt Michael Rd. Tel: 402-289-2541. Fax: 402-289-4539.
www.mountmichael.com   E-mail: admissions@mountmichael.org
David J. Peters, Head (2012). BS, MA, Creighton Univ, EdD, Univ of Nebraska-Lincoln.
Eric Crawford, Adm.
  Col Prep. AP (exams req'd)—Eng Calc Comp_Sci Bio Chem Physics Eur_Hist US_
    Hist Psych. **Feat**—Fr Span Econ Govt Relig Studio_Art Band Chorus Accounting Bus
    Journ Speech. **Supp**—Rem_Read Tut.
  Sports—B: Baseball Basket X-country Football Golf Soccer Swim Tennis Track Wres-
    tling.
  Somewhat selective adm (Gr 9-11): 48/yr. Bdg 28. Day 20. Appl fee: $25. Appl due:
    Rolling. Applied: 50. Accepted: 95%. Yield: 95%. **Tests** HSPT TOEFL.
  Enr 214. Bdg 134. Day 80. Wh 90%. Blk 3%. Native Am 1%. Asian 6%. Intl 20%. Avg
    class size: 14. Stud/fac: 8:1. Formal. **Fac 25.** M 19/F 6. FT 18/PT 7. Wh 100%. Adv
    deg: 56%. In dorms 1.
  Grad '11—46. Col—46. (Creighton, U of NE-Lincoln, U of NE-Omaha, St Louis U, GA
    Inst of Tech, Benedictine Col). **Avg SAT:** CR/M/W 1895. Avg ACT: 27.4.
  Tui '11-'12: Bdg $18,205-18,510 (+$520-635). **5-Day Bdg $15,255-15,560** (+$520-
    635). **Day $10,245-10,550** (+$1210-1325). **Intl Bdg $20,565-20,870** (+$520-635).
    Aid: Need 120 ($100,000). Work prgm 50 ($100,000).
  Endow $2,000,000. Plant val $3,000,000. Acres 400. Bldgs 2. Dorms 1. Dorm rms 40.
    Class rms 10. Lib 33,000 vols. Chapels 1. Labs 3. Art studios 3. Music studios 4.
    Gyms 2. Fields 3. Courts 2.
  Est 1956. Nonprofit. Roman Catholic (90% practice). Sem (Aug-May). **Assoc** NCA.

A Benedictine school, Mount Michael emphasizes close student-teacher relationships and
community living for highly motivated students. The Catholic, intellectual and physical aspects
of education are combined to prepare boys for college. Interscholastic and intramural sports
are provided, and family activities are planned throughout the year. The community service
requirement starts with 10 hours in grade 9, then increases by 10 hours per year.
  Students enroll from cities and towns within a 100-mile radius.

OMAHA, NE. (126 mi. W of Des Moines, IA) Urban. Pop: 390,007. Alt: 1034 ft.

BROWNELL-TALBOT SCHOOL
Day — Coed Gr PS (Age 4)-12

Omaha, NE 68132. 400 N Happy Hollow Blvd. Tel: 402-556-3772. Fax: 402-553-2994.
www.brownell.edu   E-mail: juadams@brownell.edu
Sylvia Rodriguez Vargas, Head (2012). Julie Adams, Adm.
  Col Prep. AP—Eng Fr Lat Span Calc Stats Comp_Sci Bio Chem Eur_Hist US_Hist.
    Feat—Creative_Writing Comp_Design World_Relig Sculpt Studio_Art Theater Band
    Chorus Music_Theory Orchestra Dance Journ Yoga.
  Sports—Basket X-country Golf Soccer Swim Track. B: Baseball Football Tennis. G:
    Cheer Volley.

Selective adm: 75/yr. Appl fee: $50. Appl due: Rolling. **Tests** CTP_4 IQ.
Enr 457. Elem 321. Sec 136. Avg class size: 16. Stud/fac: 8:1. Uniform. **Fac 45.**
Grad '11—27. Col—27. (Creighton, U of CO-Boulder, Wash U, U of AZ, Stanford, Yale).
     Avg SAT: CR 624. M 602. W 626. **Mid 50% SAT:** CR 550-690. M 560-630. W 580-
     680. Avg ACT: 28. Mid 50% ACT: 25-31.
Tui '12-'13: Day $12,100-17,100 (+$450-600). **Aid:** Need 69 ($448,000).
Endow $3,300,000. Plant val $6,000,000. Acres 17. Bldgs 4. Class rms 40. Lib 9000 vols.
     Auds 1. Art studios 2. Music studios 2. Dance studios 1. Arts ctrs 1. Gyms 2. Fields 2.
     Field houses 1. Pools 1. Comp labs 2. Comp/stud: 1:2 (1:1 Laptop prgm Gr 9-12).
Est 1863. Nonprofit. Sem (Sept-June). **Assoc** NCA.

Founded in 1863 by Episcopal bishop Joseph Talbot to educate children of Nebraska's early
pioneers, Brownell-Talbot is now a nonsectarian school that emphasizes college preparation.
Located on a 17-acre, wooded campus, the school offers a rigorous academic program supplemented by Advanced Placement courses. Upper school pupils (grades 9-12) perform 10 hours
of required community service annually.

Technology enhances instruction at all levels. Upper school students purchase their own
laptop computers for classroom use. Middle and lower school classes have access to two computer labs and two laptop mobile carts.

NORTH DAKOTA

FARGO, ND. (187 mi. E of Bismarck, ND) Urban. Pop: 90,599. Alt: 901 ft.

OAK GROVE LUTHERAN SCHOOL
Day — Coed Gr PS (Age 4)-12

Fargo, ND 58102. 124 N Terrace. Tel: 701-237-0210. Fax: 701-297-1993.
Other locations: 2720 32nd Ave S, Fargo 58103.
www.oakgrovelutheran.com   E-mail: oakgrove@oakgrovelutheran.com
Michael A. Slette, Pres (2011). BA, Concordia College (Moorhead). **Rachal Thompson, Adm.**

Col Prep. AP (27 exams taken, 74% 3+)—Eng Calc Bio Music_Theory. **Elem math**—Everyday Math. **Feat**—Span Stats Anat & Physiol Environ_Sci Marine_Bio/Sci Programming Civics Econ Psych Sociol Theol Studio_Art Band Chorus Accounting Culinary_Arts. **Supp**—Dev_Read Rem_Math Rem_Read Rev Tut. **Dual enr:** Concordia Col-Moorhead.

Sports—Basket X-country Golf Ice_Hockey Soccer Swim Tennis Track. B: Baseball Football. G: Gymnastics Softball Volley.

Somewhat selective adm: 50/yr. Appl fee: $50. Appl due: Rolling. Applied: 55. Accepted: 92%. Yield: 92%.

Enr 412. Elem 269. Sec 143. Wh 92%. Blk 2%. Asian 6%. Avg class size: 17. Stud/fac: 12:1. **Fac 38.** M 14/F 24. FT 28/PT 10. Wh 100%. Adv deg: 13%.

Grad '11—41. Col—40. (Concordia Col-Moorhead, ND St, MN St-Moorhead). Avg ACT: 28.1. **Col couns:** 1.

Tui '12-'13: Day $5330-7780 (+$330-370).

Endow $4,600,000. Plant val $20,000,000. Acres 5. Bldgs 5. Class rms 25. Lib 15,000 vols. Sci labs 2. Auds 1. Art studios 1. Music studios 2. Gyms 3. Athletic ctrs 1. Fields 1. Comp labs 2. Laptop prgm Gr 9-12.

Est 1906. Nonprofit. Lutheran (82% practice). Sem (Aug-May). **Assoc** NCA.

Founded as a girls' school, Oak Grove became coeducational in 1926 and consolidated with the Lutheran Bible School the next year. There is an emphasis on music with a touring concert choir, a band and five other musical groups. With prior approval, upperclassmen may earn dual credit for course work completed at Concordia College in Moorhead, MN. Independent study is available at an additional fee for pupils interested in courses not available at Oak Grove. Students in grades 9-12 receive tablet computers for use during the school year, and the north campus is equipped with a wireless network.

Serving children in grades pre-K-5, the school's south campus is located on 32nd Avenue.

Although it is essentially a day school, Oak Grove maintains a small boarding division for international pupils in grades 9-12. Boarders reside with host families.   **See Also Page 113**

South Central States

ARKANSAS

LITTLE ROCK, AR. (136 mi. W of Memphis, TN) Urban. Pop: 183,133. Alt: 300 ft.

PULASKI ACADEMY
Day — Coed Gr PS (Age 3)-12

Little Rock, AR 72212. 12701 Hinson Rd. Tel: 501-604-1910. Fax: 501-225-1974.
www.pulaskiacademy.org   E-mail: gregg.ledbetter@pulaskiacademy.org
Matthew J. Walsh, Head (2012). BA, Georgetown Univ, MA, Middlebury College. **Gregg R. Ledbetter, Sr., Adm.**

Col Prep. AP—Eng Fr Span Calc Stats Comp_Sci Bio Chem Physics World_Hist Comp_ Govt & Pol Econ Human_Geog US_Govt & Pol Art_Hist Studio_Art. **Feat**—British_ Lit Chin Anat & Physiol Ecol Microbio Organic_Chem Web_Design Intl_Relations Ceramics Photog Drama Musical_Theater Band Chorus Communications Finance Journ. **Supp**—Tut.

Sports—Basket X-country Golf Soccer Swim Tennis Track. B: Baseball Football Wrestling. G: Cheer Softball Volley. **Activities:** 43.

Selective adm: 200/yr. Appl fee: $50. Appl due: Rolling. Accepted: 81%. **Tests** IQ Stanford.

Enr 1335. Avg class size: 15. Stud/fac: 13:1. Uniform. **Fac 100.** Adv deg: 65%.

Grad '10—89. **Col**—89. (U of AR-Fayetteville 29, U of Central AR 7, U of CO-Boulder 3, Rhodes 3, Auburn 3, Hendrix 3). **Avg SAT:** CR 575. M 574. W 581. Avg ACT: 26. **Col couns:** 2.

Tui '12-'13: Day $7300 (+$800). **Aid:** Need 120 ($420,000).

Summer: Acad Enrich Rec. Sports. 1-6 wks.

Endow $500,000. Plant val $4,000,000. Acres 32. Bldgs 4. Class rms 75. 2 Libs 12,000 vols. Sci labs 4. Auds 1. Art studios 2. Music studios 2. Arts ctrs 1. Gyms 1. Fields 1. Courts 1. Comp labs 1.

Est 1971. Nonprofit. Sem (Aug-June). **Assoc** CLS NCA.

Located on a 32-acre campus in West Little Rock, Pulaski Academy was founded by a group of local citizens. The early childhood division (ages 3 and 4) provides a program that guides children through prescriptive activities in the areas of reading and math readiness, in addition to language, social and motor development. The kindergarten program stresses reading and math skills, with increasing emphasis placed on social skills, computer usage, scientific processes and thought development. In the lower school (grades 1-4), pupils take part in an interactive, developmentally appropriate curriculum. Basic skills are enriched by programs in physical education, art, music, drama and computer instruction.

The middle school (grades 5-8) provides an academic program with a strong core curriculum that emphasizes multidisciplinary units, study skills, and creative and critical thinking. The college preparatory upper school encourages the development of academic and critical-thinking skills. Advanced Placement courses are an integral part of the program. Special activities and programs include field trips, guest lecturers and performers, and dramatic productions. All upper schoolers perform community service.

SUBIACO, AR. (83 mi. WNW of Little Rock, AR) Rural. Pop: 439. Alt: 510 ft.

SUBIACO ACADEMY
Bdg and Day — Boys Gr 7-12

Subiaco, AR 72865. 405 N Subiaco Ave. Tel: 479-934-1025, 800-364-7824.
  Fax: 479-934-1033.
  www.subiacoacademy.us   E-mail: admissions@subi.org
Robert A. Loia, Head (2011). BA, Catholic Univ of America, MEd, Loyola Univ Maryland.
  Scott Breed, Adm.
  Col Prep. AP (exams req'd)—Eng Calc Stats Bio Chem US_Hist US_Govt & Pol
    Studio_Art. **Feat**—British_Lit Lat Span Comp_Sci WWII Civics Econ World_Relig
    Drama Music Journ. **Supp**—ESL Tut.
  Sports—B: Baseball Basket X-country Football Golf Soccer Tennis Track. **Activities:**
    10.
  Selective adm (Gr 7-11): 50/yr. Bdg 38. Day 12. Appl fee: $50-70. Appl due: Rolling.
    Applied: 79. Accepted: 81%. Yield: 63%. **Tests** IQ SSAT TOEFL.
  Enr 175. Bdg 115. Day 60. Elem 21. Sec 154. Wh 73%. Latino 2%. Blk 5%. Asian 19%.
    Other 1%. Intl 24%. Avg class size: 12. Stud/fac: 8:1. Uniform. **Fac 27.** M 18/F 9. FT
    15/PT 12. Wh 91%. Latino 3%. Asian 6%. Adv deg: 66%. In dorms 2.
  Grad '11—37. **Col**—36. (U of AR-Fayetteville 4, AR Tech 4, Benedictine Col 3, Lyon 2,
    St John's Col-NM 2, TX Tech 2). **Avg SAT:** CR/M/W 1772. Avg ACT: 26. **Col couns:**
    1. Alum donors: 20%.
  Tui '11-'12: Bdg $20,060 (+$495). **5-Day Bdg $17,800** (+$495). **Day $6090** (+$370).
    Intl Bdg $25,560 (+$495). **Aid:** Need 70.
  Summer: Acad. Tui Bdg $2900. 3 wks.
  Endow $3,500,000. Plant val $12,500,000. Acres 100. Bldgs 10 (7% ADA). Dorms 4.
    Dorm rms 80. Class rms 24. Libs 1. Sci labs 2. Auds 1. Theaters 1. Art studios 1. Arts
    ctrs 1. Gyms 1. Fields 3. Courts 4. Pools 1. Comp labs 2.
  Est 1887. Nonprofit. Roman Catholic (70% practice). Quar (Aug-May). **Assoc** NCA.

Benedictine monks from Switzerland founded Subiaco, which is located in the foothills
of the Ozarks some 110 miles northwest of Little Rock. Courses in Christian doctrine are
required of all students and are an integral part of the college preparatory program. The academy offers a selection of honors and Advanced Placement courses, and pupils complete compulsory course work in the arts.

All students participate either in athletics or in journalism, drama, music or community
service. The academy provides private instruction in piano, organ and other instruments.

LOUISIANA

BATON ROUGE, LA. (76 mi. WNW of New Orleans, LA) Urban. Pop: 227,818. Alt: 58 Ft.

EPISCOPAL HIGH SCHOOL
Day — Coed Gr PS (Age 4)-12

Baton Rouge, LA 70816. 3200 Woodland Ridge Blvd. Tel: 225-753-3180.
Fax: 225-756-0926.
www.ehsbr.org   E-mail: info@ehsbr.org
Hugh M. McIntosh, Head (2010). BS, Mississippi State Univ, JD, Univ of Virginia, MDiv, Harvard Univ. **Jennifer Artigue, Adm.**
Col Prep. AP (exams req'd)—Eng Fr Lat Span Calc Stats Comp_Sci Bio Chem Physics Eur_Hist US_Hist US_Govt & Pol Studio_Art Music_Theory. **Feat**—Creative_Writing Shakespeare Southern_Lit Japan Anat Botany Ecol Environ_Sci Geol Marine_Bio/Sci Econ Law Pol_Sci Psych Bible Ethics Relig Drawing Sculpt Drama Band Jazz_Ensemble Dance. **Supp**—Dev_Read Tut.
Sports—Basket X-country Golf Soccer Swim Tennis Track. B: Baseball Football Weightlifting. G: Cheer Softball Volley. **Activities:** 30.
Selective adm: 171/yr. Appl fee: $85. Appl due: Rolling. Accepted: 59%.
Enr 1034. Avg class size: 16. Stud/fac: 11:1. Uniform. **Fac 106.** M 30/F 76. FT 106. Adv deg: 53%.
Grad '10—88. Col—88. (LA St-Baton Rouge 32, U of GA 4, Tulane 3, U of AL-Tuscaloosa 3, Emory 2, Millsaps 2). **Avg SAT:** CR 589. M 611. W 596. Avg ACT: 26. **Col couns:** 2.
Tui '11-'12: Day $9000-14,900 (+$1600). **Aid:** Merit 10 ($15,000). Need 207 ($1,675,000).
Summer: Arts. Tui $175. 1 wk. Sports. Gr 3-8. 6 wks.
Endow $8,575,000. Plant val $17,573,000. Acres 55. Bldgs 15. Class rms 62. 2 Libs 32,000 vols. Chapels 1. Sci labs 9. Theaters 1. Art studios 3. Music studios 2. Dance studios 1. Perf arts ctrs 1. Gyms 2. Fields 6. Tennis courts 5. Pools 1. Tracks 1. Weight rms 1. Stadiums 1. Comp labs 7. Comp/stud: 1:2.
Est 1965. Nonprofit. Episcopal. Sem (Aug-May). **Assoc** SACS.

Founded as a college preparatory school, Episcopal now serves grades PS-12 at its 55-acre campus in the southeastern section of Baton Rouge. French and Spanish instruction begins in kindergarten, and Latin is added to the foreign language offerings in grade 4. The middle school program (grades 6-8) emphasizes study techniques, logical thinking, time management and personal responsibility. Honors sections, Advanced Placement courses and extensive elective options round out the upper school program.

Required chapel services are held once a week in the lower school and three times each week in the middle and upper schools. Upper school students perform 10 hours of community service in grade 9 and 20 hours in grades 10 and 11. In Episcopal's advisory program, pupils work closely with a faculty member throughout the upper school years.

METAIRIE, LA. (15 mi. WSW of New Orleans, LA) Suburban. Pop: 146,136. Alt: 5 ft.

METAIRIE PARK COUNTRY DAY SCHOOL
Day — Coed Gr PS (Age 4)-12

Metairie, LA 70005. 300 Park Rd. Tel: 504-837-5204. Fax: 504-837-0015.
www.mpcds.com   E-mail: admissions@mpcds.com
Carolyn Chandler, Head (2003). BA, Vanderbilt Univ, MA, Univ of Tennessee-Chattanooga. Amy White, Adm.

    Col Prep. AP (exams req'd; 163 taken)—Eng Fr Span Calc Bio Chem Physics Eur_
    Hist US_Hist Human_Geog Psych US_Govt & Pol Art_Hist. Feat—Creative_Writing
    Humanities Chin Environ_Sci Oceanog Health_Sci Computers Film Painting Photog
    Sculpt Studio_Art Acting Drama Music Dance Journ. Supp—Dev_Read Rem_Math
    Tut. Dual enr: U of New Orleans, Tulane.
    Sports—Basket X-country Golf Soccer Swim Tennis Track. B: Baseball Football. G:
    Cheer Softball Volley.
    Selective adm: 114/yr. Appl fee: $50. Appl due: Rolling. Applied: 246. Accepted: 66%.
    Yield: 70%. Tests IQ SSAT Stanford.
    Enr 721. B 383. G 338. Wh 82%. Latino 3%. Blk 7%. Asian 2%. Other 6%. Avg class size:
    13. Stud/fac: 9:1. Casual. Fac 86. M 20/F 66. FT 72/PT 14. Wh 94%. Latino 4%. Blk
    1%. Asian 1%. Adv deg: 63%.
    Grad '11—52. Col—52. (U of AL-Tuscaloosa 4, SMU 3, Wash & Lee 3, Geo Wash 2,
    Furman 2, U of NC 2). Athl schol 1. Mid 50% SAT: CR 520-660. M 540-680. W 550-
    670. Mid 50% ACT: 25-29. Col couns: 1. Alum donors: 21%.
    Tui '12-'13: Day $13,010-17,660 (+$1250-1450). Aid: Need 141 ($1,055,455).
    Summer: Enrich. Art. Tui Day $1200. 5 wks.
    Endow $7,400,000. Plant val $38,000,000. Acres 14. Bldgs 30 (100% ADA). Class rms
    50. 2 Libs 88,534 vols. Theater/auds 1. Art studios 7. Music studios 3. Dance studios
    1. Gyms 1. Fields 1. Comp/stud: 1:2 (1:1 Laptop prgm Gr 9-12).
    Est 1929. Nonprofit. Sem (Aug-May). Assoc CLS.

The first country day school in the region, MPCDS is of interest for its varied curriculum, which focuses on the individual and society. The college preparatory program emphasizes academics, and the fine arts program is an integral part of the humanistic education. Faculty promote the development of writing skills and the clear expression of ideas. Advanced Placement courses and electives are available in all subject areas. Upper school students purchase tablet computers for classroom use. Pupils may engage in summer study in France or Spain. Boys and girls in grades 9-12 accumulate 50 hours of required community service.

The school occupies 14 acres, two of which provide open land for athletic playing fields. Country Day offers interscholastic competition from grade 7.

RIDGEWOOD PREPARATORY SCHOOL
Day — Coed Gr PS (Age 4)-12

Metairie, LA 70001. 201 Pasadena Ave. Tel: 504-835-2545. Fax: 504-837-1864.
www.ridgewoodprep.com   E-mail: rps@ridgewoodprep.com
M. J. Montgomery, Jr., Head (1972). BS, MEd, Loyola Univ (LA).

    Col Prep. Feat—Lib_Skills Fr Span Comp_Sci Econ Art_Hist Studio_Art Debate Journ
    Speech. Supp—Tut.
    Sports—Basket X-country Soccer Tennis Track. B: Baseball Football. G: Softball Volley.
    Activities: 5.
    Selective adm (Gr PS-11): 50/yr. Appl fee: $300. Appl due: Rolling. Accepted: 45%.
    Yield: 95%. Tests Stanford.
    Enr 275. B 145. G 130. Elem 135. Sec 140. Wh 80%. Latino 8%. Blk 7%. Asian 5%.
    Intl 15%. Avg class size: 10. Stud/fac: 9:1. Fac 31. M 10/F 21. FT 28/PT 3. Wh 91%.

Latino 5%. Asian 4%. Adv deg: 54%.
Grad '11—50. Col—50. (U of New Orleans, LA St-Baton Rouge, Tulane, Loyola U-LA, Southeastern LA, U of S MS). Athl schol 1. Avg ACT: 25.
Tui '12-'13: Day $4075-5950 (+$500).
Endow $94,000. Plant val $5,000,000. Acres 4. Bldgs 4. Class rms 24. Lib 17,000 vols. Sci labs 1. Art studios 1. Music studios 1. Gyms 1. Fields 1. Comp labs 1. Comp/stud: 1:6.
Est 1948. Nonprofit. 6 terms (Aug-May). **Assoc** SACS.

Founded as a college preparatory school for boys, Ridgewood became coeducational in 1952. The school is organized as a primary school, a middle school and a high school, with a selection of honors courses available in the upper grades. Computer science and fine arts units are required for graduation, and elective choices include French, Spanish, journalism, speech, art and library science.

ST. MARTIN'S EPISCOPAL SCHOOL

Day — Coed Gr PS (Age 2)-12

Metairie, LA 70003. 225 Green Acres Rd. Tel: 504-733-0353. Fax: 504-736-8802.
www.stmsaints.com   E-mail: lisa.sibal@stmsaints.com
Merry P. Sorrells, Head (2012). BA, Principia College, MEd, Univ of New Orleans. **Lisa N. Sibal, Adm.**

Col Prep. AP (exams req'd; 82 taken, 66% 3+)—Eng Fr Lat Span Calc Stats Bio Chem US_Hist Econ Studio_Art. **Elem math**—Everyday Math. **Elem read**—Reading Street. **Feat**—Creative_Writing Chin Comp_Sci Civics Chin_Stud World_Relig Ceramics Film Photog Drama Chorus Speech. **Supp**—Dev_Read Rem_Math Rev. Sat classes. **Dual enr:** Tulane, U of New Orleans.
Sports—Basket X-country Golf Soccer Swim Tennis Track. B: Baseball Football. G: Softball Volley. **Activities:** 30.
Somewhat selective adm: 87/yr. Usual entry: PS, K, 8 & 9. Appl fee: $50. Appl due: Rolling. Applied: 134. Accepted: 86%. Yield: 74%. **Tests** CEEB CTP_4 IQ ISEE.
Enr 559. B 309. G 250. Elem 324. Sec 235. Wh 80%. Latino 5%. Blk 6%. Native Am 1%. Asian 8%. Avg class size: 17. Stud/fac: 10:1. **Fac 67.** M 17/F 50. FT 60/PT 7. Wh 88%. Latino 3%. Blk 6%. Asian 3%. Adv deg: 43%.
Grad '11—42. Col—42. (LA St-Baton Rouge 9, Tulane 5, Loyola U-LA 2, U of TX-Austin 2, Harvard 1, Princeton 1). **Mid 50% SAT:** CR 560-630. M 590-670. W 590-650. **Col couns:** 1. Alum donors: 10%.
Tui '12-'13: Day $8900-18,250 (+$500-1550). **Aid:** Merit 9 ($79,875). Need 116 ($672,150).
Summer (enr 409): Acad Enrich Rev Rem Rec. Tui Day $480/3-wk ses. 8 wks.
Endow $6,368,000. Plant val $25,000,000. Acres 18. Bldgs 22 (25% ADA). Class rms 51. 2 Libs 46,000 vols. Chapels 1. Sci labs 6. Lang labs 1. Comp ctrs 4. Theaters 1. Art studios 4. Music studios 2. Gyms 2. Fields 2. Pools 1. Tracks 1. Weight rms 1. Laptop prgm Gr 6-12.
Est 1947. Nonprofit. Episcopal (12% practice). Quar (Aug-May). **Assoc** CLS.

Founded under the auspices of the Episcopal Church, this independent school provides a rigorous academic curriculum that features Advanced Placement and honors programs in most upper school disciplines. Graduation requirements include courses in foreign language, computer science and the fine arts, as well as a number of electives. Pupils also enroll in religion classes at all grade levels.

A two-week senior internship project exposes each student to work placements before graduation in the areas of government, business, medicine, law, the arts and nonprofit organizations. St. Martin's facilitates concurrent enrollment with Tulane University, the University of New Orleans and the New Orleans Center for the Creative Arts for academically qualified upperclassmen. St. Martin's introduces handheld computing devices in grades 3-5, and all boys and girls in grades 6-12 must possess a tablet computer for classroom use.

Middle and upper school students take life skills courses that explore issues from substance abuse and stress management to decision making and self-esteem; in the upper school, a component addresses practical skills. Service projects begin in the lower school and culminate in a graduation requirement of 50 hours of direct, hands-on volunteering.	**See Also Page 81**

NEW ORLEANS, LA. Urban. Pop: 484,674. Alt: 5 ft.

ACADEMY OF THE SACRED HEART
Day — Girls Gr PS (Age 2)-12

New Orleans, LA 70115. 4521 St Charles Ave. Tel: 504-891-1943. Fax: 504-891-9939.
Other locations: 4301 St Charles Ave, New Orleans 70115.
www.ashrosary.org   E-mail: ash@ashrosary.org
Timothy M. Burns, Head (2003). BA, John Carroll Univ, MA, Georgetown Univ, PhD, Ohio State Univ. **Christy Sevante, Adm.**
  Col Prep. AP (exams req'd; 137 taken, 91% 3+)—Eng Fr Span Calc Stats Bio Chem US_Hist World_Hist US_Govt & Pol. **Elem math**—Everyday Math. **Elem read**—Rowland Superkids. **Feat**—Anat & Physiol Ecol Genetics Zoology Comp_Sci Relig Ceramics Drawing Painting Sculpt Musical_Theater Woodworking ACT_Prep. **Dual enr:** Tulane.
  Sports—G: Basket Cheer X-country Golf Sail Soccer Softball Swim Tennis Track Volley. **Activities:** 20.
  Selective adm (Gr PS-11): 76/yr. Usual entry: PS & 9. Appl fee: $50. Appl due: Jan. Applied: 184. Accepted: 85%. Yield: 70%. **Tests** HSPT IQ SSAT Stanford.
  Enr 781. Elem 580. Sec 201. Wh 91%. Latino 3%. Blk 4%. Asian 1%. Other 1%. Avg class size: 16. Stud/fac: 11:1. Uniform. **Fac 101.** M 10/F 91. FT 77/PT 24. Wh 95%. Latino 3%. Blk 1%. Other 1%. Adv deg: 38%.
  Grad '11—66. Col—66. (LA St-Baton Rouge 19, U of GA 4, U of LA-Lafayette 4, U of AL-Tuscaloosa 3, U of VA 2, Catholic U 2). **Mid 50% SAT:** CR 540-630. M 500-620. W 560-700. Mid 50% ACT: 22-28. **Col couns:** 1. Alum donors: 35%.
  Tui '11-'12: Day $12,750-13,900 (+$500-850). **Aid:** Merit 24 ($26,995). Need 97 ($608,515).
  Summer (enr 187): Coed. Gr PS-9. Acad Enrich Rec. Art. Theater. Tui Day $390-675. 2-3 wks.
  Endow $10,138,000. Plant val $46,459,000. Acres 12. Bldgs 7 (100% ADA). Class rms 78. 2 Libs 41,586 vols. Chapels 2. Sci labs 5. Auds 2. Art studios 3. Music studios 1. Gyms 2. Fields 2. Comp labs 4. Comp/stud: 1:1.3 (1:1 Laptop prgm Gr 9-12).
  Est 1887. Nonprofit. Roman Catholic (85% practice). Sem (Aug-June). **Assoc** SACS.

Part of the international Network of Sacred Heart Schools, the school comprises five developmentally focused divisions: Little Hearts (ages 2 and 3), preschool (pre-K and K), primary (grades 1-4), preparatory (grades 5-8) and upper school (grades 9-12). A second campus operates on St. Charles Avenue.

The prekindergarten introduces basic concepts with the aid of manipulative materials and games. A thematic structure is in use, and the prekindergarten curriculum gradually integrates language arts, math, science and social studies. Kindergarten programming combines structured and unstructured activities, and teachers employ various modalities. The primary division emphasizes effective communication and seeks to develop age-appropriate study and organizational skills. Preparatory school girls engage in a broader curriculum that includes electives and an exposure to Latin and either French or Spanish.

In addition to honors and AP courses, the college preparatory upper school program features independent study options and the opportunity to take classes at Tulane University. Upper school girl must purchase a laptop or tablet computer for classroom use. Each senior delivers a compulsory speech before the upper school, and both the preparatory and the upper schools hold annual oratory competitions. Student exchange opportunities are available through the

Sacred Heart Network, with pupils traveling to Paris, France; England; Chile; Australia; and destinations within the US.

The academy's strong athletic program commences in the preschool with activities that focus on fitness. Interscholastic competition begins at the preparatory level.

ISIDORE NEWMAN SCHOOL
Day — Coed Gr PS (Age 4)-12

New Orleans, LA 70115. 1903 Jefferson Ave. Tel: 504-899-5641. Fax: 504-896-8597. www.newmanschool.org E-mail: jrosen@newmanschool.org
T. J. Locke, Head (2007). BA, MEd, Rutgers Univ, EdD, Univ of Pennsylvania. **Jennifer Rosen, Adm.**

Col Prep. AP (exams req'd; 280 taken, 60% 3+)—Fr Lat Span Calc Stats Bio Chem Environ_Sci Physics Eur_Hist US_Hist World_Hist US_Govt & Pol Studio_Art. **Elem math**—Singapore Math. **Feat**—Creative_Writing Lat-Amer_Lit Nonfiction_Writing Southern_Lit Chin Genetics Comp_Design Comp_Sci Econ Psych World_Relig Art_ Hist Filmmaking Photog Drama Music Photojourn.

Sports—Basket X-country Golf Indoor_Track Soccer Swim Tennis Track. B: Baseball Football. G: Cheer Gymnastics Softball Volley.

Selective adm: 133/yr. Usual entry: PS & 9. Appl fee: $50. Appl due: Rolling. Applied: 297. Accepted: 75%. Yield: 61%. **Tests** IQ ISEE.

Enr 920. Wh 84%. Latino 1%. Blk 9%. Asian 4%. Other 2%. Avg class size: 15. Stud/fac: 7:1. **Fac 136.** M 36/F 100. FT 136. Wh 91%. Latino 4%. Blk 4%. Asian 1%. Adv deg: 46%.

Grad '11—83. Col—83. (LA St-Baton Rouge 13, Col of Charleston 7, Rhodes 6, U of TX-Austin 4, Tulane 4, U of GA 3). Athl schol 1. **Mid 50% SAT:** CR 590-700. M 600-720. W 610-710. Mid 50% ACT: 25-30. **Col couns:** 2. Alum donors: 7%.

Tui '12-'13: Day $16,361-19,749 (+$339-1209). **Aid:** Need 175 ($1,500,000).

Summer: Acad Enrich. Tui Day $600-800/4-wk ses. Rec. Tui Day $425-750/3-wk ses. Sports. Tui Day $250/wk. 8 wks.

Endow $24,000,000. Plant val $26,000,000. Acres 11. Bldgs 14. Class rms 65. 2 Libs 70,000 vols. Sci labs 10. Lang labs 1. Sci ctrs 1. Auds 1. Theaters 1. Art studios 4. Music studios 3. Perf arts ctrs 2. Drama studios 2. Gyms 2. Fields 1. Pools 1. Tracks 1. Comp labs 4. Laptop prgm Gr 6-12.

Est 1903. Nonprofit. Sem (Aug-May). **Assoc** CLS.

Founded by Isidore Newman, a noted financier and philanthropist, Isidore Newman Manual Training School opened in 1903. As the emphasis in curriculum gradually shifted from manual training to college preparation, the name of the institution was changed to Isidore Newman School.

Located on an 11-acre campus in uptown New Orleans, Newman offers a challenging sequential curriculum addressing the humanities, the sciences and the fine arts. A focus on writing begins with exposure to various literary genres and techniques in the lower school, and all grade 9 students enroll in a writing seminar. Advanced Placement courses and independent study opportunities are available across the curriculum, and an interdisciplinary citizenship seminar is required of seniors. Computer instruction begins in kindergarten, and boys and girls in grades 6-12 use laptop computers both in class and while connecting to the schoolwide wireless network.

LOUISE S. McGEHEE SCHOOL
Day — Boys Gr PS (Age 2)-PS (Age 4), Girls PS (Age 2)-12

New Orleans, LA 70130. 2343 Prytania St. Tel: 504-561-1224. Fax: 504-525-7910. www.mcgeheeschool.com E-mail: sarahs@mcgeheeschool.com
Eileen Friel Powers, Head (1999). BS, Marymount Manhattan College, MAT, Univ of Massachusetts-Amherst. **Sarah Smith, Adm.**

Col Prep. AP—Fr Span Calc Eur_Hist. **Feat**—Poetry Comp_Sci Women's_Hist Anthro Econ Psych Art_Hist Ceramics Film Photog Studio_Art Music Journ. **Supp**—Dev_ Read Rem_Read Rev Tut.
Sports—G: Basket X-country Golf Soccer Softball Swim Tennis Track Volley.
Selective adm: 72/yr. Appl fee: $50. Appl due: Rolling. **Tests** IQ ISEE.
Enr 525. Nonwhite 18%. Avg class size: 18. Stud/fac: 8:1. Uniform. **Fac 70.**
Grad '04—29. Col—29. (U of GA, LA St-Baton Rouge, Geo Wash, Wesleyan Col, Tulane, U of AL-Tuscaloosa). **Col couns:** 1.
Tui '11-'12: Day $11,492-17,050 (+$615-1825).
Endow $5,000,000. Plant val $6,000,000. Bldgs 11. Class rms 40. Lib 20,000 vols. Sci labs 4. Lang labs 1. Auds 1. Art studios 1. Music studios 1. Gyms 1. Comp labs 2. Laptop prgm Gr 6-12.
Est 1912. Nonprofit. Sem (Aug-June).

Louise S. McGehee founded this school to insure the opportunity for young women to have an education equal to that offered men. Located in a historic residential area of New Orleans, McGehee conducts a college preparatory curriculum that includes independent study and Advanced Placement courses.

Among the school's extracurricular activities are dramatics, choral music, team sports and interest clubs. Art facilities consist of a photography lab, potter's wheels and large areas for painting. Seniors participate in a two-week internship program that is required for graduation. McGehee offers an afternoon care program and after-school enrichment classes during the academic year, in addition to a coeducational early childhood program for two- and three-year-olds.

SHREVEPORT, LA. (176 mi. SSW of Little Rock, AR) Urban. Pop: 200,145. Alt: 210 ft.

SOUTHFIELD SCHOOL

Day — Coed Gr PS (Age 2)-8

Shreveport, LA 71106. 1100 Southfield Rd. Tel: 318-868-5375. Fax: 318-869-0890.
www.southfield-school.org   E-mail: ccoburn@southfield-school.org
Jeffrey W. Stokes, Head (1990). BA, State Univ of New York-Albany, MAT, Univ of North Carolina-Chapel Hill. **Clare Coburn, Adm.**
Pre-Prep. Gen Acad. Elem math—Everyday Math. **Elem read**—Open Court/Rowland Superkids. **Feat**—Fr Span Computers Ethics Studio_Art Drama Music. **Supp**—Dev_ Read.
Sports—Basket Fencing Golf Tennis. B: Football. G: Cheer.
Somewhat selective adm: 90/yr. Usual entry: PS. Appl fee: $50. Appl due: Rolling. Applied: 152. Accepted: 89%. Yield: 67%. **Tests** Stanford.
Enr 458. B 214. G 244. Wh 81%. Latino 2%. Blk 6%. Native Am 1%. Asian 8%. Other 2%. Avg class size: 17. Stud/fac: 11:1. Casual. **Fac 44.** M 4/F 40. FT 42/PT 2. Wh 94%. Latino 3%. Native Am 3%. Adv deg: 34%.
Grad '11—34. Prep—17. (Loyola Col Prep 17). Avg SSAT: 85%. Alum donors: 4%.
Tui '12-'13: Day $9321-10,536 (+$285-375). **Aid:** Merit 5 ($30,000). Need 90 ($475,000).
Summer (enr 400): Gr PS-6. Acad Enrich Rec. Art. Sports. Tui Day $190/wk. 5 wks.
Endow $4,500,000. Plant val $9,000,000. Acres 8. Bldgs 11 (100% ADA). Class rms 27. Lib 14,000 vols. Sci labs 2. Theaters 2. Art studios 1. Music studios 2. Gyms 1. Fields 1. Courts 1. Comp labs 3. Comp/stud: 1:3.
Est 1934. Nonprofit. Quar (Aug-May).

Opened by a group of parents, Southfield is located on an eight-acre campus and has become an institution with wide influence throughout the state. The curriculum of the lower school stresses the acquisition of basic academic skills, and the middle school emphasizes study skills and the fundamentals in the major disciplines.

Southfield's extended campus provides a program of travel and on-site learning. Middle school students take a four-day Louisiana history excursion and a geology trip to Texas. An afternoon enrichment program is available to children in all grades. The school also stresses community and school service.

MISSISSIPPI

JACKSON, MS. (140 mi. NNE of Baton Rouge, LA; 156 mi. N of New Orleans, LA)
Urban. Pop: 184,256. Alt: 296 ft. Area also includes Ridgeland.

ST. ANDREW'S EPISCOPAL SCHOOL
Day — Coed Gr PS (Age 3)-12

Ridgeland, MS 39157. 370 Old Agency Rd. Tel: 601-853-6000. Fax: 601-853-6001.
Other locations: 4120 Old Canton Rd, Jackson 39216.
www.gosaints.org   E-mail: sa@gosaints.org
George D. Penick, Jr., Head (2008). BA, Davidson College, EdM, MPA, EdD, Harvard Univ.
Dawn McCarley, Adm.
   Col Prep. AP (exams req'd; 283 taken, 93% 3+)—Eng Fr Lat Span Calc Stats Bio
      Chem Physics Eur_Hist US_Hist Comp_Govt & Pol Econ Human_Geog US_Govt
      & Pol Art_Hist Studio_Art Music_Theory. **Elem math**—Singapore Math. **Feat**—Cre-
      ative_Writing Mythology Chin Ger Ital Anat & Physiol Bioethics Environ_Sci Engi-
      neering Robotics African-Amer_Hist Psych Philos Film Acting Drama Theater_Arts
      Speech. **Supp**—Dev_Read Rem_Math Rem_Read Rev Tut.
   Sports—Arch Basket Bowl X-country Golf Soccer Swim Tennis Track Weightlifting. B:
      Baseball Football. G: Cheer Softball Volley.
   Selective adm: 187/yr. Usual entry: PS & K. Appl fee: $50. Appl due: Rolling. Applied:
      297. Accepted: 85%. Yield: 75%. **Tests** ISEE.
   Enr 1184. B 565. G 619. Elem 844. Sec 340. Wh 70%. Latino 1%. Blk 12%. Asian 6%.
      Other 11%. Avg class size: 17. **Fac 130.** M 28/F 102. FT 121/PT 9. Adv deg: 46%.
   Grad '11—88. Col—88. (U of MS 16, Millsaps 7, Rhodes 7, Loyola U-LA 4, MS St 4, MS
      Col 3). **Avg SAT:** CR 657. M 626. W 660. **Mid 50% SAT:** CR 600-720. M 560-680. W
      600-720. Avg ACT: 28.2. Mid 50% ACT: 26-31. **Col couns:** 2. Alum donors: 25%.
   Tui '12-'13: Day $9975-13,790 (+$250-700). **Aid:** Merit 15 ($98,980). Need 111
      ($555,783).
   Summer (enr 1400): Acad Enrich Rev Rem Rec. Tui Day $200/wk. 10 wks.
   Endow $8,000,000. Plant val $100,000,000. Acres 108. Bldgs 15. Class rms 65. 3 Libs
      30,000 vols. Chapels 2. Sci labs 9. Observatories 1. Auds 2. Theaters 1. Art studios 6.
      Music studios 5. Dance studios 2. Gyms 2. Fields 6. Courts 6. Field houses 2. Comp
      labs 2. Laptop prgm Gr 9-12.
   Est 1947. Nonprofit. Episcopal (26% practice). Quar (Aug-May). **Assoc** CLS SACS.

   St. Andrew's offers a college preparatory curriculum that stresses the study of classical literature and the mastery of scientific and mathematical methods. Community service projects,
a fine and performing arts program that is built into the curriculum, and a number of student-
sponsored religious celebrations and activities supplement the regular program. The school
conducts a special program enabling upper schoolers to earn certification in global studies.
Students may participate in an exchange program with St. Andrew's School for boys in Osaka,
Japan. Student life is governed by a student-written and -enforced honor code.
   The lower school (grades pre-K-4) operates on a separate campus in Jackson.

OKLAHOMA

OKLAHOMA CITY, OK. (189 mi. NNW of Dallas, TX) Urban. Pop: 506,132. Alt: 1214 ft.

CASADY SCHOOL
Day — Coed Gr PS (Age 3)-12

Oklahoma City, OK 73120. 9500 N Pennsylvania Ave. Tel: 405-749-3100. Fax: 405-749-3223.
www.casady.org   E-mail: fosterc@casady.org
Christopher Charles Bright, Head (2008). BA, Trinity Univ, MA, Univ of London (England). **Curt Foster, Adm.**
Col Prep. **AP (248 exams taken, 70% 3+)**—Fr Lat Span Calc Stats Comp_Sci Bio Chem Physics Eur_Hist US_Hist Comp_Govt & Pol US_Govt & Pol Art_Hist Music_Theory. **Feat**—Creative_Writing Chin Ger Multivariable_Calc Genetics Geol Comp_Graphics African_Hist African-Amer_Hist E_Asian_Hist Middle_Eastern_Hist Russ_Hist Ceramics Photog Sculpt Studio_Art Video_Production Printmaking Acting Drama Music Orchestra Speech. **Supp**—Tut.
Sports—Basket X-country Golf Soccer Swim Tennis Track Volley. B: Baseball Football Wrestling. G: F_Hockey Softball. **Activities: 25.**
Selective adm: 116/yr. Appl fee: $50. Appl due: Rolling. Accepted: 84%. Yield: 67%.
Enr 859. Elem 563. Sec 296. Avg class size: 15. Stud/fac: 8:1. **Fac 113.** M 46/F 67. FT 106/PT 7. Adv deg: 59%.
Grad '10—74. **Col**—74. (U of OK, OK St, SMU, Brown, TX Christian, U of Tulsa). **Avg SAT:** CR/M 1213. Avg ACT: 27. **Col couns: 2.**
Tui '12-'13: Day $11,430-16,520 (+$500). **Aid:** Need 129 ($1,400,000).
Summer: Acad Enrich Rev Rem Rec. 1-6 wks.
Endow $16,000,000. Plant val $35,694,000. Acres 80. Bldgs 29. Class rms 67. 2 Libs 30,000 vols. Chapels 1. Sci labs 8. Lang labs 3. Auds 3. Theaters 1. Art studios 4. Music studios 4. Dance studios 1. Arts ctrs 1. Gyms 2. Fields 7. Courts 12. Lakes 1. Comp labs 4.
Est 1947. Nonprofit. Episcopal. Tri (Aug-June). **Assoc** CLS.

Situated on an 80-acre campus around a six-acre lake, this school was established by Rt. Rev. Thomas Casady, then Episcopal bishop of Oklahoma, and by members of the laity. Bible instruction is given in grades 1-8; kindergartners go to chapel service once a week, while students in grades 1-12 attend daily.

Conversational Spanish commences in kindergarten, and pupils have a choice of French or Spanish in grade 6; Latin is required in grades 7 and 8. The upper division (grades 9-12) offers a rigorous college preparatory education enhanced by strong arts and sports programs and an extensive activities program. Students complete courses in English, mathematics, modern or classical languages, history, laboratory sciences, computer science and the fine arts. In addition, boys and girls choose from a large selection of electives, including Advanced Placement courses in every discipline and independent studies.

Students accumulate 45 hours of required community service during the upper division years.

HERITAGE HALL SCHOOL
Day — Coed Gr PS (Age 3)-12

Oklahoma City, OK 73120. 1800 NW 122nd St. Tel: 405-749-3001. Fax: 405-751-7372.
www.heritagehall.com   E-mail: parceneaux@heritagehall.com

Guy A. Bramble, Head (1988). BA, Amherst College, EdM, Harvard Univ. **Genifer Ring, Adm.**

Col Prep. AP (exams req'd)—Eng Fr Lat Span Calc Bio Chem Environ_Sci Physics Eur_Hist US_Hist Studio_Art. **Feat**—Creative_Writing Humanities Chin Stats Programming Web_Design Econ Intl_Relations Psych African_Stud Philos Art_Hist Ceramics Photog Theater_Arts Music Debate.

Sports—Basket X-country Golf Soccer Swim Tennis Track. B: Baseball Football Wrestling. G: F_Hockey Softball Volley.

Somewhat selective adm: 124/yr. Appl fee: $35. Appl due: Mar. Applied: 196. Accepted: 89%. Yield: 71%. **Tests** CTP_4 IQ ISEE.

Enr 930. B 470. G 460. Elem 525. Sec 405. Wh 44%. Blk 5%. Native Am 3%. Asian 3%. Other 45%. Avg class size: 15. Stud/fac: 8:1. Casual. **Fac 106.** Wh 94%. Latino 1%. Blk 2%. Native Am 1%. Asian 2%. Adv deg: 48%.

Grad '10—93. Col—93. (U of OK 15, TX Christian 9, OK St 8, SMU 6, Trinity U 4, Baylor 4). Athl schol 5. **Avg SAT:** CR 641. M 581. W 592. Avg ACT: 25.6.

Tui '12-'13: Day $12,515-21,720. Aid: Need 101 ($1,900,000).

Summer: Acad Enrich Rev Rem Rec. Tui Day $100-425. 1-3 wks.

Acres 105. Bldgs 8. Libs 2. Sci labs 6. Lang labs 3. Auds 1. Art studios 4. Music studios 3. Dance studios 1. Gyms 3. Fields 5. Tennis courts 8. Ponds 2. Comp labs 3.

Est 1969. Nonprofit. Sem (Aug-May). **Assoc** CLS.

Located on a 105-acre campus in the northwestern part of the city, Heritage Hall offers a college preparatory curriculum that combines foundational core subjects with an array of enrichment courses. The lower school (grades PS-4), which commences with a three-year-old preschool, places emphasis on the acquisition of basic learning, critical thinking, problem solving, technology and communicational skills. Instructors employ various teaching methods in a setting that can accommodate children with differing learning rates and styles. Visual arts and music course work is particularly strong.

During the middle school years (grades 5-8), programming provides a foundation for the upper school by focusing on language arts, math, science and social studies, and students also gain an exposure to foreign language. Annual standardized testing diagnoses areas in need of reinforcement and assists teachers with appropriate placement and course selection.

Heritage Hall's upper school (grades 9-12) continues to stress the traditional disciplines. Freshmen and sophomores may enroll in advanced math and science courses, while able upperclassmen choose from honors and Advanced Placement offerings in the major subject areas. All upper school boys and girls perform 32 hours of required community service annually.

TULSA, OK. (101 mi. ENE of Oklahoma City, OK) Urban. Pop: 393,049. Alt: 800 ft.

HOLLAND HALL

Day — Coed Gr PS (Age 3)-12

Tulsa, OK 74137. 5666 E 81st St. Tel: 918-481-1111. Fax: 918-481-1145.
www.hollandhall.org   E-mail: rhart@hollandhall.org

John D. Marshall, Head (2011). BA, Univ of North Carolina-Chapel Hill, MBA, Duke Univ, MEd, Columbia Univ. **Richard Hart, Adm.**

Col Prep. AP (exams req'd; 77 taken, 78% 3+)—Calc Stats Comp_Sci Chem Physics. **Feat**—Creative_Writing Chin Fr Lat Span Genetics Relig Ceramics Photog Studio_Art Theater_Arts Jazz_Band. **Supp**—Rev Tut.

Sports—Basket Crew X-country Golf Soccer Tennis Track. B: Baseball Football. G: Cheer F_Hockey Softball Volley.

Somewhat selective adm: 132/yr. Appl fee: $25. Appl due: Rolling. Applied: 187. Accepted: 86%. Yield: 82%. **Tests** CTP_4.

Enr 958. B 475. G 483. Elem 633. Sec 325. Wh 86%. Latino 1%. Blk 3%. Native Am 3%. Asian 4%. Other 3%. Avg class size: 15. Stud/fac: 9:1. Uniform. **Fac 93.** M 30/F 63. FT

91/PT 2. Wh 87%. Latino 1%. Native Am 3%. Asian 4%. Other 5%. Adv deg: 49%.
Grad '10—78. Col—78. (U of Tulsa 11, U of OK 7, OK St 4, U of MO-Columbia 3, Rice 2, Vanderbilt 2). Athl schol 5. **Avg SAT:** CR 600. M 614. W 580. Avg ACT: 26.6. **Col couns:** 3. Alum donors: 11%.
Tui '11-'12: Day \$10,225-16,475 (+\$900-1500). **Aid:** Merit 23 (\$165,125). Need 77 (\$1,032,740).
Summer: Acad Enrich Rev Rec. Sports. Tui Day \$210-300/wk. 8 wks.
Endow \$62,600,000. Plant val \$64,000,000. Acres 162. Bldgs 10 (90% ADA). Class rms 89. 3 Libs 70,000 vols. Chapels 1. Sci labs 9. Lang labs 1. Photog labs 1. Theaters 2. Art studios 6. Music studios 6. Dance studios 1. Arts ctrs 1. Art galleries 1. Recording studios 1. Gyms 3. Fields 10. Courts 12. Tracks 1. Weight rms 1. Comp labs 6. Comp/stud: 1:2.
Est 1922. Nonprofit. Episcopal (10% practice). Sem (Aug-May). **Assoc** CLS.

One of the city's first independent schools, Holland Hall opened at a site near downtown Tulsa, before later moving to Birmingham Place. Realizing in the late 1960s that developments in technology, math and foreign language would soon demand additional space and technical support, the board of trustees decided to relocate the school to a 162-acre campus in a wooded area of south Tulsa in the fall of 1970.

At all grade levels, the liberal arts curriculum emphasizes critical thinking and lifetime learning skills. The primary school (grades PS-3) follows a developmentally appropriate program that encourages intellectual and open inquiry. In-depth units of study address academic, artistic, physical and social/emotional areas. These thematic units employ technology as a learning tool.

During the middle school years (grades 4-8), the interdisciplinary program balances a solid curriculum with developmental, exploratory experiences; pupils gain increasing levels of independence as they progress through grades 7 and 8. Spanish is part of the program in the earlier middle school grades, while Latin and French are both added in grade 6. Art and music classes, competitive athletics (starting in grade 6), community service projects, student-faculty plays, mini-mester courses, ecology outings and field trips are other notable aspects of middle school life.

Students in the upper school (grades 9-12) follow a flexible modular schedule that facilitates the development of time-management skills and provides opportunities for individual and small-group learning experiences. The curriculum enables boys and girls to engage in Advanced Placement and honors courses, research and experimentation in various fields, math competitions, technology projects and community service. Upper schoolers also have access to a strong advisory program. Holland Hall conducts exchanges with schools in China, France, Mexico and Spain.

TEXAS

ARLINGTON, TX. (22 mi. WSW of Dallas, TX) Urban. Pop: 332,969. Alt: 616 ft.

THE OAKRIDGE SCHOOL
Day — Coed Gr PS (Age 3)-12

Arlington, TX 76013. 5900 W Pioneer Pky. Tel: 817-451-4994. Fax: 817-457-6681.
www.theoakridgeschool.org   E-mail: jadavis@theoakridgeschool.org
Andy J. Broadus, Pres (2007). BS, Jacksonville Univ, MEd, Univ of North Florida. **Jonathan Kellam, Head.** BA, MEd, Texas Christian Univ. **Jerry A. Davis, Jr., Adm.**
Col Prep. AP (297 exams taken)—Eng Chin Fr Span Calc Stats Comp_Sci Bio Chem Environ_Sci Physics Eur_Hist US_Hist US_Govt & Pol Studio_Art. **Feat**—Creative_ Writing Anat & Physiol Anthro Econ Relig Drama Theater_Arts Music. **Dual enr:** U of TX-Arlington.
Sports (req'd)—Basket X-country Golf Soccer Swim Tennis Track. B: Baseball Football Weightlifting Wrestling. G: F_Hockey Softball Volley. **Activities:** 17.
Selective adm: 124/yr. Appl fee: $75. Appl due: Mar. Accepted: 65%. **Tests** CTP_4 IQ ISEE Stanford.
Enr 877. Elem 572. Sec 305. Wh 60%. Latino 5%. Blk 7%. Asian 12%. Other 16%. Avg class size: 15. Uniform. **Fac 84.** M 21/F 63. FT 84. Adv deg: 57%.
Grad '11—72. Col—72. (U of TX-Arlington 8, TX A&M 6, TX Christian 4, SMU 4, AZ St 4, U of OK 2). **Avg SAT:** CR 600. M 617. W 594. **Mid 50% SAT:** CR 530-680. M 540-690. W 530-650. Avg ACT: 26.6. Mid 50% ACT: 23-30. **Col couns:** 1.
Tui '12-'13: Day $10,565-18,300 (+$50-600).
Summer: Acad Enrich Rev Rec. Sports. Tui Day $160-900. 1-5 wks.
Endow $350,000. Plant val $15,000,000. Acres 82. Bldgs 10. Class rms 59. Lib 20,000 vols. Sci labs 6. Lang labs 1. Auds 1. Art studios 4. Music studios 2. Gyms 2. Fields 4. Tennis courts 2. Tracks 1. Comp labs 4.
Est 1979. Nonprofit. Sem (Aug-May).

Situated on an 82-acre campus east of Fort Worth, the school maintains a well-rounded college preparatory curriculum. The three-, four- and five-year-old kindergarten programs provide children with an introduction to math, language arts, science, social studies, Spanish, music, art and physical education. The lower school (grades 1-4) stresses the development of basic skills and conducts a strong enrichment program, while the middle school (grades 5-8) features the addition of French, geography, club activities and class trips.

Advanced Placement courses and electives supplement college preparatory course selections in the upper school (grades 9-12). Course work in all academic areas and grades incorporates computer technology. Boys and girls perform at least 60 hours of community service during the upper school years.

AUSTIN, TX. (181 mi. SSW of Dallas, TX) Urban. Pop: 656,562. Alt: 600 ft.

ST. STEPHEN'S EPISCOPAL SCHOOL
Bdg — Coed Gr 8-12; Day — Coed 6-12

Austin, TX 78746. 6500 St Stephen's Dr. Tel: 512-327-1213. Fax: 512-327-6771.
www.sstx.org   E-mail: admission@sstx.org
Robert E. Kirkpatrick, Head (2007). BA, Kenyon College, MAT, Colgate Univ. **Lawrence Sampleton, Adm.**

Col Prep. AP exams taken: 151 (85% 3+). Feat—Chin Fr Lat Span Calc Stats Environ_ Sci Geol Astrophysics Robotics Econ Law Psych Ethics Theol Art_Hist Ceramics Filmmaking Photog Studio_Art Drama Music_Hist Music_Theory. **Supp**—ESL Tut.
Sports—Basket Crew X-country Golf Soccer Swim Tennis Track. B: Baseball Football Lacrosse. G: F_Hockey Softball Volley. **Activities:** 30.
Selective adm (Bdg Gr 8-11; Day 6-11): 161/yr. Bdg 63. Day 98. Appl fee: $50. Appl due: Feb. Accepted: 49%. Yield: 76%. **Tests** ISEE SSAT TOEFL.
Enr 665. B 366. G 299. Bdg 163. Day 502. Elem 192. Sec 473. Intl 11%. Avg class size: 16. Stud/fac: 8:1. **Fac 79.** Adv deg: 63%.
Grad '10—112. Col—112. (U of TX-Austin, Boston U, TX Christian, TX A&M, Columbia, Wesleyan U). **Avg SAT:** CR 623. M 672. W 645. Avg ACT: 28.3. **Col couns:** 3.
Tui '11-'12: Bdg $37,790-44,000 (+$4165). **Day $20,320-21,970** (+$1905). **Intl Bdg $39,260-45,470** (+$3990-8595). **Aid:** Need 100 ($1,900,000).
Endow $9,000,000. Plant val $25,000,000. Acres 370. Bldgs 44. Dorms 10. Dorm rms 94. Class rms 37. Lib 17,000 vols. Chapels 1. Sci labs 6. Dark rms 1. Theaters 2. Art studios 2. Music studios 2. Arts ctrs 1. Gyms 2. Fields 7. Courts 14. Field houses 1. Pools 1. Comp labs 5. Comp/stud: 1:5.5.
Est 1950. Nonprofit. Episcopal. Tri (Aug-May). **Assoc** CLS.

The school was founded by the Diocese of Texas under the leadership of Rt. Rev. John Hines. Rev. William Brewster, formerly of St. Mark's School in Southborough, MA, was headmaster of St. Stephen's from its founding until his death in 1953.

The college preparatory curriculum stresses a thorough understanding of English, social studies, math, science and foreign language while featuring the fine arts. A course in theology is required for graduation, and independent study is available for advanced students. College counseling begins in grade 11. Private lessons in voice, instrumental music, acting, art, pottery and photography are offered. All middle schoolers complete a four-hour community service project annually, while boys and girls in grades 9-12 perform 12 hours of compulsory service each year.

Opportunities to study abroad in Spain, China, Greece, France, Great Britain and Italy constitute the Summer Adventures Program. Students also take advantage of the cultural offerings of nearby cities.

BRYAN, TX. (85 mi. NW of Houston, TX; 86 mi. ENE of Austin, TX) Suburban. Pop: 65,660. Alt: 914 ft.

ALLEN ACADEMY
Day — Coed Gr PS (Age 2)-12

Bryan, TX 77802. 3201 Boonville Rd. Tel: 979-776-0731. Fax: 979-774-7769.
www.allenacademy.org   E-mail: info@allenacademy.org
John P. Rouse, Head (2010). BA, MEd, Texas A&M Univ.
Col Prep. AP (exams req'd; 26 taken, 81% 3+)—Eng Fr Span Calc Bio Chem Physics Eur_Hist US_Hist US_Govt & Pol. **Feat**—Comp_Sci Drawing Painting Sculpt Studio_ Art Drama Chorus Music Speech Outdoor_Ed. **Supp**—ESL Tut.
Sports—Basket X-country Golf Soccer Tennis Track. B: Baseball Football. G: Softball Volley.
Selective adm: 61/yr. Appl fee: $100-200. Appl due: Rolling. Accepted: 75%. Yield: 98%. **Tests** CTP_4 ISEE Stanford TOEFL.
Enr 310. Intl 15%. Avg class size: 15. Uniform. **Fac 36.** Adv deg: 19%.
Grad '07—16. Col—15. (TX A&M, Purdue, Baylor, SUNY-Albany, Carnegie Mellon, NYU). **Avg SAT:** CR 650. M 680. W 594. **Col couns:** 1.
Tui '06-'07: Day $6645-8615. Aid: Need 37 ($200,000).
Summer: Enrich Rec. Tui Day $110-200/wk. 10 wks. Sports. 1-6 wks.
Plant val $4,000,000. Acres 40. Bldgs 7. Class rms 35. Lib 10,000 vols. Sci labs 3. Art studios 1. Music studios 1. Gyms 1. Fields 4. Tracks 1. Comp labs 2.

Est 1886. Nonprofit. Sem (Aug-May). **Assoc** SACS.

Founded in Madisonville as Madison Academy by Mississippi educator John Hodges Allen, the school assumed its current name in 1896. After approximately 100 years of enrollment and curricular growth, the academy relocated to its 40-acre campus in Bryan in 1988. Allen evolved over the years from a boys' boarding institution to a coeducational day program.

The school's college preparatory program emphasizes the liberal arts. Computer technology, foreign language and arts classes enrich the curriculum. Allen conducts a block scheduling program in which each class convenes for an extended period every other school day. Select boys and girls in grades 10-12 may attend national conferences and workshops in government and politics. Pupils satisfy a 40-hour community service requirement prior to graduation.

DALLAS, TX. Urban. Pop: 1,188,580. Alt: 475 ft. Area also includes Addison.

GREENHILL SCHOOL

Day — Coed Gr PS (Age 4)-12

Addison, TX 75001. 4141 Spring Valley Rd. Tel: 972-628-5400. Fax: 972-404-8217.
www.greenhill.org   E-mail: admission@greenhill.org
Scott A. Griggs, Head (2000). BS, Centre College, MA, Ohio State Univ. **Angela H. Woodson, Adm.**

    Col Prep. AP (exams req'd; 338 taken, 94% 3+)—Eng Fr Lat Span Calc Stats Bio Chem Physics US_Govt & Pol Studio_Art. **Elem math**—Everyday Math. **Feat**—Poetry Shakespeare Chaucer Gothic_Lit Chin Astron Botany Biotech Organic_Chem Robotics Web_Design Cold_War Modern_African_Hist Psych Sociol World_Relig Photog Video_Production Acting Theater_Arts Debate.

    Sports—Basket X-country Golf Lacrosse Soccer Swim Tennis Track Volley. B: Baseball Football. G: Cheer F_Hockey Softball. **Activities:** 27.

    Selective adm: 174/yr. Usual entry: PS, K, 1, 5 & 9. Appl fee: $100-175. Applied: 878. Accepted: 25%. Yield: 80%. **Tests** ISEE.

    Enr 1270. B 635. G 635. Elem 806. Sec 464. Wh 60%. Latino 5%. Blk 8%. Asian 18%. Other 9%. Avg class size: 16. **Fac 167.** M 71/F 96. Wh 77%. Latino 8%. Blk 10%. Asian 4%. Other 1%. Adv deg: 61%.

    Grad '11—104. Col—104. (SMU 7, U of TX-Austin 7, IN U 6, USC 4, Duke 3, NYU 3). **Avg SAT:** CR 644. M 633. W 628. **Mid 50% SAT:** CR 600-700. M 580-690. W 550-710. Avg ACT: 29.3. **Col couns:** 3.

    Tui '12-'13: Day $19,450-23,900 (+$800-1000).

    Summer (enr 1350): Acad Enrich Rec. 1-4 wks.

    Endow $28,243,000. Plant val $60,000,000. Acres 78. Bldgs 14 (100% ADA). Class rms 120. Lib 50,000 vols. Lang labs 2. Comp ctrs 1. Theaters 1. Art studios 3. Music studios 5. Dance studios 2. Gyms 2. Fields 11. Tennis courts 10. Field houses 1. Pools 1. Comp labs 1.

    Est 1950. Nonprofit. Tri (Aug-May). **Assoc** CLS.

Founded by Bernard Fulton and a group of Dallas citizens, this school opened with 60 students and a faculty of ten. In 1959, Greenhill moved to its present, 78-acre site in Addison.

Greenhill combines a creative academic program with comprehensive arts and athletics. The curriculum is sequential at all grade levels. Integrated course materials, in addition to interdisciplinary and team-teaching techniques, are utilized in support of the college preparatory program. Honors and Advanced Placement courses are available in the upper school. Competitive sports, physical education and the fine arts form part of the curriculum at all levels. Students accumulate 48 hours of required community service in grades 9-12.

THE HOCKADAY SCHOOL

Bdg — Girls Gr 8-12; Day — Girls PS (Age 4)-12

Dallas, TX 75229. 11600 Welch Rd. Tel: 214-363-6311. Fax: 214-265-1649.
www.hockaday.org   E-mail: jliggitt@mail.hockaday.org
Kim Wargo, Head (2011). BA, Louisiana State Univ-Baton Rouge, MA, Tulane Univ. **Jen Liggitt, Adm.**

Col Prep. AP (581 exams taken, 95% 3+)—Eng Chin Fr Lat Span Calc Stats Comp_Sci Bio Chem Environ_Sci Physics Eur_Hist US_Hist World_Hist Comp_Govt & Pol Econ Studio_Art. **Feat**—British_Lit Creative_Writing Humanities Poetry Multivariable_Calc Anat Astron Ecol Genetics Microbio Engineering Meteorology Web_Design Comp_ Animation Middle_Eastern_Hist Milit_Hist Law Comp_Relig Philos Art_Hist Ceramics Photog Acting Music_Hist Dance Debate. **Supp**—Dev_Read ESL.

Sports—G: Basket Crew X-country Fencing F_Hockey Golf Lacrosse Soccer Softball Swim Tennis Track Volley. **Activities:** 75.

Very selective adm (Bdg Gr 8-11; Day PS-11): 147/yr. Bdg 25. Day 122. Usual entry: PS, 5 & 9. Appl fee: $100-175. Appl due: Jan. Applied: 827. Accepted: 14%. Yield: 88%. **Tests** ISEE SSAT TOEFL.

Enr 1087. Bdg 87. Day 1000. Elem 607. Sec 480. Wh 63%. Latino 6%. Blk 6%. Native Am 1%. Asian 14%. Other 10%. Avg class size: 15. Stud/fac: 10:1. Uniform. **Fac 128.** M 24/F 104. FT 117/PT 11. Wh 84%. Latino 5%. Blk 7%. Asian 3%. Other 1%. Adv deg: 60%.

Grad '11—122. Col—122. (U of TX-Austin 9, SMU 7, Vanderbilt 4, NYU 3, USC 3, TX A&M 3). Athl schol 3. **Mid 50% SAT:** CR 600-720. M 620-740. W 620-730. Mid 50% ACT: 28-33. **Col couns:** 3. Alum donors: 32%.

Tui '12-'13: Bdg $44,473-45,623 (+$900). **Day $17,605-25,050** (+$900). **Intl Bdg $47,973-49,123** (+$900). **Aid:** Need 166 ($2,690,000).

Summer (enr 1242): Coed. Acad Enrich Rec. Sports. Tui Bdg $2100-3650. 3-6 wks. Tui Day $135-750. 1-6 wks. ESL. Tui Bdg $3450-6900. 3-6 wks.

Endow $100,000,000. Plant val $80,000,000. Acres 85. Bldgs 14 (85% ADA). Dorms 2. Dorm rms 60. Class rms 100. 2 Libs 50,000 vols. Sci labs 10. Lang labs 1. Auds 1. Theaters 2. Art studios 4. Music studios 8. Gyms 2. Fields 6. Basketball courts 3. Tennis courts 10. Racquetball courts 2. Pools 2. Tracks 1. Weight rms 1. Laptop prgm Gr 6-12.

Est 1913. Nonprofit. Sem (Aug-May). **Assoc** CLS.

The school was established by Ela Hockaday at the invitation of a group of Dallas families who wanted a college preparatory school for girls established locally. In 1942, the school was turned over to a self-perpetuating board of trustees comprising alumnae, parents and community members.

The college preparatory program is augmented by offerings in the fine arts, schoolwide humanities studies and an upper school cocurricular program with St. Mark's School of Texas, a boys' school in Dallas. Children take French or Spanish beginning in kindergarten; Latin is added in grade 7 and Mandarin Chinese in the upper school. Sophomores may spend a semester in Zermatt, Switzerland, and, through the summer session, students may earn credits on campus in various elective and academic programs. Students in grades 6-12 purchase required laptop computers through the school.

Community service is an area of emphasis throughout, and girls in grades 9-12 fulfill a 15-hour annual service commitment. Extracurricular opportunities include interest clubs and forums, eight leadership boards and a wide range of student publications. Hockaday's resident enrollment represents many states and foreign countries; a host family program matches boarders with the families of day students, alumnae and faculty.

JESUIT COLLEGE PREPARATORY SCHOOL OF DALLAS

Day — Boys Gr 9-12

Dallas, TX 75244. 12345 Inwood Rd. Tel: 972-387-8700. Fax: 972-661-9349.
www.jesuitcp.org   E-mail: thost@jesuitcp.org

Michael Earsing, Pres (2011). BS, State Univ of New York-Fredonia, MEd, Univ of North Texas. **Thomas E. Garrison, Prin.** BA, MAT, Austin College. **Tim Host, Adm.**

Col Prep. AP (exams req'd; 377 taken)—Eng Span Calc Stats Comp_Sci Bio Chem Physics US_Hist World_Hist Comp_Govt & Pol Econ US_Govt & Pol. **Feat**—Fr Lat Anat & Physiol Astron Forensic_Sci Engineering Web_Design Intl_Relations Psych Global_Stud Theol Ceramics Drawing Studio_Art Acting Theater_Arts Debate Journ Public_Speak. **Supp**—Tut. **Dual enr:** Brookhaven.

Sports—B: Baseball Basket Cheer Crew X-country Fencing Football Golf Ice_Hockey Lacrosse Rugby Soccer Swim Tennis Track Weightlifting Wrestling.

Selective adm (Gr 9-10): 270/yr. Usual entry: 9. Appl fee: $75. Applied: 490. Accepted: 65%. Yield: 90%. **Tests** ISEE.

Enr 1040. Wh 74%. Latino 12%. Blk 4%. Native Am 1%. Asian 7%. Other 2%. Avg class size: 17. Stud/fac: 9:1. Uniform. **Fac 111.** Wh 87%. Latino 6%. Blk 2%. Native Am 2%. Asian 3%. Adv deg: 55%.

Grad '09—255. Col—252. (TX A&M 27, Boston Col 14, U of TX-Austin 11, Notre Dame 9, Rice 5, Georgetown 4). **Avg SAT:** CR 600. M 620.

Tui '11-'12: Day $13,600 (+$50-485). **Aid:** Need 190 ($1,300,000).

Summer (enr 512): Acad Enrich Rem. Tui Day $400/crse. 3 wks.

Endow $25,000,000. Plant val $36,000,000. Acres 27. Bldgs 2 (100% ADA). Libs 1. Sci labs 3. Comp ctrs 1. Auds 2. Theaters 1. Art studios 3. Music studios 3. Art museums 1. Gyms 2. Fields 3. Courts 6. Comp labs 5. Comp/stud: 1:5.

Est 1942. Nonprofit. Roman Catholic (80% practice). Sem (Aug-May). **Assoc** SACS.

Originally named Jesuit High School, the school was established shortly after Rev. Joseph P. Lynch, bishop of Dallas, commissioned the Society of Jesus to found a school in Dallas based on the principles of Jesuit secondary education. In 1969, Jesuit assumed its present name to reflect the school's new emphasis on college preparation.

The rigorous curriculum features honors or Advanced Placement courses (or both) in English, foreign language, social studies, math, science and computer science. Religion and community service are integral aspects of school life. The entire Jesuit community gathers each Friday morning for a prayer service, and schoolwide liturgies are held at least once a month. Boys satisfy the following community service requirements: 10 hours in grade 9, 20 hours in grade 10, 40 hours in grade 11 and 100 hours in grade 12.

THE LAMPLIGHTER SCHOOL

Day — Coed Gr PS (Age 3)-4

Dallas, TX 75229. 11611 Inwood Rd. Tel: 214-369-9201. **Fax:** 214-369-5540. www.thelamplighterschool.org   **E-mail:** tls@thelamplighterschool.org

Joan B. Hill, Head (2011). BS, Ohio Univ, MEd, John Carroll Univ. **Matthew S. Brenner, Adm.**

Pre-Prep. Feat—Span Environ_Sci Computers Studio_Art Drama Music Horticulture.

Selective adm: 100/yr. Usual entry: PS. Appl fee: $150-200. Appl due: Oct. Accepted: 39%. Yield: 92%.

Enr 440. Wh 69%. Latino 3%. Blk 4%. Native Am 1%. Asian 7%. Other 16%. Avg class size: 15. Stud/fac: 12:1. **Fac 55.** M 7/F 48. FT 50/PT 5. Wh 89%. Latino 3%. Blk 5%. Other 3%. Adv deg: 25%.

Grad '11—34. Prep—33. (Episcopal Sch of Dallas 6, Good Shepherd-TX 6, Hockaday 5, Parish Episcopal 5, Greenhill-TX 4, St Mark's Sch of TX 2).

Tui '12-'13: Day $20,210-21,210. Aid: Need 45 ($415,421).

Summer (enr 200): Enrich Rec. Tui Day $400/2-wk ses. 4 wks.

Endow $6,846,000. Plant val $22,183,000. Acres 12. Bldgs 2. Class rms 35. Lib 30,000 vols. Auds 1. Arts ctrs 1. Gyms 2. Fields 1. Greenhouses 1. Barns 1. Comp/stud: 1:3.

Est 1953. Nonprofit. Sem (Aug-May).

Lamplighter originated with a kindergarten and a first grade housed in an old farmhouse, complete with a barn and animals that soon became an integral part of the school's program. Today's curriculum recognizes the individual differences, needs and capacities of each student and encourages intellectual curiosity, critical thinking and creativity. Pupil progress is reported by direct parental observation through one-way windows and by several parent-teacher conferences yearly. The school operates on a modified open-classroom plan, allowing for team teaching. A nature trail leading to woods and a creek enhance Lamplighter's learning environment, and the outdoor environmental science classroom includes gardens in which pupils study native plants and trees; a greenhouse and a barn also provide enrichment opportunities for students.

Peer tutoring plays an important role at Lamplighter, as it encourages leadership skills and social-emotional development. As part of the fine arts curriculum, a study of opera begins in grade 3 and culminates in grade 4, when pupils stage an original opera production at the end of the school year.

ST. MARK'S SCHOOL OF TEXAS
Day — Boys Gr 1-12

Dallas, TX 75230. 10600 Preston Rd. Tel: 214-346-8000. Fax: 214-346-8366.
www.smtexas.org   E-mail: baker@smtexas.org
Arnold E. Holtberg, Head (1993). AB, Princeton Univ, MAR, Lutheran Theological Seminary. **David P. Baker, Adm.**
Col Prep. AP (316 exams taken)—Eng Ger Japan Lat Span Calc Stats Comp_Sci Bio Chem Environ_Sci Physics Eur_Hist US_Hist Econ. **Feat**—Creative_Writing Humanities Shakespeare World_Lit Chin Astron Forensic_Sci Geol Engineering Web_Design Civil_Rights Philos Relig Art_Hist Ceramics Film Fine_Arts Graphic_Arts Photog Sculpt Acting Drama Directing Debate Journ. **Supp**—Rev Tut.
Sports—B: Baseball Basket Crew X-country Fencing Football Golf Lacrosse Soccer Swim Tennis Track Volley W_Polo Wrestling. **Activities: 42.**
Selective adm (Gr 1-11): 116/yr. Usual entry: 1, 4, 5 & 9. Appl fee: $50-125. **Tests** ISEE.
Enr 854. Elem 487. Sec 367. Avg class size: 15. Stud/fac: 8:1. Uniform. **Fac 124.** Adv deg: 68%.
Grad '11—83. Col—83. (U of TX-Austin 11, USC 7, SMU 5, TX A&M 4, U of PA 4, Duke 3). **Avg SAT:** CR 679. M 714. W 679. Avg ACT: 31.1. **Col couns:** 2. Alum donors: 48%.
Tui '12-'13: Day $20,360-25,194. Aid: Need 145 ($2,100,000).
Summer: Acad Rec. Sports. 2-6 wks.
Endow $90,333,000. Plant val $20,000,000. Acres 40. Bldgs 14. Class rms 80. 2 Libs 48,000 vols. Chapels 1. Sci labs 14. Sci ctrs 1. Observatories 1. Planetariums 1. Auds 1. Theaters 2. Art studios 3. Music studios 3. Gyms 2. Athletic ctrs 1. Fields 5. Courts 9. Pools 1. Greenhouses 1. Comp labs 4.
Est 1906. Nonprofit. Tri (Aug-May). **Assoc** CLS.

Texas Country Day School (founded in 1933) and Cathedral School for Boys (established in 1946), formerly the Terrill School (opened in 1906), consolidated in 1950 to form St. Mark's School. Though the school itself is nondenominational, chapel affiliation is with the Episcopal Church. After decades of serving residential students, the school closed its boarding division in 1959, permitting a larger day enrollment.

Instruction in computers and Spanish begins in first grade; students take Japanese and Spanish in grades 5 and 6 and choose from Chinese, Japanese, Latin and Spanish in grades 7 and 8. The humanities program integrates language arts, social studies and study skills in grades 4-8, and a senior humanities course combines Advanced Placement English and European history. The program is complemented by electives in the creative, media and industrial arts, independent tutorials at students' request and a cocurricular program with the Hockaday School.

All boys entering grade 9 spend 10 days in August in the Pecos Wilderness. Six-week summer study/travel programs to France, Spain and Mexico are available. Upper school boys complete an annual requirement of 15 hours of community service.

DENTON, TX. (36 mi. NW of Dallas, TX) Urban. Pop: 80,537. Alt: 602 ft.

SELWYN COLLEGE PREPARATORY SCHOOL
Day — Coed Gr PS (Age 2)-12

Denton, TX 76207. 3333 W University Dr. Tel: 940-382-6771. Fax: 940-383-0704.
www.selwynschool.com   E-mail: mjensen@selwynschool.com
Connie Miller, Head (2010). BA, Auburn Univ. **Talitha Ledet, Adm.**
    Col Prep. Montessori. AP (exams req'd; 31 taken, 65% 3+)—Eng Fr Span Calc Bio Environ_Sci World_Hist. **Elem math**—Everyday Math. **Feat**—Comp_Sci Studio_Art Theater Music. **Supp**—LD Rem_Math Rev Tut. Outdoor ed. **Dual enr:** U of N TX, N Central TX.
    Sports—Basket X-country Golf Soccer Tennis. G: Volley. **Activities:** 6.
    Selective adm: 37/yr. Appl fee: $100. Appl due: Rolling. Applied: 46. Accepted: 80%.
    Enr 178. B 90. G 88. Elem 137. Sec 41. Wh 83%. Latino 4%. Blk 1%. Asian 7%. Other 5%. Avg class size: 12. Uniform. **Fac 40.** M 7/F 33. FT 37/PT 3. Wh 98%. Latino 1%. Asian 1%. Adv deg: 22%.
    Grad '10—10. Col—10. (U of N TX 2, TX A&M 1, U of AZ 1, TX Christian 1, St Edward's 1, Coe 1). Alum donors: 10%.
    Tui '11-'12: Day $8400-12,800 (+$825-1200). **Aid:** Need 30 ($113,000).
    Summer: Acad Enrich Rev Rec. 1-10 wks.
    Plant val $2,500,000. Acres 90. Bldgs 9. Class rms 24. Lib 12,000 vols. Sci labs 1. Dark rms 1. Comp ctrs 1. Amphitheaters 1. Art studios 1. Music studios 2. Gyms 1. Fields 2. Tennis courts 1. Pools 1. Stables 1. Lakes 1. Comp labs 1.
    Est 1957. Nonprofit. Sem (Aug-May).

Occupying a 90-acre campus on the northern end of town, Selwyn enrolls students from over two dozen north Texas communities. The preschool utilizes a developmental approach, while Selwyn's elementary program provides the option of a Montessori curriculum for children age 3 through grade 3, as well as an academically enriched traditional approach in grades K-5. Departmentalization begins in grade 3. During the middle school years (grades 6-8), students refine their academic skills in preparation for high school. The college preparatory upper school (grades 9-12) opened with the addition of grade 9 in fall 2003.

A well-developed enrichment program supports academics. Students take part in the Perspectives Program, an educational travel adventure that consists of outdoor, academic and artistic experiences. Other enrichment opportunities are foreign language, music, art, computers, photography, rock climbing and community service projects. A competitive athletic program is available in grades 4-12. Music lessons and scouting are among Selwyn's other extracurricular offerings.

FORT WORTH, TX. (33 mi. W of Dallas, TX) Urban. Pop: 534,694. Alt: 670 ft.

FORT WORTH COUNTRY DAY SCHOOL
Day — Coed Gr K-12

Fort Worth, TX 76109. 4200 Country Day Ln. Tel: 817-732-7718, 800-732-8485. Fax: 817-377-3425.
www.fwcd.org   E-mail: yolanda.espinoza@fwcd.org
Evan D. Peterson, Head (2002). BS, West Virginia Wesleyan College, MA, Kean College of New Jersey. **Barbara Waldron Jiongo, Adm.**
    Col Prep. AP (exams req'd; 424 taken, 86% 3+)—Eng Fr Lat Span Calc Stats Comp_ Sci Bio Chem Environ_Sci Physics Eur_Hist US_Hist Psych US_Govt & Pol Art_Hist Studio_Art Music_Theory. **Elem math**—Everyday Math. **Elem read**—Harcourt.

Feat—Forensic_Sci Drama Music Journ Outdoor_Ed. **Supp**—Rev Tut. Outdoor ed. **Dual enr:** Stanford.
Sports (req'd)—Basket X-country Golf Soccer Swim Tennis Track Volley. B: Baseball Football Lacrosse Wrestling. G: F_Hockey Softball.
Selective adm: 143/yr. Usual entry: K & 9. Appl fee: $75. Applied: 311. Accepted: 55%. Yield: 84%. **Tests** CTP_4 ISEE SSAT.
Enr 1110. B 562. G 548. Elem 703. Sec 407. Wh 84%. Latino 2%. Blk 3%. Asian 5%. Other 6%. Avg class size: 20. Stud/fac: 10:1. Uniform. **Fac 123.** M 35/F 88. FT 120/PT 3. Wh 83%. Latino 3%. Blk 3%. Asian 2%. Other 9%. Adv deg: 53%.
Grad '11—96. Col—96. (TX A&M, TX Christian, U of TX-Austin, TX Tech, Wash U, Baylor). Athl schol 3. **Mid 50% SAT:** CR 580-670. M 580-690. W 560-690. Mid 50% ACT: 24-30. **Col couns:** 3. Alum donors: 16%.
Tui '12-'13: Day $16,780-18,080 (+$940-1488). **Aid:** Merit 2 ($1500). Need 155 ($1,600,000).
Summer (enr 1300): Acad Enrich Rec. Art. Photog. Sports. Tui Day $105-425. 1-3 wks. Endow $45,677,000. Plant val $38,920,000. Acres 105. Bldgs 14 (26% ADA). Class rms 92. 2 Libs 48,000 vols. Sci labs 12. Lang labs 1. Auds 1. Theaters 1. Art studios 6. Music studios 5. Dance studios 2. Arts ctrs 1. Gyms 2. Fields 8. Tennis courts 6. Tracks 1. Stadiums 1. Comp labs 5. Comp/stud: 1:2.
Est 1963. Nonprofit. Sem (Aug-May).

Modeled after Northeastern independent schools, FWCD was established by Fort Worth families to meet a local need. The program in the lower school (grades K-4) facilitates the mastery of basic language and mathematical skills. Children begin studying a foreign language in kindergarten. Reading and effective writing skills are stressed at every level, and computer studies are offered to all students. The middle school program (grades 5-8) includes accelerated math and language courses, in addition to compulsory fine arts course work.

The college preparatory upper school program (grades 9-12) offers a wide selection of courses, with an emphasis on research methods, study skills and SAT preparation. Electives supplement required courses, and students choose from Advanced Placement selections in most academic departments. All middle and upper school pupils participate in both athletics and the arts. The extensive program in the visual and performing arts includes theater, ballet, orchestra, band, chorus, painting, photography and ceramics.

Boys and girls accumulate 40 hours of compulsory community service in grades 9-12.

See Also Page 79

TRINITY VALLEY SCHOOL

Day — Coed Gr K-12

Fort Worth, TX 76132. 7500 Dutch Branch Rd. Tel: 817-321-0100. Fax: 817-321-0105.
www.trinityvalleyschool.org E-mail: tvs@trinityvalleyschool.org
Gary W. Krahn, Head (2006). BS, US Military Academy, MS, PhD, US Naval Academy.
Judith S. Kinser, Adm.
Col Prep. AP (exams req'd; 520 taken, 87% 3+)—Eng Fr Lat Span Calc Stats Comp_ Sci Bio Chem Physics US_Hist Econ Psych US_Govt & Pol. **Feat**—Creative_Writing Humanities Physiol Asian_Hist Constitutional_Law Comp_Relig Ceramics Photog Video_Production Drama Chorus Speech. **Supp**—Tut. Outdoor ed.
Sports—Basket X-country Golf Soccer Tennis Track Volley. B: Baseball Football. G: Cheer F_Hockey Softball. **Activities:** 20.
Selective adm: 115/yr. Usual entry: K & 5. Appl fee: $75. Applied: 244. Accepted: 66%. Yield: 71%. **Tests** CTP_4 ISEE.
Enr 960. Elem 619. Sec 341. Wh 73%. Latino 5%. Blk 2%. Asian 11%. Other 9%. Avg class size: 20. Stud/fac: 10:1. Uniform. **Fac 84.** M 28/F 56. FT 84. Wh 88%. Latino 4%. Native Am 2%. Other 6%. Adv deg: 80%.
Grad '10—86. Col—86. (SMU 7, TX Christian 7, TX A&M 7, OK St 3, U of AL-Tuscaloosa 3, U of TX-Austin 2). Athl schol 2. **Mid 50% SAT:** CR 580-680. M 610-680. W 580-690. Mid 50% ACT: 26-31. **Col couns:** 2. Alum donors: 15%.
Tui '12-'13: Day $17,265-18,375 (+$400). **Aid:** Need 125 ($1,326,795).

Summer (enr 200): Enrich Rec. 9 wks.
Endow $19,250,000. Plant val $32,518,000. Acres 75. Bldgs 7. Class rms 53. 2 Libs 28,000 vols. Sci labs 7. Lang labs 3. Auds 1. Theaters 1. Art studios 5. Music studios 3. Gyms 2. Fields 8. Tennis courts 8. Comp labs 3.
Est 1959. Nonprofit. Sem (Aug-May).

Founded with an enrollment of seven boys in the third-floor kitchen of St. Ignatius Academy, Trinity Valley is a traditional college preparatory school that requires pupils to take at least five major courses per year. Upper school students generally take four years of math, English and history, three years of science and a foreign language, fine arts and economics. Lower school students acquire basic skills in all subject areas.

The schoolwide outdoor education program combines workshops with overnight trips and includes hiking, indoor and outdoor rock climbing, kayaking, canoeing, backpacking, whitewater rafting and environmental education instruction. Students accumulate at least 60 hours of required community service in grades 9-12.

HARLINGEN, TX. (107 mi. SSW of Corpus Christi, TX) Suburban. Pop: 57,564. Alt: 40 ft.

MARINE MILITARY ACADEMY

Bdg — Boys Gr 8-PG

Harlingen, TX 78550. 320 Iwo Jima Blvd. Tel: 956-423-6006. Fax: 956-421-9273.
  www.mma-tx.org   E-mail: admissions@mma-tx.org
Col. **Robert G. Hill**, USMC (Ret), Supt (1995). Lt. Col. **Robert Grider**, USMC (Ret), Adm.
  Col Prep. Milit. **AP (exams req'd; 52 taken, 50% 3+)**—Eng Chin Span Calc Stats Chem Physics US_Hist. **Feat**—Fr Marine_Bio/Sci Comp_Sci Pol_Sci Photog Cinematography JROTC Aerospace_Sci. **Supp**—ESL Makeup Rem_Math Tut. **Dual enr:** U of TX-Brownsville.
  Sports (req'd)—B: Baseball Basket X-country Football Golf Soccer Swim Tennis Track Wrestling.
  Selective adm: 144/yr. Appl fee: $100. Appl due: Rolling. Accepted: 68%. **Tests** HSPT.
  Enr 222. Elem 20. Sec 200. PG 2. Intl 16%. Avg class size: 12. Stud/fac: 10:1. Uniform.
    Fac 24. M 14/F 10. FT 23/PT 1. Adv deg: 62%.
  Grad '11—50. **Col**—50. (U of Houston 4, TX A&M 3, U of TX-Austin 2, U of Tulsa 2, U of Louisville 2, U of TX-San Antonio 2). **Mid 50% SAT:** CR 420-550. M 450-620. W 400-510.
  Tui '12-'13: Bdg $33,000 (+$1400). **Intl Bdg $33,000** (+$2400). **Aid:** Need 46 ($452,280).
  Summer (enr 340): Rec. ESL. Milit Trng. Tui Bdg $3950. 4 wks.
  Endow $18,000,000. Plant val $28,556,000. Acres 142. Bldgs 43. Dorms 7. Dorm rms 200. Class rms 35. Lib 16,000 vols. Sci labs 4. Lang labs 1. Auds 1. Theaters 1. Music studios 1. Gyms 3. Fields 5. Tennis courts 6. Pools 1. Rifle ranges 2. Comp labs 3.
  Est 1965. Nonprofit. Sem (Aug-May). **Assoc** SACS.

Founded by a group of former Marine officers on the site of the former Air Force Navigation School, MMA offers a full academic program, especially in the sciences and math, while stressing competitive sports and military discipline. An English composition course is required for sophomores. The program is based on Marine Corps concepts of leadership.

The aerospace program features a full flight operation that utilizes flight schools adjacent to the campus, and a private pilot's license may be earned. Enrollment is geographically diverse, with students coming from more than 30 states and roughly half a dozen foreign countries.

HOUSTON, TX. Urban. Pop: 1,845,967. Alt: 38 ft. Area also includes The Woodlands.

THE AWTY INTERNATIONAL SCHOOL
Day — Coed Gr PS (Age 3)-12

Houston, TX 77055. 7455 Awty School Ln. Tel: 713-686-4850. Fax: 713-686-4956.
www.awty.org   E-mail: admissions@awty.org
Stephen Codrington, Head (2011). Erika Benavente, Adm.

Col Prep. IB Diploma. Fr Bac. Bilingual (Arabic Fr Ger Ital Span). Feat—Creative_ Writing Fr Ger Ital Span Norwegian Computers Fine_Arts. Supp—ESL Tut.

Sports—Basket Cheer X-country Golf Soccer Swim Tennis Track. G: Volley.

Selective adm: 261/yr. Appl fee: $100. Appl due: Dec. Accepted: 55%. Tests IQ ISEE.

Enr 1190. Wh 38%. Latino 7%. Blk 3%. Asian 5%. Other 47%. Intl 54%. Avg class size: 17. Uniform. Fac 151. Wh 79%. Latino 12%. Blk 3%. Native Am 1%. Asian 5%. Adv deg: 55%.

Grad '10—84. Col—84. (McGill-Canada 6, Boston U 4, Duke 3, Occidental 3, U of Houston 3, U of British Columbia-Canada 2). Avg SAT: CR 634. M 657. W 655. Mid 50% SAT: CR 580-680. M 610-710. W 620-700. Col couns: 3.

Tui '11-'12: Day $14,373-19,684 (+$1500). Aid: Need 43 ($256,074).

Endow $3,000,000. Plant val $16,986,000. Acres 15. Bldgs 9. Class rms 105. 3 Libs 44,141 vols. Sci labs 6. Lang labs 2. Art studios 3. Music studios 3. Gyms 3. Athletic ctrs 1. Fields 2. Courts 2. Comp labs 4.

Est 1956. Nonprofit. Tri (Aug-June).

This international school's early childhood curriculum (three-year-old prekindergarten through kindergarten) consists of completely bilingual French/English or Spanish/English instruction. Beginning in grade 1, Awty conducts parallel but separate English- and French-speaking programs. Students work toward an American high school diploma and either the International Baccalaureate or the French Baccalaureate. Well-qualified students may earn both French and American credentials.

The curriculum provides a sound foundation in English, mathematics, science, history, the fine arts and foreign languages. Community service is required, and advanced courses, physical education and electives, including extensive computer offerings, are available. Travel groups are organized during school vacations, and students may also choose to participate in exchange programs.

Students come from around the world to create a multicultural environment. An intensive English as a Second Language program is conducted, and instruction in French, Spanish, German, Arabic and Italian is available at the native-language level.

THE JOHN COOPER SCHOOL
Day — Coed Gr PS (Age 4)-12

The Woodlands, TX 77381. 1 John Cooper Dr. Tel: 281-367-0900, 800-295-1162.
Fax: 281-298-5715.
www.johncooper.org   E-mail: admission@johncooper.org
Michael F. Maher, Head (2000). BS, MA, Catholic Univ of America. Craig Meredith, Adm.

Col Prep. AP (exams req'd; 388 taken, 92% 3+)—Eng Fr Span Calc Stats Comp_ Sci Bio Chem Physics Eur_Hist US_Hist Econ Psych Art_Hist Studio_Art. Elem math—Math Connects. Feat—Creative_Writing Southern_Lit Lat Linear_Algebra Multivariable_Calc Anat & Physiol Environ_Sci Holocaust Pol_Sci World_Relig Film Photog Sculpt Video_Production Printmaking Theater_Arts Band Chorus Speech. Supp—Rev.

Sports—Basket X-country Golf Soccer Swim Tennis Track. B: Baseball. G: Softball Volley. Activities: 22.

Selective adm: 171/yr. Usual entry: PS, K, 6 & 9. Appl fee: $125. Appl due: Jan. Applied: 350. Accepted: 62%. Yield: 84%. **Tests** IQ ISEE.
Enr 999. Elem 658. Sec 341. Wh 67%. Latino 9%. Blk 3%. Native Am 1%. Asian 14%. Other 6%. Intl 14%. Avg class size: 18. Stud/fac: 11:1. Uniform. **Fac 87.** M 22/F 65. FT 81/PT 6. Adv deg: 49%.
Grad '11—84. Col—84. (U of TX-Austin 5, Tulane 4, TX Christian 4, U of CO-Boulder 4, Trinity U 4, Rice 3). **Avg SAT:** CR 663. M 672. W 656. **Mid 50% SAT:** CR 590-720. M 630-710. W 610-700. Avg ACT: 29. Mid 50% ACT: 26-31. **Col couns:** 2. Alum donors: 3%.
Tui '11-'12: Day $15,660-19,340 (+$1000-1400). **Aid:** Need 72 ($535,975).
Summer (enr 550): Acad Enrich Rem Rec. Robotics. Sports. Tui Day $295-600/wk. 5 wks.
Endow $2,050,000. Plant val $46,050,000. Acres 43. Bldgs 9 (90% ADA). Class rms 82. 2 Libs 18,700 vols. Auds 2. Art studios 3. Music studios 2. Dance studios 2. Perf arts ctrs 1. Gyms 2. Fields 4. Courts 4. Student ctrs 1. Comp labs 3.
Est 1988. Nonprofit. Quar (Aug-May). **Assoc** CLS.

Located on a 43-acre campus 27 miles northwest of Houston, this college preparatory school provides a varied elementary and secondary program. An intensive foreign language program commences with Spanish instruction at the prekindergarten level and continues with the introduction of French and Latin in the middle school.

Upper schoolers choose from a full complement of Advanced Placement courses, as well as such electives as drama, yearbook, band, choir, painting and drawing, sculpture, photography and literary magazine. Lower and middle school children receive application-specific and curriculum-integrated computer instruction, while upper school pupils choose from applications and programming courses. **See Also Page 96**

KINKAID SCHOOL

Day — Coed Gr PS (Age 4)-12

Houston, TX 77024. 201 Kinkaid School Dr. Tel: 713-782-1640. **Fax:** 713-782-3543.
www.kinkaid.org   E-mail: admission@kinkaid.org
Donald C. North, Head (1996). BA, Vanderbilt Univ, MA, Middlebury College. **Iris R. Bonet, Adm.**
Col Prep. AP (exams req'd; 503 taken, 94% 3+)—Eng Fr Lat Span Calc Stats Comp_ Sci Bio Chem Physics Eur_Hist US_Hist Studio_Art Music_Theory. **Feat**—Classics Creative_Writing Chin Multivariable_Calc Anat & Physiol Astron Environ_Sci Econ Govt Intl_Relations Psych Philos World_Relig Architect Art_Hist Film Photog Drama Chorus Dance Debate Journ Speech.
Sports—Basket X-country Golf Lacrosse Soccer Swim Tennis Track Volley. B: Baseball Football Wrestling. G: Cheer F_Hockey Softball.
Very selective adm: 175/yr. Usual entry: PS, K, 6 & 9. Appl fee: $100. Applied: 917. Accepted: 24%. Yield: 80%. **Tests** IQ ISEE.
Enr 1379. B 702. G 677. Elem 825. Sec 554. Wh 77%. Latino 3%. Blk 4%. Asian 8%. Other 8%. Avg class size: 18. Stud/fac: 8:1. Casual. **Fac 182.** M 61/F 121. FT 155/PT 27. Wh 83%. Latino 7%. Blk 7%. Asian 1%. Other 2%. Adv deg: 48%.
Grad '11—136. Col—136. (U of TX-Austin 26, Vanderbilt 9, TX Christian 7, TX A&M 5, Emory 4, Northwestern 4). Athl schol 2. **Avg SAT:** CR 641. M 661. W 646. **Mid 50% SAT:** CR 580-700. M 610-720. W 600-700. **Col couns:** 7. Alum donors: 29%.
Tui '12-'13: Day $16,000-20,530 (+$1600-1800). **Aid:** Merit 6 ($62,220). Need 118 ($1,657,010).
Summer (enr 650): Acad Enrich Rev Rem Rec. Arts. ESL. Tui Day $75-400. 1-4 wks.
Endow $91,000,000. Plant val $61,400,000. Acres 64. Bldgs 10 (100% ADA). Class rms 126. 3 Libs 119,104 vols. Sci labs 12. Auds 4. Theaters 1. Art studios 4. Music studios 5. Dance studios 1. Gyms 3. Fields 4. Courts 4. Tracks 1. Comp labs 7. Comp/stud: 1:2.
Est 1906. Nonprofit. Sem (Aug-May). **Assoc** CLS.

The oldest coeducational independent school in the city, Kinkaid was founded by Margaret Hunter Kinkaid, who originally operated the school out of her home. In 1957, the school assumed its present, 40-acre location in Piney Point Village. From its early days, the school has placed emphasis upon both academic attainment and character development.

Kinkaid combines rigorous academics with well-developed programs in athletics and the fine and performing arts. Upper schoolers take part in a three-week interim program each January that consists of various enrichment courses, independent study opportunities, internships and travel options.

ST. JOHN'S SCHOOL
Day — Coed Gr K-12

Houston, TX 77019. 2401 Claremont Ln. Tel: 713-850-0222. Fax: 713-622-2309.
www.sjs.org   E-mail: cplummer@sjs.org
Mark D. Desjardins, Head (2010). BA, Bates College, MEd, PhD, Univ of Virginia. **Cheryl Plummer, Adm.**
Col Prep. AP (654 exams taken, 96% 3+)—Fr Lat Span Calc Stats Comp_Sci Bio Chem Physics Eur_Hist US_Hist World_Hist Comp_Govt & Pol US_Govt & Pol Music_Theory. **Feat**—Chin Multivariable_Calc Anat & Physiol Astron Microbio Organic_Chem Middle_Eastern_Hist Econ Psych Philos World_Relig Architect Art_Hist Ceramics Film Painting Photog Sculpt Studio_Art Theater Chorus Music Jazz_Band Dance. **Supp**—Tut.
Sports—Basket X-country Golf Lacrosse Soccer Swim Tennis Track Volley. B: Baseball Football Wrestling. G: F_Hockey Softball. **Activities:** 39.
Very selective adm: 156/yr. Appl fee: $100. Appl due: Dec. Accepted: 20%. Yield: 86%. **Tests** IQ ISEE.
Enr 1249. Elem 696. Sec 553. Stud/fac: 8:1. Uniform. **Fac 139.** M 43/F 96. FT 130/PT 9. Adv deg: 53%.
Grad '10—133. Col—133. (Rice, Vanderbilt, U of TX-Austin, U of VA, USC, Wash U). **Mid 50% SAT:** CR 660-740. M 680-770. W 660-770. Mid 50% ACT: 29-34. **Col couns:** 5. Alum donors: 30%.
Tui '11-'12: Day $16,415-20,235 (+$100-1762). **Aid:** Need ($2,400,000).
Summer: Acad Rec. SAT Prep. 8 wks.
Endow $54,103,000. Plant val $50,728,000. Acres 28. Bldgs 9. Class rms 100. 3 Libs 43,000 vols. Sci labs 13. Lang labs 1. Auds 1. Theaters 1. Art studios 5. Music studios 4. Dance studios 2. Gyms 2. Fields 5. Tracks 1. Comp labs 3.
Est 1946. Nonprofit. Quar (Aug-May). **Assoc** CLS.

Founded under the direction of Alan Lake Chidsey, who had extensive experience in Eastern and Southwestern boys' schools, this school of interdenominational enrollment adheres to high academic standards.

St. John's provides fine arts instruction at all grade levels and maintains numerous performing arts ensembles; computer courses are available in all divisions as well. Qualified boys and girls in grades 10-12 may engage in—and help design—an independent study project. Past projects have examined glassblowing; jewelry making; the production of films, plays, animation and musical CDs; and novel writing. Students may pursue semester programs and yearlong exchanges with other independent schools, or study in France, China, Italy or Spain through the School Year Abroad program.

Schoolwide community service projects are organized in middle school. Upper school students generate and manage a yearlong calendar of service projects.

ST. THOMAS HIGH SCHOOL
Day — Boys Gr 9-12
Houston, TX 77007. 4500 Memorial Dr. Tel: 713-864-6348. Fax: 713-864-5750.

www.sths.org   E-mail: jon.moody@sths.org
Rev. Ronald G. Schwenzer, CSB, Pres (2006). BA, St John Fisher College, STB, Univ of Toronto (Canada), MS, Purdue Univ. **Rev. Patrick Fulton, CSB, Prin.** BA, Univ of Saskatchewan (Canada), BEd, Univ of Alberta (Canada), MDiv, Univ of St Michael's College (Canada). **Jon Moody, Adm.**

Col Prep. AP (exams req'd; 262 taken, 93% 3+)—Eng Span Calc Bio Chem Physics US_Hist US_Govt & Pol. **Feat**—Creative_Writing Fr Lat Astron Environ_Sci Geol Oceanog Comp_Sci Milit_Hist Econ Global_Affairs Philos Theol Art_Hist Ceramics Photog Sculpt Studio_Art Music Jazz_Band Debate Journ. **Supp**—Rev Tut.

Sports—B: Baseball Basket X-country Football Golf Lacrosse Rugby Soccer Swim Tennis Track Wrestling. **Activities:** 35.

Selective adm: 226/yr. Usual entry: 9 & 10. Appl fee: $50. Appl due: Jan. Applied: 463. Accepted: 61%. Yield: 72%. **Tests** HSPT.

Enr 730. Wh 63%. Latino 21%. Blk 7%. Asian 6%. Other 3%. Avg class size: 19. Stud/fac: 13:1. Casual. **Fac 52.** M 36/F 16. FT 52. Wh 94%. Latino 2%. Blk 2%. Other 2%. Adv deg: 55%.

Grad '11—154. Col—154. (U of Houston 24, TX A&M 22, U of TX-San Antonio 9, U of TX-Austin 7, St Edward's 7, Notre Dame 4). Athl schol 6. **Avg SAT:** CR 640. M 670. W 620. Avg ACT: 26. **Col couns:** 3. Alum donors: 22%.

Tui '12-'13: Day $13,250 (+$750-1150). **Aid:** Merit 47 ($167,000). Need 173 ($1,876,000).

Summer: Rev. Tui Day $400/crse. 3 wks.

Endow $7,500,000. Plant val $17,000,000. Acres 17. Bldgs 4 (100% ADA). Lib 10,000 vols. Sci labs 3. Amphitheaters 1. Auds 1. Art studios 2. Music studios 1. Gyms 1. Fields 2. Tracks 1. Stadiums 1. Comp labs 5. Comp/stud: 1:5.

Est 1900. Nonprofit. Roman Catholic (75% practice). Sem (Aug-May). **Assoc** SACS.

St. Thomas, Houston's oldest boys' college preparatory school, was founded by three priests of the Congregation of St. Basil on the site of a former monastery. It moved to its present, 17-acre location in 1940. Students enroll from Houston and the surrounding community.

Curriculum and activities emphasize Catholic values and teachings. The normal course load is seven subjects, with requirements in English, math, science, history and theology. Students may qualify for honors courses that include advanced studies in most subject areas.

Cultural, social and service activities complement academics. Boys assist the campus ministry by serving as lectors, altar servers and Eucharistic ministers. Freshmen perform 15 hours of community service, sophomores attend a required service retreat, and juniors and seniors complete 40 hours of service each year.

IRVING, TX. (13 mi. WNW of Dallas, TX) Urban. Pop: 191,615. Alt: 470 ft.

CISTERCIAN PREPARATORY SCHOOL

Day — Boys Gr 5-12

Irving, TX 75039. 3660 Cistercian Rd. Tel: 469-499-5400. Fax: 469-499-5440.
www.cistercian.org   E-mail: admissions@cistercian.org
Rev. Paul McCormick, OCist, Head (2012). BA, MBA, MA, Univ of Dallas. **Jim Taylor, Adm.**

Col Prep. AP (145 exams taken, 97% 3+)—Eng Fr Span Calc Stats Comp_Sci Bio Physics Eur_Hist US_Hist Psych US_Govt & Pol Studio_Art Music_Theory. **Feat**—British_Lit Creative_Writing C_S_Lewis Lat Anat Astron Forensic_Sci Robotics Civil_War WWII Econ Govt Comp_Relig Theol Architect Film Photog Video_Production Acting Music Music_Hist Debate. **Supp**—Rev Tut. **Dual enr:** Northlake CC.

Sports—B: Baseball Basket X-country Football Soccer Swim Tennis Track. **Activities:** 10.

Selective adm (Gr 5-9): 53/yr. Usual entry: 5. Appl fee: $75. Appl due: Jan. Applied: 164. Accepted: 36%. Yield: 90%. **Tests** HSPT IQ.

Enr 355. Elem 178. Sec 177. Wh 75%. Latino 5%. Blk 2%. Asian 8%. Other 10%. Avg class size: 22. Stud/fac: 7:1. Uniform. **Fac 46.** M 36/F 10. FT 39/PT 7. Wh 87%. Latino 7%. Blk 4%. Asian 2%. Adv deg: 50%.
Grad '11—42. Col—42. (Notre Dame 4, TX A&M 3, Vanderbilt 3, Rice 2, Creighton 2, Baylor 2). **Avg SAT:** CR 688. M 714. W 698. Avg ACT: 31. **Col couns:** 1. Alum donors: 29%.
Tui '12-'13: Day $15,500-16,800 (+$600-700). **Aid:** Need 69 ($640,400).
Summer (enr 125): Acad Enrich Rev Rem Rec. Tui Day $260/2-wk ses. 4 wks.
Plant val $40,000,000. Acres 85. Bldgs 7 (100% ADA). Class rms 22. Lib 23,000 vols. Labs 4. Auds 1. Theaters 1. Art studios 2. Music studios 1. Gyms 2. Fields 4. Courts 5. Comp/stud: 1:6.
Est 1962. Nonprofit. Roman Catholic (81% practice). Quar (Aug-May). **Assoc** CLS.

Cistercian Fathers founded and conduct this college preparatory school, which accepts boys of all faiths and offers a varied curriculum. Students fulfill course requirements in English, foreign languages, math, science, social studies and theology. Seniors take dual-enrollment college courses in English, calculus, American government and science through nearby Northlake Community College. Senior projects, under the direction of a faculty member, are conducted during the fourth quarter.

Although community service is not a graduation requirement, boys participate in frequent group and individual projects.

SAN ANTONIO, TX. Urban. Pop: 1,144,646. Alt: 700 ft.

KEYSTONE SCHOOL
Day — Coed Gr K-12

San Antonio, TX 78212. 119 E Craig Pl. Tel: 210-735-4022. Fax: 210-732-4905.
www.keystoneschool.org   E-mail: zwormley@keystoneschool.org
Brian Yager, Head (2010). Zina Wormley, Adm.
Col Prep. AP (148 exams taken, 93% 3+)—Eng Fr Span Calc Comp_Sci Bio Chem Environ_Sci Eur_Hist US_Hist. **Feat**—Creative_Writing Anat & Physiol Comp_Design Govt Psych Photog Studio_Art Acting Photojourn. **Supp**—Tut. Outdoor ed.
Sports—Basket Golf Tennis Track. B: Soccer. G: Softball Volley.
Selective adm: 73/yr. Appl fee: $50. Appl due: Feb. Applied: 158. **Tests** CEEB CTP_4 ISEE Stanford.
Enr 426. Elem 300. Sec 126. Wh 48%. Latino 18%. Blk 5%. Asian 11%. Other 18%. Avg class size: 14. Stud/fac: 10:1. **Fac 44.** M 13/F 31. FT 43/PT 1. Wh 89%. Latino 11%. Adv deg: 29%.
Grad '11—28. Col—28. (Harvard 3, Rice 2, U of TX-San Antonio 2, TX A&M 2, Stanford 1, Duke 1). **Avg SAT:** CR 695. M 675. W 674. Avg ACT: 29. **Col couns:** 1. Alum donors: 3%.
Tui '12-'13: Day $12,365-15,885 (+$1000). **Aid:** Need 45 ($440,000).
Endow $750,000. Plant val $6,300,000. Acres 3. Bldgs 10. Class rms 35. Libs 2. Sci labs 3. Theaters 1. Art studios 1. Music studios 1. Dance studios 1. Perf arts ctrs 1. Gyms 1. Comp labs 2.
Est 1948. Nonprofit. Sem (Aug-May).

Serving students of above-average ability, Keystone conducts a college preparatory program that emphasizes knowledge acquisition, study skills and the mastery of fundamental skills. Lower and middle schoolers (grades K-8) engage in core course work in language arts, math, science and social studies; specialists teach Spanish, studio art, music, computer applications and physical education classes. The upper school (grades 9-12) features a broad selection of honors and Advanced Placement offerings. All upper schoolers perform at least 12 total hours of community service prior to graduation.

Field trips, which provide enrichment at all grade levels, range from daylong trips to Austin and San Marcos to multi-day hiking and camping excursions to the Yellowstone, Yosemite and Olympic national parks.

SAINT MARY'S HALL
Day — Coed Gr PS (Age 4)-12

San Antonio, TX 78217. 9401 Starcrest Dr. Tel: 210-483-9234. Fax: 210-655-5211. www.smhall.org E-mail: admissions@smhall.org
Bob Windham, Head (2005). BS, Texas A&M Univ, MEd, Univ of Houston. **Julie Hellmund, Adm.**

Col Prep. Montessori. AP (exams req'd; 515 taken, 86% 3+)—Eng Fr Lat Span Calc Stats Comp_Sci Bio Chem Environ_Sci Physics Eur_Hist US_Hist World_Hist Econ US_Govt & Pol Art_Hist Studio_Art. **Elem math**—Everyday Math. **Feat**—British_Lit Creative_Writing Geol Zoology Psych Theol Photog Sculpt Video_Production Music Dance Debate Journ. **Supp**—Rev Tut.

Sports—Basket X-country Golf Soccer Swim Tennis Track. B: Baseball Lacrosse. G: F_Hockey Softball Volley. **Activities:** 35.

Selective adm: 180/yr. Usual entry: PS, K, 6 & 9. Appl fee: $50. Applied: 395. Accepted: 70%. Yield: 62%. **Tests** ISEE SSAT.

Enr 984. Elem 617. Sec 367. Avg class size: 13. Stud/fac: 12:1. Uniform. **Fac 53.** Adv deg: 64%.

Grad '10—84. Col—84. (Trinity U 9, SMU 5, U of TX-Austin 4, Princeton 3, Duke 2, Harvard 2). **Avg SAT:** CR 640. M 647. W 642. Avg ACT: 27. **Col couns:** 2. Alum donors: 6%.

Tui '11-'12: Day $10,975-20,435 (+$1000). **Aid:** Merit 72 ($462,350). Need 118 ($820,750).

Summer (enr 1000): Acad Enrich Rev Rec. Tech. Sports. Tui Day $100-500/wk. 10 wks.

Endow $31,735,000. Plant val $46,767,000. Acres 60. Bldgs 26. Class rms 118. 2 Libs 23,000 vols. Sci labs 11. Lang labs 1. Photog labs 1. Theaters 2. Art studios 3. Music studios 8. Dance studios 3. Arts ctrs 1. Gyms 2. Fields 3. Courts 7. Pools 1. Comp labs 3.

Est 1879. Nonprofit. Sem (Aug-May). **Assoc** CLS.

Saint Mary's Hall was founded by Bishop Robert W. B. Elliott, the first bishop of the Episcopal Diocese of West Texas. A school for boys and girls of all denominations, Saint Mary's Hall still has a historical affiliation with the Episcopal Church. Over the years, the school has grown by the admission of boys into all grades and the addition of primary grades, a Montessori preschool and a traditional kindergarten. In the fall of 1968, the school moved to its present site, a wooded, 60-acre campus that overlooks San Antonio.

The school conducts a traditional college preparatory curriculum that is complemented by various cocurricular options. Honors and Advanced Placement courses in many disciplines are available in the upper school. An extensive fine arts program provides opportunities in the visual and performing arts.

TMI
THE EPISCOPAL SCHOOL OF TEXAS
Bdg — Coed Gr 9-12; Day — Coed 6-12

San Antonio, TX 78257. 20955 W Tejas Trail. Tel: 210-698-7171. Fax: 210-698-0715. www.tmi-sa.org E-mail: admission@tmi-sa.org
John Cooper, Head (2012). BA, MA, Florida State Univ, PhD, Syracuse Univ. **Brenda Klaftenegger, Adm.**

Col Prep. Milit. AP (exams req'd; 141 taken, 84% 3+)—Eng Lat Span Calc Comp_Sci Bio Chem Physics Eur_Hist US_Hist US_Govt & Pol Studio_Art. **Feat**—Creative_

Writing Hemingway & Fitzgerald Mythology Playwriting Stats Astron Bioethics Genocide Milit_Hist Philos World_Relig Film Painting Photog Theater_Arts Journ JROTC. **Supp**—Tut.

Sports—Basket X-country Golf Soccer Swim Tennis. B: Baseball Football Lacrosse. G: Cheer Softball Volley. **Activities:** 27.

Selective adm: 123/yr. Bdg 20. Day 103. Appl fee: $75. Appl due: Jan. Accepted: 64%. Yield: 68%. **Tests** CEEB CTP_4 ISEE SSAT TOEFL.

Enr 423. Bdg 42. Day 381. Wh 62%. Latino 23%. Blk 2%. Asian 3%. Other 10%. Avg class size: 14. Stud/fac: 10:1. Uniform. **Fac 44.** M 34/F 10. FT 44. Wh 71%. Latino 16%. Blk 3%. Asian 3%. Other 7%. Adv deg: 63%. In dorms 10.

Grad '10—62. Col—62. (Baylor, TX A&M, SMU, U of the Incarnate Word, TX Tech, St Edward's). Athl schol 2. **Mid 50% SAT:** CR 540-680. M 520-630. W 560-660. Alum donors: 15%.

Tui '12-'13: Bdg $39,570 (+$1000). **5-Day Bdg $36,035** (+$1000). **Day $19,030-20,145** (+$1000). **Intl Bdg $47,205** (+$1000). **Aid:** Need 90 ($529,505).

Summer: Acad Enrich Rec. Sports. 6 wks.

Endow $2,834,000. Plant val $18,907,000. Acres 80. Bldgs 14 (100% ADA). Dorms 8. Dorm rms 54. Class rms 30. Lib 20,000 vols. Chapels 1. Auds 1. Theaters 2. Art studios 1. Gyms 2. Fields 3. Courts 2. Pools 1. Rifle ranges 1. Comp labs 2.

Est 1893. Inc. Episcopal. Sem (Aug-May).

The school was founded as a boys' military program by Rt. Rev. J. S. Johnston, bishop of the Diocese of West Texas of the Protestant Episcopal Church. In 1926, it merged with San Antonio Academy and the name was changed to Texas Military Institute. The Episcopal Church once again assumed ownership and direction in 1952. The school began admitting girls and expanded to include grades 6-8 in 1972. Two years later, the military program became optional. TMI assumed its current name in 2004.

The traditional college preparatory curriculum of the upper school consists of five core fields—English, mathematics, science, social studies and foreign language—supplemented by offerings in the fine arts, athletics, religion and an optional military science program. Honors and Advanced Placement courses provide an additional challenge for the exceptionally capable student. Electives are available in such areas as drama, vocal music, photography, yearbook publication and art.

TMI encourages all students to participate in service programs and requires those in grades 9-12 to complete one internal and one external service project (each involving at least fours hours of work) annually. JROTC is available to boys and girls beginning in grade 6. The curriculum includes required religion courses, and daily chapel involves both pupils and faculty.

SAN MARCOS, TX. (45 mi. NE of San Antonio, TX) Suburban. Pop: 34,733. Alt: 581 ft.

SAN MARCOS ACADEMY
Bdg and Day — Coed Gr 7-12

San Marcos, TX 78666. 2801 Ranch Rd 12. Tel: 512-753-8000, 800-428-5120. Fax: 512-753-8031.

www.smabears.org   E-mail: admissions@smba.org

John H. Garrison, Pres (2008). BA, McMurry Univ, MEd, Univ of North Texas, PhD, Univ of Texas-Austin. Jeff Baergen, Adm.

Col Prep. AP (exams req'd)—Eng Calc Comp_Sci World_Hist. **Feat**—Fr Span Bible Ceramics Photog Studio_Art Theater Band Chorus JROTC. **Supp**—Dev_Read ESL LD Rev Tut. **Dual enr:** Hardin-Simmons.

Sports—Basket X-country Golf Soccer Swim Tennis Track Weightlifting. B: Baseball Football. G: Cheer Softball Volley. **Activities:** 12.

Selective adm: 103/yr. Bdg 67. Day 36. Usual entry: 9. Appl fee: $100. Appl due: Rolling.

Accepted: 80%. Yield: 80%.

Enr 294. B 185. G 109. Bdg 180. Day 114. Elem 52. Sec 242. Wh 49%. Latino 9%. Blk 8%. Native Am 1%. Asian 29%. Other 4%. Intl 39%. Avg class size: 12. Stud/fac: 6:1. Uniform. **Fac 41.** M 22/F 19. FT 41. Wh 80%. Latino 12%. Blk 5%. Native Am 2%. Asian 1%. Adv deg: 51%. In dorms 6.

Grad '11—51. Col—46. (TX St-San Marcos, U of TX-Austin, Baylor, TX Tech, Syracuse, U of IL-Urbana). Athl schol 1. **Avg SAT:** CR 463. M 563. W 453. Avg ACT: 21. **Col couns:** 3. Alum donors: 15%.

Tui '12-'13: Bdg $28,790 (+$3387). **Day $8518-8995** (+$1938). **Intl Bdg $31,790** (+$5427). **Aid:** Need 92 ($467,600).

Endow $6,000,000. Plant val $22,000,000. Acres 220. Bldgs 8 (100% ADA). Dorms 3. Dorm rms 180. Class rms 32. Lib 17,418 vols. Theaters 2. Art studios 1. Music studios 2. Fields 4. Courts 4. Pools 1. Riding rings 1. Stables 1. Rifle ranges 1. Ropes crses 1. Comp labs 4. Comp/stud: 1:2.

Est 1907. Nonprofit. Baptist (15% practice). Sem (Aug-May). **Assoc** SACS.

Situated on a 220-acre campus, SMA is affiliated with the Baptist General Convention of Texas. The curriculum emphasizes college preparation, and honors, Advanced Placement and dual-enrollment courses are available to qualified students. All first-year upper school boys who are US citizens participate in the Junior ROTC program for at least one semester; it is optional for girls and international students.

The academy's honor program seeks the development of critical-thinking and independent research skills by means of small classes and technology-assisted learning. Course work in the fine arts, Christian studies, computer science and leadership supplements requirements in the traditional subjects. Upperclassmen may take Advanced Placement classes and may also earn college credit from Hardin-Simmons University through enrollment in dual-credit courses. A learning skills program serves students diagnosed with a mild learning disability or ADHD.

Among student activities are athletic options and fine arts offerings, in addition to an equestrian program.

Mountain States

COLORADO

ASPEN, CO. (112 mi. WSW of Denver, CO) Suburban. Pop: 5914. Alt: 7908 ft.

ASPEN COUNTRY DAY SCHOOL
Day — Coed Gr PS (Age 2)-8

Aspen, CO 81611. 3 Music School Rd. Tel: 970-925-1909. Fax: 970-925-7074.
www.aspencountryday.org   **E-mail:** info@aspencountryday.org
John Suitor, Head (1999). BA, MA, Univ of Vermont. **Gretchen Cole, Adm.**
  Pre-Prep. Gen Acad. Feat—Fr Lat Span Computers Studio_Art Drama Music Outdoor_
    Ed. **Supp**—Dev_Read Rem_Math Rem_Read Tut. Outdoor ed.
  Selective adm: 50/yr. Usual entry: PS & K. Appl fee: $50. Appl due: Feb. Accepted: 50%.
    Yield: 95%. **Tests** SSAT Stanford.
  Enr 207. B 106. G 101. Wh 90%. Latino 5%. Asian 1%. Other 4%. Avg class size: 17.
    Casual. **Fac 41.** M 11/F 30. FT 31/PT 10. Wh 100%. Adv deg: 26%.
  Grad '10—18. Prep—10. (CO Rocky Mtn 2, Milton Acad 1, Cate 1, Fountain Valley 1).
    Avg SSAT: 70%. Alum donors: 45%.
  Tui '12-'13: Day $16,290-23,230 (+$800). **Aid:** Merit 1. Need 42 ($380,000).
    Endow $9,000,000. Plant val $1,950,000. Acres 10. Bldgs 7. Class rms 18. Libs 1. Sci
    labs 1. Theaters 1. Art studios 1. Music studios 1. Gyms 1. Fields 1. Rinks 1. Comp
    labs 1. Laptop prgm Gr 6-8.
  Est 1969. Nonprofit. Sem (Sept-June).

Country Day's favorable student-teacher ratio facilitates individualized instruction throughout the school. Beginning at age 2½, the prekindergarten balances hands-on exploration with group instruction. Children gain an introduction to French and Spanish at this level. At the lower school level (grades K-5), each classroom features a full-time instructor and a part-time assistant. The middle school (grades 6-8) places particular emphasis on critical thinking and writing.

The physical and outdoor education program utilizes the school's mountain environment. The entire school community spends eight afternoons during the winter either skiing or snowboarding. Overnight trips begin in kindergarten, with each grade embarking on two trips per school year. Activities include hiking, rock climbing, backcountry skiing and mountain biking.

COLORADO SPRINGS, CO. (63 mi. S of Denver, CO) Urban. Pop: 360,890. Alt: 5978 ft.

THE COLORADO SPRINGS SCHOOL
Day — Coed Gr PS (Age 3)-12

Colorado Springs, CO 80906. 21 Broadmoor Ave. Tel: 719-475-9747.
  Fax: 719-475-9864.
  www.css.org   **E-mail:** nmadrigal@css.org
Kevin Reel, Head (2007). BA, MS, Stanford Univ. **Nori Madrigal, Adm.**
  Col Prep. AP (92 exams taken, 85% 3+)—Eng Fr Span Calc Stats Bio Environ_Sci

Eur_Hist Comp_Govt & Pol Econ US_Govt & Pol. **Feat**—Creative_Writing Anat & Physiol Astron Botany Ecol Genetics Geol Programming Lat-Amer_Hist Psych African_Stud Ethics Philos Art_Hist Photog Sculpt Studio_Art Acting Theater_Arts Music Public_Speak. Outdoor ed.

Sports—Basket X-country Soccer Tennis. B: Golf Lacrosse. G: Volley.

Selective adm: 51/yr. Appl fee: $50. Appl due: Mar. Accepted: 80%. Yield: 84%. **Tests** IQ TOEFL.

Enr 305. Intl 5%. Avg class size: 16. Stud/fac: 7:1. **Fac 49.** M 16/F 33. FT 49. Adv deg: 46%.

Grad '09—36. Col—36. (U of CO-Boulder 3, CO St 3, Ft Lewis 2, CO Col 2, Lake Forest 2, U of WA 2). **Avg SAT:** CR/M/W 1873. Avg ACT: 28. **Col couns:** 1. Alum donors: 2%.

Tui '12-'13: Day $12,750-18,275 (+$698-978). **Aid:** Merit 37 ($103,100). Need 137 ($869,409).

Summer: Acad Enrich Rec. SAT Prep. 1-6 wks.

Endow $3,200,000. Plant val $10,800,000. Acres 32. Bldgs 8. Class rms 46. Lib 15,000 vols. Sci labs 3. Theaters 1. Art studios 3. Music studios 2. Gyms 1. Fields 2. Comp labs 3. Comp/stud: 1:3.

Est 1961. Nonprofit. Sem (Aug-May).

Founded as a college preparatory school for girls, the Colorado Springs School has evolved into a coeducational day institution. The campus occupies a 32-acre site at the foot of the Rocky Mountains.

CSS' curriculum provides rigorous college preparation, including Advanced Placement courses, in a flexible block scheduling system that divides the day into 90- and 45-minute class periods and permits accelerated study; the 90-minute classes enable boys and girls to earn full-year credits in one semester. The arts program, which includes studio art, music, photography and drama, is an integral part of the curriculum.

The Experience Centered Seminar program, required of all upper school students each year, enables pupils to travel locally, nationally and internationally during the month of February under faculty supervision. Students gain the advantage of off-campus study opportunities and internships in areas of interest. Credit is offered for writing, science (Rocky Mountain ecology, marine biology and astronomy), art, foreign language and history projects completed during the program.

In addition to a full complement of interscholastic sports and extracurricular options, pupils attend local cultural events and participate in such leisure-time activities as rock climbing, downhill and cross-country skiing, and hiking. Community service is part of the curriculum in the lower grades. Then, in grades 9-12, students satisfy a 24-hour annual service requirement.

FOUNTAIN VALLEY SCHOOL OF COLORADO

Bdg and Day — Coed Gr 9-12

Colorado Springs, CO 80911. 6155 Fountain Valley School Rd. Tel: 719-390-7035. Fax: 719-391-9039.

www.fvs.edu   E-mail: admission@fvs.edu

Craig W. Larimer, Jr., Head (2007). BA, Pomona College, MA, Johns Hopkins Univ. **Randy Roach, Adm.**

Col Prep. AP (exams req'd; 239 taken, 89% 3+)—Eng Fr Span Calc Stats Comp_ Sci Bio Chem Environ_Sci Physics US_Hist World_Hist US_Govt & Pol Studio_Art. **Feat**—Creative_Writing Tolkien Chin Geol Comp_Design Ceramics Film Filmmaking Photog Theater Music Metal_Shop. **Supp**—ESL LD Rev Tut. Outdoor ed.

Sports (req'd)—Basket X-country Equestrian Lacrosse Soccer Tennis Track Volley. B: Golf Ice_Hockey. G: Swim. **Activities:** 35.

Selective adm (Gr 9-11): 91/yr. Bdg 64. Day 27. Usual entry: 9. Appl fee: $50. Appl due: Feb. Applied: 231. Accepted: 69%. Yield: 54%. **Tests** CEEB ISEE SSAT TOEFL.

Enr 244. B 115. G 129. Bdg 162. Day 82. Wh 72%. Latino 5%. Blk 3%. Native Am 1%. Asian 17%. Other 2%. Intl 22%. Avg class size: 11. Stud/fac: 5:1. Casual. **Fac 44.** M 30/F 14. FT 34/PT 10. Wh 96%. Latino 2%. Blk 1%. Asian 1%. Adv deg: 65%. In

dorms 8.
Grad '11—74. Col—74. (CO Col 6, U of CO-Boulder 6, CO St 3, CO Sch of Mines 3, Bowdoin 2, Wesleyan U 2). **Mid 50% SAT:** CR 510-640. M 540-680. W 503-650. Mid 50% ACT: 23-29. **Col couns:** 1. Alum donors: 22%.
Tui '12-'13: Bdg $46,300 (+$1000). **Day $25,100** (+$1000). **Aid:** Merit 24 ($130,600). Need 59 ($1,900,000).
Summer (enr 16): Intl Students. Acad Enrich Rec. ESL. Tui Bdg $3000. 2 wks.
Endow $30,000,000. Plant val $40,000,000. Acres 1100. Bldgs 36. Dorms 7. Dorm rms 85. Class rms 36. Lib 25,000 vols. Sci labs 6. Sci ctrs 1. Theaters 1. Art studios 6. Music studios 3. Dance studios 1. Art galleries 1. Gyms 1. Fields 5. Courts 9. Pools 1. Riding rings 4. Stables 2. Tracks 1. Weight rms 1. Student ctrs 1. Comp labs 3.
Est 1930. Nonprofit. Sem (Aug-May). **Assoc** CLS.

Located on an 1100-acre main campus, this school was founded to provide a Western alternative to the college preparatory boarding schools of the East. Originally a boys' school, Fountain Valley began operation with a board of trustees composed of prominent scientists, physicians, businesspeople and political figures from Boston, MA, Chicago, IL, Washington, DC, and Colorado Springs. The school was founded on the principles of progressive educator John Dewey. Day students were first admitted in 1951, and the school instituted full coeducation in 1975.

FVS' academic program features honors and Advanced Placement courses in the major disciplines. The program incorporates a science center and computer labs, and the school conducts a technology curriculum that culminates in advanced topics. Qualified seniors may design independent study projects during the spring term, and all 12th graders take part in a weeklong, off-campus seminar. Also available are an ESL program for international students and an interim program, involving all students, that has included trips to Baja for marine biology, the Southwest for the study of Native American archaeology, and France and Spain for language study.

Fountain Valley's performing and visual arts, outdoor education and riding programs are particularly strong. Skiing, rock climbing, hiking/backpacking and horse packing trips are part of the program. The school maintains a separate, 40-acre mountain campus for additional experiential and outdoor education opportunities. Students engage in required, class-by-class community service each year. **See Also Page 58**

DENVER, CO. Urban. Pop: 554,636. Alt: 5280 ft. Area also includes Englewood.

COLORADO ACADEMY
Day — Coed Gr PS (Age 4)-12

Denver, CO 80235. 3800 S Pierce St. Tel: 303-986-1501. Fax: 303-914-2589.
www.coloradoacademy.org   E-mail: info@coloradoacademy.org
Michael G. Davis, Head (2008). BA, College of Wooster, MA, PhD, Vanderbilt Univ. **Catherine Laskey, Adm.**
Col Prep. AP (exams req'd; 263 taken, 73% 3+)—Eng Fr Span Calc Stats Comp_Sci Bio Chem Physics Eur_Hist Econ Human_Geog US_Govt & Pol. **Feat**—Chin Physiol Web_Design Film Photog Studio_Art Drama Theater_Arts Music Dance.
Sports (req'd)—Basket X-country Golf Lacrosse Soccer Tennis Ultimate_Frisbee. B: Baseball Ice_Hockey. G: F_Hockey Swim Volley. **Activities:** 25.
Very selective adm: 122/yr. Appl fee: $60. Appl due: Feb. Accepted: 24%. Yield: 84%. **Tests** IQ ISEE SSAT.
Enr 909. B 454. G 455. Elem 564. Sec 345. Avg class size: 17. Stud/fac: 9:1. **Fac 98.** Wh 92%. Latino 5%. Blk 2%. Asian 1%. Adv deg: 67%.
Grad '10—81. Col—81. (U of CO-Boulder 10, CO Col 3, Colgate 3, CO St 3, SMU 3, SMU 3). **Avg SAT:** CR 619. M 620. W 633. Avg ACT: 27.5. **Col couns:** 2.
Tui '12-'13: Day $16,655-21,850 (+$500). **Aid:** Need 164 ($2,100,000).

Summer: Acad Enrich Rec. Arts. Sports. 8 wks.
Endow $16,400,000. Plant val $40,000,000. Acres 94. Bldgs 13. Class rms 65. 2 Libs 18,000 vols. Sci labs 14. Lang labs 1. Auds 1. Theaters 1. Art studios 4. Music studios 10. Gyms 2. Athletic ctrs 1. Fields 7. Tennis courts 8. Pools 1. Weight rms 1. Comp labs 6. Comp/stud: 1:1.5.
Est 1906. Nonprofit. Tri (Aug-June).

Located on a 94-acre campus in southwest Denver, the academy maintains three divisions to meet the developmental and learning needs of its students: a lower school (grades pre-K-5), a middle school (grades 6-8) and an upper school (grades 9-12). Each division has its own curriculum, principal, faculty, classroom building, library, and science and computer laboratories. The entire school community meets for assembly on a regular basis.

The curriculum, which is integrated throughout the school and builds on each preceding grade, emphasizes group and individual study of the liberal arts. A favorable student-teacher ratio allows faculty to work with individual students. Pupils in the lower grades take physical education, while those in grades 7-12 choose from a variety of fall, winter and spring sports. Fine arts offerings in all three divisions include instrumental and choral music, drama and visual arts. Technology is a learning tool in all subject areas.

CA schedules community service days four times a year; all students take part. Boys and girls in the upper school perform 20 hours of required community service each year. A diverse student body enrolls from throughout the metropolitan and suburban areas.

GRALAND COUNTRY DAY SCHOOL
Day — Coed Gr K-8

Denver, CO 80220. 30 Birch St. Tel: 303-399-8361. Fax: 303-336-3762.
www.graland.org   E-mail: ccraig@graland.org
Veronica A. McCaffrey, Head (2009). BA, Manhattanville College, MEd, Columbia Univ.
Kristin Ryder, Adm.
Pre-Prep. Gen Acad. Elem math—Singapore Math. **Elem read**—Houghton Mifflin. **Feat**—Lib_Skills Fr Lat Span Computers Studio_Art Visual_Arts Drama Music Health. **Supp**—Dev_Read Rem_Read Rev Tut.
Sports (req'd)—Basket Lacrosse Soccer Tennis. B: Baseball Football. G: F_Hockey Volley.
Selective adm: 120/yr. Usual entry: K & 6. Appl fee: $60. Appl due: Jan. Applied: 208. Accepted: 58%. Yield: 95%. **Tests** CTP_4 ISEE.
Enr 631. B 318. G 313. Wh 80%. Latino 3%. Blk 7%. Asian 4%. Other 6%. Avg class size: 18. Stud/fac: 8:1. Casual. **Fac 70.** M 18/F 52. FT 67/PT 3. Wh 96%. Latino 3%. Asian 1%. Adv deg: 67%.
Grad '11—63. Prep—27. (Kent Denver 8, CO Acad 8, Mullen HS 5, Regis Jesuit 3, Denver Acad 1, St Mary's Acad-CO 1). Alum donors: 8%.
Tui '12-'13: Day $19,490-21,190. Aid: Need 101 ($1,300,000).
Endow $23,400,000. Plant val $12,784,000. Acres 7. Bldgs 9 (100% ADA). Class rms 65. Lib 32,000 vols. Sci labs 4. Theaters 4. Art studios 3. Music studios 3. Gyms 1. Fields 2. Field houses 1. Laptop prgm Gr 5.
Est 1924. Nonprofit. Tri (Aug-June).

Founded by a group of parents, Graland has met the community's need for an educational program that develops a child's individual abilities. The school continues to reflect the experience of Georgia Nelson, founding head, who had been at both Francis Parker School and Shady Hill School before she came to Graland. Diversity, multiculturalism, parental education and support, integrated learning and study skills development are important aspects of the program.

The school offers a broad curriculum of academic, artistic and athletic programs, with studies in lab science, computers and foreign languages. A comprehensive trip program complements the traditional curriculum. Graland distributes tablet computers to children in grade 5 for no additional cost.

KENT DENVER SCHOOL
Day — Coed Gr 6-12

Englewood, CO 80113. 4000 E Quincy Ave. Tel: 303-770-7660. Fax: 303-770-7137.
www.kentdenver.org   E-mail: kdsadmission@kentdenver.org
Todd R. W. Horn, Head (1997). BA, Dartmouth College, MBA, Univ of Colorado-Boulder, EdM, Harvard Univ, EdD, Northern Arizona Univ. **Kelly Holley, Upper Sch Adm; Miya Dickman, Middle Sch Adm.**

Col Prep. AP (exams req'd; 309 taken, 87% 3+)—Eng Fr Span Calc Stats Chem Physics Eur_Hist US_Hist Art_Hist Music_Theory. **Feat**—Shakespeare Fiction_Writing Mythology Chin Web_Design Amer_Stud Anthro World_Relig Ceramics Drawing Filmmaking Painting Sculpt Acting Theater_Arts.

Sports—Basket X-country Golf Lacrosse Soccer Tennis Track. B: Baseball Football Ice_Hockey. G: F_Hockey Volley. **Activities:** 63.

Selective adm (Gr 6-11): 131/yr. Usual entry: 6. Appl fee: $60. Appl due: Jan. **Tests** ISEE SSAT.

Enr 664. Elem 227. Sec 437. Avg class size: 15. Stud/fac: 10:1. **Fac 84.** Adv deg: 64%.

Grad '10—105. Col—105. (U of CO-Boulder 8, USC 7, U of Denver 4, Tufts 3, SMU 3, Cornell 2). **Avg SAT:** CR 616. M 636. W 643.

Tui '11-'12: Day $21,070 (+$200-500). **Aid:** Need ($1,800,000).

Summer (enr 1100): Acad Enrich Rev Rec. Arts. 1-5 wks.

Endow $37,500,000. Plant val $26,000,000. Acres 200. Bldgs 11. Class rms 46. Lib 18,000 vols. Sci labs 6. Lang labs 1. Theaters 1. Art studios 5. Music studios 1. Dance studios 1. Photog studios 1. Gyms 2. Fields 7. Tennis courts 6. Comp labs 3.

Est 1922. Nonprofit. Sem (Aug-May). **Assoc** CLS.

Kent School for girls, founded in 1922, and Denver Country Day School for boys, founded in 1953, merged in 1974 after six years as coordinate schools. The 200-acre site, which now houses both the middle school campus for grades 6-8 and the upper school (grades 9-12), was first occupied by both schools in the mid-1960s.

The rigorous liberal arts curriculum in the upper school is based on traditional preparation for college, with Advanced Placement preparation offered in most subjects. A balance of academics, competitive sports and extracurricular activities includes required community service at all grade levels. A mandatory career intern experience, conducted in the spring, enables boys and girls to explore potential career fields. The fine and performing arts department offers a particularly broad course selection. Community service is required at all levels: Boys and girls in grades 6-10 engage in group projects, while juniors and seniors compile at least 60 total hours of individual service.

Kent Denver's middle school curriculum includes special studies, trips and a participatory sports program.

GLENWOOD SPRINGS, CO. (132 mi. W of Denver, CO) Suburban. Pop: 7736. Alt: 5747 ft. Area also includes Carbondale.

COLORADO ROCKY MOUNTAIN SCHOOL
Bdg and Day — Coed Gr 9-12

Carbondale, CO 81623. 1493 County Rd 106. Tel: 970-963-2562. Fax: 970-963-9865.
www.crms.org   E-mail: admission@crms.org
Jeffrey Leahy, Head (2005). BA, Pomona College, MA, Trinity College (CT). **Molly Dorais, Adm.**

Col Prep. AP (exams req'd; 35 taken)—Eng Stats Environ_Sci US_Hist. **Feat**—British_Lit Creative_Writing Shakespeare Environ_Lit Span Calc Geol Programming African_Hist Anthro Ceramics Photog Studio_Art Glass_Blowing Silversmithing Drama Music. **Supp**—ESL Rev Tut.

Sports—Ski Soccer.
Selective adm: 69/yr. Bdg 47. Day 22. Usual entry: 9. Appl fee: $50. Appl due: Feb. Accepted: 75%. Yield: 65%. **Tests** SSAT TOEFL.
Enr 154. B 90. G 64. Bdg 92. Day 62. Wh 88%. Latino 1%. Native Am 1%. Asian 8%. Other 2%. Intl 16%. Avg class size: 13. Stud/fac: 4:1. Casual. **Fac 34.** M 19/F 15. FT 33/PT 1. Wh 98%. Latino 2%. Adv deg: 67%. In dorms 11.
Grad '10—41. Col—41. (CO Col, Bowdoin, U of CO-Boulder, U of Puget Sound, Bates, Ft Lewis). **Avg SAT:** CR 576. M 582. W 543. Avg ACT: 24. Alum donors: 27%.
Tui '11-'12: Bdg $43,500 (+$2000). **Day $27,000** (+$1500). **Intl Bdg $47,000** (+$2000). **Aid:** Merit 17 ($110,000). Need 60 ($990,000).
Endow $13,000,000. Plant val $17,000,000. Acres 350. Bldgs 23. Dorms 6. Dorm rms 72. Class rms 16. Lib 17,000 vols. Sci labs 1. Photog labs 1. Theaters 1. Art studios 5. Music studios 1. Blacksmithing studios 3. Gyms 1. Fields 2. Courts 2. Climbing walls 1. Student ctrs 1. Comp labs 3.
Est 1953. Nonprofit. Sem (Sept-June).

Inspired by the precept and example of Eastern coeducational schools and by a desire to integrate intellectual, manual, musical, athletic and artistic skills, Ann and John Holden established this school for college-bound students.

The curriculum is college preparatory, stressing the development of basic intellectual skills, including writing, logical reasoning and research, within the context of individual courses. The program emphasizes environmental studies, energy and resources, and organic gardening. Instruction in the performing and visual arts is offered in photography, ceramics, jewelry making, studio art, silversmithing, sculpture, acting and music.

A weeklong interim in March allows undergraduates and faculty to undertake group projects. These have included filmmaking, poetry writing and the study of desert ecology on a Navajo reservation, as well as a home-stay language trip to Mexico. Seniors instead engage in a three-week project in which they apprentice in a field of professional or avocational interest. At the end of the apprenticeship, each student makes a project presentation to the school community.

Located on a 350-acre ranch, CRMS requires all students to participate in ranch, household and construction projects. Utilizing the area surrounding the campus, the school emphasizes mountain and river sports, in addition to snowboarding, tennis and soccer. Alpine and Nordic skiing, both competitive and recreational, are offered as winter sports. The wilderness session, offered to all new students prior to the start of the academic year, is an intensive 10 days of conditioning, map reading, climbing, camping and team building. Outdoor education, offered throughout the school year, includes fall and spring excursions.

LAFAYETTE, CO. (20 mi. NW of Denver, CO) Suburban. Pop: 23,197. Alt: 5236 ft.

ALEXANDER DAWSON SCHOOL
Day — Coed Gr K-12

Lafayette, CO 80026. 10455 Dawson Dr. Tel: 303-665-6679. Fax: 303-665-0757.
www.dawsonschool.org   E-mail: info@dawsonschool.org
George Moore, Head (2012). Mark Saunders, Adm.
    Col Prep. AP (exams req'd; 136 taken, 80% 3+)—Eng Chin Fr Span Calc Comp_Sci Bio Chem Physics US_Hist World_Hist Comp_Govt & Pol Human_Geog. **Feat**—Poetry Shakespeare Tolkien Environ_Sci Forensic_Sci Engineering Web_Design African_Hist Japan_Hist Russ_Hist Ceramics Photog Sculpt Printmaking Drama Music Journ. **Supp**—Tut.
Sports—Basket X-country Soccer Tennis. B: Baseball Golf Lacrosse. G: Volley.
Selective adm: 94/yr. Appl fee: $100. Appl due: Rolling. Applied: 182. Accepted: 66%. Yield: 79%. **Tests** CTP_4 IQ.
Enr 460. Elem 280. Sec 180. Wh 85%. Latino 4%. Blk 2%. Asian 5%. Other 4%. Avg

class size: 15. Stud/fac: 7:1. **Fac 58.** M 24/F 34. FT 54/PT 4. Wh 94%. Latino 1%. Blk 3%. Asian 1%. Other 1%. Adv deg: 31%.
Grad '09—44. Col—44. (CO St 3, Franklin & Marshall 2, U of CO-Boulder 2, NYU 2, Stanford 1, Princeton 1). **Avg SAT:** CR 595. M 603. W 609. Avg ACT: 26.5.
Tui '12-'13: Day $20,550 (+$300-500). **Aid:** Need 74 ($950,000).
Summer: Acad Enrich Rec. Arts. Sports. 1-7 wks.
Plant val $28,000,000. Acres 113. Bldgs 14. Class rms 43. 2 Libs 20,000 vols. Sci labs 5. Lang labs 1. Auds 1. Theaters 1. Art studios 4. Music studios 3. Dance studios 1. Photog studios 1. Wood shops 1. Gyms 2. Fields 8. Tennis courts 6. Pools 1. Comp labs 6. Laptop prgm Gr 5-6.
Est 1970. Nonprofit. Sem (Aug-June).

Located on an 113-acre campus near Boulder, Alexander Dawson provides opportunities for honors and advanced study. In addition to traditional academic subjects, students choose from a wide variety of electives in art, music, drama, dance, photography and woodworking.

The school's winterim program combines experiential education with adventure and travel. Boys and girls engage in age-appropriate community service projects at all grade levels, and sophomores complete 10 hours of required service. Dawson's experiential education program culminates in a two-week internship project for all seniors.

A sister school, Alexander Dawson School at Rainbow Mountain (separately listed), operates in Las Vegas, NV.

STEAMBOAT SPRINGS, CO. (114 mi. WNW of Denver, CO) Suburban. Pop: 9815. Alt: 6728 ft.

LOWELL WHITEMAN SCHOOL
Bdg and Day — Coed Gr 9-12

Steamboat Springs, CO 80487. 42605 County Rd 36. Tel: 970-879-1350.
Fax: 970-879-0506.
www.lws.edu   E-mail: info@lws.edu
Chris Taylor, Head (2010). BA, Univ of Rochester, MALS, Wesleyan Univ, EdM, Harvard Univ. **Derek Svennungsen, Adm.**
Col Prep. Sports (Winter). AP—Eng Fr Span Calc Environ_Sci. **Feat**—Creative_Writing Anat & Physiol Comp_Sci Film Studio_Art Drama. **Supp**—Tut.
Sports—Ski.
Selective adm: 26/yr. Bdg 16. Day 10. Usual entry: 9. Appl fee: $50. Appl due: Feb. Accepted: 72%. Yield: 82%. **Tests** CEEB Stanford.
Enr 85. B 45. G 40. Bdg 40. Day 45. Wh 98%. Blk 2%. Intl 6%. Avg class size: 8. Stud/fac: 6:1. **Fac 17.** M 8/F 9. FT 16/PT 1. Wh 100%. Adv deg: 58%. In dorms 6.
Grad '09—32. Col—29. (U of Denver 4, CO St 4, U of CO-Boulder 3, Middlebury 1, US Air Force Acad 1, Colby 1). **Avg SAT:** CR/M 1070.
Tui '11-'12: Bdg $34,900 (+$3000-4000). **Day $18,700** (+$3000-4000). **Aid:** Merit 3 ($6500). Need 27 ($291,650).
Endow $1,000,000. Plant val $10,000,000. Acres 192. Bldgs 14. Dorms 3. Dorm rms 40. Class rms 14. Lib 4500 vols. Sci labs 2. Auds 1. Theaters 1. Art studios 1. Gyms 1. Fields 2. Riding rings 1. Stables 1. Comp labs 2.
Est 1957. Nonprofit. Tri (Aug-June).

Founded by Lowell Whiteman, the school offers traditional academics and features small classes, required proctored evening study halls and a heavy emphasis on academic effort. Graduates typically matriculate at four-year colleges.

Located near a mountain resort community, the school utilizes its environment for academic and recreational purposes. In addition to a full range of college preparatory courses, further opportunities include skiing, snowboarding, ecological studies, mountaineering, horseback riding, white-water rafting and backpacking. Annual foreign travel is required of all students—except for high-ability competitive skiers and snowboarders.

LWS provides a well-balanced academic/athletic program for high school snowboarders and Alpine, Nordic and freestyle ski competitors. A number of school graduates have participated in the Winter Olympics.

VAIL, CO. (80 mi. W of Denver, CO) Suburban. Pop: 4531. Alt: 8160.

VAIL MOUNTAIN SCHOOL
Day — Coed Gr K-12

Vail, CO 81657. 3000 Booth Falls Rd. Tel: 970-476-3850. Fax: 970-476-3860.
www.vms.edu   E-mail: info@vms.edu
Peter M. Abuisi, Head (1977). Jeremy Thelen, Adm.

   Col Prep. AP (exams req'd; 76 taken, 83% 3+)—Eng Span Calc Bio Physics US_Hist Studio_Art. **Feat**—Middle_Eastern_Hist Ethics Photog Multimedia_Design. **Supp**—LD Rev Tut.
   Sports (req'd)—Ski Soccer. B: Basket. G: Tennis Volley.
   Selective adm (Gr K-11): 54/yr. Appl fee: $50-100. Appl due: Jan. Applied: 125. Accepted: 55%. Yield: 89%.
   Enr 350. B 164. G 186. Elem 240. Sec 110. Wh 88%. Latino 5%. Blk 1%. Asian 2%. Other 4%. Avg class size: 16. Stud/fac: 8:1. **Fac 38.** M 14/F 24. FT 38. Wh 95%. Latino 5%. Adv deg: 71%.
   Grad '10—22. Col—22. (U of CO-Boulder 2). **Avg SAT:** CR 582. M 589. W 595. Avg ACT: 27.5. Alum donors: 7%.
   Tui '12-'13: Day $18,610-19,990 (+$400). **Aid:** Need 100 ($1,194,345).
   Summer (enr 75): Acad Enrich Rev Rem Rec. Sports. 10 wks.
   Endow $17,711,000. Plant val $32,000,000. Acres 9. Bldgs 2 (100% ADA). Class rms 26. Lib 16,000 vols. Sci labs 5. Dark rms 1. Auds 1. Theaters 1. Art studios 2. Music studios 3. Dance studios 1. Gyms 1. Fields 1. Comp labs 3. Comp/stud: 1:1.5 (1:1 Laptop prgm Gr 10-12).
   Est 1962. Nonprofit. Tri (Aug-May).

Founded to meet the needs of early settlers of an emerging resort community, VMS changed location and mission several times in its early years. Significant alterations in the program commenced in 1978, when administrators decided to shift the academic focus to college preparation and discontinue the host family program that had been in place. The program gradually expanded to include middle school children and then younger students, with the first kindergarten class enrolled in 1984.

The school offers a broad college preparatory program with an emphasis on the liberal arts, often utilizing individualized instruction. Community service plays an important role in school life, with VMS offering a variety of age-appropriate options for its pupils. As part of the school's tripping program, older boys and girls go on excursions to locations such as Costa Rica and New York City. In addition, all students in grades 5-12 participate in backcountry hut trips in which telemark skiing is the encouraged mode of travel. The athletic program combines traditional offerings with competitive and recreational opportunities in such areas as Alpine and Nordic skiing that make use of the school's mountain setting.

IDAHO

SUN VALLEY, ID. (94 mi. E of Boise, ID) Rural. Pop: 1427. Alt: 5920 ft.

THE COMMUNITY SCHOOL
Day — Boys Gr PS (Age 2)-PS (Age 4), Girls PS (Age 2)-12

Sun Valley, ID 83353. 1 Community School Dr, PO Box 2118. Tel: 208-622-3955.
Fax: 208-622-3962.
www.communityschool.org   E-mail: info@communityschool.org
David R. Holmes, Head (2011). BA, Middlebury College, MA, Columbia Univ, PhD, Univ of Denver. **Katie Robins, Adm.**
Col Prep. AP exams taken: 26. Feat—Fr Span Arabic Calc Stats Astrophysics Comp_ Sci Pol_Sci Psych Outdoor_Ed Wilderness_Ed. **Supp**—Dev_Read LD Tut. Outdoor ed.
Sports (req'd)—Basket X-country Golf Soccer Tennis. G: Volley.
Selective adm: 64/yr. Appl fee: $40. Appl due: Feb. **Tests** SSAT.
Enr 307. B 153. G 154. Elem 198. Sec 109. Wh 92%. Latino 1%. Other 7%. Avg class size: 15. **Fac 43.** M 19/F 24. FT 36/PT 7. Wh 100%. Adv deg: 58%.
Grad '08—32. Col—32. (U of CO-Boulder, Ft Lewis, U of Denver, U of OR, Whitman, CO Col). **Avg SAT:** CR 601. M 569. W 614. Avg ACT: 26.7. **Col couns:** 1. Alum donors: 6%.
Tui '11-'12: Day $9900-23,660 (+$150-1700). **Aid:** Need 64 ($860,000).
Summer: Acad. 3-6 wks.
Endow $4,000,000. Plant val $4,000,000. Acres 38. Bldgs 6. Class rms 35. Lib 32,000 vols. Sci labs 1. Lang labs 1. Dark rms 1. Auds 1. Theaters 1. Art studios 2. Music studios 2. Gyms 1. Fields 3. Comp labs 2.
Est 1973. Nonprofit. (Aug-June).

Located between Ketchum and Sun Valley, the school lies in the Wood River Valley on Trail Creek. The core curriculum emphasizes mastery of fundamental academic skills, while enriching pupils' class schedules with electives designed to capitalize on individual interests. The school features multiple-subject primary enrichment, a college preparatory curriculum for students in grades 6-12, and an integrated outdoor education program. Seniors participate in a six-week, off-campus independent project.

Southwest States

ARIZONA

MAYER, AZ. (60 mi. N of Phoenix, AZ) Rural. Pop: 1408. Alt: 3800 ft.

ORME SCHOOL
Bdg — Coed Gr 8-12; Day — Coed 6-12

Mayer, AZ 86333. 1000 Orme School Rd, HC 63, Box 3040. Tel: 928-632-7601.
Fax: 928-632-7605.
www.ormeschool.org   E-mail: info@ormeschool.org
Keith E. Cassell, Pres (2010). BA, Hobart College, MEd, Lesley College, MBA, Regis
Univ. **Alyce M. Brownridge, Head.** BA, Univ of California-Santa Barbara, MS, Univ of
Arizona. **Michael L. McKee, Adm.**
  Col Prep. AP (55 exams taken)—Eng Span Calc Physics Eur_Hist US_Hist. Feat—Fr
    Lat Stats Anat & Physiol Astron Environ_Sci Equine_Sci Web_Design Govt Ceramics
    Drawing Photog Studio_Art Theater_Arts Band Chorus Piano. **Supp**—ESL Tut.
  Sports—Basket X-country Tennis Track. B: Baseball Football. G: Volley.
  Selective adm: 95/yr. Appl fee: $50. Appl due: Feb. Accepted: 54%. **Tests** SSAT
    TOEFL.
  Enr 124. Intl 24%. Avg class size: 10. Stud/fac: 6:1. **Fac 24.** M 13/F 11. FT 22/PT 2. Adv
    deg: 62%.
  Grad '10—31. Col—30. (AZ St, Boston U, Dartmouth, MI St, N AZ, Skidmore). **Mid 50%
    SAT:** CR 440-560. M 480-650. Avg ACT: 21. **Col couns: 1.**
  Tui '12-'13: Bdg $40,200 (+$1850). **Day $20,500** (+$1850). **Intl Bdg $41,500** (+$1850-
    6300). **Aid:** Need 31 ($1,000,000).
  Summer: Horsemanship. 2-3 wks.
  Endow $7,000,000. Plant val $10,000,000. Acres 320. Dorm rms 122. Class rms 21. Lib
    23,000 vols. Labs 4. Art studios 3. Fields 4. Courts 5. Pools 1. Riding facilities.
  Est 1929. Nonprofit. Quar (Aug-June). **Assoc** CLS NCA.

  Mr. and Mrs. Charles H. Orme founded this school for local ranch children. Beginning as a
one-room school, Orme has grown into a modern college preparatory institution on a 320-acre
campus in the middle of a 26,000-acre ranch. The high school curriculum includes honors and
Advanced Placement courses in the major disciplines. Complementing the academic program
are interscholastic athletics, horsemanship (both English and Western) and outdoor leadership
opportunities. The arts program is supported by a weeklong midwinter festival, at which time
students and faculty are joined by professional artists from all over the country. The visiting
artists teach such media as ceramics, photography, dance, music, sculpture and filmmaking.
  The course of studies prepares students for competitive colleges throughout the country. The
Southwestern environment of the school is stressed through special courses, field trips, varied
outdoor activities and an annual caravan. Orme's middle school (grades 6-8) allows students
with academic and emotional maturity to enroll in high school-level courses for credit.

PHOENIX, AZ. Urban. Pop: 1,321,045. Alt: 1082 ft. Area also includes Paradise Valley.

ALL SAINTS' EPISCOPAL DAY SCHOOL
Day — Coed Gr PS (Age 4)-8

Phoenix, AZ 85012. 6300 N Central Ave. Tel: 602-274-4866. Fax: 602-274-0365.
   www.aseds.org   E-mail: dwaage@allsaints.org
Leo P. Dressel, Head (2009). AB, MA, St Louis Univ, MDiv, Santa Clara Univ. **Dan Waage, Adm.**
   Pre-Prep. Feat—Lib_Skills Span Computers Relig Studio_Art Drama Music.
   Sports—Basket. B: Baseball. G: Softball Volley.
   Selective adm: 93/yr. Appl fee: $100. Appl due: Jan. Accepted: 78%. Yield: 75%. **Tests** CTP_4.
   Enr 519. B 243. G 276. Wh 75%. Latino 3%. Blk 3%. Asian 5%. Other 14%. Avg class size: 16. Stud/fac: 9:1. Uniform. **Fac 56.** M 7/F 49. FT 53/PT 3. Wh 96%. Blk 2%. Asian 2%. Adv deg: 55%.
   Grad '11—63. Prep—61. (Xavier-AZ 21, Brophy 19, Phoenix Co Day 4, Notre Dame Prep-AZ 2, Deerfield Acad 1, Lawrenceville 1).
   Tui '12-'13: Day $13,350-15,975 (+$200). **Aid:** Need 60 ($700,000).
   Summer: Acad Enrich Rev. 1-4 wks.
   Endow $514,000. Plant val $10,000,000. Acres 11. Bldgs 12. Class rms 40. Lib 12,143 vols. Sci labs 4. Amphitheaters 1. Auds 1. Art studios 2. Music studios 2. Gyms 1. Fields 1. Courts 2. Playgrounds 2. Comp labs 2. Comp/stud: 1:4.
   Est 1963. Nonprofit. Episcopal (20% practice). Sem (Sept-May).

All Saints' offers a comprehensive liberal arts program in a Christian setting. In grades K-4, classes are self-contained, with each grade-level teacher providing instruction in the fundamental subject areas. Beginning in grade 5, classes are departmentalized. Communication and critical-thinking skills development are points of emphasis. Courses in computers, Spanish, religion, art, music and physical education are taught at all grade levels, and pupils in grades 5-8 go on interdisciplinary field trips. The school holds chapel services twice per week.

BROPHY COLLEGE PREPARATORY SCHOOL
Day — Boys Gr 9-12

Phoenix, AZ 85012. 4701 N Central Ave. Tel: 602-264-5291. Fax: 602-234-1669.
   www.brophyprep.org   E-mail: admissions@brophyprep.org
Rev. Edward A. Reese, SJ, Pres. MA, STM, MDiv. **Robert E. Ryan, Prin.** BS, Univ of Notre Dame, MEd, Arizona State Univ. **Michael T. Ward, Adm.**
   Col Prep. AP (exams req'd; 744 taken, 62% 3+)—Eng Fr Lat Span Calc Comp_Sci Chem Environ_Sci Physics Eur_Hist US_Hist Comp_Govt & Pol Econ Psych US_Govt & Pol Art_Hist Studio_Art Music_Theory. **Feat**—Creative_Writing Humanities Shakespeare Modern_Fiction Sports_Med Relig Photog Theater_Arts. **Supp**—Tut. **Dual enr:** Rio Salado CC.
   Sports—B: Baseball Basket X-country Football Golf Ice_Hockey Lacrosse Soccer Swim Tennis Track Volley Wrestling. **Activities:** 66.
   Selective adm (Gr 9-11): 342/yr. Appl fee: $75. Appl due: Jan. Accepted: 58%. Yield: 92%. **Tests** CEEB.
   Enr 1270. Wh 76%. Latino 12%. Blk 2%. Native Am 2%. Asian 4%. Other 4%. Avg class size: 26. **Fac 91.** M 72/F 19. FT 86/PT 5. Wh 90%. Latino 6%. Blk 4%. Adv deg: 62%.
   Grad '10—301. Col—301. (AZ St 64, U of AZ 56, N AZ 18, Loyola Marymount 10, Fordham 10, Gonzaga 9). **Avg SAT:** CR 593. M 598. W 579. Avg ACT: 25.8. **Col couns:** 3. Alum donors: 6%.
   Tui '12-'13: Day $13,200 (+$50-3000). **Aid:** Need 217 ($1,953,565).

Summer: Acad Enrich. 4 wks.
Endow $19,054,000. Plant val $50,900,000. Acres 38. Bldgs 8. Class rms 48. Lib 17,000 vols. Sci labs 4. Auds 1. Theaters 1. Art studios 3. Music studios 2. Gyms 1. Fields 4. Pools 2. Comp labs 1. Laptop prgm Gr 9-12.
Est 1928. Nonprofit. Roman Catholic. Sem (Aug-May).

This Jesuit college preparatory high school was founded by Mrs. William Henry Brophy in memory of her late husband. While open only to male applicants, Brophy shares most activities and some courses with Xavier College Preparatory, a girls' school located on adjoining property.

Students follow an extensive college preparatory course of studies, including a number of Advanced Placement courses. Boys and girls fulfill course requirements in English, math, science, social studies, religious studies, fine arts, speech, computer science and health/physical education. In addition, Brophy requires community service of its students: 10 hours during freshman year, 40 hours sophomore year and 50 hours junior year.

PHOENIX COUNTRY DAY SCHOOL
Day — Coed Gr PS (Age 4)-12

Paradise Valley, AZ 85253. 3901 E Stanford Dr. Tel: 602-955-8200. Fax: 602-955-1286.
www.pcds.org   E-mail: kelsey.neal@pcds.org
Andrew M. Rodin, Head (2011). BA, Columbia Univ, MA, Stanford Univ. **Kelsey Neal, Adm.**
Col Prep. AP (exams req'd; 240 taken, 93% 3+)—Eng Chin Fr Lat Span Calc Stats Bio Chem Environ_Sci Physics US_Hist Art_Hist. **Feat**—Shakespeare African-Amer_Lit Sci_Fiction Astron Holocaust Econ Intl_Relations Psych World_Relig Photog Studio_ Art Drama Music Orchestra.
Sports—Basket Golf Lacrosse Soccer Swim Tennis. B: Baseball. G: Cheer Softball Volley.
Selective adm: 152/yr. Usual entry: PS, 5 & 9. Appl fee: $100. Appl due: Mar. Applied: 320. Accepted: 47%. Yield: 79%. **Tests** CTP_4.
Enr 722. B 329. G 393. Wh 66%. Latino 6%. Blk 3%. Asian 11%. Other 14%. Avg class size: 16. Stud/fac: 9:1. **Fac 90.** FT 89/PT 1. Wh 92%. Latino 4%. Blk 1%. Native Am 1%. Asian 2%. Adv deg: 65%.
Grad '11—57. Col—57. (AZ St 11, Duke 2, Yale 2, Tulane 2, Pomona 2, TX Christian 2). **Avg SAT:** CR 674. M 677. W 683. Avg ACT: 29. Alum donors: 10%.
Tui '12-'13: Day $18,500-23,000. Aid: Need 149 ($2,002,875).
Summer: Acad Enrich Rec. Sports. Tui Day $500/2-wk ses. 6 wks.
Endow $16,000,000. Plant val $5,000,000. Acres 40. Bldgs 19. Class rms 75. 3 Libs 28,000 vols. Sci labs 9. Art studios 7. Music studios 4. Arts ctrs 1. Fields 4. Courts 8. Pools 2. Comp labs 3. Comp/stud: 1:2.
Est 1961. Nonprofit. Sem (Aug-June). **Assoc** CLS NCA.

Situated on a 40-acre campus, the school was founded to meet the needs of a rapidly growing city. PCDS consists of three distinct school divisions, each designed to address the developmental needs of the age group involved. Conversational Spanish instruction begins in preschool, and laboratory science and computer studies both commence in kindergarten.

Music, art and drama play an important role in school life, and various other activities are available.

RIMROCK, AZ. (79 mi. NNE of Phoenix, AZ) Rural. Pop: 3203. Alt: 5400 ft.

SOUTHWESTERN ACADEMY
Bdg and Day — Coed Gr 9-PG

Rimrock, AZ 86335. HC 64, Box 235. Tel: 928-567-4581. Fax: 928-567-5036.
www.southwesternacademy.edu
E-mail: admissions@southwesternacademy.edu
Jack Leyden, Head (2009). BA, Hartwick College. Jason Blake, Adm.

Col Prep. Gen Acad. AP (exams req'd; 7 taken, 43% 3+)—Eng Calc Physics US_Hist.
Feat—British_Lit Creative_Writing Humanities Span Environ_Sci Comp_Sci Econ
Govt Art_Hist Studio_Art Drama Music Outdoor_Ed. Supp—Dev_Read ESL Rem_
Math Rem_Read Rev Tut. Outdoor ed. Sat classes.
Sports—Basket X-country Golf Soccer Volley.
Selective adm (Gr 9-12): 12/yr. Bdg 12. Day 0. Appl fee: $100. Appl due: Rolling. Applied:
26. Accepted: 60%. Yield: 90%. Tests ISEE SSAT.
Enr 40. B 21. G 19. Bdg 39. Day 1. Sec 38. PG 2. Wh 40%. Latino 6%. Blk 10%. Asian
40%. Other 4%. Intl 60%. Avg class size: 7. Stud/fac: 5:1. Casual. Fac 9. M 4/F 5. FT
8/PT 1. Wh 80%. Blk 10%. Asian 10%. Adv deg: 33%. In dorms 8.
Grad '10—12. Col—12. (U of CA-Santa Barbara 2, U of CA-San Diego 2, Syracuse 2,
U of AZ 2, U of N AZ 2). Alum donors: 31%.
Tui '11-'12: Bdg $30,700 (+$2500). Day $14,900 (+$1000). Intl Bdg $36,750 (+$2500).
Aid: Merit 13.
Summer (enr 35): Acad Enrich Rev Rec. Travel. Outdoor Ed. Tui Bdg $5500-13,920. Tui
Day $660/wk. 4-12 wks.
Endow $11,550,000. Plant val $23,400,000. Acres 180. Bldgs 19 (10% ADA). Dorms 5.
Dorm rms 20. Class rms 6. Libs 1. Sci labs 1. Auds 1. Art studios 1. Gyms 1. Fields 1.
Courts 2. Pools 1. Comp labs 1. Comp/stud: 1:1
Est 1963. Nonprofit. Sem (Sept-June).

Established as a complement to the original Southwestern campus in San Marino, CA (see separate listing), the 180-acre Beaver Creek Ranch Campus follows an experiential approach to learning. The school admits students who require additional attention to realize their potential; it is not staffed to serve boys and girls with learning disabilities, behavioral problems, chemical dependencies or defiant attitudes. Small classes increase contact between teacher and pupil while also allowing students to pursue interests beyond the curriculum.

Delivered seminar style, the integrated course of studies comprises science, math, writing and critical-thinking components. The desert wilderness is integral to the teaching process: Hands-on, experiential and project/assignment-based field trips enrich classroom study and help boys and girls apply what they have learned. Outdoor education promotes environmental responsibility.

Students have the option of dividing time between the two Southwestern campuses.

See Also Pages 104-5

SEDONA, AZ. (92 mi. N of Phoenix, AZ) Suburban. Pop: 10,192. Alt: 4000 ft.

VERDE VALLEY SCHOOL
Bdg and Day — Coed Gr 9-12

Sedona, AZ 86351. 3511 Verde Valley School Rd. Tel: 928-284-2272.
Fax: 928-284-0432.
www.vvsaz.org   E-mail: admission@verdevalleyschool.org
Graham D. Frey, Head (2011). Jenifer Gill, Adm.

Col Prep. IB Diploma. Feat—Shakespeare Middle_Eastern_Lit Chin Fr Ger Span Anthro Ceramics Photog Visual_Arts Theater_Arts Music. **Supp**—ESL Tut.

Sports—Basket Golf Soccer.

Selective adm: 53/yr. Bdg 45. Day 8. Appl fee: $50. Appl due: Feb. Applied: 125. Accepted: 60%. **Tests** CEEB IQ SSAT TOEFL.

Enr 102. Bdg 85. Day 17. Intl 50%. Avg class size: 11. Stud/fac: 6:1. Casual. **Fac 22.** M 14/F 8. FT 15/PT 7. Adv deg: 59%. In dorms 8.

Grad '10—25. Col—23. (U of AZ 2, U of Redlands 2, Colgate 1, U of San Diego 1, Drexel 1, St John's U-MN 1). **Mid 50% SAT:** CR 480-580. M 500-620. W 490-590. Mid 50% ACT: 21-24.

Tui '10-'11: Bdg $43,000 (+$1000-1250). **Day $23,750** (+$400-1200). **Intl Bdg $44,000** (+$1000-4000). **Aid:** Need 61 ($925,800).

Summer (enr 60): ESL. Tui Bdg $4500. 5 wks.

Endow $1,800,000. Plant val $7,000,000. Acres 150. Bldgs 48. Dorms 6. Dorm rms 102. Class rms 14. Lib 34,000 vols. Sci labs 2. Photog labs 1. Amphitheaters 1. Auds 1. Theaters 1. Art studios 2. Music studios 1. Dance studios 1. Fields 3. Courts 2. Pools 1. Riding rings 1. Stables 1. Climbing walls 3. Ropes crses 1. Comp labs 1. Comp/stud: 1:6.

Est 1948. Nonprofit. Sem (Sept-May). **Assoc** NCA.

Founded and developed by Hamilton and Barbara Warren with the counsel of leading educators and anthropologists here and abroad, VVS opened with 16 students and a small teaching staff. With the assistance of such advisors as noted anthropologist Margaret Mead and John Collier, commissioner of Indian affairs under Franklin Roosevelt, the Warrens sought to promote intercultural and interracial understanding through an experiential program.

Still international in scope, the college preparatory program progresses from pre-IB course work in grades 9 and 10 to the two-year International Baccalaureate program in grades 11 and 12. VVS' field trip program is integral to the curriculum. It enables students to live, work and interact with people of other cultures, while also taking advantage of opportunities for community service work. The student body features a significant percentage of pupils from other countries, which further adds to the school's international character.

During the two years of the IB Diploma Program, students select six courses from the six IB subject groups; three are studied at higher levels (courses representing 240 teaching hours) and three at standard levels (150 teaching hours). Small class sizes allow faculty to provide individualized instruction for boys and girls at all grade levels.

VVS' outdoor program comprises Western horseback riding, rock climbing, mountain biking, martial arts and archery. Competitive athletic options in several sports are available through the athletic department.

TUCSON, AZ. (115 mi. SE of Phoenix, AZ) Urban. Pop: 486,699. Alt: 2376 ft. Area also includes Oro Valley.

FENSTER SCHOOL

Bdg and Day — Coed Gr 6-PG

Tucson, AZ 85750. 8505 E Ocotillo Dr. Tel: 520-749-3340. Fax: 520-749-3349.
www.fensterschool.org   E-mail: admissions@fensterschool.org
Tony Tsang, Admin (2011). ME, Univ of Arizona. **Margaret L. Andrews, Adm.**

Col Prep. Feat—Writing Span Calc Stats Anat & Physiol Comp_Sci Web_Design Econ Pol_Sci Studio_Art Study_Skills. **Supp**—ESL LD Rem_Read Rev Tut. Outdoor ed. **Dual enr:** Pima CC.

Sports—Basket Soccer. G: Volley. **Activities:** 8.

Selective adm: 19/yr. Bdg 18. Day 1. Appl fee: $50. Appl due: Rolling. **Tests** CEEB CTP_4 IQ ISEE MAT SSAT Stanford TOEFL.

Enr 23. B 14. G 9. Bdg 22. Day 1. Wh 48%. Latino 26%. Blk 9%. Native Am 4%. Asian

13%. Intl 25%. Avg class size: 5. Stud/fac: 3:1. Casual. **Fac 12.** M 8/F 4. FT 2/PT 10. Wh 83%. Latino 17%. Adv deg: 58%.
Grad '10—17. Col—17. (U of AZ 3, N AZ 1, Pacific U 1, Portland St 1, U of OR 1, W WA 1). **Avg SAT:** CR 516. M 496. W 469. Avg ACT: 19.5.
Tui '12-'13: Bdg $37,800 (+$2000-4000). **Day $22,680** (+$1000-2000).
Summer (enr 50): Acad Enrich Rev Rem. Tui Bdg $5000. Tui Day $1500/crse. 6 wks.
Plant val $3,000,000. Acres 150. Bldgs 24. Dorms 8. Class rms 22. Lib 5000 vols. Sci labs 2. Art studios 1. Fields 1. Courts 2. Pools 1. Riding rings 2. Stables 1. Comp labs 1. Comp/stud: 1:2.
Est 1944. Nonprofit. Sem (Aug-May). **Assoc** NCA.

The first coeducational boarding school in southern Arizona, Fenster is located in the foothills of the Santa Catalina Mountains on a 150-acre site that is surrounded by the Sonoran Desert. The school offers a structured college preparatory curriculum for students of average and above-average intelligence who stand to benefit from a personalized setting. Small classes allow for individualized instruction, thereby accommodating a range of learning styles. Dual-enrollment college courses at Pima Community College enable boys and girls to earn college credits.

Noteworthy aspects of Fenster's extracurricular program include a strong equestrian program; hiking and rock climbing; and excursions to nearby cultural events, ski areas, malls and theaters.

GREEN FIELDS COUNTRY DAY SCHOOL

Day — Coed Gr K-12

Tucson, AZ 85741. 6000 N Camino de la Tierra. Tel: 520-297-2288. Fax: 520-297-2072. www.greenfields.org　E-mail: info@greenfields.org
Diana Hill, Co-Head (2012). BS, Univ of Vermont. **Rebecca Cordier, Co-Head.** BMus, Univ of Arizona, MEd, Grand Canyon Univ.
Col Prep. AP (exams req'd; 30 taken, 53% 3+)—Eng Fr Span Calc Bio Environ_Sci Physics US_Hist US_Govt & Pol Studio_Art Music_Theory. **Elem math**—Everyday Math. **Feat**—British_Lit Creative_Writing Lat Stats Anat & Physiol Astron Marine_ Bio/Sci Web_Design Acting Drama Music Journ. **Supp**—Tut.
Sports—Basket Soccer. B: Baseball. G: Softball Volley.
Selective adm: 59/yr. Usual entry: K, 6 & 9. Appl fee: $50. Appl due: Rolling. **Tests** CEEB CTP_4 IQ ISEE SSAT Stanford.
Enr 181. B 92. G 89. Wh 74%. Latino 8%. Blk 2%. Asian 1%. Other 15%. Avg class size: 12. Stud/fac: 8:1. **Fac 28.** M 12/F 16. FT 19/PT 9. Wh 78%. Latino 18%. Asian 4%. Adv deg: 64%.
Grad '11—12. Col—12. (U of AZ 3, N AZ 2, Scripps 1, U of CA-San Diego 1, Trinity U 1, U of San Diego 1). **Avg SAT:** CR 585. M 573. W 572. Avg ACT: 25. **Col couns:** 1. Alum donors: 5%.
Tui '11-'12: Day $9500-14,200 (+$500). **Aid:** Merit 7 ($75,633). Need 76 ($548,232).
Endow $960,000. Plant val $1,840,000. Acres 22. Bldgs 22. Class rms 23. Lib 7500 vols. Sci labs 2. Theaters 1. Art studios 1. Music studios 1. Gyms 1. Fields 4. Courts 4. Pools 1. Comp labs 3.
Est 1933. Nonprofit. Sem (Aug-May). **Assoc** NCA.

Established by Mr. and Mrs. George Howard Atchley as a ranch-style boarding school for boys, the school closed its boarding department in 1960 and became coeducational in 1966. The upper school curriculum includes Advanced Placement classes, along with varied academic and fine arts electives. Juniors and seniors may, with permission, enroll in courses at the University of Arizona. A weeklong spring interim period includes on-campus projects, groups that divide time between campus and local sites, and longer trips to destinations in the Southwest and abroad.

An all-day, schoolwide forum on a controversial topic is orchestrated entirely by members of the junior class, and the senior class plans and hosts an orientation at the start of each school year.

IMMACULATE HEART HIGH SCHOOL
Day — Coed Gr 9-12

Oro Valley, AZ 85704. 625 E Magee Rd. Tel: 520-297-2851. Fax: 520-797-7374.
www.immaculateheartschool.com   E-mail: nowanawood@ihhschool.org
Sr. Luisa Sanchez, IHM, Pres. Daniel V. Ethridge, Prin.
   Col Prep. AP exams taken: 6 (100% 3+). Feat—Span Comp_Sci Relig Fine_Arts
   Journ. **Supp**—ESL Tut. **Dual enr:** Pima CC.
   Sports—Basket Soccer Tennis. G: Cheer Golf Volley. **Activities:** 5.
   Somewhat selective adm: 13/yr. Appl fee: $45. Appl due: May. Accepted: 99%. Yield:
   99%. **Tests** HSPT Stanford.
   Enr 71. B 28. G 43. Wh 53%. Latino 43%. Blk 1%. Asian 3%. Intl 5%. Avg class size: 10.
   Uniform. **Fac 12.** M 3/F 9. FT 8/PT 4. Wh 90%. Latino 10%. Adv deg: 33%.
   Grad '08—8. Col—7. (U of AZ, Pima CC, AZ St, N AZ). **Avg SAT:** CR/M 1002. Avg
   ACT: 25.
   Tui '11-'12: Day $6400 (+$600-750).
   Plant val $5,000,000. Bldgs 2. Class rms 18. Lib 6500 vols. Sci labs 2. Lang labs 1. Art
   studios 1. Music studios 1. Fields 2. Courts 1. Pools 1. Comp labs 1. Comp/stud: 1:2.
   Est 1931. Nonprofit. Roman Catholic (90% practice). Quar (Aug-May). **Assoc** NCA.

Conducted by the Sisters of the Immaculate Heart of Mary, the school offers a secondary
program in the northwest part of the city. Besides offerings in language arts, math, science and
social studies, the curriculum includes courses in foreign languages, the fine arts, computers
and religion. Students also choose from a variety of online courses offered through Virtual
High School, including Advanced Placement options.

NEW MEXICO

ALBUQUERQUE, NM. (54 mi. SW of Santa Fe, NM) Urban. Pop: 448,607. Alt: 4930 ft.

ALBUQUERQUE ACADEMY
Day — Coed Gr 6-12

Albuquerque, NM 87109. 6400 Wyoming Blvd NE. Tel: 505-828-3208.
  Fax: 505-828-3128.
  www.aa.edu   E-mail: admission@aa.edu
Andrew T. Watson, Head (2000). BS, Ohio State Univ, MS, Yale Univ. **Judy D. Hudenko, Adm.**
  Col Prep. AP (491 exams taken, 92% 3+)—Chin Fr Ger Span Calc Comp_Sci Bio Chem Environ_Sci Physics Eur_Hist US_Hist World_Hist Comp_Govt & Pol Econ US_Govt & Pol Art_Hist Studio_Art. **Feat**—Creative_Writing Humanities Playwriting Japan Russ Arabic Hindi Stats Anat & Physiol Astron Ecol Forensic_Sci Genetics Geol Robotics Native_Amer_Hist Anthro Intl_Relations Ethics Philos World_Relig Fine_Arts Photog Theater_Arts Music_Theory Public_Speak. **Supp**—LD Rem_Read Rev Tut. Outdoor ed. **Dual enr:** U of NM, Central NM CC.
  Sports—Basket X-country Golf Soccer Swim Tennis Track. B: Baseball Football Wrestling. G: Softball Volley. **Activities:** 70.
  Selective adm: 201/yr. Usual entry: 6 & 9. Appl fee: $50. Appl due: Feb. Accepted: 40%. Yield: 80%. **Tests** ISEE SSAT.
  Enr 1122. B 539. G 583. Elem 459. Sec 663. Wh 51%. Latino 26%. Blk 3%. Native Am 3%. Asian 14%. Other 3%. Avg class size: 16. Stud/fac: 9:1. **Fac 152.** M 77/F 75. FT 127/PT 25. Wh 80%. Latino 13%. Blk 1%. Native Am 1%. Asian 5%. Adv deg: 76%.
  Grad '09—164. Col—164. (U of NM 30, U of TX-Austin 9, CO St 4, Notre Dame 4, Trinity U 4, Stanford 3). **Mid 50% SAT:** CR 600-720. M 620-710. W 600-700. Mid 50% ACT: 26-32. **Col couns:** 3. Alum donors: 12%.
  Tui '11-'12: Day $19,335 (+$250-500). **Aid:** Need 340 ($4,700,000).
  Summer (enr 2400): Enrich Rec. 6 wks.
  Endow $181,000,000. Plant val $164,000,000. Acres 312. Bldgs 16. Lib 96,492 vols. Sci labs 10. Lang labs 1. Dark rms 2. Amphitheaters 1. Comp ctrs 1. Auds 1. Theaters 1. Art studios 4. Music studios 4. Dance studios 1. Art galleries 1. Music ctrs 1. Gyms 2. Fields 5. Basketball courts 3. Tennis courts 10. Pools 2. Aquatic ctrs 1. Comp labs 4.
  Est 1955. Nonprofit. Sem (Aug-May). **Assoc** CLS.

The school offers a traditional college preparatory curriculum. In 1966, AA moved to a 312-acre campus, allowing for considerable expansion in plant and enrollment. The academy includes in its curriculum for grades 6-10 an outdoor experiential education requirement. Students backpack, kayak and climb into wilderness areas of the Southwest to learn through direct experience about the natural world. In addition, juniors and seniors may take an elective course in outdoor leadership.

Students satisfy the following community service requirements: two hours per semester in grades 8 and 9, six hours per year in grades 10-12. Opportunities for both domestic and international exchanges are available to sophomores and juniors. Seniors may participate in the five-week Senior Project Program, which takes the form of a off-campus internship with a professional, an on-campus seminar or a self-directed project.

MANZANO DAY SCHOOL
Day — Coed Gr PS (Age 4)-5

Albuquerque, NM 87104. 1801 Central Ave NW. Tel: 505-243-6659. Fax: 505-243-4711.
www.manzanodayschool.org   E-mail: mprokopiak@manzanodayschool.org
Neal Piltch, Head (2001). BA, Hobart College. **Madonna Prokopiak, Adm.**
  Pre-Prep. Feat—Span Computers Logic Studio_Art Music. **Supp**—Dev_Read Tut.
  Somewhat selective adm: 104/yr. Appl fee: $75. Appl due: Rolling. Accepted: 95%.
  Enr 468. Wh 60%. Latino 16%. Blk 1%. Native Am 3%. Asian 4%. Other 16%. Avg class
    size: 18. **Fac 49.** M 5/F 44. FT 47/PT 2. Adv deg: 32%.
  Grad '11—71. Prep—66. (Albuquerque Acad 27, Bosque 17, Sandia Prep 12, Menaul
    4).
  Tui '11-'12: Day $10,155-12,970. Aid: Merit 5 ($27,405).
  Summer: Ages 4-8. Rec. Tui Day $920. 6 wks.
  Endow $1,300,000. Plant val $6,000,000. Bldgs 4. Class rms 34. Libs 1. Comp labs 2.
  Est 1938. Nonprofit. Sem (Aug-May).

Small classes and an advantageous student-teacher ratio permit individualized instruction at MDS. Spanish, music, art and physical education are taught from prekindergarten, and a full technology program is offered. The campus includes a 300-year-old Spanish hacienda located in the Old Town section of Albuquerque. An environmental studies program at the school's Fenton Camp in the nearby Jemez Mountains is offered during both the school year and the summer session.

SANDIA PREPARATORY SCHOOL
Day — Coed Gr 6-12

Albuquerque, NM 87113. 532 Osuna Rd NE. Tel: 505-338-3000. Fax: 505-338-3099.
  www.sandiaprep.org   E-mail: info@sandiaprep.org
B. Steven Albert, Head (2010). BS, Haverford College, MEd, Harvard Univ, MS, Portland
  State Univ. **Ester Tomelloso, Adm.**
  Col Prep. Feat—Creative_Writing Shakespeare Irish_Lit Chin Fr Span Calc Astron
    Comp_Sci 20th-Century_Japan & Chin Econ Global_Stud Philos Art_Hist Film Film-
    making Fine_Arts Visual_Arts Drama Music Dance Journ. **Supp**—Tut. Outdoor ed.
  Sports—Basket Bowl X-country Golf Soccer Swim Tennis Track. B: Baseball. G: Softball
    Volley.
  Selective adm: 115/yr. Appl fee: $40. Appl due: Feb.
  Enr 650. Nonwhite 44%. Avg class size: 16. Stud/fac: 8:1. **Fac 80.** Adv deg: 61%.
  Grad '11—102. Col—102. (U of NM 32, U of TX-Austin 5, U of OR 3, TX Tech 3, Regis
    U 2, Coe 2). Athl schol 4. **Avg SAT:** CR 603. M 568. W 590. **Mid 50% SAT:** CR 540-
    650. M 520-610. W 500-640. Avg ACT: 27. Mid 50% ACT: 24-31. **Col couns:** 3. Alum
    donors: 8%.
  Tui '12-'13: Day $18,150 (+$400). **Aid:** Need 195 ($1,733,850).
  Summer (enr 1003): Acad Enrich Rec. Arts. Outdoor. Sports. 1-6 wks.
  Endow $5,000,000. Plant val $22,111,000. Acres 30. Bldgs 15. Class rms 45. Lib 16,000
    vols. Sci labs 7. Dark rms 1. Observatories 1. Auds 3. Theaters 1. Art studios 3. Music
    studios 1. Perf arts ctrs 2. Gyms 2. Fields 5. Tennis courts 4. Field houses 1. Tracks
    1. Comp labs 2.
  Est 1966. Nonprofit. Sem (Aug-May).

Sandia Prep originated as Sandia School, a private day and boarding school for girls that was founded by Ruth Hanna McCormick Simms in 1932. Circumstances during World War II forced the school to cease operations. Under the leadership of Mrs. Albert G. Simms II, the present school came into being in 1966. The school became coeducational in 1973.

Students are required to take courses in English, the fine arts or communications, history, mathematics, modern languages, science and physical education. An extensive communications program features newspaper and yearbook production. Students pursue academic interests in-depth in elective courses in the various disciplines. Qualified seniors may participate in an occupation or a profession that particularly interests them during the last month of the school year.

LAS VEGAS, NM. (42 mi. E of Santa Fe, NM) Urban. Pop: 14,565. Alt: 6391 ft. Area also includes Montezuma.

ARMAND HAMMER UNITED WORLD COLLEGE
Bdg — Coed Gr 11-12

Montezuma, NM 87731. Hwy 65, PO Box 248. Tel: 505-454-4200. Fax: 505-454-4274.
www.uwc-usa.org   E-mail: info@uwc-usa.org
Lisa A. H. Darling, Pres (2005). BA, George Fox College, MDiv, Princeton Theological Seminary, MLS, State Univ of New York at Albany. **Tim Smith, Adm.**
 Col Prep. IB Diploma. Feat—Fr Ger Span Environ_Sci Anthro Econ Geog Women's_ Stud Visual_Arts Theater_Arts Music. **Supp**—ESL Tut.
 Selective adm: 100/yr. Appl fee: $0. Appl due: Jan. Yield: 99%. **Tests** CEEB SSAT.
 Enr 200. B 100. G 100. Intl 75%. **Fac 26.** M 12/F 14. FT 23/PT 3. Adv deg: 69%. In dorms 6.
 Grad '08—100. Col—97. (Brown 8, Earlham 6, U of St Andrews-Scotland 5, U of FL 5, Harvard 3, Trinity Col-CT 3).
 Tui '12-'13: Bdg $0 (+$500-800).
 Endow $84,000,000. Bldgs 30. Dorms 6. Dorm rms 104. Class rms 40. Lib 18,000 vols. Chapels 1. Sci labs 2. Lang labs 1. Auds 1. Art studios 1. Music studios 1. Dance studios 1. Gyms 1. Fields 2. Courts 3. Pools 1. Comp labs 1.
 Est 1982. Nonprofit. Tri (Aug-May).

One of 12 United World colleges, the school provides an international education emphasizing the two-year International Baccalaureate curriculum and community service. Cocurricular programs addressing conflict resolution and global issues are also integral to school life. Wilderness training and a 10-day project week in March allow students to pursue community and individual interests, and boys and girls also may participate in various cross-cultural experiences. First-year students travel to cities across the Southwest to perform community service and study the region's history and culture.

The student body is predominantly international, with roughly three-quarters of UWC's pupils enrolling from other countries. All American students receive full Davis Scholarships covering tuition, room and board, and two years of study.

SANTA FE, NM. (54 mi. NE of Albuquerque, NM) Urban. Pop: 62,203. Alt: 6950 ft.

SANTA FE PREPARATORY SCHOOL
Day — Coed Gr 7-12

Santa Fe, NM 87505. 1101 Camino de la Cruz Blanca. Tel: 505-982-1829.
 Fax: 505-982-2897.
www.sfprep.org   E-mail: info@sfprep.org
James W. Leonard, Head (1999). BA, Williams College, MA, Middlebury College. **Marta M. Miskolczy, Adm.**
 Col Prep. AP (exams req'd; 80 taken)—Span Calc Bio. **Feat**—Creative_Writing Screenwriting Web_Design Psych Philos Art_Hist Ceramics Photog Studio_Art Video_Production Stained_Glass Acting Theater_Arts Chorus Jazz_Band Journ Photojourn.
 Sports—Basket X-country Fencing Lacrosse Soccer Swim Tennis Track. B: Baseball.

G: Volley.

Selective adm: 78/yr. Usual entry: 7. Appl fee: $55-70. Appl due: Mar. Applied: 160. Accepted: 68%. Yield: 60%.

Enr 311. Wh 73%. Latino 14%. Blk 2%. Native Am 4%. Asian 4%. Other 3%. Avg class size: 13. Stud/fac: 9:1. Casual. **Fac 46.** M 24/F 22. FT 46. Wh 98%. Latino 1%. Native Am 1%. Adv deg: 67%.

Grad '09—55. Col—55. (Lewis & Clark 3, U of NM 3, Columbia 2, Brown 2, Stanford 2, USC 2). Athl schol 1. **Avg SAT:** CR 609. M 599. W 622. Avg ACT: 27. **Col couns:** 2. Alum donors: 13%.

Tui '12-'13: Day $18,906 (+$505-575). **Aid:** Need 88 ($801,129).

Summer: Enrich Rec. Forensic Sci. Tui Day $250/wk. 2 wks.

Endow $6,300,000. Plant val $14,459,000. Acres 33. Bldgs 4 (50% ADA). Class rms 33. Lib 13,761 vols. Sci labs 2. Auds 1. Theaters 1. Art studios 1. Music studios 1. Gyms 1. Fields 3. Comp labs 4.

Est 1961. Nonprofit. Sem (Aug-June). **Assoc** CLS.

Combining both creative and traditional approaches to education, the school provides a thorough foundation for college work. Primary emphasis is placed on the academic curriculum and the mastery of verbal and mathematical tools of expression. An interdisciplinary approach to learning is encouraged, and the program includes senior independent study. A full program in the fine and performing arts is part of the varied curriculum.

Students in grades 7-12 perform at least 56 hours of required community service each year, with projects and activities varying by grade.

UTAH

SALT LAKE CITY, UT. Urban. Pop: 181,743. Alt: 4400 ft.

ROWLAND HALL SCHOOL
Day — Coed Gr PS (Age 2)-12

Salt Lake City, UT 84102. 843 Lincoln St. Tel: 801-355-7494. Fax: 801-355-0474.
Other locations: 720 S Guardsman Way, Salt Lake City 84108.
  www.rowlandhall.org   **E-mail: karenhyde@rowlandhall.org**
Alan C. Sparrow, Head (1992). AB, Brown Univ, MA, MS, Univ of Rochester. **Kathy Gunderson, Adm.**

  Col Prep. Sports (Winter). AP (exams req'd; 302 taken, 81% 3+)—Eng Fr Lat Span Calc Stats Bio Chem Physics Eur_Hist US_Hist Psych Studio_Art Music_Theory. **Feat**—Chin Environ_Sci Pol_Sci Ceramics Graphic_Arts Photog Theater Music Debate. **Supp**—Rev Tut. Outdoor ed.

  Sports—Basket X-country Golf Soccer Swim Tennis Track. B: Baseball. G: Softball Volley. **Activities: 28.**

  Selective adm: 151/yr. Usual entry: PS, 6 & 9. Appl fee: $50. Appl due: Mar. Applied: 272. Accepted: 73%. Yield: 76%. **Tests** CTP_4 ISEE SSAT TOEFL.

  Enr 1005. B 499. G 506. Wh 97%. Latino 1%. Blk 2%. Avg class size: 14. Stud/fac: 10:1.
    Fac 104. M 31/F 73. Wh 97%. Latino 1%. Asian 1%. Other 1%. Adv deg: 45%.

  Grad '11—63. Col—60. (U of UT 11, Whitman 3, Westminster Col of Salt Lake City 3, St Olaf 2, Wesleyan Col 2, Bates 2). **Avg SAT:** CR 620. M 620. W 610. Avg ACT: 28. **Col couns:** 2. Alum donors: 4%.

  Tui '12-'13: Day $14,815-17,895 (+$350-2300). **Aid:** Merit 6 ($54,500). Need 147 ($1,361,475).

  Summer: Enrich Rec. Tui Day $90-315/crse. 4 wks.

  Endow $6,000,000. Plant val $30,000,000. Bldgs 6 (80% ADA). Class rms 69. 2 Libs 20,000 vols. Chapels 1. Sci labs 8. Auds 1. Art studios 3. Music studios 2. Dance studios 1. Gyms 2. Fields 4. Comp labs 4. Laptop prgm Gr 9-12.

  Est 1867. Nonprofit. Episcopal (16% practice). Tri (Aug-June). **Assoc** NWAC.

The merger of Rowland Hall and St. Mark's School in 1964 created this single school offering a coeducational program. Established in 1867, St. Mark's School suspended operations about the turn of the century, reopening in 1956 as a college preparatory school for boys. Rowland Hall was founded for girls in 1880 by Rt. Rev. Daniel S. Tuttle, first missionary Episcopal bishop of Utah, with funds provided by Benjamin Rowland of Philadelphia, PA.

Rowland Hall offers a broad liberal arts curriculum with course work in the traditional subject areas. Advanced Placement classes are available in many disciplines, and both the arts and athletics are integral to the program. Small classes and a low student-teacher ratio are other characteristics of the school, which sends its graduates to colleges throughout the country. Rowmark Ski Academy, an adjunct of the school, offers an intense alpine ski-racing program.

Lower school children (age 2 through grade 5) attend classes on the McCarthey campus on South Guardsman Way.

Pacific States

CALIFORNIA

ANAHEIM, CA. (36 mi. ESE of Los Angeles, CA) Urban. Pop: 328,014. Alt: 165 ft.

ST. CATHERINE'S ACADEMY
Bdg — Boys Gr 4-8; Day — Boys K-8

Anaheim, CA 92805. 215 N Harbor Blvd. Tel: 714-772-1363. Fax: 714-772-3004.
www.stcatherinesacademy.org   E-mail: admissions@stcatherinesacademy.org
Sr. Johnellen Turner, OP, Prin (2007). Graciela Salvador, Adm.
  Pre-Prep. Milit. Feat—Span Computers Studio_Art Music. **Supp**—Dev_Read ESL
    Rem_Math Rem_Read Tut.
  Sports—B: Basket Football Soccer Volley.
  Selective adm: 94/yr. Bdg 53. Day 41. Appl fee: $100. Appl due: Rolling.
  Enr 170. Bdg 80. Day 90. Intl 30%. Avg class size: 17. Stud/fac: 14:1. Uniform. **Fac 15.**
    M 5/F 10. FT 12/PT 3. Adv deg: 33%. In dorms 4.
  Grad '09—44. Prep—37. (Servite 5, Mater Dei HS 3, Army & Navy 2, St Michael's Prep
    2, Calvary Chapel Christian 2, NM Milit 1).
  Tui '12-'13: Bdg $41,010 (+$2500). **5-Day Bdg $30,675** (+$2000). **Day $8050-11,560**
    (+$1050-1750). **Aid:** Need 85.
  Summer: Acad Enrich Rev Rec. 4 wks.
  Plant val $25,000,000. Acres 8. Bldgs 4. Dorms 4. Class rms 15. Libs 1. Chapels 1. Sci
    labs 1. Lang labs 1. Auds 1. Theaters 1. Art studios 1. Music studios 2. Gyms 1. Fields
    1. Courts 1. Pools 1. Comp labs 1.
  Est 1889. Nonprofit. Roman Catholic (65% practice). Quar (Sept-June). **Assoc** WASC.

Conducted by the Dominican Sisters, St. Catherine's offers a pre-preparatory curriculum stressing academic skills. Math is a particularly strong subject at the school, and English as a Second Language is available.

The military program, which begins in grade 3, provides training in military courtesy, discipline and leadership skills. School activities include intramural and interscholastic sports, supervised weekend field trips for boarding students, and a music program that features both band and piano.

Christian-oriented activities include sacramental preparation, weekly Mass and family-life education. The student body reflects various religious backgrounds, and graduates attend both college preparatory schools and secondary military academies.

ATHERTON, CA. (22 mi. WNW of San Jose, CA; 30 mi. SE of San Francisco, CA) Rural. Pop: 7194. Alt: 52 ft.

MENLO SCHOOL
Day — Coed Gr 6-12

Atherton, CA 94027. 50 Valparaiso Ave. Tel: 650-330-2001. Fax: 650-330-2002.
www.menloschool.org   E-mail: info@menloschool.org
Norman M. Colb, Head (1993). BA, Brandeis Univ, MAT, Harvard Univ. **Cathy Shelburne,
Upper Sch Adm; Lisa Schiavenza, Middle Sch Adm.**

Col Prep. AP (exams req'd; 704 taken, 92% 3+)—Eng Fr Japan Lat Span Calc Stats Comp_Sci Chem Physics Eur_Hist US_Hist Econ US_Govt & Pol Studio_Art Music_ Theory. **Feat**—British_Lit Shakespeare Irony & Satire Russ_Lit Chin Anat & Physiol Astron Environ_Sci Robotics Asian_Stud Philos World_Relig Art_Hist Filmmaking Photog Drama Chorus Jazz_Band Journ. **Supp**—Tut.

Sports—Basket X-country Golf Lacrosse Soccer Swim Tennis Track W_Polo. B: Baseball Football Wrestling. G: Softball Volley. **Activities:** 32.

Selective adm: 153/yr. Usual entry: 6 & 9. Appl fee: $85. Appl due: Jan. Accepted: 41%. Yield: 65%. **Tests** ISEE SSAT.

Enr 795. Elem 233. Sec 562. Avg class size: 15. Stud/fac: 10:1. **Fac 102.** M 45/F 57. FT 82/PT 20. Adv deg: 74%.

Grad '11—146. Col—146. (USC, Princeton, Stanford, U of CA-Santa Barbara, UCLA, Claremont McKenna). **Avg SAT:** CR 655. M 679. W 679. Avg ACT: 30. **Col couns:** 4. Alum donors: 10%.

Tui '11-'12: Day $34,900 (+$2000). **Aid:** Need 151 ($4,000,000).

Summer: Enrich. 3 wks.

Endow $21,300,000. Plant val $61,838,000. Acres 35. Bldgs 23. Class rms 76. Lib 20,000 vols. Sci labs 9. Auds 1. Theaters 1. Art studios 1. Music studios 3. Dance studios 1. Gyms 1. Fields 3. Courts 12. Pools 1. Weight rms 1. Comp labs 3.

Est 1915. Nonprofit. Sem (Aug-June). **Assoc** WASC.

Located on a 35-acre campus that includes separate facilities for middle and upper school students, Menlo conducts a college preparatory curriculum designed to address the specific needs of each age group.

At the middle school level (grades 6-8), the program incorporates small classes, an integrated, interdisciplinary curriculum, and a varied selection of age-appropriate athletic and extracurricular activities. Most classes meet for 95 minutes, allowing time for hands-on exercises and classroom discussions, and pupils frequently work together on projects. Art, music and drama are integral to the program.

During the upper school years (grades 9-12), students further develop their critical thinking and independent learning skills. In addition to Advanced Placement courses, Menlo offers opportunities for independent study in such areas as biotechnology research, multimedia technology, engineering and history research. Particularly strong visual arts, choral and instrumental music, and dramatic programs are available at this level, as are peer leadership and student government programs. All upper schoolers take part in Knight School, a weeklong program each March in which pupils pursue intensive study of a subject of interest. Forty hours of community service are required for graduation. Seniors complete a compulsory seven-component project.   **See Also Page 120**

CARLSBAD, CA. (23 mi. NNW of San Diego, CA) Suburban. Pop: 78,247. Alt: 42 ft.

ARMY AND NAVY ACADEMY
Bdg and Day — Boys Gr 7-12

Carlsbad, CA 92008. 2605 Carlsbad Blvd. Tel: 760-729-2385, 888-762-2338. Fax: 760-434-5948.

www.armyandnavyacademy.org   E-mail: admission@armyandnavyacademy.org

Brig. Gen. Stephen Bliss, Pres (2002). BA, US Military Academy, MS, Univ of Missouri-Columbia, MBA, Univ of Texas-Dallas. **Candace Heidenrich, Adm.**

Col Prep. Gen Acad. Milit. AP (exams req'd; 133 taken, 24% 3+)—Eng Span Calc Bio Physics US_Hist Psych Studio_Art. **Feat**—Creative_Writing Fr Astron Computers Comp_Relig Art_Hist Photog Drama Band Music Journ JROTC. **Supp**—ESL Tut.

Sports—B: Baseball Basket X-country Football Golf Soccer Swim Tennis Track W_Polo Wrestling.

Selective adm (Gr 7-11): 142/yr. Bdg 115. Day 27. Appl fee: $100. Appl due: Rolling.

Applied: 360. Accepted: 73%. Yield: 82%. **Tests** ISEE SSAT Stanford TOEFL.
Enr 320. Bdg 300. Day 20. Wh 45%. Latino 8%. Blk 5%. Native Am 1%. Asian 30%.
Other 11%. Intl 25%. Avg class size: 15. Stud/fac: 10:1. Uniform. **Fac 30.** M 15/F 15.
FT 30. Wh 98%. Blk 1%. Other 1%. Adv deg: 46%.
Grad '11—58. Col—58. (U of CA-Irvine 4, UCLA 3, U of San Francisco 2, U of AZ 2, U of
CO-Boulder 2, Marymount U 2). **Avg SAT:** CR 496. M 546. W 479. **Col couns:** 1.
Tui '12-'13: Bdg $33,600 (+$3000). **Day $19,950** (+$2800).
Summer: Acad. 2-4 wks. Rec. Surfing. 1-3 wks.
Endow $7,000,000. Plant val $10,000,000. Acres 16. Bldgs 30. Dorms 14. Dorm rms
150. Class rms 32. Lib 5000 vols. Sci labs 4. Auds 1. Art studios 1. Music studios 1.
Dance studios 1. Gyms 1. Fields 1. Courts 3. Pools 1. Rifle ranges 1. Comp labs 1.
Est 1910. Nonprofit. Sem (Sept-June). **Assoc** WASC.

Established at Pacific Beach in 1910 and relocated to Carlsbad in 1936, this military school prepares its students for both competitive colleges nationwide and the US service academies. Honors and Advanced Placement courses in the major disciplines provide qualified cadets with opportunities for acceleration. A well-developed computer program, a learning strategies program, and a fine and performing arts department that enables pupils to take part in dramatic productions, art exhibitions, concerts and marching band are other features of the academy's program.

ANA's 16-acre, oceanfront location allows for various interscholastic sports, as well as an intramural program that includes surfing, volleyball and weightlifting, among other options. In addition, the school schedules monthly dances with neighboring schools and other weekend activities. **See Also Page 115**

CLAREMONT, CA. (40 mi. E of Los Angeles, CA) Suburban. Pop: 33,998. Alt: 1144 ft. See also Los Angeles.

FOOTHILL COUNTRY DAY SCHOOL

Day — Coed Gr PS (Age 3)-8

Claremont, CA 91711. 1035 W Harrison Ave. Tel: 909-626-5681. Fax: 909-625-4251.
www.foothillcds.org   E-mail: dzondervan@foothillcds.org
Michael Silva, Head (2011). BA, Univ of California-Berkeley, MA, California State Univ-
Northridge. **Denise M. Zondervan, Adm.**
Pre-Prep. Feat—Lib_Skills Lat Span Computers Studio_Art Drama Music Dance.
Supp—Tut.
Sports—Basket Track Volley.
Selective adm: 67/yr. Usual entry: K. Appl fee: $100. Appl due: Mar. Accepted: 40%.
Yield: 82%. **Tests** CTP_4.
Enr 228. B 119. G 109. Wh 42%. Latino 9%. Blk 3%. Asian 19%. Other 27%. Avg class
size: 20. Uniform. **Fac 34.** M 7/F 27. FT 25/PT 9. Wh 89%. Latino 6%. Asian 5%. Adv
deg: 41%.
Grad '09—20. Prep—14. (Webb Schs-CA). Alum donors: 4%.
Tui '11-'12: Day $16,768-17,458 (+$500). **Aid:** Merit 44 ($75,000).
Summer: Acad Enrich. Tui Day $650. 5 wks.
Endow $1,805,000. Plant val $2,500,000. Acres 6. Bldgs 7 (100% ADA). Class rms 16.
Lib 20,000 vols. Sci labs 2. Auds 1. Theaters 1. Art studios 1. Music studios 1. Dance
studios 1. Gyms 1. Fields 2. Courts 3. Pools 1. Comp labs 2. Comp/stud: 1:1 Laptop
prgm Gr 6-8.
Est 1954. Nonprofit. Quar (Sept-June). **Assoc** WASC.

Founded by Howell and Betty Webb, FCDS provides a structured program that emphasizes a mastery of skills in reading and literature, writing, math, science, social studies, Spanish (in grades K-8) and Latin (in grade 6). Enrichment courses include computer technology, library skills, drama, music, art and physical education. Each grade produces an annual play, and pupils take active roles in the daily chapel program. In addition, students in grades K-7 participate in several community service projects, and eighth graders travel to Costa Rica to perform service at a selected school. FCDS conducts field trips for children at all grade levels, and afterschool programs are available.

Foothill also maintains a preschool division, The Seedling School, for children ages 3-5. This program balances developmentally appropriate instruction with creative play in a structured environment.

THE WEBB SCHOOLS

Bdg and Day — Coed Gr 9-12
(Coord — Bdg and Day 9-10)

Claremont, CA 91711. 1175 W Baseline Rd. Tel: 909-626-3587. Fax: 909-621-4582.
www.webb.org   E-mail: admissions@webb.org
Taylor Stockdale, Heads (2011). BA, Colorado College, MA, Univ of Delaware. Leo G. Marshall, Adm.

Col Prep. AP (exams req'd; 370 taken, 90% 3+)—Eng Fr Span Calc Stats Bio Chem Environ_Sci Physics US_Hist World_Hist. Feat—Marine_Bio/Sci Paleontology Robotics Econ Intl_Relations Psych Constitutional_Law Studio_Art Drama Music Music_Theory Journ. Supp—Rev Tut. Dual enr: Claremont McKenna, Claremont Men's.

Sports (req'd)—Badminton Basket X-country Soccer Swim Tennis Track W_Polo. B: Baseball Football Golf Wrestling. G: Softball Volley.

Selective adm (Gr 9-11): 94/yr. Bdg 60. Day 34. Appl fee: $50. Appl due: Jan. Accepted: 42%. Yield: 71%. Tests ISEE SSAT.

Enr 400. B 202. G 198. Intl 20%. Avg class size: 15. Stud/fac: 7:1. Fac 58. Adv deg: 74%. In dorms 14.

Grad '11—86. Col—86. (USC 7, NYU 3, U of CA-Berkeley 3, Wellesley 3, U of Chicago 2, Cornell 2). Avg SAT: CR 640. M 690. W 620. Avg ACT: 28. Col couns: 1. Alum donors: 34%.

Tui '10-'11: Bdg $46,690 (+$1000). Day $33,205 (+$1000). Aid: Need 117 ($2,750,000).

Summer: Gr 1-12. Acad Enrich Rev Rec. Arts. Sports. 5 wks.

Endow $14,000,000. Plant val $76,700,000. Acres 75. Bldgs 58 (15% ADA). Dorms 10. Dorm rms 186. Class rms 22. Lib 26,000 vols. Sci labs 4. Lang labs 5. Observatories 1. Auds 1. Art studios 1. Music studios 1. Museums 1. Gyms 1. Fields 4. Tennis courts 6. Pools 1. Tracks 1. Comp labs 2.

Est 1922. Nonprofit. Sem (Aug-June). Assoc CLS WASC.

The school comprises Webb School of California for boys and Vivian Webb School for girls. The former was started in 1922, when Dr. Thompson and Vivian Webb moved west from Bell Buckle, TN, to Claremont to found a boys' school in the foothills of the San Gabriel Mountains. Thompson Webb was part of a school-making tradition that had been started by his father, Sawney Webb, in Tennessee. Sawney Webb founded Webb School of Bell Buckle after the Civil War and helped it earn a national reputation based on its academic excellence and student honor code. Thompson took his father's principles to California when he founded the Webb School of California. In 1981, Vivian Webb School, a separate day school for girls, opened on the 75-acre campus and, four years later, began accepting boarding students.

The Webb Schools share faculty and facilities, while maintaining their own student governments, school traditions and graduation ceremonies. Students in grades 9 and 10 take single-gender courses in math, science, history and English, while juniors and seniors attend coeducational classes. The two schools come together for meals, social and recreational activities, fine arts productions and other campuswide events. Advanced Placement and honors courses are offered in all major disciplines, and upperclassmen with faculty approval may attend classes at one of the nearby Claremont colleges.

The Raymond M. Alf Museum of Paleontology, the only accredited paleontology museum in the country located on a secondary school campus, enables students to learn about paleontology and the scientific method. Museum-associated activities include fossil collection, organization of collections, specimen identification and display design.

Each year, the two schools collaborate on three dramatic productions and three dance productions. All students participate in interscholastic athletics at least one season per year.

CORONA DEL MAR, CA. (47 mi. SE of Los Angeles, CA) Rural. Pop: 2757. Alt: 80 ft.

HARBOR DAY SCHOOL
Day — Coed Gr K-8

Corona del Mar, CA 92625. 3443 Pacific View Dr. Tel: 949-640-1410.
Fax: 949-640-0908.
www.harborday.org   E-mail: dphelps@harborday.org
Douglas E. Phelps, Head (2006).
   Pre-Prep. **Feat**—Fr Lat Span Computers Studio_Art Music.
   Sports—Basket Soccer Track Volley.
   Selective adm: 62/yr. Appl fee: $50. Accepted: 30%. **Tests** ISEE.
   Enr 408. B 195. G 213. Avg class size: 22. Uniform. **Fac 34.** M 6/F 28. FT 32/PT 2. Adv deg: 55%.
   Grad '08—42. Prep—10. (St Margaret's Episcopal, St Paul's Sch-NH, Phillips Exeter, Choate, Phillips Acad).
   Tui '12-'13: Day $19,250 (+$200).
   Endow $10,000,000. Plant val $12,000,000. Acres 6. Bldgs 5. Class rms 30. Lib 12,000 vols. Sci labs 3. Auds 1. Art studios 3. Music studios 1. Perf arts ctrs 1. Wood shops 1. Gyms 1. Fields 2. Courts 5. Comp labs 4. Comp/stud: 1:1.8.
   Est 1952. Nonprofit. Tri (Sept-June). **Assoc** WASC.

Serving Orange Coast communities, Harbor Day moved to a six-acre campus overlooking the Pacific in 1973. The traditional curriculum features an integrated sequence of courses in math and the English language, and it includes frequent field trips and the study of foreign languages and computer technology. Spanish is available in grades K-8, with Latin and French added as language options in grades 5-8.

Community service projects are organized at all grade levels, and the student council sponsors a number of volunteer opportunities for students.

CORTE MADERA, CA. (9 mi. NNE of San Francisco, CA) Suburban. Pop: 9100. Alt: 27 ft.

MARIN COUNTRY DAY SCHOOL
Day — Coed Gr K-8

Corte Madera, CA 94925. 5221 Paradise Dr. Tel: 415-927-5900. Fax: 415-924-2224.
www.mcds.org   E-mail: info@mcds.org
Lucinda Lee Katz, Head (2004). BA, MA, San Francisco State Univ, PhD, Univ of Illinois-Urbana. **Jeffrey Escabar, Adm.**
   Pre-Prep. Elem math—TERC Investigations. **Feat**—Chin Span Computers Studio_Art Drama Music Outdoor_Ed. **Supp**—Dev_Read LD Tut.
   Sports—Basket X-country Soccer Track Volley.
   Very selective adm: 79/yr. Usual entry: K & 6. Appl fee: $100. Appl due: Jan. Applied: 429. Accepted: 21%. Yield: 89%. **Tests** CTP_4 ISEE.

Enr 560. B 280. G 280. Wh 71%. Latino 2%. Blk 4%. Asian 8%. Other 15%. Avg class size: 18. Stud/fac: 9:1. **Fac 71.** M 22/F 49. FT 63/PT 8. Wh 77%. Latino 4%. Blk 4%. Asian 14%. Other 1%. Adv deg: 59%.
Grad '11—71. Prep—64. (Marin Acad 13, Branson 11, Urban 8, Lick-Wilmerding 6, San Francisco U HS 6). Avg SSAT: 68%. Alum donors: 3%.
Tui '12-'13: Day $25,095-28,330. **Aid:** Need 91 ($1,702,566).
Endow $13,740,000. Plant val $4,970,000. Acres 35. Bldgs 20. Class rms 34. Lib 23,000 vols. Sci labs 3. Auds 1. Art studios 3. Music studios 2. Gyms 1. Fields 2. Comp labs 2. Comp/stud: 1:2.2.
Est 1956. Nonprofit. Sem (Sept-June). **Assoc** WASC.

Founded by a group of parents as the only country day school in the San Francisco Bay Area, MCDS provides a broad and balanced program. Located on a 35-acre, waterfront campus, the school enrolls students from San Francisco and Marin counties.

Students work in self-contained classroom groups in grades K-5 and in a homeroom/departmentalized arrangement in grades 6-8. The program emphasizes inquiry and experiential learning at all grade levels. Spanish and Chinese language instruction begin in grade 3. MCDS is characterized by a focus on interdisciplinary teaching, the arts and the sciences. Teachers make use of mobile laptop computer labs to integrate technology instruction across the curriculum. Community service is included in the program at all grade levels; in addition, eighth graders may engage in a three-week service learning project.

DANVILLE, CA. (32 mi. E of San Francisco, CA) Suburban. Pop: 40,975. Alt: 368 ft.

THE ATHENIAN SCHOOL

Bdg — Coed Gr 9-12; Day — Coed 6-12

Danville, CA 94506. 2100 Mt Diablo Scenic Blvd. Tel: 925-837-5375.
Fax: 925-362-7228.
www.athenian.org   E-mail: admission@athenian.org
Eric F. Niles, Head (2009). BS, Univ of Pennsylvania, JD, Univ of California-Los Angeles.
Christopher Beeson, Adm.
Col Prep. AP (154 exams taken, 85% 3+)—Eng Fr Span Calc Stats Eur_Hist World_ Hist Studio_Art. **Feat—**Creative_Writing Humanities Shakespeare African-Amer_Lit Chin Environ_Sci Chin_Hist Amer_Stud Relig Sculpt Drama Chorus Music Dance Journ. **Supp—**ESL. Outdoor ed.
Sports—Basket X-country Golf Soccer Swim Tennis Track Wrestling. B: Baseball. G: Softball Volley. **Activities:** 30.
Selective adm (Bdg Gr 9-12; Day 6-11): 110/yr. Bdg 12. Day 98. Appl fee: $75. Appl due: Jan. Applied: 600. Accepted: 37%. Yield: 49%. **Tests** ISEE SSAT TOEFL.
Enr 455. B 217. G 238. Bdg 42. Day 413. Elem 155. Sec 300. Wh 60%. Latino 5%. Blk 4%. Native Am 1%. Asian 18%. Other 12%. Intl 10%. Avg class size: 15. Stud/fac: 10:1. Casual. **Fac 71.** M 34/F 37. FT 58/PT 13. Wh 70%. Latino 8%. Blk 7%. Asian 15%. Adv deg: 94%.
Grad '11—77. Col—77. (U of WA, CA St Polytech-Pomona, Stanford, Dartmouth, Franklin & Marshall, Santa Clara). **Avg SAT:** CR 609. M 646. W 630. **Col couns:** 1.
Tui '12-'13: Bdg $50,800 (+$1000-1200). **Day $25,350-32,650** (+$1000-1200). **Intl Bdg $51,500** (+$1000-1200). **Aid:** Need 110 ($1,800,000).
Endow $7,200,000. Acres 75. Bldgs 35 (10% ADA). Dorms 2. Class rms 21. Lib 16,000 vols. Art studios 2. Music studios 1. Gyms 1. Fields 2. Pools 1. Comp/stud: 18:1.
Est 1965. Nonprofit. Sem (Sept-June). **Assoc** WASC.

Enrolling an international student body, Athenian conducts a college preparatory program that emphasizes inquiry and interactive learning. During the middle school years (grades 6-8), group projects enhance learning, often in an interdisciplinary fashion that builds upon concepts and skills previously learned and acquired.

Upper school course work (grades 9-12) stresses writing, communicational and analytical skills. The interdisciplinary freshman humanities program focuses on the history, literature and art of seven major world cultures, while the sophomore-year American studies program coordinates American literature and history courses. Athenian offers honors or Advanced Placement classes in every major discipline, and juniors and seniors select from an array of college-style humanities seminars.

All students participate in Athenian's interim program, which operates before and during spring break and lasts from three days and two weeks. The program combines local or international travel with community service activities.

Typically completed prior to senior year during spring vacation in Death Valley or during the summer in the Sierra Nevada Mountains, the Athenian Wilderness Experience is a graduation requirement. Program activities consist of extensive backpacking, navigation, first aid, low-impact camping, technical rock climbing, rappelling, peak ascents, natural history study, a solo experience and service.

Occupying 75 hilly acres at the base of Mount Diablo, the campus and nearby San Francisco provide opportunities for diverse recreational and cultural activities. In addition, the location of the Pacific Ocean and the Sierra Nevada Mountains within a few hours' drive enables boys and girls to engage in wilderness experiences.

HILLSBOROUGH, CA. (20 mi. SE of San Francisco, CA) Suburban. Pop: 10,825. Alt: 32 ft.

CRYSTAL SPRINGS UPLANDS SCHOOL
Day — Coed Gr 6-12

Hillsborough, CA 94010. 400 Uplands Dr. Tel: 650-342-4175. Fax: 650-342-7611.
www.csus.org   E-mail: admission@csus.org
Amy C. Richards, Head. BA, MA, Univ of New Hampshire. Aaron Whitmore, Adm.
Col Prep. AP (332 exams taken, 89% 3+)—Eng Fr Span Calc Comp_Sci Bio Eur_Hist US_Hist Comp_Govt & Pol US_Govt & Pol Art_Hist Studio_Art Music_Theory. Feat—Creative_Writing Chin Stats Astron Comp_Relig Ceramics Photog Video_Production Acting Dance Design. Supp—Rev.
Sports—Badminton Basket X-country Golf Soccer Swim Tennis Track. B: Baseball Football. G: Softball Volley.
Selective adm: 75/yr. Usual entry: 6 & 9. Appl fee: $85. Appl due: Jan. Tests ISEE SSAT.
Enr 350. B 175. G 175. Elem 107. Sec 243. Wh 51%. Latino 3%. Blk 4%. Asian 23%. Other 19%. Avg class size: 14. Stud/fac: 9:1. Fac 43. M 17/F 26. FT 33/PT 10. Adv deg: 88%.
Grad '11—60. Col—60. (Stanford, USC, U of CA-Davis, Tufts, U of CA-Berkeley, UCLA). Avg SAT: CR 692. M 693. W 714. Mid 50% SAT: CR 660-720. M 650-720. W 660-780. Avg ACT: 32. Mid 50% ACT: 30-34. Col couns: 2.
Tui '12-'13: Day $35,700 (+$1990-2050). Aid: Need 63 ($1,400,000).
Endow $15,000,000. Plant val $21,000,000. Acres 10. Bldgs 4. Class rms 32. Lib 10,000 vols. Sci labs 5. Lang labs 1. Theaters 1. Art studios 2. Music studios 1. Dance studios 1. Gyms 1. Fields 2. Courts 3. Comp labs 2.
Est 1952. Nonprofit. Sem (Aug-June). Assoc CLS WASC.

Crystal Springs opened as an independent school for girls. In 1956, it moved to Uplands, the former Templeton Crocker estate in Hillsborough. The school now occupies the Renaissance-style mansion, its surrounding 10 acres and an academic building, a fine arts building and a gymnasium. Boys were first admitted to the school in 1977, and today the program is fully coeducational.

The school conducts a rigorous college preparatory curriculum. Boys and girls in grades 6-8 meet English, history, math, science and foreign language requirements. Freshmen and sophomores typically take five courses per semester, while upperclassmen generally enroll in four (due to increasingly difficult course work).

HUNTINGTON BEACH, CA. (37 mi. SE of Los Angeles, CA) Suburban. Pop: 189,594. Alt: 28 ft.

THE PEGASUS SCHOOL

Day — Coed Gr PS (Age 4)-8

Huntington Beach, CA 92646. 19692 Lexington Ln. Tel: 714-964-1224.
Fax: 714-962-6047.
www.thepegasusschool.org   E-mail: nconklin@thepegasusschool.org
John Zurn, Head (2010). BA, Williams College, MSEd, Univ of Pennsylvania. Nancy Conklin, Adm.

> **Pre-Prep. Feat**—Span Environ_Sci Computers Robotics Intl_Stud Performing_Arts Photog Studio_Art Music Outdoor_Ed. **Supp**—Dev_Read Tut.
> **Sports**—Basket Soccer Volley.
> **Selective adm (Gr PS-7):** 91/yr. Appl fee: $150. Appl due: Jan. Applied: 248. Accepted: 63%. Yield: 67%. **Tests** CTP_4 ISEE.
> **Enr 565.** B 282. G 283. Wh 73%. Latino 2%. Blk 1%. Asian 17%. Other 7%. Avg class size: 20. Stud/fac: 10:1. **Fac 51.** M 9/F 42. FT 51. Adv deg: 31%.
> **Grad '11—47. Prep—30.** (Sage Hill 21, Mater Dei HS 3, St Margaret's Episcopal 2, Junipero Serra 1, Blair 1, Thacher 1).
> **Tui '11-'12: Day $16,620** (+$500). **Aid:** Need 40 ($250,000).
> **Summer (enr 300):** Enrich. Robotics. Performing Arts. Sports. Tui Day $500/2-wk ses. 6 wks.
> Endow $2,200,000. Plant val $14,000,000. Acres 14. Bldgs 10 (100% ADA). Class rms 37. Lib 20,000 vols. Sci labs 3. Auds 1. Theaters 1. Art studios 2. Music studios 1. Gyms 1. Fields 2. Courts 4. Comp labs 2.
> **Est 1984.** Nonprofit. Sem (Sept-June). **Assoc** WASC.

The school traces its origins to 1979, when a summer program entitled Pegasus Programs first operated. Its success led founder Laura S. Hathaway to open The Pegasus School in 1984. After serving 40 preschoolers in its first year, the school gradually expanded through grade 8.

During the lower school years (grades pre-K-5), the curriculum combines basic skills instruction with open-ended opportunities for children to pursue areas of interest. In addition to the core subjects, pupils take specialist-taught classes in Spanish, science, technology, art, music and physical education. Field trips, visiting guests and performers, and annual special events enrich the lower school program.

Course work at the middle school level (grades 6-8) is suitable for gifted learners. A strong science program addresses topics within the physical, life and earth sciences. The outdoor education program features weeklong expeditions designed to enhance students' understanding of the environment, demonstrate the practical applications of science and history, and illustrate the importance of teamwork. Middle school students fulfill a 15-hour annual service requirement, with five of the hours completed during the school day.

Pegasus offers an extended-day program and after-school activities for boys and girls at all grade levels.   **See Also Page 65**

IDYLLWILD, CA. (68 mi. NNE of San Diego, CA) Rural. Pop: 3504. Alt: 5400 ft.

IDYLLWILD ARTS ACADEMY
Bdg and Day — Coed Gr 9-PG

Idyllwild, CA 92549. 52500 Temecula Rd, PO Box 38. Tel: 951-659-2171.
Fax: 951-659-3168.
www.idyllwildarts.org   E-mail: admission@idyllwildarts.org
Brian D. Cohen, Pres (2011). BA, Haverford College, MFA, Univ of Washington. **Marek Pramuka, Adm.**

Col Prep. Perform_Arts Visual_Arts Creative_Writing. AP exams taken: 9 (67% 3+). Feat—Poetry Mythology Native_Amer_Lit Playwriting World_Lit Fr Span Calc Anat Environ_Sci Comp_Design Comp_Sci Econ Govt Psych Comp_Relig Philos Ceramics Sculpt Acting Theater_Arts Music_Hist Music_Theory Ballet Jazz_Dance Tap_Dance Photojourn. **Supp**—ESL Rev Tut. Sat classes.
Activities: 37.
Selective adm (Bdg Gr 9-PG; Day 9-12): 146/yr. Bdg 131. Day 15. Usual entry: 9. Appl fee: $50. Appl due: Feb. Applied: 229. Accepted: 80%. Yield: 62%. **Tests** SSAT TOEFL.
Enr 295. B 103. G 192. Bdg 269. Day 26. Sec 292. PG 3. Wh 38%. Latino 12%. Blk 3%. Native Am 2%. Asian 42%. Other 3%. Intl 42%. Avg class size: 13. Stud/fac: 5:1. **Fac 90.** M 44/F 46. FT 41/PT 49. Wh 88%. Latino 3%. Blk 3%. Native Am 1%. Asian 5%. Adv deg: 42%. In dorms 18.
Grad '11—85. Col—81. (NYU 6, Columbia Col-IL 5, USC 5, Cornish Col of the Arts 4, U of CA-San Diego 4, Boston Conservatory 3). **Col couns:** 3. Alum donors: 4%.
Tui '12-'13: Bdg $53,600 (+$2500). **Day $35,900** (+$2000). **Aid:** Need 160 ($5,400,000).
Summer (enr 1600): Acad. Arts. 9 wks.
Endow $3,200,000. Plant val $9,708,000. Acres 205. Bldgs 40 (100% ADA). Dorms 5. Dorm rms 134. Class rms 15. Lib 3000 vols. Sci labs 3. Theaters 1. Art studios 6. Music studios 14. Dance studios 3. Fields 1. Courts 1. Pools 1. Comp labs 1. Comp/stud: 1:1
Est 1986. Nonprofit. Sem (Sept-June). **Assoc** WASC.

Trees and meadows dominate this 205-acre campus, which is set in the pine forests of the San Jacinto Mountains. The academy's location offers students recreational opportunities such as hiking, rock climbing and cross-country skiing. Roads and trails in and around the campus encourage running and cycling.

Students receive demanding preprofessional training in the arts and a strong college preparatory education. Academic courses are scheduled in the mornings, balanced by arts courses that meet in the afternoons; both range from introductory to honors levels. Each student's course of study is composed of a combination of the required arts courses for each major and the academic courses necessary to meet graduation requirements in English, history/social studies, foreign language, mathematics, science, physical education and computer literacy.

Major areas of arts study include music, dance, theater, visual arts, moving pictures, fashion design, creative writing, singing and songwriting; an individualized arts major is designed for those who have demonstrated high academic achievement and have a strong interest in two or more arts major areas. Performances, publications and exhibition center openings supplement the arts program, while the academic curriculum utilizes hands-on activities, experiments, field trips, cooperative learning and group problem solving. Arts Academy graduates gain entrance into both colleges and conservatories.

LA JOLLA, CA. (8 mi. WNW of San Diego, CA) Suburban. Pop: 28,800. Alt: 110 ft.

THE BISHOP'S SCHOOL
Day — Coed Gr 6-12

La Jolla, CA 92037. 7607 La Jolla Blvd. Tel: 858-459-4021. Fax: 858-459-3914.
www.bishops.com   E-mail: admissions@bishops.com
Aimeclaire Lambert Roche, Head (2009). AB, Harvard Univ, MA, Columbia Univ. **Kim Peckham, Adm.**

> **Col Prep. AP (828 exams taken, 89% 3+)**—Eng Chin Fr Lat Span Calc Stats Bio Chem Physics Eur_Hist US_Hist Comp_Govt & Pol Econ Psych US_Govt & Pol Art_Hist Studio_Art. **Feat**—Creative_Writing Humanities Anat & Physiol Astron Forensic_Sci Genetics Comp_Sci WWI Philos Relig Photog Drama Music Dance Journ. **Supp**—Rev Tut.
> **Sports**—Basket X-country Equestrian Golf Lacrosse Soccer Swim Tennis Track Volley W_Polo. B: Baseball Football. G: F_Hockey. **Activities:** 45.
> **Selective adm (Gr 6-11):** 175/yr. Appl fee: $100. Appl due: Feb. Applied: 350. Accepted: 48%. Yield: 85%. **Tests** ISEE.
> **Enr 780.** B 393. G 387. Wh 65%. Latino 11%. Blk 3%. Asian 19%. Other 2%. Avg class size: 15. Stud/fac: 13:1. Uniform. **Fac 93.** M 43/F 50. FT 83/PT 10. Wh 89%. Latino 6%. Blk 1%. Asian 3%. Other 1%. Adv deg: 76%.
> **Grad '11—148. Col—146.** (USC 11, U of CA-Berkeley 10, Stanford 6, SMU 6, Harvard 5, NYU 5). Athl schol 11. **Avg SAT:** CR 662. M 669. W 686. **Mid 50% SAT:** CR 610-720. M 610-740. W 630-760. Avg ACT: 29.7. Mid 50% ACT: 27-33. **Col couns:** 4. Alum donors: 8%.
> **Tui '12-'13: Day $28,900** (+$1500). **Aid:** Need 160 ($3,000,000).
> **Summer:** Acad Enrich Rev Rec. Sports. 1-8 wks.
> Endow $27,038,000. Plant val $63,737,000. Acres 11. Bldgs 9 (15% ADA). Class rms 72. Lib 12,000 vols. Sci labs 11. Lang labs 1. Sci ctrs 1. Theaters 1. Art studios 3. Music studios 2. Dance studios 1. Gyms 1. Athletic ctrs 1. Fields 3. Courts 5. Pools 1. Comp labs 4. Comp/stud: 1:2.
> **Est 1909.** Nonprofit. Episcopal. Sem (Aug-May). **Assoc** CLS WASC.

The school was established by the bishop of the Los Angeles Episcopal Diocese through benefactions of land and money from Ellen and Virginia Scripps. Founded as a girls' boarding school, Bishop's became coeducational in 1971, when it merged with the San Miguel School for Boys. The boarding department closed in 1983, creating a completely coeducational day school.

Bishop's 11-acre campus is a block from the ocean. The college preparatory program offers a balance between required courses and electives; Advanced Placement courses and independent study provide opportunities for acceleration. Attendance at weekly chapel services is required, and a six-year format of community service involves all students: Middle school pupils engage in group projects, while upper schoolers perform at least 20 hours of service per year in grades 9-11 and 40 hours in grade 12.

LA JOLLA COUNTRY DAY SCHOOL
Day — Coed Gr PS (Age 3)-12

La Jolla, CA 92037. 9490 Genesee Ave. Tel: 858-453-3440. Fax: 858-453-8210.
www.ljcds.org   E-mail: admission@ljcds.org
Christopher R. Schuck, Head (2006). AB, Princeton Univ, MA, Univ of Pennsylvania. **Vincent Travaglione, Adm.**

> **Col Prep. AP (exams req'd; 459 taken, 79% 3+)**—Eng Fr Span Calc Stats Bio Chem Physics Eur_Hist US_Hist World_Hist Psych US_Govt & Pol Art_Hist Studio_Art Music_Theory. **Elem math**—Everyday Math. **Feat**—Chin Arabic Astron Programming Philos Architect_Drawing Ceramics Photog Acting Theater_Arts Orchestra

Journ Speech. **Supp**—Tut.
Sports—Basket X-country Golf Lacrosse Soccer Swim Tennis Track W_Polo. B: Baseball Football. G: Cheer Softball Volley. **Activities:** 28.
Selective adm: 198/yr. Usual entry: PS, K, 5, 7 & 9. Appl fee: $125. Appl due: Feb. **Tests** CTP_4 ISEE.
Enr 1161. B 589. G 572. Avg class size: 17. Casual. **Fac 126.** M 41/F 85. FT 115/PT 11. Adv deg: 47%.
Grad '11—113. Col—113. (U of AZ 5, U of San Diego 4, U of CO-Boulder 3, Dartmouth 3, Stanford 3, U of CA-Santa Barbara 3). Athl schol 1. **Avg SAT:** CR 600. M 600. W 622. Avg ACT: 28. **Col couns:** 3.
Tui '12-'13: Day $16,600-27,591 (+$430-2000). **Aid:** Need 187 ($2,822,322).
Summer (enr 459): Acad Rec. Tui Day $135-1140. 1-6 wks.
Endow $2,434,000. Plant val $56,341,000. Acres 24. Bldgs 19. Class rms 86. Lib 38,143 vols. Sci labs 9. Lang labs 1. Photog labs 1. Amphitheaters 1. Observatories 1. Theaters 2. Art studios 3. Music studios 7. Dance studios 1. Photog studios 1. AV rms 1. Gyms 1. Fields 4. Tennis courts 6. Comp labs 3.
Est 1926. Nonprofit. Sem (Aug-June). **Assoc** CLS WASC.

Country Day traces its origins to the Balmer School, a primary school founded by Louise C. Balmer in 1926. In 1955, seeing the need for a local independent day school with a full nursery through grade 12 curriculum, Mrs. Balmer and a group of interested parents helped bring about the formation of the current program. The school moved to its present, 24-acre campus in 1961.

In the early grades, individualized techniques dominate the teaching philosophy. Reading and phonics are stressed in all grades, and creative writing, foreign language, art, music and physical education enhance the curriculum. The middle school is designed to meet the specific needs of students in that age group.

Emphasis in the upper school program is on college preparation in the basic subject areas, with college credit available in all departments through Advanced Placement. Computer science instruction begins in grade 1. All upper school students participate in athletics, fulfill a one-year fine arts requirement and perform 30 hours of off-campus community service by the end of junior year, plus another 10 hours by the end of the first semester of senior year.

See Also Page 146

LOS ANGELES, CA. Urban. Pop: 3,694,820. Alt: 338 ft. Area also includes Calabasas, Culver City, North Hollywood, Palos Verdes Peninsula and Sherman Oaks.

THE ARCHER SCHOOL FOR GIRLS
Day — Girls Gr 6-12

Los Angeles, CA 90049. 11725 Sunset Blvd. Tel: 310-873-7000. Fax: 310-873-7070.
www.archer.org   E-mail: admissions@archer.org
Elizabeth English, Head (2008). BA, Skidmore College, MAT, Tufts Univ, EdM, Harvard Univ. **Beth Kemp, Adm.**
Col Prep. AP (exams req'd; 196 taken, 86% 3+)—Eng Fr Lat Span Calc Bio Chem Physics US_Hist Human_Geog US_Govt & Pol Art_Hist. **Feat**—Creative_Writing Chin Anat Ecol Environ_Sci Comp_Sci Robotics Psych Ceramics Photog Studio_Art Theater Theater_Arts Music Dance Communications Journ Outdoor_Ed. Outdoor ed.
Sports—G: Basket X-country Equestrian Soccer Softball Swim Tennis Track Volley. **Activities:** 30.
Selective adm (Gr 6-11): Appl fee: $115. Appl due: Jan. **Tests** ISEE.
Enr 430. Elem 184. Sec 246. Nonwhite 31%. Avg class size: 16. Stud/fac: 7:1. Uniform. **Fac 65.** M 17/F 48. Adv deg: 61%.
Grad '11—65. Col—64. (NYU 7, Geo Wash 5, U of CO-Boulder 4, USC 4, Northwestern

3, Brown 2). **Mid 50% SAT:** CR 580-670. M 530-610. W 580-690. Avg ACT: 27. **Col couns:** 2.
Tui '11-'12: Day $29,300 (+$3240-4000). **Aid:** Need 125 ($2,800,000).
Acres 5. Bldgs 1. Class rms 62. Lib 8000 vols. Sci labs 5. Lang labs 1. Auds 1. Theaters 1. Art studios 3. Music studios 1. Dance studios 2. Art galleries 3. Fields 1. Courts 2. Comp labs 5. Laptop prgm Gr 6-10.
Est 1995. Nonprofit. Sem (Sept-June). **Assoc** WASC.

Emphasizing critical-thinking skills, the college preparatory curriculum at this girls' school follows an integrated and collaborative approach. The varied curriculum includes Advanced Placement and honors courses in all major disciplines, as well as electives and programs in such areas as robotics, media technology and experiential education.

During the annual Arrow Week, every student immerses herself in a subject, a project or a theme designed to combine elements of academics, outdoor education and service learning. Girls satisfy the following community service requirements: four hours in grade 6, eight hours in grade 7, 10 hours in grade 8, 15 hours in grade 9 and 20 hours per year in grades 10-12.

THE BUCKLEY SCHOOL

Day — Coed Gr K-12

Sherman Oaks, CA 91423. 3900 Stansbury Ave. Tel: 818-783-1610.
Fax: 818-461-6714.
www.buckley.org   E-mail: admissions@buckley.org
Larry W. Dougherty, Head (2006). BA, Wesleyan Univ, MAT, EdD, Harvard Univ. **Carinne M. Barker, Adm.**

Col Prep. AP (exams req'd; 278 taken, 79% 3+)—Eng Fr Lat Span Calc Stats Comp_ Sci Bio Chem Environ_Sci Physics Eur_Hist US_Hist US_Govt & Pol Studio_Art Music_Theory. **Elem math**—Singapore Math. **Feat**—Creative_Writing Chin Astron Econ Ceramics Drawing Film Graphic_Arts Photog Sculpt Video_Production Theater Band Chorus Orchestra Dance Journ Metal_Shop. **Supp**—Rem_Math Rev Tut. Outdoor ed.
Sports—Basket X-country Equestrian Golf Soccer Swim Tennis. B: Baseball. G: Cheer Softball Volley. **Activities:** 50.
Selective adm (Gr K-11): 127/yr. Usual entry: K, 6, 7 & 9. Appl fee: $125. **Tests** ISEE.
Enr 770. B 404. G 366. Elem 468. Sec 302. Wh 63%. Latino 3%. Blk 5%. Asian 5%. Other 24%. Avg class size: 14. Stud/fac: 9:1. Uniform. **Fac 88.** M 40/F 48. FT 81/PT 7. Wh 78%. Latino 7%. Blk 6%. Asian 6%. Other 3%. Adv deg: 56%.
Grad '11—74. Col—74. (Boston U 6, USC 5, NYU 4, Stanford 3, U of MI 3, Carnegie Mellon 2). Athl schol 4. **Mid 50% SAT:** CR 550-670. M 550-680. W 600-700. **Col couns:** 2. Alum donors: 2%.
Tui '12-'13: Day $28,864-32,475 (+$1439-2460). **Aid:** Need 105 ($2,500,000).
Summer (enr 110): Acad Rem Rec. Tui Day $2200. 6 wks.
Endow $5,100,000. Acres 18. Bldgs 15 (15% ADA). Class rms 72. 2 Libs 32,000 vols. Sci labs 4. Lang labs 2. Auds 1. Art studios 4. Music studios 3. Dance studios 2. Gyms 1. Fields 1. Pools 1. Comp labs 3. Comp/stud: 1:1.4.
Est 1933. Nonprofit. Sem (Aug-June). **Assoc** WASC.

Isabelle Buckley, author of *A Guide to a Child's World* and *College Begins at Two,* founded this school. Dr. Buckley's ideas, which were influenced by her observation of educational systems while living abroad, call for a balance between the academic demands of prewar French schools and the athletic, arts and character programs of other European systems.

Situated on an 18-acre campus, Buckley adheres to the beliefs of its founder in placing equal emphasis on academic training, creative self-expression, physical education and moral education. The school conducts a rigorous liberal arts program that features Advanced Placement courses in most disciplines. A particularly strong arts curriculum, which commences with integrated art across the curriculum in the lower school, incorporates artist visits at all grade levels. Upper school students participate in an international exchange program and outdoor education.

Community service is part of Buckley's program at all grade levels. In the lower school (grades K-5), service is integrated into the curriculum, while boys and girls in the middle school (grades 6-8) engage in formal projects. Students in grades 9-12 perform at least 20 hours of required community service each year.

CAMPBELL HALL

Day — Coed Gr K-12

North Hollywood, CA 91607. 4533 Laurel Canyon Blvd. Tel: 818-980-7280. Fax: 818-505-5319.
www.campbellhall.org   E-mail: flemina@campbellhall.org
Rev. Julian P. Bull, Head (2003). BA, Dartmouth College, MA, Boston College, MDiv, Univ of Virginia. **Alice Fleming, Adm.**
   Col Prep. Gen Acad. AP (328 exams taken, 78% 3+)—Eng Fr Japan Span Calc Stats Comp_Sci Bio Chem Physics Eur_Hist US_Hist Human_Geog Psych US_Govt & Pol Art_Hist. **Feat**—Creative_Writing Astron Environ_Sci Marine_Bio/Sci Physiol Amer_ Stud Econ Philos Ceramics Drawing Painting Photog Video_Production Drama Theater Music_Hist Music_Theory Dance Journ. **Supp**—Makeup Rev Tut.
   Sports—Basket X-country Golf Soccer Tennis Track Volley. B: Baseball Football. G: Softball. **Activities: 31.**
   Selective adm (Gr K-11): 173/yr. Appl fee: $100. Appl due: Feb. **Tests** CTP_4 ISEE.
   Enr 1094. B 549. G 545. Elem 559. Sec 535. Avg class size: 14. Stud/fac: 10:1. Uniform. **Fac 113.** M 42/F 71. FT 108/PT 5. Adv deg: 53%.
   Grad '11—128. Col—128. (UCLA, Loyola Marymount, NYU, U of CA-Berkeley, U of San Diego, USC). **Avg SAT:** CR 600. M 600. **Col couns:** 3.
   Tui '12-'13: Day $24,615-29,615 (+$565-3980). **Aid:** Need 262 ($4,100,000).
   Summer: Acad Enrich Rec. Arts. 6 wks.
   Endow $6,000,000. Plant val $22,381,000. Acres 14. Bldgs 22. Class rms 60. Libs 1. Labs 5. Theaters 1. Art studios 3. Music studios 2. Dance studios 1. Gyms 2. Fields 2. Courts 7. Comp/stud: 1:2.
   Est 1944. Nonprofit. Episcopal. Sem (Sept-June). **Assoc** CLS WASC.

Founded by Rev. Alexander K. Campbell, the school provides sound preparatory training within the Judeo-Christian tradition. With its structured, enriched college preparatory curriculum, CH prepares students for an array of colleges. Chapel is held five times a week for the elementary school and twice a week for the secondary school; however, religion is not a required course.

Varied arts and music programs are part of the course of studies. Boys and girls in grades 9-12 perform at least 20 hours of annual community service (and 80 hours prior to graduation).

CHADWICK SCHOOL

Day — Coed Gr K-12

Palos Verdes Peninsula, CA 90274. 26800 S Academy Dr. Tel: 310-377-1543. Fax: 310-377-0380.
www.chadwickschool.org   E-mail: admissions@chadwickschool.org
Frederick T. Hill, Head (1998). BA, Univ of North Carolina-Chapel Hill, MA, Middlebury College, MEd, Harvard Univ. **Judith Shaw Wolstan, Adm.**
   Col Prep. AP (256 exams taken, 88% 3+)—Eng Chin Fr Span Calc Stats Comp_Sci Bio Chem Environ_Sci Physics US_Hist Art_Hist Studio_Art Music_Theory. **Feat**—Forensic_Sci Marine_Bio/Sci Engineering Robotics African_Hist Asian_Hist Middle_ Eastern_Hist Econ Law Photog Drama Music Dance Outdoor_Ed.
   Sports—Basket X-country Golf Lacrosse Soccer Swim Tennis Track Volley W_Polo. B: Baseball Football. G: Cheer Equestrian Softball. **Activities: 49.**
   Selective adm (Gr K-11): 135/yr. Usual entry: K, 6, 7 & 9. Appl fee: $125. Accepted: 30%. Yield: 75%. **Tests** CTP_4 ISEE Stanford.

Enr 825. Elem 470. Sec 355. Wh 55%. Latino 5%. Blk 8%. Asian 17%. Other 15%. Avg class size: 18. Stud/fac: 8:1. Casual. **Fac 112.** Wh 80%. Latino 6%. Blk 3%. Asian 10%. Other 1%. Adv deg: 66%.
Grad '11—96. Col—96. (USC 8, Trinity Col-CT 5, Tufts 4, U of CA-Davis 3, Wash U 2, Yale 2). **Avg SAT:** CR 634. M 665. W 664. **Col couns:** 3.
Tui '12-'13: Day $24,360-28,770 (+$450-1900). **Aid:** Need ($2,700,000).
Summer: Acad Enrich Rec. Arts. Tui Day $325-1625. Sports. Tui Day $130-6300. 1-5 wks.
Endow $20,000,000. Acres 45. Bldgs 22. 2 Libs 28,000 vols. Sci labs 7. Amphitheaters 1. Auds 1. Theaters 1. Art studios 5. Music studios 3. Dance studios 1. Perf arts ctrs 1. Gyms 1. Fields 2. Pools 1. Comp labs 5. Comp/stud: 1:4 (1:1 Laptop prgm Gr 5).
Est 1935. Nonprofit. Sem (Sept-June). **Assoc** CLS WASC.

Drawing students from Long Beach, the South Bay and Los Angeles, Chadwick conducts a college preparatory curriculum that enables boys and girls to develop talents in art, music and drama. In grades K-6, course work emphasizes fundamental learning skills, critical thinking, sound study habits and an appreciation for the arts. Foreign language instruction commences with Spanish in kindergarten; French, Mandarin and Spanish are the language options from grade 6 on.

Technology is integrated into the curriculum in every grade. Qualified upper school students may enroll in Advanced Placement courses in the major disciplines. Outdoor education, which is an integral part of the program, features exploration of the diverse Southwestern landscape through a wilderness leadership program.

While not required to do so, most boys and girls participate in Chadwick's community service program, which consists of weekly, monthly and annual outreach (representing both local and international options). Round Square exchange opportunities enable students in grade 9 and above to study at one of approximately 70 schools around the world.

See Also Page 128

CURTIS SCHOOL

Day — Coed Gr PS (Age 4)-6

Los Angeles, CA 90049. 15871 Mulholland Dr. Tel: 310-476-1251. Fax: 310-476-1542.
www.curtisschool.org   E-mail: mpetrie@curtisschool.org
Peter W. Smailes, Head (2009). Mimi W. Petrie, Adm.
   Pre-Prep. Elem math—Everyday Math. **Feat—**Computers Studio_Art Drama Music.
      Supp—Rem_Math Rem_Read Tut.
   Sports—Basket Golf Soccer Swim Track. B: Baseball. G: Volley.
   Selective adm: 99/yr. Appl fee: $150. Appl due: Nov. Accepted: 31%. **Tests** ISEE.
   Enr 497. B 251. G 246. Avg class size: 17. Uniform. **Fac 57.** M 9/F 48. FT 57. Wh 90%.
      Latino 6%. Asian 4%. Adv deg: 42%.
   Grad '10—64. Prep—64. (Harvard-Westlake 28, Brentwood Sch-CA 11, Windward-CA
      6, Campbell Hall 5, Viewpoint 4, Marlborough 3). Alum donors: 2%.
   Tui '11-'12: Day $22,950 (+$200).
   Endow $17,000,000. Plant val $20,000,000. Acres 27. Bldgs 8. Class rms 26. Lib 14,000
      vols. Sci labs 3. Auds 1. Art studios 2. Music studios 2. Gyms 1. Fields 3. Basketball
      courts 3. Tennis courts 1. Volleyball courts 1. Pools 1. Comp labs 2. Laptop prgm Gr
      3-6.
   Est 1925. Nonprofit. Tri (Sept-June). **Assoc** WASC.

Situated on a 27-acre tract at the summit of the Santa Monica Mountains, Curtis maintains a traditional elementary program for children with varying learning styles. In the lower elementary years (developmental kindergarten through grade 2), the curriculum focuses on the child's natural curiosity while providing an academic foundation for future learning. Pupils become increasingly independent in upper elementary (grades 3-6).

The visual and performing arts are integral to school life, with regularly scheduled dramatic performances and other artistic activities complementing classroom studies.

HARVARD-WESTLAKE SCHOOL
Day — Coed Gr 7-12

North Hollywood, CA 91604. 3700 Coldwater Canyon Ave. Tel: 818-980-6692. Fax: 818-487-6631.
Other locations: 700 N Faring Rd, Los Angeles 90077.
www.harvardwestlake.com   E-mail: admissions@hw.com
Thomas C. Hudnut, Pres (1987). AB, Princeton Univ, MA, Tufts Univ. **Jeanne Huybrechts, Head.** BA, Univ of Detroit, BS, California State Univ-Northridge, EdD, Univ of California-Los Angeles. **Elizabeth B. Gregory, Adm.**
Col Prep. AP (exams req'd; 1733 taken, 90% 3+)—Eng Fr Lat Span Calc Stats Bio Chem Environ_Sci Physics US_Hist World_Hist Comp_Govt & Pol Human_Geog US_Govt & Pol Art_Hist Studio_Art Music_Theory. **Feat**—Creative_Writing Shakespeare Chin Anat & Physiol Astron Genetics Geol Oceanog Comp_Sci Psych Gender_Stud Ceramics Film Photog Drama Jazz_Band Ballet Dance Debate Journ Speech.
Sports—Basket X-country Equestrian Fencing Golf Soccer Swim Tennis Track Volley W_Polo. B: Baseball Football Lacrosse Wrestling. G: Cheer F_Hockey.
Selective adm (Gr 7-11): 318/yr. Usual entry: 7 & 9. Appl fee: $200. Appl due: Jan. Accepted: 30%. **Tests** ISEE SSAT.
Enr 1600. B 815. G 785. Elem 440. Sec 1160. Wh 70%. Latino 5%. Blk 7%. Asian 18%. Avg class size: 13. Stud/fac: 8:1. **Fac 219.** M 112/F 107. FT 200/PT 19. Adv deg: 68%.
Grad '11—282. Col—281. (USC 22, U of MI 20, Cornell 16, Stanford 12, Columbia 11, NYU 11). **Avg SAT:** CR 675. M 686. W 697. Avg ACT: 28.5. **Col couns:** 9.
Tui '12-'13: Day $31,350 (+$3000-5000). **Aid:** Need 260 ($7,000,000).
Summer: Acad Enrich Rec. Tui Day $90-1500. 1-4 wks.
Endow $36,131,000. Plant val $300,000,000. Bldgs 19. Class rms 131. Lib 20,000 vols. Sci labs 7. Lang labs 1. Photog labs 2. Auds 2. Art studios 4. Music studios 3. Dance studios 2. Arts ctrs 2. Gyms 2. Fields 2. Courts 4. Pools 2. Comp labs 2. Comp/stud: 1:4.
Est 1900. Nonprofit. Episcopal. Sem (Sept-June). **Assoc** CLS WASC.

HW was formed from the 1989 merger of Harvard School (for boys), founded in 1900, and the Westlake School for Girls, established in 1904. The school occupies both former campuses, with grades 7-9 located at the Westlake campus on North Faring Road in Los Angeles and grades 10-12 conducted on the Harvard campus on Coldwater Canyon Avenue.

The college preparatory curriculum features individualized work and instruction, and it is supplemented by a variety of elective courses. A more tightly structured program is offered in the lower grades, with increased independent responsibility introduced as the student progresses.

Seniors may develop their own independent study programs. HW pupils may study abroad in France, Spain, India, Italy or China through the School Year Abroad program, or they may spend a semester at the Mountain School in Vershire, VT, or the High Mountain Institute in Leadville, CO. All boys and girls satisfy community service requirements: outreach project work in grades 7-9 and one project or 12 hours of service per year in grades 10-12.

JOHN THOMAS DYE SCHOOL
Day — Coed Gr K-6

Los Angeles, CA 90049. 11414 Chalon Rd. Tel: 310-476-2811. Fax: 310-476-8675.
www.jtdschool.com   E-mail: jhirsch@jtdschool.com
Raymond R. Michaud, Jr., Head (1980). BA, Univ of San Francisco, MA, California Lutheran College. **Judy Hirsch, Adm.**
Pre-Prep. Feat—Computers Studio_Art Music Violin. **Supp**—Rev Tut.
Sports—Basket Soccer Track. B: Baseball Football. G: Volley.
Very selective adm: 53/yr. Usual entry: K. Appl fee: $125. Appl due: Sept. Applied: 250. Accepted: 20%. Yield: 91%. **Tests** CTP_4 ISEE.

Enr 333. B 157. G 176. Wh 76%. Latino 6%. Blk 4%. Asian 11%. Other 3%. Avg class size: 22. Stud/fac: 9:1. Uniform. **Fac 46.** M 5/F 41. FT 46. Wh 98%. Asian 2%. Adv deg: 34%.

Grad '11—48. Prep—46. (Harvard-Westlake 25, Brentwood Sch-CA 8, Marlborough 8, Archer 3, Campbell Hall 1, New Roads-CA 1). Alum donors: 6%.

Tui '12-'13: Day $24,650 (+$2000). **Aid:** Need 25 ($366,950).

Summer: Acad Enrich Rec. Tui Day $1250/2-wk ses. 4 wks.

Endow $35,000,000. Plant val $26,000,000. Acres 11. Bldgs 8. Class rms 18. Lib 12,000 vols. Sci labs 2. Art studios 1. Music studios 1. Gyms 1. Fields 1. Comp labs 1.

Est 1929. Nonprofit. Sem (Sept-June). **Assoc** WASC.

In the hills overlooking the Pacific, JTD, formerly named Bel Air Town and Country School, is an outgrowth of Brentwood Town and Country School and is the oldest private elementary school in the city. The curriculum provides a rigorous academic program, along with a full program of arts, music and physical education. Computer skills are built sequentially from year to year, and laptops are available in each classroom for student use. Community service is an integral part of school life, with activities that vary by grade level.

After-school sports begin in grade 4. John Dye prepares its graduates for secondary schools throughout the Los Angeles area.

LE LYCEE FRANCAIS DE LOS ANGELES
Day — Coed Gr PS (Age 3)-12

Los Angeles, CA 90034. 3261 Overland Ave. Tel: 310-836-3464. Fax: 310-558-8069.
Other locations: 10361 W Pico Blvd, Los Angeles 90064; 16720 Marquez Ave, Pacific Palisades 90272; 3055 Overland Ave, Los Angeles 90034; 10309 W National Blvd, Los Angeles 90034.

www.lyceela.org   E-mail: generalinfo@lyceela.org

Clara-Lisa Kabbaz, Pres (2000). BA, Univ of Southern California, JD, Univ of West Los Angeles. **Josette Cole, Dir. Edwin Gerard, Adm.**

Col Prep. Bilingual (Fr). AP (72 exams taken, 90% 3+)—Eng Fr Lat Calc Bio Eur_Hist US_Hist Econ US_Govt & Pol Studio_Art. **Feat**—Ger Greek Span Film Graphic_ Arts Drama Band Music. **Supp**—ESL Rem_Math Rem_Read Tut. **Dual enr:** Santa Monica, UCLA.

Sports—Arch Basket Fencing Soccer Tennis Volley. **Activities:** 30.

Very selective adm: 141/yr. Usual entry: PS. Appl fee: $75. Appl due: Rolling. Accepted: 20%. **Tests** ISEE TOEFL.

Enr 726. B 327. G 399. Elem 574. Sec 152. Wh 65%. Latino 6%. Blk 18%. Native Am 1%. Asian 10%. Intl 46%. Avg class size: 12. Uniform. **Fac 100.** M 57/F 43. FT 100. Adv deg: 71%.

Grad '11—28. Col—28. (U of CA-Berkeley 3, USC 3, McGill-Canada 2, Loyola Marymount 2, Stanford 1, UCLA 1). **Avg SAT:** CR 561. M 567. W 597. Avg ACT: 25. **Col couns:** 2. Alum donors: 2%.

Tui '12-'13: Day $13,320-21,010 (+$2000-4000). **Aid:** Need 21 ($142,907).

Summer: Rec. Sports. Tui Day $375/wk. 6 wks.

Plant val $50,000,000. Acres 16. Bldgs 12. Class rms 87. 2 Libs 30,000 vols. Sci labs 4. Auds 1. Theaters 1. Art studios 3. Music studios 2. Dance studios 5. Basketball courts 2. Tennis courts 1. Volleyball courts 4. Pools 1. Playgrounds 5. Comp labs 6. Comp/stud: 1:7.

Est 1964. Nonprofit. Sem (Sept-June). **Assoc** WASC.

Le Lycee is an international, bicultural and bilingual institution. The curriculum follows the French national educational system, while also incorporating elements of the American system. Students in the French language section prepare for either the French Baccalaureate examination or the French-American Baccalaureate, which combines the French Baccalaureate with the College Board's Advanced Placement program. The English language section offers a European-influenced college preparatory program that adheres to California educational standards.

All first graders, along with most kindergartners, attend school at the Century City campus on West Pico Boulevard. In addition, the school conducts preschool and kindergarten programs on Overland Avenue and at the Pacific Palisades campus. A new high school campus, Raymond and Esther Kabbaz High School, opened on West National Boulevard in September 2009. **See Also Page 69**

MARLBOROUGH SCHOOL
Day — Girls Gr 7-12

Los Angeles, CA 90004. 250 S Rossmore Ave. Tel: 323-935-1147. Fax: 323-933-0542.
www.marlboroughschool.org E-mail: admissions@marlboroughschool.org
Barbara E. Wagner, Head (1990). BM, Michigan State Univ, MME, Univ of Colorado-Boulder. **Jeanette Woo Chitjian, Adm.**
  Col Prep. AP (exams req'd; 435 taken, 88% 3+)—Eng Chin Fr Lat Span Calc Stats Comp_Sci Bio Chem Environ_Sci Physics Eur_Hist US_Hist World_Hist Art_Hist Studio_Art. **Feat**—Creative_Writing Poetry African_Lit Lat-Amer_Lit Russ_Lit Multivariable_Calc Astron Microbio Chin_Hist The_1960s Amer_Stud Psych Global_Stud Ceramics Fine_Arts Photog Sculpt Video_Production Drama Music_Theory Ballet Dance Journ Yoga.
  Sports—G: Basket X-country Equestrian Golf Soccer Softball Swim Tennis Track Volley W_Polo. **Activities:** 25.
  Selective adm (Gr 7-11): 109/yr. Appl fee: $150. Appl due: Jan. Applied: 356. **Tests** ISEE.
  Enr 530. Elem 176. Sec 354. Wh 60%. Latino 5%. Blk 7%. Asian 11%. Other 17%. Avg class size: 12. Stud/fac: 8:1. Uniform. **Fac 79.** M 27/F 52. FT 66/PT 13. Wh 77%. Latino 5%. Blk 3%. Asian 5%. Other 10%. Adv deg: 75%.
  Grad '11—84. Col—84. (USC 7, U of PA 5, Emory 4, Geo Wash 4, Columbia 3, Stanford 3). **Avg SAT:** CR 680. M 680. W 720. **Col couns:** 1. Alum donors: 35%.
  Tui '12-'13: Day $32,485 (+$950-2000). **Aid:** Need 102 ($2,100,000).
  Summer (enr 550): Acad Enrich Rec. 5 wks.
  Endow $36,849,000. Plant val $57,100,000. Acres 4. Bldgs 4. Class rms 40. Lib 25,500 vols. Comp ctrs 2. Auds 1. Theaters 1. Music studios 2. Dance studios 2. Perf arts ctrs 1. Art galleries 1. Gyms 1. Fields 1. Courts 3. Pools 1.
  Est 1889. Nonprofit. Sem (Sept-June). **Assoc** CLS WASC.

Established when Maine's Mary S. Caswell took two decades of work experience in Eastern schools to the West Coast, Marlborough is the oldest independent school for girls in southern California. Originally located in downtown Los Angeles, it moved to its present, four-acre site in residential Hancock Park in 1916. The school now draws students from more than 100 area public and independent elementary schools.

At all grade levels, the curriculum incorporates discussion-based lessons, teamwork among students and hands-on learning. Marlborough maintains high academic standards, with the traditional academic program supplemented by a variety of electives, off-campus internships and community service opportunities. The school also maintains strong fine arts and performing arts programs. Through the integrated technology curriculum, girls learn to use computers efficiently and to employ them as a learning aid.

Students may pursue independent work in the humanities and social sciences in collaboration with a mentor in Greater Los Angeles and a Marlborough faculty member. Seniors gain exposure to professional laboratory research techniques through the school's honors research in science course.

MARYMOUNT HIGH SCHOOL
Day — Girls Gr 9-12

Los Angeles, CA 90077. 10643 Sunset Blvd. Tel: 310-472-1205. Fax: 310-476-0910.

www.mhs-la.org   E-mail: admission@mhs-la.org
Jacqueline L. Landry, Head (2009). BA, Eastern Mennonite College, MDiv, Wesley Theological Seminary. **Jessica E. Butler, Adm.**
   Col Prep. AP (exams req'd; 358 taken, 85% 3+)—Eng Fr Span Calc Bio Environ_Sci Physics Eur_Hist US_Hist US_Govt & Pol Art_Hist Studio_Art Music_Theory. **Feat**—Humanities Irish_Lit Anat & Physiol Oceanog Comp_Sci Robotics Econ Psych World_Relig Music.
   Sports—G: Arch Basket Crew X-country Equestrian Fencing Golf Soccer Softball Swim Tennis Track Volley W_Polo. **Activities:** 57.
   Selective adm (Gr 9-11): 102/yr. Usual entry: 9. Appl fee: $100. Appl due: Jan. Applied: 220. Accepted: 65%. Yield: 75%. **Tests** ISEE.
   Enr 368. Wh 61%. Latino 6%. Blk 7%. Native Am 1%. Asian 11%. Other 14%. Avg class size: 15. Stud/fac: 7:1. Uniform. **Fac 51.** M 13/F 38. FT 43/PT 8. Wh 82%. Latino 6%. Blk 4%. Asian 6%. Other 2%. Adv deg: 82%.
   Grad '11—95. Col—95. (Santa Clara 6, Boston U 5, SMU 5, USC 5, U of WA 5, NYU 4). Athl schol 27. **Avg SAT:** CR 611. M 590. W 661. Avg ACT: 27. **Col couns:** 2. Alum donors: 20%.
   Tui '12-'13: Day $27,650-28,250 (+$600-1100). **Aid:** Merit 8 ($8000). Need 85 ($1,125,000).
   Summer (enr 100): Acad Enrich Rev Rem. Sports. Tui Day $650. 5 wks.
   Endow $6,000,000. Acres 6. Bldgs 6. Class rms 32. Lib 15,000 vols. Sci labs 5. Lang labs 1. Photog labs 1. Auds 1. Theaters 1. Art studios 1. Music studios 1. Gyms 1. Fields 1. Tennis courts 2. Pools 1. Comp labs 2. Comp/stud: 1:1 Laptop prgm Gr 9-12.
   Est 1923. Nonprofit. Roman Catholic (67% practice). Sem (Aug-June). **Assoc** CLS WASC.

Founded by the Religious of the Sacred Heart of Mary, Marymount emphasizes critical thinking and writing at all grade levels. The curriculum includes honors or Advanced Placement courses or both in all subject areas, and qualified girls may also engage in independent study projects. An extensive elective program allows students to pursue interests in such areas as oceanography, engineering and robotics, journalism and photography. Each girl has use of a laptop computer for an annual technology fee.

Drama productions, musicals, stage crew, talent shows, chorus, dance, instrumental music, photography and studio art are among the fine arts options, and girls may also take part in coeducational social activities. In addition, an active campus ministry program features class retreats and a community service requirement of 100 cumulative hours over four years.

THE MIRMAN SCHOOL
Day — Coed Gr 1-9

Los Angeles, CA 90049. 16180 Mulholland Dr. Tel: 310-476-2868. Fax: 310-775-8433.
   www.mirman.org   E-mail: info@mirman.org
John Thomas West III, Head (2003). BA, Macalester College, MEd, Loyola Marymount Univ, MA, Univ of California-Los Angeles. **Becky Riley Fisher, Adm.**
   Pre-Prep. Feat—Creative_Writing Shakespeare Mythology Chin Fr Lat Span Computers Studio_Art Drama Chorus Music Orchestra Speech.
   Sports—Basket Soccer Track. B: Football. G: Volley.
   Selective adm (Gr 1-7): 53/yr. Appl fee: $150. Appl due: Jan. Accepted: 75%. **Tests** IQ ISEE SSAT.
   Enr 330. Wh 69%. Latino 6%. Blk 6%. Asian 6%. Other 13%. Avg class size: 18. Uniform. **Fac 35.** M 10/F 25. FT 35. Wh 86%. Latino 6%. Blk 5%. Asian 1%. Other 2%. Adv deg: 45%.
   Grad '08—24. Prep—20. (Harvard-Westlake, Viewpoint, Brentwood Sch-CA, Campbell Hall, Phillips Exeter, Thacher).
   Tui '11-'12: Day $22,775-24,750 (+$250-2000). **Aid:** Need 70 ($1,060,000).
   Endow $6,500,000. Plant val $3,000,000. Acres 3. Bldgs 4. Class rms 25. Lib 9330 vols. Sci labs 2. Auds 1. Art studios 1. Music studios 1. Fields 1. Courts 2. Comp labs 2. Comp/stud: 1:1 Laptop prgm Gr 1-9.

Est 1962. Nonprofit. Quar (Sept-June). **Assoc** WASC.

Founded by Beverly and Norman Mirman, the school provides an educational setting where academically gifted children may maximize their mental, physical, social and emotional potential. Mirman School admits only highly gifted children with IQs of 145 or above and allows students to proceed at an accelerated pace.

As the student population is gifted, the curriculum stresses depth, complexity, novelty and critical thinking at all grade levels. The well-rounded educational program encompasses the arts, computer science, foreign language and sports. All boys and girls complete five hours of service per year in grades 6 and 7, eight hours annually in grades 8 and 9. Both parents and teachers conduct after-school enrichment classes and extracurricular activities at various times during the school year.

OAKWOOD SCHOOL
Day — Coed Gr K-12

North Hollywood, CA 91601. 11600 Magnolia Blvd. Tel: 818-732-3150. Fax: 818-732-3564.
Other locations: 11230 Moorpark St, North Hollywood 91602.
www.oakwoodschool.org E-mail: ypoydras@oakwoodschool.org
James Alan Astman, Head (1979). BA, Univ of Rochester, MA, Colgate Rochester Divinity School, PhD, Claremont Graduate School. **David Lee, Gr 7-12 Adm; Nancy Goldberg, Gr K-6 Adm.**
Col Prep. AP (exams req'd; 225 taken, 73% 3+)—Eng Fr Span Calc Comp_Sci Bio Chem Environ_Sci Physics US_Hist Comp_Govt & Pol Human_Geog Psych US_ Govt & Pol Art_Hist Music_Theory. **Feat**—Creative_Writing Sci_Fiction Chin Stats Multivariable_Calc Anat & Physiol Astron Forensic_Sci Web_Design Chin_Hist Econ Gender_Stud Socialism Comp_Relig Philos Ceramics Drawing Film Photog Sculpt Drama Theater_Arts Chorus Orchestra Jazz_Band Ballet Dance. **Supp**—Tut. Outdoor ed.
Sports—Basket X-country Equestrian Soccer Tennis Track Volley. B: Baseball. G: Softball. **Activities: 20.**
Selective adm: 100/yr. Usual entry: K, 6, 7 & 9. Appl fee: $125. Appl due: Jan. **Tests** ISEE.
Enr 755. B 365. G 390. Wh 70%. Latino 6%. Blk 3%. Asian 5%. Other 16%. Avg class size: 20. Stud/fac: 9:1. **Fac 91.** M 35/F 56. FT 75/PT 16. Adv deg: 52%.
Grad '11—82. Col—82. (NYU, Tulane, Syracuse, U of MI, Stanford, Carnegie Mellon). **Mid 50% SAT:** CR 580-690. M 580-690. W 600-720. **Col couns:** 2. Alum donors: 15%.
Tui '12-'13: Day $27,370-32,050 (+$1185-2000). **Aid:** Need 128 ($2,300,000).
Summer: Gr 4-12. Enrich. Arts. 4 wks.
Endow $11,500,000. Acres 3. Bldgs 22. Class rms 49. Libs 2. Sci labs 6. Auds 2. Theaters 1. Art studios 7. Music studios 3. Dance studios 1. Gyms 2. Weight rms 1. Comp labs 2.
Est 1951. Nonprofit. Sem (Sept-June). **Assoc** WASC.

Oakwood's location in North Hollywood offers students convenient access to the cultural, intellectual and recreational advantages of the Los Angeles metropolitan area. The curriculum combines a rigorous academic program with a broad exposure to the fine and performing arts.

Opportunities beyond the traditional college preparatory curriculum are offered through electives, special studies, field trips and extracurricular activities. Juniors and seniors who wish to focus on issues and topics not covered in the curriculum may pursue independent study with faculty members or design courses on special topics. The spring immersion program, required for students in grades 7-12, offers more than 50 in-depth courses emphasizing experiential learning and field study. Students perform five hours of community service in each of the seventh and eighth grades, and a combined 50 hours in grades 9-12.

As a complement to classroom learning, Oakwood students in grades 6-11 spend a week away from school participating in an organized experiential program. Settings include Washington, DC; the mountains surrounding Big Bear Lake; the Catalina Island Marine Institute; Joshua Tree National Park; Sequoia National Park; and the Sonoran Desert, where 11th graders canoe down the Colorado River. Students may also participate in mathematics competitions, county and national science fairs, and the school's annual arts festival.

The school's two campuses consist of nearly four acres. Each location has a nearby park to use for a variety of athletic activities. The elementary school occupies quarters about one mile away on Moorpark Street.

PILGRIM SCHOOL

Bdg — Coed Gr 9-12; Day — Coed PS (Age 2)-12

Los Angeles, CA 90020. 540 S Commonwealth Ave. Tel: 213-385-7351. Fax: 213-386-7264.

www.pilgrim-school.org   E-mail: info@pilgrim-school.org

Mark A. Brooks, Head. AB, Univ of Southern California, JD, Loyola Marymount Univ. **Patricia Kong, Adm.**

Col Prep. AP—Eng Japan Span Calc Bio Chem US_Hist Art_Hist. **Feat**—Creative_Writing Humanities World_Lit Chin Lat Anat Civics Photog Studio_Art Video_Production Drama Music Music_Theory Dance Journ. **Supp**—Dev_Read ESL Makeup Rev Tut.

Sports—Basket Soccer Volley. B: Baseball Football. G: Softball.

Selective adm: 63/yr. Appl fee: $125. Appl due: Jan. **Tests** ISEE.

Enr 350. Avg class size: 14. Uniform. **Fac 49.**

Grad '08—16. Col—16. (Stanford 1, Georgetown 1, U of PA 1, UCLA 1, U of CA-Berkeley 1, Pitzer 1). **Avg SAT:** CR 574. M 601. W 582.

Tui '12-'13: Bdg $41,550-43,950. Day $14,600-22,650 (+$750-1000). **Intl Bdg $44,050-46,450. Aid:** Need 63 ($472,500).

Summer: Acad Enrich Rem Rec. 2-6 wks.

Plant val $5,000,000. Bldgs 2. Class rms 43. Lib 11,000 vols. Labs 3. Art studios 1.

Est 1958. Nonprofit. Congregational. Sem (Sept-June). **Assoc** WASC.

A division of the First Congregational Church of Los Angeles, Pilgrim School offers a college preparatory program that emphasizes the mastery of fundamental skills. Preschoolers, who may enroll prior to age 3, meet weekly with specialists in the areas of music, storytelling, athletics and library usage. Kindergartners and first graders receive instruction in reading, arithmetic, phonics and penmanship. The program in grades 2-6 includes English grammar, history, geography, social science and math. Foreign language study begins in kindergarten, and a foundation Latin course is required in grade 6. Art, music, computers and values education are conducted at all grade levels.

The secondary school (grades 7-12) provides a traditional college preparatory program that includes AP classes. Among elective courses are dance, drama, journalism, music, choir and psychology. Grade 7 students take a quarter each of Chinese, Japanese and Spanish, then spend the fourth quarter studying the language they have chosen for the remainder of high school. Physical education offerings include group and individual sports. Computers are present in every classroom, and the school issues individual laptops to students in seven grades (including grade 1).

Each year, boys and girls in grades 9-12 satisfy a 20-hour community service requirement.

TURNING POINT SCHOOL

Day — Coed Gr PS (Age 2)-8

Culver City, CA 90232. 8780 National Blvd. Tel: 310-841-2505. Fax: 310-841-5420.

www.turningpointschool.org   E-mail: info@turningpointschool.org

Deborah Richman, Head (1989). BSE, Stephen F Austin State Univ, MEd, Univ of Hous-

ton. **Amy Calvert, Adm.**
Pre-Prep. Montessori. Elem math—Everyday Math. **Elem read**—Guided Read. **Feat**—Lat Span Environ_Sci Studio_Art Drama Music Jazz_Band. **Supp**—Dev_Read Tut.
Sports—Basket X-country Soccer Track Volley. B: Baseball Football. G: Softball.
Selective adm (Gr PS-7): 68/yr. Usual entry: PS & K. Appl fee: $100. **Tests** ISEE.
Enr 373. Nonwhite 45%. Avg class size: 18. Stud/fac: 9:1. Casual. **Fac 47.** M 11/F 36. FT 47. Adv deg: 40%.
Grad '11—24. Prep—21. (Harvard-Westlake 5, Marymount HS 3, Wildwood 2, Crossroads-CA 2).
Tui '12-'13: Day $22,650-27,175.
Summer: Acad Enrich Rec. 8 wks.
Acres 1. Bldgs 1. Class rms 41. Lib 10,000 vols. Sci labs 4. Lang labs 2. Auds 1. Theaters 2. Art studios 1. Music studios 1. Dance studios 1. Art galleries 2. Gyms 1. Fields 1. Courts 1. Comp labs 3.
Est 1970. Nonprofit. Sem (Sept-June).

Founded as Montessori of Los Angeles by a group of local educators and business professionals who adhered to the teachings of Maria Montessori, the school assumed its present name in October 1989. The Montessori-based primary division leads to an elementary division (grades K-5) that provides a skill-based curriculum and includes specialist-taught classes in art, music, Spanish, science and athletics. In all subjects, teachers deliver skill instruction in a sequential and interrelated manner. Turning Point's interdisciplinary middle school program (grades 6-8) seeks to further develop students' interests while preparing them for secondary education.

Beginning in the elementary school, study tours augment classroom instruction. These tours may include field trips to museums, cultural centers, regions of geographical interest and other educational destinations. Activities frequently incorporate current events and relevant social issues.

VIEWPOINT SCHOOL
Day — Coed Gr K-12

Calabasas, CA 91302. 23620 Mulholland Hwy. Tel: 818-340-2901. Fax: 818-591-0834.
www.viewpoint.org   E-mail: info@viewpoint.org
Robert J. Dworkoski, Head (1986). BA, George Washington Univ, MA, New York Univ, MA, PhD, Columbia Univ. **Laurel Baker Tew, Adm.**
Col Prep. AP (exams req'd; 478 taken, 90% 3+)—Eng Chin Fr Lat Span Calc Comp_Sci Bio Chem Environ_Sci Physics Eur_Hist US_Hist World_Hist Comp_Govt & Pol Psych Art_Hist Studio_Art Music_Theory. **Feat**—Creative_Writing Humanities Poetry Stats Ecol Oceanog Neurosci Robotics Asian_Hist African_Hist Middle_Eastern_Hist Archaeol Econ Intl_Relations Pol_Sci Ceramics Film Photog Sculpt Band Chorus Orchestra Dance Journ Outdoor_Ed.
Sports—Basket Equestrian Fencing Soccer Swim Tennis Volley. B: Baseball Football Golf. G: Cheer X-country Softball. **Activities:** 50.
Selective adm: 170/yr. Appl fee: $125. Appl due: Jan. Accepted: 35%. Yield: 75%. **Tests** ISEE.
Enr 1215. B 605. G 610. Elem 730. Sec 485. Avg class size: 18. Stud/fac: 10:1. **Fac 154.** M 58/F 96. FT 154. Adv deg: 35%.
Grad '11—117. Col—117. (U of CA-Santa Barbara, USC, UCLA, U of CA-Berkeley, Loyola Marymount, U of CA-Santa Cruz). **Avg SAT:** CR/M/W 1952. **Mid 50% SAT:** CR 580-690. M 580-720. W 610-730. Avg ACT: 28.5. Mid 50% ACT: 27-31. **Col couns:** 4.
Tui '12-'13: Day $25,800-30,550 (+$655-2215). **Aid:** Need 182 ($1,149,935).
Summer: Acad Enrich Rec. 6 wks.
Endow $6,000,000. Plant val $30,300,000. Acres 25. Bldgs 24. Class rms 94. 3 Libs 20,000 vols. Sci labs 9. Lang labs 9. Theaters 2. Art studios 6. Music studios 6. Dance studios 2. Gyms 1. Fields 2. Courts 4. Pools 3. Weight rms 1. Comp labs 6.
Est 1961. Nonprofit. Sem (Sept-June). **Assoc** CLS WASC.

Leading Private Schools

Viewpoint provides an enriched, traditional program for children in the elementary grades, and a comprehensive, college preparatory curriculum for students in grades 6-12 that includes an array of honors and Advanced Placement courses. In addition to increasing factual knowledge, the school's academic program further develops pupils' critical-thinking skills. Viewpoint's small-class setting enables teachers to work closely with each student.

Upper school pupils (grades 9-12) perform 45 hours of community service prior to graduation.

WILDWOOD SCHOOL
Day — Coed Gr K-12

**Los Angeles, CA 90064. 11811 W Olympic Blvd. Tel: 310-478-7189.
Fax: 310-478-6875.**
Other locations: 12201 Washington Pl, Los Angeles 90066.
www.wildwood.org   E-mail: advance@wildwood.org
Landis Green, Head (2007). BS, Kutztown Univ of Pennsylvania, MS, Univ of Pennsylvania. **Chantelle Pierre, Adm.**

Col Prep. Elem math—TERC Investigations. **Feat**—British_Lit Creative_Writing Humanities Span Calc Stats Anat & Physiol Environ_Sci Microbio Psych Ceramics Drawing Film Sculpt Theater.

Sports—Basket X-country Equestrian Golf Sail Soccer Swim Tennis Track. B: Baseball. G: Volley. **Activities:** 42.

Selective adm: 95/yr. Usual entry: K, 3, 6 & 7. Appl fee: $125. Appl due: Dec. Applied: 400. Accepted: 60%. Yield: 62%. **Tests** ISEE.

Enr 716. B 350. G 366. Elem 488. Sec 228. Wh 77%. Latino 2%. Blk 5%. Asian 1%. Other 15%. Avg class size: 16. Casual. **Fac 102.** M 29/F 73. FT 97/PT 5. Wh 63%. Latino 13%. Blk 10%. Asian 7%. Other 7%. Adv deg: 49%.

Grad '11—60. Col—59. (NYU 3, Pitzer 3, UCLA 2, USC 2, Wesleyan U 2, Sarah Lawrence 2). Athl schol 1. **Mid 50% SAT:** CR 510-660. M 520-620. W 570-680. **Col couns:** 2. Alum donors: 10%.

Tui '11-'12: Day $24,985-31,175 (+$90-850). **Aid:** Need 98 ($2,040,826).

Summer (enr 115): Acad Enrich Rec. Tui Day $475-2250. 1-8 wks.

Endow $2,062,000. Plant val $18,500,000. Acres 5. Bldgs 4 (100% ADA). Class rms 53. 2 Libs 30,000 vols. Sci labs 10. Auds 2. Theaters 2. Art studios 4. Music studios 3. Perf arts studios 2. Comp labs 4.

Est 1971. Nonprofit. Sem (Sept-June). **Assoc** WASC.

This college preparatory school employs project-based learning and a student-centered approach. In the middle and upper schools, 50 minutes per day are devoted to advising. Advisors—who are also teachers—work one-on-one with students on academic planning, tutorials, portfolio development, and group activities such as seminars and community involvement. Wildwood utilizes narrative assessments and pupil-led family conferences rather than letter grades to assess student performance.

During the high school years, boys and girls complete four years of compulsory Spanish study. Honors course work is available in the major disciplines, and advanced courses in several areas allow particularly able students to advance beyond honors level. Wildwood does not offer Advanced Placement classes.

The elementary campus (grades K-5) is located two and a half miles from the main campus on Washington Place (310-397-3134). **See Also Page 78**

LOS GATOS, CA. (8 mi. SW of San Jose, CA; 51 mi. SE of San Francisco, CA) Suburban. Pop: 28,592. Alt: 428 ft.

HILLBROOK SCHOOL

Day — Coed Gr PS (Age 4)-8

Los Gatos, CA 95032. 300 Marchmont Dr. Tel: 408-356-6116. Fax: 408-358-1286.
www.hillbrook.org   E-mail: info@hillbrook.org
Mark Silver, Head (2009). BA, Amherst College, AM, Stanford Univ, PhD, Univ of San Diego. **Tesha Poe, Adm.**
   Pre-Prep. Feat—Chin Span Computers Robotics Ceramics Studio_Art Music Jazz_ Ensemble Woodworking. **Supp**—Tut.
   Sports—Basket Softball. G: Volley.
   Selective adm (Gr PS-7): 44/yr. Appl fee: $100. Appl due: Feb. Accepted: 25%. Yield: 98%. **Tests** ISEE.
   Enr 315. B 155. G 160. Wh 66%. Latino 6%. Blk 1%. Native Am 1%. Asian 16%. Other 10%. Avg class size: 15. Stud/fac: 8:1. Uniform. **Fac 40.** M 9/F 31. FT 35/PT 5. Adv deg: 40%.
   Grad '10—35. Prep—30. (Bellarmine 12, Presentation 4, Castilleja 2, Harker 1, Menlo 1, Woodside Priory 1).
   Tui '11-'12: Day $24,500. Aid: Need 75 ($800,000).
   Acres 14. Bldgs 16. Class rms 21. Libs 2. Sci labs 2. Photog labs 1. Art studios 3. Music studios 2. Wood shops 1. Gyms 1. Fields 5. Courts 2. Pools 1. Comp labs 1. Comp/stud: 1:1.9.
   Est 1935. Nonprofit. Tri (Sept-June).

Located on a 14-acre campus in the foothills of the Santa Cruz Mountains, Hillbrook offers a balanced program that combines academic rigor with active and experiential elements. In the lower school (junior kindergarten through grade 4), cross-age grouping enriches flexibility and skill development in language arts and mathematics. Specialists instruct students in physical education, art, music, science and Spanish. English becomes a departmentalized course in grade 5, and Mandarin Chinese is offered in grades 4-8.

Music, visual and performing arts and service learning are often integrated into the thematic studies of each grade. Seventh- and eighth-graders choose from a selection of cocurricular electives, and interscholastic sports begin in grade 5.

LOS OLIVOS, CA. (28 mi. NW of Santa Barbara, CA; 105 mi. WNW of Los Angeles, CA) Rural. Pop: 800. Alt: 1000 ft.

DUNN SCHOOL

Bdg — Coed Gr 9-12; Day — Coed 6-12

Los Olivos, CA 93441. 2555 W Hwy 154, PO Box 98. Tel: 805-688-6471, 800-287-9197. Fax: 805-686-2078.
www.dunnschool.org   E-mail: admissions@dunnschool.org
Mike Beck, Head (2008). BS, US Naval Academy, MS, National War College. **Ann Greenough, Adm.**
   Col Prep. AP (exams req'd)—Eng Span Calc Stats Bio Chem Environ_Sci US_Hist World_Hist Studio_Art. **Feat**—Creative_Writing Dystopian_Lit Chin Anat & Physiol Comp_Sci African-Amer_Stud Ceramics Photog Drama Music Outdoor_Ed. **Supp**—LD Tut. Outdoor ed.
   Sports—Basket X-country Golf Lacrosse Soccer Volley. B: Baseball Football. **Activities: 13.**
   Selective adm (Bdg Gr 9-11; Day 6-10): 70/yr. Bdg 46. Day 24. Usual entry: 9. Appl fee:

$50. Appl due: Feb. Accepted: 53%. Yield: 68%. **Tests** ISEE SSAT TOEFL.
Enr 229. B 116. G 113. Bdg 109. Day 120. Elem 63. Sec 166. Wh 68%. Latino 6%. Blk 3%. Native Am 1%. Asian 17%. Other 5%. Intl 24%. Avg class size: 15. Stud/fac: 7:1. Casual. **Fac 33.** Wh 88%. Latino 9%. Asian 3%. Adv deg: 51%. In dorms 10.
Grad '10—46. Col—45. (UCLA 3, U of CA-Santa Barbara 3, Pepperdine 1, Duke 1, Bowdoin 1, U of CA-Berkeley 1). Athl schol 3. **Avg SAT:** CR 550. M 601. W 572. **Col couns:** 2.
Tui '11-'12: Bdg $47,000. Day $17,600-21,200. Intl Bdg $47,000 (+$2500). **Aid:** Need ($780,000).
Summer: Enrich Rec. 6 wks.
Endow $3,000,000. Plant val $5,400,000. Acres 65. Bldgs 15. Dorms 4. Dorm rms 112. Class rms 40. Lib 10,000 vols. Sci labs 3. Theaters 1. Art studios 2. Music studios 1. Ceramics studios 1. Gyms 1. Fields 4. Courts 4. Pools 1. Comp labs 1.
Est 1957. Nonprofit. Sem (Sept-June). **Assoc** CLS WASC.

The English-born and -educated Anthony B. Dunn established this preparatory school as a boys' program providing a rigorous academic program in a family atmosphere. Girls were admitted as day students in 1971, and, in 1990, Dunn opened its boarding facilities to girls for the first time.

Located in the Santa Ynez Valley, the school borders on the Los Padres National Forest. The approach is traditional and the curriculum college preparatory. The school also operates an well-developed outdoor education program. Class sizes average 10 to 12 students.

Dunn offers a learning skills program at an additional cost for high-ability students with learning disabilities. Limited to 34 pupils, this program allows students to participate in the regular curriculum and also receive daily, one-on-one remediation with specialists in language skills.

Required for all students, Dunn's outdoor education program is a four-year experiential curriculum modeled after the National Outdoor Leadership School. Boys and girls from all grade levels participate in seven- to 12-day wilderness excursions. Students assist in maintaining the school through a daily jobs program.

MIDLAND SCHOOL

Bdg — Coed Gr 9-12

Los Olivos, CA 93441. 5100 Figueroa Mountain Rd, PO Box 8. Tel: 805-688-5114. Fax: 805-686-2470.
    www.midland-school.org   E-mail: admissions@midland-school.org
William L. Graham, Head (2006). BA, MA, Middlebury College. **Amy Graham, Adm.**
    Col Prep. Feat—Creative_Writing Span Geol Holocaust Anthro Sociol Ceramics Music_ Theory Metal_Shop. **Supp**—Tut. Outdoor ed. Sat classes.
    Sports (req'd)—Basket X-country Lacrosse Soccer. G: Volley.
    Selective adm (Gr 9-11): 35/yr. Appl fee: $30. Appl due: Rolling. Accepted: 40%. **Tests** ISEE SSAT Stanford TOEFL.
    Enr 88. Wh 60%. Latino 15%. Blk 5%. Asian 12%. Other 8%. Intl 12%. Avg class size: 12. Stud/fac: 5:1. **Fac 20.** M 10/F 10. FT 18/PT 2. Wh 60%. Latino 15%. Blk 5%. Native Am 5%. Asian 12%. Other 3%. Adv deg: 70%.
    Grad '11—21. Col—19. (Willamette, Parsons Sch of Design, Columbia Col-CA, Drew, Earlham, Northeastern U). **Col couns:** 1.
    Tui '11-'12: Bdg $38,600 (+$500). **Intl Bdg $40,600** (+$500). **Aid:** Need 32 ($535,000).
    Endow $3,000,000. Plant val $30,000,000. Acres 2860. Libs 1. Sci labs 2. Lang labs 1. Art studios 1. Music studios 1. Gyms 1. Fields 2. Riding rings 1. Gardens 1. Comp labs 1.
    Est 1932. Nonprofit. Sem (Sept-June). **Assoc** WASC.

With an outdoor ranch life that utilizes opportunities provided by the school's setting, Midland retains the rugged simplicity that has characterized the school since its inception. Influential in the region, this successful college preparatory school was the creation of Paul and Louise Squibb, its founders and heads for 20 years.

Midland's curriculum provides a solid liberal arts grounding in the core disciplines and allows qualified pupils to engage in independent study. Academic classes meet Monday through Saturday, with each specific course generally assembling on five of the six days; students attend four or five classes per day. Elective choice varies annually depending upon student interest.

All boarding pupils live on campus in wood cabins. As the school is a working ranch, students grow and harvest their own food in a 12-acre organic garden. Boys and girls also share various other chores on the ranch. Seniors oversee the work program with the supervision of faculty, thereby developing leadership skills.

In addition to the integrated communal projects, students take part in such activities as cultural excursions and athletics. A popular equestrian program consists of horse husbandry and both English and Western riding. Situated on a 2860-acre tract in the Santa Ynez Valley, the school also provides students with many opportunities for camping and hiking.

MONTEREY, CA. (48 mi. S of San Jose, CA; 90 mi. SSE of San Francisco, CA) Urban. Pop: 29,674. Alt: 40 ft.

SANTA CATALINA SCHOOL
Bdg and Day — Girls Gr 9-12

Monterey, CA 93940. 1500 Mark Thomas Dr. Tel: 831-655-9356. Fax: 831-655-7535.
www.santacatalina.org   E-mail: admission@santacatalina.org
Sr. Claire Barone, Head (2002). BA, Univ of San Francisco. **Jamie Buffington Browne, Adm.**
Col Prep. AP (exams req'd; 218 taken, 72% 3+)—Eng Fr Lat Span Calc Bio Chem Environ_Sci Physics Eur_Hist US_Hist Econ Art_Hist Studio_Art Music_Theory. **Feat**—Creative_Writing Humanities Chin Marine_Bio/Sci Comp_Sci Philos World_ Relig Ceramics Photog Drama Dance. **Supp**—Tut.
Sports—G: Basket X-country Equestrian F_Hockey Golf Lacrosse Soccer Softball Swim Tennis Track Volley W_Polo. **Activities:** 30.
Selective adm (Gr 9-11): 63/yr. Bdg 29. Day 34. Usual entry: 9. Appl fee: $75. Appl due: Feb. Applied: 170. Accepted: 70%. Yield: 53%. **Tests** ISEE SSAT TOEFL.
Enr 243. Bdg 113. Day 130. Wh 53%. Latino 9%. Blk 4%. Asian 17%. Other 17%. Intl 12%. Avg class size: 12. Stud/fac: 7:1. Uniform. **Fac 34.** M 16/F 18. FT 27/PT 7. Wh 99%. Latino 1%. Adv deg: 79%. In dorms 7.
Grad '11—61. Col—61. (Santa Clara 3, U of AZ 3, U of San Francisco 3, Notre Dame 2, NYU 2, U of Chicago 2). **Avg SAT:** CR 603. M 583. W 605. **Col couns:** 1.
Tui '12-'13: Bdg $46,000 (+$1000). **Day $29,900** (+$700).
Summer (enr 205): Gr 3-9. Rec. Tui Bdg $2310-5150. Tui Day $1225-2950. 2-5 wks.
Endow $24,000,000. Acres 36. Bldgs 21. Dorms 3. Dorm rms 92. Class rms 26. Lib 33,000 vols. Sci labs 4. Lang labs 3. Theaters 1. Art studios 2. Music studios 6. Dance studios 1. Recital halls 1. Gyms 1. Fields 1. Courts 6. Pools 1. Comp labs 3.
Est 1950. Nonprofit. Roman Catholic (40% practice). Sem (Aug-June). **Assoc** CLS WASC.

Sr. Margaret Thompson, Mother General of the Dominican Sisters of San Rafael, founded SCS as a Dominican school for girls. This school opened nearly a century after a previous Dominican school, Santa Catalina Convent and School in Monterey, became the first Catholic school in California upon its establishment in 1850. The academic curriculum concentrates in all the traditional college preparatory areas, with particular emphasis placed on the arts and sciences. Girls choose from electives, Advanced Placement courses or both in most subject areas, and computer technology is an important aspect of the program.

The location of the school on the Monterey Peninsula and the 36-acre campus afford many opportunities for outdoor activities. **See Also Page 93**

YORK SCHOOL
Day — Coed Gr 8-12

Monterey, CA 93940. 9501 York Rd. Tel: 831-372-7338. Fax: 831-372-8055.
  www.york.org   E-mail: csmith@york.org
Chuck Harmon, Head (2002). AB, Davidson College, MDiv, Yale Univ, MFA, Warren Wilson College. **Catha Smith, Adm.**
  Col Prep. AP (exams req'd; 252 taken, 81% 3+)—Eng Chin Fr Lat Span Calc Bio Chem Physics US_Hist Psych US_Govt & Pol Studio_Art Music_Theory. **Feat**—Greek Anat & Physiol Environ_Sci Marine_Bio/Sci Comp_Sci Asian_Hist Econ Art_Hist Film Drama Band Chorus Music Orchestra Jazz_Ensemble Speech. **Supp**—Tut.
  Sports—Basket X-country Golf Soccer Swim Tennis Track. B: Lacrosse. G: F_Hockey Softball Volley.
  Selective adm: 66/yr. Usual entry: 8 & 9. Appl fee: $75. Appl due: Feb.
  Enr 229. B 113. G 116. Elem 18. Sec 211. Wh 62%. Latino 10%. Blk 3%. Asian 20%. Other 5%. Avg class size: 13. Stud/fac: 8:1. **Fac 31.** Adv deg: 83%.
  Grad '11—54. Col—54. (U of CA-Berkeley 4, U of Puget Sound 2, Stanford 2, Geo Wash 2, CA St Polytech-San Luis Obispo 2). **Avg SAT:** CR 681. M 666. W 666. **Mid 50% SAT:** CR 630-730. M 610-700. W 590-730. Avg ACT: 28. Mid 50% ACT: 25-30. **Col couns:** 1.
  Tui '12-'13: Day $27,600 (+$400). **Aid:** Need 106 ($1,429,100).
  Libs 1. Sci labs 1. Theaters 1. Art studios 2. Music studios 1. Gyms 1. Fields 3. Comp labs 1.
  Est 1959. Nonprofit. Episcopal. Sem (Aug-May). **Assoc** WASC.

York's traditional college preparatory program features Advanced Placement courses in all disciplines (including most languages), as well as a variety of independent study options. The school also offers a number of music, drama and studio art electives. Students and faculty meet three out of every seven days for Break, a student-led assembly to share announcements, celebrate accomplishments and build community.

Almost half of York's energy needs are produced by renewable solar energy on campus, and all students participate in a campuswide recycling program. Boys and girls accumulate 40 hours of required community service in grades 9-12.

OAKLAND, CA. (18 mi. E of San Francisco, CA) Urban. Pop: 399,484. Alt: 155 ft.

THE COLLEGE PREPARATORY SCHOOL
Day — Coed Gr 9-12

Oakland, CA 94618. 6100 Broadway. Tel: 510-652-0111. Fax: 510-652-7467.
  www.college-prep.org   E-mail: info@college-prep.org
Monique L. DeVane, Head (2011). BA, Brown Univ, MS, Case Western Reserve Univ. **Jonathan Zucker, Adm.**
  Col Prep. AP (269 exams taken, 95% 3+)—Fr Japan Lat Span Calc Stats Bio Chem Environ_Sci Physics Music_Theory. **Feat**—Chin Astron Comp_Sci Psych Women's_ Stud Philos Studio_Art Debate Health. **Supp**—Tut.
  Sports—Basket X-country Golf Soccer Swim Tennis Track Volley. B: Baseball. G: Softball. **Activities:** 46.
  Selective adm (Gr 9-11): 97/yr. Appl fee: $75. Appl due: Jan. Accepted: 39%. Yield: 70%. **Tests** ISEE SSAT.
  Enr 355. B 167. G 188. Wh 61%. Latino 5%. Blk 6%. Native Am 1%. Asian 21%. Other

6%. Avg class size: 14. Stud/fac: 8:1. **Fac 55.** M 19/F 36. FT 36/PT 19. Wh 80%.
Latino 2%. Blk 5%. Asian 13%. Adv deg: 78%.
Grad '11—87. Col—87. (Stanford 7, U of CA-Berkeley 6, Columbia 4, Swarthmore 4,
Harvard 3, U of PA 3). **Avg SAT:** CR 701. M 721. W 729. Avg ACT: 29.8. **Col couns:**
3. Alum donors: 13%.
Tui '12-'13: Day $33,800 (+$1500). **Aid:** Need 82 ($1,555,285).
Summer (enr 96): Acad Enrich Rec. Tui Day $0. 4 wks.
Endow $12,000,000. Plant val $12,681,000. Acres 6. Bldgs 14 (14% ADA). Class rms
25. Lib 15,000 vols. Sci labs 5. Lang labs 1. Dark rms 1. Theater/auds 1. Art studios 2.
Music studios 1. Dance studios 1. Gyms 1. Comp labs 3. Comp/stud: 1:3 (1:1 Laptop
prgm Gr 9).
Est 1960. Nonprofit. Sem (Sept-June). **Assoc** CLS WASC.

Founded by Mary H. Jenks and Ruth M. Willis, this day school with a strong academic
emphasis prepares students in small classes for colleges throughout the country. The program,
which emphasizes the development of both communicational skills and historical perspective,
includes offerings in art, drama, dance, photography, music and debate. Advanced Placement
courses in most subjects are available to qualified juniors and seniors.

College Prep's weeklong spring interim program, Intraterm, enables students to choose
from minicourses, internships and trips that address a range of topics and interests.

HEAD-ROYCE SCHOOL

Day — Coed Gr K-12

Oakland, CA 94602. 4315 Lincoln Ave. Tel: 510-531-1300. Fax: 510-530-8329.
www.headroyce.org   E-mail: lkoven@headroyce.org
Robert Anthony Lake, Head (2010). BA, Williams College, AM, Dartmouth College. **Cath-**
erine Epstein, Adm.
Col Prep. AP (exams req'd; 369 taken, 88% 3+)—Eng Fr Lat Span Calc Stats Comp_
Sci Bio Physics Eur_Hist US_Hist Art_Hist Studio_Art Music_Theory. **Feat**—Shake-
speare Chin Astron Marine_Bio/Sci Psych Film Photog Video_Production Theater
Music. **Supp**—Tut. **Dual enr:** Stanford, U of CA-Berkeley.
Sports—Basket X-country Soccer Swim Tennis Track Volley. B: Baseball Golf Lacrosse.
G: Softball. **Activities:** 40.
Selective adm (Gr K-11): 142/yr. Usual entry: K, 6 & 9. Appl fee: $100. Appl due: Jan.
Tests ISEE SSAT.
Enr 832. B 416. G 416. Elem 492. Sec 340. Wh 52%. Latino 4%. Blk 9%. Asian 16%.
Other 19%. Avg class size: 15. Stud/fac: 9:1. Casual. **Fac 120.** M 38/F 82. FT 110/PT
10. Wh 69%. Latino 6%. Blk 8%. Native Am 1%. Asian 14%. Other 2%. Adv deg:
55%.
Grad '11—85. Col—84. (UCLA 4, USC 4, U of PA 3, Stanford 3, MIT 2, U of CA-Berke-
ley 2). **Avg SAT:** CR 674. M 679. W 701. Avg ACT: 28. **Col couns:** 2. Alum donors:
12%.
Tui '12-'13: Day $22,410-31,475 (+$2000). **Aid:** Need 190 ($2,670,000). Work prgm 30
($15,000).
Summer (enr 800): Gr K-8. Acad Enrich Rev Rec. 3-6 wks.
Endow $16,000,000. Plant val $60,800,000. Acres 14. Bldgs 7 (100% ADA). Class rms
46. Libs 2. Sci labs 6. Lang labs 1. Auds 1. Theaters 1. Art studios 4. Music studios 2.
Dance studios 1. Gyms 1. Fields 2. Pools 1. Comp labs 3. Comp/stud: 1:2.
Est 1887. Nonprofit. Quar (Aug-June). **Assoc** CLS WASC.

Founded in Berkeley as the Anna Head School for Girls, this school relocated in 1964 to
its present campus. The Josiah Royce School for Boys opened at an adjacent site in 1971 as a
coordinate school. Since 1978, Head-Royce has been fully coeducational.

Head-Royce's college preparatory curriculum allows graduates to gain admittance to leading colleges. The cocurricular program is stressed, and there are many interest clubs, publications, and drama, art and music offerings. All boys and girls perform at least 40 hours of

community service prior to graduation. Students may also participate in and earn credits for an academic year abroad program or a student exchange program.

OJAI, CA. (27 mi. E of Santa Barbara, CA; 53 mi. WNW of Los Angeles, CA) Suburban. Pop: 7862. Alt: 750 ft.

BESANT HILL SCHOOL
Bdg and Day — Coed Gr 9-12

Ojai, CA 93024. 8585 Ojai Santa Paula Rd, PO Box 850. Tel: 805-646-4343.
Fax: 805-646-4371.
www.besanthill.org   E-mail: admissions@besanthill.org
Randy Bertin, Head (2011). BS, Univ of New Hampshire, MS, Univ of Massachusetts-Amherst. **Terra R. Furguiel, Adm.**
> **Col Prep. AP (exams req'd)**—Eng Span Calc US_Hist. **Feat**—Fr Environ_Sci Geol Comp_Sci 20th-Century_Hist Psych Comp_Relig Ethics Ceramics Filmmaking Photog Studio_Art Digital_Arts Drama Music_Theory. **Supp**—ESL LD Tut. Outdoor ed.
> **Sports**—Basket X-country Soccer Tennis Volley. G: Lacrosse.
> **Selective adm:** 50/yr. Bdg 40. Day 10. Appl fee: $100. Appl due: Feb. Accepted: 50%. Yield: 50%. **Tests** SSAT TOEFL.
> **Enr 100.** B 55. G 45. Bdg 84. Day 16. Wh 55%. Latino 3%. Blk 5%. Asian 30%. Other 7%. Intl 35%. Avg class size: 10. Stud/fac: 4:1. Casual. **Fac 24.** M 12/F 12. FT 12/PT 12. Wh 93%. Latino 5%. Blk 1%. Asian 1%. Adv deg: 41%. In dorms 8.
> **Grad '11—17. Col—16.** (N AZ, Otis Col of Art & Design, San Francisco Art, UCLA, Bard-NY, U of CA-Irvine). Athl schol 2. **Avg SAT:** CR 479. M 557. W 486. Avg ACT: 25. **Col couns:** 2. Alum donors: 25%.
> **Tui '12-'13: Bdg $44,550** (+$2820). **Day $20,900** (+$2820). **Intl Bdg $44,550** (+$2820-10,000). **Aid:** Need 19 ($450,000).
> **Summer (enr 20):** Acad Enrich Rev. ESL. Tui Bdg $8000. 6 wks.
> Endow $2,000,000. Plant val $50,000,000. Acres 450. Bldgs 9. Dorms 3. Class rms 17. Lib 10,000 vols. Labs 2. Theaters 1. Art studios 3. Music studios 2. Perf arts ctrs 1. Fields 1. Courts 3. Comp/stud: 1:1
> **Est 1946.** Nonprofit. Sem (Sept-June). **Assoc** WASC.

A project of the Happy Valley Foundation, a cultural organization established by political activist Annie Besant for educational purposes, this school occupies a rural campus on a 450-acre tract. After being known for 60 years as the Happy Valley School, Besant Hill assumed its present name, in honor of Dr. Besant, in July 2007.

The varied program provides sound academic preparation, and Besant Hill maintains a community setting that stresses responsibility and mutual consideration. An active fine arts program supplements course work in the core subjects and constitutes an integral part of the school curriculum. Community service work consists of mandatory participation in service learning projects.

OJAI VALLEY SCHOOL
Bdg — Coed Gr 3-12; Day — Coed PS (Age 3)-12

Ojai, CA 93023. 723 El Paseo Rd. Tel: 805-646-1423. Fax: 805-646-0362.
Other locations: 10820 Reeves Rd, Ojai 93023.
www.ovs.org   E-mail: admission@ovs.org
Michael Hall-Mounsey, Pres (2009). BEd, King Alfred's College (England), MA, California Lutheran Univ. **Tracy Wilson, Adm.**
> **Col Prep. AP**—Eng Span Calc Stats Comp_Sci Bio Chem Environ_Sci Psych Studio_

Art. **Feat**—Humanities Geol Econ Law Philos Ceramics Drawing Photog Drama Music_Hist Music_Theory Journ Equitation. **Supp**—ESL Rem_Math Rem_Read Tut.
Sports—Basket X-country Lacrosse Soccer Track Volley. B: Baseball Football Tennis.
Selective adm (Bdg Gr 3-11; Day PS-11): 75/yr. Bdg 48. Day 27. Appl fee: $50. Appl due: Jan. Accepted: 70%. **Tests** ISEE SSAT Stanford TOEFL.
Enr 296. Bdg 116. Day 180. Elem 190. Sec 106. Intl 24%. Avg class size: 13. Stud/fac: 6:1. **Fac 59.** M 23/F 36. FT 56/PT 3. Adv deg: 30%.
Grad '10—40. Col—40. (Marymount Col-CA 3, San Francisco St 2, U of CA-Riverside 2, U of CA-San Diego 2, U of WA 2, Chapman 2). **Mid 50% SAT:** CR 520-580. M 500-650. W 470-610.
Tui '12-'13: Bdg $43,700-47,950 (+$2005). **5-Day Bdg $41,700-43,700** (+$945). **Day $14,900-19,500** (+$945-1175). **Intl Bdg $47,950** (+$2005-11,055).
Summer: Acad Enrich Rev Rem Rec. ESL. Riding. Soccer. 2-6 wks.
Endow $1,000,000. Plant val $7,300,000. Acres 209. Bldgs 26. Dorms 4. Dorm rms 173. Class rms 26. Lib 12,000 vols. Sci labs 3. Lang labs 1. Amphitheaters 1. Comp ctrs 2. Art studios 2. Music studios 1. Shops 1. Fields 5. Courts 7. Pools 2. Riding rings 2. Stables 2. Ropes crses 1.
Est 1911. Nonprofit. Sem (Sept-June). **Assoc** WASC.

Ojai Valley was founded by Mr. and Mrs. Walter Bristol as the Bristol School, which conducted tutorials for elementary students. Edward Yeomans, a businessman interested in education, purchased the school in 1922. Under his direction, the school was renamed Ojai Valley and its program was expanded using Mr. Yeomans' progressive philosophy of "learning by doing." During the tenure of headmaster Wallace Burr (1943 to 1970), the school changed in character from a small country day program to a predominantly boarding school. Mr. Burr also built an upper school campus in the East End of Ojai Valley, and today the school encompasses 200 acres bordering national forest property. The upper school is located on Reeves Road, six miles from the lower school.

Academic work and life experiences are integrated at Ojai, and emphasis is placed on the development of leadership and decision-making skills. Motivated students benefit from the college preparatory curriculum, which includes Advanced Placement classes. Among school activities is an extensive equestrian program. Weekend excursions throughout southern California provide students with entertainment options, as well as cultural and recreational activities.

A five-day boarding option is available to students in grades 3-8, who may also enroll as full boarders.

THE THACHER SCHOOL
Bdg and Day — Coed Gr 9-12

Ojai, CA 93023. 5025 Thacher Rd. Tel: 805-646-4377. **Fax:** 805-646-9490.
www.thacher.org   E-mail: info@thacher.org
Michael K. Mulligan, Head (1993). BA, MA, Middlebury College, EdM, Harvard Univ. **William P. McMahon, Adm.**
Col Prep. AP (300 exams taken, 93% 3+)—Eng Span Calc Stats Comp_Sci Bio Chem Environ_Sci Physics US_Hist Human_Geog Psych Art_Hist Studio_Art Music_Theory. **Feat**—Shakespeare African-Amer_Lit Dante Chin Fr Lat Anat & Physiol Astron Geol Marine_Bio/Sci Civil_War Holocaust Lat-Amer_Hist Econ Pol_Sci Philos Ceramics Photog Drama Chorus Public_Speak. **Supp**—Rev Tut.
Sports—Basket X-country Lacrosse Soccer Tennis Track. B: Baseball Football. G: Volley.
Very selective adm (Gr 9-11): 69/yr. Appl fee: $75. Appl due: Feb. Applied: 500. Accepted: 17%. Yield: 80%. **Tests** ISEE SSAT.
Enr 240. Bdg 220. Day 20. Wh 64%. Latino 11%. Blk 8%. Native Am 1%. Asian 14%. Other 2%. Intl 10%. Avg class size: 11. Stud/fac: 6:1. **Fac 45.** Adv deg: 71%. In dorms 12.
Grad '08—64. Col—64. (Dartmouth 4, U of CO-Boulder 4, Stanford 3, USC 3, Wesleyan

U 3, Tufts 3). **Avg SAT:** CR 662. M 650. W 670. **Col couns:** 2. Alum donors: 50%.
Tui '11-'12: Bdg $45,900 (+$1500). **Day $30,400** (+$1500). **Aid:** Need 72 ($2,004,400).
Endow $100,000,000. Plant val $35,000,000. Acres 425. Bldgs 85. Dorms 9. Dorm rms 167. Class rms 31. Lib 26,000 vols. Chapels 2. Sci labs 3. Lang labs 1. Observatories 1. Auds 1. Theaters 1. Art studios 3. Music studios 2. Gyms 1. Fields 4. Courts 10. Pools 1. Riding facilities. Rifle ranges 1. Comp labs 2.
Est 1889. Nonprofit. Tri (Sept-May). **Assoc** CLS WASC.

The school was founded by Sherman Thacher, who combined the New England boarding school tradition with Western character, emphasizing the value of the outdoors. Thacher is situated on the old Casa de Piedra Ranch: 400 acres nestled at the east end of the Ojai Valley at the foot of the Los Padres National Forest.

The academic program includes a core curriculum of requirements in English, mathematics, foreign language, the sciences, history and the fine arts. Students expand beyond this core through a rich array of electives and Advanced Placement courses, independent study and senior exhibitions (interdisciplinary research and demonstration projects). Several exchange programs provide learning opportunities beyond the school.

Competitive athletics are offered at several levels. Dance and general fitness/weightlifting are also available. All students take part each season in either a team sport, the horse program or the outdoor program, which features such activities as rock and ice climbing, telemarking, downhill and cross-country skiing, winter camping, sea and river kayaking, and snowshoeing. While ninth graders may participate in athletics, their primary afternoon focus is on the horse program, a century-long tradition that requires each student to ride and care for one of Thacher's horses. The first-year experience culminates in the Big Gymkhana—games and races conducted on horseback.

The fine arts program includes musical, studio art, dance and dramatic instruction.

VILLANOVA PREPARATORY SCHOOL
Bdg and Day — Coed Gr 9-12

Ojai, CA 93023. 12096 N Ventura Ave. Tel: 805-646-1464. Fax: 805-646-4430.
www.villanovaprep.org E-mail: admissions@villanovaprep.org
Rev. Gregory Heidenblut, OSA, Pres (2008). BA, St Gregory Seminary, MA, MBA, National Univ (CA), MDiv, Washington Theological Union, MA, Univ of San Diego. **Tyler Hart, Adm.**
Col Prep. AP (exams req'd; 149 taken, 83% 3+)—Eng Lat Span Calc Stats Chem Physics US_Hist World_Hist Psych US_Govt & Pol. **Feat**—Japan Astron Marine_Bio/ Sci Comp_Design Econ Sociol Relig Drawing Film Painting Photog Drama Chorus Speech. **Supp**—ESL Tut.
Sports—Basket X-country Golf Soccer Swim Tennis Track W_Polo. B: Baseball Football. G: Softball Volley. **Activities:** 20.
Selective adm (Gr 9-11): 90/yr. Bdg 30. Day 60. Appl fee: $50-125. Appl due: Jan. Applied: 200. Accepted: 60%. Yield: 66%. **Tests** HSPT SSAT TOEFL.
Enr 274. B 154. G 120. Bdg 96. Day 178. Intl 33%. Avg class size: 16. Stud/fac: 10:1. Casual. **Fac 28.** M 11/F 17. FT 25/PT 3. Wh 78%. Latino 6%. Blk 5%. Asian 4%. Other 7%. Adv deg: 82%.
Grad '11—79. Col—75. (UCLA 7, U of IL-Urbana 4, U of CA-Irvine 3, Pepperdine 3, U of WA 3, U of CA-San Diego 2). **Avg SAT:** CR 553. M 624. W 576. Avg ACT: 25. **Col couns:** 2.
Tui '12-'13: Bdg $45,400. Day $15,800. Intl Bdg $45,400 (+$3000-5000). **Aid:** Merit 22 ($120,924). Need 92 ($645,786).
Summer: Gr 3-8. Rec. 5 wks.
Acres 123. Bldgs 10. Dorms 2. Class rms 19. Libs 1. Sci labs 3. Lang labs 1. Art studios 1. Music studios 1. Gyms 1. Fields 3. Courts 7. Pools 1. Comp labs 3.
Est 1924. Nonprofit. Roman Catholic (42% practice). Sem (Aug-June). **Assoc** WASC.

This college preparatory school remains the only Augustinian Catholic boarding and day school in the United States. After operating as a boys' school for nearly 50 years, Villanova Prep first admitted girls in 1970, partly to offset a decrease in enrollment caused by the proliferation of Catholic high schools built in the region during the 1950s and 1960s. In 1987, the administration of the school changed to reflect the lower number of Augustinians available for school governance; since then, lay heads of school have guided Villanova.

Enrolling day students from Ventura and Santa Barbara counties, as well as boarders from throughout the US and approximately 10 other countries, Villanova conducts a varied college preparatory program that includes honors courses in all disciplines (beginning in grade 10), AP classes, foreign languages and electives. Taught entirely in English, ESL classes serve international pupils lacking fluency in the language.

Community service requirements are as follows: 10 hours in grade 9 and 20 hours per year in grades 10-12 (at least five of which must involve direct service).

ORANGE, CA. (40 mi. ESE of Los Angeles, CA) Urban. Pop: 128,821. Alt: 176 ft.

ELDORADO EMERSON SCHOOL
Day — Coed Gr PS (Age 2)-12

Orange, CA 92869. 4100 E Walnut Ave. Tel: 714-633-4774. Fax: 714-744-3304.
www.eldoradoemerson.org
Glory B. Ludwick, Dir (1958). AB, Univ of California-Berkeley, MD, Univ of California-San Francisco.
    Col Prep. AP—Eng Span Calc Bio. **Feat**—Fr Japan Arabic Programming Drama Chorus Music Orchestra Fitness & Nutrition. **Supp**—Dev_Read ESL Rem_Math Rem_Read Tut.
    Sports—X-country Soccer.
    Selective adm: 31/yr. Appl due: Rolling. Accepted: 75%. Yield: 100%. **Tests** Stanford TOEFL.
    Enr 180. B 99. G 81. Elem 125. Sec 55. Intl 30%. Avg class size: 15. **Fac 27.** M 7/F 20. FT 27.
    Grad '08—14. Col—12. (U of CA, CA St U-Fullerton, Chapman, USC, NYU, Fashion Inst of Design). **Avg SAT:** CR/M 1300.
    Tui '09-'10: Day $9440-12,640 (+$900-1100).
    Summer: Acad Enrich Rev Rem. Tui Day $1000. 4½ wks.
    Plant val $5,000,000. Acres 5. Bldgs 10. Class rms 25. Lib 25,000 vols. Sci labs 1. Lang labs 2. Theater/auds 1. Art studios 2. Music studios 3. Dance studios 1. Art galleries 3. Gyms 1. Fields 1. Courts 2. Pools 2. Comp labs 1.
    Est 1958. Nonprofit. Sem (Sept-July). **Assoc** WASC.

Eldorado Emerson provides instruction for elementary students in ungraded achievement groups. The curriculum comprises English, math, computer, foreign languages, science, social studies, physical education, music and art. High school students choose from a variety of honors and Advanced Placement courses, and they may earn college credit in several disciplines. The music program includes orchestral and choral instruction. Spanish instruction begins in kindergarten, and in grade 5 students choose to continue studying that language or pursue French or Japanese.

Drama, martial arts and strength training are among Eldorado Emerson's extracurricular options. Home stay accommodations and an ESL program are available for international students.

PALO ALTO, CA. (17 mi. WNW of San Jose, CA; 35 mi. SE of San Francisco, CA) Urban. Pop: 58,598. Alt: 63 ft. Area also includes Portola Valley.

CASTILLEJA SCHOOL
Day — Girls Gr 6-12

Palo Alto, CA 94301. 1310 Bryant St. Tel: 650-328-3160. Fax: 650-326-8036.
www.castilleja.org   E-mail: admission@castilleja.org
Nanci Z. Kauffman, Head (2010). AB, Vassar College, MA, Columbia Univ. Jill V. W. Lee, Adm.
  Col Prep. AP (281 exams taken, 93% 3+)—Eng Fr Lat Span Calc Stats Bio Chem Physics Eur_Hist US_Hist Studio_Art. **Feat**—British_Lit Creative_Writing Poetry Shakespeare Short_Fiction Chin Ital Astron Marine_Bio/Sci Physiol Biotech Programming Russ_Hist Econ Intl_Relations Pol_Sci African_Stud Philos Art_Hist Drawing Film Photog Sculpt Acting Chorus Music_Hist Dance.
  Sports—G: Basket X-country Golf Lacrosse Soccer Softball Swim Tennis Track Volley W_Polo. **Activities:** 50.
  Very selective adm (Gr 6-11): 81/yr. Usual entry: 6 & 9. Appl fee: $75. Appl due: Jan. Applied: 386. Accepted: 25%. Yield: 82%. **Tests** ISEE SSAT.
  Enr 425. Elem 192. Sec 233. Wh 57%. Latino 8%. Blk 4%. Asian 27%. Other 4%. Avg class size: 15. Stud/fac: 6:1. Uniform. **Fac 60.** M 10/F 50. FT 55/PT 5. Adv deg: 85%.
  Grad '11—63. Col—63. (Stanford 11, Princeton 4, Bucknell 4, Harvard 2, Dartmouth 2, Pomona 2). **Mid 50% SAT:** CR 670-770. M 640-740. W 700-780. Mid 50% ACT: 29-32. **Col couns:** 1.
  Tui '12-'13: Day $36,750 (+$705-3055). **Aid:** Need 79 ($1,800,000).
  Summer: Gr 2-6. Rec. Tui Day $950/2-wk ses. 8 wks.
  Endow $41,000,000. Plant val $62,000,000. Acres 5. Bldgs 7. Lib 12,000 vols. Sci labs 6. Lang labs 1. Theaters 1. Art studios 2. Music studios 2. Dance studios 1. Art galleries 1. Gyms 2. Fields 1. Pools 1. Comp labs 3. Comp/stud: 1:1.3 (1:1 Laptop prgm Gr 6-12).
  Est 1907. Nonprofit. Sem (Aug-June). **Assoc** CLS WASC.

Castilleja was founded by Stanford graduate Mary Ishbel Lockey, who was encouraged by David Starr Jordan, the university's first president, to establish a school that would provide girls with a comprehensive educational program.

The college preparatory curriculum combines individual and collaborative learning opportunities. Girls have access to a varied course selection that includes advanced classes and independent study options. Students fulfill course requirements in a strong visual and performing arts department. A global perspective permeates the curriculum throughout the year, and each January the school devotes a week to an in-depth examination of global issues through speakers, workshops, readings, films and panel discussions.

An array of clubs and activities complements academics. Competitive athletics begin in the middle school, which follows a no-cut policy. Community service is an integral part of school life, with Castilleja strongly encouraging all girls to participate in service projects.

INTERNATIONAL SCHOOL OF THE PENINSULA
Day — Coed Gr PS (Age 2)-8

Palo Alto, CA 94303. 151 Laura Ln. Tel: 650-251-8500. Fax: 650-251-8501.
Other locations: 3233 Cowper St, Palo Alto 94306.
  www.istp.org   E-mail: admissions@istp.org
Philippe Dietz, Head (2004). Maile Uohara, Adm.
  Pre-Prep. Bilingual (Chin Fr). **Feat**—Humanities Chin Fr Span Computers Studio_Art Music. **Supp**—ESL Rem_Math Rem_Read Rev Tut.
  Selective adm: 114/yr. Usual entry: PS. Appl fee: $100. Appl due: Jan. Applied: 225. Accepted: 80%. Yield: 69%. **Tests** CTP_4 SSAT.

Enr 585. B 276. G 309. Wh 43%. Latino 1%. Blk 1%. Asian 29%. Other 26%. Intl 46%. Avg class size: 22. **Fac 93.** M 15/F 78. FT 89/PT 4. Wh 76%. Latino 2%. Asian 22%. Adv deg: 48%.
Grad '11—19. Prep—8. (Intl HS 3, St Francis HS-CA 2, Bellarmine 1, Sacred Heart HS-CA 1, King's Acad-CA 1). Avg SSAT: 90%.
Tui '12-'13: Day $22,100-23,050 (+$650-975). **Aid:** Need 78 ($650,000).
Summer: Enrich Rec. Fr. Chin. Tui Day $730/2-wk ses. 6 wks.
Endow $2,100,000. Plant val $10,000,000. Acres 5. Bldgs 2 (100% ADA). Class rms 30. 3 Libs 12,000 vols. Sci labs 1. Studios 1. Gyms 1. Fields 1. Courts 2. Comp labs 1. Laptop prgm Gr 6-8.
Est 1979. Nonprofit. Tri (Sept-June). **Assoc** WASC.

ISTP opened its doors as the Peninsula French-American School and, in 1996, became the International School of the Peninsula, adding a Chinese-American section, a middle school and a second campus. Providing immersion-based bilingual and multicultural education, the lower campus on Cowper Street serves children in nursery through kindergarten, while the main campus on Laura Lane offers instruction for pupils in grades 1-8.

The school maintains two language-immersion programs that serve children in nursery school through grade 5: Mandarin Chinese/English and French/English. To gain entry into either program at the elementary school level, students must be proficient in the target language. Those without experience in Chinese or French may enroll only at the nursery, prekindergarten or kindergarten levels. Pupils in the Chinese section spend 50 percent of their time immersed in Chinese, while students in the French program devote 70 to 80 percent of their time to French immersion.

ISTP's middle school program joins boys and girls from both immersion programs for classes that are conducted in English, then separates the respective groups for courses that employ Mandarin or French as the language of instruction. ISTP's middle school addresses the needs of students planning to attend an American public or private high school, as well as those wishing to enroll in a French or international institution.

In addition to language and cultural immersion, the school conducts strong technology, arts and music programs. Boys and girls may also engage in cultural exchange trips to such countries as France, China and Costa Rica.

WOODSIDE PRIORY SCHOOL
Bdg — Coed Gr 9-12; Day — Coed 6-12

Portola Valley, CA 94028. 302 Portola Rd. Tel: 650-851-8223. Fax: 650-851-2839.
    www.prioryca.com   E-mail: prioryadmissions@yahoo.com
Timothy Molak, Head (1999). BA, Christian Brothers Univ, MA, St Mary's Univ, MAEd, St Thomas Univ. **Al D. Zappelli, Adm.**
Col Prep. AP (exams req'd; 252 taken, 85% 3+)—Eng Fr Japan Span Calc Stats Comp_Sci Bio Chem Environ_Sci Physics US_Hist Econ Human_Geog Psych US_Govt & Pol Art_Hist Studio_Art Music_Theory. **Feat**—Creative_Writing Chin Anat & Physiol Astron Bioethics Marine_Bio/Sci Oceanog Sports_Med Lat-Amer_Hist Anthro Criminology Philos Relig Architect Ceramics Film Photog Drama Theater_ Arts Dance Journ Speech. **Supp**—Tut.
Sports—X-country Swim Tennis Track. B: Baseball Basket Golf W_Polo. G: Soccer Softball Volley. **Activities:** 22.
Selective adm (Bdg Gr 9-11; Day 6-11): 107/yr. Bdg 19. Day 88. Usual entry: 6, 9 & 10. Appl fee: $75. Appl due: Jan. Applied: 420. Accepted: 51%. Yield: 52%. **Tests** HSPT ISEE SSAT TOEFL.
Enr 371. B 206. G 165. Bdg 46. Day 325. Elem 101. Sec 270. Wh 73%. Latino 7%. Blk 2%. Native Am 1%. Asian 5%. Other 12%. Intl 11%. Avg class size: 18. Stud/fac: 9:1. Casual. **Fac 73.** M 43/F 30. FT 73. Adv deg: 71%. In dorms 7.
Grad '09—69. Col—69. (U of CA-Davis 5, U of CA-Santa Barbara 4, U of CA-Berkeley 2, Boston Col 2, Stanford 2, Yale 1). Athl schol 3. **Avg SAT:** CR 610. M 621. W 613. Avg ACT: 28. **Col couns:** 2. Alum donors: 9%.

Tui '12-'13: Bdg $49,500 (+$1600). **Day $34,250** (+$700). **Aid:** Need 79 ($1,693,030). Endow $10,000,000. Acres 50. Bldgs 15. Dorms 2. 2 Libs 20,000 vols. Chapels 1. Sci labs 5. Lang labs 3. Auds 1. Theaters 1. Art studios 1. Music studios 1. Dance studios 1. Gyms 1. Fields 4. Tennis courts 4. Pools 1. Comp labs 2. **Est 1957.** Nonprofit. Roman Catholic (35% practice). Sem (Aug-June). **Assoc** WASC.

Begun by a group of Benedictine monks, Priory operated as a boys' boarding and day school until 1991, when girls were first admitted as day students. In fall 2003, the school expanded its boarding program to include girls. Faculty direct a rigorous academic program supplemented with athletics, the fine arts, community service and a strong program of cocurricular activities.

Students receive a solid academic grounding in English, science, math, social studies, the fine and performing arts, and foreign language. A broad range of elective, honors and Advanced Placement classes supplements the curriculum. Approved students may pursue directed individual study, and specially gifted students may arrange to take college-level courses. Among the graduation requirements are foreign language, computer science, theology, the fine and performing arts, and electives. In addition, freshmen, sophomores and juniors perform 10 hours of compulsory community service each year, while seniors complete a service-oriented project.

PASADENA, CA. (16 mi. ENE of Los Angeles, CA) Urban. Pop: 133,936. Alt: 829 ft. Area also includes La Canada Flintridge. See also Los Angeles.

FLINTRIDGE PREPARATORY SCHOOL

Day — Coed Gr 7-12

La Canada Flintridge, CA 91011. 4543 Crown Ave. Tel: 818-790-1178. Fax: 818-952-6247.
www.flintridgeprep.org   **E-mail: admissions@flintridgeprep.org**
Peter H. Bachmann, Head (1991). AB, Univ of California-Berkeley, MA, Univ of Virginia. **G. Arthur Stetson, Adm.**

Col Prep. AP (591 exams taken, 93% 3+)—Fr Lat Span Calc Stats Comp_Sci Physics US_Hist US_Govt & Pol Art_Hist Studio_Art Music_Theory. **Feat**—British_Lit Shakespeare Anat & Physiol Sports_Med Econ Intl_Relations Psych Chin_Stud Ceramics Drawing Photog Drama Theater_Arts Chorus Music Dance Debate. **Supp**—Rev Tut. Outdoor ed.

Sports—Basket X-country Equestrian Soccer Swim Tennis Track Volley W_Polo. B: Baseball Football Golf. G: Softball. **Activities:** 43.

Selective adm (Gr 7-11): 105/yr. Usual entry: 7 & 9. Appl fee: $85. Appl due: Jan. **Tests** ISEE.

Enr 506. B 242. G 264. Elem 110. Sec 396. Avg class size: 13. Casual. **Fac 66.** Adv deg: 65%.

Grad '11—104. Col—104. (USC, U of CA-Berkeley, Cornell, Tufts, U of CA-Santa Barbara, UCLA). **Mid 50% SAT:** CR 630-730. M 630-740. W 660-750. **Col couns:** 3.

Tui '12-'13: Day $27,200-27,800 (+$1000-1640).

Summer: Acad Enrich. Sports. 1-6 wks.

Endow $12,000,000. Plant val $10,000,000. Acres 8. Bldgs 12. Class rms 35. Lib 20,000 vols. Photog labs 1. Auds 1. Theaters 1. Music studios 1. Dance studios 1. Perf arts ctrs 1. Gyms 1. Fields 1. Courts 2. Pools 1. Weight rms 1. Comp labs 3. Comp/stud: 1:10.

Est 1933. Nonprofit. Sem (Sept-May). **Assoc** CLS WASC.

Founded as Flintridge School for Boys and originally serving a student body of 22, the school occupies an eight-acre site at the base of the San Gabriel Mountains. Girls were first admitted in 1979, at which time the school assumed its current name.

Boys and girls in grades 7 and 8 receive a thorough grounding in study techniques; reading, writing and oral communication; and critical thinking. Flintridge Prep assigns each seventh grader with a peer counselor early in the school year, and a trip in the fall enables students to become better acquainted with their classmates. Eighth graders, who also have a mentor, continue to develop fundamental learning skills. In grade 8, math and foreign language courses are at the high school level.

During the upper school years (grades 9-12), academic demands gradually increase. Sophomores gain their first exposure to standardized testing, college counseling, and such school-wide responsibilities as fundraising and event planning. All twelfth graders participate in Senior Initiative, which involves peer tutoring, peer counseling, service as Senior Buddies to eighth graders, or the pursuit of academic or artistic independent study. Toward the end of senior year, recent graduates, college educators and community professionals come to campus to share their insights on college life and career opportunities.

Students engage in community service at all grade levels. Upper schoolers fulfill the following requirements: seven hours in grade 9, 10 hours annually in grades 10 and 11, and 24 hours off campus with a single agency in grade 12.

POLYTECHNIC SCHOOL
Day — Coed Gr K-12

Pasadena, CA 91106. 1030 E California Blvd. Tel: 626-392-6300. Fax: 626-796-2249.
www.polytechnic.org E-mail: admissions@polytechnic.org
Deborah E. Reed, Head (2002). BA, Univ of Massachusetts-Amherst. Sally Jeanne McKenna, Adm.

Col Prep. AP (exams req'd; 588 taken, 95% 3+)—Eng Fr Lat Span Calc Bio Chem Physics US_Hist Studio_Art. Elem math—Singapore Math. Feat—Creative_Writing Stats Anat & Physiol Astron Environ_Sci Forensic_Sci Engineering Comp_Sci Vietnam_War Econ Intl_Relations Psych Ethics World_Relig Art_Hist Ceramics Drawing Film Fine_Arts Painting Photog Sculpt African_Art Enameling Acting Theater_Arts Chorus Music_Theory Orchestra Jazz_Ensemble Dance Woodworking Outdoor_Ed. Supp—Tut. Outdoor ed.

Sports—Badminton Basket X-country Fencing Soccer Swim Tennis Track Volley W_ Polo. B: Baseball Football Golf. G: Equestrian Softball. Activities: 45.

Very selective adm: 117/yr. Usual entry: K, 6, 7 & 9. Appl fee: $100. Applied: 743. Accepted: 18%. Tests ISEE.

Enr 861. Avg class size: 17. Fac 100. M 31/F 69. FT 88/PT 12. Adv deg: 56%.

Grad '11—91. Col—92. (U of CA-Berkeley 7, Duke 5, Stanford 4, USC 4, UCLA 4, U of CO-Boulder 4. Col couns: 4. Alum donors: 21%.

Tui '12-'13: Day $22,420-30,180 (+$400-800). Aid: Need 176 ($2,930,610).

Summer (enr 400): Acad Enrich Rev. Tui Day $200/3-wk ses. 6 wks.

Endow $50,000,000. Acres 15. Bldgs 27. Class rms 80. 2 Libs 44,000 vols. Labs 5. Auds 2. Theaters 2. Art studios 5. Music studios 3. Dance studios 1. Arts ctrs 1. Gyms 2. Fields 1. Pools 1. Comp/stud: 1:2.

Est 1907. Nonprofit. Quar (Sept-June). Assoc CLS WASC.

Poly was the first elementary school in California to be incorporated as a nonprofit institution and is today one of the larger independent schools in the state. Like its neighbor, the California Institute of Technology, the school evolved from the Throop Polytechnic Institute, which had offered since its 1891 establishment an academic program extending from the primary grades through college. A road divides Poly's 15-acre campus, separating the upper school classrooms to the south from the lower and middle school classrooms to the north.

Poly offers a broad educational program that includes Advanced Placement and honors classes, performing and visual arts offerings, and an electives program in the upper grades. The school's outdoor education program features off-campus trips to various wilderness areas in the West. All students participate in community service: Younger pupils engage in project work, while upper schoolers meet formal requirements of eight service hours in grade 9 and

Leading Private Schools

the completion of a 30-hour service project during sophomore or junior year. Exchange opportunities are available through the American Field Service.

WESTRIDGE SCHOOL

Day — Girls Gr 4-12

Pasadena, CA 91105. 324 Madeline Dr. Tel: 626-799-1153. Fax: 626-799-9236.
www.westridge.org E-mail: admissions@westridge.org
Elizabeth J. McGregor, Head (2009). MEd, Columbia Univ. **Helen Varlas Hopper, Adm.**
Col Prep. AP (exams req'd; 291 taken, 87% 3+)—Eng Fr Lat Span Calc Stats Comp_ Sci Bio Chem Environ_Sci Physics Eur_Hist US_Hist Art_Hist Studio_Art. **Feat**— Creative_Writing Shakespeare Chin Ecol Physiol Molecular_Bio Middle_Eastern_ Hist Psych Comp_Relig Photog Theater Music Music_Hist Music_Theory Dance. **Supp**—Tut.
Sports (req'd)—G: Basket X-country Golf Lacrosse Soccer Softball Swim Tennis Track Volley W_Polo. **Activities:** 60.
Selective adm (Gr 4-11): 83/yr. Usual entry: 4, 7 & 9. Appl fee: $85. Appl due: Feb. Applied: 229. Accepted: 59%. Yield: 62%. **Tests** ISEE.
Enr 487. Elem 208. Sec 279. Wh 41%. Latino 7%. Blk 5%. Asian 20%. Other 27%. Avg class size: 16. Stud/fac: 8:1. Uniform. **Fac 58.** M 14/F 44. FT 56/PT 2. Wh 75%. Latino 9%. Blk 3%. Asian 10%. Other 3%. Adv deg: 68%.
Grad '11—65. Col—65. (USC 7, U of CA-Santa Barbara 3, Carnegie Mellon 2, Emerson 2, NYU 2, U of PA 2). **Mid 50% SAT:** CR 620-700. M 600-690. W 650-750. Mid 50% ACT: 25-29. **Col couns:** 2. Alum donors: 21%.
Tui '12-'13: Day $25,550-30,600 (+$725-1725). **Aid:** Need 150 ($2,583,450).
Summer (enr 60): Performing Arts. Tui Day $790-1590. 5 wks.
Endow $16,243,000. Plant val $33,353,000. Acres 10. Bldgs 18 (88% ADA). Class rms 48. Lib 16,189 vols. Sci labs 8. Auds 1. Theaters 1. Art studios 4. Music studios 2. Dance studios 1. Gyms 1. Fields 1. Comp labs 2. Comp/stud: 1:1
Est 1913. Nonprofit. Sem (Sept-June). **Assoc** CLS WASC.

Westridge was founded when two mothers concerned that there was no school for their daughters on Pasadena's west side convinced noted area architect Mary Lowther Ranney to open a girls' school in her home. From the start, enrollment exceeded expectations, leading Miss Ranney to purchase a larger home on Madeline Drive and move the school to the Tudor building that now serves as the campus centerpiece. Upon Miss Ranney's retirement in 1936, a group of parents purchased the school and chartered it as a nonprofit institution with a board of trustees.

The structured lower school curriculum (grades 4-6) emphasizes independent learning and the development of sound study skills. Westridge's middle school (grades 7 and 8) provides a transitional program that readies girls for more intensive course work in the higher grades. Students choose from an array of honors and Advanced Placement courses in the upper school (grades 9-12), while also taking part in performing arts activities, athletics and experiential education. Field trips to various points of interest provide enrichment.

Girls perform 40 hours of community service during their high school years, at least 20 of which must be completed with the same agency or in the same area of concern. Participation in the athletic program is also compulsory.

PEBBLE BEACH, CA. (57 mi. S of San Jose, CA; 101 mi. SSE of San Francisco, CA) Suburban. Pop: 4700.

STEVENSON SCHOOL
Bdg — Coed Gr 9-12; Day — Coed PS (Age 4)-12

Pebble Beach, CA 93953. 3152 Forest Lake Rd. Tel: 831-625-8300. Fax: 831-625-5208. Other locations: 24800 Dolores St, Carmel 93923.
www.stevensonschool.org   E-mail: info@stevensonschool.org
Joseph E. Wandke, Pres (1983). BA, St Olaf College, MA, Stanford Univ. **Thomas W. Sheppard, Adm.**
Col Prep. AP—Eng Fr Lat Span Calc Bio Chem Environ_Sci Physics Eur_Hist US_Hist Econ Studio_Art Music_Theory. **Feat**—Poetry Shakespeare Irish_Lit Mythology Sci_ Fiction Japan Multivariable_Calc Marine_Bio/Sci Sports_Med Biochem Ornithology Comp_Sci Middle_Eastern_Hist Psych Ethics World_Relig Architect Ceramics Film Photog Radio Acting Drama Jazz_Band Dance Journ Outdoor_Ed. Outdoor ed.
Sports—Basket X-country Golf Lacrosse Sail Soccer Swim Tennis Track W_Polo. B: Baseball Football. G: F_Hockey Softball Volley. **Activities:** 65.
Selective adm (Bdg Gr 9-11; Day PS-11): 194/yr. Bdg 82. Day 112. Usual entry: 9. Appl fee: $75. Appl due: Feb. Applied: 182. Accepted: 41%. Yield: 60%. **Tests** SSAT TOEFL.
Enr 730. B 377. G 353. Bdg 270. Day 460. Elem 199. Sec 531. Wh 68%. Latino 2%. Blk 2%. Native Am 1%. Asian 16%. Other 11%. Intl 14%. Avg class size: 14. Stud/fac: 10:1. Casual. **Fac 62.** M 44/F 18. FT 61/PT 1. Wh 95%. Latino 1%. Blk 2%. Asian 2%. Adv deg: 64%. In dorms 19.
Grad '11—148. Col—148. (NYU 13, U of CA-Berkeley 5, USC 5, U of CO-Boulder 5, Loyola Marymount 4, Boston U 4). Athl schol 4. **Avg SAT:** CR 630. M 625. W 617. **Col couns:** 3.
Tui '12-'13: Bdg $51,900 (+$2000). **Day $16,600-31,600** (+$2000). **Aid:** Need 141 ($2,750,000).
Summer: Enrich Rec. Tui Bdg $5500. Tui Day $2500. 5 wks.
Endow $20,000,000. Plant val $55,000,000. Acres 60. Bldgs 37. Dorms 6. Dorm rms 171. Class rms 41. Lib 17,000 vols. Labs 7. Theaters 1. Art studios 2. Dance studios 2. Gyms 1. Fields 3. Courts 8. Pools 1. Student ctrs 1. Laptop prgm Gr 6-12.
Est 1952. Nonprofit. Tri (Sept-May). **Assoc** CLS WASC.

Stevenson offers a rigorous college preparatory liberal arts program. The traditional curriculum emphasizes trust and self-reliance. Basic skills courses are supplemented by opportunities for exploring special interests in depth. Boys and girls choose from beginning and advanced courses in all of the fine arts. Subjects such as studio art, ceramics, photography, stagecraft, acting and voice are available. Students in grades 6-12 use required laptop computers in class.

A broad range of athletic programs and several student exchange programs complement academics. The school is located in the Del Monte Forest and shares in the climatic and scenic advantages of the Monterey Peninsula. The lower and middle school campus occupies a separate campus in nearby Carmel.

REDLANDS, CA. (71 mi. E of Los Angeles, CA) Urban. Pop: 63,591. Alt: 1351 ft.

VALLEY PREPARATORY SCHOOL
Day — Coed Gr PS (Age 3)-8

Redlands, CA 92373. 1605 Ford St. Tel: 909-793-3063. Fax: 909-798-5963.
www.valleyp) predlands.org   E-mail: info@vpredlands.org

Roy Cencirulo, Head (2011). BA, MA, Univ of Redlands, EdD, La Sierra Univ. **Karen Johnson, Adm.**
Pre-Prep. Gen Acad. Feat—Lib_Skills Fr Span Computers Studio_Art Drama Music. **Supp**—Tut.
Sports—Basket Track. G: Volley.
Somewhat selective adm: 45/yr. Appl fee: $100. Appl due: Rolling. Accepted: 90%. **Tests** CTP_4.
Enr 170. Wh 50%. Latino 7%. Blk 3%. Native Am 3%. Asian 20%. Other 17%. Avg class size: 12. Stud/fac: 9:1. Uniform. **Fac 23.** M 3/F 20. FT 23. Wh 87%. Latino 7%. Blk 1%. Native Am 2%. Asian 3%. Adv deg: 47%.
Grad '11—18. Prep—3. (Cate, Aquinas HS-CA, Arrowhead Christian,]).
Tui '11-'12: Day $8950-10,600 (+$200). **Aid:** Merit 4 ($6000). Need 11 ($82,000).
Summer (enr 245): Acad Enrich Rev Rem Rec. Tui Day $115. 2 wks.
Endow $250,000. Plant val $2,500,000. Bldgs 7. Class rms 25. Libs 1. Sci labs 1. Art studios 1. Music studios 1. Fields 1. Comp labs 1. Comp/stud: 1:2 (1:1 Laptop prgm Gr 2-8).
Est 1957. Nonprofit. Sem (Aug-June). **Assoc** WASC.

Founded by a group of parents, VPS provides a traditional elementary program for average and above-average students living in Redlands and the surrounding areas. Self-contained classrooms in the lower school (grades PS-5) are enriched by a variety of cocurricular offerings taught by specialists. The middle school (grades 6-8) is departmentally organized to accommodate the academic and social needs of students with the ability and motivation to participate in a pre-collegiate curriculum. Foreign language instruction in French and Spanish begins in preschool.

VPS' extended-day program features cooking, crafts and physical education.

ROSS, CA. (12 mi. N of San Francisco, CA) Rural. Pop: 2329. Alt: 23 ft.

THE BRANSON SCHOOL
Day — Coed Gr 9-12

Ross, CA 94957. 39 Fernhill Ave, PO Box 887. Tel: 415-454-3612. Fax: 415-454-4669.
www.branson.org E-mail: annie_tsang@branson.org
Thomas W. Price, Head (2007). BA, Lake Forest College, MA, Columbia Univ, EdD, Univ of Pennsylvania. **Annie Tsang, Adm.**
Col Prep. AP (exams req'd)—Fr Lat Span Calc Stats Chem Physics US_Hist World_Hist Art_Hist. **Feat**—Shakespeare African-Amer_Lit Chin Ital Marine_Bio/Sci Biotech Comp_Design Programming Cold_War Middle_Eastern_Hist Modern_Chin_Hist Econ Psych Comp_Relig Philos Architect Ceramics Photog Acting Music Music_Theory Study_Skills.
Sports—Basket X-country Fencing Golf Sail Soccer Swim Tennis Track. B: Baseball Lacrosse. G: Softball Volley. **Activities:** 33.
Selective adm: 79/yr. Appl fee: $100. Appl due: Jan. Accepted: 28%. Yield: 63%. **Tests** ISEE SSAT.
Enr 319. B 140. G 179. Wh 80%. Latino 3%. Blk 6%. Native Am 1%. Asian 7%. Other 3%. Avg class size: 13. Stud/fac: 8:1. **Fac 49.** M 24/F 25. FT 40/PT 9. Wh 84%. Latino 6%. Blk 4%. Asian 6%. Adv deg: 51%.
Grad '11—80. Col—80. (Stanford 5, Dartmouth 4, NYU 4, U of PA 3, USC 3, Princeton 2). **Avg SAT:** CR 655. M 630. W 670. **Col couns:** 2. Alum donors: 14%.
Tui '12-'13: Day $36,225 (+$2000). **Aid:** Need 66 ($1,357,000).
Summer: Acad Rec. SAT Prep. Sports. Tui Day $325-1600. 1-6 wks.
Endow $1,500,000. Plant val $4,100,000. Acres 18. Bldgs 31. Lib 12,000 vols. Sci labs 5. Lang labs 1. Photog labs 1. Amphitheaters 1. Auds 1. Theaters 3. Art studios 7. Music studios 2. Drama studios 1. Art galleries 1. Gyms 2. Athletic ctrs 1. Fields 1. Basketball courts 2. Pools 1. Weight rms 1.

Est 1920. Nonprofit. Tri (Sept-June). **Assoc** CLS WASC.

In 1920, Katharine F. Branson reorganized the Little Gray School, established in 1917 in San Rafael, California. Renamed the Katherine Branson School, in 1922 the school moved to its present location in Ross. KBS trustees in 1972 established Mount Tamalpais School, a coordinate day program for boys on the KBS campus, and in 1985 the schools were united under the name The Branson School. The campus is located on 18 wooded acres, 15 miles north of San Francisco. The college preparatory curriculum offers Advanced Placement and other rigorous courses, a wide selection of termlong electives, fine arts programs, independent study and a five-week work-study intern program for all seniors. Educational technology includes wireless Internet access across campus and multimedia projection systems in every classroom. Boys and girls perform 15 hours of required computer service in grade 9, 25 hours per year in grades 10-12.

SACRAMENTO, CA. (80 mi. NE of San Francisco, CA) Urban. Pop: 407,018. Alt: 30 ft. Area also includes Fair Oaks.

SACRAMENTO COUNTRY DAY SCHOOL

Day — Coed Gr PS (Age 4)-12

Sacramento, CA 95864. 2636 Latham Dr. Tel: 916-481-8811. Fax: 916-481-6016.
www.saccds.org   E-mail: lbloedau@saccds.org
Stephen T. Repsher, Head (2003). BA, Union College (NY), MA, New York Univ. **Lonna Bloedau, Adm.**
   Col Prep. AP (156 exams taken, 81% 3+)—Eng Fr Lat Span Calc Bio Chem Physics Eur_Hist US_Hist Econ Art_Hist Studio_Art. **Elem math**—Everyday Math.
   Feat—Creative_Writing Great_Books Playwriting Japan Anat & Physiol Comp_Sci Robotics Ceramics Drawing Drama Orchestra Jazz_Band Public_Speak Nutrition. **Supp**—Tut.
   Sports—Basket X-country Golf Ski Soccer Swim Tennis Track. B: Lacrosse Wrestling. G: Softball Volley.
   Selective adm (Gr PS-11): 71/yr. Appl fee: $25. Appl due: Rolling. Applied: 137. Accepted: 76%. Yield: 85%.
   Enr 479. Elem 345. Sec 134. Wh 63%. Latino 6%. Blk 6%. Asian 9%. Other 16%. Avg class size: 15. Stud/fac: 8:1. **Fac 64.** Adv deg: 59%.
   Grad '11—37. **Col**—37. (Occidental, U of CA-San Diego, Columbia, Duke, Geo Wash, Reed). **Avg SAT:** CR 622. M 619. W 638. **Col couns:** 2.
   Tui '12-'13: Day $16,970-20,960 (+$25-1000). **Aid:** Need ($1,400,000).
   Summer: Acad Enrich Rev Rec. Sports. Tui Day $225-450. 1-2 wks.
   Acres 11. Bldgs 20. Class rms 36. 2 Libs 15,000 vols. Sci labs 4. Art studios 1. Music studios 1. Gyms 1. Fields 4. Weight rms 1. Comp labs 2. Comp/stud: 1:1.6.
   Est 1964. Nonprofit. Sem (Sept-June). **Assoc** CLS WASC.

Established by Herbert H. Matthews, SCDS has grown steadily since its founding. Students in grades 7-12 participate in an enrichment program that offers courses in art, drama, debate, journalism, computers, music, yearbook and poetry. During the high school years, boys and girls accumulate 50 hours of required community service.

SACRAMENTO WALDORF SCHOOL

Day — Coed Gr PS (Age 4)-12

Fair Oaks, CA 95628. 3750 Bannister Rd. Tel: 916-961-3900. Fax: 916-961-3970.
www.sacwaldorf.org   E-mail: info@sacwaldorf.org
Elizabeth Beaven, Admin. BA, MA, Univ of Auckland (New Zealand). **Clare Andrews,**

Adm.
Col Prep. Waldorf. Feat—Ger Span Ecol Studio_Art Drama Music Dance Eurythmy Gardening. **Supp**—Makeup Rem_Math Tut.
Sports—Basket Golf Soccer. B: Baseball. G: Volley. **Activities:** 23.
Selective adm: 63/yr. Appl fee: $50. Appl due: Jan. Accepted: 82%.
Enr 400. Avg class size: 22. **Fac 56.** M 18/F 38. FT 35/PT 21. Adv deg: 23%.
Grad '08—24. Col—20. (Stanford, U of CA-Berkeley, Occidental, Lewis & Clark, Clark U). **Avg SAT:** CR 639. M 576. W 627.
Tui '12-'13: Day $9350-14,150 (+$250-550).
Summer: Rec. Tui Day $350/2-wk ses. 6 wks.
Endow $294,000. Plant val $4,000,000. Acres 22. Bldgs 16. Class rms 25. Lib 2500 vols. Labs 2. Auds 1. Theaters 1. Art studios 5. Music studios 2. Gyms 2. Fields 3. Climbing walls 1.
Est 1959. Nonprofit. Sem (Sept-June). **Assoc** WASC.

Through its artistic approach to education, the basis of the Waldorf philosophy, the school provides a firm foundation in the arts, the humanities and the sciences. With main lessons studied in blocks for several weeks at a time, objective scientific subjects are alternated with the humanities to give variety and rhythm to the school year.

In grades 1-8, a teacher remains with his or her class as it advances each year, thereby giving each child security and confidence while deepening the teacher's responsibility for and knowledge of the pupil. Specialist teachers provide instruction in grades 9-12. Foreign language instruction commences in grade 1, when both German and Spanish are introduced.

Students often attend Waldorf or other specialty schools in Europe, particularly Germany, for a quarter or semester. Sacramento Waldorf schedules field trips to local points of interest, and students in grades 4-12 take camping trips. Older pupils engage in 25 hours of required community service each year.

SAN ANSELMO, CA. (13 mi. N of San Francisco, CA) Suburban. Pop: 12,378. Alt: 45 ft.

SAN DOMENICO SCHOOL

Bdg — Girls Gr 9-12; Day — Boys PS (Age 4)-8, Girls PS (Age 4)-12

San Anselmo, CA 94960. 1500 Butterfield Rd. Tel: 415-258-1905. Fax: 415-258-1906.
www.sandomenico.org　E-mail: admissions@sandomenico.org
David G. Behrs, Head (2011). BS, Elizabethtown College, MS, Shippensburg Univ, PhD, American Univ. **Sean Kenney, Adm.**
Col Prep. AP (exams req'd; 133 taken, 66% 3+)—Eng Fr Span Calc Stats Bio Chem Environ_Sci US_Hist Psych Studio_Art Music_Theory. **Feat**—Chin Amer_Stud Intl_Relations Ethics Philos Relig Art_Hist Photog Theater_Arts Music Music_Hist Dance. **Supp**—ESL LD Tut.
Sports—G: Badminton Basket X-country Soccer Swim Tennis Volley. **Activities:** 12.
Selective adm (Bdg Gr 9-11; Day PS-11): 136/yr. Bdg 35. Day 101. Appl fee: $100. Appl due: Jan. Applied: 356. Accepted: 60%. Yield: 64%. **Tests** HSPT ISEE SSAT TOEFL.
Enr 580. B 179. G 401. Bdg 93. Day 487. Elem 426. Sec 154. Wh 74%. Latino 4%. Blk 2%. Asian 12%. Other 8%. Intl 8%. Avg class size: 15. Stud/fac: 7:1. **Fac 84.** M 17/F 67. FT 78/PT 6. Wh 98%. Latino 1%. Blk 1%. Adv deg: 39%. In dorms 2.
Grad '11—38. Col—38. (U of CA-Berkeley 3, UCLA 2, Pepperdine 2, Chapman 2, MIT 1, USC 1). **Avg SAT:** CR 574. M 649. W 620. Avg ACT: 27.4. **Col couns:** 1. Alum donors: 16%.
Tui '12-'13: Bdg $49,000 (+$1500). **Day $23,200-33,650** (+$1000). **Aid:** Need 162 ($2,900,000).
Summer: Rec. 1-9 wks.
Endow $8,500,000. Plant val $25,000,000. Acres 515. Bldgs 10. Dorms 3. Dorm rms 35.

Class rms 55. Lib 23,000 vols. Sci labs 5. Auds 2. Theaters 1. Art studios 3. Dance studios 1. Conservatories 1. Gyms 1. Fields 2. Courts 6. Pools 1. Riding rings 3. Stables 1. Comp labs 3. Laptop prgm Gr 9-12. **Est 1850.** Nonprofit. Roman Catholic. Sem (Aug-June). **Assoc** WASC.

The school was founded in Monterey by Sr. Mary Goemaere, a Dominican nun from Paris, France, and later relocated to Benicia. In 1889, the school moved again, this time to San Rafael, where, as Dominican Convent, it provided preparatory and elementary education for 76 years. Renamed San Domenico in 1965, when it shifted operations to its present, 515-acre campus, the school is the oldest independent school in California. The primary and middle schools enroll both girls and boys, while the upper school accepts girls only. Although the program is sponsored by the Dominican Sisters of San Rafael, approximately half of the students come from non-Catholic families.

San Domenico's primary and middle school curricula provide a firm grounding in the basic skills. In addition to the core courses of math, English, science, social studies and religion, young students receive instruction in foreign language, computer, physical education, music and art.

At the high school level, girls follow an integrated curriculum that features honors and Advanced Placement classes in all subject areas. San Domenico offers many opportunities for involvement in athletics, the performing arts and service learning. Particularly noteworthy is the school's music conservatory, which provides music and voice instruction for students of all ages, as well as preprofessional music training for high schoolers. A preprofessional theater program allows girls to act, direct and participate in all aspects of technical design.

SAN DIEGO, CA. Urban. Pop: 1,223,400. Alt: 687 ft.

FRANCIS PARKER SCHOOL
Day — Coed Gr PS (Age 4)-12

San Diego, CA 92111. 6501 Linda Vista Rd. Tel: 858-569-7900. Fax: 858-569-0621.
Other locations: 4201 Randolph St, San Diego 92103.
   www.francisparker.org E-mail: admission@francisparker.org
Kevin Yaley, Head (2010). BA, MA, Univ of Notre Dame, MEd, San Diego State Univ. **Judy Conner, Upper & Middle Sch Adm; Dori Rodi, Lower Sch Adm.**
   Col Prep. AP (569 exams taken, 87% 3+)—Eng Fr Lat Span Calc Stats Comp_Sci Bio Chem Environ_Sci Physics Eur_Hist US_Hist World_Hist Econ Human_Geog US_Govt & Pol Art_Hist Studio_Art. **Elem math**—Singapore Math. **Feat**—British_Lit Creative_Writing Shakespeare Great_Books Chin Multivariable_Calc Marine_Bio/ Sci Physiol Biotech Epidemiology Anthro Psych Lat-Amer_Stud Video_Production Drama Music Journ Speech Woodworking. **Supp**—Rev Tut.
   Sports—Basket X-country Golf Lacrosse Soccer Tennis Track Volley. B: Baseball Football. G: Softball. **Activities:** 78.
   Selective adm: 183/yr. Appl fee: $125. Appl due: Feb. Accepted: 35%. Yield: 88%. **Tests** ISEE.
   Enr 1237. B 624. G 613. Elem 751. Sec 486. Wh 66%. Latino 8%. Blk 3%. Native Am 1%. Asian 6%. Other 16%. Avg class size: 18. Stud/fac: 10:1. Uniform. **Fac 118.** Wh 71%. Latino 6%. Blk 3%. Asian 6%. Other 14%. Adv deg: 58%.
   Grad '10—120. Col—120. (USC, Stanford, Duke, Villanova, Yale, U of MI). Athl schol 5. **Avg SAT:** CR 626. M 650. W 668. Avg ACT: 28. **Col couns:** 3.
   Tui '11-'12: Day $17,700-24,400 (+$935-3635). **Aid:** Need ($2,650,000).
   Summer: Acad Enrich Rev. Tui Day $425-1700. 3-6 wks. Sports. Tui Day $115-230/wk. 8 wks.
   Endow $11,100,000. Plant val $100,000,000. Acres 26. Bldgs 21. Class rms 68. 2 Libs 26,000 vols. Sci labs 14. Auds 1. Theaters 1. Art studios 6. Music studios 6. Gyms 2. Fields 3. Courts 5. Comp labs 3. Comp/stud: 1:1.6.

Est 1912. Nonprofit. Tri (Sept-June). **Assoc** CLS WASC.

Parker conducts a college preparatory education that blends a traditional curriculum with the arts and athletics. Each semester, students in the upper school must take five academic courses, one or two electives, and physical education or athletics. In addition, courses in computer, the arts and speech are required. Qualified pupils choose from a selection of AP and honors classes. All boys and girls at this level perform community service: 10 hours during freshman year and 20 hours thereafter. The upper school interim week in February provides an opportunity for in-depth explorations of academic or community service themes and activities.

Middle schoolers supplement a traditional academic program with selections from the visual and performing arts and physical education or interscholastic sports. The lower school, which is located on Randolph Street in Mission Hills, emphasizes basic academic and study skills in combination with hands-on experiences. The study of a foreign language begins in junior kindergarten with Spanish.

SAN FRANCISCO, CA. Urban. Pop: 776,733. Alt: to 155 ft.

CATHEDRAL SCHOOL FOR BOYS

Day — Boys Gr K-8

San Francisco, CA 94108. 1275 Sacramento St. Tel: 415-771-6600. Fax: 415-771-2547. www.cathedralschool.net   E-mail: madison@cathedralschool.net
Michael Ferreboeuf, Head (1999). BA, Univ of California-Berkeley, MA, Univ of San Francisco. **Catherine K. Madison, Adm.**
Pre-Prep. Feat—Chin Span Computers Ethics Philos World_Relig Drama Band Chorus Music Public_Speak. **Supp**—Dev_Read Rev Tut.
Sports—B: Baseball Basket X-country Golf Soccer Volley.
Selective adm: 51/yr. Usual entry: K & 5. Appl fee: $100. Appl due: Jan. Accepted: 84%. Yield: 81%.
Enr 270. Wh 66%. Latino 4%. Blk 5%. Asian 11%. Other 14%. Avg class size: 15. Stud/fac: 9:1. Uniform. **Fac 58.** M 21/F 37. FT 49/PT 9. Wh 90%. Latino 4%. Blk 2%. Asian 4%. Adv deg: 32%.
Grad '11—30. Prep—27. (Lick-Wilmerding, San Francisco U HS, St Ignatius-CA, Urban).
Tui '12-'13: Day $25,700 (+$50). **Aid:** Merit 1 ($24,725).
Summer: Enrich Rec. 3-6 wks.
Endow $15,000,000. Plant val $6,500,000. Acres 2. Bldgs 2 (100% ADA). Class rms 23. Lib 12,000 vols. Sci labs 1. Media labs 2. Auds 1. Theaters 1. Art studios 1. Music studios 3. Gyms 1. Fields 1. Courts 2. Comp labs 1. Comp/stud: 1:1 Laptop prgm Gr 5-8.
Est 1957. Nonprofit. Episcopal (20% practice). Quar (Sept-June). **Assoc** WASC.

Cathedral provides a traditional pre-preparatory program. The literature-based language arts program features a reading specialist and a developmental approach to reading (with small reading groups across grade levels), while the math curriculum progresses from a manipulative approach to a more abstract one that emphasizes computational and thinking skills. Spanish and Mandarin courses begin in grade 5, while all boys study Latin in grades 7 and 8. CSB's curriculum also includes an English language structures class for fifth and sixth graders. A full science lab and a technology lab further enrich Cathedral's program.

Music and art programs are integral to school life. Some boys enter the Grace Cathedral choir in grade 4, although most take part in the regular music program, which includes a handbell choir and voice training. Band, string ensemble and instrumental music lessons are also available. A well-developed art program, taught in both classroom and studio settings, is integrated at all grade levels.

Other notable aspects of the program are electives in grades 3-8, no-cut athletic teams, regular field trips, weeklong environmental excursions and international travel during intersession and winter break. In addition, community service is part of the curriculum at all grade levels. An extended-day program serving children in grades K-6 operates before and after school.

DREW SCHOOL
Day — Coed Gr 9-12

San Francisco, CA 94115. 2901 California St. Tel: 415-409-3739. Fax: 415-346-0720.
www.drewschool.org   E-mail: et@drewschool.org
Samuel M. Cuddeback III, Head. AB, MALS, Dartmouth College. **Elizabeth Tilden Baier, Adm.**
Col Prep. AP (120 exams taken, 81% 3+)—Eng Fr Span Calc Chem. **Feat**—Poetry ASL Chin Anat & Physiol Marine_Bio/Sci Comp_Sci Econ Psych Art_Hist Filmmaking Photog Sculpt Studio_Art Video_Production Printmaking Music_Hist Music_Theory. **Supp**—ESL Rev Tut.
Sports—Badminton Basket X-country Soccer Tennis Volley. B: Baseball Golf. **Activities: 18.**
Somewhat selective adm: 85/yr. Appl fee: $75. Appl due: Jan. **Tests** SSAT.
Enr 250. B 125. G 125. Intl 5%. Avg class size: 14. Stud/fac: 8:1. **Fac 35.** M 14/F 21. FT 32/PT 3. Adv deg: 51%.
Grad '11—**58. Col**—**58.** (U of CA-Berkeley, U of CA-Santa Cruz, U of CO-Boulder, San Francisco St, Brandeis). **Mid 50% SAT:** CR 510-630. M 500-640. W 530-660. Mid 50% ACT: 25-29. **Col couns:** 2.
Tui '12-'13: Day $36,400 (+$2000). **Aid:** Need 100 ($1,000,000).
Summer: Acad Rem Rec. 4-6 wks.
Bldgs 1. Class rms 15. Lib 15,000 vols. Sci labs 2. Lang labs 1. Theaters 1. Art studios 1. Music studios 1. Dance studios 1. Comp labs 1.
Est 1908. Nonprofit. Sem (Aug-June). **Assoc** WASC.

Founded by John S. Drew, the school combines college preparation with a variety of electives, arts and athletics. The full preparatory curriculum includes Advanced Placement courses in the major disciplines, as well as French and Spanish language classes. Each semester Drew students are required to take two electives, which meet every Friday and include fine and performing arts, sports and fitness, social/political activities and academic enrichment. All freshmen participate in a special class designed to ease the transition into high school. Seniors conclude their high school years with a three-week individual project, supported by a faculty member and an outside mentor. The Global Awareness, Inquiry and Action program integrates perspectives on global issues into the curriculum.

As students from outside the US constitute roughly five percent of its enrollment, Drew provides intermediate and advanced English as a Second Language instruction. An outdoor education program organizes day hikes and overnight camping trips throughout the year. All faculty members serve as student advisors and participate in cocurricular or extracurricular activities.

FRENCH AMERICAN INTERNATIONAL SCHOOL AND INTERNATIONAL HIGH SCHOOL
Day — Coed Gr PS (Age 3)-12

San Francisco, CA 94102. 150 Oak St. Tel: 415-558-2000. Fax: 415-558-2024.
Other locations: 66 Page St, San Francisco 94102.
www.internationalsf.org   E-mail: admissions@internationalsf.org
Jane Camblin, Head (1994). BA, Univ of Bristol (England), MA, Univ of Sydney (Australia), MA, Stanford Univ. **Betsy Brody, HS Adm; Andrew Brown, Gr PS-8 Adm.**
Col Prep. IB Diploma. Fr Bac. Bilingual (Fr). Feat—Chin Fr Ger Ital Span Econ Geog

Philos Film Visual_Arts Theater_Arts Music. **Supp**—ESL LD.
Sports—Badminton Basket X-country Soccer Swim Tennis Track. B: Baseball. G: Volley.
Activities: 20.
Selective adm: 181/yr. Usual entry: PS, K & 9. Appl fee: $75-100. Appl due: Jan.
Accepted: 72%. Yield: 25%. **Tests** CTP_4 ISEE SSAT.
Enr 1008. Elem 665. Sec 343. Wh 68%. Latino 6%. Blk 6%. Native Am 1%. Asian 11%.
Other 8%. Avg class size: 20. **Fac 125.** M 46/F 79. FT 125. Adv deg: 43%.
Grad '11—95. Col—92. (U of CA-Davis 5, U of CA-Berkeley 4, McGill-Canada 3, Boston
U 3, USC 3, U of CA-Santa Cruz 3). Athl schol 1. **Avg SAT:** CR 631. M 610. W 616.
Col couns: 2. Alum donors: 5%.
Tui '12-'13: Day $22,130-32,290 (+$500). **Aid:** Need 239 ($3,221,893).
Endow $4,900,000. Plant val $60,000,000. Acres 2. Bldgs 3. Lib 18,000 vols. Sci labs
5. Theaters 1. Art studios 2. Music studios 2. Film studios 1. Gyms 1. Playgrounds 3.
Comp labs 4. Comp/stud: 1:15.
Est 1962. Nonprofit. Sem (Sept-June). **Assoc** WASC.

Founded as the French-American Bilingual School, French American changed its name in 1984 to reflect its growing international focus and established the International High School in 1976. In 1997, French American and International High School moved from rented facilities at the University of California Extension complex to their present location at the International Schools Campus in San Francisco's Civic Center. Approximately 70 percent of French American's students are American; the remaining 30 percent represent numerous countries and languages. No previous French language background is required to enter the lower school at the prekindergarten or kindergarten level or the ninth grade of International High School. English as a Second Language and French as a Second Language are available, in addition to Spanish and Mandarin at the high school level.

French is the language of instruction 80 percent of the time throughout the early childhood immersion program, while, in grades 3-5, students are taught academic subjects half the time in French and half in English. A third language (Mandarin, German, Italian or Spanish) is introduced in sixth grade. Students at International High School choose between the French Baccalaureate and the International Baccalaureate programs; in addition, they may prepare for Advanced Placement exams. Graduates matriculate at universities throughout the world, and those enrolling at American universities may enter with up to a full year of college credit.

All high school students participate in a cocurricular program consisting of such "creative, action and service" activities as drama, art, theater, sports and various community service programs. In addition, each pupil at this level satisfies a 25-hour annual service requirement. Exchange trips allow participants to live and learn with students and families of the host country. Opportunities also exist for extended study abroad.

THE HAMLIN SCHOOL
Day — Girls Gr K-8

San Francisco, CA 94115. 2120 Broadway. Tel: 415-922-0300. Fax: 415-674-5409.
www.hamlin.org   E-mail: aquino@hamlin.org
Wanda M. Holland Greene, Head (2008). BA, MA, Columbia Univ. **Lisa Lau Aquino,
Adm.**
Pre-Prep. Feat—Fr Span Computers Studio_Art Drama Music Dance.
Sports—G: Basket X-country Soccer Volley.
Selective adm (Gr K-7): 60/yr. Usual entry: K, 5 & 6. Appl fee: $100. Applied: 250. **Tests**
ISEE.
Enr 404. Wh 61%. Latino 1%. Blk 3%. Asian 24%. Other 11%. Stud/fac: 10:1. Uniform.
Fac 60. M 9/F 51. FT 48/PT 12. Wh 77%. Latino 1%. Blk 1%. Asian 1%. Other 20%.
Adv deg: 55%.
Grad '11—50. Prep—47. (San Francisco U HS 9, Branson 6, Drew 6, Urban 5, Lick-
Wilmerding 3, St Ignatius-CA 3).
Tui '12-'13: Day $27,400. Aid: Need 88 ($1,320,000).
Summer: Enrich Rec. Tui Day $550-1100. 1-2 wks.

Endow $13,000,000. Plant val $14,000,000. Bldgs 3 (100% ADA). Class rms 25. Lib 15,000 vols. Sci labs 2. Comp ctrs 1. Amphitheaters 1. Auds 1. Art studios 2. Music studios 2. Gyms 1. Fields 1. Comp/stud: 1:1.7. **Est 1863.** Nonprofit. Sem (Sept-June).

As the first nonsectarian school for girls in California, Hamlin continues to provide leadership in the education of young girls. Situated in Pacific Heights, overlooking San Francisco Bay and the Marin Headlands, Hamlin reflects the diversity and the traditions of San Francisco. Hamlin offers a progressive academic program balanced by the fine arts and physical education, with electives in dance, chorus and drama.

French is the foreign language choice in grades K-4, and students take either French or Spanish in grades 5-8. Before- and after-school care and an extensive after-school activities program are available. Middle school girls may engage in club or interscholastic sports.

KATHERINE DELMAR BURKE SCHOOL
Day — Girls Gr K-8

San Francisco, CA 94121. 7070 California St. Tel: 415-751-0177. Fax: 415-666-0535.
www.kdbs.org   E-mail: renee@kdbs.org
Michele Williams, Head (2012). Renee Thompson, Adm.
Pre-Prep. Feat—Chin Fr Span Studio_Art Drama Music Public_Speak Outdoor_Ed.
   Supp—Dev_Read Tut.
Sports—G: Basket Soccer Softball Volley.
Selective adm: 66/yr. Usual entry: K. Appl fee: $100. Appl due: Dec. Accepted: 40%.
   Tests CTP_4 ISEE.
Enr 400. Wh 68%. Latino 5%. Blk 3%. Asian 10%. Other 14%. Avg class size: 20. Stud/
   fac: 8:1. Uniform. **Fac 63.** M 5/F 58. FT 40/PT 23. Wh 70%. Latino 10%. Blk 6%. Asian
   10%. Other 4%. Adv deg: 36%.
Grad '11—46. Prep—42. (San Francisco U HS 6, Urban 6, Marin Acad 5, St Ignatius-
   CA 5, Lick-Wilmerding 4, Cate 2).
Tui '11-'12: Day $25,000-26,000 (+$510). **Aid:** Need 72 ($1,090,000).
Endow $11,000,000. Plant val $10,437,000. Acres 3. Bldgs 10. Class rms 35. Lib 35,000
   vols. Sci labs 3. Theater/auds 1. Art studios 2. Music studios 2. Gyms 1. Fields 1.
   Courts 2. Comp labs 2.
Est 1908. Nonprofit. Tri (Sept-June).

Founded by Katherine Delmar Burke, a native San Franciscan and gifted teacher, this school moved several times during the early years to increasingly large quarters in the city. Upon Miss Burke's death in 1929, the school passed to the direction of her young niece, Barbara Burke, under whose guidance it continued to grow until her retirement in 1960. During this period, the school expanded to the present campus in Sea Cliff, splitting the primary school into two distinct campuses. In 1975, Burke School terminated its high school program and moved its entire operation to the Sea Cliff campus, which today occupies three and a half acres.

The curriculum includes a demanding academic program; a rich variety of music, art and drama offerings; and a comprehensive athletic and sports program. All grade 7 students take a trimester of public speaking, and eighth graders choose a poem, speech or passage from literature to memorize and recite before the upper school during assembly. Outdoor education is an integral part of the curriculum for grades 3-8. Older students travel to such sites as Yosemite and Joshua Tree.

Upper school students participate in student government, and throughout there are both opportunities and requirements for service to the school community and others. All Burke students, faculty and staff participate in "family" groups, which consist of at least one adult and one student from each grade, that work and play together. After school, a study hall serves children in grades 5 and 6 and a sports program is available to those in grades 5-8.

LICK-WILMERDING HIGH SCHOOL
Day — Coed Gr 9-12

San Francisco, CA 94112. 755 Ocean Ave. Tel: 415-333-4021. Fax: 415-333-9443.
www.lwhs.org   E-mail: lwadmit@lwhs.org
Eric J. Temple, Head (2011). BA, Boston College, MA, Univ of Massachusetts-Amherst, MEd, Columbia Univ. **Lisa Wu, Adm.**
Col Prep. Feat—African-Amer_Lit Immigrant_Lit Chin Fr Span Calc Stats Anat & Physiol Genetics Marine_Bio/Sci Comp_Sci Cold_War Women's_Hist Psych Architect Ceramics Film Photog Studio_Art Acting Theater_Arts Directing Chorus Music Jazz_Combo Dance Drafting Woodworking Electronics.
Sports—Basket X-country Lacrosse Swim Tennis Track Wrestling. B: Baseball Golf. G: Soccer Volley.
Very selective adm (Gr 9-11): 115/yr. Appl fee: $95. Appl due: Jan. Applied: 794. Accepted: 22%. Yield: 68%. **Tests** ISEE SSAT.
Enr 444. B 208. G 236. Avg class size: 15. **Fac 67.** M 32/F 35. FT 67. Adv deg: 85%.
Grad '10—106. Col—106. (NYU 7, U of CA-Davis 7, USC 5, Cornell 4, Brown 4, Boston U 4). **Avg SAT:** CR 667. M 673. W 688. Avg ACT: 28. **Col couns:** 2. Alum donors: 12%.
Tui '10-'11: Day $33,365. Aid: Need 181 ($3,049,000).
Endow $38,000,000. Plant val $14,700,000. Acres 4. Bldgs 7. Class rms 28. Lib 13,500 vols. Sci labs 4. Theaters 1. Art studios 2. Music studios 1. Dance studios 1. Tech arts shops 4. Gyms 1. Comp labs 3.
Est 1895. Nonprofit. Sem (Sept-June). **Assoc** WASC.

Founded by James Lick and Jellis Wilmerding, the school offers a curriculum that integrates the liberal, technical and performing arts. Students select from a variety of Advanced Placement courses, including French and Spanish language and literature classes. A variety of technical and fine arts offerings is also available. L-W offers a flexible tuition program that allows families who would not expect to be eligible for financial aid to apply for reduced tuition, thus enabling pupils from varying economic backgrounds to attend.

During Jellis Block, all grade 11 students participate in a technical arts or visual and performing arts experience in which students work in groups with a faculty member. Junior projects are hands-on and feature real-world application of skills and knowledge.

The school runs a five-week summer outreach program that provides tuition-free academic enrichment for local middle school children from low-income households and allows Lick-Wilmerding students to serve as teaching assistants.

PRESIDIO HILL SCHOOL
Day — Coed Gr K-8

San Francisco, CA 94118. 3839 Washington St. Tel: 415-751-9318. Fax: 415-751-9334.
www.presidiohill.org   E-mail: info@presidiohill.org
Scott Duyan, Head (2009). BA, Univ of California-Los Angeles, MA, Univ of Northern Colorado. **Kelly Dees, Adm.**
Pre-Prep. Feat—Span Studio_Art Drama Music.
Sports—Basket X-country Soccer Volley.
Selective adm: 41/yr. Usual entry: K & 6. Appl fee: $75. Appl due: Jan.
Enr 193. B 92. G 101. Wh 55%. Latino 9%. Blk 5%. Asian 6%. Other 25%. Avg class size: 18. Stud/fac: 8:1. Casual. **Fac 26.** Wh 88%. Blk 7%. Asian 3%. Other 2%.
Grad '11—30. Prep—24. (Urban 6, St Ignatius-CA 4, Lick-Wilmerding 3, Bay Sch of San Francisco 2, San Francisco U HS 2, Drew 2).
Tui '12-'13: Day $22,880-23,994 (+$0-1000). **Aid:** Need 43.
Plant val $11,000,000. Acres 1. Bldgs 1. Class rms 13. Libs 1. Sci labs 1. Theaters 1.
Est 1918. Nonprofit. Tri (Sept-June).

Established by a group of local parents as the Presidio Open Air School, this progressive program has an enrollment policy aimed at reflecting the cultural, economic and ethnic diversity of the city.

The project-based curriculum places an emphasis on writing across the disciplines. Music and the visual arts are considered fundamental. Spanish is introduced in third grade and continues through grade 8. Physical education includes intramural sports in the upper grades, as well as creative movement and games in the lower grades. Students participate in as many as three outdoor education experiences per year.

Parental involvement is encouraged and is considered essential. After-school care is available for an additional fee.

SAN FRANCISCO DAY SCHOOL

Day — Coed Gr K-8

San Francisco, CA 94118. 350 Masonic Ave. Tel: 415-931-2422. Fax: 415-931-1753.
www.sfds.net   E-mail: admission@sfds.net
David E. Jackson, Head (2007). BA, Williams College, EdD, Columbia Univ. **Homa Hanjani, Adm.**
   Pre-Prep. Feat—Lib_Skills Lat Span Computers Studio_Art Music. **Supp**—Dev_Read Rem_Read Tut.
   Sports—Basket X-country Soccer Volley.
   Very selective adm: 56/yr. Usual entry: K. Appl fee: $95. Appl due: Dec. Applied: 391. Accepted: 19%. Yield: 71%. **Tests** ISEE.
   Enr 400. B 196. G 204. Avg class size: 22. Stud/fac: 12:1. **Fac 67.** M 22/F 45. FT 58/PT 9.
   Grad '11—45. Prep—42. (San Francisco U HS 8, Urban 7, Marin Acad 5, San Francisco Waldorf 4, Drew 3, Bay Sch of San Francisco 3).
   Tui '12-'13: Day $26,540. Aid: Need 77 ($1,294,000).
   Endow $14,801,000. Plant val $28,000,000. Bldgs 1. Lib 15,500 vols. Sci labs 2. Art studios 2. Music studios 2. Gyms 1. Comp labs 1.
   Est 1981. Nonprofit. Sem (Sept-June).

Founded by a group of parents, this school originally opened for kindergartners through second graders, adding one grade each year until reaching its current grade range. Strong emphasis is placed on such basic skills as reading, writing, computation and problem solving. The school offers an outdoor education program to students in grades 3-8 that involves a weeklong, off-campus course of study each year.

An afternoon enrichment program, available to children at all grade levels, provides sports, art, music, drama and computer programs after school hours. At all grade levels, students may also select special instruction classes in such areas as typing, karate, orchestra, ceramics and computers.

THE SAN FRANCISCO SCHOOL

Day — Coed Gr PS (Age 3)-8

San Francisco, CA 94134. 300 Gaven St. Tel: 415-239-5065. Fax: 415-239-4833.
www.sfschool.org   E-mail: info@sfschool.org
Steve Morris, Head (2007). BA, College of Wooster, MA, Stanford Univ. **Nina Wang, Adm.**
   Pre-Prep. Gen Acad. Montessori. Feat—Span Environ_Sci Computers Studio_Art Drama Music Dance. **Supp**—Dev_Read Tut.
   Sports—Basket X-country Soccer Volley.
   Very selective adm: 56/yr. Appl fee: $75. Appl due: Jan. Accepted: 23%. Yield: 74%. **Tests** CTP_4 ISEE Stanford.
   Enr 276. Wh 43%. Latino 13%. Blk 15%. Asian 29%. Avg class size: 19. **Fac 39.** M 9/F 30. FT 34/PT 5. Wh 61%. Latino 10%. Blk 9%. Asian 20%. Adv deg: 23%.

Grad '09—31. Prep—26. (Lick-Wilmerding, Urban, Drew, Menlo, Schs of the Sacred Heart-CA).
Tui '11-'12: Day $20,510-22,120 (+$200). **Aid:** Need 74 ($709,740).
Summer: Acad Enrich Rec. 2-6 wks.
Endow $2,000,000. Plant val $4,246,000. Acres 1. Bldgs 3. Libs 1. Sci labs 1. Lang labs 2. Auds 1. Art studios 1. Music studios 1. Dance studios 1. Playgrounds 3. Comp labs 1.
Est 1966. Nonprofit. Sem (Sept-June).

Interested in establishing a school based on the principles of Italian physicist and educator Maria Montessori, a small group of preschool teachers and parents formed the San Francisco Montessori School in a church basement in the city's Portola District. Its rapid growth led to the school's move to its present location and the addition of grade 1 in 1969. Organic growth continued through the 1970s, and the school consciously shifted from the Montessori method to a progressive approach that combined Montessori ideals with current teaching practices. In the 1980s, the school added a middle school program and assumed its current name.

SFS' increasingly demanding educational program is integrated and articulated across grade levels, with specific goals and objectives set for each subject area. The preschool combines traditional Montessori teaching tools with blocks of various sizes and shapes, a playhouse, toys, board games and manipulative materials. In the elementary program (grades 1-5), children compile journals, assume classroom responsibilities, embark on field trips and overnight excursions, and engage in environmental studies. Spanish is introduced in grade 2.

Students in the middle school (grades 6-8) follow an integrated curriculum that emphasizes the development of study and organizational skills. Boys and girls choose from elective minicourses in such areas as painting, video production and book discussion. Seventh graders explore areas of vocational interest by undertaking a field experience that enables them to spend up to three days in the workplace.

SAN FRANCISCO UNIVERSITY HIGH SCHOOL
Day — Coed Gr 9-12

San Francisco, CA 94115. 3065 Jackson St. Tel: 415-447-3100. Fax: 415-447-5801.
www.sfuhs.org   E-mail: admissions@sfuhs.org
Michael Diamonti, Head (2002). BA, Seton Hall Univ, MEd, Rutgers Univ, PhD, Boston College. **Rachel E. Skiffer, Adm.**
Col Prep. AP (497 exams taken, 94% 3+)—Fr Lat Span Calc Stats Comp_Sci Chem Environ_Sci Physics Eur_Hist US_Hist Econ Art_Hist Studio_Art Music_Theory. **Feat**—Poetry Shakespeare Russ_Lit S_African_Lit Chin Astron Genetics Marine_ Bio/Sci Microbio Molecular_Bio Psych African-Amer_Stud Ceramics Drawing Film Photog Acting Chorus Music Jazz_Ensemble. **Supp**—Tut.
Sports—Badminton Basket X-country Fencing Golf Lacrosse Soccer Swim Tennis Track. B: Baseball. G: F_Hockey Softball Volley. **Activities:** 50.
Selective adm (Gr 9-11): 102/yr. Appl fee: $90. Appl due: Jan. Accepted: 41%. Yield: 56%. **Tests** SSAT.
Enr 396. B 185. G 211. Wh 62%. Latino 4%. Blk 2%. Asian 22%. Other 10%. Avg class size: 15. Stud/fac: 8:1. **Fac 53.** M 22/F 31. FT 51/PT 2. Wh 60%. Latino 13%. Blk 4%. Asian 17%. Other 6%. Adv deg: 73%.
Grad '11—102. Col—102. (Harvard 4, Middlebury 4, U of CA-Santa Barbara 4, Stanford 3, U of Chicago 3, U of CA-Berkeley 3). **Mid 50% SAT:** CR 660-760. M 640-760. W 700-760. **Col couns:** 2. Alum donors: 14%.
Tui '12-'13: Day $35,440 (+$700-800). **Aid:** Need 83 ($1,908,750).
Summer (enr 108): Gr 6-8. Acad Enrich. HS Prep. 6 wks.
Endow $26,232,000. Plant val $35,000,000. Acres 1. Bldgs 5 (100% ADA). Class rms 23. Lib 18,000 vols. Sci labs 6. Lang labs 1. Theater/auds 1. Art studios 3. Music studios 2. AV studios 1. Gyms 1. Courts 1. Comp labs 2. Comp/stud: 1:1 Laptop prgm Gr 9-12.
Est 1973. Nonprofit. Sem (Aug-June). **Assoc** WASC.

UHS' campus extends through two city blocks in the northern section of San Francisco. The majority of students come from the city, though some commute from East Bay cities, Marin County and the Peninsula. The college preparatory course of study combines a core of required courses with numerous electives aimed at meeting special needs and interests. Advanced Placement courses are available in the major disciplines. The arts program makes use of extensive facilities that include music practice rooms, a MIDI lab and digital recording studio, photography darkrooms, a ceramics studio, and facilities for digital imaging and film production. Among other elective subjects are classical literature, economics, contemporary world issues and computer programming. Community service is part of the curriculum at all grade levels.

Each student belongs to an advising cluster consisting of peers from their grade and led by a faculty adviser. Students participate in semester and yearlong off-campus learning opportunities, including study in China, France, Italy or Spain through School Year Abroad. A rich program of independent study awards transcript credit for a variety of student-initiated projects.

The physical education program provides a climbing wall and such activities as tae kwon do, flag football and tennis. Students may participate in independent study projects. UHS schedules frequent field trips to areas of interest.

SCHOOLS OF THE SACRED HEART

Coord — Day Gr K-12

San Francisco, CA 94115. 2222 Broadway. Tel: 415-563-2900. Fax: 415-292-3183.
Other locations: 1715 Octavia St, San Francisco 94109.
www.sacredsf.org   E-mail: information@sacredsf.org
Gordon Sharafinski, Dir (2009). BA, St Mary's Univ of Minnesota, MA, Univ of St Thomas (MN). **Pamela A. Thorp, Adm.**
Col Prep. AP (exams req'd; 303 taken, 62% 3+)—Eng Chin Fr Lat Span Calc Stats Comp_Sci Bio Chem Environ_Sci Physics Eur_Hist US_Hist Comp_Govt & Pol Psych US_Govt & Pol Art_Hist Studio_Art. **Feat**—Creative_Writing Japan Econ Philos Ceramics Film Fine_Arts Photog Animation Drama Chorus Journ. **Supp**—Rev Tut.
Sports—Basket X-country Fencing Golf Soccer Swim Tennis Track. B: Baseball Lacrosse. G: Badminton Volley.
Selective adm (Gr K-11): 188/yr. Usual entry: K & 9. Appl fee: $75-100. Appl due: Jan. Applied: 749. Accepted: 55%. Yield: 46%. **Tests** CTP_4 HSPT SSAT.
Enr 996. B 478. G 518. Elem 648. Sec 348. Wh 71%. Latino 6%. Blk 4%. Asian 14%. Other 5%. Avg class size: 15. Uniform. **Fac 157.** M 44/F 113. FT 131/PT 26. Wh 86%. Latino 4%. Blk 2%. Asian 8%. Adv deg: 50%.
Grad '11—102. Col—102. (U of CA-Berkeley, USC, Regis Col, U of San Francisco, San Francisco St, Santa Clara). Athl schol 1.
Tui '12-'13: Day $24,770-35,100 (+$300-900). **Aid:** Need 231 ($3,429,975).
Summer: Coed. Acad Enrich Rev Rec. Sports. Driver Ed. 3 wks.
Endow $10,175,000. Plant val $82,000,000. Bldgs 7 (55% ADA). Class rms 72. 3 Libs 35,603 vols. Sci labs 4. Auds 2. Theaters 1. Art studios 5. Music studios 4. Gyms 2. Comp labs 3. Comp/stud: 1:2.
Est 1887. Nonprofit. Roman Catholic (57% practice). Sem (Aug-June). **Assoc** WASC.

Founded by the Religious of the Sacred Heart, SSH comprises two girls' schools, Convent of the Sacred Heart High School (grades 9-12) and Convent of the Sacred Heart Elementary School (grades K-8), and two boys' schools, Stuart Hall for Boys (grades K-8) and Stuart Hall High School (grades 9-12). The boys' high school occupies a separate campus on Octavia Street (415-345-5811).

Among the oldest and largest independent schools in the West, Schools of the Sacred Heart employ a coordinate approach that enables boys and girls to learn in single-gender classes within a coeducational community. The rigorous academic program features a strong computer curriculum, art, ceramics, photography, chorus, music, drama and sports. Honors and Advanced Placement classes are available in most disciplines.

Pupils in grades 7-12 serve the community in outreach programs. Boys accumulate 75 hours of required community service in grades 9-11, while girls compile 100 hours of compulsory service in grades 9-12. Boys and girls are encouraged to pursue leadership opportunities through student council, the classroom and student activities.

As a member of the Network of Sacred Heart Schools in the United States, SSH participates in a student exchange program that offers eligible high school students the opportunity to study at another Sacred Heart school.

TOWN SCHOOL FOR BOYS

Day — Boys Gr K-8

San Francisco, CA 94115. 2750 Jackson St. Tel: 415-921-3747. Fax: 415-921-2968.
www.townschool.com   E-mail: mckannay@townschool.com
W. Brewster Ely IV, Head (1989). BA, Ithaca College, MA, Middlebury College. Lynn McKannay, Adm.
Pre-Prep. Elem math—Everyday Math. Feat—Lat Span Computers Econ Photog Studio_Art Music Woodworking. Supp—Dev_Read Rev Tut.
Sports—B: Basket X-country Golf Lacrosse Soccer Volley.
Selective adm (Gr K-7): 63/yr. Usual entry: K. Appl fee: $100. Appl due: Jan. Applied: 193. Tests CTP_4.
Enr 404. Avg class size: 22. Stud/fac: 11:1. Fac 65. M 25/F 40. FT 65.
Grad '10—38. Prep—38. (San Francisco U HS 8, St Ignatius-CA 4, Branson 3, Lick-Wilmerding 2, Urban 2, College Prep 2).
Tui '12-'13: Day $25,670-26,650. Aid: Need 61 ($1,088,034).
Endow $17,401,000. Plant val $22,063,000. Bldgs 1. Class rms 28. Lib 23,000 vols. Sci labs 1. Sci ctrs 1. Theaters 1. Art studios 1. Music studios 2. Wood shops 1. Gyms 1. Fields 2. Courts 1. Comp labs 1. Laptop prgm Gr 5-8.
Est 1939. Nonprofit. Sem (Sept-June). Assoc WASC.

The upper school curriculum includes study in literature, composition and creative writing; ancient and modern history; mathematics; social sciences; geography; global economics; and the earth, life and physical sciences. Beginning in grade 5, students take Spanish, and Latin is a required course in grade 6. A laptop learning program requires every boy in grades 5-8 to purchase a laptop computer for classroom use, and the school also has a technology lab.

Complementing the core academic program are opportunities in art, music, community service, athletics, drama, journalism, student council, desktop publishing, digital photography and public speaking. Town School also offers students a broad range of hands-on projects, outdoor activities, school and grade-level assemblies and performances, after-school activities, and field trips around and beyond the Bay Area.

With sound elementary work, the school sends its graduates to competitive secondary schools throughout the country. Fine arts offerings and athletics supplement an intensive academic program.

THE URBAN SCHOOL OF SAN FRANCISCO

Day — Coed Gr 9-12

San Francisco, CA 94117. 1563 Page St. Tel: 415-626-2919. Fax: 415-626-1125.
www.urbanschool.org   E-mail: info@urbanschool.org
Mark Salkind, Head (1986). BA, Yale Univ. Bobby Ramos, Adm.
Col Prep. Feat—Shakespeare Chin Fr Span Calc Stats Anat & Physiol Botany Environ_ Sci Genetics Marine_Bio/Sci Neurobio Programming Civil_War Constitutional_Law Comp_Relig Art_Hist Photog Sculpt Studio_Art Theater Music.
Sports—Basket X-country Fencing Soccer Tennis Track Volley. B: Baseball Golf. G: Softball. Activities: 35.
Selective adm (Gr 9-11): 106/yr. Usual entry: 9. Appl fee: $75. Appl due: Jan. Tests

SSAT.
Enr 377. B 167. G 210. Nonwhite 32%. Avg class size: 14. Stud/fac: 10:1. Casual. **Fac 51.** M 25/F 26. FT 27/PT 24. Nonwhite 16%. Adv deg: 52%.
Grad '11—77. Col—77. (NYU 5, Occidental 4, Stanford 3, U of CA-Santa Cruz 3, U of CA-Davis 3, Cornell 2). **Avg SAT:** CR 658. M 622. W 667. **Col couns:** 2. Alum donors: 10%.
Tui '12-'13: Day $34,700 (+$620). **Aid:** Need 104 ($2,400,000).
Endow $5,750,000. Bldgs 2 (100% ADA). Class rms 22. Lib 13,000 vols. Sci labs 4. Theaters 1. Art studios 3. Gyms 1. Student ctrs 1. Comp/stud: 1:1 Laptop prgm Gr 9-12. **Est 1966.** Nonprofit. Tri (Aug-June). **Assoc** WASC.

Urban's program is designed to develop individual responsibility, student initiative and cooperative work habits. The school's block system, which divides the school year into three 12-week periods of intensive work, allows for the in-depth study of each subject through discussions, films, projects, research and fieldwork.

The variety of topics explored includes constitutional law, Latin-American and African literature, the Civil War, Russian history, neurobiology, marine biology, painting, music composition and circus movement. Advanced work in the humanities, math, science and the arts is required for graduation. In addition, each student is expected to undertake a yearly project that combines a personal interest with service to the community.

Among activities, the school offers students the opportunity to serve on the board of trustees and on other committees, as well as to assist the faculty in planning new courses and special programs. Participation in physical activities, which range from rock climbing, backpacking and competitive athletic teams to nature hiking, jogging and tennis in Golden Gate Park, is encouraged. Urban organizes various outdoor activities and trips throughout the year. The school also hosts a tuition-free summer program for middle school students from low-income families.

SAN JOSE, CA. (51 mi. SE of San Francisco, CA) Urban. Pop: 894,943. Alt: 118 ft.

HARKER SCHOOL
Day — Coed Gr K-12
San Jose, CA 95129. 500 Saratoga Ave. Tel: 408-249-2510, 800-342-7537.
Fax: 408-984-2325.
Other locations: 4300 Bucknall Rd, San Jose 95130; 3800 Blackford Ave, San Jose 95117.
www.harker.org E-mail: communications@harker.org
Christopher Nikoloff, Head (2005). BA, MAT, Boston Univ. **Nan Nielsen, Adm.**
Col Prep. AP (exams req'd; 1079 taken)—Eng Fr Japan Lat Span Calc Stats Comp_ Sci Bio Chem Environ_Sci Physics Eur_Hist US_Hist Econ Psych US_Govt & Pol Art_Hist Studio_Art Music_Theory. **Feat**—Shakespeare Asian_Lit Gothic_Lit Holocaust_Lit Satire Sci_Fiction Chin Linear_Algebra Multivariable_Calc Number_Theory Anat & Physiol Astron Ecol Engineering Electronics Comp_Animation Law Philos Architect Film Sculpt Drama Theater_Arts Music Debate. **Supp**—Rev Tut.
Sports—Basket X-country Golf Soccer Swim Tennis W_Polo. B: Baseball Football Wrestling. G: Lacrosse Softball Track Volley. **Activities:** 30.
Very selective adm (Gr K-11): 262/yr. Appl fee: $75-125. Appl due: Jan. **Tests** CTP_4 IQ ISEE SSAT.
Enr 1790. Elem 1076. Sec 714. Wh 20%. Latino 2%. Blk 1%. Asian 70%. Other 7%. Avg class size: 18. Stud/fac: 10:1. **Fac 187.** Adv deg: 60%.
Grad '10—166. Col—164. (U of CA-Berkeley, Santa Clara, USC, Stanford, U of CA-San Diego, U of CA-Davis). **Avg SAT:** CR 708. M 735. W 731. **Col couns:** 4.
Tui '12-'13: Day $26,560-37,500 (+$500-1400).
Summer: Gr K-8. Acad Enrich Rec. Tui Day $1103-2675. 2-4 wks. Gr 9-12. Acad. Tui Day

$698-1345/crse. 6 wks.
Plant val $90,000,000. Acres 66. Bldgs 37. Class rms 119. 3 Libs 28,500 vols. Sci labs 27. Art studios 6. Music studios 8. Dance studios 3. Gyms 4. Fields 9. Courts 8. Pools 2. Tracks 1. Archery ranges 1. Comp labs 8. Laptop prgm Gr 6-12. **Est 1893.** Nonprofit. Sem (Aug-June). **Assoc** CLS WASC.

Manzanita Hall, established in 1893 as a boys' preparatory school for Stanford University, and the Harker School, founded in 1902 for girls, were merged under the same management in 1959. In 1972, the two schools began joint operations at the Saratoga Avenue location, which now serves pupils in grades 9-12; children in grades K-5 attend classes at a second campus on Bucknall Road; and students in the middle school (grades 6-8) learn on a third site on Blackford Avenue that opened in the fall of 2005. An inter-campus shuttle serves the three locations, which are proximate to each other.

Situated in the heart of the Santa Clara Valley, Harker provides a traditional college preparatory program enriched with offerings in the fine arts, computer science and athletics. Technology, through wired and wireless networks, is an integral aspect of the program and is interwoven into many courses. All boys and girls in grades 9-11 perform at least 10 hours of community service annually. Both daylong and extended field trips enhance the curriculum.

The Harker Research Program holds an annual research symposium exhibiting upper school student projects and arranges internships with local universities and laboratories. Students collaborate on research projects with schools in Costa Rica and Russia, and Harker maintains partnerships with schools in seven countries.

SAN JUAN CAPISTRANO, CA. (61 mi. SE of Los Angeles, CA) Urban. Pop: 33,826. Alt: 120 ft.

ST. MARGARET'S EPISCOPAL SCHOOL
Day — Coed Gr PS (Age 3)-12
San Juan Capistrano, CA 92675. 31641 La Novia Ave. Tel: 949-661-0108.
Fax: 949-240-1748.
www.smes.org   E-mail: admission@smes.org
Marcus D. Hurlbut, Head (2003). BA, Union College (NY), MA, Dartmouth College.
Phoebe Larson, Adm.
Col Prep. AP (exams req'd; 193 taken, 88% 3+)—Eng Fr Japan Lat Span Calc Stats Comp_Sci Bio Chem Environ_Sci Physics Eur_Hist US_Hist World_Hist US_Govt & Pol Art_Hist Studio_Art Music_Theory. **Elem math**—Everyday Math/Sadlier-Oxford. **Feat**—Creative_Writing Humanities Poetry Chin Anat & Physiol Astron Anthro Econ Intl_Relations Psych Philos Relig Photog Drama Music Dance Journ.
Sports—Basket X-country Golf Lacrosse Soccer Swim Tennis Track Volley. B: Baseball Football Wrestling. G: Cheer Equestrian.
Selective adm: 177/yr. Usual entry: PS, K, 6 & 9. Appl fee: $75. Appl due: Jan. Applied: 378. Accepted: 61%. Yield: 77%. **Tests** ISEE.
Enr 1221. Elem 798. Sec 423. Wh 65%. Latino 5%. Blk 1%. Native Am 1%. Asian 10%. Other 18%. Stud/fac: 14:1. Uniform. **Fac 105.** M 40/F 65. FT 100/PT 5. Wh 91%. Latino 2%. Blk 2%. Asian 5%. Adv deg: 46%.
Grad '09—85. Col—84. (USC 5, AZ St 4, UCLA 4, Northwestern 3, Notre Dame 3, SMU 3). **Avg SAT:** CR 610. M 621. W 638. **Mid 50% SAT:** CR 530-640. M 520-660. W 560-680. **Col couns:** 2.
Tui '12-'13: Day $19,278-23,872 (+$130-2380). **Aid:** Need 187 ($2,900,000).
Summer (enr 700): Acad Enrich Rec. Tui Day $280-1700. 2½-5 wks.
Endow $2,192,000. Plant val $49,598,000. Acres 20. Bldgs 13. Class rms 81. Lib 40,000 vols. Chapels 1. Sci labs 7. Auds 1. Art studios 3. Music studios 2. Dance studios 1. Gyms 2. Fields 3. Comp labs 4. Comp/stud: 1:1.7.
Est 1979. Nonprofit. Episcopal (13% practice). Sem (Sept-June). **Assoc** CLS WASC.

St. Margaret's Episcopal School, named for Scotland's patron of education, was founded through the efforts of Canon Ernest D. Sillers, an Episcopal priest who persuaded the bishop of the diocese to acquire land on which a church and a school could be built. Chapel has been a part of St. Margaret's since its founding, and worship services, religion classes and a service program provide the structure of the school community.

In the upper school, Advanced Placement courses are offered, and all students take an elective each semester. Graduation requirements include courses in foreign language, the fine arts, religion or philosophy, history and computer science, as well as a year of advanced history, mathematics, science or language. Freshmen and sophomores perform 15 hours of required community service per year, while juniors and seniors provide 40 hours of service to a single nonprofit organization over two years.

SAN MARINO, CA. (17 mi. E of Los Angeles, CA) Suburban. Pop: 12,945. Alt: 557 ft. See also Los Angeles.

SOUTHWESTERN ACADEMY

Bdg and Day — Coed Gr 6-PG

San Marino, CA 91108. 2800 Monterey Rd. Tel: 626-799-5010. Fax: 626-799-0407.
www.southwesternacademy.edu
E-mail: admissions@southwesternacademy.edu
Kenneth R. Veronda, Head (1961). BA, MA, Stanford Univ. **Joseph Blake, Adm.**
Col Prep. Gen Acad. AP (exams req'd; 21 taken, 33% 3+)—Eng Calc Chem Physics US_Hist World_Hist. **Feat**—British_Lit Creative_Writing ASL Chin Span Environ_Sci Comp_Sci Anthro Econ Govt Pol_Sci Psych Sociol Art_Hist Photog Studio_Art Drama Music Speech Driver_Ed Outdoor_Ed. **Supp**—Dev_Read ESL Rem_Math Rem_Read Rev Tut. Outdoor ed. Sat classes. **Dual enr:** Pasadena City.
Sports—Basket X-country Soccer Volley. B: Baseball. **Activities:** 16.
Selective adm (Bdg Gr 6-PG; Day 6-12): 34/yr. Bdg 34. Day 0. Usual entry: 9. Appl fee: $100. Appl due: Mar. Applied: 63. Accepted: 50%. Yield: 90%. **Tests** CEEB SSAT.
Enr 153. B 83. G 70. Bdg 114. Day 39. Elem 18. Sec 133. PG 2. Wh 46%. Latino 12%. Blk 10%. Native Am 6%. Asian 22%. Other 4%. Intl 53%. Avg class size: 10. Stud/fac: 6:1. Casual. **Fac 26.** M 16/F 10. FT 22/PT 4. Wh 76%. Latino 4%. Blk 8%. Native Am 4%. Asian 4%. Other 4%. Adv deg: 34%. In dorms 2.
Grad '10—42. Col—40. (U of CA-Irvine 3, U of CA-San Diego 3, U of CA-Santa Barbara 2, Syracuse 2, St Louis U 2, CA St Polytech-San Luis Obispo 2). **Avg SAT:** CR/M/W 1445. Alum donors: 7%.
Tui '12-'13: Bdg $33,750 (+$2000). **Day $16,550** (+$1000). **Intl Bdg $41,000** (+$2000). **Aid:** Need 31 ($712,500).
Summer (enr 79): Acad Enrich Rev Rem Rec. ESL. Travel. Tui Bdg $1340/wk. Tui Day $660/wk. 14 wks.
Endow $22,600,000. Plant val $27,725,000. Acres 8. Bldgs 10. Dorm rms 48. Class rms 18. Lib 17,000 vols. Chapels 1. Sci labs 3. Lang labs 2. Amphitheaters 1. Auds 1. Theaters 2. Art studios 1. Music studios 1. Gyms 1. Fields 1. Basketball courts 2. Tennis courts 1. Volleyball courts 2. Greenhouses 1. Student ctrs 1. Comp labs 2. Comp/stud: 1:1.2.
Est 1924. Nonprofit. Sem (Sept-June). **Assoc** WASC.

Southwestern was founded by Maurice Veronda, who personally directed its growth until his death in 1961. Kenneth Veronda has been headmaster since his father's death. Southwestern occupies separate campuses in San Marino and Rimrock, AZ (see separate listing), each with a distinct learning environment. The school admits students who require additional attention to realize their potential; it is not staffed to serve boys and girls with learning disabilities, behavioral problems, chemical dependencies or defiant attitudes. Small classes increase contact between teacher and pupil while also allowing students to pursue interests beyond the curriculum. Students are grouped by achievement, not by age. The San Marino campus is located in an eight-acre, suburban setting. The program features achievement grouping, honors and Advanced Placement courses, as well as English as a Second Language instruction. Students in grades 9-12 may divide time between the two Southwestern campuses, both of which follow University of California curricular guidelines. Boys and girls in grades 9-12 accumulate 100 hours of required community service.

See Also Pages 104-5

SAN RAFAEL, CA. (13 mi. NNE of San Francisco, CA) Urban. Pop: 56,063. Alt: 7 ft.

MARIN ACADEMY
Day — Coed Gr 9-12

San Rafael, CA 94901. 1600 Mission Ave. Tel: 415-453-4550. Fax: 415-453-8538.
www.ma.org   E-mail: dbabior@ma.org
Travis Brownley, Head (2008). BA, Univ of Virginia, MALS, Dartmouth College. **Dan Babior, Adm.**
Col Prep. AP (exams req'd; 149 taken, 80% 3+)—Comp_Sci Environ_Sci. **Feat**—British_Lit Poetry Shakespeare African-Amer_Lit Playwriting Chin Fr Span Calc Stats Discrete_Math Multivariable_Calc Astron Physiol Astrophysics Russ_Hist Intl_Relations Pol_Sci Asian_Stud Middle_Eastern_Stud Ceramics Drawing Photog Theater Music Jazz_Band Dance Journ.
Sports—Basket X-country Soccer Tennis Track W_Polo. B: Baseball Golf Lacrosse. G: Softball Swim Volley. **Activities:** 30.
Selective adm: 109/yr. Appl fee: $100. Appl due: Jan. Applied: 460. Accepted: 39%. Yield: 59%. **Tests** CEEB CTP_4 ISEE SSAT Stanford.
Enr 409. B 200. G 209. Wh 72%. Latino 4%. Blk 5%. Asian 5%. Other 14%. Avg class size: 15. Stud/fac: 9:1. **Fac 52.** M 21/F 31. FT 46/PT 6. Adv deg: 65%.
Grad '08—100. **Col**—100. (NYU 8, Boston U 6, Stanford 6, Oberlin 5, USC 5, U of CA-Berkeley 4). **Mid 50% SAT:** CR 580-700. M 590-700. W 590-720. **Col couns:** 2.
Tui '12-'13: Day $36,080 (+$600-900). **Aid:** Need 91 ($2,500,000).
Endow $10,300,000. Plant val $38,612,000. Acres 10. Bldgs 11 (80% ADA). Class rms 34. Lib 16,000 vols. Sci labs 5. Lang labs 2. Sci bldgs 1. Auds 1. Theaters 2. Art studios 4. Music studios 3. Dance studios 1. Arts ctrs 1. Gyms 2. Fields 1. Pools 1. Comp labs 3.
Est 1971. Nonprofit. Sem (Aug-June). **Assoc** CLS WASC.

Located on a 10-acre campus 12 miles north of San Francisco, MA draws students from throughout the Bay Area. Its college preparatory curriculum features honors courses in all disciplines, as well as numerous electives. The school maintains a favorable student-teacher ratio and a small average class size. Opportunities for independent study, senior projects and study abroad are available. Juniors and seniors strongly interested in global education may choose to pursue an emphasis in international studies in tandem with their regular course of studies. Practicing artists teach in the performing arts and visual arts department.

All students participate in interdisciplinary and experiential programs at year's end. Freshmen draw on their modern world history and English classes in a study of World War II, while sophomores conduct mock trials based upon subjects with a global emphasis and derived from their investigations in contemporary world history. Juniors work together to present the Conference of American Possibilities, which expands on individual pupils' American history research papers. Finally, seniors choose from extended overnight camping trips; a civic engagement; community-based, off-campus project work; or a reflective program called Vision Quest.

A wilderness education program offers weekend opportunities for individual sports, while cultivating an appreciation of the outdoors. Through this program, students may pursue backpacking, cross-country skiing, scuba diving and rock climbing.

SANTA BARBARA, CA. (78 mi. WNW of Los Angeles, CA) Urban. Pop: 92,325. Alt: 100 ft. Area also includes Carpinteria.

CATE SCHOOL
Bdg and Day — Coed Gr 9-12

Carpinteria, CA 93013. 1960 Cate Mesa Rd. Tel: 805-684-4127. Fax: 805-684-2279. www.cate.org E-mail: admission@cate.org
Benjamin D. Williams IV, Head (1997). BA, Williams College, MA, Brown Univ. **Charlotte Brownlee, Adm.**
Col Prep. AP (exams req'd; 293 taken, 85% 3+)—Eng Fr Span Calc Stats Comp_Sci Bio Chem Environ_Sci Physics US_Hist Comp_Govt & Pol US_Govt & Pol Art_Hist Studio_Art. **Feat**—Humanities Chin Japan Anat & Physiol Astron Genetics Marine_ Bio/Sci Oceanog African-Amer_Hist Middle_Eastern_Hist Econ Intl_Relations Ceramics Filmmaking Photog Sculpt Acting Chorus Music Dance.
Sports (req'd)—Basket X-country Golf Soccer Squash Tennis Track Volley. B: Baseball Football Lacrosse Softball. G: W_Polo. **Activities:** 29.
Selective adm (Gr 9-11): 70/yr. Bdg 57. Day 13. Appl fee: $75. Appl due: Jan. Applied: 450. Accepted: 30%. Yield: 58%. **Tests** CEEB ISEE SSAT TOEFL.
Enr 265. B 133. G 132. Bdg 220. Day 45. Wh 59%. Latino 10%. Blk 8%. Asian 19%. Other 4%. Intl 20%. Avg class size: 12. Stud/fac: 5:1. **Fac 55.** Adv deg: 74%.
Grad '11—63. Col—63. (USC, U of CA-Berkeley, NYU, Columbia, U of CO-Boulder, Stanford). **Mid 50% SAT:** CR 610-710. M 610-710. W 630-720. **Col couns:** 3. Alum donors: 41%.
Tui '11-'12: Bdg $45,900 (+$750). **Day $36,550** (+$500). **Aid:** Need 79 ($2,512,000). Endow $70,000,000. Plant val $20,000,000. Acres 150. Bldgs 20. Dorms 8. Dorm rms 136. Class rms 17. Lib 30,000 vols. Comp ctrs 1. Theaters 1. Art studios 3. Music studios 4. Gyms 2. Fields 4. Courts 8. Pools 1.
Est 1910. Nonprofit. Sem (Aug-June). **Assoc** CLS WASC.

Curtis Wolsey Cate was a graduate of Harvard who journeyed west to teach. In 1910, he founded the Miramar School in Santa Barbara's Mission Canyon. The following year, Mr. Cate moved the school to the foot of a rural mesa bounded by Lillingston and Gobernador canyons in the Carpinteria Valley. He changed its name to the Santa Barbara School. In 1929, he moved it again, this time to the top of "the Mesa," as the 150-acre campus has come to be known. In 1950, the school was formally renamed Cate School to honor its founder, who served as headmaster until that year. Originally, the school featured grades 6-12, but the younger classes were gradually phased out. Girls were admitted for the first time in 1981.

Boys and girls in grades 9 and 10 are required to take a course in each of six academic departments—the arts, English, foreign language, history, mathematics and science—in addition to a human development curriculum. Those students in grades 11 and 12 choose electives in all disciplines, including honors and Advanced Placement sections, and may take noncredit enrichment classes. Directed studies permit students to pursue a particular interest by designing a course not offered in the regular curriculum; these offerings may combine academic study with fieldwork. Seniors may spend the final marking period working on individually designed projects, either on or off campus.

Athletics are integral to the overall program at Cate. All students take part in after-school options during each of the three seasons. An extensive selection of interscholastics and intramurals is available; an outdoor program and recreational sports provide an alternative to competitive teams. Other extracurriculars include clubs, services, special events and publications. Public service is strongly encouraged through participation in local community projects and involvement outside the school, and all but seniors perform daily chores ranging from kitchen duty to dormitory and campus cleanup.

The entire school community convenes each week for convocations, and individual classes spend time together during an outing week in the early fall. Five-week summer language and culture programs based in Spain, China and Japan enable participants to improve their foreign language skills by living, traveling and studying in a foreign country.

LAGUNA BLANCA SCHOOL
Day — Coed Gr K-12

Santa Barbara, CA 93110. 4125 Paloma Dr. Tel: 805-687-2461. Fax: 805-682-2553.
Other locations: 260 San Ysidro Rd, Santa Barbara 93108.
www.lagunablanca.org   E-mail: admissions@lagunablanca.org
Paul Slocombe, Head (2009). BS, MS, Univ of Warwick (England). **Joyce Balak, Adm.**
  Col Prep. AP (exams req'd; 404 taken, 73% 3+)—Eng Fr Lat Span Calc Stats Bio Chem Environ_Sci Physics US_Hist Econ Human_Geog Psych US_Govt & Pol.
  Feat—Creative_Writing Shakespeare Chin Greek Astron Marine_Bio/Sci Comp_Sci Vietnam_War Law African_Stud Women's_Stud Philos Art_Hist Film Drama Music Journ. **Supp**—Rev Tut.
  Sports (req'd)—Basket X-country Golf Lacrosse Soccer Tennis Volley. B: Baseball Football. G: Softball.
  Selective adm: 86/yr. Appl fee: $100. Appl due: Feb. Accepted: 73%. Yield: 72%. **Tests** ISEE.
  Enr 350. Avg class size: 14. Stud/fac: 12:1. **Fac 54.** M 19/F 35. FT 46/PT 8. Adv deg: 62%.
  Grad '11—51. Col—51. (Wheaton-IL, Miami U-OH, Stanford, U of CA-Berkeley, UCLA, USC). **Avg SAT:** CR 624. M 589. W 646. Avg ACT: 24.7. **Col couns:** 1.
  Tui '11-'12: Day $21,840-25,812 (+$750-1550). **Aid:** Need 76 ($994,650).
  Summer: Acad Enrich Rev. 1-6 wks.
  Endow $3,300,000. Plant val $11,444,000. Acres 33. Bldgs 31. Class rms 25. 2 Libs 15,000 vols. Sci labs 6. Auds 1. Theaters 1. Art studios 4. Music studios 2. Gyms 1. Fields 6. Courts 2. Comp labs 3.
  Est 1933. Nonprofit. Sem (Sept-June). **Assoc** CLS WASC.

Offered in a small-class setting, Laguna Blanca's program combines college preparatory academics with ample opportunities in leadership, community service, the visual and performing arts, interscholastic athletics and student publications. One-on-one advising and college counseling are integral aspects of school life.

Off-campus study options enrich the curriculum. Students in grades 5-8 take weeklong trips that focus on natural science; ninth graders embark on a two-day southern California cultural excursion that incorporates visits to monuments and museums, as well as attendance at theatrical productions; and seniors participate in a required, three-week professional internship. Laguna Blanca also conducts an upper school exchange with a school in Trowbridge, England. Boys and girls perform 16 cumulative hours of required community service in grades 5-8, and another 16 total hours in grades 9-12.

Grades K-4 convene on San Ysidro Road in Montecito, while grades 5-12 are conducted at Hope Ranch Park in Santa Barbara.

SANTA MONICA, CA. (8 mi. SW of Los Angeles, CA) Urban. Pop: 84,084. Alt: 64 ft. See also Los Angeles.

CROSSROADS SCHOOL FOR ARTS AND SCIENCES
Day — Coed Gr K-12

Santa Monica, CA 90404. 1714 21st St. Tel: 310-829-7391. Fax: 310-828-5636.
Other locations: 1715 Olympic Blvd, Santa Monica 90404.
www.xrds.org
Bob Riddle, Head (2009). BS, BA, Pennsylvania State Univ, MA, Columbia Univ. **Celia Lee, Adm.**
  Col Prep. AP exams taken: 15 (100% 3+). Elem math—TERC Investigations. **Feat**—Creative_Writing Fr Greek Japan Lat Span Stats Ecol Marine_Bio/Sci Comp_Sci Human_Dev Gender_Stud Ethics Film Photog Studio_Art Drama Chorus Dance Journ Outdoor_Ed. **Supp**—Tut. Outdoor ed.

Sports—Basket X-country Golf Soccer Swim Tennis Track Volley. **B:** Baseball. **G:** Softball. **Activities:** 40.
Selective adm: 176/yr. Usual entry: K, 6, 7 & 9. Appl fee: $125. Applied: 782. Accepted: 32%. Yield: 72%. **Tests** ISEE.
Enr 1147. B 549. G 598. Elem 647. Sec 500. Wh 57%. Latino 6%. Blk 6%. Asian 6%. Other 25%. Avg class size: 19. Stud/fac: 8:1. **Fac 152.** M 61/F 91. FT 120/PT 32. Wh 72%. Latino 8%. Blk 7%. Native Am 1%. Asian 5%. Other 7%. Adv deg: 47%.
Grad '11—129. Col—128. (USC 10, NYU 6, U of MI 6, Boston U 6, Harvard 4, U of Chicago 4). **Avg SAT:** CR 620. M 609. W 655. **Mid 50% SAT:** CR 550-680. M 560-670. W 590-730. Avg ACT: 27.3. Mid 50% ACT: 24-30. Alum donors: 12%.
Tui '12-'13: Day $26,600-31,900 (+$400-800). **Aid:** Merit 3 ($50,000). Need 247 ($5,323,036).
Summer (enr 917): Acad Enrich. Arts. Sports. Tui Day $140-1500. 1-6 wks.
Endow $15,936,000. Plant val $41,896,000. Bldgs 22. Class rms 87. Libs 2. Sci labs 8. Lang labs 1. Theaters 1. Art studios 3. Music studios 2. Dance studios 2. Gyms 1. Fields 1. Pools 1. Comp labs 3. Comp/stud: 1:3.
Est 1971. Nonprofit. Sem (Sept-June). **Assoc** CLS WASC.

Located on the West Side of Los Angeles, Crossroads provides a college preparatory curriculum consisting of English, mathematics, science, foreign languages, history, classics and the arts. Physical education, human development and community service are required parts of each student's program. In 2007, the school replaced its Advanced Placement curriculum with internally designed advanced courses.

The middle school stresses composition and reading skills in all areas. The upper school supplements the fundamentals with courses in the visual arts, classical music, film, journalism, chorus and dance. Required community service projects include gerontology studies and fieldwork, and government and community internships in grades 11 and 12; middle schoolers perform 10 hours of service annually, while students in grades 9-12 satisfy a 45-hour service requirement prior to graduation. Crossroads also offers performing arts majors in art, music and drama, in addition to a classics program.

Crossroads' elementary school (located on Olympic Boulevard) offers a curriculum for children in grades K-5. It features courses in science, computer studies, art, drama, music, dance and service learning.

WATSONVILLE, CA. (27 mi. S of San Jose, CA; 74 mi. SE of San Francisco, CA) Suburban. Pop: 44,265. Alt: 25 ft.

MONTE VISTA CHRISTIAN SCHOOL
Bdg — Coed Gr 9-12; Day — Coed 6-12

Watsonville, CA 95076. 2 School Way. Tel: 831-722-8178. Fax: 831-722-6003.
www.mvcs.org E-mail: info@mvcs.org
Stephen J. Sharp, Head (2004). BA, Central Bible College. **Peter C. Gieseke, Res Adm; Kim Dawes, Day Adm.**
Col Prep. Gen Acad. AP (exams req'd)—Eng Span Calc Stats Comp_Sci Bio Chem Physics Eur_Hist US_Hist Econ Psych US_Govt & Pol Studio_Art Music_Theory.
Feat—Fr Japan Anat & Physiol Marine_Bio/Sci Web_Design Sociol Bible World_ Relig Ceramics Photog Sculpt Video_Production Drama Music Journ Culinary_Arts.
Supp—ESL.
Sports—Basket X-country Golf Soccer Swim Tennis Track. **B:** Baseball Football. **G:** Softball Volley.
Selective adm (Bdg Gr 9-11; Day 6-11): 170/yr. Bdg 45. Day 125. Appl fee: $60-80. Appl due: Feb. Accepted: 75%. **Tests** SSAT TOEFL.
Enr 629. Bdg 511. Day 118. Intl 17%. Avg class size: 17. Stud/fac: 13:1. **Fac 62.** Adv deg: 25%.

Grad '08—173. Col—154. (U of CA-Berkeley, U of CA-Davis, St Mary's Col of CA, Santa Clara, CA St Polytech-San Luis Obispo, Stanford). **Avg SAT:** CR 534. M 581. W 553. Avg ACT: 24.6. **Col couns:** 6. **Tui '12-'13: Bdg $36,750. Day $8730-9510** (+$400-600). **Intl Bdg $39,050** (+$0-3750). **Aid:** Need ($500,000). **Summer:** Acad. 3-6 wks. ESL. 5 wks. Plant val $12,000,000. Acres 100. Bldgs 25. Dorms 2. Dorm rms 55. Class rms 26. Lib 10,000 vols. Sci labs 2. Lang labs 1. Art studios 1. Music studios 2. Gyms 2. Fields 2. Courts 2. Pools 1. Riding rings 2. Stables 1. Comp labs 1. **Est 1926.** Nonprofit. Evangelical. Sem (Aug-May). **Assoc** WASC.

Serving an international student body, this central California school emphasizes problem-solving and critical-thinking skills. The curriculum, which follows a modified block schedule, features honors and Advanced Placement course work in the upper grades. Monte Vista's one-year English as a Second Language program serves students from other countries who have intermediate to advanced English skills.

All pupils take part in Jan Term, a weeklong program at the beginning of the second semester. During this week, boys and girls take a minicourse or embark on a domestic or international excursion. To fulfill another graduation requirement, high school students (grades 9-12) complete 24 hours of annual community service.

HAWAII

HONOLULU, HI. Urban. Pop: 371,657. Alt: 18 ft.

HANAHAUOLI SCHOOL
Day — Coed Gr PS (Age 4)-6

Honolulu, HI 96822. 1922 Makiki St. Tel: 808-949-6461. Fax: 808-941-2216.
www.hanahauoli.org   E-mail: bcrum@hanahauoli.org
Robert G. Peters, Head. BA, MA, EdD, Univ of Massachusetts-Amherst. **Beverly Crum, Adm.**
Pre-Prep. Feat—Lib_Skills Fr Computers Studio_Art Music Indus_Arts. **Supp**—Dev_ Read Tut.
Very selective adm: 26/yr. Appl fee: $100. Appl due: Dec. Accepted: 20%.
Enr 208. B 101. G 107. Wh 31%. Blk 1%. Asian 68%. Avg class size: 25. **Fac 24.** M 4/F 20. FT 22/PT 2. Adv deg: 33%.
Grad '11—26. Prep—26. (Punahou 16, Iolani 4, Mid-Pacific 3, La Pietra 1).
Tui '12-'13: Day $18,110.
Summer: Acad Enrich Rev. Tui Day $740. 6 wks.
Endow $4,000,000. Bldgs 8. Class rms 8. Lib 14,000 vols. Sci labs 1. Lang labs 1. Tech labs 1. Art studios 1. Music studios 1. Shops 1. Comp/stud: 1:3.5.
Est 1918. Nonprofit. (Aug-June). **Assoc** WASC.

Established by George and Sophie Cooke to fill the need for a small school with a developmental perspective, Hanahauoli utilizes an experiential learning approach based on the ideas of John Dewey. The broad program encourages children to experiment and solve problems in a variety of integrated subject areas. A foundation in traditional academic subjects is offered, with basic skills balanced by an emphasis on concept development. Students receive in-depth instruction in art, music, woodworking, physical education, French, social studies, science, literature and computers.

Hanahauoli traditions are celebrated throughout the school year to bring students together and to enhance their sense of community. The "makahiki" is celebrated by the students at Thanksgiving in ancient Hawaiian fashion in honor of Lono, the god of agriculture. At the school's Olympic games and oratory, sixth graders retell Greek myths and compete in various track and field events. Stepping Stone Day commemorates each sixth grader's contribution to the school. Each graduating student's own stepping stone is unveiled before the school and remains on campus as a permanent symbol of the child.

Parental involvement plays an important role in the workings of the school. Parents accompany students on field trips and contribute to classroom units as lecturers on their particular professions or cultural traditions. The parent organization sponsors numerous events during the year that serve to raise funds for the school and bring families together. Hanahauoli conducts an optional after-school care program and several enrichment programs at an additional cost.

IOLANI SCHOOL
Day — Coed Gr K-12

Honolulu, HI 96826. 563 Kamoku St. Tel: 808-949-5355. Fax: 808-943-2375.
www.iolani.org   E-mail: admission@iolani.org
Val T. Iwashita, Head (1995). BEd, MEd, Univ of Hawaii, EdD, Brigham Young Univ. **Kelly Monaco, Adm.**
Col Prep. AP (exams req'd; 821 taken, 98% 3+)—Eng Fr Japan Lat Span Calc Stats Comp_Sci Bio Chem Physics Eur_Hist US_Hist Econ Psych US_Govt & Pol Studio_

Art. Feat—Shakespeare Chin Forensic_Sci African-Amer_Stud Asian_Stud Hawaiian_Culture Relig Theater Chorus Music Dance. **Supp**—Tut.
Sports—Basket Bowl X-country Golf Sail Soccer Swim Tennis Track Volley W_Polo. **B:** Baseball Football Wrestling. **G:** Cheer Softball. **Activities:** 85.
Very selective adm (Gr K-11): 270/yr. Appl fee: $125. Appl due: Dec. Applied: 1381. Accepted: 22%. Yield: 72%. **Tests** IQ SSAT.
Enr 1870. Wh 18%. Latino 2%. Blk 1%. Native Am 2%. Asian 68%. Other 9%. Avg class size: 16. **Fac 180.** M 64/F 116. FT 167/PT 13. Adv deg: 71%.
Grad '11—231. Col—231. (U of HI-Manoa 19, U of WA 13, USC 11, OR St 9, Santa Clara 8, Willamette 8). **Mid 50% SAT:** CR 530-650. M 600-720. W 560-690. Mid 50% ACT: 26-31.
Tui '11-'12: Day $16,900 (+$500). **Aid:** Need 231 ($1,960,500).
Summer (enr 2685): Acad Enrich Rev Rem Rec. Tui Day $140-575. 3-6 wks.
Endow $120,000,000. Acres 25. Bldgs 25. Class rms 101. Lib 25,000 vols. Labs 5. Art studios 4. Music studios 4. Dance studios 2. Gyms 2. Fields 3. Courts 6. Pools 1. Weight rms 1.
Est 1863. Nonprofit. Episcopal. Quar (Aug-June). **Assoc** CLS WASC.

Situated on a 25-acre campus within one mile of Waikiki Beach, this school was founded during the reign of King Kamehameha IV. Iolani emphasizes Christian values and serves students of diverse religious and racial backgrounds.

Iolani's college-oriented academic program places a special emphasis on English, mathematics and science, with five foreign languages being offered in the upper school. An accelerated academic program has been established, with Advanced Placement offered in all major areas of study.

The school introduces art in the lower grades and later conducts elective studio art courses in glass, oil painting, sculpture, ceramics, metal sculpture and photography. The performing arts program consists of band, chorus, dance, orchestra, stage band and theater.

MID-PACIFIC INSTITUTE

Day — Coed Gr PS (Age 3)-12

Honolulu, HI 96822. 2445 Kaala St. Tel: 808-973-5000. Fax: 808-973-5099.
www.midpac.edu　E-mail: admissions@midpac.edu
Joe C. Rice, Pres (1996). BA, Univ of Washington, MA, Central Washington Univ. **Scott Siegfried, Adm.**
Col Prep. IB Diploma. AP (187 exams taken, 68% 3+)—Eng Calc Stats Bio Chem Environ_Sci Physics US_Hist. **Feat**—Chin Fr Japan Lat Span Astron Oceanog Comp_Sci Robotics Web_Design E_Asian_Hist Asian_Stud HI_Stud Ceramics Photog Studio_ Art Video_Production Digital_Media Acting Theater_Arts Music_Hist Music_Theory Orchestra Jazz_Band Ballet Dance Journ. **Supp**—ESL Tut.
Sports—Basket Bowl X-country Golf Sail Soccer Swim Tennis Track Volley W_Polo Wrestling. **B:** Baseball Football. **G:** Cheer Softball. **Activities:** 94.
Selective adm: 313/yr. Usual entry: PS, K, 6, 7 & 9. Appl fee: $100. Appl due: Dec. Applied: 1054. Accepted: 50%. Yield: 55%. **Tests** CEEB SSAT TOEFL.
Enr 1550. B 778. G 772. Elem 710. Sec 840. Intl 10%. Avg class size: 18. Casual. **Fac 124.** M 44/F 80. FT 105/PT 19. Adv deg: 75%.
Grad '11—198. Col—198. (U of HI-Manoa 41, OR St 9, Seattle U 9, Pacific U 5, U of OR 5, USC 4). Athl schol 6. **Col couns:** 3. Alum donors: 6%.
Tui '12-'13: Day $18,300 (+$700). **Aid:** Merit 36 ($377,500). Need 360 ($2,171,606).
Summer: Acad Enrich Rev Rec. ESL. Tui Day $375-1070/crse. 4-6 wks.
Endow $12,000,000. Plant val $130,000,000. Acres 35. Bldgs 28 (80% ADA). Libs 1. Sci labs 8. Lang labs 2. Auds 1. Theaters 2. Art studios 4. Music studios 3. Dance studios 3. Fine arts ctrs 1. Gyms 1. Fields 3. Courts 2. Pools 1. Comp labs 6. Laptop prgm Gr PS-12.
Est 1864. Nonprofit. Quar (Aug-May). **Assoc** WASC.

MPI dates back to 1908, when Kawaiaha'o Seminary for Girls (established in 1864) merged with Mills Institute for Boys (founded in 1892) and moved to Manoa from the schools' previous downtown locations. Although officially incorporated as a single entity, the two schools kept their separate names and programs for another 15 years. Today, Mid-Pacific serves a culturally diverse, international student body that includes boys and girls from Hawaii, Asia, Europe and the US Mainland.

The curriculum is particularly noteworthy for inclusion of the two-year International Baccalaureate program; MPI was the first independent school in the state to prepare students for the IB Diploma. Another feature of the curriculum is the Mid-Pacific Institute School of the Arts (MPSA), a preprofessional arts training program that pupils may take part in as a complement to college preparatory academics. MPSA offers rigorous conservatory training in theater, musical theater, dance, hula and instrumental music, in addition to comprehensive programming in media and the visual arts. A well-developed technology center enables Mid-Pacific to enhance student learning with current computer technology.

Available for an additional annual fee, the school's ESL program provides intensive, broad-based instruction designed to facilitate the pupil's transition into the standard college preparatory curriculum.

Boys and girls accumulate 120 hours of required community service prior to graduation.

PUNAHOU SCHOOL
Day — Coed Gr K-12

Honolulu, HI 96822. 1601 Punahou St. Tel: 808-944-5711. Fax: 808-943-3602.
www.punahou.edu   E-mail: admission@punahou.edu
James K. Scott, Pres (1994). AB, Stanford Univ, MA, Univ of San Francisco, MEd, EdD, Harvard Univ. **Betsy S. Hata, Adm.**
   Col Prep. AP (exams req'd; 1034 taken, 90% 3+)—Fr Span Calc Stats Comp_Sci Bio Chem Environ_Sci Physics Eur_Hist US_Hist Psych US_Govt & Pol Studio_Art. **Feat**—Shakespeare World_Lit Chin Japan Hawaiian Bioethics Asian_Hist Amer_Stud Sports_Psych Buddhist_Philos Ceramics Photog Video_Production Glass_Blowing Jewelry Printmaking Theater Band Chorus Music_Theory Orchestra Journ JROTC. **Supp**—Tut. Outdoor ed.
   Sports—Basket Bowl Cheer X-country Golf Sail Soccer Swim Tennis Track Volley W_ Polo Wrestling. B: Baseball Football. G: Softball. **Activities:** 55.
   Very selective adm: 481/yr. Usual entry: K, 4, 6, 7 & 9. Appl fee: $100. Appl due: Dec. Applied: 2186. Accepted: 28%. Yield: 78%. **Tests** CEEB CTP_4 IQ SSAT.
   Enr 3743. B 1841. G 1902. Elem 2029. Sec 1714. Avg class size: 22. Stud/fac: 12:1. **Fac 359.** M 132/F 227. FT 315/PT 44. Adv deg: 63%.
   Grad '11—428. Col—424. (U of HI-Manoa 31, Creighton 22, Santa Clara 17, USC 17, Boston U 16, Seattle U 15). Athl schol 13. **Mid 50% SAT:** CR 550-670. M 600-710. W 550-670. Avg ACT: 26.4. **Col couns:** 7.
   Tui '12-'13: Day $19,200 (+$500-1000). **Aid:** Merit 12. Need 482.
   Summer (enr 4032): Acad Enrich Rec. Tui Day $475-1500. 1-6 wks.
   Endow $187,537,000. Plant val $125,756,000. Acres 76. Bldgs 71 (80% ADA). Class rms 231. 3 Libs 115,000 vols. Chapels 1. Auds 3. Theaters 1. Art studios 6. Music studios 16. Dance studios 1. Arts ctrs 1. Gyms 2. Fields 6. Tennis courts 9. Racquetball courts 6. Pools 1. Comp labs 3. Laptop prgm Gr 4-12.
   Est 1841. Nonprofit. (Aug-June). **Assoc** WASC.

Established by New England Congregational missionary families for their own children, Punahou was the first American college preparatory school west of the Rocky Mountains. For over a century, the school served descendants of the early missionaries, as well as island children of various races and religions and, later, arrivals from the mainland. Today, Punahou serves as the largest independent, coeducational college preparatory school in the United States. The student body reflects Hawaii's ethnic, cultural and socioeconomic diversity. Located on a 76-acre campus, the school maintains a particularly well-developed school plant.

   The junior school (grades K-8) comprises three smaller, self-contained sections designed to meet the specific needs of children of different ages. Outdoor and camp experiences provide supplemental learning opportunities during these years. In the academy (grades 9-12), pupils fulfill requirements in English, science, social studies, math, foreign language, physical education and the performing arts. In addition, seniors fulfill a 26-hour community service requirement. Boys and girls participate in a modular system in which classes vary in length and size according to the needs of instruction, allowing for significant individualization in scheduling.

ST. ANDREW'S PRIORY SCHOOL
Day — Girls Gr K-12
Honolulu, HI 96813. 224 Queen Emma Sq. Tel: 808-536-6102. Fax: 808-538-1035.
www.priory.net　E-mail: admissions@priory.net
Sandra J. Theunick, Head (2007). BA, Newton College of the Sacred Heart, MDiv, Washington Theological Union. **Sue Ann Wargo, Adm.**
Col Prep. AP (exams req'd)—Eng Fr Japan Span Calc Bio Chem Physics US_Hist US_Govt & Pol. **Elem math**—Harcourt. **Elem read**—Houghton Mifflin. **Feat**—Creative_Writing Hawaiian Stats Astron Ecol Microbio Oceanog Physiol Comp_Sci Web_Design HI_Hist Econ Psych Sociol Women's_Stud Relig Studio_Art Music Journ. **Supp**—ESL Tut. **Dual enr:** HI Pacific.
Sports—G: Basket Bowl X-country Golf Sail Soccer Softball Swim Tennis Track Volley W_Polo.
Selective adm (Gr K-11): 45/yr. Usual entry: K, 6, 7 & 9. Appl fee: $50. Appl due: Rolling. Accepted: 75%. Yield: 63%. **Tests** SSAT.
Enr 450. Wh 7%. Blk 1%. Asian 92%. Intl 10%. Avg class size: 15. Stud/fac: 8:1. Uniform.
Fac 69. M 15/F 54. FT 59/PT 10. Wh 53%. Latino 4%. Asian 26%. Other 17%. Adv deg: 50%.
Grad '09—44. Col—44. (U of HI-Manoa, Seattle U, USC, Brown, Carnegie Mellon, U of San Francisco). **Col couns:** 1.
Tui '11-'12: Day $15,000 (+$2000). **Aid:** Merit 21 ($120,345). Need 124 ($346,722).
Summer: Coed. Acad Enrich Rev Rec. Sports. Tui Day $395-700/crse. 10 wks.
Endow $3,120,000. Plant val $13,000,000. Acres 3. Bldgs 11. Class rms 44. 2 Libs 25,000 vols. Sci labs 5. Art studios 5. Music studios 6. Dance studios 2. Gyms 1. Courts 1. Comp labs 1. Laptop prgm Gr 5-12.
Est 1867. Nonprofit. Episcopal. Sem (Aug-June). **Assoc** WASC.

St. Andrew's Priory School, Hawaii's first school for girls, was founded by Anglican sisters and Queen Emma, wife of King Kamehameha IV. Curricular offerings include extensive visual and performing arts selections, computer, foreign languages and Advanced Placement preparation. St. Andrew's is affiliated with Hawaii Pacific University through the sharing of libraries, facilities, faculty and staff and ESL programs for international students. Qualified juniors and seniors may enroll in freshman-level courses at HPU at no additional cost. Each student in grades 5-12 purchases an Apple notebook computer, and elementary school classes utilize mobile laptop carts.

Located in downtown Honolulu, the Priory is easily accessible to all parts of Oahu. Students may participate in interscholastic sports, drama, science fair, and speech and math competitions. In addition to the regular day school program, the Priory offers educational opportunities to the larger community from preschool to adults.

KAILUA, HI. (7 mi. NE of Honolulu, HI) Urban. Pop: 36,818. Alt: 10 ft.

LE JARDIN ACADEMY
Day — Coed Gr PS (Age 3)-12
Kailua, HI 96734. 917 Kalanianaole Hwy. Tel: 808-261-0707. Fax: 808-262-9339.
www.lejardinacademy.org　E-mail: staylor@lejardinacademy.org

Adrian Allan, Pres (1998). BS, Univ of Leeds (England), MA, Univ of Alabama. **Susan Taylor, Adm.**

Col Prep. IB PYP. IB MYP. AP (exams req'd; 63 taken, 63% 3+)—Eng Fr Calc Bio Chem Physics US_Hist Psych Studio_Art. **Feat**—Chin Japan Span Anat & Physiol Comp_Sci Econ Sociol Drama Music Dance Bus Journ. **Supp**—Rev Tut.

Sports—Basket Golf Sail Soccer Swim. B: W_Polo. G: Volley.

Selective adm: 179/yr. Appl fee: $75. Appl due: Dec. Accepted: 50%. Yield: 40%. **Tests** MAT SSAT.

Enr 800. B 390. G 410. Elem 600. Sec 200. Wh 63%. Blk 1%. Asian 20%. Other 16%. Avg class size: 21. Stud/fac: 10:1. Uniform. **Fac 120.** M 10/F 110. FT 120. Adv deg: 21%.

Grad '09—48. Col—47. (Geo Wash, U of San Francisco, U of HI-Manoa, CA Maritime, Chaminade, Purdue). **Avg SAT:** CR 547. M 562. W 543. **Col couns:** 1.

Tui '11-'12: Day $15,540 (+$200-950). **Aid:** Need 90 ($200,000).

Summer: Acad Enrich Rev Rec. Soccer. Tui Day $350/crse. 5-6 wks.

Endow $2,000,000. Acres 50. Bldgs 10 (100% ADA). Class rms 45. Libs 2. Sci labs 4. Auds 2. Theaters 1. Art studios 2. Music studios 2. Fields 2. Pools 1. Comp labs 2. Laptop prgm Gr 9-12.

Est 1961. Nonprofit. Quar (Aug-June). **Assoc** WASC.

Founded as a one-room preschool by Henriette D. Neal, a native of France, the academy experienced significant growth in enrollment and grade range during the 1970s. By the end of the decade, the school's program extended through grade 8. After many years as an elementary school, Le Jardin added a high school division in the fall of 2002.

The academy provides a strong academic base in all subjects and an enriching fine arts program. In the early grades, basic communicational skills are taught using the Spalding method, a multisensory approach to the teaching of reading, writing and spelling. The interdisciplinary middle school program employs a flexible schedule that allows for long time blocks. An increasing number of electives are available during these years. Qualified high school pupils have Advanced Placement course options in every major discipline, as well as several foreign language choices. In addition to fulfilling a 30-hour community service requirement, all seniors write an extended essay or report on an approved topic of original scientific research.

Field trips provide enrichment at every grade level.   **See Also Page 103**

KAMUELA, HI. (42 mi. WNW of Hilo, HI) Rural. Pop: 5972. Alt: 2600 ft.

HAWAII PREPARATORY ACADEMY
Bdg — Coed Gr 6-12; Day — Coed K-12

Kamuela, HI 96743. 65-1692 Kohala Mountain Rd. Tel: 808-885-7321. Fax: 808-881-4003.

Other locations: 65-1274 Kawaihae Rd, Kamuela 96743.

www.hpa.edu   E-mail: admissions@hpa.edu

Lindsay R. Barnes, Jr., Head (2008). BA, Hampden-Sydney College, MA, Univ of Georgia, JD, Univ of Virginia. **Joshua D. Clark, Adm.**

Col Prep. AP (78 exams taken, 72% 3+)—Eng Fr Japan Span Calc Stats Bio Chem Environ_Sci Physics US_Hist World_Hist Psych Art_Hist Studio_Art. **Feat**—Creative_Writing Anat & Physiol Astron Forensic_Sci Geol Marine_Bio/Sci Engineering Comp_Sci Robotics HI_Hist Econ Ceramics Performing_Arts Drama Music Music_ Theory. **Supp**—ESL Tut. Sat classes.

Sports—Basket X-country Golf Soccer Swim Tennis Track Volley. B: Baseball Football Wrestling. G: Softball W_Polo.

Selective adm: 129/yr. Bdg 59. Day 70. Appl fee: $25. Appl due: Feb. Accepted: 42%. Yield: 90%. **Tests** ISEE SSAT TOEFL.

Enr 600. Elem 250. Sec 350. Intl 16%. Avg class size: 13. Stud/fac: 10:1. **Fac 69.** M 29/F 40. FT 52/PT 17. Adv deg: 59%. In dorms 15.

Grad '09—85. Col—85. (Santa Clara, USC). **Avg SAT:** CR 532. M 572. W 525. **Mid 50% SAT:** CR 460-600. M 520-640. W 450-580. **Col couns:** 1.
Tui '12-'13: Bdg $41,200-42,800. **5-Day Bdg** $37,200-38,700. **Day** $16,800-21,600.
Intl Bdg $50,500. **Aid:** Need 152 ($1,600,000).
Summer (enr 100): Enrich. Tui Bdg $4300. Tui Day $550-1650. 4 wks.
Endow $21,130,000. Plant val $38,000,000. Acres 209. Bldgs 40. Dorms 4. Dorm rms 116. Class rms 55. 2 Libs 17,000 vols. Sci labs 5. Art studios 2. Music studios 2. Dance studios 1. Gyms 1. Fields 7. Basketball courts 2. Tennis courts 4. Volleyball courts 1. Pools 1. Comp labs 5. Comp/stud: 1:5.
Est 1949. Nonprofit. Sem (Aug-May). **Assoc** CLS WASC.

HPA has two campuses in the town of Waimea (Kamuela) on the island of Hawaii. The upper school is situated on 200 acres at the foot of the Kohala Mountains, in the heart of Hawaii's ranching country; the campus housing the lower and middle schools occupies nine acres near the center of Waimea. Students come from the Hawaiian Islands, more than a dozen mainland states and territories, and a similar number of foreign countries.

Among the graduation requirements are modern language, fine arts and computer science courses, as well as electives. Advanced Placement classes are available in all disciplines. Students are required to participate in the cocurricular component of athletics and may choose interscholastic competition, intramurals or noncompetitive activities each weekday.

Some of the weekend activities scheduled are camping trips, scuba diving, shopping trips, excursions and hikes to points of interest on the island, surfing outings and regular Sunday trips to the beach. HPA operates a compulsory work program that consists of two hours of on-campus chores each week.

OREGON

PORTLAND, OR. Urban. Pop: 529,121. Alt: 175 ft.

CATLIN GABEL SCHOOL
Day — Coed Gr PS (Age 4)-12

Portland, OR 97225. 8825 SW Barnes Rd. Tel: 503-297-1894. Fax: 503-297-0139.
www.catlin.edu   E-mail: braunm@catlin.edu
Lark P. Palma, Head (1995). BA, George Mason Univ, MEd, PhD, Univ of South Carolina.
Sara Nordhoff, Adm.

Col Prep. AP exams taken: 48 (96% 3+). Feat—Creative_Writing Chin Fr Japan Span Calc Stats Astron Environ_Sci Geol Comp_Sci Anthro Econ Ethics Philos Art_Hist Ceramics Drawing Photog Studio_Art Theater_Arts Music Music_Theory Woodworking. **Supp**—Tut.

Sports—Basket X-country Golf Racquet Soccer Tennis. B: Baseball. G: Track Volley.

Very selective adm: 100/yr. Appl fee: $75. Accepted: 25%. **Tests** CEEB ISEE SSAT.

Enr 746. Elem 451. Sec 295. Avg class size: 13. Stud/fac: 7:1. **Fac 91.** M 40/F 51. FT 79/PT 12. Adv deg: 73%.

Grad '11—74. Col—74. (Chapman, Emory, Williams, Oberlin, Rensselaer Polytech, Bryn Mawr). **Avg SAT:** CR 639. M 640. W 639. Avg ACT: 28. **Col couns:** 2.

Tui '12-'13: Day $18,350-24,750 (+$200-4150). **Aid:** Need 209 ($2,900,000).

Summer: Acad Enrich Rec. 1-4 wks.

Endow $17,000,000. Acres 54. Bldgs 23. Class rms 60. Lib 35,000 vols. Lang labs 5. Theaters 1. Art studios 6. Music studios 2. Gyms 3. Fields 4. Tennis courts 4. Tracks 1. Weight rms 1. Comp labs 5. Laptop prgm Gr 9-12.

Est 1911. Nonprofit. Tri (Sept-June). **Assoc** NWAC.

This well-regarded school was founded by Ruth Catlin. She and her assistant and successor, Jessie Thain Powers, directed the school for many years, merging with the Cady School of Music Education to form the Hillside School for Boys and Girls. Both retired in 1942.

In 1957, the Catlin-Hillside School merged with the Gabel Country Day School (derived from the old Portland Academy, founded in 1851). The following year, the upper school (grades 9-12) moved from the urban campus to the 54-acre Honey Hollow Farm site, where all four divisions have been located since 1967.

Catlin Gabel offers a diverse curriculum that emphasizes the mastery of reading, writing and analytical skills. The academic program also includes training in fundamental mathematical and scientific techniques. Students may take advantage of an extensive arts program. While no courses carry the Advanced Placement designation, many honors courses are available for advanced study, and pupils prepare for AP exams in certain subjects.

For four days each March, the upper school suspends regular classes and offers various experiential learning opportunities outside of the regular curriculum. Students generate ideas and collaborate with faculty and alumni to create Winterim offerings. Faculty and other school personnel and community members (assisted by faculty advisors) conduct these courses.

Boys and girls complete class community service projects at all grade levels, and older pupils satisfy the following requirements: monthly service program participation in grades 6-8 and 15 hours of annual service in grades 9-12.

OREGON EPISCOPAL SCHOOL
Bdg — Coed Gr 9-12; Day — Coed PS (Age 4)-12

Portland, OR 97223. 6300 SW Nicol Rd. Tel: 503-246-7771. Fax: 503-768-3140.
www.oes.edu   E-mail: admit@oes.edu

Mo Copeland, Head (2011). BS, Reed College. **Susan Gundle, Adm.**
  Col Prep. AP (173 exams taken, 88% 3+)—Eng Fr Japan Span Calc Stats Comp_ Sci US_Hist. **Elem math**—Everyday Math. **Feat**—Poetry Shakespeare Playwriting Urban_Lit Chin Anat Ecol Geol Microbio Engineering Intl_Relations Psych Constitutional_Law Relig Digital_Arts Drama Music Study_Skills. **Supp**—ESL.
  Sports—Basket X-country Fencing Lacrosse Ski Soccer Tennis Track. G: Volley.
  Selective adm (Bdg Gr 9-12; Day PS-11): 141/yr. Bdg 16. Day 125. Usual entry: PS, K, 6 & 9. Appl fee: $75. Appl due: Feb. Applied: 443. Accepted: 49%. Yield: 66%. **Tests** CTP_4 ISEE SSAT TOEFL.
  Enr 844. B 426. G 418. Bdg 58. Day 786. Wh 70%. Latino 2%. Blk 2%. Asian 16%. Other 10%. Intl 5%. Avg class size: 14. Stud/fac: 7:1. **Fac 121.** M 43/F 78. FT 94/PT 27. Wh 92%. Latino 1%. Blk 3%. Asian 4%. Adv deg: 77%. In dorms 8.
  Grad '11—77. Col—77. (Boston U, Carleton, U of SC, Stanford, U of WA, U of OR). **Avg SAT:** CR 658. M 673. W 679. **Mid 50% SAT:** CR 550-730. M 630-740. W 570-720. Avg ACT: 28. Mid 50% ACT: 25-30. **Col couns:** 2. Alum donors: 7%.
  Tui '12-'13: Bdg $48,410 (+$600-800). **Day $17,170-25,340** (+$500-700). **Aid:** Need 150 ($1,830,791).
  Summer (enr 1550): Acad Enrich Rec. Tui Day $220-465. 1-2 wks.
  Endow $21,000,000. Plant val $28,000,000. Acres 59. Bldgs 14. Dorms 2. Dorm rms 42. Class rms 89. 3 Libs 35,000 vols. Sci labs 5. Art studios 6. Music studios 3. Gyms 2. Fields 3. Courts 7. Tracks 1. Skiing facilities. Comp labs 6. Laptop prgm Gr 6-8.
  Est 1869. Nonprofit. Episcopal. Sem (Sept-June). **Assoc** CLS NWAC.

The school traces its origin to a pioneer institution founded by the Episcopal Church in 1861. In 1869, St. Helens Hall for girls was formally established by Bishop Benjamin Wistar Morris and Miss Mary Rodney. From 1903 to 1944, it was directed by the Episcopal Sisters of St. John Baptist. In 1965, after St. Helens Hall had relocated to its present, 59-acre campus, Bishop Dagwell Hall for boys was added as a coordinate institution. In 1968, the two schools merged as Oregon Episcopal School, becoming fully coeducational in 1972.

Educational objectives and admissions criteria are demanding, and students are prepared for college through a balanced curriculum in English, history, math, science, foreign languages and religion/philosophy. Global studies are emphasized, and English as a Second Language is offered to international pupils. All students participate in an age-appropriate service program; boys and girls perform 120 hours of service prior to graduation. Art, music, drama and sports are an integral part of the overall program, with cocurricular activities offered in many areas. OES integrates an outdoor/experiential program into the curriculum, and an on-campus wetland area is used as a field biology lab.

PORTLAND LUTHERAN SCHOOL

Day — Coed Gr PS (Age 3)-12

Portland, OR 97233. 740 SE 182nd Ave. Tel: 503-667-3199. Fax: 503-667-4520.
  www.portland-lutheran.org   E-mail: sschlimpert@portland-lutheran.org
Donn Maier, Exec Dir. BA, Pacific Lutheran Univ, MEd, Concordia Univ (OR). **Scott Schlimpert, Adm.**
  Col Prep. AP—Eng Calc. **Elem math**—Bridges in Math. **Elem read**—Open Court. **Feat**—Span Comp_Sci Econ Pol_Sci Psych Relig Studio_Art Drama Music. **Supp**—ESL Tut. Outdoor ed. **Dual enr:** Concordia U-OR.
  Sports—Basket X-country Track. B: Golf. G: Volley.
  Somewhat selective adm: 64/yr. Usual entry: PS, K, 1, 6-10. Appl fee: $0. Appl due: Rolling. Applied: 90. Accepted: 95%. Yield: 71%. **Tests** HSPT Stanford TOEFL.
  Enr 245. B 112. G 133. Elem 160. Sec 85. Wh 77%. Latino 2%. Blk 3%. Asian 16%. Other 2%. Intl 11%. Avg class size: 15. Stud/fac: 11:1. **Fac 19.** M 5/F 14. FT 14/PT 5. Wh 100%. Adv deg: 52%.
  Grad '11—25. Col—24. (Mt Hood CC, Portland CC, Pacific Lutheran, Valparaiso U, U of Portland). Athl schol 2. **Avg SAT:** CR 553. M 582. W 519. Avg ACT: 22. Alum donors: 15%.
  Tui '12-'13: Day $5950-9220 (+$500). **Aid:** Merit 30 ($54,000). Need 93 ($246,000).

Endow $410,000. Plant val $7,300,000. Acres 14. Bldgs 6 (50% ADA). Class rms 23. Lib 10,000 vols. Sci labs 2. Auds 1. Art studios 1. Music studios 2. Gyms 2. Fields 2. Comp labs 2. **Est 1905.** Nonprofit. Lutheran (25% practice). Sem (Aug-June). **Assoc** NWAC.

Founded as Concordia Academy to prepare young men for the Lutheran ministry, PLS gradually evolved into a Christian, coeducational elementary and secondary school, culminating in the assumption of its present name in 1989. The school now offers a broad education in the humanities, math, science, language arts and the fine arts.

As part of the college preparatory high school curriculum, qualified students in grades 10-12 may enroll in honors or Advanced Placement classes, as well as in college-level courses at the nearby Concordia University. Religious education is part of everyday school life. In addition, all high schoolers fulfill a 20-hour annual community service requirement.

For an additional fee, PLS maintains a program for middle and high school international students. ESL instruction assists international pupils with English pronunciation, grammar, vocabulary development, writing skills and conversational skills.

WASHINGTON

REDMOND, WA. (12 mi. ENE of Seattle, WA) Suburban. Pop: 45,256. Alt: 42 ft.

THE OVERLAKE SCHOOL
Day — Coed Gr 5-12

Redmond, WA 98053. 20301 NE 108th St. Tel: 425-868-1000. Fax: 425-868-5771. www.overlake.org E-mail: questions@overlake.org
Matthew P. Horvat, Head (2012). BA, Univ of Pennsylvania, MAT, Boston Univ. Lori Maughan, Adm.
Col Prep. AP (186 exams taken, 94% 3+)—Eng Fr Japan Lat Span Calc Stats Comp_ Sci Bio Chem Physics Art_Hist. Feat—Chin Bioethics Econ Race & Ethnicity Photog Studio_Art Drama Theater_Arts Chorus Music Dance Outdoor_Ed. Supp—Rev Tut. Outdoor ed.
Sports—Basket X-country Golf Lacrosse Soccer Tennis. B: Baseball. G: Volley. Activities: 35.
Selective adm: 60/yr. Usual entry: 5, 6, 7 & 9. Appl fee: $50-60. Appl due: Jan. Applied: 349. Accepted: 39%. Yield: 70%. Tests ISEE.
Enr 535. B 283. G 252. Elem 233. Sec 302. Nonwhite 27%. Avg class size: 13. Stud/fac: 9:1. Fac 58. M 22/F 36. FT 46/PT 12. Adv deg: 63%.
Grad '11—69. Col—69. (U of WA 9, USC 4, U of CO-Boulder 4, U of Puget Sound 3, Santa Clara 3, Whitman 3). Mid 50% SAT: CR 600-690. M 620-720. W 580-710. Mid 50% ACT: 27-32. Col couns: 2. Alum donors: 5%.
Tui '12-'13: Day $26,856 (+$800-2500). Aid: Need 99 ($1,100,000).
Endow $16,000,000. Plant val $35,000,000. Acres 75. Bldgs 17 (75% ADA). Class rms 47. Lib 16,000 vols. Sci labs 1. Lang labs 1. Auds 1. Theaters 2. Art studios 4. Music studios 4. Arts ctrs 2. Gyms 2. Fields 4. Tennis courts 4. Comp labs 11. Comp/stud: 4:1.
Est 1967. Nonprofit. Sem (Aug-June). Assoc NWAC.

Overlake, located on a wooded, 75-acre campus, offers a rigorous college preparatory curriculum. Sports, a strong arts program, and Advanced Placement and honors courses in all major disciplines complement traditional course offerings. Service days and projects are part of the curriculum at all grade levels, and boys and girls in grades 9-12 perform 15 compulsory hours of community service annually. College counseling services are available.

An important element of the curriculum is the annual Project Week, in which boys and girls participate in one of more than 30 experiential projects, ranging from Southwest backpacking to automobile engine rebuilding. Seniors complete an independent internship or community service project.

Overlake provides opportunities for travel and exchange with schools in Italy, Spain, France, China and Japan. In addition, boys and girls may engage in global service projects in Cambodia and Uruguay.

SEATTLE, WA. Urban. Pop: 563,374. Alt: to 123 ft.

THE BUSH SCHOOL
Day — Coed Gr K-12

Seattle, WA 98112. 3400 E Harrison St. Tel: 206-322-7978. Fax: 206-860-3876. www.bush.edu E-mail: admissions@bush.edu

Frank E. Magusin, Head (2000). BA, Pomona College, MA, Harvard Univ. **Polly Fredlund, Adm.**
Col Prep. Feat—Creative_Writing Shakespeare Fr Span Stats Multivariable_Calc Anat & Physiol Astron Programming Japan_Hist Psych Lat-Amer_Stud Women's_Stud Ethics Ceramics Drawing Painting Photog Sculpt Acting Theater_Arts Wilderness_ Ed. **Supp**—Dev_Read ESL Makeup Rem_Math Rev Tut.
Sports—Basket Bowl X-country Golf Ski Soccer Tennis Track Ultimate_Frisbee. B: Baseball. G: Volley.
Selective adm (Gr K-11): 84/yr. Usual entry: K, 6 & 9. Appl fee: $60-75. Appl due: Jan. **Tests** ISEE.
Enr 575. B 277. G 298. Elem 343. Sec 232. Wh 71%. Latino 2%. Blk 4%. Native Am 1%. Asian 8%. Other 14%. Avg class size: 15. **Fac 85.**
Grad '11—65. Col—65. (Willamette 5, Santa Clara 4, U of WA 3, W WA 3, Yale 2, U of Chicago 2). **Mid 50% SAT:** CR 600-710. M 600-690. W 590-680. Mid 50% ACT: 26-32. **Col couns:** 2. Alum donors: 10%.
Tui '11-'12: Day $20,090-26,535 (+$100-750). **Aid:** Need 86 ($1,800,000).
Summer: Acad Enrich Rec. 1-2 wks.
Endow $10,783,000. Plant val $36,000,000. Acres 6. Bldgs 10. Class rms 64. Lib 19,000 vols. Sci labs 7. Lang labs 1. Theaters 1. Art studios 7. Music studios 5. Dance studios 1. Gyms 2. Fields 1. Comp labs 5.
Est 1924. Nonprofit. Tri (Sept-June). **Assoc** NWAC NEASC.

To fill a local need, Helen Taylor Bush founded this well-organized school and established a tradition of experiential education. Lower, middle and upper divisions of the school share the resources of a single campus in the Madison Park neighborhood of the city.

Utilizing the city and outlying wilderness areas, interdisciplinary programs and field trips supplement academic work. While Bush does not offer honors or Advanced Placement courses, pupils may prepare for AP exams. Instruction in science, math and art makes significant use of technology. Community service is part of the curriculum at all grade levels, and students must complete two service projects prior to graduation.

The school's Action Module Program enables boys and girls to select from various offerings outside of the standard curriculum every Thursday during the fall and winter trimesters, and for a full week each spring. AMP provides real-world experience while allowing students to assist with course design and assume leadership roles. Trimester-long international study programs provide opportunities abroad for community service, independent research and home stays. Also part of the curriculum are senior projects, which last for three weeks and require pupils to propose and design projects that tie into at least one of three educational foundations at Bush.

LAKESIDE SCHOOL

Day — Coed Gr 5-12

Seattle, WA 98125. 14050 1st Ave NE. Tel: 206-368-3600. Fax: 206-368-3638.
Other locations: 14510 1st Ave NE, Seattle 98125.
www.lakesideschool.org   E-mail: admissions@lakesideschool.org
Bernard Noe, Head. BA, Boston Univ, MA, Georgetown Univ, MPh, George Washington Univ. **Booth D. Kyle, Adm.**
Col Prep. AP exams taken: 471 (94% 3+). Feat—Poetry African-Amer_Lit Asian-Amer_Lit Russ_Lit Chin Fr Lat Span Calc Stats Chaos_Theory Anat & Physiol Astron Bioethics Environ_Sci Forensic_Sci Marine_Bio/Sci Organic_Chem Comp_Sci Web_ Design African-Amer_Hist Cold_War Vietnam_War Amer_Stud Anthro Gender_Stud Philos World_Relig Art_Hist Ceramics Film Photog Sculpt Studio_Art Drama Jazz_ Band. **Supp**—Tut.
Sports—Basket Crew X-country Golf Lacrosse Soccer Swim Tennis Track Wrestling. B: Baseball Football. G: Softball Volley.
Very selective adm (Gr 5-11): 141/yr. Appl fee: $25. Appl due: Jan. Applied: 951. Accepted: 18%. Yield: 90%. **Tests** ISEE.
Enr 796. B 399. G 397. Elem 267. Sec 529. Wh 51%. Latino 7%. Blk 11%. Native Am 2%.

Asian 27%. Other 2%. Avg class size: 16. Stud/fac: 9:1. **Fac 91.** M 44/F 47. FT 82/PT 9. Wh 81%. Latino 2%. Blk 3%. Native Am 1%. Asian 7%. Other 6%. Adv deg: 71%. **Grad '11—127. Col—127.** (Columbia, Stanford, USC, U of WA, Wash U, Whitman). **Avg SAT:** CR 712. M 705. W 707. **Mid 50% SAT:** CR 670-770. M 670-750. W 660-750. Avg ACT: 31. **Col couns:** 8. Alum donors: 22%.
Tui '12-'13: Day $27,250 (+$250-3200). **Aid:** Need 230 ($4,600,000).
Summer (enr 590): Acad Enrich Rec. Tui Day $350-1500/crse. 3-6 wks.
Endow $188,000,000. Plant val $49,600,000. Acres 33. Bldgs 22. Class rms 75. 2 Libs 37,500 vols. Sci labs 8. Comp ctrs 2. Auds 2. Theaters 2. Art studios 7. Music studios 2. Perf arts ctrs 2. AV ctrs 2. Gyms 2. Fields 4. Field houses 1. Comp labs 6. Laptop prgm Gr 7-12.
Est 1919. Nonprofit. (Sept-June). **Assoc** NWAC.

Located at the northern edge of Seattle, the school draws its enrollment from King and Snohomish counties. Originally a boys' boarding and day school, Lakeside discontinued its boarding department in 1964. The school became coeducational in 1971 after effecting a merger with St. Nicholas School for girls. Lakeside's campus consists of the upper school (grades 9-12) and, a block away, the middle school (grades 5-8).

The school's academic program provides students with a strong foundation in the arts, the humanities and the sciences, while also allowing them to pursue individual interests through a wide variety of curricular offerings. Both school divisions have ample facilities to support course work in the sciences and the visual and performing arts. Outdoor education, community service and physical education programs complement academics. All students in grades 7-12 utilize laptop computers.

In addition to fulfilling diploma requirements in the traditional subject areas, upper school pupils take an outdoor education trip and complete 80 hours of community service. Students have the opportunity to travel internationally to locations in Europe, South America and Asia through the Lakeside Intercultural Program and the Global Service Learning Program.

THE NORTHWEST SCHOOL

Bdg — Coed Gr 9-12; Day — Coed 6-12

Seattle, WA 98122. 1415 Summit Ave. Tel: 206-682-7309. Fax: 206-467-7353.
www.northwestschool.org   E-mail: admissions@northwestschool.org
Michael J. McGill, Head (2011). BA, Santa Clara Univ, MEd, Harvard Univ. **Anne Smith, Adm.**
Col Prep. Feat—Humanities Chin Fr Span Asian_Stud Global_Stud Lat-Amer_Stud Philos Ceramics Film Photog Studio_Art Visual_Arts Theater Chorus Orchestra Jazz_Band Dance. **Supp**—ESL. Outdoor ed.
Sports—Basket X-country Soccer Track Ultimate_Frisbee. G: Volley.
Selective adm: 120/yr. Bdg 12. Day 108. Usual entry: 6 & 9. Appl fee: $70. Appl due: Jan. Applied: 378. Accepted: 65%. Yield: 39%. **Tests** ISEE SSAT TOEFL.
Enr 474. B 239. G 235. Bdg 41. Day 433. Elem 124. Sec 350. Wh 59%. Latino 4%. Blk 8%. Native Am 1%. Asian 28%. Intl 15%. Avg class size: 17. Stud/fac: 9:1. **Fac 68.** M 25/F 43. FT 40/PT 28. Adv deg: 64%.
Grad '11—81. Col—78. (U of WA 6, Carleton 4, Santa Clara 4, Whitman 3, USC 2, Bard-NY 2). **Col couns:** 2.
Tui '12-'13: Bdg $43,655. Day $27,865-29,930. Aid: Need 68 ($1,585,955).
Summer (enr 325): Acad Enrich Rev Rem Rec. Arts. ESL. Tui Bdg $2100/2-wk ses. Tui Day $820/2-wk ses. 6 wks.
Endow $663,000. Plant val $25,338,000. Bldgs 3 (50% ADA). Dorms 1. Dorm rms 30. Class rms 30. Libs 1. Sci labs 4. Lang labs 3. Auds 1. Theaters 1. Art studios 3. Music studios 2. Dance studios 1. Courts 1. Comp labs 1. Comp/stud: 1:3.
Est 1978. Nonprofit. 5 terms (Sept-June). **Assoc** NWAC.

Northwest's sequential college preparatory curriculum comprises academic, arts, international and athletic programs. The academic studies program, which seeks to improve critical-thinking, articulation and synthesizing skills, consists of math, science, language and humanities components. Pupils in all grades receive credit for both English and history through the core humanities program; students in grades 9-12 follow a chronological history of civilization sequence that progresses from 3000 BC to the present day. The arts program features required music, dance, theater and visual arts courses, all of which are taught by practicing artists. The boarding division serves international students only. The international program offers ESL courses and foreign exchange opportunities.

The school operates an environment program in which all students clean and maintain the campus, each grade level goes on at least one major camping trip per year, and frequent wilderness excursions are offered.

UNIVERSITY PREPARATORY ACADEMY
Day — Coed Gr 6-12

Seattle, WA 98115. 8000 25th Ave NE. Tel: 206-525-2714. Fax: 206-525-5320.
www.universityprep.org   E-mail: admissionoffice@universityprep.org
Erica L. Hamlin, Head. BA, Smith College, MALS, Wesleyan Univ. **Kathy O'Neal, Adm.**
Col Prep. AP exams taken: 55 (69% 3+). Feat—Creative_Writing Chin Fr Japan Span
   Stats Astron Web_Design Japan_Hist Econ Govt Psych Philos Photog Music Music_
   Theory Orchestra Dance Media. **Supp**—Tut. Outdoor ed.
Sports—Basket X-country Soccer Tennis Track Ultimate_Frisbee. B: Baseball. G: Soft-
   ball Volley. **Activities:** 25.
Selective adm: 100/yr. Usual entry: 6 & 9. Appl fee: $70. Appl due: Jan. Applied: 485.
   Accepted: 39%. Yield: 53%. **Tests** ISEE.
Enr 510. B 271. G 239. Elem 211. Sec 299. Wh 65%. Latino 2%. Blk 4%. Asian 11%.
   Other 18%. Avg class size: 16. Stud/fac: 9:1. Casual. **Fac 60.** M 28/F 32. FT 53/PT 7.
   Wh 75%. Latino 6%. Blk 2%. Asian 8%. Other 9%. Adv deg: 78%.
Grad '11—70. Col—70. (U of WA 21, Santa Clara 13, U of PA 8, Chapman 7, Whittier
   7, Dartmouth 6). **Avg SAT:** CR 613. M 618. W 630. **Mid 50% SAT:** CR 550-660. M
   570-670. W 570-680. Avg ACT: 28. Mid 50% ACT: 25-29. **Col couns:** 2. Alum donors:
   7%.
Tui '11-'12: Day $25,950-27,150 (+$850). **Aid:** Need 96 ($1,984,339).
   Endow $5,400,000. Plant val $20,082,000. Acres 6. Bldgs 3 (100% ADA). Class rms 23.
   Libs 1. Sci labs 7. Lang labs 7. Theaters 1. Art studios 3. Music studios 6. Gyms 1.
   Fields 1. Comp labs 3. Comp/stud: 1:1
Est 1976. Nonprofit. Sem (Sept-June). **Assoc** NWAC.

The college preparatory curriculum at University Prep emphasizes the liberal arts and sciences and integrates technology at all grade levels. Boys and girls engage in global learning activities at all grade levels. During the middle school years, pupils use the Internet and E-mail to collaborate with classrooms overseas on projects that deal with new technologies, cultural awareness and community issues.

The upper school global education immersion program, Global Link, combines extensive predeparture training with subsequent travel overseas. Upon their return, upper schoolers share their experiences with University Prep and the international community through projects and theses.

Students in grades 9-12 complete 15 hours of direct community service per year, and each senior composes a required thesis that incorporates independent research.

SPOKANE, WA. (230 mi. E of Seattle, WA) Urban. Pop: 195,629. Alt: 1943 ft.

SAINT GEORGE'S SCHOOL
Day — Coed Gr K-12

Spokane, WA 99208. 2929 W Waikiki Rd. Tel: 509-466-1636. Fax: 509-467-3258.
www.sgs.org   E-mail: debbie.duvoisin@sgs.org
Joe Kennedy, Head (2011). BA, Washington State Univ, MEd, Central Washington Univ.
Debbie Duvoisin, Adm.
  Col Prep. AP (exams req'd; 175 taken, 88% 3+)—Eng Chin Fr Span Calc Bio Chem
    Environ_Sci Physics Eur_Hist US_Hist Econ Studio_Art. **Feat**—Engineering Comp_
    Sci Govt Intl_Relations Drama Music_Hist. **Supp**—Dev_Read Rev Tut. **Dual enr:**
    Whitworth.
  Sports—Basket X-country Tennis Track. B: Baseball Soccer. G: Softball Volley.
  Selective adm: 48/yr. Appl fee: $50. Appl due: Rolling. Applied: 106. Accepted: 72%.
    Yield: 70%. **Tests** CEEB ISEE TOEFL.
  Enr 381. B 208. G 173. Elem 243. Sec 138. Wh 84%. Latino 1%. Blk 2%. Asian 7%. Other
    6%. Avg class size: 15. Stud/fac: 9:1. **Fac 44.** M 20/F 24. FT 41/PT 3. Wh 85%. Latino
    9%. Blk 2%. Asian 2%. Other 2%. Adv deg: 70%.
  Grad '10—46. Col—46. (W WA, Rensselaer Polytech, E WA, Princeton, Macalester,
    Georgetown). **Avg SAT:** CR 630. M 633. W 608. Alum donors: 15%.
  Tui '12-'13: Day $14,600-17,480 (+$440-1020). **Aid:** Merit 3 ($27,506). Need 76
    ($731,543).
  Summer: Enrich. 1-2½ wks.
  Endow $3,000,000. Plant val $2,000,000. Acres 120. Bldgs 10. Class rms 29. 2 Libs
    10,000 vols. Labs 6. Theaters 1. Art studios 2. Music studios 2. Gyms 2. Fields 6.
    Courts 3. Comp/stud: 1:2.
  Est 1955. Nonprofit. Sem (Aug-June). **Assoc** CLS NWAC.
    Located on a 120-acre campus, this rigorous school conducts a full elementary and second-
ary program while preparing its graduates for competitive colleges nationwide. Nearly three-
quarters of the juniors and seniors at Saint George's take at least one Advanced Placement
course. The curriculum also features a full complement of electives. Community service is
a part of the program in the lower and middle schools, and upper school students satisfy an
eight-hour annual community service requirement.

TACOMA, WA. (26 mi. SSW of Seattle, WA) Urban. Pop: 193,556. Alt: 75 ft.

ANNIE WRIGHT SCHOOL
Bdg — Girls Gr 9-12; Day — Boys PS (Age 3)-8, Girls PS (Age 3)-12

Tacoma, WA 98403. 827 N Tacoma Ave. Tel: 253-272-2216, 800-847-1582.
Fax: 253-572-3616.
www.aw.org   E-mail: admission@aw.org
Christian Sullivan, Head (2010). BA, Univ of Durham (England), MA, Univ of Bath (Eng-
land). **Stacey Guadnola, Adm.**
  Col Prep. IB Diploma. AP exams taken: 20 (70% 3+). Elem math—Everyday Math.
    Elem read—Houghton Mifflin. **Feat**—Fr Japan Span Calc Stats Anat & Physiol Film
    Theater Music. **Supp**—ESL Rem_Read Rev Tut.
  Sports—Basket X-country Golf Soccer Tennis Track. G: Volley. **Activities:** 15.
  Selective adm (Bdg Gr 9-11; Day PS-12): 106/yr. Appl fee: $80-100. Appl due: Feb.
    Applied: 274. **Tests** TOEFL.
  Enr 441. B 104. G 337. Elem 285. Sec 156. Wh 57%. Latino 6%. Blk 3%. Native Am 2%.
    Asian 14%. Other 18%. Intl 33%. Avg class size: 11. Stud/fac: 7:1. Uniform. **Fac 87.** M

25/F 62. Wh 89%. Latino 3%. Blk 4%. Asian 4%. Adv deg: 54%. In dorms 6.
Grad '11—34. Col—34. (U of WA 2, U of San Diego 2, U of CO-Boulder 1, Wellesley 1, U of CA-Berkeley 1, Georgetown 1). **Avg SAT:** CR/M 1150. Avg ACT: 28. Alum donors: 11%.
Tui '12-'13: Bdg $44,000 (+$2000). **5-Day Bdg $35,000** (+$1700). **Day $22,000** (+$1700). **Intl Bdg $44,000-46,000** (+$3000). **Aid:** Merit ($500,000). Need ($1,200,000). **Summer (enr 335):** Acad Enrich Rec. 10 wks.
Endow $14,000,000. Plant val $24,000,000. Acres 10. Bldgs 2 (55% ADA). Dorm rms 56. Class rms 45. Lib 19,000 vols. Chapels 1. Sci labs 4. Auds 1. Theaters 1. Art studios 3. Music studios 3. Dance studios 1. Gyms 2. Fields 1. Courts 3. Pools 1. Comp labs 2. Laptop prgm Gr 6-12.
Est 1884. Nonprofit. Episcopal. Tri (Sept-June). **Assoc** NWAC.

The school was founded by Rt. Rev. John A. Paddock, first Episcopal bishop of the Washington Territory, and Charles B. Wright, with the aim that "not only the intellect, but the character, manners and morals of the pupil are subjects of earnest care and solicitude." Located in Tacoma's historic North End, Annie Wright offers a curriculum that combines a rigorous academic program with varied athletic and extracurricular offerings. English as a Second Language classes are available in grades 9-12. In the fall of 2009, the school began offering the International Baccalaureate Diploma Program to its juniors and seniors.

Community service is an important aspect of school life. Boys and girls in the lower and middle schools engage in annual service projects, while students in grades 9-12 engage in required community service blocks that demand 35 to 50 hours annually. An upper school interim week between the second and third trimesters features enrichment activities and college tours.

CHARLES WRIGHT ACADEMY
Day — Coed Gr PS (Age 4)-12

Tacoma, WA 98467. 7723 Chambers Creek Rd W. Tel: 253-620-8373.
Fax: 253-620-8357.
www.charleswright.org E-mail: admissions@charleswright.org
Robert A. Camner, Head (1996). BA, Oberlin College, MS, Ohio State Univ. **Steve Saalfeld, Adm.**
Col Prep. AP (251 exams taken, 90% 3+)—Eng Fr Span Calc Stats Comp_Sci Chem Physics Eur_Hist US_Hist US_Govt & Pol. **Feat**—Japan Environ_Sci Forensic_Sci Psych Sociol Ceramics Photog Studio_Art Theater Band Chorus Orchestra Guitar Journ Outdoor_Ed. **Supp**—Tut. Outdoor ed.
Sports—Basket X-country Golf Soccer Tennis Track. B: Baseball Football. G: Volley.
Selective adm: 103/yr. Appl fee: $40-80. Appl due: Rolling. **Tests** ISEE SSAT TOEFL.
Enr 676. B 367. G 309. Elem 401. Sec 275. Wh 65%. Latino 2%. Blk 5%. Asian 14%. Other 14%. Avg class size: 16. Stud/fac: 8:1. **Fac 85.** M 34/F 51. FT 85. Adv deg: 52%.
Grad '10—76. Col—76. Mid 50% SAT: CR 562-578. M 566-690. W 551-713. **Col couns:** 2.
Tui '11-'12: Day $15,950-21,500 (+$100-700). **Aid:** Need 154 ($1,900,000).
Endow $12,000,000. Plant val $8,000,000. Acres 100. Bldgs 10. Class rms 50. Lib 40,000 vols. Sci labs 7. Lang labs 2. Art studios 8. Music studios 3. Gyms 3. Fields 4. Courts 6. Comp labs 3.
Est 1957. Nonprofit. Sem (Aug-June). **Assoc** CLS NWAC.

Located on a suburban, 100-acre campus, CWA was founded by parents interested in providing a rigorous curriculum in the liberal arts for their sons. In 1970, the school became coeducational.

Elective courses in all disciplines, computer science, an Advanced Placement program and the opportunity for independent study complement the traditional college preparatory course of studies. The academy also offers complete arts, athletic and outdoor education programs. The five-day winterim enables upper school students to engage in experiential programming not found in the regular curriculum. Boys and girls in grades 9-12 satisfy a 15-hour community service requirement each year.

CONCISE SCHOOL
LISTINGS

The following schools complement those in the Leading Private Schools chapter. They are arranged geographically by state, progressing from east to west across the country. Within each state, schools are listed alphabetically by city or town.

These are, in many ways, schools similar to those found in Leading Private Schools. Schools that have been listed in the *Handbook* for fewer than five consecutive years appear in this section, as do those institutions that have failed to respond regularly to annual update questionnaires. This section also includes schools that offer a more limited curriculum and those that enroll students from a strictly local area.

New England States

CONNECTICUT

ACADEMY OF THE HOLY FAMILY
Baltic, CT 06330. 54 W Main St, PO Box 691.
Tel: 860-822-9272. Fax: 860-822-1318.
www.ahfbaltic.org   E-mail: principal@ahfbaltic.org
Sr. Mary Loreto, SCMC, Prin.

Bdg & Day
Girls Gr 9-12

Col Prep. Gen Acad. AP (exams req'd)—Eng Calc Physics. **Feat**—Creative_Writing Span Environ_Sci Comp_Sci Psych Relig Music Accounting Finance Speech Home_Ec. **Supp**—ESL Tut. **Comp:** Comp/Stud: 1:2. **Sports**— G: Basket Soccer Softball. Activities: 11. **Somewhat selective adm:** 27/yr. Appl fee: $100. Appl due: Rolling. Accepted: 90%. **Enr 58.** Bdg 8. Day 50. Intl 8%. Avg class size: 10. Uniform. **Fac 18.** M 3/F 15. FT 12/PT 6. Wh 88%. Blk 6%. Asian 6%. Adv deg: 44%. In Dorms 2. **Grad '06—14.** Col—13. **Avg SAT:** CR 554. M 481. W 530. **Tui '12-'13:** Bdg $24,000. Day $7000. Intl Bdg $30,000. **Est 1874.** Nonprofit. Roman Catholic (80% practice). Quar (Aug-June). **Assoc** NEASC. Founded by the Sisters of Charity, the academy conducts its educational program from a traditional Catholic perspective. The program of studies includes history, languages, religion, math and science, in addition to art, family studies, business skills, computer science and physical education. Boarding students attend prescribed study periods, weekday activity periods and weekend activities.

BESS AND PAUL SIGEL HEBREW ACADEMY
Bloomfield, CT 06002. 53 Gabb Rd.
Tel: 860-243-8333. Fax: 860-243-3986.
www.sigelacademy.org   E-mail: cmello@sigelacademy.org
Rabbi Mordechai Weiss, Prin (2005). BA, Yeshiva Univ (NY), MA, New School for Social Research. Claudette G. Mello, Adm.

Day Coed Gr PS (Age 2)-8

Pre-Prep. Gen Acad. Feat—Hebrew Computers Judaic_Stud Studio_Art Music. **Supp**—Dev_Read ESL Rem_Math Rem_Read. **Comp:** Comp/Stud: 1:3. **Sports**—Basket. G: Soccer. **Nonselective adm:** 11/yr. Appl due: Rolling. Accepted: 100%. **Tests** CTP_4. **Enr 95.** B 55. G 40. Wh 100%. Avg class size: 9. Formal dress. **Fac 22.** M 5/F 17. FT 7/PT 15. Adv deg: 50%. **Grad '11—9.** Prep—6. (Hebrew HS 6). **Tui '11-'12:** Day $13,300-15,150 (+$2750). Aid: Need 32 ($150,000). **Est 1940.** Nonprofit. Jewish (100% practice). Tri (Aug-June). The academy offers a Judaic studies program integrated with a curriculum in the language arts, the social sciences, math and the physical sciences, and supplemented by music, art, physical education and computer literacy. The Judaic curriculum combines Bible study, Hebrew language, and Jewish history, beliefs and practices. Students in grades 6-8 complete an independent study project.

ST. PAUL CATHOLIC HIGH SCHOOL
Bristol, CT 06010. 1001 Stafford Ave.
Tel: 860-584-0911. Fax: 860-585-8815.
www.spchs.com   E-mail: mcrowley@spchs.com
Cary Dupont, Pres (2008). BA, Univ of Notre Dame. Matthew Crowley, Adm.

Day Coed Gr 9-12

Col Prep. AP (46 exams taken, 59% 3+)—Eng Lat Span Comp_Sci Bio US_Hist Psych US_Govt & Pol Studio_Art Music_Theory. **Feat**—Fr Anat & Physiol Environ_Sci Forensic_Sci Marine_Bio/Sci Comp_Design Econ Sociol Relig Painting Drama Band Chorus Accounting. **Supp**—Tut. **Comp:** Comp/Stud: 1:5. **Dual enr:** U of CT. **Sports**—Basket X-country Soccer Track. B: Baseball Football Golf. G: Cheer Softball Swim Tennis Volley. **Somewhat**

selective adm (Gr 9-11): 96/yr. Appl fee: $25. Appl due: Rolling. Accepted: 85%. **Tests** HSPT. **Enr 331.** B 168. G 163. Wh 85%. Latino 4%. Blk 4%. Asian 3%. Other 4%. Intl 7%. Avg class size: 15. Stud/fac: 11:1. Uniform. **Fac 30.** M 13/F 17. FT 24/PT 6. Wh 93%. Latino 3%. Blk 3%. Other 1%. Adv deg: 66%. **Grad '10—81.** Col—78. (U of CT 11, Tunxis CC 5, Providence 4, U of Hartford 3, Mt Ida 3, NYU 3). **Avg SAT:** CR 520. M 500. W 510. **Col Couns:** 3. **Tui '11-'12:** Day $9450 (+$1000). Aid: Merit 30 ($70,000). Need 105 ($185,000). **Est 1966.** Nonprofit. Roman Catholic. Sem (Sept-June). **Assoc** NEASC. Situated on a 27-acre campus in central Connecticut, St. Paul Catholic offers a faith-based college preparatory program to boys and girls from approximately 30 communities. Particularly able pupils may enroll in Advanced Placement courses, as well as in dual-credit courses at the University of Connecticut. All students satisfy a 15-hour annual community service requirement.

IMMACULATE HIGH SCHOOL   **Day Coed Gr 9-12**
Danbury, CT 06810. 73 Southern Blvd.
Tel: 203-744-1510. Fax: 203-744-1275.
www.immaculatehs.org   E-mail: ihsmailbox@immaculatehs.org
    Kathleen D. Casey, Pres (2009). Joe Carmen, Prin.

    Col Prep. AP (110 exams taken, 74% 3+)—Eng Fr Span Calc Bio Chem Physics US_ Hist Psych US_Govt & Pol Studio_Art. **Feat**—Lat Anat & Physiol Environ_Sci Web_Design Govt Sociol Relig Sculpt Drama Band Chorus Dance Journ Public_Speak. **Supp**—Rev Tut. **Dual enr:** U of CT. **Sports**—Basket X-country Ice_Hockey Lacrosse Soccer Tennis Track. B: Baseball Football Golf Wrestling. G: F_Hockey Softball. **Selective adm (Gr 9-11):** 104/yr. Appl due: Rolling. Accepted: 70%. Yield: 60%. **Enr 352.** Avg class size: 19. Stud/fac: 13:1. Uniform. **Fac 33.** M 14/F 19. FT 27/PT 6. Adv deg: 96%. **Grad '08—79.** Col—78. **Avg SAT:** CR 538. M 534. W 542. **Tui '11-'12:** Day $9850 (+$150). Aid: Merit 40 ($76,000). Need 55 ($60,000). **Est 1962.** Nonprofit. Roman Catholic (80% practice). Quar (Aug-June). **Assoc** NEASC. College preparation at this Catholic high school includes Advanced Placement and honors course work in the major disciplines. Students perform 25 hours of compulsory community service annually.

ENFIELD MONTESSORI SCHOOL   **Day Coed Gr PS (Age 2)-6**
Enfield, CT 06082. 1370 Enfield St.
Tel: 860-745-5847. Fax: 860-745-2010.
www.enfieldmontessorischool.org   E-mail: info@enfieldmontessorischool.org
    Cliona Beaulieu, Prin (2011). Elizabeth Page, Adm.

    Gen Acad. Montessori. Feat—Computers Studio_Art Music. **Supp**—Rem_Math Rem_ Read Tut. **Comp:** Comp/Stud: 1:4. **Nonselective adm (Gr PS-3):** 18/yr. Appl fee: $100. Appl due: Apr. Accepted: 100%. **Enr 120.** B 57. G 63. Wh 75%. Latino 1%. Blk 7%. Asian 7%. Other 10%. Avg class size: 24. Stud/fac: 20:1. Uniform. **Fac 6.** M 1/F 5. FT 5/PT 1. Wh 83%. Blk 17%. Adv deg: 50%. **Grad '11—9. Tui '12-'13:** Day $4800. Aid: Need 19 ($25,000). **Est 1965.** Nonprofit. Roman Catholic (51% practice). Quar (Sept-June). **Assoc** NEASC. EMS' course of studies, which follows the Montessori method, also includes a continuous and structured program of religious education. Computer instruction is integrated into the curriculum, as it incorporates typing, word processing and tutorial applications into classroom lessons. Children receive art and music instruction at all grade levels.

EAGLE HILL SCHOOL   **5-Day Bdg Coed Ages 10-16**
Greenwich, CT 06831. 45 Glenville Rd.   **Day Coed 6-16**
Tel: 203-622-9240. Fax: 203-622-0914.
www.eaglehillschool.org   E-mail: info411@eaglehill.org
    Marjorie E. Castro, Head (2009). BS, Bucknell Univ, MA, EdD, Columbia Univ. Thomas Cone, Adm.

    Pre-Prep. LD. Feat—Computers Study_Skills. **Supp**—Rem_Math Rem_Read Rev Tut.

Comp: Laptop prgm Ages 11-16. **Sports**—Basket X-country Ice_Hockey Lacrosse Soccer Tennis. B: Baseball. G: Cheer F_Hockey Softball. **Selective adm:** 58/yr. Bdg 4. Day 54. Appl fee: $50. Appl due: Rolling. **Tests** IQ. **Enr 250.** B 157. G 93. Bdg 35. Day 215. Avg class size: 6. **Fac 80.** M 20/F 60. FT 75/PT 5. Adv deg: 90%. In Dorms 7. **Grad '11—58.** Prep—34. (Harvey 7, Forman 4, Marvelwood 4, York Prep 3). **Col Couns:** 1. **Tui '12-'13:** 5-Day Bdg $78,075 (+$500). Day $59,125. Aid: Need 46 ($1,650,000). **Est 1975.** Nonprofit. Sem (Sept-June). The school offers boys and girls of average or above-average intelligence remediation for learning disabilities. Students have typically failed to reach potential in traditional educational environments. Eagle Hill also provides speech and language services, motor training, adaptive physical education classes and counseling services. In addition to various after-school activities, EHS offers an hourlong, proctored study hall on weekday afternoons.

See Also Pages 110-1

THE STANWICH SCHOOL Day Coed Gr PS (Age 4)-11
Greenwich, CT 06830. 257 Stanwich Rd.
Tel: 203-542-0000. Fax: 203-542-0025.
Other locations: 200 Strawberry Hill Ave, Stamford 06902.
www.stanwichschool.org   E-mail: info@stanwichschool.org
Paul G. Geise, Head (2012). BA, Colgate Univ, MAT, Montclair State College, MEd, Harvard Univ. Tom Faxon, Adm.

Gen Acad. Feat—Fr Lat Span Computers Ethics Fine_Arts Drama Music Public_Speak. **Supp**—Dev_Read. **Comp:** Laptop prgm Gr 7-11. **Sports (req'd)**—Basket X-country Ice_ Hockey Lacrosse Soccer Squash Tennis. B: Baseball Football. G: F_Hockey Softball. **Selective adm (Gr PS-9):** 51/yr. Appl fee: $75. Appl due: Dec. Accepted: 68%. Yield: 77%. **Tests** ISEE. **Enr 375.** Wh 86%. Latino 2%. Blk 3%. Asian 6%. Other 3%. Intl 5%. Avg class size: 15. Stud/fac: 7:1. Uniform. **Fac 64.** Adv deg: 100%. **Grad '08—12.** Prep—9. **Tui '11-'12:** Day $21,361-31,574 (+$600-1300). Aid: Need 44 ($696,350). **Est 1998.** Nonprofit. (Sept-June). In a small-class setting, Stanwich conducts a demanding curriculum while utilizing both traditional and contemporary teaching methods. Notable features of the program include accelerated math and language arts groupings; a foreign language program that begins with French in kindergarten; a fully integrated fine arts and performing arts program; individualized scheduling and assigned academic advisors starting in grade 7; a focus on technology that culminates in a laptop program; and a directed study hall. Field trips, clubs and after-school programs enrich the curriculum, and all boys and girls engage in community service throughout the school year. Upper school classes convene on the Stamford campus.

SACRED HEART ACADEMY Day Girls Gr 9-12
Hamden, CT 06514. 265 Benham St.
Tel: 203-288-2309. Fax: 203-230-9680.
www.sacredhearthamden.org   E-mail: elamboley@sacredhearthamden.org
Sr. Sheila O'Neill, ACSJ, Pres (2010). BA, Albertus Magnus College, MA, Fordham Univ, MA, PhD, St Louis Univ. Sr. Maureen Flynn, ACSJ, Prin. Elaine M. Lamboley, Adm.

Col Prep. AP (exams req'd; 190 taken, 75% 3+)—Eng Fr Lat Span Calc Stats Comp_Sci Bio Chem Physics US_Hist Psych US_Govt & Pol. **Feat**—British_Lit Mythology Women's_ Lit Anat & Physiol Genetics Microbio Econ Law Relig Painting Studio_Art Music_Theory Accounting Finance. **Comp:** Comp/Stud: 1:1 Laptop prgm Gr 9-12. **Sports**— G: Basket Cheer X-country F_Hockey Golf Indoor_Track Lacrosse Soccer Softball Swim Tennis Track Volley. Activities: 40. **Selective adm (Gr 9-10):** 140/yr. Appl fee: $40. Appl due: Nov. Accepted: 60%. Yield: 80%. **Tests** HSPT. **Enr 490.** Wh 90%. Latino 3%. Blk 3%. Asian 2%. Other 2%. Avg class size: 20. Stud/fac: 8:1. Uniform. **Fac 55.** Wh 93%. Latino 1%. Asian 4%. Other 2%. Adv deg: 72%. **Grad '10—120.** Col—120. **Tui '11-'12:** Day $11,650 (+$1000). Aid: Need 98. **Est 1946.** Nonprofit. Roman Catholic (90% practice). Sem (Aug-June). **Assoc** NEASC. Sacred Heart's traditional college preparatory curriculum provides girls with a strong foundation in the humanities and the arts and sciences. All freshmen take a noncredit seminar course that addresses such topics as time management, decision making, substance abuse and stress. AP and honors classes are available to qualified girls, and electives enable pupils to further explore areas of interest. Sophomores perform 25 hours of required community service.

THE COUNTRY SCHOOL   Day Coed Gr PS (Age 3)-8
Madison, CT 06443. 341 Opening Hill Rd.
Tel: 203-421-3113. Fax: 203-421-4390.
www.thecountryschool.org   E-mail: admission@thecountryschool.org
    Laurie Bottiger, Head (2011). BS, Edinboro Univ of Pennsylvania, MA, Northwest Missouri State Univ, PhD, Univ of Kansas. Claire Kinkade, Adm.
    Pre-Prep. Feat—Creative_Writing Fr Lat Span Computers Studio_Art Drama Music Outdoor_Ed. **Supp**—Dev_Read Rev Tut. Outdoor Ed. **Sports**—Basket X-country Lacrosse Soccer Swim Tennis. B: Baseball. G: Softball. **Selective adm:** 31/yr. Appl fee: $50. Appl due: Feb. Accepted: 50%. **Tests** ISEE. **Enr 220.** B 124. G 96. Wh 89%. Latino 2%. Blk 6%. Asian 3%. Avg class size: 16. Stud/fac: 7:1. **Fac 36.** Adv deg: 61%. **Grad '11—35.** Prep—25. (Choate 5, Williams-CT 5, Pomfret 3, Hopkins 2, Loomis Chaffee 2, Suffield 1). **Tui '11-'12:** Day $14,050-24,760 (+$275). Aid: Need 41 ($412,000). **Est 1955.** Nonprofit. (Sept-June). TCS' elementary-level curriculum combines work in the traditional disciplines (including technology and world languages) with experiential learning and outdoor experiences. Studio art, music and drama programs represent the creative arts options. During the middle school years, students transition from self-contained classrooms with a homeroom teacher in grade 5 to fully departmentalized classrooms and an advisor system in grades 6-8. The school's outdoor education program culminates in a 10-day adventure trek in the Southwest for eighth graders.

GROVE SCHOOL   Bdg & Day
Madison, CT 06443. 175 Copse Rd.   Coed Gr 7-PG
Tel: 203-245-2778. Fax: 203-245-6098.
www.groveschool.org   E-mail: mainoffice@groveschool.org
    Richard L. Chorney, Pres (2000). BA, Bard College, MS, Southern Connecticut State Univ. Peter J. Chorney, Exec Dir. BA, Bucknell Univ, MS, Southern Connecticut State Univ. Lauren Seltzer, Adm.
    Col Prep. Gen Acad. LD. Underachiever. AP—Calc Bio US_Hist. **Feat**—Creative_Writing Span Botany Marine_Bio/Sci Biochem Comp_Networking Econ Psych Sociol Philos Ceramics Filmmaking Graphic_Arts Photog Sculpt Video_Production Stained_Glass. **Supp**—Dev_Read ESL Makeup Rem_Math Rem_Read Rev Tut. **Sports**—Baseball Basket Soccer. Activities: 20. **Selective adm:** 30/yr. Appl fee: $200. Appl due: Rolling. Accepted: 60%. **Tests** IQ. **Enr 126.** B 76. G 50. Bdg 105. Day 21. Intl 10%. Avg class size: 6. Stud/fac: 4:1. **Fac 30.** Adv deg: 50%. In Dorms 24. **Grad '11—39.** Col—35. **Avg SAT:** CR/M 1000. **Tui '12-'13:** Bdg $109,980 (+$3400). Day $80,900 (+$500). **Est 1934.** Inc. Year-round. Grove serves adolescents who have social, emotional and learning challenges through a therapeutic program that focuses on interpersonal relationships. The school's year-round program includes four two-week vacation periods; boys and girls complete intensive, individualized work during both the summer months and the traditional school year. Grove's clinical approach to psychodynamic psychotherapy features biweekly individual sessions, weekly group therapy, and family and milieu therapy. Boarders attend mandatory evening study periods and, if supplementary academic assistance is necessary, an after-school study hall.

MERCY HIGH SCHOOL   Day Girls Gr 9-12
Middletown, CT 06457. 1740 Randolph Rd.
Tel: 860-346-6659. Fax: 860-344-9887.
www.mercyhigh.com   E-mail: info@mercyhigh.com

Sr. Mary A. McCarthy, RSM, Pres (2012). MA, Trinity College (CT). Melissa Bullock, Prin. BA, Saint Joseph's College of Maine, MA, Fordham Univ. Diane Santostefano, Adm.

Col Prep. AP (exams req'd; 159 taken, 47% 3+)—Eng Fr Lat Span Calc Stats Bio Chem Physics Eur_Hist US_Hist Psych. **Feat**—Creative_Writing Ital Physiol Neurosci Govt Law Relig Photog Studio_Art Theater_Arts Music Accounting Bus Public_Speak. **Comp:** Comp/Stud: 1:3.5. **Dual enr:** U of CT. **Sports**— G: Basket Cheer X-country F_Hockey Golf Lacrosse Soccer Softball Swim Tennis Track Volley. Activities: 40. **Somewhat selective adm:** 171/yr. Appl fee: $50. Appl due: Dec. Accepted: 93%. Yield: 62%. **Tests** HSPT. **Enr 651.** Wh 91%. Latino 3%. Blk 4%. Asian 2%. Avg class size: 21. Stud/fac: 13:1. Uniform. **Fac 53.** M 9/F 44. FT 48/PT 5. Wh 94%. Blk 4%. Asian 2%. Adv deg: 75%. **Grad '11—170.** Col—170. (Sacred Heart 8, S CT St 6, Quinnipiac 6, Gateway CC 5, E CT St 5, Salve Regina 4). **Avg SAT:** CR 532. M 512. W 540. Avg ACT: 22.6. **Col Couns:** 4. Alum donors: 10%. **Tui '11-'12:** Day $10,350-10,850 (+$800-1800). **Est 1963.** Nonprofit. Roman Catholic (85% practice). Quar (Sept-June). **Assoc** NEASC. Mercy High features the liberal arts, offering students honors and college preparatory programs and focusing on college and career preparation. Electives and AP classes are available, and students take a compulsory religion course each year. Field trips, retreats, Masses and other celebrations complement the curriculum. In addition, all girls perform at least 100 hours of Christian service prior to graduation. Mercy High engages in various activities with Xavier High School, a nearby boys' school.

XAVIER HIGH SCHOOL   **Day Boys Gr 9-12**
Middletown, CT 06457. 181 Randolph Rd.
Tel: 860-346-7735. Fax: 860-346-6859.
www.xavierhighschool.org   E-mail: brfahey@xavierhighschool.org
  Br. Brian J. Davis, CFX, Head (2009). BA, Catholic Univ of America, MALS, Wesleyan Univ, EdS, Spalding Univ. Brendan Donohue, Prin. Br. Thomas Fahey, CFX, Adm.

Col Prep. AP (exams req'd; 217 taken, 62% 3+)—Eng Lat Calc Bio Chem Environ_Sci Physics Eur_Hist US_Hist World_Hist US_Govt & Pol Studio_Art. **Feat**—Humanities Poetry Chin Fr Span Anat & Physiol Ecol Genetics Microbio Engineering Computers CT_Hist Law Psych Sociol African-Amer_Stud Relig Film Music Bus Speech SAT_Prep. **Supp**—Dev_Read Makeup Rem_Math Rem_Read Tut. **Dual enr:** U of CT. **Sports**— B: Baseball Basket Crew X-country Football Golf Ice_Hockey Indoor_Track Lacrosse Sail Soccer Swim Tennis Track Volley Wrestling. Activities: 37. **Selective adm (Gr 9-11):** 227/yr. Appl fee: $0. Appl due: Dec. **Tests** HSPT. **Enr 866.** Wh 90%. Latino 2%. Blk 4%. Asian 1%. Other 3%. Avg class size: 24. Formal dress. **Fac 60.** M 48/F 12. FT 59/PT 1. Wh 96%. Latino 3%. Other 1%. Adv deg: 63%. **Grad '10—208.** Col—203. **Avg SAT:** CR 524. M 534. W 518. Avg ACT: 20.9. Alum donors: 9%. **Tui '11-'12:** Day $10,700 (+$800). Catholic $10,250-10,500 (+$800-900). Aid: Merit 65 ($169,000). Need 233 ($770,350). **Est 1963.** Nonprofit. Roman Catholic (80% practice). Quar (Sept-June). **Assoc** NEASC. Xavier provides academic, religious, service, athletic and extracurricular programs. Three distinct curricula—college prep, accelerated and honors—are offered. Boys perform 30 hours of community service by the end of junior year. Xavier engages in various activities with Mercy High School, a nearby girls' school.

ACADEMY OF OUR LADY OF MERCY   **Day Girls Gr 9-12**
LAURALTON HALL
Milford, CT 06460. 200 High St.
Tel: 203-877-2786. Fax: 203-876-9760.
www.lauraltonhall.org   E-mail: kshine@lauraltonhall.org
  Antoinette Iadarola, Pres (2009). BA, Saint Joseph College (CT), MA, PhD, Georgetown Univ. Ann M. Pratson, Prin. BA, Univ of Connecticut, MAT, Sacred Heart Univ. Kathleen O. Shine, Adm.

Col Prep. AP (exams req'd)—Eng Fr Lat Span Calc Bio Chem Environ_Sci Physics Eur_Hist US_Hist Music_Theory. **Feat**—British_Lit Shakespeare Chin Stats Anat & Physiol Forensic_Sci Marine_Bio/Sci Sports_Med Engineering Comp_Sci Econ Women's_Stud

Relig Art_Hist Ceramics Drawing Film Studio_Art Chorus Music Bus. **Dual enr:** U of CT. **Sports—** G: Basket Cheer X-country F_Hockey Golf Gymnastics Indoor_Track Lacrosse Ski Soccer Softball Swim Tennis Track Volley. Activities: 37. **Selective adm:** 125/yr. Appl fee: $60. Appl due: Nov. Accepted: 33%. **Tests** HSPT. **Enr 460.** Avg class size: 18. Uniform. **Fac 38.** Adv deg: 76%. **Grad '11—108.** Col—108. **Avg SAT:** CR 561. M 539. W 566. **Col Couns:** 4. **Tui '12-'13:** Day $16,175. **Est 1905.** Nonprofit. Roman Catholic (77% practice). Quar (Aug-June). **Assoc** NEASC. The oldest girls' Catholic college preparatory school in the state, Lauralton Hall provides a varied liberal arts curriculum that includes Advanced Placement and honors courses. All students take religion classes and fulfill a 60-hour community service requirement.

WASHINGTON MONTESSORI SCHOOL   Day Coed Gr PS (Age 3)-8
New Preston, CT 06777. 240 Litchfield Tpke.
Tel: 860-868-0551. Fax: 860-868-1362.
www.washingtonmontessori.org   E-mail: lmartin@washingtonmontessori.org
    Patricia D. Werner, Head. BA, Drew Univ, MS, Western Connecticut State Univ. Laura Eanes Martin, Adm.

    Pre-Prep. Montessori. Feat—Lat Span Animal_Sci Computers Studio_Art Music. **Sports—**Basket X-country Soccer Tennis. B: Baseball. **Selective adm:** 54/yr. Appl fee: $40-50. Appl due: Rolling. **Enr 241.** Wh 95%. Latino 2%. Blk 1%. Asian 2%. Avg class size: 24. Stud/fac: 12:1. **Fac 56.** M 5/F 51. FT 52/PT 4. **Grad '11—19.** Prep—17. (Kent Sch-CT 5, Taft 3, Westover 2, Canterbury-CT 2, Berkshire Sch 1, Miss Porter's 1). **Tui '11-'12:** Day $15,050-20,350 (+$65-550). Aid: Need ($600,000). **Est 1965.** Nonprofit. (Sept-June). Washington Montessori provides an individualized and structured, academically oriented curriculum based on the Montessori principles of child-centered teaching. Children study in ungraded, mixed-age groups that span three years, enabling students of varying ages and developmental stages to learn from each other.

SOUTHERN CONNECTICUT HEBREW ACADEMY   Day Coed Gr PS (Age 3)-8
Orange, CT 06477. 261 Derby Ave.
Tel: 203-795-5261. Fax: 203-891-9719.
www.schacademy.org   E-mail: info@schacademy.org
    Rabbi Sheya Hecht, Head (1992).

    Pre-Prep. Gen Acad. Feat—Hebrew Computers Judaic_Stud Studio_Art. **Supp—**ESL Rem_Math Rem_Read Tut. **Sports—**Basket. **Nonselective adm:** 17/yr. Appl fee: $50. Appl due: Rolling. Accepted: 100%. Yield: 100%. **Enr 173.** Avg class size: 15. Uniform. **Fac 26.** M 6/F 20. FT 26. **Grad '05—12. Tui '12-'13:** Day $11,000 (+$1525). **Est 1944.** Nonprofit. Jewish. (Sept-June). SCHA combines a general academic program with a traditional Judaic studies curriculum. Language arts, science, math, world and American history, geography and social studies are core elements of the general studies program, and students take weekly classes in art and computers as well. The Judaic portion of the school day features study of the Torah and on Jewish history, laws and traditions. Instructors place strong emphasis on Hebrew language skills and Israel's history and culture. An affiliated high school for girls, Beth Chana Academy, serves students in grades 9-12.

RIDGEFIELD ACADEMY   Day Coed Gr PS (Age 3)-8
Ridgefield, CT 06877. 223 W Mountain Rd.
Tel: 203-894-1800. Fax: 203-894-1810.
www.ridgefieldacademy.com   E-mail: lmattson@ridgefieldacademy.org
    James P. Heus, Head. BA, Hobart College, MA, Columbia Univ. Libby B. Mattson, Adm.

    Pre-Prep. Feat—Fr Span Computers Robotics Studio_Art Drama Music Music_Hist Study_Skills. **Sports—**Basket X-country Lacrosse Soccer. B: Baseball. G: F_Hockey Softball. **Selective adm:** 107/yr. **Tests** ISEE. **Enr 336.** Nonwhite 13%. Avg class size: 15. Uniform. **Fac 46.** M 5/F 41. FT 36/PT 10. Wh 94%. Latino 2%. Asian 2%. Other 2%. Adv deg: 63%. **Grad '11—24. Tui '12-'13:** Day $25,750-29,810. **Est 1975.** Nonprofit. Tri (Sept-June). French, science, music and arts and crafts are integrated into Ridgefield's preschool program. An extensive fine and performing arts curriculum that consists of music, art, theater and dance complements academics. Sports, computers, chess and cooking are among the after-school activities.

EAGLE HILL-SOUTHPORT   Day Coed Ages 6-14
Southport, CT 06890. 214 Main St.
Tel: 203-254-2044. Fax: 203-255-4052.
www.eaglehillsouthport.org   E-mail: info@eaglehillsouthport.org
    Leonard Tavormina, Head (1984). BA, Boston Univ, MA, Fairfield Univ. Carolyn Lavender, Adm.
    LD. Feat—Studio_Art Study_Skills. **Supp**—Rem_Math Rem_Read Rev Tut. **Comp:** Comp/Stud: 1:4. **Sports**—Baseball Basket X-country Soccer Softball. **Somewhat selective adm:** 27/yr. Appl fee: $100. Appl due: Rolling. Accepted: 66%. Yield: 81%. **Tests** IQ. **Enr 112.** B 82. G 30. Wh 95%. Blk 1%. Asian 1%. Other 3%. Avg class size: 4. Stud/fac: 4:1. Uniform. **Fac 27.** M 6/F 21. FT 26/PT 1. Wh 100%. Adv deg: 74%. **Grad '11—27.** Prep—14. (Wooster 3, Cheshire 2, Forman 2, Unquowa 1, Marvelwood 1, King Low Heywood Thomas 1). **Tui '11-'12:** Day $40,700. Aid: Need 20 ($463,900). **Est 1985.** Nonprofit. Sem (Aug-June). Eagle Hill offers a linguistically based language arts curriculum for children of average or above-average intelligence with language/learning disabilities. Each child receives small-group tutorial instruction and small skills classes in a structured yet flexible environment. Students generally attend for two or three years, as the school aims to place children in a more traditional setting.   **See Also Page 84**

BI-CULTURAL DAY SCHOOL   Day Coed Gr K-8
Stamford, CT 06903. 2186 High Ridge Rd.
Tel: 203-329-2186. Fax: 203-329-0464.
www.bcds.org   E-mail: office@bcds.org
    Jacqueline Herman, Head. Joanne Karow, Adm.
    Gen Acad. Feat—Hebrew Span Computers Judaic_Stud Studio_Art Music. **Supp**—LD Tut. **Sports**—Basket Soccer. G: Gymnastics Softball Volley. **Somewhat selective adm:** 63/yr. Appl fee: $75. Appl due: Rolling. Accepted: 85%. **Tests** IQ. **Enr 395.** Avg class size: 16. **Fac 82.** M 20/F 62. FT 60/PT 22. Wh 100%. Adv deg: 65%. **Grad '08—36.** Prep—18. **Tui '11-'12:** Day $10,500-14,550 (+$1000). **Est 1956.** Nonprofit. Jewish. Sem (Sept-June). The BCDS academic program represents a full curriculum of secular and Judaic subject matter, with instruction in small groups. The academic program is balanced by trips and assemblies that expose children to theater, museums and historical sights. Students in grade 8 spend three weeks in March traveling and studying in Israel.

MEAD SCHOOL   Day Coed Gr PS (Age 2)-8
Stamford, CT 06903. 1095 Riverbank Rd.
Tel: 203-595-9500. Fax: 203-595-0735.
www.meadschool.org   E-mail: admissions@meadschool.org
    Karen Biddulph, Dir (2006). Brooke Wachtel, Adm.
    Pre-Prep. Gen Acad. Feat—Span Computers Visual_Arts Drama Music Movement. **Supp**—Dev_Read Rev. **Sports**—Basket Soccer Softball. **Selective adm:** 21/yr. Appl fee: $50. Appl due: Mar. Accepted: 73%. Yield: 65%. **Enr 127.** B 65. G 62. Wh 79%. Latino 4%. Blk 4%. Asian 13%. Stud/fac: 6:1. **Fac 25.** M 6/F 19. FT 23/PT 2. Wh 99%. Asian 1%. Adv deg: 60%. **Grad '05—13.** Prep—6. **Tui '10-'11:** Day $7790-31,260 (+$250-1100). Aid: Need 33 ($500,000). **Est 1969.** Nonprofit. Sem (Sept-June). Mead's two-teacher system features a traditional curriculum supplemented by expressive arts such as drama, music, art and dance.

Negotiation and mediation skills are emphasized, and all boys and girls participate in community service. Interscholastic sports commence in grade 3.

TRINITY CATHOLIC HIGH SCHOOL   Day Coed Gr 9-12
Stamford, CT 06905. 926 Newfield Ave.
Tel: 203-322-3401. Fax: 203-322-5330.
www.trinitycatholic.org   E-mail: admissions@trinitycatholic.org
Joseph Quinn, Pres. Anthony Paul Pavia III, Prin. Connie McGoldrick, Adm.

Col Prep. AP (exams req'd)—Eng Span Calc Chem Physics Eur_Hist US_Hist. **Feat**—Shakespeare Fr Ital Anat & Physiol Environ_Sci Comp_Sci Econ Law Psych Relig Film Fine_Arts Music_Theory Bus Journ. **Supp**—Rem_Read Tut. **Sports**—Basket Soccer Tennis Track. B: Baseball Football Golf Ice_Hockey Lacrosse. G: Cheer Softball Volley. Activities: 23. **Somewhat selective adm:** 125/yr. Appl fee: $50. Appl due: Rolling. Accepted: 90%. **Enr 430.** Avg class size: 19. Stud/fac: 13:1. Uniform. **Fac 37.** Adv deg: 97%. **Grad '10—124.** Col—120. **Avg SAT:** CR 491. M 490. W 518. **Col Couns:** 3. **Tui '12-'13:** Day $10,850 (+$600). Aid: Merit 8 ($62,000). Need 40 ($120,000). **Est 1957.** Nonprofit. Roman Catholic (75% practice). Quar (Aug-June). **Assoc** NEASC. Situated on a 26-acre campus, this regional high school offers classes in numerous subjects, among them religion, fine arts and business. AP and honors courses are available, and student activities include clubs and organizations, publications and interscholastic sports. All freshmen fulfill a 28-hour community service requirement through work with local churches, hospitals or charitable organizations.

CHRISTIAN HERITAGE SCHOOL   Day Coed Gr K-12
Trumbull, CT 06611. 575 White Plains Rd.
Tel: 203-261-6230. Fax: 203-452-1531.
www.kingsmen.org   E-mail: molson@kingsmen.org
Brian Modarelli, Head (2011). Martha Olson, Adm.

Col Prep. Gen Acad. AP (55 exams taken, 93% 3+)—Eng Span Calc Comp_Sci Bio Physics US_Hist US_Govt & Pol. **Feat**—Shakespeare Lat Stats Anat & Physiol Forensic_Sci Econ Bible Philos Studio_Art Band Chorus Music_Hist Journ Public_Speak. **Supp**—ESL Rem_Read Tut. **Comp:** Comp/Stud: 1:5. **Sports**—Basket X-country Soccer Tennis. B: Baseball. G: Softball Volley. Activities: 8. **Selective adm:** 96/yr. Appl fee: $50-75. Appl due: Rolling. Accepted: 68%. **Tests** IQ ISEE Stanford. **Enr 470.** Avg class size: 17. Stud/fac: 14:1. **Fac 50.** M 16/F 34. FT 43/PT 7. Adv deg: 60%. **Grad '09—50.** Col—50. **Avg SAT:** CR 572. M 561. W 570. Alum donors: 7%. **Tui '12-'13:** Day $9900-15,900 (+$600). Aid: Need 231 ($1,101,950). **Est 1977.** Nonprofit. Nondenom Christian. Quar (Sept-June). **Assoc** NEASC. This college preparatory school emphasizes Christian values and requires each class to participate in one community service project during the year. Electives offered include art, band, chorus, painting, computer science, drafting and word processing. Students in grades 9-12 satisfy a 20-hour annual community service requirement.

THE GLENHOLME SCHOOL   Bdg & Day
A DEVEREUX CENTER   Coed Gr 5-PG
Washington, CT 06793. 81 Sabbaday Ln.
Tel: 860-868-7377. Fax: 860-868-7413.
www.theglenholmeschool.org   E-mail: admissions@theglenholmeschool.org
Maryann Campbell, Exec Dir. Kathi Fitzherbert, Adm.

LD. Underachiever. Feat—Span Studio_Art Music. **Supp**—Dev_Read Rem_Math Rem_Read Rev Tut. **Comp:** Comp/Stud: 1:1 Laptop prgm Gr 5-PG. **Sports**—Basket X-country Soccer Softball Tennis. **Somewhat selective adm:** 15/yr. Bdg 13. Day 2. Appl fee: $150. Appl due: Rolling. **Enr 89.** B 72. G 17. Bdg 83. Day 6. Intl 7%. Avg class size: 10. Stud/fac: 10:1. Uniform. **Fac 21.** M 3/F 18. FT 20/PT 1. Adv deg: 57%. **Grad '11—12.** Col—5. (Wm Jessup 1, Norwalk CC 1, CA Col San Diego 1). **Tui :** **Est 1968.** Nonprofit. Spons: The Devereux

Foundation. Sem (Sept-June). **Assoc** NEASC. Glenholme uses an evidence-based treatment milieu in a structured therapeutic setting. The 12-month program serves boys and girls who have been diagnosed with such conditions as Asperger's, ADHD, PDD, OCD, Tourette's, depression and anxiety, as well as various learning differences. The program builds competence socially and academically and integrates a learning approach into all activities, including the arts, an equestrian program, sports and various other interests. While providing a strong academic curriculum, Glenholme utilizes a positive behavior support model to promote relationships among peers, an understanding of boundaries and appropriate social behaviors. The supportive, small-class learning environment and individualized services are designed with higher education in mind.   **See Also Page 51**

HARTFORD CHRISTIAN ACADEMY   Day Coed Gr K-12
West Hartford, CT 06107. 155 Mountain Rd.
Tel: 860-521-8380. Fax: 860-521-8336.
www.hartfordchristianacademy.com   E-mail: academy@ctfabc.org
   Mark Cronemeyer, Prin (2003). BA, Bob Jones Univ, MEd, EdD, Bethany Theological Seminary.
   Col Prep. Feat—Fr Computers Bible. **Supp**—Tut. **Comp:** Comp/Stud: 1:6. **Sports**— B: Basket Soccer. G: Volley. **Somewhat selective adm:** 16/yr. Appl fee: $20. Appl due: Rolling. Accepted: 100%. Yield: 100%. **Tests** Stanford. **Enr 70.** Wh 83%. Latino 4%. Blk 13%. Avg class size: 8. **Fac 16.** M 3/F 13. FT 13/PT 3. Wh 100%. Adv deg: 18%. **Grad '11—7.** Col—7. (Bob Jones 4, Pensacola Christian 2, U of CT 1). **Tui '12-'13:** Day $4500 (+$500-750). **Est 1976.** Nonprofit. Baptist. Quar (Sept-June). A ministry of Farmington Avenue Baptist Church, this school utilizes the Bob Jones University Press Curriculum for Christian Schools in all grades. A wide range of subjects, centered around Bible study, is offered at varying levels. Reading instruction follows a phonetic approach, math a conceptual one.

HEBREW HIGH SCHOOL OF NEW ENGLAND   Day Coed Gr 9-12
West Hartford, CT 06117. 300 Bloomfield Ave.
Tel: 860-231-0317. Fax: 860-236-7623.
www.hhne.org   E-mail: info@hhne.org
   Rabbi Daniel Loew, Head (2005). BA, MS, Yeshiva Univ (NY). Rabbi Shimmy Trencher, Adm.
   Col Prep. AP (exams req'd; 50 taken, 70% 3+)—Eng Calc Bio Eur_Hist US_Hist. **Feat**—British_Lit Hebrew Israeli_Hist Govt Bible Judaic_Stud Talmud Studio_Art Drama. **Supp**—Rem_Math Rem_Read Rev. **Sports**—Baseball Basket Soccer Tennis. Activities: 27. **Somewhat selective adm:** 19/yr. Appl fee: $50. Appl due: Jan. Accepted: 88%. Yield: 86%. **Enr 79.** B 34. G 45. Wh 97%. Blk 3%. Avg class size: 10. Stud/fac: 3:1. **Fac 27.** M 15/F 12. FT 6/PT 21. Wh 100%. Adv deg: 85%. **Grad '10—14.** Col—14. (U of Hartford 2, Yeshiva-NY 2, MIT 1, Brandeis 1, Rochester Inst of Tech 1, U of CT 1). **Avg SAT:** CR 598. M 586. W 604. **Col Couns:** 1. Alum donors: 10%. **Tui '12-'13:** Day $20,750 (+$1000). **Est 1996.** Nonprofit. Jewish (100% practice). Quar (Sept-June). HHNE conducts a dual curriculum of college preparatory courses and Judaic studies. Following a daily community breakfast, students attend Judaic studies courses. Boys and girls also enroll in five college preparatory, honors or AP courses chosen from the disciplines of English, math, science, history and world language. Arts classes and various electives round out the curriculum. All students perform 15 hours of compulsory service annually. Subsidized bus transportation for families from Greater New Haven and western Massachusetts is available.

NORTHWEST CATHOLIC HIGH SCHOOL   Day Coed Gr 9-12
West Hartford, CT 06117. 29 Wampanoag Dr.
Tel: 860-236-4221. Fax: 860-586-0911.
www.northwestcatholic.org   E-mail: nbannon@nwcath.org

Margaret R. Williamson, Prin (2009). BA, College of New Rochelle, MA, Catholic Univ of America. Nancy Scully Bannon, Adm.

Col Prep. AP (exams req'd; 193 taken)—Eng Fr Lat Span Calc Comp_Sci Bio Chem Physics US_Hist US_Govt & Pol Studio_Art Music_Theory. **Feat**—Creative_Writing Astron Geol Oceanog Econ Psych Theol Jazz_Band Dance Outdoor_Ed. **Supp**—Tut. **Dual enr:** St Joseph Col-CT, U of Hartford. **Sports**—Basket X-country Golf Indoor_Track Lacrosse Soccer Tennis Track. B: Baseball Football Ice_Hockey Swim. G: Cheer F_Hockey Softball Volley. Activities: 21. **Selective adm (Gr 9-11):** 188/yr. Appl fee: $25-30. Appl due: Jan. **Tests** HSPT. **Enr 625.** Wh 72%. Latino 5%. Blk 18%. Native Am 1%. Asian 3%. Other 1%. Avg class size: 18. Stud/fac: 12:1. Uniform. **Fac 57.** M 27/F 30. FT 49/PT 8. Wh 92%. Blk 8%. Adv deg: 89%. **Grad '10—160.** Col—158. **Avg SAT:** CR 552. M 559. W 560. **Col Couns:** 4. **Tui '12-'13:** Day $13,200 (+$700). Aid: Need 300 ($1,325,000). **Est 1961.** Nonprofit. Roman Catholic (79% practice). Quar (Aug-June). **Assoc** NEASC. The school offers honors courses in math, English, history, languages and science, as well as classes in the arts and business. An AP program is also available. Sophomores perform 25 hours of required community service.

NOTRE DAME HIGH SCHOOL   Day Boys Gr 9-12
West Haven, CT 06516. 24 Ricardo St.
Tel: 203-933-1673. Fax: 203-933-2474.
www.notredamehs.com   E-mail: info@notredamehs.com

Br. James Branigan, CSC, Pres. BA, Stonehill College, MS, St John's Univ (NY), MA, Fordham Univ. Patrick Clifford, Prin. BA, MA, Fairfield Univ. Pasquale G. Izzo, Adm.

Col Prep. AP—Calc Physics US_Hist US_Govt & Pol Studio_Art. **Feat**—British_Lit Fr Ital Lat Span Anat & Physiol Forensic_Sci Marine_Bio/Sci Web_Design Holocaust Econ Law Psych Sociol Comp_Relig Photog Band Chorus Music_Theory Guitar Accounting Marketing Speech. **Supp**—Dev_Read LD Rem_Math Rem_Read Rev Tut. **Dual enr:** U of New Haven, S CT St, Yale. **Sports**— B: Baseball Basket X-country Football Golf Ice_Hockey Indoor_Track Lacrosse Soccer Swim Tennis Track. Activities: 35. **Selective adm (Gr 9-11):** 204/yr. Appl fee: $40. Appl due: Nov. **Enr 650.** Nonwhite 19%. Avg class size: 22. Stud/fac: 12:1. Uniform. **Fac 59.** M 36/F 23. FT 56/PT 3. Wh 97%. Latino 3%. Adv deg: 88%. **Grad '11—173.** Col—170. **Col Couns:** 3. **Tui '12-'13:** Day $11,400 (+$500). Aid: Need 195 ($650,000). **Est 1946.** Nonprofit. Roman Catholic (75% practice). Tri (Aug-May). **Assoc** NEASC. Sponsored by the Brothers of Holy Cross, the school offers a variety of Advanced Placement, honors and college preparatory courses. Community service and Christian retreats are important aspects of a well-developed campus ministry program. Service requirements are as follows: an in-class project in grade 9, 15 hours of service in grade 10 and 30 hours of service in grade 11.

EZRA ACADEMY   Day Coed Gr K-8
Woodbridge, CT 06525. 75 Rimmon Rd.
Tel: 203-389-5500. Fax: 203-387-5607.
www.ezraacademy.net   E-mail: info@ezraacademy.net

Rabbi Amanda Brodie, Head (2008). MA, Jewish Theological Seminary. Marni Smith Katz, Adm.

Pre-Prep. Gen Acad. Feat—Lib_Skills Hebrew Span Computers Bible Judaic_Stud Studio_Art Music. **Supp**—Dev_Read ESL Rem_Math Rem_Read Tut. **Sports**—Basket Soccer Tennis Ultimate_Frisbee. **Somewhat selective adm:** 34/yr. Appl fee: $50. Appl due: Jan. Accepted: 95%. **Enr 165.** B 95. G 70. Wh 98%. Blk 1%. Asian 1%. Avg class size: 10. Stud/fac: 9:1. Uniform. **Fac 35.** M 5/F 30. FT 32/PT 3. Adv deg: 20%. **Grad '08—15.** Prep—10. **Tui '11-'12:** Day $13,950 (+$2550). Aid: Need 64 ($370,000). **Est 1966.** Nonprofit. Jewish (100% practice). Sem (Sept-June). A Solomon Schechter day school, Ezra integrates secular and Judaic studies within a community environment. The academy's secular studies curriculum includes language arts, literature, math, science and social studies; Spanish instruction commences in grade 7. Hebrew language study, Bible, prayer, Rabbinics and Jewish history constitute the Judaic studies program. Computers, music, art, library and field trips enrich the curriculum.

MAINE

JOHN BAPST MEMORIAL HIGH SCHOOL   **Bdg & Day**
Bangor, ME 04401. 100 Broadway.   **Coed Gr 9-12**
Tel: 207-947-0313. Fax: 207-941-2474.
www.johnbapst.org   E-mail: info@johnbapst.org
Melville G. MacKay III, Head (2007). AB, Harvard Univ, MAT, Univ of North Carolina-Chapel Hill.

Col Prep. AP (exams req'd; 309 taken)—Eng Fr Lat Span Calc Stats Comp_Sci Bio Chem Physics Eur_Hist US_Hist Human_Geog US_Govt & Pol Studio_Art. **Feat**—Creative_Writing Chin Anat & Physiol Astron Ecol Web_Design Anthro Econ Psych Sociol Ceramics Sculpt Band Chorus Jazz_Band Journ. **Supp**—ESL Tut. **Sports**—Basket Cheer X-country Ice_Hockey Indoor_Track Ski Soccer Swim Tennis Track Wrestling. B: Baseball Football Golf. G: F_Hockey Softball. Activities: 25. **Somewhat selective adm:** 120/yr. Appl fee: $50. Appl due: Mar. Accepted: 91%. Yield: 84%. **Tests** MAT SSAT Stanford. **Enr 440.** B 208. G 232. Wh 96%. Native Am 1%. Asian 2%. Other 1%. Avg class size: 17. Stud/fac: 11:1. Casual dress. **Fac 38.** M 18/F 20. FT 38. Wh 96%. Latino 2%. Asian 2%. Adv deg: 63%. **Grad '10—102.** Col—100. (U of ME-Orono 36, U of S ME 7, Husson 6, U of ME-Farmington 4, E ME Tech 3, UNH 3). **Avg SAT:** CR 545. M 557. W 542. **Col Couns:** 2. **Tui '10-'11:** Bdg $36,750 (+$690). 5-Day Bdg $31,500 (+$690). Day $9600 (+$690). Aid: Need 19 ($93,120). **Est 1928.** Nonprofit. Sem (Aug-June). **Assoc** NEASC. After 52 years as a Catholic school, John Bapst reestablished itself as a nonsectarian institution in 1980. Emphasizing both college preparation and skill development, the school offers a varied curriculum that comprises the humanities, the arts and sciences, and technology. Honors and Advanced Placement courses are available in all major disciplines. In addition to five- and seven-day boarding options, John Bapst offers a home stay program for international pupils.

GEORGE STEVENS ACADEMY   **Bdg & Day**
Blue Hill, ME 04614. 23 Union St.   **Coed Gr 9-12**
Tel: 207-374-2808. Fax: 207-374-2982.
www.georgestevensacademy.org   E-mail: admissions@georgestevens.org
Paul B. Perkinson, Head (2011). BA, Earlham College, MA, Univ of Pennsylvania. Libby Irwin, Adm.

Col Prep. Gen Acad. AP (exams req'd)—Eng Calc Stats Environ_Sci US_Hist Human_Geog Studio_Art. **Feat**—Creative_Writing ME_Writers Fr Span Forensic_Sci Marine_Bio/Sci Comp_Sci Holocaust Anthro Law Psych Philos Drawing Photog Acting Band Chorus Music_Theory Dance Journ Indus_Arts Woodworking. **Supp**—Dev_Read ESL LD Rem_Math Rem_Read. **Sports**—Basket X-country Golf Indoor_Track Sail Soccer Swim Tennis Track Wrestling. B: Baseball. G: Cheer Softball. Activities: 19. **Selective adm (Bdg Gr 9-11; Day 9-12):** 106/yr. Bdg 21. Day 85. Appl fee: $75. Appl due: Mar. **Tests** SSAT TOEFL. **Enr 300.** B 150. G 150. Bdg 25. Day 275. Intl 14%. Avg class size: 14. Stud/fac: 8:1. Casual dress. **Fac 38.** M 18/F 20. FT 29/PT 9. Adv deg: 55%. In Dorms 2. **Grad '11—81.** Col—74. (E ME CC 9, U of ME-Orono 8, Husson 5, Am U 2, Bowdoin 2, ME Maritime 2). **Avg SAT:** CR 533. M 547. W 526. **Mid 50% SAT:** CR 440-640. M 480-630. W 440-610. **Col Couns:** 2. **Tui '12-'13:** Bdg $37,400 (+$2400). Day $9240. Intl Bdg $37,400 (+$7400). Aid: Need 2 ($30,000). **Est 1803.** Nonprofit. Sem (Sept-June). **Assoc** NEASC. In addition to the regular college preparatory curriculum, the school provides honors and Advanced Placement courses, ESL instruction and special education classes and support for students with dyslexia. Most students spend at least one period per day in the academic support center, which provides assistance with homework and research projects. Opportunities for two-week internships or independent study are available for pupils in grades 11 and 12. The academy added a boarding division in the fall of 2008.

FOXCROFT ACADEMY　　　　　　　　　　　　　　　　　　　　**Bdg & Day**
Dover-Foxcroft, ME 04426. 975 W Main St.　　　　　　　　　　**Coed Gr 9-12**
Tel: 207-564-8351. Fax: 207-564-8394.
www.foxcroftacademy.org　E-mail: chris.mcgary@foxcroftacademy.org
　Arnold Shorey, Head (2010). BA, Univ of Maine-Farmington, MEd, Univ of Maine-Orono. Chris McGary, Adm.

　Col Prep. AP (85 exams taken)—Eng Calc Stats Bio Chem Physics US_Hist Econ Studio_ Art. **Feat**—Creative_Writing Humanities Chin Fr Lat Span Comp_Sci Intl_Relations Art_Hist Ceramics Visual_Arts Chorus Woodworking Culinary_Arts. **Supp**—ESL Tut. **Comp:** Comp/ Stud: 1:3. **Sports**—Basket X-country Indoor_Track Soccer Swim Tennis Track. B: Baseball Football Golf Wrestling. G: Cheer F_Hockey Softball. Activities: 20. **Selective adm (Bdg Gr 9-11; Day 9-10):** 144/yr. Bdg 46. Day 98. Appl fee: $50. Appl due: Mar. Accepted: 60%. Yield: 66%. **Tests** CEEB SSAT TOEFL. **Enr 430.** B 220. G 210. Bdg 92. Day 338. Wh 80%. Latino 4%. Blk 1%. Asian 15%. Intl 20%. Avg class size: 16. Stud/fac: 11:1. **Fac 46.** M 30/F 16. FT 41/PT 5. Wh 90%. Latino 5%. Asian 5%. Adv deg: 54%. In Dorms 12. **Grad '10—128.** Col—74. (U of ME-Orono 15, ME Maritime 4, Boston U 2, Wentworth Inst of Tech 2, U of CT 1, Northeastern U 1). **Avg SAT:** CR 560. M 680. W 530. Alum donors: 12%. **Tui '12-'13:** Bdg $36,720 (+$2100). Day $11,500 (+$2100). Intl Bdg $36,720 (+$4500). Aid: Need 2 ($42,000). **Est 1823.** Nonprofit. Sem (Aug-June). **Assoc** NEASC. One of the country's oldest private boarding and day schools, FA offers a college preparatory program on a 120-acre tract along the Piscataquis River. Math and science programs make use of the latest technology, and the foreign language program comprises four levels each of four languages. Boys and girls perform at least six hours of required community service in grade 9, a minimum that increases by two hours per year through grade 12. The academy sponsors an annual trip abroad to a country such as France, England, Spain or Greece.

WASHINGTON ACADEMY　　　　　　　　　　　　　　　　　　**Bdg & Day**
East Machias, ME 04630. 66 Cutler Rd, PO Box 190.　　　　　　**Coed Gr 9-12**
Tel: 207-255-8301. Fax: 207-255-8303.
www.washingtonacademy.org　E-mail: admissions@washingtonacademy.org
　Judson McBrine, Head (1997). BS, MEd, Univ of Maine-Orono. Robin Moloff-Gautier, Adm.

　Col Prep. Voc. AP (79 exams taken, 57% 3+)—Eng Lat Span Calc Stats Bio Chem Eur_ Hist US_Hist Studio_Art. **Feat**—Creative_Writing Chin Fr Ecol Environ_Sci Econ Psych Sociol Photog Video_Production Music Journ Design Culinary_Arts. **Supp**—Dev_Read ESL LD Makeup Rem_Math Rem_Read Tut. **Dual enr:** U of ME-Machias, Husson. **Sports**— Basket Cheer X-country Golf Soccer Swim Tennis Track Wrestling. B: Baseball Football. G: Softball Volley. Activities: 50. **Somewhat selective adm (Bdg Gr 9-11; Day 9-12):** 146/yr. Bdg 41. Day 105. Appl fee: $50. Appl due: Rolling. Accepted: 98%. Yield: 38%. **Tests** SSAT TOEFL. **Enr 430.** B 215. G 215. Bdg 104. Day 326. Wh 74%. Latino 1%. Blk 4%. Native Am 3%. Asian 17%. Intl 22%. Avg class size: 16. Stud/fac: 11:1. Casual dress. **Fac 39.** M 17/F 22. FT 30/PT 9. Wh 96%. Asian 4%. Adv deg: 33%. In Dorms 12. **Grad '11—103.** Col—90. **Tui '12-'13:** Bdg $33,500 (+$3000). Day $12,000. Aid: Need 62 ($413,108). Work prgm 23 ($23,750). **Est 1792.** Nonprofit. Sem (Aug-June). **Assoc** NEASC. In addition to the traditional academic subjects, Washington Academy offers hands-on programs in boat building and environmental science. Electives such as video production, music appreciation, creative writing, computer programming and Web design are part of a curriculum that includes honors and Advanced Placement courses. Qualified juniors and seniors may take tuition-free classes at Husson College and the University of Maine-Machias. All students perform 15 hours of required community service annually.

DECK HOUSE SCHOOL

Bdg Boys Gr 9-12

Edgecomb, ME 04556. 124 Deck House Rd.
Tel: 207-882-7055. Fax: 207-882-8151.
www.deckhouseschool.org   E-mail: admissions@deckhouseschool.org
  Melinda Evelyn Browne, Head (2011). BS, Univ of Bridgeport, MSEd, Saint Joseph's College of Maine, EdD, Univ of Exeter (England).

  Col Prep. Underachiever. Feat—Creative_Writing Fr Span Marine_Bio/Sci Govt Film Studio_Art Drama Study_Skills. **Supp**—Rem_Math Tut. **Somewhat selective adm:** 6/yr. Appl due: Rolling. Accepted: 75%. **Enr 12.** Avg class size: 3. **Fac 6.** M 3/F 3. FT 4/PT 2. Adv deg: 33%. In Dorms 1. **Grad '07**—3. Col—3. (Hartwick 1, Acad of Art U 1, U of UT 1). **Avg SAT:** CR/M 1040. Alum donors: 50%. **Tui '08-'09:** Bdg $49,500 (+$900). **Est 1979.** Nonprofit. Tri (Sept-June). **Assoc** NEASC. The school's program is designed for boys who have not had success in other school settings. Each student is involved in maintaining the 180-acre campus and its facilities. The school combines a standard college preparatory curriculum with daily support, positive peer pressure and a disciplined, highly structured community environment. Maximum enrollment remains at 12 pupils, thereby facilitating individual attention, and boys have frequent opportunities to explore areas of interest outside the classroom. Students devote two to three hours per week to community outreach activities.

RILEY SCHOOL

Day Coed Gr PS (Age 4)-9

Glen Cove, ME 04846. 73 Warrenton Rd.
Tel: 207-596-6405. Fax: 207-596-7200.
www.rileyschool.org   E-mail: info@rileyschool.org
  Glenna W. Plaisted, Dir (1972). BA, Boston Univ.

  Gen Acad. Feat—Creative_Writing Humanities Lat Span Environ_Sci Philos Photog Studio_Art Theater Music. **Supp**—Dev_Read Rev Tut. **Somewhat selective adm (Gr PS-8):** 12/yr. Appl fee: $50. Appl due: Rolling. Accepted: 90%. **Tests** SSAT Stanford. **Enr 80.** B 47. G 33. Wh 97%. Latino 3%. Avg class size: 9. Stud/fac: 8:1. Casual dress. **Fac 15.** M 3/F 12. FT 13/PT 2. Wh 99%. Latino 1%. Adv deg: 20%. **Grad '11**—12. Prep—2. Avg SSAT: 90%. Alum donors: 3%. **Tui '12-'13:** Day $6250-9000 (+$600). Aid: Need 43 ($98,000). **Est 1972.** Nonprofit. Sem (Sept-June). **Assoc** NEASC. The school's curriculum emphasizes the fundamentals in reading, language arts and writing, in addition to the basic principles of mathematics, foreign language and scientific inquiry. Creative activities are offered at all levels. Electives and extracurricular activities include community service, pottery, photography, field trips, softball, swimming, skiing, skating, camping trips, music, soccer, sewing, a special-interest fair and art. **See Also Page 43**

BREAKWATER SCHOOL

Day Coed Gr PS (Age 2)-8

Portland, ME 04102. 856 Brighton Ave.
Tel: 207-772-8689. Fax: 207-772-1327.
www.breakwaterschool.org   E-mail: info@breakwaterschool.org
  David D. Sullivan, Head (2007). BA, Hampshire College, MAT, Harvard Univ. Abbie Carter, Adm.

  Pre-Prep. Gen Acad. Feat—Fr Studio_Art Music Outdoor_Ed. **Supp**—Dev_Read. **Selective adm:** 44/yr. Appl fee: $45. Appl due: Feb. Accepted: 80%. **Enr 130.** Elem 151. Wh 93%. Latino 2%. Blk 2%. Asian 3%. Avg class size: 14. **Fac 26.** M 7/F 19. FT 16/PT 10. Wh 100%. Adv deg: 38%. **Grad '08**—18. Prep—8. **Tui '11-'12:** Day $14,850-19,460. Aid: Need ($321,000). **Est 1956.** Nonprofit. Sem (Sept-June). **Assoc** NEASC. Breakwater's program includes French, computers, art, music, field trips and community service opportunities. Children study literature and develop their writing skills through the school's language arts program. In grades 1-6, students improve their spelling and grammar by writing and editing original stories, then sharing them in a workshop setting. Fifth graders complete a compulsory service project. The middle school (grades 6-8) employs an exploratory, integrated curriculum.

CATHERINE McAULEY HIGH SCHOOL   Day Girls Gr 9-12
Portland, ME 04103. 631 Stevens Ave.
Tel: 207-797-3802. Fax: 207-797-3804.
www.mcauleyhs.org   E-mail: admissions@mcauleyhs.org
    Margaret Downing, Prin (2011). BA, Trinity College (VT). Ericka Prefontaine Sanborn, Adm.

    Col Prep. AP (exams req'd)—Eng Calc Bio US_Hist US_Govt & Pol. **Feat**—Creative_Writing Fr Lat Span Anat & Physiol Ecol Environ_Sci Comp_Sci Econ Psych Theol World_Relig Studio_Art Theater_Arts Chorus Dance. **Comp:** Comp/Stud: 1:1 Laptop prgm Gr 9-12. **Sports**— G: Basket Cheer X-country F_Hockey Golf Lacrosse Soccer Softball Swim Tennis Track. Activities: 19. **Somewhat selective adm:** 68/yr. Appl fee: $50. Appl due: Feb. Accepted: 90%. Yield: 90%. **Tests** HSPT SSAT Stanford. **Enr 200.** Avg class size: 14. Stud/fac: 9:1. Uniform. **Fac 27.** M 4/F 23. FT 16/PT 11. Adv deg: 37%. **Grad '10—53.** Col—53. **Avg SAT:** CR 540. M 504. W 538. Avg ACT: 22.9. **Col Couns:** 1. Alum donors: 15%. **Tui '12-'13:** Day $13,780 (+$756-806). **Est 1969.** Nonprofit. Roman Catholic (60% practice). Quar (Sept-June). **Assoc** NEASC. The college preparatory program at this girls' school integrates daily prayer, religion courses and retreat days. Social justice and ethical issues are taught from a Christian perspective. Each year, juniors take part in a weeklong career exploration program that exposes students to jobs in education, medicine, business and communication, among others. All girls fulfill a 15-hour annual community service requirement.

CHEVERUS HIGH SCHOOL   Day Coed Gr 9-12
Portland, ME 04103. 267 Ocean Ave.
Tel: 207-774-6238. Fax: 207-321-0004.
www.cheverus.org   E-mail: admissions@cheverus.org
    Rev. William R. Campbell, SJ, Pres. BA, College of the Holy Cross, MDiv, Weston Jesuit School of Theology. John H. R. Mullen, Prin. BA, Univ of Southern Maine, MA, Middlebury College. Philip J. Dawson, Adm.

    Col Prep. AP (exams req'd; 203 taken, 70% 3+)—Eng Lat Span Calc Stats Bio Chem Environ_Sci Eur_Hist US_Hist Econ. **Feat**—Fr Greek Comp_Design Comp_Sci Theol Studio_Art Music_Theory. **Supp**—LD Tut. **Sports**—Basket X-country Ice_Hockey Indoor_Track Lacrosse Sail Ski Soccer Tennis Track. B: Baseball Football Golf Wrestling. G: F_Hockey Softball Volley. Activities: 22. **Selective adm:** 165/yr. Appl fee: $50. Appl due: Apr. Accepted: 81%. Yield: 80%. **Enr 497.** Avg class size: 21. **Fac 38.** M 23/F 15. Adv deg: 60%. **Grad '11—120.** Col—117. **Avg SAT:** CR 536. M 535. W 537. **Col Couns:** 2. **Tui '12-'13:** Day $15,835 (+$500). Aid: Need 318 ($2,000,000). **Est 1917.** Nonprofit. Roman Catholic (67% practice). Sem (Sept-June). **Assoc** NEASC. Sponsored by the Society of Jesus, the school conducts a rigorous program that emphasizes college preparation. Gifted students choose from honors and Advanced Placement courses in most subjects, and Cheverus addresses study skill development for pupils who have a demonstrated need in this area. Up-to-date computer labs are an integral part of the school's strong technology program. Seniors complete a compulsory project comprising 120 hours of community service and two 500-word reflection papers.

CHOP POINT SCHOOL   Bdg Coed Gr 8-12
Woolwich, ME 04579. 420 Chop Point Rd.   Day Coed K-12
Tel: 207-443-3080. Fax: 207-443-6760.
www.choppoint.org   E-mail: school@choppoint.org
    Peter Willard, Dir (1987). BA, Baylor Univ, MS, Univ of Wyoming. Jean Willard, Prin.

    Col Prep. Gen Acad. AP (4 exams taken, 50% 3+)—Eng Calc. **Feat**—Span Zoology Comp_Sci Archaeol Econ Psych Studio_Art Music. **Supp**—ESL Rev Tut. **Comp:** Comp/Stud: 1:2. **Sports**—Basket Soccer. **Somewhat selective adm:** 28/yr. Bdg 4. Day 24. Appl due: Rolling. Accepted: 90%. Yield: 85%. **Tests** Stanford. **Enr 95.** B 50. G 45. Bdg 3. Day 92. Elem 45. Sec 50. Wh 85%. Latino 14%. Blk 1%. Avg class size: 8. Stud/fac: 8:1. Casual dress. **Fac 16.** M 4/F 12. FT 13/PT 3. Wh 90%. Latino 10%. Adv deg: 31%. In Dorms 2.

Grad '11—7. Col—4. (Hillsborough CC 1, Sch of the Museum of Fine Arts 1, St Michael's 1, U of S ME 1). **Avg SAT:** CR 650. M 650. **Col Couns:** 1. Alum donors: 10%. **Tui '12-'13:** Bdg $18,500 (+$2000). 5-Day Bdg $14,500 (+$2000). Day $6200 (+$765). Intl Bdg $20,500 (+$4000). Aid: Need 10 ($10,000). **Est 1987.** Nonprofit. Nondenom Christian (35% practice). Sem (Aug-May). This Christian school limits its classes to 15 students, thereby allowing staff to provide individual attention and to cover material at a faster pace. In the lower grades, Chop Point emphasizes reading and math skills, and children have several periods of Spanish, art, music and computer each week. The high school program features typical college preparatory course requirements and a choice of electives. Juniors and seniors spend two to three weeks performing community service in Nicaragua.

MASSACHUSETTS

WARING SCHOOL   Day Coed Gr 6-12
Beverly, MA 01915. 35 Standley St.
Tel: 978-927-8793. Fax: 978-921-2107.
www.waringschool.org   E-mail: dwang@waringschool.org
   Peter Laird Smick, Head (1991). BA, Webster Univ, MA, Gordon-Conwell Theological Seminary. Dorothy Wang, Adm.
   Col Prep. Bilingual (Fr). AP—Fr Calc. **Feat**—Creative_Writing Humanities Amer_Stud Art_Hist Drawing Graphic_Arts Photog Studio_Art Theater Chorus Music_Theory. **Sports**—Basket X-country Lacrosse Soccer. **Selective adm:** 25/yr. Appl fee: $50. Appl due: Feb. **Enr 151.** Nonwhite 5%. Avg class size: 14. Stud/fac: 8:1. **Fac 50. Grad '10—25.** Col—25. **Avg SAT:** CR 690. M 620. W 670. **Mid 50% SAT:** CR 670-720. M 580-680. W 630-730. **Col Couns:** 1. **Tui '12-'13:** Day $26,378 (+$420-736). **Est 1972.** Nonprofit. Tri (Sept-June). **Assoc** NEASC. Waring's college preparatory program integrates French immersion at all grade levels. The core curriculum consists of math, science, humanities (a combination of history and literature), writing, French, music and art. In French class, pupils develop language fluency, while also gaining familiarity with French literature, history and culture. An intensive independent study program enables seniors to modify their curricula to allow for more depth and individualization.

GLEN URQUHART SCHOOL   Day Coed Gr K-8
Beverly Farms, MA 01915. 74 Hart St.
Tel: 978-927-1064. Fax: 978-921-0060.
www.gus.org   E-mail: lmarchesseault@gus.org
   David Provost, Head (2012). BA, Union College, MEd, Lesley College. Leslie Marchesseault, Adm.
   Pre-Prep. Feat—Lat Span Computers Drawing Visual_Arts Theater Chorus Music Orchestra. **Supp**—Tut. **Comp:** Laptop prgm Gr 6-8. **Sports (req'd)**—Basket X-country Lacrosse Soccer. **Selective adm:** 46/yr. Appl fee: $35. Appl due: Jan. Accepted: 32%. Yield: 70%. **Tests** CTP_4. **Enr 232.** B 116. G 116. Avg class size: 18. **Fac 36.** M 6/F 30. FT 20/PT 16. Adv deg: 80%. **Grad '07—33.** Prep—25. (Pingree 6, St John's Prep-MA 5, Governor's Acad 3, Waring 3, Phillips Acad 2, Phillips Exeter 1). Alum donors: 5%. **Tui '12-'13:** Day $16,700-24,850 (+$200). Aid: Need 60 ($500,000). **Est 1977.** Nonprofit. Tri (Sept-June). Glen Urquhart's thematic, interdisciplinary curriculum emphasizes problem solving and critical thinking. The school's program utilizes experiential and traditional learning modes, as well as the arts. Students participate in community service projects at all grade levels.

BOSTON COLLEGE HIGH SCHOOL   **Day Boys Gr 7-12**
Boston, MA 02125. 150 Morrissey Blvd.
Tel: 617-436-3900. Fax: 617-474-5105.
www.bchigh.edu   E-mail: admissions@bchigh.edu
   William J. Kemeza, Pres. BA, Temple Univ, MA, Andover Newton Theological School.
Stephen P. Hughes, Prin. BA, Univ of Massachusetts-Amherst, MEd, Boston College. Jim
Nicoletti, Adm.
   Col Prep. AP (exams req'd; 859 taken, 77% 3+)—Eng Fr Lat Span Calc Stats Comp_
Sci Bio Chem Environ_Sci Physics Eur_Hist US_Hist Econ US_Govt & Pol Music_Theory.
Feat—Creative_Writing Irish_Lit Chin Greek Japan Anat & Physiol Astron Forensic_Sci
Marine_Bio/Sci WWII Psych Ethics Relig World_Relig Art_Hist Studio_Art Drama Music
Journ. **Supp**—ESL Tut. **Sports**— B: Baseball Basket Crew X-country Football Golf Ice_
Hockey Lacrosse Rugby Sail Ski Soccer Swim Tennis Track Wrestling. Activities: 40. **Selec-
tive adm (Gr 7-11):** 350/yr. Appl fee: $0. Appl due: Dec. Accepted: 50%. Yield: 65%. **Tests**
HSPT ISEE SSAT. **Enr 1604.** Elem 311. Sec 1293. Wh 83%. Latino 3%. Blk 5%. Asian 4%.
Other 5%. Avg class size: 21. Stud/fac: 12:1. Casual dress. **Fac 136.** M 83/F 53. FT 136. Adv
deg: 88%. **Grad '11—268.** Col—266. (Boston Col 24, Fordham 12, Fairfield 12, Loyola U
MD 9, U of MA-Amherst 9, Holy Cross 7). **Avg SAT:** CR 608. M 617. W 599. **Col Couns:**
8. Alum donors: 26%. **Tui '12-'13:** Day $16,900 (+$400). Aid: Need 465 ($4,500,000). **Est
1863.** Nonprofit. Roman Catholic. Quar (Sept-June). **Assoc** NEASC. This college preparatory school, founded as a department of Boston College, became independent in 1913. Ample
opportunities for Advanced Placement and honors work are part of the college preparatory curriculum. After serving strictly as a high school for almost 150 years, the school added grades 7
and 8 to its program in the fall of 2007. BC High emphasizes spiritual growth and development
through religion courses, Masses, retreats and community service; all students perform at least
150 hours of service prior to graduation.

THE NEWMAN SCHOOL   **Day Coed Gr 9-PG**
Boston, MA 02116. 247 Marlborough St.
Tel: 617-267-4530. Fax: 617-267-7070.
www.newmanboston.org   E-mail: pridge@newmanboston.org
   J. Harry Lynch, Head (1985). BA, College of the Holy Cross, MBA, Northeastern Univ.
Patricia Lynch, Adm.
   Col Prep. IB Diploma. Feat—Classics Creative_Writing Nonfiction_Writing Fr Lat Span
Boston_Hist Civil_War Anthro Econ Intl_Relations Psych Sociol Bus_Law Philos Studio_Art
Chorus Music. **Supp**—Dev_Read ESL Makeup Rev Tut. **Comp:** Comp/Stud: 1:10. **Dual enr:**
Suffolk, Emmanuel. **Sports**—Basket Crew X-country Sail Soccer Tennis Track. B: Baseball.
G: Softball. **Selective adm (Gr 9-12):** 75/yr. Appl fee: $40. Appl due: Rolling. Accepted: 60%.
Yield: 66%. **Tests** HSPT SSAT. **Enr 230.** B 119. G 111. Sec 228. PG 2. Wh 68%. Latino 5%.
Blk 9%. Native Am 1%. Asian 17%. Intl 17%. Avg class size: 14. Stud/fac: 14:1. **Fac 26.** M
14/F 12. FT 22/PT 4. Wh 90%. Asian 5%. Other 5%. Adv deg: 53%. **Grad '10—90.** Col—90.
(Boston U 7, U of IL-Urbana 3, U of MA-Amherst 3, Suffolk 3, Cornell 1, Northeastern U
1). **Avg SAT:** CR 610. M 570. W 590. **Col Couns:** 3. **Tui '12-'13:** Day $18,000. Aid: Merit
25 ($125,000). Need 55 ($500,000). **Est 1945.** Nonprofit. Sem (Sept-June). **Assoc** NEASC.
Newman's college preparatory program features the two-year International Baccalaureate
Diploma Program. Students may take between four and seven courses per year, progressing
as rapidly as capability dictates. An extensive ESL program, offered for an additional tuition
fee, serves the school's international pupils, and Newman also offers a home stay option to
these students.

CAMBRIDGE MONTESSORI SCHOOL　　　**Day Coed Gr PS (Age 2)-8**
Cambridge, MA 02138. 161 Garden St.
Tel: 617-492-3410. Fax: 617-576-5154.
Other locations: 129 Sherman St, Cambridge 02140; 96 Sherman St, Cambridge 02140.
www.cambridgemontessori.org　E-mail: info@cambridgemontessori.org
　Ingrid W. Tucker, Head (2011). BA, Ohio Wesleyan Univ, MPA, Clark Atlanta Univ, EdD, Boston College. Nicole Pascarelli O'Brien, Adm.
　Pre-Prep. Gen Acad. Montessori. Feat—Span Film Studio_Art Theater_Arts Music. **Supp**—Dev_Read Rem_Math Rem_Read Rev Tut. **Comp:** Comp/Stud: 1:2 (1:1 Laptop prgm Gr 7-8). **Sports**—Basket X-country Soccer Track. **Selective adm (Gr PS-7):** 60/yr. Appl fee: $50. Appl due: Feb. Accepted: 68%. Yield: 41%. **Enr 220.** Wh 65%. Latino 4%. Blk 3%. Asian 10%. Other 18%. Avg class size: 23. Stud/fac: 8:1. Casual dress. **Fac 44.** M 2/F 42. FT 36/PT 8. Wh 71%. Latino 14%. Blk 8%. Asian 5%. Other 2%. Adv deg: 34%. **Grad '11—6.** Prep—3. (Cambridge Sch-MA 1, Intl Sch of Boston 1, Landmark Sch 1). **Tui '11-'12:** Day $20,395-23,020 (+$500). Aid: Need 48 ($550,000). **Est 1963.** Nonprofit. Tri (Sept-June). CMS' Montessori curriculum offers developmentally based learning experiences in language arts, math, social studies, science, Spanish and the arts. Children may enter the hands-on toddler program at age 21 months. The primary program (ages 3-5) introduces boys and girls to music, art, gym and field trips, while the elementary program (grades 1-6) seeks to build strong foundations in the core academic subjects. Serving grades 7 and 8, a middle school program based on education for sustainability opened in the fall of 2007. A learning center staffed by specialists and tutors provides support services when necessary. The school occupies three buildings adjacent to Danehy Park in North Cambridge.

THE CLARK SCHOOL　　　**Day Coed Gr K-12**
Danvers, MA 01923. 487 Locust St.
Tel: 978-777-4699. Fax: 978-777-7116.
www.clarkschool.com　E-mail: clarkschool@clarkschool.com
　Jeffrey K. Clark, Head. Heather Tripp, Adm.
　Col Prep. Gen Acad. Feat—Creative_Writing Shakespeare Fr Ital Lat Span Comp_Sci Geog Studio_Art Drama Chorus Music Study_Skills. **Supp**—Dev_Read Tut. **Comp:** Laptop prgm Gr 7-12. **Somewhat selective adm:** 8/yr. Appl fee: $50. Appl due: Rolling. Accepted: 90%. Yield: 95%. **Tests** Stanford. **Enr 90.** B 43. G 47. Elem 78. Sec 12. Avg class size: 15. **Fac 18.** M 5/F 13. FT 12/PT 6. Adv deg: 44%. **Grad '08—5.** Alum donors: 8%. **Tui '11-'12:** Day $12,950 (+$800-1100). **Est 1978.** Nonprofit. Sem (Sept-June). Featuring multi-age grouping and stressing history and the arts, the school provides individual diagnostic assessments twice yearly. Computer use is integral to the writing program, while science courses deal with aspects of life science, physics and chemistry. Frequent field trips enrich academic work.

URSULINE ACADEMY　　　**Day Girls Gr 7-12**
Dedham, MA 02026. 85 Lowder St.
Tel: 781-326-6161. Fax: 781-326-4898.
www.ursulineacademy.net　E-mail: ursuline@ursulineacademy.net
　Rosann M. Whiting, Pres. BA, Creighton Univ, MA, Our Lady of the Lake Univ, MA, Univ of Notre Dame. Mary Jo Keaney, Prin. AB, Bowdoin College, MEd, Harvard Univ. Catherine Spencer, Adm.
　Col Prep. AP (exams req'd)—Eng Span Calc Bio Chem US_Hist. **Feat**—Fr Lat Anat & Physiol Environ_Sci Comp_Sci Govt Psych Relig Studio_Art Communications Public_Speak Study_Skills. **Sports**— G: Basket X-country F_Hockey Golf Ice_Hockey Lacrosse Soccer Softball Swim Tennis Track Volley. Activities: 29. **Selective adm (Gr 7-10):** 71/yr. Appl fee: $30. Appl due: Dec. **Tests** HSPT. **Enr 396.** Elem 100. Sec 296. Avg class size: 20. Stud/fac: 11:1. Uniform. **Fac 36.** M 5/F 31. Adv deg: 63%. **Grad '11—64.** Col—64. (Boston Col 9, Boston U 4, Northeastern U 4, Fairfield 3, Harvard 2, Syracuse 2). **Avg SAT:** CR 639. M 611. W 659. **Col Couns:** 3. **Tui '11-'12:** Day $14,000 (+$300-500). Aid: Need 55 ($110,000). **Est**

1946. Nonprofit. Roman Catholic. Sem (Sept-June). **Assoc** NEASC. Ursuline complements a solid college preparatory curriculum with a varied athletic program and a selection of extracurricular activities. Each student satisfies a service requirement: 30 hours per year in grades 7-9, 40 hours per year in grades 10-12. Transportation to the school is available from neighboring communities.

EPIPHANY SCHOOL   **Day Coed Gr 5-8**
Dorchester, MA 02124. 154 Centre St.
Tel: 617-326-0425. Fax: 617-326-0424.
www.epiphanyschool.com   E-mail: jfinley@epiphanyschool.com
    Rev. John H. Finley IV, Head. AB, Harvard Univ.
    Pre-Prep. Gen Acad. Feat—Relig Studio_Art Music. **Supp**—Dev_Read LD Rem_Math Rem_Read Rev Tut. **Comp:** Comp/Stud: 1:1 **Sports**—Basket Soccer. B: Baseball. G: Softball. **Selective adm (Gr 5-6):** 22/yr. Appl due: Apr. Accepted: 35%. Yield: 95%. **Enr 85.** Wh 1%. Latino 14%. Blk 81%. Asian 2%. Other 2%. Avg class size: 10. Stud/fac: 4:1. Uniform. **Fac 19.** M 8/F 11. FT 19. Wh 50%. Latino 5%. Blk 20%. Other 25%. Adv deg: 21%. **Grad '09—15.** Prep—13. (Noble & Greenough 2, St Andrew's Sch-RI 2, Newman 2, Commonwealth Sch 1, St Mark's Sch-MA 1, Thayer 1). Alum donors: 1%. **Tui '12-'13:** Day $0. **Est 1997.** Nonprofit. Episcopal (10% practice). Tri (Sept-June). This tuition-free middle school serves children of diverse religious and racial backgrounds who come from economically disadvantaged families. Conducted in a small-class environment, the individualized program makes use of an extended school day. Students in each grade participate in two service trips per year. All applicants must reside in one of Boston's neighborhoods and must qualify for free or reduced-cost school lunches in Massachusetts.

POPE JOHN XXIII HIGH SCHOOL   **Day Coed Gr 9-12**
Everett, MA 02149. 888 Broadway.
Tel: 617-389-0240. Fax: 617-389-2201.
www.popejohnhs.org   E-mail: info@popejohnhs.org
    Kathleen F. Donovan, Pres (2007). Mary-Anne DiMarco, Prin. Mary-Anne DiMarco, Adm.
    Col Prep. AP (exams req'd; 59 taken)—Eng Span Calc Bio Chem Physics Eur_Hist US_Hist. **Feat**—British_Lit Ital Anat & Physiol Astron Marine_Bio/Sci Theol Fine_Arts Theater_Arts Music Journ SAT_Prep. **Supp**—ESL Tut. **Comp:** Comp/Stud: 1:2. **Sports**—Basket Soccer Tennis. B: Baseball Football Golf Ice_Hockey Lacrosse. G: Cheer Softball Volley. Activities: 19. **Somewhat selective adm:** 82/yr. Appl fee: $0. Appl due: Jan. Accepted: 85%. Yield: 45%. **Tests** HSPT. **Enr 280.** B 144. G 136. Wh 41%. Latino 13%. Blk 13%. Asian 33%. Intl 28%. Avg class size: 17. Stud/fac: 12:1. Uniform. **Fac 31.** M 16/F 15. FT 30/PT 1. Wh 100%. Adv deg: 64%. **Grad '11—47.** Col—43. (Boston U 5, Bunker Hill CC 4, U of MA-Amherst 3, U of MA-Dartmouth 3, Regis Col 2, MA Col of Pharmacy 2). **Avg SAT:** CR/M/W 1600. Avg ACT: 28. **Col Couns:** 2. Alum donors: 7%. **Tui '11-'12:** Day $8400 (+$400). **Est 1966.** Nonprofit. Roman Catholic (73% practice). **Assoc** NEASC. Founded by Cardinal Richard Cushing to serve Everett and nearby cities and towns, this school provides college preparation in a Catholic setting. The basic program, which includes four years of theology, is combined with supplementary courses at each grade level, among them College Board math and English, fine arts and online classes. Community service is part of the curriculum at all grade levels. A small boarding program serves international students.

ANTIOCH SCHOOL   **Day Coed Gr PS (Age 4)-8**
Fall River, MA 02720. 618 Rock St.
Tel: 508-673-6767. Fax: 508-676-9597.
www.antioch-school.org   E-mail: office@antioch-school.org
    John M. Frost, Prin. BA, Univ of Lowell, BS, MS, MA, Salve Regina Univ.

Pre-Prep. Feat—Span Studio_Art Music. **Supp**—Tut. **Somewhat selective adm (Gr PS-7):** 27/yr. Appl fee: $50. Appl due: Mar. Accepted: 94%. Yield: 89%. **Enr 87.** B 52. G 35. Wh 96%. Blk 3%. Asian 1%. Avg class size: 10. Stud/fac: 10:1. **Fac 13.** M 3/F 10. FT 9/PT 4. Wh 93%. Blk 7%. Adv deg: 15%. **Grad '11—6.** Prep—6. (Bishop Stang 3, La Salle Acad 2, Bishop Connolly 1). **Tui '10-'11:** Day $4325-4600 (+$275). **Est 1978.** Nonprofit. Quar (Sept-June). A limited enrollment and a low student-teacher ratio enable this structured school to address the abilities, needs and interests of each child. In addition to instruction in the standard subjects, Antioch's program includes Portuguese, music, art and after-school enrichment. Guest speakers and performers, in addition to off-campus excursions to museums and other sites of interest, complement in-class study.

THE SAGE SCHOOL Day Coed Gr PS (Age 4)-8
Foxboro, MA 02035. 171 Mechanic St.
Tel: 508-543-9619. Fax: 508-543-1152.
www.sageschool.org E-mail: admission@sageschool.org
  Timothy S. Monroe, Head (2008). BA, Tufts Univ, MEd, Lesley Univ. Kathy Trogolo, Adm.
  Pre-Prep. Feat—Humanities Span Computers Studio_Art Music. **Sports**—Basket Soccer. **Selective adm (Gr PS-7):** 50/yr. Appl fee: $50. Appl due: Jan. Accepted: 75%. Yield: 83%. **Tests IQ. Enr 163.** B 100. G 63. Avg class size: 16. Stud/fac: 5:1. **Fac 29.** M 8/F 21. FT 28/PT 1. Adv deg: 79%. **Grad '11—21.** Prep—16. (Boston U Acad 6, Boston Col HS 2, Milton Acad 2, Phillips Acad 1, Commonwealth Sch 1, Groton 1). **Tui '12-'13:** Day $21,740-25,670. Aid: Need 38 ($416,000). **Est 1990.** Nonprofit. Tri (Sept-June). Specializing in the education of academically gifted children, the school serves high-ability boys and girls in the Greater Boston area. Sage utilizes three school divisions: prime (ages 4-7), junior (ages 8-10) and middle (ages 11-14). The curriculum's flexibility provides depth and room for acceleration.

SACRED HEART HIGH SCHOOL Day Coed Gr 7-12
Kingston, MA 02364. 399 Bishops Hwy.
Tel: 781-585-7511. Fax: 781-585-1249.
www.sacredheartkingston.com E-mail: info@sacredheartkingston.com
  Pamela Desmarais, Pres. BA, College of the Holy Cross, MBA, Northeastern Univ. Michael Gill, Prin. Ann Taylor, Adm.
  Col Prep. AP—Eng Span Calc Bio US_Hist. **Feat**—Shakespeare Mythology Fr Ger Lat Astron Marine_Bio/Sci Oceanog Comp_Sci Boston_Hist Irish_Hist Civics Econ Psych Foreign_Policy Relig Film Sculpt Studio_Art Theater Music Journ Speech. **Supp**—Tut. **Comp:** Comp/Stud: 1:4. **Sports**—Basket X-country Golf Ice_Hockey Ski Soccer Swim Tennis Track. B: Baseball Lacrosse. G: Cheer Gymnastics Softball Volley. **Selective adm (Gr 7-11):** 20/yr. Appl fee: $45. Appl due: Jan. **Tests** Stanford. **Enr 412.** Elem 127. Sec 285. Wh 96%. Latino 1%. Blk 2%. Asian 1%. Avg class size: 20. Stud/fac: 14:1. Uniform. **Fac 55. Grad '10—89.** Col—89. **Avg SAT:** CR 567. M 536. W 573. **Tui '12-'13:** Day $12,350 (+$500). **Est 1953.** Nonprofit. Roman Catholic. Quar (Aug-June). **Assoc** NEASC. Sacred Heart offers a wide range of advance courses and organizes annual trips abroad. A strong campus ministry program organizes liturgies, class retreats and prayer services.

OAK MEADOW MONTESSORI SCHOOL Day Coed Gr PS (Age 3)-8
Littleton, MA 01460. 2 Old Pickard Ln.
Tel: 978-486-9874. Fax: 978-486-3269.
www.oakmeadow.org E-mail: info@oakmeadow.org
  William S. Perrine, Head (2012). BA, Hamilton College, MA, Univ of San Francisco. Erin Palmer, Adm.
  Pre-Prep. Montessori. Feat—Span Studio_Art Drama Music. **Supp**—Dev_Read LD Rem_Math Rem_Read Tut. **Comp:** Comp/Stud: 1:2.5. **Sports**—Basket Soccer. **Selective adm**

(Gr PS-7): 68/yr. Appl fee: $75. Appl due: Rolling. Accepted: 81%. Yield: 64%. **Enr 253.** B 117. G 136. Wh 56%. Latino 2%. Blk 1%. Native Am 1%. Asian 30%. Other 10%. Avg class size: 17. Stud/fac: 13:1. Casual dress. **Fac 35.** M 3/F 32. FT 28/PT 7. Wh 86%. Latino 6%. Asian 8%. Adv deg: 37%. **Grad '11—13.** Prep—9. (Lawrence Acad 4, Middlesex 1, Putney 1, Gould 1, St Bernard's 1, Cambridge Sch-MA 1). Avg SSAT: 84%. Alum donors: 4%. **Tui '12-'13:** Day $15,620-16,760 (+$555-4255). Aid: Need 33 ($220,000). **Est 1977.** Nonprofit. Sem (Sept-June). Oak Meadow's curriculum follows a sequential approach to learning that builds upon itself from year to year. Children's House, which accommodates children ages 3-5, utilizes multi-age groupings to explore five areas of study: practical life, sensorial, language, math and culture. Multi-age classes continue in grades 1-3, when boys and girls learn abstract concepts while working with Montessori materials. Grades 4-6 emphasize problem solving, information synthesis, collaborative work, critical and analytical thinking, and clear verbal and written communication. The middle school program (grades 7 and 8) combines class work with out-of-classroom experiences and other experiential learning opportunities.

MALDEN CATHOLIC HIGH SCHOOL   Day Boys Gr 9-12
Malden, MA 02148. 99 Crystal St.
Tel: 781-322-3098. Fax: 781-397-0573.
www.maldencatholic.org   E-mail: info@maldencatholic.org
Edward C. Tyrrell, Head (2009). BS, MS, Univ of Akron. Br. Thomas Puccio, CFX, Prin. EdD. Hazel Kochocki, Adm.

Col Prep. AP—Eng Span Calc Stats Chem Physics Eur_Hist US_Hist Econ US_Govt & Pol. **Feat**—Creative_Writing Humanities Chin Lat Marine_Bio/Sci Engineering Robotics Web_Design Amer_Stud Theol. **Supp**—ESL Rev Tut. **Sports**— B: Baseball Basket X-country Football Golf Ice_Hockey Lacrosse Rugby Soccer Swim Tennis Track Wrestling. Activities: 30. **Selective adm:** Appl fee: $0. Appl due: Dec. Accepted: 75%. **Tests** HSPT SSAT TOEFL. **Enr 600.** Wh 90%. Latino 2%. Blk 3%. Asian 5%. Avg class size: 22. Stud/fac: 13:1. Casual dress. **Fac 50.** M 34/F 16. FT 49/PT 1. Adv deg: 74%. **Grad '11—139.** Col—135. **Avg SAT:** CR 535. M 572. W 544. Avg ACT: 23. **Col Couns:** 4. **Tui '12-'13:** Day $12,700 (+$175). Aid: Need ($1,600,000). **Est 1932.** Nonprofit. Roman Catholic. Sem (Sept-June). **Assoc** NEASC. Sponsored by the Xaverian Brothers, Malden Catholic requires participation in its religious program. Honors and Advanced Placement courses in all major disciplines are available to qualified students.

MONTROSE SCHOOL   Day Girls Gr 6-12
Medfield, MA 02052. 29 North St.
Tel: 508-359-2423. Fax: 508-359-2597.
www.montroseschool.org   E-mail: admissions@montroseschool.org
Karen E. Bohlin, Head (2003). BA, Boston College, EdM, EdD, Boston Univ. Deborah M. Convery, Adm.

Col Prep. AP (exams req'd)—Eng Calc Bio Eur_Hist. **Feat**—British_Lit World_Lit Fr Span Programming 20th-Century_Hist Civics Philos Theol Studio_Art Drama Music. **Supp**— Tut. **Sports**— G: Basket X-country Lacrosse Soccer. **Selective adm (Gr 6-10):** 34/yr. Appl fee: $50. Appl due: Feb. Accepted: 60%. **Tests** ISEE SSAT. **Enr 172.** Wh 89%. Latino 6%. Blk 1%. Asian 4%. Avg class size: 14. Stud/fac: 7:1. Uniform. **Fac 27.** M 2/F 25. FT 27. **Grad '10—18.** Col—18. **Avg SAT:** CR 630. M 610. W 660. **Tui '11-'12:** Day $19,518 (+$700). Aid: Need 52. **Est 1979.** Nonprofit. Roman Catholic (75% practice). Quar (Sept-June). Montrose supplements its traditional liberal arts curriculum with Catholic theology courses, choral music, art, drama and computer programming. The middle school (grades 6-8) prepares girls for high school by stressing study skills and the mastery of basic concepts, while the college preparatory high school (grades 9-12) emphasizes critical thinking, sound reasoning and clear expression.

DELPHI ACADEMY Day Coed Gr PS (Age 2)-8
Milton, MA 02186. 564 Blue Hill Ave.
Tel: 617-333-9610. Fax: 617-333-9613.
www.delphiboston.org E-mail: info@delphiboston.org
Corinne Perkins, Head. Jeff Rouelle, Adm.
Pre-Prep. Feat—Fr Span Computers Govt Studio_Art Drama Music. **Selective adm:** 28/yr. Appl fee: $45. Appl due: Feb. Accepted: 50%. **Enr 150.** B 80. G 70. Avg class size: 15. **Fac 24. Grad '05**—7. Prep—6. **Tui '11-'12:** Day $11,200-11,600 (+$900). **Est 1979.** Nonprofit. Quar (Sept-June). Applying the principles of L. Ron Hubbard, Delphi conducts small, seminar-style classes designed to increase group interaction and communication. Teachers work with new students to formulate a suitable individual program based upon age, interests, and strengths and weaknesses. The school places particular emphasis on reading skills and requires pupils to read in great volume.

SOLOMON SCHECHTER DAY SCHOOL Day Coed Gr K-8
OF GREATER BOSTON
Newton, MA 02459. 125 Wells Ave.
Tel: 617-928-9100. Fax: 617-964-9401.
Other locations: 60 Stein Cir, Newton 02459.
www.ssdsboston.org E-mail: info@ssdsboston.org
Arnold Zar-Kessler, Head (2000). BA, Univ of Illinois-Urbana, MA, Univ of Massachusetts-Amherst. Carol Rumpler, Adm.
Pre-Prep. Gen Acad. Feat—Hebrew Span Judaic_Stud Studio_Art Music Dance. **Supp**—Dev_Read. **Sports**—Basket Soccer. B: Baseball. G: Softball. **Selective adm:** 75/yr. Appl fee: $100. Appl due: Feb. **Enr 465.** Wh 100%. Avg class size: 15. Stud/fac: 8:1. **Fac 65.** M 18/F 47. FT 65. Adv deg: 29%. **Grad '09**—48. Prep—18. (Buckingham Browne & Nichols 1, Concord Acad 1). **Tui '12-'13:** Day $21,725-24,695 (+$150). Aid: Need 165 ($1,500,000). **Est 1961.** Nonprofit. Jewish (100% practice). Sem (Sept-June). This Jewish school enrolls students from more than two dozen Greater Boston communities. SSDS' academic program comprises both secular and Judaic studies, and courses in art, music, drama and physical education are part of the curriculum. A schoolwide community service day brings together students, faculty, parents and alumni to serve more than 40 organizations. The school has two locations: Grades K-3 are conducted on Stein Circle, while grades 4-8 take place on Wells Avenue.

BISHOP STANG HIGH SCHOOL Day Coed Gr 9-12
North Dartmouth, MA 02747. 500 Slocum Rd.
Tel: 508-996-5602. Fax: 508-994-6756.
www.bishopstang.com E-mail: admits@bishopstang.com
Theresa E. Dougall, Pres (1988). BS, Stonehill College, MEd, Bridgewater State College. Peter Shaughnessy, Prin. BA, Canisius College, MA, Loyola Univ of Chicago, MEd, Benedictine Univ. Christine Payette, Adm.
Col Prep. AP (exams req'd; 187 taken, 76% 3+)—Eng Calc Bio Chem Physics Eur_Hist Psych. **Feat**—Fr Lat Portuguese Span Stats Bioethics Ecol Marine_Bio/Sci Physiol Web_Design Sociol Photog Studio_Art Music Accounting Bus Mech_Drawing. **Supp**—Rem_Math Rem_Read Tut. **Sports**—Basket X-country Golf Ice_Hockey Lacrosse Soccer Swim Tennis Track Volley Weightlifting. B: Baseball Football. G: Cheer F_Hockey Softball. Activities: 24. **Somewhat selective adm:** 185/yr. Appl fee: $0. Appl due: Rolling. Accepted: 94%. Yield: 81%. **Tests** HSPT SSAT. **Enr 707.** B 324. G 383. Wh 94%. Latino 1%. Blk 1%. Asian 2%. Other 2%. Avg class size: 19. Stud/fac: 13:1. Uniform. **Fac 58.** M 22/F 36. FT 56/PT 2. Wh 96%. Latino 2%. Blk 2%. Adv deg: 51%. **Grad '11**—188. Col—188. (Bristol CC 13, U of MA-Dartmouth 10, U of MA-Amherst 10, Providence 8, URI 8, Bryant 6). **Avg SAT:** CR 535. M 531. W 525. **Col Couns:** 6. **Tui '12-'13:** Day $8300 (+$600). Aid: Merit 15 ($1250). Need 300 ($555,000). **Est 1959.** Nonprofit. Roman Catholic (85% practice). Sem (Sept-June). **Assoc** NEASC. Bishop Stang offers a variety of courses at four levels (AP, honors, college

preparatory and standard). Electives may be chosen from among the different disciplines. A campus ministry program and a Christian service program—in which juniors and seniors must participate—are available.

AUSTIN PREPARATORY SCHOOL   Day Coed Gr 6-12
Reading, MA 01867. 101 Willow St.
Tel: 781-944-4900. Fax: 781-942-0918.
www.austinprepschool.org   E-mail: kdriscoll@austinprepschool.org
    Paul J. Moran, Head (1989). BA, College of the Holy Cross, MEd, Boston Univ, MA, Univ of Massachusetts-Boston. Kevin J. Driscoll, Adm.
    Col Prep. AP (exams req'd; 180 taken, 56% 3+)—Eng Fr Lat Span Calc Stats Bio Chem Environ_Sci Physics Eur_Hist US_Hist World_Hist Econ Psych US_Govt & Pol. **Feat**—British_Lit Creative_Writing Greek Ital Russ Anat & Physiol Marine_Bio/Sci Law Sociol Theol World_Relig Graphic_Arts Studio_Art Music Choreography Accounting Journ. **Supp**—Rev Tut. **Dual enr:** Merrimack. **Sports**—Basket X-country Golf Ice_Hockey Indoor_Track Lacrosse Ski Soccer Swim Tennis Track Volley. B: Baseball Football. G: Cheer Softball. Activities: 65. **Selective adm (Gr 6-11):** 160/yr. Appl fee: $0. Appl due: Dec. Accepted: 65%. Yield: 60%. **Tests** HSPT ISEE SSAT. **Enr 700.** B 235. G 465. Elem 200. Sec 500. Wh 96%. Latino 2%. Blk 1%. Asian 1%. Avg class size: 16. Stud/fac: 10:1. Uniform. **Fac 78.** M 38/F 40. FT 75/PT 3. Wh 98%. Latino 1%. Other 1%. Adv deg: 75%. **Grad '11—124.** Col—124. (U of MA-Amherst 10, Boston Col 6, Boston U 6, Northeastern U 6, UNH 5). **Avg SAT:** CR 588. M 586. W 592. **Col Couns:** 3. **Tui '12-'13:** Day $15,400 (+$750). Aid: Need 140. **Est 1961.** Nonprofit. Roman Catholic (75% practice). Quar (Sept-June). **Assoc** NEASC. Established as a boys' high school, Austin opened a middle school division (grades 6-8) in 1987, then admitted girls for the first time in 1992. The school combines a 45-minute daily activity period with three 90-minute academic blocks, offered in a six-day rotation. Strong athletic, arts and drama programs complement academics. A partnership with a school in Buenos Aires, Argentina, provides an opportunity for study abroad; in addition, Austin Prep organizes several cultural trips abroad each year. Seniors complete a required community service project.

SAINT JOHN'S HIGH SCHOOL   Day Boys Gr 9-12
Shrewsbury, MA 01545. 378 Main St.
Tel: 508-842-8934. Fax: 508-842-3670.
www.stjohnshigh.org   E-mail: admissions@stjohnshigh.org
    Michael W. Welch, Head (2001). BA, Marquette Univ, MA, Boston College. Jacob Conca, Prin. John D. Morse, Adm.
    Col Prep. AP (exams req'd; 796 taken)—Eng Chin Fr Calc Stats Comp_Sci Bio Chem Environ_Sci Physics Eur_Hist US_Hist World_Hist Comp_Govt & Pol Econ US_Govt & Pol Art_Hist Music_Theory. **Feat**—Span Anat & Physiol Web_Design Russ_Hist Psych Relig Studio_Art Theater Directing Music. **Sports**— B: Baseball Basket Crew X-country Football Golf Ice_Hockey Lacrosse Ski Soccer Swim Tennis Track Volley Wrestling. Activities: 49. **Selective adm (Gr 9-11):** 288/yr. Appl fee: $20. Appl due: Nov. Accepted: 75%. Yield: 75%. **Tests** HSPT. **Enr 1036.** Avg class size: 26. Formal dress. **Fac 70.** M 57/F 13. FT 68/PT 2. Adv deg: 81%. **Grad '10—212.** Col—210. **Avg SAT:** CR 584. M 606. W 585. **Tui '12-'13:** Day $10,875 (+$700-1300). **Est 1894.** Nonprofit. Roman Catholic. Quar (Aug-June). **Assoc** NEASC. Founded in Worcester by the Xaverian Brothers and moved to its present location in 1961, Saint John's is staffed by both religious and lay faculty. The liberal arts curriculum features an extensive selection of Advanced Placement courses. The campus ministry office coordinates many service projects.

PIONEER VALLEY CHRISTIAN SCHOOL   Day Coed Gr PS (Age 3)-12
Springfield, MA 01119. 965 Plumtree Rd.
Tel: 413-782-8031. Fax: 413-782-8033.
www.pvcs.org   E-mail: info@pvcs.org
Timothy Duff, Head. BA, Univ of Maine-Orono, MRE, Grand Rapids Baptist Seminary.
Pat Sterlacci, Adm.

Col Prep. AP (exams req'd; 17 taken, 53% 3+)—Eng Calc. **Feat**—British_Lit Fr Span Anat Sociol Govt/Econ Bible Graphic_Arts Drama Music Speech. **Supp**—Dev_Read LD Makeup Rem_Math Rem_Read Tut. **Sports**—Basket Soccer. B: Baseball Golf Tennis. G: Softball Volley. **Somewhat selective adm:** 57/yr. Appl fee: $80. Appl due: Rolling. Accepted: 92%. Yield: 88%. **Tests** IQ Stanford. **Enr 263.** B 138. G 125. Elem 176. Sec 87. Wh 66%. Latino 10%. Blk 18%. Asian 5%. Other 1%. Avg class size: 14. Uniform. **Fac 32.** M 9/F 23. FT 25/PT 7. Wh 97%. Blk 3%. Adv deg: 53%. **Grad '10**—35. Col—33. (Springfield Tech CC 5, Holyoke CC 2, Messiah 2, Cedarville 2, U of MA-Amherst 1, Mt Holyoke 1). **Avg SAT:** CR 512. M 473. W 499. Alum donors: 4%. **Tui '11-'12:** Day $7200-9900 (+$4800). Aid: Need ($600,000). **Est 1972.** Nonprofit. Evangelical. Sem (Aug-June). **Assoc** NEASC. Located on a 25-acre campus, the school offers a college preparatory curriculum that incorporates Christian values and ethics. Advanced Placement courses are available, as is a program for students with learning differences. PVCS' interim program comprises a week of extracurricular activities and enrichment and skills classes. Boys and girls perform 16 hours of compulsory service in the school and the community in grades 9 and 10, followed by 20 hours in grades 11 and 12.

THE CORWIN-RUSSELL SCHOOL   Day Coed Gr 6-PG
AT BROCCOLI HALL
Sudbury, MA 01776. 142 North Rd.
Tel: 978-369-1444. Fax: 978-369-1026.
www.corwin-russell.org   E-mail: brochall@corwin-russell.org
Jane-Elisabeth Jakuc, Head (1970). AB, Boston Univ, MEd, Framingham State College.
Chesley Wendth, Adm.

Col Prep. LD. Underachiever. Feat—Fr Ger Japan Span Comp_Sci Studio_Art Drama Music Outdoor_Ed SAT_Prep Study_Skills. **Supp**—Makeup Rem_Math Tut. **Comp:** Comp/Stud: 1:2. Outdoor Ed. **Dual enr:** Harvard, Sch of the Museum of Fine Arts. Activities: 7. **Very selective adm (Gr 6-11):** 11/yr. Appl due: Rolling. Accepted: 12%. **Tests** IQ. **Enr 55.** Wh 95%. Asian 5%. Avg class size: 10. Stud/fac: 3:1. **Fac 22.** M 10/F 12. FT 17/PT 5. Wh 100%. Adv deg: 45%. **Grad '11**—7. Col—7. (Emerson 2, Sarah Lawrence 1, Lesley 1, Quinnipiac 1, U of MA-Boston 1, Brandeis 1). **Avg SAT:** CR 660. M 550. W 610. Avg ACT: 31. **Col Couns:** 5. **Tui '12-'13:** Day $33,950 (+$400). **Est 1970.** Nonprofit. Sem (Sept-June). This small school serves college-bound students of superior intelligence who display a variety of learning styles. Multi-modal instruction is available in all traditional academic areas, and CRS also offers foreign language study, career education and social service opportunities. Students engage in visual and performing arts activities, technology, outdoor education and study partnerships with area cultural institutions and colleges. A tutorial program assists boys and girls with organizational needs and provides opportunities for course replacement, SAT preparation and skill advancement.

ACADEMY OF NOTRE DAME   Day Boys Gr PS (Age 3)-8
Tyngsboro, MA 01879. 180 Middlesex Rd.   Girls PS (Age 3)-12
Tel: 978-649-7611. Fax: 978-649-2909.
www.ndatyngsboro.org   E-mail: admissions@ndatyngsboro.org
Jocelyn M. Mendonsa, Adm.

Col Prep. AP—Eng Span Calc Bio Chem US_Hist US_Govt & Pol. **Feat**—British_Lit Creative_Writing Poetry Fr Lat Stats Anat & Physiol Forensic_Sci Comp_Sci Web_Design Ethics World_Relig Studio_Art Music Piano Accounting Finance Marketing. **Supp**—Tut. **Sports**— G: Basket Cheer X-country Soccer Softball Swim Tennis Track Volley. Activities:

19. **Selective adm (Gr PS-11):** 172/yr. Appl fee: $25. Appl due: Dec. **Tests** HSPT Stanford. **Enr 611.** B 146. G 465. Elem 417. Sec 194. Wh 73%. Latino 3%. Blk 3%. Native Am 2%. Asian 12%. Other 7%. Avg class size: 20. Uniform. **Fac 55.** M 4/F 51. FT 55. Adv deg: 49%. **Grad '11—31.** Col—31. (U of MA-Amherst 4, Clark U 2, Boston Col 2). **Avg SAT:** CR 543. M 513. W 561. Avg ACT: 24.2. **Col Couns:** 2. **Tui '12-'13:** Day $6510-10,730. Aid: Merit 83 ($201,000). Need 73 ($140,800). **Est 1854.** Nonprofit. Roman Catholic. Quar (Aug-June). **Assoc** NEASC. The school, originally established in Lowell, is under the direction of the Sisters of Notre Dame de Namur. A variety of honors and Advanced Placement courses is available. After-school activities (which vary according to student interest) and athletic teams supplement academics.

ATRIUM SCHOOL   **Day Coed Gr PS (Age 4)-6**
Watertown, MA 02472. 69 Grove St.
Tel: 617-923-4156. Fax: 617-923-1061.
www.atrium.org   E-mail: admissions@atrium.org
Linda Echt, Co-Dir. BA, Michigan State Univ, MEd, Lesley Univ. Susan Diller, Co-Dir.

Pre-Prep. Gen Acad. Feat—Span Studio_Art Music. **Supp**—Tut. **Selective adm:** 34/yr. Appl fee: $50. Appl due: Jan. **Enr 100.** Wh 75%. Latino 5%. Blk 10%. Asian 10%. **Fac 20.** M 2/F 18. FT 18/PT 2. Wh 100%. Adv deg: 80%. **Grad '10—14.** Prep—8. **Tui '11-'12:** Day $20,900-22,200. Aid: Need 35 ($250,000). **Est 1982.** Nonprofit. Sem (Sept-June). Language arts, history and culture, math, science, the creative arts and physical education are viewed as interdependent components of Atrium's progressive curriculum. Two teachers in each classroom jointly formulate lesson plans and work with the students. The school's collaborative, hands-on approach leads to the development of critical-thinking and problem-solving skills. In addition to work in the core subjects, all boys and girls learn Spanish, play violin in a partnership with New England Conservatory and study urban wildlife at the adjacent Mt. Auburn Cemetery.

CATHOLIC MEMORIAL SCHOOL   **Day Boys Gr 7-12**
West Roxbury, MA 02132. 235 Baker St.
Tel: 617-469-8000. Fax: 617-325-0888.
www.catholicmemorial.org   E-mail: information@catholicmemorial.org
Paul Sheff, Pres (2008). BA, Catholic Univ of America, MEd, Boston Univ. Richard Chisholm, Prin. BS, MEd, Boston State College. Thomas Ryan, Adm.

Col Prep. AP (111 exams taken, 82% 3+)—Eng Chin Fr Lat Calc Stats Comp_Sci Bio Environ_Sci Physics Eur_Hist US_Hist Econ US_Govt & Pol Studio_Art. **Feat**—Ital Span Irish_Stud Theol Jazz_Ensemble Journ. **Supp**—Rem_Math Rem_Read. **Sports**— B: Baseball Basket X-country Football Golf Ice_Hockey Lacrosse Rugby Soccer Tennis Track Volley. Activities: 16. **Selective adm:** 185/yr. Appl fee: $0. Appl due: Dec. Accepted: 70%. Yield: 55%. **Tests** HSPT ISEE. **Enr 745.** Elem 145. Sec 600. Wh 80%. Latino 4%. Blk 10%. Asian 5%. Other 1%. Avg class size: 21. Stud/fac: 12:1. Uniform. **Fac 65.** Adv deg: 87%. **Grad '09—148.** Col—138. **Avg SAT:** CR 513. M 547. W 531. Mid 50% ACT: 20-23. **Tui '12-'13:** Day $15,440 (+$250). Aid: Need 253 ($1,000,000). **Est 1957.** Nonprofit. Roman Catholic. Quar (Sept-June). **Assoc** NEASC. Founded by the Congregation of Christian Brothers, CM continues to operate in their tradition. Boys from approximately 90 communities enroll in a program that emphasizes academic development and college preparation. As part of the school's well-developed campus ministry curriculum, seniors work on a mandatory community service project one day per week in the spring.

XAVERIAN BROTHERS HIGH SCHOOL   **Day Boys Gr 9-12**
Westwood, MA 02090. 800 Clapboardtree St.
Tel: 781-326-6392. Fax: 781-320-0458.
www.xbhs.com   E-mail: xaverian@xbhs.com

Br. Daniel Skala, CFX, Head (1991). BA, MA, PhD, Boston College. Domenic Lalli, Prin. BS, Boston Univ, MEd, Boston State College. Andrew O'Brien, Adm.

Col Prep. AP (exams req'd; 167 taken, 87% 3+)—Eng Fr Span Calc Stats Comp_Sci Bio Chem Physics Eur_Hist US_Hist Econ Studio_Art. **Feat**—Ger Anat & Physiol Forensic_Sci Marine_Bio/Sci Robotics Web_Design Vietnam_War Intl_Relations Psych Theol Architect_ Drawing Film Theater Chorus Music Music_Theory Accounting. **Comp:** Comp/Stud: 1:3. **Sports**— B: Baseball Basket X-country Football Golf Ice_Hockey Indoor_Track Lacrosse Rugby Ski Soccer Swim Tennis Track Volley Wrestling. Activities: 50. **Selective adm:** 275/yr. Appl fee: $0. Appl due: Dec. **Tests** HSPT. **Enr 978.** Wh 94%. Latino 1%. Blk 2%. Asian 2%. Other 1%. Avg class size: 22. Stud/fac: 14:1. **Fac 86.** M 72/F 14. FT 86. Adv deg: 73%. **Grad '08—230.** Col—223. **Avg SAT:** CR 562. M 600. W 554. Alum donors: 16%. **Tui '12-'13:** Day $15,700 (+$300). Aid: Need 293 ($1,400,000). **Est 1963.** Nonprofit. Roman Catholic (85% practice). Sem (Sept-June). **Assoc** NEASC. Offering a traditional college preparatory program, Xaverian groups students according to ability and features a strong foreign language department. Theology is a mandatory part of the program, and an active campus ministry conducts retreats and other activities.

CHILDREN'S OWN SCHOOL   Day Coed PS (Age 3)-K
Winchester, MA 01890. 86 Main St.
Tel: 781-729-2689. Fax: 781-729-4192.
www.childrensown.org   E-mail: information@childrensown.org
Rosina Orr Cullinane, Dir (1977). MEd.

Gen Acad. Montessori. Feat—Fr Studio_Art Music Movement. **Selective adm:** 25/yr. Appl fee: $40. Appl due: Jan. **Enr 80.** B 31. G 49. Avg class size: 20. Stud/fac: 10:1. **Fac 11.** FT 8/PT 3. Adv deg: 18%. **Grad '05—25. Tui '06-'07:** Day $5985-7670. **Est 1942.** Nonprofit. Tri (Sept-June). Located on the former Russell Farm, Children's Own is the oldest Montessori school in New England. Within a noncompetitive environment, the school utilizes a multisensory approach to address varying learning needs.

HOLY NAME CENTRAL CATHOLIC   Day Coed Gr 7-12
JUNIOR/SENIOR HIGH SCHOOL
Worcester, MA 01604. 144 Granite St.
Tel: 508-753-6371. Fax: 508-831-1287.
www.holyname.net
Edward Reynolds, Head. BA, Univ of Massachusetts-Amherst, MEd, Worcester State College. Jacqueline Norgren, Adm.

Col Prep. Gen Acad. AP (exams req'd; 142 taken, 73% 3+)—Eng Calc Comp_Sci Physics US_Hist US_Govt & Pol. **Feat**—Fr Span Anat & Physiol Web_Design Psych Theol Art_Hist Studio_Art Theater Band Chorus Bus. **Supp**—Rev Tut. **Sports**—Basket X-country Soccer Track. B: Baseball Football Lacrosse. G: Cheer F_Hockey Softball Swim Tennis. Activities: 20. **Somewhat selective adm (Gr 7-11):** 130/yr. Appl due: Feb. Accepted: 85%. Yield: 75%. **Enr 620.** B 295. G 325. Elem 106. Sec 514. Wh 76%. Latino 4%. Blk 7%. Asian 7%. Other 6%. Intl 10%. Avg class size: 22. Stud/fac: 15:1. Uniform. **Fac 40.** M 14/F 26. FT 38/PT 2. Wh 95%. Blk 2%. Asian 2%. Other 1%. Adv deg: 55%. **Grad '09—129.** Col—129. (U of MA-Amherst 11, Quinsigamond CC 10, Anna Maria 9, Worcester St 8, Westfield St 6, Framingham St 5). **Avg SAT:** CR 530. M 510. W 520. Avg ACT: 22. Alum donors: 7%. **Tui '11-'12:** Day $6305-6785 (+$315). Aid: Merit 33 ($16,500). Need 215 ($712,169). **Est 1942.** Nonprofit. Roman Catholic (74% practice). Quar (Aug-June). **Assoc** NEASC. Founded by the Sisters of St. Anne, Holy Name stresses academics, the arts and athletics. The art program includes sculpture, ceramics, art history and graphic design. Students take part in service projects in Maine and Worcester.

NEW HAMPSHIRE

ST. THOMAS AQUINAS HIGH SCHOOL   **Day Coed Gr 9-12**
Dover, NH 03820. 197 Dover Point Rd.
Tel: 603-742-3206. Fax: 603-749-7822.
www.stalux.org   E-mail: sta@stalux.org
    Kevin J. Collins, Prin (2009). BS, MFA. Scott Rafferty, Adm.
    Col Prep. AP (exams req'd; 249 taken)—Eng Calc Stats Bio Chem Environ_Sci Physics US_Hist US_Govt & Pol. **Feat**—20th-Century_Lit Fr Lat Span Anat & Physiol Marine_ Bio/Sci Computers Econ Psych Sociol Theol World_Relig Fine_Arts Music Accounting Bus. **Supp**—Tut. **Comp:** Comp/Stud: 1:6. **Sports**—Basket X-country Golf Ice_Hockey Indoor_ Track Lacrosse Ski Soccer Swim Tennis Track. B: Baseball Football Wrestling. G: F_Hockey Softball Volley. Activities: 30. **Selective adm:** Appl fee: $40. Appl due: Dec. **Tests** HSPT. **Enr 640.** B 323. G 317. Nonwhite 4%. Avg class size: 19. Stud/fac: 5:1. **Fac 49.** M 24/F 25. FT 49. Wh 96%. Latino 2%. Asian 2%. Adv deg: 55%. **Grad '11—177.** Col—174. (UNH 28, St Anselm 12, Boston Col 5, MT St-Bozeman 5, St Michael's 4, U of Miami 4). **Avg SAT:** CR 553. M 544. W 541. Avg ACT: 24. **Col Couns:** 4. **Tui '12-'13:** Day $10,700 (+$200). Aid: Need ($500,000). **Est 1960.** Nonprofit. Roman Catholic. Quar (Aug-June). **Assoc** NEASC.
    St. Thomas Aquinas provides honors-level courses in most subject areas, and Advanced Placement classes are also available. All students enroll in a theology course each year. Between the first and second semesters, St. Thomas sponsors a weeklong academic program during which students and teachers concentrate on specialized and intensive courses. As part of the campus ministry program, boys and girls complete a mandatory project involving at least 40 hours of community service.

OLIVERIAN SCHOOL   **Bdg Coed Gr 9-PG**
Haverhill, NH 03765. 2274 Mount Moosilauke Hwy, PO Box 98.
Tel: 603-989-5100. Fax: 603-989-3055.
www.oliverianschool.org   E-mail: bmackinnon@oliverianschool.org
    Randy Richardson, Head (2009). BA, Hamilton College, MALS, Wesleyan Univ. Barclay E. Mackinnon, Jr., Adm.
    Col Prep. LD. Underachiever. AP (exams req'd; 3 taken, 0% 3+)—Span. **Feat**—Geol Programming Robotics Psych Fine_Arts Furniture_Making Culinary_Arts. **Supp**—ESL Makeup Rem_Math Rem_Read Rev Tut. Outdoor Ed. **Dual enr:** Plymouth St. **Sports**—Soccer. Activities: 12. **Selective adm:** 25/yr. Appl fee: $75. Appl due: Rolling. Accepted: 50%. Yield: 50%. **Tests** CEEB CTP_4 IQ ISEE SSAT Stanford TOEFL. **Enr 50.** B 30. G 20. Wh 80%. Blk 5%. Asian 15%. Intl 15%. Avg class size: 6. Stud/fac: 3:1. **Fac 15.** M 9/F 6. FT 15. Wh 100%. Adv deg: 46%. In Dorms 12. **Grad '09—23.** Col—20. **Avg SAT:** CR 550. M 550. W 550. Avg ACT: 22. **Col Couns:** 1. Alum donors: 25%. **Tui '10-'11:** Bdg $69,950 (+$500).Aid: Need 15 ($200,000). **Est 2004.** Nonprofit. Quar (Sept-May). This boarding school conducts an alternative college preparatory program for boys and girls who have not succeeded in traditional academic settings. Small classes provide opportunities for individualized instruction, including assistance for those with mild learning disabilities. Requirements in experiential education, health and physical education, and the fine arts supplement core course work. Oliverian's compulsory senior project enables students to explore an area of interest by designing and executing an educational program; in the process, seniors demonstrate their problem solving, time management, organizational, researching and communicational skills. The school schedule includes periodic community service days for the entire student body.

WATERVILLE VALLEY ACADEMY   **Bdg & Day**
Waterville Valley, NH 03215. 92 Boulder Path Rd, PO Box 270.   **Coed Gr 6-12**
Tel: 603-236-4246. Fax: 603-236-9906.
www.wvbbts.org/wva   E-mail: wva@wvbbts.org

Robert Sampson, Head (2008). BS, MEd, Plymouth State Univ. Kimberly Berman, Adm. **Col Prep. Sports (Winter). AP**—Eng Calc Stats Bio Chem Physics. **Feat**—Fr Ger Lat Span Anat & Physiol Comp_Sci Web_Design Psych Sociol Ceramics Studio_Art. **Supp**— Rem_Math Rem_Read Rev Tut. **Comp:** Comp/Stud: 1:1 Laptop prgm Gr 6-12. **Sports**—Ski. **Selective adm:** 10/yr. Bdg 3. Day 7. Appl fee: $40. Appl due: Rolling. **Enr 60.** B 40. G 20. Bdg 25. Day 35. Wh 98%. Blk 2%. Avg class size: 1. Stud/fac: 1:1. **Fac 34.** M 17/F 17. FT 32/PT 2. Wh 98%. Blk 2%. Adv deg: 26%. In Dorms 2. **Grad '09—11.** Col—11. **Tui '11- '12:** Bdg $25,800-27,450 (+$1000). Day $20,050-21,675 (+$1000). **Est 1972.** Nonprofit. Sem (Nov-Mar). This five-month snow sports academy offers coaching in Alpine and freestyle skiing, as well as in snowboarding. The academic program operates as an individual teaching program that follows the syllabus sent by the home school. Monday is an extended academic day with no athletic training. On Tuesday through Friday afternoons, students split their time between academics, on-hill training and conditioning activities, and weekends are devoted to training sessions and competitions. Students have access to Plymouth State University laboratory facilities and other resources.

PINE HILL WALDORF SCHOOL   Day Coed Gr PS (Age 2)-8
Wilton, NH 03086. 77 Pine Hill Dr.
Tel: 603-654-6003. Fax: 603-654-5012.
www.pinehill.org   E-mail: info@pinehill.org
Kate Knuth, Mgr (2010). BFA, California Institute of the Arts.
Pre-Prep. Gen Acad. Waldorf. Feat—Fr Ger Drawing Painting Drama Music Eurythmy Woodworking. **Supp**—Rem_Math Rem_Read Tut. **Sports**—Basket. **Selective adm:** 35/yr. Appl fee: $85. Appl due: Rolling. **Enr 187.** B 90. G 97. Avg class size: 18. **Fac 24.** M 6/F 18. FT 19/PT 5. Wh 100%. Adv deg: 45%. **Grad '10—16.** Prep—6. **Tui '11-'12:** Day $11,905- 12,650 (+$1500). **Est 1972.** Nonprofit. (Sept-June). Pine Hill incorporates such artistic activities as handwork and crafts, music, movement and the arts into its Waldorf curriculum. Students play the recorder beginning in grade 1 and learn music notation in grade 4. Although language arts preparation begins in preschool with an introduction to the oral tradition, formal reading instruction is deferred until grade 2. The school's rural setting provides access to mountains, ponds, forests and farmland.

RHODE ISLAND

MERCYMOUNT COUNTRY DAY SCHOOL   Day Coed Gr PS (Age 4)-8
Cumberland, RI 02864. 35 Wrentham Rd.
Tel: 401-333-5919. Fax: 401-333-5150.
www.mercymount.org   E-mail: rid07181@ride.ri.net
Sr. Martha Mulligan, RSM, Prin (1992). BA, Salve Regina Univ, MEd, Bridgewater State Univ.
Pre-Prep. Feat—Lib_Skills Span Computers Studio_Art Music. **Supp**—LD Rem_Math Rem_Read Rev Tut. **Comp:** Comp/Stud: 1:3. **Sports**—Basket X-country Tennis Track Volley. **Nonselective adm:** 64/yr. Appl fee: $150. Appl due: Feb. Accepted: 99%. Yield: 90%. **Enr 463.** B 242. G 221. Wh 80%. Latino 5%. Blk 1%. Asian 10%. Other 4%. Avg class size: 20. Uniform. **Fac 36.** M 8/F 28. FT 36. Wh 99%. Latino 1%. Adv deg: 41%. **Grad '11—15.** Prep—15. (Bishop Feehan 9, St Mary Acad-Bay View 3, Xaverian Bros 2, Ursuline Acad-MA 1). Alum donors: 2%. **Tui '12-'13:** Day $7150-7600 (+$400). Aid: Need 35 ($42,000). **Est 1948.** Nonprofit. Roman Catholic. Tri (Aug-June). **Assoc** NEASC. Sponsored by the Sisters of Mercy of the Americas, Mercymount offers a traditional Catholic elementary program to pupils from roughly two dozen towns in northern Rhode Island and Massachusetts. Spanish commences in prekindergarten, computer classes begin in kindergarten and the use of laptop computers is integrated into the curriculum in grades 4-8. Middle schoolers participate in a

three-day trip as part of the environmental education curriculum. Students in grades 7 and 8 take part in monthly outreach service activities.

THE PENNFIELD SCHOOL　　　　　　　　　　　**Day Coed Gr PS (Age 3)-8**
Portsmouth, RI 02871. 110 Sandy Point Ave.
Tel: 401-849-4646. Fax: 401-847-6720.
www.pennfield.org　E-mail: kemory@pennfield.org
Robert A. Kelley, Head (2005). BA, MA, Tufts Univ. Kristin Emory, Adm.
Pre-Prep. Feat—Span Computers Studio_Art Music. **Supp**—Tut. **Comp:** Comp/Stud: 1:4. **Sports**—Basket X-country Lacrosse Soccer. **Somewhat selective adm:** 41/yr. Appl fee: $50. Appl due: Feb. Accepted: 97%. Yield: 99%. **Tests** CTP_4 MAT. **Enr 184.** B 99. G 85. Wh 97%. Blk 1%. Asian 1%. Other 1%. Avg class size: 15. Stud/fac: 8:1. Casual dress. **Fac 38.** M 7/F 31. FT 38. Wh 99%. Blk 1%. Adv deg: 34%. **Grad '11—24.** Prep—19. (Portsmouth 9, Prout 3, Moses Brown 2, St George's Sch-RI 2, Proctor 1, Lincoln 1). Alum donors: 22%. **Tui '12-'13:** Day $15,905-18,195 (+$500). Aid: Merit 12 ($47,500). Need 64 ($360,073). **Est 1971.** Nonprofit. Tri (Sept-June). Pennfield utilizes traditional and modern teaching methods to develop artistic, intellectual and athletic potential in its students. Instruction in French and Spanish begins in kindergarten. The school's curriculum places strong emphasis on the arts at all grade levels. Boys and girls in grades 6-8 deliver a five-minute assembly speech each year, and eighth graders also satisfy a 20-hour community service requirement.

COMMUNITY PREPARATORY SCHOOL　　　　　　　　　**Day Coed Gr 3-8**
Providence, RI 02907. 126 Somerset St.
Tel: 401-521-9696. Fax: 401-521-9715.
www.communityprep.org　E-mail: pluca@communityprep.org
Daniel Corley, Head (1984). AB, Brown Univ. Azikiwe Husband, Adm.
Pre-Prep. Feat—Span Computers Creative_Arts Public_Speak. **Supp**—Dev_Read Tut. **Comp:** Comp/Stud: 1:1.7. **Sports**—Basket Golf Soccer Track. B: Baseball. **Selective adm:** 40/yr. Appl due: Feb. Accepted: 30%. **Tests** Stanford. **Enr 152.** B 76. G 76. Wh 18%. Latino 30%. Blk 27%. Native Am 3%. Asian 6%. Other 16%. Avg class size: 18. Uniform. **Fac 19.** M 5/F 14. FT 14/PT 5. Wh 47%. Latino 26%. Blk 21%. Asian 5%. Other 1%. Adv deg: 26%. **Grad '09—33.** Prep—16. (Providence Co Day 3, Lincoln 2, Rocky Hill 2, St Andrew's Sch-RI 1, Deerfield Acad 1, Walnut Hill 1). Alum donors: 8%. **Tui '11-'12:** Day $13,200 (+$250). Aid: Merit 3 ($10,000). Need 132 ($1,000,000). **Est 1984.** Nonprofit. Tri (Sept-June). Community Prep provides promising students from diverse cultural and economic backgrounds with the preparation necessary for a college preparatory high school. After-school electives, including photography, computer science and languages, are available to those who qualify academically. Group and individual tutoring sessions with tutors, mentors and a reading specialist convene before, during and after school. Community Prep organizes various service projects in the surrounding neighborhoods.

THE FRENCH-AMERICAN SCHOOL　　　　　　　　　**Day Coed Gr PS-8**
OF RHODE ISLAND
Providence, RI 02906. 75 John St.
Tel: 401-274-3325. Fax: 401-455-3437.
www.fasri.org　E-mail: admin@fasri.org
Dominique Velociter, Head (1994). BEd, Univ of Paris-Sorbonne (France).
Pre-Prep. Gen Acad. Bilingual (Fr). Feat—Fr Span Computers Studio_Art Music. **Selective adm (Gr PS-6):** 21/yr. Appl fee: $75. Appl due: Jan. Accepted: 50%. Yield: 45%. **Enr 170.** Intl 35%. Avg class size: 17. **Fac 11.** FT 11. **Grad '09—12.** Alum donors: 25%. **Tui '12-'13:** Day $11,930-13,990 (+$250-825). **Est 1994.** Nonprofit. Tri (Sept-June). This bilingual school combines elements of the American and French educational systems. In preschool and kindergarten, children take part in a French immersion program; afterward, students engage

in a bilingual curriculum. In grade 1, 80 percent of instruction is in French; in grades 2-8, 60 percent is in French. Depending on the discipline, courses may be taught in French, English or both.

LA SALLE ACADEMY — Day Coed Gr 7-12
Providence, RI 02908. 612 Academy Ave.
Tel: 401-351-7750. Fax: 401-444-1782.
www.lasalle-academy.org   E-mail: info@lasalle-academy.org
   Br. A. Michael McKenery, FSC, Pres. BA, Catholic Univ of America, MA, St Mary's Univ. George Aldrich, Adm.
   Col Prep. AP (488 exams taken, 82% 3+)—Eng Fr Span Calc Comp_Sci Bio Chem Physics US_Hist Human_Geog US_Govt & Pol Studio_Art Music_Theory. **Feat**—Creative_ Writing Ital Stats Anat & Physiol Bioethics Environ_Sci Forensic_Sci Microbio Engineering Web_Design Econ Law Psych Sociol Philos World_Relig Architect Ceramics Drawing Film Photog Sculpt Video_Production Acting Theater_Arts Accounting Bus Journ Public_Speak. **Supp**—Dev_Read Makeup Rem_Math Rem_Read Rev Tut. **Sports**—Basket X-country Ice_Hockey Lacrosse Soccer Swim Tennis Track Volley. B: Baseball Football Golf Wrestling. G: Cheer Gymnastics Softball. Activities: 50. **Selective adm (Gr 7-11):** 412/yr. Appl fee: $25. Appl due: Jan. Accepted: 54%. Yield: 95%. **Tests** HSPT. **Enr 1477.** B 709. G 768. Elem 87. Sec 1390. Wh 96%. Latino 1%. Blk 2%. Other 1%. Avg class size: 21. Stud/fac: 12:1. Uniform. **Fac 103.** M 53/F 50. FT 96/PT 7. Adv deg: 70%. **Grad '11—337.** Col—334. **Tui '12-'13:** Day $13,400 (+$300). Aid: Need 503 ($1,400,000). **Est 1871.** Nonprofit. Roman Catholic (83% practice). Sem (Aug-June). **Assoc** NEASC. Conducted by the Brothers of the Christian Schools, La Salle offers a college preparatory curriculum in grades 9-12 and an early enrollment program for gifted seventh and eighth graders. A transitional program in grade 9 reinforces basic concepts and study skills. Advanced Placement courses are part of the high school curriculum.

PROUT SCHOOL — Day Coed Gr 9-12
Wakefield, RI 02879. 4640 Tower Hill Rd.
Tel: 401-789-9262. Fax: 401-782-2262.
www.theproutschool.org   E-mail: kneed@theproutschool.org
   David J. A. Carradini, Prin (2012). Kristen P. Need, Adm.
   Col Prep. IB Diploma. AP (exams req'd)—Calc Chem Environ_Sci US_Hist Studio_Art. **Feat**—Creative_Writing Fr Ital Span Anat & Physiol Oceanog Comp_Sci Web_Design Econ Psych World_Relig Art_Hist Painting Sculpt Acting Drama Chorus Music_Theory Dance. **Sports**—Basket X-country Golf Lacrosse Soccer Swim Tennis Track. B: Baseball Ice_Hockey. G: Softball Volley. **Selective adm:** 147/yr. Appl fee: $25. Accepted: 50%. **Tests** HSPT. **Enr 647.** Avg class size: 23. Stud/fac: 14:1. Uniform. **Fac 50.** M 22/F 28. FT 50. Adv deg: 48%. **Grad '11—162.** Col—162. **Col Couns:** 1. **Tui '11-'12:** Day $11,200 (+$555-705). **Est 1966.** Nonprofit. Roman Catholic. Quar (Aug-June). **Assoc** NEASC. Within a college preparatory environment, Prout supplements its core courses with work in art, music, philosophy and economics. The curriculum is especially noteworthy for its inclusion of the rigorous International Baccalaureate Diploma Program, which often leads to college credit and is recognized by universities throughout the world. Boys and girls perform 25 hours of required community service each year.

MOUNT SAINT CHARLES ACADEMY — Day Coed Gr 7-12
Woonsocket, RI 02895. 800 Logee St.
Tel: 401-769-0310. Fax: 401-762-2327.
www.mountsaintcharles.org   E-mail: admissions@mountsaintcharles.org
   Herve E. Richer, Pres (2009). BA, Assumption College, MEd, Providence College. Edwin Burke, Jr., Prin. BA, St Anselm College, MEd, Providence College. Joseph J. O'Neill, Adm.

Col Prep. AP (300 exams taken)—Eng Fr Span Calc Bio Chem Environ_Sci Eur_Hist US_Hist Comp_Govt & Pol Psych US_Govt & Pol Studio_Art Music_Theory. **Feat**—Anat & Physiol Comp_Sci Econ Intl_Relations Relig Architect Film Drama Band Chorus Dance. **Supp**—Dev_Read. **Sports**—Basket X-country Golf Ice_Hockey Indoor_Track Lacrosse Soccer Swim Tennis Track Volley. B: Baseball. G: Cheer Softball. **Selective adm (Gr 7-11):** 175/yr. Appl fee: $25. Appl due: Mar. Accepted: 40%. **Tests** HSPT. **Enr 873.** B 399. G 474. Elem 150. Sec 723. Wh 97%. Blk 1%. Asian 2%. Avg class size: 25. Stud/fac: 14:1. Uniform. **Fac 60.** M 29/F 31. FT 53/PT 7. Adv deg: 61%. **Grad '11—172.** Col—172. **Tui '12-'13:** Day $11,500 (+$400). **Est 1924.** Nonprofit. Roman Catholic (85% practice). Sem (Aug-June). **Assoc** NEASC. Administered by the Brothers of the Sacred Heart, Mount Saint Charles offers honors and Advanced Placement courses, in addition to its regular high school curriculum. The school places particular emphasis on athletics and the fine arts. Community service is part of the curriculum at all grade levels.

VERMONT

LYNDON INSTITUTE   **Bdg & Day**
Lyndon Center, VT 05850. 168 Institute Cir, PO Box 127.   **Coed Gr 9-12**
Tel: 802-626-5232. Fax: 802-626-6138.
www.lyndoninstitute.org   E-mail: admissions@lyndoninstitute.org
    Richard D. Hilton, Head (1999). BS, Univ of Notre Dame, MEd, Villanova Univ. Mary B. Thomas, Adm.

    Col Prep. Gen Acad. Voc. Bus. AP (exams req'd)—Eng Calc Chem Environ_Sci Physics Eur_Hist US_Hist Studio_Art. **Feat**—Creative_Writing Sci_Fiction Fr Japan Lat Span Anat & Physiol Animal_Sci Comp_Design VT_Hist Econ Asian_Stud Architect_Drawing Photog Theater Music Music_Theory Dance Accounting Drafting Indus_Arts Metal_Shop Culinary_ Arts. **Supp**—ESL Rem_Math Rem_Read. **Comp:** Laptop prgm Gr 9-12. **Dual enr:** Lyndon St, CC of VT. **Sports**—Basket X-country Golf Ice_Hockey Ski Soccer Track Ultimate_Frisbee. B: Baseball Football. G: Cheer F_Hockey Softball. Activities: 30. **Selective adm (Gr 9-11):** 152/yr. Bdg 32. Day 120. Appl fee: $50. Appl due: Rolling. **Tests** CEEB SSAT TOEFL. **Enr 600.** B 300. G 300. Bdg 105. Day 495. Intl 11%. Avg class size: 12. Stud/fac: 10:1. **Fac 70.** M 34/F 36. FT 61/PT 9. Adv deg: 37%. In Dorms 2. **Grad '11—121.** Col—102. (Lyndon St 24, U of VT 7, S VT 5, MI St 4, Purdue 4, Johnson St 4). **Col Couns:** 2. **Tui '12-'13:** Bdg $42,570 (+$850). 5-Day Bdg $30,400 (+$850). Day $14,713. Intl Bdg $42,570 (+$1950). **Est 1867.** Nonprofit. Sem (Aug-June). **Assoc** NEASC. LI offers courses at four levels: general education, honors, Advanced Placement and technical education. Students in the technical education program prepare for careers or continued study in a variety of fields, and they may take classes in conjunction with college preparatory courses. Skiing is a notable feature of the extracurricular program, with Alpine and Nordic opportunities available nearby.

BURR AND BURTON ACADEMY   **Bdg & Day**
Manchester, VT 05254. 57 Seminary Ave, PO Box 498.   **Coed Gr 9-12**
Tel: 802-362-1775. Fax: 802-362-0574.
www.burrburton.org   E-mail: panton@burrburton.org
    Mark H. Tashjian, Head (2008). BA, Yale Univ, MBA, Univ of Pennsylvania, MEd, Columbia Univ. Philip G. Anton, Adm.

    Col Prep. Gen Acad. Voc. AP (exams req'd; 260 taken, 80% 3+)—Eng Fr Ger Span Calc Bio US_Hist Psych Studio_Art Music_Theory. **Feat**—Creative_Writing Econ Govt Art_Hist Film Drama Music Dance Accounting TV_Production Drafting Woodworking. **Supp**—Dev_ Read ESL LD Makeup Rem_Math Rem_Read Rev Tut. **Sports**—Basket X-country Golf Ice_Hockey Lacrosse Ski Soccer Tennis Track. B: Baseball Football. G: Softball. **Selective adm (Bdg Gr 9-11; Day 9-12):** 200/yr. Bdg 50. Day 150. Appl fee: $25. Appl due: Feb. **Tests**

TOEFL. **Enr 682.** Wh 95%. Latino 1%. Blk 1%. Asian 3%. Intl 6%. Avg class size: 16. Casual dress. **Fac 70.** M 33/F 37. FT 66/PT 4. Adv deg: 57%. In Dorms 2. **Grad '11—166.** Col—149. **Mid 50% SAT:** CR 470-630. M 480-620. W 450-620. **Tui '12-'13:** Day $14,450-15,450. Intl Bdg $38,800 (+$2000-3700). **Est 1829.** Nonprofit. Sem (Aug-June). **Assoc** NEASC. Burr and Burton operates under a block scheduling system of four classes per semester, with Advanced Placement courses available. All boys and girls must complete two annual community service projects. The small boarding program accommodates international students who reside either with a local family or in one of the three faculty-supervised houses on campus.

MOUNT SAINT JOSEPH ACADEMY   **Day Coed Gr 9-12**
Rutland, VT 05701. 127 Convent Ave.
Tel: 802-775-0151. Fax: 802-775-0424.
www.msjvermont.org   E-mail: guidance@msjvermont.org
   Paolo Erminio Zancanaro, Prin (2006). BA, Jesuit Univ of Detroit, MA, Univ of Windsor (Canada), MS, Johns Hopkins Univ.
   Col Prep. Bus. AP (exams req'd; 16 taken, 12% 3+)—Eng Calc Bio Physics World_Hist Art_Hist Studio_Art. **Feat**—British_Lit Creative_Writing Fr Span Anat & Physiol Environ_Sci Web_Design Psych Theol Band Chorus Music_Theory. **Supp**—ESL Rev Tut. **Comp:** Comp/Stud: 1:1 Laptop prgm Gr 9-12. **Dual enr:** CC of VT, Castleton St. **Sports**—Basket X-country Soccer Tennis Track. B: Baseball Football Lacrosse. G: Softball. Activities: 9. **Somewhat selective adm:** 42/yr. Appl fee: $125-175. Appl due: Mar. Accepted: 95%. Yield: 95%. **Tests** HSPT. **Enr 95.** B 54. G 41. Intl 10%. Avg class size: 13. Stud/fac: 5:1. Uniform. **Fac 18.** M 10/F 8. FT 9/PT 9. Wh 100%. Adv deg: 55%. **Grad '11—12.** Col—12. **Avg SAT:** CR 505. M 561. Avg ACT: 25. **Col Couns:** 1. Alum donors: 35%. **Tui '11-'12:** Day $5500 (+$400). **Est 1882.** Nonprofit. Roman Catholic (65% practice). Tri (Aug-June). **Assoc** NEASC. In a Catholic setting, MSJ offers Advanced Placement courses in the major disciplines. International students, who reside with host families, enroll at additional cost in both diploma and nondiploma programs that may include English as a Second Language instruction. Incoming freshmen each receive a netbook computer. All boys and girls satisfy a 25-hour annual community service requirement.

RICE MEMORIAL HIGH SCHOOL   **Day Coed Gr 9-PG**
South Burlington, VT 05403. 99 Proctor Ave.
Tel: 802-862-6521. Fax: 802-864-9931.
www.rmhsvt.org   E-mail: bahrenburg@rmhsvt.org
   Rev. Bernard W. Bourgeois, Prin (2007). AB, MA, MDiv, St John's Seminary. Christy Bahrenburg, Adm.
   Col Prep. AP (167 exams taken)—Eng Calc Bio Physics Eur_Hist US_Hist US_Govt & Pol. **Feat**—British_Lit Creative_Writing Fr Lat Span Anat & Physiol Environ_Sci Web_Design Econ Relig Ceramics Drawing Film Filmmaking Sculpt Studio_Art Acting Band Chorus Orchestra Accounting Journ Speech. **Supp**—ESL Tut. **Comp:** Comp/Stud: 1:3. **Sports**—Basket X-country Golf Ice_Hockey Indoor_Track Lacrosse Ski Soccer Tennis Track. B: Baseball Football. G: F_Hockey Softball. Activities: 26. **Somewhat selective adm:** 100/yr. Appl fee: $150. Appl due: Feb. Accepted: 97%. Yield: 97%. **Tests** TOEFL. **Enr 370.** Sec 365. PG 5. Wh 91%. Blk 3%. Asian 3%. Other 3%. Intl 10%. Avg class size: 20. Stud/fac: 11:1. Uniform. **Fac 31.** M 15/F 16. FT 27/PT 4. Wh 94%. Latino 3%. Blk 3%. Adv deg: 64%. **Grad '11—111.** Col—95. (U of VT 24, St Michael's 6, CC of VT 3, VT Tech 3, St Lawrence 2, Denison 2). **Avg SAT:** CR 547. M 543. W 542. Avg ACT: 23.8. **Col Couns:** 2. Alum donors: 10%. **Tui '12-'13:** Day $8540 (+$150-225). Aid: Merit 29 ($35,000). Need 160 ($500,000). Work prgm 50 ($20,000). **Est 1959.** Nonprofit. Roman Catholic (75% practice). Quar (Aug-June). **Assoc** NEASC. Boys and girls enroll at Rice High School from approximately 50 communities throughout northwest and central Vermont. The variety of courses offered in each discipline enables students to meet graduation and college-entrance requirements, while also allowing the school to serve pupils of differing ability levels. Boys and girls satisfy the follow-

ing community service requirements: eight hours in grade 9, 20 hours in grade 10, 25 hours in grade 11 and 30 hours in grade 12.

STRATTON MOUNTAIN SCHOOL   **Bdg Coed Gr 7-PG**
Stratton Mountain, VT 05155. World Cup Cir.   **Day Coed 7-12**
Tel: 802-297-1886. Fax: 802-297-0020.
www.gosms.org   E-mail: admissions@gosms.org
     Christopher G. Kaltsas, Head (1996). BS, Univ of Denver, JD, New England School of Law. Kate Nolan Joyce, Adm.
     Col Prep. Sports (Winter). Feat—Fr Lat Span Calc Environ_Sci Sports_Med Web_Design Studio_Art Drama Journ Nutrition. **Supp**—ESL Tut. **Sports**—X-country Golf Lacrosse Ski Soccer. **Selective adm:** 40/yr. Bdg 26. Day 14. Appl fee: $100. Appl due: Mar. Accepted: 70%. **Enr 140.** Bdg 75. Day 65. Avg class size: 10. Stud/fac: 4:1. **Fac 18.** M 10/F 8. FT 12/PT 6. Adv deg: 38%. In Dorms 4. **Grad '11—25.** Col—23. **Tui '12-'13:** Bdg $44,500 (+$5000). Day $32,500 (+$5000). **Est 1972.** Nonprofit. Quar (Sept-May). **Assoc** NEASC. SMS offers a strong college preparatory curriculum to competitive winter sports athletes who wish to specialize in Alpine skiing, Nordic skiing or snowboarding. The school year and daily schedules are designed to maximize training time and accommodate competition schedules. Students entering grades 7-9 may attend for the winter term only. Residential students participate in weekly evening workshops and field trips. All boys and girls satisfy a five-hour community service requirement annually. A postgraduate alpine program, which may or may not include an academic component, serves high school graduates aspiring to college or national competition.

Middle Atlantic States

DELAWARE

THE INDEPENDENCE SCHOOL Day Coed Gr PS (Age 3)-8
Newark, DE 19711. 1300 Paper Mill Rd.
Tel: 302-239-0330. Fax: 302-239-3696.
www.theindependenceschool.org E-mail: cbrechter@tisde.org
Victoria C. Yatzus, Head (2008). BSc, Univ of Newcastle (England), MEd, Univ of Delaware. Claire Brechter, Adm.

Pre-Prep. Gen Acad. Feat—Lib_Skills Fr Lat Span Computers Art_Hist Studio_Art Music. **Supp**—Tut. **Sports**—Basket X-country Lacrosse Soccer Tennis Track. B: Baseball Golf Wrestling. G: F_Hockey Volley. **Selective adm:** 207/yr. Appl fee: $75. Appl due: Jan. Accepted: 51%. **Tests** IQ. **Enr 675.** Avg class size: 19. Stud/fac: 13:1. **Fac 57.** Adv deg: 50%. **Grad '04—65.** Prep—54. **Tui '12-'13:** Day $11,227-13,272 (+$500). **Est 1978.** Nonprofit. Tri (Sept-June). **Assoc** MSA. Occupying a 89-acre campus in the Pike Creek Valley, the school's curriculum emphasizes the basics, with all pupils in grades 1-8 required to study a foreign language. Field trips, special projects, guest speakers and one-on-one assistance enrich classroom instruction.

THE PILOT SCHOOL Day Coed Gr K-8
Wilmington, DE 19803. 100 Garden of Eden Rd.
Tel: 302-478-1740. Fax: 302-478-1746.
www.pilotschool.org E-mail: info@pilotschool.org
Kathleen B. Craven, Dir (1998). BS, McPherson College, MEd, Millersville Univ.

LD. Feat—Lib_Skills Computers. **Supp**—Dev_Read Rem_Math Rem_Read Rev Tut. **Comp:** Comp/Stud: 1:1.7. **Selective adm (Gr K-7):** 29/yr. Appl fee: $75. Appl due: Rolling. **Tests** IQ. **Enr 153.** B 103. G 50. Wh 84%. Latino 3%. Blk 5%. Asian 3%. Other 5%. Avg class size: 7. Stud/fac: 5:1. Casual dress. **Fac 31.** M 6/F 25. FT 30/PT 1. Wh 100%. Adv deg: 87%. **Grad '11—43.** Prep—26. (Archmere 5, St Mark's HS 3, Concord HS 2, Salesianum 2, Tower Hill 1). Alum donors: 15%. **Tui '11-'12:** Day $23,340. Aid: Need 58 ($757,040). **Est 1957.** Nonprofit. (Aug-June). **Assoc** MSA. Pilot, which maintains a low student-teacher ratio, offers intensive small-group and individual remedial-developmental instruction to students of average or above potential who have learning differences. Language, occupational and physical therapy are part of the program. Applicants must take a series of psychological, educational and language tests prior to acceptance.

SAINT EDMOND'S ACADEMY Day Boys Gr PS (Age 4)-8
Wilmington, DE 19810. 2120 Veale Rd.
Tel: 302-475-5370. Fax: 302-475-2256.
www.stedmondsacademy.org E-mail: bdamato@stedmondsacademy.org
Br. Michael A. Smith, CSC, Head (2010). BA, St Edward's Univ, MAT, Univ of Rhode Island, MA, Univ of Notre Dame. Bill D'Amato, Adm.

Pre-Prep. Feat—Span Relig Studio_Art Drama Music. **Supp**—Rem_Math Tut. **Sports**— B: Baseball Basket X-country Lacrosse Soccer Track Wrestling. **Selective adm:** 47/yr. Appl fee: $100. Appl due: Dec. Accepted: 80%. **Tests** CTP_4. **Enr 286.** Wh 90%. Latino 2%. Blk 5%. Native Am 1%. Asian 2%. Avg class size: 17. Uniform. **Fac 30.** M 12/F 18. FT 29/PT 1. Wh 91%. Latino 3%. Blk 3%. Asian 3%. Adv deg: 60%. **Grad '09—49.** Prep—47. (Salesianum 29, Archmere 9, St Mark's HS 4, Church Farm 1, Sanford 1, Portsmouth 1). **Tui '11-'12:** Day $9230-14,850. Aid: Need 76 ($408,068). **Est 1959.** Nonprofit. Roman Catholic (81%

practice). Tri (Sept-June). **Assoc** MSA. This boys' school, which was founded in the educational tradition of the Brothers of Holy Cross, places particular emphasis on the development of fundamental academic skills. A rotating six-day schedule incorporates academics, physical and social activities, music, art and spiritual pursuits.

SAINT MARK'S HIGH SCHOOL   Day Coed Gr 9-12
Wilmington, DE 19808. 2501 Pike Creek Rd.
Tel: 302-738-3300. Fax: 302-738-5132.
www.stmarkshs.net   E-mail: mdriscoll@stmarkshs.net
   Mark J. Freund, Prin (1998). BA, Towson Univ, MEd, Loyola College. Clarice Gambacorta Kwasnieski, Adm.

   Col Prep. AP (exams req'd; 441 taken, 83% 3+)—Eng Fr Ger Span Calc Stats Bio Chem Environ_Sci Physics Eur_Hist US_Hist Comp_Govt & Pol Econ Psych US_Govt & Pol Studio_Art Music_Theory. **Feat**—British_Lit Creative_Writing Ital Anat Astron Forensic_Sci Engineering Programming Web_Design Law Theol World_Relig Architect_Drawing Drawing Photog Acting Directing Band Chorus Accounting TV_Production Nutrition. **Supp**—LD Tut. **Sports**—Basket Crew X-country Golf Ice_Hockey Indoor_Track Lacrosse Soccer Swim Tennis Track Volley. B: Baseball Football Wrestling. G: Cheer F_Hockey Softball. Activities: 50. **Selective adm (Gr 9-11):** 250/yr. Appl fee: $100. Appl due: Rolling. **Tests** HSPT. **Enr** 1100. Wh 84%. Latino 5%. Blk 7%. Asian 4%. Avg class size: 24. Stud/fac: 15:1. Uniform. **Fac 101.** M 46/F 55. FT 99/PT 2. Adv deg: 61%. **Grad '11—354.** Col—348. (U of DE 125, Wilmington-DE 17, Neumann 9, PA St 9, Towson 6, York Col of PA 6). **Avg SAT:** CR 545. M 532. W 535. Avg ACT: 23. **Col Couns:** 2. Alum donors: 10%. **Tui '11-'12:** Day $9999 (+$800-1000). Aid: Merit 175 ($500,000). Need 372 ($1,000,000). **Est 1969.** Inc. Roman Catholic (73% practice). Quar (Sept-June). **Assoc** MSA. Serving the Delaware Valley, Saint Mark's conducts college preparatory courses at five distinct ability levels. Notable elements of school life are an extensive Advanced Placement curriculum and well-established technology, service, athletic, and fine and performing arts programs. Mastery of written communications is an area of emphasis. In addition to formal religious education, this Catholic school also offers liturgies for special occasions, penance services and annual retreats.

SALESIANUM SCHOOL   Day Boys Gr 9-12
Wilmington, DE 19802. 1801 N Broom St.
Tel: 302-654-2495. Fax: 302-654-7767.
www.salesianum.org   E-mail: admissions@salesianum.org
   Brendan P. Kennealey, Pres (2011). BA, Boston College, MBA, Harvard Univ. Rev. J. Christian Beretta, OSFS, Prin. BA, Allentown College of St Francis de Sales, MDiv, DeSales Hall School of Theology, MS, Univ of Maryland-College Park, MEd, Univ of Notre Dame. Mark J. Winchell, Adm.

   Col Prep. AP (228 exams taken, 82% 3+)—Eng Fr Ger Lat Span Calc Stats Comp_Sci Bio Chem Environ_Sci Physics Eur_Hist US_Hist World_Hist Econ Psych US_Govt & Pol Studio_Art. **Feat**—20th-Century_Lit Anat & Physiol Ecol Biotech Anthro Sports_Psych Relig. **Supp**—Rev Tut. **Sports**— B: Baseball Basket X-country Football Golf Ice_Hockey Lacrosse Soccer Swim Tennis Track Volley Wrestling. Activities: 58. **Selective adm (Gr 9-11):** 250/yr. Appl fee: $65. Appl due: Dec. **Tests** HSPT. **Enr 980.** Avg class size: 20. Stud/fac: 13:1. **Fac 80.** M 57/F 23. FT 80. Adv deg: 65%. **Grad '11—261.** Col—259. (U of DE 70, PA St 19, St Joseph's U 10, Drexel 9, U of Pittsburgh 8, U of SC 8). **Avg SAT:** CR 574. M 580. W 558. **Tui '11-'12:** Day $12,000 (+$500). **Est 1903.** Nonprofit. Roman Catholic. Quar (Sept-June). **Assoc** MSA. At Salesianum, governed by the Oblates of St. Francis de Sales, boys follow a core college preparatory program that includes four years of religious studies and three consecutive years of a foreign language. A fine arts program and religious activities are among the school's offerings. Exchange courses are offered with two local girls' schools, Padua Academy and Ursuline Academy. Boys have access to a wireless Internet network. Students perform 80 hours of community service over four years.

URSULINE ACADEMY **Day Boys Gr PS (Age 3)-3**
Wilmington, DE 19806. 1106 Pennsylvania Ave. **Girls PS (Age 3)-12**
Tel: 302-658-7158. Fax: 302-658-4297.
www.ursuline.org E-mail: lwong@ursuline.org
   Cathie Field Lloyd, Pres (2008). BA, MEd, Univ of Delaware. Lynn Haggerty Wong, Adm.

   Col Prep. Montessori. AP (149 exams taken, 80% 3+)—Eng Fr Span Calc Stats Bio Chem Physics Eur_Hist US_Hist Psych US_Govt & Pol Art_Hist Studio_Art. **Feat**—Creative_Writing Lat Environ_Sci Comp_Sci Archaeol Law Theol World_Relig Drawing Painting Acting Theater Chorus Marketing. **Comp:** Comp/Stud: 1:1 Laptop prgm Gr 7-12. **Sports**— G: Basket Cheer X-country F_Hockey Lacrosse Soccer Swim Tennis Track Volley. **Selective adm:** 124/yr. Appl fee: $75. Appl due: Rolling. Accepted: 70%. **Tests** CTP_4. **Enr 650.** B 50. G 600. Elem 430. Sec 220. Avg class size: 18. Stud/fac: 10:1. Uniform. **Fac 81.** M 11/F 70. FT 79/PT 2. Adv deg: 55%. **Grad '08—56.** Col—56. (U of DE 13, PA St 3, U of Pittsburgh 3, Loyola U of Chicago 2, Fairfield 2, St Joseph's U 2). **Avg SAT:** CR 571. M 541. W 586. **Col Couns:** 2. Alum donors: 18%. **Tui '12-'13:** Day $13,665-17,340 (+$45-3500). Aid: Merit 41 ($87,000). Need 68 ($327,530). **Est 1893.** Nonprofit. Roman Catholic. Quar (Sept-June). **Assoc MSA.**
A Montessori program is conducted for children ages 3-5, with a traditional class structure employed beginning in grade 1. All students in grades 7-12 must purchase a laptop computer through the school, and upper schoolers choose from a variety of honors and Advanced Placement courses. Girls complete 80 hours of community service by the end of sophomore year, followed by 50 hours both junior and senior years. An exchange program with Salesianum School allows upper school students to experience coeducational classrooms. Compulsory religion course work, a fine arts curriculum and varied athletics round out the program.

DISTRICT OF COLUMBIA

BRITISH SCHOOL OF WASHINGTON **Day Coed Gr PS (Age 3)-12**
Washington, DC 20007. 2001 Wisconsin Ave NW.
Tel: 202-829-3700. Fax: 202-829-6522.
www.britishschoolofwashington.org E-mail: admissionsbsw@britishschool.org
   Peter Harding, Head (2008). Anna Ellenbogen, Adm.

   Col Prep. IB Diploma. Feat—Fr Lat Span Film Studio_Art Music Design. **Supp**—Tut. **Sports**—Basket X-country Rugby Soccer Swim Volley. **Somewhat selective adm (Gr PS-11):** Appl fee: $150. Appl due: Rolling. **Enr 452.** Intl 50%. Avg class size: 20. **Fac 45. Grad '11—19.** Col—19. **Col Couns:** 1. **Tui '11-'12:** Day $20,300-25,470 (+$2150). **Est 1998.** Tri (Sept-July). Founded to meet the needs of British citizens living in Greater Washington, BSW now enrolls students from America and several dozen other countries. French language instruction begins at age 3 with short lessons and songs. The program for students ages 5-16 follows the British National Curriculum and the International Primary Curriculum. Latin and Spanish commence in grade 3, and drama is offered as an extracurricular activity. Classes leading to the International General Certificate of Secondary Education begin at age 14, and 16-year-olds pursue the International Baccalaureate Diploma. The school occupies quarters near Georgetown University.

CAPITOL HILL DAY SCHOOL **Day Coed Gr PS (Age 4)-8**
Washington, DC 20003. 210 S Carolina Ave SE.
Tel: 202-547-2244. Fax: 202-543-4597.
www.chds.org E-mail: admissions@chds.org
   Jason Gray, Head (2010). BA, College of Wooster, MEd, Columbia Univ. Priscilla A. Lund, Adm.

   Pre-Prep. Gen Acad. Feat—Poetry Fr Span Computers Studio_Art Drama Music.

Supp—Dev_Read Rev Tut. **Comp:** Comp/Stud: 1:4 (1:1 Laptop prgm Gr 6). **Sports**—Basket X-country Soccer. G: Softball. **Selective adm (Gr PS-6):** 38/yr. Appl fee: $50. Appl due: Jan. Accepted: 38%. Yield: 67%. **Tests** IQ. **Enr 214.** B 107. G 107. Wh 54%. Latino 2%. Blk 30%. Asian 8%. Other 6%. Avg class size: 24. **Fac 34.** M 6/F 28. FT 25/PT 9. Wh 79%. Latino 6%. Blk 9%. Asian 6%. Adv deg: 61%. **Grad '10—22.** Prep—13. (Georgetown Day 5, Edmund Burke 2, St John's Col HS 2, Sidwell Friends 2, Field 1, Maret 1). **Tui '11-'12:** Day $25,050-26,330. Aid: Need 45 ($480,000). **Est 1968.** Nonprofit. Tri (Sept-June). CHDS offers a strong academic curriculum in a supportive environment. The arts are integrated into mathematics, literature, science and social studies classes. French and Spanish instruction begins in pre-kindergarten. The school utilizes the resources of Greater Washington to augment classroom work with frequent field trips: On any given day, at least one class is making an off-campus excursion.

THE FIELD SCHOOL   Day Coed Gr 6-12
Washington, DC 20007. 2301 Foxhall Rd NW.
Tel: 202-295-5800. Fax: 202-295-5858.
www.fieldschool.org   E-mail: admissions@fieldschool.org
    Dale T. Johnson, Head (2004). BA, Williams College, MS, Johns Hopkins Univ. Maureen Miesmer, Adm.

    Col Prep. Feat—Creative_Writing Fr Lat Span Calc Stats Environ_Sci Comp_Sci Psych Philos Art_Hist Ceramics Filmmaking Photog Studio_Art Video_Production Theater Music Journ. **Supp**—Rev Tut. **Sports (req'd)**—Basket X-country Indoor_Track Soccer Tennis Track Ultimate_Frisbee. B: Baseball Wrestling. G: Lacrosse Softball Volley. Activities: 26. **Selective adm:** 81/yr. Appl fee: $80. Appl due: Jan. **Tests** SSAT. **Enr 320.** Elem 75. Sec 245. Avg class size: 11. Stud/fac: 6:1. **Fac 50.** Adv deg: 36%. **Grad '10—63.** Col—63. **Col Couns:** 2. **Tui '11-'12:** Day $35,200 (+$475-575). Aid: Need 64. **Est 1972.** Nonprofit. Quar (Sept-June). **Assoc** MSA. In addition to an academic curriculum, this school emphasizes its extensive studio arts offerings, which include ceramics, drama, music, painting and drawing, photography, digital arts and video, and journalism. Students perform community service work as part of a two-week internship program each winter, and boys and girls accumulate 60 hours of required community service in grades 9-12. In alternate years, the school sponsors a two-week trip to a Spanish- or French-speaking country.

GONZAGA COLLEGE HIGH SCHOOL   Day Boys Gr 9-12
Washington, DC 20001. 19 Eye St NW.
Tel: 202-336-7100. Fax: 202-454-1188.
www.gonzaga.org   E-mail: abattaile@gonzaga.org
    Rev. Vincent G. Conti, SJ, Head (2009). BA, Loyola College, MA, Saint Louis Univ, MDiv, Weston Jesuit School of Theology. Andrew Battaile, Adm.

    Col Prep. AP (exams req'd; 803 taken, 85% 3+)—Eng Fr Lat Span Calc Stats Comp_Sci Bio Chem Environ_Sci Physics Eur_Hist US_Hist Comp_Govt & Pol Econ Human_Geog Psych US_Govt & Pol Art_Hist Studio_Art. **Feat**—Creative_Writing African-Amer_Lit Irish_Lit Chin Ger Greek Govt Russ_Stud Ethics Philos Relig Film Fine_Arts Photog Band Chorus Music Music_Theory Communications. **Sports**— B: Baseball Basket Crew X-country Football Golf Ice_Hockey Lacrosse Rugby Soccer Squash Swim Tennis Track W_Polo Wrestling. **Selective adm (Gr 9-11):** 241/yr. Appl fee: $35. Appl due: Dec. Accepted: 44%. Yield: 78%. **Tests** HSPT. **Enr 957.** Wh 80%. Latino 5%. Blk 12%. Asian 3%. Avg class size: 28. Stud/fac: 14:1. **Fac 73.** M 53/F 20. FT 73. Adv deg: 72%. **Grad '11—228.** Col—225. **Avg SAT:** CR 623. M 632. W 615. Avg ACT: 27. **Col Couns:** 2. **Tui '12-'13:** Day $18,550 (+$500). Aid: Need ($2,200,000). **Est 1821.** Nonprofit. Roman Catholic (80% practice). Quar (Aug-June). **Assoc** MSA. Operated by the Society of Jesus, Gonzaga offers advanced courses in the core academic subjects, as well as in the arts. Additional requirements for boys include religious studies, computer programming and community service participation. The school's urban setting enables students to interact with the larger Washington community while also taking advantage of the cultural and educational amenities of the city.

THE LAB SCHOOL OF WASHINGTON   **Day Coed Gr 1-12**
Washington, DC 20007. 4759 Reservoir Rd NW.
Tel: 202-965-6600. Fax: 202-944-3088.
Other locations: 1550 Foxhall Rd NW, Washington 20007.
www.labschool.org   E-mail: alexandra.freeman@labschool.org
    Katherine A. Schantz, Head (2009). BA, Kalamazoo College, MEd, Harvard Univ. Susan F. Feeley, Adm.
    Col Prep. LD. Supp—Dev_Read Makeup Rem_Math Rem_Read Rev Tut. **Comp:** Comp/Stud: 1:1 **Sports**—Basket Golf Lacrosse Soccer Swim Tennis Track. G: Cheer Volley. Activities: 23. **Selective adm:** 55/yr. Appl fee: $100. Appl due: Feb. Accepted: 48%. Yield: 62%. **Tests** IQ. **Enr 340.** B 219. G 121. Elem 215. Sec 125. Wh 76%. Latino 5%. Blk 12%. Asian 4%. Other 3%. Avg class size: 12. Casual dress. **Fac 77.** M 20/F 57. FT 73/PT 4. Wh 77%. Latino 4%. Blk 9%. Asian 4%. Other 6%. Adv deg: 66%. **Grad '11—30.** Col—28. (U of AZ 2, E Carolina 2, U of Mary Wash 2, Savannah Col of Art & Design 2, Guilford 1, Goucher 1). **Col Couns:** 1. **Tui '12-'13:** Day $35,000-38,000. Aid: Need 18 ($150,000). **Est 1967.** Nonprofit. Sem (Aug-June). **Assoc** MSA. The Lab School primarily serves children of average to superior intelligence who have language-based learning disabilities and attentional disorders. The arts are central to the curriculum, and teaching methods are differentiated, experiential and multisensory. In the lower grades, the school's Academic Club Method utilizes visual, concrete activities to present topics in history, geography, civics, archaeology, literature and economics. High school students complete 100 hours of required community service prior to graduation. The elementary division operates on Foxhall Road, with grades 5-12 conducted on the Reservoir Road campus.

LOWELL SCHOOL   **Day Coed Gr PS (Age 3)-8**
Washington, DC 20012. 1640 Kalmia Rd NW.
Tel: 202-577-2000. Fax: 202-577-2001.
www.lowellschool.org   E-mail: admissions@lowellschool.org
    Debbie Gibbs, Head (2007). BA, Pomona College, BS, Univ of Minnesota-Twin Cities, MA, Univ of San Francisco. Liz Yee, Adm.
    Pre-Prep. Feat—Span Computers Geog Studio_Art Drama Music Dance Outdoor_Ed. **Sports**—Basket X-country Soccer Swim Track Ultimate_Frisbee. G: Lacrosse. **Selective adm:** 65/yr. Appl fee: $65. Appl due: Jan. **Tests** IQ SSAT. **Enr 300.** Avg class size: 16. Stud/fac: 6:1. **Fac 49. Grad '08—20.** Prep—20. (Georgetown Day 5, Maret 2, Sandy Spring Friends 2, Field 2, Bullis 1, Landon 1). **Tui '12-'13:** Day $25,498-29,524 (+$2000). Aid: Need 100. **Est 1965.** Nonprofit. (Sept-June). Founded as a nursery school in Cleveland Park, this progressive school gradually expanded its program and moved to a new, eight-acre campus near Rock Creek Park in 1999. Children enroll from throughout the city and from Maryland and Virginia as well. The curriculum emphasizes project learning and developmentally appropriate course work. Frequent field trips complement classroom instruction.

NATIONAL PRESBYTERIAN SCHOOL   **Day Coed Gr PS (Age 3)-6**
Washington, DC 20016. 4121 Nebraska Ave NW.
Tel: 202-537-7500. Fax: 202-537-7568.
www.nps-dc.org   E-mail: school@nps-dc.org
    James T. Neill, Head (2006). AB, Harvard Univ, MBA, Northwestern Univ. Katy Harvey, Adm.
    Pre-Prep. Feat—Span Computers Studio_Art Drama Music. **Supp**—Dev_Read Tut. **Sports**—Basket Lacrosse Soccer. G: Softball. **Selective adm:** 54/yr. Appl fee: $60. Appl due: Jan. Accepted: 60%. Yield: 61%. **Tests** IQ. **Enr 276.** B 134. G 142. Wh 74%. Latino 3%.

Blk 10%. Asian 2%. Other 11%. Avg class size: 12. Stud/fac: 7:1. Casual dress. **Fac 41.** M 3/F 38. FT 41. Wh 95%. Blk 5%. Adv deg: 60%. **Grad '11—24.** Prep—23. (Sidwell Friends 4, St Andrew's Sch-DE 3, Potomac 2, Holton-Arms 2, Natl Cathedral 2, St Albans 1). **Tui '11-'12:** Day $24,450 (+$100). **Est 1969.** Nonprofit. Presbyterian. Quar (Sept-June). **Assoc** MSA. Core courses at NPS typically feature two classroom teachers each. Students learn from specialist instructors in math, science, technology, reading, Spanish, music, art, drama and physical education. All children attend weekly chapel services that convene at the National Presbyterian Church. Before- and after-school classes supplement the NPS curriculum, and a flexible extended-day program is also available.

PARKMONT SCHOOL   Day Coed Gr 6-12
Washington, DC 20011. 4842 16th St NW.
Tel: 202-726-0740. Fax: 202-726-0748.
www.parkmont.org   E-mail: info@parkmont.org
    Ron McClain, Head. AB, Harvard Univ. Willa Reinhard, Adm.

    Col Prep. LD. Feat—British_Lit Span Anat & Physiol Ecol Robotics Govt World_Relig Film Studio_Art. **Selective adm:** 24/yr. Appl fee: $50. Appl due: Rolling. Accepted: 80%. **Enr 52.** B 35. G 17. Elem 15. Sec 37. Avg class size: 9. Stud/fac: 7:1. Casual dress. **Fac 11.** M 5/F 6. FT 8/PT 3. Adv deg: 18%. **Tui '11-'12:** Day $27,800. **Est 1972.** Nonprofit. 5 terms (Sept-June). Enrolling an ethnically diverse student body that is kept quite small, Parkmont employs a modular scheduling system consisting of five annual terms that reduces the pupil's academic load to three courses at a time and increases opportunities for teachers to incorporate experiential activities and field trips into the curriculum. Classes comprise multi-age groups of students with differing learning styles. At the high school level (grades 9-12), boys and girls devote 180 hours per year to internships that may involve one or two placements; one placement must be a community service project.

ST. JOHN'S COLLEGE HIGH SCHOOL   Day Coed Gr 9-12
Washington, DC 20015. 2607 Military Rd NW.
Tel: 202-363-2316. Fax: 202-363-2916.
www.stjohnschs.org   E-mail: admissions@stjohnschs.org
    Jeffrey W. Mancabelli, Pres (2010). BA, Univ of Scranton, MA, George Washington Univ. Br. Michael Andrejko, FSC, Prin. Susan Hinton, Adm.

    Col Prep. AP (339 exams taken, 56% 3+)—Eng Fr Span Calc Comp_Sci Bio Chem Environ_Sci Physics Eur_Hist US_Hist US_Govt & Pol Art_Hist Studio_Art. **Feat**—British_Lit Creative_Writing Shakespeare Women's_Lit Lat Anat & Physiol Astron Sports_Med Web_Design Econ Relig Chorus Music Dance Accounting Bus Journ JROTC. **Supp**—LD Tut. **Sports**—Basket X-country Lacrosse Soccer Swim Tennis Track. B: Baseball Football Golf Ice_Hockey Rugby Wrestling. G: F_Hockey Softball Volley. Activities: 51. **Selective adm:** 297/yr. Appl fee: $60. Appl due: Dec. Accepted: 55%. Yield: 60%. **Tests** HSPT. **Enr 1046.** B 596. G 450. Wh 55%. Latino 8%. Blk 28%. Asian 4%. Other 5%. Avg class size: 23. Stud/fac: 12:1. Uniform. **Fac 84.** Adv deg: 70%. **Grad '09—247.** Col—243. (U of MD-Col Park 21, Salisbury 7, VA Polytech 7, Towson 7, Catholic U 7, Mt St Mary's-MD 6). **Mid 50% SAT:** CR 510-610. M 500-600. **Col Couns:** 2. Alum donors: 20%. **Tui '12-'13:** Day $15,950 (+$500). **Est 1851.** Nonprofit. Roman Catholic (68% practice). Quar (Aug-June). **Assoc** MSA. The second-oldest Christian Brothers school in the US, St. John's offers a comprehensive program of academics, arts and service opportunities. The school's elective Junior ROTC program seeks to develop teamwork and leadership skills through daily activities. Interdisciplinary science and technology studies are integral to the curriculum. Students perform 90 hours of required community service during their four years.

ST. PATRICK'S EPISCOPAL DAY SCHOOL　　　Day Coed Gr PS (Age 2)-8
Washington, DC 20007. 4700 Whitehaven Pky NW.
Tel: 202-342-2805. Fax: 202-342-7001.
Other locations: 4925 MacArthur Blvd NW, Washington 20007.
www.stpatsdc.org　　E-mail: admission@stpatsdc.org
　　Peter A. Barrett, Head (1994). BA, Trinity College, MAT, Northwestern Univ. Jennifer S. Danish, Adm.
　　Pre-Prep. Feat—Humanities Span Computers Relig Studio_Art Music. **Supp**—Dev_Read Tut. **Comp:** Laptop prgm Gr 7-8. **Sports**—Basket X-country Lacrosse Soccer Track. G: Softball. **Selective adm:** 87/yr. Appl due: Jan. Accepted: 38%. **Tests** IQ SSAT. **Enr 500.** Nonwhite 23%. Avg class size: 17. Casual dress. **Fac 72.** Adv deg: 59%. **Grad '08—21.** Prep—21. (Georgetown Day 3, Bullis 3, Madeira 2, Sidwell Friends 1, Maret 1, Deerfield Acad 1). **Tui '11-'12:** Day $27,998-29,384 (+$155-2035). Aid: Need ($1,600,000). **Est 1956.** Nonprofit. Episcopal. Tri (Sept-June). **Assoc** MSA. Located on two campuses northwest of Georgetown in the Palisades section of the city, St. Patrick's enriched curriculum includes computer, religion, music, art, video production and library skills. Community service opportunities, sports and after-school programs supplement academics. Laptop computers are issued to students in grades 7 and 8, who attend classes at the MacArthur Boulevard campus.

MARYLAND

ALEPH BET JEWISH DAY SCHOOL　　　Day Coed Gr K-5
Annapolis, MD 21403. 1125 Spa Rd.
Tel: 410-263-9044. Fax: 410-263-5740.
www.alephbet.org　　E-mail: info@alephbet.org
　　Nan Jarashow, Head. BA, Carleton College, MAT, George Washington Univ.
　　Pre-Prep. Gen Acad. Feat—Hebrew Judaic_Stud Studio_Art Drama Music. **Somewhat selective adm:** Appl fee: $100. Appl due: Jan. Accepted: 96%. **Enr 34.** Avg class size: 10. **Fac 9.** Wh 100%. Adv deg: 22%. **Grad '08—9.** Prep—4. **Tui '10-'11:** Day $10,325 (+$350). **Est 1989.** Nonprofit. Jewish. Tri (Aug-June). Aleph Bet's dual curriculum combines general academics with course work in Judaic studies. Hebrew language study and instruction in Jewish values, ethics and history are among the topics addressed in the Judaic studies curriculum. Enrichment classes in music, art and drama round out the program.

ANNAPOLIS AREA CHRISTIAN SCHOOL　　　Day Coed Gr PS (Age 4)-12
Annapolis, MD 21401. 716 Bestgate Rd.
Tel: 410-266-8251. Fax: 410-573-6866.
Other locations: 710 Ridgely Ave, Annapolis 21401; 109 Burns Crossing Rd, Severn 21144.
www.aacsonline.org　　E-mail: admissions@aacsonline.org
　　George J. W. Lawrence, Jr., Supt (2009). BA, Covenant College, MA, Univ of California-Berkeley. Caroline Stone, Adm.
　　Col Prep. AP (exams req'd)—Eng Span Calc Stats Bio Physics US_Hist Econ US_Govt & Pol Studio_Art. **Feat**—British_Lit Creative_Writing Sci_Fiction World_Lit Fr Hebrew Anat & Physiol Engineering Comp_Sci Civil_War Bible Drama Music Finance Journ. **Supp**—LD Rem_Math Rem_Read. **Comp:** Comp/Stud: 1:38. **Dual enr:** Anne Arundel CC. **Sports**—Basket X-country Lacrosse Soccer Tennis Volley. B: Baseball Football Golf Wrestling. G: Cheer F_Hockey. Activities: 12. **Selective adm:** 166/yr. Appl fee: $100. Appl due: Rolling. Accepted: 81%. Yield: 87%. **Tests** Stanford. **Enr 886.** B 446. G 440. Elem 407. Sec 479. Wh 77%. Latino 2%. Blk 12%. Asian 1%. Other 8%. Avg class size: 23. Uniform. **Fac 80.** M 27/F 53. FT 71/PT 9. Wh 94%. Latino 1%. Blk 1%. Other 4%. Adv deg: 48%. **Grad '10—103.** Col—101. (Anne Arundel CC 24, U of MD-Col Park 3, U of MD-Baltimore County 3, Liberty 3, Geneva 3, Eastern U 2). **Mid 50% SAT:** CR 530-640. M 500-620. W 520-610.

Col Couns: 1. **Tui '11-'12:** Day $8987-14,960 (+$300-500). Aid: Need 125 ($455,868). **Est 1971.** Nonprofit. Nondenom Christian. Sem (Aug-June). **Assoc** MSA. Adhering to a Christian worldview, AACS emphasizes basic academic skills, college preparation and arts appreciation. Seventh graders perform five hours of required community service per quarter, while students in grades 9-12 complete eight hours of off-campus service annually. The lower school (grades PS-5) is located on Ridgeley Avenue, the middle school (grades 6-8) on Bestgate Road and the upper school (grades 9-12) on Burns Crossing Road in Severn.

ST. ANNE'S SCHOOL OF ANNAPOLIS   **Day Coed Gr PS (Age 2)-8**
Annapolis, MD 21403. 3112 Arundel on the Bay Rd.
Tel: 410-263-8650. Fax: 410-280-8720.
www.st.annesschool.org   E-mail: admissions@st.annesschool.org
      Lisa Nagel, Head (1992). BA, Oberlin College, MEd, John Carroll Univ. Caroline Cather Aras, Adm.
      Pre-Prep. Feat—Span Relig Studio_Art Music. **Sports**—Basket X-country Lacrosse Soccer Tennis. **G:** F_Hockey. **Selective adm:** 76/yr. Appl fee: $50. Appl due: Feb. **Tests** ISEE. **Enr 200.** Avg class size: 13. Stud/fac: 7:1. Uniform. **Fac 34.** M 2/F 32. FT 31/PT 3. Adv deg: 38%. **Grad '11—22.** Prep—16. **Tui '12-'13:** Day $16,400-17,400 (+$250-375). Aid: Need 95 ($715,000). **Est 1992.** Nonprofit. Episcopal. Tri (Sept-June). Lower schoolers (grades 1-4) take part in a lab-based science program at St. Anne's that focuses on experimentation and research skill development. At the middle school level (grades 5-8), boys and girls participate in a hands-on program that emphasizes critical-thinking and problem-solving skills. The visual and performing arts play an important role in the middle school, with students taking music and art classes all four years. A competitive sports program commences in grade 5.

CHESAPEAKE ACADEMY   **Day Coed Gr PS (Age 3)-5**
Arnold, MD 21012. 1185 Baltimore-Annapolis Blvd.
Tel: 410-647-9612. Fax: 410-647-6088.
www.chesapeakeacademy.com   E-mail: srichburg@chesapeakeacademy.com
      Jason Scheurle, Head (2006). BS, Indiana Univ, MEd, Columbia Univ. Sue Richburg, Adm.
      Pre-Prep. Feat—Lib_Skills Span Computers Performing_Arts Visual_Arts. **Supp**—Dev_ Read Rev Tut. **Selective adm:** 66/yr. Appl fee: $75. Appl due: Rolling. Accepted: 79%. **Tests** CTP_4 IQ. **Enr 321.** B 165. G 156. Avg class size: 16. Uniform. **Fac 35.** M 1/F 34. FT 31/PT 4. Adv deg: 25%. **Grad '05—43.** Prep—33. Alum donors: 4%. **Tui '12-'13:** Day $13,620-16,840 (+$770-800). **Est 1980.** Nonprofit. Tri (Sept-June). The academy offers an early childhood program, in addition to its pre-preparatory core curriculum. Each grade level completes at least one service learning project. Before- and after-school care is available.

THE CATHOLIC HIGH SCHOOL OF BALTIMORE   **Day Girls Gr 9-12**
Baltimore, MD 21213. 2800 Edison Hwy.
Tel: 410-732-6200. Fax: 410-732-7639.
www.thecatholichighschool.org   E-mail: chsb@thecatholichighschool.org
      Barbara D. Nazelrod, Pres. BA, MEd, Loyola College (MD), PhD, Univ of Maryland-College Park. Marsha Meyd, Prin. BS, Univ of Maryland-College Park, MA, MEd, Johns Hopkins Univ. Brooke Sterrett, Adm.
      Col Prep. AP (41 exams taken, 71% 3+)—Eng Calc Comp_Sci US_Hist Psych US_Govt & Pol Studio_Art. **Feat**—Creative_Writing Nonfiction_Writing World_Lit Fr Ger Lat Span Anat & Physiol Environ_Sci Engineering Russ_Hist Human_Dev Theol Drama Music Speech. **Supp**—Dev_Read Rem_Math Rem_Read Rev Tut. **Comp:** Comp/Stud: 1:2. **Dual enr:** Anne Arundel CC, Neumann. **Sports**— G: Basket Cheer X-country F_Hockey Golf Indoor_Track Lacrosse Soccer Softball Swim Tennis Track Volley. **Selective adm:** 85/yr. Appl fee: $40. Appl due: Dec. Accepted: 83%. **Tests** HSPT. **Enr 308.** Wh 76%. Blk 20%. Asian 1%. Other 3%.

Avg class size: 17. Stud/fac: 12:1. Uniform. **Fac 33.** M 12/F 21. FT 32/PT 1. Wh 99%. Latino 1%. Adv deg: 57%. **Grad '11—77.** Col—69. (CC of Baltimore Co 21, Stevenson 8, Salisbury 4, Harford CC 2, Anne Arundel CC 2, Towson 1). **Avg SAT:** CR/M 1001. Avg ACT: 17. **Col Couns:** 2. Alum donors: 21%. **Tui '12-'13:** Day $11,300 (+$850). Aid: Merit 88 ($230,300). Need 106 ($145,875). **Est 1939.** Nonprofit. Roman Catholic (83% practice). Sem (Aug-June). **Assoc** MSA. Four years of theology, as well as an honors program and Advanced Placement courses, enrich the curriculum. The school also conducts an integrated humanities and fine arts program. Catholic High offers annual mentorship opportunities, in addition to a dual-enrollment program that enables seniors to earn college credit through local community colleges. Girls perform 30 hours of required community service each year.

THE CONSERVATORY   **Day Coed Gr K-12**
BALTIMORE ACTORS' THEATRE
Baltimore, MD 21212. 300 Dumbarton Rd.
Tel: 410-337-8519. Fax: 410-337-8582.
www.baltimoreactorstheatre.org/conservatory.html
E-mail: batpro@baltimoreactorstheatre.org
    Walter E. Anderson, Head. MDS, MLA, Johns Hopkins Univ.

Col Prep. Perform_Arts. AP—Eng Fr Bio Eur_Hist US_Hist World_Hist Music_Theory.
Feat—Lat Acting Theater Musical_Theater Chorus Music_Hist Ballet Dance. **Supp**—Tut.
Comp: Comp/Stud: 1:1 Laptop prgm Gr 3-12. **Dual enr:** Towson, Goucher, U of NE-Lincoln.
Selective adm (Gr K-11): 6/yr. Appl fee: $50. Appl due: Apr. Accepted: 7%. Yield: 7%. **Tests**
IQ Stanford. **Enr 30.** B 12. G 18. Elem 15. Sec 15. Avg class size: 6. Stud/fac: 5:1. Uniform.
Fac 15. M 2/F 13. FT 3/PT 12. Adv deg: 100%. **Grad '10—1.** Col—1. **Avg SAT:** CR 675. M
550. Avg ACT: 32. Alum donors: 10%. **Tui '11-'12:** Day $10,000. Aid: Need 12 ($30,000).
Work prgm 2 ($8000). **Est 1979.** Tri (Sept-June).   The Conservatory combines a college pre-
paratory academic curriculum with a professional performing arts program. Preparing students
for careers in music, drama and dance, the program is also structured for pupils with a strong
arts avocation who plan to pursue other areas of study in college. Year-round performance
opportunities in adult and children's theater are available through the Oregon Ridge Dinner
Theatre. Professional development programs focus upon music, drama, dance and musical
theater.

THE DAY SCHOOL AT BALTIMORE HEBREW   **Day Coed Gr PS (Age 2)-8**
Baltimore, MD 21208. 7401 Park Heights Ave.
Tel: 410-764-1867. Fax: 410-764-8138.
www.thedayschoolbh.org   E-mail: admissions@bhcds.org
    Gerri Chizeck, Head (2008). BA, Antioch College, MA, Pacific Oaks College, EdD, Univ
of Southern California. Becca Gould, Adm.

Pre-Prep. Feat—Creative_Writing Shakespeare Hebrew Jewish_Hist Judaic_Stud Studio_
Art Music. **Supp**—Dev_Read Rem_Math Rem_Read Rev Tut. **Comp:** Comp/Stud: 1:2.
Sports—Basket Soccer Track. B: Baseball. **Selective adm:** 14/yr. Appl fee: $50. Appl due:
Rolling. Accepted: 80%. Yield: 60%. **Tests** ISEE Stanford. **Enr 80.** B 50. G 30. Wh 90%. Blk
5%. Asian 5%. Avg class size: 8. Stud/fac: 6:1. Uniform. **Fac 21.** M 1/F 20. FT 16/PT 5. Non-
white 2%. Adv deg: 57%. **Grad '10—10.** Prep—10. **Tui '12-'13:** Day $14,995-17,150. Aid:
Need ($300,000). **Est 1991.** Nonprofit. Jewish (98% practice). Quar (Aug-June).   Students at
the Day School attend Judaic studies courses and receive Hebrew language instruction at all
grade levels. Beginning in grade 6, boys and girls take lessons in Torah reading, chanting and
Hebrew prayer book interpretation. The school's language arts program, which incorporates
Jewish and historical theme-based literature, seeks to develop pupils' research and writing
skills.

MERCY HIGH SCHOOL   Day Girls Gr 9-12
Baltimore, MD 21239. 1300 E Northern Pky.
Tel: 410-433-8880. Fax: 410-323-8816.
www.mercyhighschool.com   E-mail: mercy@mercyhighschool.com
   Sr. Carol E. Wheeler, RSM, Pres (1977). BA, Maryville Univ, MA, Georgetown Univ, MA,
Univ of Chicago. Pegeen D'Agostino, Prin. Jaqueline Stilling, Adm.
   Col Prep. AP—Eng Calc US_Hist Psych. **Feat**—Creative_Writing Women's_Lit Fr Lat
Span Stats Bioethics Marine_Bio/Sci Zoology Comp_Design Comp_Sci Web_Design Sociol
Lat-Amer_Stud Relig Ceramics Drawing Photog Studio_Art Acting Theater Music_Theory
Journ Public_Speak. **Supp**—LD Rev Tut. **Sports**— G: Basket Cheer X-country F_Hockey
Lacrosse Soccer Softball Track Volley. Activities: 23. **Selective adm (Gr 9-11):** 80/yr. Appl
fee: $35. Appl due: Jan. **Tests** HSPT. **Enr 400.** Wh 82%. Latino 1%. Blk 14%. Asian 3%. Avg
class size: 20. Uniform. **Fac 41.** M 3/F 38. FT 41. Wh 93%. Latino 1%. Blk 1%. Asian 3%.
Other 2%. Adv deg: 58%. **Grad '08**—128. Col—127. **Tui '12-'13:** Day $11,950 (+$500).
Est 1960. Nonprofit. Roman Catholic. Quar (Aug-June). **Assoc** MSA. Mercy's curriculum
features independent studies in career fields, college-level writing workshops, and a model college and career planning program. Students have daily contact with a faculty advisor. Elective
courses include environmental science, philosophy and economics. Juniors satisfy a 50-hour
community service requirement. The school organizes trips abroad.

MOUNT ST. JOSEPH HIGH SCHOOL   Day Boys Gr 9-12
Baltimore, MD 21229. 4403 Frederick Ave.
Tel: 410-644-3300. Fax: 410-646-6220.
www.msjnet.edu   E-mail: mhoffman@admin.msjnet.edu
   George E. Andrews, Jr., Pres (2012). BA, Wheeling Jesuit Univ, MA, Duquesne Univ.
Barry J. Fitzpatrick, Prin. BA, Catholic Univ of America, MA, Loyola Univ, MEd, Harvard
Univ. Marc Hoffman, Adm.
   Col Prep. AP (exams req'd; 364 taken, 70% 3+)—Eng Fr Span Calc Stats Comp_Sci
Bio Chem Environ_Sci Physics Eur_Hist US_Hist Econ Psych US_Govt & Pol Studio_Art
Music_Theory. **Feat**—African-Amer_Lit Lat Genetics Robotics Web_Design Relig Photog
Drama Music. **Supp**—LD Tut. **Comp:** Comp/Stud: 1:2.5. **Sports**— B: Baseball Basket X-
country Football Golf Ice_Hockey Lacrosse Soccer Swim Tennis Track Volley W_Polo Wres-
tling. Activities: 50. **Somewhat selective adm (Gr 9-11):** 290/yr. Appl fee: $0. Appl due: Jan.
Accepted: 85%. Yield: 64%. **Tests** HSPT. **Enr 1085.** Wh 76%. Latino 2%. Blk 18%. Native
Am 1%. Asian 3%. Avg class size: 19. Stud/fac: 12:1. Formal dress. **Fac 98.** M 72/F 26. FT
94/PT 4. Wh 97%. Latino 2%. Blk 1%. Adv deg: 65%. **Grad '11**—267. Col—254. **Avg SAT:**
CR 526. M 535. W 521. **Col Couns:** 8. Alum donors: 16%. **Tui '12-'13:** Day $12,400 (+$450-
1000). Aid: Merit 47 ($403,000). Need 198 ($936,050). **Est 1876.** Nonprofit. Roman Catholic. Quar (Aug-June). **Assoc** MSA. Mount St. Joseph functions under the sponsorship of the
Brothers of St. Francis Xavier. The academic curriculum features both Advanced Placement
and honors courses. Juniors complete 40 hours of community service work as part of the religion curriculum, while seniors perform another 20 hours of service. Available for an additional
fee, the DePaul Program serves college-bound students with mild learning disabilities.

SETON KEOUGH HIGH SCHOOL   Day Girls Gr 9-12
Baltimore, MD 21227. 1201 Caton Ave.
Tel: 410-646-4444. Fax: 443-573-0107.
www.setonkeough.com   E-mail: dmoran@setonkeough.com
   Karen Hanrahan, Pres (2010). BA, Capital Univ, MPA, National Univ. Angela Calamari,
Prin. BA, City Univ of New York, MA, Loyola Univ Maryland. Danielle Moran, Adm.
   Col Prep. AP (exams req'd)—Eng Fr Span Calc Comp_Sci Bio US_Hist Studio_Art
Music_Theory. **Feat**—Lat Forensic_Sci Biomed_Sci Engineering. **Supp**—LD Rev Tut.
Sports— G: Basket Cheer X-country F_Hockey Golf Indoor_Track Lacrosse Soccer Softball
Swim Track Volley. Activities: 25. **Somewhat selective adm (Gr 9-11):** 100/yr. Appl fee:

$30. Appl due: Jan. **Tests** HSPT. **Enr 400.** Avg class size: 15. Stud/fac: 12:1. Uniform. **Fac 44.** M 12/F 32. FT 41/PT 3. Wh 92%. Blk 2%. Native Am 3%. Asian 1%. Other 2%. Adv deg: 100%. **Grad '11—108.** Col—104. **Avg SAT:** CR 530. M 500. **Col Couns:** 2. **Tui '12-'13:** Day $11,400. **Est 1988.** Nonprofit. Roman Catholic. Sem (Sept-June). **Assoc** MSA. The school resulted from the merger of Seton High School, established in 1926, and Archbishop Keough High School, established in 1965. A broad curriculum that comprises a wide range of required and elective courses is offered. In addition to an honors program leading to Advanced Placement courses in the junior and senior years, the school conducts a special program for students with mild learning disabilities (available for an additional fee). A four-year advanced science program offers tracks in engineering and biomedical science. Girls perform 45 hours of required community service during their four years at Seton Keough.

THE BARNESVILLE SCHOOL   **Day Coed Gr PS (Age 3)-8**
Barnesville, MD 20838. 21830 Peach Tree Rd, PO Box 404.
Tel: 301-972-0341. Fax: 301-972-4076.
www.barnesvilleschool.org   E-mail: sjohnson@barnesvilleschool.org
    John Huber, Head (2006). BA, Cornell Univ, MA, Villanova Univ. Susanne Johnson, Adm.
    Pre-Prep. Gen Acad. Feat—Span Studio_Art Chorus Music. **Supp**—Dev_Read Rev Tut. **Comp:** Comp/Stud: 1:2.3 (1:1 Laptop prgm Gr 8). **Sports**—Basket X-country Lacrosse Soccer. **Selective adm:** 32/yr. Appl fee: $75. Appl due: Jan. **Tests** ISEE SSAT. **Enr 182.** B 78. G 104. Wh 80%. Latino 3%. Blk 5%. Asian 5%. Other 7%. Avg class size: 11. Stud/fac: 8:1. **Fac 23.** M 3/F 20. FT 19/PT 4. Wh 90%. Latino 10%. Adv deg: 60%. **Grad '11—11.** Prep—6. **Tui '11-'12:** Day $12,560-17,970 (+$150-675). **Est 1969.** Nonprofit. Tri (Sept-June). This country school offers a strong academic program in a flexible, supportive atmosphere that emphasizes hands-on activities. Particularly strong science and music programs enhance the basic curriculum. All boys and girls take part in the school's community service program. Barnesville encourages parents to become involved in school activities.

JOHN CARROLL SCHOOL   **Day Coed Gr 9-12**
Bel Air, MD 21014. 703 Churchville Rd.
Tel: 410-838-8333. Fax: 410-836-8514.
www.johncarroll.org   E-mail: jroberts@johncarroll.org
    Richard J. O'Hara, Pres (2007). BA, Williams College, MEd, Univ of Virginia. Madelyn Ball, Prin. Jesse Roberts, Adm.
    Col Prep. AP—Eng Fr Ger Span Calc Bio Chem Environ_Sci Physics Eur_Hist US_Hist Human_Geog Psych US_Govt & Pol. **Feat**—Creative_Writing Chin Lat Russ Marine_Bio/Sci Sports_Med Comp_Sci Web_Design Anthro Econ Philos World_Relig Ceramics Drawing Photog Studio_Art Animation Acting Band Chorus Music_Theory Orchestra Journ Speech. **Supp**—Dev_Read Makeup Rem_Math Rem_Read Rev Tut. **Comp:** Laptop prgm Gr 9-12. **Sports**—Basket X-country Indoor_Track Lacrosse Soccer Swim Tennis Track Volley. B: Baseball Football Golf Rugby Wrestling. G: Badminton F_Hockey Softball. Activities: 30. **Selective adm:** 250/yr. Appl fee: $35. Appl due: Jan. **Tests** HSPT. **Enr 691.** Avg class size: 19. Stud/fac: 17:1. Uniform. **Fac 67.** M 33/F 34. FT 63/PT 4. Adv deg: 55%. **Grad '10—237.** Col—237. **Tui '11-'12:** Day $13,700 (+$500). **Est 1964.** Nonprofit. Roman Catholic. Quar (Aug-June). **Assoc** MSA. Affiliated with the Archdiocese of Baltimore, this community-oriented day school features flexible modular scheduling, independent study and elective senior intern experiences. In addition, John Carroll conducts one-month exchange programs with schools in Spain, France, Germany and Russia. Each student must purchase a tablet computer for school use.

WORCESTER PREPARATORY SCHOOL   Day Coed Gr PS (Age 4)-12
Berlin, MD 21811. 508 S Main St, PO Box 1006.
Tel: 410-641-3575. Fax: 410-641-3586.
www.worcesterprep.org   E-mail: tbecker@worcesterprep.org
     Barry W. Tull, Head (1985). BS, MEd, Salisbury Univ, EdD, Univ of Maryland-College Park. Tara Becker, Adm.
     Col Prep. AP (exams req'd; 167 taken, 83% 3+)—Eng Calc Stats Bio Chem Physics US_Hist. **Feat**—Fr Lat Span Comp_Sci Robotics Milit_Hist Photog Music Debate. **Supp**—Tut. **Comp:** Comp/Stud: 1:2. Outdoor Ed. **Sports**—Basket Golf Soccer Tennis. G: F_Hockey Volley. **Selective adm (Gr PS-11):** 57/yr. Appl fee: $50. Appl due: Rolling. Accepted: 64%. Yield: 91%. **Tests** CEEB HSPT IQ SSAT Stanford. **Enr 540.** B 299. G 241. Elem 330. Sec 210. Wh 86%. Latino 2%. Blk 1%. Native Am 1%. Asian 5%. Other 5%. Avg class size: 15. Stud/fac: 10:1. Uniform. **Fac 58.** M 18/F 40. FT 53/PT 5. Wh 94%. Latino 6%. Adv deg: 77%. **Grad '11—39.** Col—39. (Clemson 3, Duke 2, Wake Forest 2, Johns Hopkins 2, Col of Charleston 2, Yale 1). **Avg SAT:** CR 632. M 636. W 657. **Col Couns:** 1. Alum donors: 28%. **Tui '11-'12:** Day $10,910-11,490 (+$800). Aid: Need 1 ($11,500). **Est 1970.** Nonprofit. Sem (Sept-June). **Assoc** CLS MSA. Worcester Prep's college preparatory curriculum comprises four years of language instruction in French and Spanish, as well as one year of Latin. Lab science and advanced mathematics courses are other noteworthy features of the program. Faculty in all disciplines and at all grade levels emphasize the development of sound writing skills.

FRENCH INTERNATIONAL SCHOOL   Day Coed Gr PS (Age 3)-12
Bethesda, MD 20814. 9600 Forest Rd.
Tel: 301-530-8260. Fax: 301-564-5779.
Other locations: 3200 Woodbine St, Chevy Chase 20815; 7108 Bradley Blvd, Bethesda 20817.
www.rochambeau.org   E-mail: finucana@rochambeau.org
     Eric Veteau, Prin. Agnes Finucan, Adm.
     Col Prep. Fr Bac. Bilingual (Fr). Feat—Fr Ger Ital Span Philos. **Supp**—ESL. **Selective adm:** 300/yr. **Enr 1040.** Wh 74%. Latino 2%. Blk 24%. Intl 85%. Avg class size: 22. **Fac 92. Grad '11—69.** Col—69. **Avg SAT:** CR/M 1200. **Tui '12-'13:** Day $14,600-19,480 (+$500). **Est 1962.** Nonprofit. Tri (Sept-June). Located on 18 acres, the school follows the French system of instruction and enrolls students from approximately 50 countries. The French academic program, supplemented by English and American history classes, leads to both the French Baccalaureate and the US high school diploma. No prior knowledge of French is required for admission to the nursery school.

THE HARBOR SCHOOL   Day Coed Gr PS (Age 3)-2
Bethesda, MD 20817. 7701 Bradley Blvd.
Tel: 301-365-1100. Fax: 301-365-7491.
www.theharborschool.org   E-mail: info@theharborschool.org
     Valaida Wise, Head (2008). BA, Syracuse Univ, MAT, Trinity College (CT), EdD, George Washington Univ. Steven D. Greisdorf, Adm.
     Pre-Prep. Feat—Lib_Skills Span Studio_Art Music Dance. **Supp**—Dev_Read Rem_Read. **Comp:** Comp/Stud: 1:10. **Selective adm:** 36/yr. Appl fee: $60. Appl due: Feb. Accepted: 82%. Yield: 64%. **Enr 109.** B 56. G 53. Wh 77%. Blk 3%. Asian 6%. Other 14%. Avg class size: 14. Stud/fac: 5:1. **Fac 23.** FT 19/PT 4. Wh 74%. Latino 9%. Blk 9%. Asian 4%. Other 4%. Adv deg: 47%. **Tui '11-'12:** Day $18,260 (+$890). Aid: Need 15 ($116,000). **Est 1972.** Nonprofit. Sem (Sept-June). Harbor's program features art, reading, handwriting, math, science and social studies. Primary grades emphasize reading and math skill development. All children attend twice-weekly music, Spanish and physical education classes. The nursery school program includes creative movement.

NORWOOD SCHOOL Day Coed Gr K-8
Bethesda, MD 20817. 8821 River Rd.
Tel: 301-365-2595. Fax: 301-841-4636.
www.norwoodschool.org E-mail: info@norwoodschool.org
    Richard T. Ewing, Jr., Head (1983). BA, Yale Univ, MEd, Univ of Virginia, EdD, Harvard Univ. Mimi Mulligan, Adm.
    Pre-Prep. Feat—Chin Fr Lat Span Computers Studio_Art Drama Music. **Supp**—Tut. **Comp:** Comp/Stud: 1:1 Laptop prgm Gr 5-8. **Sports (req'd)**—Basket X-country Lacrosse Soccer. B: Baseball Track. G: F_Hockey Softball. **Selective adm (Gr K-7):** 90/yr. Appl fee: $60. Appl due: Feb. Accepted: 50%. Yield: 73%. **Tests** IQ ISEE SSAT. **Enr 480.** B 240. G 240. Wh 66%. Latino 4%. Blk 8%. Asian 8%. Other 14%. Avg class size: 12. Stud/fac: 7:1. Casual dress. **Fac 98.** M 22/F 76. FT 92/PT 6. Wh 70%. Latino 8%. Blk 10%. Native Am 1%. Asian 8%. Other 3%. Adv deg: 61%. **Grad '11—62.** Prep—55. (Potomac 8, Landon 5, Holton-Arms 5, Sidwell Friends 4, Georgetown Day 4, St Albans 4). **Tui '12-'13:** Day $25,530-28,850 (+$40-1140). Aid: Need 81 ($1,500,000). **Est 1952.** Nonprofit. Quar (Sept-June). **Assoc** MSA. Composed of a lower school (grades K-4) and a middle school (grades 5-8), Norwood supplements course work in the traditional disciplines with classes in art, drama, technology and physical education at all grade levels. Spanish is available from kindergarten, French from grade 5, Latin in grades 7 and 8, Chinese in grades 5-8, and instrumental or choral music in grades 5-8. Children in grades K-6 engage in required community service projects throughout the year, while pupils in grades 7 and 8 take part in six daylong service experiences each year.

THE PRIMARY DAY SCHOOL Day Coed Gr PS (Age 4)-2
Bethesda, MD 20817. 7300 River Rd.
Tel: 301-365-4355. Fax: 301-469-8611.
www.theprimarydayschool.org E-mail: admission@theprimarydayschool.org
    Louise Plumb, Dir (1998). BA, State Univ of New York-Oneonta. Julie McCaffery, Adm.
    Pre-Prep. Feat—Creative_Writing Lib_Skills Computers Studio_Art Music. **Supp**—Rem_Math Rem_Read Tut. **Selective adm:** 39/yr. Appl fee: $65. Appl due: Jan. **Tests** IQ. **Enr 146.** B 64. G 82. Wh 58%. Latino 1%. Blk 4%. Asian 12%. Other 25%. Avg class size: 18. Stud/fac: 9:1. **Fac 25.** FT 20/PT 5. Wh 99%. Asian 1%. Adv deg: 28%. **Grad '11—38.** Prep—33. **Tui '12-'13:** Day $17,000-21,000. **Est 1944.** Nonprofit. Sem (Sept-June). Primary Day's traditional curriculum emphasizes fundamental skills, sound work habits and an appreciation for the arts. Music, art, computer, creative writing, literature and physical education classes complement instruction in the core subjects. Weekly assemblies and class performances augment the arts program and help students develop poise and public-speaking skills. Before- and after-school programs are available.

WASHINGTON EPISCOPAL SCHOOL Day Coed Gr PS (Age 3)-8
Bethesda, MD 20816. 5600 Little Falls Pky.
Tel: 301-652-7878. Fax: 301-652-7255.
www.w-e-s.org E-mail: admissions@w-e-s.org
    Kirk Duncan, Head (2011). BA, Occidental College, MS, Univ of Southern California. Debra Duff, Adm.
    Pre-Prep. Feat—Fr Span Computers Studio_Art Drama Music. **Supp**—Tut. **Comp:** Comp/Stud: 1:1.6. **Sports**—Basket X-country Lacrosse Soccer Track. **Selective adm:** 57/yr. Appl fee: $60. Appl due: Feb. Accepted: 75%. Yield: 47%. **Tests** IQ ISEE SSAT. **Enr 280.** Avg class size: 16. Stud/fac: 6:1. Uniform. **Fac 54.** M 12/F 42. FT 46/PT 8. Adv deg: 40%. **Grad '09—24.** Prep—20. (Georgetown Day 4, Madeira 2, Sidwell Friends 2, St Albans 2, Natl Cathedral 1, Holton-Arms 1). **Tui '12-'13:** Day $24,025-28,975 (+$535-1610). **Est 1986.** Nonprofit. Episcopal. Tri (Sept-June). **Assoc** MSA. WES features small classes and a rigorous academic program. French or Spanish study begins in prekindergarten, while Latin is first offered in grade 6. After-school enrichment classes and an extended-day program are also

available, and interscholastic sports begin in grade 5. A study trip program sends sixth graders to Utah to study desert history and geology. Seventh graders travel to Italy for 10 days in the spring, and eighth graders spend two weeks in either France or Spain. All students participate in community outreach activities, and in grades 7 and 8 students perform 10 hours of individual service.

THE WOODS ACADEMY									**Day Coed Gr PS (Age 3)-8**
Bethesda, MD 20817. 6801 Greentree Rd.
Tel: 301-365-3080. Fax: 301-469-6439.
www.woodsacademy.org   E-mail: info@woodsacademy.org
		Joseph E. Powers, Head (2011). BA, Le Moyne College, MEd, Johns Hopkins Univ. Jodie A. Shoemaker, Adm.
		Pre-Prep. Montessori. Feat—Fr Span Computers Studio_Art Drama Music. **Comp:** Comp/Stud: 1:4 (1:1 Laptop prgm Gr 5-8). **Sports**—Basket Lacrosse Soccer. B: Baseball. G: Softball. **Selective adm:** 55/yr. Appl fee: $75. Appl due: Feb. Accepted: 76%. Yield: 70%. **Tests** ISEE SSAT. **Enr 295.** B 156. G 139. Intl 8%. Avg class size: 15. Stud/fac: 8:1. Uniform. **Fac 43.** M 6/F 37. FT 43. **Grad '11—21.** Prep—19. **Tui '11-'12:** Day $17,750-18,790. **Est 1975.** Nonprofit. Roman Catholic (70% practice). Tri (Sept-June). **Assoc** MSA. The Woods conducts a Montessori preschool and kindergarten. Students develop foundational skills in mathematics, reading, writing and foreign language, with an emphasis on problem solving, critical thinking and creativity. Both French and Spanish are taught at all grade levels, four days per week in kindergarten and five times per week in grades 1-8. Children may participate in an extended-day program.

ELIZABETH SETON HIGH SCHOOL							**Day Girls Gr 9-12**
Bladensburg, MD 20710. 5715 Emerson St.
Tel: 301-864-4532. Fax: 301-864-8946.
www.setonhs.org   E-mail: admin@setonhs.org
		Sr. Ellen Marie Hagar, Pres (2009). BA, MTh, Mount Saint Mary's Univ, MEd, Boston College, MA, West Virginia Univ. Sharon Pasterick, Prin. BA, Daemen College, MA, Manhattan College, MEd, Bowie State Univ. Melissa Davey, Adm.
		Col Prep. AP (exams req'd; 186 taken, 58% 3+)—Eng Calc Stats Bio Chem Environ_Sci US_Hist Psych US_Govt & Pol. **Feat**—British_Lit Creative_Writing Fr Span Anat & Physiol Comp_Design Comp_Sci Econ Sociol African-Amer_Stud Relig Ceramics Photog Studio_ Art Band Chorus Dance Journ. **Supp**—LD Rem_Math Rem_Read Tut. **Comp:** Comp/Stud: 1:3. **Sports**— G: Basket Crew X-country F_Hockey Lacrosse Soccer Softball Swim Tennis Track Volley. Activities: 20. **Selective adm (Gr 9-11):** 138/yr. Appl fee: $50. Accepted: 63%. Yield: 58%. **Tests** HSPT Stanford. **Enr 608.** Wh 24%. Latino 4%. Blk 49%. Asian 1%. Other 22%. Avg class size: 17. Stud/fac: 12:1. Uniform. **Fac 50.** M 3/F 47. FT 46/PT 4. Wh 81%. Latino 7%. Blk 2%. Native Am 1%. Asian 2%. Other 7%. Adv deg: 72%. **Grad '11—160.** Col—160. (U of MD-Col Park 16, Towson 8, Montgomery Col 6, St John's Col-MD 5, VA Commonwealth 5, U of MD-Baltimore County 4). **Avg SAT:** CR 533. M 502. W 548. Avg ACT: 21. **Col Couns:** 5. Alum donors: 6%. **Tui '11-'12:** Day $10,950 (+$600-700). Aid: Merit 98 ($122,250). Need 204 ($418,525). Work prgm 30 ($24,000). **Est 1959.** Nonprofit. Roman Catholic (41% practice). Quar (Aug-June). **Assoc** MSA. Established by the Daughters of Charity, Elizabeth Seton provides a college preparatory program for students drawn largely from area Catholic elementary and middle schools. Small classes, honors and Advanced Placement offerings, and an emphasis on community service are noteworthy elements of the program. The service program requires students to complete 10 hours of community service per year with a disadvantaged population.

MARYVALE PREPARATORY SCHOOL
Day Girls Gr 6-12

Brooklandville, MD 21022. 11300 Falls Rd.
Tel: 410-252-3366. Fax: 410-308-1497.
www.maryvale.com   E-mail: info@maryvale.com
  Tracey Ford, Pres (2012). BA, Univ of Virginia, MAS, Johns Hopkins Univ. Donna Bridickas, Prin. BS, Towson Univ, MEd, Loyola College. Monica C. Graham, Adm.

  Col Prep. AP (exams req'd)—Eng Fr Span Calc Stats Comp_Sci Bio Chem US_Hist World_Hist. **Feat**—Shakespeare Lat Anat & Physiol Forensic_Sci Marine_Bio/Sci Web_ Design Holocaust Anthro Psych Sociol Relig Graphic_Arts Photog Studio_Art Drama Music. **Comp:** Laptop prgm Gr 6-12. **Dual enr:** Anne Arundel CC. **Sports**— G: Basket X-country F_Hockey Lacrosse Soccer Track Volley. Activities: 20. **Selective adm:** 88/yr. Appl fee: $50. Appl due: Jan. **Tests** HSPT ISEE. **Enr 365.** Wh 88%. Latino 3%. Blk 5%. Asian 2%. Other 2%. Stud/fac: 9:1. Uniform. **Fac 43.** M 6/F 37. FT 40/PT 3. Wh 99%. Latino 1%. Adv deg: 69%. **Grad '09—72.** Col—72. (High Pt 7, U of MD-Col Park 7, Towson 5, Stevenson 3, U of SC 2, Drexel 2). **Avg SAT:** CR 602. M 550. W 613. Avg ACT: 25. Alum donors: 24%. **Tui '11-'12:** Day $15,950 (+$500). **Est 1945.** Inc. Roman Catholic. Quar (Sept-May). **Assoc** MSA. Owned by the Sisters of Notre Dame de Namur, Maryvale occupies a 113-acre former estate. The college preparatory curriculum is conducted in small classes. Semester-long elective courses enable girls to explore such areas of interest as digital photography, forensic science and the Holocaust. Each pupil receives an iPad for school and home use. Students accumulate 100 hours of required community service in grades 9-12.

KENT SCHOOL
Day Coed Gr PS (Age 3)-8

Chestertown, MD 21620. 6788 Wilkins Ln.
Tel: 410-778-4100. Fax: 410-778-7357.
www.kentschool.org   E-mail: admissions@kentschool.org
  Christopher Gorycki, Head (2011). BA, Long Island Univ, MA, Columbia Univ. Beth Collins, Adm.

  Pre-Prep. Feat—Span Environ_Sci Computers Drama. **Supp**—Dev_Read Rev. **Sports**— Basket Lacrosse Soccer. G: F_Hockey. **Selective adm:** 31/yr. Appl fee: $35. Appl due: Rolling. Accepted: 70%. Yield: 86%. **Enr 192.** B 104. G 88. Avg class size: 18. Stud/fac: 8:1. **Fac 24.** M 3/F 21. FT 23/PT 1. Adv deg: 25%. **Grad '09—16.** Prep—14. (Gunston Day 4, St Andrew's Sch-DE 3, Lawrenceville 1, Oldfields 1, St Timothy's 1, Tower Hill 1). Alum donors: 10%. **Tui '12-'13:** Day $8225-13,495 (+$105-495). **Est 1967.** Nonprofit. Tri (Sept-June). Kent places strong emphasis on language arts, mathematics, the arts and athletics. Critical-thinking, research, and organizational skills are taught across disciplines, and an integrated language arts and history program is offered in grades 5 and 6. The school schedules frequent field trips to area museums and the Smithsonian Institute. Interscholastic sports begin in grade 6.

MOUNT AVIAT ACADEMY
Day Coed Gr PS-8

Childs, MD 21916. 399 Childs Rd.
Tel: 410-398-2206. Fax: 410-398-8063.
www.mountaviat.org   E-mail: school@mountaviat.org
  Sr. John Elizabeth Callaghan, OSFS, Prin. BS, Lincoln Univ, MEd, Loyola College.

  Pre-Prep. Feat—Fr Computers Relig Studio_Art Drama Music Speech. **Supp**—Rem_ Read Tut. **Sports**—Basket. G: Softball Volley. **Selective adm:** 32/yr. Appl fee: $10. Appl due: Rolling. Accepted: 20%. **Enr 250.** B 120. G 130. Wh 92%. Latino 2%. Blk 1%. Asian 3%. Other 2%. Avg class size: 26. Stud/fac: 18:1. Uniform. **Fac 19.** M 1/F 18. FT 11/PT 8. Wh 89%. Blk 2%. Asian 4%. Other 5%. Adv deg: 31%. **Grad '11—24.** Prep—21. **Tui '12-'13:** Day $5175 (+$325-350). Aid: Need 35 ($44,000). **Est 1969.** Nonprofit. Roman Catholic. Tri (Sept-June). **Assoc** MSA. Located on 22 acres of rolling countryside, Mount Aviat offers instruction in the basic subjects as well as religion and French at all levels. Elective programs include musical and dramatic presentations, academic competitions, and health and speech courses in grades 5-8. An accelerated math program is offered in grades 5-8.

TRINITY SCHOOL   **Day Coed Gr PS (Age 3)-8**
Ellicott City, MD 21043. 4985 Ilchester Rd.
Tel: 410-744-1524. Fax: 410-744-3617.
www.trinityschoolmd.org   E-mail: admintrin@trinityschoolmd.org
    Sr. Catherine Phelps, SND, Prin (1971). BS, Trinity College (DC), MS, Fordham Univ.
Joan Voshell, Adm.
    Pre-Prep. Feat—Fr Lat Span Relig Studio_Art Drama Music. **Supp**—Dev_Read Rem_
Read Tut. **Comp:** Comp/Stud: 1:3. **Sports**—Basket X-country Soccer. **Selective adm:** 82/yr.
Appl fee: $75. Appl due: Rolling. Accepted: 60%. Yield: 82%. **Enr 382.** B 172. G 210. Wh
58%. Latino 4%. Blk 20%. Asian 13%. Other 5%. Avg class size: 18. Stud/fac: 11:1. Uniform.
Fac 30. M 6/F 24. FT 29/PT 1. Wh 91%. Blk 9%. Adv deg: 56%. **Grad '11—37.** Prep—30.
(Calvert Hall 10, Mt de Sales-MD 4, Our Lady of Good Counsel-MD 4, Mt St Joseph HS 3,
Loyola Blakefield 3, Gilman 1). **Tui '12-'13:** Day $8075-11,995 (+$202-300). Aid: Need 73
($305,590). **Est 1941.** Nonprofit. Roman Catholic (63% practice). Sem (Sept-June). **Assoc**
MSA. The pre-preparatory elementary curriculum at Trinity places particular emphasis upon
reading and writing. Students develop critical-thinking skills through problem-solving techniques, avenues of creative expression and use of the scientific method. Foreign language
classes begin in the primary school, and religion, art, music, drama and athletics are available at all grade levels. Computerized library facilities and science and computer laboratories
enrich the program.

THE BANNER SCHOOL   **Day Coed Gr PS (Age 3)-8**
Frederick, MD 21701. 1730 N Market St.
Tel: 301-695-9320. Fax: 301-695-9336.
www.bannerschool.org   E-mail: lwebb@bannerschool.org
    Stephen R. Parnes, Head (2010). BA, Carleton College, MEd, MA, Harvard Univ. Lauren
Webb, Adm.
    Pre-Prep. Gen Acad. Feat—Span Computers Performing_Arts Studio_Art Music Health.
Supp—Dev_Read Tut. **Comp:** Comp/Stud: 1:3. **Sports**—Basket Soccer Track. G: Volley.
Selective adm: 36/yr. Appl fee: $50. Appl due: Rolling. Accepted: 83%. Yield: 81%. **Enr**
167. Wh 79%. Latino 1%. Blk 7%. Asian 4%. Other 9%. Avg class size: 15. Casual dress.
Fac 23. FT 22/PT 1. Wh 92%. Latino 4%. Other 4%. Adv deg: 39%. **Grad '11—12.** Prep—
7. (St John's Catholic 3, Ss John Neumann & Maria Goretti 3, Acad of the Holy Cross 1).
Alum donors: 1%. **Tui '12-'13:** Day $11,650 (+$250). Aid: Need 65 ($290,175). **Est 1982.**
Nonprofit. Tri (Aug-June). In a small-class environment, Banner conducts a differentiated
program that emphasizes basic skill development, critical thinking and problem solving. The
school's liberal arts course of studies incorporates the arts, world languages and technology.
Students explore interdisciplinary subject matter beyond the curriculum through published
works, at school assemblies and in the community.

SAINT JOHN'S CATHOLIC PREP   **Day Coed Gr 9-12**
Frederick, MD 21703. 889 Butterfly Ln.
Tel: 301-662-4210. Fax: 301-662-5166.
www.saintjohnsprep.org   E-mail: mschultz@saintjohnsprep.org
    Gordon J. Oliver, Pres (2010). Christopher Cosentino, Prin. Michael Schultz, Adm.
    Col Prep. AP (exams req'd; 131 taken, 72% 3+)—Eng Fr Lat Span Calc Stats Bio Chem
Physics Eur_Hist US_Hist Econ US_Govt & Pol Art_Hist Studio_Art. **Feat**—Creative_Writ-
ing Forensic_Sci Sports_Med Comp_Sci Web_Design Civil_War Philos Theol Drawing
Painting Video_Production Band Music_Theory Guitar Finance Journ Nutrition. **Supp**—Tut.
Sports—Basket X-country Lacrosse Soccer Tennis Track. B: Baseball Football. G: Cheer
Softball Volley. Activities: 30. **Somewhat selective adm:** 92/yr. Appl fee: $65. Appl due: Roll-
ing. Accepted: 95%. Yield: 65%. **Tests** HSPT. **Enr 274.** Intl 7%. Avg class size: 15. Stud/fac:
9:1. Uniform. **Fac 26.** M 13/F 13. FT 26. Adv deg: 61%. **Grad '11—50.** Col—50. (Frederick
CC 6, Mt St Mary's-MD 4, Cornell 2, Am U 2, James Madison 2, Towson 2). **Avg SAT:** CR/

M/W 1665. **Tui '12-'13:** Day $13,645 (+$800). **Est 1829.** Nonprofit. Roman Catholic (75% practice). Sem (Aug-June). **Assoc** MSA. The traditional college preparatory program of Saint John's features a full complement of honors and Advanced Placement courses. Technology is an important aspect of the program: Boys and girls develop proficiency in word processing, database management, spreadsheet composition and basic programming. Students perform a minimum of 80 hours of service prior to graduation, with at least 20 hours to be served each year.

HOLY TRINITY EPISCOPAL DAY SCHOOL   Day Coed Gr PS (Age 3)-8
Glenn Dale, MD 20769. 11902 Daisey Ln.
Tel: 301-464-3215. Fax: 301-464-9725.
Other locations: 13106 Annapolis Rd, Bowie 20720.
www.htrinity.org   E-mail: admissions@htrinity.org
Michael S. Mullin, Head (2011). BS, West Chester Univ, MS, Johns Hopkins Univ. Rosalyn Cruz-Williams, Adm.

Pre-Prep. Feat—Span Computers Studio_Art Drama Band Music. **Supp**—Dev_Read Rev. **Comp:** Comp/Stud: 1:3. **Sports**—Basket Soccer Track. **Selective adm:** Appl fee: $75. Appl due: Rolling. **Tests** IQ MAT. **Enr 520.** Wh 9%. Latino 1%. Blk 82%. Asian 2%. Other 6%. Avg class size: 20. Stud/fac: 15:1. Uniform. **Fac 57.** M 9/F 48. FT 54/PT 3. Wh 91%. Blk 9%. Adv deg: 26%. **Grad '10—61.** Prep—50. **Tui '12-'13:** Day $8670-11,530. **Est 1963.** Nonprofit. Episcopal. Sem (Sept-June). **Assoc** MSA. HT offers an integrated academic program complemented by an outdoor education program, Spanish (beginning in kindergarten), computer, music, art, library, chapel and team sports, as well as visits to area cultural and scientific centers. An extended-day program is available. The lower school campus is located on Annapolis Road in Bowie, while the preschool and the middle school hold classes at the Daisy Lane address in Glenn Dale.

THE CALVERTON SCHOOL   Day Coed Gr PS (Age 3)-12
Huntingtown, MD 20639. 300 Calverton School Rd.
Tel: 410-535-0216, 888-678-0216. Fax: 410-535-6934.
www.calvertonschool.org   E-mail: jsimpson@calvertonschool.org
Daniel M. Hildebrand, Head (2004). BA, MEd, Univ of Chicago. Amy Brady, Adm.

Col Prep. AP (exams req'd)—Eng Fr Span Calc Bio Chem Physics US_Hist Psych Studio_Art Music_Theory. **Feat**—Humanities Lat Environ_Sci Ceramics Photog Music. **Supp**—Tut. **Comp:** Laptop prgm Gr 9-12. Outdoor Ed. **Sports**—Basket X-country Golf Lacrosse Soccer Tennis. G: F_Hockey Softball. **Selective adm (Gr PS-11):** 95/yr. Appl fee: $100. Appl due: Rolling. Accepted: 80%. Yield: 60%. **Enr 385.** Wh 80%. Latino 1%. Blk 9%. Asian 3%. Other 7%. Avg class size: 16. Stud/fac: 10:1. Uniform. **Fac 48.** M 14/F 34. FT 46/PT 2. Wh 93%. Blk 6%. Other 1%. Adv deg: 75%. **Grad '10—38.** Col—38. **Tui '12-'13:** Day $14,081-18,998 (+$300). Aid: Merit ($40,000). Need ($300,000). **Est 1967.** Nonprofit. Tri (Sept-June). Calverton's academic program includes Advanced Placement classes in the major disciplines, as well as electives in Chesapeake Bay studies, computer and the arts. The school maintains an active interscholastic sports program and, at the middle and upper school levels, provides students with various opportunities in the visual and performing arts.

DeMATHA CATHOLIC HIGH SCHOOL   Day Boys Gr 9-12
Hyattsville, MD 20781. 4313 Madison St.
Tel: 240-764-2200. Fax: 240-764-2275.
www.demath.org   E-mail: psmith@demath.org
Rev. James Day, OSST, Rector (2011). BA, St Mary's College of Maryland, MEd, Bowie State Univ, MDiv, Oblate College. Daniel J. McMahon, Prin. BA, Mount Saint Mary's College, MA, PhD, Univ of Maryland-College Park. Patrick Smith, Adm.

Col Prep. AP (205 exams taken, 82% 3+)—Eng Fr Ger Lat Span Calc Comp_Sci Bio

Chem Environ_Sci Physics US_Hist US_Govt & Pol Studio_Art. **Feat**—Creative_Writing Mythology Chin Greek Stats Anat & Physiol Astron Forensic_Sci Geol Biotech African-Amer_Hist Psych Theol Ceramics Film Photog Chorus Music Bus Journ. **Supp**—Dev_Read Rev Tut. **Comp:** Comp/Stud: 1:10. **Sports**— B: Baseball Basket Crew X-country Football Golf Ice_Hockey Lacrosse Rugby Soccer Swim Tennis Track Wrestling. Activities: 39. **Selective adm (Gr 9-11):** 277/yr. Appl fee: $50. Appl due: Dec. Accepted: 79%. Yield: 63%. **Tests** HSPT. **Enr 900.** Wh 42%. Latino 4%. Blk 47%. Asian 2%. Other 5%. Avg class size: 20. Stud/fac: 12:1. Uniform. **Fac 78.** M 58/F 20. FT 78. Wh 87%. Latino 3%. Blk 7%. Other 3%. Adv deg: 48%. **Grad '11—231.** Col—227. **Avg SAT:** CR 543. M 551. W 524. **Col Couns:** 1. Alum donors: 6%. **Tui '11-'12:** Day $13,200 (+$250-575). Aid: Merit 219 ($429,150). Need 247 ($740,104). **Est 1946.** Nonprofit. Roman Catholic (68% practice). Quar (Aug-June). **Assoc** MSA. DeMatha's college preparatory curriculum, which accommodates boys of varying ability levels, interests and backgrounds, comprises Advanced Placement, honors and standard courses. A compulsory religious studies program incorporates historical, ethical and psychological viewpoints. Students perform at least 55 hours of community service over four years. The school's athletic and instrumental and choral music programs are quite well regarded.

GRACE EPISCOPAL DAY SCHOOL Day Coed Gr PS (Age 3)-5
Kensington, MD 20895. 9411 Connecticut Ave.
Tel: 301-949-5860. Fax: 301-949-8398.
www.geds.org   E-mail: bhouse@geds.org
  Malcolm C. Lester, Head (2012). BA, Springfield College, MA, College of William and Mary, MA, Trinity Washington Univ. John L. Bonhom II, Adm.
  Pre-Prep. Feat—Lib_Skills Span Computers Studio_Art Music. **Supp**—Dev_Read Rem_ Read. **Sports**—Basket Soccer Track. **Selective adm:** 76/yr. Appl fee: $75. Appl due: Feb. Accepted: 76%. Yield: 80%. **Tests** IQ. **Enr 239.** B 124. G 115. Wh 51%. Latino 7%. Blk 34%. Asian 1%. Other 7%. Avg class size: 16. Stud/fac: 6:1. Uniform. **Fac 35.** M 5/F 30. FT 24/PT 11. Adv deg: 37%. **Grad '08—23.** Prep—21. (St Andrew's Episcopal-MD 2, Bullis 2, Potomac 1, Woods 1, Holton-Arms 1, Field 1). **Tui '12-'13:** Day $16,600-19,535 (+$165). **Est 1960.** Nonprofit. Episcopal (33% practice). Tri (Sept-June). Founded by the Women of Grace Church, this elementary school serves a diverse student body in Metropolitan Washington. All students at Grace attend weekly chapel services. Before- and after-school programming is available.

ST. VINCENT PALLOTTI HIGH SCHOOL Day Coed Gr 9-12
Laurel, MD 20707. 113 St Mary's Pl.
Tel: 301-725-3228. Fax: 301-776-4343.
www.pallottihs.org   E-mail: admissions@pallottihs.org
  David Mackenzie, Pres (2011). Kelly Hawse, Adm.
  Col Prep. AP (exams req'd)—Eng Calc Comp_Sci Bio Chem Eur_Hist US_Hist. **Feat**—British_Lit Fr Lat Span Stats Anat Oceanog Web_Design Psych Sociol Women's_Stud Relig Photog Sculpt Drama Chorus Journ. **Supp**—LD Tut. **Comp:** Laptop prgm Gr 9-12. **Sports**—X-country Lacrosse Soccer Swim Tennis. B: Baseball Football Golf Wrestling. G: Basket Cheer Softball Volley. Activities: 25. **Selective adm (Gr 9-11):** Appl fee: $100. Appl due: Dec. Accepted: 70%. Yield: 50%. **Tests** HSPT. **Enr 510.** B 255. G 255. Avg class size: 18. Uniform. **Fac 38. Grad '08—108.** Col—105. **Col Couns:** 2. **Tui '11-'12:** Day $12,585 (+$400). Aid: Merit 12 ($120,000). Need ($300,000). **Est 1921.** Nonprofit. Roman Catholic. Quar (Sept-June). **Assoc** MSA. Sponsored by the Pallottine Sisters, St. Vincent Pallotti offers both honors and college preparatory tracks, and it also maintains a learning center for college-bound students who have been diagnosed with mild learning disabilities. As part of the campus ministry program, boys and girls perform 80 hours of compulsory community service over their four years. St. Vincent Pallotti draws the majority of its pupils from roughly 60 schools in the Baltimore/Washington, DC, area.

LEONARD HALL JUNIOR NAVAL ACADEMY Day Coed Gr 6-12
Leonardtown, MD 20650. 41740 Baldridge St.
Tel: 301-475-8029. Fax: 301-475-8518.
www.lhjna.com E-mail: suzanne.wisnieski@lhjna.com
Suzanne C. Wisnieski, Head (1996).
  Col Prep. Gen Acad. Milit. Feat—Span Relig SAT_Prep Milit_Sci Naval_Sci. **Supp**—Dev_Read Makeup Tut. **Comp:** Comp/Stud: 1:4. **Sports**—Basket Soccer. Activities: 5. **Somewhat selective adm:** 11/yr. Appl fee: $50. Appl due: Rolling. Accepted: 95%. **Tests** IQ Stanford. **Enr 50.** B 40. G 10. Elem 24. Sec 26. Wh 80%. Latino 5%. Blk 15%. Avg class size: 9. Stud/fac: 9:1. Uniform. **Fac 8.** M 3/F 5. FT 6/PT 2. Wh 100%. Adv deg: 37%. **Grad '11—5.** Col—4. (Col of S MD 2, N GA Col & State U 1, Eckerd 1). Alum donors: 5%. **Tui '11-'12:** Day $7650 (+$400). **Est 1909.** Nonprofit. Sem (Aug-June). LHJNA provides military drill instruction and a full scholastic program that includes religious education. The military curriculum, which mirrors that of the Naval Junior Reserve Officer Training Corps (NJROTC), includes practical classroom work, leadership training, life skills training, military drill and ceremonies, guest speakers and field trips.

ST. JAMES ACADEMY Day Coed Gr K-8
Monkton, MD 21111. 3100 Monkton Rd.
Tel: 410-771-4816. Fax: 410-771-4842.
www.saintjamesacademy.org E-mail: info@saintjamesacademy.org
Karl Adler, Head (2012). MEd, Goucher College. Dianne Fowler, Adm.
  Pre-Prep. IB MYP. Feat—Lib_Skills Fr Lat Span Computers Relig Studio_Art Drama Music. **Supp**—Tut. **Comp:** Laptop prgm Gr 7-8. **Sports**—Basket X-country Lacrosse Soccer. B: Baseball. **Selective adm (Gr K-7):** 57/yr. Appl fee: $60-90. Appl due: Jan. Accepted: 70%. **Tests** IQ. **Enr 349.** Nonwhite 6%. Avg class size: 20. Stud/fac: 8:1. Uniform. **Fac 42.** M 10/F 32. FT 37/PT 5. Adv deg: 35%. **Grad '11—24.** Prep—22. (St Paul's Sch-MD 6, McDonogh 3, St Paul's Sch for Girls 3, Roland Park 3, Loyola Blakefield 2, John Carroll 1). **Tui '12-'13:** Day $13,275-15,500 (+$700-750). **Est 1957.** Nonprofit. Episcopal. Tri (Sept-June). With small classes and individualized instruction, the school emphasizes a firm foundation in English, social studies, math, world languages and information technology. Students in grades 6-8 take part in the International Baccalaureate Middle Years Program. A sports and recreation program, field trips and assemblies supplement the academic curriculum. St. James conducts a weekly chapel service.

THE TOME SCHOOL Day Coed Gr K-12
North East, MD 21901. 581 S Maryland Ave.
Tel: 410-287-2050. Fax: 410-287-8999.
www.tomeschool.org E-mail: e.wohner@tomeschool.org
Elizabeth Wohner, Int Dir (2011). BS, Towson State Univ, MEd, Loyola College (MD).
  Col Prep. AP (37 exams taken, 78% 3+)—Calc. **Feat**—British_Lit Fr Lat Span Environ_Sci Computers Econ Geog Govt Studio_Art Music. **Dual enr:** Cecil CC. **Sports**—Basket X-country Soccer Tennis. B: Baseball. G: F_Hockey Softball. **Selective adm:** 60/yr. Appl due: Rolling. **Tests** Stanford. **Enr 495.** Elem 344. Sec 151. Avg class size: 20. Uniform. **Fac 41.** M 7/F 34. FT 32/PT 9. Adv deg: 24%. **Grad '11—32.** Col—30. **Avg SAT:** CR 598. M 599. W 619. **Tui '11-'12:** Day $6700 (+$200). Aid: Need 148. **Est 1889.** Nonprofit. Quar (Aug-May). Founded by local philanthropist Jacob Tome, the school received its first students in 1894 and has been in continuous operation ever since. In the summer of 1971, the school moved to the 100-acre campus in North East. The curriculum is nonelective and college preparatory. Dual-enrollment college courses are available through Cecil Community College.

THE FOURTH PRESBYTERIAN SCHOOL   **Day Coed Gr PS (Age 3)-8**
Potomac, MD 20854. 10701 S Glen Rd.
Tel: 301-765-8133. Fax: 301-765-8138.
www.fourthschool.org   E-mail: info@fourthschool.org
    John A. Murray, Head (2008). BA, Vanderbilt Univ, MA, Dartmouth College. Karen A.
Janes, Adm.
    Pre-Prep. Gen Acad. Feat—Lat Span Computers Civics Bible Art_Hist Studio_Art The-
ater Music Guitar. **Comp:** Comp/Stud: 1:4. **Sports**—Basket X-country Soccer. B: Baseball.
G: Softball. **Somewhat selective adm:** Appl fee: $100-300. Appl due: Rolling. Accepted:
96%. Yield: 87%. **Tests** CTP_4. **Enr 105.** B 45. G 60. Wh 60%. Latino 2%. Blk 3%. Asian
18%. Other 17%. Avg class size: 12. Stud/fac: 6:1. Uniform. **Fac 20.** M 3/F 17. FT 20. Wh
95%. Blk 5%. Adv deg: 35%. **Grad '11—12. Tui '11-'12:** Day $15,900 (+$50). Aid: Need
31 ($273,000). **Est 1999.** Nonprofit. Presbyterian (23% practice). Tri (Sept-June). Fourth
Presbyterian's curriculum is taught from a Christian worldview. Spanish language instruction commences in kindergarten, with Latin first available in grade 4. Technology instruction
initially addresses basic skills development and interactive lessons and expands to include
keyboarding, Internet research and multimedia publishing applications.

THE GERMAN SCHOOL   **Day Coed Gr PS (Age 2)-12**
Potomac, MD 20854. 8617 Chateau Dr.
Tel: 301-365-4400. Fax: 301-365-3905.
www.dswashington.org   E-mail: mail@dswash.org
    Waldemar Gries, Head (2009). Julia Merck-Rocha, Adm.
    Col Prep. Bilingual (Ger). AP (5 exams taken, 60% 3+)—Eng Fr Ger Span Calc Bio
Chem Physics. **Feat**—Lat Studio_Art Music. **Supp**—Tut. **Sports**—Basket Soccer Swim
Track Volley. **Somewhat selective adm (Gr PS-11):** 132/yr. Appl due: Rolling. Accepted:
90%. **Enr 565.** B 261. G 304. Intl 80%. Avg class size: 20. Casual dress. **Fac 73.** M 17/F 56.
Adv deg: 60%. **Grad '11—27.** Col—27. (Cornell 1, U of VA 1, Tulane 1, U of CA-Berkeley
1, James Madison 1, Loyola U MD 1). **Avg SAT:** CR 640. M 635. W 639. **Tui '11-'12:** Day
$11,850-13,250 (+$2000-3800). **Est 1961.** Nonprofit. Sem (Aug-June). Serving an international student body, the school follows the curricular guidelines set by the German Ministry of
Education, and the Maryland State Department of Education. The secondary school comprises
three sections: entry level (grade 5), intermediate level (grades 6-10) and upper level (grades
11 and 12). Upper level students work toward the German Abitur.

THE HEIGHTS SCHOOL   **Day Boys Gr 3-12**
Potomac, MD 20854. 10400 Seven Locks Rd.
Tel: 301-365-4300. Fax: 301-365-4303.
www.heights.edu   E-mail: rconaty@heights.edu
    Alvaro J. de Vicente, Head (2002). BA, JD, Georgetown Univ. Rich Moss, Adm.
    Col Prep. AP (213 exams taken, 70% 3+)—Eng Lat Span Calc Stats Comp_Sci Bio
Chem Physics Eur_Hist US_Hist Econ US_Govt & Pol Art_Hist Music_Theory. **Feat**—Greek
Multivariable_Calc Anat & Physiol Environ_Sci Cold_War Russ_Hist Ethics Philos Relig
Studio_Art Music_Hist Woodworking. **Supp**—Tut. **Sports**— B: Baseball Basket X-country
Golf Lacrosse Soccer Squash Swim Tennis Track Ultimate_Frisbee Wrestling. Activities: 27.
Selective adm: 98/yr. Appl fee: $50. Appl due: Jan. **Tests** SSAT. **Enr 460.** Avg class size: 15.
Stud/fac: 7:1. Formal dress. **Fac 60.** M 58/F 2. FT 60. Adv deg: 71%. **Grad '11—54. Tui '12-
'13:** Day $16,400-21,950 (+$350-600). Aid: Need 138. **Est 1969.** Nonprofit. Roman Catholic.
Quar (Sept-June). **Assoc** MSA. A largely male staff leads this Catholic boys' school's liberal
arts, college preparatory curriculum. Students in the upper school (grades 9-12) engage in
Crescite Week, an enrichment program that consists of on-campus classes and domestic and
international travel options. At all grade levels, each boy attends a monthly meeting with his
advisor; in addition, he meets with the headmaster at least once during the year to discuss his
schedule for the following school year.

CHARLES E. SMITH JEWISH DAY SCHOOL   **Day Coed Gr K-12**
Rockville, MD 20852. 1901 E Jefferson St.
Tel: 301-881-1400. Fax: 301-984-7834.
Other locations: 11710 Hunters Ln, Rockville 20852.
www.cesjds.org   E-mail: cesjds@cesjds.org
    Jonathan Cannon, Head (2001). BS, Univ of Leeds (England), MA, Univ of London (England). Robin Shapiro, Upper Sch Adm; Pam Shrock, Int Lower Sch Adm.
    Col Prep. AP exams taken: 71 (93% 3+).

Feat—Creative_Writing Shakespeare Hebrew Span Arabic Calc Stats Genetics Sports_Med Comp_Sci Bible Comp_Relig Ethics Judaic_ Stud Rabbinics Ceramics Photog Studio_Art Music Journ. **Supp**—ESL. **Sports**—Basket X-country Golf Soccer Tennis Track. B: Baseball Volley. G: Softball. Activities: 26. **Somewhat selective adm:** 187/yr. Appl fee: $100. Appl due: Jan. Accepted: 90%. **Enr 1514.** Elem 1076. Sec 438. Wh 97%. Latino 1%. Blk 1%. Asian 1%. Avg class size: 17. Stud/fac: 8:1. **Fac 134.** Adv deg: 79%. **Grad '11—112.** Col—111. **Mid 50% SAT:** CR 580-690. M 570-710. W 590-700. Mid 50% ACT: 24-30. **Col Couns:** 3. **Tui '11-'12:** Day $20,490-26,290 (+$65-385). **Est 1966.** Nonprofit. Jewish. (Sept-June). **Assoc** MSA.   Drawing its students from the Metropolitan Washington, DC, area, this school offers a rigorous college preparatory curriculum featuring Hebrew instruction at all grade levels, as well as Judaic studies classes. The school observes Jewish religious practices. Pupils may participate in a five-month academic and travel program to Israel after graduation. The upper school occupies a separate campus on Hunters Lane.

MELVIN J. BERMAN HEBREW ACADEMY   **Day Coed Gr PS (Age 2)-12**
Rockville, MD 20853. 13300 Arctic Ave.
Tel: 301-962-9400. Fax: 301-962-3991.
www.mjbha.org   E-mail: butlers@mjbha.org
    Joshua Levisohn, Head (2006). BA, PhD, Harvard Univ. Sharon Butler, Adm.
    Col Prep. AP (124 exams taken, 82% 3+)—Eng Calc Stats Comp_Sci Bio Chem Physics Eur_Hist Econ Psych Studio_Art. **Feat**—Hebrew Arabic Bible Judaic_Stud Ceramics Photog Journ. **Supp**—Dev_Read LD Makeup Rem_Math Rem_Read Rev Tut. **Sports**—Basket Soccer Tennis Track Volley. B: Baseball. **Selective adm:** 109/yr. Appl fee: $50. Appl due: Apr. **Enr 700.** Elem 526. Sec 174. Wh 100%. Intl 8%. Avg class size: 18. Casual dress. **Fac 120.** Adv deg: 36%. **Grad '11—31.** Col—31. **Avg SAT:** CR 597. M 588. W 584. Avg ACT: 22. **Tui '12-'13:** Day $13,750-20,200 (+$1150-1330). **Est 1944.** Nonprofit. Jewish (100% practice). Sem (Aug-June).   The academy's curriculum provides religious and secular education, including Hebrew for pupils in grades K-12 and a selection of Advanced Placement and accelerated courses. Pupils may also engage in independent or off-campus study of accelerated classes. Boys and girls attend single-gender Judaic studies courses in grades 6-12. Most students enter competitive colleges upon graduation, although some defer college admission to spend a year in Israel.

THE SALISBURY SCHOOL   **Day Coed Gr PS (Age 3)-12**
Salisbury, MD 21804. 6279 Hobbs Rd.
Tel: 410-742-4464. Fax: 410-912-0896.
www.thesalisburyschool.org   E-mail: info@thesalisburyschool.org
    James G. Landi, Head (2009). BA, Ohio Northern Univ, MA, Montclair St College. Gail Carozza, Adm.
    Col Prep. AP (exams req'd; 64 taken)—Eng Lat Span Calc Stats Bio Environ_Sci US_ Hist World_Hist Human_Geog Psych US_Govt & Pol Art_Hist Studio_Art. **Feat**—Humanities Fr Comp_Relig Philos Video_Production Stained_Glass Drama Band Chorus. **Supp**—LD Tut. **Comp:** Laptop prgm Gr 9-12. **Sports**—Basket X-country Golf Lacrosse Soccer Tennis. Activities: 24. **Selective adm:** 45/yr. Appl fee: $75. Appl due: Rolling. Accepted: 77%. **Tests** ISEE. **Enr 345.** Elem 242. Sec 103. Wh 71%. Latino 8%. Blk 5%. Asian 6%. Other 10%. Intl 18%. Avg class size: 12. **Fac 66.** M 20/F 46. Wh 89%. Latino 4%. Blk 7%. Adv deg: 43%. **Grad '11—22.** Col—22. **Avg SAT:** CR/M 1196. **Col Couns:** 1. **Tui '11-'12:** Day $5800-

13,950. Aid: Need 50 ($199,000). **Est 1970.** Nonprofit. Tri (Sept-June). Situated on 45 acres, Salisbury has a modified open-learning environment and traditional college preparatory academics. All upper school students use laptop computers, and every pupil satisfies a 40-hour community service requirement prior to graduation.

ARCHBISHOP SPALDING HIGH SCHOOL   **Day Coed Gr 9-12**
Severn, MD 21144. 8080 New Cut Rd.
Tel: 410-969-9105. Fax: 410-969-1026.
www.archbishopspalding.org   E-mail: millert@archbishopspalding.org
  Kathleen K. Mahar, Pres (2011). MA, George Washington Univ. Lewis R. Van Wambeke, Prin. MA, College of Notre Dame of Maryland. Thomas E. Miller, Adm.

  Col Prep. AP (exams req'd; 568 taken, 87% 3+)—Eng Lat Span Calc Stats Comp_Sci Bio Chem Environ_Sci Physics Eur_Hist US_Hist Econ Psych US_Govt & Pol Studio_Art. **Feat**—Fr Forensic_Sci Marine_Bio/Sci Sports_Med Engineering Bus_Law Graphic_Arts Orchestra. **Supp**—LD Rev Tut. **Comp:** Comp/Stud: 1:3.3. **Dual enr:** Anne Arundel CC. **Sports**—Basket X-country Lacrosse Soccer Swim Tennis Track Volley. B: Baseball Football Golf Ice_Hockey Rugby Wrestling. G: Cheer F_Hockey Softball. Activities: 15. **Selective adm (Gr 9-11):** 315/yr. Appl fee: $100. Appl due: Jan. Accepted: 54%. Yield: 88%. **Tests** HSPT. **Enr 1230.** B 632. G 598. Wh 86%. Latino 3%. Blk 7%. Native Am 1%. Asian 3%. Avg class size: 21. Uniform. **Fac 90.** M 55/F 35. FT 89/PT 1. Wh 90%. Latino 4%. Blk 5%. Asian 1%. Adv deg: 63%. **Grad '11—285.** Col—284. **Avg SAT:** CR 547. M 546. **Tui '12-'13:** Day $12,950 (+$500). Aid: Merit 48 ($216,000). Need 308 ($1,600,000). **Est 1966.** Nonprofit. Roman Catholic (78% practice). Quar (Aug-June). **Assoc** MSA. Spalding offers a broad selection of Advanced Placement, honors and college preparatory courses. Extensive music and fine arts options are part of the curriculum. The school's Aquinas Program, available for an additional fee, serves college-bound students with varying information processing skills in the areas of reading and language. Students accumulate 60 hours of required community service during their four years.   **See Also Page 70**

CHELSEA SCHOOL   **Day Coed Gr 5-12**
Silver Spring, MD 20910. 711 Pershing Dr.
Tel: 301-585-1430. Fax: 301-585-0245.
www.chelseaschool.edu   E-mail: information@chelseaschool.edu
  Katherine Fedalen, Head (2012). MEd. Deborah Lourie, Adm.

  Col Prep. LD. AP—Eng Comp_Sci. **Feat**—Span Anat & Physiol Govt Ceramics Graphic_ Arts Performing_Arts Studio_Art Video_Production Music_Theory. **Supp**—Dev_Read Rem_ Math Rem_Read Tut. Sat classes. **Sports**—Basket Soccer Softball Track. **Selective adm:** 18/yr. Appl fee: $50. Appl due: Rolling. Accepted: 52%. **Tests** IQ. **Enr 74.** Elem 15. Sec 59. Wh 36%. Latino 5%. Blk 58%. Native Am 1%. Avg class size: 8. **Fac 19.** M 10/F 9. FT 19. Wh 74%. Latino 5%. Blk 21%. Adv deg: 52%. **Grad '11—23.** Col—21. **Tui '12-'13:** Day $36,060. Aid: Need 13 ($240,203). **Est 1976.** Nonprofit. Quar (Sept-June). Learning strategies are integral to the education this school offers to students with learning disabilities. The curriculum focuses on academic preparation for college and career transition. Students incur additional hourly fees for counseling, speech-language therapy and occupational therapy. All boys and girls fulfill a 60-hour community service requirement prior to graduation.

THE NORA SCHOOL   **Day Coed Gr 9-12**
Silver Spring, MD 20910. 955 Sligo Ave.
Tel: 301-495-6672. Fax: 301-495-7829.
www.nora-school.org   E-mail: janette.patterson@faculty.nora-school.org
  David E. Mullen, Head (1991). BMus, New England Conservatory of Music, MEd, Univ of Maryland-College Park. Marcia Miller, Adm.

  Col Prep. Feat—Creative_Writing Shakespeare African-Amer_Lit Sci_Fiction Ger Span

Astron Environ_Sci Comp_Sci Pol_Sci Psych African_Stud Peace_Stud Comp_Relig Ethics World_Relig Art_Hist Photog Sculpt Music. **Supp**—LD Rem_Math Rev Tut. **Comp:** Comp/ Stud: 1:2. **Sports**—Basket Soccer Softball. **Selective adm (Gr 9-11):** 20/yr. Appl fee: $75. Appl due: Rolling. Accepted: 70%. Yield: 85%. **Enr 53.** B 30. G 23. Wh 56%. Latino 15%. Blk 25%. Asian 4%. Avg class size: 8. Stud/fac: 5:1. **Fac 9.** M 6/F 3. FT 8/PT 1. Wh 72%. Latino 7%. Blk 14%. Asian 7%. Adv deg: 88%. **Grad '10—16.** Col—15. **Avg SAT:** CR 600. M 520. W 565. Avg ACT: 29. **Tui '12-'13:** Day $24,550 (+$800). Aid: Need ($101,250). **Est 1964.** Nonprofit. Sem (Aug-June). **Assoc MSA.** This small school limits its classes to 12 students, thereby enabling instructors to formulate appropriate learning strategies for boys and girls with various learning styles. All pupils participate in community service one school day per month. The junior and senior classes embark on retreats, and Nora schedules school-sponsored trips during spring break. The school's proximity to Washington, DC, provides experiential learning opportunities for students at museums, galleries and government facilities.

LOYOLA BLAKEFIELD   Day Boys Gr 6-12
Towson, MD 21285. PO Box 6819.
Tel: 443-841-3680. Fax: 443-841-3105.
www.loyolablakefield.org   E-mail: plondon@loyolablakefield.org
Rev. Thomas A. Pesci, SJ, Pres (2005). BA, Fordham Univ, MA, Univ of North Carolina-Chapel Hill, MDiv, Weston Jesuit School of Theology. Anthony I. Day, Prin. BA, St Peter's College, MEd, Fordham Univ, MLitt, Drew Univ. Michael R. Breschi, Adm.

Col Prep. AP (338 exams taken, 91% 3+)—Eng Fr Ger Lat Span Calc Stats Comp_Sci Bio Chem Environ_Sci Physics Eur_Hist US_Hist US_Govt & Pol. **Feat**—Creative_Writing Greek Engineering Econ Relig Photog Music Accounting. **Supp**—LD Rev Tut. **Comp:** Comp/ Stud: 1:3. **Sports**— B: Baseball Basket X-country Football Golf Ice_Hockey Indoor_Track Lacrosse Rugby Soccer Squash Swim Tennis Track Volley W_Polo Wrestling. Activities: 30. **Somewhat selective adm (Gr 6-11):** 217/yr. Appl fee: $35. Appl due: Dec. Accepted: 86%. Yield: 58%. **Tests** HSPT ISEE. **Enr 1000.** Elem 259. Sec 741. Wh 85%. Latino 2%. Blk 9%. Asian 3%. Other 1%. Avg class size: 20. Stud/fac: 10:1. Formal dress. **Fac 93.** M 67/F 26. FT 87/PT 6. Wh 92%. Latino 4%. Blk 4%. Adv deg: 84%. **Grad '11—169.** Col—166. (U of MD-Col Park 17, VA Polytech 12, U of SC 8, Loyola U MD 7, James Madison 5, Col of Charleston 5). **Avg SAT:** CR 610. M 615. W 592. **Col Couns:** 5. Alum donors: 63%. **Tui '12-'13:** Day $16,935 (+$725). Aid: Need 320 ($2,608,178). **Est 1852.** Nonprofit. Roman Catholic (80% practice). Quar (Sept-June). The traditional college preparatory curriculum at Blakefield offers honors and Advanced Placement courses, as well as electives for qualified juniors and seniors. All students must complete a program in social service, computer instruction, art, music appreciation and religious studies. A compulsory project consisting of 40 hours of Christian service commences halfway through junior year and concludes by early May of senior year.

NOTRE DAME PREPARATORY SCHOOL   Day Girls Gr 6-12
Towson, MD 21286. 815 Hampton Ln.
Tel: 410-825-6202. Fax: 410-825-0982.
www.notredameprep.com   E-mail: admissions@notredameprep.com
Sr. Patricia McCarron, SSND, Head (2005). PhD, Catholic Univ of America. Laurie Jones, Prin. Katherine R. Goetz, Adm.

Col Prep. AP (313 exams taken, 85% 3+)—Eng Fr Span Calc Stats Comp_Sci Bio Chem Physics US_Hist Econ US_Govt & Pol Art_Hist Studio_Art Music_Theory. **Feat**—Creative_Writing Shakespeare Japan Anat & Physiol Environ_Sci Forensic_Sci Marine_Bio/Sci Relig Architect_Drawing Photog Music Journ. **Supp**—Tut. **Comp:** Laptop prgm Gr 9-12. **Sports**— G: Badminton Basket X-country F_Hockey Golf Lacrosse Soccer Softball Tennis Track Volley. Activities: 22. **Selective adm (Gr 6-11):** 155/yr. Appl fee: $75. Appl due: Dec. Accepted: 45%. Yield: 65%. **Tests** HSPT ISEE Stanford. **Enr 773.** Elem 169. Sec 604. Wh 84%. Latino 6%. Blk 2%. Asian 5%. Other 3%. Avg class size: 17. Stud/fac: 9:1. Uniform.

Fac 91. FT 80/PT 11. Wh 93%. Latino 3%. Blk 2%. Asian 1%. Other 1%. Adv deg: 80%. **Grad '11—133.** Col—133. (U of MD-Col Park 26, VA Polytech 8, U of DE 7, Salisbury 6, Elon 5, U of SC 5). **Avg SAT:** CR 613. M 611. W 637. Avg ACT: 26.3. **Col Couns:** 3. Alum donors: 19%. **Tui '11-'12:** Day $16,300 (+$1000-3000). Aid: Need 185 ($1,116,560). **Est 1873.** Nonprofit. Roman Catholic (85% practice). Sem (Sept-June). **Assoc** CLS MSA. The school utilizes a multi-phase approach in which the academic needs of all students are met. NDP, which is owned and operated by the School Sisters of Notre Dame, gears classes in each discipline toward college preparation by grade 9. All grades participate in appropriate social service activities, and several upper-grade courses combine classroom instruction with direct service within the Baltimore community. Seniors devote 40 hours toward direct service work with the disadvantaged (work may begin during the last quarter of junior year).

NEW JERSEY

THE KING'S CHRISTIAN SCHOOL   Day Coed Gr PS (Age 3)-12
Cherry Hill, NJ 08003. 5 Carnegie Plz.
Tel: 856-489-6724. Fax: 856-489-6727.
www.tkcs.org   E-mail: info@tkcs.org
    John Walsh, Co-Prin. MA, Glassboro State College. Jane Fort, Co-Prin. BS, King's College (NY), MEd, Rutgers Univ. Sue Trimble, Adm.
    Col Prep. AP (exams req'd)—Eng Calc Bio US_Hist Music_Theory. **Feat**—Span Anat & Physiol Environ_Sci Comp_Sci Global_Stud Bible Studio_Art Chorus Handbells Accounting Speech SAT_Prep. **Supp**—ESL LD Makeup Rem_Math Rem_Read Tut. **Comp:** Comp/Stud: 1:7. **Dual enr:** IN Wesleyan, Davis Col-NY. **Sports**—Basket X-country Soccer Track. B: Baseball. G: Cheer Softball. **Somewhat selective adm:** 60/yr. Appl fee: $200. Appl due: Rolling. **Tests** IQ SSAT Stanford TOEFL. **Enr 321.** Elem 161. Sec 160. Avg class size: 16. Uniform. **Fac 36.** M 9/F 27. FT 27/PT 9. Adv deg: 30%. **Grad '10—28.** Col—23. **Avg SAT:** CR 561. M 546. W 554. Avg ACT: 23. **Tui '12-'13:** Day $6900-8115 (+$450-900). **Est 1946.** Nonprofit. Nondenom Christian (100% practice). Quar (Sept-June). **Assoc** MSA. The elementary years (grades PS-5) provide children with a foundation in reading and math and, beginning in grade 4, an introduction to Spanish. In the middle school (grades 6-8), students take special courses in art, music, library and foreign language on a rotating basis; each pupil must also take a fine arts elective. High schoolers (grades 9-12) choose from honors and Advanced Placement courses, as well as various online options. Students satisfy the following community service requirements: 10 hours annually in grades 6-8, 15 hours in grade 9, 20 hours in grade 10, and 25 hours per year in grades 11 and 12.

HOLY CROSS HIGH SCHOOL   Day Coed Gr 9-12
Delran, NJ 08075. 5035 Rte 130 S.
Tel: 856-461-5400. Fax: 856-764-0806.
www.holycrosshighschool.org   E-mail: kevin.esmond@holycrosshighschool.org
    Dennis M. Guida, Prin (2006). BA, Univ of Scranton, MAT, Marygrove College. Kevin Esmond, Adm.
    Col Prep. AP (119 exams taken, 34% 3+)—Eng Calc Bio Chem US_Hist Econ. **Feat**—Creative_Writing Shakespeare Mythology Ger Lat Stats Anat & Physiol Environ_Sci Forensic_Sci Geol Marine_Bio/Sci Milit_Hist Geog Govt Law Psych Sociol Film Photog Acting Music Music_Theory Accounting Journ. **Supp**—Tut. **Comp:** Comp/Stud: 1:1 Laptop prgm Gr 9-12. **Dual enr:** Burlington County, Seton Hall. **Sports**—Basket Bowl X-country Lacrosse Soccer Swim Tennis Track. B: Baseball Football Golf Wrestling. G: Cheer F_Hockey Softball. Activities: 36. **Selective adm:** 148/yr. Appl fee: $40-55. Appl due: Dec. **Tests** HSPT. **Enr 601.** B 315. G 286. Wh 73%. Latino 3%. Blk 14%. Asian 2%. Other 8%. Avg class size: 25. Stud/fac: 16:1. Uniform. **Fac 39.** M 23/F 16. FT 38/PT 1. Wh 95%. Latino 5%. Adv deg: 61%.

Grad '11—186. Col—184. (Rutgers 18, PA St 8, Monmouth U 6, Neumann 6, St Joseph's U 6, Holy Family 4). **Avg SAT:** CR 509. M 503. W 513. Avg ACT: 21.5. **Col Couns: 2. Tui '11-'12:** Day $8850 (+$690-955). Aid: Need 174. **Est 1957.** Nonprofit. Roman Catholic (85% practice). Sem (Sept-June). **Assoc MSA.** Emphasizing Christian values, HCHS supplements its curriculum with art, music, clubs and community work. Students lease tablet computers for classroom use. Boys and girls satisfy the following community service requirements: 10 hours in grade 9, 15 hours in grade 10, 20 hours in grade 11 and 25 hours in grade 12.

ACADEMY OF THE HOLY ANGELS   Day Girls Gr 9-12
Demarest, NJ 07627. 315 Hillside Ave.
Tel: 201-768-7822. Fax: 201-768-6933.
www.holyangels.org   E-mail: info@holyangels.org
Sr. Virginia Bobrowski, SSND, Pres (2005). MS. Jennifer Moran, Prin. MA. Michele Sovak, Adm.

Col Prep. AP (exams req'd; 235 taken)—Eng Fr Lat Span Calc Bio Chem Physics US_Hist US_Govt & Pol Art_Hist Studio_Art. **Feat**—Creative_Writing Ger Ital Stats Anat & Physiol Comp_Sci Web_Design Film Theater_Arts Journ. **Supp**—Tut. **Comp:** Comp/Stud: 1:1 Laptop prgm Gr 9-12. **Dual enr:** Fairleigh Dickinson. **Sports**— G: Basket Bowl X-country Fencing Golf Lacrosse Soccer Softball Tennis Track Volley. Activities: 55. **Selective adm (Gr 9-10):** 154/yr. Appl fee: $20-75. Appl due: Nov. Accepted: 52%. Yield: 82%. **Enr 550.** Wh 63%. Latino 16%. Blk 7%. Asian 14%. Avg class size: 19. Stud/fac: 11:1. Uniform. **Fac 55.** M 10/F 45. FT 52/PT 3. Wh 100%. Adv deg: 72%. **Grad '10—125.** Col—125. **Avg SAT:** CR 607. M 590. W 627. **Col Couns: 3. Tui '11-'12:** Day $13,900 (+$1450). Aid: Merit 42 ($30,000). Need 81 ($45,000). **Est 1879.** Nonprofit. Roman Catholic. Quar (Sept-June). **Assoc MSA.** Located on a well-equipped, 24-acre campus, this school provides a college prep program including Advanced Placement and honors courses in most disciplines, extensive fine arts offerings and enrichment day trips to nearby New York City. Each girl must purchase a tablet computer for school use. Opportunities for European travel and study abroad are available.

BENEDICTINE ACADEMY   Day Girls Gr 9-12
Elizabeth, NJ 07208. 840 N Broad St.
Tel: 908-352-0670. Fax: 908-352-0698.
www.benedictineacad.org   E-mail: abranco@benedictineacad.org
Sr. Germaine Fritz, OSB, Pres. Kenneth Jennings, Prin. Analisa Branco, Adm.

Col Prep. AP (63 exams taken, 38% 3+)—Eng Fr Span Bio Chem Environ_Sci US_Hist Psych US_Govt & Pol. **Feat**—British_Lit Lat Calc Anat & Physiol Comp_Sci Web_Design Theol Art_Hist Drawing Painting Photog Studio_Art Music. **Supp**—Rem_Math Rem_Read Tut. **Comp:** Laptop prgm Gr 9-12. **Sports**— G: Basket Cheer Soccer Softball Track Volley. Activities: 28. **Selective adm (Gr 9-11):** 62/yr. Appl due: Feb. Accepted: 50%. Yield: 75%. **Enr 170.** Wh 16%. Latino 29%. Blk 43%. Asian 8%. Other 4%. Avg class size: 14. Uniform. **Fac 20.** M 5/F 15. FT 20. Wh 70%. Latino 10%. Blk 10%. Asian 10%. Adv deg: 70%. **Grad '04—43.** Col—43. **Avg SAT:** CR 493. M 486. W 530. **Col Couns: 1. Tui '12-'13:** Day $6950 (+$500). **Est 1915.** Nonprofit. Roman Catholic. Quar (Sept-June). **Assoc MSA.** Conducted in the Benedictine tradition, the academy places significant emphasis on Christian values. The diverse student population, which enrolls from Union and Essex counties, follows a college preparatory liberal arts program that includes Advanced Placement course work. Each student receives a laptop computer for school and home use.

VILLA VICTORIA ACADEMY   Day Girls Gr PS (Age 3)-12
Ewing, NJ 08628. 376 W Upper Ferry Rd.
Tel: 609-882-1700. Fax: 609-882-8421.
www.villavictoria.org   E-mail: admissions@villavictoria.org

Sr. Lillian Harrington, MPF, Pres. BS, Trenton State College, MS, Univ of Notre Dame.
Col Prep. AP (exams req'd; 68 taken, 54% 3+)—Eng Fr Span Calc Chem US_Hist US_Govt & Pol Studio_Art. **Feat**—Creative_Writing Anat & Physiol Comp_Sci Psych Sociol Relig World_Relig Art_Hist Film Painting Chorus Music. **Comp:** Comp/Stud: 1:2. **Sports**— G: Basket X-country Soccer Softball Tennis Track. Activities: 13. **Very selective adm (Gr K-10):** 40/yr. Appl fee: $50. Appl due: Rolling. Accepted: 15%. **Tests** SSAT. **Enr 221.** Elem 140. Sec 81. Avg class size: 20. Uniform. **Fac 30.** M 6/F 24. FT 24/PT 6. Adv deg: 40%. **Grad '08—19.** Col—19. (Villanova 2, Johns Hopkins 1, NYU 1, Catholic U 1, Geo Wash 1, UNC-Chapel Hill 1). **Avg SAT:** CR 617. M 608. W 639. Alum donors: 50%. **Tui '12-'13:** Day $8240-11,850 (+$400). Aid: Merit 55 ($50,450). Need 25 ($50,000). **Est 1933.** Nonprofit. Roman Catholic (64% practice). Sem (Sept-June). **Assoc** MSA. Multimedia instruction; private music, dance, acting and art lessons; student government; and athletics supplement the traditional curriculum at Villa Victoria. The school offers Spanish instruction beginning in kindergarten; an extensive fine arts curriculum in grades 7-12; art, music and computer discovery classes in grade 9; and Advanced Placement courses for juniors and seniors. Girls satisfy the following community service requirements: nine hours per year in grades 7 and 8, 18 hours annually in grades 9-12.

BAPTIST REGIONAL SCHOOL   Day Coed Gr K-12
Haddon Heights, NJ 08035. 3rd & Station Aves.
Tel: 856-547-2996. Fax: 856-547-6584.
www.baptistregional.org   E-mail: bhs@baptistregional.org
Lynn L. Conahan, Admin. BS, Cedarville College.
    Col Prep. Gen Acad. AP—Eng Calc US_Hist World_Hist Music_Theory. **Feat**—Creative_Writing Fr Span Stats Anat & Physiol Programming Civics Econ Bible Studio_Art Drama Chorus Music Accounting. **Supp**—Rem_Math Rem_Read Tut. **Sports**—Basket X-country Soccer Track. B: Baseball Golf. G: Cheer Softball. **Nonselective adm:** 62/yr. Appl fee: $100. Appl due: Rolling. Accepted: 100%. **Tests** Stanford. **Enr 300.** Avg class size: 25. **Fac 20.** M 8/F 12. FT 16/PT 4. Wh 95%. Blk 5%. Adv deg: 25%. **Grad '08—48.** Col—43. **Avg SAT:** CR/M 1090. Avg ACT: 22. **Tui '11-'12:** Day $7050-7800 (+$225). **Est 1972.** Nonprofit. Baptist. Sem (Sept-June). **Assoc** MSA. Founded to assist parents in the religious teaching of their children, the school enrolls a large number of Baptist students, as well as Christians of other denominations. Advanced courses in math, science, English and foreign languages are complemented by business and general programs. Bible study is a curricular requirement.

HADDONFIELD FRIENDS SCHOOL   Day Coed Gr PS (Age 3)-8
Haddonfield, NJ 08033. 47 N Haddon Ave.
Tel: 856-429-6786. Fax: 856-429-6376.
www.haddonfieldfriends.org   E-mail: strezza@haddonfieldfriends.org
Sharon Dreese, Head (2007). BS, Bloomsburg Univ, MA, Lehigh Univ. Sandy Trezza, Adm.
    Pre-Prep. Feat—Span Environ_Sci Studio_Art Music. **Sports**—X-country. **Selective adm:** 43/yr. Appl fee: $100. Appl due: Rolling. Accepted: 80%. **Enr 154.** B 76. G 78. Avg class size: 11. Stud/fac: 8:1. **Fac 23. Grad '05—8.** Prep—6. **Tui '12-'13:** Day $13,700-14,900 (+$150). **Est 1786.** Nonprofit. Religious Society of Friends. Tri (Sept-June). **Assoc** MSA. This Quaker school provides instruction in language arts, math, science, social studies, art, music, Spanish and physical education. HFS organizes service projects for its student body throughout the year, some of which are sponsored and managed by individual classes, others of which are handled by a service committee. The extended day program, which includes activity clubs, offers student care before and after school for an additional fee.

NEWGRANGE SCHOOL OF PRINCETON   **Day Coed Ages 7-21**
Hamilton, NJ 08629. 526 S Olden Ave.
Tel: 609-584-1800. Fax: 609-584-6166.
www.thenewgrange.org   E-mail: info@thenewgrange.org
    Gordon F. Sherman, Exec Dir (2000). PhD, Univ of Connecticut. Bob Hegedus, Prin. MA.
    Col Prep. Gen Acad. LD. Feat—Comp_Sci Studio_Art Music Study_Skills. **Supp**—
Dev_Read Rem_Math Rem_Read Tut. **Comp:** Comp/Stud: 1:1 **Selective adm:** Appl fee: $0.
Appl due: Rolling. **Enr 120.** Wh 64%. Latino 5%. Blk 30%. Asian 1%. Avg class size: 15.
Stud/fac: 2:1. **Fac 55.** M 12/F 43. FT 50/PT 5. Wh 98%. Blk 1%. Other 1%. Adv deg: 40%.
Grad '07—3. Col—1. **Tui '11-'12:** Day $46,134. **Est 1977.** Nonprofit. Sem (Sept-June).
Newgrange offers an individualized, intensive and full-time academic program for students
with learning difficulties. Basic skills and problem solving are stressed, and a full remedial and
tutorial program is available. The average length of stay is three years; some students remain
until graduation, while others move on to district or other schools.

THE HUDSON SCHOOL   **Day Coed Gr 5-12**
Hoboken, NJ 07030. 601 Park Ave.
Tel: 201-659-8335. Fax: 201-222-3669.
www.thehudsonschool.org   E-mail: hudson@thehudsonschool.org
    Suellen F. Newman, Dir (1978). BA, Oberlin College, MA, Univ of Chicago.
    Col Prep. AP (exams req'd; 12 taken, 33% 3+)—Fr Ger Japan Lat Span Calc Comp_Sci
Bio Chem Physics US_Hist Psych Art_Hist. **Feat**—Classics Creative_Writing Mythology
Greek Anat & Physiol Environ_Sci Microbio Web_Design Anthro Comp_Relig Philos Film
Photog Studio_Art Video_Production Drama Chorus Music Music_Theory. **Supp**—ESL Tut.
Sports—Basket Soccer Track. G: Softball. **Selective adm:** 55/yr. Appl fee: $50. Appl due:
Dec. Accepted: 33%. **Tests** ISEE SSAT. **Enr 182.** B 74. G 108. Wh 57%. Latino 11%. Blk
14%. Asian 8%. Other 10%. Avg class size: 18. **Fac 40.** M 15/F 25. FT 22/PT 18. Wh 84%.
Latino 8%. Blk 3%. Asian 5%. Adv deg: 60%. **Grad '11—20.** Col—19. (Tufts 1, Marquette
1, Lewis & Clark 1, Prescott 1, U of WI-Madison 1, Col of NJ 1). **Avg SAT:** CR 601. M 588.
W 633. **Col Couns:** 1. **Tui '12-'13:** Day $15,870-17,130. Aid: Need 54 ($472,030). **Est 1978.**
Nonprofit. Quar (Sept-June). **Assoc** MSA. The school draws its student body predominantly
from Hudson, Union, Essex, Monmouth, Bergen, Morris and Passaic counties. Hudson's rigorous program emphasizes the study of modern and classical languages. Electives include
acting, yoga, journalism, chess, video, creative writing, calligraphy, painting, chorus, sculpture, cooking and dance. Students are encouraged to spend one year studying abroad. All high
school students perform 20 hours of community service each year at food and clothing drives,
neighborhood cleanups and charitable organizations.   **See Also Page 147**

SAINT DOMINIC ACADEMY   **Day Girls Gr 9-12**
Jersey City, NJ 07304. 2572 Kennedy Blvd.
Tel: 201-434-5938. Fax: 201-434-2603.
www.stdominicacad.com   E-mail: aapruzzese@stdominicacad.com
    Barbara C. Griffin, Head (2010). BA, College of Saint Elizabeth, MA, Fairleigh Dickinson
Univ, MEd, Rutgers Univ. Thomas Corbo, Prin. BS, State Univ of New York-Cortland, MS,
Univ of New Hampshire, MA, New Jersey City Univ. Andrea Apruzzese, Adm.
    Col Prep. AP (exams req'd)—Eng Fr Span Calc Physics US_Hist Psych Art_Hist. **Feat**—
Chin Lat Stats Anat & Physiol Environ_Sci Forensic_Sci Programming Econ Law Pol_Sci
Sociol Middle_Eastern_Stud Comp_Relig Studio_Art. **Supp**—Tut. **Dual enr:** St Peter's.
Sports— G: Basket X-country Indoor_Track Soccer Softball Swim Tennis Track Volley.
Activities: 21. **Selective adm (Gr 9-11):** 82/yr. Appl fee: $40. Appl due: Nov. Accepted: 70%.
Enr 354. Wh 29%. Latino 27%. Asian 22%. Other 13%. Avg class size: 23. Stud/fac:
12:1. Uniform. **Fac 28.** M 10/F 18. FT 26/PT 2. Wh 80%. Latino 3%. Blk 3%. Asian 14%.
Adv deg: 57%. **Grad '11—126.** Col—126. (Rutgers 21, St Peter's 13, NJ City 12, Fairleigh
Dickinson 8, Seton Hall 7). **Avg SAT:** CR 485. M 481. W 505. **Col Couns:** 2. **Tui '12-'13:** Day

$8625 (+$750). **Est 1878.** Nonprofit. Roman Catholic (70% practice). Sem (Sept-June). **Assoc** MSA. A Catholic academy operated in the Dominican tradition, Saint Dominic includes honors (beginning freshman year) and Advanced Placement courses as part of its curriculum. Qualified seniors may enroll in classes at nearby Saint Peter's College. Girls perform 40 hours of required community service prior to graduation.

NOTRE DAME HIGH SCHOOL   Day Coed Gr 9-12
Lawrenceville, NJ 08648. 601 Lawrence Rd.
Tel: 609-882-7900. Fax: 609-882-5723.
www.ndnj.org   E-mail: rileyb@ndnj.org
     Barry Edward Breen, Pres (2011). BA, Univ of Notre Dame, MA, Univ of California-Berkeley, MEd, Seton Hall Univ. Mary Liz Ivins, Prin. Peggy Miller, Adm.
     Col Prep. AP **(265 exams taken, 81% 3+)**—Eng Fr Span Calc Bio Chem Environ_Sci Physics Eur_Hist US_Hist Psych US_Govt & Pol. **Feat**—Creative_Writing Etymology Ger Ital Japan Lat Anat & Physiol Sports_Med Comp_Sci Econ Relig Ceramics Photog Acting Accounting Journ Public_Speak. **Supp**—Rev Tut. **Sports**—Basket X-country Golf Indoor_ Track Lacrosse Soccer Swim Tennis Track. B: Baseball Football Ice_Hockey Wrestling. G: Cheer F_Hockey Softball. **Selective adm (Gr 9-11):** 348/yr. Appl fee: $50. Appl due: Nov. Accepted: 84%. Yield: 66%. **Tests** HSPT. **Enr 1266.** B 671. G 595. Wh 79%. Latino 4%. Blk 14%. Native Am 1%. Asian 1%. Other 1%. Avg class size: 23. Stud/fac: 15:1. Uniform. **Fac 96.** M 35/F 61. FT 91/PT 5. Wh 97%. Latino 2%. Blk 1%. Adv deg: 43%. **Grad '10—315.** Col—312. **Avg SAT:** CR 551. M 557. W 554. **Tui '10-'11:** Day $10,400 (+$600). Catholic $9900 (+$600). Aid: Need ($180,000). **Est 1957.** Nonprofit. Roman Catholic (88% practice). Sem (Sept-June). **Assoc** MSA. Affiliated with the Religious Sisters of Mercy, Notre Dame combines a solid college preparatory curriculum with service opportunities and cocurricular activities. Honors and Advanced Placement courses are available in all disciplines, and instructors employ various teaching strategies to address different learning styles. Boys and girls follow a block schedule, consisting of four 80-minute periods per day, that enables pupils to complete a yearlong course in one semester. A senior project and a professional internship are notable curricular elements in grade 12.

CHRISTIAN BROTHERS ACADEMY   Day Boys Gr 9-12
Lincroft, NJ 07738. 850 Newman Springs Rd.
Tel: 732-747-1959. Fax: 732-747-1643.
www.cbalincroftnj.org   E-mail: admissions@cbalincroftnj.org
     Br. Frank Byrne, FSC, Pres (2009). BBA, Univ of Notre Dame, MS, Fordham Univ. Br. James Butler, FSC, Prin.
     Col Prep. AP **(exams req'd; 428 taken, 81% 3+)**—Eng Fr Lat Span Calc Stats Comp_Sci Bio Chem Environ_Sci Physics Eur_Hist US_Hist World_Hist Econ Human_Geog Psych. **Feat**—Creative_Writing Astron Marine_Bio/Sci 20th-Century_Hist Govt Relig Bus. **Supp**—Tut. **Sports**— B: Baseball Basket Bowl X-country Golf Ice_Hockey Lacrosse Soccer Swim Tennis Track Volley Wrestling. Activities: 32. **Selective adm (Gr 9-11):** 257/yr. Appl fee: $75. Appl due: Rolling. Accepted: 50%. **Enr 948.** Wh 93%. Latino 3%. Asian 3%. Other 1%. Avg class size: 18. Stud/fac: 12:1. **Fac 64.** M 45/F 19. FT 64. Wh 99%. Latino 1%. Adv deg: 59%. **Grad '11—220.** Col—220. (St Joseph's U 10, Rutgers 10, Fairfield 9, Manhattan Col 9, PA St 8, Providence 8). **Avg SAT:** CR 588. M 600. W 592. Alum donors: 10%. **Tui '12-'13:** Day $13,100 (+$800). Aid: Merit 32 ($260,000). Need 150 ($950,000). **Est 1959.** Nonprofit. Roman Catholic. Sem (Sept-June). **Assoc** MSA. The academy is conducted by the Brothers of the Christian Schools. Honors and Advanced Placement courses are available in the major disciplines, and French, Spanish and Latin constitute the foreign language offerings. Spiritual life is emphasized through religious instruction and daily prayer. Boys satisfy the following community service requirements: 10 hours per year in grades 9 and 10, 15 hours annually in grades 11 and 12.

ST. JOSEPH HIGH SCHOOL   Day Boys Gr 9-12
Metuchen, NJ 08840. 145 Plainfield Ave.
Tel: 732-549-7600. Fax: 732-549-0664.
www.stjoes.org   E-mail: admissions@stjoes.org
    Lawrence N. Walsh, Pres (2006). BS, MA, Seton Hall Univ, MS, Fordham Univ. John A. Anderson, Prin. BA, MA, St Peter's College. Thomas Bacsik, Adm.
    Col Prep. AP (exams req'd; 389 taken, 65% 3+)—Eng Calc Comp_Sci Bio Chem Physics Eur_Hist US_Hist US_Govt & Pol. **Feat**—Fr Ger Lat Span Astron Meteorology Web_Design Civil_War Econ Pol_Sci Constitutional_Law Relig Drawing Film Photog Finance Journ Public_Speak. **Supp**—Tut. **Comp:** Comp/Stud: 1:8. **Dual enr:** Seton Hall. **Sports**— B: Baseball Basket Bowl Crew X-country Football Golf Ice_Hockey Indoor_Track Lacrosse Soccer Swim Tennis Track Volley. Activities: 52. **Selective adm (Gr 9-11):** 215/yr. Appl fee: $0. Appl due: Nov. Accepted: 70%. Yield: 80%. **Tests** HSPT. **Enr 755.** Wh 74%. Latino 7%. Blk 5%. Asian 12%. Other 2%. Avg class size: 25. Stud/fac: 17:1. Uniform. **Fac 52.** M 34/F 18. FT 43/PT 9. Wh 96%. Latino 3%. Blk 1%. Adv deg: 59%. **Grad '11—185.** Col—185. (Rutgers 34, Seton Hall 10, St Joseph's U 7, Col of NJ 6, Notre Dame 4). **Avg SAT:** CR 551. M 587. W 551. **Col Couns:** 4. Alum donors: 5%. **Tui '12-'13:** Day $11,850 (+$800-1050). Aid: Merit 60 ($200,000). Need 103 ($168,000). **Est 1961.** Nonprofit. Roman Catholic. Sem (Aug-June). **Assoc** MSA. Conducted by the Brothers of the Sacred Heart, St. Joseph provides a college preparatory curriculum that encourages critical and creative thinking. Students from more than 90 central New Jersey public, parochial and private elementary schools enroll in a varied program that features an array of accelerated and Advanced Placement courses. Freshmen and sophomores satisfy community service requirements: 20 hours within the boy's local parish in grade 9, 25 hours in the local community in grade 10.   **See Also Page 145**

MONTCLAIR COOPERATIVE SCHOOL   Day Coed Gr PS (Age 2)-8
Montclair, NJ 07042. 65 Chestnut St.
Tel: 973-783-4955. Fax: 973-783-1316.
www.montclaircoop.org   E-mail: catherines@montclaircoop.org
    Margaret Rourke Granados, Head (2010). BA, College of the Holy Cross, MA, Columbia Univ. Catherine W. Sweeney, Adm.
    Pre-Prep. Feat—Span Studio_Art Drama Music Dance. **Supp**—Dev_Read Rem_Math Rem_Read Tut. **Very selective adm:** 36/yr. Appl fee: $75. Appl due: Rolling. Accepted: 25%. **Enr 201.** B 92. G 109. Avg class size: 17. **Fac 42.** M 3/F 39. FT 38/PT 4. **Grad '07—8.** Prep—6. **Tui '12-'13:** Day $15,960-18,585 (+$500). **Est 1963.** Nonprofit. Sem (Sept-June). Utilizing the open classroom approach, the school emphasizes the integrated development of basic skills, creative ability and social interaction. Art, Spanish, music, ice skating and dance are also offered. Parents participate in both the classroom and school administration.

VILLA WALSH ACADEMY   Day Girls Gr 7-12
Morristown, NJ 07960. 455 Western Ave.
Tel: 973-538-3680. Fax: 973-538-6733.
www.villawalsh.org   E-mail: villawalsh@aol.com
    Sr. Doris Lavinthal, MPF, Dir (1990). BS, MS. Sr. Patricia Pompa, MPF, Prin. BA, MA.
    Col Prep. AP (exams req'd; 175 taken, 87% 3+)—Eng Fr Span Calc Stats Comp_Sci Bio Chem Physics Eur_Hist US_Hist Music_Theory. **Feat**—Anat & Physiol Econ Pol_Sci Psych Philos Theol Art_Hist Fine_Arts Chorus. **Supp**—Rev Tut. **Comp:** Comp/Stud: 1:2. **Sports**— G: Basket X-country Lacrosse Soccer Softball Swim Tennis Track Volley. Activities: 25. **Selective adm (Gr 7-9):** 60/yr. Appl fee: $25. Appl due: Feb. Accepted: 40%. Yield: 37%. **Tests** IQ. **Enr 257.** Elem 30. Sec 227. Wh 90%. Latino 5%. Blk 2%. Asian 3%. Avg class size: 12. Stud/fac: 8:1. Uniform. **Fac 35.** M 4/F 31. FT 29/PT 6. Wh 90%. Latino 3%. Blk 2%. Asian 5%. Adv deg: 71%. **Grad '11—57.** Col—57. (Boston Col 4, Villanova 4, U of PA 3, Holy Cross 3, Boston U 3, Cornell 2). **Avg SAT:** CR 660. M 660. W 690. Avg ACT: 28. **Col Couns:** 2. Alum donors: 70%. **Tui '11-'12:** Day $16,600 (+$800). Aid: Merit 5 ($15,000).

Need 27 ($125,000). **Est 1967.** Nonprofit. Roman Catholic (95% practice). Tri (Sept-June). **Assoc MSA.** Villa Walsh's curriculum features honors sections and an emphasis on the fine arts. Students fulfill course requirements in theology, modern foreign language and the fine arts. Advanced Placement courses and independent study options are available to gifted students.

OUR LADY OF MERCY ACADEMY   Day Girls Gr 9-12
Newfield, NJ 08344. 1001 Main Rd.
Tel: 856-697-2008. Fax: 856-697-2887.
www.olmanj.org   E-mail: info@olmanj.org
   Sr. Grace Marie Scandale, DM, Prin (1980).

   Col Prep. Feat—British_Lit Fr Span Anat & Physiol Botany Econ Sociol Relig Photog Studio_Art Drama. **Supp**—Tut. **Dual enr:** Camden County. **Sports**— G: Basket Cheer Crew Lacrosse Soccer Softball Swim Tennis Volley. Activities: 12. **Nonselective adm:** 46/yr. Appl fee: $200. Appl due: Jan. Accepted: 100%. Yield: 75%. **Tests** HSPT. **Enr 170.** Stud/fac: 10:1. Uniform. **Fac 21.** FT 21. Adv deg: 28%. **Grad '10—47.** Col—47. (Immaculata 5, Richard Stockton 5, Gwynedd Mercy 2, Rowan 2, La Salle 2, High Pt 1). **Avg SAT:** CR 531. M 503. W 537. **Tui '10-'11:** Day $9544 (+$1000). **Est 1962.** Nonprofit. Roman Catholic. Sem (Sept-June). This Catholic school enrolls girls from throughout Atlantic, Camden, Cape May, Cumberland, Gloucester and Salem counties. OLMA's college preparatory program includes honors courses and a dual-enrollment program in several subject areas with Camden County College. The curriculum emphasizes technology and independent-thinking skills.

YAVNEH ACADEMY   Day Coed Gr PS (Age 4)-8
Paramus, NJ 07652. 155 N Farview Ave.
Tel: 201-262-8494. Fax: 201-262-0463.
www.yavnehacademy.org   E-mail: yavnehacademy@yavnehacademy.org
   Joel Kirschner, Exec Dir. Jonathan Knapp, Prin.

   Gen Acad. Feat—Lib_Skills Hebrew Computers Holocaust Judaic_Stud Studio_Art Drama Music. **Supp**—Dev_Read LD Rem_Math Rem_Read Tut. **Comp:** Comp/Stud: 1:7. **Selective adm:** 94/yr. Appl fee: $750. Appl due: Rolling. **Enr 695.** B 363. G 332. Nonwhite 1%. Avg class size: 19. **Fac 88.** M 10/F 78. FT 65/PT 23. **Grad '11—80. Tui '11-'12:** Day $11,850-13,875 (+$1825-4567). Aid: Need 147 ($947,655). **Est 1942.** Nonprofit. Orthodox Jewish. Quar (Sept-June). Students receive both Judaic and secular education. The language of instruction in Judaic studies is modern Hebrew. The general studies curriculum is enhanced through programs in computer technology, art, music, physical education and library science.

TIMOTHY CHRISTIAN SCHOOL   Day Coed Gr K-12
Piscataway, NJ 08854. 2008 Ethel Rd.
Tel: 732-985-0300. Fax: 732-985-8008.
www.timothychristian.org   E-mail: tcs@timothychristian.org
   Mark A. Stanton, Supt (2010).

   Col Prep. AP (exams req'd)—Eng Calc Comp_Sci Bio. **Feat**—British_Lit Creative_ Writing Chin Fr Span Anat & Physiol Robotics Psych Sociol Bible Studio_Art Drama Theater_Arts Band Chorus Music_Hist Music_Theory Accounting Journ Health. **Supp**—ESL LD Tut. **Sports**—Basket Golf Soccer Track. B: Baseball. G: Cheer Softball Volley. **Somewhat selective adm:** 147/yr. Appl fee: $95. Appl due: Rolling. Accepted: 88%. Yield: 87%. **Tests** IQ SSAT Stanford. **Enr 491.** Elem 302. Sec 189. Avg class size: 19. Uniform. **Fac 53.** M 17/F 36. FT 43/PT 10. Adv deg: 39%. **Grad '08—54.** Col—48. **Avg SAT:** CR 528. M 514. W 516. **Tui '09-'10:** Day $4490-8950 (+$235-285). **Est 1949.** Nonprofit. Evangelical. Sem (Sept-June). **Assoc MSA.** With a teaching staff consisting entirely of born-again Christians, TCS bases its elementary and secondary programs on Biblical principles. Honors and AP course work is available in the upper grades, as is a full complement of electives.

PRINCETON ACADEMY OF THE SACRED HEART   **Day Boys Gr PS (Age 4)-8**
Princeton, NJ 08540. 1128 Great Rd.
Tel: 609-921-6499. Fax: 609-921-9198.
www.princetonacademy.org   E-mail: tvonoehsen@princetonacademy.org
    Olen Kalkus, Head (1998). BA, Colby College, MA, Salve Regina Univ, MEd, Columbia
Univ. Tom von Oehsen, Adm.
    Pre-Prep. Feat—Span Relig Studio_Art Music. **Supp**—Dev_Read. **Sports**— B: Baseball
Basket X-country Lacrosse Soccer Squash Tennis Wrestling. **Selective adm:** 54/yr. Appl fee:
$75. Appl due: Jan. Accepted: 82%. Yield: 76%. **Tests** CTP_4 SSAT. **Enr 228.** Wh 82%. Latino
5%. Blk 7%. Asian 3%. Other 3%. Avg class size: 13. Uniform. **Fac 30.** M 12/F 18. FT 30. Wh
86%. Latino 7%. Asian 7%. Adv deg: 40%. **Grad '10—29.** Prep—26. (Pennington 3, Avon 3,
Notre Dame HS-NJ 3, Lawrenceville 2, Hun 2, Peddie 2). **Tui '11-'12:** Day $21,650-26,200
(+$300). Aid: Need 47 ($553,123). **Est 1998.** Nonprofit. Roman Catholic (50% practice). Tri
(Sept-June). **Assoc** MSA. The curriculum at this boys' school, which emphasizes reading,
writing and discussion, provides frequent opportunities for hands-on learning. Spanish instruction begins in junior kindergarten and becomes a daily part of the program in grade 1; music,
drama and the visual arts are also integrated into the lower school curriculum. Experiential
teaching and a focus on independent thought are characteristics of the upper school program.
As social awareness is integral to school life, the academy encourages students to engage in
age-appropriate community service.

PRINCETON FRIENDS SCHOOL   **Day Coed Gr PS (Age 4)-8**
Princeton, NJ 08540. 470 Quaker Rd.
Tel: 609-683-1194. Fax: 609-252-0686.
www.princetonfriendsschool.org   E-mail: shushu@princetonfriendsschool.org
    Jane Fremon, Head (1987). AB, Princeton Univ, MEd, Bank Street College of Education.
Shu Shu Costa, Adm.
    Pre-Prep. Feat—Lib_Skills Chin Span Visual_Arts Music. **Supp**—Tut. **Selective adm (Gr
PS-7):** 30/yr. Appl fee: $50. Appl due: Jan. Accepted: 60%. Yield: 66%. **Enr 135.** Avg class
size: 12. **Fac 25.** M 7/F 18. FT 17/PT 8. Adv deg: 60%. **Grad '07—14.** Prep—10. (George
Sch 4, Pennington 2). **Tui '11-'12:** Day $21,750. **Est 1987.** Nonprofit. Religious Society of
Friends. Sem (Sept-June). In a collaborative environment, the school's integrated curriculum focuses upon a yearly central theme that students explore in multi-age groupings. Pupils
receive weekly instruction in Spanish and Mandarin Chinese in grades pre-K-2, then choose
one of these languages as a focus in grades 3-8. The curriculum also exposes students to art,
music and dance. Community service is integral to the program in grades 1-8.

HILLTOP COUNTRY DAY SCHOOL   **Day Coed Gr PS (Age 2)-8**
Sparta, NJ 07871. 32 Lafayette Rd.
Tel: 973-729-5485. Fax: 973-729-9057.
www.hilltopcds.org   E-mail: ltsemberlis@hilltopcds.org
    Laura E. McGee, Head (2011). Lisa A. Tsemberlis, Adm.
    Pre-Prep. Gen Acad. Feat—Lib_Skills Fr Span Computers Studio_Art Chorus Music.
Supp—Dev_Read Rem_Read Rev. **Selective adm:** Appl fee: $75. Appl due: Rolling. **Enr
230.** B 119. G 111. Avg class size: 10. **Fac 32.** Adv deg: 18%. **Grad '10—11. Tui '11-'12:** Day
$8550-15,986 (+$500). **Est 1967.** Nonprofit. Tri (Sept-June). Hilltop's traditional preschool
and elementary program places particular emphasis upon the arts, including both art and music
appreciation. Foreign language instruction commences in preschool with the introduction of
both French and Spanish. After-school enrichment offerings range from activities in the arts
(painting, instrumental music, and arts and crafts) to athletics (soccer, karate and basketball) to
academics (computer enrichment and SSAT preparation).

COMMUNITY SCHOOL   **Day Coed Gr 9-12**
Teaneck, NJ 07666. 1135 Teaneck Rd.
Tel: 201-862-1796. Fax: 201-862-1791.
www.communityhighschool.org   E-mail: tbraunstein@communityhighschool.org
Dennis Cohen, Co-Dir (1981). BA, MA. Toby Braunstein, Co-Dir. MA.

Col Prep. LD. Underachiever. Feat—Span Comp_Design Psych Photog Studio_Art Video_Production Drama Music Bus Journ. **Supp**—Rem_Math Rem_Read. **Sports**—Basket Golf Soccer Tennis. B: Baseball. G: Cheer Softball Volley. **Somewhat selective adm:** 47/yr. Appl fee: $65. Appl due: Rolling. **Enr 185.** Stud/fac: 3:1. **Fac 80.** M 15/F 65. FT 80. **Grad '08—46.** Col—40. **Tui '09-'10:** Day $40,901. **Est 1967.** Nonprofit. Quar (Sept-June). **Assoc** MSA. This college preparatory curriculum is designed for students with learning and attentional difficulties. Individualized attention is integral to the program: In addition to small-group instruction within classes, the school offers remedial classes for specific skill development. An enriched elementary program, conducted on Forest Avenue, closely resembles that of the high school.   **See Also Page 90**

LACORDAIRE ACADEMY   **Day Boys Gr PS (Age 4)-8**
Upper Montclair, NJ 07043. 155 Lorraine Ave.   **Girls PS (Age 4)-12**
Tel: 973-744-1156. Fax: 973-783-9521.
Other locations: 153 Lorraine Ave, Upper Montclair 07043.
www.lacordaire.net   E-mail: admissions@lacordaire.net
Brian F. Morgan, Head. BA, East Stroudsburg Univ, MA, Villanova Univ. Joan Hearst, Adm.

Col Prep. AP (exams req'd)—Eng Fr Span Calc. **Feat**—Shakespeare Anat & Physiol Comp_Graphics Intl_Relations Psych World_Relig SAT_Prep. **Supp**—Dev_Read Makeup Rem_Math Rem_Read Rev Tut. **Comp:** Comp/Stud: 1:2. **Dual enr:** Seton Hall, Fairleigh Dickinson, Caldwell. **Sports**— G: Basket Cheer Lacrosse Soccer Softball Tennis Volley. Activities: 11. **Selective adm (Day Girls Gr PS-11):** 42/yr. Appl fee: $50. Appl due: Nov. **Enr 240.** B 61. G 179. Elem 152. Sec 88. Wh 71%. Latino 6%. Blk 15%. Asian 8%. Avg class size: 14. Stud/fac: 7:1. Uniform. **Fac 32.** M 5/F 27. FT 31/PT 1. **Grad '08—34.** Col—34. **Avg SAT:** CR 560. M 510. W 560. **Tui '11-'12:** Day $7800-11,500 (+$975-1500). Aid: Merit 15 ($16,750). Need 76 ($117,201). **Est 1920.** Nonprofit. Roman Catholic (75% practice). Quar (Sept-June). **Assoc** MSA. Founded by the Sisters of St. Dominic, Lacordaire conducts a coeducational elementary school and a girls' high school. The elementary curriculum (grades pre-K-8) provides a foundation in the fundamental disciplines and an emphasis on basic skills, independent learning, critical thinking, decision making and the use of technology. In the college preparatory secondary division, qualified girls may take dual-enrollment classes through Seton Hall University, Fairleigh Dickinson University and Caldwell College.

THE ELLISON SCHOOL   **Day Coed Gr PS (Age 2)-8**
Vineland, NJ 08361. 1017 S Spring Rd.
Tel: 856-691-1734. Fax: 856-794-8361.
www.ellisonschool.org   E-mail: cchapman@ellisonschool.org
Caroline C. Chapman, Head (2009). BA, Hood College, MA, Rowan Univ, EdS, George Washington Univ. Mary Jane Kinkade, Adm.

Pre-Prep. Gen Acad. Feat—Lib_Skills Span Computers Ethics Relig Studio_Art Music Study_Skills. **Supp**—Dev_Read ESL Rem_Math Rem_Read Tut. **Comp:** Comp/Stud: 1:2. **Sports**—Basket Soccer. **Somewhat selective adm:** 50/yr. Appl fee: $100. Appl due: Rolling. Accepted: 97%. Yield: 90%. **Enr 152.** B 84. G 68. Wh 85%. Latino 5%. Blk 6%. Asian 4%. Avg class size: 11. Casual dress. **Fac 16.** M 2/F 14. FT 16. Wh 90%. Latino 5%. Blk 5%. Adv deg: 25%. **Grad '09—13.** Prep—5. **Tui '09-'10:** Day $6995-10,150. Aid: Need 10 ($17,100). **Est 1959.** Nonprofit. Tri (Sept-June). **Assoc** MSA. This elementary school serves children from Vineland, Millville, Hammonton, Mays Landing, the shore area and surrounding communities. Beginning in the lower grades, Ellison emphasizes sound study habits, the ability to work independently, personal responsibility, and organizational and critical-thinking skills. Departmentalization begins in grade 5. Students in grades 5-8 perform 10 hours of required community service annually.

GOLDA OCH ACADEMY   Day Coed Gr PS (Age 4)-12
West Orange, NJ 07052. 1418 Pleasant Valley Way.
Tel: 973-602-3600. Fax: 973-669-5921.
Other locations: 122 Gregory Ave, West Orange 07052.
www.goldaochacademy.org   E-mail: admissions@goldaochacademy.org
Joyce Raynor, Head (2007). BA, Rutgers Univ, MA, Univ of Judaism, PhD, Duke Univ. Gail Shapiro, Adm.

Col Prep. AP (exams req'd; 77 taken, 82% 3+)—Eng Span Calc US_Hist. **Feat**—World_ Lit Fr Hebrew Arabic Comp_Sci Modern_Israeli_Hist Econ Psych Bible Judaic_Stud Relig Film Photog Studio_Art Drama Music Public_Speak. **Supp**—ESL Tut. **Sports**—Basket X-country Soccer Swim Tennis Volley. B: Baseball. G: Softball. Activities: 20. **Somewhat selective adm (Gr PS-11):** 80/yr. Appl fee: $100. Appl due: Jan. Accepted: 88%. Yield: 86%. **Tests** ISEE. **Enr 554.** Elem 366. Sec 188. Wh 98%. Latino 1%. Asian 1%. Avg class size: 16. **Fac 136.** M 20/F 116. FT 84/PT 52. Adv deg: 52%. **Grad '10—41.** Col—41. (U of MD-Col Park 8, Muhlenberg 7, Brandeis 4, U of MI 1, Emory 1, Tufts 1). **Avg SAT:** CR 638. M 648. W 656. **Mid 50% SAT:** CR 540-710. M 570-710. W 590-730. Avg ACT: 27.1. Mid 50% ACT: 25-30. **Tui '11-'12:** Day $9000-24,875 (+$2000). Aid: Need 300 ($2,500,000). **Est 1965.** Nonprofit. Jewish (100% practice). Sem (Sept-June). **Assoc** MSA.   Formerly the Solomon Schechter Day School of Essex and Union, GOA offers a dual curriculum of general and Judaic studies. The latter comprises courses in Bible, Hebrew language, Rabbinics, and Jewish history, literature and philosophy. AP and honors courses and creative individualized research are aspects of the general curriculum. The school operates at two sites: a lower school campus (serving grades pre-K-5) on Gregory Avenue and a middle school and upper school location (grades 6-12) on Pleasant Valley Way.

SETON HALL PREPARATORY SCHOOL   Day Boys Gr 9-12
West Orange, NJ 07052. 120 Northfield Ave.
Tel: 973-325-7737. Fax: 973-731-3920.
www.shp.org   E-mail: mcannizzo@shp.org
Msgr. Michael E. Kelly, Head (1980). AB, MA, Seton Hall Univ. Matthew Cannizzo, Adm.

Col Prep. AP—Eng Lat Span Calc Stats Comp_Sci Bio Chem Environ_Sci Physics Eur_ Hist US_Hist Econ Human_Geog Psych US_Govt & Pol Art_Hist Studio_Art Music_Theory. **Feat**—Creative_Writing Fr Ital Global_Stud Theol Video_Production Theater_Arts Speech. **Sports**— B: Baseball Basket Bowl X-country Football Golf Ice_Hockey Indoor_Track Lacrosse Soccer Swim Tennis Track Wrestling. Activities: 42. **Selective adm (Gr 9-11):** 325/ yr. Appl fee: $50. Appl due: Feb. Accepted: 65%. **Enr 950.** Avg class size: 18. Uniform. **Fac 86.** Adv deg: 75%. **Grad '07—226.** Col—226. **Avg SAT:** CR 584. M 590. W 580. **Col Couns:** 1. **Tui '11-'12:** Day $13,000 (+$800-1300). Aid: Need 285. **Est 1856.** Nonprofit. Roman Catholic. Tri (Aug-June). **Assoc** MSA.   Students enroll at the Prep, the oldest Catholic college preparatory school in New Jersey, from a wide area that includes more than 120 towns. After boys have completed a traditional core program in their first two years, Seton Hall enables them to design a curriculum geared toward their college and career plans. Course work integrates technology and emphasizes writing skills across the curriculum. Class retreats are a compulsory part of the campus ministry program.

BARNSTABLE ACADEMY   **Day Coed Gr 5-12**
Oakland, NJ 07436. 8 Wright Way.
Tel: 201-651-0200. Fax: 201-337-9797.
www.barnstableacademy.com   E-mail: lcoyne@barnstableacademy.com
   Lizanne M. Coyne, Head (2009). BA, Providence College, MEd, Norwich Univ.
   Col Prep. LD. Feat—Fr Lat Span Comp_Sci Psych Fine_Arts Performing_Arts. **Supp**—
ESL Makeup Rem_Math Tut. **Comp:** Comp/Stud: 1:3. **Dual enr:** Wm Paterson. **Sports**—
Basket Soccer. B: Baseball. G: Cheer Softball. Activities: 13. **Selective adm (Gr 5-11):** 40/yr.
Appl due: Rolling. Accepted: 50%. Yield: 25%. **Enr 103.** Elem 22. Sec 81. Avg class size:
10. **Fac 14.** M 7/F 7. **Grad '08—31.** Col—30. (Montclair St 3, Villanova 1, Curry 1, NYU 1,
Wm Paterson 1, SUNY-Albany 1). **Avg SAT:** CR 530. M 520. W 550. Alum donors: 5%. **Tui
'11-'12:** Day $22,500-28,750. **Est 1978.** Inc. Tri (Sept-June). **Assoc** MSA. Barnstable offers
college preparatory academics for boys and girls with learning differences. Major subjects
take place prior to lunch, with afternoons devoted to electives in athletics, physical education,
the fine and performing arts, and photography. The Early College Program enables qualified
juniors and seniors to earn college credit in one or more classes through William Paterson
University. Children with Asperger's syndrome and other pervasive developmental disorders
participate in the mainstream program.

NEW YORK

CHRISTIAN BROTHERS ACADEMY   **Day Boys Gr 6-12**
Albany, NY 12205. 12 Airline Dr.
Tel: 518-452-9809. Fax: 518-452-9804.
www.cbaalbany.org   E-mail: info@cbaalbany.org
   James P. Schlegel, Prin (2008). BA, State Univ of New York-Albany, MEd, Univ of Mis-
souri-Columbia. Brian O'Connell, Adm.
   Col Prep. Milit. AP (exams req'd; 95 taken)—Eng Calc Stats Bio Chem Physics US_Hist
World_Hist. **Feat**—Creative_Writing Fr Ital Lat Span Forensic_Sci Geol Comp_Sci Web_
Design Econ Law Psych Sociol Philos Relig Drawing Sculpt Studio_Art Music Jazz_Band
Accounting Bus Marketing Mech_Drawing JROTC. **Supp**—Rem_Math Rem_Read Rev Tut.
Sports— B: Baseball Basket Bowl X-country Football Golf Ice_Hockey Lacrosse Soccer
Tennis Track Wrestling. **Somewhat selective adm (Gr 6-11):** 102/yr. Appl due: Rolling.
Accepted: 98%. Yield: 95%. **Tests** IQ. **Enr 510.** Elem 132. Sec 378. Avg class size: 22. Uni-
form. **Fac 33.** M 25/F 8. FT 33. Adv deg: 45%. **Grad '08—87.** Col—87. **Avg SAT:** CR 550.
M 555. W 532. **Tui '11-'12:** Day $8200-11,200 (+$450-500). **Est 1859.** Nonprofit. Roman
Catholic. Sem (Sept-June). **Assoc** MSA. CBA provides a junior high school and a senior
military high school. Both AP and honors courses are available, and graduation requirements
include art or music, religion, military science and electives. Boys fulfill a 70-hour cumulative
community service requirement during their high school years.

MAPLEBROOK SCHOOL   **Bdg & Day**
Amenia, NY 12501. 5142 Rte 22.   **Coed Gr 6-PG**
Tel: 845-373-9511. Fax: 845-373-7029.
www.maplebrookschool.org   E-mail: admissions@maplebrookschool.org
   Donna M. Konkolics, Head. MA, State Univ of New York-New Paltz. Jennifer L. Scully,
Adm.
   Gen Acad. Voc. LD. Underachiever. Feat—Span Computers Econ Govt Psych Perform-
ing_Arts Studio_Art Journ Home_Ec. **Supp**—Dev_Read Rem_Math Rem_Read Tut. Sat
classes. **Sports (req'd)**—X-country Equestrian Soccer Swim Tennis Track. B: Basket. G:
Cheer F_Hockey Softball. **Selective adm (Gr 6-11):** 37/yr. Bdg 34. Day 3. Appl fee: $0. Appl
due: Rolling. **Tests** IQ Stanford. **Enr 116.** B 56. G 60. Bdg 109. Day 7. Sec 79. PG 37. Wh

87%. Latino 4%. Blk 7%. Asian 2%. Avg class size: 8. **Fac 30.** M 11/F 19. FT 27/PT 3. Adv deg: 53%. In Dorms 10. **Grad '09—25.** Col—6. **Tui '11-'12:** Bdg $56,700 (+$400). 5-Day Bdg $52,200 (+$400). Day $35,850 (+$200). Aid: Need 29 ($150,000). **Est 1945.** Nonprofit. Sem (Sept-June). **Assoc MSA.** Maplebrook offers academic and social programs to adolescents who are unable to thrive in traditional school settings or whose learning differences require more individual attention. The program emphasizes multisensory instruction and the development of social skills and self-esteem. CAPS (The Center for the Advancement of Post Secondary Studies), a postsecondary program providing either vocational or college programming, is available to students ages 18-21 for an additional fee. All students in CAPS use laptop computers, purchased independently or through the school.

ACADEMY OF MOUNT ST. URSULA   Day Girls Gr 9-12
Bronx, NY 10458. 330 Bedford Park Blvd.
Tel: 718-364-5353. Fax: 718-364-2354.
www.amsu.org   E-mail: lharrison@amsu.org
    Rev. John A. Vigilanti, Pres (2008). BA, MDiv, MA, St Joseph's Seminary, JCL, Catholic Univ, MS, Iona College, MA, EdD, Fordham Univ. Lisa Harrison, Prin. BS, MA, New York Univ, MA, St John's Univ (NY). Julia Myers Bartley, Adm.
    Col Prep. AP (exams req'd; 113 taken, 57% 3+)—Eng Span Calc Bio US_Hist. **Feat**—Fr Ital Lat Anat & Physiol Forensic_Sci Comp_Sci Anthro Sociol Bus_Law World_Relig Studio_Art Music Accounting Public_Speak. **Supp**—Dev_Read Rem_Math Rev Tut. **Comp:** Comp/Stud: 1:3. **Dual enr:** St John's U-NY. **Sports (req'd)**— G: Basket Soccer Softball Volley. **Selective adm (Gr 9-11):** 90/yr. Appl due: Nov. Accepted: 60%. Yield: 27%. **Tests** TACHS. **Enr 350.** Wh 1%. Latino 48%. Blk 32%. Asian 7%. Other 12%. Avg class size: 25. Stud/fac: 14:1. Uniform. **Fac 25.** M 8/F 17. FT 23/PT 2. Wh 85%. Latino 6%. Blk 3%. Asian 6%. Adv deg: 100%. **Grad '08—101.** Col—99. (CUNY 34, SUNY 12, Col of Mt St Vincent 6, Pace 4, PA St 4, NYU 3). Alum donors: 12%. **Tui '12-'13:** Day $6975 (+$825). Aid: Merit 74 ($165,455). Need 85 ($219,180). **Est 1855.** Nonprofit. Roman Catholic (60% practice). Sem (Sept-June). **Assoc MSA.** The oldest continuously operated Catholic girls' school in New York State, MSU is conducted by the Ursuline Sisters of the Roman Union. Advanced Placement courses allow qualified juniors and seniors to earn college credit, and an internship program is also available. Service activities are a school focus: Girls typically perform substantially more than the 10 compulsory annual service hours.

BISHOP KEARNEY HIGH SCHOOL   Day Girls Gr 9-12
Brooklyn, NY 11204. 2202 60th St.
Tel: 718-236-6363. Fax: 718-236-7784.
www.bishopkearneyhs.org   E-mail: admissions@bishopkearneyhs.org
    Sr. Thomasine Stagnitta, CSJ, Prin. BS, City Univ of New York, MA, Pace Univ. Christine LoMacchio, Adm.
    Col Prep. AP—Eng Calc Bio Physics Eur_Hist US_Hist Psych Studio_Art. **Feat**—Shakespeare Fr Ital Lat Span Stats Anat & Physiol Environ_Sci Marine_Bio/Sci Comp_Sci Econ Law Relig Drawing Chorus Music_Hist Music_Theory Nutrition. **Dual enr:** St Joseph's Col-NY, St John's U-NY. **Sports**— G: Basket Cheer Golf Soccer Softball Swim Tennis Track Volley. Activities: 30. **Somewhat selective adm (Gr 9-11):** 257/yr. Appl fee: $0. Appl due: Jan. Accepted: 93%. **Tests** TACHS. **Enr 674.** Avg class size: 32. Uniform. **Fac 46. Grad '03—280.** Col—270. **Col Couns: 1. Tui '11-'12:** Day $8500 (+$300-725). **Est 1961.** Nonprofit. Roman Catholic. Sem (Sept-June). **Assoc MSA.** Enrolling a diverse student body comprising girls from throughout Brooklyn and Queens, Kearney provides a college preparatory curriculum that has at its core religion courses, liturgical celebrations and retreat experiences. Qualified pupils may take Advanced Placement classes during the junior and senior years, and college-credit courses are available through St. Joseph's College and St. John's University. Girls accumulate 90 hours of required Christian service prior to graduation.

BISHOP LOUGHLIN MEMORIAL HIGH SCHOOL   **Day Coed Gr 9-12**
Brooklyn, NY 11238. 357 Clermont Ave.
Tel: 718-857-2700. Fax: 718-398-4227.
www.bishoploughlin.org   E-mail: egonzalez@blmhs.org
    Br. Dennis J. Cronin, FSC, Pres (2008). BS, St Francis College (NY), MEd, Hofstra Univ.
James Dorney, Prin. BS, St Francis College (NY), MEd, Fordham Univ. Edwin Gonzalez,
Adm.
    Col Prep. AP—Eng US_Hist. **Feat**—Fr Span Calc Environ_Sci Web_Design Econ Psych
African-Amer_Stud Relig Drawing Painting Photog Studio_Art Video_Production Chorus
Music Accounting Public_Speak. **Supp**—Dev_Read Makeup Rem_Read Rev Tut. **Comp:**
Comp/Stud: 1:8.5. **Sports**—Basket Bowl X-country Hand Indoor_Track Track. B: Baseball.
G: Cheer Softball Volley. Activities: 24. **Somewhat selective adm (Gr 9-11):** 275/yr. Appl fee:
$0. Appl due: Oct. Accepted: 95%. Yield: 93%. **Tests** TACHS. **Enr 880.** B 490. G 390. Avg
class size: 20. Uniform. **Fac 44.** M 22/F 22. FT 44. Adv deg: 68%. **Grad '10—224.** Col—218.
Tui '12-'13: Day $8200 (+$780). Aid: Merit ($500,000). Need ($250,000). **Est 1851.** Nonprofit. Roman Catholic. Sem (Sept-June). **Assoc** MSA.   Bishop Loughlin is staffed by De La
Salle Christian Brothers, Dominican Sisters and Catholic lay teachers. Each pupil studies religion two quarters per year. Community service includes campus ministry and Lasallian Youth
projects and support for Bishop Loughlin's sister school in Kenya, St. Mary's School. A small
boarding program serves up to 25 young men from various parts of New York City; boarders
reside in an adjacent dormitory Sunday evening through Friday afternoon and participate in a
required after-school program.

BROOKLYN HEIGHTS MONTESSORI SCHOOL   **Day Coed Gr PS (Age 2)-8**
Brooklyn, NY 11201. 185 Court St.
Tel: 718-858-5100. Fax: 718-858-0500.
www.bhmsny.org   E-mail: info@bhmsny.org
    Dane L. Peters, Head. BA, Central Connecticut State Univ, MEd, Pepperdine Univ. Elise
Mattia, Adm.
    Pre-Prep. Gen Acad. Montessori. Feat—Span Ceramics Photog Studio_Art Chorus
Music Dance. **Supp**—LD. **Sports**—Basket Soccer Squash. **Selective adm:** 63/yr. Appl fee:
$75. Appl due: Jan. Accepted: 47%. Yield: 65%. **Tests** ISEE. **Enr 223.** Avg class size: 16.
Fac 44. M 11/F 33. FT 35/PT 9. Adv deg: 40%. **Grad '08—6.** Prep—5. **Tui '12-'13:** Day
$29,750-32,500 (+$250-500). **Est 1965.** Nonprofit. (Sept-June).   Children work in multi-age
classes structured to develop practical skills and enhance learning. Preschool, kindergarten
and lower elementary (grades 1-3) students build an academic foundation in the core courses,
while upper elementary pupils (grades 4-6) explore concentrated topics in math, science, technology, Spanish, literature and the arts. In the middle school (grades 7 and 8), boys and girls
further develop their skills in writing, language arts and the social sciences.

LONG ISLAND LUTHERAN   **Day Coed Gr 6-12**
MIDDLE AND HIGH SCHOOL
Brookville, NY 11545. 131 Brookville Rd.
Tel: 516-626-1700. Fax: 516-622-7459.
www.luhi.org   E-mail: info@luhi.org
    David Hahn, Head (1987). BA, Concordia Univ (IL), MEd, Towson State Univ, PhD, Univ
of Minnesota-Twin Cities. Barbara Ward, Adm.
    Col Prep. AP (exams req'd; 214 taken)—Eng Fr Span Calc Comp_Sci Bio Physics
World_Hist Econ US_Govt & Pol Music_Theory. **Feat**—Creative_Writing Chin Environ_Sci
Sports_Med Law Psych Sociol Ethics Relig Studio_Art Bus Journ Marketing Entrepreneur-
ship. **Supp**—Tut. **Dual enr:** Concordia Col-NY. **Sports**—Basket X-country Golf Lacrosse
Soccer Tennis Track. B: Baseball Football Wrestling. G: Cheer Softball Volley. Activities: 30.
Selective adm (Gr 6-11): 140/yr. Appl fee: $100. Appl due: Rolling. Accepted: 76%. Yield:
72%. **Tests** IQ. **Enr 600.** B 326. G 274. Elem 188. Sec 412. Wh 70%. Latino 1%. Blk 25%.

Asian 2%. Other 2%. Avg class size: 18. Stud/fac: 14:1. Uniform. **Fac 57.** M 22/F 35. FT 50/PT 7. Wh 99%. Latino 1%. Adv deg: 84%. **Grad '11—102.** Col—102. **Avg SAT:** CR 559. M 562. W 592. Avg ACT: 24. **Tui '11-'12:** Day $10,475-11,990 (+$580). Aid: Merit 24 ($24,000). Need ($325,000). **Est 1960.** Nonprofit. Lutheran. Sem (Sept-June). **Assoc MSA.** Situated on a 32-acre estate, the school operates in the Lutheran-Christian tradition. LuHi's strong academic curriculum features advanced studies, as well as Advanced Placement and honors classes in all academic disciplines.

CANISIUS HIGH SCHOOL   Day Boys Gr 9-12
Buffalo, NY 14209. 1180 Delaware Ave.
Tel: 716-882-0466. Fax: 716-883-1870.
www.canisiushigh.org E-mail: weislo@canisiushigh.org
John M. Knight, Pres (2008). MRE, Loyola Univ of Chicago. Timothy K. Fitzgerald, Sr., Prin. Thomas H. Weislo, Adm.

Col Prep. AP—Eng Fr Span Calc Stats Comp_Sci Bio Chem Environ_Sci Physics Eur_ Hist US_Hist World_Hist Econ Psych US_Govt & Pol. **Feat**—Creative_Writing Ger Lat Anat Astron Anthro Philos Relig Architect Drawing Film Graphic_Arts Sculpt Studio_Art Acting Drama Chorus Music Music_Theory Jazz_Ensemble Journ. **Supp**—Tut. **Comp:** Comp/Stud: 1:6 (1:1 Laptop prgm Gr 9-12). **Sports**— B: Baseball Basket Bowl Crew X-country Football Golf Ice_Hockey Lacrosse Rugby Soccer Squash Swim Tennis Track Volley Wrestling. Activities: 40. **Selective adm:** 235/yr. Appl due: Rolling. **Enr 826.** Avg class size: 18. Stud/fac: 12:1. **Fac 62.** Adv deg: 66%. **Grad '09—197.** Col—192. **Avg SAT:** CR 587. M 600. W 576. **Tui '10-'11:** Day $10,595 (+$550). **Est 1870.** Nonprofit. Roman Catholic. Quar (Sept-June). **Assoc MSA.** Honors and accelerated courses are offered all four years; college-level and AP courses are available in virtually all subjects. The Christian service program requires participation in schoolwide projects and 30 hours of outside service in each grade. Every student is encouraged to engage in at least one cocurricular activity annually.

NARDIN ACADEMY   Day Boys Gr PS (Age 2)-8
Buffalo, NY 14222. 135 Cleveland Ave.   Girls PS (Age 3)-12
Tel: 716-881-6262. Fax: 716-881-4190.
Other locations: 700 W Ferry St, Buffalo 14222.
www.nardin.org E-mail: admissions@nardin.org
Marsha Joy Sullivan, Pres (2008). Kathleen McHale, Gr 9-12 Adm; Victoria Boreanaz, Gr PS-8 Adm.

Col Prep. Montessori. AP (exams req'd; 296 taken, 88% 3+)—Eng Fr Lat Span Calc Bio Chem Eur_Hist US_Hist US_Govt & Pol Art_Hist. **Feat**—Creative_Writing Stats Environ_Sci Marine_Bio/Sci Comp_Sci Web_Design Econ Law Philos Relig Drawing Photog Studio_Art Theater Chorus Music_Theory Dance Journ Public_Speak. **Supp**—Rem_Read Rev Tut. **Sports**— G: Basket Bowl Crew X-country Golf Indoor_Track Lacrosse Soccer Softball Squash Swim Tennis Track Volley. Activities: 33. **Selective adm:** 194/yr. Appl fee: $50. Appl due: Jan. **Enr 922.** Elem 455. Sec 469. Wh 94%. Latino 1%. Blk 2%. Asian 2%. Other 1%. Avg class size: 18. Stud/fac: 10:1. **Fac 112.** M 11/F 101. FT 84/PT 28. Adv deg: 78%. **Grad '11—113.** Col—113. (SUNY-Buffalo 11, Duquesne 8, SUNY-Geneseo 7, Canisius 4, Hobart/Wm Smith 3, St Lawrence 3). **Avg SAT:** CR 600. M 600. W 615. Avg ACT: 26. **Col Couns:** 1. **Tui '12-'13:** Day $9700-10,325 (+$800). **Est 1857.** Nonprofit. Roman Catholic. Quar (Sept-June). **Assoc MSA.** The academy comprises three divisions: a coed Montessori program (the majority of which operates at a separate campus on West Ferry Street) for children age 18 months through grade 3, a coed elementary school (grades 1-8) and an all-girls high school. All pupils, regardless of religious orientation, take compulsory religious studies courses each year. The high school curriculum features AP courses, as well as both required and elective computer classes. High schoolers fulfill a 15-hour annual service commitment.

ST. JOSEPH'S COLLEGIATE INSTITUTE   **Day Boys Gr 9-12**
Buffalo, NY 14223. 845 Kenmore Ave.
Tel: 716-874-4024. Fax: 716-874-4956.
www.sjci.com   E-mail: sjci@sjci.com
    Robert T. Scott, Pres (2001). BA, Marist College, MA, Canisius College. Jeffery D. Hazel,
Prin. Peter Kennedy, Adm.
    Col Prep. AP (exams req'd; 300 taken, 80% 3+)—Eng Fr Ger Span Calc Stats Bio Chem
Physics Eur_Hist US_Hist World_Hist Econ US_Govt & Pol Studio_Art. **Feat**—British_Lit
Environ_Sci Comp_Sci Web_Design Psych Philos Relig Drawing Photog Sculpt Video_Pro-
duction Theater Band Chorus Music_Theory Accounting Journ Public_Speak. **Supp**—Tut.
Comp: Comp/Stud: 1:2.2. **Dual enr:** Niagara. **Sports**— B: Baseball Basket Bowl Crew X-
country Football Golf Ice_Hockey Indoor_Track Lacrosse Soccer Swim Tennis Track Volley
Wrestling. Activities: 49. **Selective adm (Gr 9-11):** 195/yr. Appl due: Rolling. **Tests** HSPT.
Enr 722. Wh 88%. Latino 2%. Blk 6%. Asian 2%. Other 2%. Avg class size: 26. Stud/fac:
14:1. **Fac 50.** M 45/F 5. FT 46/PT 4. **Grad '11—188.** Col—188. **Avg SAT:** CR 553. M 584.
W 546. **Tui '11-'12:** Day $10,500 (+$590). Aid: Merit 160 ($291,000). Need 373 ($748,200).
Work prgm 240 ($100,000). **Est 1861.** Nonprofit. Roman Catholic. Sem (Sept-June). **Assoc**
MSA. Sponsored by the De La Salle Christian Brothers, St. Joe's offers four levels of courses:
Advanced Placement, honors, New York State Board of Regents and basic. The academic program features various electives, among them creative arts, music, theater and environmental
science. All students complete four years of religion courses, in addition to 20 hours of community service per year.

GREEN MEADOW WALDORF SCHOOL   **Day Coed Gr PS (Age 3)-12**
Chestnut Ridge, NY 10977. 307 Hungry Hollow Rd.
Tel: 845-356-2514. Fax: 845-356-2921.
www.gmws.org   E-mail: info@gmws.org
    Tari Steinrueck, Admin (2010). Patricia Owens, Adm.
    Col Prep. Waldorf. Feat—Shakespeare Fr Ger Span Anat Astron Botany Zoology Comp_
Sci Studio_Art Drama Chorus Music Gardening. **Supp**—ESL Rem_Math Rem_Read Tut.
Sports—Basket X-country Tennis. B: Baseball. G: Softball Volley. **Selective adm:** 35/yr. Appl
fee: $50. Appl due: Rolling. **Enr 382.** Elem 302. Sec 80. Wh 91%. Latino 3%. Blk 1%. Asian
5%. Avg class size: 30. **Fac 50.** Adv deg: 44%. **Grad '11—23.** Col—19. (Bennington 3, CT Col
1, Mt Holyoke 1, NY Inst of Tech 1, Ithaca 1, Adelphi 1). **Tui '12-'13:** Day $14,700-20,750.
Aid: Need 131 ($483,700). **Est 1950.** Nonprofit. Sem (Sept-June). The elementary program
combines required handwork, woodworking, foreign language, chorus and orchestra classes
with humanities, math and science course work. The high school program features course
work in literature, math and science. All disciplines emphasize artistic elements. German and
Spanish instruction begins in grade 1, and French is an added option in grade 8. Community
service begins in the lower school and continues in grade 9, when students spend two periods
per week on required off-campus projects; students in grades 10-12 fulfill their requirements
outside of school. Seniors may participate in a full-time internship program in February. A
small number of boarding students live with host families in the community.

ST. AGNES ACADEMIC HIGH SCHOOL   **Day Girls Gr 9-12**
College Point, NY 11356. 13-20 124th St.
Tel: 718-353-6276. Fax: 718-353-6068.
www.stagneshs.org   E-mail: jmartin@stagneshs.org
    Sr. Joan Martin, OP, Prin (1999). BSEd, St John's Univ (NY), MSEd, Fordham Univ, PhD,
Long Island Univ.
    Col Prep. AP (exams req'd; 72 taken, 50% 3+)—Eng Span US_Hist Studio_Art. **Feat**—
British_Lit Fr Ecol Forensic_Sci Comp_Sci Econ Law Psych Relig Drawing Chorus Music_
Hist. **Supp**—Dev_Read ESL Rem_Math Tut. **Comp:** Comp/Stud: 1:5. **Dual enr:** St John's U-
NY, SUNY-Albany. **Sports**— G: Basket Bowl Cheer Soccer Softball Track Volley. Activities:

20. **Somewhat selective adm (Gr 9-11):** 105/yr. Appl due: Feb. Accepted: 95%. Yield: 90%. **Tests** CEEB TACHS. **Enr 390.** Wh 53%. Latino 32%. Blk 9%. Asian 6%. Avg class size: 23. Stud/fac: 14:1. Uniform. **Fac 27.** M 2/F 25. FT 25/PT 2. Wh 99%. Latino 1%. **Grad '10—97.** Col—96. **Col Couns:** 2. Alum donors: 18%. **Tui '10-'11:** Day $7600. Aid: Merit ($119,000). **Est 1908.** Nonprofit. Roman Catholic (90% practice). Tri (Sept-June). **Assoc** MSA. Sponsored by the Sisters of St. Dominic, St. Agnes is a traditional girls' Catholic school that emphasizes college preparation. In addition to honors classes, academically talented students may participate in Advanced Placement courses in most major disciplines. Computer technology is an integral aspect of the curriculum.

THE BROOKWOOD SCHOOL   Day Coed Gr PS (Age 3)-6
Cooperstown, NY 13326. 687 County Rte 59.
Tel: 607-547-4060. Fax: 607-547-2835.
www.thebrookwoodschool.org   E-mail: info@thebrookwoodschool.org
    Gina M. Reeves, Head (2009). BSEd, MEd, Univ of Delaware. Vera Sosnowski, Adm.
    Gen Acad. Montessori. Feat—Fr Computers Studio_Art Music. **Supp**—Tut. **Comp:** Comp/Stud: 1:2. **Nonselective adm:** 42/yr. Appl fee: $60. Appl due: Rolling. Accepted: 95%. Yield: 90%. **Enr 111.** B 52. G 59. Wh 88%. Latino 2%. Blk 2%. Native Am 3%. Asian 5%. Avg class size: 12. **Fac 9.** M 1/F 8. FT 6/PT 3. Adv deg: 44%. **Grad '08—4.** Alum donors: 30%. **Tui '12-'13:** Day $7200-9600 (+$250). **Est 1981.** Nonprofit. Sem (Sept-June). Preschoolers and kindergartners at this Montessori school gain an introduction to children's literature and natural science. In grades 1 and 2, Brookwood focuses on reading, mathematics and basic concepts in physical science. Older pupils (grades 3-6) address such social studies topics as mythology, government and geography. Students may also explore bookmaking, origami and other art forms.

LAUREL HILL SCHOOL   Day Coed Gr PS (Age 2)-8
East Setauket, NY 11733. 201 Old Town Rd.
Tel: 631-751-1154. Fax: 631-751-2421.
www.laurelhillschool.org   E-mail: info@laurelhillschool.org
    Robert H. Stark, Head (1973). BA, New York Univ, MA, City Univ of New York. Helen Stark, Ed Dir. Yosefa Klein-Karchmar, Adm.
    Pre-Prep. Gen Acad. Feat—Lib_Skills Fr Lat Span Computers Drama Music. **Supp**— Rem_Math Rem_Read Tut. **Selective adm:** 32/yr. Appl fee: $75. Appl due: Jan. **Enr 450.** B 218. G 232. Avg class size: 16. Uniform. **Fac 60.** M 3/F 57. FT 37/PT 23. **Grad '10—18.** Prep—12. **Tui '11-'12:** Day $10,450-14,750 (+$460-485). **Est 1973.** Inc. Tri (Sept-June). Laurel Hill's structured infant (ages six weeks to 24 months), preschool (ages 2-4) and elementary program includes small classes and independent learning opportunities. The school assigns an educational assistant to each class, and specialists teach such subjects as computers, foreign language and physical education. LHS employs varying teaching methods to address different learning styles, with students encouraged to progress at an appropriate pace. The computer lab enables boys and girls to develop computer skills through multimedia projects and Web design workshops.

CATHEDRAL PREPARATORY SEMINARY   Day Boys Gr 9-12
Elmhurst, NY 11373. 56-25 92nd St.
Tel: 718-592-6800. Fax: 718-592-5574.
www.cathedralprepseminary.com   E-mail: dokeefe@cathedralprepseminary.com
    Rev. Fred Marano, Prin (2009). BA, Cathedral College of the Immaculate Conception, MA, Seminary of the Immaculate Conception. Rev. James Kuroly, Adm.
    Col Prep. AP—Eng Eur_Hist US_Hist. **Feat**—Creative_Writing Humanities Ital Lat Span Calc Comp_Sci Global_Stud Govt/Econ Theol Film Studio_Art Drama Music. **Supp**—Rev Tut. **Sports**— B: Baseball Basket X-country Golf Soccer Track. Activities: 11. **Selective adm**

(Gr 9-11): 57/yr. Accepted: 61%. Yield: 36%. **Tests** TACHS. **Enr 182.** Stud/fac: 10:1. **Fac 13.** M 11/F 2. FT 13. Adv deg: 69%. **Grad '08—44.** Col—44. **Avg SAT:** CR 520. M 510. W 530. **Tui '07-'08:** Day $6200 (+$600-900). **Est 1914.** Nonprofit. Roman Catholic. Sem (Sept-June). **Assoc** MSA. Cathedral Prep provides a college preparatory curriculum, including honors and Advanced Placement classes and senior electives, for those considering the priesthood. A writing course available to seniors focuses upon college-level essay composition. Boys perform 20 to 40 hours of compulsory community service annually, depending upon their grade level.

ST. FRANCIS PREPARATORY SCHOOL   **Day Coed Gr 9-12**
Fresh Meadows, NY 11365. 6100 Francis Lewis Blvd.
Tel: 718-423-8810. Fax: 718-224-2108.
www.sfponline.org   E-mail: 21stcentury@sfponline.org
    Br. Leonard Conway, OSF, Prin (1983). BS, St Francis College (NY), MS, Pratt Institute. Theodore Jahn, Adm.

    Col Prep. AP (exams req'd; 572 taken, 65% 3+)—Eng Span Calc Bio Chem Environ_Sci Physics Eur_Hist US_Hist World_Hist Psych US_Govt & Pol Art_Hist Studio_Art Music_ Theory. **Feat**—Poetry Shakespeare Gothic_Lit Fr Ger Ital Stats Anat & Physiol Astron Forensic_Sci Marine_Bio/Sci Biotech Web_Design NY_Hist WWII Econ Sociol Relig World_Relig Film Graphic_Arts Painting Photog Acting Theater_Arts Music Music_Hist Dance Accounting Bus. **Supp**—Rev Tut. **Dual enr:** St John's U-NY, St Francis Col-NY, Pace. **Sports (req'd)**—Basket Bowl Cheer X-country Golf Hand Ice_Hockey Indoor_Track Lacrosse Soccer Swim Tennis Track Volley. B: Baseball Football. G: Gymnastics Softball. Activities: 100. **Selective adm (Gr 9-11):** 712/yr. Appl fee: $0. Appl due: Feb. Accepted: 50%. Yield: 26%. **Tests** TACHS. **Enr 2639.** B 1204. G 1435. Wh 52%. Latino 19%. Blk 10%. Asian 5%. Other 14%. Avg class size: 34. Uniform. **Fac 160.** M 78/F 82. FT 154/PT 6. Wh 92%. Latino 5%. Blk 2%. Asian 1%. Adv deg: 80%. **Grad '11—651.** Col—646. (CUNY 175, St John's U-NY 75, SUNY-Stony Brook 24, Adelphi 24, Long Island 22, Hofstra 14). **Avg SAT:** CR 534. M 545. W 542. **Col Couns:** 10. **Tui '11-'12:** Day $7500 (+$750). **Est 1858.** Nonprofit. Roman Catholic. Quar (Sept-June). **Assoc** MSA. Founded by the Franciscan Brothers, this large high school conducts a college preparatory program with a variety of electives. Honors and Advanced Placement courses are available in the major disciplines, and St. Francis operates a college-credit program in conjunction with St. John's University, St. Francis College and Pace University. In addition, qualified pupils may pursue an advanced science track. A junior-year elective offering allows students to perform community service at local nursing homes, shelters and hospitals.

WALDORF SCHOOL OF GARDEN CITY   **Day Coed Gr PS (Age 3)-12**
Garden City, NY 11530. 225 Cambridge Ave.
Tel: 516-742-3434. Fax: 516-742-3457.
www.waldorfgarden.org   E-mail: walshs@waldorfgarden.org
    Susan Braun, Admin (1998). BA, Bucknell Univ. Christine Bleecker, Adm.

    Col Prep. Waldorf. Feat—Shakespeare Russ_Lit Fr Ger Span Calc Botany Zoology African_Hist Econ World_Relig Studio_Art Drama Music Eurythmy Woodworking. **Supp**—Tut. **Dual enr:** Adelphi. **Sports**—Basket Soccer. B: Baseball. G: Softball. **Selective adm (Gr PS-11):** 68/yr. Appl fee: $50. Appl due: Rolling. Accepted: 43%. Yield: 92%. **Tests** SSAT. **Enr 350.** Avg class size: 29. **Fac 51.** M 12/F 39. FT 31/PT 20. Adv deg: 33%. **Grad '09—21.** Col—21. (Boston U 2, NYU 2, Oberlin 1, Swarthmore 1, Rice 1, U of VA 1). **Avg SAT:** CR 551. M 579. W 539. Avg ACT: 23. **Tui '12-'13:** Day $11,225-21,370 (+$500). Aid: Need 120 ($385,000). **Est 1947.** Nonprofit. Quar (Sept-June). Basing its program on the educational philosophy of Dr. Rudolf Steiner, the school integrates the fine and performing arts into its liberal arts curriculum. A varied foreign language program is part of the college preparatory program: French and German classes begin in grade 1 and continue through high school, while Spanish commences in grade 8. Qualified seniors may take courses for college credit at Adelphi University. Students enroll from many communities in Nassau and Queens counties.

THE GREEN VALE SCHOOL Day Coed Gr PS (Age 3)-9
Glen Head, NY 11545. 250 Valentine's Ln.
Tel: 516-621-2420. Fax: 516-621-1317.
www.greenvaleschool.org E-mail: awatters@greenvaleschool.org
  Stephen H. Watters, Head (1995). BA, Denison Univ, MAT, Univ of Massachusetts-Amherst. Anne Bailey Watters, Adm.
  Pre-Prep. Feat—Fr Lat Span Computers Studio_Art Chorus Music Woodworking. **Supp**—Dev_Read Rem_Math Rem_Read Rev Tut. **Sports**—Basket Lacrosse Soccer. B: Baseball Football Ice_Hockey. G: F_Hockey Softball. **Selective adm:** 72/yr. Appl fee: $75. Appl due: Rolling. Accepted: 65%. **Enr 466.** Elem 454. Sec 12. Wh 82%. Latino 1%. Blk 4%. Asian 5%. Other 8%. Avg class size: 14. **Fac 69.** M 14/F 55. FT 62/PT 7. Adv deg: 91%. **Grad '11—46.** Prep—43. (Friends Acad-NY 11, Portledge 4, Pomfret 3, St George's Sch-RI 3, Choate 3, Deerfield Acad 2). **Tui '11-'12:** Day $12,800-26,300 (+$300-1150). Aid: Need 25 ($360,000). **Est 1923.** Nonprofit. Tri (Sept-June). Green Vale, which provides a traditional liberal arts-based education, is divided into three divisions: the early childhood department (PS-K), the lower school (grades 1-5) and the upper school (grades 6-9). The arts and computer education are integral components of the school's curriculum, and students participate in interscholastic sports starting in grade 5.

SOLOMON SCHECHTER SCHOOL OF WESTCHESTER Day Coed Gr K-12
Hartsdale, NY 10530. 555 W Hartsdale Ave.
Tel: 914-948-8333. Fax: 914-948-7979.
Other locations: 30 Dellwood Rd, White Plains 10605.
www.solomon-schechter.com E-mail: syossem@solomon-schechter.com
  Elliot Spiegel, Head (1980). EdD, Univ of Southern California. Leora Kalikow, Upper Sch Adm; Diana Schutt, Lower Sch Adm.
  Col Prep. Bilingual (Hebrew). AP—Calc. **Feat**—Shakespeare Hebrew Lat Span Arabic Astron Forensic_Sci Econ Govt Law Judaic_Stud Visual_Arts Theater Music Dance. **Supp**—Rev. **Sports**—Basket Bowl X-country Ski Soccer Tennis. B: Baseball. G: Softball Track Volley. Activities: 24. **Selective adm:** 151/yr. Appl fee: $100. Appl due: Jan. **Tests** ISEE. **Enr 874.** B 429. G 445. Elem 596. Sec 278. Avg class size: 18. **Fac 161.** M 32/F 129. FT 150/PT 11. Adv deg: 12%. **Grad '11—83.** Col—82. (U of MD-Col Park 10, Syracuse 9, Cornell 6, U of MI 3, Lehigh 3, U of PA 3). **Avg SAT:** CR 642. M 643. W 665. **Mid 50% SAT:** CR 580-700. M 600-700. W 610-720. Avg ACT: 27.3. Mid 50% ACT: 24-31. **Col Couns:** 2. **Tui '12-'13:** Day $19,300-32,800 (+$120-3680). Aid: Need 303 ($2,789,935). **Est 1966.** Nonprofit. Jewish (100% practice). Tri (Sept-June). Beginning in the early grades, SSSW offers a bilingual (Hebrew and English) curriculum within a Jewish setting. Eighth graders spend two weeks traveling to Biblical sites and various cities in Israel, while seniors engage in an Israel Experience that comprises a week of travel in Poland, followed by two months of travel and study in Israel. Academics during this time provide boys and girls with an extensive examination of the history of Israel. Students in the high school (grades 9-12) perform 40 hours of required community service per year. The lower school (grades K-5) occupies a separate campus on Dellwood Road in White Plains (914-948-3111).

HOUGHTON ACADEMY Bdg Coed Gr 9-PG
Houghton, NY 14744. 9790 Thayer St. Day Coed 6-12
Tel: 585-567-8115. Fax: 585-567-8048.
www.houghtonacademy.org E-mail: admissions@houghtonacademy.org
  Scott Frazier, Int Co-Head (2011). BA, Grove City College. Dale Shatto, Int Co-Head. BSEd, Univ of Pittsburgh, MA, Grace Theological Seminary. Ronald J. Bradbury, Adm.
  Col Prep. AP (exams req'd; 66 taken, 68% 3+)—Physics US_Hist Econ. **Feat**—Span Environ_Sci Geog Govt Bible Studio_Art Band Chorus Music_Theory Accounting Driver_Ed Health. **Supp**—ESL Tut. **Comp:** Comp/Stud: 1:4. **Dual enr:** Houghton. **Sports**—Basket Golf. B: Soccer. G: Cheer Volley. Activities: 5. **Selective adm:** 48/yr. Bdg 31. Day 17. Appl fee: $50.

Appl due: Feb. Accepted: 58%. Yield: 50%. **Tests** CEEB SSAT TOEFL. **Enr 138.** B 74. G 64. Bdg 68. Day 70. Elem 27. Sec 111. Wh 46%. Blk 6%. Asian 45%. Other 3%. Intl 44%. Avg class size: 16. Stud/fac: 6:1. Casual dress. **Fac 22.** M 11/F 11. FT 9/PT 13. Wh 96%. Blk 4%. Adv deg: 63%. In Dorms 3. **Grad '11—43.** Col—43. (Houghton 6, MI St 4, SUNY-Binghamton 2, Drexel 2, Grove City 2, IN Wesleyan 2). **Avg SAT:** CR 496. M 600. **Col Couns:** 1. **Tui '12-'13:** Bdg $24,435. Day $6930. Intl Bdg $26,385. Aid: Need 38 ($150,000). **Est 1883.** Nonprofit. Wesleyan. Sem (Aug-June). **Assoc** MSA. The academy's college preparatory program follows a modular schedule. Dual-credit college courses are offered to qualified upperclassmen at nearby Houghton College. During the weeklong Winterim session, boys and girls engage in various nontraditional and enrichment pursuits; options vary by year.

LONG ISLAND SCHOOL FOR THE GIFTED   Day Coed Gr PS (Age 4)-9
Huntington Station, NY 11746. 165 Pidgeon Hill Rd.
Tel: 631-423-3557. Fax: 631-423-4368.
www.lisg.org   E-mail: info@lisg.org
Roberta Tropper, Head of School (1980). Carol Yilmaz, Adm.

Pre-Prep. Feat—Fr Span Computers Global_Stud Studio_Art Music Study_Skills. **Comp:** Comp/Stud: 1:4. **Selective adm:** 60/yr. Appl fee: $50. Appl due: Rolling. **Tests** IQ. **Enr 315.** Elem 297. Sec 18. Wh 57%. Latino 1%. Blk 10%. Asian 20%. Other 12%. Avg class size: 16. Stud/fac: 6:1. **Fac 39.** M 2/F 37. FT 35/PT 4. Adv deg: 97%. **Grad '09—14.** Alum donors: 5%. **Tui '11-'12:** Day $14,350-16,250 (+$400). **Est 1980.** Nonprofit. Tri (Sept-June). LISG's curriculum is individualized for the gifted student, with emphasis on creative thinking, problem solving and acceleration. Candidates for admission must have an IQ of 130 or above. Students work from one to three years above grade level in all subjects, completing most high school courses by the completion of ninth grade.

THE MARY LOUIS ACADEMY   Day Girls Gr 9-12
Jamaica Estates, NY 11432. 176-21 Wexford Ter.
Tel: 718-297-2120. Fax: 718-739-0037.
www.tmla.org   E-mail: admissions@tmla.org
Sr. Kathleen McKinney, CSJ, Prin (1971). BA, St Joseph's College, MS, Adelphi Univ, EdD, St John's Univ (NY). Sr. Filippa Luciano, CSJ, Adm.

Col Prep. AP (exams req'd; 312 taken, 57% 3+)—Eng Fr Lat Span Calc Stats Bio Chem Physics Eur_Hist US_Hist World_Hist Studio_Art Music_Theory. **Feat**—British_Lit Creative_Writing Shakespeare Ital Environ_Sci Programming Econ Law Psych Sociol World_Relig Drawing Painting Sculpt Music Orchestra Driver_Ed. **Supp**—Rev Tut. **Comp:** Comp/Stud: 1:5. **Dual enr:** St John's U-NY. **Sports**— G: Basket Golf Lacrosse Soccer Softball Swim Tennis Track Volley. Activities: 40. **Selective adm (Gr 9-11):** 255/yr. Appl fee: $300. Appl due: Dec. Accepted: 48%. Yield: 52%. **Tests** TACHS. **Enr 962.** Avg class size: 28. Stud/fac: 13:1. Uniform. **Fac 79.** M 17/F 62. FT 79. Adv deg: 86%. **Grad '10—219.** Col—219. **Avg SAT:** CR 536. M 536. Avg ACT: 23. Alum donors: 10%. **Tui '10-'11:** Day $7900 (+$850). Aid: Merit ($250,000). Need ($30,200). **Est 1936.** Nonprofit. Roman Catholic (77% practice). Tri (Sept-June). **Assoc** MSA. Established by the Sisters of Saint Joseph, Brentwood, the academy enables seniors to earn college credit through an affiliation with St. John's University. Sequences are offered in art, languages, mathematics, music and science. Community service is a required element of the religious studies curriculum.

NATIONAL SPORTS ACADEMY   Bdg & Day
Lake Placid, NY 12946. 821 Mirror Lake Dr.   Coed Gr 8-PG
Tel: 518-523-3460. Fax: 518-523-3488.
www.nationalsportsacademy.com   E-mail: grand@nationalsportsacademy.com
David Wenn, Head (1979). BA, State Univ of New York-Cortland. Gun Rand, Adm.

Col Prep. Sports (Winter). AP (exams req'd)—Eng Calc Stats Bio US_Hist Psych.

Feat—British_Lit Fr Span Environ_Sci Physiol Econ Govt. **Supp**—LD Tut. **Sports (req'd)**—Ice_Hockey Ski. **Selective adm:** 38/yr. Bdg 33. Day 5. Appl fee: $60. Appl due: Rolling. Accepted: 60%. Yield: 85%. **Tests** SSAT. **Enr 75.** B 51. G 24. Bdg 61. Day 14. Elem 3. Sec 61. PG 11. Intl 19%. Avg class size: 7. Stud/fac: 6:1. **Fac 16.** M 8/F 8. FT 16. Adv deg: 50%. In Dorms 8. **Grad '07—18.** Col—12. **Avg SAT:** CR 528. M 541. W 509. **Col Couns:** 1. Alum donors: 28%. **Tui '12-'13:** Bdg $30,740 (+$1500-6250). Day $14,340 (+$1500-6250). **Est 1979.** Nonprofit. Sem (Sept-June). NSA accepts student-athletes who are training and competing in such Olympic winter sports as Alpine, Nordic and freestyle skiing; ski jumping; snowboarding; biathlon; luge; figure and speed skating; and ice hockey. Seven- and nine-month programs are available. During the spring term, boys and girls choose from various intensive arts electives, among them cinematography, drama, drawing and music. Students perform 10 hours of required community service annually.

FRENCH-AMERICAN SCHOOL OF NEW YORK   Day Coed Gr PS (Age 3)-12
Larchmont, NY 10538. 111 Larchmont Ave.
Tel: 914-250-0000. Fax: 914-698-8696.
Other locations: 145 New St, Mamaroneck 10543; 85 Palmer Ave, Scarsdale 10580.
www.fasny.org   E-mail: aagopian@fasny.org
    Robert M. Leonhardt, Head. Antoine Agopian, Adm.

    Col Prep. Fr Bac. Bilingual (Fr). Feat—Fr Ger Lat Span Econ Philos Studio_Art Chorus Music. **Supp**—ESL Rev Tut. **Sports**—Basket Soccer Tennis. B: Baseball Rugby. G: Softball. **Selective adm (Gr PS-11):** 192/yr. Appl fee: $80. Appl due: Rolling. Accepted: 74%. Yield: 75%. **Enr 797.** B 369. G 428. Elem 688. Sec 109. Intl 90%. Avg class size: 18. Stud/fac: 9:1. Casual dress. **Fac 93.** Adv deg: 84%. **Grad '11—25.** Col—25. **Col Couns:** 2. **Tui '12-'13:** Day $22,350-25,600 (+$0-3250). Aid: Need 72 ($662,000). **Est 1980.** Nonprofit. Tri (Sept-June). Offering bilingual instruction (French and English), FAS offers a dual curriculum that emphasizes critical-thinking skills and problem solving. The preschool, which focuses on verbal skills, books, art and music, is conducted in both languages. In the upper and lower schools, math is taught in French, while science and social studies instruction is in English. Students satisfy the following community service requirements: 7 hours per year in grades 6 and 7, 10 hours annually in grades 8-10, and 12 hours per year in grades 11 and 12. The preschool operates in Scarsdale, while the lower school (grades 1-5) is housed on the Larchmont campus and the upper school (grades 6-12) is located in Mamaroneck.

SAINT GREGORY'S SCHOOL   Day Boys Gr PS (Age 3)-8
Loudonville, NY 12211. 121 Old Niskayuna Rd.   Girls PS (Age 3)-K
Tel: 518-785-6621. Fax: 518-782-1364.
www.saintgregorysschool.org   E-mail: marrao@saintgregorysschool.org
    Jeffrey P. Loomis, Head (2009). BA, Siena College, MS, La Salle Univ.

    Pre-Prep. Feat—Lat Span Computers Relig Music Handbells. **Comp:** Laptop prgm Gr 5-8. **Sports**— B: Baseball Basket X-country Lacrosse Soccer Track. **Selective adm:** 31/yr. Appl fee: $25. Appl due: Rolling. **Enr 140.** B 125. G 15. Wh 89%. Blk 6%. Asian 5%. Avg class size: 15. Uniform. **Fac 24.** M 6/F 18. FT 21/PT 3. Adv deg: 58%. **Grad '11—10.** Prep—8. (Albany Acad 5, La Salle Inst 2, Loudonville Christian 1). **Tui '11-'12:** Day $9945-12,581 (+$350-450). Aid: Need 30 ($155,000). **Est 1962.** Nonprofit. Roman Catholic. Tri (Sept-June). Enrolling girls in nursery (age 3) through kindergarten and boys at all levels, Saint Gregory's maintains a structured learning program that provides opportunities for acceleration. Well-developed computer, physical science and life science programs are integral to the curriculum. French instruction begins in prekindergarten, Spanish and Latin in grade 7. The French program culminates in a four-day learning experience in Quebec, Canada.

MARTIN LUTHER HIGH SCHOOL   **Day Coed Gr 9-12**
Maspeth, NY 11378. 60-02 Maspeth Ave.
Tel: 718-894-4000. Fax: 718-894-1469.
www.martinluthernyc.org   E-mail: info@martinluthernyc.org
    Randal C. Gast, Head (2010). MA, MS, Adelphi Univ. Elizabeth Crowe, Prin. MS. Robert
Lowig, Adm.
    Col Prep. AP (exams req'd; 209 taken)—Eng Ger Span Calc Bio Chem Environ_Sci
Eur_Hist US_Hist. **Feat**—British_Lit Mythology Fr Marine_Bio/Sci Computers Psych Theol
Photog Studio_Art Chorus Music Accounting Bus. **Supp**—Rem_Math Tut. **Comp:** Comp/
Stud: 1:4. **Dual enr:** St John's U-NY, Adelphi. **Sports**—Basket X-country Soccer Tennis
Track. B: Baseball Wrestling. G: Cheer Softball Volley. Activities: 13. **Selective adm:** 79/yr.
Appl fee: $50. Appl due: Rolling. Accepted: 60%. Yield: 80%. **Enr 223.** B 114. G 109. Wh
32%. Latino 26%. Blk 10%. Asian 17%. Other 15%. Avg class size: 16. Stud/fac: 12:1. Uni-
form. **Fac 20.** M 11/F 9. FT 18/PT 2. Wh 85%. Latino 5%. Blk 10%. Adv deg: 55%. **Grad
'11—86.** Col—83. (CUNY 18, SUNY 11, St John's U-NY 4, Concordia Col-NY 2, St Francis
Col-NY 2, St Joseph's Col-NY 2). **Avg SAT:** CR 458. M 458. W 459. **Col Couns:** 1. Alum
donors: 10%. **Tui '12-'13:** Day $8150 (+$700). Aid: Merit 25 ($60,000). Need 118 ($231,000).
Est 1960. Nonprofit. Lutheran (20% practice). Quar (Sept-June). **Assoc** MSA. In addition to a
college preparatory academic program that includes Advanced Placement courses, the school
offers an array of interscholastic sports and other activities. Under a special program with St.
John's and Adelphi universities, seniors may take college-credit courses in English, history,
science and math. Students satisfy a 30-hour community service requirement over their four
years.

GRACE DAY SCHOOL   **Day Coed Gr PS (Age 2)-8**
Massapequa, NY 11758. 23 Cedar Shore Dr.
Tel: 516-798-1122. Fax: 516-799-0711.
www.gracedayschool.org   E-mail: info@gracedayschool.org
    Frank J. Fallon, Head (2011). Katherine Licari, Adm.
    Pre-Prep. Feat—Fr Span Computers Relig Music. **Supp**—Dev_Read LD. **Sports**—Basket
Soccer Track. G: Volley. **Somewhat selective adm:** 97/yr. Appl fee: $40. Appl due: Rolling.
Accepted: 95%. Yield: 80%. **Enr 290.** B 145. G 145. Wh 89%. Latino 1%. Blk 7%. Asian
2%. Other 1%. Avg class size: 15. Uniform. **Fac 34.** M 3/F 31. FT 18/PT 16. Wh 100%.
Adv deg: 50%. **Grad '10—22.** Prep—22. **Tui '11-'12:** Day $9100-9750. **Est 1955.** Nonprofit.
Episcopal. Tri (Sept-June). The school provides a Christian education for students who are at
or above grade level. The program emphasizes basic skills acquisition, and problem-solving
activities and creative opportunities are part of the curriculum. Pupils study French and Spanish concurrently in grades K-2, then take French through grade 8. Departmentalization begins
in grade 5. Computer instruction is integrated into the curriculum as students learn about basic
applications and Internet research through classroom tutorials and independent projects.

CHAMINADE HIGH SCHOOL   **Day Boys Gr 9-12**
Mineola, NY 11501. 340 Jackson Ave.
Tel: 516-742-5555. Fax: 516-742-1989.
www.chaminade-hs.org   E-mail: admissions@chaminade-hs.org
    Br. Thomas J. Cleary, SM, Pres (2011). BA, St John's Univ (NY), MA, Hofstra Univ. Br.
Joseph Dominick Belizzi, SM, Prin. BA, St John's Univ (NY), MA, New York Univ.
    Col Prep. Feat—Chin Fr Ger Lat Span Comp_Sci Relig Studio_Art Music. **Supp**—Tut.
Sports— B: Baseball Basket Crew X-country Football Ice_Hockey Lacrosse Soccer Swim
Tennis Track Volley Wrestling. Activities: 30. **Selective adm (Gr 9):** 450/yr. Appl due: Dec.
Tests TACHS. **Enr 1700.** Wh 90%. Latino 5%. Blk 3%. Asian 2%. Uniform. **Fac 74.** M 67/F 7.
FT 71/PT 3. Adv deg: 85%. **Grad '11—433.** Col—432. (Fordham 32, U of DE 19, Holy Cross
16, Villanova 15, U of Scranton 13, Manhattan Col 10). **Avg SAT:** CR 632. M 649. **Tui '11-
'12:** Day $9230. Aid: Merit 50 ($100,000). Need 45 ($125,025). Work prgm 75 ($40,000). **Est**

1930. Nonprofit. Roman Catholic (100% practice). Tri (Sept-June). **Assoc** MSA. Conducted by Marianist priests and brothers, Chaminade complements work in the traditional academic disciplines with various cocurricular and extracurricular programs. The varied liberal arts curriculum features an array of foreign languages.

IONA PREPARATORY SCHOOL   **Day Boys Gr 9-12**
New Rochelle, NY 10804. 255 Wilmot Rd.
Tel: 914-632-0714. Fax: 914-632-9760.
www.ionaprep.org   E-mail: admissions@ionaprep.org
    Br. Thomas R. Leto, CFC, Pres (2010). Maureen Kiers, Prin. BA, Molloy College, MS, St John's Univ (NY). Judy Musho, Adm.
    Col Prep. AP (exams req'd; 178 taken, 55% 3+)—Eng Span Calc Stats Bio Chem Physics Eur_Hist US_Hist World_Hist Psych US_Govt & Pol. **Feat**—Chin Fr Ital Lat Astron Forensic_Sci Meteorology Robotics Milit_Hist Econ Relig Studio_Art Music Accounting. **Supp**—Tut. **Comp:** Laptop prgm Gr 9-12. **Sports**— B: Baseball Basket Crew X-country Football Golf Ice_Hockey Indoor_Track Lacrosse Soccer Swim Tennis Track Volley Wrestling. Activities: 35. **Selective adm (Gr 9-11):** 212/yr. Appl due: Dec. Accepted: 65%. Yield: 50%. **Tests** HSPT ISEE SSAT TACHS. **Enr 750.** Avg class size: 26. Uniform. **Fac 65.** Wh 94%. Latino 2%. Blk 2%. Asian 2%. Adv deg: 89%. **Grad '11—173.** Col—173. **Avg SAT:** CR/M 1100. **Col Couns:** 2. **Tui '12-'13:** Day $15,300. **Est 1916.** Nonprofit. Roman Catholic (87% practice). Sem (Sept-June). **Assoc** MSA. This independent Catholic school's college preparatory curriculum offers courses at four different levels: Regents, honors, accelerated and Advanced Placement. Students complete four-year course requirements in English, math, science and social studies; the core curriculum also includes foreign language, computer, fine arts and health classes. In addition, Iona Prep features a range of electives for seniors as a supplement to compulsory course work.

URSULINE SCHOOL   **Day Girls Gr 6-12**
New Rochelle, NY 10804. 1354 North Ave.
Tel: 914-636-3950. Fax: 914-636-3949.
www.ursulinenewrochelle.org   E-mail: admin@ursulinenewrochelle.org
    Eileen F. Davidson, Pres (2012). BA, Mercy College, MA, Iona College. Denise Moore, Int Prin. Rose Trapani, Adm.
    Col Prep. AP (exams req'd; 152 taken, 89% 3+)—Eng Fr Lat Span Calc Stats Bio Environ_Sci Physics Eur_Hist US_Hist Econ US_Govt & Pol Studio_Art. **Feat**—British_Lit Creative_Writing Greek Ital Anat & Physiol Marine_Bio/Sci Engineering Comp_Sci Law Psych Relig World_Relig Music Journ. **Supp**—Dev_Read Rev Tut. **Comp:** Comp/Stud: 1:1 Laptop prgm Gr 6-12. **Sports**— G: Basket Crew X-country F_Hockey Golf Lacrosse Soccer Softball Swim Tennis Track Volley. Activities: 81. **Selective adm (Gr 6-11):** 196/yr. Appl due: Jan. Accepted: 70%. Yield: 40%. **Tests** ISEE TACHS. **Enr 792.** Avg class size: 22. Uniform. **Fac 80.** Adv deg: 90%. **Grad '09—143.** Col—142. **Avg SAT:** CR 590. M 580. W 610. Alum donors: 8%. **Tui '12-'13:** Day $16,600. Aid: Need ($1,350,000). **Est 1897.** Nonprofit. Roman Catholic (80% practice). Quar (Sept-June). **Assoc** MSA. Enrolling girls from Westchester County, the Bronx, Manhattan and Connecticut, Ursuline offers a selection of honors and Advanced Placement courses. Religious instruction, which is compulsory at all grade levels, includes some semester-long elective options for juniors and seniors. Pupils use laptop computers to develop multimedia presentations, create graphs of data and connect to the school-wide wireless network. Science students in grades 10-12 may conduct independent research in biology, chemistry, mathematics, physics or psychology.

ABRAHAM JOSHUA HESCHEL SCHOOL   **Day Coed Gr PS (Age 3)-12**
New York, NY 10023. 20 W End Ave.
Tel: 212-246-7717. Fax: 212-595-7252.
Other locations: 314 W 91st St, New York 10024; 270 W 89th St, New York 10024.
www.heschel.org
    Roanna Shorofsky, Head. BA, City Univ of New York. Marsha Feris, Adm.
    Col Prep. Feat—Shakespeare Holocaust_Lit Middle_Eastern_Lit Fr Hebrew Lat Span Calc
Genetics Programming Econ Bible Theol Art_Hist Ceramics Photog Studio_Art Theater_Arts
Music Music_Hist Journ. **Supp**—ESL Rem_Math Rem_Read. **Comp:** Laptop prgm Gr 9-12.
Sports—Basket Soccer Tennis. G: Volley. Activities: 38. **Selective adm:** 113/yr. Appl due:
Dec. **Tests** CTP_4 ISEE. **Enr 793.** B 386. G 407. Elem 510. Sec 283. Wh 98%. Latino 1%. Blk
1%. Avg class size: 23. **Fac 151.** M 30/F 121. FT 135/PT 16. Adv deg: 65%. **Grad '08—68.**
Col—68. **Col Couns:** 1. **Tui '11-'12:** Day $23,850-36,500. **Est 1983.** Nonprofit. Jewish. Sem
(Sept-June). Named for Rabbi Heschel, a prominent scholar, philosopher and theologian, the
school integrates Jewish tradition and history into its secular curriculum. Students come from a
variety of Jewish backgrounds. High schoolers (grades 9-12) participate in a one-to-one laptop
program. The middle school is located on West 91st Street, while the lower school operates on
West 89th Street. The high school division opened on West End Avenue in 2002.

THE CAEDMON SCHOOL   **Day Coed Gr PS (Age 2)-5**
New York, NY 10075. 416 E 80th St.
Tel: 212-879-2296. Fax: 212-879-0627.
www.caedmonschool.org   E-mail: admissions@caedmonschool.org
    Honor Taft, Int Head (2011). BA, William Smith College, MS, MEd, Columbia Univ. Erica
L. Papir, Adm.
    Pre-Prep. Montessori. Feat—Lib_Skills Writing Span Computers Art_Hist Studio_Art
Music Yoga. **Supp**—Rev Tut. **Selective adm:** 57/yr. Appl fee: $50. Appl due: Nov. **Tests**
CTP_4 ISEE. **Enr 275.** B 139. G 136. Wh 64%. Latino 17%. Asian 18%. Other 1%. Intl 20%.
Avg class size: 20. Stud/fac: 10:1. **Fac 49.** M 11/F 38. FT 37/PT 12. Wh 88%. Latino 3%. Blk
9%. Adv deg: 46%. **Grad '10—19.** Prep—19. **Tui '11-'12:** Day $27,000-32,000. Aid: Need
48 ($793,000). **Est 1962.** Nonprofit. Sem (Sept-June). Caedmon offers a Montessori-based
curriculum in the early program (through age 4). Throughout the elementary program, the
school combines elements of Montessori with a varied curriculum that features instruction by
specialists in science, library, computer, Spanish, art, music, physical education, Latin, violin
and yoga two to three times a week. Field trips throughout the city, an instrumental music
program, after-school classes and clubs, and schoolwide theatrical productions provide further
enrichment.

THE CHILDREN'S STOREFRONT SCHOOL   **Day Coed Gr PS (Age 4)-8**
New York, NY 10035. 70 E 129th St.
Tel: 212-427-7900. Fax: 212-348-2988.
www.thechildrensstorefront.org
    Wendy Reynoso, Head (2011).
    Pre-Prep. Montessori. Feat—Computers Fine_Arts. **Very selective adm:** 25/yr. Appl due:
Apr. Accepted: 2%. **Enr 174.** Latino 5%. Blk 95%. Avg class size: 18. Stud/fac: 7:1. **Fac 25.** M
7/F 18. FT 21/PT 4. Wh 45%. Latino 5%. Blk 45%. Other 5%. Adv deg: 28%. **Grad '09—15.**
Prep—15. Alum donors: 5%. **Tui '10-'11:** Day $0. **Est 1966.** Nonprofit. Sem (Sept-June).
Providing tuition-free schooling for children from Harlem, Storefront offers a Montessori-
based preschool that emphasizes language and vocabulary skills. In the lower school (grades
1-4), students focus on the basic skills of English and math and begin their study of history, science, social studies and the arts. Upper schoolers (grades 5-8) study more concentrated topics
in science and literature, while also exploring computers and the fine arts.

CORLEARS SCHOOL
Day Coed Gr PS (Age 2)-5
New York, NY 10011. 324 W 15th St.
Tel: 212-741-2800. Fax: 212-807-1550.
www.corlearsschool.org E-mail: office@corlearsschool.org
Thya Merz, Head (2003). BA, Norwich Univ, MS, Johns Hopkins Univ. Anita Haber, Adm.

Pre-Prep. Feat—Lib_Skills Span Studio_Art Drama Music Movement Woodworking. **Supp**—Dev_Read. **Comp:** Comp/Stud: 1:5 (1:1 Laptop prgm Gr 5). **Selective adm (Gr PS-4):** 41/yr. Appl fee: $50. Appl due: Dec. Accepted: 49%. Yield: 37%. **Tests** CTP_4. **Enr 165.** B 79. G 86. Wh 74%. Latino 4%. Blk 2%. Asian 3%. Other 17%. Avg class size: 18. Casual dress. **Fac 31.** M 1/F 30. FT 29/PT 2. Wh 69%. Latino 17%. Blk 14%. Adv deg: 54%. **Grad '08—6. Tui '11-'12:** Day $25,475-29,740 (+$600). Aid: Need 28 ($570,129). **Est 1968.** Nonprofit. (Sept-June). Situated in two townhouses, Corlears offers special courses in science, art, movement, Spanish, music and physical education. Thematic studies with strong links between social studies and science form the core curriculum. Utilizing multi-age groupings, the progressive program emphasizes creative problem solving and allows for the exploration of individual interests.

DOMINICAN ACADEMY
Day Girls Gr 9-12
New York, NY 10065. 44 E 68th St.
Tel: 212-744-0195. Fax: 212-744-0375.
www.dominicanacademy.org E-mail: bkane@dominicanacademy.org
Sr. Barbara Kane, OP, Prin (2009). BA, College of Mount St Joseph, MS, Indiana Univ, MBA, Butler Univ, MRE, Loyola Univ of Chicago, MA, Univ of Notre Dame. Jo Ann Fannon, Adm.

Col Prep. AP (exams req'd; 103 taken, 69% 3+)—Eng Lat Calc Bio Chem Physics Eur_Hist US_Hist Econ US_Govt & Pol Art_Hist. **Feat**—Shakespeare Fr Span Stats Forensic_Sci Psych Drama Chorus Dance Debate. **Supp**—Rev Tut. **Comp:** Comp/Stud: 1:3. **Sports**— G: Basket X-country Soccer Softball Tennis Track Volley. Activities: 35. **Selective adm (Gr 9-11):** 50/yr. Appl due: Jan. **Tests** TACHS. **Enr 225.** Wh 59%. Latino 20%. Blk 8%. Native Am 1%. Asian 12%. Avg class size: 20. Stud/fac: 8:1. Uniform. **Fac 27.** M 5/F 22. FT 22/PT 5. Wh 82%. Latino 4%. Blk 7%. Asian 7%. Adv deg: 88%. **Grad '11—52.** Col—52. **Col Couns:** 1. **Tui '11-'12:** Day $11,000 (+$650). Aid: Need ($296,000). **Est 1897.** Nonprofit. Roman Catholic (89% practice). Quar (Sept-June). **Assoc** MSA. The curriculum at Dominican includes two compulsory years of Latin study and Advanced Placement courses in all major disciplines. The academy schedules a cultural trip abroad annually, and an enrichment series features at least two trips per year to nearby museums and performing arts centers. Community service is part of the religion curriculum, with each girl encouraged to volunteer in her local community and parish; in addition, seniors satisfy a 30-hour service requirement. Students may also embark on service trips to Ecuador and Camden, NJ.

LEMAN MANHATTAN PREPARATORY SCHOOL
Bdg Coed Gr 9-12
Day Coed PS (Age 3)-12
New York, NY 10004. 41 Broad St.
Tel: 212-232-0266. Fax: 212-232-0284.
Other locations: 1 Morris St, New York 10004.
www.lemanmanhattan.org E-mail: info@lemanmanhattan.org
Drew Alexander, Head. Janet Barrett, Adm.

Col Prep. Feat—NYC_Lit Chin Fr Span Calc Stats Astron Forensic_Sci Comp_Sci African_Hist Asian_Hist Comp_Relig Film Graphic_Arts Photog Studio_Art Acting Music Woodworking. **Comp:** Comp/Stud: 1:2. **Sports**—Basket X-country Golf Swim Track. B: Soccer. G: Volley. Activities: 20. **Selective adm:** 125/yr. Appl fee: $60. Appl due: Dec. **Tests** CTP_4 ISEE. **Enr 490.** B 259. G 231. Elem 430. Sec 60. Wh 63%. Latino 6%. Blk 9%. Asian 7%. Other 15%. Avg class size: 18. Stud/fac: 5:1. **Fac 84.** M 19/F 65. FT 75/PT 9. Wh 83%. Latino 5%. Blk 5%. Asian 7%. Adv deg: 98%. **Col Couns:** 1. **Tui '12-'13:** Bdg $67,000. Day

$33,800-36,400. Aid: Need 158. **Est 2005.** Inc. Spons: Meritas. Sem (Sept-June). **Assoc** MSA. Located in the city's Financial District, Leman Manhattan conducts a full elementary and secondary program for an international student body. Programming emphasizes problem solving and the exchange of ideas at all grade levels, and the school encourages student participation in the studio and performing arts. Boys and girls engage in compulsory, age-appropriate community service projects. The middle and upper schools (grades 5-12) occupy separate quarters on Morris Street.   **See Also Pages 38-9**

MANHATTAN DAY SCHOOL   **Day Coed Gr PS (Age 2)-8**
New York, NY 10023. 310 W 75th St.   **(Coord 4-8)**
Tel: 212-376-6800. Fax: 212-376-6389.
www.mdsweb.org   E-mail: office@mdsweb.org
    Rabbi Mordechai Besser, Prin (1999). BA, MA, Yeshiva Univ (NY), MS, Hofstra Univ. Cindy Sherman, Adm.
    Gen Acad. Feat—Lib_Skills Hebrew Computers Judaic_Stud Studio_Art Music. **Supp**—Dev_Read LD Rem_Math Rem_Read Rev Tut. **Sports**—Basket. **Selective adm:** 80/yr. Appl fee: $250. Appl due: Dec. Accepted: 80%. Yield: 90%. **Enr 540.** B 270. G 270. Wh 95%. Asian 5%. Avg class size: 18. **Fac 100.** Adv deg: 46%. **Grad '08—40. Tui '08-'09:** Day $12,925-16,615. **Est 1943.** Nonprofit. Jewish (100% practice). Sem (Sept-June). Small classes and individualized instruction are characteristics of the school's curriculum. Grades PS-3 are coeducational, while grades 4-8 feature coordinate, single-gender classes. MDS maintains an enrichment program for all students, and a special-education program for children with learning disabilities is also available. Seventh and eighth graders satisfy community service requirements: 15 hours in grade 7, 30 hours in grade 8.

METROPOLITAN MONTESSORI SCHOOL   **Day Coed Gr PS (Age 3)-6**
New York, NY 10024. 325 W 85th St.
Tel: 212-579-5525. Fax: 212-579-5526.
www.mmsny.org   E-mail: mmsadmissions@mmsny.org
    Brenda Mizel, Head (2011). Heidi Morrison, Adm.
    Pre-Prep. Montessori. Feat—Fr Span Visual_Arts Music Orchestra. **Supp**—Dev_Read Rem_Math Rem_Read Rev Tut. **Selective adm (Gr PS-4):** 42/yr. Appl fee: $40. Appl due: Dec. **Enr 206.** B 108. G 98. Wh 74%. Latino 5%. Blk 9%. Native Am 1%. Asian 6%. Other 5%. Intl 25%. Avg class size: 23. Stud/fac: 12:1. **Fac 36.** M 5/F 31. FT 34/PT 2. Wh 64%. Latino 14%. Blk 11%. Asian 8%. Other 3%. Adv deg: 66%. **Grad '10—11.** Prep—9. (Horace Mann 2, Collegiate-NY 1, Riverdale 1, Trevor 1). **Tui '12-'13:** Day $29,850-31,900 (+$2600). Aid: Need 32 ($436,344). **Est 1964.** Nonprofit. Sem (Sept-June). In the school's primary program (ages 3-6), boys and girls gain an exposure to basic concepts in mathematics and language development. Social studies, science and foreign language course work commences in grade 1. Enrichment classes in music and visual arts are integral to the program. Upper elementary course work emphasizes preparation for competitive secondary schools.

PHILOSOPHY DAY SCHOOL   **Day Coed Gr PS (Age 3)-5**
New York, NY 10075. 12 E 79th St.
Tel: 212-744-7300. Fax: 212-744-6088.
www.philosophyday.org   E-mail: secretary@philosophyday.org
    William Fox, Head (2004). BA, Skidmore College, DipEd, Univ of Sydney (Australia). Elizabeth Katz, Adm.
    Pre-Prep. Gen Acad. Feat—Greek Sanskrit Studio_Art Drama Music. **Supp**—Dev_Read Tut. **Selective adm:** Appl fee: $50. Appl due: Dec. **Tests** CTP_4. **Enr 110.** Avg class size: 14. Stud/fac: 6:1. Uniform. **Fac 21.** M 4/F 17. FT 16/PT 5. Wh 71%. Latino 9%. Blk 9%. Other 11%. Adv deg: 57%. **Grad '10—9. Tui '11-'12:** Day $25,000. **Est 1994.** Nonprofit. Sem (Sept-June). Founded as the Abraham Lincoln School, PDS was established by a group of

parents wishing to combine classical education with the principles of The School of Practical Philosophy. The preschool program, which begins at age 3, follows a two-year curriculum. Children in grades K-5 meet twice a week with an arts specialist. Kindergartners receive Sanskrit instruction once a week, while older pupils have two weekly classes in the ancient language. The program features regular trips to nearby museums and cultural institutions, as well as to the school's rural property in Wallkill.

RODEPH SHOLOM SCHOOL   **Day Coed Gr PS (Age 2)-8**
New York, NY 10024. 10 W 84th St.
Tel: 646-438-8600. Fax: 212-874-0117.
Other locations: 168 W 79th St, New York 10024; 7 W 83rd St, New York 10024.
www.rodephsholomschool.org   E-mail: rssadmissions@rssnyc.org
     Paul Druzinsky, Head (2007). BA, Claremont McKenna College, MEd, Harvard Univ. Erin Woodhams, Adm.
     Pre-Prep. Feat—Fr Hebrew Span Computers Judaic_Stud Studio_Art Media_Arts Drama Band Chorus Music Dance. **Supp**—Dev_Read Rem_Math Rem_Read Tut. **Comp:** Comp/ Stud: 1:5. **Sports**—Basket X-country Soccer Tennis Track. B: Baseball. G: Softball Volley. **Selective adm (Gr PS-7):** 80/yr. Appl fee: $60. Appl due: Dec. **Tests** CTP_4 ISEE. **Enr 660.** B 333. G 327. Wh 95%. Latino 2%. Asian 2%. Other 1%. Avg class size: 16. Stud/fac: 6:1. **Fac 138.** M 25/F 113. FT 137/PT 1. Wh 96%. Latino 2%. Asian 1%. Other 1%. Adv deg: 63%. **Grad '10—39.** Prep—33. (Columbia Grammar & Prep 8, Horace Mann 4, Fieldston 3, Dalton 3, Spence 2, Trinity Sch-NY 2). **Tui '12-'13:** Day $35,700-38,700. Aid: Need 59 ($936,000). **Est 1970.** Nonprofit. Jewish. Sem (Sept-June). This Reform Jewish school's developmentally based curriculum integrates secular and Judaic studies. Language arts and mathematics form the core components of the elementary program, and specialists provide instruction in science, art, music, physical education, computers, Hebrew and Jewish studies. French and Spanish instruction begins in grade 6. The nursery division (ages 2 and 3) is located on West 83rd Street; classes for children in prekindergarten, kindergarten and grade 1 convene on West 84th Street; and grades 2-8 are conducted on West 79th Street.

SAINT VINCENT FERRER HIGH SCHOOL   **Day Girls Gr 9-12**
New York, NY 10065. 151 E 65th St.
Tel: 212-535-4680. Fax: 212-988-3455.
www.saintvincentferrer.com   E-mail: gmorgan@saintvincentferrer.com
     Sr. Gail Morgan, OP, Prin.
     Col Prep. Gen Acad. AP—Eng Fr Span Calc Chem Eur_Hist US_Hist. **Feat**—Humanities Shakespeare Stats Forensic_Sci Programming Econ Law Psych Sociol Relig Art_Hist Drawing Studio_Art Theater Chorus Handbells Accounting Finance. **Supp**—Rev Tut. **Sports**— G: Basket Soccer Softball Volley. Activities: 20. **Selective adm (Gr 9-11):** 120/yr. Appl due: Dec. **Tests** TACHS. **Enr 494.** Stud/fac: 14:1. Uniform. **Fac 35. Col Couns:** 1. **Tui '11-'12:** Day $7900 (+$400-600). **Est 1909.** Nonprofit. Roman Catholic (80% practice). Sem (Sept-June). **Assoc** MSA. SVF's college preparatory curriculum features a number of AP courses, and classes in foreign language, religion and the fine arts are among the graduation requirements. Girls may apply for the school's Scholars Program, which allows able students to receive a two-thirds scholarship for four years tuition.

SOLOMON SCHECHTER SCHOOL OF MANHATTAN   **Day Coed Gr K-8**
New York, NY 10025. 805 Columbus Ave.
Tel: 212-427-9500. Fax: 212-427-5300.
www.sssm.org   E-mail: amandanoodell@sssm.org
     Steven C. Lorch, Head (1995). BA, Rutgers College, EdM, Harvard Univ, PhD, Columbia Univ. Amanda Noodell, Adm.
     Pre-Prep. Gen Acad. Bilingual (Hebrew). Feat—Hebrew Judaic_Stud Studio_Art Music.

Supp—ESL. **Comp:** Comp/Stud: 1:3. **Sports**—Basket Soccer. **Selective adm (Gr K-7):** 30/ yr. Appl fee: $100. Appl due: Dec. **Tests** ISEE. **Enr 135.** B 65. G 70. Avg class size: 16. Stud/ fac: 9:1. Uniform. **Fac 32.** M 10/F 22. FT 26/PT 6. Adv deg: 81%. **Grad '11—11.** Prep—3. (Birch Wathen Lenox 1, Beekman 1, Rudolf Steiner 1). Avg SSAT: 90%. **Tui '11-'12:** Day $32,950-34,600 (+$80-3385). Aid: Need 65 ($1,500,000). **Est 1996.** Nonprofit. Jewish (100% practice). Sem (Sept-June). This Conservative Jewish school offers a thematic, interdisciplinary curriculum that features two bilingual teachers in each classroom. In addition to completing course work in the core disciplines, students develop fluency in Hebrew and an understanding of Jewish culture. Boys and girls choose topics of study based upon their interests, then explore these topics from a variety of perspectives. Both English and Hebrew are used on a daily basis, with the school's goal being for all children to be Hebrew speakers by the end of kindergarten and to be literate in the language by the end of grade 1.

STEPHEN GAYNOR SCHOOL   **Day Coed Ages 5-14**
New York, NY 10024. 148 W 90th St.
Tel: 212-787-7070. Fax: 212-787-3312.
www.stephengaynor.org   E-mail: admissions@stephengaynor.org
Scott Gaynor, Head. PhD. Yvette Siegel-Herzog, Ed Dir. Jackie Long, Adm.

Gen Acad. LD. Feat—Writing Computers Photog Studio_Art Drama Music Speech. **Supp**—Rem_Math Rem_Read Tut. **Selective adm:** 37/yr. Appl fee: $150. Appl due: Rolling. **Enr 199.** Avg class size: 10. Stud/fac: 3:1. **Fac 70.** M 12/F 58. FT 70. Adv deg: 42%. **Grad '07—22. Tui '08-'09:** Day $41,800. Aid: Need 20 ($195,900). **Est 1962.** Nonprofit. Sem (Sept-June). The program addresses the needs of children of average to above-average intelligence with language-based learning differences. The curriculum, which emphasizes the mastery of basic subjects, employs a remedial approach that features multisensory teaching methods. Individual support supplements small-group instruction in ungraded classrooms. Teachers, speech and language therapists, reading and math specialists, and occupational therapists work together to return the student to a mainstream environment.

WINSTON PREPARATORY SCHOOL   **Day Coed Gr 6-12**
New York, NY 10011. 126 W 17th St.
Tel: 646-638-2705. Fax: 646-638-2706.
Other locations: 57 W Rocks Rd, Norwalk, CT 06851.
www.winstonprep.edu   E-mail: admissions@winstonprep.edu
Scott Bezsylko, Exec Dir. BS, La Salle Univ, MA, Columbia Univ. William DeHaven, Head. BA, Emory Univ, MA, Columbia Univ. Kristin Wisemiller, Adm.

Col Prep. Gen Acad. LD. Feat—Filmmaking Photog Studio_Art. **Supp**—Dev_Read Rem_Math Rem_Read Rev Tut. Outdoor Ed. **Dual enr:** NYU. **Sports**—Basket X-country Soccer Track. B: Golf. Activities: 18. **Selective adm (Gr 6-11):** 44/yr. Appl fee: $70. Appl due: Rolling. **Tests** IQ. **Enr 198.** B 133. G 65. Elem 42. Sec 156. Wh 50%. Latino 13%. Blk 15%. Native Am 1%. Asian 3%. Other 18%. Avg class size: 11. Stud/fac: 3:1. **Fac 61.** M 19/F 42. **Grad '11—39.** Col—30. **Avg SAT:** CR 613. M 587. W 531. **Col Couns:** 1. **Tui '11-'12:** Day $49,000. Aid: Need 48 ($500,000). **Est 1981.** Nonprofit. Sem (Sept-June). Winston Prep provides a language-based curriculum with a multisensory approach for students of average to above-average intelligence who have learning differences such as dyslexia, nonverbal learning disabilities and executive functioning difficulties. The skills-based curriculum offers intensive instruction with a favorable student-teacher ratio in academics, organizational skills and study strategies. Winston Prep's College Preview Program enables juniors and seniors to take college-level courses at New York University. A second campus operates in Norwalk, CT.

See Also Page 56

XAVIER HIGH SCHOOL Day Boys Gr 9-12
New York, NY 10011. 30 W 16th St.
Tel: 212-924-7900. Fax: 212-924-0303.
www.xavierhs.org E-mail: admissions@xavierhs.org
John R. Raslowsky II, Pres (2009). BA, Univ of Vermont, MA, Harvard Univ, MA, Seton Hall Univ. Michael V. LiVigni, Head. BA, MA, State Univ of New York-Buffalo, MEd, Fordham Univ. Benjamin Hamm, Adm.
Col Prep. AP (exams req'd; 478 taken, 67% 3+)—Eng Span Calc Bio Physics Eur_Hist US_Hist World_Hist US_Govt & Pol Studio_Art. **Feat**—Creative_Writing Fr Ital Lat Arabic Physiol Comp_Sci Robotics Web_Design Constitutional_Law Relig Film Filmmaking Acting Band Chorus Music_Theory JROTC. **Supp**—Rev Tut. **Comp:** Comp/Stud: 1:3. **Sports**— B: Baseball Basket Bowl X-country Football Golf Ice_Hockey Rugby Soccer Swim Tennis Track Wrestling. Activities: 50. **Selective adm (Gr 9-11):** 261/yr. Appl fee: $0. Appl due: Dec. Accepted: 55%. Yield: 36%. **Tests** ISEE SSAT TACHS TOEFL. **Enr 1050.** Wh 70%. Latino 16%. Blk 6%. Asian 6%. Other 2%. Avg class size: 23. Stud/fac: 15:1. Uniform. **Fac 77.** M 56/F 21. FT 77. Adv deg: 84%. **Grad '11—245.** Col—245. (Manhattan Col 11, St John's U-NY 10, St Joseph's U 9, Syracuse 7, Fordham 7, Loyola U MD 7). **Avg SAT:** CR 579. M 583. W 594. **Col Couns:** 2. Alum donors: 30%. **Tui '11-'12:** Day $12,925 (+$550). Aid: Merit 83 ($300,000). Need 300 ($900,000). **Est 1847.** Nonprofit. Roman Catholic (85% practice). Quar (Sept-June). **Assoc** MSA. Xavier offers a broad and varied curriculum with many electives. Advanced Placement courses are available in the major disciplines. Religious education includes both course work and community service projects. Students who meet criteria for the Ignatian Scholars Program take honors classes and participate in special cultural and intellectual activities in grades 9 and 10. Community service requirements are as follows: 10 hours per year in grades 10 and 11, 70 hours in grade 12.

WOODLAND HILL MONTESSORI SCHOOL Day Coed Gr PS (Age 3)-8
North Greenbush, NY 12144. 100 Montessori Pl.
Tel: 518-283-5400. Fax: 518-283-4861.
www.woodlandhill.org E-mail: info@woodlandhill.org
Susan Kambrich, Head (2000). MEd, Kent State Univ. Kris Gernert-Dott, Adm.
Pre-Prep. Gen Acad. Montessori. Feat—Span Studio_Art Music. **Supp**—Rem_Read. **Sports**—Basket X-country Soccer Volley. **Selective adm:** 44/yr. Appl fee: $50. Appl due: Feb. Accepted: 80%. Yield: 90%. **Enr 245.** B 120. G 125. Wh 76%. Latino 3%. Blk 5%. Asian 15%. Other 1%. Avg class size: 18. Stud/fac: 9:1. **Fac 30.** M 4/F 26. FT 26/PT 4. Wh 88%. Latino 4%. Blk 4%. Asian 4%. Adv deg: 26%. **Grad '10—11.** Prep—7. (Emma Willard 5, Albany Acad 1, Darrow 1). **Tui '11-'12:** Day $10,350-11,400 (+$300-1000). Aid: Need 46 ($100,000). **Est 1965.** Nonprofit. Sem (Sept-June). **Assoc** MSA. Woodland Hill follows an integrated Montessori approach while uniting thematically linked topics in literature, arts, history, social issues, government, economics, architecture, medicine, science and technology. A schoolwide practical life skills program progresses from basic tasks to more advanced skills for older children. Elementary and middle school students conduct library and field research both inside and outside of school, and middle schoolers perform 15 hours of required community service each year.

HOLY CHILD ACADEMY Day Coed Gr PS (Age 2)-8
Old Westbury, NY 11568. 25 Store Hill Rd.
Tel: 516-626-9300. Fax: 516-626-7914.
www.holychildacademy.org E-mail: cbowen@holychildacademy.org
Michael O'Donoghue, Head. BS, MA, MS, Adelphi Univ. Corrie Bowen, Adm.
Pre-Prep. Feat—Fr Lat Span Computers Relig Studio_Art Music Dance. **Supp**—Dev_ Read Rem_Math Rem_Read Rev Tut. **Sports (req'd)**—Basket Lacrosse Soccer. **Selective adm:** 15/yr. Appl fee: $50. Appl due: Rolling. **Enr 245.** B 120. G 125. Wh 80%. Latino 2%. Blk 10%. Asian 4%. Other 4%. Avg class size: 15. Stud/fac: 8:1. Uniform. **Fac 45.** M 5/F

40. FT 43/PT 2. Adv deg: 77%. **Grad '09—24.** Prep—24. **Tui '11-'12:** Day $13,225-19,400 (+$380-1345). Aid: Need 35 ($225,000). **Est 1959.** Nonprofit. Roman Catholic. Tri (Sept-June). **Assoc** MSA. Holy Child is part of the international network of SHCJ schools. Foreign language instruction begins in kindergarten with French and Spanish; older students continue their studies in either language or begin Latin. The program combines rigorous academics with the arts, athletics and service to the community. Religious studies and liturgical celebrations are integral aspects of school life. All children compete in intramural sports in grades 3 and 4 and interscholastic athletics in grades 5-8.

SETON CATHOLIC CENTRAL   **Bdg & Day**
Plattsburgh, NY 12903. 206 New York Rd.   **Coed Gr 7-12**
Tel: 518-561-4031. Fax: 518-563-1193.
www.setoncatholic.net   E-mail: info@setoncatholic.net
    Catherine Russell, Prin (2010). Derek Payne, Adm.

Col Prep. AP—Eng Fr Span Calc Chem US_Hist. **Feat**—Ecol Environ_Sci Comp_Sci Psych Sociol Bus_Law Relig Sculpt Studio_Art Music Bus. **Dual enr:** Paul Smith's, Clinton CC. **Sports**—Basket X-country Ice_Hockey Soccer Tennis Track. B: Baseball Football Golf. G: Softball. **Selective adm:** 88/yr. Appl fee: $50. **Enr 157.** Bdg 23. Day 134. Wh 83%. Latino 4%. Asian 12%. Other 1%. Intl 18%. Avg class size: 15. Stud/fac: 12:1. **Fac 24.** M 8/F 16. FT 23/PT 1. Wh 99%. Asian 1%. **Grad '10—42.** Col—38. **Avg SAT:** CR/M 1097. **Tui '12-'13:** Day $5000 (+$200-250). Parishioners $4200 (+$200-250). **Est 1989.** Nonprofit. Roman Catholic (80% practice). Sem (Sept-June). **Assoc** MSA. The school offers a Catholic education with a college preparatory curriculum. Course offerings include business, music, French, Spanish and computers. Course work in religion is a graduation requirement. A boarding program serves mostly international students who reside in host homes.

AQUINAS INSTITUTE AND   **Day Coed Gr PS (Age 4)-12**
NAZARETH SCHOOLS
Rochester, NY 14613. 1127 Dewey Ave.
Tel: 585-254-2020. Fax: 585-254-7401.
Other locations: 1001 Lake Ave, Rochester 14613.
www.aquinasinstitute.com   E-mail: info@aquinasinstitute.com
    Michael R. Daley, Pres. Joseph B. Knapp, Adm.

Col Prep. AP (195 exams taken)—Eng Calc Stats Comp_Sci Bio Chem Physics US_Hist World_Hist Psych US_Govt & Pol. **Feat**—Creative_Writing Fr Span Econ Law Ceramics Drawing Photog Sculpt Studio_Art Acting Theater_Arts Music_Theory Dance Accounting Bus Journ Public_Speak. **Supp**—Rem_Math Rev Tut. **Dual enr:** Monroe CC. **Sports**—Basket Bowl X-country Indoor_Track Lacrosse Soccer Swim Tennis Track. B: Baseball Football Golf Ice_Hockey. G: Cheer Softball Volley. Activities: 30. **Selective adm (Gr PS-11). Tests** HSPT. **Enr 1417.** Elem 460. Sec 957. Wh 73%. Latino 4%. Blk 17%. Asian 2%. Other 4%. Avg class size: 25. Stud/fac: 15:1. Formal dress. **Fac 117. Avg SAT:** CR 539. M 527. Avg ACT: 23.4. **Col Couns:** 2. **Tui '12-'13:** Day $5900-8150 (+$150). Aid: Need 567 ($1,000,000). **Est 1871.** Nonprofit. Roman Catholic (72% practice). Sem (Sept-June). **Assoc** MSA. This Catholic school resulted from the 2010 partnership between Aquinas Institute, a coed junior high and high school founded in 1902, and the nearby Nazareth Schools (which served girls in grades pre-K-12). Aquinas' Dewey Avenue campus hosts grades 7-12, and boys and girls in preschool through grade 6 attend classes at the former Nazareth campus on Lake Avenue. The high school curriculum allows students to major in two core subjects, and pupils satisfy an the following community service requirements: 12 hours in grade 9, 16 hours per year in grades 10 and 11, and 20 hours in grade 12.

BISHOP KEARNEY HIGH SCHOOL   Day Coed Gr 7-12
Rochester, NY 14617. 125 Kings Hwy S.
Tel: 585-342-4000. Fax: 585-342-4694.
www.bkhs.org   E-mail: ftillinghast@bkhs.org
Thomas O'Neil, Pres (2011). Julie A. Locey, Prin. Fred Tillinghast, Adm.
    Col Prep. AP—Eng Span Calc Bio Chem Eur_Hist US_Hist US_Govt & Pol Studio_Art.
Feat—Ital Anat & Physiol Astron Environ_Sci Forensic_Sci Econ Psych Sociol Genocide_
Stud Drama Music_Theory Journ TV_Production. **Supp**—Rev Tut. **Comp:** Comp/Stud: 1:1
Laptop prgm Gr 9-12. **Sports**—Basket Bowl Soccer Tennis Track. B: Baseball Football Golf
Ice_Hockey Lacrosse Wrestling. G: Cheer Softball Volley. Activities: 23. **Selective adm (Gr
7-11):** 142/yr. Appl fee: $0. Appl due: Rolling. Accepted: 65%. Yield: 85%. **Tests** TACHS.
Enr 413. B 223. G 190. Elem 89. Sec 324. Wh 77%. Latino 3%. Blk 15%. Asian 4%. Other
1%. Avg class size: 22. Stud/fac: 13:1. Uniform. **Fac 32.** M 12/F 20. FT 29/PT 3. Wh 98%.
Blk 2%. Adv deg: 100%. **Grad '11—120.** Col—120. (Rochester Inst of Tech 3, Fordham 2,
Colgate 1, Syracuse 1, Rutgers 1, Villanova 1). **Avg SAT:** CR 512. M 500. W 508. Avg ACT:
23. **Col Couns:** 2. Alum donors: 27%. **Tui '11-'12:** Day $3950-8000 (+$200). Aid: Merit 87
($100,400). Need 91 ($117,050). **Est 1962.** Nonprofit. Roman Catholic (85% practice). Quar
(Sept-June). **Assoc** MSA. Established by the Congregation of Christian Brothers and School
Sisters of Notre Dame, Bishop Kearney provides a Catholic education that emphasizes leadership development and community service. A college preparatory curriculum is supplemented
by activities in art, music and sports. In 2006, the school expanded to include a junior high
school (grades 7-8), where advanced students have the opportunity to enroll in high school
courses. All boys and girls in grades 9-12 are issued laptop computers.

McQUAID JESUIT HIGH SCHOOL   Day Boys Gr 7-12
Rochester, NY 14618. 1800 S Clinton Ave.
Tel: 585-473-1130. Fax: 585-256-6171.
www.mcquaid.org   E-mail: mcquaid@mcquaid.org
Edward F. Salmon, SJ, Int Pres (2010). Rev. James Coughlin, SJ, Prin. BA, St John Fisher
College, MA, Fordham Univ, MDiv, Weston Jesuit School of Theology, MS, New York Univ.
Christopher A. Parks, Adm.
    Col Prep. AP (exams req'd; 543 taken, 87% 3+)—Eng Span Calc Stats Comp_Sci Bio
Chem Environ_Sci Physics Eur_Hist US_Hist World_Hist Econ Psych Music_Theory. **Feat**—
Poetry Shakespeare Fr Ger Ital Lat Russ Gaelic Web_Design Govt Law Philos World_Relig
Art_Hist Film Studio_Art Drama Chorus Journ Public_Speak. **Supp**—Tut. **Sports**— B:
Baseball Basket Bowl Crew X-country Football Golf Ice_Hockey Lacrosse Rugby Sail Ski
Soccer Swim Tennis Track Volley Wrestling. **Somewhat selective adm (Gr 7-11):** 184/yr.
Appl due: Dec. Accepted: 88%. Yield: 83%. **Tests** HSPT. **Enr 838.** Elem 169. Sec 669. Wh
90%. Latino 2%. Blk 3%. Asian 4%. Other 1%. Avg class size: 19. Formal dress. **Fac 68.** M
49/F 19. FT 58/PT 10. Wh 97%. Blk 3%. Adv deg: 88%. **Grad '10—151.** Col—150. (U of
Rochester 11, Rochester Inst of Tech 8, Georgetown 5, Boston Col 5, Cornell 5, Notre Dame
4). **Avg SAT:** CR 619. M 634. W 608. **Tui '10-'11:** Day $10,050 (+$100-275). Aid: Need 291
($1,200,000). **Est 1954.** Nonprofit. Roman Catholic (77% practice). Sem (Sept-June). **Assoc**
MSA. This Jesuit school accepts students of all faiths. Electives in the academic program
include Advanced Placement courses. All students complete 100 cumulative hours of required
community service in grades 9-12, and seniors leave school for two weeks to work at off-
campus service sites.

JOHN F. KENNEDY CATHOLIC HIGH SCHOOL   Day Coed Gr 9-12
Somers, NY 10589. 54 Rte 138.
Tel: 914-232-5061. Fax: 914-232-3416.
www.kennedycatholic.org   E-mail: admissions@kennedycatholic.org

Rev. Mark G. Vaillancourt, Pres (2008). BE, State Univ of New York-Maritime, ME, Manhattan College, STB, MDiv, MA, St Joseph's Seminary, MPhil, PhD, Fordham Univ. Sr. Barbara Heil, RDC, Adm.

Col Prep. AP (exams req'd; 250 taken)—Eng Span Calc Bio Environ_Sci US_Hist World_ Hist US_Govt & Pol Studio_Art. **Feat**—Creative_Writing Linguistics Ital Lat Marine_Bio/Sci Econ Law Psych Philos Relig Drawing Painting Band Chorus Music Dance Accounting Bus Health Marketing. **Supp**—Rev Tut. **Dual enr:** St John's U-NY, Iona. **Sports**—Basket Bowl X-country Indoor_Track Lacrosse Soccer Swim Track. B: Baseball Football Golf Ice_Hockey. G: Cheer F_Hockey Softball Tennis Volley. Activities: 17. **Selective adm (Gr 9-11):** 165/yr. Appl fee: $100. Appl due: Nov. Tests TACHS. **Enr 610.** B 300. G 310. Wh 92%. Latino 5%. Blk 2%. Asian 1%. Avg class size: 29. Uniform. **Fac 46.** M 20/F 26. FT 33/PT 13. Wh 99%. Latino 1%. Adv deg: 73%. **Grad '08—162.** Col—161. (Westchester CC 14, Sacred Heart 12, Quinnipiac 9, Pace 8, Manhattanville 6, SUNY-Albany 6). **Avg SAT:** CR 531. M 537. W 530. Avg ACT: 24.3. Alum donors: 13%. **Tui '12-'13:** Day $7350 (+$300). **Est 1966.** Nonprofit. Roman Catholic. Quar (Sept-June). JFK's curriculum includes both Advanced Placement and honors courses. Students are required to complete 120 hours of community service during their four-year stay at the school. In addition, all students take four years of religious studies courses that focus on prayer, worship, morality and lifestyle. Boys and girls enroll from New York's Westchester, Putnam and Dutchess counties, as well as from neighboring Connecticut.

SAINT ANTHONY'S HIGH SCHOOL   Day Coed Gr 9-12
South Huntington, NY 11747. 275 Wolf Hill Rd.
Tel: 631-271-2020. Fax: 631-351-1507.
www.stanthonyshs.org
    Br. Gary Cregan, OSF, Prin (2004). BA, St John's Univ (NY), MA, New York Univ. Paul Washington, Adm.

Col Prep. AP—Eng Fr Span Calc Stats Bio Chem Physics Eur_Hist US_Hist Econ. **Feat**— Chin Ital Lat Anat & Physiol Environ_Sci Forensic_Sci Microbio Comp_Sci Govt Psych Sociol Philos Relig Ceramics Drawing Painting Photog Studio_Art Drama Music Music_Theory Orchestra Accounting Journ Public_Speak. **Dual enr:** St John's U-NY. **Sports**—Basket Bowl Crew X-country Golf Indoor_Track Lacrosse Sail Soccer Tennis Track Volley. B: Baseball Football Wrestling. G: Badminton Cheer Softball Swim. Activities: 62. **Selective adm:** 750/ yr. Appl fee: $40. Accepted: 60%. **Enr 2250.** B 1250. G 1000. Avg class size: 29. Uniform. **Fac 146.** M 66/F 80. FT 146. Adv deg: 57%. **Grad '10—558.** Col—552. **Avg SAT:** CR/M/W 1642. **Mid 50% SAT:** CR 490-590. M 500-620. W 480-600. Avg ACT: 24. Mid 50% ACT: 21-27. **Tui '09-'10:** Day $7500 (+$200). **Est 1933.** Nonprofit. Roman Catholic. Quar (Sept-June). **Assoc** MSA. Curricular features at Saint Anthony's include computer math, accounting, public speaking, music, art and drama. Students enroll from approximately 100 school districts in Nassau and Suffolk counties.

STELLA NIAGARA EDUCATION PARK   Day Coed Gr PS (Age 3)-8
Stella Niagara, NY 14144. 4421 Lower River Rd.
Tel: 716-754-4314. Fax: 716-754-2964.
www.stellaniagara.org   E-mail: snepoffice@stellaniagara.org
    Sr. Margaret Sullivan, OSF, Prin. BA, Daemen College, MSEd, Niagara Univ. Kristen deGuehery, Adm.

Pre-Prep. Montessori. Feat—Fr Span Relig Studio_Art Music. **Supp**—Dev_Read Rev Tut. **Comp:** Comp/Stud: 1:4. **Sports**—Basket Soccer Swim. **Nonselective adm:** 30/yr. Appl fee: $50. Appl due: Mar. Accepted: 96%. Yield: 68%. **Enr 158.** B 73. G 85. Wh 87%. Latino 1%. Blk 5%. Asian 7%. Avg class size: 15. Stud/fac: 12:1. Uniform. **Fac 23.** M 4/F 19. FT 22/PT 1. Wh 100%. Adv deg: 60%. **Grad '10—15.** Prep—12. (Canisius 6, Sacred Heart Acad-CT 2, Nardin 2, St Joseph's Collegiate 1). **Tui '11-'12:** Day $5300 (+$200). Aid: Need 76 ($92,275). **Est 1908.** Nonprofit. Roman Catholic (70% practice). Quar (Sept-June). **Assoc** MSA. Sponsored by the Sisters of St. Francis, Stella Niagara begins its program with a multi-age Montessori classroom for children ages 3-5. The kindergarten curriculum includes Spanish, library, art, music, ballet and computer. In grades 1-8, the program emphasizes the mastery of skills and the development of higher-order thinking skills. Coordinated by SNEP's campus ministry, religious instruction and activities take place at all grade levels.

CHRISTIAN BROTHERS ACADEMY   **Day Coed Gr 7-12**
Syracuse, NY 13214. 6245 Randall Rd.
Tel: 315-446-5960. Fax: 315-446-3393.
www.cbasyracuse.org   E-mail: hdowd@cbasyracuse.org
     Br. Joseph Jozwiak, FSC, Prin (2009). BA, Catholic Univ of America, MS, California Lutheran Univ, MA, Univ of San Francisco. Holly Dowd, Adm.
     Col Prep. AP (exams req'd)—Eng Fr Span Calc Stats Bio Chem Physics Eur_Hist US_Hist US_Govt & Pol Studio_Art. **Feat**—British_Lit Creative_Writing Shakespeare Anat & Physiol Environ_Sci Comp_Sci Econ Law Psych Sociol Relig Ceramics Drama Music Music_Theory Accounting Bus Journ Marketing Drafting. **Supp**—LD Rev Tut. **Comp:** Comp/Stud: 1:7. **Sports**—Basket X-country Ice_Hockey Lacrosse Soccer Swim Tennis Track. B: Baseball Football Wrestling. G: Cheer Softball Volley. Activities: 26. **Selective adm (Gr 7-11):** 148/yr. Appl fee: $50. Appl due: Dec. Accepted: 80%. Yield: 85%. **Tests** HSPT. **Enr 754.** B 439. G 315. Elem 252. Sec 502. Avg class size: 20. Uniform. **Fac 60.** M 34/F 26. FT 49/PT 11. Adv deg: 78%. **Grad '10—118.** Col—116. **Avg SAT:** CR 580. M 592. W 563. **Col Couns:** 2. **Tui '12-'13:** Day $8570-8920 (+$230). **Est 1900.** Nonprofit. Roman Catholic (80% practice). Sem (Sept-June). **Assoc** MSA. Operated by the De La Salle Christian Brothers and serving a largely Catholic student body, CBA enrolls qualified boys and girls of all faiths. Students pursue course work in the traditional disciplines, while also choosing from an array of electives and Advanced Placement offerings. Seniors satisfy a 36-hour community service requirement.

FAITH HERITAGE SCHOOL   **Day Coed Gr PS (Age 4)-12**
Syracuse, NY 13205. 3740 Midland Ave.
Tel: 315-469-7777. Fax: 315-492-7440.
www.faithheritageschool.org   E-mail: fhs@faithheritageschool.org
     Neal Capone, Head (2011). Sandra Morrison, Prin.
     Col Prep. AP—Eng Span Calc US_Hist. **Feat**—Environ_Sci Programming Web_Design Econ Pol_Sci Bible Drawing Photog Studio_Art Music_Theory Driver_Ed. **Supp**—Rem_Math Rem_Read. **Sports**—Indoor_Track Soccer Track. B: Baseball Basket. G: Cheer Volley. **Somewhat selective adm:** 100/yr. Appl fee: $100. Appl due: Rolling. Accepted: 90%. **Tests** Stanford. **Enr 300.** Avg class size: 22. Casual dress. **Fac 45. Grad '02—48.** Col—48. **Avg SAT:** CR 569. M 550. W 518. **Tui '12-'13:** Day $6566-7760 (+$360-468). **Est 1972.** Nonprofit. Evangelical. Sem (Sept-June). **Assoc** MSA. Faith Heritage's Bible-based academic program incorporates an evangelical Christian worldview. Academics at the elementary level include reading, spelling, handwriting, mathematics, social studies and science. High school students choose from college preparatory courses, Advanced Placement classes, and electives in technology and the fine arts.

LA SALLE INSTITUTE   **Day Boys Gr 6-12**
Troy, NY 12180. 174 Williams Rd.
Tel: 518-283-2500. Fax: 518-283-6265.
www.lasalleinstitute.org   E-mail: admissions@lasalleinstitute.org
     Br. Carl Malacalza, FSC, Prin. Gerald Washington, Adm.
     Col Prep. Milit. AP (exams req'd)—Eng Span Calc Stats Physics Eur_Hist US_Hist Econ US_Govt & Pol. **Feat**—Lat-Amer_Lit Fr Anat & Physiol Relig Fine_Arts Music JROTC Milit_Sci. **Supp**—Tut. **Dual enr:** SUNY-Albany, Hudson Valley CC. **Sports**— B: Baseball Basket Bowl X-country Football Golf Ice_Hockey Indoor_Track Lacrosse Ski Soccer Tennis

Track Wrestling. **Somewhat selective adm:** 151/yr. Appl due: Rolling. Accepted: 89%. **Tests** HSPT. **Enr 400.** Avg class size: 24. Uniform. **Fac 44. Grad '10—89.** Col—88. **Avg SAT:** CR 548. M 552. W 536. Avg ACT: 24.3. **Tui '12-'13:** Day $8700-11,400 (+$375-440). **Est 1850.** Nonprofit. Roman Catholic. 6 terms (Sept-June). **Assoc** MSA. Operated by the Brothers of the Christian Schools, La Salle accommodates students of varying learning styles. The school offers French and Spanish beginning in grade 7, as well as an accelerated mathematics sequence that commences in grade 7 and later allows eligible pupils to take advanced courses at Hudson Valley Community College. Advanced high school students may enroll in intensive Spanish classes at the State University of New York at Albany.

REDEMPTION CHRISTIAN ACADEMY Bdg Coed Gr 7-12
Troy, NY 12181. 192 9th St, PO Box 753. Day Coed PS (Age 4)-12
Tel: 518-272-6679. Fax: 518-270-8039.
www.info@redemptionchristianacademy.org
E-mail: info@redemptionchristianacademy.org
John Massey, Jr., Head (1979).

Col Prep. Feat—Comp_Sci. **Supp**—Dev_Read ESL LD Rem_Math Rem_Read Tut. **Sports**—Basket. **Selective adm:** Appl fee: $40. Appl due: Rolling. **Enr 150.** Elem 114. Sec 36. Blk 93%. Other 7%. Intl 10%. Avg class size: 15. Stud/fac: 10:1. Uniform. **Fac 12.** M 1/F 11. FT 10/PT 2. Adv deg: 16%. In Dorms 2. **Tui '12-'13:** Bdg $24,500. 5-Day Bdg $19,500. Day $7000. Intl Bdg $28,000. **Est 1979.** Nonprofit. Nondenom Christian. Sem (Sept-June). One of only four African-American boarding schools in the US, RCA offers a college preparatory program in a small-class setting. Both remedial and advanced courses are part of the technology-based curriculum. Boarders take part in various evening and weekend activities.

WESTBURY FRIENDS SCHOOL Day Coed Gr PS (Age 3)-5
Westbury, NY 11590. 550 Post Ave.
Tel: 516-333-3178. Fax: 516-333-1353.
www.westburyfriends.org   E-mail: naranda@westburyfriends.org
Geraldine A. Faivre, Head (2008). BS, Marywood Univ, MS, Long Island Univ. Nancy Aranda, Adm.

Pre-Prep. Feat—Lib_Skills Span Studio_Art Music Violin. **Comp:** Comp/Stud: 1:4. **Selective adm:** 31/yr. Appl fee: $50. Appl due: Jan. Accepted: 83%. Yield: 91%. **Tests** CTP_4. **Enr 85.** B 41. G 44. Wh 32%. Latino 6%. Blk 32%. Asian 6%. Other 24%. Avg class size: 12. **Fac 15.** M 1/F 14. FT 10/PT 5. Wh 82%. Latino 12%. Blk 6%. Adv deg: 73%. **Grad '09—7.** Prep—7. (E Woods 2, Friends Acad-NY 2, Portledge 2, Long Island Lutheran 1). **Tui '12-'13:** Day $12,800-14,100 (+$440). Aid: Merit 8 ($36,100). Need 22 ($83,355). **Est 1957.** Nonprofit. Religious Society of Friends (1% practice). (Sept-June). Under the care of Westbury Friends Meeting, the school conducts a program characterized by inquiry-based, hands-on learning. Components of the curriculum include a literature-based reading program, writing instruction, computers, art and music. An extended day program operates before and after school. The school's 17-acre campus provides opportunities for environmental study.

ARCHBISHOP STEPINAC HIGH SCHOOL Day Boys Gr 9-12
White Plains, NY 10605. 950 Mamaroneck Ave.
Tel: 914-946-4800. Fax: 914-684-2591.
www.stepinac.org   E-mail: stepinac@stepinac.org
Msgr. Anthony Marchitelli, Pres. Paul Carty, Prin. BA, College of New Rochelle, MA, MS, Fordham Univ. Sr. Margaret Morrissey, RSHM, Adm.

Col Prep. AP (exams req'd)—Eng Calc Comp_Sci Bio Eur_Hist US_Hist US_Govt & Pol. **Feat**—Ital Lat Span Marine_Bio/Sci Electronics Web_Design Bible Relig Studio_Art Band Chorus Music_Hist. **Supp**—Dev_Read Rem_Math Rev Tut. **Sports**— B: Baseball Basket Bowl Football Golf Ice_Hockey Lacrosse Soccer Swim Tennis Track Wrestling. **Selec-**

tive adm: 236/yr. Appl fee: $50. Appl due: May. Accepted: 85%. **Tests** TACHS. **Enr 685.** Wh 72%. Latino 11%. Blk 11%. Asian 6%. Avg class size: 25. **Fac 44.** M 32/F 12. FT 42/PT 2. Wh 94%. Latino 5%. Blk 1%. Adv deg: 77%. **Grad '10—168.** Col—164. **Tui '11-'12:** Day $7900 (+$400). **Est 1948.** Nonprofit. Roman Catholic. Quar (Sept-June). **Assoc** MSA. Curricular features at Stepinac include computer studies, religion, orchestra and drama. The school also offers a pre-engineering program.

WOODSTOCK DAY SCHOOL   **Day Coed Gr PS (Age 2)-12**
Woodstock, NY 12498. PO Box 1.
Tel: 845-246-3744. Fax: 845-246-0053.
www.woodstockdayschool.org   E-mail: info@woodstockdayschool.org
     James Handlin, Head (2007). MEd, Bank Street College of Education, PhD, Columbia Univ. Marie Kropp, Adm.
     Gen Acad. Feat—Chin Fr Span Studio_Art Theater Music Study_Skills. **Supp**—Dev_Read Makeup Rem_Math Rem_Read Rev Tut. **Sports**—Basket Lacrosse Soccer Ultimate_Frisbee. Activities: 8. **Selective adm:** 39/yr. Appl fee: $50. Appl due: Rolling. **Enr 186.** Elem 124. Sec 62. Wh 91%. Blk 6%. Asian 3%. Avg class size: 15. **Fac 24.** M 8/F 16. FT 19/PT 5. Wh 93%. Latino 7%. Adv deg: 75%. **Grad '11—6.** Col—6. (Landmark 1, Bennington 1, Evergreen St 1, NY Inst of Tech 1, SUNY-Purchase 1, SUNY-Ulster 1). **Tui '11-'12:** Day $10,500-16,200 (+$800). **Est 1972.** Nonprofit. Tri (Sept-June). Enrichment classes in Spanish, science, music and art are scheduled throughout the week beginning in kindergarten. In grades 5-8, students enroll in a weekly two-hour elective in a topic such as sculpture, theater, dance and choreography, gardening or carpentry. All boys and girls take part in the school's library program beginning in preschool. In addition to course work in the core subjects, high schoolers are encouraged to take classes in the arts each year. Students in grades 7-12 must perform 50 hours of annual community service, divided into 25 on-campus hours and 25 off-campus hours.

STEIN YESHIVA OF LINCOLN PARK   **Day Coed Gr PS (Age 2)-8**
Yonkers, NY 10704. 287 Central Park Ave.   **(Coord 1-8)**
Tel: 914-965-7082. Fax: 914-965-1902.
www.steinyeshiva.org   E-mail: sspingarn@steinyeshiva.org
     Sharon Pollock, Admin. Sandra Spingarn, Adm.
     Gen Acad. Feat—Hebrew Computers Judaic_Stud. **Supp**—LD Rem_Math Rem_Read Tut. **Somewhat selective adm:** 20/yr. Appl due: Rolling. Accepted: 85%. **Enr 125.** B 61. G 64. Wh 99%. Blk 1%. Avg class size: 12. Uniform. **Fac 26.** M 2/F 24. FT 23/PT 3. Wh 100%. Adv deg: 61%. **Grad '08—6. Tui '09-'10:** Day $8000-9500 (+$375). **Est 1986.** Nonprofit. Orthodox Jewish (95% practice). Tri (Sept-June). Providing instruction in both general studies and Judaic studies, Stein Yeshiva emphasizes Orthodox Jewish learning and Hebrew language. Computer instruction, trips, physical education, parent/child education and after-school programs are also provided.

OUR MONTESSORI SCHOOL   **Day Coed Gr PS (Age 2)-6**
Yorktown Heights, NY 10598. PO Box 72.
Tel: 914-962-9466. Fax: 914-962-9470.
www.ourmontessorischool.com   E-mail: admin@ourmontessorischool.com
     Betty M. Hengst, Dir (1972). BA, Univ of Florida, MEd, Long Island Univ. June Willis, Adm.
     Pre-Prep. Montessori. Feat—Fr Japan Lat Span Computers Studio_Art Drama Music Dance. **Supp**—Dev_Read Rem_Math Rem_Read Rev Tut. **Comp:** Comp/Stud: 1:8. **Somewhat selective adm:** 120/yr. Appl fee: $100. Appl due: Rolling. Accepted: 90%. Yield: 100%. **Enr 250.** B 130. G 120. Wh 80%. Latino 7%. Blk 6%. Asian 7%. Intl 10%. Avg class size: 12. Stud/fac: 7:1. **Fac 48.** M 1/F 47. FT 27/PT 21. Wh 90%. Latino 4%. Asian 6%. Adv deg: 12%. **Grad '10—5.** Prep—4. **Tui '11-'12:** Day $3150-14,150. **Est 1972.** Inc. (Sept-June). The

school emphasizes individualized instruction and experiential learning. French is introduced in the nursery division, and the arts, field trips and visitors from outside the classroom are central to the program. The curriculum includes courses in critical thinking and hands-on science, as well as programs for both gifted and average children. An experimental multilingual exposure program introduces boys and girls to Russian, Japanese, Arabic and Spanish.

SOUNDVIEW PREPARATORY SCHOOL   Day Coed Gr 6-12
Yorktown Heights, NY 10598. 370 Underhill Ave.
Tel: 914-962-2780. Fax: 914-302-2769.
www.soundviewprep.org   E-mail: info@soundviewprep.org
    W. Glyn Hearn, Head (1989). BA, MA, Univ of Texas-Austin. Mary E. Ivanyi, Adm.

Col Prep. AP (27 exams taken, 70% 3+)—Fr Span Calc Bio Chem Physics Eur_Hist US_Hist US_Govt & Pol Studio_Art. **Feat**—Creative_Writing Ital Lat Environ_Sci Forensic_ Sci Psych Philos Photog Drama. **Comp:** Comp/Stud: 1:5. **Sports**—Basket Soccer Ultimate_ Frisbee. Activities: 12. **Selective adm (Gr 6-11):** 25/yr. Appl fee: $50. Appl due: Rolling. Accepted: 60%. Yield: 95%. **Tests** ISEE. **Enr 70.** B 34. G 36. Elem 13. Sec 57. Wh 88%. Blk 10%. Asian 2%. Avg class size: 7. Stud/fac: 5:1. Casual dress. **Fac 16.** M 4/F 12. FT 13/PT 3. Wh 94%. Latino 6%. Adv deg: 81%. **Grad '11—21.** Col—21. (Duke 1, Oberlin 1, Bard-NY 1, Rensselaer Polytech 1, Sarah Lawrence 1, Muhlenberg 1). **Avg SAT:** CR 611. M 562. W 574. Avg ACT: 22. **Col Couns:** 1. Alum donors: 9%. **Tui '11-'12:** Day $32,100-33,200 (+$1500). Aid: Need 25 ($494,400). **Est 1989.** Nonprofit. Sem (Sept-June). Soundview's college preparatory curriculum includes four foreign languages and both honors and Advanced Placement courses. Among the school's electives are art, creative writing, environmental science, drama and psychology, among others. Students enroll from Westchester, Putnam and Rockland counties; New York City; and Connecticut's Fairfield County.

PENNSYLVANIA

ALLENTOWN CENTRAL CATHOLIC HIGH SCHOOL   Day Coed Gr 9-12
Allentown, PA 18102. 301 N 4th St.
Tel: 610-437-4601. Fax: 610-437-6760.
www.acchs.info   E-mail: ymccarthy@acchs.info
    Yvonne G. McCarthy, Prin. MEd.

Col Prep. AP (exams req'd; 154 taken)—Eng Span Calc Physics US_Hist US_Govt & Pol. **Feat**—Creative_Writing ASL Fr Ger Lat Forensic_Sci Programming Web_Design Amer_ Stud Law Psych Theol Fine_Arts Theater Music Music_Theory Accounting. **Supp**—Makeup Tut. **Dual enr:** Alvernia. **Sports**—Basket X-country Lacrosse Soccer Swim Tennis Track. B: Baseball Football Golf Wrestling. G: Cheer F_Hockey Softball Volley. **Somewhat selective adm:** Appl fee: $250. Appl due: Rolling. **Enr 900.** B 450. G 450. **Fac 77.** **Avg SAT:** CR 539. M 549. **Tui '12-'13:** Day $6650 (+$1150). **Est 1926.** Nonprofit. Roman Catholic. Quar (Sept-June). **Assoc** MSA. ACCHS' program includes honors and Advanced Placement courses in the major disciplines. Dual-credit opportunities are offered through Alvernia University. Pupils enroll primarily from 18 schools in Lehigh and Northampton counties.

BISHOP GUILFOYLE CATHOLIC HIGH SCHOOL   Day Coed Gr 9-12
Altoona, PA 16602. 2400 Pleasant Valley Blvd.
Tel: 814-944-4014. Fax: 814-944-8695.
www.bishopguilfoyle.org   E-mail: bgpublicrelations@atlanticbb.net
    Bernard G. Kubitza, Pres (2009). BA, MA, California Univ of Pennsylvania.

Col Prep. AP—Eng Calc Bio. **Feat**—Fr Span Stats Anat & Physiol Environ_Sci Comp_Sci Psych Sociol Relig Studio_Art Music_Theory Accounting Journ Public_Speak. **Dual enr:** PA

Highlands CC, Mt Aloysius Col, St Francis U. **Sports**—Basket X-country Golf Soccer Tennis Track. B: Baseball Football. G: Softball Volley. **Nonselective adm:** 99/yr. Appl due: Rolling. Accepted: 100%. **Enr 320.** Stud/fac: 15:1. Uniform. **Fac 24.** M 9/F 15. FT 24. Wh 100%. **Grad '10—89.** Col—87. **Tui '11-'12:** Day $5325 (+$125). **Est 1922.** Nonprofit. Roman Catholic. Quar (Aug-June). **Assoc** MSA. BG provides a varied secondary program that emphasizes critical-thinking skills and problem-solving strategies. Older students have dual-enrollment course options at three local colleges. Boys and girls satisfy a 25-hour community service requirement each year. Serving pupils from roughly two dozen area parishes, the faculty comprises a blend of clergy, religious and laypeople.

QUIGLEY CATHOLIC HIGH SCHOOL   Day Coed Gr 9-12
Baden, PA 15005. 200 Quigley Dr.
Tel: 724-869-2188. Fax: 724-869-3091.
www.qchs.org   E-mail: office@qchs.org
    Rita McCormick, Prin. Adrianne Kaminsky, Adm.
    Col Prep. AP—Eng Calc Eur_Hist US_Hist. **Feat**—Span Comp_Sci Relig Ceramics Studio_Art Chorus. **Supp**—Tut. **Dual enr:** La Roche, Carlow, U of Pittsburgh. **Sports**—Basket Soccer. B: Baseball Golf Ice_Hockey. G: Softball Tennis. **Nonselective adm:** 40/yr. Appl fee: $30. Appl due: Rolling. Accepted: 100%. **Tests** HSPT. **Enr 178.** B 81. G 97. Wh 80%. Latino 2%. Blk 5%. Asian 7%. Other 6%. Avg class size: 20. Stud/fac: 10:1. Uniform. **Fac 18.** M 8/F 10. FT 18. Wh 100%. Adv deg: 83%. **Grad '09—38.** Col—38. **Avg SAT:** CR 529. M 532. W 539. **Tui '10-'11:** Day $8800 (+$400-500). Catholic $7800 (+$400-500). **Est 1967.** Nonprofit. Roman Catholic. Quar (Aug-June). **Assoc** MSA. QCHS offers a college preparatory curriculum with accelerated and advanced courses in most disciplines. Christian values are emphasized, and students take part in compulsory community service: five to 25 hours per year on campus and 15 to 25 hours per year off campus.

BEAVER COUNTY CHRISTIAN SCHOOL   Day Coed Gr K-12
Beaver Falls, PA 15010. 3601 Short St.
Tel: 724-843-8331. Fax: 724-891-3315.
Other locations: 510 37th St, Beaver Falls 15010.
www.beavercountychristian.org   E-mail: bccs-wp@comcast.net
    Mary Lou Capan, Prin (2009). BA, Carlow College, MEd, Covenant College. Rose McChesney, Adm.
    Col Prep. AP (13 exams taken, 69% 3+)—Eng Calc Chem. **Feat**—Fr Span Astron Environ_Sci Oceanog Studio_Art Theater_Arts Band Chorus. **Supp**—Rem_Read. **Dual enr:** Geneva. **Sports**—Basket Volley. B: Soccer. **Somewhat selective adm:** 38/yr. Appl fee: $25. Appl due: Rolling. Accepted: 100%. Yield: 100%. **Tests** Stanford. **Enr 214.** B 116. G 98. Elem 126. Sec 88. Wh 94%. Blk 5%. Asian 1%. Avg class size: 16. **Fac 21.** M 4/F 17. FT 14/PT 7. Wh 100%. Adv deg: 38%. **Grad '10—21.** Col—19. (Geneva 9, CC of Beaver Co 3, Malone 2, Eastern U 1). **Avg SAT:** CR 540. M 523. W 496. Alum donors: 4%. **Tui '11-'12:** Day $5467-6203. Aid: Need 32 ($102,659). **Est 1969.** Nonprofit. Sem (Aug-June). BCCS offers a full elementary and secondary program that reflects a Christian worldview. Students attend trips to points of historical and literary interest as part of their course of study. Seniors may earn college credits for courses taken at Geneva College. The high school operates at the Merriman Campus building on 37th Street.

HOLY GHOST PREPARATORY SCHOOL   Day Boys Gr 9-12
Bensalem, PA 19020. 2429 Bristol Pike.
Tel: 215-639-2102. Fax: 215-639-4225.
www.holyghostprep.org   E-mail: rabramson@holyghostprep.org
    Rev. Jeffrey T. Duaime, CSSp, Pres (2002). BA, Duquesne Univ, MDiv, Catholic Theological Union. Ryan T. Abramson, Adm.

Col Prep. AP (exams req'd; 333 taken, 86% 3+)—Eng Fr Lat Span Calc Comp_Sci Bio Chem Physics Eur_Hist US_Hist World_Hist US_Govt & Pol Studio_Art Music_Theory. **Feat**—Creative_Writing Stats Anat & Physiol Astron Ecol Genetics Microbio Web_Design Intl_Relations Psych Middle_Eastern_Stud Bible Philos World_Relig Filmmaking Drama Journ. **Comp:** Comp/Stud: 1:3. **Sports**— B: Baseball Basket Bowl X-country Golf Ice_Hockey Indoor_Track Lacrosse Soccer Swim Tennis Track. Activities: 60. **Selective adm (Gr 9-11):** 120/yr. Appl fee: $50. Appl due: Dec. **Tests** HSPT. **Enr 498.** Avg class size: 17. Stud/fac: 10:1. **Fac 50.** M 31/F 19. FT 50. Adv deg: 86%. **Grad '11—120.** Col—120. **Avg SAT:** CR 610. M 630. W 620. **Tui '12-'13:** Day $16,700. Aid: Merit 70 ($500,000). Need 90 ($500,000). **Est 1897.** Nonprofit. Roman Catholic. Sem (Aug-May). **Assoc** MSA. Founded by members of the Congregation of the Holy Ghost, this Catholic school offers a college preparatory curriculum that features Advanced Placement work in every major discipline. A comprehensive humanities program and an emphasis on technology are important aspects of academic life. Freshmen and sophomores complete 10 hours of annual community service, while juniors and seniors fulfill a 20-hour commitment.

ST. ALOYSIUS ACADEMY   Day Boys Gr K-8
Bryn Mawr, PA 19010. 401 S Bryn Mawr Ave.
Tel: 610-525-1670. Fax: 610-525-5140.
www.staloysiusacademy.org   E-mail: admissions@staloysiusacademy.org
    Sr. Stephen Anne M. Roderiguez, IHM, Prin. Sr. Maryann Weidner, Adm.

Pre-Prep. Montessori. Feat—Lib_Skills Lat Span Computers Relig Studio_Art Band Chorus Music. **Supp**—Rem_Read Tut. **Sports**— B: Baseball Basket Football Lacrosse Soccer Track. **Somewhat selective adm:** 40/yr. Appl fee: $50. Appl due: Jan. Accepted: 95%. **Tests** IQ. **Enr 228.** Avg class size: 18. Stud/fac: 10:1. Uniform. **Fac 39.** M 6/F 33. FT 34/PT 5. Adv deg: 23%. **Grad '10—25.** Prep—24. (Malvern Prep 3, Salesianum 3, Archmere 1). **Tui '12-'13:** Day $10,700 (+$250). **Est 1895.** Nonprofit. Roman Catholic. Tri (Sept-June). **Assoc** MSA. St. AA emphasizes basic skills in all areas; religion and moral development are also stressed. Children in grades K-5 study Spanish, while pupils in grades 6-8 study Latin. A strong music program features piano lessons, jazz band, marching band, Archdiocesan band and a choral program.

DEVON PREPARATORY SCHOOL   Day Boys Gr 6-12
Devon, PA 19333. 363 N Valley Forge Rd.
Tel: 610-688-7337. Fax: 610-688-2409.
www.devonprep.com   E-mail: pparsons@devonprep.com
    Rev. James J. Shea, SchP, Head (1994). BEE, Villanova Univ, MA, MDiv, Oblate College. Patrick Parsons, Adm.

Col Prep. AP (exams req'd; 302 taken, 74% 3+)—Eng Fr Ger Span Calc Comp_Sci Bio Chem Physics Eur_Hist US_Hist Human_Geog US_Govt & Pol. **Feat**—Fiction & Poetry_Writing Screenwriting Ital Lat Anat & Physiol Forensic_Sci Civil_War Vietnam_War Econ Philos Relig Art_Hist Studio_Art Music Accounting. **Supp**—Dev_Read. **Comp:** Comp/Stud: 1:8.5. **Sports**— B: Baseball Basket X-country Golf Lacrosse Soccer Tennis Track. Activities: 25. **Selective adm (Gr 6-10):** 62/yr. Appl fee: $50. Appl due: Rolling. Accepted: 77%. Yield: 48%. **Tests** HSPT. **Enr 259.** Elem 69. Sec 190. Wh 90%. Latino 1%. Blk 1%. Asian 6%. Other 2%. Avg class size: 15. Stud/fac: 10:1. Formal dress. **Fac 32.** M 24/F 8. FT 32. Wh 100%. Adv deg: 68%. **Grad '11—60.** Col—60. (PA St 6, St Joseph's U 5, La Salle 4, Loyola U MD 3, Catholic U 3, U of DE 2). **Avg SAT:** CR 643. M 635. W 633. **Col Couns:** 1. Alum donors: 13%. **Tui '12-'13:** Day $17,800-19,800 (+$1755-1945). Aid: Merit 108 ($475,000). Need 54 ($250,000). **Est 1956.** Nonprofit. Roman Catholic (84% practice). Quar (Sept-June). **Assoc** MSA. Founded by the Piarist Fathers, the school offers a college preparatory curriculum with Advanced Placement courses and opportunities for field study. All boys satisfy a community service requirement—15 hours per year in the middle school (grades 6-8) and 25 hours per year in the upper school (grades 9-12)—by sponsoring food and clothing drives, visiting nursing homes or homeless shelters, and so on.

HOLY CHILD ACADEMY Day Coed Gr PS (Age 3)-8
Drexel Hill, PA 19026. 475 Shadeland Ave.
Tel: 610-259-2712. Fax: 610-259-1862.
www.holychildacademy.com E-mail: info@holychildacademy.com
  Anita P. Coll, Head. BA, Rosemont College, MA, Villanova Univ. Christine McLaughlin, Adm.
  Pre-Prep. Feat—Fr Span Computers Relig Studio_Art Drama Music. **Supp**—Dev_Read Rem_Math Rem_Read Rev Tut. **Sports**—Basket Soccer Track. G: Softball Volley. **Selective adm (Gr PS-7):** 36/yr. Appl fee: $40. Appl due: Rolling. Accepted: 82%. Yield: 88%. **Tests** IQ. **Enr 225.** Wh 85%. Latino 2%. Blk 9%. Asian 4%. Avg class size: 14. Stud/fac: 8:1. Uniform. **Fac 28.** FT 18/PT 10. Wh 99%. Latino 1%. Adv deg: 46%. **Grad '10—22.** Prep—21. (Friends' Central 3, Haverford 2, Archmere 2, Baldwin 2, Shipley 1, Episcopal Acad 1). **Tui '12-'13:** Day $10,500-12,825 (+$1000). Aid: Need 40 ($116,900). **Est 1927.** Nonprofit. Roman Catholic (82% practice). Sem (Sept-June). **Assoc MSA.** Holy Child complements its curricular basics with computer, religion, foreign language and field trips. Well-developed performing arts and athletic programs are integral to school life. The academy emphasizes small-group instruction and close student-teacher rapport. Boys and girls work on an annual community service project.

BISHOP CARROLL CATHOLIC HIGH SCHOOL Bdg & Day
Ebensburg, PA 15931. 728 Ben Franklin Hwy. Coed Gr 9-12
Tel: 814-472-7500. Fax: 814-472-8020.
www.bishopcarroll.com E-mail: info@bishopcarroll.com
  Tim Lucko, Prin (2010). Jonathan Nagy, Adm.
  Col Prep. AP—Eng Comp_Sci Bio US_Govt & Pol. **Feat**—Creative_Writing Fr Lat Span Anat & Physiol Ecol Zoology Psych Sociol Relig Studio_Art Chorus Music_Theory Accounting Finance Public_Speak. **Supp**—Dev_Read ESL Rem_Read Tut. **Comp:** Comp/Stud: 1:3. **Dual enr:** PA Highlands CC, St Francis U, Mt Aloysius Col. **Sports**—Basket X-country Soccer Swim Track. B: Baseball Football Golf Wrestling. G: Cheer Softball Volley. **Somewhat selective adm:** 70/yr. Appl fee: $20. Appl due: Mar. Accepted: 95%. Yield: 95%. **Enr 240.** Wh 93%. Latino 2%. Blk 2%. Asian 3%. Intl 7%. Avg class size: 15. Stud/fac: 10:1. **Fac 25.** M 10/F 15. FT 22/PT 3. Nonwhite 4%. Adv deg: 56%. **Grad '08—64.** Col—53. (St Francis U 10, St Vincent 6, U of Pittsburgh 5, PA St 5, IN U of PA 4, Mt Aloysius Col 4). **Avg SAT:** CR 495. M 478. W 488. Alum donors: 10%. **Tui '10-'11:** Bdg $25,000. Day $5400 (+$600). Aid: Need 211 ($418,000). Work prgm 12 ($3000). **Est 1959.** Nonprofit. Roman Catholic (85% practice). Sem (Aug-May). **Assoc MSA.** The curriculum at Bishop Carroll includes Advanced Placement courses and dual-credit options at local colleges. Students perform 20 hours of community service each year, five of which assist the pupil's home parish. A small boarding division opened in August 2009.

ERIE DAY SCHOOL Day Coed Gr PS (Age 2)-8
Erie, PA 16505. 1372 W 6th St.
Tel: 814-452-4273. Fax: 814-455-5184.
www.eriedayschool.org E-mail: ktyler@eriedayschool.org
  Karen K. Tyler, Head (2011). BS, MEd, Edinboro Univ, EdD, Indiana Univ.
  Pre-Prep. Feat—Fr Span Computers Robotics Studio_Art Drama Music. **Supp**—Rem_ Math Rem_Read. **Sports**—Basket X-country Soccer Tennis. **Selective adm (Gr PS-7):** 44/yr. Appl due: Rolling. Accepted: 80%. **Enr 154.** Avg class size: 15. Stud/fac: 7:1. Uniform. **Fac 22.** M 3/F 19. FT 17/PT 5. Adv deg: 27%. **Grad '08—22. Tui '11-'12:** Day $7800-12,700 (+$1000). **Est 1929.** Nonprofit. Sem (Sept-June). EDS' curriculum combines course work

in the standard subjects with instruction in music, art, drama, foreign language and physical education. Children receive technology and computer training beginning in early childhood. Students in the middle school (grades 6-8) take part in a noteworthy program that replaces traditional grade levels with a mixed-grade curriculum that consists of five core subjects and five special programs. In addition to working toward graduation requirements, middle schoolers also have the scheduling flexibility to pursue course areas of interest and strength.

MOUNT SAINT JOSEPH ACADEMY   **Day Girls Gr 9-12**
Flourtown, PA 19031. 120 W Wissahickon Ave.
Tel: 215-233-3177. Fax: 215-233-4734.
www.msjacad.org   E-mail: admiss@msjacad.org
   Sr. Kathleen Brabson, SSJ, Pres. BA, Chestnut Hill College, MA, Villanova Univ. Judith A. Caviston, Prin. EdD, Immaculata Univ. Carol Finney, Adm.
   Col Prep. AP (exams req'd; 398 taken, 87% 3+)—Eng Fr Lat Span Calc Stats Bio Physics Eur_Hist US_Hist Psych US_Govt & Pol Music_Theory. **Feat**—British_Lit Genetics Physiol Comp_Sci Web_Design Relig Art_Hist Theater_Arts. **Supp**—Tut. **Comp:** Comp/Stud: 1:2. **Sports**— G: Basket Cheer Crew X-country F_Hockey Golf Lacrosse Soccer Softball Swim Tennis Track Volley. Activities: 26. **Selective adm (Gr 9-11):** 143/yr. Appl fee: $75. Appl due: Oct. Accepted: 50%. Yield: 64%. **Tests** HSPT. **Enr 568.** Avg class size: 20. Stud/fac: 10:1. Uniform. **Fac 57.** M 13/F 44. FT 55/PT 2. Wh 100%. Adv deg: 80%. **Grad '08—134.** Col—134. (Temple 12, Fordham 10, U of PA 7, Drexel 7, PA St 7, St Joseph's U 7). **Avg SAT:** CR 632. M 610. W 655. **Col Couns:** 1. Alum donors: 19%. **Tui '11-'12:** Day $13,800 (+$1130). **Est 1858.** Nonprofit. Roman Catholic. Quar (Sept-June). **Assoc** MSA.   MSJA's program provides opportunities for course work at area colleges, Advanced Placement programs and independent study. The school's 78-acre campus is easily accessible to downtown Philadelphia.

AQUINAS ACADEMY OF PITTSBURGH   **Day Coed Gr PS (Age 3)-12**
Gibsonia, PA 15044. 2308 W Hardies Rd.
Tel: 724-444-0722. Fax: 724-444-0750.
www.aquinasacademy-pittsburgh.org   E-mail: info@aquinasacademy.info
   Leslie M. Mitros, Head. BA, St Mary's College (IN), MEd, Univ of Pittsburgh. Juan Mata, Adm.
   Col Prep. AP (49 exams taken, 84% 3+)—Eng Lat Calc Stats Physics Eur_Hist US_Hist US_Govt & Pol. **Feat**—British_Lit Greek Span Anat & Physiol Programming Web_Design Philos Relig Studio_Art Journ. **Sports**—Basket Crew X-country Soccer. G: F_Hockey. **Somewhat selective adm (Gr PS-10):** 45/yr. Appl fee: $50. Appl due: Rolling. Accepted: 90%. **Enr 315.** Elem 244. Sec 71. Avg class size: 16. Uniform. **Fac 35.** M 9/F 26. FT 27/PT 8. **Grad '08—12.** Col—12. **Avg SAT:** CR 665. M 610. W 650. **Mid 50% SAT:** CR 610-780. M 550-670. W 570-740. **Tui '12-'13:** Day $5954-8684 (+$350-575). **Est 1996.** Nonprofit. Roman Catholic. Quar (Aug-June). **Assoc** MSA.   Conducted in the Catholic educational tradition, the academy encourages the development of critical-thinking and independent learning skills. Children build an academic foundation in the early years in phonics, reading, writing, spelling, math, history and science. Beginning in middle school, students take six major subjects (including foreign languages and religion) and four auxiliary courses (art, music, health and physical education, and computer). Advanced Placement course work is available in the upper grades.

GLADWYNE MONTESSORI SCHOOL   **Day Coed Gr PS (Age 2)-6**
Gladwyne, PA 19035. 920 Youngsford Rd.
Tel: 610-649-1761. Fax: 610-649-7978.
www.gladwyne.org   E-mail: mail@gladwyne.org
   Abigail Miller, Head (2006). BA, Middlebury College, MA, Univ of New York-Albany. Robyn Stearne, Adm.

Pre-Prep. Montessori. Feat—Lib_Skills Span Computers Studio_Art Music. **Somewhat selective adm:** 90/yr. Appl fee: $50. Appl due: Rolling. Accepted: 90%. Yield: 85%. **Enr 270.** Wh 76%. Latino 12%. Blk 3%. Asian 9%. Avg class size: 20. Stud/fac: 8:1. **Fac 39.** M 3/F 36. FT 20/PT 19. Wh 97%. Latino 2%. Other 1%. Adv deg: 12%. **Grad '10—4.** Prep—4. (Shipley 2, Haverford 1, Wm Penn Charter 1). **Tui '11-'12:** Day $16,848-18,109. **Est 1962.** Nonprofit. Sem (Sept-June). This Montessori school emphasizes individualized instruction and experiential learning. The arts, field trips, drama, ecology and community service are important parts of the program, and French instruction begins in the primary division (ages 3-6). In both the primary and the elementary units, children work with the same teacher and peer group in the same classroom for three consecutive years.

UPATTINAS SCHOOL Day Coed Gr K-12
Glenmoore, PA 19343. 429 Greenridge Rd.
Tel: 610-458-5138. Fax: 610-458-8688.
www.upattinas.org E-mail: office@upattinas.org
Sandra M. Hurst, Dir (1971). BME, Oberlin College.

Col Prep. Gen Acad. Feat—Fr Ital Japan Span Comp_Design Outdoor_Ed. **Supp**—ESL Makeup Rev Tut. **Somewhat selective adm:** 15/yr. Appl due: Rolling. Accepted: 95%. **Enr 112.** B 60. G 52. Elem 44. Sec 68. Avg class size: 6. **Fac 14.** M 6/F 8. FT 9/PT 5. Adv deg: 14%. **Grad '10—30.** Col—21. **Tui '11-'12:** Day $10,680-13,020 (+$750). **Est 1971.** Nonprofit. Sem (Sept-June). This small community school features independent study, a travel program and an academic curriculum leading to a high school diploma. A resource center provides full- and part-time programs, as well as home education services. International students may reside with a host family for an additional fee.

GWYNEDD MERCY ACADEMY Day Girls Gr 9-12
Gwynedd Valley, PA 19437. 1345 Sumneytown Pike, PO Box 902.
Tel: 215-646-8815. Fax: 215-646-4361.
www.gmahs.org E-mail: kscott@gmahs.org
Sr. Patricia Flynn, RSM, Prin (2011). BA, Gwynedd Mercy College, MA, Villanova Univ.
Kimberly D. Scott, Adm.

Col Prep. AP (exams req'd; 104 taken, 81% 3+)—Eng Lat Span Calc Physics US_Hist US_Govt & Pol. **Feat**—Fr Zoology Comp_Sci 20th-Century_Hist Econ Theol Studio_Art Music Accounting Bus Communications. **Supp**—Rem_Math Rem_Read. **Comp:** Comp/Stud: 1:3. **Sports**— G: Basket X-country F_Hockey Golf Indoor_Track Lacrosse Soccer Softball Swim Tennis Track Volley. **Selective adm (Gr 9-10):** 101/yr. Appl fee: $50. Appl due: Nov. **Tests** HSPT. **Enr 387.** Wh 96%. Latino 1%. Blk 1%. Asian 1%. Other 1%. Avg class size: 18. Stud/fac: 10:1. Uniform. **Fac 45.** M 5/F 40. FT 43/PT 2. Wh 99%. Latino 1%. Adv deg: 60%. **Grad '10—95.** Col—95. (St Joseph's U 8, PA St 6, Drexel 6, U of Pittsburgh 5, Loyola U MD 4, Notre Dame 3). **Avg SAT:** CR 578. M 563. W 579. Avg ACT: 26. **Tui '11-'12:** Day $14,100 (+$600). Aid: Merit 28 ($133,840). Need 21 ($76,000). **Est 1861.** Nonprofit. Roman Catholic (98% practice). Quar (Sept-June). **Assoc** MSA. In addition to required course work, GMA offers an extensive program of electives. Honors and Advanced Placement courses are available for qualified students. Students take four years of theology courses, each of which has a specific focus.

MILTON HERSHEY SCHOOL Bdg Coed Gr PS (Age 4)-12
Hershey, PA 17033. PO Box 830.
Tel: 717-520-2100, 800-322-3248. Fax: 717-520-2117.
www.mhs-pa.org E-mail: mhs-admissions@mhs-pa.org
Anthony J. Colistra, Pres (2009). Mark Seymour, Adm.

Col Prep. Voc. AP (exams req'd; 152 taken, 36% 3+)—Eng Fr Span Calc Stats Bio Physics Eur_Hist US_Hist US_Govt & Pol Studio_Art Music_Theory. **Feat**—Anat & Physiol

Animal_Sci African-Amer_Hist Bus Design Drafting Culinary_Arts. **Supp**—Dev_Read Makeup Rem_Math Rem_Read Rev Tut. **Comp:** Comp/Stud: 1:1 Laptop prgm Gr 11-12. **Dual enr:** Harrisburg Area CC. **Sports**—Basket Soccer Swim Track. B: Baseball Football Ice_Hockey Wrestling. G: F_Hockey Softball Volley. Activities: 20. **Very selective adm (Gr PS-10):** 393/yr. Appl fee: $0. Appl due: Rolling. Accepted: 15%. Yield: 95%. **Tests** IQ. **Enr 1838.** B 891. G 947. Elem 947. Sec 891. Wh 44%. Latino 12%. Blk 29%. Other 15%. Avg class size: 15. Casual dress. **Fac 195.** M 80/F 115. FT 182/PT 13. Wh 88%. Latino 3%. Blk 7%. Asian 2%. Adv deg: 68%. **Grad '10—163.** Col—144. (Harrisburg Area CC 19, Kutztown 7, Northampton County CC 7, CA U of PA 6, IN U of PA 6, Lebanon Valley 6). **Avg SAT:** CR 460. M 453. W 447. **Col Couns:** 9. **Tui '11-'12: Bdg** $0. **Est 1909.** Nonprofit. Nondenom Christian. Quar (Aug-June). **Assoc** MSA. MHS was founded by chocolate magnate Milton S. Hershey and his wife, Catherine. To be considered for enrollment, students must come from families with limited income. Pupils are provided with an educational program, clothing, meals and lodging, and assistance with health care and dental expenses during their enrollment. Each student home on campus has a married couple in residence. The extensive counseling program includes both job placement and follow-up. Students in grades 11 and 12 are assigned a laptop computer for individual and group course work, research, homework and communications. All school services are provided at no charge.

JOHNSTOWN CHRISTIAN SCHOOL   Day Coed Gr PS (Age 4)-12
Hollsopple, PA 15935. 125 Christian School Rd.
Tel: 814-288-2588. Fax: 814-288-1447.
www.johnstownchristianschool.org   E-mail: t.even@atlanticbbn.net
    Kathy A. Keafer, Admin (2008). BS, MSEd, Indiana Univ of Pennsylvania, EdD, Regent Univ. Joy Yoder, Adm.
    Col Prep. Feat—Span Environ_Sci Studio_Art Drama Chorus Music_Theory Agriculture. **Supp**—LD Rem_Math Rem_Read. **Comp:** Comp/Stud: 1:2. **Dual enr:** PA Highlands CC. **Sports**—Basket X-country Soccer Track. **Somewhat selective adm:** 34/yr. Appl fee: $50. Appl due: Aug. Accepted: 95%. Yield: 88%. **Enr 224.** Wh 98%. Blk 1%. Asian 1%. Avg class size: 19. Stud/fac: 9:1. **Fac 26.** M 5/F 21. FT 17/PT 9. Wh 100%. Adv deg: 19%. **Grad '09—22.** Col—22. (U of Pittsburgh 5, PA Highlands CC 3, IN U of PA 3, Allegheny 2, Taylor-Fort Wayne 1, Wheaton-IL 1). **Avg SAT:** CR/M 1110. Avg ACT: 22. **Tui '09-'10:** Day $4260 (+$200-270). Aid: Need ($70,000). **Est 1944.** Nonprofit. Nondenom Christian. Sem (Aug-June). **Assoc** MSA. Founded by a group of Mennonite families, this Christian school conducts a college preparatory curriculum that emphasizes spiritual growth and development. Elementary students receive daily instruction in music, art, science and physical education, while older pupils attend eight rotating academic periods. JCS' music program enables younger boys and girls to develop fundamental musical skills, while providing concert and choral performance opportunities for high schoolers.

CHRISTOPHER DOCK MENNONITE HIGH SCHOOL   Day Coed Gr 9-12
Lansdale, PA 19446. 1000 Forty Foot Rd.
Tel: 215-362-2675. Fax: 215-362-2943.
www.dockhs.org   E-mail: lboaman@dockhs.org
    Conrad Swartzentruber, Prin (2009). BS, Morehead State Univ, MS, Virginia Polytechnic Univ, EdD, Duquesne Univ. Lois A. Boaman, Adm.
    Col Prep. Gen Acad. Voc. AP (exams req'd)—Eng Span Calc Stats Bio. **Feat**—Creative_Writing Anat & Physiol Astron Environ_Sci Forensic_Sci Genetics Geol Programming Web_Design Econ Govt Psych Bible Art_Hist Ceramics Painting Photog Sculpt Studio_Art Chorus Music Accounting Bus Culinary_Arts. **Supp**—Tut. **Sports**—Basket X-country Soccer Tennis Track. B: Baseball Golf. G: Cheer F_Hockey Softball Volley. **Somewhat selective adm:** 125/yr. Appl fee: $50. Appl due: Rolling. Accepted: 95%. Yield: 95%. **Enr 365.** Intl 10%. Avg class size: 21. Stud/fac: 13:1. **Fac 36.** M 17/F 19. FT 35/PT 1. Wh 100%. Adv deg: 58%. **Grad '10—96.** Col—89. **Avg SAT:** CR 525. M 555. W 518. **Tui '12-'13:** Day $14,585

(+$100). Mennonite $11,975 (+$100). Aid: Need 85 ($400,000). **Est 1952**. Nonprofit. Mennonite (55% practice). Quar (Aug-June). **Assoc MSA**. The school was named for an early Mennonite schoolmaster and draws most of its students from the North Penn, Souderton and Pennridge areas. Pupils choose from three curricula: academic, general and vocational/technical. Chapel services, Bible study and projects in the community are among Dock's spiritual activities.

MALVERN PREPARATORY SCHOOL — Day Boys Gr 6-12
Malvern, PA 19355. 418 S Warren Ave.
Tel: 484-595-1100. Fax: 484-595-1124.
www.malvernprep.org   E-mail: admissions@malvernprep.org
James H. Stewart, Pres (2006). BA, La Salle College, MA, Middlebury College, MA, Villanova Univ. Rev. James R. Flynn, OSA, Head. BA, MA, Villanova Univ, MA, Washington Theological Union, MA, Duquesne Univ. William R. Gibson, Adm.

Col Prep. AP (exams req'd; 186 taken)—Eng Fr Span Calc Stats Comp_Sci Bio Chem Environ_Sci Physics US_Hist Econ US_Govt & Pol. **Feat**—British_Lit Lat Anat & Physiol Astron Marine_Bio/Sci Sports_Med Web_Design E_Asian_Hist Law Comp_Relig Philos Theol Ceramics Fine_Arts Graphic_Arts Photog Sculpt Studio_Art Chorus Music. **Supp**—Rev Tut. **Comp:** Comp/Stud: 1:3. **Sports**— B: Baseball Basket Crew X-country Football Golf Ice_ Hockey Indoor_Track Lacrosse Rugby Soccer Squash Swim Tennis Track W_Polo Wrestling. **Very selective adm (Gr 6-11):** 133/yr. Appl fee: $25. Appl due: Jan. Accepted: 25%. **Tests** HSPT ISEE SSAT. **Enr 622.** Elem 142. Sec 480. Wh 92%. Latino 1%. Blk 4%. Asian 2%. Other 1%. Avg class size: 19. Stud/fac: 8:1. Uniform. **Fac 81.** M 57/F 24. FT 81. Wh 97%. Blk 2%. Other 1%. Adv deg: 65%. **Grad '09—107.** Col—107. (Villanova 10, Drexel 9, St Joseph's U 9, U of DE 7, PA St 5, Bucknell 5). **Mid 50% SAT:** CR 530-640. M 540-670. W 520-640. Mid 50% ACT: 20-27. Alum donors: 17%. **Tui '10-'11:** Day $24,950-25,650 (+$200-600). Aid: Merit 53 ($354,500). Need 118 ($1,540,600). **Est 1842.** Nonprofit. Roman Catholic (85% practice). Quar (Sept-May). **Assoc MSA.** Conducted in the Augustinian tradition, Malvern provides a rigorous curriculum that incorporates a full complement of Advanced Placement and honors courses. Beginning in grade 6, students acquire basic computer skills and choose from a variety of computer classes, including AP computer science. Art and music electives, as well as photography, printmaking and graphic design, represent some of the arts options. Boys satisfy the following community service requirements: 10 hours in grades 9, plus engagement in three service weekends; one outside activity in grades 10 and 11, in addition to participation in three service weekends; and three service weekends in grade 12. In addition, seniors may devote a week to a community service project in Ivanhoe, VA, or Robbins, TN.

THE PHELPS SCHOOL — Bdg & Day
Malvern, PA 19355. 583 Sugartown Rd. — Boys Gr 7-PG
Tel: 610-644-1754. Fax: 610-644-6679.
www.thephelpsschool.org   E-mail: admis@thephelpsschool.org
Michael J. Reardon, Head (2011). BA, Fairfield Univ. Ira Miles, Adm.

Col Prep. LD. Underachiever. AP (exams req'd)—Calc US_Hist. **Feat**—British_Lit Span Stats Environ_Sci Comp_Sci Geog Govt Psych Sociol Ethics Sculpt Public_Speak Culinary_Arts Health Study_Skills. **Supp**—Dev_Read ESL Rem_Math Rem_Read Rev Tut. **Sports**— B: Baseball Basket X-country Golf Lacrosse Soccer Tennis. **Selective adm (Bdg Gr 7-12; Day 7-11):** 60/yr. Bdg 45. Day 15. Appl fee: $50. Appl due: Rolling. Accepted: 75%. Yield: 62%. **Enr 120.** Intl 20%. Avg class size: 8. Stud/fac: 5:1. Formal dress. **Fac 28.** M 20/F 8. FT 28. Adv deg: 50%. Co ed. Tuition 12. **Grad '11—33.** Col—32. **Col Couns:** 1. Alum donors: 25%. **Tui '12-'13:** Bdg $41,500 (+$500-860). Day $22,500 (+$500-860). Intl Bdg $41,500 (+$2000-9360). **Est 1946.** Nonprofit. Quar (Sept-June). **Assoc MSA.** The school offers a college preparatory program to boys who are underachieving or who have a specific learning disability such as dyslexia or attention deficit disorder. Phelps features small classes and an academic support program. All students choose an afternoon activity; options include various sports, as well as arts and crafts, wood shop, photography, drama and computers.

BENCHMARK SCHOOL   Day Coed Gr 1-8
Media, PA 19063. 2107 N Providence Rd.
Tel: 610-565-3741. Fax: 610-565-3872.
www.benchmarkschool.org   E-mail: benchmarkinfo@benchmarkschool.org
   Robert W. Gaskins, Head (2007). BA, Duke Univ, MS, PhD, State Univ of New York-Albany. Adam Lemisch, Adm.
   Pre-Prep. LD. Underachiever. Feat—Lat Studio_Art Music. **Supp**—Dev_Read Rem_Math Rem_Read Tut. **Sports**—Basket Soccer. **Selective adm (Gr 1-5):** 39/yr. Appl fee: $125. Appl due: Rolling. Accepted: 46%. Yield: 95%. **Tests** IQ. **Enr 155.** Wh 91%. Latino 1%. Blk 7%. Asian 1%. Avg class size: 11. Stud/fac: 3:1. Uniform. **Fac 76.** M 15/F 61. FT 76. Wh 98%. Asian 2%. Adv deg: 71%. **Grad '11—12.** Prep—10. **Tui '11-'12:** Day $28,000 (+$300-550). Aid: Need 35 ($297,326). **Est 1970.** Nonprofit. Tri (Sept-June).   Benchmark serves bright underachievers, providing a complete curriculum of social studies, math, science, art, music, physical education and health, in addition to reading and language arts. Instruction in all subjects is individualized according to the student's needs. The program includes professional guidance in helping students to overcome social and emotional problems that may accompany academic underachievement. The successful return of each student to mainstream education is a school goal.

MERION MERCY ACADEMY   Day Girls Gr 9-12
Merion Station, PA 19066. 511 Montgomery Ave.
Tel: 610-664-6655. Fax: 610-664-6322.
www.merion-mercy.com   E-mail: admissions@merion-mercy.com
   Sr. Barbara Buckley, RSM, Prin (2007). BS, Univ of Dayton, MA, Temple Univ, MS, Univ of Pennsylvania. Eileen Daly Killeen, Adm.
   Col Prep. AP (exams req'd; 118 taken, 74% 3+)—Eng Calc Stats Bio Chem Environ_Sci US_Hist Econ US_Govt & Pol. **Feat**—Fr Lat Span Astron Bioethics Women's_Hist Psych Sociol Relig Studio_Art Drama Music Journ. **Supp**—Rev Tut. **Sports**— G: Basket Crew X-country F_Hockey Golf Lacrosse Soccer Softball Swim Tennis Track Volley. Activities: 45. **Selective adm:** 133/yr. Appl fee: $35. Appl due: Nov. Accepted: 50%. **Tests** HSPT. **Enr 481.** Wh 91%. Latino 3%. Blk 4%. Asian 1%. Other 1%. Avg class size: 17. Stud/fac: 9:1. Uniform. **Fac 53.** M 6/F 47. FT 53. Wh 96%. Latino 4%. Adv deg: 77%. **Grad '09—119.** Col—119. **Mid 50% SAT:** CR 520-660. M 510-630. W 560-660. **Col Couns:** 2. **Tui '12-'13:** Day $15,700 (+$400). Aid: Merit 74 ($125,000). Need 175 ($310,000). **Est 1884.** Nonprofit. Roman Catholic. Quar (Sept-June). **Assoc** MSA.   MMA draws its student body from Delaware, Montgomery, and Philadelphia counties, as well as southern New Jersey. Advanced Placement and honors courses in the major disciplines complement electives in contemporary fiction, drama, journalism, speech, psychology and computer.

WALDRON MERCY ACADEMY   Day Coed Gr PS (Age 4)-8
Merion Station, PA 19066. 513 Montgomery Ave.
Tel: 610-664-9847. Fax: 610-664-6364.
www.waldronmercy.org   E-mail: wma@waldronmercy.org
   Steve Stritch, Prin. Sr. Joellen McDonnell, RSM, Adm.
   Pre-Prep. Montessori. Feat—Lib_Skills Lat Span Computers Relig Studio_Art Drama Chorus Music. **Supp**—Tut. **Sports**—Basket Soccer Swim Track. B: Baseball Football. G: F_Hockey Lacrosse Softball Volley. **Somewhat selective adm:** 110/yr. Appl fee: $100. Appl due: Rolling. Accepted: 91%. **Tests** IQ. **Enr 514.** B 257. G 257. Avg class size: 18. Stud/fac: 8:1. Uniform. **Fac 55.** M 7/F 48. FT 55. Adv deg: 60%. **Grad '09—61.** Prep—61. (La Salle Col HS 3, Haverford 2, Mt St Joseph Acad-PA 2, Agnes Irwin 1, Friends' Central 1, Wm

Penn Charter 1). **Tui '12-'13:** Day $11,100-11,300 (+$150-300). **Est 1923.** Nonprofit. Roman Catholic (77% practice). Tri (Sept-June). **Assoc** MSA. WMA's focus on religious education features religion classes and community service projects. The academy provides instruction in computers and three foreign languages and conducts strong music, art and drama programs. Students publish their own works as part of the English program.

DELAWARE COUNTY CHRISTIAN SCHOOL   Day Coed Gr PS (Age 2)-12
Newtown Square, PA 19073. 462 Malin Rd.
Tel: 610-353-6522. Fax: 610-356-9684.
Other locations: 985 S Waterloo Rd, Devon 19333.
www.dccs.org   E-mail: admissions@dccs.org
    Stephen P. Dill, Head (2002). BA, Wheaton College (IL), MA, Villanova Univ, EdD, Temple Univ. Betty Ellsworth, Adm.
    Col Prep. AP (exams req'd; 154 taken, 82% 3+)—Eng Ger Span Calc Stats Bio Chem Physics US_Hist US_Govt & Pol. **Feat**—British_Lit Creative_Writing Forensic_Sci Microbio Psych Sociol Theol Film Photog Drama Theater_Arts Debate Journ. **Supp**—ESL LD Rem_Math Rem_Read Tut. **Sports**—Basket X-country Golf Indoor_Track Soccer Tennis Track. B: Baseball Ice_Hockey Wrestling. G: Cheer F_Hockey Softball. Activities: 10. **Selective adm:** 162/yr. Appl fee: $50. Appl due: Rolling. **Enr 795.** Elem 475. Sec 320. Intl 9%. Avg class size: 19. Stud/fac: 11:1. Uniform. **Fac 87.** Adv deg: 66%. **Grad '11—87.** Col—87. **Avg SAT:** CR 571. M 588. W 571. **Tui '12-'13:** Day $7997-13,288 (+$325-600). Aid: Need 239. **Est 1950.** Nonprofit. Nondenom Christian. Sem (Sept-June). **Assoc** MSA. DC integrates honors and Advanced Placement courses into a curriculum that also features, for an additional fee, individualized therapy and small-group resource rooms for students with learning differences. Pupils enroll from five Delaware Valley counties within a 25-mile radius of the school. The elementary division (grades pre-K-5) is located at a separate campus on South Waterloo Road.

STRATFORD FRIENDS SCHOOL   Day Coed Gr K-8
Newtown Square, PA 19073. 2 Bishop Hollow Rd.
Tel: 610-355-9580. Fax: 610-355-9585.
www.stratfordfriends.org   E-mail: gvare@stratfordfriends.org
    Timothy P. Madigan, Head (2007). BA, Allegheny College, MEd, PhD, State Univ of New York-Buffalo. Gretchen S. Vare, Adm.
    Pre-Prep. LD. Feat—Studio_Art Music Speech Woodworking. **Supp**—Dev_Read Rem_Math Rem_Read Rev Tut. **Comp:** Laptop prgm Gr 7-8. **Selective adm:** 18/yr. Appl fee: $75. Appl due: Rolling. Accepted: 80%. Yield: 75%. **Tests** IQ. **Enr 78.** B 52. G 26. Wh 58%. Latino 4%. Blk 30%. Asian 3%. Other 5%. Avg class size: 6. **Fac 19.** M 3/F 16. FT 17/PT 2. Wh 86%. Blk 14%. Adv deg: 84%. **Grad '11—2.** Prep—2. Alum donors: 10%. **Tui '12-'13:** Day $33,960 (+$50). Aid: Need 26 ($330,000). **Est 1976.** Nonprofit. Religious Society of Friends (4% practice). Sem (Sept-June). Stratford Friends enrolls children of average to above-average intelligence who have language-based learning differences. The multisensory program includes speech, math and reading instruction. The reading program utilizes the Orton-Gillingham approach. An extended-day option is available.

DELAWARE VALLEY FRIENDS SCHOOL   Day Coed Gr 6-12
Paoli, PA 19301. 19 E Central Ave.
Tel: 610-640-4150. Fax: 610-296-9970.
www.dvfs.org   E-mail: admissions@dvfs.org
    Pritchard Garrett, Head (2011). BA. Mary Ellen Trent, Adm.
    Col Prep. LD. Feat—Span Asian_Stud Photog Studio_Art Music Outdoor_Ed. **Supp**—Dev_Read Rem_Math Rem_Read Tut. **Comp:** Comp/Stud: 1:1 Laptop prgm Gr 6-12. Outdoor Ed. **Sports**—Basket X-country Golf Lacrosse Soccer Tennis Ultimate_Frisbee. Activities: 17.

Selective adm (Gr 6-11): 41/yr. Appl fee: $100. Appl due: Rolling. Accepted: 68%. Yield: 53%. **Enr 176.** B 102. G 74. Elem 29. Sec 147. Wh 83%. Latino 2%. Blk 6%. Asian 5%. Other 4%. Avg class size: 9. Casual dress. **Fac 39.** M 14/F 25. FT 34/PT 5. Wh 88%. Blk 8%. Other 4%. Adv deg: 61%. **Grad '10—45.** Col—41. (La Salle 2, Am U 2, DE Col of Art & Design 2). **Mid 50% SAT:** CR 440-550. M 370-490. W 420-560. Mid 50% ACT: 16-25. **Tui '11-'12:** Day $36,300. Aid: Need 48 ($667,600). **Est 1986.** Nonprofit. Religious Society of Friends (5% practice). Sem (Sept-June). Enrolling intelligent students with learning disabilities, DVFS features language arts learning skills laboratories that provide small-group remedial and developmental assistance. All students take part in a daily reading and writing lab, and the school conducts an adaptive Outward Bound-type program that includes courses in rock climbing, backpacking, bicycle touring, ropes and hiking. Seniors participate in a compulsory, off-campus work-study internship, and each pupil is required to perform community service.

ARCHBISHOP RYAN HIGH SCHOOL   Day Coed Gr 9-12
Philadelphia, PA 19154. 11201 Academy Rd.
Tel: 215-637-1800. Fax: 215-637-8833.
www.archbishopryan.com   E-mail: pmcpeak@archbishopryan.com
    Michael J. McArdle, Pres. Helen Chaykowsky, Prin. Pamela McPeak, Adm.

Col Prep. Gen Acad. AP (exams req'd)—Eng Calc Stats Bio Chem Physics Eur_Hist US_Hist US_Govt & Pol. **Feat**—Fr Ger Ital Lat Span Anat & Physiol Environ_Sci Comp_ Sci Econ Law Psych Relig Band Chorus Music Communications Journ. **Supp**—Dev_Read LD Rem_Math Rem_Read Tut. **Comp:** Comp/Stud: 1:1.8. **Sports**—Basket Bowl X-country Indoor_Track Soccer Swim Tennis Track. B: Baseball Football Golf Ice_Hockey Lacrosse Rugby Wrestling. G: Cheer F_Hockey Softball Volley. Activities: 33. **Selective adm:** 629/yr. Appl due: Mar. **Enr 1611.** B 767. G 844. Stud/fac: 22:1. Uniform. **Fac 82.** Adv deg: 36%. **Grad '08—517.** Col—439. **Avg SAT:** CR/M 1050. **Tui '11-'12:** Day $6750 (+$970). Catholic $5600 (+$970). **Est 1966.** Nonprofit. Roman Catholic. Sem (Sept-June). **Assoc** MSA. Archbishop Ryan is a full-spectrum high school offering college preparatory courses, business education and opportunities for technical training. Honors courses are available in English and religion, while AP courses are provided in four areas. Particularly able seniors may take college classes for credit at area Catholic colleges.

FATHER JUDGE HIGH SCHOOL   Day Boys Gr 9-12
Philadelphia, PA 19136. 3301 Solly Ave.
Tel: 215-338-9494. Fax: 215-338-0250.
www.fatherjudge.com   E-mail: info@fatherjudge.com
    Rev. Joseph Campellone, OSFS, Pres (2001). BA, DeSales School of Theology, MDiv, DeSales Univ. Rev. James E. Dalton, OSFS, Prin. Thomas Coyle, Adm.

Col Prep. Gen Acad. AP—Eng Calc Bio Physics Eur_Hist US_Govt & Pol. **Feat**—Fr Lat Span Anat & Physiol Psych Theol Studio_Art Music Bus Drafting. **Supp**—Tut. **Dual enr:** Manor Col. **Sports**— B: Baseball Basket Bowl Cheer Crew X-country Football Golf Ice_Hockey Lacrosse Rugby Soccer Swim Tennis Track Wrestling. Activities: 22. **Somewhat selective adm (Gr 9-11):** 346/yr. Appl fee: $50. Appl due: Rolling. Accepted: 95%. **Enr 1143.** Avg class size: 29. Stud/fac: 20:1. Uniform. **Fac 65.** M 50/F 15. FT 65. Adv deg: 35%. **Grad '11—345.** Col—323. **Tui '12-'13:** Day $7050 (+$425). Parishioners $5850 (+$425). **Est 1954.** Nonprofit. Roman Catholic. Quar (Sept-June). **Assoc** MSA. Father Judge teaches courses at different levels of academic difficulty, ranging from advanced to remedial. AP courses are available, and qualified seniors may take dual-enrollment classes through Manor College for university credit.

GIRARD COLLEGE   5-Day Bdg Coed Gr 1-12
Philadelphia, PA 19121. 2101 S College Ave.
Tel: 215-787-2620, 877-344-7273. Fax: 215-787-4402.
www.girardcollege.edu   E-mail: admissions@girardcollege.edu
    Clarence D. Armbrister, Int Pres (2012). BA, Univ of Pennsylvania, JD, Univ of Michigan.
Tamara LeClair, Adm.

Col Prep. AP (exams req'd)—Eng US_Hist. **Feat**—Fr Span Calc Psych Philos Studio_
Art Video_Production. **Supp**—Dev_Read Rem_Math Rem_Read Tut. **Dual enr:** CC of Phila-
delphia, Philadelphia U. **Sports**—Basket X-country Indoor_Track Soccer Tennis Track. B:
Baseball Wrestling. G: Cheer Softball. Activities: 40. **Very selective adm (Gr 1-10):** 24/yr.
Appl due: June. Accepted: 5%. **Tests** CEEB IQ Stanford. **Enr 475.** B 218. G 257. Elem 175.
Sec 300. Latino 5%. Blk 80%. Asian 7%. Other 8%. Avg class size: 18. Uniform. **Fac 51.** M
19/F 32. FT 51. Wh 82%. Latino 2%. Blk 14%. Asian 2%. Adv deg: 58%. In Dorms 1. **Grad
'11—55.** Col—53. (Temple 6, PA St 5, CC of Philadelphia 5, W Chester 3, Manor Col 3,
Millersville 2). **Avg SAT:** CR/M 990. Avg ACT: 19. **Col Couns:** 2. **Tui '12-'13:** 5-Day Bdg
$0. **Est 1848.** Nonprofit. Tri (Sept-June). **Assoc** MSA.   Stephen Girard, an early American
businessman, endowed this five-day boarding school to educate orphaned boys. Today, Girard
College enrolls boys and girls from limited-income families without one or both parents; the
school furnishes full scholarships for its students. In addition to providing a college preparatory curriculum, Girard provides instruction in the following five areas: respect, responsibility,
integrity, self-discipline and compassion. Juniors satisfy a 40-hour community service requirement. Students participate in recreational and enrichment activities at local museums, parks,
historical sites, theaters, universities and sporting facilities.

JOHN W. HALLAHAN   Day Girls Gr 9-12
CATHOLIC GIRLS' HIGH SCHOOL
Philadelphia, PA 19103. 311 N 19th St.
Tel: 215-563-8930. Fax: 215-563-3809.
www.jwhallahan.org   E-mail: kirbym@jwhallahan.com
    Sandra Young, Pres. Mary Kirby, Prin.

Col Prep. Gen Acad. AP (exams req'd)—Eng Calc Bio Chem US_Hist. **Feat**—Span Anat
& Physiol Environ_Sci Forensic_Sci Comp_Sci Psych Govt/Econ Theol Studio_Art Music
Accounting. **Supp**—Dev_Read Rem_Read. **Sports**— G: Basket Bowl Cheer X-country Golf
Soccer Softball Track Volley. Activities: 27. **Selective adm (Gr 9-11):** 210/yr. Appl fee: $100.
Appl due: Rolling. **Enr 650.** Avg class size: 30. Uniform. **Fac 33.** M 5/F 28. FT 33. Adv deg:
48%. **Tui '12-'13:** Day $7050 (+$620). Catholic $5850 (+$620). **Est 1901.** Nonprofit. Roman
Catholic. Quar (Sept-June). **Assoc** MSA. At Hallahan, standard, honors and Advanced Placement classes provide students with both college and career preparation. The school emphasizes
a foundation in theology, math, science and the humanities and offers electives such as foreign
languages, environmental science and fine arts. In addition, a work experience program prepares students for the business world by introducing them to current technology and providing
on-the-job training at Center City firms.

NAZARETH ACADEMY HIGH SCHOOL   Day Girls Gr 9-12
Philadelphia, PA 19114. 4001 Grant Ave.
Tel: 215-637-7676. Fax: 215-637-8523.
www.nazarethacademyhs.org   E-mail: makowski@nazarethacademyhs.org
    Sr. Mary Joan Jacobs, CSFN, Prin (2003). BA, Holy Family Univ, MA, Villanova Univ,
EdD, St Joseph's Univ. Jacqui McClernan Makowski, Adm.

Col Prep. AP (exams req'd; 175 taken, 70% 3+)—Eng Fr Lat Span Calc Stats Bio US_
Hist Psych US_Govt & Pol Art_Hist Music_Theory. **Feat**—Creative_Writing Poetry Shake-
speare Irish_Lit Mythology Women's_Lit ASL Greek Ital Anat & Physiol Environ_Sci Comp_
Design Programming Web_Design Law Sociol Theol Film Photog Studio_Art Theater_Arts
Music Accounting Bus Finance Public_Speak SAT_Prep Study_Skills. **Supp**—Tut. **Comp:**

Comp/Stud: 1:2. **Dual enr:** Holy Family. **Sports—** G: Basket Cheer X-country F_Hockey Golf Indoor_Track Lacrosse Soccer Softball Swim Tennis Track Volley. Activities: 35. **Selective adm:** 100/yr. Appl due: Nov. **Tests** HSPT. **Enr 415.** Avg class size: 20. Stud/fac: 9:1. Uniform. **Fac 46.** M 11/F 35. FT 36/PT 10. Adv deg: 78%. **Grad '11—123.** Col—123. **Col Couns:** 1. Alum donors: 8%. **Tui '12-'13:** Day $11,500 (+$400). Aid: Need ($80,000). **Est 1928.** Nonprofit. Roman Catholic (95% practice). Sem (Aug-June). **Assoc** MSA. NAHS' curriculum features Advanced Placement and honors courses, in addition to a variety of electives. In addition to requirements in the standard subjects, pupils complete four years of theology course work. Girls perform 20 hours of annual community service as part of the theology curriculum.

THE PHILADELPHIA SCHOOL
Day Coed Gr PS (Age 4)-8
Philadelphia, PA 19146. 2501 Lombard St.
Tel: 215-545-5323. Fax: 215-546-1798.
www.thephiladelphiaschool.org   E-mail: fhoover@tpschool.org
Amy Purcell Vorenberg, Head (2006). BA, Univ of New Hampshire, MS, Wheelock College. Frances Hoover, Adm.

Pre-Prep. Gen Acad. Feat—Lat Span Studio_Art Drama Music. **Supp—**Dev_Read Rem_Math Rem_Read Rev Tut. **Comp:** Comp/Stud: 1:2.8. **Sports—**Basket Soccer Tennis Track. G: Volley. **Selective adm (Gr PS-7):** 75/yr. Appl fee: $60. Appl due: Rolling. Accepted: 52%. Yield: 75%. **Enr 387.** B 188. G 199. Wh 73%. Latino 3%. Blk 10%. Asian 9%. Other 5%. Stud/fac: 8:1. **Fac 49.** M 9/F 40. FT 43/PT 6. Adv deg: 61%. **Grad '11—28.** Prep—18. (Friends Select 5, Germantown Friends 3, Wm Penn Charter 2, Springside 2). **Tui '11-'12:** Day $17,100-21,500 (+$25). Aid: Need 92 ($1,000,000). **Est 1970.** Nonprofit. Sem (Sept-June). TPS' progressive program emphasizes active, experiential learning. Mixed-age classrooms combine grades 1 and 2, 4 and 5, and 7 and 8. The school makes use of the cultural resources of Philadelphia, and K-8 students spend a day per week in the fall and the spring at Shelly Ridge, a 125-acre environmental center in Miquon. Service projects are integrated into the curriculum at all grade levels. After-school daycare, sports and activities (including instrumental music lessons) are available.

SAINTS JOHN NEUMANN AND
Day Coed Gr 9-12
MARIA GORETTI CATHOLIC HIGH SCHOOL
Philadelphia, PA 19148. 1736 S 10th St.
Tel: 215-465-8437. Fax: 215-462-2410.
www.neumanngorettihs.org
John Murawski, Pres. Patricia C. Sticco, Prin. Veronica Oster, Adm.

Col Prep. Gen Acad. Bus. AP (exams req'd)—Eng Calc US_Hist US_Govt & Pol Studio_Art. **Feat—**British_Lit Fr Ital Lat Span Kinesiology Comp_Sci Econ Psych Sociol Theol Theater Music Dance Accounting Health. **Supp—**Dev_Read ESL Rem_Math Rem_Read Tut. **Sports—**Basket Bowl Soccer Track. B: Baseball Football Golf Lacrosse. G: Softball Volley. Activities: 28. **Selective adm. Enr 1091.** B 523. G 568. Uniform. **Fac 52.** M 32/F 20. FT 52. Adv deg: 34%. **Grad '04—315.** Col—283. **Tui '11-'12:** Day $6750 (+$750). Catholic $5600 (+$750). **Est 1936.** Nonprofit. Roman Catholic. Quar (Sept-June). **Assoc** MSA. Tailoring its curriculum to students' specific needs, Neumann-Goretti offers five programs of study: Advanced Placement, honors, college placement, general and remedial support. The school's business and technology department allows pupils to take such courses as economics and business technology, business law and accounting. A strong computer program is part of the curriculum, and fine arts offerings include instrumental and vocal music, dance and art.

WEST PHILADELPHIA CATHOLIC HIGH SCHOOL   Day Coed Gr 9-12
Philadelphia, PA 19139. 4501 Chestnut St.
Tel: 215-386-2244. Fax: 215-222-1651.
www.westcatholic.org   E-mail: info@westcatholic.org
    Br. Richard Kestler, FSC, Pres (2012). MA, La Salle Univ, MA, Villanova Univ, MA, St John's Univ (NY). Sr. Mary E. Bur, IHM, Prin. John Jenkins, Adm.
    Col Prep. Gen Acad. AP (exams req'd; 30 taken)—Eng Calc US_Hist US_Govt & Pol Studio_Art. **Feat**—Fr Span Comp_Design Comp_Sci Econ Intl_Relations Relig Chorus Music Bus Mech_Drawing Culinary_Arts. **Supp**—Dev_Read Rem_Math Rem_Read Rev Tut. **Comp:** Comp/Stud: 1:5. **Sports**—Basket Indoor_Track Soccer Track. B: Baseball Football. G: X-country Softball Volley. **Somewhat selective adm:** 148/yr. Appl fee: $20. Appl due: Nov. Accepted: 95%. Yield: 100%. **Tests** SSAT. **Enr 487.** B 284. G 203. Wh 18%. Latino 2%. Blk 71%. Asian 9%. Intl 12%. Avg class size: 34. Stud/fac: 25:1. Uniform. **Fac 36.** M 18/F 18. FT 30/PT 6. Wh 98%. Blk 2%. Adv deg: 36%. **Grad '10—129.** Col—123. **Avg SAT:** CR/M 800. **Col Couns:** 1. **Tui '10-'11:** Day $6450 (+$500). Catholic $5350 (+$500). Aid: Merit 92 ($165,640). Need 480 ($719,101). **Est 1916.** Nonprofit. Roman Catholic. Sem (Sept-June). **Assoc** MSA. The school's liberal arts curriculum comprises honors, college prep and remedial programs of study. West Catholic participates in a program that allows seniors to take classes at area Catholic colleges for college credit. Technology is integral to the program. Students satisfy a 20-hour community service requirement each year.

FOX CHAPEL COUNTRY DAY SCHOOL   Day Coed Gr PS (Age 3)-5
Pittsburgh, PA 15238. 620 Squaw Run Rd E.
Tel: 412-963-8644. Fax: 412-963-7123.
www.foxchapelcountryday.com   E-mail: ssmith@foxchapelcountryday.com
    Nan Solow, Head. BA, Chatham College. Sharon Smith, Adm.
    Pre-Prep. Gen Acad. Feat—Span Studio_Art Drama Music. **Supp**—LD Tut. **Selective adm:** 22/yr. Appl fee: $0. Appl due: Rolling. Accepted: 70%. Yield: 80%. **Enr 90.** Avg class size: 18. Stud/fac: 8:1. Uniform. **Fac 19.** M 2/F 17. FT 19. **Grad '06—16.** Prep—12. **Tui '12-'13:** Day $12,650-16,950 (+$125-225). **Est 1948.** Nonprofit. Episcopal. Tri (Aug-June). Beginning in prekindergarten, Country Day places balanced emphasis on academics and the arts. The traditional elementary-level curriculum features small classes and ample flexibility to address pupils' varying needs. Although the program is nonsectarian, all children attend weekly chapel. Opportunities for outdoor play and exploration of the school's environs complement academics.

PLYMOUTH MEETING FRIENDS SCHOOL   Day Coed Gr PS (Age 3)-6
Plymouth Meeting, PA 19462. 2150 Butler Pike.
Tel: 610-828-2288. Fax: 610-828-2390.
www.pmfs1780.org   E-mail: pmfs@pmfs1780.org
    Deborah Kost, Head (2011). BS, Univ of Arizona, MEd, Lehigh Univ. Sarah Sweeney-Denham, Adm.
    Pre-Prep. Feat—Lib_Skills Span Studio_Art Theater Music. **Selective adm:** 39/yr. Appl fee: $45. Appl due: Rolling. Accepted: 68%. Yield: 76%. **Tests** IQ. **Enr 145.** B 79. G 66. Avg class size: 20. **Fac 26.** M 5/F 21. FT 17/PT 9. Adv deg: 38%. **Grad '08—18.** Prep—14. Alum donors: 15%. **Tui '12-'13:** Day $13,050-16,900 (+$280-360). Aid: Need 62. **Est 1780.** Nonprofit. Religious Society of Friends. Tri (Sept-June). This Quaker school draws roughly half of its enrollment from Philadelphia, with the remaining children coming from townships in Montgomery County. The integrated, developmentally sequenced curriculum is built around language arts, math and social studies. PMFS integrates computer use into the curriculum, and service learning activities, field trips and travel beyond the immediate community are important aspects of the program.

PORTERSVILLE CHRISTIAN SCHOOL   **Day Coed Gr PS (Age 4)-12**
Portersville, PA 16051. 343 E Portersville Rd.
Tel: 724-368-8787. Fax: 724-368-3100.
www.portersvillechristianschool.org   E-mail: pcsschooloffice@zoominternet.net
   R. Lee Saunders, Jr., Admin.
   Col Prep. AP—Calc Stats. **Feat**—British_Lit Creative_Writing Fr Russ Span Comp_Sci
Econ Sociol Bible Ethics Studio_Art Drama Chorus Music. **Sports**—Basket Track. B: Soccer.
G: Cheer Volley. **Selective adm:** 67/yr. Appl fee: $25. Appl due: Rolling. Accepted: 75%.
Yield: 75%. **Enr 262.** Elem 181. Sec 81. Wh 96%. Blk 4%. **Fac 31. Grad '07—33.** Col—31.
Avg SAT: CR 541. M 561. W 525. **Tui '11-'12:** Day $3882-5330 (+$150). **Est 1963.** Non-
profit. Evangelical. Quar (Aug-June). **Assoc** MSA. From a Christian perspective, PCS offers
honors courses in most disciplines. Eligible students may enroll in college courses in English
and communications. The school schedules frequent community service projects for boys and
girls in grades 7-12.

UNITED FRIENDS SCHOOL   **Day Coed Gr PS (Age 3)-8**
Quakertown, PA 18951. 1018 W Broad St.
Tel: 215-538-1733. Fax: 215-538-1239.
www.unitedfriendsschool.org   E-mail: frontoffice@unitedfriendsschool.org
   Nancy Donnelly, Head (2007). MEd, Univ of Pennsylvania. Marie Knapp, Adm.
   Pre-Prep. Gen Acad. Feat—Span Studio_Art Music. **Sports**—Basket X-country Soccer
Track. **Somewhat selective adm:** 28/yr. Appl fee: $45. Appl due: Rolling. Accepted: 95%.
Yield: 92%. **Enr 118.** B 57. G 61. Avg class size: 16. **Fac 18.** M 2/F 16. FT 13/PT 5. Adv deg:
16%. **Grad '08—8.** Prep—3. (Hill Sch-PA 1, Peddie 1, Christopher Dock 1). **Tui '12-'13:** Day
$12,775-13,400. **Est 1983.** Nonprofit. Religious Society of Friends (10% practice). Sem (Sept-
June). UFS places emphasis upon cooperative learning through open-ended, student-centered
exploratory activities and an integrated curriculum. The middle school program is enhanced by
community mentoring opportunities and a more advanced approach to research, independent
study, computer access and academic evaluation. Each year, students take part in various service projects, and the school community participates in weekly Meeting for Worship.

HILL TOP PREPARATORY SCHOOL   **Day Coed Gr 5-12**
Rosemont, PA 19010. 737 S Ithan Ave.
Tel: 610-527-3230. Fax: 610-527-7683.
www.hilltopprep.org   E-mail: mfitzpatrick@hilltopprep.org
   Thomas W. Needham, Head (2007). BA, Eastern Connecticut State Univ, MEd, Lesley Col-
lege. Meredith R. Fitzpatrick, Adm.
   Col Prep. LD. Feat—Span Psych Ceramics Film Photog Studio_Art Fiber_Arts Drama
Public_Speak Woodworking. **Supp**—Dev_Read Rem_Math Rem_Read. **Comp:** Laptop prgm
Gr 6-12. **Sports**—Basket Golf Soccer Tennis. B: Wrestling. **Selective adm (Gr 6-11):** 13/yr.
Appl fee: $75. Appl due: Rolling. Accepted: 25%. Yield: 85%. **Enr 71.** B 57. G 14. Elem
18. Sec 53. Wh 93%. Blk 7%. Avg class size: 6. Stud/fac: 2:1. Casual dress. **Fac 25.** M 12/F
13. FT 23/PT 2. Adv deg: 76%. **Grad '11—16.** Col—14. (Cabrini 2, Lebanon Valley 2, DE
County CC 2, Mitchell 2, W Chester 1, Ursinus 1). **Col Couns:** 1. **Tui '11-'12:** Day $36,850.
Aid: Need 21 ($127,000). **Est 1971.** Nonprofit. Quar (Sept-June). **Assoc** MSA. Founded on
the campus of Cabrini College, Hill Top moved to its current 25-acre Rosemont campus in
1976. For students of average and above-average intelligence who have learning disabilities or
attention deficit disorder, the specially designed program utilizes individualized instruction to
prepare students for college and employment. Reality-oriented group counseling sessions are
integral to the program.

ROSEMONT SCHOOL OF THE HOLY CHILD
Day Coed Gr PS (Age 3)-8

Rosemont, PA 19010. 1344 Montgomery Ave.
Tel: 610-922-1000. Fax: 610-922-1030.
www.rosemontschool.org   E-mail: info@rosemontschool.org
Sr. Mary Broderick, SHCJ, Head (1983). BA, Villanova Univ, MA, Marywood Univ. Jeanne Marie Blair, Adm.

Pre-Prep. Feat—Lat Span Computers Relig Studio_Art Drama Music. **Comp:** Comp/Stud: 1:3 (1:1 Laptop prgm Gr 6-8). **Sports**—Basket Swim Track. B: Football. G: F_Hockey. **Somewhat selective adm (Gr PS-7):** 44/yr. Appl fee: $50. Appl due: Oct. Accepted: 95%. Yield: 90%. **Tests** IQ. **Enr 323.** B 167. G 156. Wh 87%. Latino 4%. Blk 6%. Asian 3%. Avg class size: 17. Stud/fac: 8:1. Uniform. **Fac 36.** M 5/F 31. FT 36. Wh 98%. Latino 1%. Asian 1%. Adv deg: 75%. **Grad '10—30.** Prep—30. (Agnes Irwin 5, Episcopal Acad 3, Haverford 2, Malvern Prep 2). Alum donors: 18%. **Tui '12-'13:** Day $15,780-19,860 (+$600). Aid: Need 39 ($470,000). **Est 1949.** Nonprofit. Roman Catholic (92% practice). Tri (Sept-June). Rosemont's traditional curriculum and religious training are augmented by enrichment opportunities in art, music, computers and drama. Networked computers and wireless laptops are available in classrooms, libraries and labs, and the school issues netbook computers to boys and girls in grades 6-8. Students in grades 5-8 take part in an annual community service day each January.

WOODLYNDE SCHOOL
Day Coed Gr 1-12

Strafford, PA 19087. 445 Upper Gulph Rd.
Tel: 610-687-9660. Fax: 610-687-4752.
www.woodlynde.org   E-mail: frazier@woodlynde.org
Christopher M. Fulco, Head (2009). BA, College of the Holy Cross, MA, Johns Hopkins Univ, EdD, Seton Hall Univ. Dorinda Shank, Adm.

Col Prep. AP—Eng Studio_Art. **Feat**—Poetry Fr Span Pol_Sci Psych Sociol Photog Drama Music. **Supp**—Dev_Read Rem_Math Rem_Read Tut. **Comp:** Comp/Stud: 1:2 (1:1 Laptop prgm Gr 5-12). **Dual enr:** Cabrini. **Sports**—Basket X-country Golf Lacrosse Soccer Tennis. G: Softball Volley. **Selective adm (Gr 1-11):** 28/yr. Appl fee: $100. Appl due: Rolling. Accepted: 78%. Yield: 55%. **Tests** IQ. **Enr 240.** Wh 85%. Latino 2%. Blk 8%. Asian 4%. Other 1%. Avg class size: 12. Stud/fac: 3:1. Casual dress. **Fac 56.** M 15/F 41. FT 55/PT 1. Nonwhite 1%. Adv deg: 87%. **Grad '11—28.** Col—27. (Fairleigh Dickinson 3, Albright 1, Widener 1, PA St 1, Bloomsburg 1). **Col Couns:** 1. **Tui '12-'13:** Day $14,000-29,900 (+$725-1850). Aid: Need 78 ($884,420). **Est 1976.** Nonprofit. Tri (Sept-June). Woodlynde provides a standard college preparatory curriculum that includes honors sections in each discipline. Students are required to participate in one extracurricular activity. Seniors take a full-time, unpaid position for two weeks as participants in a project program, in addition to performing 60 hours of independent community service during the year.

WEST CHESTER FRIENDS SCHOOL
Day Coed Gr PS (Age 3)-5

West Chester, PA 19380. 415 N High St.
Tel: 610-696-2937. Fax: 610-431-1457.
www.wcfriends.org   E-mail: admissions@wcfriends.org
Matthew H. Bradley, Head (2001). BA, Univ of Notre Dame, MA, Columbia Univ. Barbara B. Rowe, Adm.

Pre-Prep. Gen Acad. Feat—Lib_Skills Span Computers Quakerism Art_Hist Studio_Art Music Health. **Selective adm:** Appl fee: $50. Appl due: Rolling. **Enr 110.** Wh 75%. Latino 5%. Blk 3%. Asian 8%. Other 9%. Avg class size: 14. Stud/fac: 6:1. **Fac 17.** M 1/F 16. FT 10/PT 7. Adv deg: 41%. **Grad '10—12. Tui '12-'13:** Day $18,425. **Est 1836.** Nonprofit. Religious Society of Friends (12% practice). Tri (Sept-June). All children at this Quaker school study Spanish, technology, library, studio art, music, health, physical education and core courses. Weekly community service is part of the curriculum. Before- and after-school care is available.

CHRISTIAN SCHOOL OF YORK   Day Coed Gr PS (Age 2)-12
York, PA 17404. 907 Greenbriar Rd.
Tel: 717-767-6842. Fax: 717-767-4904.
www.csyonline.com   E-mail: info@csyonline.com
    Kevin Hofer, Head (2009). BA, MEd, South Dakota State Univ. Christine Ingari, Adm.
    Col Prep. Gen Acad. AP (10 exams taken, 90% 3+)—Eng. **Feat**—Span Comp_Sci Psych
Bible Graphic_Arts Studio_Art Drama Music Music_Theory Accounting. **Supp**—ESL LD
Rem_Math Rem_Read. **Comp:** Comp/Stud: 1:3 (1:1 Laptop prgm Gr 9-10). **Dual enr:** PA St,
York Col of PA, Harrisburg Area CC. **Sports**—Basket X-country Golf Indoor_Track Soccer
Track. B: Baseball. G: Cheer Volley. Activities: 12. **Somewhat selective adm:** 96/yr. Appl fee:
$50. Appl due: Rolling. Accepted: 95%. Yield: 98%. **Tests** ISEE Stanford. **Enr 378.** B 183.
G 195. Elem 279. Sec 99. Wh 88%. Latino 2%. Blk 5%. Asian 3%. Other 2%. Avg class size:
20. Stud/fac: 9:1. **Fac 46.** M 7/F 39. FT 28/PT 18. Wh 99%. Latino 1%. Adv deg: 21%. **Grad
'11—26.** Col—25. (York Col of PA 7, Lancaster Bible 3, Messiah 2, Eastern U 2, Liberty
2, MI St 1). **Avg SAT:** CR 539. M 528. W 518. **Tui '11-'12:** Day $6800-8350 (+$300). Aid:
Need 106. **Est 1956.** Nonprofit. Nondenom Christian (98% practice). Quar (Aug-June). **Assoc**
MSA. Emphasis is placed on a Christian education at CSY. Christian service projects are
incorporated into the curriculum. A supplemental learning disabilities program serves students
in grades 1-12. Students in grades 10-12 who have studied at least one year of Spanish may
participate in an annual educational and recreational trip to Mexico. Community service is
required for graduation.

Southern States

ALABAMA

ADVENT EPISCOPAL SCHOOL   Day Coed Gr PS (Age 4)-8
Birmingham, AL 35203. 2019 6th Ave N.
Tel: 205-252-2535. Fax: 205-252-3023.
www.adventepiscopalschool.org   E-mail: ubattles@adventepiscopalschool.org
Una S. Battles, Head (1970). BS, MA, Univ of Alabama.
Pre-Prep. Gen Acad. Feat—Fr Computers Relig Studio_Art Music. **Supp**—Tut. **Sports**—
Basket Golf Soccer Volley. **Selective adm:** 56/yr. Appl fee: $25. Appl due: Rolling. Accepted:
66%. Yield: 70%. **Tests** Stanford. **Enr 319.** Wh 85%. Latino 1%. Blk 11%. Asian 1%. Other
2%. Avg class size: 16. Stud/fac: 16:1. **Fac 30.** M 2/F 28. FT 25/PT 5. Wh 96%. Blk 3%.
Other 1%. Adv deg: 73%. **Grad '10—19.** Prep—5. (Indian Springs 8, John Carroll-AL 3,
Altamont 2, Darlington 1). Avg SSAT: 92%. **Tui '11-'12:** Day $5094-8118 (+$500). Aid: Need
53 ($219,000). **Est 1951.** Nonprofit. Episcopal (32% practice). Sem (Aug-May). **Assoc** SACS.
The elementary curriculum at Advent includes foreign language, science, music and computer
instruction at all levels. The school's kindergarten program begins at age 4, and departmentalization commences in grade 5. Fifth grade also marks the start of English composition, religion
and lab science classes, while the study of ancient world history begins the following year.

HIGHLANDS SCHOOL   Day Coed Gr PS (Age 4)-8
Birmingham, AL 35213. 4901 Old Leeds Rd.
Tel: 205-956-9731. Fax: 205-951-8127.
www.highlandsschool.org   E-mail: jmcdonald@highlandsschool.org
Kathryn Woodson Barr, Head (2006). BA, Rhodes College, MA, Univ of Memphis. Judy
Ladden McDonald, Adm.
Pre-Prep. Feat—Chin Fr Span Studio_Art Drama Music Outdoor_Ed. **Supp**—Tut.
Sports—Basket Soccer Track. **Selective adm:** 61/yr. Appl fee: $75. Appl due: Feb. Accepted:
70%. Yield: 72%. **Tests** CTP_4 IQ ISEE Stanford. **Enr 280.** B 148. G 132. Avg class size: 16.
Fac 37. M 6/F 31. FT 37. Adv deg: 43%. **Grad '08—10.** Prep—8. **Tui '11-'12:** Day $11,400
(+$600). **Est 1958.** Nonprofit. Tri (Aug-June). **Assoc** SACS. The school places emphasis on
advanced academic preparation, as well as on foreign language, art and music. Instructors
commonly provide individualized and small-group instruction. An extended-day program is
available.

LYMAN WARD MILITARY ACADEMY   Bdg Boys Gr 6-12
Camp Hill, AL 36850. 174 Ward Cir, PO Drawer 550.
Tel: 256-896-4127, 800-798-9151. Fax: 256-896-4661.
www.lwma.org   E-mail: info@lwma.org
Brig. Gen. David R. Brown, Pres (2012). BS, MS, Auburn Univ. Maj. Joe Watson, Adm.
Col Prep. Milit. Feat—Span Anat & Physiol Comp_Sci Econ Govt Psych Band. **Supp**—
Dev_Read Rem_Read Tut. **Comp:** Comp/Stud: 1:5. **Dual enr:** Central AL CC. **Sports**— B:
Baseball Basket Football Soccer. **Selective adm:** 60/yr. Appl fee: $250. Appl due: Rolling.
Accepted: 80%. Yield: 98%. **Tests** Stanford. **Enr 122.** Elem 35. Sec 87. Wh 80%. Latino 2%.
Blk 17%. Asian 1%. Avg class size: 12. Stud/fac: 10:1. Uniform. **Fac 14.** M 10/F 4. FT 14.
Wh 93%. Blk 7%. Adv deg: 57%. In Dorms 1. **Grad '11—26.** Col—22. **Col Couns:** 1. Alum
donors: 25%. **Tui '11-'12:** Bdg $15,695-16,495 (+$2200).Intl Bdg $18,295 (+$2200). Aid:
Need 37 ($40,000). **Est 1898.** Nonprofit. Sem (Aug-May). **Assoc** SACS. Offering a college
preparatory program within a military setting, LWMA also provides special help in reading

and study skills. The academic program is supplemented by a full sports program, in addition to rifle and drill teams. Although they are not part of the regular curriculum, Advanced Placement courses are available online for an additional fee. Seniors may pursue college credit through dual-enrollment courses at Central Alabama Community College. Graduates attend a variety of Southern colleges.

BAYSIDE ACADEMY   Day Coed Gr PS (Age 4)-12
Daphne, AL 36526. 303 Dryer Ave.
Tel: 251-338-6415. Fax: 251-338-6310.
www.baysideacademy.org   E-mail: afoster@baysideacademy.org
     Peter B. Huestis, Head (2012). BA, Bishop's Univ (Canada), MS, Barry Univ. Alan M. Foster, Adm.
     Col Prep. AP (exams req'd; 267 taken, 60% 3+)—Eng Fr Span Calc Bio Chem Physics Eur_Hist US_Hist Studio_Art. **Feat**—Ger Anat Environ_Sci Genetics Marine_Bio/Sci Comp_Design Programming Econ Psych Ceramics Film Sculpt. **Supp**—LD. **Sports**—Basket X-country Golf Soccer Swim Tennis Track. B: Baseball Football. G: Softball Volley. **Selective adm:** 80/yr. Appl fee: $100. Appl due: Rolling. Accepted: 70%. Yield: 95%. **Tests** Stanford. **Enr 750.** B 375. G 375. Elem 502. Sec 248. Wh 95%. Latino 2%. Blk 1%. Asian 2%. Avg class size: 18. Uniform. **Fac 110.** M 26/F 84. FT 102/PT 8. Adv deg: 64%. **Grad '09**—69. Col—66. **Avg SAT:** CR 570. M 580. W 580. **Tui '12-'13:** Day $7500-10,500 (+$800). Aid: Need ($250,000). **Est 1967.** Nonprofit. Sem (Aug-May). **Assoc** SACS. The academy's campus occupies a 22-acre site on Mobile Bay. The lower school offers art, music, physical education, computer and conversational Spanish. A learning resource center assists students with attention deficits and mild learning disabilities.

MARS HILL BIBLE SCHOOL   Day Coed Gr PS (Age 4)-12
Florence, AL 35630. 698 Cox Creek Pky.
Tel: 256-767-1203. Fax: 256-718-8579.
www.mhbs.org   E-mail: kbarfield@mhbs.org
     Kenny Barfield, Pres (2000). EdD, Univ of Alabama-Tuscaloosa. Jeannie Garrett, Adm.
     Col Prep. AP—Eng Calc US_Hist US_Govt & Pol. **Feat**—Span Anat & Physiol Ecol Marine_Bio/Sci Comp_Sci Econ Psych Bible Drama Chorus Bus Debate. **Supp**—Tut. **Dual enr:** U of N AL, Northwest-Shoals CC. **Sports**—Basket X-country Soccer Tennis Track. B: Baseball Golf. G: Softball Volley. **Somewhat selective adm:** 83/yr. Appl fee: $100. Appl due: Aug. Accepted: 95%. Yield: 98%. **Enr 598.** B 298. G 300. Elem 365. Sec 233. Wh 92%. Blk 6%. Asian 2%. Avg class size: 22. Stud/fac: 13:1. **Fac 41.** M 11/F 30. FT 39/PT 2. Wh 100%. Adv deg: 56%. **Grad '10**—47. Col—47. (U of N AL 7, Auburn 6, Harding 5, Freed-Hardeman 5, U of AL-Tuscaloosa 4). **Avg SAT:** CR/M 1143. Avg ACT: 23.8. **Col Couns:** 2. Alum donors: 25%. **Tui '11-'12:** Day $5725-5952 (+$400). Aid: Need 105 ($155,000). **Est 1947.** Nonprofit. Nondenom Christian (80% practice). Quar (Aug-May). **Assoc** SACS. As part of MHBS' curriculum, all students fulfill yearly Bible study and community service requirements. Older high school pupils choose from honors, Advanced Placement and dual-enrollment courses.

MADISON ACADEMY   Day Coed Gr PS (Age 3)-12
Madison, AL 35758. 325 Slaughter Rd.
Tel: 256-971-1620. Fax: 256-971-1436.
www.macademy.org   E-mail: msmith@macademy.org
     Robert F. Burton, Pres (1995). BS, David Lipscomb Univ, MEd, Alabama A&M Univ. John Bryson, Adm.
     Col Prep. AP (exams req'd; 28 taken, 25% 3+)—Eng Calc US_Hist. **Feat**—Creative_Writing Great_Books Lat Span Physiol Comp_Sci Web_Design Econ Govt Psych Bible Studio_Art Drama Bus Finance Photojourn. **Supp**—Makeup Rem_Math Rem_Read Tut. **Comp:** Comp/Stud: 1:2 (1:1 Laptop prgm Gr 9-12). **Dual enr:** Calhoun CC, U of AL-Hunts-

ville. **Sports**—Basket X-country Golf Soccer Tennis. B: Baseball Football. G: Cheer Softball Volley. Activities: 20. **Somewhat selective adm:** 113/yr. Appl fee: $75. Appl due: Dec. Accepted: 90%. Yield: 90%. **Tests** CEEB IQ MAT Stanford TOEFL. **Enr 899.** B 435. G 464. Elem 620. Sec 279. Wh 83%. Latino 1%. Blk 12%. Native Am 1%. Asian 1%. Other 2%. Stud/fac: 7:1. Uniform. **Fac 68.** M 16/F 52. Wh 100%. Adv deg: 47%. **Grad '11—65.** Col—65. (U of N AL 10, U of AL-Huntsville 9, Auburn 9, Calhoun CC 7, U of AL-Birmingham 4, U of AL-Tuscaloosa 4). **Avg SAT:** CR 573. M 567. W 578. Avg ACT: 23.9. **Col Couns:** 1. **Tui '11-'12:** Day $5925-6850 (+$450). Aid: Need 41 ($91,514). **Est 1955.** Nonprofit. Nondenom Christian. Sem (Aug-May). **Assoc** SACS. The academy's college preparatory curriculum includes a dual-enrollment option for qualified juniors and seniors that enables them to earn college credit through one of two area colleges. Daily Bible study and chapel attendance are required, and community service is a compulsory part of the Bible program.

McGILL-TOOLEN CATHOLIC HIGH SCHOOL — Day Coed Gr 9-12
Mobile, AL 36604. 1501 Old Shell Rd.
Tel: 251-445-2900. Fax: 251-433-8356.
www.mcgill-toolen.org   E-mail: haasm@mcgill-toolen.org
Rev. W. Bry Shields, Jr., Pres. MDiv, Yale Univ, MEd, Univ of South Alabama. Michelle T. Haas, Prin. BA, Univ of South Alabama, MEd, Sam Houston Univ. Paul Knapstein, Adm.

Col Prep. AP (275 exams taken, 78% 3+)—Eng Fr Span Calc Bio Chem Environ_Sci Physics Eur_Hist US_Hist World_Hist US_Govt & Pol Studio_Art. **Feat**—British_Lit Lat Anat & Physiol Marine_Bio/Sci Comp_Sci Psych Theol World_Relig Art_Hist Ceramics Band Chorus Music Music_Theory Speech Video_Journ. **Supp**—Dev_Read LD Makeup Rem_Math Rem_Read Rev Tut. **Comp:** Comp/Stud: 1:3. **Sports (req'd)**—Basket X-country Golf Soccer Swim Tennis Track. B: Baseball Football. G: Cheer Softball Volley. Activities: 25. **Selective adm:** 298/yr. Appl fee: $100. Appl due: Jan. Yield: 98%. **Enr 1130.** B 580. G 550. Wh 85%. Blk 14%. Other 1%. Avg class size: 23. Uniform. **Fac 85.** M 42/F 43. FT 79/PT 6. Wh 96%. Latino 1%. Blk 1%. Asian 2%. Adv deg: 67%. **Grad '11—225.** Col—210. (U of S AL 56, U of AL-Tuscaloosa 33, Auburn 27, Spring Hill 9, U of S MS 8, LA St-Baton Rouge 8). **Avg SAT:** CR 590. M 600. W 570. Avg ACT: 23. **Col Couns:** 3. **Tui '12-'13:** Day $7780 (+$530). Catholic $6500 (+$530). Aid: Need ($332,450). **Est 1896.** Nonprofit. Roman Catholic (89% practice). Sem (Aug-June). **Assoc** SACS. Serving Mobile and Baldwin counties and Jackson County, MS, this Catholic school requires students to take four years of religion or theology courses, in addition to work in the core disciplines of science, math, English and social studies. Pupils enroll in at least two electives from the following areas: the humanities, business and technology, the fine arts and foreign language.

ST. LUKE'S EPISCOPAL SCHOOL — Day Coed Gr PS (Age 3)-12
Mobile, AL 36693. 3975 Japonica Ln.
Tel: 251-666-2991. Fax: 251-666-2996.
Other locations: 1400 University Blvd S, Mobile 36609.
www.stlukesmobile.com   E-mail: pkennedy@stlukesmobile.com
W. Palmer Kennedy, Head (2005). Anita Roberson, Adm.

Col Prep. Gen Acad. AP—Eng Calc Bio Chem Physics Eur_Hist US_Hist US_Govt & Pol. **Feat**—Lib_Skills Lat Span Anat & Physiol Marine_Bio/Sci Comp_Sci Studio_Art Music. **Supp**—Rem_Read Rev Tut. **Sports**—Basket X-country Soccer Swim Tennis Track. B: Baseball Football Golf. G: Cheer Softball Volley. Activities: 16. **Somewhat selective adm (Gr PS-10):** 134/yr. Appl fee: $0. Appl due: Nov. Accepted: 90%. **Tests** CTP_4 Stanford. **Enr 696.** Wh 90%. Latino 2%. Blk 5%. Asian 3%. Avg class size: 17. Uniform. **Fac 71.** M 13/F 58. FT 62/PT 9. Wh 100%. Adv deg: 42%. **Col Couns:** 1. **Tui '12-'13:** Day $6006-8855 (+$520-620). Aid: Need 28 ($35,000). **Est 1961.** Nonprofit. Episcopal. Quar (Aug-May). **Assoc** SACS. The core elementary subjects of reading, English, math, science, social studies and physical education are supplemented by courses in art, music, Spanish, writing and computer. The college preparatory upper school curriculum includes both honors and Advanced Placement courses.

All pupils and teachers attend compulsory weekly chapel services. Students perform 20 hours of required community service by the end of grade 8 and 80 hours before graduation.

ALABAMA CHRISTIAN ACADEMY   **Day Coed Gr PS (Age 4)-12**
Montgomery, AL 36109. 4700 Wares Ferry Rd.
Tel: 334-277-1985. Fax: 334-279-0604.
www.alabamachristian.com   E-mail: hparker@alabamachristian.com
    Ronnie C. Sewell, Pres (2002). BA, MA, Univ of Alabama-Birmingham. Milton C. Slauson, Supt. BA, MA, PhD, Univ of Alabama-Tuscaloosa. Harriett Parker, Adm.
    Col Prep. AP (exams req'd)—Eng Calc Bio Eur_Hist US_Hist. **Feat**—Span Anat & Physiol Comp_Sci Econ Psych Bible Studio_Art Theater Band Chorus Music Music_Theory ACT_Prep. **Supp**—Tut. **Comp:** Comp/Stud: 1:15. **Sports**—Basket X-country Soccer Track. B: Baseball Football. G: Cheer Softball Volley. **Somewhat selective adm:** 185/yr. Appl fee: $75. Appl due: Rolling. Accepted: 90%. Yield: 95%. **Tests** IQ Stanford. **Enr 987.** Wh 88%. Latino 1%. Blk 8%. Asian 2%. Other 1%. Avg class size: 24. Stud/fac: 17:1. Uniform. **Fac 61.** M 18/F 43. FT 60/PT 1. Wh 98%. Latino 2%. Adv deg: 49%. **Grad '09**—79. Col—78. (Auburn-Montgomery 20, Faulkner U 12, U of AL-Tuscaloosa 6, Auburn 5, Huntingdon 5). Avg ACT: 21. **Tui '12-'13:** Day $5640-6098 (+$250-650). Aid: Need 48 ($82,175). **Est 1942.** Nonprofit. Nondenom Christian. Sem (Aug-May). **Assoc** SACS. ACA offers a college preparatory program, with Bible study being an integral part of the curriculum. Honors and Advanced Placement courses are available, as are electives in music, art, Spanish, computer and theater.

SAINT JAMES SCHOOL   **Day Coed Gr PS (Age 3)-12**
Montgomery, AL 36116. 6010 Vaughn Rd.
Tel: 334-277-8033. Fax: 334-277-2542.
www.stjweb.org   E-mail: asteineker@stjweb.org
    Melba B. Richardson, Head (2009). BA, Univ of Alabama, MA, Auburn Univ at Montgomery. Aimee B. Steineker, Adm.
    Col Prep. AP—Eng Calc Bio Chem Eur_Hist US_Hist Econ US_Govt & Pol Art_Hist Studio_Art. **Feat**—Creative_Writing Fr Lat Span Anat & Physiol Botany Programming Psych World_Relig Fine_Arts Photog Theater_Arts Chorus Music Music_Theory Guitar Debate Journ Speech. **Supp**—Tut. **Sports**—Basket X-country Soccer Swim Tennis Track. B: Baseball Football Golf Wrestling. G: Cheer Softball Volley. **Selective adm:** 160/yr. Appl fee: $25-75. Appl due: Rolling. Accepted: 80%. **Tests** CTP_4 IQ Stanford. **Enr 1112.** B 539. G 573. Elem 790. Sec 322. Avg class size: 19. Uniform. **Fac 88.** M 13/F 75. FT 88. Wh 100%. Adv deg: 52%. **Grad '08**—82. Col—82. **Avg SAT:** CR 608. M 606. W 625. Avg ACT: 24.8. **Col Couns:** 2. **Tui '12-'13:** Day $7390-9840 (+$200-500). **Est 1955.** Nonprofit. Sem (Aug-May). **Assoc** SACS. The city's oldest and largest nonsectarian independent school, Saint James provides a college preparatory curriculum that features honors courses in grades 7-9, as well as Advanced Placement offerings in grades 10-12. The school offers strong visual and performing arts programs, as well as competitive athletics for boys and girls grades 6-12.

TUSCALOOSA ACADEMY   **Day Coed Gr PS (Age 3)-12**
Tuscaloosa, AL 35406. 420 Rice Valley Rd N.
Tel: 205-758-4462. Fax: 205-758-4418.
www.tuscaloosaacademy.org   E-mail: taknights@tuscaloosaacademy.org
    Jeffrey L. Mitchell, Head (2009). BA, Univ of Winnipeg (Canada), MEd, PhD, Univ of British Columbia (Canada). Anne Huffaker, Adm.
    Col Prep. AP (exams req'd; 64 taken, 38% 3+)—Eng Fr Lat Span Calc Bio Chem Physics US_Hist Psych Studio_Art. **Feat**—Creative_Writing Linguistics Stats Anat & Physiol Comp_Sci Sociol Art_Hist Music. **Supp**—Dev_Read ESL Rev Tut. **Comp:** Comp/Stud: 1:2 (1:1 Laptop prgm Gr 7-12). Outdoor Ed. **Dual enr:** U of AL-Tuscaloosa. **Sports**—Basket X-

country Soccer Tennis Track. B: Baseball Football Golf. G: Cheer Softball Volley. **Somewhat selective adm:** 123/yr. Appl fee: $75. Appl due: Rolling. Accepted: 90%. Yield: 90%. **Tests** CEEB. **Enr 400.** Elem 280. Sec 120. Wh 95%. Blk 2%. Asian 3%. Intl 22%. Avg class size: 16. Stud/fac: 12:1. Casual dress. **Fac 57.** M 11/F 46. FT 55/PT 2. Wh 98%. Blk 2%. Adv deg: 31%. **Grad '10—33.** Col—31. **Avg SAT:** CR 550. M 500. W 540. Avg ACT: 25. Alum donors: 3%. **Tui '10-'11:** Day $7334-8792 (+$400). Aid: Need 36 ($115,000). **Est 1967.** Nonprofit. Quar (Aug-May). **Assoc** SACS. The academy's college preparatory program places emphasis on reading and composition. Independent study is encouraged. During the middle school years, boys and girls fulfill a 10-hour annual community service commitment; in the upper school, students perform 20 hours annually. Students in grades 7-12 purchase tablet computers for classroom use.

FLORIDA

BOCA RATON CHRISTIAN SCHOOL Day Coed Gr PS (Age 3)-12
Boca Raton, FL 33432. 315 NW 4th St.
Tel: 561-391-2727. Fax: 561-226-0617.
www.bocachristian.org E-mail: bocachristian@bocachristian.org
   Robert H. Tennies, Head (1977). BS, Wheaton College (IL), MA, Univ of South Florida, EdS, EdD, Florida Atlantic Univ. Eileen L. Travasos, Adm.
   Col Prep. AP (exams req'd; 64 taken, 45% 3+)—Eng Calc Bio Chem Eur_Hist Psych Music_Theory. **Feat**—British_Lit World_Lit Fr Span Ecol Environ_Sci Marine_Bio/Sci Comp_Sci Web_Design Econ Govt Sociol Bible Philos Drama Debate. **Supp**—Tut. **Comp:** Comp/Stud: 1:2 (1:1 Laptop prgm Gr 10-12). **Dual enr:** FL Atlantic, Palm Beach Atlantic, Palm Beach St. **Sports**—Basket X-country Golf Soccer Tennis Track. B: Baseball Football. G: Cheer Softball Volley. **Somewhat selective adm:** 170/yr. Appl fee: $175. Appl due: Rolling. Accepted: 85%. Yield: 95%. **Enr 535.** Wh 66%. Latino 23%. Blk 5%. Asian 3%. Other 3%. Avg class size: 22. Uniform. **Fac 54.** Wh 73%. Latino 18%. Blk 3%. Asian 3%. Other 3%. Adv deg: 35%. **Grad '11—26.** Col—26. **Avg SAT:** CR 535. M 520. W 519. **Tui '11-'12:** Day $7524-10,307 (+$110-500). **Est 1973.** Nonprofit. Nondenom Christian (100% practice). Sem (Aug-May). BRCS' elementary program emphasizes mastery and application of basic skills and includes enrichment and remedial activities. The high school offers three diplomas: standard, college and advanced. Students in the three diploma programs take varying amounts of math, science, social studies and foreign language. Boys and girls may participate in dual-enrollment, credit-bearing courses at Florida Atlantic University, Palm Beach State College or Palm Beach Atlantic University. High schoolers perform at least 25 hours of required community service per year.

DONNA KLEIN JEWISH ACADEMY Day Coed Gr K-12
Boca Raton, FL 33428. 9701 Donna Klein Blvd.
Tel: 561-852-3300. Fax: 561-852-3327.
www.dkja.org E-mail: info@dkja.org
   Karen Feller, Head. BA, Newark State College, MA, Kean College of New Jersey. Hilary Arenstein, Adm.
   Col Prep. AP—Eng Calc Stats Chem Environ_Sci US_Hist World_Hist. **Feat**—Hebrew Span Anat & Physiol Econ Govt Law Psych Judaic_Stud Studio_Art Debate SAT_Prep. **Dual enr:** Palm Beach CC, Broward CC. **Sports**—Basket X-country Soccer. B: Golf. G: Volley. Activities: 12. **Selective adm:** 125/yr. Appl fee: $100-115. Appl due: Rolling. **Tests** SSAT. **Enr 702.** B 344. G 358. Elem 617. Sec 85. Avg class size: 18. **Fac 141.** Adv deg: 35%. **Grad '11—23.** Col—23. **Avg SAT:** CR 513. M 546. W 552. Avg ACT: 24. **Tui '12-'13:** Day $18,255-19,980 (+$268-2468). Aid: Need 280 ($2,500,000). **Est 1979.** Nonprofit. Jewish. Sem (Aug-June). **Assoc** SACS. DKJA's elementary and secondary program integrates the

arts, science, math, Judaic studies and the humanities. Importance is placed on the Jewish religious heritage and an understanding of other cultures. Utilizing a hands-on method, the school seeks to develop problem-solving and independent and collaborative learning skills. Instructors employ a cross-disciplinary approach that allows students to gain a greater depth of knowledge by recognizing connections between different subjects. All upper school students fulfill community service requirements: 40 hours in grade 9, 50 hours in grade 10, 60 hours in grade 11 and 75 hours in grade 12.

GRANDVIEW PREPARATORY SCHOOL				**Day Coed Gr PS (Age 3)-12**
Boca Raton, FL 33431. 336 Spanish River Blvd NW.
Tel: 561-416-9737. Fax: 561-416-9739.
www.grandviewprep.net   E-mail: lkubach@grandviewprep.net
   Jacqueline R. Westerfield, Head (2002). BA, Univ of Iowa, JD, Univ of Illinois-Urbana. Lori Kubach, Adm.
   Col Prep. AP (exams req'd)—Eng Span Calc Bio Chem Physics Eur_Hist US_Hist US_ Govt & Pol Studio_Art. **Feat**—British_Lit Playwriting Women's_Lit Anat & Physiol Astron Environ_Sci Marine_Bio/Sci Web_Design Econ Intl_Relations Psych Sociol Philos World_ Relig Art_Hist Drama Chorus Music Music_Hist Dance Journ Speech SAT_Prep Nutrition. **Supp**—Tut. **Comp:** Laptop prgm Gr 9-12. **Dual enr:** FL Atlantic, Palm Beach St. **Sports**— Basket Swim Tennis. B: Baseball Golf Soccer. G: Softball Volley. **Somewhat selective adm:** 50/yr. Appl fee: $100. Appl due: Rolling. Accepted: 95%. Yield: 58%. **Tests** SSAT Stanford. **Enr 250.** Intl 21%. Avg class size: 12. Stud/fac: 8:1. Uniform. **Fac 34.** M 10/F 24. FT 30/PT 4. Adv deg: 52%. **Grad '09—26.** Col—26. (U of Central FL 2, FL Atlantic 2, U of FL 1, U of Miami 1, FL St 1, U of CO-Boulder 1). **Avg SAT:** CR 487. M 500. W 457. **Mid 50% SAT:** CR 450-550. M 460-550. W 410-510. Avg ACT: 21. Mid 50% ACT: 17-26. **Col Couns:** 1. **Tui '10-'11:** Day $11,640-15,315 (+$850-1925). **Est 1997.** Inc. Quar (Aug-June). Grandview's traditional liberal arts program places considerable emphasis on technology. Hands-on activities are prominent during the lower school years (grades K-5), while the middle school program (grades 6-8) prepares students for future academic work and integrates a critical-thinking skills sequence. Advanced Placement courses and dual-enrollment opportunities at two nearby colleges are elements of the comprehensive upper school curriculum.

BRADENTON CHRISTIAN SCHOOL				**Day Coed Gr PS (Age 3)-12**
Bradenton, FL 34209. 3304 43rd St W.
Tel: 941-792-5454. Fax: 941-795-7190.
www.bcspanthers.org   E-mail: dcobb@bcspanthers.org
   Dan van der Kooy, Supt. BA, Calvin College, MA, Univ of Redlands. Jannon Pierce, Adm.
   Col Prep. AP (32 exams taken, 56% 3+)—Eng Calc Bio Eur_Hist US_Hist Psych. **Feat**— Fr Span Comp_Sci Econ Bible Studio_Art Music. **Supp**—Dev_Read Rem_Math Rem_Read Rev Tut. **Dual enr:** Manatee CC. **Sports**—Basket Soccer Tennis Track. B: Baseball Football Golf. G: Cheer Softball Swim Volley. **Selective adm:** 100/yr. Appl due: Rolling. Accepted: 50%. Yield: 98%. **Tests** Stanford. **Enr 540.** Wh 88%. Latino 5%. Blk 2%. Other 5%. Avg class size: 16. Stud/fac: 15:1. Uniform. **Fac 48.** M 15/F 33. FT 44/PT 4. Wh 96%. Blk 4%. Adv deg: 39%. **Grad '08—35.** Col—35. **Avg SAT:** CR 530. M 500. W 520. Avg ACT: 23. **Col Couns:** 1. **Tui '11-'12:** Day $6375-9795 (+$350-550). **Est 1960.** Nonprofit. Nondenom Christian. Quar (Aug-June). **Assoc** SACS. Students at BCS, who enroll from Manatee and Sarasota counties, are required to participate in community service (totaling 75 hours in grades 9-12) and senior projects, while off-campus and independent study is also offered. Spanish instruction is available in grades pre-K-12. In alternate years, BCS conducts a weeklong interim program that features special-interest courses.

BRANDON ACADEMY Day Coed Gr PS (Age 3)-8
Brandon, FL 33510. 801 Limona Rd.
Tel: 813-689-1952. Fax: 813-651-4278.
www.brandon-academy.com E-mail: info@brandon-academy.com
Robert Rudolph, Head (2005). BA, Southeastern Louisiana Univ. Sondra Cliggitt, Adm.

Pre-Prep. Gen Acad. Feat—Lib_Skills Ger Span Computers Web_Design Econ Psych Ceramics Studio_Art Music Journ. **Supp**—Rev Tut. **Sports**—Basket X-country Golf Soccer Volley. B: Football. G: Cheer. **Somewhat selective adm:** 63/yr. Appl fee: $75. Appl due: Rolling. Accepted: 98%. Yield: 88%. **Tests** IQ SSAT. **Enr 264.** B 135. G 129. Wh 86%. Latino 2%. Blk 2%. Native Am 3%. Asian 2%. Other 5%. Avg class size: 18. Uniform. **Fac 25.** M 5/F 20. FT 23/PT 2. Wh 95%. Latino 1%. Blk 2%. Other 2%. Adv deg: 12%. **Grad '08—25.** Prep—4. Avg SSAT: 81%. **Tui '10-'11:** Day $6900-7200 (+$585-680). Aid: Need 5. **Est 1969.** Quar (Aug-May). At all grade levels, this elementary school balances its emphasis on reading, math and science with instruction in Spanish, computers, writing and physical education. The developmentally appropriate lower school provides a foundation for future learning, while the middle school serves average and above-average students who have mastered the fundamentals. All middle schoolers choose yearlong electives as a supplement to core courses. Off-campus field trips and guest speakers are elements of the middle school program.

SAINT PAUL'S SCHOOL Day Coed Gr PS (Age 3)-8
Clearwater, FL 33764. 1600 St Paul's Dr.
Tel: 727-536-2756. Fax: 727-531-2276.
www.st.pauls.edu E-mail: admissions@st.pauls.edu
Angel W. Kytle, Head (2008). PhD. Colleen Smith, Adm.

Pre-Prep. Gen Acad. Feat—Fr Span Environ_Sci Studio_Art Drama Music Study_Skills. **Supp**—Dev_Read Rem_Math Rem_Read Rev Tut. **Comp:** Comp/Stud: 1:3. **Sports**—Basket Golf Soccer Track Volley. B: Baseball. G: Softball. **Selective adm:** 39/yr. Appl fee: $75. Appl due: Feb. Accepted: 82%. Yield: 87%. **Tests** CTP_4 SSAT. **Enr 346.** B 192. G 154. Wh 87%. Latino 4%. Blk 1%. Asian 2%. Other 6%. Avg class size: 16. Stud/fac: 7:1. Uniform. **Fac 51.** M 11/F 40. FT 48/PT 3. Wh 94%. Latino 6%. Adv deg: 43%. **Grad '11—47.** Prep—29. (Berkeley Prep 12, Calvary Christian HS 7, Clearwater Central Catholic 6, Shorecrest 2, Tampa Prep 1, Jesuit HS-FL 1). Alum donors: 3%. **Tui '11-'12:** Day $14,100-15,580 (+$150-500). Aid: Need 37 ($249,694). **Est 1968.** Nonprofit. Episcopal. Tri (Aug-May). **Assoc** SACS. Located on a 10-acre campus, the school enrolls students of above-average ability. The curriculum is supplemented by foreign languages, study skills, the fine arts and technology. Eighth graders participate in Wolfcreek, a weeklong outdoor adventure program. Boys and girls in grades 6-8 satisfy a 15-hour annual community service requirement.

NORTH BROWARD PREPARATORY SCHOOL Bdg Coed Gr 6-12
Coconut Creek, FL 33073. 7600 Lyons Rd. Day Coed PS (Age 3)-12
Tel: 954-247-0011. Fax: 954-247-0012.
www.nbps.org E-mail: admission@nbps.org
Elise R. Ecoff, Head (2012). Jackie Fagan, Adm.

Col Prep. IB Diploma. LD. AP (exams req'd; 551 taken, 55% 3+)—Eng Fr Span Calc Stats Comp_Sci Bio Chem Physics Eur_Hist US_Hist Econ Human_Geog Psych US_Govt & Pol Art_Hist Studio_Art Music_Theory. **Feat**—Creative_Writing Chin Anat & Physiol Ecol Marine_Bio/Sci Robotics Web_Design Drawing Film Painting Acting Theater_Arts Band Chorus Jazz_Ensemble Dance Debate Journ SAT_Prep. **Supp**—ESL Rev Tut. **Comp:** Laptop prgm Gr 6-12. **Sports**—Basket Bowl X-country Fencing Golf Lacrosse Soccer Swim Tennis Track. B: Baseball Football Ice_Hockey Rugby. G: Cheer Softball Volley. **Somewhat selective adm:** 304/yr. Bdg 91. Day 213. Appl fee: $150. Appl due: Rolling. Accepted: 90%. Yield: 80%. **Tests** CEEB CTP_4 ISEE MAT SSAT TOEFL. **Enr 1381.** Bdg 187. Day 1194. Elem 649. Sec 732. Avg class size: 18. Stud/fac: 9:1. Uniform. **Fac 149.** Adv deg: 53%. **Grad '10—167.** Col—166. (U of FL 17, FL St 15, U of N FL 13, FL Atlantic 10, U of Miami 7, U of

CO-Boulder 3). **Avg SAT:** CR 522. M 560. W 533. Avg ACT: 22.8. **Col Couns:** 5. **Tui '12-'13:** Bdg $46,500. Day $17,500-33,500 (+$1500). **Est 1957.** Inc. Spons: Meritas. Tri (Aug-June). **Assoc** SACS. Serving Palm Beach and Broward counties, NBPS comprises two programs: a traditional elementary and secondary division and Lighthouse Point Academy, which offers a similar college preparatory education to pupils with mild learning disabilities. Features of the high school program include a varied selection of Advanced Placement courses and the IB Diploma Program. Boys and girls satisfy the following community service requirements: 15 hours in grade 9, 25 hours in grade 10, and 30 hours in both grade 11 and grade 12.

ST. PHILIP'S EPISCOPAL SCHOOL   **Day Coed Gr PS-5**
Coral Gables, FL 33134. 1121 Andalusia Ave.
Tel: 305-444-6366. Fax: 305-442-0236.
www.saintphilips.net   E-mail: admissions@saintphilips.net
   Greg Blackburn, Head (2011). BA, MA, PhD.
   Pre-Prep. Feat—Fr Span Computers Relig Studio_Art Music. **Supp**—Dev_Read Rem_ Math Rem_Read Tut. **Comp:** Comp/Stud: 1:1 Laptop prgm Gr 4-5. **Selective adm:** 33/yr. Appl fee: $150. Appl due: Rolling. **Tests** Stanford. **Enr 180.** B 91. G 89. Wh 44%. Latino 53%. Blk 2%. Asian 1%. Avg class size: 22. Stud/fac: 11:1. Uniform. **Fac 30.** M 7/F 23. FT 24/PT 6. Wh 53%. Latino 40%. Blk 3%. Asian 3%. Other 1%. Adv deg: 16%. **Grad '11—** 22. Prep—21. (Ransom Everglades 12, Palmer Trinity 6, Carrollton Sch 2, Gulliver 1). **Tui '12-'13:** Day $13,700-15,600 (+$3000-5090). Aid: Need 7 ($45,000). **Est 1953.** Nonprofit. Episcopal. Tri (Aug-June). The school serves children of average and above-average ability. Features of the program are character education, chapel, foreign language instruction, physical education/tennis lessons, before- and after-school care, a full range of enrichment courses and a summer camp.

ST. THOMAS EPISCOPAL PARISH SCHOOL   **Day Coed Gr PS (Age 3)-5**
Coral Gables, FL 33156. 5692 N Kendall Dr.
Tel: 305-665-4851. Fax: 305-669-9449.
www.stepsmia.org   E-mail: admission@stepsmia.org
   Kris M. Charlton, Head (2000). BA, Long Island Univ, MS, Southern Connecticut State Univ. Valerie C. Douberley, Adm.
   Pre-Prep. Feat—Span Computers Studio_Art Music Dance. **Comp:** Laptop prgm Gr 4-5. **Selective adm (Gr PS-4):** 78/yr. Appl fee: $135. Appl due: Jan. **Tests** Stanford. **Enr 425.** B 221. G 204. Avg class size: 18. Uniform. **Fac 61.** M 3/F 58. FT 61. Adv deg: 36%. **Grad '11—58.** Prep—56. Alum donors: 6%. **Tui '11-'12:** Day $10,360-13,740 (+$625-750). **Est 1953.** Nonprofit. Episcopal. Tri (Aug-June). Language arts, science and social studies form the core of the St. Thomas curriculum. In addition, students receive specialized instruction in Spanish, art, music, dance, physical education, library skills and computers. Electronic whiteboards are present in all classrooms, and fourth and fifth graders purchase tablet computers for school use. In addition, the school conducts a well-regarded robotics program and maintains a STEM (science, technology, engineering and mathematics) lab.

ZION LUTHERAN CHRISTIAN SCHOOL   **Day Coed Gr PS (Age 2)-12**
Deerfield Beach, FL 33441. 959 SE 6th Ave.
Tel: 954-421-3146. Fax: 954-421-5465.
www.zion-lutheran.org   E-mail: jcunningham@zion-lutheran.org
   Jayne A. Cunningham, Prin (2010).
   Col Prep. AP (exams req'd)—Eng Environ_Sci Eur_Hist US_Govt & Pol. **Feat**—Creative_Writing Chin Fr Ital Japan Portuguese Span Anat & Physiol Comp_Sci Econ Geog Psych Sociol Relig Architect Ceramics Drawing Film Studio_Art Drama Musical_Theater Chorus Dance Journ. **Supp**—Dev_Read LD Makeup Rem_Math Rem_Read Rev Tut. **Comp:** Comp/Stud: 1:2 (1:1 Laptop prgm Gr 9-12). **Dual enr:** FL Atlantic. **Sports**—Basket X-country

Golf Soccer Swim Tennis Track. **B:** Baseball Football. **G:** Cheer Softball Volley. Activities: 50. **Somewhat selective adm:** 100/yr. Appl fee: $50. Appl due: Feb. Accepted: 96%. Yield: 99%. **Tests** CEEB Stanford. **Enr 506.** Elem 385. Sec 121. Wh 55%. Latino 15%. Blk 25%. Asian 2%. Other 3%. Avg class size: 15. Stud/fac: 9:1. Uniform. **Fac 56.** M 10/F 46. FT 56. Wh 81%. Latino 9%. Blk 7%. Asian 2%. Other 1%. Adv deg: 7%. **Grad '11—24.** Col—23. **Avg SAT:** CR/M 1100. Avg ACT: 26. **Col Couns:** 1. Alum donors: 1%. **Tui '12-'13:** Day $6835-9465 (+$550-985). Aid: Merit 3 ($10,000). Need 166 ($166,000). **Est 1964.** Nonprofit. Lutheran (40% practice). Quar (Aug-May). **Assoc** SACS. Zion Lutheran offers a college preparatory program, with honors and Advanced Placement classes constituting part of a special curriculum for advanced pupils. Spanish instruction at the school begins in kindergarten. Qualified seniors may take courses at Florida Atlantic University for both high school and college credit. Students perform 20 hours of community service each year in grades 9-12.

FORT LAUDERDALE PREPARATORY SCHOOL   Day Coed Gr PS (Age 4)-12
Fort Lauderdale, FL 33311. 3275 W Oakland Park Blvd.
Tel: 954-485-7500. Fax: 954-485-1732.
www.flps.com   E-mail: admissions@flps.com
Anita Lonstein, Dir. BA, City Univ of New York. Lawrence Berkowitz, Head. EdD, Nova Southeastern Univ.

Col Prep. AP (exams req'd)—Eng Span Calc World_Hist US_Govt & Pol. **Feat**—Comp_ Sci Fine_Arts Music Speech. **Supp**—Dev_Read ESL LD Makeup Rem_Math Rem_Read Rev Tut. **Comp:** Comp/Stud: 1:6. **Somewhat selective adm:** 45/yr. Appl fee: $50. Appl due: Rolling. Accepted: 95%. Yield: 75%. **Tests** IQ Stanford TOEFL. **Enr 185.** B 120. G 65. Elem 80. Sec 105. Wh 25%. Latino 10%. Blk 55%. Native Am 3%. Asian 5%. Other 2%. Intl 5%. Avg class size: 13. Stud/fac: 7:1. Uniform. **Fac 21.** M 6/F 15. FT 18/PT 3. Wh 55%. Latino 10%. Blk 30%. Other 5%. Adv deg: 42%. **Grad '09—10.** Col—9. **Avg SAT:** CR/M 1100. **Tui '10-'11:** Day $8500-10,500 (+$750-4500). Aid: Merit 11 ($87,000). Need 37 ($250,000). **Est 1986.** Inc. Quar (Aug-June). **Assoc** SACS. FLP features individualized academic programs within small classes and an integrated computer curriculum. Advanced Placement and honors programs are also part of the curriculum, and a remedial program for academic underachievers is provided for an additional fee.

ST. MARK'S EPISCOPAL SCHOOL   Day Coed Gr PS (Age 3)-8
Fort Lauderdale, FL 33334. 1750 E Oakland Park Blvd.
Tel: 954-563-4508. Fax: 954-563-0504.
www.saintmarks.com   E-mail: info@saintmarks.com
Rev. Robert G. Trache, Rector (2008). BA, MA, George Washington Univ, MDiv, Harvard Divinity School. Alice M. Hendrickson, Adm.

Pre-Prep. Feat—Lib_Skills Span Computers Relig Studio_Art Band Chorus Music. **Supp**—Tut. **Comp:** Comp/Stud: 1:3. **Sports**—Basket X-country Golf Soccer Tennis. **B:** Baseball. **G:** Cheer Softball Volley. **Selective adm:** 84/yr. Appl fee: $100. Appl due: Rolling. Accepted: 80%. Yield: 75%. **Tests** CTP_4 MRT. **Enr 443.** B 241. G 202. Wh 85%. Latino 7%. Blk 3%. Asian 2%. Other 3%. Avg class size: 16. Stud/fac: 10:1. Uniform. **Fac 44.** M 5/F 39. FT 36/PT 8. Wh 89%. Latino 10%. Blk 1%. Adv deg: 34%. **Grad '11—52.** Prep—50. (Cardinal Gibbons 25, St Thomas Aquinas-FL 17, Pine Crest 4, Am Heritage 2, U Sch of Nova 1). Avg SSAT: 73%. Alum donors: 5%. **Tui '12-'13:** Day $11,970-16,360 (+$1600). Aid: Merit 1 ($1000). Need 29 ($203,714). **Est 1959.** Nonprofit. Episcopal (4% practice). Quar (Aug-June). **Assoc** SACS. St. Mark's offers an academic curriculum designed to prepare students for selective secondary schools. Field trips and cocurricular activities, together with music, art, Spanish, computers, yearbook and chapel services, supplement the academic program.

ST. THOMAS AQUINAS HIGH SCHOOL   Day Coed Gr 9-12
Fort Lauderdale, FL 33312. 2801 SW 12th St.
Tel: 954-581-0700. Fax: 954-581-8263.
www.aquinas-sta.org   E-mail: tjones@aquinas-sta.org
    Rev. Vincent T. Kelly, Supvg Prin (1970). MS, Univ of Nebraska-Lincoln. Tina Jones, Prin.
BA, State Univ of New York, MA, Florida Atlantic Univ.
    Col Prep. AP (exams req'd; 1641 taken)—Eng Fr Lat Span Calc Stats Comp_Sci Bio
Chem Environ_Sci Physics Eur_Hist US_Hist World_Hist Comp_Govt & Pol Econ Human_
Geog Psych US_Govt & Pol Studio_Art. **Feat**—Creative_Writing Ital Anat & Physiol Ecol
Genetics Marine_Bio/Sci Global_Stud Philos Theol Film Animation Acting Theater_Arts
Music_Theory Dance Debate Journ Public_Speak TV_Production. **Supp**—Dev_Read Makeup
Rem_Read Rev Tut. **Sports**—Basket X-country Lacrosse Soccer Swim Tennis Track Volley
W_Polo. B: Baseball Football Golf Ice_Hockey Wrestling. G: Cheer Softball. Activities: 54.
Selective adm: 595/yr. Appl fee: $50. Appl due: Feb. Accepted: 80%. Yield: 78%. **Tests** HSPT.
Enr 2190. Avg class size: 25. Stud/fac: 18:1. Uniform. **Fac 101.** M 47/F 54. FT 101. Adv deg:
59%. **Grad '09—537.** Col—536. (FL St 104, FL Atlantic 104, U of FL 56, U of Central FL 54,
FL Gulf Coast 24, U of Miami 16). **Avg SAT:** CR 573. M 572. W 582. Avg ACT: 24.4. **Tui '11-
'12:** Day $10,200 (+$1400-2075). Parishioners $8200 (+$1400-2075). **Est 1936.** Nonprofit.
Roman Catholic. Quar (Aug-June). **Assoc** SACS. Enrolling students from three counties, this
Catholic school conducts classes at three levels: Advanced Placement, honors and college preparatory. In addition to the core subjects, the curriculum features courses in business, the fine
arts, physical education, theology and computer science. Class Masses, penitential services,
retreats, and speakers from the Archdiocese of Miami and the community supplement theology course material. In addition, students satisfy a 20-hour community service requirement
each year.

WESTMINSTER ACADEMY   Day Coed Gr PS (Age 2)-12
Fort Lauderdale, FL 33308. 5601 N Federal Hwy.
Tel: 954-771-4600. Fax: 954-491-3021.
www.wacad.edu   E-mail: westminster@wacad.edu
    Leo Orsino, Head (2009). BS, New York Institute of Technology, MS, City Univ of New
York, PhD, Ohio State Univ. Jeffrey Jacques, Adm.
    Col Prep. AP (exams req'd; 148 taken, 80% 3+)—Eng Span Calc Bio Chem Physics
Eur_Hist US_Hist US_Govt & Pol. **Feat**—Lat Stats Anat & Physiol Marine_Bio/Sci Econ
Bible Fine_Arts Visual_Arts Drama Chorus Orchestra Jazz_Band. **Supp**—LD Makeup Rem_
Math Rem_Read. **Dual enr:** Broward CC. **Sports**—Basket Crew X-country Golf Soccer Swim
Tennis Track W_Polo. B: Baseball Football Wrestling. G: Cheer Softball Volley. Activities: 34.
Somewhat selective adm: 224/yr. Appl fee: $100. Appl due: Rolling. Accepted: 90%. Yield:
85%. **Tests** MRT Stanford. **Enr 1000.** Elem 635. Sec 365. Avg class size: 22. Uniform. **Fac 83.**
M 24/F 59. FT 79/PT 4. Adv deg: 69%. **Grad '11—76.** Col—74. **Mid 50% SAT:** CR 520-610.
M 500-590. Avg ACT: 24. **Col Couns:** 3. Alum donors: 9%. **Tui '12-'13:** Day $7310-13,350
(+$450-1025). **Est 1971.** Nonprofit. Presbyterian. Quar (Aug-June). **Assoc** SACS. The cur-
riculum at Westminster, conducted within a Christian environment, features Advanced Placement and honors courses. Fine arts and athletic offerings are available. Students in grades 9-12
perform 20 hours of required community service annually.

BISHOP VEROT CATHOLIC HIGH SCHOOL   Day Coed Gr 9-12
Fort Myers, FL 33919. 5598 Sunrise Dr.
Tel: 239-274-6700. Fax: 239-274-6798.
www.bvhs.org   E-mail: information@bvhs.org
    John Cavell, Jr., Prin (2010). BS, MS, MEd, Louisiana State Univ. Deanna Breen, Adm.
    Col Prep. AP (exams req'd; 270 taken, 81% 3+)—Eng Span Calc Bio Chem Physics
Eur_Hist US_Hist Comp_Govt & Pol US_Govt & Pol. **Feat**—British_Lit ASL Fr Stats Anat
& Physiol Environ_Sci Marine_Bio/Sci Web_Design Econ Law Psych Theol World_Relig

Ceramics Photog Video_Production Theater Music_Theory Bus Journ. **Supp**—LD Tut. **Dual enr:** FL Gulf Coast, Edison. **Sports**—Basket X-country Golf Lacrosse Soccer Swim Tennis Track. B: Baseball Football Weightlifting. G: Cheer Softball Volley. **Selective adm:** Appl fee: $50. Appl due: Dec. Accepted: 75%. Yield: 90%. **Tests** CEEB HSPT. **Enr 650.** Wh 92%. Latino 6%. Blk 1%. Asian 1%. Avg class size: 23. Stud/fac: 19:1. Uniform. **Fac 46.** Wh 98%. Blk 2%. **Grad '11—155.** Col—154. **Avg SAT:** CR 545. M 543. W 529. Avg ACT: 23.5. **Tui '12-'13:** Day $10,650. Aid: Merit 25 ($100,000). Need 115 ($900,000). **Est 1962.** Nonprofit. Roman Catholic (70% practice). Sem (Aug-May). **Assoc** SACS. Bishop Verot's college preparatory curriculum includes honors and Advanced Placement courses, in addition to opportunities for dual enrollment at Florida Gulf Coast University and Edison College. Teachers are available for after-school tutoring on Tuesdays and Thursdays, and peer tutoring is also part of the program. The school's campus ministry program facilitates student involvement in Masses, retreats, penance services, prayer sessions and other spiritual exercises. All students accrue 60 community service points per year.

OAK HALL SCHOOL   Day Coed Gr PS (Age 3)-12
Gainesville, FL 32607. 8009 SW 14th Ave.
Tel: 352-332-3609. Fax: 352-332-4975.
Other locations: 7715 SW 14th Ave, Gainesville 32607.
www.oakhall.org   E-mail: oakhall@oakhall.org
    Richard H. Gehman, Head (1993). AB, Princeton Univ, MEd, Univ of Massachusetts-Amherst. Alice Garwood, Upper & Middle Sch Adm; Nancy Coleman, Lower Sch Adm.
    Col Prep. AP (134 exams taken, 80% 3+)—Eng Lat Span Calc Bio Chem Environ_Sci Physics US_Hist World_Hist Comp_Govt & Pol Econ US_Govt & Pol Studio_Art. **Feat**—ASL Chin Ceramics Filmmaking Photog Sculpt Video_Production Acting Music. **Comp:** Comp/Stud: 1:2. **Dual enr:** U of FL, Santa Fe CC. **Sports**—Basket X-country Golf Soccer Tennis Track. B: Baseball Football Lacrosse. G: Softball Volley. **Selective adm:** 110/yr. Appl fee: $50. Appl due: Feb. **Tests** Stanford TOEFL. **Enr 784.** B 382. G 402. Elem 580. Sec 204. Wh 83%. Latino 6%. Blk 3%. Asian 8%. Avg class size: 13. **Fac 97.** M 25/F 72. FT 93/PT 4. Wh 88%. Latino 6%. Blk 2%. Asian 4%. Adv deg: 47%. **Grad '09—43.** Col—43. **Mid 50% SAT:** CR 580-640. M 600-670. Alum donors: 10%. **Tui '12-'13:** Day $8710-12,675 (+$300). Aid: Need 44 ($520,000). **Est 1970.** Nonprofit. Sem (Aug-May). **Assoc** CLS SACS. Oak Hall offers a traditional liberal arts program of study. Beyond the core curriculum, elective opportunities are available. Qualified upper school students are encouraged to enroll in honors and Advanced Placement courses, and may also earn college credit through dual enrollment at the University of Florida or Santa Fe Community College. Pupils in grades 9-12 accumulate 40 hours of required community service. Grades pre-K-5 are held at 7715 S.W. 14th Ave., while grades 6-12 convene at 8009 S.W. 14th Ave.

CHAMINADE-MADONNA COLLEGE PREPARATORY   Day Coed Gr 9-12
Hollywood, FL 33021. 500 E Chaminade Dr.
Tel: 954-989-5150. Fax: 954-983-4663.
www.cmlions.org   E-mail: info@cmlions.org
    Rev. Larry Doersching, SM, Pres (2008). BA, Saint Mary's Univ of Minnesota, MA, St Louis Univ, DMin, Eden Theological Seminary. Teresita Vasquez Wardlow, Prin. Richard Pulido, Adm.
    Col Prep. AP (exams req'd; 138 taken, 41% 3+)—Eng Fr Calc Bio Chem Physics Eur_ Hist US_Hist Econ US_Govt & Pol Studio_Art. **Feat**—Span Anat & Physiol Sports_Med Web_Design Intl_Relations Law Theol Video_Production Theater Band Dance Bus. **Supp**—Dev_Read LD Makeup Rem_Math Rem_Read Tut. **Comp:** Comp/Stud: 1:5. **Dual enr:** St Thomas U-FL. **Sports**—Basket X-country Golf Soccer Swim Tennis Track Volley. B: Baseball Football Wrestling. G: Cheer Lacrosse Softball. Activities: 37. **Selective adm:** 230/yr. Appl fee: $50. Appl due: Rolling. **Enr 565.** B 333. G 232. Wh 47%. Latino 28%. Blk 14%. Other 11%. Avg class size: 24. Stud/fac: 12:1. Uniform. **Fac 45.** M 20/F 25. FT 45. Adv deg:

53%. **Grad '11—144.** Col—144. (Broward 32, FL Intl 20, FL St 11, FL Gulf Coast 11, U of FL 8, FL Atlantic 7). **Col Couns:** 4. **Tui '11-'12:** Day $9700. Catholic $8200. Aid: Need 211 ($400,000). **Est 1960.** Nonprofit. Roman Catholic (67% practice). Sem (Aug-May). **Assoc** SACS. The result of a 1988 merger between Chaminade High School and its sister school, Madonna Academy, this school is operated by priests and brothers from the Society of Mary (the Marianists). Qualified seniors can dually enroll in St. Thomas University, and pupils may earn college credit in a dozen courses. Boys and girls in grades 9-12 satisfy a 20-hour annual community service requirement. Religious retreats and service groups complement the traditional selection of activities.

ST. JOHN'S EPISCOPAL SCHOOL   Day Coed Gr PS (Age 3)-8
Homestead, FL 33030. 145 NE 10th St.
Tel: 305-247-5445. Fax: 305-245-4063.
www.stjohnshomestead.com   E-mail: stjohns1@bellsouth.net
   Rev. George Ronkowitz, Head. Lakshmi Nair, Adm.
   Gen Acad. Feat—Span Computers Studio_Art Theater Music. **Supp**—Dev_Read Rem_ Math Rem_Read Tut. **Sports**—Basket Volley. G: Softball. **Selective adm (Gr PS-7):** 37/yr. Appl due: Rolling. **Tests** Stanford. **Enr 172.** Wh 27%. Latino 53%. Blk 17%. Asian 3%. Avg class size: 15. Uniform. **Fac 17.** M 4/F 13. FT 14/PT 3. Wh 30%. Latino 68%. Blk 1%. Asian 1%. Adv deg: 17%. **Grad '10—9. Tui '11-'12:** Day $3400-4155 (+$515). Aid: Need 13 (26,000). **Est 1973.** Nonprofit. Episcopal. Quar (Aug-June). Using multi-age groupings instead of traditional grade levels, St. John's Episcopal is equipped to accommodate children with varying learning styles. Twice-weekly Spanish classes and weekly computer instruction are part of the curriculum, and teachers frequently utilize the computer lab to enhance classroom work. Daily chapel attendance is mandatory.

HENDRICKS DAY SCHOOL   Day Coed Gr PS (Age 3)-8
Jacksonville, FL 32216. 1824 Dean Rd.
Tel: 904-720-0398. Fax: 904-720-0435.
www.hendricksdayschool.org   E-mail: admissions@hendricksdayschool.org
   Sally D. Lott, Head.
   Pre-Prep. Gen Acad. Feat—Lat Span Computers Studio_Art Theater Music. **Supp**—Tut. **Sports**—Basket Soccer. B: Baseball. G: Softball Volley. **Somewhat selective adm:** 84/yr. Appl fee: $100. Appl due: Rolling. Accepted: 92%. Yield: 100%. **Enr 291.** Avg class size: 23. Uniform. **Fac 38.** M 3/F 35. FT 38. **Grad '08—43.** Prep—43. **Tui '12-'13:** Day $4910-10,260 (+$550). **Est 1970.** Tri (Aug-May). This progressive elementary school prepares its children for high school through an emphasis on critical-thinking and study skills development. HMDS utilizes various techniques to address differing learning styles. The enrichment program, which begins at age 5, allows students to gain an introduction to music, art, technology, health, theater and foreign language. Each class takes part in one community service project per year.

ST. MARK'S EPISCOPAL DAY SCHOOL   Day Coed Gr PS (Age 2)-6
Jacksonville, FL 32210. 4114 Oxford Ave.
Tel: 904-388-2632. Fax: 904-387-5647.
www.stmarksdayschool.org   E-mail: smeds@stmarksdayschool.org
   Cathy Hardage, Head. BA, Sweet Briar College, MEd, EdS, Univ of Florida. Susan C. Kwartler, Adm.
   Pre-Prep. Feat—Lib_Skills Span Computers Relig Studio_Art Music. **Supp**—Dev_Read Rem_Math Rem_Read Rev Tut. **Comp:** Comp/Stud: 1:1 **Somewhat selective adm:** 60/yr. Appl fee: $50. Appl due: Rolling. Accepted: 98%. Yield: 84%. **Tests** ISEE. **Enr 415.** Avg class size: 18. Stud/fac: 11:1. Uniform. **Fac 39.** M 2/F 37. FT 39. Adv deg: 46%. **Grad '08—32.** Prep—32. (Episcopal HS-FL 23, Bolles 8). **Tui '12-'13:** Day $8750-10,680 (+$250-450). Aid: Need ($200,000). **Est 1970.** Nonprofit. Episcopal. Tri (Aug-May). This parish school's cur-

riculum, which emphasizes independent study skills, includes art, music, computers, physical education, Spanish, library and Christian education. Special events and after-school opportunities supplement class work, and extended-day and summer programs are available. An early learning program for one- and two-year-olds is also offered. Sixth graders perform 10 hours of required community service.

BEACHES EPISCOPAL SCHOOL   Day Coed Gr PS (Age 4)-6
Jacksonville Beach, FL 32250. 1150 5th St N.
Tel: 904-246-2466. Fax: 904-246-1626.
www.beachesepiscopalschool.org   E-mail: info@beachesepiscopalschool.org
    Jackie Busse, Head (2001). BS, Western Illinois Univ, MEd, Univ of North Florida. Heather Galloway, Adm.
    Gen Acad. Feat—Lib_Skills Span Computers Relig Studio_Art Music. **Supp**—Dev_Read Rem_Math Rem_Read Rev Tut. **Somewhat selective adm:** 84/yr. Appl fee: $100. Appl due: Rolling. Accepted: 95%. **Tests** Stanford. **Enr 270.** Avg class size: 16. Uniform. **Fac 27.** FT 27. Adv deg: 11%. **Grad '08—39.** Prep—32. **Tui '12-'13:** Day $9100-10,650 (+$1175). **Est 1952.** Nonprofit. Episcopal. Tri (Aug-May). The school provides a well-rounded curriculum of traditional academic subjects, religious education, the fine arts, Spanish, computer science, library and physical education in a Christian setting. Christian education consists of classroom instruction, chapel services and outreach. An extended-day program is available.

JUPITER CHRISTIAN SCHOOL   Day Coed Gr PS (Age 3)-12
Jupiter, FL 33458. 700 S Delaware Blvd.
Tel: 561-746-7800. Fax: 561-746-1955.
www.jupiterchristian.org   E-mail: info@jupiterchristian.org
    Jim Colman, Pres (2011).
    Col Prep. AP (exams req'd)—Eng Span Calc Stats Bio Chem US_Hist World_Hist Psych US_Govt & Pol. **Feat**—British_Lit Anat Environ_Sci Marine_Bio/Sci Microbio Comp_Sci Econ Bible Visual_Arts Band Chorus Journ Speech. **Supp**—Rev Tut. **Dual enr:** Palm Beach Atlantic. **Sports**—Basket X-country Soccer Tennis Track Wrestling. B: Baseball Football Golf. G: Cheer Softball Volley. **Selective adm:** 100/yr. Appl fee: $575. Appl due: Rolling. **Tests** Stanford. **Enr 600.** Elem 350. Sec 250. Avg class size: 18. Uniform. **Fac 45.** M 10/F 35. FT 45. Adv deg: 17%. **Grad '07—63.** Col—63. **Avg SAT:** CR 590. M 608. Avg ACT: 25. **Col Couns:** 2. **Tui '12-'13:** Day $9414-10,717 (+$550). **Est 1963.** Nonprofit. Nondenom Christian. Sem (Aug-May). **Assoc** SACS. Jupiter offers a traditional college preparatory program in a Christian setting. Academic subjects are integrated with Bible study, and communicational skills are stressed. A weeklong program in March, required for all students, features field trips, service activities, internships and enrichment workshops. All children in grades 6-8 perform 20 hours of annual community service, while pupils in grades 9-12 complete 30 hours of compulsory service each year.

LAKE MARY PREPARATORY SCHOOL   Bdg Coed Gr 9-12
Lake Mary, FL 32746. 650 Rantoul Ln.   Day Coed PS (Age 3)-12
Tel: 407-805-0095. Fax: 407-322-3872.
www.lakemaryprep.com   E-mail: admissions@lakemaryprep.com
    Spencer Taintor, Head (2008). BA, MBA, Univ of Miami, PhD, Capella Univ. Jennifer Clary-Grundorf, Adm.
    Col Prep. AP (exams req'd)—Eng Calc Stats Bio Chem Environ_Sci Physics Eur_Hist US_Hist World_Hist US_Govt & Pol. **Feat**—Humanities Chin Lat Span Anat Marine_Bio/ Sci Econ Psych Ceramics Film Photog Sculpt Studio_Art Band Music Dance Bus Debate. **Sports**—Basket X-country Golf Soccer Swim Tennis Track. B: Baseball Football. G: Softball Volley. **Selective adm (Gr PS-11):** 150/yr. Appl fee: $100. Appl due: Rolling. Accepted: 75%. Yield: 95%. **Tests** IQ ISEE. **Enr 680.** Avg class size: 15. Stud/fac: 13:1. Uniform. **Fac 59.** M

12/F 47. FT 52/PT 7. Adv deg: 32%. **Grad '05—21.** Col—21. **Avg SAT:** CR 607. M 576. W 511. **Tui '12-'13:** Bdg $42,500 (+$1625-3825). Day $9000-13,050 (+$270-1770). **Est 1999.** Spons: Meritas. Quar (Aug-May). In a small-class setting, Lake Mary Prep blends traditional college preparatory course work with interdisciplinary teaching techniques. Compulsory community service begins in grade 8 with a 10-hour annual requirement; boys and girls in grades 9-12 perform 20 hours per year, at least 10 of which must be completed off campus. Students choose from various artistic, athletic and technological offerings. A small boarding program enables older students to reside in a dormitory or with host families in the community.

LAKELAND CHRISTIAN SCHOOL   **Day Coed Gr PS (Age 4)-12**
Lakeland, FL 33803. 1111 Forest Park St.
Tel: 863-688-2771. Fax: 863-682-5637.
www.lcsonline.org   E-mail: info@lcsonline.org
    Michael M. Sligh, Head (1996). BA, MEd, Univ of Florida, MEd, Univ of South Florida, EdD, Nova Southeastern Univ. Julie Rice, Adm.

    Col Prep. AP (exams req'd; 146 taken, 63% 3+)—Eng Span Calc Bio US_Hist Econ Studio_Art Music_Theory. **Feat**—Greek Lat Environ_Sci Marine_Bio/Sci Physiol Comp_Sci Govt Psych Sociol Bible Graphic_Arts Music Piano Journ Mech_Drawing Home_Ec. **Supp**— LD Makeup Rem_Math Tut. **Comp:** Comp/Stud: 1:3. **Dual enr:** Polk St. **Sports**—Basket X-country Golf Soccer Swim Tennis Track. B: Baseball Football. G: Cheer Softball Volley. Activities: 15. **Somewhat selective adm:** 149/yr. Appl fee: $50-150. Appl due: Mar. Accepted: 85%. Yield: 98%. **Tests** Stanford. **Enr 985.** B 479. G 506. Elem 646. Sec 339. Wh 88%. Latino 5%. Blk 3%. Native Am 1%. Asian 1%. Other 2%. Avg class size: 25. Stud/fac: 14:1. Uniform. **Fac 83.** M 22/F 61. FT 73/PT 10. Wh 89%. Latino 5%. Blk 3%. Asian 1%. Other 2%. Adv deg: 28%. **Grad '11—80.** Col—77. (Polk St 12, U of FL 9, FL St 7, U of S FL 7, FL Southern 4, Santa Fe Col 4). **Avg SAT:** CR 523. M 523. W 525. Avg ACT: 23.3. **Col Couns:** 1. Alum donors: 5%. **Tui '12-'13:** Day $7600-8650 (+$500-1000). Aid: Need 150 ($465,850). **Est 1954.** Nonprofit. Nondenom Christian. Quar (Aug-June). **Assoc** SACS. LCS offers a traditional academic curriculum in which Bible study is compulsory. The school emphasizes athletics and the arts through interscholastic and intramural sports, dramatic and musical productions, and piano lessons. Honor society students fulfill a community service requirement.

PACE-BRANTLEY HALL SCHOOL   **Day Coed Gr 1-12**
Longwood, FL 32779. 3221 Sand Lake Rd.
Tel: 407-869-8882. Fax: 407-869-8717.
www.mypbhs.org   E-mail: info@mypbhs.org
    Kathleen Shatlock, Dir (2005). BSE, Saint John's College (MD), MEd, Xavier Univ. Nicole Castelluccio, Adm.

    Gen Acad. LD. Feat—ASL Span Environ_Sci Comp_Sci Studio_Art Speech. **Supp**—Dev_ Read Rem_Math Rem_Read. **Dual enr:** Seminole CC, Valencia CC. **Sports**—Basket Soccer Volley. **Somewhat selective adm:** 39/yr. Appl fee: 0. Funding. Accepted: 85%. Yield: 85%. **Enr 150.** Avg class size: 10. Uniform. **Fac 26.** M 4/F 22. FT 26. Adv deg: 26%. **Grad '08—10.** Col—6. **Avg SAT:** CR 401. M 379. W 393. Avg ACT: 18. **Tui '11-'12:** Day $13,385-13,855 (+$800-1000). **Est 1972.** Nonprofit. Sem (Aug-May). PACE provides reading, language arts and math programs for the child with learning disabilities whose needs have not been met in traditional school settings. Teaching methods combine three distinct learning approaches: auditory, visual and tactile. Frequently scheduled field trips enhance classroom learning.

SWEETWATER EPISCOPAL ACADEMY   **Day Coed Gr PS (Age 4)-5**
Longwood, FL 32779. 251 E Lake Brantley Dr.
Tel: 407-862-1882. Fax: 407-788-1714.
www.sweetwaterepiscopal.org   E-mail: kbailey@sweetwaterepiscopal.org

Janet Stroup, Head (2004). BA, Grove City College, MEd, Millersville Univ of Pennsylvania. Kimberly P. Bailey, Adm.

Pre-Prep. Feat—Creative_Writing Lib_Skills Span Computers Relig Studio_Art Music. **Supp**—Tut. **Comp:** Comp/Stud: 1:2.2. **Somewhat selective adm:** 38/yr. Appl fee: $150. Appl due: Rolling. Accepted: 90%. **Tests** SSAT. **Enr 181.** Wh 83%. Latino 1%. Blk 5%. Asian 5%. Other 6%. Avg class size: 20. Uniform. **Fac 21.** M 3/F 18. FT 20/PT 1. Wh 89%. Latino 11%. Adv deg: 38%. **Grad '11—29.** Prep—29. (Trinity Prep 20, Annunciation Catholic-FL 2, Windermere Prep 1, Lake Mary Prep 1, Geneva Sch-FL 1, Orangewood Christian 1). **Tui '12-'13:** Day $7900-10,200 (+$900-1500). **Est 1974.** Nonprofit. Episcopal (12% practice). Quar (Aug-May). Computer instruction begins in prekindergarten at this Christian school. Other enrichment classes include art, library, music, religion and Spanish. For an additional fee, students may take part in such after-school offerings as chess club, art, music, science and sports.

PARK MAITLAND SCHOOL   Day Coed Gr PS (Age 4)-6
Maitland, FL 32794. PO Box 941095.
Tel: 407-647-3038. Fax: 407-645-4755.
www.parkmaitland.org   E-mail: info@parkmaitland.org
Cindy Moon, Head. Kirsten Telan, Adm.

Gen Acad. Feat—Lib_Skills Span Computers Studio_Art Drama Music. **Supp**—Tut. **Selective adm:** 100/yr. Appl fee: $75. Appl due: Feb. **Enr 625.** Avg class size: 16. Uniform. **Fac 54.** M 6/F 48. FT 52/PT 2. Adv deg: 25%. **Grad '08—54. Tui '12-'13:** Day $9500-12,750 (+$550-600). **Est 1968.** Inc. Sem (Aug-May). Serving the communities of Winter Park and Maitland, the school provides a fully departmentalized elementary program beginning at age 4. Spanish instruction begins in kindergarten, and Park Maitland also conducts strong fine and performing arts programs. Field trip destinations include St. Augustine; the Kennedy Space Center; Williamsburg, VA; and Washington, DC.

HOLY TRINITY EPISCOPAL ACADEMY   Day Coed Gr PS (Age 3)-12
Melbourne, FL 32940. 5625 Holy Trinity Dr.
Tel: 321-723-8323. Fax: 321-308-9077.
Other locations: 50 W Strawbridge Ave, Melbourne 32901.
www.htacademy.org
Catherine A. Ford, Head (1988). BS, MS, Auburn Univ. Patricia Craig, Upper Sch Adm; Rebecca Cacciatore, Lower Sch Adm.

Col Prep. AP (exams req'd; 211 taken, 70% 3+)—Eng Lat Span Calc Stats Comp_Sci Bio Chem Physics Eur_Hist US_Hist World_Hist Econ Psych US_Govt & Pol Studio_Art Music_Theory. **Feat**—Creative_Writing Chin Fr Japan Anat & Physiol Ecol Web_Design Film Theater Music Dance Journ. **Supp**—Tut. **Sports**—Basket X-country Golf Soccer Swim Tennis Track. B: Baseball Football Lacrosse. G: Cheer Softball Volley. **Selective adm:** 88/yr. Appl fee: $50. Appl due: Rolling. **Tests** CEEB Stanford. **Enr 854.** Elem 531. Sec 323. Wh 91%. Latino 3%. Blk 2%. Asian 4%. Avg class size: 16. Uniform. **Fac 79.** M 16/F 63. FT 71/PT 8. Wh 95%. Latino 1%. Blk 2%. Asian 1%. Other 1%. Adv deg: 27%. **Grad '10—82.** Col—82. (FL St 10, U of FL 9, FL Gulf Coast 6, U of Central FL 6, Broward 5, Auburn 4). **Mid 50% SAT:** CR 540-680. M 540-670. W 520-650. Mid 50% ACT: 23-30. **Tui '11-'12:** Day $8225-11,375 (+$1000). Aid: Merit 3 ($2200). Need 19 ($763,070). **Est 1957.** Nonprofit. Episcopal. Sem (Aug-May). **Assoc** SACS. Holy Trinity complements its traditional curriculum with full extracurricular, physical education and interscholastic sports programs. Christian living and life management courses are important elements of the program. All high schoolers fulfill community service requirements: 15 hours per semester in grades 9-12, 120 hours prior to graduation. The lower school (grades PS-6) occupies a separate campus on West Strawbridge Avenue.

ALEXANDER MONTESSORI SCHOOL   Day Coed Gr PS (Age 2)-5
Miami, FL 33143. 6050 SW 57th Ave.
Tel: 305-665-6274. Fax: 305-665-7726.
Other locations: 14850 SW 67th Ave, Miami 33158; 14400 Old Cutler Rd, Miami 33158; 17800 Old Cutler Rd, Miami 33157.
www.alexandermontessori.com   E-mail: school@alexandermontessori.com
    James R. McGhee II, Head (1999). BA, Trinity College (CT). Joyce McGhee, Head. BS, Trinity College (CT), MSEd, PhD, Univ of Miami.
    Pre-Prep. Montessori. Feat—Span Computers Studio_Art Music. **Supp**—Dev_Read ESL Rem_Math Rem_Read Rev Tut. **Comp:** Comp/Stud: 1:1 **Somewhat selective adm:** 100/yr. Appl fee: $0. Appl due: Rolling. Accepted: 95%. Yield: 85%. **Enr 560.** B 252. G 308. Avg class size: 16. Uniform. **Fac 38.** M 2/F 36. FT 36/PT 2. Adv deg: 31%. **Grad '09—35.** Prep—35. (Palmer Trinity 15, Ransom Everglades 9, Gulliver 6, Westminster Christian-FL 2). **Tui '12-'13:** Day $14,230-17,200 (+$380). **Est 1963.** Inc. Quar (Aug-June). **Assoc** SACS. Conducted on four campuses in Miami-Dade County, the school follows a traditional Montessori curriculum. Private lessons are available in violin, cello, piano and tennis. Alexander encourages parental involvement.

ATLANTIS ACADEMY   Day Coed Gr K-12
Miami, FL 33176. 9600 SW 107th Ave.
Tel: 305-271-9771. Fax: 305-271-7078.
Other locations: 10193 NW 31 St, Coral Springs 33065; 1950 Prairie Rd, West Palm Beach 33406.
www.miami.atlantisacademy.com   E-mail: esmith@esa-education.com
    Carlos R. Aballi, Dir. BA, MS, Indiana State Univ, EdS, Indiana Univ. Eric Smith, Adm.
    LD. Feat—Fr Span Computers Studio_Art. **Supp**—Dev_Read ESL Rem_Math Rem_Read Tut. **Sports**—Basket Bowl Golf Soccer Tennis Track. B: Football. G: Softball Volley. **Selective adm:** 35/yr. Appl due: Rolling. Accepted: 60%. **Tests** IQ. **Enr 180.** Elem 96. Sec 84. Stud/fac: 8:1. Uniform. **Fac 27.** M 4/F 23. FT 27. Adv deg: 33%. **Grad '05—10.** Col—8. **Tui '06-'07:** Day $14,200-16,330 (+$550). **Est 1976.** Inc. Quar (Aug-June). **Assoc** SACS. Students with reading and learning difficulties receive individualized instruction in small classes and a clinical setting at Atlantis. All students have access to computers, and pupils in grade 3 and above receive formal instruction in computer usage.

CARROLLTON SCHOOL OF THE SACRED HEART   Day Girls Gr PS (Age 3)-12
Miami, FL 33133. 3747 Main Hwy.
Tel: 305-446-5673. Fax: 305-446-4160.
Other locations: 3645 Main Hwy, Miami 33133.
www.carrollton.org   E-mail: aroye@carrollton.org
    Sr. Suzanne Cooke, RSCJ, Head (1998). BA, Manhattanville College, MA, Univ of Chicago. Ana J. Roye, Adm.
    Col Prep. Montessori. IB Diploma. AP—Eng Calc Comp_Sci Bio Environ_Sci Physics Studio_Art. **Feat**—Anat & Physiol Relig Photog Drama Music Dance. **Supp**—Rev Tut. **Comp:** Laptop prgm Gr 6-12. **Sports**— G: Basket Crew X-country Golf Sail Soccer Softball Swim Tennis Track Volley. **Selective adm (Gr PS-11):** 99/yr. Appl fee: $100. Appl due: Feb. Accepted: 40%. **Tests** ISEE. **Enr 800.** Elem 497. Sec 303. Wh 34%. Latino 60%. Blk 5%. Asian 1%. Avg class size: 15. Stud/fac: 15:1. Uniform. **Fac 74.** M 10/F 64. FT 65/PT 9. Adv deg: 47%. **Grad '10—66.** Col—66. **Avg SAT:** CR 590. M 582. Avg ACT: 24. **Col Couns:** 2. **Tui '12-'13:** Day $16,300-26,000 (+$900). Aid: Need 100 ($2,100,000). **Est 1961.** Nonprofit. Roman Catholic. Quar (Aug-June). **Assoc** SACS. Carrollton's two campuses are on Biscayne Bay, within walking distance of each other: The Barat campus at 3747 Main Hwy. serves grades 4-6 and 9-12, while the Duchesne campus at 3645 Main Hwy. houses girls in the remaining grades. Features of the school's program include a Montessori preschool, honors and Advanced Placement course work and the International Baccalaureate Diploma program,

pursued by more than half of the senior class. Students in grades 5-12 purchase laptop computers through the school. All high schoolers fulfill community service requirements. Carrollton conducts quarter-, semester- and yearlong exchanges with other Sacred Heart schools.

CUSHMAN SCHOOL   Day Coed Gr PS (Age 3)-8
Miami, FL 33137. 592 NE 60th St.
Tel: 305-757-1966. Fax: 305-757-1632.
www.cushmanschool.org E-mail: srentzepis@cushmanschool.org
    Arvi Balseiro, Head (2012). Sheri Rentzepis, Adm.
    Pre-Prep. Gen Acad. Feat—Fr Lat Span Ecol Computers Studio_Art Video_Production Drama Music Public_Speak Speech. **Supp**—LD. **Comp:** Laptop prgm Gr 5-8. **Sports**—Basket X-country Soccer Tennis. B: Baseball. G: Cheer Volley. **Selective adm:** 106/yr. Appl fee: $150. Appl due: Rolling. **Enr 487.** B 270. G 217. Intl 10%. Avg class size: 20. Uniform. **Fac 78.** M 7/F 71. FT 73/PT 5. Adv deg: 44%. **Grad '08—36.** Prep—22. **Tui '12-'13:** Day $14,100-20,975 (+$800-1050). **Est 1924.** Nonprofit. Sem (Aug-June). Cushman offers conversational Spanish throughout, and two other foreign languages are also available. The school uses computer instruction (featuring laptops in grades 5-8) to develop students' reading and reasoning skills. The Laura Cushman Academy, available for an additional tuition fee, provides an alternative program for pupils with auditory or visual processing difficulties, sensory-integration issues and language difficulties.

DADE CHRISTIAN SCHOOL   Day Coed Gr PS (Age 2)-12
Miami, FL 33015. 6601 NW 167th St.
Tel: 305-822-7690. Fax: 305-826-4072.
www.dadechristian.org E-mail: mrodriguez@dadechristian.org
    Stan Stone, Head. BA, Tennessee Temple Univ, MS, Baptist Univ of America. Margie Rodriguez, Adm.
    Col Prep. Gen Acad. AP—Eng Span Calc Bio Chem US_Hist World_Hist Psych US_Govt & Pol Studio_Art. **Feat**—Stats Anat & Physiol Astron Marine_Bio/Sci Programming Econ Bible Ceramics Chorus Accounting. **Supp**—Makeup Rem_Math Tut. **Sports**—Basket X-country Soccer Tennis Track. B: Baseball Wrestling. G: Cheer Softball Volley. Activities: 9. **Selective adm:** 226/yr. Appl due: Rolling. Accepted: 80%. Yield: 70%. **Enr 924.** Elem 608. Sec 316. Avg class size: 20. Uniform. **Fac 63. Grad '08—76.** Col—74. **Avg SAT:** CR 530. M 524. W 526. Avg ACT: 23.3. **Col Couns:** 1. **Tui '12-'13:** Day $8172-11,148 (+$1125-1375). **Est 1961.** Nonprofit. Baptist. Quar (Aug-May). **Assoc** SACS. Dade Christian's Christ-centered elementary curriculum (age 3 kindergarten through grade 6) emphasizes cooperative and experiential learning in the early years, and later stresses critical-thinking skills. Geared toward college preparation, the secondary school (grades 7-12) features honors and Advanced Placement courses, as well as a strong fine arts program. Technology is an important aspect of the curriculum, as computer science instruction begins in kindergarten and continues through grade 12.

IMMACULATA-LA SALLE HIGH SCHOOL   Day Coed Gr 9-12
Miami, FL 33133. 3601 S Miami Ave.
Tel: 305-854-2334. Fax: 305-858-5971.
www.ilsroyals.com E-mail: principal@ilsroyals.com
    Col Prep. AP—Eng Span Calc Comp_Sci Physics Eur_Hist US_Hist US_Govt & Pol Studio_Art. **Feat**—Creative_Writing Humanities Fr Ital Anat & Physiol Web_Design Psych Sociol Theol Ceramics Video_Production Drama Music Accounting Finance Journ Marketing. **Sports**—Basket Soccer Swim. B: Football. G: Softball Volley. **Selective adm:** 230/yr. Appl fee: $50. Appl due: Jan. Accepted: 75%. **Tests** HSPT. **Enr 630.** B 250. G 380. Intl 10%. Avg class size: 27. Stud/fac: 15:1. Uniform. **Fac 41.** M 18/F 23. FT 40/PT 1. Adv deg: 51%. **Grad '07—143.** Col—143. **Avg SAT:** CR 499. M 477. W 498. Avg ACT: 20. **Tui '10-'11:** Day

$9150 (+$1460-1660). Catholic $8150 (+$1460-1660). **Est 1959.** Nonprofit. Roman Catholic. Sem (Aug-June). **Assoc** SACS. Administered by the Salesian Sisters of Saint John Bosco and staffed by lay teachers, ILS occupies a 13-acre site on Biscayne Bay. The school's curriculum features a selection of Advanced Placement classes, in addition to business and technology offerings. An integral component of school life, the youth ministry program encourages students to participate in youth encounters and retreats and serve as liturgical ministers. All boys and girls perform 20 hours of required community service each year.

PINEWOOD ACRES SCHOOL   Day Coed Gr PS (Age 3)-8
Miami, FL 33176. 9500 SW 97th Ave.
Tel: 305-271-3211. Fax: 305-271-3212.
www.pinewoodacres.org   E-mail: pwa@pinewoodacres.org
    Jennifer Lones, Dir (1998). BA, Palm Beach Atlantic Univ, MS, PhD, Univ of Miami.

    Pre-Prep. Feat—Span Computers Studio_Art Band Chorus. **Supp**—Dev_Read Tut. **Selective adm (Gr PS-7):** 30/yr. Appl fee: $300. Appl due: Mar. Accepted: 40%. Yield: 35%. **Tests** Stanford. **Enr 280.** B 150. G 130. Wh 34%. Latino 60%. Blk 2%. Native Am 2%. Asian 2%. Stud/fac: 15:1. Uniform. **Fac 25.** M 1/F 24. FT 24/PT 1. Wh 90%. Latino 10%. Adv deg: 24%. **Grad '11—14.** Prep—8. Alum donors: 5%. **Tui '11-'12:** Day $9800-11,800 (+$250). Aid: Merit 2 ($5000). Need 4 ($8000). **Est 1952.** Inc. Quar (Aug-May). This pre-preparatory school's program places a significant emphasis on the arts. Pinewood Acres' location between the Atlantic Ocean and the Everglades allows children to readily study and observe nature and the environment. Spanish classes begin in kindergarten, and the school offers two levels of the language in grades 2-6.

MONTVERDE ACADEMY   Bdg Coed Gr 7-PG
Montverde, FL 34756. 17235 7th St.   Day Coed PS (Age 3)-12
Tel: 407-469-2561. Fax: 407-469-3711.
www.montverde.org   E-mail: admissions@montverde.org
    Kasey C. Kesselring, Head (1999). BA, Dickinson College, MEd, Middle Tennessee State Univ. Robin Revis-Pyke, Adm.

    Col Prep. AP (exams req'd)—Eng Chin Fr Span Calc Stats Comp_Sci Bio Chem Physics Eur_Hist US_Hist World_Hist Econ US_Govt & Pol Art_Hist Studio_Art Music_Theory. **Feat**—Creative_Writing Anat & Physiol Environ_Sci Marine_Bio/Sci Civil_War Holocaust Psych World_Relig Graphic_Arts Photog Video_Production Acting Theater Directing Band Chorus Music_Hist Orchestra Accounting Finance Marketing Speech. **Supp**—ESL Tut. **Comp:** Laptop prgm Gr 9-12. **Sports**—Basket X-country Golf Soccer Swim Tennis Track. B: Baseball. G: Equestrian Volley. Activities: 46. **Somewhat selective adm:** 125/yr. Bdg 80. Day 45. Appl fee: $50. Appl due: Rolling. Accepted: 88%. Yield: 90%. **Tests** ISEE SSAT TOEFL. **Enr 705.** B 387. G 318. Bdg 245. Day 460. Elem 313. Sec 392. Intl 59%. Avg class size: 20. Uniform. **Fac 42.** M 19/F 23. FT 37/PT 5. Adv deg: 64%. **Grad '05—41.** Col—40. **Avg SAT:** CR 502. M 506. **Tui '12-'13:** Bdg $35,000 (+$2635-3985). Day $9250-11,250 (+$1285-2785). **Est 1912.** Nonprofit. Sem (Aug-June). **Assoc** CLS SACS. Offering a varied college preparatory curriculum that includes honors classes and Advanced Placement work in all major subject areas, Montverde enrolls a substantial percentage of international pupils and offers three levels of English as a second language instruction. The academy schedules a tutorial period every Monday through Thursday at the end of the class day; extra help is also available after school. Students may take certain noncredit courses on an extracurricular basis, among them SAT preparation, photography and dance.

NAPLES CHRISTIAN ACADEMY   Day Coed Gr PS (Age 3)-8
Naples, FL 34116. 3161 Santa Barbara Blvd.
Tel: 239-455-1080. Fax: 239-455-5225.
www.napleschristian.net   E-mail: info@ncanaples.com

Phil Tingle, Int Head (2011). BS, Georgetown College, MA, Arizona State Univ, MS, EdD, Indiana Univ.

Gen Acad. Feat—Span Computers Visual_Arts Music. **Comp:** Comp/Stud: 1:3. **Sports**—Basket Golf Soccer Volley. G: Cheer. **Selective adm:** 15/yr. Appl fee: $150. Appl due: Rolling. Accepted: 75%. Yield: 80%. **Tests** Stanford. **Enr 160.** Wh 77%. Latino 7%. Blk 1%. Asian 1%. Other 14%. Avg class size: 15. Uniform. **Fac 22.** M 2/F 20. FT 16/PT 6. Wh 96%. Asian 4%. Adv deg: 27%. **Grad '10—15.** Prep—3. (Community Sch of Naples 1, St John Neumann-FL 1, First Baptist Acad 1). **Tui '11-'12:** Day $8500-11,400 (+$400). Aid: Need 50 ($275,000). **Est 1973.** Nonprofit. Nondenom Christian (85% practice). Quar (Aug-May). **Assoc** SACS. NCA's curriculum fully incorporates the Bible and its principles. The literature-based reading program blends phonics with writing skills. Spanish, art, music, library skills and computer complement core subjects in the elementary program, and the school offers an enrichment program for gifted children. The middle school (grades 6-8) places particular emphasis on writing, research and study skills in preparation for high school. Eighth graders complete 20 hours of required community service.

BENJAMIN SCHOOL Day Coed Gr PS (Age 3)-12
North Palm Beach, FL 33408. 11000 Ellison Wilson Rd.
Tel: 561-472-3451. Fax: 561-472-3410.
Other locations: 4875 Grandiflora Rd, Palm Beach Gardens 33418.
www.thebenjaminschool.org   E-mail: mprimm@thebenjaminschool.org
   Robert S. Goldberg, Head (2008). BA, Temple Univ, MAT, Rutgers Univ. Mary Lou Primm, Adm.

Col Prep. AP (exams req'd; 379 taken, 88% 3+)—Eng Fr Span Calc Stats Comp_Sci Bio Chem Physics Eur_Hist US_Hist Econ US_Govt & Pol Studio_Art. **Feat**—Chin Anat & Physiol Ecol Genetics Marine_Bio/Sci Psych Drawing Photog Video_Production Drama Music Dance Debate. **Supp**—Dev_Read Makeup Rem_Math Rem_Read Rev Tut. **Comp:** Laptop prgm Gr 6-12. **Sports (req'd)**—Basket Bowl X-country Golf Lacrosse Soccer Swim Tennis Track. B: Baseball Football Wrestling. G: Cheer Softball Volley. Activities: 35. **Somewhat selective adm:** 168/yr. Appl fee: $100. Appl due: Feb. Accepted: 90%. Yield: 74%. **Tests** CEEB ISEE SSAT. **Enr 1144.** B 571. G 573. Elem 711. Sec 433. Wh 88%. Latino 4%. Blk 2%. Asian 2%. Other 4%. Avg class size: 14. Stud/fac: 7:1. Uniform. **Fac 136.** M 29/F 107. FT 132/PT 4. Wh 85%. Latino 10%. Blk 3%. Asian 2%. Adv deg: 43%. **Grad '10—92.** Col—92. (U of FL 9, U of Central FL 7, FL St 7, U of AL-Tuscaloosa 5, Rollins 3, U of CO-Boulder 3). **Avg SAT:** CR 571. M 587. W 583. Avg ACT: 26.1. **Col Couns:** 2. Alum donors: 7%. **Tui '11-'12:** Day $13,900-23,000 (+$400). Aid: Merit 6 ($12,500). Need 137 ($1,515,405). **Est 1960.** Nonprofit. Sem (Aug-June). **Assoc** SACS. Benjamin provides a college preparatory program with an English curriculum that emphasizes grammar/composition, literature, speech and expository writing. Honors and Advanced Placement courses are available in many areas. French, Spanish and Mandarin classes begin in prekindergarten. Community service includes class projects grades pre-K-5, required individual service in grades 6-8, and student-directed programs and activities in grades 9-12. Lower school intramural sports precede compulsory interscholastic sports in grades 6-12. The upper school (grades 9-12) operates at a separate campus in Palm Beach Gardens.

BISHOP MOORE CATHOLIC HIGH SCHOOL Day Coed Gr 9-12
Orlando, FL 32804. 3901 Edgewater Dr.
Tel: 407-293-7561. Fax: 407-296-8135.
www.bishopmoore.org   E-mail: admissions@bishopmoore.org
   Thomas Doyle, Pres (2012). BA, MA, Hofstra Univ. Scott Brogan, Prin.

Col Prep. Gen Acad. AP—Eng Fr Lat Span Calc Stats Comp_Sci Bio Chem Environ_Sci Physics Eur_Hist US_Hist World_Hist Econ Human_Geog Psych US_Govt & Pol Art_Hist Studio_Art Music_Theory. **Feat**—Anat Marine_Bio/Sci Law Sociol Theol Drawing Fine_Arts Sculpt. **Supp**—Tut. **Sports**—Basket Bowl X-country Golf Lacrosse Soccer Swim Tennis

Track Volley W_Polo. B: Baseball Football Weightlifting Wrestling. G: Cheer Softball. Activities: 30. **Selective adm:** Appl fee: $75. **Enr 1100.** Avg class size: 22. Uniform. **Fac 75.** M 28/F 47. FT 74/PT 1. Adv deg: 56%. **Grad '08—287.** Col—281. **Avg SAT:** CR/M 1070. Avg ACT: 23. **Col Couns:** 4. **Tui '12-'13:** Day $13,116 (+$450). Catholic $9480 (+$450). **Est 1954.** Nonprofit. Roman Catholic. Sem (Aug-May). **Assoc** SACS. Situated on 54 acres along Little Lake Fairview, BMHS combines academic studies with religious education. Advanced Placement and honors courses are available, as are electives in business and the fine arts. Each student performs 100 hours of community service with one or more nonprofit organizations prior to graduation.

LAKE HIGHLAND PREPARATORY SCHOOL   Day Coed Gr PS (Age 4)-12
Orlando, FL 32803. 901 N Highland Ave.
Tel: 407-206-1900. Fax: 407-206-1933.
www.lhps.org   E-mail: admissions@lhps.org
Warren Hudson, Pres (2001). BA, Vanderbilt Univ, MEd, Tulane Univ, MPA, Harvard Univ. Ann B. Mills, Adm.

Col Prep. AP (exams req'd; 884 taken, 76% 3+)—Eng Fr Lat Span Calc Stats Comp_Sci Bio Chem Environ_Sci Physics Eur_Hist US_Hist Psych US_Govt & Pol Studio_Art Music_Theory. **Feat**—Creative_Writing Humanities Shakespeare Chin Forensic_Sci Marine_Bio/Sci Engineering Web_Design Bus_Law Comp_Relig Photog Video_Production Drama Debate. **Supp**—Dev_Read Rem_Math Rem_Read Rev Tut. **Sports**—Basket Bowl X-country Golf Lacrosse Soccer Swim Tennis Track. B: Baseball Football Weightlifting Wrestling. G: Cheer Softball Volley. Activities: 46. **Selective adm:** 289/yr. Appl fee: $90. Appl due: Rolling. Accepted: 56%. Yield: 76%. **Tests** ISEE SSAT Stanford. **Enr 2030.** Elem 1234. Sec 796. Wh 75%. Latino 5%. Blk 2%. Asian 6%. Other 12%. Avg class size: 19. Uniform. **Fac 159.** M 41/F 118. FT 159. Adv deg: 54%. **Grad '10—196.** Col—196. **Mid 50% SAT:** CR 530-680. M 550-670. W 550-660. Mid 50% ACT: 23-30. **Col Couns:** 6. **Tui '11-'12:** Day $9000-16,500 (+$2000). Aid: Need 53. **Est 1970.** Nonprofit. Sem (Aug-May). **Assoc** CLS SACS. LHPS offers a diversified curriculum and small, seminar-style classes. In the lower school, a daily enrichment period features art, drama, music, computers, Spanish and library skills. Students in the upper school may take honors courses beginning in grade 7, and Advanced Placement classes are available starting in grade 9. All pupils study composition, speech, the humanities and computers.

NEW SCHOOL PREPARATORY   Day Coed Gr K-8
Orlando, FL 32803. 832 Irma Ave.
Tel: 407-246-0556. Fax: 407-246-0822.
www.newschoolprep.org   E-mail: director@newschoolprep.org
Morris Sorin, Dir. BS, MA, Case Western Reserve Univ.

Pre-Prep. Feat—Span Studio_Art Drama Music Dance. **Sports**—Basket Soccer Tennis Track. G: Softball Volley. **Selective adm:** 11/yr. Appl due: Rolling. Accepted: 80%. Yield: 80%. **Enr 129.** B 51. G 78. Avg class size: 18. Stud/fac: 15:1. Uniform. **Fac 16.** M 3/F 13. FT 15/PT 1. Adv deg: 62%. **Grad '07—12.** Prep—8. **Tui '12-'13:** Day $9700 (+$700). **Est 1995.** Inc. Sem (Aug-May). New School Prep bases its inquiry-based approach on Multiple Intelligences Theory. The school's literature-based language arts program draws on varying genres, time periods and cultures, while a progressive math program incorporates measurement, data manipulation and graphing. Units on earth science, physical science, biology and astronomy are part of a science curriculum that stresses logic, conceptual thinking and problem solving.

WESTMINSTER CHRISTIAN SCHOOL   Day Coed Gr PS (Age 3)-12
Palmetto Bay, FL 33157. 6855 SW 152nd St.
Tel: 305-233-2030. Fax: 305-253-9623.
www.wcsmiami.org   E-mail: lnorth@wcsmiami.org

A. J. West, Supt (2009). BA, Marshall Univ, MEd, Univ of Miami. Lisa North, Adm.

Col Prep. AP (268 exams taken, 66% 3+)—Eng Fr Span Calc Stats Bio Chem Environ_Sci Physics US_Hist World_Hist Econ Human_Geog US_Govt & Pol Studio_Art. **Feat**—Creative_Writing Anat & Physiol Marine_Bio/Sci Programming Robotics Web_Design Intl_Relations Psych Sociol Bible Philos World_Relig Drama Theater_Arts Musical_Theater Band Chorus Orchestra Debate. **Supp**—Rem_Math Rem_Read Rev Tut. **Sports**—Basket X-country Golf Soccer Swim Tennis Track Volley. B: Baseball Football Wrestling. G: Cheer Softball. Activities: 100. **Selective adm (Gr PS-11):** 179/yr. Appl fee: $125. Appl due: Feb. Accepted: 61%. Yield: 85%. **Enr 1040.** B 510. G 530. Elem 616. Sec 424. Wh 37%. Latino 58%. Blk 3%. Asian 1%. Other 1%. Avg class size: 18. Stud/fac: 12:1. Uniform. **Fac 82.** M 25/F 57. FT 78/PT 4. Adv deg: 64%. **Grad '11—112.** Col—112. (FL Intl 24, FL St 11, Miami Dade 7, U of Central FL 6, FL Gulf Coast 5, U of Miami 3). **Avg SAT:** CR 531. M 536. W 534. Avg ACT: 23. **Col Couns:** 3. Alum donors: 15%. **Tui '12-'13:** Day $11,600-16,300 (+$1300). Aid: Need 184 ($950,000). **Est 1961.** Nonprofit. Nondenom Christian (100% practice). Sem (Aug-May). **Assoc** SACS. Taught from a Christian perspective, the thematic curriculum in Westminster's preschool and elementary school (grades K-5) integrates Bible, language arts, math, music, Spanish, social studies, art, computer and physical education. At the middle school level (grades 6-8), the school employs interdisciplinary units to facilitate development in the areas of problem solving, creativity, decision making and critical thinking. Honors and Advanced Placement offerings enrich the high school years (grades 9-12), as do strong fine arts and athletic programs. Support for students who are experiencing academic difficulties is available both during the school day and after school.

PENSACOLA CATHOLIC HIGH SCHOOL   Day Coed Gr 9-12
Pensacola, FL 32505. 3043 W Scott St.
Tel: 850-436-6400. Fax: 850-436-6405.
www.pensacolachs.org   E-mail: kmartin@pensacolahs.org
Sr. Kierstin Martin, Prin (1988). BS, Duquesne Univ, MALS, Wesleyan Univ. Mary Adams, Adm.

Col Prep. AP (37 exams taken, 68% 3+)—Eng Calc Econ US_Govt & Pol. **Feat**—Creative_Writing Fr Span Stats Anat & Physiol Botany Environ_Sci Genetics Marine_Bio/Sci Comp_Sci FL_Hist Law Philos Theol World_Relig Ceramics Photog Video_Production Band Chorus Marketing. **Supp**—Rev Tut. **Comp:** Comp/Stud: 1:1 Laptop prgm Gr 9-12. **Dual enr:** Pensacola St. **Sports**—Basket X-country Golf Soccer Swim Tennis Track. B: Baseball Football Weightlifting. G: Cheer Softball Volley. Activities: 25. **Somewhat selective adm:** 199/yr. Appl fee: $0. Appl due: Mar. Accepted: 97%. Yield: 99%. **Tests** HSPT. **Enr 565.** B 315. G 250. Wh 81%. Latino 5%. Blk 8%. Asian 2%. Other 4%. Avg class size: 20. Stud/fac: 15:1. Casual dress. **Fac 39.** M 16/F 23. FT 37/PT 2. Wh 95%. Latino 5%. Adv deg: 48%. **Grad '11—128.** Col—126. (U of FL 25, Pensacola St 20, FL St 17, U of S AL 8, U of AL-Tuscaloosa 7, LA St-Baton Rouge 5). **Avg SAT:** CR 514. M 499. W 535. Avg ACT: 22.5. **Col Couns:** 1. Alum donors: 15%. **Tui '12-'13:** Day $6852 (+$500). Parishioners $5220 (+$500). Aid: Merit 7 ($11,500). Need 122 ($184,219). Work prgm ($6001). **Est 1941.** Nonprofit. Roman Catholic (66% practice). Sem (Aug-May). **Assoc** SACS. After evaluating standardized test results and past academic achievement, CHS places entering students into one of four ability levels: honors, accelerated college prep, college prep or general studies. Dual-enrollment and Advanced Placement courses are open to qualified pupils. Boys and girls satisfy the following community service requirements: 20 hours in grades 9 and 10, 30 hours in grade 11 and 40 hours in grade 12.

AMERICAN HERITAGE SCHOOL   Day Coed Gr PS (Age 3)-12
Plantation, FL 33325. 12200 W Broward Blvd.
Tel: 954-472-0022. Fax: 954-472-3088.
Other locations: 6200 Linton Blvd, Delray Beach 33484.
www.ahschool.com   E-mail: admissions@ahschool.com

William R. Laurie, Pres (1965). BA, Univ of the South, MEd, Univ of Florida. Lauren G. Johnston, Adm.

Col Prep. AP (exams req'd; 477 taken, 92% 3+)—Eng Fr Span Calc Comp_Sci Bio Chem Environ_Sci Physics Eur_Hist US_Hist World_Hist Econ Psych US_Govt & Pol Art_Hist Studio_Art Music_Theory. **Feat**—Sci_Fiction Women's_Lit Chin Multivariable_Calc Forensic_Sci Sports_Med Engineering Organic_Chem Law Sociol World_Relig Architect Photog Drama. **Supp**—Dev_Read ESL LD Makeup Rem_Math Rem_Read Tut. **Comp:** Comp/Stud: 1:6. **Sports**—Basket X-country Golf Lacrosse Soccer Swim Tennis Track Volley. B: Baseball Football Wrestling. G: Cheer Softball. **Somewhat selective adm:** 461/yr. Appl fee: $100. Appl due: Rolling. Accepted: 90%. Yield: 70%. **Tests** IQ Stanford. **Enr 2541.** B 1355. G 1186. Elem 1272. Sec 1269. Wh 69%. Latino 20%. Blk 6%. Asian 4%. Other 1%. Intl 9%. Avg class size: 18. Stud/fac: 16:1. Uniform. **Fac 202.** M 49/F 153. FT 189/PT 13. Wh 90%. Latino 8%. Blk 1%. Asian 1%. Adv deg: 43%. **Grad '10**—**292.** Col—290. **Avg SAT:** CR 590. M 570. W 560. Avg ACT: 22. **Col Couns:** 4. **Tui '11-'12:** Day $17,494-22,019 (+$1000). Aid: Merit 350 ($3,500,000). Need 500 ($3,500,000). **Est 1965.** Inc. Sem (Aug-May). **Assoc** SACS. American Heritage serves students in grades PS-12 on two campuses: a 35-acre location in Plantation and a 40-acre site in Delray Beach (561-495-7272). Children gain an introduction to Spanish at age 4, while the school introduces Chinese in grade 4 and French in grade 7. Extensive fine arts offerings are available in the high school, as is a special track for students interested in pursuing a legal or health-related career. Boys and girls complete 120 hours of mandatory community service in grades 9-12. The school's American Academy program, available for an additional fee, serves pupils with moderate learning disabilities who are working below grade level.

ST. JOSEPH ACADEMY   Day Coed Gr 9-12
St Augustine, FL 32084. 155 State Rd 207.
Tel: 904-824-0431. Fax: 904-826-4477.
www.sjaweb.org   E-mail: info@sjaweb.org

Rev. Michael R. Houle, Pres (2000). BA, MA, Pontifical College Josephinum, MA, Univ of North Florida. Michael Heubeck, Prin. BA, MA, Manhattan College. Patrick M. Keane, Adm.

Col Prep. AP (exams req'd; 46 taken, 59% 3+)—Eng Span Calc Bio Psych Studio_Art. **Feat**—ASL Anat & Physiol Environ_Sci Programming Econ Theol Drawing Drama. **Supp**—Tut. **Dual enr:** St Johns River CC. **Sports**—Basket X-country Soccer Swim Tennis Track. B: Baseball Football Golf Wrestling. G: Cheer Softball Volley. Activities: 16. **Somewhat selective adm:** 91/yr. Appl fee: $0. Appl due: Feb. Accepted: 88%. **Enr 275.** B 131. G 144. Wh 86%. Latino 5%. Blk 2%. Native Am 1%. Asian 5%. Other 1%. Intl 5%. Avg class size: 14. Stud/fac: 12:1. Uniform. **Fac 24.** M 12/F 12. FT 23/PT 1. Nonwhite 7%. Adv deg: 66%. **Grad '10**—**80.** Col—80. (U of N FL 18, U of FL 12, U of Central FL 10, Flagler 10, FL St 6, U of W FL 4). **Avg SAT:** CR 540. M 520. W 535. Avg ACT: 22. **Tui '11-'12:** Day $9780 (+$350). Catholic $7665 (+$350). Aid: Merit 3 ($6000). Need 46 ($90,400). **Est 1866.** Nonprofit. Roman Catholic (90% practice). Quar (Aug-May). **Assoc** SACS. Florida's oldest Catholic high school, the academy was founded by the Sisters of St. Joseph of St. Augustine. In addition to honors and Advanced Placement courses, advanced students may take dual-enrollment classes offered by St. Johns River Community College in four subjects: world civilizations, English composition, US history and Spanish. All boys and girls perform 20 hours of annual community service with a nonprofit organization, at least 10 of which must involve direct contact with people or animals in need.

KESWICK CHRISTIAN SCHOOL   Day Coed Gr PS (Age 2)-12
St Petersburg, FL 33708. 10101 54th Ave N.
Tel: 727-393-9100. Fax: 727-397-5378.
www.keswickchristian.org   E-mail: swilliams@keswickchristian.org

Nick Stratis, Supt (2012). BS, Univ of Florida, MEd, Liberty Univ. Sue Williams, Adm.

Col Prep. AP (exams req'd; 49 taken, 61% 3+)—Eng Span Calc Bio US_Hist Studio_ Art Music_Theory. **Feat**—Lat Marine_Bio/Sci Comp_Sci Bible. **Supp**—Dev_Read Rem_ Read Tut. **Comp:** Comp/Stud: 1:15. **Dual enr:** St Petersburg Col. **Sports**—Basket X-country Soccer Swim Track. B: Baseball Football Golf. G: Cheer Softball Volley. **Selective adm:** 84/ yr. Appl fee: $50-225. Appl due: Rolling. **Tests** CEEB Stanford. **Enr 487.** B 242. G 245. Wh 87%. Latino 4%. Blk 1%. Asian 2%. Other 6%. Avg class size: 16. Uniform. **Fac 37.** M 6/F 31. FT 35/PT 2. Wh 100%. Adv deg: 21%. **Grad '11—28.** Col—28. (St Petersburg Col 9, U of S FL 4, FL Atlantic 3). **Avg SAT:** CR 532. M 515. W 498. Avg ACT: 22.4. **Col Couns:** 1. **Tui '11-'12:** Day $6625-9900 (+$30-125). Aid: Need 157 ($344,794). **Est 1953.** Nonprofit. Nondenom Christian (99% practice). Sem (Aug-June). **Assoc** SACS. Keswick Christian offers a college preparatory curriculum that emphasizes Christian values. Advanced Placement courses are part of the high school curriculum.

CARDINAL MOONEY HIGH SCHOOL Day Coed Gr 9-12
Sarasota, FL 34232. 4171 Fruitville Rd.
Tel: 941-371-4917. Fax: 941-371-6924.
www.cmhs-sarasota.org   E-mail: blees@cmhs-sarasota.org
Sr. Lucia Haas, SND, Pres. BS, Notre Dame College (OH), MTS, College of William and Mary. Stephen J. Christie, Prin. BS, Manhattan College, MS, Hofstra Univ. Bob Lees, Adm.
Col Prep. AP—Eng Fr Span Calc Stats Comp_Sci Bio Chem US_Hist US_Govt & Pol. **Feat**—Creative_Writing Anat & Physiol Environ_Sci Marine_Bio/Sci Web_Design Econ Govt Psych Sociol Theol Ceramics Studio_Art Drama Music Dance Accounting Journ Speech. **Supp**—LD Rem_Math Rem_Read Tut. **Sports**—Basket X-country Golf Lacrosse Soccer Swim Tennis Track. B: Baseball Football Weightlifting. G: Cheer Softball Volley. Activities: 18. **Nonselective adm (Gr 9-11):** 180/yr. Appl due: Mar. Accepted: 100%. **Tests** HSPT. **Enr 477.** Avg class size: 25. Stud/fac: 13:1. Uniform. **Fac 38.** FT 34/PT 4. **Grad '08—121.** Col—119. **Avg SAT:** CR 530. M 524. W 526. Avg ACT: 23.3. **Col Couns:** 1. **Tui '12-'13:** Day $11,330 (+$500). Parishioners $8870 (+$500). **Est 1959.** Nonprofit. Roman Catholic. Quar (Aug-June). **Assoc** SACS. As part of its college preparatory curriculum, Cardinal Mooney offers honors and Advanced Placement courses and a full complement of electives. In addition to engaging in a four-year religious studies curriculum, students also complete at least 100 hours of required community service prior to graduation. A learning strategies curriculum assists those who require special help.

JULIE ROHR ACADEMY Day Coed Gr PS (Age 2)-8
Sarasota, FL 34232. 4466 Fruitville Rd.
Tel: 941-371-4979. Fax: 941-379-5816.
www.julierohracademy.com   E-mail: cblankenship@julierohracademy.com
Julie Rohr McHugh, Dir (1974). BM, MM, Univ of Miami. Cecilia R. Blankenship, Adm.
Pre-Prep. Gen Acad. Feat—Span Performing_Arts Studio_Art Music. **Supp**—Dev_Read LD Rem_Math Rem_Read Rev Tut. **Somewhat selective adm:** 51/yr. Appl due: Rolling. Accepted: 98%. **Enr 190.** Wh 91%. Latino 1%. Blk 1%. Asian 1%. Other 6%. Avg class size: 12. **Fac 17.** M 2/F 15. FT 17. Wh 100%. Adv deg: 17%. **Grad '11—8.** Prep—3. (Cardinal Mooney-FL 3). **Tui '12-'13:** Day $7300-9290 (+$500-650). **Est 1974.** Inc. Sem (Aug-May). Children at JRA are placed according to academic ability. Students take enrichment classes in Spanish, art, music and physical education. Developmental learning activities are used in nursery school through kindergarten, and a strong performing arts curriculum includes chorus for students at all grade levels. Interested boys and girls may take private or group music lessons after school.

HOLY COMFORTER EPISCOPAL SCHOOL   **Day Coed Gr PS (Age 3)-8**
Tallahassee, FL 32308. 2001 Fleischmann Rd.
Tel: 850-383-1007. Fax: 850-383-1021.
www.holy-comforter.org   E-mail: nmartinez@holy-comforter.org
Peter Klekamp, Head (2011). BA, Univ of Cincinnati, MA, Univ of Detroit Mercy. Nena Martinez, Adm.

Gen Acad. Feat—Fr Lat Span Computers Relig Studio_Art Musical_Theater Band Music. **Comp:** Laptop prgm Gr 7-8. **Sports**—Basket X-country Golf Soccer Tennis Track. B: Baseball Lacrosse. G: Cheer Softball Volley. **Nonselective adm:** 65/yr. Appl fee: $75. Appl due: Rolling. Accepted: 100%. Yield: 95%. **Enr 595.** Wh 81%. Latino 4%. Blk 5%. Asian 3%. Other 7%. Avg class size: 20. Stud/fac: 19:1. Uniform. **Fac 57.** M 2/F 55. FT 50/PT 7. Wh 96%. Latino 4%. Adv deg: 49%. **Grad '11—50.** Prep—4. (Maclay 4). **Tui '12-'13:** Day $9132-9584. Aid: Need 81 ($322,400). **Est 1955.** Nonprofit. Episcopal (14% practice). Sem (Aug-May). **Assoc** SACS. The Christian emphasis at Holy Comforter is first evident in the lower school (grades PS-5), where children participate in classroom devotionals twice a week and attend chapel services three times per week. Weekly Spanish, music, art and physical education classes enrich the curriculum. The middle school program (grades 6-8) features advanced math, science and foreign language courses, as well as electives. Held while classes are suspended, the weeklong ACE program enables students and faculty to join together in multi-grade groups to study a topic intensively; photography, veterinary science, crime scene investigation, sports management, veterinary science, and the visual and dramatic arts are representative topics.

ACADEMY OF THE HOLY NAMES   **Day Boys Gr PS (Age 4)-8**
Tampa, FL 33629. 3319 Bayshore Blvd.   **Girls PS (Age 4)-12**
Tel: 813-839-5371. Fax: 813-839-1486.
www.holynamestpa.org   E-mail: jwilson@holynamestpa.org
Art Raimo, Pres (2011). BA, St Francis College (NY), MEd, Loyola Univ Maryland. Pam Doherty, Adm.

Col Prep. AP (exams req'd; 262 taken, 63% 3+)—Eng Lat Span Calc Bio Chem Physics US_Hist US_Govt & Pol Art_Hist Studio_Art. **Feat**—Fr Anat & Physiol Marine_Bio/Sci Comp_Sci Econ Law Ethics World_Relig Photog Theater Dance Accounting Journ Marketing. **Supp**—Dev_Read Tut. **Sports**— G: Basket Crew X-country Golf Soccer Softball Swim Track Volley. Activities: 30. **Somewhat selective adm (Gr PS-11):** 136/yr. Appl fee: $50. Appl due: Jan. Accepted: 90%. Yield: 62%. **Tests** HSPT Stanford. **Enr 855.** B 203. G 652. Elem 540. Sec 315. Wh 70%. Latino 21%. Blk 2%. Native Am 1%. Asian 3%. Other 3%. Avg class size: 16. Stud/fac: 15:1. Uniform. **Fac 95.** M 9/F 86. FT 95. Adv deg: 43%. **Grad '10—75.** Col—75. **Avg SAT:** CR 570. M 569. W 588. **Mid 50% SAT:** CR 510-630. M 500-630. W 520-650. Avg ACT: 25.1. **Tui '11-'12:** Day $9690-15,280 (+$700). Aid: Merit 15 ($43,900). Need 92 ($481,115). Work prgm 17 ($11,900). **Est 1881.** Nonprofit. Roman Catholic (72% practice). Quar (Aug-June). **Assoc** SACS. Courses in music, computer science, religion and speech supplement core subject offerings at Academy of the Holy Names. Spanish instruction begins in prekindergarten. Students perform at least 100 hours of required community service prior to graduation.

BAYSHORE CHRISTIAN SCHOOL   **Day Coed Gr PS (Age 2)-12**
Tampa, FL 33611. 3909 S MacDill Ave.
Tel: 813-839-4297. Fax: 813-835-1404.
www.bayshorechristianschool.org   E-mail: info@bayshorechristianschool.org
Herman J. Valdes, Head (2009). BS, MEd, Univ of South Florida. Kathy Mollett, Adm.

Col Prep. AP (exams req'd; 29 taken, 38% 3+)—Eng Calc Econ Art_Hist. **Feat**—Span Anat Comp_Design Programming Web_Design Bible Performing_Arts Studio_Art Music. **Supp**—Makeup Tut. **Comp:** Comp/Stud: 1:5. **Dual enr:** Hillsborough CC. **Sports**—Basket Bowl X-country Swim Track. B: Baseball Golf. G: Cheer Softball Volley. **Somewhat selective**

adm: 75/yr. Appl fee: $75. Appl due: Rolling. Accepted: 95%. Yield: 90%. **Tests** Stanford. **Enr 215.** B 110. G 105. Elem 162. Sec 53. Wh 67%. Latino 17%. Blk 13%. Asian 2%. Other 1%. Avg class size: 15. Uniform. **Fac 28.** M 4/F 24. FT 25/PT 3. Wh 88%. Latino 8%. Blk 4%. Adv deg: 21%. **Grad '10—27.** Col—27. **Avg SAT:** CR/M 1090. Avg ACT: 21. Alum donors: 1%. **Tui '11-'12:** Day $7322-8732 (+$250). Aid: Need 43 ($137,500). **Est 1971.** Nonprofit. United Methodist. Sem (Aug-May). **Assoc** SACS.   Bayshore offers such enrichment courses as computer, library, art, music and physical education beginning in grade 1, and daily Bible study is an integral part of the academic program at all grade levels. Honors and advanced courses begin in grade 7. Pupils in grades 9-12 perform 40 hours of compulsory community service annually.

CAMBRIDGE CHRISTIAN SCHOOL   Day Coed Gr PS (Age 3)-12
Tampa, FL 33614. 6101 N Habana Ave.
Tel: 813-872-6744. Fax: 813-872-6013.
www.cambridge-christian.com
   G. Boyd Chitwood, Head (2007). BS, Rhodes College, MDiv, Vanderbilt Univ, MEd, EdD, Univ of Arkansas-Little Rock. Lisa Brennan, Adm.
   Col Prep. AP (exams req'd)—Eng Span Calc Bio Chem Eur_Hist US_Hist World_Hist Psych. **Feat**—Shakespeare Fr Stats Anat & Physiol Environ_Sci Comp_Sci Econ Bible Film Studio_Art Band Chorus Music. **Sports**—Basket X-country Soccer Swim Tennis Track. B: Baseball Football Golf. G: Softball Volley. **Selective adm:** 60/yr. Appl due: Rolling. Accepted: 82%. Yield: 81%. **Tests** Stanford. **Enr 579.** Elem 399. Sec 180. Avg class size: 18. Uniform. **Fac 66.** M 13/F 53. FT 64/PT 2. Adv deg: 31%. **Grad '10—49.** Col—49. **Avg SAT:** CR/M 1105. Avg ACT: 21. **Tui '12-'13:** Day $9996-13,509 (+$950-1200). **Est 1964.** Nonprofit. Non-denom Christian. Sem (Aug-June).   CCS integrates the classical model of education (logic and rhetoric) with traditional college preparatory academics. The core curriculum comprises English, science, mathematics, foreign language, social studies, fine arts and practical arts. Advanced Placement courses and an honors track in English and math are available for qualified students, and formal computer instruction begins in grade 1. Religious programs include student-led Bible study groups and weekly chapel services. Boys and girls in the lower grades engage in community service projects, while high schoolers satisfy the following requirements: 15 hours of service in grade 9 and an additional five hours of service per year thereafter.

CARROLLWOOD DAY SCHOOL   Day Coed Gr PS (Age 2)-12
Tampa, FL 33613. 1515 W Bearss Ave.
Tel: 813-920-2288. Fax: 813-920-8237.
Other locations: 12606 Casey Rd, Tampa 33618.
www.carrollwooddayschool.org   E-mail: kperez@carrollwooddayschool.org
   Mary L. Kanter, Head (1998). BA, State Univ of New York-Stony Brook, MA, Temple Univ. Dawn Schweitzer, Adm.
   Col Prep. IB Diploma. IB PYP. IB MYP. Feat—Fr Span Econ Govt Psych Ceramics Photog Studio_Art Visual_Arts Drama Theater_Arts Music Dance. **Supp**—Tut. **Comp:** Laptop prgm Gr 9-12. **Sports**—Basket X-country Soccer Tennis Track. B: Baseball Football Golf. G: Cheer Softball Volley. Activities: 25. **Somewhat selective adm (Gr PS-11):** Appl fee: $75. Appl due: Jan. Accepted: 95%. Yield: 93%. **Tests** SSAT. **Enr 799.** B 431. G 368. Elem 629. Sec 170. Avg class size: 16. Uniform. **Fac 76.** M 12/F 64. FT 58/PT 18. Adv deg: 59%. **Grad '10—21.** Col—21. **Tui '11-'12:** Day $9800-14,900 (+$250-2300). Aid: Need ($270,957). **Est 1981.** Quar (Aug-May).   Founded as an early childhood center, CDS eventually grew to include elementary, middle school and high school divisions. Beginning at age 3, the curriculum centers around the three components of the International Baccalaureate Organization, culminating with the IB Diploma in grades 11 and 12. Boys and girls accumulate 75 hours of required community service in grades 9-12. The early childhood program occupies a separate campus on Casey Road.

JESUIT HIGH SCHOOL   **Day Boys Gr 9-12**
Tampa, FL 33614. 4701 N Himes Ave.
Tel: 813-877-5344. Fax: 813-872-1853.
www.jesuittampa.org   E-mail: pmack@jesuittampa.org
    Rev. Richard C. Hermes, SJ, Pres (2008). BA, St Louis Univ, MA, City Univ of New York,
MDiv, Weston Jesuit School of Theology. Barry J. Neuburger, Prin. MBA, Florida Institute of
Technology, MEd, Univ of New Orleans. Steve Matesich, Adm.
    Col Prep. AP (exams req'd; 262 taken)—Eng Span Calc Chem Physics US_Hist World_
Hist US_Govt & Pol Studio_Art. **Feat**—Fr Lat Anat & Physiol Marine_Bio/Sci Comp_Sci
Intl_Relations Psych Theol Chorus Music Speech. **Comp:** Comp/Stud: 1:4. **Sports**— B: Base-
ball Basket Bowl X-country Football Golf Lacrosse Soccer Swim Tennis Track Wrestling.
Activities: 43. **Selective adm (Gr 9-10):** 199/yr. Appl fee: $50. Appl due: Dec. Accepted: 74%.
Yield: 75%. **Tests** HSPT. **Enr 733.** Wh 70%. Latino 21%. Blk 5%. Native Am 1%. Asian 3%.
Avg class size: 24. Stud/fac: 13:1. Formal dress. **Fac 55.** M 41/F 14. FT 55. Wh 83%. Latino
15%. Blk 1%. Asian 1%. Adv deg: 76%. **Grad '11—151.** Col—151. (FL St 21, U of FL 17, U
of Central FL 11, U of S FL 7, FL Atlantic 4, FL Gulf Coast 4). **Avg SAT:** CR 600. M 617. W
595. Avg ACT: 27. **Col Couns:** 4. **Tui '11-'12:** Day $12,400 (+$1280-1480). Aid: Need 182
($1,300,000). **Est 1899.** Nonprofit. Roman Catholic (77% practice). Sem (Aug-May). **Assoc**
SACS. JHS' college preparatory curriculum includes honors and Advanced Placement courses
in most academic departments. Students take four years of theology and participate in regularly scheduled religious functions such as chapel services and retreats. Each boy performs 150
hours of compulsory community service during his four years.

ST. JOHN GREEK ORTHODOX DAY SCHOOL   **Day Coed Gr PS (Age 3)-8**
Tampa, FL 33609. 2418 W Swann Ave.
Tel: 813-258-5646. Fax: 813-258-5654.
www.stjohntampa.com   E-mail: info@stjohntampa.com
    Cynthia J. Strickland, Head (2009). BS, Pennsylvania State Univ. Karen Ciao, Adm.
    Pre-Prep. Feat—Creative_Writing Lib_Skills Span Computers Relig Studio_Art Music
Guitar. **Supp**—Dev_Read Rev Tut. **Sports**—Basket X-country Soccer Track. B: Lacrosse. G:
Softball Volley. **Somewhat selective adm:** 13/yr. Appl fee: $25-50. Appl due: Mar. Accepted:
100%. Yield: 80%. **Tests** Stanford. **Enr 125.** B 64. G 61. Wh 90%. Latino 9%. Blk 1%. Avg
class size: 11. Stud/fac: 11:1. Uniform. **Fac 21.** M 3/F 18. FT 15/PT 6. Wh 98%. Latino 2%.
Adv deg: 28%. **Grad '10—17.** Prep—7. (Jesuit HS-FL 4, Acad of the Holy Names 2, Canterbury Sch of FL 1). Alum donors: 2%. **Tui '10-'11:** Day $8700-9200 (+$1000). Aid: Merit 1
($8700). Need 4 ($4000). **Est 1967.** Nonprofit. Greek Orthodox. Quar (Aug-May). St. John,
which runs from early childhood through middle school, features Spanish, music, art and a
strong technology program. Classroom focus shifts from learning to read in the early elementary years to knowledge acquisition in the upper elementary grades. The middle school (grades
6-8) prepares students for college preparatory high schools by emphasizing skill development
in English, math, science, history/geography and Spanish.

ST. JOHN'S EPISCOPAL PARISH DAY SCHOOL   **Day Coed Gr PS (Age 4)-8**
Tampa, FL 33606. 906 S Orleans Ave.
Tel: 813-849-5200. Fax: 813-258-2548.
Other locations: 240 Plant Ave, Tampa 33606; 1002 Rome Ave, Tampa 33606.
www.stjohnseagles.org   E-mail: cfenlon@stjohnseagles.org
    Gordon R. Rode, Head (2005). BA, Johns Hopkins Univ, MST, Rutgers Univ. Cindy M.
Fenlon, Adm.
    Pre-Prep. Gen Acad. Feat—Lat Span Computers Relig Art_Hist Studio_Art Music
Music_Theory. **Comp:** Comp/Stud: 1:6. **Sports**—Basket X-country Soccer Tennis Track. B:
Baseball Lacrosse. G: Cheer Softball Volley. **Selective adm:** 80/yr. Appl fee: $100. Appl due:
Rolling. Accepted: 78%. Yield: 75%. **Tests** CTP_4 ISEE. **Enr 586.** B 316. G 270. Wh 92%.
Latino 2%. Blk 2%. Asian 4%. Avg class size: 20. Stud/fac: 12:1. Uniform. **Fac 50.** M 11/F 39.

FT 48/PT 2. Wh 97%. Latino 3%. Adv deg: 40%. **Grad '11—61.** Prep—15. (Berkeley Prep 6, Jesuit HS-FL 3, Acad of the Holy Names 2, Tampa Prep 2). Alum donors: 7%. **Tui '12-'13:** Day $9900-10,160 (+$900). Aid: Need 42 ($175,000). **Est 1951.** Nonprofit. Episcopal (21% practice). Quar (Aug-May). St. John's conducts a rigorous elementary program that prepares graduates for private and public high schools in the Tampa area. In the middle division, many pupils follow the honors curriculum, which enables them to earn high school credit in algebra, science, Latin and history. Each grade undertakes an annual community service project. St. John's maintains three campuses: The primary division (grades pre-K and K) on Rome Avenue, the lower division (grades 1-4) on South Orleans Avenue and the middle division (grades 5-8) on Plant Avenue. See Also Page 84

UNIVERSAL ACADEMY OF FLORIDA   Day Coed Gr PS (Age 3)-12
Tampa, FL 33610. 6801 Orient Rd.
Tel: 813-664-0695. Fax: 813-664-4506.
www.uaftampa.org   E-mail: office@uaftampa.org
Kem Hussain, Supt. May Khdeir, Prin.

    Col Prep. Gen Acad. AP—Eng Calc Bio US_Hist World_Hist Psych. **Feat**—Arabic Islamic_Stud. **Supp**—Rem_Math Rem_Read Tut. **Dual enr:** U of S FL, Hillsborough CC. **Sports**—Soccer. B: Basket. Activities: 10. **Somewhat selective adm:** 56/yr. Appl fee: $50. Appl due: Rolling. Accepted: 98%. **Tests** Stanford. **Enr 359.** Avg class size: 20. Stud/fac: 10:1. Uniform. **Fac 25.** M 4/F 21. FT 18/PT 7. Adv deg: 32%. **Grad '05—16.** Col—16. **Avg SAT:** CR 550. M 550. W 500. Avg ACT: 22. **Tui '12-'13:** Day $4900-5600 (+$210-390). **Est 1992.** Nonprofit. Islamic. Quar (Aug-May). **Assoc** SACS. Serving Hillsborough, Pinellas, Pasco and Hernando counties, this Islamic school requires its students to take Islamic studies, Arabic and Quran classes. Dual-enrollment programs are in place with the University of South Florida and two community colleges. Pupils complete 75 hours of community service prior to graduation.

FLORIDA COLLEGE ACADEMY   Day Coed Gr PS (Age 4)-9
Temple Terrace, FL 33637. 7032 Temple Terrace Hwy.
Tel: 813-899-6800. Fax: 813-984-8301.
www.floridacollegeacademy.net   E-mail: academy@floridacollege.edu
Lynn Wade, Prin (2008).

    Gen Acad. Feat—Span Bible Studio_Art Music Journ Public_Speak Study_Skills. **Supp**—Rem_Math Rem_Read Tut. **Sports**—Basket X-country Golf Soccer Volley. B: Baseball. G: Cheer. **Somewhat selective adm:** 45/yr. Appl due: Rolling. Accepted: 85%. Yield: 85%. **Enr 150.** B 64. G 86. Elem 146. Sec 4. Avg class size: 20. Stud/fac: 13:1. Uniform. **Fac 17.** M 6/F 11. FT 15/PT 2. Nonwhite 1%. Adv deg: 29%. **Tui '11-'12:** Day $4700-5100 (+$500). Aid: Need 39 ($187,000). **Est 1958.** Nonprofit. Nondenom Christian. Quar (Aug-May). Children at FCA attend Bible classes and daily chapel. Frequent field trips to local cultural events and educational resource centers enrich academic work.

ARTHUR I. MEYER JEWISH ACADEMY   Day Coed Gr K-8
West Palm Beach, FL 33409. 3261 N Military Trail.
Tel: 561-686-6520. Fax: 561-686-8522.
www.meyeracademy.org   E-mail: office@meyeracademy.org
Nehemia Ichilov, Head (2010). MA, Jewish Theological Seminary of America. Susan Lord, Adm.

    Gen Acad. Feat—Hebrew Span Computers Judaic_Stud Studio_Art Drama Music. **Supp**—Tut. **Comp:** Comp/Stud: 1:2. **Sports**—Basket Golf Lacrosse Soccer Tennis. G: Volley. **Somewhat selective adm:** 56/yr. Appl fee: $250. Appl due: Feb. Accepted: 96%. Yield: 93%. **Tests** Stanford. **Enr 340.** Wh 100%. Avg class size: 18. Uniform. **Fac 50.** M 3/F 47. FT 46/ PT 4. Wh 100%. Adv deg: 42%. **Grad '10—36.** **Tui '11-'12:** Day $13,100. Aid: Need 158 ($812,817). **Est 1973.** Nonprofit. Jewish. Sem (Aug-June). Meyer Academy provides a bilingual Hebrew and English education for Jewish children of the Palm Beach area. Knowledge acquisition and information processing are particular points of emphasis. Through the Judaic studies program, boys and girls study the Bible, prayer, holidays and rituals, values and Jewish social studies. Located on the campus of the Jewish Community Center, the academy makes use of many JCC facilities.

CARDINAL NEWMAN HIGH SCHOOL   Day Coed Gr 9-12

West Palm Beach, FL 33409. 512 Spencer Dr.
Tel: 561-683-6266. Fax: 561-683-7307.
www.cardinalnewman.com   E-mail: jclarke@cardinalnewman.com
     Rev. David W. Carr, Pres (1995). BA, Univ of Notre Dame, MEd, Florida Atlantic Univ. John F. Clarke, Prin. BA, St John's Univ (NY), MA, Hofstra Univ, EdS, Florida Atlantic Univ. Julie Carr & Jan Joy, Adms.
     Col Prep. IB Diploma. AP—Eng Fr Span Calc Environ_Sci US_Hist Econ. **Feat**—Creative_Writing Stats Anat & Physiol Comp_Sci World_Relig Studio_Art Visual_Arts Band Chorus Music Journ Speech. **Supp**—Dev_Read Makeup Rem_Math Rem_Read Tut. **Dual enr:** Palm Beach St, St Thomas U-FL, FL Atlantic. **Sports**—Basket Bowl X-country Golf Lacrosse Soccer Swim Tennis Track. B: Baseball Football Wrestling. G: Cheer Softball Volley. **Selective adm (Gr 9-11):** 165/yr. Appl fee: $50-100. Appl due: Rolling. **Tests** HSPT. **Enr 572.** B 271. G 301. Wh 84%. Latino 10%. Blk 4%. Asian 1%. Other 1%. Avg class size: 25. Uniform. **Fac 45.** M 13/F 32. FT 43/PT 2. Wh 99%. Latino 1%. Adv deg: 80%. **Grad '11—184.** Col—182. **Col Couns:** 2. **Tui '11-'12:** Day $10,650 (+$1375). Parishioners $9650 (+$1375). **Est 1961.** Nonprofit. Roman Catholic. Sem (Aug-June). **Assoc** SACS. Cardinal Newman offers a college preparatory curriculum that features International Baccalaureate, Advanced Placement, honors and regular classes. In addition to course work in the basic disciplines (English, foreign language, mathematics, science and social studies), all pupils take religion classes. The International Baccalaureate Diploma Program is open to qualified juniors and seniors. All boys and girls perform at least 25 hours of community service annually.

WINDERMERE PREPARATORY SCHOOL   Bdg Coed Gr 9-12

Windermere, FL 34786. 6189 Winter Garden-Vineland Rd.   **Day Coed PS (Age 3)-12**
Tel: 407-905-7737. Fax: 407-905-7710.
www.windermereprep.com   E-mail: carol.riggs@windermereprep.com
     Tom Marcy, Head (21). BA, MEd, EdD, Univ of Florida. Carol A. Riggs, Adm.
     Col Prep. IB Diploma. AP (exams req'd; 141 taken, 56% 3+)—Calc Environ_Sci Eur_Hist US_Hist World_Hist Econ Human_Geog US_Govt & Pol. **Feat**—Creative_Writing Fr Lat Span Psych Fine_Arts Graphic_Arts Performing_Arts Photog Studio_Art Drama Music Dance Journ Speech SAT_Prep. **Supp**—ESL Tut. **Comp:** Comp/Stud: 1:1 Laptop prgm Gr 5-12. **Sports**—Basket Golf Soccer Swim Tennis Track. B: Baseball Football Lacrosse. G: Softball Volley. **Somewhat selective adm:** 298/yr. Bdg 51. Day 247. Appl fee: $100. Appl due: Rolling. Accepted: 95%. Yield: 95%. **Tests** CEEB CTP_4 IQ ISEE SSAT Stanford TOEFL. **Enr 1068.** B 540. G 528. Bdg 83. Day 985. Elem 719. Sec 349. Wh 60%. Latino 10%. Blk 5%. Asian 12%. Other 13%. Intl 12%. Avg class size: 18. Stud/fac: 12:1. Uniform. **Fac 94.** M 21/F 73. Wh 90%. Latino 5%. Blk 3%. Asian 2%. Adv deg: 48%. **Grad '11—54.** Col—52. (U of FL 7, U of Central FL 3, Rollins 3, PA St 2, Northeastern U 2, FL St 2). **Avg SAT:** CR 532. M 554. W 533. Avg ACT: 25. **Col Couns:** 2. **Tui '12-'13:** Bdg $45,500 (+$5800). Day $11,500-16,275 (+$1500). Aid: Merit 4 ($12,000). Need 24 ($230,082). **Est 2000.** Inc. Spons: Meritas. Quar (Aug-June). **Assoc** SACS. The liberal arts curriculum at WPS focuses on four main areas: intellectual, technological, cultural and personal. For academic, developmental and social reasons, grade levels are grouped into forms intended to mark the passage from one important stage to another. In addition to Advanced Placement course work, the school offers the International Baccalaureate Diploma Program in grades 11 and 12. Students perform 60 hours of community service in four years beginning in grade 5, then another 75 hours over four years starting in grade 9.

GEORGIA

DEERFIELD-WINDSOR SCHOOL　　　　　　**Day Coed Gr PS (Age 4)-12**
Albany, GA 31707. 2500 Nottingham Way.
Tel: 229-435-1301. Fax: 229-888-6085.
Other locations: 1733 Beattie Rd, Albany 31721.
www.deerfieldwindsor.com　E-mail: laurie.allen@deerfieldwindsor.com
　David L. Davies, Head (2009). BS, MSEd, Wilkes College, MS, Univ of Pennsylvania.
Sharon Evans, Adm.
　Col Prep. AP (exams req'd; 129 taken, 53% 3+)—Eng Span Calc Bio Physics US_Hist
US_Govt & Pol Studio_Art. **Feat**—Southern_Lit Fr Lat Environ_Sci Comp_Sci Psych Bible
Ethics Film Fine_Arts Drama Theater Band Communications Debate Journ Speech. **Supp**—
Dev_Read Tut. **Dual enr:** Darton. **Sports**—Basket X-country Soccer Swim Tennis Track. B:
Baseball Football Golf Wrestling. G: Softball. **Somewhat selective adm:** 160/yr. Appl fee:
$50. Appl due: Mar. Accepted: 98%. Yield: 99%. **Tests** CEEB IQ ISEE MAT. **Enr 832.** Elem
587. Sec 245. Wh 89%. Blk 7%. Asian 4%. Avg class size: 15. **Fac 72.** M 16/F 56. FT 69/PT
3. Wh 99%. Latino 1%. Adv deg: 66%. **Grad '10—55.** Col—55. **Avg SAT:** CR 576. M 527.
W 587. Avg ACT: 28. **Col Couns:** 1. Alum donors: 35%. **Tui '12-'13:** Day $6452-10,966
(+$350). Aid: Merit 7 ($80,000). Need 99 ($465,000). **Est 1964.** Nonprofit. Sem (Aug-May).
Assoc SACS. Deerfield-Windsor enrolls college-bound children of above-average intelligence. Emphasis is placed on math and language arts in the elementary division, while upper
schoolers may enroll in honors and Advanced Placement courses. Dual-enrollment courses
are offered through Darton College. Students in grades 10-12 accumulate 40 hours of required
community service. The 10-acre lower school campus hosts grades K-5 on Beattie Road, while
grades 6-12 are located at the 15-acre Nottingham Way location.

ATHENS ACADEMY　　　　　　**Day Coed Gr PS (Age 3)-12**
Athens, GA 30604. 1281 Spartan Ln, PO Box 6548.
Tel: 706-549-9225. Fax: 706-354-3775.
www.athensacademy.org　E-mail: academy@athensacademy.org
　J. Robert Chambers, Jr., Head (1984). BS, MEd, Univ of Georgia. Stuart Todd, Adm.
　Col Prep. AP (exams req'd; 182 taken, 96% 3+)—Eng Fr Lat Span Calc Bio Chem
Eur_Hist US_Hist. **Feat**—Stats Comp_Sci Econ Pol_Sci Psych World_Relig Photog Sculpt
Studio_Art Drama Music. **Supp**—Rev Tut. **Comp:** Laptop prgm Gr 7-12. **Sports**—Basket
X-country Golf Soccer Swim Tennis Track. B: Baseball Football. G: Cheer Volley. **Selective
adm:** 135/yr. Appl fee: $85. **Tests** IQ ISEE. **Enr 957.** B 482. G 475. Wh 82%. Latino 2%. Blk
5%. Asian 7%. Other 4%. Avg class size: 18. **Fac 120. Grad '10—66.** Col—66. (U of GA 16,
GA Inst of Tech 4, Auburn 4, GA Col & State U 3, Clemson 2, Berry 2). **Avg SAT:** CR 632. M
638. W 615. **Col Couns:** 3. **Tui '12-'13:** Day $13,775-15,600 (+$1000). **Est 1967.** Nonprofit.
Sem (Aug-May). **Assoc** CLS SACS. Middle school students may participate in instrumental
lessons, performing arts groups or athletics. In the upper school, Advanced Placement courses
are offered in most subjects. The fine arts curriculum includes drama, visual arts and music,
and the arts are integrated into other academic subjects.

THE GALLOWAY SCHOOL　　　　　　**Day Coed Gr PS (Age 3)-12**
Atlanta, GA 30342. 215 W Wieuca Rd NW.
Tel: 404-252-8389. Fax: 404-252-7770.
www.gallowayschool.org　E-mail: info@gallowayschool.org
　Suzanna Jemsby, Head (2012). MA, Univ of Cambridge (England). Polly Williams, Adm.
　Col Prep. AP (116 exams taken, 78% 3+)—Eng Fr Lat Span Calc Stats Bio Chem
Environ_Sci Physics Eur_Hist US_Hist Comp_Govt & Pol US_Govt & Pol Music_Theory.
Feat—British_Lit Creative_Writing Playwriting Anat & Physiol Ecol Genetics Comp_Design

Comp_Sci Robotics Anthro Econ Psych African-Amer_Stud Comp_Relig Philos Filmmaking Photog Animation Theater Chorus Music Orchestra Dance Journ Public_Speak. **Supp**—Rev Tut. **Dual enr:** Oglethorpe. **Sports**—Basket Golf Soccer Tennis Track. B: Baseball. G: Softball Swim Volley. **Selective adm:** 105/yr. Appl fee: $75. Appl due: Feb. Accepted: 58%. Yield: 47%. **Tests** SSAT. **Enr 725.** Elem 465. Sec 260. Nonwhite 25%. Avg class size: 15. Stud/fac: 8:1. Casual dress. **Fac 87.** Adv deg: 51%. **Grad '11—58.** Col—58. **Mid 50% SAT:** CR 620-730. M 570-680. W 610-710. **Col Couns:** 2. Alum donors: 7%. **Tui '12-'13:** Day $18,700-21,370. Aid: Need 130. **Est 1969.** Nonprofit. Sem (Aug-June). **Assoc** SACS. Galloway offers a college preparatory curriculum that features Advanced Placement courses in all disciplines. Academic emphasis is placed upon small-group instruction and close teacher-student interaction.

HOLY INNOCENTS' EPISCOPAL SCHOOL   Day Coed Gr PS (Age 3)-12
Atlanta, GA 30327. 805 Mt Vernon Hwy NW.
Tel: 404-255-4026. Fax: 404-250-0815.
www.hies.org   E-mail: chris.pomar@hies.org
    Gene Bratek, Head (2011). BA, Univ of Virginia, MA, Trenton State College, MEd, Rutgers Univ. Christopher Pomar, Adm.

    Col Prep. AP (exams req'd; 350 taken, 78% 3+)—Eng Fr Lat Span Calc Stats Bio Chem Environ_Sci Physics Eur_Hist US_Hist World_Hist Human_Geog Psych US_Govt & Pol Studio_Art. **Feat**—Poetry Shakespeare Mythology Greek Anat & Physiol Astron Sports_Med Comp_Relig Ethics Drawing Photog Video_Production Theater_Arts Music Journ Broadcast_ Journ SAT_Prep. **Supp**—Dev_Read Rev Tut. **Comp:** Comp/Stud: 1:1.6 (1:1 Laptop prgm Gr 5-12). Outdoor Ed. **Sports**—Basket X-country Golf Lacrosse Soccer Swim Tennis Track. B: Baseball Football Wrestling. G: Cheer Softball Volley. Activities: 33. **Selective adm (Gr PS-11):** 165/yr. Appl fee: $95. Appl due: Feb. Accepted: 50%. Yield: 76%. **Tests** SSAT. **Enr 1300.** B 602. G 698. Elem 855. Sec 445. Wh 90%. Latino 1%. Blk 6%. Asian 1%. Other 2%. Avg class size: 9. Stud/fac: 9:1. Uniform. **Fac 180.** M 42/F 138. FT 150/PT 30. Nonwhite 9%. Adv deg: 38%. **Grad '11—90.** Col—90. **Avg SAT:** CR 581. M 600. W 606. Avg ACT: 25. **Col Couns:** 3. Alum donors: 5%. **Tui '11-'12:** Day $17,270-20,510 (+$1000). Aid: Need 151 ($1,800,000). **Est 1959.** Nonprofit. Episcopal (26% practice). Sem (Aug-May). **Assoc** CLS SACS. Holy Innocents' combines college preparatory academics, the arts and athletics with a Judeo-Christian worldview. Language instruction begins in kindergarten with the introduction of Spanish. A laptop computer program in grades 5-12 highlights HIES' integrated technology curriculum. Chapel services and religion classes supplement the educational program. Students in grade 8 satisfy a five-hour community service requirement, while boys and girls in grades 9-12 perform 10 hours of required service per year.

HOLY SPIRIT PREPARATORY SCHOOL   Day Coed Gr PS (Age 2)-12
Atlanta, GA 30327. 4449 Northside Dr.
Tel: 678-904-2811. Fax: 678-904-4983.
Other locations: 4820 Long Island Dr, Atlanta 30342; 4465 Northside Dr, Atlanta 30327.
www.holyspiritprep.org   E-mail: shiggins@holyspiritprep.org
    Gareth N. Genner, Pres. Jamie Arthur, Head. BBA, MEd, Univ of South Carolina, PhD, Georgia State Univ. Sharon Higgins, Adm.

    Col Prep. AP—Eng Lat Span Calc Stats Comp_Sci Bio Chem Environ_Sci Physics Eur_ Hist US_Hist Econ Human_Geog US_Govt & Pol Studio_Art Music_Theory. **Feat**—British_Lit Fr Ger Greek Ital Portuguese Anat & Physiol Astron Genetics Robotics Law Psych Philos Theol Ceramics Film Photog Acting Theater_Arts Chorus Dance Journ Public_Speak. **Supp**—Rev Tut. **Sports**—Basket X-country Soccer Swim Tennis Track. B: Baseball Football Golf. G: Cheer Volley. Activities: 36. **Selective adm:** 176/yr. Appl fee: $100. Appl due: Rolling. **Enr 787.** Avg class size: 20. Uniform. **Fac 109.** M 22/F 87. FT 109. Wh 92%. Latino 7%. Blk 1%. Adv deg: 31%. **Grad '07—37.** Col—36. (GA Inst of Tech 5, GA St 5, U of GA 2, Emory 2, Harvard 1, US Air Force Acad 1). **Mid 50% SAT:** CR 540-640. M 480-630. W 520-

660. Mid 50% ACT: 26-30. **Tui '12-'13:** Day $16,543-18,671. Aid: Need ($2,500,000). **Est 1996.** Nonprofit. Roman Catholic. Sem (Aug-May). **Assoc** SACS. Holy Spirit Prep's hands-on preschool program, which commences at age 2 and operates near the upper school on Northside Drive, employs multisensory activities and weekly, age-specific thematic units. The lower school program on Long Island Drive (grades K-8) includes music and drama classes, as well as a comprehensive program in the visual arts. The junior high curriculum (grades 7 and 8) features the interdisciplinary Lyceum program, which consists of introductory modules in Latin, Greek, art and philosophy. High school students (grades 9-12) choose from honors, Advanced Placement, college-level and college courses. Compulsory community service begins in grade 7, with service hour requirements increasing annually through senior year.

HORIZONS SCHOOL   **Bdg Coed Gr 8-12**
Atlanta, GA 30307. 1900 DeKalb Ave NE.   **Day Coed K-12**
Tel: 404-378-2219. Fax: 404-378-8946.
www.horizonsschool.com   E-mail: horizonsschool@horizonsschool.com
    Les Garber, Admin (1978). BA, Emory Univ, MEd, Georgia State Univ.

    Col Prep. AP—Eng Calc US_Hist. **Feat**—Fr Ger Japan Span Studio_Art Drama Music Bus. **Supp**—Dev_Read ESL Makeup Rem_Math Rem_Read Tut. **Comp:** Comp/Stud: 1:3. Outdoor Ed. **Dual enr:** GA Perimeter, GA St. **Sports**—Basket Soccer Volley. Activities: 3. **Selective adm:** 30/yr. Bdg 5. Day 25. Appl fee: $50. Appl due: Rolling. Accepted: 70%. Yield: 95%. **Enr 122.** B 63. G 59. Bdg 8. Day 114. Elem 48. Sec 74. Wh 35%. Latino 5%. Blk 52%. Asian 8%. Intl 28%. Avg class size: 14. **Fac 18.** M 4/F 14. FT 13/PT 5. Wh 62%. Blk 38%. Adv deg: 22%. In Dorms 4. **Grad '11—13.** Col—12. **Avg SAT:** CR/M 1125. **Col Couns:** 3. Alum donors: 2%. **Tui '10-'11:** Bdg $26,500 (+$450). Day $12,500 (+$250). Intl Bdg $26,500 (+$3500). Aid: Need 30 ($90,000). Work prgm 38 ($30,400). **Est 1978.** Nonprofit. Sem (Aug-May). In Horizons' elementary division (grades K-5), teachers employ different approaches to suit individual learning styles. The transitional middle school program (grades 6 and 7) combines course work in the fundamentals with instruction in research, note-taking, communicational and study skills. Geared primarily toward college preparation, the high school (grades 8-12) encourages active participation and offers flexible scheduling and opportunities for special academic credit. A three-week short term in the fall provides a break from regular classes and enables students to engage in seminars pertaining to such subjects as finance, art and philosophy.

MOUNT VERNON PRESBYTERIAN SCHOOL   **Day Coed Gr PS (Age 2)-12**
Atlanta, GA 30328. 471 Mt Vernon Hwy NE.
Tel: 404-252-3448. Fax: 404-252-7154.
Other locations: 510 Mt Vernon Hwy NE, Atlanta 30328.
www.mountvernonschool.org   E-mail: chouston@mountvernonschool.org
    J. Brett Jacobsen, Head (2009). BA, Texas Tech Univ, MEd, Univ of Houston, EdD, Baylor Univ. Kirsten Beard, Adm.

    Col Prep. AP—Eng Fr Span Calc Bio Chem Environ_Sci Physics US_Hist Studio_Art. **Feat**—British_Lit Creative_Writing Chin Lat Stats Sports_Med Govt Ethics Drama Band Chorus Debate Journ Public_Speak. **Supp**—Tut. **Comp:** Laptop prgm Gr 9-12. **Sports**—Basket X-country Golf Soccer Swim Tennis Track. B: Baseball Football Weightlifting Wrestling. G: Volley. Activities: 22. **Selective adm (Gr PS-11):** 144/yr. Appl fee: $100. Appl due: Feb. Accepted: 75%. **Tests** IQ SSAT. **Enr 740.** Nonwhite 12%. Avg class size: 16. Stud/fac: 10:1. Uniform. **Fac 96.** M 18/F 78. FT 77/PT 19. Adv deg: 38%. **Grad '11—52.** Col—52. (U of GA 6, U of AL-Tuscaloosa 5, GA Inst of Tech 4, Auburn 3, Col of Charleston 2, Auburn 2). **Tui '12-'13:** Day $11,925-16,925 (+$0-750). Aid: Need 155. **Est 1972.** Nonprofit. Presbyterian. Sem (Aug-May). **Assoc** SACS. The school's curriculum for children age 3 through kindergarten balances readiness skills in language arts and math with course work in science, social studies, art, music and foreign language. The lower school (grades 1-5) emphasizes the mastery of basic skills in a small-class environment, while the middle school (grades 6-8) combines continued study in the core subjects with exploratory classes and the choice of study hall or an elective. Students in the upper school (grades 9-12) choose from a varied selection of AP courses and electives. Pupils in grades 7-12 attend classes at 510 Mt. Vernon Highway Northeast.

ST. MARTIN'S EPISCOPAL SCHOOL   Day Coed Gr PS (Age 3)-8
Atlanta, GA 30319. 3110-A Ashford Dunwoody Rd NE.
Tel: 404-237-4260. Fax: 404-237-9311.
www.stmartinschool.org   E-mail: bmarsau@stmartinschool.org
Rev. James E. Hamner IV, Head (2004). BA, Washington and Lee Univ, MDiv, Univ of the South, MPhil, PhD, Oxford Univ (England). Blythe Marsau, Adm.

Pre-Prep. Feat—Fr Span Computers Relig Studio_Art Drama Music Public_Speak. **Supp**—Dev_Read Rev Tut. **Sports**—Basket X-country Golf Soccer Tennis Track. B: Baseball. G: Volley. **Selective adm:** 101/yr. Appl fee: $75. Appl due: Feb. **Tests** IQ SSAT. **Enr 575.** Nonwhite 8%. Uniform. **Fac 72.** M 10/F 62. FT 55/PT 17. Adv deg: 41%. **Grad '09—42.** Prep—34. **Tui '12-'13:** Day $14,900-16,500 (+$900-950). Aid: Need ($300,000). **Est 1959.** Nonprofit. Episcopal (31% practice). Sem (Aug-May). **Assoc** SACS. St. Martin's supplements its core curriculum with computer, religion, art, speech and drama, and music classes. In addition, French and Spanish instruction begins in prekindergarten. Advanced math grouping is available in grades 7 and 8.

ST. PIUS X CATHOLIC HIGH SCHOOL   Day Coed Gr 9-12
Atlanta, GA 30345. 2674 Johnson Rd NE.
Tel: 404-636-3023. Fax: 404-633-8387.
www.spx.org   E-mail: mfree@spx.org
Stephen W. Spellman, Prin (2000). EdS, Univ of Georgia. Charles L. Byrd, Adm.

Col Prep. AP (exams req'd; 635 taken)—Eng Fr Span Calc Stats Comp_Sci Bio Chem Physics Eur_Hist US_Hist World_Hist Comp_Govt & Pol Econ Psych US_Govt & Pol Studio_Art. **Feat**—British_Lit Lat Anat & Physiol Marine_Bio/Sci Holocaust Sociol Bus_Law Comp_Relig Band Music_Theory Guitar Dance Accounting Journ. **Supp**—Tut. **Sports**—Basket X-country Golf Lacrosse Soccer Swim Tennis Track. B: Baseball Football Wrestling. G: Cheer Softball Volley. Activities: 25. **Selective adm (Gr 9-11):** 290/yr. Appl fee: $100. Appl due: Feb. Accepted: 60%. **Tests** CEEB SSAT. **Enr 1100.** Wh 79%. Latino 6%. Blk 10%. Asian 2%. Other 3%. Avg class size: 20. Stud/fac: 12:1. Uniform. **Fac 95.** M 44/F 51. Wh 90%. Latino 5%. Blk 5%. Adv deg: 64%. **Grad '11—261.** Col—260. **Avg SAT:** CR/M 1200. **Col Couns:** 5. **Tui '12-'13:** Day $11,430 (+$650-850). Aid: Merit 36 ($45,650). Need 22 ($141,750). Work prgm 147 ($483,174). **Est 1958.** Nonprofit. Roman Catholic (85% practice). Sem (Aug-June). **Assoc** SACS. St. Pius complements its core curriculum with extensive offerings in the fine arts, computer, journalism and business. Academic departments generally offer courses at three levels: Advanced Placement, honors and college preparatory. Each student must complete five two-hour projects annually as part of the theology curriculum.

TRINITY SCHOOL   Day Coed Gr PS (Age 3)-6
Atlanta, GA 30327. 4301 Northside Pky NW.
Tel: 404-231-8100. Fax: 404-231-8111.
www.trinityatl.org   E-mail: kwatts@trinityatl.org
Stephen G. Kennedy, Head (2002). BA, MA, Univ of Tulsa. Kristin Watts, Adm.

Pre-Prep. Feat—Environ_Sci Computers Music Outdoor_Ed. **Supp**—Dev_Read. **Comp:** Comp/Stud: 1:1.7 (1:1 Laptop prgm Gr 5-6). **Selective adm:** 123/yr. Appl fee: $75. Appl due: Jan. **Tests** SSAT. **Enr 627.** Wh 80%. Latino 2%. Blk 8%. Asian 5%. Other 5%. Avg class size: 18. Stud/fac: 6:1. Uniform. **Fac 103.** Wh 91%. Latino 1%. Blk 6%. Asian 1%. Other 1%. Adv deg: 54%. **Grad '11—39.** Prep—39. **Tui '12-'13:** Day $19,750. **Est 1951.** Nonprofit. Sem (Aug-May). **Assoc** SACS. Trinity's developmental academic program emphasizes reading, writing, math and science, and it is enhanced by a fine arts program. The school's world language program, which commences at age 4, enables children to gain an introduction to one or more of approximately two dozen languages.

AQUINAS HIGH SCHOOL   Day Coed Gr 9-12
Augusta, GA 30904. 1920 Highland Ave.
Tel: 706-736-5516. Fax: 706-736-2678.
www.aquinashigh.org E-mail: aquinas@aquinashigh.org
    Chris Paul, Prin (2009). BS, Kent State Univ, MEd, Cleveland State Univ, MA, Ashland Univ.
    Col Prep. AP—Eng Calc Eur_Hist US_Hist Econ. **Feat**—Fr Lat Span Horticulture. **Supp**—LD Tut. **Sports**—Basket Golf Soccer Swim Tennis Track. B: Baseball Football. G: Cheer Softball Volley. **Somewhat selective adm:** 110/yr. Appl fee: $20. Appl due: Rolling. Accepted: 95%. Tests HSPT. **Enr 320.** Avg class size: 19. **Fac 24.** M 11/F 13. FT 20/PT 4. Adv deg: 41%. **Grad '11—65.** Col—65. (Augusta St 14, GA Southern 9, U of SC 6, U of GA 4, U of SC-Aiken 4, Savannah Col of Art & Design 2). **Avg SAT:** CR/M/W 1626. **Col Couns:** 1. **Tui '09-'10:** Day $8250 (+$475). Parishioners $6650 (+$475). Aid: Need ($269,000). **Est 1957.** Nonprofit. Roman Catholic. Sem (Aug-May). **Assoc** SACS. AHS opened following the merger of Boy's Catholic High School, operated by the Marist Brothers under the Diocese of Savannah, and Mt. St. Joseph's Academy, owned and operated by the Sisters of St. Joseph of Carondelet. The curriculum includes an honors program and Advanced Placement courses.

EPISCOPAL DAY SCHOOL   Day Coed Gr PS (Age 3)-8
Augusta, GA 30904. 2248 Walton Way.
Tel: 706-733-1192. Fax: 706-733-1388.
www.edsaugusta.com E-mail: klilly@edsaugusta.com
    Ned R. Murray, Head (2003). BA, Univ of the South, MEd, Univ of Tennessee-Chattanooga. Karen B. Lilly, Adm.
    Pre-Prep. Gen Acad. Feat—Span Computers Relig Studio_Art Music. **Supp**—Dev_Read Rem_Math Rem_Read Rev Tut. **Sports**—Basket X-country Golf Soccer Swim Tennis. B: Baseball Football. G: Cheer Volley. **Somewhat selective adm:** 52/yr. Appl fee: $75. Appl due: Rolling. Accepted: 90%. Tests CEEB. **Enr 450.** B 244. G 206. Wh 91%. Latino 1%. Blk 7%. Asian 1%. Avg class size: 16. Uniform. **Fac 70.** M 7/F 63. FT 58/PT 12. Wh 93%. Latino 3%. Blk 3%. Asian 1%. Adv deg: 21%. **Grad '11—36.** Prep—15. (Augusta Prep 10, Aquinas HS 3, Westminster Schs of Augusta 1, St Andrew's Sch-DE 1). **Tui '12-'13:** Day $10,950-11,050 (+$325). Aid: Merit 1 ($500). Need 61 ($229,718). **Est 1944.** Nonprofit. Episcopal (33% practice). Quar (Aug-May). **Assoc** SACS. Students at the school receive mathematics enrichment beginning in grade 1. Instruction in music, art, computer, religion and research skills is available at all grade levels. Pupils in grades 6-8 satisfy a 15-hour community service requirement each year.

WESTMINSTER SCHOOLS OF AUGUSTA   Day Coed Gr PS (Age 4)-12
Augusta, GA 30909. 3067 Wheeler Rd.
Tel: 706-731-5260. Fax: 706-731-7786.
www.wsa.net E-mail: info@wsa.net
    Stephen D. O'Neil, Head (2008). BA, Wheaton College (IL), MA, Univ of Colorado-Boulder. Aimee Lynch, Adm.
    Col Prep. AP (exams req'd; 152 taken, 75% 3+)—Eng Fr Lat Span Calc Stats Bio Chem Environ_Sci Eur_Hist US_Hist US_Govt & Pol Studio_Art. **Feat**—Greek Comp_Sci Econ Govt Psych Bible Drama Music Debate. **Supp**—Rev Tut. Outdoor Ed. **Sports**—Basket X-country Soccer Swim Tennis Track. B: Baseball Football Golf. G: Cheer Softball. Activities: 37. **Somewhat selective adm:** 100/yr. Appl fee: $75. Appl due: Rolling. Accepted: 94%. Yield: 82%. **Tests CTP_4. Enr 598.** B 305. G 293. Elem 423. Sec 175. Wh 90%. Blk 5%. Asian 2%.

Other 3%. Avg class size: 18. **Fac 52.** M 17/F 35. FT 50/PT 2. Wh 100%. Adv deg: 51%. **Grad '11—34.** Col—34. (GA Col & State U 5, GA Southern 4, U of GA 3, Col of Charleston 3, GA Inst of Tech 2, Wofford 2). **Avg SAT:** CR 602. M 583. W 612. **Mid 50% SAT:** CR 530-630. M 550-640. W 560-660. Avg ACT: 25.3. **Col Couns:** 1. Alum donors: 10%. **Tui '12-'13:** Day $8500-12,200 (+$375). Aid: Merit 2 ($17,500). Need 150 ($650,000). **Est 1972.** Nonprofit. Nondenom Christian. Sem (Aug-May). **Assoc** SACS. WSA is comprised of three divisions: Westminster Lower School (grades pre-K-5), Westminster Middle School (grades 6-8) and Westminster Upper School (grades 9-12). The curriculum is based on a Christian worldview at all grade levels. Lower School children develop a foundation in the basic content areas and take cocurricular classes in music, library, art and physical education. The transitional Middle School program features increasing student independence in organizational and learning strategies. A broad selection of Advanced Placement courses enhances the Upper School curriculum.

OAK MOUNTAIN ACADEMY   Day Coed Gr PS (Age 4)-12
Carrollton, GA 30116. 222 Cross Plains Rd.
Tel: 770-834-6651. Fax: 770-834-6785.
www.oakmountain.us   E-mail: admissions@oakmountain.us
    Paula J. Gillispie, Head (2010). BS, Univ of Arkansas-Fayetteville, MEd, George Washington Univ. Rhyne Owenby, Adm.
    Col Prep. AP (exams req'd; 52 taken, 50% 3+)—Eng Calc Bio Chem US_Hist. **Feat**—Lat Span Forensic_Sci Comp_Sci Econ Govt Bible Studio_Art Drama Musical_Theater Chorus Music. **Supp**—Rev Tut. **Comp:** Comp/Stud: 1:2. **Dual enr:** U of W GA. **Sports**—Basket X-country Golf Soccer Swim Tennis Track. B: Baseball. G: Cheer Softball Volley. Activities: 17. **Selective adm:** 40/yr. Appl fee: $75. Appl due: Rolling. Accepted: 84%. Yield: 70%. **Tests** CTP_4. **Enr 184.** B 90. G 94. Elem 123. Sec 61. Wh 80%. Latino 1%. Blk 4%. Asian 4%. Other 11%. Avg class size: 10. Stud/fac: 7:1. **Fac 29.** M 7/F 22. FT 23/PT 6. Wh 94%. Latino 3%. Blk 3%. Adv deg: 62%. **Grad '11—15.** Col—15. (U of GA 3, Auburn 3, U of W GA 2, Mercer U 2, St John's U-NY 1, Shorter 1). **Avg SAT:** CR 566. M 573. W 542. Avg ACT: 27. **Col Couns:** 1. **Tui '11-'12:** Day $6500-11,925 (+$350). Aid: Need 22 ($62,000). **Est 1962.** Nonprofit. Nondenom Christian. Tri (Aug-May). **Assoc** SACS. This nondenominational Christian school offers a variety of AP courses and electives. OMA works with advanced students desiring college credits through a cooperative program with the University of West Georgia. Boys and girls in grades 9-12 satisfy a 15-hour annual community service requirement. All seniors complete an independent project consisting of five phases: research, paper, product, presentation and internship.

LANDMARK CHRISTIAN SCHOOL   Day Coed Gr PS (Age 4)-12
Fairburn, GA 30213. 50 SE Broad St.
Tel: 770-306-0647, 877-834-6644. Fax: 770-969-6551.
Other locations: 777 Robinson Rd, Peachtree City 30269.
www.landmarkchristianschool.org   E-mail: admissions@landmark-cs.org
    Leanne Messer, Int Head (2011). BS, Texas Wesleyan College, MA, Univ of New Mexico, JD, Georgia College and State Univ. Tammy McCurry, Adm.
    Col Prep. AP (exams req'd; 102 taken)—Eng Span Calc Bio Chem Physics US_Hist World_Hist US_Govt & Pol Studio_Art. **Feat**—Comp_Sci Bible Drawing Fine_Arts Photog Theater. **Supp**—Tut. **Dual enr:** Truett-McConnell. **Sports**—Basket X-country Golf Soccer Swim Tennis Track Volley. B: Football Wrestling. G: Cheer Softball. Activities: 20. **Selective adm:** 121/yr. Appl fee: $100. Appl due: Rolling. Accepted: 56%. Yield: 92%. **Enr 807.** B 416. G 391. Elem 583. Sec 224. Wh 74%. Latino 1%. Blk 24%. Asian 1%. Avg class size: 17. Uniform. **Fac 72.** M 18/F 54. FT 72. Wh 99%. Blk 1%. Adv deg: 31%. **Grad '11—51.** Col—51. (Mercer U 5, Samford 4, Kennesaw St 4, Auburn 3, U of W GA 3, GA Southern 3). **Avg SAT:** CR 542. M 555. W 534. Avg ACT: 23. **Col Couns:** 2. **Tui '12-'13:** Day $6875-13,500 (+$100-400). **Est 1989.** Nonprofit. Nondenom Christian. Quar (Aug-May). **Assoc** SACS. A nonde-

nominational school that operates according to a Christian worldview, Landmark provides a comprehensive elementary and secondary program for college-bound students. In addition to the main, 62-acre campus in Fairburn, the school offers a second elementary school option (grades PS-5) at an 18-acre site in Peachtree City.

VALWOOD SCHOOL   **Day Coed Gr PS (Age 3)-12**
Hahira, GA 31632. 4380 Old US Hwy 41 N.
Tel: 229-242-8491. Fax: 229-245-7894.
www.valwood.org   E-mail: info@valwood.org
     Darren J. Pascavage, Head (2011). BA, Georgia Institute of Technology, MEd, Univ of Georgia, PhD, Georgia State Univ. Ginger Holley, Adm.
     Col Prep. AP (exams req'd; 69 taken, 61% 3+)—Eng Fr Span Calc Bio Chem Environ_Sci Physics US_Hist World_Hist Studio_Art. **Feat**—Anat & Physiol Comp_Sci Psych Govt/Econ Drama Chorus Speech. **Sports**—Basket X-country Soccer Track. B: Baseball Football Golf Wrestling. G: Cheer Softball Tennis. **Somewhat selective adm:** 98/yr. Appl fee: $50. Appl due: Rolling. Accepted: 85%. **Tests** CEEB IQ Stanford. **Enr 394.** B 207. G 187. Elem 280. Sec 114. Avg class size: 18. Stud/fac: 9:1. **Fac 44.** M 9/F 35. FT 36/PT 8. Adv deg: 34%. **Grad '03—18.** Col—18. **Mid 50% SAT:** CR 510-650. M 470-600. W 480-620. Mid 50% ACT: 23-30. **Col Couns:** 2. **Tui '03-'04:** Day $6500 (+$250). **Est 1968.** Nonprofit. Quar (Aug-May). **Assoc** SACS. Valwood's curriculum focuses on the core academic skills necessary for college success. In addition to the academic program, which features an array of Advanced Placement and enrichment courses, the school provides students with opportunities in athletics and the arts.

NORTH COBB CHRISTIAN SCHOOL   **Day Coed Gr PS (Age 3)-12**
Kennesaw, GA 30144. 4500 Lakeview Dr.
Tel: 770-975-0252. Fax: 770-975-9051.
www.ncchristian.org   E-mail: bwright@ncchristian.org
     Todd Clingman, Head (2007). BS, Liberty Univ, MA, Florida Atlantic Univ. Beth Wright, Adm.
     Col Prep. AP (exams req'd)—Eng Calc Comp_Sci Eur_Hist US_Hist Comp_Govt & Pol Econ US_Govt & Pol. **Feat**—Fr Span Stats Anat & Physiol Environ_Sci Web_Design Anthro Law Psych Bible Graphic_Arts Studio_Art Theater Band Chorus Orchestra Speech. **Supp**—LD Tut. **Sports**—Basket X-country Golf Soccer Swim Tennis Track Volley. B: Baseball. G: Cheer Softball. Activities: 7. **Somewhat selective adm:** 178/yr. Appl fee: $100. Appl due: Rolling. Accepted: 85%. Yield: 89%. **Tests** Stanford. **Enr 779.** Elem 531. Sec 248. Avg class size: 21. Uniform. **Fac 68.** M 19/F 49. FT 63/PT 5. Adv deg: 50%. **Grad '11—73.** Col—73. **Avg SAT:** CR 567. M 561. W 558. **Tui '12-'13:** Day $5705-11,545 (+$305-785). **Est 1983.** Nonprofit. Nondenom Christian. Sem (Aug-May). **Assoc** SACS. Honors and Advanced Placement courses, Bible classes and an extensive fine arts department are noteworthy features of this Christian school's program. High school students follow a modified block schedule in which classes meet every other day for 90 minutes. In addition to meeting graduation requirements in various subject areas, upper school pupils accumulate 46 hours of mandatory community service during their four years.

LaGRANGE ACADEMY   **Day Coed Gr K-12**
LaGrange, GA 30240. 1501 Vernon Rd.
Tel: 706-882-8097. Fax: 706-882-8640.
www.lagrangeacademy.org   E-mail: lagrangeacademy@lagrangeacademy.org
     Matt Walsh, Head (2006). BS, Georgetown Univ, MA, Middlebury College. Amanda Smallwood, Adm.
     Col Prep. AP (exams req'd; 44 taken, 52% 3+)—Eng Span Calc Bio Chem US_Hist. **Feat**—Lat Forensic_Sci Comp_Sci Art_Hist Drama Chorus Music_Theory Health. **Supp**—

Rev Tut. **Dual enr:** LaGrange, Auburn, Faulkner U. **Sports**—Basket Golf Soccer Tennis. B: Baseball. G: Softball Volley. Activities: 12. **Selective adm (Gr K-10):** 21/yr. Appl fee: $50. Appl due: Rolling. **Tests** CEEB CTP_4 IQ Stanford. **Enr 198.** Bdg 86. Day 112. Elem 123. Sec 75. Wh 78%. Latino 2%. Blk 7%. Native Am 1%. Asian 9%. Other 3%. Intl 10%. Avg class size: 15. Stud/fac: 8:1. **Fac 26.** M 5/F 21. FT 21/PT 5. Wh 96%. Latino 4%. Adv deg: 53%. **Grad '10—15.** Col—15. (Anderson U 2, LaGrange 1, Emory 1, Mercer U 1, Berry 1, Auburn 1). **Avg SAT:** CR 510. M 516. W 523. **Tui '11-'12:** Day $5955-8486 (+$1500). Aid: Merit 14 ($41,800). Need 33 ($128,834). **Est 1970.** Nonprofit. Quar (Aug-May). **Assoc** SACS. The traditional academic curriculum is supplemented by Spanish, Latin, choir, drama, forensics and computer programming. Juniors and seniors in good standing may pursue dual enrollment at three local colleges. Each semester, students satisfy the following community service requirements: eight hours in grade 9, 10 hours in grade 10, and 15 hours in grades 11 and 12.

WHITEFIELD ACADEMY   **Day Coed Gr PS (Age 4)-12**
Mableton, GA 30126. 1 Whitefield Dr SE.
Tel: 678-305-3000. Fax: 678-305-3010.
www.whitefieldacademy.com   E-mail: lindas@whitefieldacademy.com
     John H. Lindsell, Head (2008). AB, Wheaton College (IL), MTS, Gordon-Conwell Theological Seminary, MEd, EdD, Harvard Univ. Linda Simpson, Adm.
     Col Prep. AP (exams req'd)—Eng Fr Span Calc Stats Comp_Sci Bio Chem Physics Eur_Hist US_Hist Studio_Art. **Feat**—Lat Fine_Arts Theater Public_Speak. **Supp**—Tut. **Sports**—Basket X-country Golf Soccer Swim Tennis Track. B: Baseball Football Wrestling. G: Cheer Softball Volley. Activities: 25. **Selective adm:** 114/yr. Appl fee: $65. Appl due: Feb. **Tests** SSAT. **Enr 654.** Nonwhite 24%. Avg class size: 17. Stud/fac: 8:1. Uniform. **Fac 76.** M 19/F 57. FT 73/PT 3. Wh 86%. Latino 3%. Blk 8%. Asian 3%. Adv deg: 40%. **Grad '11—67.** Col—67. **Mid 50% SAT:** CR 500-640. M 540-650. W 510-650. **Col Couns:** 1. **Tui '12-'13:** Day $14,480-19,410 (+$800-900). **Est 1996.** Nonprofit. Nondenom Christian (100% practice). Sem (Aug-May). **Assoc** SACS. This Christ-centered preparatory school provides honors and AP courses, as well as classes in the visual arts, drama and music. Juniors and seniors take a life and career planning course.

FIRST PRESBYTERIAN DAY SCHOOL   **Day Coed Gr PS (Age 3)-12**
Macon, GA 31210. 5671 Calvin Dr.
Tel: 478-477-6505. Fax: 478-477-2804.
Other locations: 682 Mulberry St, Macon 31201.
www.fpdmacon.org   E-mail: cheri.frame@fpdmacon.org
     Gregg Thompson, Head (1997). BS, Wheaton College (IL), MEd, Reformed Theological Seminary. Cheri Frame, Adm.
     Col Prep. AP (exams req'd; 255 taken, 64% 3+)—Eng Fr Lat Span Calc Bio Physics Eur_Hist US_Hist US_Govt & Pol Studio_Art. **Feat**—British_Lit Environ_Sci Comp_Sci Web_Design Econ Govt Bible Comp_Relig Drama Band Chorus Dance Accounting Journ Public_Speak. **Supp**—LD Tut. **Comp:** Comp/Stud: 1:3.3. **Sports**—X-country Soccer Swim Tennis Track. B: Baseball Football Golf Wrestling. G: Cheer Softball. **Somewhat selective adm:** 136/yr. Appl fee: $60. Appl due: Jan. Accepted: 94%. **Tests** CTP_4. **Enr 972.** Elem 632. Sec 340. Wh 93%. Latino 1%. Blk 5%. Asian 1%. Avg class size: 20. Stud/fac: 16:1. Uniform. **Fac 92.** M 30/F 62. FT 86/PT 6. Wh 97%. Latino 1%. Blk 1%. Asian 1%. Adv deg: 67%. **Grad '11—78.** Col—78. **Avg SAT:** CR 600. M 610. W 600. **Col Couns:** 1. **Tui '12-'13:** Day $11,250-12,100 (+$400). Aid: Merit 9 ($35,500). Need 198 ($329,600). **Est 1970.** Inc. Presbyterian (20% practice). Sem (Aug-May). **Assoc** SACS. In addition to fulfilling core academic requirements, elementary students at FPD enroll in arts classes each semester. High school pupils select from a full complement of honors and Advanced Placement courses. Boys and girls with diagnosed learning disabilities may take part in the school's learning assistance program. Students in grades 9-12 satisfy a 30-hour community service requirement each year.

A satellite elementary campus on Mulberry Street opened with prekindergarten programming in fall 2011.

MOUNT DE SALES ACADEMY   **Day Coed Gr 6-12**
Macon, GA 31201. 851 Orange St.
Tel: 478-751-3240. Fax: 478-751-3241.
www.mountdesales.net   E-mail: lcardwell@mountdesales.net
    David Held, Pres (2010). BA, Univ of the South, MEd, Univ of Tennessee-Chattanooga. Linda D. Cardwell, Adm.
    Col Prep. AP (exams req'd; 374 taken, 71% 3+)—Eng Span Calc Stats Comp_Sci Bio Chem Eur_Hist US_Hist World_Hist Psych US_Govt & Pol Studio_Art. **Feat**—British_Lit Fr Lat Anat & Physiol Astron Civil_War Econ Govt African-Amer_Stud Women's_Stud Comp_ Relig Philos Fine_Arts Theater_Arts Chorus Music Debate Journ Speech. **Supp**—Tut. **Comp:** Comp/Stud: 1:4. **Dual enr:** Macon St, Mercer U. **Sports**—Basket X-country Golf Soccer Swim Tennis Track. B: Baseball Football Wrestling. G: Cheer Softball Volley. **Selective adm:** 133/yr. Appl fee: $50. Appl due: Mar. Accepted: 81%. Yield: 72%. **Tests** Stanford. **Enr 658.** B 306. G 352. Elem 225. Sec 433. Wh 65%. Latino 5%. Blk 23%. Asian 3%. Other 4%. Avg class size: 20. Uniform. **Fac 70.** M 37/F 33. FT 70. Wh 96%. Blk 4%. Adv deg: 31%. **Grad '11—101.** Col—101. **Col Couns:** 3. Alum donors: 4%. **Tui '12-'13:** Day $10,515-10,645 (+$100). Aid: Merit 30 ($122,000). Need 191 ($813,771). **Est 1876.** Nonprofit. Roman Catholic (51% practice). Sem (Aug-May). **Assoc** SACS. This Catholic school is ecumenical in nature, enrolling students of other faiths and of diverse racial and economic backgrounds. An exploratory language course in grade 6 introduces elements of Spanish, French, Latin, Italian, German, and Japanese, and students choose either French or Spanish in grade 7. Religious education includes required courses in middle school and electives in the upper school. Students in grades 9-12 perform 20 hours of compulsory community service each year.

STRATFORD ACADEMY   **Day Coed Gr PS (Age 4)-12**
Macon, GA 31220. 6010 Peake Rd.
Tel: 478-477-8073. Fax: 478-477-0299.
www.stratford.org   E-mail: johnpaul.gaddy@stratford.org
    Robert Veto, Head (2008). BA, MA, Univ of North Carolina-Chapel Hill, PhD, Carnegie Mellon Univ. John Paul Gaddy, Adm.
    Col Prep. AP (exams req'd; 257 taken, 73% 3+)—Eng Fr Lat Span Calc Stats Comp_Sci Bio Chem Eur_Hist US_Hist Econ Human_Geog US_Govt & Pol Studio_Art Music_Theory. **Feat**—Humanities Greek Anat & Physiol Environ_Sci Genetics Web_Design Holocaust Comp_Relig Art_Hist Drawing Graphic_Arts Photog Video_Production Acting Theater. **Supp**—Dev_Read ESL Rem_Math Rem_Read Rev Tut. **Sports**—Basket X-country Soccer Swim Tennis Track. B: Baseball Football Golf Wrestling. G: Cheer Softball. Activities: 23. **Selective adm:** 130/yr. Appl fee: $50. Appl due: Rolling. Accepted: 84%. Yield: 83%. **Tests** CTP_4. **Enr 935.** Wh 92%. Latino 1%. Blk 2%. Asian 4%. Other 1%. Uniform. **Fac 135.** M 35/F 100. FT 115/PT 20. Wh 95%. Latino 3%. Blk 2%. **Grad '09—72.** Col—72. (U of GA 24, Auburn 9, GA Inst of Tech 5). **Col Couns:** 2. **Tui '12-'13:** Day $8115-12,516 (+$100). Aid: Need 120 ($588,000). **Est 1960.** Nonprofit. Sem (Aug-May). **Assoc** SACS. Stratford's curriculum includes an array of Advanced Placement classes, as well as courses in instrumental and choral music, drama and physical education.

TATTNALL SQUARE ACADEMY   **Day Coed Gr PS (Age 3)-12**
Macon, GA 31210. 111 Trojan Trail.
Tel: 478-477-6760. Fax: 478-474-7887.
www.tattnall.org   E-mail: admissions@tattnall.org
    Michael Drake, Head. BA, Univ of Virginia, MEd, Vanderbilt Univ, EdD, Tennessee State Univ. Lynne Adams, Adm.

Col Prep. AP—Eng Calc Stats Bio US_Hist US_Govt & Pol Studio_Art. **Feat**—Fr Lat Span Anat & Physiol Environ_Sci Sports_Med Programming Econ Bible Ethics Journ. **Supp**—ESL Tut. **Sports**—Basket X-country Soccer Swim Tennis Track. B: Baseball Football Golf Wrestling. G: Cheer Softball. **Selective adm:** 102/yr. Appl fee: $50. Appl due: Rolling. Accepted: 82%. **Enr 700.** B 350. G 350. Wh 98%. Blk 1%. Asian 1%. Avg class size: 15. Stud/fac: 12:1. Uniform. **Fac 77.** M 18/F 59. FT 64/PT 13. Adv deg: 55%. **Grad '09—72.** Col—72. **Avg SAT:** CR/M/W 1560. **Col Couns:** 1. **Tui '12-'13:** Day $5157-10,632 (+$630). **Est 1968.** Nonprofit. Nondenom Christian. Quar (Aug-May). **Assoc** SACS. Tattnall provides a structured curriculum in a Christian atmosphere. In the elementary grades, emphasis is placed on acquiring proficiency in language and numerical skills. High school students are offered a traditional college preparatory program, as well as an AP program and courses in the fine arts and computer programming. Boys and girls in grades 9-12 perform 20 hours of required community service annually.

THE WALKER SCHOOL   Day Coed Gr PS (Age 4)-12
Marietta, GA 30062. 700 Cobb Pky N.
Tel: 770-427-2689. Fax: 770-514-8122.
www.thewalkerschool.org   E-mail: patty.mozley@thewalkerschool.org
   Jack Hall, Head (2011). BA, Davidson College, MS, Georgia State Univ, MA, Columbia Univ. Patricia H. Mozley, Adm.

   Col Prep. AP (exams req'd; 448 taken, 77% 3+)—Eng Fr Ger Lat Span Calc Stats Comp_ Sci Bio Chem Physics Eur_Hist US_Hist World_Hist Comp_Govt & Pol Econ US_Govt & Pol Studio_Art Music_Theory. **Feat**—Anat Astron Botany Forensic_Sci Genetics Oceanog Zoology Epidemiology Film Painting Sculpt Drama Directing Chorus Music Dance Finance Study_Skills. **Supp**—Tut. **Comp:** Comp/Stud: 1:3. **Sports**—Basket X-country Golf Soccer Swim Tennis Track. B: Baseball Football Wrestling. G: Cheer Softball Volley. Activities: 25. **Selective adm:** 179/yr. Appl fee: $75. Appl due: Feb. Accepted: 76%. Yield: 67%. **Tests** IQ SSAT Stanford. **Enr 1049.** B 530. G 519. Elem 669. Sec 380. Wh 79%. Latino 2%. Blk 5%. Asian 9%. Other 5%. Avg class size: 14. Stud/fac: 12:1. **Fac 135.** M 38/F 97. FT 107/PT 28. Wh 88%. Latino 4%. Blk 5%. Other 3%. Adv deg: 53%. **Grad '11—102.** Col—102. **Mid 50% SAT:** CR 540-655. M 540-680. W 530-650. Mid 50% ACT: 23-30. **Col Couns:** 2. Alum donors: 3%. **Tui '11-'12:** Day $14,525-17,950 (+$150-650). Aid: Need 150 ($800,000). **Est 1957.** Nonprofit. Sem (Aug-May). **Assoc** SACS. In Walker's prekindergarten for four-year-olds, children develop motor skills, visual perception and social skills while also working toward reading and math readiness. Foreign languages, drama, art, computer, library skills and music supplement basic academic subjects in the lower school (grades 1-5); middle school students (grades 6-8) take exploratory art, music, drama, computer and foreign language courses, in addition to work in the core subjects; and upper schoolers choose from Advanced Placement classes in all disciplines.

GREATER ATLANTA CHRISTIAN SCHOOL   Day Coed Gr PS (Age 3)-12
Norcross, GA 30093. 1575 Indian Trail Rd.
Tel: 770-243-2274. Fax: 770-243-2213.
www.greateratlantachristian.org   E-mail: lclovis@greateratlantachristian.org
   David Fincher, Pres (1998). BA, Harding Univ, MAT, Georgia State Univ, EdD, PhD, Univ of Georgia. Jill Morris, Adm.

   Col Prep. AP (exams req'd; 398 taken, 80% 3+)—Eng Lat Calc Stats Comp_Sci Bio Chem Environ_Sci Physics Eur_Hist US_Hist World_Hist Econ Psych US_Govt & Pol Studio_Art Music_Theory. **Feat**—British_Lit Fr Span Anat & Physiol Sociol Bible Comp_ Relig Photog Drama Accounting Speech. **Comp:** Comp/Stud: 1:1 Laptop prgm Gr 6-12. Outdoor Ed. **Sports**—Basket X-country Golf Lacrosse Soccer Swim Tennis Track. B: Baseball Football Wrestling. G: Cheer Softball Volley. Activities: 20. **Somewhat selective adm:** 247/yr. Appl fee: $160. Appl due: Feb. Accepted: 87%. Yield: 67%. **Enr 1850.** B 932. G 918. Elem 1131. Sec 719. Wh 69%. Latino 3%. Blk 16%. Asian 9%. Other 3%. Avg class size: 15. Stud/

fac: 13:1. Uniform. **Fac 150.** M 57/F 93. FT 148/PT 2. Wh 92%. Latino 1%. Blk 7%. Adv deg: 63%. **Grad '10—151.** Col—151. (U of GA 32, GA Southern 11, U of AL-Tuscaloosa 8, GA Inst of Tech 7, Auburn 6, Lipscomb 6). **Avg SAT:** CR 576. M 588. W 566. Avg ACT: 26. **Tui '12-'13:** Day $13,010-15,490 (+$295-1050). Aid: Need 113 ($773,126). **Est 1961.** Nonprofit. Sem (Aug-May). **Assoc** SACS. Located on a 74-acre campus 10 miles northeast of Atlanta, GACS conducts daily Bible classes. Students may participate in service activities, retreats and mission trips. A one-to-one laptop program commences in grade 6. Honors and Advanced Placement courses are available in the upper grades.

HIGH MEADOWS SCHOOL   **Day Coed Gr PS (Age 3)-8**
Roswell, GA 30075. 1055 Willeo Rd.
Tel: 770-993-2940. Fax: 770-993-8331.
www.highmeadows.org   E-mail: info@highmeadows.org
     Jay Underwood, Head (2010). BA, Guilford College, MEd, Rutgers Univ. Laura Nicholson, Adm.
     Pre-Prep. Gen Acad. IB PYP. Feat—Span Environ_Sci Performing_Arts Visual_Arts Debate Outdoor_Ed Study_Skills. **Supp**—Tut. **Selective adm:** 115/yr. Appl fee: $100. Appl due: Feb. Accepted: 71%. Yield: 80%. **Enr 400.** B 198. G 202. Avg class size: 20. Stud/fac: 18:1. **Fac 52.** M 9/F 43. FT 44/PT 8. Wh 90%. Latino 8%. Blk 2%. Adv deg: 38%. **Grad '10—31.** Prep—14. **Tui '12-'13:** Day $12,160-16,030. Aid: Need ($15,000). **Est 1973.** Nonprofit. Tri (Aug-May). **Assoc** SACS. Following the International Baccalaureate Primary Years Program, High Meadows utilizes thematic units in arts, language, math, science, technology and social science classes. As early as kindergarten, children begin working on projects that involve teamwork and technology and further develop presentational, organizational, problem-solving and time-management skills. The school conducts a highly regarded outdoor education program that features archery, ropes courses, stargazing, white-water rafting and hiking in the Appalachian Mountains.

THE ST. FRANCIS SCHOOLS   **Day Coed Gr K-12**
Roswell, GA 30075. 9375 Willeo Rd.
Tel: 770-641-8257. Fax: 770-641-0283.
Other locations: 13440 Cogburn Rd, Alpharetta 30004.
www.stfranschool.com   E-mail: ebrown@stfranschool.com
     Drew Buccellato, Head (1981). BS, MA, Fordham Univ, MS, Pace Univ. Ellen V. Brown, Adm.
     Col Prep. AP (exams req'd)—Eng US_Hist US_Govt & Pol Studio_Art. **Feat**—British_ Lit Creative_Writing Lat Span Forensic_Sci Sports_Med Computers Civil_War Russ_Hist Econ Psych Drawing Painting Sculpt Drama Music Journ. **Supp**—Dev_Read Rem_Math Rem_Read Rev Tut. **Sports**—Basket X-country Golf Soccer Tennis Track Wrestling. B: Base-ball Football. G: Cheer Equestrian Softball Volley. **Selective adm:** 171/yr. Appl fee: $100. Appl due: Rolling. **Enr 700.** Elem 440. Sec 260. Wh 90%. Latino 2%. Blk 5%. Asian 3%. Avg class size: 12. Stud/fac: 8:1. Uniform. **Fac 110.** M 34/F 76. FT 110. Adv deg: 40%. **Grad '11—59.** Col—58. (Valdosta St 10, Berry 6, U of Miami 2, Auburn 2, GA St 2, Oglethorpe 2). **Col Couns:** 1. **Tui '12-'13:** Day $9900-17,600 (+$750). **Est 1976.** Nonprofit. Sem (Aug-June). **Assoc** SACS. St. Francis offers a comprehensive academic program that addresses the needs of students requiring a smaller teacher-pupil ratio than is available at most schools. Competitive athletics begin at the middle school level. The high school occupies a separate campus in Alpharetta.

FREDERICA ACADEMY   **Day Coed Gr PS (Age 4)-12**
St Simons Island, GA 31522. 200 Murray Way.
Tel: 912-638-9981. Fax: 912-638-1442.
www.fredericaacademy.org   E-mail: julieackerman@fredericaacademy.org

Greg Griffeth, Head (2011). BS, Univ of Georgia, MS, Vanderbilt Univ, MS, Columbia Univ. Julie Ackerman, Adm.

Col Prep. AP (exams req'd; 89 taken, 56% 3+)—Eng Span Calc Bio Physics US_Hist World_Hist. **Feat**—British_Lit Lat Astron Ecol Comp_Sci Econ Govt Psych Sociol Photog Studio_Art Chorus Debate. **Supp**—Tut. **Dual enr:** Coastal GA CC. **Sports**—Basket Crew X-country Golf Soccer Tennis. B: Baseball. G: Volley. Activities: 16. **Selective adm (Gr PS-11):** 72/yr. Appl fee: $75. Appl due: Mar. Accepted: 80%. Yield: 96%. **Tests** CEEB IQ SSAT Stanford. **Enr 400.** Avg class size: 16. Uniform. **Fac 46.** M 9/F 37. FT 40/PT 6. Adv deg: 47%. **Grad '11—31.** Col—31. **Avg SAT:** CR/M/W 1795. **Col Couns:** 1. **Tui '11-'12:** Day $9840-15,300 (+$1000-1500). **Est 1969.** Nonprofit. Sem (Aug-June). **Assoc** SACS. Frederica provides a structured curriculum, with paid attention to college preparation in the high school years. The school encourages all students to take part in service opportunities, the arts and athletics.

ST. ANDREW'S SCHOOL   Day Coed Gr PS (Age 3)-12
Savannah, GA 31410. 601 Penn Waller Rd.
Tel: 912-897-4941. Fax: 912-897-4943.
www.saintschool.com   E-mail: admissions@saintschool.com

Mark Toth, Head (2012). BS, MS, Michigan State Univ. Beth Aldrich, Adm.

Col Prep. IB Diploma. Feat—Creative_Writing Fr Span Stats Anat Ecol Environ_Sci Marine_Bio/Sci Comp_Sci Econ Psych Philos Relig Ceramics Drawing Studio_Art Drama. **Supp**—Tut. **Dual enr:** Armstrong Atlantic. **Sports**—Basket X-country Soccer Tennis Track. B: Baseball Football Golf. G: Cheer Softball Swim Volley. **Selective adm:** 100/yr. Appl fee: $100. Appl due: Rolling. Accepted: 80%. Yield: 77%. **Tests** CEEB CTP_4 IQ ISEE SSAT Stanford. **Enr 450.** Intl 7%. Avg class size: 15. Stud/fac: 9:1. Casual dress. **Fac 70.** M 18/F 52. FT 63/PT 7. Wh 96%. Latino 2%. Other 2%. Adv deg: 45%. **Grad '11—41.** Col—41. **Mid 50% SAT:** CR 460-600. M 450-590. W 440-580. **Col Couns:** 1. **Tui '12-'13:** Day $7650-11,125 (+$500). **Est 1947.** Nonprofit. Sem (Aug-May). **Assoc** SACS. Located on Wilmington Island, St. Andrew's offers a college preparatory program. The school awards the International Baccalaureate Diploma, and IB courses are open to students pursuing a traditional degree. All students in grades 9-12 perform 30 hours of community service annually. Second-semester seniors complete a work project with a professional in a field of interest.

ST. VINCENT'S ACADEMY   Day Girls Gr 9-12
Savannah, GA 31401. 207 E Liberty St.
Tel: 912-236-5508. Fax: 912-236-7877.
www.svaga.net

Mary Anne Hogan, Prin (2010). BA, Michigan State Univ, MEd, Nova Southeastern Univ. Mary Anne Butler, Adm.

Col Prep. AP (exams req'd)—Eng Fr Lat Span Calc Bio US_Hist US_Govt & Pol Studio_Art. **Feat**—Anat Comp_Sci Holocaust Psych Relig Photog Music. **Supp**—Rev Tut. **Comp:** Comp/Stud: 1:10. **Dual enr:** Armstrong Atlantic, GA St. **Sports**— G: Basket X-country Golf Soccer Softball Swim Tennis Track Volley. Activities: 26. **Somewhat selective adm:** 115/yr. Appl fee: $100. Appl due: May. Accepted: 95%. Yield: 98%. **Tests** HSPT. **Enr 300.** Wh 85%. Latino 2%. Blk 11%. Asian 2%. Avg class size: 12. Uniform. **Fac 30.** M 7/F 23. FT 27/PT 3. Wh 85%. Latino 5%. Blk 5%. Other 5%. Adv deg: 33%. **Grad '06—73.** Col—66. **Col Couns:** 1. **Tui '12-'13:** Day $9055 (+$400). Catholic $7640 (+$400). Aid: Need 113 ($148,715). **Est 1845.** Nonprofit. Roman Catholic. Sem (Aug-May). **Assoc** SACS. Founded by the Sisters of Mercy, St. Vincent's offers dual-enrollment courses in conjunction with Armstrong Atlantic University and Georgia State University. Interest clubs, school activities, publications and interscholastic athletic competition supplement academics.

BULLOCH ACADEMY　　　　Day Coed Gr PS (Age 4)-12
Statesboro, GA 30458. 873 Westside Rd.
Tel: 912-764-6297. Fax: 912-764-3165.
www.bullochacademy.com　E-mail: rhutcheson@bullochacademy.com
　Leisa Houghton, Int Head.
　Col Prep. AP (exams req'd; 41 taken, 76% 3+)—Eng Calc Bio US_Hist US_Govt & Pol Studio_Art. **Feat**—Creative_Writing Span Physiol Comp_Sci 20th-Century_Hist Psych Comp_Relig Ethics Fine_Arts Journ Speech. **Supp**—Makeup Rev Tut. **Dual enr:** GA Southern, Ogeechee Tech. **Sports**—Basket X-country Soccer Tennis Track. B: Baseball Football Golf Wrestling. G: Cheer Softball. **Somewhat selective adm:** 40/yr. Appl fee: $375. Appl due: Rolling. Accepted: 95%. **Tests** CEEB CTP_4. **Enr 494.** Wh 95%. Blk 3%. Asian 2%. Intl 5%. Avg class size: 12. Stud/fac: 12:1. **Fac 46.** M 5/F 41. FT 42/PT 4. Wh 100%. Adv deg: 21%. **Grad '10—28.** Col—28. (GA Southern 12, U of GA 9, E GA 3, GA Col & State U 2, U of AL-Tuscaloosa 1, SUNY-Albany 1). **Avg SAT:** CR 571. M 583. W 584. **Tui '11-'12:** Day $5709-6515 (+$500). **Est 1971.** Nonprofit. Sem (Aug-May). **Assoc** SACS.　Bulloch's curriculum stresses college preparation in the upper grades, and emphasis is placed on math and language skills, in addition to sound study habits. The lower school curriculum features a phonics-based approach to reading, writing and vocabulary; math instruction that stresses real-world applications; and an independent reading program. Spanish instruction begins in the middle school. Upper school students have dual-enrollment options at Georgia Southern University and Ogeechee Technical College.

GEORGIA CHRISTIAN SCHOOL　　　　Day Coed Gr PS (Age 3)-12
Valdosta, GA 31601. 4359 Dasher Rd.
Tel: 229-559-5131. Fax: 229-559-7401.
www.georgiachristian.org　E-mail: gcsregistration@bellsouth.net
　Brad L. Lawson, Head (2008). BA, Harding Univ, MEd, Univ of Maryland.
　Col Prep. Voc. AP—Calc. **Feat**—Creative_Writing Span Web_Design Pol_Sci Sociol Bible Studio_Art Chorus Finance. **Sports**—Basket Soccer. B: Baseball Softball Wrestling. G: Cheer. **Selective adm:** 42/yr. Appl fee: $0. **Enr 206.** Elem 139. Sec 67. Avg class size: 17. **Fac 28.** M 8/F 20. FT 20/PT 8. Adv deg: 10%. **Grad '08—12.** Col—11. **Avg SAT:** CR/M 1170. **Tui '12-'13:** Day $3240-4995 (+$190-450). **Est 1914.** Nonprofit. Nondenom Christian. Sem (Aug-May).　A Christian atmosphere pervades all activities at the school, including the curriculum. Bible lessons and memorization begin in preschool and continue through grade 12. The high school curriculum allows students to choose from college and vocational preparatory programs.

KENTUCKY

ST. HENRY DISTRICT HIGH SCHOOL　　　　Day Coed Gr 9-12
Erlanger, KY 41018. 3755 Scheben Dr.
Tel: 859-525-0255. Fax: 859-525-5855.
www.shdhs.org　E-mail: dmotte@shdhs.org
　David M. Otte, Prin. BA, Thomas More College, MEd, Xavier Univ.
　Col Prep. AP (224 exams taken, 79% 3+)—Eng Ger Lat Span Calc Comp_Sci Bio Chem Eur_Hist US_Hist World_Hist Comp_Govt & Pol Psych US_Govt & Pol Art_Hist Studio_Art. **Feat**—Stats Anat & Physiol Astron Web_Design Econ Theol Painting Drama Chorus Music Accounting Bus Journ Study_Skills. **Supp**—Dev_Read Rev Tut. **Sports**—Basket Bowl Cheer X-country Golf Soccer Swim Tennis Track Volley. B: Baseball. G: Softball. Activities: 33. **Nonselective adm:** 160/yr. Appl due: Rolling. Accepted: 100%. **Enr 477.** Avg class size: 19. Stud/fac: 13:1. Casual dress. **Fac 39.** M 16/F 23. FT 35/PT 4. Adv deg: 43%. **Grad '11—109.** Col—106. **Avg SAT:** CR 615. M 586. W 580. Avg ACT: 24.4. **Col Couns:** 1. **Tui '11-'12:**

Day $7200 (+$600). Parishioners $6200 (+$600). **Est 1933.** Nonprofit. Roman Catholic. Quar (Aug-May). **Assoc** SACS. Christian values and religious instruction receive priority at this college preparatory school. Students may pursue business, vocational or general studies as well. Boys and girls engage in required community service as part of the theology curriculum.

CAPITAL DAY SCHOOL   Day Coed Gr PS (Age 3)-8
Frankfort, KY 40601. 120 Deepwood Dr.
Tel: 502-227-7121. Fax: 502-227-7558.
www.capitaldayschool.net   E-mail: office@capitaldayschool.net
   Debra K. Atkins, Head (2011). BS, BSEd, Eastern Kentucky Univ.
   Gen Acad. Feat—Fr Span Computers Studio_Art Drama Music. **Supp**—Tut. **Comp:** Comp/Stud: 1:5. **Sports**—Arch Basket Crew Golf Track. **Somewhat selective adm (Gr PS-6):** 24/yr. Appl fee: $50. Appl due: Rolling. Accepted: 91%. Yield: 87%. **Tests** CTP_4. **Enr 156.** B 80. G 76. Wh 84%. Latino 1%. Blk 5%. Asian 10%. Intl 5%. Avg class size: 10. Stud/fac: 7:1. Casual dress. **Fac 19.** M 4/F 15. FT 13/PT 6. Wh 100%. Adv deg: 15%. **Grad '11—10.** Alum donors: 2%. **Tui '12-'13:** Day $6250 (+$200). Aid: Merit 3 ($9000). Need 22 ($33,200). **Est 1955.** Nonprofit. Quar (Aug-May). **Assoc** SACS. CDS' curriculum emphasizes reading, language arts, mathematics, science and social studies. Art, music, computer technology, foreign languages and physical education constitute the enrichment program. The middle school field studies program (grades 5-8) includes springtime overnight trips for each grade. Students participate in academic competitions, interest clubs and interscholastic sports and attend theater productions, musical performances and art exhibits.

ASSUMPTION HIGH SCHOOL   Day Girls Gr 9-12
Louisville, KY 40205. 2170 Tyler Ln.
Tel: 502-458-9551. Fax: 502-454-8411.
www.ahsrockets.org
   Elaine Salvo, Pres. BA, Immaculata Univ, MA, Univ of Louisville. Rebecca Henle, Prin. BS, Univ of Dayton, MEd, Univ of Arkansas-Little Rock. Elisabeth Russo, Adm.
   Col Prep. AP—Eng Fr Span Calc Stats Bio Chem Environ_Sci Physics US_Hist World_ Hist Human_Geog Psych US_Govt & Pol Art_Hist Studio_Art Music_Theory. **Feat**—Creative_Writing Humanities Mythology Astron Forensic_Sci Holocaust Econ Law Theol Ceramics Drawing Fine_Arts Graphic_Arts Sculpt Acting Band Chorus Accounting Debate Journ Public_Speak. **Supp**—LD Rem_Math. **Comp:** Comp/Stud: 1:2. **Dual enr:** Bellarmine. **Sports**— G: Basket Cheer Crew X-country F_Hockey Golf Ice_Hockey Lacrosse Soccer Softball Swim Tennis Track Volley. Activities: 60. **Somewhat selective adm (Gr 9-11):** 300/yr. Appl due: Dec. **Tests** HSPT. **Enr 947.** Avg class size: 17. Stud/fac: 10:1. Uniform. **Fac 93.** M 13/F 80. FT 83/PT 10. Adv deg: 90%. **Grad '08—232.** Col—229. **Avg SAT:** CR/M 1120. Avg ACT: 23.5. **Col Couns:** 1. **Tui '11-'12:** Day $9750 (+$100). Aid: Need ($400,000). **Est 1955.** Nonprofit. Roman Catholic (85% practice). Sem (Aug-June). **Assoc** SACS. AHS' varied curriculum includes Advanced Placement, honors and college preparatory classes in a range of academic subjects, as well as college-credit course work for juniors and seniors through Bellarmine University. Individualized attention and special testing services are provided for pupils with diagnosed learning differences. Juniors satisfy a 15-hour community service requirement, while seniors complete a weeklong mission trip; service is part of the theology curriculum in the earlier grades.

HAYFIELD MONTESSORI SCHOOL   Day Coed Gr PS (Age 3)-5
Louisville, KY 40205. 2000 Tyler Ln.
Tel: 502-454-7122. Fax: 502-479-8716.
www.hayfieldmontessori.com   E-mail: hayfield-montessori1@insightbb.com
   Aline M. Abell, Head (2009). BA, Earlham College, MEd, Loyola College.

Gen Acad. Montessori. Feat—Fr Span Music. **Supp**—Tut. **Somewhat selective adm (Gr PS-1):** 40/yr. Appl fee: $125. Appl due: Rolling. Accepted: 95%. **Enr 100.** Wh 85%. Latino 2%. Blk 3%. Asian 10%. Avg class size: 22. Stud/fac: 11:1. **Fac 12.** M 1/F 11. FT 7/PT 5. Wh 100%. Adv deg: 16%. **Tui '12-'13:** Day $7650-7850 (+$50-200). **Est 1967.** Nonprofit. Sem (Aug-May). The school's program relies upon Montessori methods and tools of teaching. Spanish is taught at all grade levels. The elementary section accepts new students into grade 1 only.

ST. XAVIER HIGH SCHOOL   Day Boys Gr 9-12
Louisville, KY 40217. 1609 Poplar Level Rd.
Tel: 502-637-4712. Fax: 502-634-2171.
www.saintx.com   E-mail: kwoodward@saintx.com
     Perry E. Sangalli, Pres. BA, Bellarmine Univ, MAT, Univ of Louisville, EdD, Spalding Univ. Br. Edward Driscoll, CFX, Prin. BA, Catholic Univ of America, MEd, Spalding Univ. Kevin S. Woordward, Adm.
     Col Prep. AP (495 exams taken, 95% 3+)—Eng Fr Ger Span Calc Stats Comp_Sci Bio Chem Environ_Sci Physics Eur_Hist US_Hist Comp_Govt & Pol Psych US_Govt & Pol Art_ Hist Studio_Art Music_Theory. **Feat**—Chin Forensic_Sci Engineering Web_Design Econ Philos Theol Film Filmmaking Acting Theater Music_Hist Finance Journ Speech. **Supp**— Dev_Read Rem_Math Rem_Read Tut. **Comp:** Comp/Stud: 1:4 (1:1 Laptop prgm Gr 9). **Dual enr:** Bellarmine. **Sports**— B: Baseball Basket X-country Football Golf Ice_Hockey Lacrosse Soccer Swim Tennis Track Volley Weightlifting Wrestling. Activities: 48. **Somewhat selective adm (Gr 9-11):** 385/yr. Appl due: Feb. Accepted: 96%. Yield: 95%. **Tests** HSPT. **Enr 1455.** Wh 96%. Latino 1%. Blk 2%. Asian 1%. Avg class size: 20. Stud/fac: 12:1. Uniform. **Fac 120.** M 92/F 28. FT 117/PT 3. Wh 99%. Latino 1%. Adv deg: 83%. **Grad '09—333.** Col—326. **Avg SAT:** CR 587. M 592. W 585. Avg ACT: 24.6. **Col Couns:** 2. Alum donors: 37%. **Tui '12-'13:** Day $11,325 (+$250-795). Aid: Need 364 ($1,600,000). **Est 1864.** Nonprofit. Roman Catholic (88% practice). Sem (Aug-May). **Assoc** SACS. Sponsored by the Xaverian Brothers, St. X conducts three distinct programs of study to meet students' needs: honors, academic and traditional. Placement is determined by entrance test scores, previous grades and teacher recommendations. Full honors and Advanced Placement programs are available. Juniors satisfy a 20-hour community service requirement.

TRINITY HIGH SCHOOL   Day Boys Gr 9-12
Louisville, KY 40207. 4011 Shelbyville Rd.
Tel: 502-736-2119. Fax: 502-899-2052.
www.trinityrocks.com   E-mail: porter@thsrock.net
     Robert J. Mullen, Pres (2000). BS, Bellarmine Univ, EdD, Spalding Univ. Daniel Zoeller, Prin. BA, Eastern Kentucky Univ, MAT, Univ of Louisville. Jennifer Browning, Adm.
     Col Prep. AP (245 exams taken)—Eng Fr Span Calc Bio Chem Environ_Sci Physics Eur_Hist US_Hist Econ Psych Studio_Art. **Feat**—Creative_Writing Ger Forensic_Sci Web_ Design Sociol Relig Art_Hist Film Photog Video_Production Journ. **Supp**—Dev_Read LD Rem_Math Rem_Read Tut. **Comp:** Comp/Stud: 1:4. **Sports**— B: Baseball Basket Bowl Cheer Crew X-country Fencing Football Golf Ice_Hockey Lacrosse Soccer Swim Tennis Track Volley Weightlifting Wrestling. Activities: 100. **Somewhat selective adm:** 400/yr. Appl fee: $75. Appl due: Mar. Accepted: 95%. Yield: 95%. **Tests** HSPT. **Enr 1320.** Wh 90%. Latino 3%. Blk 6%. Asian 1%. Avg class size: 20. Stud/fac: 12:1. Uniform. **Fac 118.** M 90/F 28. FT 117/PT 1. Wh 90%. Latino 5%. Blk 3%. Native Am 1%. Asian 1%. Adv deg: 88%. **Grad '11—287.** Col—281. **Avg SAT:** CR 630. M 628. W 596. Avg ACT: 23.4. **Col Couns:** 2. **Tui '11-'12:** Day $10,825 (+$500). Aid: Merit 60 ($80,000). Need 420 ($1,800,000). Work prgm 100 ($51,500). **Est 1953.** Nonprofit. Roman Catholic (84% practice). Sem (Aug-June). **Assoc** SACS. Trinity's academic curriculum features advanced credit for college and independent study, and technology is an important learning and teaching tool at the school. Boys satisfy the

following community service requirements: 15 hours in grade 9, 20 hours in grade 10 and 25 hours in grade 11. THS conducts a program for students with learning differences.

ONEIDA BAPTIST INSTITUTE   **Bdg & Day**
Oneida, KY 40972. 11 Mulberry St, PO Box 67.   **Coed Gr 6-12**
Tel: 606-847-4111. Fax: 606-847-4496.
www.oneidaschool.org   E-mail: admissions@oneidaschool.org
    W. F. Underwood, Pres (1994). Wanita Bortell, Adm.
    Col Prep. Gen Acad. AP (34 exams taken, 15% 3+)—Eng Calc Bio US_Hist US_Govt & Pol. **Feat**—Ger Span Child_Dev Bible Studio_Art Drama Theater_Arts Band Chorus Guitar Piano Auto_Mechanics Culinary_Arts Agriculture. **Supp**—Dev_Read ESL Makeup Rem_Math Rem_Read Rev Tut. **Comp:** Comp/Stud: 1:5. **Sports**—Basket X-country Soccer Softball Swim Tennis Track. B: Baseball. G: Cheer Volley. **Selective adm:** 90/yr. Bdg 80. Day 10. Appl fee: $35. Appl due: Rolling. Accepted: 80%. Yield: 95%. **Tests** CEEB SSAT Stanford. **Enr 300.** B 150. G 150. Bdg 250. Day 50. Elem 50. Sec 250. Intl 20%. Avg class size: 11. Stud/fac: 11:1. Casual dress. **Fac 44.** M 21/F 23. FT 40/PT 4. Wh 99%. Latino 1%. Adv deg: 36%. **Grad '11—53.** Col—45. (U of KY 5, Lindsey Wilson 3, Hazard Community & Tech 3, Berea 1). Avg ACT: 18. **Col Couns:** 1. **Tui '12-'13:** Bdg $5750 (+$515-575). Day $0. Intl Bdg $10,200 (+$2000). Aid: Need 92 ($205,518). **Est 1899.** Nonprofit. Southern Baptist (15% practice). Quar (Aug-May). OBI's Christian program features small classes, a tutoring lab, a nightly study hall and an ESL program. Advanced Placement courses meet the needs of the college-bound pupil, while vocational and fine arts classes enable boys and girls to pursue their talents and interests. An important aspect of school life is Oneida's work program, which requires students to work or engage in certain cocurricular activities one and a half hours each weekday and four hours on weekends. The school also operates a working farm and offers agricultural classes.

COVINGTON CATHOLIC HIGH SCHOOL   **Day Boys Gr 9-12**
Park Hills, KY 41011. 1600 Dixie Hwy.
Tel: 859-491-2247. Fax: 859-448-2242.
www.covcath.org   E-mail: tbarczak@covcath.org
    Robert J. Rowe, Prin (2008). BA, Northern Kentucky Univ, MEd, Xavier Univ (OH). Tony Barczak, Adm.
    Col Prep. AP (exams req'd; 131 taken)—Eng Span Calc Chem Physics Eur_Hist US_ Hist Psych. **Feat**—Creative_Writing Ger Lat Stats Anat & Physiol Programming Web_Design Sociol Relig Film Studio_Art Chorus Music Orchestra Accounting. **Supp**—LD Rev. **Comp:** Comp/Stud: 1:4.4. **Sports**— B: Baseball Basket Bowl X-country Football Golf Lacrosse Soccer Swim Tennis Track. Activities: 40. **Nonselective adm:** 133/yr. Appl fee: $20. Appl due: Rolling. Accepted: 100%. **Tests** HSPT. **Enr 502.** Wh 97%. Latino 1%. Blk 1%. Asian 1%. Stud/fac: 16:1. Casual dress. **Fac 36.** FT 29/PT 7. Wh 97%. Blk 1%. Asian 2%. **Grad '11—118.** Col—116. **Avg SAT:** CR 607. M 628. W 582. Avg ACT: 24.8. **Col Couns:** 1. **Tui '11-'12:** Day $6590 (+$725). Parishioners $5985 (+$725). Aid: Need ($270,000). **Est 1925.** Nonprofit. Roman Catholic (95% practice). Sem (Aug-May). **Assoc** SACS. The only boys' high school in northern Kentucky, Covington Catholic offers a college preparatory curriculum that includes Advanced Placement options in English, foreign language, math, science, history and computer science. Religious education is required for four years. All students perform 15 hours of community service each year.

NOTRE DAME ACADEMY   **Day Girls Gr 9-12**
Park Hills, KY 41011. 1699 Hilton Dr.
Tel: 859-261-4300. Fax: 859-292-7722.
www.ndapandas.org   E-mail: koehll@ndapandas.org

Sr. Lynette Shelton, Pres (2011). Laura Dickman Koehl, Prin. EdD, Univ of Cincinnati. Sr. Mary Paul Ann Hanneken, SND, Adm.

Col Prep. AP (144 exams taken, 76% 3+)—Eng Fr Lat Span Calc Bio Physics Eur_ Hist US_Hist Studio_Art. **Feat**—British_Lit Ecol Marine_Bio/Sci Physiol Comp_Sci Women's_Hist Econ Govt Psych Sociol Theol Visual_Arts Theater_Arts Band Music Accounting. **Supp**—Dev_Read LD Rem_Math Tut. **Comp:** Comp/Stud: 1:2.5. **Dual enr:** Thomas More, N KY. **Sports**— G: Basket Bowl X-country Golf Lacrosse Soccer Softball Swim Tennis Track Volley. Activities: 22. **Nonselective adm:** 148/yr. Appl fee: $200. Accepted: 100%. **Tests** HSPT. **Enr 605.** Wh 96%. Latino 1%. Blk 1%. Native Am 1%. Asian 1%. Avg class size: 25. Stud/fac: 14:1. Uniform. **Fac 44.** M 6/F 38. FT 44. Wh 98%. Latino 1%. Blk 1%. Adv deg: 63%. **Grad '11—150.** Col—150. (N KY 26, U of KY 22, U of Louisville 22, U of Cincinnati 15, E KY 12, U of Dayton 5). **Avg SAT:** CR/M/W 1737. Avg ACT: 24.9. **Col Couns:** 1. **Tui '11-'12:** Day $6500 (+$650). Parishioners $5700 (+$650). Aid: Merit 23 ($39,300). Need 96 ($277,500). Work prgm 72 ($102,000). **Est 1876.** Nonprofit. Roman Catholic. Sem (Aug-June). **Assoc** SACS. A strong religion program is integral to Notre Dame's Christian atmosphere. Modified scheduling allows for extended art and science labs, as well as community service. A learning differences program and student mentoring are also available.

VILLA MADONNA ACADEMY   Day Coed Gr K-12
Villa Hills, KY 41017. 2500 Amsterdam Rd.
Tel: 859-331-6333. Fax: 859-331-8615.
www.villamadonna.net   E-mail: vma@villamadonna.net
Donna Klus, Adm.

Col Prep. AP—Eng Fr Lat Span Calc Comp_Sci Bio Chem Physics US_Hist Psych Studio_Art. **Feat**—Web_Design Econ Sociol Theol Art_Hist Drama Band Chorus Music_Hist Accounting Bus Finance Journ Public_Speak. **Supp**—Rev Tut. **Dual enr:** Thomas More. **Sports**—Basket X-country Golf Lacrosse Soccer Swim Tennis Track. B: Baseball. G: Cheer Softball Volley. Activities: 14. **Somewhat selective adm:** 89/yr. Appl fee: $0. Appl due: Rolling. Accepted: 90%. **Tests** HSPT. **Enr 510.** B 228. G 282. Elem 334. Sec 176. Avg class size: 18. Stud/fac: 9:1. Uniform. **Fac 40.** M 2/F 38. FT 37/PT 3. Wh 100%. Adv deg: 32%. **Grad '09—56.** Col—56. **Avg SAT:** CR 640. M 628. W 615. Avg ACT: 26.9. **Tui '12-'13:** Day $7100-10,700 (+$565-1080). **Est 1904.** Nonprofit. Roman Catholic (65% practice). Sem (Aug-June). **Assoc** SACS. Overlooking the Ohio River, VMA offers Advanced Placement classes to qualified students. Music, art, speech, computer and foreign language courses are compulsory. The school offers a dual-credit course in modern European history in association with Thomas More College.

NORTH CAROLINA

BURLINGTON DAY SCHOOL   Day Coed Gr PS (Age 3)-8
Burlington, NC 27215. 1615 Greenwood Ter.
Tel: 336-228-0296. Fax: 336-226-6249.
www.burlingtondayschool.org   E-mail: pscott@burlingtondayschool.org
Stephen E. Switzer, Head (2009). BA, Hanover College, MA, Oberlin College. Penny Scott, Adm.

Pre-Prep. Gen Acad. Feat—Span Computers Visual_Arts Drama Band Music. **Supp**—Tut. **Comp:** Comp/Stud: 1:4 (1:1 Laptop prgm Gr 6-8). **Sports**—Basket X-country Golf Soccer Tennis. G: Cheer Volley. **Somewhat selective adm:** 37/yr. Appl fee: $75. Appl due: Jan. Accepted: 95%. Yield: 86%. **Tests** IQ Stanford. **Enr 200.** Avg class size: 16. **Fac 33.** M 1/F 32. FT 25/PT 8. Adv deg: 15%. **Grad '07—17.** Prep—7. Alum donors: 5%. **Tui '12-'13:** Day $7400-11,100 (+$300). **Est 1954.** Nonprofit. Quar (Aug-May). **Assoc** SACS. The school offers an accelerated traditional curriculum supplemented by music, drama, technology, publications, athletics and various field trips. Spanish instruction begins in first grade, with an emphasis placed on basic language skills and cultural understanding. Boys and girls in grades 6-8 must each supply a laptop for school use. Students participate in group community service projects, including fundraising and volunteering for local charitable organizations.

CHARLOTTE CATHOLIC HIGH SCHOOL   **Day Coed Gr 9-12**
Charlotte, NC 28226. 7702 Pineville-Matthews Rd.
Tel: 704-543-1127. Fax: 704-543-1217.
www.charlottecatholic.org   E-mail: bvacitelli@charlottecatholic.com
     Gerald S. Healy, Prin (2003). BA, Belmont Abbey College, MEd, Univ of North Carolina-Charlotte.
     Col Prep. AP (exams req'd; 587 taken, 61% 3+)—Eng Fr Lat Span Calc Stats Bio Chem Environ_Sci Physics Eur_Hist US_Hist Econ US_Govt & Pol. **Feat**—Ger Comp_Sci Relig Band Bus. **Supp**—Rev Tut. **Sports**—Basket Cheer X-country Golf Lacrosse Soccer Swim Tennis Track. B: Baseball Football Ice_Hockey Wrestling. G: Softball Volley. Activities: 58. **Somewhat selective adm:** 420/yr. Appl fee: $100. Appl due: Rolling. Accepted: 90%. **Enr 1392.** B 698. G 694. Wh 87%. Latino 4%. Blk 3%. Native Am 1%. Asian 5%. Avg class size: 19. Uniform. **Fac 103.** M 31/F 72. FT 93/PT 10. Wh 87%. Latino 4%. Blk 4%. Native Am 3%. Other 2%. Adv deg: 34%. **Grad '10—335.** Col—334. **Mid 50% SAT:** CR 520-640. M 520-640. W 510-640. Avg ACT: 25. **Tui '11-'12:** Day $11,398 (+$1025). Catholic $7874 (+$1025). **Est 1887.** Nonprofit. Roman Catholic (94% practice). Sem (Aug-June). **Assoc** SACS. Charlotte Catholic's varied course of studies features several foreign languages, as well as a full complement of Advanced Placement classes. Daily religion classes are also part of the school's curriculum. All students fulfill a 10-hour community service requirement each semester.

CHARLOTTE CHRISTIAN SCHOOL   **Day Coed Gr PS (Age 4)-12**
Charlotte, NC 28270. 7301 Sardis Rd.
Tel: 704-366-5657. Fax: 704-366-5678.
www.charlottechristian.com   E-mail: cathie.broocks@charchrist.com
     Barry F. Giller, Head (2010). BA, Wheaton College (IL), MS, Nova Southeastern Univ. Cathie Broocks, Adm.
     Col Prep. AP—Eng Fr Lat Span Calc Stats Comp_Sci Bio Chem Environ_Sci Physics Eur_Hist US_Hist US_Govt & Pol Art_Hist Studio_Art Music_Theory. **Feat**—British_Lit Astron Sports_Med Web_Design Civil_War Psych Sociol Theol Painting Photog Acting Dance Bus Public_Speak. **Supp**—Tut. **Sports**—Basket X-country Soccer Swim Tennis Track. B: Baseball Football Golf Wrestling. G: Cheer Softball Volley. Activities: 40. **Selective adm:** 174/yr. Appl fee: $90. Appl due: Jan. Accepted: 50%. **Tests** CTP_4 HSPT IQ ISEE TOEFL. **Enr 1002.** Elem 628. Sec 374. Avg class size: 20. Stud/fac: 10:1. **Fac 86.** M 24/F 62. FT 82/PT 4. Adv deg: 36%. **Grad '10—93.** Col—93. **Avg SAT:** CR/M/W 1758. Avg ACT: 25. **Tui '11-'12:** Day $11,240-16,125 (+$500). Aid: Need ($452,389). **Est 1950.** Nonprofit. Nondenom Christian. Quar (Aug-June). **Assoc** SACS. This interdenominational school combines academics, service opportunities, athletics, the performing and fine arts, and computer technology. Foreign language study begins in junior kindergarten with Spanish and continues through the elementary grades; during the middle and upper school years, French and Latin are added.

CHARLOTTE PREPARATORY SCHOOL   **Day Coed Gr PS (Age 2)-8**
Charlotte, NC 28211. 212 Boyce Rd.
Tel: 704-366-5994. Fax: 704-366-0221.
www.charlotteprep.com   E-mail: info@charlotteprep.com
     Maura Leahy-Tucker, Exec Dir (1971). BA, Univ of Ireland, MBA, Queens Univ of Charlotte. Blair Fisher, Head. BA, College of William and Mary, MEd, George Mason Univ, MEd, Kennesaw State Univ. Vicky Wilkison, Adm.

Pre-Prep. Montessori. Feat—Span Computers Robotics Web_Design Studio_Art Drama Band Chorus. **Supp**—Rev Tut. **Comp:** Comp/Stud: 1:1 **Sports**—Basket X-country Golf Soccer Tennis. B: Lacrosse. G: Cheer Volley. **Selective adm:** 50/yr. Appl fee: $90. Appl due: Jan. **Tests** CTP_4 IQ ISEE TOEFL. **Enr 350.** B 169. G 181. Wh 60%. Latino 5%. Blk 12%. Asian 11%. Other 12%. Intl 38%. Avg class size: 15. Casual dress. **Fac 39.** M 6/F 33. FT 34/PT 5. Wh 86%. Latino 5%. Other 9%. Adv deg: 46%. **Grad '11—19.** Prep—15. (Providence Day 5, Charlotte Co Day 3, Charlotte Latin 2, Charlotte Christian 1, McCallie 1, Asheville 1). **Tui '11-'12:** Day $11,900-16,380 (+$1000). **Est 1971.** Inc. Tri (Aug-June). **Assoc** SACS. Located on an eight-acre, wooded campus in the southeastern part of the city, Charlotte Prep commences its program with a Montessori preschool. The lower school (grades K-4) establishes a foundation in language arts, math, science and social studies, with additional instruction in computers, music, Spanish, art, band and drama. Middle school students (grades 5-8) attend weekly leadership classes, join after-school clubs, and play interscholastic and intramural sports. Charlotte Prep facilitates community service involvement by organizing developmentally appropriate group activities at each grade level. The school arranges an exchange program for middle school pupils to study with a sister school in Ocotlan, Mexico.

NORTHSIDE CHRISTIAN ACADEMY Day Coed Gr PS (Age 3)-12
Charlotte, NC 28262. 333 Jeremiah Blvd.
Tel: 704-599-9015. Fax: 704-921-1384.
www.ncaknights.com   E-mail: pamela.starkey@northsidecharlotte.com
   Tony Fajardo, Head (2010). BS, Barry Univ, MS, Nova Southeastern Univ. Pamela Starkey, Adm.

   Col Prep. Gen Acad. AP (exams req'd; 21 taken, 86% 3+)—Eng Calc Bio US_Hist. **Feat**—Creative_Writing Span Anat & Physiol Comp_Sci Govt/Econ Bible Studio_Art Drama Music Speech. **Supp**—Dev_Read Rem_Math Rem_Read Tut. **Comp:** Comp/Stud: 1:7. **Sports**—Basket X-country Soccer Track. B: Baseball Golf Wrestling. G: Cheer Softball Volley. Activities: 35. **Somewhat selective adm:** 79/yr. Appl fee: $300. Appl due: Rolling. Accepted: 89%. **Tests** IQ Stanford. **Enr 540.** Elem 410. Sec 130. Wh 58%. Latino 1%. Blk 39%. Asian 2%. Avg class size: 16. Stud/fac: 12:1. Uniform. **Fac 54.** M 13/F 41. FT 49/PT 5. Wh 95%. Latino 1%. Blk 4%. Adv deg: 18%. **Grad '11—40.** Col—37. **Avg SAT:** CR 530. M 543. W 543. **Col Couns:** 1. Alum donors: 20%. **Tui '12-'13:** Day $5460-6755 (+$275-990). Aid: Need 56 ($82,217). **Est 1961.** Nonprofit. Baptist (28% practice). Sem (Aug-May). The academy's high school offers subject matter on two academic levels: advanced college preparatory and general studies. One unit of Bible is required each year of attendance, and students in grades 6-12 are involved in an annual community service project. NCA holds compulsory weekly chapel programs.

CAMELOT ACADEMY Day Coed Gr K-12
Durham, NC 27707. 809 Proctor St.
Tel: 919-688-3040. Fax: 919-682-4320.
www.camelotacademy.org   E-mail: camelotacad@aol.com
   Thelma DeCarlo-Glynn, Dir (1982). BA, Johns Hopkins Univ, MA, Univ of North Carolina-Chapel Hill. Scott Mitchell, Adm.

   Col Prep. AP—Eng Calc Stats US_Hist World_Hist US_Govt & Pol. **Feat**—Span Anat & Physiol Environ_Sci Civics Studio_Art Music. **Supp**—ESL Rem_Math. **Sports**—Soccer. B: Basket. G: Volley. **Selective adm (Gr K-11):** 28/yr. Appl fee: $50. Appl due: Rolling. Accepted: 40%. Yield: 60%. **Tests** ISEE TOEFL. **Enr 95.** Nonwhite 18%. Avg class size: 11. Stud/fac: 10:1. Casual dress. **Fac 17.** FT 11/PT 6. Wh 93%. Asian 7%. **Grad '11—3.** Col—3. **Avg SAT:** CR 690. M 677. W 660. **Tui '12-'13:** Day $8300-11,950 (+$1800-2000). Aid: Need 47. **Est 1982.** Sem (Aug-May). Camelot's favorable student-to-teacher ratio enables the academy to tailor its curriculum to the pupil's aptitudes and needs. Each school year begins with diagnostic testing of all students: Teachers follow a period of assessment with a staff retreat.

The mastery-based learning approach requires boys and girls to demonstrate mastery of previously covered material before instructors will introduce new concepts.

GASTON DAY SCHOOL   Day Coed Gr PS (Age 3)-12
Gastonia, NC 28056. 2001 Gaston Day School Rd.
Tel: 704-864-7744. Fax: 704-865-3813.
www.gastonday.org   E-mail: kpaxton-shaw@gastonday.org
   Richard Rankin, Head (2001). BA, Univ of Virginia, PhD, Univ of North Carolina-Chapel Hill. Martha Jayne Rhyne, Adm.
   Col Prep. AP (exams req'd; 133 taken, 82% 3+)—Eng Span Calc Stats Bio Chem Environ_Sci US_Hist US_Govt & Pol Studio_Art. **Feat**—Fr Lat Anat & Physiol Performing_Arts Visual_Arts Theater_Arts. **Supp**—LD Makeup Tut. **Sports**—Basket X-country Golf Soccer Swim Tennis Track. B: Baseball. G: Cheer Softball Volley. Activities: 34. **Somewhat selective adm (Gr PS-11):** 90/yr. Appl fee: $50. Appl due: Rolling. Accepted: 82%. Yield: 62%. **Tests** CEEB CTP_4 ISEE. **Enr 503.** B 243. G 260. Elem 359. Sec 144. Wh 81%. Latino 2%. Blk 6%. Asian 4%. Other 7%. Avg class size: 14. Stud/fac: 10:1. **Fac 50.** M 10/F 40. FT 50. Wh 96%. Blk 2%. Other 2%. Adv deg: 40%. **Grad '11**—40. Col—40. (NC St 4, UNC-Chapel Hill 4, Appalachian St 3, Auburn 2, Lynchburg 2, VA Polytech 2). **Avg SAT:** CR 603. M 606. W 613. **Col Couns:** 1. **Tui '11-'12:** Day $11,575-13,140. Aid: Merit ($119,300). Need ($469,262). **Est 1967.** Nonprofit. Sem (Aug-June). **Assoc** SACS. Spanish, computers, art, music and physical education classes begin in prekindergarten at Gaston Day. A language acquisitions course is part of the grade 6 curriculum, Latin is required in grade 7, and French and Spanish are the foreign language choices starting in grade 8. Academics also include honors and Advanced Placement classes, as well as curriculum-based class trips. Students in grades 9-12 fulfill a 25-hour annual community service requirement.

WAYNE COUNTRY DAY SCHOOL   Day Coed Gr PS (Age 2)-12
Goldsboro, NC 27530. 480 Country Day Rd.
Tel: 919-736-1045. Fax: 919-583-9493.
www.waynecountryday.com   E-mail: wcds@waynecountryday.com
   Todd Anderson, Head. BA, Williams College, MEd, Harvard Univ. Elidia Eason, Adm.
   Col Prep. AP (exams req'd)—Eng Fr Calc Bio Chem US_Hist World_Hist. **Feat**—Women's_Lit Span Ecol Marine_Bio/Sci Comp_Sci Psych Photog Studio_Art Drama Music. **Supp**—Dev_Read Tut. **Sports**—Basket Golf Soccer Tennis. B: Baseball. G: F_Hockey Softball Volley. **Selective adm:** 40/yr. Appl due: Rolling. **Tests** CTP_4 ISEE TOEFL. **Enr 252.** Elem 170. Sec 82. Wh 84%. Blk 6%. Asian 5%. Other 5%. Avg class size: 12. **Fac 41.** M 6/F 35. FT 39/PT 2. Wh 96%. Blk 4%. Adv deg: 29%. **Grad '11**—17. Col—17. **Avg SAT:** CR/M 1067. **Tui '12-'13:** Day $7600-8900 (+$700). **Est 1968.** Nonprofit. Sem (Aug-May). **Assoc** SACS. Wayne Country Day's primary emphasis is intensive college preparation. In the Upper School, Advanced Placement courses and other electives supplements a foundation of college prep and honors courses.

AMERICAN HEBREW ACADEMY   Bdg & Day
Greensboro, NC 27410. 4334 Hobbs Rd.   Coed Gr 9-12
Tel: 336-217-7100. Fax: 336-217-7011.
www.americanhebrewacademy.org   E-mail: info@americanhebrewacademy.org
   Glenn A. Drew, Exec Dir. BA, Univ of Maryland-College Park, JD, Univ of Miami. Gary M. Grandon, Prin. BS, Univ of Michigan, MEd, Wayne State Univ, PhD, Univ of Connecticut. Leslie Grossman, Adm.
   Col Prep. AP (exams req'd; 151 taken, 65% 3+)—Eng Calc Comp_Sci Bio Chem Environ_Sci Physics Psych Studio_Art. **Feat**—Hebrew Arabic Stats Comp_Relig Ethics Judaic_ Stud Film Photog Acting Theater Music_Theory. **Supp**—ESL Rev Tut. **Comp:** Comp/Stud: 1:1 Laptop prgm Gr 9-12. **Sports**—Basket X-country Soccer Swim Tennis Track. B: Baseball

Wrestling. G: Volley. **Selective adm:** 43/yr. Appl fee: $50. Appl due: May. Yield: 85%. **Tests** CEEB IQ ISEE SSAT Stanford TOEFL. **Enr 156.** B 81. G 75. Bdg 128. Day 28. Intl 12%. Avg class size: 12. Casual dress. **Fac 48.** Adv deg: 50%. In Dorms 8. **Grad '10—34.** Col—34. **Avg SAT:** CR 594. M 614. W 588. **Tui '10-'11:** Bdg $30,000. Day $18,000. Intl Bdg $30,500. Aid: Merit ($10,000). Need ($1,120,383). **Est 2001.** Nonprofit. Jewish (100% practice). Tri (Aug-June). **Assoc** SACS. The country's only pluralistic Jewish boarding school, AHA enrolls students from roughly two dozen states and a host of foreign countries. Pupils follow a curriculum that combines secular college preparatory academics with a Jewish studies program. Boys and girls typically take up to seven core classes per trimester: five secular courses, two Jewish studies. Juniors spend a trimester abroad at Alexander Muss High School in Israel, enabling them to practice their Hebrew with native speakers while continuing to receive instruction in the core disciplines. Seniors perform 10 hours of required community service.

CANTERBURY SCHOOL Day Coed Gr K-8
Greensboro, NC 27455. 5400 Old Lake Jeanette Rd.
Tel: 336-288-2007. Fax: 336-288-1933.
www.canterburysch.org E-mail: info@canterburygso.org
A. Burns Jones, Head (2008). BA, Univ of the South, JD, Univ of South Carolina, MA, Middlebury College. Kathy R. Creekmuir, Adm.

Pre-Prep. Gen Acad. Feat—Creative_Writing Lib_Skills Lat Span Computers Robotics Theol Studio_Art Drama Band Music Handbells Health Gardening. **Supp**—Dev_Read Rem_ Read Tut. **Sports**—Basket Golf Soccer Tennis. B: Baseball. G: Volley. **Selective adm:** 63/yr. Appl fee: $75. Appl due: Rolling. Accepted: 80%. Yield: 79%. **Tests** CTP_4. **Enr 337.** B 152. G 185. Wh 87%. Blk 11%. Asian 1%. Other 1%. Avg class size: 20. **Fac 41.** M 8/F 33. FT 32/PT 9. Wh 93%. Latino 2%. Blk 5%. Adv deg: 63%. **Grad '09—40.** Prep—11. (Greensboro Day 6, Episcopal HS-VA 2, Blair 1, Christ Sch 1, Woodberry Forest 1). **Tui '10-'11:** Day $13,300. Aid: Need 77 ($561,704). **Est 1993.** Nonprofit. Episcopal. Sem (Aug-May). **Assoc** SACS. During the lower school years (grades K-5), the school's broad-based approach to instruction emphasizes skill development in the fundamentals. In the middle school (grades 6-8), Latin and Spanish join the core curriculum and departmentalization begins. At all levels, Canterbury offers art, music, library, physical education and computer, and the extensive use of reference materials, audio-visual aids, computers, math manipulatives and current texts facilitates the learning process. An on-site outdoor education center provides experiential learning and leadership opportunities. Frequent chapel attendance is integral to school life.

NEW GARDEN FRIENDS SCHOOL Day Coed Gr PS (Age 3)-12
Greensboro, NC 27410. 1128 New Garden Rd.
Tel: 336-299-0964. Fax: 336-292-0347.
Other locations: 2015 Pleasant Ridge Rd, Greensboro 27410.
www.ngfs.org E-mail: admissions@ngfs.org
David R. Tomlin, Head. BA, Guilford College. Chris Winchester, Adm.

Col Prep. Gen Acad. Feat—British_Lit Creative_Writing Span Calc Discrete_Math Environ_Sci Robotics Middle_Eastern_Hist Amer_Stud Econ Quakerism Drawing Film Filmmaking Photog Sculpt Studio_Art Acting Music Guitar Finance Speech SAT_Prep. **Supp**— Dev_Read Rem_Math Rem_Read Tut. **Dual enr:** UNC-Greensboro, Guilford, Greensboro. **Sports**—Basket X-country. B: Golf. G: Soccer Softball Volley. **Selective adm:** 69/yr. Appl fee: $25-60. Appl due: Rolling. Accepted: 65%. **Enr 275.** Elem 210. Sec 65. Avg class size: 21. Casual dress. **Fac 34.** M 10/F 24. FT 27/PT 7. Adv deg: 32%. **Grad '09—17.** Col—17. **Tui '12-'13:** Day $12,615-16,710 (+$250-650). **Est 1971.** Nonprofit. Religious Society of Friends. Sem (Aug-June). **Assoc** SACS. NGFS maintains for a cooperative atmosphere and small classes with a strong sense of community. It is appropriate for students who wish to be actively involved in their own learning. Students work in multi-grade groups; interdisciplinary units, individualized and computer-aided instruction, field trips and weekly community service are important elements of the curriculum. The upper school (grades 9-12) occupies a separate campus on Pleasant Ridge Road.

HARRELLS CHRISTIAN ACADEMY   Day Coed Gr K-12
Harrells, NC 28444. 360 Tomahawk Hwy, PO Box 88.
Tel: 910-532-4575. Fax: 910-532-2958.
www.harrellschristianacademy.com   E-mail: drm@harrellsca.org
      Ronald L. Montgomery, Head (2002). BS, EdD, Campbell Univ, MS, North Carolina Agricultural and Technical State Univ, EdS, Appalachian State Univ. Susan Frederick, Adm.
      Col Prep. AP (exams req'd; 37 taken, 51% 3+)—Eng Calc Chem Physics US_Hist. **Feat**—Creative_Writing Lat Span Anat & Physiol Animal_Sci Comp_Sci Web_Design Civics Bible Philos Relig Photog Studio_Art Drama Chorus Accounting Bus. **Supp**—Dev_Read. **Comp:** Comp/Stud: 1:4.5. **Dual enr:** Sampson CC. **Sports**—Basket Golf Soccer. B: Baseball Football. G: Cheer Softball Tennis Volley. Activities: 7. **Somewhat selective adm (Gr K-11):** 30/yr. Appl fee: $35. Appl due: Rolling. Accepted: 83%. Yield: 95%. **Tests** Stanford. **Enr 396.** B 209. G 187. Elem 253. Sec 143. Wh 98%. Latino 1%. Blk 1%. Avg class size: 15. Stud/fac: 9:1. Casual dress. **Fac 45.** M 8/F 37. FT 41/PT 4. Wh 100%. Adv deg: 22%. **Grad '11—31.** Col—31. (UNC-Wilmington 10, NC St 4, Campbell 3, UNC-Chapel Hill 2, Mt Olive 2). **Avg SAT:** CR 520. M 490. W 496. Avg ACT: 23. Alum donors: 7%. **Tui '12-'13:** Day $6710-7370 (+$330). Aid: Need 72 ($186,000). **Est 1969.** Nonprofit. Nondenom Christian (98% practice). Sem (Aug-June). **Assoc** SACS. Provisions for the total development of the student are made through a regular academic curriculum that is supplemented by religious studies, the fine arts and regular chapel services.

KERR-VANCE ACADEMY   Day Coed Gr PS (Age 2)-12
Henderson, NC 27537. 700 Vance Academy Rd.
Tel: 252-492-0018. Fax: 252-438-4652.
www.kerrvance.com   E-mail: rirvin@kerrvance.com
      Paul Villatico, Head (2006). BA, MEd, Worcester State College. Rebecca Irvin, Adm.
      Col Prep. AP (45 exams taken, 73% 3+)—Eng Calc Bio Chem US_Hist Psych. **Feat**—Lat Span Environ_Sci Comp_Sci Art_Hist Studio_Art Journ. **Supp**—Rev Tut. **Comp:** Comp/Stud: 1:6. **Dual enr:** Vance-Granville CC. **Sports**—Basket X-country Golf Soccer Tennis Track. B: Baseball Lacrosse Wrestling. G: Cheer Softball Volley. **Selective adm (Gr PS-11):** 54/yr. Appl fee: $50. Appl due: Feb. **Tests** CEEB Stanford. **Enr 430.** Elem 300. Sec 130. Wh 96%. Blk 2%. Asian 1%. Other 1%. Avg class size: 15. **Fac 48.** M 8/F 40. FT 48. Wh 98%. Blk 1%. Other 1%. Adv deg: 27%. **Grad '11—45.** Col—45. **Avg SAT:** CR 533. M 535. W 520. **Tui '12-'13:** Day $8100-8800 (+$200). Aid: Need 18 ($63,950). **Est 1968.** Nonprofit. Sem (Aug-May). **Assoc** SACS. This college preparatory school follows a liberal arts approach. All students in grades 9-12 perform 10 hours of community service per year. Seniors work for one week in an area they are considering for a future career.

HICKORY DAY SCHOOL   Day Coed Gr PS (Age 4)-8
Hickory, NC 28601. 2535 21st Ave NE.
Tel: 828-256-9492. Fax: 828-256-1475.
www.hickoryday.org   E-mail: jdollar@hickoryday.org
      Janice T. Dollar, Head (2005). BS, BA, Appalachian State Univ, MA, East Tennessee State Univ.
      Pre-Prep. IB PYP. Feat—Humanities Span Computers Studio_Art Visual_Arts Theater_Arts Music. **Supp**—Rem_Math Rem_Read Tut. **Selective adm:** Appl fee: $75. Appl due: Rolling. **Tests** CTP_4. **Enr 68.** Wh 84%. Latino 1%. Blk 1%. Native Am 1%. Asian 11%. Other 2%. Avg class size: 7. Stud/fac: 7:1. **Fac 13.** M 2/F 11. FT 11/PT 2. Wh 99%. Latino 1%. Adv deg: 23%. **Tui '10-'11:** Day $5350-8350. **Est 1993.** Nonprofit. Quar (Aug-June). HDS' developmentally appropriate lower school (grades pre-K-6) stresses basic skills development

while gradually shifting the learning focus from the concrete to the abstract. Children at this level take part in the IB Primary Years Program. During the middle school years (grades 7 and 8), children gain increasing levels of independence as they prepare for public and independent high schools. Computers are present in all classrooms, in accordance with the school's emphasis on technology. Boys and girls in grades 6-8 satisfy a 20-hour community service requirement each year.

HOBGOOD ACADEMY
Day Coed Gr K-12

Hobgood, NC 27843. 201 S Beech St.
Tel: 252-826-4116. Fax: 252-826-2265.
www.hobgoodacademy.com   E-mail: goraiders@hobgoodacademy.com
William H. Whitehurst, Head. BS, Atlantic Christian College.

Col Prep. Feat—Span Environ_Sci Comp_Sci Psych Sociol Film Studio_Art Music Journ Woodworking Study_Skills. **Supp**—Rem_Math Rem_Read Tut. **Dual enr:** Halifax CC. **Sports**—Basket. B: Baseball Football Golf. G: Cheer Softball Volley. **Somewhat selective adm:** 30/yr. Appl due: Apr. Accepted: 98%. Yield: 100%. **Enr 220.** Avg class size: 21. Casual dress. **Fac 19.** M 3/F 16. **Grad '07—26.** Col—25. **Avg SAT:** CR/M 1140. **Tui '07-'08:** Day $3710 (+$500). **Est 1970.** Nonprofit. Sem (Aug-June). This traditional elementary and secondary school draws students from Edgecombe, Halifax, Martin, Nash and Pitt counties. In addition to classes in the core subjects, boys and girls may enroll in electives in such areas as horticulture, technology and the arts. Each year, pupils in grades 9-12 perform 25 hours of required community service.

CHESTERBROOK ACADEMY
Day Coed Gr PS (Age 3)-5

Raleigh, NC 27615. 10200 Strickland Rd.
Tel: 919-847-3120, 877-638-8131. Fax: 919-847-2120.
http://northraleigh.chesterbrookacademy.com   E-mail: megan.coleman@nlcinc.com
Michael Williams, Prin.

Gen Acad. Feat—Span Studio_Art Drama Music. **Supp**—Rev Tut. **Somewhat selective adm:** 60/yr. Appl due: Rolling. Accepted: 98%. Yield: 98%. **Enr 145.** Avg class size: 12. **Fac 14. Tui '04-'05:** Day $7100-7200 (+$300-1350). **Est 1985.** Inc. Spons: Nobel Learning Communities. Quar (Aug-May). Children in Chesterbrook's kindergarten program gain an introduction to reading and language arts, in addition to basic mathematical and scientific concepts. First grade offers a chance for the student to acquire fundamental abilities through a skill-based curriculum. In grades 2-5, teachers emphasize problem solving and critical-thinking skills. The creative arts, Spanish, music and physical education provide enrichment opportunities.

ST. DAVID'S SCHOOL
Day Coed Gr K-12

Raleigh, NC 27609. 3400 White Oak Rd.
Tel: 919-782-3331. Fax: 919-571-3330.
www.sdsw.org   E-mail: twilson@sdsw.org
Kevin J. Lockerbie, Head. Teresa Wilson, Adm.

Col Prep. AP (196 exams taken, 90% 3+)—Eng Fr Lat Span Calc Stats Bio Chem Physics Eur_Hist US_Hist World_Hist Psych Art_Hist Studio_Art Music_Theory. **Feat**—British_ Lit Greek Anat Geol Programming Web_Design Philos Ceramics Drawing Painting Performing_Arts Sculpt Acting Theater_Arts Chorus Public_Speak. **Supp**—Makeup Rev Tut. **Comp:** Comp/Stud: 1:4. **Sports**—Basket X-country Indoor_Track Soccer Swim Tennis Track. B: Baseball Football Golf Wrestling. G: Cheer Volley. Activities: 23. **Somewhat selective adm:** 130/yr. Appl fee: $75. Appl due: Feb. Accepted: 92%. Yield: 75%. **Tests** ISEE. **Enr 622.** B 326. G 296. Elem 424. Sec 198. Stud/fac: 8:1. **Fac 77.** M 36/F 41. FT 75/PT 2. Wh 97%. Latino 1%. Blk 1%. Asian 1%. Adv deg: 46%. **Grad '09—61.** Col—61. (UNC-Chapel Hill 8, NC St 5, Elon 4, Furman 3, Hampden-Sydney 3, Meredith 3). **Mid 50% SAT:** CR 550-670.

M 570-690. W 560-670. **Col Couns:** 2. **Tui '11-'12:** Day $13,950-16,650 (+$100-1600). Aid: Need 87 ($358,300). **Est 1972.** Nonprofit. Episcopal. Sem (Aug-May). **Assoc** SACS. A broad, accelerated curriculum is provided at this Christian school, which conducts daily chapel services. Designed for the college-bound student of average to above-average ability, the upper school program features Advanced Placement courses in the major disciplines. Boys and girls accumulate 80 hours of required community service in grades 9-12.

ROCKY MOUNT ACADEMY   Day Coed Gr PS (Age 4)-12
Rocky Mount, NC 27803. 1313 Avondale Ave.
Tel: 252-443-4126. Fax: 252-937-7922.
www.rmacademy.com   E-mail: mwalker@rmacademy.com
     Beth Barbour Covolo, Head (2011). BS, MSA, East Carolina Univ. Millie H. Walker, Adm.

     Col Prep. AP (96 exams taken, 80% 3+)—Eng Calc Stats Chem Environ_Sci Eur_Hist US_Hist Comp_Govt & Pol Econ Psych US_Govt & Pol Studio_Art. **Feat**—Creative_Writing Poetry Mythology Fr Span Anat & Physiol Forensic_Sci Marine_Bio/Sci Comp_Sci Women's_Hist WWII Philos World_Relig Ceramics Film Photog Music Public_Speak SAT_Prep. **Supp**—Tut. **Dual enr:** NC Wesleyan, Nash CC. **Sports**—Basket X-country Soccer Swim Tennis. B: Baseball Football Golf. G: Cheer Softball Volley. **Selective adm:** 69/yr. Appl fee: $90. Accepted: 80%. Yield: 95%. **Tests** IQ. **Enr 414.** B 211. G 203. Elem 284. Sec 130. Nonwhite 13%. Avg class size: 13. Stud/fac: 8:1. **Fac 52.** M 12/F 40. Adv deg: 46%. **Grad '11—23.** Col—23. **Avg SAT:** CR/M/W 1740. Alum donors: 8%. **Tui '06-'07:** Day $4095-9790 (+$450-725). Aid: Need 103. **Est 1968.** Nonprofit. Tri (Aug-June). **Assoc** SACS. RMA's college preparatory curriculum includes honors and Advanced Placement courses during the high school years, in addition to a well-established technology program. Students perform 50 cumulative hours of compulsory community service in grades 9-12.

THE O'NEAL SCHOOL   Day Coed Gr PS (Age 3)-12
Southern Pines, NC 28388. 3300 Airport Rd, PO Box 290.
Tel: 910-692-6920. Fax: 910-692-6930.
www.onealschool.org   E-mail: adroppers@onealschool.org
     Alan K. Barr, Head (2009). BA, Hampden-Sydney College, MS, Longwood Univ. Alice Droppers, Adm.

     Col Prep. AP (exams req'd; 185 taken, 65% 3+)—Eng Calc Stats Bio Chem Environ_Sci Physics Eur_Hist US_Hist US_Govt & Pol Studio_Art. **Feat**—Creative_Writing Sci_Fiction Fr Lat Span Comp_Sci Econ Sociol Philos Ceramics Film Photog Drama Music Public_Speak. **Supp**—LD Rev Tut. **Sports**—Basket X-country Golf Soccer Swim Tennis Track. B: Baseball. G: Cheer Volley. Activities: 29. **Somewhat selective adm:** 96/yr. Appl fee: $75. Appl due: Rolling. Accepted: 86%. Yield: 81%. **Tests** CEEB Stanford. **Enr 430.** B 201. G 229. Elem 272. Sec 158. Wh 89%. Latino 2%. Blk 3%. Asian 3%. Other 3%. Avg class size: 15. Stud/fac: 12:1. Casual dress. **Fac 56.** M 14/F 42. FT 47/PT 9. Wh 100%. Adv deg: 33%. **Grad '11—43.** Col—43. **Avg SAT:** CR 600. M 600. W 585. Avg ACT: 27. **Col Couns:** 1. Alum donors: 10%. **Tui '12-'13:** Day $9400-15,500 (+$500). Aid: Merit 3 ($33,525). Need 101 ($660,410). **Est 1971.** Nonprofit. Tri (Aug-May). **Assoc** CLS SACS. Serving students of average and above-average ability, O'Neal draws boys and girls from six counties to its 40-acre campus. The traditional, structured curriculum enables pupils to accelerate in grade 8 by enrolling in high school mathematics and foreign language classes, then to take Advanced Placement courses in the upper school (grades 9-12). All boys and girls accumulate 36 hours of community service during the upper school years.

FRIENDS SCHOOL OF WILMINGTON   **Day Coed Gr PS (Age 2)-8**
Wilmington, NC 28409. 350 Peiffer Ave.
Tel: 910-792-1811, 888-644-3769. Fax: 910-792-9274.
Other locations: 207 Pine Grove Dr, Wilmington 28403.
www.fsow.org   E-mail: info@fsow.org
    Ethan D. Williamson, Head (1997). BS, Guilford College. Ann M. Souder, Adm.
    Gen Acad. Montessori. Feat—Span Computers Quakerism Studio_Art Drama Music Dance Study_Skills. **Supp**—Dev_Read Tut. **Comp:** Comp/Stud: 1:3. **Sports**—Basket Lacrosse Soccer Tennis. **Selective adm:** 31/yr. Appl fee: $100. Appl due: Rolling. Accepted: 78%. Yield: 63%. **Enr 181.** B 89. G 92. Wh 96%. Blk 1%. Asian 2%. Other 1%. Avg class size: 15. Stud/fac: 12:1. Casual dress. **Fac 22.** M 2/F 20. FT 15/PT 7. Nonwhite 4%. Adv deg: 27%. **Grad '11—13.** Prep—2. (Cape Fear 2). **Tui '11-'12:** Day $9189 (+$950). Aid: Merit 15 ($52,900). Need 30 ($108,350). **Est 1994.** Nonprofit. Religious Society of Friends (3% practice). Quar (Aug-June). FSOW places significant emphasis on Quaker values and traditions, with students attending Meeting for Worship daily and engaging in an extended class period devoted to on- or off-campus community service projects each week; the curriculum also includes a Quakerism class. Whenever possible, instructors make connections across the academic disciplines in the basic subjects of language arts, math, science and social studies. Field trips and school visitors form an important component of these integrated theme units. The preschool/elementary campus is located on Pine Grove Drive.

SOUTH CAROLINA

MEAD HALL EPISCOPAL SCHOOL   **Day Coed Gr PS (Age 3)-12**
Aiken, SC 29801. 129 Pendleton St SW.
Tel: 803-644-1122. Fax: 803-644-1122.
Other locations: 619 Barnwell Ave NW, Aiken 29801.
www.meadhallschool.org   E-mail: meadhall@meadhallschool.org
    Katherine B. Gordon, Head. BS, College of William and Mary, MS, Univ of Virginia. Ferris Delionbach, Adm.
    Col Prep. AP—Eng Calc US_Hist Studio_Art. **Feat**—Creative_Writing Span Environ_Sci Comp_Sci Web_Design Econ Psych Sociol Theater Music Finance Public_Speak. **Supp**—Tut. **Sports**—Soccer Tennis. B: Baseball Basket Golf. G: Volley. **Somewhat selective adm:** 89/yr. Appl fee: $40. Appl due: Rolling. Accepted: 90%. Yield: 98%. **Tests** MAT Stanford. **Enr 356.** B 162. G 194. Wh 86%. Latino 1%. Blk 12%. Asian 1%. Avg class size: 12. Stud/fac: 8:1. Uniform. **Fac 57.** M 8/F 49. FT 36/PT 21. Wh 94%. Latino 3%. Blk 3%. **Grad '11—9.** Col—9. (Clemson 3, U of SC-Aiken 2, Wofford 1, U of SC 1, Savannah Col of Art & Design 1, Coastal Carolina CC 1). **Avg SAT:** CR 561. M 606. W 567. Avg ACT: 25. **Tui '12-'13:** Day $4825-12,700 (+$0-1150). Aid: Merit 7 ($7250). Need 31 ($76,250). **Est 1955.** Nonprofit. Episcopal. Quar (Aug-June). **Assoc** SACS. After serving elementary children for more than five decades, Mead Hall effected a merger with Aiken Preparatory School in June 2012, in the process adding a high school program. The high school division occupies the 12-acre former Aiken Prep campus on Barnwell Avenue Northwest.
    During the early years, Mead Hall introduces Spanish to its three-year-old children as a weekly enrichment class. The school places particular emphasis on cognitive and language/literacy skills during the primary grades. For older pupils, instructors teach the writing process through expressive, informative, persuasive and descriptive writing, as well as a discussion of comparison, classification, argumentation and definition. Boys and girls engage in various community outreach activities at all grade levels.
    Offerings in foreign language, art, computer and music complement the secondary students' foundation in the core academic subject areas. Honors classes in all core subjects are part of the high school curriculum, as are certain Advanced Placement courses. A tutorial program is available for those in need of additional academic support.

In addition to its interscholastic sports program, Mead Hall conducts a nontraditional physical education program. Horseback riding is also available in the nearby, 2000-acre Hitchcock Woods.

MASON PREPARATORY SCHOOL   **Day Coed Gr 1-8**
Charleston, SC 29401. 56 Halsey Blvd.
Tel: 843-723-0664. Fax: 843-723-1104.
www.masonprep.org   E-mail: mainoffice@masonprep.org
     John Horlbeck, Head (2009). BS, The Citadel, MEd, Old Dominion Univ. Lynn Kornya, Adm.
     Pre-Prep. Feat—Fr Span Computers Studio_Art Drama Music Public_Speak. **Supp**—Dev_Read Rem_Math Rev Tut. **Comp:** Comp/Stud: 1:1 **Sports**—Basket Golf Tennis. G: Volley. **Selective adm:** 30/yr. Appl fee: $100. Appl due: Feb. **Enr 330.** Avg class size: 21. Stud/fac: 14:1. **Fac 36.** FT 32/PT 4. Adv deg: 27%. **Grad '05—46.** Prep—46. **Tui '11-'12:** Day $10,030-10,450 (+$700). **Est 1964.** Nonprofit. Quar (Aug-May). **Assoc** SACS. In grades 1-6, Mason Prep's curriculum emphasizes the core subjects of language arts, math, the natural sciences and social studies. Frequent field trips and guest speakers enrich the program during these years. Preparation for secondary school is of primary importance in grades 7 and 8, and advanced students may earn high school credit in algebra, French and Spanish. Eighth graders satisfy a 20-hour community service requirement.

BEN LIPPEN SCHOOL   **Bdg Coed Gr 6-12**
Columbia, SC 29203. 7401 Monticello Rd.   **Day Coed PS (Age 4)-12**
Tel: 803-807-4100. Fax: 803-744-1387.
Other locations: 500 St Andrews Rd, Columbia 29210.
www.benlippen.com   E-mail: kelly.adams@benlippen.com
     Mickey Bowdon, Head. Kelly Adams & Debbie Austin, Adms.
     Col Prep. AP (exams req'd; 350 taken)—Eng Calc Bio Chem Physics US_Hist Studio_Art. **Feat**—Fr Lat Span Anat & Physiol Comp_Sci Amer_Stud Sociol Bible Philos Music Accounting Speech. **Supp**—ESL Rem_Math Rem_Read Tut. **Comp:** Comp/Stud: 1:3.3. **Dual enr:** Columbia Intl. **Sports**—Basket X-country Soccer Swim Tennis Track. B: Baseball Football Golf Wrestling. G: Cheer Softball Volley. Activities: 13. **Selective adm:** 171/yr. Bdg 43. Day 128. Appl fee: $50-100. Appl due: Rolling. Accepted: 77%. Yield: 71%. **Tests** Stanford TOEFL. **Enr 777.** B 405. G 372. Bdg 93. Day 684. Wh 81%. Blk 4%. Asian 11%. Other 4%. Intl 10%. Avg class size: 24. Uniform. **Fac 55.** M 22/F 33. FT 47/PT 8. Wh 92%. Blk 6%. Asian 1%. Other 1%. Adv deg: 52%. In Dorms 2. **Grad '10—92.** Col—90. (Clemson 15, U of SC 15, Midlands Tech 5, N Greenville 4, MI St 2, MA Col of Pharmacy 2). **Avg SAT:** CR 550. M 595. W 536. Avg ACT: 22. **Col Couns:** 4. **Tui '11-'12:** Bdg $29,770 (+$1200). Day $7420-11,165 (+$400-600). Aid: Need 104 ($173,055). **Est 1940.** Nonprofit. Nondenom Christian (80% practice). Spons: Columbia International University. Sem (Aug-May). **Assoc** SACS. Ben Lippen's structured program combines academic and Bible curricula. Elementary students (grades pre-K-5) receive computer tutoring and attend art and music classes weekly. Upper school pupils (grades 9-12) may enroll in honors and Advanced Placement courses. Seniors fulfill a 30-hour community service requirement. The school maintains a second elementary division (grades pre-K-5) on St. Andrews Road.

HAMMOND SCHOOL   **Day Coed Gr PS (Age 4)-12**
Columbia, SC 29209. 854 Galway Ln.
Tel: 803-776-0295. Fax: 803-776-0122.
www.hammondschool.org   E-mail: admission@hammondschool.org
     Christopher B. Angel, Head. BS, Univ of Georgia, MA, Columbia Univ. Matthew W. Radtke, Adm.
     Col Prep. AP (exams req'd; 215 taken, 74% 3+)—Eng Fr Lat Span Calc Stats Bio Chem

Environ_Sci Physics Eur_Hist US_Hist Psych Studio_Art. **Feat**—British_Lit Shakespeare Anat & Physiol Astron Ecol Holocaust Econ Intl_Relations Art_Hist Ceramics Film Filmmaking Drama Theater_Arts Chorus Dance Journ Public_Speak. **Supp**—Tut. **Comp:** Laptop prgm Gr PS-12. **Sports**—Basket X-country Equestrian Golf Soccer Swim Tennis Track. B: Baseball Football Wrestling. G: Cheer Softball Volley. Activities: 30. **Selective adm:** 133/yr. Appl fee: $75. Appl due: Rolling. Accepted: 50%. Yield: 96%. **Tests** CEEB IQ ISEE SSAT Stanford. **Enr 902.** B 451. G 451. Wh 86%. Latino 1%. Blk 10%. Asian 2%. Other 1%. Stud/fac: 8:1. Uniform. **Fac 105.** M 26/F 79. FT 99/PT 6. Wh 93%. Latino 3%. Blk 3%. Asian 1%. Adv deg: 70%. **Grad '11—61.** Col—59. **Avg SAT:** CR/M 1178. **Col Couns:** 2. **Tui '12-'13:** Day $11,626-15,365 (+$250-400). Aid: Need ($1,200,000). **Est 1966.** Nonprofit. Sem (Aug-May). **Assoc** CLS SACS. With an educational approach that focuses on academic skills, Hammond places particular emphasis on reading and written expression, while also providing students with a grounding in math and science. In each division, the school's program allows pupils who have mastered the core curriculum to undertake accelerated or advanced work in every discipline, and college preparation and admission become primary objectives during the upper school years. Visits from speakers, writers, painters and poets from around the world enrich the fine arts program.

THE BYRNES SCHOOLS　　　Day Coed Gr PS (Age 3)-12
Florence, SC 29506. 1201 E Ashby Rd.
Tel: 843-662-0131. Fax: 843-669-2466.
www.byrnesschools.org　E-mail: contact@byrnesschools.org
　Brandis Winstead, Head (212). BEd, MEd, Francis Marion Univ, MS, South Carolina State Univ. Kelley Byrd, Adm.

　Col Prep. AP (exams req'd; 45 taken, 44% 3+)—Eng Span Calc Bio Chem Eur_Hist US_Hist. **Feat**—British_Lit World_Lit Comp_Sci Econ Govt Psych Studio_Art Drama. **Comp:** Comp/Stud: 1:8. **Dual enr:** Francis Marion. **Sports**—Basket Golf Soccer Tennis. B: Baseball Football. G: Cheer Softball Volley. Activities: 8. **Somewhat selective adm:** 35/yr. Appl fee: $50. Appl due: Rolling. Accepted: 92%. Yield: 100%. **Tests** CEEB IQ Stanford. **Enr 200.** B 111. G 89. Elem 132. Sec 68. Wh 84%. Latino 1%. Blk 12%. Native Am 1%. Asian 1%. Other 1%. Avg class size: 9. Stud/fac: 9:1. **Fac 28.** Nonwhite 5%. Adv deg: 39%. **Grad '11—12.** Col—12. (Francis Marion 3, Col of Charleston 2, U of AL-Tuscaloosa 1, U of the South 1, U of SC 1, Florence Darlingon Tech 1). **Avg SAT:** CR 475. M 515. W 434. Avg ACT: 21. Alum donors: 12%. **Tui '12-'13:** Day $5900-7050 (+$500). Aid: Need 47 ($125,775). **Est 1966.** Nonprofit. Sem (Aug-May). In addition to the standard course work, supplemental programs are available in computers, art and foreign languages beginning at the elementary level. Juniors and seniors may take honors and Advanced Placement courses in most subjects. Seventh-period enrichment elective courses meet twice each week.

BOB JONES ACADEMY　　　Bdg Coed Gr 9-12
Greenville, SC 29614. 1700 Wade Hampton Blvd.　　　Day Coed PS (Age 3)-12
Tel: 864-770-1395. Fax: 864-271-7278.
www.bobjonesacademy.net　E-mail: bja@bobjonesacademy.net
　Dan Nelson, Admin (2011). BS, MA, Bob Jones Univ, MS, Marshall Univ. Ben Yarborough, Adm.

　Col Prep. Feat—Fr Ger Lat Span Programming Econ Govt Bible Studio_Art Band Chorus Orchestra Handbells Accounting Journ Public_Speak Speech Indus_Arts Driver_Ed. **Supp**—Dev_Read Tut. **Sports**—Basket. B: Soccer. G: Volley. Activities: 14. **Selective adm:** Appl fee: $0. Appl due: Rolling. **Tests** Stanford TOEFL. **Enr 1178.** Bdg 21. Day 1157. Elem 812. Sec 366. Stud/fac: 13:1. **Fac 91.** M 26/F 65. FT 76/PT 15. Wh 98%. Latino 2%. Adv deg: 58%. **Grad '11—114.** Col—108. (Bob Jones 87, Anderson-SC 6, Greenville Tech 5, N Greenville 2, U of SC 2). Avg ACT: 23. **Col Couns:** 1. **Tui '12-'13:** Bdg $10,330 (+$370). Day $3890-4900 (+$370). **Est 1927.** Inc. Nondenom Christian. Sem (Aug-May). Students at this Christian school have frequent opportunities to perform community service. Graduation requirements reflect the admissions requirements for Bob Jones University.

ST. JOSEPH'S CATHOLIC SCHOOL   **Day Coed Gr 6-12**
Greenville, SC 29607. 100 St Joseph's Dr.
Tel: 864-234-9009, 866-510-7527. Fax: 864-234-5516.
www.sjcatholicschool.org   E-mail: info@sjcatholicschool.org
   Keith F. Kiser, Head (2000). BA, Grove City College, MEd, Duquesne Univ. Barbara McGrath, Adm.
   Col Prep. AP (exams req'd; 185 taken, 85% 3+)—Eng Fr Lat Span Calc Stats Comp_Sci Bio Chem Physics Eur_Hist US_Hist Econ US_Govt & Pol. **Feat**—Anat & Physiol Forensic_Sci Theol Fine_Arts Theater_Arts Chorus Dance Journ. **Supp**—LD Tut. **Sports**—Basket X-country Golf Soccer Swim Tennis. B: Baseball Football Wrestling. G: Cheer Softball Volley. **Activities:** 47. **Somewhat selective adm:** 138/yr. Appl fee: $125. Appl due: Feb. Accepted: 88%. Yield: 83%. **Tests** HSPT. **Enr 611.** B 295. G 316. Elem 256. Sec 355. Wh 86%. Latino 5%. Blk 3%. Asian 2%. Other 4%. Avg class size: 19. Stud/fac: 13:1. Uniform. **Fac 54.** M 24/F 30. FT 47/PT 7. Wh 89%. Latino 8%. Asian 3%. Adv deg: 42%. **Grad '11—76.** Col—76. (U of SC 14, Clemson 13, Col of Charleston 10, U of AL-Tuscaloosa 4, Furman 2, Coastal Carolina CC 2). **Avg SAT:** CR 615. M 611. W 598. Avg ACT: 27. **Col Couns:** 1. **Tui '11-'12:** Day $7490-9280 (+$1800-2010). Aid: Need 249 ($585,000). **Est 1993.** Nonprofit. Roman Catholic (75% practice). Sem (Aug-May). St. Joseph's traditional liberal arts curriculum comprises the arts and sciences, the humanities and a complete Catholic theology program. In addition to an array of college preparatory, honors and Advanced Placement courses, high schoolers have access to a comprehensive college guidance program. The school conducts a program for college-bound boys and girls with mild language or learning disabilities. All high school students perform 65 hours of community service prior to graduation.

SHANNON FOREST CHRISTIAN SCHOOL   **Day Coed Gr PS (Age 3)-12**
Greenville, SC 29615. 829 Garlington Rd.
Tel: 864-678-5107. Fax: 864-281-9372.
www.shannonforest.com   E-mail: admissions@shannonforest.com
   Bob Collins, Pres (2010). BA, Mars Hill Bible College, MA, Clemson Univ. Lynn Pittman, Adm.
   Col Prep. AP—Eng Calc Comp_Sci Bio Eur_Hist US_Hist. **Feat**—Fr Span Web_Design Psych Sociol Bible Photog Studio_Art Drama Chorus Journ. **Supp**—LD Tut. **Comp:** Comp/Stud: 1:4. **Sports**—Basket X-country Soccer Swim Track. B: Baseball Football Golf. G: Cheer Volley. **Somewhat selective adm:** Appl fee: $150. Appl due: Rolling. **Tests** CEEB IQ Stanford. **Enr 424.** Stud/fac: 9:1. Uniform. **Fac 48.** M 6/F 42. Adv deg: 41%. **Grad '10—21.** Col—20. **Avg SAT:** CR/M/W 1674. Avg ACT: 23. **Tui '12-'13:** Day $6200-8900 (+$300-450). **Est 1968.** Nonprofit. Nondenom Christian. Sem (Aug-May). **Assoc** SACS. Providing a Christian college preparatory education, Shannon Forest offers chapel services and Bible study. Honors and Advanced Placement courses are available, as is a program (for an additional fee) for students in grades 1-12 with learning differences. Boys and girls perform 30 cumulative hours of required community service in grades 9-12.

CAMBRIDGE ACADEMY   **Day Coed Gr PS (Age 3)-8**
Greenwood, SC 29649. 103 Eastman Dr.
Tel: 864-229-2875. Fax: 864-229-6712.
www.cambridgecougars.org   E-mail: mprice@cambridgeacademy.org
   Jody Gable, Head (2011). BS, Ball State Univ. Mandy Price, Adm.
   Pre-Prep. Gen Acad. Feat—Span Computers Studio_Art Chorus Music. **Supp**—Dev_Read Rev Tut. **Comp:** Comp/Stud: 1:4. **Sports**—Basket X-country Swim Tennis. B: Football Golf. G: Cheer. **Somewhat selective adm:** 40/yr. Appl fee: $75. Appl due: Mar. Accepted:

90%. Yield: 92%. **Tests** Stanford. **Enr 167.** B 87. G 80. Avg class size: 12. **Fac 19.** M 3/F 16. FT 19. Adv deg: 15%. Alum donors: 10%. **Tui '12-'13:** Day $5009-7530 (+$575-835). **Est 1968.** Nonprofit. Sem (Aug-May). **Assoc** SACS. The early and lower school programs (grades pre-K-5) emphasize basic skills in reading, writing and math. Music, art, Spanish, computer, library, health and physical education are included for each grade. Students in grades 6-8 perform 20 hours of compulsory community service annually.

HILTON HEAD PREPARATORY SCHOOL   **Day Coed Gr PS (Age 4)-12**
Hilton Head Island, SC 29928. 8 Fox Grape Rd.
Tel: 843-671-2286. Fax: 843-671-7624.
www.hhprep.org   E-mail: bsomerville@hhprep.org
    Anthony Kandel, Head (2009). BA, Pomona College, MA, PhD, Univ of Southern California. Bobbie Somerville, Adm.

    Col Prep. AP—Eng Fr Span Calc Stats Bio Chem Physics US_Hist US_Govt & Pol Studio_Art. **Feat**—British_Lit Chin Marine_Bio/Sci Econ Chorus Orchestra. **Supp**—Dev_ Read LD Tut. **Sports**—Basket X-country Soccer Tennis. B: Baseball Football Golf. G: Volley. Activities: 26. **Selective adm:** 77/yr. Appl fee: $75. Appl due: Rolling. Accepted: 75%. Yield: 90%. **Tests** SSAT Stanford. **Enr 440.** B 220. G 220. Elem 289. Sec 151. Avg class size: 12. **Fac 57.** Adv deg: 59%. **Grad '11—49.** Col—49. **Avg SAT:** CR 544. M 528. W 537. Avg ACT: 24. **Col Couns:** 1. **Tui '12-'13:** Day $7950-16,575 (+$325). **Est 1965.** Nonprofit. Tri (Aug-May). **Assoc** SACS. Hilton Head Prep conducts an honors program in grades 6-12, as well as Advanced Placement courses in the upper school. Graduation requirements include computer literacy and the delivery of a senior speech. In addition, boys and girls in grades 9-12 perform 10 hours of required community service per year. A travel program and career internships are available. The school's learning center offers student and professional tutoring.

TRIDENT ACADEMY   **Day Coed Gr K-12**
Mount Pleasant, SC 29464. 1455 Wakendaw Rd.
Tel: 843-884-3494. Fax: 843-884-1483.
www.tridentacademy.com   E-mail: admissions@tridentacademy.com
    Joe Ferber, Head (2007). BA, George Washington Univ, MEd, American Univ. Patty Held, Adm.

    Col Prep. Gen Acad. LD. Feat—Span Speech. **Supp**—Dev_Read Rem_Math Rem_Read Rev Tut. **Sports**—Basket Golf Soccer Tennis Track. G: Cheer Volley. **Somewhat selective adm:** 15/yr. Appl fee: $150. Appl due: Rolling. Accepted: 99%. Yield: 100%. **Tests** IQ. **Enr 100.** B 74. G 26. Wh 97%. Blk 1%. Asian 2%. Avg class size: 8. Stud/fac: 3:1. **Fac 30.** M 4/F 26. FT 30. Nonwhite 2%. Adv deg: 30%. **Grad '10—7.** Col—7. **Col Couns:** 1. **Tui '11-'12:** Day $24,780-24,930 (+$900-2650). Aid: Merit 3 ($3500). Need 21 ($240,000). **Est 1972.** Nonprofit. Sem (Aug-May). **Assoc** SACS. This college preparatory school serves children with learning disabilities who possess average to above-average intelligence. Diagnosis of a learning disability is required for admission. The academy utilizes a multisensory teaching approach within a structured, individualized environment. Students in grades 10-12 perform community service. A limited number of boarders reside with local families.

LOWCOUNTRY PREPARATORY SCHOOL   **Day Coed Gr PS (Age 3)-12**
Pawleys Island, SC 29585. 300 Blue Stem Dr.
Tel: 843-237-4147. Fax: 843-237-4543.
www.lowcountryprep.org   E-mail: info@lowcountryprep.org
    Scott K. Gibson III, Head.

    Col Prep. AP (18 exams taken, 44% 3+)—Eng Fr Calc Bio Environ_Sci Eur_Hist US_ Govt & Pol. **Feat**—Lat Span Forensic_Sci Computers Relig Studio_Art Drama Music. **Dual enr:** Coastal Carolina CC. **Sports**—Basket Soccer Swim Tennis. B: Golf. G: Cheer Volley. **Selective adm:** 36/yr. Appl fee: $40. Appl due: Mar. Accepted: 80%. Yield: 95%. **Tests** IQ

Stanford. **Enr 160.** Wh 89%. Blk 5%. Asian 1%. Other 5%. Avg class size: 13. **Fac 24.** M 5/F 19. FT 22/PT 2. Wh 99%. Asian 1%. Adv deg: 58%. **Grad '10—9.** Col—9. (U of VA 1, Loyola U-LA 1, U of TN-Knoxville 1, UNC-Wilmington 1, Winthrop 1, Presbyterian 1). **Avg SAT:** CR 634. M 608. W 615. **Tui '10-'11:** Day $6500-8700 (+$450-750). Aid: Need 29 ($125,000). **Est 1995.** Nonprofit. Sem (Aug-May). **Assoc** SACS. In addition to core academics classes, students at LPS are encouraged to pursue course work in the arts. The lower school (grades PS-5) provides a solid foundation in the standard subjects. During the middle and upper school years (grades 6-12), pupils have enrichment options in the fields of music, drama, chorus, dance and computers. All boys and girls compile 80 hours of community service in grades 9-12.

PINEWOOD PREPARATORY SCHOOL   Day Coed Gr PS (Age 3)-12
Summerville, SC 29483. 1114 Orangeburg Rd.
Tel: 843-873-1643. Fax: 843-821-4257.
www.pinewoodprep.com   E-mail: admissions@pinewoodprep.com
   Stephen M. Mandell, Head (2011). Nicole Bailey, Adm.

   Col Prep. AP (145 exams taken, 80% 3+)—Eng Span Calc Stats Bio Chem Environ_Sci Physics Eur_Hist US_Hist Human_Geog US_Govt & Pol Studio_Art. **Feat**—British_Lit Zoology Comp_Sci Robotics Econ Psych Drama Chorus Music Dance Journ Marketing Public_Speak. **Supp**—Rem_Read Tut. Outdoor Ed. **Dual enr:** Trident Tech. **Sports**—Basket X-country Equestrian Fencing Golf Soccer Swim Tennis. B: Baseball Football. G: Cheer Softball Volley. Activities: 20. **Selective adm (Gr PS-11):** 175/yr. Appl fee: $50. Appl due: Rolling. Accepted: 70%. Yield: 90%. **Tests** IQ Stanford. **Enr 800.** Wh 89%. Latino 2%. Blk 5%. Asian 2%. Other 2%. Intl 5%. Avg class size: 15. Stud/fac: 12:1. **Fac 77.** M 15/F 62. FT 75/PT 2. Wh 98%. Blk 2%. **Grad '11—69.** Col—69. **Mid 50% SAT:** CR 510-620. M 530-640. W 480-580. **Tui '12-'13:** Day $8475-10,990 (+$450-800). Aid: Need 122 ($450,000). **Est 1952.** Nonprofit. Quar (Aug-June). **Assoc** SACS. Pinewood's college preparatory program features advanced-level instruction in math, English, science, history and foreign language. Art, music, study skills and physical education complement the core curriculum. A community service program requires students to complete five hours of service per year in grades 6-8, 10 hours in grades 9-11, and 30 hours in grade 12. Pinewood teachers who serve as adjunct faculty at Trident Technical College teach courses offering dual high school and college credit.

WILSON HALL   Day Coed Gr PS (Age 4)-12
Sumter, SC 29150. 520 Wilson Hall Rd.
Tel: 803-469-3475. Fax: 803-469-3477.
www.wilsonhall.org   E-mail: sean_hoskins@hotmail.com
   Frederick B. Moulton, Head (1988). BS, MEd, Univ of South Carolina. Sean P. Hoskins, Adm.

   Col Prep. AP (174 exams taken, 67% 3+)—Eng Fr Lat Span Calc Stats Comp_Sci Bio Chem Physics Eur_Hist US_Hist US_Govt & Pol Studio_Art Music_Theory. **Feat**—Creative_ Writing Southern_Lit Anat Environ_Sci Psych Sociol Philos Theol World_Relig Art_Hist Ceramics Photog Journ. **Supp**—Tut. **Comp:** Comp/Stud: 1:7. **Sports**—Basket Bowl X-country Golf Soccer Swim Tennis Track. B: Football. G: Cheer Equestrian Softball Volley. Activities: 30. **Selective adm (Gr PS-11):** 106/yr. Appl fee: $150. Appl due: Rolling. Accepted: 67%. Yield: 67%. **Tests** CEEB IQ Stanford. **Enr 838.** B 438. G 400. Elem 588. Sec 250. Wh 92%. Blk 3%. Asian 2%. Other 3%. Avg class size: 13. **Fac 74.** M 15/F 59. FT 64/PT 10. Wh 98%. Latino 2%. Adv deg: 41%. **Grad '10—63.** Col—63. (U of SC 13, Clemson 12, Col of Charleston 5, Wofford 4, U of MS 2, Winthrop 2). **Avg SAT:** CR 574. M 591. W 566. Avg ACT: 23.8. **Tui '12-'13:** Day $5175-5995 (+$500). Aid: Need 5 ($10,000). **Est 1966.** Nonprofit. Quar (Aug-June). **Assoc** SACS. Instruction at Wilson Hall is in small classes to provide each student with individual attention. The school offers all courses at the college preparatory level or higher, including Advanced Placement courses in most subjects. Boys and girls accumulate 30 hours of required community service prior to graduation.

TENNESSEE

BRENTWOOD ACADEMY   **Day Coed Gr 6-12**
Brentwood, TN 37027. 219 Granny White Pike.
Tel: 615-373-0611. Fax: 615-377-3709.
www.brentwoodacademy.com   E-mail: admission@brentwoodacademy.com
Curtis G. Masters, Head (2000). BA, Wheaton College (IL), MS, Univ of Puget Sound.
Susan Gering, Adm.

Col Prep. AP (exams req'd; 106 taken)—Eng Fr Lat Span Calc Bio Chem Physics
Eur_Hist US_Hist. **Feat**—British_Lit Humanities Greek Stats Anat & Physiol Marine_Bio/
Sci Comp_Sci African-Amer_Hist Econ Psych Relig Photog Studio_Art Visual_Arts The-
ater_Arts Music Journ Speech. **Supp**—Rev Tut. **Sports**—Basket Bowl X-country Golf Soccer
Swim Tennis Track. B: Baseball Football Wrestling. G: Cheer Softball Volley. Activities: 25.
Somewhat selective adm: 150/yr. Appl fee: $25. Appl due: Rolling. Accepted: 85%. Yield:
61%. **Tests** Stanford. **Enr 765.** Wh 88%. Blk 11%. Asian 1%. Avg class size: 17. Stud/fac:
10:1. **Fac 84.** M 38/F 46. FT 69/PT 15. Wh 94%. Blk 6%. Adv deg: 72%. **Grad '11—106.**
Col—106. (U of TN-Knoxville 28, Belmont U 8, Samford 8, U of TN-Chattanooga 6, TN Tech
6, Auburn 4). **Mid 50% SAT:** CR 490-620. M 470-620. W 480-610. Mid 50% ACT: 22-28.
Col Couns: 2. Alum donors: 10%. **Tui '11-'12:** Day $18,950 (+$500-1000). Aid: Need 150
($1,170,000). **Est 1969.** Nonprofit. Nondenom Christian. Sem (Aug-May). **Assoc** SACS. This
nondenominational school emphasizes traditional Christian values and ethics. Weekly Bible
study and weekend retreats are popular features, although participation in religious activities is
voluntary. An upper school interim program provides enrichment through cultural exchanges,
community service and internships. Community service is part of the curriculum at all grade
levels.

CURREY INGRAM ACADEMY   **Day Coed Gr K-12**
Brentwood, TN 37027. 6544 Murray Ln.
Tel: 615-507-3242, 877-507-3242. Fax: 615-507-3170.
www.curreyingram.org   E-mail: cindy.burch@curreyingram.org
Kathleen G. Rayburn, Head (1995). BS, Saint Mary-of-the-Woods College, MA, Butler
Univ. Amber Cathey, Adm.

Col Prep. LD. Feat—Creative_Writing Span Calc Environ_Sci Econ Govt Ethics Studio_
Art Theater Music Music_Theory Dance Finance Health ACT_Prep. **Supp**—Dev_Read
Rem_Math Rem_Read Tut. **Comp:** Comp/Stud: 1:1 Laptop prgm Gr K-12. **Sports**—Basket
X-country Soccer. B: Baseball. G: Football Softball Volley. Activities: 26. **Selective adm:**
45/yr. Appl fee: $250. Appl due: Rolling. Accepted: 82%. Yield: 92%. **Tests** IQ. **Enr 340.** Wh
94%. Latino 1%. Blk 3%. Asian 2%. Stud/fac: 4:1. Uniform. **Fac 91.** M 14/F 77. FT 76/PT
15. Wh 96%. Latino 2%. Blk 2%. Adv deg: 68%. **Grad '11—9.** Col—8. (U of AZ 2, Trevecca
Nazarene 2, W KY 1, Mitchell 1, Syracuse 1, Belmont U 1). **Col Couns:** 2. **Tui '12-'13:**
Day $33,070-36,690 (+$300). Aid: Need 119 ($1,200,000). **Est 1968.** Nonprofit. Quar (Aug-
May). **Assoc** SACS. Currey Ingram provides an individualized elementary and secondary
program for students of average to above-average intelligence who have learning differences.
The school's college preparatory program assists pupils in developing effective learning strate-
gies. In a setting that encourages active participation in the learning process, course work balances the acquisition of knowledge and skills with the meeting of individual and group needs.
Children in kindergarten and grade 1 each receive an iPad for school use, while a one-to-one
laptop program serves those in grades 2-12.

BOYD-BUCHANAN SCHOOL   **Day Coed Gr PS (Age 4)-12**
Chattanooga, TN 37411. 4650 Buccaneer Trail.
Tel: 423-622-6177. Fax: 423-508-2218.
www.bbschool.org   E-mail: lwitt@bbschool.org

Lanny Witt, Pres (2007). BS, Abilene Christian Univ, MEd, East Texas State Univ.

Col Prep. AP (92 exams taken, 48% 3+)—Eng Span Calc Bio Chem US_Hist Studio_Art. **Feat**—Fr Engineering Web_Design Psych Sociol Bible Photog Video_Production Graphic_ Design Drama Music_Theory Journ Speech. **Supp**—Dev_Read Rem_Math Rem_Read Tut. **Comp:** Laptop prgm Gr 6-12. **Dual enr:** Lipscomb. **Sports**—Basket X-country Golf Soccer Tennis. B: Baseball Football Wrestling. G: Softball Volley. **Selective adm (Gr PS-11):** 106/yr. Appl fee: $25. Appl due: Rolling. Accepted: 50%. Yield: 90%. **Enr 898.** Wh 90%. Blk 9%. Asian 1%. Avg class size: 15. Uniform. **Fac 72.** M 17/F 55. FT 70/PT 2. Wh 95%. Blk 5%. Adv deg: 26%. **Grad '11—52.** Col—52. **Col Couns:** 1. Alum donors: 30%. **Tui '12-'13:** Day $6750-9160 (+$200). Aid: Need ($113,800). **Est 1952.** Nonprofit. Nondenom Christian (36% practice). Sem (Aug-May). **Assoc** SACS. In addition to core courses, Boyd-Buchanan offers exploratory classes in sign language, journalism, drama and other areas of interest. Music, art and drama are integral parts of the school's curriculum, and all students attend daily Bible classes. Each student performs nine hours of community service per nine-week grading period.

CHATTANOOGA CHRISTIAN SCHOOL   Day Coed Gr K-12

Chattanooga, TN 37409. 3354 Charger Dr.
Tel: 423-265-6411. Fax: 423-756-4044.
www.ccsk12.com   E-mail: kcash@ccsk12.com

Chad Dirkse, Pres (2009). BA, Covenant College, MBA, LeTourneau Univ. Debbie Grisham, Adm.

Col Prep. AP (exams req'd; 53 taken, 83% 3+)—Eng Calc Eur_Hist Studio_Art. **Feat**— Fr Ger Lat Span Anat & Physiol Astron Environ_Sci Geol Kinesiology Programming Web_ Design Civil_Rights WWII Econ Govt Psych Bible Art_Hist Theater Chorus Music Music_ Theory Ballroom_Dancing Modern_Dance Finance Drafting Indus_Arts. **Supp**—Dev_Read LD Makeup Rem_Math Rev Tut. **Comp:** Comp/Stud: 1:1 Outdoor Ed. **Dual enr:** Bryan, Covenant. **Sports**—Basket Bowl X-country Golf Soccer Tennis Track. B: Baseball Football Wrestling. G: Cheer Softball Volley. Activities: 19. **Somewhat selective adm (Gr K-11):** 195/ yr. Appl fee: $100. Appl due: Feb. Accepted: 95%. Yield: 83%. **Tests** Stanford TOEFL. **Enr 1147.** B 574. G 573. Elem 688. Sec 459. Wh 84%. Latino 2%. Blk 10%. Asian 4%. Avg class size: 17. **Fac 95.** M 38/F 57. FT 77/PT 18. Wh 98%. Latino 1%. Blk 1%. Adv deg: 33%. **Grad '11—104.** Col—98. (U of TN-Chattanooga 28, Covenant 11, Chattanooga St CC 8, U of TN-Knoxville 6, Berry 5, E TN St 4). **Avg SAT:** CR 578. M 519. W 540. Avg ACT: 23. **Col Couns:** 1. **Tui '11-'12:** Day $6300-9059 (+$200). Aid: Merit 1 ($8709). Need 184 ($371,444). Work prgm 39 ($169,544). **Est 1970.** Nonprofit. Nondenom Christian. Sem (Aug-May). **Assoc** SACS. Serving children from Christian families, CCS teaches its educational program from a Biblical perspective. In the elementary years (grades K-5), children develop fundamental learning skills. CCS' middle school curriculum (grades 6-8) includes advanced courses at each level. The college preparatory high school course of studies features AP and advanced courses; dual-enrollment classes through two nearby colleges; and strong sports, fine arts, computer and industrial arts programs. A February interim program enables high schoolers to engage in educational travel or special studies for three days or longer.

NOTRE DAME HIGH SCHOOL   Day Coed Gr 9-12

Chattanooga, TN 37404. 2701 Vermont Ave.
Tel: 423-624-4618. Fax: 423-624-4621.
www.myndhs.com   E-mail: admissions@myndhs.com

Perry L. Storey, Prin (1996). BS, MEd, Univ of Tennessee-Chattanooga, EdS, Lincoln Memorial Univ. Jenny Rittgers, Adm.

Col Prep. AP—Bio Chem Physics Eur_Hist US_Hist Studio_Art. **Feat**—Fr Lat Span Stats Anat & Physiol Ecol Forensic_Sci Genetics Comp_Sci Econ Govt Psych Relig Film Theater Chorus Music Dance Journ. **Supp**—Dev_Read LD Makeup Rem_Math Rev Tut. **Dual enr:** Chattanooga St Tech CC. **Sports**—Basket Bowl X-country Soccer Swim Track. B: Baseball

Football Golf Wrestling. G: Cheer Softball Tennis Volley. Activities: 45. **Selective adm:** 165/ yr. Appl fee: $100. Appl due: Rolling. **Enr 471.** Avg class size: 15. Stud/fac: 11:1. Uniform. **Fac 67.** M 24/F 43. FT 67. Adv deg: 58%. **Grad '11—124.** Col—122. **Avg SAT:** CR/M 1080. Avg ACT: 21. **Col Couns:** 1. **Tui '11-'12:** Day $11,444. Catholic $8502. **Est 1876.** Non-profit. Roman Catholic (70% practice). Sem (Aug-May). **Assoc** SACS. Located on a 20-acre campus in the city's Glenwood section, the school provides a structured college preparatory program that features honors and Advanced Placement course work. In addition, dual-enrollment classes are offered in several disciplines in conjunction with Chattanooga State Technical Community College. As roughly 10 percent of enrolled pupils have been diagnosed with a learning disability, Notre Dame conducts an individualized LD program.

COLUMBIA ACADEMY   **Day Coed Gr PS (Age 2)-12**
Columbia, TN 38401. 1101 W 7th St.
Tel: 931-388-5363. Fax: 931-380-8506.
Other locations: 756 Beechcroft Rd, Spring Hill 37174.
www.columbia-academy.net   E-mail: emily.lansdell@cabulldogs.org
     James Thomas, Pres (2009). BA, Freed-Hardeman Univ, MA, EdD, Univ of Memphis. Emily Lansdell, Adm.
     Col Prep. AP (exams req'd; 18 taken, 39% 3+)—Eng US_Hist. **Feat**—Span Calc Anat Comp_Sci Econ Bible Studio_Art Band Chorus Accounting Journ. **Supp**—Tut. **Comp:** Comp/Stud: 1:1 Laptop prgm Gr 7-12. **Dual enr:** Columbia St CC. **Sports**—Basket Bowl X-country Golf Soccer Tennis Track. B: Baseball Football. G: Cheer Softball Volley. Activities: 20. **Somewhat selective adm:** 95/yr. Appl fee: $75. Appl due: Rolling. Accepted: 98%. Yield: 86%. **Tests** IQ. **Enr 706.** B 373. G 333. Elem 533. Sec 173. Wh 93%. Latino 1%. Blk 2%. Asian 1%. Other 3%. Avg class size: 18. Stud/fac: 17:1. **Fac 51.** M 14/F 37. FT 39/PT 12. Wh 100%. Adv deg: 47%. **Grad '11—50.** Col—49. (David Lipscomb 17, Columbia St CC 9, Harding 5, Freed-Hardeman 4, E TN St 3, U of TN-Knoxville 2). Avg ACT: 24. Alum donors: 6%. **Tui '12-'13:** Day $5350-6380 (+$300-500). Aid: Need 94 ($158,595). Work prgm 52 ($28,720). **Est 1905.** Nonprofit. Nondenom Christian (60% practice). Sem (Aug-May). **Assoc** SACS. Founded as Columbia Military Academy, the school changed its name and focus in 1979. The program emphasizes basic academics and Bible study, and CA also offers particularly strong fine arts and athletics programs. Qualified juniors and seniors may take dual-credit courses at Columbia State Community College. Students in grades 9-12 perform 16 hours of required community service each year. A one-to-one tablet computer program serves students in grades 7-12. In the fall of 2010, CA opened a second campus in Spring Hill for children in junior kindergarten through grade 5.

EVANGELICAL CHRISTIAN SCHOOL   **Day Coed Gr PS (Age 4)-12**
Cordova, TN 38088. 7600 Macon Rd, PO Box 1030.
Tel: 901-754-7217. Fax: 901-754-8123.
Other locations: 735 Ridge Lake Blvd, Memphis 38120; 1920 Forest Hill-Irene Rd, German-town 38139; 11893 Macon Rd, Eads 38028.
www.ecseagles.net   E-mail: plittrell@ecseagles.com
     J. Bryan Miller, Pres. BS, Millsaps College. Paul Norby, Head. Patty Littrell, Adm.
     Col Prep. AP (exams req'd; 84 taken, 77% 3+)—Eng Fr Lat Span Calc Bio Eur_Hist US_Hist US_Govt & Pol Studio_Art. **Feat**—Anat & Physiol Comp_Sci Bible Drama Finance Speech. **Supp**—Rev Tut. **Dual enr:** U of Memphis. **Sports**—Basket X-country Golf Soccer Swim Tennis Track. B: Baseball Football. G: Cheer Softball Volley. Activities: 50. **Somewhat selective adm (Gr PS-11):** 150/yr. Appl fee: $50. Appl due: Rolling. Accepted: 92%. Yield: 89%. **Tests** CTP_4 ISEE Stanford. **Enr 1068.** B 534. G 534. Elem 608. Sec 460. Wh 91%. Blk 4%. Asian 2%. Other 3%. Avg class size: 22. Stud/fac: 12:1. Uniform. **Fac 145.** M 27/F 118. FT 123/PT 22. Wh 99%. Asian 1%. Adv deg: 35%. **Grad '10—115.** Col—115. **Avg SAT:** CR 600. M 580. Avg ACT: 26. **Col Couns:** 2. Alum donors: 3%. **Tui '11-'12:** Day $8595-12,630. Aid: Need 246 ($810,451). **Est 1965.** Nonprofit. Evangelical. Sem (Aug-May). **Assoc** SACS.

During the lower school years (grades K-5) at this Bible-based school, children develop a foundation for future learning as they gain an introduction to Spanish and receive basic instruction in music and art. ECS' middle school program (grades 6-8) features an expanded curriculum and discussion-based classes. Upper schoolers choose from Advanced Placement and enrichment courses, in addition to standard offerings. The middle and upper schools operate in Cordova, while ECS maintains lower school campuses in Memphis, Germantown and Eads.

BATTLE GROUND ACADEMY   Day Coed Gr K-12
Franklin, TN 37065. PO Box 1889.
Tel: 615-794-3501. Fax: 615-595-7374.
Other locations: 150 Franklin Rd, Franklin 37064; 336 Ernest Rice Ln, Franklin 37069.
www.battlegroundacademy.org   E-mail: admissions@mybga.org
    John W. Griffith, Head (2009). BA, Middlebury College, MA, Columbia Univ, MPhil, DPhil, Oxford Univ (England). Robin Goertz, Adm.
    Col Prep. AP—Eng Fr Lat Span Stats Bio Chem Eur_Hist US_Hist US_Govt & Pol Studio_Art. **Feat**—Anat & Physiol Environ_Sci Comp_Sci Econ Govt Theater_Arts Music_ Hist Music_Theory. **Supp**—Makeup Tut. **Comp:** Laptop prgm Gr 9-12. **Sports**—Basket Bowl X-country Golf Soccer Swim Tennis Track. B: Baseball Football Wrestling. G: Cheer Softball Volley. **Selective adm:** 180/yr. Appl fee: $50. Appl due: Rolling. **Tests** IQ ISEE Stanford. **Enr 886.** Elem 529. Sec 357. Wh 90%. Blk 8%. Other 2%. Avg class size: 18. Stud/fac: 9:1. Uniform. **Fac 100.** M 37/F 63. FT 100. Wh 93%. Latino 2%. Blk 5%. Adv deg: 66%. **Grad '11—90.** Col—90. **Avg SAT:** CR 607. M 622. W 618. Avg ACT: 26. **Col Couns:** 1. **Tui '12-'13:** Day $14,760-17,930 (+$500-2495). Aid: Need 175. **Est 1889.** Nonprofit. Sem (Aug-May). **Assoc** CLS SACS. BGA's college preparatory program includes both honors and Advanced Placement courses. A comprehensive fine arts program and competitive athletics are also available. Students gain an introduction to community service in the lower school (grades K-4), then satisfy 10- and 20-hour annual requirements in the middle (grades 5-8) and upper (grades 9-12) schools, respectively. The academy operates on two campuses in proximity to one another: The lower school occupies quarters on Franklin Road, while both the middle school and the upper school are located on Ernest Rice Lane.

SUMNER ACADEMY   Day Coed Gr PS (Age 4)-8
Gallatin, TN 37066. 464 Nichols Ln.
Tel: 615-452-1914. Fax: 615-452-1923.
www.sumneracademy.org   E-mail: information@sumneracademy.org
    William E. Hovenden, Head (1991). BA, Cornell College, MS, Indiana Univ, PhD, Florida State Univ. Gillian Gaetano, Adm.
    Pre-Prep. Feat—Span Computers Studio_Art Music. **Supp**—Tut. **Sports**—Basket X-country Golf Soccer Tennis. G: Cheer. **Somewhat selective adm:** 52/yr. Appl fee: $50. Appl due: Rolling. Accepted: 90%. Yield: 91%. **Tests** IQ. **Enr 212.** B 95. G 117. Wh 90%. Blk 3%. Asian 4%. Other 3%. Stud/fac: 15:1. Uniform. **Fac 31.** M 3/F 28. FT 29/PT 2. Wh 92%. Blk 4%. Asian 4%. Adv deg: 48%. **Grad '11—23.** Prep—18. (Pope John Paul II 18). **Tui '11-'12:** Day $8282-10,121 (+$300). Aid: Need 76 ($244,336). **Est 1973.** Nonprofit. Quar (Aug-May). **Assoc** SACS. In addition to a curriculum that offers advanced standing at every grade level, the academy provides special learning activities in music, art, computer, physical education and Spanish. Students are ability grouped for reading and math. The school schedule alternates nine weeks of classes with two weeks of vacation. Sumner schedules frequent guest lectures, concerts, films and field trips.

POPE JOHN PAUL II HIGH SCHOOL   Day Coed Gr 9-12
Hendersonville, TN 37075. 117 Caldwell Dr.
Tel: 615-822-2375. Fax: 615-822-6226.
www.jp2hs.org   E-mail: info@jp2hs.org

Faustin N. Weber, Head (2008). BA, MA, Univ of Notre Dame. Patrick Weaver, Adm. **Col Prep. AP (513 exams taken, 73% 3+)**—Eng Calc Stats Bio Chem Environ_Sci Physics Eur_Hist US_Hist Comp_Govt & Pol Econ Psych US_Govt & Pol. **Feat**—Creative_Writing Fr Lat Span Anat & Physiol Civil_War Theol Drawing Photog Studio_Art Theater_Arts Chorus Music_Hist Orchestra Debate Journ Public_Speak. **Supp**—Tut. **Sports**—Basket Bowl X-country Lacrosse Soccer Swim Tennis Track. B: Baseball Football Ice_Hockey Wrestling. G: Cheer Golf Softball Volley. Activities: 29. **Selective adm (Gr 9-11):** Appl fee: $60. Appl due: Rolling. **Enr 615.** Wh 86%. Latino 2%. Blk 8%. Asian 2%. Other 2%. Stud/fac: 13:1. Uniform. **Fac 55.** Adv deg: 54%. **Grad '09—162.** Col—162. **Avg SAT:** CR 597. M 584. W 572. **Mid 50% SAT:** CR 540-640. M 500-680. W 490-630. Avg ACT: 26.6. Mid 50% ACT: 23-30. **Col Couns:** 2. **Tui '11-'12:** Day $12,075 (+$1175-1425). Catholic $10,600 (+$1175-1425). Aid: Need 141 ($455,923). **Est 2002.** Nonprofit. Roman Catholic (61% practice). Quar (Aug-May). **Assoc** SACS. Located on a 66-acre campus north of Nashville, JPII conducts a classical curriculum that combines work in the core disciplines and electives with the following annual course requirements: a Great Books seminar and four quarter-long Renaissance classes that are designed to expose students to nontraditional subjects. The college counseling office sponsors a college tour program. All boys and girls satisfy a 40-hour community service requirement each year.

EPISCOPAL SCHOOL OF KNOXVILLE   **Day Coed Gr K-8**
Knoxville, TN 37932. 950 Episcopal School Way.
Tel: 865-777-9032. Fax: 865-777-9034.
www.esknoxville.org   E-mail: info@esknoxville.org
James J. Secor III, Head (1999). BA, Virginia Wesleyan College, MEd, James Madison Univ.

Pre-Prep. Feat—Lib_Skills Fr Lat Span Computers Relig Studio_Art Band Music. **Supp**—Dev_Read Rem_Math Rem_Read Tut. **Comp:** Comp/Stud: 1:2 (1:1 Laptop prgm Gr 2-5). **Sports**—Basket X-country Golf Soccer Tennis Track. B: Football. G: Volley. **Somewhat selective adm:** 75/yr. Appl fee: $85. Appl due: Feb. Accepted: 91%. Yield: 85%. **Enr 321.** B 174. G 147. Wh 92%. Latino 3%. Blk 2%. Asian 2%. Other 1%. Avg class size: 15. Stud/fac: 9:1. Uniform. **Fac 50.** M 9/F 41. FT 28/PT 22. Wh 94%. Latino 3%. Other 3%. Adv deg: 52%. **Grad '10—35.** Prep—27. (Webb Sch of Knoxville 7, Webb Sch-Bell Buckle 1, McCallie 1). **Tui '11-'12:** Day $12,080-13,190 (+$400). Aid: Need 50 ($190,000). **Est 1998.** Nonprofit. Episcopal (23% practice). Sem (Aug-May). **Assoc** SACS. Foreign language, art, music and religion classes are core components of each student's education. In both the lower school (grades K-5) and the middle school (grades 6-8), programming focuses on the fundamentals of literature, math, science and social studies, as well as on critical-thinking and study skills. Five times a week, all pupils receive instruction in computer technology and the visual and performing arts. Middle schoolers satisfy the following community service requirements: six hours per year in grade 6, seven hours per year in grade 7 and eight hours per year in grade 8. Boys and girls attend daily chapel services.

FRIENDSHIP CHRISTIAN SCHOOL   **Day Coed Gr PS (Age 3)-12**
Lebanon, TN 37087. 5400 Coles Ferry Pike.
Tel: 615-449-1573. Fax: 615-449-2769.
www.friendshipchristian.org   E-mail: info@fcsweb.net
Jon Shoulders, Pres. BBA, Freed-Hardeman Univ, MEd, David Lipscomb Univ. Terresia Williams, Adm.

Col Prep. AP—Calc. **Feat**—British_Lit Greek Span Anat & Physiol Environ_Sci Comp_ Sci Econ Psych Bible Studio_Art Drama Band Chorus Music. **Supp**—Tut. **Dual enr:** Cumberland U. **Sports**—Basket Bowl X-country Golf Soccer Softball Swim Tennis Track Volley. B: Baseball Football Wrestling. G: Cheer. **Somewhat selective adm:** 123/yr. Appl fee: $75. Appl due: Rolling. Accepted: 96%. Yield: 96%. **Tests** IQ. **Enr 600.** Elem 400. Sec 200. Wh 95%. Blk 2%. Asian 3%. Avg class size: 16. Stud/fac: 12:1. **Fac 75.** M 23/F 52. FT 72/PT 3.

Wh 96%. Blk 2%. Asian 2%. Adv deg: 40%. **Grad '11—50.** Col—50. (TN Tech 14, U of TN-Knoxville 10, Cumberland U 9, Middle TN St 5, Volunteer St CC 5, US Naval Acad 2). Avg ACT: 24.6. **Col Couns: 1. Tui '12-'13:** Day $5945-7895 (+$375). **Est 1973.** Nonprofit. Nondenom Christian. Sem (Aug-May). **Assoc** SACS. FCS' curriculum features extensive Bible instruction. Qualified students in the upper grades may take dual-enrollment courses through Cumberland University.

HARDING ACADEMY OF MEMPHIS   Day Coed Gr PS (Age 2)-12
Memphis, TN 38117. 1100 Cherry Rd.
Tel: 901-767-4494. Fax: 901-763-4949.
Other locations: 8350 Macon Rd, Cordova 38018; 8360 Macon Rd, Cordova 38018; 8220 E
    Shelby Dr, Memphis 38125; 1106 Colonial Rd, Memphis 38117.
www.hardingacademymemphis.org   E-mail: copeland.betty@hardingacademymemphis.org
    Trent Williamson, Pres (2012). BA, Harding Univ, MA, Univ of Memphis. Betty Copeland, Adm.

    Col Prep. AP (61 exams taken, 75% 3+)—Eng Calc Bio US_Hist Studio_Art. **Feat**—Humanities Etymology Fr Span Stats Anat & Physiol Comp_Sci Sociol Bible Drama Accounting Journ Speech. **Supp**—Tut. **Comp:** Comp/Stud: 1:7. **Sports**—Basket Bowl X-country Soccer Tennis Track. B: Baseball Football Golf Wrestling. G: Cheer Softball Volley. **Selective adm (Gr PS-11):** 230/yr. Appl fee: $50. Appl due: Rolling. Accepted: 74%. Yield: 80%. **Tests** IQ MAT Stanford. **Enr 1475.** Elem 1108. Sec 367. Avg class size: 17. Stud/fac: 13:1. Uniform. **Fac 111.** M 20/F 91. FT 110/PT 1. Adv deg: 36%. **Grad '11—64.** Col—64. Avg ACT: 23.6. **Col Couns:** 1. **Tui '12-'13:** Day $8195-11,195 (+$100-300). **Est 1952.** Nonprofit. Nondenom Christian. Quar (Aug-May). **Assoc** SACS. The school's four elementary campuses are located throughout Greater Memphis, while the junior/senior school on Cherry Road (grades 7-12) shares its campus with Harding Graduate School of Religion. Extensive fine arts electives augment the Christ-centered college preparatory curriculum. Daily Bible study is required.

WOODLAND PRESBYTERIAN SCHOOL   Day Coed Gr PS (Age 3)-8
Memphis, TN 38119. 5217 Park Ave.
Tel: 901-685-0976. Fax: 901-761-2406.
www.woodlandschool.org   E-mail: info@woodlandschool.org
    Adam Moore, Head (2008). BSEd, Mississippi College, EdM, EdS, Union Univ. Tim Tatum, Adm.

    Pre-Prep. Feat—Lat Span Computers Studio_Art Music. **Supp**—Dev_Read LD Rem_ Math Rem_Read Tut. **Sports**—Basket X-country Soccer Tennis Track. B: Football Golf. G: Cheer Volley. **Selective adm:** 70/yr. Appl fee: $75. Appl due: Rolling. Accepted: 70%. Yield: 91%. **Tests** IQ MRT Stanford. **Enr 362.** B 201. G 161. Wh 95%. Blk 3%. Native Am 1%. Asian 1%. Avg class size: 18. Uniform. **Fac 42.** M 4/F 38. FT 34/PT 8. Wh 98%. Blk 2%. Adv deg: 40%. **Grad '10—27.** Prep—19. (Christian Bros-TN 8, St Benedict-TN 5, Briarcrest Christian 2, Harding-Memphis 2, Lausanne 1, St Mary's Episcopal Sch 1). **Tui '11-'12:** Day $8675-10,135 (+$200). Aid: Need 30 ($120,000). **Est 1957.** Nonprofit. Presbyterian. Sem (Aug-May). **Assoc** SACS. At all age levels, Woodland provides students with specialized instruction in foreign languages and the laboratory sciences. The school also features a gifted program designed around critical thinking and inquiry. Remediation based upon contemporary research assists pupils of average or above-average ability who have mild learning difficulties.

MIDDLE TENNESSEE CHRISTIAN SCHOOL   Day Coed Gr PS (Age 3)-12
Murfreesboro, TN 37129. 100 E MTCS Rd.
Tel: 615-893-0601. Fax: 615-895-8815.
www.mtcscougars.org   E-mail: cindysiler@mtcscougars.org
    J. Lynn Watson, Pres (1992). Cindy Siler, Adm.

Col Prep. AP (exams req'd)—Eng Bio Eur_Hist US_Hist. **Feat**—Creative_Writing Fr Span Anat Bible Studio_Art Drama Chorus. **Supp**—Tut. **Sports**—Basket Bowl X-country Golf Soccer Tennis Track. B: Baseball Football. G: Cheer Softball Volley. Activities: 47. **Somewhat selective adm:** 120/yr. Appl fee: $50. Accepted: 98%. **Enr 696.** Avg class size: 19. Stud/fac: 18:1. Casual dress. **Fac 59.** FT 55/PT 4. Adv deg: 45%. **Grad '11—63.** Col—59. Avg ACT: 23. **Col Couns:** 1. **Tui '12-'13:** Day $5100-7480. **Est 1962.** Nondenom Christian (50% practice). Quar (Aug-May). **Assoc** SACS. The MTCS curriculum features daily Bible instruction at all levels. The high school program provides college preparation with an emphasis on oral and written communication skills. Students perform 20 annual hours of required community service in grades 9-11, then 40 hours during senior year.

DAVID LIPSCOMB CAMPUS SCHOOL   Day Coed Gr PS (Age 4)-12
Nashville, TN 37204. 3901 Granny White Pike.
Tel: 615-966-1828, 800-333-4358. Fax: 615-966-7633.
Other locations: 4517 Granny White Pike, Nashville 37204.
www.dlcs.lipscomb.edu   E-mail: cheryl.pittard@lipscomb.edu
    Michael P. Hammond, Head (2008). BA, David Lipscomb Univ, MS, Middle Tennessee State Univ, PhD, Vanderbilt Univ. Michael L. Roller, Adm.

Col Prep. AP (exams req'd; 63 taken)—Span Calc Bio Chem. **Feat**—Fr Lat Bible Theater_Arts Chorus Accounting. **Supp**—Rev Tut. **Comp:** Comp/Stud: 1:11. **Dual enr:** David Lipscomb. **Sports**—Basket Bowl X-country Golf Soccer Tennis Track. B: Baseball Football Wrestling. G: Cheer Softball Volley. Activities: 29. **Selective adm:** 221/yr. Appl fee: $0. Appl due: Rolling. Accepted: 73%. Yield: 95%. **Enr 1386.** Elem 848. Sec 538. Avg class size: 20. Uniform. **Fac 103.** Wh 98%. Blk 2%. Adv deg: 48%. **Grad '08—122.** Col—120. (David Lipscomb 55, U of TN-Knoxville 11, Harding 7, Middle TN St 6, U of TN-Chattanooga 6, TN Tech 4). **Avg SAT:** CR 569. M 566. W 551. Avg ACT: 23.7. **Tui '11-'12:** Day $9075-9975 (+$200-360). Aid: Need 74 ($140,063). **Est 1891.** Nonprofit. Nondenom Christian. Sem (Aug-May). **Assoc** SACS. Operated by David Lipscomb University, the school bases its program on the principles of obedience to parents, government and God. DLCS' supplements its core curriculum with course work in art, computers, music, foreign languages and physical education. The school's dual-enrollment program, operated in conjunction with the university, enables participating students to earn college credit. Students in grades 9-12 accumulate 60 hours of community service.

FRANKLIN ROAD ACADEMY   Day Coed Gr PS (Age 4)-12
Nashville, TN 37220. 4700 Franklin Rd.
Tel: 615-832-8845, 877-216-2013. Fax: 615-834-4137.
www.franklinroadacademy.com   E-mail: wynnk@franklinroadacademy.com
    Margaret W. Wade, Head (2001). BA, EdD, Vanderbilt Univ, MEd, Middle Tennessee State Univ. Kenyetta Wynn, Adm.

Col Prep. AP (exams req'd; 113 taken, 83% 3+)—Eng Fr Lat Span Calc Stats Bio Chem Physics Eur_Hist US_Hist World_Hist Studio_Art. **Feat**—Shakespeare Mythology Anat & Physiol Environ_Sci Comp_Sci Econ World_Relig Art_Hist Visual_Arts Drama Band Music_ Hist. **Supp**—Rev Tut. **Comp:** Laptop prgm Gr 7-12. **Sports**—Basket Bowl Cheer X-country Golf Soccer Swim Tennis Track. B: Baseball Football Ice_Hockey Wrestling. G: Softball Volley. **Selective adm (Gr PS-11):** 165/yr. Appl fee: $25-40. Appl due: Jan. Accepted: 75%. Yield: 60%. **Tests** ISEE. **Enr 800.** Elem 571. Sec 229. Wh 90%. Latino 1%. Blk 3%. Asian 3%. Other 3%. Avg class size: 15. Stud/fac: 8:1. Uniform. **Fac 120.** Wh 90%. Latino 1%. Blk 3%. Asian 3%. Other 3%. Adv deg: 53%. **Grad '10—56.** Col—56. **Avg SAT:** CR 580. M 580. Mid 50% ACT: 23-28. **Tui '11-'12:** Day $14,460-16,560 (+$400). Aid: Merit 3 ($46,000). Need 134 ($945,614). **Est 1971.** Nonprofit. Nondenom Christian. Sem (Aug-May). **Assoc** SACS. In an inclusive nondenominational Christian setting, FRA offers honors and Advanced Placement courses in many traditional subjects as part of its college preparatory program. Considerable emphasis is placed on the fine and performing arts. Each March, pupils in grades

9-12 participate in a weeklong interim program that features enrichment classes, and these same boys and girls accumulate 20 hours of required community service over four years.

HARDING ACADEMY   Day Coed Gr K-8
Nashville, TN 37205. 170 Windsor Dr.
Tel: 615-356-5510. Fax: 615-356-0441.
www.hardingacademy.org   E-mail: arnoldb@hardingacademy.org
     Ian L. Craig, Head (2006). BA, Syracuse Univ, MA, New York Univ. Rebecca Arnold, Adm.
     Pre-Prep. Feat—Fr Lat Span Computers Studio_Art Drama Music Dance. **Supp**—Tut. **Comp:** Comp/Stud: 1:2. **Sports**—Basket X-country Golf Lacrosse Soccer Swim Tennis Track. B: Baseball Football Wrestling. G: Cheer Volley. **Selective adm:** 67/yr. Appl fee: $100. Appl due: Dec. Accepted: 78%. Yield: 83%. **Tests** ISEE. **Enr 482.** B 245. G 237. Wh 95%. Blk 2%. Asian 1%. Other 2%. Avg class size: 18. Uniform. **Fac 60.** M 10/F 50. FT 60. Wh 96%. Latino 3%. Asian 1%. Adv deg: 50%. **Grad '11—48.** Prep—46. (Ensworth 15, Harpeth Hall 9, Montgomery Bell 7). Alum donors: 10%. **Tui '11-'12:** Day $15,310 (+$500). Aid: Need 23 ($197,985). **Est 1971.** Nonprofit. Tri (Aug-May). **Assoc** SACS. Harding's traditional academic curriculum features Spanish and computer studies from kindergarten, arts and physical education throughout, and athletics in the middle school. After their early exposure to Spanish, children in grade 6 spend a trimester each studying Latin, Spanish and French, then choose a language to specialize in during their final two years at the school. Eighth graders embark on a five-day trip to Washington, DC, as the culmination of the social studies program.

OAK HILL SCHOOL   Day Coed Gr PS (Age 4)-6
Nashville, TN 37220. 4815 Franklin Rd.
Tel: 615-297-6544. Fax: 615-298-9555.
www.oakhillschool.org   E-mail: countert@oakhillschool.org
     Jennifer Hinote, Head. BSEd, Western Carolina Univ, MEd, Winthrop Univ. E. Todd Counter, Adm.
     Pre-Prep. Feat—Lib_Skills Lat Span Computers Bible Studio_Art Drama Music. **Supp**—Dev_Read LD Rem_Math Rem_Read Tut. **Selective adm:** 72/yr. Appl fee: $100. Accepted: 35%. **Tests** ISEE. **Enr 513.** Avg class size: 16. Uniform. **Fac 65.** Adv deg: 53%. **Grad '06—63.** Prep—60. Alum donors: 5%. **Tui '11-'12:** Day $14,659 (+$450-1150). **Est 1961.** Nonprofit. Nondenom Christian. Sem (Aug-May). **Assoc** SACS. The comprehensive course of studies at this Christian elementary school emphasizes the development of critical-thinking skills. Foreign language, drama, art, music/band and computer enrich the core curriculum. Oak Hill faculty take a hands-on, developmentally suitable approach at all grade levels, and children gradually gain more independence in learning. Sixth graders embark on a study trip to Williamsburg, VA, and Washington, DC, each year.

OVERBROOK SCHOOL   Day Coed Gr PS (Age 4)-8
Nashville, TN 37205. 4210 Harding Rd.
Tel: 615-292-5134. Fax: 615-783-0560.
www.overbrook.edu   E-mail: admissions-os@overbrook.edu
     Sr. Mary Gertrude Blankenhagen, OP, Prin. BA, Middle Tennessee State Univ, MEd, Christian Brothers Univ. Ellen Butler Fernandez, Adm.
     Pre-Prep. Gen Acad. Feat—Span Computers Relig Studio_Art Music Handbells. **Supp**—Dev_Read. **Sports**—Basket X-country Golf Soccer. B: Football. G: Volley. **Selective adm:** 66/yr. Appl fee: $60. Appl due: Jan. **Tests** ISEE. **Enr 331.** Wh 82%. Latino 6%. Asian 2%. Other 6%. Avg class size: 18. Uniform. **Fac 38.** M 6/F 32. FT 34/PT 4. Wh 100%. Adv deg: 50%. **Grad '08—35. Tui '12-'13:** Day $11,700. **Est 1936.** Nonprofit. Roman Catholic. Quar (Aug-May). **Assoc** SACS. Owned and operated by the Dominican Sisters of St. Cecilia Congregation, Overbrook shares its 83-acre campus with two other institutions, St. Cecilia

Academy and Aquinas College. At all grade levels, the program includes religion, art, foreign language, music, computer and physical education, as well as an advanced core curriculum. Each class participates in at least one annual community service project. Parental involvement is an important element of the program.

ST. CECILIA ACADEMY   Day Girls Gr 9-12
Nashville, TN 37205. 4210 Harding Rd.
Tel: 615-298-4525. Fax: 615-783-0561.
www.stcecilia.edu   E-mail: info@stcecilia.edu
    Sr. Mary Thomas, OP, Prin. Betty Bader, Adm.

Col Prep. AP (exams req'd; 170 taken, 83% 3+)—Eng Fr Span Calc Bio Chem Physics Eur_Hist US_Hist Psych Art_Hist Studio_Art Music_Theory. **Feat**—Humanities Lat Stats Multivariable_Calc Anat & Physiol Ecol Environ_Sci Comp_Sci Econ Govt Asian_Stud Relig Photog Visual_Arts Drama Chorus Music Dance Bus Journ. **Supp**—Tut. **Dual enr:** Aquinas-TN. **Sports**— G: Basket Bowl X-country Golf Lacrosse Soccer Softball Swim Tennis Track Volley. Activities: 16. **Selective adm:** Appl fee: $60. Appl due: Jan. Accepted: 82%. Yield: 81%. **Tests** ISEE. **Enr 259.** Nonwhite 15%. Avg class size: 13. Stud/fac: 12:1. Uniform. **Fac 33.** M 5/F 28. Wh 92%. Latino 2%. Blk 2%. Asian 4%. Adv deg: 81%. **Grad '11—56.** Col—56. (U of TN-Knoxville 4, U of TN-Chattanooga 3, U of the South 2, Furman 2, Samford 2, Wash U 2). **Avg SAT:** CR 629. M 576. W 633. **Mid 50% SAT:** CR 570-690. M 510-640. W 580-680. Avg ACT: 26.3. Mid 50% ACT: 23-29. **Col Couns:** 1. **Tui '12-'13:** Day $15,250 (+$680). Aid: Merit 2. Need 106. **Est 1860.** Nonprofit. Roman Catholic (70% practice). Quar (Aug-May). **Assoc** SACS. Established and operated by the Dominican Sisters of St. Cecilia Congregation, this college preparatory school offers Advanced Placement and honors courses, as well as a comprehensive arts program that offers both participatory and competitive opportunities in the visual arts, dance, drama, forensics and music. A weeklong winter interim program provides such travel opportunities as Broadway theater and art tours, marine biology courses in Florida, wilderness studies in Utah and Arizona, and tours of Europe. Girls in grades 10-12 fulfill a 20-hour community service each year. St. Cecilia is affiliated with Overbrook School, an elementary school for boys and girls in grades pre-K-8.

THE KING'S ACADEMY   Bdg Coed Gr 6-12
Seymour, TN 37865. 202 Smothers Rd.   Day Coed PS (Age 4)-12
Tel: 865-573-8321, 877-378-1880. Fax: 865-573-8323.
www.thekingsacademy.net   E-mail: admissions@thekingsacademy.net
    Walter Grubb, Pres (1987). BA, California Baptist College, MS, California State Univ.
Janice S. Mink, Adm.

Col Prep. AP (exams req'd; 12 taken, 92% 3+)—Eng Span Calc Bio Chem Environ_Sci Physics Studio_Art. **Feat**—Creative_Writing Chin Greek Anat & Physiol Econ Govt Psych Sociol Bible Photog Drama Chorus Music Bus Finance Journ. **Supp**—ESL Tut. **Dual enr:** Carson-Newman. **Sports**—Basket Bowl X-country Golf Soccer Tennis. B: Football. G: Cheer Volley. Activities: 1. **Somewhat selective adm (Bdg Gr 6-10; Day PS-10):** 115/yr. Bdg 18. Day 97. Appl fee: $50. Appl due: Rolling. Accepted: 95%. Yield: 95%. **Tests** IQ TOEFL. **Enr 455.** B 241. G 214. Bdg 50. Day 405. Elem 298. Sec 157. Wh 80%. Latino 1%. Blk 2%. Native Am 1%. Asian 12%. Other 4%. Intl 39%. Avg class size: 14. Stud/fac: 14:1. Uniform. **Fac 39.** M 12/F 27. FT 34/PT 5. Wh 98%. Asian 2%. Adv deg: 53%. In Dorms 1. **Grad '11—32.** Col—30. (U of TN-Knoxville 8, Carson-Newman 4, E TN St 2, Maryville Col 2, U of WA 1, PA St 1). **Avg SAT:** CR 360. M 560. W 400. Avg ACT: 23. Alum donors: 30%. **Tui '12-'13:** Bdg $22,260-23,390 (+$1200). 5-Day Bdg $15,970-16,680 (+$1200). Day $5500-6600 (+$250-350). Intl Bdg $26,680-27,390 (+$1200). Aid: Need 95 ($136,615). **Est 1880.** Nonprofit. Southern Baptist (87% practice). Sem (Aug-May). **Assoc** SACS. Emphasizing a Christian worldview, the school is located 12 miles south of Knoxville. Instruction in Bible study and wellness begins in elementary school and continues through high school. Older students complete 25 hours of required community service annually.

VIRGINIA

ALEXANDRIA COUNTRY DAY SCHOOL   Day Coed Gr K-8
Alexandria, VA 22301. 2400 Russell Rd.
Tel: 703-548-4804. Fax: 703-549-9022.
www.acdsnet.org   E-mail: hhartge@acdsnet.org
　　Scott Baytosh, Head (2012). BA, Wesleyan Univ, MA, Carnegie Mellon Univ, MSEd, Johns Hopkins Univ. Holly Hartge, Adm.

　　Pre-Prep. Feat—Lib_Skills Span Computers Studio_Art Drama Music Outdoor_Ed. **Sports**—Basket X-country Soccer Softball Swim Tennis. **Selective adm:** 40/yr. Appl fee: $75. Appl due: Jan. Accepted: 70%. Yield: 51%. **Tests** IQ ISEE SSAT. **Enr 228.** Avg class size: 13. Stud/fac: 8:1. Uniform. **Fac 38.** M 12/F 26. Adv deg: 44%. **Grad '11—35.** Prep—27. **Tui '11-'12:** Day $22,089-23,988 (+$0-350). Aid: Need ($600,000). **Est 1983.** Nonprofit. Tri (Sept-June). Focusing on basic skills development, the primary division (grades K-2) offers specialist-taught enrichment classes in art, music, library, computer, Spanish and physical education. Enrichment courses continue in the elementary division (grades 3-5). Computer use is integral to the interdisciplinary middle school (grades 6-8). Intensive computer, art and music classes enable middle schoolers to complete major projects in these areas. Community service begins in the primary division, and all students take part in an experiential outdoor learning program.

BISHOP IRETON HIGH SCHOOL   Day Coed Gr 9-12
Alexandria, VA 22314. 201 Cambridge Rd.
Tel: 703-751-7606. Fax: 703-212-8173.
www.bishopireton.org   E-mail: info@bishopireton.org
　　Timothy Hamer, Prin (2008). BA, DeSales Univ, MA, Univ of Virginia. Peter J. Hamer, Adm.

　　Col Prep. AP (exams req'd; 421 taken, 62% 3+)—Eng Fr Span Calc Stats Comp_Sci Bio Chem Eur_Hist US_Hist Human_Geog US_Govt & Pol Studio_Art. **Feat**—Creative_Writing Shakespeare Ger Lat Russ Web_Design WWI WWII Govt Relig Film Music Public_Speak. **Supp**—Tut. **Sports**—Basket Crew X-country Lacrosse Soccer Swim Tennis Track. B: Baseball Football Golf Ice_Hockey Wrestling. G: F_Hockey Softball Volley. **Selective adm:** 212/yr. Appl fee: $50. Appl due: Jan. Accepted: 88%. Yield: 56%. **Tests** HSPT. **Enr 828.** B 393. G 435. Wh 63%. Latino 11%. Blk 8%. Asian 6%. Other 12%. Avg class size: 24. Stud/fac: 13:1. Uniform. **Fac 65.** M 29/F 36. FT 58/PT 7. Adv deg: 76%. **Grad '11—206.** Col—204. **Avg SAT:** CR 574. M 562. W 580. **Mid 50% SAT:** CR 520-640. M 500-610. W 530-640. Avg ACT: 24.6. Mid 50% ACT: 23-28. **Col Couns:** 3. Alum donors: 10%. **Tui '11-'12:** Day $16,065 (+$850-1100). Catholic $11,928-13,535 (+$850-1100). Aid: Merit ($128,000). Need ($622,588). **Est 1964.** Nonprofit. Roman Catholic (85% practice). Quar (Aug-June). **Assoc** SACS. Founded by and affiliated with the Oblates of St. Francis de Sales, Bishop Ireton offers honors, Advanced Placement and college prep courses. A symphonic wind ensemble, an academic enrichment program and a full sports program complement the curriculum. Each student fulfills a 60-hour community service commitment over four years.

BROWNE ACADEMY   Day Coed Gr PS (Age 3)-8
Alexandria, VA 22310. 5917 Telegraph Rd.
Tel: 703-960-3000. Fax: 703-960-7325.
www.browneacademy.org   E-mail: ssalvo@browneacademy.org
　　Margot N. Durkin, Head (2006). BA, Salve Regina Univ, MSA, Trinity Univ. Stephen G. Salvo, Adm.

　　Pre-Prep. Feat—Lib_Skills Fr Span Computers Studio_Art Music. **Supp**—Tut. **Sports**—Basket Soccer. G: Softball. **Selective adm:** 75/yr. Appl fee: $60. Appl due: Feb. **Tests** IQ

ISEE SSAT. **Enr 300.** B 150. G 150. Wh 58%. Latino 6%. Blk 19%. Asian 5%. Other 12%. Avg class size: 13. Stud/fac: 7:1. **Fac 44.** M 12/F 32. FT 44. Adv deg: 45%. **Grad '10—20.** Prep—17. (St Stephen's & St Agnes 5, Bishop Ireton 4, Flint Hill 2, Bishop O'Connell 2). **Tui '11-'12:** Day $14,540-24,100 (+$1200-1500). Aid: Need 43 ($250,000). **Est 1941.** Nonprofit. Quar (Sept-June). At the academy, major subjects are introduced in preschool and are developed through grade 8. The school's individualized, interdisciplinary curriculum helps students develop their problem solving and critical-thinking skills. French begins in preschool, while Spanish commences in grade 3.

COMMONWEALTH ACADEMY   Day Coed Gr 3-12
Alexandria, VA 22301. 1321 Leslie Ave.
Tel: 703-548-6912. Fax: 703-548-6914.
www.commonwealthacademy.org   E-mail: josh_gwilliam@commonwealthacademy.org
    Susan J. Johnson, Head (2002). BA, MPA, New York Univ, MAT, EdS, Trenton State College, PhD, Newport Univ. Josh Gwilliam, Adm.

    Col Prep. LD. Feat—Span Stats Environ_Sci Comp_Sci Web_Design Studio_Art Drama Music SAT_Prep ACT_Prep. **Supp**—Dev_Read Rem_Math Rem_Read Rev. **Comp:** Comp/Stud: 1:1 **Sports**—Basket Soccer Track. **Somewhat selective adm (Gr 3-11):** 35/yr. Appl fee: $100. Appl due: Mar. Accepted: 95%. Yield: 68%. **Tests** IQ. **Enr 138.** B 85. G 53. Elem 54. Sec 84. Wh 79%. Latino 2%. Blk 16%. Asian 3%. Avg class size: 8. Casual dress. **Fac 28.** M 18/F 10. FT 25/PT 3. Wh 85%. Latino 5%. Blk 10%. Adv deg: 53%. **Grad '11—8.** Col—8. **Avg SAT:** CR 520. M 530. W 500. **Col Couns:** 2. **Tui '12-'13:** Day $31,000 (+$900). Aid: Need 21. **Est 1997.** Nonprofit. Quar (Sept-June). The school serves intelligent students who have mild to moderate learning differences or attentional challenges. A college preparatory curriculum serves pupils in grades 6-12, while an elementary program for children in grades 3-5 features reading and math remediation. The academy maintains small class sizes and tailors instruction to individual learning styles, with the goal of preparing graduates for four-year college attendance. Honors courses and graphic and visual arts offerings are part of the high school curriculum. Boys and girls satisfy the following community service requirements: five hours per year in grades 6-8, 10 hours annually in grades 9-12.

OAKWOOD SCHOOL   Day Coed Gr K-8
Annandale, VA 22003. 7210 Braddock Rd.
Tel: 703-941-5788. Fax: 703-941-4186.
www.oakwoodschool.com   E-mail: mjedlicka@oakwoodschool.com
    Robert C. McIntyre, Head (1971). BA, MA, Wheaton College (IL). Muriel A. Jedlicka, Adm.

    Gen Acad. LD. Feat—Computers Studio_Art. **Supp**—Dev_Read Rem_Math Rem_Read. **Selective adm:** 27/yr. Appl fee: $50. Appl due: Rolling. **Tests** IQ. **Enr 106.** B 79. G 27. Intl 8%. Avg class size: 12. Stud/fac: 4:1. Casual dress. **Fac 35.** M 4/F 31. FT 34/PT 1. Adv deg: 71%. **Grad '11—12. Tui '12-'13:** Day $29,900 (+$150-300). Aid: Need 13 ($114,325). **Est 1971.** Nonprofit. Sem (Sept-June). Serving pupils with mild to moderate learning differences, Oakwood conducts a program that includes adaptive physical education, individualized education planning, speech-language and occupational therapies, and psycho-educational evaluations. Offered in a small-class setting, the school's individualized program follows a multisensory approach.

POWHATAN SCHOOL   Day Coed Gr K-8
Boyce, VA 22620. 49 Powhatan Ln.
Tel: 540-837-1009. Fax: 540-837-2558.
www.powhatanschool.org   E-mail: info@powhatanschool.org
    Susan C. Scarborough, Head (2011). Michael A. Hatfield, Adm.

    Pre-Prep. Gen Acad. Feat—Fr Lat Span Computers Studio_Art Drama Music. **Supp**—

Dev_Read Rem_Read Tut. **Sports**—Basket X-country Lacrosse Soccer Track. G: F_Hockey Volley. **Somewhat selective adm:** 38/yr. Appl fee: $50. Appl due: Jan. Accepted: 86%. Yield: 52%. **Tests** CTP_4. **Enr 235.** Wh 91%. Blk 2%. Asian 2%. Other 5%. Avg class size: 15. Stud/fac: 8:1. **Fac 32.** M 8/F 24. FT 32. Wh 97%. Blk 3%. Adv deg: 53%. **Grad '10—31.** Prep—10. Alum donors: 7%. **Tui '12-'13:** Day $10,000-15,375 (+$560-660). Aid: Need 46 ($235,000). **Est 1948.** Nonprofit. Tri (Aug-June). Powhatan's elementary and middle school program—which serves pupils from Frederick, Loudoun, Clarke and Warren counties, as well as Winchester, Martinsburg and Charles Town—places particular emphasis on the development of sound study habits and oral and written communicational skills. Children study Spanish in grades K-4, Latin in grades 5 and 6, and either Spanish or French in grades 6-8. Older students fulfill a community service requirement: 10 hours in grade 7, 15 hours in grade 8.

LINTON HALL SCHOOL   Day Coed Gr PS (Age 4)-8
Bristow, VA 20136. 9535 Linton Hall Rd.
Tel: 703-368-3157. Fax: 703-368-3036.
www.lintonhall.edu   E-mail: info@lintonhall.edu
   Elizabeth A. Poole, Prin (2007). BA, Univ of Kent (England), MEd, George Mason Univ. Erika Marks, Adm.

   Gen Acad. Feat—Span Ecol Computers Relig Studio_Art Music Outdoor_Ed. **Supp**—Tut. **Sports**—Basket Golf Soccer. **Selective adm:** 38/yr. Appl fee: $75. Appl due: Rolling. **Enr 196.** B 88. G 108. Avg class size: 22. Uniform. **Fac 24.** M 3/F 21. FT 14/PT 10. Adv deg: 29%. **Grad '06—14. Tui '12-'13:** Day $8960 (+$170-330). **Est 1922.** Nonprofit. Roman Catholic. Quar (Aug-June). Linton Hall provides an independent Catholic program on a rural, 120-acre site located 35 miles southwest of Washington, DC. The school offers small classes, opportunities for advanced study and an accelerated reading program. The core curriculum comprises science, history, religion, computer science and language arts, and music, art, outdoor education and Spanish are also part of the program. Extended-day care is available.

THE COVENANT SCHOOL   Day Coed Gr PS (Age 4)-12
Charlottesville, VA 22902. 175 Hickory St.
Tel: 434-220-7329. Fax: 434-220-7346.
Other locations: 1000 Birdwood Rd, Charlottesville 22903.
www.covenantschool.org   E-mail: dharris@covenantschool.org
   George Sanker, Head (2011). BA, Colgate Univ. Donna B. Harris, Adm.

   Col Prep. AP (195 exams taken, 90% 3+)—Eng Fr Lat Span Calc Bio Chem Environ_Sci Eur_Hist US_Hist Comp_Govt & Pol US_Govt & Pol Studio_Art. **Feat**—Bible Drama Journ Study_Skills. **Supp**—Rem_Read. **Sports**—Basket X-country Golf Lacrosse Soccer Swim. B: Baseball Football Wrestling. G: F_Hockey Tennis Volley. Activities: 25. **Somewhat selective adm:** 80/yr. Appl fee: $50. Appl due: Mar. Accepted: 95%. **Tests** CEEB SSAT. **Enr 507.** Elem 274. Sec 233. Nonwhite 15%. Avg class size: 13. Casual dress. **Fac 64.** M 27/F 37. Wh 98%. Blk 2%. Adv deg: 45%. **Grad '11—64.** Col—64. **Mid 50% SAT:** CR 510-690. M 510-680. W 500-700. **Col Couns:** 1. **Tui '12-'13:** Day $6930-14,520 (+$0-450). Aid: Need 152 ($800,000). **Est 1985.** Nonprofit. Nondenom Christian. (Aug-May). **Assoc** CLS SACS. Covenant's lower school (grades pre-K-6)—which occupies separate quarters on Birdwood Road (434-220-7309)—offers course work in foreign language, language arts, math, science, the fine arts, history, Bible and physical education. An enrichment program assists children in grades K-4, while a resource teacher aids students in grades 1-6 who have reading or spelling difficulties. Honors and Advanced Placement courses are features of the upper school program. Students in grades 7-12 satisfy a 30-hour annual community service requirement.

MILLER SCHOOL **Bdg & Day**
Charlottesville, VA 22903. 1000 Samuel Miller Loop. **Coed Gr 8-PG**
Tel: 434-823-4805. Fax: 434-823-6617.
www.millerschool.org E-mail: dgregory@millerschool.org
 Patrick L. France, Pres (2010). AB, Transylvania Univ, MA, Middlebury College.
 Col Prep. AP—Eng Fr Span Calc Environ_Sci Eur_Hist US_Hist US_Govt & Pol. **Feat**—Creative_Writing Lat Econ Photog Studio_Art Drama Chorus Music Woodworking. **Supp**—ESL Tut. **Sports (req'd)**—Basket Golf Soccer Tennis. B: Baseball Lacrosse Wrestling. G: Volley. **Selective adm:** 67/yr. Appl fee: $50. Appl due: Feb. Accepted: 72%. **Tests** CEEB SSAT TOEFL. **Enr 150.** B 90. G 60. Bdg 90. Day 60. Intl 20%. Avg class size: 10. Stud/fac: 6:1. **Fac 30.** Adv deg: 53%. **Grad '08—42.** Col—40. **Avg SAT:** CR 517. M 554. W 514. **Tui '10-'11:** Bdg $36,980 (+$200-350). 5-Day Bdg $33,165 (+$200-350). Day $15,865 (+$200-350). Intl Bdg $44,940 (+$200-350). Aid: Need 53. **Est 1878.** Nonprofit. Sem (Sept-May). The Miller School of Albemarle, which was established under the will of Samuel Miller, occupies 1600 acres and offers a traditional college preparatory curriculum. Courses emphasize experiential learning, group work and an interdisciplinary perspective. Upper school students satisfy requirements in English, mathematics, foreign language, science, social studies and the fine arts and choose among a number of electives. Boys and girls must participate in competitive team sports in two of Miller's three athletic seasons annually.

TANDEM FRIENDS SCHOOL **Day Coed Gr 5-12**
Charlottesville, VA 22902. 279 Tandem Ln.
Tel: 434-296-1303. Fax: 434-296-1886.
www.tandemfs.org E-mail: contact@tandemfs.org
 Andy Jones-Wilkins, Head (2011). BA, Hamilton College, MA, Villanova Univ. Louise Cole, Adm.
 Col Prep. AP (exams req'd; 96 taken, 83% 3+)—Eng Fr Lat Span Calc Stats Bio Chem Physics US_Hist Studio_Art Music_Theory. **Feat**—Bioethics Govt Drama Band Jazz_Ensemble. **Supp**—Rem_Math Rem_Read Tut. **Comp:** Comp/Stud: 1:1.6. **Dual enr:** Piedmont VA CC. **Sports**—Basket X-country Golf Lacrosse Soccer Tennis. G: F_Hockey Volley. **Selective adm (Gr 5-11):** 56/yr. Appl fee: $50. Appl due: Mar. Accepted: 80%. **Enr 197.** B 99. G 98. Elem 88. Sec 109. Wh 90%. Latino 1%. Blk 5%. Asian 2%. Other 2%. Avg class size: 15. Stud/fac: 8:1. **Fac 38.** M 19/F 19. FT 29/PT 9. Wh 91%. Latino 3%. Blk 3%. Other 3%. Adv deg: 63%. **Grad '11—36.** Col—36. (Temple 3, Geo Mason 2, Guilford 2, Wm & Mary 2, Dartmouth 1, NYU 1). **Avg SAT:** CR 648. M 611. W 635. Avg ACT: 26. **Col Couns:** 1. Alum donors: 2%. **Tui '12-'13:** Day $15,300-17,900 (+$300-400). **Est 1970.** Nonprofit. Religious Society of Friends. Sem (Sept-June). Tandem Friends' curriculum integrates humanities studies and offers math, science, foreign language, and the performing and visual arts. Internships and classes at local colleges are also available to students. The entire community gathers for a Quaker Meeting once a week, and each afternoon students participate in the upkeep of the buildings and the grounds. Community service is part of the curriculum throughout; projects vary by year and class.

SOUTHAMPTON ACADEMY **Day Coed Gr PS (Age 3)-12**
Courtland, VA 23837. 26495 Old Plank Rd.
Tel: 757-653-2512. Fax: 757-653-0011.
www.southamptonacademy.org E-mail: apittman@southamptonacademy.org
 Mercer Neale, Head. BA, Hampden-Sydney College, MEd, Towson Univ, MLA, Johns Hopkins Univ, EdD, Univ of Maryland-College Park. Anne Pittman, Adm.
 Col Prep. AP—Eng Calc Physics US_Hist US_Govt & Pol. **Feat**—British_Lit Fr Span Environ_Sci Studio_Art Drama Music. **Supp**—Rev Tut. **Sports**—Basket. B: Baseball Football Golf Soccer. G: Cheer Softball Tennis Volley. **Selective adm:** 57/yr. Appl fee: $25. Appl due: Rolling. Accepted: 81%. **Tests** MAT Stanford. **Enr 368.** Elem 254. Sec 114. Wh 97%. Blk 1%. Asian 1%. Other 1%. Avg class size: 15. **Fac 41.** M 5/F 36. FT 36/PT 5. Adv deg:

24%. **Grad '09—16.** Col—14. **Col Couns:** 1. **Tui '09-'10:** Day $5390-6370 (+$200-1000). **Est 1969.** Nonprofit. Quar (Aug-May). **Assoc** SACS. Located on a 30-acre tract in the state's largest peanut-producing county, the academy's demanding curriculum includes AP classes in the upper grades. Students may earn an honors diploma by completing additional science and foreign language course work.

ST. LUKE'S SCHOOL   Day Coed Gr PS (Age 2)-9
Culpeper, VA 22701. 1211 E Grandview Ave.
Tel: 540-825-8890. Fax: 540-825-4471.
www.stlukes-school.org   E-mail: info@stlukes-school.org
    Roger Mello, Head (2012). Robin F. Schools, Adm.

    Col Prep. Feat—Lib_Skills Lat Span Computers Relig Studio_Art Drama. **Sports**—Basket Soccer. **B:** Lacrosse. **G:** Volley. **Selective adm:** Appl fee: $50. Appl due: Rolling. **Enr 93.** Elem 90. Sec 3. Avg class size: 7. **Fac 17.** M 4/F 13. FT 17. **Tui '12-'13:** Day $4800-7200 (+$150). **Est 1979.** Nonprofit. Sem (Aug-May). Founded as a mission of St. Luke's Lutheran Church, this Christian school became fully independent from the church in summer 2010. St. Luke's—which enrolls students from Culpeper, Fauquier, Madison, Orange and Rappahannock counties—complements the core subjects with resource classes in art, drama, foreign language, library, music, technology, religion and physical education. Boys and girls in grades 1-9 engage in a winter sports program on several days in January and February; it enhances the physical education curriculum with such pursuits as skiing, snowboarding, martial arts and cheerleading.

BROADWATER ACADEMY   Day Coed Gr PS (Age 3)-12
Exmore, VA 23350. 3500 Broadwater Rd, PO Box 546.
Tel: 757-442-9041. Fax: 757-442-9615.
www.broadwateracademy.org   E-mail: info@broadwateracademy.org
    Jeremy McLean, Head (2008). Carol G. Bowen, Adm.

    Col Prep. AP (exams req'd)—Eng Fr Lat Span Calc US_Hist Comp_Govt & Pol US_ Govt & Pol. **Feat**—Marine_Bio/Sci Oceanog Comp_Sci Architect Study_Skills. **Supp**—Tut. **Sports**—Basket X-country Golf. **B:** Baseball Football. **G:** Cheer Softball Volley. Activities: 18. **Selective adm:** 70/yr. Appl fee: $100. Appl due: Rolling. **Tests** IQ. **Enr 388.** Avg class size: 15. Stud/fac: 7:1. Casual dress. **Fac 45.** M 7/F 38. FT 42/PT 3. Adv deg: 22%. **Grad '10—27.** Col—27. **Avg SAT:** CR 576. M 586. W 597. **Col Couns:** 1. **Tui '12-'13:** Day $5100-8625 (+$150). **Est 1966.** Nonprofit. Sem (Sept-June). Broadwater's liberal arts curriculum includes Advanced Placement courses, and computer instruction is available in every grade. Pupils in grades 9-11 perform 12 compulsory hours of community service annually.

THE NEW SCHOOL OF NORTHERN VIRGINIA   Day Coed Gr 4-12
Fairfax, VA 22031. 9431 Silver King Ct.
Tel: 703-691-3040. Fax: 703-691-3041.
www.newschoolva.com   E-mail: johnp@newschoolva.com
    John Potter, Head (1989).

    Col Prep. AP—Eng Calc US_Hist Human_Geog US_Govt & Pol. **Feat**—Creative_Writing African_Lit Russ_Lit Fr Ger Span Stats Genetics Microbio Physiol Comp_Sci Web_ Design Econ Sociol Philos Architect Filmmaking Sculpt Studio_Art Theater_Arts Music Journ. **Supp**—ESL LD. **Sports**—Basket Soccer. **G:** Softball. **Selective adm:** Appl fee: $75. Appl due: Rolling. **Enr 150. Fac 22.** M 9/F 13. FT 22. **Tui '10-'11:** Day $17,800-23,200 (+$300-375). **Est 1989.** Quar (Sept-June). **Assoc** SACS. The New School's liberal arts program follows the principles of Howard Gardner's Theory of Multiple Intelligences. Points of emphasis include effective communication, independent and collaborative work, research skills, and organizational and problem-solving abilities, among others. In grade 12, all students complete the project-oriented Senior Exhibition, which consists of three five-week rounds and progresses from a series of benchmarks through a concluding, 50-minute presentation. Boys and girls work with a three-person faculty committee to establish their benchmarks.

THE CONGRESSIONAL SCHOOLS OF VIRGINIA Day Coed Gr PS (Age 3)-8
Falls Church, VA 22042. 3229 Sleepy Hollow Rd.
Tel: 703-533-9711. Fax: 703-532-5467.
www.congressionalschools.org E-mail: info@csov.org
  Janet F. Marsh, Exec Dir (2012). BS, Pace Univ. Karen H. Weinberger, Adm.

  Pre-Prep. Feat—Fr Lat Span Computers Studio_Art Drama Music Speech. **Supp**—Dev_ Read Rev Tut. **Comp:** Laptop prgm Gr 8. **Sports**—Basket X-country Soccer Track. B: Baseball. G: Softball. **Selective adm:** 65/yr. Appl fee: $75. Appl due: Rolling. Accepted: 80%. Yield: 75%. **Tests** CTP_4 IQ ISEE SSAT Stanford. **Enr 412.** B 192. G 220. Wh 55%. Latino 8%. Blk 10%. Native Am 2%. Asian 16%. Other 9%. **Fac 50.** M 10/F 40. FT 47/PT 3. Adv deg: 40%. **Grad '11—18.** Prep—15. **Tui '12-'13:** Day $20,040-22,100 (+$1000). **Est 1939.** Nonprofit. Tri (Sept-June). **Assoc** SACS. The strong core curriculum of English, social studies, math, science, foreign languages and technology is complemented by art, music, physical education, health, library and study skills. Boys and girls participate in schoolwide and individual class service projects at all grade levels. Extended hours, transportation and enrichment programs are available. The school's 40-acre, wooded campus is 15 minutes from Washington, DC.

FUQUA SCHOOL Day Coed Gr PS (Age 3)-12
Farmville, VA 23901. 605 Fuqua Dr, PO Drawer 328.
Tel: 434-392-4131, 800-214-3460. Fax: 434-392-5062.
www.fuquaschool.com E-mail: murphycm@fuquaschool.com
  Ruth S. Murphy, Pres (1994). BA, Univ of North Carolina-Chapel Hill, MEd, Univ of North Carolina-Greensboro. Christy M. Murphy, Adm.

  Col Prep. AP—Calc US_Hist US_Govt & Pol. **Feat**—Span Anat Environ_Sci Zoology Econ Psych Ethics Studio_Art Theater Band Chorus. **Supp**—Tut. **Comp:** Comp/Stud: 1:2. **Sports**—Basket X-country Golf Soccer Swim Tennis Track. B: Baseball Football. G: Softball Volley. Activities: 10. **Somewhat selective adm (Gr PS-11):** 63/yr. Appl fee: $100. Appl due: Apr. Accepted: 98%. Yield: 97%. **Tests** CEEB IQ Stanford. **Enr 472.** B 233. G 239. Elem 341. Sec 131. Wh 93%. Latino 2%. Blk 3%. Asian 2%. Avg class size: 17. Stud/fac: 15:1. Uniform. **Fac 42.** M 9/F 33. FT 41/PT 1. Adv deg: 28%. **Grad '11—41.** Col—41. **Avg SAT:** CR 529. M 541. W 544. **Mid 50% SAT:** CR 490-630. M 510-630. W 480-640. Avg ACT: 24. Mid 50% ACT: 21-26. **Col Couns:** 1. Alum donors: 17%. **Tui '12-'13:** Day $5055-7325 (+$350). **Est 1959.** Nonprofit. Sem (Aug-June). **Assoc** CLS SACS. Serving students from 13 counties within a 50-mile radius, the developmentally based program at Fuqua enables each pupil to advance at an appropriate rate of learning, as the school does not utilize traditional grade-level caps. The multi-age lower school (grades pre-K-5) enables boys and girls to remain with the same teacher for two years; specialists teach weekly art, music, media, computer and physical education classes. At the middle school level (grades 6-8), planning teams deliver instruction to monitor learning and allow for flexible scheduling. Semester block scheduling during the high school years (grades 9-12) enables students to complete a traditional yearlong course in one semester by taking four classes at a time instead of seven.

WARE ACADEMY Day Coed Gr PS (Age 3)-8
Gloucester, VA 23061. 7936 John Clayton Memorial Hwy.
Tel: 804-693-3825. Fax: 804-694-0695.
www.wareacademy.org E-mail: info@wareacademy.org
  Thomas L. Thomas III, Head (2004). BA, Univ of Richmond, MA, Virginia Polytechnic Institute. Ginger James, Adm.

  Pre-Prep. Gen Acad. Feat—Lib_Skills Span Computers Fine_Arts Performing_Arts

Music. **Supp**—Dev_Read Rem_Read Rev Tut. **Sports**—Basket X-country Golf Lacrosse Soccer. G: Volley. **Somewhat selective adm:** 28/yr. Appl fee: $75. Appl due: Rolling. Accepted: 95%. Yield: 99%. **Tests** CTP_4. **Enr 140.** Avg class size: 14. Uniform. **Fac 17.** M 2/F 15. FT 14/PT 3. Adv deg: 11%. **Grad '11—18.** Prep—8. (Christchurch Sch 6, Putney 1, St Mary's Sch 1). **Tui '12-'13:** Day $6808-9280. **Est 1949.** Nonprofit. Sem (Sept-June). The academy's primary school (grades pre-K-2) introduces children to the fundamentals of reading, writing, speaking and listening. By second grade, boys and girls have gained exposure to creative writing and logically formed sentences, as well as computation and math problem solving. Pupils further develop language arts and math skills in the lower school (grades 3-5), with greater content depth evident in all subject areas. Ware's middle school curriculum, which prepares students for high school academics, includes such electives as forensics, art, journalism and music.

NYSMITH SCHOOL FOR THE GIFTED   Day Coed Gr PS (Age 3)-8
Herndon, VA 20171. 13625 EDS Dr.
Tel: 703-713-3332. Fax: 703-713-3336.
www.nysmith.com   E-mail: info@nysmith.com
Kenneth Nysmith, Dir (2007). Marian White, Adm.

Pre-Prep. Gen Acad. Feat—Fr Lat Span Computers Logic Studio_Art Music. **Comp:** Comp/Stud: 1:2.5. **Selective adm:** 85/yr. Appl fee: $250. Appl due: Jan. **Tests** IQ. **Enr 620.** Avg class size: 18. Stud/fac: 9:1. **Fac 142.** M 12/F 130. FT 83/PT 59. Adv deg: 13%. **Grad '04—44. Tui '11-'12:** Day $19,070-28,100 (+$250). **Est 1983.** Inc. Quar (Aug-June). **Assoc** SACS. This elementary school provides an individualized, accelerated curriculum for able students. As reading and math are considered the foundation of future learning, they are introduced at an early age. While children remain with their classmates, they progress at their own rates, with four to eight grade-level plans implemented in a typical classroom. The curriculum includes spelling, vocabulary, grammar, punctuation and math drills.   See Also Page 83

CHESAPEAKE ACADEMY   Day Coed Gr PS (Age 3)-8
Irvington, VA 22480. 107 Steamboat Rd, PO Box 8.
Tel: 804-438-5575. Fax: 804-438-6146.
www.chesapeakeacademy.org   E-mail: hscott@chesapeakeacademy.org
Deborah M. Cook, Head (2007). BS, College of New Jersey, MA, Rider Univ. Hilary Scott, Adm.

Pre-Prep. Gen Acad. Feat—Lib_Skills Lat Span Computers Studio_Art Music Study_Skills. **Supp**—Tut. **Comp:** Comp/Stud: 1:1.5. **Sports**—Basket X-country Golf Soccer Tennis Track Volley. **Somewhat selective adm:** 15/yr. Appl fee: $50. Appl due: Rolling. Accepted: 95%. Yield: 75%. **Tests** CTP_4. **Enr 108.** B 60. G 48. Wh 88%. Blk 7%. Asian 1%. Other 4%. Avg class size: 12. Stud/fac: 8:1. Uniform. **Fac 16.** M 2/F 14. FT 11/PT 5. Nonwhite 6%. Adv deg: 43%. **Grad '10—11.** Prep—8. Alum donors: 9%. **Tui '12-'13:** Day $9425-9960. Aid: Merit 4 ($2250). Need 40 ($158,445). **Est 1889.** Nonprofit. Sem (Sept-June). Pupils at the academy follow a broad-based, sequential liberal arts curriculum that progresses from a hands-on early childhood division (prekindergarten and kindergarten) to a lower school featuring unit classrooms (grades 1-4) to a departmentalized middle school (grades 5-8). The foreign language program features Spanish from kindergarten and Latin in grade 6. Chesapeake conducts field study excursions to south Florida and service trips for seventh and eighth graders, and boys and girls in grades 5-8 take part in Inward Bound, an overnight trip to a local camp. Students enroll from Lancaster, Northumberland, Middlesex, Mathews and Gloucester counties.

LITTLE KESWICK SCHOOL   Bdg Boys Ages 10-17
Keswick, VA 22947. 500 Little Keswick Ln, PO Box 24.
Tel: 434-295-0457. Fax: 434-977-1892.
www.littlekeswickschool.net   E-mail: lksinfo@littlekeswickschool.net

Marc J. Columbus, Head (1990). MEd, Univ of Virginia. Terry Columbus, Dir. MEd, Univ of Virginia.

LD. Underachiever. Feat—Studio_Art Music Woodworking. **Supp**—Rem_Math Rem_ Read Tut. **Sports**— B: Basket Soccer. **Somewhat selective adm:** 9/yr. Appl fee: $350. Appl due: Rolling. **Tests** IQ. **Enr 34.** Intl 9%. Avg class size: 7. **Fac 7.** M 3/F 4. FT 7. Adv deg: 71%. **Grad '11—10.** Prep—10. **Tui '12-'13:** Bdg $103,131. **Est 1963.** Inc. Quar (Sept-June). This therapeutic, special-education boarding school serves boys of below-average to superior intelligence who have one or more of the following: learning problems, emotional disorders or behavioral disorders. While highly structured, the program operates in a small, open setting. LKS also offers specialized academics; an independent living program; individual and family counseling; and speech and language, occupational and art therapies. All students must attend the school's five-week summer session.

OAKLAND SCHOOL   **Bdg & Day**
Keswick, VA 22947. Boyd Tavern.   **Coed Gr 1-9**
Tel: 434-293-9059. Fax: 434-296-8930.
www.oaklandschool.net   E-mail: information@oaklandschool.net
Carol Williams, Dir. BA, MEd, Univ of Virginia. Amanda Baber, Adm.

LD. Feat—Computers Study_Skills. **Supp**—Dev_Read Rem_Math Rem_Read Rev Tut. **Comp:** Comp/Stud: 1:2. **Sports**—Basket X-country Soccer. **Somewhat selective adm (Gr 1-8):** 22/yr. Appl fee: $0. Appl due: Rolling. Accepted: 90%. Yield: 95%. **Tests** IQ. **Enr 54.** Bdg 29. Day 25. Wh 83%. Latino 6%. Blk 8%. Native Am 1%. Asian 1%. Other 1%. Intl 9%. Avg class size: 5. Casual dress. **Fac 14.** M 4/F 10. FT 14. Wh 93%. Blk 7%. Adv deg: 64%. **Grad '10—16.** Prep—8. **Tui '11-'12:** Bdg $44,975 (+$500). Day $26,850 (+$100). Aid: Need 10 ($75,000). **Est 1950.** Nonprofit. (Sept-Aug). Accepting children of average to above-average ability with dyslexia and other learning disabilities, Oakland provides a year-round academic curriculum stressing basic skills in one-on-one and small-class settings. The school specializes in the teaching of reading, math, written language and study skills. A full recreational program, team sports, daily physical education and horseback riding are also provided. Those receiving ninth grade credits perform 20 hours of required community service per semester. Most students return to a traditional educational setting after two to four years.

LOUDOUN COUNTRY DAY SCHOOL   **Day Coed Gr PS (Age 4)-8**
Leesburg, VA 20175. 20600 Red Cedar Dr.
Tel: 703-777-3841. Fax: 703-771-1346.
www.lcds.org   E-mail: info@lcds.org
Randall Hollister, Head (1993). BS, St Bonaventure Univ, MEd, Plymouth State College, EdM, PhD, State Univ of New York-Buffalo. Pam Larimer, Adm.

Pre-Prep. Gen Acad. Feat—Fr Span Computers Studio_Art Chorus Music Orchestra. **Supp**—Tut. **Comp:** Comp/Stud: 1:3. **Sports**—Basket X-country Lacrosse Swim Tennis. B: Soccer. G: F_Hockey. **Selective adm:** 50/yr. Appl fee: $75. Appl due: Rolling. Accepted: 40%. Yield: 90%. **Tests** IQ. **Enr 296.** Wh 82%. Latino 3%. Blk 3%. Asian 12%. Avg class size: 15. Stud/fac: 6:1. Uniform. **Fac 50.** M 3/F 47. FT 38/PT 12. Adv deg: 34%. **Grad '11—21.** Prep—9. (Flint Hill 3, Foxcroft Sch 2, Georgetown Prep 1, Madeira 1, Highland-VA 1, Middleburg 1). **Tui '11-'12:** Day $17,650-19,150 (+$150). **Est 1953.** Nonprofit. Tri (Sept-June). LCDS stresses proficiency in English and math skills, as well as science and technology. French and Spanish are taught from prekindergarten. A diversified art program, music instruction (including chorus and orchestra) and physical education are part of the curriculum. Although not compulsory, community service is an area of emphasis.

JAMES RIVER DAY SCHOOL   **Day Coed Gr K-8**
Lynchburg, VA 24503. 5039 Boonsboro Rd.
Tel: 434-384-7385. Fax: 434-384-5937.
www.jamesriverdayschool.org   E-mail: email@jamesriverdayschool.org
     Mary Riser, Head (2007). BA, Georgetown Univ, MFA, Univ of Oregon. Kirstin McHenry, Adm.
     Pre-Prep. Gen Acad. Feat—Lib_Skills Fr Lat Span Computers Studio_Art Chorus Music Study_Skills. **Supp**—Dev_Read Rem_Math Rem_Read Tut. **Sports**—Basket X-country Lacrosse Soccer. G: Volley. **Somewhat selective adm:** 42/yr. Appl fee: $50. Appl due: Rolling. Accepted: 85%. Yield: 90%. **Tests** CTP_4 IQ. **Enr 253.** Avg class size: 16. Casual dress. **Fac 30.** M 6/F 24. FT 25/PT 5. Adv deg: 46%. **Grad '11—18.** Prep—8. **Tui '12-'13:** Day $8740-9090 (+$325). **Est 1971.** Nonprofit. Quar (Sept-June). James River's curriculum stresses basic academic skills and provides enrichment programs in computers, music, art, French and Spanish. The program is designed for the child of average to above-average intelligence.

CARLISLE SCHOOL   **Bdg Coed Gr 8-12**
Martinsville, VA 24115. 300 Carlisle Rd, PO Box 5388.   **Day Coed PS (Age 2)-12**
Tel: 276-632-7288. Fax: 276-632-9545.
Other locations: 179 Piney Forest Rd, Danville 24540; 956 Woodlawn Academy Rd, Chatham 24531.
www.carlisleschool.org   E-mail: admissions@carlisleschool.org
     Simon Owen-Williams, Head (2004). BA, Univ of Exeter (England), MA, Columbia Univ. Lee Probst, Adm.
     Col Prep. IB Diploma. IB PYP. IB MYP. AP (76 exams taken, 63% 3+)—Eng Calc Stats Chem Eur_Hist US_Hist US_Govt & Pol Studio_Art. **Feat**—Span Programming Econ Psych Comp_Relig Philos Art_Hist Theater Dance. **Supp**—ESL LD Rev Tut. **Dual enr:** Patrick Henry CC. **Sports**—Basket X-country Soccer Tennis. B: Baseball Football Golf. G: Cheer F_Hockey Softball Volley. Activities: 35. **Selective adm (Bdg Gr 8-11; Day PS-11):** 60/yr. Appl fee: $50. Appl due: Rolling. Accepted: 82%. Yield: 86%. **Tests** Stanford. **Enr 436.** B 234. G 202. Bdg 26. Day 410. Wh 81%. Latino 1%. Blk 9%. Asian 3%. Other 6%. Intl 6%. Avg class size: 14. Stud/fac: 14:1. Casual dress. **Fac 57.** M 5/F 52. FT 57. Wh 89%. Latino 1%. Blk 5%. Other 5%. Adv deg: 15%. **Grad '10—47.** Col—47. (Roanoke Col 4, Radford 3, U of VA 3, VA Polytech 3, Emory & Henry 2, Lynchburg 2). **Avg SAT:** CR 503. M 571. W 518. **Tui '11-'12:** Bdg $29,900 (+$2700). Day $6000-9575. Aid: Need 140 ($1,082,925). **Est 1968.** Nonprofit. Sem (Aug-May). **Assoc** SACS. In addition to offering the International Baccalaureate Diploma, Carlisle maintains a selection of Advanced Placement courses. The school also conducts the IB Primary Years and Middle Years programs. Students in grades 9-12 perform 21 hours of required community service annually. A small boarding program for high school boys and girls is offered. The Danville campus provides additional classrooms for children in grades PS-2, while the Woodlawn campus in Chatham hosts grades PS-8.

MIDDLEBURG ACADEMY   **Day Coed Gr 9-12**
Middleburg, VA 20117. 35321 Notre Dame Ln.
Tel: 540-687-5581. Fax: 540-687-3552.
www.middleburgacademy.org   E-mail: info@middleburgacademy.org
     Charles E. Britton, Jr., Adm.
     Col Prep. AP (exams req'd; 140 taken, 39% 3+)—Eng Span Calc Physics US_Hist World_Hist US_Govt & Pol Studio_Art. **Feat**—Fr Lat Stats Anat & Physiol Environ_Sci Comp_Sci Anthro Archaeol Econ Psych Philos Relig Architect Art_Hist Drawing SAT_Prep. **Supp**—LD Tut. **Comp:** Comp/Stud: 1:2. **Sports**—Basket X-country Golf Lacrosse Soccer Swim Tennis. B: Baseball. G: F_Hockey Volley. Activities: 15. **Selective adm:** 60/yr. Appl fee: $50. Appl due: Feb. Accepted: 80%. Yield: 90%. **Tests** ISEE SSAT. **Enr 172.** Nonwhite 26%. Intl 10%. Avg class size: 15. Stud/fac: 8:1. Uniform. **Fac 23.** Adv deg: 73%. **Grad '09—60.** Col—60. **Avg SAT:** CR 560. M 600. W 580. **Col Couns:** 1. **Tui '11-'12:** Day $20,370 (+$500-

850). **Est 1965.** Nonprofit. Quar (Aug-June). **Assoc** SACS. Founded as Notre Dame Academy, a Catholic girls' boarding school, this coeducational school assumed its current name in 2010 to better reflect its independent, nonsectarian status. The college preparatory program features Advanced Placement courses, an annual schoolwide retreat, tutorial services, off-campus independent study opportunities for qualified students, a career internship for seniors and required community service. Middleburg's music program provides instruction in voice, piano, guitar and orchestral instruments.

AYLETT COUNTRY DAY SCHOOL   Day Coed Gr PS (Age 3)-8
Millers Tavern, VA 23115. PO Box 70.
Tel: 804-443-3214. Fax: 804-443-3064.
www.acdspatriots.net   E-mail: info@acdspatriots.net
     Nancy W. Haynes, Head (2008). BS, Radford Univ, MEd, Virginia Commonwealth Univ, MEd, EdS, Univ of Virginia. Robin Taylor, Adm.
     Pre-Prep. Gen Acad. Feat—Fr Span Computers Civics Studio_Art Drama Music Debate. **Supp**—Rev Tut. **Sports**—Basket Soccer Track. B: Golf. **Selective adm:** 24/yr. Appl fee: $25. Appl due: Rolling. Accepted: 80%. Yield: 95%. **Tests** IQ Stanford. **Enr 163.** Wh 87%. Latino 5%. Blk 1%. Asian 2%. Other 5%. Avg class size: 16. Casual dress. **Fac 20.** M 2/F 18. FT 20. Nonwhite 5%. Adv deg: 10%. **Grad '09—15.** Prep—3. (St Margaret's Sch 2, Episcopal HS-VA 1). **Tui '10-'11:** Day $6675-7300 (+$375). **Est 1966.** Nonprofit. Sem (Sept-June). ACDS provides a flexible learning structure and emphasizes the development of independence and self-reliance. The curriculum includes programs in physical education, art, music, Spanish, technology and science.

ST. ANDREW'S EPISCOPAL SCHOOL   Day Coed Gr PS (Age 4)-5
Newport News, VA 23601. 45 Main St.
Tel: 757-596-6261. Fax: 757-596-7218.
www.standrewsschool.com   E-mail: standrews@standrewsschool.com
     Valerie Migliore, Head (2011). BA, Albertus Magnus College, MEd, Southern Connecticut State Univ.
     Gen Acad. Feat—Fr Computers Studio_Art Music. **Comp:** Comp/Stud: 1:1.5. **Sports**—Track. **Selective adm:** 52/yr. Appl fee: $75. Appl due: Rolling. **Enr 132.** Wh 82%. Latino 5%. Blk 10%. Asian 2%. Other 1%. Avg class size: 15. Stud/fac: 13:1. Uniform. **Fac 20.** M 1/F 19. FT 19/PT 1. Wh 96%. Latino 4%. Adv deg: 30%. **Grad '10—27.** Prep—3. (Hampton Rds 1, Nansemond-Suffolk 1, Trinity Lutheran 1). **Tui '11-'12:** Day $5750-7280 (+$950). Aid: Need 19 ($36,000). **Est 1946.** Nonprofit. Episcopal. Quar (Aug-June). St. Andrew's provides sound academic training within a Christian environment. Programs in French, art, music, physical education and computer provide enrichment. Small classes, field trips and the use of community resources are integral features of the program.

FLINT HILL SCHOOL   Day Coed Gr PS (Age 4)-12
Oakton, VA 22124. 3320 Jermantown Rd.
Tel: 703-584-2300. Fax: 703-584-2369.
Other locations: 10409 Academic Dr, Oakton 22124.
www.flinthill.org   E-mail: cpryor@flinthill.org
     John M. Thomas, Head. BA, Randolph-Macon College, MA, Towson State Univ. Chris Pryor, Adm.
     Col Prep. AP—Eng Fr Lat Span Calc Stats Bio Chem Environ_Sci Physics Eur_Hist US_Hist Econ Psych US_Govt & Pol Studio_Art Music_Theory. **Feat**—Creative_Writing Shakespeare Satire Chin Greek Multivariable_Calc Ecol Forensic_Sci Marine_Bio/Sci Ornithology Programming Robotics Middle_Eastern_Hist Russ_Stud World_Relig Ceramics Drawing Sculpt Drama Band Chorus Orchestra Ballet Dance. **Supp**—LD. **Comp:** Laptop prgm Gr PS-12. **Sports**—Basket X-country Golf Lacrosse Soccer Swim Tennis Track. B: Baseball

Football. G: Softball Volley. **Selective adm:** 207/yr. Appl fee: $75. Appl due: Jan. Accepted: 47%. Yield: 71%. **Tests** IQ SSAT. **Enr 1097.** Elem 617. Sec 480. Intl 6%. Avg class size: 18. Uniform. **Fac 133.** M 54/F 79. FT 105/PT 28. Adv deg: 47%. **Grad '11—124.** Col—123. (U of VA 6, VA Polytech 6, High Pt 5, James Madison 4, U of CO-Boulder 4, Christopher Newport 4). **Avg SAT:** CR 610. M 630. W 600. Avg ACT: 26. **Col Couns:** 3. **Tui '12-'13:** Day $27,050-30,950. Aid: Need 165 ($3,100,000). **Est 1956.** Nonprofit. Sem (Sept-June). **Assoc** CLS. Enrolling able students from Greater Washington, Flint Hill conducts a rigorous curriculum that prepares boys and girls for college through a combination of Advanced Placement courses and electives. Course work emphasizes learning skills development in the areas of critical thinking, problem solving and writing, and a learning center offers support for pupils with different learning styles. Varied arts offerings, an experiential education program and an athletic program that features competitive sports at the upper school level are important aspects of school life. The lower and middle schools (junior kindergarten through grade 8) occupy a separate campus on Academic Drive.

BLESSED SACRAMENT HUGUENOT　　　　　Day Coed Gr PS (Age 3)-12
CATHOLIC SCHOOL
Powhatan, VA 23139. 2501 Academy Rd.
Tel: 804-598-4211. Fax: 804-598-1053.
www.bshknights.org　E-mail: admissions@bshknights.org
　Tracy Bonday-deLeon, Prin (2011). MEd, Univ of Miami. Christy Polster, Adm.

　Col Prep. Feat—Lat Span Calc Anat & Physiol Comp_Sci Govt Studio_Art Drama Music Debate Journ. **Sports**—Basket X-country Soccer Swim Tennis. B: Baseball Football. G: Softball Volley. **Selective adm:** 60/yr. Appl fee: $50. Appl due: Rolling. **Tests** IQ. **Enr 365.** Elem 241. Sec 124. Avg class size: 18. Stud/fac: 10:1. Uniform. **Fac 51.** M 14/F 37. FT 49/PT 2. Adv deg: 17%. **Grad '09—24.** Col—24. **Tui '10-'11:** Day $6700-10,725 (+$300). Aid: Need 34 ($61,000). **Est 1959.** Nonprofit. Roman Catholic (40% practice). Sem (Aug-June). **Assoc** SACS. BSH emphasizes individual attention in a family-like atmosphere. Interscholastic athletic competition begins in grade 6. Students in grades 9-12 perform at least six hours of community service each year, with juniors completing an additional 30-hour outreach project.

THE NEW COMMUNITY SCHOOL　　　　　　　Day Coed Gr 6-12
Richmond, VA 23227. 4211 Hermitage Rd.
Tel: 804-266-2494. Fax: 804-264-3281.
www.tncs.org　E-mail: info@tncs.org
　Nancy L. Foy, Head (2012). BA, Millikin Univ, MEd, Univ of Richmond. Gita Morris, Adm.

　Col Prep. LD. Feat—Creative_Writing Stats Govt Ethics Fine_Arts Photog Drama Health SAT_Prep. **Supp**—Dev_Read Rem_Math Rem_Read Rev Tut. **Comp:** Comp/Stud: 1:2. **Sports**—Basket Soccer. B: Baseball Golf. G: Volley. **Selective adm (Gr 6-11):** 21/yr. Appl fee: $75. Appl due: Rolling. Accepted: 79%. Yield: 78%. **Tests** IQ Stanford. **Enr 90.** B 58. G 32. Elem 32. Sec 58. Wh 89%. Latino 1%. Blk 8%. Asian 1%. Other 1%. Avg class size: 7. Stud/fac: 3:1. **Fac 30.** M 7/F 23. FT 27/PT 3. Wh 100%. Adv deg: 56%. **Grad '11—11.** Col—10. (Marshall 2, Davis & Elkins 2, Randolph Col 2, Savannah Col of Art & Design 1, Goucher 1, NC Wesleyan 1). **Avg SAT:** CR 520. M 470. W 510. **Col Couns:** 1. Alum donors: 3%. **Tui '12-'13:** Day $25,360-26,600. Aid: Need 25 ($315,650). **Est 1974.** Nonprofit. Sem (Sept-June). Providing college preparation for students with dyslexia, TNCS offers a highly structured, individualized educational environment that allows pupils to work at an appropriate intellectual level while developing language skills that help compensate for their learning difficulties. The curriculum includes both remediation of language skills and sufficient academic challenge for students of average to above-average intelligence. Once the pupil's reading, writing and spelling skills are commensurate with his or her intelligence level, the school may recommend a transfer to a less-specialized setting.

TRINITY EPISCOPAL SCHOOL   Day Coed Gr 8-12
Richmond, VA 23235. 3850 Pittaway Dr.
Tel: 804-272-5864. Fax: 804-272-4652.
www.trinityes.org   E-mail: robshort@trinityes.org
     Thomas G. Aycock, Head (1990). BS, Barton College, MAT, PhD, Univ of North Carolina-Chapel Hill. Emily H. McLeod, Adm.
     Col Prep. IB Diploma. AP (253 exams taken)—Eng Fr Ger Span Calc Stats Bio Chem Physics Eur_Hist US_Hist US_Govt & Pol Studio_Art. **Feat**—Creative_Writing Southern_Lit Lat Environ_Sci Programming Robotics Web_Design Econ World_Relig Ceramics Drawing Film Photog Sculpt Drama Chorus Music_Theory Journ. **Sports**—Baseball Basket X-country Golf Indoor_Track Lacrosse Soccer Swim Tennis Track Volley Weightlifting. B: Football. G: F_Hockey Softball. Activities: 29. **Somewhat selective adm:** 116/yr. Appl fee: $50. Accepted: 89%. **Tests** IQ. **Enr 445.** Avg class size: 13. Stud/fac: 10:1. **Fac 55.** Adv deg: 61%. **Grad '10—95.** Col—94. (VA Polytech 14, VA Commonwealth 9, VA Milit 6, Wm & Mary 5, Hampden-Sydney 5, U of Mary Wash 5). **Avg SAT:** CR 568. M 589. W 558. **Col Couns:** 2. **Tui '11-'12:** Day $18,750. Aid: Need 112. **Est 1972.** Nonprofit. Episcopal. Sem (Aug-May). Trinity, which draws its pupils from more than 60 schools in central Virginia, was the first school in Metropolitan Richmond to offer the International Baccalaureate Diploma. The school also offers Advanced Placement courses in all major disciplines. All boys and girls satisfy community service requirements, and seniors complete a compulsory project. Student exchange opportunities are available.

GREEN HEDGES SCHOOL   Day Coed Gr PS (Age 3)-8
Vienna, VA 22180. 415 Windover Ave NW.
Tel: 703-938-8323. Fax: 703-938-1485.
www.greenhedges.org   E-mail: ldixon@greenhedges.org
     Robert E. Gregg III, Head. BA, Univ of New Hampshire, MBA, Univ of Wisconsin-Madison. Leslie Dixon, Adm.
     Pre-Prep. Montessori. Feat—Fr Lat Span Computers Studio_Art Drama Chorus Music Public_Speak. **Sports**—Basket X-country Soccer Softball. **Selective adm:** 39/yr. Appl fee: $75. Appl due: Feb. Yield: 65%. **Tests** IQ. **Enr 190.** B 97. G 93. Nonwhite 32%. Avg class size: 15. Stud/fac: 8:1. Uniform. **Fac 34.** M 7/F 27. FT 26/PT 8. Adv deg: 55%. **Grad '08—15.** Prep—9. (Flint Hill 1, Madeira 1, Wakefield 1, Episcopal HS-VA 1, Potomac 1, Cate 1). **Tui '11-'12:** Day $22,320-22,850 (+$250-315). Aid: Need 34 ($432,900). **Est 1942.** Nonprofit. Tri (Sept-June). A Montessori-based program in the early school (ages 3-5) transitions to a more traditional primary program in the elementary school (grades 1-5). All classes in the middle school (grades 6-8) are departmentalized. French instruction begins in the preschool, while Spanish and Latin are added in grades 5-8. Music, art, literature, drama and physical education are taught at all grade levels, and technology is integral to the program.

TIDEWATER ACADEMY   Day Coed Gr PS (Age 3)-12
Wakefield, VA 23888. 217 Church St, PO Box 1000.
Tel: 757-899-5401. Fax: 757-899-2521.
www.tidewateracademy-pvt-va.us   E-mail: r_croft@tidewateracademy-pvt-va.us
     Rodney Taylor, Head. Robyn Croft, Adm.
     Col Prep. AP—Eng Calc US_Hist US_Govt & Pol. **Feat**—Shakespeare Southern_Lit Span Comp_Sci Photog Music Dance Bus. **Supp**—Tut. **Sports**—Basket Tennis. B: Baseball Football. G: Cheer Softball Volley. **Selective adm:** 36/yr. Appl fee: $25. Appl due: Apr. Accepted: 75%. **Enr 227.** B 127. G 100. Elem 149. Sec 78. Avg class size: 16. **Fac 29.** M 9/F 20. FT 21/PT 8. Adv deg: 13%. **Grad '04—15.** Col—14. **Avg SAT:** CR/M 1184. **Col Couns:** 1. **Tui '12-'13:** Day $6375-6575 (+$400-500). **Est 1964.** Nonprofit. Quar (Aug-May). The curriculum at this school includes college preparatory instruction and independent study opportunities. Lower schoolers (grades pre-K-6) attend classes at a second campus near Dendron. Tidewater

assigns each student in grades 7-12 a faculty advisor who provides both academic and non-academic mentoring.

WALSINGHAM ACADEMY
Day Coed Gr PS (Age 3)-12

Williamsburg, VA 23187. 1100 Jamestown Rd, PO Box 8702.
Tel: 757-229-6026. Fax: 757-259-1401.
www.walsingham.org   E-mail: amagliola@walsingham.org
Sr. Mary Jeanne Oesterle, RSM, Pres. MEd, St Michael's College. Anita Magliola, Adm.

Col Prep. AP (exams req'd; 183 taken)—Eng Fr Lat Span Calc Stats Bio Chem US_Hist US_Govt & Pol Studio_Art Music_Theory. **Feat**—Programming. **Supp**—Dev_Read Rem_ Read Tut. **Sports**—Basket X-country Golf Sail Soccer Swim Tennis Track Volley. B: Baseball Lacrosse. G: F_Hockey Softball. **Selective adm:** 50/yr. Appl fee: $100. Appl due: Rolling. **Enr 755.** Elem 455. Sec 300. Intl 5%. Avg class size: 18. Uniform. **Fac 70.** M 6/F 64. FT 67/ PT 3. Adv deg: 67%. **Grad '11—52.** Col—52. **Avg SAT:** CR 537. M 577. W 528. **Col Couns:** 1. **Tui '12-'13:** Day $7235-12,534 (+$800). **Est** 1947. Nonprofit. Roman Catholic (50% practice). Quar (Aug-June). **Assoc** SACS. The college preparatory program at this school is conducted by the Sisters of Mercy. In the lower school, language instruction begins with Spanish in kindergarten. Advanced Placement courses and fine and performing arts offerings are part of the upper school curriculum. All students perform community service.

WILLIAMSBURG CHRISTIAN ACADEMY
Day Coed Gr PS (Age 4)-12

Williamsburg, VA 23188. 101 Schoolhouse Ln.
Tel: 757-220-1978. Fax: 757-741-4009.
www.williamsburgchristian.org   E-mail: marting@williamsburgchristian.org
Gwen Martin, Head (2002). BS, MAEd, College of William and Mary.

Col Prep. AP (exams req'd; 23 taken, 74% 3+)—Eng Span Calc Bio Eur_Hist US_Hist Psych Studio_Art. **Feat**—British_Lit ASL Anat & Physiol Comp_Design Comp_Sci Econ Govt Bible Philos Music Bus Speech SAT_Prep. **Supp**—Dev_Read LD Rem_Math Tut. **Dual enr:** Thomas Nelson CC, Wm & Mary. **Sports**—Basket Golf Soccer Tennis. B: Baseball. G: Cheer Softball Volley. Activities: 3. **Somewhat selective adm:** 36/yr. Appl fee: $160. Appl due: Rolling. Accepted: 100%. Yield: 100%. **Tests** CEEB Stanford. **Enr 265.** B 122. G 143. Elem 181. Sec 84. Wh 84%. Latino 3%. Blk 11%. Asian 1%. Other 1%. Avg class size: 15. Stud/fac: 13:1. Uniform. **Fac 39.** M 6/F 33. FT 26/PT 13. Wh 98%. Latino 1%. Other 1%. Adv deg: 17%. **Grad '11—21.** Col—21. (Thomas Nelson CC 5, VA Polytech 3, Liberty 2, Wm & Mary 1, VA Milit 1, U of Mary Wash 1). **Avg SAT:** CR 610. M 600. W 600. Avg ACT: 62. Alum donors: 5%. **Tui '12-'13:** Day $6200-9950 (+$500-1000). Aid: Need 50 ($250,000). **Est** 1978. Nonprofit. Nondenom Christian (99% practice). Sem (Aug-June). **Assoc** SACS. WCA's elementary school (grades pre-K-5) maintains a strong phonics curriculum while offering both resource and accelerated classes. Focusing on study skills, middle school course work (grades 6-8) includes opportunities for advancement in all subject areas, as well as foreign language instruction in grade 8. High school students (grades 9-12) follow a college preparatory curriculum that includes both Advanced Placement courses and electives. Boys and girls in grades 6-12 perform 20 hours of required community service annually.

WEST VIRGINIA

NOTRE DAME HIGH SCHOOL
Day Coed Gr 7-12

Clarksburg, WV 26301. 127 E Pike St.
Tel: 304-623-1026. Fax: 304-623-1026.
www.notredamewv.org
Carroll K. Morrison, Prin (1998). BA, Transylvania Univ, MA, EdD, West Virginia Univ.

Col Prep. Bus. AP—Eng Calc Bio Chem US_Hist Psych US_Govt & Pol Studio_Art. **Feat**—Fr Span Anat & Physiol Relig Theater Chorus. **Supp**—Rem_Math Rem_Read Tut. **Sports**—Basket Golf Soccer Swim Tennis Track. B: Baseball Football. G: Cheer Softball. **Selective adm:** 28/yr. **Enr 149.** B 52. G 97. Avg class size: 20. Stud/fac: 9:1. Uniform. **Fac 18.** M 8/F 10. FT 12/PT 6. Adv deg: 44%. **Grad '04—20.** Col—19. **Tui '09-'10:** Day $5244 (+$150-255). Catholic $3984 (+$150-255). **Est 1955.** Nonprofit. Roman Catholic. Sem (Aug-June). **Assoc** NCA. Notre Dame's curriculum includes Advanced Placement classes and such electives as speech, journalism and accounting. Course work in religion is compulsory. The affiliated St. Mary's Grade School (grades K-6) is located on Pike Street.

THE COUNTRY DAY SCHOOL   Day Coed Gr PS (Age 3)-8
Kearneysville, WV 25430. 449 Rose Hill Dr.
Tel: 304-725-1438. Fax: 304-728-8394.
www.thecountrydayschool.com   E-mail: admissions@thecountrydayschool.com
  Leslie C. Steeley, Head (2010). MA.

Pre-Prep. Feat—Classics Creative_Writing Poetry Lat Span Computers Studio_Art Music. **Supp**—Dev_Read Rev Tut. **Somewhat selective adm:** 53/yr. Appl fee: $50. Appl due: Rolling. Accepted: 90%. **Enr 110.** Avg class size: 15. Uniform. **Fac 30.** M 3/F 27. FT 30. Adv deg: 23%. **Grad '06—5.** Prep—4. **Tui '11-'12:** Day $8750 (+$1000). **Est 1982.** Nonprofit. Sem (Sept-June). Located on a 30-acre campus, the school draws students from a wide tri-state area that includes Virginia, West Virginia and western Maryland. Field trips are planned throughout the year, for children at all grade levels, to such places as Washington, DC, and Williamsburg, VA. Sports, current events, art, music and computer science complement the curriculum.

Great Lakes States

ILLINOIS

SAINT VIATOR HIGH SCHOOL

Day Coed Gr 9-12

Arlington Heights, IL 60004. 1213 E Oakton St.
Tel: 847-392-4050. Fax: 847-392-4101.
www.saintviator.com   E-mail: bsanford@saintviator.com
    Rev. Robert M. Egan, CSV, Pres. Eileen Manno, Prin. Bill Sanford, Adm.

Col Prep. AP (exams req'd; 221 taken, 83% 3+)—Eng Fr Span Calc Bio Chem Physics Eur_Hist US_Hist Comp_Govt & Pol. **Feat**—British_Lit Chin Stats Anat & Physiol Astron Environ_Sci Comp_Sci Web_Design Psych Sociol Urban_Stud Ethics World_Relig Ceramics Film Painting Photog Studio_Art Theater_Arts Music Music_Theory Accounting Study_ Skills. **Supp**—Tut. **Sports**—Basket X-country Golf Soccer Swim Tennis Track Volley W_ Polo. B: Baseball Football Ice_Hockey Lacrosse Wrestling. G: Cheer Softball. Activities: 35. **Selective adm (Gr 9-11):** 304/yr. Appl fee: $50. **Enr 1000.** B 530. G 470. Avg class size: 25. Stud/fac: 13:1. Casual dress. **Fac 73.** M 30/F 43. FT 70/PT 3. Adv deg: 78%. **Grad '11—288.** Col—285. (U of IL-Urbana 25, U of IA 14, IN U 13, DePaul 12, St Norbert 11, Northwestern 9). Avg ACT: 25.7. **Tui '12-'13:** Day $11,400 (+$400). Aid: Need 270 ($1,200,000). **Est 1961.** Nonprofit. Roman Catholic. Quar (Aug-June). **Assoc** NCA. Emphasizing religious education, Saint Viator supplements its college preparatory curriculum with school publications, athletics, the arts, clubs, organizations and other extracurricular activities. All students perform 25 hours of community service per year, for a required total of 100 hours. Boys and girls enroll from approximately 50 nearby towns.

QUEEN OF PEACE HIGH SCHOOL

Day Girls Gr 9-12

Burbank, IL 60459. 7659 S Linder Ave.
Tel: 708-458-7600. Fax: 708-458-5734.
www.queenofpeacehs.org   E-mail: info@queenofpeacehs.org
    Anne O'Malley, Pres (2010). BA, Marquette Univ. Mary Kay Nickels, Prin. BS, Northern Illinois Univ, MS, Dominican Univ. Mary Kate Love, Adm.

Col Prep. AP (exams req'd)—Eng Span Calc Bio Chem US_Hist World_Hist Psych. **Feat**—Creative_Writing Fr Stats Anat & Physiol Environ_Sci Engineering Web_Design Amer_Stud Econ Sociol Women's_Stud Relig World_Relig Ceramics Drawing Painting Sculpt Studio_Art Acting Drama Music_Theory Ballet Accounting Bus Journ. **Supp**—Tut. **Comp:** Comp/Stud: 1:1 Laptop prgm Gr 9-12. **Dual enr:** Moraine Valley CC. **Sports**— G: Basket X-country Golf Soccer Softball Tennis Track Volley. Activities: 38. **Somewhat selective adm (Gr 9-11):** 95/yr. Appl fee: $0. Appl due: Rolling. Accepted: 95%. **Tests** HSPT. **Enr 400.** Wh 50%. Latino 35%. Blk 12%. Native Am 1%. Asian 1%. Other 1%. Avg class size: 22. Stud/fac: 13:1. Uniform. **Fac 30.** M 2/F 28. FT 26/PT 4. Wh 89%. Latino 7%. Native Am 2%. Asian 2%. Adv deg: 90%. **Grad '11—121.** Col—119. **Tui '11-'12:** Day $9250 (+$300). Aid: Need ($350,000). **Est 1962.** Nonprofit. Roman Catholic. Quar (Aug-June). **Assoc** NCA. Peace offers a complete college preparatory curriculum that includes Advanced Placement course work. The school places particular emphasis on technology and the disciplines of science, math and engineering. The school's collaboration with Moraine Valley Community College enables qualified students to enroll in dual-enrollment courses in certain subjects. Girls perform 60 hours of required community service over their four years.

BROTHER RICE HIGH SCHOOL Day Boys Gr 9-12
Chicago, IL 60655. 10001 S Pulaski Rd.
Tel: 773-429-4300. Fax: 773-779-5239.
www.brotherrice.org E-mail: toconnell@brrice.org
Kevin G. Burns, Pres (2010). James P. Antos, Prin. Tim O'Connell, Adm.

Col Prep. AP (155 exams taken, 77% 3+)—Eng Fr Span Calc Comp_Sci Chem Eur_Hist US_Hist Econ Psych. **Feat**—Ger Anat & Physiol Vietnam_War Law Sociol Theol Studio_Art Accounting Journ. **Supp**—LD. **Comp:** Comp/Stud: 1:2.6. **Dual enr:** Moraine Valley CC. **Sports**— B: Baseball Basket Bowl Cheer X-country Football Golf Ice_Hockey Lacrosse Rugby Soccer Swim Tennis Track Volley W_Polo Wrestling. **Selective adm. Tests** HSPT. **Enr 887. Fac 70.** Adv deg: 60%. **Grad '10—302.** Col—288. **Avg SAT:** CR 590. M 600. Avg ACT: 22.6. **Tui '11-'12:** Day $9150. **Est 1956.** Nonprofit. Roman Catholic. Quar (Aug-May). **Assoc** NCA. The Congregation of Christian Brothers conducts this school, which draws its students from the southwest side of Chicago and the surrounding suburbs. Brother Rice provides several special options for academically gifted pupils: a selective program for gifted students, honors and Advanced Placement classes, and a program for juniors and seniors wishing to take dual-credit college courses. In addition, the school offers assistance to boys in need of individualized strategies to improve their academic skills and prepare for college. Students satisfy the following community service requirements: 10 hours per year in grades 9 and 10, 20 hours annually in grades 11 and 12.

CHICAGO WALDORF SCHOOL Day Coed Gr PS (Age 3)-12
Chicago, IL 60626. 1300 W Loyola Ave.
Tel: 773-465-2662. Fax: 773-465-6648.
www.chicagowaldorf.org E-mail: info@chicagowaldorf.org
Leukos Goodwin, Admin Dir (2008). BA, Davidson College, MEd, Antioch Univ of New England. Lisa Payton, Adm.

Col Prep. Waldorf. Feat—Russ_Lit Ger Span Astron Geol Marine_Bio/Sci Drawing Drama Chorus Eurythmy Journ Metal_Shop Agriculture. **Supp**—Dev_Read Rem_Math Rem_ Read Tut. **Comp:** Comp/Stud: 1:3. Outdoor Ed. **Sports**—Basket Soccer Track. G: Volley. Activities: 11. **Selective adm (Gr PS-11):** 61/yr. Appl fee: $75. Appl due: Dec. Accepted: 78%. Yield: 65%. **Enr 353.** B 158. G 195. Elem 286. Sec 67. Wh 73%. Latino 6%. Blk 3%. Asian 2%. Other 16%. Avg class size: 22. Stud/fac: 7:1. **Fac 52.** M 16/F 36. FT 37/PT 15. Wh 94%. Latino 4%. Blk 2%. Adv deg: 23%. **Grad '11—21.** Col—21. (U of IL-Urbana 2, Eckerd 2, U of IL-Chicago 1, Hobart/Wm Smith 1, St Olaf 1, Bennington 1). **Tui '11-'12:** Day $14,826-16,808 (+$530-2555). Aid: Need 135 ($777,616). **Est 1974.** Nonprofit. Sem (Sept-June). **Assoc** NCA. Offering a full early childhood through high school program, this urban school follows the Waldorf curriculum and approach pioneered by Rudolf Steiner. As Chicago Waldorf's curriculum integrates academics and the arts, such special subjects as handwork and eurythmy complement traditional music and art classes. The language program features Spanish from grade 1 and a choice between Spanish and German during the high school years. Students in grades 9-12 participate in four annual community service days.

DE LA SALLE INSTITUTE Day Coord Gr 9-12
Chicago, IL 60616. 3434 S Michigan Ave.
Tel: 312-842-7355. Fax: 312-842-5640.
Other locations: 1040 W 32nd Pl, Chicago 60608.
www.dls.org
Rev. Paul E. Novak, OSM, Pres (2008). BA, St Louis Univ, MDiv, Catholic Theological Union. Chuck Kuhn, Adm.

Col Prep. AP (15 exams taken, 20% 3+)—Eng Fr Span Calc US_Hist US_Govt & Pol Studio_Art. **Feat**—British_Lit Creative_Writing Anat & Physiol Environ_Sci Comp_Sci Psych World_Relig Film Drama Chorus Accounting Bus Finance Mech_Drawing. **Supp**— Dev_Read Rem_Math Rem_Read Rev Tut. **Comp:** Comp/Stud: 1:1 Laptop prgm Gr 9-12.

Dual enr: St Mary's U of MN. **Sports**—Basket Bowl X-country Soccer Swim Tennis Track Volley. B: Baseball Football Golf Ice_Hockey W_Polo Wrestling. G: Cheer Softball. Activities: 32. **Selective adm (Gr 9-11):** 337/yr. Appl fee: $25. Appl due: Rolling. Accepted: 95%. Yield: 65%. **Tests** HSPT. **Enr 1122.** B 669. G 453. Wh 36%. Latino 24%. Blk 33%. Asian 3%. Other 4%. Avg class size: 28. Uniform. **Fac 75.** M 50/F 25. FT 74/PT 1. Wh 80%. Latino 11%. Blk 8%. Asian 1%. Adv deg: 60%. **Grad '10—286.** Col—268. (Lewis 18, DePaul 13, E IL 11, U of IL-Urbana 11, U of IL-Chicago 10, Columbia Col-IL 9). **Avg SAT:** CR 455. M 450. W 446. Avg ACT: 20. **Col Couns:** 6. Alum donors: 35%. **Tui '11-'12:** Day $8950 (+$500). Aid: Merit 141 ($170,000). Need 502 ($1,060,000). Work prgm 19 ($25,000). **Est 1889.** Nonprofit. Roman Catholic (74% practice). Sem (Aug-May). **Assoc** NCA. This Catholic high school offers coordinated single-gender programs at two distinct locations: the boys' campus on South Michigan Avenue and the girls' campus on West 32nd Place. All pursuits aside from academics—activities, sporting events and Masses, for example—are conducted in a coeducational setting. The varied college preparatory curriculum enables qualified students to take both Advanced Placement courses and classes for college credit through St. Mary's University of Minnesota. Boys and girls perform 100 hours of required community service prior to graduation.

HOLY TRINITY HIGH SCHOOL   Day Coed Gr 9-12
Chicago, IL 60642. 1443 W Division St.
Tel: 773-278-4212. Fax: 773-278-0144.
www.holytrinity-hs.org   E-mail: admissions@holytrinity-hs.org
     Timothy M. Bopp, Pres (2007). Anne Rog, Prin. BA, St Louis Univ, MEd, Dominican College (NY). Allison Thurman, Adm.

     Col Prep. AP—Calc. **Feat**—British_Lit Creative_Writing Fr Span Anat & Physiol Astron Comp_Sci Holocaust Econ Govt Psych Philos World_Relig Ceramics Film Sculpt Studio_Art Animation Acting Theater_Arts Band Music Speech. **Supp**—Dev_Read Rem_Math Rem_Read Rev Tut. **Comp:** Comp/Stud: 1:4. **Sports**—Basket X-country Soccer Track Volley. B: Baseball. G: Softball. Activities: 17. **Selective adm:** 150/yr. Appl fee: $25. Appl due: Jan. Accepted: 80%. **Enr 324.** Avg class size: 23. Uniform. **Fac 30.** M 16/F 14. FT 30. Adv deg: 70%. **Grad '08—95.** Col—95. **Col Couns:** 1. **Tui '12-'13:** Day $6950 (+$450-550). Aid: Need ($750,000). **Est 1910.** Nonprofit. Roman Catholic. Quar (Aug-June). **Assoc** NCA. Conducted by the Brothers of Holy Cross, Holy Trinity offers a structured college preparatory and general education curriculum. Among the courses required for graduation are religion, humanities, computers and consumer education. Beyond academics, students participate in required community service within their local neighborhoods.

LUTHER NORTH COLLEGE PREP   Day Coed Gr 9-12
Chicago, IL 60634. 5700 W Berteau Ave.
Tel: 773-286-3600. Fax: 773-286-0304.
www.luthernorth.org   E-mail: admissions@luthernorth.org
     Sheri Meyer, Exec Dir. JoAnne Rzadzki, Adm.

     Col Prep. Gen Acad. AP—Eng Calc Chem US_Govt & Pol. **Feat**—Span Anat & Physiol Environ_Sci Comp_Sci Econ Sociol Theol World_Relig Fine_Arts Accounting Bus Public_Speak. **Supp**—Dev_Read LD Rem_Math Rem_Read Tut. **Dual enr:** Concordia U-IL. **Sports**—Basket X-country Track. B: Baseball Football. G: Soccer Softball Volley. **Somewhat selective adm:** 53/yr. Appl fee: $150. Appl due: Rolling. Accepted: 100%. Yield: 43%. **Tests** IQ Stanford. **Enr 174.** B 93. G 81. Wh 54%. Latino 25%. Blk 7%. Asian 1%. Other 13%. Avg class size: 16. Stud/fac: 14:1. **Fac 17.** M 7/F 10. FT 13/PT 4. Wh 98%. Blk 1%. Asian 1%. Adv deg: 82%. **Grad '10—70.** Col—66. Avg ACT: 20.4. **Col Couns:** 2. Alum donors: 20%. **Tui '12-'13:** Day $8500 (+$800-900). Aid: Merit 62 ($100,000). Need 60 ($75,000). Work prgm 15 ($20,000). **Est 1909.** Nonprofit. Lutheran-Missouri Synod (40% practice). Quar (Aug-June). **Assoc** NCA. Luther North offers two diplomas, each with distinct graduation requirements. Boys and girls typically select their program of study in the spring of sophomore year. Band, chorus and drama are among the school's arts electives. An 11-day interim program enables students to take a half-credit course not offered in the regular curriculum.

SAINT IGNATIUS COLLEGE PREP Day Coed Gr 9-12
Chicago, IL 60608. 1076 W Roosevelt Rd.
Tel: 312-421-5900. Fax: 312-421-7124.
www.ignatius.org   E-mail: elizabeth.cummings@ignatius.org
Rev. Michael P. Caruso, SJ, Pres (2010). BA, Conception Seminary College, MDiv, STB, Univ of Saint Mary of the Lake, EdD, Univ of San Francisco. Catherine Karl, Prin. PhD. Elizabeth Cummings, Adm.

Col Prep. AP (exams req'd; 963 taken, 77% 3+)—Eng Fr Lat Span Calc Stats Comp_ Sci Bio Chem Environ_Sci Physics Eur_Hist US_Hist Comp_Govt & Pol Econ Studio_Art Music_Theory. **Feat**—British_Lit Creative_Writing Shakespeare Chicago_Lit Irish_Lit Chin Greek Anat & Physiol Astron Genetics African-Amer_Hist Amer_Stud Psych World_Relig Film Photog Acting Chorus Music Dance Journ. **Supp**—Tut. **Comp:** Comp/Stud: 1:6.4. **Sports**—Basket Bowl Crew X-country Golf Lacrosse Sail Soccer Tennis Track Volley W_ Polo. B: Baseball Football Ice_Hockey Rugby Wrestling. G: Cheer Softball Swim. Activities: 60. **Selective adm:** 345/yr. Appl fee: $25. Appl due: Jan. **Tests** HSPT. **Enr 1383.** B 692. G 691. Avg class size: 18. Stud/fac: 14:1. Casual dress. **Fac 82.** M 46/F 36. FT 74/PT 8. Adv deg: 84%. **Grad '10—328.** Col—328. **Avg SAT:** CR 612. M 604. W 604. Avg ACT: 27.7. **Col Couns:** 4. **Tui '11-'12:** Day $13,620 (+$800-1000). Aid: Need ($3,000,000). **Est 1869.** Nonprofit. Roman Catholic. Sem (Aug-June). St. Ignatius' curriculum reflects a liberal arts tradition in which mandatory foreign language and religious studies courses are supplemented by required classes in speech, the fine arts and computers. Juniors and seniors may take honors and AP courses. Freshmen and sophomores participate in required community service projects.

SAINT PATRICK HIGH SCHOOL Day Boys Gr 9-12
Chicago, IL 60634. 5900 W Belmont Ave.
Tel: 773-282-8844. Fax: 773-282-2361.
www.stpatrick.org   E-mail: info@stpatrick.org
Br. Konrad Diebold, FSC, Pres (1983). BA, MEd, St Mary's College (MN). Joseph Schmidt, Prin. BA, MS, EdS, EdD, Northern Illinois Univ. Robert McMillin, Adm.

Col Prep. AP (49 exams taken, 80% 3+)—Eng Fr Span Calc Bio US_Hist US_Govt & Pol. **Feat**—British_Lit Chin Comp_Sci Web_Design Econ Psych Sociol Relig Fine_Arts Acting Theater_Arts Music Accounting Bus Journ. **Supp**—Dev_Read ESL Rem_Math Rem_ Read Tut. **Comp:** Comp/Stud: 1:4. **Dual enr:** St Mary's U of MN. **Sports**— B: Baseball Basket Bowl X-country Football Golf Soccer Swim Tennis Track Volley W_Polo Wrestling. Activities: 28. **Somewhat selective adm:** 232/yr. Appl fee: $0. Appl due: Rolling. Accepted: 99%. Yield: 76%. **Enr 816.** Wh 62%. Latino 28%. Blk 6%. Asian 4%. Avg class size: 23. Stud/fac: 17:1. Casual dress. **Fac 63.** M 46/F 17. FT 63. Adv deg: 61%. **Grad '11—197.** Col—190. (U of IL-Chicago 17, U of IL-Urbana 16, Northeastern IL 12, St Mary's U of MN 7, Lewis 6, Loyola U of Chicago 5). Avg ACT: 22. **Col Couns:** 6. Alum donors: 11%. **Tui '11- '12:** Day $8890 (+$400). Aid: Need 378 ($1,000,000). **Est 1861.** Nonprofit. Roman Catholic (74% practice). Sem (Aug-June). **Assoc** NCA. Course work at this boys' Catholic school emphasizes college preparation, and Advanced Placement examinations are given each year. A special, limited-enrollment program is available to students who are ill prepared for the college preparatory program or who are working below grade level, and a computer education facility integrates all curricula with computer applications and software. Qualified students may earn college credit through St. Mary's University of Minnesota. Freshmen perform 10 hours of required community service, while sophomores and juniors donate 20 hours per year.

SCIENCE AND ARTS ACADEMY   Day Coed Gr PS (Age 3)-8
Des Plaines, IL 60016. 1825 Miner St.
Tel: 847-827-7880. Fax: 847-827-7716.
www.scienceandartsacademy.org   E-mail: info@scienceandartsacademy.org
   Thomas A. Mikolyzk, Head (2009). Amanda Davey, Adm.

   Pre-Prep. Feat—Fr Lat Span Computers Logic Philos Studio_Art Music. **Selective adm:** Appl fee: $100. Appl due: Rolling. **Tests** IQ. **Enr 220.** Avg class size: 14. Stud/fac: 7:1. **Fac 30.** M 8/F 22. FT 30. **Tui '11-'12:** Day $16,900 (+$1500). **Est 1992.** Nonprofit. Quar (Sept-June). **Assoc** NCA. The academy's accelerated liberal arts curriculum emphasizes creative and critical thinking, inquiry and discovery strategies, problem solving and rapid pacing. In grades 1-4, Science & Arts organizes educational experiences according to students' individual profiles and areas of strength; ability groupings are utilized in math and language arts. Fifth grade serves as a transitional period to increased academic independence. The departmentalized middle school program (grades 6-8) features an adaptable curriculum that offers course work at the high school level as needed. Classical study of Latin, philosophy and logic supplements work in the traditional academic disciplines at this level.

THE WILLOWS ACADEMY   Day Girls Gr 6-12
Des Plaines, IL 60016. 1012 Thacker St.
Tel: 847-824-6900. Fax: 847-824-7089.
www.willowsacademy.org   E-mail: info@willowsacademy.org
   Mary J. Keenley, Head. BA, Northwestern Univ, MSEd, Northeastern Illinois Univ. Stephanie Sheffield, Adm.

   Col Prep. AP (95 exams taken, 77% 3+)—Eng Fr Lat Span Calc Bio Eur_Hist US_Hist. **Feat**—British_Lit Stats Anat & Physiol Programming Econ Pol_Sci Philos Theol Studio_Art Chorus Music_Theory Speech. **Supp**—Tut. **Sports**— G: Basket X-country Soccer Softball Swim Volley. Activities: 16. **Selective adm:** 75/yr. Appl fee: $50. Appl due: Rolling. Accepted: 80%. **Tests** ISEE. **Enr 272.** Elem 94. Sec 178. Wh 88%. Latino 8%. Blk 1%. Asian 3%. Avg class size: 19. Stud/fac: 12:1. Uniform. **Fac 27.** FT 25/PT 2. Wh 99%. Latino 1%. Adv deg: 55%. **Grad '11—35.** Col—35. (U of IL-Urbana 2, IN Wesleyan 2, Boston Col 1, Villanova 1, Lake Forest 1, Notre Dame 1). **Avg SAT:** CR 654. M 663. W 660. Avg ACT: 27. **Col Couns:** 1. Alum donors: 11%. **Tui '11-'12:** Day $8250-13,000 (+$1000). **Est 1974.** Nonprofit. Roman Catholic (95% practice). Sem (Aug-June). With its classic liberal arts orientation, Willows' college preparatory curriculum offers courses at the honors or AP level in most disciplines. A favorable student-teacher ratio characterizes the program at all grade levels. Girls satisfy the following community service requirements: 20 hours in grade 6, 40 hours of in grades 9-12. Students enroll from roughly 40 communities in Metropolitan Chicago.

DA VINCI ACADEMY   Day Coed Gr PS (Age 3)-8
Elgin, IL 60124. 37W080 Hopps Rd.
Tel: 847-841-7532. Fax: 847-841-7546.
www.dvacademy.org   E-mail: admissions@dvacademy.org
   Scott Etters, Head (2012). BA, Bradley Univ, MEd, Aurora Univ. Rebecca Malotke-Meslin, Adm.

   Pre-Prep. Gen Acad. Feat—Span Computers Studio_Art Music. **Comp:** Comp/Stud: 1:2.5. **Sports**—Basket Soccer Volley. **Somewhat selective adm (Gr PS-7):** 30/yr. Appl fee: $50. Appl due: Rolling. Accepted: 86%. Yield: 76%. **Tests** IQ. **Enr 130.** B 85. G 45. Wh 77%. Latino 8%. Blk 1%. Asian 13%. Other 1%. Avg class size: 13. Stud/fac: 8:1. Uniform. **Fac 20.** M 4/F 16. FT 14/PT 6. Wh 83%. Latino 11%. Asian 6%. Adv deg: 60%. **Grad '11—11.** Prep—5. (Wheaton 2, Elgin 1, Hotchkiss 1, St Francis HS-IL 1). **Tui '12-'13:** Day $13,125-16,800. Aid: Need 37 ($256,800). **Est 2000.** Nonprofit. Tri (Aug-June). Founded to serve gifted students, the academy addresses the needs of these students by providing an accelerated curriculum that features project-based and hands-on learning experiences, and also by employing flexible teaching strategies to accommodate various learning styles. The curriculum, which is designed to be one grade level ahead, combines work in the core disciplines with Spanish, art, music, computers and physical education. Each year, middle school students (grades 5-8) organize a community service project over the course of one trimester.

JOLIET CATHOLIC ACADEMY   Day Coed Gr 9-12
Joliet, IL 60435. 1200 N Larkin Ave.
Tel: 815-741-0500. Fax: 815-741-8825.
www.jca-online.org   E-mail: admissions@jca-online.org
    Jeffrey R. Budz, Prin. BA, MA, St Xavier Univ. Diane Nowaczyk, Adm.

    Col Prep. AP (88 exams taken, 36% 3+)—Eng Calc Bio Chem Eur_Hist US_Hist US_ Govt & Pol. **Feat**—Holocaust_Lit Fr Lat Span Anat & Physiol Environ_Sci Comp_Design Comp_Sci Econ Intl_Relations Psych Sociol Relig Studio_Art Music Handbells Journ. **Supp**—LD Tut. **Dual enr:** U of St Francis. **Sports**—Basket X-country Golf Soccer Tennis Track Volley. B: Baseball Football Ice_Hockey Wrestling. G: Cheer Softball. Activities: 50. **Somewhat selective adm:** 225/yr. Appl fee: $30. Appl due: Jan. Accepted: 90%. **Enr 702.** Wh 56%. Latino 25%. Blk 15%. Native Am 1%. Asian 3%. Avg class size: 24. Stud/fac: 15:1. **Fac 51.** M 19/F 32. FT 49/PT 2. Wh 98%. Latino 2%. Adv deg: 33%. **Grad '10—217.** Col—207. Avg ACT: 24. **Col Couns:** 4. Alum donors: 20%. **Tui '10-'11:** Day $8850 (+$525-1600). Aid: Merit 3 ($70,000). Need 320 ($2,500,000). **Est 1990.** Nonprofit. Roman Catholic. Sem (Aug-June). **Assoc** NCA. The school resulted from the 1990 merger of Joliet Catholic High School for boys (founded in 1918) and St. Francis Academy for girls (established in 1869). JCA's college preparatory curriculum includes a four-year honors program and Advanced Placement courses in the major disciplines. Students satisfy community service requirements at each grade level: five hours in grade 9, 10 hours in grade 10, 15 hours in grade 11 and 30 hours in grade 12.

MOUNT ASSISI ACADEMY   Day Girls Gr 9-12
Lemont, IL 60439. 13860 Main St.
Tel: 630-257-7844. Fax: 630-257-6362.
www.mtassisi.org   E-mail: mtadros@mtassisi.org
    Kimberly Johnson Quinn, Pres (2011). BA, Lewis Univ, MBA, St Xavier Univ. Sr. Mary Francis Werner, SSFCR, Prin. BA, Univ of St Francis, MSA, Concordia Univ Chicago, MRE, Loyola Univ of Chicago. Marina Tadros, Adm.

    Col Prep. Gen Acad. AP (exams req'd)—Eng Calc US_Hist US_Govt & Pol. **Feat**—British_Lit Creative_Writing Fr Lat Span Anat & Physiol Environ_Sci Forensic_Sci Comp_Sci Econ Govt Psych Sociol Theol Studio_Art Music Accounting Journ Health. **Supp**—Dev_ Read Makeup Rem_Math Rem_Read Rev Tut. **Comp:** Comp/Stud: 1:1 Laptop prgm Gr 9-12. **Sports**— G: Basket Cheer X-country Golf Soccer Softball Swim Tennis Track Volley. **Somewhat selective adm:** 90/yr. Appl due: Aug. Accepted: 99%. Yield: 100%. **Tests** CTP_4. **Enr 220.** Wh 94%. Latino 4%. Other 2%. Avg class size: 22. Uniform. **Fac 28.** M 2/F 26. FT 21/PT 7. Adv deg: 75%. **Grad '11—67.** Col—65. Avg ACT: 22. **Col Couns:** 1. Alum donors: 5%. **Tui '12-'13:** Day $8140 (+$400-500). **Est 1951.** Nonprofit. Roman Catholic. Sem (Aug-May). **Assoc** NCA. Established by the School Sisters of St. Francis of Christ the King, this girls' school continues to emphasize Franciscan ideals. Students pursue course work in three distinct programs: basic, academic and honors. Advanced Placement courses are part of the curriculum, and girls take two semesters of religion per year. Each girl leases a tablet laptop computer from the school.

BENET ACADEMY   Day Coed Gr 9-12
Lisle, IL 60532. 2200 Maple Ave.
Tel: 630-969-6550. Fax: 630-719-2849.
www.benet.org   E-mail: jbrown@benet.org
    Rev. Jude D. Randall, OSB, Pres. Stephen A. Marth, Prin. James E. Brown, Adm.

Col Prep. AP (639 exams taken, 87% 3+)—Eng Calc Stats Comp_Sci Bio Physics Eur_Hist US_Hist Econ US_Govt & Pol. **Feat**—Creative_Writing Humanities Fr Ger Lat Span Multivariable_Calc Relig Band Chorus Bus. **Dual enr:** Benedictine U. **Sports**—Basket X-country Golf Soccer Swim Tennis Track Volley. B: Baseball Football. G: Cheer Softball. **Selective adm:** 352/yr. Appl fee: $35. Appl due: Jan. Accepted: 66%. **Tests** HSPT. **Enr 1350.** Avg class size: 26. Stud/fac: 17:1. Uniform. **Fac 70.** Adv deg: 87%. **Grad '10—321.** Col— 319. (Notre Dame 23, U of IL-Urbana 21, Marquette 20, Miami U-OH 16, IN U 15, St Louis U 14). **Avg SAT:** CR 632. M 647. W 622. Avg ACT: 28.7. **Col Couns:** 3. **Tui '12-'13:** Day $9400 (+$86-157). **Est 1887.** Nonprofit. Roman Catholic. Sem (Aug-June). **Assoc** NCA. This Benedictine academy is closely affiliated with Benedictine University, which provides additional educational opportunities, advanced courses, increased library facilities and other collegiate advantages. Students may earn up to 24 college credits while still attending the academy by enrolling in courses at the university. All students take four years of religion. Benet draws its pupils from DuPage, Kane, Will and Cook counties.

MONTINI CATHOLIC HIGH SCHOOL   Day Coed Gr 9-12
Lombard, IL 60148. 19W070 16th St.
Tel: 630-627-6930. Fax: 630-627-0537.
www.montini.org   E-mail: info@montini.org
    James F. Segredo, Pres (2004). BA, Lewis Univ, MEd, Univ of Illinois-Chicago. Maryann O'Neill, Prin. BS, Univ of Illinois-Urbana, MA, Lewis Univ. Michael Bukovsky, Adm.

Col Prep. AP (128 exams taken, 74% 3+)—Eng Fr Span Calc Bio Chem US_Hist World_Hist US_Govt & Pol. **Feat**—Creative_Writing Stats Anat & Physiol Programming Web_Design Psych Sociol Theol Film Graphic_Arts Studio_Art Acting Music Accounting Marketing. **Supp**—Dev_Read Rem_Math Rem_Read Rev Tut. **Comp:** Comp/Stud: 1:3. **Dual enr:** Col of DuPage. **Sports**—Basket X-country Lacrosse Soccer Tennis Track Volley. B: Baseball Football Golf Ice_Hockey Rugby Wrestling. G: Cheer Softball. Activities: 26. **Somewhat selective adm (Gr 9-11):** 182/yr. Appl fee: $30. Appl due: Jan. Accepted: 92%. Yield: 90%. **Tests** HSPT. **Enr 700.** B 387. G 313. Wh 85%. Latino 3%. Blk 2%. Asian 8%. Other 2%. Avg class size: 20. Stud/fac: 14:1. Uniform. **Fac 52.** M 25/F 27. FT 45/PT 7. Wh 97%. Latino 3%. Adv deg: 59%. **Grad '10—155.** Col—151. (U of IL-Urbana 8, Loyola U of Chicago 7, DePaul 6, U of IA 6, N IL 6). Avg ACT: 22.9. **Col Couns:** 2. Alum donors: 9%. **Tui '11-'12:** Day $9175 (+$600). Aid: Merit 12 ($10,000). Need 199 ($469,535). **Est 1966.** Nonprofit. Roman Catholic (88% practice). Sem (Aug-May). **Assoc** NCA. This college preparatory school, named for Pope Paul VI (whose family name was Montini), offers students a traditional curriculum supplemented by four years of religion. All freshmen attend a day of recollection; sophomores complete a day of service and prayer; juniors participate in a two-day retreat program consisting of prayer, community building, confession, Mass and recreation; and seniors take part in an optional retreat. Boys and girls fulfill a 40-hour community service requirement (10 hours per year) prior to graduation.

CHRISTIAN HERITAGE ACADEMY   Day Coed Gr PS (Age 2)-12
Northfield, IL 60093. 315 Waukegan Rd.
Tel: 847-446-5252. Fax: 847-446-5267.
Other locations: 1001 N Crosby St, Chicago 60610.
www.christianheritage.org   E-mail: admissions@christianheritage.org
    David L. Roth, CEO. EdD. Cynthia Strull, Adm.

Gen Acad. Feat—Span Computers Bible Fine_Arts Music Speech Study_Skills. **Supp**— Dev_Read Rem_Math Rem_Read Rev Tut. **Comp:** Laptop prgm Gr 9-12. **Sports**—Basket Soccer Track Volley. **Somewhat selective adm:** 76/yr. Appl fee: $125. Appl due: Rolling. Accepted: 97%. Yield: 83%. **Enr 453.** B 227. G 226. Elem 408. Sec 45. Wh 58%. Latino 5%. Blk 4%. Asian 30%. Other 3%. Avg class size: 17. Stud/fac: 11:1. Casual dress. **Fac 47.** M 7/F 40. FT 29/PT 18. Wh 82%. Latino 2%. Asian 16%. Adv deg: 29%. **Grad '11—40. Tui '12-'13:** Day $8480-13,400. Aid: Merit 4 ($20,000). Need 113 ($405,000). **Est 1983.** Nonprofit. Evangelical. Quar (Aug-June). **Assoc** NCA. This nondenominational, parent-governed, evangelical Christian school integrates Bible instruction into all subject areas. Students attend weekly chapel services and convene once a month for all-school chapel. Middle school pupils take thematic annual trips: A sixth-grade excursion to Eagle River, WI, focuses on outdoor science education; a seventh-grade trek to Springfield enables boys and girls to study Illinois state history; and an eighth-grade trip to Washington, DC, and Gettysburg, VA, enhances social studies and literature study. CHA's Chicago campus hosts students in preschool through grade 1.

FENWICK HIGH SCHOOL   Day Coed Gr 9-12
Oak Park, IL 60302. 505 W Washington Blvd.
Tel: 708-386-0127. Fax: 708-386-3052.
www.fenwickfriars.com   E-mail: frabchuk@fenwickfriars.com
    Rev. DePorres Durham, OP, Pres. BA, Wadhams Hall Seminary College, BTh, Saint Paul Univ (Canada), MA, St Louis Univ. Peter Groom, Prin. Francesca Rabchuk, Adm.
    Col Prep. AP (exams req'd; 711 taken, 67% 3+)—Eng Fr Span Calc Stats Comp_Sci Bio Chem Environ_Sci Physics Eur_Hist US_Hist World_Hist Econ US_Govt & Pol Art_Hist. **Feat**—British_Lit Creative_Writing Ger Ital Lat Anat & Physiol Asian_Hist Lat-Amer_Hist Theol Music_Hist Orchestra Journ. **Supp**—Tut. **Sports**—Basket Bowl X-country Golf Lacrosse Soccer Swim Tennis Track Volley W_Polo. B: Baseball Football Ice_Hockey Wrestling. G: Cheer Softball. Activities: 35. **Selective adm (Gr 9-11):** 310/yr. Appl due: Jan. Accepted: 65%. Yield: 83%. **Tests** HSPT. **Enr 1196.** B 665. G 531. Wh 83%. Latino 8%. Blk 7%. Asian 1%. Other 1%. Avg class size: 23. Uniform. **Fac 85.** M 45/F 40. FT 80/PT 5. Wh 94%. Latino 1%. Blk 3%. Native Am 1%. Other 1%. Adv deg: 76%. **Grad '10—291.** Col—291. (U of IL-Urbana 34, Notre Dame 22, IN U 20, Marquette 17, DePaul 12, Loyola U of Chicago 11). Avg ACT: 27.1. Alum donors: 11%. **Tui '12-'13:** Day $12,500. Aid: Merit 62 ($91,500). Need 286 ($1,336,049). **Est 1929.** Nonprofit. Roman Catholic. Sem (Aug-June). **Assoc** NCA. Founded and still sponsored by the Dominican Friars, Fenwick provides students with a thorough grounding in English, math, computer science, foreign language, history and theology. Boys and girls take theology each year, and each junior fulfills a 40-hour Christian service requirement; half of this commitment may be completed during the summer prior to junior year.

CHICAGO CHRISTIAN HIGH SCHOOL   Day Coed Gr 9-12
Palos Heights, IL 60463. 12001 S Oak Park Ave.
Tel: 708-388-7650. Fax: 708-388-0154.
www.swchristian.org   E-mail: wpersenaire@swchristian.org
    Robert D. Payne, Prin. Wilma Persenaire, Adm.
    Col Prep. Gen Acad. AP (155 exams taken, 54% 3+)—Eng Span Calc Bio US_Hist US_Govt & Pol. **Feat**—Creative_Writing Shakespeare Stats Ecol Web_Design Chicago_Hist Econ Psych Sociol Bible Ceramics Drawing Painting Sculpt Studio_Art Drama Chorus Music_Theory Accounting Bus. **Supp**—Rev. **Dual enr:** Moraine Valley CC. **Sports**—Basket Soccer Tennis Track. B: Baseball Football Golf. G: Bowl Cheer X-country Softball Volley. Activities: 12. **Somewhat selective adm (Gr 9-11):** 93/yr. Appl due: June. Accepted: 90%. Yield: 95%. **Tests** IQ. **Enr 365.** B 173. G 192. Wh 84%. Latino 4%. Blk 9%. Asian 2%. Other 1%. Avg class size: 18. Casual dress. **Fac 31.** FT 26/PT 5. Wh 100%. Adv deg: 48%. **Grad '11—99.** Col—94. (Trinity Christian 18, Moraine Valley CC 12, Calvin 9, DePaul 7, Olivet Nazarene 5, IN Wesleyan 2). Avg ACT: 23.2. **Col Couns:** 1. **Tui '11-'12:** Day $8710 (+$300). **Est 1901.** Nonprofit. Nondenom Christian (100% practice). Quar (Aug-June). **Assoc** NCA. This college preparatory school serves a student body consisting entirely of practicing Christians from many different churches. Bible is part of the daily curriculum, and all pupils attend chapel with staff twice a week. Students devote 10 hours to community service annually, then prepare a follow-up report on their service work. Seniors may earn credit through internships or courses at Moraine Valley Community College.

QUINCY NOTRE DAME HIGH SCHOOL	Day Coed Gr 9-12
Quincy, IL 62301. 1400 S 11th St.
Tel: 217-223-2479. Fax: 217-223-0023.
www.quincynotredame.org   E-mail: rheilmann@quincynotredame.org
  Mark McDowell, Prin (2012). BA, Quincy Univ, MEd, William Woods Univ.
  Col Prep. AP—Calc US_Hist. **Feat**—British_Lit Ger Span Physiol Comp_Sci Govt Psych
Relig Drawing Painting Chorus Accounting. **Supp**—Rem_Math Rem_Read Tut. **Dual enr:**
Quincy, John Wood CC. **Sports**—Basket X-country Golf Soccer Tennis. B: Baseball Football
Wrestling. G: Cheer Softball Volley. Activities: 11. **Somewhat selective adm:** 120/yr. Appl
due: Rolling. **Tests** HSPT. **Enr 387.** B 206. G 181. Avg class size: 22. Stud/fac: 17:1. Casual
dress. **Fac 33.** Wh 99%. Latino 1%. Adv deg: 57%. **Grad '06—126.** Col—119. Avg ACT:
23.1. **Col Couns:** 1. **Tui '12-'13:** Day $4800 (+$330). Aid: Need 286. **Est 1959.** Nonprofit.
Roman Catholic (90% practice). Sem (Aug-May). **Assoc** NCA. Students at QND participate
in a wide range of activities. Upper-level college preparatory offerings, as well as business, art
and vocational courses, are available. Pupils take four years of compulsory religion classes,
and they also perform 10 hours of required service annually.

TRINITY HIGH SCHOOL	Day Girls Gr 9-12
River Forest, IL 60305. 7574 W Division St.
Tel: 708-771-8383. Fax: 708-488-2014.
www.trinityhs.org   E-mail: trinity@trinityhs.org
  Sr. Michelle Germanson, OP, Pres. BA, Edgewood College, MS, Loras College, MPS,
Loyola Univ of Chicago. Antonia C. Bouillette, Prin. PhD, Loyola Univ of Chicago. Mary
Tansey, Adm.
  Col Prep. IB Diploma. Feat—Humanities Fr Ital Span Stats Econ Pol_Sci Psych Sociol
Bus_Law Women's_Stud Theol World_Relig Ceramics Drawing Film Sculpt Drama Chorus
Dance Accounting Journ Marketing Speech. **Supp**—Tut. **Sports**— G: Basket Bowl X-country
Golf Soccer Softball Swim Tennis Track Volley. Activities: 53. **Somewhat selective adm:**
163/yr. Appl due: Rolling. Accepted: 95%. **Tests** HSPT. **Enr 534.** Wh 66%. Latino 14%. Blk
15%. Asian 1%. Other 4%. Avg class size: 20. Stud/fac: 14:1. Uniform. **Fac 34.** M 3/F 31.
FT 32/PT 2. Wh 98%. Latino 2%. Adv deg: 91%. **Grad '11—107.** Col—107. Avg ACT: 23.
Tui '12-'13: Day $9500. Aid: Merit 24 ($21,700). Need 121 ($182,500). Work prgm 100
($4000). **Est 1918.** Nonprofit. Roman Catholic (80% practice). Quar (Aug-June). **Assoc** NCA.
Drawing girls from Chicago and approximately 30 other communities, Trinity employs block
scheduling, which allows students to meet for extended class periods while focusing on fewer
classes at a time. Another noteworthy feature of the curriculum is the school's International
Baccalaureate Program. Qualified juniors and seniors may take part in this program, which
combines rigorous academics with a 150-hour community service requirement and often leads
to advanced standing in college. Juniors who meet a GPA requirement may enroll in a summer
course for college credit at Dominican University.

WHEATON ACADEMY	Day Coed Gr 9-12
West Chicago, IL 60185. 900 Prince Crossing Rd.
Tel: 630-562-7500. Fax: 630-231-0842.
www.wheatonacademy.org   E-mail: paul.ferguson@wheatonacademy.org
  Gene Frost, Head. BA, Wheaton College (IL), MDiv, Northern Baptist Theological Semi-
nary, EdD, Northern Illinois Univ. Steve Bult, Prin. BA, Calvin College, MA, Governors State
Univ. Paul Ferguson, Adm.
  Col Prep. AP (289 exams taken, 72% 3+)—Eng Fr Span Calc Stats Chem Physics US_
Hist World_Hist Comp_Govt & Pol Psych US_Govt & Pol. **Feat**—Creative_Writing Shake-
speare Chin Anat & Physiol Comp_Sci Web_Design Milit_Hist Econ Bible Ceramics Draw-
ing Painting Photog Studio_Art Video_Production Theater_Arts Music Music_Theory Dance
Accounting Bus Journ Marketing. **Supp**—LD Rev Tut. **Dual enr:** Col of DuPage. **Sports**—
Basket X-country Soccer Tennis Track. B: Baseball Football Golf Wrestling. G: Cheer Softball

Volley. Activities: 36. **Selective adm:** 183/yr. Appl fee: $25-50. Appl due: Jan. **Tests** Stanford. **Enr 639.** Wh 92%. Latino 2%. Blk 2%. Asian 2%. Other 2%. Avg class size: 20. Stud/fac: 15:1. **Fac 44.** M 24/F 20. FT 40/PT 4. Adv deg: 70%. **Grad '11—163.** Col—161. Avg ACT: 25.2. **Col Couns:** 1. **Tui '12-'13:** Day $13,030 (+$1205). **Est 1853.** Nonprofit. Evangelical. Sem (Aug-June). **Assoc** NCA. This Christian school offers traditional academic and college preparatory curricula. Between semesters, a two-and-a-half-week interim period allows for concentrated and in-depth study, trips and internships. Six credits of Bible study are required, and all courses are interspersed with relevant Biblical themes. Students may take college-credit courses through the College of DuPage. Weekly devotional chapels are compulsory. A limited number of international pupils reside with host families.

ST. FRANCIS HIGH SCHOOL   Day Coed Gr 9-12
Wheaton, IL 60187. 2130 W Roosevelt Rd.
Tel: 630-668-5800. Fax: 630-668-5893.
www.sfhsnet.org   E-mail: tlynch@sfhsnet.org
    Thomas V. Bednar, Pres. BA, MDiv, Univ of Notre Dame. Raeann Huhn, Prin. BS, Eastern Illinois Univ, MS, Northern Illinois Univ. Dan Tuskey, Adm.

    Col Prep. AP (250 exams taken, 73% 3+)—Eng Calc Stats Bio Chem Physics US_Hist Psych US_Govt & Pol Studio_Art Music_Theory. **Feat**—Creative_Writing Fr Span Anat & Physiol Programming Web_Design Econ Sociol Relig World_Relig Theater_Arts Music Accounting. **Supp**—Tut. **Sports**—Basket X-country Golf Soccer Swim Tennis Track Volley. B: Baseball Football. G: Cheer Softball. Activities: 29. **Selective adm (Gr 9-11):** 202/yr. Appl fee: $35. Appl due: Jan. **Tests** HSPT. **Enr 769.** Stud/fac: 14:1. Uniform. **Fac 58.** Wh 99%. Latino 1%. Adv deg: 68%. **Grad '11—195.** Col—195. **Avg SAT:** CR 581. M 596. W 575. Avg ACT: 26. **Tui '12-'13:** Day $10,095 (+$240-540). **Est 1956.** Nonprofit. Roman Catholic. Quar (Aug-May). **Assoc** NCA. Operated by the Diocese of Joliet, St. Francis offers both honors and Advanced Placement courses. The curriculum includes various class and social activities, and all boys and girls perform 15 hours of annual community service (for a four-year total of 60 hours). French and Spanish classes alternately take a summer trip to Europe.

LOYOLA ACADEMY   Day Coed Gr 9-12
Wilmette, IL 60091. 1100 Laramie Ave.
Tel: 847-256-1100. Fax: 847-853-4512.
www.goramblers.org   E-mail: gatwood@loy.org
    Rev. Patrick E. McGrath, SJ, Pres (2009). BA, Univ of Notre Dame, MDiv, Jesuit School of Theology at Berkeley, MA, Northwestern Univ. David K. McNulty, Prin. Genevieve Atwood, Adm.

    Col Prep. AP (exams req'd; 870 taken, 82% 3+)—Eng Fr Lat Span Calc Stats Comp_ Sci Bio Chem Environ_Sci Physics Eur_Hist US_Hist World_Hist Comp_Govt & Pol Psych US_Govt & Pol Art_Hist Studio_Art Music_Theory. **Feat**—British_Lit Creative_Writing Shakespeare Chin Ger Greek Anat & Physiol Astron Genetics Geol Sociol Ethics Theol Drawing Film Fine_Arts Architect_Design Theater Chorus Music Dance Communications Journ. **Supp**—LD Tut. **Sports**—Basket Bowl Crew X-country Golf Ice_Hockey Lacrosse Sail Soccer Swim Tennis Track Volley W_Polo. B: Baseball Football Wrestling. G: Cheer F_Hockey Softball. **Selective adm:** 500/yr. Appl fee: $25. Appl due: Jan. **Tests** HSPT. **Enr 2000.** B 1050. G 950. Uniform. **Fac 150.** Adv deg: 76%. **Grad '11—465.** Col—460. **Avg SAT:** CR 606. M 601. W 596. **Mid 50% SAT:** CR 530-660. M 530-660. W 530-660. Avg ACT: 25.8. Mid 50% ACT: 25-29. **Col Couns:** 4. **Tui '12-'13:** Day $13,725 (+$600). Aid: Need 600 ($4,000,000). **Est 1909.** Nonprofit. Roman Catholic. Sem (Aug-June). **Assoc** NCA. Founded by Rev. Henry J. Dumbach, SJ on the present campus of Loyola University of Chicago and later moved to Wilmette, the academy offers an education in the classical liberal arts. Special features of its curriculum are the Dumbach Scholars Program, for gifted and talented students, and the O'Shaughnessy Program of developmental learning, for students who need a more integrated, structured and sequential learning program. Boys and girls enroll from approximately 250 elementary and junior high schools throughout Chicago and its suburbs.

INDIANA

UNIVERSITY HIGH SCHOOL OF INDIANA   Day Coed Gr 9-12
Carmel, IN 46032. 2825 W 116th St.
Tel: 317-733-4475. Fax: 317-733-4484.
www.universityhighschool.org   E-mail: nwebster@universityhighschool.org
    Charles Webster, Head (2000). BA, MA, Oakland Univ. Nancy Webster, Adm.

    Col Prep. AP (exams req'd; 138 taken, 72% 3+)—Eng Fr Span Calc Stats Comp_Sci Bio Chem Physics US_Hist Art_Hist Studio_Art. **Feat**—Creative_Writing Etymology Anat & Physiol Astron Environ_Sci Organic_Chem Web_Design Econ Psych Ethics Photog Theater_Arts Journ Public_Speak Design. **Supp**—Tut. **Comp**: Comp/Stud: 1:1 Laptop prgm Gr 9-12. **Sports**—Basket X-country Golf Soccer Tennis Track. B: Baseball. G: Cheer Volley. **Somewhat selective adm:** 84/yr. Appl fee: $50. Appl due: Rolling. Accepted: 92%. Yield: 90%. **Tests** ISEE. **Enr 278.** B 139. G 139. Wh 82%. Latino 2%. Blk 9%. Asian 7%. Avg class size: 15. Stud/fac: 10:1. Casual dress. **Fac 35.** M 19/F 16. FT 24/PT 11. Wh 88%. Latino 11%. Blk 1%. Adv deg: 54%. **Grad '11—34.** Col—34. (DePauw 7, IN U 4, Butler U 2, Purdue 2, IN U-Purdue Indianapolis 2). **Avg SAT:** CR/M/W 1703. Avg ACT: 25. **Col Couns:** 2. **Tui '11-'12:** Day $16,200 (+$1000). Aid: Merit 81 ($133,000). Need 62 ($554,940). **Est 2000.** Nonprofit. Sem (Aug-May). **Assoc** CLS NCA. Situated on 115 acres on the north side of Indianapolis, University High School complements its two semesters with a January Term. During this term, boys and girls study one subject intensively for three weeks. The school's academic program emphasizes creative and critical thinking while incorporating class discussions, debate, analysis, group projects and experimentation. All boys and girls purchase laptop computers for use in class and at home.

BISHOP DWENGER HIGH SCHOOL   Day Coed Gr 9-12
Fort Wayne, IN 46825. 1300 E Washington Center Rd.
Tel: 260-496-4700, 877-393-6437. Fax: 260-496-4702.
www.bishopdwenger.com   E-mail: bdhs@bishopdwenger.com
    Jason Schiffli, Prin (2010). BA, MEd, Indiana Univ-Purdue Univ Fort Wayne. Cindy Johnson, Adm.

    Col Prep. AP (exams req'd; 246 taken, 73% 3+)—Eng Calc Stats Bio Chem US_Hist. **Feat**—Fr Lat Span Anat & Physiol Genetics Marine_Bio/Sci Econ Theol Ceramics Fine_Arts Chorus Music Bus. **Supp**—Dev_Read Rem_Math Rem_Read Rev Tut. **Comp:** Comp/Stud: 1:3. **Dual enr:** St Francis Col-IN, IN U-Purdue Ft Wayne. **Sports**—Basket X-country Golf Soccer Swim Tennis Track. B: Baseball Football Wrestling. G: Cheer Gymnastics Softball Volley. Activities: 45. **Nonselective adm:** 264/yr. Appl fee: $0. Appl due: Rolling. Accepted: 100%. **Tests** TOEFL. **Enr 1019.** Avg class size: 28. Stud/fac: 17:1. Uniform. **Fac 58.** Adv deg: 36%. **Grad '08—269.** Col—250. **Avg SAT:** CR 526. M 524. W 516. Avg ACT: 23.6. **Col Couns:** 2. **Tui '12-'13:** Day $7500-7625. Parishioners $6000-6125. Aid: Need 316 ($650,000). **Est 1963.** Nonprofit. Roman Catholic (97% practice). Sem (Aug-May). **Assoc** NCA. Bishop Dwenger's weighted curriculum offers remedial, honors and Advanced Placement courses. All boys and girls fulfill community service requirements: three hours in grade 9, five hours in grade 10, 10 hours in grade 11 and 15 hours in grade 12.

BISHOP LUERS HIGH SCHOOL — Day Coed Gr 9-12
Fort Wayne, IN 46816. 333 E Paulding Rd.
Tel: 260-456-1261. Fax: 260-456-1262.
www.bishopluers.org   E-mail: mzwick@bishopluers.org
Mary Keefer, Prin (1996). BA, MA, Indiana Univ–Purdue Univ Fort Wayne. Jenny Andorfer, Adm.

Col Prep. AP—Eng Calc Bio Chem US_Hist Psych US_Govt & Pol. **Feat**—Creative_Writing Fr Lat Span Anat & Physiol Comp_Sci Sociol Theol Drawing Sculpt Studio_Art Theater_Arts Band Chorus Accounting Bus Design. **Supp**—LD Rem_Math Tut. **Dual enr:** IN U-Purdue Ft Wayne. **Sports**—Basket Bowl X-country Golf Lacrosse Soccer Swim Tennis Track Volley. B: Baseball Football Wrestling. G: Softball. Activities: 12. **Somewhat selective adm:** 175/yr. Appl fee: $120. Appl due: Jan. Accepted: 95%. Yield: 95%. **Enr 567.** Nonwhite 26%. Stud/fac: 18:1. Casual dress. **Fac 41.** Adv deg: 51%. **Grad '08**—127. Col—120. **Tui '11-'12:** Day $6703 (+$935-1060). Parishioners $5520 (+$935-1060). **Est 1958.** Nonprofit. Roman Catholic (80% practice). Sem (Aug-May). **Assoc** NCA. BLHS offers courses at three levels: honors, academic and basic. The college preparatory curriculum includes advanced classes in math, science, social studies and English, and students take theology each semester. Vocational training is also available at Bishop Luers through a cooperative program with the Fort Wayne Community Schools' Anthis Career Center.

CONCORDIA LUTHERAN HIGH SCHOOL — Day Coed Gr 9-12
Fort Wayne, IN 46805. 1601 St Joe River Dr.
Tel: 260-483-1102. Fax: 260-471-0180.
www.clhscadets.com   E-mail: krista@clhscadets.com
Terry Breininger, Exec Dir. John Marks, Prin. MA, Eastern Michigan Univ. Krista Friend, Adm.

Col Prep. Voc. AP—Eng Calc Stats Bio Chem Physics US_Hist Econ US_Govt & Pol. **Feat**—Creative_Writing Humanities Fr Ger Lat Span Environ_Sci Comp_Sci Web_Design Psych Sociol Relig Ceramics Drawing Video_Production Theater Chorus JROTC Nutrition. **Supp**—Tut. **Sports**—Basket X-country Golf Soccer Swim Tennis Track. B: Baseball Football Wrestling. G: Cheer Gymnastics Softball Volley. **Somewhat selective adm:** 160/yr. Appl fee: $35. Appl due: Rolling. Accepted: 95%. **Enr 697.** Avg class size: 24. Stud/fac: 15:1. **Fac 44.** M 22/F 22. FT 40/PT 4. Adv deg: 63%. **Grad '11**—151. Col—142. **Avg SAT:** CR 538. M 549. Avg ACT: 22. **Col Couns:** 3. **Tui '11-'12:** Day $8275 (+$600). Assoc Members $6825 (+$600). **Est 1935.** Nonprofit. Lutheran-Missouri Synod (80% practice). Sem (Aug-May). **Assoc** NCA. Concordia's curriculum includes JROTC, remedial courses and courses for the gifted, as well as honors classes in all academic areas. The fine arts department offers courses in visual arts, media, theater and music.

BREBEUF JESUIT PREPARATORY SCHOOL — Day Coed Gr 9-12
Indianapolis, IN 46268. 2801 W 86th St.
Tel: 317-524-7050. Fax: 317-524-7144.
www.brebeuf.org   E-mail: admissions@brebeuf.org
Rev. Jack Dennis, SJ, Pres (2012). BA, Villanova Univ, MEd, Harvard Univ, MDiv, Jesuit School of Theology. LaTonya Turner, Prin. BS, Missouri Valley College, MS, Indiana Univ-Purdue Univ Indianapolis. Patrick Orr, Int Adm.

Col Prep. AP (523 exams taken)—Eng Fr Lat Span Calc Stats Comp_Sci Bio Chem Environ_Sci Physics Eur_Hist US_Hist Comp_Govt & Pol Econ US_Govt & Pol Studio_Art. **Feat**—Etymology Anat Zoology Holocaust African-Amer_Stud Sports_Psych World_Relig Eastern_Relig Ceramics Drawing Painting Sculpt Theater_Arts Music. **Supp**—Rev Tut. **Comp:** Comp/Stud: 1:2.3. **Dual enr:** IN U. **Sports**—Basket Crew X-country Golf Lacrosse Soccer Swim Tennis Track. B: Baseball Bowl Football Ice_Hockey Wrestling. G: Cheer Softball Volley. **Selective adm (Gr 9-11):** 201/yr. Appl fee: $50. Appl due: Dec. **Tests** HSPT. **Enr 785.** B 402. G 383. Wh 81%. Latino 1%. Blk 9%. Asian 3%. Other 6%. Avg class size: 25.

Stud/fac: 11:1. **Fac 69.** M 32/F 37. FT 66/PT 3. Wh 91%. Latino 4%. Blk 1%. Asian 1%. Other 3%. Adv deg: 75%. **Grad '10—202.** Col—202. (IN U 58, Purdue 14, Xavier-OH 10, Butler U 7, Ball St 6, DePauw 5). **Avg SAT:** CR 603. M 629. W 599. Avg ACT: 27. **Col Couns:** 4. Alum donors: 6%. **Tui '12-'13:** Day $14,675 (+$300). Aid: Merit 12 ($17,000). Need 254 ($1,498,681). Work prgm 67 ($67,000). **Est 1962.** Nonprofit. Roman Catholic. Sem (Aug-May). Enrolling pupils from close to 50 Greater Indianapolis schools, Brebeuf Jesuit conducts a varied college preparatory program that features Advanced Placement course work in all major disciplines. All boys and girls perform 40 hours of community service during a single semester in junior or senior year, 10 of which are completed as part of the religion curriculum. Qualified students may earn college credits in any of three subject areas through a joint program conducted with Indiana University.

HERITAGE CHRISTIAN SCHOOL   **Day Coed Gr PS (Age 4)-12**
Indianapolis, IN 46250. 6401 E 75th St.
Tel: 317-849-3441. Fax: 317-594-5863.
www.heritagechristian.net   E-mail: emily.iglendza@heritagechristian.net
    Jeffrey D. Wilcox, Supt (2011). BA, Cornerstone Univ, BA, Calvin College, MEd, Cleveland State Univ. Emily A. Iglendza, Adm.
    Col Prep. AP (exams req'd; 200 taken, 77% 3+)—Eng Calc Stats Bio Chem US_Hist. **Feat**—British_Lit Fr Span Physiol Zoology Comp_Sci Web_Design Sociol Bible Studio_Art Video_Production Drama Music Speech. **Supp**—ESL LD Rev Tut. **Dual enr:** IN Wesleyan. **Sports**—Basket X-country Golf Lacrosse Soccer Swim Tennis Track. B: Baseball Football. G: Cheer Softball Volley. **Somewhat selective adm:** 255/yr. Appl fee: $50. Appl due: Rolling. Accepted: 90%. Yield: 97%. **Tests** Stanford TOEFL. **Enr 1371.** Elem 883. Sec 488. Wh 86%. Latino 1%. Blk 8%. Asian 4%. Other 1%. Avg class size: 18. **Fac 103.** M 29/F 74. FT 100/PT 3. Wh 98%. Latino 1%. Other 1%. Adv deg: 38%. **Grad '11—119.** Col—116. (IN U 19, Purdue 18, IN U-Purdue Indianapolis 10, Anderson-IN 10, Ball St 9, IN Wesleyan 5). **Avg SAT:** CR/M/W 1684. Avg ACT: 25.2. **Col Couns:** 2. **Tui '12-'13:** Day $6611-9306 (+$250). Aid: Need ($600,000). **Est 1965.** Nonprofit. Nondenom Christian. Sem (Aug-May). **Assoc** NCA. Enrolling students predominantly from Marion, Indianapolis, Lawrence, Noblesville and Carmel, HCS provides a full elementary and secondary program on a 38-acre campus. In addition to taking Advanced Placement courses, qualified pupils may enroll in college-credit distance-learning classes through Indiana Wesleyan University. Boys and girls attend daily Bible classes and weekly chapel. The school's community service program requires all high schoolers to perform 20 hours of annual service.

LUTHERAN HIGH SCHOOL OF INDIANAPOLIS   **Day Coed Gr 9-12**
Indianapolis, IN 46237. 5555 S Arlington Ave.
Tel: 317-787-5474. Fax: 317-787-2794.
www.lhsi.org   E-mail: lhsi@lhsi.org
    Michael Brandt, Head (2011). Christie Hampton, Adm.
    Col Prep. Gen Acad. Bus. AP (exams req'd; 84 taken, 36% 3+)—Eng Span Calc Bio Chem US_Hist Studio_Art. **Feat**—British_Lit Humanities ASL Stats Anat & Physiol Environ_Sci Psych Sociol Relig Ceramics Sculpt Music_Theory. **Supp**—Dev_Read Makeup Rem_ Math Rem_Read Rev Tut. **Comp:** Comp/Stud: 1:1 Laptop prgm Gr 9-12. **Sports**—Basket X-country Golf Soccer Tennis Track. B: Baseball Football. G: Softball Volley. **Nonselective adm:** 65/yr. Appl fee: $150. Appl due: Mar. Accepted: 100%. **Enr 237.** B 121. G 116. Wh 91%. Blk 2%. Asian 5%. Other 2%. Intl 5%. Avg class size: 17. Uniform. **Fac 17.** M 12/F 5. FT 11/PT 6. Wh 100%. Adv deg: 70%. **Grad '11—65.** Col—60. **Avg SAT:** CR 510. M 503. W 499. Avg ACT: 23. **Col Couns:** 1. **Tui '12-'13:** Day $9150 (+$375). Assoc Members $8350 (+$375). Aid: Need 73 ($168,000). Work prgm 5 ($5000). **Est 1976.** Nonprofit. Lutheran-Missouri Synod (65% practice). Sem (Aug-May). **Assoc** NCA. Advanced Placement and honors courses are part of LHSI's college preparatory program, as is a one-to-one laptop program at

all grade levels. Seniors may pursue independent study for credit in an area of academic interest. Boys and girls accumulate 16 hours of required community service over four years.

FOREST RIDGE ACADEMY   **Day Coed Gr PS (Age 3)-8**
Schererville, IN 46375. 7300 Forest Ridge Dr.
Tel: 219-756-7300. Fax: 219-756-2365.
www.fra.edu   E-mail: dshultz@fra.edu
    Cindy J. Arnold, Head. BS, Ball State Univ. Diane Shultz, Adm.

    Pre-Prep. Feat—Lib_Skills ASL Span Computers Studio_Art Chorus Music Orchestra Piano. **Comp:** Laptop prgm Gr 5-8. **Sports**—Basket Soccer. **Selective adm:** 66/yr. Appl fee: $50. Appl due: Apr. **Tests** IQ. **Enr 155.** Wh 58%. Latino 3%. Blk 19%. Asian 20%. Avg class size: 15. Stud/fac: 5:1. Uniform. **Fac 25.** M 5/F 20. FT 25. Adv deg: 52%. **Grad '09—12.** Prep—8. (La Lumiere 3, Marian Catholic 2, Morgan Park 1, St Ignatius-IL 1, Culver 1). **Tui '10-'11:** Day $12,240 (+$650). **Est** 1982. Nonprofit. Sem (Aug-June). **Assoc** NCA.   FRA's academic program comprises a core curriculum of language arts, mathematics, social studies and science that is supplemented by Spanish, computer, physical education, art and music classes at all grade levels. Beginning in grade 5, boys and girls perform eight hours of required community service per year. Forest Ridge students participate in a number of field trips each year.

MICHIGAN

SUMMERS-KNOLL SCHOOL   **Day Coed Gr K-8**
Ann Arbor, MI 48104. 2015 Manchester Rd.
Tel: 734-971-7991. Fax: 734-971-9663.
www.summers-knoll.org   E-mail: info@summers-knoll.org
    Joanna Hastings, Head (2007). BA, MA, Univ of York (England).

    Pre-Prep. Feat—Fr Lat Studio_Art Music. **Supp**—Tut. **Comp:** Laptop prgm Gr 4-8. **Selective adm (Gr K-5):** 16/yr. Appl fee: $40. Appl due: Rolling. Accepted: 74%. Yield: 80%. **Tests** IQ. **Enr 58.** B 35. G 23. Wh 71%. Latino 3%. Blk 1%. Asian 3%. Other 22%. Avg class size: 12. Stud/fac: 5:1. Casual dress. **Fac 11.** M 4/F 7. FT 5/PT 6. Wh 90%. Blk 10%. Adv deg: 63%. **Grad '11—4.** Prep—4. **Tui '11-'12:** Day $14,350-16,100. Aid: Need 14. **Est** 1994. Nonprofit. Tri (Aug-June).   The progressive curriculum at Summers-Knoll, which is geared toward bright and creative children, incorporates thematic units and allows for acceleration. Themes addressed span content areas, grade levels and classrooms. Technology and the arts enrich the program throughout, and pupils in grades 4-8 must purchase laptop computers for classroom use. Students select from a variety of block electives throughout the year.

OUR LADY QUEEN OF MARTYRS SCHOOL   **Day Coed Gr PS (Age 3)-8**
Beverly Hills, MI 48025. 32460 Pierce Rd.
Tel: 248-642-2616. Fax: 248-642-3671.
www.olqmcatholicschool.org   E-mail: jvincler@olqm-parish.org
    Joseph Vincler, Prin.

    Pre-Prep. Gen Acad. Feat—Lib_Skills Span Computers Relig Studio_Art Music Journ Study_Skills. **Supp**—Rem_Read Tut. **Sports**—Basket Soccer Track. B: Baseball Football. G: Cheer Volley. **Somewhat selective adm:** 35/yr. Appl fee: $25. Appl due: May. Accepted: 90%. **Enr 235.** Stud/fac: 22:1. **Fac 21.** M 5/F 16. **Grad '06—41.** Prep—34. **Tui '12-'13:** Day $5865 (+$420-465). Parishioners $4195 (+$420-465). **Est** 1954. Nonprofit. Roman Catholic. Quar (Sept-June).   Founded by the Sisters of Charity of Cincinnati, OH, the school conducts a Catholic-centered elementary curriculum. French language courses begin in grade 6, as does an electives program that includes computer, journalism, drama and study skills. Graduates typically matriculate at area Catholic high schools.

BROTHER RICE HIGH SCHOOL   **Day Boys Gr 9-12**
Bloomfield Hills, MI 48301. 7101 Lahser Rd.
Tel: 248-647-2526. Fax: 248-647-8170.
www.brrice.edu   E-mail: sofran@brrice.edu
    John Birney, Pres. Br. Michael Segvich, CFC, Prin. BA, Lewis College, MEd, Iona College, MS, Univ of San Francisco. David Sofran, Adm.
    Col Prep. AP (exams req'd; 300 taken, 67% 3+)—Eng Fr Ger Span Calc Comp_Sci Chem Physics US_Govt & Pol. **Feat**—ASL Lat Anat & Physiol Engineering Theol Speech. **Supp**—Rem_Math Rev Tut. **Sports**— B: Baseball Basket X-country Football Golf Ice_ Hockey Lacrosse Ski Soccer Swim Tennis Track Wrestling. **Selective adm (Gr 9-11):** 183/yr. Appl fee: $0. Appl due: Rolling. Accepted: 70%. Yield: 65%. **Tests** HSPT SSAT. **Enr 685.** Wh 79%. Latino 1%. Blk 12%. Asian 3%. Other 5%. Avg class size: 20. Stud/fac: 15:1. Formal dress. **Fac 47.** M 33/F 14. FT 46/PT 1. Wh 98%. Asian 2%. Adv deg: 63%. **Grad '11—174.** Col—172. (U of MI 25, MI St 20, Central MI 20). **Avg SAT:** CR 601. M 615. W 569. Avg ACT: 25.2. **Col Couns:** 2. Alum donors: 9%. **Tui '12-'13:** Day $11,050 (+$500). **Est 1960.** Nonprofit. Roman Catholic (75% practice). Quar (Aug-June). **Assoc** NCA.   Brother Rice's college preparatory course of studies features a four-year theology program and a Christian service requirement of 15 hours annually. The core curriculum is supplemented by honors and AP courses. Pupils satisfy requirements in English, math, science, computer science, social studies, modern languages, speech, health, theology and physical education.

DETROIT WALDORF SCHOOL   **Day Coed Gr PS (Age 2)-8**
Detroit, MI 48214. 2555 Burns Ave.
Tel: 313-822-0300. Fax: 313-822-4030.
www.detroitwaldorf.org   E-mail: admissions@detroitwaldorf.org
    Linda Brooks, Admin. BA, Eastern Michigan Univ. Charis Calender, Adm.
    Pre-Prep. Waldorf. Feat—Ger Span Drawing Painting Music Eurythmy. **Supp**—Dev_ Read Rem_Math Rem_Read Tut. **Somewhat selective adm:** 34/yr. Appl fee: $50. Appl due: Mar. Accepted: 90%. Yield: 45%. **Enr 127.** B 62. G 65. Wh 60%. Latino 3%. Blk 36%. Other 1%. Avg class size: 15. Casual dress. **Fac 20.** M 3/F 17. FT 9/PT 11. Wh 90%. Latino 5%. Blk 5%. Adv deg: 25%. **Grad '11—9.** Prep—7. (Rudolf Steiner Sch of Ann Arbor 5, Roeper 2). **Tui '12-'13:** Day $8650-12,075 (+$400). Aid: Need 70 ($365,000). **Est 1965.** Nonprofit. (Sept-June). **Assoc** NCA. One of the nation's oldest Waldorf schools, Detroit Waldorf offers a broad academic program that integrates music and the arts. Course work emphasizes creativity and critical-thinking skills. The foreign language curriculum begins with German and Spanish in grade 1, the same year that vocal and instrumental music classes also commence.

FRIENDS SCHOOL IN DETROIT   **Day Coed Gr PS (Age 3)-8**
Detroit, MI 48207. 1100 St Aubin Blvd.
Tel: 313-259-6722. Fax: 313-259-8066.
www.friendsschool.org   E-mail: mrheajohnson@friendsschool.org
    Edwin Harris, Head (2011). Marta Rhea-Johnson, Adm.
    Pre-Prep. Feat—Chin Fr Span Computers Studio_Art Drama Music. **Supp**—Dev_Read Rem_Math Tut. **Sports**—Basket. G: Volley. **Selective adm:** Appl fee: $50. Appl due: Rolling. Accepted: 80%. **Tests** ISEE. **Enr 110.** Avg class size: 15. Casual dress. **Fac 14.** M 4/F 10. FT 12/PT 2. Adv deg: 42%. **Grad '11—10. Tui '11-'12:** Day $9750-11,525. **Est 1965.** Nonprofit. Religious Society of Friends. Sem (Sept-June). Founded by Detroit business and commu-nity leaders and educators, FSD enrolls students whose backgrounds reflect the diversity of the community racially, religiously and economically. Chinese is part of the school's foreign

language program. Boys and girls in grades 5-8 take required human rights and community service classes each week.

MERCY HIGH SCHOOL   Day Girls Gr 9-12
Farmington Hills, MI 48336. 29300 W 11 Mile Rd.
Tel: 248-476-8020. Fax: 248-476-3691.
www.mhsmi.org   E-mail: mhs@mhsmi.org
   Cheryl Delaney Kreger, Pres (2010). BS, MA, Eastern Michigan Univ, EdD, Wayne State Univ. Carolyn R. Witte, Prin. BS, Eastern Michigan Univ, MA, Michigan State Univ. Maureen Weiss, Adm.
   Col Prep. AP (220 exams taken, 64% 3+)—Calc Bio Chem Physics Eur_Hist US_Hist US_Govt & Pol. **Feat**—Fr Lat Span Comp_Sci Econ Relig Studio_Art Drama Theater_Arts Chorus Orchestra. **Supp**—Rem_Math Tut. **Comp:** Comp/Stud: 1:1 Laptop prgm Gr 9-12. **Sports**— G: Basket Bowl X-country Equestrian F_Hockey Golf Ice_Hockey Lacrosse Ski Soccer Softball Swim Tennis Track Volley. Activities: 25. **Somewhat selective adm (Gr 9-11):** 217/yr. Appl fee: $0. Appl due: Rolling. Accepted: 95%. **Tests** HSPT. **Enr 742.** Wh 71%. Latino 3%. Blk 17%. Asian 3%. Other 6%. Avg class size: 25. Uniform. **Fac 45.** M 11/F 34. FT 45. Wh 98%. Latino 1%. Blk 1%. Adv deg: 73%. **Grad '11—191.** Col—191. **Avg SAT:** CR 604. M 576. W 612. Avg ACT: 24. **Tui '12-'13:** Day $10,895 (+$325). **Est 1945.** Nonprofit. Roman Catholic (75% practice). Sem (Sept-June). **Assoc** NCA. The college preparatory program encompasses the humanities, the sciences, religious studies and the fine arts. A semester of computer science study is required, and girls perform at least 40 hours of community service prior to graduation. All students purchase tablet computers for use in class and to connect to the school's wireless network.

THE VALLEY SCHOOL   Day Coed Gr PS (Age 4)-12
Flint, MI 48507. 2474 S Ballenger Hwy.
Tel: 810-767-4004. Fax: 810-767-0841.
www.valleyschool.org   E-mail: email@valleyschool.org
   Kaye Panchula, Head. Minka Owens, Adm.
   Col Prep. Feat—Fr Span Physiol Comp_Sci Robotics Art_Hist Drawing Painting Photog Studio_Art Chorus. **Supp**—Tut. **Dual enr:** U of MI-Flint, Mott CC. **Sports (req'd)**—Basket Soccer. B: Tennis. G: Volley. **Somewhat selective adm:** 15/yr. Appl due: Rolling. Accepted: 95%. **Enr 54.** Elem 34. Sec 20. Wh 69%. Latino 1%. Blk 9%. Other 21%. Avg class size: 6. Stud/fac: 8:1. **Fac 10.** M 5/F 5. FT 7/PT 3. Wh 100%. **Grad '08—6.** Col—6. **Avg SAT:** CR 513. M 536. Avg ACT: 26. **Tui '09-'10:** Day $2900-9800 (+$500). Aid: Merit 12 ($7620). Need 41 ($182,416). **Est 1970.** Nonprofit. Quar (Sept-June). The school allows qualified juniors and seniors to dually enroll at the University of Michigan-Flint or Mott Community College. Valley offers an unusually broad arts curriculum, as professional artists from the community (many from the Flint Institute of the Arts) teach in their specialty areas on a part-time basis. The school schedules eight class periods per day, allowing boys and girls to take two courses from the same department in a given semester. Students in grades 9-12 perform 40 hours of required community service annually.

GRAND RAPIDS CHRISTIAN SCHOOLS   Day Coed Gr PS (Age 3)-12
Grand Rapids, MI 49506. 1508 Alexander St SE.
Tel: 616-574-6000. Fax: 616-574-6010.
www.grcs.org   E-mail: eburgess@grcs.org
   Thomas J. DeJonge, Supt.
   Col Prep. AP—Eng Calc Stats Bio Chem Physics Eur_Hist US_Hist US_Govt & Pol. **Feat**—Creative_Writing Chin Fr Ger Lat Span Anat & Physiol Astron Environ_Sci Comp_ Sci Econ Govt Law Psych Sociol Relig Drawing Painting Studio_Art Acting Theater Chorus Music Dance Bus Debate Journ Speech Indus_Arts Home_Ec. **Supp**—Dev_Read ESL

Makeup Rem_Math Rem_Read Tut. **Sports**—Basket Bowl X-country Golf Lacrosse Ski Soccer Swim Tennis Track. B: Baseball Football Ice_Hockey Wrestling. G: Cheer Equestrian Softball Volley. Activities: 21. **Nonselective adm:** 355/yr. Appl due: Rolling. Accepted: 100%. **Enr 2100.** Elem 1154. Sec 946. Wh 78%. Latino 3%. Blk 12%. Asian 5%. Other 2%. Avg class size: 24. **Fac 179.** M 52/F 127. FT 136/PT 43. Adv deg: 56%. **Grad '11—225.** Col—218. Avg ACT: 24.6. **Tui '11-'12:** Day $7595-9475 (+$120-670). **Est 1891.** Nonprofit. Nondenom Christian. Sem (Aug-June). **Assoc** NCA. This Christian school system serves students from the Greater Grand Rapids area, operating four primary schools, a high school, and a center for worship and the arts at locations throughout the city. The schools provide a comprehensive and rigorous curriculum that includes math, science, English, social science, foreign language, religion, art, music, computer and physical education.

HILLSDALE ACADEMY   Day Coed Gr K-12
Hillsdale, MI 49242. 1 Academy Ln.
Tel: 517-439-8644. Fax: 517-607-2794.
www.hillsdale.edu/academy   E-mail: piszler@hillsdale.edu
    Kenneth Calvert, Head (2002). MDiv, Gordon-Conwell Theological Seminary, ThM, Harvard Univ, PhD, Miami Univ (OH).

    Col Prep. Feat—Fr Lat Comp_Sci Econ Studio_Art Theater Music. **Comp:** Comp/Stud: 1:20. **Dual enr:** Hillsdale. **Sports**—Basket X-country Golf Track. B: Soccer. G: Volley. Activities: 2. **Somewhat selective adm (Gr K-11):** 29/yr. Appl fee: $25. Appl due: Jan. Accepted: 85%. Yield: 99%. **Enr 183.** Elem 104. Sec 79. Wh 89%. Latino 2%. Blk 2%. Asian 3%. Other 4%. Avg class size: 20. Uniform. **Fac 19.** M 7/F 12. FT 8/PT 11. Wh 100%. Adv deg: 31%. **Grad '10—20.** Col—19. (Hillsdale 8, Alma 1, Franciscan 1, Huntington 1, U of AL-Huntsville 1, U of Dayton 1). **Avg SAT:** CR 640. M 619. W 617. Avg ACT: 27. **Tui '12-'13:** Day $3550-5610 (+$500). Aid: Need 20 ($21,000). **Est 1990.** Nonprofit. Tri (Aug-June). Founded as an elementary school, the academy added an upper school (grades 9-12) in 1998. As part of language study at the school, all students take French in grades 1-6 and Latin in grades 7-12. In addition to work in the core subjects, course requirements in the college preparatory upper school include two or more years of electives in the areas of art, music and physical education, as well as civics/economics in grade 12.   **See Also Page 43**

MONSIGNOR JOHN R. HACKETT   Day Coed Gr 9-12
CATHOLIC CENTRAL HIGH SCHOOL
Kalamazoo, MI 49008. 1000 W Kilgore Rd.
Tel: 269-381-2646. Fax: 269-381-3919.
www.hackettcc.org   E-mail: hackett@hackettcc.org
    Timothy Eastman, Prin (2002). BA, Kalamazoo College, MA, Western Michigan Univ.

    Col Prep. AP (117 exams taken)—Eng Calc Stats Bio US_Hist World_Hist. **Feat**—Creative_Writing Fr Lat Span Anat & Physiol Environ_Sci Forensic_Sci Web_Design Econ Govt Psych Sociol Theol Drawing Photog Sculpt Studio_Art Acting Band Chorus Bus. **Supp**—Dev_Read LD Rem_Math Rem_Read Tut. **Sports**—Basket X-country Golf Ski Soccer Swim Tennis Track. B: Baseball Football. G: Cheer Volley. Activities: 15. **Somewhat selective adm:** 90/yr. Appl fee: $125. Appl due: Mar. Accepted: 95%. **Enr 321.** B 164. G 157. Avg class size: 28. Uniform. **Fac 27.** M 7/F 20. FT 23/PT 4. Adv deg: 40%. **Grad '09—100.** Col—97. (Kalamazoo Valley CC 22, MI St 12, W MI 9, Aquinas-MI 6, U of MI 5, Grand Valley St 5). **Avg SAT:** CR 591. M 587. W 537. Avg ACT: 24.4. **Tui '11-'12:** Day $9703. **Est 1964.** Nonprofit. Roman Catholic. Sem (Aug-June). Hackett Catholic Central conducts three programs of study: general studies, college preparatory and honors. Requirements include courses in religion, government, economics, foreign language and fine arts. Catholic traditions and values are stressed through daily prayer, liturgies, service projects in the community, religious retreats and the campus ministry. Tuition for subsidized parish families is determined along a sliding scale according to family income.

LANSING CATHOLIC HIGH SCHOOL   Day Coed Gr 9-12
Lansing, MI 48912. 501 Marshall St.
Tel: 517-267-2100. Fax: 517-267-2135.
www.lansingcatholic.org   E-mail: gates@lcchs.org
     Thomas P. Maloney, Prin. BS, Alma College, MA, Michigan State Univ. Mary Gates, Adm.

     Col Prep. AP—Eng Span Calc Bio Environ_Sci Physics US_Govt & Pol Studio_Art. **Feat**—Creative_Writing Fr Greek Lat Comp_Design Comp_Sci Econ Psych Sociol Philos Theol Fine_Arts Music Music_Theory Journ Speech. **Sports**—Basket Bowl X-country Golf Lacrosse Soccer Swim Tennis Track. B: Baseball Football Ice_Hockey Wrestling. G: Cheer Softball Volley. Activities: 34. **Somewhat selective adm (Gr 9-11):** 170/yr. Appl fee: $25. Appl due: Dec. Accepted: 99%. Yield: 94%. **Enr 490.** Avg class size: 24. Stud/fac: 16:1. Uniform. **Fac 33.** M 11/F 22. FT 26/PT 7. Adv deg: 51%. **Grad '08—120.** Col—110. **Avg SAT:** CR 612. M 605. Avg ACT: 23.2. **Col Couns:** 1. **Tui '12-'13:** Day $6045 (+$800-1000). Aid: Need 147 ($230,000). **Est 1970.** Nonprofit. Roman Catholic. Quar (Aug-June). Lansing Catholic provides a comprehensive secondary program that emphasizes college preparation and enables students to earn college credits through honors and Advanced Placement course work. Community service is an integral part of school life, with all pupils fulfilling a service requirement of five hours per quarter.

LADYWOOD HIGH SCHOOL   Day Girls Gr 9-12
Livonia, MI 48154. 14680 Newburgh Rd.
Tel: 734-591-1544. Fax: 734-591-4214.
www.ladywood.org   E-mail: admissions@ladywood.org
     Joan L. Fitzgerald, Pres (2011). BA, MA, Madonna Univ, MS, Univ of Detroit Mercy. Kristine Sanders, Adm.

     Col Prep. AP (exams req'd; 106 taken, 67% 3+)—Eng Fr Span Calc Bio Environ_Sci Eur_Hist US_Hist Studio_Art. **Feat**—Humanities Mythology Ital Stats Genetics Microbio Comp_Sci Econ Psych Sociol Asian_Stud Theol Film Theater_Arts Music_Hist Accounting Bus Home_Ec. **Supp**—Tut. **Comp:** Comp/Stud: 1:2. Outdoor Ed. **Sports**— G: Basket Bowl Cheer X-country Equestrian F_Hockey Golf Ice_Hockey Lacrosse Ski Soccer Softball Swim Tennis Track Volley. Activities: 20. **Somewhat selective adm (Gr 9-11):** 65/yr. Appl due: Rolling. Accepted: 91%. Yield: 42%. **Tests** HSPT. **Enr 322.** Wh 86%. Latino 3%. Blk 2%. Native Am 1%. Asian 3%. Other 5%. Avg class size: 22. Stud/fac: 12:1. Uniform. **Fac 29.** M 6/F 23. FT 26/PT 3. Wh 97%. Blk 2%. Native Am 1%. Adv deg: 62%. **Grad '11—86.** Col—86. (MI St 11, U of MI 10, U of MI-Dearborn 9, Wayne St 8, Schoolcraft Col 8, Grand Valley St 7). **Avg SAT:** CR 556. M 527. W 543. Avg ACT: 23.6. **Col Couns:** 2. **Tui '12-'13:** Day $8650 (+$550-600). Aid: Merit 2 ($12,500). **Est 1950.** Nonprofit. Roman Catholic (92% practice). Sem (Sept-June). **Assoc** NCA. Located on a 60-acre campus and owned and operated by the Felician Sisters, Ladywood provides a full college preparatory program. Students are required to take four years of theology and to attend religious services and retreats. Freshmen perform 15 hours of community service annually, sophomores 20 hours, and juniors and seniors 25 hours.

ST. MARY CATHOLIC CENTRAL HIGH SCHOOL   Day Coed Gr 9-12
Monroe, MI 48162. 108 W Elm Ave.
Tel: 734-241-7622. Fax: 734-241-9042.
www.smccmonroe.com   E-mail: jlinster@smccmonroe.com
     Sean Jorgensen, Pres (2008). BS, Siena Heights Univ, MA, Univ of Notre Dame. Jenny M. Biler, Prin. MA, Siena Heights Univ. Jason Linster, Adm.

     Col Prep. AP (30 exams taken, 43% 3+)—Eng Calc US_Hist US_Govt & Pol. **Feat**—Fr Span Comp_Sci Theol Ceramics Graphic_Arts Studio_Art Drama Band Chorus Music Bus. **Supp**—Tut. **Comp:** Comp/Stud: 1:2.5. **Sports**—Baseball Basket Cheer X-country Equestrian Football Golf Ice_Hockey Soccer Softball Swim Tennis Track Volley Wrestling. **Nonselec-**

tive adm: 126/yr. Appl due: Apr. Accepted: 100%. **Tests** HSPT. **Enr 430.** B 235. G 195. Wh 93%. Latino 3%. Blk 1%. Native Am 1%. Asian 2%. Avg class size: 22. Stud/fac: 14:1. Uniform. **Fac 28.** M 9/F 19. FT 25/PT 3. Wh 100%. Adv deg: 39%. **Grad '09—90.** Col—89. (Monroe CC 13, MI St 5, Grand Valley St 5, U of Toledo 4, U of MI 3, E MI 3). **Avg SAT:** CR/M 1150. Avg ACT: 21.7. Alum donors: 20%. **Tui '11-'12:** Day $7350 (+$1000). Aid: Need 258 ($600,000). **Est 1986.** Nonprofit. Roman Catholic. Sem (Aug-June). **Assoc** NCA. St. Mary's comprehensive curriculum offers programs for all levels of academic ability and includes honors and Advanced Placement courses and four years of required theology classes. In the Christian tradition, daily prayer and monthly liturgies, as well as retreats for all grades, are available. Students accumulate 40 hours of required community service during their four years at the school.

ORCHARD LAKE ST. MARY'S PREPARATORY   Bdg & Day
                                        Boys Gr 9-12
Orchard Lake, MI 48324. 3535 Indian Trl.
Tel: 248-683-0514. Fax: 248-683-1740.
www.stmarysprep.com   E-mail: cknight@stmarysprep.com
    James M. Glowacki, Head (2000). Candace Knight & Tony Koterba, Adms.

    Col Prep. AP—Eng Calc Stats Chem US_Hist World_Hist. **Feat—**Chin Fr Span Anat Environ_Sci Zoology Engineering Comp_Sci Robotics WWII Psych Govt/Econ Ethics World_ Relig Drawing Fine_Arts Painting Studio_Art Chorus Music_Theory Accounting Bus Debate Journ Speech Drafting. **Supp—**ESL Tut. **Dual enr:** Madonna. **Sports—** B: Baseball Basket Crew X-country Football Golf Ice_Hockey Lacrosse Ski Soccer Track Wrestling. Activities: 35. **Somewhat selective adm (Gr 9-11):** 150/yr. Bdg 25. Day 125. Appl fee: $35. Appl due: Rolling. Accepted: 81%. Yield: 96%. **Tests** HSPT. **Enr 500.** Bdg 84. Day 416. Intl 10%. Avg class size: 16. Stud/fac: 11:1. Uniform. **Fac 57.** M 31/F 26. FT 57. Adv deg: 71%. In Dorms 5. **Grad '11—116.** Col—116. **Avg SAT:** CR/M 1150. Avg ACT: 25.9. **Tui '12-'13:** Bdg $27,350 (+$350-750). 5-Day Bdg $23,700 (+$350-750). Day $10,500 (+$350-750). **Est 1885.** Nonprofit. Roman Catholic (60% practice). Sem (Aug-May). SMPS students supplement required course work with electives that reflect their interests. Seniors and selected juniors may enroll in classes for college credit at nearby St. Mary's College. Boys take four years of theology in the classroom and attend chapel services twice weekly. Class retreats and outdoor recreation are among the extracurricular options.

SPRING VALE ACADEMY   Bdg & Day
                                        Coed Gr 9-12
Owosso, MI 48867. 4150 S M-52.
Tel: 989-725-2391. Fax: 989-729-6408.
www.springvale.us   E-mail: lmolinar@springvale.us
    Mark Caswell, Dir. BS, Cornerstone Univ, MS, Walden Univ. Leticia Molinar, Adm.

    Col Prep. Gen Acad. Feat—Creative_Writing Span Anat & Physiol Econ Govt Psych Bible Drama Music Accounting Bus Journ Speech. **Supp—**Tut. **Sports—**Basket. B: Soccer. G: Volley. **Nonselective adm:** 14/yr. Bdg 13. Day 1. Appl fee: $50. Appl due: July. Accepted: 95%. **Enr 48.** Avg class size: 12. Stud/fac: 6. **Fac 8.** M 2/F 6. FT 5/PT 3. Adv deg: 12%. **Grad '06—9.** Col—8. Alum donors: 50%. **Tui '10-'11:** Bdg $9300 (+$800). Day $4228 (+$500). **Est 1948.** Nonprofit. Church of God (Seventh-Day). Sem (Aug-May). SVA's campus occupies 147 acres in the central portion of the state. Bible study, music, drama, writing and athletics are available. All boys and girls engage in one service project per semester. An on-campus work-study program is required of all students.

NOTRE DAME PREPARATORY SCHOOL   Day Coed Gr 9-12
Pontiac, MI 48340. 1300 Giddings Rd.
Tel: 248-373-5300. Fax: 248-373-8024.
www.ndpma.org   E-mail: gsimon@ndpma.org

Rev. Leon Olszamowski, SM, Pres (1993). BA, Boston College, MA, Univ of Notre Dame, MDiv, Weston School of Theology, PhD, Catholic Univ of America. Rev. Joseph C. Hindelang, SM, Prin. BA, Assumption College, MDiv, Weston School of Theology. Gregory P. Simon, Adm.

Col Prep. IB Diploma. LD. AP (exams req'd)—Eng Span Calc Stats Bio Chem Physics Eur_Hist US_Hist Econ Psych US_Govt & Pol Art_Hist Studio_Art Music_Theory. **Feat**—British_Lit Chin Anat & Physiol Astron Environ_Sci Sports_Med Comp_Sci Web_Design WWII Sociol World_Relig Drawing Painting Photog Band Chorus Music Accounting Marketing Public_Speak Health. **Supp**—Tut. **Sports**—Basket X-country Golf Lacrosse Ski Soccer Swim Tennis Track. B: Baseball Football Ice_Hockey Wrestling. G: Softball Volley. Activities: 36. **Selective adm:** 187/yr. Appl fee: $40. Appl due: Jan. Accepted: 80%. Yield: 75%. **Tests** HSPT. **Enr 699.** Avg class size: 24. Uniform. **Fac 56.** M 26/F 30. FT 50/PT 6. Adv deg: 76%. **Grad '11—160.** Col—160. Avg ACT: 26.6. **Col Couns:** 3. **Tui '12-'13:** Day $12,052 (+$600). **Est 1994.** Nonprofit. Roman Catholic (85% practice). Sem (Aug-June). As nearly every graduate of Notre Dame Prep will attend college, the school offers two academic tracks: college preparatory and accelerated. In the upper grades, pupils choose from an array of Advanced Placement courses and may also pursue the two-year International Baccalaureate Diploma. Boys and girls perform 10 hours of compulsory service annually.

KALAMAZOO COUNTRY DAY SCHOOL   Day Coed Gr PS (Age 3)-8
Portage, MI 49002. 4221 E Milham Rd.
Tel: 269-329-0116. Fax: 269-329-1850.
www.kalamazoocountryday.org
    Nicholas M. Edgerton, Head (2010). AB, Brown Univ, MA, Columbia Univ. Joanne Stewart, Adm.

Pre-Prep. Gen Acad. Feat—Span Botany Computers Studio_Art Drama Band Music Dance. **Supp**—LD Rem_Math Rem_Read Tut. **Sports**—Basket. G: Volley. **Selective adm:** 55/yr. Appl due: Rolling. **Tests** CTP_4. **Enr 180.** Wh 77%. Latino 4%. Blk 7%. Asian 6%. Other 6%. Avg class size: 20. **Fac 23.** M 3/F 20. FT 22/PT 1. Wh 100%. Adv deg: 43%. **Grad '11—15.** Prep—2. (Monsignor John R Hackett 2). Alum donors: 5%. **Tui '11-'12:** Day $8900 (+$55). Aid: Need 15 ($40,000). **Est 1979.** Nonprofit. Tri (Sept-June). In addition to addressing the basic skills, this school offers courses in music, studio art, band and computers. A special program for students with learning differences is also available. The Orton-Gillingham approach, as well as multisensory integrated learning, is used.

SHRINE CATHOLIC HIGH SCHOOL   Day Coed Gr 9-12
Royal Oak, MI 48073. 3500 W 13 Mile Rd.
Tel: 248-549-2925. Fax: 248-549-2953.
www.shrineschools.com   E-mail: info@shrineschools.com
    Gabrielle A. Erken, Prin. Meg Armstrong, Adm.

Col Prep. AP (exams req'd; 96 taken, 70% 3+)—Eng Calc Chem Physics US_Hist World_Hist. **Feat**—Humanities Fr Span Anat & Physiol Astron Environ_Sci Comp_Sci Econ Relig Film Studio_Art Drama Music Music_Theory Public_Speak. **Supp**—ESL Tut. **Sports**—Basket Bowl X-country Soccer Track. B: Baseball Football Golf Ice_Hockey Tennis. G: Softball Swim Volley. Activities: 19. **Selective adm:** 103/yr. Appl fee: $500. Appl due: Apr. Accepted: 65%. **Tests** HSPT. **Enr 280.** Avg class size: 20. Uniform. **Fac 28.** Adv deg: 53%. **Grad '11—70.** Col—70. Avg ACT: 23.8. **Col Couns:** 1. **Tui '09-'10:** Day $9900 (+$675-725). Parishioners $7850 (+$675-725). **Est 1942.** Nonprofit. Roman Catholic. Quar (Sept-June). Drawing students from parochial and public schools in the Metropolitan Detroit area, Shrine Catholic gears its program toward college preparation. Honors and Advanced Placement courses are available, and electives allow pupils to pursue areas of interest. An extensive arts program prepares some graduates for future careers in such areas as vocal and instrumental music, drama and graphic design. Pupils perform 10 hours of required community service per year.

MICHIGAN LUTHERAN SEMINARY   Bdg & Day
Saginaw, MI 48602. 2777 Hardin St.   Coed Gr 9-12
Tel: 989-793-1041. Fax: 989-793-4213.
www.mlsem.org   E-mail: info@mlsem.org
     Rev. Daniel Sims, Pres (2011). Norval Kock, Adm.

     Col Prep. Feat—British_Lit Ger Lat Span Anat & Physiol Environ_Sci Comp_Sci Econ Govt Bible Band Music_Theory. **Supp**—ESL Tut. **Sports**—Basket X-country Track. B: Baseball Football Wrestling. G: Softball Volley. **Selective adm:** 76/yr. Bdg 55. Day 21. Appl fee: $0. Appl due: Apr. Accepted: 76%. Yield: 90%. **Tests** HSPT Stanford. **Enr 234.** B 120. G 114. Bdg 149. Day 85. Intl 10%. Avg class size: 21. **Fac 29.** M 21/F 8. FT 20/PT 9. Adv deg: 55%. In Dorms 4. **Grad '07—59.** Col—59. (Martin Luther 37, Lansing CC 4, Bethany Lutheran 3, Delta Col 2, Mott CC 2, Central MI 2). Avg ACT: 24. Alum donors: 12%. **Tui '12-'13:** Bdg $8900. Day $5500. Aid: Need ($380,000). **Est 1910.** Nonprofit. Lutheran (100% practice). Sem (Aug-May). MLS' enrollment is restricted to students preparing to work in the Wisconsin Evangelical Lutheran synod as pastors or teachers. The school schedules late afternoon or early evening study halls for all dormitory pupils. Qualified students may complete summer study in Italy, Mexico or Germany.

DE LA SALLE COLLEGIATE HIGH SCHOOL   Day Boys Gr 9-12
Warren, MI 48088. 14600 Common Rd.
Tel: 586-778-2207. Fax: 586-778-6016.
www.delasallehs.com   E-mail: padams@delasallehs.com
     Br. Thomas Lackey, FSC, Pres (2011). BA, Catholic Univ of America, MA, Univ of Michigan, MEd, Univ of San Francisco. Patrick R. Adams, Jr., Prin. BA, Univ of Detroit, MA, EdS, Wayne State Univ. William Burkhardt, Adm.

     Col Prep. AP (exams req'd; 347 taken, 77% 3+)—Eng Fr Span Calc Comp_Sci Bio Chem Physics Eur_Hist US_Hist US_Govt & Pol. **Feat**—Chin Astron Ecol Comp_Graphics Psych Constitutional_Law Philos Relig Photog Studio_Art Band Chorus Accounting Journ Mech_Drawing. **Supp**—Rem_Read Tut. **Comp:** Comp/Stud: 1:13. **Sports**— B: Baseball Basket Bowl X-country Football Golf Ice_Hockey Lacrosse Soccer Swim Tennis Track Wrestling. Activities: 28. **Somewhat selective adm (Gr 9-11):** 227/yr. Appl fee: $250. Appl due: Dec. Accepted: 98%. Yield: 68%. **Tests** HSPT. **Enr 778.** Wh 88%. Latino 1%. Blk 3%. Asian 4%. Other 4%. Avg class size: 26. Stud/fac: 18:1. Uniform. **Fac 46.** M 31/F 15. FT 45/PT 1. Wh 98%. Latino 1%. Other 1%. Adv deg: 41%. **Grad '11—219.** Col—219. (MI St 34, U of MI 21, Macomb CC 20, Wayne St U 17, Central MI 13, Oakland U 12). **Avg SAT:** CR 605. M 657. W 610. Avg ACT: 23.5. **Col Couns:** 4. Alum donors: 5%. **Tui '12-'13:** Day $9600 (+$500-600). Aid: Merit 62 ($81,750). Need 275 ($782,610). **Est 1926.** Nonprofit. Roman Catholic (85% practice). Sem (Aug-June). **Assoc** NCA. Conducted by the Christian Brothers, De La Salle offers an honors and a regular college prep curriculum, in addition to AP courses. Four years of religion classes are complemented by an active campus ministry program. In addition, all boys perform community service: 10 hours in grade 9, 15 hours in grade 10, 20 hours in grade 11 and 25 hours in grade 12.

OHIO

THE LIPPMAN SCHOOL   Day Coed Gr K-8
Akron, OH 44320. 750 White Pond Dr.
Tel: 330-836-0419. Fax: 330-869-2514.
www.thelippmanschool.org   E-mail: info@thelippmanschool.org
     Sam Chestnut, Head (2011). BA, Kenyon College, MA, Univ of Akron. Linda Brotsky, Adm.

     Gen Acad. Feat—Lib_Skills Hebrew Span Computers Judaic_Stud Visual_Arts Drama

Music. **Supp**—Dev_Read Tut. **Comp:** Comp/Stud: 1:1 Laptop prgm Gr 4-8. **Somewhat selective adm:** 21/yr. Appl fee: $100. Appl due: Rolling. Accepted: 90%. Yield: 90%. **Enr 63.** B 34. G 29. Wh 80%. Latino 3%. Blk 13%. Asian 2%. Other 2%. Avg class size: 8. Stud/fac: 8:1. **Fac 15.** M 2/F 13. FT 9/PT 6. Wh 94%. Asian 6%. Adv deg: 33%. **Grad '10—6.** Prep—2. (Hawken 1). **Tui '10-'11:** Day $7200 (+$100). Aid: Need 42 ($168,770). **Est 1965.** Nonprofit. Jewish (50% practice). Tri (Aug-June). Lippman offers two dual-curriculum options: Judaic studies and the Hebrew language and world cultures and the Spanish language. Each student pursues general studies along with one of the dual curricula. The experiential program includes visual and performing arts offerings, technology and science labs, and cultural celebrations. Skill building addresses higher-order thinking, social and cross-cultural skills, economic literacy, creative thinking and problem solving, technology and media skills, leadership and teamwork, self-direction, flexibility and adaptability, and global awareness.

OLNEY FRIENDS SCHOOL
Barnesville, OH 43713. 61830 Sandy Ridge Rd.
Tel: 740-425-3655, 800-302-4291. Fax: 740-425-3202.
www.olneyfriends.org   E-mail: mainoffice@olneyfriends.org

Bdg & Day
Coed Gr 9-12

Charles F. Szumilas, Head (2011). BS, Yale Univ, MEd, Univ of Vermont. Musa Hamideh, Adm.

Col Prep. AP (exams req'd)—Eng Span Calc Physics Psych. **Feat**—Humanities Environ_ Sci Amer_Stud Anthro Peace_Stud Women's_Stud Relig Photog Studio_Art Chorus Music_ Theory Woodworking Outdoor_Ed. **Supp**—ESL Rev Tut. Outdoor Ed. **Sports**—Basket Soccer. **Somewhat selective adm (Bdg Gr 9-12; Day 9):** 26/yr. Bdg 25. Day 1. Appl fee: $50. Appl due: Feb. **Enr 52.** B 23. G 29. Bdg 50. Day 2. Intl 45%. Avg class size: 10. Stud/fac: 5:1. Casual dress. **Fac 13.** M 7/F 6. FT 7/PT 6. Wh 84%. Blk 8%. Other 8%. In Dorms 5. **Grad '11—15.** Col—12. **Avg SAT:** CR/M/W 1510. **Col Couns:** 1. **Tui '12-'13:** Bdg $28,900 (+$500). Day $14,450 (+$250). Aid: Merit 2 ($1000). Need 35 ($75,000). **Est 1837.** Nonprofit. Religious Society of Friends. Quar (Aug-June). Emphasizing college preparation, this small Quaker school accepts students of all denominations and enrolls a substantial number of international pupils. Course work at all levels emphasizes critical-thinking skills, and Olney provides opportunities for acceleration through its AP program. The closely knit community life is supported by a low student-faculty ratio. Silent Meetings for Worship are held twice a week, and all students perform 20 hours of community service per year. The senior humanities program exposes students to college-level texts and seminar-style discussions. All students complete a 20-page formal research paper during senior year.

AGNON SCHOOL
Beachwood, OH 44122. 26500 Shaker Blvd.
Tel: 216-464-4055. Fax: 216-464-3229.
www.agnon.org   E-mail: agnon@agnon.org

Day Coed Gr PS (Age 2)-8

Jerry D. Isaak-Shapiro, Head. MA, George Washington Univ. Laura Simon, Adm.

Pre-Prep. Gen Acad. Feat—Lib_Skills Hebrew Computers Judaic_Stud Drama Chorus Music. **Supp**—ESL. **Selective adm:** 93/yr. Appl fee: $75. Appl due: Feb. Accepted: 75%. **Enr 357.** Avg class size: 15. **Fac 50.** M 6/F 44. FT 50. Wh 100%. **Grad '08—24. Tui '12-'13:** Day $7900-11,400 (+$665). **Est 1969.** Nonprofit. Jewish. Sem (Aug-June). In the primary and elementary divisions, children at this Jewish school develop research and editing skills, learn problem-solving strategies, participate in a Hebrew curriculum that progresses from listening to speaking to reading and writing, and have access to computers in every classroom. Employing a thematic approach to learning, the middle school features daily access to science and computer labs; reading, writing and researching across the curriculum; a well-developed fine arts program; and annual retreats and trips.

LAWRENCE SCHOOL   Day Coed Gr K-12
Broadview Heights, OH 44147. 1551 E Wallings Rd.
Tel: 440-526-0003. Fax: 440-526-0595.
Other locations: 10036 Olde 8 Rd, Sagamore Hills 44067.
www.lawrenceschool.org   E-mail: admissions@lawrenceschool.org
     Lou Salza, Head (2007). BA, Univ of Massachusetts-Amherst, MEd, Harvard Univ. Doug-
las W. Hamilton, Adm.

     Col Prep. LD. AP—World_Hist. **Feat**—Creative_Writing Mythology ASL Span Astron
Environ_Sci Forensic_Sci Geol Marine_Bio/Sci Comp_Sci Robotics Comp_Animation Civil_
War Econ Law Psych Sociol Art_Hist Graphic_Arts Painting Studio_Art Video_Production
Drama Chorus Music Finance Journ Speech Culinary_Arts. **Supp**—Dev_Read Rem_Math
Rem_Read Rev Tut. **Comp:** Comp/Stud: 1:1 Laptop prgm Gr 7-12. **Sports**—Basket X-country Golf Soccer. B: Baseball Football. G: Volley. Activities: 25. **Selective adm:** 59/yr. Appl
fee: $100. Appl due: Rolling. Accepted: 73%. Yield: 80%. **Tests** IQ. **Enr 289.** Elem 151. Sec
138. Nonwhite 16%. Avg class size: 10. Uniform. **Fac 54.** M 15/F 39. FT 46/PT 8. Wh 90%.
Latino 2%. Blk 8%. **Grad '11—37.** Col—31. (Notre Dame Col-OH 5, Kent St 3, Muskingum
3, John Carroll 1, U of CT 1, Valparaiso U 1). **Avg SAT:** CR/M 977. **Col Couns:** 1. **Tui '11-
'12:** Day $15,375-19,475 (+$500-2000). Aid: Need 95 ($900,000). **Est 1969.** Nonprofit. Quar
(Aug-June). In addition to college preparatory academics, this state-chartered school provides
remediation in the areas of academics and organizational and study skills for bright students
with learning differences and attentional disorders from approximately a dozen counties and
70 communities throughout Greater Cleveland and Akron. Lawrence employs ability grouping in a small-class setting to enable the student to progress at a suitable pace. The carefully
sequenced curriculum places particular emphasis on language arts and mathematics, but also
includes course work in social studies, science, art, music and physical education. A separate
campus in Sagamore Hills serves students in grades 7-12.

NOTRE DAME-CATHEDRAL LATIN SCHOOL   Day Coed Gr 9-12
Chardon, OH 44024. 13000 Auburn Rd.
Tel: 440-286-6226. Fax: 440-286-7199.
www.ndcl.org   E-mail: ndcl@lgca.org
     Sr. Jacqueline Gusdane, SND, Pres (2007). BA, Notre Dame College (OH), MA, Univ of
Minnesota-Twin Cities, MA, DMin, John Carroll Univ. Joseph A. Waler, Prin. BA, MA, John
Carroll Univ, MEd, Cleveland State Univ. Keith Corlew, Adm.

     Col Prep. AP—Eng Calc Stats Comp_Sci Physics US_Hist US_Govt & Pol Studio_Art.
Feat—Creative_Writing Chin Fr Ger Span Anat & Physiol Environ_Sci Forensic_Sci Genet-
ics Web_Design Econ Sociol Theol Ceramics Drawing Film Photog Theater Chorus Music_
Theory Accounting Bus Speech. **Supp**—Rem_Math Rem_Read Rev Tut. **Sports**—Basket
Bowl X-country Golf Soccer Swim Tennis Track. B: Baseball Football Ice_Hockey Wrestling.
G: Cheer Gymnastics Softball Volley. Activities: 22. **Selective adm (Gr 9-10):** 213/yr. Appl
due: Feb. Accepted: 75%. **Tests** HSPT. **Enr 747.** B 366. G 381. Wh 92%. Blk 4%. Asian
2%. Other 2%. Avg class size: 23. Stud/fac: 14:1. Uniform. **Fac 60.** Adv deg: 60%. **Grad
'08—180.** Col—178. **Avg SAT:** CR 538. M 511. W 509. Avg ACT: 24. **Col Couns:** 4. **Tui '12-
'13:** Day $10,200. Aid: Need 269. **Est 1878.** Nonprofit. Roman Catholic (90% practice). Sem
(Aug-June). Both general and college preparatory courses are offered, as are fine arts, home
economics, computer, sports and a full extracurricular program. Students satisfy a 20-hour
annual community service requirement.

ARCHBISHOP McNICHOLAS HIGH SCHOOL   Day Coed Gr 9-12
Cincinnati, OH 45230. 6536 Beechmont Ave.
Tel: 513-231-3500. Fax: 513-231-1351.
www.mcnhs.org   E-mail: csherrick@mcnhs.org
     Patricia A. Beckert, Prin (2011). BA, Ohio Univ, MA, Wright State Univ. Lizanne Ingram,
Adm.

Col Prep. AP (220 exams taken, 65% 3+)—Eng Fr Lat Span Calc Comp_Sci Bio Physics Eur_Hist US_Hist Comp_Govt & Pol US_Govt & Pol Studio_Art Music_Theory. **Feat**—Creative_Writing Anat & Physiol Web_Design Law Native_Amer_Stud Relig Ceramics Photog Video_Production Theater Band Chorus Accounting Bus Communications Journ. **Supp**—LD Tut. **Comp:** Laptop prgm Gr 9. **Sports**—Basket Bowl X-country Golf Soccer Swim Tennis Track Volley. B: Baseball Football Wrestling. G: Cheer Softball. **Selective adm:** Appl fee: $0. Appl due: Dec. **Tests** HSPT. **Enr 660.** Avg class size: 19. Stud/fac: 14:1. Uniform. **Fac 51.** M 19/F 32. FT 51. Adv deg: 47%. **Grad '10—183.** Col—181. **Col Couns:** 3. Alum donors: 9%. **Tui '11-'12:** Day $8675 (+$1700). **Est 1951.** Nonprofit. Roman Catholic (92% practice). Quar (Aug-June). **Assoc** NCA. Drawing its enrollment from throughout southwestern Ohio, this Catholic school features Advanced Placement courses in the major disciplines and a particularly broad selection of fine arts and technology electives. The SAIL Program helps pupils with learning differences cope more effectively with high school academics. Students perform 40 cumulative hours of required community service prior to graduation, at least 20 of which must be with an agency that serves individuals in need.

CINCINNATI HILLS CHRISTIAN ACADEMY   Day Coed Gr PS (Age 3)-12
Cincinnati, OH 45249. 11525 Snider Rd.
Tel: 513-247-0900. Fax: 513-247-0950.
Other locations: 11300 Snider Rd, Cincinnati 45259; 11312 Snider Rd, Cincinnati 45259;
   140 W 9th St, Cincinnati 45202.
www.chca-oh.org   E-mail: admissions@chca-oh.org
   T. Randall Brunk, Head (2003). BS, Colorado State Univ, MEd, Regent Univ. Natalie Pfister, Adm.

   Col Prep. AP (exams req'd; 223 taken, 91% 3+)—Eng Chin Lat Span Calc Stats Bio Chem Environ_Sci Physics Eur_Hist US_Hist Econ US_Govt & Pol Studio_Art Music_ Theory. **Feat**—Creative_Writing Anat & Physiol Web_Design Sociol Bible Ceramics Photog Drama Journ Speech. **Supp**—LD. **Comp:** Comp/Stud: 1:1.5. **Sports**—Basket X-country Lacrosse Soccer Swim Tennis Track. B: Baseball Football Golf Wrestling. G: Softball Volley. **Selective adm:** 246/yr. Appl fee: $25-100. Appl due: Rolling. Accepted: 85%. Yield: 72%. **Tests** ISEE Stanford. **Enr 1520.** Elem 1065. Sec 455. Nonwhite 26%. Stud/fac: 13:1. **Fac 131.** M 40/F 91. FT 104/PT 27. Adv deg: 71%. **Grad '11—92.** Col—90. **Avg SAT:** CR 571. M 585. W 568. Avg ACT: 26. **Col Couns:** 2. **Tui '12-'13:** Day $8250-12,795 (+$160-250). Aid: Need 334. **Est 1989.** Nonprofit. Nondenom Christian (100% practice). Quar (Aug-June). In a Christian setting, the school emphasizes development of the basic skills: reading, writing, comprehension, problem solving, study skills and critical thinking. In addition to work in the core subjects, the middle school curriculum includes several electives; various activities, including intramural and (in grades 7 and 8) interscholastic athletics, supplement academics. AP offerings and mandatory community service (120 hours prior to graduation) are features of the high school curriculum, as is a two-week interim program each January that features academic enrichment, arts, athletics, internships, travel and missionary work opportunities.

ELDER HIGH SCHOOL   Day Boys Gr 9-12
Cincinnati, OH 45205. 3900 Vincent Ave.
Tel: 513-921-3744. Fax: 513-921-8123.
www.elderhs.org   E-mail: regan.m@elderhs.org
   Thomas R. Otten, Prin (1997). BA, Thomas More College, MEd, Xavier Univ (OH). Maureen Regan, Adm.

   Col Prep. AP (exams req'd; 181 taken, 61% 3+)—Eng Calc Stats Comp_Sci Chem Physics US_Hist US_Govt & Pol Studio_Art. **Feat**—Shakespeare Fr Ger Lat Span Astron Physiol Cincinnati_Hist Psych Relig Film Graphic_Arts Music_Theory Accounting Finance. **Supp**—LD Makeup Rem_Math Rem_Read Tut. **Comp:** Laptop prgm Gr 9-11. **Dual enr:** Thomas More, Xavier-OH, U of Cincinnati. **Sports**— B: Baseball Basket Bowl X-country Football Golf Ice_Hockey Lacrosse Soccer Swim Tennis Track Volley Wrestling. Activities:

45. Somewhat selective adm (Gr 9-11): 250/yr. Appl due: Dec. Accepted: 99%. **Tests** HSPT. **Enr 932.** Wh 94%. Latino 1%. Blk 3%. Other 2%. Avg class size: 18. **Fac 64.** FT 61/PT 3. Wh 95%. Latino 1%. Blk 3%. Other 1%. Adv deg: 57%. **Grad '11—210.** Col—203. **Avg SAT:** CR 515. M 528. W 486. Avg ACT: 23. **Col Couns:** 5. Alum donors: 20%. **Tui '12-'13:** Day $8900-9400. Aid: Need 541 ($2,000,000). **Est 1922.** Nonprofit. Roman Catholic. Quar (Aug-June). The school's curriculum, which incorporates Christian values, ranges from basic level to Advanced Placement courses, with a variety of electives. Independent study and community service are special features of the religion department.

THE SCHILLING SCHOOL FOR GIFTED CHILDREN   Day Coed Gr K-12
Cincinnati, OH 45249. 8100 Cornell Rd.
Tel: 513-489-8940. Fax: 513-489-8941.
www.schillingschool.org   E-mail: lmink@schillingschool.org
     Sandra D. Kelly-Schilling, Head (1997). BA, MPA, JD, Univ of Cincinnati.

     Col Prep. AP—US_Hist Econ. **Feat**—Ital_Lit ASL Chin Fr Ger Japan Lat Russ Span Stats Robotics Naval_Milit_Hist. **Comp:** Comp/Stud: 1:3. **Dual enr:** U of Cincinnati, Xavier-OH, Miami U-OH. **Sports**—Fencing. Activities: 3. **Selective adm:** 17/yr. Appl fee: $0. Appl due: Rolling. Accepted: 95%. Yield: 100%. **Tests** IQ. **Enr 45.** B 34. G 11. Elem 36. Sec 9. Wh 82%. Blk 2%. Native Am 2%. Asian 13%. Other 1%. Avg class size: 5. Stud/fac: 6:1. **Fac 25.** M 9/F 16. FT 3/PT 22. Wh 84%. Native Am 8%. Asian 8%. Adv deg: 64%. **Grad '11—6.** Col—6. (Rose-Hulman Inst of Tech 1, Miami U-OH 1, U of San Francisco 1, Bradley U 1, St Thomas Aquinas 1, U of CO-Boulder 1). **Tui '11-'12:** Day $12,750. **Est 1997.** Nonprofit. Quar (Aug-June). This small, unusual school serves only those students who have an IQ of 130 or higher. Academic programs are accelerated throughout, and Schilling considers all upper school classes to be at the honors level. Classes are formed according to student ability, not grade level. Many courses, such as differential equations, discrete math, advanced Chinese, and 20th century European and Russian literature, are taught at the college level. Foreign language instruction begins in kindergarten and comprises nine languages (including sign language).

URSULINE ACADEMY   Day Girls Gr 9-12
Cincinnati, OH 45242. 5535 Pfeiffer Rd.
Tel: 513-791-5791. Fax: 513-791-5802.
www.ursulineacademy.org   E-mail: mmcclarnon@ursulineacademy.org
     Sharon L. Redmond, Pres (2005). BA, MA, Northern Kentucky Univ. Molly McClarnon, Adm.

     Col Prep. AP (326 exams taken, 87% 3+)—Eng Fr Ger Lat Span Calc Bio Chem Physics Eur_Hist US_Hist US_Govt & Pol. **Feat**—Chin Anat & Physiol Engineering Programming Web_Design Amer_Women's_Hist Amer_Stud Econ Law Psych Relig Photog Studio_Art Video_Production Drama Music Accounting Journ Public_Speak. **Supp**—Tut. **Sports**— G: Basket X-country F_Hockey Golf Soccer Softball Swim Tennis Track Volley. **Selective adm:** 180/yr. Appl fee: $0. Appl due: Nov. Accepted: 33%. **Tests** HSPT. **Enr 649.** Wh 92%. Blk 5%. Asian 3%. Avg class size: 18. Stud/fac: 12:1. Uniform. **Fac 80.** Wh 98%. Latino 1%. Blk 1%. Adv deg: 63%. **Grad '10—179.** Col—178. **Avg SAT:** CR 607. M 600. Avg ACT: 27. **Tui '10-'11:** Day $10,800 (+$450). **Est 1896.** Nonprofit. Roman Catholic (80% practice). Quar (Aug-June). **Assoc** NCA. Ursuline offers honors classes and Advanced Placement work for qualified girls. Although community service participation is optional, the academy conducts an extensive service program.

BENEDICTINE HIGH SCHOOL   Day Boys Gr 9-12
Cleveland, OH 44104. 2900 Martin Luther King Jr Dr.
Tel: 216-421-2080. Fax: 216-421-0107.
www.cbhs.net   E-mail: cbhs@cbhs.net

Rev. Gerard Gonda, OSB, Pres. BA, John Carroll Univ, MA, Univ of Notre Dame, MEd, Bowling Green State Univ. Joseph Gressock, Prin. MA, Lake Erie College, MA, St Mary's Univ of Minnesota. Kieran Patton, Adm.

Col Prep. AP (148 exams taken, 28% 3+)—Eng Calc Bio Chem Eur_Hist US_Hist Human_Geog Psych US_Govt & Pol. **Feat**—British_Lit Fr Ger Greek Lat Russ Span Programming Sociol Relig Studio_Art Chorus Music Journ. **Supp**—Rev Tut. **Comp:** Comp/Stud: 1:3 (1:1 Laptop prgm Gr 9-10). **Dual enr:** Cleveland St, Case Western Reserve, Cuyahoga CC. **Sports**— B: Baseball Basket Bowl X-country Football Golf Ice_Hockey Lacrosse Soccer Swim Track Wrestling. **Selective adm:** 134/yr. Appl due: Rolling. Accepted: 76%. Yield: 75%. **Tests** HSPT. **Enr 380.** Wh 70%. Blk 30%. Avg class size: 18. Stud/fac: 11:1. Uniform. **Fac 38.** M 36/F 2. FT 38. Adv deg: 65%. **Grad '08—101.** Col—99. (John Carroll 9, U of Akron 9, Kent St 8, U of Dayton 7, Bowling Green St 4, Case Western Reserve 2). **Avg SAT:** CR/ M 1047. Alum donors: 16%. **Tui '11-'12:** Day $8900 (+$100). **Est 1927.** Nonprofit. Roman Catholic. Sem (Aug-June). **Assoc** NCA. Operated by the Benedictine monks of Saint Andrew Abbey, this Catholic school offers college preparatory courses in the arts, the sciences, languages and business administration. A one-to-one tablet computer program serves freshmen and sophomores. Boys enroll from throughout northeastern Ohio.

SAINT IGNATIUS HIGH SCHOOL   Day Boys Gr 9-12
Cleveland, OH 44113. 1911 W 30th St.
Tel: 216-651-0222. Fax: 216-651-6313.
www.ignatius.edu   E-mail: contactus@ignatius.edu
    Rev. William J. Murphy, SJ, Pres (2009). BA, DePauw Univ, MDiv, Weston Jesuit School of Theology. Peter H. Corrigan, Jr., Prin. AB, Xavier Univ (OH), MA, Fordham Univ. Pat O'Rourke, Adm.

Col Prep. AP (exams req'd; 772 taken, 81% 3+)—Eng Fr Lat Span Calc Stats Bio Chem Physics Eur_Hist US_Hist US_Govt & Pol Art_Hist Studio_Art Music_Theory. **Feat**—Creative_Writing Shakespeare Etymology Mythology Greek Comp_Design Web_Design Econ Psych Theol Drawing Sculpt Theater_Arts Chorus. **Supp**—Tut. **Sports**— B: Baseball Basket Bowl Crew X-country Football Golf Ice_Hockey Lacrosse Soccer Swim Tennis Track Volley Wrestling. **Selective adm:** Appl fee: $20. Appl due: Jan. **Enr 1461.** Formal dress. **Fac 107.** Adv deg: 85%. **Grad '11—331.** Col—328. **Mid 50% SAT:** CR 510-640. M 530-640. W 500-620. Mid 50% ACT: 23-29. **Col Couns:** 4. **Tui '12-'13:** Day $13,220 (+$300-420). Aid: Need 731 ($4,700,000). **Est 1886.** Nonprofit. Roman Catholic (90% practice). Sem (Aug-June). **Assoc** NCA. Founded by German Jesuits, SIHS conducts a traditional college preparatory curriculum for boys from seven counties and some 100 cities and towns. A learning center offers various resources for students in need of extra help. Sophomores devote at least 45 hours to community service as part of Saint Ignatius' theology curriculum. Further service opportunities are available through the Arrupe Neighborhood Partnership Program, a three-component undertaking sponsored by Saint Ignatius that focuses on education, housing and recreation.

BEAUMONT SCHOOL   Day Girls Gr 9-12
Cleveland Heights, OH 44118. 3301 N Park Blvd.
Tel: 216-321-2954. Fax: 216-321-3947.
www.beaumontschool.org   E-mail: admissions@beaumontschool.org
    Sr. Gretchen Rodenfels, OSU, Pres. BSE, Saint John College of Cleveland, MEd, John Carroll Univ. Mary Whelan, Prin. Kaitlin Daly, Adm.

Col Prep. AP (exams req'd; 76 taken)—Eng Fr Lat Span Bio Chem Physics US_Hist US_Govt & Pol. **Feat**—British_Lit Engineering Comp_Sci Robotics Pol_Sci Women's_Stud Theol Art_Hist Fine_Arts Studio_Art. **Supp**—Rem_Math Tut. **Comp:** Comp/Stud: 1:1.5. **Sports**— G: Basket X-country Golf Indoor_Track Lacrosse Soccer Softball Swim Tennis Track Volley. Activities: 31. **Selective adm (Gr 9-11):** 107/yr. Appl fee: $0. Appl due: Rolling. Accepted: 80%. Yield: 61%. **Tests** HSPT. **Enr 442.** Wh 79%. Latino 1%. Blk 17%. Asian 2%. Other 1%. Avg class size: 22. Stud/fac: 12:1. Uniform. **Fac 51.** M 4/F 47. FT 36/PT 15.

Wh 90%. Latino 2%. Blk 4%. Asian 4%. Adv deg: 72%. **Grad '07—117.** Col—111. (OH St 11, Kent St 10, John Carroll 8, Xavier-OH 8, U of Dayton 6, Miami U-OH 6). **Avg SAT:** CR 559. M 548. W 560. Avg ACT: 26. **Col Couns:** 3. **Tui '11-'12:** Day $11,200. Aid: Merit 34 ($62,900). Need 141 ($260,150). Work prgm 68 ($36,000). **Est 1850.** Nonprofit. Roman Catholic (81% practice). Quar (Aug-June). **Assoc** NCA. The oldest chartered school in Cleveland, Beaumont offers a rigorous liberal arts curriculum that features a strong technology component. Block scheduling enables students to take four 90-minute classes a day; one day per week, 45 minutes is built into each class for personal study time. Girls accumulate 80 hours of required community service by the end of junior year.

BISHOP WATTERSON HIGH SCHOOL   **Day Coed Gr 9-12**
Columbus, OH 43214. 99 E Cooke Rd.
Tel: 614-268-8671. Fax: 614-268-0551.
www.bishopwatterson.com   E-mail: ccampbel@cdeducation.org
    Marian A. Hutson, Prin (2000). BS, MS, Ohio State Univ. Chris Campbell, Adm.

    Col Prep. AP (161 exams taken, 84% 3+)—Eng Fr Lat Span Calc Stats Comp_Sci Chem US_Hist Comp_Govt & Pol Econ Psych US_Govt & Pol. **Feat**—Ital Anat & Physiol Relig Architect_Design Graphic_Design Music Bus. **Supp**—Tut. **Comp:** Laptop prgm Gr 9-12. **Dual enr:** OH Dominican. **Sports**—Basket Bowl X-country Golf Lacrosse Soccer Swim Tennis Track Volley. B: Baseball Football Ice_Hockey Wrestling. G: F_Hockey Softball. **Selective adm:** 278/yr. Appl fee: $100. Appl due: Feb. **Enr 1019.** B 389. G 630. Wh 92%. Latino 3%. Blk 1%. Asian 1%. Other 3%. Uniform. **Fac 77.** M 41/F 36. FT 75/PT 2. Adv deg: 58%. **Grad '11—248.** Col—244. **Avg SAT:** CR 572. M 564. W 553. Avg ACT: 25.4. **Col Couns:** 4. **Tui '11-'12:** Day $8500. Parishioners $7500. **Est 1954.** Nonprofit. Roman Catholic (90% practice). Quar (Aug-June). The school's curriculum includes five years of French and Spanish, four years of Latin and Italian instruction, and an array of art, music and business courses. Each August, interested students may attend the Shakespeare Festival in Stratford, Ontario (Canada). In addition to enrolling in on-site honors, Advanced Placement and dual-enrollment courses (through Ohio Dominican University), Bishop Watterson pupils may take advanced classes at local colleges. All seniors, as well as younger students in select courses, receive tablet computers for use in class and at home.

MARBURN ACADEMY   **Day Coed Gr 1-12**
Columbus, OH 43229. 1860 Walden Dr.
Tel: 614-433-0822. Fax: 614-433-0812.
www.marburnacademy.org   E-mail: marburnadmission@marburnacademy.org
    Earl B. Oremus, Head (1986). BA, Univ of Kentucky, MEd, Harvard Univ. Scott B. Burton, Adm.

    Col Prep. LD. Underachiever. Feat—Span Computers Studio_Art Drama Music Study_ Skills. **Supp**—Dev_Read Rem_Math Rem_Read Tut. **Comp:** Comp/Stud: 1:1 Laptop prgm Gr 9-12. Outdoor Ed. **Sports**—Basket X-country Golf Soccer Tennis Volley. **Very selective adm (Gr 1-11):** 48/yr. Appl fee: $100. Appl due: Rolling. Accepted: 15%. Yield: 97%. **Tests** IQ. **Enr 152.** B 100. G 52. Elem 109. Sec 43. Wh 93%. Latino 1%. Blk 5%. Asian 1%. Avg class size: 16. Stud/fac: 4:1. Uniform. **Fac 27.** M 7/F 20. FT 25/PT 2. Wh 100%. Adv deg: 22%. **Grad '11—9.** Col—9. **Col Couns:** 1. **Tui '11-'12:** Day $18,900-20,900 (+$50). Aid: Merit 7 ($10,000). Need 48 ($200,000). **Est 1981.** Nonprofit. Quar (Aug-June). Enrolling pupils with learning disabilities from approximately 30 central Ohio communities, Marburn provides a full primary and secondary program that seeks to remediate students with academic problems in a college preparatory setting. The academy's typical student possesses average to superior intelligence and has previously unremediated problems caused by dyslexia, ADHD or another specific learning disability. The program addresses academic skills, social interaction and problem solving.

CUYAHOGA VALLEY CHRISTIAN ACADEMY   Day Coed Gr 7-12
Cuyahoga Falls, OH 44224. 4687 Wyoga Lake Rd.
Tel: 330-929-0575. Fax: 330-929-0156.
www.cvcaroyals.org   E-mail: cvca@cvcaroyals.org
    Roger Taylor, Pres (2001). BA, Mount Vernon Nazarene College, MA, PhD, Kent State Univ. Mike Bova, Head. BA, Georgetown College, MA, Univ of Akron. Mindy Fullerton, Adm.

    Col Prep. AP (exams req'd; 175 taken, 84% 3+)—Eng Span Calc Stats Bio Eur_Hist US_Hist Econ Music_Theory. **Feat**—Creative_Writing Poetry Fr Ger Lat Engineering Comp_Sci Web_Design Govt Psych Sociol Global_Stud Bible Logic Graphic_Arts Studio_Art Video_Production Theater Band Chorus Handbells Accounting Journ. **Supp**—Rev Tut. **Comp:** Comp/Stud: 1:6. **Sports**—Basket X-country Golf Lacrosse Soccer Swim Tennis Track. B: Baseball Football Ice_Hockey Wrestling. G: Cheer Softball Volley. Activities: 47. **Somewhat selective adm (Gr 7-11):** 217/yr. Appl fee: $70. Appl due: Rolling. Accepted: 91%. Yield: 96%. **Tests** HSPT. **Enr 850.** B 410. G 440. Elem 223. Sec 627. Wh 82%. Latino 1%. Blk 14%. Asian 3%. Avg class size: 18. Stud/fac: 9:1. Uniform. **Fac 77.** M 40/F 37. FT 67/PT 10. Wh 94%. Blk 5%. Asian 1%. Adv deg: 51%. **Grad '11—155.** Col—153. (U of Akron 24, Cedarville 6, IN Wesleyan 6, Bowling Green St 6, Grove City 5, Gordon 5). **Avg SAT:** CR 560. M 555. W 565. Avg ACT: 25. Alum donors: 35%. **Tui '12-'13:** Day $8975 (+$125-210). Aid: Merit 45 ($55,700). Need 329 ($850,000). **Est 1968.** Nonprofit. Nondenom Christian (100% practice). Quar (Aug-June). As an evangelical school, CVCA provides a curriculum centered in historical, Bible-based Christianity. All students are required to take Bible courses each semester, and pupils also take several compulsory electives. Advanced Placement and honors courses provide qualified students with opportunities for acceleration. J-Term, which operates for eight days each January, combines intensive, credit-bearing course work with domestic or international travel. Boys and girls enroll from Summit, Portage, Cuyahoga, Medina, Stark, Geauga and Lake counties.

WALSH JESUIT HIGH SCHOOL   Day Coed Gr 9-12
Cuyahoga Falls, OH 44224. 4550 Wyoga Lake Rd.
Tel: 330-929-4205, 800-686-4694. Fax: 330-929-9749.
www.walshjesuit.org   E-mail: moorej@walshjesuit.org
    Karl Ertle, Pres (2010). BA, MA, John Carroll Univ. Mark Hassman, Prin. BS, Marietta College, MEd, Ashland Univ. Rob Eubank, Adm.

    Col Prep. AP (377 exams taken, 62% 3+)—Eng Calc Stats Bio Chem Environ_Sci Physics Eur_Hist US_Hist Econ US_Govt & Pol. **Feat**—British_Lit Irish_Lit Chin Fr Ger Lat Span Anat & Physiol Ecol Genetics Psych Sociol Theol Art_Hist Drawing Graphic_Arts Painting Studio_Art Acting Theater_Arts Chorus Music Music_Theory Accounting Journ Speech. **Supp**—Tut. **Sports**—Basket Bowl X-country Golf Lacrosse Soccer Swim Tennis Track Volley. B: Baseball Football Ice_Hockey Wrestling. G: Cheer Softball. Activities: 47. **Selective adm (Gr 9-11):** 250/yr. Appl due: Jan. Accepted: 70%. **Tests** Stanford. **Enr 936.** Avg class size: 24. Stud/fac: 14:1. Uniform. **Fac 76.** Adv deg: 78%. **Grad '11—217.** Col—215. (U of Dayton 24, OH St 21, U of Akron 15, Miami U-OH 13, John Carroll 10, Kent St 10). **Avg SAT:** CR 556. M 558. W 553. **Mid 50% SAT:** CR 500-610. M 490-620. W 500-600. Avg ACT: 26.3. Mid 50% ACT: 23-29. **Col Couns:** 1. **Tui '12-'13:** Day $9935 (+$350-1215). **Est 1964.** Nonprofit. Roman Catholic (85% practice). Sem (Aug-June). **Assoc** NCA. This Jesuit school conducts a varied college preparatory program that includes an array of electives and Advanced Placement classes. Grade 12 ends with the Senior Experience Program, in which seniors undertake a three-week career or volunteer field experience in an area of interest (under the guidance of a teacher). At the conclusion of the program, each student writes a paper and defends it before a faculty board. Walsh Jesuit pupils satisfy the following community service requirements: 15 hours of service in grades 9 and 12, 20 hours in grade 10 and 25 hours in grade 11.

ST. JOHN'S HIGH SCHOOL   Day Coed Gr 9-12
Delphos, OH 45833. 515 E 2nd St.
Tel: 419-692-5371. Fax: 419-879-6874.
www.delphosstjohns.org   E-mail: huysman@delphosstjohns.org
    Donald P. Huysman, Prin (2000). BS, Ohio State Univ, MS, Univ of Dayton.

    Col Prep. Voc. Bus. Feat—Fr Span Stats Anat Comp_Sci Econ Govt Psych Sociol Relig Film Studio_Art Music_Theory Accounting Bus Speech. **Supp**—Rem_Math Rem_Read Tut. **Dual enr:** Wright St, Bluffton. **Sports**—Basket X-country Golf Track. B: Baseball Football Wrestling. G: Soccer Volley. **Somewhat selective adm. Enr 259.** Wh 98%. Latino 1%. Blk 1%. Uniform. **Fac 22.** M 9/F 13. FT 21/PT 1. Wh 100%. Adv deg: 31%. **Grad '09—73.** Col—68. **Tui '11-'12:** Day $2652 (+$288). **Est 1912.** Nonprofit. Roman Catholic (98% practice). Quar (Aug-May). **Assoc** NCA. St. John's offers a Catholic secondary education that includes course work in business and the practical arts. All juniors take part in a compulsory community service project.

STEPHEN T. BADIN HIGH SCHOOL   Day Coed Gr 9-12
Hamilton, OH 45013. 571 New London Rd.
Tel: 513-863-3993. Fax: 513-785-2844.
www.badinhs.org   E-mail: bpendergest@badinhs.org
    Brian D. Pendergest, Prin (2011). BA, MA, Xavier Univ (OH). Dirk Q. Allen, Adm.

    Col Prep. AP (exams req'd; 109 taken, 63% 3+)—Eng Calc Bio US_Hist US_Govt & Pol. **Feat**—British_Lit Etymology Fr Lat Span Stats Physiol Comp_Sci Psych World_Relig Ceramics Painting Photog Studio_Art Band Music Music_Theory Accounting Bus Journ Marketing Speech Design. **Supp**—Dev_Read LD Makeup Rem_Math Tut. **Comp:** Comp/Stud: 1:1 Laptop prgm Gr 9-12. **Dual enr:** Xavier-OH, Miami U-OH. **Sports**—Basket Bowl X-country Golf Soccer Swim Tennis Track Volley. B: Baseball Football Wrestling. G: Gymnastics Softball. Activities: 25. **Somewhat selective adm:** 109/yr. Appl fee: $0. Appl due: Rolling. Accepted: 99%. Yield: 95%. **Tests** HSPT. **Enr 450.** Wh 98%. Blk 1%. Asian 1%. Avg class size: 22. Stud/fac: 15:1. Uniform. **Fac 39.** M 21/F 18. FT 39. Adv deg: 71%. **Grad '09—138.** Col—134. (Miami U Hamilton 27, U of Cincinnati 24, Miami U-OH 12, Xavier-OH 7, U of Dayton 6, Wright St 6). **Avg SAT:** CR 520. M 520. W 502. Avg ACT: 22. Alum donors: 55%. **Tui '12-'13:** Day $7900 (+$370-720). Aid: Need 113 ($300,000). **Est 1966.** Nonprofit. Roman Catholic (90% practice). Quar (Aug-June). **Assoc** NCA. The result of a merger between Hamilton Catholic for boys and Notre Dame High School for girls, Badin takes its name from the first priest ordained in the US. For the cost of an annual technology fee, each pupil receives an iPad for school use. Boys and girls perform 15 hours of required community service annually. Students may participate in academic school year abroad or student exchange programs.

ST. EDWARD HIGH SCHOOL   Day Boys Gr 9-12
Lakewood, OH 44107. 13500 Detroit Ave.
Tel: 216-221-3776. Fax: 216-221-4609.
www.sehs.net   E-mail: admission@sehs.net
    James P. Kubacki, Pres (2010). AB, Harvard Univ, MA, Fordham Univ. K. C. McKenna, Adm.

    Col Prep. IB Diploma. AP (258 exams taken, 74% 3+)—Eng Lat Span Calc Stats Comp_Sci Bio Chem Physics US_Hist Comp_Govt & Pol US_Govt & Pol. **Feat**—Creative_Writing Mythology Chin Fr Ital Engineering Robotics Web_Design Econ Law Psych World_Relig Film Painting Sculpt Studio_Art Theater_Arts Chorus Music_Theory Orchestra Public_Speak Health. **Supp**—Dev_Read Rem_Math Tut. **Comp:** Comp/Stud: 1:10. **Sports**— B: Baseball Basket Bowl Crew X-country Football Golf Ice_Hockey Lacrosse Rugby Soccer Swim Tennis Track Volley Wrestling. **Selective adm:** 250/yr. Appl due: Jan. Accepted: 70%. **Enr 828.** Stud/fac: 17:1. Uniform. **Fac 70.** Adv deg: 84%. **Grad '08—214.** Col—208. **Avg SAT:** CR 535. M 566. W 536. **Mid 50% SAT:** CR 470-590. M 490-640. W 480-590. Avg ACT: 23.3. **Col Couns:** 3. **Tui '12-'13:** Day $12,350 (+$50). **Est 1949.** Nonprofit. Roman Catholic (85%

practice). Quar (Aug-May). **Assoc** NCA. Founded and sponsored by the Brothers of Holy Cross, St. Edward's offers a traditional college preparatory curriculum that features honors and Advanced Placement courses, as well as the two-year IB Diploma Program. Students develop critical-thinking and study skills in all classes. The school's Pre-Engineering Program enables boys who are considering a career in engineering to receive classroom instruction in the discipline while partaking of mentoring and networking opportunities from St. Edward alumni and others currently employed in various engineering fields.

TUSCARAWAS CENTRAL CATHOLIC   Day Coed Gr 7-12
JUNIOR/SENIOR HIGH SCHOOL
New Philadelphia, OH 44663. 777 3rd St NE.
Tel: 330-343-3302. Fax: 330-343-6388.
www.tccsaints.com   E-mail: tccsaints@cdeducation.org
   Scott Power, Prin.

   Col Prep. AP—Eng Calc Chem. **Feat**—Fr Span Anat Comp_Sci Web_Design Econ Govt Relig Studio_Art Music. **Supp**—Tut. **Sports**—Basket X-country Golf Swim Track. B: Baseball Football Wrestling. G: Softball Volley. **Nonselective adm:** 42/yr. Appl due: Rolling. Accepted: 100%. **Enr 184.** Elem 58. Sec 126. Avg class size: 24. Uniform. **Fac 15.** M 7/F 8. **Grad '07—31.** Col—31. Avg ACT: 24. **Tui '08-'09:** Day $4895 (+$62). Parishioners $3995 (+$62). **Est 1970.** Nonprofit. Roman Catholic. Quar (Aug-June). This Roman Catholic school offers a college preparatory education. Students accumulate 120 hours of community service prior to graduation.

PADUA FRANCISCAN HIGH SCHOOL   Day Coed Gr 9-12
Parma, OH 44134. 6740 State Rd.
Tel: 440-845-2444. Fax: 440-845-5710.
www.paduafranciscan.com   E-mail: padua@paduafranciscan.com
   Rev. Ted Haag, OFM, Pres (2003). BA, Quincy Univ, MDiv, Catholic Theological Union, MSSA, Case Western Reserve Univ. David G. Stec, Prin. BA, Borromeo College of Ohio, MA, John Carroll Univ, MA, Ursuline College. Lillian J. Gathers, Adm.

   Col Prep. AP—Eng Calc Bio Chem Physics US_Hist US_Govt & Pol Studio_Art. **Feat**—Creative_Writing Fr Ger Greek Ital Lat Span Comp_Sci Econ Govt Law Psych Sociol Child_Dev Theol Photog Drama Music Accounting Bus Marketing. **Supp**—Dev_Read LD Tut. **Comp:** Comp/Stud: 1:4. **Dual enr:** Cuyahoga CC. **Sports**—Basket X-country Golf Soccer Swim Track. B: Baseball Football Ice_Hockey Lacrosse Tennis Wrestling. G: Softball Volley. Activities: 30. **Somewhat selective adm (Gr 9-11):** 231/yr. Appl fee: $0. Appl due: Jan. Accepted: 95%. Yield: 84%. **Tests** HSPT. **Enr 837.** Wh 96%. Latino 1%. Blk 1%. Asian 2%. Avg class size: 25. Stud/fac: 17:1. Formal dress. **Fac 56.** M 24/F 32. FT 50/PT 6. Adv deg: 71%. **Grad '11—202.** Col—200. **Avg SAT:** CR 538. M 534. W 525. Avg ACT: 23.2. **Col Couns:** 5. **Tui '11-'12:** Day $8975. Aid: Merit 403 ($201,500). Need 147 ($125,300). **Est 1961.** Nonprofit. Roman Catholic (90% practice). Sem (Aug-June). **Assoc** NCA. Padua's program of study offers selections in business, English, life skills, mathematics, science and social studies, with requirements in theology, foreign language, fine arts and computer science. Honors and AP classes and electives are part of the curriculum. Foreign exchange opportunities and community involvement are other elements of the program. Students in each grade complete annual community service projects.

THE LILLIAN AND BETTY RATNER SCHOOL   Day Coed Gr PS (Age 2)-8
Pepper Pike, OH 44124. 27575 Shaker Blvd.
Tel: 216-464-0033. Fax: 216-464-0031.
www.theratnerschool.org   E-mail: ddriggs@theratnerschool.org
   Larry Goodman, Head (2011). PhD, Univ of Chicago. Dawn Driggs, Adm.

   Pre-Prep. Gen Acad. Montessori. Feat—Hebrew Span Computers Judaic_Stud Studio_Art

Music. **Supp**—LD Rem_Read. **Selective adm:** 90/yr. Appl fee: $75. Appl due: Rolling. **Enr 217.** Avg class size: 15. **Fac 34.** M 8/F 26. FT 27/PT 7. **Grad '08—20.** Prep—10. (Hawken 2, Beaumont 2, Benedictine HS-OH 1, Hotchkiss 1). **Tui '12-'13:** Day $12,676-15,618 (+$470-2030). **Est 1963.** Nonprofit. Jewish (40% practice). Tri (Aug-June). Ratner offers a Montessori curriculum in preschool and kindergarten and features Jewish studies and Hebrew language instruction in the later grades. The elementary school (grades 1-4) emphasizes academic and social development through age-blended classrooms, integrated arts instruction, and a combination of individual, small- and large-group learning activities. Middle school students (grades 5-8) spend eight days exploring marine biology at The Island School in the Bahamas.

LUTHERAN HIGH SCHOOL WEST   Day Coed Gr 9-12
Rocky River, OH 44116. 3850 Linden Rd.
Tel: 440-333-1660. Fax: 440-333-1729.
www.lutheranwest.org   E-mail: info@lutheranwest.org
    Dale Wolfgram, Prin. BS, MS, Concordia Univ Nebraska. Stephanie Zehnder, Adm.

    Col Prep. AP—Eng Ger Span Calc Bio Chem US_Hist US_Govt & Pol. **Feat**—Chin Lat Stats Comp_Sci Web_Design Econ Psych Sociol Relig Photog Studio_Art Video_Production Drama Band Chorus Journ Speech Woodworking. **Supp**—Tut. **Comp:** Comp/Stud: 1:4. **Sports**—Basket Bowl X-country Golf Soccer Track. B: Baseball Football Wrestling. G: Softball Volley. Activities: 8. **Selective adm:** 130/yr. Appl fee: $100. Appl due: Mar. **Enr 450.** Avg class size: 21. Stud/fac: 12:1. Casual dress. **Fac 39. Grad '08—113.** Col—110. **Avg SAT:** CR 554. M 540. W 547. **Tui '12-'13:** Day $8906 (+$150-210). Aid: Need 360 ($1,000,000). **Est 1948.** Nonprofit. Lutheran (67% practice). Quar (Aug-June). **Assoc** NCA. Advanced Placement classes are part of Lutheran West's curriculum, as is a specialized reading program. Community service is a point of emphasis, with the school requiring boys and girls to perform at least 15 hours of service in grade 9, 18 hours in grade 10, 24 hours in grade 11 and 30 hours in grade 12.

MAGNIFICAT HIGH SCHOOL   Day Girls Gr 9-12
Rocky River, OH 44116. 20770 Hilliard Blvd.
Tel: 440-331-1572. Fax: 440-331-7257.
www.magnificaths.org   E-mail: info@magnificaths.org
    Sr. Carol Anne Smith, HM, Pres (2007). BA, Ursuline College, MEd, John Carroll Univ. Heather Schwager, Adm.

    Col Prep. AP (267 exams taken, 80% 3+)—Eng Fr Span Calc Stats Bio Chem US_Hist World_Hist Econ US_Govt & Pol Art_Hist. **Feat**—British_Lit Women's_Lit Chin Arabic Astron Environ_Sci Psych Sociol Comp_Relig Theol Drawing Graphic_Arts Photog Studio_Art Drama Theater_Arts Band Orchestra Piano Dance Accounting Finance. **Supp**—Rem_Math Rem_Read Tut. **Sports**— G: Basket X-country F_Hockey Golf Gymnastics Indoor_Track Lacrosse Soccer Softball Swim Tennis Track Volley. Activities: 45. **Selective adm (Gr 9-11):** 217/yr. Appl fee: $150. Appl due: Jan. **Tests** HSPT. **Enr 774.** Wh 90%. Latino 5%. Blk 1%. Asian 4%. Avg class size: 22. Stud/fac: 12:1. Uniform. **Fac 74.** Adv deg: 56%. **Grad '09—202.** Col—202. (OH U 20, Miami U-OH 15, OH U 15, John Carroll 15, Kent St 14, U of Dayton 12). **Avg SAT:** CR 554. M 544. W 557. Avg ACT: 25.5. **Col Couns:** 4. **Tui '11-'12:** Day $10,900. Aid: Need 356. **Est 1955.** Nonprofit. Roman Catholic (93% practice). Sem (Aug-June). **Assoc** NCA. Staffed by the Sisters of the Humility of Mary, this school conducts a college preparatory curriculum. Honors and Advanced Placement classes are offered in many subject areas. Magnificat maintains four-year programs in art, English, modern languages, math, science and theology, and computers are used extensively in all academic departments. Sophomores satisfy a 30-hour community service requirement.

ST. FRANCIS DE SALES HIGH SCHOOL   Day Boys Gr 9-12
Toledo, OH 43607. 2323 W Bancroft St.
Tel: 419-531-1618. Fax: 419-531-9740.
www.sfstoledo.org   E-mail: sfs@sfstoldeo.org
 Rev. Ronald Olszewski, OSFS, Pres. Eric J. Smola, Prin. MA, Univ of Toledo. Rick Michalak, Adm.

 Col Prep. AP (389 exams taken, 57% 3+)—Eng Fr Lat Span Calc Stats Comp_Sci Bio Chem Physics US_Hist World_Hist Econ Psych Studio_Art. **Feat**—British_Lit Chin Anat & Physiol Environ_Sci Engineering Web_Design Comp_Animation Govt Law Sociol Theol World_Relig Ceramics Drawing Chorus Journ Public_Speak. **Supp**—Tut. **Comp:** Comp/Stud: 1:4.75. **Dual enr:** U of Toledo. **Sports**— B: Baseball Basket Crew X-country Football Golf Ice_Hockey Lacrosse Soccer Swim Tennis Track W_Polo Wrestling. Activities: 26. **Somewhat selective adm:** 167/yr. Appl due: Dec. Accepted: 90%. Yield: 93%. **Tests** HSPT. **Enr 606.** Wh 85%. Latino 4%. Blk 10%. Asian 1%. Avg class size: 25. Stud/fac: 12:1. Formal dress. **Fac 54.** M 42/F 12. FT 47/PT 7. Adv deg: 59%. **Grad '11—136.** Col—136. **Avg SAT:** CR 551. M 577. W 535. Avg ACT: 24. **Col Couns:** 1. Alum donors: 15%. **Tui '11-'12:** Day $9240 (+$500-675). Aid: Need 394. **Est 1955.** Inc. Roman Catholic. Quar (Aug-June). Staffed by the Oblates of St. Francis de Sales, this school offers AP courses in every academic area and shares classes in some areas with a nearby girls' school. A retreat program is mandatory for all students. In addition, boys satisfy the following community service requirements: 20 hours of annual service in grades 9 and 10, 30 in grades 11 and 12.

CARDINAL MOONEY HIGH SCHOOL   Day Coed Gr 9-12
Youngstown, OH 44507. 2545 Erie St.
Tel: 330-788-5007. Fax: 330-788-4511.
www.cardinalmooney.com   E-mail: jcarneysmith@youngstowndiocese.org
 Rev. Gerald DeLucia, Pres (2012). John Young, Prin. Joanne Carney Smith, Adm.

 Col Prep. AP—Eng Calc Bio Chem US_Hist. **Feat**—Creative_Writing Fr Ger Lat Span Stats Anat & Physiol Astron Environ_Sci Genetics Oceanog Programming African-Amer_Hist Econ Govt Psych Sociol Theol World_Relig Photog Studio_Art Drama Chorus Music Music_Theory Accounting Journ Indus_Arts Study_Skills. **Supp**—Dev_Read Rem_Math Rem_Read Tut. **Sports**—Basket Bowl X-country Golf Lacrosse Soccer Swim Tennis Track. B: Baseball Football Ice_Hockey. G: Cheer Softball Volley. Activities: 30. **Somewhat selective adm (Gr 9-11):** 161/yr. Appl due: Feb. **Enr 590.** B 309. G 281. Avg class size: 25. Stud/fac: 13:1. Casual dress. **Fac 47.** Adv deg: 55%. **Grad '11—149.** Col—145. **Avg SAT:** CR/M 1076. Avg ACT: 22. **Col Couns:** 1. **Tui '04-'05:** Day $4775. Aid: Need 295 ($400,000). **Est 1956.** Nonprofit. Roman Catholic (73% practice). Sem (Aug-June). Cardinal Mooney's traditional college preparatory curriculum is enhanced by training in the practical and performing arts. Christian values are integrated into all aspects of the program, and students take theology every semester.

WISCONSIN

CATHOLIC CENTRAL HIGH SCHOOL   Day Coed Gr 9-12
Burlington, WI 53105. 148 McHenry St.
Tel: 262-763-1510. Fax: 262-763-1509.
www.cchsnet.org   E-mail: jkresken@cchsnet.org
 Greg Groth, Prin (2007). BS, Southern Illinois Univ, MS, National-Louis Univ. Joannie Kresken, Adm.

 Col Prep. AP—Eng Calc. **Feat**—Chin Fr Span Arabic Stats Anat & Physiol Botany Environ_Sci Forensic_Sci Geol Zoology Web_Design Econ Psych Sociol Philos Theol World_Relig Drawing Painting Photog Studio_Art Animation Chorus Music_Theory Bus Marketing

Speech. **Supp**—Tut. **Comp:** Comp/Stud: 1:3. **Dual enr:** Gateway Tech. **Sports**—Basket X-country Swim Track. B: Baseball Bowl Football Golf Wrestling. G: Cheer Gymnastics Softball Tennis Volley. **Somewhat selective adm:** 43/yr. Appl fee: $80. Appl due: Nov. Accepted: 96%. Yield: 96%. **Enr 148.** B 84. G 64. Wh 92%. Latino 1%. Blk 2%. Native Am 1%. Asian 2%. Other 2%. Avg class size: 14. Stud/fac: 9:1. Casual dress. **Fac 18.** M 11/F 7. FT 16/PT 2. Wh 95%. Latino 5%. Adv deg: 27%. **Grad '09—42.** Col—42. (Marquette 6, Carroll 3, U of WI-La Crosse 3, U of WI-Stevens Point 3, Milwaukee Sch of Engineering 2, U of WI-Madison 2). Avg ACT: 24.7. Alum donors: 25%. **Tui '10-'11:** Day $7610 (+$640-1790). Parishioners $6960 (+$640-1790). Aid: Need 46 ($139,006). **Est 1920.** Nonprofit. Roman Catholic (85% practice). Sem (Sept-June). **Assoc** NCA. Serving southeastern Wisconsin, Central Catholic combines college preparatory academics with varied athletic and activities programs. Three years of Chinese and two years of Arabic are among the language courses available. A course offered by nearby Gateway Technical College enrolls pupils interested in becoming certified nursing assistants. Students perform 10 hours of compulsory annual service as part of the theology curriculum.

IMMANUEL LUTHERAN HIGH SCHOOL

Bdg & Day
Coed Gr 9-12

Eau Claire, WI 54701. 501 Grover Rd.
Tel: 715-836-6621. Fax: 715-836-6634.
www.ilc.edu   E-mail: john.pfeiffer@ilc.edu
     John K. Pfeiffer, Pres (1997). BA, Univ of Massachusetts-Amherst, MDiv, Immanuel Lutheran Seminary. Jeffrey A. Schierenbeck, Prin.

     Col Prep. Feat—Span Comp_Sci Comp_Relig Relig Studio_Art Music Hymnology Bus. **Supp**—Rem_Math Rem_Read Tut. **Dual enr:** Immanuel Lutheran. **Sports**—Basket X-country Soccer. B: Baseball. G: Softball Volley. **Somewhat selective adm:** 34/yr. Bdg 20. Day 14. Appl due: Rolling. Accepted: 99%. Yield: 95%. **Enr 121.** B 60. G 61. Bdg 72. Day 49. Wh 97%. Asian 3%. Avg class size: 30. Stud/fac: 10:1. **Fac 15.** M 13/F 2. FT 12/PT 3. Wh 100%. Adv deg: 60%. **Grad '10—23.** Col—15. (Immanuel Lutheran 4, U of WI-Eau Claire 3). Avg ACT: 24. **Tui '12-'13:** Bdg $6400-8400 (+$400). Day $3200-5200 (+$400). Aid: Merit 28 ($8400). Need 29 ($34,600). Work prgm 42 ($30,000). **Est 1959.** Nonprofit. Church of the Lutheran Confession (97% practice). Sem (Aug-May). Religion courses are part of this school's curriculum. All seniors perform 10 hours of mandatory community service per semester. In addition to the high school division, Immanuel Lutheran operates a four-year college and a three-year, postgraduate theological seminary.

NOTRE DAME DE LA BAIE ACADEMY

Day Coed Gr 9-12

Green Bay, WI 54303. 610 Maryhill Dr.
Tel: 920-429-6100. Fax: 920-429-6168.
www.notredameacademy.com   E-mail: kkonop@notredameacademy.com
     Robert C. Pauly, Pres (2010). MA, Univ of Notre Dame. John Ravizza, Prin. BA, Santa Clara Univ, MEd, Boston College, EdD, Cardinal Stritch Univ. Karen Konop, Adm.

     Col Prep. IB Diploma. Feat—Creative_Writing Fr Ger Russ Span Calc Stats Environ_Sci Kinesiology Econ Govt Pol_Sci Psych Sociol Theol World_Relig Painting Studio_Art Drama Chorus Music Music_Theory Journ Metal_Shop. **Supp**—Rem_Math Tut. **Comp:** Comp/Stud: 1:2.5. **Dual enr:** St Norbert. **Sports**—Basket X-country Golf Ice_Hockey Soccer Softball Tennis Track. B: Baseball Football. G: Cheer Volley. Activities: 43. **Somewhat selective adm:** 179/yr. Appl fee: $50. Appl due: Rolling. Accepted: 95%. Yield: 83%. **Enr 740.** Nonwhite 9%. Avg class size: 25. Uniform. **Fac 48.** M 21/F 27. Adv deg: 41%. **Grad '11—184.** Col—182. Avg ACT: 25.2. **Col Couns:** 1. **Tui '11-'12:** Day $5950 (+$255-390). Parishioners $4950 (+$255-390). Aid: Need 287 ($602,038). **Est 1990.** Nonprofit. Roman Catholic (88% practice). Quar (Aug-June). **Assoc** NCA. Notre Dame provides both college preparatory and general academic programs for high school students. College-credit courses are offered through St. Norbert College. An accelerated curriculum comprises honors and advanced classes, and qualified students may pursue the International Baccalaureate Diploma in grades 11 and 12.

ARMITAGE ACADEMY Day Coed Gr K-8
Kenosha, WI 53143. 6032 8th Ave.
Tel: 262-654-4200. Fax: 262-654-4737.
www.armitageacademy.org   E-mail: armitage@armitageacademy.org
Rose Parquette, Head (2009). Nadia Dreger, Adm.

Pre-Prep. Gen Acad. Feat—Fr Ger Computers Studio_Art Drama Chorus. Supp—Dev_ Read Tut. Somewhat selective adm: 10/yr. Appl fee: $50. Appl due: Rolling. Accepted: 90%. Yield: 99%. Enr 71. B 35. G 36. Wh 81%. Latino 1%. Blk 4%. Asian 3%. Other 11%. Avg class size: 16. Uniform. Fac 13. M 2/F 11. FT 11/PT 2. Wh 100%. Adv deg: 69%. Grad '10—8. Prep—5. Tui '11-'12: Day $6695-8000 (+$1080-1150). Aid: Need 35 ($380,000). Est 1975. Nonprofit. Quar (Sept-June). Armitage offers a liberal arts curriculum emphasizing a strong foundation in the basic learning skills. Cultural enrichment programs in the fine arts include music, art and drama classes. Computer literacy training and French instruction begin in kindergarten.

LAKESIDE LUTHERAN HIGH SCHOOL Day Coed Gr 9-12
Lake Mills, WI 53551. 231 Woodland Beach Rd.
Tel: 920-648-2321. Fax: 920-648-5625.
www.llhs.org   E-mail: info@llhs.org
James C. Grasby, Prin. BSE, Dr Martin Luther College, MCM, Concordia Univ Wisconsin, MAR, Wisconsin Lutheran Seminary, MAE, Marian College of Fond du Lac. Steve Lauber, Adm.

Col Prep. Gen Acad. AP—Eng Calc. Feat—British_Lit Ger Lat Span Anat & Physiol Environ_Sci Programming Econ Psych Sociol Relig Studio_Art Band Chorus Indus_Arts. Supp—Dev_Read Rem_Math Rem_Read Tut. Sports—Basket X-country Soccer Track. B: Baseball Football Wrestling. G: Golf Softball Volley. Activities: 26. Somewhat selective adm: 150/yr. Appl due: Aug. Enr 424. B 216. G 208. Avg class size: 25. Stud/fac: 14:1. Fac 34. Grad '10—93. Col—81. Avg ACT: 24.5. Tui '11-'12: Day $9025 (+$390-675). Assoc Members $5300-8500 (+$390-675). Est 1958. Nonprofit. Lutheran. Quar (Aug-May). Serving families from communities throughout south-central Wisconsin, Lakeside offers a religiously centered program that readies students primarily for four-year colleges, and, to a lesser degree, for technological studies, employment or the military. Business, foreign language, computer, industrial arts and home economics electives complement required courses in English, math, science, social studies, religion and music.

EDGEWOOD HIGH SCHOOL Day Coed Gr 9-12
Madison, WI 53711. 2219 Monroe St.
Tel: 608-257-1023. Fax: 608-257-9133.
www.edgewoodhs.org   E-mail: kotzaly@edgewood.k12.wi.us
Judd T. Schemmel, Pres. BA, JD, Marquette Univ. Robert D. Growney, Prin. BA, Loras College, MA, Edgewood College. Alyssa Kotzian, Adm.

Col Prep. AP (exams req'd; 246 taken, 75% 3+)—Eng Fr Lat Span Calc Bio Chem Environ_Sci Physics Eur_Hist US_Hist. Feat—British_Lit Creative_Writing Anat & Physiol Astron Comp_Sci Web_Design Econ Law Psych World_Relig Architect_Drawing Ceramics Drawing Painting Photog Sculpt Acting Theater_Arts Band Chorus Orchestra Handbells Dance Bus Public_Speak Aviation. Supp—Dev_Read LD Makeup Rev Tut. Dual enr: Edgewood, U of WI-Madison. Sports—Basket X-country Golf Ski Soccer Swim Tennis Track. B: Baseball Football Ice_Hockey. G: Softball Volley. Activities: 25. Somewhat selective adm: 201/yr. Appl fee: $30. Appl due: Dec. Accepted: 98%. Yield: 94%. Tests TOEFL. Enr 650. Nonwhite 14%. Avg class size: 19. Stud/fac: 12:1. Fac 58. FT 39/PT 19. Adv deg: 67%. Grad '10—150. Col—146. Avg ACT: 25. Alum donors: 12%. Tui '12-'13: Day $9980 (+$0-333). Aid: Need 266 ($591,083). Est 1881. Nonprofit. Roman Catholic. Quar (Aug-May). Assoc NCA. Operated by the Dominican Sisters of Sinsinawa, this school bases instruction on Christian values. A summer environmental science course is available. Students may take courses at Edgewood

College and the University of Wisconsin. Boys and girls satisfy a 100-hour community service requirement prior to graduation.

MARQUETTE UNIVERSITY HIGH SCHOOL   **Day Boys Gr 9-12**
Milwaukee, WI 53208. 3401 W Wisconsin Ave.
Tel: 414-933-7220, 800-831-6847. Fax: 414-937-8588.
www.muhs.edu   E-mail: admissions@muhs.edu
   Rev. Warren Sazama, SJ, Pres. BA, MA, St Louis Univ, MA, San Francisco Theological Seminary, MDiv, Jesuit School of Theology at Berkeley. Jeff Monday, Prin. BS, Creighton Univ, MEd, Marquette Univ. Sean O'Brien, Adm.
   Col Prep. AP (exams req'd; 481 taken, 86% 3+)—Eng Lat Span Calc Stats Comp_Sci Bio Chem Eur_Hist US_Hist Econ Studio_Art. **Feat**—Creative_Writing Poetry Shakespeare Irish_Lit Sci_Fiction Ger Geol Middle_Eastern_Hist Govt Intl_Relations Law Psych Sociol Philos Theol Architect_Drawing Ceramics Painting Photog Sculpt Theater Chorus. **Supp**— Rev Tut. **Sports**— B: Baseball Basket X-country Football Golf Ice_Hockey Ski Soccer Swim Tennis Track Volley Wrestling. Activities: 45. **Selective adm (Gr 9-10):** 274/yr. Appl fee: $25. Appl due: Nov. **Tests** HSPT. **Enr 1064.** Wh 80%. Latino 8%. Blk 6%. Asian 3%. Other 3%. Avg class size: 21. Stud/fac: 13:1. **Fac 86.** Adv deg: 77%. **Grad '11—251.** Col—251. (U of WI-Madison 58, Marquette 37, U of WI-Milwaukee 30, St Louis U 8, U of WI-La Crosse 8, Boston Col 7). **Mid 50% SAT:** CR 540-650. M 560-680. Avg ACT: 27.7. **Col Couns:** 1. Alum donors: 21%. **Tui '11-'12:** Day $10,235 (+$300-500). Aid: Need 295 ($1,400,000). **Est 1857.** Nonprofit. Roman Catholic (84% practice). Sem (Aug-May). **Assoc** NCA. In the Jesuit tradition, MUHS emphasizes a comprehensive study of the liberal arts and a commitment to social responsibility. An honors program is available, and both accelerated courses and the AP program provide college-credit options. Student service is required of all sophomores, juniors and seniors: 24 hours in grade 10, 65 hours in grade 11 and 80 hours in grade 12.

MILWAUKEE LUTHERAN HIGH SCHOOL   **Day Coed Gr 9-12**
Milwaukee, WI 53222. 9700 W Grantosa Dr.
Tel: 414-461-6000. Fax: 414-461-2733.
www.milwaukeelutheranhs.org   E-mail: mpankow@milwaukeelutheranhs.org
   Matthew D. Pankow, Prin (2011). Paul Gnan, Adm.
   Col Prep. Gen Acad. Bus. AP (125 exams taken, 68% 3+)—Eng Span Calc Physics US_Hist World_Hist. **Feat**—Ger Lat Stats Anat & Physiol Forensic_Sci Comp_Sci Robotics Web_Design Econ Govt Psych Relig Ceramics Photog Studio_Art Music Accounting Bus Speech Indus_Arts. **Supp**—LD Makeup Rem_Math Rem_Read Tut. **Comp:** Comp/Stud: 1:5. **Sports**—Basket X-country Golf Soccer Swim Tennis Track. B: Baseball Football Wrestling. G: Softball Volley. Activities: 15. **Selective adm:** 140/yr. Appl fee: $200. Appl due: Jan. **Enr 622.** B 295. G 327. Wh 46%. Latino 3%. Blk 44%. Asian 1%. Other 6%. Avg class size: 24. Stud/fac: 17:1. **Fac 38.** M 26/F 12. FT 36/PT 2. Wh 98%. Latino 1%. Blk 1%. Adv deg: 55%. **Grad '11—175.** Col—158. (U of WI-Milwaukee 34, Concordia U Chicago 13, Concordia U WI 9, U of WI-Oshkosh 8, U of WI-Whitewater 7). Avg ACT: 20.8. **Col Couns:** 4. **Tui '11-'12:** Day $9449 (+$500). Assoc Members $7349 (+$500). Aid: Merit 19 ($12,600). Need 82 ($150,000). **Est 1903.** Nonprofit. Lutheran-Missouri Synod (42% practice). Sem (Aug-May). **Assoc** NCA. Milwaukee Lutheran offers four basic courses of study—college preparatory, preministerial, business education and general education—in addition to a special-needs program for at-risk students. Spiritual life consists of regular chapel and prayer services, Bible study and a weekend retreat for seniors.

PIUS XI HIGH SCHOOL   **Day Coed Gr 9-12**
Milwaukee, WI 53213. 135 N 76th St.
Tel: 414-290-7000, 800-516-9974. Fax: 414-290-7001.
www.piusxi.org   E-mail: cwinfrey@piusxi.org

Melinda Skrade, Admin (2006). MA, PhD, Marquette Univ. Nathan Sheets, Adm.

Col Prep. Gen Acad. AP—Eng Span Calc Bio Environ_Sci Physics US_Hist World_Hist Econ Psych Studio_Art Music_Theory. **Feat**—Fr Forensic_Sci Genetics Oceanog Theol Bus Debate. **Supp**—Dev_Read ESL Rem_Math Rem_Read Tut. **Sports**—Basket X-country Golf Ski Soccer Swim Tennis Track Volley. B: Baseball Football Ice_Hockey Wrestling. G: Cheer Softball. Activities: 36. **Somewhat selective adm:** 250/yr. Appl fee: $25. Appl due: Jan. Accepted: 98%. **Enr 992.** Avg class size: 20. Stud/fac: 15:1. **Fac 87.** M 39/F 48. FT 87. Adv deg: 45%. **Grad '08—313.** Col—279. **Avg SAT:** CR 575. M 570. Avg ACT: 24. Alum donors: 4%. **Tui '11-'12:** Day $9150 (+$450). **Est 1929.** Nonprofit. Roman Catholic (75% practice). Sem (Aug-June). **Assoc** NCA. Pius' college preparatory curriculum enables students to focus on specific subjects beyond their basic academic and religious requirements. In-depth courses are offered in literature, world languages, science, mathematics, social science, business education, engineering, and the creative and performing arts.

ST. LAWRENCE SEMINARY HIGH SCHOOL   Bdg Boys Gr 9-12
Mount Calvary, WI 53057. 301 Church St.
Tel: 920-753-7570. Fax: 920-753-7507.
www.stlawrence.edu   E-mail: admissions@stlawrence.edu
Rev. Dennis Druggan, Pres. BA, Univ of Detroit, MDiv, Catholic Theological Union, MA, Boston College. Dave Bartel, Adm.

Col Prep. Feat—Humanities Ger Lat Span Calc Stats Comp_Sci Econ Psych Theol World_Relig Studio_Art Band Chorus Music_Theory Accounting Woodworking. **Supp**—Tut. **Comp:** Comp/Stud: 1:2. **Dual enr:** Marian U. **Sports**— B: Baseball Basket X-country Soccer Tennis Track Wrestling. Activities: 15. **Selective adm (Gr 9-11):** 80/yr. Appl fee: $50. Appl due: Rolling. Accepted: 94%. Yield: 97%. **Enr 196.** Wh 28%. Latino 33%. Blk 5%. Native Am 1%. Asian 29%. Other 4%. Intl 15%. Avg class size: 12. Stud/fac: 9:1. Casual dress. **Fac 24.** M 20/F 4. FT 23/PT 1. Wh 96%. Latino 4%. Adv deg: 54%. In Dorms 2. **Grad '11—47.** Col—46. **Avg SAT:** CR 550. M 600. W 540. Avg ACT: 23.7. **Tui '12-'13:** Bdg $10,300 (+$1500). **Est 1860.** Nonprofit. Roman Catholic (100% practice). Quar (Aug-May). **Assoc** NCA. Founded by the Capuchin Franciscans, SLS prepares Catholic boys academically and spiritually and for a life in the Church as laymen, deacons, brothers or priests. College preparation is paramount, and the school conducts a program of advanced study with Marian University that provides dual-credit opportunities in literary genres, modern world literature, calculus, chemistry and US history. Boys satisfy the following community service requirements: five hours freshmen year; 10 hours sophomore year, including at least one off-campus project; 20 hours junior year, at least half of which must be performed off campus; 30 hours senior year, at least half of which take place off campus.

PRAIRIE HILL WALDORF SCHOOL   Day Coed Gr PS (Age 2)-8
Pewaukee, WI 53072. N14 W29143 Silvernail Rd.
Tel: 262-646-7497. Fax: 262-646-7495.
www.prairiehillwaldorf.org   E-mail: info@prairiehillwaldorf.org
Anita Rodriguez, Admin (2009). Maia Wilson, Adm.

Pre-Prep. Gen Acad. Waldorf. Feat—Span Studio_Art Drama Music Woodworking. **Supp**—Rem_Math Rem_Read Tut. **Sports**—Basket Track. G: Volley. **Nonselective adm (Gr PS-7):** 34/yr. Appl fee: $50. Appl due: Rolling. Accepted: 100%. Yield: 98%. **Enr 160.** B 87. G 73. Wh 90%. Latino 5%. Blk 1%. Asian 4%. Avg class size: 15. **Fac 19.** M 2/F 17. FT 11/ PT 8. Wh 100%. **Grad '11—10.** Prep—4. (Chicago Waldorf 2, U Lake 1). **Tui '12-'13:** Day $8850 (+$325-375). Aid: Need 34 ($153,000). **Est 1987.** Nonprofit. Sem (Aug-May). **Assoc** NCA. Part of the worldwide network of Waldorf schools, Prairie Hill operates early childhood programs and a full elementary-level program. Instruction in French and German begins in grade 1. The integrated curriculum incorporates vocal and instrumental music increasingly as students age. Handwork, a characteristic of Waldorf education, serves as an important instructional tool.

DOMINICAN HIGH SCHOOL   **Day Coed Gr 9-12**
Whitefish Bay, WI 53217. 120 E Silver Spring Dr.
Tel: 414-332-1170. Fax: 414-332-4101.
www.dominicanhighschool.com   E-mail: abelongea@dominicanhighschool.com
   Colleen K. Brady, Head (2010). BA, Carroll College, MA, Univ of Wisconsin-Milwaukee.
Jonathan Friday, Adm.
   Col Prep. AP—Eng Calc Stats Comp_Sci Bio Eur_Hist US_Hist. **Feat**—Fr Span Ecol
Econ Law Psych Relig Ceramics Drawing Film Painting Photog Studio_Art Stained_Glass
Acting Theater_Arts Band Chorus Music_Theory Journ. **Supp**—Rev Tut. **Dual enr:** Mt Mary
Col. **Sports**—Basket X-country Golf Soccer Track Volley. B: Baseball Football Ice_Hockey
Wrestling. G: Softball Tennis. **Selective adm (Gr 9-11):** 126/yr. Appl fee: $25. Appl due:
Rolling. Accepted: 65%. Yield: 75%. **Tests** HSPT. **Enr 278.** Nonwhite 40%. Avg class size: 15.
Stud/fac: 13:1. Casual dress. **Fac 33.** M 13/F 20. FT 32/PT 1. Adv deg: 60%. **Grad '07—84.**
Col—82. (U of WI-Madison 13, U of WI-Milwaukee 10, Marquette 8, Cardinal Stritch 2,
Loyola U of Chicago 2, U of WI-Green Bay 2). Avg ACT: 23.4. **Col Couns:** 2. **Tui '11-
'12:** Day $10,200 (+$0-100). Aid: Merit 10 ($10,000). Need ($500,000). **Est 1956.** Nonprofit.
Roman Catholic. Sem (Aug-May). **Assoc** NCA. Sponsored by the Sinsinawa Dominican Sisters, the school emphasizes college preparation and provides opportunities for acceleration
in English, math and science. Students also have various options in religion, social studies,
foreign languages, the fine arts, computer science, communications, business and physical
education. Calculus course work leads to direct college credit at nearby Mount Mary College.

Plains States

IOWA

MAHARISHI SCHOOL OF THE　　　　　　　Day Coed Gr PS (Age 2)-12
AGE OF ENLIGHTENMENT　　　　　　　　(Coord Gr PS (Age 2)-12)
Fairfield, IA 52556. 804 Dr Robert Keith Wallace Dr.
Tel: 641-472-9400, 866-472-6723. Fax: 641-472-1211.
www.maharishischooliowa.org　E-mail: admissions@msae.edu
　Richard Beall, Head (2008). PhD, Maharishi Univ of Management. Jane Deans, Adm.

　Col Prep. Feat—Span Sanskrit Ceramics Photog Studio_Art Drama Music Speech.
Supp—Dev_Read ESL LD Rem_Math Rem_Read Tut. Sat classes. **Comp:** Comp/Stud:
1:1.7. **Sports**—Basket Tennis Track. B: Golf Soccer. G: Cheer Volley. Activities: 11. **Selective
adm:** 46/yr. Appl due: Rolling. Accepted: 75%. Yield: 61%. **Tests** TOEFL. **Enr 212.** B 118. G
94. Elem 127. Sec 85. Nonwhite 29%. Intl 18%. Avg class size: 11. Uniform. **Fac 48.** M 18/F
30. FT 20/PT 28. Wh 89%. Latino 2%. Blk 2%. Asian 7%. Adv deg: 39%. **Grad '11—20.**
Col—19. (Maharishi U 3, DePaul 2, U of IA 2, U of CA-Berkeley 1, Georgetown 1, Bennington 1). **Avg SAT:** CR 587. M 618. W 585. Avg ACT: 28. **Col Couns:** 1. **Tui '11-'12:** Day
$8700-12,500. **Est 1973.** Nonprofit. Quar (Aug-June). Maharishi School employs hands-on
experiments, projects, field trips and workshops as part of the learning process. The school's
early childhood program seeks to build a foundation for future learning, and older pupils practice meditation each day to assist in academic achievement. At every grade level, all classes
are single gender. Students in grades 10-12 perform 10 hours of required community service
annually. A small boarding program places international and nonlocal boys and girls in grades
9-12 with host families.

DOWLING HIGH SCHOOL　　　　　　　　　　　Day Coed Gr 9-12
West Des Moines, IA 50265. 1400 Buffalo Rd.
Tel: 515-225-3000. Fax: 515-222-1056.
www.dowlingcatholic.org　E-mail: teischei@dowlingcatholic.org
　Jerry M. Deegan, Pres. EdD, Drake Univ. James M. Dowdle, Prin. PhD. Tatia Eischeid,
Adm.

　Col Prep. Gen Acad. AP (145 exams taken, 78% 3+)—Eng Span Calc Comp_Sci Bio
Chem Physics Eur_Hist US_Hist US_Govt & Pol. **Feat**—British_Lit Creative_Writing Fr Ger
Stats Environ_Sci Physiol Engineering Econ Sociol World_Relig Ceramics Fine_Arts Photog
Sculpt Studio_Art Acting Music_Hist Music_Theory Accounting Journ Marketing Speech.
Supp—Dev_Read Rem_Math Rem_Read Tut. **Dual enr:** St Louis U. **Sports**—Basket X-
country Golf Soccer Swim Tennis Track. B: Baseball Football Wrestling. G: Cheer Softball
Volley. **Somewhat selective adm (Gr 9-11):** 387/yr. Appl due: June. Accepted: 99%. **Enr
1150.** B 588. G 562. Nonwhite 13%. Avg class size: 20. Stud/fac: 17:1. Uniform. **Fac 85.**
Adv deg: 52%. **Grad '11—313.** Col—311. **Avg SAT:** CR/M 1166. Avg ACT: 25. **Col Couns:**
1. **Tui '12-'13:** Day $8676 (+$120). Catholic $6526 (+$120). Aid: Need 518 ($1,000,000).
Est 1972. Nonprofit. Roman Catholic (95% practice). Sem (Aug-May). Advanced Placement
courses are provided, and courses in vocational/technical subjects are available to juniors and
seniors through the Des Moines public schools. Each semester, all students are required to take
religion and to perform 10 hours of community service.

KANSAS

MAUR HILL-MOUNT ACADEMY   **Bdg Coed Gr 7-12**
Atchison, KS 66002. 1000 Green St.   **Day Coed 9-12**
Tel: 913-367-5482. Fax: 913-367-5096.
www.mh-ma.com   E-mail: admissions@mh-ma.com
    Phil Baniewicz, Pres (2010). Monika King, Prin. Deke Nolan, Adm.

    Col Prep. Feat—Span Anat & Physiol Comp_Sci Psych Relig Fine_Arts Drama Journ. **Supp**—ESL Tut. **Comp:** Comp/Stud: 1:3. **Dual enr:** Benedictine Col. **Sports**—Basket Bowl X-country Golf Soccer Tennis Track. B: Baseball Football Wrestling. G: Cheer Softball Swim Volley. Activities: 29. **Somewhat selective adm (Bdg Gr 7-11; Day 9-12):** 75/yr. Appl fee: $50. Appl due: Rolling. Accepted: 85%. **Tests** HSPT TOEFL. **Enr 190.** B 98. G 92. Bdg 80. Day 110. Wh 58%. Latino 18%. Blk 1%. Native Am 1%. Asian 22%. Intl 33%. Avg class size: 18. Stud/fac: 9:1. Uniform. **Fac 20.** M 12/F 8. FT 19/PT 1. Adv deg: 55%. In Dorms 2. **Grad '11—50.** Col—49. **Col Couns:** 1. **Tui '12-'13:** Bdg $20,500 (+$500). 5-Day Bdg $18,900 (+$500). Day $4975 (+$500). Parishioners $4575 (+$500). Intl Bdg $27,150 (+$500). **Est 1863.** Nonprofit. Roman Catholic (60% practice). Sem (Aug-May). **Assoc** NCA. This Benedictine boarding and day school assumed its present name upon the 2003 merger of Maur Hill Preparatory School, a boys' school founded in 1919 by the monks of St. Benedict's Abbey, and Mount St. Scholastica Academy, a girls' school established in 1863 by the Benedictine Sisters. The college preparatory curriculum combines grade-level requirements with various electives. Spiritual activities form an integral component of school life: MH-MA conducts a schoolwide Mass at least once a month, and each class embarks on an annual retreat. Students in grades 9-12 satisfy a 20-hour community service requirement each year.

THOMAS MORE PREP—MARIAN HIGH SCHOOL   **Bdg Coed Gr 9-12**
Hays, KS 67601. 1701 Hall St.   **Day Coed 7-12**
Tel: 785-625-6577. Fax: 785-625-3912.
www.tmp-m.org   E-mail: fairbankm@tmp-m.org
    Bill DeWitt, Prin (2009). BA, MS, Univ of Kansas. Michelle Fairbank, Adm.

    Col Prep. AP—Eng Chem Physics. **Feat**—Humanities Ger Japan Lat Span Calc Stats Anat & Physiol Ecol Electronics Comp_Sci Econ Govt Psych Sociol Relig Architect Art_ Hist Ceramics Drawing Fine_Arts Painting Photog Sculpt Studio_Art Drama Band Chorus Accounting Bus Debate Speech Study_Skills. **Supp**—Dev_Read ESL. **Sports**—Basket X-country Soccer Swim Track. B: Baseball Football Golf Wrestling. G: Softball Volley. Activities: 11. **Somewhat selective adm:** 80/yr. Bdg 22. Day 58. Appl fee: $35-100. Appl due: Rolling. Accepted: 99%. **Tests** TOEFL. **Enr 240.** Bdg 62. Day 178. Intl 15%. Avg class size: 15. Stud/fac: 11:1. Uniform. **Fac 28.** Adv deg: 60%. **Grad '10—52.** Col—51. **Avg SAT:** CR 410. M 653. W 448. Avg ACT: 23. **Col Couns:** 1. **Tui '12-'13:** Bdg $22,750 (+$0-100). Day $9500. Intl Bdg $26,400 (+$0-100). **Est 1908.** Nonprofit. Roman Catholic. Quar (Aug-May). **Assoc** NCA. Advanced Placement, fine and performing arts, and business courses are all aspects of the school's curriculum. A small boarding division primarily serves international students from such countries as South Korea, Mexico, Taiwan, China and Nepal.

HYMAN BRAND HEBREW ACADEMY   **Day Coed Gr K-12**
Overland Park, KS 66211. 5801 W 115th St.
Tel: 913-327-8150. Fax: 913-327-8180.
www.hbha.edu   E-mail: information@hbha.edu
    Howard Haas, Head (2007). BS, Univ of Wisconsin-Milwaukee, MA, Pepperdine Univ. Tamara Lawson Schuster, Adm.

    Col Prep. AP (exams req'd; 9 taken, 89% 3+)—Eng Calc Stats US_Hist US_Govt & Pol. **Feat**—Hebrew Anat & Physiol Comp_Sci Econ Judaic_Stud Relig Drama Music. **Supp**—Tut.

Dual enr: Johnson County CC. **Sports**—Basket X-country Soccer Tennis. **Somewhat selective adm (Gr K-11):** 48/yr. Appl fee: $50. Appl due: Rolling. **Enr 241.** Elem 193. Sec 48. Wh 93%. Latino 2%. Blk 4%. Asian 1%. Avg class size: 15. Stud/fac: 7:1. Formal dress. **Fac 41.** M 9/F 32. FT 29/PT 12. Nonwhite 8%. Adv deg: 63%. **Grad '11—12.** Col—12. (U of KS 3, Johnson County CC 3, Tulane 1, Geo Wash 1, Yeshiva-NY 1, Clark U 1). **Tui '11-'12:** Day $6800 (+$175-600). **Est 1966.** Nonprofit. Jewish. Quar (Aug-May). HBHA's college preparatory program combines Jewish, Hebrew and secular studies within a Jewish environment. The weeklong winterim program enables middle school and high school students to choose from an array of electives not part of the regular curriculum. All high schoolers fulfill community service requirements: 10 hours during freshman year, 15 hours sophomore year, 20 hours junior year and 25 hours senior year.

TOPEKA COLLEGIATE SCHOOL   Day Coed Gr PS (Age 3)-8
Topeka, KS 66614. 2200 SW Eveningside Dr.
Tel: 785-228-0490. Fax: 785-228-0504.
www.topekacollegiate.org   E-mail: lkehres@topekacollegiate.org
    Mary Beth Marchiony, Head (2011). BA, Iona College, MA, Univ of Missouri-Kansas City. Linda Kehres, Adm.

    Gen Acad. Feat—Lat Span Computers Studio_Art. **Supp**—Dev_Read Rem_Math Rem_Read Tut. **Sports**—Basket Soccer Track Volley. **Somewhat selective adm:** 34/yr. Appl fee: $75. Appl due: Rolling. Accepted: 90%. **Tests** MAT. **Enr 212.** B 107. G 105. Wh 66%. Latino 2%. Blk 4%. Native Am 1%. Asian 11%. Other 16%. Avg class size: 15. Stud/fac: 15:1. Casual dress. **Fac 27.** M 5/F 22. FT 21/PT 6. Wh 98%. Latino 2%. Adv deg: 62%. **Grad '11—16.** Prep—3. (Bishop O'Dowd 1, Bishop Seabury 1, Laurel Springs 1). Alum donors: 3%. **Tui '11-'12:** Day $8175-9275 (+$85-195). Aid: Need 78 ($282,496). **Est 1982.** Nonprofit. Quar (Aug-May). **Assoc** NCA. Basic skills development takes place in the lower grades. TCS offers accelerated math and science classes in grades 5-8, in addition to physical education, music, art and computer courses. Spanish instruction begins in prekindergarten, Latin in grade 7.

THE INDEPENDENT SCHOOL   Day Coed Gr PS (Age 4)-12
Wichita, KS 67207. 8317 E Douglas Ave.
Tel: 316-686-0152. Fax: 316-686-3918.
www.theindependentschool.com   E-mail: danielle.dankey@theindependentschool.com
    Mary Dickerson, Head (2010). BME, Univ of Kansas, MEd, Lesley College, EdM, Harvard Univ, PhD, Boston College. Danielle Dankey, Adm.

    Col Prep. AP (153 exams taken, 78% 3+)—Eng Calc Stats Bio Chem Physics US_Hist Psych US_Govt & Pol Music_Theory. **Feat**—Creative_Writing Humanities Lib_Skills Lat Span Anat & Physiol Astron Environ_Sci Engineering Health_Sci Comp_Sci Econ Law Drawing Photog Studio_Art Drama Theater_Arts Music Dance Debate Journ. **Supp**—Rev Tut. **Comp:** Comp/Stud: 1:5. **Sports**—Basket X-country Soccer Swim Tennis Track. B: Baseball Football Golf Wrestling. G: Cheer Softball Volley. Activities: 12. **Somewhat selective adm:** 115/yr. Appl fee: $40. Appl due: Rolling. Accepted: 90%. Yield: 85%. **Tests** IQ Stanford. **Enr 550.** Elem 336. Sec 214. Avg class size: 15. Stud/fac: 9:1. **Fac 61.** M 19/F 42. FT 57/PT 4. Adv deg: 47%. **Grad '10—51.** Col—49. (U of KS 15, KS St 7, Creighton 3, Wichita St 3, Butler CC 2). **Avg SAT:** CR/M 1264. Avg ACT: 26. **Tui '12-'13:** Day $8200-10,400 (+$300-525). Aid: Need 127. **Est 1980.** Nonprofit. Sem (Aug-May). Located in the eastern section of the city, the school conducts a full elementary and secondary curriculum that emphasizes a strong foundation in basic skills, problem-solving and critical-thinking abilities, and study skills development. The arts are integral to school life, and Independent features notable computer and library programs. Students in grades 9-12 accumulate 50 hours of compulsory community service.

MINNESOTA

MARANATHA CHRISTIAN ACADEMY   Day Coed Gr PS (Age 3)-12
Brooklyn Park, MN 55428. 9201 75th Ave N.
Tel: 763-488-7900. Fax: 763-315-7294.
www.maranathachristianacademy.org   E-mail: info@mca.lwcc.org
    Brian J. Sullivan, Admin. BA, Hamline Univ. Jane Wallen, Adm.

    Col Prep. Gen Acad. AP (exams req'd)—Eng Calc Bio US_Hist. **Feat**—Span Stats
Astron Oceanog Meteorology Programming Robotics Econ Psych Bible World_Relig Ceram-
ics Drawing Painting Sculpt Studio_Art Acting Theater Chorus Accounting Journ. **Supp**—
Makeup Tut. **Comp:** Comp/Stud: 1:4. **Sports**—Basket X-country Soccer Track. B: Baseball
Golf. G: Cheer Softball Volley. Activities: 15. **Somewhat selective adm:** 87/yr. Appl fee:
$125. Appl due: Rolling. Accepted: 98%. **Tests** CEEB. **Enr 660.** Wh 73%. Latino 3%. Blk
14%. Asian 3%. Other 7%. Avg class size: 18. Stud/fac: 15:1. Uniform. **Fac 56.** M 8/F 48.
FT 47/PT 9. Adv deg: 35%. **Grad '09—49.** Col—42. **Avg SAT:** CR/M 1300. Avg ACT: 24.
Tui '12-'13: Day $7036-8580 (+$500). **Est 1978.** Nonprofit. Nondenom Christian (98% practice). Quar (Sept-June). **Assoc** NCA. A ministry of Living Word Christian Center, this nondenominational school provides a traditional prekindergarten through grade 12 program from
a Christian perspective. Notable aspects of MCA's curriculum are an emphasis on computer
technology and a variety of electives.

MARSHALL SCHOOL   Day Coed Gr 4-12
Duluth, MN 55811. 1215 Rice Lake Rd.
Tel: 218-727-7266. Fax: 218-727-1569.
www.marshallschool.org   E-mail: sperryspears@marshallschool.org
    Michael Ehrhardt, Head (2010). BA, St Olaf College, MA, Columbia Univ, MEd, Univ of
Massachusetts-Lowell, EdD, Univ of Minnesota-Twin Cities. Sarah Perry-Spears, Adm.

    Col Prep. AP—Eng Fr Ger Span Calc Bio Chem Physics US_Hist. **Feat**—Stats Anat &
Physiol Environ_Sci Zoology Comp_Design Econ Govt Law Sociol Relig Ceramics Draw-
ing Painting Photog Sculpt Studio_Art Drama Band Chorus Orchestra Speech. **Supp**—Tut.
Comp: Comp/Stud: 1:3. **Sports**—Basket X-country Golf Ice_Hockey Ski Soccer Tennis
Track. B: Baseball Football. G: Softball Volley. Activities: 40. **Selective adm:** 94/yr. Appl
fee: $50. Appl due: Feb. **Tests** CTP_4. **Enr 460.** Nonwhite 20%. Avg class size: 16. Stud/fac:
12:1. **Fac 45. Grad '11—64.** Col—64. **Avg SAT:** CR 622. M 665. W 641. Avg ACT: 26. **Col
Couns:** 1. **Tui '11-'12:** Day $12,500-13,900 (+$200). Aid: Need 184 ($1,300,000). **Est 1904.**
Nonprofit. Sem (Aug-June). **Assoc** NCA. Marshall provides a liberal arts education complete
with honors and AP courses. Foreign language, religion and fine arts courses are among the
graduation requirements. In addition, students complete requirements in community service
and outdoor education. Competitive sports teams are available beginning in grade 7.

BETHLEHEM ACADEMY   Day Coed Gr 7-12
Faribault, MN 55021. 105 3rd Ave SW.
Tel: 507-334-3948. Fax: 507-334-3949.
www.bacards.org   E-mail: cseidel@bacards.org
    Sherri Langfeldt, Pres. Celese Seidel, Adm.

    Col Prep. Gen Acad. Feat—Creative_Writing Span Calc Stats Anat & Physiol Ecol Econ
Psych Sociol Theol World_Relig Drawing Film Painting Studio_Art Theater_Arts Music
Woodworking. **Supp**—Tut. **Comp:** Comp/Stud: 1:1 Laptop prgm Gr 7-12. **Dual enr:** U of
MN-Twin Cities. **Sports**—Basket Golf Soccer Swim Track. B: Baseball Football Wrestling.
G: Softball Volley. **Selective adm:** Appl due: Rolling. **Enr 281.** Avg class size: 18. Stud/fac:
15:1. **Fac 22.** M 8/F 14. FT 15/PT 7. Adv deg: 31%. **Grad '08—48.** Col—48. Avg ACT: 21.4.
Mid 50% ACT: 18-25. **Tui '12-'13:** Day $6955 (+$750-850). Aid: Need 169 ($453,500). **Est**

'ootball Wrestling. G: Cheer Softball Swim Volley. Activities: 16. **Selective adm:** pl due: Feb. Accepted: 60%. Yield: 74%. **Tests** HSPT. **Enr 630.** B 308. G 322. Avg 23. Uniform. **Fac 47.** M 25/F 22. FT 44/PT 3. Adv deg: 82%. **Grad '04—127.** Avg ACT: 25. **Tui '12-'13:** Day $11,295 (+$300-750). Aid: Need ($2,000,000). Nonprofit. Roman Catholic. Sem (Aug-June). **Assoc** NCA. The first Catholic high the city, De La Salle requires students to take religion courses, engage in prayer is, take part in liturgies and fulfill a cumulative community service requirement of Students enroll not only from the Twin Cities, but also from approximately 30 area

)UNTRY SCHOOL   Day Coed Gr PS (Age 3)-9

lis, MN 55409. 3755 Pleasant Ave S.
27-3707. Fax: 612-827-1332.
:ountryschool.org   E-mail: admissions@lakecountryschool.org
e Zoe, Prin (2004). Lucinda Anderson, Adm.

ep. **Gen Acad. Montessori. Feat**—Humanities Fr Lat Philos Studio_Art Drama
•odworking. **Supp**—Dev_Read Rem_Math Rem_Read Rev Tut. **Very selective**
r. Appl fee: $75. Accepted: 12%. **Enr 300.** Avg class size: 27. **Fac 34. Grad '06—**
-13. **Tui '12-'13:** Day $12,140-15,330 (+$75). Aid: Need 61 ($294,752). **Est 1976.**
Sem (Sept-June). Founded to address the need for an urban Montessori school in
:ities, Lake Country emphasizes critical thinking and independent learning. Begin-
: 6, the course of studies incorporates overnight trips that provide boys and girls with
lucational experiences. The junior high curriculum (grades 7-9) follows a three-year
hich students focus attention on their own research and projects.

LUTHER HIGH SCHOOL   Day Coed Gr 9-12

MN 56075. 315 Martin Luther Dr, PO Box 228.
36-5249. Fax: 507-436-5240.
inlutherhs.com   E-mail: margethiesse@martinlutherhs.com
B. Patrick, Prin. BME, Valparaiso Univ, MM, Butler Univ, MS, Minnesota State
kato.

ep. **AP (exams req'd)**—Calc Comp_Sci. **Feat**—Span Relig Drama Band Chorus
iction. **Supp**—Rem_Math Rev Tut. **Comp:** Comp/Stud: 1:3.5. **Dual enr:** Concor-
•aul. **Sports**—Basket X-country Golf Ice_Hockey Soccer Track. B: Baseball Foot-
heer Softball Volley. **Nonselective adm:** 24/yr. Appl fee: $50. Appl due: Rolling.
100%. **Enr 71.** B 33. G 38. Avg class size: 16. Stud/fac: 9:1. Casual dress. **Fac 14.**
·T 6/PT 8. Wh 100%. Adv deg: 21%. **Grad '11—19.** Col—16. Avg ACT: 23.8. **Tui**
ay $5671 (+$225). Parishioners $4400 (+$225). Aid: Need 21. **Est 1983.** Nonprofit.
Missouri Synod. Quar (Aug-May). MLHS offers college preparatory course work in
bjects. English and social studies students may earn college credit for courses taken
oncordia University-St. Paul.

ENCE ACADEMY   Day Coed Gr PS (Age 4)-12

MN 55446. 15100 Schmidt Lake Rd.
.58-2500. Fax: 763-258-2501.
·idenceacademy.org   E-mail: info@providenceacademy.org
R. Flanders, Head (2000). BA, Univ of Chicago, MA, Truman State Univ, PhD,
illege. Sarah L. Hogan, Adm.

ep. **AP exams taken: 25 (60% 3+). Feat**—British_Lit Chin Fr Lat Span Engineer-
_Sci Robotics Econ Sociol Philos Relig Photog Studio_Art Theater Music Debate
tal_Shop Culinary_Arts. **Supp**—Tut. **Comp:** Comp/Stud: 1:7. **Sports**—Basket X-
olf Ice_Hockey Soccer Swim Tennis Track. B: Baseball Football. G: Softball Volley.
45. **Somewhat selective adm (Gr PS-11):** 132/yr. Appl fee: $100. Appl due: Jan.

1865. Nonprofit. Roman Catholic. Sem (Aug-May). **Assoc** NC/
compulsory theology course each year as part of the core acade
sion, qualified eighth graders may take algebra I and Spanish.

HILLCREST LUTHERAN ACADEMY
Fergus Falls, MN 56537. 610 Hillcrest Dr.
Tel: 218-739-3371. Fax: 218-739-3372.
www.ffhillcrest.org   E-mail: office@ffhillcrest.org
Rev. Steven J. Brue, Pres. BA, Bethel College, MS, Minne
MDiv, Lutheran Brethren Seminary, Prin. Jeffrey Isaac, Prin. BA,
State Univ-Fullerton.

Col Prep. AP (exams req'd)—Eng Calc Eur_Hist US_Hist
Programming Bible. **Supp**—ESL Rev Tut. **Sports**—Basket X-cou
ball Football. G: Softball Volley. **Nonselective adm:** 90/yr. Bdg 52
Appl due: Rolling. Accepted: 99%. **Tests** TOEFL. **Enr 197.** Elem
class size: 22. **Fac 16.** M 10/F 6. FT 12/PT 4. Wh 100%. Adv deg:
36. **Avg SAT:** CR/M 1185. Avg ACT: 24. **Col Couns:** 1. **Tui '12**
495). Day $3970-8125 (+$200-495). Intl Bdg $17,400 (+$200-
Lutheran. Sem (Aug-May). Hillcrest provides college preparation
ment. Private voice, piano, organ and instrumental lessons are part

MAYER LUTHERAN HIGH SCHOOL
Mayer, MN 55360. 305 5th St NE.
Tel: 952-657-2251. Fax: 952-657-2344.
www.lhsmayer.org   E-mail: info@lhsmayer.org
Joel P. Landskroener, Exec Dir (2006). BS, Concordia College (
land-College Park, MS, Johns Hopkins Univ. Kevin Wilaby, Prin
(NE), MA, Saginaw Valley State Univ.

Col Prep. AP—Eng US_Hist. **Feat**—British_Lit Creative_Writin
ron_Sci Comp_Sci Econ Psych Comp_Relig Ethics Ceramics Drawi
Art Drama Music_Theory Jazz_Hist Woodworking. **Dual enr:** Con
western Col-MN. **Sports**—Basket X-country Golf Track. B: Baseb
Wrestling. G: Gymnastics Soccer Softball Volley. **Somewhat selecti**
$100. Appl due: Feb. **Enr 252.** B 143. G 109. Avg class size: 16. S
13/F 9. FT 22. Adv deg: 31%. **Grad '09—44.** Col—40. (Bethel U
2, U of WI-River Falls 2, Mankato St 2, U of Sioux Falls 2). Avg A
60%. **Tui '11-'12:** Day $8900 (+$480-680). Assoc Members $7150-
Need ($170,000). **Est 1961.** Nonprofit. Lutheran-Missouri Synod. Se
students from roughly 50 communities within a 30-mile radius, May
college preparatory program within a Lutheran setting. Technology
element of the curriculum, and qualified pupils may pursue Advanced
in several disciplines. The flexible nature of the program allows the
student needs and interests through postsecondary opportunities, ind
and individualized programming.

DE LA SALLE HIGH SCHOOL
Minneapolis, MN 55401. 1 De La Salle Dr.
Tel: 612-676-7600. Fax: 612-362-9641.
www.delasalle.com   E-mail: mike.okeefe@delasalle.com
Barry C. Lieske, Int Pres (2011). Mike O'Keefe, Adm.

Col Prep. AP (exams req'd)—Eng Calc Eur_Hist US_Hist. **Feat-**
Ger Span Astron Forensic_Sci Web_Design WWII Anthro Econ Psyc
Theol Drawing Photog Chorus Bus. **Sports**—Basket X-country Golf Sc

Accepted: 93%. Yield: 90%. **Tests** SSAT. **Enr 910.** B 429. G 481. Avg class size: 19. Uniform. **Fac 75.** M 28/F 47. FT 73/PT 2. Adv deg: 58%. **Grad '11—62.** Col—62. (U of St Thomas-MN 8, Gustavus Adolphus 4, Benedictine Col 4, Boston Col 3, St Olaf 3). **Mid 50% SAT:** CR 530-650. M 550-670. W 550-660. Avg ACT: 27. Mid 50% ACT: 24-29. **Col Couns:** 1. **Tui '12-'13:** Day $12,455-15,855 (+$150-350). Aid: Need 265 ($1,505,000). **Est 2000.** Nonprofit. Roman Catholic (64% practice). Quar (Sept-June). **Assoc** NCA. Providence combines formal Catholic education with an instructional approach that emphasizes essential facts, skills and content across each grade level. Daily religion courses commence in grades pre-K-5 and are required through grade 12. The foreign language program includes twice-weekly Spanish in grades pre-K-2 and French in grades 3-5, daily Latin instruction in grades 6 and 7, and three years of required language study in the upper school. Electives address such areas as engineering, studio art, photography, music and culinary arts.

BENILDE-ST. MARGARET'S SCHOOL　　　　Day Coed Gr 7-12
St Louis Park, MN 55416. 2501 Hwy 100 S.
Tel: 952-927-4176. Fax: 952-920-8889.
www.bsmschool.org E-mail: admissions@bsmschool.org
　　Bob Tift, Pres (2002). BA, MA, Arizona State Univ, EdS, EdD, Univ of St Thomas (MN). Kate Leahy, Adm.
　　Col Prep. AP (325 exams taken)—Eng Fr Span Calc Stats Bio Eur_Hist US_Hist Comp_ Govt & Pol Econ US_Govt & Pol. **Feat**—British_Lit Creative_Writing Mythology Lat Astron Ecol Environ_Sci Engineering Comp_Sci Law Psych Theol World_Relig Ceramics Drawing Film Painting Photog Studio_Art Drama Chorus Music_Theory Accounting Debate Journ Marketing. **Comp:** Comp/Stud: 1:1 Laptop prgm Gr 7-12. **Sports**—Basket X-country Golf Ice_Hockey Lacrosse Ski Soccer Swim Tennis Track. B: Baseball Football Wrestling. G: Softball Volley. **Selective adm:** 218/yr. Appl fee: $0. Appl due: Jan. **Enr 1184.** Elem 264. Sec 920. Avg class size: 22. Stud/fac: 11:1. **Fac 104.** Adv deg: 66%. **Grad '11—222.** Col—215. **Avg SAT:** CR 590. M 596. W 598. Avg ACT: 25.7. **Tui '12-'13:** Day $10,350-12,000 (+$200-600). Aid: Need 199 ($1,300,000). **Est 1907.** Nonprofit. Roman Catholic (72% practice). Sem (Aug-June). **Assoc** NCA. Formed by the 1974 merger of St. Margaret's Academy, a girls' school founded in 1907 and operated by the Sisters of St. Joseph, and Benilde High School, a Catholic boys' school that was founded in 1956, Benilde-St. Margaret's enrolls students from Minneapolis and 20 suburban areas. Juniors take a career and college planning class as a graduation requirement. Among the school's special offerings are summer retreats and peer ministry, mission trips, study abroad opportunities, community tutoring programs, service learning and environmental programs.

GROVES ACADEMY　　　　Day Coed Gr 1-12
St Louis Park, MN 55416. 3200 Hwy 100 S.
Tel: 952-920-6377. Fax: 952-920-2068.
www.grovesacademy.org E-mail: info@grovesacademy.org
　　John Alexander, Head (2005). MEd, Harvard Univ. Teresa Smith, Upper & Middle Sch Adm; Debbie Moran, Lower Sch Adm.
　　Col Prep. Gen Acad. LD. Feat—Studio_Art Theater Music Health Home_Ec. **Supp**—Dev_Read Rem_Math Rem_Read Tut. **Comp:** Comp/Stud: 1:1 Laptop prgm Gr 7-12. Outdoor Ed. **Selective adm (Gr 1-11):** 55/yr. Appl fee: $75. Appl due: Rolling. Accepted: 68%. Yield: 87%. **Tests** IQ. **Enr 207.** B 128. G 79. Elem 139. Sec 68. Wh 79%. Latino 3%. Blk 6%. Native Am 1%. Asian 6%. Other 5%. Avg class size: 8. Stud/fac: 5:1. **Fac 48.** M 13/F 35. FT 44/PT 4. Wh 97%. Asian 3%. Adv deg: 39%. **Grad '10—15.** Col—15. **Col Couns:** 2. **Tui '12-'13:** Day $22,500-23,400. Aid: Need 75 ($812,000). **Est 1972.** Nonprofit. Sem (Aug-June). Groves offers diagnostic assessment and highly individualized programming for students with specific learning or language disabilities or attention deficit disorder. In addition to the day school, the academy conducts a summer program, tutoring, social skills groups and specialty workshops.

FRIENDS SCHOOL OF MINNESOTA   **Day Coed Gr K-8**
St Paul, MN 55104. 1365 Englewood Ave.
Tel: 651-917-0636. Fax: 651-917-0708.
www.fsmn.org   E-mail: admissions@fsmn.org
   Lili Herbert, Head (2006). BA, Boston Univ, MEd, Univ of Minnesota-Twin Cities. Susan A. Nagel, Adm.
   Pre-Prep. Gen Acad. Feat—Span Studio_Art Drama Music. **Selective adm:** 26/yr. Appl fee: $60. Accepted: 46%. Yield: 72%. **Enr 162.** Avg class size: 17. **Fac 14.** M 5/F 9. FT 14. **Grad '11—20. Tui '12-'13:** Day $12,560-13,755 (+$150-250). Aid: Need 50. **Est 1988.** Nonprofit. Religious Society of Friends. Sem (Sept-June). While providing no direct religious education, this elementary school adheres to the values of the Religious Society of Friends. Instructors employ a hands-on approach to learning, and children learn to gather information through different sources, then synthesize and apply what they have learned. The weekly Quaker Meeting is an important aspect of school life, as is a well-developed conflict resolution program that teaches children alternatives to violence.

SAINT AGNES SCHOOL   **Day Coed Gr K-12**
St Paul, MN 55103. 530 Lafond Ave.
Tel: 651-925-8700. Fax: 651-925-8708.
www.saintagnesschool.org   E-mail: jhoughton@saintagnesschool.org
   Rev. Mark Moriarty, Supt (2012). James Morehead, Prin. MA, Univ of St Thomas (MN). Jean Houghton, Adm.
   Col Prep. AP (exams req'd; 64 taken)—Eng Calc Bio Chem Eur_Hist US_Hist. **Feat**—Fr Lat Span Environ_Sci Comp_Sci Civics Econ Psych Relig Studio_Art Chorus Bus. **Supp**—Dev_Read LD Rem_Math Tut. **Comp:** Comp/Stud: 1:6. **Dual enr:** St Mary's U of MN. **Sports**—Basket Ice_Hockey Soccer Track. B: Baseball Football Golf. G: Cheer Softball Swim Volley. **Somewhat selective adm:** 85/yr. Appl fee: $100. Appl due: Rolling. Accepted: 94%. **Enr 516.** B 263. G 253. Elem 295. Sec 221. Wh 80%. Latino 3%. Blk 9%. Asian 8%. Avg class size: 13. Stud/fac: 13:1. Uniform. **Fac 52.** M 25/F 27. FT 46/PT 6. Wh 95%. Latino 1%. Blk 1%. Asian 1%. Other 2%. Adv deg: 21%. **Grad '11—51.** Col—54. **Tui '11-'12:** Day $3350-8700 (+$300). Aid: Merit 9 ($55,300). Need 113 ($433,117). **Est 1888.** Nonprofit. Roman Catholic (90% practice). Sem (Sept-June). **Assoc** NCA. Saint Agnes provides a traditional education, with religion being an integral part of the curriculum. Both honors and Advanced Placement courses are available. Students put on a spring musical each year.

COTTER SCHOOLS   **Bdg Coed Gr 9-12**
Winona, MN 55987. 1115 W Broadway.   **Day Coed 7-12**
Tel: 507-453-5000. Fax: 507-453-5006.
www.cotterschools.org   E-mail: admissions@cotterschools.org
   Jennifer Elfering, Pres (2010). MA, St Norbert College, MA, Ave Maria Univ. Sandra Blank, Prin. MA. Will Gibson, Adm.
   Col Prep. AP (exams req'd; 94 taken)—Eng Calc Chem Environ_Sci Physics US_Hist Econ US_Govt & Pol. **Feat**—Ger Span Linear_Algebra Comp_Sci Robotics Relig Video_Production. **Supp**—ESL Rem_Read Tut. **Comp:** Comp/Stud: 1:3. **Dual enr:** St Mary's U of MN. **Sports**—Basket X-country Golf Ice_Hockey Ski Soccer Swim Tennis Track. B: Baseball Football Wrestling. G: Gymnastics Softball Volley. Activities: 30. **Selective adm:** 86/yr. Bdg 35. Day 51. Appl fee: $35. Appl due: Rolling. Accepted: 75%. Yield: 65%. **Tests** CEEB TOEFL. **Enr 380.** Bdg 92. Day 288. Wh 70%. Latino 5%. Blk 2%. Asian 23%. Intl 28%. Avg class size: 20. Stud/fac: 11:1. **Fac 37.** M 16/F 21. FT 29/PT 8. Wh 94%. Asian 3%. Other 3%. Adv deg: 59%. In Dorms 2. **Grad '09—92.** Col—88. (Winona St 8, U of MN-Twin Cities 7, St Mary's U of MN 5, St John's U-MN 4, St Cloud St 4). Avg ACT: 23.5. **Col Couns:** 3. **Tui '12-'13:** Bdg $25,700. 5-Day Bdg $22,850. Day $6075. Intl Bdg $30,700. **Est 1911.** Nonprofit. Roman Catholic. Sem (Aug-June). **Assoc** NCA. Emphasizing a Catholic worldview, Cotter offers an academic program that follows a liberal arts approach and integrates the humani-

ties, math, science and the arts. The college preparatory curriculum features Advanced Placement and honors courses, a strong technology component and three college-credit programs. A learning center is available to students who require additional academic support. Boys and girls perform 20 hours of required community service annually.

NEW LIFE ACADEMY   Day Coed Gr PS (Age 3)-12
Woodbury, MN 55129. 6758 Bailey Rd.
Tel: 651-459-4121. Fax: 651-459-6194.
www.newlifeacademy.org   E-mail: info@newlifeacademy.org
    Cade M. Lambert, Head (2011). Velma Vigar, Adm.

    Col Prep. AP (109 exams taken, 55% 3+)—Eng Calc Stats Bio Chem Eur_Hist US_ Hist. **Feat**—British_Lit Shakespeare Sports_Lit Ger Span Anat & Physiol Civics Econ Psych Sociol Bible Sculpt Studio_Art Drama Band Chorus Journ Design. **Supp**—Dev_Read LD Tut. **Comp:** Comp/Stud: 1:2.5. **Dual enr:** Bethel U, U of MN-Twin Cities. **Sports**—Basket X-country Soccer Tennis Track. B: Baseball Football Golf. G: Cheer Softball Volley. Activities: 10. **Somewhat selective adm:** Appl fee: $100. Appl due: Rolling. Accepted: 94%. Yield: 95%. **Tests** Stanford TOEFL. **Enr 647.** B 320. G 327. Wh 90%. Latino 2%. Blk 2%. Asian 6%. Avg class size: 25. Uniform. **Fac 52.** M 12/F 40. FT 40/PT 12. Wh 98%. Latino 2%. Adv deg: 19%. **Grad '11**—69. Col—69. (Century 8, Bethel U 7, U of MN-Twin Cities 6, U of WI-River Falls 4, Northwestern Col-MN 3, U of WI-Madison 3). Avg ACT: 24.6. **Col Couns:** 2. Alum donors: 1%. **Tui '12-'13:** Day $7824-8640. Aid: Merit 17. **Est 1977.** Nonprofit. Nondenom Christian (100% practice). Quar (Sept-June). **Assoc** NCA. The curriculum at this nondenominational academy integrates a Christian worldview into all subject areas. Advanced Placement and honors courses provide students with opportunities for acceleration. Girls and boys satisfy the following community service requirements: class projects in grades 7 and 8, then at least five hours of service per semester in grades 9-12. Cocurricular activities allow students to pursue individual interests and develop aptitudes.

MISSOURI

CHESTERFIELD DAY SCHOOL   Day Coed Gr PS (Age 2)-6
Chesterfield, MO 63017. 1100 White Rd.
Tel: 314-469-6622. Fax: 314-469-7889.
www.chesterfielddayschool.org   E-mail: jbryzeal@chesterfielddayschool.org
    Matthew Virgil, Head (2011). BA, Vanderbilt Univ, MA, Columbia Univ, MEd, Harvard Univ. Alicia Noddings, Prin. BM, BS, Baylor Univ, MA, Concordia Univ, PhD, St Louis Univ. Julie Bryzeal, Adm.

    Pre-Prep. Montessori. Feat—Lib_Skills Span Computers Studio_Art Drama Music. **Somewhat selective adm:** 50/yr. Appl fee: $75. Appl due: Rolling. Accepted: 95%. Yield: 95%. **Tests** IQ. **Enr 190.** B 95. G 95. Nonwhite 33%. Avg class size: 12. **Fac 27.** M 4/F 23. FT 21/PT 6. Wh 89%. Blk 7%. Asian 4%. Adv deg: 62%. **Grad '11**—18. Prep—17. **Tui '12-'13:** Day $16,275 (+$500). **Est 1962.** Nonprofit. Sem (Aug-May). **Assoc** NCA. Chesterfield Day's toddler through grade 1 programs are Montessori based; traditional approaches prevail thereafter. The personalized educational program includes courses in science, Spanish, music, art and library skills, and computers are integrated into all subjects. Departmentalization begins in grade 4. Student participation in service activities and assistance with the maintenance of the community promotes personal responsibility and initiative.

OAKHILL DAY SCHOOL   **Day Coed Gr PS (Age 2)-8**
Gladstone, MO 64118. 7019 N Cherry St.
Tel: 816-436-6228. Fax: 816-436-0184.
www.oakhilldayschool.org   E-mail: office@oakhilldayschool.org
     Suzanne McCanles, Head. BA, William Jewell College, MEd, Univ of Missouri-Kansas City. Leah Gipe, Adm.
     Gen Acad. Feat—Span Computers Studio_Art Music. **Supp**—Tut. **Sports**—Basket X-country Soccer Track. G: F_Hockey. **Somewhat selective adm (Gr PS-7):** 72/yr. Appl fee: $25. Appl due: Rolling. Accepted: 98%. Yield: 100%. **Enr 295.** Wh 89%. Latino 1%. Blk 3%. Native Am 2%. Asian 3%. Other 2%. Avg class size: 16. **Fac 38.** M 2/F 36. FT 27/PT 11. **Grad '11—7.** Prep—1. (St Pius X-MO 1). **Tui '12-'13:** Day $9724-9823 (+$200). Aid: Need 35 ($65,225). **Est 1947.** Nonprofit. Quar (Aug-May). **Assoc** NCA. Oakhill Day's toddler through middle school programs are enhanced by special enrichment classes, individualized learning, environmental study opportunities and community-building activities. The summer program includes tutoring, sports, and classes in science and cooking.

ARCHBISHOP O'HARA HIGH SCHOOL   **Day Coed Gr 9-12**
Kansas City, MO 64138. 9001 James A Reed Rd.
Tel: 816-763-4800. Fax: 816-763-0156.
www.oharahs.org   E-mail: ajulich@oharahs.org
     John O'Connor, Prin (2011). Ann Julich, Adm.
     Col Prep. AP (100 exams taken)—Eng Calc Bio Chem Physics US_Hist US_Govt & Pol Studio_Art. **Feat**—Span Anat & Physiol Environ_Sci Programming Web_Design Holocaust Econ Law Psych Philos Theol Photog Drama Music_Theory Accounting Debate Journ. **Supp**—Rem_Math Rem_Read Tut. **Comp:** Laptop prgm Gr 9-12. **Dual enr:** U of MO-Kansas City, Rockhurst. **Sports**—Basket X-country Golf Soccer Swim Tennis Track. B: Baseball Football Wrestling. G: Softball Volley. Activities: 35. **Selective adm:** 100/yr. Appl fee: $0. Appl due: Rolling. **Enr 353.** B 207. G 146. Wh 67%. Latino 4%. Blk 23%. Asian 4%. Other 2%. Avg class size: 25. Stud/fac: 14:1. Uniform. **Fac 37.** Adv deg: 64%. **Grad '11—98.** Col—98. Avg ACT: 23. **Col Couns:** 2. **Tui '12-'13:** Day $7400 (+$600). Parishioners $7100 (+$300). **Est 1965.** Nonprofit. Roman Catholic (75% practice). Quar (Aug-June). **Assoc** NCA. Sponsored by the Christian Brothers, O'Hara provides a college preparatory curriculum that includes honors courses and a basic skills track. Advanced Placement courses are available in the major disciplines. Students perform 65 hours of community service over four years: 10 during freshman year, 15 sophomore year, 30 junior year and 10 senior year.

LUTHERAN HIGH SCHOOL   **Day Coed Gr 9-12**
Kansas City, MO 64145. 12411 Wornall Rd.
Tel: 816-241-5478. Fax: 816-876-2069.
www.lhskc.com   E-mail: lkettler@lhskc.com
     Karl Birnstein, Int Exec Dir (2012). BA, Concordia Teachers College, MA, California Lutheran Univ. Chris Domsch, Prin. BSEd, MA, Concordia Univ Nebraska. Paula Meier, Adm.
     Col Prep. Feat—Creative_Writing Ger Span Calc Anat & Physiol Govt Psych Sociol Comp_Relig Ceramics Drawing Film Photog Sculpt Studio_Art Band Chorus Handbells Journ. **Supp**—Rem_Math Tut. **Comp:** Comp/Stud: 1:4. **Dual enr:** U of Central MO, U of MO-Kansas City. **Sports**—Basket X-country Soccer Tennis Track. B: Baseball Golf. G: Cheer Volley. Activities: 4. **Nonselective adm:** 28/yr. Appl fee: $200-275. Appl due: Rolling. Accepted: 100%. Yield: 100%. **Tests** HSPT. **Enr 108.** B 41. G 67. Wh 80%. Latino 7%. Blk 6%. Asian 4%. Other 3%. Avg class size: 20. Stud/fac: 10:1. Uniform. **Fac 13.** M 5/F 8. FT 8/PT 5. Wh 84%. Latino 8%. Other 8%. Adv deg: 38%. **Grad '11—32.** Col—28. (U of Central MO 5, Concordia U NE 4, Metro CC 4, Truman St 2, Avila 2, U of MO-Columbia 2). Avg ACT: 25. **Col Couns:** 1. Alum donors: 10%. **Tui '11-'12:** Day $7300 (+$625). **Assoc** Members $6400-6850 (+$625). Aid: Need 31 ($59,000). **Est 1980.** Nonprofit. Lutheran-Missouri

Synod (73% practice). Sem (Aug-May). LHS' curriculum offers a performance-oriented fine arts program. Students accumulate 40 hours of required community service in grades 9-12. The school is located in a suburban residential area in the southern part of the city.

NOTRE DAME DE SION SCHOOL OF KANSAS CITY   **Day Boys Gr PS (Age 3)-8**
Kansas City, MO 64114. 10631 Wornall Rd.   **Girls PS (Age 3)-12**
Tel: 816-942-3282. Fax: 816-942-4052.
Other locations: 3823 Locust St, Kansas City 64109.
www.ndsion.edu
    Alice J. Munninghoff, Head. MA, Univ of Missouri-Kansas City. Sharon Radovich, HS Adm; Carla Maloney, Gr PS-8 Adm.
    Col Prep. Montessori. AP—Eng Fr Span Calc Chem Eur_Hist US_Hist Studio_Art. **Feat**—Creative_Writing Anat & Physiol Bioethics Environ_Sci Forensic_Sci Web_Design Holocaust Econ Psych Sociol Philos World_Relig Art_Hist Ceramics Drawing Painting Drama Chorus Debate Public_Speak. **Dual enr:** Rockhurst. **Sports**— G: Basket X-country F_Hockey Golf Soccer Softball Swim Tennis Track Volley. **Selective adm:** Appl fee: $50. Appl due: Feb. **Tests** HSPT. **Enr 754.** Elem 320. Sec 434. Avg class size: 18. Stud/fac: 12:1. Uniform. **Grad '08—107.** Col—107. **Tui '11-'12:** Day $10,240-10,690 (+$150-250). Aid: Need 269 ($450,000). **Est 1912.** Nonprofit. Roman Catholic (61% practice). Sem (Aug-May). **Assoc** NCA. This Catholic school's coeducational elementary program, which commences with a Montessori preschool, focuses on fundamental skills development. Emphasizing college preparation, the girls-only high school features dual-enrollment biology, psychology, French and Spanish courses through nearby Rockhurst University. High school girls perform 100 hours of required community service over four years, at least 40 of which are to be spent working directly with people who are disadvantaged or suffering. The elementary school occupies a separate campus on Locust Street.

ROCKHURST HIGH SCHOOL   **Day Boys Gr 9-12**
Kansas City, MO 64114. 9301 State Line Rd.
Tel: 816-363-2036. Fax: 816-363-3764.
www.rockhursths.edu   E-mail: jreichme@rockhursths.edu
    Rev. Terrence A. Baum, SJ, Pres (2003). BS, Xavier Univ (OH), MS, Fordham Univ, MDiv, Weston School of Theology. Gregory Harkness, Prin. BA, Georgia State Univ, MA, Manhattan College. Jack Reichmeier, Adm.
    Col Prep. AP (exams req'd; 419 taken, 79% 3+)—Eng Fr Lat Span Calc Stats Bio Chem Physics US_Hist World_Hist Comp_Govt & Pol US_Govt & Pol Studio_Art. **Feat**—Greek Environ_Sci Physiol Comp_Sci Econ Bus_Law Theol Architect Drawing Photog Acting Theater_Arts Chorus Orchestra Jazz_Band Journ Public_Speak. **Supp**—Rev Tut. **Comp:** Comp/Stud: 1:6. **Dual enr:** Rockhurst, U of MO-Kansas City. **Sports**— B: Baseball Basket X-country Football Golf Lacrosse Soccer Swim Tennis Track Wrestling. Activities: 3740. **Somewhat selective adm (Gr 9-11):** 316/yr. Appl fee: $15. Appl due: Dec. Accepted: 93%. Yield: 87%. **Tests** HSPT. **Enr 1089.** Wh 85%. Latino 4%. Blk 6%. Asian 1%. Other 4%. Avg class size: 25. Stud/fac: 17:1. Casual dress. **Fac 78.** M 68/F 10. FT 77/PT 1. Wh 95%. Latino 3%. Blk 1%. Other 1%. Adv deg: 74%. **Grad '11—253.** Col—252. (U of KS 46, U of MO-Columbia 36, KS St 24, St Louis U 15, Creighton 11, U of AR-Fayetteville 9). **Avg SAT:** CR 646. M 662. W 651. **Mid 50% SAT:** CR 550-680. M 560-690. W 530-680. Avg ACT: 27. **Col Couns:** 3. Alum donors: 19%. **Tui '11-'12:** Day $10,650 (+$700). Aid: Merit 23 ($22,000). Need 324 ($1,534,750). Work prgm 294 ($620,725). **Est 1910.** Nonprofit. Roman Catholic (77% practice). Sem (Aug-May). **Assoc** NCA. Sponsored by the Jesuits, Rockhurst provides a varied college preparatory program for students from Greater Kansas City. Qualified students may earn college credit. Boys perform 25 hours of compulsory annual service in grades 9-11, while seniors commit two and a half weeks to full-time service in January.

ST. PAUL'S EPISCOPAL DAY SCHOOL
Day Coed Gr PS (Age 2)-8

Kansas City, MO 64111. 4041 Main St.
Tel: 816-931-8614. Fax: 816-931-6860.
www.speds.org E-mail: mzavagnin@speds.org
  Elizabeth Barnes, Head (2004). BS, Southern Methodist Univ, MA, Southwest Texas State Univ. Miriam Zavagnin, Adm.

  Pre-Prep. Feat—Fr Span Computers Comp_Relig Studio_Art Music Speech. **Supp**—Tut. **Sports**—Basket Lacrosse Soccer Tennis Volley. **Selective adm:** 70/yr. Appl fee: $75. Appl due: Jan. **Enr 475.** Avg class size: 20. Stud/fac: 11:1. **Fac 60.** M 6/F 54. FT 40/PT 20. Wh 88%. Latino 5%. Blk 2%. Native Am 1%. Asian 2%. Other 2%. Adv deg: 36%. **Grad '06—40.** Prep—36. (Pembroke Hill 14, St Teresa's Acad 8, Rockhurst 6, Notre Dame de Sion 4, Barstow 3). **Tui '12-'13:** Day $10,340-11,049 (+$390-535). Aid: Need 45 ($260,000). **Est 1963.** Nonprofit. Episcopal (15% practice). Sem (Aug-May). **Assoc** NCA. Academic basics are supplemented by enrichment in computers, French, Spanish, music, art, speech, drama and physical education. Community service projects are an integral part of the program, and middle school students support the church food pantry and raise scholarship money for a sister school in Haiti. St. Paul's conducts a daily chapel service.

JOHN F. KENNEDY CATHOLIC HIGH SCHOOL
Day Coed Gr 9-12

Manchester, MO 63011. 500 Woods Mill Rd.
Tel: 636-227-5900. Fax: 636-227-0298.
www.jfk-catholic-high.org E-mail: info@kennedycatholic.net
  Rev. Bob Suit, Pres (2012). Mary Hey, Prin. Jeannie Kihn, Adm.

  Col Prep. AP (10 exams taken)—Calc Comp_Sci. **Feat**—Mythology Span Anat & Physiol Environ_Sci Web_Design Psych Sociol World_Relig Ceramics Drawing Painting Sculpt Studio_Art Drama Chorus Music_Theory Accounting Bus ACT_Prep. **Supp**—Dev_ Read Makeup Rem_Math Rem_Read Rev Tut. **Comp:** Laptop prgm Gr 9-12. **Sports**—Basket X-country Soccer Swim Tennis Track. B: Baseball Football. G: Cheer Golf Softball Volley. Activities: 20. **Somewhat selective adm:** 120/yr. Appl due: Jan. Accepted: 97%. Yield: 90%. **Tests** Stanford. **Enr 400.** B 160. G 240. Wh 96%. Latino 1%. Blk 1%. Asian 1%. Other 1%. Avg class size: 23. Uniform. **Fac 40.** M 14/F 26. FT 40. Wh 97%. Blk 3%. Adv deg: 55%. **Grad '06—122.** Col—122. (MO St 11, Truman St 11, U of MO-Columbia 9, U of Dayton 6, Lindenwood 6). **Tui '12-'13:** Day $10,050 (+$950). **Est 1968.** Nonprofit. Roman Catholic. Sem (Aug-May). JFK offers both advanced and honors courses. To obtain college credits, juniors and seniors may participate in a program at a nearby university. Religion classes, liturgical celebrations and retreats are important elements of school life. Students complete 30 compulsory hours of community service prior to grade 11, then perform two weeks of service during junior year.

BISHOP DuBOURG HIGH SCHOOL
Day Coed Gr 9-12

St Louis, MO 63109. 5850 Eichelberger St.
Tel: 314-832-3030. Fax: 314-832-0529.
www.bishopdubourg.org E-mail: rsykora@bishopdubourg.org
  Kermit V. Boschert, Pres (2006). MEd, Univ of Missouri-St Louis, MA, Naval War College, MEd, South Dakota State Univ. Bridget Timoney, Prin. MEd, St Louis Univ. Ryan Sykora, Adm.

  Col Prep. Gen Acad. Feat—Fr Span Relig Fine_Arts. **Supp**—LD. **Comp:** Comp/Stud: 1:2.25. **Dual enr:** St Louis U, U of MO-St Louis. **Sports**—Basket X-country Soccer Tennis Track Volley. B: Baseball Football Golf. G: Cheer Softball Swim. **Somewhat selective adm:** 152/yr. Appl fee: $0. Appl due: Jan. Accepted: 96%. Yield: 99%. **Enr 575.** B 271. G 304. Wh 85%. Latino 2%. Blk 12%. Asian 1%. Avg class size: 22. Stud/fac: 15:1. Uniform. **Fac 53.** M 23/F 30. FT 45/PT 8. Wh 96%. Latino 2%. Blk 2%. Adv deg: 73%. **Grad '09—163.** Col—148. Avg ACT: 21. **Tui '11-'12:** Day $8400-8600 (+$300). Aid: Merit 15 ($15,000). Need 238 ($168,000). Work prgm 14 ($14,000). **Est 1950.** Nonprofit. Roman Catholic (85% practice).

Sem (Aug-June). **Assoc** NCA. Bishop DuBourg's comprehensive curriculum provides honors, college prep and skills classes, and a wide array of courses includes advanced and college-credit courses in most departments. An active campus ministry plans regular liturgies, prayer services and days of prayer for all students; all seniors participate in a three-day retreat. Pupils in grades 9-11 accumulate 80 hours of required community service, while seniors complete a two-week, 70-hour service project.

CHRISTIAN BROTHERS COLLEGE HIGH SCHOOL — Day Boys Gr 9-12
St Louis, MO 63141. 1850 De La Salle Dr.
Tel: 314-985-6100. Fax: 314-985-6115.
www.cbchs.org   E-mail: brockmanj@cbchs.org
   Michael F. England, Pres (2007). BA, Southern Illinois Univ-Edwardsville, MA, Univ of Missouri-St Louis. Br. David Poos, FSC, Prin. MA, Univ of St Thomas (MN), MA, St Louis Univ. James Brockman, Adm.

   Col Prep. AP—Eng Span Calc Stats Bio Chem Physics Eur_Hist US_Hist US_Govt & Pol Art_Hist. **Feat**—Classics Creative_Writing Fr Anat & Physiol Ecol Forensic_Sci Zoology Engineering Programming Web_Design Civil_War Psych African_Stud E_Asian_Stud World_Relig Ceramics Drawing Painting Photog Sculpt Acting Theater_Arts Band Chorus Guitar Piano Accounting Bus Journ Marketing. **Comp:** Comp/Stud: 1:1 Laptop prgm Gr 9-12. **Dual enr:** St Louis U, U of MO-St Louis. **Sports**— B: Baseball Basket Bowl X-country Football Ice_Hockey Lacrosse Racquet Rugby Soccer Swim Tennis Track Ultimate_Frisbee Volley Wrestling. **Somewhat selective adm (Gr 9-11):** 280/yr. Appl fee: $7. Appl due: Dec. Accepted: 90%. Yield: 80%. **Enr 940.** Wh 82%. Latino 2%. Blk 14%. Asian 1%. Other 1%. Avg class size: 20. Stud/fac: 14:1. Casual dress. **Fac 67.** Adv deg: 85%. **Grad '11—220.** Col—217. Avg ACT: 24.1. **Col Couns:** 5. **Tui '12-'13:** Day $12,625 (+$450). Aid: Need 301 ($1,500,000). **Est 1850.** Nonprofit. Roman Catholic. Quar (Aug-May). **Assoc** NCA. Operated by the Brothers of the Christian Schools, CBC tracks pupils in the core academic areas and provides additional learning support where necessary; flexibility in scheduling enables students to follow different tracks in different subjects. Academically talented boys may earn college credit through Advanced Placement course work and dual-enrollment opportunities with two local universities. Students satisfy the following community service requirements: 16 hours per year in grades 9 and 10, 50 hours in grade 11 and 32 hours in grade 12.

COR JESU ACADEMY — Day Girls Gr 9-12
St Louis, MO 63123. 10230 Gravois Rd.
Tel: 314-842-1546. Fax: 314-842-6061.
www.corjesu.org   E-mail: admissions@corjesu.org
   Sr. Barbara Thomas, ASCJ, Pres. Sr. Kathleen Mary Coonan, ASCJ, Prin.

   Col Prep. AP—Eng Fr Lat Span Calc Stats Bio Chem Physics US_Hist Comp_Govt & Pol Psych US_Govt & Pol Art_Hist Studio_Art Music_Theory. **Feat**—British_Lit Shakespeare Engineering Programming Amer_Stud Pol_Sci Relig Fine_Arts Accounting. **Supp**—Tut. **Comp:** Comp/Stud: 1:1 Laptop prgm Gr 9-12. **Dual enr:** St Louis U. **Sports**— G: Basket Cheer X-country F_Hockey Golf Lacrosse Soccer Softball Swim Tennis Track Volley. Activities: 24. **Selective adm (Gr 9-11):** 146/yr. Appl due: Dec. **Tests** MAT. **Enr 575.** Stud/fac: 12:1. Uniform. **Fac 68.** Adv deg: 85%. **Grad '11—146.** Col—146. **Avg SAT:** CR 697. M 645. W 675. Avg ACT: 28.8. **Tui '11-'12:** Day $10,875 (+$325). **Est 1956.** Nonprofit. Roman Catholic. Sem (Aug-May). **Assoc** NCA. Serving the Archdiocese of St. Louis, Cor Jesu offers a full range of electives in English, the arts, social studies, languages, math, sciences, computer and business. CJA utilizes an eight-block schedule in which courses meet for 85 minutes every other class day, thereby giving students more time to discuss topics and develop critical-thinking skills. Juniors and seniors may take courses for college credit through St. Louis University.

CROSSROADS COLLEGE PREPARATORY SCHOOL Day Coed Gr 7-12
St Louis, MO 63112. 500 DeBaliviere Ave.
Tel: 314-367-8085. Fax: 314-367-9711.
www.crossroadscollegeprep.org E-mail: maggie@crossroadscollegeprep.org
  Clark J. Daggett, Head (2011). BA, Johns Hopkins Univ, MLitt, Drew Univ. Maggie
Baisch, Adm.
  Col Prep. AP (exams req'd; 126 taken, 80% 3+)—Eng Calc Bio Environ_Sci US_Hist
World_Hist Psych Art_Hist Studio_Art. **Feat**—Creative_Writing Shakespeare Fr Span Stats
Anat & Physiol Comp_Sci Econ Pol_Sci Philos Ceramics Drawing Photog Acting Music
Dance. **Supp**—Dev_Read. **Dual enr:** Wash U, U of MO-St Louis, Harris-Stowe St. **Sports**—
Basket Soccer Track. B: Baseball. G: Tennis Volley. **Selective adm:** 60/yr. Appl fee: $40. Appl
due: Jan. Accepted: 80%. **Tests** ISEE SSAT. **Enr 233.** B 118. G 115. Wh 54%. Latino 2%. Blk
33%. Asian 4%. Other 7%. Stud/fac: 9:1. **Fac 39. Grad '09—33.** Col—33. (Col of Wooster 2,
Syracuse 2, U of MO-Columbia 2, Columbia 1, U of PA 1, U of Chicago 1). **Avg SAT:** CR 701.
M 625. W 689. **Mid 50% SAT:** CR 670-750. M 610-670. W 630-780. Avg ACT: 27. Mid 50%
ACT: 24-31. **Col Couns:** 2. **Tui '11-'12:** Day $17,500 (+$500-600). Aid: Need 94 ($767,007).
Est 1974. Nonprofit. Sem (Aug-May). **Assoc** NCA. This small college preparatory school
features a variety of Advanced Placement courses. The program emphasizes critical-thinking
skills and aesthetic appreciation, and students have outreach opportunities in the city. Intern-
ships are required in grade 12, and seniors must complete a college-level class each semester.
Crossroads College Prep schedules a schoolwide community service day each year.

DeSMET JESUIT HIGH SCHOOL Day Boys Gr 9-12
St Louis, MO 63141. 233 N New Ballas Rd.
Tel: 314-567-3500. Fax: 314-567-1519.
www.desmet.org E-mail: admissions@desmet.org
  Rev. Walter T. Sidney, SJ, Pres (2007). Gregory Densberger, Prin. BA, Univ of Memphis,
MA, Univ of Missouri-Kansas City, PhD, St Louis Univ. Anthony T. Fior, Adm.
  Col Prep. AP (exams req'd)—Calc Stats Comp_Sci Bio Chem Physics US_Hist World_
Hist Psych US_Govt & Pol. **Feat**—Fr Lat Span Anat Forensic_Sci Econ Intl_Relations Theol
Film Music. **Supp**—Rev Tut. **Comp:** Laptop prgm Gr 9-12. **Dual enr:** St Louis U. **Sports**—
B: Baseball Basket X-country Football Golf Ice_Hockey Racquet Rugby Soccer Swim Track
W_Polo Wrestling. Activities: 51. **Somewhat selective adm:** 336/yr. Appl due: Dec. Accepted:
89%. Yield: 90%. **Tests** CEEB HSPT. **Enr 1103.** Avg class size: 22. Stud/fac: 14:1. **Fac 108.**
M 90/F 18. FT 103/PT 5. Adv deg: 53%. **Grad '08—236.** Col—232. (U of MO-Columbia 64,
St Louis U 21, Truman St 13, MO St 11, St Louis CC 11, U of Central MO 7). Avg ACT: 25.
Alum donors: 30%. **Tui '11-'12:** Day $11,690 (+$500). **Est 1967.** Nonprofit. Roman Catholic.
Sem (Aug-May). **Assoc** NCA. Conducted by the Society of Jesus, DeSmet provides an honors
program and AP courses in addition to its college prep curriculum, and courses are offered for
college credit through St. Louis University to juniors and seniors in good academic standing.
Students purchase tablet computers for use in class. Boys in grades 10-12 engage in mandatory
community service projects.

INCARNATE WORD ACADEMY Day Girls Gr 9-12
St Louis, MO 63121. 2788 Normandy Dr.
Tel: 314-725-5850. Fax: 314-725-2308.
www.iwacademy.org E-mail: mcrain@iwacademy.org
  Randy Berzon-Mikolas, Pres. BA, Drake Univ, MA, PhD, St Louis Univ. Mary Maguire,
Prin. MA. Megan Crain, Adm.
  Col Prep. AP—Calc Bio Chem Environ_Sci. **Feat**—British_Lit Creative_Writing Fr Span
Stats Ecol Genetics Physiol Zoology Web_Design Econ Law Pol_Sci Psych Women's_Stud
Theol World_Relig Ceramics Drawing Painting Studio_Art Acting Drama Music Dance
Accounting. **Supp**—Tut. **Comp:** Comp/Stud: 1:2. **Dual enr:** St Louis U, U of MO-St Louis.
Sports— G: Basket Cheer X-country Golf Soccer Softball Swim Tennis Track Volley. Activi-

ties: 20. **Somewhat selective adm:** Appl due: Nov. **Enr 450.** Wh 81%. Latino 4%. Blk 15%. Avg class size: 20. Stud/fac: 11:1. Uniform. **Fac 45.** Wh 97%. Latino 1%. Blk 2%. Adv deg: 60%. **Grad '07—140.** Col—139. **Col Couns:** 2. **Tui '11-'12:** Day $10,400 (+$50). **Est 1932.** Nonprofit. Roman Catholic (85% practice). Sem (Aug-May). **Assoc** NCA. The school's curriculum encompasses required courses, electives and the fine arts within a strong religious foundation. IWA offers an Advanced Placement program and a full range of advanced college courses through St. Louis University and the University of Missouri-St. Louis, which is located nearby. Girls accumulate 120 hours of community service during their four years at the academy.

LOGOS SCHOOL   **Day Coed Gr 6-12**
St Louis, MO 63132. 9137 Old Bonhomme Rd.
Tel: 314-997-7002. Fax: 314-997-6848.
www.logosschool.org   E-mail: skolker@logosschool.org
    Kathy Boyd-Fenger, Head. BA, MA, Webster Univ. Stephanie Kolker, Adm.
    Col Prep. LD. Underachiever. AP—Eng. **Feat**—Span Computers Ceramics Fine_Arts Mosaic_Art Mural_Painting. **Supp**—Dev_Read Rem_Math Rev Tut. **Sports**—Basket Soccer. B: Baseball. G: Volley. **Somewhat selective adm:** 75/yr. Appl due: Rolling. Accepted: 90%. **Tests** Stanford. **Enr 150.** B 90. G 60. Elem 30. Sec 120. Avg class size: 8. Stud/fac: 6:1. **Fac 23.** M 9/F 14. FT 23. Adv deg: 34%. Avg ACT: 27.4. **Tui '08-'09:** Day $22,000 (+$2000). **Est 1970.** Nonprofit. Year-round. **Assoc** NCA. Logos provides a program of therapeutic counseling, accredited academics and parental involvement to students who have had difficulty succeeding in traditional school settings. Features include a favorable student-teacher ratio, individualized education, and therapeutic treatment plans specializing in ADHD, learning disabilities, behavioral disorders and emotional problems. Boys and girls perform 120 hours of community service prior to graduation. Students may enroll at any time during the 12-month school year.

LUTHERAN HIGH SCHOOL NORTH   **Day Coed Gr 9-12**
St Louis, MO 63121. 5401 Lucas & Hunt Rd.
Tel: 314-389-3100. Fax: 314-389-3103.
www.lhsn.org   E-mail: pendorf@lhsn.org
    Timothy J. Brackman, Prin (2011). Paul Endorf, Adm.
    Col Prep. AP—Eng Calc US_Hist. **Feat**—Fr Span Anat & Physiol Organic_Chem Pol_ Sci Psych Comp_Relig Theol Ceramics Painting Photog Studio_Art Drama Band Chorus Accounting Bus Journ Marketing. **Supp**—Tut. **Comp:** Comp/Stud: 1:3. **Dual enr:** St Louis U. **Sports**—Basket X-country Soccer Tennis Track. B: Baseball Football Golf. G: Cheer Softball Volley. Activities: 26. **Somewhat selective adm:** 100/yr. Appl fee: $100. Appl due: May. Accepted: 88%. Yield: 90%. **Enr 314.** B 165. G 149. Wh 35%. Blk 58%. Asian 4%. Other 3%. Avg class size: 20. Uniform. **Fac 30.** M 16/F 14. Adv deg: 86%. **Grad '11—93.** Col—91. (U of MO-Columbia 17, MO U of Sci & Tech 6, St Louis CC 6, S IL-Carbondale 5, Truman St 4, Lindenwood 4). **Avg SAT:** CR 580. M 553. W 587. Avg ACT: 22. **Col Couns:** 2. **Tui '11-'12:** Day $10,725. Assoc Members $9525. Aid: Merit 61 ($62,200). Need 207 ($676,395). Work prgm 11 ($11,000). **Est 1946.** Nonprofit. Lutheran. Sem (Aug-May). **Assoc** NCA. Lutheran North conducts a college preparatory program within a Christian setting that includes daily chapel, theology courses and peer ministry. Teachers employ various instructional strategies to accommodate individual learning styles. The hands-on curriculum features Advanced Placement courses, academic lab periods and an emphasis on technology. Students may earn more than 20 hours of college credit through St. Louis University. Boys and girls accumulate 60 hours of required community service during their four years.

NEW CITY SCHOOL   **Day Coed Gr PS (Age 3)-6**
St Louis, MO 63108. 5209 Waterman Ave.
Tel: 314-361-6411. Fax: 314-361-1499.
www.newcityschool.org   E-mail: trhoerr@newcityschool.org
    Thomas R. Hoerr, Head (1981). BA, Harris-Stowe State College, MEd, Univ of Missouri-
St Louis, PhD, Washington Univ. Melanie Harmon, Adm.
    Pre-Prep. Feat—Lib_Skills Span Computers Performing_Arts Studio_Art Music. **Supp**—
Rem_Math Rem_Read. **Selective adm:** 76/yr. Appl fee: $100. Appl due: Feb. Accepted: 75%.
Yield: 73%. **Enr 350.** Avg class size: 13. **Fac 42.** M 3/F 39. FT 41/PT 1. Adv deg: 52%. **Grad
'10—38.** Prep—30. **Tui '10-'11:** Day $14,750. Aid: Need 127 ($585,000). **Est 1969.** Nonprofit. Sem (Sept-June). Students at the school develop traditional academic skills through an
experience-based learning approach. The integrated, thematic curriculum is based on Howard
Gardner's theory of multiple intelligences and focuses on linguistic, spatial-artistic, bodily-
kinesthetic, musical, logical-mathematical, interpersonal and intrapersonal skills. An appreciation for diversity is stressed at all grade levels.

NOTRE DAME HIGH SCHOOL   **Day Girls Gr 9-12**
St Louis, MO 63125. 320 E Ripa Ave.
Tel: 314-544-1015. Fax: 314-544-8003.
www.ndhs.net   E-mail: emmem@ndhs.net
    Sr. Gail Guelker, SSND, Pres. MA, St Louis Univ. Sr. Michelle Emmerich, SSND, Prin.
MA, Univ of Notre Dame, EdD, St Louis Univ. Katie Peroutka, Adm.
    Col Prep. AP—Fr Span. **Feat**—British_Lit Creative_Writing Calc Stats Anat & Physiol
Astron Environ_Sci Forensic_Sci Web_Design Econ Law Pol_Sci Sociol Women's_Stud Relig
Ceramics Drawing Film Painting Photog Studio_Art Acting Theater_Arts Chorus Music Journ
Public_Speak Culinary_Arts. **Supp**—Rev Tut. **Comp:** Comp/Stud: 1:2. **Dual enr:** St Louis U.
Sports— G: Basket Cheer X-country Golf Racquet Soccer Softball Swim Track Volley. **Some-
what selective adm (Gr 9-11):** 68/yr. Appl due: Dec. Accepted: 98%. Yield: 95%. **Enr 320.**
Wh 97%. Latino 2%. Asian 1%. Avg class size: 23. Stud/fac: 10:1. Uniform. **Fac 35.** M 5/F
30. FT 33/PT 2. Nonwhite 1%. Adv deg: 88%. **Grad '08—95.** Col—95. (MO St 23, Southeast
MO St 12, St Louis CC 10, U of MO-Columbia 7, St Louis U 5, Lindenwood 5). Avg ACT:
22. **Col Couns:** 1. **Tui '12-'13:** Day $10,200 (+$400). **Est 1934.** Nonprofit. Roman Catholic
(95% practice). Sem (Aug-May). **Assoc** NCA. In addition to its strong core curriculum, Notre
Dame offers advanced classes and college-credit opportunities through St. Louis University.
Electives in art, business, communications, computer, consumer science, math, music, science
and social studies complement required course work. Girls may meet one-on-one with teachers between class periods for extra help, and each student convenes with her advisor every 10
school days to track academic progress and gain support.

ROHAN WOODS SCHOOL   **Day Coed Gr PS (Age 2)-6**
St Louis, MO 63122. 1515 Bennett Ave.
Tel: 314-821-6270. Fax: 314-821-6878.
www.rohanwoods.org   E-mail: spage@rohanwoods.org
    Sam Templin-Page, Head (2011). BEd, Univ of Nebraska. Jana Allen, Adm.
    Pre-Prep. Feat—Lib_Skills Fr Span Computers Studio_Art Music. **Comp:** Laptop prgm
Gr 4-6. **Sports**—Soccer Track. **Selective adm:** 17/yr. Appl fee: $75. Appl due: Rolling.
Accepted: 60%. Yield: 80%. **Tests** CTP_4. **Enr 100.** B 60. G 40. Wh 83%. Latino 2%. Blk
10%. Other 5%. Avg class size: 14. Stud/fac: 8:1. **Fac 18.** M 1/F 17. FT 11/PT 7. Wh 99%.
Latino 1%. Adv deg: 27%. **Grad '11—10.** Prep—10. **Tui '11-'12:** Day $15,950-16,450. Aid:
Merit 4 ($25,0000). Need ($320,000). **Est 1937.** Nonprofit. Tri (Aug-May). **Assoc** NCA. In
the early years, children at RWS develop basic skills as a foundation for future learning. As the
student ages, the developmentally based program places additional emphasis on independence
and responsibility, and an ethics is integrated into the curriculum. Art, music, technology and

foreign languages are among Rohan Woods' specialty subjects. For an additional fee, boys and girls may take part in an afternoon enrichment program.

ROSATI-KAIN HIGH SCHOOL **Day Girls Gr 9-12**
St Louis, MO 63108. 4389 Lindell Blvd.
Tel: 314-533-8513. Fax: 314-533-1618.
www.rosati-kain.org   E-mail: rkoffice@rosati-kain.org
    Sr. Joan Andert, SSND, Pres (1989). BS, Notre Dame College, MAT, Southeast Missouri State Univ. Judy Mohan, Prin. BA, Northwestern Univ, MA, St Louis Univ. Kelly Albright, Adm.
    Col Prep. AP—Calc Stats Bio Physics US_Hist. **Feat**—Shakespeare Women's_Lit World_ Lit Fr Span Anat & Physiol Web_Design Econ Psych Theol World_Relig Film Fine_Arts Painting Theater_Arts Music_Hist Music_Theory Accounting Bus Finance Media. **Supp**— Tut. **Comp:** Comp/Stud: 1:3. **Dual enr:** St Louis U, U of MO-St Louis. **Sports**— G: Basket Cheer X-country F_Hockey Soccer Softball Swim Tennis Track Volley. Activities: 25. **Selective adm:** 95/yr. Appl fee: $5. Appl due: Nov. **Enr 408.** Wh 84%. Latino 3%. Blk 11%. Asian 1%. Other 1%. Avg class size: 20. Stud/fac: 12:1. Uniform. **Fac 34.** M 3/F 31. FT 32/PT 2. Wh 94%. Latino 3%. Blk 3%. Adv deg: 67%. **Grad '11—83.** Col—83. **Avg SAT:** CR 659. M 608. W 601. Avg ACT: 25.6. **Col Couns:** 2. **Tui '11-'12:** Day $8400 (+$500). Catholic $7900 (+$500). **Est 1911.** Nonprofit. Roman Catholic (87% practice). Sem (Aug-June). **Assoc** NCA. Required courses at Rosati-Kain include four years of religion and one year each of fine arts and practical arts course work. Advanced classes carrying college credit are offered through St. Louis University and the University of Missouri-St. Louis in history, English, French, Spanish and science. Girls accumulate 75 hours of required community service prior to graduation.

ST. ELIZABETH ACADEMY **Day Girls Gr 9-12**
St Louis, MO 63118. 3401 Arsenal St.
Tel: 314-771-5134. Fax: 314-771-3528.
www.seahs.org   E-mail: jkeuss@seahs.org
    Sr. Susan Borgel, CPPS, Pres. BA, Fontbonne Univ, MS, St Louis Univ. Christina R. Cheak, Prin. BA, Harris-Stowe State Univ. Jane F. Keuss, Adm.
    Col Prep. AP—Studio_Art. **Feat**—Creative_Writing Fr Span Calc Ecol Comp_Sci Women's_Hist Psych Theol Film Photog Drama Music_Theory Bus Marketing Nutrition. **Supp**— Dev_Read ESL LD Rem_Math Tut. **Comp:** Comp/Stud: 1:2. **Dual enr:** St Louis U. **Sports**— G: Basket Soccer Softball Track Volley. Activities: 15. **Somewhat selective adm:** 45/yr. Appl fee: $0. Appl due: Rolling. Accepted: 98%. Yield: 90%. **Enr 150.** Wh 50%. Latino 10%. Blk 35%. Asian 2%. Other 3%. Stud/fac: 8:1. Uniform. **Fac 20.** M 4/F 16. FT 20. Adv deg: 50%. **Grad '11—54.** Col—51. (U of MO-Columbia 6, St Louis U 3, Benedictine U 3, Fontbonne 3, Webster 3, Xavier-OH 2). **Tui '12-'13:** Day $8900 (+$500). **Est 1882.** Nonprofit. Roman Catholic. Sem (Aug-May). **Assoc** NCA. Girls at this Catholic school, who represent different faiths and backgrounds, select from a varied curriculum that features at least two levels of difficulty in most subjects. Levels are distinguished by the degree of higher-order thinking demanded, not by the work load required. Three weeks into each semester, instructors help the student decide whether to pursue course work at the regular, advanced or honors level. Girls satisfy an 80-hour community service requirement during their four years at SEA.

ST. JOHN VIANNEY HIGH SCHOOL **Day Boys Gr 9-12**
St Louis, MO 63122. 1311 S Kirkwood Rd.
Tel: 314-965-4853. Fax: 314-965-1950.
www.vianney.com   E-mail: tmulvihill@vianney.com
    Michael E. Loyet, Pres (2007). BBA, Southeast Missouri State Univ, MBA, Webster Univ, MEd, St Louis Univ. Tom Dilg, Prin. EdD, St Louis Univ. Tom Mulvihill, Adm.
    Col Prep. AP (exams req'd)—Calc Stats Bio Chem Environ_Sci Econ. **Feat**—ASL

Ger Span Forensic_Sci Programming Web_Design Govt Architect_Drawing Drawing Film Fine_Arts Drama Theater_Arts Music Music_Theory Accounting Journ Speech. **Supp**—Tut. **Comp:** Comp/Stud: 1:2. **Dual enr:** U of MO-St Louis, St Louis U. **Sports**— B: Baseball Basket X-country Football Golf Ice_Hockey Lacrosse Soccer Swim Tennis Track Volley Wrestling. **Somewhat selective adm:** 165/yr. Appl due: Nov. Accepted: 98%. **Tests** HSPT. **Enr 603.** Wh 98%. Blk 1%. Other 1%. Avg class size: 22. Stud/fac: 12:1. **Fac 48.** M 39/F 9. FT 48. Adv deg: 72%. **Grad '09—165.** Col—160. Avg ACT: 23. **Tui '12-'13:** Day $11,775 (+$300-500). Aid: Need ($500,000). **Est 1960.** Nonprofit. Roman Catholic (85% practice). Sem (Aug-May). **Assoc** NCA. Operated in the Marianist tradition, Vianney offers college preparation in a Christ-centered environment. Honors and Advanced Placement course work is available, and seniors may also earn college credit in certain classes through St. Louis University or the University of Missouri-St. Louis. Community service requirements are as follows: 20 hours annually in grades 9 and 10, 60 hours in grade 11.

ST. JOSEPH'S ACADEMY   Day Girls Gr 9-12
St Louis, MO 63131. 2307 S Lindbergh Blvd.
Tel: 314-965-7205. Fax: 314-965-9114.
www.stjosephacademy.org   E-mail: pdunphy@stjosephacademy.org
     Anita Reznicek, Pres. Sr. Pat Dunphy, CSJ, Prin. BA, Fontbonne Univ, MA, Univ of Northern Colorado. Sr. Carol Gerondale, CSJ, Adm.
     Col Prep. AP (exams req'd; 65 taken)—Eng Fr Span Calc Eur_Hist US_Hist US_Govt & Pol. **Feat**—Chin Lat Anat & Physiol Astron Environ_Sci Forensic_Sci Genetics Zoology Govt Psych Theol Drawing Music_Theory. **Comp:** Comp/Stud: 1:1 Laptop prgm Gr 9-12. **Dual enr:** St Louis U, Fontbonne. **Sports**— G: Basket X-country F_Hockey Golf Lacrosse Racquet Soccer Softball Swim Tennis Track Volley. Activities: 25. **Selective adm (Gr 9-11):** 136/yr. Appl due: Nov. Accepted: 69%. **Enr 630.** Wh 98%. Latino 1%. Blk 1%. Avg class size: 19. Stud/fac: 12:1. Uniform. **Fac 52.** Wh 98%. Latino 1%. Asian 1%. **Grad '10—173.** Col—173. **Avg SAT:** CR 632. M 615. W 663. Avg ACT: 26. **Col Couns:** 2. **Tui '12-'13:** Day $11,630 (+$1335-1760). Aid: Need ($39,314). Work prgm ($71,500). **Est 1840.** Nonprofit. Roman Catholic. Sem (Aug-May). Sponsored by the Sisters of St. Joseph of Carondelet, the school offers a wide selection of honors classes, as well as some Advanced Placement offerings. SJA leases laptop computers to all students for use during class projects and research. Community service requirements are as follows: 10 hours in grade 9, 14 hours in grade 10, 18 hours in grade 11, and completion of a 90-hour service project in grade 12.

VISITATION ACADEMY   Day Boys PS (Age 2)-K
St Louis, MO 63131. 3020 N Ballas Rd.   Girls Gr PS (Age 2)-12
Tel: 314-625-9100. Fax: 314-432-7210.
www.visitationacademy.org   E-mail: agiljum@visitationacademy.org
     Rosalie Henry, Head. Ashley M. Giljum, Adm.
     Col Prep. Montessori. AP (195 exams taken, 95% 3+)—Eng Fr Span Calc Stats Bio Chem Physics Eur_Hist US_Hist US_Govt & Pol. **Feat**—Lat Anat & Physiol Environ_Sci Genetics Programming Psych World_Relig Photog Studio_Art Theater_Arts Music Dance. **Supp**—Rev Tut. **Comp:** Comp/Stud: 1:1 Laptop prgm Gr 7-12. **Dual enr:** St Louis U. **Sports**— G: Basket Cheer X-country F_Hockey Golf Lacrosse Racquet Soccer Softball Swim Tennis Track Volley. Activities: 33. **Somewhat selective adm (Gr PS-11):** 134/yr. Appl fee: $75. Appl due: Jan. Accepted: 93%. Yield: 74%. **Tests** CEEB HSPT ISEE SSAT. **Enr 633.** B 20. G 613. Elem 307. Sec 326. Wh 87%. Latino 2%. Blk 2%. Asian 6%. Other 3%. Avg class size: 18. Stud/fac: 9:1. Uniform. **Fac 83.** M 9/F 74. FT 83. Adv deg: 66%. **Grad '11—88.** Col—88. (U of MO-Columbia 13, St Louis U 8, IN U 4, Wash U 3, U of Dayton 3, Auburn 3). **Avg SAT:** CR 613. M 621. W 623. Avg ACT: 29. **Col Couns:** 3. **Tui '12-'13:** Day $15,535-16,720 (+$0-1000). **Est 1833.** Nonprofit. Roman Catholic. Quar (Aug-May). **Assoc** NCA. This Catholic school conducts a coeducational Montessori preschool and kindergarten and all-girls elementary and secondary programs. Visitation's college preparatory curriculum is enhanced by elective offer-

ings in technology, the fine and performing arts, and athletics. Students in grades 7-12 take part in the school's laptop program. During grades 9-12, girls perform 120 hours of compulsory community service.

WHITFIELD SCHOOL   **Day Coed Gr 6-12**
St Louis, MO 63141. 175 S Mason Rd.
Tel: 314-434-5141. Fax: 314-434-6193.
www.whitfieldschool.org   E-mail: admissions@whitfieldschool.org
    John Delautre, Head (2012). BA, Western Kentucky Univ, MA, Vanderbilt Univ, MDiv, Princeton Theological Seminary. Cynthia Crum Alverson, Adm.
    Col Prep. AP (exams req'd)—Fr Span Calc Chem. **Feat—**Lat Environ_Sci Zoology Econ Ceramics Drawing Film Painting Photog Theater_Arts Music. **Comp:** Laptop prgm Gr 6-12. **Sports—**Basket X-country Soccer Tennis Track. B: Baseball Golf Ice_Hockey Wrestling. G: Cheer F_Hockey Lacrosse Volley. Activities: 20. **Selective adm:** 98/yr. Appl fee: $75. Appl due: Jan. Accepted: 73%. Yield: 65%. **Enr 380.** Elem 122. Sec 258. Nonwhite 22%. Avg class size: 10. Stud/fac: 8:1. Casual dress. **Fac 56.** FT 56. Wh 80%. Latino 5%. Blk 6%. Asian 3%. Other 6%. Adv deg: 48%. **Grad '11—75.** Col—75. Avg ACT: 27. **Col Couns:** 2. **Tui '12-'13:** Day $22,700 (+$1035). Aid: Need 80 ($1,288,000). **Est 1952.** Nonprofit. Sem (Aug-June). **Assoc** NCA.   At this research-based institution, students must display mastery of subject matter through traditional testing and exhibitions. Upon faculty recommendation, pupils may enroll in Advanced Placement courses, which are available in several disciplines. Technology is integral to school life, highlighted in all grades by a one-to-one laptop program. Particularly able students may pursue independent study in foreign language, math or science.

WESTMINSTER CHRISTIAN ACADEMY   **Day Coed Gr 7-12**
Town and Country, MO 63017. 800 Maryville Centre Dr.
Tel: 314-997-2900. Fax: 314-997-2903.
www.wcastl.org   E-mail: info@wcastl.org
    James C. Marsh, Jr., Head (1985). BA, Calvin College, MEd, Florida Atlantic Univ. Peggy M. Johnson, Adm.
    Col Prep. AP (exams req'd; 288 taken, 63% 3+)—Eng Fr Span Calc Stats Bio Chem Physics Eur_Hist US_Hist US_Govt & Pol Art_Hist. **Feat—**Chin Anat & Physiol Forensic_Sci Bible Ethics Fine_Arts Study_Skills. **Supp—**LD Rem_Math Tut. **Comp:** Comp/Stud: 1:2.5. Outdoor Ed. **Dual enr:** MO Baptist. **Sports—**Basket X-country Golf Soccer Swim Tennis Volley. B: Baseball Football Ice_Hockey Wrestling. G: Cheer Lacrosse Softball. Activities: 14. **Selective adm:** 264/yr. Appl fee: $50. Appl due: Rolling. Accepted: 75%. Yield: 94%. **Enr 940.** B 474. G 466. Elem 270. Sec 670. Wh 81%. Latino 2%. Blk 10%. Asian 1%. Other 6%. Avg class size: 19. Stud/fac: 13:1. Uniform. **Fac 89.** M 46/F 43. FT 74/PT 15. Wh 95%. Blk 3%. Other 2%. Adv deg: 65%. **Grad '11—146.** Col—146. (U of MO-Columbia 25, Truman St 8, Covenant 7, MO U of Sci & Tech 4, TX Christian 4, U of MS 4). **Avg SAT:** CR 590. M 637. W 574. Avg ACT: 26. **Col Couns:** 1. Alum donors: 2%. **Tui '12-'13:** Day $13,400 (+$250-500). Aid: Need 175 ($1,800,000). **Est 1976.** Nonprofit. Nondenom Christian. Quar (Aug-May). **Assoc** NCA.   Located in suburban St. Louis County, WCA enrolls students from Metropolitan St. Louis and western Illinois. The comprehensive college preparatory program—which includes AP and honors courses—has competency requirements in Bible, English, the fine arts, foreign language, history, math, science, the practical arts and physical education. Seniors fulfill a 60-hour community service requirement in which they each keep a weekly journal and write a final paper.

NERINX HALL   **Day Girls Gr 9-12**
Webster Groves, MO 63119. 530 E Lockwood Ave.
Tel: 314-968-1505. Fax: 314-968-0604.
www.nerinxhs.org   E-mail: broche@nerinxhs.org

Sr. Barbara Roche, SL, Pres (1986). BA, Webster Univ. Jane W. Kosash, Prin. BA, St Louis Univ, MAT, Webster Univ. Mary Ann Gentry, Adm.

Col Prep. AP (56 exams taken, 64% 3+)—Calc Stats Studio_Art. **Feat**—Creative_Writing Humanities Poetry Shakespeare Mythology Chin Fr Ger Lat Span Anat & Physiol Astron Bioethics Geol Programming Web_Design Holocaust Anthro Econ Psych Theol World_Relig Ceramics Drawing Fine_Arts Painting Photog Acting Drama Theater_Arts Accounting Bus Debate Finance Marketing Public_Speak. **Comp:** Comp/Stud: 1:1 Laptop prgm Gr 9-12. **Dual enr:** St Louis U, U of MO-St Louis. **Sports**— G: Basket X-country F_Hockey Golf Lacrosse Racquet Soccer Softball Swim Tennis Track Volley. **Selective adm (Gr 9-11):** 170/yr. Appl due: Dec. Accepted: 82%. Yield: 94%. **Enr 625.** Wh 91%. Latino 2%. Blk 3%. Asian 3%. Other 1%. Avg class size: 20. Stud/fac: 10:1. Uniform. **Fac 56.** M 14/F 42. FT 46/PT 10. Wh 98%. Blk 2%. Adv deg: 76%. **Grad '08**—152. Col—152. (U of MO-Columbia 31, Truman St 10, St Louis U 9, Loyola U of Chicago 5, MO St 5, U of KS 5). Avg ACT: 27. **Col Couns:** 1. Alum donors: 15%. **Tui '12-'13:** Day $11,300 (+$1300). Aid: Merit 7 ($3500). Need 130 ($475,000). Work prgm 94 ($94,000). **Est 1924.** Nonprofit. Roman Catholic (95% practice). Quar (Aug-May). **Assoc** NCA. Nerinx offers a college preparatory curriculum that includes honors courses and electives in the major disciplines, as well as in theology, the arts, business and computer technology. Girls may enroll in college-credit courses offered through St. Louis University and the University of Missouri-St. Louis. Pupils must lease laptop computers through the school. All students devote 40 hours to community service between the fourth quarter of junior year and the second quarter of senior year.

NEBRASKA

MESSIAH LUTHERAN SCHOOL   Day Coed Gr PS (Age 3)-5
Lincoln, NE 68506. 1800 S 84th St.
Tel: 402-489-3024. Fax: 402-489-3093.
www.messiahlincoln.org   E-mail: aable@messiahlincoln.org
Matthew Stueber, Prin. MEd, Univ of Houston. Amanda Able, Adm.

Gen Acad. Feat—Computers Relig Studio_Art Music. **Supp**—Dev_Read Rem_Math Rem_Read. **Comp:** Comp/Stud: 1:4. **Somewhat selective adm:** 78/yr. Appl due: Rolling. Accepted: 99%. **Enr 315.** B 150. G 165. Avg class size: 20. Casual dress. **Fac 13.** FT 13. Adv deg: 30%. **Grad '08**—24. **Tui '12-'13:** Day $3975 (+$200). Parishioners $3180 (+$200). **Est 1930.** Nonprofit. Lutheran (90% practice). Sem (Aug-May). Messiah's elementary curriculum emphasizes reading, writing, arithmetic and religion. Daily Bible-based religion classes and weekly all-school chapel services are part of the program, as are after-school athletics and clubs.

SOUTH DAKOTA

FREEMAN ACADEMY   Bdg Coed Gr 9-12
Freeman, SD 57029. 748 S Main St, PO Box 1000.   Day Coed 5-12
Tel: 605-925-4237. Fax: 605-925-4271.
www.freemanacademy.org   E-mail: info@freemanacademy.org
Pam Tieszen, Supt (2008). BA, Jamestown College. Bonnie Young, Adm.

Col Prep. Feat—British_Lit Span Calc Stats Anat & Physiol Web_Design Psych Bible Visual_Arts Theater Music Music_Theory Speech. **Comp:** Comp/Stud: 1:2. **Sports**—Basket X-country Golf Soccer Track. G: Cheer Volley. Activities: 9. **Selective adm:** 16/yr. Bdg 4. Day 12. Appl fee: $0. Appl due: Rolling. Accepted: 88%. Yield: 100%. **Enr 67.** Bdg 7. Day 60. Wh 81%. Latino 4%. Blk 3%. Asian 12%. Intl 10%. Avg class size: 8. Stud/fac: 6:1. Casual dress.

Fac 10. M 4/F 6. FT 8/PT 2. Wh 80%. Latino 20%. Adv deg: 40%. **Grad '11—16.** Col—15. (Augustana 2, U of Sioux Falls 2, Bethel Col 2, Goshen 1, Dakota St 1, Hesston 1). Avg ACT: 25. Alum donors: 10%. **Tui '11-'12:** Bdg $11,085 (+$400). Day $5115-6135 (+$400). Intl Bdg $16,550-18,550 (+$400). Aid: Merit 5 ($3000). Need 10 ($27,000). **Est 1903.** Mennonite (53% practice). Tri (Aug-May). **Assoc** NCA. This small Mennonite school has a particularly strong creative arts curriculum, with the vast majority of the student body participating in Freeman's choir. Instruction and academy activities conform to a Christian worldview. All boys and girls attend chapel twice weekly, and class devotions, required Bible courses, and informal discussions among students and faculty are other aspects of the program. International pupils need not be Christian to enroll.

ST. THOMAS MORE HIGH SCHOOL
Day Coed Gr 9-12
Rapid City, SD 57701. 300 Fairmont Blvd.
Tel: 605-343-8484. Fax: 605-343-1315.
www.rccss.net   E-mail: mwerner@rccss.net
Wayne Sullivan, Prin. Marcia Werner, Adm.

Col Prep. AP (exams req'd)—Eng Calc Bio Chem Physics US_Hist US_Govt & Pol. **Feat**—Fr Span Stats Anat & Physiol Astron Forensic_Sci Comp_Sci Web_Design Psych Sociol World_Relig Studio_Art Drama Band Chorus Orchestra Jazz_Band Accounting Debate Journ Speech. **Supp**—Tut. **Sports**—Basket Cheer X-country Football Golf Soccer Tennis Track Volley Wrestling. **Somewhat selective adm:** 33/yr. Appl due: Mar. Accepted: 90%. **Tests** Stanford. **Enr 234.** B 108. G 126. Avg class size: 18. Uniform. **Fac 18.** Adv deg: 16%. **Grad '05—55.** Col—53. Avg ACT: 25.2. **Col Couns:** 1. **Tui '12-'13:** Day $6491 (+$150). Parishioners $5156 (+$150). **Est 1991.** Nonprofit. Roman Catholic. Sem (Aug-May). Options for acceleration at the school include AP and advanced classes. A community service project is required during senior year, and daily prayer and weekly Mass complement the curriculum.

SIOUX FALLS CHRISTIAN SCHOOLS
Day Coed Gr PS (Age 3)-12
Sioux Falls, SD 57108. 6120 S Charger Ave.
Tel: 605-334-1422. Fax: 605-334-6928.
www.siouxfallschristian.org   E-mail: sfchristian@sfchristian.org
Jay Woudstra, Supt (2004). BA, Dordt College, MEd, Univ of Sioux Falls.

Col Prep. Gen Acad. AP—Span Calc Bio Physics US_Govt & Pol. **Feat**—British_Lit Creative_Writing Fr Anat & Physiol Environ_Sci Comp_Sci Econ Govt Psych Sociol Bible Studio_Art Chorus Accounting. **Supp**—Rem_Math Rem_Read Tut. **Comp:** Comp/Stud: 1:5. **Sports**—Basket X-country Golf Soccer Track. B: Football. G: Volley. **Somewhat selective adm:** 30/yr. Appl fee: $60. Appl due: Rolling. Accepted: 98%. **Tests** Stanford. **Enr 875.** B 465. G 410. Elem 638. Sec 237. Wh 95%. Latino 2%. Blk 3%. Avg class size: 25. **Fac 48.** M 10/F 38. FT 33/PT 15. Wh 100%. Adv deg: 31%. **Grad '09—56.** Col—48. Avg ACT: 24. Alum donors: 10%. **Tui '12-'13:** Day $5250-6580 (+$600). **Est 1977.** Nonprofit. Nondenom Christian. Quar (Aug-May). Such enrichment and exploratory classes as art, band, choir, computers, keyboarding, Spanish and physical education complement core curricular offerings in SFCS' middle school (grades 6-8). To meet varying needs and abilities, the high school (grades 9-12) provides both college preparatory and general education curricula.

South Central States

ARKANSAS

ANTHONY SCHOOL   Day Coed Gr PS (Age 3)-8
Little Rock, AR 72227. 7700 Ohio St.
Tel: 501-225-6629. Fax: 501-225-2149.
www.anthonyschool.org   E-mail: tas@anthonyschool.org
  Sharon Morgan, Head (2004). MAEd, Univ of Arkansas-Monticello. Ann Vanhook, Gr 1-8 Adm; Kenda White, PS-K Adm.
  Pre-Prep. Gen Acad. Feat—Lib_Skills Fr Span Computers Studio_Art Drama Chorus Music Speech. **Supp**—Tut. **Comp:** Comp/Stud: 1:8.2. **Sports**—Basket Bowl X-country Golf Soccer Tennis Track Volley. B: Football. G: Cheer. **Somewhat selective adm:** 80/yr. Appl due: Rolling. Accepted: 90%. Yield: 95%. **Tests** Stanford. **Enr 415.** Avg class size: 13. Casual dress. **Fac 41.** M 3/F 38. FT 37/PT 4. Adv deg: 31%. **Grad '05**—**35.** Prep—18. **Tui '05-'06:** Day $5300 (+$1000). **Est 1944.** Nonprofit. Quar (Aug-May). The oldest nonsectarian independent school in the state, Anthony begins both Spanish and computer classes at age 3. In addition, students pursue age-appropriate course work in reading, language arts, math, science, social studies and physical education.

MOUNT ST. MARY ACADEMY   Day Girls Gr 9-12
Little Rock, AR 72205. 3224 Kavanaugh Blvd.
Tel: 501-664-8006. Fax: 501-666-4382.
www.mtstmary.edu   E-mail: cmccarroll@mtstmary.edu
  Sr. Deborah Troillett, RSM, Pres (1990). BA, St Louis Univ, MSEd, Univ of Dayton. Diane Wolfe, Prin. BS, MS. Chelle McKenzie McCarroll, Adm.
  Col Prep. IB Diploma. Feat—Fr Lat Span Anat & Physiol Intl_Relations Law Psych Theol Studio_Art Drama Theater_Arts Chorus Music_Theory Accounting Speech Nutrition. **Supp**—Tut. **Sports**— G: Basket Bowl Cheer X-country Golf Soccer Softball Swim Tennis Track Volley. **Nonselective adm:** 160/yr. Appl fee: $0. Appl due: Jan. Accepted: 100%. **Enr 500.** Avg class size: 21. Stud/fac: 13:1. Uniform. **Fac 43.** M 4/F 39. FT 33/PT 10. Adv deg: 58%. **Grad '09**—**126.** Col—123. **Tui '10-'11:** Day $6480 (+$1150-1300). Catholic $5880 (+$1150-1300). Aid: Need 135 ($407,113). **Est 1851.** Nonprofit. Roman Catholic. Quar (Aug-May). **Assoc** NCA. The only girls' secondary school in the state, Mount St. Mary enrolls students from Greater Little Rock, Benton, England, Roland, Hot Springs, Cabot and Pine Bluff. Particularly able girls may take honors courses and may also enroll in the International Baccalaureate Diploma Program. Seniors perform 30 hours of required community service.

CENTRAL ARKANSAS CHRISTIAN SCHOOLS   Day Coed Gr PS (Age 3)-12
North Little Rock, AR 72113. 1 Windsong Dr.
Tel: 501-758-3160. Fax: 501-791-7975.
Other locations: 10900 Rodney Parham Rd, Little Rock 72212; 117 W Maryland Ave, Sherwood 72120.
www.cacmustangs.org   E-mail: ctappe@cacmustangs.org
  Carter E. Lambert, Pres. PhD. Chad Tappe, Adm.
  Col Prep. AP (exams req'd; 78 taken, 68% 3+)—Eng Calc Eur_Hist US_Hist World_Hist. **Feat**—Greek Lat Span Stats Comp_Sci Web_Design Psych Bible Photog Studio_Art Theater_Arts Journ. **Supp**—Tut. **Dual enr:** Pulaski Tech, U of Central AR. **Sports**—Basket X-country Golf Soccer Swim Tennis Track. B: Baseball Football. G: Softball Volley. **Somewhat selective adm:** 45/yr. Appl fee: $0. Appl due: Feb. Accepted: 95%. Yield: 95%. **Tests**

CEEB Stanford. **Enr 985.** B 537. G 448. Wh 91%. Latino 1%. Blk 6%. Asian 1%. Other 1%. Avg class size: 25. Uniform. **Fac 63.** M 21/F 42. FT 60/PT 3. Wh 99%. Latino 1%. **Grad '11—81.** Col—80. (Harding 22, U of Central AR 16, U of AR-Fayetteville 13, U of AR-Little Rock 7, Ouachita Baptist 4, AR St 4). Avg ACT: 24.2. **Tui '12-'13:** Day $5850-6900 (+$550-1000). Aid: Need 75 ($250,000). **Est 1971.** Nonprofit. Nondenom Christian. Quar (Aug-May). **Assoc** NCA. The school combines two elementary campuses in outlying sections of the metropolitan area with a central secondary campus serving pupils in grades 7-12. The college preparatory curriculum includes chemistry, Spanish, calculus, physics, fine arts and accounting, in addition to AP courses, and all students attend a daily Bible class.

LOUISIANA

HOLY SAVIOR MENARD CENTRAL HIGH SCHOOL　　　　**Day Coed Gr 7-12**
Alexandria, LA 71303. 4603 Coliseum Blvd.
Tel: 318-445-8233. Fax: 318-448-8170.
www.holysaviormenard.com　　E-mail: dkelly@holysaviormenard.com
　　Joel Desselle, Prin (2007). BS, Louisiana State Univ-Baton Rouge, MEd, Northwestern State Univ.

　　Col Prep. AP (14 exams taken, 71% 3+)—Eng Calc Stats Bio. **Feat**—Fr Span Anat & Physiol Comp_Sci LA_Hist Amer_Stud Econ Law Psych Sociol Philos Relig Studio_Art Theater_Arts Journ. **Supp**—Rem_Math Rem_Read Tut. **Comp:** Comp/Stud: 1:4. **Dual enr:** LA St-Alexandria, LA Tech. **Sports**—Basket X-country Golf Soccer Swim Tennis Track. B: Baseball Football. G: Cheer Softball. Activities: 19. **Somewhat selective** Appl fee: $250. Appl due: Mar. Accepted: 98%. Yield: 95%. **Tests** Stanford. **Enr 481.** B 234. G 247. Elem 182. Sec 299. Wh 90%. Latino 2%. Blk 6%. Asian 1%. Other 1%. Avg class size: 18. Stud/fac: 14:1. Uniform. **Fac 34.** M 14/F 20. FT 32/PT 2. Wh 94%. Latino 6%. Adv deg: 35%. **Grad '11—82.** Col—77. (LA St-Baton Rouge 22, LA St-Alexandria 11, U of LA-Lafayette 7, Northwestern St 7, LA Tech 5, LA Col 4). **Avg SAT:** CR 615. M 530. W 610. Avg ACT: 23.2. **Col Couns:** 1. Alum donors: 35%. **Tui '11-'12:** Day $5500 (+$750-800). Catholic $4400 (+$750-800). Aid: Merit 5 ($5000). Need 60 ($135,000). **Est 1893.** Nonprofit. Roman Catholic (87% practice). Quar (Aug-May). **Assoc** SACS. While Catholic faith courses are compulsory in all grades, the school serves both the Catholic and the non-Catholic communities in the area. Students may pursue either the Menard diploma or the diocesan diploma. Pupils in grades 7 and 8 compile six hours of required community service per semester, while boys and girls in grades 9-12 accumulate eight hours per semester.

CATHOLIC HIGH SCHOOL　　　　**Day Boys Gr 8-12**
Baton Rouge, LA 70806. 855 Hearthstone Dr.
Tel: 225-383-0397. Fax: 225-383-0381.
www.catholichigh.org　　E-mail: info@catholichigh.org
　　Gerald E. Tullier, Pres (2006). BA, St Joseph Seminary College, MTS, Notre Dame Seminary, MEd, Univ of New Orleans. Lisa Harvey, Prin. BA, Louisiana State Univ-Baton Rouge, MRelEd, Loyola Univ (LA). Sherie LeBlanc, Adm.

　　Col Prep. AP (exams req'd; 142 taken, 82% 3+)—Eng Calc Stats Bio US_Hist World_Hist. **Feat**—Fr Lat Span Comp_Sci Web_Design Law Psych Relig Architect_Drawing Studio_Art Chorus Music Accounting Bus Finance Speech. **Supp**—Dev_Read Tut. **Dual enr:** LA St-Baton Rouge. **Sports**— B: Baseball Basket Bowl X-country Football Golf Soccer Swim Tennis Track Wrestling. Activities: 30. **Somewhat selective adm (Gr 8-11):** 308/yr. Appl fee: $45. Appl due: Dec. Accepted: 92%. **Enr 1028.** Elem 26. Sec 1002. Wh 92%. Latino 1%. Blk 6%. Asian 1%. Avg class size: 24. Stud/fac: 12:1. **Fac 86.** M 56/F 30. FT 78/PT 8. Wh 97%. Blk 2%. Other 1%. Adv deg: 60%. **Grad '11—243.** Col—243. (LA St-Baton Rouge 141, Baton Rouge CC 17, Southeastern LA 16, U of LA-Lafayette 9, LA Tech 8, U of New

Orleans 8). **Avg SAT:** CR 628. M 651. W 629. Avg ACT: 25.8. Alum donors: 8%. **Tui '12-'13:** Day $7590 (+$450-550). **Est 1894.** Nonprofit. Roman Catholic. Sem (Aug-May). **Assoc** SACS. The curriculum at CHS offers both honors and AP courses, and graduation requirements include religion, computer literacy, fine arts and general electives. Community service is an important aspect of school life. In addition to scheduling various schoolwide service projects, the school maintains the following requirements: five service hours in grade 8, 10 hours in grade 9, 15 hours in grade 10, completion of a 60-hour service experience in grade 11 and 20 service hours in grade 12.

THE DUNHAM SCHOOL   Day Coed Gr PS (Age 4)-12
Baton Rouge, LA 70810. 11111 Roy Emerson Dr.
Tel: 225-767-7097. Fax: 225-767-3475.
www.dunhamschool.org   E-mail: linda.spear@dunhamschool.org
    Robert W. Welch, Head (2006). BBA, William Carey College, MA, Univ of Louisiana-Monroe. Linda Spear, Adm.
    Col Prep. AP (exams req'd; 31 taken, 68% 3+)—Eng Fr Lat Span Calc Comp_Sci Bio Chem Physics US_Hist World_Hist US_Govt & Pol Studio_Art. **Feat**—Anat Forensic_Sci Kinesiology Psych Relig Fine_Arts Photog Drama Chorus Music Ballet Dance Journ Speech ACT_Prep. **Supp**—LD Rem_Math Rem_Read Rev Tut. **Comp:** Comp/Stud: 1:1 Laptop prgm Gr 2-12. **Sports**—Basket X-country Golf Soccer Swim Tennis Track. B: Baseball Football Wrestling. G: Cheer Softball Volley. Activities: 7. **Selective adm:** 146/yr. Appl fee: $125. Appl due: Jan. Accepted: 85%. Yield: 94%. **Tests** CTP_4. **Enr 802.** B 423. G 379. Elem 544. Sec 258. Wh 86%. Latino 3%. Blk 8%. Asian 2%. Other 1%. Avg class size: 14. Stud/fac: 7:1. Uniform. **Fac 104.** M 21/F 83. FT 88/PT 16. Wh 100%. Adv deg: 40%. **Grad '11—61.** Col—59. (LA St-Baton Rouge 26, TX A&M 3, Southeastern U 2, U of AL-Tuscaloosa 2, U of CO-Boulder 2, U of MS 2). **Avg SAT:** CR 581. M 542. W 531. Avg ACT: 24.7. Alum donors: 11%. **Tui '11-'12:** Day $8330-12,255 (+$825). Aid: Need 244 ($1,096,173). **Est 1981.** Nonprofit. Nondenom Christian (90% practice). Sem (Aug-May). **Assoc** SACS. Dunham offers college preparatory academics, creative opportunities in the fine arts, and various athletic and recreational activities within a Christian environment. The school's advisory program matches middle and upper school students with faculty members in groups of eight to 10 pupils; during these meetings, faculty work with boys and girls on academic and nonacademic issues. Pupils in grades 9-12 perform 25 hours of required community service each year, six of which come during a schoolwide, two-day service project.

EPISCOPAL SCHOOL OF ACADIANA   Day Coed Gr PS (Age 3)-12
Cade, LA 70519. PO Box 380.
Tel: 337-365-1416. Fax: 337-367-9841.
Other locations: 1557 Smede Rd, Broussard 70518; 721 E Kaliste Saloom Rd, Lafayette 70508.
www.esacadiana.com   E-mail: admissions@esacadiana.com
    Charles Skipper, Head (2009). BA, Old Dominion Univ, MA, PhD, George Mason Univ. Jon Berthelot, Adm.
    Col Prep. AP (exams req'd; 57 taken, 70% 3+)—Eng Fr Calc Stats Bio Physics Eur_Hist US_Hist. **Feat**—British_Lit Mythology Span Comp_Sci Comp_Relig Philos Architect Art_Hist Ceramics Photog Sculpt Drama Public_Speak. **Supp**—Dev_Read Rem_Read Tut. **Comp:** Comp/Stud: 1:2. **Sports**—X-country Soccer Swim Tennis Track. B: Baseball Basket Golf Rugby. G: Cheer Volley. **Selective adm (Gr PS-11):** 110/yr. Appl fee: $50. Appl due: Rolling. Accepted: 83%. Yield: 76%. **Tests** CTP_4 IQ. **Enr 530.** B 276. G 254. Elem 355. Sec 175. Wh 79%. Blk 9%. Other 12%. Avg class size: 16. Uniform. **Fac 76.** M 26/F 50. FT 71/PT 5. Wh 96%. Latino 4%. Adv deg: 57%. **Grad '11—58.** Col—58. (LA St-Baton Rouge 16, U of LA-Lafayette 11, Loyola U-LA 4, Tulane 3, U of MS 3, SMU 2). **Avg SAT:** CR 610. M 620. W 600. Avg ACT: 27. **Col Couns:** 1. **Tui '12-'13:** Day $8650-15,050 (+$100-1100). Aid: Merit 1 (7175). Need 130 ($624,000). **Est 1979.** Nonprofit. Episcopal (18% practice). Quar

(Aug-June). In ESA's lower school, one-on-one instruction and group enrichment projects of the children's choosing enable pupils to pursue their interests and learn in an efficient manner. The transitional middle school places emphasis on the learning skills and processes that will assist them with future learning. The upper school curriculum, which features honors and Advanced Placement courses in every discipline, follows the liberal arts model and stresses critical thinking and problem solving. Grades 6-12 are held in Broussard, while the earlier grades convene in Lafayette.

SCHOOLS OF THE SACRED HEART **Bdg Girls Gr 7-12**
Grand Coteau, LA 70541. 1821 Academy Rd, PO Box 310. **Day Boys PS (Age 3)-9**
Tel: 337-662-5275. Fax: 337-662-3011. **Girls PS (Age 3)-12**
www.sshcoteau.org   E-mail: admission@sshcoteau.org **(Coord PS (Age 3)-9)**
    Sr. Lynne Lieux, RSCJ, Head (2008). MA, Washington Univ. D'Lane Wimberley Thomas, Adm.

Col Prep. AP—Eng Fr Span Calc. **Feat**—Environ_Sci Comp_Sci Relig Ceramics Photog Studio_Art Drama Chorus Dance. **Supp**—ESL Rev Tut. **Sports**— G: Basket X-country Equestrian Soccer Swim Tennis Track Volley. **Somewhat selective adm:** 80/yr. Appl fee: $100. Appl due: Rolling. Accepted: 93%. **Enr 476.** Avg class size: 13. Uniform. **Fac 60. Grad '10—31.** Col—31. Avg ACT: 27. Mid 50% ACT: 24-29. **Tui '11-'12:** Bdg $27,650-28,350 (+$3000-3900). 5-Day Bdg $26,350-27,050 (+$3000-3900). Day $8450-11,350 (+$300-900). Intl Bdg $33,700-35,000 (+$3000-3900). **Est 1821.** Nonprofit. Roman Catholic. Quar (Aug-May). Schools of the Sacred Heart comprises two single-gender institutions. Academy of the Sacred Heart offers girls a college preparatory curriculum that features Advanced Placement courses and local and national service programs. Seniors participate in volunteer service projects in a chosen field or career interest. An exchange program with other Sacred Heart schools is open to sophomores or juniors for one quarter. English riding and piano are optional courses. St. John Berchmans School, a day program for boys, opened in 2006 on the north side of campus.

ARCHBISHOP SHAW HIGH SCHOOL **Day Boys Gr 8-12**
Marrero, LA 70072. 1000 Barataria Blvd.
Tel: 504-340-6727. Fax: 504-347-9883.
www.archbishopshaw.org   E-mail: ducote4@archbishopshaw.us
    Rev. Louis Molinelli, SDB, Pres (2011). Rev. Louis Konopelski, Prin. Matthew Ducote, Adm.

Col Prep. AP—Calc Comp_Sci US_Hist World_Hist US_Govt & Pol. **Feat**—Fr Span Econ Psych Sociol Relig Studio_Art Accounting SAT_Prep Study_Skills. **Comp:** Laptop prgm Gr 8-12. **Dual enr:** Our Lady of Holy Cross. **Sports**— B: Baseball Basket Bowl X-country Football Golf Soccer Track Wrestling. **Selective adm:** Appl fee: $20. Appl due: Jan. Accepted: 82%. **Tests** HSPT. **Enr 491.** Elem 39. Sec 452. Avg class size: 24. Stud/fac: 20:1. Uniform. **Fac 36.** M 26/F 10. FT 36. **Grad '04—115.** Col—112. Avg ACT: 24. **Tui '12-'13:** Day $6900 (+$1000-1200). **Est 1962.** Nonprofit. Roman Catholic. Quar (Aug-May). **Assoc** SACS. Operated by the Salesians of Don Bosco, the school offers both college preparatory and honors tracks in grades 8 and 9. Various honors classes are available in the higher grades, as are Advanced Placement courses in several areas and a college-level math class (offered in conjunction with Our Lady of Holy Cross College). Spirituality is integral to school life, with Archbishop Shaw conducting daily religion classes, liturgical celebrations on feast days, retreat programs at each grade level, peer ministry and an optional service program.

CRESCENT CITY CHRISTIAN SCHOOL **Day Coed Gr PS (Age 3)-12**
Metairie, LA 70006. 4828 Utica St.
Tel: 504-885-4700. Fax: 504-885-4703.
http://cccs.publishpath.com   E-mail: billr@celebrationchurch.org

Bill Rigsby, Admin.

Col Prep. Feat—Span Computers Bible Studio_Art Drama Music Speech. **Supp**—Dev_ Read ESL Tut. **Sports**—Basket. B: Baseball Football. G: Softball Volley. **Somewhat selective adm:** 69/yr. Appl fee: $100. Appl due: Rolling. Accepted: 85%. **Tests** Stanford. **Enr 325.** Avg class size: 24. Uniform. **Fac 37.** M 9/F 28. FT 34/PT 3. Adv deg: 8%. **Grad '03—37.** Col—34. Avg ACT: 20. **Tui '12-'13:** Day $4300-5900 (+$725-875). **Est 1956.** Nonprofit. Nondenom Christian. Quar (Aug-June). The program at CCCS includes college preparatory courses. The school is nonsectarian in enrollment. Students in grades 8-12 perform 10 hours of required community service each year.

HOLY CROSS SCHOOL   Day Boys Gr 5-12
New Orleans, LA 70122. 5500 Paris Ave.
Tel: 504-942-3100. Fax: 504-286-5665.
www.holycrosstigers.com   E-mail: contacthc@holycrosstigers.com
    Charles J. DiGange, Head (2004). BS, Loyola Univ (LA), MEd, Tulane Univ. Brian J. Kitchen, Adm.

Col Prep. AP—Eng Calc Environ_Sci US_Govt & Pol Studio_Art. **Feat**—Anat & Physiol Geol Comp_Sci Civics Law Psych Sociol Relig Film Band Chorus Music Bus Journ Speech. **Supp**—Makeup Tut. **Comp:** Laptop prgm Gr 7-12. **Sports**— B: Baseball Basket Bowl X-country Football Golf Soccer Swim Tennis Track Weightlifting Wrestling. Activities: 36. **Selective adm (Gr 5-10):** 200/yr. Appl fee: $20. Accepted: 65%. **Enr 747.** Elem 390. Sec 357. Avg class size: 25. Uniform. **Fac 70.** M 53/F 17. FT 70. Adv deg: 54%. **Grad '08—79.** Col— 74. **Tui '12-'13:** Day $5755-7277 (+$1527-1727). **Est 1879.** Nonprofit. Roman Catholic. Sem (Aug-May). **Assoc** SACS. The school is under the direction of the Brothers of the Congregation of Holy Cross. In addition to a traditional four-year college preparatory program, Holy Cross conducts four- and five-year honors programs. The curriculum features independent study, business and journalism courses, instrumental music and religious studies.

JESUIT HIGH SCHOOL   Day Boys Gr 8-12
New Orleans, LA 70119. 4133 Banks St.
Tel: 504-486-6631. Fax: 504-483-3942.
www.jesuitnola.org   E-mail: info@jesuitnola.org
    Michael A. Giambelluca, Prin. BA, JD, Tulane Univ. Jack S. Truxillo, Adm.

Col Prep. AP (318 exams taken, 92% 3+)—Eng Lat Bio Chem. **Feat**—Creative_Writing Fr Greek Span Calc Astron Environ_Sci Comp_Sci LA_Hist Milit_Hist Econ Law Psych Sociol Theol Film Theater_Arts Band Jazz_Band Public_Speak Speech TV_Production JROTC. **Supp**—Tut. **Comp:** Comp/Stud: 1:3. **Dual enr:** U of NE-Omaha, Creighton. **Sports**— B: Baseball Basket X-country Football Golf Soccer Swim Tennis Track Wrestling. Activities: 42. **Somewhat selective adm:** 309/yr. Appl fee: $20. Appl due: Nov. Accepted: 91%. Yield: 94%. **Tests** HSPT. **Enr 1358.** Elem 256. Sec 1102. Wh 85%. Latino 4%. Blk 5%. Asian 5%. Other 1%. Avg class size: 24. Stud/fac: 12:1. Uniform. **Fac 113.** Wh 94%. Latino 4%. Blk 1%. Other 1%. Adv deg: 47%. **Grad '11—264.** Col—264. **Avg SAT:** CR 635. M 639. W 643. Avg ACT: 27. **Col Couns:** 2. Alum donors: 40%. **Tui '12-'13:** Day $7700 (+$300-700). Aid: Need ($425,000). **Est 1847.** Nonprofit. Roman Catholic. Quar (Aug-May). **Assoc** SACS. Jesuit offers a five-year accelerated academic program, with advanced courses available in all major subjects. All upperclassmen perform 100 hours of community service between the middle of junior year and the middle of senior year. Students in grades 9-12 may join the Marine Corps Junior Reserve Officer Training Corps.

MOUNT CARMEL ACADEMY   Day Girls Gr 8-12
New Orleans, LA 70124. 7027 Milne Blvd.
Tel: 504-288-7626. Fax: 504-288-7629.
www.mcacubs.org   E-mail: mca@mcacubs.org

Sr. Camille Anne Campbell, OCarm, Pres (1980). BA, Dominican College, MS, Univ of Notre Dame, MEd, Univ of Dayton, MA, Mundelein College. Michelle Rigney, Adm.

Col Prep. AP (exams req'd; 198 taken, 79% 3+)—Eng Calc US_Hist US_Govt & Pol. **Feat**—Fr Lat Span Comp_Sci Web_Design Econ Law Psych Sociol Women's_Stud Theol Ceramics Sculpt Studio_Art Drama Theater Music Accounting Communications Speech. **Supp**—Tut. **Comp:** Comp/Stud: 1:4. **Sports**— G: Basket Bowl X-country Golf Soccer Softball Swim Tennis Track Volley. Activities: 28. **Selective adm (Gr 8-11):** 250/yr. Appl fee: $20. Appl due: Nov. Yield: 100%. **Tests** HSPT Stanford. **Enr 1172.** Wh 88%. Latino 3%. Blk 5%. Native Am 1%. Asian 2%. Other 1%. Avg class size: 17. Stud/fac: 11:1. Uniform. **Fac 110.** M 17/F 93. FT 110. Wh 95%. Latino 2%. Blk 1%. Asian 1%. Other 1%. Adv deg: 36%. **Grad '09—214.** Col—214. (LA St-Baton Rouge 111, U of New Orleans 26, U of LA-Lafayette 17, Loyola U-LA 10, Southeastern LA 8, U of MS 7). **Mid 50% SAT:** CR 450-590. M 440-570. W 500-570. Avg ACT: 24.1. Mid 50% ACT: 22-27. Alum donors: 25%. **Tui '10-'11:** Day $5800 (+$2115). Aid: Merit 41 ($20,500). Need 10 ($42,000). Work prgm 54 ($203,000). **Est 1896.** Nonprofit. Roman Catholic (95% practice). Sem (Aug-May). **Assoc** SACS. Mount Carmel offers a college preparatory curriculum that integrates technology and is enriched by Advanced Placement and honors courses, as well as by various electives. Theology classes and prayer are part of the students' daily routine. Cocurricular activities such as a closed-circuit television station and computer-assisted instruction supplement the classroom experience. Girls perform 45 hours of required community service annually.

ST. ANDREW'S EPISCOPAL SCHOOL   **Day Coed Gr PS (Age 4)-8**
New Orleans, LA 70118. 8012 Oak St.
Tel: 504-861-3743. Fax: 504-861-3973.
www.standrewsepiscopalschool.org   E-mail: office@standrewsepiscopalschool.org
Mason Lecky, Head (2009). BA, Univ of Virginia, MEd, Harvard Univ. Lisa Witter, Adm.

Pre-Prep. Feat—Lib_Skills Chin Span Computers Studio_Art Drama Music. **Supp**—Rem_Read Tut. **Comp:** Comp/Stud: 1:1 **Sports**—X-country Soccer. B: Basket. G: Volley. **Selective adm:** 39/yr. Appl fee: $45. Appl due: Rolling. Accepted: 70%. Yield: 61%. **Tests** IQ. **Enr 177.** B 106. G 71. Wh 82%. Latino 1%. Blk 9%. Asian 1%. Other 7%. Avg class size: 16. Stud/fac: 5:1. **Fac 28.** M 5/F 23. FT 22/PT 6. Wh 89%. Latino 7%. Blk 1%. Asian 1%. Other 2%. Adv deg: 50%. **Grad '11—3.** Prep—3. (De La Salle HS-LA 1, New Orleans Ctr for Creative Arts 1, Metairie Park Co Day 1). **Tui '11-'12:** Day $8734-11,278 (+$335-810). Aid: Need ($149,750). **Est 1957.** Nonprofit. Episcopal (26% practice). Tri (Aug-May). The oldest Episcopal school in New Orleans, St. Andrew's emphasizes learning and thinking skills, in addition to good work habits, at all levels. Computer programs supplement most areas of the basic curriculum, and students in grades 2-8 use classroom-based wireless laptop computers. Students attend chapel services two to three times per week. Spanish is taught at all levels and Chinese in grades 7 and 8.

ST. MARY'S DOMINICAN HIGH SCHOOL   **Day Girls Gr 8-12**
New Orleans, LA 70125. 7701 Walmsley Ave.
Tel: 504-865-9401. Fax: 504-866-5958.
www.stmarysdominican.org   E-mail: crice@stmarysdominican.org
Cynthia A. Thomas, Pres. BA, Nicholls State Univ, MRE, Loyola Univ (LA), MEd, Our Lady of Holy Cross College. Carolyn Favre, Prin. Cathy Rice, Adm.

Col Prep. AP—Eng Fr Span Calc Chem US_Hist US_Govt & Pol. **Feat**—Creative_Writing Women's_Lit Lat Anat & Physiol Comp_Sci Law Psych Relig Fine_Arts Studio_Art Band Chorus Music Journ. **Supp**—Rev Tut. **Sports**— G: Basket X-country Golf Soccer Softball Swim Tennis Track Volley. Activities: 33. **Selective adm:** 275/yr. Appl fee: $20. Appl due: Jan. Accepted: 80%. **Tests** HSPT Stanford. **Enr 919.** Elem 152. Sec 767. Uniform. **Fac 76.** M 11/F 65. FT 68/PT 8. Adv deg: 38%. **Grad '08—147.** Col—147. Mid 50% ACT: 22-27. **Tui '12-'13:** Day $8200 (+$1600-1725). **Est 1860.** Nonprofit. Roman Catholic. Sem (Aug-May). **Assoc** SACS. Founded by the Dominican Sisters as the New Orleans Female Dominican

Academy, Dominican supplements its college preparatory curriculum with various extracurricular activities. An active parents' club sponsors many parent-daughter activities.

STUART HALL SCHOOL FOR BOYS Day Boys Gr PS (Age 3)-7
New Orleans, LA 70118. 2032 S Carrollton Ave.
Tel: 504-861-1954. Fax: 504-861-5389.
www.stuarthall.org E-mail: fmckenna@stuarthall.org
   Kevin R. Avin, Head. MEd. Cissy LaForge, Prin. PhD. Katherine Morrill Diliberto, Adm.
   Pre-Prep. Feat—Lib_Skills Fr Span Computers Relig Studio_Art Music. **Sports**— B: Baseball Basket X-country Soccer Tennis. **Selective adm:** Appl fee: $35. **Enr 332.** Avg class size: 18. Uniform. **Fac 42.** M 9/F 33. FT 41/PT 1. Adv deg: 42%. **Grad '10**—33. Prep—33. (Jesuit HS-LA 31, Br Martin 2). **Tui '11-'12:** Day $7400-10,000 (+$1000-2000). **Est 1984.** Nonprofit. Roman Catholic. Tri (Aug-May). As boys progress at Stuart Hall, focus shifts from concrete to abstract learning concepts. Specialized instruction in art, library, music, computer, French and physical education complements core course work.

TRINITY EPISCOPAL SCHOOL Day Coed Gr PS (Age 4)-8
New Orleans, LA 70130. 1315 Jackson Ave.
Tel: 504-525-8661. Fax: 504-523-4837.
www.trinitynola.com E-mail: msorrells@trinitynola.com
   Rev. Michael C. Kuhn, Head (2001). BA, Univ of the South, MDiv, General Theological Seminary, DMin, Episcopal Divinity School. Merry Sorrells, Adm.
   Pre-Prep. Feat—Fr Span Computers Relig Fine_Arts Visual_Arts Drama Music. **Supp**—Dev_Read Rem_Math Rem_Read Rev Tut. **Sports**—Basket Soccer Tennis Track. B: Baseball. G: Softball Volley. **Selective adm:** 42/yr. Appl fee: $50. Appl due: Jan. Accepted: 43%. Yield: 72%. **Tests** IQ. **Enr 331.** B 180. G 151. Avg class size: 15. Casual dress. **Fac 56.** M 9/F 47. FT 42/PT 14. Adv deg: 75%. **Grad '08**—29. Prep—24. Alum donors: 20%. **Tui '12-'13:** Day $16,260-17,160 (+$800-1500). **Est 1960.** Nonprofit. Episcopal. (Aug-May). Trinity's traditional elementary program balances core course work in language arts, math, science, social studies and foreign language with fine arts, computer, religious studies and physical education classes. Technology is an important element of the program: Lower school children develop word processing skills and learn to create Web pages, multimedia presentations and spreadsheets; at the middle school level (grades 5-8), technology is integrated into the curriculum and is used as a tool to broaden and strengthen skills in all subject areas. Boys and girls attend daily chapel, study religion formally in grades 1-8 and, in middle school, participate in age-appropriate community service projects.

URSULINE ACADEMY Day Girls Gr PS (Age 2)-12
New Orleans, LA 70118. 2635 State St.
Tel: 504-861-9150. Fax: 504-861-7392.
www.ursulineneworleans.org E-mail: info@ursulineneworleans.org
   Glenn Gennaro, Int Pres (2012). Mary Antee, Adm.
   Col Prep. AP—Eng Bio US_Hist US_Govt & Pol. **Feat**—Southern_Lit Fr Lat Span Calc Anat & Physiol Environ_Sci Comp_Sci Civics Law Psych Theol Drawing Graphic_Arts Painting Sculpt Studio_Art Drama Theater_Arts Chorus Music Speech. **Supp**—Rev Tut. **Sports**—G: Basket X-country Golf Soccer Softball Swim Tennis Track Volley. Activities: 24. **Selective adm (Gr PS-11):** Appl fee: $25-50. Appl due: Jan. **Tests** HSPT. **Enr 754.** Elem 329. Sec 425. Wh 74%. Latino 3%. Blk 19%. Native Am 1%. Asian 3%. Stud/fac: 11:1. Uniform. **Fac 82.** M 9/F 73. FT 76/PT 6. Adv deg: 31%. **Grad '11**—74. Col—74. Avg ACT: 22.3. **Col Couns:** 2. **Tui '12-'13:** Day $8200 (+$800). Aid: Need 75. **Est 1727.** Nonprofit. Roman Catholic (81% practice). Quar (Aug-May). **Assoc** SACS. The oldest continuously operating girls' school in the country, Ursuline provides an intensive study of the liberal arts, in addition to a strong technology program and a diverse fine arts program. Prekindergarten and kindergarten chil-

dren gain an exposure to French, music, art and computer literacy. Girls in grades 5-7 receive accelerated instruction in the core subjects, and the high school curriculum includes honors and Advanced Placement classes. Christian service is an integral part of the program at all grade levels, with girls in grades 9-12 performing 25 hours of required service each year.

WESTMINSTER CHRISTIAN ACADEMY   **Day Coed Gr PS (Age 3)-12**
Opelousas, LA 70570. 186 Westminster Dr.
Tel: 337-948-8607. Fax: 337-948-8983.
Other locations: 163 Westminster Dr, Opelousas 70570; 111 Goshen Ln, Lafayette 70508; 4015 Moss St, Lafayette 70507.
www.wcala.org   E-mail: mnezat@wcala.org
    Merida Brooks, Supt (2007). Michelle Nezat, Adm.

    Col Prep. AP—Eng Chem Eur_Hist. **Feat**—Linguistics Fr Lat Span Calc Comp_Sci Bible Graphic_Arts Photog Studio_Art Theater. **Supp**—LD. **Comp:** Laptop prgm Gr 11-12. **Sports**—Basket X-country Swim Track. B: Baseball Football Soccer. G: Cheer Softball Volley. **Selective adm (Gr PS-10):** 124/yr. Appl fee: $150. Appl due: Rolling. Accepted: 73%. **Tests** Stanford. **Enr 1039.** B 532. G 507. Elem 813. Sec 226. Wh 80%. Latino 2%. Blk 17%. Asian 1%. Avg class size: 24. Uniform. **Fac 68.** M 15/F 53. FT 62/PT 6. Wh 92%. Blk 8%. Adv deg: 14%. **Grad '10—44.** Col—43. (U of LA-Lafayette 18, LA St-Baton Rouge 12, LA St-Eunice 5, LA Tech 2, Northwestern St 2, Olivet Nazarene 1). **Avg SAT:** CR 680. M 581. Avg ACT: 24.2. **Col Couns:** 1. **Tui '12-'13:** Day $4340-5935 (+$325-550). Aid: Need 70 ($71,144). **Est 1978.** Nonprofit. Nondenom Christian. Quar (Aug-May). WCA's preschool program emphasizes play and discovery as learning tools, while the lower school (grades 1-6) focuses on academic skills development. The transitional middle school (grades 7 and 8) features an expanded curriculum designed to ready students for high school. Two separate honors curricula and an array of electives are important aspects of the upper school program (grades 9-12). A campus serving children in grades PS-6 operates on Goshen Lane in Lafayette; preschool children may also attend school at 163 Westminster Dr. (adjacent to the main Opelousas campus) or at the Calvary campus on Moss Street in Lafayette.

CEDAR CREEK SCHOOL   **Day Boys Gr PS (Age 4)-12**
Ruston, LA 71270. 2400 Cedar Creek Dr.   **Girls PS (Age 3)-12**
Tel: 318-255-7707. Fax: 318-251-2846.
www.cedarcreekschool.org   E-mail: info@cedarcreekschool.org
    Andrew Yepson, Int Head (2012). BS, MS, Louisiana Tech Univ. Susan Everett, Adm.

    Col Prep. AP (exams req'd; 49 taken, 39% 3+)—Eng Calc Bio Chem. **Feat**—Creative_Writing Fr Span Comp_Sci Civics Econ Sociol Studio_Art Music Journ Speech. **Supp**—Rev Tut. **Sports**—Basket X-country Golf Tennis Track. B: Baseball Football Weightlifting. G: Cheer Softball. **Somewhat selective adm:** 72/yr. Appl fee: $100. Appl due: May. Accepted: 97%. Yield: 99%. **Tests** IQ. **Enr 682.** B 349. G 333. Elem 469. Sec 213. Avg class size: 17. Stud/fac: 17:1. Uniform. **Fac 68.** M 14/F 54. FT 65/PT 3. Wh 98%. Latino 1%. Blk 1%. Adv deg: 33%. **Grad '09—44.** Col—41. (LA Tech 20, LA St-Baton Rouge 10, U of LA-Monroe 2, U of LA-Lafayette 1, Emory 1, Millsaps 1). **Avg SAT:** CR/M/W 2027. Avg ACT: 24.3. **Tui '11-'12:** Day $5990-6270 (+$250-1250). **Est 1970.** Nonprofit. Sem (Aug-May). **Assoc** SACS. During the lower school years (grades pre-K-5), all children at Cedar Creek receive instruction in music, art, computer, library and Spanish each week; frequent field trips provide enrichment at this level. The junior high school (grades 6-8) blends traditional, self-contained and departmentalized courses in the major disciplines. This division also features an advisory program and interdisciplinary projects. CCS' high school program, which includes college preparatory, honors and AP courses, enables the student to progress at an appropriate pace. Programming for gifted pupils begins in junior high. Students enroll from a 50-mile radius that covers the north-central part of the state.

MISSISSIPPI

SAINT STANISLAUS COLLEGE   **Bdg Boys Gr 7-PG**
Bay St Louis, MS 39520. 304 S Beach Blvd.   **Day Boys 7-12**
Tel: 228-467-9057. Fax: 228-466-2972.
www.ststan.com   E-mail: admissions@ststan.com
    Br. Bernard Couvillion, Pres. Patrick McGrath, Prin. John Thibodeaux, Adm.
    Col Prep. AP (80 exams taken)—Eng Calc Comp_Sci Bio Chem Physics Eur_Hist
US_Hist. **Feat**—Creative_Writing Fr Span Stats Anat & Physiol Astron Environ_Sci Geol
Marine_Bio/Sci Econ Govt Law MS_Stud Relig Ceramics Chorus Accounting Health. **Supp**—
Dev_Read ESL LD Rem_Math Rem_Read. **Sports**— B: Baseball Basket X-country Football
Golf Sail Soccer Swim Tennis Track Weightlifting. Activities: 24. **Selective adm:** 165/yr. Bdg
77. Day 88. Appl fee: $100. Appl due: Rolling. Accepted: 80%. Yield: 90%. **Enr 414.** Bdg
90. Day 324. Elem 114. Sec 300. Intl 10%. Avg class size: 23. Uniform. **Fac 34.** M 22/F 12.
FT 34. Adv deg: 55%. In Dorms 2. **Grad '10**—77. Col—74. Avg ACT: 22. **Tui '11-'12:** Bdg
$21,500-26,275 (+$1375). Day $5680 (+$375). Intl Bdg $24,375-27,225 (+$1375-2575). **Est**
1854. Nonprofit. Roman Catholic. Sem (Aug-May). **Assoc** SACS. The college preparatory
curriculum at St. Stanislaus includes advanced French and Spanish language study, as well
as Advanced Placement courses in several other disciplines. Business, computer education,
physical education and religion programs round out the curriculum. Students with diagnosed
learning differences may enroll in an academic assistance program.

JACKSON ACADEMY   **Day Coed Gr PS (Age 3)-12**
Jackson, MS 39236. 4908 Ridgewood Rd, PO Box 14978.
Tel: 601-362-9676. Fax: 601-364-5722.
www.jacksonacademy.org   E-mail: ja@jacksonacademy.org
    J. Peter Jernberg, Jr., Pres (1988). BA, MSE, EdS, Delta State Univ. Pat Taylor, Head. BS,
MEd, PhD. DeLeslie Porch, Adm.
    Col Prep. AP (exams req'd; 183 taken, 63% 3+)—Eng Calc Bio Chem Physics US_Hist
Comp_Govt & Pol US_Govt & Pol Studio_Art. **Feat**—Creative_Writing Fr Lat Span Anat &
Physiol Econ Psych Sociol Music Accounting Speech. **Supp**—LD. **Comp:** Comp/Stud: 1:9.
Sports—Basket X-country Golf Soccer Swim Tennis Track. B: Baseball Football. G: Cheer
Softball. **Somewhat selective adm:** 159/yr. Appl fee: $50. Appl due: Rolling. Accepted: 97%.
Yield: 91%. **Tests** Stanford. **Enr 1263.** Elem 924. Sec 339. Wh 94%. Blk 3%. Asian 1%. Other
2%. Avg class size: 22. Stud/fac: 18:1. Uniform. **Fac 100.** M 13/F 87. FT 97/PT 3. Wh 96%.
Latino 2%. Blk 2%. Adv deg: 44%. **Grad '10**—86. Col—85. (U of MS 34, MS St 32, MS Col
5, U of AL-Tuscaloosa 4, Auburn 2, Delta St 2). **Avg SAT:** CR 650. M 650. W 650. Avg ACT:
28. **Col Couns:** 4. Alum donors: 6%. **Tui '12-'13:** Day $8340-11,760 (+$400-700). Aid: Need
183 ($521,310). **Est 1959.** Nonprofit. Sem (Aug-May). **Assoc** CLS SACS. The school, located
on 48 acres in northeast Jackson, offers a traditional curriculum supplemented by honors and
Advanced Placement courses. Art, music, physical education and foreign language instruction
commences in grade 1.

JACKSON PREPARATORY SCHOOL   **Day Coed Gr 6-12**
Jackson, MS 39232. 3100 Lakeland Dr.
Tel: 601-939-8611. Fax: 601-936-4068.
www.jacksonprep.net   E-mail: lmorton@jacksonprep.net
    Susan R. Lindsay, Head (2004). BS, Memphis Univ, MEd, Mississippi College. Lesley
Morton, Adm.
    Col Prep. AP (exams req'd; 208 taken, 77% 3+)—Eng Fr Lat Span Calc Bio Chem Envi-
ron_Sci Physics US_Hist US_Govt & Pol Studio_Art. **Feat**—British_Lit Creative_Writing
Chin Greek Stats Programming MS_Stud World_Relig Film Drama Band Chorus Account-

ing Debate Finance Speech. **Supp**—LD. **Comp:** Comp/Stud: 1:4. **Sports**—Basket X-country Golf Soccer Swim Tennis Track. B: Baseball. G: Softball. Activities: 16. **Somewhat selective adm:** 208/yr. Appl fee: $40. Appl due: Rolling. Accepted: 92%. Yield: 94%. **Enr 805.** Avg class size: 17. Uniform. **Fac 86.** Adv deg: 53%. **Grad '09—112.** Col—112. (U of MS 50, MS St 28, MS Col 5, Samford 3, Belmont U 2, Col of Charleston 2). **Avg SAT:** CR 644. M 630. W 615. **Mid 50% SAT:** CR 590-710. M 550-690. W 550-670. Avg ACT: 26. Mid 50% ACT: 23-29. **Col Couns:** 3. **Tui '12-'13:** Day $10,818-11,818 (+$850-2350). **Est 1970.** Nonprofit. Sem (Aug-May). **Assoc** CLS SACS. Jackson Prep's curriculum, designed for the average to above-average student, features the Classical Heritage Program, which allows students to receive a diploma with an emphasis in classical studies. Program participants must complete at least six courses in Latin, Greek and classical civilization and must carry a 95 average in these classes.

CATHEDRAL SCHOOL   Day Coed Gr PS (Age 3)-12
Natchez, MS 39120. 701 Martin Luther King Jr St.
Tel: 601-442-2531. Fax: 601-442-0960.
www.cathedralgreenwave.com   E-mail: pat.sanguinetti@cathedralgreenwave.com
    Patrick Sanguinetti, Admin (2002). BA, Univ of Mississippi, MEd, William Carey College.
    Col Prep. AP (exams req'd)—Eng Calc. **Feat**—Lib_Skills Fr Span Anat & Physiol Environ_Sci Comp_Sci Econ Psych MS_Stud Relig Studio_Art Chorus Music Accounting Study_Skills. **Supp**—LD Tut. **Sports**—Basket Bowl X-country Golf Soccer Swim Tennis Track. B: Baseball Football Weightlifting. G: Cheer Softball. **Somewhat selective adm:** 65/yr. Appl due: Rolling. Accepted: 95%. **Enr 625.** Elem 425. Sec 200. Wh 75%. Latino 5%. Blk 17%. Asian 3%. Avg class size: 20. Uniform. **Fac 70.** M 10/F 60. FT 70. Wh 90%. Latino 5%. Blk 5%. Adv deg: 40%. **Grad '09—33.** Col—33. (MS St 9, U of MS 7, Copiah-Lincoln CC 6, LA St-Baton Rouge 2, U of S MS 2, Hinds CC 2). Avg ACT: 22.6. **Col Couns:** 1. **Tui '12-'13:** Day $4100-5355 (+$100-275). **Est 1847.** Nonprofit. Roman Catholic (47% practice). Quar (Aug-May). **Assoc** SACS. The college preparatory curriculum at Cathedral, which includes honors and Advanced Placement courses, is enhanced by strong foreign language and fine arts programs. Students take religion classes in all grades, and daily prayer is an important element of the school environment. Computer training begins in kindergarten. Students in grades 9-12 perform 20 hours of required community service each year.

OXFORD UNIVERSITY SCHOOL   Day Coed Gr PS (Age 3)-5
Oxford, MS 38655. 2402 S Lamar Blvd.
Tel: 662-234-2200. Fax: 662-234-3505.
www.ouschool.com   E-mail: oxford@bellsouth.net
    Tommy Naron, Head (2010). Emily Grace Ames, Adm.
    Gen Acad. Feat—Span Computers Bible Art_Hist Studio_Art Music. **Supp**—Tut. **Comp:** Comp/Stud: 1:5. **Sports**—Swim. **Somewhat selective adm:** 48/yr. Appl fee: $50. Appl due: Feb. Accepted: 92%. Yield: 85%. **Tests** IQ Stanford. **Enr 140.** B 72. G 68. Avg class size: 10. Stud/fac: 8:1. **Fac 19.** M 1/F 18. FT 15/PT 4. **Tui '12-'13:** Day $5810-6546 (+$500-1200). **Est 1984.** Nonprofit. Quar (Aug-May). Children at OUS gain an introduction to computers and the arts while also developing research skills. The foreign language program commences in grade 4. Field trips provide enrichment at all grade levels.

CHAMBERLAIN-HUNT ACADEMY   Bdg & Day
Port Gibson, MS 39150. 124 McComb Ave.   Boys Gr 7-12
Tel: 601-437-8855. Fax: 601-437-4313.
www.chamberlain-hunt.com   E-mail: admissions@chamberlain-hunt.com

Col. John Gardner West, Pres (2008). MEd, Reformed Theological Seminary, MDiv, Covenant Theological Seminary, JD, Univ of Notre Dame. Lt. Col. Quentin Johnston, Prin. MDiv, PhD, Whitefield Theological Seminary. Stephen C. Allen, Adm.

Col Prep. Milit. AP—Eng. **Feat**—Fr Lat Span Calc Comp_Sci Econ Govt MS_Stud Bible. **Supp**—Dev_Read ESL Makeup Rem_Math Rem_Read Rev Tut. **Comp:** Comp/Stud: 1:4. Outdoor Ed. **Sports**— B: Basket X-country Football Golf Soccer Tennis Track. Activities: 20. **Selective adm (Gr 7-11):** 56/yr. Bdg 52. Day 4. Appl fee: $50. Appl due: Aug. Accepted: 75%. Yield: 85%. **Enr 120.** B 110. G 10. Bdg 100. Day 20. Elem 45. Sec 75. Wh 80%. Latino 4%. Blk 10%. Asian 2%. Other 4%. Avg class size: 5. Stud/fac: 5:1. Uniform. **Fac 18.** M 13/F 5. FT 17/PT 1. Wh 95%. Latino 5%. Adv deg: 61%. **Grad '11—10.** Col—7. Avg ACT: 23. **Col Couns:** 1. **Tui '12-'13:** Bdg $25,000. Day $13,500. Intl Bdg $29,000. Aid: Merit 6 ($12,500). Need 30 ($400,000). Work prgm 1 ($6500). **Est 1879.** Nonprofit. Nondenom Christian (90% practice). Sem (Aug-May). CHA's Christian military program features small classes and a structured environment. The college preparatory curriculum includes an annual Bible unit; in addition, cadets receive scripture instruction each weekday and attend Wednesday chapel services. Students generally devote Saturday mornings to on-campus work or community projects. The academy's wilderness program utilizes a 70-acre site adjoining the main campus. Although Chamberlain-Hunt is primarily a boys' school, the day division enrolls a small number of girls.   **See Also Page 80**

OKLAHOMA

ST. JOHN'S EPISCOPAL SCHOOL   Day Coed Gr PS (Age 3)-8
Oklahoma City, OK 73112. 5401 N Brookline Ave.
Tel: 405-943-8583. Fax: 405-943-8584.
www.stjohnsokc.com   E-mail: knelson@stjohnsokc.com
Joe Norton, Head (2011).

Pre-Prep. Gen Acad. Feat—Span Computers Relig Studio_Art Drama Music Speech. **Supp**—Tut. **Sports**—Soccer Track. **Somewhat selective adm:** 9/yr. Appl fee: $0. Appl due: Rolling. Accepted: 95%. **Tests** Stanford. **Enr 120.** B 50. G 70. Wh 89%. Latino 1%. Blk 7%. Native Am 1%. Asian 2%. Avg class size: 12. Uniform. **Fac 11.** M 2/F 9. FT 9/PT 2. Wh 100%. Adv deg: 45%. **Grad '10—6.** Prep—2. Alum donors: 25%. **Tui '11-'12:** Day $5850 (+$300). Aid: Need 12 ($21,825). **Est 1951.** Nonprofit. Episcopal (40% practice). Sem (Aug-May). Based on Christian principles, the school's course of studies provides solid preparation for high school. The curriculum includes such enrichment classes as foreign languages, art, music, physical education and computer science.

WESTMINSTER SCHOOL   Day Coed Gr PS (Age 3)-8
Oklahoma City, OK 73118. 600 NW 44th St.
Tel: 405-524-0631. Fax: 405-528-4412.
www.westminsterschool.org   E-mail: mail@westminsterschool.org
Robert S. Vernon, Head (1992). BA, Yale Univ, MEd, Univ of Oklahoma. Paul Arceneaux, Adm.

Pre-Prep. Feat—Span Engineering Computers Amer_Stud Studio_Art. **Supp**—Rev Tut. **Comp:** Comp/Stud: 1:2. **Sports**—Basket Soccer Tennis Track. G: Volley. **Somewhat selective adm:** 89/yr. Appl fee: $0. Appl due: Rolling. **Enr 537.** B 263. G 274. Wh 80%. Latino 4%. Blk 3%. Native Am 3%. Asian 4%. Other 6%. Avg class size: 17. Stud/fac: 13:1. **Fac 55.** M 8/F 47. FT 45/PT 10. Wh 84%. Blk 2%. Native Am 4%. Asian 8%. Other 2%. Adv deg: 49%. **Grad '11—55.** Prep—34. (Bishop McGuinness 22, Heritage Hall 14, Casady 10). Alum donors: 6%. **Tui '12-'13:** Day $10,300-11,580 (+$400-900). Aid: Need 11 ($106,640). **Est 1963.** Nonprofit. Sem (Aug-May). Drawing students from throughout Metropolitan Oklahoma City, Westminster employs a team-teaching approach that provides opportunities for curriculum integration across subject lines. Westminster comprises three divisions—primary (prekindergarten and kindergarten), lower school (grades 1-5) and middle school (grades 6-8)—each of which addresses the particular learning needs of its age group. Grade-level interdisciplinary classes in such areas as science and math, American studies and engineering enrich the middle school curriculum; various electives complement core courses during these years.

BISHOP KELLEY HIGH SCHOOL   **Day Coed Gr 9-12**
Tulsa, OK 74135. 3905 S Hudson Ave.
Tel: 918-627-3390. Fax: 918-664-2134.
www.bkelleyhs.org   E-mail: mgabel@bkelleyhs.org
     Rev. Brian O'Brien, Pres (2009). BA, Boston College, MEd, Univ of Notre Dame, MA, MDiv, Saint Meinrad School of Theology. Curt Feilmeier, Prin. BA, Univ of Nebraska-Lincoln, MA, Wayne State College. Jane Oberste, Adm.
     Col Prep. AP (exams req'd; 324 taken, 64% 3+)—Eng Fr Span Calc Bio Chem Environ_Sci Physics Eur_Hist US_Hist Econ Psych US_Govt & Pol Studio_Art. **Feat**—Creative_Writing Chin Ger Lat Stats Engineering Programming Russ_Hist Intl_Relations Sociol Women's_Stud Theol Accounting Debate Journ. **Supp**—LD Rem_Math Tut. **Sports**—Basket X-country Golf Soccer Swim Tennis Track. B: Baseball Football Wrestling. G: Cheer Softball Volley. Activities: 38. **Selective adm (Gr 9-11):** 250/yr. Appl fee: $20. Appl due: Rolling. **Tests** HSPT. **Enr 807.** B 421. G 386. Wh 81%. Latino 8%. Native Am 4%. Asian 3%. Other 2%. Avg class size: 13. Stud/fac: 12:1. Uniform. **Fac 82.** FT 72/PT 10. Adv deg: 54%. **Grad '10—207.** Col—197. (U of OK 47, OK St 32, Tulsa CC 21, U of AR-Fayetteville 11, U of Tulsa 11, U of CO-Boulder 7). **Avg SAT:** CR 576. M 561. W 553. Avg ACT: 24. **Col Couns:** 2. **Tui '12-'13:** Day $10,600 (+$645). Catholic $8300 (+$645). **Est 1960.** Nonprofit. Roman Catholic (71% practice). Quar (Aug-May). **Assoc** NCA. Bishop Kelley offers a selection of courses designed to meet students' varying needs and abilities. The school follows a block-scheduling format that includes both honors and Advanced Placement course work. A pre-engineering program allows students to gain hands-on experience in the laboratory. As part of Bishop Kelley's Christian service program, each student performs 25 hours of community service annually, some of which must involve work with the economically disadvantaged.

CASCIA HALL PREPARATORY SCHOOL   **Day Coed Gr 6-12**
Tulsa, OK 74114. 2520 S Yorktown Ave.
Tel: 918-746-2604. Fax: 918-746-2640.
www.casciahall.org   E-mail: info@casciahall.org
     Roger C. Carter, Head (2010). Carol A. Bradley, Adm.
     Col Prep. AP (exams req'd; 302 taken, 68% 3+)—Eng Ger Span Calc Stats Bio Chem Physics Eur_Hist US_Govt & Pol Studio_Art. **Feat**—Creative_Writing Chin Fr Lat Calc Astron Comp_Sci Russ_Hist Geog Psych Philos Theol World_Relig Photog Acting Theater_Arts Chorus Journ Speech Driver_Ed. **Supp**—LD Rev Tut. **Dual enr:** Tulsa CC, U of Tulsa, OK St. **Sports**—Basket X-country Golf Soccer Tennis Track. B: Baseball Football Wrestling. G: Cheer Softball Volley. Activities: 25. **Selective adm:** 111/yr. Appl fee: $25. Appl due: Rolling. Accepted: 75%. Yield: 75%. **Tests** SSAT. **Enr 579.** B 300. G 279. Elem 204. Sec 375. Wh 83%. Latino 5%. Blk 3%. Native Am 5%. Asian 3%. Other 1%. Avg class size: 20. Stud/fac: 12:1. Uniform. **Fac 50.** M 25/F 25. FT 39/PT 11. Wh 89%. Latino 4%. Native Am 5%. Asian 1%. Other 1%. Adv deg: 78%. **Grad '10—88.** Col—88. (U of OK 17, U of KS 7, U of Tulsa 7, OK St 6, U of AR-Fayetteville 3, U of TX-Austin 2). **Avg SAT:** CR 611. M 602. W 600. **Mid 50% SAT:** CR 560-650. M 530-650. W 540-660. Avg ACT: 26.5. Alum donors: 25%. **Tui '11-'12:** Day $11,800 (+$500). Aid: Need 85 ($400,000). **Est 1926.** Nonprofit. Roman Catholic (50% practice). Quar (Aug-May). **Assoc** NCA. Located on a 40-acre campus in an urban setting. Cascia Hall is conducted by the Order of St. Augustine. The middle school program (grades 6-8) emphasizes the mastery of fundamental skills as it readies students for the higher grades. In the upper school (grades 9-12), the liberal arts curriculum includes Advanced Placement offerings, and a four-week term in January enables freshmen and sophomores to

participate in a variety of activities, lectures and field trips. Boys and girls accumulate 80 hours of required community service during the upper school years.

MONTE CASSINO SCHOOL   **Day Coed Gr PS (Age 3)-8**
Tulsa, OK 74114. 2206 S Lewis Ave.
Tel: 918-742-3364. Fax: 918-742-5206.
www.montecassino.org   E-mail: mfitzpatrick@montecassino.org
Matthew Vereecke, Dir (2010). MEd, Univ of Notre Dame. Mary Fitzpatrick, Adm.

Pre-Prep. Feat—Fr Lat Span Relig Performing_Arts Studio_Art Music. **Supp**—Rev Tut. **Comp:** Comp/Stud: 1:1.3 (1:1 Laptop prgm Gr 5-8). **Sports**—Basket Golf Tennis. B: Baseball Wrestling. G: Cheer Softball Volley. **Selective adm:** 146/yr. Appl fee: $35. Appl due: Rolling. **Enr 904.** B 431. G 473. Wh 84%. Latino 3%. Blk 1%. Native Am 5%. Asian 5%. Other 2%. Avg class size: 18. Uniform. **Fac 81.** M 2/F 79. FT 75/PT 6. Wh 98%. Native Am 2%. **Grad '10—91.** Prep—74. (Bishop Kelley 46, Cascia Hall 21, Holland Hall 6). **Tui '11-'12:** Day $7832 (+$575). **Est 1926.** Nonprofit. Roman Catholic (50% practice). Sem (Aug-May). **Assoc** NCA. Monte Cassino's developmentally appropriate preschool program, which commences at age 3, combines play, guided exploration and hands-on activities. Elementary school children (grades K-4) follow a curriculum organized around grade-wide themes that require students to demonstrate mastery of skills and content. The curriculum at the middle school level (grades 5-8), which continues to center around grade-level themes, supplements required course work with pre-Advanced Placement classes.

UNIVERSITY SCHOOL   **Day Coed Gr PS (Age 3)-8**
Tulsa, OK 74104. 800 S Tucker Dr.
Tel: 918-631-5060. Fax: 918-631-5065.
www.uschool.utulsa.edu   E-mail: debra-price@utulsa.edu
Patricia L. Hollingsworth, Dir (1982). BS, Florida State Univ, MAT, EdD, Univ of Tulsa. Debra Price, Adm.

Gen Acad. Feat—Chin Span Computers Geog Studio_Art Drama Music. **Comp:** Comp/ Stud: 1:10. **Somewhat selective adm:** 41/yr. Appl fee: $25. Appl due: Rolling. **Tests** IQ. **Enr 235.** B 126. G 109. Wh 84%. Latino 1%. Blk 5%. Native Am 5%. Asian 5%. Avg class size: 21. **Fac 42.** M 3/F 39. FT 32/PT 10. Wh 84%. Latino 1%. Blk 5%. Native Am 5%. Asian 5%. Adv deg: 19%. **Grad '11—14. Tui '12-'13:** Day $9318-9535. Aid: Need ($135,000). **Est 1982.** Nonprofit. Spons: University of Tulsa. Sem (Aug-May). The school's curriculum emphasizes active learning within an interdisciplinary structure. Course work focuses on academic achievement, personal responsibility, and the development of students' creativity and problem-solving abilities. Older pupils take part in required community service projects; annual participation is 10 hours in grade 5, 12 hours in grade 6, 14 hours in grade 7 and 16 hours in grade 8. The school is situated on the University of Tulsa campus.

TEXAS

AUSTIN INTERNATIONAL SCHOOL   **Day Coed Gr PS (Age 3)-5**
Austin, TX 78759. 12001 Oak Knoll Dr.
Tel: 512-331-7806. Fax: 512-219-5201.
www.austininternationalschool.org   E-mail: info@austininternationalschool.org
Christophe Bonnet, Exec Dir (2010). Christine Christy, Adm.

Pre-Prep. Gen Acad. Bilingual (Fr Span). Feat—Fr Span Computers Geog Studio_Art. **Supp**—ESL Rem_Math Rem_Read Tut. **Comp:** Comp/Stud: 1:5. **Somewhat selective adm:** 42/yr. Appl fee: $100. Appl due: Feb. Accepted: 100%. Yield: 99%. **Enr 150.** B 67. G 83. Intl 37%. Avg class size: 16. Uniform. **Fac 18.** M 2/F 16. FT 11/PT 7. Wh 89%. Latino 11%. Adv deg: 22%. **Grad '09—5.** Prep—3. **Tui '11-'12:** Day $9400-10,300 (+$1200). Aid: Need 8 ($60,000). **Est 2001.** Nonprofit. Tri (Aug-June). Accredited by the French Ministry of Education, AIS conducts a trilingual immersion program in Spanish, French and English that combines elements of the American and French public school curricula. Boys and girls develop a solid foundation in the basic academic areas while gaining proficiency in these three languages. Programming at the school prepares graduates for future pursuit of either the International Baccalaureate or the French Baccalaureate. Native speakers provide all language instruction.

HYDE PARK BAPTIST SCHOOLS — Day Coed Gr K-12
Austin, TX 78751. 3901 Speedway Ave.
Tel: 512-465-8331. Fax: 512-371-1433.
Other locations: 11400 N Mopac Expressway, Austin 78759.
www.hpbs.org   E-mail: jshaver@hpbs.org
James Grunert, Supt (2009). BS, MEd, Stephen F. Austin Univ, EdD, East Texas State Univ. Lisa Thomas, HS Adm & Becky Fenlaw, K-8 Adm.

Col Prep. Gen Acad. AP (182 exams taken, 66% 3+)—Eng Fr Span Calc Stats Bio Chem Physics US_Hist Econ US_Govt & Pol. **Feat**—Creative_Writing Lat Comp_Sci Psych Bible Studio_Art Drama Theater_Arts Chorus Dance Journ Speech. **Supp**—ESL Tut. **Sports**—Basket X-country Soccer Tennis Track. B: Baseball Football Golf. G: Softball Volley. Activities: 10. **Selective adm:** 145/yr. Appl fee: $75-125. Appl due: Rolling. **Tests** ISEE Stanford. **Enr 524.** Elem 291. Sec 233. Wh 99%. Latino 1%. Stud/fac: 9:1. Uniform. **Fac 69.** M 17/F 52. FT 57/PT 12. Adv deg: 21%. **Grad '11—72.** Col—72. **Avg SAT:** CR 583. M 613. W 579. Avg ACT: 24.8. **Col Couns:** 1. **Tui '12-'13:** Day $7350-12,550 (+$1000). **Est 1968.** Nonprofit. Baptist. Sem (Aug-May). **Assoc** SACS. HPBS consists of a junior/senior high and on elementary school. The school maintains a strong Christian emphasis: Biblical studies classes and weekly chapel attendance are required. Junior high students perform at least five hours of community service annually.

KIRBY HALL SCHOOL — Day Coed Gr PS (Age 4)-12
Austin, TX 78705. 306 W 29th St.
Tel: 512-474-1770. Fax: 512-474-1117.
www.kirbyhallschool.org   E-mail: admissions@khs.org
Beverly Rase, Dir (1976). BA, Wellesley College. Helen Roberts, Adm.

Col Prep. AP (28 exams taken, 79% 3+)—Eng Span Calc Stats Bio Eur_Hist US_Hist US_Govt & Pol. **Feat**—Comp_Sci Film Studio_Art Drama Music Debate Health. **Supp**—Rev Tut. **Dual enr:** U of TX-Austin. Activities: 18. **Selective adm:** 29/yr. Appl fee: $50. Appl due: Rolling. Accepted: 84%. Yield: 97%. **Enr 105.** B 51. G 54. Elem 95. Sec 10. Wh 76%. Latino 5%. Blk 1%. Asian 14%. Other 4%. Avg class size: 10. **Fac 19.** FT 11/PT 8. Wh 89%. Latino 10%. Other 1%. Adv deg: 52%. **Grad '11—6.** Col—6. (U of St Andrews-Scotland 1, U of Chicago 1, U of TX-Austin 1, TX St-San Marcos 1, Middlebury 1). **Avg SAT:** CR 650. M 610. W 620. **Col Couns:** 1. Alum donors: 2%. **Tui '12-'13:** Day $7700-10,320 (+$700-845). Aid: Need 2 ($12,202). **Est 1976.** Nonprofit. Nondenom Christian. Quar (Aug-May). **Assoc** SACS. Kirby Hall's elementary curriculum features innovative approaches to phonics, grammar and composition, and math. In the upper school, students choose from a selection of Advanced Placement courses beginning in grade 10. The school makes extensive use of its proximity to the University of Texas-Austin: Starting in grade 4, pupils conduct research at the university's library and in its databases, and boys and girls attend various exhibits and performances at the institution as well. Upper schoolers may travel abroad to such locations as Australia, Italy, Costa Rica, France, Spain, England and Greece.

1136   Concise School Listings

REGENTS SCHOOL OF AUSTIN   Day Coed Gr K-12
Austin, TX 78735. 3230 Travis Country Cir.
Tel: 512-899-8095. Fax: 512-899-8623.
www.regentsschool.com   E-mail: btucci@regents-austin.com
Rod Gilbert, Head (2008). BS, MDiv. Becky Tucci, Adm.

Col Prep. AP—Lat Calc Stats. **Feat**—Humanities Fr Span Anat & Physiol Econ Bible Drama Band Chorus Orchestra Dance Speech. **Supp**—Tut. **Sports**—Basket X-country Golf Soccer Swim Tennis. B: Baseball Football. G: Cheer Volley. **Selective adm:** 142/yr. Appl fee: $125. Appl due: Feb. **Tests** ISEE. **Enr 900.** Avg class size: 14. Stud/fac: 7:1. Uniform. **Fac 69.** M 15/F 54. FT 62/PT 7. Adv deg: 28%. **Grad '10—39.** Col—39. **Mid 50% SAT:** CR 600-700. M 600-690. W 600-720. Avg ACT: 26. **Col Couns:** 1. Alum donors: 25%. **Tui '05-'06:** Day $7450-9750. Aid: Need 126 ($530,000). **Est 1992.** Nonprofit. Nondenom Christian. Sem (Aug-May). Located on an 82-acre campus in the southwestern part of the city, Regents conducts a classical liberal arts program that incorporates a Christian worldview. At all grade levels, course content conforms to the student's ability to process facts, analyze concepts and express themselves as they synthesize material. Boys and girls spend much of their classroom time in grades 9-12 sitting at oval Harkness tables that encourage discussion. Field trips that may involve travel to other cities or other countries are included in the standard tuition fee.

ALL SAINTS EPISCOPAL SCHOOL   Day Coed Gr PS (Age 3)-8
Beaumont, TX 77706. 4108 Delaware St.
Tel: 409-892-1755. Fax: 409-892-0166.
www.allsaints-beaumont.org   E-mail: sclark@allsaints-beaumont.org
Catherine Clark, Head (2005). BA, Stephens College. Kathy Fisher, Adm.

Pre-Prep. Feat—Lat Span Studio_Art Drama Chorus Music Health. **Supp**—ESL Rem_ Read Rev Tut. **Comp:** Comp/Stud: 1:4. **Sports**—Basket X-country Golf Soccer Tennis Track. G: Softball Volley. **Selective adm:** 52/yr. Appl fee: $125. Appl due: Rolling. Accepted: 79%. Yield: 62%. **Tests** IQ Stanford. **Enr 396.** B 189. G 207. Wh 82%. Latino 5%. Blk 5%. Asian 3%. Other 5%. Avg class size: 20. Stud/fac: 20:1. Uniform. **Fac 45.** M 6/F 39. FT 39/PT 6. Wh 92%. Latino 5%. Blk 3%. Adv deg: 13%. **Grad '10—34.** Prep—28. (Monsignor Kelly HS 26, St Stephen's Episcopal Sch-TX 2). **Tui '11-'12:** Day $7690-8200 (+$480). Aid: Need 27 ($87,592). **Est 1954.** Nonprofit. Episcopal (27% practice). Sem (Aug-May). **Assoc** CLS. All Saints offers individualized instruction, team teaching and classroom learning, with particular emphasis placed upon phonetics and linguistics. Pupils must study two foreign languages.

EPISCOPAL HIGH SCHOOL   Day Coed Gr 9-12
Bellaire, TX 77401. 4650 Bissonnet St.
Tel: 713-512-3400. Fax: 713-512-3603.
www.ehshouston.org   E-mail: akoehler@ehshouston.org
C. Edward Smith, Head (2007). AB, Princeton Univ, MA, Middlebury College. Audrey S. Koehler, Adm.

Col Prep. AP (exams req'd)—Eng Fr Lat Span Calc Stats Bio Environ_Sci Physics Eur_ Hist US_Hist World_Hist Econ Psych US_Govt & Pol Studio_Art. **Feat**—Creative_Writing Shakespeare Chin Geol Oceanog Comp_Sci Chin_Hist WWII Relig World_Relig Photog Theater Music Dance. **Supp**—Rev Tut. **Comp:** Comp/Stud: 1:1 Laptop prgm Gr 9-12. **Sports**—Basket X-country Golf Lacrosse Soccer Swim Tennis Track. B: Baseball Football Wrestling. G: Cheer F_Hockey Softball Volley. Activities: 28. **Selective adm (Gr 9-11):** 182/yr. Appl fee: $60. Appl due: Jan. Accepted: 67%. Yield: 55%. **Tests** ISEE. **Enr 672.** B 305. G 367. Wh 78%. Latino 6%. Blk 8%. Asian 3%. Other 5%. Avg class size: 15. Stud/fac: 8:1. Uniform. **Fac 90.** M 40/F 50. FT 88/PT 2. Wh 90%. Latino 4%. Blk 2%. Asian 2%. Other 2%. Adv deg: 58%. **Grad '11—156.** Col—156. (U of TX-Austin 28, TX Christian 16, U of MS 8, U of GA 7, TX A&M 6, TX Tech 6). **Avg SAT:** CR 580. M 602. W 570. **Col Couns:** 4. **Tui '12-'13:** Day $21,880 (+$5075). Aid: Need 105 ($1,700,000). **Est 1982.** Nonprofit. Episcopal (23% practice). Sem (Aug-May). Drawing students primarily from the Houston metropolitan area, the school features a college preparatory curriculum and a favorable student-faculty ratio. Technology instruction is integrated into the curriculum, with all students using laptop computers in class and at home. For a week each January, boys and girls in grades 9-11 choose a grade-level course and an elective course from a variety of subject areas. Student groups organize regular community service projects, and seniors may substitute two weeks of intensive outreach activities for classes. **See Also Page 92**

CARROLLTON CHRISTIAN ACADEMY Day Coed Gr PS (Age 4)-12
Carrollton, TX 75010. 2205 E Hebron Pky.
Tel: 972-242-6688. Fax: 972-245-0321.
www.ccasaints.org   E-mail: jfunk@ccasaints.org
David Culpepper, Head (2012). Jane Funk, Adm.

Col Prep. AP—Calc. **Feat**—Span Econ Govt Bible Photog Studio_Art Theater_Arts Band Chorus Orchestra Debate Photojourn. **Supp**—LD Tut. **Comp:** Comp/Stud: 1:2. **Dual enr:** Brookhaven. **Sports**—Basket X-country Golf Soccer Tennis Track. B: Baseball Football. G: Cheer Softball Volley. **Somewhat selective adm:** 103/yr. Appl fee: $100. Appl due: Rolling. Accepted: 85%. **Tests** CEEB ISEE SSAT Stanford. **Enr 325.** B 180. G 145. Elem 225. Sec 100. Wh 66%. Latino 6%. Blk 6%. Native Am 2%. Asian 15%. Other 5%. Intl 6%. Avg class size: 18. Uniform. **Fac 41.** M 8/F 33. FT 35/PT 6. Wh 91%. Latino 7%. Blk 2%. Adv deg: 41%. **Grad '09—49.** Col—49. (Abilene Christian 8, TX A&M 5, U of OK 2, Baylor 2, SMU 1, Northwestern 1). **Avg SAT:** CR 534. M 578. W 529. **Col Couns:** 1. **Tui '12-'13:** Day $6500-11,250 (+$1100). **Est 1980.** Nonprofit. Nondenom Christian (95% practice). Sem (Aug-May). **Assoc** SACS. CCA integrates Biblical principles into all aspects of school life. A phonics-intensive reading curriculum is employed during the elementary years, while the college preparatory high school offers a dual-credit program with Brookhaven College. Students choose from various academic electives, musical and artistic pursuits, school publications and athletic options. High schoolers perform 10 hours of required community service per semester. The affiliated First United Methodist Church offers before- and after-school care for CCA children in grades pre-K-5, as well as after-school supervision for boys and girls in grades 7-12.

INCARNATE WORD ACADEMY Day Coed Gr PS (Age 3)-12
Corpus Christi, TX 78404. 2920 S Alameda St.
Tel: 361-883-0857. Fax: 361-883-2185.
www.iwacc.org   E-mail: iwacc@iwacc.org
Charles D. Imbergamo, Pres (2010). BA, St Joseph's College, MA, St Mary's Univ of San Antonio. Colette Rye, Adm.

Col Prep. Montessori. AP (136 exams taken, 62% 3+)—Eng Span Calc Bio Chem Physics US_Hist Econ US_Govt & Pol Studio_Art. **Feat**—Fr Comp_Sci Web_Design Psych Sociol Relig Fine_Arts Band Chorus Journ. **Supp**—Rev Tut. **Comp:** Comp/Stud: 1:3. **Dual enr:** Del Mar Col. **Sports**—Basket X-country Golf Soccer Swim Tennis Track. B: Baseball. G: Cheer Softball Volley. **Selective adm (Gr PS-11):** 172/yr. Appl due: Rolling. **Enr 889.** B 417. G 472. Elem 577. Sec 312. Wh 56%. Latino 40%. Blk 2%. Asian 2%. Uniform. **Fac 104.** M 34/F 70. FT 79/PT 25. Wh 50%. Latino 49%. Blk 1%. Adv deg: 34%. **Grad '10—72.** Col—72. (TX A&M-Corpus Christi 11, Del Mar Col 10, U of TX-San Antonio 8, TX A&M 6, U of the Incarnate Word 5, Trinity U 3). **Avg SAT:** CR 533. M 514. W 526. Avg ACT: 22.9. Alum donors: 30%. **Tui '11-'12:** Day $7250-7800 (+$500-650). Aid: Merit 136 ($243,700). Need 139 ($953,463). **Est 1871.** Nonprofit. Roman Catholic (75% practice). Sem (Aug-May). **Assoc** SACS. IWA's college preparatory high school curriculum features Advanced Placement and honors courses and dual-credit opportunities through Del Mar College. The middle school program includes electives in such areas as art, life skills and mediation training, while the elementary grades utilize both Montessori and traditional methods of instruction. The academy integrates technology into the curriculum at all grade levels. Boys and girls perform 12 hours of community service per year in grades 6-8, and 24 hours per year in grades 9-12.

ST. JAMES EPISCOPAL SCHOOL   Day Coed Gr PS (Age 2)-8
Corpus Christi, TX 78401. 602 S Carancahua St.
Tel: 361-883-0835. Fax: 361-883-0837.
www.sjes.org   E-mail: stjames@sjes.org
     Walter Spencer, Head (2012). BA, MA, Univ of Texas-San Antonio. Alison Relkin, Adm.
     Gen Acad. Feat—Lib_Skills Span Computers Studio_Art Drama Outdoor_Ed. **Supp**—
Dev_Read Rem_Math Rem_Read Rev Tut. **Comp:** Laptop prgm Gr 6-8. Outdoor Ed.
Sports—Basket X-country Golf Soccer Tennis Track Volley. **Somewhat selective adm:** 25/yr.
Appl fee: $50. Appl due: Rolling. Accepted: 90%. Yield: 90%. **Tests** ISEE. **Enr 214.** B 107.
G 107. Wh 90%. Latino 8%. Blk 1%. Asian 1%. Avg class size: 16. Stud/fac: 11:1. Uniform.
Fac 25. M 2/F 23. Wh 88%. Latino 12%. Adv deg: 36%. **Grad '11**—**17.** Prep—5. (Incarnate
Word-TX 2, Pope John Paul II-FL 1). **Tui '11-'12:** Day $7000-8575 (+$350-1180). Aid: Merit
6 ($5500). Need 34 ($125,000). **Est 1946.** Nonprofit. Episcopal (30% practice). Sem (Aug-
May).   St. James' program, built around central themes, stresses a strong academic base in
reading, language arts, process writing, spelling, mathematics, history and the sciences. Computer literacy is required. Music, studio and theater arts, and physical education complement
the academic curriculum. Students in grades 5-8 perform 25 hours of required community
service each year.

ANN AND NATE LEVINE ACADEMY   Day Coed Gr PS (Age 2)-8
Dallas, TX 75252. 18011 Hillcrest Rd.
Tel: 972-248-3032. Fax: 972-248-0695.
www.levineacademy.org   E-mail: info@levineacademy.org
     Mark Stolovitsky, Head (2010). BCL, LLB, McGill Univ (Canada), MEd, Univ of Calgary
(Canada). Mireille Brisebois-Allen, Adm.
     Pre-Prep. Feat—Hebrew Computers Judaic_Stud Studio_Art Drama Music Study_Skills.
Supp—ESL Rem_Math Rem_Read Tut. **Sports**—Basket Soccer. G: Volley. **Somewhat selec-
tive adm:** 83/yr. Appl fee: $100-200. Appl due: Jan. Accepted: 90%. **Tests** CTP_4. **Enr 400.**
Wh 94%. Latino 5%. Asian 1%. Avg class size: 15. Stud/fac: 5:1. Uniform. **Fac 98.** M 4/F 94.
FT 49/PT 49. Wh 95%. Latino 5%. Adv deg: 25%. **Grad '10**—**23.** Prep—12. (Episcopal Sch
of Dallas 1, Greenhill-TX 1). **Tui '11-'12:** Day $13,900-19,900 (+$50). **Est 1979.** Nonprofit.
Jewish (100% practice). Tri (Aug-May). **Assoc** SACS.   As part of its curriculum, Levine Academy emphasizes Jewish studies and the Hebrew language. Judaic teachings and Torah lessons
are integrated into the elementary school program (grades K-4), while older students engage
in an advanced-level program of rabbinical text study that includes the Talmud. Science, math,
the humanities, computer science and the arts are among the general subject areas. Boys and
girls in grades 5-8 perform 10 hours of required community service per year.

DALLAS INTERNATIONAL SCHOOL   Day Coed Gr PS (Age 3)-12
Dallas, TX 75230. 6039 Churchill Way.
Tel: 972-991-6379. Fax: 972-991-6608.
www.dallasinternationalschool.org   E-mail: admissions@dallasinternationalschool.org
     Pierre Vittoz, Head (2004). Mea Ahlberg, Adm.
     Col Prep. IB Diploma. Fr Bac. Bilingual (Fr Span). Feat—Chin Fr Span Geol Econ
Philos. **Supp**—ESL Tut. **Comp:** Comp/Stud: 1:15. **Dual enr:** U of TX-Dallas. **Sports**—
Basket Soccer Swim Tennis. Activities: 5. **Selective adm:** 70/yr. Appl fee: $170. Appl due:
Jan. Accepted: 70%. Yield: 65%. **Tests** ISEE. **Enr 600.** Elem 530. Sec 70. Intl 30%. Avg class
size: 18. Uniform. **Fac 70.** M 10/F 60. FT 70. Wh 90%. Latino 10%. Adv deg: 41%. **Grad
'11**—**6.** Col—4. (U of TX-Austin 1, McGill-Canada 1, Hendrix 1). **Col Couns:** 1. **Tui '12-'13:**
Day $11,870-18,900 (+$200). Aid: Need 17 ($50,000). **Est 1991.** Nonprofit. Tri (Aug-June).
Students at this multilingual, multicultural school attend classes taught in French, Spanish
and English, enabling them to achieve fluency in all three languages. (Chinese is an additional
curricular choice.) In addition to receiving American college preparation, high school pupils
prepare for the French Baccalaureate or the International Baccalaureate. Boys and girls per-

form 10 hours of required community service each year in grades 9-12, or 75 hours annually for those enrolled in the IB Diploma Program.

DALLAS LUTHERAN SCHOOL Day Coed Gr 7-12
Dallas, TX 75243. 8494 Stults Rd.
Tel: 214-349-8912. Fax: 214-340-3095.
www.dallaslutheranschool.com E-mail: betsybronkhorst@dallaslutheranschool.com
David Bangert, Exec Dir. BA, Concordia Univ River Forest, MA, Univ of Wisconsin-Milwaukee. Betsy Bronkhorst, Adm.

Col Prep. AP—Eng Calc World_Hist. **Feat**—Shakespeare Mythology Span Stats Anat & Physiol Programming TX_Hist Econ Govt Psych Relig Studio_Art Drama Chorus Music Speech. **Supp**—Dev_Read Makeup Rem_Math Rem_Read Rev Tut. **Comp:** Comp/Stud: 1:1 **Sports**—Basket X-country Golf Soccer Track. B: Baseball Football. G: Cheer Softball Volley. **Somewhat selective adm:** Appl fee: $100. Appl due: Feb. **Enr 200.** Avg class size: 16. Stud/fac: 9:1. Uniform. **Fac 21.** M 11/F 10. FT 21. Adv deg: 61%. **Grad '11—42.** Col—40. **Avg SAT:** CR 483. M 480. W 485. Avg ACT: 23.7. **Tui '12-'13:** Day $10,400-12,550 (+$300). **Est 1974.** Nonprofit. Lutheran-Missouri Synod. Sem (Aug-May). DLS conducts a college preparatory program that emphasizes efficient work habits, critical-thinking ability and sound study skills. Electives and several Advanced Placement options are part of the curriculum. Students accumulate 80 hours of required community service between the end of sophomore year and graduation.

EPISCOPAL SCHOOL OF DALLAS Day Coed Gr PS (Age 3)-12
Dallas, TX 75229. 4100 Merrell Rd.
Tel: 214-358-4368. Fax: 214-353-5872.
Other locations: 4344 Colgate Ave, Dallas 75225.
www.esdallas.org E-mail: info@esdallas.org
Rev. Stephen B. Swann, Head (1974). BA, Northeastern Oklahoma State Univ, MDiv, Church Divinity School of the Pacific. Ruth Burke, Adm.

Col Prep. AP (exams req'd; 256 taken, 88% 3+)—Eng Fr Lat Span Calc Stats Comp_Sci Bio Chem Physics Eur_Hist US_Hist World_Hist Econ US_Govt & Pol Art_Hist Studio_Art Music_Theory. **Feat**—Creative_Writing Chin Forensic_Sci Geol Microbio Oceanog Biochem Relig World_Relig Ceramics Film Photog Drama Music Journ Outdoor_Ed Wilderness_Ed. **Supp**—Tut. **Sports**—Basket Crew X-country Lacrosse Soccer Tennis Track. B: Baseball Football Golf Wrestling. G: F_Hockey Softball Volley. **Selective adm (Gr PS-11):** 161/yr. Appl fee: $100-200. Appl due: Jan. Accepted: 32%. Yield: 68%. **Tests** CEEB CTP_4 IQ ISEE SSAT. **Enr 1170.** B 580. G 590. Wh 86%. Latino 4%. Blk 3%. Native Am 1%. Asian 3%. Other 3%. Avg class size: 15. Uniform. **Fac 145.** M 32/F 113. FT 133/PT 12. Wh 94%. Latino 1%. Blk 1%. Native Am 1%. Asian 1%. Other 2%. Adv deg: 56%. **Grad '11—96.** Col—96. (U of TX-Austin 11, SMU 6, U of AL-Tuscaloosa 6, TX Christian 5, TX A&M 5, Rhodes 3). **Mid 50% SAT:** CR 570-690. M 610-700. W 610-680. **Col Couns:** 3. **Tui '12-'13:** Day $13,870-24,150 (+$110-2075). Aid: Need ($2,700,000). **Est 1974.** Nonprofit. Episcopal. Quar (Aug-May). **Assoc** CLS. At ESD, the academic curriculum is complemented by artistic and athletic programs, as well as extracurricular offerings. Pupils must attend daily chapel services, participate in a wilderness program and perform community service (50 hours during the upper school years). The lower school holds classes at a separate campus on Colgate Avenue (214-353-5818).

FIRST BAPTIST ACADEMY Day Coed Gr PS (Age 4)-12
Dallas, TX 75221. 1606 Patterson St.
Tel: 214-969-7861. Fax: 214-969-7797.
www.fbacademy.com E-mail: smoney@firstdallas.org
Brian Littlefield, Head (2010). MEd. Elizabeth Gore, Adm.

Col Prep. AP—Eng Calc Eur_Hist US_Hist World_Hist Econ US_Govt & Pol. **Feat**—ASL Lat Span Anat Forensic_Sci Bible Architect Drawing Painting Photog Studio_Art Theater Debate Journ. **Supp**—LD. **Sports**—Basket Golf Swim Tennis Track Weightlifting. B: Baseball Football Wrestling. G: Softball Volley. **Selective adm:** Appl due: Rolling. **Tests** CTP_4 ISEE Stanford. **Enr 285.** Stud/fac: 10:1. Uniform. **Fac 31. Tui '12-'13:** Day $9050-13,015 (+$650). **Est 1972.** Nonprofit. Evangelical. Quar (Aug-May). **Assoc** SACS. FBA's college preparatory program emphasizes critical-thinking and problem-solving skills. During the spring interim week, middle and upper school students attend spiritual retreats, mission trips and educational excursions. Boys and girls attend weekly chapel and daily Bible classes.

LAKEHILL PREPARATORY SCHOOL
Day Coed Gr K-12

Dallas, TX 75214. 2720 Hillside Dr.
Tel: 214-826-2931. Fax: 214-826-4623.
Other locations: 7401 Ferguson Rd, Dallas 75228.
www.lakehillprep.org   E-mail: hwalker@lakehillprep.org
    Roger L. Perry, Head (1982). BS, MEd, Univ of North Texas. Holly Walker, Adm.

Col Prep. AP (exams req'd; 79 taken, 46% 3+)—Eng Fr Span Calc Stats Comp_Sci Bio Environ_Sci Eur_Hist US_Hist Studio_Art. **Feat**—Creative_Writing Shakespeare Lat Comp_Graphics Art_Hist Sculpt Drama Musical_Theater Music Public_Speak. Outdoor Ed. **Sports**—Basket X-country Golf Tennis Track. B: Baseball Football. G: Cheer Softball Volley. Activities: 35. **Selective adm:** 71/yr. Appl fee: $150. Appl due: Jan. **Tests** CTP_4 ISEE Stanford. **Enr 400.** B 190. G 210. Elem 294. Sec 106. Wh 81%. Latino 3%. Blk 7%. Asian 6%. Other 5%. Avg class size: 16. Stud/fac: 10:1. **Fac 44.** M 14/F 30. FT 43/PT 1. Wh 83%. Latino 3%. Blk 3%. Native Am 3%. Asian 3%. Other 5%. Adv deg: 63%. **Grad '11—32.** Col—32. (TX Christian 3, TX A&M 2, Duke 1, Morehouse 1, Brown 1, Tufts 1). **Avg SAT:** CR 643. M 594. W 604. **Mid 50% SAT:** CR 535-630. M 520-600. W 518-604. Avg ACT: 24. Mid 50% ACT: 20-27. **Col Couns:** 1. **Tui '11-'12:** Day $12,672-16,725 (+$900). Aid: Need 65 ($500,000). **Est 1971.** Nonprofit. Sem (Aug-May). **Assoc** SACS. Lakehill's curriculum features Advanced Placement courses in the major disciplines. Speech, drama, musical theater and choir are among the performing arts options. Senior projects are required. The Ferguson Road campus hosts athletic facilities and an environmental science center.

THE PARISH EPISCOPAL SCHOOL
Day Coed Gr PS (Age 3)-12

Dallas, TX 75244. 4101 Sigma Rd.
Tel: 972-239-8011, 800-909-9081. Fax: 972-991-1237.
Other locations: 14115 Hillcrest Rd, Dallas 75254.
www.parishepiscopal.org   E-mail: mmclean@parishepiscopal.org
    David W. Monaco, Head (2009). BA, Hamilton College, MA, Columbia Univ. Marci M. McLean, Adm.

Col Prep. AP—Eng Fr Lat Span Calc Stats Comp_Sci Bio Chem Physics Eur_Hist US_Hist Psych Studio_Art Music_Theory. **Feat**—Creative_Writing Satire Sci_Fiction Women's_Lit Anat & Physiol Environ_Sci Engineering Govt/Econ Philos World_Relig Existentialism Ceramics Drawing Film Photog Acting Theater_Arts Music Dance Journ Speech. **Sports**—Basket Cheer X-country Golf Soccer Swim Tennis Track. B: Baseball Football Weightlifting. G: Softball Volley. **Selective adm:** Appl fee: $100-150. Appl due: Jan. **Tests** ISEE. **Enr 1150.** Avg class size: 18. Uniform. **Fac 163.** M 39/F 124. FT 152/PT 11. Adv deg: 17%. **Grad '11—103.** Col—102. (U of TX-Austin 11, U of OK 6, TX Christian 5, SMU 4, Rhodes 3, U of AZ 3). **Col Couns:** 2. **Tui '12-'13:** Day $18,300-22,390 (+$500-1000). **Est 1972.** Nonprofit. Episcopal (70% practice). Tri (Aug-May). Religious services and practices form a significant part of Parish Episcopal's daily schedule. The curriculum's structure enables students to attend chapel services and devote time to community service activities. Advanced Placement courses are offered in most disciplines. Pupils choose from various electives in drama, art and music. Boys and girls in grades 9-12 perform 15 hours of required community service per year. A second campus, serving grades pre-K-2, operates on Hillcrest Road.

ST. THOMAS AQUINAS SCHOOL
Dallas, TX 75214. 3741 Abrams Rd.

Day Coed Gr PS (Age 3)-8

Tel: 214-826-0566. Fax: 214-826-0251.
Other locations: 6255 Mockingbird Ln, Dallas 75214.
www.staschool.org   E-mail: jlimber@staschool.org
Patrick Magee, Prin (2004). Joyce Limber, Adm.

Pre-Prep. Feat—Span Computers Relig Studio_Art Drama Music. **Supp**—Dev_Read LD Rem_Math Rem_Read Rev Tut. **Sports**—Basket Soccer Swim Track Volley. B: Baseball Football. G: Cheer Softball. **Nonselective adm:** 70/yr. Appl fee: $75. Appl due: Feb. Accepted: 100%. **Enr 875.** Avg class size: 25. Uniform. **Fac 49.** M 7/F 42. FT 37/PT 12. Adv deg: 22%. **Grad '11**—71. Prep—61. (Bishop Lynch 39, Ursuline Acad of Dallas 10, Jesuit Col Prep 10, Bishop Dunne 1, John Paul II HS 1). **Tui '12-'13:** Day $8650 (+$525). Parishioners $6050 (+$525). Aid: Need 30 ($40,000). **Est 1947.** Nonprofit. Roman Catholic. Quar (Aug-June). With an early childhood program (ages 3-5) in addition to grades PS-8, the school offers a full elementary program in a Catholic setting. Language and learning skills specialists provide support to pupils in need of academic assistance. The lower school (469-341-0911) operates on Mockingbird Lane.

SHELTON SCHOOL
Dallas, TX 75248. 15720 Hillcrest Rd.

Day Coed Gr PS (Age 3)-12

Tel: 972-774-1772. Fax: 972-991-3977.
www.shelton.org   E-mail: wdeppe@shelton.org
Suzanne Stell, Exec Dir (2010). BS, Univ of Texas-Austin, MEd, Dallas Baptist Univ. Linda Kneese, Head. MEd. Diann Slaton, Adm.

LD. Feat—ASL Lat Span Computers Econ Govt Psych Ethics Studio_Art Theater_Arts Music Speech Design. **Supp**—Dev_Read Rem_Math Rem_Read Rev Tut. **Comp:** Laptop prgm Gr 7-12. **Sports**—Basket X-country Golf Tennis Track. B: Baseball Football. G: Cheer Softball Volley. **Selective adm (Gr PS-10):** 154/yr. Appl fee: $50. Appl due: Rolling. Accepted: 48%. Yield: 89%. **Tests** IQ. **Enr 853.** B 536. G 317. Elem 618. Sec 235. Avg class size: 8. Stud/fac: 6:1. Uniform. **Fac 169.** M 28/F 141. FT 165/PT 4. Adv deg: 55%. **Grad '09**—**49.** Col—47. (U of AR-Fayetteville 5, Savannah Col of Art & Design 4, TX Tech 3, TX Christian 3, U of AZ 3, U of OK 2). **Tui '11-'12:** Day $11,625-22,790. **Est 1976.** Nonprofit. Sem (Aug-May). The school offers specialized training for children with learning differences through multisensory instruction. Highly structured, small classes provide ongoing work in study skills. Supplementary offerings include perceptual-motor training, physical education and intramural athletic competition, computer classes and a variety of extracurricular activities. Students in grades 7-12 lease laptop computers from the school for classroom work and homework assignments. The Shelton Evaluation Center provides assessment services for the evaluation and referral of children and adults. A speech, language and hearing clinic is also available.

URSULINE ACADEMY OF DALLAS
Dallas, TX 75229. 4900 Walnut Hill Ln.

Day Girls Gr 9-12

Tel: 469-232-1800. Fax: 469-232-1836.
www.ursulinedallas.org   E-mail: msnyder@ursulinedallas.org
Gretchen Zibilich Kane, Pres (2012). BS, MME, Univ of New Orleans. Elizabeth C. Bourgeois, Prin. BA, College of New Rochelle, MA, Creighton Univ. Michele L. Snyder, Adm.

Col Prep. AP (364 exams taken, 85% 3+)—Eng Fr Lat Span Calc Stats Comp_Sci Bio Environ_Sci Physics Eur_Hist US_Hist Econ Psych US_Govt & Pol Studio_Art Music_Theory. **Feat**—Creative_Writing Shakespeare Chin Arabic Anat & Physiol Web_Design Comp_Relig Theol Ceramics Drawing Painting Photog Jewelry Theater Chorus Dance Journ. **Supp**—Rev Tut. **Comp:** Comp/Stud: 1:1 Laptop prgm Gr 9-12. **Sports**— G: Basket Cheer Crew X-country Golf Lacrosse Soccer Softball Swim Tennis Track Volley. Activities: 42. **Selective adm (Gr 9-11):** 200/yr. Appl fee: $60. Appl due: Jan. Accepted: 60%. **Tests** ISEE. **Enr 800.** Wh

75%. Latino 14%. Blk 3%. Native Am 1%. Asian 5%. Other 2%. Avg class size: 19. Stud/fac: 10:1. Uniform. **Fac 84.** M 12/F 72. FT 84. Wh 84%. Latino 8%. Blk 1%. Native Am 1%. Asian 5%. Other 1%. Adv deg: 67%. **Grad '10—191.** Col—191. **Avg SAT:** CR 614. M 608. W 619. **Mid 50%** SAT: CR 570-680. M 560-670. W 570-680. Avg ACT: 27.8. Mid 50% ACT: 25-30. **Col Couns:** 3. **Tui '11-'12:** Day $15,750 (+$500-1300). Aid: Need 158 ($732,000). **Est 1874.** Nonprofit. Roman Catholic (83% practice). Sem (Aug-June). **Assoc** SACS. Sponsored by the Ursuline Sisters of Dallas, this Catholic school provides a college preparatory program that emphasizes critical thinking and the further development of individual talents and interests. Each girl must have a laptop computer for daily class use. All students perform 100 hours of required community service prior to graduation.

THE WINSTON SCHOOL   **Day Coed Gr 1-12**
Dallas, TX 75229. 5707 Royal Ln.
Tel: 214-691-6950. Fax: 214-691-1509.
www.winston-school.org   E-mail: stefanie_whitworth@winston-school.org
   Polly A. Peterson, Head (2007). BSW, Southern Connecticut State Univ, MSW, Univ of Maryland-Baltimore County, PhD, Univ of Southern California. Stefanie Whitworth, Adm.
   Col Prep. LD. Feat—Lat Span Engineering Ceramics Fine_Arts Studio_Art Drama Music. **Supp**—Rem_Math Rem_Read Tut. **Comp:** Comp/Stud: 1:1.5 (1:1 Laptop prgm Gr 7-12). **Dual enr:** Brookhaven, Richland. **Sports**—Basket Bowl Golf Soccer Tennis. B: Baseball Football. G: Cheer Softball Volley. **Selective adm:** 43/yr. Appl fee: $150. Appl due: Rolling. Accepted: 64%. Yield: 67%. **Tests** IQ. **Enr 200.** B 137. G 63. Elem 106. Sec 94. Wh 86%. Latino 4%. Blk 8%. Other 2%. Avg class size: 8. **Fac 34.** M 18/F 16. FT 32/PT 2. Wh 82%. Latino 9%. Blk 9%. Adv deg: 55%. **Grad '09—30.** Col—30. (TX Tech 4, U of Denver 2, Westminster-MO 2, Eckerd 2, St Edward's 1). **Avg SAT:** CR 547. M 510. W 530. Avg ACT: 24.5. **Tui '11-'12:** Day $18,687-23,743 (+$2290-2990). Aid: Need 43 ($415,075). **Est 1975.** Nonprofit. Sem (Aug-May). Winston's program provides individual attention, a low student-teacher ratio and small-group instruction for able boys and girls who have learning differences. Pupils develop computer literacy and word processing skills, and course requirements include reading, writing, spelling, grammar, math, social studies, foreign language and the sciences. Students are encouraged to take such electives as music, drama, art, journalism and photography. Boys and girls engage in schoolwide service projects.

CANTERBURY EPISCOPAL SCHOOL   **Day Coed Gr K-12**
DeSoto, TX 75115. 1708 N Westmoreland Rd.
Tel: 972-572-7200. Fax: 972-572-7400.
www.thecanterburyschool.org   E-mail: admissions@thecanterburyschool.org
   Sandy Doerge, Head. BA, Stanford Univ, MTS, Harvard Univ, MA, Middlebury College. Libby Tadlock, Adm.
   Col Prep. AP (36 exams taken, 75% 3+)—Eng Span Calc Bio Chem Environ_Sci Physics Eur_Hist US_Hist Art_Hist. **Feat**—Creative_Writing Lat Anat & Physiol Web_Design Govt Ethics Philos Theol Film Performing_Arts Studio_Art Drama Debate Journ. **Supp**—Rev Tut. **Comp:** Comp/Stud: 1:2.7. **Sports**—Basket Soccer Swim Tennis Track. B: Baseball. G: Cheer Softball Volley. Activities: 6. **Somewhat selective adm (Gr K-11):** 55/yr. Appl fee: $150. Appl due: Rolling. Accepted: 85%. Yield: 90%. **Tests** IQ Stanford. **Enr 265.** B 115. G 150. Elem 182. Sec 83. Wh 37%. Latino 5%. Blk 47%. Native Am 1%. Asian 3%. Other 7%. Avg class size: 11. Stud/fac: 9:1. Uniform. **Fac 37.** M 12/F 25. FT 22/PT 15. Wh 83%. Latino 3%. Blk 11%. Asian 3%. Adv deg: 35%. **Grad '11—22.** Col—22. **Avg SAT:** CR 588. M 558. W 571. Avg ACT: 25. **Col Couns:** 1. Alum donors: 1%. **Tui '12-'13:** Day $11,900-14,400 (+$300). Aid: Need 79 ($308,000). **Est 1992.** Nonprofit. Episcopal (12% practice). Sem (Aug-May). Serving southwest Dallas County and northern Ellis County, Canterbury provides a full elementary and secondary program in a small-class setting. During the primary years (grades K-3), children develop basic learning skills in self-contained classrooms. Departmentalization begins in the upper elementary division (grades 4-6), where students follow an accelerated,

integrated curriculum that comprises composition, humanities, math, science, Spanish, art, music and physical education. Consisting of the middle school (grades 7 and 8) and the upper school (grades 9-12), the upper division emphasizes social responsibility and spiritual development, in addition to mastery of material and critical-thinking skill development.

MARY IMMACULATE CATHOLIC SCHOOL   Day Coed Gr K-8
Farmers Branch, TX 75234. 14032 Dennis Ln.
Tel: 972-243-7105. Fax: 972-241-7678.
www.mischool.org   E-mail: smcgrenaghan@mischool.org
   Matthew Krause, Prin (2010). BS, Angelo State Univ, MEd, Univ of North Texas. Sandy McGrenaghan, Adm.
   Pre-Prep. Gen Acad. Feat—Lib_Skills Span Computers Studio_Art Drama Chorus Speech Study_Skills. **Supp**—Dev_Read. **Comp:** Comp/Stud: 1:10. Outdoor Ed. **Sports**—Basket X-country Golf Soccer Swim Tennis Track. B: Baseball Football. G: Softball Volley. **Selective adm:** 86/yr. Appl fee: $100. Appl due: Rolling. **Enr 510.** Wh 53%. Latino 30%. Blk 1%. Asian 9%. Other 7%. Uniform. **Fac 41.** M 1/F 40. FT 34/PT 7. Wh 95%. Latino 5%. **Grad '11—60.** Prep—32. (Jesuit Col Prep 10, Ursuline Acad of Dallas 9, John Paul II HS-TX 5, Bishop Lynch 4, Parish Episcopal 3, Highlands-TX 1). Alum donors: 1%. **Tui '12-'13:** Day $7670 (+$391). Catholic $5040 (+$391). Aid: Need ($200,000). **Est 1959.** Nonprofit. Roman Catholic. Quar (Aug-June). Serving northwest Dallas County and southern Denton County, MIS admits students of all faiths and backgrounds. Daily religion classes are part of the schedule at all grade levels. Each month, boys and girls participate in a required community service project during school hours; in addition, confirmation candidates in grades 7 and 8 must complete three projects outside of school hours.

FORT WORTH ACADEMY   Day Coed Gr K-8
Fort Worth, TX 76132. 7301 Dutch Branch Rd.
Tel: 817-370-1191. Fax: 817-294-1323.
www.fwacademy.org   E-mail: info@fwacademy.org
   William M. Broderick, Head (1999). BA, Boston College, MEd, Antioch Institute of Open Education. Nancy Palmer, Adm.
   Pre-Prep. Feat—Span Computers Studio_Art Drama Music Speech. **Comp:** Laptop prgm Gr 2-8. **Sports**—Basket Soccer Track Volley. B: Baseball Football. G: Softball. **Selective adm:** 55/yr. Appl fee: $75. Appl due: Rolling. Accepted: 75%. **Tests** CTP_4 IQ ISEE. **Enr 240.** Wh 77%. Latino 9%. Blk 4%. Asian 4%. Other 6%. Avg class size: 15. Stud/fac: 8:1. Uniform. **Fac 27.** M 6/F 21. FT 25/PT 2. Wh 92%. Latino 8%. Adv deg: 40%. **Grad '10—29.** Prep—23. **Tui '12-'13:** Day $14,995 (+$300-500). Aid: Need 30 ($124,600). **Est 1982.** Nonprofit. Quar (Aug-May). **Assoc** SACS. The academy's elementary program allows for acceleration and includes various electives and enrichment classes in Spanish, art, the performing arts and physical education. The school issues laptop computers to boys and girls in grades 5-8 for use in class and at home, while younger students use both desktop and laptop computers. FWA conducts a three-day winterim program for middle school students in which they undertake in-depth exploration of areas of interest beyond the curriculum.

HOLY FAMILY CATHOLIC SCHOOL   Day Coed Gr PS (Age 3)-8
Fort Worth, TX 76107. 6146 Pershing Ave.
Tel: 817-737-4201. Fax: 817-738-1542.
www.hfsfw.org   E-mail: secretary@hfsfw.org
   Albert Herrera, Prin (2011). BA, Texas A&M Univ, MEd, Univ of Texas-Arlington. Pearl Middleton, Adm.
   Pre-Prep. Feat—Span Computers Relig Studio_Art Music Dance. **Supp**—Tut. **Comp:** Comp/Stud: 1:9.3. **Sports**—Basket Soccer Track Volley. B: Baseball. G: Softball. **Selective adm (Gr PS-7):** 49/yr. Appl due: Rolling. Accepted: 70%. Yield: 70%. **Enr 232.** Wh 68%.

Latino 24%. Blk 3%. Native Am 1%. Asian 3%. Other 1%. Avg class size: 24. Uniform. **Fac 17.** FT 13/PT 4. Wh 95%. Latino 5%. Adv deg: 5%. **Grad '11—21.** Prep—19. (Nolan 19). **Tui '11-'12:** Day $6400 (+$300). Parishioners $5900 (+$300). **Est 1945.** Nonprofit. Roman Catholic (85% practice). Quar (Aug-May). Founded as St. Alice School, the school assumed its current name in 1970, at which time it was under the direction of the Sisters of the Incarnate Word. Holy Family's faculty has consisted entirely of lay staff since 1979. Academics account for the student's level of achievement, allowing children to work above, at or below grade level in each subject.

NOLAN CATHOLIC HIGH SCHOOL   **Day Coed Gr 9-12**
Fort Worth, TX 76103. 4501 Bridge St.
Tel: 817-457-2920. Fax: 817-496-9775.
www.nolancatholichs.org   E-mail: office@nchstx.org
     Rev. Richard Villa, SM, Pres (2009). BA, St Mary's Univ of San Antonio, BST, Univ of Wales, MS, Univ of Notre Dame. Catherine Buckingham, Prin. BS, Michigan State Univ, MS, Johns Hopkins Univ. Rene Ramirez, Adm.
     Col Prep. AP (329 exams taken, 83% 3+)—Eng Fr Ger Span Calc Stats Bio Chem Physics Eur_Hist US_Hist World_Hist Econ Psych US_Govt & Pol Art_Hist. **Feat**—British_Lit Lat Anat & Physiol Environ_Sci Engineering Comp_Sci Web_Design Law Sociol Relig World_Relig Film Photog Studio_Art Theater_Arts Band Chorus Music_Theory Dance Accounting Journ. **Supp**—Dev_Read Rem_Math Rem_Read Rev Tut. **Comp:** Comp/Stud: 1:11. **Sports**—Basket X-country Soccer Swim Tennis Track. B: Baseball Football. G: Cheer Golf Softball Volley. Activities: 23. **Selective adm (Gr 9-10):** 250/yr. Appl fee: $50. Appl due: Jan. **Tests** HSPT. **Enr 956.** Wh 61%. Latino 21%. Blk 2%. Native Am 1%. Asian 10%. Other 5%. Avg class size: 25. Stud/fac: 14:1. Uniform. **Fac 91.** M 43/F 48. FT 88/PT 3. Wh 83%. Latino 10%. Blk 2%. Native Am 1%. Asian 3%. Other 1%. Adv deg: 51%. **Grad '11—252.** Col—249. (U of TX-Arlington 33, TX A&M 21, TX Christian 14, U of N TX 13, OK St 12, U of TX-Austin 12). **Avg SAT:** CR 560. M 565. W 555. Avg ACT: 25.1. **Col Couns:** 2. **Tui '12-'13:** Day $12,760 (+$600-725). Catholic $10,640 (+$600-725). Aid: Need 221 ($781,000). **Est 1961.** Nonprofit. Roman Catholic (93% practice). Sem (Aug-May). **Assoc** SACS. Located on a 65-acre campus, the school offers honors and Advanced Placement courses as part of its college preparatory program. Nolan Catholic's fine arts curriculum is particularly strong. Religious studies are required, and boys and girls perform 75 hours of compulsory Christian ministry work during their four years.

ST. IGNATIUS COLLEGE PREPARATORY SCHOOL   **Day Coed Gr 9-12**
Fort Worth, TX 76120. 8109 Shelton Dr.
Tel: 817-801-4801.
www.ignatiusofloyola.org   E-mail: principal@sicps.org
     Victor Nguyen, Prin. BS, Univ of Texas-Austin.
     Col Prep. Feat—Lat Span Calc Comp_Sci Econ Bible Studio_Art Drama Guitar Health. **Supp**—Tut. **Selective adm:** Appl fee: $45. Appl due: July. **Enr 38.** Stud/fac: 2:1. Uniform. **Fac 19.** M 12/F 7. FT 19. Adv deg: 52%. **Avg SAT:** CR/M 1275. **Tui '11-'12:** Day $7000 (+$1250). **Est 1989.** Nonprofit. Roman Catholic. Quar (Sept-May). Conducted in the Roman Catholic tradition, this very small school's classical liberal arts curriculum places particular emphasis on the development of effective speaking and writing skills. The works addressed in history, literature, religion, music and art are actively related to each other throughout the year. Field trips to cultural centers, businesses and science facilities complement class work.

ST. RITA CATHOLIC SCHOOL   **Day Coed Gr PS (Age 3)-8**
Fort Worth, TX 76112. 712 Weiler Blvd.
Tel: 817-451-9383. Fax: 817-446-4465.
www.saintritaschool.net   E-mail: srsoffice54@yahoo.com

Kathleen Krick, Prin (2009).

Pre-Prep. Gen Acad. Feat—Lib_Skills Span Geol Computers Relig Studio_Art Chorus Music. **Supp**—Dev_Read Rem_Math Rem_Read Rev Tut. **Comp:** Comp/Stud: 1:4. **Sports**— Basket Soccer Track. B: Baseball. G: Softball Volley. **Nonselective adm (Gr PS-7):** 48/yr. Appl fee: $90. Appl due: Rolling. Accepted: 99%. **Enr 200.** B 94. G 106. Avg class size: 21. Uniform. **Fac 18.** M 1/F 17. FT 13/PT 5. Wh 78%. Latino 22%. Adv deg: 16%. **Grad '10—20.** Prep—15. (Nolan 12, Cassata HS 1, St Ignatius-TX 1, Highlands 1). **Tui '11-'12:** Day $5875 (+$590). Parishioners $5130 (+$590). Aid: Need 85 ($94,750). **Est 1954.** Nonprofit. Roman Catholic (89% practice). Quar (Aug-May). St. Rita provides a Christian education in a multi-cultural setting. The curriculum includes basic instruction in English grammar and composition, reading and spelling, as well as more intensive courses in religion, music and Spanish. The school conducts tutorials in content areas and in study and organizational skills. Instrumental band is part of the program in grades 6-8, as are interscholastic athletics.

TRINITY EPISCOPAL SCHOOL   **Day Coed Gr PS (Age 2)-8**
Galveston, TX 77550. 720 Tremont St.
Tel: 409-765-9391. Fax: 409-762-7000.
www.tesgalv.org   E-mail: tstrimple@tesgalv.org
    Rev. David C. Dearman, Head (2002). BS, Univ of the South, MDiv, Virginia Theological Seminary, MEd, Mississippi College. Thomala L. Walker, Adm.

Pre-Prep. Gen Acad. Feat—Span Computers Studio_Art Music. **Supp**—Dev_Read Tut. **Sports**—Basket Soccer Volley. G: Softball. **Somewhat selective adm (Gr PS-7):** 34/yr. Appl fee: $50. Appl due: Rolling. Accepted: 97%. **Tests** Stanford. **Enr 200.** B 87. G 113. Wh 82%. Latino 12%. Blk 2%. Asian 2%. Other 2%. Avg class size: 14. Uniform. **Fac 26.** M 2/F 24. FT 21/PT 5. Wh 86%. Latino 14%. Adv deg: 15%. **Grad '11—18.** Prep—2. **Tui '12-'13:** Day $5450-8700 (+$600). Aid: Need 36 ($78,000). **Est 1952.** Nonprofit. Episcopal (17% practice). Sem (Aug-May). Chapel enriches this school's program, as do field trips to local, state and national destinations. Middle school students (grades 6-8) satisfy a five-hour annual community service commitment.

ALEXANDER-SMITH ACADEMY   **Day Coed Gr 9-12**
Houston, TX 77042. 10255 Richmond Ave.
Tel: 713-266-0920. Fax: 713-266-8857.
www.alexandersmith.com   E-mail: darnold@alexandersmith.com
    J. David Arnold, Pres (1968). Margaret Waldner De La Garza, Prin. BA, Univ of Houston, MLA, Univ of St Thomas (TX).

Col Prep. AP—Eng Calc US_Hist US_Govt & Pol. **Feat**—Span Forensic_Sci Marine_ Bio/Sci Web_Design Econ Psych Sociol Studio_Art Speech. **Supp**—Tut. **Selective adm:** 28/ yr. Appl fee: $300. Appl due: Apr. Accepted: 47%. Yield: 95%. **Tests** CEEB SSAT Stanford. **Enr 70.** B 38. G 32. Stud/fac: 7:1. **Fac 16.** M 2/F 14. FT 16. Adv deg: 68%. **Grad '07—28.** Col—27. (U of St Thomas-TX 6, St Edward's 5, U of TX-Austin 2, TX A&M 2, Pratt 1, Eckerd 1). **Avg SAT:** CR 600. M 595. W 590. **Tui '12-'13:** Day $26,600. **Est 1968.** Inc. Sem (Sept-May). **Assoc** SACS. ASA offers both college preparatory subjects and a more general academic program. The school maintains a low student-teacher ratio in all subject areas. Online learning options expand the curriculum.

ANNUNCIATION ORTHODOX SCHOOL   **Day Coed Gr PS (Age 3)-8**
Houston, TX 77006. 3600 Yoakum Blvd.
Tel: 713-470-5600. Fax: 713-470-5605.
www.aoshouston.org   E-mail: admissions@aoshouston.org
    Mark H. Kelly, Head (1996). BA, St Lawrence Univ, MEd, Univ of New Orleans. Maria Newton, Adm.

Pre-Prep. Feat—Creative_Writing Greek Span Computers Relig Studio_Art Drama Music. **Supp**—Dev_Read. **Comp:** Comp/Stud: 1:2. **Sports**—Basket X-country Lacrosse Soccer Track Volley. B: Football. G: F_Hockey Softball. **Selective adm:** 140/yr. Appl fee: $75. Appl due: Dec. Accepted: 64%. Yield: 67%. **Tests** IQ ISEE Stanford. **Enr 669.** B 316. G 353. Wh 73%. Latino 4%. Blk 2%. Asian 4%. Other 17%. Avg class size: 20. Uniform. **Fac 79.** M 12/F 67. FT 69/PT 10. Wh 80%. Latino 6%. Blk 4%. Asian 3%. Other 7%. Adv deg: 30%. **Grad '11—66.** Prep—53. (Episcopal HS-TX 18, St Agnes Acad 15, St John's Sch 9, Strake Jesuit 5, Kinkaid 2). Alum donors: 4%. **Tui '12-'13:** Day $15,500-18,135 (+$500-2000). Aid: Merit 81 ($119,766). Need 35 ($309,660). **Est 1970.** Nonprofit. Greek Orthodox (13% practice). Quar (Aug-May). This Christian school enriches its curriculum with offerings in art, drama, foreign languages, music and technology. During the middle school years, a daily assembly program enables the school community to convene for prayer, the pledge of allegiance and student speeches. Pupils each write a short speech (with the assistance of a language arts teacher) on a topic of interest, then gain public speaking experience during speech presentation. Field trips, competitive team sports, student publications and interest clubs complement academics.

DUCHESNE ACADEMY OF THE SACRED HEART   Day Girls Gr PS (Age 4)-12
Houston, TX 77024. 10202 Memorial Dr.
Tel: 713-468-8211. Fax: 713-465-9809.
www.duchesne.org   E-mail: admissions@duchesne.org
Sr. Jan Dunn, RSCJ, Head (1996). BA, Maryville College, MA, St Louis Univ, MEd, Univ of Houston. Beth Lowry Speck, Adm.

Col Prep. AP (exams req'd; 172 taken, 90% 3+)—Eng Fr Span Calc Stats Bio Chem Eur_Hist US_Hist US_Govt & Pol Art_Hist Studio_Art. **Feat**—British_Lit Creative_Writing Shakespeare Lat Bioethics Environ_Sci Programming Robotics Econ Psych Relig Drawing Painting Photog Theater_Arts Music Music_Theory. **Supp**—Rem_Math. **Comp:** Laptop prgm Gr 6-12. **Sports**— G: Basket X-country F_Hockey Soccer Softball Swim Track Volley. **Selective adm:** 124/yr. Appl fee: $80. Appl due: Jan. Accepted: 71%. Yield: 61%. **Tests** IQ ISEE. **Enr 674.** Elem 436. Sec 238. Wh 64%. Latino 16%. Blk 5%. Native Am 1%. Asian 3%. Other 11%. Avg class size: 17. Stud/fac: 9:1. Uniform. **Fac 95.** M 3/F 92. FT 84/PT 11. Wh 69%. Latino 17%. Blk 4%. Native Am 7%. Asian 3%. Adv deg: 51%. **Grad '11—58.** Col—58. **Avg SAT:** CR 611. M 599. W 639. Avg ACT: 27. **Col Couns:** 1. Alum donors: 26%. **Tui '12-'13:** Day $14,302-20,047 (+$400-4150). Aid: Merit 8 ($50,000). Need 100 ($1,130,000). **Est 1960.** Nonprofit. Roman Catholic (63% practice). Sem (Aug-May). The academy is named for Saint Philippine Duchesne, who opened the first Sacred Heart school in the US in 1818. The college preparatory program requires students in grades 6-12 to purchase tablet computers for use in class and to connect to the campus wireless network. Girls in grades 9-12 participate in mandatory community service projects. Students enroll from throughout Greater Houston.

HOLY SPIRIT EPISCOPAL SCHOOL   Day Coed Gr PS (Age 2)-8
Houston, TX 77024. 12535 Perthshire Rd.
Tel: 713-468-5138. Fax: 713-465-6972.
www.hses.org   E-mail: admissions@hses.org
Lori A. Preston, Head.

Pre-Prep. Feat—Fr Span Relig Studio_Art Theater_Arts Outdoor_Ed. **Supp**—Rev Tut. **Sports**—Basket Soccer Track. B: Baseball. G: Softball Volley. **Selective adm:** 56/yr. Appl fee: $75. Appl due: Feb. Accepted: 80%. Yield: 75%. **Tests** IQ ISEE. **Enr 330.** Intl 26%. Avg class size: 11. Uniform. **Fac 34.** M 3/F 31. FT 24/PT 10. **Grad '06—17.** Prep—15. **Tui '12-'13:** Day $10,495-14,920 (+$225-1300). **Est 1962.** Nonprofit. Episcopal. Quar (Aug-May). Holy Spirit enrolls infants as young as six weeks old into the Child Enrichment Center, and accepts boys and girls ages 3-5 into its early childhood program. The lower school (grades K-4) features integrated technology, fine arts activities, hands-on math and science programs, access to a learning center and semiweekly chapel services. Holy Spirit's middle school program (grades 5-8) includes electives, outdoor education trips and a Costa Rican exchange opportunity.

PRESBYTERIAN SCHOOL   **Day Coed Gr PS (Age 2)-8**
Houston, TX 77004. 5300 Main St.
Tel: 713-520-0284. Fax: 713-620-6390.
Other locations: 9100 South Freeway, Houston 77051.
www.pshouston.org   E-mail: kbrown@pshouston.org
    Mark Carleton, Head (2009). BA, Centenary College of Louisiana, MA, Louisiana State
Univ, EdD, Univ of Tennessee-Knoxville. Kristin Brown, Adm.
    Pre-Prep. Gen Acad. Feat—Lib_Skills Span Computers Bible Ethics Studio_Art Music.
Comp: Laptop prgm Gr 8. **Sports**—Basket X-country Lacrosse Soccer Track. B: Football. G:
F_Hockey Volley. **Selective adm:** 90/yr. Appl fee: $100. Appl due: Feb. **Tests** IQ ISEE Stan-
ford. **Enr 521.** Avg class size: 18. Uniform. **Fac 85.** Wh 93%. Latino 2%. Blk 3%. Asian 2%.
Grad '09—58. Tui '12-'13: Day $14,260-18,770 (+$500). **Est 1988.** Nonprofit. Presbyterian.
(Aug-May). **Assoc** SACS. The school's curriculum places significant emphasis on language
arts, practical math and individualized instruction. Spanish begins in kindergarten, and weekly
chapel services are conducted for each grade. Participation in a comprehensive parent education program is required.

RIVER OAKS BAPTIST SCHOOL   **Day Coed Gr PS (Age 2)-8**
Houston, TX 77027. 2300 Willowick Rd.
Tel: 713-623-6938. Fax: 713-626-0650.
www.robs.org   E-mail: admissions@robs.org
    Leanne Reynolds, Head (2012). BS, Univ of Texas-Austin, MEd, EdD, Univ of Houston.
Kristin Poe, Adm.
    Pre-Prep. Gen Acad. Feat—Span Computers Bible Visual_Arts Theater_Arts Music.
Supp—Tut. **Sports**—Basket X-country Lacrosse Soccer Tennis Track Volley. B: Football. G:
F_Hockey Softball. **Very selective adm:** 114/yr. Appl fee: $100. Appl due: Dec. Accepted:
24%. Yield: 96%. **Tests** IQ ISEE Stanford. **Enr 852.** B 422. G 430. Wh 83%. Latino 2%.
Blk 4%. Asian 4%. Other 7%. Avg class size: 20. Stud/fac: 10:1. Uniform. **Fac 76.** M 9/F
67. FT 63/PT 13. Wh 87%. Latino 5%. Blk 4%. Native Am 1%. Asian 3%. Adv deg: 36%.
Grad '11—77. Prep—75. (Episcopal HS-TX 35, St John's Sch 9, Strake Jesuit 9, Kinkaid 8,
Houston Christian 3, St Thomas HS 2). **Tui '11-'12:** Day $10,055-19,335 (+$875-1250). Aid:
Need 65 ($819,405). **Est 1955.** Nonprofit. Baptist (9% practice). Quar (Aug-May). ROBS
comprises three distinct divisions: primary school (ages 2-5), lower school (grades K-4) and
middle school (grades 5-8). Frequently scheduled field trips supplement the school's academic
program. Bible classes, weekly chapel services and daily morning devotionals are important
aspects of the program. Each class takes part in a community service project. Interscholastic
athletics begin in grade 6.   **See Also Page 86**

ST. AGNES ACADEMY   **Day Girls Gr 9-12**
Houston, TX 77036. 9000 Bellaire Blvd.
Tel: 713-219-5400. Fax: 713-219-5499.
www.st-agnes.org   E-mail: judi.cox@st-agnes.org
    Sr. Jane Meyer, OP, Head (1981). BA, Dominican College, MS, Texas Woman's Univ,
MRE, Univ of St Thomas (TX). Deborah Whalen, Prin. BA, Santa Clara Univ, MS, California
State Univ. Brigid Schiro, Adm.
    Col Prep. AP (exams req'd; 418 taken, 94% 3+)—Eng Lat Span Calc Bio Chem
US_Hist World_Hist US_Govt & Pol. **Feat**—Fr Astron Environ_Sci Geol Marine_Bio/Sci
Physiol Comp_Sci Web_Design Econ Law Psych Philos Theol Art_Hist Drawing Film Paint-
ing Photog Studio_Art Acting Theater_Arts Chorus Music_Theory Dance Accounting Journ
Speech TV_Production. **Comp:** Laptop prgm Gr 9-12. **Sports**— G: Basket X-country Golf
Soccer Softball Swim Tennis Track Volley W_Polo. Activities: 52. **Selective adm (Gr 9-11):**
222/yr. Appl fee: $50. Appl due: Jan. Accepted: 65%. Yield: 75%. **Tests** ISEE. **Enr 872.** Avg
class size: 20. Stud/fac: 13:1. Uniform. **Fac 60.** M 15/F 45. FT 60. Adv deg: 65%. **Grad '11—
209.** Col—209. (U of TX-Austin 31, TX A&M 19, Notre Dame 9, TX Christian 9, Trinity U

7, Baylor 7). **Mid 50% SAT:** CR 570-680. M 590-680. W 590-690. Mid 50% ACT: 26-31. **Col Couns:** 4. **Tui '12-'13:** Day $14,550 (+$200-4600). Aid: Need 89 ($685,000). **Est 1906.** Nonprofit. Roman Catholic (79% practice). Quar (Aug-May). **Assoc** SACS. As part of SAA's college preparatory curriculum, students fulfill course requirements in theology, the fine arts and computer competency, in addition to the traditional disciplines. Upon admission, each girl purchases a laptop computer for school use.

ST. FRANCIS EPISCOPAL DAY SCHOOL   Day Coed Gr PS (Age 2)-8
Houston, TX 77024. 335 Piney Point Rd.
Tel: 713-458-6100. Fax: 713-782-4720.
www.sfedshouston.org   E-mail: sdalal@sfedshouston.org
   Susan B. Lair, Head. BS, Univ of North Texas, MS, Texas Christian Univ, PhD, Univ of Texas-Austin. Margaret Ann Casseb, Adm.
   Pre-Prep. Feat—Span Computers Relig Ceramics Painting Sculpt Studio_Art Drama Band Music Music_Hist. **Sports**—Basket X-country Lacrosse Soccer Track. B: Football Wrestling. G: F_Hockey Softball Volley. **Selective adm:** 147/yr. Appl fee: $75. Appl due: Jan. Accepted: 73%. Yield: 69%. **Tests** IQ ISEE Stanford. **Enr 807.** B 430. G 377. Avg class size: 18. Uniform. **Fac 78.** M 13/F 65. FT 78. Adv deg: 23%. **Grad '09—82.** Prep—64. (Episcopal HS-TX 30, Strake Jesuit 8, Kinkaid 6, St Agnes Acad 6, St John's Sch 2, Deerfield Acad 1). Alum donors: 1%. **Tui '12-'13:** Day $12,230-19,960 (+$0-711). **Est 1952.** Nonprofit. Episcopal. Sem (Aug-May). Enrolling children beginning at age 18 months, St. Francis offers a full elementary program that readies students for competitive area preparatory schools. Community outreach and religious education are integral to the program. Extensive art, music and drama programs allow pupils to pursue interests in these areas. The school's outdoor education sequence combines class study with outdoor awareness and enables students to apply what they have learned in a natural setting.

ST. PIUS X HIGH SCHOOL   Day Coed Gr 9-12
Houston, TX 77091. 811 W Donovan St.
Tel: 713-692-3581. Fax: 713-692-5725.
www.stpiusx.org   E-mail: admissions@stpiusx.org
   Sr. Donna M. Pollard, OP, Head. BS, Univ of Houston, MA, Aquinas Institute of Philosophy and Theology, MEd, Boston College. Susie Kramer, Adm.
   Col Prep. AP (102 exams taken)—Eng Lat Span Calc Comp_Sci Bio US_Hist US_Govt & Pol. **Feat**—Fr Ital Web_Design Painting Photog Sculpt Theater Band Chorus Dance Journ. **Supp**—Dev_Read LD Rem_Math Tut. **Comp:** Comp/Stud: 1:10. **Sports**—Basket X-country Golf Soccer Swim Tennis Track. B: Baseball Football. G: Cheer Softball Volley. **Selective adm (Gr 9-11):** 211/yr. Appl fee: $35. Appl due: Feb. Accepted: 73%. Yield: 72%. **Tests** HSPT ISEE. **Enr 692.** B 377. G 315. Wh 47%. Latino 30%. Blk 16%. Asian 4%. Other 3%. Avg class size: 20. Stud/fac: 14:1. Uniform. **Fac 52.** M 20/F 32. FT 49/PT 3. Wh 85%. Latino 9%. Blk 2%. Asian 4%. Adv deg: 44%. **Grad '10—156.** Col—150. (TX A&M 22, U of Houston 22, U of Houston-Downtown 13, U of TX-San Antonio 11, Blinn 8, St Edward's 6). **Avg SAT:** CR 527. M 537. Avg ACT: 23. **Col Couns:** 4. Alum donors: 3%. **Tui '11-'12:** Day $10,800 (+$800). Aid: Merit 20 ($20,000). Need 191 ($693,695). **Est 1956.** Nonprofit. Roman Catholic (71% practice). Sem (Aug-May). **Assoc** SACS. Among St. Pius' available electives are sociology, psychology, philosophy, multimedia, art, photography, band, choir, drama and yearbook. The theology department provides opportunities for service, retreats and days of prayer. All students accumulate at least 100 hours of community service in grades 11 and 12.

STRAKE JESUIT COLLEGE PREPARATORY   Day Boys Gr 9-12
Houston, TX 77036. 8900 Bellaire Blvd.
Tel: 713-490-8113. Fax: 713-272-4300.
www.strakejesuit.org   E-mail: admissions@strakejesuit.org

Rev. Daniel K. Lahart, SJ, Pres (2001). BS, Georgetown Univ, MDiv, Weston Jesuit School of Theology, MEd, Boston College, MBA, Stanford Univ. Richard C. Nevle, Prin. BA, MEd, Univ of St Thomas. Ken Lojo, Adm.

Col Prep. AP (301 exams taken, 74% 3+)—Span Calc Comp_Sci Bio Chem US_Hist US_Govt & Pol. **Feat**—Fr Lat Oceanog Physiol Vietnam_War Psych Philos Theol World_Relig Drawing Film Studio_Art Chorus Music Music_Theory Accounting Debate TV_Production. **Supp**—Tut. **Comp:** Comp/Stud: 1:5. **Dual enr:** Houston CC. **Sports**— B: Baseball Basket X-country Football Golf Lacrosse Rugby Soccer Swim Tennis Track W_Polo Wrestling. Activities: 80. **Selective adm:** 239/yr. Appl fee: $50. Appl due: Jan. **Tests** HSPT. **Enr 895.** Wh 61%. Latino 15%. Blk 9%. Asian 14%. Other 1%. Avg class size: 25. **Fac 81.** M 61/F 20. FT 81. Wh 75%. Latino 15%. Blk 5%. Asian 4%. Other 1%. Adv deg: 72%. **Grad '10—218.** Col—216. (TX A&M 35, U of TX-Austin 18, U of TX-San Antonio 14, LA St-Baton Rouge 12, U of TX-Dallas 7, TX Christian 7). **Avg SAT:** CR 630. M 640. W 631. Avg ACT: 27.9. **Tui '11-'12:** Day $15,100 (+$500). Aid: Merit 5 ($33,625). Need 117 ($1,105,650). Work prgm 115 ($56,250). **Est 1961.** Nonprofit. Roman Catholic (75% practice). Quar (Aug-May). **Assoc** SACS. Participation in religious activities is an essential component of Strake Jesuit's college preparatory curriculum. Advanced Placement and dual-credit options are offered, as well as electives in the arts, theology, history and science. All classrooms feature multimedia projectors and interactive whiteboards. As a graduation requirement, all boys perform 100 hours of community service between the spring of junior year and the end of the first semester of senior year.

THE VILLAGE SCHOOL   Day Coed Gr PS (Age 4)-12
Houston, TX 77077. 13077 Westella Dr.
Tel: 281-496-7900. Fax: 281-496-7799.
Other locations: 2005 Gentryside Dr, Houston 77077.
www.thevillageschool.com   E-mail: info@thevillageschool.com
Monica Garza, Int Head (2011). BA, MA, Univ of Monterrey (Mexico). Erik Srnka, Gr 5-12 Adm; Zoe Anderson, Gr PS-4 Adm.

Col Prep. IB Diploma. Feat—Humanities Fr Span Computers Econ Studio_Art Theater_ Arts Band Music Orchestra. **Supp**—Tut. **Sports**—Basket X-country Soccer Tennis Track. B: Baseball Football. G: Lacrosse Softball Volley. Activities: 14. **Selective adm:** 195/yr. Appl fee: $100. Appl due: Rolling. Accepted: 60%. Yield: 90%. **Tests** IQ ISEE. **Enr 795.** B 477. G 318. Intl 20%. Avg class size: 18. Uniform. **Fac 80.** M 14/F 66. FT 49/PT 31. Adv deg: 25%. **Col Couns:** 1. **Tui '12-'13:** Day $16,375-21,275 (+$675). **Est 1966.** Spons: Meritas. Sem (Aug-May). The school offers a particularly strong math and science curriculum and also emphasizes reading, phonics, grammar and writing. Computer lab is available beginning in kindergarten. Music is presented as a participatory art, and theater, choir, band and orchestra are important elements of the curriculum in the lower grades. In fall 2008, Village opened a high school division on Gentryside Drive that offers preparation for the International Baccalaureate Diploma.

ALL SAINTS EPISCOPAL SCHOOL   Day Coed Gr PS (Age 3)-9
Lubbock, TX 79423. 3222 103rd St.
Tel: 806-745-7701. Fax: 806-748-0454.
www.allsaintsschool.org   E-mail: pmckay@allsaintsschool.org
Mike Bennett, Head. BS, MacMurray College, MEd, Abilene Christian Univ, EdD, Texas Tech Univ. Paige McKay, Adm.

Pre-Prep. Feat—Lat Span Computers Relig Studio_Art. **Supp**—Dev_Read Tut. **Sports**— Basket X-country Soccer Swim Tennis Track. B: Football Golf. G: Softball Volley. **Somewhat selective adm:** Appl fee: $50-125. Appl due: Rolling. **Tests** IQ. **Enr 351.** Avg class size: 15. Stud/fac: 7:1. Uniform. **Fac 44.** M 4/F 40. FT 37/PT 7. Adv deg: 31%. **Grad '08—15.** Prep—15. **Tui '05-'06:** Day $4900-7770 (+$200). **Est 1956.** Nonprofit. Episcopal. Sem (Aug-May). All Saints stresses classical education, as well as independent or self-directed learning through individualized instruction. Students participate in compulsory community service at all grade levels.

TRINITY SCHOOL   **Day Coed Gr PS (Age 2)-12**
Midland, TX 79707. 3500 W Wadley Ave.
Tel: 432-697-3281. Fax: 432-697-7403.
www.trinitymidland.org   E-mail: a_clifton@trinitymidland.org
     Rev. Walter L. Prehn, Head (2010). BA, Texas A&M Univ, MDiv, Nashotah House Theological Seminary, PhD, Univ of Virginia. Adrianne Clifton, Adm.
     Col Prep. Montessori. AP (exams req'd; 129 taken, 73% 3+)—Eng Fr Lat Span Calc Comp_Sci Bio Chem Physics Eur_Hist US_Hist World_Hist US_Govt & Pol Studio_Art. **Feat**—World_Relig Film Photog Drama Music Music_Theory. **Supp**—Tut. **Comp:** Comp/Stud: 1:3 (1:1 Laptop prgm Gr 5-12). **Dual enr:** Midland Col. **Sports**—Basket X-country Track. B: Baseball Football Golf. G: Cheer Tennis Volley. Activities: 10. **Somewhat selective adm (Gr PS-11):** 80/yr. Appl fee: $75. Appl due: Rolling. Accepted: 88%. Yield: 63%. **Tests** Stanford. **Enr 535.** Elem 368. Sec 167. Wh 74%. Latino 6%. Blk 2%. Asian 6%. Other 12%. Intl 5%. Avg class size: 15. Stud/fac: 8:1. **Fac 77.** M 18/F 59. FT 58/PT 19. Wh 72%. Latino 7%. Blk 1%. Native Am 1%. Asian 1%. Other 18%. Adv deg: 35%. **Grad '11—36.** Col—36. (TX A&M 6, TX Tech 4, U of TX-Austin 3, Auburn 3, TX Christian 3, Rice 2). **Avg SAT:** CR 592. M 599. W 604. Avg ACT: 26. **Col Couns:** 1. Alum donors: 10%. **Tui '12-'13:** Day $9995-16,395 (+$50-600). Aid: Merit 23 ($55,000). Need 43 ($445,000). **Est 1958.** Nonprofit. Episcopal. Sem (Aug-May). This college preparatory school offers a sequential curriculum that emphasizes the liberal arts. Program features include Advanced Placement courses, computer studies, fine arts, foreign languages and competitive athletics. All students attend daily chapel services and take part in community service activities, both on and off campus; pupils in grades 9-12 accumulate 90 hours of compulsory service. Preschool classes follow the Montessori approach.

FORT WORTH CHRISTIAN SCHOOL   **Day Coed Gr PS (Age 4)-12**
North Richland Hills, TX 76180. 6200 Holiday Ln.
Tel: 817-281-6504, 888-281-3927. Fax: 817-281-7063.
www.fwc.org   E-mail: info@fwc.org
     Kelly Moore, Pres. Kelly Cantrell, Adm.
     Col Prep. AP (exams req'd; 101 taken)—Eng Calc Bio US_Hist World_Hist Econ US_Govt & Pol. **Feat**—ASL Lat Span Comp_Sci Bible Studio_Art Drama Music. **Supp**—Dev_Read Makeup Rev Tut. **Comp:** Comp/Stud: 1:2 (1:1 Laptop prgm Gr 6-12). **Dual enr:** Tarrant County. **Sports**—Basket X-country Golf Soccer Tennis Track. B: Baseball Football. G: Cheer Softball Volley. **Selective adm:** 270/yr. Yield: 86%. **Enr 880.** Elem 566. Sec 314. Avg class size: 18. Stud/fac: 14:1. Uniform. **Fac 73.** M 17/F 56. FT 65/PT 8. Nonwhite 2%. Adv deg: 28%. **Grad '08—66.** Col—66. **Avg SAT:** CR/M/W 1630. Avg ACT: 24.4. Alum donors: 12%. **Tui '11-'12:** Day $7300-11,100 (+$400-1500). Aid: Need 26 ($65,000). **Est 1958.** Nonprofit. Nondenom Christian. Sem (Aug-May). **Assoc** SACS. FWCS teaches Bible at each grade level, and students attend daily chapel. As part of a strong technology program, the school issues laptops to all middle and high school pupils. Juniors fulfill a 100-hour community service requirement.

THE ALEXANDER SCHOOL   **Day Coed Gr 7-12**
Richardson, TX 75081. 409 International Pky.
Tel: 972-690-9210. Fax: 972-690-9284.
www.alexanderschool.com   E-mail: admissions@alexanderschool.com
     David B. Bowlin, Dir (1975). BS, Texas Tech Univ. Andrew E. Cody, Prin. BSEd, Texas Tech Univ, MEd, Univ of North Texas.
     Col Prep. AP—Eng Span Calc Bio Chem Physics US_Hist World_Hist. **Feat**—Mythology

Comp_Graphics African-Amer_Hist Civil_War Ethics Yoga. **Supp**—Makeup Rem_Read Rev Tut. **Dual enr:** SMU, U of TX-Dallas, Collin County CC. **Sports**—Golf Tennis. **Selective adm:** 10/yr. Appl due: Rolling. Accepted: 75%. Yield: 75%. **Enr 30.** B 20. G 10. Elem 4. Sec 26. Wh 85%. Latino 3%. Blk 11%. Asian 1%. Avg class size: 6. Stud/fac: 4:1. Casual dress. **Fac 7.** M 4/F 3. FT 5/PT 2. Wh 57%. Blk 29%. Asian 14%. Adv deg: 85%. **Grad '11—11.** Col—9. (U of N TX 2, MS St 2, Collin County CC 2, Dallas County CC 2, Clemson 1). **Avg SAT:** CR 615. M 605. W 550. Avg ACT: 26. **Col Couns:** 1. **Tui '11-'12:** Day $20,000 (+$500). Aid: Need 7 ($80,000). **Est 1975.** Inc. Sem (Aug-May). **Assoc** SACS. The school's college preparatory curriculum comprises core courses in the traditional disciplines and a full complement of electives. Limited enrollment and small classes facilitate hands-on learning and enable students to receive individualized instruction. Juniors and seniors perform 20 hours of required community service per year.

ST. LUKE'S EPISCOPAL SCHOOL   Day Coed Gr PS (Age 3)-8
San Antonio, TX 78209. 15 St Luke's Ln.
Tel: 210-826-0664. Fax: 210-826-8520.
www.sles-sa.org   E-mail: admission@sles-sa.org
   Mark Reford, Head (2009). BA, MA, DPhil, Univ of Oxford (England). Steve Bradley, Adm.

   Pre-Prep. Gen Acad. Feat—Lib_Skills Lat Span Computers Web_Design Photog Studio_Art Radio Music Journ. **Supp**—Dev_Read Tut. **Comp:** Comp/Stud: 1:2 (1:1 Laptop prgm Gr 5-8). **Sports**—Basket X-country Golf Soccer Tennis Track Volley. B: Baseball Football. G: Softball. **Somewhat selective adm:** 78/yr. Appl fee: $50. Appl due: Rolling. Accepted: 86%. Yield: 90%. **Tests** ISEE Stanford. **Enr 340.** B 130. G 210. Wh 77%. Latino 15%. Blk 2%. Asian 6%. Avg class size: 13. Stud/fac: 13:1. Uniform. **Fac 39.** M 7/F 32. FT 32/PT 7. Wh 84%. Latino 16%. Adv deg: 25%. **Grad '11—23.** Prep—12. (TX Milit 9, St Mary's Hall-TX 4, Central Catholic-TX 1). **Tui '12-'13:** Day $12,971-16,416 (+$50-200). Aid: Need 72 ($548,425). **Est 1947.** Nonprofit. Episcopal. Sem (Aug-May). The school provides an interdisciplinary program for students from age 3 through middle school. Spalding phonics and Texas Journeys for writing and grammar complement the core curriculum. All boys and girls take Spanish, music, art, library, computer and physical education classes, and middle schoolers use laptop computers and choose from such courses as Latin, geometry and percussion band. Students perform 50 hours of required community service prior to graduation.

SAN ANTONIO ACADEMY   Day Boys Gr PS (Age 4)-8
San Antonio, TX 78212. 117 E French Pl.
Tel: 210-733-7331. Fax: 210-734-0711.
www.sa-academy.org   E-mail: tmcwilliams@sa-academy.org
   John Webster, Head (1985). BA, Gettysburg College. Mary Wilde, Adm.

   Gen Acad. Feat—Lib_Skills Span Computers Fine_Arts Music. **Supp**—Tut. **Comp:** Comp/Stud: 1:1.7. **Sports**—B: Basket X-country Football Golf Lacrosse Soccer Tennis Track. **Selective adm:** 53/yr. Appl fee: $50. Appl due: Rolling. **Tests** Stanford. **Enr 335.** Wh 74%. Latino 16%. Blk 2%. Asian 3%. Other 5%. Avg class size: 17. Stud/fac: 10:1. Uniform. **Fac 42.** M 15/F 27. FT 32/PT 10. Adv deg: 40%. **Grad '10—36.** Prep—24. **Tui '12-'13:** Day $12,400-18,700 (+$500). Aid: Merit 6 ($100,210). Need 31 ($331,229). **Est 1886.** Nonprofit. Sem (Aug-May). The only private boys' elementary school in the state, SAA offers accelerated courses and a small-class setting. Detailed online progress reports every three weeks keep parents updated on the student's academic performance. After-school activities include a wide selection of interscholastic and intramural sports and enrichment classes.

Mountain States

COLORADO

REGIS JESUIT HIGH SCHOOL   Day Coord Gr 9-12
Aurora, CO 80016. 6300 S Lewiston Way.
Tel: 303-269-8000. Fax: 303-221-4772.
www.regisjesuit.com
    Rev. Philip G. Steele, SJ, Pres (2006). BA, St Louis Univ, MFA, Temple Univ, MDiv, Jesuit School of Theology. Paul Muller, Boys' Adm; Patricia Long, Girls' Adm.
    Col Prep. AP (725 exams taken, 66% 3+)—Eng Fr Lat Span Calc Stats Bio Chem Physics Eur_Hist US_Hist World_Hist Comp_Govt & Pol US_Govt & Pol Studio_Art. **Feat**—British_Lit Shakespeare Fiction_Writing Women's_Lit Geol Programming Web_Design Comp_ Graphics Amer_Stud Econ Psych Sociol Theol Architect Ceramics Video_Production Theater Music_Theory Journ. **Supp**—Rem_Math Rem_Read Tut. **Dual enr:** Regis U. **Sports**—Basket X-country Golf Lacrosse Soccer Swim Tennis Track Volley. B: Baseball Football Ice_Hockey Wrestling. G: Cheer F_Hockey Softball. Activities: 80. **Selective adm (Gr 9-11):** 444/yr. Appl due: Dec. **Tests** HSPT. **Enr 1599.** B 905. G 694. Wh 78%. Latino 8%. Blk 4%. Native Am 1%. Asian 4%. Other 5%. Avg class size: 25. Stud/fac: 24:1. Casual dress. **Fac 140.** M 64/F 76. FT 124/PT 16. Wh 94%. Latino 4%. Blk 1%. Other 1%. Adv deg: 72%. **Grad '11—346.** Col— 342. **Avg SAT:** CR 576. M 575. W 572. Avg ACT: 25.3. Alum donors: 7%. **Tui '12-'13:** Day $12,075 (+$800-950). Aid: Merit 37 ($53,550). Need 329 ($2,099,435). **Est 1877.** Nonprofit. Roman Catholic (70% practice). Sem (Aug-May). **Assoc** NCA. Conducted as co-divisional single-gender high schools, this Jesuit school offers boys and girls a rigorous curriculum that features Advanced Placement and honors courses, in addition to opportunities for transferable college credit from Regis University. A pastoral ministry program and extensive junior and senior service and leadership experiences are important components of school life. Boys and girls satisfy the following service requirements: 10 hours in the local community in grade 9; 20 hours (including five at school) in grade 10; 60 hours during the two-week interim program in grade 11; and 60 interim hours plus another 25 hours in grade 12.

FRIENDS' SCHOOL   Day Coed Gr PS (Age 3)-5
Boulder, CO 80303. 5465 Pennsylvania Ave.
Tel: 303-499-1999. Fax: 303-499-1365.
www.friendsschoolboulder.org   E-mail: info@friendsschoolboulder.org
    Steve de Beer, Head (2011). BA, Univ of York (England), MEd, Univ of Massachusetts-Amherst. Mari Engle Friedman, Adm.
    Pre-Prep. Gen Acad. Feat—Lib_Skills Span Computers Studio_Art Music. **Supp**—Rem_ Math Rem_Read Tut. **Outdoor Ed. Selective adm:** 54/yr. Appl fee: $50. Appl due: Rolling. Accepted: 58%. Yield: 71%. **Enr 172.** B 92. G 80. Wh 84%. Latino 6%. Native Am 1%. Asian 8%. Other 1%. Avg class size: 18. Stud/fac: 9:1. **Fac 26.** M 2/F 24. FT 6/PT 20. Wh 88%. Latino 4%. Native Am 4%. Asian 4%. Adv deg: 50%. **Grad '11—20.** Prep—2. (Alexander Dawson 1, Macintosh Acad 1). **Tui '11-'12:** Day $6199-14,075. Aid: Need 45 ($250,000). **Est 1987.** Nonprofit. Sem (Aug-May). Preschool classes at the school emphasize social, emotional, cognitive and physical development through play. The elementary program includes one-on-one and small-group instruction, and Spanish, art and music classes enhance the curriculum. Boys and girls devote three to five days each school year to service learning. Tuition is determined along a sliding scale.

SHINING MOUNTAIN WALDORF SCHOOL
Day Coed Gr PS (Age 3)-12
Boulder, CO 80304. 999 Violet Ave.
Tel: 303-444-7697. Fax: 303-444-7701.
www.smwaldorf.org E-mail: info@smwaldorf.org
Sue Levine, Dir (2010). BM, Univ of Rochester, MM, Univ of Illinois-Urbana, MA, Bentley College. Erin Lawinski, Adm.

Col Prep. Waldorf. Feat—Shakespeare Russ_Lit Ger Span Calc Anat & Physiol Astron Botany Environ_Sci Native_Amer_Hist Comp_Relig Architect Art_Hist Drawing Fine_Arts Studio_Art Batik Stone_Carving Drama Chorus Music Music_Hist Eurythmy Woodworking Blacksmithing. **Supp**—Dev_Read Rem_Math Rem_Read Tut. **Sports**—Basket X-country. G: Volley. **Selective adm:** 58/yr. Appl fee: $50-65. Appl due: Rolling. Accepted: 75%. Yield: 50%. **Enr 295.** Avg class size: 15. **Fac 40.** M 17/F 23. FT 25/PT 15. Adv deg: 22%. **Grad '08—22.** Col—22. **Tui '11-'12:** Day $13,100-15,600 (+$350-900). Aid: Need ($450,000). **Est 1983.** Nonprofit. Quar (Aug-June). Based on Rudolf Steiner's holistic educational principles, this school's curriculum blends the humanities and sciences with art, handwork, foreign languages, music, movement and practical activities. A broad range of opportunities for participating in the performing arts is offered. Seniors engage in a three-week community service project, and the curriculum integrates service at all grade levels.

HOLY FAMILY HIGH SCHOOL
Day Coed Gr 9-12
Broomfield, CO 80023. 5195 W 144th Ave.
Tel: 303-410-1411. Fax: 303-466-1935.
www.holyfamilyhs.com E-mail: jennifer.wilcomb@holyfamilyhs.com
Tim Gallic, Prin (2010). Eric Nakayama & Jennifer Wilcomb, Adms.

Col Prep. AP (exams req'd; 217 taken, 55% 3+)—Eng Calc Bio Chem Eur_Hist US_Hist US_Govt & Pol. **Feat**—Creative_Writing Fr Lat Span Theol Ceramics Photog Studio_Art Drama Music Journ. **Supp**—Rev Tut. **Dual enr:** Regis U. **Sports**—Basket X-country Golf Soccer Track. B: Baseball Football Wrestling. G: Softball Tennis Volley. Activities: 30. **Selective adm:** 200/yr. Appl due: Jan. **Tests** HSPT. **Enr 580.** B 280. G 300. Wh 76%. Latino 12%. Blk 1%. Native Am 1%. Asian 3%. Other 7%. Avg class size: 25. Stud/fac: 13:1. Uniform. **Fac 47.** M 25/F 22. FT 44/PT 3. Wh 90%. Latino 5%. Asian 5%. Adv deg: 36%. **Grad '10—145.** Col—144. **Avg SAT:** CR 547. M 553. W 527. **Mid 50% SAT:** CR 466-628. M 470-636. W 441-613. **Col Couns:** 4. Alum donors: 20%. **Tui '11-'12:** Day $9300 (+$350). Catholic $8000 (+$350). Aid: Merit 20 ($75,000). Need 170 ($525,000). **Est 1922.** Nonprofit. Roman Catholic (90% practice). Sem (Aug-June). **Assoc** NCA. Holy Family's college preparatory curriculum includes both honors and Advanced Placement courses, and qualified students may earn college credit through the University of Colorado or Regis University. The foreign language program consists of four years of Latin, five of French and six of Spanish. Boys and girls take theology each semester.

ST. MARY'S HIGH SCHOOL
Day Coed Gr 9-12
Colorado Springs, CO 80909. 2501 E Yampa St.
Tel: 719-635-7540. Fax: 719-471-7623.
www.smhscs.org E-mail: rcross@smhscs.org
Ky McCarty, Int Pres (2011). Mike Biondini, Prin. Robyn Cross, Adm.

Col Prep. AP—Eng Span Calc Chem US_Hist Studio_Art. **Feat**—Fr Stats Anat & Physiol Ecol Programming Web_Design Econ Psych Theol Ceramics Theater_Arts Band Chorus Guitar Speech. **Supp**—Tut. **Sports**—Basket X-country Golf Soccer Track. B: Baseball Football Lacrosse Wrestling. G: Cheer Softball Swim Tennis Volley. **Somewhat selective adm:** 102/yr. Appl fee: $50. Accepted: 95%. Yield: 96%. **Tests** CEEB HSPT SSAT Stanford. **Enr 340.** Stud/fac: 13:1. **Fac 31.** FT 27/PT 4. Adv deg: 70%. **Grad '11—91.** Col—91. **Avg SAT:** CR 572. M 563. W 558. Avg ACT: 25.1. **Col Couns:** 2. **Tui '12-'13:** Day $8300 (+$500). Aid: Need ($225,000). **Est 1885.** Nonprofit. Roman Catholic. Sem (Aug-May). **Assoc** NCA. Advanced Placement courses are part of SMHS' college preparatory curriculum, and religion courses are mandatory. Spiritual activities are an integral part of school life: St. Mary's schedules monthly all-school Masses, regular prayer services and an annual class retreat for each grade level. Students accumulate at least 150 hours of community service prior to graduation.

DENVER ACADEMY   **Day Coed Gr 1-12**
Denver, CO 80222. 4400 E Iliff Ave.
Tel: 303-777-5870. Fax: 303-777-5893.
www.denveracademy.org   E-mail: admissions@denveracademy.org
    Kevin M. Smith, Head (2008). BS, Univ of Dayton, MA, Bowling Green State Univ. Janet Woolley, Adm.

    Col Prep. Gen Acad. Voc. LD. Underachiever. Feat—Span Calc Anat Astron Ecol Anthro Sociol Film Drama. **Supp**—Dev_Read Rem_Math Rem_Read Rev Tut. **Sports**—Basket X-country Golf Soccer. B: Baseball Wrestling. G: Volley. Activities: 9. **Somewhat selective adm:** 76/yr. Appl fee: $75. Appl due: Rolling. Accepted: 95%. Yield: 86%. **Tests** IQ. **Enr 387.** B 293. G 94. Elem 161. Sec 226. Wh 87%. Latino 6%. Blk 4%. Asian 2%. Other 1%. Avg class size: 13. **Fac 69.** M 35/F 34. FT 69. Wh 93%. Latino 1%. Blk 6%. **Grad '10**—**53.** Col—50. Avg ACT: 20. **Tui '12-'13:** Day $23,025-24,900 (+$50). Aid: Need 117 ($1,100,000). **Est 1972.** Nonprofit. Quar (Aug-June). The school's curriculum is designed to meet the needs of children with learning differences or other problems that lead to underachievement. In the elementary and middle schools, instruction focuses on language skills and mathematics in a structured, nurturing environment. High school students can choose either the Core program or the Progressive track, which includes experiential, hands-on learning and the following community service requirements: 20 hours annually in grades 9-11 and 25 hours during senior year. The academy's 22-acre campus is located near downtown; the Rocky Mountains provide opportunities for field trips and activities.

DENVER JEWISH DAY SCHOOL   **Day Coed Gr K-12**
Denver, CO 80231. 2450 S Wabash St.
Tel: 303-369-0663. Fax: 303-369-0664.
www.denverjds.org   E-mail: sfriedman@denverjds.org
    Avi Halzel, Head. Shayna Friedman, Adm.

    Col Prep. AP—Eng Calc. **Feat**—Creative_Writing Hebrew Span Astron Environ_Sci Judaic_Stud Studio_Art Drama Public_Speak. **Supp**—ESL Rev. **Sports**—Baseball Basket Soccer Volley. **Selective adm:** 57/yr. Appl fee: $100. Appl due: Rolling. **Enr 361.** B 189. G 172. Elem 218. Sec 143. Wh 100%. Avg class size: 20. **Fac 61.** M 14/F 47. FT 46/PT 15. Wh 100%. Adv deg: 32%. **Grad '10**—**15.** Col—15. **Tui '11-'12:** Day $13,865-16,390 (+$150). **Est 1976.** Nonprofit. Jewish. Sem (Aug-June). Formed by the 1999 union of Theodor Herzl Jewish Day School (grades K-5) and Rocky Mountain Hebrew Academy (grades 6-12), this institution combines rigorous secular studies with Judaic studies. At this, the largest Jewish day school in the Rocky Mountain region, instructors place strong emphasis on language arts, math, science and social studies. Elective classes at DJDS include public speaking, drama, creative writing, sign language and art. Judaic studies, which address differing Jewish perspectives, focus on history, ethics and values, and Israel. Pupils learn Hebrew, study traditional and modern texts, and celebrate and learn more about holidays.

DENVER MONTCLAIR INTERNATIONAL SCHOOL   **Day Coed Gr PS (Age 3)-7**
Denver, CO 80230. 206 Red Cross Way.
Tel: 303-340-3647. Fax: 303-360-9426.
www.dmischool.com   E-mail: info@dmischool.com
    Adam T. Sexton, Exec Dir (2007). BA, Univ of Colorado-Boulder, MSc, King's College London (England). Mieke Bushhouse, Adm.

    Pre-Prep. IB MYP. Feat—Chin Fr Span Computers Visual_Arts Drama Music. **Supp**—Rem_Math Rem_Read Rev Tut. **Comp:** Comp/Stud: 1:5. **Sports**—X-country Tennis. **Selec-**

tive adm: Appl fee: $150. Appl due: Rolling. **Enr 472.** Wh 64%. Latino 5%. Blk 18%. Asian 9%. Other 4%. Avg class size: 16. Stud/fac: 9:1. **Fac 68.** FT 62/PT 6. Adv deg: 8%. **Grad '08—12.** Prep—12. **Tui '12-'13:** Day $12,150-14,000 (+$300). Aid: Need ($320,000). **Est 1977.** Nonprofit. Tri (Aug-June). Resulting from the 2009 merger of Denver International School and Montclair Academy, DMIS inhabits Montclair's six-acre campus in the Lowry neighborhood. The school offers full-immersion language education in French, Mandarin and Spanish throughout, as well as an English-language section. A middle school division, featuring the International Baccalaureate Middle Years Program, opened in fall 2011 with the addition of grade 6. The comprehensive program includes computer-integrated instruction, physical education, outdoor education, field trips and overnight excursions, and supervised after-school study and enrichment opportunities.

THE LOGAN SCHOOL FOR CREATIVE LEARNING Day Coed Gr K-8
Denver, CO 80230. 1005 Yosemite St.
Tel: 303-340-2444. Fax: 303-340-2041.
www.theloganschool.org E-mail: info@theloganschool.org
 Mark Niedermier, Head. Becky Godec, Adm.

 Pre-Prep. Gen Acad. Feat—Fr Lat Span Visual_Arts Theater Music. **Selective adm:** 33/ yr. Appl fee: $75. Appl due: Jan. Accepted: 32%. Yield: 86%. **Tests** IQ. **Enr 286.** Avg class size: 19. Stud/fac: 6:1. **Fac 45.** Adv deg: 60%. **Grad '08—25.** Prep—6. **Tui '12-'13:** Day $16,264 (+$275-2575). Aid: Need 57. **Est 1981.** Nonprofit. Tri (Aug-June). Founded as The Denver School for Gifted and Creative, the school assumed its present name in 1989. A full-time assistant instructor aids each core class teacher. Multi-age classrooms enable boys and girls to study at an appropriate academic level while learning with their social and emotional peers. Logan's technology program features a computer lab and campuswide Internet access. Pupils take part in an extensive field trip curriculum that displays an environmental emphasis; trips vary in length according to age and grade level.

ST. ANNE'S EPISCOPAL SCHOOL Day Coed Gr PS (Age 3)-8
Denver, CO 80210. 2701 S York St.
Tel: 303-756-9481. Fax: 303-756-5512.
www.st-annes.org E-mail: lfrank@st-annes.org
 Alan Smiley, Head (2006). BA, Middlebury College, MEd, Univ of Virginia. Lori Frank, Adm.

 Pre-Prep. Feat—Fr Span Environ_Sci Computers Relig Studio_Art Drama Band Music. **Supp**—Dev_Read Rem_Math Rem_Read Rev Tut. **Sports**—Basket Soccer Track. B: Lacrosse. G: Volley. **Selective adm (Gr PS-6):** 65/yr. Appl fee: $75. Appl due: Dec. Accepted: 60%. **Tests** ISEE. **Enr 423.** B 211. G 212. Wh 79%. Latino 4%. Blk 2%. Asian 2%. Other 13%. Avg class size: 22. Stud/fac: 8:1. **Fac 57.** M 16/F 41. FT 54/PT 3. Wh 99%. Asian 1%. Adv deg: 40%. **Grad '11—44.** Prep—28. **Tui '11-'12:** Day $17,236-17,962. Aid: Need 80 ($868,000). **Est 1950.** Nonprofit. Tri (Aug-June). Located on an 8-acre campus in southeast Denver, St. Anne's features an extended-day program. Spanish instruction begins in preschool, while French joins the curriculum in grade 5. The middle school program (grades 6-8) includes weekly community service projects.

COLORADO TIMBERLINE ACADEMY Bdg & Day
Durango, CO 81301. 35554 US Hwy 550. Coed Gr 9-PG
Tel: 970-247-5898. Fax: 970-259-8067.
www.ctaedu.org E-mail: fishlotsdurango@yahoo.com
 Daniel J. Coey, Dir (1994). Alexander J. Schuhl, Adm.

 Col Prep. Gen Acad. Underachiever. Feat—Creative_Writing Fr Span Anat & Physiol Astron Botany Ecol Environ_Sci Comp_Sci Robotics Psych Philos World_Relig Photog Studio_Art Drama Music Journ Woodworking. **Supp**—Dev_Read ESL Rem_Math Rem_

Read Rev Tut. Sat classes. **Sports**—Basket Soccer. B: Football. **Somewhat selective adm:** 9/yr. Bdg 8. Day 1. Appl fee: $25. Appl due: Rolling. Accepted: 90%. Yield: 90%. **Enr 42.** B 30. G 12. Bdg 40. Day 2. Intl 6%. Avg class size: 8. Stud/fac: 4:1. **Fac 10.** M 7/F 3. FT 8/PT 2. Adv deg: 40%. In Dorms 2. **Grad '07—12.** Col—10. **Tui '10-'11:** Bdg $26,700 (+$800). **Est 1975.** Nonprofit. 7 terms (Aug-May). CTA offers an unusual college-oriented program in small classes. The school year comprises seven four- or five-week blocks, with students taking three classes per block. Each class meets for 90 minutes daily. Rather than receiving a specific number of credits for various subjects, students must pass seven basic academic goals. During each block, students select a nonacademic pursuit from such offerings as guitar, photography, art and cooking. Among the recreational activities are skiing, fishing, snowboarding, rock climbing, and fall and winter wilderness trips.

EVERGREEN COUNTRY DAY SCHOOL   Day Coed Gr PS (Age 2)-8

Evergreen, CO 80439. 1093 Swede Gulch Rd.
Tel: 303-674-3400. Fax: 303-670-7957.
www.ecdschool.org   E-mail: info@ecdschool.org
    Benjamin J. Jackson, Head (2005). BA, Hobart College, MA, Providence College. Cynthia Mitchell, Adm.

    Pre-Prep. Feat—Span Computers Studio_Art Music. **Supp**—Tut. **Comp:** Comp/Stud: 1:2 (1:1 Laptop prgm Gr 4-8). **Sports**—Basket Soccer Volley. **Somewhat selective adm:** 56/yr. Appl fee: $75. Appl due: Rolling. Accepted: 90%. Yield: 85%. **Enr 215.** B 112. G 103. Wh 88%. Latino 2%. Blk 2%. Asian 8%. Avg class size: 14. Stud/fac: 7:1. **Fac 29.** M 7/F 22. FT 21/PT 8. Wh 90%. Latino 8%. Other 2%. Adv deg: 34%. **Grad '11—8.** Prep—8. **Tui '12-'13:** Day $11,500-14,250 (+$225-475). Aid: Merit 5 ($64,750). Need 44 ($180,425). **Est 1971.** Nonprofit. Tri (Sept-June). Enrolling children as young as 18 months old, the early childhood program combines socialization, life skills and foundation academics. The self-contained elementary school (grades K-5) emphasizes critical and creative thinking and includes specialist-taught Spanish, science, art, music and physical education classes. Departmentalization begins in the middle school (grades 6-8), where advisors replace homeroom teachers as the student's main source of support. Eighth graders perform 20 hours of required community service.

BEACON COUNTRY DAY SCHOOL   Day Coed Gr PS (Age 3)-8

Greenwood Village, CO 80111. 6100 E Belleview Ave.
Tel: 303-771-3990. Fax: 303-290-6462.
www.beaconcountrydayschool.com   E-mail: cwallace@beaconcountrydayschool.com
    Cynthia A. Wallace, Prin (1977). MA, JD, PhD, Univ of Denver. Tracy Rogers, Adm.

    Pre-Prep. Feat—Fr Computers Studio_Art Drama Music. **Supp**—Dev_Read. **Comp:** Comp/Stud: 1:2 (1:1 Laptop prgm Gr 4-8). **Somewhat selective adm:** 25/yr. Appl due: Rolling. Accepted: 90%. Yield: 90%. **Tests** IQ. **Enr 152.** Wh 84%. Latino 2%. Blk 2%. Native Am 2%. Asian 10%. Avg class size: 15. Stud/fac: 11:1. Casual dress. **Fac 18.** M 4/F 14. FT 17/PT 1. Wh 94%. Latino 6%. Adv deg: 33%. **Grad '11—3.** Prep—3. (Regis Jesuit 3). Alum donors: 20%. **Tui '11-'12:** Day $6000-15,000 (+$500-750). **Est 1954.** Nonprofit. Tri (Sept-June). **Assoc** NCA. Located in suburban Greenwood Village, BCDS utilizes small learning groups to meet the specific needs of gifted students. Children develop fundamental skills during the early years through a program that incorporates music, games, puppets and play. In grades 1-8, traditional courses are supplemented by computers, higher-level thinking skills, research skill development, enrichment seminars, music and art. Middle schoolers may participate in an International Baccalaureate preparation program that readies students for IB course work at the high school level.

CAMPION ACADEMY   **Bdg & Day**
Loveland, CO 80537. 300 SW 42nd St.   **Coed Gr 9-12**
Tel: 970-667-5592. Fax: 970-667-5104.
www.campion.net   E-mail: info@campion.net
   John Winslow, Prin (2006). MA, Walla Walla College. Lynne Eagan, Adm.

   Col Prep. Gen Acad. AP (21 exams taken, 71% 3+)—Eng. **Feat**—Span Anat & Physiol Comp_Sci Govt Bible Studio_Art Music Music_Theory. **Supp**—Dev_Read Rem_Math Rem_Read Tut. **Comp:** Comp/Stud: 1:3. **Dual enr:** Union Col-NE. **Sports**—Basket Soccer. B: Baseball. G: Volley. **Somewhat selective adm:** 60/yr. Bdg 47. Day 13. Appl fee: $25. Appl due: Rolling. Accepted: 98%. Yield: 92%. **Tests** TOEFL. **Enr 151.** B 73. G 78. Bdg 116. Day 35. Wh 78%. Latino 11%. Blk 3%. Asian 4%. Other 4%. Intl 5%. Avg class size: 20. Stud/fac: 10:1. **Fac 17.** M 10/F 7. FT 8/PT 9. Wh 95%. Latino 5%. Adv deg: 47%. **Grad '11—50.** Col—50. Avg ACT: 22.3. **Tui '11-'12:** Bdg $14,530 (+$300). Day $9275 (+$300). Aid: Merit ($12,000). Work prgm 202 ($255,000). **Est 1906.** Nonprofit. Seventh-day Adventist. Sem (Aug-May). **Assoc** NCA. Campion provides three separate curricula: general high school, college preparatory and honors. Subject requirements include Bible, vocational/technical, keyboarding/word processing and fine arts, and all students are expected to work a portion of each weekday. The academy conducts regular religious services and sponsors various campus ministry activities. Boys and girls engage in required community service projects, and Campion schedules a service day.

IDAHO

BISHOP KELLY HIGH SCHOOL   **Day Coed Gr 9-12**
Boise, ID 83709. 7009 Franklin Rd.
Tel: 208-375-6010. Fax: 208-375-3626.
www.bk.org   E-mail: kshockey@bk.org
   Richard Raimondi, Pres (2010). Robert R. Wehde, Prin. BA, Northwest Missouri State Univ, MA, Idaho State Univ, EdS, Univ of Idaho. Kelly Shockey, Adm.

   Col Prep. AP (156 exams taken, 65% 3+)—Eng Span Calc Stats Comp_Sci Bio Chem Physics US_Hist. **Feat**—British_Lit Creative_Writing ASL Fr Ecol Geol Sports_Med Psych Comp_Relig Theol Ceramics Drawing Painting Studio_Art Theater_Arts Band Chorus Guitar Speech Study_Skills. **Supp**—Dev_Read Rev Tut. **Dual enr:** Boise St. **Sports**—Basket X-country Golf Lacrosse Ski Soccer Swim Tennis Track. B: Baseball Football Ice_Hockey Wrestling. G: Cheer Softball Volley. Activities: 34. **Nonselective adm:** Appl fee: $205. Appl due: Mar. Accepted: 100%. **Enr 675.** B 342. G 333. Wh 80%. Latino 8%. Blk 1%. Asian 6%. Other 5%. Intl 5%. Avg class size: 21. Stud/fac: 18:1. Casual dress. **Fac 46.** M 24/F 22. FT 35/PT 11. Wh 80%. Latino 8%. Blk 1%. Asian 6%. Other 5%. Adv deg: 60%. **Grad '11—153.** Col—150. **Avg SAT:** CR 551. M 570. W 540. Avg ACT: 25.1. **Col Couns:** 3. **Tui '11-'12:** Day $6890. Parishioners $6090. Aid: Need ($956,077). **Est 1964.** Nonprofit. Roman Catholic (80% practice). Sem (Aug-May). **Assoc** NWAC. Bishop Kelly's college preparatory curriculum features Advanced Placement course work in every major discipline, as well as two foreign languages and an array of electives. All students fulfill a 90-hour service learning requirement prior to graduation, including 30 hours in grade 12.

GEM STATE ADVENTIST ACADEMY   **Bdg & Day**
Caldwell, ID 83607. 16115 S Montana Ave.   **Coed Gr 9-12**
Tel: 208-459-1627. Fax: 208-454-9079.
www.gemstate.org   E-mail: kdavies@gemstate.org
   Peter J. McPherson, Prin (2008). Karen Davies, Adm.

   Col Prep. Gen Acad. AP—Calc. **Feat**—Span Anat & Physiol Comp_Sci Relig Studio_Art Band Chorus Music_Hist Music_Theory Piano Bus Health. **Supp**—Tut. **Sports**—Basket. G:

Volley. **Selective adm:** 33/yr. Bdg 18. Day 15. Appl due: Rolling. **Enr 115.** Avg class size: 17. **Fac 11.** M 8/F 3. Wh 77%. Blk 15%. Asian 8%. In Dorms 2. **Grad '07—39.** Col—34. Avg ACT: 22. **Tui '12-'13:** Bdg $15,343. 5-Day Bdg $13,732. Day $9707. Intl Bdg $22,007. **Est 1918.** Nonprofit. Seventh-day Adventist. Sem (Aug-May). **Assoc** NWAC. This small school offers a standard curriculum that prepares boys and girls for college. Spiritual activities include Friday evening vespers, Sunday worship services, outreach, designated prayer weeks, Bible study and prayer groups, and mission trips. A well-established work-study program enables students to reduce school expenses.

MONTANA

HEADWATERS ACADEMY
Day Coed Gr 6-8
Bozeman, MT 59715. 418 W Garfield St.
Tel: 406-585-9997. Fax: 406-585-9992.
www.headwatersacademy.org   E-mail: admissions@headwatersacademy.org
 Tim McWilliams, Head (2003). BA, Eastern Washington Univ. Lydia Elgas, Adm.

 Gen Acad. Feat—Span Computers Studio_Art Music Outdoor_Ed. **Supp**—Tut. **Somewhat selective adm:** 5/yr. Appl fee: $50. Appl due: Rolling. Accepted: 90%. **Enr 26.** B 17. G 9. Wh 99%. Asian 1%. Avg class size: 8. Stud/fac: 3:1. **Fac 9.** M 2/F 7. FT 2/PT 7. Wh 100%. Adv deg: 44%. **Grad '11—10. Tui '12-'13:** Day $9600 (+$100-200). **Est 1990.** Nonprofit. Sem (Aug-June). Headwaters combines middle school academics with a noteworthy outdoor education program. The academy's proximity to Montana State University enables students to conduct research there. Each year, the school organizes a weeklong field study tour. Boys and girls engage in class discussions and research prior to the tour, then compose and present a project based upon their experiences. Foreign language study begins in grade 7.

LUSTRE CHRISTIAN HIGH SCHOOL
Bdg & Day
Coed Gr 9-12
Lustre, MT 59225. 294 Lustre Rd.
Tel: 406-392-5735. Fax: 406-392-5765.
www.lustrechristian.com   E-mail: lchs@nemont.net
 Al Leland, Supervisor.

 Col Prep. Feat—British_Lit Span Comp_Sci Govt Bible Drama Band Chorus Journ. **Supp**—Tut. **Comp:** Comp/Stud: 1:2. **Sports**—Basket Track. B: Football. G: Volley. Activities: 6. **Selective adm:** 8/yr. Bdg 7. Day 1. Appl due: Rolling. Accepted: 80%. **Tests** CEEB. **Enr 31.** B 14. G 17. Bdg 15. Day 16. Wh 55%. Latino 3%. Blk 6%. Native Am 3%. Asian 29%. Other 4%. Intl 32%. Avg class size: 8. **Fac 7.** M 2/F 5. FT 4/PT 3. Wh 100%. Adv deg: 14%. **Grad '11—8.** Col—7. (Minot St 2, E Los Angeles Col 1, Austin CC-TX 1, Dawson CC 1, U of WA 1, Nashville St CC 1). **Avg SAT:** CR 570. M 520. W 480. Avg ACT: 23. **Col Couns:** 1. Alum donors: 20%. **Tui '12-'13:** Bdg $6950 (+$700). Day $2500 (+$450). Intl Bdg $12,750 (+$700). **Est 1948.** Nonprofit. Nondenom Christian. Tri (Aug-May). Lustre offers elective courses in many subject areas, in addition to its traditional academic program. Bible classes are required, and chapel services are held once a week. Students participate in various music competitions.

LOYOLA SACRED HEART CATHOLIC HIGH SCHOOL
Day Coed Gr 9-12
Missoula, MT 59801. 320 Edith St.
Tel: 406-549-6101. Fax: 406-542-1432.
www.missoulacatholicschools.org   E-mail: info@missoulacatholicschools.org
 Jeremy Beck, Pres. EdM. Kathy Schneider, Prin.

 Col Prep. AP—Eng US_Hist. **Feat**—Creative_Writing Humanities Fr Japan Lat Span Calc Stats Astron Ecol Environ_Sci Geol Programming Middle_Eastern_Hist MT_Hist Econ

Law Pol_Sci Psych Theol Fine_Arts Studio_Art Chorus Accounting Marketing Study_Skills. **Sports**—Basket X-country Soccer Tennis Track. B: Football Golf. G: Softball Volley. **Selective adm:** Appl fee: $0. **Enr 205.** Stud/fac: 15:1. Casual dress. **Fac 25.** Adv deg: 32%. **Grad '09—39.** Col—37. **Avg SAT:** CR 543. M 555. W 550. Avg ACT: 24. **Tui '12-'13:** Day $8975. **Est 1893.** Nonprofit. Roman Catholic (70% practice). Quar (Aug-June). **Assoc** NWAC. Students at this diocesan high school take eight courses annually in a block-schedule system. Loyola maintains graduation requirements in theology, health, practical arts, fine arts and the humanities, in addition to the standard subjects. Boys and girls satisfy the following community service requirements: 10 hours in grade 9, 20 hours in grade 10, 30 hours in grade 11 and 40 hours in grade 12.

WYOMING

JOURNEYS SCHOOL   Day Coed Gr PS (Age 4)-12
Jackson, WY 83001. 700 Coyote Canyon Rd.
Tel: 307-733-3729. Fax: 307-733-3340.
www.journeysschool.org   E-mail: info@journeysschool.org
Nate McClennen, Head (2006). BS, Bowdoin College, MS, Univ of Wyoming. Tammie Van Holland, Adm.

Col Prep. IB Diploma. Feat—Chin Lat Span Calc Ecol Environ_Sci Robotics Architect Film Studio_Art Drama Music. **Comp:** Laptop prgm Gr 6-12. **Sports**—Basket X-country Golf Ski Soccer Swim Tennis Track. B: Football Wrestling. G: Volley. **Selective adm (Gr PS-11):** 30/yr. Appl fee: $50. Appl due: Feb. Accepted: 80%. Yield: 73%. **Enr 176.** Avg class size: 10. Stud/fac: 10:1. Casual dress. **Fac 32.** M 11/F 21. FT 31/PT 1. Adv deg: 62%. **Grad '10—7.** Col—7. **Tui '12-'13:** Day $18,900 (+$150-3000). Aid: Need 70. **Est 2001.** Nonprofit. (Sept-June). Operated under the auspices of Teton Science Schools, Journeys' place-based approach integrates community, leadership and ecology. The high school curriculum centers around the two-year International Baccalaureate Diploma Program, which begins in grade 11. Journeys plans age-appropriate community service projects at all grade levels, and compulsory independent service hours range from 10 hours in grade 5 to 50 hours in grade 12. A small boarding division serves high school pupils from abroad who are interested in pursuing the IB Diploma.

Southwest States

ARIZONA

PARADISE VALLEY CHRISTIAN PREPARATORY   Day Coed Gr PS (Age 4)-12
Phoenix, AZ 85028. 11875 N 24th St.
Tel: 602-992-8140. Fax: 602-992-8152.
www.paradisevalleychristian.org   E-mail: tabernethy@pvcp.org
   Sheryl J. Temple, Head. BS, Grand Canyon Univ, MA, Univ of Phoenix. Tammy Abernethy, Adm.
   Gen Acad. Feat—Lat Span Comp_Sci Bible Studio_Art Drama Band Music Dance. **Supp**—Dev_Read Rem_Math Rem_Read Rev Tut. **Comp:** Comp/Stud: 1:4. **Sports**—Basket X-country Soccer. B: Baseball. G: Softball Volley. **Somewhat selective adm:** 64/yr. Appl fee: $250. Appl due: Mar. Accepted: 90%. Yield: 90%. **Tests** Stanford. **Enr 335.** Elem 290. Sec 45. Wh 85%. Latino 7%. Blk 3%. Native Am 1%. Asian 4%. Intl 6%. Avg class size: 18. Uniform. **Fac 35.** M 10/F 25. FT 28/PT 7. Wh 90%. Latino 10%. Adv deg: 42%. **Grad '11—30. Tui '12-'13:** Day $8128 (+$175). **Est 1974.** Nonprofit. Nondenom Christian. Sem (Aug-May). **Assoc** NCA. Among noteworthy aspects of PVCP's academic program are an honors language arts track and advanced math placement from grade 4 on. Pupils study Spanish at all grade levels. Boys and girls may play on organized athletic teams beginning in grade 6. Students in grades 9-12 fulfill a 20-hour community service requirement each year.

PHOENIX CHRISTIAN UNIFIED SCHOOLS   Day Coed Gr PS (Age 2)-12
Phoenix, AZ 85015. 1751 W Indian School Rd.
Tel: 602-265-4707. Fax: 602-277-7170.
Other locations: 4002 N 18th Ave, Phoenix 85015.
www.phoenixchristian.org   E-mail: contact@phoenixchristian.org
   Phil Adams, Supt (2012). BA, Arizona College of the Bible, MA, EdD, Arizona State Univ, MA, Grace Theological Seminary. Brandon Harris, Adm.
   Col Prep. AP (exams req'd; 111 taken, 49% 3+)—Eng Span Calc Bio Eur_Hist US_Hist US_Govt & Pol. **Feat**—Creative_Writing Stats Anat & Physiol Comp_Sci Psych Sociol Bible Philos Relig Photog Studio_Art Band Chorus Culinary_Arts Study_Skills. **Supp**—ESL Makeup Rev Tut. **Comp:** Comp/Stud: 1:3. **Dual enr:** Glendale CC, AZ Christian. **Sports**—Basket Soccer Swim Tennis Track. B: Baseball Football Golf Wrestling. G: Cheer Softball Volley. **Activities:** 4. **Somewhat selective adm:** 103/yr. Appl fee: $200. Appl due: Rolling. Accepted: 96%. Yield: 95%. **Tests** IQ Stanford TOEFL. **Enr 571.** B 280. G 291. Elem 350. Sec 221. Wh 58%. Latino 11%. Blk 4%. Asian 6%. Other 21%. Intl 7%. Avg class size: 17. Stud/fac: 12:1. Uniform. **Fac 50.** M 13/F 37. FT 47/PT 3. Wh 98%. Latino 1%. Blk 1%. Adv deg: 34%. **Grad '11—63.** Col—55. **Avg SAT:** CR 506. M 552. W 504. Alum donors: 5%. **Tui '12-'13:** Day $5750-8100 (+$200). Aid: Need 70 ($135,000). **Est 1949.** Nonprofit. Nondenom Christian. Sem (Aug-May). **Assoc** NCA. This nondenominational school provides a Christian education, complete with daily Bible studies and weekly chapel services. The multitrack diploma program (general education, college prep and honors) allows students to match their interests with a desired career goal. Qualified pupils choose from honors and AP courses. Pupils in grades 7-12 satisfy a 10-hour community service requirement each semester. Phoenix Christian maintains an elementary campus on North 18th Avenue (grades PS-5).

SAINT MARY'S CATHOLIC HIGH SCHOOL   Day Coed Gr 9-12
Phoenix, AZ 85004. 2525 N 3rd St.
Tel: 602-251-2500. Fax: 602-251-2595.
www.smknights.org   E-mail: rrogers@smknights.org

Suzanne M. Fessler, Prin (2009). BA, MAEd, Arizona State Univ. Robert Rogers, Adm.

Col Prep. AP (114 exams taken, 42% 3+)—Eng Span Calc US_Hist US_Govt & Pol. **Feat**—Fr Anat & Physiol Programming Web_Design Holocaust Psych Theol Ceramics Painting Studio_Art Acting Dance Journ. **Supp**—ESL Makeup Rem_Math Rem_Read Rev Tut. **Comp:** Comp/Stud: 1:5. **Dual enr:** Rio Salado CC, Grand Canyon. **Sports**—Basket X-country Golf Soccer Swim Tennis Track Volley. B: Baseball Football. G: Softball. Activities: 17. **Somewhat selective adm:** 160/yr. Appl fee: $35. Appl due: Rolling. Accepted: 90%. Yield: 95%. **Tests** HSPT. **Enr 503.** B 242. G 261. Wh 13%. Latino 62%. Blk 7%. Native Am 2%. Asian 5%. Other 11%. Intl 5%. Avg class size: 25. Stud/fac: 15:1. Uniform. **Fac 33.** M 11/F 22. FT 22/PT 11. Wh 77%. Latino 13%. Blk 5%. Native Am 2%. Asian 2%. Other 1%. Adv deg: 87%. **Grad '11**—112. Col—108. **Avg SAT:** CR 540. M 520. W 530. Avg ACT: 21. **Col Couns:** 2. Alum donors: 35%. **Tui '12-'13:** Day $11,748 (+$800-1000). Catholic $9108 (+$800-1000). Aid: Need 400 ($2,500,000). Work prgm 50 ($8000). **Est 1917.** Nonprofit. Roman Catholic (85% practice). Sem (Aug-May). **Assoc** NCA. Students at Saint Mary's take a Catholic theology course each semester, while also fulfilling course requirements in English, math, science, social studies, world languages, the fine arts and physical education/health. At the freshman level, the admissions committee recommends course selections; older pupils develop their schedules in cooperation with an academic advisor, with consideration given to postsecondary goals. Freshmen, sophomores and juniors perform 30 hours of Christian service per year, and all boys and girls take part in various retreats, mission trips and faith experiences.

SCOTTSDALE CHRISTIAN ACADEMY   **Day Coed Gr PS (Age 4)-12**
Phoenix, AZ 85032. 14400 N Tatum Blvd.
Tel: 602-992-5100. Fax: 602-992-0575.
www.scottsdalechristian.org   E-mail: info@scottsdalechristian.org
   Timothy J. Hillen, Supt (2008). BS, Taylor Univ, MA, Eastern Michigan Univ, EdS, Univ of Wisconsin-Milwaukee. Kathy Bruch, Gr 7-12 Adm; Sheri Moy, Gr PS-6 Adm.

Col Prep. AP (exams req'd; 123 taken, 60% 3+)—Eng Physics US_Hist. **Feat**—ASL Span Anat & Physiol Comp_Sci Web_Design Econ Govt Bible Philos Studio_Art Drama Music Speech. **Supp**—LD Rev Tut. **Dual enr:** Rio Salado CC. **Sports**—Basket X-country Golf Soccer Swim Tennis Track. B: Baseball Football. G: Cheer Softball Volley. **Selective adm:** 157/yr. Appl fee: $100. Appl due: Apr. Accepted: 80%. Yield: 90%. **Tests** CTP_4 IQ Stanford. **Enr 850.** Elem 550. Sec 300. Wh 96%. Latino 1%. Blk 1%. Asian 1%. Other 1%. Avg class size: 25. Uniform. **Fac 65.** M 19/F 46. FT 51/PT 14. Wh 97%. Blk 1%. Asian 1%. Other 1%. Adv deg: 1%. **Grad '10**—75. Col—70. (AZ St 21, Paradise Valley CC 6, N AZ 5, Southwestern Col 4, Biola 3, U of AZ 3). **Avg SAT:** CR 565. M 559. W 551. Avg ACT: 25.2. **Col Couns:** 3. Alum donors: 15%. **Tui '11-'12:** Day $8404-10,186 (+$2000). Aid: Need 30 ($36,500). **Est 1968.** Nonprofit. Nondenom Christian. Quar (Aug-May). **Assoc** NCA. As part of SCA's Bible-based curriculum, computer instruction begins in prekindergarten. All elementary children attend a weekly computer class that emphasizes keyboarding, and electives in the junior high and high school address such topics as word processing and the Internet. Students in grades 9-12 satisfy an 18-hour annual community service commitment.

CAMELBACK DESERT SCHOOL   **Day Coed Gr PS (Age 2)-8**
Scottsdale, AZ 85260. 9606 E Kalil Dr.
Tel: 480-451-3130. Fax: 480-451-8197.
www.camelbackdesertschools.com   E-mail: info@camelbackdesertschools.com
   Jen Estes, Prin. BA, MA, Arizona State Univ.

Pre-Prep. Feat—Span Computers Studio_Art Music. **Comp:** Comp/Stud: 1:2. **Sports (req'd)**—Lacrosse Softball Volley. **Nonselective adm:** 22/yr. Appl fee: $0. Appl due: Rolling. Accepted: 99%. **Enr 176.** Wh 97%. Latino 1%. Blk 1%. Asian 1%. Avg class size: 11. Uniform. **Fac 20.** M 3/F 17. FT 20. Wh 95%. Latino 5%. Adv deg: 20%. **Grad '08**—13. Prep—11. **Tui '11-'12:** Day $11,593-13,558 (+$1000). Aid: Need 2 ($16,762). **Est 1950.** Inc. Quar (Aug-May). CDS' curriculum emphasizes language arts and individualized instruction. Computer applications are taught at all grade levels. Students in grades 5-8 receive typing instruction. Boys and girls take part in an active sports program.

ST. GREGORY COLLEGE PREPARATORY SCHOOL   **Day Coed Gr 6-12**
Tucson, AZ 85712. 3231 N Craycroft Rd.
Tel: 520-327-6395. Fax: 520-327-8276.
www.stgregoryschool.org   E-mail: admissions@stgregoryschool.org
      Rick Belding, Head (2012). BA, Princeton Univ. Christine Thornton, Adm.
      Col Prep. AP (101 exams taken, 69% 3+)—Eng Fr Lat Span Calc Stats Bio Chem Physics Eur_Hist US_Hist US_Govt & Pol Studio_Art Music_Theory. **Feat**—Creative_Writing Anat & Physiol Environ_Sci Programming Econ Comp_Relig Photog Drama Theater_Arts Music Journ. **Comp:** Laptop prgm Gr 6-12. **Sports**—Basket X-country Soccer Swim Tennis Track Volley. B: Baseball. G: Golf Softball. **Selective adm:** 71/yr. Appl fee: $45. Appl due: Feb. **Tests** CEEB CTP_4 ISEE SSAT. **Enr 304.** B 158. G 146. Elem 125. Sec 179. Wh 76%. Latino 12%. Blk 1%. Native Am 1%. Asian 5%. Other 5%. Avg class size: 16. Stud/fac: 9:1. **Fac 35.** M 16/F 19. FT 30/PT 5. Adv deg: 85%. **Grad '11—29.** Col—28. **Mid 50% SAT:** CR 520-660. M 510-670. W 520-660. Mid 50% ACT: 23-28. **Col Couns:** 1. **Tui '12-'13:** Day $14,950-15,950 (+$950-1175). Aid: Merit 5 ($25,000). Need 100 ($744,648). **Est 1980.** Nonprofit. Quar (Aug-May). St. Gregory's middle and high school program emphasizes leadership and innovation, writing skills, communicational skills, articulateness, logical thinking and effective argumentation. In a small-class setting, the school offers lab and fieldwork experiences, Advanced Placement courses in all disciplines and a senior internship program. Boys and girls satisfy the following community service requirements: eight hours per year in grades 6 and 7, 10 hours annually in grades 8-10, and 15 hours per year in grades 11 and 12.

ST. MICHAEL'S PARISH DAY SCHOOL   **Day Coed Gr K-8**
Tucson, AZ 85711. 602 N Wilmot Rd.
Tel: 520-722-8478. Fax: 520-886-0851.
www.stmichael.net   E-mail: school@stmichael.net
      Barry Bedrick, Head (2006). BS, MA, Trinity College (CT). James Franks, Adm.
      Pre-Prep. Gen Acad. Feat—Lat Span Computers Relig Fine_Arts Music. **Supp**—Tut. **Comp:** Comp/Stud: 1:4. **Sports**—Basket Soccer Track. G: Softball Volley. **Somewhat selective adm (Gr K-7):** 63/yr. Appl fee: $75. Appl due: Mar. Accepted: 85%. Yield: 88%. **Tests** Stanford. **Enr 337.** B 144. G 193. Avg class size: 14. Stud/fac: 11:1. Uniform. **Fac 30.** M 6/F 24. FT 27/PT 3. Wh 97%. Latino 3%. Adv deg: 43%. **Grad '09—50.** Prep—27. (Salpointe 14, St Gregory Col Prep 2). Avg SSAT: 87%. **Tui '11-'12:** Day $6970-7310 (+$300-900). Aid: Need 81 ($230,000). **Est 1958.** Episcopal (16% practice). Sem (Aug-May). This traditional Episcopal elementary school combines pre-preparatory academics with a varied fine arts curriculum. The exploratory elementary program in the early years supplements core instruction with art, music, Spanish enrichment and, beginning in grade 2, computer classes; all classrooms are self-contained at this level. The departmentalized middle school program (grades 6-8) features daily English, math, social studies and science, as well as two to three days per week of Spanish; Latin instruction begins in grade 7. Boys and girls in grades 4-7 participate in two annual service days, while eighth graders engage in three such days per year and also complete an independent service project.

SALPOINTE CATHOLIC HIGH SCHOOL   **Day Coed Gr 9-12**
Tucson, AZ 85719. 1545 E Copper St.
Tel: 520-327-6581. Fax: 520-327-8477.
www.salpointe.org   E-mail: jcotter@salpointe.org
      Kay G. Sullivan, Pres (2011). BA, Spring Hill College, MA, Univ of Alabama-Birmingham. Sr. Helen Timothy, IBVM, Prin. BA, California State Univ-Sacramento, MSA, Univ of Notre Dame. Meg Rother-Gossmann, Adm.

Col Prep. AP (exams req'd; 522 taken)—Eng Fr Lat Span Calc Stats Bio Chem Physics US_Hist World_Hist Econ US_Govt & Pol Art_Hist Studio_Art. **Feat**—British_Lit Humanities Amer_Stud Theol Fine_Arts. **Supp**—Dev_Read Rem_Math Rem_Read Rev Tut. **Comp:** Comp/Stud: 1:3. **Dual enr:** Seton Hill. **Sports**—Basket X-country Golf Soccer Swim Tennis Track Volley. B: Baseball Football Lacrosse Wrestling. G: Softball. Activities: 30. **Somewhat selective adm (Gr 9-11):** 306/yr. Appl fee: $60. Appl due: Jan. Accepted: 99%. Yield: 84%. **Tests** HSPT. **Enr 1117.** B 618. G 499. Wh 77%. Latino 4%. Blk 3%. Native Am 6%. Asian 4%. Other 6%. Avg class size: 24. Stud/fac: 22:1. Uniform. **Fac 80.** M 36/F 44. FT 70/PT 10. Wh 86%. Latino 13%. Blk 1%. Adv deg: 53%. **Grad '11—297.** Col—296. **Avg SAT:** CR 546. M 536. W 528. Avg ACT: 24. **Col Couns:** 1. Alum donors: 2%. **Tui '11-'12:** Day $8000 (+$500). Catholic $7300 (+$500). Aid: Need 391 ($1,500,000). **Est 1950.** Nonprofit. Roman Catholic (75% practice). Sem (Aug-May). **Assoc** NCA. Operated in the Carmelite tradition, Salpointe offers a traditional college preparatory curriculum that includes standard, honors, humanities and Advanced Placement courses, as well as a strong, four-year elective program. Classes in the integrated program build upon one another in scope, sequence, skills, content and experiences. Qualified students may take dual-credit classes through Seton Hill University. The school's retreat program and theology sequence form an important component of school life.

OAK CREEK RANCH SCHOOL   Bdg Coed Gr 7-12
West Sedona, AZ 86340. PO Box 4329.
Tel: 928-634-5571, 877-554-6277. Fax: 928-634-4915.
www.ocrs.com   E-mail: dwick@ocrs.com
   David Wick, Jr., Head. BA, Univ of Arizona, JD, Oklahoma City Univ. Nadine O'Brien, Prin. BA, Michigan State Univ, MS, Purdue Univ.

Col Prep. Gen Acad. LD. Underachiever. Feat—Span Comp_Sci Photog. **Supp**—Dev_ Read ESL Makeup Rem_Math Rem_Read Rev Tut. **Sports**—Basket X-country Golf Soccer. G: Softball Volley. **Somewhat selective adm:** 32/yr. Appl due: Rolling. Accepted: 90%. **Enr 90.** B 60. G 30. Elem 22. Sec 68. Intl 8%. Avg class size: 8. **Fac 15.** M 8/F 7. FT 15. Adv deg: 73%. **Grad '09—25.** Col—22. **Avg SAT:** CR/M 1100. **Tui '08-'09:** Bdg $36,500 (+$1000). **Est 1972.** Sem (Sept-May). **Assoc** NCA. OCRS' academic program is designed for students who have not succeeded in usual school settings. In addition to the regular nine-month program, Oak Creek offers a year-round program. Emphasis is placed on both basic learning skills and college preparation. Academics address individual needs, and the school maintains a program for pupils with learning disabilities. Activities include camping, fishing, horseback riding, skiing and other sports.

NEVADA

LAKE TAHOE SCHOOL   Day Coed Gr PS (Age 3)-8
Incline Village, NV 89451. 995 Tahoe Blvd.
Tel: 775-831-5828. Fax: 775-831-5825.
www.laketahoeschool.org   E-mail: mszerman@laketahoeschool.org
   Ruth Huyler Glass, Head (2011). BA, Univ of Arizona, MEd, Univ of Ashland. Millie Szerman, Adm.

Pre-Prep. Gen Acad. Feat—Span Computers Photog Studio_Art Music. **Comp:** Comp/ Stud: 1:5. Outdoor Ed. **Sports**—Basket X-country Track. G: Volley. **Selective adm:** 21/yr. Appl fee: $100. Appl due: Rolling. **Enr 164.** B 88. G 76. Wh 86%. Latino 8%. Blk 2%. Native Am 1%. Asian 3%. Avg class size: 13. **Fac 25.** M 8/F 17. FT 17/PT 8. Wh 100%. Adv deg: 32%. **Grad '09—14.** Prep—2. (Phillips Exeter 1, Taft 1). Alum donors: 25%. **Tui '11-'12:** Day $17,092. Aid: Need 25 ($350,000). **Est 1995.** Nonprofit. Tri (Aug-June). **Assoc** NWAC. The school combines its skill-based curriculum with hands-on learning activities both in the classroom and on outdoor education experiences. Small class sizes enable teachers to accommodate different learning styles and provide differentiated instruction when it is indicated. In grades 2-8, students embark on multi-night camping trips as part of the experiential education program. An integrated program for the gifted serves qualified boys and girls.

THE ALEXANDER DAWSON SCHOOL   Day Coed Gr PS (Age 3)-8
AT RAINBOW MOUNTAIN
Las Vegas, NV 89135. 10845 W Desert Inn Rd.
Tel: 702-949-3600. Fax: 702-838-1818.
www.adsrm.org   E-mail: info@adsrm.org
    Michael Imperi, Head (2007). BA, John Carroll Univ, MA, Cleveland State Univ. Julie Lepere, Adm.
    Pre-Prep. Gen Acad. Feat—Chin Fr Hebrew Lat Span Computers Ceramics Photog Visual_Arts Theater Band Chorus. **Supp**—Rem_Math Rem_Read Rev Tut. **Comp:** Comp/Stud: 1:1.5 (1:1 Laptop prgm Gr 7-8). **Sports**—Basket X-country Soccer Swim Tennis Track. G: Cheer Volley. **Selective adm:** 118/yr. Appl fee: $100. Appl due: Rolling. **Enr 600.** Avg class size: 15. Stud/fac: 8:1. Uniform. **Fac 86.** M 14/F 72. FT 75/PT 11. Wh 91%. Latino 4%. Blk 2%. Other 3%. Adv deg: 50%. **Grad '10**—60. Prep—39. (Bishop Gorman 21, Meadows 13, Faith Lutheran 2, Thacher 1, Choate 1, Stevenson 1). **Tui '11-'12:** Day $13,900-20,100. Aid: Merit 4 ($80,000). Need 120 ($1,670,000). **Est 2000.** Nonprofit. Quar (Aug-June). **Assoc** NWAC. Dawson occupies a 35-acre site in the desert mountains near Red Rock Canyon. The lower school curriculum features the thematic integration of units of study. Foreign language instruction commences with Spanish in grades K-4; French, Latin, Mandarin and Hebrew are available in the middle school (grades 5-8). Science, technology, engineering and mathematics are part of the middle school program. A sister school, the original Alexander Dawson School (separately listed), operates in Lafayette, CO.

BISHOP GORMAN HIGH SCHOOL   Day Coed Gr 9-12
Las Vegas, NV 89148. 5959 S Hualapai Way.
Tel: 702-732-1945. Fax: 702-732-2856.
www.bishopgorman.org   E-mail: admissions@bishopgorman.org
    John Kilduff, Pres (2009). Kevin P. Kiefer, Prin. Ann Wozniak, Adm.
    Col Prep. AP (exams req'd; 444 taken, 57% 3+)—Eng Span Calc Stats Bio Chem Physics US_Hist World_Hist Econ. **Feat**—Fr Lat Physiol Psych Sociol Criminal_Justice World_Relig Drawing Photog Studio_Art Theater Music Music_Theory. **Sports**—Basket Bowl X-country Golf Soccer Swim Tennis Track Volley. B: Baseball Football Wrestling. G: Softball. **Activities:** 25. **Somewhat selective adm:** 386/yr. Appl fee: $50. Appl due: Rolling. Accepted: 96%. Yield: 75%. **Tests** HSPT. **Enr 1267.** B 648. G 619. Wh 64%. Latino 13%. Blk 7%. Native Am 1%. Asian 10%. Other 5%. Avg class size: 25. Uniform. **Fac 67.** M 29/F 38. FT 66/PT 1. Wh 64%. Latino 13%. Blk 6%. Native Am 1%. Asian 10%. Other 6%. Adv deg: 56%. **Grad '11**—249. Col—237. (U of NV-Las Vegas 45, U of NV-Reno 22, U of AZ 7, Loyola Marymount 7, U of CO-Boulder 6, San Diego St 6). **Avg SAT:** CR 543. M 542. W 541. **Avg ACT:** 24. **Col Couns:** 1. **Tui '12-'13:** Day $12,100 (+$1000-1150). Parishioners $10,700 (+$1000-1150). Aid: Merit 105 ($178,200). Need 205 ($744,996). **Est 1954.** Nonprofit. Roman Catholic (75% practice). Sem (Aug-May). **Assoc** NWAC. In addition to traditional honors and Advanced Placement courses, Bishop Gorman conducts a high honors program that allows qualified students to take the maximum possible number of AP classes during their four years at the school. Pupils involved in the program must take some summer or independent study courses to meet state and school requirements. Boys and girls perform 25 hours of required community service per year.

FAITH LUTHERAN JR./SR. HIGH SCHOOL Day Coed Gr 6-12
Las Vegas, NV 89117. 2015 S Hualapai Way.
Tel: 702-804-4400. Fax: 702-804-4488.
www.faithlutheranlv.org E-mail: info@faithlutheranlv.org
Steven Buuck, Chief Exec (2011). BA, Concordia Univ Wisconsin, PhD, Marquette Univ. Julie Buuck, Adm.

Col Prep. AP (142 exams taken)—Eng Span Calc Bio US_Hist US_Govt & Pol Studio_ Art. **Feat**—Fr Anat & Physiol Forensic_Sci Comp_Sci Robotics NV_Hist Psych Sociol Relig Drama Chorus Music Journ Home_Ec. **Supp**—Tut. **Comp:** Comp/Stud: 1:1 Laptop prgm Gr 9-12. **Dual enr:** Concordia U NE. **Sports**—Basket X-country Golf Swim Track. B: Baseball Football Wrestling. G: Cheer Softball Volley. **Somewhat selective adm:** 340/yr. Appl fee: $350-450. Appl due: Rolling. **Tests** SSAT. **Enr 1360.** B 667. G 693. Elem 654. Sec 706. Wh 75%. Latino 5%. Blk 3%. Native Am 1%. Asian 10%. Other 6%. Avg class size: 25. Uniform. **Fac 81.** M 35/F 46. FT 75/PT 6. Wh 94%. Latino 2%. Blk 2%. Asian 2%. Adv deg: 56%. **Grad '11—159.** Col—157. **Avg SAT:** CR 538. M 543. W 524. Avg ACT: 24.6. Alum donors: 1%. **Tui '11-'12:** Day $9375 (+$920). Aid: Need 188 ($461,000). **Est 1979.** Nonprofit. Lutheran (23% practice). Quar (Aug-June). **Assoc** NWAC. Serving southern Nevada, Faith provides a Christian middle and high school program that features strong fine arts offerings, particularly in music. The varied curriculum includes two foreign languages and computer instruction.

THE MEADOWS SCHOOL Day Coed Gr PS (Age 3)-12
Las Vegas, NV 89128. 8601 Scholar Ln.
Tel: 702-254-1610. Fax: 702-254-2452.
www.themeadowsschool.org E-mail: hchanin@themeadowsschool.org
Henry L. Chanin, Head (2008). BA, Hiram Scott College, MA, Univ of Nevada-Las Vegas.

Col Prep. AP (exams req'd; 269 taken, 89% 3+)—Eng Fr Lat Span Calc Stats Comp_Sci Bio Chem Physics Eur_Hist US_Hist World_Hist Econ Human_Geog Psych US_Govt & Pol Art_Hist Studio_Art. **Feat**—British_Lit Shakespeare Arabic Anat & Physiol Environ_Sci Genetics Engineering Organic_Chem Robotics African_Hist E_Asian_Hist Sci_Hist Anthro Intl_Relations Terror_Policy Architect Ceramics Film Fine_Arts Photog Sculpt Theater Theater_Arts Finance Journ. **Supp**—Tut. **Sports**—Basket Bowl X-country Soccer Swim Tennis Track. B: Baseball Football Golf Wrestling. G: Cheer Softball Volley. Activities: 34. **Selective adm (Gr PS-11):** 94/yr. Appl fee: $100. Appl due: Rolling. **Tests** CEEB CTP_4 IQ ISEE SSAT. **Enr 900.** B 423. G 477. Elem 635. Sec 265. Wh 58%. Latino 5%. Blk 3%. Native Am 1%. Asian 20%. Other 13%. Avg class size: 12. Stud/fac: 11:1. Uniform. **Fac 87.** M 25/F 62. FT 84/PT 3. Wh 89%. Latino 4%. Blk 4%. Asian 3%. Adv deg: 74%. **Grad '11—44.** Col—44. (Chapman 4, USC 4, U of San Diego 3, U of CA-San Diego 2, Am U 2, Cornell 2). **Avg SAT:** CR 662. M 670. W 690. Avg ACT: 29. **Col Couns:** 2. Alum donors: 8%. **Tui '12-'13:** Day $16,190-21,110 (+$730-1640). Aid: Need 82 ($1,022,770). **Est 1984.** Nonprofit. Sem (Aug-June). **Assoc** CLS NWAC. After gaining an introduction to many disciplines in its beginning school, children at Meadows progress to an integrated lower school program that stresses reading, writing, mathematics, science and research skills, with Spanish and computer instruction beginning in kindergarten. The middle school offers opportunities for acceleration and departmentalized courses, while the upper school provides a diverse academic and elective program that features Advanced Placement classes in the major disciplines. Upper schoolers fulfill community service requirements of 16 hours per semester in grades 9-11, 24 hours per semester in grade 12.

SAGE RIDGE SCHOOL Day Coed Gr 5-12
Reno, NV 89511. 2515 Crossbow Ct.
Tel: 775-852-6222. Fax: 775-852-6228.
www.sageridge.org E-mail: lbecker@sageridge.org
Colburn Shindell, Dean (2011). Laurice Antoun-Becker, Adm.

Col Prep. AP (exams req'd; 109 taken, 80% 3+)—Eng Lat Span Calc Stats Comp_Sci Bio Chem Physics Eur_Hist US_Hist US_Govt & Pol Studio_Art. **Feat**—Anat & Physiol Environ_Sci Art_Hist Ceramics Theater Chorus Music_Hist Public_Speak. **Supp**—Tut. **Comp:** Comp/Stud: 1:1 Laptop prgm Gr 6-12. Outdoor Ed. **Sports (req'd)**—Basket X-country Ski Soccer Swim Track. B: Golf Wrestling. G: Volley. Activities: 22. **Somewhat selective adm (Gr 5-11):** 46/yr. Appl fee: $50. Appl due: Rolling. **Tests** ISEE. **Enr 227.** Elem 146. Sec 81. Avg class size: 14. Stud/fac: 9:1. Uniform. **Fac 24.** M 14/F 10. FT 23/PT 1. Adv deg: 87%. **Grad '10—15.** Col—15. (U of NV-Reno 2, Rensselaer Polytech 1, Rose-Hulman Inst of Tech 1, Syracuse 1, U of CA-Davis 1, Wellesley 1). **Avg SAT:** CR 612. M 660. W 636. Avg ACT: 27.2. **Tui '09-'10:** Day $17,000-17,500 (+$325-2550). Aid: Need 45. **Est 1998.** Nonprofit. Sem (Aug-June). Each SRS student utilizes a laptop computer as a learning aid. Honors and Advanced Placement courses are available in the core disciplines. A two-week interim program each January enables pupils to pursue course work outside the normal curriculum. Boys and girls in grades 10-12 satisfy a 15-hour annual community service requirement.

NEW MEXICO

BOSQUE SCHOOL   Day Coed Gr 6-12
Albuquerque, NM 87120. 4000 Learning Rd NW.
Tel: 505-898-6388. Fax: 505-922-0392.
www.bosqueschool.org   E-mail: jan.garrett@bosqueschool.org
    William Handmaker, Head (2011). BA, George Washington Univ, MA, Washington Univ in St Louis. Jan Garrett, Adm.

    Col Prep. Feat—Humanities Lat Span Calc Environ_Sci Drawing Film Studio_Art Drama Theater_Arts Chorus Music. **Supp**—Rev. **Sports**—Basket X-country Golf Lacrosse Soccer Swim Tennis Track. G: Volley. **Selective adm:** Appl fee: $40. Appl due: Feb. Accepted: 30%. **Enr 548.** Avg class size: 16. Stud/fac: 9:1. Casual dress. **Fac 61.** Adv deg: 55%. **Grad '09—64.** Col—64. **Avg SAT:** CR 590. M 582. W 574. **Col Couns:** 2. **Tui '12-'13:** Day $18,200 (+$740). Aid: Need 159 ($1,500,000). **Est 1994.** Nonprofit. Sem (Aug-May). Providing an independent middle and high school education for the Greater Albuquerque community, Bosque utilizes a block schedule that combines traditional 45-minute classes with courses that meet for 90 to 180 minutes at a time. The arts are integral to the school's program at all grade levels: Middle schoolers study art and music daily, and art and music constitute a major part of the humanities program during the high school years. The weeklong Winterim program, conducted each March, provides students with domestic and international travel opportunities.

MENAUL SCHOOL   Bdg Coed Gr 9-12
Albuquerque, NM 87107. 301 Menaul Blvd NE.   Day Coed 6-12
Tel: 505-345-7727. Fax: 505-344-2517.
www.menaulschool.com   E-mail: jthayer@menaulschool.com
    Lindsey R. Gilbert, Jr., Pres (2006). BA, Wheaton College (IL), MEd, Univ of Utah. Rebecca Toevs, Adm.

    Col Prep. Feat—Span Calc Astron Botany Environ_Sci Robotics Web_Design Amer_Stud Econ Govt Law Psych Ethics Relig Drawing Painting Photog Studio_Art Drama Theater_Arts Chorus Music SAT_Prep. **Supp**—ESL Tut. **Comp:** Comp/Stud: 1:2. **Sports**—Basket Golf Soccer Track. B: Football. G: Volley. **Somewhat selective adm:** 58/yr. Bdg 10. Day 48. Appl fee: $30. Appl due: Feb. Accepted: 90%. Yield: 70%. **Tests** ISEE SSAT TOEFL. **Enr 200.** B 101. G 99. Bdg 15. Day 185. Elem 79. Sec 121. Wh 30%. Latino 45%. Blk 3%. Native Am 16%. Asian 6%. Intl 10%. Avg class size: 12. Stud/fac: 6:1. Uniform. **Fac 29.** M 17/F 12. FT 29. Wh 65%. Latino 19%. Blk 12%. Native Am 3%. Other 1%. Adv deg: 51%. **Grad '09—18.** Col—18. (U of NM 8, NM Inst of Mining & Tech 2, NYU 1, CO St 1, Purdue 1, TX Tech 1). **Avg SAT:** CR/M 1100. Avg ACT: 23. Alum donors: 70%. **Tui '10-'11:** Bdg $26,778 (+$1175).

Day $13,100 (+$875). Intl Bdg $26,778 (+$2100). Aid: Need 62 ($403,000). **Est 1896.** Non-profit. Presbyterian. Sem (Aug-May). Founded by Presbyterian missionaries to serve the educational needs of Native Americans from New Mexico, Menaul now enrolls many Hispanic and Native American pupils. The curriculum emphasizes the acquisition of basic skills, critical-thinking and reasoning abilities, and facility with technology. Spirituality is an important aspect of school life: Each student attends daily chapel services and takes a religion class one semester per year. Seniors satisfy a 40-hour community service requirement.

ST. PIUS X HIGH SCHOOL   **Day Coed Gr 9-12**
Albuquerque, NM 87120. 5301 St Joseph's Dr NW.
Tel: 505-831-8400. Fax: 505-831-8413.
www.saintpiusx.com   E-mail: bducaj@spx.k12.nm.us
    Barbara Rothweiler, Prin (1992). BA, Univ of Missouri-St Louis, MA, Univ of Texas-San Antonio, EdS, Univ of New Mexico. Barbara Ducaj, Adm.
    Col Prep. AP exams taken: 208 (70% 3+). Supp—Tut. **Comp:** Comp/Stud: 1:4. **Sports**—Baseball Basket Cheer X-country Football Golf Soccer Softball Swim Tennis Track Volley Wrestling. **Selective adm (Gr 9-11):** 248/yr. Appl fee: $0. Appl due: Rolling. Accepted: 78%. Yield: 97%. **Tests** HSPT. **Enr 818.** B 406. G 412. Wh 23%. Latino 66%. Blk 2%. Native Am 6%. Asian 3%. Avg class size: 22. Stud/fac: 11:1. Uniform. **Fac 60.** M 28/F 32. FT 54/PT 6. Wh 67%. Latino 33%. Adv deg: 68%. **Grad '11—200.** Col—197. (U of NM 107, NM Inst of Mining & Tech 13, NM St 11, Central NM CC 7, Regis U 3, U of AZ 3). Avg ACT: 24.1. **Col Couns:** 5. Alum donors: 8%. **Tui '12-'13:** Day $11,975 (+$605-770). Catholic $9975 (+$605-770). Aid: Merit 16 ($32,500). Need 310 ($1,100,000). **Est 1956.** Nonprofit. Roman Catholic (95% practice). Sem (Aug-May). **Assoc** NCA. Administered by the Archdiocese of Santa Fe, St. Pius provides a varied college preparatory curriculum. Advanced Placement courses, theology classes and campus ministry, including yearly retreats, enrich the academic program. Students satisfy the following community service requirements: 20 hours in grades 9, 25 hours in grade 10, 30 hours in grade 11 and 40 hours in grade 12.

McCURDY SCHOOL   **Day Coed Gr PS (Age 4)-12**
Espanola, NM 87532. 261 S McCurdy Rd.
Tel: 505-753-7221. Fax: 505-753-7830.
www.mccurdy.org   E-mail: eromero@mccurdy.org
    Patricia Alvarado, Supt (2010).
    Col Prep. Gen Acad. AP (21 exams taken, 19% 3+)—Eng. **Feat**—Mythology Span Calc Relig Ceramics Drawing Drama. **Supp**—Rem_Math Rem_Read Tut. **Comp:** Comp/Stud: 1:2. **Sports**—Basket Bowl X-country Track. B: Baseball Football. G: Cheer Softball Volley. **Somewhat selective adm:** 69/yr. Appl fee: $25. Appl due: Rolling. Accepted: 95%. **Enr 270.** Elem 164. Sec 106. Wh 10%. Latino 77%. Blk 1%. Native Am 7%. Asian 1%. Other 4%. Stud/fac: 13:1. **Fac 27.** M 5/F 22. FT 27. Wh 26%. Latino 74%. Adv deg: 51%. **Grad '10—31.** Col—31. (U of NM 11, NM St 9, NM NM 5, U of NM-Los Alamos 2, U of San Diego 1). **Avg SAT:** CR 535. M 471. W 532. Avg ACT: 18.5. Alum donors: 16%. **Tui '10-'11:** Day $3750-5250 (+$300). **Est 1912.** Nonprofit. United Methodist (10% practice). Sem (Aug-May). **Assoc** NCA. This Christian school offers college preparatory and practical arts courses. The arts program explores both traditional art of northern New Mexico (such as weaving and painting) and contemporary art forms as well. Religious instruction incorporates daily devotions, chapel services, Bible study and formal classes.

REHOBOTH CHRISTIAN SCHOOL   **Day Coed Gr PS (Age 4)-12**
Rehoboth, NM 87322. PO Box 41.
Tel: 505-863-4412, 800-657-9345. Fax: 505-863-2185.
www.rcsnm.org   E-mail: adminsec@rcsnm.org
    Carol Bremer-Bennett, Int Dir (2010). Lorretta Smith, Adm.

Col Prep. AP—Eng Bio Eur_Hist Studio_Art. **Feat**—Span Navajo_Lang Computers SW_Stud Navajo_Govt Music. **Supp**—Rem_Math Rem_Read Rev Tut. **Sports**—Basket X-country Soccer Tennis Track. G: Softball Volley. **Somewhat selective adm (Gr K-11):** 102/yr. Appl fee: $25. Appl due: July. Accepted: 90%. Yield: 88%. **Enr 487.** B 238. G 249. Elem 289. Sec 198. Wh 21%. Latino 6%. Blk 1%. Native Am 69%. Asian 1%. Other 2%. Avg class size: 22. Stud/fac: 13:1. **Fac 38.** Wh 90%. Native Am 10%. Adv deg: 57%. **Grad '09—51.** Col—46. Avg ACT: 22. **Tui '11-'12:** Day $7575 (+$50). Aid: Need 300 ($695,000). **Est 1903.** Nonprofit. Nondenom Christian (75% practice). Sem (Aug-May). Founded by the Christian Reformed Church as a boarding school for Native American students, Rehoboth now enrolls day boys and girls only and serves a diverse student body that continues to include a large percentage of Native American pupils. The school's academic program emphasizes a core curriculum while also providing extra help in different subjects through a learning center (grades 1-8) and a resource room (grades 9-12).

NEW MEXICO MILITARY INSTITUTE   Bdg Coed Gr 9-PG

Roswell, NM 88201. 101 W College Blvd.
Tel: 575-624-8065, 800-421-5376. Fax: 575-624-8058.
www.nmmi.edu   E-mail: admissions@nmmi.edu
   Maj. Gen. Jerry Grizzle, USA (Ret), Pres (2009). BS, Southwestern Oklahoma State Univ, MBA, Central State Univ, PhD, Oklahoma State Univ. Sonya Rodriguez, Adm.

Col Prep. Milit. Feat—Fr Ger Span Econ Psych Sociol Studio_Art Music Accounting Bus Journ Speech TV_Production Mech_Drawing JROTC. **Supp**—Tut. Sat classes. **Sports**—Basket X-country Tennis Track. B: Baseball Football Golf Soccer Wrestling. G: Swim Volley. **Selective adm (Gr 9-PG):** 512/yr. Appl fee: $85. Appl due: Rolling. Accepted: 60%. **Tests** CEEB SSAT. **Enr 893.** B 737. G 156. Sec 402. PG 491. Intl 17%. Avg class size: 15. Stud/fac: 12:1. Uniform. **Fac 53.** M 31/F 22. FT 53. Adv deg: 88%. **Grad '06—151.** Col—142. **Avg SAT:** CR/M 1019. Avg ACT: 23. **Tui '11-'12:** Bdg $10,660-14,935.Intl Bdg $15,135. Aid: Need ($1,200,000). **Est 1891.** Nonprofit. Sem (Aug-May). **Assoc** NCA. NMMI is an academic institution operating within the framework of a military environment. All high school cadets participate in the Junior ROTC program, and athletic participation is required each semester. An affiliated two-year junior college offers a basic or advanced course of Senior ROTC that allows cadets to receive an Army commission.

RIO GRANDE SCHOOL   Day Coed Gr PS (Age 3)-6

Santa Fe, NM 87505. 715 Camino Cabra.
Tel: 505-983-1621. Fax: 505-986-0012.
www.riograndeschool.org   E-mail: barbara_bentree@riograndeschool.org
   Kelly R. Horn, Head (2011). BA, MA, Truman State Univ. Barbara Bentree, Adm.

Pre-Prep. Feat—Lib_Skills Span Studio_Art Drama Music. **Selective adm:** 36/yr. Appl fee: $75. Appl due: Rolling. **Enr 160.** B 82. G 78. Nonwhite 25%. Avg class size: 18. **Fac 24.** M 4/F 20. **Grad '07—22.** Prep—22. **Tui '10-'11:** Day $16,325 (+$300). Aid: Need 30 ($211,000). **Est 1978.** Nonprofit. Tri (Aug-June). At all grade levels, Rio Grande's elementary program includes math, science, social studies, research projects, literature studies and extensive writing opportunities. The school follows a thematic approach, with course work in each grade revolving around a core theme. Beginning in kindergarten, children meet weekly with music, art and drama instructors, and all academic subjects integrate the arts.

UTAH

WASATCH ACADEMY

Bdg & Day
Coed Gr 7-12

Mount Pleasant, UT 84647. 120 S 100 W.
Tel: 435-462-1400, 800-634-4690. Fax: 435-462-1450.
www.wasatchacademy.org   E-mail: admissions@wasatchacademy.org
   Joseph R. Loftin, Head (1989). BS, Univ of Texas-Austin, MEd, Utah State Univ. Carol Reeve, Adm.

   Col Prep. AP (exams req'd; 153 taken, 48% 3+)—Eng Calc Stats Bio Chem Physics Eur_Hist US_Hist Psych. **Feat**—Chin Lat Span Environ_Sci Comp_Design Robotics Econ Sociol Philos Ceramics Film Fine_Arts Photog Studio_Art Glass_Art Drama Music Dance Debate Speech Outdoor_Ed. **Supp**—Dev_Read ESL LD Rev Tut. **Comp:** Comp/Stud: 1:1 Laptop prgm Gr 7-12. Outdoor Ed. **Sports (req'd)**—Basket Cheer X-country Equestrian Golf Ski Soccer Tennis Track. B: Baseball. G: Volley. Activities: 33. **Selective adm:** 126/yr. Appl fee: $75. Appl due: Rolling. Accepted: 80%. Yield: 80%. **Tests** IQ ISEE SSAT Stanford TOEFL. **Enr 250.** B 135. G 115. Bdg 210. Day 40. Elem 4. Sec 246. Wh 60%. Latino 5%. Blk 5%. Native Am 5%. Asian 20%. Other 5%. Intl 40%. Avg class size: 13. Stud/fac: 10:1. Casual dress. **Fac 39.** M 22/F 17. FT 26/PT 13. Wh 84%. Latino 3%. Blk 5%. Asian 8%. Adv deg: 43%. **Grad '11—68.** Col—67. (UT St 4, U of WA 3, U of UT 2, Case Western Reserve 2, U of CA-Irvine 2, Quest U-Canada 2). **Avg SAT:** CR/M 1110. **Col Couns:** 2. **Tui '12-'13:** Bdg $44,700 (+$3000). 5-Day Bdg $41,700 (+$3000). Day $24,500 (+$2000). Intl Bdg $50,200 (+$3000). Aid: Merit 23 ($49,000). Need 81 ($2,435,725). **Est 1875.** Nonprofit. Quar (Sept-May). **Assoc** NWAC. Wasatch offers a traditional college preparatory curriculum with small classes. The academy's outdoor recreation program provides opportunities for hiking, mountain biking, rock climbing, backpacking, skiing and snowboarding at nearby national parks and ski resorts. The equine science program provides instruction in stable management, horse healthcare and nutrition, and English and Western riding. Students have access to the cultural pursuits and artistic performances of Salt Lake City, which is 90 miles from campus.

PARK CITY DAY SCHOOL

Day Coed Gr PS (Age 3)-9

Park City, UT 84098. 3120 Pinebrook Rd.
Tel: 435-649-2791. Fax: 435-649-6759.
www.parkcitydayschool.org   E-mail: info@parkcitydayschool.org
   Charles Sachs, Head (2007). BA, Colgate Univ, MA, Middlebury College. Diana Kaps, Adm.

   Pre-Prep. Gen Acad. Feat—Span Studio_Art Visual_Arts Music Outdoor_Ed. **Comp:** Comp/Stud: 1:3. **Sports**—Basket X-country Soccer Volley. **Somewhat selective adm:** 49/yr. Appl fee: $75. Appl due: Feb. Accepted: 86%. Yield: 86%. **Tests** CTP_4. **Enr 175.** B 85. G 90. Elem 168. Sec 7. Wh 95%. Latino 1%. Blk 2%. Asian 2%. Avg class size: 17. Uniform. **Fac 25.** M 3/F 22. FT 23/PT 2. Wh 92%. Latino 4%. Asian 4%. Adv deg: 28%. **Grad '09—8.** Prep—7. (Rowland Hall 1). **Tui '12-'13:** Day $12,995-15,050 (+$200-500). **Est 1989.** Nonprofit. Tri (Aug-June). **Assoc** NWAC. Employing an interdisciplinary, holistic approach, PCDS combines art, music and service learning with work in the standard academic disciplines. The lower school (grades K-5), which emphasizes the development of decision-making and problem-solving skills, features environmental education, field trips and community service. Students in the middle school program (grades 6-9) prepare for competitive high schools through a curriculum that includes hands-on, experiential learning opportunities and integrated technology. Research and project work are important elements of the middle school program, and boys and girls engage in the performing and visual arts, outdoor education and service learning. **See Also Page 125**

REID SCHOOL   Day Coed Gr PS (Age 2)-9
Salt Lake City, UT 84109. 2965 E 3435 S.
Tel: 801-466-4214. Fax: 801-466-4214.
www.reidschool.com   E-mail: ereid@xmission.com
Ethna R. Reid, Dir (1986). PhD, Univ of Utah.

Pre-Prep. Gen Acad. Feat—Chin Greek Lat Span Computers Archaeol Fine_Arts Photog Music Journ TV_Production Study_Skills. **Supp**—Dev_Read ESL Rem_Math Rem_Read Tut. **Comp:** Comp/Stud: 1:2.3. **Selective adm (Gr PS-8):** 15/yr. Appl fee: $75. Appl due: Feb. **Enr 212.** B 104. G 108. Elem 207. Sec 5. Wh 98%. Asian 2%. Intl 8%. Avg class size: 12. Uniform. **Fac 31.** M 5/F 26. FT 14/PT 17. Wh 100%. Adv deg: 16%. **Grad '09—22.** Prep—8. Avg SSAT: 90%. **Tui '10-'11:** Day $8856 (+$340-590). Aid: Need 5 ($50,000). **Est 1987.** Inc. Quar (Sept-May). **Assoc** NWAC. This unusual school employs the instructional methods of Exemplary Center for Reading Instruction. At all grade levels, the program is characterized by a strong emphasis on reading skills. Features of the curriculum include hands-on instruction in math, science, social studies and health; a focus on comprehension and study skills in reading, writing and speaking; specialist teachers in the fine arts, crafts and physical fitness; and a program flexible enough to allow students to work beyond grade level. In the middle school (grades 6-9), boys and girls perform three hours of required community service each week.

THE WATERFORD SCHOOL   Day Coed Gr PS (Age 3)-12
Sandy, UT 84093. 1480 E 9400 S.
Tel: 801-572-1780. Fax: 801-572-1787.
www.waterfordschool.org   E-mail: admissions@waterfordschool.org
Nancy M. Heuston, Head (1981). Todd Winters, Adm.

Col Prep. AP (exams req'd; 231 taken, 87% 3+)—Eng Fr Ger Span Calc Stats Comp_Sci Bio Chem Physics Eur_Hist US_Hist Studio_Art. **Feat**—Poetry African-Amer_Lit Southern_ Lit Japan Marine_Bio/Sci Molecular_Bio Japan_Hist Ceramics Photog Sculpt Acting Chorus Dance. **Supp**—Tut. **Comp:** Comp/Stud: 1:8. **Sports**—Basket Crew Golf Lacrosse Racquet Soccer Tennis. G: Volley. **Selective adm:** 130/yr. Appl fee: $35. Appl due: Apr. Accepted: 70%. Yield: 92%. **Tests** CTP_4. **Enr 900.** B 447. G 453. Elem 657. Sec 243. Wh 84%. Latino 3%. Blk 4%. Native Am 1%. Asian 8%. Avg class size: 20. Stud/fac: 8:1. Uniform. **Fac 114.** M 43/F 71. FT 114. Wh 94%. Latino 1%. Asian 5%. Adv deg: 58%. **Grad '11—69.** Col—69. **Avg SAT:** CR 622. M 607. W 608. Avg ACT: 26. **Col Couns:** 2. **Tui '11-'12:** Day $11,450-18,500 (+$150-500). Aid: Need ($675,000). **Est 1981.** Nonprofit. Tri (Sept-June). **Assoc** CLS NWAC. Waterford conducts a liberal arts program in a small-class setting. The school offers an unusually varied curriculum, particular in the areas of foreign language and the arts. An interim program allows boys and girls to choose among such options as mountain climbing and biking excursions, art exhibits, college visits and museum tours.

Pacific States

ALASKA

GRACE CHRISTIAN SCHOOL   Day Coed Gr K-12
Anchorage, AK 99516. 12407 Pintail St.
Tel: 907-345-4814. Fax: 907-644-2260.
www.gracechristianalaska.org   E-mail: admissions@gracechristianalaska.org
   J. Nathan Davis, Supt (2002). BS, BEd, Univ of Alaska-Anchorage, MA, Seattle Pacific
Univ. Carrie Schliesing, Adm.
   Col Prep. AP (85 exams taken, 91% 3+)—Eng Span Calc Bio Chem Studio_Art Music_
Theory. **Feat**—ASL Bible Band Music Orchestra Study_Skills. **Supp**—LD Tut. **Dual enr:**
Southwest Baptist. **Sports**—Basket X-country Ski Soccer Track. B: Wrestling. G: Volley.
Somewhat selective adm: 93/yr. Appl fee: $50. Appl due: Rolling. Accepted: 100%. Yield:
100%. **Tests** Stanford. **Enr 577.** Elem 368. Sec 209. Wh 93%. Blk 1%. Native Am 4%. Asian
2%. Avg class size: 16. Casual dress. **Fac 42.** M 15/F 27. FT 35/PT 7. Wh 94%. Latino 2%.
Asian 2%. Other 2%. Adv deg: 47%. **Grad '11—58.** Col—57. (U of AK-Anchorage 15, Seattle Pacific 4, OR St 4, Corban 2, Geo Fox 2, CO St 2). **Avg SAT:** CR 577. M 550. W 535.
Avg ACT: 24.7. Alum donors: 2%. **Tui '11-'12:** Day $6150-7750 (+$350-400). Aid: Need
82 ($243,000). **Est 1980.** Nonprofit. Nondenom Christian (95% practice). Sem (Aug-May).
Assoc NWAC. Grace teaches academic subjects within a biblical context, emphasizing Christian values and beliefs. The curriculum includes advanced courses, and Spanish and French
are taught in the upper grades. Older students perform 10 hours of community service per
semester. Parental involvement is an important component of the school's program.

PACIFIC NORTHERN ACADEMY   Day Coed Gr PS (Age 4)-8
Anchorage, AK 99508. 550 Bragaw St.
Tel: 907-333-1080. Fax: 907-333-1652.
www.pacificnorthern.org   E-mail: admissions@pacificnorthern.org
   Arnold Cohen, Head (2011). MA, PhD, Ohio State Univ. Krystal Meuleners, Adm.
   Gen Acad. Feat—Humanities Span Stats Computers Econ Graphic_Arts Photog Studio_
Art Drama Chorus Music Health. **Selective adm:** 42/yr. Appl fee: $50. Appl due: Rolling.
Tests CTP_4 SSAT. **Enr 135.** B 59. G 76. Wh 70%. Latino 4%. Blk 4%. Native Am 7%.
Asian 10%. Other 5%. Intl 6%. Avg class size: 13. Stud/fac: 9:1. Uniform. **Fac 17.** M 4/F 13.
FT 17. Wh 57%. Latino 4%. Blk 4%. Native Am 13%. Asian 14%. Other 8%. Adv deg: 41%.
Grad '10—7. Tui '12-'13: Day $11,859-14,905 (+$500). Aid: Merit 6 ($60,536). Need 22
($219,049). **Est 1996.** Nonprofit. Quar (Aug-May). In the lower school (grades PS-5) students
focus on math, science and English, and also develop basic computer skills. Middle schoolers (grades 6-8) devote mornings to the core disciplines, while afternoons are spent rotating
among Spanish, art, music, choir, physical education and other elective offerings. Boys and
girls perform both school and community service, and PNA conducts an extensive outdoor
education and travel program.

CALIFORNIA

RAMONA CONVENT SECONDARY SCHOOL   Day Girls Gr 7-12
Alhambra, CA 91803. 1701 W Ramona Rd.
Tel: 626-282-4151. Fax: 626-281-0797.
www.ramonaconvent.org   E-mail: mbarnheiser@ramonaconvent.org

Sr. Kathleen Callaway, Pres. Tina D. Bonacci, Prin. Mary Anne Barnheiser, Adm.

Col Prep. AP—Eng Fr Span Calc Bio Chem Eur_Hist US_Hist Psych US_Govt & Pol Studio_Art. **Feat**—Comp_Sci Relig Fine_Arts Speech. **Supp**—Rev Tut. **Sports**— G: Basket X-country Soccer Softball Swim Tennis Track Volley. Activities: 33. **Selective adm:** 161/yr. Appl fee: $75. Appl due: Mar. Accepted: 80%. **Tests** HSPT. **Enr 392.** Wh 4%. Latino 68%. Blk 1%. Asian 9%. Other 18%. Avg class size: 22. Stud/fac: 10:1. Uniform. **Fac 44. Grad '08—115.** Col—114. **Avg SAT:** CR 556. M 521. W 570. **Tui '12-'13:** Day $12,000 (+$1080-1480). Aid: Need 125 ($299,000). **Est 1889.** Nonprofit. Roman Catholic (88% practice). Sem (Aug-June). **Assoc** WASC. Ramona Convent is conducted by the Sisters of the Holy Names. Girls, who take seven courses per semester, choose from a wide selection of electives and Advanced Placement and honors courses. The well-equipped, 15-acre campus is easily accessible to Los Angeles.

PASADENA WALDORF SCHOOL   Day Coed Gr PS (Age 3)-8
Altadena, CA 91001. 209 E Mariposa St.
Tel: 626-794-9564. Fax: 626-794-4704.
www.pasadenawaldorf.org   E-mail: admissions@pasadenawaldorf.org
Carolyn Leach, Admin (2007). Diane Kelly LaSalle, Adm.

Pre-Prep. Gen Acad. Waldorf. Feat—Classical_Lit & Mythology Japan Span Studio_Art Drama Music Movement Woodworking. **Supp**—Dev_Read Rev Tut. **Sports**—Basket Volley. **Selective adm:** 34/yr. Appl fee: $100. Appl due: Rolling. Accepted: 57%. Yield: 90%. **Enr 220.** B 97. G 123. Wh 70%. Latino 17%. Blk 6%. Asian 6%. Other 1%. Avg class size: 19. **Fac 32.** M 7/F 25. FT 18/PT 14. Wh 70%. Latino 15%. Asian 5%. Other 10%. **Grad '10—16.** Prep—11. (La Salle HS-CA 4, Mayfield Sr 2, St Francis HS-CA 2, Flintridge Sacred Heart 1, Dunn 1, Immaculate Heart HS-CA 1). Alum donors: 30%. **Tui '11-'12:** Day $13,885-17,245 (+$825-1100). Aid: Need 56 ($345,500). **Est 1979.** Nonprofit. Sem (Sept-June). Pasadena Waldorf follows the curriculum and the educational philosophy of Rudolf Steiner by taking a variety of approaches to learning. Instructors integrate academics and the arts in a developmentally appropriate manner. The middle school curriculum includes a community service component. **See Also Page 129**

CORNELIA CONNELLY SCHOOL   Day Girls Gr 9-12
Anaheim, CA 92804. 2323 W Broadway.
Tel: 714-776-1717. Fax: 714-776-2534.
www.connellyhs.org   E-mail: admissions@connellyhs.org
Sr. Francine Gunther, SHCJ, Head. AB, Rosemont College, MA, George Washington Univ. Margaret Meland, Adm.

Col Prep. Gen Acad. AP (exams req'd; 89 taken, 67% 3+)—Eng Fr Span Calc Bio Chem US_Hist Art_Hist Studio_Art. **Feat**—British_Lit Chin Lat Comp_Sci Relig Fine_Arts Theater Music. **Supp**—Rev Tut. **Sports**— G: Basket X-country Golf Soccer Softball Swim Tennis Track Volley W_Polo. **Somewhat selective adm:** 58/yr. Appl fee: $50. Appl due: Jan. Accepted: 85%. Yield: 72%. **Tests** HSPT TOEFL. **Enr 259.** Wh 34%. Latino 23%. Blk 2%. Native Am 1%. Asian 20%. Other 20%. Intl 5%. Avg class size: 17. Stud/fac: 8:1. Uniform. **Fac 29.** M 4/F 25. FT 25/PT 4. Wh 80%. Latino 17%. Asian 3%. Adv deg: 55%. **Grad '11—72.** Col—72. (CA St U-Fullerton 5, Loyola Marymount 4, Chapman 3, UCLA 3, U of CA-Riverside 3, Pepperdine 2). **Avg SAT:** CR 549. M 562. W 582. Avg ACT: 24. **Col Couns:** 1. **Tui '12-'13:** Day $14,400 (+$600-1200). Aid: Merit 13 ($27,900). Need 64 ($217,850). **Est 1961.** Nonprofit. Roman Catholic (75% practice). Sem (Sept-June). **Assoc** WASC. Established by the Sisters of the Holy Child Jesus, Connelly offers a college preparatory curriculum augmented by electives in the arts. All students perform community service: 16 hours per year in grades 9 and 10, 24 hours annually in grades 11 and 12. An exchange program is available with other Holy Child schools in the US.

FAIRMONT PRIVATE SCHOOLS
Day Coed Gr PS (Age 2)-12

Anaheim, CA 92802. 1575 W Mable St.
Tel: 714-765-6300. Fax: 714-234-2794.
Other locations: 2200 W Sequoia Ave, Anaheim 92801; 121 S Citron St, Anaheim 92805;
5310 E La Palma Ave, Anaheim 92807; 12421 Newport Ave, North Tustin 92705.
www.fairmontschools.com E-mail: info@fairmontschools.com
David R. Jackson, Pres (1979). Michelle Lowe, Adm.

Col Prep. Gen Acad. IB Diploma. AP—Eng Fr Span Calc Comp_Sci Bio Chem Environ_
Sci Physics Eur_Hist US_Hist Econ Psych US_Govt & Pol Studio_Art Music_Theory. **Feat**—
Music. **Supp**—Tut. **Sports**—Basket X-country Golf Soccer. B: Baseball Football. G: Tennis
Volley. **Somewhat selective adm:** 448/yr. Appl fee: $50-100. **Tests** ISEE SSAT TOEFL. **Enr**
2230. Intl 20%. Uniform. **Fac 148.** M 32/F 116. FT 148. **Grad '11—160.** Col—160. **Avg**
SAT: CR 529. M 665. W 575. **Tui '12-'13:** Day $11,620-17,400 (+$66-792). **Est 1953.** Inc.
Tri (Aug-June). **Assoc** WASC. Fairmont comprises six campuses at five locations throughout
Orange County. The high school offers honors classes, Advanced Placement courses and the
International Baccalaureate diploma and certificates. Special programs in medical and engineering tracks provide advanced and individualized math and science instruction. Among the
graduation requirements are foreign language, computer and fine arts courses. The International Academy (grades 7-11) on West Sequoia Avenue offers four hours of daily ESL instruction plus courses in mathematics, physical education and American culture. International students live with host families.

SERVITE HIGH SCHOOL
Day Boys Gr 9-12

Anaheim, CA 92801. 1952 W La Palma Ave.
Tel: 714-774-7575. Fax: 714-774-1404.
www.servitehs.org E-mail: admissions@servitehs.org
Peter S. Bowen, Pres. BA, Univ of Notre Dame, MA, Duke Univ. Michael P. Brennan, Prin.
BA, MS, Chapman Univ. Bill Brundige, Adm.

Col Prep. AP—Eng Lat Span Calc Stats Comp_Sci Bio Chem Physics Eur_Hist US_Hist
World_Hist Econ US_Govt & Pol. **Feat**—Fr Greek Anat & Physiol Marine_Bio/Sci Sports_
Med Ethics Theol Art_Hist Drawing Film Painting Theater Chorus Music_Hist Music_Theory
Guitar Journ. **Supp**—Makeup Tut. **Comp:** Laptop prgm Gr 10-12. **Dual enr:** CA St U-Ful-
lerton. **Sports**— B: Baseball Basket X-country Football Golf Lacrosse Soccer Swim Tennis
Track Volley W_Polo Wrestling. Activities: 24. **Selective adm:** 260/yr. Appl fee: $65. Appl
due: Jan. Accepted: 72%. Yield: 94%. **Tests** HSPT. **Enr 957.** Avg class size: 19. Casual dress.
Fac 58. M 38/F 20. FT 58. Adv deg: 55%. **Grad '11—215.** Col—213. **Avg SAT:** CR 540. M
559. W 536. Avg ACT: 24. **Tui '12-'13:** Day $12,700 (+$600-2075). Catholic $11,950 (+$600-
2075). **Est 1958.** Nonprofit. Roman Catholic. Sem (Aug-June). **Assoc** WASC. Located on a
15-acre campus, this boys' school offers course work at the college preparatory, honors and
Advanced Placement levels. Servite's active performing arts program operates in conjunction
with two sister schools. Also noteworthy is the school's classical guitar program. The tablet
computer program in grades 10-12 integrates technology across the curriculum. Freshmen and
sophomores perform 30 hours of required community service annually, juniors and seniors 20
hours per year.

NOTRE DAME HIGH SCHOOL
Day Girls Gr 9-12

Belmont, CA 94002. 1540 Ralston Ave.
Tel: 650-595-1913. Fax: 650-595-2643.
www.ndhsb.org E-mail: admissions@ndhsb.org
Rita L. Gleason, Prin. BA, College of Notre Dame (CA), MA, Univ of Santa Clara, MA,
San Francisco State Univ. Alison Bianchetti, Adm.

Col Prep. AP (exams req'd; 205 taken, 78% 3+)—Eng Fr Span Calc Bio Chem US_
Hist US_Govt & Pol Art_Hist Studio_Art. **Feat**—Creative_Writing Environ_Sci Sports_Med
Comp_Sci Psych Relig Photog Sculpt Band Chorus Orchestra Dance TV_Production. **Supp**—

LD. **Sports**— G: Basket X-country Golf Soccer Softball Swim Tennis Track W_Polo. Activities: 20. **Selective adm (Gr 9-11):** 120/yr. Appl fee: $100. Appl due: Jan. **Tests** HSPT. **Enr 450.** Wh 72%. Latino 12%. Blk 2%. Native Am 1%. Asian 13%. Avg class size: 21. Stud/fac: 14:1. Uniform. **Fac 58.** Adv deg: 74%. **Grad '10—138.** Col—138. (Sonoma St 11, Col of San Mateo 8, U of CA-Davis 6, U of CA-Irvine 6, U of OR 6, San Jose St 5). **Avg SAT:** CR 540. M 519. W 561. **Col Couns:** 4. **Tui '11-'12:** Day $17,400 (+$450-1200). Aid: Merit 78 ($142,125). Need 96 ($534,845). **Est 1922.** Nonprofit. Roman Catholic. Sem (Aug-June). **Assoc** WASC. Sponsored by the Sisters of Notre Dame de Namur, this independent Catholic school provides a college preparatory program for a student body drawn largely from San Mateo County. Advanced Placement and honors courses are available, and students may take certain classes not offered at NDB at either Junipero Serra High School or Mercy High School through the Tri-School Program. Girls perform 100 hours of compulsory community service prior to graduation.

ECOLE BILINGUE DE BERKELEY   Day Coed Gr PS (Age 3)-8
Berkeley, CA 94710. 1009 Heinz Ave.
Tel: 510-549-3867. Fax: 510-845-3209.
www.eb.org   E-mail: bbastrenta@eb.org
    Frederic Canadas, Head (2002). BS, MEd. Brigitte Bastrenta, Adm.
    Pre-Prep. Bilingual (Fr). Feat—Fr Lat Computers Studio_Art Drama Music. **Supp**—ESL Rem_Read Tut. **Comp:** Laptop prgm Gr 6-8. **Sports**—Basket Volley. **Selective adm:** 85/yr. Appl fee: $150. Appl due: Feb. Accepted: 80%. Yield: 65%. **Enr 546.** Nonwhite 38%. Avg class size: 16. Stud/fac: 11:1. **Fac 50.** M 12/F 38. FT 40/PT 10. **Grad '09—38.** Prep—25. (Head-Royce 6, Intl HS 5, College Prep 4, Bentley 2, Athenian 1, Lick-Wilmerding 1). **Tui '12-'13:** Day $20,695-23,440 (+$2000-3900). Aid: Need 246. **Est 1977.** Nonprofit. Sem (Sept-June). **Assoc** WASC. Ecole Bilingue de Berkeley, formerly known as East Bay French-American School, provides a rigorous elementary course of study, set in a multicultural environment, in both English and French. In grades pre-K-2, children receive French immersion 80 percent of the school day, in addition to an hour of English instruction daily. Then, in grades 3-8, immersion is split equally between the two languages. Specialists teach science, computer, music, art, drama, physical education and gardening. Field trips and international exchange opportunities enrich the program.

PROVIDENCE HIGH SCHOOL   Day Coed Gr 9-12
Burbank, CA 91505. 511 S Buena Vista St.
Tel: 818-846-8141. Fax: 818-843-8421.
www.providencehigh.org   E-mail: paul.kaminski@providencehigh.org
    Joe Sciuto, Head (2011). BA, California State Univ-Northridge, MA, Pepperdine Univ. Judy Egan Umeck, Adm.
    Col Prep. AP (exams req'd; 199 taken)—Eng Fr Span Calc Stats Bio Chem Physics US_Hist Econ US_Govt & Pol Studio_Art. **Feat**—British_Lit Chin Lat Anat & Physiol Environ_Sci Comp_Sci Anthro Law Psych Sociol Ethics World_Relig Ceramics Film Photog Video_Production Animation Music Accounting Communications Journ TV_Production. **Supp**—Tut. **Comp:** Comp/Stud: 1:4. **Sports**—Basket X-country Golf Soccer Track Volley. B: Baseball. G: Softball. Activities: 30. **Somewhat selective adm:** 125/yr. Appl fee: $65. Appl due: Jan. Accepted: 90%. Yield: 62%. **Enr 400.** B 195. G 205. Wh 17%. Latino 12%. Blk 1%. Native Am 1%. Asian 20%. Other 49%. Avg class size: 24. Stud/fac: 15:1. Uniform. **Fac 43.** M 17/F 26. FT 42/PT 1. Wh 67%. Latino 27%. Asian 1%. Other 5%. Adv deg: 65%. **Grad '11—99.** Col—99. **Avg SAT:** CR 529. M 524. W 538. **Col Couns:** 3. Alum donors: 10%. **Tui '12-'13:** Day $12,900 (+$550). Aid: Merit 14 ($54,000). Need 110 ($350,000). **Est 1955.** Nonprofit. Roman Catholic (75% practice). Sem (Sept-June). **Assoc** WASC. Providence's curriculum includes honors and AP classes, electives and required courses in art, computer science, foreign language, music and religious studies. In addition to the college preparatory course of study, qualified students may enroll in one of three four-year focus programs in

medical careers, technology and media communications. Boys and girls complete mandatory Christian service projects. **See Also Page 68**

ALL SAINTS' EPISCOPAL DAY SCHOOL — Day Coed Gr PS (Age 4)-8
Carmel, CA 93923. 8060 Carmel Valley Rd.
Tel: 831-624-9171. Fax: 831-624-3960.
www.asds.org   E-mail: info@asds.org
Michele M. Rench, Head (2003). BA, Univ of California-Berkeley, MA, College of Notre Dame (CA). Anne Crisan, Adm.

Pre-Prep. Gen Acad. Feat—Shakespeare Fr Lat Span Relig Art_Hist Studio_Art Theater Music. **Supp**—Tut. **Comp:** Comp/Stud: 1:2.2. **Sports**—Basket Golf Soccer Tennis. G: Volley. **Selective adm:** 34/yr. Appl fee: $50. Appl due: Jan. Accepted: 72%. Yield: 69%. **Tests** CTP_4. **Enr 215.** B 108. G 107. Wh 79%. Latino 4%. Blk 2%. Asian 8%. Other 7%. Avg class size: 23. Stud/fac: 7:1. Uniform. **Fac 31.** M 5/F 26. FT 15/PT 16. Wh 100%. **Grad '11—26.** Prep—20. (Robert Louis Stevenson-CA 11, Santa Catalina 4, York Sch 2, Phillips Acad 1, Palma HS 1, Trinity Christian-CA 1). **Tui '12-'13:** Day $15,199-18,396. Aid: Need ($636,059). **Est 1961.** Nonprofit. Episcopal (27% practice). Sem (Aug-June). All Saints' complements its core curriculum with course work in religion, art, music, foreign language, technology, performing arts and physical education. The foreign language program features Spanish and French in grades 1-8, as well as Latin from grade 8. Team sports and leadership opportunities complement academics in grades 6-8, while field trips and class projects provide enrichment at all grade levels. Eighth graders perform 10 hours of compulsory independent service.

JESUIT HIGH SCHOOL — Day Boys Gr 9-12
Carmichael, CA 95608. 1200 Jacob Ln.
Tel: 916-482-6060. Fax: 916-482-2310.
www.jesuithighschool.org   E-mail: admissions@jhssac.org
Rev. David Suwalsky, SJ, Pres (2011). PhD, St Louis Univ. Brianna Latko, Prin. BA, Univ of Iowa, MEd, Loyola Univ of Chicago. Gerald C. Lane, Adm.

Col Prep. AP (432 exams taken, 85% 3+)—Eng Lat Span Calc Bio Chem Physics US_ Hist Econ US_Govt & Pol Art_Hist Music_Theory. **Feat**—Fr Ger Anat & Physiol Comp_Sci Holocaust Psych Comp_Relig Ethics Theol Studio_Art Chorus. **Supp**—Tut. **Sports**— B: Baseball Basket X-country Football Golf Rugby Soccer Swim Tennis Track Volley W_Polo Wrestling. **Selective adm (Gr 9-11):** 290/yr. Accepted: 70%. **Tests** HSPT. **Enr 1065.** Nonwhite 32%. Avg class size: 26. Casual dress. **Fac 72.** M 53/F 19. FT 62/PT 10. Adv deg: 62%. **Grad '08—252.** Col—247. **Avg SAT:** CR 575. M 587. W 582. Avg ACT: 25.4. **Col Couns:** 6. **Tui '11-'12:** Day $12,010 (+$700-1000). Aid: Need 199. **Est 1963.** Nonprofit. Roman Catholic. Sem (Aug-May). **Assoc** WASC. Jesuit's college preparatory curriculum is supplemented by programs in music, drama, journalism and the fine arts. Both Advanced Placement and honors courses are available. Boys in grades 9-11 perform 16 hours of community service per year, while seniors take part in a semester-long Christian service course that includes 50 hours of service and 10 hours of class time.

ST. MICHAEL'S EPISCOPAL DAY SCHOOL — Day Coed Gr PS (Age 4)-8
Carmichael, CA 95608. 2140 Mission Ave.
Tel: 916-485-3418. Fax: 916-485-9084.
www.smeds.net   E-mail: maryheise@smeds.net
Rev. Jesse Vaughan, Head. MTh, Episcopal Theological Seminary. Mary D. Heise, Adm.

Gen Acad. Feat—Lat Span Computers Robotics Civics Relig Studio_Art Drama Music. **Supp**—Dev_Read Tut. **Sports**—Basket Golf Track. G: Volley. **Selective adm:** Appl fee: $75. Appl due: Rolling. **Enr 231.** Avg class size: 22. Stud/fac: 6:1. Uniform. **Fac 42.** M 8/F 34. FT 24/PT 18. **Grad '10—27. Tui '11-'12:** Day $8945-10,520 (+$600). Aid: Need ($95,000). **Est 1963.** Nonprofit. Episcopal. (Sept-June). **Assoc** WASC. SMEDS' preschool and kindergarten focus on concept and motor development, social and motor skills, reading, math and the arts. Daily chapel is part of a curriculum that also includes Spanish, Latin, music, drama, computers and physical education.

CHAMINADE COLLEGE PREPARATORY   Day Coed Gr 6-12
Chatsworth, CA 91311. 10210 Oakdale Ave.
Tel: 818-360-4211. Fax: 818-363-0127.
Other locations: 7500 Chaminade Ave, West Hills 91304; 19800 Devonshire St, Chatsworth 91311.
www.chaminade.org   E-mail: ecelaya@chaminade.org
     James V. Adams, Pres. Esther Bonino Bennett, Gr 9-12 Adm; Barbara Willick, Gr 6-8 Adm.

     Col Prep. AP (722 exams taken, 72% 3+)—Eng Fr Lat Span Calc Stats Bio Chem Environ_Sci Physics US_Hist World_Hist Comp_Govt & Pol Econ Human_Geog Psych US_Govt & Pol Studio_Art. **Feat**—British_Lit Creative_Writing Shakespeare Chin Anat & Physiol Ecol Geol Sports_Med Programming Robotics Women's_Stud Philos World_Relig Film Sculpt Acting Theater_Arts Chorus Dance Debate Journ. **Comp:** Laptop prgm Gr 9-10. **Sports**—Basket X-country Equestrian Fencing Golf Lacrosse Soccer Swim Tennis Track Volley. B: Baseball Football Wrestling. G: Cheer F_Hockey. **Selective adm:** Appl fee: $100. Appl due: Jan. **Enr 1320.** Avg class size: 27. Stud/fac: 14:1. Uniform. **Fac 87.** Adv deg: 54%. **Grad '08—277.** Col—274. (CA St U-Northridge 17, U of CA-Santa Cruz 16, U of CA-Santa Barbara 14, U of CO-Boulder 13, USC 10, U of CA-Davis 10). **Avg SAT:** CR 565. M 574. W 582. Avg ACT: 25.5. **Col Couns:** 3. **Tui '12-'13:** Day $12,925 (+$1570-2375). **Est 1952.** Non-profit. Roman Catholic. Sem (Sept-June). **Assoc** WASC. Founded as Chaminade High School for Boys by Marianists seeking to expand their educational mission in southern California, the school added a middle school program in 1969 and a girls' division three years later. In addition to meeting course requirements in the traditional disciplines, students earn credits in such areas as critical thinking and composition, religious studies and expository composition. Boys and girls, who must perform community service each year, compile 60 cumulative hours prior to graduation. The middle school (grades 6-8) operates on Devonshire Street, while the upper school campus (grades 9-12) is in West Hills.

CHATSWORTH HILLS ACADEMY   Day Coed Gr PS (Age 2)-8
Chatsworth, CA 91313. PO Box 5077.
Tel: 818-998-4037. Fax: 818-998-4062.
www.chaschool.org   E-mail: info@chaschool.org
     Ann Gillinger, Head (2009). BA, MA, Univ of Washington. Nancy Salyers, Adm.

     Pre-Prep. Feat—Span Computers Studio_Art Drama Music Journ. **Supp**—Tut. **Sports**—Basket Soccer Volley. **Selective adm:** Appl fee: $25-75. Appl due: Feb. Accepted: 80%. Yield: 79%. **Tests** ISEE. **Enr 250.** B 130. G 120. Avg class size: 15. Stud/fac: 9:1. **Fac 30.** M 6/F 24. FT 29/PT 1. Adv deg: 66%. **Grad '08—15.** Prep—13. **Tui '12-'13:** Day $12,250-18,650 (+$500-2000). **Est 1977.** Nonprofit. Quar (Sept-June). **Assoc** WASC. Enrolling children from age 2½, the academy conducts a spiral curriculum that continually introduces new material, while also reinforcing previous content and skills. The early childhood through grade 4 programs focus on integrating all subjects, and the middle school program (grades 5-8) employs a liberal arts approach that emphasizes both skill acquisition and content. Main course areas are English, math, history, science, modern language, and the visual and performing arts. Middle school students satisfy a nine-hour annual service requirement.

SIERRA CANYON SCHOOL
Day Coed Gr PS (Age 4)-12
Chatsworth, CA 91311. 11052 Independence Ave.
Tel: 818-882-8121. Fax: 818-882-4953.
Other locations: 20801 W Rindaldi St, Chatsworth 91311.
www.sierracanyonschool.org   E-mail: jskrumbis@sierracanyonschool.org
James P. Skrumbis, Head (2004). BA, California State Univ-Long Beach, MA, Univ of Southern California. Kendall Pillsbury, Adm.

Col Prep. AP (exams req'd; 99 taken)—Eng Fr Lat Span Calc Bio Chem Physics Eur_ Hist US_Hist Studio_Art Music_Theory. **Feat**—Creative_Writing Gothic_Lit Satire Chin Programming Holocaust Geog Law Social_Psych Philos Ceramics Fine_Arts Photog Animation Theater Dance. **Supp**—Tut. **Sports**—Basket X-country Soccer Swim Tennis Track. B: Baseball Football. G: Softball Volley. **Selective adm:** 202/yr. Appl fee: $150. Appl due: Feb. **Tests** ISEE. **Enr 922.** B 472. G 450. Wh 60%. Latino 4%. Blk 10%. Asian 6%. Other 20%. Avg class size: 20. Casual dress. **Fac 135.** Adv deg: 12%. **Grad '11—72.** Col—72. **Tui '12-'13:** Day $21,750-28,600 (+$500). Aid: Need ($500,000). **Est 1977.** Nonprofit. Sem (Sept-June). **Assoc** WASC. Sierra Canyon features small-group math instruction, hands-on science courses and a social studies curriculum that incorporates frequent field trips. After-school enrichment and sports are available. The middle and upper schools (grades 7-12) operate on a separate campus on West Rindaldi Street.

HILLDALE SCHOOL
Day Coed Gr PS (Age 4)-8
Daly City, CA 94014. 79 Florence St.
Tel: 650-756-4737. Fax: 650-756-3162.
www.hilldaleschool.org   E-mail: info@hilldaleschool.org
Sasha Clayton, Prin (2007). BA, Drake Univ, MA, Concordia Univ (IL).

Pre-Prep. Feat—Span Studio_Art Music. **Supp**—Rev Tut. **Comp:** Comp/Stud: 1:1 **Selective adm:** 30/yr. Appl fee: $25. Appl due: Jan. Accepted: 60%. Yield: 80%. **Enr 93.** B 49. G 44. Wh 45%. Latino 18%. Blk 11%. Asian 19%. Other 7%. Avg class size: 14. Stud/fac: 8:1. Uniform. **Fac 12.** M 3/F 9. FT 9/PT 3. Wh 67%. Asian 33%. Adv deg: 50%. **Grad '11—8.** Prep—6. (Mercy HS-Burlingame 2, San Francisco U HS 1, Lick-Wilmerding 1, Lisa Kampner Hebrew 1). Avg SSAT: 98%. Alum donors: 5%. **Tui '11-'12:** Day $13,500. Aid: Need 22. **Est 1948.** Inc. Quar (Aug-June). Designed for gifted students and those of above-average intelligence, Hilldale maintains a 195-day school year. Hands-on experiences, experiments, projects and field trips enrich the comprehensive, accelerated curriculum. Programming emphasizes the presentation and the mastery of basic skills and subject content in phonics, reading, grammar, composition, spelling, math, science, geography and history, thereby providing the necessary foundation for higher-level study. Children engage in service learning projects at all grade levels.

CHRISTIAN UNIFIED SCHOOLS OF SAN DIEGO
Day Coed Gr K-12
El Cajon, CA 92019. 2100 Greenfield Dr.
Tel: 619-201-8800. Fax: 619-201-8898.
Other locations: 211 S 3rd St, El Cajon 92019.
www.christianunified.org   E-mail: admissions@christianunified.org
Chuck Leslie, Supt (2006). BS, Univ of California-San Diego. Kimberly Johnston, Adm.

Col Prep. AP (exams req'd; 111 taken, 75% 3+)—Eng Span Calc Stats Bio Chem Physics US_Hist World_Hist US_Govt & Pol Studio_Art. **Feat**—Anat & Physiol Comp_Sci Econ Bible Comp_Relig Film Drama Band Chorus Speech Health Home_Ec Study_Skills Nutrition. **Supp**—ESL Rem_Math Rem_Read Tut. **Comp:** Comp/Stud: 1:10. **Sports**—Basket X-country Golf Soccer Swim Tennis Track Volley. B: Baseball Football Wrestling. G: Cheer Softball. **Somewhat selective adm (Gr K-11):** 135/yr. Appl fee: $150. Appl due: Feb. Accepted: 95%. Yield: 90%. **Tests** CEEB Stanford. **Enr 820.** B 419. G 401. Elem 318. Sec 502. Wh 68%. Latino 8%. Blk 4%. Native Am 3%. Asian 11%. Other 6%. Intl 10%. Avg class size: 15. Stud/fac: 14:1. Uniform. **Fac 67.** M 18/F 49. FT 67. Wh 95%. Latino 3%. Blk 1%. Asian

1%. Adv deg: 31%. **Grad '10—98.** Col—91. (Pt Loma Nazarene 6, Biola 4, Baylor 3, CA Baptist 3). **Avg SAT:** CR 505. M 577. W 510. Avg ACT: 23. **Col Couns:** 2. **Tui '11-'12:** Day $7716-11,352 (+$600-3500). **Est 1965.** Nonprofit. Baptist. Sem (Aug-May). CUSSD conducts a college preparatory program that includes Advanced Placement course work in the major disciplines. Technology, vocal and instrumental music, art, drama and foreign language classes complement the core curriculum. Christian Unified teaches all subjects from a Biblical perspective. An additional elementary school campus serving grades K-6 operates on South 3rd Street.

PROSPECT SIERRA SCHOOL   Day Coed Gr K-8
El Cerrito, CA 94530. 2060 Tapscott Ave.
Tel: 510-236-5800. Fax: 510-232-7615.
Other locations: 960 Avis Dr, El Cerrito 94530.
www.prospectsierra.org   E-mail: admissions@prospectsierra.org
   Katherine M. Dinh, Head (2007). BA, Univ of Virginia, MEd, Harvard Univ. Lily Shih, Adm.

   Pre-Prep. Gen Acad. Feat—Fr Span Computers Studio_Art Drama Orchestra Jazz_Band. **Comp:** Comp/Stud: 1:4. **Sports**—Basket X-country Track Ultimate_Frisbee. G: Volley. **Selective adm:** 87/yr. Appl fee: $100. Appl due: Jan. Accepted: 70%. Yield: 68%. **Tests** ISEE. **Enr 479.** B 226. G 253. Wh 58%. Latino 4%. Blk 3%. Asian 6%. Other 29%. Avg class size: 24. Casual dress. **Fac 68.** M 15/F 53. FT 50/PT 18. Wh 83%. Latino 6%. Blk 6%. Asian 5%. Adv deg: 60%. **Grad '11—61.** Prep—23. (Bishop O'Dowd 5, Athenian 4, College Prep 3, Head-Royce 2, Lick-Wilmerding 2, Marin Acad 2). **Tui '11-'12:** Day $20,975-22,975 (+$550). Aid: Need ($1,503,524). **Est 1981.** Nonprofit. Sem (Aug-June). Prospect Sierra's curriculum encompasses the humanities, math, science, technology, art, music, drama and physical education. Beginning in grade 5, children study either French or Spanish. Service learning is part of the curriculum at all grade levels. A second campus, one mile away on Avis Drive, houses the middle school (grades 5-8).

THE GRAUER SCHOOL   Day Coed Gr 6-12
Encinitas, CA 92024. 1500 S El Camino Real.
Tel: 760-944-6777. Fax: 760-944-6784.
www.grauerschool.com   E-mail: info@grauerschool.com
   Stuart R. Grauer, Dir (1991). MS, Long Island Univ, EdD, Univ of San Diego. Dana Abplanalp-Diggs, Prin.

   Col Prep. AP—Span. **Feat**—Creative_Writing Humanities ASL Chin Fr Japan Lat Calc Stats Comp_Sci Anthro Psych Govt/Econ Peace_Stud World_Relig Art_Hist Film Photog Studio_Art Drama Journ. **Supp**—ESL Rev Tut. **Comp:** Comp/Stud: 1:3. **Dual enr:** Mira-Costa, U of CA-San Diego. **Sports**—Basket Tennis. G: Volley. **Selective adm:** 50/yr. Appl fee: $100. Appl due: Rolling. Accepted: 30%. Yield: 98%. **Tests** CEEB ISEE Stanford. **Enr 150.** B 75. G 75. Elem 65. Sec 85. Intl 8%. Avg class size: 8. Stud/fac: 6:1. Casual dress. **Fac 32.** M 13/F 19. FT 17/PT 15. Adv deg: 68%. **Grad '09—13.** Col—13. **Avg SAT:** CR 580. M 560. W 570. Avg ACT: 28. Alum donors: 25%. **Tui '12-'13:** Day $19,900-20,600 (+$1700-2200). **Est 1991.** Nonprofit. Sem (Aug-June). **Assoc** WASC. Located in northern San Diego County, this small school employs a modified block schedule in which students attend a pair of two-hour class sessions each morning, then follow a 50-minute elective by a 100-minute elective each afternoon. Grauer offers well-developed arts and multimedia technology program, and boys and girls embark on enrichment field trips each semester. Private tutoring (for an additional fee), independent studies opportunities and internships are available to interested students. Pupils accumulate 50 hours of required community service in grades 9-12.

CALVIN CHRISTIAN SCHOOL
Day Coed Gr PS (Age 2)-12

Escondido, CA 92026. 2000 N Broadway.
Tel: 760-489-6430. Fax: 760-489-7055.
Other locations: 1868 N Broadway, Escondido 92026.
www.calvinchristianescondido.org   E-mail: admissions@calvinchristianescondido.org
    Terry Kok, Supt (2002). BA, Seattle Pacific Univ, MA, Central Washington Univ. Cindi
Glossop, Adm.

    Col Prep. AP (exams req'd; 68 taken, 85% 3+)—Eng Span Calc Bio US_Hist. **Feat**—
Creative_Writing Anat & Physiol Ecol Programming Robotics Web_Design Civil_War Psych
Sociol Bible Ethics Art_Hist Photog Studio_Art Drama Bus Journ. **Supp**—ESL Rem_Math
Rem_Read Tut. **Comp:** Comp/Stud: 1:5. **Sports**—Basket X-country Golf Soccer Track. B:
Baseball Football. G: Volley. Activities: 10. **Selective adm:** 60/yr. Appl fee: $300. Appl due:
Rolling. Accepted: 80%. Yield: 90%. **Tests** Stanford TOEFL. **Enr 517.** Elem 366. Sec 151. Wh
79%. Latino 12%. Blk 3%. Asian 6%. Avg class size: 18. Stud/fac: 17:1. **Fac 35.** M 13/F 22.
FT 33/PT 2. Wh 94%. Latino 3%. Asian 3%. Adv deg: 34%. **Grad '11—32.** Col—32. (Dordt
6, Trinity Christian 5, CA St U-Monterey Bay 3, Pt Loma Nazarene 2, U of CA-Santa Barbara
1, Pepperdine 1). **Avg SAT:** CR 568. M 570. W 542. Avg ACT: 25.1. **Col Couns:** 1. Alum
donors: 10%. **Tui '11-'12:** Day $6879-8515 (+$200). Aid: Need 58 ($230,000). **Est 1960.**
Nonprofit. Nondenom Christian (100% practice). Quar (Aug-June). **Assoc** WASC. Calvin
Christian's elementary and secondary programs adhere to a Biblical worldview. Classes range
from Advanced Placement to remedial education classes. Spiritual activities consist of weekly
chapel, Bible study and special events. Service learning is integrated into the curriculum in
grades K-12.

NAWA ACADEMY
Bdg Coed Gr 7-12

French Gulch, CA 96033. 17351 Trinity Mountain Rd.
Tel: 530-359-2215, 800-358-6292. Fax: 530-359-2229.
www.nawaacademy.org   E-mail: info@nawaacademy.org
    David W. Hull, Pres (1994). BA, Chapman Univ, MRel, School of Theology at Claremont.
Jan Kells, Prin. BA, Univ of Exeter (England). Jason T. Hull, Adm.

    Col Prep. Gen Acad. Voc. LD. Underachiever. Sports (Winter). Feat—Span Computers
Studio_Art Music Metal_Shop Wilderness_Ed. **Supp**—Dev_Read ESL Makeup Rem_Math
Rem_Read Tut. **Selective adm:** 14/yr. Appl fee: $0. Appl due: Rolling. **Enr 50.** B 37. G 13.
Elem 8. Sec 42. Intl 5%. Avg class size: 8. **Fac 10.** M 4/F 6. FT 10. Adv deg: 30%. **Grad '08—
12.** Col—10. (Suffolk 1, Humboldt St 1, Marymount Col-CA 1, Butte 1, Shimer 1, Cabrillo 1).
Tui '10-'11: Bdg $40,820 (+$1500-3500).Aid: Need 15 ($80,000). **Est 1988.** Nonprofit. Quar
(Sept-June). **Assoc** WASC. The academy offers experiential education through three nine-
month boarding options: California Academy is an on-campus, structured program of academic and vocational classes, group projects, wilderness and rescue training, and recreational
and social activities; International Academy combines academics and intercultural experiences
with travel throughout the world; and Snowboard USA blends academics with competitive and
noncompetitive snowboarding. All programs include high academic standards and training in
outdoor skills. Students engage in community service projects on certain weekends.

ROSARY HIGH SCHOOL
Day Girls Gr 9-12

Fullerton, CA 92831. 1340 N Acacia Ave.
Tel: 714-879-6302. Fax: 714-879-0853.
www.rosaryhs.org   E-mail: rosary@rosaryhs.org
    Annette Zaleski, Prin. Natalie Benson, Adm.

    Col Prep. AP (exams req'd; 361 taken, 68% 3+)—Eng Fr Span Calc Bio Chem US_Hist
Psych US_Govt & Pol. **Feat**—Playwriting Comp_Sci Web_Design Amer_Stud Econ Relig
Performing_Arts Visual_Arts Orchestra Handbells Journ Speech. **Supp**—LD Rem_Math Tut.
Sports— G: Basket X-country Golf Soccer Softball Swim Tennis Track Volley W_Polo. **Selec-
tive adm:** 200/yr. Appl fee: $70. Appl due: Jan. **Tests** HSPT. **Enr 684.** Wh 51%. Latino 33%.

Blk 1%. Asian 11%. Other 4%. Avg class size: 25. Uniform. **Fac 45.** M 5/F 40. FT 45. Wh 86%. Latino 5%. Blk 2%. Asian 2%. Other 5%. Adv deg: 40%. **Grad '10—166.** Col—166. **Avg SAT:** CR 534. M 518. W 546. Avg ACT: 24. **Tui '11-'12:** Day $12,780 (+$1500). Parishioners $11,280 (+$1500). Aid: Merit 5 ($2500). Need 91 ($144,980). **Est 1965.** Nonprofit. Roman Catholic (85% practice). Sem (Aug-June). **Assoc** WASC. Rosary's college preparatory curriculum features a selection of honors and Advanced Placement courses. Students must take four years of religion courses to graduate. Campus ministry opportunities and community service are among the cocurricular options.

ST. LUCY'S PRIORY HIGH SCHOOL Day Girls Gr 9-12
Glendora, CA 91741. 655 W Sierra Madre Ave.
Tel: 626-335-3322. Fax: 626-335-4373.
www.stlucys.com
Sr. Monica Collins, OSB, Prin (1982). BA, Univ of San Diego, MA, Loyola Marymount Univ, MA, Univ of San Francisco. Katie Rossi, Adm.

Col Prep. AP (exams req'd; 360 taken, 79% 3+)—Eng Span Calc Bio Eur_Hist US_Hist US_Govt & Pol. **Feat**—Fr Physiol Kinesiology Relig Art_Hist Film Visual_Arts Theater_Arts Music Dance. **Sports**— G: Basket X-country Soccer Softball Swim Tennis Track Volley W_ Polo. Activities: 15. **Selective adm (Gr 9-11):** 182/yr. Appl fee: $60. Appl due: Jan. Accepted: 80%. Yield: 72%. **Tests** HSPT. **Enr 700.** Wh 39%. Latino 28%. Blk 3%. Asian 11%. Other 19%. Avg class size: 27. Stud/fac: 21:1. Uniform. **Fac 34.** M 6/F 28. FT 34. Wh 70%. Latino 26%. Asian 3%. Other 1%. Adv deg: 35%. **Grad '10—195.** Col—195. **Avg SAT:** CR 541. M 526. W 548. Avg ACT: 23.2. **Col Couns:** 3. **Tui '12-'13:** Day $7800 (+$1000). Aid: Merit 15 ($6000). Need 25 ($60,000). **Est 1962.** Nonprofit. Roman Catholic (82% practice). Quar (Aug-June). **Assoc** WASC. Established by the Benedictine Sisters, the school emphasizes a Catholic education in the tradition of a college preparatory program. Girls choose from a broad selection of honors and Advanced Placement courses.

MOREAU CATHOLIC HIGH SCHOOL Day Coed Gr 9-12
Hayward, CA 94544. 27170 Mission Blvd.
Tel: 510-881-4300. Fax: 510-582-8405.
www.moreaucatholic.org E-mail: admissions@moreaucatholic.org
Terry Lee, Pres (2008). BA, Fordham Univ, MA, San Francisco State Univ. Lauren Lek, Prin. BA, Univ of California-San Diego, MEd, St Mary's College of California.

Col Prep. AP (exams req'd; 378 taken, 70% 3+)—Eng Fr Span Calc Stats Comp_Sci Bio Chem Physics US_Hist Econ US_Govt & Pol Studio_Art. **Feat**—Creative_Writing Women's_ Lit Chin Lat Psych Theol Video_Production Theater Band Orchestra Dance Bus. **Supp**—Tut. **Comp:** Laptop prgm Gr 9-12. **Sports**—Badminton Basket X-country Golf Soccer Swim Tennis Track Volley. B: Baseball Football. G: Softball. **Somewhat selective adm (Gr 9-11):** 278/yr. Appl fee: $65. Appl due: Dec. **Tests** HSPT SSAT. **Enr 930.** B 459. G 471. Wh 22%. Latino 15%. Blk 4%. Native Am 1%. Asian 39%. Other 19%. Avg class size: 30. **Fac 51.** M 25/F 26. FT 51. Wh 76%. Latino 6%. Asian 8%. Other 10%. Adv deg: 41%. **Grad '08—225.** Col—223. **Avg SAT:** CR 555. M 559. Avg ACT: 23. **Tui '11-'12:** Day $13,356 (+$300). **Est 1965.** Nonprofit. Roman Catholic (73% practice). Sem (Aug-June). **Assoc** WASC. Sponsored by the Brothers of Holy Cross, Moreau offers a college preparatory curriculum. A strong arts program includes extensive opportunities in visual arts, theater productions and musical ensembles. Students at all grade levels fulfill a 20-hour annual service requirement.

HEBREW ACADEMY Day Coed Gr PS (Age 2)-12
Huntington Beach, CA 92647. 14401 Willow Ln.
Tel: 714-898-0051. Fax: 714-898-0633.
www.hebrewacademyhb.com E-mail: admin@hebrewacademyhb.com

Rabbi Yitzchok Newman, Head. MA, Pepperdine Univ. Megan M. Carlson, Prin. EdD, Univ of California-Los Angeles. Alex Greenberg, Adm.

Col Prep. AP (exams req'd; 14 taken, 71% 3+)—Eng Bio US_Hist Psych US_Govt & Pol Art_Hist. **Feat**—Hebrew Comp_Sci Child_Dev Judaic_Stud Performing_Arts Visual_ Arts. **Supp**—Dev_Read Rem_Math Rem_Read Rev Tut. **Selective adm:** 21/yr. Appl fee: $100. Appl due: Apr. Accepted: 78%. Yield: 75%. **Enr 275.** Wh 97%. Latino 1%. Blk 1%. Asian 1%. Avg class size: 12. Stud/fac: 8:1. Uniform. **Fac 36.** M 5/F 31. FT 17/PT 19. Wh 89%. Latino 7%. Blk 1%. Asian 3%. **Grad '09—11.** Col—11. **Avg SAT:** CR/M 1175. Alum donors: 21%. **Tui '10-'11:** Day $12,100-14,000 (+$1750). Aid: Need 124 ($478,000). Work prgm 150 ($232,000). **Est 1969.** Nonprofit. Jewish (100% practice). Sem (Sept-June). **Assoc** WASC. Students at the academy follow a dual general studies/Judaic curriculum. Instruction focuses upon communicational and thinking skills and the use of technology. Specialists teach art, music, physical education and computer classes. The comprehensive program fosters traditional Judaic values through study of the Bible, the Hebrew language, and Jewish philosophy and ethics. Boys and girls in grades 9-12 perform eight hours of required community service per quarter, 32 hours per year.

FLINTRIDGE SACRED HEART ACADEMY
Bdg & Day
La Canada Flintridge, CA 91011. 440 St Katherine Dr.   **Girls Gr 9-12**
Tel: 626-685-8300. Fax: 626-685-8305.
www.fsha.org   E-mail: info@fsha.org

Sr. Carolyn McCormack, OP, Pres (2003). Sr. Celeste Marie Botello, OP, Prin. MA, Univ of San Francisco. Luana Castellano, Adm.

Col Prep. AP (exams req'd)—Eng Fr Lat Span Calc Bio Environ_Sci Eur_Hist US_Hist Psych US_Govt & Pol Art_Hist Studio_Art Music_Theory. **Feat**—Creative_Writing Stats Anat & Physiol Astron Forensic_Sci Sports_Med Robotics Econ Lat-Amer_Stud Ethics World_Relig Ceramics Sculpt Theater_Arts Music Dance Journ Design. **Supp**—ESL Rev Tut. **Comp:** Comp/Stud: 1:11.5. **Sports**— G: Basket X-country Equestrian Golf Soccer Softball Swim Tennis Track Volley W_Polo. Activities: 22. **Selective adm (Gr 9-10):** 118/yr. Bdg 19. Day 99. Appl fee: $130-255. Appl due: Jan. **Tests** HSPT TOEFL. **Enr 400.** Bdg 52. Day 348. Wh 53%. Latino 17%. Blk 2%. Native Am 1%. Asian 27%. Intl 10%. Avg class size: 20. Stud/ fac: 10:1. Uniform. **Fac 40.** M 11/F 29. FT 39/PT 1. Adv deg: 67%. **Grad '11—96.** Col—96. (UCLA 6, USC 4, SMU 4, Pasadena City 4, U of CO-Boulder 3, San Diego St 3). **Col Couns:** 2. Alum donors: 11%. **Tui '11-'12:** Bdg $42,450. Day $19,500. Aid: Need 97 ($585,000). **Est 1931.** Nonprofit. Roman Catholic. Sem (Aug-June). **Assoc** WASC. Founded by the Dominican Sisters of Mission San Jose, FSHA offers a varied college preparatory program to day students from approximately 30 local communities and boarders from both the US and overseas. Girls fulfill course requirements in theology, liberal arts, science, math, visual and performing arts, computer studies and physical education. All students perform 15 hours of community service per year, with seniors also taking part in two mandatory service weeks.

ST. FRANCIS HIGH SCHOOL
Day Boys Gr 9-12
La Canada Flintridge, CA 91011. 200 Foothill Blvd.
Tel: 818-790-0325. Fax: 818-790-5542.
www.sfhs.net   E-mail: jmonarrez@sfhs.net

Rev. Antonio Marti, OFMCap, Pres (2008). Thomas G. Moran, Prin. BA, MEd, California State Univ-Northridge. Joe K. Monarrez, Adm.

Col Prep. AP—Eng Lat Span Calc Stats Comp_Sci Bio Chem Physics Eur_Hist US_Hist Econ Human_Geog US_Govt & Pol. **Feat**—British_Lit Kinesiology Psych Sociol Comp_ Relig Visual_Arts Theater_Arts Chorus. **Sports**— B: Baseball Basket X-country Football Golf Soccer Tennis Track Volley. Activities: 54. **Selective adm:** Appl fee: $75. Appl due: Jan. **Tests** HSPT. **Enr 600.** Wh 51%. Latino 23%. Blk 2%. Native Am 1%. Asian 9%. Other 14%. Stud/fac: 13:1. **Fac 53.** M 43/F 10. FT 53. Adv deg: 58%. **Grad '11—108.** Col—106. (CA St U-Northridge 12, U of CA-Santa Barbara 8, Santa Clara 7, CA St Polytech-San Luis Obispo

6, Loyola Marymount 6, CA St Polytech-Pomona 5). **Col Couns:** 3. **Tui '12-'13:** Day $12,400 (+$650). Aid: Need 120. **Est 1946.** Nonprofit. Roman Catholic. Quar (Aug-June). Founded by the Capuchin Franciscan Friars, St. Francis prepares its graduates for entry into the California university system, as well as two- and four-year institutions around the country. The curriculum features Advanced Placement course options in all major disciplines, in addition to such electives as media studies and kinesiology. Boys accumulate 100 hours of required community service prior to graduation.

THE GILLISPIE SCHOOL   Day Coed Gr PS (Age 2)-6
La Jolla, CA 92037. 7380 Girard Ave.
Tel: 858-459-3773. Fax: 858-459-3834.
www.gillispie.org   E-mail: lmoyer@gillispie.org
     Alison Fleming, Head (2008). BA, Univ of Pennsylvania, MBA, Univ of San Diego.

   Pre-Prep. Feat—Span Computers Studio_Art Music. **Supp**—Dev_Read. **Comp:** Laptop prgm Gr 3-6. **Very selective adm:** 35/yr. Appl fee: $125. Appl due: Feb. Accepted: 18%. **Tests** ISEE. **Enr 292.** B 142. G 150. Wh 78%. Latino 6%. Blk 7%. Asian 2%. Other 7%. Avg class size: 20. **Fac 40.** M 6/F 34. FT 40. Wh 93%. Latino 2%. Blk 5%. Adv deg: 25%. **Grad '11—12.** Prep—12. (Bishop's 5, Francis Parker-CA 4, All Hallows Acad-CA 1). **Tui '12-'13:** Day $16,660-18,810. Aid: Need 9 ($35,000). **Est 1952.** Nonprofit. Sem (Sept-June). **Assoc** WASC. Cocurricular activities such as music, art, library, creative movement, cooking, physical education and Spanish complement Gillispie's academic program of science, social studies, mathematics and language arts. Teachers make frequent use of resources within the community: La Jolla's coastline; the Museum of Contemporary Art; and local galleries, libraries, restaurants, shops and parks. The integrated digital curriculum supports learning and teaching through research, presentations, graphic arts and multimedia projects.

SAN DIEGO FRENCH-AMERICAN SCHOOL   Day Coed Gr PS (Age 2)-8
La Jolla, CA 92037. 6550 Soledad Mountain Rd.
Tel: 858-456-2807. Fax: 858-459-2670.
www.sdfrenchschool.org   E-mail: admin@sdfrenchschool.org
     Christian Jarlov, Head (2010). Virginia Berracasa, Adm.

   Pre-Prep. Bilingual (Fr). Feat—Fr Span Computers Studio_Art Music. **Supp**—ESL Tut. **Selective adm:** 86/yr. Appl fee: $125. Appl due: Feb. **Enr 345.** Intl 13%. Avg class size: 12. **Fac 35.** M 8/F 27. FT 33/PT 2. Adv deg: 80%. **Grad '07—6.** Prep—3. **Tui '12-'13:** Day $13,250-14,250 (+$700-1900). **Est 1988.** Nonprofit. Quar (Sept-June). **Assoc** WASC. Seventy to 80 percent of the course work at this bilingual, multicultural school is in French and follows the curricular guidelines of the French Ministry of Education; the remainder is taught in English. Boys and girls study Spanish as a compulsory third language beginning in grade 5. Students in grades 6-8 perform 10 hours of required community service each year.

VILLAGE CHRISTIAN SCHOOLS   Day Coed Gr K-12
La Tuna Canyon, CA 91352. 8950 Village Ave.
Tel: 818-767-8382. Fax: 818-768-2006.
www.villagechristian.org   E-mail: vcs@villagechristian.org
     Tom Konjoyan, Head (2010). AB, Harvard Univ, MBA, Pepperdine Univ. Andrea Newton & Jon Shaw, Adms.

   Col Prep. AP (exams req'd; 219 taken)—Eng Span Calc Stats Bio Environ_Sci Eur_Hist US_Govt & Pol Studio_Art Music_Theory. **Feat**—Chin Anat & Physiol Web_Design Econ Bible Ceramics Photog Video_Production Music Journ. **Supp**—LD Tut. **Comp:** Comp/Stud: 1:6. **Sports**—Basket X-country Equestrian Soccer Tennis Track Volley. B: Baseball Football Golf. G: Cheer Softball. **Selective adm:** 110/yr. Appl fee: $50. Appl due: Feb. Accepted: 80%. Yield: 90%. **Tests** MRT. **Enr 1088.** B 530. G 558. Elem 679. Sec 409. Wh 54%. Latino 18%. Blk 4%. Asian 15%. Other 9%. Avg class size: 24. Stud/fac: 17:1. Uniform. **Fac 64.** M 23/F

41. FT 64. Adv deg: 37%. **Grad '10—127.** Col—124. **Avg SAT:** CR 502. M 490. W 500. **Col Couns:** 2. **Tui '12-'13:** Day $9890-11,400 (+$626-950). **Est 1949.** Nonprofit. Nondenom Christian (50% practice). Sem (Sept-June). **Assoc** WASC. Bible courses and weekly chapel are important elements of Village Christian's program. The elementary curriculum (grades K-5) combines core courses with work in art, technology, Spanish, music and physical education, while the middle school program (grades 6-8) features electives in economics, Spanish, and the fine and performing arts. Both honors and AP courses are part of the college preparatory high school curriculum (grades 9-12). Educational support is available to those requiring academic assistance.

DAMIEN HIGH SCHOOL   Day Boys Gr 9-12
La Verne, CA 91750. 2280 Damien Ave.
Tel: 909-596-1946. Fax: 909-596-6112.
www.damien-hs.edu   E-mail: info@damien-hs.edu
     Rev. Peadar Cronin, SSCC, Pres (2011). Sam Pearsall, Prin. BS, Loyola Marymount Univ, MA, California State Univ-San Bernardino, MS, California State Univ-Fullerton. Michael Williams, Adm.
     Col Prep. AP (875 exams taken, 65% 3+)—Eng Fr Ger Span Calc Stats Comp_Sci Bio Chem Environ_Sci Physics Eur_Hist Comp_Govt & Pol Econ Psych US_Govt & Pol Art_Hist Studio_Art. **Feat**—British_Lit Creative_Writing Chin Anat & Physiol Ecol World_Relig Drama. **Comp:** Comp/Stud: 1:5. **Sports**— B: Baseball Basket X-country Football Golf Ice_Hockey Soccer Swim Tennis Track W_Polo Wrestling. Activities: 30. **Nonselective adm:** 265/yr. Appl fee: $75. Appl due: May. Accepted: 100%. Yield: 85%. **Tests** HSPT. **Enr 950.** Wh 40%. Latino 35%. Blk 5%. Native Am 1%. Asian 4%. Other 15%. Stud/fac: 25:1. Uniform. **Fac 52.** M 43/F 9. FT 52. Wh 64%. Latino 33%. Blk 3%. Adv deg: 90%. **Grad '11—269.** Col—269. **Avg SAT:** CR 525. M 531. **Mid 50%** SAT: CR 460-570. M 480-620. **Col Couns:** 4. **Tui '12-'13:** Day $7600 (+$875). Aid: Merit 104 ($64,000). Need 207 ($363,580). **Est 1959.** Nonprofit. Roman Catholic (66% practice). Quar (Aug-May). The college preparatory curriculum at this Archdiocesan Catholic boys' school features an expansive Advanced Placement program. Damien's technology program progresses from literacy classes through programming and computer systems and analysis courses. Each boy accumulates 100 required community service hours over four years.

LUTHERAN HIGH SCHOOL   Day Coed Gr 9-12
La Verne, CA 91750. 3960 Fruit St.
Tel: 909-593-4494. Fax: 909-596-3744.
www.lhslv.org   E-mail: lebel@lhslv.org
     Lance Ebel, Prin. BS, Concordia Univ (OR), MAEd, Univ of Northern Colorado.
     Col Prep. AP (35 exams taken, 51% 3+)—Eng Span Calc Chem Physics US_Hist. **Feat**—Comp_Sci Psych Relig Studio_Art Drama Band Chorus JROTC. **Supp**—ESL Tut. **Comp:** Comp/Stud: 1:6. **Sports**—Basket Soccer Track. B: Baseball Football Golf Wrestling. G: Cheer Softball Volley. Activities: 5. **Somewhat selective adm:** 48/yr. Appl fee: $75. Appl due: May. Accepted: 94%. Yield: 90%. **Tests** Stanford. **Enr 140.** Wh 48%. Latino 17%. Blk 15%. Asian 5%. Other 15%. Intl 10%. Avg class size: 15. Stud/fac: 9:1. Uniform. **Fac 14.** M 5/F 9. FT 7/PT 7. Wh 75%. Latino 20%. Blk 2%. Asian 3%. Adv deg: 50%. **Grad '11—38.** Col—35. (Concordia U-CA 4, Azusa Pacific 3). **Avg SAT:** CR 650. M 643. W 600. **Col Couns:** 1. Alum donors: 3%. **Tui '11-'12:** Day $7050 (+$1075). Assoc Members $6500 (+$1075). Aid: Merit 15 ($40,000). Need 25 ($104,000). **Est 1973.** Nonprofit. Lutheran-Missouri Synod. Sem (Aug-June). **Assoc** WASC. Historical and doctrinal theology, naval JROTC, and a variety of electives and activities, in addition to the college preparatory curriculum, are offered. Students may earn academic credit in theology for participating in a chapel service program. Boys and girls complete at least 25 hours of community service per year.

MARIN PRIMARY & MIDDLE SCHOOL   **Day Coed Gr PS (Age 2)-8**
Larkspur, CA 94939. 20 Magnolia Ave.
Tel: 415-924-2608. Fax: 415-924-9351.
www.mpms.org   E-mail: info@mpms.org
     Julie Elam, Head (2006). BA, Univ of California-Davis, MEd, Univ of Minnesota-Twin
Cities. Donna Fanfelle, Adm.
     Pre-Prep. Gen Acad. Feat—Span Computers Studio_Art Drama Music Woodworking
Outdoor_Ed. **Supp**—Dev_Read LD Rev Tut. **Sports**—Basket X-country Soccer Track. **Selective adm (Gr PS-7):** 91/yr. Appl fee: $50-75. Appl due: Jan. Accepted: 60%. Yield: 69%.
Tests ISEE. **Enr 348.** Wh 82%. Latino 3%. Blk 2%. Native Am 1%. Asian 6%. Other 6%. Intl
7%. Avg class size: 25. Stud/fac: 7:1. **Fac 50.** M 15/F 35. FT 42/PT 8. Wh 84%. Latino 6%.
Asian 2%. Other 8%. Adv deg: 14%. **Grad '10—30.** Prep—20. (Branson 5, Marin Acad 2,
San Francisco U HS 1, Urban 1). **Tui '11-'12:** Day $21,450-25,200 (+$1000). Aid: Need 15
($275,533). **Est 1975.** Nonprofit. Sem (Sept-June). **Assoc** WASC. Preschoolers at MP&MS
are introduced to core academic subjects while also participating in such classes as gymnastics, piano, dance and computer. Language instruction in Spanish and French commences in
preschool. An after-school program at all grade levels offers course work in Chinese, carpentry, writing, Web design, drama and sports, among others.

WESTERLY SCHOOL   **Day Coed Gr K-8**
Long Beach, CA 90806. 2950 E 29th St.
Tel: 562-981-3151. Fax: 562-981-3153.
www.westerlyschool.org   E-mail: admission@westerlyschool.org
     Chris J. Rodenhizer, Head (2009). BA, California State Univ-Long Beach, MA, California
State Univ-Dominguez Hills. Crystal Barnwell, Adm.
     Pre-Prep. Gen Acad. Feat—Humanities Span Computers Visual_Arts Music Outdoor_
Ed. **Supp**—Rev Tut. **Comp:** Comp/Stud: 1:2 (1:1 Laptop prgm Gr 6-8). **Selective adm:** 30/yr.
Appl fee: $100. Appl due: Jan. Accepted: 75%. **Tests** CTP_4 ISEE. **Enr 121.** Avg class size:
13. Stud/fac: 10:1. Uniform. **Fac 15.** M 6/F 9. FT 12/PT 3. Wh 50%. Latino 40%. Asian 5%.
Other 5%. Adv deg: 40%. **Grad '10—16.** Prep—7. (Cornelia Connelly 2, Chadwick 2, Loyola
HS-CA 1, Fairmont 1, Rolling Hills Prep 1). Alum donors: 5%. **Tui '11-'12:** Day $17,100
(+$400-1850). Aid: Need 28 ($188,807). **Est 1993.** Nonprofit. Tri (Sept-June). **Assoc** WASC.
Westerly's elementary curriculum combines work in the core subjects of language arts, social
studies, math, science and computer with art, music, Spanish and physical education classes.
The hands-on, experiential program assists children with basic skills mastery, as well as creative and independent thinking skills, and the school seeks to instill in students an appreciation
for the arts. Boys and girls in grades 6-8 satisfy a 15-hour annual community service requirement.

BERKELEY HALL SCHOOL   **Day Coed Gr PS (Age 3)-8**
Los Angeles, CA 90049. 16000 Mulholland Dr.
Tel: 310-476-6421. Fax: 310-476-5748.
www.berkeleyhall.org   E-mail: info@berkeleyhall.org
     Lisle Staley, Head (2011). BA, Principia College, MA, PhD, Univ of California-Los Angeles. Nathalie Miller, Adm.
     Pre-Prep. Feat—Span Computers Photog Studio_Art Video_Production Drama Music
Woodworking. **Supp**—Tut. **Comp:** Comp/Stud: 1:2. Outdoor Ed. **Sports**—Basket Soccer
Swim Track Volley. B: Baseball. G: Softball. **Selective adm (Gr PS-7):** 60/yr. Appl fee: $125.
Appl due: Jan. Accepted: 78%. Yield: 54%. **Tests** ISEE. **Enr 260.** B 125. G 135. Wh 50%.
Latino 7%. Blk 13%. Asian 8%. Other 22%. Intl 6%. Avg class size: 22. Stud/fac: 8:1. Uniform. **Fac 30.** M 7/F 23. FT 27/PT 3. Wh 94%. Latino 3%. Asian 3%. Adv deg: 30%. **Grad
'10—33.** Prep—30. (Pacifica Christian 5, Viewpoint 5, Harvard-Westlake 4, Campbell Hall 2,
New Roads 2). Alum donors: 2%. **Tui '11-'12:** Day $21,600-23,200 (+$1500). Aid: Need 62
($856,750). **Est 1911.** Nonprofit. Tri (Sept-June). **Assoc** WASC. At BHS, preschoolers and

kindergartners gain an introduction to basic academic concepts in math, reading preparation and handwriting. During the elementary years (grades 1-6), specialists teach science, music, art, technology, drama and woodworking courses. Weeklong outdoor education experiences are part of the junior high curriculum (grades 7 and 8).

BISHOP CONATY Day Girls Gr 9-12
OUR LADY OF LORETTO HIGH SCHOOL
Los Angeles, CA 90006. 2900 W Pico Blvd.
Tel: 323-737-0012. Fax: 323-737-1749.
www.bishopconatyloretto.org E-mail: rspicer@bishopconatyloretto.org
    Richard A. Spicer, Prin (2007). BA, Univ of California-Santa Barbara, MSEd, Mount Saint Mary's College (CA). Sr. Harriet Stellern, SSND, Adm.
    Col Prep. Gen Acad. AP (exams req'd)—Fr Span US_Govt & Pol. **Feat**—Comp_Sci Relig Visual_Arts Music Dance. **Supp**—Dev_Read Rem_Math Rem_Read Tut. **Comp:** Comp/Stud: 1:7. **Sports**— G: Basket X-country Soccer Softball Volley. Activities: 19. **Somewhat selective adm:** 96/yr. Appl fee: $55. Appl due: Rolling. Accepted: 100%. Yield: 70%. **Tests** HSPT. **Enr 313.** Wh 1%. Latino 86%. Blk 4%. Native Am 6%. Asian 3%. Avg class size: 21. Uniform. **Fac 22.** M 9/F 13. FT 17/PT 5. Adv deg: 86%. **Grad '09—91.** Col—84. (Santa Monica 14, CA St U-Los Angeles 10, Pasadena City 8, CA St U-Northridge 7, Mt St Mary's-CA 6, CA St U-Dominguez Hills 5). **Avg SAT:** CR 432. M 424. W 427. Avg ACT: 17.9. Alum donors: 14%. **Tui '12-'13:** Day $6325-8350 (+$900-1525). **Est 1923.** Nonprofit. Roman Catholic (91% practice). Sem (Aug-June). **Assoc** WASC. Resulting from the 1989 merger of Bishop Conaty Memorial High School (formerly Los Angeles Catholic Girls' High School) and Our Lady of Loretto High School, this Catholic school emphasizes college preparation. All girls take four years of religion courses while also accumulating 100 hours of community service.

LOYOLA HIGH SCHOOL Day Boys Gr 9-12
Los Angeles, CA 90006. 1901 Venice Blvd.
Tel: 213-381-5121. Fax: 213-368-3819.
www.loyolahs.edu E-mail: hutley@loyolahs.edu
    Rev. Gregory M. Goethals, SJ, Pres (2006). BA, Santa Clara Univ, MDiv, Jesuit School of Theology at Berkeley, MTh, Weston Jesuit School of Theology, MA, Univ of San Francisco. Frank Kozakowski, Prin. BS, MA, Univ of California-Los Angeles. Heath Utley, Adm.
    Col Prep. AP (exams req'd; 1100 taken, 84% 3+)—Eng Fr Lat Span Calc Stats Comp_Sci Chem Environ_Sci Physics Eur_Hist US_Hist Econ Psych US_Govt & Pol Art_Hist Music_ Theory. **Feat**—Shakespeare Ger Anat & Physiol Oceanog African-Amer_Stud Theol World_ Relig Fine_Arts Photog Acting Design. **Supp**—Tut. **Comp:** Comp/Stud: 1:2. **Sports**— B: Baseball Basket X-country Football Golf Lacrosse Soccer Swim Tennis Track Volley W_Polo. **Selective adm (Gr 9-11):** 315/yr. Appl fee: $75. Appl due: Jan. Accepted: 42%. Yield: 88%. **Tests** HSPT. **Enr 1256.** Wh 49%. Latino 26%. Blk 11%. Native Am 1%. Asian 12%. Other 1%. Avg class size: 26. Stud/fac: 15:1. **Fac 101.** Wh 80%. Latino 10%. Blk 5%. Asian 5%. Adv deg: 74%. **Grad '09—292.** Col—291. **Avg SAT:** CR 605. M 618. W 614. **Tui '11-'12:** Day $13,810 (+$1000). Aid: Need ($2,100,000). **Est 1865.** Nonprofit. Roman Catholic (85% practice). Sem (Sept-June). **Assoc** CLS WASC. Conducted by the Jesuits, Loyola offers elective courses, as well as Advanced Placement and honors classes. Each student performs at least 135 hours of community service prior to graduation, a total that includes a three-week, 85-hour service immersion experience during senior year.

LYCEE INTERNATIONAL DE LOS ANGELES   Day Coed Gr PS-12
Los Angeles, CA 90027. 4155 Russell Ave.
Tel: 323-665-4526. Fax: 323-665-2607.
Other locations: 30 N Marion Ave, Pasadena 91106; 2625 N Tustin Ave, Santa Ana 92705;
    5933 Lindley Ave, Tarzana 91356.
www.lilaschool.com   E-mail: deborah.thornburg@lilaschool.com
    Elizabeth Chaponot, Head (2006). PhD, Univ of Southern California.
    Col Prep. IB Diploma. Bilingual (Fr). Feat—Fr Span Geol Comp_Sci Econ Govt Philos
Visual_Arts Music. **Supp**—Tut. **Sports**—Basket X-country Soccer Track Volley. B: Baseball.
Somewhat selective adm (Gr PS-11): 60/yr. Appl fee: $100. Appl due: Rolling. Accepted:
85%. Yield: 95%. **Enr 900.** Elem 798. Sec 102. Avg class size: 20. **Fac 75. Grad '07—19.**
Col—19. **Avg SAT:** CR 580. M 614. W 584. **Tui '12-'13:** Day $13,200-16,000 (+$175-2500).
Est 1978. Nonprofit. Quar (Sept-June). **Assoc** WASC. LILA pupils learn to read, write and
speak both English and French by the end of grade 5. In preschool, all children learn in a traditional French classroom setting, regardless of their language proficiency. English is added to
the curriculum gradually beginning in kindergarten, and by grade 5 classes are conducted in
equal parts French and English. Boys and girls take the French Brevet exam at the end of grade
9. High schoolers pursue the International Baccalaureate diploma. Students complete 150
hours of community service in grades 11 and 12. The Russell Avenue campus houses grades
PS-12; additional primary school locations operate on North Marion Avenue in Pasadena, on
North Tustin Avenue in Santa Ana and on Lindley Avenue in Tarzana.

NOTRE DAME ACADEMY   Day Girls Gr 9-12
Los Angeles, CA 90064. 2851 Overland Ave.
Tel: 310-839-5289. Fax: 310-839-7957.
www.ndala.com   E-mail: admissions@ndala.com
    Nancy J. Coonis, Pres. Joan Gumaer Tyhurst, Prin. BA, Mount Saint Mary's College (CA),
MA, Univ of San Francisco. Brigid Williams, Adm.
    Col Prep. AP (exams req'd; 343 taken, 70% 3+)—Eng Fr Span Calc Bio Chem US_
Hist World_Hist Psych US_Govt & Pol Art_Hist Studio_Art. **Feat**—British_Lit Japan Anat
& Physiol Law Theol Photog Drama Chorus Dance. **Sports**— G: Basket X-country Soccer
Softball Swim Track Volley. Activities: 23. **Selective adm (Gr 9-11):** 105/yr. Appl fee: $75.
Appl due: Jan. **Tests** HSPT. **Enr 400.** Wh 33%. Latino 30%. Blk 10%. Asian 13%. Other 14%.
Avg class size: 23. Stud/fac: 12:1. Uniform. **Fac 31.** M 7/F 24. Adv deg: 48%. **Grad '11—99.**
Col—99. **Avg SAT:** CR 571. M 552. W 597. **Col Couns:** 3. **Tui '11-'12:** Day $10,950. **Est
1949.** Nonprofit. Roman Catholic (86% practice). Sem (Aug-June). **Assoc** WASC. Sponsored
by the Congregation of the Sisters of Notre Dame, NDA serves students from a wide radius
on its West Los Angeles campus. The school's college preparatory curriculum features a full
complement of honors and Advanced Placement courses. Girls perform at least 25 hours of
community service per year.

PAGE PRIVATE SCHOOL   Day Coed Gr PS (Age 2)-8
Los Angeles, CA 90004. 565 N Larchmont Blvd.
Tel: 323-463-5118. Fax: 323-465-9964.
Other locations: 419 S Robertson Blvd, Beverly Hills 90211; 12111 Buaro St, Garden Grove
    92840; 657 Victoria St, Costa Mesa 92627.
www.pageschool.com
    Charles J. Vaughan, Pres.
    Pre-Prep. Gen Acad. Feat—Span Computers Studio_Art Drama. **Supp**—Rev Tut.
Sports—Basket Volley. **Somewhat selective adm:** 40/yr. Appl due: Rolling. Accepted:
90%. **Tests** Stanford. **Enr 250.** Avg class size: 20. Uniform. **Fac 20.** M 5/F 15. FT 20. **Grad
'05—19.** Prep—16. **Tui '10-'11:** Day $7920-15,565 (+$1000). **Est 1908.** Nonprofit. Quar
(Aug-June). Page operates schools on six campuses—four in southern California and two
in central Florida—continuously operated by succeeding generations of the Vaughan family.

The Hancock Park (North Larchmont Boulevard) and Costa Mesa locations accept children in grades PS-8, the Beverly Hills location enrolls students in grades PS-4, and the Garden Grove campus accommodates grades PS-6. A selection of enrichment classes supplements the traditional academic program. Enrichment weeks interspersed throughout the year expose students to subjects that are not traditionally taught during the academic sessions.

SACRED HEART HIGH SCHOOL — Day Girls Gr 9-12
Los Angeles, CA 90031. 2111 Griffin Ave.
Tel: 323-225-2209. Fax: 323-225-5046.
www.shhsla.org   E-mail: mainoffice@shhsla.org
   Sr. Angelica Velez, OP, Prin (2008). Juan Carlos Montenegro, Adm.

   Col Prep. AP (exams req'd)—Eng Fr Span Calc Eur_Hist US_Hist Art_Hist. **Feat**—Computers Relig Video_Production Dance Study_Skills. **Supp**—Tut. **Sports**— G: Basket X-country Soccer Softball Track Volley. Activities: 8. **Somewhat selective adm:** 106/yr. Appl fee: $45. Appl due: Feb. Accepted: 84%. **Enr 370.** Wh 3%. Latino 94%. Other 3%. Avg class size: 26. Uniform. **Fac 22.** M 3/F 19. FT 21/PT 1. Wh 88%. Latino 11%. Other 1%. Adv deg: 90%. **Grad '08—77.** Col—70. **Avg SAT:** CR/M 850. Avg ACT: 19. **Tui '11-'12:** Day $6460 (+$600). Aid: Need 222 ($70,000). **Est 1907.** Nonprofit. Roman Catholic. Sem (Aug-June). **Assoc** WASC. Administered by the Dominican Sisters of Mission San Jose, this school is staffed by both members of the religious order and lay faculty. Honors and Advanced Placement courses are offered. The entire student body takes part by grade level in a retreat program. Girls perform 20 hours of required community service each year.

WINDWARD SCHOOL — Day Coed Gr 7-12
Los Angeles, CA 90066. 11350 Palms Blvd.
Tel: 310-391-7127. Fax: 310-397-5655.
www.windwardschool.org   E-mail: communications@windwardschool.org
   Thomas W. Gilder, Head (1986). BA, Univ of California-Santa Barbara, MS, Pepperdine Univ. Sharon Pearline, Adm.

   Col Prep. AP (exams req'd; 323 taken, 83% 3+)—Eng Fr Span Calc Stats Bio Chem Environ_Sci Physics Eur_Hist US_Hist US_Govt & Pol. **Feat**—Creative_Writing World_Lit Chin Lat Govt Philos Relig Fine_Arts. **Sports**—Basket X-country Equestrian Golf Soccer Tennis Track Volley. B: Baseball Football. G: Softball. **Very selective adm (Gr 7-11):** 95/yr. Appl fee: $100. Appl due: Dec. Accepted: 20%. **Tests** ISEE. **Enr 525.** Elem 160. Sec 365. Wh 72%. Latino 4%. Blk 8%. Asian 4%. Other 12%. Avg class size: 15. **Fac 68.** M 34/F 34. FT 68. Adv deg: 76%. **Grad '08—83.** Col—83. **Avg SAT:** CR 630. M 640. W 660. **Mid 50% SAT:** CR 570-680. M 590-690. W 590-720. **Tui '10-'11:** Day $30,141 (+$1250). **Est 1971.** Nonprofit. Tri (Sept-June). **Assoc** CLS WASC. Special programs offered at Windward include instrumental and vocal music, musical theater, Japanese and marine biology. Students choose from an array of Advanced Placement courses. Service learning is a core component of the program, and upper school students are required to complete two separate and extensive projects prior to graduation.

THE PHILLIPS BROOKS SCHOOL — Day Coed Gr PS (Age 3)-5
Menlo Park, CA 94025. 2245 Avy Ave.
Tel: 650-854-4545. Fax: 650-854-6532.
www.phillipsbrooks.org   E-mail: amadden@phillipsbrooks.org
   Scott Erickson, Head (2011). BA, North Park Univ, DTh, Uppsala Univ (Sweden).

   Pre-Prep. Feat—Lib_Skills Chin Span Computers Studio_Art Music. **Supp**—Dev_Read. **Comp:** Laptop prgm Gr 3-5. **Selective adm:** 66/yr. Appl fee: $85. Appl due: Jan. Accepted: 62%. Yield: 66%. **Tests** CTP_4. **Enr 276.** B 143. G 133. Wh 61%. Latino 1%. Blk 2%. Asian 10%. Other 26%. Avg class size: 18. Stud/fac: 9:1. **Fac 40.** M 3/F 37. FT 40. **Grad '09—37.** Prep—31. **Tui '11-'12:** Day $25,800 (+$400). Aid: Need 33 ($323,040). **Est 1978.** Nonprofit.

Sem (Sept-June). The sequential basic skills curriculum is enriched with courses in world languages, technology, art, music and physical education. In addition, all students take weekly classes that focus upon the basic skills of communication: eye contact, tone of voice, body language and so on. Each grade participates in one community service project, and Phillips Brooks also organizes schoolwide projects.

MARIN HORIZON SCHOOL   Day Coed Gr PS (Age 2)-8
Mill Valley, CA 94941. 305 Montford Ave.
Tel: 415-388-8408. Fax: 415-388-7831.
www.marinhorizon.org   E-mail: admissions@marinhorizon.org
    Luis A. Ottley, Head (2011). Sharman M. Bonus, Adm.

    Pre-Prep. Gen Acad. Montessori. Feat—Lib_Skills Span Computers Studio_Art Music Outdoor_Ed. **Supp**—Tut. **Sports**—Basket X-country Soccer Softball Track. **Selective adm:** 51/yr. Appl fee: $75. Appl due: Jan. **Enr 287.** Wh 72%. Latino 6%. Blk 6%. Asian 10%. Other 6%. Avg class size: 24. Stud/fac: 9:1. **Fac 36.** Adv deg: 36%. **Grad '10—23.** Prep—21. **Tui '11-'12:** Day $19,090-25,400. Aid: Need ($652,000). **Est 1977.** Nonprofit. (Aug-June). Serving families throughout Marin County, San Francisco, and the North and East Bay areas, MHS conducts a Montessori-based, interdisciplinary program that utilizes multi-age grouping. Staff specialists provide learning support and teach art, Spanish, music, technology, library science and physical education. Ideas and concepts that are introduced to young children are revisited and explored in greater detail as the students mature. Instructors help boys and girls to develop critical-thinking skills and to identify and solve problems.

MOUNT TAMALPAIS SCHOOL   Day Coed Gr K-8
Mill Valley, CA 94941. 100 Harvard Ave.
Tel: 415-383-9434. Fax: 415-383-7519.
www.mttam.org   E-mail: admissions@mttam.org
    Kathleen M. Mecca, Dir (1976). MA, MSEd, Univ of California-Los Angeles, PhD, Univ of California-San Francisco, PhD, Stanford Univ. Daphne Opperman, Adm.

    Pre-Prep. Feat—Chin Fr Japan Lat Span Astron Computers Geog Art_Hist Drama Music Dance. **Supp**—Dev_Read Rev. **Comp:** Comp/Stud: 1:2. **Sports**—Basket X-country Track Volley. **Very selective adm (Gr K-6):** 35/yr. Appl fee: $175. Appl due: Jan. Accepted: 10%. Yield: 99%. **Tests** CTP_4 ISEE SSAT. **Enr 260.** B 130. G 130. Wh 84%. Latino 3%. Blk 5%. Asian 6%. Other 2%. Avg class size: 12. Stud/fac: 8:1. Uniform. **Fac 46.** M 13/F 33. FT 40/PT 6. Wh 94%. Latino 2%. Blk 1%. Native Am 1%. Asian 1%. Other 1%. Adv deg: 52%. **Grad '10—30.** Prep—29. (Branson 6, Schs of the Sacred Heart-CA 6, St Ignatius-CA 4, San Francisco U HS 2, Marin Acad 2). Avg SSAT: 93%. Alum donors: 59%. **Tui '11-'12:** Day $23,050 (+$150). Aid: Need ($625,000). **Est 1976.** Nonprofit. Tri (Aug-June). **Assoc** WASC. Mount Tamalpais offers a departmentalized curriculum for students in grades K-8. Complementing the core curriculum are such courses as French, Spanish, Latin, Mandarin, Japanese, drama, literature, art history and dance. Extended outdoor education classes for children in grades 4-8 complement the program of nature study, which begins in kindergarten.

CENTRAL CATHOLIC HIGH SCHOOL   Day Coed Gr 9-12
Modesto, CA 95351. 200 S Carpenter Rd.
Tel: 209-524-9611. Fax: 209-524-4913.
www.cchsca.org   E-mail: tybor@cchsca.org
    Jim Pecchenino, Pres. BA, Univ of the Pacific, MA, California State Univ-Stanislaus. Melissa J. Bengtson, Prin. Jodi Tybor, Adm.

    Col Prep. AP—Eng Span Calc Bio Chem Eur_Hist US_Hist. **Feat**—Fr Astron Comp_Sci Comp_Graphics Psych Philos Theol World_Relig Graphic_Arts Visual_Arts Drama Dance Speech. **Supp**—Rem_Read. **Sports**—Basket X-country Golf Soccer Swim Tennis Track W_ Polo. B: Baseball Football Wrestling. G: Cheer Softball Volley. Activities: 21. **Selective adm:**

122/yr. Appl fee: $45. Appl due: Rolling. **Tests** CEEB IQ. **Enr 410.** Avg class size: 25. Stud/fac: 17:1. **Fac 28.** M 7/F 21. Adv deg: 32%. **Grad '11—112.** Col—112. **Avg SAT:** CR/M/W 1590. Avg ACT: 22. **Tui '12-'13:** Day $9566 (+$630-800). Catholic $9175 (+$650). Aid: Need 100 ($360,000). **Est 1966.** Nonprofit. Roman Catholic. Quar (Aug-June). **Assoc** WASC. The school offers college preparatory classes and electives in the fine arts, computers, journalism and yearbook. In addition, CCHS provides college-level courses in psychology, anthropology, sociology, philosophy and agriculture. Catholic values are emphasized and community service is a graduation requirement.

THE SAKLAN SCHOOL
Day Coed Gr PS (Age 4)-8

Moraga, CA 94556. 1678 School St.
Tel: 925-376-7900. Fax: 925-376-1156.
www.saklan.org   E-mail: dhague@saklan.org
Laroilyn H. Davis, Int Head (2011). BS, Wittenberg Univ, MA, Stanford Univ. Melissa Zippin, Adm.

Pre-Prep. Gen Acad. Feat—Chin Fr Computers Studio_Art Music. **Comp:** Laptop prgm Gr 6-8. **Selective adm:** 15/yr. Appl fee: $75. Appl due: Feb. Accepted: 70%. Yield: 75%. **Tests** CTP_4 ISEE. **Enr 110.** B 60. G 50. Wh 74%. Latino 10%. Blk 3%. Asian 13%. Avg class size: 13. Stud/fac: 7:1. Uniform. **Fac 24.** M 5/F 19. FT 18/PT 6. Wh 90%. Blk 10%. Adv deg: 25%. **Grad '10—13. Tui '12-'13:** Day $16,500-22,000 (+$75-100). Aid: Need 25 ($180,000). **Est 1954.** Nonprofit. Tri (Aug-June). **Assoc** WASC. Starting in prekindergarten, children have access to the library and gain exposure to language concepts, math and science, music, art and Spanish. Utilizing an individualized approach that accommodates students of varying learning styles and developmental levels, the lower school (grades K-5) focuses on the basics while incorporating hands-on activities and laboratory experiences. Saklan's traditional middle school (grades 6-8) curriculum provides opportunities for problem solving, in-depth classroom discussions, the development of study skills and an experiential travel program.

JUSTIN-SIENA HIGH SCHOOL
Day Coed Gr 9-12

Napa, CA 94558. 4026 Maher St.
Tel: 707-255-0950. Fax: 707-255-0334.
www.justin-siena.org   E-mail: holquind@justin-siena.org
Robert T. Jordan, Pres (2009). BA, San Francisco State Univ, MA, St Mary's College of California. Noel Laird Hesser, Prin. MA, California State Univ-Sacramento. David J. Holquin, Adm.

Col Prep. AP (exams req'd; 188 taken, 62% 3+)—Eng Calc Bio US_Hist World_Hist US_Govt & Pol. **Feat**—British_Lit Shakespeare Fr Ital Span Stats Environ_Sci Physiol Comp_ Design Govt Law Psych Sociol Relig World_Relig Film Photog Studio_Art Theater_Arts Band Chorus Music Orchestra Jazz_Band Dance Journ. **Supp**—LD Makeup Rem_Math. **Comp:** Comp/Stud: 1:5.6. **Dual enr:** Napa Valley Col. **Sports**—Basket X-country Golf Soccer Swim Tennis Track W_Polo. B: Baseball Football Wrestling. G: Cheer Softball Volley. Activities: 21. **Somewhat selective adm:** 192/yr. Appl fee: $50. Appl due: Feb. Accepted: 85%. Yield: 89%. **Tests** HSPT. **Enr 646.** B 323. G 323. Wh 71%. Latino 13%. Blk 3%. Asian 9%. Other 4%. Avg class size: 24. Stud/fac: 13:1. Casual dress. **Fac 41.** M 24/F 17. FT 35/PT 6. Adv deg: 78%. **Grad '11—131.** Col—130. **Avg SAT:** CR/M/W 1656. Avg ACT: 23.7. **Col Couns:** 2. **Tui '12-'13:** Day $14,000 (+$775-1250). Aid: Need 194 ($1,200,000). **Est 1966.** Nonprofit. Roman Catholic (62% practice). Sem (Aug-June). **Assoc** WASC. Founded and cosponsored by the Dominican Sisters of San Rafael and the Christian Brothers of the San Francisco District, this Napa Valley school emphasizes college preparation and critical-thinking skills in a Christian setting. Justin-Siena's curriculum features honors and Advanced Placement courses, computer and technology labs, and a strong religious studies program. In addition, qualified upperclassmen may earn transferable college credit through Napa Valley College in philosophy.

SAGE HILL SCHOOL   Day Coed Gr 9-12
Newport Coast, CA 92657. 20402 Newport Coast Dr.
Tel: 949-219-0100. Fax: 949-219-1399.
www.sagehillschool.org   E-mail: admission@sagehillschool.org
    Gordon J. McNeill, Head (2008). BA, Univ of California-San Diego, MA, Columbia Univ.
Elaine Mijalis-Kahn, Adm.
    Col Prep. AP (exams req'd; 145 taken, 85% 3+)—Eng Span Calc Stats Comp_Sci Bio
Chem Environ_Sci Physics Eur_Hist US_Hist Econ US_Govt & Pol Art_Hist Studio_Art
Music_Theory. **Feat**—British_Lit Chin Fr Lat Multivariable_Calc Forensic_Sci Marine_Bio/
Sci Intl_Relations Psych Ceramics Film Theater Chorus Dance. **Sports**—Basket X-country
Golf Lacrosse Soccer Swim Tennis Track Volley W_Polo. B: Baseball Football. Activities:
50. **Selective adm:** Appl fee: $100. Appl due: Feb. **Tests** ISEE. **Enr 444.** B 205. G 239. Avg
class size: 15. Casual dress. **Fac 44.** M 22/F 22. FT 34/PT 10. Adv deg: 52%. **Grad '11—114.**
Col—113. (USC 7, Boston U 6, Stanford 5, Chapman 4, Emory 4, NYU 4). **Avg SAT:** CR
639. M 664. W 666. **Mid 50% SAT:** CR 570-690. M 610-710. W 590-740. **Col Couns:** 2.
Tui '11-'12: Day $29,140 (+$700). Aid: Need 66 ($1,800,000). **Est 2000.** Nonprofit. Sem
(Aug-June). Sage Hill's rigorous college preparatory curriculum emphasizes independent and
critical thinking. The school's freshman program features weekly one-on-one advisory meetings, a fall retreat and a yearlong service learning program. All students take part in a weeklong
experiential learning program at year's end that includes global travel, intensive on-campus
seminars, internships and independent study opportunities.   **See Also Page 40**

SUGAR BOWL ACADEMY   Bdg & Day
Norden, CA 95724. 19195 Donner Pass Rd, PO Box 68.   Coed Gr 8-12
Tel: 530-426-1844. Fax: 530-426-1860.
www.sbacademy.org   E-mail: tkeller@sbacademy.org
    Tracy Keller, Head. BA, Dartmouth Univ, MA, Univ of Nevada-Reno.
    Col Prep. Sports (Winter). AP—Eng Calc US_Hist Human_Geog. **Feat**—British_Lit
Span Stats Astron Econ Film Photog Studio_Art Health. **Sports**—Ski. **Somewhat selective
adm:** 17/yr. Bdg 9. Day 8. Appl fee: $50. Appl due: Rolling. Accepted: 90%. Yield: 75%. **Tests**
ISEE. **Enr 44.** B 27. G 17. Bdg 19. Day 25. Elem 12. Sec 32. Avg class size: 5. **Fac 11.** M
6/F 5. FT 11. Adv deg: 54%. In Dorms 4. **Grad '11—7.** Col—5. **Col Couns:** 1. **Tui '12-'13:**
Bdg $36,175 (+$4000). Day $19,350 (+$4000). **Est 1995.** Nonprofit. Sem (Sept-June). **Assoc**
WASC. Students at the state's only college preparatory skiing academy take part in a rigorous
academic program during the school day, while also participating in ski training before and
after school and on weekends. A shorter school day during the winter months facilitates on-hill
training and enables boys and girls to meet racing schedules. Programs accommodate Alpine,
Nordic and freestyle skiers.

BENTLEY SCHOOL   Day Coed Gr K-12
Oakland, CA 94618. 1 Hiller Dr.
Tel: 510-843-2512. Fax: 510-845-6516.
Other locations: 1000 Upper Happy Valley Rd, Lafayette 94549.
www.bentleyschool.net   E-mail: msanchez@bentleyschool.net
    Arlene Hogan, Head (2009). BS, City Univ of New York, MST, Univ of Illinois-Urbana.
Marcia Levin, Gr 9-12 Adm; Michele Sanchez, Gr K-8 Adm.
    Col Prep. AP (exams req'd; 161 taken, 75% 3+)—Fr Lat Span Calc Comp_Sci Bio Chem
Physics US_Hist World_Hist Art_Hist Studio_Art Music_Theory. **Feat**—Classics Satire Chin
Multivariable_Calc Ecol Civil_War Medieval_Hist Milit_Hist Film Sculpt Video_Production
Theater Study_Skills. **Supp**—Tut. **Sports**—Basket X-country Golf Soccer Swim Tennis. B:
Baseball Lacrosse. G: Softball Volley. Activities: 32. **Selective adm:** 138/yr. Appl fee: $75.
Appl due: Jan. Accepted: 43%. Yield: 84%. **Tests** ISEE SSAT. **Enr 617.** B 316. G 301. Elem
332. Sec 285. Wh 69%. Latino 2%. Blk 5%. Asian 19%. Other 5%. Avg class size: 18. Casual
dress. **Fac 78.** M 31/F 47. FT 65/PT 13. Wh 79%. Latino 10%. Blk 5%. Asian 5%. Other

1%. Adv deg: 58%. **Grad '10—83.** Col—82. (USC 5, U of CA-Davis 4, Chapman 3, CA St Polytech-Pomona 3, Stanford 2, Carnegie Mellon 2). **Avg SAT:** CR 630. M 640. W 620. Avg ACT: 27. **Col Couns:** 1. **Tui '12-'13:** Day $23,025-30,890 (+$500-1000). Aid: Need 135 ($2,400,000). **Est 1920.** Nonprofit. Tri (Sept-June). **Assoc** WASC. Within a small-class environment, Bentley complements its traditional core curriculum with electives and independent study opportunities. Honors and Advanced Placement courses provide additional challenge for qualified students, while peer tutors, faculty advisors, scheduled study halls, a study skills workshop and extra-help periods allow pupils to receive academic support when necessary. The school places a strong emphasis on the arts both within the curriculum and during after-school activities. High schoolers perform 15 hours of community service each year. The upper school program (grades 9-12) operates on a separate campus in Lafayette.

BISHOP O'DOWD HIGH SCHOOL   **Day Coed Gr 9-12**
Oakland, CA 94605. 9500 Stearns Ave.
Tel: 510-577-9100. Fax: 510-638-3259.
www.bishopodowd.org   E-mail: tkreitz@bishopodowd.org
  Stephen Phelps, Pres (2005). EdD. Pamela Shay, Prin. MSA. Tyler Kreitz, Adm.
  Col Prep. AP (500 exams taken, 64% 3+)—Eng Fr Span Calc Stats Comp_Sci Bio Chem Environ_Sci US_Hist Comp_Govt & Pol Psych US_Govt & Pol Studio_Art. **Feat**—Women's_Lit Chin Ital Anat Marine_Bio/Sci Sports_Med Cold_War Holocaust Lat-Amer_Hist Econ Law Relig World_Relig Ceramics Painting Photog Drama Theater_Arts Chorus Orchestra. **Supp**—LD Tut. **Comp:** Comp/Stud: 1:1 Laptop prgm Gr 9-12. **Sports**—Basket X-country Golf Lacrosse Soccer Swim Tennis Track W_Polo. B: Baseball Football. G: Softball Volley. Activities: 40. **Selective adm (Gr 9-11):** 340/yr. Appl fee: $120. Appl due: Jan. Accepted: 82%. **Tests** HSPT. **Enr 1130.** Wh 43%. Latino 12%. Blk 19%. Native Am 1%. Asian 12%. Other 13%. Avg class size: 24. Stud/fac: 15:1. Uniform. **Fac 76.** M 40/F 36. FT 76. Wh 74%. Latino 7%. Blk 10%. Asian 8%. Other 1%. Adv deg: 65%. **Grad '10—296.** Col—294. **Avg SAT:** CR 561. M 566. W 576. **Col Couns:** 6. **Tui '12-'13:** Day $15,220 (+$1650-2650). Aid: Need 345 ($2,100,000). **Est 1951.** Nonprofit. Roman Catholic. Sem (Aug-June). **Assoc** WASC. Bishop O'Dowd's college preparatory program features honors and Advanced Placement courses, in addition to a variety of electives and fine arts offerings. Boys and girls accumulate 100 hours of service learning work prior to graduation. Incoming freshmen purchase or lease tablet computers for school use.

HOLY NAMES HIGH SCHOOL   **Day Girls Gr 9-12**
Oakland, CA 94618. 4660 Harbord Dr.
Tel: 510-450-1110. Fax: 510-547-3111.
www.hnhsoakland.org   E-mail: hnhs@hnhsoakland.org
  Sr. Sally Slyngstad, Prin. BA, Univ of California-Berkeley, MA, Univ of San Francisco. Emily Burns, Adm.
  Col Prep. AP (exams req'd; 93 taken, 56% 3+)—Eng Fr Span Calc Bio Chem US_Hist Studio_Art Music_Theory. **Feat**—Physiol Comp_Sci Psych Relig Drama Chorus Orchestra Dance. **Supp**—Rem_Math Tut. **Comp:** Comp/Stud: 1:2. Outdoor Ed. **Sports**— G: Basket X-country Golf Soccer Softball Swim Tennis Track Volley. **Selective adm (Gr 9-11):** 62/yr. Appl fee: $75. Appl due: Jan. Accepted: 80%. Yield: 60%. **Tests** HSPT. **Enr 200.** Wh 27%. Latino 20%. Blk 35%. Asian 15%. Other 3%. Avg class size: 25. Stud/fac: 11:1. Uniform. **Fac 28.** M 4/F 24. FT 22/PT 6. Wh 78%. Latino 7%. Blk 7%. Native Am 4%. Asian 4%. Adv deg: 75%. **Grad '11—59.** Col—59. (CA St U-E Bay 8, San Jose St 6, U of CA-Davis 5, San Francisco St 4, Hampton 3, Holy Names 3). Alum donors: 40%. **Tui '11-'12:** Day $12,300 (+$1050). Aid: Merit 2 ($5000). **Est 1868.** Nonprofit. Roman Catholic. Sem (Aug-June). **Assoc** WASC. HNHS offers a diverse curriculum for students of all aptitude levels. Qualified girls enroll in competitive honors and Advanced Placement courses, while pupils in need of additional help may receive tutorial services in math and science. Options in the visual and performing arts include instrumental and vocal music, drawing and painting, and drama. Girls

display their artistic talents in plays, musicals, art exhibits and concerts. Community service is integrated into the religion curriculum throughout, and seniors perform 15 hours of independent service.

SAINT ELIZABETH HIGH SCHOOL   Day Coed Gr 9-12
Oakland, CA 94601. 1530 34th Ave.
Tel: 510-532-8947. Fax: 510-532-9754.
www.stliz-hs.org   E-mail: rtroper@stliz-hs.org
     Sr. Mary Liam Brock, OP, Prin (1999). MA, San Jose State Univ, MA, St Mary's College.
     Col Prep. Gen Acad. AP (exams req'd; 18 taken)—Eng Span. **Feat**—Creative_Writing Calc Anat & Physiol Comp_Design Comp_Sci Psych Relig Fine_Arts. **Supp**—LD Tut. **Comp:** Comp/Stud: 1:3. **Sports**—Basket Soccer Volley. B: Baseball Football. **Somewhat selective adm:** 52/yr. Appl fee: $75. Appl due: Jan. Accepted: 88%. Yield: 65%. **Tests** HSPT. **Enr 165.** Latino 64%. Blk 22%. Native Am 1%. Asian 8%. Other 5%. Avg class size: 20. Stud/fac: 11:1. **Fac 14.** M 7/F 7. FT 13/PT 1. Wh 72%. Latino 14%. Blk 7%. Other 7%. Adv deg: 35%. **Grad '11—36.** Col—34. (San Francisco St 5, CA St U-E Bay 4, U of CA 3, St Mary's Col of CA 3, Holy Names 2, CA St U-Sacramento 1). **Avg SAT:** CR 409. M 418. W 401. Avg ACT: 17.3. Alum donors: 12%. **Tui '12-'13:** Day $11,200 (+$1200). Aid: Merit ($103,000). Need ($980,000). **Est 1921.** Nonprofit. Roman Catholic (80% practice). Sem (Aug-June). **Assoc** WASC. Saint Elizabeth provides a college preparatory curriculum that features Advanced Placement courses and electives in the arts and sciences. Students complete 100 hours of community service by graduation. More than half of the pupils come from single-parent households.

ST. PAUL'S EPISCOPAL SCHOOL   Day Coed Gr K-8
Oakland, CA 94610. 116 Montecito Ave.
Tel: 510-285-9600. Fax: 510-899-7297.
Other locations: 262 Grand Ave, Oakland 94610.
www.spes.org   E-mail: info@spes.org
     Karan A. Merry, Head (1999). BA, Salem State College, MEd, Lesley College. Khadija A. Fredericks, Adm.
     Pre-Prep. Gen Acad. Feat—Span Computers Fine_Arts Drama Music. **Supp**—Tut. **Comp:** Comp/Stud: 1:1 **Sports**—Basket X-country Ultimate_Frisbee Volley. **Selective adm:** 59/yr. Appl fee: $75. Appl due: Jan. Accepted: 50%. Yield: 59%. **Tests** ISEE. **Enr 354.** B 184. G 170. Wh 42%. Latino 8%. Blk 19%. Asian 7%. Other 24%. Avg class size: 20. Stud/fac: 10:1. **Fac 38.** M 11/F 27. FT 31/PT 7. Wh 70%. Latino 14%. Blk 12%. Asian 4%. Adv deg: 36%. **Grad '11—40.** Prep—28. (Bishop O'Dowd 21, College Prep 3, Lick-Wilmerding 2, St Mary's Col HS 1, Bentley 1). **Tui '11-'12:** Day $20,725-22,330 (+$200-400). Aid: Need 139 ($2,200,000). **Est 1975.** Nonprofit. Episcopal (5% practice). Quar (Aug-June). **Assoc** WASC. Instructors at St. Paul's lower school (grades K-6) teach core courses through an interactive program of learning centers, individual and group presentations, discussions, and research and writing projects. At the middle school level (grades 7 and 8), students supplement core classes with course work in computers, art and music, service learning, drama, study skills or high school planning, and electives. The school takes advantage of its urban setting by utilizing the city's resources and scheduling frequent field trips to local museums, parks and historical sites. A second campus on Grand Avenue hosts grade 6 and the middle school.

OAK GROVE SCHOOL   Bdg Coed Gr 9-12
Ojai, CA 93023. 220 W Lomita Ave.   Day Coed PS (Age 3)-12
Tel: 805-646-8236. Fax: 805-646-6509.
www.oakgroveschool.com   E-mail: info@oakgroveschool.com
     Meredy Benson Rice, Head (2008). BA, Sussex Univ (England), MA, Columbia Univ. Joy Maguire-Parsons, Adm.

Col Prep. AP—Eng Span Chem. **Feat**—Ceramics Film Photog Studio_Art Drama Music Outdoor_Ed. **Supp**—ESL. **Comp:** Laptop prgm Gr 4-6. Outdoor Ed. **Sports (req'd)**—Basket Equestrian Soccer Tennis Volley. **Selective adm:** 40/yr. Bdg 10. Day 30. Appl fee: $35-100. Appl due: Rolling. Accepted: 80%. Yield: 40%. **Tests** SSAT TOEFL. **Enr 200.** B 103. G 97. Bdg 15. Day 185. Elem 140. Sec 60. Wh 80%. Latino 4%. Blk 4%. Asian 12%. Intl 15%. Avg class size: 14. Stud/fac: 7:1. Casual dress. **Fac 29.** M 12/F 17. FT 24/PT 5. Wh 80%. Latino 10%. Asian 10%. Adv deg: 34%. **Grad '09—13.** Col—12. (NYU 1, U of CA-Berkeley 1, Middlebury 1, USC 1, Wesleyan U 1, CA Inst of the Arts 1). **Avg SAT:** CR 540. M 562. W 565. **Col Couns:** 3. **Tui '12-'13:** Bdg $36,200. Day $8650-16,000. Aid: Need 44 ($208,000). **Est 1975.** Nonprofit. Sem (Sept-June). **Assoc** WASC. The school was founded on the philosophical ideals of author and educator J. Krishnamurti. Located on 150 acres, the school balances college preparatory academics with studio art, ceramics, photography, music, drama, physical education, sports, life skills, outdoor education and travel. High school pupils satisfy a 25-hour annual community service requirement.

ORINDA ACADEMY   Day Coed Gr 6-12
Orinda, CA 94563. 19 Altarinda Rd.
Tel: 925-254-7553. Fax: 925-254-4768.
www.orindaacademy.org   E-mail: admission@orindaacademy.org
    Ron Graydon, Head (1982). BS, Univ of California-Berkeley. Laurel Evans, Adm.

    Col Prep. AP (5 exams taken, 40% 3+)—Eng Span. **Feat**—Fr Calc Environ_Sci Computers Web_Design Civics Econ Studio_Art Visual_Arts Multimedia Drama Music Jazz_Ensemble. **Supp**—ESL LD Tut. **Comp:** Comp/Stud: 1:1.8. Outdoor Ed. **Dual enr:** Diablo Valley, Contra Costa. **Sports**—Basket Soccer. B: Baseball. Activities: 4. **Selective adm:** 23/yr. Appl fee: $75. Appl due: Jan. Accepted: 66%. Yield: 75%. **Tests** ISEE TOEFL. **Enr 100.** B 50. G 50. Elem 10. Sec 90. Wh 74%. Latino 5%. Blk 10%. Asian 11%. Intl 5%. Avg class size: 9. Stud/fac: 8:1. **Fac 13.** M 6/F 7. FT 13. Wh 90%. Latino 10%. Adv deg: 53%. **Grad '11—14.** Col—14. (Humboldt St 4, Acad of Art U 1, Willamette 1, U of MO-Columbia 1, U of CA-Davis 1, San Jose St 1). **Avg SAT:** CR 549. M 534. W 554. **Col Couns:** 2. Alum donors: 5%. **Tui '12-'13:** Day $30,475 (+$675). Aid: Need 27 ($200,000). **Est 1982.** Nonprofit. Quar (Aug-June). **Assoc** WASC. Drawing Bay Area students within a 50-mile radius, OA conducts a college preparatory program that emphasizes organization, time management and self-advocacy. Honors and Advanced Placement courses provide additional challenge for qualified boys and girls. An annual dramatic production, musical performances, a student talent show, and vocal and instrumental opportunities are among the academy's performing arts options. Boys and girls accumulate 40 hours of required community service prior to graduation.

See Also Page 57

ST. MATTHEW'S PARISH SCHOOL   Day Coed Gr PS (Age 3)-8
Pacific Palisades, CA 90272. 1031 Bienveneda Ave, PO Box 1710.
Tel: 310-454-1350. Fax: 310-573-7423.
www.stmatthewsschool.com   E-mail: lquiring@stmatthewsschool.com
    Stuart Work, Head (2011). AB, Bowdoin College. A. Lee Quiring, Adm.

    Pre-Prep. Feat—Creative_Writing Shakespeare Lat Span Environ_Sci Computers Art_Hist Studio_Art Drama Music Speech. **Comp:** Comp/Stud: 1:2.7. **Sports**—Basket Golf Soccer Swim Tennis Track Volley. G: Softball. **Selective adm:** 46/yr. Appl fee: $125. Appl due: Jan. Accepted: 28%. Yield: 80%. **Tests** ISEE. **Enr 325.** B 163. G 162. Wh 86%. Latino 1%. Blk 4%. Asian 8%. Other 1%. Avg class size: 28. Stud/fac: 11:1. Uniform. **Fac 41.** M 9/F 32. FT 38/PT 3. Wh 98%. Latino 1%. Other 1%. Adv deg: 48%. **Grad '10—38.** Prep—38. (Harvard-Westlake 10, Loyola HS-CA 6, Brentwood Sch-CA 4, Windward-CA 3, Crossroads-CA 2). Alum donors: 2%. **Tui '11-'12:** Day $22,300-27,000 (+$1800). Aid: Need 26 ($402,959). **Est 1949.** Nonprofit. Episcopal. Tri (Sept-June). **Assoc** WASC. Located on 33 acres in the Santa Monica Mountains, the school emphasizes math and language arts instruction. All pupils take at least one year of Latin, and Spanish is a second foreign language option. Boys and girls fulfill a community service requirement at all grade levels.

THE GIRLS' MIDDLE SCHOOL   Day Girls Gr 6-8
Palo Alto, CA 94303. 3400 W Bayshore Rd.
Tel: 650-968-8338. Fax: 650-968-4775.
www.girlsms.org   E-mail: mmiller@girlsms.org
   Deborah Hof, Head (2005). BA, Univ of Southern California, MS, Pepperdine Univ. Megan R. Miller, Adm.

   Pre-Prep. Gen Acad. Feat—Humanities Span Computers Ceramics Photog Studio_Art Drama Study_Skills. **Comp:** Comp/Stud: 1:1 Laptop prgm Gr 6-8. **Sports**— G: Basket X-country Soccer Softball Tennis Track Volley. **Selective adm:** 64/yr. Appl fee: $75. Appl due: Jan. **Tests** ISEE. **Enr 150.** Avg class size: 16. Stud/fac: 7:1. Uniform. **Fac 25.** M 6/F 19. **Grad '11—46.** Prep—26. (Notre Dame-San Jose 8, Menlo 2, Woodside Priory 2, Archbishop Mitty 2, Kehillah 2, Pinewood Sch-CA 1). **Tui '12-'13:** Day $23,400 (+$1000). Aid: Need 25 ($368,020). **Est 1998.** Nonprofit. Quar (Sept-June). **Assoc** WASC. Founded to provide local girls with a single-gender learning environment during their middle school years, GMS emphasizes problem solving and self-directed study through project-based, hands-on and multidisciplinary projects that combine group work with individual research. A study skills class designed to teach time management, organizational and goal-setting skills meets weekly. The school's entrepreneurial studies program allows seventh graders to create and run their own businesses, from formulating a business plan through marketing a product. Each year, GMS' weeklong intersession enables girls to take half- or full-day courses in areas not covered in the regular curriculum.

KEHILLAH JEWISH HIGH SCHOOL   Day Coed Gr 9-12
Palo Alto, CA 94303. 3900 Fabian Way.
Tel: 650-213-9600. Fax: 650-213-9601.
www.kehillah.org   E-mail: info@kehillah.org
   Lillian Howard, Head (2007). BA, Scripps College, MA, Univ of Texas-Austin. Marily Lerner, Adm.

   Col Prep. AP—Eng Lat Span Calc Stats Comp_Sci Bio Chem Physics US_Hist Studio_Art Music_Theory. **Feat**—Jewish_Lit Satire Hebrew Anat & Physiol Robotics Web_Design Psych Bible Judaic_Stud Philos Ceramics Photog Theater. **Comp:** Comp/Stud: 1:6. **Sports**—Basket X-country Soccer Swim Tennis Ultimate_Frisbee. G: Volley. **Selective adm (Gr 9-11):** 46/yr. Appl fee: $75. Appl due: Jan. **Tests** ISEE SSAT. **Enr 135.** B 67. G 68. Wh 97%. Latino 1%. Blk 1%. Asian 1%. Avg class size: 12. **Fac 25.** M 13/F 12. FT 14/PT 11. Adv deg: 92%. **Grad '10—27.** Col—27. **Avg SAT:** CR 597. M 587. W 605. **Mid 50% SAT:** CR 520-670. M 510-620. W 540-650. **Tui '11-'12:** Day $31,650. **Est 2002.** Nonprofit. Jewish. Quar (Aug-June). **Assoc** WASC. Kehillah offers a college preparatory program comprising general and Jewish studies. Students satisfy course requirements in Hebrew language, Jewish studies, technology and fine arts, as well as the traditional disciplines. Each class takes an annual service-oriented trip, with the culminating trip for juniors and seniors being a three-week excursion to Israel. In addition, students fulfill an 80-hour service requirement prior to graduation.

MARANATHA HIGH SCHOOL   Day Coed Gr 9-12
Pasadena, CA 91105. 169 S St John Ave.
Tel: 626-817-4000. Fax: 626-817-4040.
www.maranatha-hs.org   E-mail: l_diamond@mhs-hs.org
   Charles E. Crane, Head (2002). BS, Univ of Pittsburgh, MTS, Fuller Theological Seminary. John Rouse, Adm.

   Col Prep. AP (exams req'd; 489 taken, 70% 3+)—Eng Span Calc Bio Chem Physics US_Hist World_Hist Psych US_Govt & Pol Studio_Art Music_Theory. **Feat**—ASL Fr Lat

Anat & Physiol Comp_Sci Econ Sociol Bible Drawing Photog Theater_Arts Dance. **Supp—** LD. **Dual enr:** Pasadena City, Citrus, Glendale CC. **Sports—**Basket X-country Equestrian Golf Soccer Swim Tennis Track. B: Baseball Football. G: Cheer Softball Volley. Activities: 19. **Somewhat selective adm:** 188/yr. Appl fee: $75. Appl due: Feb. Accepted: 95%. **Tests** ISEE. **Enr 623.** Wh 53%. Latino 12%. Blk 12%. Asian 21%. Other 2%. Avg class size: 20. Stud/fac: 13:1. Uniform. **Fac 47.** FT 46/PT 1. Adv deg: 53%. **Grad '11—155.** Col—155. **Avg SAT:** CR/M 1046. **Col Couns:** 3. **Tui '12-'13:** Day $16,750 (+$500). Aid: Merit 6 ($2200). Need 110 ($271,000). **Est 1965.** Nonprofit. Nondenom Christian. Sem (Aug-May). **Assoc** WASC. Maranatha conducts a Christian program that emphasizes acquisition of the skills and knowledge necessary for further education and successful employment. In addition to Advanced Placement course work in the major disciplines, the school offers a special program for a limited number of students with learning differences. Freshmen and sophomores devote 10 hours per year to community service, juniors and seniors 20 hours annually.

MAYFIELD JUNIOR SCHOOL   Day Coed Gr K-8
OF THE HOLY CHILD JESUS
Pasadena, CA 91101. 405 S Euclid Ave.
Tel: 626-796-2774. Fax: 626-796-5753.
www.mayfieldjs.org   E-mail: thalpin@mayfieldjs.org
     Joseph J. Gill, Head (2008). BS, Springfield College, MS, Indiana Univ.

     Pre-Prep. Feat—Fr Span Computers Relig Studio_Art Drama Music. **Comp:** Comp/Stud: 1:2. **Sports—**Basket Golf Soccer Swim Tennis Track Volley. B: Baseball Football. G: Softball. **Selective adm:** 68/yr. Appl fee: $100. Appl due: Dec. Accepted: 30%. Yield: 80%. **Tests** CTP_4 ISEE. **Enr 508.** B 243. G 265. Wh 63%. Latino 18%. Blk 3%. Asian 15%. Other 1%. Avg class size: 18. Stud/fac: 18:1. Uniform. **Fac 56.** M 14/F 42. FT 51/PT 5. Wh 64%. Latino 20%. Blk 5%. Asian 9%. Other 2%. Adv deg: 32%. **Grad '10—58.** Prep—58. (Mayfield Sr 20, Loyola HS-CA 9, St Francis-La Canada 7, Flintridge Sacred Heart 6, Flintridge Prep 5, Polytech Sch 4). **Tui '11-'12:** Day $16,980 (+$3000). Aid: Need 83 ($647,000). **Est 1931.** Nonprofit. Roman Catholic (80% practice). (Sept-June). **Assoc** WASC. A member of the Holy Child Network of Schools, Mayfield offers a developmentally appropriate program that enriches its core curriculum with foreign language and the visual, musical and performing arts. Children first gain exposure to technology and Spanish in the lower school (grades K-4). During the middle school years (grades 5-8), students assume increasing levels of independence and take part in sequential programs in language arts, math, science, social studies and foreign language.

MAYFIELD SENIOR SCHOOL   Day Girls Gr 9-12
OF THE HOLY CHILD JESUS
Pasadena, CA 91105. 500 Bellefontaine St.
Tel: 626-799-9121. Fax: 626-799-8576.
www.mayfieldsenior.org   E-mail: clemmie.phillips@mayfieldsenior.org
     Rita Curasi McBride, Head (2002). BA, Univ of California-Santa Barbara, MALS, Wesleyan Univ. Clemmie Phillips, Adm.

     Col Prep. AP (exams req'd; 193 taken, 76% 3+)—Eng Fr Lat Span Calc Bio Physics Eur_Hist US_Hist Art_Hist Studio_Art Music_Theory. **Feat—**Creative_Writing Women's_ Lit Astron Environ_Sci Intl_Relations Law Psych World_Relig Photog Theater Theater_Arts Music. **Supp—**Tut. **Comp:** Comp/Stud: 1:1.5. **Sports—** G: Badminton Basket X-country Equestrian Golf Soccer Softball Swim Tennis Track Volley W_Polo. Activities: 28. **Somewhat selective adm:** 81/yr. Appl fee: $100. Appl due: Jan. Accepted: 93%. Yield: 50%. **Tests** ISEE. **Enr 304.** Wh 60%. Latino 16%. Blk 4%. Native Am 3%. Asian 6%. Other 11%. Avg class size: 16. Stud/fac: 8:1. Uniform. **Fac 35.** M 11/F 24. FT 24/PT 11. Wh 90%. Latino 2%. Blk 1%. Other 7%. Adv deg: 80%. **Grad '11—76.** Col—76. (Santa Clara 7, U of CA-Santa Barbara 3, NYU 3, Seattle U 3, USC 3, TX Christian 3). **Avg SAT:** CR 633. M 592. W 612. **Mid 50% SAT:** CR 590-680. M 540-640. W 590-640. Avg ACT: 28. Mid 50% ACT: 26-30. **Col Couns:**

2. Alum donors: 11%. **Tui '11-'12:** Day $21,200 (+$900-1900). Aid: Merit 33 ($203,600). Need 63 ($581,600). **Est 1931.** Nonprofit. Roman Catholic (80% practice). Sem (Sept-June). **Assoc** WASC. Mayfield's college preparatory curriculum, which includes Advanced Placement and honors classes, is supplemented by many electives. Theology courses and monthly liturgies are important aspects of the school program. All girls perform community service: Freshmen and sophomores complete at least four three-hour projects, while juniors and seniors work on a yearlong, 20-hour project.

WALDEN SCHOOL   Day Coed Gr PS (Age 3)-6
Pasadena, CA 91107. 74 S San Gabriel Blvd.
Tel: 626-792-6166. Fax: 626-792-1335.
www.waldenschool.net   E-mail: sgill@waldenschool.net
   Matt Allio, Dir (2005). BA, Univ of San Francisco, MA, California State Univ-Northridge. Sarah Lougheed-Gill, Adm.
   Pre-Prep. Feat—Lib_Skills Span Computers Visual_Arts Music Dance Outdoor_Ed. **Selective adm (Gr PS-5):** 47/yr. Appl fee: $70. Appl due: Feb. Accepted: 78%. Yield: 45%. **Enr 215.** B 108. G 107. Nonwhite 49%. Avg class size: 20. Stud/fac: 10:1. Casual dress. **Fac 34.** M 6/F 28. FT 28/PT 6. Wh 33%. Latino 14%. Blk 10%. Native Am 2%. Asian 12%. Other 29%. Adv deg: 23%. **Grad '11—28.** Prep—25. (Chandler Sch-CA 6, Flintridge Prep 5, Westridge 3, Waverly Sch-CA 3, Oakwood Sch-CA 2, Barnhart Sch-CA 2). Alum donors: 2%. **Tui '12-'13:** Day $18,263 (+$0-500). Aid: Need 41 ($336,134). **Est 1970.** Nonprofit. Sem (Sept-June). **Assoc** WASC. Walden, which employs a hands-on approach, conducts multi-age classes that often span two grade levels. Field trips, science projects, art, music, Spanish, library skills, storytelling sessions and physical education complement the curriculum.

ST. JOHN'S EPISCOPAL SCHOOL   Day Coed Gr PS (Age 2)-8
Rancho Santa Margarita, CA 92688. 30382 Via Con Dios.
Tel: 949-858-5144. Fax: 949-858-1403.
www.stjohns-es.org   E-mail: jlusby@stjohns-es.org
   James S. Lusby, Head (1996). BA, Trinity College (CT), MEd, Boston College. Gwen Croce, Adm.
   Pre-Prep. Feat—Span Computers Relig Studio_Art Chorus Music. **Supp**—Rem_Read Tut. **Comp:** Comp/Stud: 1:12. **Sports**—Basket Lacrosse Soccer Track Volley. **Somewhat selective adm:** 109/yr. Appl fee: $50. Appl due: Rolling. Accepted: 90%. **Enr 650.** B 309. G 341. Wh 87%. Latino 2%. Blk 1%. Asian 3%. Other 7%. Avg class size: 23. Stud/fac: 13:1. Uniform. **Fac 58.** M 3/F 55. FT 53/PT 5. Wh 96%. Latino 4%. Adv deg: 22%. **Grad '11—78.** Prep—72. (Santa Margarita Catholic 61, St Margaret's Episcopal 6, Junipero Serra 4, Crean Lutheran 1). **Tui '11-'12:** Day $10,400-13,405 (+$400). Aid: Need 105 ($378,623). **Est 1988.** Nonprofit. Episcopal (10% practice). Tri (Sept-June). **Assoc** WASC. All children in grades K-8 attend chapel, and religion is taught throughout the school. A field studies program complements the curriculum. After-school competitive sports begin in grade 5.

MERCY HIGH SCHOOL   Day Coed Gr 9-12
Red Bluff, CA 96080. 233 Riverside Way.
Tel: 530-527-8314. Fax: 530-527-3058.
www.mercy-high.org   E-mail: mercy@mercy-high.org
   Cheryl Ramirez, Prin. BA, Humboldt State Univ, MS, Univ of La Verne.
   Col Prep. AP (exams req'd)—Eng Span Calc Bio US_Hist US_Govt & Pol. **Feat**—Comp_ Sci Econ World_Relig Studio_Art Drama Chorus. **Dual enr:** Butte, Shasta. **Sports**—Basket Ski Soccer Swim Tennis Track. B: Baseball Football Golf. G: Cheer Softball Volley. **Nonselective adm:** 40/yr. Appl fee: $50. Appl due: Mar. Accepted: 100%. **Enr 91.** Avg class size: 15. Stud/fac: 13:1. **Fac 11.** M 4/F 7. FT 10/PT 1. Adv deg: 18%. **Grad '08—28.** Col—27. **Tui '09-'10:** Day $6950-8100 (+$250). **Est 1882.** Nonprofit. Roman Catholic. Sem (Aug-June).

Assoc WASC. Mercy places emphasis on the development of faith, community awareness and college preparation. Enrichment, Advanced Placement and honors courses are offered. Students perform 80 hours of compulsory community service prior to graduation.

ALPHA BEACON CHRISTIAN SCHOOL   Day Coed Gr PS (Age 3)-12
Redwood City, CA 94065. 384 Montserrat Dr.
Tel: 650-592-1803. Fax: 650-212-1026.
www.alphabeacon.org   E-mail: info@alphabeacon.org
Lillian G. Mark, Supt (1969). BA, Univ of California-Berkeley, MS, Pensacola Christian College, PhD, Shasta Bible College. Christopher Chu, Prin. BA, San Jose State Univ. Eleanor Chan, Adm.

Col Prep. AP (exams req'd)—Calc. **Feat**—Span Econ Govt Bible Ethics Performing_Arts Drama Chorus Speech Home_Ec. **Supp**—ESL Makeup Tut. Outdoor Ed. **Sports**—Basket. B: Baseball Football Soccer. G: Softball Volley. **Somewhat selective adm:** 35/yr. Appl fee: $100. Appl due: Mar. Accepted: 90%. Yield: 90%. **Tests** ISEE SSAT Stanford. **Enr 150.** Elem 90. Sec 60. Wh 28%. Latino 13%. Blk 3%. Asian 43%. Other 13%. Intl 5%. Avg class size: 11. Uniform. **Fac 20.** M 9/F 11. FT 16/PT 4. Wh 43%. Latino 17%. Asian 40%. Adv deg: 10%. **Grad '11—10.** Col—10. (Biola 3, Acad of Art U 2, Col of San Mateo 2, U of CA-Berkeley 1, UCLA 1). **Col Couns:** 3. **Tui '11-'12:** Day $6900-10,000 (+$200-500). Aid: Need 10 ($20,000). **Est 1969.** Nonprofit. Nondenom Christian (85% practice). Quar (Aug-June). Alpha Beacon provides a Bible-based curriculum that emphasizes college preparation and character development in a Christian environment. Student council, retreats, educational trips, performing arts offerings, and intramural and interscholastic athletics supplement academics. Older boys and girls perform at least 20 hours of community service per year.

PENINSULA HERITAGE SCHOOL   Day Coed Gr K-6
Rolling Hills Estates, CA 90274. 26944 Rolling Hills Rd.
Tel: 310-541-4795. Fax: 310-541-8264.
www.peninsulaheritage.org   E-mail: admin@peninsulaheritage.org
Patricia Cailler, Head (2002). Debbie Schwartz, Adm.

Pre-Prep. Gen Acad. Feat—Fr Span Computers Studio_Art Drama Music. **Supp**—Dev_ Read Rem_Math Rem_Read Rev Tut. **Selective adm:** Appl fee: $135. Appl due: Feb. **Enr 110.** Avg class size: 20. **Fac 22.** Adv deg: 27%. **Grad '10—25.** Prep—10. **Tui '12-'13:** Day $18,720-22,050. Aid: Need ($283,000). **Est 1962.** Nonprofit. Tri (Sept-June). The school conducts a pre-preparatory program in a rural setting. In addition to its academic curriculum, Peninsula Heritage offers art, music, drama, computer, a library program and physical education. An extended-day program is available.

ROLLING HILLS COUNTRY DAY SCHOOL   Day Coed Gr K-8
Rolling Hills Estates, CA 90274. 26444 Crenshaw Blvd.
Tel: 310-377-4848. Fax: 310-377-9651.
www.rhcds.com   E-mail: lburrows@rhcds.com
Karen Shipherd, Exec Dir (2004). BA, Harvard Univ, MBA, Univ of California-Los Angeles. Laura Horowitz, Adm.

Pre-Prep. Gen Acad. Feat—Span Environ_Sci Computers Econ Fine_Arts Studio_Art Music. **Supp**—Rem_Math Rev Tut. **Comp:** Comp/Stud: 1:5. **Sports**—Basket Soccer Swim Volley W_Polo. **Selective adm:** 60/yr. Appl fee: $125. Appl due: Rolling. Accepted: 48%. **Tests** ISEE. **Enr 375.** Wh 70%. Latino 4%. Blk 3%. Asian 21%. Other 2%. Intl 5%. Avg class size: 19. Stud/fac: 12:1. Uniform. **Fac 41.** M 9/F 32. FT 36/PT 5. Wh 98%. Blk 1%. Other 1%. Adv deg: 48%. **Grad '11—49.** Prep—19. **Tui '11-'12:** Day $16,100-16,800 (+$1500). **Est 1961.** Inc. Tri (Sept-June). **Assoc** WASC. RHCDS offers a traditional academic curriculum enriched by creative teaching and learning techniques. The core course work is enriched with computer studies, Spanish, drama, art and music. Children in grades K-5 complete grade-level projects, while pupils in grades 6-8 perform 10 hours of annual service. A full physical education and sports program provides swimming for all students and interscholastic offerings for children in grades 5-8. A diverse outdoor experiential education program includes weeklong trips. **See Also Page 134**

BROOKFIELD SCHOOL   Day Coed Gr K-8
Sacramento, CA 95822. PO Box 22220.
Tel: 916-442-1255. Fax: 916-443-5477.
www.brookfieldschool.org   E-mail: info@brookfieldschool.org
     Josephine Gonsalves, Prin (2007). BA, MA, Univ of California-Davis, EdD, St Mary's College of California.
     Pre-Prep. Gen Acad. Feat—Fr Environ_Sci Computers Geog Studio_Art Music. **Supp**— Tut. **Sports**—Basket X-country Golf Soccer Track Volley. B: Baseball. **Selective adm:** 33/yr. Appl fee: $75. Appl due: Rolling. Accepted: 80%. Yield: 80%. **Tests** DAT IQ. **Enr 150.** B 64. G 86. Wh 71%. Latino 5%. Blk 2%. Asian 22%. Avg class size: 14. Uniform. **Fac 15.** M 3/F 12. FT 10/PT 5. Wh 94%. Blk 6%. Adv deg: 53%. **Grad '11—10.** Prep—6. (Christian Bros HS-CA 4, Jesuit HS-CA 1). Avg SSAT: 88%. **Tui '11-'12:** Day $10,100 (+$200-350). **Est 1962.** Inc. 6 terms (Aug-June). In the lower grades, Brookfield provides an accelerated and enriched program that emphasizes fundamental learning skills. Acceleration continues in the upper grades with algebra and formal grammar study, as well as a French program that enables children to study at a high school level in grades 7 and 8. The computer is an important learning tool in grades 1-8. Music and the arts are integral to the program.

ACADEMY OF OUR LADY OF PEACE   Day Girls Gr 9-12
San Diego, CA 92116. 4860 Oregon St.
Tel: 619-297-2266. Fax: 619-297-2473.
www.aolp.org   E-mail: admissions@aolp.org
     Sr. Dolores Anchondo, CSJ, Prin. BA, MA, Mount St Mary's College, MEd, Univ of San Diego. Susan DeWinter, Adm.
     Col Prep. AP—Eng Fr Span Calc Bio Chem US_Hist US_Govt & Pol Studio_Art Music_ Theory. **Feat**—Astron Genetics Marine_Bio/Sci Oceanog Comp_Sci Econ Psych Relig Fine_ Arts Speech. **Supp**—Tut. **Sports**— G: Basket Cheer X-country Golf Soccer Softball Tennis Volley. **Somewhat selective adm:** 210/yr. Appl fee: $50. Appl due: Jan. Accepted: 90%. Yield: 98%. **Tests** HSPT. **Enr 750.** Avg class size: 28. Stud/fac: 13:1. Uniform. **Fac 47.** Wh 99%. Latino 1%. Adv deg: 70%. **Grad '11—161.** Col—160. **Avg SAT:** CR 555. M 524. W 573. Avg ACT: 24.2. **Tui '12-'13:** Day $13,780. Catholic $13,360. **Est 1882.** Nonprofit. Roman Catholic. Quar (Aug-June). **Assoc** WASC. OLP offers a traditional college preparatory curriculum, with Advanced Placement offerings in English, calculus, biology, US history, government and Spanish. Requirements include religion, 25 hours of community service per year, and active participation in fine arts course work. Students select classes in dance, music, drama and art.

ST. AUGUSTINE HIGH SCHOOL   Day Boys Gr 9-12
San Diego, CA 92104. 3266 Nutmeg St.
Tel: 619-282-2184. Fax: 619-282-1203.
www.sahs.org   E-mail: mhaupt@sahs.org
     Edwin J. Hearn, Pres (2005). BA, Loyola Marymount Univ, MA, California State Univ-Los Angeles. James Horne, Prin. BA, Univ of California-San Diego, MBA, California State Univ-Long Beach, MA, Univ of San Francisco. Michael Haupt, Adm.
     Col Prep. AP (536 exams taken)—Eng Fr Lat Span Calc Stats Bio Chem Physics US_ Hist World_Hist Econ Psych US_Govt & Pol Art_Hist Music_Theory. **Feat**—Anat & Physiol Web_Design Govt Ethics Philos Relig Graphic_Arts Studio_Art Drama Theater_Arts Music. **Supp**—Rev Tut. **Sports**— B: Baseball Basket X-country Football Golf Lacrosse Rugby Soccer Swim Tennis Track Volley Wrestling. Activities: 15. **Selective adm:** 205/yr. Appl fee: $50.

emphasize logical thinking, clear writing and expression, public speaking, creative expression and critical thinking. Students satisfy a 25-hour annual community service requirement.

LIVE OAK SCHOOL   **Day Coed Gr K-8**
San Francisco, CA 94107. 1555 Mariposa St.
Tel: 415-861-8840. Fax: 415-861-7153.
www.liveoaksf.org   E-mail: info@liveoaksf.org
    Virginia Paik, Head (2009). BA, Pomona College, MA, Columbia Univ. Tracey Gersten, Adm.

    Pre-Prep. Gen Acad. Feat—Span Computers Ceramics Sculpt Drama Chorus Music Movement. **Supp**—Rev Tut. **Comp:** Comp/Stud: 1:2.5. **Sports**—Basket X-country Volley. **Selective adm:** 51/yr. Appl fee: $85. Appl due: Dec. Accepted: 26%. Yield: 69%. **Tests** CTP_4 ISEE. **Enr 272.** B 129. G 143. Wh 66%. Latino 4%. Blk 4%. Asian 3%. Other 23%. Avg class size: 22. Stud/fac: 8:1. Casual dress. **Fac 35.** M 12/F 23. FT 27/PT 8. Wh 77%. Blk 11%. Asian 9%. Other 3%. Adv deg: 25%. **Grad '11—30.** Prep—18. (Lick-Wilmerding 4, Schs of the Sacred Heart-CA 4, Urban 2, Drew 2, St Ignatius-CA 2). Avg SSAT: 64%. **Tui '12-'13:** Day $23,500 (+$1500). Aid: Need 66 ($847,000). **Est 1971.** Nonprofit. Tri (Sept-June). Live Oak's developmentally oriented elementary curriculum emphasizes the arts and sciences and the humanities. Students frequently work in small groups on experiential, hands-on projects designed to promote skill mastery. The school follows an interdisciplinary approach in the core subjects; art, music, drama, Spanish and physical education classes complement the standard courses.

MERCY HIGH SCHOOL   **Day Girls Gr 9-12**
San Francisco, CA 94132. 3250 19th Ave.
Tel: 415-334-0525. Fax: 415-334-9726.
www.mercyhs.org   E-mail: admissions@mercyhs.org
    Dorothy McCrea, Prin (1998). BA, EdD, Univ of San Francisco, MA, Univ of Santa Clara. Liz Belonogoff, Adm.

    Col Prep. AP (exams req'd; 170 taken)—Eng Fr Span Calc Bio Chem Physics US_Hist Studio_Art. **Feat**—Creative_Writing Shakespeare Environ_Sci Physiol Comp_Sci Web_Design Govt World_Relig Drama Music Dance Bus Speech. **Supp**—LD Tut. **Sports**— G: Basket Cheer X-country Soccer Softball Swim Tennis Track Volley. Activities: 35. **Selective adm:** 103/yr. Appl fee: $80. Appl due: Dec. **Tests** HSPT TOEFL. **Enr 450.** Wh 27%. Latino 19%. Blk 3%. Asian 34%. Other 17%. Avg class size: 25. Stud/fac: 16:1. Uniform. **Fac 43.** M 7/F 36. FT 40/PT 3. Wh 92%. Latino 4%. Asian 4%. Adv deg: 72%. **Grad '11—126.** Col—124. (U of CA 21, U of San Francisco 12, San Francisco St 12, City Col of San Francisco 9, San Jose St 8). **Col Couns:** 3. **Tui '12-'13:** Day $14,200 (+$1000). **Est 1952.** Nonprofit. Roman Catholic (63% practice). Sem (Aug-May). **Assoc** WASC. Mercy offers a four-year sequence of courses in religion, English, math, science, foreign language, social science and the fine arts; students choose additional course work from electives. The school schedules liturgies and retreats. Girls perform 100 compulsory hours of community service over four years.

ST. IGNATIUS COLLEGE PREPARATORY SCHOOL   **Day Coed Gr 9-12**
San Francisco, CA 94116. 2001 37th Ave.
Tel: 415-731-7500. Fax: 415-682-5064.
www.siprep.org   E-mail: kgrady@siprep.org
    Rev. Robert T. Walsh, SJ, Pres (2006). BA, Gonzaga Univ, MDiv, Jesuit School of Theology, MEd, Univ of San Francisco. Patrick Ruff, Prin. BA, Georgetown Univ, MEd, Loyola Marymount Univ. John J. Grealish, Adm.

    Col Prep. AP (1352 exams taken, 81% 3+)—Eng Fr Japan Lat Span Calc Stats Comp_Sci Bio Chem Physics US_Hist Psych US_Govt & Pol. **Feat**—Shakespeare Mythology World_Lit Anat & Physiol Astron Environ_Sci Engineering Econ Ethics Relig Architect Photog Sculpt

Studio_Art Acting Theater Music Dance Health. **Supp**—LD. **Sports (req'd)**—Basket Crew X-country Golf Lacrosse Soccer Swim Tennis Track Volley W_Polo. B: Baseball Football. G: F_Hockey Softball. Activities: 60. **Very selective adm:** 350/yr. Appl fee: $20. Appl due: Dec. Accepted: 29%. **Tests** HSPT. **Enr 1446.** B 714. G 732. Wh 64%. Latino 10%. Blk 4%. Asian 21%. Other 1%. Avg class size: 25. Stud/fac: 14:1. **Fac 164.** Wh 88%. Latino 4%. Blk 1%. Asian 5%. Other 2%. Adv deg: 54%. **Grad '10**—351. Col—349. **Avg SAT:** CR 611. M 606. W 621. Avg ACT: 26.2. **Tui '10-'11:** Day $15,810 (+$550). Aid: Need 289 ($1,300,000). **Est 1855.** Nonprofit. Roman Catholic (78% practice). Quar (Aug-May). **Assoc** WASC. This Jesuit school, located in the Sunset District of San Francisco, draws students not only from the city but also from Marin County, the Oakland-Berkeley area and the San Francisco Peninsula. Honors and Advanced Placement courses are available in all disciplines except religious studies. A well-developed campus ministry program features annual class retreats and special liturgies. Boys and girls accumulate 100 hours of required community service prior to graduation.

CLAIRBOURN SCHOOL   Day Coed Gr PS (Age 3)-8
San Gabriel, CA 91775. 8400 Huntington Dr.
Tel: 626-286-3108. Fax: 626-286-1528.
www.clairbourn.org   E-mail: admissions@clairbourn.org
    Robert W. Nafie, Head (1979). BA, Univ of Minnesota-Twin Cities, MS, Univ of Wisconsin-Madison, PhD, Claremont Graduate School. Janna Hawes, Adm.
    Pre-Prep. Feat—Lib_Skills Fr Lat Span Computers Studio_Art Drama Music Orchestra. **Comp:** Comp/Stud: 1:2 (1:1 Laptop prgm Gr 6-8). **Sports**—Basket Golf Soccer Swim Tennis Track Volley. B: Baseball Football. G: Softball. **Selective adm:** 60/yr. Appl fee: $75. Appl due: Jan. **Tests** CTP_4 ISEE MRT. **Enr 351.** B 183. G 168. Wh 40%. Latino 7%. Blk 3%. Asian 30%. Other 20%. Avg class size: 17. Stud/fac: 10:1. Uniform. **Fac 36.** M 7/F 29. FT 35/PT 1. Wh 97%. Latino 3%. Adv deg: 33%. **Grad '11**—26. Prep—23. (La Salle HS-CA 5, St Francis HS-CA 4, Maranatha HS 3, Flintridge Prep 2, Flintridge Sacred Heart 2, Loyola HS-CA 2). **Tui '12-'13:** Day $15,250-19,450 (+$80-460). Aid: Merit 4 ($2500). Need 64 ($432,830). **Est 1926.** Nonprofit. Christian Science (9% practice). Sem (Sept-June). **Assoc** WASC. Although the school's staff are all Christian Scientists, the student body at Clairbourn represents various denominations. The curriculum focuses on the basics and is designed to teach children creative-thinking, problem-solving and fundamental academic skills. Foreign languages, computers, library, art, music and physical education enrich the program. Accelerated English and math courses are available at the middle school level. Each class completes a community service project.

BELLARMINE COLLEGE PREPARATORY   Day Boys Gr 9-12
San Jose, CA 95126. 960 W Hedding St.
Tel: 408-294-9224, 888-462-3557. Fax: 408-294-4086.
www.bcp.org   E-mail: tcouncil@bcp.org
    Rev. Paul Sheridan, SJ, Pres. Chris Meyercord, Prin. Bill Colucci, Adm.
    Col Prep. AP (991 exams taken, 90% 3+)—Eng Chin Fr Lat Span Calc Stats Comp_Sci Bio Chem Environ_Sci Physics Eur_Hist US_Hist World_Hist Human_Geog Psych Art_Hist Studio_Art. **Feat**—British_Lit Creative_Writing Shakespeare African-Amer_Lit Sci_Fiction Screenwriting Multivariable_Calc Anat & Physiol Marine_Bio/Sci Web_Design Econ Comp_ Relig Ethics Ceramics Fine_Arts Photog Video_Production Acting Theater_Arts Dance Journ. **Sports**— B: Baseball Basket X-country Football Golf Lacrosse Soccer Swim Tennis Track Volley W_Polo Wrestling. **Selective adm:** 400/yr. Appl fee: $75. Appl due: Dec. Accepted: 43%. **Tests** HSPT. **Enr 1600.** Avg class size: 25. Stud/fac: 13:1. **Grad '11**—393. Col—390. **Avg SAT:** CR 611. M 641. W 617. Avg ACT: 26.7. **Col Couns:** 5. **Tui '12-'13:** Day $16,770. Aid: Need ($3,200,000). **Est 1851.** Nonprofit. Roman Catholic. Sem (Aug-May). **Assoc** WASC. The oldest Jesuit school west of the Mississippi River, Bellarmine enrolls boys from a wide geographical area: north to Burlingame and San Francisco, east to Fremont and Liver-

more, west to Scotts Valley and Santa Cruz, and south to Watsonville and Gilroy. Advanced Placement offerings are available throughout the curriculum, including in all four foreign languages. Performing and visual arts course work is extensive. Students in grades 9-11 perform 15 hours of required community service annually (with target population varying by grade), while seniors compile 30 hours.

PRESENTATION HIGH SCHOOL   Day Girls Gr 9-12
San Jose, CA 95125. 2281 Plummer Ave.
Tel: 408-264-1664. Fax: 408-266-3028.
www.presentationhs.org   E-mail: dcollins@pres-net.com
   Mary Miller, Prin. BA, MA. Dina Collins, Adm.
   Col Prep. AP (347 exams taken, 66% 3+)—Eng Fr Span Calc Bio Environ_Sci US_Hist Econ Psych. **Feat**—Shakespeare Stats Anat & Physiol Bioethics Programming Web_Design Civics Relig World_Relig Ceramics Drawing Photog Acting Dance. **Supp**—Tut. **Comp:** Comp/Stud: 1:3. **Sports**— G: Basket X-country F_Hockey Golf Soccer Softball Swim Tennis Track Volley W_Polo. Activities: 20. **Selective adm (Gr 9-11):** 200/yr. Appl fee: $70. Appl due: Jan. **Tests** HSPT. **Enr 750.** Wh 52%. Latino 11%. Blk 1%. Asian 8%. Other 28%. Avg class size: 28. Uniform. **Fac 54.** M 12/F 42. FT 42/PT 12. Adv deg: 57%. **Grad '11—204.** Col—204. (Loyola Marymount 13, Santa Clara 9, Sonoma St 9, U of CA-Berkeley 8, San Jose St 8, U of San Diego 7). **Col Couns:** 2. **Tui '11-'12:** Day $14,750. Aid: Need 150 ($1,400,000). **Est 1962.** Nonprofit. Roman Catholic (74% practice). Sem (Aug-May). **Assoc** WASC. Focusing primarily on college preparation, Presentation conducts a varied curriculum that includes offerings in the disciplines of religious studies, the visual and performing arts, modern languages and computer technology. A well-developed technology program features computer labs, wireless Internet access and an electronic library collection. While community service involvement is elective, the vast majority of the school's students volunteer in the San Jose community.

CHINESE CHRISTIAN SCHOOLS   Day Coed Gr K-12
San Leandro, CA 94579. 750 Fargo Ave.
Tel: 510-351-4957. Fax: 510-351-1789.
Other locations: 1801 N Loop Rd, Alameda 94502.
www.ccs-rams.org   E-mail: info@ccs-rams.org
   Robin S. Hom, Supt (1988). AB, Univ of California-Berkeley, JD, Univ of the Pacific, MA, Biola Univ. Cindy Loh, Adm.
   Col Prep. AP (227 exams taken, 74% 3+)—Eng Chin Calc Bio Chem Physics Eur_Hist US_Hist Econ Psych US_Govt & Pol Studio_Art. **Feat**—British_Lit Span Stats Comp_Sci Bible Drama Music Home_Ec. **Supp**—ESL Tut. **Comp:** Comp/Stud: 1:9. Outdoor Ed. **Sports**—Basket X-country Soccer Tennis Track Volley. Activities: 20. **Somewhat selective adm:** 126/yr. Appl fee: $50. Appl due: Rolling. Accepted: 90%. Yield: 95%. **Tests** Stanford. **Enr 695.** B 360. G 335. Elem 480. Sec 215. Wh 4%. Latino 1%. Blk 2%. Asian 88%. Other 5%. Intl 5%. Avg class size: 20. Stud/fac: 10:1. Uniform. **Fac 85.** M 26/F 59. FT 85. Wh 10%. Blk 1%. Asian 85%. Other 4%. Adv deg: 15%. **Grad '11—49.** Col—49. (U of CA-Irvine 8, U of CA-Riverside 5, U of CA-Davis 4, U of the Pacific 4, U of CA-Berkeley 3, U of CA-Santa Cruz 3). **Avg SAT:** CR 591. M 644. W 594. **Col Couns:** 3. **Tui '11-'12:** Day $7400-9300 (+$1600). Aid: Merit 20. **Est 1979.** Nonprofit. Nondenom Christian (20% practice). Quar (Aug-June). **Assoc** WASC. Originally inhabiting two one-bedroom Oakland apartments, CCS relocated to the 10-acre San Leandro location in 1985. The college preparatory high school program includes Advanced Placement and honors courses, elective and extracurricular options, and Mandarin language study. A second campus in Alameda, which opened in 2003, hosts additional pupils in grades K-8.

JUNIPERO SERRA HIGH SCHOOL   **Day Boys Gr 9-12**
San Mateo, CA 94403. 451 W 20th Ave.
Tel: 650-345-8207. Fax: 650-573-6638.
www.serrahs.com   E-mail: padres@serrahs.com

Lars Lund, Pres (2007). BA, Santa Clara Univ, MA, Univ of San Francisco. Barry Thornton, Prin. BS, California State Polytechnic Univ-San Luis Obispo, MA, St Patrick's Seminary & Univ, EdD, Univ of San Francisco. Randy Vogel, Adm.

Col Prep. AP (exams req'd; 344 taken, 83% 3+)—Eng Fr Span Calc Comp_Sci Bio Physics US_Hist US_Govt & Pol Art_Hist. **Feat**—ASL Chin Ger Anat & Physiol Environ_Sci Bioengineering CA_Hist Econ Psych Theol Ceramics Film Photog Sculpt Architect_Design Drama Band Chorus Orchestra Dance Journ. **Supp**—LD. **Sports**— B: Baseball Basket Crew X-country Football Golf Lacrosse Soccer Swim Tennis Track Volley W_Polo Wrestling. Activities: 37. **Selective adm (Gr 9-11):** 233/yr. Appl fee: $75. Appl due: Jan. Accepted: 82%. Yield: 66%. **Tests** HSPT. **Enr 900.** Wh 52%. Latino 13%. Blk 2%. Asian 16%. Other 17%. Avg class size: 24. Casual dress. **Fac 73.** M 53/F 20. FT 63/PT 10. Adv deg: 80%. **Grad '11—226.** Col—226. **Col Couns:** 5. **Tui '12-'13:** Day $17,120 (+$700). Aid: Need 285 ($2,100,000). **Est 1944.** Nonprofit. Roman Catholic (72% practice). Sem (Aug-May). **Assoc** WASC. Serra's college preparatory program includes dozens of accelerated, honors and Advanced Placement courses. The Tri School Program, a collaborative effort among Serra and two other local private schools (Mercy and Notre Dame high schools), offers the following: classes on each campus in which students from the three schools can learn together; coeducational retreats, prayer services and community service opportunities; and various coed extracurricular activities. The school's Academic Resource Center serves boys of average to gifted levels of intelligence who have been diagnosed with a learning difference. Students accumulate 80 hours of required community service over four years.

ROLLING HILLS PREPARATORY SCHOOL   **Day Coed Gr 6-12**
San Pedro, CA 90732. 1 Rolling Hills Prep Way.
Tel: 310-791-1101. Fax: 310-373-4931.
www.rollinghillsprep.org   E-mail: bfisco@rollinghillsprep.org

Peter McCormack, Head (1993). BA, York Univ (England), MSc, Oxford Univ (England). Bryonna Fisco, Adm.

Col Prep. AP (exams req'd; 68 taken, 57% 3+)—Eng Fr Span Calc Bio Chem Physics Eur_Hist US_Hist. **Feat**—ASL Anat Horticulture Robotics Econ Govt Photog Studio_Art Video_Production Drama Music. **Supp**—ESL Rev Tut. **Comp:** Comp/Stud: 1:4. **Sports**— Basket X-country Golf Soccer Track. B: Baseball Football. G: Softball Volley. Activities: 24. **Selective adm:** 51/yr. Appl fee: $150. Appl due: Rolling. Accepted: 65%. Yield: 80%. **Tests** ISEE TOEFL. **Enr 225.** B 115. G 110. Elem 100. Sec 125. Wh 77%. Latino 2%. Blk 5%. Asian 16%. Intl 10%. Avg class size: 15. Stud/fac: 11:1. **Fac 38.** M 13/F 25. FT 27/PT 11. Wh 82%. Latino 1%. Blk 10%. Native Am 2%. Asian 5%. Adv deg: 26%. **Grad '11—33.** Col—33. (USC 2, UCLA 2, U of AZ 2, Swarthmore 1, NYU 1, Hampshire 1). **Avg SAT:** CR 542. M 528. W 544. **Col Couns:** 1. Alum donors: 5%. **Tui '12-'13:** Day $24,750 (+$700-3060). Aid: Need 69 ($910,000). **Est 1981.** Nonprofit. Tri (Sept-June). **Assoc** WASC. All courses within the traditional liberal arts curriculum are college preparatory, with electives, Advanced Placement options and honors classes provided. Qualified students may complete a yearlong independent study, and seniors are offered two-week internships before graduation. Rolling Hills Prep provides various community service options; freshmen serve 10 compulsory hours per year, sophomores 20 hours, juniors 30 hours and seniors 40 hours.

SAINT MARK'S SCHOOL   **Day Coed Gr K-8**
San Rafael, CA 94903. 39 Trellis Dr.
Tel: 415-472-8000. Fax: 415-472-0722.
www.saintmarksschool.org   E-mail: admissions@saintmarksschool.org

Joseph M. Harvey, Head (2011). BA, Harvard Univ, MA, Middlebury College. Wendy Broderick, Adm.

Pre-Prep. Feat—Chin Fr Span Computers Studio_Art Drama Music Gardening. **Supp**—Dev_Read Rem_Math Rem_Read Rev Tut. **Comp:** Comp/Stud: 1:2.5 (1:1 Laptop prgm Gr 6-8). **Sports**—Basket X-country Track. G: Volley. **Selective adm (Gr K-7):** 53/yr. Appl fee: $100. Appl due: Jan. Accepted: 44%. Yield: 70%. **Tests** CTP_4 ISEE. **Enr 380.** B 200. G 180. Wh 71%. Latino 9%. Blk 1%. Asian 5%. Other 14%. Avg class size: 20. Stud/fac: 10:1. **Fac 38.** M 9/F 29. FT 32/PT 6. Wh 81%. Latino 5%. Blk 3%. Asian 11%. **Grad '10—42.** Prep—38. (Branson 13, Marin Acad 10, San Francisco U HS 2, Sonoma Acad 2, Urban 2). **Tui '11-'12:** Day $23,700 (+$300-2600). Aid: Need 91 ($1,300,000). **Est 1980.** Nonprofit. Sem (Aug-June). All students at Saint Mark's receive instruction in world languages, computer, art, drama, music and physical education. Tutoring is available for those with learning differences. Seventh graders perform one week of required community service. Extracurricular activities include fine arts and interscholastic and intramural athletic offerings. After-school care is available.

MATER DEI HIGH SCHOOL   **Day Coed Gr 9-12**
Santa Ana, CA 92707. 1202 W Edinger Ave.
Tel: 714-754-7711. Fax: 714-754-1880.
www.materdei.org   E-mail: admissions@materdei.org
    Patrick Murphy, Pres (1990). BE, Simon Fraser Univ (Canada), MA, San Diego State Univ. Frances Clare, Prin. BA, MA, California State Univ-Long Beach, MA, Univ of San Francisco. Anne Welsh-Treglia, Adm.

Col Prep. AP (exams req'd; 644 taken, 81% 3+)—Eng Fr Lat Span Calc Comp_Sci Bio Physics Eur_Hist US_Hist US_Govt & Pol Art_Hist Studio_Art. **Feat**—Web_Design Econ Bus_Law Photog Theater Band Chorus Music_Theory Dance Speech TV_Production. **Supp**—Dev_Read LD Rem_Math Rem_Read Tut. **Comp:** Comp/Stud: 1:1 Laptop prgm Gr 9-12. **Sports**—Basket Cheer X-country Golf Lacrosse Soccer Swim Tennis Track Volley W_Polo. B: Baseball Football Wrestling. G: Softball. Activities: 50. **Somewhat selective adm:** 625/yr. Appl fee: $60. Appl due: Jan. Accepted: 90%. Yield: 65%. **Tests** HSPT. **Enr 2049.** B 1007. G 1042. Wh 47%. Latino 21%. Blk 2%. Asian 14%. Other 16%. Avg class size: 28. Uniform. **Fac 141.** M 48/F 93. FT 141. Adv deg: 51%. **Grad '11—515.** Col—515. (CA St U-Fullerton 39, UCLA 23, USC 23, U of CA-Irvine 16, Loyola Marymount 10, U of San Diego 9). **Avg SAT:** CR 520. M 540. W 530. Avg ACT: 23.7. **Col Couns:** 5. **Tui '11-'12:** Day $11,950 (+$1000). Catholic $10,725 (+$1000). Aid: Need 820 ($3,100,000). **Est 1950.** Nonprofit. Roman Catholic (85% practice). Sem (Sept-June). **Assoc** WASC. Mater Dei offers a traditional college preparatory curriculum, with Advanced Placement opportunities provided in most disciplines. Various electives, business courses and athletics are also available. Students fulfill an 80-hour community service requirement over their four years.

CRANE COUNTRY DAY SCHOOL   **Day Coed Gr K-8**
Santa Barbara, CA 93108. 1795 San Leandro Ln.
Tel: 805-969-7732. Fax: 805-969-3635.
www.craneschool.org   E-mail: dwilliams@craneschool.org
    Joel J. Weiss, Head (2000). BA, Swarthmore College, MEd, Harvard Univ. Debbie Williams, Adm.

Pre-Prep. Gen Acad. Feat—Span Marine_Bio/Sci Computers Geog Studio_Art Drama Music. **Comp:** Comp/Stud: 1:2. **Sports**—Basket Soccer Volley. **Selective adm:** 62/yr. Appl fee: $100. Appl due: Feb. Accepted: 40%. Yield: 97%. **Tests** ISEE. **Enr 250.** B 125. G 125. Wh 82%. Latino 13%. Blk 1%. Asian 4%. Avg class size: 17. Casual dress. **Fac 37.** M 11/F 26. FT 29/PT 8. Wh 99%. Latino 1%. Adv deg: 27%. **Grad '11—48.** Prep—23. (Cate 7, Laguna Blanca 6, Bishop Garcia Diego 5, Robert Louis Stevenson 2, Phillips Acad 1). Alum donors: 2%. **Tui '11-'12:** Day $21,975-22,975 (+$50-1500). Aid: Need 49 ($728,104). **Est 1928.** Nonprofit. Tri (Sept-June). **Assoc** WASC. While stressing the fundamentals within a traditional curriculum, the school also places emphasis upon the visual arts, drama, music and athletics. Community service, another important element of Crane's program, is incorporated into the school day. Spanish instruction begins in kindergarten.

MARYMOUNT OF SANTA BARBARA   Day Coed Gr PS (Age 4)-8
Santa Barbara, CA 93103. 2130 Mission Ridge Rd.
Tel: 805-569-1811. Fax: 805-569-0573.
www.marymountsb.org   E-mail: mseguel@marymountsb.org
    Andrew Wooden, Head (2011). BA, Univ of Maine, MA, Yale Divinity School. Molly Seguel, Adm.
    Pre-Prep. Gen Acad. Feat—Span Computers Relig World_Relig Studio_Art Drama Music. **Supp**—Tut. **Very selective adm:** 49/yr. Appl fee: $150. Appl due: Feb. Accepted: 18%. **Tests** ISEE. **Enr 216.** B 104. G 112. Avg class size: 20. Stud/fac: 9:1. **Fac 29.** M 9/F 20. FT 24/PT 5. **Grad '11**—26. Prep—13. (Bishop Garcia Diego 9, Laguna Blanca 1, Cate 1, St Paul's Sch-NH 1, Dunn 1). **Tui '12-'13:** Day $18,380-20,940. Aid: Need 64 ($750,000). **Est 1938.** Nonprofit. Tri (Sept-June). The pre-preparatory program at Marymount emphasizes fundamental learning and critical-thinking skills. Noteworthy program features include particularly strong language arts and math curricula, a program for gifted and talented children, a full-time learning specialist and community service opportunities. Computer, Spanish, art and music classes begin in kindergarten, and the middle school curriculum (grades 6-8) includes more than 20 electives.

ST. LAWRENCE ACADEMY   Day Coed Gr 9-12
Santa Clara, CA 95051. 2000 Lawrence Ct.
Tel: 408-296-3013. Fax: 408-296-3794.
www.saintlawrenceacademy.com   E-mail: mdixon@saintlawrence.org
    Christie H. Filios, Prin. BA, Loyola Marymount Univ, MA, Stanford Univ. Mary Dixon, Adm.
    Col Prep. AP—Eng Calc US_Hist Studio_Art. **Feat**—British_Lit Creative_Writing ASL Fr Span Stats Anat & Physiol Ecol Comp_Design Econ Govt Sociol World_Relig Drama Study_Skills. **Supp**—LD Tut. **Comp:** Comp/Stud: 1:1 Laptop prgm Gr 9-12. **Sports**—Basket X-country Swim Tennis Track. B: Baseball Softball. G: Golf Soccer Volley. Activities: 17. **Selective adm (Gr 9-11):** 70/yr. Appl fee: $65. Appl due: Jan. **Tests** HSPT. **Enr 260.** Avg class size: 21. Stud/fac: 15:1. Uniform. **Fac 24.** M 13/F 11. FT 20/PT 4. Adv deg: 70%. **Grad '08**—74. Col—74. **Tui '11-'12:** Day $14,020 (+$500). **Est 1975.** Nonprofit. Roman Catholic (70% practice). Quar (Aug-June). **Assoc** WASC. The academy's college preparatory program provides several forms of learning support: a library/multimedia information resource center, reading labs, before- and after-school study halls, and a formal program for high-functioning students with diagnosed learning disabilities. The school encourages pupils to take part in the campus ministry program: All students perform 25 hours of community service annually, and full-class retreats and liturgical celebrations are integral aspects of school life.

CARLTHORP SCHOOL   Day Coed Gr K-6
Santa Monica, CA 90402. 438 San Vicente Blvd.
Tel: 310-451-1332. Fax: 310-451-8559.
www.carlthorp.org
    Dorothy Menzies, Head (1983). BS, MA, California State Polytechnic Univ-San Luis Obispo. Lynn Wagmeister, Adm.
    Pre-Prep. Feat—Span Computers Studio_Art Music. **Supp**—Dev_Read Rev Tut. **Comp:** Comp/Stud: 1:2. **Sports**—Basket Soccer Volley. **Very selective adm:** 44/yr. Appl fee: $100. Appl due: Nov. Accepted: 22%. Yield: 95%. **Enr 280.** B 140. G 140. Avg class size: 20. Stud/fac: 10:1. Uniform. **Fac 53.** M 7/F 46. FT 45/PT 8. Wh 79%. Latino 1%. Blk 1%. Native Am 1%. Asian 17%. Other 1%. Adv deg: 56%. **Grad '10**—40. Prep—38. **Tui '11-'12:** Day

$21,023 (+$850). Aid: Need 28. **Est 1939.** Nonprofit. Tri (Sept-June). **Assoc** WASC. The oldest independent elementary school in the city, Carlthorp complements its core subjects of English, math, social studies and reading with specialist-taught Spanish, science, technology, arts and physical education classes. Interscholastic athletics begin in grade 4. The school integrates the use of technology into all classes. Although participation is voluntary, Carlthorp maintains an active community service program.

PS #1 ELEMENTARY SCHOOL
Day Coed Gr K-6

Santa Monica, CA 90404. 1454 Euclid St.
Tel: 310-394-1313. Fax: 310-395-1093.
www.psone.org   E-mail: admissions@psone.org
Joel M. Pelcyger, Head (1971). BA, Univ of Rochester. Amanda Perla, Adm.

Pre-Prep. Feat—Visual_Arts Drama Music. **Supp**—Dev_Read. **Selective adm (Gr K-5):** 43/yr. Appl fee: $125. Appl due: Jan. Accepted: 50%. **Enr 215.** Wh 72%. Latino 7%. Blk 8%. Asian 10%. Other 3%. Avg class size: 25. Stud/fac: 13:1. **Fac 22.** M 5/F 17. Wh 68%. Latino 14%. Asian 18%. Adv deg: 54%. **Grad '11—26.** Prep—2. (Windward-CA 8, Crossroads-CA 4, Harvard-Westlake 2, Marlborough 2, Wildwood 2, Brentwood Sch-CA 1). **Tui '12-'13:** Day $23,950 (+$1250). Aid: Need 38 ($534,235). **Est 1971.** Nonprofit. (Sept-June). This progressive school enriches its curriculum with multicultural experiences, community and environmental studies, science and arts programs, and field trips. Pupils at PS #1 acquire academic and life skills in multi-age classes that are each led by two master teachers. Faculty members continually evaluate the student's progress through observation and portfolio assessment.

SONOMA ACADEMY
Day Coed Gr 9-12

Santa Rosa, CA 95404. 2500 Farmers Ln.
Tel: 707-545-1770. Fax: 707-636-2474.
www.sonomaacademy.org   E-mail: info@sonomaacademy.org
Janet Durgin, Head (2000). BA, Evergreen State College, MA, School for International Training. Sandy Stack, Adm.

Col Prep. AP (90 exams taken, 83% 3+)—Eng Span Calc Stats Chem Physics. **Feat**—CA_Lit Expository_Writing Chin Fr Multivariable_Calc Anat & Physiol Genetics Oceanog Engineering Programming Econ African_Stud Constitutional_Law Comp_Relig Filmmaking Photog Studio_Art Music_Theory. **Supp**—LD Tut. **Comp:** Comp/Stud: 1:1 Laptop prgm Gr 9-12. Outdoor Ed. **Sports**—Basket X-country Lacrosse Soccer Track. B: Baseball. G: Volley. Activities: 15. **Selective adm:** 76/yr. Appl fee: $85. Appl due: Jan. **Tests** SSAT. **Enr 237.** B 118. G 119. Wh 67%. Latino 6%. Asian 5%. Other 22%. Avg class size: 15. Stud/fac: 12:1. **Fac 24.** M 9/F 15. FT 17/PT 7. Nonwhite 1%. Adv deg: 79%. **Grad '11—63.** Col—59. (Sarah Lawrence 4, USC 3, CA St Polytech-San Luis Obispo 2, NYU 2, Middlebury 2, Lewis & Clark 2). **Avg SAT:** CR 598. M 571. W 610. **Mid 50% SAT:** CR 510-640. M 520-610. W 540-640. Avg ACT: 27. **Col Couns:** 1. **Tui '11-'12:** Day $32,550 (+$1250). Aid: Need 127 ($2,520,000). **Est 2001.** Nonprofit. Quar (Aug-May). **Assoc** WASC. With a focus on college preparation, SA conducts a varied liberal arts program. The curriculum includes global and environmental leadership concentrations that enable students to pursue an area of focus through a combination of course work, service and independent projects. A two-week intersession, held each January, offers students an opportunity to either travel abroad or immerse themselves in a topic of interest. The community service program requires all boys and girls to engage in project work once a week.

SONOMA COUNTRY DAY SCHOOL
Day Coed Gr K-8

Santa Rosa, CA 95403. 4400 Day School Pl.
Tel: 707-284-3200. Fax: 707-284-3254.
www.scds.org   E-mail: scds@scds.org

Bradley L. Weaver, Head (2009). BA, Wake Forest Univ, MEd, Univ of North Carolina-Chapel Hill, EdD, Boston College. Dana Nelson-Isaacs, Adm.

Pre-Prep. Feat—Chin Span Environ_Sci Computers Studio_Art Drama Band Chorus Public_Speak Outdoor_Ed. **Sports**—Basket Lacrosse Track Volley. **Somewhat selective adm:** 53/yr. Appl fee: $150. Appl due: Feb. **Tests** MRT Stanford. **Enr 250.** B 131. G 119. Avg class size: 19. Stud/fac: 10:1. Uniform. **Fac 30. Grad '11—36.** Prep—26. (Sonoma Acad 17, Cardinal Newman 5, Justin-Siena 1, Brentwood Sch-CA 1, Midland 1, Eagle Hill-MA 1). **Tui '11-'12:** Day $19,950-22,260 (+$500-1500). Aid: Need ($510,000). **Est 1983.** Nonprofit. Sem (Sept-June). **Assoc** WASC. The core curriculum at SCDS is enhanced by integrated instruction in philosophy and ethics. The liberal arts course of studies features a wide selection of visual and performing arts offerings. Children are expected to take advantage of leadership opportunities and also to devote parts of three days per year to community service.

BAYMONTE CHRISTIAN SCHOOL

Day Coed Gr PS (Age 2)-8

Scotts Valley, CA 95066. 5000-B Granite Creek Rd.
Tel: 831-438-0100. Fax: 831-438-0715.
Other locations: 4901 Scotts Valley Dr, Scotts Valley 95066; 800 Bethany Dr, Scotts Valley 95066.
www.baymonte.org   E-mail: steve@baymonte.org
    Steve Patterson, Prin (1991). BA, California State Univ-Sacramento, MA, US International Univ. Teri Hillenga, Adm.

Gen Acad. Feat—Span Computers Robotics Bible Studio_Art Video_Production Music. **Supp**—Dev_Read Rem_Math. **Sports**—Basket Soccer Softball. G: Volley. **Somewhat selective adm:** 64/yr. Appl fee: $75. Appl due: Apr. Accepted: 98%. **Enr 450.** Wh 78%. Latino 11%. Blk 3%. Native Am 1%. Asian 7%. Avg class size: 22. **Fac 30.** M 5/F 25. FT 27/PT 3. Wh 100%. Adv deg: 20%. **Grad '10—41. Tui '12-'13:** Day $6450 (+$200-300). Aid: Need 30. **Est 1968.** Nonprofit. Nondenom Christian. Sem (Sept-June). **Assoc** WASC. Baymonte's curriculum includes daily Bible and basic computer instruction. Middle school students participate in community service trips to New Orleans and Mexico. In addition to one at the main location, the school conducts preschool programs on Scotts Valley Drive and Bethany Drive.

NOTRE DAME HIGH SCHOOL

Day Coed Gr 9-12

Sherman Oaks, CA 91423. 13645 Riverside Dr.
Tel: 818-933-3600. Fax: 818-501-0507.
www.ndhs.org   E-mail: moss@ndhs.org
    Brian A. Lowart, Pres. Stephanie Connelly, Prin. Alec Moss, Adm.

Col Prep. AP (exams req'd)—Eng Fr Japan Lat Span Calc Stats Comp_Sci Bio Chem Physics Eur_Hist US_Hist Econ US_Govt & Pol Art_Hist Studio_Art. **Feat**—Humanities Playwriting Anat & Physiol Sports_Med Web_Design Law Psych Sociol World_Relig Painting Photog Acting Band Chorus Dance Debate Journ Speech TV_Production. **Supp**—Tut. **Sports**—Basket X-country Golf Soccer Swim Tennis Track W_Polo. B: Baseball Football. G: Cheer Equestrian Volley. Activities: 52. **Selective adm (Gr 9-11):** 330/yr. Appl fee: $100. Appl due: Jan. Accepted: 50%. **Tests** HSPT. **Enr 1200.** Wh 57%. Latino 21%. Blk 5%. Native Am 1%. Asian 6%. Other 10%. Avg class size: 28. Uniform. **Fac 93.** Adv deg: 73%. **Grad '08—265.** Col—262. **Avg SAT:** CR 539. M 541. W 549. **Col Couns:** 2. **Tui '12-'13:** Day $12,200 (+$1600-1800). Aid: Need ($1,300,000). **Est 1947.** Nonprofit. Roman Catholic. Sem (Sept-June). **Assoc** WASC. Founded by the Brothers of the Holy Cross, Notre Dame offers a college preparatory curriculum that features honors and Advanced Placement courses and a variety of electives. Freshmen spend 20 compulsory hours in service to their families, sophomores spend 20 in service to their parishes, juniors complete 30 hours in service to the school, and seniors spend another 30 in off-campus Christian service to organizations and institutions that assist the underprivileged.

ST. MICHAEL'S PREPARATORY SCHOOL

5-Day Bdg Boys Gr 9-12

Silverado, CA 92676. 19292 El Toro Rd.
Tel: 949-858-0222. Fax: 949-858-7365.
www.stmichaelsprep.org   E-mail: admissions@stmichaelsprep.org
Rev. Gabriel D. Stack, OPraem, Head (1997). EdD, Pepperdine Univ.

Col Prep. AP (exams req'd)—Eng Calc Physics US_Hist Econ. **Feat**—Humanities World_Lit Greek Lat Marine_Bio/Sci Philos Relig Art_Hist Fine_Arts. **Supp**—Tut. **Dual enr:** Brigham Young, Keystone. **Sports**— B: Baseball X-country Football Soccer. **Selective adm:** 26/yr. Appl fee: $100. **Tests** HSPT Stanford TOEFL. **Enr 65.** Wh 71%. Latino 11%. Asian 18%. Avg class size: 10. Uniform. **Fac 23.** M 21/F 2. FT 14/PT 9. Wh 85%. Latino 3%. Blk 1%. Asian 8%. Other 3%. Adv deg: 69%. In Dorms 2. **Grad '05—11.** Col—11. **Tui '12-'13:** 5-Day Bdg $21,700 (+$3000).Aid: Merit 1 ($8000). **Est 1961.** Nonprofit. Roman Catholic. Sem (Aug-June). **Assoc** WASC. Catholic principles are an important element of school life. All students take religion, attend chapel and perform daily maintenance jobs on campus. Boys who choose to spend weekends on campus pay an additional fee.

BRIDGES ACADEMY

Day Coed Gr 5-12

Studio City, CA 91604. 3921 Laurel Canyon Blvd.
Tel: 818-506-1091. Fax: 818-506-8094.
www.bridges.edu   E-mail: info@bridges.edu
Carl Sabatino, Head (2005). Doug Lenzini, Adm.

Col Prep. LD. Feat—Playwriting Japan Span Anat & Physiol Ecol Genetics Geol Programming Robotics Web_Design Comp_Animation Film Photog Visual_Arts Drama Theater_Arts Music. **Supp**—Rev. **Comp:** Laptop prgm Gr 5-12. Outdoor Ed. **Sports**—X-country Track. B: Basket. **Selective adm:** 35/yr. Appl fee: $150. Appl due: Rolling. **Tests** CTP_4 IQ Stanford. **Enr 130.** B 110. G 20. Elem 50. Sec 80. Avg class size: 8. **Fac 38.** FT 32/PT 6. Adv deg: 57%. **Grad '11—15.** Col—13. **Tui '12-'13:** Day $32,432 (+$700). **Est 1994.** Nonprofit. Sem (Aug-May). **Assoc** WASC. Bridges' program serves gifted students with nonverbal learning differences, organizational challenges, and such other issues as attentional disorders, auditory or visual processing problems, and dysgraphia. Above-average students who have not succeeded in traditional academic environments also enroll. Academic programming incorporates social skills instruction. The school's laptop program compels all boys and girls to purchase a computer for classroom work, research and communication. Pupils satisfy a 30-hour community service requirement prior to graduation.

WOODCREST SCHOOL

Day Coed Gr K-5

Tarzana, CA 91356. 6043 Tampa Ave.
Tel: 818-345-3002. Fax: 818-345-7880.
www.woodcrestschool.com   E-mail: info@woodcrestschool.com
Luanne Paglione, Prin. BS, Seton Hall Univ.

Pre-Prep. Gen Acad. Feat—Span Computers Fine_Arts Drama Music Dance. **Supp**—Dev_Read Rem_Math Rem_Read. **Sports**—Basket Soccer. G: Cheer. **Selective adm:** 55/yr. Appl fee: $35. Appl due: Rolling. **Enr 161.** Avg class size: 17. Uniform. **Fac 13.** M 3/F 10. **Grad '08—19. Tui '11-'12:** Day $9190-9240 (+$350-400). **Est 1969.** Quar (Sept-June). **Assoc** WASC. In addition to the basic educational program, this school also offers enrichment and gifted programs. Spanish instruction begins in grade 2, computer courses in kindergarten. The school has a computer lab, and each class has its own computer. An extended-day program is available.

LAURENCE SCHOOL

Day Coed Gr K-6

Valley Glen, CA 91401. 13639 Victory Blvd.
Tel: 818-782-4001. Fax: 818-782-4004.
www.laurenceschool.com   E-mail: office@laurenceschool.com

Lauren Wolke, Head (2010). JD. Gary Stern, Prin.

Pre-Prep. Feat—Lib_Skills Chin Span Studio_Art Drama Music Orchestra. **Sports**—Basket Soccer. **B**: Baseball. **G**: Volley. **Selective adm:** 53/yr. Appl fee: $125. Appl due: Jan. **Enr 315.** Wh 73%. Latino 4%. Blk 6%. Asian 7%. Other 10%. Avg class size: 20. Stud/fac: 8:1. Uniform. **Fac 47.** M 7/F 40. Wh 76%. Latino 4%. Blk 8%. Asian 6%. Other 6%. Adv deg: 51%. **Grad '11—29.** Prep—29. **Tui '12-'13:** Day $23,000 (+$500). **Est 1953.** Nonprofit. Sem (Sept-June). **Assoc** WASC. Laurence emphasizes developmentally appropriate academics, enrichment opportunities and character formation. Children in grades K-4 take Spanish twice a week, and each classroom adopts a sister country for the school year as part of the global education program. Technology is integrated across the curriculum and features a technology center, the availability of laptops and tablet computers, and the presence of interactive white-boards in all classrooms and specialty labs. Boys and girls engage in schoolwide and grade-specific community service projects.

MONTCLAIR COLLEGE PREPARATORY SCHOOL   Day Coed Gr 7-12
Van Nuys, CA 91402. 8071 Sepulveda Blvd.
Tel: 818-787-5290. Fax: 818-786-3382.
www.montclairprep.net   E-mail: mcpneumann@yahoo.com
    Mark Simpson, Exec Dir. Walter Steele, Prin.

Col Prep. AP (exams req'd)—Eng Span Calc Eur_Hist US_Hist Econ US_Govt & Pol. **Feat**—Creative_Writing Fr Hebrew Stats Environ_Sci Comp_Sci Philos Filmmaking Studio_Art Drama Music Bus Journ. **Supp**—ESL Tut. **Sports**—Basket X-country Golf Soccer Tennis Track. **B**: Baseball Football. **G**: Softball Volley. **Selective adm:** 60/yr. Appl fee: $100. Appl due: Rolling. Accepted: 60%. Yield: 40%. **Tests** ISEE. **Enr 350.** Stud/fac: 20:1. Uniform. **Fac 34.** M 20/F 14. FT 32/PT 2. Adv deg: 44%. **Grad '08—110.** Col—110. (U of CA-Santa Cruz 5, U of CA-Berkeley 5, USC 5, UCLA 5, U of CO-Boulder 4, U of San Diego 3). **Avg SAT: CR** 503. **M** 535. **W** 525. **Tui '11-'12:** Day $15,000 (+$1200-1500). **Est 1956.** Nonprofit. Sem (Sept-June). **Assoc** WASC. Montclair's middle school program (grades 6-8), which is designed to meet the needs of early adolescents, stresses basic skills competency and includes time for group counseling and guidance activities and team planning among the teaching staff. The upper school program (grades 9-12) features small classes and displays increased flex-ibility due to an array of electives. Boys and girls satisfy the following community service requirements: 10 hours in grade 8, 20 hours per year in grades 9-12. A small boarding division serves international students only.

THE DORRIS-EATON SCHOOL   Day Coed Gr PS (Age 3)-8
Walnut Creek, CA 94595. 1847 Newell Ave.
Tel: 925-933-5225. Fax: 925-256-9710.
Other locations: 1286 Stone Valley Rd, Alamo 94507.
www.dorriseaton.com   E-mail: admissions@dorriseaton.com
    Gerald F. Ludden, Head. Nancee Watson, Dir. Trina M. Spencer, Gr 6-8 Adm; Jeannie Maoggi, Gr PS-5 Adm.

Pre-Prep. Gen Acad. Feat—Span Computers Studio_Art Music Violin. **Sports**—Basket. **B**: Football. **G**: Volley. **Selective adm:** 60/yr. Appl fee: $200. Appl due: Rolling. **Tests** ISEE. **Enr 425.** B 225. G 200. Avg class size: 18. Stud/fac: 12:1. Uniform. **Fac 39.** FT 39. **Grad '11—36.** Prep—15. (College Prep 6, Head-Royce 4, Cate 2, Bentley 2, Carondelet HS 1). **Tui '11-'12:** Day $19,370-19,870. **Est 1954.** Quar (Sept-June). Dorris-Eaton's curriculum empha-sizes critical-thinking skills and creativity at all grade levels. Spanish, computer science, art, music and physical education classes complement work in the core subjects. An after-school activities program includes team sports, band and performing arts offerings. The preschool occupies a separate campus in Alamo.

SEVEN HILLS SCHOOL   Day Coed Gr PS (Age 2)-8
Walnut Creek, CA 94598. 975 N San Carlos Dr.
Tel: 925-933-0666. Fax: 925-933-6271.
www.sevenhillsschool.org   E-mail: sgoldman@sevenhillsschool.org
    William H. Miller, Head (1992). BA, Univ of Notre Dame, MA, Univ of San Francisco. Susanne Goldman, Adm.

    Pre-Prep. Gen Acad. Feat—Lib_Skills Fr Span Computers Studio_Art Drama Music. **Supp**—Dev_Read Tut. **Sports**—Basket X-country Golf Lacrosse Track. G: Volley. **Selective adm:** 67/yr. Appl fee: $100. Appl due: Jan. Accepted: 44%. Yield: 76%. **Tests** CTP_4 ISEE MAT SSAT. **Enr 375.** Avg class size: 18. Stud/fac: 10:1. **Fac 39.** M 5/F 34. FT 31/PT 8. Adv deg: 33%. **Grad '08—38.** Prep—13. (Athenian 3, Bentley 3, College Prep 2, Robert Louis Stevenson-CA 1, Phillips Exeter 1). **Tui '12-'13:** Day $20,535-22,720 (+$2000). Aid: Need 71. **Est 1962.** Nonprofit. Sem (Sept-June). **Assoc** WASC. Seven Hills' well-equipped, nine-acre campus is adjacent to a wildlife refuge. The curriculum combines traditional and innovative methods, and a year-round enriched daycare program is available. Middle school pupils perform at least 10 hours of community service annually. Spanish instruction begins in kindergarten and continues through grade 5; students choose either Spanish or French in grades 6-8.

PACIFIC HILLS SCHOOL   Day Coed Gr 6-12
West Hollywood, CA 90069. 8628 Holloway Dr.
Tel: 310-276-3068. Fax: 310-657-3831.
www.phschool.org   E-mail: lbradshaw@phschool.org
    Peter Temes, Head (2010). BA, State Univ of New York, MFA, MA, MPhil, PhD, Columbia Univ. Lynne Bradshaw, Adm.

    Col Prep. AP (exams req'd)—Eng Span Calc Environ_Sci Physics Eur_Hist US_Hist US_Govt & Pol Art_Hist Studio_Art. **Feat**—Fr Lat Stats Anat Comp_Sci Econ Filmmaking Photog Theater_Arts Music Journ Speech. **Supp**—Tut. **Comp:** Laptop prgm Gr 6-12. Outdoor Ed. **Sports**—Basket X-country Soccer Track Volley. B: Baseball. G: Cheer Softball. **Selective adm:** Appl fee: $100. Appl due: Rolling. **Tests** ISEE. **Enr 180.** B 95. G 85. Elem 55. Sec 125. Intl 8%. Avg class size: 13. **Fac 23.** M 16/F 7. FT 19/PT 4. Wh 70%. Latino 17%. Blk 13%. Adv deg: 39%. **Grad '11—30.** Col—30. (UCLA 3, CA St U-Northridge 2, Mt St Mary's-CA 2, Amherst 1, NYU 1, Notre Dame 1). **Col Couns:** 1. **Tui '11-'12:** Day $22,950 (+$4000-5000). **Est 1983.** Nonprofit. Sem (Aug-June). **Assoc** WASC. The developmentally appropriate middle school program (grades 6-8) combines work in the core curriculum with semester-long art, study skills, computer science and theater arts classes. During the high school years, instructors teach theory, history and practical application in each subject. Beginning in grade 10, Advanced Placement courses provide additional challenge for qualified boys and girls. Students accumulate 30 hours of required community service in grades 9-12.

HERITAGE OAK PRIVATE EDUCATION   Day Coed Gr PS (Age 3)-8
Yorba Linda, CA 92886. 16971 Imperial Hwy.
Tel: 714-524-1350. Fax: 714-524-1352.
www.heritageoak.org   E-mail: pcygan@heritageoak.org
    Phyllis M. Cygan, Exec Dir (1992). Shawna Rhebergen, Adm.

    Gen Acad. Feat—Fr Span Computers Studio_Art Band. **Supp**—Tut. **Comp:** Laptop prgm Gr 6-8. **Sports**—Basket Soccer. G: Volley. **Selective adm:** 121/yr. Appl fee: $500. Appl due: Rolling. **Enr 515.** Avg class size: 20. Stud/fac: 20:1. **Fac 37.** M 4/F 33. FT 37. **Grad '09—51.** **Tui '11-'12:** Day $9636-12,617 (+$1089-1386). **Est 1966.** Quar (Sept-June). Established as Carden Country Day School, a small preschool program, Heritage Oak assumed its current name in 1995 after moving from its original eight-classroom facility in Fullerton. Instructors teach math, language and reading in small groups, and specialty teachers lead instruction in art, music, French, Spanish, computers, physical education and etiquette. The middle school program (grades 6-8) features semester-long elective courses and a laptop immersion program. Interscholastic sports begin in grade 4.

HAWAII

HOLY NATIVITY SCHOOL   Day Coed Gr PS (Age 3)-6

Honolulu, HI 96821. 5286 Kalanianaole Hwy.
Tel: 808-373-3232. Fax: 808-377-9618.
www.holynativityschool.org   E-mail: admissions@holynativityschool.org
   Timothy P. Spurrier, Head (2012). Kelly Goheen, Adm.

   Pre-Prep. Feat—Computers Relig Studio_Art Music. **Supp**—Tut. **Selective adm:** 41/yr.
Appl fee: $100. Appl due: Dec. **Tests** Stanford. **Enr 147.** B 76. G 71. Wh 44%. Blk 1%. Asian
50%. Other 5%. Avg class size: 18. Stud/fac: 9:1. Uniform. **Fac 23.** M 3/F 20. FT 21/PT 2. Adv
deg: 21%. **Grad '11—9.** Prep—8. (Punahou 4, Maryknoll 2, Mid-Pacific 1, La Pietra 1). **Tui
'11-'12:** Day $12,900. **Est 1949.** Nonprofit. Episcopal. Quar (Aug-June). **Assoc** WASC. Holy
Nativity's research-based, sequential curriculum features Orton-Gillingham language instruction and enrichment classes in art, music, computers, religious studies and physical education.
In addition to studying the core disciplines with a classroom teacher, boys and girls attend
weekly music, art, religion, computer and physical education classes with specialist teachers.
The school prepares a culturally and ethnically diverse student body for entrance into local
independent secondary schools.

LA PIETRA-HAWAII SCHOOL FOR GIRLS   Day Girls Gr 6-12

Honolulu, HI 96815. 2933 Poni Moi Rd.
Tel: 808-922-2744. Fax: 808-923-4514.
www.lapietra.edu   E-mail: info@lapietra.edu
   Mahina E. Hugo, Head. BA, MEd, Univ of Hawaii-Manoa. Sumoha Jani, Adm.

   Col Prep. AP—Eng Calc Bio US_Hist. **Feat**—British_Lit Creative_Writing Shakespeare
Chin Fr Japan Span Stats Anat & Physiol Environ_Sci Forensic_Sci Geol Marine_Bio/Sci Pro-
gramming Web_Design Psych HI_Stud Ethics Art_Hist Ceramics Photog Studio_Art Acting
Theater Chorus Music Speech. **Comp:** Laptop prgm Gr 6. **Sports**— G: Basket Bowl Cheer
X-country Golf Soccer Softball Swim Tennis Track Volley W_Polo Wrestling. **Selective adm:**
54/yr. Appl fee: $50. Appl due: Rolling. **Tests** SSAT TOEFL. **Enr 233.** Elem 88. Sec 145.
Stud/fac: 10:1. Uniform. **Fac 36.** M 4/F 32. FT 36. **Grad '11—25.** Col—25. **Avg SAT:** CR
553. M 562. **Col Couns:** 1. **Tui '12-'13:** Day $17,100. **Est 1964.** Nonprofit. Quar (Aug-May).
Assoc WASC. Located on the slopes of Diamond Head, La Pietra offers a college preparatory
program for girls that includes Advanced Placement courses. A strong fine arts program of art,
music and theater provides balance to the academic load; locally and nationally acclaimed artists enrich this program with seminars and master classes.

MARYKNOLL SCHOOL   Day Coed Gr PS (Age 4)-12

Honolulu, HI 96822. 1526 Alexander St.
Tel: 808-952-7330. Fax: 808-952-7331.
Other locations: 1722 Dole St, Honolulu 96822; 1402 Punahou St, Honolulu 96822.
www.maryknollschool.org   E-mail: admission@maryknollschool.org
   Perry K. Martin, Pres (2008). Lori A. K. Carlos, Adm.

   Col Prep. AP—Eng Calc Stats Bio Chem Physics US_Hist Econ. **Feat**—British_Lit Cre-
ative_Writing Mythology World_Lit Chin Fr Japan Span Hawaiian Forensic_Sci Asian_Hist
HI_Hist Govt Law Psych Sociol Philos World_Relig Graphic_Arts Studio_Art Ukulele Journ.
Sports—Basket Bowl X-country Sail Soccer Swim Tennis Track Volley W_Polo. B: Baseball
Football Wrestling. G: Cheer Softball. Activities: 35. **Selective adm:** 247/yr. Appl fee: $75.
Appl due: Dec. Accepted: 60%. Yield: 55%. **Tests** SSAT Stanford. **Enr 1400.** B 710. G 690.
Elem 820. Sec 580. Avg class size: 18. Stud/fac: 11:1. Uniform. **Fac 104.** M 35/F 69. FT
101/PT 3. Adv deg: 54%. **Grad '11—136.** Col—136. **Avg SAT:** CR 514. M 555. W 520. Avg
ACT: 22. **Col Couns: 3.** **Tui '12-'13:** Day $12,990-14,250 (+$200-400). **Est 1927.** Nonprofit.

Roman Catholic. (Aug-June). **Assoc** WASC. This Catholic school offers a college preparatory curriculum that features Advanced Placement courses and a world language immersion program. In addition to offering a selection of extracurricular activities, the school operates a mission experience in the Marshall Islands and student exchange programs in Japan, France, Spain and China. Seniors complete a weeklong project in March. The school occupies seven buildings on two campuses, with grades PS-8 on Dole Street and the high school three blocks away on Punahou Street.

SACRED HEARTS ACADEMY   Day Girls Gr PS (Age 3)-12
Honolulu, HI 96816. 3253 Waialae Ave.
Tel: 808-734-5058. Fax: 808-737-7867.
www.sacredhearts.org   E-mail: info@sacredhearts.org
  Betty White, Head. BA, Mary Washington College, MA, College of William and Mary, MA, Univ of Hawaii-Manoa. Karen Muramoto, Adm.
  Col Prep. AP (exams req'd)—Eng Calc US_Hist Econ Art_Hist. **Feat**—Chin Japan Span Hawaiian Stats Physiol Computers Programming Govt Asian_Stud World_Relig Ceramics Studio_Art Video_Production Band Chorus Accounting Journ. **Supp**—ESL Rev Tut. **Sports**— G: Basket Bowl X-country Golf Sail Soccer Softball Swim Tennis Track Volley W_Polo. Activities: 26. **Selective adm (Gr PS-11):** 285/yr. Appl fee: $35. Appl due: Feb. Accepted: 40%. Yield: 60%. **Tests** CEEB CTP_4 IQ SSAT. **Enr 1150.** Elem 400. Sec 750. Avg class size: 25. Uniform. **Fac 84.** M 6/F 78. FT 78/PT 6. Adv deg: 38%. **Grad '07—146.** Col—146. **Avg SAT:** CR 505. M 523. Avg ACT: 21. **Col Couns:** 1. Alum donors: 15%. **Tui '12-'13:** Day $8714-11,607 (+$1000). **Est 1909.** Nonprofit. Roman Catholic (70% practice). Sem (Aug-May). **Assoc** WASC. The academy offers Advanced Placement courses as part of a varied college preparatory program. Each girl in grades 7-12 contributes at least 25 hours of required community service per year.

SAINT FRANCIS SCHOOL   Day Coed Gr PS (Age 2)-12
Honolulu, HI 96822. 2707 Pamoa Rd.
Tel: 808-988-4111. Fax: 808-988-5497.
www.stfrancis-oahu.org   E-mail: kcurry@stfrancis-oahu.org
  Sr. Joan of Arc Souza, Head. BA, St Joseph's College (IN), MA, La Salle Univ. Karen A. Curry, Adm.
  Col Prep. AP (exams req'd; 62 taken)—Eng Span Calc Bio US_Hist US_Govt & Pol. **Feat**—Creative_Writing ASL Chin Japan Programming Web_Design HI_Hist World_Relig Ceramics Filmmaking Drama Band Chorus Journ Photojourn JROTC. **Supp**—Dev_Read ESL Makeup Rem_Math Rem_Read Rev Tut. **Comp:** Comp/Stud: 1:10. Outdoor Ed. **Sports**— Basket Bowl X-country Golf Tennis Track Wrestling. B: Baseball Football. G: Cheer Soccer Softball Swim Volley. **Selective adm:** 152/yr. Appl fee: $40. Appl due: Rolling. Accepted: 60%. Yield: 70%. **Tests** SSAT. **Enr 497.** B 172. G 325. Elem 218. Sec 279. Avg class size: 20. Uniform. **Fac 51.** M 15/F 36. FT 39/PT 12. Wh 77%. Latino 2%. Asian 20%. Other 1%. Adv deg: 45%. **Grad '11—41.** Col—41. Avg ACT: 23. **Col Couns:** 1. Alum donors: 7%. **Tui '11-'12:** Day $6300-9400 (+$600). Aid: Merit ($173,000). Need ($317,000). **Est 1924.** Nonprofit. Roman Catholic. Sem (July-June). **Assoc** WASC. St. Francis offers an unusual year-round program that begins in late July and ends in early June. In addition to Christmas and summer vacations, the school schedules two-week intersessions in both fall and spring that enable boys and girls to either relax or prepare for the next quarter by participating in special workshops for enrichment or academic credit. A Great Books seminar, an honors program and AP classes are available during the high school years. Students in grades 9-12 perform 100 compulsory hours of community service.

ISLAND SCHOOL   Day Coed Gr PS (Age 4)-12
Lihue, HI 96766. 3-1875 Kaumualii Hwy.
Tel: 808-246-0233. Fax: 808-245-6053.
www.ischool.org   E-mail: info@ischool.org
   Robert Springer, Head (1997). BA, Occidental College, MA, Univ of the Americas
(Mexico). Sean Magoun, Adm.
   Col Prep. Feat—British_Lit Creative_Writing Span Computers Comp_Design Ceramics
Fine_Arts Performing_Arts Drama. **Supp**—Tut. **Sports**—Basket X-country Golf Soccer Swim
Tennis Track. G: Volley. **Selective adm:** 95/yr. Appl fee: $75. Appl due: Rolling. Accepted:
80%. **Tests** CEEB Stanford. **Enr 365.** Wh 50%. Latino 3%. Blk 1%. Native Am 1%. Asian
33%. Other 12%. Avg class size: 18. **Fac 41.** M 13/F 28. FT 41. **Grad '09—22.** Col—22. **Avg
SAT:** CR/M 1108. **Tui '11-'12:** Day $11,500-12,100 (+$800). Aid: Need 160 ($550,000). **Est
1977.** Nonprofit. Tri (Aug-May). **Assoc** WASC. Physical education, music, drama, computer,
Spanish, Hawaiian studies and art classes supplement the academic program at this school,
which is located on the island of Kauai.

LANAKILA BAPTIST SCHOOLS   Day Coed Gr K-12
Waipahu, HI 96797. 94-1250 Waipahu St.
Tel: 808-677-0731. Fax: 808-677-0733.
Other locations: 91-1219 Renton Rd, Ewa 96706.
www.lanakilabaptist.org   E-mail: lanakilabaptist@hotmail.com
   Steven C. Wygle, Pres. BA, Baptist Bible College, MBA, PhD, California Coast Univ.
   Col Prep. Gen Acad. Feat—Span. **Supp**—Makeup Rev Tut. **Sports**—Basket X-country
Golf Swim Track Volley. B: Baseball. **Somewhat selective adm:** Appl fee: $25. Appl due:
Aug. Accepted: 90%. **Tests** IQ SSAT Stanford. **Enr 250.** Elem 160. Sec 90. Avg class size: 19.
Uniform. **Fac 23.** M 7/F 16. FT 17/PT 6. Adv deg: 8%. **Grad '08—18.** Col—13. **Avg SAT:**
CR/M 1100. **Tui '10-'11:** Day $5800-6300 (+$250). **Est 1969.** Nonprofit. Baptist. Sem (Aug-
May). The elementary and junior/senior high schools present an academic curriculum with a
Scriptural foundation. The senior high offers both college preparatory and general academic
programs, and all students study the Bible. The junior/senior high is located on Renton Road
in Ewa (808-681-3146).

OREGON

VALLEY CATHOLIC SCHOOL   Day Coed Gr PS (Age 2)-12
Beaverton, OR 97007. 4275 SW 148th Ave.
Tel: 503-644-3745. Fax: 503-646-4054.
Other locations: 4420 SW St Mary's Dr, Beaverton 97007; 4450 SW St Mary's Dr, Beaver-
ton 97007.
www.valleycatholic.org   E-mail: rthomas@ssmo.org
   Bob Weber, Pres. BA, Univ of Oregon, MAT, Pacific Univ. Claudia Thomas, Adm.
   Col Prep. AP (152 exams taken, 80% 3+)—Eng Calc Comp_Sci Bio Chem Physics
Studio_Art Music_Theory. **Feat**—Creative_Writing Fr Japan Span Environ_Sci Civil_War
Vietnam_War WWII Econ Psych Sociol Ethics World_Relig Fine_Arts Drama Band Chorus
Orchestra Jazz_Band Health. **Supp**—ESL Tut. **Sports**—Basket X-country Golf Soccer Swim
Tennis Track. B: Baseball Football. G: Softball Volley. Activities: 9. **Selective adm:** 145/yr.
Appl fee: $50. **Tests** CEEB TOEFL. **Enr 716.** Intl 5%. Avg class size: 20. Stud/fac: 14:1.
Uniform. **Fac 55.** Adv deg: 45%. **Grad '11—79.** Col—77. **Avg SAT:** CR 569. M 554. W 540.
Col Couns: 1. **Tui '12-'13:** Day $6325-10,900 (+$200-345). **Est 1902.** Nonprofit. Roman
Catholic. Sem (Sept-June). **Assoc** NWAC. Located on a 42-acre campus in Willamette Valley,
Valley Catholic conducts a college preparatory program that features particularly strong pro-
grams in the fine arts, international studies and athletics. Students perform 15 hours of annual

community service in designated areas. The school effected a 2008 merger with St. Mary of the Valley School, in the process adding grades PS-6. Grades K-8 are hosted near the early learning center on Southwest St. Mary's Drive, while the high school occupies a campus on Southwest 148th Avenue.

MILO ADVENTIST ACADEMY
Bdg & Day
Coed Gr 9-12

Days Creek, OR 97429. 324 Milo Dr, PO Box 278.
Tel: 541-825-3200. Fax: 541-825-3723.
www.miloacademy.net   E-mail: miloinfo@miloacademy.org
 Randy Bovee, Prin (2000). BA, Walla Walla College, MS, Univ of Oregon.

 Col Prep. AP (exams req'd)—Eng. **Feat**—British_Lit Lat Span Calc Anat & Physiol Geol Web_Design Econ Govt Global_Stud Bible Photog Studio_Art Chorus Handbells Woodworking. **Supp**—ESL. **Sports**—Basket Soccer. B: Baseball. G: Softball Volley. **Selective adm:** Appl fee: $25. Appl due: Rolling. **Tests** TOEFL. **Enr 103.** Avg class size: 20. **Fac 13.** M 8/F 5. FT 9/PT 4. **Grad '07—36.** Col—28. **Avg SAT:** CR/M 1097. **Avg ACT:** 23. **Tui '11-'12:** Bdg $14,990-15,015. Day $8620. Seventh-day Adventist $7750. **Est 1954.** Seventh-day Adventist. Quar (Aug-May). **Assoc** NWAC. Bible classes, fine arts and technology electives complement MAA's college preparatory curriculum, which also includes advanced classes in the core subjects. A student work program emphasizes strong work habits and service.

OAK HILL SCHOOL
Day Coed Gr K-12

Eugene, OR 97405. 86397 Eldon Schafer Dr.
Tel: 541-744-0954. Fax: 541-741-6968.
www.oakhillschool.net   E-mail: admission@oakhillschool.net
 Elliott Grey, Head (2005). MBA, Marylhurst Univ. Lauren Moody, Adm.

 Col Prep. AP—Eng Fr Lat Span Calc Bio Chem Environ_Sci Physics Eur_Hist US_Hist Econ US_Govt & Pol Studio_Art Music_Theory. **Feat**—Creative_Writing Chin Stats Ecol Comp_Sci Web_Design Psych World_Relig Drawing Film Painting Sculpt Theater_Arts Music Dance Finance Journ Speech. **Supp**—ESL Tut. **Comp:** Comp/Stud: 1:3 (1:1 Laptop prgm Gr 11-12). **Sports**—Basket X-country Golf Track Volley. **Somewhat selective adm:** 29/yr. Appl fee: $100. Appl due: Feb. Accepted: 95%. Yield: 78%. **Tests** TOEFL. **Enr 115.** B 55. G 60. Elem 81. Sec 34. Wh 75%. Latino 8%. Blk 6%. Native Am 1%. Asian 7%. Other 3%. Intl 27%. Avg class size: 10. **Fac 22.** M 6/F 16. FT 8/PT 14. Wh 92%. Latino 6%. Asian 2%. **Grad '09—12.** Col—12. (Lane CC 2, Dartmouth 1, Pitzer 1, GA Inst of Tech 1, Berklee Col of Music 1, U of San Francisco 1). **Avg SAT:** CR 660. M 680. W 710. Alum donors: 2%. **Tui '10-'11:** Day $12,650-15,000. Aid: Merit 3 ($14,000). Need 42 ($340,000). **Est 1994.** Nonprofit. Sem (Sept-June). **Assoc** NWAC. Oak Hill's full elementary and secondary program places emphasis upon higher-order thinking skills, sound study habits and organizational skills, and individual student interests. Students perform 70 hours of required community service in grades 9-12. For an additional fee, the school offers a home stay option to international pupils.

NESKOWIN VALLEY SCHOOL
Day Coed Gr PS (Age 3)-8

Neskowin, OR 97149. 10005 Slab Creek Rd.
Tel: 503-392-3124. Fax: 503-392-3928.
www.neskowinvalleyschool.com   E-mail: nvs@oregoncoast.com
 Julie Fiedler, Head (2009). BA, Univ of Puget Sound, MA, Univ of Washington.

 Gen Acad. Feat—Chin Studio_Art Drama Chorus Music Gardening. **Comp:** Comp/Stud: 1:8. **Sports**—Soccer Swim Tennis. **Nonselective adm:** 11/yr. Appl fee: $50. Appl due: Rolling. **Enr 45.** B 23. G 22. Wh 92%. Latino 4%. Blk 4%. Avg class size: 10. **Fac 6.** M 2/F 4. FT 5/PT 1. Wh 100%. Adv deg: 33%. **Grad '11—3.** Alum donors: 10%. **Tui '12-'13:** Day $6900-7200 (+$60). Aid: Need 22 ($60,000). **Est 1972.** Nonprofit. (Sept-June). **Assoc** NWAC. NVS was established to provide a personally tailored education for elementary students. The curriculum is designed around core subjects, and special emphasis is placed on the arts and environmental studies. The school's rural campus on the Oregon coast provides opportunities for ecological field study.

CENTRAL CATHOLIC HIGH SCHOOL   Day Coed Gr 9-12
Portland, OR 97214. 2401 SE Stark St.
Tel: 503-235-3138. Fax: 503-233-0073.
www.centralcatholichigh.org   E-mail: pomalley@centralcatholichigh.org
     John Harrington, Pres. John Garrow, Prin. Paul O'Malley, Adm.

     Col Prep. AP (exams req'd; 259 taken, 73% 3+)—Eng Span Calc Chem Physics US_Hist US_Govt & Pol. **Feat**—Creative_Writing Playwriting Fr Japan Stats Anat & Physiol Marine_ Bio/Sci Sports_Med Programming Web_Design Econ Psych Sociol Global_Stud Relig Ceramics Photog Studio_Art Stained_Glass Acting Theater_Arts Journ Speech. **Sports**—Basket X-country Golf Soccer Swim Tennis. B: Baseball Football Softball. G: Cheer Track Volley. **Selective adm:** 225/yr. Appl fee: $50. Appl due: Jan. **Enr 830.** B 473. G 357. Wh 71%. Latino 4%. Blk 6%. Asian 5%. Other 14%. Avg class size: 23. Stud/fac: 15:1. **Fac 55.** Adv deg: 76%. **Grad '08—208.** Col—197. **Avg SAT:** CR 544. M 540. W 532. Avg ACT: 24. **Col Couns:** 1. **Tui '11-'12:** Day $10,300 (+$520-680). Aid: Need ($1,500,000). **Est 1939.** Nonprofit. Roman Catholic (75% practice). Sem (Sept-June). **Assoc** NWAC. Central Catholic's traditional curriculum includes a selection of Advanced Placement classes. Religion course work combines the study of Catholic doctrine and scriptures with an examination of other religious traditions. Boys and girls accumulate at least 80 hours of Christian service over their four years at the school.

THE INTERNATIONAL SCHOOL   Day Coed Gr PS (Age 3)-5
Portland, OR 97201. 025 SW Sherman St.
Tel: 503-226-2496. Fax: 503-525-0142.
www.intlschool.org   E-mail: admissions@intlschool.org
     Alfonso Orsini, Head (2009). BA, Hamilton College, MA, Long Island Univ, EdD, Columbia Univ. Jan Williams, Adm.

     Pre-Prep. Gen Acad. IB PYP. Bilingual (Chin Japan Span). Feat—Chin Japan Span Studio_Art Music. **Nonselective adm (Gr PS-4):** 110/yr. Appl fee: $50. Appl due: Rolling. **Enr 465.** Wh 49%. Latino 3%. Blk 4%. Native Am 1%. Asian 25%. Other 18%. Avg class size: 13. Stud/fac: 7:1. **Fac 60. Grad '11—25.** Prep—11. (Fr Amer Intl Sch-OR 5, Northwest Acad 4, OR Episcopal 1). **Tui '12-'13:** Day $12,900 (+$300). Aid: Need 80 ($237,325). **Est 1990.** Nonprofit. Sem (Sept-June). **Assoc** NWAC. This unusual elementary school offers an American-style curriculum taught by means of total-immersion language programs in Spanish, Japanese and Chinese, making it one of the few schools in the US that offers immersion tracks in more than one language. Children may enroll in both the preschool and kindergarten classes with no prior knowledge of the target language; students entering TIS after kindergarten must display proficiency in the language of immersion. Children are encouraged to remain at the school through grade 5.

JESUIT HIGH SCHOOL   Day Coed Gr 9-12
Portland, OR 97225. 9000 SW Beaverton-Hillsdale Hwy.
Tel: 503-292-2663. Fax: 503-291-5464.
www.jesuitportland.org   E-mail: pchambers@jesuitportland.org
     John J. Gladstone, Pres (2005). Sandra L. Satterberg, Prin. Erin DeKlotz, Adm.

     Col Prep. AP (422 exams taken, 90% 3+)—Eng Fr Span Calc Bio Chem Physics US_Hist Comp_Govt & Pol Econ. **Feat**—Creative_Writing Chin Stats Linear_Algebra Multivariable_ Calc Anat & Physiol Intl_Stud Comp_Relig Ethics Theol Photog Studio_Art Drama Band Chorus Journ. **Supp**—Rem_Math Rev Tut. **Sports**—Basket X-country Golf Lacrosse Ski Soccer Swim Tennis Track. B: Baseball Football. G: Softball Volley. **Selective adm (Gr 9-**

11): 312/yr. Appl fee: $50. Accepted: 50%. **Tests** HSPT. **Enr 1260.** B 640. G 620. Nonwhite 23%. Avg class size: 24. Stud/fac: 18:1. Casual dress. **Fac 94.** Adv deg: 68%. **Grad '11—286.** Col—281. **Avg SAT:** CR 595. M 603. W 589. Avg ACT: 27.4. **Tui '12-'13:** Day $11,525 (+$500). Aid: Need ($2,015,000). **Est 1956.** Nonprofit. Roman Catholic (76% practice). Sem (Sept-June). **Assoc** NWAC. Jesuit features accelerated and Advanced Placement courses in most major disciplines. Students perform 65 hours of required community service over four years.

NORTHWEST ACADEMY   Day Coed Gr 6-12
Portland, OR 97205. 1130 SW Main St.
Tel: 503-223-3367. Fax: 503-402-1043.
www.nwacademy.org   E-mail: lettinger@nwacademy.org
    Mary Vinton Folberg, Head (1997). BA, San Francisco State Univ. Lainie Ettinger, Adm.

    Col Prep. Perform_Arts Visual_Arts. Feat—Creative_Writing Chin Fr Span Ecol Geol Philos Film Photog Sculpt Visual_Arts Theater Music Dance. **Dual enr:** Portland St. **Selective adm (Gr 6-11):** 35/yr. Appl fee: $100. Appl due: Feb. **Enr 121.** B 45. G 76. Elem 62. Sec 59. Avg class size: 15. Stud/fac: 10:1. **Fac 31.** M 17/F 14. FT 8/PT 23. Adv deg: 22%. **Grad '10—19.** Col—19. (Georgetown 1, Emerson 1, Worcester Polytech 1, CA Col of the Arts 1, Pitzer 1). **Avg SAT:** CR 655. M 592. W 617. **Col Couns:** 1. **Tui '11-'12:** Day $16,250-18,250 (+$300). Aid: Need 23 ($220,000). **Est 1997.** Nonprofit. Sem (Sept-June). **Assoc** NWAC. The academy's college preparatory curriculum emphasizes creative thinking and the arts. Middle school students (grades 6-8) develop basic skills in English, social studies, math and science, and choose from a variety of arts electives. The interdisciplinary high school program (grades 9-12) combines studies in language and literature with history, economics, philosophy and other subjects. Foreign languages offered typically include French, Spanish and Chinese. Conservatory-style arts courses, which take place both during and after school, include varied offerings in the visual, performing, media and literary arts. High schoolers complete 30 hours of required community service prior to graduation.

ST. MARY'S ACADEMY   Day Girls Gr 9-12
Portland, OR 97201. 1615 SW 5th Ave.
Tel: 503-228-8306. Fax: 503-223-0995.
www.stmaryspdx.org   E-mail: admissions@stmaryspdx.org
    Christina Friedhoff, Pres (1992). BS, Lewis and Clark College. Patricia Barr, Prin. BA, Portland State Univ, MA, Lewis and Clark College. Lauren A. Kawa, Adm.

    Col Prep. AP (187 exams taken, 81% 3+)—Eng Fr Span Calc US_Hist US_Govt & Pol Studio_Art. **Feat**—Creative_Writing Lat Stats Comp_Sci Web_Design Econ Relig Ceramics Drawing Filmmaking Graphic_Arts Photog Acting Theater_Arts Chorus Music_Theory Dance Bus Journ. **Supp**—Tut. **Comp:** Comp/Stud: 1:2. **Dual enr:** Portland St. **Sports—** G: Basket X-country Golf Lacrosse Ski Soccer Swim Tennis Track Volley. Activities: 30. **Somewhat selective adm:** 186/yr. Appl fee: $50. Appl due: Jan. Accepted: 90%. Yield: 62%. **Tests** HSPT TOEFL. **Enr 640.** G 600. Wh 68%. Latino 7%. Blk 8%. Native Am 1%. Asian 10%. Other 6%. Avg class size: 20. Stud/fac: 16:1. **Fac 51.** M 10/F 41. FT 42/PT 9. Wh 94%. Latino 4%. Blk 2%. Adv deg: 82%. **Grad '11—129.** Col—128. (U of OR 13, Seattle U 8, U of Portland 6, Gonzaga 5, Whitman 5, NYU 4). **Avg SAT:** CR 627. M 588. W 619. **Mid 50% SAT:** CR 560-700. M 540-630. W 560-690. Avg ACT: 26.8. Mid 50% ACT: 24-29. **Col Couns:** 2. Alum donors: 20%. **Tui '11-'12:** Day $10,375 (+$100). Aid: Merit 67. Need 250 ($1,100,000). **Est 1859.** Nonprofit. Roman Catholic (48% practice). Sem (Sept-June). **Assoc** NWAC. Oregon's oldest continuously operating independent school, St. Mary's maintains a particularly strong religion curriculum that includes campus ministry, retreats and service opportunities. In addition, the college preparatory program addresses human development, Catholic theology, world religions, ethics and social justice. The school's downtown location places it within several blocks of Portland State University, Portland Art Museum and the Portland Center for the Performing Arts, among other cultural and educational institutions.

BLANCHET CATHOLIC SCHOOL   Day Coed Gr 6-12
Salem, OR 97301. 4373 Market St NE.
Tel: 503-391-2639. Fax: 503-399-1259.
www.blanchetcatholicschool.com   E-mail: info@blanchetcatholicschool.com
    Charles E. Lee, Pres (1997). BA, Univ of Washington, MA, Seattle Univ. Anthony Guevara, Prin. BA, Humboldt State Univ, MEd, Univ of San Francisco. Cathleen McClaughry, Adm.

    Col Prep. AP (exams req'd)—Eng US_Hist. **Feat**—Fr Span Calc Anat & Physiol Psych Sociol Ceramics Fine_Arts Photog Studio_Art Drama Band Chorus Orchestra Finance Marketing Public_Speak. **Supp**—ESL Tut. **Comp:** Comp/Stud: 1:9. **Dual enr:** Chemeketa CC. **Sports**—Basket X-country Golf Soccer Swim Tennis Track. B: Baseball Football. G: Softball Volley. Activities: 13. **Somewhat selective adm:** 90/yr. Appl fee: $100. Appl due: Feb. Accepted: 95%. Yield: 99%. **Enr 372.** B 185. G 187. Elem 116. Sec 256. Wh 72%. Latino 9%. Blk 1%. Native Am 1%. Asian 7%. Other 10%. Avg class size: 19. Stud/fac: 17:1. Casual dress. **Fac 25.** M 8/F 17. Wh 96%. Latino 4%. Adv deg: 80%. **Grad '11—65.** Col—63. **Avg SAT:** CR 535. M 525. W 521. Avg ACT: 24.2. **Col Couns:** 1. Alum donors: 15%. **Tui '12-'13:** Day $5570-7450 (+$525). Aid: Merit 27 ($34,300). Need 117 ($284,500). **Est 1995.** Nonprofit. Roman Catholic (70% practice). Sem (Sept-June). **Assoc** NWAC. Blanchet's curriculum includes religion and foreign language requirements, as well as elective options in computers, art and drama. Seventh graders take six weeks of music, art, study skills and keyboarding courses in their first semester. Students in grades 7 and 8 perform 10 hours of compulsory community service per year, while boys and girls in grades 9-12 engage in 20 service hours annually.

WESTERN MENNONITE SCHOOL   Bdg Coed Gr 9-12
Salem, OR 97304. 9045 Wallace Rd NW.   Day Coed 6-12
Tel: 503-363-2000. Fax: 503-370-9455.
www.westernmennoniteschool.org   E-mail: rmartin@westernmennoniteschool.org
    Darrel J. Camp, Prin. BS, MS, Western Oregon Univ. Rich Martin, Adm.

    Col Prep. Gen Acad. Feat—Span Calc Anat & Physiol Programming Web_Design Econ Govt Psych Sociol Bible Ceramics Photog Drama Theater_Arts Chorus Music Accounting Woodworking. **Supp**—ESL Tut. Outdoor Ed. **Sports**—Basket Soccer. B: Baseball X-country. G: Softball Volley. **Somewhat selective adm:** 62/yr. Bdg 10. Day 52. Appl fee: $50. Appl due: Aug. Accepted: 90%. Yield: 99%. **Tests** TOEFL. **Enr 250.** B 90. G 160. Bdg 25. Day 225. Intl 8%. Avg class size: 20. Stud/fac: 16:1. Casual dress. **Fac 26.** M 12/F 14. FT 22/PT 4. Adv deg: 46%. **Grad '10—51.** Col—48. **Avg SAT:** CR 563. M 540. W 528. **Col Couns:** 2. **Tui '11-'12:** Bdg $13,701 (+$550). 5-Day Bdg $12,018 (+$550). Day $6645-7970 (+$550). Intl Bdg $22,925 (+$550). Aid: Need 108. **Est 1945.** Nonprofit. Mennonite (18% practice). Sem (Aug-June). **Assoc** NWAC. Advanced courses at WMS are conducted in math, science, computers and foreign language. All students attend chapel services and participate in group community service projects. The school schedules occasional academic field trips, and travel opportunities are available through the choir program and during a weeklong mini-term that occurs at the end of second semester.

DELPHIAN SCHOOL   Bdg Coed Gr 3-12
Sheridan, OR 97378. 20950 SW Rock Creek Rd.   Day Coed K-12
Tel: 503-843-3521, 800-626-6610. Fax: 503-843-4158.
www.delphian.org   E-mail: info@delphian.org
    Rosemary Didear, Head (1999). BA, Barnard College.

    Col Prep. AP—Eng Calc Econ. **Feat**—Fr Span Genetics Comp_Sci Civics Ethics World_Relig Art_Hist Music_Hist Bus Study_Skills. **Supp**—Dev_Read ESL Makeup Rem_Math Rem_Read Rev. **Comp:** Comp/Stud: 1:2.7. **Sports (req'd)**—Basket. B: Baseball Soccer. G: Volley. **Selective adm:** 60/yr. Appl fee: $100. Appl due: Rolling. **Tests** IQ SSAT Stanford. **Enr 272.** Bdg 231. Day 41. Wh 85%. Latino 4%. Asian 10%. Other 1%. Intl 21%. Avg class size: 17. Stud/fac: 7:1. Casual dress. **Fac 56.** M 22/F 34. FT 46/PT 10. In Dorms 15. **Grad**

'09—30. Col—28. **Avg SAT:** CR/M/W 1779. **Tui '10-'11:** Bdg $36,770-38,890 (+$1650). Day $12,245-21,220 (+$1100). **Est 1976.** Nonprofit. Tri (Sept-June). Delphian emphasizes high academic standards and integrity. The school uses study methods developed by L. Ron Hubbard. Individualized programs of study, coupled with the drilling of math basics and a high quantity of reading, lead rapidly to the ability to do independent research. Facilities are available for advanced work in all subject areas.

WASHINGTON

COLUMBIA ADVENTIST ACADEMY   Day Coed Gr 9-12
Battle Ground, WA 98604. 11100 NE 189th St.
Tel: 360-687-3161. Fax: 360-687-9856.
www.caaschool.org   E-mail: hendde@caaschool.org
   Matthew Butte, Prin. BA, Newbold College (England), MEd, Boston College.

   Col Prep. Gen Acad. AP (exams req'd; 8 taken, 75% 3+)—Eng Calc. **Feat**—Span Comp_Sci Govt Relig Studio_Art Music Accounting. **Supp**—Tut. **Sports**—Basket. B: Soccer. G: Volley. **Nonselective adm:** 28/yr. Appl due: Aug. Accepted: 100%. Yield: 99%. **Enr 108.** Wh 94%. Latino 6%. Avg class size: 20. **Fac 16.** M 7/F 9. FT 11/PT 5. Wh 99%. Latino 1%. Adv deg: 43%. **Grad '08—27.** Col—26. **Avg SAT:** CR/M 1100. Avg ACT: 25. **Col Couns:** 1. Alum donors: 27%. **Tui '11-'12:** Day $9115 (+$350-500). Parishioners $8115 (+$350-500). **Est 1903.** Nonprofit. Seventh-day Adventist (93% practice). Sem (Aug-June). **Assoc** NWAC. To meet varying learning needs, CAA offers three diplomas: a general high school diploma program; a vocational program that operates in conjunction with Clark County Skills Center; and a college prep diploma that carries additional math, science and foreign language requirements. Thrice-weekly chapel services, monthly community service activities, semiannual prayer weeks, mission trips, and Bible study and prayer groups are important elements of school life.

THE LITTLE SCHOOL   Day Coed Gr PS (Age 3)-6
Bellevue, WA 98004. 2812 116th Ave NE.
Tel: 425-827-4609. Fax: 425-827-3814.
www.thelittleschool.org   E-mail: info@thelittleschool.org
   Peter Berner-Hays, Head (2010). MEd, Lesley College, MEd, Univ of Washington. Barb Cartmell, Adm.

   Gen Acad. Feat—Span Drama Music Outdoor_Ed. **Supp**—Rem_Read Tut. **Comp:** Comp/Stud: 1:2.9. **Selective adm:** 57/yr. Appl fee: $75. Appl due: Feb. **Enr 165.** Wh 83%. Latino 4%. Blk 3%. Asian 8%. Other 2%. Avg class size: 13. Stud/fac: 6:1. **Fac 18.** M 4/F 14. FT 11/PT 7. Wh 79%. Latino 6%. Blk 13%. Asian 2%. Adv deg: 27%. **Grad '07—12.** Prep—4. (U Prep 2, Overlake 1, Northwest Sch 1). Alum donors: 3%. **Tui '11-'12:** Day $16,900 (+$200). Aid: Need 20 ($200,000). **Est 1959.** Nonprofit. (Sept-June). **Assoc** NWAC. The school's developmentally based curriculum, which includes Spanish, world cultures and creative movement, features a variety of hands-on learning experiences in art, music and science. Children learn in small, multi-age classes. Field trips supplement academic work.

SPRING STREET INTERNATIONAL SCHOOL   Day Coed Gr 6-12
Friday Harbor, WA 98250. 505 Spring St.
Tel: 360-378-6393. Fax: 360-378-4220.
www.springstreet.org   E-mail: jriley@springstreet.org
   Louis O'Prussack, Head (2008). BA, Oberlin College, MA, Columbia Univ. Jerome Riley, Adm.

   Col Prep. AP—Calc Environ_Sci Eur_Hist Human_Geog Psych US_Govt & Pol Studio_

Art. **Feat**—Creative_Writing Shakespeare Span Biotech Philos World_Relig Art_Hist Film Photog Drama Music. **Somewhat selective adm (Gr 6-11):** 21/yr. Appl fee: $0. Appl due: Apr. Accepted: 90%. Yield: 85%. **Enr 76.** B 38. G 38. Intl 16%. Stud/fac: 8:1. **Fac 13.** FT 7/PT 6. **Tui '12-'13:** Day $12,000 (+$500). **Est 1995.** Nonprofit. Sem (Sept-June). **Assoc** NWAC. This experiential school combines college preparation with travel and community service opportunities. As part of the curriculum, middle schoolers (grades 6-8) perform 25 hours of annual service and also travel in Washington State and to New York City and Washington, DC, while high schoolers (grades 9-12) spend four to eight weeks studying and doing service work in remote villages in Asia or Latin America. A four-week winterim in the middle school enables boys and girls to take enrichment courses in such areas as first aid, cooking, Chinese and technology. A small boarding program serves international students.

ST. THOMAS SCHOOL   Day Coed Gr PS (Age 2)-7
Medina, WA 98039. 8300 NE 12th St.
Tel: 425-454-5880. Fax: 425-454-1921.
www.stthomasschool.org   E-mail: info@stthomasschool.org
   Kirk M. Wheeler, Head (2005). BA, Univ of Northern Colorado, MA, Framingham State College, EdD, Univ of Minnesota-Twin Cities. Lyn-Felice Calvin, Adm.
   Pre-Prep. Feat—Lib_Skills Lat Span Computers Studio_Art Music. **Supp**—Tut. **Comp:** Comp/Stud: 1:2 (1:1 Laptop prgm Gr 4-6). **Selective adm:** 71/yr. Appl fee: $60. Appl due: Jan. Accepted: 70%. Yield: 80%. **Tests** ISEE. **Enr 284.** B 140. G 144. Wh 77%. Latino 1%. Blk 3%. Asian 9%. Other 10%. Avg class size: 16. Stud/fac: 8:1. Uniform. **Fac 33.** M 6/F 27. FT 25/PT 8. Wh 85%. Latino 3%. Blk 3%. Asian 6%. Other 3%. Adv deg: 54%. **Grad '11—8.** Prep—7. (Overlake 3, Lakeside Sch 2, Eastside Catholic 2). Alum donors: 1%. **Tui '12-'13:** Day $21,930 (+$300). Aid: Need 29 ($293,613). **Est 1951.** Nonprofit. Tri (Sept-June). **Assoc** NWAC. St. Thomas provides a solid foundation in basic skills of literacy and computation, while also emphasizing inquiry and hands-on math and science course work. The curriculum comprises social sciences, technology, music, art, Spanish, Latin and language arts. Daily chapel incorporates world religions and provides a forum for public speaking.

THE BEAR CREEK SCHOOL   Day Coed Gr PS (Age 3)-12
Redmond, WA 98053. 8905 208th Ave NE.
Tel: 425-898-1720. Fax: 425-898-1430.
Other locations: 19315 NE 95th St, Redmond 98053.
www.tbcs.org   E-mail: info@tbcs.org
   Patrick Carruth, Pres (2007). BA, Univ of Georgia, MA, Univ of Memphis. Christie Hazeltine, Adm.
   Col Prep. AP (exams req'd; 171 taken, 84% 3+)—Eng Calc Stats Bio Chem Physics Eur_Hist US_Hist. **Feat**—British_Lit World_Lit Fr Lat Span Bible Logic Relig Art_Hist Drawing Painting Photog Sculpt Drama Music_Theory Bus Debate Journ Culinary_Arts. **Supp**—ESL Tut. Outdoor Ed. **Sports**—Basket X-country Golf Soccer Tennis Track. B: Baseball. G: Volley. Activities: 20. **Selective adm (Gr PS-11):** 171/yr. Appl fee: $75. Appl due: Rolling. Accepted: 73%. Yield: 78%. **Tests** ISEE Stanford TOEFL. **Enr 756.** B 383. G 373. Elem 542. Sec 214. Wh 76%. Latino 2%. Blk 2%. Asian 16%. Other 4%. Avg class size: 18. Stud/fac: 8:1. Uniform. **Fac 86.** M 22/F 64. FT 86. Adv deg: 47%. **Grad '10—47.** Col—47. **Avg SAT:** CR 637. M 623. W 624. **Tui '11-'12:** Day $15,490-17,340 (+$1050-1250). Aid: Merit 12 ($46,500). Need 75 ($468,900). **Est 1988.** Nonprofit. Nondenom Christian. Quar (Aug-June). **Assoc** NWAC. Bear Creek offers a classical education taught from a Christian worldview. In a small-class setting, the lower school curriculum (preschool through grade 6) is designed to build a solid foundation in skills and knowledge while improving children's critical-thinking and problem-solving abilities. Latin and Christian studies are among the core requirements in middle school (grades 7 and 8), which features single-gender core classes. Upper schoolers (grades 9-12) follow a college preparatory program that includes a selection of honors and Advanced Placement courses. Grade 12 pupils develop and present a manda-

tory senior project prior to graduation. Students accumulate 100 hours of community service in grades 9-12. The Redmond campus on 208th Avenue Northeast accommodates students in grades K-12, while the Valley campus on Northeast 95th Street serves children from preschool through grade 6.

BERTSCHI SCHOOL Day Coed Gr PS (Age 4)-5
Seattle, WA 98102. 2227 10th Ave E.
Tel: 206-324-5476. Fax: 206-329-4806.
www.bertschi.org   E-mail: info@bertschi.org
Brigitte Bertschi, Head (1975). Pam Lauritzen, Adm.

Pre-Prep. Feat—Lib_Skills Span Computers Studio_Art Drama Music Dance. **Supp**—Dev_Read LD Rem_Math Rem_Read Tut. **Selective adm:** 47/yr. Appl fee: $100. Appl due: Jan. Accepted: 33%. **Enr 235.** B 113. G 122. Wh 68%. Latino 3%. Blk 6%. Asian 6%. Other 17%. Avg class size: 17. Stud/fac: 8:1. **Fac 24.** M 6/F 18. FT 18/PT 6. Wh 95%. Latino 1%. Blk 1%. Asian 3%. Adv deg: 50%. **Grad '11—36.** Prep—31. (Seattle Acad of Arts & Sciences 7, Northwest Sch 6, U Prep 3, Bush 2, Hyla Middle Sch 2, Morningside Acad 2). **Tui '11-'12:** Day $20,150 (+$500). Aid: Need 26 ($350,000). **Est 1975.** Nonprofit. (Sept-June). **Assoc** NWAC. The school's integrated curriculum stretches across disciplines and grade levels, allowing children to make connections while learning. Students remain with the grade-level teacher for language arts, math and social studies; specialists provide instruction in art, music, science, library, computers, Spanish and physical education. Various class activities and field trips complement academics.

EPIPHANY SCHOOL Day Coed Gr PS (Age 4)-5
Seattle, WA 98122. 3710 E Howell St.
Tel: 206-323-9011. Fax: 206-324-2127.
www.epiphanyschool.org   E-mail: gjones@epiphanyschool.org
Matt Neely, Head (2008). BA, Yale Univ, MA, Stanford Univ. Greg Jones, Adm.

Pre-Prep. Feat—Lib_Skills Fr Lat Studio_Art Drama Music. **Supp**—Dev_Read Rem_Math Rem_Read Rev Tut. **Comp:** Comp/Stud: 1:3. **Selective adm:** 49/yr. Appl fee: $65. Appl due: Feb. Accepted: 40%. Yield: 80%. **Enr 233.** Wh 79%. Blk 4%. Asian 2%. Other 15%. Avg class size: 16. Stud/fac: 8:1. Uniform. **Fac 36.** M 9/F 27. FT 27/PT 9. Adv deg: 33%. **Grad '11—28.** Prep—27. (Northwest Sch 6, Seattle Acad of Arts & Sci 5, U Prep 2, Bush 2, Evergreen Sch 2, Lakeside Sch 1). Alum donors: 8%. **Tui '12-'13:** Day $15,078-19,005. Aid: Need 31 ($466,527). **Est 1958.** Nonprofit. Tri (Sept-June). **Assoc** NWAC. Located in the city's Madrona neighborhood, Epiphany offers a traditional elementary program that emphasizes the fundamentals and addresses critical-thinking and problem-solving skills. Children gain an introduction to French in the early grades; Latin joins the curriculum in grades 4 and 5. A learning skills program (available for an additional fee) provides remedial academic support for boys and girls requiring assistance with their studies.

HOLY NAMES ACADEMY Day Girls Gr 9-12
Seattle, WA 98112. 728 21st Ave E.
Tel: 206-323-4272. Fax: 206-323-5254.
www.holynames-sea.org   E-mail: admissions@holynames-sea.org
Elizabeth A. Swift, Head. BA, MA, Univ of Washington. Eileen Denby, Adm.

Col Prep. AP (exams req'd; 796 taken)—Eng Fr Span Calc Comp_Sci Bio Physics Eur_Hist US_Hist Psych Art_Hist Studio_Art Music_Theory. **Feat**—Creative_Writing Environ_Sci Amer_Stud Intl_Relations Law Theol Film Photog Drama Music. **Sports**— G: Basket Crew X-country Golf Gymnastics Lacrosse Soccer Softball Swim Tennis Track Ultimate_Frisbee Volley. Activities: 35. **Selective adm:** 180/yr. Appl fee: $25. Appl due: Jan. Accepted: 60%. Yield: 72%. **Tests** MAT. **Enr 675.** Wh 66%. Latino 6%. Blk 9%. Asian 17%. Other 2%. Avg class size: 22. Stud/fac: 14:1. Casual dress. **Fac 52.** M 12/F 40. FT 52. Wh 76%. Latino 4%.

Blk 12%. Asian 8%. Adv deg: 98%. **Grad '11—159.** Col—159. (U of WA 21, Gonzaga 17, W WA 9, WA St 8, U of OR 6, Seattle U 6). **Col Couns:** 1. Alum donors: 22%. **Tui '12-'13:** Day $12,972 (+$685-885). Aid: Merit 15 ($20,000). Need 211 ($985,360). **Est 1880.** Nonprofit. Roman Catholic (74% practice). Sem (Aug-June). **Assoc** NWAC. Holy Names offers a college prep curriculum that includes Advanced Placement courses in most disciplines. Students enroll in four years of theology courses and contribute to community service projects each year. The fine arts program comprises academic courses and cocurricular activities in music, drama and dance.

JOHN F. KENNEDY MEMORIAL HIGH SCHOOL   Day Coed Gr 9-12
Seattle, WA 98168. 140 S 140th St.
Tel: 206-246-0500. Fax: 206-242-0831.
www.kennedyhs.org   E-mail: info@kennedyhs.org
     Michael L. Prato, Prin (2003). BA, MA, Central Washington Univ. Sarah Dahleen, Adm.

     Col Prep. AP—Eng Stats US_Hist. **Feat**—Creative_Writing ASL Fr Lat Span Environ_ Sci Comp_Sci Econ Govt Pol_Sci Psych Relig Art_Hist Studio_Art Video_Production Drama Music Jazz_Ensemble Accounting Bus Journ Speech Design Drafting. **Supp**—Dev_Read ESL LD Makeup Rem_Math Rem_Read Rev Tut. **Sports**—Basket X-country Golf Soccer Swim Tennis Track. B: Baseball Football Wrestling. G: Cheer Gymnastics Softball. Activities: 63. **Selective adm:** 240/yr. Appl fee: $25. Appl due: Rolling. Accepted: 78%. Yield: 64%. **Tests** HSPT TOEFL. **Enr 865.** Wh 67%. Latino 4%. Blk 6%. Native Am 1%. Asian 18%. Other 4%. Intl 14%. Avg class size: 19. Stud/fac: 16:1. Casual dress. **Fac 62.** M 31/F 31. FT 60/PT 2. Adv deg: 50%. **Grad '11—256.** Col—247. (U of WA 31, WA St 16, Seattle U 13, Gonzaga 11, Central WA 10, W WA 5). **Col Couns:** 4. **Tui '12-'13:** Day $10,878 (+$200-400). Parishioners $9785 (+$200-400). Aid: Merit 10 ($5000). Need 146 ($392,000). **Est 1966.** Nonprofit. Roman Catholic (70% practice). Sem (Aug-June). **Assoc** NWAC. Kennedy offers a curriculum that covers a wide range of academic levels and learning styles. Two advanced programs, operating in conjunction with the University of Washington and Mateo Ricci College at Seattle University, offer juniors and seniors the opportunity to earn college credits while still in high school. The campus ministry sponsors several retreats and liturgies, along with daily Mass. All students complete a service project in the context of junior religion and senior English and social studies classes. Kennedy provides boarding options for a limited number of international students: Boys may board on campus, while girls may live in a home stay setting.

SEATTLE COUNTRY DAY SCHOOL   Day Coed Gr K-8
Seattle, WA 98109. 2619 4th Ave N.
Tel: 206-284-6220. Fax: 206-283-4251.
www.seattlecountryday.org   E-mail: info@seattlecountryday.org
     Michael G. Murphy, Head (2004). BA, Wabash College, BS, Univ of Wisconsin-Madison, MALS, Univ of Detroit. Kathy McCann, Adm.

     Pre-Prep. Gen Acad. Feat—Span Computers Studio_Art Music. **Sports**—Basket X-country Soccer Tennis Ultimate_Frisbee Volley. **Selective adm:** 59/yr. Appl fee: $60. Appl due: Jan. **Tests** IQ ISEE. **Enr 334.** B 168. G 166. Avg class size: 16. **Fac 40.** M 11/F 29. FT 35/PT 5. Adv deg: 85%. **Grad '11—35.** **Tui '11-'12:** Day $19,559-22,870 (+$300). **Est 1964.** Nonprofit. Sem (Sept-June). **Assoc** NWAC. This school for highly capable children incorporates foreign language, computers and science as part of its curriculum from kindergarten. Daily laboratory-based science courses begin in grade 4. The school's Winterim program, conducted on six successive Fridays in January and February, enables students to participate in a nonacademic, off-campus activity as a supplement to classroom learning.

SEATTLE PREPARATORY SCHOOL   **Day Coed Gr 9-12**
Seattle, WA 98102. 2400 11th Ave E.
Tel: 206-324-0400. Fax: 206-323-6509.
www.seaprep.org   E-mail: kgoodwin@seaprep.org
     Kent Hickey, Pres. BA, MA, JD, Marquette Univ. Matt Barmore, Prin. BA, Santa Clara Univ, MA, EdD, Univ of San Francisco. Kate Goodwin, Adm.
     Col Prep. AP—Eng Span Calc Eur_Hist. **Feat**—Creative_Writing Shakespeare Fr Ger Japan Stats Anat & Physiol Bioethics Web_Design Econ Govt African_Stud Asian_Stud World_Relig Ceramics Photog Visual_Arts Drama Music. **Comp:** Comp/Stud: 1:4.3. **Sports**—Basket X-country Golf Lacrosse Soccer Swim Tennis Track. B: Baseball Football. G: Cheer Softball Volley. Activities: 15. **Selective adm (Gr 9-11):** 180/yr. Appl fee: $40. Accepted: 50%. **Tests** ISEE. **Enr 702.** B 351. G 351. Nonwhite 27%. Avg class size: 24. **Fac 53.** Adv deg: 81%. **Grad '11—161.** Col—161. **Avg SAT:** CR 599. M 605. W 604. Avg ACT: 26.3. **Tui '12-'13:** Day $14,700 (+$700-1000). Aid: Need ($1,250,000). **Est 1891.** Nonprofit. Roman Catholic (76% practice). Sem (Sept-June). **Assoc** NWAC. Seattle Prep's strictly defined sequence of courses emphasizes hands-on learning and the integration of various disciplines across the curriculum. Boys and girls in grades 9-11 enroll in Collegio, a course combining the study of social studies, English and religious themes. The curriculum prepares all students for the Matteo Ricci College program, a partnership with Seattle University that allows participants to earn an undergraduate degree in six years: three years at Seattle Prep and three years at the university. Alternatively, students may remain at Seattle Prep for a traditional college preparatory senior year. Pupils complete 20 to 30 hours of school, church or community service each year.

SEATTLE WALDORF SCHOOL   **Day Coed Gr PS (Age 3)-12**
Seattle, WA 98125. 2728 NE 100th St.
Tel: 206-524-5320. Fax: 206-523-3920.
Other locations: 160 John St, Seattle 98109; 4919 Woodlawn Ave N, Seattle 98103.
www.seattlewaldorf.org   E-mail: mpetty@seattlewaldorf.org
     Tracy Bennett, Head (2011). BA, Dartmouth College, MEd, Univ of Washington. Meg Petty, Adm.
     Col Prep. Waldorf. Feat—Shakespeare Mythology Japan Span Anat Astron Environ_Sci Geol Computers WA_Hist Econ Comp_Relig Philos Drawing Filmmaking Painting Drama Music Music_Hist Eurythmy Woodworking. **Supp**—Dev_Read LD Rem_Math Rem_Read Tut. **Selective adm:** Appl fee: $60. Appl due: Jan. **Enr 360.** Wh 84%. Latino 4%. Asian 4%. Other 8%. Avg class size: 22. Casual dress. **Fac 34.** M 13/F 21. FT 28/PT 6. Adv deg: 47%. **Grad '09—8.** Col—8. (U of WA 1, Sch of the Art Inst of Chicago 1, U of CA-Berkeley 1, Wheelock 1, Whitman 1, Guilford 1). **Tui '12-'13:** Day $10,350-19,400 (+$250-500). Aid: Need 108. **Est 1980.** Nonprofit. (Sept-June). Seattle Waldorf's curriculum, which integrates the arts, includes foreign languages, music, handwork, community service and physical education. A limited special-needs program is available. The main campus on Northeast 100th Street serves students in grades PS-8, while kindergartners may also attend school on Woodlawn Avenue North (206-545-9001). After a summer 2007 merger with a local high school, Seattle Waldorf added grades 9-12; this division operates at a separate campus on John Street (206-522-2644).

THE EVERGREEN SCHOOL   **Day Coed Gr PS (Age 3)-8**
Shoreline, WA 98133. 15201 Meridian Ave N.
Tel: 206-364-2650. Fax: 206-365-1827.
www.evergreenschool.org   E-mail: admission@evergreenschool.org
     Margaret Wagner, Head (2000). BA, Univ of Cape Town (South Africa), MEd, Univ of New Orleans. Eric Barber, Adm.
     Pre-Prep. Feat—Chin Fr Ger Span Environ_Sci Computers Drawing Photog Sculpt Studio_Art Drama Music Dance. **Supp**—Tut. **Comp:** Comp/Stud: 1:1 Laptop prgm Gr 6-8.

Sports—Basket X-country Golf Soccer Tennis Ultimate_Frisbee. G: Volley. **Selective adm:** 61/yr. Appl fee: $65. Appl due: Jan. Accepted: 39%. Yield: 80%. **Tests** IQ ISEE. **Enr 455.** Wh 69%. Latino 1%. Blk 3%. Asian 11%. Other 16%. Avg class size: 16. Stud/fac: 9:1. **Fac 44.** M 11/F 33. FT 44. Wh 85%. Latino 2%. Blk 7%. Asian 5%. Other 1%. Adv deg: 50%. **Grad '10—31.** Prep—24. **Tui '12-'13:** Day $20,400-22,600. Aid: Need 61 ($774,000). **Est 1963.** Nonprofit. Sem (Sept-June). Evergreen tailors its program to the needs of children with advanced and creative learning potential. The academically focused basic skills program features individual and small-group instruction, thereby allowing children to progress at an appropriate rate. French, Spanish, German, Mandarin, art, music and computer classes begin in the primary grades, while fine arts electives start in grade 6. The school's global education program, which is integrated into the entire curriculum, culminates in a three-week trip abroad for eighth graders.

GONZAGA PREPARATORY SCHOOL   Day Coed Gr 9-12
Spokane, WA 99207. 1224 E Euclid Ave.
Tel: 509-483-8511. Fax: 509-483-3124.
www.gprep.com   E-mail: office@gprep.com
   Al Falkner, Pres. BA, MAT, MEd, Whitworth College. Rev. Kevin Connell, SJ, Prin. BA, Gonzaga Univ, MDiv, Weston Jesuit School of Theology, MEd, Lewis and Clark College. Corrina O'Brien, Adm.
   Col Prep. AP (exams req'd; 364 taken, 74% 3+)—Eng Fr Span Calc Bio Chem Eur_Hist US_Hist World_Hist US_Govt & Pol Studio_Art. **Feat**—Lat Holocaust Law Psych Theol Ceramics Photog Visual_Arts Drama Music Home_Ec. **Supp**—Makeup Rem_Math Tut. **Dual enr:** Gonzaga. **Sports**—Basket X-country Golf Lacrosse Soccer Tennis Track. B: Baseball Football Wrestling. G: Cheer Softball Volley. Activities: 50. **Selective adm:** Appl due: Dec. **Tests** HSPT. **Enr 902.** Wh 84%. Latino 3%. Blk 2%. Native Am 2%. Asian 5%. Other 4%. Avg class size: 18. Casual dress. **Fac 65. Grad '11—217.** Col—212. **Avg SAT:** CR 559. M 550. W 536. Avg ACT: 24. **Col Couns:** 2. **Assoc** NWAC. Founded as a boys' college preparatory division of Gonzaga University, the school moved to its current site in 1954 and became coeducational in 1975. An extensive curriculum provides courses in standard, college prep and honors programs, as well as Advanced Placement and limited remedial offerings. Juniors and seniors may earn dual-enrollment credit through Gonzaga University or the Spokane Area Vocational Skills Center. Seniors fulfill a community service requirement through project work.

TERM PROGRAMS

This section describes secondary-level academic term programs (usually operating on a semester system) that combine credit-bearing course work with experiential learning. Programs may have an environmental focus and typically employ the local environs as a significant teaching tool. Curricula are designed to promote academic continuity between the student's home school and the term program.

Term Programs

MAINE

OCEAN CLASSROOM HIGH SCHOOL SEMESTER
Bdg — Coed Gr 10-PG

Boothbay Harbor, ME 04538. 1 Oak St, PO Box 205. Tel: 207-633-2750, 800-724-7245. Fax: 207-633-4337.
www.oceanclassroom.org   E-mail: mail@oceanclassroom.org
Greg Belanger, Exec Dir (2012). Alyson Graham, Adm.
  Feat—Maritime_Lit Marine_Bio/Sci Oceanog Maritime_Hist.
  Applied: 42 Accepted: 60%. Yield: 50%.
  Enr 22. B 11. G 11. Stud/fac: 2:1. Fac 10. M 4/F 6. FT 2/PT 8. Wh 60%. Latino 10%. Blk 10%. Asian 20%. Adv deg: 60%. In dorms 8.
  Tui '12-'13: Bdg $19,500/sem (+$1000). Aid: Merit 3 ($24,000). Need 9 ($78,000).
  Est 1996. Nonprofit. Sem (Feb-June).

Ocean Classroom's 17-week spring semester program combines seamanship and nautical arts instruction with an integrated academic program. Topics in each course correspond with the voyage itinerary, as boys and girls learn about the maritime heritage and the culture of coastal and island communities. Students, who need have no previous sailing experience, are considered crew members and split into three groups for daily rotating watch duty. Programs progress from St. Thomas (US Virgin Islands) to New England.

CHEWONKI SEMESTER SCHOOL
Bdg — Coed Gr 11-12

Wiscasset, ME 04578. 485 Chewonki Neck Rd. Tel: 207-882-7323. Fax: 207-882-4074.
www.chewonki.org/mcs   E-mail: admissions@chewonki.org
Ann Carson, Head (2011). BA, Univ of California-Berkeley, MEd, Lesley College.
  AP (47 exams taken)—Fr Span Calc US_Hist. Feat—Chin Ger Lat Environ_Sci Ethics Outdoor_Ed.
  Accepted: 60%. Yield: 90%.
  Enr 72. B 17. G 55. Intl 5%. Avg class size: 8. Stud/fac: 3:1. Fac 16. M 7/F 9. FT 14/PT 2. Adv deg: 56%.
  Tui '11-'12: Bdg $22,300/sem (+$600). Aid: Need 23 ($260,000).
  Endow $2,800,000. Plant val $8,156,000. Acres 400. Bldgs 10. Dorms 5. Class rms 7. Lib 8352 vols. Sci labs 1. Art studios 1. Fields 3. Courts 2.
  Est 1988. Nonprofit. Spons: The Chewonki Foundation. Sem (Aug-May). Assoc NEASC.

This semester-long school is open to high school juniors and seniors. Natural science and one of two English classes form the core curriculum. In addition, students choose three optional courses from the following: environmental issues, art and the natural world, and multiple levels of mathematics, American history and foreign language. Boys and girls may prepare for Advanced Placement examinations in various subject areas, and all courses are taught at the honors or college level. Students and faculty participate together in an afternoon work program to maintain the buildings and grounds, and, at some point during the semester, every student completes early morning farm chores.

VERMONT

THE MOUNTAIN SCHOOL

Bdg — Coed Gr 11

Vershire, VT 05079. 151 Mountain School Rd. Tel: 802-685-4520. Fax: 802-685-3317.
www.mountainschool.org   E-mail: info@mountainschool.org
Alden Smith, Dir (2001). BA, Davidson College, MA, Middlebury College. **Missy Smith, Adm.**
AP—Chin Fr Lat Span Calc US_Hist. **Feat**—Humanities Studio_Art.
Enr 45. B 18. **G** 27. Avg class size: 11. Stud/fac: 2:1. **Fac 22. M** 11/**F** 11. **FT** 11/**PT** 11. Wh 100%. Adv deg: 54%. In dorms 10.
Tui '11-'12: Bdg $22,850/sem (+$450).
Acres 300. Bldgs 11. Dorms 5. Dorm rms 21. Class rms 6. Libs 1. Art studios 1. Comp labs 1.
Est 1983. Nonprofit. Sem (Aug-May).

Enrolling 45 high-achieving juniors from private and public schools throughout the US, the Mountain School of Milton Academy combines college preparatory academics with life on a working organic farm in Vermont. The integrated curriculum, which makes use of small class sizes and the mountain campus, emphasizes individual and communal responsibility, simplicity and sustainability. All classes are taught at the Advanced Placement or honors level. Students live with teachers in small houses and participate in decision making that pertains to communal life and farm management.

NEW YORK

CITYterm

Bdg — Coed Gr 11-12

Dobbs Ferry, NY 10522. c/o The Masters School, 49 Clinton Ave. Tel: 914-479-6502.
Fax: 914-693-6905.
www.cityterm.org   E-mail: info@cityterm.org
Erica Chapman, Dir (2012). BA, Sarah Lawrence College. **Patrick McGettigan, Adm.**
AP—Fr Span Calc. **Feat**—Humanities NYC_Lit Stats NYC_Hist Urban_Stud.
Accepted: 45%. Yield: 85%.
Enr 30. B 12. **G** 18. **Fac 9. M** 3/**F** 6. **FT** 6/**PT** 3. Wh 85%. Blk 15%. Adv deg: 55%. In dorms 6.
Tui '10-'11: Bdg $22,750/sem (+$550).
Dorm rms 16. Class rms 3. Auds 1. Theaters 1. Gyms 1. Fields 1. Courts 1.
Est 1996. Nonprofit. Spons: The Masters School. Sem (Aug-May).

This unusual, experiential semester program exposes able juniors and seniors to an intensive study of New York City. Students spend three days of each six-day academic week in the classroom on the campus of The Masters School, and the remaining three days in the city engaged in fieldwork. CITYterm's integrated, interdisciplinary curriculum encourages boys and girls to connect classroom learning with their city experiences. Core courses explore the history, literature and urban environment of New York City. To support ongoing academic work at the student's home school, courses in other subject areas (some at the honors or Advanced Placement level) are also available.

NORTH CAROLINA

THE OUTDOOR ACADEMY
Bdg — Coed Gr 10-11

Pisgah Forest, NC 28768. 43 Hart Rd. Tel: 828-877-4349. Fax: 828-884-2788.
www.enf.org/outdoor_academy   E-mail: oaadmissions@enf.org
Mark Meyer-Braun, Head. BA, MA, Wesleyan Univ, PhD, Brown Univ. **Laura Belanger, Adm.**
Feat—Fr Span Environ_Sci Appalachian_Hist Visual_Arts Music Outdoor_Ed. **Supp**—Rev Tut.
Enr 30. B 16. G 14. Wh 94%. Latino 3%. Blk 3%. **Fac 9.** M 3/F 6. FT 6/PT 3. Wh 90%. Latino 10%. Adv deg: 44%.
Tui '11-'12: Bdg $19,000/sem (+$500). **Aid:** Need 14 ($154,265).
Acres 185. Bldgs 10. Dorms 4. Class rms 5. Libs 1. Art studios 2. Music studios 1. Dance studios 1. Fields 1. Courts 2.
Est 1995. Nonprofit. Spons: Eagle's Nest Foundation. Sem (Aug-May). **Assoc** SACS.

This semester-long program primarily serves sophomores, although select juniors also enroll. The academy combines a college preparatory curriculum with environmental education, regional studies, arts programming and outdoor leadership training. Making use of its location in the Blue Ridge Mountains, the school holds class both indoors and in the forest; the outdoor education program teaches hiking, backpacking, caving, canoeing and rock climbing skills.

COLORADO

HIGH MOUNTAIN INSTITUTE SEMESTER
Bdg — Coed Gr 11-12

Leadville, CO 80461. PO Box 970. Tel: 719-486-8200. Fax: 719-486-8201.
www.hminet.org   E-mail: info@hminet.org
Molly P. Barnes, Co-Head (1998). BA, Colgate Univ, MBA, Univ of Denver. **Christopher Barnes, Co-Head.** BA, Colorado College. **Laura Dougherty, Adm.**
AP—Span US_Hist. **Feat**—Calc Wilderness_Ed. Outdoor ed.
Enr 42. B 19. G 23. Avg class size: 10. **Fac 9.** M 5/F 4. FT 9. Wh 100%. Adv deg: 22%.
Tui '12-'13: Bdg $24,750/sem (+$1500). **Aid:** Merit 2 ($49,500). Need 21 ($337,460).
Plant val $2,500,000. Acres 40. Bldgs 8. Dorms 5. Class rms 4. Lib 500 vols. Sci labs 1. Fields 1. Climbing walls 1. Comp labs 1.
Est 1998. Nonprofit. Sem (Aug-May).

This semester-long program for juniors and seniors focuses on experiential education, both in the classroom and in the wilderness. Students take five or six courses, one of which pertains to ethics in the natural world. Instructors assist pupils in making connections between what they learn in class and what they learn in the wilderness. Each semester, boys and girls embark on three two-week expeditions, with backpacking in the mountains and canyons, a community service trip and a winter trek during the spring semester being some of the options.

CALIFORNIA

THE OXBOW SCHOOL
Bdg — Coed Gr 11-PG

Napa, CA 94559. 530 3rd St. Tel: 707-255-6000. Fax: 707-255-6006.
www.oxbowschool.org   E-mail: mail@oxbowschool.org
Stephen Thomas, Head (1998). Holly McVeigh, Adm.
   Feat—Fr Span Drawing Painting Photog Sculpt.
   Enr 96. B 24. G 72. Sec 94. PG 2. Avg class size: 16. **Fac 10.** M 3/F 7. FT 7/PT 3. Wh
   80%. Blk 10%. Other 10%.
   Tui '12-'13: Bdg $23,000/sem. Aid: Need 40 ($500,000).
   Acres 3. Bldgs 14 (40% ADA). Dorms 2. Dorm rms 28. Class rms 4. Comp labs 1.
   Comp/stud: 1:3.
   Est 1998. Nonprofit. Sem (Aug-May).

Oxbow's semester-long program for high school upperclassmen and postgraduates combines a strong program in the visual arts with interdisciplinary humanities. Students undergo intensive training in painting, sculpture, printmaking and photography/digital media. Each art discipline occupies a fully equipped studio that is open in the evening and on weekends, and instructors encourage boys and girls to supplement assigned projects with creative independent work. A full academic program accompanies visual arts programming, thereby enabling pupils to fulfill graduation requirements in the traditional disciplines.   **See Also Page 52**

THE WOOLMAN SEMESTER
Bdg — Coed Gr 11-PG

Nevada City, CA 95959. 13075 Woolman Ln. Tel: 530-273-3183. Fax: 530-273-9028.
www.woolman.org   E-mail: admissions@woolman.org
Dorothy Henderson, Head (2008). Samantha Sommers, Adm.
   Feat—Environ_Sci Global_Stud Peace_Stud Ethics. **Supp**—Tut. Outdoor ed.
   Applied: 18.
   Enr 15. B 6. G 9. **Fac 3.** M 1/F 2. FT 3. Adv deg: 66%.
   Tui '10-'11: Bdg $17,000/sem (+$500). **Aid:** Need 10 ($110,000).
   Acres 230.
   Est 2003. Nonprofit. Religious Society of Friends. Spons: College Park Friends
   Educational Association. Sem (Aug-May).

Conducted on a 230-acre campus in the foothills of the Sierra Nevada Mountains, Woolman Semester is an intense, 16-week academic program for 16- to 19-year-olds that focuses on peace, social justice and environmental sustainability. Students spend the morning attending classes, then devote the afternoon to hands-on work in the garden and orchard, the kitchen and the forest. All boys and girls take the following inquiry-driven core courses: world issues, peace studies, humanities and ethics, and environmental science. Foreign language and math classes are available as independent study options.

ASSOCIATIONS AND ORGANIZATIONS

The list that follows comprises organizations and associations that offer information or services pertinent to nonpublic elementary or secondary education. Accrediting Associations conduct formal evaluations of schools interested in gaining accreditation; in some cases, accredited institutions are eligible for membership benefits. Advocacy Organizations provide assistance and active support for members of a specified population. Professional Organizations offer membership and benefits to specified professionals. School Membership Associations provide benefits for member schools, but do not have a formal accreditation process. Student Exchange Organizations dispense information and provide resources associated with intercultural learning. Testing Organizations compose and, in many cases, oversee and administer examinations given for the purpose of school admission or placement.

ACCREDITING ASSOCIATIONS

CUM LAUDE SOCIETY
4100 Springdale Rd, Louisville, KY 40241. Tel: 502-814-4361. Fax: 502-423-0445.
E-mail: cumlaude@kcd.org. Web: www.cumlaudesociety.org.

MIDDLE STATES ASSOCIATION OF COLLEGES AND SCHOOLS
Commission on Elementary and Secondary Schools, 3624 Market St, Philadelphia, PA
19104. Tel: 267-284-5000. Fax: 215-662-0957. E-mail: info@css-msa.org.
Web: www.middlestates.org.

NEW ENGLAND ASSOCIATION OF SCHOOLS AND COLLEGES
209 Burlington Rd, Ste 201, Bedford, MA 01730. Tel: 781-271-0022.
Fax: 781-271-0950. Web: www.neasc.org.

NORTH CENTRAL ASSOCIATION
COMMISSION ON ACCREDITATION AND SCHOOL IMPROVEMENT
c/o Arizona State Univ, PO Box 871008, Tempe, AZ 85287. Tel: 480-773-6900,
800-525-9517. Fax: 480-773-6901. E-mail: nca@ncacasi.org. Web: www.ncacasi.org.

NORTHWEST ACCREDITATION COMMISSION
1510 Robert St, Ste 103, Boise, ID 83705. Tel: 208-493-5077. Fax: 208-334-3228.
E-mail: info@northwestaccreditation.org. Web: www.northwestaccreditation.org.

SOUTHERN ASSOCIATION OF COLLEGES AND SCHOOLS
COUNCIL ON ACCREDITATION AND SCHOOL IMPROVEMENT
2520 Northwinds Pky, Ste 600, Alpharetta, GA 30009. Tel: 888-413-3669.
E-mail: membership-info@advanc-ed.org. Web: www.sacscasi.org.

WESTERN ASSOCIATION OF SCHOOLS AND COLLEGES
533 Airport Blvd, Ste 200, Burlingame, CA 94010. Tel: 650-696-1060.
Fax: 650-696-1867. E-mail: mail@acswasc.org. Web: www.acswasc.org.

ADVOCACY ORGANIZATIONS

A BETTER CHANCE
253 W 35th St, 6th Fl, New York, NY 10001. Tel: 646-346-1310, 800-562-7865.
Fax: 646-346-1311. Web: www.abetterchance.org.

AMERICAN ASSOCIATION FOR GIFTED CHILDREN
c/o Duke Univ, Box 90539, Durham, NC 27708. Tel: 919-783-6152.
Fax: 919-683-1742. E-mail: megayle@aol.com. Web: www.aagc.org.

ASSOCIATION FOR CHILDHOOD EDUCATION INTERNATIONAL
17904 Georgia Ave, Ste 215, Olney, MD 20832. Tel: 301-570-2111, 800-423-3563.
Fax: 301-570-2212. E-mail: headquarters@acei.org. Web: www.acei.org.

ASSOCIATION FOR EXPERIENTIAL EDUCATION
3775 Iris Ave, Ste 4, Boulder, CO 80301. Tel: 303-440-8844, 866-522-8337.
Fax: 303-440-9581. E-mail: admin@aee.org. Web: www.aee.org.

COUNCIL FOR AMERICAN PRIVATE EDUCATION
13017 Wisteria Dr, PMB 457, Germantown, MD 20874. Tel: 301-916-8460.
Fax: 301-916-8485. E-mail: cape@capenet.org. Web: www.capenet.org.

THE EDUCATION TRUST
1250 H St NW, Ste 700, Washington, DC 20005. Tel: 202-293-1217.
Fax: 202-293-2605. E-mail: lsingleton@edtrust.org. Web: www.edtrust.org.

GAY, LESBIAN AND STRAIGHT EDUCATION NETWORK
90 Broad St, 2nd Fl, New York, NY 10004. Tel: 212-727-0135. Fax: 212-727-0254.
E-mail: glsen@glsen.org. Web: www.glsen.org.

INDEPENDENT SCHOOL ALLIANCE FOR MINORITY AFFAIRS
1545 Wilshire Blvd, Ste 711, Los Angeles, CA 90017. Tel: 213-484-2411.
Fax: 213-484-2545. E-mail: info@thealliance-la.org. Web: www.thealliance-la.org.

JEWISH EDUCATION SERVICE OF NORTH AMERICA
318 West 39th St, 5th Fl, New York, NY 10018. Tel: 212-284-6950.
Fax: 212-284-6951. E-mail: info@jesna.org. Web: www.jesna.org.

NATIONAL ASSOCIATION FOR GIFTED CHILDREN
1331 H St NW, Ste 1001, Washington, DC 20005. Tel: 202-785-4268.
Fax: 202-785-4248. E-mail: nagc@nagc.org. Web: www.nagc.org.

NATIONAL ASSOCIATION FOR THE EDUCATION OF YOUNG CHILDREN
1313 L St NW, Ste 500, Washington, DC 20005. Tel: 202-232-8777.
Fax: 202-328-1846. Web: www.naeyc.org.

NATIONAL ASSOCIATION OF PARENTS WITH CHILDREN IN SPECIAL EDUCATION
1431 W South Fork Dr, Phoenix, AZ 85045. Tel: 800-754-4421. Fax: 800-424-0371.
E-mail: contact@napcse.org. Web: www.napcse.org.

NATIONAL ASSOCIATION OF PRIVATE SPECIAL EDUCATION CENTERS
601 Pennsylvania Ave, Ste 900, South Bldg, Washington, DC 20004.
Tel: 202-434-8225. Fax: 202-434-8224. E-mail: napsec@aol.com.
Web: www.napsec.org.

NATIONAL COALITION OF ALTERNATIVE COMMUNITY SCHOOLS
PO Box 1451, Ann Arbor, MI 48106. Tel: 734-483-7040. Fax: 734-482-1867.
E-mail: office@ncacs.org. Web: www.ncacs.org.

NATIONAL EDUCATION ASSOCIATION
1201 16th St NW, Washington, DC 20036. Tel: 202-833-4000. Fax: 202-822-7974. Web: www.nea.org.

NATIONAL PTA
1250 N Pitt St, Alexandria, VA 22314. Tel: 703-518-1200, 800-307-4782. Fax: 703-836-0942. E-mail: info@pta.org. Web: www.pta.org.

PARENTS LEAGUE OF NEW YORK
115 E 82nd St, New York, NY 10028. Tel: 212-737-7385. Fax: 212-737-7389. E-mail: info@parentsleague.org. Web: www.parentsleague.org.

PRINCETON CENTER FOR LEADERSHIP TRAINING
911 Commons Way, Princeton, NJ 08540. Tel: 609-252-9300. Fax: 609-252-9393. E-mail: princetoncenter@princetonleadership.org. Web: www.princetonleadership.org.

RELIGIOUS EDUCATION ASSOCIATION
c/o Yale Divinity School, 409 Prospect St, New Haven, CT 06511. Tel: 765-225-8836. Fax: 203-432-5356. E-mail: secretary@religiouseducation.net. Web: www.religiouseducation.net.

VENTURES SCHOLARS PROGRAM
15 Maiden Ln, Ste 200, New York, NY 10038. Tel: 212-566-2522, 800-947-6278. Fax: 212-566-2536. E-mail: mbleich@vesc-education.com. Web: www.venturescholar.org.

PROFESSIONAL ASSOCIATIONS

AMERICAN ASSOCIATION OF TEACHERS OF FRENCH
Mailcode 4510, Southern Illinois Univ, Carbondale, IL 62901. Tel: 618-453-5731. Fax: 618-453-5733. E-mail: abrate@siu.edu. Web: www.frenchteachers.org.

AMERICAN ASSOCIATION OF TEACHERS OF GERMAN
112 Haddontowne Ct, Ste 104, Cherry Hill, NJ 08034. Tel: 856-795-5553. Fax: 856-795-9398. E-mail: headquarters@aatg.org. Web: www.aatg.org.

AMERICAN ASSOCIATION OF TEACHERS OF SPANISH AND PORTUGUESE
900 Ladd Rd, Walled Lake, MI 48390. Tel: 248-960-2180. Fax: 248-960-9570. E-mail: aatspoffice@aatsp.org. Web: www.aatsp.org.

AMERICAN COUNCIL ON THE TEACHING OF FOREIGN LANGUAGES
1001 N Fairfax St, Ste 200, Alexandria, VA 22314. Tel: 703-894-2900. Fax: 703-894-2905. E-mail: headquarters@actfl.org. Web: www.actfl.org.

AMERICAN COUNSELING ASSOCIATION
5999 Stevenson Ave, Alexandria, VA 22304. Tel: 703-823-9800, 800-347-6647. TTY: 703-823-6862. Fax: 800-473-2329. E-mail: membership@counseling.org. Web: www.counseling.org.

AMERICAN EDUCATIONAL STUDIES ASSOCIATION
Univ of Alabama-Huntsville, Dept of Education, 235 Morton Hall, Huntsville, AL 35899. E-mail: philip.kovacs@uah.edu. Web: www.educationalstudies.org.

AMERICAN LIBRARY ASSOCIATION
50 E Huron St, Chicago, IL 60611. Tel: 312-944-6780, 800-545-2433. Fax: 312-280-3255. E-mail: library@ala.org. Web: www.ala.org.

AMERICAN SCHOOL COUNSELOR ASSOCIATION
1101 King St, Ste 625, Alexandria, VA 22314. Tel: 703-683-2722, 800-306-4722. Fax: 703-683-1619. E-mail: asca@schoolcounselor.org. Web: www.schoolcounselor.org.

ASSOCIATION FOR EDUCATIONAL COMMUNICATIONS AND TECHNOLOGY
1800 N Stonelake Dr, Ste 2, Bloomington, IN 47408. Tel: 812-335-7675. E-mail: aect@aect.org. Web: www.aect.org.

ASSOCIATION FOR SUPERVISION & CURRICULUM DEVELOPMENT
1703 N Beauregard St, Alexandria, VA 22311. Tel: 703-578-9600, 800-933-2723. Fax: 703-575-5400. Web: www.ascd.org.

ASSOCIATION FOR SCIENCE TEACHER EDUCATION
113 Radcliff Dr, Pittsburgh, PA 15237. Tel: 412-624-2861. E-mail: executivedirector@theaste.org. Web: http://theaste.org.

ASSOCIATION OF CALIFORNIA SCHOOL ADMINISTRATORS
1029 J St, Ste 500, Sacramento, CA 95814. Tel: 916-444-3216, 800-890-0325. Fax: 916-444-3739. Web: www.acsa.org.

ASSOCIATION OF COLLEGE COUNSELORS IN INDEPENDENT SCHOOLS
16 Brookdale Ln, Pepperell, MA 01463. Tel: 978-809-2829. E-mail: info@accisnet.org. Web: www.accisnet.org.

ASSOCIATION OF INDEPENDENT SCHOOL ADMISSION PROFESSIONALS
170 Boston Post Rd, Ste 160, Madison, CT 06443. Tel: 203-421-7051. E-mail: info@aisap.org. Web: www.aisap.org.

ASSOCIATION OF INDEPENDENT SCHOOL LIBRARIANS
c/o Darlington School, 1014 Cave Spring Rd, Rome, GA 30161. Tel: 706-236-0465. Fax: 706-236-0456. E-mail: meholmes@darlingtonschool.org. Web: www.aislnews.org.

ASSOCIATION OF TEACHER EDUCATORS
PO Box 793, Manassas, VA 20113. Tel: 703-331-0911. Fax: 703-331-3666. E-mail: info@ate1.org. Web: www.ate1.org.

COUNCIL FOR ADVANCEMENT AND SUPPORT OF EDUCATION
1307 New York Ave NW, Ste 1000, Washington, DC 20005. Tel: 202-328-2273. Fax: 202-387-4973. E-mail: memberservicecenter@case.org. Web: www.case.org.

COUNTRY DAY SCHOOL HEADMASTERS' ASSOCIATION OF THE UNITED STATES
966 Harbortowne Rd, Charleston, SC 29412. Tel: 843-795-7947. Fax: 843-762-9204. E-mail: gebond@comcast.net.

ELEMENTARY SCHOOL HEADS ASSOCIATION
33 Ralyn Rd, Cotuit, MA 02635. Tel: 774-238-8416. E-mail: info@elementaryschoolheads.org. Web: www.elementaryschoolheads.org.

INDEPENDENT EDUCATIONAL CONSULTANTS ASSOCIATION
3251 Old Lee Hwy, Ste 510, Fairfax, VA 22030. Tel: 703-591-4850. Fax: 703-591-4860. E-mail: info@iecaonline.com. Web: www.iecaonline.com.

INSTITUTE OF INTERNATIONAL EDUCATION
809 United Nations Plz, New York, NY 10017. Tel: 212-883-8200. Fax: 212-984-5452. Web: www.iie.org.

INSTITUTE ON RELIGION AND CIVIC VALUES
PO Box 20186, Fountain Valley, CA 92728. Tel: 714-839-2929. Fax: 714-839-2714. E-mail: info@ircv.org. Web: www.ircv.org.

INTERNATIONAL COUNCIL FOR HEALTH, PHYSICAL EDUCATION, RECREATION, SPORT AND DANCE
1900 Association Dr, Reston, VA 20191. Tel: 703-476-3462. Fax: 703-476-9527. E-mail: ichper@aahperd.org. Web: www.ichpersd.org.

INTERNATIONAL COUNCIL ON EDUCATION FOR TEACHING
c/o National-Louis Univ, 1000 Capitol Dr, Wheeling, IL 60090. Tel: 847-947-5881. Fax: 847-947-5881. E-mail: icet@icet-online.org. Web: www.icet-online.org.

INTERNATIONAL READING ASSOCIATION
800 Barksdale Rd, PO Box 8139, Newark, DE 19714USA. Tel: 302-731-1600. Fax: 302-731-1057. Web: www.reading.org.

KLINGENSTEIN CENTER FOR INDEPENDENT SCHOOL LEADERSHIP
c/o Teachers College, Columbia Univ, 525 W 120th St, 204 Zankel Bldg, Box 125, New York, NY 10027. Tel: 212-678-3156. Fax: 212-678-3254. E-mail: klingenstein@tc.columbia.edu. Web: www.klingenstein.org.

NAFSA: ASSOCIATION OF INTERNATIONAL EDUCATORS
1307 New York Ave NW, 8th Fl, Washington, DC 20005. Tel: 202-737-3699. Fax: 202-737-3657. E-mail: inbox@nafsa.org. Web: www.nafsa.org.

NATIONAL ASSOCIATION FOR COLLEGE ADMISSION COUNSELING
1050 N Highland St, Ste 400, Alexandria, VA 22201. Tel: 703-836-2222, 800-822-6285. Fax: 703-243-9375. E-mail: info@nacacnet.org. Web: www.nacacnet.org.

NATIONAL ASSOCIATION OF BIOLOGY TEACHERS
1313 Dolley Madison Blvd, Suite 402, McLean, VA 22101. Tel: 703-264-9696, 888-501-6228. Fax: 800-883-0698. E-mail: office@nabt.org. Web: www.nabt.org.

NATIONAL ASSOCIATION OF ELEMENTARY SCHOOL PRINCIPALS
1615 Duke St, Alexandria, VA 22314. Tel: 703-684-3345, 800-386-2377.
Fax: 800-396-2377. E-mail: naesp@naesp.org. Web: www.naesp.org.

NATIONAL ASSOCIATION OF PRINCIPALS OF SCHOOLS FOR GIRLS
23490 Caraway Lakes Dr, Bonita Springs, FL 34135. Tel: 239-947-6196.
Fax: 855-390-3245. E-mail: napsg@mac.com. Web: www.napsg.org.

NATIONAL ASSOCIATION OF SECONDARY SCHOOL PRINCIPALS
1904 Association Dr, Reston, VA 20191. Tel: 703-860-0200, 800-253-7746.
Fax: 703-476-5432. Web: www.nassp.org.

NATIONAL ASSOCIATION OF SPECIAL EDUCATION TEACHERS
1250 Connecticut Ave NW, Ste 200, Washington, DC 20036. Tel: 800-754-4421.
Fax: 800-424-0371. E-mail: info@naset.org. Web: www.naset.org.

NATIONAL COUNCIL FOR GEOGRAPHIC EDUCATION
1145 17th St NW, Rm 7620, Washington, DC 20036. Tel: 202-857-7695.
Fax: 202-618-6249. E-mail: ncge@ncge.org. Web: www.ncge.org.

NATIONAL COUNCIL FOR PRIVATE SCHOOL ACCREDITATION
PO Box 13686, Seattle, WA 98198. Tel: 253-874-3408. Fax: 253-874-3409.
E-mail: ncpsaexdr@aol.com. Web: www.ncpsa.org.

NATIONAL COUNCIL FOR THE SOCIAL STUDIES
8555 16th St, Ste 500, Silver Spring, MD 20910. Tel: 301-588-1800.
Fax: 301-588-2049. E-mail: publications@ncss.org. Web: www.ncss.org.

NATIONAL COUNCIL OF TEACHERS OF ENGLISH
1111 W Kenyon Rd, Urbana, IL 61801. Tel: 217-328-3870, 800-369-6283.
Fax: 217-328-9645. E-mail: public_info@ncte.org. Web: www.ncte.org.

NATIONAL COUNCIL OF TEACHERS OF MATHEMATICS
1906 Association Dr, Reston, VA 20191. Tel: 703-620-9840. Fax: 703-476-2970.
E-mail: nctm@nctm.org. Web: www.nctm.org.

NATIONAL SCIENCE TEACHERS ASSOCIATION
1840 Wilson Blvd, Arlington, VA 22201. Tel: 703-243-7100. Fax: 703-243-7177.
Web: www.nsta.org.

SCHOOL SCIENCE AND MATHEMATICS ASSOCIATION
c/o Oklahoma State Univ, College of Education, 245 Willard Hall, Stillwater, OK
74078. Tel: 405-744-8018. E-mail: office@ssma.org. Web: www.ssma.org.

SCHOOL MEMBERSHIP ASSOCIATIONS

ALABAMA INDEPENDENT SCHOOL ASSOCIATION
1500 E Fairview Ave, Montgomery, AL 36106. Tel: 334-833-4080.
Fax: 334-833-4086. E-mail: aisa@aisaonline.org. Web: www.aisaonline.org.

AMERICAN ASSOCIATION OF CHRISTIAN SCHOOLS
602 Belvoir Ave, East Ridge, TN 37412. Tel: 423-629-4280. Fax: 423-622-7461.
E-mail: info@aacs.org. Web: www.aacs.org.

AMERICAN MONTESSORI SOCIETY
116 E 16th St, New York, NY 10003. Tel: 212-358-1250. Fax: 212-358-1256.
E-mail: ams@amshq.org. Web: www.amshq.org.

ARIZONA ASSOCIATION OF INDEPENDENT SCHOOLS
c/o Tesseract School, 4800 E Doubletree Ranch Rd, Paradise Valley, AZ 85253.
Tel: 480-991-1770. Fax: 480-991-1954. E-mail: president@azais.org.
Web: www.azais.org.

THE ASSOCIATION OF BOARDING SCHOOLS
1 N Pack Sq, Ste 301, Asheville, NC 28801. Tel: 828-258-5354. Fax: 828-258-6428.
Web: www.boardingschools.com.

ASSOCIATION OF CHRISTIAN SCHOOLS INTERNATIONAL
PO Box 65130, Colorado Springs, CO 80962. Tel: 719-528-6906, 800-367-0798.
Fax: 719-531-0631. E-mail: info@acsi.org. Web: www.acsi.org.

ASSOCIATION OF COLORADO INDEPENDENT SCHOOLS
1702 Sumac Ave, Boulder, CO 80304. Tel: 303-444-2201. Fax: 303-265-9776.
E-mail: lquinby@acischools.org. Web: www.acischools.org.

ASSOCIATION OF DELAWARE VALLEY INDEPENDENT SCHOOLS
701 W Montgomery Ave, Bryn Mawr, PA 19010. Tel: 610-527-0130.
Fax: 610-527-4332. E-mail: info@advis.org. Web: www.advis.org.

ASSOCIATION OF INDEPENDENT MARYLAND & DC SCHOOLS
890 Airport Park Rd, Ste 103, Glen Burnie, MD 21061. Tel: 410-761-3700.
Fax: 410-761-5771. E-mail: info@aimsmddc.org. Web: www.aimsmddc.org.

ASSOCIATION OF INDEPENDENT MICHIGAN SCHOOLS
Eton Academy, 1755 Melton Rd, Birmingham, MI 48009. Tel: 248-642-1150.
E-mail: ppullen@etonacademy.org. Web: www.aims-mi.org.

ASSOCIATION OF INDEPENDENT SCHOOLS IN NEW ENGLAND
222 Forbes Rd, Ste 106, Braintree, MA 02184. Tel: 781-843-8440. Fax: 781-843-3933.
E-mail: info@aisne.org. Web: www.aisne.org.

ASSOCIATION OF WALDORF SCHOOLS OF NORTH AMERICA
2344 Nicollet Ave S, Minneapolis, MN 55404. Tel: 612-870-8310. Fax: 612-870-8316.
E-mail: awsna@awsna.org. Web: www.whywaldorfworks.org.

ATLANTA AREA ASSOCIATION OF INDEPENDENT SCHOOLS
c/o The Atlanta Speech School, 3610 Northside Pky NW, Atlanta, GA 30327.
Tel: 404-233-5332. Fax: 404-266-2175. Web: www.aaais.org.

CALIFORNIA ASSOCIATION OF INDEPENDENT SCHOOLS
4450 Lakeside Dr, Ste 375, Burbank, CA 91505. Tel: 818-845-0800.
Fax: 818-845-0888. E-mail: cais@caisca.org. Web: www.caisca.org.

CATHOLIC BOARDING SCHOOLS ASSOCIATION
c/o Maur Hill-Mount Academy, 1000 Green St, Atchison, KS 66002.
Tel: 913-367-5482. Fax: 913-367-5096. Web: www.cbsa.org.

CENTER FOR SPIRITUAL AND ETHICAL EDUCATION
PO Box 19807, Portland, OR 97280. Tel: 503-232-1531, 800-298-4599.
Fax: 678-623-5634. E-mail: info@csee.org. Web: www.csee.org.

CHURCH SCHOOLS IN THE DIOCESE OF VIRGINIA
110 W Franklin St, Richmond, VA 23220. Tel: 804-288-6045.
E-mail: khenderson@thediocese.net. Web: www.thediocese.net.

CLEVELAND COUNCIL OF INDEPENDENT SCHOOLS
1088 Dorsch Rd, Cleveland, OH 44121. Tel: 440-893-9585. Fax: 440-338-3471.
E-mail: linda.ccis@gmail.com. Web: www.ccis-ohio.org.

COALITION OF ESSENTIAL SCHOOLS
c/o Great Schools Partnership, 482 Congress St, Ste 500, Portland, ME 04101.
Tel: 510-433-1912. E-mail: inquiries@essentialschools.org.
Web: www.essentialschools.org.

CONNECTICUT ASSOCIATION OF INDEPENDENT SCHOOLS
28A Cottrell St, PO Box 159, Mystic, CT 06355. Tel: 860-572-2950.
Fax: 860-415-0835. E-mail: lyons@caisct.org. Web: www.caisct.org.

DELAWARE ASSOCIATION OF INDEPENDENT SCHOOLS
c/o The Pilot School, 100 Garden of Eden Rd, Wilmington, DE 19803.
Tel: 302-478-1740. Fax: 302-478-1746. Web: www.daisschools.org.

FLORIDA COUNCIL OF INDEPENDENT SCHOOLS
1211 N Westshore Blvd, Ste 612, Tampa, FL 33607. Tel: 813-287-2820.
Fax: 813-286-3025. E-mail: fcisoffice@aol.com. Web: www.fcis.org.

FRIENDS COUNCIL ON EDUCATION
1507 Cherry St, Philadelphia, PA 19102. Tel: 215-241-7245. Fax: 215-241-7299.
E-mail: info@friendscouncil.org. Web: www.friendscouncil.org.

GEORGIA INDEPENDENT SCHOOL ASSOCIATION
PO Box 1057, Thomaston, GA 30286. Tel: 706-938-1400. Fax: 706-938-1401.
E-mail: info@gisaschools.org. Web: www.gisaschools.org.

HAWAII ASSOCIATION OF INDEPENDENT SCHOOLS
1585 Kapiolani Blvd, Ste 1212, Honolulu, HI 96814. Tel: 808-973-1540.
Fax: 808-973-1545. E-mail: info@hais.org. Web: www.hais.org.

INDEPENDENT CURRICULUM GROUP
1217 Courtyard Dr, Charlottesville, VA 22903.
E-mail: bhammond@independentcurriculum.org.
Web: www.independentcurriculum.org.

INDEPENDENT EDUCATION
1524 35th St NW, Washington, DC 20007. Tel: 202-625-9223. Fax: 202-625-9225.
E-mail: info@independenteducation.org. Web: www.independenteducation.org.

INDEPENDENT SCHOOL HEALTH ASSOCIATION
PO Box 482, Byfield, MA 01922. Tel: 978-462-1368. E-mail: ishaoffice@comcast.net.
Web: www.ishanet.org.

INDEPENDENT SCHOOLS ASSOCIATION OF NORTHERN NEW ENGLAND
38 Clark Cove Rd, Bowerbank, ME 04426. Tel: 207-564-2333. Fax: 207-564-2422.
E-mail: dcummings@isanne.org. Web: www.isanne.org.

INDEPENDENT SCHOOLS ASSOCIATION OF RHODE ISLAND
c/o Moses Brown School, 250 Lloyd Ave, Providence, RI 02906. Tel: 401-831-7350.
Fax: 401-755-8854. Web: www.isari.org.

INDEPENDENT SCHOOLS ASSOCIATION OF THE CENTRAL STATES
1165 N Clark St, Ste 311, Chicago, IL 60610. Tel: 312-255-1244. Fax: 312-255-1278.
E-mail: info@isacs.org. Web: www.isacs.org.

INDEPENDENT SCHOOLS ASSOCIATION OF THE SOUTHWEST
505 N Big Spring St, Ste 505, Midland, TX 79701. Tel: 432-684-9550.
Fax: 432-684-9401. E-mail: rdurham@isasw.org. Web: www.isasw.org.

INDEPENDENT SCHOOLS OF ST. LOUIS
425 S Lindbergh Blvd, St Louis, MO 63131. Tel: 314-567-9229. Fax: 314-567-4074.
E-mail: gnewport@independentschools.org. Web: www.independentschools.org.

INTERNATIONAL BACCALAUREATE ORGANIZATION
Rte des Morillons 15, Grand-Saconnex, 1218 Geneva, Switzerland.
Tel: 41-22-791-7740. Fax: 41-22-791-0277. E-mail: ibhq@ibo.org. Web: www.ibo.org.

INTERNATIONAL BOYS' SCHOOLS COALITION
700 Rte 22, Pawling, NY 12564. Tel: 207-841-7441. E-mail: adams@theibsc.org.
Web: www.theibsc.org.

INTERNATIONAL MONTESSORI SOCIETY
9525 Georgia Ave, Ste 200, Silver Spring, MD 20910. Tel: 301-589-1127.
Fax: 301-589-0733. E-mail: havis@imsmontessori.org. Web: www.imsmontessori.org.

JESUIT SECONDARY EDUCATION ASSOCIATION
1016 16th St NW, Ste 200, Washington, DC 20036. Tel: 202-667-3888.
Fax: 202-387-6305. E-mail: jsea@jsea.org. Web: www.jsea.org.

JUNIOR BOARDING SCHOOLS ASSOCIATION
c/o Hillside School, 404 Robin Hill St, Marlborough, MA 01752. Tel: 508-485-2824.
Fax: 508-485-4420. E-mail: admission@hillsideschool.net. Web: www.jbsa.org.

KENTUCKY ASSOCIATION OF INDEPENDENT SCHOOLS
c/o St. Francis School, 11000 US 42, Goshen, KY 40026. Tel: 502-228-1197.
Web: www.mykais.org.

LAKE MICHIGAN ASSOCIATION OF INDEPENDENT SCHOOLS
PO Box 381, Grayslake, IL 60030. Web: www.lmais.com.

LUTHERAN EDUCATION ASSOCIATION
7400 Augusta St, River Forest, IL 60305. Tel: 708-209-3343. Fax: 708-209-3458.
E-mail: lea@lea.org. Web: www.lea.org.

MIDWEST BOARDING SCHOOLS
PO Box 218, Faribault, MN 55021. Tel: 800-799-6927. Web: www.mwbs.org.

MINNESOTA INDEPENDENT SCHOOL FORUM
445 Minnesota St, Ste 505, St Paul, MN 55101. Tel: 651-297-6716.
Fax: 651-297-6718. E-mail: info@misf.org. Web: www.misf.org.

MISSOURI INDEPENDENT SCHOOL ASSOCIATION
10631 Wornall Rd, Kansas City, MO 64114. Tel: 816-942-3282. Fax: 816-942-4052.
E-mail: amunninghoff@ndsion.edu.

**NATIONAL ALLIANCE OF CONCURRENT
ENROLLMENT PARTNERSHIPS**
126 Mallette St, Chapel Hill, NC 27516. Tel: 919-593-5205. Fax: 877-572-8693.
E-mail: alowe@nacep.org. Web: www.nacep.org.

NATIONAL ASSOCIATION OF EPISCOPAL SCHOOLS
815 2nd Ave, Ste 819, New York, NY 10017. Tel: 212-716-6134, 800-334-7626.
Fax: 212-286-9366. E-mail: info@episcopalschools.org. Web: www.naes.org.

NATIONAL ASSOCIATION OF INDEPENDENT SCHOOLS
1129 20th St NW, Ste 800, Washington, DC 20036. Tel: 202-973-9700.
Fax: 202-973-9790. E-mail: info@nais.org. Web: www.nais.org.

NATIONAL CATHOLIC EDUCATIONAL ASSOCIATION
1005 N Globe Rd, Ste 525, Arlington, VA 22201. Tel: 571-257-0010.
Fax: 703-243-6025. E-mail: nceaadmin@ncea.org. Web: www.ncea.org.

NATIONAL COALITION OF GIRLS' SCHOOLS
50 Leonard St, Ste 2C, Belmont, MA 02478. Tel: 617-489-0013. Fax: 617-489-0024.
E-mail: ncgs@ncgs.org. Web: www.ncgs.org.

NEW JERSEY ASSOCIATION OF INDEPENDENT SCHOOLS
118 Washington St, Morristown, NJ 07960. Tel: 888-472-3491. Fax: 973-898-3630.
E-mail: info@njais.org. Web: www.njais.org.

NEW YORK STATE ASSOCIATION OF INDEPENDENT SCHOOLS
17 Elk St, Albany, NY 12207. Tel: 518-694-5500. Fax: 518-694-5501.
Web: www.nysais.org.

NORTH CAROLINA ASSOCIATION OF INDEPENDENT SCHOOLS
13000 S Tryon St, Ste F, Box 235, Charlotte, NC 28278. Tel: 704-461-7602.
Fax: 866-442-0515. E-mail: lnelson@ncais.org. Web: www.ncais.org.

OHIO ASSOCIATION OF INDEPENDENT SCHOOLS
PO Box 400, Hebron, OH 43025. E-mail: dandodd@oais.org. Web: www.oais.org.

PACIFIC NORTHWEST ASSOCIATION OF INDEPENDENT SCHOOLS
5001 California Ave SW, Ste 112, Seattle, WA 98136. Tel: 206-323-6137.
Fax: 206-324-4863. E-mail: mthayer@pnais.org. Web: www.pnais.org.

PALMETTO ASSOCIATION OF INDEPENDENT SCHOOLS
PO Box 30145, Charleston, SC 29417. Tel: 843-556-4395. Fax: 843-556-6536.
E-mail: pais-sc@bellsouth.net. Web: www.scpais.net.

PENNSYLVANIA ASSOCIATION OF INDEPENDENT SCHOOLS
37 E Germantown Pike, Ste 302, Plymouth Meeting, PA 19462. Tel: 610-567-2960.
Fax: 610-567-2963. E-mail: lphelps@paispa.org. Web: www.paispa.org.

SMALL BOARDING SCHOOL ASSOCIATION
c/o Landmark School, 412 Hale St, Prides Crossing, MA 01965.
Web: www.smallboardingschools.org.

SOUTH CAROLINA INDEPENDENT SCHOOL ASSOCIATION
PO Box 690, Orangeburg, SC 29116. Tel: 803-535-4820. Fax: 803-535-4840.
E-mail: administration@scisa.org. Web: www.scisa.org.

SOUTHERN ASSOCIATION OF INDEPENDENT SCHOOLS
5901 Peachtree-Dunwoody Rd NE, Ste B-200, Atlanta, GA 30328. Tel: 404-918-8850.
Fax: 404-633-2433. E-mail: sais@sais.org. Web: www.sais.org.

SOUTHWESTERN ASSOCIATION OF EPISCOPAL SCHOOLS
1420 4th Ave, Ste 29, Canyon, TX 79015. Tel: 806-655-2400, 866-655-7237.
Fax: 806-655-2426. E-mail: cwootton@swaes.org. Web: www.swaes.org.

TENNESSEE ASSOCIATION OF INDEPENDENT SCHOOLS
6544 Murray Ln, Brentwood, TN 37027. Tel: 615-321-2800. Fax: 615-321-2827.
E-mail: info@taistn.com. Web: www.taistn.com.

VIRGINIA ASSOCIATION OF INDEPENDENT SCHOOLS
6802 Paragon Pl, Ste 525, Richmond, VA 23230. Tel: 804-282-3592.
Fax: 804-282-3596. E-mail: info@vais.org. Web: www.vais.org.

WISCONSIN ASSOCIATION OF INDEPENDENT SCHOOLS
c/o St John's Northwestern Military Academy, 1101 N Genesee St, Delafield, WI
53018. Tel: 262-646-7111. Fax: 262-646-7128. E-mail: jalbert@sjnma.org.

STUDENT EXCHANGE ORGANIZATIONS

AFS INTERNATIONAL PROGRAMS
71 W 23rd St, 17th Fl, New York, NY 10010. Tel: 212-352-9810. Fax: 212-352-9826.
E-mail: info@afs.org. Web: www.afs.org.

NETWORK OF COMPLEMENTARY SCHOOLS
112 Lakeridge Rd, Quinter, KS 67752. Tel: 785-754-2287.
E-mail: youcan@ruraltel.net. Web: www.netcompsch.org.

TESTING ORGANIZATIONS

ACT
500 ACT Dr, PO Box 168, Iowa City, IA 52243. Tel: 319-337-1000.
Fax: 319-339-3021. Web: www.act.org.

THE COLLEGE BOARD
45 Columbus Ave, New York, NY 10023. Tel: 212-713-8000. Fax: 212-713-8282.
Web: www.collegeboard.org.

EDUCATIONAL RECORDS BUREAU
470 Park Ave, 2nd Fl, New York, NY 10016. Tel: 212-672-9800, 800-989-3721.
Fax: 212-370-4096. E-mail: info@erblearn.org. Web: www.erblearn.org.
See *Display Ad* **on page 1245**

EDUCATIONAL TESTING SERVICE
Rosedale Rd, Princeton, NJ 08541. Tel: 609-921-9000. Fax: 609-734-5410.
E-mail: etsinfo@ets.org. Web: www.ets.org.

SECONDARY SCHOOL ADMISSION TEST BOARD
CN 5339, Princeton, NJ 08543. Tel: 609-683-4440. Fax: 609-683-1702.
E-mail: info@ssat.org. Web: www.ssat.org.

WHEN QUALITY MATTERS, FAMILIES CHOOSE THE ISEE®

 **ERB** | **ISEE**® INDEPENDENT SCHOOL ENTRANCE EXAM

FREE ONLINE STUDY GUIDE

The most advanced admission testing available for independent schools worldwide, for students entering Grades 2–12.

Registration Available Online at:
www.ISEEtest.org
(800) 446-0320

www.erblearn.org

CLASSIFIED LISTINGS OF FIRMS AND AGENCIES

INDEX TO FIRMS AND AGENCIES

EDUCATIONAL CONSULTANTS

EILEEN ANTALEK, Ed.D.
33 Lyman St, Ste 200, Westboro, MA 01581. Tel: 508-870-1515. 73 Lexington St, Newton 02466. E-mail: eileen@educationaldirections.com. APA AANE IDA IECA. Day, Boarding, College, LD, Therapeutic, Psyched Evaluations.

CAMILLE M. BERTRAM EDUCATIONAL CONSULTANTS
120 Riders Lane, Fairfield, CT 06824. Tel: 203-255-2577.
Web: www.cmbertram.com. E-mail: cmbertram@cmbertram.com.
Camille M. Bertram, Certified Educational Planner; Member, IECA, SSATB

KIMBERLY DAVIS, MA, MS, Certified Educational Planner
Member IECA, SSATB, SBSA, LDA, NAGC, NACAC, NATSAP
Boarding and Day Schools, Colleges, Educational concerns (LD, ADD, Gifted)
P.O. Box 383, Huntersville NC 28070 Tel: 704-458-8929. Fax 704-631-4993.
E-mail: kim@daviseducationalconsulting.com. Twitter: @EduConsultCEP

DOBSON EDUCATIONAL SERVICES, INC.
8238 Germantown Ave, Philadelphia, PA 19118. Tel: 215-242-3587.
Fax: 215-242-3588. E-mail: jpd@dobconsult.com. Web: www.dobconsult.com.
Joseph P. Dobson, MA, Director. Member IECA, LDA, IDA, SSATB.
Counseling and referral services for students and families seeking day, boarding, and special needs schools.

GREENWICH PRIVATE SCHOOL ADMISSIONS ADVISORS
Dr. Paul R. Lowe, Dir; Veronica Hanley, and Emily Zhao.
Specializes in helping families who reside in Greenwich, CT and Lower Fairfield Cty.
Specializes in admissions/placement to elite boarding and day schools.
Partners with Ivy League Admissions Advisors for college admissions.
Located on Route 1: 500 West Putnam Ave, Ste. 400, Greenwich, CT 06830
Tel: 203-542-7288. E-mail: info@greenwichprivateschooladmissions.com

JEAN P. HAGUE, MA, Certified Educational Planner, IECA, SSATB
400 Colony Sq., Ste. 200, 1201 Peachtree St. NE, Atlanta, GA 30361.
Tel: 404-872-9128. Fax: 404-870-9093. E-mail: jeanhague@aol.com.
Boarding, College, Summer, Alternative Educational Options.

HOWLAND, SPENCE & McMILLAN, IECA
266 Beacon St., Boston, MA 02116. Tel: 617 536-4319. Fax: 617-536-9031.
E-mail: dmcmillan@howlandspence.com. Web: www.howlandspence.com.
Located in the heart of Boston's Back Bay for more than 50 years, Howland,
Spence & McMillan helps families in New England, nationally, and
worldwide with independent boarding and day school, college, and graduate
program planning.

MANHATTAN PRIVATE SCHOOL ADMISSIONS ADVISORS
Dr. Paul R. Lowe, Dir; Veronica Hanley, and Elizabeth Vandenburg.
Specializes in helping families who reside in Manhattan, Riverdale and West-
chester County.
Specializes in admissions/placement to elite boarding and day schools.
Partners with Ivy League Admissions Advisors for college admissions.
Located in Midtown Manhattan: 405 Lexington Ave, 26th Flr, NY, NY 10174
Tel: 212- 829-4341. E-mail: info@manhattanprivateschooladmissions.com

MASON ASSOCIATES
PO Box 59, 2687 Greenbush Rd, Charlotte, VT 05445
Tel: 802-425-7600. Fax: 802-425-7601. Email: ben@masonconsult.com.
Web: www.masonconsult.com.

DR. STEPHEN MIGDEN AND ASSOCIATES
Offices in Roslyn Heights, NY, and Manhattan. Tel: 516-625-0824.
Email: drmigden@verizon.net. www.DrStephenMigdenandAssociates.com.
Specializes in ADHD, learning disabilities and emotional-behavioral problems.

PRIVATE SCHOOL ADMISSIONS ADVISORS, Dr. Paul R. Lowe, President.
Specializes in admissions/placement to elite boarding and day schools.
Partners with Ivy League Admissions Advisors for college admissions.
Woodbridge, CT; Tel: 203-387-1574. Greenwich, CT; Tel: 203-542-7288.
Manhattan; Tel: 212-829-4341. info@privateschooladmissionsadvisors.com

JUDI ROBINOVITZ
See *Display Ad* on page 1295

SCHOOL PLACEMENT SERVICES, Tutoring & Test Prep
Elissa Sommerfield, MA, Certified Educational Planner, Member IECA
6126 Averill Way, #109W, Dallas, TX 75225. Tel: 214-363-7043.
Fax: 214-363-0146. E-mail: esom@techrack.com.
Web: www.elissasommerfield.com.

STEINBRECHER & PARTNERS, LLC, Educational Consultants
Diederik J. van Renesse, Richard Avitabile, and Meghan Lahey.
College, Boarding, Special and Alternative Counseling.
225 Main St., Ste. 203, Westport, CT 06880. Tel: 203-227-3190.
Fax: 203-221-0182. E-mail: edcon225@steinbrecherconsulting.com.
Web: www.steinbrecherconsulting.com.

IMY F. WAX, MS, LCPC, Certified Educational Planner
1320 Carol Ln, Deerfield, IL 60015. Tel:847-945-0913. Fax: 847-945-6475.
E-mail: imy@imywaxcom. Web: www.imywax.com.
IECA, APA, ICA, NACAC, NATSAP, ACA, AMHCA
Offices in U.S. and Canada. International consulting; traditional, non-traditional
and special needs boarding; college alternatives; summer options; therapeutic
and wilderness programs; counseling and psychotherapy.

INSURANCE

A.W.G. DEWAR, INC.
Four Batterymarch Park, Quincy, MA 02169-7468. Tel: 617-774-1555.
Fax: 617-774-1715. E-mail: trp@dewarinsurance.com.
Representatives throughout North America
TUITION REFUND PLANS
Our specialized work for over 80 years has won complete confidence nationwide
for these voluntary or required-participation plans.
See Also *Display Ad* on page 1296

FUNDRAISING AND
PUBLIC RELATIONS COUNSEL

BARNES & ROCHE INC.
Rosemont Business Campus, 919 Conestoga Rd., Building One, Suite 101,
Rosemont, PA 19010-1352. Tel: 610-527-3244.
E-mail: consult@brnsrche.com. Web: www.barnesroche.com.
Consultants providing strategic and operational consultation for fund-raising;
program assessments; capital campaigns; feasibility studies; planned giving;
electronic screening; and communications services.

MANAGEMENT CONSULTING

CARNEY, SANDOE AND ASSOCIATES
44 Bromfield St, Boston, Massachusetts 02108. Tel: 617-542-0260.
Fax: 617-592-9200. Email: recruitment@carneysandoe.com.
Web: www.carneysandoe.com.

SCHOOL SUPPLIERS

BOOKHOUSE GROUP, INC.
818 Marietta St NW, Atlanta, GA 30318. Tel: 404-885-9515. Fax: 404-885-1976.
Email: rob@bookhouse.net. Web: www.bookhouse.net.

INDEX OF SCHOOLS

INDEX OF SCHOOLS

Schools are referenced by page number. Boldface page numbers refer to the optional Featured Schools section of schools that subscribe for space. To facilitate the use of this section, refer to the separate index preceding the Featured Schools. Cross-references to Featured Schools also appear at the end of the free descriptive listings of subscribing schools.

Yes, send me the most recent editions of:

Title	Price	Qty	Total
The Handbook of Private Schools (Hardcover)	$99.00		
Guide to Private Special Education (Paperback)	$32.00		
Guide to Programs (Paperback)	$27.00		
Guide to Programs (Hardcover)	$45.00		

Order Amount	Shipping		
		Subtotal	
$1-$50	$6.95	US shipping (*see rates at left*)	
$51-$200	$15.95	**TOTAL**	
$201-$300	$19.95		
$300+	6% of total		

☐ Check or money order enclosed (payable on a US bank)

☐ Bill me (organizations only)

☐ Visa   ☐ MasterCard

Card # _____ Exp. Date _____

3-digit Security Code _____

Card Holder_____

Signature _____

Charge on your statement will read "ALY*ALLOYEDUCATION"

First Name   Last Name
_____

Company Name
_____

Street Address (no P.O. Boxes, please)
_____

City   State   Zip
_____

Country   Postal Code
_____

E-mail _____

Daytime phone _____   HPS12

PORTER SARGENT HANDBOOKS
A division of Carnegie Communications

2 LAN Dr   Ste 100   Westford, MA 01886   USA
Tel: 978-842-2812   Fax: 978-692-2304
info@portersargent.com   www.portersargent.com

Judi Robinovitz

Certified Educational Planner

Offices in
Palm Beach & Broward counties:
(877) 438-2400 or
(561) 241-1610

Email: judi@ScoreAtTheTop.com
Web: www.ScoreAtTheTop.com

- Member: IECA, HECA, NACAC, SSATB, LDA, NATSAP (associate)
- Accredited by the Southern Association of Colleges & Schools
- Comprehensive guidance for private day & boarding schools world-wide (traditional, LD/ADHD, therapeutic)
- College & grad/med/law/business school admission
- Authorized SSAT Flex Test site
- Private tutoring in our 6 Florida locations or "virtually"
- Full-time 1-on-1 private-school in Florida or "virtually"

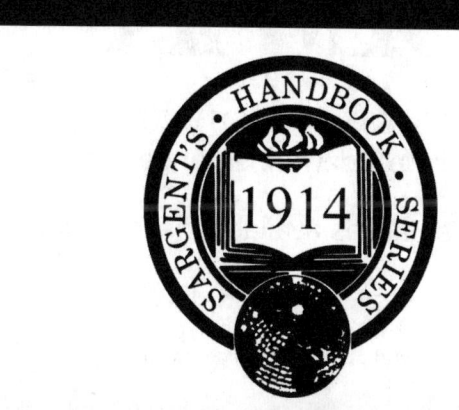

www.portersargent.com

THE TUITION REFUND PLAN

This unique program, which we originated over 80 years ago, is now in use at 1,200 schools and colleges. The Plan provides benefits which refund tuition for class time lost due to absence, dismissal or withdrawal for almost any reason. This assures a school its budgeted tuition income while mitigating the parents financial loss. It is available to schools and colleges throughout North America.

ORIGINATORS OF THE TUITION REFUND PLAN

DEWAR

Since 1930

(617) 774-1555   Fax (617) 774-1715
Email: trp@dewarinsurance.com

Representatives available nationwide.

A.W.G. DEWAR, INC.

Four Batterymarch Park, Quincy, Massachusetts 02169-7468